Practice makes perfect in accounting.

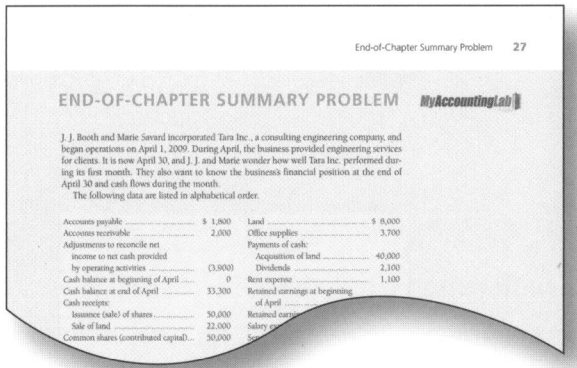

The algorithmic engine that drives MyAccountingLab means you can practise questions any number of times and actually master the content, not just memorize it!

88% of students surveyed found the algorithmic practice to be either very helpful or extremely helpful

You will have more "I get it" moments in and out of the classroom!

MyAccountingLab doesn't just provide opportunities for limitless practice – it recreates the "I get it" moments of the classroom by providing clear guidance when you need it most.

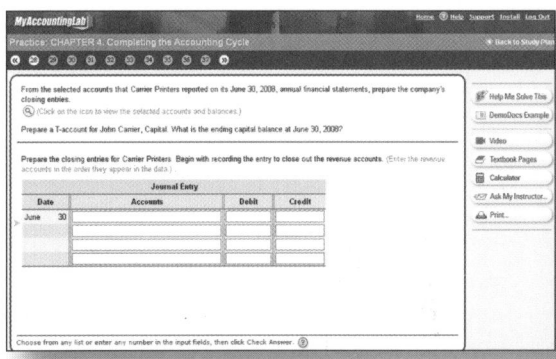

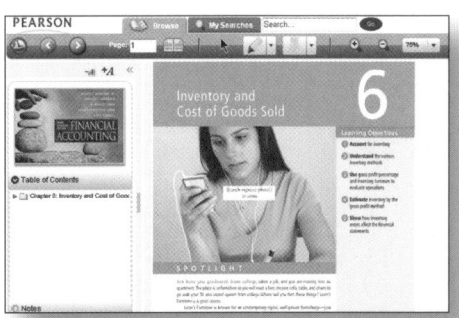

Having difficulty solving a question?

Click the *Help Me Solve This* button anytime and a pop-up window will appear with tips to help you solve the specific part of the problem you are working on. It's just like having a friend standing over your shoulder helping you—right in the middle of the problem— so that you can get through it and understand how to solve it.

Want to view the textbook while you work?

MyAccountingLab contains an *online version of the textbook.* By clicking on the ebook link, you are immediately taken right to the section of the textbook related to the problem you are working to solve. You can even take notes and highlight key passages in the ebook.

www.myaccountinglab.com

MyAccountingLab

To your success!

To help you achieve your goals in this course and beyond, here are some valuable study tools that can also be found on MyAccountingLab.

THE ACADIA|PEARSON
BUSINESSINSIDER
SERIES

Get the big picture. Listen to interviews with industry leaders and top executives from Canada and abroad. Interview topics range from entrepreneurship and advertising to human resource management. A wide range of industries and areas of interest are also featured, including wine, oil and gas, finance, mining, fruit growing, advertising, and Canadians working in Japan.

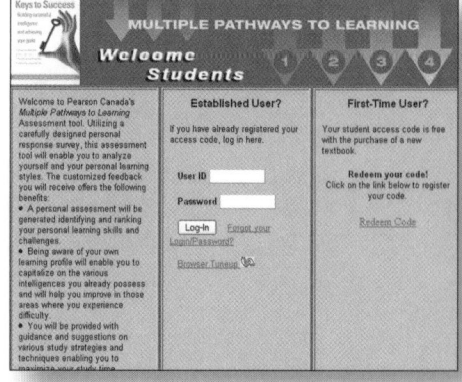

Multiple Pathways to Learning, a learning style assessment quiz, allows you to identify your preferred learning style by completing a quick quiz. You will then receive personalized feedback to help you strengthen your study skills.

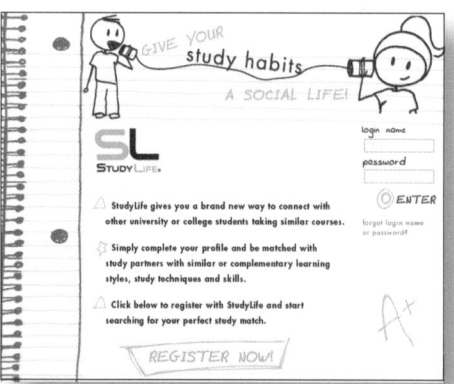

StudyLife is Pearson Canada's new social networking application that allows you to make new connections with other students studying in similar programs. Improve your grades and make friends with classmates or those across Canada studying in similar programs.

www.myaccountinglab.com

Cost Accounting

A Managerial Emphasis Fifth Canadian Edition

Charles T. Horngren
Stanford University

George Foster
Stanford University

Srikant M. Datar
Stanford University

Maureen P. Gowing
University of Windsor

Pearson Canada
Toronto

Cataloguing information is available from Library and Archives Canada.

ISBN-13: 978-0-13-500493-7
ISBN-10: 0-13-500493-4

Vice President, Editorial Director: Gary Bennett
Sponsoring Editor: Carolin Sweig
Executive Marketing Manager: Cas Shields
Developmental Editor: Anita Smale
Production Editors: Laura Neves, Cheryl Jackson
Copy Editors: Susan Bindernagel, Anita Smale, Laura Neves
Proofreaders: Kelli Howey, Nancy Mucklow
Production Coordinator: Sarah Lukaweski
Compositor: Integra
Photo and Permissions Researcher: Sandy Cooke
Art Director: Julia Hall
Cover Designer: Miguel Acevedo
Interior Designer: Anthony Leung
Cover Image: Getty Images

The globe image that appears on pages 13, 58, 162, 319, 391, 435, 483, 536, 545, 612, 719, 753, 813, 841, 982, 1025, 1069, 1111, 1116, and 1146 is courtesy of Getty Images.

1 2 3 4 5   13 12 11 10 09

Printed and bound in the United States of America.

I would like to recognize a wonderful champion of this text and, more importantly, a friend whom I still keenly miss, Samantha Scully. The friendship and tireless, consummate professional support Sam provided with gentle humour and generosity of spirit cannot be replaced. I dedicate this text in her memory.

M.P.G.

BRIEF CONTENTS

CONTENTS

PART SEVEN
MANAGEMENT CONTROL SYSTEMS

23 **Management Control Systems, Transfer Pricing, and Multinational Considerations**   1091

24 **Performance Measurement, Compensation, and Multinational Considerations**   1137

PREFACE

In the for-profit domain, business managers must accept responsibility for making important, ethical decisions that respect social values and maximize profit. The decision processes within organizations are complex. Excellent decision making is, ironically, most important when uncertainty about the future is highest and information is incomplete. Reasonable estimates of quantitative financial and nonfinancial data are an elegant, effective, and efficient way to communicate information about any business process. Quantitative reports are the language of business. This information is vital to the survival of companies whether they compete in a regulated (e.g., milk production and sale) or free (e.g., automobile production and sale) market. Each phase of management, from planning product and service design through to delivery and customer service, requires quantitative data used to organize, monitor, and control actions. The goal is to improve the probability that actual social and business results meet or exceed expectations.

Students face several learning challenges as they develop the skills required to more accurately estimate costs, profitable prices, inventory valuation, and return on investments in long-term projects. By surmounting these challenges, they will be able both to produce more accurate estimates, and to understand that these estimates are often used as future performance thresholds to which managers are held accountable. This text will support instructors as students learn how to apply their understanding of these estimation techniques to explain the causes of performance shortfalls. Students will also grasp how the choice of costing techniques affects amounts reported on the income statement, cash flow, and balance sheet.

Similar to financial accounting, there are different techniques of estimation appropriate to different costing, pricing, and valuation situations—this is the central theme of the text. The difference from financial accounting is that no formal standards constrain managers' choices. However, financial failure will claim those who make inappropriate choices and consistently act on inappropriate estimates. Management is about solving problems—it is rare that an executive calls a management meeting to announce everything is going according to plan or better than planned. Cost estimation techniques cannot solve problems in and of themselves. This text emphasizes that people solve problems through analysis of cost information and other relevant nonfinancial and qualitative factors. The text presents a comprehensive set of techniques but emphasizes that students should never lose sight of the objective, which is to provide the most accurate information possible upon which to make ethical, profitable, and socially responsible management decisions.

HALLMARK FEATURES

The first thirteen chapters are the basis of a one-semester course that follows immediately after an introductory course in financial accounting. There is ample material in the remaining chapters to sustain either a two-term course or another one-term advanced topics course. Reviewers continue to praise the hallmark features of this text:

- ◆ Balanced emphasis on both the preparation and use of cost information through extensive use of real-world examples
- ◆ Critical and reflective approach as cost procedures are developed
- ◆ Clear contrast of relevant cost information for use in both strategic and operating decisions

- Emphasis on the importance of different cost information to measure progress towards the achievement of different goals
- Clarity in the logic used to teach different cost estimation techniques
- In-depth explanation and analysis of alternative cost estimation techniques
- Excellent integration of modern methods of data collection and analysis
- Flexibility in sequencing the order of topics taught
- Excellent quantity, quality, and scope of assignment material

This text organizes the presentation of topics in a modular way that gives instructors the independence to teach the topics in a sequence customized to their students' needs. For example, Exhibit 2-10 of Chapter 2 presents the heart of the explanation of how choosing different cost allocation methods in different manufacturing contexts affects the income statement and balance sheet. Once students understand this content, instructors can move on to a simple application where there is only one cost object, cost pool, and cost allocation base using the material in Chapter 17 on process costing. The format of Exhibit 2-10 is used again in Chapter 17 to link cost allocation in the context of process costing with its objectives—the estimate of cost of goods sold on the income statement, and the valuation of inventory on the balance sheet. Instructors could decide to follow Chapter 2 with an exploration of improved accuracy of cost estimation and pricing arrived at by changing from one cost object to another and delve into the contrast of job-order and activity-based costing (Chapters 4 and 5). Others may prefer teaching in the order presented in the text. The framework of Exhibit 2-10 is also an excellent template to introduce line-by-line budgeting (Chapter 6), variance analyses (Chapters 7, 8, and 16), and inventory valuation (Chapters 6–9).

NEW TO THIS EDITION

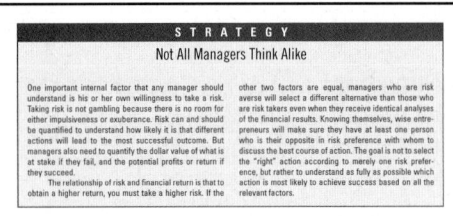

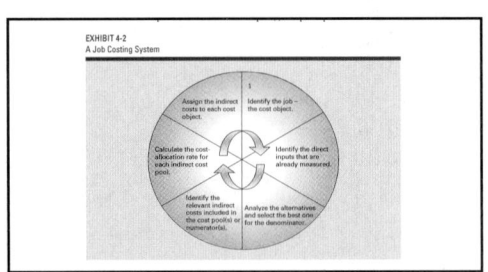

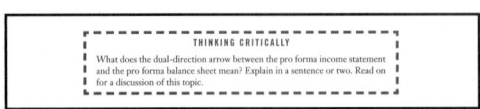

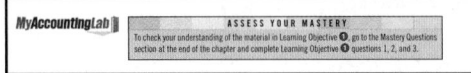

- Strategy and good decision-making abilities are what set great managers apart. This edition introduces the concept of strategy in Chapter 1, and applies cost-management techniques throughout the text to improve strategic as well as operating decisions. New Strategy boxes highlight the importance of strategic decision making in real business situations.
- Decision making is the reason for producing cost estimates. To emphasize that making decisions is more than a step-by-step exercise, new decision pie charts provide a means to focus on both the balance and thoughtfulness required of managers who use cost information and make decisions.
- Critical-thinking skills are crucial in today's business world and this edition of *Cost Accounting* offers students numerous opportunities to think about and discuss what they have just learned. Thinking Critically boxes have been added throughout the text to highlight the thoughtful application of cost-estimation techniques to resolve cost-management problems.
- The material has been organized to follow a competency-based-method of teaching, which allows students to test their level of mastery of a topic after the completion of each Learning Objective. Assess Your Mastery boxes direct students to Mastery Questions at the end of the chapter. Solutions to these questions are available on MyAccountingLab. This enables students to diagnose how competently they can apply their newly acquired cost-estimation, cost-management, and decision-making skills before moving on to the next concept.

- Each chapter opens with a Business Matters box, a short vignette that reports how real companies apply techniques and deal with the challenges presented in the chapter to engage students actively with the material. When coupled with the other pedagogical features, Business Matters encourages critical reflection on actual practices.

- Governance Issues boxes link the chapter content to issues of governance—an enterprise's requirement to pursue its mission without harming individuals, society, or the environment by voluntarily following legal and ethical norms, while at the same time improving the welfare of or producing profit for the owners of the enterprise. This feature explores behavioural and ethical issues by presenting the consequences of both appropriate and inappropriate management decisions.

- The Real Companies feature informs students about how widespread the managerial use of cost estimation, pricing, and inventory valuation practices is. Examples of multinational companies in industries including electronics, retailing, financial services, and manufacturing give students ample evidence that what they are learning is practised across the globe.

- MyAccountingLab offers students the opportunity to practise and perfect the technical skills that they require for the management-accounting profession. With this new edition of *Cost Accounting*, students gain access to MyAccountingLab with the purchase of a new textbook. By making use of the resources available in MyAccountingLab, students will soon find themselves moving beyond just "crunching numbers" and into insightful analysis of data. See the inside front cover to learn more about MyAccountingLab.

- The relevant Learning Objective numbers appear beside each Exercise and Problem in the Assignment Material at the end of each chapter. When appropriate, check figures appear next to questions to help students verify that they are on the right track.

- A List of Abbreviations appears at the very end of the book for convenient student reference.

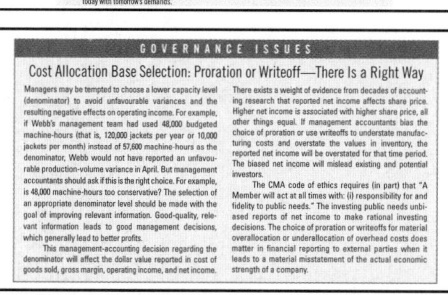

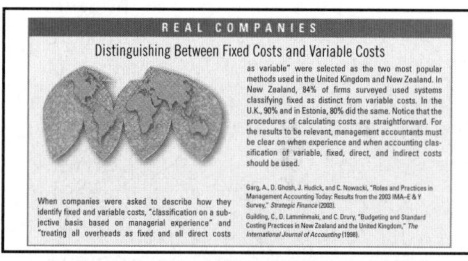

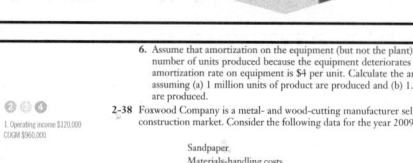

The procedures introduced in this text tend to be straightforward in practice, especially with the help of computer programs, such as Excel's simple regression and matrix algebra, which do all the calculations at the push of a button, even if the underlying theory is somewhat complex. It is not the ability to do the arithmetic that distinguishes excellent managers and management accountants from the rest. What distinguishes them is their ability to a) understand what the financial data are telling them about how profitable they have been and b) make excellent decisions about how to improve in the future, often in a team setting. The goal of this text is to create these excellent management accountants.

A number of changes have been made throughout the text to help create excellent management accountants. One broad change was to ensure that relevance was introduced early in Chapter 2 and emphasized through the textbook, with corresponding problems provided to illustrate this key concept. Another broad change was to introduce new opportunities to make strategic decisions in almost every chapter, and to highlight existing strategic decision-making opportunities. A third broad change was to streamline and integrate the topical content of the text to achieve specific learning objectives rather than to present material topic by topic.

A significant and noticeable change was to apply a specific pedagogy similar to that used in the Certified Management Accountants' Competency Map Entrance Requirements. The CMA Competencies include strategic management, risk management and governance, performance management and measurement, financial resource management, and financial reporting. These are core functional competencies of the CMA profession and this text provides the content necessary to apply costing techniques appropriate to the management decision or task at hand. The CMA also emphasises the fundamental achievements of the profession: the goals of management. These are the enabling management competencies of problem solving and decision making, leadership and group dynamics, professionalism and ethical behaviour, and communication.

At the end of each Learning Objective in a chapter, the Assess Your Mastery box directs students to relevant Mastery Questions at the end of the chapter. There are three levels Mastery Questions—elementary, intermediate, and advanced. Elementary questions are procedural and include verbs such as identify, describe, and at a slightly higher CMA entrance level of skill, the verb explain. The CMA language of the more advanced level of skill consistently uses verbs such as evaluate, formulate, analyze, assess, distinguish, allocate, perform, prepare, calculate, compute, and interpret. This text splits this higher level of mastery into intermediate and advanced mastery questions. In essence, elementary questions are purely procedural, intermediate questions are analytical, and advanced questions are far more difficult procedurally, and require some judgment and interpretation. Since some Learning Objectives are very procedural, especially in early chapters, there may be a large number of procedural Mastery Questions. Instructors can suggest or assign more or fewer questions depending on the level of mastery they desire from their students. This text consistently applies the CMA language when both expressing and linking the Learning Objectives to the level of mastery required to complete the Mastery Questions.

Another significant broad change was to eliminate the "recipe" approach of some techniques (for example, Step 1, Step 2, and so on in developing the procedures in the job-costing process). Some students are very literal in their logic and in fact most of the techniques are not linear but reflexive—one step forward, then two steps back—and sometimes steps are simultaneous—one can't happen without another happening at the same time. Taking the step approach confused both the least and most mathematically adept students. Instead, a pie-chart graphic of these cognitive processes shows the decisions to be made and the challenges of the techniques, without making them too confusing or complex.

Another broad change was to reduce or eliminate detailed descriptions of arithmetic procedures and replace them with explanations of how to analyze the results of the arithmetic. This alone rebalances the content away from rather straightforward arithmetic procedures that are assisted handily by readily accessible spreadsheet programs.

For visual learners, and for pedagogical consistency, we have changed the colours in many exhibits to tie into the colours used in the value chain of business functions introduced in Chapter 1. For example, the Production function appears in blue in the value chain. In subsequent chapters, production-function items appear in blue in exhibits. The consistent use of colours gives students visual cues about how things fit in the "big picture"—the value chain— when they are introduced to new concepts.

These broad changes are reflected throughout this book. Specific chapter-by-chapter changes are described in the next section.

SELECTED CHAPTER-BY-CHAPTER CONTENT CHANGES IN THIS EDITION

Chapter 1: Management Accountants: Their Vital Role in Strategic and Operating Decisions

- ◆ The new chapter title highlights the distinct contribution of management accountants.
- ◆ Exhibit 1-2, The Value Chain of Business Functions and Costs, is introduced and provides a recurring framework throughout the all chapters of the text.

- The colours in Exhibit 1-2 have a pedagogical purpose and are repeated throughout subsequent chapters to indicate what business functions various costs are related to.
- New material about corporate social responsibility and environmental sustainability augments and draws a distinction from the material on corporate governance.

Chapter 2: An Introduction to Cost Terms and Purposes

- All the content is now oriented around a single cost object—the output unit—to focus on the idea that cost drivers cause costs. Material about different cost objects causing different costs to be classified as direct or indirect has been left for Chapter 4. Similarly, material about value-added activities has been left for Chapter 5.
- This chapter begins with a familiar accounting-function classification, then expands to management-accounting–classification systems. This is the first, but not the last, time the interdependence of financial and management accounting is emphasized. The chapter then presents the input from management accounting information systems that results in the Cost of Goods Sold line on the income statement in Exhibit 2-2.
- Exhibit 2-10 expands on the management accounting detail contained in the Cost of Goods Manufactured schedule and its contribution to the Cost of Goods Sold.
- The calculation and limitations to the use of average unit cost are introduced. This is the foundation for ongoing discussion of the unavoidable reduced quality of information based on simple averages.
- Learning Objective 5 asks students to apply management accounting logic to classify costs for use in managerial decisions. This "think like a management accountant" approach is encouraged from this early chapter onward. It requires students to exercise strategic thinking and critical thinking about the chapter content rather than to simply proceed through calculations.
- New exhibits use the financial-accounting approach of T-accounts with the management-accounting approach of flow charts to illustrate that raw materials, work-in-process, and finished goods inventories flow parallel with their respective costs.

Chapter 3: Cost-Volume-Profit Analysis

- The chapter begins with financial-accounting logic, then shows how management-accounting logic, classifications, and summaries of costs differ but generate relevant information for CVP analysis.
- The effect of the time horizon on the classification of costs is moved forward to the beginning of the chapter to explain cost-behaviour constraints.
- The decision-process pie chart (Exhibit 3-6) is introduced in the context of making choices about relevant costs, plans, and performance evaluation. This format highlights that procedures are meaningless without the cognitive process accompanying them. The double arrows emphasize the reflection required in decisions.
- Decision models and uncertainty, topics previously presented in an appendix, have been moved into the body of the chapter and revised to emphasize the benefits of quantitative modelling using probabilities to communicate ideas about various risks. Relevant cost problems have been added.

Chapter 4: Job Costing Services and Goods

- Wildfire-suppression cost data are presented in two ways to illustrate how the same data can lead people to opposite assessments of the relative costs and benefits of the service. The uncertainty introduced in Chapter 2 is augmented with the concept of ambiguity in the interpretation of cost information.
- A decision-process pie chart illustrates the point that no allocation process provides an accurate result—all results depend on the quality of the decisions

made prior to undertaking the calculations. This is applied to wildfire suppression services as well as a new manufacturing job-costing scenario.

◆ Another concept, planning, is introduced with the technique of normal costing in comparison with actual costing.

◆ The chapter concludes with a return to financial accounting methods to record allocated costs and adjustments for any difference between expected and actual costs.

◆ Together, the first four chapters of the text illustrate how interdependent the financial and management accounting processes actually are and distinguish the contributions made by each to the overall quality of financial information used in decision making.

Chapter 5: Activity-Based Costing and Activity-Based Management

◆ The chapter has a coffee theme, with a new chapter-opening Business Matters box and an extensive chapter-wide example centred on coffee production and ABC costing methods.

◆ The Problem for Self-Study touches on all five of the learning objectives and gives students another opportunity to review the technique of ABC in a service (supermarket) setting rather than a product setting.

Chapter 6: Master Budget and Responsibility Accounting

◆ The cash-budget material follows logically from preparing the master budget and its supporting schedules. This material has been moved into the body of the chapter as part of the development of the top line of the income statement—a forecast of revenue.

Chapter 7: Flexible Budgets, Variances, and Management Control: I

◆ All the analytical processes are now included in Learning Objective 2.

◆ The ABC application of variance analysis is included in Learning Objective 3 to clearly indicate the managerial importance of ABC methods of indirect cost allocation.

◆ The interpretive processes are now gathered in Learning Objective 4. Colour coding in the exhibits distinguish production cost variances from period cost variances symbolized as marketing costs.

◆ The decision pie chart introduces benchmarking. This expanded section adds a new application of benchmarking: an engineering study of environmental costs informs a strategic decision to choose paper cups or plastic cups (you may be surprised).

Chapter 8: Flexible Budgets, Variances, and Management Control: II

◆ The long-term variances arising from fixed cost commitments are presented again within the context of decisions made prior to calculating the variance.

◆ Material was reorganized so that variance calculations are immediately followed by their related journal entries, demonstrating again the interdependence of management accounting and financial accounting.

◆ Learning Objective 5 contains new material on nonfinancial performance measures, and introduces the concept of agility and the need to combine strategies of product differentiation and cost leadership. This leads to the idea that there can be problems if companies ignore what their customers really want.

Chapter 9: Income Effects of Denominator Level on Inventory Valuation

◆ The denominator-level discussion is now at the beginning of the chapter to put the easier concept first and improve the flow of the chapter. New art is added to illustrate this discussion.

◆ New material on the cognitive process of decision making in Exhibit 9-1 builds on the foundation laid in Chapter 3 on risk. The interdependence of one set of decisions underlying the implementation and application of a variance analysis to important strategic decisions such as pricing is introduced.

♦ The chapter concludes with an analysis of the effects of three costing methods on breakeven points.

Chapter 10: Quantitative Analyses of Cost Functions

♦ The new chapter title reflects that regression analysis tools are a focus of the chapter and a key way to determine the factors that can explain changes in costs. The chapter applies a standard statistical tool to resolve a standard management accounting issue: What is the best choice of cost driver?

♦ Concepts are described so that students can focus on interpreting the results of regression analysis. This is consistent with the approach in previous chapters to set either the quantitative techniques or the arithmetic procedures in a cognitive context.

♦ New assignment material requires students to interpret the results of data produced by Excel's OLS regression analysis feature. Other less-technical methods, along with their limitations, are also presented.

♦ The chapter content presents progressively more complex material, such as discontinuous linear cost functions and curvilinear cost functions, in a sequence permitting instructors to select only the material they believe best suits the needs of their students.

Chapter 11: Decision Making and Relevant Information

♦ Material has been streamlined, with the decision pie chart motivating most of the presentation of content in this chapter. The concepts of uncertainty introduced in Chapter 3 and expanded upon in Chapter 9 are now given a Bayesian context to emphasize the importance of accurate and timely information.

♦ The recursive nature of decisions is emphasized in Exhibit 11-2, which visually presents a limited series of interdependencies among various value-chain business functions.

♦ Linear programming as a technique to readily respond to decision-making needs has been placed within the body of the chapter to encourage a progression to more mathematically rigorous analysis.

Chapter 12: Pricing Decisions, Product Profitability Decisions, and Cost Management

♦ A pricing question is placed within a broader context of corporate social responsibility. It starkly compares the goal of maximizing profit to the goal of saving lives and the practical reconciliation of these two goals.

♦ Reclamation and pollution costs as well as government demands for companies to fully remediate environmental damage illustrate the importance and relevance of non-quantitative factors.

♦ The chapter concludes with an illustration of how performance measures of corporate social responsibility have been developed by Dow Chemical Company. These are compared to international corporate governance measures.

Chapter 13: Strategy, Balanced Scorecard, and Strategic Profitability Analysis

♦ The balanced scorecard is introduced earlier, with Exhibit 13-1 emphasizing the interconnected rather than disconnected nature of nonfinancial and financial performance measures.

♦ The importance of internal control and use of the balanced scorecard in enterprise risk management are applied to supply-chain strategy, along with a quantitative example to illustrate what motivates a move to the supply-chain strategy to manage costs of resource acquisition. Exhibit 13-3 illustrates how balanced scorecard information will influence the decisions made by one key element of the internal control and governance structure of any company—the Board of Directors.

◆ An example of the triple-bottom-line measure of economic, environmental, and social achievement—a different application of a balanced scorecard—is illustrated using the Dow Jones Sustainability Index.

Chapter 14: Cost Allocation

◆ New colours in the illustrations remind students that indirect period costs are only part of the total costs.

◆ New material on methods of justification of choices has been added to emphasize the importance of making reasonable and feasible decisions.

◆ New material shows how Excel and matrix algebra can be used for reciprocal allocation of support department costs. Two new Problems illustrate how important this technique is to more complex costing. The three strategic choices of cost-allocation methods and their effects on product costing are quantified and discussed.

Chapter 15: Cost Allocation: Joint Products and Byproducts

◆ The chapter now begins with the "why" of joint costing, which was previously found later in the chapter.

Chapter 16: Revenues, Sales Variances, and Customer Profitability Analysis

◆ New material on how government allocates charitable gambling revenue to Aboriginal peoples in Alberta extends the importance of revenue allocation beyond the strategic and operating goals of for-profit companies.

◆ Strategic implications of the techniques of revenue allocation are presented first in a for-profit, then in a not-for-profit context.

◆ New governance material emphasizes the most recent changes in governance legislation.

◆ The chapter concludes with another strategy, the assessment of customer profitability rather than customer cost, as a method to improve the effectiveness of corporate activity.

◆ There are three parts to this chapter accompanied by three Problems for Self-Study to comprehensively review the learning objectives.

Chapter 17: Process Costing

◆ Instructors may choose to place this material very early in the course. The revised presentation emphasizes the simplicity of cost assignment when there is only one indirect cost pool, one cost-allocation base (equivalent units) and one cost object.

◆ New material connects the results of cost allocation in a government-regulated context (milk processing) to the presentation of financial results in the cost of goods manufactured.

◆ The chapter concludes with a discussion of the flow of financial costs that previously appeared in the chapter appendix.

Chapter 18: Spoilage, Rework, and Scrap

◆ Material on inspection and spoilage at intermediate stages of completion now appears in Learning Objective 3, rather than in an appendix.

◆ The Problem for Self-Study is a comprehensive review of process costing.

Chapter 20: Supply-Chain Strategies: JIT, MRP, and Backflush Costing

◆ Learning Objective 1 now introduces the EOQ decision model and applies it to JIT in retailing and manufacturing.

◆ All backflush costing material is now in Learning Objective 5.

Chapter 21: Capital Budgeting: Methods of Investment Analysis

◆ Material was added to Learning Objective 1 to review the difference between income and cash flow, and there is new material on the capital-budgeting decision.

Chapter 22: Capital Budgeting: A Closer Look

◆ Material on CCA classes and rates now appears in Learning Objective 1, rather than in an appendix.

◆ A new Governance box outlines Canada Revenue Agency's authority to undertake criminal and civil proceedings and the results of its Special Enforcements Program.

Chapter 23: Management Control Systems, Transfer Pricing, and Multinational Considerations

◆ Learning Objective 1 now focuses on Canadian legislation and includes a CoCo exhibit and a new Governance box.

◆ The chapter-wide example has been revised.

Chapter 24: Performance Measurement, Compensation, and Multinational Considerations

◆ Steps for designing an accounting-based performance measure are now represented in a pie diagram to emphasize the nonlinearity of the key decisions.

◆ New governance material addresses earnings management and professional codes of conduct.

ASSIGNMENT MATERIAL

The fifth edition tightly links new chapter content to assignment material, a precedent set in previous editions. Assignment material presents increasing levels of difficulty from less difficult questions and exercises to more difficult problems and collaborative learning cases. Short-Answer Questions test how well students understand key terms and content, while Exercises are short, structured calculations to test the development of basic skills. Problems present students with more difficult challenges to develop their ability to assess alternatives and make the most appropriate choice among techniques of estimation. The Collaborative Learning Cases ending each chapter's assignment material require students to gather information and critically reflect on a specific issue or situation. Each chapter's assignment material also contains a relevant question related to either governance, social responsibility, or both. Check figures have now been provided for most Exercises and Problems, as appropriate, and the Learning Objectives addressed by each Exercise and Problem are indicated in the margin beside the question.

TEACHING AND LEARNING SUPPORT

MyAccountingLab. See the inside front cover to learn more about MyAccountingLab. **MyAccountingLab**

Supplements available to students include the following:

◆ *Student Solutions Manual:* (0-13-611021-5) Designed to enable students to monitor their progress, this supplement contains fully worked-out solutions for all of the even-numbered questions, exercises, and problems in the textbook. This supplement may be purchased with the instructor's permission.

Supplements available to instructors include the following:

◆ *Instructor's Resource CD-ROM:* (0-13-815249-7) This CD-ROM contains the Instructor's Solutions Manual and Instructor's Resource Manual in Word and PDF formats, Pearson TestGen software, and PowerPoint Lecture Slides. This makes it extremely easy for faculty to customize supplements, access supplements on a computer, and transport a large supplement package from home, to class, to office.

- *Instructor's Solutions Manual:* In addition to fully worked-out solutions for every question, exercise, and problem in the text, the Instructor's Solutions Manual also provides suggested alternative chapter sequences and categorization of assignment material. The solutions are available in both PDF and Word formats

- *Instructor's Resource Manual:* This resource manual provides a chapter overview, outline, additional examples, alternative means of presenting topics, chapter quiz/demonstration exercises with solutions, and suggested readings. For Chapter 18, additional questions and solutions are provided that take some topics beyond the coverage in the text. The IRM is available in both PDF and Word formats.

- *Pearson TestGen:* The TestGen test bank for *Cost Accounting* offers a comprehensive suite of tools for testing and assessment. TestGen allows educators to easily create and distribute tests for their courses, either by printing and distributing through traditional methods or by online delivery via a Local Area Network (LAN) server. The more than 2,200 items are linked to the Learning Objectives; ranked in difficulty as elementary, intermediate, or advanced; and identified as either an application, comprehension, or knowledge question type. This supplement is also available for instructors from the Pearson Canada online catalogue (http://vig.pearsoned.ca).

- *PowerPoint Lecture Slides:* At least 25 slides have been prepared in PowerPoint for each chapter of the text. The interactive presentation offers helpful graphics that illustrate key figures and concepts from the text, chapter outlines, and additional examples. This supplement is also available for instructors from the Pearson Canada online catalogue (http://vig.pearsoned.ca).

- *Technology Specialists:* Pearson's Technology Specialists work with faculty and campus course designers to ensure that Pearson technology products, assessment tools, and online course materials are tailored to meet your specific needs. This highly qualified team is dedicated to helping schools take full advantage of a wide range of educational resources by assisting in the integration of a variety of instructional materials and media formats. Your local Pearson Education sales representative can provide you with more details on this service program.

- *CourseSmart:* CourseSmart is a new way for instructors and students to access textbooks online anytime from anywhere. With thousands of titles across hundreds of courses, CourseSmart helps instructors choose the best textbook for their class and give their students a new option for buying the assigned textbook as a lower cost eTextbook. For more information, visit www.coursesmart.com.

ACKNOWLEDGMENTS

I would like to acknowledge the excellent assistance I have received from many people. This fifth Canadian edition is based upon the twelfth US edition by Charles Horngren, George Foster, and Srikant M. Datar. I thank them for their willingness to share their work with me. Their knowledge and experience have significantly contributed to this book. I also acknowledge David Gowing, who revised the presentation of material in Chapter 10 and the added matrix algebra case material and solutions in Chapter 14. Mr. Thomas Haddrath has provided ongoing informal support for this text as he applied his tax expertise to hone the accuracy of the materials in Chapters 22 and 23.

The following valued team members developed some excellent end-of-chapter assignment material and solutions:

Lawrence Tenenbaum, McGill University	Chapters 6–10, 14–20, 22
Judith Watson, Capilano College	Chapters 3–5, 11–13
Marcela Porporato, York University	Chapters 21, 23, 24
Anita Smale, C.A.	Chapters 1, 2

I also extend my sincere appreciation to my colleagues at Pearson Education Canada. This textbook would not be produced without their expertise, patience, and diligence. Thank you—Carolin Sweig, Acquisitions Editor; Anita Smale, Developmental Editor; and Laura Neves and Cheryl Jackson, Production Editors. Thanks also to Anita Smale, Laura Neves, and Susan Bindernagel for their copy-editing expertise, and Kelli Howey and Nancy Mucklow, the proofreaders. And a special thanks to Ross Meacher and Ian Farmer for their careful technical reviews. Both individually and collectively, your input has greatly improved the accuracy, content, and flow of this text. My thanks go as well to Bill Todd for his unfailing ability to find appropriate sources for me as I developed the new material in this revision.

I am grateful to the Odette School of Business at the University of Windsor for providing an environment that supports the development of teaching materials.

My appreciation goes as well to the Certified Management Accountants Association of Canada and, in particular, to Deborah Clarke, the Southwestern Ontario Regional Director of Marketing and Communication. I express my appreciation as well to the Certified General Accountants Association of Canada and many other individuals, publishers, and companies for their generous permission to quote from their publications. Problems from the Certified Management Accountant examination are designated (CMA); problems from the Certified General Accountants Association examination are designated (CGA). These problems have been adapted to highlight specific points. I am also grateful to professors and individuals in the industry who contributed both chapter content and assignment material for this edition. I thank the reviewers and other contributors to this project for their patient, timely, and meticulous reviews that provided me with valuable insights and suggestions, especially:

Hilary Becker, Carleton University

Brent Bertrand, University of Toronto

Donald Drury, McGill University

Susan Ferris, CGA-Canada

Clinton Free, Queen's University

Barbara Katz, Kwantlen University College

Richard Lowe, Durham College

Elin Maher, University of New Brunswick

Winston Marcellin, George Brown College

Jaime Morales, Trent University

Debbie Musil, Kwantlen University College

Andrews Oppong, Dalhousie University

Marcela Porporato, York University

Jeffrey Power, Saint Mary's University

Randy Robinson, British Columbia Institute of Technology

David Scallen, Wilfred Laurier University

Harry Soltermann, Northern Alberta Institute of Technology

Lawrence Tenenbaum, McGill University

Judith Watson, Capilano College

Most importantly, I would like to recognize a wonderful champion of this text and, more importantly, a friend whom I still keenly miss, Samantha Scully. The friendship and tireless, consummate professional support Sam provided with gentle humour and generosity of spirit cannot be replaced. I dedicate this text in her memory.

Comments are most welcome.

Maureen P. Gowing

ABOUT THE AUTHORS

CHARLES T. HORNGREN is the Edmund W. Littlefield Professor of Accounting, Emeritus, at Stanford University. A Graduate of Marquette University, he received his MBA from Harvard University and his Ph.D. from the University of Chicago. He is also the recipient of honorary doctorates from Marquette University and DePaul University.

A Certified Public Accountant, Horngren served on the Accounting Principles Board for six years, the Financial Accounting Standards Board Advisory Council for five years, and the Council of the American Institute of Certified Public Accountants for three years. For six years, he served as a trustee of the Financial Accounting Foundation, which oversees the Financial Accounting Standards Board and the Government Accounting Standards Board.

Horngren is a member of the Accounting Hall of Fame.

A member of the American Accounting Association, he has been its President and its Director of Research. He received its first annual Outstanding Accounting Educator Award.

The California Certified Public Accounts Foundation gave Horngren its Faculty Excellence Award and its Distinguished Professor Award. He is the first person to have received both awards.

The American Institute of Certified Public Accountants presented its first Outstanding Educator Award to Horngren.

Horngren was named Accountant of the Year, Education, by the national professional accounting fraternity, Beta Alpha Psi.

Professor Horngren is also a member of the Institute of Management Accountants, from whom he received its Distinguished Service Award. He was also a member of the Institutes' Board of Regents, which administers the Certified Management Accountant examinations.

Horngren is the author of other accounting books published by Prentice Hall: Introduction to Management Accounting, 13th ed. (2005, with Sundem and Stratton); Introduction to Financial Accounting, 9th ed. (2005, with Sundem and Elliott); Accounting, 6th ed. (2005, with Harrison and Bamber); and Financial Accounting, 6th ed. (2005, with Harrison).

Horngren is the Consulting Editor for the Charles T. Horngren Series in Accounting.

GEORGE FOSTER is the Paul L. and Phyllis Wattis Professor of Management at Stanford University. He graduated with a university medal from the University of Sydney and has a Ph.D. from Stanford University. He has been awarded honorary doctorates from the University of Ghent, Belgium, and from the University of Vaasa, Finland. He has received the Outstanding Educator Award from the American Accounting Association.

Foster has received the Distinguished Teaching Award at Stanford University and the Faculty Excellence Award from the California Society of Certified Public Accountants. He has been a Visiting Professor to Mexico for the American Accounting Association.

Research awards Foster has received include the Competitive Manuscript Competition Award of the American Accounting Association, the Notable Contribution to Accounting Literature Award of the American Institute of Certified

Public Accountants, and the Citation for Meritorious Contribution to Accounting Literature Award of the Australian Society of Accountants.

He is the author of Financial Statement Analysis, published by Prentice Hall. He is co-author of Activity-Based Management Consortium Study (APQC and CAM-I) and Marketing, Cost Management and Management Accounting (CAM-I). He is also co-author of two monographs published by the American Accounting Association: Security Analyst Multi-Year Earnings Forecasts and The Capital Market and Market Microstructure and Capital Market Information Content Research. Journals publishing his articles include Abacus, The Accounting Review, Harvard Business Review, Journal of Accounting and Economics, Journal of Accounting Research, Journal of Cost Management, Journal of Management Accounting Research, Management Accounting, and Review of Accounting Studies.

Foster works actively with many companies, including Apple Computer, ARCO, BIIP, Digital Equipment Corp., Exxon, Frito-Lay Corp., Hewlett-Packard, McDonalds Corp., Octel Communications, PepsiCo, Santa Fe Corp., and Wells Fargo. He also has worked closely with Computer Aided Manufacturing-International (CAM-I) in the development of a framework for modern cost-management practices. Foster has presented seminars on new developments in cost accounting in North and South America, Asia, Australia, and Europe.

SRIKANT M. DATAR is the Arthur Lowes Dickinson Professor of Business Administration and Senior Associate Dean at Harvard University. A graduate with distinction from the University of Bombay, he received gold medals upon graduation from the Indian Institute of Management, Ahmedabad, and the Institute of Cost and Works Accountants of India. A Chartered Accountant, he holds two masters degrees and a Ph.D. from Stanford University.

Cited by his students as a dedicated and innovative teacher, Datar received the George Leland Bach Award for Excellence in the Classroom at Carnegie Mellon University and the Distinguished Teaching Award at Stanford University.

Datar has published his research in leading accounting, marketing, and operations management journals, including The Accounting Review, Contemporary Accounting Research, Journal of Accounting, Auditing and Finance, Journal of Accounting and Economics, Journal of Accounting Research, and Management Science. He has also served on the editorial board of several journals and presented his research to corporate executives and academic audiences in North America, South America, Asia, Africa, Australia, and Europe.

Datar is a member of the Board of Directors of Novartis A. G., ICF International, and KPIT Cummins Infosystems Ltd., and has worked with many organizations, including Apple Computer, AT&T, Boeing, Du Pont, Ford, General Motors, Hewlett-Packard, Kodak, Morgan Stanley, PepsiCo, Stryker, TRW, Visa, and the World Bank. He is a member of the American Accounting Association and the Institute of Management Accountants.

MAUREEN P. GOWING is an Assistant Professor in the Odette School of Business at the University of Windsor. Prior to being appointed at Odette, she worked as an assistant professor at the John Molson School of Business at Concordia University. She received her BA (psychology) from Carleton University, her MBA from the University of Toronto, and her Ph.D. from Queen's University. Dr. Gowing received the Award of Excellence from the Administrative Sciences Association of Canada for her doctoral dissertation.

She has co-authored many journal articles and published in the Journal of Business Ethics and the Canadian Journal of Higher Education, among others. In addition to co-authoring, with Charles Horngren, George Foster, Srikant Datar, and Howard Teal, Cost Accounting: A Managerial Emphasis, Fourth Canadian Edition, Dr. Gowing has also co-authored an introductory financial accounting textbook with Dr. George Kanaan.

Dr. Gowing obtained both her BA and MBA while working full time. She has worked as a financial analyst with an upstream oil exploration and development company that was controlled by Noranda, and a boutique Canadian investment banker, Pemberton Securities Ltd., now part of the Royal Bank. Her research portfolio of companies newly listed on the Toronto Stock Exchange included Westar, Ballard Technologies, and QLT Pharmaceuticals. She has also consulted for Discovery Foundation of British Columbia, and just prior to her return to university to obtain her Ph.D, she did forensic analysis for the Vancouver Stock Exchange.

Management Accountants: Their Vital Role in Strategic and Operating Decisions

1

GOOD MANAGEMENT IN HARD TIMES

Companies such as Research In Motion (RIM), at the forefront with versatile, secure communications technology products such as the BlackBerry Bold, face difficult economic times. Until October 2008, most consumers could readily use credit cards to purchase wireless communications devices. But across the globe, people began to worry whether or not credit-card companies would demand immediate payment of their balances, and their demand for consumer products decreased. Widespread uncertainty affects demand for consumer products manufactured and sold by companies such as RIM.

Management accountants play a key role as providers of readily understandable information necessary for companies such as RIM to adjust their long-term strategies and their short-term operations to cope today with tomorrow's demands.

After studying this chapter, you should be able to

1. Describe how cost accounting supports financial, management, and strategic decisions

2. Explain how the value-chain concept relates to the dimensions of performance customers expect

3. Identify differences between the planning and control decisions of managers, and the different roles of relevant accounting information

4. Describe three guidelines management accountants follow in supporting managers, and describe the profession's role in an organization

5. Explain how professional accounting codes of ethics relate to corporate governance

Chapter 1 describes the role of management accountants in the process of management decision making. Modern management accounting serves business managers who require relevant information to make good decisions that result in growth and success for their companies. This book focuses on the challenges of producing timely, relevant financial and nonfinancial information to assist managers as they make a wide variety of business decisions. These decisions are most difficult when little is known with certainty about future consequences. Members of the profession of management accounting can apply a wide variety of techniques to quantitatively clarify the nature of problems and the scope of most likely remedial actions.

COST ACCOUNTING, FINANCIAL ACCOUNTING, AND MANAGEMENT ACCOUNTING

1 Describe how cost accounting supports financial, management, and strategic decisions

This section explains the relationship among cost accounting, financial accounting, and management accounting. Large domestic and multinational companies in Canada such as GlaxoSmithKline Inc., Rogers Communications Inc., Hewlett Packard (Canada) Co., and Kraft Canada Inc. employ senior executives who are professional Certified Management Accountants (CMAs). Some apply techniques to cost products, services, processes, and customers. Managers who understand the techniques, especially their limitations, can use this information to improve their decisions.

Accounting systems take economic events and business transactions that have occurred and process these data into information helpful to users such as sales representatives, production supervisors, and senior managers. Processing any economic transaction entails collecting, categorizing, summarizing, and analyzing data for a specified time period. For example, costs are collected by cost categories (materials, labour, and shipping); summarized to determine total costs by month, quarter, or one year; and analyzed to evaluate how costs have changed relative to revenues, say, from one period to the next.

Accounting systems provide information such as financial statements (the income statement, balance sheet, and statement of cash flows) and performance reports (such as the cost of operating a plant or providing a service). Managers use financial and cost accounting information to:

1. Administer each of the activity or functional areas for which they are responsible, and
2. Coordinate those activities or functions within the framework of the organization as a whole.

This book focuses on the management accountant's role in these tasks.

Managers often require the information from an accounting system to be presented or reported differently because the decisions they must make vary. Consider, for example, sales order information. A sales manager needs the total dollar amount of sales to determine the commissions to be paid. A distribution manager needs the sales order quantities by geographic region and customer-requested delivery dates to ensure timely deliveries. A manufacturing manager needs the quantities of various products and their desired delivery dates to schedule production.

An ideal management information system (MIS) comprises databases—sometimes called data warehouses or infobarns—consisting of detailed bits of information that can be used for multiple purposes. For example, the sales order database will contain detailed information about the product, quantity ordered, selling price, and delivery (place and date) for each sales order. The data warehouse stores information in a way that allows managers to access exactly what they need. Many companies build their own Enterprise Resource Planning (ERP) systems, single databases to collect data and feed it into applications that support each business activity, such as purchasing, production, distribution, sales, and customer service.

Cost accounting measures and reports financial and nonfinancial information, which relates to the cost of either acquiring or utilizing resources in an organization.

For example, financial accountants must conform with generally accepted accounting principles (GAAP) when they report the cost of goods sold (COGS) on an income statement. Cost accountants apply various techniques to provide reliable estimates of the cost of a product: those not yet complete, those completed but not yet sold, and those both completed and sold. Financial accountants need this information not only to produce GAAP-compliant income statements, but also for inventory valuation on the balance sheet.

Financial accounting focuses on reporting to external parties in a standardized format. Members of the financial accounting profession apply their expertise in accounting standards to record business transactions and report aggregate results to external readers in a GAAP-compliant format.

Managers are responsible for issuing financial statements that are free from material misstatement to investors, government regulators, and other parties outside the organization. Executive compensation is often directly affected by the net income reported in these financial statements. It is easy to see that managers are interested in both management accounting and financial accounting. Exhibit 1-1 summarizes the major differences between management accounting and financial accounting.

Management accounting focuses on reporting to internal parties. Members of the management accounting profession have expertise in both cost and financial accounting practices. They measure and report financial and nonfinancial information in a customized format that is most useful for managers when making decisions. In some, but by no means all, cases this will be the standard financial-reporting format. Managers use this information to plan, choose, communicate, and implement strategy. They also use management accounting information to both monitor actual performance and coordinate interdependent product design, production, and marketing decisions to improve profit and achieve strategic goals.

Unfortunately the term **cost management** has no uniform definition. We use cost management to describe the approaches and activities of managers who undertake both short-run and long-run planning and control decisions intended to lower the costs of products and services, and increase value for customers. Examples include decisions regarding the amounts and kinds of materials being used, changes in plant processes, and changes in product designs. Information from accounting

EXHIBIT 1-1

Major Differences Between Management Accounting and Financial Accounting

	Management Accounting	**Financial Accounting**
Purpose of information	Help managers make decisions to fulfill an organization's goals	Communicate organization's financial position to investors, banks, regulators, and other outside parties
Primary users	Managers of the organization	External users such as investors, banks, regulators, and suppliers
Focus and emphasis	Future-oriented (budget for 2011 prepared in 2010)	Past-oriented (reports on 2010 performance prepared in 2011)
Rules of measurement and reporting	Internal measures and reports do not have to follow GAAP but are based on cost-benefit analysis	Financial statements must be prepared in accordance with GAAP and be certified by external, independent auditors
Time span and type of reports	Varies from hourly information to 15 to 20 years, with financial and nonfinancial reports on products, departments, territories, and strategies	Annual and quarterly financial reports, primarily on the company as a whole, and presented as consolidated financial statements
Behavioural implications	Designed to influence the behaviour of managers and other employees	Primarily reports economic events but also influences behaviour because manager's compensation is often based on reported financial results

systems helps managers to manage costs, but the information and the accounting systems themselves are not cost management.

Cost management has a broad focus. It includes, but is not confined to, the continuous reduction of costs because the planning and control of costs is usually inextricably linked with revenue and profit planning. For example, to increase revenues and profits, managers can decide to increase costs for advertising and product modifications. Other examples include programs that enhance customer satisfaction and quality, as well as programs that promote "blockbuster" new-product development. The examples illustrate that cost management is not practised in isolation. It is an integral part of general management strategies and their implementation.

STRATEGIC DECISIONS

A company earns profit by attracting customers willing to pay more for the goods and services it offers than the costs to design and deliver them. A company succeeds by both creating value for customers and differentiating itself from its competitors. This is what strategy is all about. But a great strategy can be defeated by ineffective implementation. Management accountants provide input to aid in both developing and implementing strategy, as well as building resources and capabilities. To understand the management accountant's role, we must first understand the manager's tasks.

Strategy "is . . . a way of thinking that relies on hypothesis generation and testing. In hypothesizing, you ask the creative 'what if' questions. To test your hypothesis, you ask the analytic 'if . . . , then . . .' questions. You adopt a mindset that treats your method of accomplishing your purpose as an experiment. If that experiment fails, you try something else. . . . It is intelligently opportunistic in search of its goals . . . while leaving room for new and unintended strategies to emerge."[1] Formally, strategy:

- Specifies how an organization accomplishes its objectives by matching its own capabilities with the predicted opportunities in the marketplace.
- Describes how a company will compete, and the opportunities its employees should seek and pursue.

Companies follow one of two broad strategies. Some companies, such as WestJet and Costco, compete on the basis of providing quality products or services at low prices. Others, such as Research In Motion (developer of the BlackBerry) and Genetech (a biopharmaceutical company), compete on their ability to offer unique, new, or higher–value-added products or services that are priced higher than the older products or services of competitors.

Deciding between these strategies is a big part of what managers do. Management accountants work closely with managers in formulating strategy by providing information about the sources of competitive advantage. Examples include information about cost, productivity, or efficiency advantages of their company relative to competitors, and the premium prices a company can charge relative to the costs of adding features that make its products or services distinctive. Management accountants also help formulate a strategy by answering questions such as:

- Who are our most important customers, and how do we deliver value to them to retain their loyalty (CRM, or customer-relationship management)? How sensitive are their purchases to price, quality, and service?
- Who are our most important suppliers, and how do we ensure timely access to appropriate quality and cost (SCM, or supply-chain management)?
- What substitute products exist in the marketplace, and how do they differ from our product in terms of price and quality?

[1]Jeanne Leidtka, "Everything I Need to Know about Strategy I Learned at the National Zoo," *The Journal of Business Strategy*, 18.1 (January/February 1997): 8–11.

- What is our most critical resource—technology, production, or marketing? What demands will be made on this critical resource by the new strategic initiatives?
- Will adequate cash be available to fund the strategy, or will additional funds need to be raised?

Strategic management often describes cost management that focuses on strategic issues such as these. Successful companies design strategies to respond to the opportunities and threats in the marketplace with appropriate resources and capabilities. Sometimes companies see opportunities and threats that require them to build capabilities. For example, after Amazon.com's success in selling books online, Indigo Books & Music Inc. also developed capabilities to sell online through its Chapters.Indigo.ca website.

At other times, companies use their existing capabilities to create new opportunities. For example, in Toyota's computer-integrated manufacturing (CIM) plants, computers instruct robotic equipment to set up and complete tasks. Manufacturing labour in CIM plants is largely computer programming, engineering support, and machine maintenance. CIM technology enables plants to quickly make major design modifications, such as switching from manufacturing a two-door to a four-door car. In CIM plants, computers also monitor and directly control the manufacturing process to achieve high-quality output. Continuous monitoring and control enables reports of real-time information about process parameters (such as temperature and pressure), units produced, defects, and product costs. The best-designed strategies and the best-developed capabilities are useless, however, unless they are effectively executed.

ASSESS YOUR MASTERY

To check your understanding of the material in Learning Objective ❶, go to the *Mastery Questions* section at the end of this chapter and complete Learning Objective ❶ questions 1, 2, and 3.

MyAccountingLab

THE VALUE CHAIN OF BUSINESS FUNCTIONS LEADS TO THE CUSTOMER

Explain how the value-chain concept relates to the dimensions of performance customers expect ❷

Managers implement strategy by translating it into action. As they build action plans, managers seek input from customers, and evaluate and assess how competitors will react. They answer questions such as:

- Are the right executives in place to execute the plans?
- Do the executives have the necessary cash and human and physical resources to implement the plans?
- Should the company sell more products to existing customers or find new customers?
- What can go wrong?
- What contingency plans does the company have if things do go wrong?

Questions such as these must be freely debated if managers are to create a good strategic plan and implement it effectively to create value for customers. **Value** is the usefulness a customer gains from a company's product or service. We now discuss how a company goes about creating this value.

VALUE-CHAIN AND ANALYSIS

Value chain refers to the sequence of business functions in which customer usefulness is added to products or services. Exhibit 1-2 shows six business functions: research and development (R&D), design, production, marketing, distribution, and customer service. We illustrate these business functions using Sony Corporation's television division. For each business function, adding value also generates costs,

EXHIBIT 1-2
The Value Chain of Business Functions and Costs

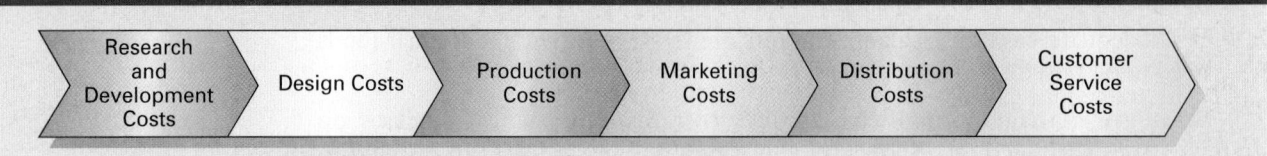

which must be recovered from the revenue arising when the finished goods are sold to the customer. Management accountants provide both cost and revenue information managers need to make decisions in each of these six business functions:

◆ **Research and development (R&D)**—Generating and experimenting with ideas related to new products, services, or processes. At Sony, this function includes research on alternative signal transmission technologies (analoge, digital, high-definition), on the clarity of different shapes and thicknesses of television screens, and on portability.

◆ **Design of products, services, or processes**—Detailed planning and engineering of products, services, or processes. Design at Sony includes determining the number of component parts in a television set, and the effect of alternative product designs on quality and manufacturing costs.

◆ **Production**—Acquiring, coordinating, and assembling resources to produce a product or deliver a service. Production of a Sony television set includes the acquisition and assembly of the electronic parts, the cabinet, and the packaging used for shipping.

◆ **Marketing**—Promoting and selling products or services to customers or prospective customers. Sony markets its televisions through trade shows, advertisements in newspapers and magazines, and on the Internet.

◆ **Distribution**—Delivering products or services to customers. Distribution for Sony includes shipping to retail outlets, catalogue vendors, direct sales via the Internet, and other channels through which customers purchase televisions.

◆ **Customer service**—Providing after-sale support to customers. Sony provides customer service on its televisions in the form of customer-help telephone lines, support on the Internet, and warranty repair work.

Examples of some of Sony's value-chain costs are shown in Exhibit 1-3.

Each function in the value chain sequence is essential if Sony is to satisfy its customers and keep them satisfied (and loyal) over time. Customer relationship

EXHIBIT 1-3
Value Chain for Sony Business Functions and Costs

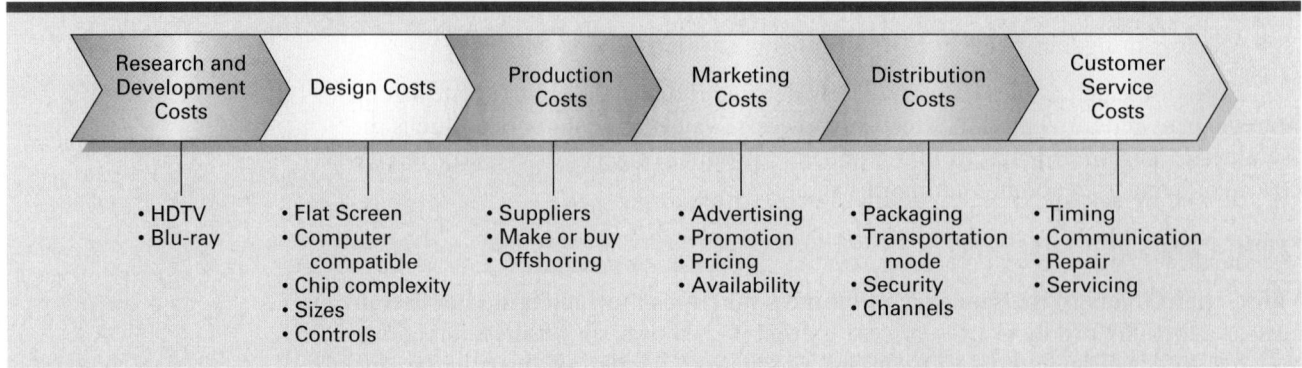

management (CRM) describes a strategy that integrates people and technology in all business functions to enhance relationships with customers, partners, and distributors. CRM initiatives use technology to coordinate the research, design, and production activities necessary to put the product or service in the customers' hands, as well as all customer-facing activities (marketing, sales calls, distribution, and customer support).

Exhibit 1-2 depicts different business-function activities as if they occur in a linear sequence, but this is not the case. It would be inefficient and ineffective if managers always planned and managed activities by proceeding step-by-step through the value chain. Companies accelerate the development of new products if two or more individuals from different business functions of the value chain work concurrently as a team. For example, when production, marketing, distribution, and customer service managers discuss product design together, they have the opportunity to make design choices that reduce total costs to the company instead of to only one business function.

The colours in the value chain of business functions are used consistently throughout the text. For example, in Chapter 2, which focuses on the various components of cost of goods sold (production costs), most of the exhibits will have the same blue as the Production segment in Exhibits 1-2 and 1-3.

SUPPLY-CHAIN MANAGEMENT (SCM)

Companies can also implement strategy, cut costs, and create value by improving the management of their **supply chain**.

The supply chain describes the flow of goods, services, and information from the initial sources of materials and services to the delivery of products to consumers, regardless of whether those activities occur in the same organization or in other organizations. Consider companies such as RIM and Motorola. Many companies from around the world produce and ship materials and supplies to be assembled in the manufacturing facilities of RIM and Motorola. Other companies ensure cost-efficient and effective distribution of RIM's and Motorola's finished products, while still others provide advertising and promotion services. **Supply-chain management (SCM)** emphasizes integrating and coordinating activities across all companies in the supply chain, as well as across each business function in an individual company's value chain, to reduce costs and improve reliability. For example, both RIM and Motorola will obtain computer chips from their suppliers in small quantities, just in time to deliver to the production process to ensure continuous production is not interrupted. This reduces handling and inventory storage costs. To reduce inventory levels in their supply chains, companies such as Rogers Communications, which supplies wireless services, ask RIM and Motorola to manage delivery of finished products, such as the BlackBerry Bold and the Motorola RAZR, to outlets just in time for sale.

KEY SUCCESS FACTORS

Customers are demanding that companies use the value chain and supply chain to deliver ever-improving levels of performance regarding several (or even all) of the following:

◆ **Cost and efficiency**—Companies face continuous pressure to reduce the cost of the products or services they sell. Understanding the tasks or activities (such as setting up machines or distributing products) that cause costs is useful for calculating and managing the cost of products.

To set cost-reduction targets, managers start by scanning the market to discover prices that customers are willing to pay for products or services. From this "target price," managers subtract the operating income they want to earn to arrive at the target cost. Managers strive to achieve the target cost by eliminating some activities (such as rework) and by reducing the costs of performing activities (Chapter 12). They do so across all value-chain functions and over the entire life cycle of the product—from its initial R&D to customer support including products that are no longer offered. North American companies now outsource not only their manufacturing labour but also customer service, technical support, and software development to countries such as Taiwan, Mexico, and India.

◆ **Quality**—Customers expect high levels of quality management. Total quality management (TQM) is a management process undertaken to improve operations throughout the value chain to produce and deliver products and services that exceed customers' expectations with zero or minimal defects and waste.

Outsourcing production and service support to other countries and the accelerating pace of international trade agreements have led to the increasing importance of consistent quality and safety standards. The International Organization for Standardization (ISO) develops not only technical but also environmental and social standards. Companies worldwide can become accredited as ISO compliant to show their customers and suppliers that the company meets global standards of quality. Management accountants evaluate the costs and revenue benefits of TQM initiatives, including ISO compliance.

◆ **Time**—Time has many components. *New-product development time* is the time to develop and bring new products to market. The increasing pace of technological innovation has led to shorter product life cycles and the need for companies to bring new products to market more rapidly.

Customer-response time describes the speed at which an organization responds to customer requests. To increase customer satisfaction, organizations must complete activities faster and meet promised delivery dates reliably. Delays or bottlenecks occur when the work to be performed exceeds the available capacity. To increase output, managers need to increase the capacity of the bottleneck operation. The management accountant's role is to quantify the cost and benefits of relieving the bottleneck constraints.

◆ **Innovation**—A constant flow of innovative products or services is the basis for ongoing company success. Management accountants help managers evaluate alternative investment decisions and R&D decisions.

Management accountants help managers track performance of key success factors relative to the performance of competitors. Tracking improvements that competitors are making, and implementing those that are appropriate, lead to continuous improvement in the key business functions of the value chain. The best practice in industry is the benchmark. Benchmarking is the process of measuring the company's performance on key success factors against the best levels of performance found in competing companies. These key factors differ across industries. For example, WestJet seeks improvement in the percentage of flights arriving and departing on time, while RIM seeks to reduce wireless service interruptions and increase online security.

At times, a company may have to make more fundamental changes in its operations and restructure, often referred to as reengineering its processes to improve cost, quality, timeliness, or service. Management accountants provide the financial and nonfinancial information that helps managers make decisions about reengineering and continuous improvement.

E-business is an example of how technological change presented opportunities to many industries to improve on the speed with which they could convey up-to-date information. Global manufacturers and service providers have designed websites on which they post information of interest to many users. Others, however, have invented entirely new ways to fulfill their customers' value proposition. For example, eBay, the auction site that enables individuals to buy and sell goods online, created an entirely new online industry. Google established its superiority as an online search engine. Facebook and MySpace founded commercially viable social networking systems and sell data to advertisers based on their customers' personal profiles.

E-business—Old Wine in New Bottles, Some New Wine

E-business meant nothing a decade ago, and it is only through what companies have done using Internet capabilities that we now understand what the term means.

Companies, such as RIM, have been careful to use the web for a variety of business functions, none of which are critical to the company's success. These companies have adopted a strategy of *rational experimentation* to ensure they understand the downside of innovation before taking too much risk.

Other companies have pursued a strategy of *operational excellence*, such as Dell, which uses the Internet to complete almost all of its customer transactions electronically, from order taking through to payment. FedEx is a similar example. Via the web, FedEx gives customers full access to information about where their packages are in transit.

Finally, companies such as eBay, Facebook, and MySpace have used *breakthrough strategies* and invented new services for new and profitable customer groups.

At the other extreme, some companies have used a strategy of *new fundamentals* to communicate the same old information via the web to reduce costs with only a small investment. For example, companies put information about employee benefits on their internal websites and post career opportunities on their external websites, reducing human resource and recruiting costs.

Source: A. Hartman, J. Sifonis, and J. Kador, *Net Ready* (New York: McGraw Hill, 2000); Google Inc., S-1: Registration Statement, April 29, 2004 (Mountain View, CA: Google Inc., 2004); various company financial reports.

ASSESS YOUR MASTERY

MyAccountingLab

To check your understanding of the material in Learning Objective ❷, go to the *Mastery Questions* section at the end of this chapter and complete Learning Objective ❷ questions 1, 2, and 3.

PLANNING AND CONTROL SYSTEMS

Is Magna's management control system better than Linamar's? Is RIM's better than Motorola's? This section provides an overview of management control systems, illustrating the role of management accounting information.

There are countless definitions of planning and control. We define **planning** as choosing goals, predicting results under various ways of achieving those goals, deciding how to attain the desired goals, and then communicating the goals and how to achieve them throughout the organization. The most important planning tool is a budget. Why? Because a budget is a benchmark against which actual performance can be compared.

A **budget** is the quantitative expression of a proposed plan of action by management. The budgeting process aids coordination of what needs to be done to implement that plan. The information used to project budgeted amounts includes past financial and nonfinancial information routinely recorded in accounting systems. The budget expresses the strategy by describing the sales goals; the production, distribution, and customer-service costs that would be needed to achieve sales goals; the anticipated cash flows; and the potential financing needs. Because the process of preparing a budget crosses business functions in the value chain, it forces coordination and communication throughout the company, as well as with the company's suppliers and customers (see Chapter 6). Management accountants play a valuable role in the budgeting process because they have an overview of the organization as a whole and understand the financial consequences of different actions.

Study the left side of Exhibit 1-4, which uses planning and control at the *Calgary Herald* as an illustration. For example, one goal of the *Calgary Herald* may be to increase operating income. Three main alternatives are considered to achieve this goal:

Identify differences between the planning and control decisions of managers, and the different roles of relevant accounting information ❸

◆ Change the price per newspaper
◆ Change the rate per page charged to advertisers
◆ Reduce labour costs by increasing automation of the printing process

EXHIBIT 1-4
How Accounting Facilitates Planning and Control

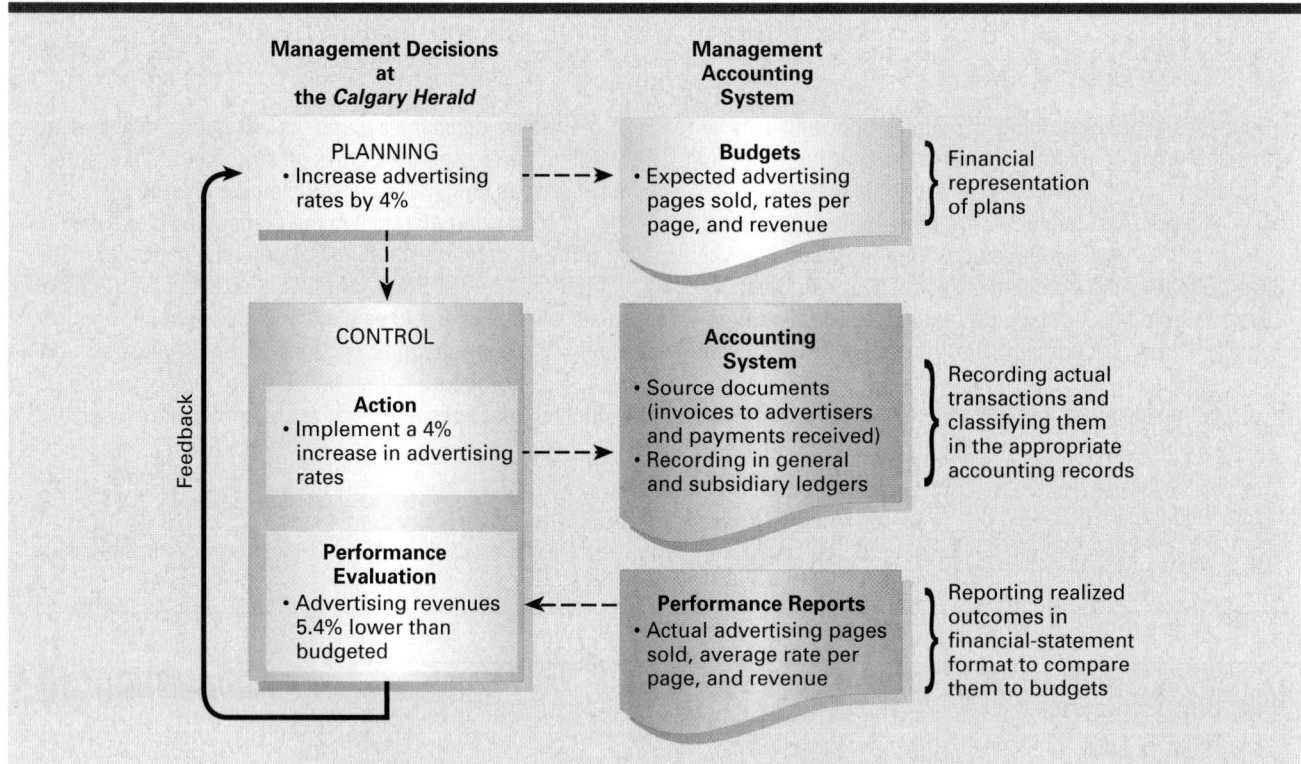

Analyzing the effects of choosing alternative 2, assume that the publisher increases advertising budgeted rates by 4% to $5,200 per page for the month. Total budgeted advertising revenue is the product of the expected pages sold and the budgeted rate per page, which equals $4,160,000 ($5,200 × 800).

Control (the bottom box in Exhibit 1-4) covers both the action that implements the planning decision and the performance evaluation of the personnel and operations. Control requires that companies take coordinated action to implement their planning decisions, evaluate actual against expected performance, and provide timely feedback on current results. With our example, the action would include communicating the new advertising rate schedule to marketing sales representatives and advertisers.

During the month, the *Calgary Herald* sells advertising, sends out invoices, and receives payments. These invoices and receipts are recorded in the accounting system. Exhibit 1-5 shows the advertising revenue performance report for the *Calgary Herald*. This report indicates that 760 pages of advertising (40 pages fewer than the budgeted 800 pages) were sold in the month. The average rate per page was $5,080, compared with the budgeted $5,200 rate, yielding actual advertising revenue in the month of $3,860,800. The actual advertising revenue is $299,200 less than the budgeted $4,160,000. Understanding the reasons for any difference between actual results and budgeted results is an important part of **management by exception**, which is the practice of concentrating on areas not operating as expected (such as a cost overrun on a project) and placing less attention on areas operating as expected. The term **variance** in Exhibit 1-5 refers to the difference between the actual results and the budgeted amounts.

The performance report in Exhibit 1-5 should spur investigation. For example, did other newspapers experience a comparable decline in advertising revenue? Did the marketing department make sufficient efforts to convince advertisers that, even with the new rate of $5,200 per page, advertising was a good buy? Why was the actual average rate per page $5,080 instead of the budgeted rate of $5,200? Did sales representatives offer discounted rates? Did a major advertiser threaten to transfer its

EXHIBIT 1-5
Advertising Revenue Performance Report at the *Calgary Herald*

	Actual Results (1)	Variance (difference) (1) − (3)	Budgeted Amounts (3)
Advertising pages sold	760	(40) U	800
Average rate per page	$ 5,080	$ (120) U	$ 5,200
Advertising revenue	$3,860,800	$(299,200) U	$4,160,000

advertising to another newspaper unless it was given a large rate reduction? Answers to these questions could prompt the publisher to take subsequent actions, including, for example, pushing marketing personnel to renew efforts to promote advertising to existing and potential advertisers.

A well-conceived plan includes enough flexibility so that managers can seize opportunities unforeseen at the time the plan is formulated. A plan is made as a *possible* response to anticipated events but never as a *necessary* response. If actual events differ from those anticipated (fewer advertising pages were sold), then the plan should change. The best actual response will provide the best profitability for the company.

Planning and control are so strongly intertwined that managers do not spend time drawing artificially rigid distinctions between them. Unless otherwise stated, we use control in its broadest sense to denote the entire management process of both planning and control. For example, instead of referring to a management planning and control system, we will refer to a management control system. Similarly, we will often refer to the control purpose of accounting instead of the awkward planning and control purpose of accounting.

FEEDBACK: LINKING PLANNING AND CONTROL

Exhibit 1-4 shows a feedback loop from control back to planning. Feedback involves managers examining past performance and systematically exploring alternative ways to improve future performance. It can lead to a variety of responses, including the following:

USE OF FEEDBACK	EXAMPLE
◆ Changing goals	◆ Air Canada increases emphasis on cash flow, rather than income, after emerging from bankruptcy protection.
◆ Changing how decision alternatives are identified	◆ Chrysler adopts a team-based new-product development process with input from both manufacturing and marketing.
◆ Changing the range of information collected in order to make predictions	◆ Bell Canada incorporates average inflation forecasts for wages when predicting future labour costs.
◆ Changing how the company operates	◆ Wal-Mart Canada Corp. has Coca-Cola store and deliver its products as needed instead of building its own warehouse.
◆ Changing reward systems	◆ Research In Motion (RIM) considers basing its marketing bonuses on the profitability of sales rather than on the dollar amount of sales.
◆ Changing managers	◆ Royal Dutch/Shell dismisses its chairman Sir Philip Watts after a huge writedown in the value of oil reserves.

PROBLEM-SOLVING, SCOREKEEPING, AND ATTENTION-DIRECTING FUNCTIONS

Management accountants contribute to the company's decisions about strategy, planning, and control by problem solving, scorekeeping, and attention directing.

◆ **Problem solving**: Comparative analysis serves to reduce the scope of and identify the best available alternatives to achieve the company's goals. The *Calgary Herald*, for example, could compare the expected additional revenues and costs of outsourcing the production of an online version of the newspaper.

◆ **Scorekeeping**: Accumulating data and reporting reliable results to all levels of management. An example, Exhibit 1-5, illustrates the importance of comparing actual to expected performance in order for the *Calgary Herald* to clarify the causes for its failure.

◆ **Attention directing**: Clarifying and sorting out situations that require management attention from those that do not. For example, the *Calgary Herald* could report daily the number of unsold newspapers compared to the printing press costs. Establishing an acceptable threshold of costs per returned newspaper would then direct attention to exceptions requiring some remedy. Attention directing should also focus on all opportunities to add value to an organization and not just on cost-reduction opportunities.

Different decisions place different emphases on these three roles. For strategic decisions and planning decisions, the problem-solving role is most prominent. Consider the *Calgary Herald*'s strategic decision to try to increase revenues by increasing advertising rates per page (Exhibit 1-5). The newspaper's management accountants serve as problem solvers to help make this strategic decision. They provide information about past increases or decreases in advertising rates and the subsequent changes in advertising revenue. They also collect and analyze information about past increases or decreases in advertising rates charged by competing media outlets (including other newspapers). The manager works with the management accountant to make the best decision about whether to increase the advertising rate per page and by how much to increase the rate.

For control decisions at the *Calgary Herald* (which include both actions to implement planning decisions and decisions about performance evaluation), the management accountant's scorekeeping and attention-directing roles are most prominent because they provide feedback to managers. For example, recording the details of advertising revenues and writing up a summary in the monthly income statement show how scorekeeping aids control. An example of control via attention directing would be a report highlighting the reduced year-to-date advertising revenues, with details of the specific advertisers that cut back or stopped advertising after the rate increase went into effect. This feedback helps managers decide which advertisers to target for intensive follow-up by sales representatives.

Feedback from scorekeeping and attention directing often leads managers to revise planning decisions and sometimes to make new strategic decisions. Information that prompts a planning decision is frequently reanalyzed and supplemented by the management accountant in the problem-solving and business-partner roles. The ongoing interaction among strategic decisions, planning decisions, and control decisions means that management accountants often are simultaneously doing problem-solving, scorekeeping, and attention-directing activities. The Real Companies box indicates the increasingly important roles management accountants are playing in helping managers develop and implement strategy.

Many organizations now have management accountants who concentrate solely on the attention-directing or problem-solving function. The titles of these individuals differ. For instance, Clorox has special staff positions for "cost systems and financial reporting," "planning and analysis," "forecasting," and "manufacturing analysis and support." The Yoplait Company, a French yogurt company, has staff positions for "operations analysis," "budget analysis and reporting," and "marketing and sales analysis," while Siemens VDO has "senior cost price analysts."

REAL COMPANIES

Today's Management Accountant

What do management accountants do? The following table, based on a survey of U.S. certified management accountants,[a] shows the percentage of respondents who named a particular work activity in their top five work activities (out of 29 activities identified to them) in terms of time devoted to the activity.

Accounting systems and financial reporting	62%
Managing accounting/finance functions	42%
Internal consulting	42%
Short-term budgeting	37%
Long-term strategic planning	25%
Financial and economic analysis	24%
Computer systems and operations	21%
Process improvement	20%
Performance evaluation	17%
Tax compliance	14%
Accounting policy	13%
Consolidations	11%

In recent years, management accounting has reached a critical juncture. Shifts in perceptions mean management accountants are seen as business partners increasingly focused on key strategic issues, well beyond the boundaries of the traditional finance functions. A recent survey of 2,000 Institute of Management

Accountants (IMA) members identified the following seven priorities facing today's management accountants:[b]

1. Generating cost information
2. Cost reduction
3. Improving processes
4. Contributing to core strategy
5. Setting standards
6. Reducing risk
7. Automating processes

Similar changes are also occurring globally within the profession. One survey of United Kingdom accounting professionals predicted the following tasks would be the most vital to the management accountant's job in the next five years:[c]

1. Business performance evaluation
2. Cost/financial control
3. Interpreting/presenting management accounts
4. Profit improvement
5. Planning/managing budgets
6. Strategic planning and decision making
7. Implementing business strategy

Another survey of Irish accountants noted several trends within management accounting practice.[d] Among these were management reliance on traditional accounting techniques (with only supplemental use of new methods) and movement toward accountants as business partners. Similarly, U.S. respondents identified the demand for "actionable" cost information and continued use of traditional management accounting tools.

[a] G. Siegel and J. Sorensen, "The Practice Analysis of Management Accounting," *Management Accounting* (1999).

[b] Ernst & Young, *2003 Survey of Management Accounting* (New York: Ernst & Young, March 2003).

[c] J. Burns and H. Yazdifar, "Tricks or Treats?" *Financial Management* (2001).

[d] B. Pierce, "Management Accounting Without Accountants?" *Accountancy Ireland* (2001).

ASSESS YOUR MASTERY

To check your understanding of the material in Learning Objective ③, go to the *Mastery Questions* section at the end of this chapter and complete Learning Objective ③ questions 1, 2, and 3.

Three important guidelines help management accountants provide the most value in performing their problem-solving, scorekeeping, and attention-directing functions: (1) employ a cost–benefit approach, (2) give full recognition to behavioural as well as technical considerations, and (3) adopt the different-costs-for-different-purposes theme.

COST–BENEFIT APPROACH

Management accountants continually face resource-allocation decisions, such as whether to purchase a new software package or whether to employ a new associate. A **cost–benefit approach** should be used in these decisions—resources should be spent if they promote decision making that better attains organization goals in relation to the costs of those resources. The perceived net benefits from spending those resources should exceed their perceived expected costs. The expected benefits and costs may not be easy to quantify, and although the benefits may take many forms, they can be summarized as the collective set of decisions that will better attain the organization's goals.

Consider the installation of a company's first budgeting system. Previously, the company had probably been using some historical record keeping and little formal planning. A major benefit of installing the budgeting system is that it compels managers to plan more formally. They can make a different, more profitable set of decisions than they would have made using only a historical system. Thus, the expected benefits exceed the expected costs of the new budgeting system. These costs include investments in physical assets, in training people, and in ongoing operating costs of the system.

BEHAVIOURAL AND TECHNICAL CONSIDERATIONS

The cost–benefit test is the overarching criterion that assists managers in deciding whether, say, to install a proposed budgeting system instead of using an existing historical system. Note the human side of why budgeting is used. As was just mentioned, budgets induce a different set of collective decisions because of compelled collaborative planning. A management accounting system should have two simultaneous missions for providing information: (1) to help managers make wise economic decisions and (2) to help motivate managers and other employees to aim and strive for the goals of the organization. In other words, the technical information by itself might guide managers to wise economic decisions, but it is worthless if managers fail to understand and use it.

Do not underestimate the role of individuals and groups in management planning and control systems. Both accountants and managers should always remember that management systems are not confined exclusively to technical matters such as the type of computer software systems used and the frequency with which reports are prepared. Management is primarily a human activity that should focus on how to help individuals do their jobs better. For example, it is often better for managers to speak personally with underperforming workers about how to improve performance than to send those workers a report highlighting their underperformance.

DIFFERENT COSTS FOR DIFFERENT PURPOSES

This book discusses alternative ways to estimate costs. That is because there are different costs for different purposes. This is the management accountant's version of the "one size does not fit all" notion. A cost concept used for external reporting may not be the appropriate concept for internal reporting to managers. Consider the advertising costs associated with launching a major new Microsoft product. The product is expected to have a useful life of two years or more. For external reporting to shareholders, advertising costs are fully expensed in the income statement in the year in which they are incurred. This immediate expensing is a requirement of GAAP governing external reporting to shareholders.

In contrast, for evaluating management performance (an example of the internal routine-reporting purpose), the advertising costs could be capitalized and then written off as expenses over several years. Microsoft could capitalize these advertising costs if it believed this treatment would better represent the performance of the managers launching the new product. In short, immediate-period expensing of advertising costs for external reporting does not imply it is always the ideal cost treatment for other purposes of an accounting system.

A management accountant following these guidelines operates within a given organization structure. We now discuss how organization structure affects the reporting responsibilities of a management accountant.

ORGANIZATION STRUCTURE—LINE AND STAFF RELATIONSHIPS

We focus first on broad management functions, and then examine the accounting and finance functions in more detail. Most organizations distinguish between line and staff management. **Line management** is directly responsible for attaining the objectives of the organization. For example, managers of manufacturing divisions may have objectives for a specified amount of operating income plus targets for product quality, safety, and compliance with environmental laws.

Staff management, such as management accountants, exist to provide advice and assistance to line management. Increasingly, however, organizations such as DaimlerChrysler Canada Inc. and GlaxoSmithKline use teams to achieve their objectives. These teams include both line and staff management so that all inputs into a decision are available simultaneously. As a result, the traditional distinctions between line and staff have become less clear-cut than they were a decade ago. Line management and staff management designations are best viewed as different ends of a spectrum.

The **chief financial officer (CFO)**—also called the **finance director**—is the senior officer empowered with overseeing the financial operations of an organization. The responsibilities of the CFO vary among organizations, but they almost always encompass the following four areas:

◆ **Controllership** includes providing financial information for both internal reports to managers and external reports to investors, as well as overseeing the overall operations of the accounting system.

◆ **Treasury** includes short-term and long-term financing and investments; banking; and cash, foreign exchange, and derivatives management.

◆ **Tax** includes income taxes, sales taxes, and domestic and international tax planning.

◆ **Investor relations** includes responding to and interacting with shareholders.

In some organizations, the CFO also has responsibility for information systems. In other organizations, an officer of equivalent rank to the CFO, who is called the *chief information officer*, or CIO, has responsibility for information systems.

The **controller** is the financial executive primarily responsible for both management accounting and financial accounting. This book focuses on the management accounting function of the controller. The modern controller does not do any controlling in terms of line authority except over his or her own department. Yet the modern concept of controllership maintains that the controller does control in a special sense. That is, by reporting and interpreting relevant data, the controller exerts a force or influence that impels management toward making better-informed decisions.

Exhibit 1-6 presents an organization chart depicting the reporting relationships for the CFO and the corporate controller at Nike. The CFO is a staff management function that reports to the most senior line managers (who in turn report to the board of directors). As in most organizations, the corporate controller at Nike reports to the CFO. Organization charts, like that in Exhibit 1-6, show formal reporting relationships. In most organizations, informal relationships also exist that must be understood when managers attempt to implement their decisions. Examples of informal relationships are friendships among managers (of a professional or

EXHIBIT 1-6
The Nike Company: Reporting Relationships for the CFO and the Corporate Controller

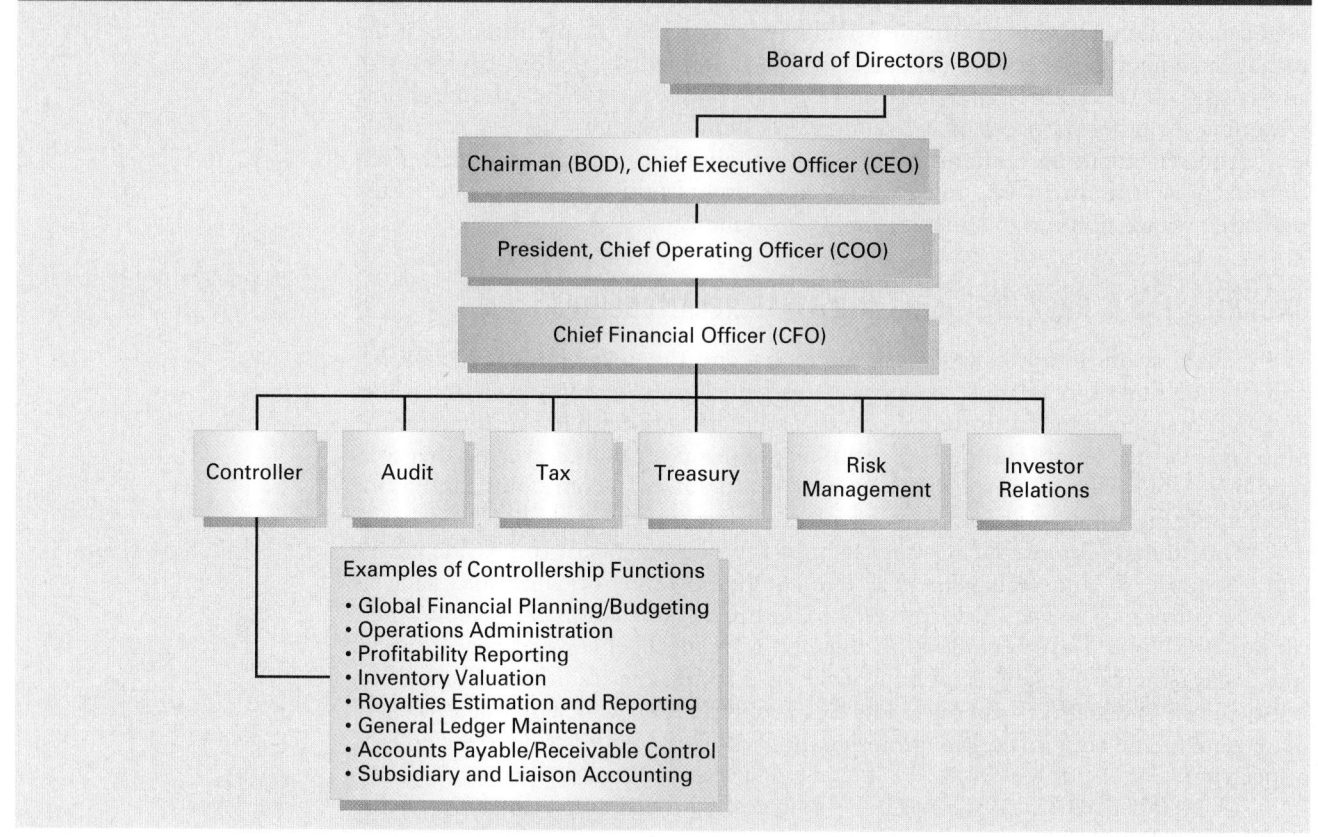

personal kind) and the personal preferences of senior managers for the type of managers they choose to rely on in decision making.

The CFO at Nike is one of 13 corporate officers. These include the chief executive officer (CEO), the president and chief operating officer (COO), the treasurer, and ten vice-presidents (such as for its geographic regions in the United States, Asia–Pacific, and Europe; for its products of apparel and footwear; for its brand management; for its global human resources; and a chief legal counsel). Exhibit 1-6 provides examples of the functions undertaken in the controller's group. Each of Nike's major geographic groups (United States, Asia–Pacific, and Europe) has its own group controller. Many individual countries within each geographic group also have a country controller.

MyAccountingLab

ASSESS YOUR MASTERY

To check your understanding of the material in Learning Objective ❹, go to the *Mastery Questions* section at the end of this chapter and complete Learning Objective ❹ questions 1, 2, and 3.

PROFESSIONAL ETHICS, CORPORATE SOCIAL RESPONSIBILITY, AND CORPORATE GOVERNANCE

❺ Explain how professional accounting codes of ethics relate to corporate governance

Ponder what managers do to design and implement strategies, and the organizational structures within which they operate. Reflect on the management accountant's and controller's roles. Clearly, successful management accountants possess both technical and analytical competence, as well as behavioural and interpersonal skills. The Governance Issues box on page 18 lists some desirable values and behaviours. We will elaborate on corporate social responsibility and corporate governance as we discuss different topics in subsequent chapters of this book. **Corporate social**

responsibility (CSR) is the voluntary integration by companies of social and environmental concerns into their business operation.[2] **Corporate governance**, in contrast, is mandatory. Corporate governance requires compliance with existing laws, regulations, and standards.

A strategy of corporate social responsibility indicates a company's commitment to the broader social environment in which they operate. Issues that companies have voluntarily addressed include how to establish the moral price of HIV/AIDS retroviral drugs sold to Sub-Saharan and other African countries where 28.5 million of the 38 million afflicted worldwide reside.[3] It is a difficult question when effective drugs can take up to 12 years to develop and cost $800 million. But corporate social responsibility implies that some companies are willing to broaden their scope of interest beyond maximizing profit.

Oxfam and Médecins Sans Frontière, among others, applied global pressure to remedy the problem. UNAIDS and five pharmaceutical companies accepted the accelerating access initiative (AAI) to provide these drugs at a substantial reduction. In the U.S., one effective drug costing US $10,000–$15,000 annually is provided by an offshore generic drug manufacturer for US $250 per year. Other pharmaceutical companies took legal action to prevent these sales under the AAI because the generics infringe on the intellectual property rights of the manufacturers. A global settlement provided licenses to a single distribution company, and the cost is approximately US $1.97 per patient for each day's dosage, or $719 per year.

In fact, research has provided evidence that exercising corporate social responsibility results in improved financial performance, stronger customer relationships, improved product quality, and various internal benefits arising from stronger employee commitment.[4] In marketing, corporate social responsibility has translated into a strategy of branding, which links brands to social responsiveness and the needs of the community. Rather than reflecting the core attributes of the product, corporate social responsibility has translated into a strategy of brands reflecting the core values of the community.

At no time has the focus on appropriate corporate governance been sharper than it is today. Corporate scandals at Nortel, Enron, WorldCom, Bre-X, Cinar Corp., Livent, and YBM Magnex have seriously eroded the public's confidence in corporations. All employees in a company, whether in line management or staff management, must comply with the organization's—and, more broadly, society's—expectations of corporate governance.

Accountants have special obligations regarding ethics, given that they are responsible for the integrity of the financial information provided to internal and external parties. Recent securities legislation in the United States, the *Sarbanes-Oxley Act of 2002*, as well as international and Canadian counterparts (such as MI 52-109), require companies listed on stock exchanges to create, enforce, and publish a formal code of ethical and business conduct. Clauses in the new legislation focus on improving internal control, corporate governance, monitoring of managers, and disclosure practices of public corporations. These regulations make tough ethical standards into laws and provide a process for employees to report wrongdoing (whether unethical, illegal, or both).

ETHICAL GUIDELINES

Professional accounting organizations representing management accountants exist in many countries. Appendix B discusses professional organizations in Canada, the United States, Australia, Japan, and the United Kingdom. Each of these organizations provides certification programs. For example, the **Society of Management Accountants of**

---

[2]D. Silberhorn and R. C. Warren, "Defining Corporate Social Responsibility," *European Business Review* (2007), 352–372.

[3]C. Soares, "The HIV/AIDS Crisis and Corporate Moral Responsibility in Light of the Levinasian Notions of Proximity and the Third World," *Business Ethics: A European Review* (2007), 278–285; R. Brennan and P. Baines, "Is There a Morally Right Price for Anti-Retroviral Drugs in the Developing World?" *Business Ethics: A European Review* (2006), 29–43.

[4]M. J. Polonsky and C. Jevons, "Understanding Issue Complexity When Building a Socially Responsible Brand," *Business Ethics: A European Review* (2006), 340–349.

Numbers Are Trivial—It's About Professional Trust

Management accountants cannot claim to be professional by simply focusing on "the numbers." One reason is that the techniques used to manipulate data are not very complex, and technique does not constitute professional expertise. Engineers use far more complex manipulations. For both professions, it is the interpretation and presentation of estimated values within a more comprehensive context that adds value. To do so effectively, the profession must be trustworthy. Managers inside the company must trust the management accountants to have applied their techniques in a way consistent with their professional ethics. More importantly, however, is their professional judgment to look up and look out to understand how decisions can infringe on or even harm others outside the company.

Members of the management accounting profession work in cross-functional teams and are often the ones who must raise tough questions to consider with the intent of improving plans and decisions. They work at developing and implementing innovation, and this is a difficult process of planning, communication, and training. Management accountants communicate relevant information openly and in a straightforward way based on appropriate and professional application of their expertise.

Without a strong sense of integrity and the courage to do the right things as well as do things right, management accountants can too readily succumb to pressures to manipulate information. Their professional commitment is to the organization and the stakeholders dependent upon it, not its managers.

Source: A. Serwer, "The Hole Story," *Fortune,* July 7, 2003; M. Green, J. Garrity, A. Gumbus, and B. Lyons, "Pitney Bowes Calls for New Metrics," *Strategic Finance,* May 2002.

Canada (SMAC)—the largest association of management accountants in Canada—provides a program leading to the **Certified Management Accountant (CMA)** certificate. This certificate signals that the holder has passed the admission criteria and demonstrated the competency of technical knowledge and skills required by the SMAC.

Professional accounting organizations play an important role in promoting a high standard of ethics. The SMAC has issued a Code of Professional Ethics (see Exhibit 1-7). As you can see, the first duty of management accountants is to act in the public interest, then in the interests of the profession, clients, and employers.

EXHIBIT 1-7
Excerpts from the Society of Management Accountants of Ontario Code of Professional Ethics

All Members will adhere to the following "Code of Professional Ethics" of the Society:

(1) A Member will act at all times with:
   (a) responsibility for and fidelity to public needs;
   (b) fairness and loyalty to such Member's associates, clients and employers; and
   (c) competence through devotion to high ideals of personal honour and professional integrity.

(2) A Member will:
   (a) maintain at all times independence of thought and action;
   (b) not express her or his opinion on financial reports or statements without first assessing her or his relationship with her or his client to determine whether such Member might expect her or his opinion to be considered independent, objective and unbiased by one who has knowledge of all the facts; and
   (c) when preparing financial reports or statements or expressing an opinion on financial reports or statements, disclose all material facts known to such Member in order not to make such financial reports or statements misleading, acquire sufficient information to warrant an expression of opinion and report all material misstatements or departures from generally accepted accounting principles.

(Continued)

EXHIBIT 1-7 (*continued*)

(3) A Member will:

(a) not disclose or use any confidential information concerning the affairs of such Member's employer or client unless acting in the course of his or her duties or except when such information is required to be disclosed in the course of any defence of himself or herself or any associate or employee in any lawsuit or other legal proceeding or against alleged professional misconduct by order of lawful authority of the Board or any committee of the Society in the proper exercise of their duties but only to the extent necessary for such purpose;

(b) inform his or her employer or client of any business connections or interests of which such Member's employer or client would reasonably expect to be informed;

(c) not, in the course of exercising his or her duties on behalf of such Member's employer or client, hold, receive, bargain for or acquire any fee, remuneration or benefit without such employer's or client's knowledge and consent; and

(d) take all reasonable steps, in arranging any engagement as a consultant, to establish a clear understanding of the scope and objectives of the work before it is commenced and will furnish the client with an estimate of cost, preferably before the engagement is commenced, but in any event as soon as possible thereafter.

(4) A Member will:

(a) conduct himself or herself toward other Members with courtesy and good faith;

(b) not commit an act discreditable to the profession;

(c) not engage in or counsel any business or occupation which, in the opinion of the Society, is incompatible with the professional ethics of a management accountant;

(d) not accept any engagement to review the work of another Member for the same employer except with the knowledge of that Member, or except where the connection of that Member with the work has been terminated, unless the Member reviews the work of others as a normal part of his or her responsibilities;

(e) not attempt to gain an advantage over other Members by paying or accepting a commission in securing management accounting work;

(f) uphold the principle of adequate compensation for management accounting or public accounting work; and

(g) not act maliciously or in any other way which may adversely reflect on the public or professional reputation or business of another Member.

(5) A Member will:

(a) at all times maintain the standards of competence expressed by the Board from time to time;

(b) disseminate the knowledge upon which the profession of management accounting is based to others within the profession and generally promote the advancement of the profession;

(c) undertake only such work as he or she is competent to perform by virtue of his or her training and experience and will, where it would be in the best interests of an employer or client, engage, or advise the employer or client to engage, other specialists;

(d) expose before the proper tribunals of the Society any incompetent, unethical, illegal or unfair conduct or practice of a Member which involves the reputation, dignity or honour of the Society; and

(e) endeavour to ensure that a professional partnership or company, with which such Member is associated as a partner, principal, director or officer, associate or employee abides by the Code of Professional Ethics and the rules of professional conduct established by the Society.

Source: *Management Accounting Handbook: Bylaw 20* (The Society of Management Accountants of Ontario). Reproduced with permission of The Society of Management Accountants of Ontario.

It is important to understand what a profession *is* to understand why professional ethics are important. A profession is distinguished by certain characteristics:

◆ Mastery of a specific intellectual skill acquired by education and training
◆ Acceptance of duties to society (i.e., protection of the public) as a whole in addition to duties to the employer or client
◆ An outlook that is essentially objective or neutral
◆ A high standard in the conduct and performance of personal service

A professional provides a service (e.g., advice regarding legal, financial, or medical issues) rather than producing a specific product (e.g., furniture, vehicles). Thus it is difficult, if not impossible, for the public (i.e., a layperson) to assess the quality of a professional service, because the public lacks the specialized knowledge and skills that are necessary to assess that quality. This lack of skills is what sends the public to the professional in the first place, but it leaves the public vulnerable to those professionals. Because of this vulnerability, the public must be protected by standards established by those who have the appropriate knowledge and skills. Since the members themselves establish the standards and then monitor other members for adherence to those standards, this is considered "self-governance."

An important component of a profession's self-governance is that it is responsible for disciplining its members found guilty of "unprofessional conduct." By setting out what constitutes "unprofessional conduct," the profession ensures that the public will be protected by acceptable minimum standards and disciplinary processes. For example, for CMAs in Alberta, "unprofessional conduct" would include

◆ conduct that is detrimental to the best interest of the public or harms the integrity of the accounting profession;
◆ conduct that contravenes this Act, the regulations, or the bylaws;
◆ conduct that contravenes the rules of professional conduct or practice standards;
◆ conduct that displays a lack of competence.[5]

To strengthen the protection of the public, provincial governments pass legislation to establish limits on the self-governance of professional organizations and to set out governance criteria. These criteria require, among other things, that members of the profession set standards for the knowledge and skills necessary for entry into the profession, for continuing competency, and for discipline. In this way the public is assured no profession may operate as if it is above the law.

TYPICAL ETHICAL CHALLENGES

Ethical issues can confront management accountants in many ways. The following examples are illustrative.

◆ **Case 1** A management accountant, knowing that reporting a loss for a software division will result in yet another "rightsizing initiative" (a euphemism for layoffs), has concerns about the commercial viability of software for which development costs are currently being capitalized. The division manager argues vehemently that the new product will be a "winner" but has no credible evidence to support the opinion. The last two products from this division have not been successful in the market. The management accountant has friends in the division and wants to avoid a personal confrontation with the division manager. Should the management accountant require the development to be expensed immediately because of the lack of evidence as to its commercial viability?

◆ **Case 2** A packaging supplier, bidding for a new contract, offers the management accountant of its customer an all-expenses-paid weekend to the Grey Cup. The supplier does not mention the new contract when making the invitation. The

[5]Excerpt from Section 91(1) of the *Regulated Accounting Profession Act*, Alberta.

accountant is not a personal friend of the supplier. He knows operating-cost issues are critical in approving the new contract and is concerned that the supplier will ask for details about bids by competing packaging companies.

In each case, the management accountant is faced with an ethical challenge. Case 1 involves competence, objectivity, and integrity, whereas case 2 involves confidentiality and integrity. Ethical issues are not always black and white. For example, the supplier in case 2 may have no intention of raising issues associated with the bid. However, the appearance of a conflict of interest in case 2 is sufficient for many companies to prohibit employees from accepting free "favours" from suppliers.

Most professional accounting organizations around the globe issue statements about professional ethics. Although these statements include many of the same issues discussed by the Society of Management Accountants of Ontario outlined in Exhibit 1-7, differences do exist in their content. For example, the Chartered Institute of Management Accountants (CIMA) in the United Kingdom identifies four fundamental principles of competency, confidentiality, integrity, and objectivity. A statement by the Institute of Management Accountants in the United States goes further by providing guidance on the resolution of ethical conflict.

ASSESS YOUR MASTERY

To check your understanding of the material in Learning Objective ⑤, go to the *Mastery Questions* section at the end of this chapter and complete Learning Objective ⑤ questions 1, 2, and 3.

PULLING IT ALL TOGETHER—PROBLEM FOR SELF-STUDY

(Try to solve this problem before examining the solution that follows.)

PROBLEM

The Campbell Soup Company incurs the following costs:

a. Purchase of tomatoes by the canning plant for Campbell's tomato soup products.

b. Materials purchased for redesigning Mr. Christie biscuit containers to make biscuits stay fresh longer.

c. Payment to Bates, the advertising agency for the Healthy Request line of soup products.

d. Salaries of food technologists researching feasibility of a Prego pizza sauce that has zero calories.

e. Payment to Sobeys for shelf space to display Campbell's food products.

f. Cost of a toll-free telephone line used for customer inquiries about possible taste problems with Campbell's soups.

g. Cost of gloves used by line operators on the Swanson Fiesta breakfast food production line.

h. Cost of hand-held computers used by Campbell Soup Company delivery staff serving major supermarket accounts.

REQUIRED

1. Identify two costs incurred most likely as a result of strategic decisions.

2. Classify each cost item (a) to (h) into a component of the value chain shown in Exhibit 1-2 (p. 6).

3. How would the treatment of (c) by a financial accountant differ from that by a management accountant?

4. How could Campbell Soup Company use corporate social responsibility to brand its products?

SOLUTION

1. Costs incurred for materials for redesign in (b) are likely the result of a strategic decision, as are those from (d).
2. The items should be classified as:
   a. Production
   b. Design of products, services, or processes
   c. Marketing
   d. Research and development
   e. Marketing
   f. Customer service
   g. Production
   h. Distribution
3. Advertising is an expense, a period cost that financial accountants must record during the period it is incurred. For internal purposes of management evaluation, advertising costs are likely based on a strategic decision and would be capitalized by management accountants producing a performance report.
4. A strategy of corporate social responsibility would link the attributes of a product to the core values of the customers to whom the product is sold. Campbell's could advertise the wholesome method in which raw materials were produced (e.g., chicken for soup) or its use of organic vegetables. The strategy will only be effective, however, if it is true.

DECISION POINTS

The following decision guidelines use a question-and-answer format to summarize the chapter's main points. Each decision presents a key question. The guideline is the answer to that question.

DECISIONS	GUIDELINES
1. What information does cost accounting provide?	Cost accounting measures, analyzes, and reports financial and nonfinancial information related to the cost of acquiring or using resources in an organization. Cost accounting provides information for both management accounting and financial accounting. Management accountants contribute to strategic decisions by providing information about the sources of competitive advantage.
2. How do companies add value?	Companies add value through research and development (R&D); design of products, services, or processes; production; marketing; distribution; and customer service. Managers in all business functions of the value chain are customers of management accounting information. Customers are expecting companies to deliver performance through cost, efficiency, quality, timeliness, and innovation.
3. How do planning and control differ, and what roles do management accountants play?	Planning is undertaken prior to action while control is an evaluation of how well plans have been implemented. Management accountants perform multiple roles to implement strategies: problem solving (comparative analyses for decision making), scorekeeping (accumulating data and reporting reliable results), and attention directing (helping managers properly focus their attention).
4. What guidelines do management accountants use?	Three guidelines that help management accountants increase their value to managers are (a) employ a cost–benefit approach, (b) recognize behavioural as well as technical considerations, and (c) identify different costs for different purposes. Management accounting is an integral part of the controller's function in an organization. In most organizations, the controller reports to the chief financial officer, who is a key member of the top management team.
5. What are the ethical responsibilities of management accountants?	Management accountants have ethical responsibilities that are related to competence, confidentiality, integrity, and objectivity.

Each chapter will include this section. Like all technical subjects, accounting contains many terms with precise meanings. Pin down the definitions of new terms when you initially encounter them. The meaning of each of the following terms is explained in this chapter. The definitions are collected in the Glossary at the end of this book.

attention directing (p. 12)
budget (p. 9)
Certified Management Accountant (CMA) (p. 18)
chief financial officer (CFO) (p. 15)
control (p. 10)
controller (p. 15)
controllership (p. 15)
corporate governance (p. 16)
corporate social responsibility (p. 16)
cost accounting (p. 2)
cost–benefit approach (p. 14)
cost management (p. 3)
customer service (p. 6)

design of products, services, or processes (p. 6)
distribution (p. 6)
finance director (p. 15)
financial accounting (p. 3)
investor relations (p. 15)
line management (p. 15)
management accounting (p. 3)
management by exception (p. 10)
marketing (p. 6)
planning (p. 9)
problem solving (p. 12)
production (p. 6)
research and development (R&D) (p. 6)

scorekeeping (p. 12)
Society of Management Accountants of Canada (SMAC) (p. 17)
staff management (p. 15)
strategic management (p. 5)
strategy (p. 4)
supply chain (p. 7)
supply-chain management (p. 7)
tax (p. 15)
treasury (p. 15)
value (p. 5)
value chain (p. 5)
variance (p. 10)

MASTERY QUESTIONS

The Mastery Questions are rated by proficiency level: elementary, intermediate, and advanced. The solutions appear in the Mastery Question Solutions section of MyAccountingLab.

LEARNING OBJECTIVE 1

1. **Cost, financial, and management accounting—Elementary.** Members of the accounting profession possess different expertise.

   REQUIRED
   1. What is the key link between a cost accountant and a financial accountant?
   2. What is the key source of information for management accountants?
   3. How do cost and management accountants differ?

2. **Cost, financial, and management accounting—Intermediate.** Strategy is a way of thinking by hypothesizing about two types of questions. It is experimentation: if one experiment fails, you try something else.

   REQUIRED
   1. Identify two types of questions asked when strategizing.
   2. What can defeat a great strategy?

3. **Cost, financial, and management accounting—Advanced.** Albert Einstein, a physicist and Nobel Prize winner, has been quoted as saying, "We cannot solve our problems with the same thinking we used when we created them."

   REQUIRED
   1. As business managers, what is Einstein trying to tell us?
   2. What is your opinion about choosing between differentiation and cost leadership?

LEARNING OBJECTIVE 2

1. **Value chain and customer expectations—Elementary.** A recent annual report of Ford Motor Company included the following comments: "Delivering great value to our customers. That's our passion . . . Throughout Ford Motor Company, we're focused on improving the quality and value of our products and speeding delivery to market."

REQUIRED

1. Who are the customers of management accounting?
2. How may the value of management accounting systems to the customers of management accounting be enhanced?

2. **Value chain and customer expectations—Intermediate.** QLT Inc., a Canadian biopharmaceutical company, incurs the following costs:

   a. Cost of redesigning blister packs to make drug containers more tamper-proof
   b. Cost of videos sent to doctors to promote sales of a new drug
   c. Cost of a toll-free telephone line used for customer inquiries about usage, side-effects of drugs, and so on
   d. Equipment purchased by a scientist to conduct experiments on drugs awaiting approval by the government
   e. Payment to actors in an infomercial to be shown on television promoting Visudyne, a new treatment for age-related progressive blindness
   f. Labour costs of workers in the packaging area of a production facility
   g. Bonus paid to a salesperson for exceeding monthly sales quota
   h. Cost of the Purolator courier services to deliver drugs to hospitals

   REQUIRED
   Classify each cost item in parts (a) to (h) as belonging to a component of the value chain shown in Exhibit 1-2 (p. 6).

3. **Value chain and customer expectations—Advanced.** Apple Computer incurs the following costs:
   a. Electricity costs for the plant assembling the Macintosh computer line of products
   b. Transportation costs for shipping Macintosh software to a retail chain
   c. Payment to David Kelley Designs for design of the Powerbook carrying case
   d. Salary of a computer scientist working on the next generation of laptops
   e. Cost of a visit by Apple employees to a major customer to demonstrate Apple's ability to interconnect with other computers
   f. Purchase of competitors' products for testing against potential future Apple products
   g. Payment to a television station for running Apple advertisements
   h. Cost of cables purchased from an outside supplier to be used with the Macintosh printer

   REQUIRED
   Classify each cost item in parts (a) to (h) as belonging to a component of the value chain shown in Exhibit 1-2 (p. 6).

LEARNING OBJECTIVE 3

1. **Different activities, different relevant information—Elementary.** For each of the following activities, identify the major function (problem solving, scorekeeping, and attention directing) the accountant is performing.

   a. Preparing a monthly statement of Australian sales for the IBM marketing vice-president
   b. Interpreting differences between actual results and budgeted amounts on a performance report for the customer warranty department of General Electric
   c. Preparing a schedule of amortization for forklift trucks in the receiving department of a Hewlett Packard plant in Scotland
   d. Analyzing, for a Mitsubishi international manufacturing manager, the desirability of buying some auto parts made in Korea
   e. Interpreting why a Birmingham distribution centre did not adhere to its delivery costs budget
   f. Explaining a Xerox shipping department's performance report
   g. Preparing, for the manager of production control of a U.S. steel plant, a cost comparison of two computerized manufacturing control systems
   h. Preparing a scrap report for the finishing department of a Toyota parts plant
   i. Preparing the budget for the maintenance department of Mount Sinai Hospital
   j. Analyzing, for a General Motors product designer, the impact on product costs of some new headlight lamps

   REQUIRED
   Identify each activity in parts (a) to (j) as a problem-solving, scorekeeping, or attention-directing function.

2. **Different activities, different relevant information—Intermediate.** Indigo is a book retailing company. The majority of its sales are made at its own stores. These stores are often located in shopping malls or in the downtown central business districts of cities. A small but increasing percentage of sales are made via its Internet shopping division.

The following five reports were recently prepared by the management accounting group at Indigo:

a. Annual financial statements included in the annual report sent to its shareholders
b. Weekly report to the vice-president of operations for each Indigo store—includes revenue, gross margin, and operating costs
c. Study for vice-president of new business development of the expected revenue and expected costs of the Indigo Internet Division selling music products as well as books
d. Weekly report to book publishers and trade magazines on the sales of the top-ten fiction and nonfiction books at both its own stores and in the Internet Division
e. Report to its insurance company on losses Indigo suffered at three of its Toronto stores resulting from a storm

REQUIRED

For each report, identify how a manager might use it to make both a planning decision and a control decision (either at Indigo or another company).

3. **Different activities, different relevant information—Advanced.** WebNews.com offers its subscribers several services, such as an annotated TV guide and local-area information on weather, restaurants, and movie theatres. Its main revenue sources are fees for banner advertisements and fees from subscribers. Recent data are:

Month/Year	Advertising Revenues	Actual Number of Subscribers	Monthly Fee per Subscriber
June 2008	$ 481,186	28,642	$17.94
December 2008	999,790	54,813	23.94
June 2009	1,033,241	58,178	23.94
December 2009	1,773,686	86,437	23.94
June 2010	3,500,354	146,581	23.94

The following decisions were made from June through October 2010:

a. June 2010: Raised subscription fee to $29.94 per month from July 2010 onward. The budgeted number of subscribers for this monthly fee is shown in the table below.
b. June 2010: Informed existing subscribers that from July onward, monthly fee would be $29.94.
c. July 2010: Offered email service to subscribers and upgraded other online services.
d. October 2010: Dismissed the vice-president of marketing after significant slowdown in subscribers and subscription revenues, based on July through September 2010 data in table.
e. October 2010: Reduced subscription fee to $26.34 per month from November 2010 onward. Results for July–September 2010 are:

Month/Year	Budgeted Number of Subscribers	Actual Number of Subscribers	Monthly Fee per Subscriber
July 2010	140,000	128,933	$29.94
August 2010	150,000	139,419	29.94
September 2010	160,000	143,131	29.94

REQUIRED

1. Classify each of the decisions (a) to (e) as either a planning or a control decision.
2. Give two examples of other planning decisions and two examples of other control decisions that may be made at WebNews.com

LEARNING OBJECTIVE 4

1. **Management accountants' guidelines and roles in a company—Elementary.** Consider the five decisions made by Webnews.com in the Mastery Question above.

REQUIRED

1. For each of the five decisions (a) to (e), provide an example of pertinent information that an accountant could provide, and indicate whether the accountant would be acting in a problem-solving, scorekeeping, or attention-directing role.
2. Identify one decision that WebNews.com made as a result of feedback from the control system.
3. What further action might WebNews.com take based on the feedback from the July through September 2010 subscriber information?

2. **Management accountants' guidelines and roles in a company—Intermediate.** For each of the following items, identify which of the management guidelines applies: cost–benefit approach, behavioural and technical considerations, or different costs for different purposes.

1. Analyzing whether to keep the customer-service function within the organization or outsourcing it
2. Including costs of all the value-chain functions before deciding to launch a new product but including only its manufacturing costs in determining its inventory valuation
3. Considering the desirability of hiring one more accounts receivable clerk
4. Selecting the costliest photocopier after considering two other models
5. Installing a participatory budgeting system in which managers set their own performance targets, instead of top management imposing performance targets on them
6. Introducing a health-club plan for employees

3. **Management accountants' guidelines and roles in a company—Advanced.** Karen Phillipson is the new corporate controller of a multinational company that has just overhauled its organizational structure. The company is now decentralized. Each division is under an operating vice-president who, within wide limits, has responsibility and authority to run the division like a separate company.

Phillipson has a number of bright staff members. One of them, Bob Garrett, is in charge of a newly created performance analysis staff. Garrett and staff members prepare monthly division performance reports for the company president. These reports are division income statements, showing budgeted performance and actual results, and they are accompanied by detailed written explanations and appraisals of variances. In the past, each of Garrett's staff members was responsible for analyzing one division; each consulted with division line and staff executives and became generally acquainted with the division's operations.

After a few months, Bill Whisler, vice-president in charge of Division C, stormed into the controller's office. The gist of his complaint follows:

"Your staff are trying to take over part of my responsibility. They come in, snoop around, ask hundreds of questions, and take up plenty of our time. It's up to me, not you and your detectives, to analyze and explain my division's performance to central headquarters. If you don't stop trying to grab my responsibility, I'll raise the whole issue with the president."

REQUIRED
1. What events or relationships may have led to Whisler's outburst?
2. As Phillipson, how would you answer Whisler's contentions?
3. What alternative actions can Phillipson take to improve future relationships?

LEARNING OBJECTIVE 5

1. **Professional ethics and corporate governance—Elementary.** Marcia Miller is division controller and Tom Maloney is division manager of the Sports Shoe Company. Miller has line responsibility to Maloney, but she also has staff responsibility to the company controller.

Maloney is under severe pressure to achieve budgeted division income for the year. He has asked Miller to book $240,000 of sales on December 31. The customers' orders are firm, but the shoes are still in the production process. They will be shipped on or about January 4. Maloney said to Miller, "The key event is getting the sales order, not shipping of the shoes. You should support me, not obstruct my reaching division goals."

REQUIRED
1. Describe Miller's ethical responsibilities.
2. What should Miller do if Maloney gives her a direct order to book the sales?

2. **Professional ethics and corporate governance—Intermediate.** Jorge Michaels is the Winnipeg-based controller of Mexa Foods, a rapidly growing manufacturer and marketer of Mexican food products. Michaels is currently considering the purchase of a new cost management package for use by each of its six manufacturing plants and its many marketing personnel. Four major competing products are being considered by Michaels.

Horizon 1-2-3 is an aggressive software developer. It views Mexa as a target of opportunity. Every six months Horizon has a three-day users' conference in a Caribbean location. Each conference has substantial time left aside for "rest and recreation." Horizon offers Michaels an all-expenses-paid visit to the upcoming conference in Cancun, Mexico. Michaels accepts the offer, believing that it will be very useful to talk to other users of Horizon software. He is especially looking forward to the visit as he has close relatives in the Cancun area.

Before leaving, Michaels receives a visit from the president of Mexa. She shows him an anonymous letter sent to her. It argues that Horizon is receiving unfair favourable treatment in the Mexa software decision-making process. The letter specifically mentions Michaels's upcoming "all-expenses-paid trip to Cancun during Winnipeg's deep winter." Michaels is deeply offended. He says he has made no decision and believes he is very capable of making a software choice on the merits of each product. Mexa currently does not have a formal written code of ethics.

1. Do you think Michaels faces an ethical problem as regards his forthcoming visit to the Horizon users' group meeting? Refer to Exhibit 1-7 (pp. 18–19). Explain.
2. Should Mexa allow executives to attend users' meetings while negotiating with other vendors about a purchase decision? Explain. If yes, what conditions on attending should apply?
3. Would you recommend that Mexa develop its own code of ethics to handle situations such as this one? What are the pros and cons of having such a written code?

3. **Professional ethics and corporate governance—Advanced.** Shell Oil Company operates in many parts of the globe. These operations include oil exploration, production, transportation, refining, and marketing. One challenge faced by Shell is how to handle requests for "bribes" and "facilitating payments." The chair of Shell's operations recently gave an address where he "claimed that Shell loses valuable business because it refuses to pay bribes."

One form of bribe is a payment to a private bank account that is portrayed as a charitable donation. Shell's chair noted that "on occasion it has been suggested to me that Shell's cause would be much helped by a donation to a national cultural or humanitarian fund—which just happens to have a bank account in Switzerland." Another form of a bribe is a payment to an "intermediary" in which a company pays a third party for a "go-between" role that could be more efficiently handled without the third party. The "intermediary" handles the bribery payment plus takes an extra facilitating payment.

The Shell chair concluded the address as follows: "We do not bribe. We do not sanction any type of illegal payment of any kind anywhere, directly or indirectly, and any employee who is found to have done so will be dismissed and, if possible, prosecuted. The principle employees have to follow is simple: 'Just say no.'"

REQUIRED

1. Suppose you are a shareholder of Shell. Would you prefer Shell to pay bribes if it meant "gaining valuable business"?
2. Suppose you are the CFO of Shell. You suspect that one of your overseas subsidiaries is making payments to a local law firm for being an "intermediary" as well as for legal services. This subsidiary also makes payments to several Swiss-based "humanitarian funds" of questionable nature. How would you examine whether bribery is occurring? If you discovered it was, what actions would you take?

ASSIGNMENT MATERIAL

MyAccountingLab Make the grade with MyAccountingLab: The questions, exercises, and problems marked in red can be found on MyAccountingLab at **www.myaccountinglab.com.** You can practise them as often as you want, and most feature step-by-step guided instructions to help you find the right answer. Exercises and problems with an Excel icon in the margin have an accompanying Excel template on MyAccountingLab.

SHORT-ANSWER QUESTIONS

1-1 How does management accounting differ from financial accounting?

1-2 "Management accounting should not fit the straitjacket of financial accounting." Explain and give an example.

1-3 How can a management accountant help formulate a strategy?

1-4 Describe the business functions in the value chain.

1-5 Explain the term "supply chain" and its importance to cost management.

1-6 "Management accounting deals only with costs." Do you agree? Explain.

1-7 How can management accountants help improve quality and achieve timely product deliveries?

1-8 Distinguish planning decisions from control decisions.

1-9 What are the three roles management accountants perform?

1-10 What three guidelines help management accountants provide the most value to managers?

1-11 "Knowledge of technical issues such as computer technology is necessary but not sufficient to becoming a successful accountant." Do you agree? Why?

1-12 As a new controller, reply to this comment by a plant manager: "As I see it, our accountants may be needed to keep records for shareholders and Canada Revenue Agency—but I don't want them sticking their noses in my day-to-day operations. I do the best I know how. No pencil-pushing bean counter knows enough about my responsibilities to be of any use to me."

1-13 As used in accounting, what do "SMAC" and "CMA" stand for?

1-14 Name the four areas in which standards of ethical conduct exist for management accountants in Canada. What organization sets forth these standards?

1-15 What steps should a management accountant take if established written policies provide insufficient guidance on how to handle an ethical conflict?

EXERCISES

1-16 Cost, management, and financial accounting. Financial accountants use estimates of financial value differently than either cost or management accountants.

REQUIRED
1. Identify two differences in use.
2. Identify a similarity among accountants.

1-17 Strategy. Strategy usually includes some formal processes.

REQUIRED
1. How can managers choose between different strategies?
2. How is strategy different from an operating decision?

1-18 Value chain, supply chain, and key success factors. A survey on the ways organizations are changing their management accounting systems reported the following:

a. Company A now prepares a value-chain income statement for each brand it sells.
b. Company B now presents in a single report all costs related to achieving high quality levels in its products.
c. Company C now presents in its performance reports estimates of the manufacturing costs of its two most important competitors, in addition to its own manufacturing costs.
d. Company D now contracts with its suppliers to frequently deliver small quantities of materials directly to the production floor.
e. Company E now reports the percentage of times it fails to meet delivery dates that it has promised to customers.

REQUIRED
Link each of these changes to value-chain or supply-chain analysis or to the key success factors that are important to managers.

1-19 Value chain and classification of costs, computer company. Compaq Computer incurs the following costs:

a. Electricity costs for the plant assembling the Presario computer line of products
b. Transportation costs for shipping the Presario line of products to a retail chain
c. Payment to Eileen Donan Designs for design of the Armada Notebook
d. Salary of a computer scientist working on the next generation of minicomputers
e. Cost of a visit by Compaq employees to a major customer to demonstrate Compaq's multimedia capabilities
f. Purchase of competitors' products for testing against potential future Compaq products
g. Payment to a television station for running Compaq advertisements
h. Cost of cables purchased from an outside supplier to be used with the Compaq scanner

REQUIRED
Classify each cost item in parts (a) to (h) as belonging to a component of the value chain shown in Exhibit 1-2 (p. 6).

1-20 Value chain and classification of costs, fast food restaurant. Burger King, a hamburger fast food restaurant, incurs the following costs:

a. Cost of oil for the deep fryer
b. Wages of the counter help who give customers the food they order
c. Cost of the costume for the King on the Burger King television commercials
d. Cost of children's toys given away free with kids' meals
e. Cost of posters advertising a new dessert
f. Costs of frozen onion rings and french fries
g. Salaries of the food specialists who create new sandwiches for the restaurant chain
h. Cost of "to-go" bags requested by customers who do not eat their meals in the restaurant

Classify each cost item in parts (a) to (h) as belonging to a component of the value chain shown in Exhibit 1-2 (p. 6).

1-21 Planning and control decisions. Conner Company makes and sells brooms and mops. It takes the following actions, not necessarily in the order given below.

REQUIRED
For each action (a) to (e) below, state whether it is a planning decision or a control decision.

a. Conner asks its marketing team to consider ways to get back market share from its competitor, Swiffer
b. Conner calculates market share after introducing its newest product
c. Conner compares costs it actually incurred with costs it expected to incur for the production of a new product
d. Conner's design team proposes a new product to compete directly with the Swiffer
e. Conner estimates the costs it will incur to sell 30,000 units of the new product in the first quarter of next fiscal year

1-22 Problem solving, scorekeeping, and attention directing. Each of the following activities is a function accountants perform.

a. Interpreting differences between actual results and budgeted amounts on a shipping manager's performance report at a Sony distribution centre
b. Preparing a report showing the benefits of leasing motor vehicles versus owning them
c. Preparing adjusting journal entries for amortization on the personnel manager's office equipment at Bank of Nova Scotia
d. Preparing a customer's monthly statement for a Hudson's Bay store
e. Processing the weekly payroll for the University of Toronto maintenance department
f. Explaining the product design manager's performance report at a DaimlerChrysler division
g. Analyzing the costs of several different ways to blend materials in the foundry of a General Electric plant
h. Tallying sales, by branches, for the sales vice-president of Unilever
i. Analyzing, for the president of RIM, the impact of a contemplated new product on net income
j. Interpreting why an IBM sales district did not meet its sales quota

REQUIRED
Identify each of the activities in parts (a) to (j) as a problem-solving, scorekeeping, or attention-directing function.

1-23 Problem solving, scorekeeping, and attention directing. The Home Improvements Group Inc. (HIGI) produces home-improvement magazines and home-show events. Its managers are currently examining the following reports and accounting statements:

a. Five-year projections for expanding into home-improvement shows for cable television
b. Income statement to be included in a six-month interim report to be sent to investors and filed with the securities regulators
c. Profitability comparison of home shows directed by different managers, each of whom receives a percentage of their event's profits
d. Monthly reports of office costs for each of the six HIGI offices in Canada
e. Statement showing the revenues HIGI earns from different types of activities (magazines and home shows)

REQUIRED
Identify each of the activities in parts (a) to (e) as a problem-solving, scorekeeping, or attention-directing function.

1-24 Management accounting guidelines. For each of the following items, identify which of the management guidelines applies: cost–benefit approach, behavioural and technical considerations, or different costs for different purposes.

1. Considering the desirability of hiring one more sales representative
2. Installing a participatory system in which factory workers set their own production targets, instead of managers imposing performance targets on them
3. Deciding to give bonuses for superior performance to the employees who remained with the company during difficult times
4. Recording the costs of an advertising campaign as an expense for financial reporting purposes but capitalizing and expensing these costs over a longer period to evaluate the performance of the marketing manager
5. Introducing a dental plan for employees
6. Analyzing whether to keep the payroll function within the organization or outsourcing it

1-25 Professional ethics and reporting divisional performance. Sue Stevenson is division controller and John Jonas is division manager of the Silver Sandal Company. Stevenson has line responsibility to Jonas, but she also has staff responsibility to the company controller.

Jonas is under severe pressure to achieve budgeted division income for the year. He has asked Stevenson to book $200,000 of sales on December 31. The customers' orders are firm, but the shoes are still in the production process. They will be shipped on or about January 4. Jonas said to Stevenson, "The key event is getting the sales order, not shipping of the shoes. You should support me, not obstruct my reaching division goals."

REQUIRED
1. Describe Stevenson's ethical responsibilities.
2. What should Stevenson do if Jonas gives her a direct order to book the sales?

PROBLEMS

1-26 Planning and control decisions. Softmoc is a shoe retailing company. The majority of its sales are made at its own stores. These stores are often located in shopping malls or in the downtown shopping districts of cities. A small but increasing percentage of sales are made via its Internet shopping division.

The following five reports were recently prepared by the management accounting group at Softmoc:
1. Annual financial statements included in the annual report sent to its shareholders
2. Weekly report to the vice-president of operations for each Softmoc store—includes revenue, gross margin, and operating costs
3. Report to insurance company on losses Softmoc suffered at its new Toronto store resulting from a storm
4. Weekly report to a new supplier on the sales of that supplier's products at both the Softmoc stores and by the Internet Division
5. Study for vice-president of new business development of the expected revenue and expected costs of the Softmoc Internet Division selling foot-health products (arch supports, heel inserts, etc.) as well as shoes

REQUIRED
1. For each report, identify how a manager would use it to make both a planning decision and a control decision (either at Softmoc or another company).

1-27 Planning and control, feedback. In April 2009, Sheri Campbell, editor of the *Daily Shopping News* (*DSN*), decides to reduce the price per newspaper from $0.84 to $0.70, starting May 1, 2009. Actual paid circulation in April is 4,200,000 (140,000 per day × 30 days). Campbell estimates that the $0.14 price reduction will increase paid circulation in May to 6,200,000 (200,000 × 31 days). The actual May circulation turns out to be 6,820,000 (220,000 × 31 days). Assume that one goal of *DSN* is to increase operating income. The budgeted increase in circulation would enable *DSN* to charge higher advertising rates in later months of 2009 if those budgeted gains actually occur. The actual price paid in May 2009 was the budgeted $0.70 per newspaper.

REQUIRED
1. Distinguish between planning and control at *DSN*, giving an example of each.
2. Prepare a newspaper revenue performance report for *DSN* for May 2009 showing the actual results, budgeted amounts, and the variance.
3. Give two types of action Campbell might take based on feedback on the May 2009 circulation revenue.

1-28 Planning and control decisions: Internet company. WebInfo.com offers its subscribers several services, such as an annotated TV guide and local-area information on weather, restaurants, and movie theatres. Its main revenue sources are fees for banner advertisements and fees from subscribers. Recent data are:

Month/Year	Advertising Revenues	Actual Number of Subscribers	Monthly Fee per Subscriber
June 2008	$ 400,988	28,642	$14.95
December 2008	833,158	54,813	19.95
June 2009	861,034	58,178	19.95
December 2009	1,478,072	86,437	19.95
June 2010	2,916,962	146,581	19.95

The following decisions were made from June through October 2010:

a. June 2010: Raised subscription fee to $24.95 per month from July 2010 onward. The budgeted number of subscribers for this monthly fee is shown in the table below.

b. June 2010: Informed existing subscribers that from July onward, monthly fee would be $24.95.

c. July 2010: Offered email service to subscribers and upgraded other online services.

d. October 2010: Dismissed the vice-president of marketing after significant slowdown in subscribers and subscription revenues, based on July through September 2010 data in table.

e. October 2010: Reduced subscription fee to $21.95 per month from November 2010 onward. Results for July–September 2010 are:

Month/Year	Budgeted Number of Subscribers	Actual Number of Subscribers	Monthly Fee per Subscriber
July 2010	140,000	128,933	$24.95
August 2010	150,000	139,419	24.95
September 2010	160,000	143,131	24.95

REQUIRED

1. Classify each of the decisions (a) to (e) as either a planning or a control decision.

2. Give two examples of other planning decisions and two examples of other control decisions that may be made at WebInfo.com.

1-29 Strategic decisions and management accounting. A series of independent situations in which a company is about to make a strategic decision follow.

DECISIONS:

a. Major Phones is about to decide whether to launch production and sale of a cell phone with standard features.

b. Computer Magic is trying to decide whether to produce and sell a new home computer software package that includes the ability to interface with a sewing machine and a vacuum cleaner. There is no such software currently on the market.

c. Christina Cosmetics has been asked to provide a "store brand" lip gloss that will be sold at discount retail stores.

d. Marcus Meats is entertaining the idea of developing a special line of gourmet bologna made with sun-dried tomatoes, pine nuts, and artichoke hearts.

REQUIRED

1. For each decision, state whether the company is following a low price or a differentiated product strategy.

2. For each decision, discuss what information the management accountant can provide about the source of competitive advantage for these firms.

1-30 Management accounting guidelines. For each of the following items, identify which of the management guidelines applies: cost–benefit approach, behavioural and technical considerations, or different costs for different purposes.

1. Analyzing whether to keep the billing function within the organization or outsourcing it

2. Deciding to give bonuses for superior performance to the employees in a Japanese subsidiary and extra vacation time to the employees in a Swedish subsidiary

3. Including costs of all the value-chain functions before deciding to launch a new product but including only its manufacturing costs in determining its inventory valuation

4. Considering the desirability of hiring one more salesperson

5. Giving each salesperson the compensation option of choosing either from a low salary and high-percentage sales commission or a high salary and a low-percentage sales commission

6. Selecting the costlier computer system after considering two systems

7. Installing a participatory budgeting system in which managers set their own performance targets, instead of top management imposing performance targets on them

8. Recording research costs as an expense for financial reporting purposes but capitalizing and expensing them over a longer period for management performance-evaluation purposes

9. Introducing a profit-sharing plan for employees

1-31 Role of controller; role of chief financial officer. George Perez is the controller at Allied Electronics, a manufacturer of devices for the computer industry. He is being considered for a promotion to chief financial officer.

1. In this table, indicate which executive is primarily responsible for each activity.

Activity	Controller	CFO
Managing accounts payable		
Communicating with investors		
Strategic review of different lines of businesses		
Budgeting funds for a plant upgrade		
Managing the company's short-term investments		
Negotiating fees with auditors		
Assessing profitability of various products		
Evaluating the costs and benefits of a new product design		

2. Based on this table and your understanding of the two roles, what types of training or experience will George find most useful for the CFO position?

1-32 **Governance and end-of-year actions.** Janet Taylor is the new division controller of the snack-foods division of Gourmet Foods. Gourmet Foods has reported a minimum 15% growth in annual earnings for each of the past five years. The snack-foods division has reported annual earnings growth of more than 20% each year in this same period. During the current year, the economy went into a recession. The corporate controller estimates a 10% annual earnings growth rate for Gourmet Foods in this year. One month before the December 31 fiscal year-end of the current year, Taylor estimates the snack-foods division will report an annual earnings growth of only 8%. Warren Ryan, the snack-foods division president, is not happy, but he notes that "end-of-year actions" still need to be taken.

Taylor makes some inquiries and is able to compile the following list of end-of-year actions that were more or less accepted by the prior division controller:

a. Deferring December's routine monthly maintenance on packaging equipment by an independent contractor until January of next year

b. Extending the close of the current fiscal year beyond December 31 so that some sales of next year are included in the current year

c. Altering dates of shipping documents of next January's sales to record them as sales in December of the current year

d. Giving salespeople a double bonus to exceed December sales targets

e. Deferring the current period's advertising by reducing the number of television spots run in December and running more than planned in January of next year

f. Deferring the current period's reported advertising costs by having Gourmet Foods' outside advertising agency delay billing December advertisements until January of next year or by having the agency alter invoices to conceal the December date

g. Persuading carriers to accept merchandise for shipment in December of the current year although they normally would not have done so

REQUIRED

1. Why might the snack-foods division president want to take these end-of-year actions?

2. The division controller is deeply troubled and reads the Code of Professional Ethics in Exhibit 1-7 (pp. 18–19). Classify each of the end-of-year actions as (i) acceptable or (ii) unacceptable according to that document.

3. What should Taylor do if Ryan suggests that these end-of-year actions are taken in every division of Gourmet Foods and that she will greatly harm the snack-foods division if she does not cooperate and paint the rosiest picture possible of the division's results?

1-33 **Governance and earnings management.** Harvest Day Corporation is a publishing company that produces trade magazines. The company's stakeholders are awaiting the announcement of Harvest Day's earnings for the fiscal year, which ends on December 31. Market analysts have predicted earnings to be around $1.34 per share. The CEO of Harvest Day expects earnings to be only $1.20 per share, and knows this will cause the price of the stock to drop. The CEO suggests the following ideas to various managers to try to increase reported earnings by the end of the fiscal year:

a. Delaying recording of cancelled subscriptions for December until January

b. Waiting until the new fiscal year to update the software on office computers

c. Recognizing unearned subscription revenue (cash received in advance for magazines that will be sent in the future) as revenue when received in the current month (just before fiscal year end) instead of booking it as a liability

d. Delay recording purchases of office supplies on account until after year end

e. Booking advertising revenues that relate to January in December

f. Waiting until after fiscal year end to do building repairs

g. Switching from declining-balance to straight-line amortization to reduce amortization expense in the current year

REQUIRED

1. Why would Harvest Day Corporation's CEO want to "manage" earnings?
2. From the point of view of the Code of Professional Ethics in Exhibit 1-7 (pp. 18–19), which of the items in (a) to (g) above are acceptable to Harvest Day's controller? Which are unacceptable?
3. What should the controller do about the CEO's suggestions? What should the controller do if the CEO refuses to change the suggestions?

COLLABORATIVE LEARNING CASES

1-34 Responding to allegations of fraud. You are the controller of Maple Ridge Finance Corp. (MRFC). MRFC is an investment banking company that has recently encountered severe financial difficulties and has had to lay off more than 100 employees. The only bright spot in this picture is MRFC's bond trading division, but you have just received the following anonymous letter:

Dear Sir,

Last year's reported earnings for the bond trading division are fictitious. The top three managers of the division recently received bonuses of more than $14 million, based on their share of last year's reported earnings. The head of bond trading has been inventing bond trades that are supposed to be highly profitable. They are not. The division profits are like a house of cards about to collapse. The head of bond trading cares only about "how much you reportedly made" and nothing about how you made it. The auditors don't understand the complexity of today's bond trading operations. This problem will blow up in your face unless handled quickly and carefully. I am sending a copy of this letter to the Ontario Securities Commission, the *Financial Post*, *Canadian Business*, *The Globe and Mail*, and all members of Maple Ridge's board of directors.

Sincerely,
Concerned Ex-employee

INSTRUCTIONS

Form groups of three or more students. One will be the chief financial officer, one the president, and one the chairperson of the board of directors. Other members are on the board of directors.

REQUIRED

Develop a group consensus on how you should respond to this letter. Like many firms in the financial services industry, MRFC has no formal code of ethics. Should MRFC formalize a code of ethics statement?

1-35 Global company, ethical challenges with bribery. In June 2009, the government of Vartan invited bids for construction of a cellular telephone network. ZenTel, an experienced communications company, was eager to enter the growing field of cellular telephone networks in countries with poor infrastructures for land lines. If ZenTel won a few of these early contracts, it would be sought after for its field experience and expertise. After careful analysis, it prepared a detailed bid for the Communications Ministry of Vartan, building in only half of its usual profit margin and providing a contractual guarantee that the project would be completed in two years or less. The multimillion-dollar bid was submitted before the deadline, and ZenTel received notification that it had reached the Vartan government. Then, despite repeated faxes, emails, and phone calls to the ministry, there was no news on the bids or the project from the Vartan government.

Steve Cheng, vice-president of global operations for ZenTel, contacted the Canadian commercial attaché in Vartan, who told him that his best chance was to go to Vartan and try to meet the deputy minister of communications in person. Cheng prepared for the trip, rereading the proposal and making sure that he understood the details.

At the commercial attaché's office in Vartan's capital, Cheng waited nervously for the deputy minister and his assistant. Cheng had come to Vartan with a clear negotiating strategy to try to win the bid. Soon the deputy minister and his staff arrived, introductions were made, and pleasantries were exchanged. The deputy minister asked a few questions about ZenTel and the bid and then excused himself, leaving his assistant to talk to Cheng. After clearly indicating that many other compelling bids had been made by firms from around the world, the assistant said, "Mr. Cheng, I guarantee that ZenTel's bid will be accepted if you pay a $1 million commission. Of course, your excellent proposal doesn't have to be altered in any way." It was clear to Cheng that the "commission" was, in fact, a bribe. Tactfully, he pointed out that government laws and ZenTel's corporate policy prohibited such a payment. The assistant wished him a good day and a pleasant flight home and left.

REQUIRED

1. As a shareholder of ZenTel, would you prefer that ZenTel executives agree to the payment of the "commission"?
2. When Cheng described his experience to his friend Hank Shorn, who managed international business development for another company, Hank said that his own "personal philosophy" was to make such payments if they were typical in the local culture. Do you agree with Hank's point of view? Explain.
3. Why would ZenTel have a corporate policy against such payments?
4. What should Steve Cheng do next?

An Introduction to Cost Terms and Purposes

BUSINESS MATTERS

Cost Classification: Accounting Logic for Cost Management

Times change but Motorola's leadership in customer satisfaction, with its cutting-edge cell phones, has not. In 2007, the company tied for the highest ranking on design, operation, features, handset durability, and battery function. By any performance measure—$43 billion in net sales, net income of $3.7 billion, and 75 million units sold of its newest product, MOTORAZR[2] (pictured)—this global corporation is a success. Designs incorporating new technology reliably will fuel increased revenue. Motorola improves its profit because it continues to examine and reduce costs by discontinuing product lines, exiting less-profitable businesses, outsourcing manufacturing, combining manufacturing operations, and reducing the number of employees.

LEARNING OBJECTIVES

After studying this chapter, you should be able to

1. Identify and distinguish the logic underlying three cost classification systems derived from financial accounting information: period and inventoriable, direct and indirect, prime and conversion

2. Apply cost information to produce detailed financial schedules to illustrate how the asset value of inventories expires into cost of goods sold reported on the income statement

3. Differentiate fixed costs from variable costs using the management-accounting cost-classification system

4. Explain the limitations that the use of average or unit costs impose on managerial decision making

5. Apply management-accounting logic to classify costs for use in managerial decisions

COSTS AND TERMINOLOGY

Cost is a resource sacrificed or foregone to achieve a specific objective. The resource sacrificed is usually measured and recorded as a monetary amount paid or contracted to be paid to acquire inputs that will be consumed. For example, the cost of $23 million of raw materials in one month is a cash resource sacrificed. Giving up the opportunity to use the $23 million for another purpose such as research and development is a resource foregone. This basic transaction, a payment or promise to pay, is a fundamental input to a useful cost management information system.

Managers use this cost information to solve an enormous variety of problems that put at risk the profitability of their companies. The reason for distinguishing among different classification methods is that different, relevant cost information is needed to identify and remedy different cost management problems. **Relevant information** is that information that will change a decision. The same cost classification will not be appropriate for all problems. Different classification methods for the same set of costs filter out and then report relevant information in a form that supports good managerial decisions. The goal of each classification system is to produce information relevant to identify and decide how to remedy a specific set of cost management problems.

We begin with the logic of financial accountants with which you are already familiar, then move to two logics of cost classification used by management accountants. Financial accountants primarily examine business transactions undertaken in the past, then estimate, record, and report the **actual costs** incurred during some specific time period. These past payments and obligations to pay are referred to on the income statement as either costs or expenses, and on the balance sheet as either current or long-term liabilities. What financial accountants list on the income statement as operating expenses, management accountants term period costs. **Period costs** are all costs incurred to generate revenue during a specific time period except the costs of manufacturing accumulated as cost of goods sold. **Revenue** is an actual or promised inflow of assets, most often cash, from customers paying for the output provided by the seller.

PERIOD AND INVENTORIABLE COSTS

Period costs are expensed because accountants cannot find sufficient evidence that they will generate any benefit in future time periods. By expensing these period costs or operating expenses, accountants can match costs or sacrifices to the benefit of the revenues realized and reported as recognized in a specific time period. Period costs shown in Exhibit 2-1 include research and development, design, marketing, distribution, and customer service. In Exhibit 2-1 the Production Costs in blue are *excluded* from period costs (or operating expenses) on the income statement.

The word *cost* appears on the income statement in reference to a subset of total costs incurred in a time period. If the company is a manufacturer, all the costs of manufacturing are accumulated in inventory accounts until the goods are sold. The **cost of goods sold (COGS)** is the accumulation of all costs incurred to manufacture the finished products that have been sold. Merchandising companies such as Danier Leather do not manufacture their products but purchase them for resale.

EXHIBIT 2-1

Costs According to a Timeline from Idea to After-Sales Service (The Value Chain of Business Functions)

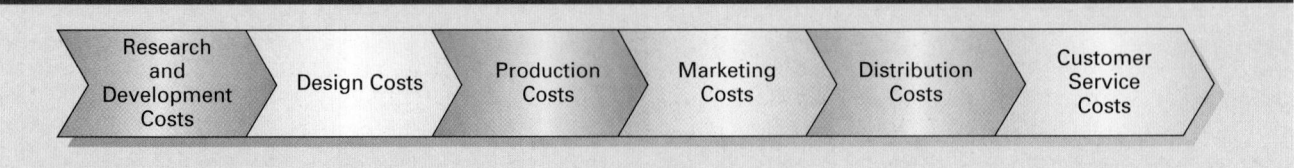

Research and Development Costs → Design Costs → Production Costs → Marketing Costs → Distribution Costs → Customer Service Costs

Often merchandisers still refer to this as COGS, although you will also see the term *cost of sales*. **Cost of sales (COS)** includes all the accumulated purchase costs for merchandise sold for companies such as Danier Leather, a merchandiser that simply purchases then resells finished goods.

In this chapter, to emphasize the difference between value-chain business functions, we use COGS in reference only to manufacturers and COS in reference only to merchandisers. The sale of the goods in a specific time period is the event that triggers the matching and recognition of either COGS or COS on the income statement. You may recall that in Canada, the dollar value of the cost outflow from the finished goods inventory to COGS or COS is determined by either the first-in, first-out (FIFO), weighted-average, or specific-identification method. Management accountants refer to the COGS or COS as inventoriable costs. **Inventoriable cost** is the accumulation of all costs incurred to either manufacture (for manufacturers) or purchase inventory for resale (for merchandisers) the finished products that have been sold during a specific time period.

In contrast to COGS, the **cost of goods manufactured (COGM)** is the costs of all finished goods transferred into finished goods inventory, whether sold or unsold, irrespective of the time period when work was begun. The completion and transfer of goods in a specific time period is the event that triggers the recognition of COGM. The unsold finished goods remain in inventory where their costs have been accumulated as the **cost of goods available for sale (COGAS)**. Notice that production events trigger COGM and COGAS but a *sales* event triggers the transfer of costs from COGAS to COGS. Service companies sell intangible services such as audit, legal, or technical support, which have no physical presence and no inventory accounts. Instead, service-company costs almost always appear as period costs or operating expenses matched to revenue generated during a specific time period.

Inventoriable costs are all estimated according to generally accepted accounting principles (GAAP). The specific inventoriable costs comprising COGS and COGM, also known as **production costs**, are those to purchase and transform raw material inputs into outputs using labour and equipment. In the example illustrated in Exhibits 2-3 through 2-5, the accumulation and flow of costs through various inventory accounts is illustrated for a single model of cell phone for Motorola for the month of January 2009.

According to GAAP, similar transactions should be treated similarly, and this is the basis for summing the costs into general ledger accounts that describe the transactions, for example raw (or direct) materials, manufacturing (direct) labour, fuel, heat, power, light, plant rent or lease, plant amortization, plant insurance, plant property taxes, maintenance supplies, supervisory and executive salaries of plant employees, and so on. Notice that all of the costs listed are incurred to manufacture the cell phone but some are more directly associated with the outputs from the manufacturing process than are others. We will explain this difference more fully later in the chapter. Now, the focus is on how to identify the COGM and COGS as they accumulate in and flow through the raw (direct) materials, work-in-process, and finished goods accounts. COGM and COGS are the production, or inventoriable, costs of manufacturing goods.

Before focusing exclusively on the product costs reported as components of COGS and inventory, an income statement is illustrated in Exhibit 2-2. Exhibit 2-2 links the financial-accounting information to the management-accounting logic of the value chain of business functions. Financial accountants classify similar transactions, which have already occurred, in the same account. In this chapter, the basis of constructing the COGS is the financial information in the company's management information system (MIS). All inventoriable costs are production costs, and in Exhibit 2-2 they are shown in blue. Period costs are shown in the colours that match the value-chain costs introduced in Chapter 1, Exhibit 1-2 (p. 6). Operations managers and management accountants are concerned with accounting for and managing COGS and operating costs. Costs such as interest and taxes are not controlled by operations managers but rather by financial managers in the organization. At the end of this chapter, you will see in Exhibit 2-10 the detail of the components of COGS. The dollar values of the accounts in Exhibit 2-2 are identical to those in Exhibit 2-10.

EXHIBIT 2-2
The Relationship between Value-Chain Management-Cost Classifications and Financial-Cost Classifications

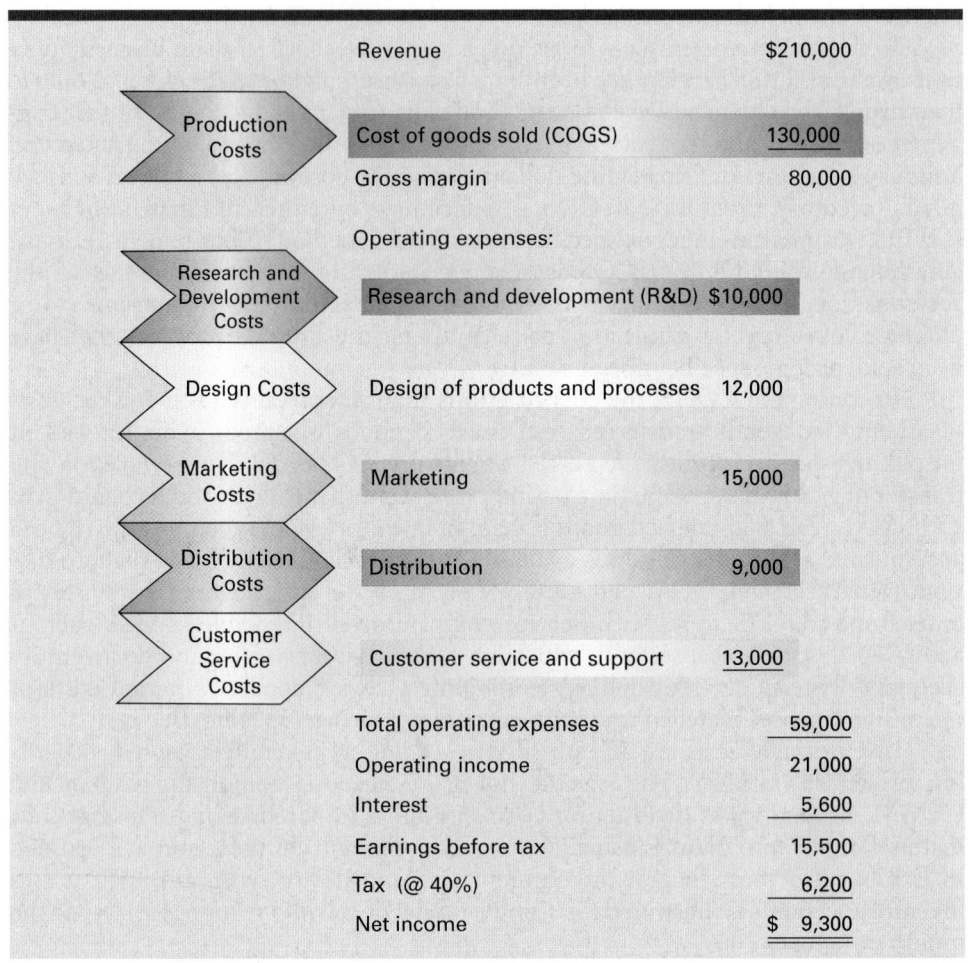

Revenue	$210,000
Cost of goods sold (COGS)	130,000
Gross margin	80,000
Operating expenses:	
Research and development (R&D)	$10,000
Design of products and processes	12,000
Marketing	15,000
Distribution	9,000
Customer service and support	13,000
Total operating expenses	59,000
Operating income	21,000
Interest	5,600
Earnings before tax	15,500
Tax (@ 40%)	6,200
Net income	$ 9,300

In the classification of costs, we assume that raw physical materials are transformed by an orderly sequence of activities performed by either people or machines. The full sequence of activities is a production process. When the production process is complete, the result is a product that is available for sale. The flow of costs matches the flow of the raw or direct materials through the production process. The classification starts with the purchase cost of direct materials; then costs in the production process are accumulated.

The direct materials account is the beginning of the sequence of cost accumulation. The cost accumulation and production process is actually circular and continuous but is presented in stages to illustrate how important inventoriable costs are identified. The ending inventory values for December 31, 2008 are also the beginning inventory values for January 1, 2009, and that is what is meant by a continuous flow of costs in the production process. The time period for which the inventoriable costs are accounted is one month ending January 31, 2009. It is assumed that Motorola has the equipment and labour available to transform raw materials into finished goods. Because labour costs incurred directly to produce a cell phone are relatively easy to accumulate in separate accounts, we are also going to assume that the costs of transformation accumulated in the inventory accounts exclude labour costs. Other costs include many manufacturing overhead support (indirect) costs such as utilities, supervision, maintenance, insurance, taxes, and amortization of the equipment or lease costs that can also be readily identified and accumulated into separate accounts. For purposes of this example and to avoid double-counting any costs, we are assuming that the transformation cost is fuel for the equipment. The direct labour and manufacturing overhead costs are accumulated and will be reported separately as the remaining inventoriable costs for January 2009.

The beginning balance for the cost of all direct materials available for use on January 1, 2009 in the raw (direct) materials inventory is $11 million. During the month, additional purchases of direct materials of $23 million bring the total cost of direct materials available for use in January to $34 million ($11 million + $23 million = $34 million). Throughout the month, the transactions representing costs of direct materials transferred out of inventory have been summarized in the general ledger inventory T-account as debits and credits. The cost of direct materials used during the month was $12 million, leaving an ending balance remaining in this inventory account on January 31, 2009 of $22 million. This is summarized in Exhibit 2-3.

The cost of direct materials is a sacrifice or obligation to sacrifice resources. The value of materials used to assemble cell phones was $12 million; the remaining $22 million in ending inventory has not yet been of benefit to Motorola. This $22 million is now or shortly will be a cash flow out of Motorola. In this case, the dollar value accumulated in inventory of $22 million could have been used in a different, perhaps more beneficial, way by Motorola.

THINKING CRITICALLY

Of what use is it to consider costs as a sacrifice that might better have been made elsewhere? Explain in a sentence or two. Read on for an assessment of this situation.

The initial cost flows listed in this example have meaning because they report on actual events, in this case the purchase of direct materials. Good, timely financial accounting of these events is one accurate basis upon which others in the company can manage operations to reduce costs and improve profit. Management accountants understand not only how to calculate these costs, but what they mean. In the short term, these costs alone cannot identify an issue, but they are attention-getting and signal the need to assess why so much raw (direct) material was purchased but not used. Possibilities include:

◆ There was an error in the quantity of materials purchased
◆ Planned production processes were unexpectedly interrupted
◆ An anticipated interruption in future supply led to a build-up in inventory

EXHIBIT 2-3
Schedule of Direct (Raw) Materials Inventory to Generate the Cost of Goods Manufactured Schedule

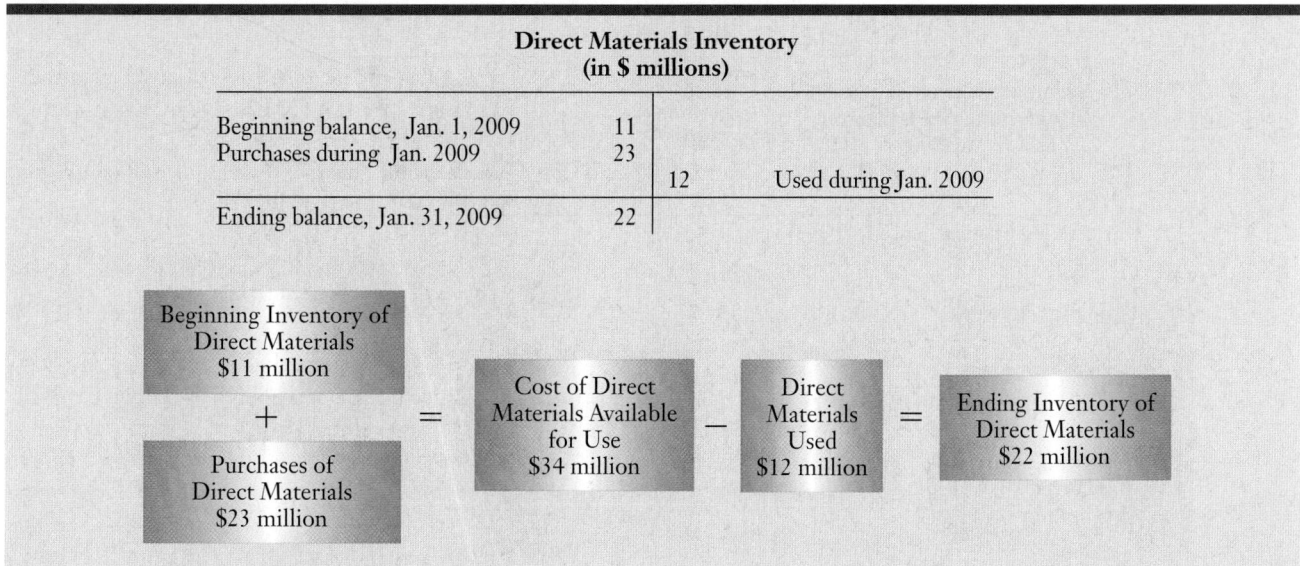

During January, the beginning balance for costs accumulated in the work-in-process (WIP) inventory was $6 million for this model of cell phone, which was the ending balance on December 31, 2008. Of all the direct materials transferred into WIP inventory in December 2008, some remained incompletely transformed into finished goods. Transformation costs include those of labour, which we have noted are readily accumulated separately. During January 2009, the cost of direct materials transferred to WIP was $12 million and additional transformation costs for fuel to run the equipment were $2 million, for a total manufacturing cost to be accounted for of $20 million ($6 million + $12 million + $2 million). The total cost of goods finished and transferred out to the finished goods inventory in January 2009 was $5 million, and this is the cost of goods manufactured (COGM). The WIP ending inventory was $15 million ($20 million - $5 million), as shown in Exhibit 2-4.

This analysis of costs through the WIP inventory partially confirms that there may be problems in the production process because only $5 million of cell phones were completed and transferred to finished goods during January 2009. Consider the second possible potential problem mentioned, an unexpected interruption in the production process. Perhaps the supply of fuel, rather than direct materials, was interrupted to some of Motorola's plants around the world. If true, then the company would not have been able to continue using its equipment for the entire month because it would not have had the fuel to keep its equipment running. With 2007 annual sales of 75 million units for one model of cell phone, it seems unlikely this could be achieved with $5 million spent on monthly production costs unless the costs per unit were extremely low. More information, such as the quantity of units produced, is required before any conclusive identification of the problem can be made. The WIP accounts have helped to focus on one problem for either confirmation or elimination, and also led to understanding that relevant information in addition to costs must be provided before the cost control problem can be identified.

On December 31, 2008, the balance in finished goods (FG) inventory was $25 million, meaning that not all the cell phones completed and available for sale during December were actually sold. In January 2009, an additional $5 million of cell phones were completed and the total costs of completion were transferred from WIP to FG. This is the exact amount of COGM shown in Exhibit 2-4. The sum of the costs accumulated in the FG beginning balance plus the COGM is the cost of goods available for sale (COGAS) of $30 million ($25 million + $5 million = $30 million). The costs of the finished goods that were actually sold (COGS) during January 2009

EXHIBIT 2-4

Schedule of Work-in-Process Inventory to Generate the Cost of Goods Manufactured Schedule

Work-in-Process (WIP) Inventory (in $ millions)			
Beginning balance, Jan. 1, 2009	6		
Manufacturing costs incurred during Jan. 2009	14		
		5	Cost of goods manufactured during Jan. 2009
Ending balance, Jan. 31, 2009	15		

Beginning Inventory of WIP $6 million

+

Manufacturing Costs Incurred $14 million

=

Total Manufacturing Costs to be Accounted for $20 million

−

Costs of Goods Manufactured (COGM) $5 million

=

Ending Inventory of WIP $15 million

EXHIBIT 2-5
Schedule of Finished Goods Inventory to Generate the Cost of Goods Manufactured Schedule

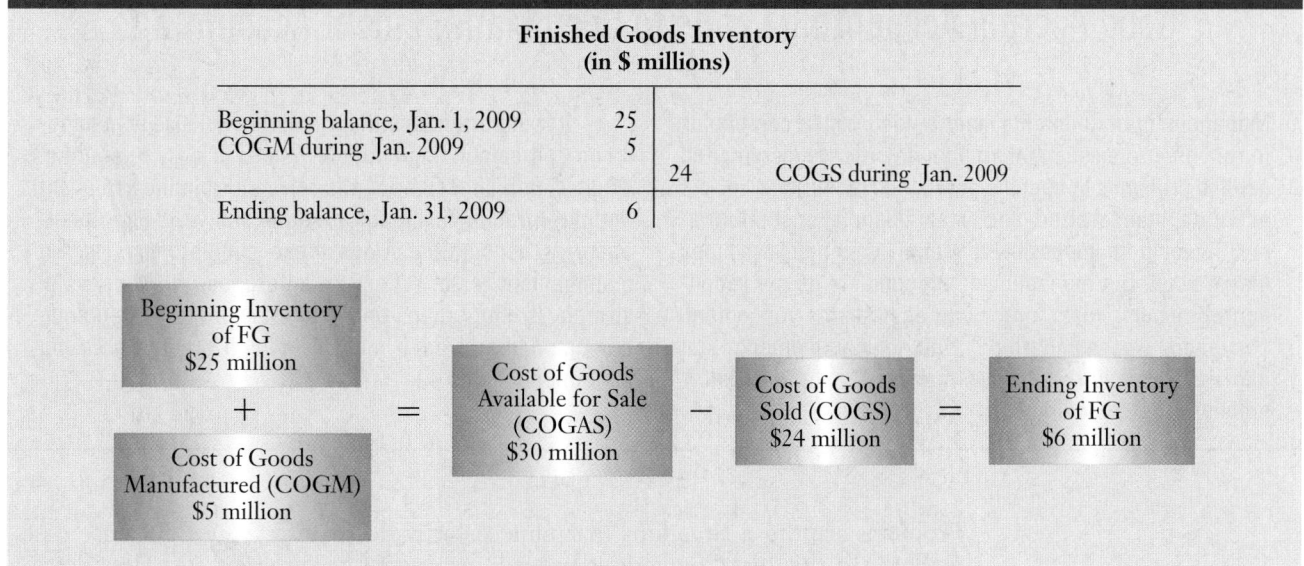

Finished Goods Inventory
(in $ millions)

Beginning balance, Jan. 1, 2009	25		
COGM during Jan. 2009	5		
		24	COGS during Jan. 2009
Ending balance, Jan. 31, 2009	6		

Beginning Inventory of FG $25 million
+
Cost of Goods Manufactured (COGM) $5 million
=
Cost of Goods Available for Sale (COGAS) $30 million
−
Cost of Goods Sold (COGS) $24 million
=
Ending Inventory of FG $6 million

was $24 million, leaving a balance of costs of $6 million in ending finished goods inventory. This is shown in Exhibit 2-5.

January's demand for the cell phones was $24 million of production (as shown by the COGS in the Finished Goods Inventory account), yet only $5 million of production actually occurred (as shown by the COGM in the Work-in-Process Inventory account). No additional manufacturing costs accumulate in the FG inventory. This situation suggests an imminent shortfall of supply. If demand continues for production costing $24 million and actual production costs continue at $5 million, then Motorola will lose a lot of potential sales. It is the revenue from sales that represents the benefit realized from the costs of production. Thus, the costs recorded in the three inventory accounts suggest that Motorola's managers need to identify the problem quickly and remedy it.

Inventoriable costs, which financial accountants refer to as COGS, can be classified according to management-accounting logic. Management-accounting logic supports the managerial goal of identifying a wide variety of sets of costs. Rather than use similar transactions as the basis for classification, management accountants use the cost object. A **cost object** is anything for which it is desirable to measure the costs. In the Motorola example, the unit of finished goods, the cell phone, is a cost object. But there may be no problems with the costs per cell phone; in the example, one potential problem was identified as an unplanned interruption to the production process. To clarify the financial effect of the interruption, managers would want information on the costs of the interruption. Thus, the interruption becomes the cost object. Should remedying the interruption require a reconfiguration of the production process and alternatives are available, managers would want cost information on each alternative process. Thus, the process becomes the cost object.

A second possible problem was that too much direct material was purchased. To clarify the financial effect of this error, managers would want information on the costs of possible ways to change the purchasing process to remedy the problem. One possibility might be to outsource the entire purchasing activity and eliminate this department to save costs. Thus, the cost object becomes either the activity or the department. This logic differs fundamentally from that of financial accountants, for whom there is only one basis of classification: the similarity of transactions. Their standardized estimation and recording process, however, enables management accountants to feel confident that when they access the management information system, the relevant costs they retrieve for the cost object will be reliable. As you may have noticed, the task of managers is to identify problems and remedy them.

Good Accrual Accounting Leads to Good Management Accounting

Management accountants meet a need within companies to reconfigure existing information in order to identify and resolve problems in both the short and long terms. Without accurate, standardized, and timely financial cost information, it would be impossible to identify which dollar values meant what. But management accountants do not reconfigure financial costs in any way that seems convenient. They, too, use standardized and logical methods that can be explained to business managers, who may know nothing about accounting.

It is important to understand that the skill of manipulating and calculating financial values is easy to acquire. What is difficult is filtering the relevant from the irrelevant and interpreting results in a meaningful way. Each management accountant brings these competencies to the management team. Within an enterprise, the successful strategy is cooperation and mutual respect for the unique competencies of each member, which creates a strong accounting team.

Problems are those situations that unnecessarily decrease revenues, increase costs, or both. In this text, the various procedures, including different cost classification systems, are primarily directed at how to provide and analyze relevant cost information and remedy cost control problems.

DIRECT AND INDIRECT COSTS

The management-accounting logic of using a cost object to filter out and retrieve only the relevant costs from a management information system can explain two types of costs. The first is **direct costs** of production that can be traced to a cost object—a single output unit—in an economically feasible way. Another way of understanding this is that the existence of the cost object causes the direct cost. Many different cost objects can be specified according to the management problem at hand, but in this section, the focus is on how to separate inventoriable costs into those that are direct, or economically traced to a single output unit, and those that are indirect. For example, if a labour contract states all rates per hour paid to workers of different status and seniority, then it is not expensive to extract the cost information from existing payroll records at any level of detail required to help trace direct labour costs to each output unit. This information helps managers identify and solve labour cost-control problems. If a product requires a specified amount of some unique direct material, then it is not expensive to extract this cost information from existing purchasing records to help identify and solve a direct materials cost-control problem. In both these situations, the production cost of the input can be readily and inexpensively traced directly to a specific cost object—an output unit.

Direct materials (DM) costs are inventoriable costs to acquire production materials that can be traced economically to an output unit as the cost object. The recorded cost of DM includes freight-in, sales tax, and customs duties. **Direct manufacturing labour (DML)** costs are *inventoriable* costs to compensate production labour that can be traced economically to an output unit as the cost object. DML are a part of COGS. We will use the term **direct labour (DL)** costs in this chapter to distinguish all *period* labour costs that can be traced economically to a specified cost object but are *not* part of COGS. To illustrate, an example of DL would be the labour costs to undertake research and development, while the labour costs of those performing the manufacturing activity would be DML. The extent to which costs can be readily and inexpensively traced to a range of cost objects will depend upon the level of detail and flexibility of the management information system, as well as the ingenuity of management accountants trying to extract relevant information in a consistent and logical way.

Many production costs, however, cannot be readily traced to an output unit even though these costs are related to its production. For example, acquiring a piece of equipment that is expected to last 10 years causes the cost of that equipment.

Because financial accountants record the acquisition cost, it is not expensive to extract this information. For this equipment, the benefit in use realized over 10 years by the purchaser will be the revenue realized from the sale of products produced by the equipment during that time. Different products and different production processes may be used over the lifetime of the equipment. This means that it is not immediately obvious what the accurate cost of using the equipment might be for a single product or process.

Another example is the supervisor of a production process in Motorola that produces a subassembly used for both cell phones and wireless hubs. It is not obvious what the accurate cost of supervision is for a single product. A final example is Motorola's purchase of one type of lubricant used in hundreds of different pieces of equipment that manufacture a variety of products worldwide. It is not obvious what the cost of this material is for a single piece of equipment, a process, or a product. Management accountants classify costs such as these as indirect costs.

Indirect costs of production cannot be readily traced to specific output units in an economically feasible way. Management accountants also use the term **manufacturing overhead (MOH)** in reference to all indirect inventoriable costs. One contributor to MOH could be indirect materials costs such as lubricants for a variety of equipment. Other MOH costs include supplies used for scheduled equipment maintenance, supplies for a security system, and janitorial supplies. These MOH costs arise because maintenance, security, and custodial services are a normal cost of running all production processes, not of producing a specific output unit. Indirect manufacturing labour costs often include fringe and statutory benefits of all manufacturing labour as well as specific labour costs, such as

◆ Materials handling (e.g., forklift truck operators)
◆ Custodial (janitorial) costs in production plants
◆ Security in the production plants
◆ Maintenance labour
◆ Rework
◆ Overtime
◆ Idle time

These various labour costs are caused by similar transactions and therefore are accumulated in specific general ledger accounts. This means that the cost of these activities can be readily accessed but they cannot be readily and economically traced to an output unit as a cost object. The logic of classifying an inventoriable cost as direct or indirect depends on identifying the cost object as an output unit of production. Remember, however, that this classification method is intended to identify and solve cost-control issues for output units. Other types of cost-control problems require identification of different cost objects, and this in turn will require the classification of costs as direct or indirect according to whether or not they can be readily and economically traced to the cost object.

Overtime costs are all wages in excess of straight-time wages paid for all manufacturing labour. The reason this is considered an indirect rather than a direct cost is that it is normally incurred due to heavy workload volume or rework when quality-control problems arise. Most manufacturers hire enough labour for a normal workload and during higher peak workload pay overtime. Often this decision is made because it is less expensive to pay an overtime premium rather than the permanent costs of fringe and statutory benefits to additional people who will be idle for most of the normal production time period. **Idle time** or downtime arises when production is interrupted because of equipment breakdown, material shortages, poor scheduling of work orders, or lack of work orders.

Most manufacturing labour contracts require that employees be paid during unproductive idle time because the causes are beyond the employees' control. Unproductive idle time and overtime do not arise because a specific product has been produced. Thus these costs are considered indirect manufacturing labour costs. None of these indirect costs can be traced to output units. As you will learn in

Chapter 4, however, there are a variety of procedures that management accountants use to allocate indirect costs to output units. All the costs identified as indirect labour costs are accounted for in accounts separate from the inventory accounts.

Employees such as supervisors and managers of a manufacturing plant are paid salaries. These labour costs are accumulated in separate accounts and often reported as miscellaneous indirect manufacturing costs. Exhibit 2-6 presents a way to organize production costs already identified according to whether or not they are inventoriable or period, direct or indirect. The diagram combines and organizes costs based on the management-accounting terminology and management-accounting logic.

On the left are the inventoriable or production costs in the blue chevron. The shape is to remind you of Exhibit 2-1 where production is only one element in the value chain of business functions. Within this section, the direct and indirect costs are identified and separated in different boxes. You will see these colours again when you construct an income statement. On the right are the period costs shown in the same form and colours as Exhibit 2-1.

So far, two cost classification methods have been presented that would be impossible without cost inputs estimated and recorded according to financial-accounting

EXHIBIT 2-6
Management-Accounting Logic of Cost Classification and the Value Chain of Business Functions

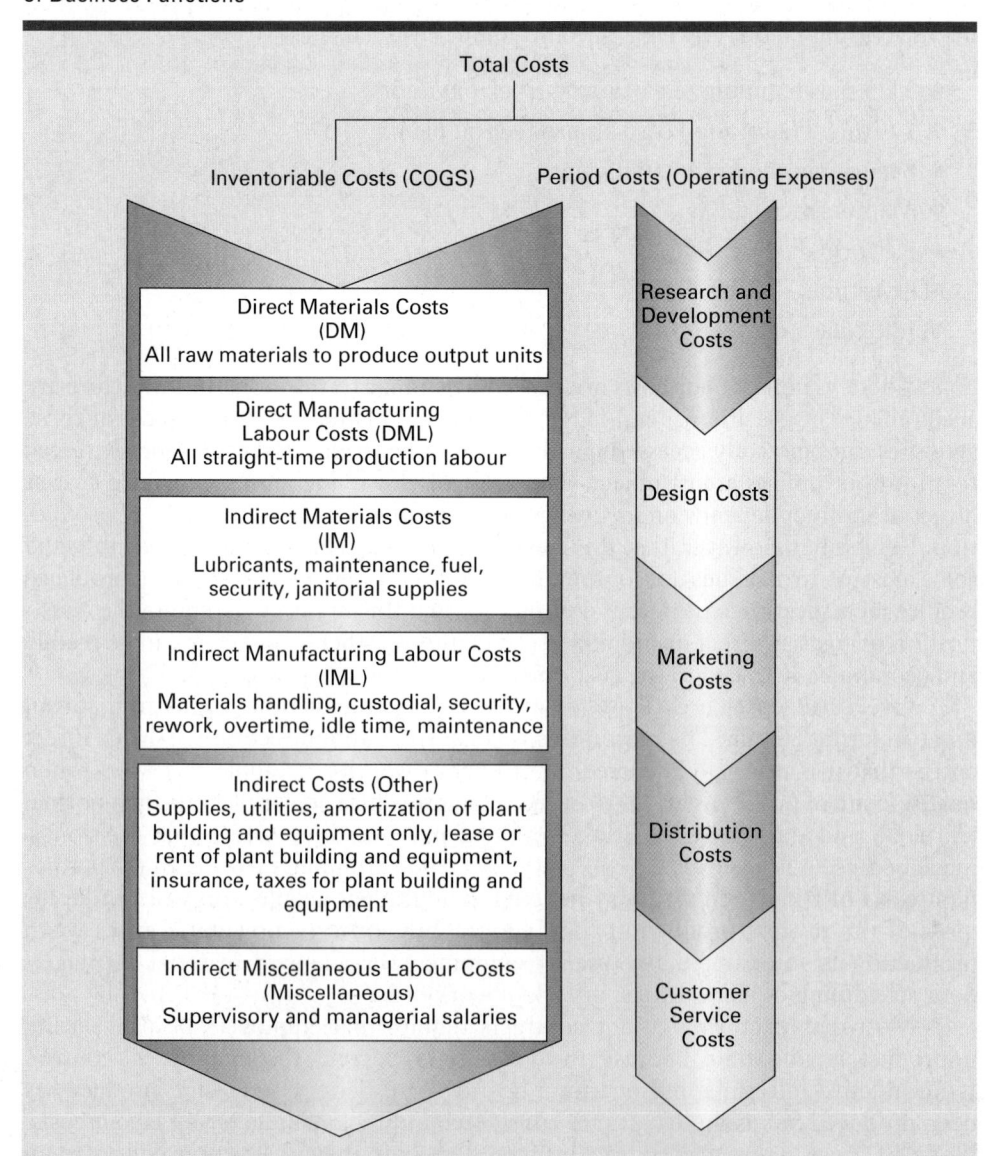

standards. Whether a company traces costs directly to an output unit or not depends upon:

◆ Materiality of the contribution a cost makes to the total cost per output unit. For Motorola, the costs contributed by different computer chips installed in its different cell phone models are probably material and should be traced, but the cost of the colour of dye added to each plastic handset is probably a small fraction of $0.01 and not material. Motorola may trace the cost of each chip to each handset but not the cost of the dye used to colour a single handset cover.

◆ Information technology available to create and maintain a management information system. Integrated computer information management systems such as SAP link data from production to data from accounting systems, and bar-code scanning technology makes tracing more costs economically feasible.

◆ Production process or operation's designs that differ according to the type of transformation of inputs required. Some transformations depend more on human labour, while others depend more on equipment and technology. The classification of costs will also depend on the type of production process, as illustrated below in the next classification system.

PRIME COSTS AND CONVERSION COSTS

The emphasis so far has been on product costing as a framework to understand the components of COGS. Another framework is process costing. Process costing is also based on the same financial accounting information provided in the company's management information system. The difference, however, is the logic of how to partition the COGS. As you will learn later in detail, the reason for using a process-costing framework is that the units produced cannot be separated one from the other. Think about a hectolitre of milk—one litre is identical to another until the milk is packaged. The input-conversion-output process is continuous, identical for each litre, and cannot be stopped to measure how much milk is finished without ruining all the unfinished work in process.

Using the process framework, or logic, accountants partition all inventoriable costs into either of two classifications, prime or conversion. **Prime costs** may include only DM, or may record DM separate from DML. All remaining indirect costs are accumulated into one classification called **conversion costs**. The first column in Exhibit 2-7 illustrates the product-costing framework for inventoriable COGS and is identical to Exhibit 2-6. The second and third columns classify inventoriable COGS using the process-costing logic of either prime or conversion. For some processes, it is sensible to include only DM costs as prime; this is illustrated in the second column. These continuous processes are generally highly mechanized and DML is immaterial in comparison with DM. DML and all other inventoriable costs, both direct and indirect, are included in conversion costs. This logic helps managers focus on controlling DM, the most material of the production costs.

For other continuous processes, DML may also be a material (significant) cost requiring close monitoring and control. For these processes, the prime costs are separated into two; this is illustrated in the third column. DM is separate from DML, and all other conversion costs include only indirect inventoriable costs. Irrespective of the classification method used for inventoriable costs, ultimately the outputs must be sold at a price that covers total costs, both inventoriable and period. The use of different classification methods also helps managers accomplish the important task of pricing for profitability. The product-costing system and both process-costing systems for inventoriable COGS are shown in Exhibit 2-7.

Assume the management-accounting system accumulates all DM costs separately from DML and all indirect costs, a three-part classification. This would be useful in a modern computer-integrated manufacturing (CIM) environment. CIM enables a management information system to include, among other things, detailed data about quantity of inputs, equipment time, labour time, specific quantities of outputs, as well as costs of each input. This situation is highly likely for a large,

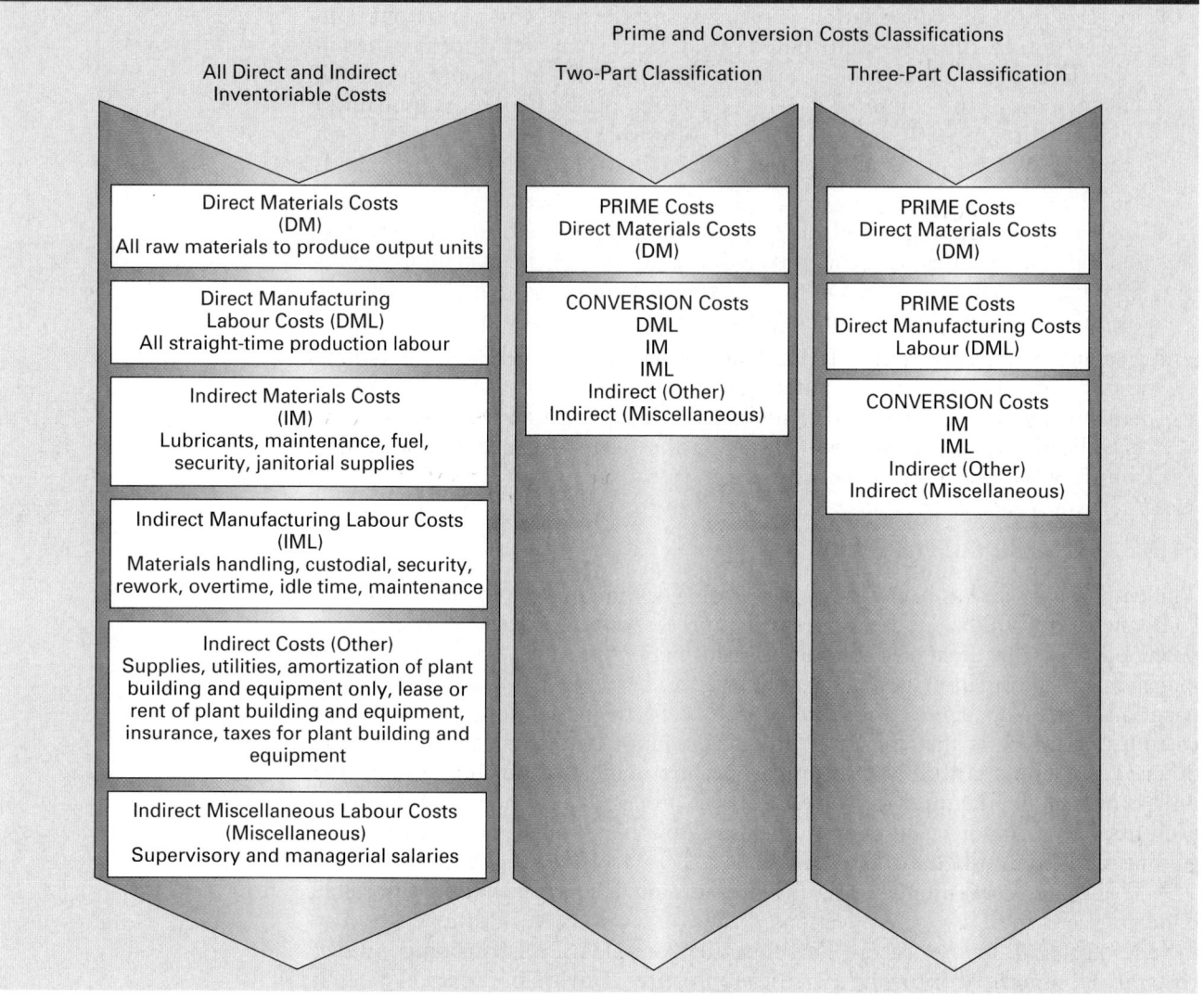

global, and technology-dependent company such as Motorola. With CIM, some indirect costs can be inexpensively measured and traced to a single output unit. For example, during a specified time period, if the indirect cost of power is measured for each piece of equipment and if the time that each model of cell phone is manufactured on that piece of equipment is also measured (the time of a production run), then it is possible to trace the cost of power to each model of output unit. To trace the cost per unit requires knowing the quantity of each model completed in each production run during a specified time period. One inexpensive way (among many) to identify models of cell phone is bar-code scanning at the beginning and end of a production run.

The higher the proportion of prime costs, the more confident managers can be about the accuracy of their unit product costs. Advantages of accurate costs include

- More focused attention-getting on potential cost-control problems
- More accurate identification of cost-control problems
- More relevant information available to resolve cost-control problems
- More flexibility and accuracy in product pricing to achieve a target profit
- More reliable predictions of performance improvement in cost control

As with all management-accounting procedures, the goal of this cost classification is to provide information that will improve Motorola's ability to achieve improved profits. Improved accuracy of cost inputs also improves the predictability of profit outcomes.

Two-part classification systems are appropriate for continuous manufacturing processes, such as the refining of salt, oil, and mineral ore, or the production of milk, wine, juices, or beer. There is no easy way to identify one output unit from another during the conversion process. Refining and fermentation processes are usually equipment-intensive rather than labour-intensive.

This means that DML costs are very low relative to other conversion costs. Tracing DML to each output unit would not make a material difference in the unit cost of producing a tonne of salt or a hectolitre of milk. Costs of DM, however, are easy to trace during a specified time period, and engineers who design these conversion processes can readily measure the yield or completed output units per unit of input. The difference between DM inputs and outputs must be in WIP. In this type of continuous-process situation, a two-part classification of costs into DM prime costs and conversion (all remaining) costs including DML provides sufficient relevant information to managers who must quickly identify and remedy cost-management problems. This method of cost classification will be important to understanding the material in Chapter 17 on process costing.

An important advantage of accurate and relevant costs is to improve predicted profit performance. When financial accountants report income-statement information, it is historical-cost or actual-cost information. Management accountants, however, use past information not only to identify and remedy existing problems, but also to predict and estimate the cost and dollar value of benefits from anticipated changes in the future. To do so, they often transform their cost analyses back into the financial-accounting format of the income statement. This is done because ultimately the company, for example Motorola, must reveal the financial results of its operations to its owners, the shareholders, in this standardized format.

When management accountants produce predicted income statements, they are referred to as operating budgets or pro forma income statements. **Pro forma income statements** classify and report predicted revenue and costs in the standardized format of a financial-accounting income statement. Budgeted revenue is an estimate of future revenue for a specified time period. **Budgeted costs** are an estimate of probable future costs, in contrast to actual or historical costs reported on an income statement.

STRATEGY

So far we have used different cost-classification methods to identify and perhaps remedy different cost-management problems that usually require a quick solution. What we have overlooked is the possibility that the best solution can be the result of a long-term decision. Strategy begins with defining the mission and then the vision of the future for an enterprise. **Strategy** is ". . . a way of thinking that relies on hypothesis generation and testing. In hypothesizing, you ask the creative 'what if' questions. To test your hypothesis, you ask the analytic 'if . . . , then . . . ' questions. You adopt a mindset that treats your method of accomplishing your purpose as an experiment. If that experiment fails, you try something else. . . . It is intelligently opportunistic in search of its goals . . . while leaving room for new and unintended strategies to emerge."[1] Each decision made can be tested with respect to how well it will implement or execute the mission, and how consistent it is with the company's vision of the future. In its 2006 Annual Report, Motorola begins with a statement of mission and vision. It concludes with a statement of the value

[1]Jeanne Leidka, "Everything I Need to Know about Strategy I Learned at the National Zoo," *The Journal of Business Strategy*, 18 (January/February 1997): pp. 8–11.

proposition it delivers to its customers. A **value proposition** is a distinct benefit for which customers will pay:

> We build, market and sell products, services and applications that make simple and seamless connections to people, information and entertainment possible through broadband, embedded systems and wireless networks. Our vision is to provide cutting-edge technologies that empower mobile consumers to go anywhere and do anything without sacrificing connectivity. This is seamless mobility.[2]

Strategy will differ depending on the mission of a company—roughly a choice between creating a new, uncontested market for its products or becoming the strongest competitor in an existing market. This choice, like other strategic choices, will depend on managerial skill at analyzing the environment and the company's abilities to exploit opportunities. Some managers cannot imagine new markets but are exceptional at discovering opportunities to profit very well in existing markets, such as those of communication and entertainment. In contrast to Motorola, which distributes existing entertainment through various wireless channels, Cirque du Soleil stated its entertainment mission in terms of its value proposition and invented a new form of live entertainment:

> To invoke the imagination, provoke the senses and evoke the emotions of people around the world, this is *Cirque du Soleil's* mission. . . . *Cirque du Soleil* produces live shows that combine, in an innovative way, acrobatics, theatre, dance and music.[3]

Motorola and Cirque du Soleil compete in the entertainment industry, but their missions, visions, value propositions, and strategies for success differ. Motorola discovers and applies technology to produce products that can transmit entertainment that has already been created. Cirque du Soleil creates entertainment that combines people, music, dance, and original themes for the viewer to experience live. With such different visions, the strategy that will guide each company will differ. Motorola does not need to create interesting stories and costumes, and Cirque du Soleil does not need to manufacture handsets for cell phones.

THINKING CRITICALLY

Motorola's mission is to market and sell seamless communication, whereas Cirque du Soleil's is to invoke the imagination, provoke the senses, and evoke the emotions. Which enterprise provides a service and which provides a product? Explain in a sentence or two. Read on for a discussion of this situation.

Both companies produce and sell an output—one produces cell phones, the other theatre spectacles. What is easy to understand is that the Motorola product is tangible. Its benefit can be reused, even traded in for a sharper, edgier model. Cirque du Soleil's product is intangible and a unique experience that cannot be inventoried, traded, or resold. On that basis, its output is an entertainment service with huge production costs. Management accountants can systematically associate costs with

[2]Motorola Inc., *2006 Annual Report*, p. 1, accessed online on October 26, 2008, at http://media. corporater.net/media_files/irol/90/90829/reports/2006%20Motorola%20Annual%20Report%20on%20Form%2010K.pdf.

[3]Cirque du Soleil website, accessed online on October 26, 2008, at www.cirquedusoleil.com/CirqueDuSoleil/en/showstickets/saltimbanco/intro/about.htm.

each type of output despite their differences. The management-accounting processes of filtering relevant costs can be applied across a very wide variety of cost objects.

Where there is collaboration, there is no need for a competitive strategy. Views differ about what constitutes a winning competitive strategy, but there is no doubt that companies competing in the same market are adversaries, not collaborators, and each is trying to be the best. There are barriers to entry, rules that cannot be broken, and only one winner—the rest are not. Universal measures to establish the winner are few: who earned the highest profit, and who harmed the fewest in so doing. The first measure explains in part why it is so important to predict and control both revenue and cost—to maximize the positive difference between them. The second measure explains why governance is so important. **Governance** includes, at a minimum, compliance with laws, regulations, standards, conventions, traditions, and ethical norms to avoid doing harm in pursuit of profit. Compliance costs can be high but failure costs can be higher. Compliance improves the probability the company will survive, but often decreases profit.

ASSESS YOUR MASTERY

To check your understanding of the material in Learning Objective ❶, go to the Mastery Questions section at the end of the chapter and complete Learning Objective ❶ questions 1 to 9.

MyAccountingLab

MERCHANDISING IN CONTRAST TO MANUFACTURING

Motorola's products are sold around the world. Suppliers of wireless services, such as Telus, COGECO, Bell Enterprises, Vidéotron, and Rogers tie the sale of Motorola's cell phones to the service contract. Rogers, for example, does no more than purchase the cell phone at a wholesale price from Motorola's distributor, then resells the cell phone from inventory. There is only one finished goods inventory account in which the costs to purchase the cell phones (including freight-in, and taxes) accumulate. Similar to the manufacturing company, the total cost of unsold finished goods inventory is the COGAS. Once a cell phone is sold, its cost becomes a cost of sales (COS). The revenue or benefit from the sale minus the COS is a Rogers' merchandising gross margin, sometimes referred to as gross profit.

Assume a Rogers wireless services supplier sells $4,500 of services, cell phones, and accessories in the month of January 2009 (the numbers in this example are kept small for illustrative purposes). Rogers' cost to purchase the finished goods merchandise remaining in inventory from December 2008 is the beginning inventory value of $2,000 for January 1, 2009. During January 2009, the local Rogers supplier ordered a further $3,000 of cell phones, and the total cost of the cell phones sold during January (the COS) was $4,000. The ending inventory on January 31, 2009 must be $1,000 ($2,000 + $3,000 − $4,000 = $1,000). Exhibit 2-8 presents the general ledger T-account balances, a flow of costs through merchandise inventory, all period costs, and an income statement for the month of January 2009 for this Rogers service and cell phone merchandiser.

All of the general ledger T-accounts and the flow of costs through the DM, WIP, and FG inventory accounts have already been illustrated in Exhibits 2-3 through 2-5 for a manufacturing company. Exhibit 2-9 contrasts a merchandising company with a manufacturing company. In Exhibit 2-9, the top of the exhibit shows the flow of costs through the general ledger to the balance sheet inventory account and then to the income statement of a merchandising company. The bottom of the exhibit shows the same for a manufacturing company. Notice that the two-part classification system accumulates many different indirect costs, plus DML into a single conversion cost general ledger account.

A numerical example of the income statement for the month of January 2009 for Motorola Inc. is shown in Panel A of Exhibit 2-10. Panel B illustrates in detail

Apply cost information to produce detailed financial schedules to illustrate how the asset value of inventories expires into cost of goods sold reported on the income statement ②

EXHIBIT 2-8
Rogers Wireless Service Provider's Merchandise Inventory Account and Income Statement

Merchandise Inventory

Beginning balance, Jan. 1, 2009	2,000		
Purchases during Jan. 2009	3,000		
		4,000	COS during Jan. 2009
Ending balance, Jan. 31, 2009	1,000		

Beginning Merchandise Inventory $2,000

+

Purchases in January $3,000

=

Cost of Goods Available for Sale (COGAS) $5,000

−

Costs of Sales (COS) $4,000

=

Ending Merchandise Inventory $1,000

Rogers Wireless Service Provider
Income Statement
For the Month Ended January 31, 2009

Revenue		$4,500
Cost of Sales (COS):		
Beginning merchandise inventory, January 1, 2009	$2,000	
Purchases of merchandise inventory in January	3,000	
Cost of goods available for sale (COGAS)	5,000	
Ending merchandise inventory, January 31, 2009	1,000	4,000
Gross margin (or gross profit)		500
Operating expenses (period costs):		
Salaries and wages	70	
Sales commissions	50	
General and administrative	40	
Amortization of property and equipment	15	
Customer service and technical support	12	187
Earnings before interest and taxes (operating income)		313
Interest expense		8
Earnings before tax		305
Tax expense (@ 40%)		122
Net income		$ 183

the schedule of the cost of goods manufactured for that month. This exhibit shows how financial accountants formally present the information illustrated in Exhibit 2-9, Panel B.

DIFFERENT COSTS FOR DIFFERENT CONTRACTS

A lot of detailed discussion has been presented to introduce two different cost-classification processes used by management accountants to identify and remedy cost-control problems. There are, however, other useful applications of these different methods that arise because of the nature of business contracts for products and services. For example, some countries provide income-tax relief for companies locating manufacturing plants there. Often to qualify, DML must achieve a specific threshold percentage of total inventoriable or manufacturing costs (COGM). Management cost-classification systems permit considerable flexibility in how some manufacturing labour costs are classified.

Earlier it was stated that all fringe and statutory benefits were indirect costs or manufacturing overhead; however, specific contracts may permit their inclusion in

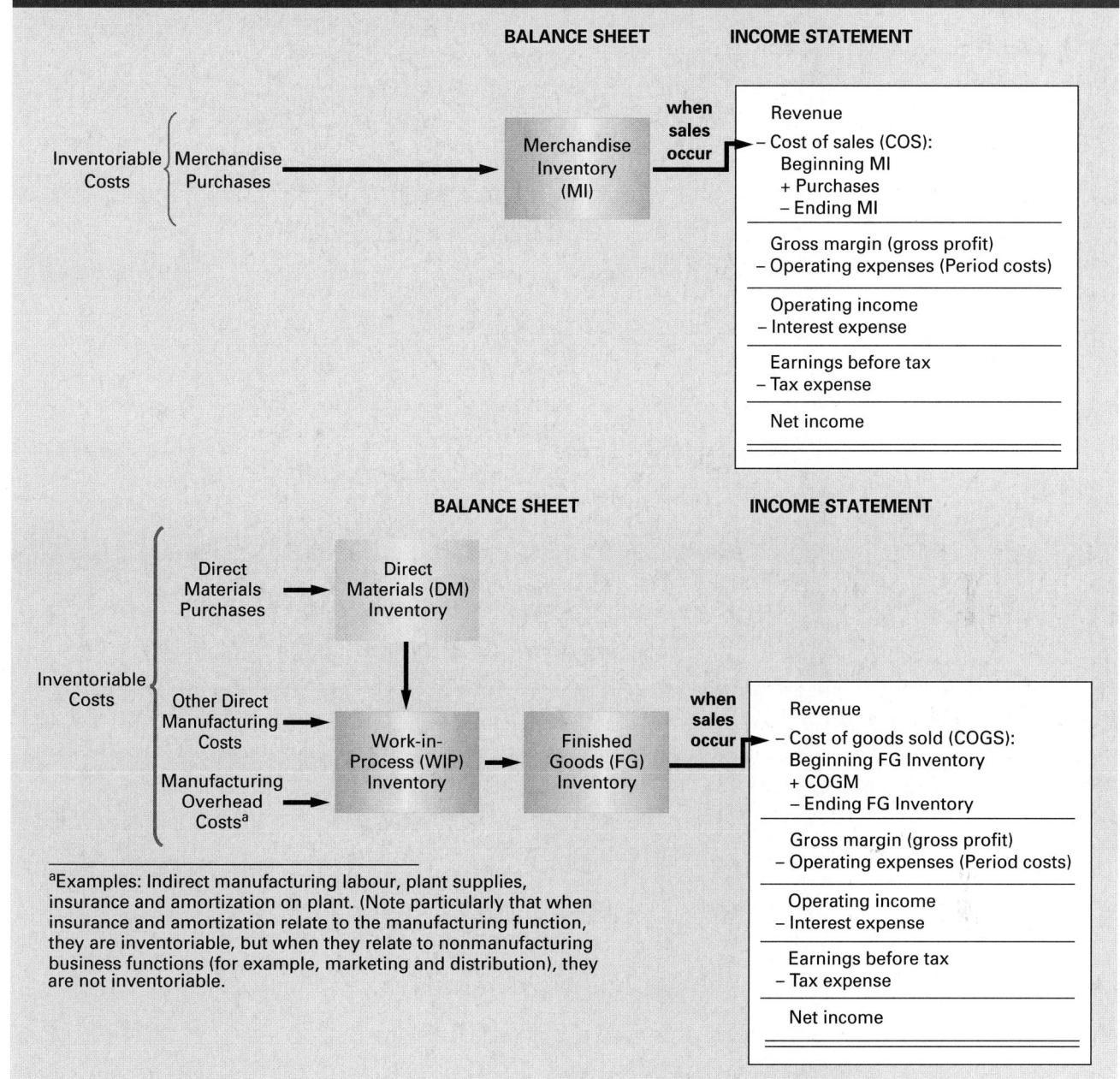

aExamples: Indirect manufacturing labour, plant supplies, insurance and amortization on plant. (Note particularly that when insurance and amortization relate to the manufacturing function, they are inventoriable, but when they relate to nonmanufacturing business functions (for example, marketing and distribution), they are not inventoriable.)

DML. While internal management reports would include these costs, financial accountants would have to report them to comply with GAAP, regardless of the contract terms. The example below applies a three-part classification of prime and conversion costs, with the costs reported in millions of dollars.

Assume your company intends to establish an overseas manufacturing plant where, to qualify for a tax subsidy, DML must equal or exceed 25%. A tax subsidy provides qualifying companies with lower tax rates. Also assume that, legally, there is flexibility in classifying fringe and statutory benefit costs of labour. Total MOH is $40 million, of which $8 million is the cost of fringe and statutory benefits. Under Method A, fringe and statutory costs are classified as conversion costs and are part of indirect costs or MOH. Under Method B, fringe and statutory costs are classified as DML. Under Method A, your company would not qualify for the tax subsidy, but under Method B it would.

EXHIBIT 2-10
Income Statement and Schedules of Cost of Goods Sold and Cost of Goods Manufactured

	A	B	C
1	**PANEL A: Income Statement**		
2	**Motorola Inc.**		
3	**Income Statement**		
4	**For the Month Ended January 31, 2009 (in thousands)**		
5	Revenue		$210,000
6	Cost of Goods Sold (COGS):		
7	Beginning finished goods inventory (FG), January 1, 2009	$ 25,000	
8	Cost of goods manufactured (COGM—see below, Panel B)	54,000	
9	Cost of goods available for sale (COGAS)	79,000	
10	Ending finished goods inventory (FG), January 31, 2009	6,000	
11	Cost of goods sold		73,000
12	Gross margin (or gross profit)		137,000
13	Operating expenses (period costs):		
14	Research and development	10,000	
15	Design of products	12,000	
16	Marketing	15,000	
17	Distribution	9,000	
18	Customer service and technical support	13,000	
19	Total operating costs for the month ended January 31, 2009		59,000
20	Earnings before interest and tax (operating income)		78,000
21	Interest expense		5,500
22	Earnings before tax		72,500
23	Tax expense @ 40%		29,000
24	Net income for the month ended January 31, 2009		$ 43,500
25	**PANEL B: Cost of Goods Manufactured (COGM) (in thousands)**		
26	Direct Materials:		
27	Beginning direct materials inventory, January 1, 2009	$11,000	
28	Purchases of direct materials	23,000	
29	Cost of direct materials available for use	34,000	
30	Ending direct materials inventory, January 31, 2009	22,000	
31	Direct materials used		$ 12,000
32	Direct Manufacturing Labour (straight-time wages)		10,000
33	Indirect Manufacturing Costs:		
34	Indirect manufacturing labour (custodial, security, rework,		
35	maintenance, idle time)	12,000	
36	Indirect manufacturing costs (fuel)	2,000	
37	Supplies (lubricants, security, janitorial)	500	
38	Utilities (heat, light, power)	5,000	
39	Amortization—plant, building	2,000	
40	Lease–equipment	4,000	
41	Insurance—plant building and manufacturing equipment	1,500	
42	Property taxes—plant building, land	200	
43	Indirect miscellaneous (supervisory and management salaries)	1,800	
44	Total indirect manufacturing costs (manufacturing overhead)		29,000
45	Manufacturing costs incurred for the month ended		
46	January 31, 2009		51,000
47	Beginning Work-in-Process Inventory, January 1, 2009		6,000
48	Total manufacturing costs to account for		57,000
49	Ending Work-in-Process Inventory, January 31, 2009		3,000
50	Cost of goods manufactured (COGM)		$54,000

	Method A		Method B	
	Costs	Percentage	Costs	Percentage
Prime: Direct materials	$ 40	40%	$ 40	40%
Prime: Direct manufacturing labour	20	20	28	28
Conversion: All direct costs, manufacturing overhead	40	40	32	32
Total inventoriable (COGM) manufacturing costs	$100	100%	$100	100%

GOVERNANCE ISSUES—DIFFERENT COST CLASSIFICATIONS

Flexibility in cost classification, intended to help with internal diagnosis and remedying of cost control problems, can be misused. For example, the U.S. Department of Defense (DoD) has contracts with private companies, such as Lockheed Martin, General Dynamics, and Boeing. These companies supply military equipment such as fighter jets, submarines, and tanks. As is the case for many government contracts, the DoD paid its suppliers on a cost-plus basis. This means that given the total costs of the project, the DoD added some percentage and established the sum of the two as the purchase price.

Through its own internal Defense Contract Audit Agency (DCAA), the DoD discovered that some of its equipment suppliers had funneled costs from other projects into the defense projects. The effect was to classify ineligible indirect costs to the DoD products and fewer indirect costs to their other commercial products. The higher the costs the supplier classified to the DoD business, the higher the revenues the supplier earned. Management cost-classification systems are not intended as a method to incorporate ineligible costs into manufacturing overhead, but rather as a method to sort eligible costs in a useful way.

GOVERNANCE ISSUES

Overcharging the Government

In a recent case, the Pentagon, through its normal audit process, identified overcharging in excess of US $1.03 billion by Halliburton KBR for fuel sold to Iraq as part of the US government's rebuilding contract. A whistleblower inside Halliburton KBR said:

"I can unequivocally state that the abuse related to contracts awarded to KBR (Kellogg Brown and Root) represents the most blatant and improper contract abuse I have witnessed during the course of my professional career," said Bunny Greenhouse, the whistleblower and a procurement veteran of more than 20 years.

Management cost-classification systems are not intended as a method to inflate or make up and claim imaginary costs. In general, the governments awarding contracts rely on the management accountants to adhere to their professional code of ethics. In Chapter 1, the Code of Professional Ethics states that management accountants must act with responsibility for and fidelity to public needs as well as fairness to clients (among others). Defrauding the government is certainly not fair to clients. When the client is the government, fraud is the theft of tax dollars paid by the public. Even using as simplistic a measure as money, fraud does not serve the public need. Monitoring and enforcement systems, such as the audits conducted by the Pentagon and the Defense Contract Audit Agency (DCAA) are ways that purchasers discover when their trust in individual professional accountants is misplaced. Governments are very protective of their tax dollars. Penalties imposed for fraud can be in the hundreds of millions of dollars for companies, and individuals have been formally prosecuted, convicted, and jailed for fraud.

Sources: For Halliburton and DCAA: Lawrence DiRita, Acting ASD (Public Affairs) Thursday, December 11, 2003; www.defenselink.mil/transcripts/2003/ tr20031211-0985.html.

ASSESS YOUR MASTERY

To check your understanding of the material in Learning Objective ❷, go to the Mastery Questions section at the end of the chapter and complete Learning Objective ❷ questions 1 to 3.

COST DRIVERS AND COST MANAGEMENT

Achieving lower costs is simply a means to an end—to achieve higher profits. But engaging in any business requires the transformation of some inputs into outputs for which customers will pay. The input acquisition and transformation requires a sacrifice of resources, usually money. The intent is to generate more money in revenue than was sacrificed. Notice that without purchasers, the best cost-control system will fail to maximize profit because no benefit from sales will be realized. Without a cost-control system, the company selling the most popular and expensive goods and services will fail because its sales will not exceed its costs. To succeed, competitors cannot ignore customers, costs, or each other. Analyzing customers and other competitors requires an understanding of what affects external factors beyond the control of a company's managers. Analyzing cost and benefit tradeoffs requires understanding what affects internal factors within the control of a company's managers. Matching both very well contributes to successful strategies.

Thoroughly understanding what customers prefer and the price they are willing to pay will help managers develop an appropriate mission and value proposition. To succeed, managers must identify important external factors. This has been called in the past the product differentiation, activity-based management (ABM), value-added, and now the *lean-management* strategy. **Lean management** means reducing or, preferably, eliminating those activities and their accompanying costs that fail to add value from the customer's point of view. The lean approach is intended to open up opportunities to create quicker, uninterrupted transformation of inputs or costs to output sales or revenue, and minimize wasted resources and their costs. This approach leads to the classification of costs within a company using a basis that is outside rather than inside the company. The classification depends upon separating activities and their accompanying costs that contribute to adding value from the customer's point of view from those that do not.

Assuming a company adopts the lean-management approach, the managers then need to assess what causes the huge array of costs of transformation. Fortunately, management accountants understand the meaning of materiality and can help other managers direct their attention towards identifying and controlling the most material or most significant costs. The **Pareto principle** expresses materiality in a straightforward way: for many events, 80% of the effects arise from 20% of the causes.

COST DRIVERS: DIFFERENT NAMES FOR DIFFERENT CAUSES

Understanding the management-accounting method to classify costs into fixed and variable depends upon understanding that inputs are not acquired and activities are not undertaken for their own sake but rather for their consequences or effects. Management accountants who understand the Pareto principle will examine those 20% of causes of 80% of the costs first. A **cost driver** causes a cost. If the quantity of the cost driver changes, the cost will change for a specific cost object. To understand how to classify fixed and variable costs, the cost object is specified as the unit of output. Similar to the classification of direct from indirect costs, if the cost object changes, so too can the definition of fixed and variable cost.

It is helpful to specify types of causes, and it was Aristotle who created this classification. One type is the *material cause*, or those inputs of material needed to produce the output (for example, the computer chips are input transformed to create a MOTORAZR² cell phone, the unit of output or cost object). The second is the *efficient cause*, or the process whereby the input becomes the output. The cause of the process arises from applying knowledge about how to transform the material inputs into a unit of output. As knowledge improves, so too will the process. DM costs are the consequence of the material cause. DML and indirect inventoriable costs are the consequence of the efficient cause.

Notice, however, that research and development as well as product design are activities that cause period costs. These activities are undertaken earlier than those of production, but the goal is to create the unit of output that is the specified cost object. Not all cost drivers or causes of the costs of output are classified as inventoriable. Financial accounting standards require that these costs be expensed during the time period they are incurred. Management accountants, however, must use their judgment to decide if, when, and how to include period costs as cost drivers or causes of the cost of the cost object during a specific time period. The inclusion or exclusion of these costs will depend upon whether they are relevant to identifying and solving a cost-control problem.

Production is not undertaken for its own sake but rather is the material cause of sales. Production is the material or output from which sales are created. Activities such as marketing, distribution, and customer service cause costs but they also cause sales. Notice, however, they do not drive the cost of producing the unit of output. Instead, these period costs drive the cost of a different cost object, the unit sold. Nevertheless, sales are the final consequence or benefit of undertaking all the activities of production and sales. Merchandising and service companies have no production process to intervene between purchases of the unit of sale, finished goods. The purchase is the material cause of the sale of those goods. Period costs are the efficient cause of the sale of the unit sold of finished goods.

COST MANAGEMENT

The discussion of cost is the context within which to understand different procedures of cost management. **Cost management** describes actions taken by managers to continuously control and reduce costs yet satisfy customers. Unfortunately, the cost consequence of any change in a cause is uncertain. This is because, in reality, many factors combine to cause a single cost. It is not merely the quantity of a DM but also the unit cost of the DM that causes the purchasing cost. The process that fails to apply knowledge of production well, will cause waste of DM and this affects the quantity of DM used, and therefore, the cost. It may also cause rework of poor-quality output and this will cause increased DML costs.

Poorly designed products lead to unnecessarily complex production processes that are more likely to fail. Poor application of knowledge of production processes causes inefficiency of design. Achieving the continuous-flow goal of lean management from product design to production can result in excess cost if any part of that flow is poorly executed. The reason is that failure to execute one function well, such as design, will cause increased costs in all the functions following it.

In order to simplify the explanation of how variable and fixed costs differ with respect to their cause, the focus will begin with inventoriable costs. The discussion will use the example illustrated in Exhibits 2-3 to 2-5. Assume that the research and development and product design activities have resulted in reasonable material and efficient causes of costs. The management accounting task is to determine how to classify those costs as either variable or fixed.

COST BEHAVIOUR: VARIABLE AND FIXED COSTS

Management cost-accounting systems classify costs already recorded using financial-accounting logic in a systematic way to identify and remedy cost-control problems. Inventoriable costs are caused either directly or indirectly by the production of the unit of output, the cost object. As the material and efficient causes change, so too do the costs. The causes are called cost drivers. A **variable cost (VC)** changes in proportion to the change in quantity of a cost driver of an output unit. A **fixed cost (FC)** remains unchanged despite changes in the quantity of output units produced.

MAJOR ASSUMPTIONS

The definitions of variable costs and fixed costs have five important underlying assumptions:

◆ Costs are defined as variable or fixed with respect to a specific cost object. In this discussion of inventoriable costs, the cost object is a unit of output.

◆ The time horizon must be specified because all costs are variable in the long run but most costs are fixed in the short run.

◆ Total costs (TC) are the sum of all VC + FC and are linear. The TC can be represented in an equation of the form y = a + bx, where y is the TC, a is the FC that is incurred even if there is no unit of output, and bx represents the VC that changes as x, the quantity (Q) of output units produced, changes. When plotted on ordinary graph paper, the TC relationship to the cost driver will appear as an unbroken straight line sloping upwards to the right.

◆ There is only one cost driver for each cost. The influences of other possible cost drivers on total costs are held constant or are judged as immaterial and irrelevant.

◆ The relevant range of output units (cost object) must be specified to assure there is a stable basis upon which to compare costs over a specified time horizon. All production processes have a limited capacity or maximum quantity of output units beyond which the process must change. **Relevant range** is the range of quantity of output units through which a specific relationship between cost and its material or efficient cost driver is valid.

VC and FC are the two most frequently recognized cost-behaviour patterns in management-accounting systems. Assumption 3 states, however, that in total, inventoriable costs have both FC (a) components and VC (bx) components. The reason for separating FC and VC components is that in the short run, a fixed cost cannot be changed or controlled. In the short run, the way to reduce or eliminate a variable cost is to reduce or stop its cause. Separating the two types of costs will focus attention on those costs that can be quickly controlled from those that cannot. Benefits of controlling VC are realized quickly, reported on the income statement, and all other things equal, as the inventoriable costs decrease, profits will increase.

For example, assume that one of the computer chips for a cell phone costs Motorola $1.20. The material cause of this cost is the purchase of the DM, a computer chip. Each cell phone requires one of these computer chips. Further assume that the unit cost of each computer chip does not change. As the quantity (Q) of cell phones or output units increases, the quantity of DM increases. The quantity of computer chips is the cost driver of the DM costs of the cell phone. Clearly, however, with a DM cost of $12 million, there are several other materials required to produce a cell phone.

Now, assume that the cost per hour of DML straight time is $11 and it takes 30 seconds to position, snap the computer chip into place, and test it for each handset. If there is no idle time or overtime, then one efficient cause will cause a DML cost of approximately $0.09167 per handset ($11.00/hr ÷ 3,600 sec/hr = $0.00306/sec; $0.00306/sec × 30 sec = $0.09167 per handset).

From the annual report, Motorola produced and sold 72 million cell phones in 2007 or approximately 6 million per month. But the total COGM for January 2009 was only $5 million while the COGS was $24 million, or almost five times higher. Motorola relied on its finished goods inventory, not the amount produced in the month, to meet demand. Assume that in January 2009, the company produced only 1 million cell phones and these were transferred into finished goods. The material cause of costs of a single computer chip was therefore the quantity used Q multiplied by the unit cost of $1.20, making the cost $1.2 million (1 million × $1.20 = $1.2 million), which is 10% of total DM costs of $12 million. For simplicity, we will assume zero defective chips, and zero waste and rework.

The efficient cause of costs of a single computer chip was the quantity of cell phones produced multiplied by the DML cost per cell phone, or $91,670 for the month of January (1 million × $0.09167). But the income statement in Exhibit 2-10 on page 52 reports the DML cost was $10 million; therefore, the cost of snapping a single computer chip into place was an extremely small component of the total DML for the month. In total, the efficient cause of the direct cost of DML was the total DML cost divided by Q, or $10 per cell phone ($10 million ÷ 1 million = $10). But there were more costs incurred in January—all the indirect costs, or MOH, that amount to $29 million as shown in Exhibit 2-10.

While the Q of DM per handset and the Q of DML hours are examples of direct, variable-cost drivers, some of the indirect costs also had identifiable material and efficient causes. Identifying these causes is discussed fully in Chapter 4 and, for purposes of this example, we will assume that all the lease, amortization, insurance, property taxes, and indirect miscellaneous costs amounting to $9.5 million are fixed. The remaining indirect VCs amount to $19.5 million, which when divided by the quantity of cell phones produced results in $19.50 per cell phone produced ($19.5 million ÷ 1 million = $19.50). We have assumed the cost object is identical for all of the variable direct and indirect costs, and we can sum them. Panel A of Exhibit 2-11 presents the numerical Motorola data for the production of 0 to 7 million cell phones. Panel B of Exhibit 2-11 presents these data in graph form. In Panel B, the left diagram illustrates how the total variable cost changes as the quantity of cell phones produced changes. **Total variable cost (TVC)** is calculated by multiplying the quantity of input by its unit cost (or price). The middle panel illustrates the behaviour of the fixed costs as the quantity of cell phones produced changes over the relevant range Q = 0 to 7 million cell phones. The panel to the right illustrates

EXHIBIT 2-11
Cost Behaviour of Variable, Fixed, and Total Inventoriable Costs

	A	B	C	D	E	F	G	H	I
1	**PANEL A: MOTOROLA INC. NUMERICAL DATA**								
2		**Per Unit**	**Q Cell Phones**		**VC**		**Average Unit**		**Total Unit**
3	DM VC	$ 1.20000	**Produced**	**TVC**	**Per Unit**	**FC**	**Cost (FC)**	**TC**	**Cost (TC)**
4	DML VC	0.09167	0	$ -	$20.79167	$9,500,000	$ -	$ 9,500,000	$ -
5	Indirect VC	19.50000	500,000	10,395,835	20.79167	9,500,000	19.00	19,895,835	39.79
6	TVC	$ 20.79167	1,000,000	20,791,670	20.79167	9,500,000	9.50	30,291,670	30.29
7			1,500,000	31,187,505	20.79167	9,500,000	6.33	40,687,505	27.13
8	FC	$9,500,000	2,000,000	41,583,340	20.79167	9,500,000	4.75	51,083,340	25.54
9			2,500,000	51,979,175	20.79167	9,500,000	3.80	61,479,175	24.59
10			3,000,000	62,375,010	20.79167	9,500,000	3.17	71,875,010	23.96
11			3,500,000	72,770,845	20.79167	9,500,000	2.71	82,270,845	23.51
12			4,000,000	83,166,680	20.79167	9,500,000	2.38	92,666,680	23.17
13			4,500,000	93,562,515	20.79167	9,500,000	2.11	103,062,515	22.90
14			5,000,000	103,958,350	20.79167	9,500,000	1.90	113,458,350	22.69
15			5,500,000	114,354,185	20.79167	9,500,000	1.73	123,854,185	22.52
16			6,000,000	124,750,020	20.79167	9,500,000	1.58	134,250,020	22.38
17			6,500,000	135,145,855	20.79167	9,500,000	1.46	144,645,855	22.25
18			7,000,000	145,541,690	20.79167	9,500,000	1.36	155,041,690	22.15

PANEL B:

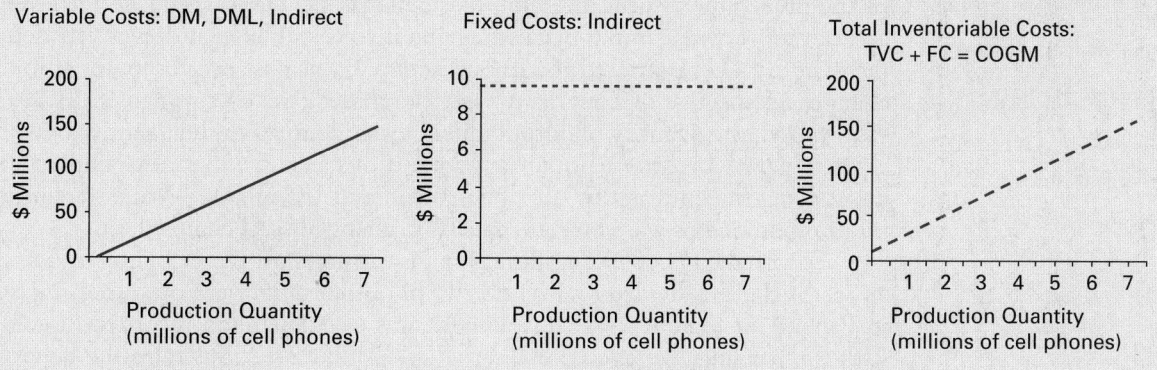

Distinguishing Between Fixed Costs and Variable Costs

When companies were asked to describe how they identify fixed and variable costs, "classification on a subjective basis based on managerial experience" and "treating all overheads as fixed and all direct costs

as variable" were selected as the two most popular methods used in the United Kingdom and New Zealand. In New Zealand, 84% of firms surveyed used systems classifying fixed as distinct from variable costs. In the U.K., 90% and in Estonia, 80% did the same. Notice that the procedures of calculating costs are straightforward. For the results to be relevant, management accountants must be clear on when experience and when accounting classification of variable, fixed, direct, and indirect costs should be used.

Garg, A., D. Ghosh, J. Hudick, and C. Nowacki, "Roles and Practices in Management Accounting Today: Results from the 2003 IMA–E & Y Survey," *Strategic Finance* (2003).

Guilding, C., D. Lamminmaki, and C. Drury, "Budgeting and Standard Costing Practices in New Zealand and the United Kingdom," *The International Journal of Accounting* (1998).

the behaviour of total costs $y = a + bx$ where x is the quantity Q produced. Note that this example has been simplified so that the unit cost of both the material and efficient causes, or the cost drivers, of the variable costs have been calculated per output unit (the cost object).

Should the cost object change, the classification of a cost as variable or fixed will change. For example, if the cost object is a piece of equipment and several manufacturing facilities have that piece of equipment, then the total equipment cost will vary as the number of pieces of equipment change. When the cost object is a unit of output, however, the total equipment cost is fixed within the relevant range over a specified time horizon, whether zero output units or billions are produced.

MyAccountingLab

ASSESS YOUR MASTERY

To check your understanding of the material in Learning Objective ③, go to the Mastery Questions section at the end of the chapter and complete Learning Objective ③ questions 1 to 3.

UNIT COSTS ARE AN AVERAGE

④ Explain the limitations that the use of average or unit costs impose on managerial decision making

In the preceding section, the unit cost of DM and DML could be retrieved from accounting records simply by reading the invoices. The cost object was defined as the quantity Q of output units. In our example, this cost per computer chip did not change; irrespective of how many were purchased, the cost remained $1.20. In the case of DM, the quantity of output units Q was identical to the quantity of computer chips required, but this is not always true. It was a simple matter to understand that multiplying the unit cost by the Q equalled the TVC of DM. While the unit cost of the computer chips was constant, the TVC changed as Q changed.

For fixed costs of $9.5 million, what is the unit cost per cell phone? The correct answer is the FC divided by whatever Q of output units were produced. Notice that in Panel A of Exhibit 2-11, this amount was calculated and recorded in column G with the heading Average Unit Cost (FC). Exhibit 2-12 illustrates the behaviour of the average or unit FC that results. The graph of this cost behaviour in no way resembles that of either a variable cost or a fixed cost. It is not linear and there is a material decrease in the unit cost between the Q = 1 output unit (or $9.5 million/unit) and

EXHIBIT 2-12
Cost Behaviour of the Average Unit Cost (FC)

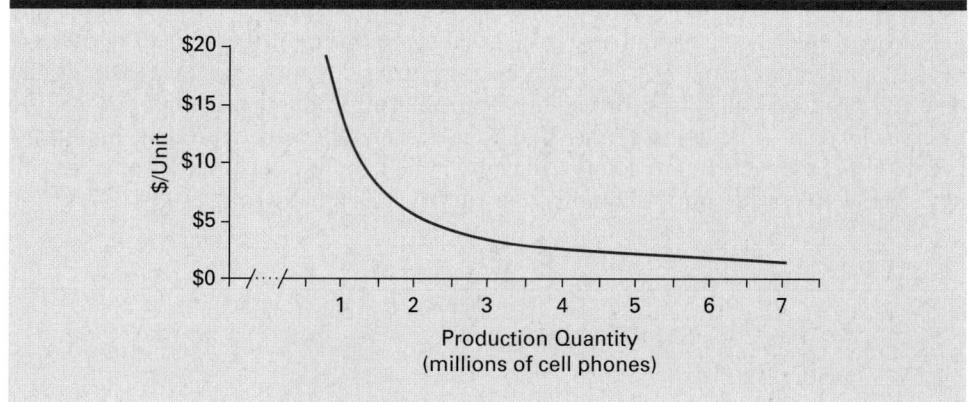

Q = 500,000 output units (of $19/unit). While the total FC remains constant at $9.5 million, the average unit FC changes as the denominator Q changes. The proper management accounting methods to address this issue are discussed in Chapter 9.

USE UNIT AVERAGE FIXED COSTS CAUTIOUSLY

Unit costs are averages. As we will see, they must be interpreted with caution. For decision making, it is best to think in terms of total fixed costs rather than unit costs. Nevertheless, unit-cost numbers are frequently used in many situations. Consider what would happen if 500,000 units were produced and the resulting average unit FC of $19.00 was mistaken for a unit VC. When forecasting the cost of a cell phone at the average monthly output of 6 million cell phones (based on Motorola's annual report), this average cost will not change if it is treated as a unit VC. At Q = 6 million, the average unit FC should be recalculated as approximately $1.58 per cell phone (from Panel A in Exhibit 2-11). The difference between the two average unit FCs is $17.42 per cell phone. The forecasted TC of each cell phone would be overstated by this amount. Instead of calculating the TC per unit as approximately $22.37 ($20.79 + $1.58 = $22.37), it would be calculated at $39.79 ($20.79 + $19.00 = $39.79), approximately 78% too high [($39.79 − $22.37) ÷ $22.37 = 77.87%].

In the extremely competitive domain of wireless mobile communications, an overstatement of costs of 78% would almost certainly lead to foolish decisions. Managers might choose to reduce the quality of DM, for example, in an effort to reduce costs. The reduction of the unit variable cost of DM will reduce total costs but it will *not* reduce the average unit fixed cost. Managers may decide to raise the price per cell phone to cover the additional cost that was incorrectly calculated and lose sales to other cell-phone manufacturers offering equal or better quality at a lower price based on a more accurate TC forecast. Managers may lay off workers or perhaps even close a manufacturing facility if the mistake is not caught and remedied. The reason it is important to understand the behaviour of fixed, variable, and average costs is that both strategic and accounting decisions are made on the basis of this information. If the information directs attention to a non-existent problem, or to the wrong problem, then decisions to remedy the problem will be ineffective.

THINKING CRITICALLY

Many times the objective of filtering relevant costs is to identify and solve an operating-cost-control problem. Are fixed costs controllable by the managers of an enterprise? Explain in a sentence or two. Read on for an assessment of this question.

If fixed costs are incurred primarily to purchase the capital assets that are the source of production capacity throughout their lifetime, then once the asset is acquired, the cost is no longer controllable. What can happen is that the higher the quantity produced by a capital asset, the greater the economies of scale. *Economies of scale* is simply another way to say the average fixed cost per unit decreases as the quantity produced increases. But added quantities of production cannot control the total fixed cost—that is why it is fixed. Also remember an extremely important point—costs are incurred to acquire benefits. The benefit of economies of scale will never arise unless and until the units in inventory are actually sold.

MyAccountingLab

DIFFERENT COSTS FOR DIFFERENT PURPOSES

⑤ Apply management-accounting logic to classify costs for use in managerial decisions

An important theme of this book is "different costs for different purposes." This theme can be illustrated with respect to product costing. A **product cost** is the sum of the costs assigned to a product for a specific purpose, which could be:

1. **Cost-control-problem identification and management.** Cost control is not restricted to just one of inventoriable or period, direct or indirect, variable or fixed costs. To maximize revenue, managers want relevant information to identify cost-control problems no matter where they arise.

2. **Product pricing and product emphasis.** To execute a lean management strategy that will continue to produce a product with an appropriate value proposition, the features of the product must match what is demanded at the price customers are willing to pay. Managers need appropriate historical costs to ensure that, in their effort to maximize revenue through the unit price at the point of sale, they remain competitive, or they will lose sales. They require detailed information matching costs to features to ensure appropriate pricing. Managers also use current information to forecast pro forma or budgeted income statements. Once the budget is accepted, it becomes a performance target for which managers are held accountable.

3. **Contracting with government agencies.** Typically, government contracts are awarded to the lowest bidder. A mistake in total product-cost estimation will unnecessarily exclude a company from a successful bid. Government agencies frequently provide detailed guidelines on the allowable and nonallowable items in a product-cost amount. Some government agencies explicitly exclude specific period costs, such as marketing, from reimbursement and may reimburse only a portion of research and development costs.

   Good governance requires that the classification of costs will be authentic and withstand scrutiny by external auditors. This means that managers cannot play games by switching costs from other projects into a government project, nor can they disguise costs as something they are not. While there may be some flexibility with respect to prime and conversion costs, the degree of flexibility will be determined by the government-contract terms. Contracts are legal documents that oblige the supplier to produce according to the covenants in the contract, with penalties should the supplier fail to do so.

4. **Financial statements.** According to GAAP, COGS must include only inventoriable manufacturing costs when reported publicly on financial statements. The remaining costs must be recorded and reported as period costs, either matched to the revenue generated or incurred during a specific time period.

A telecommunications giant such as Motorola lists its shares on a stock exchange. This means that every three months, managers must issue financial statements for the time period along with cumulative financial results. But Motorola competes against Ericsson of Sweden, Alcatel-Lucent of France, and ZTE of China. Ultimately, the net income reported each quarter will affect the share price of all these companies. For existing owners of shares, the higher the share price rises, the greater the return they will earn if they sell their shares. To impress investors, Motorola must improve on its profits in part by controlling its costs.

THINKING CRITICALLY

In one of the examples in this chapter, the cost of a computer chip and the cost of DML per handset for a specific activity were calculated. If the 80/20 rule of thumb applies in this instance, would you identify the computer chip or the DML as part of the set of 20% of inputs that causes 80% of the cost? Which of the two process costing systems would you choose? Explain in a sentence or two. Read on for an assessment of this situation.

Of course, if the cost of a computer chip and the cost of DML per handset for a specific activity were the only cost drivers, you would choose the DM and focus attention on controlling the cost of computer chips during a specific time period, not the cost of DML. You would choose a two-part system and include DML as part of conversion costs along with all other indirect costs because DML is not material if these were the only two costs.

But these were not the only two costs of DM and DML. As the analysis unfolded, it turned out that from Exhibit 2-10, the total DM costs of 1 million cell phones during the month of January were $11 million. If the unit cost of DM per cell phone remained constant, then January's cost was $12 ($12 million ÷ 1 million = $12). Similarly, the total DML straight-time wages were $10 million and, assuming cost of labour per cell phone was constant, then January's cost was $10 per cell phone for DML. The data provided for Exhibit 2-11 stated that the straight-time DML wage was $11 per hour. What is the total straight-time it takes to assemble a cell phone? The answer is $10/$11 = 0.91 hours, or approximately 54.5 minutes (0.91 hours 60 × minutes/hour = 54.51 minutes).

If Motorola's workers are in the manufacturing facilities for 7 working hours per day for 5 days per week, how many cell phones can 1 labourer complete in a normal week? The answer is approximately 38.5 cell phones [(60 minutes, 7 hours, 5 days) + 54.5 = 38.5 cell phones]. To make 1 million cell phones, how many workers were required for the month of January? The answer is 5,865.1 (38.5 cell phones per worker per week × 4.48 weeks in January [31 + 7 days = 4.48 weeks]). In the month of January, each person will be able to make 170.5 cell phones and 1,000,000 cell phones were completed (1,000,000 + 170.5 cell phones = 5,865.1). At this rate, if Motorola had completed the average production target of 6 million cell phones, 35, 191 workers would have been needed (6 × 5,865.1 = 35,190.6, but you must round up). The DML cost would have been approximately $60 million (6 × $10 million).

As the facts have become known, it does not appear that there was a problem with fuel that interrupted the production in January, but rather an interruption in the supply of labour. The reason is that Motorola is a good corporate citizen and its global union contracts prohibit laying-off so many employees. It is also illogical that Motorola would have laid-off so many workers when they forecast a robust market demand for their phones. If Motorola had suffered idle time, then the DML cost would have been far higher because union contracts also specify payment for idle time. The DML cost was, however, only $10 million and Motorola paid no additional $50 million in idle time. It is more likely that workers voluntarily stopped work, in which case Motorola would not have had to pay for their time away from production.

The incentive for Motorola to resolve the problem quickly is to get production back to normal and avoid losing sales. Assuming that revenue was almost all due to cell phone sales, each lost sale will decrease revenue by $210, the unit sales price of a cell phone. Overall, demand was approximately 4.8 times January's production ($24 million COGS ÷ $5 million COGM = 4.8). If $24 million in COGS generated $210 million in revenue, then each $1 million of COGS generates $8.75 million of revenue.

Currently, the company is producing at only $5 million in COGM per month with only $6 million in finished goods. In February, it can expect to have a COGS of only $11 million ($6 million FG + $5 million COGM = $11 million COGS), and if all units are sold, the revenue will be only $96.25 million ($11 COGS × $8.75 million). The company will lose $113.75 million in revenue in February and more in March because it will begin the month with no inventory in FG. With a little bit of arithmetic and a little bit of basic business knowledge, a few accurate pieces of data can tell an experienced manager how to pinpoint the cost-control problem. The remedy for the problem in this case, however, is beyond the control of those responsible for production. The remedy is in the control of human resources, which normally negotiates union contracts.

To understand how to calculate a conversion cost or a total variable cost is a small part of becoming competent at managing. The larger and more important competency is analyzing and interpreting what the numbers mean. In particular, the results are useful to pinpoint cost-control problems, their remedy, and improve the probability that forecast or budgeted revenue and cost targets will materialize in future.

MyAccountingLab

ASSESS YOUR MASTERY

To check your understanding of the material in Learning Objective **5**, go to the Mastery Questions section at the end of the chapter and complete Learning Objective **5** question 1.

PULLING IT ALL TOGETHER—PROBLEM FOR SELF-STUDY

(*Try to solve this problem before examining the solution that follows.*)

PROBLEM

A distraught employee, Guy Arson, put a torch to a manufacturing plant on a blustery February 26, 2009. The resulting blaze completely destroyed the plant and its contents. Fortunately, certain accounting records were kept in another building. They revealed the following for the period from January 1, 2009 to February 26, 2009:

Direct materials (DM) purchased in January 2009	$192,000
Work in process, January 1, 2009	$ 40,800
Direct materials (DM), January 1, 2009	$ 19,200
Finished goods, January 1, 2009	$ 36,000
Indirect manufacturing costs	40% of conversion costs
Revenues	$600,000
Direct manufacturing labour (DML)	$216,000
Prime costs	$352,800
Gross margin percentage based on sales	20%
Cost of goods available for sale	$540,000

REQUIRED

1. Calculate the cost of finished goods inventory on February 26, 2009.
2. Calculate the cost of work-in-process inventory on February 26, 2009.
3. Calculate the cost of direct materials inventory on February 26, 2009.

SOLUTION

1. $60,000
2. $33,600
3. $74,400

This problem is not as easy as it first appears. These answers are obtained by working from the known figures to the unknowns in the schedule below. Use the two-part classification system for prime and conversion costs, which includes DML in conversion costs. The basic relationships between categories of costs are:

Prime costs (given)		= $352,800
Direct materials used	= $352,800 − Direct manufacturing labour costs	
	= $352,800 − $216,000	= $136,800
Conversion costs	= Direct manufacturing labour costs ÷ 0.6	
	= $216,000 ÷ 0.6	= $360,000
Indirect manuf. costs	= $360,000 − $216,000	= $144,000
	(or 0.40 × $360,000)	

Schedule of Computations:

Direct materials, Jan. 1, 2009		$ 19,200
Direct materials purchased		192,000
Direct materials available for use		211,200
Direct materials, Feb. 26, 2009	3. =	74,400
Direct materials used ($352,800 − $216,000)		136,800
Direct manufacturing labour costs		216,000
Prime costs		352,800
Indirect manufacturing costs		144,000
Manufacturing costs incurred during the current period		496,800
Add work in process, Jan. 1, 2009		40,800
Manufacturing costs to account for		537,600
Deduct work in process, Feb. 26, 2009	2. =	33,600
Cost of goods manufactured		504,000
Add finished goods, Jan. 1, 2009		36,000
Cost of goods available for sale (given)		540,000
Deduct finished goods, Feb. 26, 2009	1. =	60,000
Cost of goods sold (80% of $600,000)		$480,000

It may be helpful to follow the key amounts through the Work-in-Process Inventory, Finished Goods Inventory, and Cost of Goods Sold T-accounts. All amounts are in thousands of dollars:

Work-in-Process Inventory				Finished Goods Inventory				Cost of Goods Sold		
BI	40.8			BI	36					
DM used	136.8	COGM 504.0			→ 504	COGS 480			→ 480	
DML	216.0									
OH	144.0			*(Available*						
(To account for	537.6)			*for sale*	540)*					
EI	33.6			EI	60			COGS	480	

The following decision guidelines use a question-and-answer format to summarize the chapter's main points. Each decision presents a key question. The guideline is the answer to that question.

DECISIONS	GUIDELINES
1. How does the logic underlying three cost-classification systems derived from financial accounting information differ among the systems?	The logic of inventoriable and period costs is identical to the financial logic that classifies the cost of goods sold (COGS) separately from operating expenses of a specified time period. The logic of direct and indirect costs depends on the specific cost object for which costs are being identified. Direct costs are readily and inexpensively traced to a cost object while indirect costs are not. Prime and conversion costs segment only the inventoriable costs into two classifications, roughly the same as direct and indirect but not always.
2. How does the asset value of inventories expire into the cost of goods sold (COGS) reported on the income statement for a manufacturing company and a merchandising company?	For a manufacturing company, the asset value of unused, unfinished, and unsold inventories as well as those used and finished are collected in the cost of goods manufactured general ledger account. The total costs to complete those finished goods that are sold are accumulated in the cost of goods sold account and reported on the income statement. Merchandising companies do not produce the goods they sell. They purchase finished goods. The purchase cost constitutes the cost of sales. The goods unsold remain in ending inventory at the lower of their cost or net realizable value.
3. What is the logic of the management-accounting cost-classification system?	The logic of the management-accounting cost-classification system depends on the behaviour of costs relative to the specific cost object, the output unit. The cost behaviour is linear with respect to the quantity of the output units produced.
4. What limitations are imposed by the use of average or unit costs?	Average unit costs are an arithmetic result obtained by dividing a fixed numerator by a changing denominator. This means the denominator must be specified to estimate the appropriate average cost per output unit. The average unit cost is non-linear with respect to the quantity of the output units produced.
5. How can cost-classification information be used to make managerial decisions?	Cost-classification systems separate the same costs in one of four different ways. The reason for doing so is to highlight those costs that are relevant to identifying and controlling a cost-control issue, and filtering out those that are not.

TERMS TO LEARN

This chapter contains more basic terms than any other in this book. Do not proceed before you check your understanding of the following terms. You will find definitions of these terms in this chapter and in the Glossary.

actual cost (p. 36)
budgeted cost (p. 47)
conversion cost (p. 45)
cost (p. 36)
cost driver (p. 54)
cost management (p. 55)
cost object (p. 41)
cost of goods available for sale (COGAS) (p. 37)
cost of goods manufactured (COGM) (p. 37)
cost of goods sold (COGS) (p. 36)
cost of sales (COS) (p. 37)

direct cost (p. 42)
direct labour (DL) (p. 42)
direct manufacturing labour (DML) (p. 42)
direct materials (DM) (p. 42)
fixed cost (p. 55)
governance (p. 49)
idle time (p. 43)
indirect cost (p. 43)
inventoriable cost (p. 37)
lean management (p. 54)
manufacturing overhead (p. 43)
overtime cost (p. 43)

Pareto principle (p. 54)
period cost (p. 36)
prime cost (p. 45)
pro forma income statement (p. 47)
product cost (60)
production cost (p. 37)
relevant information (p. 36)
relevant range (p. 56)
revenue (p. 36)
strategy (p. 47)
total variable cost (p. 57)
value proposition (p. 48)
variable cost (p. 55)

MASTERY QUESTIONS

The Mastery Questions are rated by proficiency level—elementary, intermediate, and advanced. The solutions appear in the Mastery Question Solutions section of MyAccountingLab.

LEARNING OBJECTIVE 1

1. Inventoriable costs versus period costs—Elementary. Each of the following cost items pertains to one of the following companies: General Electric (a manufacturing-sector company), Loblaws (a merchandising-sector company), and Excite (a service-sector company):

a. Perrier mineral water purchased by Loblaws for sale to its customers
b. Electricity used to provide lighting for assembly-line workers at a General Electric refrigerator assembly plant
c. Amortization on computer equipment at Excite used to update website directories.
d. Electricity used to provide lighting for Loblaws store aisles
e. Amortization on computer equipment at General Electric used for quality testing of refrigerator components during the assembly process
f. Salaries of Loblaws marketing personnel planning local newspaper advertising campaigns
g. Perrier mineral water purchased by Excite for consumption by its software engineers
h. Salaries of Excite marketing personnel selling banner advertising

REQUIRED
1. Distinguish among manufacturing-sector, merchandising-sector, and service-sector companies. Which of these have inventories of goods for sale?
2. Distinguish between inventoriable costs and period costs.
3. Classify each of the (a) to (h) cost items as an inventoriable cost or a period cost. Explain your answers.

2. Inventoriable costs versus period costs—Intermediate. Regina Office Equipment manufactures and sells metal shelving. It began operations on January 1, 2009. Costs incurred for 2009 are as follows (V stands for variable; F stands for fixed):

Direct materials used costs	$168,000 V
Direct manufacturing labour costs	36,000 V
Plant energy costs	6,000 V
Indirect manufacturing labour costs	12,000 V
Indirect manufacturing labour costs	19,200 F
Other indirect manufacturing costs	9,600 V
Other indirect manufacturing costs	28,800 F
Marketing, distribution, and customer-service costs	147,420 V
Marketing, distribution, and customer-service costs	48,000 F
Administrative costs	60,000 F

Variable manufacturing costs are variable with respect to units produced. Variable marketing, distribution, and customer-service costs are variable with respect to units sold.

Inventory data are as follows:

	Beginning, January 1, 2009	Ending, December 31, 2009
Direct materials	0 kilograms	2,000 kilograms
Work in process	0 units	0 units
Finished goods	0 units	? units

Production in 2009 was 100,000 units. Two kilograms of direct materials are used to make one unit of finished product.

Revenues in 2009 were $524,160. The selling price per unit and the purchase price per kilogram of direct materials were stable throughout the year. The company's ending inventory of finished goods is carried at the average unit manufacturing costs for 2009. Finished goods inventory at December 31, 2009, was $25,164.

REQUIRED
1. Direct materials inventory, total cost, December 31, 2009
2. Finished goods inventory, total units, December 31, 2009
3. Selling price per unit, 2009
4. Operating income, 2009 (show your computations)

3. Inventoriable costs versus period costs; continuation of Mastery Question 2—Advanced. Assume management predicts that the selling price per unit and variable cost per unit will be the same in 2010 as in 2009. Fixed manufacturing costs and marketing, distribution, and customer-service costs in 2010 are also predicted to be the same as in 2009. Sales in 2010 are forecast to be 122,000 units. The desired ending inventory of finished goods, December 31, 2010, is 12,000 units. Assume zero ending inventories of both direct materials and work in process. The company's ending inventory of finished goods is carried at the average unit manufacturing costs for 2010. The company uses the first-in, first-out inventory method. Management has asked that you prepare a budgeted income statement for 2010. December 31, 2009, Finished Goods Inventory is 9,000 units.

REQUIRED
1. Units of finished goods produced in 2010
2. Budgeted income statement for 2010

4. Direct costs versus indirect costs—Elementary. Finnish Forest Products (FFP) produces three different paper products at its Vaasa lumber plant—supreme, deluxe, and regular. Each product has its own dedicated production line at the plant. FFP currently uses the following three-part classification for its manufacturing costs: direct materials, direct manufacturing labour, and indirect manufacturing costs. Indirect manufacturing costs are allocated to each product line on the basis of direct manufacturing labour costs on each line. Summary data for the most recent month (July 2009) are (in millions):

	Supreme	Deluxe	Regular
Direct materials cost	$100.80	$ 64.80	$ 74.40
Direct manufacturing labour costs	16.80	33.60	9.60
Indirect manufacturing costs	50.40	100.80	28.80
Kilograms produced	80	120	100

REQUIRED
Compute the unit manufacturing cost per kilogram for each product produced in July 2009.

5. Direct costs versus indirect costs; continuation of Mastery Question 4—Intermediate. Finnish Forest Products (FFP) employs a consultant to help reduce energy costs at its Vaasa plant. Currently, FFP does not trace energy costs to each product line. The energy consultant notes that each production line at the Vaasa plant has multiple energy meters and that tracing energy costs to each line is possible. Of the $180 million of indirect manufacturing costs in July 2009, $108 million is for energy costs traceable to individual production lines and $24 million is fixed cost. Using this information, FFP's cost analyst reports the following revised numbers for July 2009 (in millions):

	Supreme	Deluxe	Regular
Direct materials cost	$100.80	$ 64.80	$ 74.40
Direct manufacturing labour costs	16.80	33.60	9.60
Direct energy costs	47.76	24.84	35.40
Indirect manufacturing costs	20.16	40.32	11.52
Kilograms produced	80	120	100

REQUIRED
1. What is the difference between a direct cost and an indirect cost?
2. Why might FFP's managers prefer energy costs to be traced as a direct cost rather than included as part of indirect manufacturing costs?
3. Compute the revised unit manufacturing cost per kilogram for each product produced in July 2009. Compare these costs with those computed in Mastery Question 4. Comment on any differences in the unit cost numbers.

6. Direct costs versus indirect costs—Advanced. Gwen Benson, Ian Blacklaw, and Eduardo Cabrera are sales representatives for Electronic Manufacturing Inc. (EMI). EMI specializes in low-volume production orders for the research groups of major companies. Each sales representative receives a base salary plus a bonus based on 20% of the actual profit of each order they sell. Before this year, the bonus was 5% of the revenues of each order they sold. Actual profit in the revised system was defined as actual revenue minus actual manufacturing cost. EMI uses a three-part classification of manufacturing costs—direct materials, direct manufacturing labour, and indirect manufacturing costs. Indirect manufacturing costs are determined as 200% of actual direct manufacturing labour cost.

Benson receives a report on an EMI job for BBC Inc. She is dismayed by the low profit on the BBC job. She prided herself on not discounting the price BBC would pay by convincing BBC of the quality of EMI's work. Benson discussed the issue with Blacklaw and Cabrera. They share with her details of their most recent jobs. Summary data are as follows:

Customer Sales Representative	Westec Blacklaw	La Electricidad Cabrera	BBC Benson
Revenues	$504	$984	$576
Direct materials	300	492	324
Direct manuf. labour	48	120	72
Indirect manufacturing	96	240	144
Direct labour-hours	2 hours	5 hours	2 hours

Benson asks Hans Brunner, EMI's manufacturing manager, to explain the different labour costs charged on the Westec and BBC jobs, given both used two direct labour-hours. She was told the BBC job was done in overtime and that the actual overtime rate ($36) was 50% higher than the $24 per hour straight-time rate. Benson noted that she brought the BBC order to EMI one week ago and that there was no rush order on the job. In contrast, the Westec order was a "hot-hot" one with a request it be done by noon the day after the order was received. Brunner said that the "actual cost" he charged to the BBC job was actually paid to the workers on that job.

REQUIRED
1. Using both the actual straight-time and overtime rates paid for direct labour, what is the actual profit EMI would report on each of the three jobs?
2. Assume that EMI charges each job for direct labour at the $24 straight-time rate (and that the indirect-manufacturing rate of 200% includes an overtime premium). What would be the revised profit EMI would report on each of the three jobs? Comment on any differences from requirement 1.
3. Discuss the pros and cons of charging the BBC job the $36 labour rate per hour.
4. Why might EMI adopt the 20% profit incentive instead of the prior 5% of revenue incentive? How might EMI define "profit" to reduce possible disagreements with its sales representatives?

7. **Prime costs versus conversion costs—Elementary.** Assume there is no beginning balance in any of Microchip Manufacturing Ltd.'s inventories. The company completed a total of 15,000 microchips during August 2009. Each microchip is assembled from direct materials. The total assembly costs for the month of August 2009 were:

Direct materials (DM) used	$ 990,000
Conversion costs	1,350,000
Total inventoriable costs	$2,340,000

REQUIRED
1. Calculate the DM as a percentage of total inventoriable costs.
2. What is the most likely reason that no direct manufacturing labour (DML) costs are specified?
3. What inventory accounts are included in conversion costs?
4. What was the unit cost per completed microchip in August?
5. If the company had finished manufacturing 24,000 microchips in August at a cost of $2,934,000, what would you infer about the cost behaviour of conversion costs?

8. **Prime costs versus conversion costs—Intermediate.** The following items (in millions) pertain to the Chan Corporation:

For Specific Date		For Year 2009	
Work in process, January 1, 2009	$12.00	Plant utilities	$ 6.00
Direct materials, December 31, 2009	6.00	Indirect manufacturing labour	24.00
Finished goods, December 31, 2009	14.40	Amortization—plant, building, and equipment	10.80

(Continued)

For Specific Date		For Year 2009	
Accounts payable, December 31, 2009	$24.00	Revenues	$420.00
Accounts receivable, January 1, 2009	60.00	Miscellaneous manufacturing overhead	12.00
Work in process, December 31, 2009	2.40	Marketing, distribution, and customer-service costs	108.00
Finished goods, January 1, 2009	48.00	Purchases of direct materials	96.00
Accounts receivable, December 31, 2009	36.00	Direct manufacturing labour	48.00
Accounts payable, January 1, 2009	48.00	Plant supplies used	7.20
Direct materials, January 1, 2009	36.00	Property taxes on plant	1.20

Chan's manufacturing cost system uses a three-part classification of manufacturing costs. There are two prime costs and one conversion cost: direct materials, direct manufacturing labour, and indirect manufacturing costs.

REQUIRED
1. Identify the prime costs. Identify the conversion costs.
2. Prepare an income statement and a supporting schedule of cost of goods manufactured.

9. **Prime costs versus conversion costs; continuation of Mastery Question 8—Advanced.** Refer to Mastery Question 8.

REQUIRED
1. How would the answer to Mastery Question 8 be modified if you were asked for a schedule of cost of goods manufactured and sold instead of a schedule of cost of goods manufactured? Be specific.
2. Would the sales manager's salary (included in marketing, distribution, and customer-service costs) be accounted for any differently if the Chan Corporation were a merchandising company instead of a manufacturing company? Using the flow of costs outlined in Exhibit 2-1 (p. 36), describe how the wages of an assembler in the plant would be accounted for in this manufacturing company.
3. Plant supervisory salaries are usually regarded as indirect manufacturing costs. Under what conditions might some of these costs be regarded as direct manufacturing costs? Give an example.

LEARNING OBJECTIVE 2

1. **Computing cost of goods manufactured and cost of goods sold—Elementary.** The following are account balances relating to 2009 (in thousands):

Property tax on plant building	$ 3,600
Marketing, distribution, and customer-service costs	44,400
Finished goods inventory, January 1, 2009	32,400
Plant utilities	20,400
Work-in-process inventory, December 31, 2009	31,200
Amortization of plant building	10,800
General and administrative costs (nonplant)	51,600
Direct materials used	104,400
Finished goods inventory, December 31, 2009	40,800
Amortization of plant equipment	13,200
Plant repairs and maintenance	19,200
Work-in-process inventory, January 1, 2009	24,000
Direct manufacturing labour	40,800
Indirect manufacturing labour	27,600
Indirect materials used	13,200
Miscellaneous plant overhead	4,800

REQUIRED
Compute cost of goods manufactured and cost of goods sold.

2. Income statement and schedule of cost of goods manufactured—Intermediate. The Howell Corporation has the following account balances (in millions):

For Specific Date		For Year 2009	
Direct materials, January 1, 2009	$ 18	Purchases of direct materials	$ 390
Work in process, January 1, 2009	12	Direct manufacturing labour	120
Finished goods, January 1, 2009	84	Amortization—plant, building,	
Direct materials, December 31, 2009	24	and equipment	96
Work in process, December 31, 2009	6	Plant supervisory salaries	6
Finished goods, December 31, 2009	66	Miscellaneous plant overhead	42
		Revenues	1,140
		Marketing, distribution, and	
		customer-service costs	288
		Plant supplies used	12
		Plant utilities	36
		Indirect manufacturing labour	72

Prepare an income statement and a supporting schedule of cost of goods manufactured for the year ended December 31, 2009.

3. Interpretation of statements—Advanced. Refer to the preceding Mastery Question 2.

REQUIRED

1. How would the answer to the preceding Mastery Question 2 be modified if you were asked for a schedule of cost of goods manufactured and sold instead of a schedule of cost of goods manufactured? Be specific.
2. Would the sales manager's salary (included in marketing, distribution, and customer-service costs) be accounted for differently if the Howell Corporation were a merchandising company instead of a manufacturing company? Using the flow of costs outlined in Exhibit 2-1 (p. 36), describe how the wages of an assembler in the plant would be accounted for in this manufacturing company.
3. Plant supervisory salaries are usually regarded as indirect manufacturing costs. Under what conditions might some of these costs be regarded as direct manufacturing costs? Give an example.

LEARNING OBJECTIVE 3

1. Variable costs and fixed costs behaviour—Elementary. Consolidated Minerals (CM) owns the rights to extract minerals from beach sands on Fraser Island. CM has costs in three areas:

a. Payment to a mining subcontractor who charges $96 per tonne of beach sand mined and returned to the beach (after being processed on the mainland to extract three minerals: ilmenite, rutile, and zircon).
b. Payment of a government mining and environmental tax of $60 per tonne of beach sand mined.
c. Payment to a barge operator. This operator charges $180,000 per month to transport batches of beach sand—up to 100 tonnes per batch per day to the mainland and then return to Fraser Island (i.e., 0–100 tonnes per day = $180,000 per month; 101–200 tonnes = $360,000, and so on). Each barge operates 25 days per month. The $180,000 monthly charge must be paid even if fewer than 100 tonnes are transported on any day and even if Consolidated Minerals requires fewer than 25 days of barge transportation in that month.

CM is currently mining 180 tonnes of beach sand per day for 25 days per month.

REQUIRED

1. What is the variable cost per tonne of beach sand mined? What is the fixed cost to CM per month?
2. Plot one graph of the variable costs and another graph of the fixed costs of CM. Your plots should be similar to Exhibit 2-11 (pp. 57). Is the concept of relevant range applicable to your plots?
3. What is the unit cost per tonne of beach sand mined (a) if 180 tonnes are mined each day and (b) if 220 tonnes are mined each day? Explain the difference in the unit-cost figures.

2. Variable costs and fixed costs behaviour—Intermediate. Consumer Focus is a marketing research firm that organizes focus groups for consumer-product companies. Each focus group has eight individuals who are paid $50 per session to provide comments on new products. These focus groups meet in hotels and are led by a trained independent marketing specialist hired by Consumer Focus. Each specialist is paid a fixed retainer to conduct a minimum number of sessions at a per-session fee of $2,000. A Consumer Focus staff member attends each session to ensure that all the logistical aspects run smoothly.

REQUIRED

Classify each of the following cost items as:

a. Direct or indirect (D or I) costs with respect to each individual focus group.

b. Variable or fixed (V or F) costs with respect to how the total costs of Consumer Focus change as the number of focus groups changes. (If in doubt, select the cost type based on whether the total costs will change substantially if a large number of groups are conducted.)

You will have two answers (D or I, and V or F) for each of the following items:

Cost Item	D or I	V or F
A. Payment to individuals in each focus group to provide comments on new products		
B. Annual subscription of Consumer Focus to *Consumer Reports* magazine		
C. Phone calls made by Consumer Focus staff member to confirm individuals will attend a focus group session (records of individual calls are not kept)		
D. Retainer paid to focus group leader to conduct 20 focus groups per year on new medical products		
E. Hotel meals provided to participants in each focus group		
F. Lease payment by Consumer Focus for corporate office		
G. Cost of tapes used to record comments made by individuals in a focus group session (these tapes are sent to the company whose products are being tested)		
H. Gasoline costs of Consumer Focus staff for company-owned vehicles (staff members submit monthly bills with no breakdowns)		

3. **Variable costs and fixed costs behaviour—Advanced.** Woody Company manufactures slippers and sells them for $11 a pair. Variable manufacturing costs are $4.95 a pair, and indirect fixed manufacturing costs are $1.65 a pair. The company can accept a one-time-only special order of 20,000 pairs of slippers at $6.60 a pair because the extra quantity is within the relevant range of production, so indirect fixed manufacturing costs will not increase due to this special order. Woody will not incur any marketing or other period costs as a result of the special order. What would the effect on operating income be if the special order could be accepted without affecting normal sales? Choose the correct answer.

(a) $0

(b) $33,000 increase

(c) $99,000 increase

(d) $132,000 increase.

LEARNING OBJECTIVE 4

1. **Using unit costs for making decisions—Intermediate.** Finnish Forest Products (FFP) produces three different paper products at its Vaasa lumber plant—supreme, deluxe, and regular. Each product has its own dedicated production line at the plant. FFP currently uses the following three-part classification for its manufacturing costs: direct materials, direct manufacturing labour, and indirect manufacturing costs. Indirect manufacturing costs are allocated to each product line on the basis of direct manufacturing labour costs on each line. Summary data for March 2009 are (in millions):

	Supreme	Deluxe	Regular
Direct materials cost	$100.80	$ 64.80	$ 74.40
Direct manufacturing labour costs	16.80	33.60	9.60
Indirect manufacturing costs	50.40	100.80	28.80
Total cost per kilogram	1.87	1.81	0.81
Kilograms produced	90	110	140

Suppose that in April 2009, production was 120 kilograms of Supreme, 160 kilograms of Deluxe, and 180 kilograms of Regular.

Why would the March 2009 unit manufacturing cost information be misleading when predicting total manufacturing costs in April 2009?

2. **Using unit costs for making decisions—Advanced.** Susan Wang is a well-known software engineer. Her specialty is writing software code used in maintaining the security of credit card information. Wang is approached by the Electronic Commerce Group (ECG). They offer to pay her $120,000 for the right to use her code under licence in their e-procurement software package. Wang rejects this offer because it provides her with no additional benefits if the e-procurement package is a runaway success. Both parties eventually agree to a contract in which ECG pays Wang a flat fee of $120,000 for the right to use her code in up to 10,000 packages. If e-procurement sells more than 10,000 packages, Wang receives $9.60 for each package sold beyond the 10,000 level.

REQUIRED

1. What is the unit cost of ECG for Wang's software code included in its e-procurement package if it sells (a) 2,000, (b) 6,000, (c) 10,000, and (d) 20,000 packages? Comment on the results.
2. For prediction of ECG's total cost of using Wang's software code in e-procurement, which unit cost (if any) of (a) to (d) in requirement 1 would you recommend ECG use? Explain.

LEARNING OBJECTIVE 5

1. **Classifying costs for managerial decisions—Advanced.** Kamal Diamond is the owner of the Galaxy chain of four-star prestige hotels. These hotels are in Chicago, London, Los Angeles, Montreal, New York, Seattle, Tokyo, and Vancouver. Diamond is currently struggling to set weekend rates for the Vancouver hotel (the Vancouver Galaxy). From Sunday through Thursday, the Galaxy has an average occupancy rate of 90%. On Friday and Saturday nights, however, average occupancy declines to less than 30%. Galaxy's *major customers* are business travellers who stay mainly Sunday through Thursday.

The current room rate at the Galaxy is $180 a night for single occupancy and $216 a night for double occupancy. These rates apply seven nights a week. For many years, Diamond has resisted having rates for Friday and Saturday nights that are different from those for the remainder of the week. Diamond has long believed that price reductions convey a "nonprestige" impression to his guests. The Vancouver Galaxy highly values its reputation for treating its guests as "royalty."

Most room costs at the Galaxy are fixed on a short-stay (per-night) basis. Diamond estimates the variable costs of servicing each room to be $24 a night per single occupancy and $26.40 a night per double occupancy.

Many prestige hotels in Vancouver offer special weekend rate reductions (Friday and/or Saturday) of up to 50% of their Sunday-through-Thursday rates. These weekend rates also include additional items such as a breakfast for two, a bottle of champagne, and discounted theatre tickets.

REQUIRED

1. Would you recommend that Diamond reduce room rates at the Vancouver Galaxy on Friday and Saturday nights? What factors to protect the value proposition should be considered in his decision?
2. In six months' time, the Grey Cup is to be held in Vancouver. Diamond observes that several four-star prestige hotels have already advertised a Friday-through-Sunday rate for Grey Cup weekend of $360 a night. Should Diamond charge extra for the Grey Cup weekend? Explain.

ASSIGNMENT MATERIAL

Make the grade with MyAccountingLab: The questions, exercises, and problems marked in red can be found on MyAccountingLab at **www.myaccountinglab.com**. You can practise them as often as you want, and most feature step-by-step guided instructions to help you find the right answer. Exercises and problems with an Excel icon in the margin have an accompanying Excel template on MyAccountingLab.

SHORT-ANSWER QUESTIONS

2-1 Define *relevant cost information*, and state two reasons why it is needed.

2-2 Define *cost object* and give three examples.

2-3 Define *period costs*. What is the equivalent term used by financial accountants? What is the importance of period costs as a cause of sales? Define *inventoriable costs*. What is the equivalent term used by financial accountants?

2-4 Define *direct costs* and *indirect costs*.

2-5 Name three factors that affect the classification of a cost as direct or indirect.

2-6 Define the following: *direct materials costs, direct manufacturing labour costs, indirect manufacturing costs, prime costs,* and *conversion costs.* What two groups of costs can be conversion costs, and why are there two groups?

2-7 What is the difference between cost of goods sold, cost of goods available for sale, and cost of goods manufactured? What is the difference between cost of goods sold and cost of sales?

2-8 Do service-sector companies have inventoriable costs? Explain.

2-9 What are three different types of inventory that manufacturing companies hold?

2-10 Define a *cost driver*. How does a cost driver relate to the Pareto principle?

2-11 Define *variable* cost and *fixed* cost. Give an example of each.

2-12 What is the *relevant range*? What role does the relevant-range concept play in explaining how costs behave?

2-13 Explain why *unit costs* must often be interpreted with caution.

2-14 What is key to successful execution of a *lean management* strategy?

2-15 Why do management accountants need to understand financial accounting?

EXERCISES

2-16 Inventoriable costs versus period costs. Each of the following cost items pertains to one of the following companies: Toyota (a manufacturing-sector company), Sobeys (a merchandising-sector company), and Google (a service-sector company):

a. Spring water purchased by Sobeys for sale to its customers

b. Electricity used to provide lighting for assembly-line workers at a Toyota truck-assembly plant

c. Amortization on computer equipment at Google used to update directories of websites.

d. Electricity used to provide lighting for Sobeys store aisles

e. Amortization on computer equipment at Toyota used for quality testing of truck components during the assembly process

f. Salaries of Sobeys marketing personnel planning local newspaper advertising campaigns

g. Spring water purchased by Google for consumption by its software engineers

h. Salaries of Google marketing personnel selling banner advertising

REQUIRED

1. Distinguish among manufacturing-sector, merchandising-sector, and service-sector companies. Which of these have inventories of goods for sale?

2. Distinguish between inventoriable costs and period costs.

3. Classify each of the (a) to (h) cost items as an inventoriable cost or a period cost. Explain your answers.

2-17 Direct and indirect costs; computing and interpreting unit manufacturing costs. Maximum Office Products (MOP) produces three different paper products at its Vernon lumber plant—Supreme, Deluxe, and Regular. Each product has its own dedicated production line at the plant. MOP currently uses the following three-part classification for its manufacturing costs: direct materials, direct manufacturing labour, and indirect manufacturing costs. Total indirect manufacturing costs of the plant in May 2009 are $150 million ($20 million of which are fixed). This total amount is allocated to each product line on the basis of direct manufacturing labour costs of each line. Summary data (in millions) for May 2009 are:

	Supreme	Deluxe	Regular
Direct materials cost	$84	$54	$62
Direct manufacturing labour costs	$14	$28	$ 8
Indirect manufacturing costs	$42	$84	$24
Kilograms produced	80	120	100

1. Supreme $1.75
Deluxe $1.3833
Regular $0.94

1. Compute the manufacturing cost per Kilogram for each product produced in May 2009.
2. Suppose that in June 2009, production was 120 million Kilograms of Supreme, 160 million Kilograms of Deluxe, and 180 million Kilograms of Regular. Why might the May 2009 information on manufacturing cost per Kilogram be misleading when predicting total manufacturing costs in June 2009?

2-18 Direct and indirect costs, effect of changing the classification of a cost item (continuation of 2-17). Maximum Office Products (MOP) employs a consultant to help reduce energy costs at its Vernon plant. Currently, MOP does not trace energy costs to each product line. The energy consultant notes that each production line at the Vernon plant has multiple energy meters and that tracing of energy costs to each line is possible. Of the $150 million of indirect manufacturing costs in May 2009, $108 million is for energy costs traceable to individual production lines and $20 million is fixed cost allocated to each product line on the basis of direct manufacturing labour costs of each line. Using this information, MOP's cost analyst reports the following revised numbers for May 2009 (in millions):

	Supreme	Deluxe	Regular
Direct materials cost	$84	$54	$ 62
Direct manufacturing labour cost	$14	$28	$ 8
Direct energy costs	$45	$25	$ 38
Indirect manufacturing costs	$20	$15	$ 7
Kilograms produced	80	120	100

REQUIRED

1. What is the difference between a direct cost and an indirect cost?
2. Why might MOP's managers prefer energy costs to be traced as a direct cost rather than included as part of indirect manufacturing costs?
3. Compute the revised unit manufacturing cost per kilogram for each product produced in May 2009. Compare these costs with those computed in requirement 1 of Exercise 2-17. Comment on any differences in the unit cost numbers.

2-19 Direct and indirect costs, fixed and variable costs. Ceramica Company manufactures three kinds of handpainted ceramic figurines in a two-step process. The first step is automated; in the Baking Department, a machine presses the clay figurines into moulds and bakes them. In the Painting Department, the baked figurines are carefully removed from their moulds and hand painted. After they dry, the figurines are packed and shipped to customers. Ceramica's two departments, Baking and Painting, are in a single factory building. Packaging takes place in the Painting Department.

REQUIRED

1. Costs involved in the process are listed below. For each cost below, indicate whether it is a direct variable, direct fixed, indirect variable, or indirect fixed cost, assuming "units of production of each kind of figurine" is the cost object.

Costs:
Clay
Paint
Packaging materials
Amortization on machinery and moulds
Rent on factory
Insurance on factory
Factory utilities
Painters
Painting Department manager
Baking Department manager
Materials handlers
Custodian in factory
Night guard in factory
Machinist (running the baking machine)
Machine maintenance personnel
Maintenance supplies for factory
Cleaning supplies for factory

3. Supreme $1.9675
Deluxe $0.9233
Regular $1.1180

2. If the cost object were "Baking Department" rather than output, which costs above would now be direct instead of indirect costs?

2-20 Classification of costs, merchandising sector. Home Entertainment Centre (HEC) operates a large store in Halifax. The store has both a DVD section and a musical section (compact discs, mp3 players, etc.). HEC reports revenues for the DVD section separately from the musical section.

REQUIRED

Classify each of the following cost items as

a. Direct or indirect (D or I) costs with respect to the DVD section.

b. Variable or fixed (V or F) costs with respect to how the total costs of the DVD section change as the number of DVDs sold changes. (If in doubt, select the cost type based on whether the total costs will change substantially if a large number of DVDs are sold.) You will have two answers (D or I; V or F) for each of the following items:

Cost Item	D or I	V or F
A. Annual retainer paid to a DVD distributor		
B. Electricity costs of HEC store (single bill covers entire store)		
C. Costs of DVDs purchased for sale to customers		
D. Subscription to *DVD Trends* magazine		
E. Leasing of computer software used for financial budgeting at HEC store		
F. Cost of popcorn provided free to all HEC customers		
G. Fire insurance policy for HEC store		
H. Freight-in costs of DVDs purchased by HEC		

2-21 Classification of costs, manufacturing sector. The Fremont, California, plant of NUMMI (New United Motor Manufacturing, Inc.), a joint venture of General Motors and Toyota, assembles two types of cars (Corollas and Geo Prisms). A separate assembly line is used for each type of car.

REQUIRED

Classify each of the following cost items as

a. Direct or indirect (D or I) costs with respect to the type of car assembled (Corolla or Geo Prism).

b. Variable or fixed (V or F) costs with respect to how the total costs of the plant change as the number of cars assembled changes. (If in doubt, select the cost type based on whether the total costs will change substantially if a large number of cars are assembled.) You will have two answers (D or I, and V or F) for each of the following items:

Cost Item	D or I	V or F
A. Cost of tires used on Geo Prisms		
B. Salary of public relations manager for NUMMI plant		
C. Annual awards dinner for Corolla suppliers		
D. Salary of engineer who monitors design changes on Geo Prism		
E. Freight costs of Corolla engines shipped from Toyota City, Japan, to Fremont, California		
F. Electricity costs for NUMMI plant (single bill covers entire plant)		
G. Wages paid to temporary assembly-line workers hired in periods of high production (paid on an hourly basis)		
H. Annual fire-insurance policy cost for NUMM1 plant		

2-22 Computing cost of goods manufactured and cost of goods sold. The following are account balances relating to 2009 (in thousands):

Property tax on plant building	$ 4,200
Marketing, distribution, and customer-service costs	44,400
Finished goods inventory, January 1, 2009	37,400
Plant utilities	20,400

COGM $250,800
COGS $242,400

Work-in-process inventory, December 31, 2009	32,200
Amortization of plant building	14,700
General and administrative costs (nonplant)	51,600
Direct materials used	106,800
Finished goods inventory, December 31, 2009	44,800
Amortization of plant equipment	14,700
Plant repairs and maintenance	19,200
Work-in-process inventory, January 1, 2009	25,000
Direct manufacturing labour	38,400
Indirect manufacturing labour	27,600
Indirect materials used	12,200
Miscellaneous plant overhead	5,200

REQUIRED

Compute cost of goods manufactured and cost of goods sold.

2-23 **Computing cost of goods purchased and cost of sales.** The data below are for Marvin Department Store. The account balances (in thousands) are for 2009.

(a) COG Purchased $152,000
(b) COS $145,000

Marketing, distribution, and customer-service costs	$ 37,000
Merchandise inventory, January 1, 2009	27,000
Utilities	17,000
General and administrative costs	43,000
Merchandise inventory, December 31, 2009	34,000
Purchases	155,000
Miscellaneous costs	4,000
Transportation-in	7,000
Purchase returns and allowances	4,000
Purchase discounts	6,000

REQUIRED

Compute (a) cost of goods purchased and (b) cost of sales.

2-24 **Variable costs and fixed costs behaviour.** TwinkleToes Company manufactures beach sandals and sells them for $22 a pair. Variable manufacturing costs are $9.90 a pair, and indirect fixed manufacturing costs are $3.30 a pair. The company can accept a one-time-only special order of 20,000 pairs of sandals at $13.20 a pair because the extra quantity is within the relevant range of production, so indirect fixed manufacturing costs will not increase due to this special order. Woody will not incur any marketing or other period costs as a result of the special order. What would the effect on operating income be if the special order could be accepted without affecting normal sales?

REQUIRED

Choose the correct answer.

a. $0
b. $66,000 increase
c. $198,000 increase
d. $264,000 increase.

2-25 **Variable costs, fixed costs, relevant range.** Yumball Candies manufactures jaw-breaker candies in a fully automated process. The machine that produces candies was purchased recently and can make 4,000 per month. The machine costs $6,000 and is amortized using straight-line amortization over ten years assuming zero residual value. Rent for the factory space and warehouse, and other fixed manufacturing overhead costs total $1,000 per month.

Yumball currently makes and sells 3,000 jaw-breakers per month. Yumball buys just enough materials each month to make the jaw-breakers it needs to sell. Materials cost 10 cents per jawbreaker.

Next year Yumball expects demand to increase by 100%. At this volume of materials purchased, it will get a 10% discount on price. Rent and other fixed manufacturing overhead costs will remain the same.

2. Variable manufacturing cost $3,600 for the year

REQUIRED

1. What is Yumball's current annual relevant range of output?
2. What is Yumball's current annual fixed manufacturing cost within the relevant range? What is the variable manufacturing cost?

3. What will Yumball's relevant range of output be next year? How, if at all, will fixed and variable manufacturing costs change next year?

2-26 Total costs and unit costs. A student association has hired a musical group for a graduation party. The cost will be a fixed amount of $4,800.

REQUIRED

1. Suppose 500 people attend the party. What will be the total cost of the musical group; the unit cost per person?
2. Suppose 2,000 people attend. What will be the total cost of the musical group; the unit cost per person?
3. For prediction of total costs, should the manager of the party use the unit cost in requirement 1; the unit cost in requirement 2? What is the major lesson of this problem?

2-27 Total and unit costs, decision making. Graham's Glassworks makes glass flanges for scientific use. Materials cost $1 per flange, and the glass blowers are paid a wage rate of $20 per hour. A glass blower blows 10 flanges per hour. Fixed manufacturing costs for flanges are $20,000 per period. Period (nonmanufacturing) costs associated with flanges are $10,000 per period, and are fixed.

REQUIRED

1. Graph the fixed, variable and total manufacturing cost for flanges, using units (number of flanges) on the x-axis.
2. Fred's Flasks sells flanges for $8.25 each. Can Graham sell below Fred's price and still make a profit on the flanges? Assume Graham produces and sells 5,000 flanges this period.
3. How would your answer to requirement 2 differ if Graham's Glassworks made and sold 10,000 flanges this period? Why? What does this indicate about the use of unit cost in decision making?

PROBLEMS

2-28 Labour cost, overtime, and idle time. Len Lippart is a line worker in the assembly department of Maxart Manufacturing. He normally earns $12 per hour, but gets time and a half ($18 per hour) for overtime, over 40 hours per week. He earns double time if he works holidays even if he has not worked 40 hours that week.

Sometimes the assembly line equipment goes down and Len has to wait for the mechanics to repair the equipment or there is a scheduling mix-up. Len is paid for this time and Maxart considers this idle time.

In May, Len worked two 42-hour weeks, one 43-hour week, and the last week he worked 40 hours, but one of those days was a national holiday. During regular hours, the assembly-line equipment was down 4.2 hours in May, and Len had one hour of idle time because of a scheduling mix-up.

REQUIRED

1. Calculate (a) direct manufacturing labour, (b) idle time, (c) overtime holiday premium, and (d) total earnings for Len in May.
2. Is idle time and overtime premium a direct or indirect cost of the jobs that Len worked on in May? Explain.

2-29 Comprehensive problem on unit costs, product costs. Soo Office Equipment manufactures and sells metal shelving. It began operations on January 1, 2009. Costs incurred for 2009 are as follows (V stands for variable; F stands for fixed):

Direct materials used costs	$140,000 V
Direct manufacturing labour costs	30,000 V
Plant energy costs	5,000 V
Indirect manufacturing labour costs	10,000 V
Indirect manufacturing labour costs	16,000 F
Other indirect manufacturing costs	8,000 V
Other indirect manufacturing costs	24,000 F
Marketing, distribution, and customer-service costs	122,850 V
Marketing, distribution, and customer-service costs	40,000 F
Administrative costs	50,000 F

Variable manufacturing costs are variable with respect to units produced. Variable marketing, distribution, and customer-service costs are variable with respect to units sold.

Inventory data are as follows:

	Beginning, January 1, 2009	Ending, December 31, 2009
Direct materials	0 kilograms	2,000 kilograms
Work in process	0 units	0 units
Finished goods	0 units	? units

Production in 2009 was 100,000 units. Two kilograms of direct materials are used to make one unit of finished product.

Revenues in 2009 were $436,800. The selling price per unit and the purchase price per kilogram of direct materials were stable throughout the year. The company's ending inventory of finished goods is carried at the average unit manufacturing costs for 2009. Finished goods inventory at December 31, 2009, was $20,970.

REQUIRED
1. Calculate direct materials inventory, total cost, December 31, 2009.
2. Calculate finished goods inventory, total units, December 31, 2009.
3. Calculate selling price per unit in 2009.
4. Calculate operating income for 2009 (show your computations).

2-30 Budgeted income statement (continuation of 2-29). Assume management predicts that the selling price per unit and variable cost per unit will be the same in 2010 as in 2009. Fixed manufacturing costs and marketing, distribution, and customer-service costs in 2010 are also predicted to be the same as in 2009. Sales in 2010 are forecast to be 122,000 units. The desired ending inventory of finished goods, December 31, 2010, is 12,000 units. Assume zero ending inventories of both direct materials and work in process. The company's ending inventory of finished goods is carried at the average unit manufacturing costs for 2010. The company uses the first-in, first-out inventory method. Management has asked that you prepare a budgeted income statement for 2010. On December 31, 2009, finished goods inventory is 9,000 units.

1. 125,000 units

REQUIRED
1. Units of finished goods produced in 2010
2. Budgeted income statement for 2010

2-31 Cost of goods manufactured. Consider the following account balances (in thousands) for the Canseco Company:

1. COGM $136,000

	Beginning of 2009	End of 2009
Direct materials inventory	$22,000	$26,000
Work-in-process inventory	21,000	20,000
Finished goods inventory	18,000	23,000
Purchases of direct materials		75,000
Direct manufacturing labour		25,000
Indirect manufacturing labour		15,000
Plant insurance		9,000
Amortization—plant building and equipment		11,000
Repairs and maintenance—plant		4,000
Marketing, distribution, and customer-service costs		93,000
General and administrative costs		29,000

REQUIRED
1. Prepare a schedule of cost of goods manufactured for 2009.
2. Revenues in 2009 were $300 million. Prepare the 2009 income statement.

2-32 Flow of inventoriable costs. Hofstra Plastics Inc.'s selected data for the month of August 2009 are presented below (in millions):

1. Direct materials inventory $75

Work-in-process inventory, August 1, 2009	$ 200
Direct materials inventory, August 1, 2009	90
Direct materials purchased	360
Direct materials used	375

Variable manufacturing overhead	250
Total manufacturing overhead	480
Total manufacturing costs incurred during August 2009	1,600
Cost of goods manufactured	1,650
Cost of goods sold	1,700
Finished goods inventory, August 1, 2009	125

REQUIRED

Calculate the following costs:

1. Direct materials inventory on August 31, 2009
2. Fixed manufacturing overhead costs for August
3. Direct manufacturing labour costs for August
4. Work-in-process inventory on August 31, 2009
5. Cost of goods available for sale in August
6. Finished goods inventory on August 31, 2009

②

A = $20,700

2-33 Finding unknown balances. An auditor for Canada Revenue Agency is trying to reconstruct some partially destroyed records of two taxpayers. For each case in the accompanying list, find the unknowns designated by capital letters (figures are in thousands).

	Case 1	Case 2
Accounts receivable, December 31, 2009	$ 6,000	$ 2,100
Cost of goods sold	A	20,000
Accounts payable, January 1, 2009	3,000	1,700
Accounts payable, December 31, 2009	1,800	1,500
Finished goods inventory, December 31, 2009	B	5,300
Gross margin	11,300	C
Work in process, January 1, 2009	0	800
Work in process, December 31, 2009	0	3,000
Finished goods inventory, January 1, 2009	4,000	4,000
Direct materials used	8,000	12,000
Direct manufacturing labour	3,000	5,000
Indirect manufacturing costs	7,000	D
Purchases of direct material	9,000	7,000
Revenues	32,000	31,800
Accounts receivable, January 1, 2009	2,000	1,400

②

Operating income $50
COGM $645

2-34 Income statement and schedule of cost of goods manufactured. The Powell Corporation has the following account balances (in millions):

For Specific Date		For Year 2009	
Direct materials, January 1, 2009	$ 15	Purchases of direct materials	$ 390
Work in process, January 1, 2009	10	Direct manufacturing labour	120
Finished goods, January 1, 2009	70	Amortization—plant building and equipment	96
Direct materials, December 31, 2009	20	Plant supervisory salaries	6
Work in process, December 31, 2009	5	Miscellaneous plant overhead	42
Finished goods, December 31, 2009	55	Revenues	1,140
		Marketing, distribution, and customer-service costs	288
		Plant supplies used	12
		Plant utilities	36
		Indirect manufacturing labour	60

REQUIRED

Prepare an income statement and a supporting schedule of cost of goods manufactured for the year ended December 31, 2009. (For additional questions regarding these facts, see the next problem.)

2-35 Interpretation of statements (continuation of 2-34). Refer to the preceding problem.

4. Unit cost for direct materials $320

REQUIRED

1. How would the answer to the preceding problem be modified if you were asked for a schedule of cost of goods manufactured and sold instead of a schedule of cost of goods manufactured? Be specific.
2. Would the sales manager's salary (included in marketing, distribution, and customer-service costs) be accounted for differently if the Powell Corporation were a merchandising company instead of a manufacturing company? Using the flow of costs outlined in Exhibit 2-1 (p. 36), describe how the wages of an assembler in the plant would be accounted for in this manufacturing company.
3. Plant supervisory salaries are usually regarded as indirect manufacturing costs. Under what conditions might some of these costs be regarded as direct manufacturing costs? Give an example.
4. Suppose that both the direct materials used and the plant amortization were related to the manufacture of 1 million units of product. What is the unit cost for the direct materials assigned to those units? What is the unit cost for plant building and equipment amortization? Assume that yearly plant amortization is computed on a straight-line basis.
5. Assume that the historical, actual cost behaviour patterns in requirement 4 persist—that is, direct materials costs behave as a variable cost and amortization behaves as a fixed cost. Repeat the computations in requirement 4, assuming that the costs are being predicted for the manufacture of 1.2 million units of product. How would the total costs be affected?
6. As a management accountant, explain concisely to the president why the unit costs differed in requirements 4 and 5.

2-36 Income statement and schedule of cost of goods manufactured. The following items (in millions) pertain to the Chan Corporation:

Operating income $28
COGM $204

For Specific Date		For Year 2009	
Work in process, January 1, 2009	$10	Plant utilities	$ 5
Direct materials, December 31, 2009	5	Indirect manufacturing labour	20
Finished goods, December 31, 2009	12	Amortization—plant building and equipment	9
Accounts payable, December 31, 2009	20	Revenues	350
Accounts receivable, January 1, 2009	50	Miscellaneous manufacturing overhead	10
Work in process, December 31, 2009	2	Marketing, distribution, and customer-service costs	90
Finished goods, January 1, 2009	40	Purchases of direct materials	80
Accounts receivable, December 31, 2009	30	Direct manufacturing labour	40
Accounts payable, January 1, 2009	40	Plant supplies used	6
Direct materials, January 1, 2009	30	Property taxes on plant	1

Chan's manufacturing cost system uses a three-part classification of manufacturing costs. There are two prime costs and one conversion cost: direct materials, direct manufacturing labour, and indirect manufacturing costs.

REQUIRED

Prepare an income statement and a supporting schedule of cost of goods manufactured. (For additional questions regarding these facts, see the next problem.)

2-37 Interpretation of statements (continuation of 2-36). Refer to the preceding problem.

1. Total prime costs $145

REQUIRED

1. Calculate total prime costs and total conversion costs.
2. Compute total inventoriable costs and period costs.
3. Design costs and R&D costs are not considered product costs for financial statement purposes. When might some of these costs be regarded as product costs? Give an example.
4. Suppose that both the direct materials used and the plant amortization were related to the manufacture of 1 million units of product. What is the unit cost for the direct materials assigned to those units? What is the unit cost for plant building and equipment amortization? Assume that yearly amortization is computed on a straight-line basis.
5. Assume that the implied cost behaviour patterns in requirement 4 persist. That is, direct materials costs behave as a variable cost and plant amortization behaves as a

fixed cost. Repeat the computations in requirement 4, assuming that the costs are being predicted for the manufacture of 1.5 million units of product. How would the total costs be affected?

6. Assume that amortization on the equipment (but not the plant) is computed based on the number of units produced because the equipment deteriorates with units produced. The amortization rate on equipment is $4 per unit. Calculate the amortization on equipment assuming (a) 1 million units of product are produced and (b) 1.5 million units of product are produced.

2 3 4

1. Operating income $120,000
COGM $960,000

2-38 Foxwood Company is a metal- and wood-cutting manufacturer selling products to the home construction market. Consider the following data for the year 2009:

Sandpaper	$ 2,000
Materials-handling costs	70,000
Lubricants-handling costs	5,000
Miscellaneous indirect manufacturing labour	40,000
Direct manufacturing labour	300,000
Direct materials, January 1, 2009	40,000
Direct materials, December 31, 2009	50,000
Finished goods January 1, 2009	100,000
Finished goods December 31, 2009	150,000
Work in process, January 1, 2009	10,000
Work in process, December 31, 2009	14,000
Plant leasing costs	54,000
Amortization—plant equipment	36,000
Property taxes on plant equipment	4,000
Fire and casualty insurance on plant equipment	3,000
Direct materials purchased in 2009	460,000
Revenue	1,360,000
Marketing and promotion	60,000
Marketing salaries	100,000
Shipping costs	70,000
Customer service costs	100,000

REQUIRED

1. Prepare an income statement with a separate supporting schedule of cost of goods manufactured. For all manufacturing items, indicate by V or F whether each is basically a variable cost or a fixed cost (where the cost object is a product unit). If in doubt, decide on the basis of whether the total cost will change substantially over a wide range of production output.
2. Suppose that both the direct materials and plant leasing costs are tied to the production of 900,000 units. What is the direct materials cost assigned to each output unit produced? Assume that the plant leasing costs are a fixed cost. What is the unit cost of the plant leasing costs?
3. Repeat the computation in requirement 2 for direct materials and plant leasing costs assuming that the costs are being predicted for the manufacturing of 1 million units next year. Assume no changes in the historical or actual cost behaviour patterns.
4. As a management consultant, explain concisely to the president why the direct materials cost per output unit did not change in requirements 2 and 3 but the plant leasing costs per output unit did change.
5. Calculate what direct manufacturing labour (DML) cost is as a percentage of total cost of goods sold (COGS). In your opinion is this a material cost? Provide your reason(s). Consistent with your opinion, would you classify DML as a prime or a conversion cost?

5

1. Opportunity cost $94,680

2-39 **Inventory decision, opportunity costs.** Lawnox, a manufacturer of lawn mowers, predicts that it will purchase 240,000 spark plugs next year. Lawnox estimates that 20,000 spark plugs will be required each month. A supplier quotes a price of $9 per spark plug. The supplier also offers a special discount option: If all 240,000 spark plugs are purchased at the start of the year, a discount of 4% off the $9 price will be given. Lawnox can invest its cash at 10% per year. It costs Lawnox $200 to place each purchase order.

REQUIRED

1. What is the opportunity cost of interest forgone from purchasing all 240,000 units at the start of the year instead of in 12 monthly purchases of 20,000 units per order?

2. Would this opportunity cost be recorded in the accounting system? Why?
3. Should Lawnox purchase 240,000 units at the start of the year or 20,000 units each month? Show your calculations.

2-40 Labour-cost ethics, governance. Zix Manufacturing has recently opened a plant in Costa Melon in order to take advantage of certain tax benefits. In order to qualify for these tax benefits, the company's direct manufacturing labour costs must be at least 20% of total manufacturing costs for the period.

Zix Manufacturing normally classifies direct manufacturing labour wages as direct manufacturing labour, but classifies fringe benefits, overtime premiums, idle time, and vacation time and sick leave as indirect manufacturing labour.

During the first period of operations in Costa Melon, Zix incurs a total of $2,500,000 in manufacturing costs. Of that, $410,000 is direct manufacturing labour wages, $45,000 is overtime premium, $86,000 is fringe benefits, $20,500 is vacation time and sick leave, and $10,900 is idle time.

REQUIRED
1. Will Zix's direct manufacturing labour costs qualify them for the tax benefit?
2. Bob Zixson, the manager of the new Costa Melon plant, is concerned that he will not get a bonus this year because the plant will not get the tax benefit. What might he ask the plant controller to do to make sure Zix gets the tax benefit? How might these accounting changes be rationalized?
3. Should the plant controller do what the manager has asked in requirement 2? Why or why not?

COLLABORATIVE LEARNING CASES

2-41 Cost analysis, litigation risk, governance. Sam Nash is the head of new-product development of Forever Young (FY). Nash is currently considering Enhance, which would be FY's next major product in its beauty/cosmetics line and its estimated unit cost is currently $144. Enhance represents a new direction for FY. All FY's current products are cosmetics applied to the skin by the consumer. In contrast, Enhance is inserted via needle into the skin by a nurse after an initial meeting with a doctor. FY planned to sell Enhance at cost plus 20% to physicians. FY used an estimated treatment cost to patients of $432 to provide a financial incentive to physicians. Each treatment will last three months. Enhance is an animal-based product that fills out the skin so that fewer wrinkles are observable.

Nash, however, questions the economics of this product because FY has failed to budget for any litigation costs, which Nash estimated as $132 per unit. At present, the costs recognized are research and development, manufacturing by a third party, marketing, distribution, and a small amount for customer support. Nash's main concern is with recognizing in the current costing proposal potential future litigation costs (such as the costs of lawyers and expert witnesses in defending lawsuits against Enhance). He points to the litigation with breast implants and notes that a settlement of more than $4.80 billion is being discussed in the press. He also notes the tobacco company litigation and those proposed billion-dollar settlements. Elisabeth Savage, the CEO and president of the company, disagrees with Nash. She maintains that she has total confidence in her medical research team and directs Nash not to include any dollar amount for potential litigation cost in his upcoming presentation to the board of directors on the economics and pricing of the Enhance product. Nash was previously controller of FY and has a strong background in finance. His current job represents his first nonfinance position, and he views himself as potential CEO material.

REQUIRED
1. What reasons might Savage have for not wanting Nash to record potential future litigation costs on the product in a presentation on Enhance's economics and pricing?
2. Suppose Savage asks Nash to give her an "off-the-record" presentation on the possible magnitude of the potential litigation costs of Enhance. What is the new unit cost including the estimated litigation costs? What should the new selling price to physicians be to maintain the triple-the-cost target? What is the percentage decrease in the margin physicians could expect per unit assuming the cost to the patient cannot be changed?
3. After hearing Nash's presentation (see requirement 2), Savage directs Nash to drop any further discussion of the litigation issue. He is to focus on making Enhance the blockbuster product that field research has suggested it will be. Nash is uneasy with this directive. He tells Savage it is an "ostrich approach" (head-in-the-sand) to a real problem that could potentially bankrupt the company. Savage tells Nash to go and think about her directive. What should Nash do next?

2-42 Movie profit sharing, defining terms. Brad Fittler, first-time author of *The Sporting Life*, has just had a meeting with Bill Harrigan, a senior executive of Golden Ventures (GV). GV is a major movie studio with many successes. *The Sporting Life* is a best-selling novel about the personal and professional career of Allan Langer, a recently retired football superstar. Harrigan bubbled with excitement during the meeting. He said the book was the "best thing he had seen in many years" and would make "*Titanic* look like a minor movie." Fittler felt great about a luminary such as Harrigan being so full of praise for a film based on a book that many publishers initially rejected as "not meeting their commercial criteria."

After the meeting, Fittler called Penny Carr, a friend for many years. Carr showed Fittler some extracts from an exposé on "Accounting, Hollywood Style"—see statement below. Fittler was dismayed by the Cumulative Distribution Statement. He thought *Bill Goldberg Superstar* was a box-office success and yet it still was more than $74 million "in the red."

Golden Venture Report on *Bill Goldberg Superstar*
Cumulative Distribution Statement (in $ thousands)
From July 1, 2008 to March 31, 2009

1.	Gross receipts (a)	$192,354
2.	Less distribution fees (b)	67,324
3.	Gross after distribution fees	125,030
4.	Less distribution expenses (c)	66,076
5.	Balance	58,954
6.	Less gross participation fees of directors, screen stars, and so on (d)	38,471
7.	Balance	20,483
8.	Less negative cost (e)	(82,104)
9.	Balance	(61,621)
10.	Less interest on negative cost (f)	12,943
11.	Net profit	$ (74,564)

a. The studio's revenues from the film to date. All North American theatre screen and television revenues are included. Only 50% of non–North American revenues are included. Only 20% of the gross is included for home DVD sales. The film's video distributor, Golden Ventures Home Video (100% owned by GV), kept 80% because it was treated as a separate company. Revenues from nontheatre, nonvideo, and nontelevision sources are not included.

b. Distribution fees. Covers overhead costs of running a studio and is a flat 35% of revenues.

c. Distribution expenses. The actual costs of putting the movie in theatres, including advertising, printing copies of the film, and transportation.

d. Gross participation fees of directors, screen stars. The major "talent" on the movie receive 20% of the gross receipts for the first $240 million and 25% thereafter.

e. Negative cost is the cost of producing everything that is seen onscreen, from film and sets to up-front fees paid to cast and crew.

f. Interest on negative cost. The studio views the cost of financing a film as a loan and charges 125% of the prime rate for any negative balance in line 9 as long as the movie "remains in the red."

REQUIRED

You are asked to give advice to Brad Fittler. You should

a. Identify the weaknesses in the Golden Ventures Cumulative Distribution Statement for an author whose payment is 5% of net profits.

b. Propose ways to reduce (or even eliminate) the weaknesses you identify in (a) for a contract for Fittler.

2-43 Defining cost terms. You are the controller of the Heinz potato processing subsidiary in Ireland. This subsidiary processes potatoes for frozen dinners, fast food restaurants, and other large institutional buyers. Assume that companies setting up manufacturing facilities in Ireland receive an income tax rebate equivalent to the ratio of employment costs of Irish citizens to total manufacturing costs in Ireland. Thus, if the Irish subsidiary has a "pre-rebate" tax bill of $12 million and the ratio of employment costs to total manufacturing costs is 22%, its actual tax bill will be reduced by $2.64 million to $9.36 million.

INSTRUCTIONS
Form groups of two or more students to complete the following requirement.

REQUIRED
Develop guidelines as to how Heinz should define costs at its Irish subsidiary. Assume one aim is to minimize the income taxes that Heinz is legitimately required to pay to the Irish government.

Cost-Volume-Profit Analysis

BUSINESS MATTERS

Cost-Volume-Profit

WestJet can combine information about cost and price per seat, the number of seats sold (volume), and profit using a technique called cost-volume-profit analysis. The benefit is that WestJet can use the technique to calculate how many seats must be sold at what price to cover all costs of a flight, or, more to the point, to earn a profit on the flight. Managers learn cost-volume-profit analysis because it is a tool that helps them analyze and select the best from among many alternatives to change how they currently do business and to improve profit.

LEARNING OBJECTIVES

After studying this chapter, you should be able to

1. Classify and summarize revenue, volume, and cost data to produce relevant information for a cost-volume-profit analysis

2. Distinguish among contribution margin, gross margin, and operating margin

3. Apply cost-volume-profit analysis to determine breakeven points for a single-product company under different conditions of target operating income and net income using the appropriate equation, contribution margin, or graph method

4. Select the most appropriate strategy when the breakeven point is affected by alternative planned changes to price, volume, and/or costs

5. Analyze and select the most appropriate product mix for a two-product company, and adapt CVP analysis to multiple revenue-driver situations

6. Analyze and select the most appropriate product mix for a two-product company, and adapt CVP analysis to multiple cost-driver situations

Cost-volume-profit (CVP) analysis is a method to take a lot of data on volume, price, and costs, classify them, and then produce a meaningful summary that is used to calculate either *breakeven* volume or revenue. Both breakeven values indicate the point at which total revenue equals total costs and operating income is zero. In not-for-profit companies, the goal is to break even. In for-profit companies, the goal is to maximize the amount by which revenue exceeds all costs, which is the profit. Managers can apply CVP to analyze and clarify how to either achieve an operating income of zero or to maximize net income after tax. A CVP analysis simplifies reality because the key assumption is the volume of finished goods or services available for sale (Q) equals the volume of the finished goods or services sold. In accounting terminology, the ending inventory is zero.

Either historical or forecasted data inputs on volume, price, and costs can be used to produce a CVP analysis. Accountants often refer to forecasts as budgets. All data inputs relevant to a CVP analysis are classified and summarized according to management-accounting logic. Managers can then vary each of these inputs in turn or all of them together to understand how changes affect both operating income (OI) and net income (NI). Managers commonly use CVP to help them answer such questions as:

◆ What happens to OI and NI if we sell 1,000 more units?

◆ What happens to OI and NI if we raise or lower our selling prices?

◆ What happens to OI and NI if we increase our discretionary period costs such as advertising?

◆ What happens to OI and NI if we reduce our variable cost of raw materials?

◆ What happens to OI and NI if we increase our sales commissions?

CVP analyses help managers select the best from among many alternatives to change how they currently do business and improve profits in both the short term and long term.

Central to CVP is classifying all inventoriable and period costs as either variable or fixed costs or the cost behaviour with respect to Q available for sale and sold (see Chapter 2 p. 55–60). Fixed costs (FC), both inventoriable and period, represent the assets purchased and financing undertaken to support long-term capacity or output volume. Total variable costs (TVC), both inventoriable and period, increase or decrease as Q available for sale and sold varies. The TVC plus FC sum to the **total costs** (TC), which must be completely recovered during each time period of operations before either breakeven volume or revenue is achieved. Estimating the breakeven volume or revenue is relevant both to control operations in the short run and to decide on long-run output volume (capacity) required to achieve long-term profitability (Chapter 22).

COST-VOLUME-PROFIT ANALYSIS PROCEDURES

1 Classify and summarize revenue, volume, and cost data to produce relevant information for a cost-volume-profit analysis

As you will learn, the cost-volume-profit (CVP) relationship, although simple, provides powerful assistance to companies in all industries when managers in any business function of the value chain decide on the best changes to make to financial results from their operations. For example, in the short run, when a WestJet flight from Ottawa to Maui has empty seats and passengers arrive shortly before takeoff, WestJet managers must decide a price policy for last-minute boarding. In this situation, once a flight is scheduled, all the costs are fixed. The costs can be very high primarily because the tonnes of fuel used changes very little whether the aircraft is full or nearly empty. When an extra passenger with baggage boards late, the only additional cost to the company may be the in-flight meal, which is at most $10 per passenger. The extra passenger causes an almost negligible change in the cost of the flight. However, if WestJet permitted late passengers to board at a dramatic reduction from a normal fare of approximately $3,340 return, soon all passengers would all show up at the last minute to obtain the lower fare. If the managers decide on a dramatic increase, the passengers would choose another carrier if they can. The effect on profit of a higher volume at a lower unit sales price, or lower volume at a higher unit sales price are questions that CVP analysis would help answer and enable managers to select an appropriate last-minute price. In contrast, not long ago, WestJet had to decide if it would switch its primary Ontario airport from Hamilton to Toronto. This strategic decision would affect profitability for a long period of time, because landing fees at Toronto are far higher, in fact the highest in the world, but so too are volumes of passengers landing there. For each WestJet flight in or out of Toronto, the number of paying passengers per flight had to increase to not only cover this higher cost, but also produce a target profit.

EFFECT OF TIME HORIZON

Bear in mind that whether costs are classified as fixed or variable always depends upon a specified time horizon and relevant range or volume of sales. As the WestJet example of last-minute boarding illustrates, the shorter the time horizon, the higher the percentage of total costs that will be fixed. In contrast, if WestJet's decision is whether to add another destination to its routes, there may be a one-year planning horizon, and a higher percentage of total costs would be regarded as variable than those incurred once a flight is scheduled to take off. Whether costs are fixed depends heavily on the relevant range, the length of the time horizon in question, and the specific decision situation.

Before explaining the basics of CVP analysis, we must first review some financial accounting relationships as described in Chapter 2. Refer to the abbreviated financial income statement in equation form:

Revenue − Cost of goods sold (or cost of sales) = **Gross margin**

Gross margin − Operating expenses = **Operating income**

Operating income − Interest expense = **Taxable income**

Taxable income − Tax expense = **Net income**

In column form, these equations appear as:

Abbreviated Financial-Accounting Statement of Net Income

Revenue
    − Cost of goods sold (COGS)   variable plus fixed inventoriable costs
Gross margin (GM)
    − Operating expenses (Opex)   variable plus fixed period costs
Operating income (OI)
    − Interest expense   variable plus fixed financing costs
Taxable income
    − Tax expense   taxable income × tax rate
Net income (NI)

Notice the logic of this classification of costs is the separation of inventoriable from period costs (financial accountants refer to period costs as operating expenses, abbreviated here as Opex). One important equation to understand is the relationship of OI to NI. This permits you to calculate a target net income for use in a CVP analysis:

$$\text{NI} = (\text{OI} - \text{interest expense}) \times (1 - \text{tax rate}) = \text{Taxable income} \times (1 - \text{tax rate})$$

You may also recall from financial accounting that the gross margin divided by revenue is a ratio called the **gross margin percentage** (GM%). On the other hand, the operating income (OI) divided by total revenue is sometimes called the **operating margin percentage (OM%)**, but more often the **operating margin (OM)**. In the next section, you will learn new management accounting terms *contribution margin* (CM), *contribution margin percentage* (CM%), and a new management accounting summary, the *contribution income statement*. Unlike either the GM or OM, the contribution margin is a value for which no financial accounting standard exists, although often it is financial accounting data that are reclassified to help managers make internal operating decisions to improve profit. CVP analysis requires using a different way to classify and summarize the same set of costs reported on a financial accounting statement of net income. The new classification method permits a different summary of costs that will provide the relevant information required to calculate breakeven values. (A list of all abbreviations appears on the inside back cover of this book.)

The CVP analysis is based on the following six assumptions:

1. Cost behaviour is the management-accounting logic used to classify total costs as either fixed or variable. The reason why this new classification system is important is that it produces relevant information required for a CVP analysis that helps managers improve their profits. (We discuss methods to determine fixed and variable components of costs in Chapter 10.)

2. Changes in revenues and variable costs arise only because of changes in the volume (Q) of finished goods (or service) units both available for sale and sold (i.e., beginning and ending inventory are identical). If we assume Q finished goods (or services) available for sale = Q sales, then Q is the only *revenue* and *variable cost driver*. A **revenue driver** is any factor that affects revenues.

3. Behaviour of total revenues and total costs is linear (in a straight line, as shown later in Exhibit 3-2) in relation to changes in the volume (Q) of output units within the relevant range.

4. Unit selling price (USP), unit variable costs (UVC), and total fixed costs (FC) are known.

5. CVP analyses initially assume either a single product, or that a given revenue mix of products will remain constant as the level of total units sold (Q) changes.

6. All revenues and costs can be added and compared without taking into account the time value of money. (Chapters 21 and 22 relax this assumption.)

The six simplifying assumptions, however, do not always hold in practice when, for example, there are multiple revenue drivers (e.g., number of sales visits and number of advertisements) and cost drivers (e.g., number of batches and engineering hours of labour). More difficult analysis could represent these complex relationships more faithfully, but management accountants weigh the benefit of increased relevance against the costs of the analysis. When simplified CVP relationships generate enough information to contribute towards a profitable decision, then there is no reason to undertake more complex analyses unless these will significantly improve managers' decisions.

The management-accounting logic of assumption one requires classifying the inventoriable and period costs on the financial-accounting income statement into variable and fixed costs. The **contribution income statement** can be produced from costs classified according to their behaviour. It does not matter, however, if the financial or management classification logic is used, the costs will sum to the same **total costs** (TC). The **total variable costs** (TVC) include both inventoriable and period (e.g., raw materials and sales commission, respectively) variable costs. The **total fixed costs** (FC) include both inventoriable and period fixed costs. This means that

$$COGS + Opex = TVC + FC$$

An important relationship that the management-accounting logic reveals is the **contribution margin** (TCM), illustrated later in Exhibit 3-1. The TCM is the result of subtracting TVC from **total revenue** (TRev), or

$$TCM = TRev - TVC$$

We also assumed that quantity Q is the only cost driver and revenue driver of TVC and TRev. Based on internal information, if managers know the **unit variable cost** (UVC) and the **unit sales price** (USP), then Q(UVC) = TVC and Q(USP) = TRev. Moreover, Q(USP − UVC) = TCM. The **unit contribution margin** (UCM) is calculated as USP − UVC and the contribution margin TCM is calculated as Q(UCM).

To see how CVP analysis works, consider the following example:

Example: Carolin Smale will sell One Size Software, a home-office software package, at a heavily attended two-day computer convention in Montreal. She can purchase this software from a wholesaler at $120 per package; thus her unit VC = $120. She may return all unsold units and receive a full $120 refund per package. This arrangement is known as a consignment contract. Because Carolin can return all unsold packages, Q(Unit VC) = total VC, and the ending inventory will be zero.

Each unit or software package will be sold for $200; thus the USP = $200. The UCM = USP − UVC = $200 − $120 = $80. If ending inventory is zero, then Q is the revenue driver and Q(USP) = TRev. Carolin has already paid $2,000 to Computer Conventions Inc. to rent the booth for the two-day convention, which is a fixed cost (FC). This FC will be constant no matter what her volume of sales (Q) will be. Carolin could also use the **contribution margin percentage (CM%)**, which is defined as Total CM ÷ TRev, or identically, UCM ÷ USP.

To answer questions about possible financial results, Carolin can summarize this information in a contribution income statement, as shown in Exhibit 3-1, using different numbers of packages (Q) sold. Applying her knowledge of the arithmetic relationships among these data inputs in this new format, she can calculate either the contribution margin (total CM) or the unit contribution margin (UCM). Data will sometimes be presented in a percentage format. For example, the contribution margin can be expressed as a percentage of variable costs, say UCM = 25% UVC but UVC must be known, say UVC = $80. Based on this information alone, the unit sales price USP must equal UVC+UCM = $80 + 25% × $80 = $100. By definition the CM% = UCM ÷ USP = $20 ÷ 100 = 20%.

The abbreviations are summarized below:

◆ USP = unit selling price (price per unit)

◆ UVC = unit variable costs (includes inventoriable and period UVC)

◆ UCM = unit contribution margin (USP – UVC)

◆ CM% = contribution margin percentage (UCM ÷ USP)

◆ FC = fixed costs (includes inventoriable and period FC, and does not change with Q in the relevant range of finished goods or services available and sold)

◆ Q = quantity of output units produced or available, and sold

◆ TRev = total revenue (Q × USP)

◆ TVC = total variable costs (Q × UVC)

◆ TC = total cost; total of all variable and all fixed costs (TVC + FC)

◆ TCM = total contribution margin (TRev – TVC)

◆ OI = operating income (TCM – FC)

EXHIBIT 3-1
Contribution Income Statement for Different Quantities (Q) of One Size Software Units Sold

	Carolin Sells 5 Packages	**Carolin Sells 40 Packages**
Revenue (TRev)	$ 1,000 (5 packages × $200 per package)	$8,000 (40 packages × $200 per package)
Total variable cost (TVC)	600 (5 packages × $120 per package)	4,800 (40 packages × $120 per package)
Contribution margin (TCM)	400	3,200
Fixed cost (FC)	2,000	2,000
Operating income (OI)	$(1,600)	$1,200

As you inspect Exhibit 3-1, it is clear that both TRev and TVC vary with the Q of units available for sale and sold, which is assumption two. The unit SP and unit VC are constant but as Q increases, both TRev and total VC increase in direct proportion to the increase to Q. This illustrates how Q is both a revenue driver and a variable cost driver.

The graph in Exhibit 3-2 illustrates assumption three for the quantities (Q) of units available and sold of 0, 5, and 40. If Carolin sells Q = 0 packages, the TRev will be $Q \times USP = 0 \times \$200 = \$0$. The Total VC will be: $Q \times UVC = 0 \times \$120 = \$0$. Her Total CM = TRev – Total VC = $0. From Exhibit 3-1, you have already calculated Carolin's Total CM at Q = 5 and Q = 40; they are $400 and $3,200 respectively. But her costs include the FC = $2,000 and total costs (TC) = Total VC + FC. This FC will not change whether Carolin sells Q = 0, 5, or 40 units. This is why the cost line in the graph on the left intersects the vertical axis at $2,000 but the revenue line in the graph on the right intersects the vertical axis at $0. This is also why Carolin has a loss of $1,600 at Q = 5 and a profit of $1,200 at Q = 40.

The Q sold affects how much of her TC are recovered, and somewhere between the two quantities of 5 and 40, her OI will be $0, the **breakeven revenue** at which TRev = TC obtained at her **breakeven volume** of sales (both abbreviated as BEP, the *breakeven point*). Clearly, Carolin would prefer to sell at least enough Q to cover all her costs.

It is the difference between TRev and Total VC that contributes towards the payments of the FC; hence, this difference is the contribution margin. Before we apply our analysis to answer some important questions about profitability, let us make sure we understand what assumption three means. Based on the data summarized in the Contribution Income Statement in Exhibit 3-1, the graph in Exhibit 3-2 illustrates the two linear relationships derived from the management-accounting logic that classifies a cost by its behaviour. Assumption three is the basis for using graphs to depict the BEP.

EXHIBIT 3-2

Behaviour of Total Revenue (TRev) and Total Costs (TC = TVC + FC) is Linear in Relation to Changes in Quantity (Q)

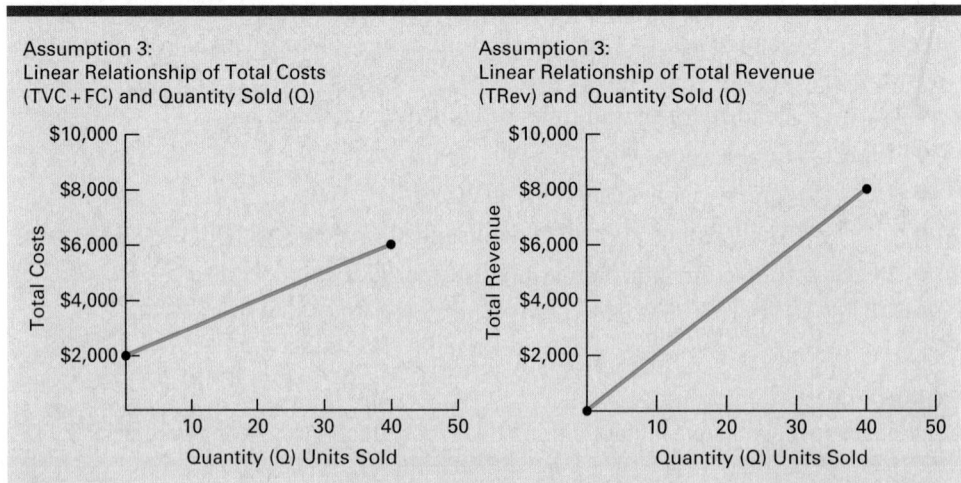

MyAccountingLab

ASSESS YOUR MASTERY

To check your understanding of the material in Learning Objective ❶, go to the Mastery Questions section at the end of the chapter and complete Learning Objective ❶ questions 1, 2, and 3.

Costs for the One Size Software example have now been classified according to how they behave and summarized in the contribution income statement (Exhibit 3-1). Another way to understand what this management-accounting logic means is to examine the definitions of three items:

Distinguish among contribution margin, gross margin, and operating margin

2

- ◆ gross margin (GM)
- ◆ operating margin (OM), and
- ◆ contribution margin (TCM).

The GM and OM are based on the financial-accounting logic of the income statement (see page 87), whereas the TCM is based on the management-accounting logic of the contribution income statement.

The definition of the GM is TRev – COGS. Financial accountants classify COGS as total inventoriable costs (both fixed and variable). For a merchandiser who simply purchases finished goods from a wholesaler and then resells them, total inventoriable cost is often called the cost of sales (COS) and then GM = TRev – COS. The definition of OM is very different because OM is a ratio OI ÷ TRev where OI = GM – Opex or total period costs (both fixed and variable). In our example of One Size Software, Carolin is a merchandiser. For purposes of the contribution income statement, however, whether she incurs a COGS or a COS based on financial-accounting logic is irrelevant. The reason is that the classification of costs is based on management-accounting logic. The relevant point is how costs behave with respect to Q of goods available and sold over a relevant range of Q for a specified time horizon. Using management-accounting logic, all the financial accounting COS or inventoriable costs are classified as either variable or fixed. Then all the period costs are classified as either variable or fixed. Finally, all the variable costs are accumulated as Total VC and the fixed costs as FC. The definition of the TCM is TRev – Total VC. The final step to calculate operating income using this management-accounting approach is to subtract fixed costs from the Total CM or (TCM – FC = OI). Below is a side-by-side comparison of the two types of income statements:

Contribution Income Statement		**Financial Income Statement**	
TRev – TVC = TCM;		TRev – COGS = GM;	
TCM – FC = OI		GM – Opex = OI	

TRev	(Q × USP)			TRev	(Q × USP)	
– TVC	(Q × UVC)			– COGS	(or COS)	
TCM	(Q × UCM)			GM		
– FC	(always a total)			– Opex	(period costs)	
OI	Operating Income		=	OI	Operating Income	

The contribution margin relationships among revenue, costs, contribution margin, and operating income—the cost-volume-profit (CVP) analysis—can now be used to help answer questions such as:

- ◆ What is the minimum Carolin must sell to ensure no losses?
- ◆ What quantity Q must she sell to earn either a target operating income (Target OI) or a target net income (Target NI)?

These questions and others can be answered by applying the CVP analysis as shown in the next section.

MyAccountingLab

ASSESS YOUR MASTERY

To check your understanding of the material in Learning Objective ② , go to the Mastery Questions section at the end of the chapter and complete Learning Objective ② questions 1 and 2.

THE BREAKEVEN POINT (BEP)

③ Apply cost-volume-profit analysis to determine breakeven points for a single-product company under different conditions of target operating income and net income using the appropriate equation, contribution margin, or graph method

Continuing with the One Size Software example, assume Carolin has produced a spreadsheet to show her forecast (or budgeted) OI at different levels of Q available for sale and sold. One convenience of her software is she can also easily present her output in graph form. Exhibit 3-3 presents her spreadsheet in contribution income statement format. Notice that the inputs appear as the quantities (Q) sold in row 2. This format for her spreadsheet would allow Carolin to change any single input or all of them to produce new forecasts of her OI. Provided she has programmed the contribution income statement values properly, these values would change automatically as she changed each input in row 2:

EXHIBIT 3-3
Contribution Income Statement for Different Quantities (Q) of One Size Software Units Sold

	A	B	C	D	E	F	G	H
1				Quantity (Q) of Software Units Sold				
2				0	2	5	25	40
3	TRev for each Q at USP =	$ 200	per pkg	$ 0	$ 400	$ 1,000	$5,000	$8,000
4	TVC for each Q at UVC =	120	per pkg	0	240	600	3,000	4,800
5	TCM for each Q at UCM =	80	per pkg	0	$ 160	400	2,000	3,200
6	Fixed Costs	2,000		2,000	2,000	2,000	2,000	2,000
7	OI			$(2,000)	$(1,840)	$(1,600)	$ 0	$1,200

In the One Size Software example, the Unit CM (UCM) = $200 – $120 = $80, and the Total CM (TCM) = Q × UCM. In a manner similar to calculating the GM% and OM, the ratio of the Total CM ÷ TRev is the contribution margin percentage or CM%. The CM% is the percentage of fixed costs Carolin covers with each unit sold. Because Q is a driver of both TRev and Total VC, it is a constant and can be factored out. The CM% can also equal Unit CM ÷ Unit SP. In this example:

Unit SP = $200

Unit CM = $200 − $120 = $80

CM% = $80 ÷ $200 = 40%

Alternatively, using Total CM ÷ TRev at Q = 5 units, the CM% = $400 ÷ $1,000 = 40%

But what does the CM% mean? It means that for every dollar someone spends to purchase a unit of software, Carolin retains $0.40 after covering her unit variable cost. This $0.40 from each $1.00 of revenue will contribute towards paying her fixed costs until the full $2,000 is paid. Another way of understanding this is that for every unit sold at $200, Carolin keeps 40%, or $200 × 40% = $80 that must be used to pay her fixed costs. Once the FC are paid, nothing is subtracted from the Unit CM, and the $80 per additional unit sold all goes towards increasing OI. The quantity Q at which no FC remain is the *breakeven volume*, and it is also the point at which OI = $0, the **breakeven point (BEP)**.

Why would managers be interested in a BEP? One reason is that a BEP is the basis to calculate the target Q required to make both a target operating income (Target OI) and target net income (Target NI). A second reason is that if something has gone wrong and the profit target was missed, the CVP analysis used to calculate the target Q compared to actual results can reveal what changes must be made to make the profit target in the future. A third reason is that if the BEP in volume is too high for the existing capacity, managers know that without changes in operations, they will go broke. In summary, the BEP is relevant information to decide on a budgeted or Target OI or Target NI. The assumptions leading to a specific BEP in a budget may not be met in reality. Examining the difference between past actual Q, Unit SP, Unit VC, FC, and OI will help diagnose and remedy what went wrong. Finally, if changing the assumptions of a previous budget leads to a BEP that exceeds current capacity, managers must either expand capacity or change future operations to remain solvent and regain profitability.

Another analytical approach is to divide all values on the contribution income statement by TRev. If Carolin had more than one product line this method would assure she compared only relevant differences in how each product contributed to her profit. Of course TRev ÷ TRev = 1, or 100%. The **variable-cost percentage** or VC% is obtained in a similar way to the CM% where either the Unit VC ÷ Unit SP or the Total VC ÷ TRev can be used. From the contribution income statement, the VC% + CM% = 100%; therefore, if you have calculated one you can easily determine the other by subtraction. Whether you use CM%, Unit CM, or Total CM to calculate the BEP will depend on the data available to you.

Using the One Size Software data inputs, we can apply three methods—equation, contribution margin, and the graph method— to calculate the BEP.

EQUATION METHOD

The first approach for computing the breakeven point (BEP) is the equation method. The equation method relies on the contribution income statement in equation form:

$$\text{Total Revenues} - \text{Total Variable costs} - \text{Fixed costs} = \text{Operating income, or}$$
$$\text{TRev} - \text{TVC} - \text{FC} = \text{OI}$$

But TRev and TVC are simply the USP and the UVC multiplied by Q. Therefore,

$$(Q \times \text{USP}) - (Q \times \text{UVC}) - \text{FC} = \text{OI} \qquad (1)$$

This equation provides the most general and easy-to-remember approach to any CVP situation. Setting operating income equal to zero in the preceding equation, we obtain the breakeven Q for Carolin's situation:

$$(Q \times \$200) - (Q \times \$120) - \$2,000 = \$0$$
$$\$80Q = \$0 + \$2,000$$
$$Q = \$2,000 \div \$80 = 25 \text{ units}$$

If Carolin sells fewer than 25 units, she will have a loss; if she sells 25 units, she will break even; if she sells more than 25 units, she will make a profit.

This BEP is expressed in units. It can also be expressed as the breakeven revenue by multiplying the Unit SP by the BEP in units: $25 \times \$200 = \$5,000$, which is exactly what Exhibit 3-3 reports. Carolin does not need to guess the Q of units she must sell to cover all her costs; she can calculate that quantity based on her knowledge of Unit SP, Unit VC, and FC.

CONTRIBUTION MARGIN METHOD

A second approach for computing the breakeven point (BEP) is the contribution margin method, which is simply an algebraic manipulation of the equation method. Using equation (1) as the starting point:

$$(Q \times USP) - (Q \times UVC) - FC = OI \qquad (1)$$

Knowing Q × (USP − UVC) − FC = OI and USP − UVC = UCM, therefore

$$(Q \times UCM) - FC = OI \qquad (2)$$

$$Q \times UCM = OI + FC$$

$$Q = \frac{OI + FC}{UCM} \qquad (3)$$

At the breakeven point (BEP), by definition, OI = \$0, so equation (3) becomes:

$$Q = \frac{\$0 + FC}{UCM}$$

$$= \frac{FC}{UCM}$$

Equation (2) can be used if you have no data on the Unit SP and Unit VC but do know the Unit CM and FC.

At the breakeven point, where OI = \$0 and substituting in the values from our example in equation (3), we obtain:

$$Q = (\$0 + \$2,000) \div \$80 = 25 \text{ units}$$

Notice that equation (2) is a straightforward restatement of equation (1) and equation (3). Equation (1) is the most general and easy-to-remember approach to any CVP situation where you know Unit SP, Unit VC, and FC.

THINKING CRITICALLY

What are the similarities and differences among equations 1, 2, and 3? In what situation would you use equation 1 rather than equation 2 or 3? In what situation would you use equation 2 rather than the others? Read on for a discussion of these issues.

The calculations in the equation method and contribution margin method are similar because one is a restatement of the other to arrive at the identical outcome, equation (3). The equation approach or contribution margin approach will be more useful depending on the input data available. Using equation 1 requires that Carolin know FC and both the Unit SP and Unit VC whereas using equation 2 requires only that she know FC and Unit CM.

We can also algebraically manipulate equation (3) to calculate breakeven in revenue dollars using the contribution margin percentage. If you do not know the Unit SP and the Unit CM, but do know TRev and Total CM, you can use CM%. You know that the CM% = Q(Unit CM ÷ Unit SP) or Total CM ÷ TRev. Multiplying both sides of equation (3) by the USP gives:

$$BEP \text{ in } \$TRev = Q \times USP$$

$$= \frac{FC \times USP}{UCM}$$

Now divide both numerator and denominator by Unit SP:

$$= \frac{FC}{UCM \div USP}$$

$$= \frac{FC}{CM\%} \quad (4)$$

In our One Size Software example, we have already calculated the CM% = 40% and know FC = $2,000. Therefore, the BEP in $TRev from equation (4) is:

$$BEP \text{ in } \$TRev = \frac{FC}{CM\%}$$

$$= \frac{\$2,000}{40\%}$$

$$= \$5,000$$

The following statement confirms the preceding breakeven calculations:

TRev	$5,000	(25 packages × $200 USP)
TVC	3,000	(25 packages × $120 UVC)
TCM	2,000	(25 packages × $80 UCM)
FC	2,000	
OI	$ 0	

GRAPH METHOD

In the graph method, we plot the total cost (TC) line and the total revenue (TRev) line together on the same graph. Recall that these were plotted in separate graphs in Exhibit 3-2 on page 90 to illustrate assumption three. Inspect Exhibit 3-4 where both lines are plotted on the same graph and you will see that the lines intersect. Their point of intersection is the breakeven point (BEP), and from the graph you can read this in both breakeven volume along the horizontal axis and breakeven revenue along the vertical axis. The breakeven volume remains 25 units and the breakeven revenue remains $5,000. Irrespective of the method you use, with the same input values, your answer will be the same.

1. **Total costs line (TC).** Recall that TC = Q(Unit VC) + FC. In our example, FC are $2,000 at all output levels within the relevant range. To plot FC, measure $2,000 on the vertical axis where Q = 0 (point A) and extend a line horizontally. Unit VC of $120 per unit must be added to the FC to plot the TC line. The TC line will slope upwards from point A where Q = 0 at a rate of $120 for each additional unit sold. Select a second point by choosing any other convenient output level (say, 40 units) and calculate the corresponding Total VC of Q × Unit VC = 40 × $120 = $4,800. At Q = 40 units available and sold, TC = Total VC + FC = $4,800 + $2,000 = $6,800, which is point B in Exhibit 3-4. The TC line is the straight line from point A passing through point B.

2. **Total revenues line (TRev).** A convenient starting point is zero revenues at Q = 0 units available and sold, which is point C in Exhibit 3-4. At Q = 40 units available and sold, TRev = Q × USP = 40 × $200 = $8,000, which is point D in Exhibit 3-4. On the graph, the TRev line is the straight line from point C passing through point D. As previously mentioned, the point of intersection of TRev and TC illustrates the breakeven point (BEP).

Exhibit 3-4 illustrates the profit or loss outlook for a wide range of Q units available and sold. This is consistent with the phrase "cost-volume-profit analysis," within which the BEP is only one interesting item. Managers often want to know how OI differs at many different combinations of output levels, fixed and variable costs, and different prices. With only one product, these can be calculated and summarized on a spreadsheet, then plotted on graphs to show visually the effect on OI of different assumptions.

EXHIBIT 3-4
Cost-Volume-Profit Graph

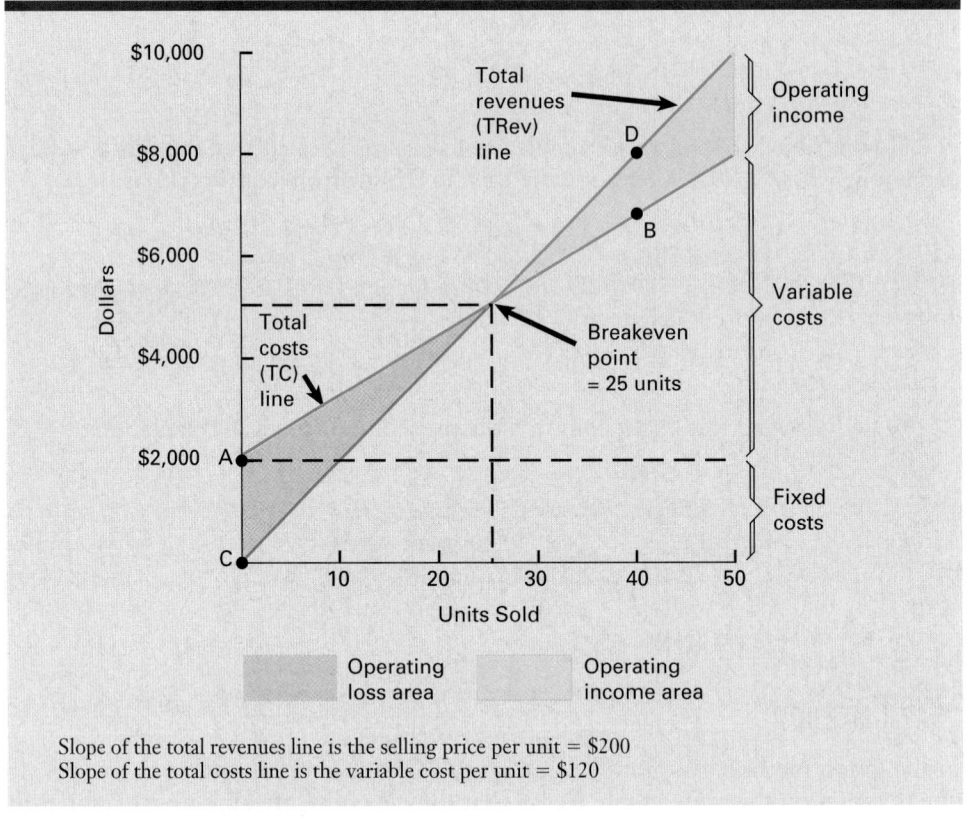

Slope of the total revenues line is the selling price per unit = $200
Slope of the total costs line is the variable cost per unit = $120

TARGET OPERATING INCOME (TARGET OI)

Like any other entrepreneur, Carolin wants to make a profit. We'll begin by calculating her Target OI, then move on to her Target NI in the next section. Assume her Target OI is $1,200; how many units must Carolin sell? Using the equation method and equation (1):

$$\text{Let Q = Number of units sold to earn Target OI}$$

$$\text{TRev} - \text{Total VC} - \text{FC} = \text{Target OI}$$

$$(Q \times \$200) - (Q \times \$120) - \$2,000 = \$1,200$$

$$\$80Q = \$1,200 + \$2,000$$

$$Q = \$3,200 \div \$80 = 40 \text{ units}$$

Using the contribution margin method and equation (3), the numerator now consists of FC + Target OI. The logic of this approach assumes that Carolin's Target OI is also fixed. This logic can be generalized to include changes to discretionary costs, which will be explained in Learning Objective 4.

$$Q = \frac{\text{Target OI} + \text{FC}}{\text{UCM}}$$

$$= \frac{\$2,000 + \$1,200}{\$80}$$

$$= 40 \text{ units}$$

Proof:	TRev, 40 × $200	$8,000
	TVC, 40 × $120	4,800
	TCM, 40 × $80	3,200
	FC	2,000
	Target OI	$1,200

The revenue in dollars to earn a Target OI of $1,200 can also be calculated directly using the approach of equation (4):

$$\text{Revenue in dollars} = \frac{\text{Target OI} + \text{FC}}{\text{CM}\%} = \frac{\$1,200 + \$2,000}{0.40}$$

$$= \frac{\$3,200}{0.40}$$

$$= \$8,000$$

The graph in Exhibit 3-4, however, is not helpful for answering the question posed at the beginning of this section about Q, the units Carolin must sell to earn a Target OI of $1,200. It is difficult to determine by inspection the point at which the difference between the TRev and TC line is $1,200. Changing Exhibit 3-4 from a CVP to a profit-volume (PV) graph focuses the information directly on OI and Q available and sold to illustrate how changes in Q affect OI. Exhibit 3-5 presents the PV graph for One Size Software. The **PV graph** shows the impact on OI when Q available and sold changes.

The PV line can be drawn using two points. One convenient point (X) is the operating loss at Q = 0, which is equal to the fixed costs of $2,000. For consistency, a second convenient point (Y) is the BEP where Q = 25 units. The PV line is the straight line sloping at a constant rate upwards from point X passing through and beyond point Y. To find the number of units Carolin must sell to earn an operating income of $1,200, draw a horizontal line corresponding to $1,200 on the y-axis. At the point where this line intersects the PV line (point A on the graph), draw a vertical line to the x-axis. The vertical line cuts the x-axis at 40 units, indicating that by selling 40 units Carolin will generate operating income of $1,200. This is illustrated in Exhibit 3-5.

EXHIBIT 3-5
The Profit-Volume Graph

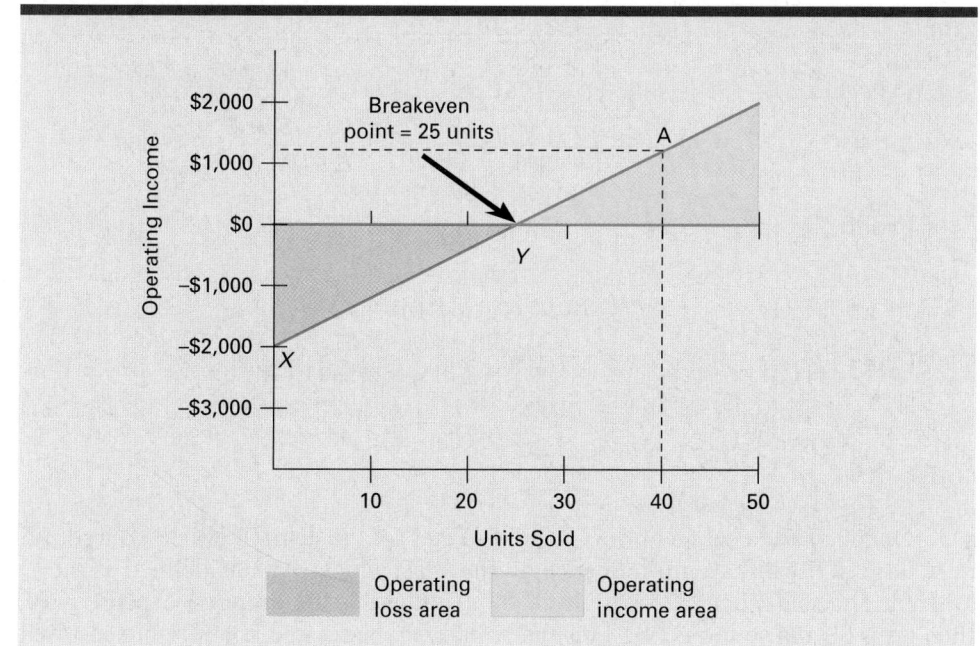

TARGET NET INCOME (TARGET NI) AND INCOME TAXES

Carolin is legally obligated to pay tax on any positive OI and, therefore, like any other manager, she will be most interested in knowing the Q required to achieve a Target NI. On page 87, we already defined NI as (OI – interest expense) × (1 – tax rate). For simplicity, assume interest expense is zero and the relationship becomes OI × (1 − tax rate). What Q will achieve a Target NI of $1,200, the amount Carolin can put in her pocket or use to grow her company? Assuming an income tax rate of 40% and using equation (1), we can substitute Target OI for OI:

$$\text{Target NI} = \text{Target OI} - [(\text{Target OI}) \times (\text{Tax rate})]$$

$$\text{Target NI} = (\text{Target OI})(1 - \text{Tax rate})$$

$$\text{Target OI} = \frac{\text{Target NI}}{(1 - \text{Tax rate})}$$

In contribution income statement format:

$$Q(\text{USP} - \text{UVC}) - \text{FC} = \frac{\text{Target OI}}{(1 - \text{Tax rate})}$$

Substituting the values from One Size Software, we have

$$(Q \times \$200) - (Q \times \$120) - \$2,000 = \frac{\$1,200}{(1 - 0.40)}$$

$$\$80Q = \frac{\$1,200}{0.60} + \$2,000$$

$$Q = \$4,000 \div \$80 \text{ per unit} = 50 \text{ units}$$

$$Q = 50 \text{ units, which is double her BEP.}$$

Alternatively, we could use the method of equation (3) and substitute

$$\text{Target OI} = \frac{\text{Target NI}}{(1 - \text{Tax rate})}, \text{ that is}$$

$$Q = \frac{\text{FC} + \dfrac{\text{Target NI}}{(1 - \text{Tax rate})}}{\text{UCM}}$$

$$Q = \frac{\$2,000 + \dfrac{\$1,200}{(1 - 0.40)}}{\$80} = \frac{\$2,000 + \$2,000}{\$80} = 50 \text{ units}$$

Proof:

TRev	$10,000 (50 packages × $200 USP)
TVC	6,000 (50 packages × $120 UVC)
TCM	4,000 (50 packages × $80 UCM)
FC	2,000
Income taxes	800 ($2,000 × 40%)
NI	$ 1,200

Of course the change in the Q available and sold to achieve either a Target NI or a Target OI will have no influence on the BEP, which remains defined at the Q available and sold when OI = $0. If OI = $0 and we assume interest expense is $0, then tax is $0 and so too is NI. This type of tax can be treated as a variable cost that increases as Q available and sold increases.

Carolin can also use the PV graph in Exhibit 3-5. For a Target NI of $1,200:

$$\text{Target OI} = \text{Target NI} \div (1 - \text{Tax rate}) = \$1,200 \div (1 - 0.40) = \$2,000$$

From Exhibit 3-5, to earn a Target OI of $2,000, Carolin will need to sell Q = 50 packages, which is double her BEP.

ASSESS YOUR MASTERY

To check your understanding of the material in Learning Objective ③, go to the Mastery Questions section at the end of the chapter and complete Learning Objective ③ questions 1 and 2.

USING CVP ANALYSIS IN PLANNING AND DECISION MAKING

Select the most appropriate strategy when the breakeven point is affected by alternative planned changes to price, volume, and/or costs

Strategy requires disciplined thinking about how best to exploit opportunities and how best to defend against threats in the environment, given the scarce resources available to a company. Strategy is important in an adversarial or competitive situation where, over the long run, one adversary will best all others, and where conditions in the environment and among competitors will change. Collecting accurate data and facts in an organized way, and thinking about them realistically helps managers both imagine possible strategies and assess which one is most likely to be successful. The challenge is that strategy becomes a framework to assure survival and growth in the long term, but the longer the term, the more uncertain the actual results will be. The reason is that relevant facts change over time, and the best strategy today can easily be a guarantee of failure five years from now. One important strategic choice any for-profit business must make is whether it will maximize profit based on unique and desirable features of the good or service it sells, or will it maximize profit based on the best possible cost control. The first strategy is called *differentiation* and the second is called *cost leadership*.[1] The techniques and procedures of CVP analysis help managers execute a cost-leadership strategy successfully.

Carolin, as an entrepreneur and sole proprietor of a start-up company, has already made some important strategic decisions:

◆ She is a for-profit business and her goal will be to maximize profit, measured as either OI or NI.

◆ She has made an informed selection of the product she will merchandise at the convention. Her decision reflected facts available on important product features and consumer demand, and her ability to generate sales.

◆ She has decided to be a distributor or merchandiser, not a producer.

She has decided to use CVP analysis to help her lower her costs, a cost leadership strategy. Her success will not arise from knowing CVP and all its procedures—after all, anyone can read that in a textbook. Her success will arise from thinking carefully about what the quantitative results from the CVP procedures mean for the company given its strategy and the important facts about its environment and internal resources.

Some rudimentary methods of calculating the BEP at various OI and NI levels have answered some basic-but-important profitability questions. Carolin, like other managers, can apply this knowledge of CVP analysis to make more complicated decisions. For example, she can:

◆ calculate whether or not an increase in discretionary, fixed period costs, such as advertising, will increase her Q enough to improve her OI.

◆ compare her current situation to reducing her price to increase her Q sold to decide the best course of action.

◆ compare different contracts offered by Computer Conventions that have fixed and variable components to make a short-run decision on her best option.

◆ examine *uncertainty* using three methods: sensitivity analysis, margin of safety, or decision models. **Uncertainty** is defined as the possibility that an actual amount will deviate from an expected or budgeted amount.

---

[1]Michael Porter of Harvard University first presented strategy as an appropriate matching of internal and external factors, as well as identifying the two generic strategies of differentiation and cost leadership.

First we will undertake independent CVP analyses of two important and common short-run operating decisions: 1. Whether to increase discretionary fixed costs, and 2. Whether to reduce the unit sales price. Then we will examine how different combinations of fixed and variable costs in a contract can affect operating profit. Finally, we will present three methods to deal with the issue of uncertainty.

DECISION TO INCREASE DISCRETIONARY PERIOD COSTS—ADVERTISING

Carolin budgeted sales of Q = 40 packages to generate OI of $1,200 (see Exhibit 3-3). What if she could advertise the benefits of her One Size Software in a brochure published by Computer Conventions for an additional $500? She knows that this discretionary period cost will remain constant irrespective of the quantity of packages available and sold. Therefore, it increases her FC from $2,000 to $2,500. She anticipates the advertising will increase her sales to Q = 45 packages. Based on the following CVP analysis, Carolin's budgeted OI decreases by $100:

	A	B	C	D	E	F	G	H
1		Inputs:		40 Packages		45 Packages		
2	USP	$ 200		sold with		sold with		
3	UVC	120		no advertising		advertising		Difference
4	UCM	$ 80						
5	Fixed cost FC	$ 2,000						
6	Discretionary advertising cost	$ 500						
7				(1)		(2)		(2) − (1)
8	TCM ($80 × 40; 45)			$ 3,200		$3,600		$ 400
9	Total fixed costs			2,000		2,500		500
10	OI			$ 1,200		$1,100		$(100)

By formatting her spreadsheet so that she can vary the advertising cost and the budgeted Q sold, Carolin can easily program the answer to her current question. But this approach also allows her to estimate what Q she must sell to improve her OI and then decide if that is a reasonable expectation. In this case, we know that for each package sold the contribution to FC will be $80; therefore, her maximum increase in TCM will be Q × UCM = 5 packages × $80 = $400, which is $100 less than the cost of advertising. Based on this logic, it is clear she must sell at least Q = 7 packages to produce a change in TCM of $560 before it would pay her to advertise. Using the contribution margin approach and the logic developed for the Target OI, Carolin can calculate this value immediately as:

$$Q = \frac{\text{FC of advertising}}{\text{UCM}}$$

$$= \frac{\$500}{\$80}$$

$$= 6.25 \text{ packages}$$

Of course, Carolin cannot sell $\frac{1}{4}$ of a unit; therefore, she must round up or else she will still lose money if she advertises. This is a general rule when calculating the breakeven volume: you must round up to a whole unit; otherwise, you will go broke, but slowly. This example also introduces the idea of sensitivity. Notice that the difference between a negative OI and a positive OI if Carolin advertises is only Q = 2. This is a very small difference, and now she must use more information, perhaps her superior knowledge of her market, to decide if she can indeed sell Q = 47 packages, or she can compare this outcome with other alternatives that may provide clearer quantitative answers.

DECISION TO REDUCE UNIT SELLING PRICE (USP)

Carolin is curious about what would happen to OI if, instead of advertising, she reduced her unit selling price (USP) from $200 to $175. She believes this will result in a sales increase of Q = 10, from 40 to 50 units. In addition, if Carolin purchases 50 units, the wholesaler will reduce the unit variable cost (UVC) to $115. Using the contribution-margin approach and focusing on the differences between her initial and the changed assumptions, she calculates the following:

Expected Total CM from lower USP of $175 and lower UVC of $115:	
50 × ($175 − $115)	$3,000
Expected Total CM from original USP of $200 and UVC of $120:	
40 × ($200 − $120)	3,200
Increase (decrease) in Total CM from lower USP and lower UVC	$ (200)

Carolin examined only those values that had changed from her initial assumptions because these are what cause the change in her OI and may cause her to change her decision. Information that causes a change in a decision is **relevant**. Another important point is that a negative Total CM means there is no contribution made towards paying FC. This is a permanent change, and her new Q to breakeven is FC ÷ UCM = $2,000 ÷ $60 = 33.33, rounded up to 34 units. (The new UCM is $175 – $115 = $60.) This is 9 units higher than her original BEP of Q = 25, or 36% higher ((34 − 25) ÷ 25 = 36%). But more importantly, once she does break even, only $60 will be added to OI each time she sells an additional package of One Size Software. If the goal is to maximize profit, then all other things equal, it is unreasonable to make a choice that will reduce that profit.

In the analysis above, we did not allow for the impossibility of a perfect prediction of the future. The future is uncertain, and in this section you will learn three common applications of CVP analyses to deal with the problem of uncertain *outcomes*. **Outcomes** are uncertain if they are possible but unidentified consequences from different combinations of actions and events. If an outcome can be identified, then the correct term to indicate it is uncertain is **risk**. A risky outcome or consequence is identifiable because there is some likelihood it will happen. If a consequence was perfectly certain, the likelihood it would happen is 100%, but if there is risk, then the likelihood is less than 100%. **Probability** quantifies the likelihood an actual or realized value, event, or outcome will differ from an expected or budgeted value, event, or outcome. When managers want to quantify the answer to questions such as "How likely is it my estimated or budgeted Q sold will differ from my actual Q sold?" they are estimating risk. If there is no uncertainty about the future, then the likelihood your budget is wrong is zero, but this is almost never the case because, by definition, no one can be certain of the future.[2]

A **sensitivity analysis** is a procedure based on CVP that Carolin can use to estimate how an actual difference in either units, dollars, or both from her initial assumptions would affect her budgeted OI. It is important because a sensitivity analysis will alert Carolin to the worst threats or risks to her financial profit. The second procedure Carolin can use is to analyze her cost structure—the percentage of her costs that is fixed and the percentage that is variable—to decide in the long run on the best risk and expected return trade-off. Finally, Carolin could use an advanced procedure, decision modeling.

SENSITIVITY ANALYSIS

Carolin has changed the inputs of her CVP analyses using whole numbers to increase or decrease her values. The examples so far demonstrate how the same 25% change to FC (($2,500 − $2,000) ÷ $2,000 = 25%) and to UCM (($80 − $60) ÷ $80 = 25%)

---

[2]Zero risk means there is a 100% probability that the future outcome will equal the expected or budgeted values; the probability of the budgeted outcome is (p) = 1. However, if there is any risk, then (p)<1. For example, if the quality of your information is excellent, then you may estimate the probability that you are correct about the budgeted value of Q is 80%, or (p) = 0.80. If the budgeted Q = 40, then incorporating risk means you expect your actual Q to be no lower than p(40) = 0.80 × 40 = 32. If your information is less than excellent, you may estimate the probability that you are correct at 0.60; then you expect your actual to be no lower than p(40) = 0.60 × 40 = 24.

cause relatively small and relatively large changes in profitability respectively. A 25% change in FC through additional advertising resulted in a BEP volume change from 25 to 32 units, or an increase of 28% ((32 − 25) ÷ 25 = 28%). A 25% change in the UCM caused a 36% change in the breakeven point ((34 − 25) ÷ 25 = 36%) and a long-term decrease in profitability. The second decision is much more clearcut than the first and is evidence that OI is more sensitive to the same percentage change in variable cost relative to fixed cost. This is consistent with the definition of FC, which are unchanged over a relevant range.

This entrepreneur could also use percentages to undertake similar analyses. A sensitivity analysis uses percentage changes to understand which changes cause the greatest effect on profit. When small percentage changes cause large profit effects, managers know their profits are highly sensitive to these changes. This analysis also helps focus attention on important differences when managers cannot agree on budgeted estimates. For example, if a 30% difference in estimates of a particular value cause a 2% change in OI, then the difference is likely irrelevant because the effect on profit is so small.

As shown below in Sensitivity Analysis 1, based on Carolin's initial CVP, she can calculate answers to questions such as: What will OI be if USP is reduced by 20%, which spurs an increase of 20% in Q sold at the same time UVC increases 20%? Carolin can vary the amounts in the Change column to obtain

	A	B	C	D	E	F	H
1	Sensitivity Analysis 1						
2		Inputs	Change	40 Packages		48 Packages	
3	Q	40	20%	sold based on		sold based on	
4	USP	$ 200	−20%	original data		new data	Difference
5	UVC	$ 120	20%				
6	UCM	$ 80					
7	FC	$2,000	0%				
8							
9				(1)		(2)	(2) − (1)
10	TRev			$8,000		$ 7,680	$ (320)
11	TVC			(4,800)		(6,912)	(2,112)
12	TCM			3,200		768	(2,432)
13	FC			(2,000)		(2,000)	0
14	OI			$1,200		$(1,232)	$(2,432)

	A	B	C	D	E	F	H
1	Sensitivity Analysis 2						
2		Inputs	Change	40 Packages		48 Packages	
3	Q	40	20%	sold based on		sold based on	
4	USP	$ 200	−20%	original data		new data	Difference
5	UVC	$ 120	0%				
6	UCM	$ 80					
7	FC	$ 2,000	20%				
8							
9				(1)		(2)	(2) − (1)
10	TRev			$8,000		$ 7,680	$ (320)
11	TVC			(4,800)		(5,760)	(960)
12	TCM			3,200		1,920	(1,280)
13	FC			(2,000)		(2,000)	0
14	OI			$1,200		$(1,232)	$(1,280)

estimates of her budgeted financial performance under different assumptions. This is a more complex application of CVP to focus managers' attention on the greatest threats or risks to their profits. The outcomes both decrease profit. More importantly, the Differences column shows a far greater decrease due to increased UVC than to reduced USP.

Overall, under the assumptions of this sensitivity analysis, Carolin knows that a declining USP is not as great a threat to her OI as an increase in UVC. She can focus her attention on avoiding this type of increase in UVC.

However, Sensitivity Analysis 2 illustrates how sensitive her profits are to an increase in FC of 20% instead of to UVC. The results indicate her profits decrease roughly half as much with the FC increase compared to the UVC increase of the same percentage. This is consistent with the fact that FC do not change over a relevant range of Q available and sold. Examining both sensitivity analyses stemming from her original CVP analysis indicates that Carolin's strategy is to control first the variable, then the fixed costs to best protect her profit.

MARGIN OF SAFETY

Another approach to sensitivity analysis is the **margin of safety**, which is the excess of forecasted or budgeted revenues over the breakeven revenues. The question Carolin can ask is: How far can revenues fall below budgeted TRev before the breakeven value is reached? Poor marketing and obsolescence can cause decreases in TRev. Refer to Exhibit 3-3. Carolin's initial assumptions led to a breakeven revenue of $5,000 for a breakeven volume of 25 packages available and sold. At her budgeted Q = 40, the TRev is $8,000. The margin of safety is $8,000 – $5,000 = $3,000 and in percent terms is $3,000 ÷ $5,000 = 60%. Under her current assumptions, Carolin has a very large margin of safety.

DECISION MODELS AND UNCERTAINTY

A third method of quantifying the uncertainty surrounding future actual outcomes and the inherent inaccuracy of estimated values is to use a **decision model**. A decision model outlines formally how to make a choice using both quantitative and qualitative analysis. Decision models are unnecessary if OI is not sensitive to possible alternative plans or if less formal CVP analysis provides a clear answer. Decision models, such as that illustrated in Exhibit 3-6, simplify a very complicated and interactive process (see Chapters 11 and 12). Usually decisions under uncertainty are made by teams of managers who must obtain relevant information about the issue. Often this information is the basis of a key decision—what are the key deciding factors? Given several alternatives, why would the team choose one rather than another? A reason to choose one alternative over another is a **choice criterion**, which is usually based on an agreed-upon quantitative threshold or goal. Two possible choice criteria are to maximize OI or minimize TC.[3]

It is important to distinguish actions from events. **Actions** *include* choices made by management—for example, the decision about what USP should be charged for the company's product (see Chapter 12 for a full discussion of pricing). **Events** are occurrences that management cannot control and are also called externalities—for example, a growing or declining economy. Uncertainty about future events causes uncontrollable risk; nevertheless, decision teams make assumptions and forecasts, often using sensitivity analyses, about what influence on the company various sets of events (or scenarios) would likely have. Events are probable occurrences.

One important question is how future events are likely to affect a key *outcome*, the OI of the company, which depends both on the action management selects

---

[3]The presentations here draw (in part) from teaching notes prepared by R. Williamson.

EXHIBIT 3-6
A Decision-Process Model

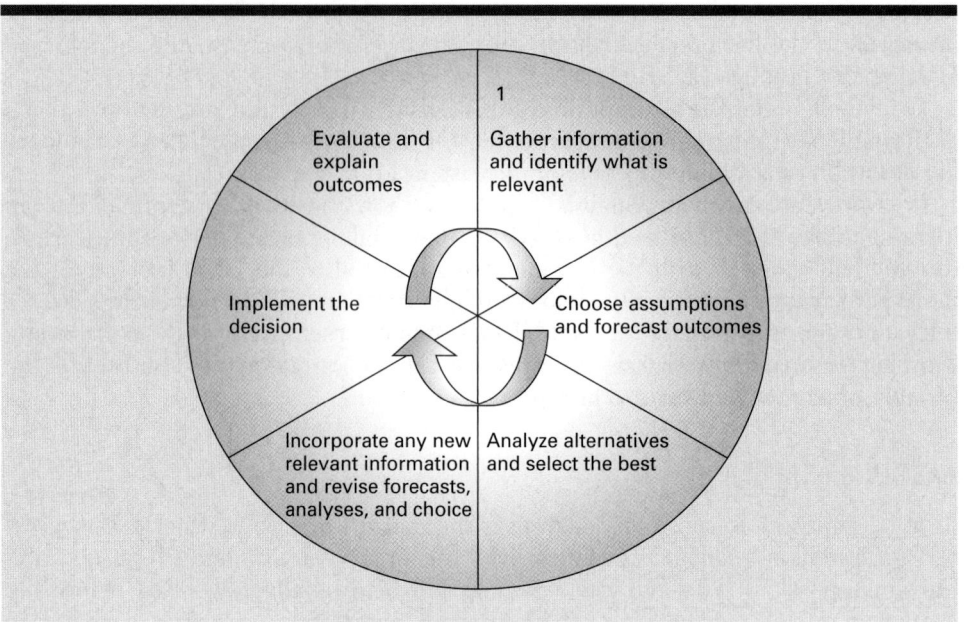

(pricing strategy) and the events that occur (how the economy performs). *Outcomes* refer to the company and are uncertain if they are possible but unidentified consequences from different combinations of actions and events. Once the forecasts are complete, additional relevant information may become available and the team will have to change various assumptions and forecasts.

At some point, however, the team must quantify risks in the form of probabilities regarding the likelihood of various externalities and the most likely outcome for the company given the realization of those externalities. The externalities, such as a robust or a failing economy, exclude one another from happening. If the economy is robust, it cannot also be failing. Also, we will assume that there are only two possible outcomes for this externality. The externalities are **mutually exclusive** and **exhaustive**. This makes assigning probabilities relatively straightforward. The team then must forecast outcomes for the company given one or the other externality is realized.

Gathering relevant information and communicating among team members means the team pools together the expertise of individual members when they revise assumptions and forecasts. Decisions affect many business functions in the value chain and that is why decision teams pool their knowledge of production, marketing, and sales to agree upon the probability or likelihood different events or outcomes will occur. Formally assigning risk requires that all probabilities of a specific value, event, or outcome sum to a total of 100%, or the sum of all (p) = 1. If all events have been specified, then the list of events must be exhaustive and that is why the sum of all (p) = 1. Because no event can occur simultaneously with another, only one (p) < 1 can be assigned to each event. Once these probabilities are agreed upon and listed, they can be graphed to illustrate a **probability distribution**. This probability distribution describes the likelihood or probability that each of the mutually exclusive and exhaustive set of events will occur.

For some events, a lot of available evidence will justify what probability is assigned to it. For example, the probability of obtaining a head in the toss of a fair coin is (p) = 0.50 and there is no other possible event if the head is the outcome. The probability of drawing one particular playing card from a standard, well-shuffled deck is 1/52 or (p) ≈ 0.019. In business, the probability of having a specified percentage of defective units may be assigned with great confidence, on the basis of production experience with thousands of units. In other cases, little evidence will exist to justify what probability is assigned to an event. For example, how many units of a new pharmaceutical product will be sold next year? This is an uncertain outcome.

The concept of uncertainty can be illustrated by a decision situation facing a software wholesaler who is deciding whether to expand the product offering by adding either a database program or a statistical-analysis program. The customers are assumed to be people like Carolin. These two choices are mutually exclusive and exhaustive events. Both require a $200,000 investment at the beginning of the year, which is a FC and, consistent with assumption 6, we ignore the time value of money. The wholesaler would consult a decision team of experts and produce the list containing the probabilities or likelihood of each cash inflow from each program. The cash inflows are also mutually exclusive and exhaustive outcomes, and the sum of all probabilities is (p) = 1. The sum of multiplying each cash inflow, a_i, by the probability results in the **expected value** or $\sum_{a=1}^{i} E(a) = \sum(p_i) \times a_i$. Arithmetically, the set of expected values is simply a weighted average of the outcomes with the probability of each outcome serving as the weight, as shown in the table below. If the sum of the weighted outcomes is measured in monetary terms, the result is often called **expected monetary value**.

Proposal A: Add a Database Program			**Proposal B: Add a Statistical Program**		
Weight	**Outcomes a_i**	**Weight × Outcome**	**Weight**	**Outcomes b_i**	**Weight × Outcome**
Probability (p)	Cash Inflows	Expected Value	Probability (p)	Cash Inflows	Expected Value
(1)	(2)	(1) × (2)	(1)	(2)	(1) × (2)
0.10	$300,000	$ 30,000	0.10	$200,000	$ 20,000
0.20	350,000	70,000	0.25	300,000	75,000
0.40	400,000	160,000	0.30	400,000	120,000
0.20	450,000	90,000	0.25	500,000	125,000
0.10	500,000	50,000	0.10	800,000	80,000
1.00	$\sum_{a=1}^{i} E(a) = \sum(p_i) \times a_i =$	$400,000	1.00	$\sum_{a=1}^{i} E(b) = \sum(p_i) \times b_i =$	$420,000

Exhibit 3-7 compares the probability distributions graphically.

EXHIBIT 3-7
Decisions under Uncertainty: Comparison of Probability Distributions

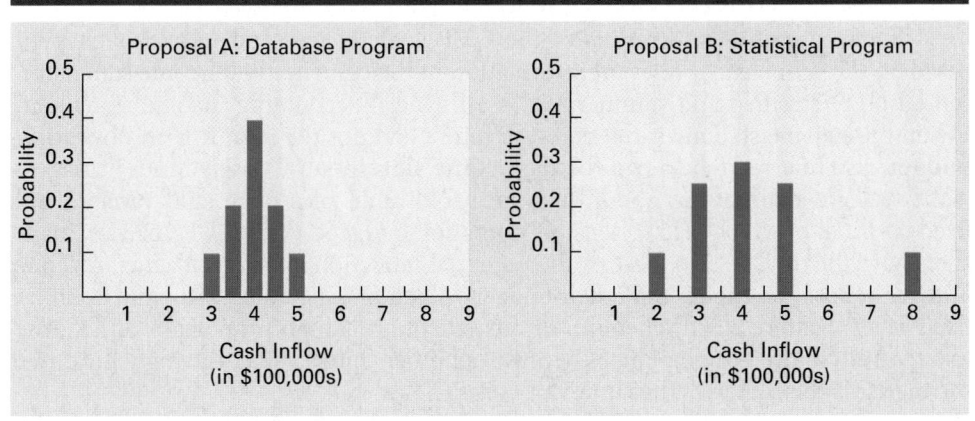

THINKING CRITICALLY

If you were the wholesaler and these expected monetary values were presented to you, would you add the database program or the statistical program? Why? Can you think of a reason that would make you change your mind and choose to add the other program? Explain why in a sentence or two. Read on for an assessment of this situation.

The expected monetary value of the cash inflows from each program are now new items of relevant information input into the analysis of which program to add. Expected monetary value is widely used as a decision criterion. For a wholesaler wanting to maximize the expected monetary value, the statistical program is preferable to the database program. Notice, however, that the difference is only 5% [($420,000 − $400,000) ÷ $400,000]. To finalize a decision on this basis, the wholesaler must have very high confidence in the quality of relevant information used by the decision team and its expertise.

But many software programs become available each year. The wholesaler would not select only one statistical program each year. What if there were 100 such programs available, each with a probability distribution of cash inflows given in Proposal B? If the wholesaler publishes Q = 100 statistical programs, it will expect to receive $42 million in total cash inflows, for an average of $420,000 per program. Many analysts favour presenting the entire probability distribution as relevant information for decision makers. Others present information in three categories: optimistic, most likely, and pessimistic. Each presentation reminds decision makers that they have quantified uncertainty as risk and their decisions carry some probability of failure that actual actions taken will result in the expected outcomes.

Good Decisions and Good Outcomes Always distinguish between a good decision and a good outcome. One can exist without the other. The uncertain future means it is impossible to rule out unfavourable events. What the different forms of CVP analysis contribute to are good actions or decisions. It is possible that bad luck will produce unfavourable outcomes even when good decisions have been made.

Suppose you are offered a one-time-only gamble tossing a fair coin. You will win $20 if the event is heads, but you will lose $1 if the event is tails. As a decision maker, you proceed through the logical phases: gathering information, assessing outcomes, and making a choice. You accept the bet because the sum of the weighted monetary outcomes in your probability distribution, the expected monetary value, is $9.50 [0.5($20) + 0.5(−$1)]. The coin is tossed and the event is tails. You lose. From your viewpoint, this was a good decision but a bad outcome.

A decision can be made only on the basis of information available at the time of the decision. Hindsight is flawless, but a bad outcome does not necessarily mean that a bad decision was made. Obtaining relevant information and conducting a good analysis contributes towards making a good decision, the best protection against a bad outcome. Major benefits of CVP analysis are improved planning and improved actions.

The information and results of the CVP analyses undertaken in this chapter, based on the summary or relevant information in the contribution income statement, can all be reclassified and summarized as a financial-accounting income statement. When the income statement refers to the future and not the past, it is an **operating budget**, also referred to as a **pro forma income statement**. Conscientious managers make realistic assumptions about quantities sold, unit sales price, and variable and fixed costs, all of which lead to sensible operating budgets. With CVP analysis, managers have the tools to also forecast the potential reduction in profits if actual revenue is lower or costs are higher than their budget. When FC, including loans and bonds at fixed rates of interest and schedules of repayment are a high proportion of TC, the risk to profitability is high. This is because, all other things equal, the higher are FC, the higher is the BEP, whether it be in Q or in TRev.

ALTERNATIVE FIXED-COST/VARIABLE-COST STRUCTURES

The sensitivity analysis below, followed by a formal decision-model analysis, focuses on transfers from FC to TVC of One Size Software. Carolin must decide among three rental agreements available from Computer Conventions Inc. You are already familiar with Option 1, the $2,000 cost to rent the booth for two days. Option 2 is a $1,400 FC with an additional 5% of revenue. The second option is similar to a revenue tax such as GST or PST because the effect is to reduce Carolin's USP and increase her UVC by 5%. The third option is a completely variable cost contract where Carolin will pay 20% of revenue.

♦ **Option 1:** FC = $2,000, change in TVC = $0; requires a BEP of Q = 25 units and TRev = $5,000. The UVC is $80; therefore, for any Q ≥ 26, the full $80 will contribute to increasing OI.

♦ **Option 2:** FC = $1,400, increase in TVC is 5% of TRev; requires a lower BEP based on a lower Unit CM because UVC will increase by $10 from $120 to $130 (or USP × 5% = $200 × 0.05 = $10). The new Unit CM will be $70 (USP − UVC = $200 − $130 = $70). Therefore, for any Q ≥ 20 (FC ÷ Unit CM = $1,400 ÷ $70 = 20), only $70 will contribute to increasing OI.

♦ **Option 3:** FC = $0, increase in TVC = 20% of TRev; requires a lower BEP based on the lowest Unit CM because UVC will increase by $40 from $120 to $160 (or USP × 20% = $200 × 0.20 = $40) and the new Unit CM will be $40 (USP − UVC = $200 − $160 = $40). Beginning with her first sale, Carolin will increase her OI by $40 per unit.

EXHIBIT 3-8
CVP Graphs for Alternative Rental Schedules for One Size Software

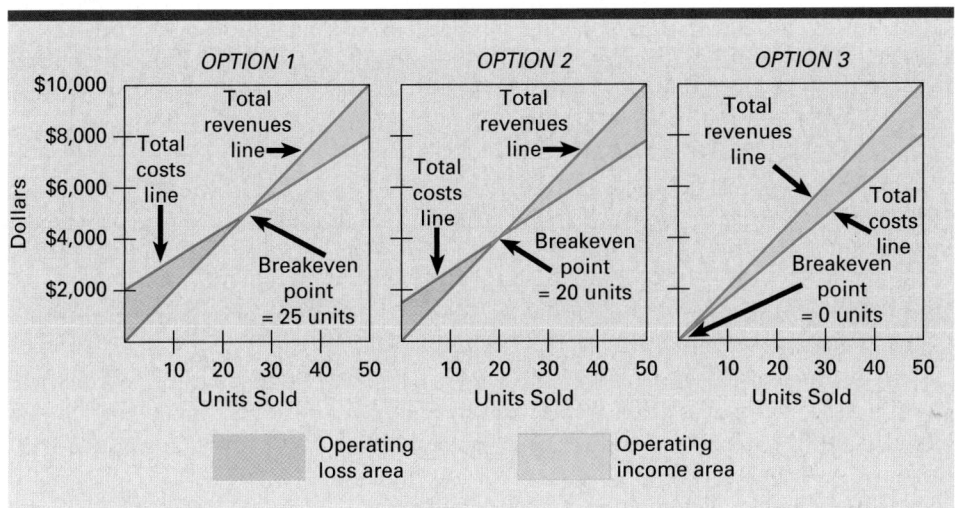

If you were a risk-averse manager, which of the three rental agreements available from Computer Conventions Inc. would you choose—Option 1, 2, or 3? If you were a manager who was a risk taker, which option would you choose? Explain your choices in a sentence or two. Read on for an assessment of this situation.

The interpretation of the result of this CVP analysis of Carolin's three options requires careful thought. If, based on her knowledge of the market for One Size Software, she believes she will not sell at least 25 packages, then she will not select Option 1.

Option 1 requires the highest Q and the greatest loss per unit of $80 if she fails. On the other hand, if Carolin is confident she will sell at least 26 packages, then this option also carries with it the highest reward, or return, because $80 per unit will contribute directly to her OI *after* she reaches her BEP. In general, if you take higher risk, you must anticipate higher return or the risk is foolish.

Option 2 is not as risky to Carolin because the BEP is lower, but so too is the contribution to OI *after* she reaches her BEP of 20 packages sold. The BEP is lower because the reduction in FC of 30% (($2,000 – $1,400) ÷ $2,000 = 0.30) is greater than the reduction in Unit CM of 12.5% (($80 – $70) ÷ $80 = 0.125). This somewhat lower risk of failure to achieve BEP is accompanied by a somewhat lower return.

Option 3 is least risky because the BEP is lowest of all three options but so too is the $40 contribution to OI for each unit sold. The lowest-risk contract is accompanied by the lowest return. The decision about what contract to choose will depend on other data inputs, including Carolin's understanding of the market at the convention, her propensity for taking risk, resources available, and other external factors.

All things equal, if Carolin is risk averse, she will choose either Option 3 or Option 2. If she is a risk taker, she will most likely choose Option 1. Notice that the risk and return do not matter until *after* the BEP has been achieved for each option.

The table below compares unit CM, Total CM, OI, and operating leverage at the sales level of 40 units for the three alternative rental options.

	Option 1	Option 2	Option 3
Contribution margin per unit	$ 80	$ 70	$ 40
Contribution margin (row 1 × 40 units)	$3,200	$2,800	$1,600
Operating income	$1,200	$1,400	$1,600
Degree of operating leverage (row 2 ÷ row 3)	2.67	2.00	1.00

The risk-return tradeoff across alternative cost structures is usefully summarized and compared using a measure called *operating leverage*. **Operating leverage** describes the effects that different FC have on changes in OI as changes occur in Q available and sold and hence in either the unit or total contribution margin. At any given level of sales, **degree of operating leverage (DOL)** equals contribution margin divided by operating income. Comparing the degree of operating leverage (DOL) requires a starting point or baseline Q of sales volume. Assume Carolin's starting point is Q = 40

$$\text{DOL for Option 1} = \frac{\text{CM}}{\text{CM} - \text{FC}} = \frac{\$80 \times 40}{(\$80 \times 40) - \$2,000}$$
$$= 2.67$$

Notice that the starting point is Q BEP because it is only after the BEP is achieved that the DOL will be relevant. The table above illustrates the different DOL associated with each option when Q = 40 units available and sold.

The important point to understand is that as the FC decrease, the DOL also decreases. This means that the risk to positive OI, Carolin's return, is also decreasing. Leverage means that the DOL has a multiplier effect. Based on a starting point of Q = 40, the result 2.67 is interpreted as: every 1% change in Total CM will produce 2.67 times that change in OI. If, for example, the Total CM increases by 20%, then the OI will change by 53.4% (2.67 × 0.20 = 0.534) under Option 1. Under Option 2, the DOL = 2.00; therefore, if Total CM increases by 20%, then the OI will change by 40%. The same logic applies to increases in sales. Based on a starting point of Q = 40, if there is a change in assumption to Q = 60 or a 50% increase in Q ((60 – 40) ÷ 40 = 20 ÷ 40 = 0.50), then the corresponding increase in OI for Option 1 will be 133.50% (2.67 × 0.50 = 1.335). This means that, given a specific starting point and known DOL, for any percentage increase in sales, the effect on profit or OI can be calculated easily.

It may seem unusual to be referring to fixed costs as something long-term when, in this example, Carolin's fixed costs refer to a two-day convention. This highlights one important feature of management-accounting logic—costs are classified as fixed or variable relative to a specific time horizon during which goods or services are available and sold. In contrast to the simple example presented here to illustrate the concept of DOL, when we refer to cost structure, the implicit time horizon is a significant period longer than one year.

Analytical tools such as CVP analyses are sufficiently flexible to provide some warning about the effects of changes to important factors external and internal to an enterprise. But the best long-term plan or strategy at one point in time will not improve success when the internal factors no longer match the opportunities and threats in a changing environment.

The opportunity to obtain exclusivity is an important contract element that would create a barrier to entry for other competitors and Carolin would need to consider this after she has thought about DOL. But, if product features must change rapidly to match demand and if Carolin does lock into a contract for a specific product for the long term, then she runs the risk of paying for access to an obsolete product. Her choice of distribution contract also has long-term effects as she considers how to grow. In case she cannot obtain exclusivity, her competitive advantage and success will depend in large part on her ability to be the lowest-cost supplier. Similarly, however, the use of CVP analyses will not guarantee Carolin will execute her cost-leadership strategy successfully. These procedures are readily available to any entrepreneur or manager. Success will depend on her superior ability to change her strategy with the goal of achieving the best match between the external and internal environment as they both change.

In the longer term, however, entrepreneurs like Carolin want their enterprises to grow, and what she has learned from her DOL analysis of the three contract options clearly show that risk is the balancing element to maximizing her return. Risk is complex because the degree of risk in a situation will be perceived differently by different people. DOL analysis based on a short time horizon will help Carolin understand two important elements in her long-term decisions. The first is her own risk preference because her choice of an option will tell her whether she is risk averse or a risk taker. The second is that cost drivers exist in the long term as well as the short term. As she executes her cost leadership strategy well and achieves her growth objectives, she will do so with a conscious awareness that the proportion of total costs that are variable and fixed tell her about the risk associated with different choices of cost structure, as well as the return.

Carolin could have undertaken a formal decision-model analysis of the cash flow outcomes of the three possible contract options with Computer Conventions Inc. She could have taken five specific steps based on the information she knows:[4]

◆ *Identify the choice criterion of the decision maker.* Assume that Carolin's choice criterion is to maximize expected OI at the convention.

---

[4]For more formal approaches, refer to G. Eppen, F. Gould, and C. Schmidt, *Introductory Management Science*, 4th Edition (Upper Saddle River, NJ: Prentice Hall, 1993).

- ◆ *Identify the set of alternative actions under consideration.* The notation for an action is *a*. Carolin has three possible actions, Option 1, 2, or 3:

  Option 1, action a_1 = Pay $2,000 fixed fee.

  Option 2, action a_2 = Pay $1,400 fixed fee plus 5% of convention revenues.

  Option 3, action a_3 = Pay 20% of convention revenues (but no fixed fee).

- ◆ *Identify the set of relevant events that can occur.* Carolin's risk arises from the events of Q = number of available units that she can sell in 48 hours. Using x_i as the notation for an event:

  Event x_1 Q = 40 units

  Event x_2 Q = 70 units

- ◆ *Assign the set of probabilities for the events Q = 40 and Q = 70 that can occur.* Carolin assesses a 60% chance that she will sell 40 units and a 40% chance that she will sell 70 units. Using $p(x_i)$ as the notation for the probability of an event, the probabilities are:

  $p(x_1)$ = 0.60 that 40 units available and sold = 0.60(40) = 24 units

  $p(x_2)$ = 0.40 that 70 units available and sold = 0.40(70) = 28 units

- ◆ *Identify the set of possible outcomes that are dependent on specific actions and events.* The outcomes in this example take the form of six possible OI. The table below summarizes the three contemplated actions, two events, and the probabilities of each event, as well as the OI outcomes. This summary is a *decision table*. A **decision table** is a summary of the contemplated actions, events, and probabilities of events as well as outcomes, for each decision.

	A	C	D	E	F	G	H	I
1	Inputs							
2	Events Q = x_i	40				70		
3	Probability (p)	60%				40%		
4	Wtd. $p(x_i)$ =	24				28		
5	Analyses	**Event x_1 Outcomes Q = 40; (p) = 0.60**				**Event x_2 Outcomes Q = 70; (p) = 0.40**		
6	Contact VC % of TRev:		5%	20%			5%	20%
7		**Option 1**	**Option 2**	**Option 3**		**Option 1**	**Option 2**	**Option 3**
8	USP	$ 200	$ 200	$ 200		$ 200	$ 200	$ 200
9	UVC	120	130	160		120	130	160
10	UCM	$ 80	$ 70	$ 40		$ 80	$ 70	$ 40
11	TRev weighted	$4,800	$ 4,800	$ 4,800		$ 5,600	$ 5,600	$ 5,600
12	TVC weighted	2,880	3,120	3,840		3,360	3,640	4,480
13	TCM weighted	1,920	1,680	960		2,240	1,960	1,120
14	FC	2,000	1,400	0		2,000	1,400	0
15	OI weighted	$ (80)	$ 280	$ 960		$ 240	$ 560	$ 1,120
16								
17	Outcome OI, a_i	$\sum_{a=1}^{i} E(a_1) = \sum (px_i) \times a_i$ = Expected OI=				$ 160	$ 840	$ 2,080

This quantitative analysis indicates a more complex choice for Carolin. Under event x_1 when Q = 40 with a 60% probability, she will not sell her breakeven volume of Q = 25 under Option 1 and, therefore, to maximize OI she will choose Option 3. While her Unit CM is lowest under this option, she will pay no FC and thus will keep $40 for every package of software available and sold. The logic of interpreting this more advanced CVP analysis is the same under event x_2 when Q = 70 with a 40% probability, although she will sell more than her breakeven volume of 25 packages of software. Carolin is risk averse and she will choose Option 3. This analysis differs from the DOL analysis because we are not comparing the effect on OI, her return, using the same Q = 40.

Today's reality is that large manufacturing companies have a global reach that makes it easier to avoid the high fixed costs of a permanent expansion in capacity. Manufacturers are temporarily leasing plant and equipment in Mexico, or they offshore their production to Haiti, Honduras, and the Dominican Republic. Service companies are also reducing fixed costs. For example, British Airways does not even hire pilots and cabin crew on its permanent payroll, but rather leases the flight and cabin crew with the aircraft. This saves the company fixed costs such as training, retirement benefits, and health benefits. Many other companies license the right to use software from application service providers (ASP) rather than create an in-house management information system. These companies pay only for the applications they use for the time used, which makes this a variable cost. Industries have also outsourced entire functions in the value chain, such as customer service, to technical support call centres in countries such as India, where labour costs are far lower. (See the Real Companies box.)

REAL COMPANIES

Influencing Cost Structures to Manage the Risk-Return Tradeoff at Amazon.com

Fixed costs, unlike variable costs, do not automatically decrease as volumes of either production or sales decline. Amazon began with a unique vision of what features book purchasers really desired. It was one of the first merchandisers to successfully use the Internet to sell its product. It designed a webpage that allowed potential, technologically savvy customers to select and purchase books online. In so doing, Amazon incurred the fixed costs of its information technology infrastructure but saved on the bricks and mortar infrastructure of purchasing and storing high volumes of books in warehouses. The normal costs generated by people taking orders from people also disappeared. Amazon simply paid the unit variable cost of acquiring books on an as-needed basis after it had received a confirmed order from a customer. The cost structure was predominantly variable—the cost of sales varied directly with the quantity sold by Amazon. But this low-risk strategy came at a price—the unit variable cost to purchase one book at a time from a wholesaler is significantly higher than purchasing larger quantities of books directly from publishers. Amazon's profits depended upon maintaining its cost leadership strategy.

It was a low-risk cost structure until 1997, when Barnes and Noble, a traditional publisher and merchandiser, decided that it had to meet Amazon's threat to its market by competing against Amazon for online sales. The costs of technology infrastructure had decreased, therefore for Barnes and Noble there was no barrier to entry into the e-business of online book sales. Barnes and

(*continued*)

(continued)

Noble already had a successful distribution network of warehouses and incurred the fixed costs to create this online network to build on its competitive advantage in bricks-and-mortar sales. Barnes and Noble paid less for its books than Amazon because it already ordered a high quantity of books into inventory to benefit from publishers' volume discounts. The unit variable costs of each book were inevitably lower than Amazon's. This meant the company could easily price its products lower than Amazon and claimed it would offer "the lowest everyday prices of any online bookseller," as well as better service, because it controlled distribution of the product, rather than having to rely on third-party wholesalers to supply it as Amazon did.

By 1998, Amazon had lost approximately $121 million and changed its sales and distribution strategy by choosing to build or acquire its own warehouses, assuming very optimistic growth in sales volumes. The choice lowered Amazon's unit variable costs, increased its unit contribution margins, but its breakeven sales volume was much higher because of its increased fixed costs. In 2000, actual sales volumes fell far short of budgeted resulting in a $1.5 billion net loss. The company adjusted its assumptions to forecast even lower sales growth in 2001, and closed two of its distribution facilities. Closing permanent capacity reduced its fixed costs and improved Amazon's opportunity to break even. Within a year its net loss was approximately $567 million. By 2003 the company had turned around to report a net profit of approximately $35 million, which grew to $588 million in 2004. The last two years have been less successful but in 2006 Amazon still reported a net profit of $190 million.

The real ups and downs of Amazon illustrate that the calculations undertaken during a CVP analysis do not guarantee year-to-year operating profit. Indeed there are no guarantees. Amazon's managers paid attention to bad news instead of ignoring it. Based on a realistic set of facts, Amazon's managers accepted that the best way to execute its cost leadership strategy and return to profitability was to imitate Barnes and Noble—and so far it has worked.

Source: Amazon.com financial statements, stock-analyst reports, and conversations with company management.

MyAccountingLab

ASSESS YOUR MASTERY

To check your understanding of the material in Learning Objective **4**, go to the Mastery Questions section at the end of the chapter and complete Learning Objective **4** question 1.

MULTIPLE REVENUE DRIVERS AND MULTIPLE COST DRIVERS

5 Analyze and select the most appropriate product mix for a two-product company, and adapt CVP analysis to multiple revenue-driver situations

MULTIPLE REVENUE DRIVERS

Continuing with the One Size Software example, Carolin has had a successful experience at the convention and has begun to plan for next year. She will have an opportunity to sell either a Basic or an Advanced product, or both. The percentage or proportion of total Q = packages available and sold for each product will be the *revenue* or *sales mix*. The **revenue mix** (also called the **sales mix**) is the relative contribution of quantities of products or services that constitutes total revenues. The calculation is straightforward because the Q_i for each product is simply divided by the total Q of sales for all products.

Unlike the single product (or service) situation, there is not a unique number of units for a multiple-product BEP. The BEP will depend on the revenue mix. The revenue mix in the example below is 66.67% Basic and 33.33% Advanced but the

	Advanced	Basic	Total
Q_i = Units sold	**60**	**120**	**180**
TRev @ USP $200; $90	$12,000	$10,800	$22,800
TVC @ UVC $120; $50	7,200	6,000	13,200
TCM @ UCM $80; $40	$ 4,800	$ 4,800	$ 9,600
FC			2,000
OI			$ 7,600

OI > \$0; therefore, these are not the BEP for the quantities of each type of product sold. The key assumption made is that budgeted revenue mix will be two units of Basic sold for every single unit of Advanced sold. Notice that FC is unchanged at \$2,000, the contract that represents Option 1, because FC is constant over a relevant range that includes $Q = 180$ units available and sold. While Carolin could use the flexibility of the software to find the BEP by trial and error, she may use an arithmetic analysis:

$$\text{Let } S = \text{BEP in Q of units available and sold of Advanced to break even}$$

$$2S = \text{BEP in Q of units available and sold of Basic to break even}$$

$$\text{TRev} - \text{TVC} - \text{FC} = \text{OI and at the BEP, OI} = \$0$$

$$[\$200(S) + 90(2S)] - [\$120(S) + \$50(2S)] - \$2,000 = \$0$$

$$\$380S - \$220S = \$2,000$$

$$\$160S = \$2,000$$

$$S = 12.5, \text{ rounded up to } 13$$

$$2S = 25$$

The BEP for Basic is $Q = 25$ units and the BEP for Advanced is $Q = 13$ units for a total BEP of $Q = 38$ units available and sold. The Unit CM for Advanced is double at \$80 than it is for Basic at \$40. At these BEP, notice that the Total CM is \$1000 for Advanced using the unrounded breakeven volume, and \$1,000 for Basic, which sum to the FC = \$2,000. The Total CM = FC; therefore, OI = \$0. Alternative revenue mixes (in units) that have a contribution margin of \$2,000 and thus result in breakeven operations include the following:

	1	2	3	4	5	6
Advanced	25	20	15	10	5	0
Basic	0	10	20	30	40	50
Total	25	30	35	40	45	50

Other things being equal, for any given total quantity of units sold, if the mix shifts or Q available and sold shifts towards the product with the higher Unit CM, the result will be an increase in OI. Thus, if the mix shifts toward Advanced, for example from 33.33% to 50%, with a Unit CM that is double Basic, Carolin's OI must increase. While the arithmetic is not complex, the quantitative result will not fully determine either her budgeted revenue mix, or the actual quantities she chooses to sell. Her knowledge of her market and the limitations on her time to sell the well-known product in contrast to the new product will all have to be carefully considered before she makes her choice.

In service organizations, the outcomes are measured in some type of unit, although often these are more complex than a straightforward quantity of product. Examples of different service output measures in different industries are:

Industry	Measure of Output
Airlines	Revenue passenger-miles
Hotels/motels	Room-nights occupied
Hospitals	Patient-days
Universities	Student course credits

CVP ANALYSIS IN NONPROFIT ORGANIZATIONS

The CVP analyses have highlighted two merchandising companies seeking to make a profit, but CVP can be applied readily to decisions by service and nonprofit organizations. The key to applying CVP analysis to these organizations is measuring their output. Consider a nonprofit service organization, for example a social welfare agency for which the government provides a specific annual revenue at the beginning of 2008 of $900,000. Assume the major purpose of this agency is to assist people with physical challenges who are seeking employment. On average, the agency supplements each physically challenged and unemployed person's income by $5,000 annually. The agency's fixed costs are $270,000. There are no other costs. The agency manager wants to know how many people could be assisted in 2008. As noted at the beginning of this chapter, the goal of this agency is not to make a profit but rather to break even at OI = $0. Let Q be the number of people to be assisted:

$$\text{Revenue} - \text{Variable costs} - \text{Fixed costs} = \$0$$
$$\$900,000 - \$5,000Q - \$270,000 = \$0$$
$$\$5,000Q = \$900,000 - \$270,000$$
$$Q = \$630,000 \div \$5,000 = 126 \text{ people}$$

Suppose the manager is concerned that the total budget appropriation for 2008 will be reduced by 15% to a new amount of $(1 - 0.15) \times \$900,000 = \$765,000$. The manager wants to know how many unemployed people with physical challenges will be assisted. Assume the same amount of monetary assistance per person:

$$\$765,000 - \$5,000Q - \$270,000 = \$0$$
$$\$5,000Q = \$765,000 - \$270,000$$
$$Q = \$495,000 \div \$5,000 = 99 \text{ people}$$

Note the following two characteristics of the CVP relationships in this nonprofit situation:

1. The percentage drop in service $((126 - 99) \div 126)$, or 21.4%, is more than the 15% reduction in the budget appropriation. Why? Because the existence of $270,000 in fixed costs means that the percentage drop in service exceeds the percentage drop in budget appropriation.

2. If the relationships were graphed, the budget appropriation (revenue) amount would be a straight horizontal line of $765,000. The manager could adjust operations to stay within the reduced appropriation in one or more of three major ways: (a) reduce the number of people assisted, (b) reduce the variable costs (the assistance per person), or (c) reduce the total fixed costs.

MyAccountingLab

MULTIPLE COST DRIVERS

⑥ Analyze and select the most appropriate product mix for a two-product company, and adapt CVP analysis to multiple cost-driver situations

Throughout this chapter we have assumed that Q, the number of units available and sold, is the only revenue and cost driver. In this section, we relax this important assumption and describe how some aspects of CVP analysis can be adapted to the more general case of multiple cost drivers.

In the One Size Software example, assume that Carolin will incur a cost of $10 for preparing documents and invoices associated with the each customer who purchases any quantity of Basic software. These documents and invoices must be prepared for each customer; therefore, the UVC = $10 per customer. The UVC per unit of Basic software remains at $120. The cost driver of document-and-invoice-preparation costs is the number of different customers while the cost driver of the purchasing costs of packages of Basic software is the quantity of packages purchased. Carolin's OI can then be expressed as

$$OI = TRev - \left(\begin{array}{c} \text{UVC per} \\ \text{Basic package} \end{array} \times \begin{array}{c} Q_1 \text{ units} \\ \text{available and sold} \end{array}\right) - \left(\begin{array}{c} \text{UVC per} \\ \text{customer invoice} \end{array} \times \begin{array}{c} Q_2 \text{ invoices} \\ \text{prepared} \end{array}\right) - FC$$

If Carolin sells $Q_1 = 40$ packages of Basic software to $Q_2 = 15$ customers, then:

$$OI = (\$200 \times 40) - (\$120 \times 40) - (\$10 \times 15) - \$2,000$$
$$= \$8,000 - \$4,800 - \$150 - \$2,000$$
$$= \$1,050$$

If Carolin sold $Q_1 = 40$ packages of Basic software to $Q_2 = 40$ customers, then:

$$OI = (\$200 \times 40) - (\$120 \times 40) - (\$10 \times 40) - \$2,000$$
$$= \$8,000 - \$4,800 - \$400 - \$2,000$$
$$= \$800$$

Carolin's OI no longer depends solely on a single cost driver but rather on the interaction of two cost drivers: $Q_1 = $ units of Basic available and sold and $Q_2 = $ customers who purchased Q_1. Just as in the case of multiple products, there is no unique breakeven point when there are multiple cost drivers. For example, Carolin will break even if she sells 26 packages to 8 customers or 27 packages to 16 customers:

$$(\$200 \times 26) - (\$120 \times 26) - (\$10 \times 8) - \$2,000 = \$5,200 - \$3,120 - \$80 - \$2,000 = \$0$$
$$(\$200 \times 27) - (\$120 \times 27) - (\$10 \times 16) - \$2,000 = \$5,400 - \$3,240 - \$160 - \$2,000 = \$0$$

CVP-type analysis can be adapted to multiple-cost-driver situations. In cases involving multiple cost drivers, however, the equation, contribution margin, and graph methods described at the beginning of Chapter 3 cannot be used.

ASSESS YOUR MASTERY

MyAccountingLab

To check your understanding of the material in Learning Objective ❻, go to the Mastery Questions section at the end of the chapter and complete Learning Objective ❻ question 1.

PULLING IT ALL TOGETHER—PROBLEM FOR SELF-STUDY

PROBLEM
The following example illustrates how to use relevant information from both the financial-accounting income statement and the contribution income statement to calculate the breakeven point (BEP). (R. Lambert, adapted)

Operating income (OI) for Anita Sweig Inc. (ASI) for the year 2008 on production and sales of 200,000 units is summarized in the financial-accounting income statement below. Additional management-accounting information is also provided regarding the inventoriable fixed costs and the period unit variable costs as follows:

Anita Sweig Inc.
Operating Income Statement
For the Year 2008

Sales	$ 3,120,000
Cost of goods sold (COGS)	1,920,000
Gross margin (GM)	1,200,000
Operating expenses (Opex)	1,380,000
Operating income (OI) (Operating loss)	$ (180,000)
Inventoriable FC	$ 600,000
Period UVC was:	$ 6.00

REQUIRED

1. Calculate ASI's variable manufacturing costs per unit in 2008.
2. Calculate ASI's fixed marketing and distribution costs in 2008.
3. Because ASI's gross margin per unit is $6 ($1,200,000 ÷ 200,000 units), ASI's president believes that if ASI had produced and sold 230,000 units, it would have covered the $1,380,000 of marketing and distribution costs ($1,380,000 ÷ $6 = 230,000) and enabled ASI to break even for the year. Calculate ASI's operating income if production and sales equal 230,000 units. Explain briefly why the president is wrong.
4. Calculate the BEP for the year 2008 in units and dollars.

SOLUTION

1. Variable manufacturing costs per unit in 2008

Total inventoriable costs (COGS)	$1,920,000	Given
Inventoriable FC	600,000	Given
Total inventoriable VC = COGS – Inventoriable FC	$1,320,000	
Q produced and sold	200,000	
Unit inventoriable VC = TVC ÷ Q	$ 6.60	

2. Fixed marketing and distribution costs in 2008

Total period costs (Opex)	$1,380,000	Given
Total period VC = Q × Unit period VC	1,200,000	Q, Unit period VC
Total period FC = Opex – Total period VC	$ 180,000	

3. Operating income if production and sales equal 230,000 units

USP for Q produced and sold = TRev ÷ Q = $3,120,000 ÷ 200,000 =		$15.60
UCM = USP – UVC inventoriable and period = $15.60 – $6.60 – $6.00 =		$3.00
TRev for Q produced and sold = USP × Q = $15.60 × 230,000 =		$3,588,000 ✓
TCM for Q produced and sold = UCM × Q = $3.00 × 230,000 =		$690,000
FC = FC inventoriable and period = $600,000 + $180,000 =		$780,000
OI = TCM – FC =		$(90,000)

The President has confused GM with TCM and assumed that the COGS consists of only variable costs while Opex or period costs consist of only fixed costs. The President does not realize that both inventoriable and period costs consist of both fixed and variable costs.

4. The BEP for the year 2008 in units (Q) and dollars (TRev).

BEP Q = FC ÷ UCM = $780,000 ÷ $3.00 = 260,000 units
BEP TRev = BEP in Q × USP = 260,000 × $15.60 = $4,056,000
Alternatively, use CM% = UCM ÷ USP = $3.00 ÷ $15.60 = 19.231%
BEP TRev = FC ÷ CM% = $780,000 ÷ 0.19231 = $4,056,000

The following decision guidelines use a question-and-answer format to summarize the chapter's main points. Each decision presents a key question. The guideline is the answer to that question.

DECISIONS	GUIDELINES
1. What assumptions must hold to apply CVP analysis?	CVP analysis requires simplifying assumptions, such as costs are either fixed or variable with respect to the number of output units (Q produced and sold), and the relationship between total revenues and total costs is linear.
2. What is the difference among contribution, gross, and operating margins?	Contribution margin is revenues minus all variable costs based on the logic of classifying all costs as either fixed or variable. Based on the logic of classifying all costs as either inventoriable or period costs, gross margin is revenues minus cost of goods sold, and operating margin is operating income divided by revenue.
3. How can CVP analysis assist managers?	CVP analysis assists managers as they select the best way to execute their strategy. CVP clearly illustrates how changes in a single product or service output level available and sold, unit selling price, unit variable costs, and fixed costs affect operating income in the short term and the long term.
4. How do companies use CVP analysis to execute a strategy successfully, calculate a breakeven point, or calculate some quantity of units or revenue required to achieve a target operating income?	The breakeven point is the quantity of output at which total revenues equal total costs. The three methods for computing the breakeven point and the quantity of output to achieve either target operating or target net income are the equation method, the contribution margin method, and the graph method, which are restatements of the same relationships. The most useful method depends on the information available. The breakeven point is unaffected by tax because at zero operating income there is no tax. Different, more complicated CVP analyses provide information on the risk-and-return tradeoff of various fixed and variable cost structures.
5. How do managers apply CVP analysis in a multiproduct company?	CVP analysis can be applied to a company producing multiple products by assuming the revenue or sales mix of products sold remains constant as the total quantity of units sold changes. There is no unique breakeven number of units for a company producing multiple products or providing multiple services.
6. Can CVP analysis be applied to a product that has multiple cost drivers?	The basic concepts of CVP analysis can be applied to multiple-cost-driver situations, but the equation, contribution margin, and graph method used in the single-cost-driver case cannot be used to calculate the breakeven point when there are multiple cost drivers.

TERMS TO LEARN

This chapter contains definitions of the following important terms:

MASTERY QUESTIONS

The Mastery Questions are rated by proficiency level—elementary, intermediate, and advanced. The solutions appear in the Mastery Question Solutions section of MyAccountingLab.

LEARNING OBJECTIVE 1

1. CVP analysis computations—Elementary. In the following data, fill in the blanks for each of the four independent cases.

Case	Revenues	Variable Costs	Fixed Costs	Total Costs	Operating Income	CM%	Contribution Margin
a	$ —	$600	$ —	$ 960	$1,440	—	$1,800
b	2,400	—	360	—	240	—	600
c	1,200	840	—	1,200	—	—	360
d	1,800	—	360	1,440	—	40%	—

2. CVP analysis computations—Intermediate. Fill in the blanks for each of the following independent cases.

Case	Selling Price	Variable Costs per Unit	Total Units Sold	Total Contribution Margin	Total Fixed Costs	Operating Income
a	$36	$24	70,000	$ —	$ —	($18,000)
b	30	—	180,000	1,080,000	960,000	—
c	—	12	150,000	360,000	264,000	—
d	24	16.80	—	144,000	—	14,000

3. CVP analysis computations—Advanced. Kamal Diamond is the owner of the Galaxy chain of four-star prestige hotels. These hotels are in Chicago, London, Los Angeles, Montreal, New York, Seattle, Tokyo, and Vancouver. Diamond is currently struggling to set weekend rates for the Vancouver hotel (the Vancouver Galaxy). From Sunday through Thursday, the Galaxy has an average occupancy rate of 90%. On Friday and Saturday nights, however, average occupancy declines to less than 30%. Galaxy's major customers are business travellers who stay mainly Sunday through Thursday.

The current room rate at the Galaxy is $180 a night for single occupancy and $216 a night for double occupancy. These rates apply seven nights a week. For many years, Diamond has resisted having rates for Friday and Saturday nights that are different from those for the remainder of the week. Diamond has long believed that price reductions convey a "nonprestige" impression to his guests. The Vancouver Galaxy highly values its reputation for treating its guests as "royalty."

Most room costs at the Galaxy are fixed on a short-stay (per-night) basis. Diamond estimates the variable costs of servicing each room to be $24 a night per single occupancy and $26.40 a night per double occupancy.

Many prestige hotels in Vancouver offer special weekend rate reductions (Friday and/or Saturday) of up to 50% of their Sunday-through-Thursday rates. These weekend rates also include additional items such as a breakfast for two, a bottle of champagne, and discounted theatre tickets.

1. Would you recommend that Diamond reduce room rates at the Vancouver Galaxy on Friday and Saturday nights? What factors should be considered in his decision?
2. In six months' time, the Grey Cup is to be held in Vancouver. Diamond observes that several four-star prestige hotels have already advertised a Friday-through-Sunday rate for Grey Cup weekend of $360 a night. Should Diamond charge extra for the Grey Cup weekend? Explain.

LEARNING OBJECTIVE 2

1. **CVP computations—Intermediate.** The Doral Company manufactures and sells pens. Present sales output is 5,000,000 units per year at a selling price of $0.60 per unit. Fixed costs are $1,080,000 per year. Variable costs are $0.36 per unit.

REQUIRED
(Consider each case separately.)
1. a. What is the present operating income for a year?
   b. What is the present breakeven point in revenues?
Compute the new operating income for each of the following changes:
2. a $0.048 per unit increase in variable costs.
3. a 10% increase in fixed costs and a 10% increase in units sold.
4. a 20% decrease in fixed costs, a 20% decrease in selling price, a 10% decrease in variable costs per unit, and a 40% increase in units sold.
Compute the new breakeven point in units for each of the following changes:
5. a 10% increase in fixed costs.
6. a 10% increase in selling price and a $24,000 increase in fixed costs.

2. **CVP computations—Advanced.** Patel Manufacturing sold 180,000 units of its product for $30 per unit in 2009. Variable cost per unit is $24 and total fixed costs are $960,000.

REQUIRED
1. Calculate (a) contribution margin and (b) operating income.
2. Patel's current manufacturing process is labour intensive. Kate Schoenen, Patel's production manager, has proposed investing in state-of-the-art manufacturing equipment, which will increase the annual fixed costs to $3,000,000. The variable costs are expected to decrease to $12 per unit. Patel expects to maintain the same sales volume and selling price next year. How would acceptance of Ms. Schoenen's proposal affect your answers to (a) and (b) in requirement 1?
3. Should Patel accept Schoenen's proposal? Explain.

LEARNING OBJECTIVE 3

1. **CVP computations with target net income—Intermediate.** The Rapid Meal has two restaurants that are open 24 hours a day. Fixed costs for the two restaurants together total $540,000 per year. Service varies from a cup of coffee to full meals. The average sales cheque for each customer is $9.60. The average cost of food and other variable costs for each customer is $3.84. The income tax rate is 30%. Target net income is $126,000.

REQUIRED
1. Compute the revenues needed to obtain the target net income.
2. How many sales cheques are needed to earn net income of $126,000? To break even?
3. Compute net income if the number of sales cheques is 150,000.

2. **CVP computations with sensitivity analysis—Advanced.** Hoot Washington is the newly elected charismatic leader of the Western Party. He is the darling of the right-wing media. His "take no prisoners" attitude has left many an opponent on a talk show feeling run over by a Mack truck.

Media Publishers is negotiating to publish Hoot's Manifesto, a new book that promises to be an instant bestseller. The fixed costs of producing and marketing the book will be $600,000. The variable costs of producing and marketing will be $4.80 per book. These costs are before any payments to Hoot. Hoot negotiates an up-front payment of $3.60 million plus a 15% royalty rate on the net sales price of each book. The net sales price is the listed book-store price of $36 minus the margin paid to the book store to sell the book. The normal book-store margin of 30% of the listed book-store price is expected to apply.

REQUIRED
1. Present a PV graph for Media Publishers.
2. How many copies must Media Publishers sell to (a) break even and (b) earn a target operating profit of $2.4 million?

3. Examine the sensitivity of the breakeven point to the following changes:
   a. Decreasing the normal book-store margin to 20% of the listed book-store price of $36
   b. Increasing the listed book-store price to $48 while keeping the book-store margin at 30%

LEARNING OBJECTIVE 4

1. **CVP and income taxes—Advanced.** R. A. Ro and Company, a manufacturer of quality handmade walnut bowls, has experienced a steady growth in sales for the past five years. However, increased competition has led Mr. Ro, the president, to believe that an aggressive marketing campaign will be necessary next year to maintain the company's present growth.

To prepare for next year's marketing campaign, the company's controller has prepared and presented Mr. Ro with the following data for the current year, 2009:

Variable costs (per bowl):	
Direct manufacturing labour	$ 9.60
Direct materials	3.90
Variable overhead (manufacturing, marketing, distribution, customer service, and administration)	3.00
Total variable costs	$ 16.50
Fixed costs:	
Manufacturing	$ 30,000
Marketing, distribution, and customer service	48,000
Administrative	84,000
Total fixed costs	$162,000
Selling price per bowl	$30.00
Expected revenues, 2009 (20,000 units)	$600,000
Income tax rate	40%

REQUIRED

1. What is the projected net income for 2009?
2. What is the breakeven point in units for 2009?
3. Mr. Ro has set the revenue target for 2010 at a level of $660,000 (or 22,000 bowls). He believes an additional marketing cost of $13,500 for advertising in 2010, with all other costs remaining constant, will be necessary to attain the revenue target. What will be the net income for 2010 if the additional $13,500 is spent and the revenue target is met?
4. What will be the breakeven point in revenues for 2010 if the additional $13,500 is spent for advertising?
5. If the additional $13,500 is spent for advertising in 2010, what is the required 2010 revenue for 2010's net income to equal 2009's net income?
6. At a sales level of 22,000 units, what maximum amount can be spent on advertising if a 2010 net income of $72,000 is desired?

LEARNING OBJECTIVE 5

1. **CVP analysis and revenue mix—Advanced.** Ronowski Company has three product lines of belts, A, B, and C, with contribution margins of $3.60, $2.40, and $1.20 respectively. The president forecasts sales of 200,000 units in the coming period, consisting of 20,000 units of A, 100,000 units of B, and 80,000 units of C. The company's fixed costs for the period are $306,000.

REQUIRED

1. What is the company breakeven point in units, assuming that the given revenue mix is maintained?
2. If the mix is maintained, what is the total contribution margin when 200,000 units are sold? What is the operating income?
3. What would operating income become if 20,000 units of A, 80,000 units of B, and 100,000 units of C were sold? What is the new breakeven point in units if these relationships persist in the next period?

LEARNING OBJECTIVE 6

1. **CVP analysis and multiple cost drivers—Advanced.** Susan Wong is a distributor of brass picture frames. During 2010, she plans to purchase frames for $36 each and sell them for $54 each. Susan's fixed costs for 2010 are expected to be $288,000. Susan's only other costs will be variable costs of $72 per shipment for preparing the invoice and delivery documents, organizing the delivery, and collecting cash. The $72 cost will be incurred each time Susan ships an order of picture frames, regardless of the number of picture frames in the order.

REQUIRED

1. Suppose Susan sells 40,000 picture frames in 1,000 shipments in 2010. Calculate Susan's 2010 operating income.
2. Suppose Susan sells 40,000 picture frames in 800 shipments in 2010. Calculate Susan's 2010 operating income.
3. Suppose Susan anticipates making 500 shipments in 2010. How many picture frames must Susan sell to break even in 2010?
4. Calculate another breakeven point for 2010, different from the one described in requirement 3. Explain briefly why Susan has multiple breakeven points.

ASSIGNMENT MATERIAL

MyAccountingLab Make the grade with MyAccountingLab: The questions, exercises, and problems marked in red can be found on MyAccountingLab at **www.myaccountinglab.com.** You can practise them as often as you want, and most feature step-by-step guided instructions to help you find the right answer. Exercises and problems with an Excel icon in the margin have an accompanying Excel template on MyAccountingLab.

SHORT-ANSWER QUESTIONS

Note: To underscore the basic CVP relationships, the assignment material ignores income taxes unless stated otherwise.

3-1 Define cost-volume-profit analysis.

3-2 Describe the assumptions underlying CVP analysis.

3-3 Distinguish between operating income and net income.

3-4 Define contribution margin, gross margin, contribution margin percentage, variable-cost percentage, and margin of safety.

3-5 Describe three methods that can be used to calculate the breakeven point.

3-6 Why is it more accurate to describe the subject matter of this chapter as CVP analysis rather than as breakeven analysis?

3-7 "CVP is both simple and simplistic. If you want realistic analysis to underpin your decisions, look beyond CVP." Do you agree? Explain.

3-8 How does an increase in the income tax rate affect the breakeven point?

3-9 Describe sensitivity analysis. How has spreadsheet software affected its use?

3-10 Give an example of how a manager can decrease variable costs while increasing fixed costs.

3-11 Give an example of how a manager can increase variable costs while decreasing fixed costs.

3-12 What is operating leverage? How is knowing the degree of operating leverage (DOL) helpful to managers?

3-13 "There is no such thing as a fixed cost. All costs can be 'unfixed' given sufficient time." Do you agree? What is the implication of your answer for CVP analysis?

3-14 How can a company with multiple products compute its breakeven point?

3-15 "Gross margin is a less useful concept than contribution margin in CVP analysis." Do you agree? Explain.

Case a CM%, 23.67%

3-16 CVP analysis computations. The following partial information is available. Complete the table by filling in all the blanks. Each case is independent.

Case	Revenues	Variable Costs	Fixed Costs	Total Costs	Operating Income	CM%
a	$ 3,000	$ —	$ 250	$—	$ 460	—
b	—	7,400	—	8,700	9,800	—
c	10,600	—	3,200	—	—	30%
d	9,450	—	2,500	8,170	—	—

Case b unit selling price, $87

3-17 CVP analysis computations. Fill in the blanks for each of the following independent cases.

Case	Unit Selling Price	Unit Variable Costs	Number of Units Sold	Total Contribution Margin	Total Fixed Costs	Operating Income
a	$ 70	$25	—	$ 900,000	$ —	$200,000
b	—	62	15,000	—	250,000	125,000
c	250	—	30,000	4,500,000	—	900,000
d	150	—	24,000	1,728,000	1,500,000	—

1. 40 cars

3-18 CVP analysis, income taxes. Diego Motors is a small car dealership. On average it sells a car for $26,000, which it purchases from the manufacturer for $22,000. Each month, Diego Motors pays $60,000 in rent and utilities and $70,000 for salespeople's salaries. In addition to their salaries, salespeople are paid a commission of $500 for each car they sell. Diego Motors also spends $10,000 each month for local advertisements. Its tax rate is 40%.

REQUIRED
1. How many cars must Diego Motors sell each month to break even?
2. Diego Motors has a target monthly net income of $63,000. What is its target operating income? How many cars must be sold each month to reach the target monthly net income of $63,000?

1. 21 mowers

3-19 CVP analysis, income taxes. (J. Watson) Orillia Equipment sells riding lawn mowers. The average price for a lawn mower is $16,000. Orillia purchases these mowers from the manufacturers at an average cost of $12,200. Orillia's monthly fixed costs are $28,000 in rent, $45,000 in salaries, $5,600 in advertising and promotion, and $1,200 in other operating expenses. It has a corporate tax rate of 25%.

REQUIRED
1. How many mowers must Orillia Equipment sell each month to break even?
2. How many mowers must be sold each month if Orillia Equipment has a target net income of $42,750?

3-20 Gross margin and contribution margin. The Museum of Art is preparing for its annual appreciation dinner for contributing members. Last year, 500 members attended the dinner. Tickets for the dinner were $20 per attendee. Last year's income statement was as follows:

Ticket sales	$10,000
Cost of dinner	11,000
Gross margin	(1,000)
Invitations and paperwork	3,000
Profit (loss)	$ (4,000)

This year the dinner committee does not want to lose money on the dinner. To help achieve its goal, the committee analyzed last year's costs. Of the $11,000 total cost of the dinner, it was determined that $6,000 were fixed costs and $5,000 were variable costs. Of the $3,000 for invitations and paperwork, $2,500 were fixed and $500 were variable.

REQUIRED
1. Prepare last year's profit report using the contribution-margin format.
2. The committee is considering expanding this year's dinner invitation to include volunteer members (in addition to contributing members). If the committee expects attendance to double, calculate the effect this will have on the profitability of the dinner.

3-21 Athletic scholarships, CVP analysis. Huron University is committed to improving access to higher education. Each year it makes $4,500,000 available for scholarships for students based on financial needs and academic achievement. The scholarship covers the full annual tuition (based on a full course load) for the recipients. Tuition fees are based on credit hours ($400 per credit hour), and a full-time student takes 30 credit hours per year. Fixed costs of administering the scholarship program are $600,000 per year.

1. 325 scholarships

REQUIRED
1. How many athletic scholarships can Huron University offer each year?
2. Suppose the total budget for the following year is reduced by 20%. Fixed costs are to remain the same. Calculate the number of scholarships that Huron can offer in the following year.
3. As in requirement 2, assume a budget reduction of 20%. Fixed costs are to remain the same. If Huron wanted to offer the same number of scholarships as it did in requirement 1, how much reduction in tuition would it be able to offer to each student who receives a scholarship?

3-22 CVP analysis, changing revenues and costs. Sunshine Tours is a travel agency specializing in cruises between Miami: and Jamaica. It books passengers on Carib Cruises. Sunshine's fixed costs are $22,000 per month. Carib charges passengers $1,000 per round trip ticket.

1. a) 489 tickets

REQUIRED
Calculate the number of tickets Sunshine must sell each month to a) break even and b) make a target operating income of $10,000 per month in each of the following independent cases.
1. Sunshine's variable costs are $35 per ticket and Carib Cruises pays Sunshine 8% commission on the ticket price.
2. Sunshine's variable costs are $29 per ticket. Carib Cruises pays Sunshine 8% commission on the ticket price.
3. Sunshine's variable costs are $29 per ticket. It receives a $48 commission per ticket from Carib Cruises. Comment on the results.
4. Sunshine's variable costs are $29 per ticket. It receives a $48 commission per ticket from Carib Cruises. It charges customers a delivery fee of $5 per ticket. Comment on the results.

3-23 Contribution margin, gross margin, and margin of safety. Mirabel Cosmetics manufactures and sells a face cream to small family-run stores in the greater Montreal area. It presents the monthly operating income statement shown here to Francois Laval, a potential investor in the business. Help Mr. Laval understand Mirabel's cost structure.

2. CM%, 40%

Mirabel Cosmetics
Operating Income Statement
For the Month of June 2009

Units Sold		10,000
Revenues		$100,000
Cost of Goods Sold		
Variable Manufacturing Costs	$55,000	
Fixed Manufacturing Costs	20,000	
Total		75,000
Gross Margin		25,000
Operating Costs		
Variable Marketing Costs	5,000	
Fixed Marketing and Administration Costs	10,000	
Total Operating Costs		15,000
Operating Income		$ 10,000

REQUIRED
1. Recast the income statement to emphasize contribution margin.
2. Calculate the contribution margin percentage and breakeven point in units and revenues for June 2009.
3. What is the margin of safety (in units) for June 2009?
4. If sales in June were only 8,000 units and Mirabel's tax rate is 30%, calculate its net income.

3-24 CVP exercises. Simple Designs owns and operates several retail outlets throughout Western Canada. You are given the following corporate budget data for next year:

Revenues	$15,000,000
Fixed costs	2,400,000
Variable costs	10,800,000

The cost driver for variable costs is the number of units sold.

REQUIRED

Compute the budgeted operating income for each of the following deviations from the original budget data. (Consider each case independently.)

1. A 12% increase in contribution margin, holding revenues constant
2. A 12% decrease in contribution margin, holding revenues constant
3. A 6% increase in fixed costs
4. A 6% decrease in fixed costs
5. A 10% increase in units sold
6. A 10% decrease in units sold
7. An 8% increase in fixed costs and 12% increase in units sold
8. A 5% increase in fixed costs and 5% decrease in variable costs

3-25 CVP exercises. (J. Watson) Beans Unlimited sells specialty coffees in 1-kilogram packages. Fixed costs are budgeted at $730,000 per year. For the upcoming year, revenues are forecasted to be $3,240,000 (selling price is $36 per kilogram) and the company has an average contribution margin percentage of 48%.

REQUIRED

1. What is the budgeted operating income given the sales forecast?
2. Beans is considering reducing its fixed costs by 15%. This would result in a lowering of the contribution margin percentage to 42%. What would be the new forecasted operating income?
3. Another alternative Beans is considering is raising its selling price by 10%. It estimates this would result in a reduction in sales volume of 5%. There would be no changes to variable or fixed costs. What would be the forecasted operating income with the new selling price and volume? What is the new contribution margin percentage?
4. Which strategy would you recommend for the company? Explain.

3-26 CVP, margin of safety. Suppose Latimer Ltd.'s breakeven point is revenues of $2,159,000. Fixed costs are $323,850.

REQUIRED

1. Compute the contribution margin percentage.
2. Compute the selling price if variable costs are $17.00 per unit.
3. Suppose 140,000 units are sold. Compute the margin of safety.

3-27 Operating leverage. Charles Rothman is an importer of silver cuff bracelets from Mexico. He has a three-month agreement with the local coffee shop, Dellano's, to set up a booth to exhibit the jewellery. Rothman is under no obligation to keep any unsold items and can return them to the Mexican silversmith at no personal cost. The average selling price of the bracelets is $125 and it costs Rothman $80 to purchase each piece. Dellano's has proposed two payment alternatives for the use of space.

◆ Option 1: A fixed payment of $435 per month.
◆ Option 2: 12% of the total revenues earned during the agreement.

REQUIRED

1. Calculate the breakeven point in units for (a) option 1 and (b) option 2.
2. At what level of sales revenue will Rothman earn the same operating income under either option?
3. **a.** For what range of unit sales will Rothman prefer option 1?
   b. For what range of unit sales will Rothman prefer option 2?
4. Calculate the degree of operating leverage at sales of 150 units for the two alternative rental options.
5. Briefly explain and interpret your answer in requirement 4.

3-28 Gross margin and contribution margin, making decisions. Saunders' Electronics had the following results for the year just ended:

Revenues		$800,000
Cost of goods sold (48% of sales)		384,000
Gross margin		416,000
Operating costs		
Salaries fixed	$212,000	
Sales commissions (12% of sales)	96,000	
Amortization of equipment and fixtures	19,200	
Store rent ($5,100 per month)	61,200	
Other operating costs	72,300	460,700
Operating income (loss)		$ (44,700)

2

1. CM, $288,000

Mr. Saunders, the owner of the store, is unhappy with the operating results. An analysis of other operating costs reveals that it includes $32,000 variable costs, for which the cost driver is sales volume, and $40,300 fixed costs.

REQUIRED:
1. Compute the contribution margin of Saunders' Electronics.
2. Compute the contribution margin percentage for the company.
3. Mr. Saunders estimates he can increase revenues by 25% by incurring additional advertising costs of $24,300. Calculate the impact on operating income of this action.

3-29 CVP, revenue mix. (J. Watson) Burdon Snowboards sells two models of snowboards—the Men's Dominator and the Ladies' Luxury. Information on the two models of snowboards follows:

5

2. Weighted-average CM, $243.70

Product	Unit Selling Price	Unit Variable Cost	Sales Commission
Dominator	$750	$475	$25
Luxury	$640	$390	$21

Of Burdon's total sales, 70% are for the Men's Dominator Model. The company's annual fixed costs are $180,000.

REQUIRED
1. Compute the unit contribution margin for each model of snowboard.
2. Compute the weighted-average contribution margin assuming a constant sales mix.
3. If the company's target operating income is $115,000, how many units of each model of snowboard must be sold to achieve the company's goals?

3-30 CVP, international cost structure differences. Kaleden Inc. is considering three countries for the sole manufacturing site of its new product: India, China, and Canada. The product will be sold to retail outlets in Canada at $47.50 per unit. These retail outlets add their own markup when selling to final customers. The three countries differ in their fixed costs and variable costs per product.

3

1. a. India unit CM, $20.50

	Annual Fixed Costs	Variable Manufacturing Costs per Unit	Variable Marketing and Distribution Costs per Unit
India	$ 6.4 million	$ 5.20	$21.80
China	4.4 million	9.50	18.40
Canada	10.2 million	19.30	6.20

REQUIRED
1. Compute the breakeven point of Kaleden Inc. in both (a) units sold and (b) revenues for each of the three countries considered.
2. If Kaleden Inc. sells 1,350,000 units in 2010, what is the budgeted operating income for each of the three countries considered?
3. What level of sales (in units) would be required to produce the same operating income in China and in Canada? What would be the operating income in India at that volume of sales?

3-31 CVP, not for profit. The Sunrise Group (SG) is an environmentally conscious organization that buys land with the objective of preserving the natural environment.

SG receives private contributions and takes no assistance from the government. Fixed costs of operating the organization are $1,000,000 per year. Variable costs of purchasing the land (including environmental impact reports, title searches, etc.) average $3,000 per hectare. For the next budget year, SG expects to receive private contributions totalling $19,000,000. All contributions in excess of costs will be used to purchase land.

REQUIRED

1. How many hectares will SG be able to purchase next year?
2. SG is considering participating in a new government program that will provide $1,000 per hectare to subsidize the purchase of environmentally sensitive land. If SG participates in this program, it estimates the organization will lose $5,000,000 in contributions from supporters who believe that accepting money from the government is not consistent with its mission. If SG does participate in the program, and its forecasts are accurate, how many hectares of land will it be able to purchase? On financial considerations alone, should SG participate in the government program?
3. SG is worried that contributions may decrease by more than the $5,000,000 it has estimated if it takes the subsidy. By how much can contributions decrease for SG to be able to buy the same amount of land if it takes the government subsidy or rejects it? (i.e., what is the point of indifference between the two options?)

3-32 **CVP, revenue mix.** (J. Watson) Zyrcon Ltd. is a computer games manufacturer. It currently has two games on the market—Alien Predators and Vegas Pokermatch. Data regarding the two products are as follows:

	Alien Predators	Vegas Pokermatch
Selling price	$89	$59
Variable manufacturing costs	$18	$12
Variable marketing costs	$27	$16

The fixed costs of Zyrcon are $18,750,000, and the current sales mix is 40% Alien Predators and 60% Vegas Pokermatch.

REQUIRED

1. Assuming no change in sales mix, costs, or revenues, what is the breakeven point in total units? How many units of Alien Predators and how many units of Vegas Pokermatch are sold at the breakeven point?
2. Assume the following sales mixes:
   a. 25% Alien Predators and 75% Vegas Pokermatch
   b. 60% Alien Predators and 40% Vegas Pokermatch
   c. 50% Alien Predators and 50% Vegas Pokermatch
   Calculate the breakeven point under each sales mix assumption.
3. For all four possible sales mixes (in requirements 1 and 2), determine operating income if total unit sales are 750,000.

3-33 **Effects on operating income, pricing decision.** Teguchi Manufacturing is a manufacturer of electronics components. Income data for one of the products (XT-107) for the month just ended are as follows:

Sales, 220,000 units at average price of $125		$27,500,000
Variable costs:		
Direct materials at $48 per unit	$10,560,000	
Direct manufacturing labour at $16 per unit	3,520,000	
Variable manufacturing overhead at $8 per unit	1,760,000	
Sales commissions at 12% of sales	3,300,000	
Other variable costs at $7 per unit	1,540,000	
Total variable costs		20,680,000
Contribution margin		6,820,000
Fixed costs		4,620,000
Operating income		$2,200,000

Teguchi has capacity to produce 250,000 units each month, and its current average sales level is 175,000 units per month.

Recently Andrew Ltd. approached one of Teguchi's sales representatives and asked if Teguchi could supply a one-time order of 5,000 units of the XT-107. Its current supplier is moving to a new factory and has temporarily suspended production. Andrews has offered a selling price of $98 per unit. Sales commissions on this order can be negotiated at a flat fee of $9,500, instead of the normal 12% of sales. All other costs would behave as with regular production.

REQUIRED

1. From a financial perspective, should Teguchi accept the order? (Calculate the change in monthly operating income if the order is accepted.)
2. The general manager of Teguchi is concerned about accepting the order at the $98 selling price. He is afraid of the precedent that might be set by cutting the price and that Andrews might expect the same price concessions in the future. He has stated that he believes the sales representative should quote the regular price of $125 and argues that the $98 is below the full cost (excluding the commission) of $100 per unit. Do you agree with the general manager? Explain.

3-34 **Alternate cost structures, uncertainty, and sensitivity analysis.** Edible Bouquets (EB) makes and sells flower bouquets. EB is considering opening a new store in the local mall. The mall has several empty shops and EB is unsure of the demand for its product. The mall has offered EB two alternative rental agreements. The first is a standard fixed-rent agreement where EB will pay the mall $5,000 per month. The second is a royalty agreement where the mall receives $10 for each bouquet sold. EB estimates that a bouquet will sell for $50 and have a variable cost of $30 to make (including the cost of the flowers and commission for the salesperson).

③ ④
1. BEP for assumption 1, 250 bouquets

REQUIRED

1. What is the breakeven point in units under each assumption?
2. For what range of sales levels will EB prefer a) the fixed-rent agreement and b) the royalty agreement?
3. If EB signs a sales agreement with a local flower stand, it will save $5 in variable costs per bouquet. How would this affect your answer in requirement 2?
4. EB estimates that the store is equally likely to sell 200, 400, 600, 800, or 1,000 arrangements. Using information from the original problem, prepare a table that shows the expected profit at each sales level under each rental agreement. What is the expected value of each rental agreement? Which rental agreement should EB choose?

3-35 **CVP analysis, multiple cost drivers.** (J. Watson) Clarke Ltd. is a manufacturer of promotional items. The majority of its revenues is from the production of promotional pens. Clarke imports these pens from China and then imprints them with corporate names. These pens are then distributed to customers, suppliers, etc., for promotional purposes. The pens are purchased in batches of 100 and each batch costs Clarke $95. Imprinting costs $0.35 per pen. Fixed costs average $275,000 per year. In addition to the variable imprinting costs, Clarke incurs set-up charges for each customer. Set-up costs average $120 per set-up, regardless of the number of pens imprinted on that production run. The selling price is $4.50 per pen. Clarke requires a minimum order of 50 pens and typically sells to customers in batches of 50, 100, 250, or 500 units.

⑥
1. OI, $425,000

REQUIRED

1. Assuming that Clarke anticipates it will sell 350,000 pens during the year and that the average order size will be 100 pens, calculate Clarke's operating income and operating margin.
2. Calculate Clarke's operating income and operating margin assuming it will sell 350,000 pens, but that the average order size will be 250 pens.
3. Calculate the breakeven points (in terms of number of orders) assuming the various batch sizes of 50, 100, 250, and 500 units.
4. What would you recommend to Clarke regarding its pricing of this product?

3-36 **Uncertainty.** Angela King is the Las Vegas promoter for Randy Couture. King is promoting a new Octagon world championship fight for Couture. The key area of uncertainty is the size of the cable pay-per-view TV market. King will pay Couture a fixed fee of $3.2 million and 25% of net cable pay-per-view revenue. Every cable TV home receiving the event pays $45, of which King receives $27. King pays Couture $6.75, 25% of the $27.

King estimates the following probability distribution for homes purchasing the pay-per-view event:

④
1. Expected value, $6,220,625

Demand	Probability
250,000	0.05
300,000	0.10
350,000	0.20
400,000	0.40
500,000	0.15
1,000,000	0.10

1. What is the expected value of the payment King will make to Couture?
2. Assume the only uncertainty is over cable TV demand for the fight. King wants to know the breakeven point given her own fixed costs of $1.3 million and her own variable costs of $2.25 per home. (Also include King's payments to Couture in your answer.)

PROBLEMS

3-37 CVP, executive teaching compensation. David Hutchinson is an internationally known Canadian professor specializing in consumer marketing. In 2009, Hutchinson and the United Kingdom Business School (UKBS) agreed to conduct a one-day seminar at UKBS for marketing executives. Each executive would pay £350 to attend. The non–speaker-related fixed costs for UKBS conducting the seminar would be

Advertising in magazines	£5,200
Mailing of brochures	2,500
Administrative labour at UKBS	3,200
Charge for UKBS lecture auditorium	1,800

The variable costs to UKBS for each participant attending the seminar would be

Food service	£38
Printed materials and binders	37

The dean at UKBS initially offered Hutchinson its regular compensation package of (a) business-class airfare and accommodation (£3,800 maximum) and (b) a £2,750 lecture fee. Hutchinson views the £2,750 lecture fee as providing him no upside potential (that is, no sharing in the potential additional operating income that arises if the seminar is highly attended). He suggests instead that he receive 50% of the operating income to UKBS (if positive) from the one-day seminar and no other payments. The dean of UKBS quickly agrees to Hutchinson's proposal after confirming that Hutchinson is willing to pay his own airfare and accommodation and deliver the seminar irrespective of the number of executives signed up to attend.

REQUIRED

1. What is UKBS's breakeven point (in number of executives attending) if
   a. Hutchinson accepts the regular compensation package of £3,800 expenses and a £2,750 lecture fee.
   b. Hutchinson receives 50% of the operating income to UKBS (if positive) from the one-day seminar and no other payments.

   Comment on the results for (a) and (b).
2. Hutchinson gave the one-day seminar at UKBS in 2006 (60 attended), 2007 (75 attended), and 2008 (120 attended). How much was Hutchinson paid by UKBS for the one-day seminar under the 50% of UKBS's operating income compensation plan in (a) 2006, (b) 2007, and (c) 2008? (Assume that the £350 charge per executive attending and UKBS's fixed and variable costs are the same each year.)
3. After the 2008 seminar, the dean at UKBS suggested to Hutchinson that the 50%–50% profit-sharing plan was resulting in Hutchinson getting excessive compensation and that a more equitable arrangement to UKBS be used in 2009. How should Hutchinson respond to this suggestion?

3-38 CVP analysis, service firm. Wildlife Escapes generates average revenue of $9,200 per person on its five-day package tours to wildlife parks in Kenya. The variable costs per person are

Airfare	$3,500
Hotel accommodations	1,200
Meals	480
Ground transportation	920
Park tickets and other costs	240

Annual fixed costs total $1,287,000.

REQUIRED

1. Calculate the number of package tours that must be sold to break even.
2. Calculate the revenue needed to earn a target operating income of $214,500.
3. If fixed costs increase by $40,500, what decrease in variable costs must be achieved to maintain the breakeven point calculated in requirement 1?

3-39 CVP, target operating and net income. (J. Watson) Carumba Inc.'s 2009 budget includes the following items:

1. Breakeven price, $34.75

Sales	80,000 units
Production	80,000 units
Direct materials used	$600,000
Direct labour	400,000
Variable overhead	720,000
Fixed overhead	400,000
Variable selling costs	260,000
Fixed selling costs	250,000
Administrative costs (all fixed)	150,000

The company's tax rate is 30%.

REQUIRED

1. At what price would the company break even?
2. If the company were to sell only 60,000 units, what price would produce a before-tax profit of 20% of sales?
3. Majestix Inc. has offered to supply Carumba with 80,000 units at a price of $28/unit. Should Carumba accept the offer? Explain.
4. What price would produce an after-tax profit of $350,000?

3-40 CVP, target income, service firm. Teddy Bear Daycare provides daycare for children Mondays through Fridays. Its monthly variable costs per child are

1. BEP 14 children

Lunch and snacks	$100
Educational supplies	75
Other supplies (paper products, toiletries, etc.)	25
Total	$200

Monthly fixed costs consist of

Rent	$2,000
Utilities	300
Insurance	300
Salaries	2,500
Miscellaneous	500
	$5,600

Teddy Bear charges each parent $600 per child.

REQUIRED

1. Calculate the breakeven point.
2. Teddy Bear's target operating income is $10,400 per month. Compute the number of children that must be enrolled to achieve the target operating income.
3. Teddy Bear lost its lease and had to move to another building. Monthly rent for the new building is $3,000. At the suggestion of parents, Teddy Bear plans to take children on field trips. Monthly costs of the field trips are $1,000. By how much should Teddy Bear increase fees per child to meet the target operating income of $10,400 per month, assuming the same number of children as in requirement 2?

3-41 CVP, income taxes, manufacturing decisions. (J. Watson) Prairie Ltd. currently manufactures a single product in its Saskatoon factory. Last year's results (based on sales volume of 25,000 units) were

1. BEP 15,433 units

Sales		$1,350,000
Variable costs	$ 742,500	
Fixed costs	375,000	1,117,500
Operating income		232,500
Income taxes (40%)		93,000
Operating income		$ 139,500

REQUIRED

1. Using last year's data, calculate Prairie's breakeven point in units and calculate the margin of safety in dollars.
2. How many units of product would Prairie have had to sell last year if it wished to earn $225,000 in net income?

3. In an attempt to improve its product quality, Prairie is considering replacing one of its current component parts. This part costs $7.50 (one component per finished unit), and Prairie is evaluating a new and better part that has a cost of $9.80 per unit. The company would simultaneously expand its production by investing in a machine that costs $25,000. This machine has no salvage value and would be amortized on a straight-line basis over five years (assume this is acceptable for both financial-statement and tax purposes). If these changes are made and selling price is held constant:
   a. Calculate the new breakeven point in units.
   b. Determine how many units of product must be sold next year to achieve the same net income after taxes as last year.

4. Instead of the changes in requirement 3, the company is considering adding a higher-quality product to its sales mix. This new product would sell for $95 and variable costs per unit would increase by 60% over the old product. Total unit sales are forecast to increase to 50,000 units (which is in the company's current capacity—no additional fixed costs are needed) and the sales mix is estimated to be 3:2 (old product to new product). If Prairie introduces this new product at the planned sales mix, calculate the new breakeven point in sales dollars.

3-42 CVP, shoe stores. The Walk Rite Shoe Company operates a chain of shoe stores. The stores sell ten different styles of inexpensive men's shoes with identical unit costs and selling prices. A unit is defined as a pair of shoes. Each store has a store manager who is paid a fixed salary. Individual salespeople receive a fixed salary and a sales commission. Walk Rite is trying to determine the desirability of opening another store, which is expected to have the following revenue and cost relationships:

Selling price	$30.00
Unit variable cost per pair:	
Cost of shoes	$19.50
Sales commissions	1.50
Total variable costs	$21.00
Annual fixed costs:	
Rent	$ 60,000
Salaries	200,000
Advertising	80,000
Other fixed costs	20,000
Total fixed costs	$360,000

REQUIRED
(Consider each question independently.)
1. What is the annual breakeven point in (a) units sold and (b) revenues?
2. If 35,000 units are sold, what will be the store's operating income (loss)?
3. If sales commissions were discontinued for individual salespeople in favour of an $81,000 increase in fixed salaries, what would be the annual breakeven point in (a) units sold and (b) revenues?
4. Refer to the original data. If the store manager were paid $0.30 per unit sold in addition to his current fixed salary, what would be the annual breakeven point in (a) units sold and (b) revenues?
5. Refer to the original data. If the store manager were paid $0.30 per unit commission on each unit sold in excess of the breakeven point, what would be the store's operating income if 50,000 units were sold? (This $0.30 is in addition to both the commission paid to the sales staff and the store manager's fixed salary.)

3-43 CVP, shoe stores (continuation of 3-42). Refer to requirement 3 of 3-42. In this problem assume the role of the owner of Walk Rite.

REQUIRED
1. Calculate the number of units sold where the operating income under (a) a fixed salary plan and (b) a lower fixed salary and commission plan (for salespeople only) would be equal. Above that number of units sold, one plan would be more profitable than the other; below that number of units sold, the reverse would occur.
2. As owner, which sales compensation plan would you choose if forecasted annual sales of the new store were at least 55,000 units? What do you think of the motivation aspects of your chosen compensation plan?

3. Suppose the target operating income is $168,000. How many units must be sold to reach the target under (a) the fixed salary plan and (b) the lower fixed salary-and-commission plan?

4. You open the new store on January 1, 2009 with the original salary-plus-commission compensation plan in place. Because you expect the cost of the shoes to rise due to inflation, you place a firm bulk order for 50,000 shoes and lock in the $19.50 per unit price. But, toward the end of the year, only 48,000 pairs of shoes are sold, and you authorize a markdown of the remaining inventory to $18 per unit. Finally all units are sold. Salespeople, as usual, get paid a commission of 5% of revenues. What is the annual operating income for the store?

3-44 Uncertainty and expected costs. Dawmart Corp., an international retail giant, is considering implementing a new business-to-business (B2B) information system for processing purchase orders. The current system costs Dawmart $1,000,000 per month and $40 per order. Dawmart has two options: a partially automated B2B and a fully automated B2B system. The partially automated B2B system will have a fixed cost of $5,000,000 per month and a variable cost of $30 per order. The fully automated B2B system will have fixed costs of $10,000,000 per month and variable costs of $20 per order.

Based on data from the last two years, Dawmart has determined the following distribution on monthly orders:

4

2. Current system expected cost, $20,600,000

Monthly Number of Orders	Probability
300,000	0.10
400,000	0.25
500,000	0.40
600,000	0.15
700,000	0.10

REQUIRED

1. Prepare a table showing the cost of each plan for each quantity of monthly orders.
2. What is the expected cost of each plan?
3. In addition to the information systems costs, what other factors should Dawmart consider before deciding to implement a new B2B system?

3-45 CVP analysis, decision making. (M. Rajan, adapted) Tocchet Company manufactures CB1, a citizens' band radio that is sold mainly to truck drivers. The company's plant in Camden has an annual capacity of 75,000 units. Tocchet currently sells 60,000 units at a selling price of $148. It has the following cost structure:

4

1. BEP 25,600 units

Variable manufacturing costs per unit	$63
Fixed manufacturing costs	$1,012,000
Variable marketing and distribution costs per unit	$5
Fixed marketing and distribution costs	$780,000

REQUIRED

(Consider each question separately.)

1. Calculate the breakeven volume in units and in dollars.
2. The marketing department indicates that decreasing the selling price to $140 would stimulate sales to 70,000 units. This strategy will require Tocchet to increase its fixed costs, although variable costs per unit will remain the same as before. What is the *maximum* increase in fixed costs for which Tocchet will find it worthwhile to reduce the selling price?
3. The manufacturing department proposes changes in the manufacturing process to add new features to the CB1 product. These changes will increase fixed manufacturing costs by $150,000 and variable manufacturing costs per unit by $3.20. At its current sales quantity of 60,000 units, what is the *minimum* selling price above which Tocchet will find it worthwhile to add these new features?

3-46 Revenue mix, two products. The Goldman Company retails two products, a standard and a deluxe version of a luggage carrier. The budgeted income statement is as follows:

5

1. BEP 160,000 total units

	Standard Carrier	Deluxe Carrier	Total
Units sold	150,000	50,000	200,000
Revenues @ $20 and $30 per unit	$3,000,000	$1,500,000	$4,500,000
Variable costs @ $14 and $18 per unit	2,100,000	900,000	3,000,000

Contribution margins @ $6 and $12 per unit	$ 900,000	$ 600,000	1,500,000
Fixed costs			1,200,000
Operating income			$ 300,000

REQUIRED

1. Compute the breakeven point in units, assuming that the planned revenue mix is maintained.
2. Compute the breakeven point in units (a) if only standard carriers are sold and (b) if only deluxe carriers are sold.
3. Suppose 200,000 units are sold, but only 20,000 are deluxe. Compute the operating income. Compute the breakeven point if these relationships persist in the next period. Compare your answers with the original plans and the answer in requirement 1. What is the major lesson of this problem?

3

1. a. BEP $34,375,000

3-47 CVP, movie production. Panther Productions has just finished production of the most recent sequel in its Illinois Jones series. The film cost $22 million to produce. Most production personnel and actors were paid a fixed salary (included in the $22 million); however, the two major stars of the film, Chevy Harrison and Sean Connelly, as well as the director and producer, Stephen Lucas and George Spielberg, all received equity interests in the film. In addition, the distributor of the film, Parimont Productions, receives royalties in exchange for its investment of $6.5 million to promote the film. The actors each receive 4% of revenues, the director and producer each receive 8% of revenues, and Parimont receives 12% of the revenues. Panther receives 65% of the total box office receipts, and out of this amount it pays the royalties to the actors, director, producer, and promoter.

REQUIRED

1. What is the breakeven point on the film to Panther Productions expressed in terms of (a) revenues received by Panther and (b) total box office receipts?
2. Assume that, in its first year of release, the box office receipts for the movie total $320 million. What is the operating income to Panther from the movie in its first year?

4

2. Contract A $ 38,120,000
Contract B $69,200,000

3-48 CVP, cost structure differences, movie production (continuation of 3-47). Panther Productions is negotiating the next sequel to its Illinois Jones series. This negotiation is proving more difficult than for the original movie. There is a risk that the series may have peaked and the total box office receipts will drop. The budgeted production cost (excluding royalty payments) is $32 million. The agent negotiating for Harrison and Connelly proposes either of two contracts:

◆ Contract A. Fixed salary component of $50 million for both (combined) with no residual interest in the revenues.

◆ Contract B. Fixed salary component of $8 million for both (combined) plus a residual of 3% each of the revenues.

The promoter, Parimont Productions, will invest a minimum of $12 million of its own money, and because of its major role in the success of the last film, it will now be paid 18% of the revenues received from the total box office receipts. Panther continues to receive 65% of the total box office receipts (out of which comes the royalty payments).

REQUIRED

1. What is the breakeven point for Panther Productions expressed in terms of (a) revenues received by that company and (b) total box office receipts—for contracts A and B? Explain the difference between the breakeven points for contracts A and B.
2. Assume the sequel achieves $280 million in box office revenues. What is the operating income to Panther under each of the contracts? Comment on the results.

5

1. BEP 7,800 units

3-49 Multi-product breakeven, decision making. Bonavista Cribs manufactures baby cribs. It currently produces one model, the Surrey crib, and it is priced at $600. Variable manufacturing costs are $210 per unit and variable shipping costs are $60 per unit. Fixed costs are $2,574,000. In 2008, it sold 9,800 units of the Surrey crib. One of Bonavista's customers, Dover Corporation, has asked if Bonavista could manufacture a new style of crib, the Shilo, for 2009. Dover will pay $350 for the Shilo. The variable costs to produce the new crib are estimated to be $180 per unit and Dover will pay for the shipping. Bonavista has sufficient manufacturing capacity and will not incur any additional fixed costs. Bonavista estimates that in 2009, it will sell 10,000 units of Surrey and 4,000 units of Shilo.

The president of Bonavista checked the impact of accepting the Dover order on the breakeven sales revenues for 2009 and was surprised to find that the dollar sales revenues required to break even using the sales mix for 2009 appeared to increase. He was not sure that his numbers were correct, but if they were, he felt inclined to reject the Dover order. He has asked for your advice.

REQUIRED

1. Calculate the breakeven point in units and sales dollars for 2008.
2. Calculate the breakeven point in units and sales dollars for 2009 at the expected sales mix.
3. Explain why the breakeven points in sales dollars calculated in requirements 1 and 2 are different.
4. What would you advise the president to do? Support your recommendations.

3-50 Choosing between compensation plans, operating leverage. (CMA, adapted) Marston Corporation manufactures pharmaceutical products that are sold through a network of sales agents. The agents are paid a commission of 18% of sales. The income statement for the year ending December 31, 2008, under two scenarios, is as follows:

1. CM% using own sales agents 37%

CM% using own sales force 45%

Marston Corporation
Income Statement
For the Year Ending December 31, 2008

	Using Sales Agents		Using Own Sales Force	
Sales		$26,000,000		$26,000,000
Cost of goods sold				
Variable	$11,700,000		$11,700,000	
Fixed	2,870,000	14,570,000	2,870,000	14,570,000
Gross margin		11,430,000		11,430,000
Marketing costs				
Commissions	$ 4,680,000		$ 2,600,000	
Fixed costs	3,420,000	8,100,000	5,500,000	8,100,000
Operating income		$ 3,330,000		$ 3,330,000

Marston is considering hiring its own sales staff to replace the network of agents. Marston will pay its salespeople a commission of 10% and incur additional fixed costs of $2,080,000.

REQUIRED

1. Calculate Marston Corporation's 2008 contribution margin percentage, breakeven revenues, and degree of operating leverage under each of the two scenarios. (You will first have to recast the 2008 income statement assuming Marston had hired its own sales staff).
2. Describe the advantages and disadvantages of each type of sales alternative.
3. In 2009, Marston uses its own salespeople who demand a 15% commission. If all other cost behaviour patterns are unchanged, how much revenue must the salespeople generate in order to earn the same operating income as in 2008?

3-51 Special-order decision. Manitoba Production Corporation (MPC) specializes in the manufacture of one-litre plastic bottles. The plastic moulding machines are capable of producing 100 bottles per hour. The firm estimates that the variable cost of producing a plastic bottle is 25 cents. The bottles are sold for 55 cents each.

1. Additional income, $46,000

Management has been approached by a local toy company that would like the firm to produce a moulded plastic toy for it. The toy company is willing to pay $3.40 per unit for the toy. The unit variable cost to manufacture the toy will be $2.70. In addition, MPC would have to incur a cost of $24,000 to construct the mould required exclusively for this order. Because the toy uses more plastic and is of a more intricate shape than a bottle, a moulding machine can produce only 40 units per hour. The customer wants 100,000 units. Assume that MPC has a total capacity of 10,000 machine-hours available during the period in which the toy company wants delivery of the toys. The firm's fixed costs, *excluding* the costs to construct the toy mould, during the same period will be $220,000.

REQUIRED

1. Suppose the demand for its bottles is 750,000 units, and the special toy order has to be either taken in full or rejected totally. Should MPC accept the special toy order? Explain your answer.
2. Suppose the demand for its bottles is 850,000 units, and the special toy order has to be either taken in full or rejected totally. Should MPC accept the special toy order? Explain your answer.
3. Suppose the demand for its bottles is 900,000 units, and the special toy order has to be either taken in full or rejected totally. Should MPC accept the special toy order? Explain your answer.

3-52 CVP, sensitivity analysis. Technology of the Past (TOP) produces old-fashioned simple corkscrews. Last year was not a good year for sales but TOP expects the market to pick up this year. Last year's income statement showed

Sales revenues ($4 per corkscrew)	$40,000
Variable cost ($3 per corkscrew)	30,000
Contribution margin	10,000
Fixed cost	6,000
Operating income	$ 4,000

To take advantage of the anticipated growth in the market, TOP is considering various courses of action:

1. Do nothing. If TOP does nothing, it expects sales to increase by 10%.
2. Spend $2,000 on a new advertising campaign that is expected to increase sales by 50%.
3. Raise the price of the corkscrew to $5. This is expected to decrease sales quantities by 20%.
4. Redesign the classic corkscrew and increase the selling price to $6 while increasing the variable costs by $1 per unit. The sales level is not expected to change from last year.

REQUIRED
Evaluate each of the alternatives considered by TOP. What should TOP do?

3-53 Nonprofit institution. The City of Vancouver makes a $850,000 lump-sum budget appropriation to run a safe injection site for a year. All the appropriation is to be spent. The variable costs average $16 per patient visit. Fixed costs are $500,000 per year.

REQUIRED
1. Compute the number of patient visits that the budget allocation will cover.
2. Suppose the total budget for the following year is reduced by 10%. Fixed costs are to remain the same. The same level of service on each patient visit will be maintained. Compute the number of visits that could be provided in a year.
3. As in requirement 2, assume a budget reduction of 10%. Fixed costs are to remain the same. By how much would variable costs have to decline in order to provide the same number of visits?

3-54 CVP, nonprofit event planning. The Windsor Chamber of Commerce is planning its annual event. There are two possible plans:

a. Hold the event at a local hotel. The fixed rental cost would be $2,700 and the charge for meals would be $110 per person.
b. Hold the event at the University of Windsor. The fixed rental fee for the facility would be much higher at $7,000, and the Chamber would also spend another $500 in permits. However, the Chamber could use the local caterer and the per-unit charge for meals would drop to $75 per person.

    The Chamber of Commerce budgets $5,000 for administration and marketing. Entertainment will cost $4,000 regardless of the venue chosen. Tickets to the event will be $175 per person. All other costs, such as door prizes and drinks, will be paid for by corporate sponsors.

REQUIRED
1. Compute the breakeven point for each plan in terms of tickets sold.
2. For each plan, compute the operating income of the event (a) if 100 people attend, (b) if 250 people attend. Comment on your results.
3. At what level of tickets sold will the two plans have the same operating income?

3-55 Review of Chapters 2 and 3. For each of the following independent cases, find the unknowns designated by the capital letters.

	Case 1	Case 2
Direct materials used	$H	$96,000
Direct manufacturing labour	45,000	60,000
Variable marketing, distribution, customer service, and administrative costs	K	T
Fixed manufacturing overhead	I	30,000
Fixed marketing, distribution, customer service, and administrative costs	J	40,000
Gross margin	50,000	84,000

Finished goods inventory, January 1, 2009	0	12,000
Finished goods inventory, December 31, 2009	0	17,000
Contribution margin (dollars)	72,000	V
Revenues	200,000	300,000
Direct materials inventory, January 1, 2009	18,000	8,700
Direct materials inventory, December 31, 2009	12,000	W
Variable manufacturing overhead	13,500	X
Work in process, January 1, 2009	0	10,800
Work in process, December 31, 2009	0	10,800
Purchases of direct materials	56,000	97,500
Breakeven point (in dollars)	120,000	Y
Cost of goods manufactured	G	U
Operating income (loss)	L	(15,000)

3-56 CVP under uncertainty. (J. Patell) In your new position as supervisor of product introduction, you have to decide on a pricing strategy for a talking doll specialty product with the following cost structure:

3 4

1. a. Probability of breaking even, 66.6%

Variable costs per unit	$ 60
Fixed costs	$240,000

The dolls are manufactured upon receipt of orders, so the inventory levels are insignificant. Your market research assistant is very enthusiastic about probability models and has presented the results of his price analysis in the following form:

a. If you set the selling price at $120 per unit, the probability distribution of revenues is uniform between $360,000 and $720,000. Under this distribution, there is a 0.50 probability of equalling or exceeding revenues of $540,000.

b. If you lower the selling price to $84 per unit, the distribution remains uniform, but it shifts up to the $720,000–$1,080,000 range. Under this distribution, there is a 0.50 probability of equalling or exceeding revenues of $900,000.

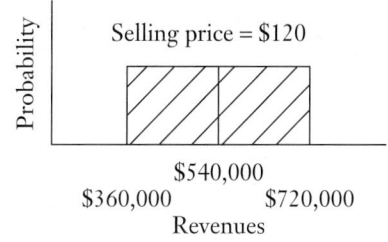
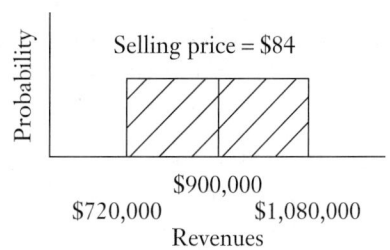

REQUIRED
1. This is your first big contract and, above all, you want to show an operating income. You decide to select the strategy that maximizes the probability of breaking even or earning a positive operating income.
   a. What is the probability of at least breaking even with a selling price of $120 per unit?
   b. What is the probability of at least breaking even with a selling price of $84 per unit?
2. Your assistant suggests that maximum expected operating income might be a better objective to pursue. Which pricing strategy would result in the higher expected operating income? (Use the expected revenues under each pricing strategy when making expected operating-income computations.)

3-57 Governance, CVP analysis. Athabaska Ltd. produces a lens used for webcams. Summary data from its year 2008 income statement are as follows:

3

1. BE revenues, $8,478,261

Revenues	$8,000,000
Variable costs	4,320,000
Fixed costs	3,900,000
Operating income	$ (220,000)

The president of Athabaska, Roberta Klein, is very concerned about the company's operations. She has discussed the situation with the Operations Manager, Roland Bell, and the controller, Clara Walton.

After two weeks, Roland returns with a proposal. After researching various component parts, he advises that he can reduce variable costs to 48% of revenues by changing both the direct materials and the production process. The downside of this proposal is that the new direct material (although cheaper) results in more waste and is more toxic to the environment. Currently, waste produced in the production process does not require any special treatment and is disposed of normally. Roland points out that there are no current specific laws governing the disposal of this waste created by the use of the new material, and therefore production costs can be cut by using this material. Clara is concerned that this would expose the company to potential environmental liabilities. She believes that these potential future costs need to be estimated and included in the analysis. Roland disagrees and reiterates that there are no laws being violated and replies, "There is some possibility that we may have to incur costs in the future, but if we bring it up now, this proposal will not go through because our senior management always assumes these costs to be larger than they are. The market is very tough and we are in danger of shutting down the company. We don't want all our colleagues to lose their jobs. The only reason our competitors are making money is because they are doing exactly what I am proposing."

REQUIRED
1. Calculate Athabaska's breakeven revenues for the year 2008.
2. Calculate Athabaska's breakeven revenues if variable costs are 48% of revenues.
3. Calculate Athabaska's operating income in 2008 if variable costs had been 48% of sales.
4. What should Roberta Klein do?

3-58 Short-run pricing, budgeting, capacity constraints. Tillsonburg Dairy, maker of specialty cheeses, produces a soft cheese from the milk of Holstein cows raised on a special corn-based diet. One kilogram of soft cheese, which has a contribution margin of $8, requires 4 litres of milk. A well-known gourmet restaurant has asked Tillsonburg to produce 2,000 kilograms of a hard cheese from the same milk of Holstein cows. Knowing that the dairy has sufficient unused capacity, the owner of the dairy calculates the cost of making one kilogram of the desired hard cheese as follows:

Milk (10 litres × $1.50 per litre)	$ 15.00
Direct manufacturing labour	5.00
Variable manufacturing overhead costs	3.00
Fixed manufacturing overhead costs allocated	6.00
Total manufacturing costs	$ 29.00

REQUIRED
1. Suppose Tillsonburg can acquire all the Holstein milk that it needs. What is the minimum price per kilogram it should charge for the hard cheese?
2. Now suppose that Holstein milk is in short supply. Every kilogram of hard cheese produced by Tillsonburg will reduce the quantity of soft cheese that it can make and sell. What is the minimum price per kilogram it should charge to produce the hard cheese?

3-59 Uncertainty. Chester Steel Fabrication (CSF) is considering submitting a bid to construct a metal bridge for a new highway. The company controller thinks that a bid of $2,500,000 will cover both the costs associated with the project, and the opportunity costs of the equipment and labour that would be used on the project. The company president figures a bid of $2,500,000 is sure to get the job and she intends to bid that amount. However, she is wondering about some of the cost estimates used in the controller's report.

After some study, the president determined that the costs associated with the proposal could range from $1,800,000 to $3,000,000. A table outlining the range of costs and probabilities is presented below:

Expected Cost	Probability
$1,800,000	0.10
2,250,000	0.30
2,500,000	0.40
3,000,000	0.20

REQUIRED
1. Create the decision table.
2. Assuming the objective is to maximize profits, what is the optimal decision? Show all calculations.

3-60 Governance, CVP, cost analysis. Ahmed Diba is the controller of the Body Products Division of World Wide Drugs (WWD). It is located in Winnipeg, which is also the head-quarters of WWD. Diba is helping develop a proposal for a new product to be called Vital Hair. This product is a cream to be rubbed on the scalp to restore hair growth. Cheryl Kelly, president of the division, and Diba are scheduled to make a presentation to the WWD execu-tive committee on the expected profitability of Vital Hair. The fixed costs associated with the development, production, and marketing of Vital Hair are $25,000,000. Each customer will pay a doctor $98 per monthly treatment, of which $68 is paid to WWD. Diba estimates WWD's variable costs per treatment to be $28.50. Included in this $28.50 is $9.25 for poten-tial product litigation costs. Kelly is livid at Diba for including the $9.25 estimate. She argues that it is imperative to get the R&D funds approved (and quickly) and that any number that increases the breakeven point reduces the likelihood of the Vital Hair project being approved. She notes that WWD has had few successful lawsuits against it, in contrast to some recent "horrendous" experiences of competitors with breast implant products. Moreover, she is furious that Diba put the $9.25 amount in writing. "How do we know there will be any litiga-tion problem?" She suggests Diba redo the report excluding the $9.25 litigation risk cost estimate. "Put it on the chalkboard in the executive committee room, if you insist, but don't put it in the report sent to the committee before the meeting. You can personally raise the issue at the executive committee meeting and have a full and frank discussion."

Diba takes Kelly's "advice." He reports a variable cost of $19.25 per treatment in the proposal. Although he feels uneasy about this, he is comforted by the fact that he will flag the $9.25 amount to the executive committee in his forthcoming oral presentation.

One month later, Kelly walks into Diba's office. She is in a buoyant mood and announces she has just come back from an executive committee meeting that approved the Vital Hair proposal. Diba asks why he was not invited to the meeting. Kelly says the meeting was held in Toronto, and she decided to save the division money by going alone. She then says to Diba that it "was now time to get behind the new venture and help make it the success the committee and her team members believe it will be."

REQUIRED
1. What is the breakeven point (in units of monthly treatments) when WWD's variable costs (a) include the $9.25 estimate and (b) exclude the $9.25 estimate for potential product litigation costs?
2. Should Diba have excluded the $9.25 estimate in his report to the executive committee of WWD? Explain your answer.
3. What should Diba do in response to Kelly's decision to make the Vital Hair presentation on her own?

3-61 Contribution approach. Air Delta is about to introduce a daily round-trip flight from New York to Los Angeles and is determining how it should price its round-trip tickets.

The market research group segments the market into business and pleasure travellers. It provides the following information on the effects of two different prices on the number of seats expected to be sold and the variable cost per ticket, including the commission paid to travel agents.

		Number of Seats Expected to Be Sold	
Ticket Price	Variable Cost/Ticket	Business	Pleasure
$ 500	$ 80	200	100
2,000	180	190	20

Pleasure travellers start their travel during one week, spend at least one weekend at their destination, and return the following week or thereafter. Business travellers usually start and complete their travel within the same work week. They do not stay over weekends.

Assume that round trip fuel costs are fixed at $24,000, and that the fixed costs allocated to the round trip flight for airplane lease costs, ground services, and flight-crew salaries total $188,000.

REQUIRED
1. If you could charge different prices to business travellers and pleasure travellers, would you? Show your computations.
2. Explain the key factor or factors for your answer in requirement 1.
3. How might Air Delta implement price discrimination? That is, what plan could the airline formulate so that business travellers and pleasure travellers each pay the price desired by the airline?

3-62 Deciding where to produce. (CMA, adapted) Domestic Engines Company produces the same power generators in two plants, a newly renovated, automated plant in Peona, and an older, less automated plant in Modine. The following data are available for the two plants:

	Peona		Modine	
Selling price		$150.00		$150.00
Variable manufacturing cost per unit	$72.00		$88.00	
Fixed manufacturing cost per unit	30.00		15.00	
Variable marketing and distribution cost per unit	14.00		14.00	
Fixed marketing and distribution cost per unit	19.00		14.50	
Total cost per unit		135.00		131.50
Operating income per unit		$ 15.00		$ 18.50
Production rate per day		400 units		240 days
Normal annual capacity usage		240 days		240 days
Maximum annual capacity		300 days		300 days

All unit fixed costs are calculated based on a normal year of 240 working days. When the number of working days exceeds 240, variable manufacturing costs increase by $3.00 per unit in Peona and $8.00 per unit in Modine.

Domestic Engines is expected to produce and sell 192,000 generators during the coming year. Wanting to maximize the higher unit profit at Modine, Domestic Engines' production manager has decided to manufacture 96,000 units at each plant. This production plan results in Modine operating at capacity (320 units per day × 300 days) and Peona operating at its normal volume (400 units per day × 240 days).

REQUIRED

1. Determine the breakeven point for the Peona and Modine plants in units.
2. Calculate the operating income that would result from the division production manager's plan to produce 96,000 units at each plant.
3. Determine how the production of the 192,000 units should be allocated between Peona and Modine to maximize operating income for Domestic Engines. Show your calculations.

COLLABORATIVE LEARNING CASE

3-63 CVP, theatre planning. *The Globe and Mail* has just published a stinging criticism of the inflation in theatre ticket prices. The article was titled, "The $100 Price Gouge: Is $150 Next?" This article has increased the concerns of a group planning Toronto's future productions. It had been planning for a $100 price for all of its seats. The up-front fixed costs to open are $12 million. Production and operating costs are $550,000 per week. The theatre has capacity for 2,000 seats with six performances per week planned. Approximately 75 seats per night are held as complimentary house seats.

INSTRUCTIONS

Form groups of two or more students to complete the following requirements.

REQUIRED

Your group is charged with exploring ways of improving the profitability of the venture and of reducing its breakeven point. Areas you should explore (but are not restricted to) include the following:

a. Increase the number of shows per week. The cast is under contract for up to eight shows a week for a fixed amount that is included in the $550,000.
b. Provide the two star performers with a $40,000 weekly salary and a percentage of revenues or operating income instead of the fixed $70,000 per week each is budgeted to receive.
c. Change the single $100 pricing policy. Whereas all seats in the 2,000-person auditorium have unobstructed views, a recent theatre reviewer referred to the back rows of the balcony section as "binocular land" (e.g., 400 seats at $125; 525 seats at $100; and 1,075 seats at $75—the policy is your choice).
d. The assumptions about attendance changes and so on (i.e., assume varying levels of attendance—80%, 90%, 100%).

Job Costing Services and Goods

What Does It Cost to Do the Job?

In the last decade, on average each year 7,445 wildfires have destroyed 2.5 million hectares of Canadian wilderness at an average annual cost of $417 million to suppress. A ferocious force of nature, wildfires killed three firefighters in 2003, two more in 2004, and three in 2006. The government estimated the financial value of 1.7 million hectares lost in the 6,518 wildfires of 2007 at approximately $3,000 per hectare or $5.1 billion. If each wildfire is considered a job, then on average each job has a cost of $56,011 and each hectare destroyed has a cost of $167. Job costing procedures refine and improve estimated average cost to focus on how best to control input costs.

After studying this chapter, you should be able to

1 Identify the job costing process, and the procedures of job cost allocation and assignment

2 Apply knowledge of direct and indirect cost pools to calculate cost-allocation rates and assign costs to a service job

3 Apply knowledge of direct and indirect cost pools to calculate cost-allocation rates and assign costs to manufacturing departments

4 Explain the usefulness of normal and actual costing procedures based on material and efficient causes of costs

5 Apply management-accounting logic to underallocation and overallocation of indirect costs arising from the use of normal costing procedures

Sources: Wildfire suppression data used throughout this chapter are from the websites http://ciffc.cricketworks.com/images/stories/pdf/2006canadareport.pdf and http://www.ciffc.ca, accessed on November 17, 2008.

The underlying assumption of this textbook is that cost identification and control are core competencies required of any successful business. If these are primary goals, then the strategy is called *cost leadership*. The idea is that the output cost equals the sum of input costs. Therefore, by identifying and controlling the material and efficient causes of costs—the inputs—the output cost can be controlled. Businesses must charge customers a high-enough price to cover all costs plus some reasonable profit to remain healthy. None of the costs are recovered until a sale is made. Not-for-profit, governmental, and non-governmental organizations (NGOs) must also account for the total costs of producing their goods and services. These organizations also must explain to donors or taxpayers, respectively, why the costs of service provision in a specific time period exceeded either the donations or the tax revenue of the provider.

In Chapter 2, the specific *cost object* was a cellphone output unit, a good. But, a **cost object** is *anything* for which it is desirable to measure the costs, inputs, activities, processes, clients, salespeople, business functions, departments where activities occur, and processes (see Chapter 17). In this chapter, we focus on a cost object we call a *job*. Process costing differs in its techniques from job costing because these are two different types of cost objects (see Chapter 2).

The **job costing system** focuses on management accounting methods to systematically link all input costs to a distinct output unit or set of units referred to as a **job**. One underlying assumption is that each job is distinguishable in some way from another because jobs either consume different resources, different quantities of the same resources, or both. One example is a job of installing a new luxury spa in a home in contrast to a job installing new faucets in a kitchen. Each job could be done by the same plumbing company, but the costs of direct materials and the costs of labour would be far higher to install the spa than the faucets. Another example would be the job of a normal audit of a long-time client in contrast to a forensic audit undertaken because fraud is suspected. Each of these services could be provided by the same accounting firm, but the cost would be far higher for the forensic audit. Notice two important things. First, it does not matter if the sale is a product or a service or some combination of both—it's called a job. Second, the jobs are different.

The **process costing system** focuses on how to average the prime and conversion costs of identical units in both finished goods and work-in-process inventories. The quantities in inventory cannot be observed and measured because to do so would interrupt a continuous process and destroy the units progressing through work-in-process. Please return to Chapter 2 to review cost classification methods if you do not recall what the terminology used in these two definitions means. One reason it is important to cost either jobs or processes is that the managers must justify how well they both understand and can control either the job or process costs. One example is the process of pasteurizing raw milk where all raw milk must reach a specific temperature before it is drawn off into containers. If the pasteurization is interrupted to try to measure either the work-in-process or observe the temperature, then the safety of the final product is compromised. The law requires all the work-in-process be destroyed to protect consumers. Notice two distinct features of process costing systems, compared to job costing systems. First, the process cannot be interrupted. Second, the output units are identical to one another.

The more clearly and accurately costs can be assigned to a job:

- ◆ the greater is the understanding of the material and efficient causes of costs of specific jobs and the better both the causes and costs can be controlled
- ◆ the more readily either a current or budgeted price can be adjusted to ensure it meets the value proposition of customers and generates reasonable profit, or achieves breakeven in not-for-profit agencies
- ◆ the more reliably managers can forecast (budget) the price of a job or a process to compete successfully for future job contracts
- ◆ the more predictable are the outcomes of decisions about what types of jobs should be either accepted or rejected in future based on their forecasted profitability.

In a job costing system, the cost object is called a job. A job is a generic term referring to a product, service, or some combination of both. Job costing matters when jobs differ in their consumption of resources. For example, a roofing company will have to work on roofs of different sizes, using different materials (shingles of clay, cedar, asphalt, tar and gravel, or copper), taking different amounts of labour time and requiring different machinery. An accounting partnership will supply audit services to its clients but each client will require different levels of accounting expertise and different amounts of time spent by people with different skills. It is very important for PricewaterhouseCoopers (PWC) to understand what it costs to audit Research in Motion (RIM) compared to Barrick Gold in order to price each audit profitably. Reasonable job costing permits PWC to estimate in advance what a job would cost and use this in a budget. It also permits PWC to bid on a new job and be assured a successful bid will also be profitable.

Each job will generate some readily traceable direct costs. A **direct cost** is one that is readily and economically traced to a cost object. The direct costs, however, are usually a small proportion of total costs. The indirect costs are not readily traceable and yet still must be included to ensure all costs are recovered for the job, plus some profit. Financial accountants must classify and report costs according to the type of transaction, and there is a big difference between an individual transaction and an entire job. But for management-accounting purposes, these same transaction costs recorded in the general ledger accounts are reclassified and recorded for each job. Instead of general ledger accounts, management accountants accumulate costs in cost pools but use a different logic that depends on the job costing system itself, not GAAP. A **cost pool** is a group of costs, and the logic of the grouping is intended to help identify and control costs of each job.

The cost pools decided upon by a business will comprise one essential part of its job costing system. Gathering the cost data can be done using the general ledger accounts, various scanning and direct-input technologies, and, for smaller businesses, even manual records. The other part of the job costing system is nonfinancial data indicating the material and efficient causes of the costs wherever it is economically feasible to do so. A variety of *source documents* are needed to verify both the causes and the costs per job, not only for the company but also for the client and Canada Revenue Agency (CRA). A **source document** is an original record that supports journal entries in an accounting system, such as a time sheet for an employee where the hours worked per job are recorded as well as the cost per hour.

For each job, a **job cost record** (or **job cost sheet**) is the document where the costs are recorded and accumulated. Jobs usually require some type of direct materials input. The materials are ordered on a **materials requisition record** and the requisition records the job for which the materials are needed. The actual quantity requisitioned, its actual cost per unit, and the total cost must also appear on the job cost record. While most businesses use computers to record and verify the requisition and receipt of inputs, our illustration shows examples of a manual record in Exhibit 4–1, Panels A and B, respectively. The sum of the total costs on all materials-requisition records for one job will provide the total direct materials cost for the job. Of course for some professional services, direct materials would be a very small portion of total costs.

Panel C illustrates a manual record of a direct labour source document. The direct labour costs are tracked electronically or manually on a **labour time record**. The type of labour, quantity of time, unit labour rate, and total cost of labour are recorded for each job. In an accounting firm such as PWC, the managing partner would track labour per client as would the junior auditor. The total cost for each job would depend on the quantity of each type of labour hours consumed by each client. The same is true of an auto-repair shop. The direct labour hours for repairs differ. Some repairs require highly skilled and highly paid labour while others do not.

There is often machinery time associated with both service provision and manufacturing. But an audit firm or a legal firm will also spend hours photocopying and most photocopiers permit the electronic input of various codes. It is not difficult to enter the time and job code to ensure these machine hours are recorded per job. In a

EXHIBIT 4-1
Source Documents at Robinson Company: Job Cost Record, Materials Requisition Record, and Labour Time Record

PANEL A:

JOB COST RECORD

JOB NO:	WPP 298		CUSTOMER:	Western Pulp and Paper	
Date Started:	Feb. 7, 2009		Date Completed:	March 1, 2009	

DIRECT MATERIALS

Date Received	Materials Requisition No.	Part No.	Quantity Used	Unit Cost	Total Costs
Feb. 7, 2009	2009: 198	MB 468–A	8	$14	$112
Feb. 7, 2009	2009: 199	TB 267–F	12	63	756
					•
					•
					•
Total					$4,606

DIRECT MANUFACTURING LABOUR

Period Covered	Labour Time Record No.	Employee No.	Hours Used	Hourly Rate	Total Costs
Feb. 7–13, 2009	LT 232	551-87-3076	25	$18	$450
Feb. 7–13, 2009	LT 247	287-31-4671	5	19	95
					•
					•
					•
Total					$1,579

MANUFACTURING OVERHEAD*

Date	Cost Pool Category	Allocation Base Dir Manuf.	Allocation Base Units Used	Allocation Base Rate	Total Costs
Dec. 31, 2009	Manufacturing	Labour-Hours	88 Hours	$45	$3,960
					•
					•
					•
Total					$3,960
TOTAL JOB COST					$10,145

PANEL B:

MATERIALS REQUISITION RECORD

Materials Requisition Record No:			2009:198	
Job No: WPP 298	Date: Feb. 7, 2009			

Part No.	Part Description	Quantity	Unit Cost	Total Cost
MB 468-A	Metal Brackets	8	$14	$112

Issued By: *B. Clyde*   Date: Feb. 7, 2009
Received By: *L. Daley*   Date: Feb. 7, 2009

PANEL C:

LABOUR TIME RECORD

Labour Time Record No: _____ LT 232 _____

Employee Name: __G.L. Cook__   Employee No: __551-87-3076__

Employee Classification Code: __Grade 3 Machinist__

Hourly Rate: $18

Week Start: ___Feb. 7, 2009___   Week End: ___Feb. 13, 2009___

Job. No.	M	T	W	Th	F	S	Su	Total
WPP 298	4	8	3	6	4	0	0	25
JL 256	3	0	4	2	3	0	0	12
Maintenance	1	0	1	0	1	0	0	3
Total	8	8	8	8	8	0	0	40

Supervisor: *R. Stuart*   Date: Feb. 14, 2009

*Robinson Company uses a single manufacturing overhead cost pool. The use of multiple overhead cost pools would mean multiple entries in the "Manufacturing Overhead" section of its job cost record.

manufacturing environment, for example car assembly, robots both weld and check the quality of welds on a vehicle. The type of vehicle determines the location of the welds and thus each job is coded into the machine before the welding and robotic quality-control hours are spent.

For services such as firefighting, direct materials would be a far larger proportion of total costs than for a legal or audit firm. Helicopters, special fire suppressant chemicals, fireproof garments, fuels, and so on are costs that legal and audit firms do not incur. It is similar in manufacturing; for manufacturers of electronic devices, the direct costs of computer chips can be very large compared to the costs of labour for assembly and packaging. Note in Exhibit 4–1 the details of the job number, the date, the type of materials and labour, and other data used to assign indirect costs. In Panel A, identifying direct costs is straightforward because that is what they are called. Manufacturing Overhead in this panel refers to indirect inventoriable costs. Please review material in Chapter 2 to refresh your understanding of these two terms. Remember that the costs recorded on these source documents are also accumulated in the financial accounting system in full compliance with GAAP. This is because inventoriable costs comprise COGS.

The machine hours (MH), direct manufacturing labour-hours (DMLH), and direct materials (DM) are readily traced. This is not the case with indirect inventoriable costs of materials and labour, for example lubricants and rework, respectively. If the job is to be reasonably costed, these indirect costs must also be recorded, then assigned to the job in a way that reasonably reflects differences in how each job consumed the indirect costs. Exhibit 4–2 illustrates a job costing system whereby the different rates of consumption of indirect inputs can be linked to different jobs.

Exhibit 4–2 illustrates the complex set of decisions required by the job costing process. Identifying the job initiates a cascade of decisions, illustrated in Exhibit 4–2, some of which are made simultaneously. That is why the arrows do not begin in segment 1. The goal is to develop a set of average rates per input unit. Each type of job consumes different quantities of inputs, but it is too expensive to trace the inputs other than direct materials and labour. Direct materials and labour are often used as indirect cost allocation bases. Some businesses will prefer to identify cost pools, then the nonfinancial quantities of inputs provided in their information system, while others will do the reverse. The order of the decisions is irrelevant provided the elements of the job costing process are identified.

Cost-effectiveness will determine how much cost and quantity detail is available and how much more will be demanded as managers develop a reasonable job costing process. What is a certainty is that not all costs can be economically traced and some costs will be collected into indirect cost pools. One difficult decision managers will have to make is which of the quantities of inputs will be the best way to estimate the indirect costs per job. The cost pools are called *indirect* cost pools precisely because any change to their financial value cannot be directly explained by any change in quantity of a specific input consumed. For a manufacturing example, the indirect cost pool(s) would be referred to as manufacturing overhead (MOH). Another set of indirect cost pools may be identified for period costs, and the indirect period cost-allocation rate would be calculated using a different total direct input quantity from that used for MOH (see Chapter 14). For services, however, very often there is no MOH because there is no inventoriable product. The indirect cost pool(s) comprises period costs.

EXHIBIT 4-2
A Job Costing System

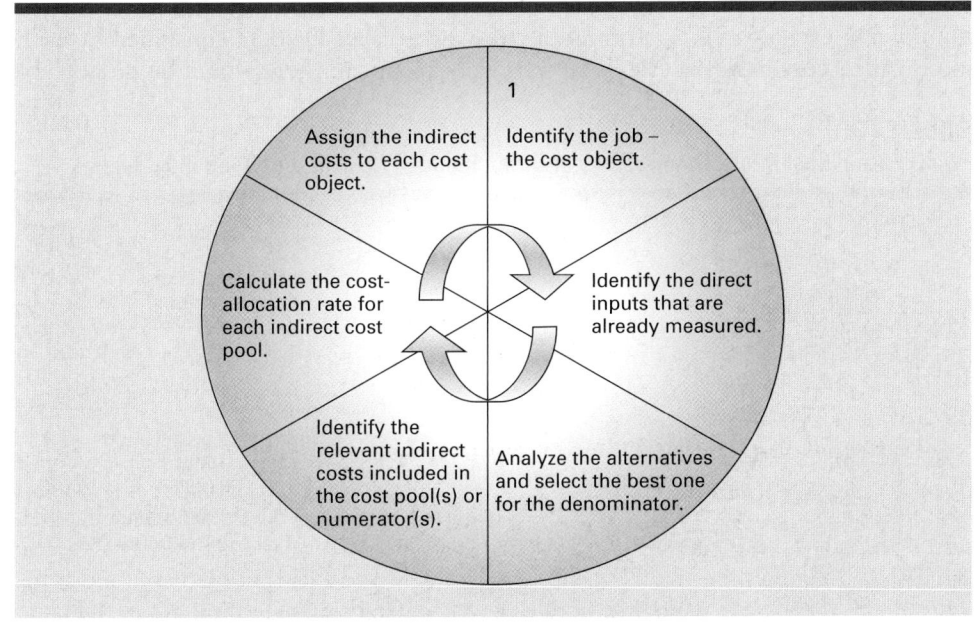

Usually managers already have a measure of an input common to all jobs, such as either DMLH or MH. These quantities, called a **cost-allocation base**, often provide a reasonable way to calculate an indirect cost-allocation rate used to distribute or *assign* indirect costs out of the cost pool to each job. When the cost object is a specific client, product, or job, the cost-allocation base is called a **cost-application base**. The **cost-allocation rate** is calculated by dividing the indirect cost pool by a quantity of total direct inputs. The division is sometimes called either **cost allocation** or **cost application**. This is the mechanical aspect of cost allocation: indirect cost pools are divided by quantities of direct total input to obtain an average rate per unit of input. The average rate per unit of input is the cost-allocation rate.

If the cost pool is a group of direct costs, then the result will be a **direct cost-allocation rate**. If the cost pool is a group of indirect costs, then the result will be an **indirect cost-allocation rate**. As illustrated in Exhibit 4–3, the identical quantity of direct total units consumed is the divisor used to calculate two different cost-allocation rates. Assume all direct manufacturing labour costs have been accumulated into one direct cost pool. The quantity of DMLH is also known. The MOH costs have also all been accumulated into one cost pool. Dividing the direct cost pool by the DMLH will give a direct labour cost-allocation rate. A business would make this choice if there were several different types of labour but the actual labour cost rates differed very little and the people working on different jobs were easily interchangeable.

Managers identify the MOH cost pool (supervisor salaries; utilities; labour from custodial, maintenance, security, and quality control activities; property tax; and so on). Exactly what costs are included will depend on each business. For example, managers could decide to group all fixed costs (e.g., supervisor and quality control salaries, taxes, insurance) in one cost pool and all variable costs (e.g., maintenance, security and custodial labour, supplies, utilities) in another. They could also decide to group all MOH in one cost pool. If period costs were not significant, managers might even decide to include them into a single indirect cost pool with MOH. Job costing systems will serve the needs of each business.

After examining all their choices, Exhibit 4–3 assumes managers decided that DMLH was the best denominator to use to calculate an indirect cost-allocation rate. The MOH cost pool and the direct manufacturing labour cost pool will never be equal; therefore, the two cost-allocation rates will never be equal even though the same denominator was used. For simplicity, all MOH costs have been grouped into one indirect cost pool. The green indirect cost pool is larger than the direct manufacturing labour cost pool, and this is realistic. The quantity of direct inputs is identical. Indirect costs as a proportion of total costs are many times larger than direct costs. The green colour indicates that all operating expenses, both inventoriable and period costs, are in a single indirect cost pool.

The cost pools must now be separated among the different jobs according to the different quantities of input each job consumed. This mechanical procedure of multiplying each cost-allocation rate by the quantity of DMLH consumed by each job is called **cost assignment**. If all jobs were identical, there would be no need to

EXHIBIT 4-3

Two Different Cost Pools, One Quantity of Direct Inputs: Two Different Allocation Rates

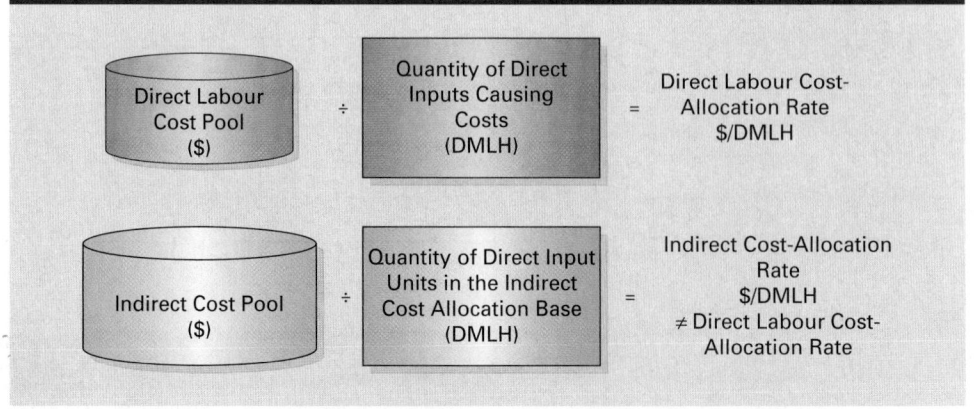

assign costs—each job cost would be identical. It must be the case that the quantity of the indirect input consumed differs from job to job for it to be sensible to assign proportions of the indirect cost pool to each job.

In practice, as illustrated in Exhibit 4–1, many businesses trace DMLH, DM, and MH to each job. This is sensible when jobs require different types and quantities of labour, materials, and machines with different costs. The costs do not need to be assigned because actual costs are traced to each job. **Actual costing** enables tracing direct costs to each job by multiplying each actual unit direct cost rate by the quantity of the direct input used. Managers have at least three denominators from which to choose when they calculate indirect cost-allocation rates. This provides opportunities to improve the accuracy of indirect cost-allocation rates at the cost of a more complex (and costly) job costing system.

ASSESS YOUR MASTERY

To check your understanding of the material in Learning Objective ❶, go to the *Mastery Questions* section at the end of this chapter and complete Learning Objective ❶ questions 1, 2, and 3.

MyAccountingLab

JOB COSTING A SERVICE

Apply knowledge of direct and indirect cost pools to calculate cost-allocation rates and assign costs for a service ❷

This section begins with how to identify and calculate relevant costs per job for a not-for-profit government service. The next section will show how to identify and calculate the relevant costs per job for manufactured goods produced by a for-profit business. The output cost object is referred to generically as a job. For the government service example, the job is a suppressed wildfire. Wildfires differ in size, destruction, and resources required to suppress them. About 45% of wildfires start from lightning strikes but cause 81% of the destruction. Only 3% of wildfires exceed 200 hectares in size but they destroy 97% of the average 2.5 million hectares annually.

Firefighters are a direct labour resource common to every job but not to every business function that comprises the service of wildfire suppression (see Exhibit 4-4). The direct and indirect costs of each business function are not identical. The total relevant input costs, however, will equal the total relevant cost per job. Wildfire

EXHIBIT 4-4
Accumulating Relevant Direct and Indirect Costs per Input for Business Functions and Assigning Them to a Suppressed Wildfire

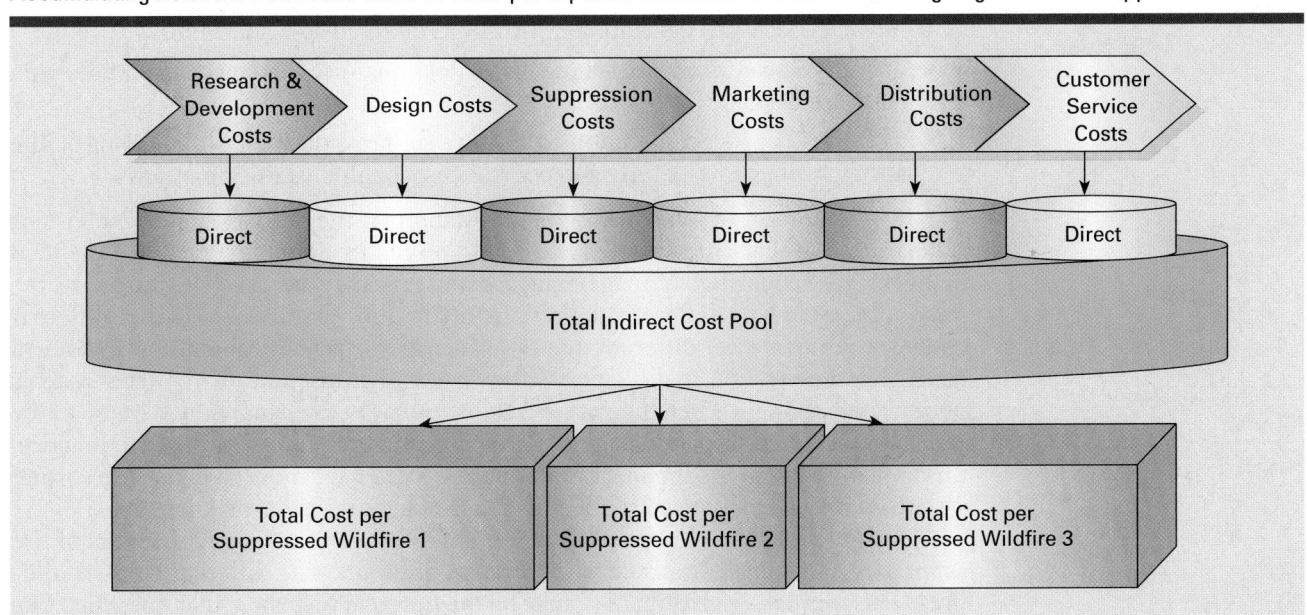

suppression is the core function or service in the same sense that production is the core function for a manufacturer, so it is shown in blue in Exhibit 4-4.

Exhibit 4-4 expands on the business functions of Exhibit 2-1 (p. 36) to illustrate the ideal costing procedures for direct and indirect costs of inputs. Except for wildfire suppression being the core function (rather than production being the core function for a manufacturer), Exhibit 4-4 shows that the business functions for a not-for-profit government service are no different than those for a manufacturer. The government service of wildfire suppression includes research and development to improve understanding of fire behaviour, improve prevention, improve communication of fire crises, and improve suppression methods. New firefighting processes are designed as new technology emerges. The production function is the activity of wildfire suppression. Marketing includes federal and provincial government websites informing Canadians, whose tax dollars fund this service, about the effectiveness and efficiency of the fire suppression service, as well as the devastation and loss of value caused by wildfires. The government also distributes brochures informing people how to prevent fires reduce their potential loss from wildfires. As an essential customer service, there is also a two-way real-time communication of wildfire information.

Tax dollars are the revenue to fund the provision of all the business functions that combine to form this service. Notice in Exhibit 4-4 that there are both direct costs (those that can be readily and economically traced to a cost object) and indirect costs, which cannot. Indirect costs are a larger proportion of total input costs than are direct costs for most services.

The costs of fighting and suppressing wildfires can be assigned to the job, defined as a single wildfire. Exhibit 4–4 illustrates how the direct suppression cost pool and the other indirect costs pools could be assigned across three different wildfires. The box sizes differ at the bottom of the diagram to show that wildfires differ in their costs of suppression. The average cost per wildfire suppressed was calculated based on the following facts. Total average annual input costs from all business functions are accumulated in a single cost pool. If the output unit is a wildfire, then the average unit cost is $56,011 per wildfire ($417 million ÷ 7,445 wildfires = $56,011 per wildfire).

Exhibit 4–5 illustrates the costs of wildfire suppression per job when the job is defined as a hectare of woodlands lost to each wildfire. If the output unit is hectares, then the average unit cost is $167/hectare ($417 million ÷ 2.5 million hectares = $167 per hectare). If, on average, the financial value of a lost hectare of wilderness habitat is $30,000 per hectare, then Canadians are obtaining a very cost-effective service. What is not considered in this approach:

◆ some wildfires are more expensive than others to suppress (production function)

◆ most research and development (R&D) is directed at large wildfires

◆ quantity of wildfires varies annually as does quantity of hectares lost, but many costs are fixed

◆ an input cost object common to wildfire suppression (the job) may not be the best cost object to identify and control costs of all business functions

It is important in job costing to understand that the definition of the job is not standardized in the same way that the definition of, for example, revenue, is defined in financial accounting. Management accountants may be asked to calculate the same job costs using different definitions of the job. One reason is that different costs per output answer different questions managers may have about how to control costs. The task is not as difficult as it once was, because automated data systems permit management accountants to readily identify the individual costs to be assigned to each cost pool depending on the information managers need. In practice, this implies that a single organization or business can have more than one job costing system approach customized to meet its management decision-making needs.

Imagine that the citizens of British Columbia whose taxes pay the costs of fire suppression are most concerned with the costs of suppressing different types of wildfires. The approach in Exhibit 4–5 may be the best one to answer that question. The cost of lost hectares for Wildfire 1 may be lower because it was readily accessible by road, whereas Wildfire 2 may have been on a mountain and required helicopters and planes to deliver the fire suppressants to quell the blaze. The lower cost was caused

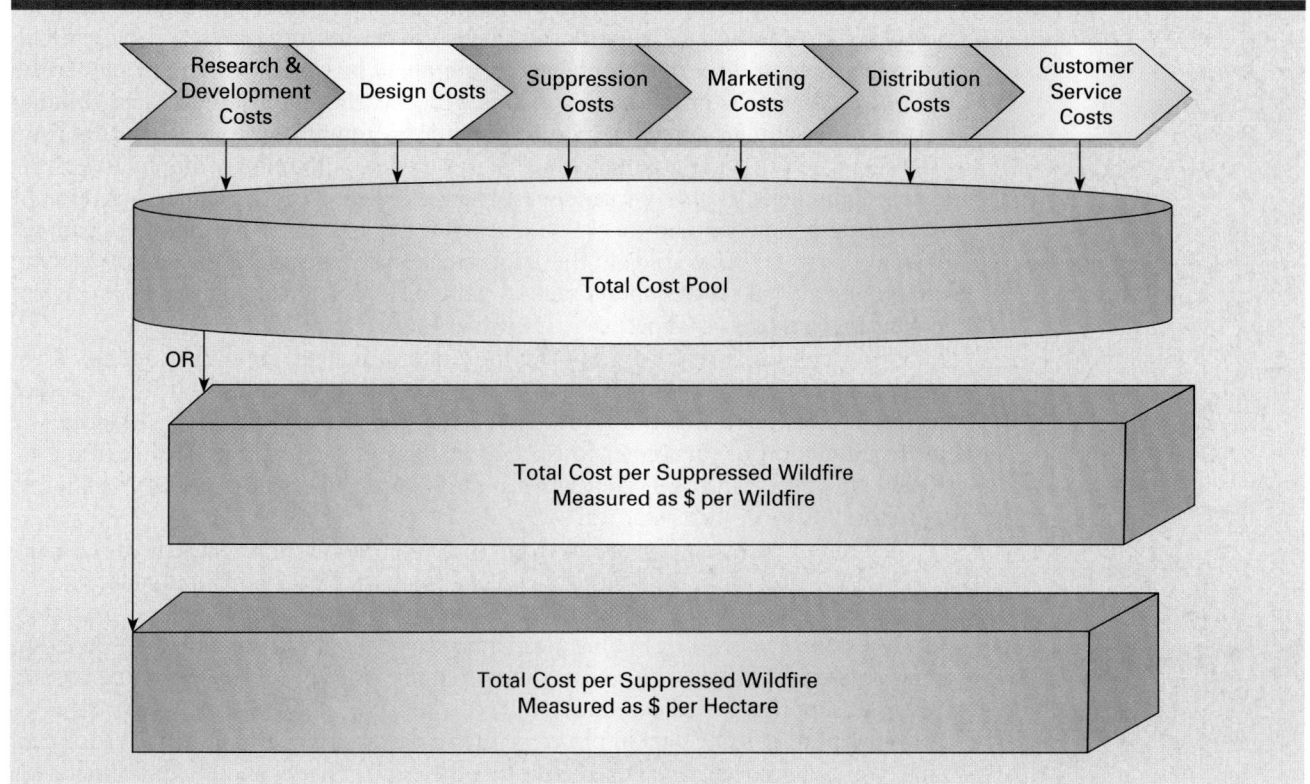

by the location of the fire, although many more hectares may have been destroyed than for Wildfire 2. The numerator or size of the total cost pool was smaller for Wildfire 1 than Wildfire 2.

In contrast, the approach in Exhibit 4–4 may be the best one to answer the question of how much more (or less) it cost to suppress a wildfire in Ontario than in Alberta or Saskatchewan. The three boxes at the bottom of the diagram represent all the wildfires suppressed in each province. If we assume that the mix of remote and accessible hectares is reasonably similar, then it could be the quantity of fires that differed among the provinces. The size of the cost pools could be very similar but the denominator for wildfire Type 2 is lower than either wildfire Types 3 or 1 because more were suppressed in that province for roughly the same cost per wildfire. Having this type of data helps managers in all three provinces to, for example, investigate whether or not they could adopt more effective and less-costly prevention methods.

As discussed in Chapter 2, the relationship of average unit costs to quantity is not linear for fixed costs. To the extent some of the total costs of fire suppression are fixed, as the quantity of either wildfires or the hectares lost fluctuates, the average unit cost and the fixed indirect cost-allocation rate will fluctuate. The fixed costs comprising part of the total costs in the numerator (the cost pool) will remain unchanged as the quantity in the denominator varies. The larger the number of fires (or hectares destroyed), the smaller the fixed indirect cost-allocation rate will be. The total fixed cost in the indirect cost pool, however, will be constant.

The use of an average rate gives rise to a *perverse incentive*. A **perverse incentive** rewards inappropriate management behaviour to present the appearance of cost-effective performance instead of to achieve actual cost-effective performance. If performance were judged on the basis of a low fixed indirect cost-allocation rate, then it would be to the advantage of the service to avoid fire prevention so that more hectares would burn and the average fixed cost per hectare would appear low. But the costs of prevention are far less than suppression, and prevention does not risk human lives. This is one reason why job cost systems need to be carefully designed.

Some technical background helps us understand other reasons why costs of wildfire suppression vary other than the design of the job costing system. Suppressing a wildfire can be done using three different firefighting crews. The different crews give rise to different labour costs. Initial attack crews of three firefighters are the first on the scene to establish an attack base when wildfires are accessible by ground transportation. Ground crews of 20 arrive later. When the fire is not accessible by ground, rappattack crews of three must rappel with equipment by rope from a helicopter to the attack base. When the ground crew of 20 is airborne, the smokejumpers parachute to remote sites. Supplies often include water, fuel to ignite controlled backfires, and power machinery. Equipment includes aircraft, heavy pumping equipment, earth-moving equipment, chainsaws, axes, and trucks. Helicopters and fixed-wing aircraft dump fire retardants and up to 11,000 litres of water in one pass in remote locations. Fire retardants, powders sold by the kilogram, usually include fertilizer to promote plant growth as well as ammonium salts to extinguish fires and a red dye to mark where the retardant has been dropped.

In developing an appropriate costing system, management accountants must understand relevance. The total costs to suppress wildfires are not linear but rather increase at a faster rate as the total destruction increases, as shown in Exhibit 4-6. The accumulation of total costs illustrated in Exhibit 4-6 assumes 15,600 firefighters, 90 helicopters, and 104 fixed-wing aircraft were the resources used to suppress the fires in 2003 in California.

A similar relationship between total costs and number of fires is true in Canada. The Canadian government service statistics indicate that 3% of the fires cause 97% of the destruction (224 wildfires destroy 2.42 million hectares annually, approximately 10,804 hectares per wildfire). This means most of the relevant costs are expended to suppress large wildfires. Large wildfires require more people, equipment, and supplies to suppress than small ones.

Now, putting some data in place, we can undertake the development of a job cost system. You will notice in the table below that there are two jobs and the direct materials cost pool is a very small proportion of total costs, slightly over 4% ($4,000 ÷ $92,344 = 0.0433). In contrast, the direct labour cost pool is slightly over 27% ($25,344 ÷ $92,344 = 0.274), and the indirect cost pool is largest of the three at almost 40% ($36,000 ÷ $92,344 = 0.39). These data show that the indirect cost pool must be allocated in a sensible way in this job costing system even though there is no readily identifiable cause that can be measured in an economically feasible way. Managers will pay careful

EXHIBIT 4-6
Cumulative Costs Compared to Wildfire Size

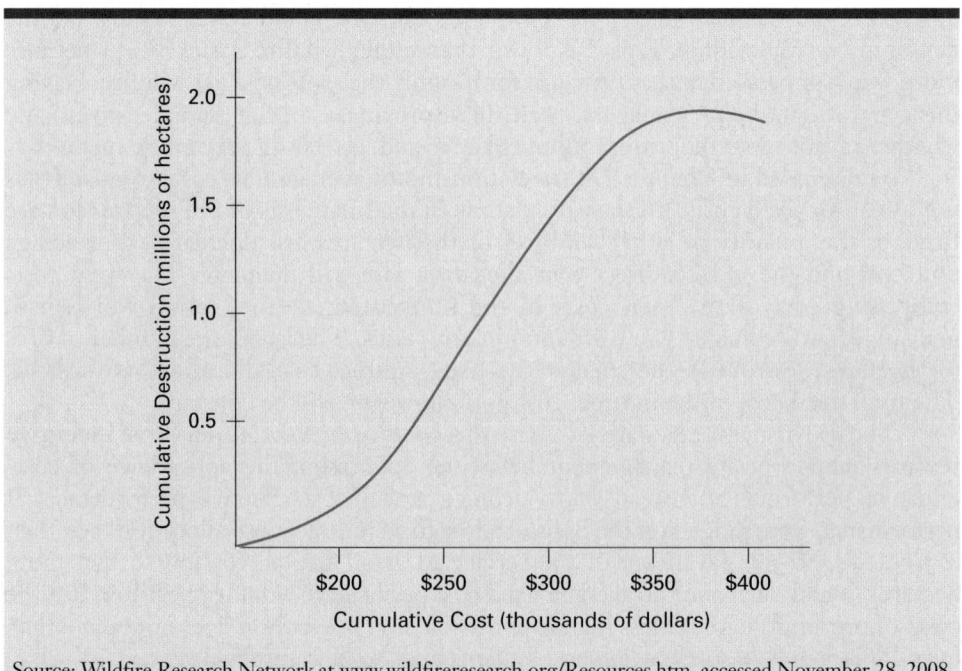

Source: Wildfire Research Network at www.wildfireresearch.org/Resources.htm, accessed November 28, 2008.

attention to how many indirect cost pools they identify and the logic of choosing a non-financial measure used in each cost-allocation base.

Beginning with the easier cost pools, the direct materials cost pool is the actual cost of fire retardant for one fire. This cost pool does not need to be assigned because it can be traced not only to the wildfire but also the hectares lost. Another fact recorded for this job is that 500 kilograms of fire retardant were actually used at a cost of $8 per kilogram. Consider how appropriate kilograms of direct material might be as an indirect cost-allocation base. You would quickly conclude it was inappropriate because no direct materials were used in the other fire. To assign a direct materials cost to the second fire could significantly distort the cost estimate for the two jobs.

The direct labour (DL) cost pool totals $25,344; however, the nonfinancial information that 450 direct labour-hours (DLH) were used in total is inadequate. Assume Job 1, ignited by a lightning strike in a remote location near Tumbler Ridge, British Columbia, required Rappattack crews and aircraft dumping water and fire retardant to suppress the fire for a total of 180 DLH. Job 2 was ignited by a campfire in a park close to Fort McMurray, Alberta and could be accessed by ground; it was suppressed using water and ground equipment, and in total consumed 270 DLH. Because the information system is limited, the tonnes of fuel, food, hygiene, and other supplies have not been tracked.

The necessary but indirect costs for fuel, food, hygiene, and other supplies totalled $36,000 (water is free), and period costs were $27,000 during the month, as shown in the table below. At this point, the management accountant could only recommend using DLH as the cost-allocation base used to assign all indirect costs. The managers still must decide how to group the indirect costs (inventoriable and period) into indirect cost pools. The last lines of the table show that the average, the rate per DLH, is $56.32 ($25,344 ÷ 450 DLH = $56.32/DLH). This is not an actual labour rate at all; it is an average. This is the reason it is called a DL cost-allocation rate. The mechanical process of dividing the DL cost pool by the total DLH is simple, as is the process of assigning the DL cost pool to each job based on the number of DLH consumed by each. The DLH cost pool assigned to Job 1 is $10,138 ($56.32/DLH × 180 DLH = $10,138) and $15,206 to Job 2 ($56.32/DLH × 270 DLH = $15,206).

Direct Cost Pool Allocation For Job 1 and Job 2

	Total Cost Pools	Input Quantity	Allocation Base Measure
Direct materials (fire retardant Job 1 only)	$ 4,000	500	kg
DL (common input across Job 1 and Job 2)	25,344	450	DLH
Indirect costs (no easily identified causes)	36,000		
Other business function costs (no common input)	27,000		
Total costs Job 1 + Job 2	$ 92,344		

	Cost-Allocation Rate	Cost pool allocated to:		
		Job 1	Job 2	Cost Pool
Common input quantity used (DLH)		180	270	
DL (common input across Job 1 and Job 2)	$ 56.32 per DLH	$10,138	$15,206	$25,344

The steps just described and the resulting assignment of the DL cost pool are illustrated in Exhibit 4–7.

Had the MIS been more sophisticated, the management accountant would have found that the actual hourly rate for a firefighter is $16/DLH irrespective of the type of crew on the ground. There is a wide range of hourly rates for pilots working in the armed forces but the actual wage rate paid was $100/DLH. A more sophisticated management information system would have also provided the fact

EXHIBIT 4-7
Cost Assignment For A Direct Cost Pool

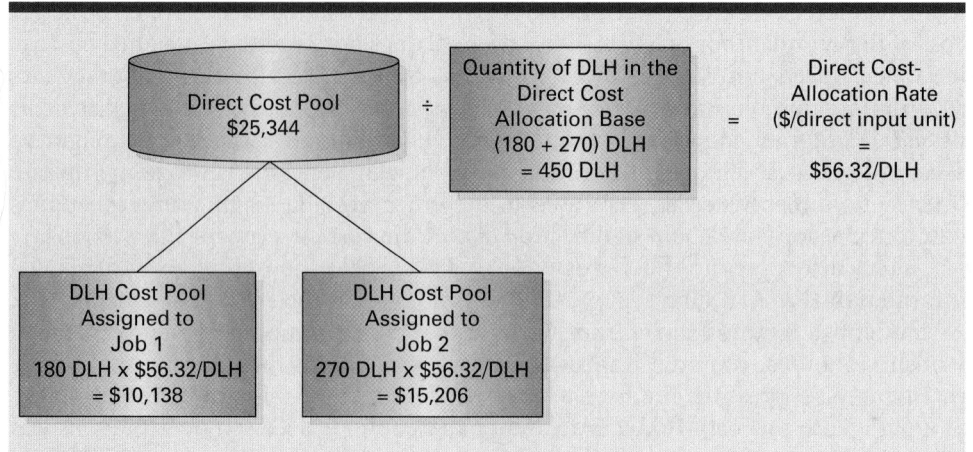

that 90% or 162 DLH for Job 1 cost $100/DLH for a total of $16,200 and 80% or 216 DLH for Job 2 cost $16/DLH or $3,456. A comparison of the job costs based on actual rates traced to the output unit, and the job costs based on the direct cost-allocation rate traced to a common input unit, is shown in the table below. The current job cost procedure applied, allocated, or assigned too low a proportion of the DL cost pool to Job 1 relative to Job 2.

Allocated and Actual Direct Job Cost Comparison

	Rates	Per	Job 1	Job 2	Cost Pool
DL actual firefighter rate	$ 16	DLH			
Pilot actual rate	$100	DLH			
Input quantity use of firefighters @ $16/DLH			18	216	
Input quantity use of pilots @ $100/DLH			162	54	
Actual cost of firefighters			$ 288	$ 3,456	
Actual cost of pilots			16,200	5,400	
Actual DL cost per job			$ 16,488	$ 8,856	$ 25,344
Allocated DL cost per job			$ 10,138	$ 15,206	$ 25,344

This highlights the difficulty of using average rates per unit instead of actual costs. There is a large discrepancy, a material difference, between the actual DL rate for the different types of labour as well as the proportion of expensive and inexpensive DL consumed by each job. While an average direct cost-allocation rate is simple, it erases differences in job cost that should be retained for purposes of relevant cost identification. Based on actual direct labour rates, Job 1 cost almost double that of Job 2, but based on the direct cost-allocation rate, Job 1 was approximately $\frac{2}{3}$ the cost of Job 2.

THINKING CRITICALLY

If you were a manager, what would these results mean to you? Explain in a sentence or two. Read on for an analysis of this situation.

A manager unfamiliar with the limitations of using averages would conclude that suppressing wildfires of similar size that are accessible by ground is approximately 50% [($15,206 − 10,138) ÷ $10,138)] more expensive than those attacked by air. This would lead to focusing on controlling the inputs used to suppress wildfires of the Job-2 type when in fact the wildfires of the Job-1 type are more expensive. Should managers act on the incorrect identification of more expensive and less expensive jobs, the outcome will be failure to both identify and control the efficient causes of costs.

This problem of materially inaccurate cost assignment worsens when allocating indirect cost pools to jobs. There is no economical way to identify and measure any common input for indirect costs—that is why they are classified as indirect. This means the indirect cost-allocation base is neither a material nor an efficient cause of the costs in the indirect cost pool. Nevertheless, all the costs of service provision must be covered by tax revenue, not just the direct costs. The numerator value of the cost pool may be very accurate, but because the denominator is often based on a common direct input that has already been measured, the result is an arbitrary average cost per unit of an arbitrarily selected cost-allocation base.

The indirect cost pool is, in total, $36,000. Now the crucial question is what to select as the denominator. The one input that most certainly is measured is DLH. If this is chosen as the cost-allocation base, then the indirect cost-allocation rate will be $80/DLH ($36,000 ÷ 450 DLH = $80/DLH). The indirect cost of Job 1 will be $14,400 (180 DLH × $80/DLH = $14,400) and for Job 2 it will be $21,600 (270 DLH × $80/DLH = $21,600). At this stage in the job costing process, because DLH is not a cause of indirect costs, there is no way to analyze whether the allocation of the indirect cost pool is reasonable or not.

One approach is to consider that fuel is one component of indirect cost. Aircraft use more expensive aviation gas than diesel-powered ground equipment. Aircraft were the primary firefighting equipment used during the 162 pilot hours flown for Job 1. It is very likely that the cost of fuel has not been correctly allocated between the two jobs. The level of inaccuracy will depend on the proportion of total inventoriable indirect costs comprised by fuel compared to all other costs. But it is a guess if the indirect cost pool is overallocated to Job 2 relative to Job 1. The table below compares "actual direct plus allocated indirect" compared to "allocated direct and indirect" cost pools of the two jobs.

Inventoriable Actual and Allocated Job Cost Comparison

	Actual DL Cost	Actual DM Cost	Allocated Indirect Cost	Inventoriable Job Cost
Job 1	$16,488	$4,000	$14,400	$34,888
Job 2	8,856	–	21,600	30,456
Inventoriable costs	$25,344	$4,000	$36,000	$65,344

	Allocated DL Cost	Actual DM Cost	Allocated Indirect Cost	Inventoriable Job Cost
Job 1	$10,138	$4,000	$14,400	$28,538
Job 2	15,206	–	21,600	36,806
Inventoriable costs	$25,344	$4,000	$36,000	$65,344

This inaccuracy is not the result of a management accounting problem but rather a MIS problem. In the case of direct costs, the remedy may be very straightforward—improve the MIS to trace direct costs to their inputs. This is not the answer, however, for indirect costs because indirect costs cannot be readily and economically traced to either their causes (inputs) or to a job (output). Often a larger proportion of organizational costs are indirect rather than direct. Indirect cost pool allocation improvements are discussed in Chapter 5.

To complete the example, the table below illustrates the allocation of indirect period costs to Job 1 and Job 2 using DLH in the cost-allocation base. The cost-allocation rate is $60/DLH ($27,000 ÷ 450 DLH = $60/DLH). Of the indirect period cost pool, $10,800 is allocated to Job 1 ($60/DLH × 180 DLH = $10,800) and $16,200 to Job 2 ($60/DLH × 270 DLH = $16,200).

If Something Is Being Done Wrong, Doing More of It Will Not Solve the Problem

In the lower half of the table above, the two job costs are diverging because the inaccuracy introduced when allocating a direct cost pool has been reinforced by allocating the indirect cost pool in the same way. There is nothing wrong with pursuing a cost leadership strategy; what is wrong here is the procedure used to implement the strategy. Examine the inventoriable job costs based on actual DL rates and actual DM cost. In the top half of the table, the cost of both jobs is converging to a similar amount. Important differences in consumption of resources have been obscured by the procedure based on one average unit cost. In this case, the implementation of cost allocation has meant that the larger the indirect cost pool is compared to the direct cost pool, the greater will be the inaccuracy.

Actual and Allocated Direct and Allocated Indirect Cost Pools

	Actual DL Cost	Actual DM Cost	Allocated Inventoriable Indirect Cost	Allocated Indirect Period Costs	Total Costs
Job 1	$16,488	$4,000	$14,400	$10,800	$45,688
Job 2	8,856	–	21,600	16,200	46,656
	$25,344	$4,000	$36,000	$27,000	$92,344

	Allocated DL Cost	Actual DM Cost	Allocated Inventoriable Indirect Cost	Allocated Indirect Period Costs	Total Costs
Job 1	$10,138	$4,000	$14,400	$10,800	$39,338
Job 2	15,206	–	21,600	16,200	53,006
	$25,344	$4,000	$36,000	$27,000	$92,344

The inaccuracy continues to worsen when the indirect period costs are allocated using DLH as the cost-allocation base. Again, the DLH spent fighting a fire clearly do not cause research and development costs or customer service costs, but the reason these business function period costs are indirect is that there is no readily and economically identifiable cause for them. In Chapter 14 there is a full discussion of how to allocate indirect period cost pools. Inevitably, job costing procedures result in some degree of inaccuracy.

A single direct and a single indirect cost pool may be too few, but hundreds of cost pools will be too many. The number of cost pools should reflect those 20% of common inputs that cause 80% of indirect costs. At least one of these common inputs or cost objects must be related to the time spent providing the core service. These few costly common inputs are often called key success factors. A **key success factor** is a *strategic* factor that requires close attention and control to ensure an organization will survive and thrive. Management accountants do not identify these factors but those responsible for the cost effectiveness of each business function do so in discussion with one another. For indirect costs, the identification of a reasonable number of cost pools and reasonable cost-allocation bases should be logically associated with one key success factor, although that factor will not cause the indirect cost pool.

The contribution made by management accountants is to understand and communicate the importance of selecting appropriate cost pools and appropriate cost-allocation bases to achieve job costing objectives. This is particularly important when considering that total indirect costs are a higher and total direct costs a lower proportion of total costs. Management accountants also help retain focus on the relevant costs in each cost pool. Their task is to create a job costing procedure to allocate all costs that cannot be readily and economically traced to the job. The allocations must reflect the costs per job of key success factors.

Strategically, however, all organizations fulfill the value proposition of customers: some benefit at least equal to the cost of the service. What is the value proposition of a hectare of wildlife habitat? The commercial financial value has been estimated at $3,000/hectare—but is there more than this financial value in a hectare of wilderness? Research from the University of Victoria, supported by a government grant, indicates the following financial value proposition of saving a hectare of wilderness for Canadians rather than simply the forestry companies harvesting timber:[1]

Financial Value Proposition to Save a Hectare of Wilderness

	$/Acre High	$/Acre Low	$/Hectare High	$/Hectare Low
Access to clean water	$ 113.00	$ 113.00	$ 279.22	$ 279.22
Access to wilderness	509.00	509.00	1,257.74	1,257.74
Reduce loss of economic timber value	1,018.00	489.00	2,515.48	1,208.32
Reduce risk of personal property loss	83.00	83.00	205.09	205.09
Reduce loss of a firefighter's life	11.00	5.00	27.18	12.36
Total financial value proposition	$1,734.00	$1,199.00	$ 4,284.71	$2,962.73

A straightforward multiplication of the hectares lost by the high and low financial value proposition results in the following for the ten-year-average value proposition per hectare and per fire compared to the 2007 actual services had the destruction been prevented:

Financial Value Proposition of Hectares Lost

	10-Year Average	Actual 2007	$/Hectare High	$/Hectare Low
Quantity of fires	7,445	6,518	$4,284.71	$2,962.73
Quantity of hectares lost, Q	2,500,000	1,700,000		
Total value proposition of hectares (high)	$10,711,775,000	$7,284,007,000		
Total value proposition of hectares (low)	$ 7,406,825,000	$5,036,641,000		
Value proposition per fire (high)	$ 1,438,787.78	$ 1,117,521.79		
Value proposition per fire (low)	$ 944,872.40	$ 772,727.98		

The second set of calculations identifies the wildfire as the cost object. The total financial value proposition for hectares destroyed is divided by the number of wildfires. As a Canadian taxpayer, the table shows that you would be content to pay at least $2,963 to save a hectare of forest that cost approximately $167 (see page 139) to save.

GOVERNANCE ISSUES

Unbiased Costs, Biased Interpretations

Accountants, by and large, do their best to provide unbiased, reliable, relevant information to help assess costs and performance. But readers can interpret this information within any context they choose. The same cost can appear as either well controlled or poorly controlled. Using the publicly available values, it appears that Canadian taxpayers are getting a bad deal.

According to the statistics, the average cost was $61,369 for 2007. Using the ten-year average cost, a political party in the opposition could provide evidence that the 2007 amount per fire signalled a disturbing cost overrun of 9.6% ($($|56,011 − 61,369|) ÷ $56,011 = 0.0957%) and a problem of cost control. But the government in power can argue, using the value proposition amounts, that $61,369 per fire was a bargain at only $167 per hectare saved.

[1]S. Peterson, "UVic Student Aims to Tally Cost of Wildfire Damage," from http://web.uvic.ca/gradstudies/greats/pdf/2004/TomHobby.pdf, accessed November 20, 2008.

MyAccountingLab

ASSESS YOUR MASTERY

To check your understanding of the material in Learning Objective ②, go to the Mastery Questions section at the end of the chapter and complete Learning Objective ② questions 1, 2, and 3.

JOB COSTING A PRODUCT

③ Apply knowledge of direct and indirect cost pools to calculate cost-allocation rates and assign costs to manufacturing departments

Our discussion of the design of a job costing system for wildfires indicated that many compromises were made in the interests of cost effectiveness. Perhaps the problem arose because the job was an intangible service rather than a tangible product job costing system. In the discussion that follows, it becomes apparent that inaccuracy is common to all job costing systems. Cost allocation and assignment are expedient but not accurate methods to cost different jobs. Organizations use inaccurate cost-allocation procedures that generate inaccurate job costs for one readily understandable reason: the cost to improve the management information system is higher than the benefit of improved accuracy. The more sophisticated the available information, the higher will be the training costs for both those who input data, and those who extract and analyze the data. Off-the-shelf job-costing software is available, ready for installation, but the costs of maintenance and upgrades, as well as the possibility the provider may go out of business, make this risky for small organizations.

When the job is a good, such as furniture, rather than a service produced, the distinction between inventoriable and period costs will be used as a logical basis for developing at least two indirect cost pools. The development of the job costing system for direct costs in the furniture example will assume the management information system tracks two common inputs for a two-stage conversion process. Inventoriable direct costs of production include direct manufacturing labour-hours (DMLH) and direct machine hours (MH) for preparation and assembly. This means that managers will have a choice of two input measures, DMLH or MH, when they decide on the cost-allocation bases for indirect inventoriable costs (e.g., rework).

Indirect inventoriable costs or manufacturing overhead (MOH) will be examined in this example. Indirect costs include labour costs for materials handling, maintenance, custodial and security activity, as well as overtime, idle time, rework, management, quality control, and supervisory salaries. Indirect supplies and various fixed costs such as amortization, utilities, and taxes also comprise MOH.

Exhibit 4-8 illustrates a generic production function for a furniture job that transforms or converts raw materials into finished goods using labour and equipment. In the first example in this chapter where the job was a service, the problem of inaccurate job costing arose because the MIS was inadequate. In this example, the MIS is far more detailed.

EXHIBIT 4-8
Generic Production Function for a Two-Phase Conversion Process

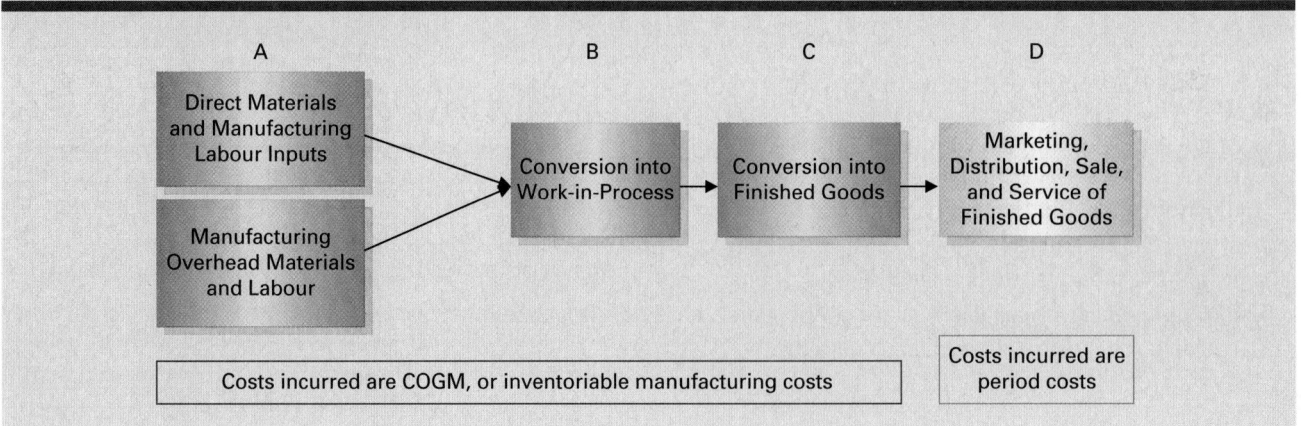

Assume that Robinson and Company transforms solid wood such as maple, oak, and cherry into furniture in a two-stage process. Each stage is undertaken in a single department that uses the same ten machines and same pool of labour. Robinson employs two carpenter apprentices, four journeymen carpenters, and four carpenter foremen. The company also employs one person who undertakes all marketing and sales, an accountant, and four administrative support staff. The core function (production) of Robinson is manufacturing furniture. To simplify the example, we will assume that all remaining value-added business functions can be represented as the marketing, distribution, sale, and servicing of the furniture. Assume these and all the period costs and actual month-end quantities and costs have been reported.

The preparation department is the first assembly stage represented in Exhibit 4-8 as B (conversion into work-in-process). Assembly, the second stage of conversion into finished goods, is C. Dining-room furniture includes a table, one extension leaf, and eight chairs made from the same wood. All components of each bed and entertainment unit are also made of the same wood. For simplicity, assume that 200 entertainment units, 150 dining-room sets, and 180 beds are completed in the month of March.

The following table reports all the labour components for each product. The A indicates apprentice time as a fraction of one DMLH per unit; the J indicates journeyman time as a fraction of one DMLH per unit; the F indicates foreman time as a fraction of one DMLH per unit. The foreman spends 3 minutes on the table in the preparation (B) stage of conversion (DMLH A/unit is 60 minutes × 0.05 = 3 minutes) and 24 minutes on each table in the assembly (C) stage of conversion. Examining the table, notice that no journeymen work during the (B) stage of conversion. Notice in the table, this means that the type of labour consumed differs between the two processes (B) and (C).

Furniture	Total Q	DMLH/unit	Preparation Conversion (B) DMLH A/unit	DMLH J/unit	DMLH F/unit	Preparation Total DMLH	Assembly Conversion (C) DMLH A/unit	DMLH J/unit	DMLH F/unit	Assembly Total DMLH
Tables	150	0.15	0.05		0.10	22.5	0.05	0.30	0.40	112.5
Chairs	1,200	0.15	0.05		0.10	180.0	0.10	0.25	0.40	900.0
Beds	180	0.10	0.05		0.05	18.0	0.05	0.25	0.60	162.0
Entertain.	200	0.10	0.05		0.05	20.0	0.05	0.30	0.60	190.0
	1,730		0.20		0.30	240.5	0.25	1.10	2.00	1,364.5

The table below reports all the direct cost pools and total direct cost pool. The controller provided necessary data on materials, labour, and unit costs to generate this table. Each cost pool represents a minimum of 9% of the total cost pool and would meet a reasonable materiality threshold. This implies that all three direct cost pools are relevant and ultimately must be allocated to the output unit, the job. The company had dried DM inventory on hand of $89,000 during the month and a total DM of $81,039 was transferred from DM inventory to WIP inventory representing DM used. Transferred value equals actual costs of the total number of board feet of each type of wood consumed for each job. Beds, for example, were ordered in curly maple, entertainment units in cherry wood, and all the dining sets in either red oak or hard

	Direct Cost Pools	Allocation Bases	Allocation Rates	% of Total
DM cost pool	$ 81,039			59.39%
DMLH cost pool	41,922	1,525*	$27.49	30.72%
MH cost pool	13,488	1,124	$12.00	9.89%
Total direct cost pool	$136,449			100.00%
Indirect cost pool	$ 2,199	80	$27.49	

*1,525 = 1,364.5 DMLH + 240.5 DMLH − 80 DMLH; the preparation plus assembly hours minus the rework hours.

maple. The woods were requisitioned prior to the date manufacturing would begin because they needed to dry before being cut.

The requisitions transferred costs of materials already purchased from the direct materials inventory to the WIP inventory. Each board foot of wood would have been requisitioned for a job code and the costs recorded for that job. The total straight time direct labour cost is $41,922, the sum of the DMLH cost of $6,312 for preparation indicated in the table below and the DMLH cost of $35,610 straight time only for assembly indicated in the next table. The DMLH excludes statutory contributions by the employer and rework (see Chapter 2 for details). Later, the use of the direct cost-allocation rate for rework will be explained. The direct machine hours (MH) total $13,488 ($8,352 + $5,136 = $13,488 from the tables below).

As soon as the dried wood is released from direct materials inventory and placed on a conveyor belt, the conversion process begins as the apprentice carpenter inputs into the computer the type and size of the direct material in board feet as well as the job code and specifications of the job. No time-in or time-out, however, is input. The computer software calculates how the various components of each job should be placed on the direct material (e.g., chair seats and backs, arms, and legs), then activates the machine to trace the patterns on the wood. The table below summarizes both DMLH and MH for the first step in conversion (B), which is preparation.

| | Direct Manufacturing Labour-Hours (DMLH) | | | | | Direct Machine Hours (MH) | | | |
| | | Preparation | | DL Allocation | | | | Preparation | |
Carpenter	DMLH $/hr	Q DMLH	Cost Pool	Rate		MH $/hr	MH/unit	MH/mo	Cost Pool
Apprentice	$16.00	86.50	$1,384		Tables	$12.00	0.30	45*	$ 540
Journeyman	25.00	–	–		Chairs	12.00	0.40	480	5,760
Foreman	32.00	154.00	4,928		Beds/Ent.	12.00	0.45	171	2,052
Total		240.50	$6,312	$26.25	Total			696	$8,352

*E.g., 150 tables × 0.30 MH/unit = 45 MH/mo

Notice in the preparation department that most of the conversion tasks are completed by machinery, although people do input the standard order specifications to the computer and do a quality check on the patterning before the wood is cut. The total cost pool for an apprentice, for example, is $1,384 ($16/DMLH × 86.5 DMLH = $1,384). The direct machine cost pool for tables is $540 ($12/MH × 0.30 MH/table × 150 tables/month = $540). The direct machine cost pool is approximately 32% larger than the direct manufacturing labour cost pool ($(8,352 − 6,312) ÷ $6,312 = 0.323). The direct inputs common to all job orders, whether customized or standardized, are direct machine hours (MH) and direct manufacturing labour-hours (DMLH), which are efficient causes. At the next conversion phase (C), which is assembly, the reverse is true because it requires more direct labour than direct machine hours to convert the work-in-process into finished goods available for sale. During assembly, machines are programmed to cut dovetail joints (which improve the strength and durability of Robinson's furniture), lathe, and sand individual components of each piece of furniture. However, journeymen and master carpenters fine-finish each piece by hand. The parts are assembled, stained or varnished, then moved out of work-in-process to be packaged and delivered to the customer.

During the assembly process, both direct labour and direct machine hours are inputs common to all jobs. These inputs remain efficient causes of their respective cost pools. The following table reports the cost pools for the assembly process described, and during this part of the conversion process, the direct labour cost pool is approximately seven times larger than the direct machine cost pool ($35,610 ÷ $5,136 = 6.93). The assembly direct labour cost pool for apprentices was $2,344 ($16/DMLH × 146.5 DMLH/month = $2,344). The direct machine hours cost pool for beds and entertainment units was $456 ($12/MH × 0.10/beds and ent. × (180 beds + 200 entertainment units) = $456). The quantities of beds and entertainment units are provided in the table on page 155.

Direct Manufacturing Labour-Hours (DMLH)

Carpenter	DMLH $/hr	Q DMLH	Assembly Cost Pool							
Apprentice	$16.00	146.5*	$ 2,344							
Journeyman	25.00	450.0	1,250							
Foreman	32.00	768.0	24,576							
Total		1,364.5	$38,170	$27.72						
Rework		80.0	$ 2,560							
Straight-time		1,284.5	$35,610							

Direct Machine Hours (MH)

	MH $/hr	MH/unit	MH/mo	QMH	Assembly Cost Pool
Tables	$12.00	0.20	30	75	$ 360
Chairs	12.00	0.30	360	840	4,320
Beds/Ent.	12.00	0.10	38	209	456
Total MH			428	1,124	$5,136

*Sum of (MH/mo for each type of furniture made × quantity of each type made/mo)

THINKING CRITICALLY

If you were a management accountant, what would the differences in use of direct machine hours and direct manufacturing labour-hours mean to you as you choose cost-allocation bases to split the direct cost pools between the two departments? Explain in a sentence or two. Read on to understand how to justify a choice of different cost-allocation bases for different departments when both consume the same set of common inputs.

Each stage of conversion consumes direct labour in different proportions. To the management accountant, the relevant indirect cost pools should be allocated differently to reflect the different intensity of use by each department working on a single job. A single average cost-allocation base and rate would obscure the different rates at which each department consumes two different direct inputs. Two different cost-allocation bases will help managers who will receive cost reports focus more clearly on what the causes of any cost problems may be in each department. Assume all rework must be done by hand. *Rework*, which is work done to unacceptable units of production to turn them into acceptable units that can be sold, is an indirect labour cost, not a direct labour cost, and is part of manufacturing overhead (see Chapter 2). Some rework is normal in most manufacturing settings; therefore, the financial accounting standard accepts this as cost of goods sold (COGS), although abnormal rework is excluded. Management accountants are not limited to the financial accounting standards, but by including an abnormal cost of rework, all job costs will be somewhat overstated.

A feature of this information also worth noting is that standard amounts of time per activity for each of the apprentice, journeymen, and foreman carpenters are used to calculate DMLH required in both preparation and in assembly. A standard rate of $12 per direct machine hour is also used. The benefits of using standard quantities and rates will be discussed more fully in Objective 4. In this example, no time-in and time-out is recorded for each individual piece of furniture, thus actual quantities of time are impossible to trace for either input. With the current information, the cost-allocation rate for direct labour in preparation is $26.25, due in large part because no journeyman labour is required ($6,312 ÷ 240.5 DMLH = $26.25/DMLH). The cost-allocation rate for direct labour in the assembly department is $27.72 ($35,610 ÷ 1,284.5 DMLH = $27.72/DMLH). The difference in the rates of $1.47 is 5.6% (($27.72 − $26.25) ÷ $26.25 = 0.056) and is not material. This suggests that a single average cost-allocation rate over both departments of $27.49/DMLH is a reasonable choice to use for both processes (($6,312 + $35,610) ÷ (240.5 DLH + 1,284.5 DMLH) = $27.49/DMLH).

	Direct Cost Pools	Allocation Bases	Allocation Rates
DM cost pool	$ 81,039		
DMLH cost pool	41,922	1,525	$27.49
MH cost pool	13,488	1,124	$12.00
Total direct cost pool	$136,449		

The final step in this direct inventoriable cost-allocation procedure is to use cost-allocation rates and cost-allocation bases to assign the direct labour and machine cost pools to each department. The next table illustrates not only the assigned costs but also compares allocated costs of direct manufacturing labour to the standard costs (see p. 163 for a discussion of standard costs) and the percentage difference. A slight overstatement of assigned costs of $299.31 or approximately 2.04% (($14,963.31 − $14,664) ÷ $14,664 = 0.0204) is an overallocation (discussed later) in the preparation department. A somewhat larger understatement in the assembly department of $(2,859.31) is an underallocation of approximately 6.60% (($40,446.69 − $43,306) ÷ $43,306 = −0.0660). These calculations may be sufficient to justify the use of the simpler cost procedure with only two cost-allocation bases and rates because the over and understatements are not material, but top management will decide.

	Direct Labour	Direct Machine	Allocated Total	Standard Total	% Difference
Preparation	$ 6,611.31	$8,352.00	$14,963.31	$14,664	2.04%
Assembly	$35,310.69	5,136.00	$40,446.69	$43,306	−6.60%
			$55,410.00		

In this example, there are no actual direct labour times upon which to base any actual direct cost pool calculations—what is available are standard times. Nevertheless, there are two possible direct manufacturing labour cost-allocation rates, one for each department. The top managers will decide if the inaccuracy caused by using a single direct manufacturing cost-allocation rate for both departments obstructs identification and control of efficient causes of costs in each department. If the answer is no, then the simpler costing procedure is less costly to implement and meets the objective of enabling identification and control of cost problems in each department.

INDIRECT COST POOL ALLOCATION PROCEDURE—MANUFACTURING OVERHEAD

The carpenter foremen spent 80 DMLH on rework. The current union contract includes the following statutory requirements of 12% vacation pay, pension benefits of $3/DMLH, medical benefits of $2/DMLH, and various administrative fees of $0.70 per hour of straight time worked. The table below reports the total indirect inventoriable cost pool for statutory benefits per the current union contract. Robinson *must* pay this component of manufacturing overhead to comply with employment law.

The total indirect cost pool in the last column of the table now includes all the statutory benefits of $9.00/DMLH plus the straight-time direct labour cost-allocation rate multiplied by the total DMLH worked. The dollar value of the added statutory benefits for the 80 DMLH of rework (80 DMLH × $9.00/DMLH = $720) generates a slight adjustment to the total indirect cost pool.

Indirect Manufacturing Labour Cost Pool

Statutory Benefits per the Contract

	Straight-time Allocation Rate	12% Vacation	Pension	Medical	Administrative	Total Added Benefits $/DMLH	Actual Q DMLH	Indirect Labour Cost Pool
	$27.49	$3.30	$3.00	$2.00	$0.70			
Straight-time (Q DMLH rounded[2])						$9.00	1,525	$13,723
Rework ($ rounded)						9.00	80	720
Total						9.00	1,605	$14,443

The various machines run eight hours per day for five days each week. In the last week, scheduled maintenance occurred on the weekend. The maintenance was out-sourced to the supplier of the machines and cost $1,000. Amortization expense was $8,000. Monthly insurance on the manufacturing building and equipment was $2,000. Local property tax costs $1,800 monthly. Head office monthly salaries for marketing and sales, administration support, and accounting were $3,000, $10,000, and $3,000, respectively. The monthly salary of the CEO is $6,000. These indirect cost pools and each as a percentage of the total indirect cost pool are summarized here:

Indirect Cost Pool Summary

Account	Amount $	% Indirect
Statutory labour benefits	$13,723	27.40%
Amortization (plant)	8,000	15.97%
Rework	2,560	5.11%
Insurance (plant)	2,000	3.99%
Property tax	1,800	3.60%
Marketing	3,000	5.99%
Administration	10,000	19.97%
Accounting	3,000	5.99%
CEO salary	6,000	11.98%
Total	$50,083	

THINKING CRITICALLY

If you were a management accountant, what cost pools would you eliminate from manufacturing overhead? How many manufacturing overhead cost pools would achieve a reasonably accurate job costing procedure for each department? What would your choice(s) be for cost-allocation base(s)? Explain in a sentence or two, then read on to understand how to justify the number of indirect cost pools and their cost-allocation bases.

The first step is to classify the indirect costs as inventoriable and period costs. Of the $50,083 total in the indirect cost pool, $22,000 are period costs (marketing, administration, accounting, and CEO salary). The total is a material amount exceeding 43% of the indirect cost pool ($22,000 ÷ $50,083 = 0.4393). To conform with the financial-accounting inventory standard, these period costs must be excluded from any allocation to the MOH cost pool, which is ultimately expensed as COGS. To include period costs in MOH could materially misstate the reported COGS.

---

[2]To use four or five decimals when doing allocations implies the rates and dollar values are accurate. They are never accurate because allocations are always estimates. In this table, using an Excel spreadsheet, both the Actual Q DMLH and the Indirect Labour Cost Pool are rounded values. The calculated values are 1,525.7933 and $13,723.1397, respectively.

There are two alternatives to consider for the remaining $28,083 in MOH. To be consistent, the first alternative is to use the materiality threshold of 9% as in the direct cost pool allocation procedure, to generate MOH cost pools. If the 9% materiality criterion is used, then there will be three indirect cost pools: statutory benefits, amortization, and other (rework, insurance, property tax). You will see this again in Chapter 6, where all amortization arises in the manufacturing property, plant, and equipment, and therefore is a component of COGS expense. These cost pools do not conform to the financial-accounting standard, which specifies how to allocate fixed MOH, but for management purposes may be sensible.

The second alternative is to examine cost behaviour. Statutory benefit and rework costs vary with the number of straight-time hours worked; amortization, insurance, and property tax are fixed. If cost behaviour is used as the criterion, then there will be two MOH cost pools. This approach would require two different cost-allocation bases, one for the variable cost pool and one for the fixed cost pool, and an opportunity to allocate fixed costs according to financial-accounting standards. MOH with their respective percentages of the total MOH cost pool are:

Cost Pool Name	MOH	% MOH
Statutory labour benefits	$13,723	48.87%
Rework	2,560	9.11%
Amortization (plant)	8,000	28.49%
Insurance (plant)	2,000	7.12%
Property tax	1,800	6.41%
Total	$28,083	

Under either of the two alternatives, the cost-allocation base for the statutory benefit cost pool is clearly the total quantity of DMLH, and the standard rate has already been calculated as $9.00/DMLH. Unless rework is consistently required each month and generates a material dollar value for the indirect cost pool, then the direct manufacturing labour rate for the carpenter foremen of $32/DMLH should not be the basis upon which to allocate all variable MOH to each department. This same reasoning applies to using the average cost-allocation rate of $14.01/DMLH. Using this average unit cost of statutory benefits and rework will obscure identification of any cost control problems arising from just one of these efficient causes.

The actual carpenter foreman's rate is over three times ($32.00 ÷ $9.00 = 3.56) higher than the actual statutory benefits rate of $9.00/DMLH, but statutory benefits will be incurred every month and generate over five times more in the cost pool than rework ($14,443 ÷ $2,560 = 5.64). On balance, from our analysis of the existing information, it appears that the cost-allocation rate that is most sensible is $9.00/DMLH. As costs directly related to the output, both statutory benefits and rework can be allocated as variable MOH and conform with financial accounting standards, providing this is a normal situation (see Chapter 18).

The fixed costs are incurred as each month passes. Job cost systems allocate even fixed MOH cost pools to departments in some reasonable way. The number of jobs is common to both departments but the number of either direct machine or manufacturing labour-hours is not. First, consider the alternative of three MOH cost pools where one cost pool consists of only statutory benefits. Notice that of the total fixed costs of $11,800, the amortization and insurance for plant and equipment amount to $10,000. If the second cost pool is amortization, then MH is a better choice of the efficient cause of this MOH cost than DMLH. It is the use of the machines that causes the wear and tear, the financial value of which is estimated as the monthly amortization expense. The cost-allocation rate will be $7.12 per MH ($8,000 ÷ 1,124 MH = $7.12/MH).

The choice of cost-allocation base for the third cost pool of $6,360 is now very difficult to make because the largest single component of this pool is rework of $2,560 or 9.12% of the total MOH cost pool. The efficient cause is clearly DMLH. The remaining two costs of $3,800, or 13.53% of the total MOH cost pool, however, are related to property tax and insurance, not DMLH. Moreover, the insurance premium and property tax expense are beyond the control of those managing the costs of the production process. In contrast, the rework cost is within their control.

From this analysis, a reasonable conclusion is that because both the statutory benefits cost pool and the rework cost pool share the same efficient cause *and* both can be controlled by those managing the production process, they should be in the same variable MOH cost pool. The conclusion, based on the facts provided, is that cost behaviour rather than a materiality threshold is the best basis upon which to generate Robinson's two manufacturing overhead cost pools.

The discussion of indirect period cost pool allocation illustrates the importance of understanding management-accounting as well as financial-accounting concepts. It does not mean this will be the appropriate decision for any other different set of facts. Allocation under each alternative is summarized in the table below.

Manufacturing Overhead Cost Pool Allocation Rates

| | Alternative 1: Use 9% | | | | Alternative 2: Behaviour | | | | |
Cost Pool Name	MOH	Cost-Allocation Base Q Hr.	Cost-Allocation Rate*	Per	Cost Pool	MOH	Cost-Allocation Base Q Hr.	Cost-Allocation Rate	Per
Benefits	$13,723.14	1,605	$8.55	DMLH	Variable	$16,283.14	1,605	–	DMLH
Amortization (plant)	8,000.00	1,124	$7.12	MH	Fixed	11,800.00	1,124	$10.50	MH
Other (includes rework)	6,360.00	1,124	$ 5.66	MH		–			
Total	$28,083.14					$28,083.14			

*$13,723.14 ÷ 1,605 = $8.55; the previously rounded amount of MOH was $13,723

The final step in the design of the job cost system is to assign the indirect costs to each department as shown below. The choice of cost pools will depend on how important it is to track amortization separately from the other indirect fixed MOH costs. One important factor would be if Robinson intends to downsize or grow in its capacity to serve its customers. Downsizing would entail selling equipment and reducing amortization expense, while growth would entail purchasing new equipment and increasing amortization expense. The insurance on equipment would decrease or increase proportional to the value of the equipment disposed of in downsizing or acquired in growth. Property tax would not change unless Robinson expanded its current plant size. If no changes are anticipated, then the simpler alternative of one variable and one fixed indirect cost pool is preferable. It is easier to understand, therefore easier to justify, and less expensive to implement than a more complicated method. It does not matter which method is chosen— the total MOH cost pool remains $28,083.14.

Manufacturing Overhead Cost Pool Departmental Allocation

| | Alternative 1: Use 9% | | | | | | Alternative 2: Behaviour | | |
Department	DMLH	MH	Statutory	Fixed 1	Fixed 2	Total	Variable	Fixed	Total
Preparation	240.5	696	$ 2,056.33	$4,953.74	$3,938.22	$ 10,948.29	$ 4,616.33	$ 7,306.76	$ 11,923.10
Assembly	1,364.5	428	11,666.81	3,046.26	2,421.78	17,134.84	11,666.81	4,493.24	16,160.04
			$13,723.14	$8,000.00	$6,360.00	$28,083.14	$16,283.14	$11,800.00	$28,083.14

Cost-Allocation Procedures

The percentages in the following table indicate how frequently particular cost-allocation bases are used in costing systems in six countries. The reason reported percentages for a country exceed 100% is that many companies surveyed use more than one cost-allocation base, as was the case in the preceding example. With the exception of the U.S., all countries report percentages exceeding 100%, showing a clear preference for using multiple cost-allocation bases and multiple indirect cost pools.

As more common inputs are readily and inexpensively measured across jobs, the change in the financial value of the indirect cost-allocation pool can be more readily explained by changes in the cost-allocation base. This is one benefit of using measures other than direct labour and machine-hours.[a]

	U.K.[b]	Australia[c]	Ireland[d]	Japan[c]	N.Z.[b]	U.S.[e]
Direct manufacturing labour-hours	73%	52%	68%	84%	78%	62%
Direct machine hours	17	22	27	53	60	12
Units of production	17	28	32	47	55	4
Direct material cost	14	7	36	44	40	5
Other	—	22	—	10	15	17

[a] T. Groot, "Activity Based Costing in U.S. and Dutch Food Companies," *Advances in Management Accounting* (1999).

[b] D. Lamminmaki and C. Drury, "A Comparison of New Zealand and British Product-Costing Practices," *International Journal of Accounting* (2001).

[c] H. Wijewardena and A. De Zoysa, "A Comparative Analysis of Management Accounting Practices in Australia and Japan: An Empirical Investigation," *International Journal of Accounting* (1999).

[d] P. Clarke, "Management Accounting Practices in Large Irish Manufacturing Firms," *Irish Journal of Management* (1997).

[e] J. Cohen and L. Paquette, "Management Accounting Practices: Perceptions of Controllers," *Journal of Cost Management* (1991).

MyAccountingLab

ASSESS YOUR MASTERY

To check your understanding of the material in Learning Objective ③ go to the Mastery Questions section at the end of the chapter and complete Learning Objective ③ questions 1, 2, and 3.

NORMAL LOOKS TO THE FUTURE, ACTUAL LOOKS AT THE PAST

④ Explain the usefulness of normal and actual costing procedures based on material and efficient causes of costs

Without an extremely detailed management information system, managers cannot trace actual job or process costs to each output unit. Moreover, tracing is only possible if either the material or efficient cause of the input costs is known, and this is never the case for indirect cost pools such as MOH. Costing procedures will always result in estimated values. In part because financial values such as work-in-process inventory are estimated over some time period, managers cannot calculate the actual costs of jobs as the jobs are completed. Managers need close approximations of the manufacturing costs of various jobs on a timely basis, not just at the end of the year or the end of a quarter.

Managers need these costs (often together with other period costs, such as marketing or customer service) for various ongoing uses, including:

◆ to choose types of profitable jobs to seek in future and unprofitable jobs to avoid
◆ to select types of profitable customers or clients to seek in future, and unprofitable customers or clients to avoid or remove
◆ to adjust the price of current jobs and services to improve profitability
◆ to control the costs of current jobs and services to improve profitability
◆ to budget or forecast future prices and costs of jobs
◆ to prepare interim financial statements.

In short, financial information must be timely, possess reasonable predictive validity, and possess reasonable evaluative validity if it is to be internally cost-beneficial. Predictive validity improves forecasts, whereas evaluative validity improves assessment of past actions. You may recall that these three elements from the conceptual framework for financial accounting comprise relevance. Relevance means the information will change decisions, and that is a key benefit of providing it.

Managers need relevant cost information that is timely, has reasonable predictive validity to forecast or budget the future, and has reasonable evaluative validity to assess past performance. Waiting for actual costs often results in too little information arriving too late to make improvements to cost management and financial performance. These are reasons why standard quantities of inputs are often used to calculate standard cost-allocation rates used to assign manufacturing overhead. Standard rates and quantities are periodically compared to actual amounts to make adjustments for material changes. Other synonyms are *predetermined indirect cost-allocation rates* and *budgeted indirect cost-allocation rates*.

Normal costing requires the use of standard, or predetermined, or budgeted indirect cost-allocation rates and actual quantities of the cost-allocation base of common inputs consumed to assign overhead costs, but actual direct cost rates and actual quantities to assign direct costs. When actual indirect and direct cost rates as well as actual quantities of inputs consumed common to all jobs or processes are known, then companies can undertake actual costing. The difference between actual costing and normal costing is normal costing uses an indirect cost rate for common inputs to assign costs to jobs or processes. Exhibit 4-9 summarizes the differences between the actual-costing and normal-costing methods. The normal indirect costing method is the only one that uses a budgeted or standard rate.

Using Robinson and Company, the following example and table below compare the assignment of manufacturing overhead cost pools to two conversion departments, and the difference or variance between using normal (budgeted indirect cost rates) and actual costing procedures. The calculations for the variable manufacturing overhead is in the top of the table and the fixed manufacturing overhead is in the bottom.

Assume that the *normal total* variable manufacturing overhead cost pool was budgeted as $15,163 with 1,600 DMLH for the month of March 2009. The standard cost rate for indirect labour has been calculated as $9.00 and by law this cannot be changed because it pays for statutory benefits. Assume that the actual variable manufacturing overhead cost pool was $17,003 and the actual direct manufacturing labour-hours were 1,605 DMLH. The preparation department

EXHIBIT 4-9
Actual Costing and Normal Costing Systems

	Actual Costing	Normal Costing
Direct Costs	*Actual direct-cost rates* × actual quantities of direct-cost inputs	*Actual direct-cost rates* × actual quantities of direct-cost inputs
Indirect Costs	*Actual indirect-cost rates* × actual quantities of cost-allocation bases	*Budgeted indirect-cost rates* × actual quantities of cost-allocation bases

budgeted 320 DMLH and actual was 240 DMLH. The assembly department budgeted for 1,290 DMLH and actual was 1,285 DMLH. Budgeted quantities are irrelevant, however, because (as Exhibit 4-9 shows) *actual* quantities are used to assign normal costs irrespective of the type of costing procedure. This is illustrated in the second quadrant on the left of Exhibit 4-10. Comparing normal to actual costs in variable manufacturing overhead will result in zero, overallocation, or underallocation of costs.

Assume that the budgeted fixed manufacturing overhead cost pool of $10,935 was the normal amount and $11,800 was the actual fixed manufacturing overhead cost pool. Comparing normal to actual costs in fixed manufacturing overhead will result in zero, overallocation, or underallocation of costs.

Comparison of Actual and Normal Manufacturing Overhead Cost Assignment for Robinson

Manufacturing Overhead Cost Pools Assigned and Variances (Budget - Actual)

	MOH Cost Pools and Cost-Allocation Bases		Preparation Department (B)			Assembly Department (C)			Total Over (under) MOH Allocation Variance
			MOH Cost Pools and Cost-Allocation Bases		Over (under) MOH Allocation Variance	MOH Cost Pools and Cost-Allocation Bases		Over (under) MOH Allocation Variance	
	Normal	Actual	Normal	Actual	Variance	Normal	Actual	Variance	Variance
Total variable MOH cost pool	$15,163	$17,003							
Total DMLH	1,600	1,605	320	240		1,290	1,285		
Carpenter foreman rate for rework	$9.00	$32.00	–	–		75	80		
Statutory cost rate for indirect labour	$9.00		$2,160	$2,160	$0	$13,003	$14,843	$(1,840)	$ (1,840)
Total fixed MOH cost pool	$10,935	$11,800							$ (865)
	$26,098	$28,803							$ (2,705)

By definition, fixed costs do not vary over a relevant range and time horizon. What does change is the budgeted and actual total direct machine hours in the first two columns. This means that the budgeted cost-allocation rate will differ from the actual direct machine hours cost-allocation rate as shown in the final line of the table. The total quantity of direct machine hours for both budgeted and actual will be the actual 1,124 MH.

In both departments, the cost pools were underallocated using normal-costing relative to actual-costing rates. An analysis of the underallocations for both cost pools and accounting procedures for overhead allocation and end-of-period adjustments is addressed in Learning Objective 5.

VARIATION OF NORMAL COSTING: A SERVICE INDUSTRY EXAMPLE

As we discussed at the start of this chapter, job costing is very useful in service industries such as accounting and consulting firms, advertising agencies, auto repair shops, and hospitals. In an accounting firm, each audit is a job. The costs of the audit are accumulated on a job cost record, much like the document used by Robinson Company, using the approach described earlier in the chapter. Based on labour time records, direct labour costs of audit partners, audit managers, and audit staff are traced to individual jobs. Other direct costs, such as travel, out-of-town meals and lodging, telephone, fax, and copying, are also traced to jobs. The costs of secretarial support, head office staff, rent, and amortization of furniture and equipment are indirect costs because these costs cannot be identified with jobs in an economically feasible way. Indirect costs are allocated to jobs, for example, using a cost-allocation base such as professional labour-hours.

In some service, merchandising, and manufacturing organizations, a variation of normal costing is helpful because actual direct-labour costs (the largest component of total cost) are difficult to trace to jobs as they are completed. For example, in our audit illustration, the actual direct-labour costs may include bonuses that are known only at the end of the year (a numerator reason). Also, the hours worked each period might vary significantly, depending on the number of working days each month and the demand from clients (a denominator reason). In these situations, to obtain timely information as a job is completed rather than wait until the end of the year, an organization may choose to use budgeted rates for some direct costs in addition to using budgeted rates for indirect costs. All budgeted rates used are calculated at the start of the accounting period. Recall that normal costing uses actual cost rates for all direct costs, and budgeted cost rates only for indirect costs.

The mechanics of using budgeted rates for direct costs are similar to the methods employed when using budgeted rates for indirect costs in normal costing. We illustrate using Lindsay and Associates, a public accounting firm. This business provides services, therefore there are no DMLH because there is no manufacturing labour. Lindsay does, however, accumulate direct labour costs. At the start of the year 2009, Lindsay budgets total direct labour costs of $14,400,000, total indirect costs of $12,960,000, and total direct (professional) labour-hours (DLH) of 288,000 for the year. In this case,

$$\text{Budgeted direct} \atop \text{labour cost rate} = \frac{\text{Budgeted total direct labour cost}}{\text{Budgeted total direct labour-hours}}$$

$$= \frac{\$14,400,000}{288,000 \text{ DLH}} = \$50/\text{DLH}$$

Assuming only one indirect-cost pool and total direct labour-hours as the cost-allocation base:

$$\text{Budgeted indirect} \atop \text{cost rate} = \frac{\text{Budgeted total costs in the indirect-cost pool}}{\text{Budgeted total quantity of cost-allocation base}}$$

$$= \frac{\$12,960,000}{288,000 \text{ DLH}} = \$45/\text{DLH}$$

Suppose an audit of Tracy Transport, a client of Lindsay and Associates, completed in March 2009, uses 800 direct labour-hours. Lindsay calculates the direct costs of the Tracy Transport audit by multiplying the budgeted direct-cost rate by the actual quantity of the direct-cost input. It allocates indirect costs to the Tracy Transport audit by multiplying the budgeted indirect-cost rate by the actual quantity of the cost-allocation base. Assuming no other direct costs for travel, outsourcing, computer work, and so on, the cost of the Tracy Transport audit is:

$$\text{Direct labour costs, } \$50 \times 800 = \$40,000$$
$$\text{Indirect costs allocated, } \$45 \times 800 = \$36,000$$
$$\text{Total} = \$76,000$$

At the end of the year, the direct costs traced to jobs using budgeted rates will rarely equal the actual direct costs because the actual and budgeted rates are developed at different points in time using different information. End-of-period adjustments for underallocated or overallocated direct costs would need to be made in the same way that adjustments were made for underallocated or overallocated indirect costs. Three methods for making these adjustments are discussed at the end of this chapter.

The Lindsay and Associates example illustrates that all costing systems do not map neatly onto either the actual costing or normal costing system described earlier in the chapter. As another example, engineering consulting firms often have some actual direct costs (cost of making blueprints or fees paid to outside experts), other direct costs traced to jobs using a budgeted rate (professional labour costs), and indirect costs allocated to jobs using a budgeted rate (engineering and office support costs).

ASSESS YOUR MASTERY

To check your understanding of the material in Learning Objective ❹, go to the Mastery Questions section at the end of the chapter and complete Learning Objective ❹ question 1.

NORMAL COSTING IS A FORECAST—ALLOCATIONS WILL BE WRONG

⑤ Apply management-accounting logic to underallocation and over-allocation of indirect costs arising from the use of normal costing procedures

The intent of Exhibit 4-10 is to depict the unobservable flow of a few typical costs through the computer MIS records at Robinson Company. Exhibit 4-10 illustrates, using arrows, how the financial transactions flow through Robinson's financial accounting general ledger accounts during March 2009. The transactions are listed and described at the top of Exhibit 4-10. For simplicity, assume beginning balances are zero. Transaction eleven does not give rise to inventoriable but rather to period costs.

There are three types of inventoriable cost pools for this job: direct materials (DM), direct manufacturing labour (DML) at straight time, and MOH (indirect materials, indirect manufacturing labour, utilities, amortization, and insurance). Fortunately, the bookkeeping is based on financial information for individual jobs, and financial accounting standards determined the logic of the management accounting decisions for the job costing system. This exhibit depicts three important features of a reasonable management information system:

♦ relevant inputs are identified with specific departments

♦ actual unit costs are recorded for some inputs, and either statutory or standard rates are recorded for others

♦ all inventoriable or production costs are separated from period costs.

EXHIBIT 4-10

Manufacturing Job Costing System Using Normal Costing: Diagram of General-Ledger Relationships for March 2009 for Robinson and Company

TRANSACTIONS TO BE JOURNALIZED IN THE GENERAL LEDGER ACCOUNTS:

1. Purchase of DM on account, $89,000
2. Transfer of DM to WIP, $81,039
3. DMLH straight-time wages, $41,922, and statutory employer contributions, $13,723 (Var MOH)
4. Rework wages $2,560 and statutory employer contributions, $720 (Var MOH)
5. Wages paid, $58,925
6. Property tax payable $1,800
   Insurance premium $2,000
   Amortization $8,000
   Total fixed MOH $11,800
7. Variable MOH allocated at normal rate, $15,163, and fixed MOH allocated at normal rate, $10,935
8. Transfer MOH allocated to WIP at normal rate, $26,098
9. Transfer WIP to FG, $149,059
10. Transfer FG to COGS, $119,297
11. Period cost salaries incurred and paid, $22,000
12. Revenues from sales all on account, $200,000

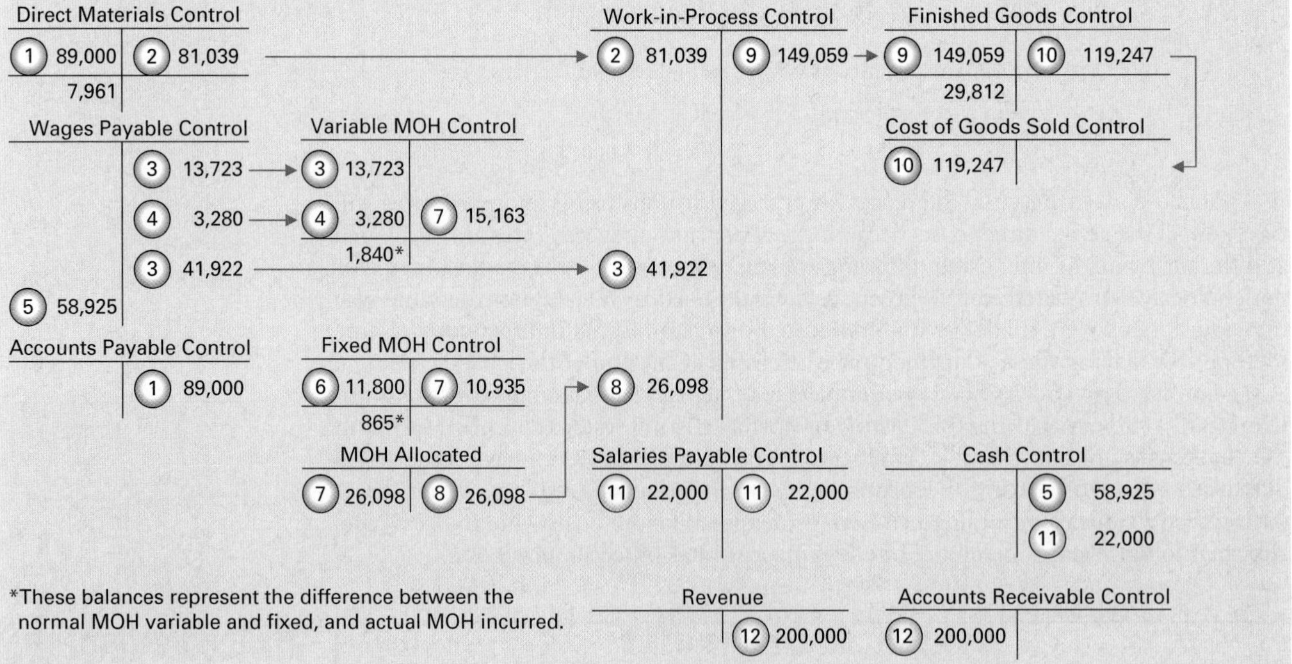

*These balances represent the difference between the normal MOH variable and fixed, and actual MOH incurred.

You will notice that with the exception of manufacturing overhead allocated and revenue, all the general ledger accounts are called *control* accounts. This financial-accounting term signifies that supporting data for each job are recorded in the subsidiary ledgers. The entries in the general ledger accounts are always financial values. But entries in subsidiary ledger accounts include nonfinancial quantities and unit cost rates as illustrated in Exhibit 4–1. For example, subsidiary ledger accounts report the information on:

- quantity of any materials received per either shipping and receiving reports or invoices
- quantity of materials issued to work-in-process per materials requisition records
- quantity of direct manufacturing labour-hours and rework hours per time sheets or a payroll analysis
- dates and quantity of direct manufacturing labour-hours by department and assigned manufacturing overhead (normal costing) per time sheets or a payroll analysis
- quantity of direct machine hours per time records
- all normal and statutory cost-allocation rates (and actual if these are part of the MIS)
- quantities of indirect materials and indirect manufacturing labour costs per shipping and receiving reports or invoices, as well as payroll analysis of statutory benefits and rework
- amortization expense, insurance premium, tax payable per special authorization

While you cannot see these financial flows in any accounting software, Exhibit 4-10 is intended to make these flows visible. The transactions are described below along with both the journal entries and the T-accounts.

Transaction 1 is the purchase of direct materials acquired at $89,000 on account. The journal entry is shown first, followed by posting to the general ledger using T-accounts for the general ledger accounts Direct Materials Control and Accounts Payable Control. Double-entry bookkeeping means the dollars debited and credited must balance. The T-account and the journal entry are two ways of understanding the same transactions.

Stage	Journal Entry:		
A	Direct Materials Control		89,000	
	Accounts Payable Control			89,000

Direct Materials Control	Accounts Payable Control
89,000			89,000

Transaction 2 involves transferring direct materials costing $81,039 to work-in-process (WIP). This begins the value-added conversion. In the subsidiary ledger, the requisitions records, which are recorded (posted) monthly, can be analyzed to separate direct materials between the phases of conversion (B, C) if required. To simplify the example, assume all direct materials move through both phases of conversion into finished goods. Note that actual costs are recorded. This means direct materials will not be allocated to preparation (B) because the cost can be traced directly to this department. The Materials Control general ledger account now has two entries accumulated. The debits and credits for this particular transaction also balance. To this point, if you were to place the Accounts Payable Control T-account beside the Direct Materials and WIP Control accounts, the debit and credit entries for the first two transactions also balance. This format of accumulation continues throughout the example.

Stage	*Journal Entry:*		
B, C	Work-in-Process Control	81,039	
	Direct Materials Control		81,039

Direct Materials Control		**Work-in-Process Control**	
89,000	81,039	81,039	

Assume Robinson uses normal costing for allocation of MOH. *Transaction 3* is the incurrence of *straight-time* wages of $41,922 for the month and statutory employer deductions that comprise part of variable MOH of $13,723. Normal costing requires that MOH be allocated based on budgeted or standard rates multiplied by actual quantities of hours worked. The variable MOH of $13,723 is an estimate, not an actual cost. The budgeted DMLH for March was 1,600 while the actual was 1,605. To simplify this example, assume the additional 5 DMLH were incurred in rework. Total of wages payable and statutory employer deductions is $55,645, the debit to the Wages Payable Control account that balances this entry.

Stage	*Journal Entry:*		
B, C	Work-in-Process Control	41,922	
	Variable Manufacturing Overhead Control	13,723	
	Wages Payable Control		55,645

Wages Payable Control		**Work-in-Process Control**	
	55,645	81,039	
		41,922	

Variable Manufacturing Overhead Control	
13,723	

Transaction 4 reports the 80 DLH of rework wages to carpenter foremen during the conversion of direct materials into finished goods. Robinson must record the *actual* rework cost in these accounts. To allocate manufacturing overhead, however, Robinson uses normal costing whereby the standard rate of $9.00/DLH is multiplied by the actual rework hours worked of 80 DLH. Actual rework and statutory employer contributions are $2,560 and $720. The normal costing rework amount is $720 ($9.00/DLH × 80 DLH = $720) and this is the amount that will be allocated to each department. The variable manufacturing overhead T-account is cumulative and now reports both transactions 3 and 4. The variable manufacturing overhead control must increase by the statutory contributions required of the employer for the hours of rework.

Stage	*Journal Entry:*		
B, C	Variable Manufacturing Overhead Control	2,560	
	Variable Manufacturing Overhead Control	720	
	Wages Payable Control		3,280

Wages Payable Control		**Variable Manufacturing Overhead Control**	
	55,645	13,723	
	3,280	2,560	
		720	

One clear consequence is that variable manufacturing overhead allocated to each department will be too low, or *underallocated*, by $1,840 ($2,560 − $720 = $1,840). The statutory employer deductions will be accurate because $9.00/DLH, the manufacturing overhead cost-allocation rate, is the statutory deductions rate.

Transaction 5 is the payment of the manufacturing payroll for the month of the $58,205 incurred, including statutory employer contributions. To simplify the example: no withholdings for *employee* contributions to statutory pension and medical plans are included; there are no accruals; and all actual rework wages incurred in March are paid in March.

Stage   *Journal Entry:*

B, C   Wages Payable Control   58,925
      Cash Control   58,925

Wages Payable Control		**Cash Control**	
58,925	55,645		58,925
	3,280		

Transaction 6 is the fixed manufacturing overhead costs of $11,800 incurred in March, consisting of amortization of $8,000, insurance of $2,000, and property tax[3] of $1,800. The subsidiary ledger account Accumulated Amortization Control is a contra-asset account to offset the amortization expense. The subsidiary ledger account Property Tax is a current-liability account. The Insurance subsidiary ledger account is a prepaid account. These fixed-cost details are recorded in the subsidiary ledger for Fixed Manufacturing Overhead Control. Assume 1,200 MH were budgeted.

Stage   *Journal Entry:*

B, C   Fixed Manufacturing Overhead Control   11,800
      Property Tax Payable Control   1,800
      Prepaid Insurance Control   2,000
      Accumulated Amortization Control   8,000

Fixed Manufacturing Overhead Control		**Property Tax Payable Control**	
11,800			1,800

Prepaid Insurance Control		**Accumulated Amortization Control**	
	2,000		8,000

[3]Property taxes are often paid quarterly, but for simplicity, this example assumes monthly payments.

Fixed costs do not vary over a relevant range for a specified time horizon. Assuming that the 1,200 budgeted MH and the 1,124 actual MH are within these relevant ranges for the month of March, actual fixed manufacturing overhead will not change. The actual fixed manufacturing overhead has been established as $11,800 resulting in the budgeted or standard fixed MOH rate of $9.83 ($11,800 ÷ 1,200 MH = $9.83/MH). The method of selecting the quantity of machine hours is fully discussed in Chapter 9. Budgeted or forecast values are used consistently to establish this budgeted fixed indirect cost rate. The total normal fixed manufacturing overhead rounded to the nearest dollar will be $11,053. The difference arises because an average unit cost-allocation rate was multiplied by a different quantity of DMH actually used than the quantity upon which this rate was initially calculated. This problem arising from the use of average rates was discussed fully in Chapter 2 and the implications will be more fully discussed in Chapter 8.

Transaction 7 reports the *allocation* of total manufacturing overhead to both departments based on normal costing. For variable MOH, the statutory rate of $9.00/DMLH is the standard rate used in normal costing. This is a variable cost pool; therefore, the actual total variable MOH will increase and decrease with the total actual DMLH consumed.

Normal costing requires multiplying the standard rate by actual DMLH consumed; therefore, this multiplier cannot possibly give rise to any overallocation or underallocation. What gives rise to a different value being allocated is the cost-allocation rate. In this case, the assumption was that rework is not planned but statutory employer contributions are. In addition, the percentage of the total indirect costs for rework was very small relative to that of statutory contributions; therefore, the standard cost-allocation rate chosen was the statutory rate of $9.00/DLH. The rework wages for normal costing are based on the standard rate of $9.00 when the actual rate per DLH for carpenter foremen is $32/DLH. This is the reason why there will be an underallocation of this variable MOH; the difference is due to the different rates. The underallocation is the balance of $1,840 remaining in the Variable Manufacturing Overhead Control account.

The standard cost-allocation rate for the fixed MOH cost pool is $9.83/MH The numerator is the budgeted total fixed cost pool while the denominator is the budgeted total MH for the month. Normal costing requires that this cost pool be allocated based on the standard rate multiplied by the *actual* quantity of MH consumed during March, which was 1,124 MH. For this cost pool, what gives rise to the inaccurate allocation is not the rate. The inaccuracy arises because the actual MH differs from the budgeted MH quantity in the cost-allocation base used to calculate the standard or budgeted fixed manufacturing cost-allocation rate. The total underallocation is $865 as shown in the remaining balance in the Fixed Manufacturing Overhead Control account. The balances with asterisks represent the difference between normal and actual MOH.

Stage	Journal Entry:		
B, C	Manufacturing Overhead Allocated	26,098	
	Variable Manufacturing OH Allocated		15,163
	Fixed Manufacturing Overhead Allocated		10,935

Manufacturing Overhead Allocated		Variable Manufacturing Overhead Control	
	26,098	17,003	15,163
		1,840*	

Fixed Manufacturing Overhead Control	
11,800	10,935
865*	

Transaction 8 is the pivotal event that transfers the costs from the two MOH (variable and fixed) control accounts into the work-in-process control account. At the end of the month, the costs accumulated in the MOH control accounts are assigned to the preparation and assembly departments using the contra account Manufacturing Overhead Allocated. Work-in-process increases by the *allocated* amounts. In total, the underallocation for the month of March was $2,705 ($1,840 + $865 = $2,705). The two MOH control accounts will be returned to zero by means of closing entries at which time adjustments will be made to reflect the actual manufacturing overhead incurred.

Stage	Journal Entry:		
B, C	Work-in-Process Control	26,098	
	Manufacturing Overhead Allocated		26,098

Work-in-Process Control		Manufacturing Overhead Allocated	
81,039		26,098	26,098
41,922			
26,098			

Be clear that transactions 3, 4, and 6 did *not* affect the Work-in-Process Control account until the variable and fixed manufacturing overhead amounts were finally transferred out of these overhead accounts into the work-in-process control account in transaction 8. The pivotal transaction that increased the inventory value of work-in-process was transferring, *not* incurring or even paying these costs, which were reported in transactions 3, 4, and 6. This emphasizes that the assigning of manufacturing overhead is a transaction separate from incurring and paying the actual costs of production.

Transaction 9 reports the transfer of all work-in-process direct material and *allocated* manufacturing overhead costs totalling $149,059 to the finished goods control account. This is an estimated, not an actual, value of the cost of goods available for sale. It is an estimate because the $26,098 in MOH is a normal value, not an actual value. Remember that it has been assumed no unfinished goods remain in work-in-process at the end of March. The ending inventory balance for work-in-process inventory will be zero because all accumulated costs have been transferred out to the finished goods inventory.

Stage	Journal Entry:		
C	Finished Goods Control	149,059	
	Work-in-Process Control		149,059

Work-in-Process Control		Finished Goods Control	
81,039	149,059	149,059	
41,922			
26,098			

In March, however, only 80% of the furniture produced and ready for sale was actually sold. *Transaction 10* is the transfer of the costs accumulated in the finished goods subsidiary ledger control account into the cost of goods sold (COGS) rounded to the nearest dollar was $119,247 ($149,059 × 80% = $119,247). The COGS includes all direct costs and normal manufacturing overhead costs. *Transaction 10* reports the sales for March and the ending inventory balance in finished goods of $29,812 ($149,059 – $119,247 = $29,812) based on allocated, not actual, dollar values. Knowing that the beginning balances in all accounts were assumed to be zero, all the information required to produce financial statements of income, cost of goods manufactured (COGM) and COGS can be extracted from these general ledger accounts. Adjustments must be made to the closing entries, however, to reconcile the allocated with the actual amounts in inventory and COGS. This is discussed in the next section.

Stage	Journal Entry:		
D	Cost of Goods Sold	119,247	
	Finished Goods Control		119,247

Finished Goods Control		Cost of Goods Sold	
149,059	119,247	119,247	
29,812			

This completes the task of understanding all inventoriable cost flows through the various general ledger control and subsidiary ledger accounts with the exception of overallocation and underallocation of MOH. Both variable and fixed manufacturing overhead have been underallocated using normal costing relative to the actual costs, and the end result has been an understatement of COGS, which all other things equal will produce an overstatement of net income for the month of March.

Transaction 11 is the period cost salaries of $22,000 that were incurred and paid. This total consists of the following salaries: marketing $3,000; administration $10,000; accounting $3,000; CEO $6,000.

Stage	Journal Entries:		
D	Marketing Expense	3,000	
	Administration Expense	10,000	
	Accounting Expense	3,000	
	CEO Expense	6,000	
	Salaries Payable Control		22,000
	Salaries Payable Control	22,000	
	Cash Control		22,000

Salaries Expense		Salaries Payable Control	
22,000		22,000	22,000

Cash Control	
	22,000

Transaction 12 is the $200,000 sales revenue for March. All sales were made on account. Transactions 11 and 12 do not affect any inventoriable accounts and will not affect the COGS.

Stage	Journal Entry:		
D	Accounts Receivable Control	200,000	
	Revenue		200,000

Accounts Receivable Control		Revenue	
200,000			200,000

This concludes the set of transactions required to complete a set of financial statements for Robinson Company for March 2009. At this stage, please be sure to trace each journal entry, by transaction number, to the general ledger accounts in Exhibit 4-10 on page 166.

END-OF-PERIOD ADJUSTMENTS FOR OVERALLOCATED AND UNDERALLOCATED MANUFACTURING OVERHEAD

The advantage of using standard or budgeted cost-allocation rates is timeliness. Throughout the month of March, manufacturing overhead can be assigned or allocated to the preparation and assembly departments as incurred. If there is a problem during one week, the managers will not have to wait until month end when the actual costs are available to identify the problem. Budgeted rates permit earlier identification and remedy of cost-control problems. The disadvantage is that inaccuracies arise and manufacturing overhead may be either underallocated or overallocated.

Underallocated indirect costs occur when the allocated amount of indirect costs in an accounting period is less than the actual (incurred) amount in that period. **Overallocated indirect costs** occur when the allocated amount of indirect costs in an accounting period exceeds the actual (incurred) amount in that period. Equivalent terms are **underapplied** (or **overapplied**) **indirect costs** and **underabsorbed** (or **overabsorbed**) **indirect costs.**

Underallocated (overallocated) indirect costs = Indirect costs incurred − Indirect costs allocated

Robinson Company has two indirect-cost pools (Variable Manufacturing Overhead and Fixed Manufacturing Overhead) in its job costing system. There are three indirect-cost accounts in its general ledger that pertain to manufacturing overhead:

◆ **Variable Manufacturing Overhead Control**, which is the record of the *actual* costs in all the individual overhead categories (such as indirect variable statutory benefits for straight-time worked, and rework and statutory benefits).

◆ **Fixed Manufacturing Overhead Control**, which is the record of the *actual* costs in all the individual overhead categories (such as statutory benefits, amortization, insurance, and property taxes).

◆ **Manufacturing Overhead Allocated**, which is the record of the manufacturing overhead allocated to each of the preparation and assembly departments based on the standard or budgeted rate multiplied by the appropriate quantities in the cost-allocation bases of either direct labour-hours or direct machine hours.

There are three main approaches to adjust the closing entries and account correctly for the $2,705 underallocation of manufacturing overhead. These approaches are (1) the adjusted allocation rate, (2) the prorated, and (3) the immediate write-off to COGS.

ADJUSTED ALLOCATION RATE APPROACH

The adjusted allocation rate approach "corrects" all manufacturing overhead (MOH) entries in the general and subsidiary ledgers to what they would have been if accountants had forecasted perfectly the actual MOH costs and the actual quantity of the allocation base. If these two values had been used when calculating the standard cost-allocation rates and quantities of common inputs consumed, the budgeted or normal manufacturing overhead costs would have been identical to the actual manufacturing overhead costs.

The adjusted allocation rate approach restates all entries in the general ledger, replacing all standard or budgeted cost-allocation rates with actual rates. As costs to improve MIS have decreased, the feasibility of this approach has increased. The table below reports the allocation to each department based on normal costing. Notice where the differences in quantity for variable manufacturing overhead occur—the actual total DLH consumed in the assembly department of 1,305 exceeds the budgeted of 1,300 due in part to more rework than anticipated. There is no difference in the preparation department, and the cost-allocation rate is also constant.

Comparison of Actual and Normal Manufacturing Overhead Cost Assignment for Robinson

Manufacturing Overhead Cost Pools Assigned and Variances (Budget - Actual)

	MOH Cost Pools and Cost-Allocation Bases		Preparation Department (B)			Assembly Department (C)			
			MOH Cost Pools and Cost-Allocation Bases		Over (under) MOH Allocation	MOH Cost Pools and Cost-Allocation Bases		Over (under) MOH Allocation	Total Over (under) MOH Allocation
	Normal	Actual	Normal	Actual	Variance	Normal	Actual	Variance	Variance
Total variable MOH cost pool	$15,163	$17,003							
Total DMLH	1,600	1,605	320	240		1,290	1,285		
Carpenter foreman rate for rework	$9.00	$32.00	–	–		75	80		
Statutory cost rate for indirect labour	$9.00		$2,160	$2,160	$0	$13,003	$14,843	$(1,840)	$ (1,840)
Total fixed MOH cost pool	$10,935	$11,800							$ (865)
	$26,098	$28,803							$ (2,705)

In the fixed manufacturing overhead cost pool in the lower half of the table, the budgeted or normal cost-allocation rate differs from the actual rate. The underallocation shown in parentheses amounts to $865, the balance in the Fixed Manufacturing Overhead Control account at the end of March.

The first step is to recalculate the actual indirect cost-allocation rates for each period by dividing the actual variable or fixed manufacturing overhead cost pool by the actual quantity of either DMLH or MH consumed in March. This transforms a normal costing into an actual costing procedure *in content*. End-of-period adjustments are made to close the temporary manufacturing overhead control accounts. In this example, the underallocation amounts to 7.07% of the total actual manufacturing overhead cost pool (($28,085 − $26,098) ÷ $28,085 = 7.07%). Software programs can use these data in the information system to complete the calculation and simply increase the allocation to each department by 7.07% for each manufacturing overhead cost pool. The benefit of timely normal costing during the time period for cost control problem identification and remedy is not lost, yet the cost of this software change would be minimal and the financial reports would be less inaccurate. The end balances for inventory general ledger accounts would reflect their actual dollar value.

PRORATION APPROACH

Proration is itself an allocation method that uses the percentages of manufacturing overhead allocated based on normal costing to allocate the underallocation or overallocation among the relevant accounts of inventories and cost of goods sold. At the end of the year, assume the following balances in the two inventory accounts (Work-in-Process and Finished Goods), the COGS expense, and the normal allocated MOH component of each balance:

	End-of-Year Balances (Before Proration)	Manufacturing Overhead Allocated Component of Year-End Balances (Before Proration)	Allocation as a Percentage of Year-End Balance Allocation in Each Account ÷ Total Normal Allocation
Work in Process	$1,430,964	$18,000	45.0%
Finished Goods	1,080,000	12,000	30.0%
Cost of Goods Sold	864,000	10,000	25.0%
	$3,374,964	$40,000	

Assume the actual MOH is $45,500 at the end of the year. The first step is to calculate the proportion of total manufacturing overhead currently allocated to the work-in-process inventory, finished goods inventory, and cost of goods sold expense accounts. The underallocated amount of $5,500 is then multiplied by each percentage and the dollar value added to each account in turn. Recall that there was zero ending work-in-process inventory. This is why the manufacturing overhead allocated to each inventory account is the same. Not all finished goods were sold, however, which is why the manufacturing overhead in this ending inventory amount is smaller than in the work-in-process ending inventory account. The assumption of a zero ending work-in-process inventory was done to simplify the financial flow of costs illustrated throughout this example.

	End-of-Year Balances (Before Proration) (1)	Manufacturing Overhead Allocated Component of Year-End Balances (Before Proration) (2)	Allocated Manufacturing Overhead Included in Each Account Balance Percent of Total (3)	Proration of $5,500 of Underallocated Manufacturing Overhead (4) = (3) × $5,500	Account Balance (After Proration) (5) = (1) + (4)
Work in Process	$1,430,964	$18,000	45.0%	$2,475	$1,433,439
Finished Goods	1,080,000	12,000	30.0%	1,650	1,081,650
Cost of Goods Sold	864,000	10,000	25.0%	1,375	865,375
	$3,374,964	$40,000		$5,500	$3,380,464

The journal entries restate the ending balances to actual dollar values at year end, which happens to be March 31, 2009. Note that if manufacturing overhead had been overallocated, the Work-in-Process, Finished Goods, and Cost of Goods Sold accounts would be decreased (credited) instead of increased (debited). The journal entry at year end would be:

Work-in-Process Control	20,475	
Finished Goods Control	13,650	
Cost of Goods Sold	11,375	
Manufacturing Overhead Control		45,500

Some companies use the proration approach but base it on column 1 of the earlier table—that is, the ending balances in Work-in-Process, Finished Goods, and Cost of Goods Sold before proration. It gives the same results as the proration approach only if the proportions of direct costs of manufacturing based on column 2 are constant in the Work-in-Process, Finished Goods, and Cost of Goods Sold accounts. If this was the case, prorating based on total costs is the same as prorating based on allocated overhead costs. Often, however, prorations based on column 1 will not be the same as the more accurate prorations based on column 2. In manual systems, proration based on total costs could be justified as less laborious; however, with low-cost technology, this is no longer a reasonable justification.

WRITE-OFF TO COST OF GOODS SOLD APPROACH

When using the write-off to cost of goods sold approach, the total underallocated or overallocated overhead is included in this year's Cost of Goods Sold. In the Robinson Company example of the $5,500 underallocation, the journal entry would be:

Cost of Goods Sold	5,500	
Manufacturing Overhead Allocated	40,000	
Manufacturing Overhead Control		45,500

Robinson's two Manufacturing Overhead accounts (MOH Control and MOH Allocated) are closed out with all the difference between them now included in cost of goods sold. The Cost of Goods Sold account is now $869,500, the balance before proration of $864,000 plus the underallocated overhead amount of $5,500.

No matter which approach is used, the underallocated overhead is not carried in the overhead accounts beyond the end of the year. That is, the ending balances in Manufacturing Overhead Control and Manufacturing Overhead Allocated are closed to Work-in-Process Control, Finished Goods, or Cost of Goods Sold, and consequently become zero at the end of each year.

CHOICE AMONG APPROACHES

In choosing among the approaches for making adjustments for the underallocation or overallocation of manufacturing overhead, managers should be guided by how the resultant information is to be used. If managers desire to develop the most accurate record of individual job costs for profitability analysis, the adjusted allocation rate approach is preferred. The proration approach does not make any adjustment to individual departmental or job cost records. If the purpose is confined to reporting the most accurate inventory and cost of goods sold figures, proration based on the indirect cost allocated component of ending balances should be used because it adjusts the balances to what they would have been under actual costing but does not adjust individual departmental or job cost records.

The write-off to Cost of Goods Sold is the simplest approach for dealing with underallocated or overallocated overhead. If the amount of underallocated (or overallocated) overhead is small—in comparison to total operating income or some other measure of materiality—the approach yields a good approximation to more accurate but more complex approaches. Modern companies are also becoming increasingly conscious of inventory control; thus, inventories are lower than they were in earlier years, and Cost of Goods Sold tends to be higher in relation to inventories of Work-in-Process and Finished Goods. Also, the inventory balances of job-costing companies are usually relatively small because goods are often made in response to specific sales orders. Consequently, as is true in the Robinson Company example, writing off underallocated or overallocated overhead instead of prorating it is unlikely to cause significant distortions in financial statements. For all these reasons, the cost-benefit test would favour the simplest method—immediate write-off to Cost of Goods Sold—because the more costly attempts at accuracy represented by the other approaches do not appear to provide additional useful information.

To implement a normal costing system with multiple overhead cost pools, Robinson Company determined the budgeted total direct manufacturing labour-hours and the budgeted total machine hours for the year 2009, and identified the associated budgeted indirect total costs for each cost pool. Robinson calculated the two indirect-cost rates, one based on direct manufacturing labour-hours and one based on machine hours. The general ledger contained two Overhead Control and Overhead Allocated amounts for each cost of the variable and fixed overhead cost pools. End-of-period adjustments for underallocated or overallocated indirect costs were made separately for each cost pool.

Management accountants must use professional judgment when presenting alternative cost-allocation bases and sets of cost pools. There is never a single right way to implement job and process costing procedures. Cost-allocation bases should be linked to the core function and the key success factors of an organization in order to control the most important costs. Those actually responsible for the performance of the core function will decide among the alternative costing procedures that management accountants present. It is important to ensure that the costing procedure avoids providing perverse incentives to managers. No job or process costing procedure will be accurate simply because it is neither easy nor economical to identify all causes of all costs. This means that job and processing costing procedures inevitably overallocate or underallocate costs.

ASSESS YOUR MASTERY

To check your understanding of the material in Learning Objective 5, go to the Mastery Questions section at the end of the chapter and complete Learning Objective 5 question 1.

Re-examine the Exhibit 4-10 illustration of a job costing system on page 166. Then try to solve the following problem, which requires consideration of many of this chapter's important points in a service-sector company.

PROBLEM

You are asked to bring the following incomplete accounts of Endeavour Printing Inc. up to date through January 31, 2010. Consider the data that appear in the T-accounts as well as the following information in items (a) through (i).

Endeavour's job costing system, which uses normal costing, has two direct-cost categories (direct materials and direct manufacturing labour) and one indirect-cost pool (manufacturing overhead, which is allocated using direct manufacturing labour costs).

Materials Control	Wages Payable Control
12-31-2009 Bal. 15,000	1-31-2010 Bal. 3,000

Work-in-Process Control	Manufacturing Overhead Control
	1-31-2010 Bal. 57,000

	Manufacturing Overhead Allocated

Finished Goods Control	Cost of Goods Control
12-31-2009 Bal. 20,000	

ADDITIONAL INFORMATION

a. Manufacturing overhead is allocated using a budgeted rate set every December. Management forecasts next year's manufacturing overhead and next year's direct manufacturing labour costs. The budget for 2010 is $400,000 of direct manufacturing labour and $600,000 of manufacturing overhead.

b. The only job unfinished on January 31, 2010, is No. 419, on which direct manufacturing labour costs are $2,000 (125 DMLH) and direct materials costs are $8,000.

c. Total materials placed into production during January are $90,000.

d. Cost of goods completed during January is $180,000.

e. Materials inventory as of January 31, 2010, is $20,000.

f. Finished goods inventory as of January 31, 2010, is $15,000.

g. All plant workers earn the same wage rate. DMLH used for January total 2,500. Other labour and supervision labour total $10,000.

h. The gross plant payroll paid in January equals $52,000. Ignore withholdings.

i. All "actual" Manufacturing Department overhead incurred during January has already been posted.

REQUIRED

Calculate the following:

1. Materials purchased during January
2. Cost of Goods Sold during January
3. Direct Manufacturing Labour Costs incurred during January
4. Manufacturing Overhead Allocated during January
5. Balance of Wages Payable Control, December 31, 2009
6. Balance of Work-in-Process Control, January 31, 2010
7. Balance of Work-in-Process Control, December 31, 2009
8. Manufacturing Overhead underallocated or overallocated for January 2010

SOLUTION

Amounts from the T-accounts are labelled "(T)".

1. From Materials Control T-account, Materials purchased: $90,000 (c) + $20,000 (e) − $15,000 (T) = $95,000
2. From Finished Goods Control T-account, Cost of Goods Sold: $20,000 (T) + $180,000 (d) − $15,000 (f) = $185,000
3. Direct manufacturing wage rate: $2,000 (b) ÷ 125 DMLH (b) = $16 per DMLH

   Direct manufacturing labour costs: 2,500 DMLH (g) × $16 = $40,000

4. Manufacturing overhead rate: $600,000 (a) ÷ $400,000 (a) = 150%

   Manufacturing Overhead Allocated: 150% of $40,000 (see 3) = $60,000

5. From Wages Payable Control T-account, Wages Payable Control, December 31, 2009: $52,000 (h) + $3,000 (T) − $40,000 (see 3) − $10,000 (g) = $5,000
6. Work-in-Process Control, January 31, 2010: $8,000 (b) + $2,000 (b) + 150% of $2,000 (b) = $13,000 (This answer is used in item 7.)
7. From Work-in-Process Control T-account, Work-in-Process Control, December 31, 2009: $180,000 (d) + $13,000 (see 6) − $90,000 (c) − $40,000 (see 3) − $60,000 (see 4) = $3,000
8. Manufacturing overhead overallocated: $60,000 (see 4) − $57,000 (T) = $3,000

Entries in T-accounts are lettered in accordance with the preceding additional information and are numbered in accordance with the requirements above.

Materials Control

December 31, 2009 Bal.	(given)	15,000			
	(1)	95,000*		(c)	90,000
January 31, 2010 Bal.	(e)	20,000			

Work-in-Process Control

December 31, 2009 Bal.	(7)	3,000		(d)	180,000
Direct materials	(c)	90,000			
Direct manufacturing labour	(b) (g) (3)	40,000			
Manufacturing overhead allocated	(g) (a) (4)	60,000			
January 31, 2010	Bal. (b) (6)	13,000			

Finished Goods Control

December 31, 2009 Bal.	(given)	20,000		(2)	185,000
	(d)	180,000			
January 31, 2010 Bal.	(f)	15,000			

Wages Payable Control

(h)		52,000	December 31, 2009	(5)	5,000
				(b) (g) (3)	40,000
				(g)	10,000
			January 31, 2010	(given)	3,000

Manufacturing Overhead Control

Total January charges	(given)	57,000	

Manufacturing Overhead Allocated

				(g) (a) (4)	60,000

Cost of Goods Sold

(2)	185,000		

*Can be computed only after all other postings in the account have been found.

The following decision guidelines use a question-and-answer format to summarize the chapter's main points. Each decision presents a key question. The guideline is the answer to that question.

DECISIONS	GUIDELINES
1. How do job costing system development, procedures, allocation, and assignment link with one another?	The development of any job costing system depends upon reliable financial and nonfinancial data. Some costs can be traced directly to a single job because it is economically feasible to do so, so no further procedures are needed. Often the link between costs and a specific job are neither readily observable nor economically measurable. A job costing procedure requires two stages. The first is allocation, which means costs are grouped into logically reasonable cost pools, then divided by the quantity of some input common to all jobs. The result, a cost-allocation rate, is the basis to assign costs from each cost pool to each job.
2. Can job costing systems be developed to assign costs to services as well as products?	The job is another general term for cost object. The job can be identified as a service, a department, or a final unit of output. The key issue is that jobs consume inputs in different amounts. If the consumption of inputs is identical per job, no assignment is required and a simple averaging of costs will be sufficient.
3. What procedures are used to calculate cost-allocation rates and assign costs to jobs when the job is a manufacturing department?	The job costing procedures of calculating allocation rates and assigning costs from a cost pool to a job are arithmetically straightforward. The first arithmetic step is division and the second is multiplication. Job cost assignment requires multiplying the cost-allocation rate by the quantity of input used by a job, in this case a department. The input used as the multiplier is the same as the input used to calculate the cost-allocation rate. Each department will use different quantities of this input; otherwise job cost assignment is not necessary.
4. With all the inaccuracies of cost procedures, what are the benefits of normal costing over actual costing?	Normal costing refers to the practice of assigning relevant costs to a job based on the standard or budgeted cost-allocation rate. This rate is forecasted for some time period and is calculated by dividing the budgeted overhead cost pool by the budgeted quantity of common inputs used (the quantity in the cost-allocation base). The budgeted rate multiplied by the actual quantity of common inputs provides a timely estimate of costs accumulated to date for each job. Managers can identify cost-control problems and begin solving them before the job is completed rather than endure unnecessary cost overruns that impair profitability. In some variations from normal costing, organizations use budgeted rates to assign direct costs, as well as indirect costs, to jobs.
5. When normal costing is used, the budgeted rate is an estimate. How are the financial accounts adjusted to include any differences between actual and normal costs?	The two theoretically correct approaches to adjusting for underallocated or overallocated overhead costs are 1. to adjust the allocation rate, and 2. to prorate based on the total amount of the allocated manufacturing overhead cost in the ending balances of Work-in-Process Control, Finished Goods Control, and Cost of Goods Sold. Many companies simply write off amounts of underallocated or overallocated manufacturing overhead to Cost of Goods Sold on the basis of practicality.

This chapter contains definitions of the following important terms:

actual costing (p. 145)
cost allocation (p. 144)
cost-allocation base (p. 144)
cost-allocation rate (p. 144)
cost application (p. 144)
cost-application base (p. 144)
cost assignment (p. 144)
cost object (p. 140)
cost pool (p. 141)

direct cost (p. 141)
direct cost-allocation rate (p. 144)
indirect cost-allocation rate (p. 144)
job (p. 140)
job cost record (job cost sheet) (p. 141)
job costing system (p. 140)
key success factor (p. 14)
labour time record (p. 141)
materials requisition record (p. 141)

normal costing (p. 163)
overallocated (overabsorbed, overapplied) indirect costs (p. 173)
perverse incentive (p. 147)
process costing system (p. 140)
proration (p. 174)
source document (p. 141)
underallocated (underabsorbed, underapplied) indirect costs (p. 173)

The Mastery Questions are rated by proficiency level—elementary, intermediate, and advanced. The solutions appear in the Mastery Question Solutions section of MyAccountingLab.

LEARNING OBJECTIVE 1

1. Differences between job costing and process costing—Elementary. Of the following items, which are relevant to job costing?

conversion costs

direct manufacturing labour

period costs

indirect costs of manufacturing

prime costs

direct materials costs

2. Job costing procedures—Intermediate. A team of top managers at Gundy and Associates Ltd. are reviewing a preliminary annual budget of expected revenue and costs for one of their projects, shown below. The revenues are based on 100,000 units sold in the year. The facilities can produce 1,000,000 units and the project has not yet begun so there are no beginning inventories. Indirect manufacturing costs are allocated on the basis of direct manufacturing labour-hours (DMLH). Gundy and Associates Ltd. expects to pay for 600,000 hours this year. Fixed manufacturing costs are allocated on the basis of the output the facility can produce.

	Total	Allocation Rate per Unit
Budgeted revenue	$90,000,000	
Budgeted COGS		
Direct materials	9,000,000	
Direct manufacturing labour	12,000,000	
Variable manufacturing overhead	15,000,000	
Fixed manufacturing overhead	18,000,000	
Total COGS	54,000,000	
Budgeted period costs		
Variable period costs	6,000,000	
Fixed period costs	8,000,000	
Total period costs	14,000,000	
Total costs	68,000,000	
Operating income	$22,000,000	

REQUIRED

1. Calculate the budgeted indirect variable manufacturing overhead (MOH) rate.
2. Calculate the fixed MOH rate.
3. At what rate is Gundy and Associates Ltd. producing units?
4. Calculate the total MOH rate.
5. If the company does no customization of its outputs for different customers, discuss the usefulness of allocation.

3. Job costing procedures—Advanced. Broadway Printers operates a printing press with a monthly capacity of 2,000 machine hours (MH). Broadway has two main customers, Taylor Corporation and Kelly Corporation. Data on each customer for January follow:

	Taylor Corporation	Kelly Corporation	Total
Revenues	$132,000	$88,000	$220,000
Variable costs	46,200	52,800	99,000
Fixed costs (allocated on the basis of revenues)	66,000	44,000	110,000
Total operating costs	112,200	96,800	209,000
Operating income (loss)	$ 19,800	$(8,800)	$ 11,000
Machine hours (MH) required	1,500 hours	500 hours	2,000 hours

Each of the following requirements refers only to the preceding data; there is *no connection* between the requirements.

REQUIRED

1. Fixed costs arise because equipment and other capacity have been purchased. What would be the allocation of fixed costs and what would the operating income and operating margin be for each job if the fixed MOH cost-allocation base were machine hours instead of revenue?
2. Should Broadway drop the Kelly Corporation business? If Broadway drops the Kelly Corporation business, its total fixed costs will decrease by 20%.
3. Kelly Corporation indicates that it wants Broadway to do an *additional* $88,000 worth of printing jobs during February. These jobs are identical to the existing business Broadway did for Kelly in January in terms of variable costs and machine hours required. Broadway anticipates that the business from Taylor Corporation in February will be the same as that in January. Broadway can choose to accept as much of the Taylor and Kelly business for February as it wants. Assume that total fixed costs for February will be the same as the fixed costs in January. What should Broadway do? What will Broadway's operating income be in February?

LEARNING OBJECTIVE 2

1. **Computing indirect cost rates, services—Elementary.** Mike Rotundo, the president of Tax Assist, is examining alternative ways to compute indirect cost rates. He collects the following information from the budget for 2011:

   ◆ Budgeted variable indirect costs: $12 per hour of professional labour time
   ◆ Budgeted fixed indirect costs: $60,000 per quarter

   The budgeted billable professional labour-hours per quarter are:

January–March	24,000 hours
April–June	12,000 hours
July–September	4,800 hours
October–December	7,200 hours

   Rotundo pays all tax professionals employed by Tax Assist on an hourly basis ($36 per hour, including all fringe benefits).

   Tax Assist's job costing system has a single direct-cost category (professional labour at $36 per hour) and a single indirect-cost pool (office support that is allocated using professional labour-hours).

   Tax Assist charges clients $78 per professional labour-hour.

   ### REQUIRED

   1. Compute budgeted indirect cost rates per professional labour-hour using
      a. Quarterly budgeted billable hours as the denominator
      b. Annual budgeted billable hours as the denominator
   2. Compute the operating income for the following four customers using
      a. Quarterly based indirect-cost rates
      b. An annual indirect-cost rate
      ◆ Stan Hansen: 10 hours in February
      ◆ Lelani Kai: 6 hours in March and 4 hours in April
      ◆ Ken Patera: 4 hours in June and 6 hours in August
      ◆ Evelyn Stevens: 5 hours in January, 2 hours in September, and 3 hours in November
   3. Comment on your results in requirement 2.

2. **Job costing, consulting firm—Intermediate.** Taylor & Partners, a consulting firm, has the following condensed budget for 2010:

Revenues		$24,000,000
Total costs:		
Direct costs: Professional labour	$ 6,000,000	
Indirect costs: Client support	15,600,000	21,600,000
Operating income		$ 2,400,000

   Taylor has a single direct-cost category (professional labour) and a single indirect-cost pool (client support). Indirect costs are allocated to jobs based on professional labour costs.

1. The markup rate for pricing jobs is intended to produce a 10% operating-income-to-revenue margin. Compute the markup rate as a percentage of professional labour costs.
2. Taylor is bidding on a consulting job for Red Rooster, a fast-food chain specializing in poultry meats. The budgeted breakdown of professional labour on the job is as follows:

Professional Labour Category	Budgeted Rate per Hour	Budgeted Hours
Director	$240	3
Partner	120	16
Manager	60	40
Assistant	36	160

Compute the budgeted cost of the Red Rooster job. How much will Taylor bid for the job if it is to earn its target operating-income-to-revenue margin of 10%?

3. **Job costing, cost-plus pricing—Advanced.** (CMA, adapted) Hall Company specializes in packaging bulk drugs. Wyant Memorial Hospital has asked Hall to bid on the packaging of one million doses of medication at full cost plus a return on full cost of no more than 9% after income taxes. Wyant defines cost as including all variable costs of performing the service, a reasonable amount of fixed overhead, and incremental administrative costs. The hospital will supply all packaging materials and ingredients. Wyant has indicated that any bid over $0.084 per dose will be rejected.

Don Greenway, the director of cost accounting, has accumulated the following information prior to the preparation of the bid:

Variable direct manufacturing labour costs	$19.20 per direct manufacturing labour-hour (DMLH)
Variable overhead costs	$7.20 per DMLH
Fixed overhead costs	$36.00 per DMLH
Incremental administrative costs	$6,000 for the order
Production rate	1,000 doses per DMLH

Hall Company is subject to an income tax rate of 40%.

REQUIRED
1. Calculate the minimum price per dose that Hall could bid for the Wyant job without changing Hall's net income.
2. Calculate Hall's bid price per dose using the full cost criterion and the maximum allowable return specified by Wyant.
3. Without considering your answer to requirement 2, assume that the price per dose that Hall calculated using the cost-plus criterion specified by Wyant is greater than the maximum bid of $0.084 per dose allowed by Wyant. Discuss the factors that Hall should consider before deciding whether or not to submit a bid at the maximum price of $0.084 per dose.

LEARNING OBJECTIVE 3

1. **Budgeted manufacturing overhead rate, allocated manufacturing overhead—Elementary.** Waheed Company allocates manufacturing overhead costs using a budgeted rate per machine hour and actual machine hours (MH). The following data are available for 2010:

Budgeted manufacturing overhead costs	$3,420,000
Budgeted machine hours (MH)	190,000
Actual manufacturing overhead costs	$3,492,000
Actual machine hours (MH)	195,000

REQUIRED
1. Calculate the budgeted manufacturing overhead rate.
2. Compute the manufacturing overhead allocated during 2010.

2. **Job costing, accounting for manufacturing overhead, budgeted rates—Intermediate.** Solomon Company's Dover plant has a Machining Department and a Finishing Department. Its job costing system has two direct-cost categories (direct materials and direct manufacturing labour) and two manufacturing overhead cost pools (the Machining Department, allocated using actual machine

hours (MH), and the Finishing Department, allocated using actual labour cost). The 2010 budget for the plant is as follows:

	Machining Department	Finishing Department
Manufacturing overhead	$12,000,000	$9,600,000
Direct manufacturing labour cost	$ 1,080,000	$4,800,000
Direct manufacturing labour-hours (DMLH)	30,000	160,000
Machine hours (MH)	200,000	33,000

REQUIRED
1. What is the budgeted overhead rate that should be used in the Machining Department? in the Finishing Department?
2. During the month of January, the cost record for Job 431 shows the following:

	Machining Department	Finishing Department
Direct material used	$16,800	$3,600
Direct manufacturing labour cost	$ 720	$1,500
Direct manufacturing labour-hours (DMLH)	30	50
Machine hours (MH)	130	10

What is the total manufacturing overhead allocated to Job 431?
3. Assuming that Job 431 consisted of 200 units of product, what is the unit product cost of Job 431?

3. **Job costing, considering three alternatives—Advanced.** (CMA) The Auer Company had just completed an order for a special machine from the Jay Company when the Jay Company declared bankruptcy, defaulted on the order, and forfeited the 10% deposit paid on the selling price of $79,750. Auer has to choose the most profitable of three courses of action.

Auer's manufacturing manager identified the total costs already incurred in the production of the special machine for Jay as follows:

Direct materials used		$18,260
Direct manufacturing labour incurred		23,540
Overhead allocated:		
Manufacturing:		
Variable	$11,770	
Fixed	5,885	17,655
Fixed marketing and administration		5,945
Total costs		$65,400

One choice is that the Kaytell Corporation would be interested in buying the special machine if it is reworked to Kaytell's specifications. It will take 30 days to complete the rework. Auer would sell the reworked machine to Kaytell as a special order for $75,240. This price is net of any discount for early payment (see below). Kaytell would pay when it takes delivery in 60 days. The additional traceable costs to rework the machine to Kaytell's specifications are as follows:

Direct materials	$ 6,820
Direct manufacturing labour	4,620
	$11,440

The second choice is to convert the customized machine for Jay to the standard model. The standard model lists for $68,750. This price is also net of any discount. The additional traceable costs to convert the special machine to the standard model are

Direct materials	$3,135
Direct manufacturing labour	3,630
	$6,765

The third choice is to sell the machine as is for a net price of $57,200. However, the potential buyer of the unmodified machine does not want it for 60 days. The buyer will pay a $7,700 down payment immediately, with final payment upon delivery.

The following additional information is available regarding Auer's operations:

◆ Auer pays its salespeople 2% commission on sales of standard models and 3% on special orders. All sales commissions are calculated on selling price minus cash discount, if any.

◆ Credit terms for sales of standard models are 2/10, n/30 (2/10 means a discount of 2% is given if payment is made within 10 days of signing the sales contract; n/30 means the full balance payable amount is due within 30 days of delivery). If they can, customers will take advantage of the discounts. Credit terms for special orders are negotiated with the customer.

◆ The allocation rates for manufacturing overhead and the fixed marketing and administration costs are

Manufacturing:	
Variable	50% of direct manufacturing labour costs
Fixed	25% of direct manufacturing labour costs
Marketing and administration:	
Fixed	10% of the total of direct materials, direct manufacturing labour costs, and manufacturing overhead costs

◆ Normal time required for rework is one month.

◆ A surcharge of 5% of the selling price is placed on all customer requests for minor modifications of standard models.

◆ Auer normally sells a sufficient number of standard models for the company to operate at a volume in excess of the breakeven point.

Auer does not consider the time value of money in its analyses of special orders whenever the period is less than one year, because the effect is not significant.

REQUIRED

1. In which of the 3 choices is the discount applicable?
2. Based on each choice, list the dollar values of the incremental costs and discounts where applicable, then calculate the dollar contribution that each of the three alternatives will add to Auer Company's operating income.
3. Consider operating leverage (see Chapter 3). Discuss the influence that fixed manufacturing overhead costs should have on the selling prices Auer quotes for special orders when (a) the firm is operating at or below the breakeven point and (b) the firm's special orders will mean efficient utilization of unused capacity above the breakeven point.

LEARNING OBJECTIVE 4

1. **Job costing, accounting for overhead costs, budgeted rates—Advanced.** Jefferson Company is a painting contractor for office and factory buildings. Jefferson uses a normal costing system to cost each job. Jefferson's normal costing system has two direct-cost categories (direct materials and direct labour) and one indirect-cost pool called *overhead costs*. Jefferson uses a budgeted overhead rate for allocating overhead costs to jobs on the basis of direct labour costs.

Jefferson provides the following additional information:

1. Budgeted overhead costs for the year 2010 $1,440,000
   Budgeted direct labour costs for the year 2010 $1,800,000
2. As of January 31, Job 101 was the only job in process, with direct materials costs of $36,000 and direct labour costs of $60,000.
3. Jobs 102, 103, and 104 were started during February.
4. Direct materials used during February equal $180,000.
5. Direct labour costs for February are $144,000.
6. Actual overhead costs for February are $122,400.
7. The only job still in process at February 28, 2010 was Job 104, with direct materials costs of $24,000 and direct labour costs of $48,000.

Jefferson maintains a Jobs-in-Process Control account in its general ledger. As a job is completed, Jefferson immediately bills the client and transfers the cost of the completed job to the Cost of Jobs Billed account to be matched against the revenues billed to the client. Consequently, unlike manufacturing companies, Jefferson does not have an account that corresponds to Finished Goods Control. Each month, Jefferson closes any underallocated or overallocated overhead to Cost of Jobs Billed.

REQUIRED

1. Calculate the budgeted overhead rate for allocating overhead costs in 2010.
2. Calculate the manufacturing overhead allocated to Job 101 as of January 31, 2010, and the manufacturing overhead allocated to Job 104 as of February 28, 2010.
3. Calculate the underallocated or overallocated overhead for February 2010.
4. Calculate the Cost of Jobs Billed by Jefferson in February 2010.

LEARNING OBJECTIVE 5

1. **Disposition of overhead underallocated or overallocated overhead—Advanced.** (Z. Iqbal, adapted) Zaf Radiator Company uses a single manufacturing overhead cost pool in its job costing system. It uses a normal costing system with actual machine hours (MH) as the allocation base. The following data are for 2010:

Budgeted manufacturing overhead (MOH)	$5,760,000
Overhead allocation base	machine hours (MH)
Budgeted machine hours (MH)	80,000
Manufacturing overhead (MOH) incurred	$5,880,000
Actual machine hours (MH)	75,000

Machine-hours data and the ending balances (before proration of underallocated or overallocated overhead) are as follows:

	Actual Machine Hours (MH)	2010 End-of-Year Balance
Cost of Goods Sold	60,000	$9,600,000
Finished Goods	11,000	1,500,000
Work-in-Process	4,000	900,000

REQUIRED
1. Compute the budgeted manufacturing overhead rate for 2010.
2. Compute the underallocated or overallocated manufacturing overhead of Zaf Radiator in 2010. Dispose of this underallocated or overallocated amount using
   a. Immediate write-off to Cost of Goods Sold
   b. Proration based on ending balances (before proration) in Work-in-Process, Finished Goods, and Cost of Goods Sold
   c. Proration based on the allocated overhead amount (before proration) in the ending balances of Work-in-Process, Finished Goods, and Cost of Goods Sold
3. Which disposition method do you prefer in requirement 2? Explain.

ASSIGNMENT MATERIAL

Make the grade with MyAccountingLab: The questions, exercises, and problems marked in red can be found on MyAccountingLab at **www.myaccountinglab.com.** You can practise them as often as you want, and most feature step-by-step guided instructions to help you find the right answer. Exercises and problems with an Excel icon in the margin have an accompanying Excel template on MyAccountingLab.

SHORT-ANSWER QUESTIONS

4-1 Define cost pool, cost tracing, cost-allocation base, and cost allocation.

4-2 How does a job costing system differ from a process costing system?

4-3 What is the benefit of creating more than one manufacturing overhead cost pool?

4-4 Why would it be of benefit to separate a conversion process into different stages or departments?

4-5 What are the two major cost objects that managers focus on in companies using job costing?

4-6 Describe the three major source documents used in job costing systems.

4-7 What is the main concern about source documents used to prepare job cost records?

4-8 Give two reasons why most organizations use an annual period rather than a weekly or monthly period to compute budgeted indirect cost-allocation rates.

4-9 How does actual costing differ from normal costing?

4-10 Describe two ways in which a house-construction company may use job cost information.

4-11 Comment on the following statement: "In a normal costing system, the amounts in the Manufacturing Overhead Control account will always equal the amounts in the Manufacturing Overhead Allocated account."

4-12 Describe three different debit entries in the Work-in-Process Control general ledger T-account.

4-13 Describe three alternative ways to dispose of underallocated or overallocated indirect costs.

4-14 When might a company use budgeted costs rather than actual costs to compute direct labour rates?

4-15 What is the right way to decide on the cost-allocation bases and number of cost pools?

EXERCISES

4-16 **Job costing, process costing.** In each of the following situations, determine whether job costing or process costing would be more appropriate.

a. A CA firm	**l.** A landscaping company
b. An oil refinery	**m.** A cola-drink-concentrate producer
c. A custom furniture manufacturer	**n.** A movie studio
d. A tire manufacturer	**o.** A law firm
e. A textbook publisher	**p.** A commercial aircraft manufacturer
f. A pharmaceutical company	**q.** A management consulting firm
g. An advertising agency	**r.** A breakfast cereal company
h. An apparel manufacturing factory	**s.** A catering service
i. A flour mill	**t.** A paper mill
j. A paint manufacturer	**u.** An auto repair garage
k. A medical care facility	

1. Budgeted is 85% of direct labour costs

4-17 **Actual costing, normal costing, manufacturing overhead.** Destin Products uses a job costing system with two direct-cost categories (direct materials and direct manufacturing labour) and one manufacturing overhead cost pool. Destin allocates manufacturing overhead costs using direct manufacturing labour costs. Destin provides the following information:

	Budget for Year 2010	Actuals for Year 2010
Direct manufacturing labour costs	$2,600,000	$2,540,000
Direct manufacturing overhead costs	$2,210,000	$2,311,400
Direct materials costs	$1,800,000	$1,740,000

REQUIRED

1. Compute the actual and budgeted manufacturing overhead rates for 2010.
2. During March, the cost record for Job 626 contained the following:

Direct materials used	$38,000
Direct manufacturing labour costs	$27,000

Compute the cost of Job 626 using (a) an actual costing system and (b) a normal costing system.

3. At the end of 2010, compute the underallocated or overallocated manufacturing overhead under Destin's normal costing system. Why is there no underallocated or overallocated overhead under Destin's actual costing system?
4. Comment briefly on the advantages and disadvantages of actual costing systems and normal costing systems.

1. a. Direct cost rate: $58 per professional labour-hour; Indirect cost rate: $48 per professional labour-hour

4-18 **Job costing; actual, normal, and variation of normal costing.** Chirac & Partners is a Quebec-based public accounting partnership specializing in audit services. Its job costing system has a single direct cost category (professional labour) and a single indirect cost pool (audit support, which contains all the costs in the Audit Support Department). Audit support costs are allocated to individual jobs using actual professional labour-hours. Chirac & Partners employs ten professionals who are involved in their auditing services.

Budgeted and actual amounts for 2010 are as follows:

Budget for 2010

Professional labour compensation	$960,000
Audit support department costs	$720,000
Professional labour-hours billed to clients	16,000 hours

Actual results for 2010

Audit support department costs	$744,000
Professional labour-hours billed to clients	15,500 hours
Actual professional labour cost rate	$58 per hour

REQUIRED

1. Identify the direct cost rate per professional labour-hour and the indirect cost rate per professional labour-hour for 2010 under (a) actual costing, (b) normal costing, and (c) variation of normal costing that uses budgeted rates for direct costs.
2. The audit of Pierre & Company done in 2010 was budgeted to take 110 hours of professional labour time. The actual professional labour time on the audit was 120 hours. Compute the 2010 job cost using (a) actual costing, (b) normal costing, and (c) variation of normal costing that uses budgeted rates for direct costs. Explain any differences in the job cost.

4-19 Job costing; actual, normal, and variation from normal costing. Thanatos & Hades (T&H) is a law firm that specializes in writing wills. Its job costing system has one direct cost pool, professional labour, and a single indirect cost pool that includes all supporting costs of running the law office. The support costs are allocated to clients on the basis of professional labour-hours. In addition to the two senior partners at T&H, there are six associates who work directly with clients. Each of the eight lawyers is expected to work for approximately 2,500 hours per year.

1. a. Direct cost rate: $60 per professional labour-hour; Indirect cost rate: $109.09 per professsional labour-hour

Budgeted and actual costs for 2009 were:

Budgeted professional labour costs	$1,100,000
Budgeted support costs	$2,000,000
Actual professional labour costs	$1,320,000
Actual support costs	$2,400,000
Actual total professional hours	22,000 hours

REQUIRED

1. Compute the direct cost rate and the indirect cost rate per professional labour-hour under
   a. Actual costing
   b. Normal costing
   c. Variation from normal costing that uses budgeted rates for direct costs.
2. The will for a rich tycoon, Ari Roos, was very complex and took four lawyers at the firm 1,000 hours each to prepare. What would be the cost of writing this will under each of the costing methods in requirement 1?

4-20 Job costing, normal and actual costing. Anderson Construction assembles residential homes. It uses a job costing system with two direct cost categories (direct materials and direct labour) and one indirect cost pool (assembly support). The allocation base for assembly support costs is direct labour-hours. In December 2009, Anderson budgets 2010 assembly support costs to be $8,000,000 and 2010 direct labour-hours to be 160,000.

1. a. $50 per direct labour-hour;
b. $42 per direct labour-hour

At the end of 2010, Anderson is comparing the costs of several jobs that were started and completed in 2010. Information for a couple of jobs follows.

Construction Period	Laguna Model February–June 2010	Mission Model May–October 2010
Direct materials	$106,450	$127,604
Direct labour	$ 36,276	$ 41,410
Direct labour-hours	900	1,010

Direct materials and direct labour are paid for on a contract basis. The costs of each are known when direct materials are used or direct labour-hours are worked. The 2010 actual assembly support costs were $6,888,000, while the actual direct labour-hours were 164,000.

REQUIRED

1. Compute the (a) budgeted and (b) actual indirect cost rate. Why do they differ?
2. What is the job cost of the Laguna Model and the Mission Model using (a) normal costing and (b) actual costing?
3. Why might Anderson Construction prefer normal costing over actual costing?

1. $31.25 per machine hour

4-21 Normal costing, manufacturing overhead. (J. Watson) Trenton Ltd. uses a normal job costing system and applies manufacturing overhead to products on the basis of machine hours. At the beginning of 2009, the company controller budgeted annual overhead at $1,500,000. She also forecast that machine hours would total 48,000. Actual costs were as follows:

Direct material (DM) used	$ 340,000
Direct labour	$ 875,000
Manufacturing overhead (MOH)	$1,605,000

Actual machine hours worked during the year were 49,200. Trenton adjusts any under-allocated or overallocated overhead to cost of goods sold. The company's records show that total sales for the year were $2,938,000 and cost of goods sold (before adjustment) equalled $2,260,000.

REQUIRED

1. Determine the company's budgeted overhead rate.
2. Determine the amount of underallocated or overallocated overhead for the year.
3. Compute the company's cost of goods sold.

1. Total MOH allocated to Job 494, $99,000

4-22 Job costing, accounting for manufacturing overhead, budgeted rates. Lynn Company uses a job costing system at its Mississauga plant. The plant has a Machining Department and an Assembly Department. Its job costing system has two direct cost categories (direct materials and direct manufacturing labour) and two manufacturing overhead cost pools (the Machining Department, allocated using actual machine hours (MH), and the Assembly Department, allocated using actual direct manufacturing labour cost). The 2010 budget for the plant is as follows:

	Machining Department	Assembly Department
Manufacturing overhead (MOH)	$1,800,000	$3,600,000
Direct manufacturing labour cost	$1,400,000	$2,000,000
Direct manufacturing labour-hours (DMLH)	100,000	200,000
Machine hours (MH)	50,000	200,000

The company uses a budgeted overhead rate for allocating overhead to production orders on a machine-hour basis in Machining and on a direct-manufacturing-labour-cost basis in Assembly.

REQUIRED

1. During February, the cost record for Job 494 contained the following:

	Machining Department	Assembly Department
Direct materials used	$45,000	$70,000
Direct manufacturing labour cost	$14,000	$15,000
Direct manufacturing labour-hours (DMLH)	1,000	1,500
Machine hours (MH)	2,000	1,000

Compute the total manufacturing overhead costs of Job 494.
2. At the end of 2010, the actual manufacturing overhead costs were $2,100,000 in Machining and $3,700,000 in Assembly. Assume that 55,000 actual machine hours were used in Machining and that actual direct manufacturing labour costs in Assembly were $2,200,000. Compute the overallocated or underallocated manufacturing overhead for each department.

4-23 Job costing, budgeted rates, unit costs. (J. Watson) Lytton Ltd. uses a normal job costing system with two direct cost categories (direct materials and direct labour) and one indirect cost pool. It allocates manufacturing overhead to jobs using a predetermined overhead rate based on direct labour-hours. At the start of the year, the company estimated that manufacturing overhead would be $632,000, and direct labour-hours were estimated at 32,000 hours for the year. In November, Job #X905 was completed. Materials costs on the job totalled $13,200 and labour costs totalled $10,120 at $22 per hour. At the end of the year, it was determined that the company worked 34,100 direct labour-hours for the year and incurred $656,125 in actual manufacturing overhead costs.

③ ④ ⑤
1. Unit cost, $64.81

REQUIRED

1. Job #X905 contained 500 units. Determine the unit cost that would appear on the job cost sheet.
2. Assuming Lytton prices its products to achieve a 25% margin, what would be the selling price of Job X905?
3. Determine the underallocated or overallocated overhead for the year.

4-24 Job costing, journal entries. The University of Toronto Press is wholly owned by the university. It performs the bulk of its work for other university departments, which pay as though the Press were an outside business enterprise. The Press also publishes and maintains a stock of books for general sale. A job costing system is used to cost each job. There are two direct cost categories (direct materials and direct manufacturing labour) and one indirect cost pool (manufacturing overhead, allocated based on direct labour costs).

③ ⑤
1. Overallocation $130

The following data (in thousands) pertain to 2010:

Direct materials and supplies purchased on account	$ 800
Direct materials used	710
Indirect materials issued to various production departments	100
Direct manufacturing labour	1,300
Indirect manufacturing labour incurred by various departments	900
Amortization on building and manufacturing equipment	400
Miscellaneous manufacturing overhead* incurred by various departments (ordinarily would be detailed as repairs, photocopying, utilities, etc.)	550
Manufacturing overhead allocated at 160% of direct manufacturing labour costs	?
Cost of goods manufactured	4,120
Revenues	8,000
Cost of goods sold	4,020
Inventories, December 31, 2009:	
Materials control	100
Work-in-process control	60
Finished goods control	500

*The term *manufacturing overhead* is not used uniformly. Other terms that are often encountered in printing companies include *job overhead* and *shop overhead*.

REQUIRED

1. Prepare general journal entries to summarize 2010 transactions. As your final entry, dispose of the year-end overallocated or underallocated manufacturing overhead as a direct write-off to Cost of Goods Sold. Number your entries. Explanations for each entry may be omitted.
2. Show posted T-accounts for all inventories, Cost of Goods Sold, Manufacturing Overhead Control, and Manufacturing Overhead Allocated.

4-25 Job costing, journal entries. Duchess Ltd. manufactures and installs kitchen cabinetry. It uses normal job costing with two direct cost categories (direct materials and direct manufacturing labour) and one indirect cost pool for manufacturing overhead (MOH), applied on the basis of machine hours (MH). At the beginning of the year, the company estimated that it would work 980,000 MH and had budgeted $73,500,000 for MOH. The following data (in millions) pertain to operations for the year 2010:

③ ⑤
1. WIP ending balance, $17.40

Materials control (beginning balance), December 31, 2009	$ 6.0
Work-in-process control (beginning balance), December 31, 2009	1.8
Finished goods control (beginning balance), December 31, 2009	7.2
Materials and supplies purchased on account	238
Direct materials used	194
Indirect materials (supplies) issued to various production departments	27
Direct manufacturing labour	123
Indirect manufacturing labour incurred by various departments	19

Amortization on plant and manufacturing equipment	21
Miscellaneous manufacturing overhead incurred (credit Various Liabilities; ordinarily would be detailed as repairs, utilities, etc.)	9
Manufacturing overhead allocated (972,000 actual MH)	?
Cost of goods manufactured	374.3
Revenues	512
Cost of goods sold	368.4

REQUIRED

1. Prepare general journal entries. Number your entries. Post to T-accounts. What is the ending balance of Work-in-Process Control?
2. Show the journal entry for disposing of overallocated or underallocated manufacturing overhead directly as a year-end write-off to Cost of Goods Sold. Post the entry to T-accounts.

4-26 Job costing, unit cost, ending work-in-process. Richmond Company worked on only two jobs during May. Information on the jobs is given below:

	Job A701	Job A702
Direct materials	$ 80,000	$ 92,000
Direct labour	287,000	219,000
Direct manufacturing labour-hours (DMLH)	20,500	14,600

At the beginning of the year, annual manufacturing overhead (MOH) was budgeted at $3,780,000 and Richmond budgeted 35,000 DMLH per month. Job A701 was completed in May.

REQUIRED

1. Compute the total cost of Job A701.
2. Calculate per unit cost for Job A701 assuming it has 2,500 units.
3. Make this journal entry transferring Job A701 to Finished Goods.
4. Determine the ending balance in the Work-in-Process account.

4-27 Job costing, various cost drivers. (J. Watson) Rochester Ltd. has budgeted $435,000 for manufacturing overhead for the upcoming year. It forecast that 72,500 machine hours will be used in the factory, and budgeted direct labour-hours were 17,400. The average direct labour rate is budgeted to be $20 Actual data for the year were:

Actual manufacturing overhead	$434,300
Actual machine hours	73,010
Actual direct labour wage rate	$ 19.60
Actual direct labour-hours worked	17,630

REQUIRED

1. Compute the budgeted manufacturing overhead rate under each of the following cost drivers:
   a. Direct labour-hours
   b. Direct labour cost
   c. Machine hours
2. Compute the amount of underallocated or overallocated manufacturing overhead under each of the cost drivers listed in requirement 1.

4-28 Job costing, journal entries, T-accounts, source documents. Production Company produces gadgets for the coveted small appliance market. The following data reflect activity for the most recent year, 2009:

Costs incurred	
Purchases of direct materials (net) on account	$124,000
Direct manufacturing labour cost	80,000
Indirect labour	54,500
Amortization, factory equipment	30,000
Amortization, office equipment	7,000
Maintenance, factory equipment	20,000
Miscellaneous factory overhead	9,500
Rent, factory building	70,000
Advertising expense	90,000
Sales commissions	30,000

Beginning and ending inventories for the year were as follows:

	January 1, 2009	December 31, 2009
Direct materials	$ 9,000	$11,000
Work-in-process	6,000	21,000
Finished goods	69,000	24,000

Production Company uses a normal job costing system and allocates overhead to work-in-process at a rate of $2.50 per direct manufacturing labour dollar. Indirect materials are insignificant, so there is no inventory account for indirect materials.

REQUIRED

1. Prepare journal entries to record the 2009 transactions including an entry to close out over-allocated or underallocated overhead to cost of goods sold. For each journal entry, indicate the source document that would be used to authorize each entry. Also note which subsidiary ledger, if any, should be referenced as backup for the entry.
2. Post the journal entries to T-accounts for all of the inventories, Cost of Goods Sold, Manufacturing Overhead Control, and Manufacturing Overhead Allocated accounts.

4-29 Accounting for manufacturing overhead. Consider the following selected cost data for Housser Inc. for 2010.

3 5
1. $22 per MH

Budgeted manufacturing overhead (MOH)	$4,180,000
Budgeted machine hours (MH)	190,000
Actual manufacturing overhead (MOH) ending balance	$4,230,000
Actual machine hours (MH)	192,000

Housser's job costing system has a single manufacturing overhead cost pool (allocated using a budgeted rate based on actual MH). Any amount of underallocation or overallocation is immediately written off to cost of goods sold.

REQUIRED

1. Compute the budgeted manufacturing overhead (MOH) rate.
2. Journalize the allocation of manufacturing overhead (MOH).
3. Compute the amount of underallocation or overallocation of MOH. Is the amount significant? Journalize the disposition of this amount based on the ending balances in the relevant accounts.

4-30 Proration of overhead. The Ride-On-Water (ROW) Company produces a line of non-motorized boats. ROW uses a normal job costing system and allocates manufacturing overhead costs using direct manufacturing labour cost. The following data are available for 2009:

3 5
1. 50% of direct manufacturing labour costs

Budgeted manufacturing overhead costs	$100,000
Budgeted direct manufacturing labour cost	$200,000
Actual manufacturing overhead costs	$106,000
Actual direct manufacturing labour cost	$220,000

Inventory balances on December 31, 2009 were:

Account	Ending Balance	2009 Direct Manufacturing Labour Cost in Ending Balance
Work-in-process	$ 50,000	$ 20,000
Finished goods	$240,000	$ 60,000
Cost of goods sold	$560,000	$140,000

REQUIRED

1. Calculate the budgeted manufacturing overhead rate.
2. Calculate the amount of underallocated or overallocated manufacturing overhead.
3. Calculate the ending balances in work-in-process, finished goods, and cost of goods sold if underallocated or overallocated overhead is:
   a. Written off to cost of goods sold
   b. Prorated based on ending balances (before proration) in each of the three accounts
   c. Prorated based on the overhead allocated in 2009 in the ending balances, before proration, in each of the three accounts.
4. Which disposition method do you prefer in requirement 3? Explain.

4-31 Job costing, solving for unknowns. (J. Watson) Osprey Ltd. manufactures designer purses. During the year, it recorded direct materials used of $684,000. Total manufacturing costs of $1,482,000 were incurred during the year. Osprey uses one indirect cost pool for all overhead costs and allocates overhead at a rate of 60% of direct labour dollars.

	January 1	December 31
Direct materials inventories	$193,000	$162,000
Work-in-process inventories	204,000	107,000
Finished goods inventories	225,000	248,000

REQUIRED

Prepare a Schedule of Cost of Goods Manufactured and Sold for the year. You will need to solve for the following unknowns:

a. Direct materials purchased
b. Direct labour costs
c. Manufacturing overhead allocated
d. Cost of goods manufactured
e. Cost of goods sold

4-32 Disposition of underallocated or overallocated overhead. (J. Watson) Princeton Manufacturing budgeted $325,000 and incurred $337,000 of overhead costs in the past year. During the year, it allocated $302,000 to its production. An extract from the company's financial records showed the following account balances:

Work-in-Process Inventory	$26,000
Finished Goods Inventory	$37,625
Cost of Goods Sold	$86,375

REQUIRED

1. Calculate the amount of underallocated or overallocated manufacturing overhead for the year.
2. Prepare the journal entry to dispose of this underallocated or overallocated overhead amount using
   a. Immediate write-off to Cost of Goods Sold
   b. Proration based on ending balances (before proration) in Work-in-Process Inventory, Finished Goods Inventory, and Cost of Goods Sold
3. Which method do you recommend for this company?

PROBLEMS

4-33 Job costing, law firm. Keating & Partners is a law firm specializing in labour relations and employee-related work. It employs 25 professionals (5 partners and 20 managers) who work directly with its clients. The average budgeted total compensation per professional for 2010 is $104,000. Each professional is budgeted to have 1,600 billable hours to clients in 2010. Keating is a highly respected firm, and all professionals work for clients to their maximum 1,600 billable hours available. All professional labour costs are included in a single direct cost category and are traced to jobs on a per-hour basis.

All costs of Keating & Partners other than professional labour costs are included in a single indirect cost pool (legal support) and are allocated to jobs using professional labour-hours as the allocation base. The budgeted level of indirect costs in 2010 is $2.2 million.

REQUIRED

1. Compute the 2010 budgeted professional labour-hour direct cost rate.
2. Compute the 2010 budgeted indirect cost rate per hour of professional labour.
3. Keating & Partners is considering bidding on two jobs
   a. Litigation work for Richardson Inc. that requires 100 budgeted hours of professional labour
   b. Labour contract work for Punch Inc. that requires 150 budgeted hours of professional labour
   Prepare a cost estimate for each job.

4-34 Job costing with two direct cost and two indirect cost categories, law firm (continuation of 4-33). Keating has just completed a review of its job costing system. This review included a detailed analysis of how past jobs used the firm's resources and interviews with personnel about what factors drive the level of indirect costs. Management concluded that a system with two direct cost categories (professional partner labour and professional manager labour) and two indirect cost categories (general support and administration support) would yield more accurate job costs. Budgeted information for 2010 related to the two direct cost categories is as follows:

1. a. $125 per hour
   b. $50 per hour

	Professional Partner Labour	Professional Manager Labour
Number of professionals	5	20
Hours of billable time per professional	1,600 per year	1,600 per year
Total compensation (average per professional)	$200,000	$80,000

Budgeted information for 2010 relating to the two indirect cost categories is

	General Support	Administration Support
Total costs	$1,800,000	$400,000
Cost-allocation base	Professional labour-hours	Partner labour-hours

REQUIRED

1. Compute the 2010 budgeted direct cost rates for (a) professional partners and (b) professional managers.
2. Compute the 2010 budgeted indirect cost rates for (a) general support and (b) administration support.
3. Compute the budgeted job costs for the Richardson and Punch jobs, given the following information:

	Richardson Inc.	Punch Inc.
Professional partners	60 hours	30 hours
Professional managers	40 hours	120 hours

4. Comment on the results in requirement 3. Why are the job costs different from those computed in Problem 4-33?

4-35 Overview of general-ledger relationships. Blakely Company is a small machine shop that uses highly skilled labour and a job costing system (using normal costing). The total debits and credits in certain accounts just before year end are as follows:

2. Overallocated, $13,800

	December 30, 2010	
	Total Debits	Total Credits
Materials Control	$134,000	$ 91,000
Work-in-Process Control	686,000	683,000
Manufacturing Department Overhead Control	204,500	—
Finished Goods Control	731,000	690,000
Cost of Goods Sold	690,000	—
Manufacturing Overhead Allocated	—	217,600

All materials purchased are for direct materials. Note that "total debits" in the inventory accounts would include beginning inventory balances, if any.

The preceding accounts *do not* include the following:

a. The manufacturing labour costs summary for the December 31 working day: direct manufacturing labour, $4,000, and indirect manufacturing labour, $1,010.
b. Miscellaneous manufacturing overhead incurred on December 30 and December 31: $850 total.

ADDITIONAL INFORMATION

◆ Manufacturing overhead has been allocated as a percentage of direct manufacturing labour costs through December 30.
◆ Direct materials purchased during 2010 were $107,000.

- ◆ There were no returns to suppliers.
- ◆ Direct manufacturing labour costs during 2010 totalled $340,000, not including the December 31 working day described previously.

REQUIRED

1. Compute the inventories (December 31, 2010) of Materials Control, Work-in-Process Control, and Finished Goods Control. Show T-accounts.
2. Prepare all adjusting and closing journal entries for the preceding accounts. Assume that all underallocated or overallocated manufacturing overhead is closed directly to Cost of Goods Sold.

1. $2,875,000

4-36 Normal costing, overhead allocation, working backwards. Gaston Ltd. uses a normal job costing system with two direct cost categories—direct materials and direct manufacturing labour—and one indirect cost category—manufacturing overhead. At the beginning of 2010, Gaston had $236,000 in work-in-process inventory. The company allocates manufacturing overhead at the rate of 180% of direct manufacturing labour costs. Total allocated manufacturing overhead for the year was $5,175,000. Manufacturing costs incurred for the year were $9,732,500 and the cost of goods manufactured for the year totalled $9,612,200.

REQUIRED

1. What was the total direct labour cost in 2010?
2. What was the total cost of direct materials used in 2010?
3. What was the dollar amount of work-in-process inventory on December 31, 2010?

2. $1,675,700

4-37 General ledger relationships, underallocation and overallocation, service industry. John Brody and Co. is an engineering consulting firm. Brody uses a variation of a normal costing system. It charges jobs for blueprints made and fees paid to outside experts at actual costs, professional direct labour costs at a budgeted direct labour rate, and engineering support overhead costs (for engineering and office support) at a budgeted indirect cost rate.

Brody maintains a Jobs-in-Process Control account in its general ledger that accumulates all costs of jobs. As a job is completed, Brody immediately bills the client and transfers the costs of the completed job to the Cost of Jobs Billed account to be matched against the revenues billed to the client. Consequently, unlike manufacturing companies, Brody has no accounts that correspond to Materials Control and Finished Goods Control accounts.

The following data pertain to the year 2010:

Cost of jobs in process on January 1, 2010	$ 198,000
Direct costs of fees and blueprints (all cash)	$ 210,000
Actual direct professional labour costs (all cash)	$2,650,000
Direct professional labour allocated at $82 per direct professional labour-hour	?
Actual direct professional labour-hours	31,600
Actual engineering support overhead costs (all cash)	$1,963,000
Engineering support overhead allocated at $0.75 per direct professional labour dollar incurred	?
Cost of jobs billed	$4,275,000
Revenues	$5,985,000

Brody incurs no marketing and business development costs.

REQUIRED

1. Summarize the year 2010 transactions by preparing T-accounts for Jobs-in-Process Control, Cost of Jobs Billed, Direct Professional Labour Control, Direct Professional Labour Allocated, Engineering Support Overhead Control, Engineering Support Overhead Allocated, and Cash Control. As your final entry, dispose of the year-end underallocated or overallocated account balances as a direct write-off to Cost of Goods Sold.
2. Calculate Brody's operating income for the year 2010.

2. Machining Department: Overallocation, $510,000; Assembly Department: Underallocation, $170,000

4-38 Disposition of overhead overallocation or underallocation, two indirect cost pools. Glavine Corporation manufactures precision equipment made to order for the semiconductor industry. Glavine uses two manufacturing overhead cost pools—one for the overhead costs incurred in its highly automated Machining Department and another for overhead costs incurred in its labour-based Assembly Department. Glavine uses a normal costing system. It allocates Machining Department overhead costs to jobs based on actual machine hours using a budgeted machine hour overhead rate. It allocates Assembly Department overhead costs to jobs based on actual direct manufacturing labour-hours using a budgeted direct manufacturing labour-hour rate.

The following data are for the year 2010:

	Machining Department	Assembly Department
Budgeted overhead	$5,850,000	$7,812,000
Budgeted machine hours (MH)	90,000	0
Budgeted direct manufacturing labour-hours (DMLH)	0	124,000
Actual manufacturing overhead costs	$5,470,000	$8,234,000

Machine hours and direct manufacturing labour-hours and the ending balances (before proration of underallocated overhead) are as follows:

	Actual Machine Hours	Actual Direct Manufacturing Labour-Hours	Balance before Proration, December 31, 2010
Cost of Goods Sold	69,000	83,200	$21,600,000
Finished Goods	6,900	12,800	2,800,000
Work-in-Process	16,100	32,000	7,600,000

REQUIRED
1. Compute the budgeted overhead rates for the year in the Machining and Assembly Departments.
2. Compute the underallocated or overallocated overhead in *each* department for the year. Dispose of the underallocated or overallocated amount in *each* department using:
   a. Immediate write-off to Cost of Goods Sold.
   b. Proration based on ending balances (before proration) in Cost of Goods Sold, Finished Goods, and Work-in-Process.
   c. Proration based on the allocated overhead amount (before proration) in the ending balances of Cost of Goods Sold, Finished Goods, and Work-in-Process.
3. Which disposition method do you prefer in requirement 2? Explain.

4-39 **Job Costing, normal versus actual, under/over applied overhead.** (J. Watson) The following information relates to the activities of King Ltd. for the year 2010.

③ ④ ⑤

1. Underallocated, $21,100

Advertising Costs	$ 62,500	Beginning Work-in-Process	$ 34,000
Direct Labour	320,000	Beginning Direct Materials	52,000
Indirect Labour	61,400	Factory Amortization	162,000
Factory Equipment Maintenance	13,300	Ending Work-in-Process	45,000
Ending Direct Materials	42,500	Factory Utilities	26,000
Office Amortization	13,000	Sales Commissions	24,000
Purchases of Direct Materials	156,000	Corporate Salaries	289,000
Factory Supplies	4,400	Insurance on Factory	22,600

The company uses normal costing and applies overhead on the basis of machine hours (MH). The company had calculated its overhead rate to be $4.25 per MH on the basis of 60,000 budgeted MH. Actual MH worked in the plant were 63,200.

REQUIRED
1. Compute the amount of overallocated or underallocated overhead for the year.
2. Prepare the journal entry to record the disposition of the amount of overallocated or underallocated overhead assuming the company writes off the difference to Cost of Goods Sold.
3. Identify and briefly outline an alternative treatment (from requirement 2) for disposing of overallocated or underallocated overhead.
4. Prepare a Schedule of Cost of Goods Manufactured for the year.
5. Briefly explain the differences between actual and normal costing, and state how the Schedule of Cost of Goods Manufactured would differ under actual costing.

4-40 Job costing and governance. Jack Halpern is the owner and CEO of Aerospace Comfort, a firm specializing in the manufacture of seats for air transport. He has just received a copy of a letter written to the Auditor General of the Canadian government. He believes it is from an ex-employee of Aerospace.

> Dear Sir,
>
> Aerospace Comfort in 2010 manufactured 100 X7 seats for the Canadian Forces. You may be interested to know the following:
> 1. Direct materials cost billed for the 100 X7 seats was $40,000.
> 2. Direct manufacturing labour cost billed for 100 X7 seats was $8,400. This cost includes 16 hours of setup labour at $50 per hour, an amount included in the manufacturing overhead cost pool as well. The $8,400 also includes 15 hours of design time at $120 an hour. Design time was explicitly identified as a cost the Canadian Forces was not to reimburse.
> 3. Manufacturing overhead cost billed for 100 X7 seats was $14,700 (175% of direct manufacturing labour costs). This amount includes the 16 hours of setup labour at $50 per hour that is incorrectly included as part of direct manufacturing labour costs.
>
> You may also want to know that over 40% of the direct materials is purchased from Frontier Technology, a company that is 51% owned by Jack Halpern's brother.
>
> For obvious reasons, this letter will not be signed.
>
> c.c.: *The Globe and Mail*
> Jack Halpern, CEO of Aerospace Comfort

Aerospace Comfort's contract states that the Canadian Forces reimburses Aerospace at 130% of manufacturing costs.

REQUIRED

Assume that the facts in the letter are correct as you answer the following questions.

1. What is the cost amount per X7 seat that Aerospace Comfort billed the Canadian Forces? Assume that the actual direct materials costs are $40,000.
2. What is the amount per X7 seat that Aerospace Comfort should have billed the Canadian Forces? Assume that the actual direct materials costs are $40,000.
3. Based on the problems highlighted in the letter, what should the Canadian Forces do to tighten its procurement procedures to reduce the likelihood of such situations recurring?

4-41 Allocation of manufacturing overhead and disposition of overallocation or underallocation. (SMA, heavily adapted) Nicole Limited is a company that produces machinery to customer order. Its job costing system (using normal costing) has two direct cost categories (direct materials and direct manufacturing labour) and one indirect cost pool (manufacturing overhead, allocated using a budgeted rate based on direct manufacturing labour costs). The budget for 2010 was:

Direct manufacturing labour	$630,000
Manufacturing overhead	$441,000

At the end of 2010, two jobs were incomplete: No. 1768B (total direct manufacturing labour costs were $15,000) and No. 1819C (total direct manufacturing labour costs were $48,000). Machine time totalled 318 hours for No. 1768B and 654 hours for No. 1819C. Direct materials issued to No. 1768B amounted to $30,600. Direct materials for No. 1819C came to $56,800.

Total charges to the Manufacturing Overhead Control account for the year were $406,200. Direct manufacturing labour charges made to all jobs were $650,000, representing 25,000 direct manufacturing labour-hours (DMLH).

There were no beginning inventories. In addition to the ending work-in-process, the ending finished goods showed a balance of $204,500 (including a direct manufacturing labour cost component of $60,000). Sales for 2010 totalled $3,124,000, cost of goods sold was $2,200,000, and marketing costs were $523,900.

Nicole prices on a cost-plus basis. It currently uses a guideline of cost plus 40% of cost.

REQUIRED

1. Prepare a detailed schedule showing the ending balances in the inventories and cost of goods sold (before considering any underallocated or overallocated manufacturing overhead). Show also the manufacturing overhead allocated to these ending balances.
2. Compute the underallocated or overallocated manufacturing overhead for 2010.

3. Prorate the amount computed in requirement 2 on the basis of:

   a. The ending balances (before proration) of work-in-process, finished goods, and cost of goods sold

   b. The allocated overhead amount (before proration) in the ending balances of work-in-process, finished goods, and cost of goods sold

4. Assume that Nicole decides to immediately write off to Cost of Goods Sold any underallocated or overallocated manufacturing overhead. Will operating income be higher or lower than the operating income that would have resulted from the proration in requirements 3(a) and 3(b)?

5. Calculate the cost of job No. 1819C if Nicole Limited had used the adjusted allocation rate approach to disposing of underallocated or overallocated manufacturing overhead in 2010.

4-42 General ledger relationships, underallocation and overallocation. (S. Sridhar, adapted) Northley Industries is a manufacturer of sailboats. The following partial information for 2010 is available:

1. $403,000

Material Control		
1-1-2010	32,000	403,000
	431,000	

Work-in-Process Control		
1-1-2010	18,000	
Direct Manufacturing Labour		
	380,000	

Finished Goods Control		
1-1-2010	12,250	1,280,000
	1,307,250	

Manufacturing Overhead Allocated	

Manufacturing Overhead Control	
543,000	

Cost of Goods Sold	

ADDITIONAL INFORMATION

1. Direct manufacturing labour wage rate was $16 per hour.
2. Manufacturing overhead (MOH) is allocated at $25 per direct manufacturing labour-hour (DMLH).
3. During the year, sales revenues were $1,664,000, and marketing and distribution expenses were $199,700.

REQUIRED

1. What was the amount of direct materials issued to manufacturing during the year?
2. What was the amount of manufacturing overhead allocated to jobs during the year?
3. What was the cost of jobs completed during the year?
4. What was the balance in work-in-process inventory on December 31, 2010?
5. What was the cost of goods sold before any proration of underallocated or overallocated overhead?
6. What was the underallocated or overallocated manufacturing overhead for the year?
7. Dispose of the underallocated or overallocated manufacturing overhead using

   a. Immediate write-off to Cost of Goods Sold

   b. Proration based on ending balances (before proration) in Work-in-Process, Finished Goods, and Cost of Goods Sold.

8. Using each of the disposition methods in requirement 7, calculate operating income for the year.
9. Which disposition method in requirement 7 do you recommend Northley use? Explain your answer briefly.

4-43 Normal costing, departments. (J. Watson) Kalor Ltd. uses a normal job costing system with two direct cost categories, direct materials and direct labour, and one indirect cost pool. Manufacturing overhead is allocated based on direct labour costs. Any overallocated or underallocated overhead is written off to Cost of Goods Sold. Each product goes through two

1. $17,829,625

departments, Fabrication and Assembly. The Fabrication process is automated whereas the Assembly Department is highly labour intensive. Kalor's budget for 2010 was as follows:

Budgeted	Fabrication	Assembly
Direct Materials (DM)	$3,500,000	$2,100,000
Direct Labour	$ 735,000	$3,825,000
Factory Overhead	$6,450,000	$1,530,000
Machine Hours (MH)	2,580,000	250,000

Kalor started the year without any work-in-process. During the year it had the following results:

Actual	Fabrication	Assembly
Direct Materials (DM)	$3,350,000	$2,200,000
Direct Labour	$ 750,000	$3,750,000
Factory Overhead	$6,390,000	$1,590,000
Machine Hours (MH)	2,610,000	260,000

At December 31, 2010, the company had only two jobs still in process, #Z438 and #Q917. Job #Z438 had $7,000 of direct materials and $1,500 of direct labour and had used 3,400 MH in fabrication. It had not yet been transferred to the Assembly Department. Job #Q917 had incurred $4,000 and $6,000 of direct materials costs in Fabrication and Assembly, respectively. It had used 1,800 MH in Fabrication and 800 MH in Assembly. Labour charges in the two departments were $9,000 and $18,000 for Fabrication and Assembly, respectively.

REQUIRED
1. Calculate Cost of Goods Manufactured for the year ended December 31, 2010 assuming the company uses its current overhead costing method.
2. Under the current costing system, what is the amount of overallocated or underallocated overhead?
3. What would be the amount of overallocated or underallocated overhead at the end of the year if the company had used departmental overhead rates with the most appropriate base for each department?

8 5

1.75% of labour cost

4-44 **Overhead allocation and proration.** Franklin & Son Printing designed and printed sales brochures, catalogues, and pamphlets. The business was dissolved in early 2010. The company had used a normal job costing system with two direct cost categories—direct materials and direct manufacturing labour—and one indirect cost category—manufacturing overhead. Overhead was charged to printing jobs on the basis of direct labour cost. The following information was known about the firm for 2009.

Budgeted direct materials costs	£1,000
Budgeted direct labour costs	£2,000
Budgeted overhead costs	£1,500
Actual direct material costs	£ 900
Actual direct labour costs	£1,800
Actual overhead costs	£1,250

There was no work-in-process at the beginning of the year and there were two jobs in process at the end of the year. The first job had used £25 of materials so far and £20 of direct labour. The second job had used £15 of materials and £32 of labour. Franklin did not carry any finished goods inventories because all printing jobs were based on orders that, when completed, were immediately transferred to cost of goods sold and delivered to the customer.

REQUIRED
1. Calculate the overhead allocation rate for 2009.
2. Calculate the balance in ending work-in-process and in cost of goods sold.
3. Calculate underallocated or overallocated overhead.
4. Calculate the ending balances in work-in-process and cost of goods sold if the underallocated or overallocated overhead amount is:
   a. Written off to cost of goods sold
   b. Prorated using the ending balance (before proration) in cost of goods sold and work-in-process.
5. Which of the methods in requirement 4 would you choose? Explain.

4-45 Disposition of underallocated or overallocated overhead—Advanced. (Z. Iqbal, adapted) Naf Radiator Company uses a normal costing system with a single manufacturing overhead (MOH) cost pool and machine hours (MH) as the cost-allocation base. The following data are for 2010:

1. $60 per machine hour

Budgeted manufacturing overhead (MOH)	$4,800,000
Overhead allocation base	machine hours (MH)
Budgeted machine hours (MH)	80,000
Manufacturing overhead (MOH) incurred	$4,900,000
Actual machine hours (MH)	75,000

Machine-hours data and the ending balances (before proration of underallocated or overallocated overhead) are as follows:

	Actual Machine Hours (MH)	2010 End-of-Year Balance
Cost of Goods Sold	60,000	$8,000,000
Finished Goods Control	11,000	1,250,000
Work-in-Process Control	4,000	750,000

REQUIRED

1. Compute the budgeted manufacturing overhead rate for 2010.
2. Compute the underallocated or overallocated manufacturing overhead of Naf Radiator in 2010. Dispose of this underallocated or overallocated amount using
   a. Write-off to Cost of Goods Sold
   b. Proration based on ending balances (before proration) in Work-in-Process Control, Finished Goods Control, and Cost of Goods Sold
   c. Proration based on the allocated overhead amount (before proration) in the ending balances of Work-in-Process Control, Finished Goods Control, and Cost of Goods Sold
3. Which method do you prefer in requirement 2? Explain.

COLLABORATIVE LEARNING CASES

4-46 Normal job costing, unit costs. (J. Watson) Pearson Ltd. uses a normal job costing system and applies overhead on the basis of direct labour-hours. At the beginning of the year, the company estimated that total overhead costs for the year would be $180,000, and it budgeted total labour-hours of 15,000. Actual labour-hours worked for the period January 1 to November 30 were 13,750.

1. $12 per direct labour-hour

On December 1, the company had three jobs in process:

Work-in-Process at December 1

Job Number	815	817	822
Direct Materials (DM)	$1,400	$2,500	$1,700
Direct Labour (DL)	$1,200	$2,400	$ 600
Overhead (OH)	$ 600	$1,350	$ 450
Total	$3,200	$6,250	$2,750

During the month of December the following costs were incurred by job:

Job #	815	817	822	823	824
DM	$500	$ 700	$1,300	$1,250	$1,500
DL	$900	$1,440	$3,060	$3,960	$5,940
DL hours	50 hours	80 hours	170 hours	220 hours	330 hours

In addition, the company incurred the following costs during the month of December (these costs have not yet been recorded in the books):

DM purchases	$7,800	Advertising expense	$5,200
Plant amortization	2,490	Factory repairs and maintenance	1,500
Factory utilities	1,800	Factory supplies	1,800
Production supervisor salary	2,200	Sales personnel salaries	9,700
Administrative salaries	3,450	Interest expense	1,400

ADDITIONAL INFORMATION
1. The balance in the Overhead Control account on December 1 was $195,010.
2. There were no jobs in Finished Goods as of December 1.
3. Jobs # 815, 822, 823 and 824 were completed during December.
4. Job 824 is the only job in Finished Goods as of December 31.
5. The company's pricing policy is 200% of total manufacturing cost.

REQUIRED
1. Calculate the budgeted overhead rate used by Pearson.
2. Calculate the unit cost of ending work-in-process inventory assuming that the number of units in the job(s) total 250 units
3. Calculate the cost of goods manufactured and the unadjusted gross margin for the month of December.
4. Calculate the amount of overallocated or underallocated overhead for the year.

② ④

1. $2,100

4-47 Job costing, service industry. Michael Scott books tours for new bands, and arranges to print T-shirts and produce demo CDs to sell on the tour. Scott's agency uses a normal costing system with two direct cost pools, labour and materials, and one indirect cost pool, general overhead. General overhead is allocated to each tour at 150% of labour cost. The following information relates to the agency for 2010:

1. As of June 1, there were tours for two bands in progress Grunge Express and Different Strokes.
2. During June, both bands finished their tours.
3. New tours were started for three bands, As I Lay Dying, Ask Me Later, and Maybe Tomorrow. Of these bands, only Maybe Tomorrow finished its tour by the end of June.

All costs incurred during the planning stage for a tour are gathered in a balance sheet account called "Tours In Process (TIP)". When a tour is completed, the costs are transferred to an income statement account called "Cost of Completed Tours (CCT)."

The following cost information is for June:

	From Beginning TIP		Incurred in June	
	Materials	**Labour**	**Materials**	**Labour**
Grunge Express	$400	$600	$ 0	$100
Different Strokes	$300	$400	$175	$300
As I Lay Dying	$ 0	$ 0	$250	$400
Ask Me Later	$ 0	$ 0	$350	$200
Maybe Tomorrow	$ 0	$ 0	$275	$400

Actual overhead in June was $2,500.

REQUIRED
1. Calculate the TIP for the end of June.
2. Calculate CCT for June.
3. Calculate underallocated or overallocated overhead at the end of June.
4. Calculate the ending balances in work-in-process and cost of goods sold if the underallocated or overallocated overhead amount is:
   a. Written off to CCT
   b. Prorated using the ending balances (before proration) in TIP and CCT.
   c. Prorated based on the overhead allocated in June in the ending balances of TIP and CCT (before proration).
5. Which of the methods in requirement 4 would you choose? Explain.

Activity-Based Costing and Activity-Based Management

BUSINESS MATTERS

Accurate Assignment = Better Profit Control

Tim Hortons: How much does a large double-double cost to produce? Starbucks: How much does a latte venti cost to produce? Should the companies sell iced cappuccino or sushi? Both companies sell hundreds of millions of cups of coffee each year. As customers, we know the price, but managers must know the costs. Coffee beans, the raw materials, cost little compared to the indirect and overhead costs of transformation and sales. In the extremely competitive world of coffee, the more accurate the assignment of indirect costs, the more likely managers will remain profitable.

LEARNING OBJECTIVES

After studying this chapter, you should be able to

1. Explain undercosting and overcosting of products or services

2. Contrast the logic of traditional cost assignment with the logic of the activities cost hierarchy

3. Apply the logic of an activity-based costing (ABC) cost hierarchy

4. Assign costs using activity-based costing (ABC)

5. Use ABC systems for activity-based management (ABM)

Chapter 4 introduced the cost pool, cost allocation base, cost allocation rate, and traditional cost assignment to a cost object. Selection of a cost allocation base was influenced by whether measures of the quantity consumed of the common input were accessible in the management information system (MIS). Cost allocation is a second-best solution, chosen because it would not be cost-beneficial to improve on cost assignment accuracy by tracing costs. In Chapter 4, we assumed that to identify and measure different input quantities and associated indirect cost pools would cost far more than the benefits of more accurate cost-allocation rates. In Chapter 5, we assume that it *would* be cost-beneficial to obtain better measurements of common inputs and indirect cost pools.

Improving indirect cost assignment requires a logic of transaction analysis different from financial-accounting logic. The focus is on classifying the scope of cost effects of activities. An **activity** is an event, task, or unit of work with a specified purpose. Some activities transform a single unit of output, such as a bowl of chilli. Some activities transform many units called a batch, such as a pot of coffee. Some activities transform an entire product, such as all mugs, and improve quality. The indirect costs of activity become a cost pool at the unit, batch, or product level. This logic results in *activity-based costing*, or *ABC*. **Activity-based costing (ABC)** systems refine costing systems by focusing on activities as the fundamental cost objects.

UNDERCOSTING AND OVERCOSTING PRODUCTS AND SERVICES

1 Explain undercosting and overcosting of products or services

Activity-based costing (ABC) is the focus of this chapter. In general, cost pools are neither purely fixed nor purely variable, but a mix. One benefit of the ABC approach is to examine costs that vary with a specific activity common to several different business functions. The cost object is the *activity level*. An **activity level** specifies the scope of changes in cost, which may cause a change in the cost of single units, batches, and entire products. The assumption is that a large proportion of the change in the dollar value of the cost pool can be explained by the change in the activity level (unit, batch, or product). A company is seen as a set of common activities that cause cost changes at different levels, rather than a set of separate business functions.

Managers implement ABC costing to improve the relevance of the information they use in management decision making by improving its accuracy. Operating decisions in the short run, such as profitable product pricing, and strategic decisions in the long run, such as add or drop a product, will be informed by more accurate costing. Improved cost estimates of units, batches, and products lead to:

- better matching of costs to their level of cause (activity), and better performance measurement and control systems
- deeper understanding of interdependencies among costs and activities occurring at different levels of unit, batch, and product
- clearer diagnoses of costing problems (per unit, batch, product) and identification of more effective remedies
- superior methods to analyze and increase value-added activity and decrease or eliminate non–value-added activity at all levels
- refined, more reliable planning for future costs (pro-forma costing)

ABC is the foundation of **activity-based management (ABM)**, a cost-leadership strategy to eliminate non–value-added activities, which are those activities failing to add value for which customers will pay. ABC is a response to a problem—the problem is twofold. First, indirect or manufacturing overhead is a large proportion of total cost; therefore, the accuracy of cost assignment is relevant; it matters to management decision making. Relevant means that because you have received the information, you will change your mind. Second, the outputs the company produces consume activities differently during the conversion of raw inputs to finished goods.

If neither problem exists, an ABC system is not cost beneficial. If either the indirect costs are a small proportion of total costs or the difference in activities' costs to convert raw materials to finished goods is uniform, then traditional costing is the appropriate approach to cost assignment. **Traditional costing, cost smoothing,** or **peanut butter costing** simply spreads the costs of conversion and inputs uniformly. As you learned in Chapter 4, this is accomplished using a single average rate to assign costs uniformly to all outputs. It is not appropriate when different levels of costs are incurred for different outputs because some outputs will be undercosted and some overcosted.

UNDERCOSTING AND OVERCOSTING

When the cost object is units of different outputs (e.g., a small green tea in contrast to a venti mocha latte), different batches of outputs (e.g., burrito wraps in contrast to sushi), or different products (coffee mugs in contrast to containers of ground coffee beans), the activities to produce each cost object are different. Using an average cost per output, for example, will result in both:

◆ **Output level undercosting.** A unit, batch, or product consumes a relatively high level of input materials and conversion activities but is reported to have a relatively low total cost.

◆ **Output level overcosting.** A unit, batch, or product consumes a relatively low level of input materials and conversion activities but is reported to have a relatively high total cost.

One threat to companies is that if their outputs are undercosted, they are likely to be underpriced relative to their actual costs to retail, and operating margin is lower than it should be. Another threat is that if companies overcost their outputs, they are likely to overprice them. In a competitive market, they will lose sales. Because these products actually cost less than what managers have estimated using peanut butter costing, the company could cut selling prices to maintain or enhance market share and still make the same profit on each sale. Recall that the COGS and COS can only be recovered by making the sale; therefore, if you can more closely match costs to their causes, you will more readily identify and remedy cost and pricing problems. Exhibit 5-1 illustrates the traditional, cost smoothing, or peanut butter approach based on three different products. Unlike Chapter 4, the indirect costs include not only COGS or COS but also period costs. That is why the colour of the overhead cost pool for design, production, and distribution is no longer the blue signifying manufacturing overhead, but green signifying a mix of both inventoriable and period overhead. Assigned amounts of indirect costs are in identical one-thirds across the three very different types of products.

COST CROSS-SUBSIDIZATION

Unfortunately, if one output, batch, or product is undercosted, another will be overcosted. Imagine two different types of unit of output and only one cost pool. Costs that are not assigned to the undercosted output remain in the pool. These costs must be assigned to the second type of output unit as illustrated in Exhibit 5-2. Think back to a time you either served or were served in a fast-food restaurant such as Tim Hortons.

The time needed to hand a customer a Tim Hortons refillable thermal cup, obtain payment, and provide change is very short. The cups themselves are manufactured by machine as large amounts of plastic pellets are melted, coloured, poured into moulds, cooled, extracted, assembled, and then stamped with the company's logo. The materials can be purchased in large quantities and will not spoil if they remain in inventory. Small, medium, and large thermal cups are produced in batches but designed with the same-sized lid to reduce batch costs. The indirect costs include primarily those to change the size of the moulds for different-sized cups, machine maintenance, custodial and security costs, quality control, plant management, utilities, and other uncontrollable fixed costs such as taxes, leases or amortization, and insurance.

In contrast, preparing and selling a sandwich incurs a very different set of costs. The sandwiches are not manufactured in advance but are prepared each day. They too are made in batches but primarily by hand as people prepare the fillings and garnishes such as lettuce and tomatoes each day. The different kinds of bread and

EXHIBIT 5-1
Traditional Cost Assignment: Large Proportion of Indirect Costs and Different Activities for Different Outputs

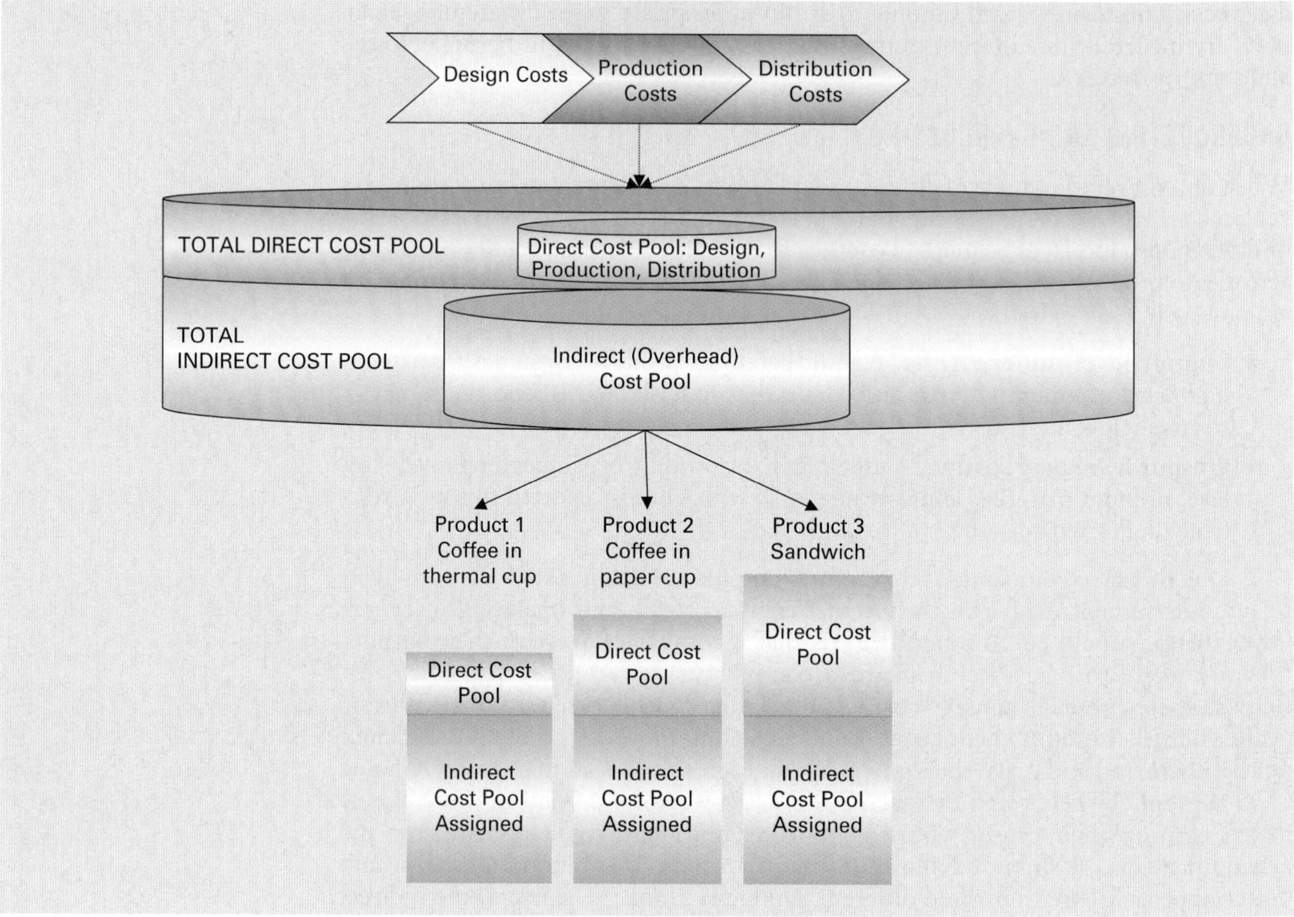

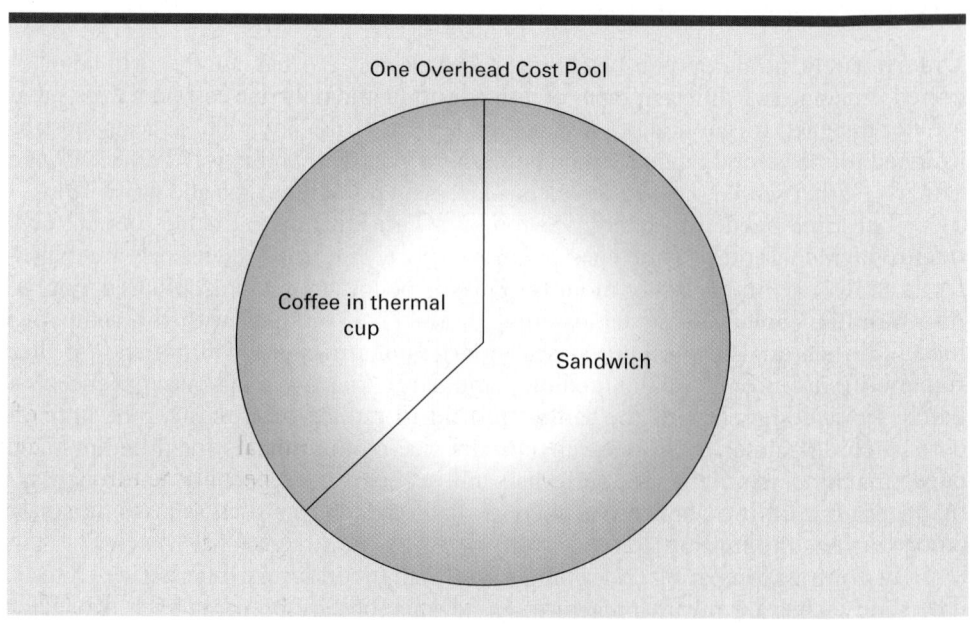

EXHIBIT 5-2
Cross-Subsidization of Costs—Costs Not Borne by One Product Must be Assigned to the Other Product

fillings are combined in batches and packaged differently before being distributed for sale from a refrigerator. A conveyor may move the bread from one person filling to the next garnishing and finally to wrapping. The indirect costs arise because of very different sets of activities compared to manufacturing mugs. To survive, these differences in producing different products must be accurately reflected in the prices Tim Hortons charges customers. This will be true whether Tim Hortons actually produces the outputs itself or merely merchandises the outputs.

When indirect costs are spread evenly despite different sets of activities that cause them, overcosting subsidizes those outputs, batches, or products that are undercosted. This is called **cost cross-subsidization**. Imagine four friends are sharing a meal in a restaurant. Assume each of them orders separate dinners, desserts, and drinks. The restaurant bill is as follows:

	Entrée	Dessert	Drinks	Total
Audra	$11	$ 0	$ 4	$ 15
Lincoln	20	8	14	42
Esai	15	4	8	27
Dan	14	4	6	24
	$60	$16	$32	$108

The $108 total restaurant bill produces a $27 average cost per dinner. This broad-average costing approach treats each diner the same. Audra would probably object to paying $27, because her actual cost is only $15. Indeed, she ordered the lowest-cost entrée, had no dessert, and had the lowest drink bill. When costs are averaged across all four diners, both Audra and Dan are overcosted, Lincoln is undercosted, and Esai is costed accurately.

The restaurant example is both simple and intuitive. The amount of cost cross-subsidization for each friend can be readily computed given that all cost items can be traced as direct costs to each diner. More complex costing issues arise, however, when there are indirect costs, when resources are used by two or more individual diners (e.g., purchasing a pitcher of beer to share instead of individual beverages). It is most likely you will notice when, as designated driver, you do not drink any beer and yet you will contribute towards paying for the pitcher—your consumption is overcosted. Your contribution is cross-subsidizing the costs of beer consumption for your friends. It is relatively easy to accurately cost the dinners by tracing each cost to each friend. But as the evening progresses, it becomes increasingly difficult and perhaps against the spirit of friendship to trace the cost of the beer consumed by each friend.

ASSESS YOUR MASTERY

MyAccountingLab

To check your understanding of the material in Learning Objective ❶, go to the *Mastery Questions* section at the end of this chapter and complete Learning Objective ❶ questions 1 and 2.

THE LOGIC OF TRADITIONAL COST ASSIGNMENT AND THE COST HIERARCHY

TRADITIONAL COSTING SYSTEM AT COFFEE BEAN INC. (CBI)

Contrast the logic of traditional cost assignment with the logic of the activities cost hierarchy ②

Coffee Bean Inc. (CBI) roasts, blends, packages, and distributes different types of coffee. The raw coffee beans are purchased through a central worldwide auction market. The raw coffee beans are sold by each farmer's co-operative to the highest bidder. While CBI purchases raw beans in 100-kg bags, it eventually sells roasted, blended, ground coffee in 1-kg bags and tins. CBI managers have focused their attention on two blends of coffee.

One blend, Mona Loa, sells in high volume. The other, a newly introduced blend, Malaysian, sells in low volume. Both blends are roasted, blended, and packaged using the same equipment, and CBI schedules production runs to produce larger batches of Mona Loa than Malaysian. This means more kilograms of Mona Loa are roasted, taking more time for the batch than for Malaysian. The transformation from raw beans to goods packaged and available for sale is highly automated, requiring very little direct manufacturing labour.

With its traditional costing system, CBI budgets its pro-forma costs including allocated overhead costs, then adds a profit mark-up of 30% to each product. Customers return to CBI because they can depend on the quality of the coffee. But they are also price-conscious and will switch if they can obtain the same quality at a lower price elsewhere. The 2009 budget for the two blends reports their pro-forma costs. Indirect costs, CBI's overhead, are $7,875,400, and this cost pool is allocated based on the pro-forma cost of direct manufacturing labour-hours (DMLH) for each product. The budgeted direct labour cost pool is $1,575,080. The budgeted direct materials (DM) cost pool totals $7,200,000. The indirect costs are the highest proportion of total costs, over 47% ($7,875,400 ÷ 16,650,480). The per-unit and total pro-forma costs are:

	Cost per Unit		
	Mona Loa (1)	Malaysian (2)	Total (3)
Direct materials (per kg)	$5.04	$3.84	$ 7,200,000
Direct manufacturing labour (per DMLH)	0.36	0.36	1,575,080
Total direct costs	$5.40	$4.20	8,775,080
Indirect costs			7,875,400
Total			$16,650,480

Based on this information, the traditional or peanut butter overhead allocation rate is the total pro-forma value of the overhead cost pool divided by the total pro-forma direct manufacturing labour cost pool:

$$\text{Traditional overhead allocation rate} = \frac{\text{Budgeted overhead cost pool}}{\text{Budgeted direct manufacturing labour cost pool}}$$

$$= \frac{\$7,875,400}{\$1,575,080}$$

$$= \$5.00 \text{ per direct manufacturing labour dollar}$$

This means that for every direct manufacturing labour dollar spent to produce either Mona Loa or Malaysian, CBI will allocate $5.00 of overhead. Therefore, the current pro-forma costs per kilogram of each blend of coffee are:

		Cost per Unit	
		Mona Loa (1)	Malaysian (2)
Direct materials (per kg)		$5.04	$3.84
Direct manufacturing labour (per DMLH)		0.36	0.36
Total direct costs		5.40	4.20
Indirect cost allocation rate per $1.00 DMLH	$5.00		
Indirect costs assigned (0.36 DMLH × $5.00)		1.80	1.80
Total unit cost per kg		$7.20	$6.00
Mark-up (assume 30%)	30%		
Pro forma price per kilogram (unit cost per kg × 1.30)		$9.36	$7.80

The controller believes that this current allocation method is misleading CBI's managers about the difference in costs to produce each blend of coffee.

The controller is aware that while CBI's products are of high quality, CBI's customers will purchase their ground coffee elsewhere at a lower price per kilogram, all other things being equal. Quality at the correct price is CBI's value proposition to its customers. If its customers cannot tell the difference between a less-expensive competitor's coffee and CBI's, then they will switch.

The controller knows that the correct price and quality trade-off is essential to CBI's long-term success. It is far more expensive to capture new customers or recapture former customers who were dissatisfied than to retain customers. CBI wants to prevent customers switching because they believe CBI's coffee is overpriced for the value they are receiving. Correct pricing will help prevent switching and all the costs to recapture former customers.

We now examine how ABC can be applied to refine a traditional costing system and reduce the miscosting of products sold to customers.

COST HIERARCHIES

A **cost hierarchy** is the name given to the management-accounting logic used to separate one indirect cost pool into four possible cost pools according to the level at which activities contribute to producing output. Clearly, it is not a financial-accounting logic, although good financial records are the necessary foundation upon which to build an ABC system. The financial-accounting method of classifying indirect or manufacturing overhead costs is logical when producing financial statements. This same logic can confuse or conceal the indirect effects of efficient causes in different business functions on the indirect costs of manufacturing. Cost hierarchy is not based on the value chain but rather on activity level. In Exhibit 5-3, notice that the indirect inventoriable and period costs from different business functions in the value chain have been gathered into a single cost pool in red, then sorted according

EXHIBIT 5-3
Accumulating Relevant Indirect Costs per Input for Business Functions and Assigning Them to a Job or Process Output Unit Cost Object

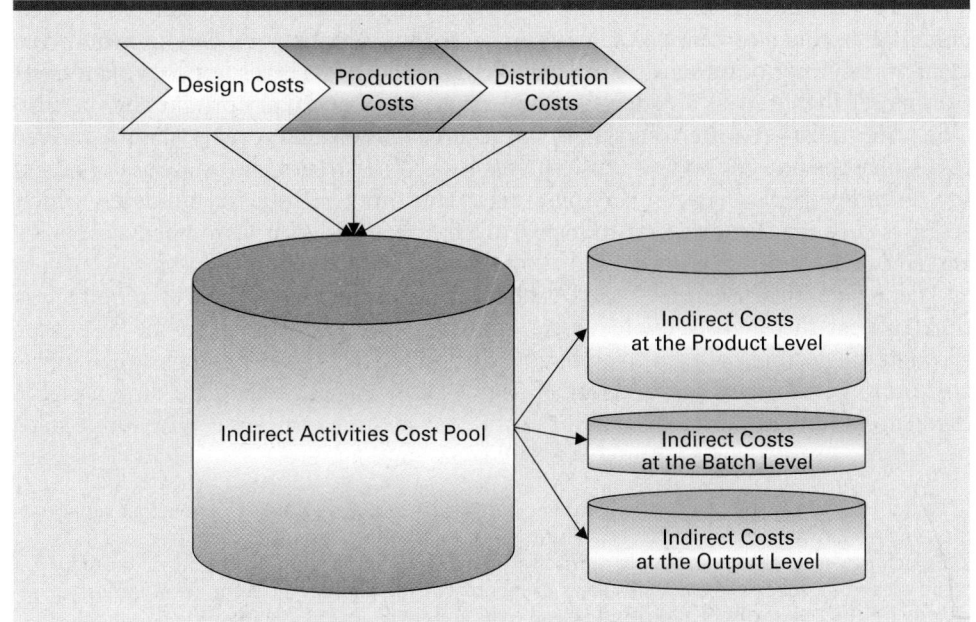

to the activity level that causes the indirect costs in green. An activity is an event, task, or unit of work with a specific purpose.

ABC systems commonly use a four-part cost hierarchy—output unit-level costs, batch-level costs, product-sustaining costs, and facility-sustaining costs—to identify cost allocation bases.[1] ABC systems call these cost allocation bases the **activity cost drivers** of costs in activity cost pools. The cost allocation base is the denominator used to calculate the cost allocation rate in traditional cost assignment. The activity cost driver is the name of the denominator used to calculate the cost allocation rate in ABC cost assignment. This simply means that the more activity undertaken, the higher the total **activity cost pool** will be in the unit, batch, or product activity cost pool. An activity cost pool is the dollar value of the cost of activities at a specified level. The lowest level affected by an activity is a single output unit, which is the foundation or base of the hierarchy. The largest unit affected is the entire organization, which is the pinnacle of the hierarchy. The larger the scope of costs affected by an activity, the higher the activity is placed in the hierarchy.

It is without doubt that reclassifying costs using the logic of the cost hierarchy will require amending the way financial costs in the current management information system (MIS) are sorted and reported for management use. Managers who decide to learn and apply the logic of the cost hierarchy need to identify key activities common to single outputs, batches, or products. Those activities critical to the success of the company are the critical success factors for which activities costs should be identified.

This is very different from the financial-accounting approach of applying a specific level of materiality. For example, a cost pool such as design may have a lower dollar value but be extremely critical to success because improved design will reduce costs for all products, batches, and units by, for example, reducing materials handling, custodial, and quality-control costs. If costs are simply classified by business functions in the value chain, then indirect design costs would be considered as a cost pool separate from manufacturing overhead and distribution overhead costs. In fact, manufacturing overhead will decrease if design is good.

The key difference between Exhibits 5-1 and 5-3 is that in Exhibit 5-3, the size of the indirect activities cost pools differs by activity level. For illustration only, the product-level activities cost pool is largest, the batch-level activities cost pool is smallest, and the output-level activities cost pool is mid-sized. The diagram has been produced so that the volume in all three green activities cost pools equals the volume in the total indirect cost pool, shown in red. The reason the total indirect cost pool has been accumulated based on design, distribution, and production is that the different levels of activities occurring in each business function affect costs at other levels of activity in other business functions. These indirect costs are relevant to each other and to decisions.

Output unit-level costs arise when activities contribute to the cost of each unit of a product or service, such as maintenance supplies and labour per direct machine hour per output unit. For example, Tim Hortons serves hot chocolate from a dispenser that brews a powdered mix of cocoa, sugar, and dairy product by the cup. The water must be hotter than that used to brew coffee, and it takes slightly longer to dissolve the powder and dispense the same sized cup of hot chocolate as coffee. As the dispenser cools between servings, sugar and other residue accumulates, which requires cleaning the dispenser to maintain a free flow of fluid. Maintenance supplies and labour are indirect costs caused by the type of output unit dispensed.

The identical dispenser used exclusively to dispense coffee will require less time to heat the slightly cooler water, and the water flowing from the dispenser through the ground coffee into a pot contains no sugar. All other things equal, it will cost more per direct machine hour of use to clean the hot-chocolate dispenser for each cup of hot chocolate sold than the coffee dispenser for each cup of coffee sold.

---

[1]The fourth level of costs, facility-sustaining costs, arises from head office activities that support the entire organization (e.g., legal costs, information technology costs, and executive salaries). This facilities-sustaining cost pool comprises primarily fixed costs and is frequently allocated on an average-cost basis to each subsidiary or manufacturing plant in different geographical locations. Other methods of allocating period costs are discussed in Chapter 14.

When hundreds of millions of cups of each are sold, this can make a difference to prices that are both competitive with Starbucks and yet profitable for Tim Hortons, and prices that are not.

Batch-level costs are resources sacrificed on activities that are related to a group of units. Again, Tim Hortons must purchase and distribute both ground coffee and powdered hot chocolate. The ground coffee is pre-packaged to provide exactly a one-litre amount of brewed coffee each batch. Each pot of coffee is a batch. These materials are not provided by the cup but rather in bags weighing several kilograms. Remember, Tim Hortons promises fresh coffee because the taste deteriorates if it is kept on a heater for too long. On the other hand, tea can be brewed by dispensing hot water into a single cup containing a tea bag.

These bags of tea and coffee do not simply appear at the Tim Hortons outlet. They must be ordered, delivered from the Tim Hortons' supplier, then paid for on time. The activities of purchasing, receiving, and paying for each bag of materials are indirect costs. It would be sensible to order these materials at the same time because with the same supplier you avoid paying more than once for the same transportation activity. While the number of bags may be different for tea and coffee, it is the activities of purchasing, transporting, and paying that generate the indirect costs. These costs can be divided up among or assigned to each batch of beverages produced from each bag of either ground coffee or tea.

Product-sustaining (or **service-sustaining**) **costs** are resources sacrificed on activities undertaken to support product lines, not batches of product lines or units of product. One example is product-design costs. Currently, the information technology used to design products, often referred to as computer-aided design (CAD), shortens design time. The same configuration of technology can be applied to design either a coffee mug or an espresso machine. If Bunn, the manufacturer of Tim Hortons' coffee makers, also manufactured its mugs, it would know that design improvements based on standardizing, reducing, and simplifying parts reduce costs across all product lines.

Facility-sustaining costs are resources sacrificed on activities that sustain the entire enterprise. These are reported in period costs as operating expenses and include labour (e.g., accounting, legal, security) and space costs. The facility-sustaining cost pool can include costs of switching to electronic documentation systems for all purchasing activities that would apply to all functional areas. The cost pool may be readily identifiable but the activity cost driver will be difficult to identify if this cost must be assigned to some output (see Chapter 10).

STRATEGY

"If Only Everything Didn't Depend On ... Everything Else"*

A tremendous benefit of refined costing systems is that they do reveal the complex dependencies among activities. But observing how types and quantities of activity affect cost also clarifies how to simplify by reducing both the variety of types and quantity of activity. Complexity is not the same as confusion. Instead of confusion, a method such as an ABC system, ironically, leads to clarity in understanding costs of activities. An effective cost leadership strategy per unit may only result from higher-level activity cost reduction.

It is important that managers understand the principle of simplicity underlying ABC. The cost hierarchy "chunks" financial information into one of four cost pools. The logic is simple—classify a cost according to the scope of activity that caused it. ABC systems are an example of the strategy of simplicity. This strategy can be applied in any business when the objective is to improve the relevance of information used to make business decisions.

* The source of this quotation is Mintzberg, Ahlstrand, and Lampel, *Strategy Bites Back*, (London: Prentice Hall, 2005), p. 67.

A **refined costing system** results in a better measure of the nonuniformity in the use of an organization's resources by products and customers. For example, the activities to deliver Automated Teller Machine (ATM) services differ tremendously from those to deliver the same services face-to-face. Improvements to the ease of transferring digital information from one medium to another have increased the use of information technology from research through to customer service. The use of direct manufacturing labour activity has decreased as robots perform these and other higher-level manufacturing activities. With improved flexibility in production of goods and services, businesses can compete globally through websites that market their outputs, track orders, take electronic payments, and confirm the shipment or the service, complete inventory entries, and record revenue in the corporate information system.

Managing complex technology and producing very diverse products requires committing an increasing amount of resources for various support functions, such as production scheduling, and product and process design and engineering. As the activities costs increase in their interdependence, companies install IT software (e.g., SAP) to coordinate among the activities, reconfiguring them to reduce costs. But costing-system refinements require more data gathering and more analysis. Benefits include improved forecasting, performance measurement, and control, and a faster, more on-target strategic response as opportunities emerge from the environment.

MyAccountingLab

ASSESS YOUR MASTERY

To check your understanding of the material in Learning Objective ❷, go to the *Mastery Questions* section at the end of this chapter and complete Learning Objective ❷ questions 1 and 2.

ACTIVITY-BASED COSTING (ABC) SYSTEMS

❸ Apply the logic of an activities-based costing (ABC) cost hierarchy

CBI REFINES ITS COSTS USING THE LOGIC OF ABC

The goal of applying a refined costing system, such as ABC, is to unlock cost savings opportunities currently hidden by the traditional costing method. The controller had obtained a professional accounting designation and recalled an alternative method of rearranging costs using the logic of the cost hierarchy. After long consultation with managers, the controller obtained their support for improving the relevance of cost information they would obtain from a refined ABC cost-assignment system. The managers identified six activities for which controlling costs were critical to CBI's success: purchasing, materials handling, quality control, roasting, blending, and packaging. The purpose of identifying the activities was to establish the foundation for the new costing system.

The controller and managers then began the task of identifying the scope of each activity. The purpose was to identify the level within the cost hierarchy at which each activity caused costs. After considerable consultation with one another, the managers identified one product-level overhead activity: purchasing. Furthermore, the manager of purchasing noted that as the number of purchase orders (P.O.s) increased, the cost of purchasing activity increased. This meant that the number of P.O.s was an activity cost driver of the indirect activity cost pool, purchasing.

The controller then analyzed the existing financial records and accumulated all the costs of purchasing the husked ripe coffee berries or green beans into one indirect activity cost pool. Next, the pro forma cost for the coming year was estimated, with the managers' help, at $2,777,600. The cost of the purchasing activity was not uniformly distributed because the manager of marketing had forecast sales of 1,050,000 kg of Mona Loa but only 350,000 kg of the new blend, Malaysian. The purchase order size for Mona Loa was 25,000 kg but it was 5,000 kg per purchase order for Malaysian.

For the coming year, CBI budgeted placement of 42 purchase orders for Mona Loa (1,050,000 kg ÷ 25,000 per P.O. = 42 P.O.s). CBI budgeted 70 purchase orders for Malaysian (350,000 kg ÷ 5,000 per P.O. = 70 P.O.s). CBI produces several blends of coffee, of which Mona Loa and Malaysian are only two. For all the blends of coffee, CBI budgeted a total placement of 448 purchase orders. The pro forma cost for each P.O. (the activity cost driver) would be $6,200 ($2,777,600 ÷ 448 P.O.s = $6,200 per P.O.). The $6,200 is called the **activity cost rate**. The activity cost rate is the activity (purchasing) cost pool divided by the total quantity consumed of the activity cost driver (P.O.s). To assign this purchasing activity cost pool to each blend of coffee, the activity cost rate must be multiplied by the quantity of POs for each blend. For Mona Loa, the assigned product-level purchasing cost is $260,400 ($6,200 × 42 P.O.s). For Malaysian, the assigned product-level purchasing cost is $434,000 ($6,200 × 70 P.O.s). As a rule, the quantity of activity cost driver consumed for each blend of coffee should differ; otherwise, CBI is as well off using the traditional method to allocate that specific cost pool.

ABC systems calculate the costs of individual activities and assign costs to cost objects such as products (or services), batches, and units based on the scope of activities undertaken. By defining activities and identifying the costs of performing each activity, ABC systems provide a greater level of detail to understand how an organization uses its resources. As we describe refinement to cost assignment, keep in mind three features:

1. *Direct-cost tracing.* A feature of ABC systems is to identify some costs or cost pools that can be reclassified as direct costs that vary with the quantity of a single activity cost driver consumed. An example at Tim Hortons could be the cost of indirect labour to clean the machines that brew either coffee or hot chocolate. If it takes a standard amount of time to clean each machine, then the cost per cleaning can be traced as direct labour instead of assigned from an indirect labour cost pool. To make this worthwhile, the cost of cleaning the machines must be material.

2. *Indirect-cost pools.* ABC systems of cost assignment create smaller cost pools (numerators) that vary with the consumption of a defined activity. Because a single activity causes costs in the pool, the cost pool is homogeneous. The amount in the cost pool varies directly as activity varies. It is a direct cost of activity but an indirect cost of production. The activity does not directly produce a unit of finished output, batch of units, or a product, but nevertheless is required for production. This is why the activity cost pool is an indirect and not a direct cost pool. In the CBI example, purchasing did not result in kilograms of ground coffee, but without purchasing direct materials, there would be nothing to transform.

3. *Activity cost drivers.* For each activity cost pool, a measure of the activity performed is required. Usually some output results from activity and it is the output that is measured. The output is called an activity cost driver. It is the denominator that is divided into the indirect cost pool to calculate the activity cost rate. In the CBI example, the output from the purchasing activity was measured as the quantity of purchase orders generated in a year.

THINKING CRITICALLY

On the basis of purchasing activity only, should CBI managers suspect that Mona Loa is underpriced or overpriced, and Malaysian is underpriced or overpriced? Explain in a sentence or two. Read on for an analysis of this situation.

The example of purchasing shows that the cost of ordering the annual supply of Malaysian coffee beans is far higher than the cost of ordering the annual supply of Mona Loa. The total difference in purchasing cost is $173,600 ($434,000 – $260,400 = $173,600). Malaysian costs 66.7% more to purchase than Mona Loa ($173,600 ÷ $260,400 = 0.667).

Notice, however, that the price per kilo of Mona Loa before the mark-up is $7.20 and that of Malaysian is $6.00. The revenue CBI is accumulating is 16.7% lower for Malaysian than it is for Mona Loa [($7.20 – $6.00) ÷ $7.20 = 0.1667] but Malaysian's indirect cost is 66.7% higher. The evidence so far is that the price of Mona Loa is cross-subsidizing the purchasing activity costs incurred by Malaysian.

On the basis of only this information, the managers at CBI should suspect that Malaysian is underpriced while Mona Loa is overpriced. A competitor who has implemented an ABC system of assigning indirect costs would know more accurately the costs of each blend. This competitor could reduce the price of coffee of similar quality and taste as Mona Loa substantially and still earn a 30% profit. CBI would lose sales but lacks the information needed to become price-competitive.

The logic of an ABC cost-assignment system produces more accurate cost allocation rates based on smaller, homogeneous activity cost pools (numerators) accompanied by appropriate measures of activities—the activity cost drivers (denominators)—that drive or cause the total cost pool to vary. The result is a more accurate cost rate per unit of activity cost driver. A more accurate rate means that assigning portions of the total cost pool to different cost objects (units, batches, or products) will be more accurate. It will be less likely that material mistakes in costing will occur among cost objects with non-uniform consumption of activities.

The goal in the CBI example, however, is not to calculate the cost per purchase order (activity cost driver) but rather the cost per kilogram of ground coffee sold for each blend, either Mona Loa or Malaysia. Calculating the cost per purchase order—the activity cost rate—is simply an intermediate step that is necessary because different quantities of purchase orders are issued for each blend. This means the purchasing activity (and cost) is not uniformly consumed. In fact this is true of each activity identified by CBI's managers. In Exhibit 5-4 in the next section are the data produced by the managers and the controller for the six activities considered critical to CBI's success.

IMPLEMENTING AN ABC COST-ASSIGNMENT SYSTEM AT CBI

4 Assign costs using activity-based costing (ABC)

Now that we understand the basic concepts of cost hierarchy and an ABC system of cost assignment, we will complete the refinement of CBI's indirect cost assignment system. Over the period of two months, the controller continued to meet regularly with the managers within whose departments the purchasing, materials handling, quality control, roasting, blending, and packaging occurred. It was through these negotiations that these six activities were isolated as causes of a material amount of costs.

The managers next had to identify the scope of output affected by each activity and, again through discussion, they also identified how to measure the quantity of the activity consumed. This measure was the activity cost driver. The denominators or activity cost drivers were now identified. The managers had always provided the nonfinancial quantities for the controller in order to produce a budget and they did so again. This year, however, they provided the budgeted quantities of each activity cost driver consumed. Based on dividing each indirect activity cost pool by the quantity of activity cost driver, the new activity cost rates were calculated. The results are shown in Exhibit 5-4.

The controller's objective was to improve the estimates of costs per kilogram of each blend of coffee. This required that managers also inform the controller of the quantity of kilograms of each blend of coffee affected by each activity. The activity cost rate could then be transformed into a cost assigned per kilogram. The batch size

EXHIBIT 5-4
Activity Cost Rates for CBI's Activity Cost Pools

Activity	Total Pro Forma Indirect Activity Cost Pool (1)	Total Pro Forma Activity Cost Driver Quantity (2)	Activity Cost Rate (3) = (1) ÷ (2)	Activity Cost Driver	Cost Hierarchy Activity Level	Relationship of the Activity Cost Driver to the Total Activity Cost
Purchasing	$2,777,600	448	$6,200 per P.O.		Product	Purchasing costs increase with number of P.O.s
Materials handling	3,465,000	15,400	225 per setup		Batch	Indirect setup costs increase with number of setups
Quality control	687,800	1,900	362 per batch		Batch	Indirect quality control costs increase with the batches inspected
Roasting	182,000	9,100	20 per roasting-hour		Batch	Indirect roasting costs increase with the hours of roasting
Blending	273,000	9,100	30 per blending-hour		Batch	Indirect blending costs increase with the hours of blending
Packaging	490,000	49,000	10 per packaging-hour		Unit	Indirect packaging costs increase with the packaging-hours
Total	$7,875,400					

or maximum number of kilograms of Mona Loa processed at any single time was 500 kg and for Malaysian was 200 kg. The batch size is limited by the equipment capacity. Exhibit 5-5 summarizes all the cost assignment and costs per kilogram for each activity for Mona Loa and Malaysian.

To produce 1,050,000 kg of Mona Loa would require 2,100 setups. To produce 350,000 kg of Malaysian would require 1,750 setups to total 3,850 setups annually. On a daily basis, assuming a 50-week year (to provide for maintenance time), CBI processed coffee for 350 days. Each day it handled enough coffee beans for 6 batches of Mona Loa and 5 batches of Malaysian. Dividing the total budgeted materials handling activity cost pool by total setups results in an activity cost rate of $225 per setup ($3,465,000 ÷ 15,400 setups = $225 per setup). The materials handling activity cost assigned to Mona Loa will be $472,500 (2,100 setups × $225 per setup = $472,500) and for Malaysian will be $393,750 (1,750 setups × $225 per setup = $393,750). But each activity cost pool for each blend must be assigned per kilogram of that specific blend of coffee to complete the indirect cost assignment task.

On a cost-per-kilogram basis, the purchasing activity costs will be $0.248/kg for Mona Loa ($260,400 ÷ 1,050,000 kg = $0.248 per kg). The materials handling activity cost for Mona Loa on a per-kilogram basis will be $0.45 per kg ($472,500 ÷ 1,050,000 kg = $0.45 per kg). The purchasing activity costs will be $1.24/kg for Malaysian ($434,000 ÷ 350,000 kg = $1.24 per kg) and the materials handling costs for Malaysian will be $1.125 per kg ($393,750 ÷ 350,000 kg = $1.125 per kg).

CBI's quality control policy was to test every 7 batches of Mona Loa and every 10 batches of Malaysian. In one year, there would be 300 quality control tests for Mona Loa and 175 quality control tests for Malaysian for a total of 475 tests. The indirect quality control activity cost pool pro forma value was $687,800 and the activity cost rate per batch tested was $362 per batch ($687,800 ÷ 1,900 batches = $362 per batch). The quality control activity costs assigned to Mona Loa would be $108,600 (300 batches × $362 per batch = $108,600) and to Malaysian would be $63,350 (175 batches × $362 per batch = $63,350) for the year. On a per-kilogram basis, the quality control activity cost assigned to Mona

EXHIBIT 5-5
Assigning Activity Cost per Unit of Output (Kilogram)

Activity Consumed	Mona Loa	Malaysian	Activity Cost Rate	Per
Purchasing	42	70	$6,200	P.O.
Materials handling	2,100	1,750	225	setup
Quality control	300	175	362	batch
Roasting	525	350	20	roasting-hour
Blending	210	175	30	blending-hour
Packaging	10,500	1,750	10	packaging-hour
Pro forma marketing demand, kg	1,050,000	350,000		

Activity costs assigned:	Assigned Activity Cost Pools		Activity Cost per kg	
	Mona Loa	Malaysian	Mona Loa	Malaysian
Purchasing ($6,200 × 42; 70)	$260,400	$434,000	$0.2480	$1.2400
Materials handling ($225 × 2,100; 1,750)	472,500	393,750	0.4500	1.1250
Quality control ($362 × 300; 175)	108,600	63,350	0.1034	0.1810
Roasting ($20 × 525; 350)	10,500	7,000	0.0100	0.0200
Blending ($30 × 210; 175)	6,300	5,250	0.0060	0.0150
Packaging ($10 × 10,500; 1,750)	105,000	17,500	0.1000	0.0500
Total assigned activity costs	$963,300	$920,850	$0.9174	$2.6310

Loa would be $0.104 per kg ($108,600 ÷ 1,050,000 kg = $0.104 per kg) and to Malaysian would be $0.181 per kg ($63,350 ÷ 350,000 kg = $0.181 per kg).

The costs included in the activity cost pool of roasting hours included utilities to power the roaster and vent the fumes, and the labour to check temperature and colour. This specialist also conducted quality-control tests. The time to roast a 500-kg batch of Mona Loa was 15 minutes and for a 200-kg batch of Malaysian was 12 minutes. In total, running 6.5 hours per day for 350 days, there was roasting capacity of 2,275 roasting hours for each of CBI's four roasters. Mona Loa consumed 525 and Malaysian 350 roasting-hours.

The total indirect roasting activity cost pool was budgeted at $182,000 and the activity cost rate at $20 per roasting-hour ($182,000 ÷ 9,100 roasting-hours = $20 per roasting-hour). The pro forma activity cost assigned to Mona Loa was $10,500 ($20 per roasting-hour × 525 roasting-hours = $10,500) and on a per-kilogram basis was $0.01 per kg ($10,500 ÷ 1,050,000 kg = $0.01 per kg). For Malaysian, the pro forma activity cost assigned was $7,000 ($20 per roasting-hour × 350 roasting hours = $7,000) and $0.02 per kg ($7,000 ÷ 350,000 kg = $0.02 per kg).

The costs included in the activity cost pool of blending hours included utilities to power the blender and the conveyor belt moving the blended beans from the roaster to the blender. Moving the beans in the open air permitted them to cool properly and stopped the roasting process. One conveyor serviced each roaster and blender pair, and if the conveyor stopped, the batch could be spoiled. The combined time to move and blend the beans limited CBI's processing capacity but the entire process consumed only six minutes or 0.10 of an hour per batch. The remaining time until the next batch moved along the conveyor was spent inspecting and either informing the roaster not to start the next batch, or switching to another conveyor-blender pair.

During the year, CBI had budgeted to process 2,100 batches of Mona Loa and 1,750 batches of Malaysian. Of the total blending hours of capacity, Mona Loa consumed 210 blending hours (2,100 batches × 0.10 blending-hours per batch = 210 blending-hours) and Malaysian 175 blending-hours (1,750 batches × 0.10 blending-hours per batch = 175 blending-hours) per year. The blending activity cost rate was based on full capacity of 9,100 hours and the pro forma blending activity cost pool was $273,000. The blending activity cost rate was $30 per blending-hour ($273,000 ÷ 9,100 blending-hours = $30 per blending-hour). The blending activity cost assigned to Mona Loa was $6,300 ($30 per blending-hour x 210 blending-hours = $6,300) and on a per-kilogram basis was $0.006 ($6,300 ÷ 1,050,000 kg = $0.006 per kg). The amount assigned to Malaysian was $5,250 ($30 per blending-hour × 175 blending-hours = $5,250) and on a per-kilogram basis $0.015 per kg ($5,250 ÷ 350,000 kg = $0.015 per kg).

THINKING CRITICALLY

Why don't the assigned activity costs equal the total activity cost pools? Explain in a sentence or two. Read on for an analysis of this situation.

The company produces several different blends of coffee, of which Mona Loa and Malaysian are only two. The unassigned costs in each activity cost pool are the proportion of activity costs consumed by producing other blends of coffee. As shown above, the roasting required attention from the Coffee Master to ensure the right colour and oiliness of each batch.

Notice that it takes a tremendous amount of information, both financial and nonfinancial, to refine this costing system. Using the traditional method, only three cost pools were required—two direct and one indirect. The indirect cost pool was assigned uniformly to all output units based on the total direct labour cost. Managers will only spend their time gathering data at this level of detail if they are convinced it is important to CBI's short-term and long-term success.

The use of the cost hierarchy is a strategic decision, not an operating decision. It is strategic because it affects the long-term understanding of how activities across the value chain interact to cause costs of each unit of output. Generally speaking, high activity cost rates will provide a very good initial signal to managers of where to begin with cost-control efforts. Those efforts will succeed either if they reduce the activity cost rate or they decrease the volume of activity undertaken (the multiplier).

The total indirect packaging activity cost pool was budgeted at $490,000 and it took approximately 36 seconds, or 0.01 hours, to fill each kilogram package of Mona Loa blended coffee beans. It took approximately 18 seconds, or 0.005 hours, to package each kilogram of Malaysian blended coffee beans. Each packaging process used a different sealing method, which accounted for the time difference. CBI had six machines.

In the exercise of refining the cost-assignment system, this was the only unit activity cost identified. The indirect cost pool value varied with the packaging hours consumed. CBI's capacity was 49,000 packaging-hours; therefore, the activity cost rate was $10 per packaging-hour ($490,000 ÷ 49,000 packaging-hours = $10 per packaging-hour). This management-costing system paid no attention whatsoever to whether or not the activity costs were inventoriable or period costs, nor to the business function giving rise to the activity.

The total time to package Mona Loa's 1,050,000 kg was 10,500 hours (1,050,000 kg × 0.01 packaging-hour per kg = 10,500 packaging-hours) and for Malaysian's 350,000 kg was 1,750 hours (350,000 kg × 0.005 packaging-hours per kg = 1,750 packaging-hours). The total packaging activity cost assigned to Mona Loa was $105,000 ($10 per packaging-hour × 10,500 packaging hours = $105,000) and to Malaysian was $17,500 ($10 per packaging-hour × 1,750 packaging-hours = $17,500). On a per-kilogram basis, the packaging cost for Mona Loa was $0.01 per kg ($105,000 ÷ 1,050,000 kg = $0.10 per kg). For Malaysian, the cost per kilogram was $0.05 per kg ($17,500 ÷ 350,000 kg = $0.05 per kg).

COMPARING ALTERNATIVE COSTING SYSTEMS

Exhibit 5-6 compares the original cost assignment and price per kilogram for Mona Loa and Malaysian using the traditional method to the refined ABC system of cost assignment. The more refined ABC system informs CBI that its Mona Loa blend is overpriced in a very competitive market. If this is not remedied, the danger is that customers will switch to a brand they perceive as being equally high quality but of lower cost. In fact, CBI can reduce its Mona Loa price to $8.21 and, all other things being equal, retain its 30% profit. Just as important, CBI also knows now that it is losing $1.08 on every kilogram it sells of Malaysian ($8.88 – $7.80 = $1.08). CBI can either increase the unit price of Malaysian to achieve its 30% mark-up, or leave the price as it is and be satisfied with a 14.2% profit [($7.80 – $6.831) ÷ $6.831 = 0.1419, rounded to 14.2%].

ABC SYSTEM AND DEPARTMENT INDIRECT COST RATES

Companies often use costing systems that have features of ABC systems—such as multiple cost pools and multiple cost-allocation bases—but fail to emphasize individual activities. Instead, separate indirect-cost rates are calculated for each department (for example, design, manufacturing, distribution, and so on) or sub-department (for example, roasting within the production department) using a cost-allocation base that best represents the usage of resources in that department or sub-department. Using the same logic that we described for ABC systems, companies prefer using department indirect-cost rates rather than a single company-wide indirect-cost rate when the drivers of costs in each department differ. In this section, we compare ABC systems and department-rate costing systems.

In the CBI example, the entire purchasing department constituted one activity cost pool. The company calculated the purchasing activity cost rate by dividing total purchasing department costs by a measure of output, which was purchase orders. CBI did not find it worthwhile to calculate separate activity rates within the purchasing department because purchase orders consume activities uniformly.

In contrast, in the production department, CBI identified two activity cost pools—a setup-cost pool and a batch-cost pool—rather than use a single production

EXHIBIT 5-6
Contrast CBI Costing and Pricing Using Traditional Costing and ABC Systems

	Traditional Costs per Unit			ABC Costs per Unit		
	Mona Loa	Malaysian		Mona Loa		Malaysian
Direct materials (per kg)	$5.04	$3.84	Direct materials (per kg)	$5.0400		$3.8400
Direct manufacturing labour (per DMLH)	0.36	0.36	Direct manufacturing labour (per DMLH)	0.3600		0.3600
Total direct costs	5.40	4.20	Total direct costs		$5.4000	$4.2000
Indirect cost allocation rate per $1.00 DMLH	$5.00		Activity costs:			
			Purchasing	0.2480		1.2400
Indirect costs assigned (0.36 DMLH × $5.00)	1.80	1.80	Materials handling	0.4500		1.1250
			Quality control	0.1034		0.1810
Total unit cost per kg	$7.20	$6.00	Roasting	0.0100		0.0200
Mark-up	30%		Blending	0.0060		0.0150
Pro forma price per kilogram (unit cost per kg × 1.30)	$9.36	$7.80	Packaging	0.1000		0.0500
			Total indirect costs		0.9174	2.6310
			Total cost		$6.3174	$6.8310
			Mark-up	30%		
			Pro forma price per kilo (unit cost per kg × 1.30)		$ 8.21	$ 8.88

department indirect-cost pool. The reasons are, first, each of these activities within production incurs significant costs and consumes different common inputs. Materials handling costs are driven by the time to set and reset the roasting machines. The roasting costs are driven by the roasting time per batch. Second, the Mona Loa and Malaysian blends do not use resources from these two activity areas in the same proportion of available hours. Using a single activity cost driver would result in overcosting one blend and undercosting the other.

It is appropriate to use a single department indirect-cost rate to allocate costs to products if:

◆ a single activity, for example contacting suppliers, accounts for a very material amount of the department's costs
◆ material costs are incurred on different activities within a department but each activity has the same cost-allocation base or
◆ material costs are incurred on different activities with different cost-allocation bases within a department but different products use resources from the different activity areas in the same proportions.

If any one of these three conditions hold, a department indirect-cost rate system is adequate. If none of the conditions hold, emphasizing activities leads to more focused and homogeneous cost pools, and aids in identifying activity cost drivers with clearer cause-and-effect relationships with the costs in activity cost pools. But the benefits of an ABC system must be balanced against its costs and limitations.

ASSESS YOUR MASTERY

To check your understanding of the material in Learning Objective ④, go to the *Mastery Questions* section at the end of this chapter and complete Learning Objective ④ questions 1 and 2.

MyAccountingLab

USING ABC SYSTEMS FOR PROFITABILITY IMPROVEMENT

Use ABC systems for activity-based management (ABM) ⑤

The emphasis of this chapter so far has been on improving the assignment of indirect costs. More accurate information is more relevant information that provides a sounder basis for both operating and strategic decisions.

Product and pricing decisions. The repricing of Mona Loa and Malaysian for CBI has already been discussed but the company must make longer-term product decisions. Based on the information from traditional cost assignment, it appears that the more kilograms sold of Mona Loa, the higher the revenue. This could lead CBI to spend more on marketing and advertising Mona Loa, anticipating it could simply increase the unit price to cover the additional cost. The cost hierarchy refinement signals the opposite to CBI.

Focusing on Mona Loa would be a mistake because it is already overpriced in the market. CBI would be more likely to increase revenue by reducing the unit price to stimulate higher sales volume. The company now knows it can reduce price as much as $1.15 and retain its 30% profit margin. How much to reduce the price will depend on what competitors charge for coffee blends of similar quality. CBI also knows that in the long run, if the market will not accept a price increase on Malaysian, then CBI must make the hard decision of dropping this blend to retain its profit margin of 30% or reducing its profit expectations to lower than 30%.

Cost-reduction decisions. The largest activity cost rate is very large indeed. At $6,200 per purchase order, this rate is almost 28 times higher than the next highest rate! This fact alone is attention-getting, and managers at CBI need to investigate ways to reduce the purchasing activity cost without impairing quality. The expensive purchasing process may be warranted if it contributes to the value of the coffee; otherwise, it must be changed to reduce the cost. One question that must be asked is, given the expense of a single purchase order, why is an order of Malaysian only 5,000 kilograms while it is 25,000 kilograms for Mona Loa? Unless there would be some deterioration in quality of raw Malaysian coffee beans, then it may be less expensive to reduce the number of purchase orders by increasing the quantity ordered each time and incur the inventory costs.

Customers anticipate a value proposition for which they are willing to pay. Activities undertaken by CBI that contribute to that value proposition are those for which customers should be willing to pay. **Value-added activity** is an activity that contributes directly to the customer's value proposition. Activities undertaken by CBI that do not contribute to the value proposition are activities for which the customer is not willing to pay. **Non–value-added activity** is an activity that fails to contribute to the customer's value proposition. This ABC system provides the opportunity for CBI to reassess expensive activities with a view to eliminating or at least reducing the non–value-added activities. Activity-based management (ABM) is a cost-leadership strategy to eliminate non–value-added activities.

Process decisions. The activity cost pools were selected by CBI managers because the activities were critical to CBI's success. Analyzing more carefully the processes that comprise each activity cost driver opens many opportunities for improving efficiency. Reducing the frequency and number of repetitions of activities can reduce the activity cost driver quantity (the denominator) causing the cost pool to decrease. For example, the number of daily setups is quite high but is a response to the capacity constraints imposed by the equipment. It may be worthwhile to purchase higher-capacity equipment to reduce the number of daily setup hours and decrease the materials handling activity cost pool.

When one activity within a process is adjusted to increase capacity, other adjustments are often required to avoid bottlenecks in production. It is also difficult, however, to cost-effectively match the production capacity throughout every stage of transformation. To enjoy lower costs on standard equipment, CBI may have to compromise by purchasing excess capacity at one stage of production. One benefit of ABC systems of cost assignment is that only the capacity used is included in operating costs. Thus the long-run cost of excess capacity is not allocated to current production. The current units of output are unburdened of excess capacity costs. If managers receive bonuses for reducing the costs of existing processes, this approach provides a financial incentive to seek and implement appropriate process improvements in a timely way.

Design decisions. Management can identify and evaluate new designs to improve performance by evaluating how product and process designs affect activities and costs. Companies can then work with their customers to evaluate the costs and prices of alternative design choices. For example, creative design decisions that decrease the complexity of blends will also affect the number of different beans for each blend. Each type of bean may require different roasting times and that will increase the number of setups.

If CBI used its traditional direct manufacturing labour-hour-based system to choose among alternative designs, which blends would CBI favour? Those designs that reduce direct manufacturing labour-hours the most, because the cost system sends an erroneous signal that reducing direct manufacturing labour-hours reduces overhead costs. In fact, the cause-and-effect relationship between direct manufacturing labour-hours and CBI's overhead costs is non-existent. Therefore, reducing direct manufacturing labour-hours would have no effect on CBI's indirect costs.

Planning and managing activities. Most companies implementing ABC systems for the first time analyze actual costs to identify activity cost pools and activity cost rates. Many then use ABC systems for planning and managing activities. They specify budgeted cost rates for activities, then, using a variation on normal costing for direct costs and normal costing for indirect costs, multiply these rates by actual quantity of activities. At year end, actual costs are compared to budgeted costs, providing feedback on how well activities were managed. Adjustments are also made for underallocated or overallocated indirect costs for each activity area, using the methods described in Chapter 4 (writeoff, proration, or adjusted allocation rate).

Our objective is to introduce activity-based management (ABM), wherein managers use ABC information to improve their decisions on pricing, design, process improvement, and cost reduction. Many variables causing cost are nonfinancial, such as complexity of blended coffee, and ABC provides the way to link nonfinancial causes to financial effects. By dividing large processes into smaller sets of activities, ABC also improves the ability of managers to identify cost-reduction opportunities by changing either the quantity of activity undertaken or the resources consumed by a product. In Chapter 6, we discuss activity-based budgeting; in Chapter 11, we discuss outsourcing and adding or dropping business segments; and in Chapter 12, we evaluate alternative design choices to improve efficiency and reduce non–value-added costs. Our discussion of ABM continues in Chapter 13, where we cover reengineering and downsizing, and in Chapter 14, where we explore managing customer profitability. We also present how to apply ABM techniques in Chapter 19, where we explain quality improvements, and in Chapter 20, where we describe how to evaluate suppliers.

ABC SYSTEMS IN MERCHANDISING AND SERVICE COMPANIES

Although many of the early examples of ABC originated in manufacturing, it has many applications in the merchandising and service areas. Companies in merchandising, such as Chapters and Amazon.com, which resell products without changing them, also have implemented ABC and ABM. Many retail and wholesale companies are working with ABC systems. Costs of activities are grouped into homogeneous cost pools and classified as output unit-level, batch-level, product- or service-sustaining, and facility-sustaining costs. The cost pools correspond to key activities. Costs are allocated to products or customers using activity drivers or cost-allocation bases that have a cause-and-effect relationship with the costs in the cost pool.

The general approach to ABC in service and even not-for-profit organizations is very similar to the approach described in this chapter. Service and not-for-profit organizations also have to confront the problems of measuring activity cost pools and identifying and measuring allocation bases. Companies in banking, insurance, accounting, and consulting industries have implemented ABC systems to define

---

GOVERNANCE ISSUES

Effective Cost Assignment Is a Fiduciary Duty

Managers act on behalf of the owners of the assets under the managers' control. They are obliged to do so in the most effective way possible. Acting in the best financial interests of another is called fiduciary duty. ABC cost assignment should only be undertaken when there is adequate reason to believe the benefits will outweigh the costs for the owners of the business.

1. Good faith must be established that a refined cost-assignment system is intended to improve managerial decision-making. Inevitably some managers will be or will perceive they will be negatively affected by the ABC information. At CBI, the managers of the Malaysian blend could feel disadvantaged when more costs are assigned to that product, especially if there is little opportunity to make changes that would reduce these costs. But CBI is not being run to benefit specific managers—it is being run by the managers to benefit the owners.

2. Managers responsible for resource use have the best knowledge about activities and cost drivers. The responsibility approach creates opportunities for coordination and cooperation to reduce costs in one function that benefits others.

3. Educating and training employees in ABC enables effective delegation to levels where knowledge resides. For example, WS Industries, an Indian manufacturer of insulators, shared ABC information with its workers and established an incentive. A percentage of cost savings was returned to employees who made the cost-saving suggestions.

4. Begin with a limited scope of activities that managers believe are critical to the success of the company. The interdependence among only three business functions may be extensive. Give managers time to learn how to best deal with interdependence.

profitable product mixes, improve efficiency, and satisfy customers. Similarly, some of the Canadian government's service providers (for example, Environment Canada, the Departments of the Auditor General of Canada, National Defence Maritime Command, the Meteorological Service, and Citizenship and Immigration) have implemented ABC and ABM.

The Co-operative Bank in the United Kingdom followed this approach when it implemented ABC in its retail banks. It calculated the costs of various activities, such as making ATM transactions, opening and closing accounts, administering mortgages, and processing VISA transactions. It then used the activity cost rates to calculate costs of various products, such as a chequing account, mortgage, and VISA card. ABC information helped the bank to improve its processes and to identify profitable products and customer segments. The Real Companies box below provides an example of how ABC can improve the information used in banks to make management decisions.

PULLING IT ALL TOGETHER—PROBLEM FOR SELF-STUDY

PROBLEM

Family Supermarkets (FS) has decided to increase the size of its St. John's store. It wants information about the profitability of individual product lines: soft drinks, fresh produce, and packaged food.

Operating personnel at FS provide the following data for each product line:

	Soft Drinks	Fresh Produce	Packaged Food
Revenue	$317,400	$840,240	$483,960
Cost of goods sold	$240,000	$600,000	$360,000
Cost of bottles returned	$ 4,800	$ 0	$ 0
Number of purchase orders placed	144	336	144
Number of deliveries received	120	876	264
Hours of shelf-stocking time	216	2,160	1,080
Items sold	50,400	441,600	122,400

FS also provides the following information for the year 2009:

Activity (1)	Description of Activity (2)	Total Costs (3)	Cost-Allocation Base (4)	
Bottle returns	Returning empty bottles to store	$ 4,800	Direct tracing to soft-drink line	
Ordering	Placing orders for purchases	$ 62,400	purchase orders =	624
Delivery	Physical delivery and receiving of merchandise	$100,800	deliveries =	1,260
Shelf-stocking	Stocking and restocking merchandise	$ 69,120	hours stocking =	3,456
Customer support	Assistance provided for customers	$122,880	items sold =	614,400
Total		$360,000		

REQUIRED

1. Family Supermarkets currently allocates store support costs (all costs other than cost of goods sold) to product lines based on cost of goods sold of each product line. Calculate the operating income and operating income as a percentage of revenues for each product line. ❶

2. If Family Supermarkets allocates store support costs (all costs other than cost of goods sold) to product lines using an activity-based costing (ABC) system, calculate the operating income and operating income as a percentage of revenues for each product line. ❷❸❹

3. Comment on your answers to requirements 1 and 2. ❺

SOLUTION

1. The following table shows the operating income and operating income as a percentage of revenues. All store support costs (that is, costs other than cost of goods sold) are allocated to product lines using cost of goods sold of each product line as the cost-allocation base. Total store support costs equal $360,000 (cost of bottles returned, $4,800 + cost of purchase orders, $62,400 + cost of deliveries, $100,800 + cost of shelf-stocking, $69,120 + cost of customer support, $122,880). If cost of goods sold is the cost-allocation base, the allocation rate for store support costs = $360,000 ÷ $1,200,000 = $0.30 per dollar of cost of goods sold. To allocate support costs to each product line, FS multiplies the cost of goods sold of each product line by 0.30. Operating income for each product line is as follows:

	Soft Drinks	Fresh Produce	Packaged Food	Total
Revenue	$317,400	$840,240	$483,960	$1,641,600
Cost of goods sold	240,000	600,000	360,000	1,200,000
Store support cost ($240,000; $600,000; $360,000 × 0.30)	72,000	180,000	108,000	360,000
Total costs	312,000	780,000	468,000	1,560,000
Operating income	$ 5,400	$ 60,240	$ 15,960	$ 81,600
Operating margin (Operating income ÷ Revenue)	1.70%	7.17%	3.30%	4.97%

2. Under an ABC system, FS identifies bottle return costs as a direct cost since these costs can be traced easily to the soft drink product line. FS then calculates cost-allocation rates for each activity area. The activity rates are as follows:

Activity (1)	Cost Hierarchy (2)	Total Costs (3)	Quantity of Cost-Allocation Base (4)	Overhead Allocation-Rate (5) = (3) ÷ (4)
Ordering	Batch level	$ 62,400	624 purchase orders	$ 100 per purchase order
Delivery	Batch level	$100,800	1,260 deliveries	$ 80 per delivery
Shelf-stocking	Unit level	$ 69,120	3,456 hours stocking	$ 20 per hour stocking
Customer support	Unit level	$122,880	614,400 items sold	$0.20 per item sold

Store support costs for each product line by activity are obtained by multiplying the total quantity of the cost-allocation base for each product line by the activity cost rate. Operating income for each product line is as follows:

	Soft Drinks	Fresh Produce	Packaged Food	Total
Revenue	$317,400	$840,240	$483,960	$1,641,600
Cost of goods sold	240,000	600,000	360,000	1,200,000
Bottle-return costs	4,800	–	–	4,800
Ordering costs (144; 336; 144) P.O. × $100	14,400	33,600	14,400	62,400
Delivery costs (120; 876; 264) del. × $80	9,600	70,080	21,120	100,800
Shelf-stocking costs (216; 2,160; 1,080) hr. × $20	4,320	43,200	21,600	69,120
Customer support costs (50,400; 441,600; 122,400) items × $0.20	10,080	88,320	24,480	122,880
Total costs	283,200	835,200	441,600	1,560,000
Operating income	$ 34,200	$ 5,040	$ 42,360	$ 81,600
Operating margin (Operating income ÷ Revenue)	10.78%	0.60%	8.75%	4.97%

3. Managers believe the ABC system is more credible than the previous costing system. It distinguishes the different types of activities at FS more precisely. It also tracks more accurately how individual product lines use their resources. Rankings of relative profitability (the percentage of operating income to revenues) of the three product lines under the previous costing system and under the ABC system are as follows:

Simple Costing System		ABC System	
1. Fresh produce	7.17%	1. Soft drinks	10.78%
2. Packaged food	3.30%	2. Packaged food	8.75%
3. Soft drinks	1.70%	3. Fresh produce	0.60%

The percentage of revenues, cost of goods sold, and activity costs for each product line are as follows:

	Soft Drinks	Fresh Produce	Packaged Food
Revenue	19.335%	51.184%	29.481%
Cost of goods sold	20.000%	50.000%	30.000%
Bottle-return costs	100.000%	0.000%	0.000%
Ordering costs	23.077%	53.846%	23.077%
Delivery costs	9.524%	69.524%	20.952%
Shelf-stocking costs	6.250%	62.500%	31.250%
Customer support costs	8.203%	71.875%	19.922%

Soft drinks consume less of all resources. Soft drinks have fewer deliveries and require less shelf-stocking than does either fresh produce or packaged food. Most major soft-drink suppliers deliver merchandise to the store shelves and stock the shelves themselves. In contrast, the fresh produce area has the most deliveries and consumes a large percentage of shelf-stocking time. It also has the highest number of individual sales items. The previous costing system assumed that each product line used the resources in each activity area in the same ratio as their respective individual cost of goods sold to total cost of goods sold ratio. Clearly, this assumption was inappropriate. The previous costing system was a classic example of broad averaging via cost smoothing.

FS managers can use the ABC information to guide decisions on how to allocate the planned increase in floor space. An increase in the percentage of space allocated to soft drinks is warranted. Note, however, that ABC information should be but one input into decisions about shelf space allocation. FS may have minimum limits on the shelf space allocated to fresh produce because of shoppers' expectations that supermarkets will carry merchandise from this product line.

Pricing decisions can also be made in a more informed way with the ABC information. For example, suppose a competitor announces a 5% reduction in soft-drink prices. Given the 10.78% margin FS currently earns on its soft-drink product line, it has flexibility to reduce prices and still make a profit on this product line. In contrast, the previous costing system erroneously implied that soft drinks only had a 1.70% margin, leaving little room to counter a competitor's pricing initiatives.

The following decision guidelines use a question-and-answer format to summarize the chapter's main points. Each decision presents a key question. The guideline is the answer to that question.

DECISIONS	GUIDELINES
1. When does product undercosting or product overcosting occur?	Product undercosting (overcosting) occurs when a product or service consumes a high (low) level of resource but is reported to have a low (high) cost. Traditional, or peanut butter costing, a common cause of undercosting or overcosting, is the result of using broad averages that uniformly assign, or spread, the cost of resources to products when the individual products use those resources in a nonuniform way. Product cost cross-subsidization exists when one undercosted (overcosted) product results in at least one other product being overcosted (undercosted).
2. How does the logic of traditional cost assignment differ from the logic of the activities cost hierarchy?	The logic of the cost hierarchy separates a single indirect cost pool into as many as four "chunks" according to the scope of activities that cause the indirect costs. The smallest scope of activity is the unit of output level and the largest is the facilities level. The second smallest is a batch level and the next largest is the product level. Traditional cost assignment separates an indirect cost pool using financial accounting-logic into an inventoriable indirect cost pool and a period cost pool.
3. How are cost assignment systems refined using ABC?	The refinement of cost assignment systems should only be undertaken when indirect costs are both material relative to total costs and indirect costs are not consumed uniformly by each output unit. Refinement requires careful discussion among managers who can identify the activities for which controlling costs is most critical to the company. Managers must also establish the scope of activity (output, batch, product, or facilities) and identify a measure of activity. The measure is called an activity cost driver. It reliably indicates that if the measure of the cost driver changes, the activity-cost-pool amount will also change. Managers also must provide enough detail to estimate each activity-cost-pool amount.
4. How are costs assigned using ABC?	Once the indirect activity cost pools and measures of the activity cost drivers are identified, an activity-cost-driver rate can be calculated. But the goal is not to assign the activity costs to a unit of output. Therefore, for the activity cost pools at the batch, product, and facilities level, calculating the activity-cost-driver rates is an intermediate step that allows costs to be assigned per batch or product or facility.
	Indirect cost pools can also be separated by either business function or department, and separate cost allocation bases selected. These are alternatives to refining cost assignment methods using ABC.
5. How can ABC systems be used to manage better?	Activity-based management (ABM) describes management decisions that use ABC information to satisfy customers and improve profits. ABC systems are used for such management decisions as pricing, product-mix, cost reduction, process improvement, product and process redesign, and planning and managing activities.

This chapter contains definitions of the following important terms:

The Mastery Questions are rated by proficiency level—elementary, intermediate, and advanced. The solutions appear in the Mastery Question Solutions section of MyAccountingLab.

LEARNING OBJECTIVE 1

1. **Explain undercosting and overcosting of products—Elementary.** For many years, five former classmates—Steve Armstrong, Lola Gonzales, Rex King, Elizabeth Poffo, and Gary Young—have had a reunion dinner at the annual meeting of the Canadian Academic Accounting Association. The bill for the most recent dinner at a Montreal restaurant was broken down as follows:

Diner	Entrée	Dessert	Drinks	Total
Armstrong	$32	$10	$29	$71
Gonzales	29	4	0	33
King	25	7	16	48
Poffo	37	7	14	58
Young	18	5	7	30

For at least the last ten dinners, King has put the total restaurant bill on his Visa card. He then mailed the other four a bill for the average cost. They shared the gratuity at the restaurant by paying cash. King continued this practice for the Montreal dinner. However, just before he sent the bill to the other diners, Young phoned him to complain. He was livid at Poffo for ordering the steak and lobster entrée ("She always does that!") and at Armstrong for having three glasses of imported champagne ("What's wrong with domestic beer?").

REQUIRED

1. Why is the average-cost approach in the context of the reunion dinner an example of peanut butter costing?
2. Compute the average cost to each of the five diners. Who is undercharged and who is overcharged under the average-cost approach? Is Young's complaint justified?
3. Give an example of a dining situation where King would find it more difficult to compute the amount of undercosting or overcosting. How might the behaviour of the diners be affected if each person paid his or her own bill instead of continuing with the average-cost approach?

2. **Explain undercosting and overcosting of services—Intermediate.** The Wolfson Group (WG) provides tax advice to multinational firms. WG charges clients for (a) direct professional time (at an hourly rate), and (b) support services (at 30% of the direct professional costs billed). The three professionals in WG and their rates per professional hour are as follows:

Professional	Billing Rate per Hour
Myron Wolfson	$600
Naomi Ku	144
John Anderson	96

WG has just prepared the May 2009 bills for two clients. The hours of professional time spent on each client are as follows:

	Hours per Client	
Professional	Winnipeg Dominion	Tokyo Enterprises
Wolfson	15	2
Ku	3	8
Anderson	22	30
Total	40	40

1. What amounts did WG bill to Winnipeg Dominion and Tokyo Enterprises for May 2009?
2. Suppose support services were billed at $60 per professional labour-hour (instead of 30% of professional labour costs). How would this change affect the amounts WG billed to the two clients for May 2009? Comment on the differences between the amounts billed in requirements 1 and 2.
3. How would you determine whether professional labour costs or professional labour-hours is the more appropriate allocation base for WG's support services?

LEARNING OBJECTIVE 2

1. **Contrast the logic of two cost assignment systems—Intermediate.** Niagara Winery makes two different grades of wine—regular wines and specialty wines. Recently, Niagara has shown small profits on its regular wines and large profits on its specialty wines. As a result, management is considering getting out of the regular wine business and concentrating on specialty wines. This is a difficult decision because Niagara had been very profitable in regular wines, its original business. In fact, the profitability of regular wines dipped substantially only after Niagara got into the specialty wine business. Before making a decision, Niagara wants to be sure that it understands what it costs to make and sell the regular and specialty wines. This question focuses on costs in the distribution area.

   Niagara distributes the regular wines and the specialty wines through completely different distribution channels. It distributes 120,000 cases of the regular wines through 10 provincial distributors and 80,000 cases of the specialty wines through 30 specialty distributors. Niagara incurs $2,556,000 in distribution costs. Under its existing costing system, Niagara allocates distribution costs to products based on cases shipped.

   To understand better the demands on its resources in the distribution area, Niagara identifies three activities and related activity costs:
   1. Promotional activity including advertising and point-of-sales material at each distributor. Niagara estimates it incurs $9,600 per distributor.
   2. Order handling costs including costs to confirm and input the order into the order-entry system, set aside the correct number of cases, organize shipment and delivery, verify order packing, ensure delivery, send invoices, and follow up for payments. Niagara estimates costs of $360 for performing all the activities pertaining to each order. Niagara's records show that distributors of regular wine placed an average of 10 orders per year, while distributors of specialty wine placed an average of 20 orders per year.
   3. Distribution costs of $10 per case for freight.

   REQUIRED
   1. Calculate the total distribution costs and distribution cost per case for the regular wine and the specialty wine using Niagara's existing costing system.
   2. a. For each activity, classify the cost of the activity as an output unit-level, batch-level, product-sustaining or service-sustaining, or facility-sustaining cost. Explain your answers.
      b. Calculate the total distribution costs and distribution cost per case for the regular wine and the specialty wine using Niagara's activity-based costing (ABC) system.
   3. Explain the cost differences and the accuracy of the product costs calculated using the existing and the ABC systems. How might Niagara's management use the information from the ABC system to manage its business better?

2. **Contrast the logic of two cost assignment systems—Advanced.** Halifax Test Laboratories does heat testing (HT) and stress testing (ST) on materials. Under its current costing system, Halifax aggregates all operating costs of $1,440,000 into a single overhead cost pool. Halifax calculates a rate per test-hour of $18 ($1,440,000 ÷ 80,000 total test-hours). HT uses 50,000 test-hours and ST uses 30,000 test-hours. Gary Celeste, Halifax's controller, believes that there is enough variation in test procedures and cost structures to establish separate costing and billing rates. The market for test services is very competitive, and without this information, any miscosting and mispricing could cause Halifax to lose business. Celeste breaks down Halifax's costs into four activity-cost categories.

   1. Direct labour costs, $288,000. These costs can be directly traced to HT, $216,000, and ST, $72,000.
   2. Equipment-related costs (rent, maintenance, energy, and so on), $480,000. These costs are allocated to HT and ST based on test-hours.
   3. Setup costs, $420,000. These costs are allocated to HT and ST based on the number of setup-hours required. HT requires 13,500 setup-hours and ST requires 4,000 setup-hours.
   4. Costs of designing tests, $252,000. These costs are allocated to HT and ST based on the time required to design the tests. HT requires 2,800 hours and ST requires 1,400 hours.

REQUIRED

1. Classify each of the activity costs as output unit level, batch level, product or service sustaining, or facility sustaining. Explain your answers.
2. Calculate the cost per test-hour for HT and ST using activity-based costing (ABC). Explain briefly the reasons why these numbers differ from the $18 per test-hour that Halifax had calculated using its existing costing system.
3. Explain the cost differences and the accuracy of the product costs calculated using the existing and the ABC systems. How might Halifax's management use the cost hierarchy and ABC information to manage its business better?

LEARNING OBJECTIVE 3

1. **Apply the logic of an ABC cost hierarchy—Intermediate.** Huey Parker produces mathematical and financial calculators. Data related to the two products are presented below.

	Mathematical	Financial
Annual production in units	50,000	100,000
Direct materials costs	$180,000	$360,000
Direct manufacturing labour costs	$ 60,000	$120,000
Direct manufacturing labour-hours	2,500	5,000
Machine-hours	25,000	50,000
Number of production runs	50	50
Inspection hours	1,000	500

Both products pass through Department 1 and Department 2. The departments' combined manufacturing overhead costs are:

	Total
Machining costs	$450,000
Setup costs	144,000
Inspection costs	126,000

REQUIRED

1. Compute the manufacturing overhead cost for each product.
2. Compute the manufacturing cost for each product.

2. **Apply the logic of an ABC cost hierarchy—Advanced.** Home Furnishings makes bookshelves, tables, and beds. The following sales and cost information is available about the profitability of each of these lines:

	Bookshelves	Tables	Beds	Total
Revenues	$825,000	$550,000	$1,100,000	$2,475,000
Direct materials	330,000	242,000	440,000	1,012,000
Direct manufacturing labour	82,500	66,000	88,000	236,500
Setups and materials handling	49,500	44,000	66,000	159,500
Amortization on tools and fixtures	55,000	52,800	79,200	187,000
Marketing and distribution	82,500	66,000	132,000	280,500
General administration and facilities	165,000	110,000	220,000	495,000
Total costs	764,500	580,800	1,025,200	2,370,500
Operating income (loss)	$ 60,500	$ (30,800)	$ 74,800	$ 104,500

Home Furnishings uses an activity-based costing (ABC) system to assign costs to products. The following additional information is available:

a. Direct materials and direct manufacturing labour costs vary with the number of units of products manufactured.
b. Setups and materials-handling costs vary with the number of batches made.
c. Tools and fixtures have one-year lives and zero disposal prices.
d. Of the total marketing and distribution costs, $123,750 are fixed costs allocated to product lines based on sales revenue. Fixed marketing and distribution costs allocated to a product line can be avoided if the line is discontinued. The remaining marketing costs vary with the number of shipments made.
e. General administration and facilities costs are fixed costs that will not change if sales of individual product lines are increased or decreased, or if product lines are added or dropped. These costs are allocated to product lines based on sales revenues.

In answering the following requirements, assume that prices of the various products do not change.

1. Should Home Furnishings discontinue the tables product line assuming the released facilities remain idle? Assume Home Furnishings has already acquired the tools and fixtures it needs to manufacture tables.

2. Suppose that if Home Furnishings discontinues the tables product line, the released facilities could be used to sell beds worth an additional $275,000. This would require Home Furnishings to purchase tools and fixtures for $4,400, which would be fully expensed in the year of purchase. Assume that there will be no change in either the number of batches in which beds are made or the number of shipments.

   a. Based on your calculations, should Home Furnishings discontinue the tables product line?

   b. What other factors should Home Furnishings consider before making a decision?

3. What would be the effect on operating income if Home Furnishings could double its sales of tables? Assume that, at the higher sales, both the number of batches and the number of shipments would be three times the current levels and purchases of tools and fixtures would be twice the current levels.

LEARNING OBJECTIVE 4

1. **Assign costs using ABC—Intermediate.** Baker's Delight (BD) has been in the food-processing business three years. For its first two years (2007 and 2008), its sole product was raisin cake. All cakes were manufactured and packaged in one-kilogram units. BD used a normal-costing system. The two direct-cost categories were direct materials and direct manufacturing labour. The sole indirect manufacturing cost category—manufacturing overhead—was allocated to products using a units-of-production allocation base. BD prices on a cost-plus basis. It currently uses a "cost plus 40% of cost" guideline.

   In its third year (2009), BD added a second product—layered carrot cake—that was packaged in one-kilogram units. This product differs from raisin cake in several ways:

   ◆ More expensive ingredients are used.
   ◆ More direct manufacturing labour time is required.
   ◆ More complex manufacturing is required.

   In 2009, BD continued to use its existing costing system where a unit of production of either cake was weighted the same.

   Direct materials costs in 2009 were $0.72 per kilogram of raisin cake and $1.08 per kilogram of layered carrot cake. Direct manufacturing labour cost in 2009 was $0.168 per kilogram of raisin cake and $0.24 per kilogram of layered carrot cake.

   During 2009, BD salespeople reported greater-than-expected sales of layered carrot cake and less-than-expected sales of raisin cake. The budgeted and actual sales volume for 2009 were as follows:

	Budgeted	Actual
Raisin cake	160,000 kilograms	120,000 kilograms
Layered carrot cake	40,000 kilograms	80,000 kilograms

   The budgeted manufacturing overhead for 2009 was $252,960.

   At the end of 2009, Jonathan Davis, the controller of BD, decided to investigate how the use of an activity-based costing (ABC) system would affect the product cost numbers. After consultation with operating personnel, the single manufacturing overhead cost pool was subdivided into five activity areas. These activity areas, their driver, their 2009 budgeted rate, and the driver units used per kilogram of each cake are as follows:

Activity	Driver	Budgeted 2009 Cost per Driver Unit	Driver Units per Kilogram of Raisin Cake	Driver Units per Kilogram of Layered Carrot Cake
1. Mixing	Labour time	$0.048	5	8
2. Cooking	Oven time	$0.168	2	3
3. Cooling	Cool room time	$0.024	3	5
4. Creaming/icing	Machine time	$0.30	0	3
5. Packaging	Machine time	$0.096	3	7

1. Compute the 2009 unit product cost of raisin cake and of layered carrot cake with the normal costing system used in the 2007 to 2009 period.

2. Compute the 2009 unit product cost per cake under the activity-based costing (ABC) system.

3. Explain the differences in unit product costs computed in requirements 1 and 2.

4. Describe three uses BD might make of the activity-based costing numbers.

2. **Assign costs using ABC—Advanced.** Uppervale Health Centre runs four programs: (1) alcoholic rehabilitation, (2) drug-addict rehabilitation, (3) children's services, and (4) after-care (counselling and support of patients after release from a psychiatric hospital). The Centre's budget for 2009 follows:

Professional salaries:

6 physicians at $120,000	$ 720,000	
19 psychologists at $60,000	1,140,000	
23 nurses at $30,000	690,000	$2,550,000
Medical supplies		360,000
General overhead (administrative salaries, rent, utilities, etc.)		1,530,000
		$4,440,000

Mrs. Muriel Clayton, the director of the Centre, is keen on determining the cost of each program. She has limited funds and feels that this information will help her to budget better and allocate resources more effectively. For example, Clayton needs to decide whether to allocate funds to alcoholic rehabilitation or to drug-addict rehabilitation. Her decision rule is that if the cost to treat a drug-addict patient for a year is more than 15% higher than the cost to treat an alcoholic patient for a year, the alcohol program would receive additional funds.

As a first step, Mrs. Clayton, who had earned uniformly high respect from the professional staff, asked the staff to fill out a form indicating the time devoted to each of the four programs. She then allocated costs of medical supplies based on physician-hours spent in each program and general overhead based on direct-labour cost (where direct labour is defined to include the time of doctors, psychologists, and nurses multiplied by the salary rate of each). Clayton compiled the following data describing employee allocations to individual programs:

	Alcohol	Drug	Children	After-Care	Total Employees
Physicians		2	4		6
Psychologists	6	4		9	19
Nurses	4	6	4	9	23

Eighty patients are in residence in the alcohol program, each staying about a half-year. Thus, the clinic provided 40 patient-years of service in the alcohol program. Similarly, 100 patients were involved in the drug program for about a half-year each. Thus the clinic provided 50 patient-years of service in the drug program.

Clayton has recently become aware of activity-based costing (ABC) as a method to refine cost systems. She asks her accountant, Huey Deluth, how she should apply this new technique. Deluth obtains the following information:

1. Consumption of medical supplies depends on the number of patients in each department and the length of their stays (that is, patient-years).
2. General overhead costs consist of

Rent and clinic maintenance	$ 240,000
Administrative costs to manage patient charts, food, laundry	960,000
Laboratory services	330,000
Total	$1,530,000

3. Other information about individual departments is

	Alcohol	Drug	Children	After-Care	Total
Square metres of space occupied by each program	9,000	9,000	10,000	12,000	40,000
Patient-years of service	40	50	50	60	200
Number of patients	80	100	200	120	500
Number of laboratory tests	400	1,400	3,000	700	5,500

REQUIRED

1. **a.** Compute indirect-cost rates for medical supplies and general overhead under Clayton's existing costing system.
   b. What is the cost of each program and the cost per patient-year of the alcohol and drug programs, using Clayton's existing costing system?
   c. Using the existing costing system, would Clayton allocate additional funds to the drug program or to the alcohol program?

2. **a.** Calculate the indirect-cost rates for medical supplies, rent and clinic maintenance, administrative costs for patient charts, food, and laundry, and laboratory services, selecting cost-allocation bases that you believe are the most appropriate for allocating indirect costs to programs.

   b. What is the cost of each program and the cost per patient-year of the alcohol and drug programs, using an activity-based costing (ABC) approach to cost analysis?

   c. Using the ABC system, would Clayton allocate additional funds to the drug program or to the alcohol program?

3. Explain the cost differences and the accuracy of program costs calculated using the existing and the ABC system. What other benefits can Uppervale Health Centre obtain by implementing the ABC system?

4. What factors, other than cost, do you think Uppervale Health Centre should consider in allocating resources to its programs?

LEARNING OBJECTIVE 5

1. **Use ABC systems for ABM—Advanced.** Family Supermarkets (FS) found that its ABC analysis (see p. 221) provided important insights. FS extends the analysis to cover three more product lines: baked goods, milk and fruit juice, and frozen products. It identifies four activities and activity cost rates for each activity as:

Ordering	$120 per purchase order
Delivery and receipt of merchandise	$96 per delivery
Shelf-stocking	$24 per hour
Customer support and assistance	$0.24 per item sold

The revenues, cost of goods sold, store support costs, and activity area usage of the three product lines are as follows:

	Baked Goods	Milk and Fruit Juice	Frozen Products
Financial data:			
Revenues	$68,400	$75,600	$62,400
Cost of goods sold	45,600	56,400	42,000
Store support	13,680	16,920	12,600
Activity area usage (cost driver):			
Ordering (purchase orders)	30	25	13
Delivery (deliveries)	98	36	28
Shelf-stocking (hours)	183	166	24
Customer support (items sold)	15,500	20,500	7,900

There are no bottle returns for any of these three product lines.

REQUIRED

1. Use the previous costing system (support costs allocated to products at the rate of 30% of cost of goods sold) to compute a product line profitability report for FS.

2. Use the ABC system (ordering at $120 per purchase order, delivery at $96 per delivery, shelf-stocking at $24 per hour, and customer support at $0.24 per item sold) to compute a product line profitability report for FS.

3. What new insights does the ABC system in requirement 2 provide to FS managers?

ASSIGNMENT MATERIAL

SHORT-ANSWER QUESTIONS

5-1 Define *cost smoothing*, and describe the consequences it can have on costs.

5-2 Why should managers worry about product overcosting or undercosting?

5-3 What is costing system refinement? Describe three guidelines for such refinement.

5-4 What is an activity-based approach to refining a cost assignment system?

5-5 Describe four levels of a cost hierarchy.

5-6 Why is it important to classify costs into a cost hierarchy?

5-7 What are the key reasons for product cost differences between traditional costing systems and ABC systems?

5-8 Describe four decisions for which ABC information is useful.

5-9 "Department indirect-cost rates are never activity cost rates." Do you agree? Explain.

5-10 Describe four ways that help indicate when ABC systems are likely to provide the most benefits.

5-11 What are the main costs and limitations of implementing ABC systems?

5-12 "ABC systems apply only to manufacturing companies." Do you agree? Explain.

5-13 "Activity-based costing is the wave of the present and the future. All companies should adopt it." Do you agree? Explain.

5-14 "Increasing the number of indirect-cost pools is guaranteed to sizably increase the accuracy of product or service costs." Do you agree? Why?

5-15 The controller of a retailer has just had a $50,000 request to implement an ABC system quickly turned down. A senior vice-president involved in rejecting the request noted, "Given a choice, I will always prefer a $50,000 investment in improving things a customer sees or experiences, such as our shelves or our store layout. How does a customer benefit by our spending $50,000 on a supposedly better accounting system?" How should the controller respond?

EXERCISES

5-16 Cost hierarchy. Teledor Inc. manufactures boom boxes (music systems with radio, cassette, and compact disc players) for different well-known companies. The boom boxes differ significantly in their complexity and the batch sizes in which they are manufactured. The following costs were incurred in 2009:

  a. Indirect manufacturing labour costs such as supervision that supports direct manufacturing labour, $1,200,000.
  b. Procurement costs of placing purchase orders, receiving materials, and paying suppliers that are related to the number of purchase orders placed, $600,000.
  c. Cost of indirect materials, $350,000.
  d. Costs incurred to set up machines each time a different product needs to be manufactured, $700,000.
  e. Designing processes, drawing process charts, making engineering process changes for products, $900,000.
  f. Machine-related overhead costs such as amortization, maintenance, production engineering, $1,200,000. These resources are related to the activity of running the machines.
  g. Plant management, plant rent, and insurance, $950,000.

  REQUIRED
  1. Classify each of the preceding costs as output unit level, batch level, product sustaining, or facility sustaining. Explain your answers.
  2. Consider two boom boxes made by Teledor Inc. One boom box is complex to make and is made in many batches. The other boom box is simple to make and is made in few batches. Suppose that Teledor needs the same number of machine-hours to make either boom box. If Teledor allocated all overhead costs using machine-hours as the only allocation base, how, if at all, would the boom boxes be miscosted? Briefly explain why.
  3. How is the cost hierarchy helpful to Teledor in managing its business?

5-17 Cost hierarchy classification. (J. Watson) The following outlines a number of activities related to operations at Nordan Manufacturing Ltd.:
  a. Engineers design new products.
  b. Production workers set up machines.
  c. Completed goods are inspected for quality assurance.
  d. Direct materials are moved from inventory to the production line.
  e. Raw materials are received from the supplier.
  f. Regular equipment maintenance is performed.
  g. The inventory management software is updated.

REQUIRED

1. Classify each of the preceding activities as output unit level, batch level, product sustaining, or facility sustaining. Explain your answers.
2. Identify a possible appropriate cost driver for each of the activities listed.

5-18 **Plantwide indirect-cost rates.** Automotive Products (AP) designs, manufactures, and sells automotive parts. Actual variable manufacturing overhead costs for 2009 were $308,600. AP's simple costing system allocates variable manufacturing overhead to its three customers based on machine hours and prices its contracts based on full costs. One of its customers has regularly complained of being charged non-competitive prices, so AP's controller, Devon Smith, realizes that it is time to examine the consumption of resources more closely. AP has three main operating departments: design, engineering, and production.

◆ *Design*—the design of parts, using state-of-the-art, computer-aided design (CAD) equipment
◆ *Engineering*—the prototyping of parts and testing of their specifications
◆ *Production*—the manufacture of parts

Interviews with the department personnel and examination of time records yield the following detailed information:

			Use of Cost Drivers by Customer		
Department	Cost Driver	Variable MOH in 2009	United Motors	Holden Motors	Leland Motors
Design	CAD design hours	$ 39,000	110	200	80
Engineering	Engineering hours	29,600	70	60	240
Production	Machine hours	240,000	120	2,800	1,080
Total		$308,600			

REQUIRED

1. Using the simple costing system, compute the plantwide variable manufacturing overhead rate for 2009 and the variable manufacturing overhead allocated to each contract in 2009.
2. Compute the variable manufacturing overhead rate for 2009 and the variable manufacturing overhead allocated to each contract in 2009 using department-based variable overhead rates.
3. Comment on your answers in requirements 1 and 2. Which customer do you think was complaining about being overcharged in the simple system? If the new department-based rates are used to price contracts, which customer(s) will be unhappy? How would you respond to these concerns?
4. How else might AP use the information available from its department-by-department analysis of variable manufacturing overhead costs?
5. AP's managers are wondering if they should further refine the department-by-department costing system into an ABC system by identifying different activities within each department. Under what conditions would it not be worthwhile to further refine the department costing system into an ABC system?

5-19 **ABC, product cross-subsidization.** (J. Watson) Noble Industries manufactures two models of tiffany-style lamps, a table-top model and a floor model. Summary data for the two products for the most recent fiscal year showed the following:

	Table-Top Model	Floor Model
Unit Costs:		
Direct material	$28	$34
Direct labour (@ $14/hour)	7	14
Manufacturing overhead	8	16

Under the company's current costing, manufacturing overhead is allocated on the basis of direct labour-hours. The company president is concerned that the use of a single overhead cost pool does not result in accurate costing of the two product lines and is wondering whether the company should implement activity-based costing (ABC).

The overhead for the year has been estimated at a total of $1,600,000. Further analysis of the overhead costs resulted in the following classification:

Materials handling	$450,000
Setups	750,000
General factory overhead	400,000

The company has identified the appropriate cost driver for each activity. Materials handling will be allocated using number of parts, setups will be allocated based on number of setups, and general factory overhead will be allocated using direct labour-hours. The company has budgeted for the production of 40,000 units of the table-top model and 80,000 units of the floor model. Consumption of the cost drivers, based on this production volume, is estimated as follows:

Cost Driver	Table-Top Model	Floor Model	Total
Number of parts	160,000	240,000	400,000
Number of setups	500	250	750
Direct labour-hours	20,000	80,000	100,000

The company currently prices its products by adding a 40% mark-up to the total manufacturing cost.

REQUIRED

1. Compute the per-unit cost and selling price of both models of lamps based on the current costing system.
2. Compute the per-unit cost and selling price of both models of lamps using an ABC costing system.
3. Compare and briefly outline the significance of your results from requirements 1 and 2.

5-20 Allocation of costs to activities, unused capacity. Harmon Academy, a private school, serves 500 students: 200 in the middle school (grades 6 to 8) and 300 in the high school (grades 9 to 12). Each school group has its own assistant principal, and there is one principal, Brian Smith, for the academy. For any single student, almost all of Harmon's costs are indirect. Harmon currently has five indirect cost categories, which are listed in the following table. Smith wants to develop an activity-based-costing system for the school. He identifies four activities—academic instruction, administration, sports training, and community relationships—related to the educational enterprise.

1. Overall cost, $15,600 per student

Smith and his team identify number of students as the cost driver of academic instruction and administration costs, and the number of team sports offered by the school as the driver of sports training costs. The cost of maintaining community relationships—dealing with the town council and participating in local activities—is a facility-sustaining cost that the school has to incur each year. The table shows the percentage of costs in each line item used by each activity.

Percentage of Costs Used by Each Activity

Indirect Cost	Academic Instruction	Administration	Sports Training	Community Relationships	2009 Expenditures
Teachers' salaries/benefits	60%	20%	8%	12%	$4,000,000
Principals' salaries and benefits	10%	60%	5%	25%	400,000
Facilities	35%	15%	45%	5%	2,600,000
Office staff salaries and benefits	5%	60%	10%	25%	300,000
Sports program staff salaries and benefits	35%	10%	45%	10%	500,000

REQUIRED

1. What is the overall cost of educating each student? Of this cost, what percentage is the cost of academic instruction? Of administration?
2. Smith is dismayed at the high cost of sports training. Further examination reveals that $300,000 of those costs are for ice hockey, a sport pursued by a total of 40 students. What would be the overall cost of educating each student if the ice hockey program is eliminated and its cost saved?
3. For the 2010 school year, Harmon charges an annual fee of $1,000 for any student who wants to play ice hockey. As a result, 10 of the less-motivated students drop the sport. Assuming the costs of the school in 2010 are the same as in 2009, what is the overall cost of educating each student in 2010?
4. Consider the costs of the academic instruction activity and assume they are fixed in the short run. At these costs, Harmon could serve 600 students. What is the cost of the academic instruction resources used by Harmon's current 500 students? What

is the cost of unused academic instruction capacity? What actions can Smith take to reduce the cost of academic instruction per student in the short run? In the long run?

5-21 Special order, activity-based costing. (CMA, adapted) The Award Plus Company manufactures medals for winners of athletic events and other contests. Its manufacturing plant has the capacity to produce 12,000 medals each month; current production and sales are 9,000 medals per month. The company normally charges $200 per medal. Cost information for the current activity level is as follows:

5

1. Operating income increase, $190,000

Variable costs (vary with units produced):	
Direct materials	$ 360,000
Direct labour	405,000
Variable costs (vary with number of batches):	
Setups, materials handling, quality control	126,000*
Fixed manufacturing costs	325,000
Fixed marketing costs	224,000
Total Costs	$1,440,000

*Costs of $126,000 are based on 180 batches at $700 per batch

Award Plus has just received a special one-time-only order for 2,500 medals at $168 per medal. Accepting the special order would not affect the company's regular business. Award Plus makes medals for its existing customers in batch sizes of 50 medals (180 batches × 50 medals per batch = 9000 medals). The special order requires Award Plus to make the medals in 25 batches of 100 each.

REQUIRED
1. Should Award Plus accept this special order? Explain briefly.
2. Suppose plant capacity was only 10,000 medals instead of 12,000 medals each month. The special order must either be taken in full or rejected totally. Should Award Plus accept the special order?
3. As in requirement 1, assume that monthly capacity is 12,000 medals. Award Plus is concerned that if it accepts the special order, its existing customers will immediately demand a price discount of $11 in the month in which the special order is being filled. They would argue that Award Plus's capacity costs are now being spread over more units and that existing customers should get the benefit of these lower costs. Should Award Plus accept the special order under these conditions? Show all calculations.

5-22 Make versus buy, activity-based costing. Svenson Corporation manufactures cellular modems. It manufactures its own cellular modem circuit boards (CMCB), an important part of the cellular modem. It reports the following cost information about the costs of making CMCBs in 2008 and the expected costs in 2009:

5

1. Expected manufacturing cost per unit, $364.50

	Current Costs in 2008	Expected Costs in 2009
Variable Manufacturing Costs:		
Direct materials cost per CMCB	$ 200	$ 194
Direct manufacturing labour cost per CMCB	76	72
Variable manufacturing costs per batch for setups, materials handling, and quality control	1,800	1,740
Fixed Manufacturing Costs:		
Fixed manufacturing overhead costs that can be avoided if CMCBs are not made	360,000	360,000
Fixed manufacturing overhead costs of plant amortization, insurance, administration that cannot be avoided if CMCBs are not made	900,000	900,000

Svenson manufactured 12,000 CMCBs in 2008 in 40 batches of 200 each. In 2009, Svenson anticipates needing 15,000 CMCBs. The CMCBs would be needed in 120 batches of 125 each.

The Minton Corporation has approached Svenson about supplying CMCBs to Svenson in 2009 at $340 per CMCB on whatever delivery schedule Svenson wants.

1. Calculate the total expected manufacturing (absorption) cost per unit of making CMCBs in 2009.
2. Suppose the capacity currently used to make CMCBs will become idle if Svenson purchases CMCBs from Minton. Should Svenson make CMCBs or buy them from Minton?
3. Now suppose that, if Svenson purchases CMCBs from Minton, its best alternative use of the capacity currently used to make CMCBs is to make and sell special circuit boards (CB3s) to the Essex Corporation. Svenson estimates the following incremental revenues and costs from CB3s:

Total expected incremental future revenues	$2,418,000
Total expected incremental future costs	$2,504,000

Should Svenson make CMCBs or buy them from Minton?

5-23 ABC, product cost cross-subsidization. PEI Potatoes processes potatoes into potato cuts at its highly automated plant. For many years, it processed potatoes for only the retail consumer market where it had a superb reputation for quality. Recently, it started selling potato cuts to the institutional market, which includes hospitals, cafeterias, and university dormitories. Its penetration into the institutional market has been slower than predicted.

PEI's existing costing system has a single direct-cost category (direct materials, which are the raw potatoes) and a single indirect-cost pool (production support). Support costs are allocated on the basis of kilograms of potato cuts processed. Support costs include packaging material. The 2009 total actual costs for producing 1,000,000 kilograms of potato cuts (900,000 for the retail market and 100,000 for the institutional market) are:

Direct materials used	$ 250,000
Production support	1,298,000

The existing costing system does not distinguish between potato cuts produced for the retail or the institutional markets.

At the end of 2009, PEI unsuccessfully bid for a large institutional contract. Its bid was reported to be 30% above the winning bid. This came as a shock, as PEI included only a minimum profit margin on its bid. Moreover, the PEI plant was widely acknowledged as the most efficient in the industry.

As part of its lost contract bid review process, PEI decided to explore several ways of refining its costing system. First, it identified that $260,000 of the $1,298,000 pertains to packaging materials that could be traced to individual jobs ($238,000 for retail and $22,000 for institutional). These will now be classified as a direct material. The $250,000 of direct materials used were classified as $225,000 for retail and $25,000 for institutional. Second, it used activity-based costing (ABC) to examine how the two products (retail potato cuts and institutional potato cuts) used the support area differently. The finding was that three activity areas could be distinguished and that different usage occurred in two of these three areas. The indirect cost per kilogram of finished product at each activity area is as follows:

Activity Area	Retail Potato Cuts	Institutional Potato Cuts
Cleaning	$0.18	$0.18
Cutting	0.30	0.20
Packaging labour	0.60	0.28

There was no beginning or ending amount of any inventory (materials, work in process, or finished goods).

REQUIRED
1. Using the current costing system, what is the cost per kilogram of potato cuts produced by PEI?
2. Using the refined costing system, what is the cost per kilogram of (a) retail market potato cuts, and (b) institutional market potato cuts?
3. Comment on the cost differences shown between the two costing systems in requirements 1 and 2. How might PEI use the information in requirement 2 to make better decisions?

④

1. Current cost, $1.548 per kg

5-24 **ABC, wholesale, customer profitability.** Villeagas Wholesalers sells furniture items to four department-store chains. Mr. Villeagas commented, "We apply ABC to determine profit line profitability. The same ideas apply to customer profitability, and we should find out our customer profitability as well." Villeagas Wholesalers sends catalogues to the corporate purchasing departments on a monthly basis. The customers are entitled to return unsold merchandise within a six-month period from the purchase date and receive a full purchase-price refund. The following data were collected from last year's operations:

	Chain 1	Chain 2	Chain 3	Chain 4
Gross sales	$50,000	$30,000	$100,000	$70,000
Sales returns:				
Number of items	100	26	60	40
Amount	$10,000	$ 5,000	$ 7,000	$ 6,000
Number of orders:				
Regular	40	150	50	70
Rush	10	50	10	30

Villeagas has calculated the following activity rates:

Activity	Cost-Driver Rate
Regular order processing	$20 per regular order
Rush order processing	$100 per rush order
Returned items processing	$10 per item
Catalogues and customer support	$1,000 per customer

REQUIRED
Determine the contribution to profit from each chain last year. Cost of goods sold is 80% of net sales. Comment on your solution.

④

1. MOH allocation rate
for equipment setup,
$550 per setup

5-25 **ABC, product line costing.** (J. Watson) PTech Ltd. manufactures two models of cordless phones. The Family Friend model has features designed for a multiple-user family, including the ability to have multiple ring tones and colour ID from different callers. The Office Assistant model is designed for use in home offices. Data regarding the two product lines are as follows:

	Family Friend	Office Assistant
Expected production	50,000 units	150,000 units
Direct material cost	$12.14 per unit	$28.64 per unit
Direct labour cost	$10.86 per unit	$10.86 per unit

PTech is considering implementing an activity-based costing (ABC) system in its plant and has identified four primary activities. Data on these activities are as follows:

	Family Friend	Office Assistant
Equipment setup	50 setups	30 setups
Machine processing	30,000 machine-hours	220,000 machine-hours
Quality control	5,000 inspection-hours	10,000 inspection-hours
Packaging/shipping	125 shipments	75 shipments

REQUIRED
1. Calculate the manufacturing overhead allocation rate for each activity using ABC.
2. Compute the unit cost of each model of phone using ABC.
3. Assume the company currently allocates overhead on the basis of direct labour costs. Compute the unit cost of each model of phone using this method.
4. Compare the unit costs of each model calculated in requirements 2 and 3. Comment on your results.

5-26 **ABC, product costing at banks, cross-subsidization.** First International Bank (FIB) is examining the profitability of its Premier Account, a combined savings and chequing account. Depositors receive a 6% annual interest rate on their average deposit. FIB earns an interest rate spread of 2.5% (the difference between the rate at which it lends money and the rate it pays depositors) by lending money for residential home loan purposes at 8.5%. Thus, FIB would gain $250 on the interest spread if a depositor has an average Premier Account balance of $10,000 in 2009 ($10,000 × 2.5% = $250).

The Premier Account allows depositors unlimited use of services such as deposits, withdrawals, chequing account, and foreign currency drafts. Depositors with Premier Account balances of $2,500 or more receive unlimited free use of services. Depositors with minimum balances of less than $2,500 pay a $35 monthly service fee for their Premier Account.

FIB recently conducted an activity-based costing study of its services. It assessed the following costs for six individual services. The use of these services in 2009 by three Premier Account customers is as follows:

	ABC Cost per Transaction	Account Usage		
		Robinson	Skerrett	Farrel
Deposits/withdrawals with teller	$ 4.00	45	55	10
Deposits/withdrawals at ATM	1.20	12	24	18
Prearranged monthly deposit/withdrawal	0.80	0	15	60
Cheques written	11.25	10	5	4
Foreign currency drafts	12.50	4	1	7
Account balance inquiries	2.50	12	20	11
Average cash balance		$2,600	$1,200	$40,000

Assume Robinson and Farrel always maintain a balance above $2,500 while Skerrett always has a balance below $2,500 in 2009.

REQUIRED
1. Compute the 2009 profitability of the Robinson, Skerrett, and Farrell Premier Accounts at FIB.
2. What evidence is there of cross-subsidization across Premier Accounts? Why might FIB worry about this cross-subsidization if the Premier Account product offering is profitable as a whole?
3. What changes at FIB would you recommend for its Premier Account?

5-27 ABC, costs of quality. (J. Watson) Stanford Industries currently uses a normal job-costing system with a single overhead cost pool. It supplies parts to the aeronautic industry, and as a result, quality control is paramount. It currently applies the indirect costs of quality control on the basis of direct labour cost at a rate of 150%. Most of the company's work is awarded by bidding on cost-plus contracts. Recently, Stanford has come under increasing pressure to justify its costs. It is concerned that its single allocation rate may be distorting some of its product bids.

In an analysis of its quality-control costs, it has determined that there are four activities, and it has determined the following cost drivers and rates based on annual projections:

Activity	Cost Driver	Activity Rate
Incoming materials testing and inspection	Number of types of part	$36 per type
In-process testing and inspection	Number of units produced	$6 per unit produced
Final product testing and inspection	Number of units inspected	$25 per unit inspected
Testing supplies	Direct materials (DM) cost	30% of DM cost

Stanford has decided to review one of its recently completed contracts. Direct labour on the job was $467,000 and the direct material cost was $392,000. A review of the job's activities showed that:
◆ 50 different types of parts were used.
◆ A total of 40,000 units were produced.
◆ 30% of all units produced were inspected upon completion.

REQUIRED
1. Calculate the amount of overhead that would be allocated to the contract
   a. Using the current costing system that allocates overhead on the basis of direct labour cost.
   b. Using an ABC system.
2. Do you recommend a switch to ABC? Why or why not?

PROBLEMS

③

2. Widnes Coal costs, $18,200

5-28 Job costing with single direct-cost category, single indirect-cost pool, law firm. Wigan Associates is a recently formed law partnership. Ellery Hanley, the managing partner of Wigan Associates, has just finished a tense phone call with Martin Offiah, president of Widnes Coal. Offiah complained about the price Wigan charged for some legal work done for Widnes Coal.

Hanley also received a phone call from its only other client (St. Helen's Glass) saying it was very pleased with both the quality of the work and the price charged on its most recent case.

Wigan Associates operates at capacity and uses a cost-based approach to pricing (billing) each job. Currently it uses a single direct-cost category (for professional labour-hours) and a single indirect-cost pool (general support). Indirect costs are allocated to cases on the basis of professional labour-hours per case. The case files show the following:

	Widnes Coal	St. Helen's Glass
Professional labour	104 hours	96 hours

Professional labour costs at Wigan Associates are $70 an hour. Indirect costs are allocated to cases at $105 an hour. Total indirect costs in the most recent period were $21,000.

REQUIRED
1. Why is it important for Wigan Partners to understand the costs associated with individual cases?
2. Compute the costs of the Widnes Coal and St. Helen's Glass cases using Wigan's simple costing system.

④

1. Revised indirect cost-allocation rate, $35 per professional labour-hour

5-29 Job costing with multiple direct-cost categories, single indirect-cost pool, law firm (continuation of 5-28). Hanley asks his assistant to collect details on those costs included in the $21,000 indirect-cost pool that can be traced to each individual case. After further analysis, Wigan is able to reclassify $14,000 of the $21,000 as direct costs:

Other Direct Costs	Widnes Coal	St. Helen's Glass
Research support labour	$1,600	$ 3,400
Computer time	500	1,300
Travel and allowances	600	4,400
Telephones/faxes	200	1,000
Photocopying	250	750
Total	$3,150	$10,850

Hanley decides to calculate the costs of each case had Wigan used six direct-cost pools and a single indirect-cost pool. The single indirect-cost pool would have $7,000 of costs and would be allocated to each case using the professional labour-hours base.

REQUIRED
1. What is the revised indirect cost-allocation rate per professional labour-hour for Wigan Associates when total indirect costs are $7,000?
2. Compute the costs of the Widnes and St. Helen's cases if Wigan Associates had used its refined costing system with multiple direct-cost categories and one indirect-cost pool.
3. Compare the costs of the Widnes and St. Helen's cases in requirement 2 with those in requirement 2 of Problem 5-28. Comment on the results.

⑤

1. Widnes Coal costs, $12,530

5-30 Job costing with multiple direct-cost categories, multiple indirect-cost pools, law firm (continuation of 5-28 and 5-29). Wigan Associates has two classifications of professional staff—partners and managers. Hanley asks his assistant to examine the relative use of partners and managers on the recent Widnes Coal and St. Helen's cases. The Widnes case used 24 partner-hours and 80 manager-hours. The St. Helen's case used 56 partner-hours and 40 manager-hours.

Hanley decides to examine how the use of separate direct-cost and indirect-cost pools for partners and managers would have affected the costs of the Widnes and St. Helen's cases. Indirect costs in each cost pool would be allocated based on total hours of that category of professional labour.

The rates per category of professional labour are as follows:

Category of Professional Labour	Direct Cost per Hour	Calculation	Indirect Cost per Hour
Partner	$100.00	$4,600/80 hours	$57.50
Manager	$ 50.00	$2,400/120 hours	$20.00

1. Compute the costs of the Widnes and St. Helen's cases with Wigan Associates' further refined system, with multiple direct-cost categories and multiple indirect-cost pools.
2. For what decisions might Wigan Associates find it more useful to use this job-costing approach rather than the approach in Problems 5-28 or 5-29?

5-31 Department and activity cost rates, service sector. Radhika's Radiology Centre (RRC) performs x-rays, ultrasounds, CT scans, and MRIs. RRC has developed a reputation as a top Radiology Centre in the area. RRC has achieved this status because it constantly re-examines its processes and procedures. RRC has been using a single, facility-wide overhead allocation rate. The VP of Finance believes that RRC can make better process improvements if it uses more disaggregated cost information. She says, "We have state-of-the-art medical imaging technology. Can't we have state-of-the-art accounting technology?"

1. Budgeted cost for service, $56.16 per X-ray

The following budgeted information is available:

Radhika's Radiology Centre
Budgeted Information
For the Year Ending May 30, 2011

	X-Rays	Ultrasound	CT Scan	MRI	Total
Technician labour	$61,440	$105,600	$ 96,000	$ 105,000	$ 368,040
Amortization	32,240	268,000	439,000	897,500	1,636,740
Materials	22,080	16,500	24,000	31,250	93,380
Administration					20,610
Maintenance					247,320
Sanitation					196,180
Utilities					134,350
Totals	$115,760	$390,100	$559,000	$1,033,750	$2,696,620
Number of procedures	3,840	4,400	3,000	2,500	
Minutes to clean after each procedure	5	5	15	35	
Minutes for each procedure	5	15	20	45	

RRC operates at capacity. The proposed allocation bases for overhead are as follows:

Administration	Number of procedures
Maintenance (including parts)	Capital cost of equipment (amortization)
Sanitation	Total cleaning minutes
Utilities	Total procedure minutes

REQUIRED
1. Calculate the budgeted cost per service for X-rays, ultrasounds, CT scans, and MRIs using the direct technician labour as the cost allocation base.
2. Calculate the budgeted cost per service for X-rays, ultrasounds, CT scans, and MRIs if RRC allocated overhead costs using activity-based costing (ABC).
3. Explain how the disaggregation of information could be helpful to RRC's intention to continuously improve its services.

5-32 Plantwide versus department overhead cost rates. (CMA, adapted) Merrick Corporation manufactures a complete line of fibreglass attaché cases and suitcases. Merrick has three manufacturing departments (moulding, component, and assembly) and two support departments (maintenance and power).

1. Plantwide overhead rate, $26.36 per DMLH

The sides of the cases are manufactured in the moulding department. The frames, hinges, locks, and so on are manufactured in the component department. The cases are completed in the assembly department. Varying amounts of materials, time, and effort are required for each of the various cases. The maintenance and power departments provide services to the three manufacturing departments.

Merrick has always used a plantwide manufacturing overhead rate. Direct manufacturing labour-hours (DMLH) are used to allocate the overhead to each product. The budgeted rate is calculated by dividing the company's total budgeted manufacturing overhead cost by the total budgeted DMLH to be worked in the three manufacturing departments.

Whit Portlock, manager of Cost Accounting, has recommended that Merrick use department overhead rates. Portlock has projected operating costs and production levels for the coming year. They are presented (in thousands) by department in the following tables:

	Manufacturing Department		
	Moulding	**Component**	**Assembly**
Department Operating Data:			
Direct labour-hours	600	3,000	1,400
Machine hours	800	200	
Department Costs:			
Direct materials	$16,400	$42,000	$ 1,800
Direct labour	5,200	28,000	16,500
Department overhead	30,000	24,000	29,000
Total departmental costs	$51,600	$94,000	$47,300
Use of Support Departments:			
Estimated usage of maintenance resources (in labour-hours)	100	30	20
Estimated usage of power (in kilowatt hours)	400	380	120

Estimated costs of the maintenance department are $12,800 and of the power department are $36,000.

REQUIRED

1. Calculate the plantwide overhead rate for Merrick Corporation for the coming year using the same method as used in the past.
2. Whit Portlock has been asked to develop department overhead rates for comparison with the plantwide rate. Follow these steps in developing the department rates:
   a. Allocate the maintenance department and power department costs to the three manufacturing departments.
   b. Calculate department overhead rates for the three manufacturing departments using a machine-hour allocation base for the moulding department and a direct manufacturing labour-hour (DMLH) allocation base for the component and assembly departments.
3. Should Merrick Corporation use a plantwide rate or department rates to allocate overhead to its products? Explain your answer.

5-33 **Activity-based costing, merchandising.** Pharmacare Inc. specializes in the distribution of pharmaceutical products. Pharmacare operates at capacity and has three main market segments:
a. General supermarket chains
b. Drugstore chains
c. "Mom and Pop" single-store pharmacies

Rick Flair, the new controller of Pharmacare, reported the following data for August 2009:

	General Supermarket Chains	Drugstore Chains	"Mom and Pop" Single Stores	Pharmacare
Revenues	$3,708,000	$3,150,000	$1,980,000	$8,838,000
Cost of goods sold	3,600,000	3,000,000	1,800,000	8,400,000
Gross margin	$ 108,000	$ 150,000	$ 180,000	438,000
Other operating costs				301,080
Operating income				$ 136,920

For many years, Pharmacare has used gross margin percentage [(Revenue − Cost of goods sold) ÷ Revenue] to evaluate the relative profitability of its different groupings of customers (distribution outlets).

Flair recently attended a seminar on activity-based costing (ABC) and decides to consider using it at Pharmacare. Flair meets with all the key managers and many staff members. People generally agree that there are five key activity areas at Pharmacare:

Activity Area	Cost Driver
Order processing	Number of customer purchase orders
Line-item processing	Number of line items ordered by customers
Delivering to stores	Number of store deliveries
Cartons shipped to store	Number of cartons shipped
Stocking of customer store shelves	Hours of shelf-stocking

Each customer order consists of one or more line items. A line item represents a single product (such as Extra-Strength Tylenol Tablets). Each product line item is delivered in one or more separate cartons. Each store delivery entails the delivery of one or more cartons of products to a customer. Pharmacare's staff stacks cartons directly onto display shelves in customers' stores. Currently, there is no additional charge to the customer for shelf-stocking, and not all customers use Pharmacare for this activity. The level of each activity in the three market segments and the total cost incurred for each activity in 2009 are shown below:

Activity	General Supermarket Chains	Drugstore Chains	"Mom and Pop" Single Stores	Total Cost of Activity in 2009
Number of orders processed	140	360	1,500	$80,000
Number of line items ordered	1,960	4,320	15,000	$63,840
Number of store deliveries made	120	360	1,000	$71,000
Number of cartons shipped to stores	36,000	24,000	16,000	$76,000
Shelf stocking (hours)	360	180	100	$10,240

REQUIRED
1. Compute the August 2009 gross margin percentage for each of Pharmacare's three market segments.
2. Compute the August 2009 per-unit cost driver rate for each of the five activity areas.
3. Use the activity-based costing (ABC) information to allocate the $301,080 of "other operating costs" to each of the market segments. Compute the operating income for each market segment.
4. Comment on the results. What new insights are available with the activity-based information?

5-34 **ABC, product cross-subsidization.** Cartwright Ltd. manufactures two models of saddles, the Jordan and the Shenandoah. The Jordan is a more basic model and sells for $750. The Shenandoah is a professional-model saddle and sells for $1,600. At the beginning of the year, the following budgeted data were available:

1. Cost of Jordan, $163.86 per unit

	Jordan	Shenandoah
Expected production (units)	15,000	5,000
Machine time (hours)	2,000	2,000
Direct material unit cost	$ 100	$ 200
Direct labour-hours	30,000	30,000
Receiving (number of orders processed)	150	650
Setups (number of setups)	15	100
Direct labour average wage rate (per hour)	$ 20	$ 20
Purchasing (number of requisitions)	50	110
Inspection (% of units inspected)	10%	20%
Maintenance hours	450	950
Design and production support (hours)	100	400

The following are the budgeted indirect costs for the year:

Equipment maintenance	$140,000
Utilities	48,000
Purchasing materials	50,000
Indirect materials	60,000

(continued)

(*continued*)

Receiving goods	35,000
Factory rental	96,000
Setting up equipment	13,800
Inspection costs	148,000
Design	50,000
Production support	75,000

Facility level costs are allocated on the basis of machine hours.

REQUIRED
1. Calculate the cost per unit for each product assuming the company uses a single overhead allocation rate based on direct labour-hours.
2. Form homogeneous cost pools and select appropriate cost drivers. Explain the rationale behind each of your groupings. Calculate the activity rates.
3. Using the activity rates calculated in requirement 2, calculate the per-unit cost for each product.
4. Compare your results from requirements 1 and 3, and comment on your results.

4 5

3. Cost for setups, $320 per batch

5-35 Choosing cost drivers, activity-based costing, activity-based management. (J. Watson) Pumpkin Bags (PB) is a designer of high-quality backpacks and purses. Each design is made in small batches. Each spring, PB comes out with new designs for the backpack and for the purse. They use these designs for one year and then move on to the next trend. The bags are all made on the same fabrication equipment that is expected to operate at capacity. The equipment must be switched over to a new design and set up to prepare for the production of each new batch of products. When completed, each batch of products is immediately shipped to a wholesaler. Shipping costs vary with the number of shipments. Budgeted information for the year is as follows:

Pumpkin Bags

Budgeted Costs and Activities for the Year Ending February 28, 2010

Direct materials—purses	$ 362,000
Direct materials—backpacks	427,000
Direct labour—purses	98,000
Direct labour—backpacks	115,597
Setup	64,960
Shipping	72,065
Design	167,000
Plant utilities and administration	225,000
Total	$1,531,622

Other information:

	Backpacks	Purses	Total
Number of bags	6,000	3,150	9,150
Hours of production	1,560	2,600	4,160
Number of batches	133	70	203
Number of designs	3	2	5

REQUIRED
1. Identify the cost hierarchy level for each cost category.
2. Identify the most appropriate cost driver for each cost category. Explain briefly your choice of cost driver.
3. Calculate the cost per unit of cost driver for each cost category.
4. Calculate the total costs and cost per unit for each product line.
5. Explain how you could use the information in requirement 4 to reduce costs.

4

1. Current overhead rate, $15.75 per direct labour-hour

5-36 Activity-based costing, product cross-subsidization. Gideon Ltd. manufactures desktop DNA machines that use glass and silicon chips in PCR testing. PCR is "polymerase chain reaction" and is used in DNA profiling. Until recently, existing DNA testing required a laboratory, but advances in technology have resulted in the production of these new chips that can be used in portable DNA-testing equipment. This "lab on a chip" technology can be used outside the laboratory in agricultural settings, in doctors' offices, and at crime scenes. Gideon specializes in manufacturing two models of the desktop DNA machine, The Diagnostic and The Profiler.

242 CHAPTER 5

The Diagnostic model is used primarily in agricultural and medical applications, while The Profiler is used for crime-scene analysis. Gideon uses the same production facilities for both machines. Each model requires different direct materials, and the production machinery must be retooled for each model. The same assembly line is used to manufacture both models, and the production processes are similar with respect to direct labour.

Gideon currently uses a normal job-costing system with a single overhead cost pool and direct labour-hours as the driver. The company is considering a switch to activity-based costing (ABC) and has gathered the following information from October's production records:

Activity	Cost	The Diagnostic	The Profiler
Materials handling	$7,200	5 setups	10 setups
Machining	9,800	210 machine hours	490 machine hours
Assembly	3,230	600 units	350 units

In addition, the company has a quality-control process. The company tests 5% of The Diagnostic units produced and 10% of The Profiler produced. The company has no beginning or ending work-in-process inventory. Quality testing costs for October were $1,820.

Direct labour costs for October totalled $39,200 at an average wage rate of $28 per hour. Direct labour costs were split equally between the two product models. The direct materials costs for October were $5.50 per unit for the 600 units produced of The Diagnostic and $26.50 per unit for the 350 units produced of The Profiler.

REQUIRED

1. Calculate the overhead rate used by Gideon under its current normal job-costing system.
2. Calculate the total manufacturing costs and the unit manufacturing cost of each product under the current costing system.
3. Calculate the activity rate for each cost pool.
4. Calculate the total manufacturing costs and the unit manufacturing cost of each product if the company switches to activity-based costing.
5. Do you recommend the company should switch to activity-based costing? Why or why not?

5-37 **Plantwide, department, and activity cost rates.** (J. Watson) (CGA, adapted) Sayther Company manufactures and sells two products, A and B. The manufacturing activity is organized in two departments. Manufacturing overhead (MOH) costs at its Calgary plant are allocated to each product using a plantwide rate of $24.80 per direct manufacturing labour-hour (DMLH). This rate is based on budgeted MOH of $595,200 and 24,000 budgeted DMLH:

4

1. a. Product A, $18,600; Product B, $55,800

Manufacturing Department	Budgeted MOH	Budgeted DMLH
1	$372,000	12,000
2	223,200	12,000
Total	$595,200	24,000

The number of DMLH required to manufacture each product is:

ManufacturingDepartment	Product A	Product B
1	4	1
2	1	4
Total	5	5

Per-unit costs for the two categories of direct manufacturing costs are:

Direct Manufacturing Costs	Product A	Product B
Direct materials	$175	$210
Direct labour	100	100

At the end of the year, there was no work in process. There were 150 finished units of product A and 450 finished units of product B on hand. Assume that the budgeted production level of the Calgary plant was exactly attained.

Sayther sets the listed selling price of each product by adding 150% to its unit manufacturing costs; that is, if the unit manufacturing costs are $100, the listed selling price is $250 ($100 + $150). This 150% markup is designed to cover costs upstream to manufacturing (for example, product design) and costs downstream from manufacturing (for example, marketing and customer service) as well as to provide an operating income.

1. What is the manufacturing cost included in the inventory of products A and B if Sayther uses (a) a plantwide overhead rate and (b) department overhead rates?
2. What difference would result in the per-unit selling prices of product A and product B from using a plantwide overhead rate instead of department overhead rates?
3. Should Sayther Company prefer plantwide or department manufacturing overhead rates?
4. Under what conditions should Sayther Company further subdivide the department cost pools into activity cost pools?

⑤

1. Difference in relevant costs, $6,000

5-38 Make or buy, activity-based costing, opportunity costs. (N. Melumad and S. Reichelstein, adapted) Ace Bicycle Company produces bicycles. This year's expected production is 10,000 units. Currently, Ace makes the chains for its bicycles. Ace's accountant reports the following costs for making the 10,000 bicycle chains:

	Costs per unit	Costs for 10,000 units
Direct materials	$6	$60,000
Direct labour	3	30,000
Variable manufacturing overhead (utilities)	2	20,000
Inspection, setup, materials handling		2,500
Equipment rental		3,500
Allocation of fixed plant facility costs (insurance, administration, etc.)		34,000

Ace has received an offer from an outside vendor to supply any number of chains Ace requires at $12.20 per chain. The following additional information is available:
a. Inspection, setup, and materials-handling costs vary with the number of batches in which the chains are produced. Ace produces chains in batch sizes of 1,000 units. Ace estimates that it will produce the 10,000 units in ten batches.
b. Ace rents the machine used to make the chains. If Ace buys all its chains from the outside vendor, it does not need to pay rent on this machine.

1. Assume that, if Ace purchases the chains from the outside supplier, the facility where the chains are currently made will remain idle. Should Ace accept the outside supplier's offer at the anticipated production (and sales) volume of 10,000 units?
2. For this question, assume that if the chains are purchased outside, the facilities where the chains are currently made will be used to upgrade the bicycles by adding mud flaps and reflectors. As a consequence, the selling price on bicycles will be raised by $25. The variable per-unit cost of the upgrade would be $20.50, and additional tooling costs of $18,500 would be incurred. Should Ace make or buy the chains, assuming that 10,000 units are produced (and sold)?
3. The sales manager at Ace is concerned that the estimate of 10,000 units may be high and believes that only 6,400 units will be sold. Production will be cut back, and this opens up work space, which can be used to add the mud flaps and reflectors whether Ace goes outside for the chains or makes them in-house. At this lower output, Ace will produce the chains in eight batches of 800 units each. Should Ace purchase the chains from the outside vendor?

⑤

1. Profitability of Regal model, $436,760 gross margin

5-39 ABC, implementation, governance. (CMA, adapted) Applewood Electronics, a division of Elgin Corporation, manufactures two large-screen television models: the Monarch, which has been produced since 2005 and sells for $1,700, and the Regal, a new model introduced in early 2008, which sells for $2,200. Based on the following income statement for the year ended November 30, 2009, senior management at Elgin have decided to concentrate Applewood's marketing resources on the Regal model and begin to phase out the Monarch model.

Applewood Electronics
Income Statement
For the Year Ended November 30, 2009

	Monarch	Regal	Total
Sales	$30,600,000	$4,400,000	$35,000,000
Cost of goods sold	19,890,000	3,080,000	22,970,000
Gross margin	10,710,000	1,320,000	12,030,000
Selling and administrative expense	8,032,500	925,000	8,957,500
Operating income	$ 2,677,500	$ 395,000	$ 3,072,500
Units sold	18,000	2,000	
Operating income per unit sold	$148.75	$ 197.50	

Unit costs for the Monarch and Regal are as follows:

	Monarch	Regal
Direct materials	$ 540.00	$1,089.00
Direct labour		
Monarch (2.5 hours × $18 per hr)	45.00	
Regal (7.0 hours × $18 per hr)		126.00
Machine costs*		
Monarch (8 hours × $25 per hr)	200.00	
Regal (5 hours × $25 per hr)		125.00
Other manufacturing overhead**	320.00	200.00
Total	$1,105.00	$1,540.00

*Machine costs include leasing of the machine, repairs, and maintenance.
**Other manufacturing overhead is allocated on the basis of machine hours at a rate of $40 per machine hour.

Applewood's controller, Susan Benzo, is advocating the use of activity-based costing (ABC) and activity-based management (ABM), and has gathered the following information about the company's manufacturing overhead costs for the year ended November 30, 2009.

Activity Centre	Total Activity Costs	Units of Cost Driver Monarch	Regal
Soldering (number of solder points)	$1,872,400	1,296,000	214,000
Shipments (number of shipments)	1,480,000	1,500	500
Quality control (number of inspections)	1,749,600	54,000	18,000
Purchase orders (number of P.O.s)	582,400	16,640	4,160
Machine power (machine hours)	61,600	144,000	10,000
Machine setups (number of setups)	414,000	360	100
Total manufacturing overhead	$6,160,000		

After completing her analysis, Benzo showed the results to Filipe Figueira, the Applewood Division President. Figueira did not like what he saw. "If you show headquarters this analysis, they are going to ask us to phase out the Regal line, which we have just introduced. This whole costing thing has been a major problem for us. First Monarch was not profitable and now Regal.

"Looking at the ABC analysis, I see two problems. We do many more activities than the ones you have listed. If you had included all activities, maybe your conclusions would have been different. Second, you used number of setups and number of inspections as allocation bases. The numbers would have been different had you used setup-hours and inspection-hours instead. I know that measurement problems precluded you from using these other cost-allocation bases, but at least you ought to make some adjustments to our current numbers to compensate for these issues. I know you can do better. We can't afford to phase out either product."

Benzo knew her numbers were fairly accurate. On a limited sample, she had calculated the profitability of Regal and Monarch using different allocation bases. The set of activities and activity rates she had chosen resulted in numbers that approximated closely those based on more detailed analyses. She was confident that headquarters, knowing that Regal was introduced only recently, would not ask Applewood to phase it out. She was also aware that a sizable portion of Figueira's bonus was based on division sales. Phasing out either product would adversely affect the bonus. Still, she felt some pressure from Figueira to do something.

REQUIRED
1. Using activity-based costing (ABC), calculate the profitability of the Regal and Monarch models.
2. Explain briefly why these numbers differ from the profitability of the Regal and Monarch models calculated using Applewood's existing costing system.
3. Comment on Figueira's concerns about the accuracy and limitations of ABC.
4. How might Applewood find the ABC information helpful in managing its business?
5. What should Susan Benzo do?

COLLABORATIVE LEARNING CASE

5-40 Using ABC for activity-based management (ABM). As you've seen in this chapter, activity-based costing (ABC) systems are useful in helping companies make better decisions about pricing, product mix, and cost management related to product design and efficiency. In fact, General Mills used ABC to identify and analyze the costs associated with the different channels used to market its Colombo frozen yogurt products.

Before performing ABC analysis, General Mills charged the same prices and provided the same promotions—$3 per case—to its customers, whether the customer was in the grocery channel (food purchased for later consumption or preparation at home) or the food-service (outside of home, immediate consumption) channel. Upon closer examination of the food-service channel, General Mills discovered segments within food service: destination yogurt shops or restaurants and impulse locations, located in business cafeterias and on college campuses and military bases. General Mills also noticed that sales dollars for frozen yogurt products were relatively constant, but profits were declining. The company sensed that destination yogurt shops might be more profitable than impulse locations, but it didn't have the information about profit differences to make changes. General Mills' logic was: Destination shops/restaurants focus on maximizing profit per square foot and managing guest cheque averages. However, impulse locations focus on cost per serving, and this segment of the business was growing at a much faster rate than the destination shop segment.

The case sales data and income statements for last year, by segment, looked like this:

Category	Impulse Location	Yogurt Shops	Total
Sales in cases	1,200,000	300,000	1,500,000
Sales revenue	$23,880,000	$5,970,000	$29,850,000
Less: Promotions	3,600,000	900,000	4,500,000
Net sales	20,280,000	5,070,000	25,350,000
Cost of goods sold	13,800,000	3,450,000	17,250,000
Gross margin	6,480,000	1,620,000	8,100,000
Less: Merchandising	1,380,000	345,000	1,725,000
Less: Selling, general, and admin. expenses	948,000	237,000	1,185,000
Net income	$ 4,152,000	$1,038,000	$ 5,190,000

Cost of goods sold includes $14,250,000 for ingredients, packaging, and storage, and $3,000,000 for picking, packing, and shipping. The product is the same across segments, so cost to produce is the same. However, picking, packing, and shipping costs vary if the order is for a full pallet. Full pallets cost $75 to pick and ship, where individual orders cost $2.25 per case. There are 75 cases in a pallet, with pallet and case usage by segment shown here:

	Segment		
	Impulse Location	Yogurt Shops	Total
Cases in full pallets	60,000	240,000	300,000
Individual cases	1,140,000	60,000	1,200,000
Total cases	1,200,000	300,000	1,500,000

For merchandising, costs consist mainly of kits selling for $500 each. A total of 3,450 kits were delivered in the period, 90 of them to yogurt shops. For selling, general, and administration, costs were allocated to products based on gross sales dollars. When a random sample of the sales force was asked to keep diaries for 60 days, the resulting data revealed they spent much more time per sales dollar on yogurt sales than other General Mills products they represented. Thus, when selling, general, and administration costs were allocated based on time, the total allocation to yogurt products jumped from $1,185,000 to $3,900,000. Of the total time spent on selling Colombo frozen yogurt, only 1% of that time was spent in shops.

REQUIRED

1. How do the two segments identified by General Mills for Colombo frozen-yogurt sales differ from each other?
2. Using ABC analysis, restate the income statements above to show new net income (*hint:* add a line item for shipping). What is "per case" net income?
3. Based on your analysis in requirement 2, what changes should General Mills make?

(IMA adapted; "Colombo Frozen Yogurt," John Guy and Jane Saly, *Cases from Management Accounting Practice*, Vol. 15, Institute of Management Accountants, 2000.) © IMA. Reprinted with permission from the Institute of Management Accountants, Montvale, N.J., www.imanet.org.)

Master Budget and Responsibility Accounting

BUSINESS MATTERS

Budgets Communicate Choices

Chrysler's budget forecasts how changes in the business and economic environment are likely to affect Chrysler's financial health. Chrysler has limited resources, and its budgets represent choices about where those resources will be used, based on experience and assumptions about the future. A budget reports pro forma or expected financial results in standard financial-statement format. The pro forma financial reports are performance targets that Chrysler's managers have committed to achieve.

LEARNING OBJECTIVES

After studying this chapter, you should be able to

1. Distinguish the long-term from the short-term benefits of budgets (pro forma financial statements)

2. Prepare a master operating budget and all supporting budgets or schedules

3. Prepare a cash budget

4. Distinguish among sensitivity analysis, Kaizen budgeting, and activity-based budgeting

5. Contrast responsibility against controllability

Budgets provide managers an opportunity to imagine how to improve financial performance by identifying potential opportunities for change. Budgets are plans. Budgets express the managerial choices that comprise strategy in a familiar financial format. The budget becomes a formal statement of both short-term operating targets and long-term strategies to improve financial performance. Budgets are plans, not commands. As one observer has said, "Few businesses plan to fail, but many of those that flop failed to plan."

This chapter presents the budgeting process used to create an operating budget (reported as a pro forma income statement) and a cash budget (presented as a statement of operating cash flow) using the direct method. The capital budget is presented in detail in Chapter 22. Topics covered in prior chapters are widely used in this discussion. Chapter 1 described some newly evolving management themes that affect management accounting. Budgets give financial expression to many of these themes. For example, budgets can quantify the planned financial effects of activities aimed at continuous improvement and cost reduction. By understanding cost behaviour (covered in Chapters 2 and 3), managers can better predict how total budgeted costs are affected by different forecasts of output levels. By understanding cost tracing and cost allocation (covered in Chapters 4 and 5), managers can show how different forecasts of revenue and cost amounts will affect the budgeted income statement and balance sheet. The material covered in this chapter is also integral to subsequent chapters. For example, Chapters 7 and 8 examine how the numbers used in budgets assist in evaluating the performance of managers or the business areas where they have responsibility.

DEFINE THE BENEFITS OF BUDGETS

① Distinguish the long-term from the short-term benefits of budgets (pro forma financial statements)

DEFINITION OF BUDGETS

A **budget** is a quantitative expression for a set time period of a proposed (future) plan of action by management. If unlimited resources were available within a company, a budget would be unnecessary. It is because resources are constrained that choices must be made to obtain the maximum benefit of the resources in use. The **budget constraint** describes the combination of limitations on nonfinancial and financial resources within a company's management control.

You are familiar with individual financial statements prepared to report the outcome of past periods. Pro forma financial statements are prepared to cover future periods—for example, a budgeted income statement, a budgeted cash flow statement, and a budgeted balance sheet. The plan or budget includes both financial and nonfinancial aspects of expected future events that are often called schedules. Well-managed organizations usually have the following **budgeting cycle**:

1. Plan the performance of the organization as a whole and of its sub-units. The entire management team must agree with what is expected.
2. Provide a frame of reference—a set of specific expectations against which actual results can be compared.
3. Implement the budget and investigate variations from plans. If necessary, corrective action follows investigation so the plan will be met in the future.
4. Plan again, considering changed conditions and feedback from investigations.

The **master budget** summarizes the financial projections of all the organization's individual schedules and sub-unit budgets. A sub-unit can be a subsidiary, a department, a value-chain function, or an activity level. Budgets report the effects of planned *operating* decisions and *financing* decisions. Operating decisions centre on the acquisition and use of scarce resources; financing decisions centre on how to pay for acquired resources. We concentrate on how accounting helps managers make operating decisions. In this chapter the focus is on the operating budget. The operating budget is a pro forma income statement (see Chapter 2, p. 47).

The term *master* in *master budget* means this is a comprehensive, organization-wide set of schedules and a budget. Consider Bombardier Inc. Each of its individual product lines, either aerospace or ground transportation, has a separate budgeted income statement, a separate budgeted cash flow statement, and so on. The master budgeted income statement for Bombardier is a single pro forma income statement that combines information from all these product-line budgeted income statements. Similarly, the master budgeted cash flow statement is a single cash flow statement that combines information from all the many product-line budgeted cash flow statements.

The terminology used to describe budgets varies among organizations. For example, budgeted financial statements are sometimes called pro forma statements. Some organizations, such as Hewlett-Packard, refer to budgeting as targeting. Indeed, to give a more positive thrust to budgeting, many organizations—for example, Nissan Canada and Bombardier—describe the budget as a *profit plan*.

ADVANTAGES OF BUDGETS

Budgets are a major feature of most management-control systems. When administered intelligently, budgets

◆ compel planning and monitoring of the implementation of plans,

◆ provide reliable performance assessment criteria, and

◆ promote communication and coordination within the organization.

Strategy is a search for ideas or hypotheses (see Chapter 2, p. 47) about what the future for an organization could be. Budgeting is most useful when done as an integral part of an organization's strategic analysis.[1] **Strategic analysis** is the evaluation of how well the organization has combined its own capabilities with the relevant features of the competitive environment to progress towards its future.

Budgets provide feedback to managers about the likely consequences of their strategic and operating plans. This feedback helps to make revisions to the less-successful plans. For example, Chrysler's strategic decision to reduce the selling prices of its Dodge Durango was intended to boost sales volume. The change increased pro forma revenue, but managers determined from the budget that, even at the predicted

---

S T R A T E G Y

A Pest, A Swot—Can't We All Just Get Along?

PESTs and SWOTs are methods of strategic analysis. A PEST analysis places the organization in its political, economic, social, and technological environment. A SWOT analysis examines the organization's internal strengths and weaknesses, and the external environment's opportunities and threats. Other analyses include sensitivity (Chapter 2), critical success factors, value chain, balanced scorecard (BSC), and benchmarking.

Critical success factor analyses examine those activities that must be accomplished well if the organization is to thrive. Value-chain analyses examine how groups of activities contribute to the value proposition to the customer. Balanced scorecard analyses examine how best to balance the achievement of nonfinancial targets,

such as customer service and improved expertise, to achieve financial targets. Benchmarking attempts to realign processes to match or exceed the known best performance. For example, emergency-room processes and aircraft turnaround between flights can be monitored and analysed to reduce the time and costs involved in these complex activities.

Other approaches to strategic analysis are available and analyses can be combined. The goals of strategic analysis are to assess where a company expected to be, where it is, and where it needs to go. Strategic analysis helps managers find at least partial answers to these questions. Comparing pro forma financial statements or budgets to actual results will provide additional guidance.

---

[1] See J. Hope and R. Fraser, *Beyond Budgeting* (Boston, MA: Harvard Business School Press, 2003) for several examples.

higher sales volume, the company would be unable to meet its profit targets. For the strategy to succeed, the company also needed to reduce operating costs. Chrysler then used cross-functional teams with members from different parts of the value chain to seek major cost reductions by streamlining operations and moving to lower-cost manufacturing regions.

OPERATING AND STRATEGIC PERFORMANCE ASSESSMENT

Budgeted performance measures can overcome two key limitations of using past performance as a basis for judging actual results. For example, past results incorporate past miscues and substandard performance. Consider a cellular telephone service company examining the 2009 performance of its sales force. The past performance in 2008 incorporated the efforts of many salespeople who left because they did not understand the marketplace. Using the sales record of those departed employees would set the performance bar for knowledgeable salespeople far too low.

Another limitation of past performance is that the anticipated future may be very different from the past. Consider again our cellular telephone company. Suppose the company had a 20% revenue increase in 2009, compared with a 10% increase in 2008. Does this indicate stellar sales performance? Before saying yes, consider two additional facts. Fact one is that, in November 2008, an industry trade association forecast that the 2009 growth rate in industry revenues would be 40%. Fact two is that, in 2009, the actual growth rate in industry revenues was 50%. The 20% actual revenue gain in 2009, although it exceeds the 2008 actual growth rate of 10%, remains below the actual industry gain of 50%. Use of the 40% figure as the budgeted rate provides a better way to evaluate the 2009 sales performance than the use of the 2008 actual rate of 10%.

Exhibit 6-1 illustrates the strategic analysis and planning processes. The dual-directional arrows indicate the interdependence among these activities and outcomes. The budgets, expressed in financial format, are outcomes of plans. The cycle of planning and budgeting is continuous as actual results provide feedback regarding how well managers forecast future results. When the feedback is negative, it is sensible for managers to reassess their long-run and short-run plans to determine where changes can be made to improve the achievement of their financial and nonfinancial goals.

A company's internal budget is not the only threshold of year-to-year accomplishment that can be used to evaluate performance. Companies must also consider their own performance relative both to their peers in the industry and the overall industry's annual performance. When companies evaluate accomplishment exclusively on their internal performance, the situation is ripe for "gaming," whereby managers set easily achieved targets;[2] but those to whom they report know this

EXHIBIT 6-1

Strategic Analysis in the Formulation of Long-Run and Short-Run Budgets

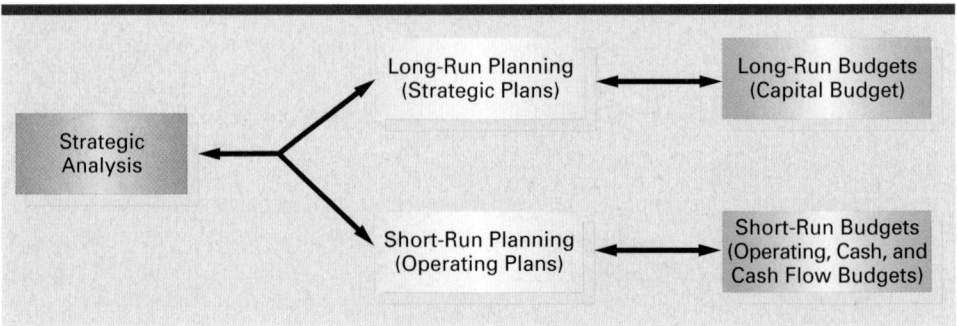

[2]For a more detailed discussion, see R. Varnick, G. Wu, and C. Heath, "Raising the Bar on Goals," Graduate School of Business Publication, University of Chicago, Spring, 1999.

game. In turn, they set more challenging targets and negotiating begins among the levels of the company's managers to decide what the budget will be. General Electric's former CEO, Jack Welch, maintained that demanding, yet achievable, goals created anxiety for managers but improved corporate performance. He perceived "stretch" goals as a way to motivate creative change and progress in existing processes of each business function.

COORDINATION AND COMMUNICATION

Coordination is the meshing and balancing of all factors of production or service and of all the departments and business functions so that the company can meet its objectives. *Communication* is getting those objectives understood and accepted by all employees.

Coordination forces executives to think of relationships and interdependencies among individual operations, departments, and the company as a whole. As we learned in Chapter 5, purchasing officers make material purchase plans based on either production, service, or merchandising requirements. Reduction in purchasing costs can improve profitability in other value-chain functions because of interdependence. In a manufacturing setting, after marketing forecasts future demand, production managers plan personnel and machinery needs to produce the number of products necessary to meet revenue forecasts.

How does a budget lead to coordination? Consider Snapple Beverage Corporation. Production managers, who are evaluated on maximizing output while keeping unit costs per bottle low, would prefer long production runs with very few changeovers of flavours. But if the output cannot be sold, Snapple may find itself awash in a costly inventory buildup of Mango Madness. The budget achieves coordination by constraining production managers to produce only what marketing forecasts. This may entail doing a changeover from Mango Madness to Lemonade partway into a production shift. This may be inconvenient but it is cost-beneficial because the COGS will only be recovered when the outputs are sold.

Communication is key to coordination. Production managers must know the sales plan. A purchasing manager must know the production plans, and so on. A formal document, such as the budget, is an effective way to communicate a consistent set of plans to the organization as a whole. Within a company, the value-chain managers must all get along to produce a budget of benefit to the entire company.

CHALLENGES IN BUDGET IMPLEMENTATION

Budgeting consumes a lot of time at all levels of an organization. Those employees on the front lines possess hands-on experience with day-to-day production and their managers possess specialized knowledge of how to control these processes. Communication from the bottom up that is reflected in the budget creates greater commitment and accountability towards its achievement among all levels. Ultimately, top management bears responsibility for producing and achieving the budget targets for the companies they lead.

The prevalence of budgets in companies of all sizes is evidence that the benefits of budgeting processes outweigh their costs (see the Real Companies on the next page). Executive support is especially critical for obtaining active line participation in the formulation of budgets and for successful administration of budgets. The "garbage in, garbage out" maxim applies to budgets. At all levels in a company, managers must understand and support both the budget and the control it imposes on their decision making.

Budgets are plans made based on assumptions about what the future will be. Changing conditions call for changes in plans. A manager may commit to the budget, but opportunities often develop where some special repairs or a special advertising program would better serve the interests of the organization. Deferring the repairs or the advertising in order to meet the budget is foolish if it will hurt the organization in the long run. Attaining the budget is never an end in itself.

Budgets: A Common Global Practice

budget goal.[a,b] In contrast, fewer division managers participate in the budget committee processes in New Zealand and Japan,[c] and Japanese companies regard sales revenue as the most important budget goal. Australian managers report that budgeting is the management-accounting process that they benefit from the most.[d] The tables below show some budgeting preferences in various parts of the world.

Of course, not all budgeting is successful. U.S. chief financial officers (CFOs) state the following reasons for ineffective budgets:[e]

1. Poorly defined strategy
2. Poor links from strategy to operating plans
3. Poor individual accountability for results
4. Poorly chosen performance measures

Budgeting practices differ around the world. U.S. and Greek companies favour participation by division managers and regard return on investment (ROI) as the most important

Two planning methodologies viewed as "significant to extremely valuable" by more than 60% of CFOs surveyed were activity-based budgeting and rolling budget forecasts.

1. Percentage of companies that prepare a complete master budget:

Australia	Finland[f]	Greece	India[g]	Japan[a]	New Zealand	Singapore[h]	Sweden[i]	U.K.	United States
100%	92%	93%	91%	93%	98%	97%	89%	95%	91%

2. Percentage of companies reporting division-manager participation in budget-committee discussions:

Greece	India	Japan	New Zealand	U.K.	United States
93%	84%	67%	70%	71%	78%

3. Ranking of the most important budget goals for division managers (1 is most important):

	United States	Japan
Return on investment	1	4
Operating income	2	2
Sales revenue	3	1
Production costs	4	3

4. Percentage of executives who place importance on the budget when appraising management performance:

	New Zealand	United Kingdom
Not important	0%	1%
Below average importance	7	4
Average importance	22	14
Above average importance	45	39
Vital importance	26	28

---

[a] T. Asada, J. Bailes, and M. Amano, *An Empirical Study of Japanese and American Budget Planning and Control Systems*, Working Paper, Tsukuba University and Oregon State University, 1989.

[b] A. Ballas and G. Venieris, "A Survey of Management Accounting Practice in Greek Firms," in A. Bhimani (ed.) *Management Accounting: European Perspectives* (Oxford: Oxford University Press, 1996).

(continued)

(*continued*)

[c] C. Guilding, D. Lamminmaki, and C. Drury, "Budgeting and Standard Costing Practices in New Zealand and the United Kingdom," *International Journal of Accounting* (1998).

[d] R. Crenhall and K. Smith, "Adoption and Benefits of Management Accounting Practices: An Australian Study," *Management Accounting Research* (1998).

[e] C. Lazere, "All Together Now," *CFO*, February 1998.

[f] B. Ekholm and J. Wallin, "Is the Annual Budget Really Dead?" *European Accounting Review* (2000).

[g] P. Joshi, "The International Diffusion of New Management Accounting Practices: The Case of India," *Journal of International Accounting, Auditing & Taxation* (2001).

[h] B. Ghosh and Y. Chan, "Management Accounting in Singapore—Well in Place?" *Managerial Auditing Journal* (1997).

[i] M. Glader, "Ekonomistyrning i Svenska Börsföretag, Rapport från Sektionen för Redovisning och Finansiering," (Stockholm: Stockholm School of Economics, 1996).

ASSESS YOUR MASTERY

To check your understanding of the material in Learning Objective ❶, go to the *Mastery Questions* section at the end of this chapter and complete Learning Objective ❶ questions 1, 2, and 3.

PREPARE THE MASTER OPERATING BUDGET

Prepare a master operating budget and all supporting budgets or schedules

TIME COVERAGE

The purpose(s) for budgeting should guide the time period chosen for the budget. Consider budgeting for a new Harley-Davidson 500-cc motorcycle. If the purpose is to budget for the total profitability of this new model, a five-year period (or more) may be appropriate because it covers design, manufacture, sales, and after-sales support. In contrast, consider budgeting for a Christmas play. If the purpose is to estimate all cash outlays, a six-month period from the planning to staging of the play may be adequate.

The most frequently used budget period is one year. The annual budget is often subdivided by months for the first quarter and by quarters for the remainder of the year. The budgeted data for a year are frequently revised as the year unfolds. For example, at the end of the first quarter, the budget for the next three quarters is changed in light of new information.

Businesses increasingly use *rolling budgets*. A **rolling budget** is a budget or plan that is always available for a specified future period by adding a month, quarter, or year in the future as the current month, quarter, or year is completed. Thus, a 12-month rolling budget for the March 2008 to February 2009 period becomes a 12-month rolling budget for the April 2008 to March 2009 period the next month, and so on. There is always a 12-month budget in place. The NEC Corporation of Japan has a one-year operating budget that is updated as each month ends. Rolling budgets motivate managers to look forward 12 months, regardless of the month at hand. Companies also frequently use rolling budgets when developing five-year budgets for long-run planning. For example, the NEC Corporation also has a five-year budget that is updated as each year ends.

STEPS IN DEVELOPING AN OPERATING BUDGET

Budgeting, like swimming, is best learned by doing. We will walk through the development of an actual master budget because it provides a comprehensive picture of the entire budgeting process. Our example is a mid-sized, owner-managed manufacturer of aircraft replacement parts, Halifax Engineering. Its job-costing system for manufacturing costs (see Chapter 4) has two direct-cost categories, direct materials and direct manufacturing labour, as well as one indirect-cost pool, manufacturing overhead. Manufacturing overhead (both variable and fixed) is allocated to output units using direct manufacturing labour-hours as the allocation base. The company manufactures specialized parts for the aerospace industry.

Exhibit 6-2 illustrates the flow among the various parts of the master budget for Halifax Engineering. The master budget summarizes the anticipated financial outcomes of all the organization's individual budgets. The result is a set of related

EXHIBIT 6-2
Overview of the Master Budget for Halifax Engineering

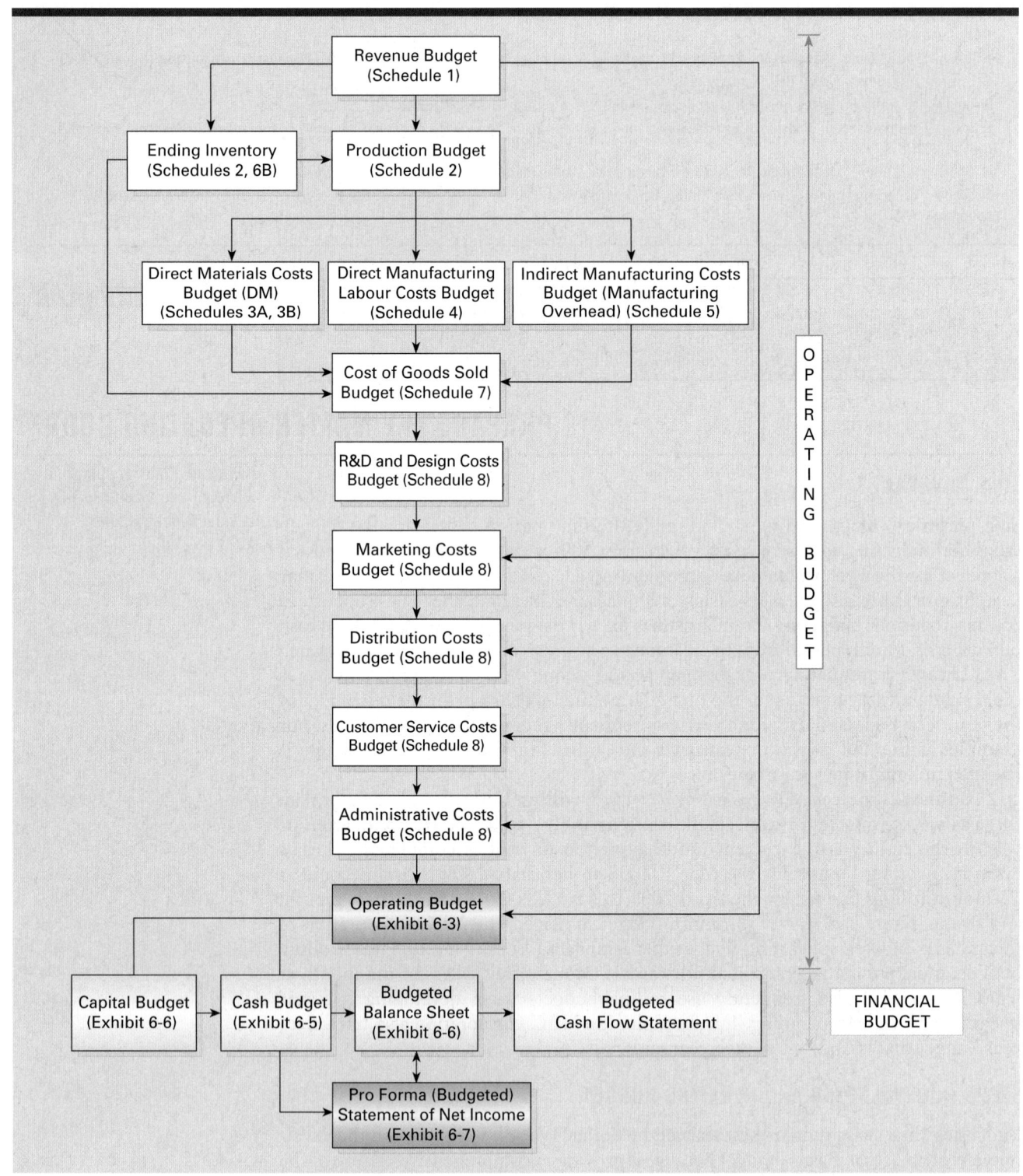

financial statements for a set time period, usually a year. The twelve schedules in Exhibit 6-2 illustrate the logical flow among budgets that together are often called the *operating budget*. The **operating budget** presents the results of operations in many value-chain business functions, prior to financing and taxes. Later in this chapter you will learn how the remaining budget information is produced to create a budgeted or pro forma income statement.

The operating budget and pro forma income statement, new elements introduced in this chapter, are coloured green, as is the arrow indicating all the schedules required in the operating budget.

The dual-direction arrows in Exhibit 6-2 indicate interdependencies among elements. For example, the operating budget will be amended to include added amortization if the demand forecast indicates a permanent increase in production is required. A permanent increase in production means the purchase of long-term assets would be recorded in the capital budget. Financing the purchase and the interest incurred would be recorded in the cash budget and would affect the pro forma income statement. If Halifax Engineering cannot access the financing to increase its capacity, then the production must be decreased and the operating budget changed. Similarly, if the interest expense on the cash budget indicates that Halifax Engineering will be "in the red" with a negative net profit, the company may decide to postpone its expansion plans.

The **financial budget** is that part of the master budget that comprises the capital budget, cash budget, budgeted balance sheet, and budgeted cash flow statement. This set of budgets is coloured yellow in Exhibit 6-2. Notice the dual-direction arrow between the financial and operating budget. This signifies that Halifax Engineering must be able to afford its operating and investing plans. The final master budget is often the result of several iterations. Each draft involves interaction across the various business functions of the value chain.

THINKING CRITICALLY

What does the dual-direction arrow between the pro forma income statement and the pro forma balance sheet mean? Explain in a sentence or two. Read on for a discussion of this topic.

The master budget reports a large amount of nonfinancial data from various value-chain functions. The managers at the company use these data to create forecasts of the drain on or contribution to financial resources each quarter.

The dual-direction arrow between the pro forma or budgeted income statement and the budgeted or pro forma balance sheet indicates familiar interdependencies. For example, net income is one of the financial elements included in owners' equity on the balance sheet. While budgeting is not financial accounting, the quality of the financial-accounting data in the management information system is crucial to good budgeting. Moreover, the structure of financial-accounting statements enables communication and coordination among managers of the different value-chain functions using a familiar and common financial language.

BASIC DATA AND REQUIREMENTS

Halifax Engineering is a machine shop that uses skilled labour and metal alloys to manufacture two types of aircraft replacement parts—Regular and Heavy-Duty. Halifax managers are ready to prepare a master budget for the year 2009. To keep our illustration manageable for clarifying basic relationships, we make the following assumptions:

1. The only source of revenues is sales of the two parts. Non-sales-related revenue, such as interest income, is assumed to be zero.

2. Work-in-process inventory is negligible and is ignored. Ending inventory is a planned quantity, not a remainder.

3. Direct materials inventory and finished goods inventory are costed using the first-in, first-out (FIFO) method.

4. Unit costs of direct materials purchased and finished goods sold remain unchanged throughout the budget year (2009).

5. Variable production (inventoriable) costs are variable with respect to direct manufacturing labour-hours. Variable nonproduction (period) costs vary with respect to revenues. These simplifying assumptions are made to keep our example relatively straightforward.

6. For calculating inventoriable costs, *all* manufacturing costs (fixed and variable) are assigned using direct manufacturing labour-hours as the cost allocation base.

After carefully examining all relevant factors, the executives of Halifax Engineering forecast the following for 2009:

A	B	C
1 Direct materials:		
2 Material 111 alloy	$ 7	per kilogram
3 Material 112 alloy	$10	per kilogram
4 Direct manufacturing labour	$20	per hour
5		
6 **Content of Each Product Unit**	**Regular**	**Heavy-Duty**
7 Direct materials 111 alloy—kilograms	12	12
8 Direct materials 112 alloy—kilograms	6	8
9 Direct manufacturing labour-hours (DLH)	4	6

All direct manufacturing costs are variable with respect to the units of output produced. Additional information regarding the year 2009 is as follows:

A	B	C
1	**Product**	
2	**Regular**	**Heavy-Duty**
3 Expected sales in units	5,000	1,000
4 Selling price per unit	$ 600	$ 800
5 Target ending inventory in units*	1,100	50
6 Beginning inventory in units	100	50
7 Beginning inventory value in dollars	$38,400	$26,200
8		
9	**Direct Materials**	
10	**111 Alloy**	**112 Alloy**
11 Beginning inventory in kilograms	7,000	6,000
12 Target ending inventory in kilograms*	8,000	2,000
13		
14 *Target inventories depend on expected sales, expected variation in demand for products, and management philosophies such as just-in-time (JIT) inventory management.		

At the anticipated output levels for the Regular and Heavy-Duty aircraft parts, management believes the manufacturing overhead costs will be incurred as shown below. Notice that under fixed costs in this schedule of inventoriable manufacturing overhead, amortization of the manufacturing plant and equipment is included. There is no remaining amortization expense reported in the non-inventoriable or period costs schedule:

A	B	C
1 **Manufacturing Overhead Costs**		
2 Variable:		
3 Supplies	$ 90,000	
4 Indirect manufacturing labour	210,000	
5 Direct and indirect manufacturing labour fringe costs	300,000	
6 Power	120,000	
7 Maintenance	60,000	$ 780,000
8 Fixed:		
9 Amortization	220,000	
10 Property taxes	50,000	
11 Property insurance	10,000	
12 Supervision	100,000	
13 Power	22,000	
14 Maintenance	18,000	420,000
15 Total		$1,200,000

The period or nonproduction overhead costs are:

	A	B	C
1	**Other (Nonproduction or Period) Costs**		
2	Variable:		
3	R&D/product design	$ 76,000	
4	Marketing	133,000	
5	Distribution	66,500	
6	Customer service	47,500	
7	Administrative	152,000	$475,000
8	Fixed:		
9	R&D/product design	60,000	
10	Marketing	67,000	
11	Distribution	33,500	
12	Customer service	12,500	
13	Administrative	222,000	395,000
14	Total		$870,000

Our task at hand is to prepare a budgeted or pro forma income statement for the year 2009. As shown in Exhibit 6-2 (p. 254), this is one component of Halifax's master budget. Other components of the master budget—the budgeted or pro forma balance sheet and the cash budget—are discussed in the next section of this chapter.

The following supporting budget schedules will be prepared when developing Halifax's budgeted income statement:

1. Revenue budget
2. Production budget (in units)
3. Direct materials usage budget and direct materials purchases budget
4. Direct manufacturing labour budget
5. Manufacturing overhead budget (includes manufacturing plant and equipment amortization. This amortization expense is also included in the cost of goods sold budget)
6. Ending inventory budget
7. Cost of goods sold (COGS) budget
8. Other (nonproduction) costs budget

Some companies prepare budget manuals; while details differ among organizations, the following sequence of events is common for developing a budgeted income statement. Beginning with the revenue budget, each budget is developed in logical fashion. In most cases, computer software speeds the budget calculations.

PREPARING A MASTER OPERATING BUDGET

◆ **Schedule 1:** *Revenue budget.* The revenue budget (Schedule 1) is the usual starting point for budgeting. Why? Because production (and hence costs) and inventory levels generally depend on the forecasted level of revenue. See the Real Companies box on p. 263 to illustrate this application.

	A	B	C	D
1		**Schedule 1: Revenue Budget**		
2		**For the Year Ended December 31, 2009**		
3			**Selling**	**Total**
4		**Units**	**Price**	**Revenues**
5	Regular	5,000	$600	$3,000,000
6	Heavy-Duty	1,000	800	800,000
7	Total			$3,800,000

The $3.8 million is the amount of revenues in the budgeted income statement. The revenue budget results from elaborate information-gathering and intense discussions among sales managers and field sales representatives.

Pressures can exist for budgeted revenues to be either overestimates or underestimates of the expected amounts. Some firms set "stretch" or "challenge" targets for revenues. These targets are actually overestimates of expected revenues intended to motivate employees to put in extra effort and achieve higher performance.

Pressure for employees to underestimate budgeted revenues can occur when a company uses the difference between actual and budget amounts to evaluate managers. These managers may respond by giving highly conservative forecasts. **Padding** the budget or introducing **budgetary slack** refers to the practice of underestimating budgeted revenues (or overestimating budgeted costs) to make budgeted targets easier to achieve. Introducing budgetary slack makes it more likely that actual revenues will exceed budgeted amounts. From the marketing manager's standpoint, budgetary slack hedges against unexpected downturns in demand.

Occasionally, revenues are limited by available production capacity. For example, unusually heavy market demand, shortages of labour or resources, or strikes may cause a company to exhaust its finished goods inventory completely. Additional sales cannot be made because no stock of the product is available. In such cases, the production capacity—the factor that limits revenue—is the starting point for preparing the revenue budget.

◆ **Schedule 2**: *Production budget (in units).* After revenues are budgeted, the production budget (schedule 2) can be prepared. The total finished goods units to be produced depends on planned sales and expected changes in inventory levels:

$$\begin{array}{c} \text{Budgeted} \\ \text{production} \\ \text{(units)} \end{array} = \begin{array}{c} \text{Budgeted} \\ \text{sales} \\ \text{(units)} \end{array} + \begin{array}{c} \text{Target ending} \\ \text{finished goods} \\ \text{inventory} \\ \text{(units)} \end{array} - \begin{array}{c} \text{Beginning} \\ \text{finished goods} \\ \text{inventory} \\ \text{(units)} \end{array}$$

	A	B	C
1	Schedule 2: Production Budget		
2	For the Year Ended December 31, 2009		
3		Product	
4		Regular	Heavy-Duty
5	Budgeted sales (schedule 1)	5,000	1,000
6	Add: Target ending finished goods inventory	1,100	50
7	Total requirements	6,100	1,050
8	Deduct: Beginning finished goods inventory	(100)	(50)
9	Units to be produced	6,000	1,000

When unit sales are not stable throughout the year, managers must decide whether (1) to adjust production levels periodically to minimize inventory held, or (2) to maintain constant production levels and let inventory rise and fall. Increasingly, managers are choosing to adjust production.

◆ **Schedules 3**: *Direct materials usage budget and direct materials purchases budget.* The decision on the quantity of each type of output unit produced (Schedule 2) provides the data required to calculate the quantities of direct materials used. Information from purchasing will provide the cost data to produce Schedule 3A.

	A	B	C	D	E
1	Schedule 3A: Direct Materials Usage Budget in Kilograms and Dollars				
2	For the Year Ended December 31, 2009				
3		Materials			
4		111 Alloy	112 Alloy	Total	
5	Direct materials to be used in production of Regular parts (6,000 units) × 12 and 6 kilograms	72,000	36,000		see Schedule 2
6	Direct materials to be used in production of Heavy-Duty (1,000 units) × 12 and 8 kilograms	12,000	8,000		see Schedule 2
7	Total direct materials to be used (in kilograms)	84,000	44,000		
8	Direct materials to be used from beginning inventory (assume FIFO cost flow)	7,000	6,000		
9	Multiply by: Cost per kilogram of beginning inventory	$ 7	$ 10		
10	Cost of direct materials to be used from beginning inventory	$ 49,000	$ 60,000	$ 109,000	(a)
11	Direct materials to be used from purchases (84,000 − 7,000; 44,000 − 6,000)	77,000	38,000		
12	Multiply by: Cost per kilogram of purchased materials	$ 7	$ 10		
13	Cost of direct materials to be used from purchases	$539,000	$380,000	$ 919,000	(b)
14	Total costs of direct materials to be used (a) + (b)	$588,000	$440,000	$1,028,000	

Schedule 3B computes the budget for direct materials purchases, which depends on the budgeted direct materials to be used, the beginning inventory of direct materials, and the target ending inventory of direct materials:

$$\begin{array}{ccccc} \text{Purchases} & & \text{Usage} & \text{Target ending} & \text{Beginning} \\ \text{of direct} & = & \text{of direct} + & \text{inventory of} - & \text{inventory of} \\ \text{materials} & & \text{materials} & \text{direct materials} & \text{direct materials} \end{array}$$

	A	B	C	D
1	Schedule 3B: Direct Materials Usage Budget in Kilograms and Dollars			
2	For the Year Ended December 31, 2009			
3		Materials		
4		111 Alloy	112 Alloy	Total
5	Direct materials to be used in production (in kilograms)	84,000	44,000	
6	Add: Target ending direct materials inventory	8,000	2,000	
7	Total requirements (in kilograms)	92,000	46,000	
8	Deduct: Beginning direct materials inventory	(7,000)	(6,000)	
9	Direct materials to be purchased (in kilograms)	85,000	40,000	
10	Multiply by: Cost per kilogram of purchased materials	$ 7	$ 10	
11	Total direct materials purchase costs	$595,000	$400,000	$995,000

◆ **Schedule 4:** *Direct manufacturing labour budget.* These costs depend on wage rates, production methods, and hiring plans. The computations of budgeted direct manufacturing labour costs appear in Schedule 4.

	A	B	C	D	E	F
1		Schedule 4: Direct Manufacturing Labour Budget				
2		For the Year Ended December 31, 2009				
3		Output	Direct			
4		Units	Manufacturing		Hourly	
5		Produced	Labour-Hours	Total	Wage	
6		(Schedule 2)	per Unit	Hours	Rate	Total
7	Regular	6,000	4	24,000	$20	$480,000
8	Heavy-Duty	1,000	6	6,000	$20	120,000
9	Total			30,000		$600,000

◆ **Schedule 5:** *Manufacturing overhead budget.* The total of these costs depends on how individual overhead costs vary with the assumed cost allocation base, direct manufacturing labour-hours. The calculations of budgeted manufacturing overhead costs appear in Schedule 5. Notice that manufacturing equipment and plant amortization has been transferred from the schedule of Manufacturing Overhead Costs (p. 256) and included in this budget. This means that some amortization expense is included in the Cost of Goods Sold (COGS) budget and is allocated to each unit of output. The remaining amortization, if any, of non-production long-term assets is included in fixed non-inventoriable or period costs, a separate schedule.

	A	B	C	D
1	Schedule 5: Manufacturing Overhead Budget*			
2	For the Year Ended December 31, 2009			
3		At Budgeted Level of 30,000 Direct		
4		Manufacturing Labour-Hours		
5	Variable manufacturing overhead costs:			
6	Supplies	$ 90,000		
7	Indirect manufacturing labour	210,000		
8	Direct and indirect manufacturing labour fringe costs	300,000		
9	Power	120,000		
10	Maintenance	60,000	$ 780,000	
11	Fixed:			
12	Amortization	220,000		
13	Property taxes	50,000		
14	Property insurance	10,000		
15	Supervision	100,000		
16	Power	22,000		
17	Maintenance	18,000	420,000	
18	Total		$1,200,000	
19				
20	NOTE: The annual amortization expense becomes part of Cost of Goods Sold (schedule 7)			
21	*Data are from p. 256.			

Schedule 5 reports two costs, power and maintenance, as both variable and fixed costs. This suggests that most of these two manufacturing overhead cost pools vary with some common input measure ($120,000 of a total power cost of $142,000; $60,000 of a total maintenance cost of $78,000). Managers at Halifax Engineering have decided that the $22,000 of fixed power costs and $18,000 of fixed maintenance costs are material and should be reported separately as a fixed manufacturing overhead cost pool. Halifax treats all manufacturing overhead as inventoriable costs.[3] It inventories manufacturing overhead at the budgeted rate of $40 per direct manufacturing labour-hour (total manufacturing overhead, $1,200,000 ÷ 30,000 budgeted direct manufacturing labour-hours). It does not use separate variable and fixed manufacturing overhead rates.

◆ **Schedule 6:** *Ending inventory budget.* Schedule 6A shows the computation of unit costs for the two products. These unit costs are used to calculate the costs of target ending inventories of direct materials and finished goods in Schedule 6B.

	A	B	C	D	E	F
1	**Schedule 6A: Computation of Units Costs of Manufacturing**					
2				**Product**		
3				**Regular**		**Heavy-Duty**
4		**Cost per Unit**				
5		**of Input***	**Inputs***	**Amount**	**Inputs***	**Amount**
6	Material 111 alloy	$ 7	12	$ 84	12	$ 84
7	Material 112 alloy	$10	6	60	8	80
8	Direct manufacturing labour	$20†	4	80	6	120
9	Manufacturing overhead	$40‡	4	160	6	240
10	Total			$384		$524
11						
12	*In kilograms or hours					
13	†Data are from p. 260.					
14	‡Direct manufacturing labour-hours is the sole allocation base for manufacturing overhead (both variable and fixed). The budgeted manufacturing overhead rate per direct manufacturing labour-hour of $40 was calculated in step 5.					

	A	B	C	D	E
1	**Schedule 6B: Ending Inventory Budget**				
2	**For the Year Ended December 31, 2009**				
3			**Cost per**		
4		**Kilograms**	**Kilogram**		**Total**
5	Direct materials				
6	111 alloy	8,000*	$ 7	$ 56,000	
7	112 alloy	2,000*	$10	20,000	$ 76,000
8			**Cost per**		
9		**Units**	**Unit**		
10	Finished goods				
11	Regular	1,100†	$384‡	$422,400	
12	Heavy-Duty	50†	$524‡	26,200	$448,600
13	Total Ending Inventory				$524,600
14					
15	*Data are from p. 256.				
16	†Data are from p. 256.				
17	‡From schedule 6A: this is based on 2009 costs of manufacturing finished goods because, under the FIFO costing method, the units in finished goods ending inventory consist of units that are produced during 2009.				

[3]This inventory costing method is termed *absorption costing* because the costs of production, including fixed manufacturing overhead, are recorded in COGS and recovered in the price of the outputs sold (see Chapter 9).

◆ **Schedule 7:** *Cost of goods sold budget.* The information from Schedules 1 to 6 leads to Schedule 7:

	A	B	C	D
1	Schedule 7: Cost of Goods Sold Budget			
2	For the Year Ended December 31, 2009			
3		**From Schedule**		**Total**
4	Beginning finished goods inventory, January 1, 2009	Given*		$ 64,600
5	Direct materials used	3A	$1,028,000	
6	Direct manufacturing labour	4	600,000	
7	Manufacturing overhead	5	1,200,000	
8	Cost of goods manufactured			2,828,000
9	Cost of goods available for sale			2,892,600
10	Deduct: Ending finished goods inventory			
11	December 31, 2009	6B		(448,600)
12	Cost of goods sold			$2,444,000
13				
14	NOTE: The annual amortization expense has been included in manufacturing overhead and therefore is part of Cost of goods sold.			
15	*Given in the description of basic data and requirements (Regular $38,400, Heavy-Duty $26,200) on p. 256.			

Note that the following holds:

$$\begin{array}{l}\text{Cost of} \\ \text{goods sold}\end{array} = \begin{array}{l}\text{Beginning} \\ \text{finished goods} \\ \text{inventory}\end{array} + \begin{array}{l}\text{Cost of goods} \\ \text{manufactured}\end{array} - \begin{array}{l}\text{Ending} \\ \text{finished goods} \\ \text{inventory}\end{array}$$

◆ **Schedule 8:** *Other (nonproduction) costs budget.* Schedules 2 to 7 cover budgeting for Halifax's production area of the value chain. For brevity, other areas of the value chain are combined into a single schedule.

	A	B	C	D	E
1	Schedule 8: Other (Nonproduction) Costs Budget				
2	For the Year Ended December 31, 2009				
3					
4	Variable costs:				
5	R&D/product design	$ 76,000			
6	Marketing	133,000			
7	Distribution	66,500			
8	Customer service	47,500			
9	Administrative	152,000	$475,000*		
10	Fixed costs:				
11	R&D/product design	60,000			
12	Marketing	67,000			
13	Distribution	33,500			
14	Customer service	12,500			
15	Administrative	222,000	395,000		
16	Total costs		$870,000		
17					
18	*Total variable cost for Schedule 8 is $0.125 per revenue dollar or $475,000 ÷ $3,800,000.				

	A	B	C	D
1	**Budgeted Income Statement for Halifax Engineering**			
2	**For the Year Ended December 31, 2009**			
3	Revenues	Schedule 1		$3,800,000
4	Costs:			
5	Cost of goods sold	Schedule 7		2,444,000
6	Gross margin			1,356,000
7	Operating (period) costs:			
8	R&D/product design costs	Schedule 8	$136,000	
9	Marketing costs	Schedule 8	200,000	
10	Distribution costs	Schedule 8	100,000	
11	Customer service costs	Schedule 8	60,000	
12	Administrative costs	Schedule 8	374,000	870,000
13	Operating income			$ 486,000
14				
15	NOTE: Unlike financial accounting, this budgeted income statement contains the noncash annual amortization expense in Cost of goods sold (see Schedule 5 and Schedule 7).			

◆ **Schedule 9:** *Budgeted income statement.* Schedules 1, 7, and 8 provide the necessary information to complete the budgeted income statement, shown in Exhibit 6-3. Of course, more details could be included in the income statement and then fewer supporting schedules would be prepared.

REAL COMPANIES

Newport Gliders and Electronic Pro Formas

In recent years, many companies have implemented comprehensive software packages to manage budgeting and forecasting functions across the organization. Newport Gliders, for example, is a fully computerized manufacturer of 3,000 wooden furniture parts. Each part is tracked using bar codes, and computer-driven machines cut each part based on a numeric code.

The company automated and integrated all of its business functions into an enterprise resource planning (ERP) system that tracks wood inventory, work in process, production times, and so on. Newport also uses computers for customer relationship management (CRM). In addition, the company uses Microsoft's FRx software for financial reporting.

This software enables the company to produce periodic reports of actual operations as standard financial statements. Pro forma data from Microsoft Excel spreadsheets can be imported directly into FRx to automate the budget preparation process. Newport can easily run reports to compare budgeted pro forma financial results with actual results for a specific time period.

Small and medium-sized enterprises that are owner-managed, such as Newport Gliders, can benefit greatly from computerizing their budgeting and performance-evaluation processes since there are systematic relationships among the different data sets, and these relationships are stable and do not change year-to-year with each budget cycle. The relationships can be programmed into the relevant software systems to make reporting more accurate, useful, and efficient.

Source: Microsoft Corporation, *Microsoft FRx: Financial Reporting and Analysis Software,* www.microsoft.com/FRx; Sage PFW, "Customer Success: Newport Gliders Rock with Sage PFW," accessed March 28, 2008, from www.sagesoftware.com/pdf/pfw/ss/pfw_NewportFurniture_ss.pdf.

Top management's strategies for achieving revenue and operating income goals influence the costs planned for the different business functions of the value chain. In particular, all direct variable costs will change as volumes change, while all indirect variable costs will change as the quantities of common inputs consumed change. If a large expansion is planned, then the amortization expense, as well as fixed costs such as insurance and taxes, will also change. The actual financial results will be compared to budgeted results. Management can then evaluate whether their operating plan has been successful and change the plan if necessary. Remember that a budget is a forecast of anticipated future performance. It can be changed.

```
┌─────────────────────────────────────────────────────────────────┐
│                     THINKING CRITICALLY                          │
│  Why is amortization expense not included above? Explain in a    │
│  sentence or two. Read on for a discussion of this situation.    │
└─────────────────────────────────────────────────────────────────┘
```

Halifax Engineering's clients are from the aerospace industry. Exhibit 6-3 illustrates a pro forma operating income statement. Almost all companies own long-term assets. These long-term assets generate amortization, depreciation, or depletion, which is reported on the income statement. You will usually see this non-cash expense reported under period, or non-inventoriable, operating expenses.

Halifax Engineering reports no amortization expense under its period costs. The reason is clear if you refer to the Manufacturing Overhead Costs and the Other (Nonproduction) Costs data (pp. 256–257). These data are reported as Schedule 5 (p. 260) and Schedule 8 (p. 262), respectively.

All amortization for Halifax Engineering, a machine shop, is for the manufacturing plant and equipment. This non-cash cost has been reported in total as an inventoriable cost and included in the Cost of Goods Sold amount in Exhibit 6-3. This is why there is no amortization expense reported in the Operating (Period) Cost section.

MyAccountingLab

ASSESS YOUR MASTERY

To check your understanding of the material in Learning Objective ❷, go to the *Mastery Questions* section at the end of this chapter and complete Learning Objective ❷ questions 1 and 2.

PREPARE THE CASH BUDGET

❸ Prepare a cash budget

This chapter features the operating budget, which reports the expected inventoriable and period costs for Halifax Engineering but does not report the interest expense, tax expense, or net income. Without these estimates, the company will not be able to complete any of its financial budgets. In this section we focus on developing the *cash budget*. The **cash budget** is a schedule of expected cash receipts and disbursements, and is essential for forecasting any expected interest expense. Once interest expense has been estimated, Halifax Engineering can prepare a pro forma income statement in proper financial format.

Assume the company's managers have budgeted quarterly cash flows as shown below. In 2009 these have been estimated given the operating forecasts that have already been prepared. Therefore, the cash budget cannot be prepared before the operating budget has been prepared. The cash budget, however, must be prepared before Halifax Engineering can produce a pro forma income statement, balance sheet, and cash flow statement. You will prepare only the pro forma cash flow from operations since a full pro forma cash flow statement is beyond the scope of this text. The method to prepare the cash budget is identical to the direct method of preparing a statement of cash flow from operations used in financial accounting.

	A	B	C	D	E
1				Quarters	
2		(1)	(2)	(3)	(4)
3	Collections from customers	$913,700	$975,600	$976,500	$918,400
4	Disbursements:				
5	Direct materials	314,360	283,700	227,880	213,800
6	Payroll	557,520	432,080	409,680	410,720
7	Income taxes	50,000	47,912	47,912	47,912
8	Other costs	184,000	156,000	151,000	149,000
9	Machinery purchase	—	—	—	35,080

The actual balance sheet for the company for the year ended December 31, 2008 is reported in Exhibit 6-4; these will be the opening balances for the 2009 cash budget. The cash budget for 2009 will affect all the amounts except that reported for land. The preparation of a capital budget, which is necessary for the preparation of the pro forma balance sheet, is covered in Chapters 21 and 22.

Assume the managers want to maintain a $35,000 minimum cash balance at the end of each quarter of their budgeted year. The company can borrow or repay exactly the amount required at an annual interest rate of 6%. The company will repay total interest owed and as much of the principal outstanding as possible, leaving the required cash balance at the end of the quarter. Interest each quarter is on an annualized rate of 0.5% per month (0.06 ÷ 12 months = 0.005, or 0.5% per month). Assume that borrowing and repayment occur at the end of the quarters in question. Interest is calculated to the nearest dollar. Tax expense has been rounded to the nearest dollar, using a 40% tax rate.

There are three facts to remember when preparing cash budgets:

◆ The ending balance (EB) of the previous quarter must be the beginning balance (BB) of the next quarter, *except*

◆ the "Year as a Whole" column reports the total cash receipts and disbursments for four quarters *but* the BB in this column is the BB from column 1. This is

EXHIBIT 6-4
Balance Sheet for Halifax Engineering as of December 31, 2008

	A	B	C
1	**Assets**		
2	Current Assets		
3	Cash	$ 30,000	
4	Accounts receivable	400,000	
5	Direct materials	109,000	
6	Finished goods	64,600	$ 603,600
7	Property, plant, and equipment		
8	Land	200,000	
9	Building and equipment	2,200,000	
10	Accumulated amortization	(685,000)	1,715,000
11	Total Assets		$2,318,600
12			
13	**Liabilities and Shareholders' Equity**		
14	Current Liabilities		
15	Accounts payable	150,000	
16	Income taxes payable	50,000	200,000
17	Shareholders' Equity		
18	Common shares, 25,000 issued and outstanding	350,000	
19	Retained earnings	1,768,600	2,118,600
20	Total Liabilities and Shareholders' Equity		$2,318,600

because the BB for quarter 1 is the *year end* balance for 2008, which becomes the BB for the *year* 2009. The EB for this "Year as a Whole" column must be the same as the EB for quarter 4 because there is no further activity in cash inflow or outflow.

◆ Amortization is not a cash disbursement and is therefore not reported in the cash budget. A sophisticated approach would be to use the actual capital cost allowance (CCA) and estimated taxes. These refinements are presented in Chapters 21 and 22.

The company now must prepare the cash budget in a logical flow:

◆ Prepare a statement of cash receipts and disbursements by quarters, including details of borrowing, repayment, and interest expense.

◆ Prepare a budgeted balance sheet.

◆ Prepare a budgeted income statement, including the effects of interest expense and income taxes. Assume that income taxes for 2009 (at a tax rate of 40%) are $193,736.

PREPARATION OF THE CASH BUDGET

1. The cash budget (Exhibit 6-5) details expected cash receipts and disbursements quarter by quarter. It predicts the effects on the cash position at the given level of operations. Each quarter, this budget clearly shows the impact of cash-flow timing on bank loans and their repayment. In practice, monthly—and sometimes weekly—cash budgets are very helpful for cash planning and control, depending on the company's needs. Cash budgets help avoid unnecessary idle cash and unexpected cash deficiencies. Ordinarily, the cash budget has the following main sections:

   a. The *beginning cash balance* plus cash receipts equals the total cash available for needs. Cash receipts depend on collections of accounts receivable, cash sales, and miscellaneous recurring sources such as rental or royalty receipts. Information on the prospective collectibility of accounts receivable is needed for accurate predictions. Key factors include bad debt (uncollectible accounts) experience, and average time lag between sales and collections.

   b. *Cash disbursements* include the following items:

      i. Direct materials purchases depend on credit terms extended by suppliers and bill-paying patterns of the buyer.

      ii. Direct labour and other wage and salary outlays depend on payroll dates.

      iii. Other costs depend on timing and credit terms. Amortization is *not* a cash outlay.

      iv. Other disbursements are cash outlays for property, plant, and equipment, as well as long-term investments.

   c. *Financing requirements* depend on how the cash balance before borrowing, keyed as (a) – (b) in Exhibit 6-5, line 14, compares with the minimum cash balance desired; keyed as (c), line 15. The financing plans will depend on the relationship between the cash balance before borrowing and the minimum cash balance desired. If there is excess cash, loans may be repaid or temporary investments made. The outlays for interest expense are usually shown in this section of the cash budget.

   d. *Ending cash balance* reports the net effect of the financing decisions on the cash budget. When the amount is negative as it is at the end of the first quarter ($162,180), the company must borrow enough to cover this shortfall plus $35,000 to achieve its desired ending balance for the quarter.

A	B	C	D	E	F
1		Quarters			Year as
2	(1)	(2)	(3)	(4)	as a Whole
3 Cash balance, beginning	$ 30,000	$ 35,000	$ 35,000	$ 35,000	$ 30,000
4 Add: Receipts:					
5 Collections from customers	913,700	975,600	976,500	918,400	3,784,200
6 Total cash available for needs: (a)	943,700	1,010,600	1,011,500	953,400	3,814,200
7 Deduct: Disbursements					
8 Direct materials	314,360	283,700	227,880	213,800	1,039,740
9 Payroll	557,520	432,080	409,680	410,720	1,810,000
10 Income taxes	50,000	47,912	47,912	47,912	193,736
11 Other costs	184,000	156,000	151,000	149,000	640,000
12 Machinery purchase	—	—	—	35,080	35,080
13 Total disbursements (b)	1,105,880	919,692	836,472	856,512	3,718,556
14 Cash balance before borrowing (a) − (b)	(162,180)	90,908*	175,028	96,888	95,644
15 Minimum cash balance desired (c)	35,000	35,000	35,000	35,000	35,000
16 Additional cash needed	197,180	—	—	—	197,180
17 Loan repayment including interest 6% per year	—	55,908	140,028	6,461	202,397
18 Cash balance end of quarter (after borrowing)	$ 35,000	$ 35,000	$ 35,000	$ 90,427	$ 90,427
19 Financing					
20 Borrowing (at end of each quarter)	$ 197,180**	$ —	$ —	$ —	$ 197,180
21 Repayment (at end of next quarter)	—	(52,950)	(137,865)	(6,365)	(197,180)
22 Interest (at 6% per year or 0.50% per month)	—	(2,958)***	(2,163)	(96)	(5,217)
23 Total effects of financing	$ 197,180	$ (55,908)	$ (140,028)	$ (6,461)	$ (5,217)
24 Cash balance end of quarter (after repayments)†	$ 35,000†	$ 35,000	$ 35,000	$ 90,427	$ 90,427
25					
26 *Excess of total cash available over total cash needed before current financing.					
27 **Note that the interest payments pertain only to the principal balance outstanding at the end of the quarter after the borrowing has occurred. For simplicity assume the company pays its loan as quickly as possible.					
28 ***Note that the interest is charged at an annualized rate of 0.50% per month for 3 months on the principal outstanding after the loan repayment is made at the end of the quarter = $197,180 × 0.005 × 3 months = $2,958.					
29 †Note: Amortization expense is noncash and excluded from the cash budget.					

The cash budget in Exhibit 6-5 shows the short-term *self-liquidating cycle* of cash loans. Seasonal peaks of production or sales often result in heavy cash disbursements for purchases, payroll, and other operating outlays as the products are produced and sold. Cash receipts from customers typically lag behind sales. The loan is self-liquidating in the sense that the borrowed money is used to acquire resources that are combined for sale, and the proceeds from sales are used to repay the loan. This **self-liquidating cycle**—sometimes called the **working capital cycle**, **cash cycle**, or **operating cycle**— is the movement of cash to produce inventories, then to receivables from sales, and back to cash from collections.

2. The budgeted balance sheet is presented in Exhibit 6-6. Each item is projected in the light of the details of the business plan as expressed in all the previous budget schedules. For example, the ending balance of accounts receivable of $415,800 is calculated by adding the budgeted revenues of $3,800,000 (from Schedule 1) to the beginning balance of $400,000 (given in the December 31, 2008 balance sheet) and subtracting cash receipts of $3,784,200 (given in Exhibit 6-5).

EXHIBIT 6-6
Halifax Engineering: Budgeted Balance Sheet as of December 31, 2009

	A	B	C	D
1	**Assets**			
2	Current Assets			
3	Cash (from Exhibit 6-5)	$ 90,427		
4	Accounts receivable (1)	415,800		
5	Direct materials (2)	76,000		
6	Finished goods (2)	448,600		$1,030,827
7	Property, plant, and equipment			
8	Land (3)		200,000	
9	Building and equipment (4)	2,235,080		
10	Accumulated amortization (5)	906,754	1,328,326	1,528,326
11	Total Assets			$2,559,153
12				
13	**Liabilities and Shareholders' Equity**			
14	Current Liabilities			
15	Accounts payable (6)		$ 105,260	
16	Income taxes payable (7)		47,876	$ 153,136
17	Shareholders' Equity			
18	Common shares, 25,000 issued and outstanding (8)		350,000	
19	Retained earnings (9)		2,056,017	2,406,017
20	Total Liabilities and Shareholders' Equity			$2,559,153
21				
22	*Notes:*			
23	Beginning balances from Exhibit 6-4 are used as the starting point for most of the following computations:			
24	(1) $400,000 + $3,800,000 revenues − $3,784,200 receipts (Exhibit 6-5) = $415,800.			
25	(2) From schedule 6B, p. 261.			
26	(3) From beginning balance sheet (Exhibit 6-4).			
27	(4) $2,200,000 + $35,080 purchases = $2,235,080.			
28	(5) $685,000 + $220,000 (schedule 5, p. 260) plus incremental amortization of $1,754 Exhibit 6-7.			
29	(6) $150,000 + $995,000 (schedule 3B, p. 259) − $1,039,740 (Exhibit 6-5) = $105,260.			
30	(7) $50,000 + $191,612 current year (Exhibit 6-7) − $193,736 payment (Exhibit 6-5) = $47,876.			
31	(8) From beginning balance sheet (Exhibit 6-4).			
32	(9) $1,768,600 + $287,417 net income (Exhibit 6-7) = $2,056,017.			

3. The budgeted income statement is presented in Exhibit 6-7. It is merely the budgeted operating income statement in Exhibit 6-3 (p. 263) expanded to include interest expense and income taxes.

Amortization is reported as a period cost in Exhibit 6-7. With the added information available from the cash budget, there is an anticipated new purchase. You know this expected acquisition of a long-term asset must not be manufacturing plant or equipment. You know because the amortization is reported as a period cost and there has been no change in the total COGS reported.

For simplicity, the cash receipts and disbursements were given explicitly in this illustration of a cash budget. Frequently, there are lags between the items reported on the accrual basis of accounting in an income statement and their related cash receipts and disbursements. In the Halifax Engineering example, collections from customers are derived under two assumptions: (1) In any month, 10% of sales are

EXHIBIT 6-7
Budgeted Income Statement for Halifax Engineering for the Year Ended December 31, 2009

	A	B	C	D
1	Revenues	Schedule 1		$3,800,000
2	Costs:			
3	Cost of goods sold	Schedule 7		2,444,000
4	Gross margin			1,356,000
5	Period costs:			
6	R&D and product design costs	Schedule 8	$136,000	
7	Marketing costs	Schedule 8	200,000	
8	Distribution	Schedule 8	100,000	
9	Customer service	Schedule 8	60,000	
10	Administrative costs	Schedule 8	374,000	
11	Amortization on new purchase*		1,754	871,754
12	Operating income			484,246
13	Interest expense			(5,217)
14	Income before tax			479,029
15	Income tax at 40%			191,612
16	Net income			$ 287,417
17				
18	*Amortization on the new purchase was excluded from the initial estimate of manufacturing overhead and cost of goods sold. Incremental expense has been calculated by applying a tax rule, the half-year rule, assuming a useful life of 10 years and no residual value.			

cash sales and 90% of sales are on credit, and (2) half the total credit sales are collected in each of the two months subsequent to the sale, as illustrated for the third quarter in the following table:

	A	B	C	D	E	F	G
1							**Cash Collections**
2							**in 3rd Quarter**
3		**May**	**June**	**July**	**August**	**September**	**as a Whole**
4	Monthly revenue budget for Halifax (given)						
5	Credit sales, 90%	$307,800	$307,800	$280,800	$280,800	$280,800	
6	Cash sales, 10%	34,200	34,200	31,200	31,200	31,200	
7	Total revenues	$342,000	$342,000	$312,000	$312,000	$312,000	
8	Cash collections from:						
9	Cash sales this month			$ 31,200	$ 31,200	$ 31,200	
10	Credit sales last month			153,900*	140,400‡	140,400$	
11	Credit sales two months ago			153,900†	153,900*	140,400‡	
12	Total collection			$339,000	$325,500	$312,000	$976,500
13							
14	*0.50 × $307,800 (June sales) = $153,900.						
15	†0.50 × $307,800 (May sales) = $153,900.						
16	‡0.50 × $280,800 (July sales) = $140,400.						
17	$0.50 × $280,800 (August sales) = $140,400.						

Of course, such schedules of cash collections depend on credit terms, collection histories, and expected bad debts. Similar monthly schedules can be prepared for operating costs and their related cash disbursements.

MyAccountingLab

ASSESS YOUR MASTERY

To check your understanding of the material in Learning Objective ③, go to the *Mastery Questions* section at the end of this chapter and complete Learning Objective ③ questions 1 and 2.

SENSITIVITY, KAIZEN, AND ACTIVITY-BASED BUDGETS: THREE BUDGET STRATEGIES

④ Distinguish among sensitivity analysis, Kaizen budgeting, and activity-based budgeting

Exhibit 6-1 (p. 254) illustrated the interrelationships among strategic analysis, planning, and budgeting. The value of budgets to managers in their strategic analysis and planning is enhanced by conducting sensitivity analysis. Sensitivity analysis is a what-if technique that examines how a result will change if the original predicted data are not achieved or if an underlying assumption changes. A hand-held calculator is adequate to do the basic budget calculations. Commercial software packages such as Microsoft FRx, however, make important tests such as sensitivity analysis, continuous improvement planning, and activity-based budgeting accessible even to small owner-managed enterprises.

The financial planning model from which the master budgets and schedules were calculated for Halifax Engineering assumes the following:

♦ Direct materials and direct manufacturing labour costs vary proportionately with the quantities of Regular and Heavy-Duty parts produced.

♦ Variable manufacturing overhead costs vary with direct manufacturing labour-hours.

♦ Variable nonmanufacturing costs vary with revenue dollars.

♦ Target ending inventories remain unchanged.

SENSITIVITY ANALYSIS: A FORM OF STRATEGIC ANALYSIS

The budget and schedules are simply quantified reports of expectations; they are not actual achievements. Some assumptions are more critical to the company's success than others. Recall that one tool for strategic analysis requires identifying critical factors. Exhibit 6-8 presents the budgeted operating income for three changes in each of three critical factors for Halifax Engineering:

♦ **Scenario 1.** A 3% decrease in the selling price of the Regular part and a 3% decrease in the selling price of the Heavy-Duty part.

♦ **Scenario 2.** A 4% decrease in units sold of the Regular part and a 4% decrease in units sold of the Heavy-Duty part.

♦ **Scenario 3.** A 5% increase in the price per kilogram of 111 alloy and a 5% increase in the price per kilogram of 112 alloy.

Exhibit 6-8 indicates that, relative to the master budget, budgeted operating income decreases by 21% under scenario 1, by 10% under scenario 2, and by 8% under scenario 3. Managers can use this information to plan actions that they can take if faced with these scenarios, rather than scrambling in a crisis if such changes occur.

KAIZEN BUDGETING: IMPLEMENTING CONTINUOUS QUALITY IMPROVEMENT STRATEGIES

Chapter 1 noted how continuous improvement is one of the key issues facing management today. **Kaizen budgeting** implements a strategy of systematic elimination of waste in every business process.[4] A key assumption is that attention is focused on eliminating activities that cause cost but add no value. The improvements gained through Kaizen budgeting arise from many small changes made during the budget

---

[4]For an overview of Japanese management accounting, see R. Cooper, "Japanese Cost Management Practices," *CMA Magazine*, October 1994.

EXHIBIT 6-8
Effect of Changes in Budget Assumptions on Budgeted Income for Halifax Engineering

| | Key Assumptions | | | | | | | Budgeted Operating Income | |
| What-if Scenario | Units Sold | | Selling Price | | Direct Materials Cost* | | | | |
	Regular	Heavy-Duty	Regular	Heavy-Duty	111 Alloy	112 Alloy	Dollars	Change from Master Budget
Master budget	5,000	1,000	$600	$800	$7.00	$10.00	$486,000†	—
Scenario 1	5,000	1,000	582	776	7.00	10.00	386,250	20.52% decrease
Scenario 2	4,800	960	600	800	7.00	10.00	438,562	9.76% decrease
Scenario 3	5,000	1,000	600	800	7.35	10.50	448,380	7.74% decrease

*Per kilogram.
†From Exhibit 6-3, p. 254

period as a result of employees' suggestions. Kaizen is most closely identified with Toyota and the strategy of lean management.

Consider our Halifax Engineering example in Schedule 4 (p. 260). The 2009 budget assumes that it will take 4.0 and 6.0 manufacturing labour-hours respectively for each Regular and Heavy-Duty aircraft part. A Kaizen budgeting approach would incorporate continual reduction in these manufacturing labour-hour requirements during 2009. Assume Halifax budgets the following labour-hour amounts:

| | Budgeted Amounts (Labour-Hours) | |
	Regular	Heavy-Duty
January–March 2009	4.00	6.00
April–June 2009	3.90	5.85
July–September 2009	3.80	5.70
October–December 2009	3.70	5.55

Unless Halifax meets these continuous improvement goals, unfavourable variances will be reported. Note that, in the Halifax budget, the implications of these direct labour-hour reductions would extend to reductions in variable manufacturing overhead costs, given that direct manufacturing labour-hours is the driver of these costs.

ACTIVITY-BASED BUDGETING

Chapter 5 explained how activity-based cost (ABC) assignment systems can lead to improved decision making. ABC principles also extend to budgeting. **Activity-based budgeting (ABB)** is a strategy that focuses on the cost of activities necessary to produce and sell products and services. The example in Exhibit 6-2 (p. 254) assumed a budget was produced for business functions in the value-chain. Exhibit 6-9 illustrates how activity-based budgeting requires schedules and budgets for different activities rather than different business functions. You will recall from Chapter 5 that activities, especially those at the batch, product, and facilities levels, will cross boundaries among business functions and highlight interdependencies among them.

The key difference, as reported by Hansen, Otley, and Van der Stede,[5] between the two approaches is that in ABB, the Operating Loop must be completed first within the resource-budget constraints. Then the financial budget is produced. Both approaches begin with the forecast demand for outputs. Managers using ABB focus their efforts on matching forecast demand to the rates at which different *activities* are

[5]Stephen C. Hansen, David T. Otley, and Wim A. Van der Stede, "Recent Developments in Budgeting: An Overview and Research Perspective," *Journal of Management Accounting Research*, 15 (2003): 95–116.

consumed at specified activity levels in order to fulfill a single unit of demand. Recall that these are conversion activities and that cost drivers measure the resources consumed during conversion. In this approach, the measure of the quantities of cost drivers will be the basis for calculating the costs of activities. The second stage is the Financial Loop, the goal of which is to match various measures of rates of return (e.g., net profit, operating profit, return on assets) with the demanded rate of return.

Activity-based budgeting also follows a logic:

◆ Determine the budgeted costs of performing each unit of activity for each activity area.

◆ Determine the demand for each individual activity at the product level based on, for example, budgeted new-product R&D, production, marketing, and so on. Budgets and schedules are also needed for existing products. Adding or dropping a product will change both the activity and the cost pool.

◆ Calculate the costs of performing each activity.

◆ Describe the budget as costs of performing various activities (rather than budgeted costs of functional or conventional value-chain spending categories).

Notice in Exhibit 6-9 that there are three opportunities to make four operating adjustments (demand, resource capacity, and both resource and activity consumption

EXHIBIT 6-9
The Activity-Based Budgeting Approach

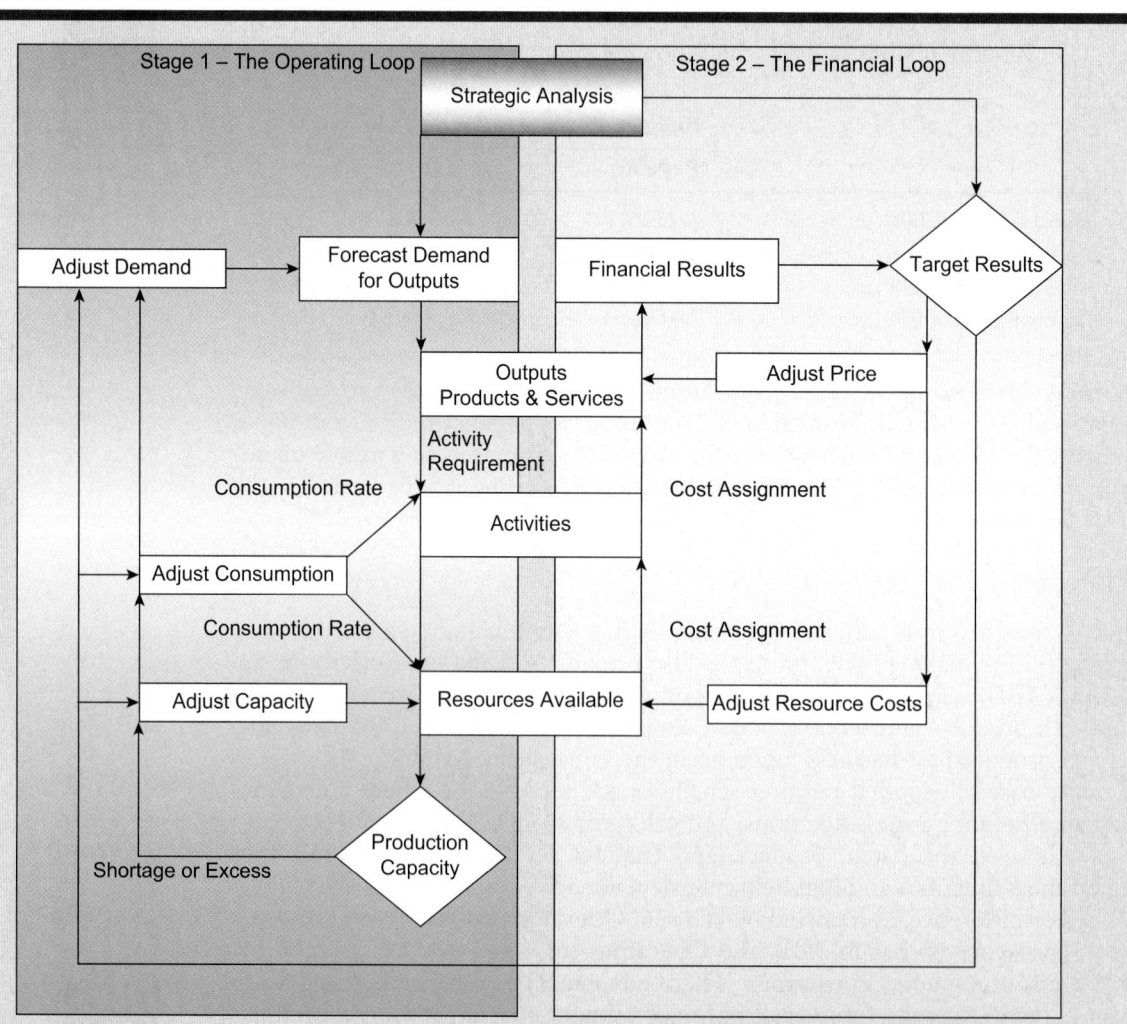

Source: Adapted from Stephen C. Hansen, David T. Otley, and Wim A. Van der Stede, "Recent Developments in Budgeting: An Overview and Research Perspective," *Journal of Management Accounting Research*, 15 (2003): 100.

rates). There are two opportunities to make financial adjustments in both the price of outputs and the costs of inputs. As Hansen and his colleagues noted, this approach highlights imbalances among demand for and supplies of resources at the unit, batch, product (or service), and facilities levels that are not readily apparent from the traditional approach. As with the ABC costing approach, ABB ensures that managers will not focus on individual business functions but rather on the interdependencies among the functions.

Consider activity-based budgeting for the R&D/product design parts of the value chain at Bradford Aerospace. Four activity areas and their cost drivers have been identified. The budgeted 2009 rates for the costs in each activity area are as follows:

Activity	Cost Driver/Budgeted Cost Rate
Computer-aided design (CAD)—using computer software to design aircraft parts	CAD hours, $80 per hour
Manual design—manually designing aircraft parts	Manual design hours, $50 per hour
Prototype development—building actual versions of aircraft parts	Prototyping hours, $60 per hour
Testing—examining how new aircraft parts "perform" in different operating conditions	Testing hours, $40 per hour
Procurement—purchasing supplies and component parts	Purchase orders, $25 per purchase order

Exhibit 6-10 presents the activity-based budget for January to December 2009. Bradford budgets usage of the cost driver in each activity area based on budgeted production and new-product development. This budgeted usage of the cost driver for each activity is multiplied by the respective budgeted costs rates per activity to obtain the budgeted activity costs. The budgeted total costs for R&D/product design is the sum of the budgeted costs of the individual activities in that part of the value chain.

The activity-based budget in Exhibit 6-10 is for one part of Bradford's value chain. In many cases, the same activity will appear in more than one part of the value chain. For example, procurement activities such as purchase ordering and supplier payment are found in most areas of the value chain. Companies using activity-based budgeting may choose to present their budgets at either the individual value-chain level or at some more basic activity level, such as procurement by combining budgeted procurement costs from different parts of the value chain.

A survey of U.K. managers reported the following ranking of the benefits from activity-based budgeting: (1) ability to set more realistic budgets, (2) better identification of resource needs, (3) linking of costs to outputs, (4) clearer linking of costs with staff responsibilities, and (5) identification of budgetary slack[6] (see the Governance Issues box on p. 276).

EXHIBIT 6-10
Activity-Based Budget for R&D/Product Design Costs of Bradford Aerospace: January to December 2009

Activity Area	Budgeted Usage of Driver	Budgeted Rate per Cost Driver	Budgeted Activity Costs
Computer-aided design	200 hours	$80	$16,000
Manual design	70 hours	50	3,500
Prototype development	80 hours	60	4,800
Testing	280 hours	40	11,200
Procurement	120 purchase orders	25	3,000
Total			$38,500

[6]J. Innes and F. Mitchell, "A Survey of Activity-Based Costing in the U.K.'s Largest Companies," *Management Accounting Research*, 6: 137–53.

RESPONSIBILITY VERSUS CONTROLLABILITY

5 Contrast responsibility against controllability

ORGANIZATIONAL STRUCTURE AND RESPONSIBILITY

Organizational structure is the arrangement of centres of responsibility within an entity. A company such as Petro-Canada may be organized primarily by business function: exploration, refining, and marketing. Another company such as Procter & Gamble, a household-products giant, may be organized by product or brand line. The managers of the individual divisions (toothpaste, soap, and so on) would each have decision-making authority concerning all the business functions (manufacturing, marketing, etc.) within that division.

Managers and executives are assigned responsibility and held accountable for achieving specific financial and nonfinancial performance targets. A **responsibility centre** is a part, segment, or sub-unit of an organization whose manager is accountable for a specified set of activities. The higher the manager's level, the broader the responsibility centre he or she manages and, generally, the larger the number of subordinates who report to him or her. **Responsibility accounting** is a system that measures the plans (by budgets) and actions (by actual results) of each responsibility centre. The complexity of the processes in a company often requires decentralizing both authority and responsibility. Four major types of responsibility centres are:

1. **Cost centre.** Manager accountable for costs only, not revenue lost or gained. Some managers may have authority over subordinate managers responsible for the outcomes of quantity, price, and scheduling decisions; others may not. The scope of authority, and therefore decentralization, will depend on the organizational structure.

2. **Revenue centre.** Manager accountable for revenues only, not costs incurred to generate the revenues. Some managers of revenue centres may have authority over subordinate managers responsible for the outcomes of quantity and unit price decisions; others may not.

3. **Profit centre.** Manager accountable for revenues and costs, and has some authority over others who decide upon key factors affecting both revenue and cost. A profit-centre manager can coordinate among those responsible for either costs or revenue; however, this increases centralization.

4. **Investment centre.** Manager accountable for investments, revenues, and costs.

The maintenance department of a Delta hotel is a cost centre if the maintenance manager is responsible only for costs; the budget would also emphasize costs. The sales department of the hotel is a revenue centre if the sales manager is responsible only for revenues, and the budget would emphasize revenues. The hotel manager might be in charge of a profit centre if the hotel manager is accountable for both revenues and costs, and the budget would then emphasize both. The regional manager responsible for investments in new hotel projects, and for revenues and costs could be in charge of an investment centre; revenues, costs, and the investment base would be emphasized in the budget for this manager.

Responsibility accounting affects behaviour. Consider the following incident:

The Sales Department requests a rush production run. The plant scheduler argues that it will disrupt his production and will cost a substantial, though not clearly determined, amount of money. The answer coming from sales is, "Do you want to take the responsibility of losing the X Company as a customer?" Of course, the production scheduler does not want to take such a responsibility and gives up, but not before a heavy exchange of arguments and the accumulation of a substantial backlog of ill feeling.

The controller proposes an innovative solution. He analyzes the payroll in the Assembly Department to determine the costs involved in getting out rush orders. This information eliminates the cause for argument. Henceforth, any rush order is accepted by the production scheduler, "no questions asked." The extra costs are duly recorded and charged to the Sales Department.

As a result, the tension created by rush orders disappears, and, somehow, the number of rush orders requested by the Sales Department is progressively reduced to an insignificant level.[7]

Responsibility accounting assigns accountability to:

◆ the individual who has the best knowledge about why the costs arose
◆ the individual undertaking the activity that caused the costs.

In this incident, the cause was the sales activity, and the resulting costs were charged to the sales department. If rush orders occur regularly, the sales department might have a budget for such costs, and the department's actual performance would then be compared against the budget.

FEEDBACK

Responsibility accounting applied to budgets provides feedback to top management about the performance relative to the budget of different responsibility-centre managers.

Differences between actual results and budgeted amounts—also called variances—if properly used, can be helpful in three ways:

1. *Early warning.* Variances alert managers early to events neither easily nor immediately evident. Managers can then take corrective actions or exploit the available opportunities. For example, is a small decline in sales this period an indication of an even steeper decline to follow later in the year or an opportunity to design a higher value-added and more competitive product?

2. *Performance evaluation.* Variances inform managers about how well the company has performed in implementing its strategies. Were materials and labour used efficiently? Was R&D spending increased as planned? Did product warranty costs decrease as planned?

3. *Evaluating strategy.* Variances sometimes signal to managers that their strategies are ineffective. For example, a company seeking to compete by reducing cost and improving quality may find that it is achieving these goals but with little effect on sales and profits. Top management may then want to reevaluate the strategy.

DEFINITION OF CONTROLLABILITY

Controllability is the degree of authority that a specific manager has over costs, revenues, or other items in question. A **controllable cost** is any cost that is primarily subject to the authorization of a specific manager of a specific responsibility centre for a specific time span. A responsibility accounting system could either exclude all uncontrollable costs from a manager's performance report or segregate such costs from the controllable costs.

Recall the separation of variable from fixed costs of manufacturing overhead. Fixed costs comprised items such as insurance, taxes, lease costs or amortization, and management salaries. These costs are rarely controllable. Insurance companies set premiums with executives of corporations rather than plant managers; and cities, provinces, and countries set tax policies independent of corporations (not to mention individuals). While some negotiation of insurance premiums may be possible year to

[7]R. Villers, "Control and Freedom in a Decentralized Company," *Harvard Business Review*, 32.2: 95.

year, governments do not negotiate tax increases. Other examples include foreign currency exchange rates, commodity prices, and interest rates. All are important factors over which individual companies have no control.

Within a corporation, for example, a machining supervisor's performance report might be confined to quantities (not costs) of direct materials, direct manufacturing labour, power, and supplies. Unless the machining supervisor has the authority to set the price at which materials are procured, this approach is fair to the supervisor. Assume the purchasing manager has the authority to decide at what price materials will be purchased. The problem of cost control arises because the supervisor may order a lower quantity than required, or incur more than the expected level of waste in a time period. To meet customer demand, the supervisor will request a rush order. The purchasing manager has no authority to refuse and knows the cost of a rush order is higher than orders with a normal delivery time. Who is responsible for any cost overrun: the supervisor who needs the materials or the purchasing manager who negotiates prices with suppliers?

In practice, controllability is difficult to pinpoint:

1. Few costs are clearly under the sole influence of one manager. For example, costs of direct materials may be influenced by a purchasing manager, but such costs also depend on market conditions beyond the manager's control. Quantities used may be influenced by a production manager, but quantities used also depend on the quality of materials purchased. Moreover, managers often work in teams. How can individual responsibility be evaluated in a team decision?

2. With a long enough time span, all costs will come under somebody's control. However, most performance reports focus on periods of a year or less. A current manager may have inherited problems and inefficiencies from his or her predecessor. For example, current managers may have to work under undesirable

Management Accounting: The Heart of the Budgeting Process

An accurate budget is essential to a company's success. But when it comes time to discuss the budget, some managers approach the negotiation process with an eye toward protecting their own interests. If managers make their budgets—or, better, improve on them—financial rewards will come their way. So managers may intentionally ask for budget amounts that will help them achieve their targets but that will not maximize the company's overall profits. Addressing this issue of budgetary slack may be the most difficult role for management accountants because they must be able to deal with conflict and argue persuasively for more realistic targets.

In addition to simplifying the budgeting process, management accountants work to ensure that managers' ideas and their resulting budgets are realistic. Management accountants must challenge faulty assumptions and incorrect logic ("let's assume a 10% increase in sales even though the overall market for the product is expected to decline") and probe for alternative approaches ("a 5% increase in sales is possible but this will require more resources to be devoted to marketing").

The CMA code of ethics states:

(a) A Member will act at all times with: (i) responsibility for and fidelity to public needs; (ii) fairness and loyalty to such Member's associates, clients and employers; and (iii) competence through devotion to high ideals of personal honour and professional integrity. (b) A Member will: (i) maintain at all times independence of thought and action . . .

It is not only sensible to persuade managers to act in the best interests of the organization but also required by the professional code of ethics. Members of the CMA are expected to fulfil their fiduciary duty to the public, act with fairness and loyalty towards employers, and act independently.

Sources: L. Gray, "Why Budgeting Kills Your Company," *Working Knowledge*, Harvard Business School, August 11, 2003; The Society of Management Accountants of Ontario, "Code of Ethics," www.cma-ontario.org/index.cfm/ci_id/7409/la_id/1.htm, accessed November 12, 2008.

contracts with suppliers or labour unions that were negotiated by their predecessors. How can we separate what the current manager actually controls from the results of decisions made by others? Exactly what is the current manager accountable for? Answers to such questions may not be clear-cut.

Senior managers differ in how they embrace the controllability notion when evaluating those reporting to them. For example, a newly appointed president took his management team on a cruise and commented, "I expect everybody to meet their budget targets no matter what happens, and those who don't should stand a little closer to the railing." Other presidents believe that a more risk-sharing approach with managers is preferable, where noncontrollable factors are taken into account when making judgments about the performance of managers who miss their budgets.

EMPHASIS ON INFORMATION AND BEHAVIOUR

Responsibility accounting focuses on information and knowledge, not control. To succeed, however, other incentive systems must be aligned to the goal of free exchange of accurate information. The key question is: Who is the best informed? To put it another way: Who is the person that can tell us the most about the specific item in question, regardless of that person's ability to exert personal control? For instance, purchasing managers may be held accountable for total purchase costs, not because of their ability to affect market prices, but because of their ability to predict uncontrollable prices and explain uncontrollable price changes. Similarly, managers at a Tim Hortons store may be held responsible for the operating income of their units, even though they do not fully control selling prices or the costs for many food items, and have minimal flexibility as to items to sell or their ingredients. These unit managers are in the best position to explain variances between their actual operating income and their budgeted operating income.

Performance reports for responsibility centres may also include uncontrollable items because this approach could change behaviour in the directions top management desires. For example, some companies have changed the accountability of a cost centre to a profit centre to motivate a change in managers' decisions and actions. A cost centre manager may emphasize production efficiency and deemphasize the pleas of sales personnel for faster service and rush orders. In a profit centre, the manager is responsible for both costs and revenues. Although the manager still has no control over sales personnel, the manager will now more likely weigh the impact of his or her decisions on costs and revenues, rather than solely on costs.

HUMAN ASPECTS OF BUDGETING

Why did we cover three major topics, master budgets, cash budgets, and responsibility accounting, in the same chapter? Primarily to emphasize that human factors are crucial parts of budgeting. Too often, students study budgeting as though it were a mechanical tool.

The budgeting techniques themselves are free of emotion; however, their administration requires education, persuasion, and intelligent interpretation. To be effective, budgeting requires "honest" communication about the business from subordinates and lower-level managers to their bosses. But subordinates may try to build in budgetary slack to hedge against unexpected adverse circumstances. The budgetary slack could mislead top management about the true profit potential of the company.

What can top management do to obtain accurate budget forecasts from lower-level managers? There are several options.

To explain one approach, let's consider the plant manager of a beverage bottler who is suspected by top management of understating the productivity potential of the bottling lines in his forecasts for the coming year. His presumed motivation is to increase the likelihood of meeting next year's production bonus targets. Suppose top management could purchase a consulting firm's study that reports productivity levels—such as the number of bottles filled per hour—at a number of comparable plants owned by other bottling companies. This report shows that their own plant manager's productivity forecasts are well below actual productivity levels being achieved at other comparable plants.

Top management could share this independent information source with their plant manager and ask him to explain why his productivity differs from that at other comparable plants. They could also base part of the plant manager's compensation on his plant's productivity relative to other "benchmark" plants rather than on the forecasts he provided. Using external benchmark performance measures reduces a manager's ability to set budget levels that are easy to achieve.[8]

Another approach to reducing budgetary slack is for managers to involve themselves regularly in understanding what their subordinates are doing. Such involvement should not result in managers dictating the decisions and actions of subordinates. Rather, a manager's involvement should take the form of providing support, challenging in a motivational way the assumptions subordinates make, and enhancing mutual learning about the operations. Regular interaction with subordinates allows managers to become knowledgeable about the operations and diminishes the ability of subordinates to create slack in their budgets.

Part of top management's responsibility is to improve organization commitment to a set of core values and norms. The values and norms describe what constitutes acceptable and unacceptable behaviour. Companies such as General Electric and Johnson & Johnson have developed values and a culture that discourage budgetary slack.

Some companies, such as IBM and Kodak, have designed innovative performance-evaluation measures that reward managers based on the subsequent accuracy of the forecasts used in preparing budgets. For example, the *higher and more accurate* the budgeted profit forecasts of division managers, the higher their incentive bonuses.

Many of the best-performing companies set "stretch" or "challenge" targets. *Stretch targets* are actually overestimates of expected performance, intended to motivate employees to exert effort and attain better performance.

Many managers regard budgets negatively. To them, the word *budget* is about as popular as, say, *downsizing*, *layoff*, or *strike*. Top managers must convince their subordinates that the budget is a tool designed to help them set and reach goals. But budgets are not remedies for weak management talent, faulty organization, or a poor accounting system.

The management style of executives is a factor in how budgets are perceived in companies. Some CEOs argue that "numbers always tell the story." An executive once noted that "you can miss your plan once, but you wouldn't want to miss it twice." Other CEOs believe "too much focus on making the numbers in a budget" can lead to poor decision making.

BUDGETING: A PROCESS IN TRANSITION

Many areas of management accounting are subject to ongoing debate. Budgeting is no exception. Advocates of new proposals invariably include criticisms of so-called "traditional budgeting." These criticisms are often exaggerations of "current worst practice." Exhibit 6-11 summarizes six proposals designed to improve traditional budgeting systems. Few of the negative features cited in the left-hand column are new; they have long been singled out for criticism. Indeed, earlier sections of this chapter have mentioned the importance of avoiding many of these problems. Nonetheless, major changes that address these problems are currently being examined by managers.

MyAccountingLab

[8]For an excellent discussion of these issues, see Chapter 14 ("Formal Models in Budgeting and Incentive Contracts") of R. S. Kaplan and A. A. Atkinson, *Advanced Management Accounting*, 3rd ed. (Upper Saddle River, NJ: Prentice Hall, 1998).

Criticism of Traditional Budgeting	Proposal for Change
Excessive reliance on extrapolating past trends	Link budgeting explicitly to strategy.
Making across-the-board fixed percentage cuts when early iterations of a budget provide "unacceptable results"	Use activity-based budgeting to identify areas for cost reduction.
Examining individual functional areas as if they are independent (so-called silos, to use a farming analogy)	Explicitly adopt a cross-functional approach where interdependencies across business function areas of the value chain are recognized.
Myopically overemphasizing a fixed time horizon such as a year. Viewing annual cost targets as a key task to be accomplished	Tailor the budget cycle to the purpose of budgeting. Events beyond current period are recognized as important when evaluating current actions. Value creation is given paramount importance.
Being preoccupied with financial aspects of events in the budget period	Balance financial aspects with nonfinancial (such as quality and time) aspects.
Not using budgets to evaluate performance until end of budget period	Signal to all employees the need for continuous improvement of performance (such as revenue enhancement and cost reduction) within the budget period.

Source: Adapted from "*Advanced Budgeting Study Group Report* for CAM-I," *Management Accounting* (U.K.).

PULLING IT ALL TOGETHER—PROBLEM FOR SELF-STUDY

PROBLEM

Consider the Halifax Engineering example described in this chapter. Suppose Halifax Engineering managers conducted sensitivity analyses not only on the cash budget (see Exhibit 6-8, p. 271) but also on the effect of a 10% price increase in material 112 alloy from $10 to $11; a 12% increase in the variable supplies cost; a 22% increase in power costs to account for an unexpected jump in oil prices; and a corresponding 22% increase in distribution costs to account for ground and air transportation cost increases in concert with an oil-price increase.

REQUIRED

1. What are the benefits of budgeting for these specific changes now?　①
2. Before preparing a budgeted income statement, identify the supporting budget schedules that will *not* change as a result of this sensitivity analysis.　②
3. Prepare the budgeted operating income statement, including all necessary supporting schedules.　②
4. Discuss the results. Focus on any important changes that can be planned should the increases described above be realized in the coming year.　④
5. Discuss how responsibility and controllability will affect Halifax Engineering's response to the events noted in the sensitivity analysis.　⑤

SOLUTION

1. In the short term, the budget constraints for Halifax have changed. Only by recalculating the affected schedules can the company's managers understand what remedies may be available to reduce the effects of these cost increases. The team can agree in advance what responses may be made to sustain operating profits. The managers are already anticipating how to protect the company from external threats over which the company itself has no control.

   In the long run, the managers can assess if their current strategy will respond to these changes in the critical success factors of their environment. If the management team believes that key input prices can increase by such a large percentage, one strategic response may be to change how its products are distributed. In the long run, existing transportation contracts can be amended to share the risk of fuel price increases and managers can undertake hedging strategies. Halifax may also be able to renegotiate contracts with its purchasers to place the burden of transportation costs on them.

2. The revenue, production, and direct manufacturing labour budgets (Schedules 1, 2, and 4, p. 257, 258, and 260) will not change as a result of this sensitivity analysis.

3. The change in the cost of 112 alloy is shown in Schedule 3A. In total, the costs of direct materials to be used has increased from $1,028,000 to $1,066,000.

	A	B	C	D	E
1	**Schedule 3A: Direct Materials Usage Budget in Kilograms and Dollars**				
2	**For the Year Ended December 31, 2009**				
3		**Materials**			
4		**111 Alloy**	**112 Alloy**	**Total**	
5	Direct materials to be used in production of Regular parts (6,000 units) × 12 and 6 kilograms	72,000	36,000		see Schedule 2
6	Direct materials to be used in production of Heavy-Duty (1,000 units) × 12 and 8 kilograms	12,000	8,000		see Schedule 2
7	Total direct materials to be used (in kilograms)	84,000	44,000		
8	Direct materials to be used from beginning inventory (assume FIFO cost flow)	7,000	6,000		
9	Multiply by: Cost per kilogram of beginning inventory	$ 7	$ 10		
10	Cost of direct materials to be used from beginning inventory	$ 49,000	$ 60,000	$ 109,000	(a)
11	Direct materials to be used from purchases (84,000 − 7,000; 44,000 − 6,000)	77,000	38,000		
12	Multiply by: Cost per kilogram of purchased materials	$ 7	$ 11		
13	Cost of direct materials to be used from purchases	$539,000	$418,000	$ 957,000	(b)
14	Total costs of direct materials to be used (a) + (b)	$588,000	$478,000	$1,066,000	

Changes to Schedule 3B, below, reflect the increase in cost of 112 alloy. The direct materials purchase cost for this alloy has increased from $400,000 to $440,000. Overall, the total direct materials purchase cost has also increased $40,000.

	A	B	C	D
1	**Schedule 3B: Direct Materials Usage Budget in Kilograms and Dollars**			
2	**For the Year Ended December 31, 2009**			
3		**Materials**		
4		**111 Alloy**	**112 Alloy**	**Total**
5	Direct materials to be used in production (in kilograms)	84,000	44,000	
6	Add: Target ending direct materials inventory	8,000	2,000	
7	Total requirements (in kilograms)	92,000	46,000	
8	Deduct: Beginning direct materials inventory	(7,000)	(6,000)	
9	Direct materials to be purchased (in kilograms)	85,000	40,000	
10	Multiply by: Cost per kilogram of purchased materials	$ 7	$ 11	
11	Total direct materials purchase costs	$595,000	$440,000	$1,035,000

In Schedule 5, the variable manufacturing overhead supplies has increased from $90,000 to $100,800 and the total manufacturing overhead budget has also increased $37,200 to $1,237,200:

	A	B	C	D
1	**Schedule 5: Manufacturing Overhead Budget**			
2	**For the Year Ended December 31, 2009**			
3		**At Budgeted Level of 30,000 Direct**		
4		**Manufacturing Labour-Hours**		
5	Variable manufacturing overhead costs:			
6	Supplies	$100,800		
7	Indirect manufacturing labour	210,000		
8	Direct and indirect manufacturing labour fringe costs	300,000		
9	Power	146,400		
10	Maintenance	60,000	$ 817,200	
11	Fixed:			
12	Amortization	220,000		
13	Property taxes	50,000		
14	Property insurance	10,000		
15	Supervision	100,000		
16	Power	22,000		
17	Maintenance	18,000	420,000	
18	Total		$1,237,200	
19				
20	NOTE: The annual amortization expense becomes part of Cost of Goods Sold (Schedule 7)			

The change in Schedule 6A reflects both the change in direct materials and in variable manufacturing overhead:

	A	B	C	D	E	F
1	**Schedule 6A: Computation of Unit Costs of Manufacturing**					
2				**Product**		
3				**Regular**		**Heavy-Duty**
4		**Cost per Unit**				
5		**of Input***	**Inputs***	**Amount**	**Inputs***	**Amount**
6	Material 111 alloy	$ 7	12	$ 84	12	$ 84
7	Material 112 alloy	$11	6	66	8	88
8	Direct manufacturing labour	$20†	4	80	6	120
9	Manufacturing overhead	$41.24‡	4	165	6	247
10	Total			$395		$539
11						
12	*In kilograms or hours					
13	†Data are from p. 260.					
14	‡Direct manufacturing labour-hours is the sole allocation base for manufacturing overhead (both variable and fixed). The budgeted manufacturing overhead rate per direct manufacturing labour-hour is $41.24 ($1,237,200 ÷ 30,000 budgeted direct manufacturing labour-hours).					

The change in Schedule 6B also reflects the change in direct materials on the value of total ending inventory:

	A	B	C	D	E
1	**Schedule 6B: Ending Inventory Budget**				
2	**For the Year Ended December 31, 2009**				
3			**Cost per**		
4		**Kilograms**	**Kilogram**		**Total**
5	Direct materials				
6	111 alloy	8,000*	$ 7	$ 56,000	
7	112 alloy	2,000*	$11	22,000	$ 78,000

8			**Cost per**		
9		**Units**	**Unit**		
10	Finished goods				
11	Regular	1,100[†]	$395	$434,500	
12	Heavy-Duty	50[†]	$539	26,950	$461,450
13	Total Ending Inventory				$539,450
14					
15	*Data are from pp. 256 and 279.				
16	[†]Data are from p. 256.				

The changes to inventoriable costs result in the following Cost of Goods Sold Budget, Schedule 7:

	A	B	C	D
1	**Schedule 7: Cost of Goods Sold Budget**			
2	**For the Year Ended December 31, 2009**			
3		**From Schedule**		**Total**
4	Beginning finished goods inventory, January 1, 2009	Given*		$ 64,600
5	Direct materials used	3A	$1,066,000	
6	Direct manufacturing labour	4	600,000	
7	Manufacturing overhead	5	1,237,200	
8	Cost of goods manufactured			2,903,200
9	Cost of goods available for sale			2,967,800
10	Deduct: Ending finished goods inventory			
11	December 31, 2009	6B		(461,450)
12	Cost of goods sold			$2,506,350
13				
14	NOTE: The annual amortization expense has been included in manufacturing overhead and therefore is part of Cost of goods sold.			
15	*Given in the description of basic data and requirements (Regular $38,400, Heavy-Duty $26,200) on p. 256.			

The change to distribution costs is reflected in the nonproduction costs budget, Schedule 8:

	A	B	C	D	E
1	**Schedule 8: Other (Nonproduction) Costs Budget**				
2	**For the Year Ended December 31, 2009**				
3					
4	Variable costs:				
5	R&D/product design	$ 76,000			
6	Marketing	133,000			
7	Distribution	81,130			
8	Customer service	47,500			
9	Administrative	152,000	$489,630*		
10	Fixed costs:				
11	R&D/product design	60,000			
12	Marketing	67,000			
13	Distribution	33,500			
14	Customer service	12,500			
15	Administrative	222,000	395,000		
16	Total costs		$884,630		
17					
18	*Total variable cost for Schedule 8 is $0.129 per revenue dollar or $489,630 ÷ $3,800,000.				

The result of these changes on operating income for Halifax Engineering is:

	A	B	C	D
1	**Budgeted Income Statement for Halifax Engineering**			
2	**For the Year Ended December 31, 2009**			
3	Revenues	Schedule 1		$3,800,000
4	Costs:			
5	Cost of goods sold	Schedule 7		2,506,350
6	Gross margin			1,293,650
7	Operating (period) costs:			
8	R&D/product design costs	Schedule 8	$136,000	
9	Marketing costs	Schedule 8	200,000	
10	Distribution costs	Schedule 8	114,630	
11	Customer service costs	Schedule 8	60,000	
12	Administrative costs	Schedule 8	374,000	884,630
13	Operating income			$ 409,020
14				
15	NOTE: Unlike financial accounting, this budgeted income statement contains the noncash annual amortization expense in Cost of goods sold (see Schedule 5 and Schedule 7).			

4. The operating margin percentage without the sensitivity was $486,000 ÷ $3,800,000 = 12.79%. With the sensitivity analysis the operating margin percentage is $409,020 ÷ $3,800,000 = 10.76%. A close comparison of the Ending Inventory Budget and the Cost of Goods Sold Budget provides the answer. The increase in direct materials, while only $1 per kilogram, increases the value of ending inventory from $448,600 to $461,450. This is a deduction from the cost of goods available for sale resulting in a larger cost of goods sold. Revenue has remained constant, therefore the gross margin decreases from $1,356,000 to $1,293,650.

The results illustrate the importance of sensitivity analysis. In the immediate one-year period, the effect is positive, however, the following year will present problems. All other things equal, and without further projected cost increases, Halifax must recover the additional costs in ending inventory of $191,400; otherwise its operating profit will decline in the second year and years following. The sensitivity analysis directs the managers to look beyond the short-term.

5. Halifax changed its assumptions about the purchase price of direct materials. If an ongoing increase in prices is forecast and if Halifax has no special bargaining power with suppliers, it has no control over price. Those in the purchasing function will have the greatest knowledge about current and likely future prices and sources of supply. In the short term, they can advise Halifax of the availability of long-term contracts and the likelihood of new suppliers entering the market for alloy 112.

The production engineers, however, will have the greatest knowledge about the current performance and safety specifications that require the use of alloy 112. The engineers can advise Halifax about the likelihood of switching to a less expensive direct material input, or of redesigning the part to use less of this alloy without jeopardizing performance and safety.

Those in the marketing function will have the greatest knowledge about the needs of customers such as Boeing. The engineering specifications in a contract require Boeing to take extreme care prior to making changes because the company sells its finished product, aircraft, to purchasers. Before Boeing can change its parts specification it must receive authorization not only from the Boeing aeronautical engineers but also from its customers. Finally, the federal government inspects all aircraft, which must conform in all respects to safety laws. The specification change process can easily take over a year to complete.

Halifax must communicate across the functions in the value chain to obtain the best advice from marketing, engineering, and purchasing. The responsibility for developing a plan to respond to the potential increase in direct materials price is spread throughout the company. The sensitivity analysis should direct Halifax to begin the consultation process and involve each responsibility centre in assessing the best strategic response.

The other changes in the sensitivity analysis to variable supplies and fuel costs, which affect costs of power and distribution, will also require input from several responsibility centres.

DECISION POINTS

The following decision guidelines use a question-and-answer format to summarize the chapter's main points. Each decision presents a key question. The guideline is the answer to that question.

DECISIONS	GUIDELINES
1. What are the long-term and short-term benefits of budgets?	Budgets look forward to the future to anticipate financial and nonfinancial achievements of the company. In the long term, an annual budget cycle is integral to strategic analysis—the evaluation of how well the company fits with its environment. In the short term, budgets provide financial targets and a framework for operating performance measurement and control.
2. Why is a master budget useful?	A master budget summarizes all the projections (plans) of the managers in different areas of the company. It presents in a familiar and standardized financial-statement format how the financial future of a company will arise, quarter by quarter, month by month, or even week by week. The familiar format coordinates and communicates where the company is, where it wants to go, and how it will get there. The output from a master budget is an operating budget.
3. What is a cash budget and why is it useful?	A cash budget summarizes the timing and amount of cash inflows and outflows for a company over a specified time period. The cash budget depends on the facts summarized in the operating budget. One result of the cash budget is anticipated interest expense, which enables companies to produce a pro forma or budgeted income statement. Input into the cash budget includes any capacity expansion requiring the acquisition of long-term assets reported in the capital budget. Together, these budgets lead to the pro forma or budgeted balance sheet and cash flow statement.
4. How do the strategies of sensitivity analysis, Kaizen budgeting, and activity-based budgeting differ?	Sensitivity analysis is a way to alter the assumptions of the master budget. This analysis permits managers to establish plans in advance of possible adverse events. Kaizen budgeting is incremental cost reduction through elimination of waste in various business processes. Activity-based budgeting is the reduction of non–value-added activities that fail to contribute to the customers' value proposition. They are all long-term strategies to reduce costs.
5. How does responsibility differ from controllability?	Responsibility refers to holding accountable for achievement of performance targets those people who know best how to do so. The complexity of most organizations means that one person cannot be responsible for every decision without slowing decision making to a halt. It is a decentralized type of budgeting that should converge with both incentives and compensation and organizational structure. Individuals responsible for achievement of organizational targets rarely control all the factors contributing towards that achievement. Controllability means the decisions about different key factors affecting cost, revenue, investment, or some combination of the three are within an individual's control, even though the individual may not be responsible for them.

The chapter contains definitions of the following important terms:

activity-based budgeting (ABB) (p. 271) cost centre (p. 274) profit centre (p. 274)
budget (p. 248) financial budget (p. 255) responsibility accounting (p. 274)
budget constraint (p. 248) investment centre (p. 274) responsibility centre (p. 274)
budgetary slack (p. 258) Kaizen budgeting (p. 270) revenue centre (p. 274)
budgeting cycle (p. 248) master budget (p. 248) rolling budget (p. 253)
cash budget (p. 264) operating budget (p. 254) self-liquidating cycle (p. 267)
cash cycle (p. 267) operating cycle (p. 267) strategic analysis (p. 249)
controllability (p. 275) organizational structure (p. 274) working capital cycle (p. 267)
controllable cost (p. 275) padding (p. 258)

MASTERY QUESTIONS

The Mastery Questions are rated by proficiency level: elementary, intermediate, and advanced. The solutions appear in the Mastery Question Solutions section of MyAccountingLab.

LEARNING OBJECTIVE 1

1. **Short-term, long-term benefits—Elementary.** When a company authorizes its operating budget, the managers and executives have made a commitment to achieve specific objectives outlined in the various schedules. How does the process of building a master budget hold executives and managers accountable to achieving these objectives?

2. **Short-term, long-term benefits—Intermediate.** The master budget output is an operating budget, which is a short-term one-year plan. What other information is required to provide long-term benefits to the company?

3. **Short-term, long-term benefits; traditional budgeting and its critics—Advanced.** Critics of traditional budgeting often make their points in a colourful way. Consider the following comments by the CEO of a multinational company with revenues of more than $36 billion and more than 200,000 employees:

> We set "stretch" goals for our people. Stretch means that we try for huge gains while having no idea how to get there—but our people figure out ways to get there. To reach these stretch goals, it takes an atmosphere where a goal doesn't become part of the old-fashioned budget. The budget is the bane of the corporate world. It never should have existed. A budget is this: If you make it, you generally get a pat on the back and a few bucks. If you miss it, you get a stick in the eye—or worse.
>
> Making a budget is an exercise in minimization. You're always trying to get the lowest out of people, because everyone is negotiating to get a lower number.
>
> If I worked for you, you would come charging into the boardroom and say, "I need four! We'd haggle all day, me making presentations, with 50 charts, saying the right number is two. In the end we'd settle on three. We'd go home and tell our families that we had a helluva day at the office. And what did we do? We ended up minimizing our activity. We weren't dreaming, reaching. I was trying to get the lowest budget number I could sell you. It's all backward.

REQUIRED
1. Do you agree that "The budget is the bane of the corporate world. It never should have existed"? Explain.
2. Assume you are the CEO of a television station. Your marketing manager shows you the preceding extract and suggests that you "dispense with the annual budget ritual." How would you respond?

LEARNING OBJECTIVE 2

1. Prepare a master operating budget; budget schedules for manufacturer—Intermediate.
Sierra Furniture is an elite desk manufacturer. It manufactures two products:

◆ Executive desks: 0.91 m × 1.5 m oak desks = 1.365 m²
◆ Chairperson desks: 1.8 m × 1.2 m red oak desks = 2.16 m²

The budgeted direct-cost inputs for each product in 2009 are as follows:

	Executive Line	Chairperson Line
Direct materials:		
Oak top	1.5 square metres	—
Red oak top	—	2.3 square metres
Oak legs	4 legs	—
Red oak legs	—	4 legs
Direct manufacturing labour	3 hours	5 hours

Unit data pertaining to the direct materials for March 2009 are as follows:

Actual Beginning Direct Materials Inventory
(March 1, 2009)

	Product	
	Executive Line	Chairperson Line
Oak top	29.8 square metres	—
Red oak top	—	13.9 square metres
Oak legs	100 legs	—
Red oak legs	—	40 legs

Target Ending Direct Materials Inventory
(March 31, 2009)

	Product	
	Executive Line	Chairperson Line
Oak top	17.9 square metres	—
Red oak top	—	18.6 square metres
Oak legs	80 legs	—
Red oak legs	—	44 legs

Unit cost data for direct-cost inputs pertaining to February 2009 and March 2009 are:

	February 2009 (Actual)	March 2009 (Budgeted)
Oak top (per square metre)	$21.60	$24.00
Red oak top (per square metre)	27.60	30.00
Oak legs (per leg)	13.20	14.40
Red oak legs (per leg)	20.40	21.60
Manufacturing labour cost per hour	36.00	36.00

Manufacturing overhead (both variable and fixed) is allocated to each desk based on budgeted direct manufacturing labour-hours per desk. The budgeted variable manufacturing overhead rate for March 2009 is $42 per direct manufacturing labour-hour. The budgeted fixed manufacturing overhead for March 2009 is $51,000. Both variable and fixed manufacturing overhead costs are allocated to each unit of finished goods.

Data relating to finished goods inventory for March 2009 are:

	Executive Line	Chairperson Line
Beginning inventory	20 units	5 units
Beginning inventory in dollars (cost)	$12,576	$5,820
Budgeted ending inventory	30 units	15 units

Budgeted sales for March 2009 are 740 units of the Executive Line and 390 units of the Chairperson Line. The budgeted selling prices per unit in March 2009 are $1,224 for an Executive Line desk and $1,920 for a Chairperson Line desk.

Assume the following in your answer:

a. Work-in-process inventories are negligible and ignored.
b. Direct materials inventory and finished goods inventory are costed using the FIFO method.
c. Unit costs of direct materials purchased and finished goods are constant in March 2009.

REQUIRED
Prepare the following budgets for March 2009:
1. Revenue budget
2. Production budget in units
3. Direct materials usage budget and direct materials purchases budget
4. Direct manufacturing labour budget
5. Manufacturing overhead budget
6. Ending inventory budget
7. Cost of goods sold budget and gross margin calculation

2. **Prepare a master operating budget—Advanced.** Slopes Inc. manufactures and sells snowboards. Slopes manufactures a single model, the Pipex. In the summer of 2008, Slopes's accountant gathered the following data to prepare budgets for 2009. These units are standard in the lumber industry. Wage rate = $25/hr.

Materials and labour requirements

Direct materials	
Wood	5 board-feet per snowboard
Fibreglass	6 yards per snowboard
Direct labour	5 hours per snowboard

Slopes's CEO expects to sell 1,200 snowboards during 2009 at an estimated retail price of $540 per board. Further, she expects 2009 beginning inventory to be 100 boards and would like to end 2009 with 200 snowboards in stock. The company follows FIFO for inventory flow.

Direct material inventories

	Beginning Inventory January 1, 2009	Ending Inventory December 31, 2009
Wood	2,000 feet	1,500 feet
Fibreglass	1,000 yards	2,000 yards

The beginning inventory of wood was purchased at $34 per board foot and fibreglass was purchased at $5.80 per yard. Prices have now risen to $36 per board foot of wood and $6 per yard of fibreglass. Variable manufacturing overhead is allocated at the rate of $8.40 per direct manufacturing labour-hour. Fixed manufacturing overhead costs are budgeted at $78,000 for 2009. Variable marketing costs are allocated at the rate of $300 per sales visit, and the marketing plan calls for 36 sales visits during 2009. Finally, fixed nonmanufacturing costs are budgeted at $36,000 for 2009.

REQUIRED
Based on the data and projections supplied by Slopes's managers,
1. Prepare the 2009 revenue budget (in dollars).
2. Prepare the 2009 production budget (in units).
3. Prepare direct materials usage and purchases budgets for 2009.

4. Prepare a direct manufacturing labour budget for 2009.
5. Prepare a manufacturing overhead budget for 2009.
6. What is the budgeted manufacturing overhead rate?
7. What is the budgeted manufacturing overhead cost per output unit?
8. Calculate the cost of a snowboard in finished goods inventory at the end of 2009.
9. Prepare an ending inventory budget for 2009.
10. Prepare a cost-of-goods-sold budget for 2009. (Opening finished goods inventory is $44,976.)
11. Prepare the budgeted income statement for Slopes Inc. for 2009.

LEARNING OBJECTIVE 3

1. **Prepare a cash budget—Intermediate.** On December 1, 2009, the Itami Wholesale Company is attempting to project cash receipts and disbursements through January 31, 2010. On January 31, 2010, a note will be payable in the amount of $120,000. This amount was borrowed in September to carry the company through the seasonal peak in November and December.

The trial balance on December 1 shows in part the following information:

Cash	$ 12,000	
Accounts receivable	336,000	
Allowance for bad debts		$ 18,960
Inventory	105,000	
Accounts payable		110,400

Sales terms call for a 2% discount if payment is made within the first ten days of the month after purchase; after that, the full amount is due by the end of the month after purchase. Experience has shown that 70% of the billings will be collected within the discount period, 20% by the end of the month after purchase, 8% in the following month, and 2% will be uncollectible. There are no cash sales.

The average selling price of the company's products is $120 per unit. Actual and projected sales are as follows:

October actual	$ 216,000
November actual	300,000
December estimated	360,000
January estimated	180,000
February estimated	144,000
Total estimated for year ended June 30, 2009	1,800,000

All purchases are payable within 15 days. Thus, approximately 50% of the purchases in a month are due and payable in the next month. The average unit purchase cost is $84. Target ending inventories are 500 units plus 25% of the next month's unit sales.

Total budgeted marketing, distribution, and customer service costs for the year are $480,000. Of this amount, $180,000 is considered fixed (and includes amortization of $36,000). The remainder varies with sales. Both fixed and variable marketing, distribution, and customer service costs are paid as incurred.

REQUIRED
Prepare a cash budget for December and January. Supply supporting schedules for collections of receivables, payments for merchandise, and marketing, distribution, and customer service costs. Will there be enough cash available on January 31, 2010 to repay the $120,000 note?

2. **Comprehensive budget, fill in schedules; prepare a cash budget—Advanced.** The following information is for the Newport Stationery Store.

Balance Sheet Information as of September 30

Current assets:	
Cash	$ 14,400
Accounts receivable	12,000
Inventory	76,320
Equipment, net	120,000
Liabilities	None

Recent and Anticipated Sales

September	$48,000
October	57,600
November	72,000
December	96,000
January	43,200

◆ **Credit sales.** Sales are 75% for cash and 25% on credit. Assume that credit accounts are all collected in the month following the sale. The accounts receivable on September 30 are the result of the credit sales for September (25% of $48,000). Gross margin averages 30% of sales. Newport treats cash discounts on purchases in the income statement as "other income."

◆ **Operating costs.** Salaries and wages average 15% of monthly sales; rent, 5%; other operating costs, excluding amortization, 4%. Assume that these costs are disbursed each month. Amortization is $1,200 per month.

◆ **Purchases.** Newport keeps a minimum inventory of $36,000. The policy is to purchase additional inventory each month in the amount necessary to provide for the following month's sales. Terms on purchases are 2/10, n/30: a 2% discount is available if the payment is made within ten days after purchase; no discount is available if payment is made beyond ten days after purchase; and the full amount is due within thirty days. Assume that payments are made in the month of purchase and that all discounts are taken.

◆ **Light fixtures.** The expenditures for light fixtures are $720 in October and $480 in November. These amounts are to be capitalized.

Assume that a minimum cash balance of $9,600 must be maintained. Assume also that all borrowing is effective at the beginning of the month and all repayments are made at the end of the month of repayment. Loans are repaid when sufficient cash is available. Interest is paid only at the time of repaying principal. The interest rate is 18% per year. Management does not want to borrow any more cash than is necessary and wants to repay as soon as cash is available.

Schedule A
Budgeted Monthly Cash Receipts

Item	September	October	November	December
Total sales	$48,000	$57,600	$72,000	$96,000
Credit sales	12,000	14,400		
Cash sales				
Receipts:				
Cash sales		$43,200		
Collections on accounts receivable		12,000		
Total		$55,200		

Schedule B
Budgeted Monthly Cash Disbursements for Purchases

Item	October	November	December	4th Quarter
Purchases	$50,400			
Deduct: 2% cash discount	1,008			
Disbursements	$49,392			

Schedule C
Budgeted Monthly Cash Disbursements
for Operating Costs

Item	October	November	December	4th Quarter
Salaries and wages	$ 8,640			
Rent	2,880			
Other cash operating costs	2,304			
Total	$13,824			

Schedule D
Budgeted Total Monthly Cash
Disbursements

Item	October	November	December	4th Quarter
Purchases	$49,392			
Cash operating costs	13,824			
Light fixtures	720			
Total	$63,936			

Schedule E
Budgeted Cash Receipts
and Disbursements

Item	October	November	December	4th Quarter
Receipts	$ 55,200			
Disbursements	63,936			
Net cash increase (decrease)	$ (8,736)			

Schedule F
Financing Required

Item	October	November	December	Total
Beginning cash balance	$14,400			
Net cash increase				
Net cash decrease	8,736			
Cash position before borrowing	5,664			
Minimum cash balance required	9,600			
Excess/(deficiency)	(3,936)			
Borrowing required	4,000			
Interest payments				
Borrowing repaid				
Ending cash balance	$ 9,664			

REQUIRED

1. Based on the preceding facts, complete schedule A.
2. Complete schedule B. Note that purchases are 70% of next month's sales.
3. Complete schedule C.
4. Complete schedule D.
5. Complete schedule E.
6. Complete schedule F (assume that borrowings must be made in multiples of $1,000).
7. What do you think is the most logical type of loan needed by Newport? Explain your reasoning.
8. Prepare a budgeted income statement for the fourth quarter and a budgeted balance sheet as of December 31. Ignore income taxes.
9. Some simplifications have been introduced in this problem. What complicating factors would be met in a typical business situation?

LEARNING OBJECTIVE 4

1. **Distinguish among sensitivity analysis, Kaizen budgeting, and activity-based budgeting—Advanced.** Dinettes Inc. operates at capacity and makes glass-topped dining tables and wooden chairs that are typically sold as sets of four chairs with one table. However, some customers purchase replacement or extra chairs, and others buy some chairs or a table only, so the sales

mix is not exactly 4:1. Dinettes Inc. is planning its annual budget for fiscal year 2009. Information for 2009 follows:

Input prices

Direct materials

Wood	$ 1.60 per board foot
Glass	$12 per sheet
Direct manufacturing labour	$15 per direct manufacturing labour-hour

Input quantities per unit of output

	Chairs	Tables
Direct materials		
Wood	5 board feet	7 board feet
Glass	—	2 sheets
Direct manufacturing labour	4 hours	8 hours
Machine-hours (MH)	3 MH	5 MH

Inventory information, direct materials

	Wood	Glass
Beginning inventory	109,200 board feet	8,750 sheets
Target ending inventory	117,500 board feet	9,000 sheets
Cost of beginning inventory	$170,352	$109,375

Dinettes Inc. accounts for direct materials using a FIFO cost flow.

Sales and inventory information, finished goods

	Chairs	Tables
Expected sales in units	172,000	45,000
Selling price	$80	$900
Target ending inventory in units	8,500	2,250
Beginning inventory in units	8,000	2,100
Beginning inventory in dollars	$760,000	$477,000

Dinettes Inc. uses a FIFO cost flow assumption for finished goods inventory.

Chairs are manufactured in batches of 500, and tables are manufactured in batches of 50. It takes three hours to set up for a batch of chairs, and two hours to set up for a batch of tables.

Dinettes Inc. uses activity-based costing and has classified all overhead costs as shown in the table below:

Cost type	Budgeted variable	Budgeted fixed	Cost driver/ Allocation base
Manufacturing:			
Materials handling	$342,840	$ 600,000	Number of board feet used
Setup	97,000	300,740	Setup hours
Processing	789,250	5,900,000	Machine hours
Nonmanufacturing:			
Marketing	2,011,200	4,500,000	Sales revenue
Distribution	54,000	380,000	Number of deliveries

Delivery trucks transport units sold in delivery sizes of 500 chairs or 500 tables.

REQUIRED

Do the following for the year 2009:
1. Prepare the revenue budget.
2. Use the revenue budget to:
   a. Find the budgeted allocation rate for marketing costs.
   b. Find the budgeted number of deliveries and allocation rate for distribution costs.
3. Prepare the production budget in units.

LEARNING OBJECTIVE 5

1. **Responsibility versus controllability; Fixing responsibility—Advanced.** (Adapted from a description by H. Bierman, Jr.) The city of Mountainvale hired its first city manager four years ago. She favoured a "management by objectives" philosophy and accordingly set up many profit responsibility centres, including a sanitation department, a utility department, and a repair shop.

For many months, the sanitation manager had been complaining to the utility manager about overhead wires being too low at one point along a city road. There was barely clearance for large sanitation trucks. The sanitation manager asked the repair shop to make changes in the clearance. The repair shop manager asked, "Should I charge the sanitation or the utility department for the $2,400 cost of making the adjustment?" Both departments refused to accept the charge, so the repair department refused to do the work.

Late one day, the top of a sanitation truck caught the wires and ripped them down. The repair department made an emergency repair at a cost of $3,120. Moreover, the city lost $1,200 of utility revenues (net of variable costs) because of the disruption of service.

Investigation disclosed that the sanitation truck had failed to clamp down its top properly. The extra two inches of height caused the wire to be caught.

Both the sanitation manager and the utility manager argued strenuously about who should bear the $3,120 cost. Moreover, the utility manager demanded reimbursement from the sanitation department of the $1,200 of lost utility income.

REQUIRED

As the city controller in charge of the responsibility accounting system, how would you favour accounting for these costs? Specifically, what would you do next? What is the proper role of responsibility accounting in assigning cost in this situation?

ASSIGNMENT MATERIAL

MyAccountingLab Make the grade with MyAccountingLab: The questions, exercises, and problems marked in red can be found on MyAccountingLab at **www.myaccountinglab.com**. You can practise them as often as you want, and most feature step-by-step guided instructions to help you find the right answer. Exercises and problems with an Excel icon in the margin have an accompanying Excel template on MyAccountingLab.

SHORT-ANSWER QUESTIONS

6-1 What are the four elements of the budgeting cycle?

6-2 Define *master budget*.

6-3 If actual results do not match the budget, what should managers do?

6-4 "Strategy, plans, and budgets are unrelated to one another." Do you agree? Explain.

6-5 "Budgeted performance is a better criterion than past performance for judging managers." Do you agree? Explain.

6-6 How might a company benefit by sharing its own internal budget information with other companies?

6-7 Define rolling budget. Give an example.

6-8 Outline the steps in preparing an operating budget.

6-9 "The revenue budget is the cornerstone for budgeting." Why?

6-10 How can the use of sensitivity analysis increase the benefits of budgeting?

6-11 Define Kaizen budgeting.

6-12 Describe how non–output-based cost drivers can be incorporated into budgeting.

6-13 Explain how the choice of the responsibility centre type (cost, revenue, profit, or investment) affects budgeting.

6-14 When governments reduce their funding to hospitals and universities, often the executives respond with a demand for an equal percentage reduction in costs by all business functions. Is this the best strategic approach?

6-15 What factors reduce the effectiveness of companies' budgeting?

EXERCISES

6-16 Budgeting and behaviour. (CMA, adapted) Many managers claim that budgets are impractical because companies experience so many uncertainties. However, it is very probable that a firm's competitors are using budgets as indispensable management tools. A major objective of budgeting is to substitute deliberate, well-conceived business judgment for accidental success or failure in enterprise management. Implicit in this objective is the confidence that a competent management team can plan for, manage, and control in large measure the relevant variables that dominate the life of a business. Managers must grapple with uncertainties, regardless of whether they have a budget.

❶

REQUIRED
1. Describe at least three benefits, other than improved cost control, that an organization can expect to realize from the implementation of budgeting.
2. Because a reliable prediction of sales is critical to the planning process, describe at least two factors that should be considered when preparing sales forecasts.

6-17 Production budget (in units), fill in the missing numbers. The following (in units) is taken from the production budget for three models of fax machines in October 2009:

❷

Model 101: 2. 17

	Model 101	Model 201	Model 301
1. Beginning finished goods inventory	13	10	?
2. Target ending finished goods inventory	?	7	40
3. Budgeted production	?	?	1,026
4. Budgeted sales	216	?	1,040
5. Total required units (2 + 4)	233	240	?

REQUIRED
Fill in the missing numbers.

6-18 Sales budget, service setting. In 2009, McGrath & Sons, a small environmental-testing firm, performed 11,000 radon tests for $250 each and 15,200 lead tests for $200 each. Because newer homes are being built with lead-free pipes, lead-testing volume is expected to decrease by 10% next year. However, awareness of radon-related health hazards is expected to result in a 5% increase in radon-test volume each year in the near future. Jim McGrath feels that if he lowers his price for lead testing to $190 per test, he will have to face only a 5% decline in lead-test sales in 2010.

❷

1. Total revenues, $5,623,500

REQUIRED
1. Prepare a 2010 sales budget for McGrath & Sons assuming that McGrath holds prices at 2009 levels.
2. Prepare a 2010 sales budget for McGrath & Sons assuming that McGrath lowers the price of a lead test to $190. Should McGrath lower the price of a lead test in 2010 if its goal is to maximize sales revenue?

6-19 Sales and production budget. The Armondo Company expects 2009 sales of 135,000 units of serving trays. Armondo's beginning inventory for 2009 is 9,700 trays; target ending inventory, 16,300 trays.

❷

REQUIRED
Compute the number of trays budgeted for production in 2009.

6-20 Direct materials budget. The wine producing company Lebeau Vineyard expects to produce 2.1 million three-litre bottles of Chablis in 2009. Lebeau purchases empty glass bottles from a reliable supplier. The target ending inventory of such bottles is 55,000; the beginning inventory is 23,700. For simplicity, ignore loss due to breakage.

❷

REQUIRED
Compute the number of bottles to be purchased in 2009.

6-21 Budgeting material purchases. In the preparation of the sales budget for the next three-month period, the Westing Company determined that 52,250 finished units would be needed to fulfill sales obligations. The company has an inventory of 27,300 units of finished goods on hand at December 31 and has a target finished goods inventory of 29,400 units at the end of the succeeding quarter.

❷

54,350 production units

It takes three litres of direct materials to make one unit of finished product. The company has an inventory of 117,350 litres of direct materials at December 31 and has a target ending inventory of 110,000 litres.

REQUIRED

How many litres of direct materials should be ordered for delivery during the three months ending March 31?

6-22 Sales and production budget. From its company-owned natural spring in northern Ontario, Fountain Springs Inc. bottles and distributes mineral water worldwide. Fountain Springs markets its product in 1-litre disposable plastic bottles and in 16-litre reusable plastic containers.

REQUIRED

1. For the year 2009, Northern marketing managers project monthly sales of 520,000 1-litre and 185,000 16-litre units. Average selling prices are estimated at $0.50 per 1-litre unit and $7.00 per 16-litre unit. Prepare a revenue budget for Fountain Springs Inc. for the year ending December 31, 2009.
2. Fountain Springs begins 2009 with 1,275,000 1-litre units in inventory (that is, beginning inventory). The VP of Operations requests that 1-litre ending inventory on December 31, 2009, be no fewer than 976,000 units. Based on sales projections as budgeted above, what is the minimum number of 1-litre units Fountain Springs must produce during 2009?
3. The VP of Operations requests that ending inventory of 16-litre units on December 31, 2009, be 265,000 units. If the production budget calls for Fountain Springs to produce 2,090,000 16-litre units during 2009, what is the beginning inventory of 16-litre units on January 1, 2009?

6-23 Budgeting revenue, cost of sales, and gross margin. Madeline Franks, the owner of a small gift and souvenir shop, expects cash sales of $14,000 for October, $16,300 for November, and $21,100 for December. In addition, she expects credit card sales of $9,800 during October and $11,200 and $15,800, respectively, during November and December. Sales returns and allowances, being historically nonexistent, can be ignored. Credit card companies such as VISA and MasterCard charge 4% on credit card sales; thus, the net sales will be 96%. Cost of goods sold traditionally averages 40% of net sales.

REQUIRED

Ms. Franks, operating under the business name Whimsy Gifts, asks you to prepare a schedule of budgeted revenue, cost of goods sold, and gross margin for each month of the last quarter. Also, she requires you to show totals for the quarter.

6-24 Revenue, production, and purchases budget. The Suzuki Company in Japan has a division that manufactures two-wheel motorcycles. Its budgeted sales for Model G in 2009 is 985,000 units. Suzuki's target ending inventory is 115,000 units, and its beginning inventory is 152,000 units. The company's budgeted selling price to its distributors and dealers is 505,000 yen (¥) per motorcycle.

Suzuki buys all its wheels from an outside supplier. No defective wheels are accepted. (Suzuki's needs for extra wheels for replacement parts are ordered by a separate division of the company.) The company's target ending inventory is 28,000 wheels and its beginning inventory is 19,000 wheels. The budgeted purchase price is ¥21,300 per wheel.

REQUIRED

1. Compute the budgeted revenue in yen.
2. Compute the number of motorcycles to be produced.
3. Compute the budgeted purchases of wheels in units and in yen.

6-25 Budgets for production and direct manufacturing labour. (CMA, adapted) The All Frame Company makes and sells artistic frames for pictures of weddings, graduations, and other special events. Martin Flack, the company controller, is responsible for preparing the master budget and has accumulated the following information for 2010:

| | 2010 | | | | |
	January	February	March	April	May
Estimated sales in units	10,000	12,000	8,000	9,000	9,000
Selling price	$54.00	$51.50	$51.50	$51.50	$51.50
Direct manufacturing labour-hours per unit	2.0	2.0	1.5	1.5	1.5
Wage per direct manufacturing labour-hour	$10.00	$10.00	$10.00	$11.00	$11.00

Direct manufacturing labour-related costs include pension contributions of $0.50 per hour, workers' compensation insurance of $0.15 per hour, employee medical insurance of $0.40 per hour, and employment insurance, in addition to wages. Assume that as of January 1, 2010, the employment insurance rates are 7.5% of wages for employers and 7.5% of wages for employees. The cost of employee benefits paid by All Frame for its employees is treated as a direct manufacturing labour cost.

All Frame has an employee labour contract that calls for a wage increase to $11.00 per hour on April 1, 2010. New labour-saving machinery has been installed and will be fully operational by March 1, 2010.

The controller has been informed that the company expects to have 16,000 frames on hand on December 31, 2009, and has a policy of carrying an end-of-month inventory of 100% of the following month's sales plus 50% of the second following month's sales.

REQUIRED

Prepare a production budget and a direct manufacturing labour budget for the All Frame Company by month and for the first quarter of 2010. The direct manufacturing labour budget should include labour-hours and show the details for each labour cost category.

6-26 **Cash flow analysis.** (CMA, adapted) TabComp Inc. is a retail distributor for MZB-33 computer hardware and related software and support services. TabComp prepares annual sales forecasts of which the first six months for 2009 are presented here. Cash sales account for 25% of TabComp's total sales, 30% of the total sales are paid by bank credit card, and the remaining 45% are on open account (TabComp's own charge accounts). The cash sales and cash from bank credit-card sales are received in the month of the sale. Bank credit-card sales are subject to a 4% discount deducted at the time of the daily deposit. The cash receipts for sales on open account are 70% in the month following the sale and 28% in the second month after the sale. The remaining accounts receivable are estimated to be uncollectible.

TabComp's month-end inventory requirements for computer hardware units are 30% of the next month's sales. A one-month lead time is required for delivery from the manufacturer. Thus, orders for computer hardware units are placed on the 25th of each month to assure that they will be in the store by the first day of the month needed. The computer hardware units are purchased under terms of n/45 (payment in full within 45 days of invoice), measured from the time the units are delivered to TabComp. TabComp's purchase price for the computer units is 60% of the selling price.

1. $429,400

TabComp Inc.
Sales Forecast for First Six Months of 2009

| | Hardware Sales | | Software Sales | Total |
	Units	Dollars	and Support	Revenues
January	130	$ 390,000	$160,000	$ 550,000
February	120	360,000	140,000	500,000
March	110	330,000	150,000	480,000
April	90	270,000	130,000	400,000
May	100	300,000	125,000	425,000
June	125	375,000	225,000	600,000
Total	675	$2,025,000	$930,000	$2,955,000

REQUIRED

1. Calculate the cash that TabComp Inc. can expect to collect during April 2009. Be sure to show all of your calculations.
2. TabComp Inc. is determining how many MZB-33 computer hardware units to order on January 25, 2009.
   a. Determine the projected number of computer hardware units that will be ordered.
   b. Calculate the dollar amount of the order that TabComp will place for these computer hardware units.
3. As part of the annual budget process, TabComp prepares a cash budget by month for the entire year. Explain why a company such as TabComp would do this.

6-27 **Activity-based budgeting.** The Chelsea location of Family Supermarket (FS), a chain of small neighbourhood grocery stores, is preparing its activity-based budget for

1. Total budgeted indirect cost
$27,147

January 2009. FS has three product categories: soft drinks, fresh produce, and packaged food. The following table shows the four activities that consume indirect resources at the Chelsea store, the cost drivers and their rates, and the cost-driver amount budgeted to be consumed by each activity in January 2009.

Activity	Cost Driver	January 2009 Budgeted Cost-Driver Rate	January 2009 Budgeted Amount of Cost Driver Used		
			Soft Drinks	Fresh Produce	Packaged Food
Ordering	Number of purchase orders	$ 90	14	24	14
Delivery	Number of deliveries	$ 82	12	62	19
Shelf-stocking	Hours of stocking time	$ 21	16	172	94
Customer support	Number of items sold	$0.18	4,600	34,200	10,750

REQUIRED
1. What is the total budgeted indirect cost at the Chelsea store in January 2009? What is the total budgeted cost of each activity at the Chelsea store for January 2009? What is the budgeted indirect cost of each product category for January 2009?
2. Which product category has the largest fraction of total budgeted indirect costs?
3. Given your answer in requirement 2, what advantage does FS gain by using an activity-based approach to budgeting over, say, allocating indirect costs to products based on cost of goods sold?

6-28 **Kaizen approach to activity-based budgeting (continuation of 6-27).** Family Supermarkets (FS) has a Kaizen (continuous improvement) approach to budgeting monthly activity area costs for each month of 2009. Each successive month, the budgeted cost-driver rate decreases by 0.2% relative to the preceding month (so, for example, February's budgeted cost-driver rate is 0.998 times January's budgeted cost-driver rate, and March's budgeted cost-driver rate is 0.998 times the budgeted February 2009 rate). FS assumes that the budgeted amount of cost-driver usage remains the same each month.

1. Total budgeted indirect cost
for March 2009 $27,025

REQUIRED
1. What is the total budgeted cost for each activity and the total budgeted indirect cost for March 2009?
2. What are the benefits of using a Kaizen approach to budgeting? What are the limitations of this approach, and how might FS management overcome them?

PROBLEMS

6-29 **Revenue and production budgets.** (CPA, adapted) Two products are manufactured by the Burlington Northern Corporation: Widget and Thingamajig. In July 2009, the controller of Burlington Northern, upon instructions from senior management, had the budgeting department gather the following data in order to prepare budgets for 2010:

2. Production Widgets
65,000 units
Thingamajigs 41,000 units

2010 Projected Sales

Product	Units	Price
Widget	60,000	$198
Thingamajig	40,000	$300

2010 Inventories in Units

Product	Expected January 1, 2010	Target December 31, 2010
Widget	22,000	27,000
Thingamajig	10,000	11,000

The following direct materials are used to produce one unit of Widget and Thingamajig:

Direct Material	Amount Used per Unit		
	Unit	Widget	Thingamajig
A	Kilograms	4	5
B	Kilograms	2	3
C	Each	0	1

Projected data for 2010 with respect to direct materials are as follows:

Direct Material	Anticipated Purchase Price	Expected Inventories, January 1, 2010	Target Inventories, December 31, 2010
A	$14	32,000 kilograms	36,000 kilograms
B	$ 7	29,000 kilograms	32,000 kilograms
C	$ 5	6,000 units	7,000 units

Projected direct manufacturing labour requirements and rates for 2010 are as follows:

Product	Hours per Unit	Rate per hour
Widget	2	$15
Thingamajig	3	$19

Manufacturing overhead is allocated at the rate of $24 per direct manufacturing labour-hour.

REQUIRED

Based on the preceding projections and budget requirements for Widgets and Thingamajigs, prepare the following budgets for 2010:

1. Revenue budget (in dollars)
2. Production budget (in units)
3. Direct materials purchases budget (in quantities)
4. Direct materials purchases budget (in dollars)
5. Direct manufacturing labour budget (in dollars)
6. Budgeted finished goods inventory at December 31, 2010 (in dollars)

6-30 **Budgeted income statement.** (CMA, adapted) Easecom Company is a manufacturer of video-conferencing products. Regular units are manufactured to meet marketing projections, and specialized units are made after an order is received. Maintaining the video-conferencing equipment is an important area of customer satisfaction. With the recent downturn in the computer industry, the video-conferencing equipment segment has suffered, leading to a decline in Easecom's financial performance. The following income statement shows results for 2010.

② Operating income $843

Easecom Company
Income Statement
For the Year Ended December 31, 2010 (in thousands)

Revenues:		
Equipment	$6,000	
Maintenance contracts	1,800	
Total revenues		$7,800
Cost of goods sold		4,600
Gross margin		3,200
Operating costs:		
Marketing	600	
Distribution	150	
Customer maintenance	1,000	
Administration	900	
Total operating costs		2,650
Operating Income		$ 550

1. Selling prices of equipment are expected to increase by 10% as the economic recovery begins. The selling price of each maintenance contract is expected to remain unchanged from 2010.
2. Equipment sales in units are expected to increase by 6%, with a corresponding 6% growth in units of maintenance contracts.
3. Cost of each unit sold is expected to increase by 3% to pay for the necessary technology and quality improvements.
4. Marketing costs are expected to increase by $250,000, but administration costs are expected to remain at 2010 levels.
5. Distribution costs vary in proportion to the number of units of equipment sold.
6. Two maintenance technicians are to be hired at a total cost of $130,000, which covers wages and related travel costs. The objective is to improve customer service and shorten response time.
7. There is no beginning or ending inventory of equipment.

REQUIRED
Prepare a budgeted income statement for the year ending December 31, 2011.

6-31 Comprehensive review of budgeting. The two soft drinks bottled by British Beverages are ginger ale and diet ginger ale. The syrup for both soft drinks is purchased from Cadbury Schweppes. Syrup for the regular brand contains a higher sugar content than the syrup for the diet brand.

British Beverages bottles the two soft drinks under licence to Cadbury Schweppes at its Manchester plant. Bottling at this plant is a highly repetitive, automated process. Empty bottles are removed from their carton, placed on a conveyor, sterilized, rinsed, dried, filled, capped, and heated (to reduce condensation). All inventory consists of direct materials and finished goods at the end of each working day. There is no work-in-process inventory.

British Beverages uses a lot size of 2,000 cases as the unit of analysis in its budgeting. (Each case contains 24 bottles.) Direct materials are expressed in terms of lots, where one lot of direct materials is the input necessary to yield one lot (2,000 cases) of beverage. In 2010, the following purchase prices are forecast for direct materials:

	Ginger Ale	**Diet Ginger Ale**
Syrup	£1,440 per lot	£1,320 per lot
Containers (bottles, caps, etc.)	£1,200 per lot	£1,200 per lot
Packaging	£ 960 per lot	£ 960 per lot

The two soft drinks are bottled using the same equipment. The equipment is sanitized daily, but it is only rinsed when a switch is made during the day between diet ginger ale and ginger ale production. Diet ginger ale is always bottled first each day to reduce the risk of sugar contamination. The only difference in the bottling process for the two soft drinks is the syrup.

Summary data used in developing budgets for 2010 are as follows:
a. Sales
   ◆ Ginger ale, 1,296 lots at £10,800 selling price per lot
   ◆ Diet ginger ale, 648 lots at £10,200 selling price per lot
b. Beginning (January 1, 2010) inventory of direct materials
   ◆ Syrup for ginger ale, 80 lots at £1,320 purchase price per lot
   ◆ Syrup for diet ginger ale, 70 lots at £1,200 purchase price per lot
   ◆ Containers, 200 lots at £1,140 purchase price per lot
   ◆ Packaging, 400 lots at £1,080 purchase price per lot
c. Beginning (January 1, 2010) inventory of finished goods
   ◆ Ginger ale, 100 lots at £6,360 per lot
   ◆ Diet ginger ale, 50 lots at £6,240 per lot
d. Target ending (December 31, 2010) inventory of direct materials
   ◆ Syrup for ginger ale, 30 lots
   ◆ Syrup for diet ginger ale, 20 lots
   ◆ Containers, 100 lots
   ◆ Packaging, 200 lots
e. Target ending (December 31, 2010) inventory of finished goods
   ◆ Ginger ale, 20 lots
   ◆ Diet ginger ale, 10 lots
f. Each lot requires 20 direct manufacturing labour-hours at the 2010 budgeted rate of £30 per hour. Indirect manufacturing labour costs are included in the manufacturing overhead forecast.

Units to be produced:
1,216 ginger ale; 608 diet ginger ale

g. Variable manufacturing overhead is forecast to be £720 per hour of bottling time; bottling time is the time the filling equipment is in operation. It takes two hours to bottle one lot of ginger ale and two hours to bottle one lot of diet ginger ale.

Fixed manufacturing overhead is forecast to be £1,440,000 for 2010.

h. Hours of budgeted bottling time is the sole allocation base for all fixed manufacturing overhead.

i. Administration costs are forecast to be 10% of the cost of goods manufactured for 2010. Marketing costs are forecast to be 12% of dollar sales for 2010. Distribution costs are forecast to be 8% of dollar sales for 2010.

REQUIRED

Assume that British Beverages applies FIFO for costing all inventories and prepare the following budgets for 2010:

1. Revenue budget (in £)
2. Production budget (in units)
3. Direct materials usage budget (in units and £)
4. Direct materials purchases budget (in units and £)
5. Direct manufacturing labour budget
6. Manufacturing overhead costs budget
7. Ending inventory budget (direct materials and finished goods)
8. Cost of goods sold budget
9. Marketing costs budget
10. Distribution costs budget
11. Administration costs budget
12. Budgeted income statement

6-32 **Cash budgeting for distributor.** (CMA) Martha Jonat, the marketing vice-president of Montrose Inc., a distributor, has completed the sales budget for 2010, shown below:

1. Ending cash balance for June $3,126,000

Montrose Inc.
2010 Budgeted Revenues (in thousands)

Month	Revenues	Month	Revenues
January	$10,800	July	$18,000
February	12,000	August	18,000
March	10,800	September	19,200
April	13,800	October	19,200
May	15,000	November	18,000
June	16,800	December	20,400

Mark Phillips, the controller, has the responsibility of preparing the cash budget. Additional information required to assist in preparing the cash budget follows:

a. Montrose's collection of accounts receivable is expected to continue as in the past: 60% of billings are collected the month after the sale and the remaining 40% two months after. Bad debts have been negligible and are expected to continue as such.

b. Purchases of the products distributed by Montrose form the largest expenditure component of the company and is traditionally 40% of revenues. The purchases are received on the following basis: 70% one month before sale and 30% during the month of sale.

c. Historically, 75% of accounts payable have been paid one month after receipt of the purchased products and the remaining 25% paid two months after receipt.

d. Hourly wages and fringe benefits, which approximate 30% of the current month's revenues, are paid in the month incurred.

e. General and administrative expenses are projected to be $18,744,000 for the year. The breakdown of these expenses is as follows:

2010 Budgeted General and Administrative Costs
(in thousands)

Salaries and fringe benefits	$ 3,840
Promotion	4,560
Property taxes	1,632
Insurance	2,400
Utilities	2,160
Amortization	4,152
Total	$18,744

All expenditures are paid uniformly throughout the year, except the property taxes, which are paid at the end of each quarter in four equal instalments.

f. Income tax payments are made at the beginning of each calendar quarter based on the income of the prior quarter. Montrose is subject to an effective income tax rate of 40%. The operating income for the first quarter of 2010 is projected to be $3,840,000. The company pays 100% of the estimated tax payment.

g. A minimum cash balance of $600,000 is maintained at all times. If the cash balance is less than $600,000 at the end of each month, the company borrows amounts necessary to maintain this balance. All amounts borrowed are repaid out of subsequent positive cash flow. The April 1, 2010 opening cash balance is expected to be $600,000.

h. There is no short-term debt as of April 1, 2010.

i. The company fiscal year corresponds with the calendar year for both financial reporting and tax purposes.

REQUIRED

1. Prepare a cash budget for Montrose by month for the second quarter of 2010. Ignore any interest expense associated with borrowing.
2. Why is cash budgeting important for Montrose?

6-33 **Cash budgeting.** UltraMag, a manufacturer of high-quality electronic components, plans a major capital investment over a six-month period starting at the beginning of the second quarter of its fiscal year ending December 31, 2010. The firm estimates the total investment cost to be $80 million with a 25% down payment at the end of the first quarter and continuing with equal instalments at the end of each month for the following six months. The firm expects to sell the replaced equipment at the end of the fourth quarter for $5 million.

The company sold $250 million 10-year 9% bonds three years previously. The interest on these bonds is payable semi-annually on May 31 and November 30. A specific covenant for these bonds requires the firm to maintain a minimum cash balance of $30 million at all times. As well, the firm is required to deposit $20 million into a sinking fund on or before May 31 of each year.

UltraMag has an open credit line with the Royal Bank for short-term loans at an interest rate of 12% per annum. The firm can draw up to $100 million at the beginning of each quarter and repay outstanding balances at the end of each quarter. All borrowings and repayments are to be made in increments of $1 million. Interest on the loans is payable at the end of each month. As of the end of the current year, UltraMag has yet to draw any funds against this line of credit.

The CFO, Martina Juarez, has determined that any excess cash on hand over $50 million should be applied to pay down short-term bank loans or should be invested in marketable securities at the end of the quarter. The firm is likely to earn a 5 percent annual return on marketable securities.

REQUIRED

Use the following data to complete UltraMag's quarterly cash budgets for the year ending December 31, 2010 (all amounts in thousands).

June cash balance, ending $30,520

	Quarter Ending				
	March	June	September	December	Year
Cash balance, beginning	$ 30,000	?	?	?	?
Add cash receipts:					
Collections from customers	425,000	?	?	460,000	?
Equipment disposal	?	?	?	?	?
Total cash available	?	$475,000	$510,000	?	?
Cash disbursements:					
Raw material purchases	$200,000	$220,000	?	$270,000	$940,000
Payroll	?	120,000	115,000	?	474,000
Selling, general, and administration expenses	60,000	62,000	58,000	64,000	?
Equipment purchase	?	?	?	?	?
Bond interest	?	?	?	?	?
Bond sinking fund	?	?	?	?	?
Income taxes	20,000	21,000	25,000	18,000	?
Total cash disbursements	?	?	?	?	?
Cash balance before borrowing	?	?	?	?	?

	Quarter Ending				
	March	June	September	December	Year
Minimum cash balance required	?	?	?	?	?
Total cash needed	?	?	?	?	?
Excess cash (cash deficiency), prior to financing	?	?	?	?	?
Short-term financing:					
Borrowing	0	?	?	?	?
Repayment (principal)	?	?	?	?	?
Interest	?	?	?	?	?
Total effects of financing	?	?	?	?	?
Cash balance, ending	$38,000	?	?	?	?

6-34 Sensitivity analysis, changing budget assumptions, and Kaizen approach. Two brands of chocolate chip cookies, Chippo and Choco, each using two ingredients, are produced by the Choco Chips Confectionary Company. The two ingredients input are chocolate chips and cookie dough. Chippo is 50% chips and 50% dough, whereas Choco is 25% chips and 75% dough.

2. Total gross margin
$2,065,500

Choco Chips's master budget projects sales of 600,000 packages of each product in 2010. According to the master budget, estimated selling prices are $3.60 per package for each product. A finished product of either brand weighs one kilogram. Forecasted 2010 ingredients costs are as follows: one kilogram of chocolate will cost $2.40, and one kilogram of cookie dough will cost $1.20. A total of 6,000 direct manufacturing labour-hours—2,400 hours for Chippo and 3,600 hours for Choco—are budgeted at the hourly rate of $24 per hour. Indirect manufacturing costs are expected to be $192,000. The indirect manufacturing costs are allocated equally between Chippo and Choco on the basis of packages produced in 2010.

(Note to students: sensitivity analysis lends itself very easily to computer analysis with the changing of one or more variables being easily evaluated.)

REQUIRED
1. Use the preceding information to calculate Choco Chips's budgeted gross margins for 2010.
2. By working with suppliers, Choco Chips was able to reduce the purchase cost of ingredients by 3%. Calculate Choco Chips's revised gross margin for 2010.
3. Assume that in addition to the 3% reduction in the purchase cost of ingredients mentioned in requirement 2, Choco Chips plans a 1% cost reduction in direct manufacturing labour-hours and a 2% cost reduction in the indirect manufacturing costs from the original data. These revisions to the original budget resulted from an analysis of all activities by a cross-functional team as a part of Choco Chips's efforts toward continuous improvement. Compute Choco Chips's revised gross margin for 2010 under these assumptions.

6-35 Activity-based budget; Kaizen improvements. Korna Company manufactures a product, gizmo, that uses the following direct inputs

5. Budgeted unit cost $74.80

	Price	Quantity	Cost per unit of output
Direct materials	$4 per gram	10 grams per unit	$40 per unit
Direct manufacturing labour-hours (DMLH)	$15 per DMLH	2 DMLH per unit	$30 per unit

Korna has no direct materials inventory. All manufacturing overhead costs are variable costs. The manufacturing overhead cost is comprised of two activities: setup and operations. The cost driver for setup is setup hours, and the cost driver for operations is direct manufacturing labour-hours. Korna allocates setup cost at a rate of $80 per setup-hour, and each setup takes two hours. Korna Company makes gizmos in batches of 100 units. Operations costs are allocated at a rate of $1.60 per direct manufacturing labour-hour.

REQUIRED
1. Korna plans to make and sell 20,000 gizmos in the first quarter of next year. The selling price for the product is $120. Prepare the revenue budget for the first quarter.
2. Prepare the direct material usage budget for the first quarter of next year.

3. Prepare the direct manufacturing labour usage budget for the first quarter of next year.
4. Prepare the manufacturing overhead cost budget for each activity for the first quarter of next year.
5. Compute the budgeted unit cost of a gizmo for the first quarter of next year.
6. Prepare the cost of goods sold budget for the first quarter of next year. Assume Korna budgets 1,000 units of beginning finished goods inventory at a cost of $72 per unit. Korna uses the LIFO cost flow assumption for finished goods inventory. Korna expects to sell all 20,000 gizmos made in the first quarter.
7. Calculate the budgeted gross margin for the first quarter of next year.
8. Korna Company managers want to implement Kaizen costing. They budget a 1% decrease in materials quantity and direct manufacturing labour-hours and a 3% decrease in setup time per unit for each subsequent quarter. Calculate the budgeted unit cost and gross margin for quarters two and three. Assume no change in budgeted output.
9. Refer to requirement 8 above. How could the reduction in materials and time be accomplished? Are there any problems with this plan?

6-36 Comprehensive problem with ABC costing. Pet Transport Company makes two pet carriers, the Cat-allac and the Dog-eriffic. They are both made of plastic with metal doors, but the Cat-allac is smaller. Information for the two products for the month of April is given in the following tables:

4

2. Production units:
Cat-allac 520
Dog-eriffic 285

Input prices

Direct materials

Plastic	$4 per kilogram
Metal	$3 per kilogram
Direct manufacturing labour	$10 per direct manufacturing labour hour

Input quantities per unit of output

	Cat-allac	Dog-eriffic
Direct materials		
Plastic	4 kilograms	6 kilograms
Metal	0.5 kilograms	1 kilogram
Direct manufacturing labour-hours (DMLH)	3 hours	5 hours
Machine-hours (MH)	10 MH	18 MH

Inventory information, direct materials

	Plastic	Metal
Beginning inventory	250 kilograms	60 kilograms
Target ending inventory	380 kilograms	55 kilograms
Cost of beginning inventory	$950	$180

Pet Transport accounts for direct materials using a FIFO cost flow assumption.

Sales and inventory information, finished goods

	Cat-allac	Dog-eriffic
Expected sales in units	500	300
Selling price	$160	$250
Target ending inventory in units	35	15
Beginning inventory in units	15	30
Beginning inventory in dollars	$1,500	$5,580

Pet Transport uses a FIFO cost flow assumption for finished goods inventory.

Pet Transport uses an activity-based costing system and classifies overhead into three activity pools: Setup, Processing, and Inspection. Activity rates for these activities are $100 per setup hour, $5 per machine hour, and $16 per inspection hour. Other information follows:

Cost driver information

	Cat-allac	Dog-eriffic
Number of units per batch	20	15
Setup time per batch	1.5 hours	1.75 hours
Inspection time per batch	0.5 hour	0.6 hour

Nonproduction fixed costs for March equal $36,000, of which half are salaries. Salaries are expected to increase 5% in April. The only variable nonproduction cost is sales commission, equal to 1% of sales revenue.

REQUIRED

Prepare the following for April:

1. Revenue budget
2. Production budget in units
3. Direct material usage budget and direct material purchases budget
4. Direct manufacturing labour cost budget
5. Manufacturing overhead cost budgets for each of the three activities
6. Budgeted unit cost of ending finished goods inventory and ending inventories budget
7. Cost of goods sold budget
8. Nonmanufacturing costs budget
9. Budgeted income statement (ignore income taxes)

6-37 Cash budget. (Continuation of 6-36) Assume the following: Pet Transport (PT) does not make any sales on credit. PT sells only to the public, and accepts cash and credit cards. Of its sales, 90% are to customers using credit cards, for which PT gets the cash right away, less a 3% transaction fee.

Ending cash balance $20,740

Purchases of materials are on account. PT pays for half the purchases in the period of the purchase and the other half in the following period. At the end of March, PT owes suppliers $8,500. PT plans to replace a machine in April at a net cash cost of $13,700. Labour, other production costs, and nonproduction costs are paid in cash in the month incurred except, of course, amortization, which is not a cash flow. For April, $20,000 of the production cost and $10,000 of the nonproduction cost is amortization.

PT currently has a $2,000 loan at an annual interest rate of 12%. The interest is paid at the end of each month. If PT has more than $10,000 cash at the end of April, it will pay back the loan. PT owes $5,000 in income taxes that need to be remitted in April. PT has cash of $5,360 on hand at the end of March.

REQUIRED

Prepare a cash budget for April for Pet Transport.

6-38 Responsibility and controllability. (Adapted from a description by R. Villers) Francois Chenier is the purchasing agent for Highlight Manufacturing Company. Marge Belvedere is head of the production planning and control department. Every six months, Belvedere gives Chenier a general purchasing program. Chenier gets specifications from the engineering department. He then selects suppliers and negotiates prices. When he took this job, Chenier was informed very clearly that he bore responsibility for meeting the general purchasing program once he accepted it from Belvedere.

During week 24, Chenier was advised that Part No. 1234—a critical part—would be needed for assembly on Tuesday morning of week 32. He found that the regular supplier could not deliver. He called everywhere and finally found a supplier in the West and accepted the commitment.

He followed up by mail. Yes, the supplier assured him, the part would be ready. The matter was so important that on Thursday of week 31, Chenier checked by phone. Yes, the shipment had left on time. Chenier was reassured and did not check further. But on Tuesday of week 32, the part had not arrived. Inquiry revealed that the shipment had been misdirected by the railroad and was stuck in Winnipeg.

REQUIRED

What department should bear the costs of time lost in the plant? Why? As the purchasing agent, do you think it fair that such costs be charged to your department?

6-39 Budgeting and governance. Delma Company manufactures a variety of products in a variety of departments, and evaluates departments and departmental managers by comparing actual costs and outputs relative to their budgets. Departmental managers help create the budgets and usually provide information about input quantities for materials, labour, and overhead costs. Wert Mimble is the manager of the department that produces Product Z. Wert has estimated these inputs for Product Z:

Input	Budget Quantity per Unit of Output
Direct material	3 kilograms
Direct manufacturing labour	20 minutes
Machine time	10 minutes

The department produces about 100 units of Product Z each day. Wert's department always gets excellent evaluations, sometimes exceeding budgeted production quantities. Each 100 units of Product Z uses, on average, about 32 hours of direct manufacturing labour (four people working eight hours each), 295 kg of material, and 16.5 machine hours.

Top management of Delma Company has decided to implement budget standards that will challenge the workers in each department and it has asked Wert to design more challenging input standards for Product Z. Wert provides top management with the following input quantities:

Input	Budget Quantity per Unit of Output
Direct material	2.95 kilograms
Direct manufacturing labour	19.2 minutes
Machine time	9.9 minutes

REQUIRED

Discuss the following:

1. Are these challenging standards for Wert's department?
2. Why do you suppose Wert picked these particular standards?
3. What steps can Delma Company top management take to make sure Wert's standards really meet the goals of the firm?

COLLABORATIVE LEARNING CASES

① ② ③ ④

3. Budgeted net income $998

6-40 Comprehensive budgeting problem; activity-based costing, operating and financial budgets. Yummi-Lik makes really big lollipops in two sizes, large and giant. Yummi-Lik sells these lollipops to convenience stores, fairs, schools for fundraisers, and in bulk on the Internet. Summer is approaching and Yummi-Lik is preparing its budget for the month of June. The lollipops are handmade, mostly out of sugar, and attached to wooden sticks. Expected sales are based on past experience. This company uses pounds of material as its standard measure.

Other information for the month of June follows:

Input prices
Direct materials

Sugar	$0.50 per pound (lb)
Sticks	$0.30 each
Direct manufacturing labour	$8 per direct manufacturing labour-hour

Input quantities per unit of output

	Large	Giant
Direct materials		
Sugar	0.25 lb	0.50 lb
Sticks	1	1
Direct manufacturing labour-hours (DMLH)	0.20 hours	0.25 hours
Setup hours per batch	0.08 hours	0.09 hours

Inventory information, direct materials

	Sugar	Sticks
Beginning inventory	125 lb	350
Target ending inventory	240 lb	480
Cost of beginning inventory	$64	$105

Yummi-Lik accounts for direct materials using a FIFO cost flow assumption.

Sales and inventory information, finished goods

	Large	Giant
Expected sales in units	3,000	1,800
Selling price	$3	$4
Target ending inventory in units	300	180
Beginning inventory in units	200	150
Beginning inventory in dollars	$500	$474

Yummi-Lik uses a FIFO cost flow assumption for finished goods inventory.

All the lollipops are made in batches of 10. Yummi-Lik incurs manufacturing overhead costs, and marketing and general administration costs, but customers pay for shipping. Other than manufacturing labour costs, monthly processing costs are very low. Yummy-Lik uses activity-based costing and has classified all overhead costs for the month of June as shown in the following chart:

Cost type	Denominator Activity	Rate
Manufacturing:		
Setup	Setup hours	$20 per setup hr
Processing	Direct manufacturing labour-hours (DMLH)	$1.70 per DMLH
Nonmanufacturing:		
Marketing and general administration	Sales revenue	10%

REQUIRED

1. Prepare each of the following for June:
   a. Revenue budget
   b. Production budget in units
   c. Direct material usage budget and direct material purchases budget
   d. Direct manufacturing labour cost budget
   e. Manufacturing overhead cost budgets for processing and setup activities
   f. Budgeted unit cost of ending finished goods inventory and ending inventories budget
   g. Cost of goods sold budget
   h. Marketing and general administration costs budget

2. Yummi-Lik's balance sheet for May 31 follows. Use it and the following information to prepare a cash budget for Yummi-Lik for June.

   ◆ 80% of sales are on account, of which half are collected in the month of the sale, 49% are collected the following month, and 1% are never collected and written off as bad debts.
   ◆ All purchases of materials are on account. Yummi-Lik pays for 70% of purchases in the month of purchase and 30% in the following month.
   ◆ All other costs are paid in the month incurred.
   ◆ Yummi-Lik is making monthly interest payments of 1% (12% per year) on a $20,000 long-term loan.
   ◆ Yummi-Lik plans to pay the $500 of taxes owed as of May 31 in the month of June. Income tax expense for June is zero.
   ◆ 40% of processing and setup costs, and 30% of marketing and general administration costs are amortization.

Yummi-Lik
Balance Sheet
May 31

Assets

Cash		$ 587
Accounts receivable	$ 4,800	
Less: Allowance for bad debts	96	4,704
Inventories:		
Direct materials		169
Finished goods		974
Fixed assets	190,000	
Less: Accumulated amortization	55,759	134,241
Total assets		$140,675

Liabilities and Equity

Accounts payable		$ 696
Taxes payable		500
Interest payable		200
Long-term debt		20,000
Common shares		10,000
Retained earnings		109,279
Total liabilities and equity		$140,675

3. Prepare a budgeted income statement for June and a budgeted balance sheet for Yummi-Lik as of June 30.

6-41 University department, budget revision options. Gary Gemst is the athletics director of Pacific University (PU). He has been director for more than ten years. PU is a men's football and basketball powerhouse. The women's athletics program, however, has had less success. Last year, the women's basketball team finally had more wins than losses.

Gemst has just had a meeting with Laura Medley, the newly appointed president of PU. It did not go well. Medley and Gemst discussed what she called "Draft I" of the 2010 athletics department budget. He had believed it was the final draft. Medley expressed four grave concerns about Draft I in particular and about the PU athletics program in general:

◆ **Concern 1.** The athletics department was budgeting a loss of more than $3.6 million in 2010. Given the tight fiscal position of the university, this was unacceptable. A budgeted loss of $1.2 million was the most she would tolerate for 2010. Draft II of the 2010 budget was due in two weeks' time. By 2011, the athletics department had to operate with a balanced budget. She told Gemst this was nonnegotiable.

◆ **Concern 2.** The low allocation of money to the women's athletics program. Frontline, a tabloid television show, recently ran a program titled "It's a Man's World at the Pacific University Athletics Program." Medley said Gemst was treating female athletes as "third-class citizens."

◆ **Concern 3.** The low academic performance of the men's football athletes, many of whom had full scholarships. Medley noted that the local TV news recently ran an interview with three football-team students, none of whom "exemplified the high academic credentials she wanted Pacific to showcase to the world." She called one student "incoherent" and another "incapable of stringing sentences together."

◆ **Concern 4.** The outrageous salary paid to Bill Madden, the football coach. Medley noted it was twice that of the highest-paid academic on campus, a Nobel Prize winner! Moreover, Madden received other payments from his "Football the Pacific Way" summer program for high-school students.

Exhibit 6-12 is a summary of the Draft I athletics department budget for 2010.

INSTRUCTIONS

Form groups of two or more students to complete the following requirement.

REQUIRED

Your group should discuss the concerns noted both from quantitative and qualitative perspectives. What should be addressed in preparing Draft II of the athletics department's 2010 budget? This draft will form the basis of a half-day meeting Gemst will have with key officials of the athletics department.

EXHIBIT 6-12
Pacific University 2010 Athletics Department Budget (in Millions)

Revenues:		
Men's athletics programs	$12.420	
Women's athletics programs	0.936	
Other (endowment income, gifts)	4.080	$ 17.436
Costs:		
Men's athletics programs	$13.248	
Women's athletics programs	3.360	
Other (not assigned to programs)	4.440	21.048
Operating income		$ (3.612)

Men's Athletics Programs

	Football	Basketball	Swimming	Other	Total
Revenues	$10.320	$1.800	$0.120	$0.180	$12.420
Costs	8.880	3.240	0.360	0.768	13.248
Full student scholarships	37	21	6	4	68

Women's Athletic Programs

	Basketball	Swimming	Other	Total
Revenues	$ 0.720	$0.096	$0.120	$ 0.936
Costs	2.160	0.240	0.960	3.360
Full student scholarships	11	4	2	17

Flexible Budgets, Variances, and Management Control: I

Keeping It Real

At McDonald's, when they ask, "Would you like fries with that?" it's part of a technique called "upselling." More often than not, diners respond "yes," and the sale contributes more to the restaurant's budgeted sales targets and profitability. Managers track both actual sales and the actual costs associated with them. Budgeted food and labour costs are compared to actual restaurant performance. Any significant differences between the budgeted (pro forma) and actual results must be explained and the appropriate remedies put into place to meet the plan in future.

After studying this chapter, you should be able to

1. Distinguish between a static budget and a flexible budget

2. Develop flexible budgets, and calculate flexible-budget and sales-volume variances, price variances, and efficiency variances for direct cost categories

3. Undertake variance analysis in activity-based costing systems

4. Describe how managers use variance analyses

5. Distinguish the strategy of benchmarking from standard costing

Managers quantify their operating and strategic plans for the future in the form of budgets. Recall that one reason budgets are necessary is that important financial and nonfinancial resources are limited. Companies cannot access more than what is available to them to achieve operating and strategic goals. This chapter focuses on the improving information available for managerial decision making after the budget is prepared. The technique is a straightforward comparison of planned or pro forma results to those actually realized in a specified time period.

The difference between actual (realized) and budgeted (pro forma) results is a **variance**. This information is important feedback, and if used well will identify potential operating and strategic problems that require remedy. **Variance analysis** is a way to focus managerial attention on discovering why actual results failed to meet expectations. It is an exceptions-based approach to management. The calculation of variances is somewhat mathematically trivial—it is the explanations that arise from the managerial analyses of the variances that are valuable.

Assume that the operating income is the point of reference from which variances are assessed as favourable or unfavourable. A **favourable (F) variance** will result in an actual operating income that exceeds the budgeted amount. An **unfavourable (U) variance** will result in an actual operating income that is less than the budgeted amount. The logic of variance analysis is clear. All other things equal, when either actual revenue is less than pro forma or when actual expenses are more than pro forma, the operating income will decrease relative to the budgeted operating income. The reverse is also true. Notice that once again, the management-accounting activity of variance analysis depends upon the availability of timely, reliable, financial-accounting information reported in good form. One important function of variance analysis is to give managers timely feedback on whether or not the actual operations are exceeding the resources available to the company. One remedy is to change actual operations.

Because budgets are plans, the demand for products and services (the starting point of a master budget) is simply an estimate. The pro forma volume of sales is based on a series of assumptions about the future that will inevitably be inaccurate. The only question is, *how* inaccurate? If the demand forecast is inaccurate, then all the subsequent schedules will also be inaccurate. The inaccuracy is the inevitable result of being unable to foretell the future. Thus, a second important function of variance analysis is to provide feedback to enable managers to adjust their assumptions to reality. A second remedy is to change the budget, and plan how to reduce or obtain more resources to respond appropriately to the real world.

In practice, companies undertake variance analyses on many of the schedules supporting the master budget in order to understand what caused the changes to the operating-budget amounts. Companies, therefore, use various points of reference appropriate to the schedule being analyzed, including:

♦ nonfinancial variables, such as defect rate or mean time between failures (MTBF)

♦ nonfinancial variables reported in industry databases, such as growth in market size

♦ financial variables reported in government and other financial databases, such as industry profitability and return on equity

♦ financial variables reported within a company, such as accounts receivable and inventory turnover ratios, return on assets, operating margin, and so on

This chapter emphasizes financial points of reference reported within a company's own accounting information system.

Organizations differ widely in how they calculate and label the budgeted amounts they report. Often, but not always, budgeted amounts are also standards. A **standard** is a carefully determined price, cost, or quantity used for judging performance; the term is frequently used to refer to amounts estimated from either engineering or time-motion studies. Standards can be set external to or within a company. Standard amounts are usually expressed on a per-unit basis (e.g., per hour, per square metre, per task, per output, etc.). The terms *standard* and *budget* are interchangeable for the purpose of calculating variances. Other methods to calculate a budgeted amount include analyses of historical costs, time-series linear regression (Chapter 10), and benchmarking (covered later in this chapter).

STATIC AND FLEXIBLE BUDGETS

Distinguish between a static budget and a flexible budget — 1

This chapter compares realized results to both static budgets and flexible budgets. A **static budget** is a budget that is based on one level of output; it is not adjusted or altered after it is set regardless of ensuing changes in either actual output or actual revenue and cost drivers. A **flexible budget** is adjusted in accordance with ensuing changes in either actual output or actual revenue and cost drivers. As we will see, a flexible budget enables managers to compute a richer set of variances than does a static budget.

The budgeted operating income is the point of reference from which to assess if the variance is favourable or unfavourable. Chapter 6 presented many schedules and budgets wherein the fixed and variable costs were clearly separated. Variable direct and indirect costs changed as the rate of consumption of either direct resources or the resource allocation bases (cost drivers for ABC) changed.

THINKING CRITICALLY

Reflect on the material covered in chapters 2 and 6—what is one problem with static budgets? Explain in a sentence or two. Read on for a discussion of this topic.

Chapter 2 explained the difference between fixed and variable costs. The variable cost pools, whether direct or indirect, change in value with a change in quantity of some input consumed. This is why they are variable. A doubling of sales will automatically result in a doubling of some variable costs. The difference between the budgeted (pro forma) and actual cost results will be reported as an unfavourable variance. These cost variances, however, are not bad news—they are a predictable result of the good news in sales. A more useful and relevant analysis is to evaluate the change in variable costs realized against the pro forma (budgeted) variable costs if the forecast of sales quantity had been perfect. This is one benefit of using a flexible, rather than static, budget. It focuses scarce (and expensive) managerial attention on comparable unfavourable variances.

Budgets, both static and flexible, can differ in their level of detail. Increasingly, organizations are developing approaches to budgeting that report summary figures yet have the capability to display more detailed breakdowns of these figures on a computer screen. In this book, the term *Level* followed by a number denotes the amount of detail indicated by the variance(s) isolated. Level 0 reports the least detail, Level 1 offers more information, and so on. Detail is also referred to as *fineness* in financial accounting. **Fineness** is a characteristic of reliable information that enables users of that information to better predict how one factor will change with a change in another factor. In fact, this is exactly what managers need to explain when actual costs differ from budgeted. Therefore, the finer the variance report, the more readily the causes of variances can be identified.

ACCOUNTING SYSTEM AT WEBB COMPANY

The example of Webb Company illustrates static budgets and flexible budgets. Webb manufactures and sells a single product, a distinctive jacket that requires many materials, tailoring, and hand operations. Sales are made to independent clothing stores and retail chains. Webb sets budgeted revenues (budgeted selling price × budgeted units sold) based on input from its marketing personnel, and an analysis of general and industry economic conditions.

The costing system at Webb includes both manufacturing costs and marketing costs. There are direct and indirect costs in each category:

	Direct Costs	**Indirect Costs**
Manufacturing	Direct materials	Variable manufacturing overhead
	Direct manufacturing labour	Fixed manufacturing overhead
Marketing	Direct marketing labour	Variable marketing overhead
		Fixed marketing overhead

All costs at Webb are either driven by output units or are fixed. We make this simplifying assumption to highlight the basic approach to flexible budgeting. Webb's inventoriable costs include direct materials (all variable), direct manufacturing labour (all variable), and manufacturing overhead (both variable and fixed). The cost driver for direct materials, direct manufacturing labour, and variable manufacturing overhead is the *number of units manufactured.*

Period costs, for example marketing costs (distribution, customer service, and advertising costs), also include direct marketing labour (primarily distribution personnel, which are all variable) and marketing overhead (both variable and fixed). The cost driver for direct marketing labour and variable marketing overhead is the *number of units sold.* The revenue driver is also the number of units sold. The relevant range for the $180 selling price per jacket, and for the inventoriable and period cost drivers is from 8,000 to 16,000 units.

STATIC-BUDGET VARIANCES

The actual results and the static-budget amounts of Webb for April 2009 are as follows:

	Actual Results	**Static Budget Amounts**
Units sold	10,000	12,000
Revenues	$1,850,000	$2,160,000
Variable costs	1,120,000	1,188,000
Fixed costs	705,000	710,000
Operating income	$ 25,000	$ 262,000

Exhibit 7-1 presents the Level 0 and Level 1 variance analyses for April 2009. Level 0 gives the least detailed comparison of the actual and budgeted operating income. The unfavourable variance of $237,000 is simply the result of subtracting the budgeted operating income of $262,000 from the actual operating income of $25,000:

$$\text{Static budget variance of operating income} = \text{Actual results} - \text{Static budget amount}$$
$$= \$25,000 - \$262,000$$
$$= \$237,000 \text{ U}$$

The *static-budget variance* is based on the operating income of $262,000 that was forecast in the static budget. The forecast failed to reflect reality: A lower realized sales level of 10,000 units actually sold in the month of April. All other things equal, the pro forma operating income was overstated. More importantly, however, the favourable variance shown for variable costs is misleading because the master budget volume was 12,000, not 10,000, units sold. The favourable cost variance most likely arose because 2,000 fewer units were produced, not because of any improved efficiency in production.

Level 1 analysis in Exhibit 7-1 provides managers with more detailed information on the static-budget variance of operating income of $237,000 U. The additional information added in Level 1 pertains to revenues, variable costs, and fixed costs. The budgeted contribution margin percentage of 45.0% ($972,000 ÷ $2,160,000) decreases to 39.5% ($730,000 ÷ $1,850,000) for the actual results.

LEVEL 0 ANALYSIS

Actual operating income	$ 25,000 F*
Budgeted operating income	262,000 F
Static-budget variance of operating income	$237,000 U

LEVEL 1 ANALYSIS

	A	B	C	D
1		**Actual**	**Static-Budget**	**Static**
2		**Results**	**Variances**	**Budget**
3		**(1)**	**(2)**	**(3)**
4	Units sold	10,000	2,000 U	12,000
5	Revenues	$1,850,000	$310,000 U	$2,160,000
6	Variable costs	1,120,000	(68,000) F	1,188,000
7	Contribution margin	730,000	242,000 U	972,000
8	Fixed costs	705,000	(5,000) F	710,000
9	Operating income	$ 25,000	$237,000 U	$ 262,000
10		↑		↑
11			$237,000 U	
12			Total static-budget variance	
13				
14	*F = favourable effect on operating income; U = unfavourable effect on operating income.			

Although Level 1 contains more information than Level 0, additional insights into the causes of variances can be gained by incorporating a flexible budget into the computation of variances. To do so requires understanding the various schedules that comprise the master budget.

ASSESS YOUR MASTERY

To check your understanding of the material in Learning Objective ❶, go to the *Mastery Questions* section at the end of this chapter and complete Learning Objective ❶ questions 1, 2, and 3.

MyAccountingLab

STEPS IN DEVELOPING A FLEXIBLE BUDGET

Webb Company's approach to developing a flexible budget is relatively straightforward, given the assumption that all costs are either fixed or variable with respect to output units. As in Chapter 3, the assumption is that revenue is the product of total units sold multiplied by the unit sales price. The **revenue driver** is the quantity of units sold of a product or service. In logical order, Webb must:

◆ Refer to the Revenue Budget (e.g., Chapter 6, p. 257) to obtain the budgeted selling price per unit.

◆ Refer to the Direct Materials Usage Budget, Direct Manufacturing Labour Budget, and the Manufacturing Overhead Budget to obtain the inventoriable budgeted variable costs per unit, and the budgeted fixed costs for the relevant range of production (e.g., Chapter 6, pp. 259–260).

◆ Refer to the Other (Nonproduction) Costs Budget to obtain the variable costs per unit and the budgeted fixed costs for the relevant range of units sold, which in this example also equals the units produced (e.g., Chapter 6, p. 262).

Develop flexible budgets, and calculate flexible-budget and sales-volume variances, price variances, and efficiency variances for direct cost categories

②

EXHIBIT 7-2
Flexible-Budget Data for Webb Company for April 2009

	A	B	C	D	E	F
1		**Budgeted**	**Flexible Budget Amounts for**			**Actual Results**
2		**Cost Amount**	**Alternative Levels of Output Units Sold**			**Results for**
3	**Line Item**	**Per Unit**	**10,000**	**12,000**	**15,000**	**10,000 units**
4	**(1)**	**(2)**	**(3)**	**(4)**	**(5)**	**(6)**
5						
6	Revenue	$ 180	$1,800,000	$2,160,000	$2,700,000	$1,850,000
7	Variable cost					
8	Direct materials	60	600,000	720,000	900,000	688,200
9	Direct manufacturing labour	16	160,000	192,000	240,000	198,000
10	Direct marketing labour	6	60,000	72,000	90,000	57,600
11	Variable manufacturing overhead	12	120,000	144,000	180,000	130,500
12	Variable marketing overhead	5	50,000	60,000	75,000	45,700
13	Total variable costs	99	990,000	1,188,000	1,485,000	1,120,000
14	Contribution margin	$ 81	810,000	972,000	1,215,000	730,000
15	Fixed costs					
16	Manufacturing overhead		276,000	276,000	276,000	285,000
17	Marketing overhead		434,000	434,000	434,000	420,000
18	Total fixed costs		710,000	710,000	710,000	705,000
19	Total costs		1,700,000	1,898,000	2,195,000	1,825,000
20	Operating Income		$ 100,000	$ 262,000	$ 505,000	$ 25,000

Each output unit (a jacket) has a budgeted selling price of $180. The budgeted variable cost is $99 per jacket. To simplify this example, amounts but no source documents (the supporting budgets) have been provided. The source documents would be similar to those referred to in Chapter 6. Column B of Exhibit 7-2 has a breakdown of this $99 (each amount would be found in source documents). The budgeted fixed costs total $710,000 ($276,000 manufacturing and $434,000 marketing).

◆ Obtain a report of the actual quantity of the revenue driver. Webb's revenue driver is the number of units sold. In April 2009, Webb sold 10,000 jackets.

◆ Calculate the flexible budget for revenue based on budgeted selling price per unit and the actual quantity of the revenue driver:

$$\text{Flexible budget revenues} = 180 \times 10,000$$
$$= \$1,800,000$$

◆ Obtain a report of the actual quantity of either the cost allocation base(s) or cost driver(s) consumed for both inventoriable and period costs.

Webb's cost driver for manufacturing costs is also units produced. The cost driver for marketing costs is units sold. In April 2009, for simplicity, assume Webb both produced and sold 10,000 jackets. This eliminates the need to value any ending inventories (Chapter 9).

◆ Calculate the flexible budget for costs based on the budgeted direct costs per unit (variable costs) and fixed costs, and the actual quantity of the cost allocation bases and/or cost driver(s).

Flexible-budget variable costs:
Manufacturing = $88 × 10,000 = $880,000
Marketing = $11 × 10,000 = 110,000
$990,000

This completes the flexible budgeting process, allowing Webb Company to move forward to a more detailed and informative Level 2 variance analysis.

FLEXIBLE-BUDGET VARIANCES AND SALES-VOLUME VARIANCES

The Level 2 analysis will help Webb Company identify not only unfavourable (U) variances but also the reasons for the $237,000 unfavourable static-budget variance of operating income. The Level 2 analysis reports the difference between realized and pro forma sales, as well as the difference between realized and pro forma costs. Exhibit 7-2 shows the flexible budget for 10,000 units (column 3) as well as for 12,000 and 15,000 units in the relevant range (columns 4 and 5).

Exhibit 7-3 presents the Level 2 flexible-budget-based variance analysis for Webb. Note that the $237,000 unfavourable static-budget variance of operating income is now split into two categories—a flexible-budget variance and a sales-volume variance. The **flexible-budget variance** is the difference between the actual (realized) results and the flexible-budget (pro forma) amount for revenue and cost drivers. The **sales-volume variance** is the difference between the flexible-budget amount and the static-budget amount; unit selling prices, unit variable costs, and fixed costs are held constant. Knowing these variances helps managers better explain the static-budget variance of $237,000 U.

FLEXIBLE-BUDGET COST AND SELLING-PRICE VARIANCES

Columns B, C, and D of Exhibit 7-3 compare the actual results with the flexible-budget amounts. Flexible-budget variances are reported in column B for four line items in the income statement:

Flexible-budget variance = Actual results – Flexible-budget amount

For the operating income line item, the flexible-budget variance is $75,000 U ($25,000 – $100,000). This variance arises because the actual selling price, unit variable costs, and

EXHIBIT 7-3
Flexible-Budget-Based Variance Analysis for Webb Company for April 2009: Level 2 Analysis

LEVEL 2 ANALYSIS

	A	B	C	D	E	F
		Actual	**Flexible-Budget**	**Flexible**	**Sales-Volume**	**Static**
		Results	**Variances**	**Budget**	**Variances**	**Budget**
		(1)	**(2) = (1) − (3)**	**(3)**	**(4) = (3) − (5)**	**(5)**
4	Units sold	10,000	–	10,000	2,000 U	12,000
5	Revenue	$1,850,000	$ 50,000 F	$1,800,000	$(360,000) U	$2,160,000
6	Variable costs	1,120,000	130,000 U	990,000	(198,000) F	1,188,000
7	Contribution margin	730,000	(80,000) U	810,000	(162,000) U	972,000
8	Fixed costs	705,000	(5,000) F	710,000	–	710,000
9	Operating income	$ 25,000	$ (75,000) U	$ 100,000	$(162,000) U	$ 262,000
10						
11			$ (75,000) U		$(162,000) U	
12			Total flexible-budget variance		Total sales-volume variance	
13						
14				$(237,000) U		
15				Total static-budget variance		

fixed costs differ from the budgeted amounts. The actual and budgeted unit amounts for the selling price and variable costs are as follows:

	Actual Unit Amount	Budgeted Unit Amount
Selling price	$185	$180
Variable cost	112	99

By analyzing the information in Exhibit 7-2, we can determine a total variable manufacturing overhead variance of $10,500 (the difference between columns 3 and 6—unfavourable because the actual exceeded budgeted costs) as well as a variable marketing overhead variance of $4,300 F, to result in a net variable overhead variance of $6,200 U. But this is not all that is included in the total variable cost variance. As Exhibit 7-2 indicates, the direct materials and total direct labour costs are also included in total variable costs. The direct materials variance is $88,200 U, while the total direct labour variance is $35,600 U. The direct labour variance is the net of both the direct manufacturing labour variance of $38,000 U and the direct marketing labour variance of $2,400 F. When you add the direct materials, total direct labour and marketing, and total variable manufacturing and marketing overhead variances, you obtain the total variable-cost variance of $130,000 U.

From Exhibit 7-3, the actual total fixed cost of $705,000 is $5,000 less than the budgeted total fixed cost of $710,000. This is a favourable change from what was expected. Refer back to Exhibit 7-2 and it is clear that the total fixed cost variance is the net result of adding the variance from fixed manufacturing overhead of $9,000 U, and fixed marketing overhead of $14,000 F.

The flexible-budget variance pertaining to revenues is often called a **selling-price variance** because it arises solely from differences between the actual selling price and the budgeted selling price:

$$\begin{aligned} \text{Selling-price variance} &= \left(\text{Actual selling price} - \text{Budgeted selling price} \right) \times \text{Actual units sold} \\ &= (\$185 - \$180) \times 10{,}000 \\ &= \$50{,}000 \text{ F} \end{aligned}$$

Webb has a favourable selling-price variance because the actual selling price exceeds the budgeted amount (by $5). Marketing managers typically are best-informed as to why a selling-price difference arises. The relationship among the levels of variance analysis is illustrated in Exhibit 7-4. The left branch of the tree diagram will be extended to include details for all three levels of cost variance analysis. Analysis of four levels of increasingly detailed sales-volume variance is presented in Chapter 16.

EXHIBIT 7-4
Relationship Among Cost Variance Analysis Levels 1 and 2

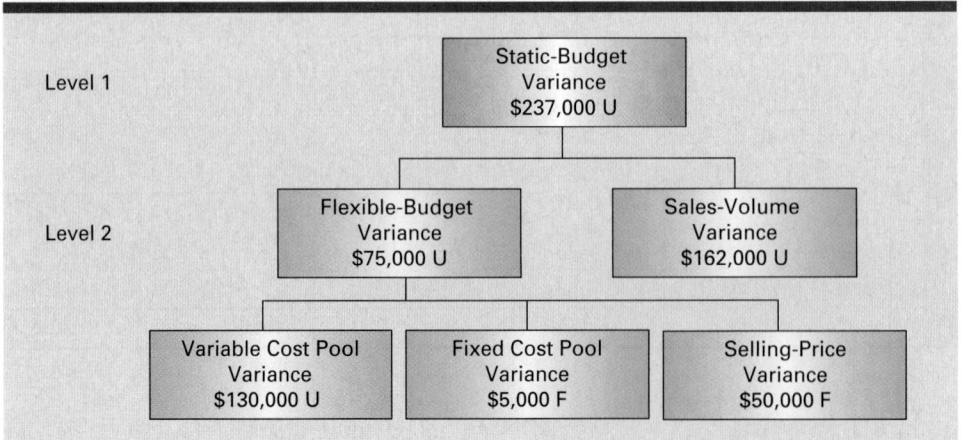

The flexible-budget variance for variable costs is unfavourable for the actual output of 10,000 jackets. It's unfavourable because either (a) Webb used more quantities of inputs (such as direct manufacturing labour-hours) relative to the budgeted quantities of inputs, or (b) Webb incurred higher prices per unit for the inputs (such as the wage rate per direct manufacturing labour-hour) relative to the budgeted prices per unit for the inputs, or (c) both (a) and (b). Higher input *quantities* relative to the budget and/or higher input *prices* relative to the budget could be the result of Webb deciding to produce a superior product to what was planned in the budget, or the result of inefficiencies in Webb's manufacturing and purchasing, or both. *You should always think of variance analysis as attention-directing. Managers use variances to indicate what requires further investigation rather than as establishing conclusive evidence of good or bad performance.*

SALES-VOLUME VARIANCES

The flexible-budget amounts in column D of Exhibit 7-3 and the static-budget amounts in column F are both computed using the budgeted selling prices and budgeted costs. This variance is labelled the "sales-volume variance" because in many contexts, the number of units sold is both the revenue driver and the cost driver. For the operating income line item,

$$\begin{aligned}\text{Sales-volume} \atop \text{variance} &= {\text{Flexible-budget} \atop \text{amount}} - {\text{Static-budget} \atop \text{amount}}\\ &= \$100,000 - \$262,000\\ &= \$162,000 \text{ U}\end{aligned}$$

In our Webb example, this sales-volume variance in operating income arises solely because Webb sold 10,000 units, which was 2,000 less than the budgeted 12,000 units. The result is reassuring in the sense that this is exactly how variable costs should behave with changes to the amount of the cost driver. This simple arithmetic, however, adds little value. The question is, *why* did Webb sell 2,000 fewer jackets? Webb's unfavourable sales-volume variance could be due to one or more of the following:

1. The overall demand for jackets is not growing at the rates that were anticipated.
2. Competitors are taking away market share from Webb.
3. Webb did not adapt quickly to changes in customer preferences and tastes.
4. Quality problems developed that led to customer dissatisfaction with Webb's jackets.
5. Budgeted sales targets were set without careful analysis of market conditions.

Webb's response to the unfavourable sales-volume variance will depend on the cause(s) of the variance. For example, if Webb believes the variance was caused by market-related reasons (reasons 1 or 2), the sales manager would be in the best position to explain what happened and to suggest corrective actions, such as sales promotions, that may be needed. If, however, the unfavourable variance was caused by quality problems, the manufacturing manager would be in the best position to analyze the causes and to suggest strategies for improvement, such as changes in the manufacturing process or investments in new machines.

THINKING CRITICALLY

What causes sales-volume and flexible-budget cost variances? Explain in a sentence or two. Read on for a discussion of this topic.

For flexible budgets, the pro forma volume of sales is adjusted to actual sales volume. In Exhibit 7-2, the realized or actual revenue was $1,850,000 while the pro forma flexible sales revenue was $1,800,000. The explanation must be that the actual unit sales price was $185 and not $180 per jacket because the volumes were identical. This sales-*price* variance is the difference between the actual revenue and the flexible budget revenue. Flexible budgets change the sales volume to match the volume that is realized. This is no guarantee, however, that changes in either the actual volumes of inputs used or the unit prices will match exactly what *should* have been used to produce the actual volume of sales realized. Therefore, variable cost variances caused by over-consumption of inputs and/or changes in unit costs are very possible. The revenue will vary if the unit price, the total volume of sales, or both varies from the pro forma amounts. The sales-*volume* variance is the difference between actual sales revenue and the static-budget revenue.

Fixed costs should not give rise to a variance over the relevant range of 8,000 to 16,000 units sold. This is why these cost pools are called "fixed." The realized sales volume is 10,000 units but shown in Exhibit 7-3, there is a fixed cost variance. The causes of fixed cost variances are explained in Chapter 8.

PRICE VARIANCES AND EFFICIENCY VARIANCES

The flexible-budget variance (Level 2) captures the difference between the actual, or realized, results and the flexible, or pro forma, budget. The sources of this variance (as regards costs) are the individual differences between actual and budgeted prices or quantities for inputs. The next two variances we discuss—price variances and efficiency variances for inputs—distinguish between such differences. This information is more refined and helps managers to better understand past performance and to plan for future performance. We call this a Level 3 analysis, as it takes a more detailed analysis of the Level 2 variances.

A **price variance** is the difference between the actual price and the budgeted price multiplied by the actual quantity of input in question (such as direct materials purchased or used). *Price variances* are sometimes called **input-price variances** or **rate variances** (especially when those variances are for direct labour). An **efficiency variance** is the difference between the actual quantity of input used (such as metres of cloth in direct materials) and the budgeted quantity of input that should have been used, multiplied by the budgeted price. *Efficiency variances* are sometimes called **input-efficiency variances** or **usage variances.** The relationship of these two variances to those we have already discussed for Webb is shown in Exhibit 7-5. Note that no indirect variances such as overhead appear in Exhibit 7-5.

In reality, managers are responsible for controlling efficiency variances and have the authority to do so. This is not usually the case with respect to price variances. Unless the company is a very large consumer (a monopsony) of direct materials, it has no power to affect the price per unit of those materials. This is especially true if there is only one supplier (a monopoly). The company depends upon astute negotiation with the supplier to obtain the lowest possible price per unit at the correct quality level and at the right time. Managers remain responsible for explaining price variance but have little control.

OBTAINING BUDGETED INPUT PRICES AND INPUT QUANTITIES

Webb's two main sources of information upon which to base the budgeted input prices and budgeted input quantities are

1. *Actual input data from past periods.* Most companies have past data on actual input prices and actual input quantities. These past amounts could be used for the budgeted amounts in a flexible budget. Past data are typically available at a relatively low cost from the company's management information system (MIS). The limitations of using this source are (a) past data include past inefficiencies and (b) past data do not incorporate any expected changes planned to occur in the budget period.

EXHIBIT 7-5
Detailed Variable-Cost Sources of Variance

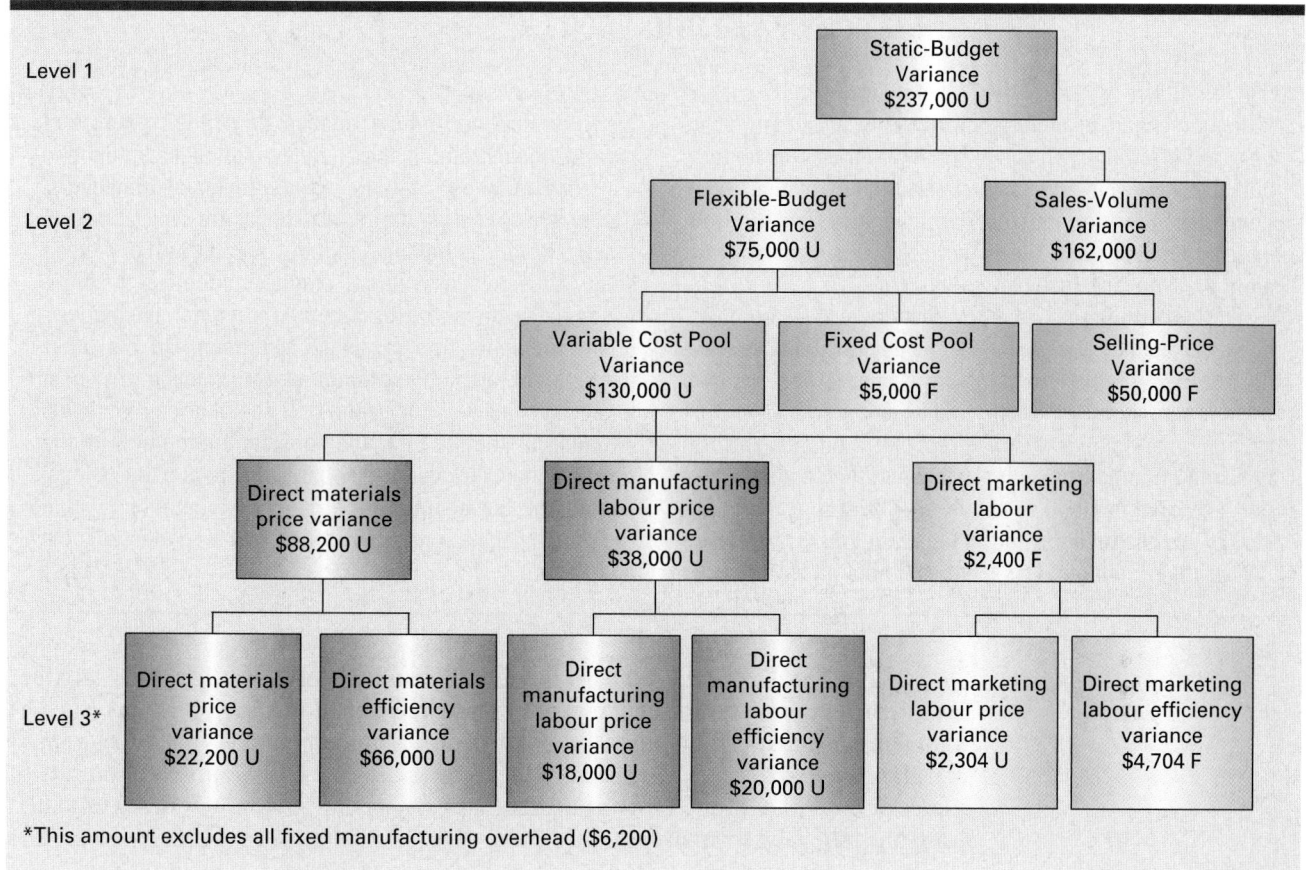

*This amount excludes all fixed manufacturing overhead ($6,200)

2. *Standards developed by Webb.* A standard is a carefully predetermined amount; it is usually expressed on a per-unit basis. A standard communicates what *should* be achieved. Assume Webb uses industry time-and-motion and engineering studies to determine its standard amounts. Each task involved in making a jacket is assigned a standard amount of time based on work by an experienced operator using equipment operating in an efficient manner.

An industry standard may be chosen as either an average or an ideal (benchmark) threshold. Ideal standards imply stretch performance targets but unless external and internal conditions match the ideal, this standard cannot be achieved. Inevitably, Webb would report unfavourable variances and part of the explanation would always be that ideal conditions did not prevail. The advantages of using average external standards are that (a) they can exclude past inefficiencies that Webb can control and (b) they can take into account expected changes in the budget period.

An example of (a) for direct materials is a supplier making dramatic improvements in its ability to consistently meet Webb's demanding quality requirements for the cloth used to make jackets. An example of (b) is the acquisition of new loom machines that operate at a faster speed and that enable work to be done with lower reject rates. For internal efficiencies in the transformation process, an example of (a) is a new process design to eliminate unnecessary steps in production and reduce the labour hours per unit. An example of (b) is the purchase of newer equipment that would replace some labourers during the budgeted time period.

Standards may be short-term or long-term thresholds of performance. If the industry or the company itself is innovative and changes are rapid, then Webb would have to review its standards more often than if the industry and the company were very stable. The standards could not be ideal because the best internal and external conditions would change too frequently. If change is very rapid, it might be better for Webb to avoid standards, and use internal data and assumptions to calculate its budgeted amounts.

Look Up and Look Out!

Managers need to understand not only how their company is performing relative to the internal plan or budget, but also how the company is performing relative to its competitors in the industry. This means looking *up* from internal analyses and *out* to the larger business environment to discover causes for variances.

Good managers connect strategy to their competitive environment. One method is to adopt an industry standard for expected or pro forma performance. For example, variance analysis for Webb could compare its own performance to some industry threshold. Students perform this kind of comparative analysis when they compare the percentage they need to obtain an "A" at their own university or college to the percentage required to receive an "A" at other schools. This gives students an idea of how well they are performing relative to *all* their peers, not merely those attending the same educational institution.

International, national, and provincial employers, the purchasers of managerial labour, are well aware of these differences among academic standards. For a given salary, an employer wants to employ students of the highest quality in the *world* (or country) rather than the highest-quality students from a single institution. On the other hand, local employers focus on purchasing the best locally available labour. Webb's choice of price thresholds (standards) need to be made consistent not only with the product quality (or value proposition) expected by its local customers, but also with the quality expectations within the provincial, national, or international market in which it competes.

Webb has developed standard inputs and standard costs for each of its variable-cost items. A **standard input** is a carefully predetermined quantity of inputs (such as kilograms of materials or hours of labour time) required for one unit of output. A **standard cost** is a carefully predetermined cost. Standard costs can relate to units of inputs or units of outputs. Webb's budgeted cost for each variable cost item is computed using the following formula:

Standard inputs allowed for one output unit × Standard cost per input unit

And the variable cost items are

- ◆ **Direct materials:** 2 square metres of cloth input allowed per output unit (jacket) manufactured, at $30 standard cost per square metre:

  Standard cost = 2 × $30 = $60 per output unit manufactured

- ◆ **Direct manufacturing labour:** 0.80 manufacturing labour-hours of input allowed per output unit manufactured, at $20 standard cost per hour:

  Standard cost = 0.80 × $20 = $16 per output unit manufactured

- ◆ **Direct marketing labour:** 0.25 marketing labour-hours of input allowed per output unit sold, at $24 standard cost per hour:

  Standard cost = 0.25 × $24 = $6 per output unit sold

- ◆ **Variable manufacturing overhead:** Allocated based on 1.20 machine-hours per output unit manufactured, at $10 standard cost per machine-hour:

  Standard cost = 1.20 × $10 = $12 per output unit manufactured

- ◆ **Variable marketing overhead:** Allocated based on 0.125 direct marketing labour-hours per output unit sold, at $40 standard cost per hour:

  Standard cost = 0.125 × $40 = $5 per output unit sold

These standard cost computations explain how Webb developed the numbers in column B of Exhibit 7-2 on p. 312 (also see the Real Companies box on the next page).

Standard Costs: Widespread Adoption Worldwide

Country	Percent of Companies Using Standard Costs	Year Reported
India[a]	77%	2004
Japan[b]	76%	2005
Korea[b]	44%	1994
Malaysia[b]	73%	2005
New Zealand[d]	74%	2000
Singapore[b]	56%	1997
Taiwan[b]	39%	1995
U.K.[c]	73%	1993
U.S.[c]	76%	2003

Surveys from around the world report widespread use of standard costs by manufacturers. Most manufacturing occurs in developing countries but, as shown in the table to the right, there is widespread use of standard costing in both developing and developed countries.

While Japan has adopted standard costing almost universally, Japanese manufacturers also use Kaizen budgeting. This means that the standards are constantly being revised as ongoing changes to production processes alter what is understood as "standard." Japan has adapted the technique of standard costing to a rapidly changing environment.

[a] M. Anand, B.S. Sahay, and S. Saha, "Cost Management Practices in India: An Empirical Study," *ASCI Journal of Management*, 33.1–2 (2004): 1–13.

[b] M. Sulaiman, N. Ahmad, and M.A. Norhayati, "Is Standard Costing Obsolete? Empirical Evidence from Malaysia," *Managerial Auditing Journal*, 20.2 (2005): 109–124.

[c] Ernst & Young, *2003 Survey of Management Accounting* (New York: Ernst & Young, 2003).

[d] R.A. Adler, A.M. Everett, and M. Waldron, "Advanced Management Accounting Techniques in Manufacturing: Utilization, Benefits, and Barriers to Implementation," *Accounting Forum*, 24.2 (2000): 131–150.

The breakdown of the flexible-budget variance into its price and efficiency components is important when evaluating individual managers. At Webb, the production manager is responsible for the efficiency variance, while the purchasing manager is responsible for the price variance. This separate computation of the price variance enables the efficiency variance to be computed using budgeted input prices. Thus, judgments about efficiency (the quantity of inputs used to produce a given level of output) are not affected by whether actual input prices differ from budgeted input prices. A word of caution, however, is appropriate. As will be discussed next, the causes of price and efficiency variances can be interrelated. For this reason, do not interpret these variances in isolation from each other.

CONTROL FEATURE OF STANDARD COSTS

We will now illustrate journal entries when standard costs are used. For illustrative purposes, we will focus on direct materials and direct manufacturing labour.

We will continue with the data in the Webb Company illustration with one exception. Assume that during April 2009 Webb purchases 25,000 square metres (m²) of materials. The actual quantity used is 22,200 m² and the standard quantity allowed for the actual output achieved is 20,000 m². The actual purchase price was $31 per m², while the standard price was $30 m².

Fundamentally this is a transaction that generates an expense. Note that in each of the following entries, unfavourable cost variances are always debits because they reduce operating income. Favourable cost variances are always credits because they increase operating income.

- ◆ **Entry 1(a).** Isolate the direct materials price variance at the time of purchase by debiting Materials Control at standard prices. This is the earliest date possible to isolate this variance.

1. a. Materials Control
    ($25,000 \text{ m}^2 \times \$30/\text{m}^2$) $750,000

    Direct Materials Price Variance
    ($25,000 \text{ m}^2 \times \$1/\text{m}^2$)   25,000

            Accounts Payable Control   775,000

    To record direct materials purchased.

- ◆ **Entry 1(b).** Isolate the direct materials efficiency variance at the time of usage by debiting Work-in-Process Control at standard input quantities allowed for actual output units achieved at standard input prices. This approach is consistent with Chapter 4 where under the actual and normal cost methods, the direct costs are calculated using actual unit costs.

1. b. Work-in-Process Control
    ($20,000 \text{ m}^2 \times \$30/\text{m}^2$) $600,000

    Direct Materials Efficiency Variance
    ($2,200 \text{ m}^2 \times \$30/\text{m}^2$)   66,000

            Materials Control
            ($22,200 \text{ m}^2 \times \$30/\text{m}^2$)   666,000

    To record direct materials used.

- ◆ **Entry 2.** Isolate the direct manufacturing labour price and efficiency variances at the time this labour is used by debiting Work-in-Process Control at standard quantities allowed for actual output units achieved at standard input prices. Note that Wages Payable Control measures the payroll liability and hence is always at actual wage rates. Because direct manufacturing labour can never be inventoried, there is only one journal entry for both the purchase and use of direct manufacturing labour.

2. Work-in-Process Control
    (8,000 hours × $20/hr) $160,000

    Direct Manufacturing Labour Price Variance
    (9,000 hours × $2/hr)   18,000

    Direct Manufacturing Labour Efficiency Variance
    (1,000 hours × $20/hr)   20,000

            Wages Payable Control
            (9,000 hours × $22/hr)   198,000

    To record liability for direct manufacturing labour costs.

A major advantage of this standard costing system is its emphasis on the control feature of standard costs. All variances are isolated at the earliest possible time, when managers can make informed decisions based on those variances.

END-OF-PERIOD ADJUSTMENTS

Chapter 4 discussed two main approaches to recognizing the underallocated or overallocated manufacturing overhead at the end of a period:

- ◆ The adjusted allocation rate approach, which adjusts every job cost record for the difference between the allocated and actual indirect cost amounts
- ◆ The proration approach, which makes adjustments to one or more of the following end-of-period account balances: materials, work in process, finished goods, and cost of goods sold

Price and efficiency variances can also be disposed of using these same two approaches.

STANDARD COSTING AND INFORMATION TECHNOLOGY

Modern information technology greatly facilitates the use of standard costing systems for product costing and control. The company's MIS can readily store bar-code scanner or RFID (radio frequency identification) information to record the receipt of materials, immediately costing each material using its stored standard price. The receipt of materials is matched with the purchase order to record Accounts Payable and to isolate the direct materials price variance.

As output is completed, the standard quantity of direct materials that should have been used is computed and compared with the actual quantity requested for direct materials that was input into the MIS by an operator on the production floor. This difference multiplied by the standard direct material price is the direct materials efficiency variance. Labour variances are calculated as employees log into production floor terminals and punch in their employee numbers, start and end times, and the quantity of the product they helped produce. Managers use this instantaneous feedback on variances to initiate immediate corrective action, as needed.

AN ILLUSTRATION OF PRICE AND EFFICIENCY VARIANCES FOR INPUTS

Consider Webb's three direct-cost categories. The actual cost for each of these three categories is as follows:

	Actual Results	Budgeted Inputs	Standard Inputs/ Unit Output
Direct materials purchased and used			
Direct materials total cost	$688,200		
Square metres of cloth purchased and used	22,200	–	2.00 sq metres
Actual price per square metre	$ 31.00	$30.00	$60.00 per output unit
Direct manufacturing labour			
Direct manufacturing labour total costs	$198,000		
Direct manufacturing total labour-hours of input consumed	9,000	–	0.80 DLH
Actual price per direct manufacturing labour-hour	$ 22.00	$20.00	$16.00 per output unit
Direct marketing labour			
Direct marketing labour total costs	$ 57,600		
Direct marketing total labour-hours of input consumed	2,304	–	0.25 marketing LH
Actual price per direct marketing labour-hour	$ 25.00	$24.00	$6.00 per output unit

Recall in Chapter 6 that this information can be found in the Direct Materials Usage Budget (p. 259) and in the detail of the Other (Nonproduction) Costs Budget (p. 262). For simplicity, we assume here that direct materials used is equal to direct materials purchased; therefore, there will be no Ending Inventory Budget (p. 261). The reason for this is that we do not want to complicate the variance analyses with questions of inventory valuation. If you refer back to Chapter 2, Exhibit 2-10 (p. 52), you will see in Panel B a calculation for cost of goods manufactured where there are dollar values for beginning and ending inventories of direct materials. As a result, the cost of direct materials purchased is incremental to the beginning inventory value to provide us with a cost of direct materials available for use from which the ending inventory of direct materials is subtracted to give us the cost of direct materials used. By assuming the beginning and ending inventories of direct materials are zero, the calculations in Panel B collapse into a simple equivalence that direct materials purchased equals direct materials used. This makes both the calculation and interpretation of direct materials variances much more straightforward.

The actual results and the flexible-budget amounts for each category of direct costs of inputs consumed to produce the 10,000 actual output units in April 2009 are as follows:

	Actual Results	Flexible Budget Variances	Flexible Budget
	(1)	**(2) = (1)−(3)**	**(3)**
Direct materials (22,200 × $31)	$688,200	$ 88,200 U	$600,000 (20,000 × $30)
Direct manufacturing labour (9,000 × $22)	198,000	38,000 U	160,000 (8,000 × $20)
Direct marketing labour (2,304 × $25)	57,600	(2,400) F	60,000 (2,500 × $24)
Total	$943,800	$123,800 U	$820,000

We now use this Webb Company data to illustrate the input-price and input-efficiency variances. Consider first the input-price variances. The materials price and efficiency variances discussed in this chapter illustrate the use of standard costs in promoting cost management or control.

PRICE VARIANCES

The formula for computing a price variance is

$$\begin{array}{c} \text{Price} \\ \text{variance} \end{array} = \left(\begin{array}{c} \text{Actual price} \\ \text{of input} \end{array} - \begin{array}{c} \text{Budgeted price} \\ \text{of input} \end{array} \right) \times \begin{array}{c} \text{Actual quantity} \\ \text{of input} \\ \text{purchased} \end{array}$$

Price variances for each of Webb's three direct cost categories are

	Actual − Budgeted Price per Input Unit	Actual Quantity of Input Units Purchased	=	Input Price Variance
	(1)	**(2)**	**=**	**(1) × (2)**
Direct materials ($31 − $30) × 22,200 m²	$1.00	22,200	=	$22,200 U
Direct manufacturing labour ($22 − $20) × 9,000 direct labour-hours	$2.00	9,000	=	18,000 U
Direct marketing labour ($25 − $24) × 2,304 direct marketing labour-hours	$1.00	2,304	=	2,304 U
				$42,504 U

All three price variances are unfavourable (they reduce operating income) because the actual price of each direct-cost input exceeds the budgeted price; that is, Webb incurred more cost per input unit than was budgeted.

Always consider a broad range of possible causes for price variances. For example, Webb's unfavourable direct materials price variance could be due to one or more of the following reasons:

◆ Webb's purchasing manager negotiated less skillfully than was assumed in the budget.

◆ Webb's purchasing manager bought in smaller lot sizes than budgeted, even though quantity discounts were available for the larger lot sizes.

◆ Materials prices unexpectedly increased because of unanticipated increases in market demand or unanticipated increases in costs of transportation from the supplier to Webb.

◆ Quality of materials purchased exceeded the production specifications, leading to higher prices.

◆ The specified quality of materials required was discontinued by suppliers.

◆ Budgeted purchase prices for Webb's materials were set without careful analysis of the market.

Webb's first response to a materials price variance will be to ascertain the cause. The reason for the unfavourable variance will affect the method used to control it. Assume Webb discovers an unfavourable variance is due to poor negotiating by its purchasing officer. Webb may decide to invest more in training this officer in negotiations, or it may decide to hire a more skillful purchasing officer.

When interpreting materials price variances, Webb's managers should consider any change in the relationship with the company's suppliers. For example, assume that Webb can negotiate fixed prices for future shipments of direct materials with its suppliers. It is likely that price variances will be minimal because they have been fixed according to a new contract.

EFFICIENCY VARIANCES

Consider now the efficiency variance. Computation of efficiency variances requires measurement of inputs for a given level of output. For any actual level of output, the efficiency variance is the difference between the input that was actually used and the input that should have been used to achieve that actual output, holding input price constant:

$$\text{Efficiency variance} = \left(\begin{array}{c} \text{Actual quantity} \\ \text{of input used} \end{array} - \begin{array}{c} \text{Budgeted quantity of input allowed} \\ \text{for actual output units achieved} \end{array} \right) \times \begin{array}{c} \text{Budgeted price} \\ \text{of input} \end{array}$$

The idea here is that an organization is inefficient if it uses more inputs than budgeted for the actual output units achieved, and it is efficient if it uses fewer inputs than budgeted for the actual output units achieved.

The efficiency variances for each of Webb's direct-cost categories are as follows:

Direct-Cost Category	(Actual Quantity of Input Used −	Budgeted Quantity of Input Allowed for Actual Output Units Achieved)	× Budgeted Price of Input]	(1)	(2)	= (3) Efficiency Variance
Direct materials	[22,200 m² −	(10,000 units of output × 2 m²) ×	$30]	2,200	$30.00	= $66,000 U
Direct manufacturing labour	[9,000 −	(10,000 units of output × 0.80) ×	$20]	1,000	$20.00	= $20,000 U
Direct marketing labour	[2,304 −	(10,000 units of output × 0.25) ×	$24]	(196)	$24.00	= $ (4,704) F
Total						= $81,296 U

The two manufacturing-efficiency variances (direct materials and direct manufacturing labour) are both unfavourable because more input was used than was budgeted, resulting in a decrease in operating income. The marketing-efficiency variance is favourable because less input was used than was budgeted, resulting in an increase in operating income (for further discussion, see the Real Companies box, "Almost Fooled," on p. 328).

As with price variances, Webb's managers need to consider a broad range of possible reasons for efficiency variances. For example, Webb's unfavourable direct manufacturing labour variance could be due to one or more of the following reasons:

◆ Webb's personnel manager hired underskilled workers or their training was inadequate (internal).

◆ Webb's production process is being reorganized or a new machine has been installed, creating additional direct manufacturing labour time per jacket as workers learn the new process (internal).

◆ Webb's production scheduler inefficiently scheduled work, resulting in more direct manufacturing labour time per jacket (internal).

◆ Webb's marketing department promised early deliveries to clients, which created too many rush-order interruptions that led to overtime (internal).

◆ Webb's maintenance department did not properly maintain machines, resulting in additional direct manufacturing labour time per jacket to avoid damage done by the machines (internal).

- ◆ Webb's jacket design became obsolete, leading to a new, more complicated design, requiring more direct manufacturing labour time (external; look up and out).
- ◆ Budgeted time standards were set without careful analysis of the operating conditions and employees' skills (external; look up and out).

Suppose Webb determines that the unfavourable variance is due to poor machine maintenance. One reasonable response is to create a team consisting of plant machine engineers and machine operators who will develop a new maintenance schedule so that, in the future, jackets can be sewn in less time.

PRESENTATION OF PRICE AND EFFICIENCY VARIANCES FOR INPUTS

Note how the sum of the price variance and the efficiency variance equals the flexible budget variance:

	Input Price Variances	Input Efficiency Variances	Flexible Budget Variance
Direct materials	$22,200 U	$66,000 U	$ 88,200 U
Direct manufacturing labour	$18,000 U	$20,000 U	$ 38,000 U
Direct marketing labour	$ 2,304 U	$ (4,704) F	$ (2,400) F
Total	$42,504 U	$81,296 U	$123,800 U

Exhibit 7-6 illustrates a convenient way to integrate the actual and budgeted input information used to compute the price and efficiency variances for direct materials. This exhibit assumes that materials purchased equals materials used.

MULTIPLE CAUSES OF VARIANCES

Often the causes of variances are interrelated. For example, an unfavourable materials-efficiency variance can be related to a favourable materials price variance because a purchasing officer purchased lower-priced, lower-quality materials. It is always best to consider possible interdependencies among variances and not to interpret variances in isolation from each other. Causes of variances can arise in different parts of the value

EXHIBIT 7-6

Columnar Presentation of Variance Analysis: Direct Materials Costs for Webb Company for April 2009

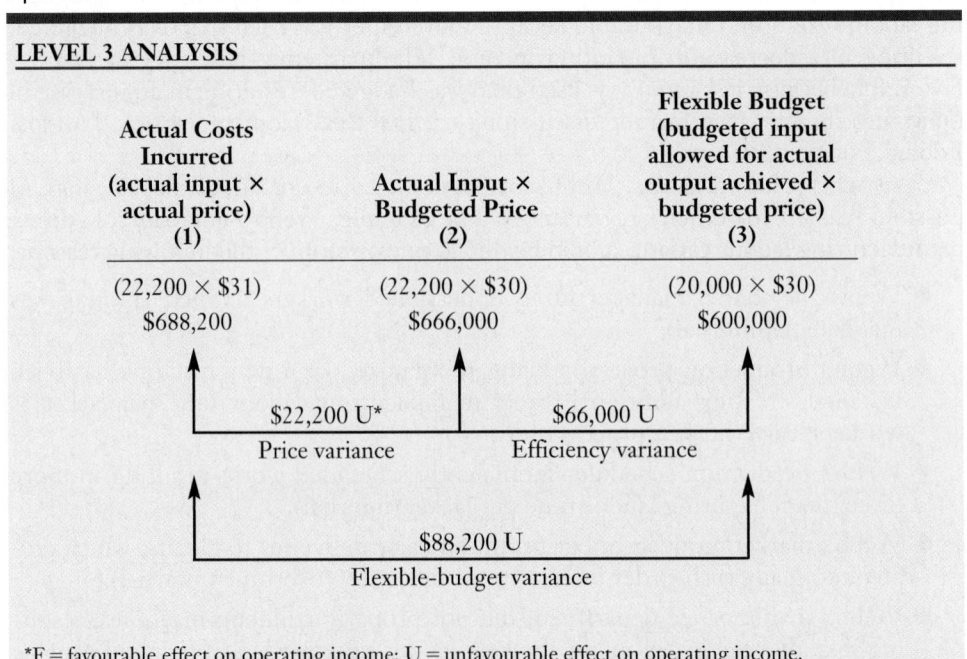

LEVEL 3 ANALYSIS

Actual Costs Incurred (actual input × actual price) (1)	Actual Input × Budgeted Price (2)	Flexible Budget (budgeted input allowed for actual output achieved × budgeted price) (3)
(22,200 × $31)	(22,200 × $30)	(20,000 × $30)
$688,200	$666,000	$600,000

$22,200 U* $66,000 U
Price variance   Efficiency variance

$88,200 U
Flexible-budget variance

*F = favourable effect on operating income; U = unfavourable effect on operating income.

chain in one organization. Consider an unfavourable materials-efficiency variance in the production area of Webb. Possible causes of this variance across the value chain of the organization are:

1. Poor design of products or processes
2. Poor work quality in the manufacturing area
3. Inadequate training of the labour force
4. Inappropriate assignment of labour or machines to specific jobs
5. Congestion due to scheduling a large number of rush orders required by Webb marketing representatives
6. Webb's suppliers do not manufacture cloth materials of uniformly high quality

An even broader perspective is to consider actions taken in the *supply chain* of an organization. A **supply chain** is an integrated system of suppliers, subcontractors, manufacturers, distributors, and retailers collaborating with the purpose of adding value to the output for the customer.[1] The supply chain for Webb Company (the manufacturer) includes

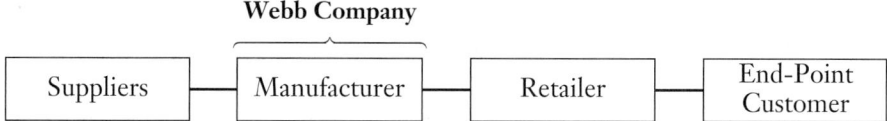

For example, actions taken by Webb's suppliers could cause unfavourable material-efficiency variances at Webb (see point 6 above).

This list of six possible causes is far from exhaustive. However, it does indicate that the cause of a variance in one part of the value chain (production in our example) can be due to actions taken in other parts of the value chain (for example, product design or marketing) and in other organizations. Note how improvements in early stages of the supply chain or value chain can sizably reduce the magnitudes of variances in subsequent stages.

ASSESS YOUR MASTERY

To check your understanding of the material in Learning Objective ❷, go to the *Mastery Questions* section at the end of this chapter and complete Learning Objective ❷ questions 1, 2, and 3.

FLEXIBLE BUDGETING AND ACTIVITY-BASED COSTING

Undertake variance analysis in activity-based costing systems ❸

Activity-based costing (ABC) systems focus on individual activities that may occur throughout the value-chain functions. ABC systems classify the costs of various activities into a cost hierarchy—output unit-level costs, batch-level costs, product-sustaining costs, and facility-sustaining costs. Webb's two direct-cost categories—direct material costs and direct manufacturing labour costs—are examples of output unit-level costs. In this section, we focus on batch-level costs to show how the basic principles and concepts of flexible budgets and variance analysis can be applied to other levels of the cost hierarchy. Batch-level costs are the costs of activities related to a group of units of products or services rather than to each individual unit of product or service.

RELATING BATCH COSTS TO PRODUCT OUTPUT

Consider Lyco Brass Works, which manufactures Jacutaps, a line of decorative brass faucets for home spas. Lyco produces Jacutaps in batches. For each product line, Lyco dedicates material-handling labour to bring materials to the manufacturing area,

---

[1] J.W.K. Chan and N.D. Burn, "Benchmarking Manufacturing Planning and Control (MPC) Systems: An Empirical Study of Hong Kong Supply Chains," *Benchmarking: An International Journal*, 9.3 (2002): 256–77.

transport work in process from one work centre to the next, and take the finished product to the shipping area. Hence, material-handling labour costs for Jacutaps are direct costs of Jacutaps. Because the materials for a batch are moved together, material-handling labour costs vary with the number of batches rather than with the number of units in a batch. Material-handling labour costs are variable direct batch-level costs.

Information regarding Jacutaps for 2009 follows:

	Static-Budget Amounts	Actual Amounts
1. Units of Jacutaps produced and sold	180,000	151,200.00
2. Batch size (units per batch)	150	140.00
3. Number of batches (Line 1 ÷ Line 2)	1,200	1,080.00
4. Material-handling labour-hours per batch	5	5.25
5. Total material-handling labour-hours (Line 3 × Line 4)	6,000	5,670.00
6. Cost per material-handling labour-hour	$ 14	$ 14.50
7. Total material-handling labour costs	$ 84,000	$ 82,215.00

To prepare the flexible budget for material-handling labour costs, Lyco starts with the actual units of output produced, 151,200 units, and proceeds in the following steps:

◆ **Step 1:** *Using budgeted batch size, calculate the number of batches that should have been used to produce the actual output.* At the budgeted batch size of 150 units per batch, Lyco should have produced the 151,200 units of output in 1,008 batches (151,200 units ÷ 150 units per batch).

◆ **Step 2:** *Using budgeted material-handling labour-hours per batch, calculate the number of material-handling labour-hours that should have been used.* At the budgeted quantity of 5 hours per batch, 1,008 batches should have required 5,040 material-handling labour-hours (1,008 batches × 5 hours per batch).

◆ **Step 3:** *Using budgeted cost per material-handling labour-hour, calculate the flexible-budget amount for material-handling labour-hours.* The flexible-budget amount is 5,040 material-handling labour-hours × $14 budgeted cost per material-handling labour-hour = $70,560.

Note how the flexible-budget calculations for material-handling costs focus on batch-level quantities (material-handling labour-hours) rather than on output unit-level amounts (such as material-handling labour-hours per unit of output). The flexible-budget variance for material-handling costs can then be calculated as:

$$
\begin{aligned}
\text{Flexible-budget variance} &= \quad\quad \text{Actual costs} \quad\quad - \quad \text{Flexible-budget costs} \\
&= (5,670 \text{ hours} \times \$14.50 \text{ per hour}) - (5,040 \text{ hours} \times \$14 \text{ per hour}) \\
&= \quad\quad\quad \$82,215 \quad\quad\quad\quad - \quad\quad\quad\quad \$70,560 \\
&= \$11,655, \text{ or } \$11,655 \text{ U}
\end{aligned}
$$

The unfavourable variance indicates that material-handling labour costs were $11,655 higher than the flexible-budget target.

PRICE AND EFFICIENCY VARIANCES

We can get some insight into the possible reasons for this $11,655 unfavourable variance by examining the price and efficiency components of the flexible-budget variance:

$$
\begin{aligned}
\frac{\text{Price}}{\text{variance}} &= \left(\begin{matrix} \text{Actual price} \\ \text{of input} \end{matrix} - \begin{matrix} \text{Budgeted price} \\ \text{of input} \end{matrix} \right) \times \begin{matrix} \text{Actual quantity} \\ \text{of input} \end{matrix} \\
&= (\$14.50 \text{ per hour} - \$14 \text{ per hour}) \times 5,670 \text{ hours} \\
&= \quad\quad \$0.50 \text{ per hour} \quad\quad\quad \times 5,670 \text{ hours} \\
&= \$2,835, \text{ or } \$2,835 \text{ U}
\end{aligned}
$$

The unfavourable price variance for material-handling labour indicates that the $14.50 actual cost per material-handling labour-hour exceeds the $14.00 budgeted cost per material-handling labour-hour. This variance could be due, for example, to (1) Lyco's human resources manager negotiating less skillfully than was planned in the budget and (2) unexpected wage rate increases due to scarcity of labour.

$$\begin{array}{rl} \text{Efficiency} \atop \text{variance} = & \left(\begin{array}{c} \text{Actual quantity} \\ \text{of input used} \end{array} - \begin{array}{c} \text{Budgeted quantity of input} \\ \text{allowed for actual output} \end{array} \right) \times \begin{array}{c} \text{Budgeted price} \\ \text{of input} \end{array} \\ = & (5{,}670 \text{ hours} - 5{,}040 \text{ hours}) \qquad \times \$14 \text{ per hour} \\ = & 630 \text{ hours} \qquad\qquad\qquad \times \$14 \text{ per hour} \\ = & \$8{,}820, \text{ or } \$8{,}820 \text{ U} \end{array}$$

The unfavourable efficiency variance indicates that the 5,670 actual material-handling labour-hours exceeded the 5,040 material-handling labour-hours that Lyco should have used for the number of units it produced. Two reasons for the unfavourable efficiency variance are:

1. Smaller actual batch sizes of 140 units, instead of the budgeted batch sizes of 150 units, resulting in Lyco producing the 151,200 units in 1,080 batches instead of 1,008 (151,200 ÷ 150) batches
2. Higher actual material-handling labour-hours per batch of 5.25 hours instead of budgeted material-handling labour-hours of 5 hours

Reasons for smaller-than-budgeted batch sizes could include:

1. Quality problems, if batch sizes exceed 140 faucets
2. High costs of carrying inventory

Reasons for higher actual material-handling labour-hours per batch could include:

1. Inefficient layout of the Jacutap production line relative to the layout proposed in the budget
2. Material-handling labour having to wait at work centres before picking up or delivering materials
3. Unmotivated, inexperienced, or underskilled employees
4. Standards for material-handling time that are too tight

Identifying the reasons for the efficiency variance will help Lyco's managers develop a plan for improving material-handling labour efficiency.

FOCUS ON HIERARCHY

The idea is to focus the flexible-budget quantity computations at the appropriate level of the cost hierarchy. For example, because material handling is a batch-level cost, the flexible-budget quantity calculations are made at the batch level—the quantity of material-handling labour-hours that Lyco should have used based on the number of batches it should have taken to produce the actual quantity of 151,200 units. If a cost had been a product-sustaining cost—such as product-design cost—the flexible-budget quantity computations would focus at the product-sustaining level, for example, by evaluating the actual complexity of product design relative to the budget.

ASSESS YOUR MASTERY

To check your understanding of the material in Learning Objective ③, go to the *Mastery Questions* section at the end of this chapter and complete Learning Objective ③ question 1.

MANAGERIAL USES OF VARIANCE ANALYSES

4 Describe how managers use variance analyses

Some managers refer to the task of proceeding through successively more detailed data as "drilling-down" (or "peeling the onion"). The growing use of online data collection is increasing the number of databases that have this drill-down capability.

A key use of variance analysis is in performance evaluation. Two attributes of performance are commonly measured:

◆ **Effectiveness:** The degree to which a predetermined objective or target is met.
◆ **Efficiency:** The relative amount of inputs used to achieve a given level of output.

To illustrate the difference, consider that killing a fly with a sledgehammer will be effective (if you hit the fly), but not efficient, since you will expend a lot of extra energy. Killing a fly with a fly swatter is both effective and efficient.

Be careful to understand the cause(s) of a variance before using it as a performance measure. Assume that a Webb purchasing manager has just negotiated a deal resulting in a favourable price variance for materials. The deal could have achieved a favourable variance for any or all of three reasons:

1. The purchasing manager bargained effectively with suppliers.
2. The purchasing manager accepted lower-quality materials at a lower price.
3. The purchasing manager secured a discount for buying in bulk. However, he or she bought higher quantities than necessary for the short run, which resulted in excessive inventories.

If the purchasing manager's performance is evaluated solely on materials price variances, then only reason 1 will be considered acceptable, and the evaluation will be positive. Reasons 2 and 3 will be considered unacceptable and will likely cause the

---

REAL COMPANIES

Almost Fooled: Analyzing Efficiency and Yield

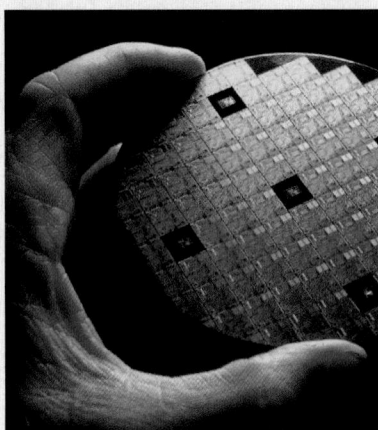

Analog Devices, Inc. (ADI) produces integrated circuits and systems used in computer disc drives, medical instruments, and customer electronics. ADI must deliver high-quality products to its customers on time and at an appropriate cost. By improving yield (a measure of effectiveness)—the quantity of good die produced on a silicon wafer divided by the total number of die that *should* be produced on the wafer for a specified quantity of inputs—ADI can control cost.

ADI's operating managers believed that if they improved yield, efficiency gain would follow. Indeed, in most periods, higher yields were associated with favourable direct materials efficiency variances. In one period, however, a puzzling thing happened—yields increased, but an unfavourable direct materials efficiency variance was also reported.

In the relevant period, ADI had changed to producing more standardized products, which have higher yields than nonstandardized products. To find out if performance improved, managers referred to the *flexible budget* quantity of wafers that should have been produced given the actual inputs consumed. The company discovered that it actually started more wafers than the flexible-budget amount, resulting in the unfavourable direct materials efficiency variance. Performance was *weak* because, although yield increased, it did not increase as much as it should have for the actual quantity and type of output produced.

Source: Analog Devices: The Half-Life System, Harvard Business School case number 9–190–061, and discussions with company management.

company to incur additional costs, such as higher inventory storage costs, higher quality inspection costs, higher costs to repair or replace defects, and higher materials scrap costs. *Managers should not automatically interpret a favourable variance as "good" news.*

FINANCIAL AND NONFINANCIAL PERFORMANCE MEASURES

Almost all organizations use a combination of financial and nonfinancial performance measures rather than relying exclusively on either type. Consider our Webb Company illustration. Exhibit 7-7 shows the manufacturing system used at Webb. At each level of this system, the functions are colour coded to be consistent with the value chain and costing exhibits in previous chapters.

In its cutting room (Cutting and assembly), fabric is laid out and cut into pieces, which are then matched together and assembled. Control is often exercised at the cutting-room level by focusing on nonfinancial measures such as the number of square metres of cloth used to produce 1,000 jackets or the percentage of jackets started and completed without requiring any rework.

Production managers at Webb also will likely use financial measures to evaluate the overall cost efficiency with which operations are being run and to help guide decisions about, say, changing the mix of inputs used in manufacturing jackets. Financial measures are often critical in an organization because they summarize the economic impact of diverse physical activities in a way managers readily understand. Moreover, managers are often evaluated on results reported using financial measures.

Performance measures should focus the managers' attention on reducing the total costs incurred by the entire company. Such a focus is central to the total value-chain analysis theme in the new management approach. In the purchasing manager example used earlier, the company may ultimately lose more money because of reasons 2 and 3 than it gains from reason 1. Conversely, manufacturing costs may be deliberately increased (for example, because higher costs are paid for better materials or more direct manufacturing labour time) to obtain better product quality. In turn, the costs of the better product quality may be more than offset by reductions in customer-service costs.

If any single performance measure (for example, a labour efficiency cost variance or a consumer rating report) receives excessive emphasis, managers tend to

EXHIBIT 7-7
Webb Company Manufacturing System

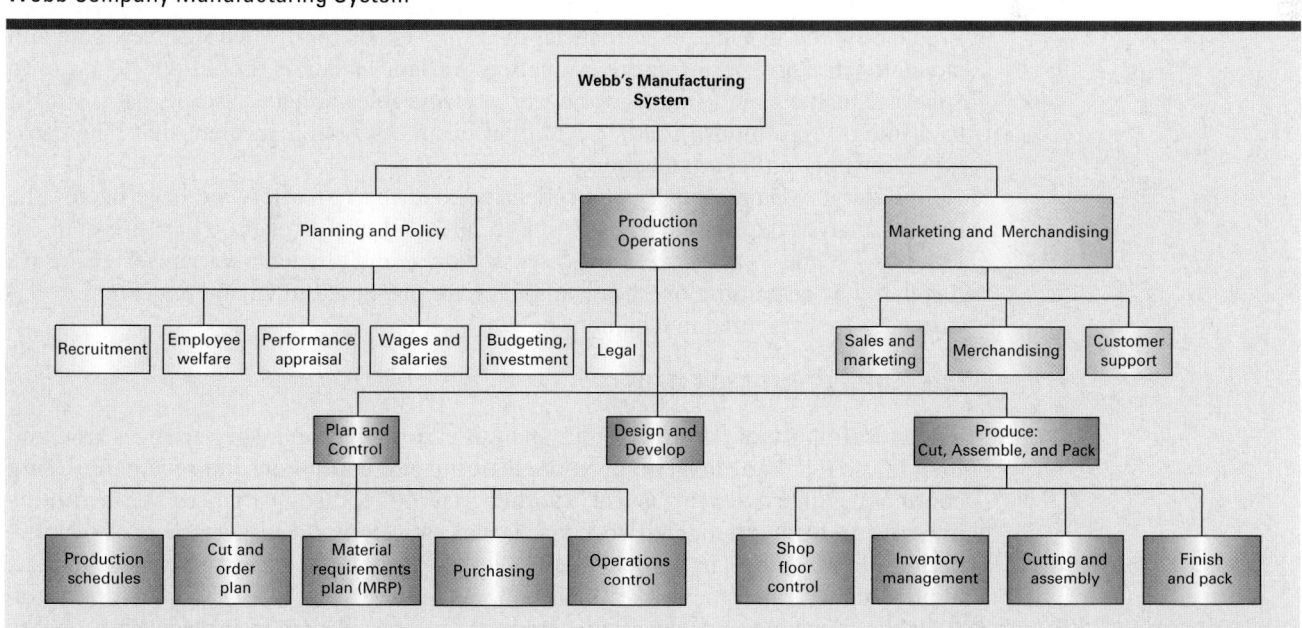

Source: Adapted from D.K. Hurreeram, "Manufacturing Strategy Auditing for Garment Making Companies," *Benchmarking: An International Journal*, 14.3 (2007): 275.

make decisions that will maximize their own reported performance in terms of that single performance measure. Such actions may conflict with the organization's overall goals. This faulty perspective on performance arises because top management has designed a performance measurement and reward system that does not adequately emphasize total organization objectives.

WHEN TO INVESTIGATE VARIANCES

When should variances be investigated? An investigation of variances requires a range of communications among all managers responsible for controlling the value-chain functions. These individuals are highly paid for their time, which is scarce. Detailed investigations are warranted only when the expected benefits will exceed the costs of the investigation.

Frequently, managers base their decisions on when to investigate on thresholds they set using either subjective judgments or rules of thumb. For critical items, a small variance may prompt follow-up. For other items, a minimum dollar variance or a certain percentage of variance from budget may prompt investigations. Of course, a 4% variance in direct materials costs of $1,000,000 may deserve more attention than a 20% variance in repair costs of $10,000. Therefore, rules such as "investigate all variances exceeding $5,000 or 25% of budgeted cost, whichever is lower" are common. Variance analysis is subject to the same cost-benefit test as all other phases of a management-control system.

Management-accounting systems have traditionally implied that a standard is a single acceptable measure. Practically, managers realize that the standard is a band or range of possible acceptable outcomes. Consequently, they expect actual outcomes to vary from budgeted or expected outcomes within some normal limits. A variance within this band is deemed to be from an in-control process and calls for no corrective action by managers. In fact, control is an ongoing task for managers. Supervisors do not wait until the periodic variance report to detect problems. Based on their experience, supervisors use their real-time personal observations and timely nonfinancial reports of actual defect rates. The use of these nonfinancial measures tends to offset the relentless focus on cost reduction. As often as not, a change to a process that reduces cost may also reduce quality below acceptable levels.

At lower levels of control, managers and supervisors depend primarily on nonfinancial performance measures to control operations. Financial measures, however, enable top management to compare variances in a common unit of measure. Frequently, the variance as a financial measure signals both when to investigate and facilitates strategic performance evaluation. Variance analysis should not be a tool to "play the blame game" (that is, for every unfavourable variance, a scapegoat is sought to blame or even punish); rather, it should be an essential ingredient that helps promote learning in the organization.

Exhibit 7-8 presents a comprehensive road map of where we have been. The Level 1 analysis depicts the analysis in Exhibit 7-1. Level 2 relies on data presented in Exhibits 7-3 and 7-4. We have just discussed price and efficiency variances, which are Level 3. The remaining overhead variances are presented in Chapter 8. The Level 4 variances are presented in Chapter 16.

CONTINUOUS IMPROVEMENT

The most important task in variance analysis is to understand why variances arise and then to use that knowledge to promote learning and continuous improvement. Using continuous improvement is yet another way to control variances. **Continuous improvement** is a budgeted cost that is successively reduced over succeeding time periods. For instance, in our list of examples on page 325, we may seek improvements in product design, in the commitment of the manufacturing labour force to do the job right the first time, in the activities undertaken by suppliers to provide high-quality materials, and so on.

Top management should recognize that this learning/continuous improvement use of variance analysis can be undermined if it places excessive (or obsessive) emphasis on meeting individual variance targets. Employees become exhausted as

EXHIBIT 7-8
Performance Measurement Using Variances

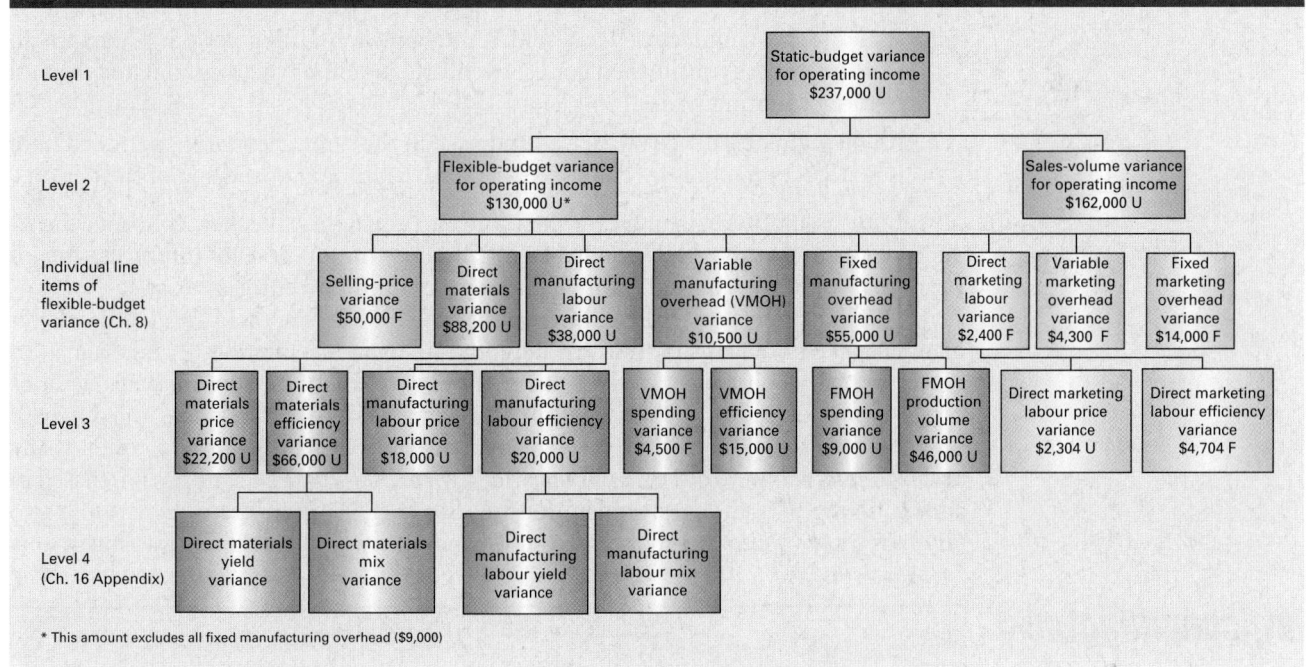

Level 1

Static-budget variance
for operating income
$237,000 U

Level 2

Flexible-budget variance
for operating income
$130,000 U*

Sales-volume variance
for operating income
$162,000 U

Individual line
items of
flexible-budget
variance (Ch. 8)

Selling-price
variance
$50,000 F

Direct
materials
variance
$88,200 U

Direct
manufacturing
labour
variance
$38,000 U

Variable
manufacturing
overhead (VMOH)
variance
$10,500 U

Fixed
manufacturing
overhead
variance
$55,000 U

Direct
marketing
labour
variance
$2,400 F

Variable
marketing
overhead
variance
$4,300 F

Fixed
marketing
overhead
variance
$14,000 F

Level 3

Direct
materials
price
variance
$22,200 U

Direct
materials
efficiency
variance
$66,000 U

Direct
manufacturing
labour price
variance
$18,000 U

Direct
manufacturing
labour efficiency
variance
$20,000 U

VMOH
spending
variance
$4,500 F

VMOH
efficiency
variance
$15,000 U

FMOH
spending
variance
$9,000 U

FMOH
production
volume
variance
$46,000 U

Direct marketing
labour price
variance
$2,304 U

Direct marketing
labour efficiency
variance
$4,704 F

Level 4
(Ch. 16 Appendix)

Direct materials
yield
variance

Direct materials
mix
variance

Direct
manufacturing
labour yield
variance

Direct
manufacturing
labour mix
variance

* This amount excludes all fixed manufacturing overhead ($9,000)

they try to meet increasingly difficult targets. Managers may engage in padding the standard input quantities or input prices so that their targets are easier to attain. Padded numbers in a budget, however, mean that management underperformance is potentially rewarded, and learning and improvement are less likely to occur.

Continuous improvement is one of the evolving management themes highlighted in this book (see the discussion of Kaizen budgeting in Chapter 6). The budgeted direct materials cost for each jacket that Webb Company manufactured in April 2009 is $60 per unit. The budgeted cost used in variance analysis for subsequent periods could be based on a targeted 1% reduction each period:

Month	Prior Month's Amount	Reduction in Budgeted Amount	Revised Budgeted Amount
April 2009	–	–	$60.00
May 2009	$60.00	$0.600 (0.01 × $60.00)	59.40
June 2009	59.40	0.594 (0.01 × $59.40)	58.81
July 2009	58.81	0.588 (0.01 × $58.81)	58.22

The source of the 1% reduction in budgeted direct materials costs could be efficiency improvements or price reductions. By using continuous improvement budgeted costs, an organization signals the importance of constantly seeking ways to reduce total costs. For example, managers could avoid unfavourable materials efficiency variances by continuously reducing materials waste.

Products in the initial months of their production may have higher budgeted improvement rates than those that have been in production for, say, three years. Improvement opportunities may be much easier to identify when products have just started in production. Once the easy opportunities have been identified ("the low-hanging fruit picked"), much more ingenuity may be required to identify successive improvement opportunities. The improvements in production that arise as people learn new processes are expanded upon in Chapter 10.

IMPACT OF INVENTORIES

Our Webb Company illustration assumed the following:

1. All units are manufactured and sold in the same accounting period. There are no work-in-process or finished goods inventories at either the beginning or the end of the accounting period.

2. All direct materials are purchased and used in the same accounting period. There is no direct materials inventory at either the beginning or the end of the period.

Both assumptions can be relaxed without changing the key concepts introduced in this chapter. However, changes in the computation or interpretation of variances would be required when beginning or ending inventories exist.

Suppose direct materials are purchased some time before their use and that direct materials inventories exist at the beginning or end of the accounting period. Managers typically want to pinpoint variances at the earliest possible time so that their decisions can be best informed by the variances. For direct materials price variances, the purchase date will almost always be the earliest possible time to isolate them. As a result, many organizations compute direct materials price variances using the quantities purchased in an accounting period. The Problem for Self-Study (p. 340) illustrates how to use two different times (purchase time and use time) to pinpoint direct materials variances.

MyAccountingLab

ASSESS YOUR MASTERY

To check your understanding of the material in Learning Objective ❹, go to the *Mastery Questions* section at the end of this chapter and complete Learning Objective ❹ question 1.

GOVERNANCE ISSUES

Management Accounting: Learn, Don't Blame

The performance-evaluation aspect of variance analysis causes anxiety for managers because they are responsible for the commitment made to achieving budgeted targets—for being effective. If targets are not met, however, the objective should not be to find people to blame, but to learn how to become more effective and efficient. Variance analyses are critical to an organization's success. Management accountants must never waver from accurately presenting the numbers and from persuading managers to be realistic about performance. Learning from past mistakes and implementing corrective action plans quickly can happen only when management accountants are successful in their roles as motivators, communicators, and team players.

Managers at Starbucks, for example, are responsible for making sure that each new store's sales meet or exceed expectations: not a small task. Management accountants at the company are intimately involved in establishing budgeted performance and monitoring actual performance for each of the company's stores. Management accountants provide managers with clear and precise explanations for variances in a thoughtful, constructive, and helpful way. Variances should be addressed by teams so that there are shared responsibilities and accumulation of ideas from all areas of the organization. McDonald's, for example, established a system-wide response to upgrading its coffee offerings due to increased competition from Starbucks.

Johnson & Johnson (J&J), a global giant in pharmaceuticals and consumer products, conducts business via hundreds of subsidiary companies within a highly decentralized structure. At J&J, management accountants bring together the senior management teams at the subsidiary companies to explain and remedy the causes of any unfavourable variances. One J&J executive remarked that "managers are forced to review their businesses in depth for costs, trends, manufacturing efficiency, marketing plans, and their competitive situation. Program and action plans result. . . . These meetings force us to think about how we should respond and to look at both the upside and downside of changes in the business. They really get our creative juices flowing."

Sources: Allison Linn, "Starbucks Lays Out Aggressive Growth Plans," *Seattle Post-Intelligence*, March 30, 2004; "Schaeffer's Market Observation Features Starbucks: SBUX," *Businesswire.com*, April 1, 2004; Andy Serwer, "Starbucks to Go," *Fortune*, January 26, 2004; R. Simons, *Codman and Shurtleff Inc.: Planning and Control System*, Harvard Business School case number 9–187–081.

The budgeted amounts in the variance formulas discussed in this chapter are baseline points of reference from which comparisons can be made. The term **benchmarking** refers to a strategy of establishing ideal standards as the baseline against which to measure actual performance. In the 1980s, Xerox successfully used benchmarking to aggressively respond to encroachment by international competitors and regain market share. Notice that market share depends on how well Xerox competes and requires that Xerox analyze its external competitors. Extending performance indicators beyond the measurement of internal value-chain functions is one way to distinguish the strategic characteristic of benchmarking as a method of setting standards. Competitive benchmarking, as it is now known, is only one form of strategic management accounting.

Benchmarking is also a useful way to set internal performance standards, especially for large multi-national companies. Companies also benchmark key competencies, quality, product or service attributes, customer profitability, intellectual capital, and environmental sustainability.[2] Benchmarking involves continuous change within a company in an effort to match or exceed the best performance in some domain. Changes in the outputs offered, design processes, speed of innovation, target markets, and customers served are often needed to achieve or exceed a benchmark. Management's choice to benchmark can either support an existing corporate mission and strategy, or signal a change. The answer to whether or not benchmarking is the best remedy depends on careful reconsideration of existing strategic choices.

Exhibit 7-9 illustrates the process of benchmarking. The process is ongoing and the cycle of activities is not sequential. The strategy of adopting excellence as a goal implies widespread change in many organizations. Simply establishing what a best practice or performance threshold *is* means little without understanding if and how an organization can change to achieve it. The broader the scope of a benchmarking target, the more dispersed the relevant data will be. For example, benchmarking a

EXHIBIT 7-9
The Benchmarking Process

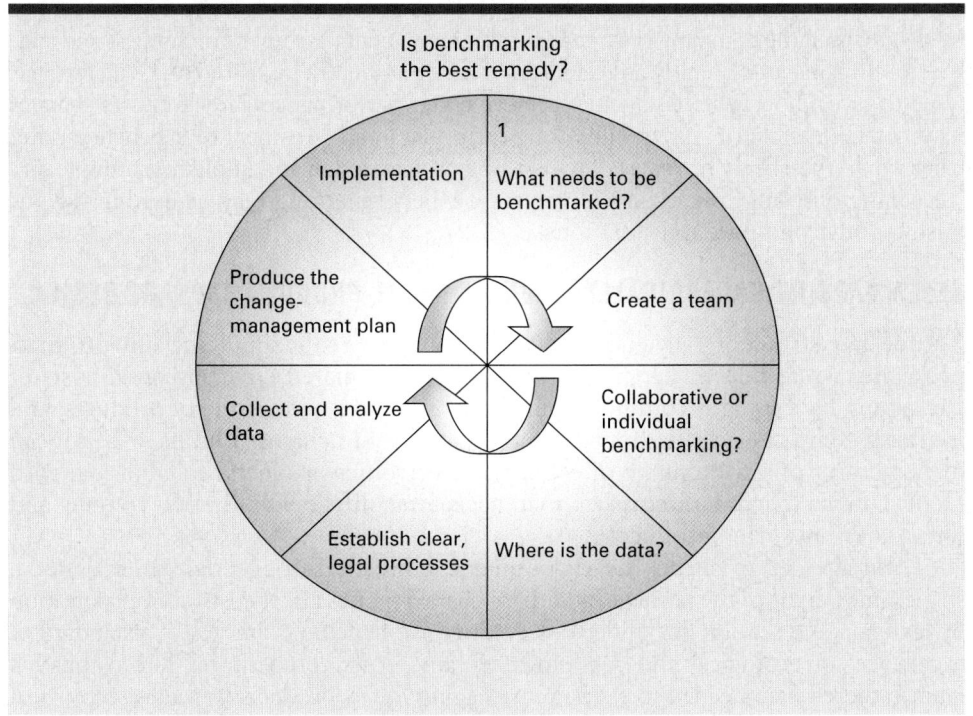

[2]W.P. Wong and K.Y. Wong, "A Review on Benchmarking of Supply Chain Performance Measures," *Benchmarking: An International Journal*, 15.1 (2008): 25–51.

What Is a Strategic Choice?

Various ways to classify strategic choices have been suggested. For example, a company may choose to compete effectively through excellent cost leadership or to differentiate the output it presents to consumers (Porter, 1980). The strategy of differentiation means that companies will undertake the appropriate research to match their products to what customers say they value. Risk arises because there can be a gap between what customers say they value and what they are willing to pay for. Apple is an example of a company that competes by differentiating its products. In contrast, Dell is an example of a company that competes using cost leadership.

A second way of thinking about strategy is the choice to use a grow or harvest strategy, an agricultural metaphor that views business itself as a life cycle dependent on external changes (Gupta and Govindarajan, 1984).

A third way of thinking about strategy is the choice to prospect for new opportunities or defend existing markets (Miles & Snow, 1978).

There is considerable similarity among the strategies of differentiation, growth, and prospecting, and among those of cost leadership, harvest, and defence. A company's choice of strategy will make that strategy a priority, but not necessarily to the exclusion of other strategies. For example, the choice to succeed competitively through prospecting would not mean that costs (or cost leadership) are completely ignored.

Sources: M. Porter, *Competitive Strategy* (New York: Free Press, 1980); R.E. Miles and C.G. Snow, *Organizational Strategy, Structure, and Process* (New York: McGraw-Hill, 1978); V. Govinderajan and J. Fisher, "Strategy, Control Systems, and Resource Sharing: Effects on Business-unit Performance," *The Academy of Management Journal,* 33.2 (1990): 259–285.

specific manufacturing process for one product is of narrower scope than benchmarking the most ecologically friendly packaging process for all products. The first is limited to applying change to a specific value-chain function within an organization. The second is almost unbounded in terms of the factors that must be considered to define and achieve the best packaging process.

For instance, if the benchmarking team undertakes preliminary investigation, it may discover that the most important data are only available from competitors. The initial decision to undertake individual benchmarking would change to a collaborative approach. The central issue, however, is that sharing some competitive information is illegal if it leads to price fixing or discourages competition in a market. If the key data cannot be shared, then the company must return to an individual benchmarking process and analyze the available information as best it can. If information can be shared, the data are analyzed to reveal how other companies achieve better performance. However, the changes may not be feasible or may require long-term planning. Members of a benchmarking team would then likely be replaced in part by a project design and implementation team.

The following discussions illustrate how benchmarking may be used in various business environments and situations.

BENCHMARKING ECOLOGICALLY FRIENDLY MULTI-PRODUCT PACKAGE DESIGN

Europe has stringent recycling and re-use laws to reduce and reclaim product-packaging waste that makes producers bear the estimated environmental costs of packaging. Packaging is common to manufacturers of a wide range of products, and it affects companies throughout the supply and value chains. Philips, a European manufacturer of a wide range of consumer electronics products, collaborated with Delft University and discovered that packaging affected both the volume and weight of transported products.

Package design affects the environment indirectly through the materials used, shape, and weight of the package, and these characteristics affect costs of transportation by land, air, and sea. Philips undertook competitive benchmarking to set a standard of excellence for ecological and cost efficiency among its competitors. The company's team gathered data needed to redesign packaging for its products to reduce ecological impact and the costs of transportation. Philips' product offerings range from light bulbs and personal shavers to TV sets and cell phones. Its team identified nine functions of packaging but not all nine were relevant for every product.

Through analyzing the gathered data, the team separated product-packaging requirements into two types. One design focused on preserving the electronic and physical integrity of some products. A set of performance indicators for ecological and cost efficiency was established for this packaging category. A different packaging design was needed for other products to prevent theft and attract customer attention. Different best-performance indicators or benchmarks were needed to choose the most ecological and cost-efficient package for these types of products. In a market with very slim margins, the overall reduction to environmental cost ranged from 1% to 2%. The result of multi-product internal benchmarking included:

◆ improved understanding of choice of packaging design
◆ reduced ecological impact for Philips' packaging designs
◆ reduced environmental costs below those of competitors[3]

BENCHMARKING THE COMPETITIVE GAP

Rather than establish a threshold level of performance, a second approach to benchmarking is to measure the gap between best and worst. The relevant performance statistics for professional sports teams are easily accessible on many public websites. What is less obvious to those who are not familiar with competitive sports is which of these statistics matter in separating the winners from the losers. In the study from which this example has been summarized, the gap between the best and worst is very small—a reflection of how competitive professional sports are.[4]

Consider the goal of a for-profit basketball franchise: To advance through progressively more intense to win the playoffs championship. As the season unfolds, the results of each game initiate efforts towards continuous improvement to better the winning performance record. This is not only the nature of sports competition but has far-reaching financial implications. Failing teams can lose millions annually in season-ticket sales, depending on the unit price and volume of sales. They lose additional revenue from failing to make it to semi-final and final playoff rounds—games for which the demand by loyal fans for tickets increases. Franchises would also lose broadcasting revenues based on the lower number of TV viewers, and players themselves might lose endorsement opportunities and bonuses if the team fails. Moreover, taxpayers and corporate sponsors are more likely to construct new arenas for winning than losing teams.

With the high involvement of fans, sports franchises like those in the NBA produce huge volumes of performance statistics. The question is, which statistics are related to improved winning performance? Nourayi (2006) established the clear association between ticket sales and the ratio of winning-to-losing performances. The higher a team's win/loss ratio, the higher its ticket sales. Top basketball teams also showed some common offensive statistics. Winning teams:

◆ shot less frequently but made more field goals (effectiveness)
◆ shot less frequently but made more 3-point shots
◆ made a higher percentage of free throws
◆ had fewer offensive rebounds

On defence, when the top teams won games, they:

◆ stole the ball more often from opponents
◆ took possession of more defensive rebounds (blocking second-shot opportunities)
◆ blocked more shots
◆ turned over the ball less frequently

[3]R. Wever, C. Boks, T. Marinelli, and A. Stevels, "Increasing the Benefits of Product-level Benchmarking for Strategic Eco-efficient Decision Making," *Benchmarking: An International Journal*, 14.6 (2007): 711–727.

[4]The NBA information presented in this section is from M. Nourayi, "Profitability in Professional Sports and Benchmarking: The Case of NBA Franchises," *Benchmarking: An International Journal*, 13.3 (2006): 252–271.

The performance gaps among the top and bottom four teams during the regular season are small. These gaps represent the difference between the best in the NBA and the worst. As such, they indicate the distance the losing teams must cover to achieve excellent winning performance. In other words, they show *how* teams need to improve and by *how much*. Team owners and managers can see from the statistics that the gap between the top and bottom performers in terms of actual performance is very small, but closing that gap has the potential to produce very large financial payoffs.

For example, the table below indicates a losing team must improve its ratio of field goals made to those attempted by 4% to perform as well offensively as a top team, and to the same end they must improve their free throw percentage by 2.3%. On defence, the top teams achieve 3.5 more assists and almost 2 more defensive rebounds per game than the losing teams and have only 1 less turnover. These slim differences between the best and worst result in almost 8 more points scored per game by the best team. These benchmarks were produced from readily available statistics and illustrate the intensity of competition among professional basketball teams in the 1995 to 1998 regular-season games.

Offense		Defence	
Statistics	Gap	Statistics	Gap
Field goals made	2.644	Assists	3.505
Field goal attempts	−1.152	Steals	0.551
Field goal %	4.0%	Offensive rebounds	−0.444
Free throws made	2.539	Defensive rebounds	1.951
Free throw attempts	2.584	Total rebounds	1.507
Free throw %	2.3%	Turnovers	−1.152
3-point shots made	0.887	Team rebounds	0.189
3-point shot attempts	1.395	Blocked shots	0.326
3-point %	0.026	Points	7.508

ENVIRONMENTAL BENCHMARKING

Increasing concern about environmental sustainability has extended the scope of consideration companies must give to their performance. While internal benchmarking based on widely available statistics can improve profitability, companies are increasingly required to avoid or minimize environmental destruction. McDonald's faced widespread criticism of its use of polystyrene clamshell containers, for example.[5]

But are polystyrene containers really worse than paper? The table below compares the resources consumed by using polystyrene and paper cups. It assumes a linear economic input–output analysis for the cups throughout their life cycles, including the pollution effects of production. Linearity means if outputs increase by 5% (for example), each input will also increase by 5%. These indicators fail to include either the paraffin (a petroleum product) or plastic coatings used on paper cups to waterproof them. The environmental cost of using paper cups also assumes no cardboard collars are used to reduce heat transferred by the hot liquid inside the cup to customers' hands. Thus, the environmental effects of using paper cups are understated.

Based on these statistics, the production of polystyrene cups consumes less energy but more non-renewable ores. Producing polystyrene cups emits less conventional pollutants but causes more toxic emissions and hazardous wastes than the production of paper cups. Overall, on an equivalent measure basis, consumption of 10 million paper cups contributes slightly less than double the amount towards global warming than does the consumption of polystyrene cups.

[5]The information in this example was adapted from H.S. Matthews and L.B. Lave, "Using Input–Output Analysis for Corporate Benchmarking," *Benchmarking: An International Journal*, 10.2 (2003): 152–167.

	A	B	C	D	E	F	G	H	I
1	Price per unit		$0.03	$0.06					
2	Output value ($mm)		$0.745	$1.463					
3	**Consumption**	**Units**	**Polystyrene**	**Paper**			**Units**	**Polystyrene**	**Paper**
4	Energy					Conventional Pollutants			
5	Coal	MT	100.04	232.6		Sulfur dioxide	MT	1.7	4.2
6	Natural gas	MT	79.72	63.6		Carbon monoxide	MT	1.4	4.4
7	Light fuel oil	MT	9.18	25.1		Nitrogen oxides	MT	> 1.5	3.5
8	Heavy fuel oil	MT	4.67	24.8		Volatile organics	MT	0.76	1.1
9	Electricity	MKWH	0.37	0.51		Hazardous wastes			
10	Total energy	TJ	9.27	13.9		Generated	MT	155	41
11	Non-renewable ore					Managed onsite	MT	151	40
12	Iron ores	MT	8.84	13.94		Shipped out	MT	4	2
13	Copper ores	MT	85.64	33.79		Summary index			
14	Toxic emissions					Global warming potential	MT CO_2	566	984
15	Air	MT	0.35	0.51					
16	Water	MT	0.04	0.05		MT = metric tons; MKWH = millions of kilowatt hours; TJ = terajoules			
17	Land	MT	0.04	0.03		Summary index MT CO_2 measured as the metric tonnes equivalent of carbon dioxide emissions			
18	Total emissions	MT	0.6	0.62					
19	Releases and transfers	MT	1.7	0.92					

The table above suggests that any decision on the cups to use will depend on the relative importance of hazardous waste and non-renewable ore compared to toxic emissions and non-renewable energy for environmental advocates. While these data estimate the relative global-warming potential, the social costs of each contribution to that potential are not indicated.

A company such as McDonald's faced the possibility of a strong consumer backlash against its use of plastic packaging. Based on historical data both for resolved legal claims against companies in polluting industries and measures of the volume of pollution of various types of industries, the social costs of pollution can be estimated.

	A	B	C	D	E
1			**Added Social**		**Added Social**
2			**Cost of Paper**		**Cost of Polystyrene**
3		**Paper %**	**at $0.06/cup**	**Polystyrene %**	**at $0.03/cup**
4	Total median cost	2.9785	0.17871	1.4912	0.044736
5	Component air pollution costs:				
6	Electric utilities	0.7151	0.042906	0.432	0.01296
7	Energy	0.323	0.01938	0.3099	0.009297
8	Transportation	0.2262	0.013572	0.0809	0.002427
9	Industrial chemicals	0.0682	0.004092	0.2618	0.007854
10	Paper, pulp mills	1.1223	0.067338	0	0
11	Paper containers	0.01571	0.0009426	0	0
12	Plastic inputs	0	0	0.1865	0.005595
13	Repair, maintenance	0	0	0.0145	0.000435
14	Other	0.3666	0.021996	0.2056	0.006168

The actual costing process is very complex and beyond the scope of this text; however, the results in the table below indicate that the social costs of air pollution from consuming polystyrene cups is approximately 25% (0.0447 ÷ 0.1787) that of paper.

One strong implication is that a public willing to consume beverages from paper containers should be willing to pay almost $0.18 more (on average) for the product. Those willing to consume beverages from a polystyrene container should be willing to pay only $0.04 more (on average) for the product. The retailer of beverages should be able to pass this cost of air pollution on to the final consumer, who is willing to reward the producer for making the environmentally friendly choice.

While $0.04 seems a very small value, when multiplied by 10 million cups it becomes a social cost of $447,360 for the consumption of polystyrene cups compared to $1,787,100 for paper cups. Notice also that the social cost of air pollution is almost 3 times the real cost of consuming paper (0.1787 ÷ 0.06 = 2.978) and is almost one-and-a-half-times the real cost of consuming polystyrene cups (0.04474 ÷ 0.03 = 1.491). Finally, the costs of waste management, re-use, recycling, reclamation, and remediation must be included before benchmarking the social cost of environmental sustainability.

Ultimately consumers demand products in preferred packages as well as environmentally sustainable production choices. Consumers who value environmental sustainability will be willing to pay appropriate prices for products that are delivered in appropriate packages.

THINKING CRITICALLY

What kind of cup do you buy your coffee in? Who bears the social cost of your choice (or who *should*)? Read on for further discussion.

Benchmarking, a strategic management-accounting method to set targets of cost excellence, speaks the universal language of dollars and cents. Management accountants are trained specifically to analyze and translate complex and diverse nonfinancial measures of resources consumed into estimates of the cost of those resources, and then to allocate costs in a reasonable way to outputs (either goods or services). Financial growth through to the harvest and consumption of resources that are then thrown away in paper and plastic cups (plus waste management costs) comprise a startlingly high social cost of environmental sustainability.

The real social cost of consuming a standard portion of coffee from an individual paper or plastic cup currently is not paid by any participant in the supply chain, in part because the cost is largely unknown or not communicated reliably through a price mechanism. Imagine the choice a consumer would make between paying $12 for a standard cup of coffee served in a disposable paper cup versus $2 for an identical portion served in a personally owned, reuseable cup. The strategic management-accounting technique of benchmarking environmental sustainability means that, ultimately, the consumer can bear the full social cost of choosing to consume beverages in disposable cups, including waste management.

NOT-FOR-PROFIT BENCHMARKING

Examples of benchmarking in the Canadian government include benchmarking trust, change, corporate development strategy, tasks, progress, and quality. The following example refers to a provincial government ministry of health initiative. The initiative was designed to allocate the total amount of tax revenue available to hospitals for health care in a different way. Health care funds also include those allocated to public care (e.g., vaccination programs) and prevention of illness.

HayGroup is a global human resources consulting organization. HayGroup, among other things, collects and analyzes cost information submitted by hospitals to provincial and federal governments to comply with financial and nonfinancial reporting regulations. From this and other data HayGroup collects privately, the target hospital can prepare benchmark reports. These reports show how costs to treat case-mix groups (CMG) in a target hospital differ from those of other comparable hospitals.

CMG is an imaginary cost object, which refers to a set of related medical diagnoses, for example stroke, respiratory disorders, etc.

Standard lengths of stay per CMG have been calculated. From these, standard costs have been estimated per length of stay for each CMG. A standard cost, however, is not a benchmark. A benchmark is the lowest cost per length of stay achieved by any hospital for treatment of a particular CMG. If a hospital's actual costs per CMG are higher than a standard cost for comparable hospitals, it will certainly be higher than the benchmark cost per CMG in that same group of hospitals.

Exhibit 7-10 illustrates a typical report for a client hospital. Panel A reports the target hospital's cost per CMG is 10% above the average for comparable hospitals. Note that the benchmark hospital is Hospital E and the target hospital's costs are 59% higher than this benchmark. Panel B reports costs for three specific CMGs. Focus for now on the costs per CMG for stroke. The problem for the target hospital is that the government that funds treatment of patients in this CMG will only pay the average amount. If the target hospital cannot reduce its costs, it will show an operating deficit.

The government has the power to replace managers of the hospital with others appointed by the government. It may be true that higher CMG costs can be justified because those admitted are more seriously ill than at other hospitals, or the treatment provided is superior, but this is rare. Moreover, the costs per CMG are adjusted for severity levels and hospitals must report these severity levels in the normal course of complying with government reporting requirements.

EXHIBIT 7-10
Cost Benchmark Reports for Client Hospital by Market Insights

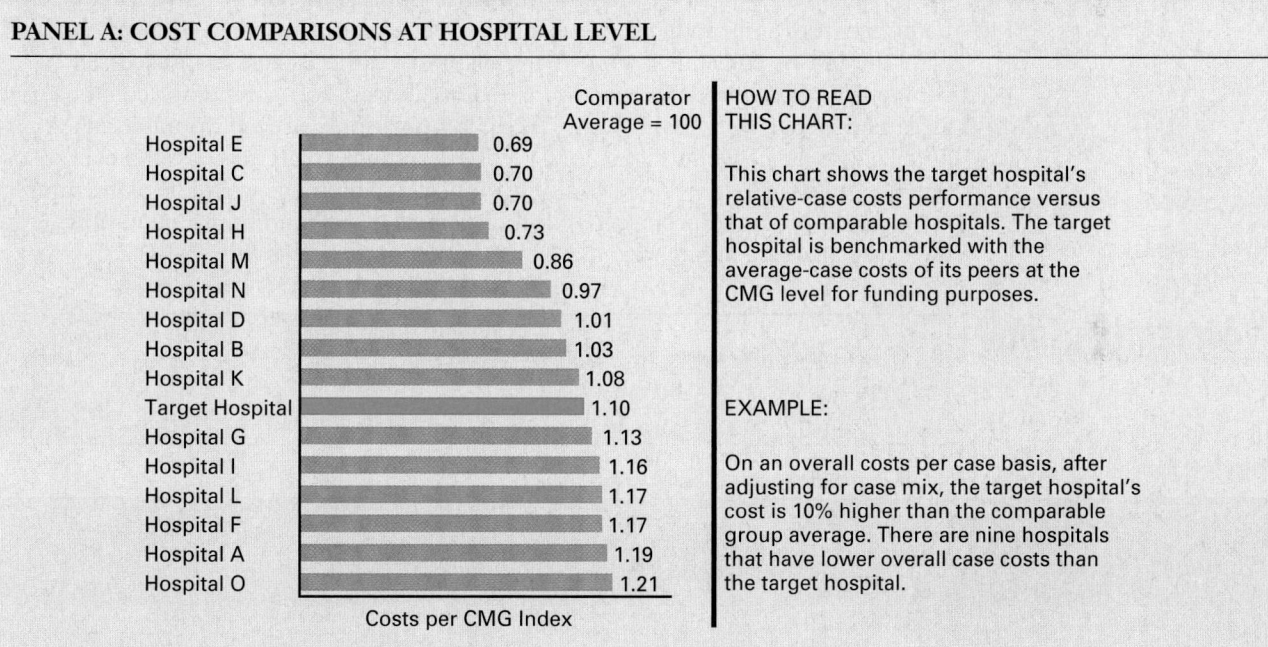

PANEL A: COST COMPARISONS AT HOSPITAL LEVEL

Comparator Average = 100

Hospital E	0.69
Hospital C	0.70
Hospital J	0.70
Hospital H	0.73
Hospital M	0.86
Hospital N	0.97
Hospital D	1.01
Hospital B	1.03
Hospital K	1.08
Target Hospital	1.10
Hospital G	1.13
Hospital I	1.16
Hospital L	1.17
Hospital F	1.17
Hospital A	1.19
Hospital O	1.21

Costs per CMG Index

HOW TO READ THIS CHART:

This chart shows the target hospital's relative-case costs performance versus that of comparable hospitals. The target hospital is benchmarked with the average-case costs of its peers at the CMG level for funding purposes.

EXAMPLE:

On an overall costs per case basis, after adjusting for case mix, the target hospital's cost is 10% higher than the comparable group average. There are nine hospitals that have lower overall case costs than the target hospital.

PANEL B: COST COMPARISONS AT DIAGNOSTIC GROUP LEVEL

Case-Mix Group	Target Hospital	Group Average	25th Percentile	Average of Lowest Cost Quartile (0–25th)
Stroke	$33,700	$31,300	$21,900	$20,500
Respiratory disorders	66,800	53,700	44,400	38,400
Simple pneumonia	37,100	29,500	23,300	22,000

Source: Market Insights (San Francisco, California).

While those managing hospitals are responsible for prudent fiscal management, their overriding concern is for the safety of their patients. That is why the managers of the target hospital must exercise caution when they change their treatment processes to become more cost-efficient. Safe treatment of patients is made more complex because many patients are not admitted until they are very close to death. Simply changing one or two activities may reduce the costs of activities but not the treatment processes as a whole. Costs saved by changing one set of activities can easily drive up the costs of a second interlinked and more expensive set of activities. The result may be higher, rather than lower, overall costs per CMG. It is also the case that hospitals are funded to provide effective and safe medical treatment, not to develop sophisticated and reliable costing systems. This means the input used to calculate costs per CMG may not be accurate. Despite these potential shortcomings, benchmarking does give managers the opportunity to investigate different, equally safe treatment processes that also reduce costs.

Cost reports like Exhibit 7-10 provide an external benchmark that forces the administrator to ask *why* cost levels differ between hospitals and *how* best practices can be transferred from the more efficient to the less efficient hospitals.

Evaluating the overall performance of a hospital or hospital personnel requires analyzing other factors in addition to costs. These factors include the perceived quality of service to patients; the success rate of operations (for example, how many patients with strokes survive?); and the morale of the doctors, nurses, and other staff. In many cases, however, cost factors have been given too little weighting in the past, in part because of the lack of reliable information on cost relationships in this sector of the economy.

Benchmark reports based on the costs of other companies can be developed for many activities and products. For example, Webb Company could estimate (possibly with the aid of consultants) the materials cost of the jackets manufactured by its competitors. The materials cost estimate of the lowest-cost competitor could be used as the budgeted amounts in its variance computations. An unfavourable materials-efficiency variance would signal that Webb has a higher materials cost than "best cost practice" in its industry. The magnitude of the cost difference would be of great interest to Webb. It could prompt Webb to do an extensive search into how to bring its own cost structure in line with that of the lowest in the industry.

MyAccountingLab

ASSESS YOUR MASTERY

To check your understanding of the material in Learning Objective ❺ , go to the *Mastery Questions* section at the end of this chapter and complete Learning Objective ❺ question 1.

PULLING IT ALL TOGETHER—PROBLEM FOR SELF-STUDY

PROBLEM

O'Shea Company manufactures ceramic vases. It uses its standard costing system when developing its flexible budget amounts. In April 2010, 2,000 finished units were produced. The following information is related to its two direct manufacturing cost categories of direct materials and direct manufacturing labour.

Direct materials used were 4,400 kilograms. The standard direct materials input allowed for one output unit is 2 kilograms at $15 per kilogram, and 5,000 kilograms of materials were purchased at $16.50 per kilogram, for a total of $82,500.

Actual direct manufacturing labour-hours were 3,250 at a total cost of $66,300. Standard manufacturing labour time allowed is 1.5 hours per output unit, and the standard direct manufacturing labour cost is $20 per hour.

1. Calculate the direct materials price and efficiency variances and the direct manufacturing labour price and efficiency variances. The direct materials price variance will be based on a flexible budget for actual quantities purchased, but the efficiency variance will be based on a flexible budget for actual quantities used.
2. Prepare journal entries for a standard-costing system that isolates variances as early as feasible.
3. Based on these results, list in order from most to least important the variances you would investigate. Explain briefly what you considered in your ranking.
4. Give three alternative explanations for the most important variance.
5. Give reasons why the flexible budget variance analysis is more helpful than a static budget variance analysis for O'Shea.
6. O'Shea likely produces vases in a variety of shapes and colours. What advantages might arise from using the strategy of ABC budgeting and variance analysis?
7. Ceramics, until very recently, were non-metallic and formed by applying heat to glazed clay. What approach would you take to benchmarking the environmental costs of producing ceramic?

SOLUTION

1. Exhibit 7-11 shows how the columnar presentation of variances introduced in Exhibit 7-8 can be adjusted for the difference in timing between the purchase and use of materials. In particular, note the two sets of computations in column 2 for direct materials. The $75,000 pertains to the direct materials purchased; the $66,000 pertains to the direct materials used.

EXHIBIT 7-11
Columnar Presentation of Variance Analysis: Direct Materials and Direct Manufacturing Labour[*]

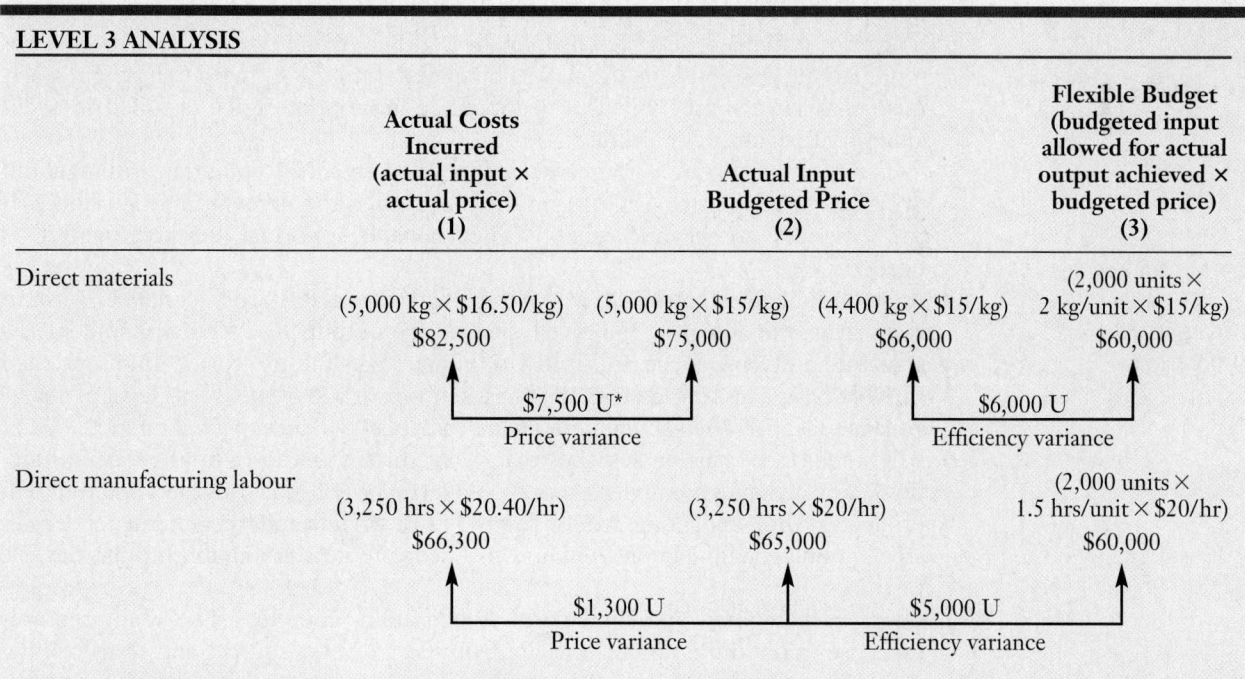

LEVEL 3 ANALYSIS

	Actual Costs Incurred (actual input × actual price) (1)	Actual Input Budgeted Price (2)		Flexible Budget (budgeted input allowed for actual output achieved × budgeted price) (3)
Direct materials	(5,000 kg × $16.50/kg) $82,500	(5,000 kg × $15/kg) $75,000	(4,400 kg × $15/kg) $66,000	(2,000 units × 2 kg/unit × $15/kg) $60,000
		$7,500 U* Price variance	$6,000 U Efficiency variance	
Direct manufacturing labour	(3,250 hrs × $20.40/hr) $66,300	(3,250 hrs × $20/hr) $65,000		(2,000 units × 1.5 hrs/unit × $20/hr) $60,000
		$1,300 U Price variance	$5,000 U Efficiency variance	

*F = favourable effect on operating income; U = unfavourable effect on operating income.

2. Materials Control

Materials Control		
(5,000 kilograms × $15/kg)	$75,000	
Direct Materials Price Variance		
(5,000 kilograms × $1.50/kg)	$ 7,500	
Accounts Payable Control		
(5,000 kilograms × $16.50/kg)		$82,500
Work-in-Process Control		
(2,000 units × 2 kg/unit × $15/kg)	$60,000	
Direct Materials Efficiency Variance		
(400 kilograms × $15/kg)	$ 6,000	
Materials Control		
(4,400 kilograms × $15/kg)		$66,000
Work-in-Process Control		
(2,000 units × 1.5 hrs/unit × $20/hr)	$60,000	
Direct Manufacturing Labour Price Variance		
(3,250 hours × $0.40/hr)	$ 1,300	
Direct Manufacturing Labour Efficiency Variance		
(250 hours × $20/hr)	$ 5,000	
Wages Payable Control		
(3,250 hours × $20.40/hr)		$66,300

3. In order, the most important variances from most to least important are: direct materials price variance of $7,500 U; direct materials efficiency variance of $6,000 U; direct manufacturing labour efficiency variance of $5,000 U; and direct manufacturing labour price variance of $1,300 U. No guidelines are provided, therefore the only reason for this ranking is the level of materiality—the highest unfavourable variance first followed by the lower unfavourable variances, in order.

4. The direct materials price variance could have several explanations. The price variance is accompanied by an almost equally high efficiency variance, which suggests the two may be linked. An explanation could be poor scheduling of production that led to emergency orders of additional material that cost more per unit. The price variance is also accompanied by a labour efficiency variance, which means more labour was consumed than was budgeted. Of course, the purchasing department may have simply failed to negotiate an appropriate price or failed to order appropriate quantities on time.

The value of the variance itself is a good signal of potential problems but provides no conclusive explanation of what caused the unfavourable variances. If the variances are beyond what O'Shea considers normal, an investigation is needed.

5. A static budget analysis may have shown a variable cost variance without comparing the actual to budgeted quantity of output produced and sold. If the actual quantity produced and sold was higher than the pro forma amounts, then variable costs must increase relative to the pro forma amounts. This level of analysis fails to signal when actual performance is outside of an expected range.

6. ABC requires a focus on activities that occur throughout a set of value-chain functions. The activities are undertaken to obtain batches of similar outputs and different products. ABC budgeting would help O'Shea understand the interdependencies among value-chain functions, and how these contribute to favourable or unfavourable variances.

7. Benchmarking environmental costs is extremely complex. The team requires expertise in obtaining imperfect data from very diverse sources and transforming the data into reasonable estimates of cost. The harvesting of clay changes the environment permanently by removing an element. The environmental degradation can be measured by various government and non-governmental groups. The team must choose what data to use and justify that the choice is reasonable. The transportation and transformation of clay into ceramic also consumes non-renewable energy, and chemicals in coloured pottery glazes affect water and air. Emissions, packaging, and waste disposal add further environmental costs.

The following decision guidelines use a question-and-answer format to summarize the chapter's main points. Each decision presents a key question. The guideline is the answer to that question.

DECISIONS	GUIDELINES
1. How do flexible budgets differ from static budgets, and why should companies use flexible budgets?	A static budget is based on the level of output planned at the start of the budget period. A flexible budget is adjusted (flexed) to recognize the actual output level of the budget period. Flexible budgets help managers gain more insight into the causes of variances than static budgets provide.
2. How can you develop a flexible budget and compute the flexible-budget variance and the sales-volume variance?	Using information from the various supporting documents for the master budget, obtain the volumes, cost allocation base quantities, unit prices, and cost allocation rates for all inventoriable and period variable costs (including overhead). Adjust each static budget variable cost to flex (increase or decrease) with the actual quantities produced and sold. The computation of more detailed variances, such as price variances and efficiency variances, helps managers gain insight into two different—but not independent—aspects of performance. The price variance focuses on the difference between the actual input price and the budgeted input price. The efficiency variance focuses on the difference between the actual quantity of input and the budgeted quantity of input allowed for the actual output.
3. Can variance analysis be used with an activity-based costing system?	Variance analysis can be applied to activity costs (such as setup costs) to gain insight into why actual activity costs differ from activity costs in the static budget or in the flexible budget. Interpreting cost variances for different activities requires understanding whether the costs are output unit-level, batch-level, product-sustaining, or facility-sustaining costs.
4. What is a standard cost, and why should a company use standard costs?	A standard cost is a carefully determined cost based on efficient operations. Standard costs aim to exclude past inefficiencies and to take into account changes expected to occur in the budget period.
5. What is benchmarking and why is it useful?	Benchmarking is a strategy to calculate standard costs based on the best performance of competitors. This strategy implies the company will undertake the continuous process of comparing its level of performance in producing products and services and executing activities against the best levels of performance. Benchmarking measures how well a company and its managers are doing relative to others.

This chapter contains definitions of the following important terms:

benchmarking (p. 333)
continuous improvement (p. 330)
effectiveness (p. 328)
efficiency (p. 328)
efficiency variance (p. 316)
favourable (F) variance (p. 308)
fineness (p. 309)
flexible budget (p. 309)
flexible-budget variance (p. 313)

input-efficiency variance (p. 316)
input-price variance (p. 316)
price variance (p. 316)
rate variance (p. 316)
revenue driver (p. 311)
sales-volume variance (p. 313)
selling-price variance (p. 314)
standard (p. 308)
standard cost (p. 318)

standard input (p. 318)
static budget (p. 309)
supply chain (p. 325)
unfavourable (U) variance (p. 308)
usage variance (p. 316)
variance (p. 308)
variance analysis (p. 308)

The Mastery Questions are rated by proficiency level—elementary, intermediate, and advanced. The solutions appear in the Mastery Question Solutions section of MyAccountingLab.

LEARNING OBJECTIVE 1

1. **Static vs. flexible budgets—Elementary.** How does static budget variance analysis mislead those assessing actual performance against pro forma performance indicators?
2. **Static vs. flexible budgets—Intermediate.** An assumption is made during static budget variance analysis. How does this assumption simplify analysis?
3. **Static vs. flexible budgets—Advanced.** Brabham Enterprises manufactures tires for the Formula I motor racing circuit. For August 2010, Brabham budgeted to manufacture and sell 3,000 tires at a variable cost of $88 per tire and a total fixed cost of $64,800. The budgeted selling price was $132 per tire. Actual results in August 2010 were 2,800 tires manufactured and sold at a selling price of $134 per tire. The actual total variable costs were $275,520, and the actual total fixed costs were $60,000.

REQUIRED

1. Prepare a performance report (similar to Exhibit 7-2, p. 312) that uses a flexible budget and a static budget.
2. Comment on the results in requirement 1.

LEARNING OBJECTIVE 2

1. **Variance procedures; flexible budget preparation, service sector—Elementary.** Meridian Finance helps prospective homeowners of substantial means to find low-cost financing and assists existing homeowners in refinancing their current loans at lower interest rates. Meridian works only for customers with excellent borrowing capacity. Hence, Meridian is able to obtain a loan for every customer with whom it decides to work.

Meridian charges clients 0.5% of the loan amount it arranges. In 2008, the average loan amount per customer was $238,800. In 2009, the average loan amount was $240,252. In its 2010 flexible budgeting system, Meridian assumes the average loan amount will be $240,000. Budgeted cost data per loan application for 2010 are

◆ Professional labour: 6 budgeted hours at a budgeted rate of $48 per hour
◆ Loan filing fees: budgeted at $120 per loan application
◆ Creditworthiness checks: budgeted at $144 per loan application
◆ Courier mailings: budgeted at $60 per loan application

Office support (the costs of leases, secretarial workers, and others) is budgeted to be $37,200 per month. Meridian Finance views this amount as a fixed cost.

REQUIRED

1. Prepare a static budget for November 2010 assuming 90 loan applications.
2. Actual loan applications in November 2010 were 120. Other actual data for November 2010 were

   ◆ Professional labour: 7.2 hours per loan application at $50.40 per hour
   ◆ Loan filing fees: $120 per loan application
   ◆ Creditworthiness checks: $150 per loan application
   ◆ Courier mailings: $64.80 per loan application

   Office support costs for November 2010 were $40,200. The average loan amount for November 2010 was $268,800. Meridian received its 0.5% fee on all loans. Prepare a Level 2 variance analysis of Meridian Finance for November 2010. Meridian's output measure in its flexible budgeting system is the number of loan applications.

2. **Variance procedures; material cost variances, use of variances for performance evaluation—Intermediate.** Katharine Stanley is the owner of Better Bikes, a company that produces high-quality cross-country bicycles. Better Bikes participates in a supply chain that consists of suppliers, manufacturers, distributors, and elite bicycle shops. For several years Better Bikes has purchased titanium from suppliers in the supply chain. Better Bikes uses titanium for the bicycle frames because it is stronger and lighter than other metals and therefore increases the quality of the bicycle. Earlier this year, Better Bikes hired Michael Scott, a recent graduate from Key University, as purchasing manager. Michael believed that he could reduce costs if he purchased titanium from an online marketplace at a lower price.

Better Bikes established the following standards based upon their experience with their previous suppliers. The standards are:

Cost of titanium	$20 per kg
Titanium used per bicycle	8 kg

Actual results for the first month using the online supplier of titanium are:

Bicycles produced	500
Titanium purchased	6,000 kg for $108,000
Titanium used in production	5,000 kg

REQUIRED

1. Compute the direct materials price and efficiency variances.
2. What factors can explain the variances identified in requirement 1? Could any other variances be affected?
3. Was switching suppliers a good idea for Better Bikes? Explain why or why not.
4. Should Michael Scott's performance evaluation be based solely on price variances? Should the production manager's evaluation be based solely on efficiency variances? Why it is important for Katharine Stanley to understand the causes of a variance before she evaluates performance?
5. Other than performance evaluation, what reasons are there for calculating variances?
6. What future problems could result from Better Bikes' decision to buy a lower quality of titanium from the online marketplace?

3. **Variance procedures; price and efficiency variances, journal entries—Advanced.** The Monroe Corporation manufactures lamps. It has set up the following standards per finished unit for direct materials and direct manufacturing labour:

Direct materials: 10 kg at $4.50 per kg	$45.00
Direct manufacturing labour: 0.5 hour at $30 per hour	15.00

The number of finished units budgeted for January 2009 was 10,000; 9,850 units were actually produced.

Actual results in January 2009 were:
Direct materials: 98,055 kg used
Direct manufacturing labour: 4,900 hours $154,350

Assume that there was no beginning inventory of either direct materials or finished units.

During the month, materials purchases amounted to 100,000 kg, at a total cost of $465,000. Input price variances are isolated upon purchase. Input-efficiency variances are isolated at the time of usage.

REQUIRED

1. Compute the January 2009 price and efficiency variances of direct materials and direct manufacturing labour.
2. Prepare journal entries to record the variances in requirement 1.
3. Comment on the January 2009 price and efficiency variances of Monroe Corporation.
4. Why might Monroe calculate direct materials price variances and direct materials efficiency variances with reference to different points in time?

LEARNING OBJECTIVE 3

1. **Variance analysis with activity-based costing and batch-level direct costs—Advanced.** Electric Eels Company produces high quality electric eels for museums and aquaria to sell in their gift shops. It accounts for the production of these eels with an ABC system. For 2009, Electric Eels expected to produce and sell 16,000 units, but actual output was only 15,000 units.

You are a new management accountant at the company. You have been asked to calculate the variances for the batch-level costs. The two main batch-level costs are setup and quality inspection. Quality inspection is driven by inspection hours, and setup is driven by the number of setup hours.

		Setup	Quality Inspection
Static budget:	Batch size (units per batch)	100	120
	Cost driver (hours) per batch	8	10
	Cost per hour	$10.75	$17.50
Actual results:	Batch size (units per batch)	75	100
	Cost driver (hours) per batch	7	9
	Cost per hour	$12.00	$15.50

1. Calculate the flexible-budget, price, and efficiency variances for both batch activities.
2. Write a short memo to your boss, the Controller, explaining the variances that you calculated.

LEARNING OBJECTIVE 4

1. **Managerial uses; when to investigate variances—Advanced.** (CMA, adapted) Windsor Injection Moulding Ltd. (WIM) knows that when its injection process is out of control, a materials variance larger than normal will occur and the whole production line must be shut down. Last month there was an unfavourable direct materials variance totalling $229,600 as follows:

	Budget	Actual
Production volume (units)	40,000	39,000
Direct materials at 2 g per unit	2	2.2
Direct materials for production, in g	80,000	85,800
Cost per g of direct materials	$10.00	$12.00

Either this variance was caused by random factors or the injector device was out of control. If there is no investigation, the expected cost until the next scheduled shut down is $90,000. There is a 10% probability, however, the device is out of control and needs repairs. If repairs are necessary, the cost will be $90,000 (see Chapter 2 for a discussion of probability and expected outcomes). Lost contribution margin will be $1,000 per hour of downtime.

If the production manager shuts down production, the costs will be as follows:

	Budget	
	Hours	**Rate/Hour**
Inspection	10	$300
Repair hours	20	$300

1. What other information would be important to the production manager who is deciding whether or not to shut down the line?
2. Calculate the total flexible-budget materials price and efficiency variances.
3. Calculate the expected pro forma cost if the variance is investigated.
4. What is the cost of investigating the variance?
5. What is the expected cost of repair?
6. What is your decision? Should the line be shut down?

LEARNING OBJECTIVE 5

1. **Benchmarking, hospital cost comparisons—Advanced.** Julie Leung is the newly appointed president of Provincial University. Provincial University Hospital (PUH) is a major problem for her, because it is running large deficits. While it is not-for-profit, the province will reduce funding if hospitals fail to meet their budgets. Sam Horn, the chairman of the hospital, tells Leung that he and his staff have cut costs to the bare bone. Any further cost cutting, he argues, would destroy the culture of the hospital. He also argues that the use of detailed cost studies is totally inappropriate for a medical institution because of (a) the inability to have well-defined relationships between inputs and outputs and (b) the problem of defining what a good output for a hospital is. He notes that he is "fed up with people equating continuous improvement at PUH with continued cost reduction. This is only a cost accountant's view of the world. Our top priority is to help doctors save lives and to help people recover their health."

Leung hears about a new benchmark cost analysis service offered by Market Insights (MI). She asks Horn to hire Market Insights to provide a benchmark cost report that pertains to PUH.

Horn is not enthusiastic about doing so, but he complies with her request. The report includes the following:

a. Aggregate Hospital Cost Comparison
(average = 1.00)

Hospital E	0.69
Hospital C	0.70
Hospital J	0.70
.	.
.	.
.	.
Hospital A	1.19
Provincial University Hospital	1.20
Hospital O	1.21

b. Diagnostic Group Cost Comparison

Diagnostic Group	Provincial University Hospital	Market Average	25th Percentile	Average of Best Quartile (0–25th)
Angina, chest pain	$27,600	$24,600	$20,760	$18,360
Asthma, bronchitis	18,480	15,720	12,480	10,800
Skin disorders, cellulitis	11,520	11,040	7,800	6,960
Renal failure and dialysis	9,120	6,600	5,040	4,320
Diabetes	8,040	6,120	4,440	3,720
Gastroenteritis	14,400	22,200	19,200	15,360

REQUIRED

1. Do you agree with Horn that the use of detailed cost studies at PUH is totally inappropriate? Explain your answer and comment on Horn's reasoning.
2. What inferences can you draw from the MI benchmark cost report on PUH?
3. What use might Leung make of the MI benchmark cost report?
4. What criticisms might you anticipate Horn would make of the MI benchmark cost report?
5. What factors other than cost might Leung consider in evaluating Horn's performance and that of PUH?

ASSIGNMENT MATERIAL

SHORT-ANSWER QUESTIONS

7-1 What is the relationship between *management by exception* and *variance analysis*?

7-2 Distinguish between a *favourable variance* and an *unfavourable variance*.

7-3 What is the key difference between a *static budget* and a *flexible budget*?

7-4 What master budget schedules (illustrated in Chapter 6) are relevant to the development of a flexible budget?

7-5 Describe the steps in developing a flexible budget.

7-6 If the calculation of variances is straightforward, what provides value-added information?

7-7 List reasons for using industry-based standard costs.

7-8 List three causes of a favourable materials-price variance.

7-9 Describe why direct materials price variance and direct materials efficiency variance may be computed with reference to different points in time.

7-10 Why does merely understanding the arithmetic relationship among materials and efficiency variances fail to explain the flexible budget variance?

7-11 How might the continuous improvement theme be incorporated into the process of setting budgeted costs?

7-12 Why might an analyst examining variances in the production area look beyond that business function for explanations of those variances?

7-13 Comment on the following statement made by a plant supervisor: "Meetings with my plant accountant are frustrating. All he wants to do is pin the blame for the many variances he reports."

7-14 How can variances be used to analyze costs in individual activity areas?

7-15 "Benchmarking against other companies enables a company to identify the lowest-cost producer. This amount should become the performance measure for the next year." Do you agree?

EXERCISES

Flexible-budget variance
$23,470 U

7-16 Flexible budget. The budgeted prices for direct materials, direct manufacturing labour, and direct marketing (distribution) labour per attaché case are $46, $10.40, and $14.20, respectively. The president is pleased with the following performance report:

	Actual costs	Static Budget	Variance
Direct materials	$436,800	$460,000	$23,200 F
Direct manufacturing labour	93,600	104,000	10,400 F
Direct marketing (distribution) labour	132,000	142,000	10,000 F

REQUIRED

Actual output was 9,050 attaché cases. Is the president's pleasure justified? Prepare a revised performance report that uses a flexible budget and a static budget. Assume all three direct-cost items are variable costs.

Total sales-volume variance
$2,757,500 F

7-17 Flexible budget. Sugar Candy Company sells sweets in bulk over the Internet. Sugar Candy's budgeted operating income for the year ended December 31, 2010, was $5,870,000. As a result of continued explosive growth in Internet sales, actual operating income totalled $7,985,300.

REQUIRED

1. Calculate the total static-budget variances.
2. Flexible-budget operating income was $8,627,500. Calculate the total flexible-budget and total sales-volume variances.
3. Comment on the total flexible-budget variance in the light of Sugar Candy's explosive growth.

7-18 Benchmarking. (CMA adapted) Syed and Shabnam Ltd. (S&S) have analyzed historical data to establish the following cost benchmarks in their industry:

Budget Item	Quantity	Units	Unit Price	Standard Cost per Unit
Direct materials	2.50	kg	$ 85.00	$ 212.50
Direct labour	5.00	DLH	50.00	250.00
Variable manufacturing overhead	5.00	DLH	65.00	325.00
Fixed manufacturing overhead	5.00	DLH	70.00	350.00
Total standard cost per unit				$1,137.50

During the month, the following variances for direct materials and direct labour were reported:

	Efficiency Variance	Price Variance
Direct materials	$ 850 F	$2,995 F
Direct labour	$1,500 U	$ 115 F

REQUIRED

1. Summarize what these variances mean to S&S.
2. Explain the difference between a benchmark and a standard set using industry information.

7-19 Flexible budget variance analysis. (CMA adapted) Todd and Smale Company Ltd. (T&S) is a small manufacturer of auto parts. The total production capacity is 100,000 units per year. T&S currently produces and sells 80,000 units, which completely satisfies current market demand. This demand has been constant for five years, and with the current downturn in the auto industry, it is not likely that demand will change in the near future. The unit price has also been constant for the last five years. Below is a flexible budget statement over the relevant range of 80,000 to 100,000 units.

1. Direct materials price variance $3,660 F

	A	B	C	D	E	F	G	H	I	J
1	Total units produced and sold:		80,000			90,000			100,000	
2		Unit Price	Unit cost	Total	Unit Price	Unit cost	Total	Unit Price	Unit cost	Total
3	Revenue	$10.00		$800,000	$10.00		$900,000	$10.00		$1,000,000
4	Production:									
5	Direct materials		$1.50	120,000		$1.50	135,000		$1.50	150,000
6	Direct manufacturing labour		1.00	80,000		1.00	90,000		1.00	100,000
7	Manufacturing overhead									
8	Variable		1.50	120,000		1.50	135,000		1.50	150,000
9	Fixed		3.50	280,000		3.11	279,900		2.80	280,000
10	Total inventoriable cost		7.50	600,000		7.11	639,900		6.80	680,000
11	Period costs									
12	Variable		0.80	64,000		0.80	72,000		0.80	80,000
13	Fixed		0.70	56,000		0.62	55,800		0.56	56,000
14	Total period costs		1.50	120,000		1.42	127,800		1.36	136,000
15	Total costs		$9.00	720,000		$8.53	767,700		$8.16	816,000
16	Operating income			$ 80,000			$132,300			$ 184,000
17										

Assume that actual production was 79,000 units, and actual input quantities and costs were:

Raw materials purchased and used (122,000 kg)	$118,340
Direct labour used (7,950 DLH)	82,680
Variable manufacturing overhead	121,635
Fixed manufacturing overhead	280,450

T&S uses standards based on engineering information available from specialized industry databases. These standards are shown below:

		Rate ($)	
Direct materials in kg per unit	1.5	$ 1.00	$ 1.50
Direct labour (DLH)	0.1	10.00	1.00
Variable manufacturing overhead (DLH)	0.1	15.00	1.50
Fixed manufacturing overhead (DLH)	0.1	35.00	3.50
Standard inventoriable cost per unit			$ 7.50

REQUIRED
1. Calculate the price and efficiency variances for direct costs.
2. Comment on the results in requirement 1.

2. Price variance $2,040 F

7-20 **Price and efficiency variances.** Peterson Foods manufactures pumpkin scones. For January 2010, it budgeted to purchase and use 16,000 kilograms of pumpkin at $1.11 per kilogram; budgeted output was 60,000 scones. Actual purchases and use for January 2010 was 17,000 kilograms at 0.99 per kilogram; actual output was 60,800 scones.

REQUIRED
1. Calculate the flexible-budget variance.
2. Calculate the price and efficiency variances
3. Comment on the results in requirements 1 and 2.

Direct manufacturing labour/
efficiency variance $6,000 U

7-21 **Materials and manufacturing-labour variances.** Consider the following data collected for Great Homes Inc.:

	Direct Materials	Direct Manufacturing Labour
Costs incurred: Actual inputs × actual prices	$200,000	$90,000
Actual inputs × standard prices	214,000	86,000
Standard inputs allowed for actual outputs × standard prices	225,000	80,000

REQUIRED
Compute the price, efficiency, and flexible-budget variances for direct materials and direct manufacturing labour.

1. Total flexible budget
variance $8,672 F

7-22 **Comprehensive variance analysis.** Sol Electronics, a fast-growing electronic device producer, uses a standard costing system, with standards set at the beginning of each year.

In the second quarter of 2009, Sol faced two challenges: it had to negotiate and sign a new short-term labour agreement with its workers' union, and it also had to pay a higher rate to its suppliers for direct materials. The new labour contract raised the cost of direct manufacturing labour relative to the company's 2009 standards. Similarly, the new rate for direct materials exceeded the company's 2009 standards. However, the materials were of better quality than expected, so Sol's management was confident that there would be less waste and less rework in the manufacturing process. They also speculated that the per-unit direct manufacturing labour cost might decline as a result of the materials' improved quality.

At the end of the second quarter, Sol's CFO, Terence Shaw, reviewed the following results:

Variable Costs	Standard		Variable Costs per Unit First-Quarter 2009 Actual Results		Second-Quarter 2009 Actual Results	
Direct materials	2.2 kg at $5.70/kg	$12.54	2.3 kg at $5.80/kg	$13.34	2.0 kg at $6.00/kg	$12.00
Direct manufacturing labour	0.5 hrs at $12/hr	$ 6.00	0.52 hrs at $12/hr	$ 6.24	0.45 hrs at $14/hr	$ 6.30
Other variable costs		$10.00		$10.00		$ 9.85
		$28.54		$29.58		$28.15

	Static Budget for Each Quarter Based on 2009	First-Quarter 2009 Results	Second-Quarter 2009 Results
Units	4,000	4,400	4,800
Selling price per unit	$ 70	$ 72	$ 71.50
Sales	$280,000	$316,800	$343,200
Variable costs:			
Direct materials	50,160	58,696	57,600
Direct manufacturing labour	24,000	27,456	30,240
Other variable costs	40,000	44,000	47,280
Total variable costs	114,160	130,152	135,120
Contribution margin	165,840	186,648	208,080
Fixed costs	68,000	66,000	68,400
Operating income	$ 97,840	$120,648	$139,680

Shaw was relieved to see that the anticipated savings in material waste and rework seemed to have materialized. But, he was concerned that the union would press hard for higher wages, given that actual unit costs came in below standard unit costs and operating income continued to climb.

REQUIRED

1. Prepare a detailed variance analysis of the second-quarter results relative to the static budget. Show how much of the improvement in operating income arose due to changes in sales volume and how much arose for other reasons. Calculate variances that isolate the effects of price and usage changes in direct materials and direct manufacturing labour.
2. Use the results of requirement 1 to prepare a rebuttal to the union's anticipated demands in light of the second-quarter results.
3. Terence Shaw thinks that the company can negotiate better if it changes the standards. Without performing any calculations, discuss the pros and cons of immediately changing the standards.

7-23 Flexible budgets, variance analysis. You have been hired as a consultant by Harriet Fletcher, the president of a small manufacturing company that makes specialty automobile parts. Fletcher is an excellent engineer, but she has been frustrated by working with inadequate cost data.

1. Total flexible-budget $115,200 U

You had previously helped install flexible budgeting and standard costs for Fletcher's company. She has now asked you to consider the following data for May and recommend how variances might be computed and presented in performance reports:

Static budget in output units	20,000
Actual output units produced and sold	23,000
Budgeted selling price per output unit	$ 48
Budgeted variable costs per output unit	$ 30
Budgeted total fixed costs per month	$ 240,000
Actual revenue	$1,048,800
Actual variable costs	$ 756,000
Favourable variance in fixed costs	$ 6,000

Fletcher is disappointed in the May data. Although output units sold exceeded expectations, operating income did not. Assume that there was no beginning or ending inventory.

REQUIRED

1. You decide to present Fletcher with alternative ways to analyze variances so that she can decide what level of detail she prefers. The reporting system can then be designed accordingly. Prepare an analysis similar to Levels 1 and 2 in Exhibit 7-8 (p. 33).
2. What are some likely causes for the variances you report in requirement 1?

1. Total flexible-budget
variance for both inputs
$2,469.50 U

7-24 Direct materials and direct manufacturing labour variances. GloriaDee Inc. designs and manufactures T-shirts. It sells its T-shirts to brand-name clothing retailers in lots of one dozen. GloriaDee's May 2009 static budget and actual results for direct inputs are:

Static Budget	
Number of T-shirt lots (1 lot = 1 dozen)	500
Per lot of T-shirts:	
Direct materials	12 metres at $1.50 per metre = $18.00
Direct manufacturing labour	2 hours at $8.00 per hour = $16.00
Actual Results	
Number of T-shirt lots sold	550
Total direct inputs:	
Direct materials	7,260 metres at $1.75 per metre = $12,705.00
Direct manufacturing labour	1,045 hours at $8.10 per hour = $8,464.50

GloriaDee has a policy of analyzing all input variances when they add up to more than 10% of the total cost of materials and labour in the flexible budget, and this is true in May 2009. The production manager discusses the sources of the variances: "A new type of material was purchased in May. This led to faster cutting and sewing, but the workers used more material than usual as they learned to work with it. For now, the standards are fine."

REQUIRED
1. Calculate the direct materials and direct manufacturing labour price and efficiency variances in May 2009. What is the total flexible-budget variance for both inputs (direct materials and direct manufacturing labour) combined? What percentage is this variance of the total cost of direct materials and direct manufacturing labour in the flexible budget?
2. Gloria Denham, the CEO, is concerned about the input variances. However, she likes the quality and feel of the new material and agrees to use it for one more year. In May 2010, GloriaDee again produces 550 lots of T-shirts. Relative to May 2009, 2% less direct material is used, direct material price is down 5%, and 2% less direct manufacturing labour is used. Labour price has remained the same as in May 2009. Calculate the direct materials and direct manufacturing labour price and efficiency variances in May 2010. What is the total flexible-budget variance for both inputs (direct materials and direct manufacturing labour) combined? What percentage is this variance of the total cost of direct materials and direct manufacturing labour in the flexible budget?
3. Comment on the May 2010 results. Would you continue the "experiment" of using the new material?

7-25 Flexible-budget preparation and analysis. Bank Management Printers Inc. produces luxury chequebooks with three cheques and stubs per page. Each chequebook is designed for an individual customer and is ordered through the customer's bank. The company's operating budget for September 2010 included these data:

Number of chequebooks	15,000
Selling price per book	$ 20
Variable costs per book	$ 8
Total fixed costs for the month	$145,000

The actual results for September 2010 were

Number of chequebooks produced and sold	12,000
Average selling price per book	$ 21
Variable costs per book	$ 7
Total fixed costs for the month	$150,000

The executive vice-president of the company observed that the operating income for September was much less than anticipated, despite a higher-than-budgeted selling price and a lower-than-budgeted variable cost per unit. You have been asked to provide explanations for the disappointing September results.

Bank Management develops its flexible-budget-based budgeted revenue per output unit and variable costs per output unit without a detailed analysis of budgeted inputs.

REQUIRED

1. Prepare a Level 1 analysis of the September performance.
2. Prepare a Level 2 analysis of the September performance.
3. Why might Bank Management find the Level 2 analysis more informative than the Level 1 analysis? Explain your answer.

7-26 Flexible budget, working backward. The Specialty Bearings Company designs and manufactures ball bearings for extreme performance machinery. The following table is a partially completed variance analysis of Specialty Bearings' budgeted and actual results from sales of platinum bearings for the year ended December 31, 2010.

Variance Analysis for Specialty Bearings for 2010, Incomplete

	Actual Results (1)	Flexible-Budget Variances (2) = (1) − (3)	Flexible Budget (3)	Sales-Volume Variances (4) = (3) − (5)	Static Budget (5)
Units sold	650,000				600,000
Revenues (sales)	$4,290,000				$2,520,000
Variable costs	3,090,000				1,440,000
Contribution margin	1,200,000				1,080,000
Fixed costs	840,000				720,000
Operating income	$ 360,000				$ 360,000

Total flexible-budget variance   Total sales-volume variance

Total static-budget variance

REQUIRED

1. Complete the variance analysis. Calculate all the required variances. If your work is accurate, you will find that the total static-budget variance is $0 (zero).
2. What are the actual and budgeted prices per unit? What are the actual and budgeted costs per unit?
3. Specialty Bearings' CEO was delighted with the lack of a static-budget variance. Was his reaction appropriate? Review the variances you have calculated and discuss possible causes and potential problems.

7-27 Activity-based costing, flexible-budget variances for finance function activities. Martin Weber is the chief financial officer of Bouquets.com, an Internet company that enables customers to order deliveries of flowers through its website. Weber is concerned with the efficiency and effectiveness of the finance function. He collects the following information for three activities in 2010:

			Rate per Unit of Cost Driver	
Activity	Activity Level	Cost Driver	Static Budget	Actual
Receivables	Output unit	Remittances	$0.767	$0.90
Payables	Batch	Invoices	3.480	3.36
Travel expenses	Batch	Travel claims	9.120	8.88

The output measure is the number of deliveries, which is the same as the number of remittances. The following is additional information.

	Static-Budget Amounts	Actual Amounts
Number of deliveries	1,000,000	948,000
Batch size in terms of deliveries:		
Payables	5	4.46801
Travel expenses	500	501.587

REQUIRED

1. Calculate the flexible-budget variance for each activity in 2010.
2. Calculate the price and efficiency variances for each activity in 2010.

7-28 Finance function activities, benchmarking (continuation of 7-27). Martin Weber, CFO of Bouquets.com, engages The Hackett Group, a consulting firm specializing in benchmarking. He asks Hackett to provide benchmark data of the finance function at "world-class" retail companies (both traditional retail and Internet-based retail). Hackett's cost benchmarks for Bouquet.com's three finance activities are

Finance Activity	"World-Class" Cost Performance
Receivables	$0.12 per remittance
Payables	$0.85 per invoice
Travel expenses	$1.90 per travel claim

REQUIRED

1. What new insights might arise with the Hackett benchmark data using the amounts in Exercise 7-27?
2. Assume you are in charge of travel-claim processing. What concerns might you have with Weber using the Hackett benchmark of $1.90 per travel claim as the key to evaluate your performance next period?

7-29 Materials and manufacturing labour variances, standard costs. Dunn Inc. is a privately held furniture manufacturer. For August 2009, Dunn had the following standards for one of its products, a wicker chair:

	Standards per Chair
Direct materials	2 square metres of input at $5 per square metre
Direct manufacturing labour	0.5 hour of input at $10 per hour

The following data were compiled regarding actual performance: actual output units (chairs) produced, 2,000; square metres of input purchased and used, 3,700; price per square metre, $5.10; direct manufacturing labour costs, $8,820; actual hours of input, 900; labour price per hour, $9.80.

REQUIRED

1. Show your computations on the price and efficiency variances for direct materials and for direct manufacturing labour. Give a plausible explanation of why the variances occurred.
2. Suppose 6,000 square metres of materials were purchased (at $5.10 per square metre) even though only 3,700 square metres were used. Suppose further that variances are identified with their most likely control point; accordingly, direct materials price variances are isolated and traced to the purchasing department rather than to the production department. Compute the price and efficiency variances under this approach.

7-30 Journal entries and T-accounts (continuation of 7-29). Prepare journal entries and post them to T-accounts for all transactions in Exercise 7-29, including requirement 2. Summarize how these journal entries differ from the normal costing entries described in Chapter 5.

7-31 Flexible budget (continuation of 7-29 and 7-30). Suppose the static budget was for 2,500 units of output. Actual output was 2,000 units. The variances are shown in the following report:

	Actual Results	Static Budget	Variance
Direct materials	$18,870	$25,000	$6,130 F
Direct manufacturing labour	8,820	12,500	3,680 F

REQUIRED

What are the price, efficiency, and sales-volume variances for direct materials and direct manufacturing labour? Based on your results, explain why the static budget was not achieved.

7-32 Activity-based costing, flexible-budget variances for finance-function activities. Fast-Grocery.com, an online company that delivers groceries to its customers, has the following information for its three finance activities in 2009:

1. Receivables flexible-budget variance $152,145 U

Activity	Activity Level	Cost Driver	Rate per Unit of Cost Driver Static Budget	Rate per Unit of Cost Driver Actual
Receivables	Output unit	Remittances	$0.639	$0.80
Payables	Batch	Invoices	2.900	2.85
Travel expenses	Batch	Travel claims	7.600	7.45

The output measure is the number of deliveries, which is the same as the number of remittances. The following is additional information.

	Static-Budget Amounts	Actual Amount
Number of deliveries	1,000,000	945,000
Batch size in terms of deliveries:		
Payables	5	4.468
Travel expenses	500	501.587

REQUIRED
1. Calculate the flexible-budget variance for each activity in 2009.
2. Calculate the price and efficiency variances for each activity in 2009.

7-33 Variance analysis, nonmanufacturing setting. Stevie McQueen has run Lightning Car Detailing for the past ten years. His static budget and actual results for June 2011 are provided below. Stevie has one employee who has been with him for all ten years that he has been in business. He has not been as lucky with his second and third employees. Stevie is hiring new employees in those positions almost every second month. It usually takes 2 hours to detail a vehicle. It takes as long for the seasoned employee as for the new ones, as the former tends to put more into the job. Stevie pays his long-term employee $20 per hour and the other two employees $10 per hour. Stevie pays all employees for 2 hours of work on each car, regardless of how long the work actually takes them. There were no wage increases in June.

2. Flexible budget variance for labour $30 F

Lightning Car Detailing
Actual and Budgeted Income Statements
For the Month Ending June 30, 2011

	Budget	Actual
Cars detailed	200	225
Revenue	$30,000	$ 39,375
Variable costs:		
Costs of supplies	1,500	2,250
Labour	5,600	6,000
Total variable costs	7,100	8,250
Contribution margin	22,900	31,125
Fixed costs	9,500	9,500
Operating income	$13,400	$ 21,625

REQUIRED
1. Prepare a statement of the static budget variances that Stevie would be interested in.
2. Compute any flexible budget variances that you believe would be appropriate.
3. What information, in addition to that provided in the income statements, would you want Stevie to gather if you wanted to improve operational efficiency?
4. How many cars, on average, did Stevie budget for each employee? How many cars did they actually detail?
5. What advice would you give Stevie about motivating his employees?

PROBLEMS

③

1. Direct materials efficiency variance for January $5,760 U

7-34 Direct-materials variances, long-term agreement with supplier. For its manufacturing facility in Montreal, Quebec, Metalmoulder has a long-term contract with Osaka Metals. Metalmoulder manufactures large-scale machining systems that are sold to other industrial companies. Each machining system has a sizable direct materials cost, consisting primarily of the purchase price for a metal compound. Osaka will supply to Metalmoulder up to 2,400 kilograms of metal per month at a fixed purchase price of $144 per kilogram for each month in 2010. For purchases above 2,400 kilograms in any month, Metalmoulder renegotiates the price for the additional amount with Osaka Metals (or another supplier). The standard price per kilogram is $144 for each month in the January to December 2010 period.

Production data, direct materials actual usage in dollars, and direct materials actual price per kilogram for the January to May 2010 period, are

	Number of Machining Systems Produced	Total Actual Direct Materials Usage	Average Actual Direct Materials Purchase Price per Kilogram of Metal
January	10	$290,880	$144.00
February	12	343,872	144.00
March	18	530,712	151.20
April	16	474,317	153.60
May	11	304,128	144.00

The average actual direct materials purchase price is for all units purchased in that month. Assume that (a) the direct materials purchased in each month are all used in that month and (b) each machining system is started and completed in the same month.

The Montreal facility is one of three plants that Metalmoulder operates to manufacture large-scale machining systems. The other plants are in Worcester, U.K., and Tokyo, Japan.

REQUIRED
1. Assume that Metalmoulder's standard materials input per machining system is 198 kilograms of metal. Compute the direct materials price variance and direct materials efficiency variance for each month of the January to May 2010 period.
2. How does the signing of a long-term agreement with a supplier—an agreement that includes a fixed-purchase-price clause—affect the interpretation of a materials price variance?

1. Standard DMLH for actual output achieved, 2,000 hours

7-35 Direct materials and manufacturing labour variances, solving unknowns. (CPA, adapted) On May 1, 2010, Bovar Company began the manufacture of a new Internet paging device known as Dandy. The company installed a standard costing system to account for manufacturing costs. The standard costs for a unit of Dandy are as follows:

Direct materials (3 kg at $5 per kg)	$15.00
Direct manufacturing labour (0.5 hours at $20 per hour)	10.00
Manufacturing overhead (75% of direct manufacturing labour costs)	7.50
	$32.50

The following data were obtained from Bovar's records for the month of May:

	Debit	Credit
Revenues		$125,000
Accounts payable control (for May's purchases of direct materials)		68,250
Direct materials price variance	$3,250	
Direct materials efficiency variance	2,500	
Direct manufacturing labour price variance	1,900	
Direct manufacturing labour efficiency variance		2,000

Actual production in May was 4,000 units of Dandy, and actual sales in May were 2,500 units. The amount shown for direct materials price variance applies to materials purchased during May. There was no beginning inventory of materials on May 1, 2010.

Compute each of the following items for Bovar for the month of May. Show your computations.

1. Standard direct manufacturing labour-hours (DMLH) allowed for actual output achieved
2. Actual direct manufacturing labour-hours (DMLH) worked
3. Actual direct manufacturing labour wage rate
4. Standard quantity of direct materials allowed (in kg)
5. Actual quantity of direct materials used (in kg)
6. Actual quantity of direct materials purchased (in kg)
7. Actual direct materials price per kg

7-36 Direct manufacturing labour and direct materials variances, missing data. (CMA, adapted). Morro Bay Surfboards is a California company that manufactures fibreglass surfboards. The standard cost of direct materials and direct manufacturing labour is $100 per board. This includes 20 pounds of direct materials, at the budgeted price of $2 per pound, and 5 hours of direct manufacturing labour, at the budgeted rate of $12 per hour. Following are additional data for the month of July:

1. Direct manufacturing labour price variance, $16,000 F

Units completed	6,000	units
Direct material purchases	150,000	pounds
Cost of direct material purchases	$292,500	
Actual direct manufacturing labour-hours	32,000	hours
Actual direct-labour cost	$368,000	
Direct materials efficiency variance	$ 12,500	U

There were no beginning inventories.

REQUIRED
1. Compute direct manufacturing labour variances for July.
2. Compute the actual pounds of direct materials used in production in July.
3. Calculate the actual price per pound of direct materials purchased.
4. Calculate the direct materials price variance.

7-37 Activity-based costs, variance analysis. A manufacturer of a variety of pastry products, Tasty Pastry has one of its plants producing five different fruit-cake products. Each cake product differs in terms of material inputs (different fruits, flour, and liquor). They are identical in terms of both the cooking and the setup processes.

1. Flexible-budget variance $6,600 F

    Tasty Pastry prefers to make long production runs of each cake product. A major benefit is that fewer changeovers are made. A changeover is the process of switching the production line from the manufacture of one product to another product. The costs of a changeover are a batch cost. They comprise the labour cost of the workers who clean the mixing equipment so that the contents of each different product are not mixed together. The following information pertains to March 2010.

	Static-Budget Amounts	Actual Amounts
Units of cakes produced and sold	270,000	330,000
Average number of cakes per production run	6,000	10,000
Changeover labour-hours per production run	20 hours	24 hours
Changeover labour cost per hour	$24	$25

REQUIRED
1. Compute the flexible-budget variance for total changeover labour costs in March 2010. Comment on the results.
2. Compute the price and efficiency variance for total changeover labour costs in March 2010. Comment on the results.
3. Provide two explanations for each of the price and efficiency variances in requirement 2.

7-38 Direct materials and manufacturing labour variances, journal entries. Shayna's Smart Shawls Inc. is a small business that Shayna developed while in college. She began hand-knitting shawls for her dorm friends to wear while studying. As demand grew, she hired some workers and began to manage the operation. Shayna's shawls require wool and labour. She experiments with the type of wool that she uses, and she has great variety in the shawls she produces. Shayna has bi-modal turnover in her labour—she has some employees who have been with her for a very long time and others who are new and inexperienced.

1. Price variance for the wool $395 U

Shayna uses standard costing for her shawls. She expects that a typical shawl should take 3.5 hours to produce, and the standard wage rate is $10.50 per hour. An average shawl uses 12 skeins of wool. Shayna shops around for good deals and expects to pay $3.00 per skein.

Shayna uses a just-in-time inventory system, as she has clients tell her what type and colour of wool they would like her to use.

For the month of April, Shayna's workers produced 230 shawls using 836 hours and 2,633.50 skeins of wool. Shayna bought wool for $8,295.50 (and used the entire quantity), and incurred labour costs of $7,814.50.

REQUIRED
1. Calculate the price and efficiency variances for the wool, and the price and efficiency variances for direct manufacturing labour.
2. Record the journal entries for the variances incurred.
3. Discuss logical explanations for the combination of variances that Shayna experienced.

② ④

1. a. Selling price variance
$54,000 U

7-39 Comprehensive variance analysis. (CMA, adapted) Aunt Molly's Old Fashioned Cookies bakes cookies for a chain of retail stores. The company's best-selling cookie is chocolate nut supreme, which is marketed as a gourmet cookie and regularly sells for $9.60 per kilogram. The standard input cost per kilogram of chocolate nut supreme, based on Aunt Molly's normal monthly production of 400,000 kilograms, is calculated as follows:

Cost Item	Standard Quantity	Unit Cost	Total Cost
Direct materials:			
Cookie mix	625 g	$0.384 per kg	$0.24
Milk chocolate	312.5 g	$2.88 per kg	0.90
Almonds	62.5 g	$9.60 per kg	0.60
1,000 g = 1 kg			$1.74
Direct labour			
Mixing	1 minute	$17.28 per hour	$0.288
Baking	2 minutes	$21.60 per hour	0.720
			$1.008

Aunt Molly's management accountant, Karen Blair, prepares monthly budget reports based on these standard costs. Presented here is April's report, which compares budgeted and actual performance.

Performance Report
April 2009

	Budget	Actual	Variance
Units (in kilograms)*	400,000	450,000	50,000 F
Revenue	$3,840,000	$4,266,000	$ 426,000 F
Direct material	$ 696,000	$1,017,365	$ 321,365 U
Direct labour	$ 403,200	$ 453,600	$ 50,400 U

* Units produced and sold

Usage Report
April 2009

Cost Item	Quantity	Actual Cost
Direct materials:		
Cookie mix	290,000 kg	$111,360
Milk chocolate	161,720 kg	$621,005
Almonds	29,688 kg	$285,000
1,000 g = 1 kg		
Direct labour		
Mixing	450,000 minutes	129,600
Baking	800,000 minutes	288,000

1. Compute the following variances:

   a. Selling-price variance
   b. Material-price variance
   c. Material-efficiency variance
   d. Labour-price variance
   e. Labour-efficiency variance

2. What explanations might exist for the variances in requirement 1?

7-40 Comprehensive variance analysis, responsibility issues. (CMA, adapted) Styles Inc. manufactures a full line of well-known sunglasses frames and lenses. Styles uses a standard costing system to set attainable standards for direct materials, labour, and overhead costs. Styles reviews and revises standards annually, as necessary. Department managers, whose evaluations and bonuses are affected by their department's performance, are held responsible to explain variances in their department performance reports.

1. a. Selling price variance $14,550 F

Recently, the manufacturing variances in the Image prestige line of sunglasses have caused some concern. For no apparent reason, unfavourable materials and labour variances have occurred. At the monthly staff meeting, Jack Barton, manager of the Image line, will be expected to explain his variances and suggest ways of improving performance. Barton will be asked to explain the following performance report for 2009:

	Actual Results	**Static-Budget Amounts**
Units sold	7,275	7,500
Revenues	$596,550	$600,000
Variable manufacturing costs	$351,965	$324,000
Fixed manufacturing costs	$108,398	$112,500
Gross margin	$136,187	$163,500

Barton collected the following information:

Three items comprised the standard variable manufacturing costs in 2009:

◆ Direct materials: Frames. Static budget cost of $49,500. The standard input for 2009 is 3.00 g per unit.

◆ Direct materials: Lenses. Static budget costs of $139,500. The standard input for 2009 is 6.00 g per unit.

◆ Direct manufacturing labour: Static budget costs of $135,000. The standard input for 2009 is 1.20 hours per unit.

Assume there are no variable manufacturing overhead costs.

The actual variable manufacturing costs in 2009 were:

◆ Direct materials: Frames. Actual costs of $55,872. Actual grams used were 3.20 g per unit.

◆ Direct materials: Lenses. Actual costs of $150,738. Actual grams used were 7.00 g per unit.

◆ Direct manufacturing labour: Actual costs of $145,355. The actual labour rate was $14.80 per hour.

REQUIRED

1. Prepare a report that includes:

   a. Selling-price variance
   b. Sales-volume variance and flexible-budget variance for operating income in the format of the analysis in Exhibit 7-3
   c. Price and efficiency variances for:
      ◆ Direct materials: frames
      ◆ Direct materials: lenses
      ◆ Direct manufacturing labour

2. Give three possible explanations for each of the three price and efficiency variances at Styles in requirement 1c.

7-41 Possible causes for price and efficiency variances. You are a student preparing for a job interview with a large Canadian consumer products manufacturer. You are applying for a job in the Finance Department. This company is known for its rigorous case-based interview process. One of the students who successfully obtained a job with the company upon graduation last year advised you to "know your variances cold!" When you inquired further, she told you that she had been asked to pretend that she was investigating wage and materials variances. Per her advice, you have been studying the causes and consequences of variances. You are

1. Direct materials price variance $25,000 U

excited when you get to the interview and find that the first case you are presented with deals with variance analysis. You are given the following data for May for a detergent bottling plant:

Actual

Bottles filled	360,000
Direct materials used in production	60,000,000 g
Actual direct material cost	$ 2,125,000
Actual direct manufacturing labour-hours	22,040 hours
Actual direct labour cost	$ 664,940

Standards

Purchase price of direct materials	$ 0.035 per g
Bottle materials used	150 g
Wage rate	$29.30 per hour
Bottles per minute	0.5

REQUIRED

Please respond to the following questions as if you were in an interview situation:

1. Calculate the materials efficiency and price variance, and the wage and labour efficiency variances for the month of May.
2. You are given the following context: "Union organizers are targeting our detergent bottling plant for a union." Can you provide a better explanation for the variances that you have calculated on the basis of this information?

④

1. Hergonia purchase price variance $400,000 U

7-42 Procurement costs, variance analysis, governance. Rashid Daley is the manager of the athletic shoe division of Raider Products. Raider is a European-based company that has just purchased Fastfoot, a leading European shoe company. Fastfoot has long-term production contracts with suppliers in two East European countries, Hergonia and Tanista. Daley receives a request from Kevin Neal, president of Raider Products. Daley and his controller, Brooke Mullins, are to make a presentation to the next board of directors' meeting on the cost competitiveness of its Fastfoot subsidiary. This should include budgeted and actual procurement costs for 2010 at its Hergonia and Tanista supply sources.

Mullins decides to visit the two supply operations. The budgeted average procurement cost for 2010 was $14 per pair of shoes. This includes payments to the shoe manufacturer and all other payments to conduct business in each country. Mullins reports the following to Daley:

◆ **Hergonia.** Total 2010 procurement costs for 250,000 pairs of shoes were $3,900,000. Payment to the shoe manufacturer was $3,108,000. Very few receipts exist for the remaining $792,000. Kickback payments are viewed as common in Hergonia.

◆ **Tanista.** Total 2010 procurement costs for 900,000 pairs of shoes were $12,300,000. Payment to the shoe manufacturer was $10,136,000. Receipts exist for $827,000 of the other costs, but Mullins is skeptical of their validity. Kickback payments are a "way of business" in Tanista.

At both the Hergonia and Tanista plants, Mullins is disturbed by the employment of young children (many of them under 15 years). She is told that all major shoe-producing companies have similar low-cost employment practices in both countries.

Daley is uncomfortable about the upcoming presentation to the board of directors. He was a leading advocate of the acquisition. A recent business magazine reported that the Fastfoot acquisition would make Raider Products the global low-cost producer in its market lines. The stock price of Raider Products jumped 21% the day the Fastfoot acquisition was announced. Mullins, likewise, is widely identified as a proponent of the acquisition. She is seen as a rising star due for promotion to a division management post in the near future.

REQUIRED

1. What summary procurement cost variances could be reported to the board of directors of Raider Shoes?
2. What ethical issues do (a) Daley and (b) Mullins face when preparing and making a report to the board of directors?
3. How should Mullins address the issues you identify in requirement 2?

7-43 Comprehensive variance analysis review. Memflash Inc. manufactures 500 megabyte flash drives that are compatible with a popular portable storage device. Memflash sells flash drives directly to computer retail chains and to direct marketing organizations that resell flash drives under their house brands. The flash drives retail for an average of $9.60 per unit, and compete with well-known brands that retail for between $12.00 and $14.40 per flash drive.

2

2. Total static-budget variance $652,280 U

Memflash's CFO has provided you with the following budgeted standards for the month of February 2010:

Budgeted average wholesale selling price per unit	$4.80
Total direct material standard cost per drive	$1.02
Direct manufacturing labour	
Direct manufacturing labour standard cost per hour	$18.00
Average labour productivity (drives per hour)	300
Direct marketing cost per unit	$0.36
Total fixed overhead	$1,080,000

The VP of Marketing forecasts sales of 1,660,500 units for the month.

On March 7, the VP of Planning and Control meets with the executive committee to discuss February results. He reports as follows:

- Unit sales totalled 1,400,000 units.
- Actual average selling price declined to $4.86.
- Productivity dropped to 280 drives/hour; however, because of favourable market conditions, the actual price per unit dropped to $0.94.
- Fixed costs came in $33,000 below plan.
- All other costs were incurred at their standard rates.

REQUIRED

As the senior financial analyst, you are asked to calculate the following:

1. Static-budget and actual operating income
2. Total static-budget variance
3. Flexible-budget operating income
4. Total flexible-budget variance
5. Total sales-volume variance
6. Price and efficiency variances
7. What is the material-price variance? What is the labour-price variance?
8. What is the material-efficiency variance? What is the labour-efficiency variance?

COLLABORATIVE LEARNING CASE

7-44 Price and efficiency variances, problems in standard-setting, benchmarking. New Fashions Inc. manufactures shirts for retail chains. Andy Jorgenson, the controller, is becoming increasingly disenchanted with New Fashions' standard costing system. The budgeted and actual amounts for direct materials and direct manufacturing labour for June 2009 were:

2 4 5

1. Direct-materials price variance $306 F

	Budgeted Amounts	Actual Amounts
Shirts manufactured	6,000	6,732
Direct material costs	30,000	$30,294
Direct material units (rolls of cloth)	600	612
Direct manufacturing labour costs	$27,000	$27,693
Direct manufacturing labour-hours (DMLH)	1,500	1,530

There were no beginning or ending inventories of materials.

Standard costs are based on a study of the operations conducted by an independent consultant six months earlier. Jorgenson observes that, since that study, he has rarely seen an unfavourable variance of any magnitude. He notes that even at their current output levels, the workers seem to have a lot of time for sitting around and gossiping. Jorgenson is concerned that the production manager, Charlie Fenton, is aware of this but does not want to tighten up the standards because the lax standards make his performance look good.

REQUIRED

1. Compute the price and efficiency variances of New Fashions for direct materials and direct manufacturing labour in June 2009.
2. Describe the types of actions the employees at New Fashions may have taken to reduce the accuracy of the standards set by the independent consultant. Why would employees take those actions? Is this behaviour ethical?
3. If Jorgenson does nothing about the standard costs, will his behaviour violate any of the ethical conduct characteristics described in Chapter 1?
4. What actions should Jorgenson take?
5. Jorgenson can obtain benchmarking information about the estimated costs of New Fashions' major competitors from Benchmarking Clearing House (BCH). Discuss the pros and cons of using the BCH information to compute the variances in requirement 1.

Flexible Budgets, Variances, and Management Control: II

Tracking Performance

In mature industries it is extremely important to be cost competitive. Overhead, the indirect costs of running any company, often comprises a large proportion of total costs. For extraction industries such as oil, gold, and iron ore, the costs to build or purchase refining operations are very high. These refining plants are used for many years and their costs are called fixed overhead costs of production.

Barrick Gold Corporation, a Canadian gold producer, explores for, refines, and produces gold, which are captial intensive activities. Barrick has high operating leverage. Fixed costs are very high in comparison with variable costs. Changes in production volumes have an impact on the unit fixed costs of gold mined and refined, and therefore on the profitability of Barrick's operations.

After studying this chapter, you should be able to

1 Establish fixed overhead cost-allocation rates; calculate and analyze flexible budget variances

2 Establish variable overhead cost-allocation rates; calculate and analyze flexible budget variances

3 Calculate ABC overhead variances

4 Integrate the fixed and variable overhead cost variance analyses to reconcile the actual overhead incurred with overhead allocated

5 Analyze nonfinancial and nonmanufacturing variance

This chapter completes the Level 3 flexible-budget variance fixed and variable overhead analyses for Webb Company. Overhead, or indirect costs, is a major cost area for many organizations. Chemical, paper, steel, and telecommunications companies, for example, incur hundreds of millions of dollars of fixed cost to construct and maintain both their physical plant and equipment and other aspects of their infrastructure. These investments are made to ensure a capacity level of production that is appropriate to existing and expected future demand for outputs and are often incurred long before a specified operating budget period. Fixed costs may be either inventoriable overhead (for example, a new factory accounted for in cost of goods sold) or period overhead (for example, a new head-office building accounted for as an expense).

Variable indirect costs also contribute to overhead. For service companies such as airlines, up to 50% of their total costs are indirect, passenger-related costs such as ticketing, security, and landing fees. These costs vary with the quantity of passengers or their baggage. Indirect costs are allocated to the individual products or services companies produce and sell.

FLEXIBLE-BUDGET FIXED OVERHEAD COST VARIANCES

1 Establish fixed overhead cost-allocation rates; calculate and analyze flexible budget variances

Chapter 8 focuses on understanding flexible-budget variances for overhead costs and the causes of these variances. We continue the analysis of Webb Company begun in Chapter 7 and simplify the example by examining only inventoriable overhead. Referring back to Exhibit 7-2, p. 312 this discussion includes only the variable manufacturing overhead of $120,000 budgeted for the 10,000-jackets level of output and fixed manufacturing overhead of $276,000 budgeted for the relevant range including 10,000 jackets. To ease the discussion, we will refer to these costs simply as either fixed overhead or variable overhead.

Webb's cost structure illustrates why planning and control of overhead costs is important. The following percentages of total static-budget costs (see column D of Exhibit 7-2, p. 312) are based on Webb's static budget for 12,000 jackets for April 2009:

	Variable Overhead Costs	Fixed Overhead Costs	Total Overhead Costs
Manufacturing[1]	7.59%	14.54%	22.13%
Marketing	3.16	22.87	26.03
Total	10.75%	37.41%	48.16%

Total overhead costs amount to almost half (48.16%) of Webb's total budgeted costs at 12,000 output units for April 2009. Based on its overhead, Webb may be classified as a high operating leverage company because of its high proportion of fixed (37.41%) relative to variable costs (10.75%), although this judgment depends on the specific industrial context. High operating leverage means that Webb must sell many jackets to cover its fixed costs. After breakeven, however, every dollar of revenue from selling a jacket will create an additional $0.3741 in operating profit. Clearly, Webb's control of fixed overhead is important. The variable costs actually incurred in comparison to those planned for the actual quantity of jackets produced consume another $0.1075 in variable overhead costs from every revenue dollar earned.

[1]Manufacturing variable overhead as a percentage of total costs is $144,000 ÷ $1,898,000 = 7.59% and manufacturing fixed overhead is $276,000 ÷ 1,898,000 = 14.54%. Total manufacturing overhead is $420,000 ÷ $1,898,000 = 22.13%. Similar calculations will result in the percentages shown for marketing overhead costs. The total variable marketing and manufacturing overhead costs as a percentage of total costs is ($144,000 + $60,000) ÷ $1,898,000 = 10.75% and similar calculations can be made for the fixed manufacturing and marketing overhead as a percentage of total costs.

For Webb, any unfavourable variances in either fixed or variable overhead will either increase the number of jackets that need to be sold to reach breakeven or, after breakeven, will decrease the amount that each dollar of revenue from selling one jacket will contribute to operating profit. This is why variances are relevant to both operating and strategic decisions—if Webb is not profitable in the short run, there will be no long run to strategize about. Since fixed overhead costs are a high proportion of indirect costs, our discussion begins with fixed overhead variance planning and control through variance calculation and analyses.

PLANNING FIXED OVERHEAD COSTS

Effective planning of fixed overhead costs is basically a capacity planning issue. **Capacity** refers to the quantity of outputs that can be produced from long-term resources available to the company. The alternatives that managers consider in capacity decisions are covered in Chapter 9. However, regardless of the alternative chosen, capacity is acquired through the purchase or lease of long-term assets. This means that decisions about capacity are *strategic* decisions. Decisions would include consideration of current capacity, forecasted future demand and risks, potential alternative uses of idle capacity, and ease of disposal of excess capacity.

The fixed overhead issue is that either the lease or acquisition cost of capacity must be recovered through the sale of outputs (goods or services) if the company is to be profitable. The key question in overhead allocation and cost assignment is: the cost of what? Chapters 4 and 5 presented two approaches to cost allocation and stressed that both methods provide *estimates* of the cost of a unit of some common input, whether material, labour, or activities. Ultimately these costs per unit of common input were assigned to a cost per unit of output to help managers price those outputs in a profitable way.

Capacity cost is a fixed overhead cost. In a cost system, it could be sensible to group all fixed overhead costs into a single fixed overhead cost pool. Decisions about the design of the costing system are the responsibility of top management. While this chapter focuses on inventoriable capacity costs, period capacity costs also exist. It is often more readily apparent what is the most informative grouping of capacity costs into overhead cost pools for refining and other manufacturing industries than for service industries. Please review Chapters 2 and 4 if you need to refresh your understanding of the meaning of the terms fixed cost, inventoriable cost, and overhead cost.

In service industries for example, the same building often houses both those whose activities generate revenue as well as all service-support activities. Capacity is related to the people and their intangible skills rather than to tangible equipment and property. Where the acquisition cost of tangible equipment and property is reported by financial accountants, the labour expense of people and the financial value of their skills will fluctuate. These are considered expenses rather than assets and therefore are not capacity costs. The standards of financial accounting separate fixed (capacity) costs from variable costs or expenses. The management accounting approach also separates these costs based on their effect on the contribution margin.

Assume that Webb's managers have decided to lease rather than purchase sewing machines at a fixed annual lease rate. The initial decision would have entailed estimates of how many elements (sleeves, backs, fronts) of each jacket could be produced by a reasonably skilled operator during some specific time period. This would allow the managers to estimate the output. With good information on both market demand (market size) and Webb's market share, the managers could estimate how many sewing machines (the capacity) would be required to retain its market share. If the managers leased too few machines, capacity would be insufficient to meet demand, resulting in lost sales. If the managers leased too many machines, then Webb would have unutilized or idle capacity. The competitive problem of unutilized capacity is that, to remain profitable, Webb's price must recover the cost of all capacity, idle or productive. Competitors may not have any or as much idle capacity, and so might achieve profitability at a lower price per jacket.

┌─ ┐

THINKING CRITICALLY

Is idle capacity necessarily a sign of bad management? Explain in a sentence or two. Read on for an assessment of this situation.

└─ ┘

It may seem strange to think that any idle capacity would arise in a well-managed and well-planned company. In reality, machines require maintenance to refurbish and repair the wear and tear arising from normal use. Many manufacturers run two or three shifts twenty-four hours every day of the week. Without scheduled idle or down time for maintenance, the machines would break down. Good capacity management requires excess capacity to minimize output lost during maintenance. Finally, government regulations in many industries (such as the airline industry) legislate scheduled maintenance at specific times, which companies must comply with.

The goal is to assign a proportion of fixed overhead costs to each product or service sold. The identification of the fixed costs accumulated in each fixed overhead cost pool is one step and the other is the identification of inputs. The inputs are usually a nonfinancial measure and are the cost allocation base. Assume the lease costs represent the fixed overhead cost pool and machine-hours (MH) the cost allocation base. The cost pool divided by the cost allocation base will be the fixed overhead cost-allocation rate. Had Webb purchased the machines, then this numerator would comprise amortization rather than lease expense.

Webb, however, would have leased or acquired far more than merely one type of fixed manufacturing asset. Webb's top management must decide how many fixed overhead cost pools would provide enough relevant information to make good operating and strategic decisions. Some fixed overhead would best be allocated based on MH (a direct input), some based on shifts worked, and some on plant value (facilities level). If Webb's managers decide on a single fixed overhead cost pool, all other fixed costs will be accumulated or grouped in one cost pool.

Recall that tax and insurance are also fixed costs and these costs are incurred regardless of the number of machine-hours or shifts used, and most likely would be allocated based on some measure of output capacity. Webb could legitimately choose to put these costs in a fixed period overhead cost pool. But to simplify this example, Webb's managers have chosen a single fixed overhead cost pool that is composed of all fixed costs of running the manufacturing plant.

Fixed-cost decisions influence operating-management decisions. The day-to-day operating responses to unplanned events can produce either favourable or unfavourable fixed overhead variances. This is discussed in detail in the analysis of production-volume variance. Total fixed costs are usually included in flexible budgets, and they remain the same total amount (within the relevant range) regardless of the output level chosen (in contrast, variable costs and revenues are "flexed" depending on the chosen output level). A development process for Webb Company's budgeted fixed overhead rate is illustrated in Exhibit 8-1.

Similar to the process of benchmarking, the development of fixed cost rates is not a linear, step-by-step process. One reason is that neither all relevant information nor all managers are available at the same time. A second reason is that the processes are interdependent—one step cannot occur without an understanding of the other steps in the process. For example, the selection of homogeneous fixed overhead cost pools would best occur simultaneously with the analysis and discussion of the cost allocation bases (or cost driver rates) and capacity level. A third reason is that the strategy of using benchmark, standard, or budgeted costs may differ from one cost pool to another. Finally, technological advances may change the timing of the budgeting period.

When choosing the appropriate time period for analysis, a longer time period will better reflect the nature of capacity costs for long-term fixed costs. A simple monthly average, however, will give rise to predictable variances due to quarterly seasonal effects and the varying number of days in each month. This can be partially offset if managers take the time to establish a range of results that would be considered a normal or anticipated variance due to these predictable effects. Establishing a

EXHIBIT 8-1
Developing Fixed Overhead Rates

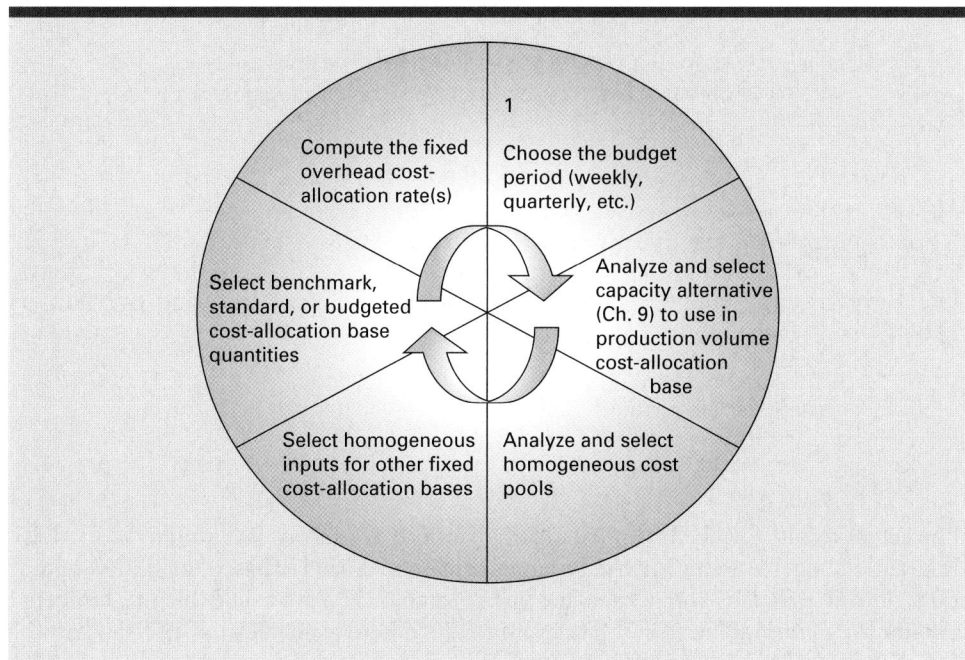

- Choose the budget period (weekly, quarterly, etc.) **1**
- Analyze and select capacity alternative (Ch. 9) to use in production volume cost-allocation base
- Analyze and select homogeneous cost pools
- Select homogeneous inputs for other fixed cost-allocation bases
- Select benchmark, standard, or budgeted cost-allocation base quantities
- Compute the fixed overhead cost-allocation rate(s)

normal range of variance will save valuable management time and improve the attention-getting function of variance reports.

The selection of a **production denominator level** (or **volume**) is intended to convey a measure of capacity. This choice gives rise to a **specific production-volume variance**, and the denominator can be one of four choices. Arithmetically, when a numerator is constant, the smaller the denominator level, the higher will be the result from the division (the fixed overhead rate), and vice versa. An inappropriate choice of denominator level will generate a fixed overhead rate that is too low or too high. This, in turn, gives rise to variances that are completely unpredictable, impair the attention-getting function of variance reports, and reduce relevance.

Assume Webb's managers have decided the cost allocation base, the production denominator volume, will be direct machine-hours. The production denominator level is assumed to be the master budget value of 57,600 machine-hours (MH) required for a budgeted output of 144,000 jackets.[2] Each jacket requires 0.40 MH (57,600 MH ÷ 144,000 = 0.40 MH) or 24 machine minutes per jacket. Other cost allocation bases, or perhaps facilities-level cost drivers if Webb is using ABC, must be chosen for each remaining fixed overhead cost pool. Webb has budgeted for 12,000 jackets manufactured in April 2009. Webb's budget reports 4,800 MH to manufacture 12,000 jackets (12,000 × 0.40 MH/jacket = 4,800 MH).

Concurrently, the managers would choose those costs comprising each homogeneous fixed overhead cost pool. This is the numerator. Webb's managers have decided fixed manufacturing overhead costs, which include amortization, plant leasing costs, property taxes, plant manager's salary, and some manufacturing administrative costs, will comprise a single cost pool. Webb's budget is $276,000 for April 2009. This cost pool will remain unchanged over the relevant range of output.

Dividing the fixed overhead cost pool of $276,000 by the quantity of homogeneous inputs in the cost allocation base of 4,800 MH gives the fixed overhead cost allocation rate. For simplicity we have assumed that Webb's managers are satisfied with the information provided by pooling all fixed costs into one cost pool. Had

[2]Because Webb plans its capacity over multiple periods, anticipated demand in 2009 is less than capacity. Companies vary in the denominator levels they choose, but the basic approach and analysis presented in this chapter is unchanged. Chapter 9 discusses choosing a denominator level and its implications in more detail.

there been more than one fixed cost pool, the process would be carried out for each pool. As shown, the budgeted fixed overhead rate per unit in the cost allocation base is $57.50 per machine hour, or $57.50/MH.

$$\text{Budgeted fixed overhead rate per unit of allocation base} = \frac{\text{Budgeted fixed overhead costs}}{\text{Budgeted quantity of allocation base units}}$$

$$= \$276,000 \div 4,800 \text{ MH}$$

$$= \$57.50 \text{ per MH}$$

FIXED OVERHEAD COST VARIANCE CALCULATION AND ANALYSIS

The Level 1 static-budget variance for Webb's fixed manufacturing overhead is $9,000 U:

$$\text{Fixed overhead static-budget variance} = \text{Actual results} - \text{Static-budget amount}$$

$$= \$285,000 - \$276,000$$

$$= \$9,000 \text{ U}$$

The actual results for fixed manufacturing overhead are shown in Exhibit 7-2 (p. 312). The static budget amount for fixed manufacturing overhead is based on 12,000 output units. Given that it is for a fixed cost, this same $276,000 would be the budgeted amount for all output levels in the relevant range. There is no "flexing" of fixed costs.

One possible cause of the variance when there is only one overhead cost pool is an increase in taxes or insurance premiums. These are generally not controllable by individual managers nor are they caused by any flaw in the production process. The $9,000 unfavourable variance simply means that Webb spent more on fixed manufacturing overhead in April 2009 than the lump sum pro forma (budgeted) amount, and the result was a decrease in the month's gross margin and operating income of $9,000. This is why it is called a **fixed overhead spending variance**. The $9,000 is, however, only a part of the total flexible budget overhead variance. It excludes another source of fixed overhead variance and all variable overhead variances.

┌───┐

THINKING CRITICALLY

Why is it important to find the relevant range for fixed overhead variance analysis? Explain in a sentence or two. Read on for an assessment of this situation.

└───┘

The fixed overhead flexible-budget variance is the same as the fixed overhead static-budget variance. There is no "flexing" of fixed costs. For Level 3 analysis (decomposing the flexible-budget variance into its efficiency and spending components), the total flexible-budget variance is attributed to spending variance because this is the only cause. The quantity in the cost allocation base remains unchanged over a relevant range. Unless the actual quantity consumed exceeds the relevant range, any difference compared to the quantity in the cost-allocation base is irrelevant. Exceeding the relevant range implies new equipment must be acquired or leased, which is a decision with long-term implications.

The arithmetic involved here is trivial—the value of variance analysis arises from finding the cause or causes of the variance. Reasons for the unfavourable spending variance could include an unplanned salary increase to retain the plant manager, increased insurance premiums, or increased taxes. Assume Webb investigated this variance and found that there was a $9,000 per month unexpected increase in its equipment leasing costs. However, management concluded that the new lease rates were competitive with lease rates available elsewhere. If this were not competitive, management could look to lease equipment from other suppliers.

Exhibit 8-2 shows a summary of the Levels 1, 2, and 3 variance analyses for Webb's fixed manufacturing overhead in April 2009, but it is not yet consistent with

EXHIBIT 8-2
Static-Budget and Flexible-Budget Analysis of Fixed Manufacturing Overhead
Spending Variance for Webb Company for April 2009

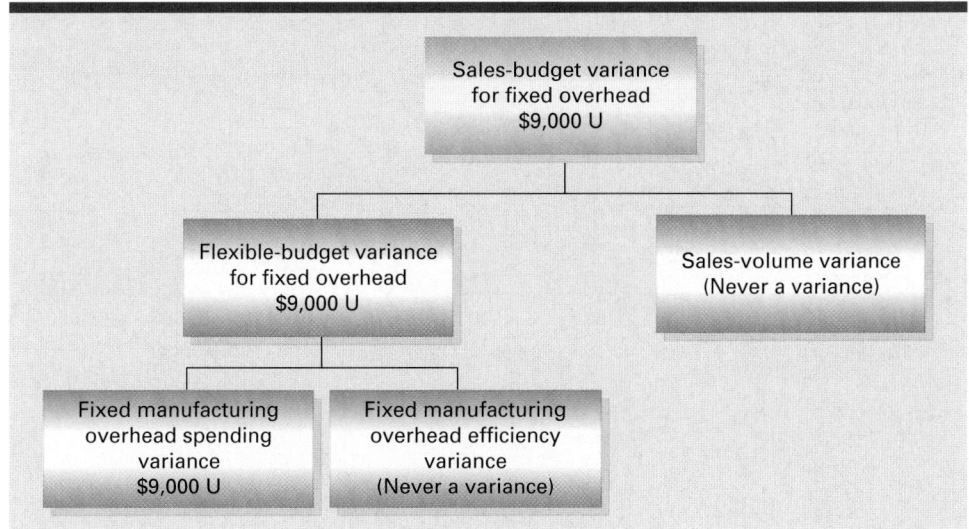

Exhibit 7-8 because neither the production-volume variance nor the variable overhead variances have yet been analyzed. Together, the spending and production-volume variances sum to the flexible-budget fixed overhead variance.

THINKING CRITICALLY

Why is there never a sales-volume variance? Explain in a sentence or two. Read on for an assessment of this situation.

Budgeted fixed costs are, by definition, unaffected by sales-volume changes. Sales and production volumes are assumed to be identical. Within a relevant range, there will never be a sales-volume variance because the sales-volume variance arises only for costs affected by changes in the volume of sales. Similarly, there is never an efficiency variance in Level 3 for fixed overhead costs because within the relevant range, differences in output levels do not affect fixed costs. Managers cannot be more or less efficient in dealing with a specified amount of fixed costs.

PRODUCTION-VOLUME VARIANCE CALCULATION AND ANALYSIS

The *production-volume variance* is a denominator-level variance. Other terms for this variance include **denominator-level variance** and **output-level overhead variance.** The **production-volume variance** is the difference between budgeted fixed overhead and the fixed overhead that should have been assigned for the actual quantity of outputs. Assigned fixed overhead is calculated by multiplying the budgeted fixed overhead rate by two factors: first, the quantity of the actual output and second, the result is multiplied by the budgeted input of the cost allocation base for the actual output level.

Using standard costs, Webb budgeted its fixed overhead cost rate of $57.50 per standard MH. The standard quantity of the cost allocation base (machine-hours) required per jacket is 0.40 MH. The fixed overhead is therefore $23 for each jacket (0.40 MH/jacket × $57.50/MH = $23/jacket). Webb *actually* produced 10,000 jackets, so its allocation is $230,000 ($23/jacket × 10,000 jackets = $230,000). Of course, if Webb actually produced 12,000 jackets, then the allocation would be $276,000 ($23/jacket × 12,000 jackets = $276,000).

The graph in Exhibit 8-3 illustrates the costs associated with the different quantities of jackets that might actually be produced. Assuming that this overhead cost pool is

EXHIBIT 8-3
Production-Volume Allocated Cost Behaviour

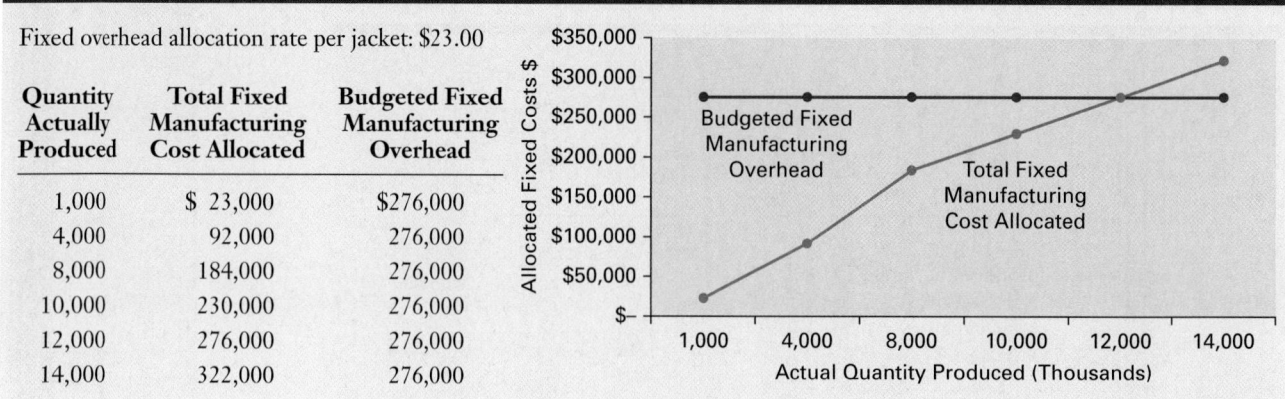

Quantity Actually Produced	Total Fixed Manufacturing Cost Allocated	Budgeted Fixed Manufacturing Overhead
1,000	$ 23,000	$276,000
4,000	92,000	276,000
8,000	184,000	276,000
10,000	230,000	276,000
12,000	276,000	276,000
14,000	322,000	276,000

Fixed overhead allocation rate per jacket: $23.00

fixed over the relevant range of 1,000 to 14,000 jackets, the budgeted fixed cost pool is the straight line at the top of the graph. The sloped line is the amount of fixed overhead cost that would be allocated to inventories using the per-unit rate of $23 per jacket at different levels of actual production. The only quantity at which no production-volume variance will arise is 12,000 jackets, where the two lines intersect. At any other volume, a production-volume variance will be reported.

There will almost inevitably be a production-volume variance reported. The denominator level to calculate this fixed overhead rate is a capacity decision among four alternatives. Only one alternative is the master budget capacity, which was assumed for this example. The actual volume produced will vary around the master-budget level for Webb. If there is an unfavourable production-volume variance, then allocated fixed overhead will be less than budgeted. Actual production achieved failed to reach the budgeted capacity, so the production-volume variance represents an opportunity cost of unused capacity. Again, the arithmetic is not as important as a careful reflection on what caused an unfavourable variance.

The formula for the production-volume variance, expressed in terms of allocation base units (MH for Webb), is

$$\text{Production-volume variance} = \begin{pmatrix} \text{Budgeted} \\ \text{fixed} \\ \text{overhead} \end{pmatrix} - \begin{pmatrix} \text{Fixed overhead allocated using} \\ \text{budgeted input allowed for} \\ \text{actual output units achieved} \end{pmatrix} \times \begin{pmatrix} \text{Budgeted fixed} \\ \text{overhead rate} \end{pmatrix}$$

$$= \$276,000 - (0.40 \text{ MH per jacket} \times 10,000 \text{ jackets} \times \$57.50 \text{ per MH})$$

$$= \$276,000 - (4,000 \text{ MH} \times \$57.50 \text{ per MH})$$

$$= \$276,000 - \$230,000$$

$$= \$46,000 \text{ U}$$

The amount used for budgeted fixed overhead will be the same lump sum shown in the static budget and also in any flexible budget within the relevant range. Fixed overhead costs allocated is the sum of the individual fixed overhead costs allocated to each of the products manufactured during the accounting period.

The production-volume variance results from "unitizing" fixed costs. Be careful when attributing economic significance to this variance. The most common misinterpretation is to assume this variance measures the economic cost of producing and selling 10,000 units rather than the 12,000 budgeted for April. This assumption does not consider why Webb sold only 10,000 units. Exhibit 8-4 illustrates the fixed overhead variance relationships.

The report of unfavourable variances should trigger an analysis of how the variances arose. Assume that Webb's managers have found out that a new competitor had gained market share by pricing below what Webb charges its customers. To sell the budgeted 12,000 units, Webb may have had to reduce its own selling price on all

EXHIBIT 8-4
Static-Budget and Flexible-Budget Analysis of Fixed Manufacturing Overhead Costs for
Webb Company for April 2009

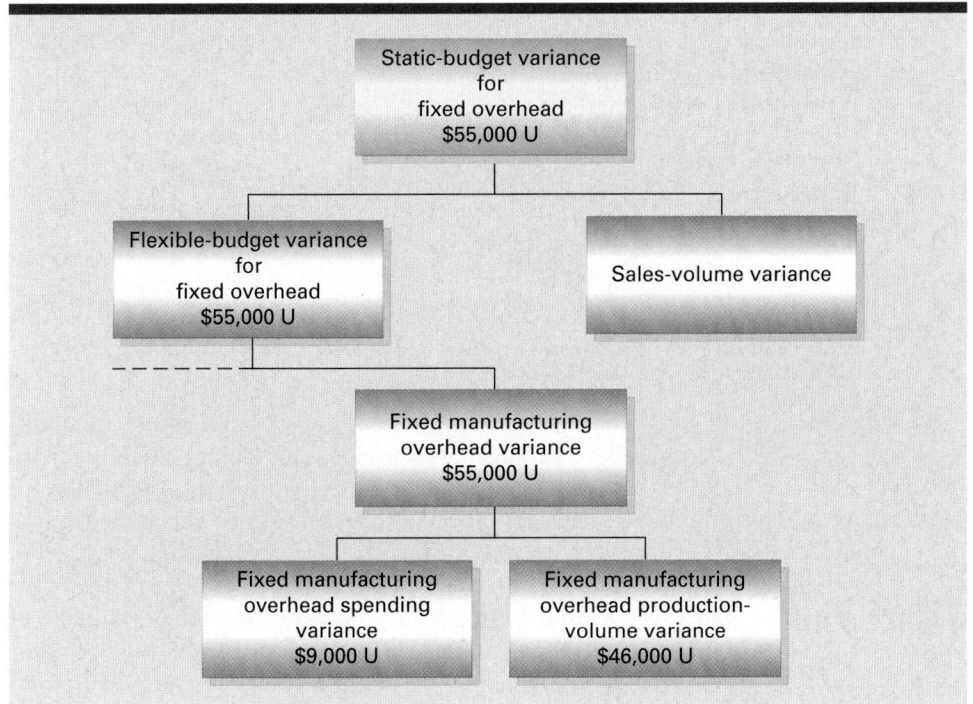

12,000 units. Suppose managers decided that selling 10,000 units at a higher price yielded higher operating income than selling 12,000 units at a lower price. The production-volume variance does not take into account such information. Hence, it would be misleading to interpret the $46,000 unfavourable amount as Webb's economic cost of selling 2,000 units fewer than the budgeted quantity of 12,000 units for April. The variance arises from the *overuse of MH* for the 10,000 jackets produced.

If there is almost always a variance, then the attention-getting function of variance analysis is questionable. Why companies must compute this variance is that some contracts and GAAP standards require that fixed overhead costs be calculated on a unit-of-output basis as well as for inventory valuation purposes. When allocating fixed overhead for inventory, the average unit cost is multiplied by the quantity remaining in various inventories to produce an inventory valuation.

The way in which capacity is added is another factor to consider when analyzing a production-volume variance. For example, imagine that Webb only had capacity to create 8,000 jackets and needed to increase capacity to meet an anticipated permanent increase in demand of 10,000 jackets. It may be the case that capacity can only be added in 4,000-jacket increments. Assume Webb increases its capacity to 12,000 jackets. Until the actual demand for jackets increases to 12,000, Webb may choose 12,000 as its denominator level, which will create a predictable production-volume variance. The idle capacity is beyond Webb's control and does not indicate poor management. Partial discussion of the sales-volume variance is undertaken later in this section and is completed in Chapter 16.

JOURNAL ENTRIES FOR FIXED OVERHEAD COSTS AND VARIANCES

The journal entries are illustrated below for the month of April 2009 using the Fixed Overhead Control and the contra account Fixed Overhead Allocated. These data are identical to those in Exhibit 8-12 Panel B. The fixed manufacturing overhead variances are the same as those shown in Exhibit 8-4. The reconciliation of the two data sets will be explained by the variable cost variances in the next section.

1.	Fixed Overhead Control	285,000	
	Salaries, lease, tax, insurance payable		285,000
	To record actual fixed overhead costs incurred		
2.	WIP Control	230,000	
	Fixed Overhead Allocated		230,000
	To record fixed overhead costs allocated (0.40 MH/jacket × 10,000 jackets × $57.50/MH)		
	The costs accumulated in WIP control are transferred to Finished Goods Control when production is completed and into Cost of Goods Sold Control when the goods are sold (Ch. 4)		
3.	Fixed Overhead Allocated	230,000	
	Fixed Overhead Spending Variance	9,000	
	Fixed Overhead Production-Volume Variance	46,000	
	Fixed Overhead Control		285,000
	Records variances for the accounting period		

The fixed overhead spending variance and production-volume variance record the $55,000 ($285,000 − $230,000 = $55,000) of fixed overhead costs that were incurred according to the budget but not allocated to the jackets produced. These are the underallocated fixed overhead costs from normal costing (introduced in Chapter 4).

How the fixed overhead spending variance is treated at the end of the fiscal year depends on its materiality. If it is immaterial, it may be either written off to Cost of Goods Sold or prorated among the Work-In-Process Control, Finished Goods Control, and Cost of Goods Sold accounts on the basis of the fixed overhead allocated to these accounts. This process was described in detail in Chapter 4 in Learning Objective 5. Some companies combine the write-off and proration methods. They write off the portion of variance arising from inefficiency that could have been avoided, and then prorate the portion that was unavoidable. If the balance in the Fixed Overhead Spending Variance account at the end of April 2009 is also the year-end balance in December and is immaterial, then the following journal entry records the write-off to Cost of Goods Sold:

Cost of Goods Sold	9,000	
Fixed Overhead Spending Variance		9,000

Also assume that the balance in the Fixed Overhead Spending Variance account at the end of April 2009 is the year-end balance in December. Assume there is some WIP and finished goods inventory at December 31, 2009. There is some argument about the appropriate treatment of an unfavourable production-volume variance. Some accountants contend that the $46,000 U measures the cost of resources expended in anticipation of 2,000 jackets that were not produced ($23/jacket × 2,000 jackets = $46,000).

Prorating would inappropriately allocate fixed overhead costs incurred for jackets not produced to those that were produced. In principle, the jackets produced already bear their fair share of the burden of overhead incurred during the year. This favours charging the unfavourable production-volume variance against the year's revenue to ensure the fixed costs of unused capacity are not carried in the WIP and finished goods inventories. This avoids an understatement of cost of goods sold from an overstated inventory valuation.

Alternatively, some accountants look at the choice of a denominator level as merely an estimate of the fixed capacity needed to produce jackets. Unforeseen events happen randomly, which can cause the actual capacity to differ from the denominator level. Such random events in April led to the production of 10,000 jackets, rather than the planned 12,000. We know this because there is no systematic and repeated unfavourable production-volume variance in other months. The budgeted $276,000 supported the cost of manufacturing the 10,000 jackets. Therefore, it is appropriate to prorate this fixed overhead cost to the jackets to properly allocate the costs to the remaining WIP and finished goods inventories.

Favourable production-volume variances could also arise. Assume Webb had manufactured and sold 13,800 jackets in April 2009:

$$\begin{aligned}
\text{Production volume variance} &= \begin{array}{c}\text{Budgeted}\\\text{fixed}\\\text{overhead}\end{array} - \begin{array}{c}\text{Fixed overhead allocated using}\\\text{the budgeted cost per output unit overhead}\\\text{allowed for the actual output produced}\end{array}\\
&= \$276{,}000 - (\$23/\text{jacket} \times 13{,}800 \text{ jackets})\\
&= \$276{,}000 - \$317{,}400\\
&= \$41{,}400 \text{ F}
\end{aligned}$$

The fixed overhead costs of \$276,000 in this situation supported the production of all 13,800 jackets and must be allocated to the actual production volume. The more conservative approach to prorating the favourable production-volume variance of \$41,400 is to prorate it to reduce the value of WIP and finished goods inventories because this will increase the cost of goods sold, which reduces the reported gross margin and in turn the operating income. Crediting the entire amount to cost of goods sold would result in a higher reported operating income.

Recall that the process of setting standards is complex and if variances were always written off to cost of goods sold, there would be temptation for managers to set standards to affect financial reports rather than to improve operating and strategic management decisions. The denominator level could be chosen to increase (for financial-reporting purposes) or decrease (for tax purposes) the reported operating income. Webb could generate a favourable (or unfavourable) production-volume variance by setting the denominator level to allocate fixed overhead costs either low (or high) to either increase (or decrease) reported operating income.

Each approach has its strengths and weaknesses and the procedure is a matter of professional judgment assessed case by case. If Webb wrote off the production-volume variance to Cost of Goods Sold, the journal entry would be:

Fixed Overhead Production-Volume Variance	41,400	
Cost of Goods Sold		41,400

GOVERNANCE ISSUES

Cost Allocation Base Selection: Proration or Writeoff—There Is a Right Way

Managers may be tempted to choose a lower capacity level (denominator) to avoid unfavourable variances and the resulting negative effects on operating income. For example, if Webb's management team had used 48,000 budgeted machine-hours (that is, 120,000 jackets per year or 10,000 jackets per month) instead of 57,600 machine-hours as the denominator, Webb would not have reported an unfavourable production-volume variance in April. But management accountants should ask if this is the right choice. For example, is 48,000 machine-hours too conservative? The selection of an appropriate denominator level should be made with the goal of improving relevant information. Good-quality, relevant information leads to good management decisions, which generally lead to better profits.

This management-accounting decision regarding the denominator will affect the dollar value reported in cost of goods sold, gross margin, operating income, and net income.

There exists a weight of evidence from decades of accounting research that reported net income affects share price. Higher net income is associated with higher share price, all other things equal. If management accountants bias the choice of proration or use writeoffs to understate manufacturing costs and overstate the values in inventory, the reported net income will be overstated for that time period. The biased net income will mislead existing and potential investors.

The CMA code of ethics requires (in part) that "A Member will act at all times with: (i) responsibility for and fidelity to public needs." The investing public needs unbiased reports of net income to make rational investing decisions. The choice of proration or writeoffs for material overallocation or underallocation of overhead costs does matter in financial reporting to external parties when it leads to a material misstatement of the actual economic strength of a company.

MyAccountingLab

> ### ASSESS YOUR MASTERY
>
> To check your understanding of the material in Learning Objective **1**, go to the *Mastery Questions* section at the end of this chapter and complete Learning Objective **1** questions 1, 2, and 3.

FLEXIBLE-BUDGET VARIABLE OVERHEAD VARIANCES

2 Establish variable overhead cost-allocation rates; calculate and analyze flexible budget variances

PLANNING VARIABLE OVERHEAD COSTS

Among Webb's variable manufacturing overhead costs are energy, machine maintenance, engineering support, indirect materials, and indirect manufacturing labour.

Webb uses standard costing. The development of standards for Webb's direct-cost categories was described in Chapter 7. This chapter discusses Webb's indirect-cost categories. In the context of indirect costs, standard costing means that Webb will allocate indirect costs on the basis of the standard indirect rates multiplied by the standard quantities of the allocation bases allowed for the actual outputs produced.

With a standard-costing system, the standard costs of every product or service budgeted as output during the period can be computed at the start of that period. This feature of standard costing makes the recording system a simple one. In addition to the standard direct costs, the standard indirect cost rates for variable and fixed overhead are also required. These rates can be calculated because the standard quantities in the allocation bases are known, and the total fixed and total variable overhead costs have been budgeted. Once standards have been set, the costs of operating a standard-costing system can be low relative to the costs of operating either an actual-costing or a normal-costing system.

The process of developing budgeted variable overhead cost rates, as outlined in Exhibit 8-5, is slightly less complex because no denominator level needs to be chosen.

We know that Webb has selected a 12-month, or fiscal year, budget period. With an additional simplification, we will assume the managers have decided

EXHIBIT 8-5
Developing Variable Overhead Rates

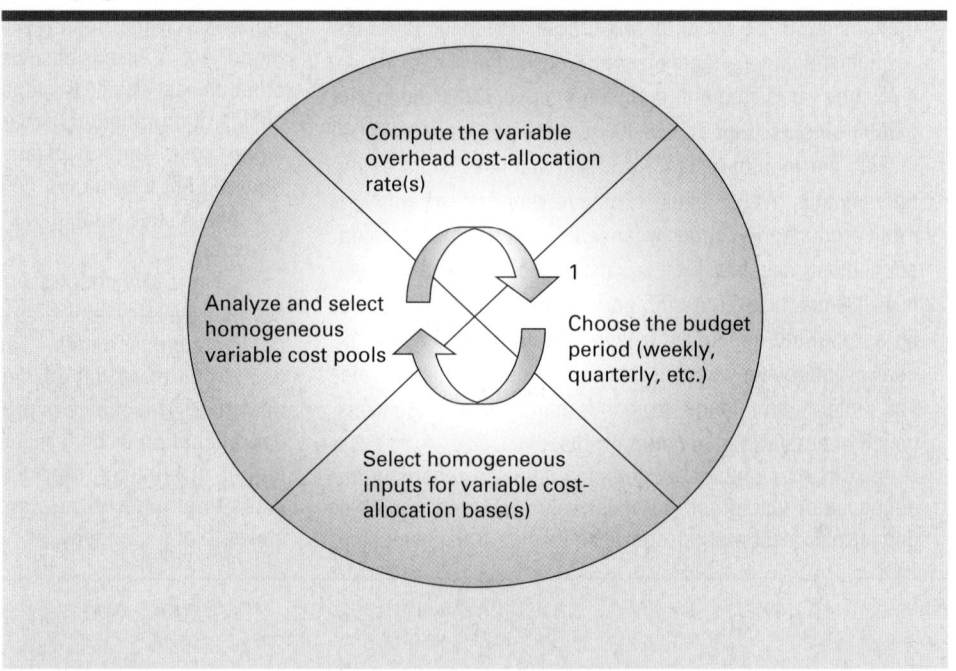

that machine-hours (MH) is a reasonable variable-cost allocation base as well. The Webb Company summary information for April 2009 that we will use in this chapter is as follows:

Overhead Category	Actual Results	Flexible Budget Amount (for 10,000 Output Units)	Static Budget Amount (for 12,000 Output Units)
Variable manufacturing overhead	$130,500	$120,000	$144,000
Fixed manufacturing overhead	285,000	276,000	276,000
Variable marketing overhead	45,700	50,000	60,000
Fixed marketing overhead	420,000	434,000	434,000

Also assume Webb's managers have decided to group all variable overhead costs (utilities, indirect materials, indirect manufacturing labour [e.g., quality inspection wages], sewing machine maintenance labour and supplies) into a single variable overhead cost pool for the year budgeted at $1,728,000.[3]

The variable overhead cost per input unit is simply the total budgeted variable overhead cost pool of $1,728,000 divided by the budgeted total of 57,600 MH in the cost allocation base. The amount in the cost allocation base is a standard quantity of machine-hours to produce 144,000 jackets per year. The variable overhead cost rate is $30 per standard machine-hour to allocate these costs. Thus, the cost per homogeneous unit of input is $30/MH. But the variable overhead cost per jacket is far lower because Webb has also budgeted a standard of 0.40 MH/jacket. The variable overhead cost per *output* unit is $12/jacket ($30/MH × 0.40 MH/jacket = $12/jacket). This budgeted variable overhead cost rate will be used both in the static budget for 2009 and the monthly performance reports prepared during 2009.

$$\frac{\text{Budgeted variable overhead}}{\text{cost rate per output unit}} = \frac{\text{Budgeted inputs allowed}}{\text{per output unit}} \times \frac{\text{Budgeted variable overhead}}{\text{cost rate per input unit}}$$

$$= 0.40 \text{ hour per jacket} \times \$30 \text{ per hour}$$

$$= \$12 \text{ per jacket}$$

VARIABLE OVERHEAD COST VARIANCE CALCULATIONS AND ANALYSES

We now illustrate how the budgeted variable manufacturing overhead rate is used in computing Webb's variable manufacturing overhead cost variances. The following data are for April 2009:

Item	Actual Results	Flexible Budget Amount (for 10,000 output units)	Static Budget Amount (for 12,000 output units)
1. Variable overhead costs	$130,500	$120,000	$144,000
2. MH	4,500	4,000	4,800
3. Output, jackets	10,000	10,000	12,000
4. MH/jacket (2 ÷ 3)	0.45	0.40	0.40
5. Variable overhead cost (1 ÷ 2)	$ 29.00	$ 30.00	$ 30.00
6. Variable overhead cost/jacket (1 ÷ 3)	$ 13.05	$ 12.00	$ 12.00

The key to understanding flexible budget variance calculations is to remember that the appropriate comparison is between what should have been spent per jacket for the actual quantity produced and what was actually spent. The first column of costs per unit reports the actual amounts spent and the second column reports the pro forma amounts spent, or what should have been spent, for the actual outputs produced.

---

[3]The budgeted variable manufacturing overhead per 10,000 jackets is $120,000 and the budgeted output is 144,000 jackets. Therefore, the budgeted amount is 144,000 ÷ 10,000 × $120,000 = $1,728,000.

The Level 0 static-budget variance is not sufficiently informative; therefore, this discussion begins with the Level 1 static-budget analysis. The Level 1 analysis for the static budget is shown in Exhibit 8-6 for variable manufacturing overhead. The calculation is:

$$\frac{\text{Variable overhead}}{\text{static-budget variance}} = \frac{\text{Actual}}{\text{results}} - \frac{\text{Static-budget}}{\text{amount}}$$
$$= \$130{,}500 - \$144{,}000$$
$$= \$13{,}500 \text{ F}$$

Unfortunately, the result of a simple subtraction provides no insight into what caused the variance, although if it was a material amount and unfavourable, it would capture attention.

Additional insight into the ability of Webb's managers to control variable manufacturing overhead can be gained by moving to the Level 2 flexible-budget analysis, also shown in Exhibit 8-6. The budgeted amounts in Level 2 recognize that 10,000 output units were produced instead of the budgeted 12,000 output units. The April 2009 flexible budget for variable manufacturing overhead is $120,000 (0.4 × 10,000 × $30).

EXHIBIT 8-6
Static-Budget and Flexible-Budget Analysis of Variable Manufacturing Overhead Costs for Webb Company for April 2009

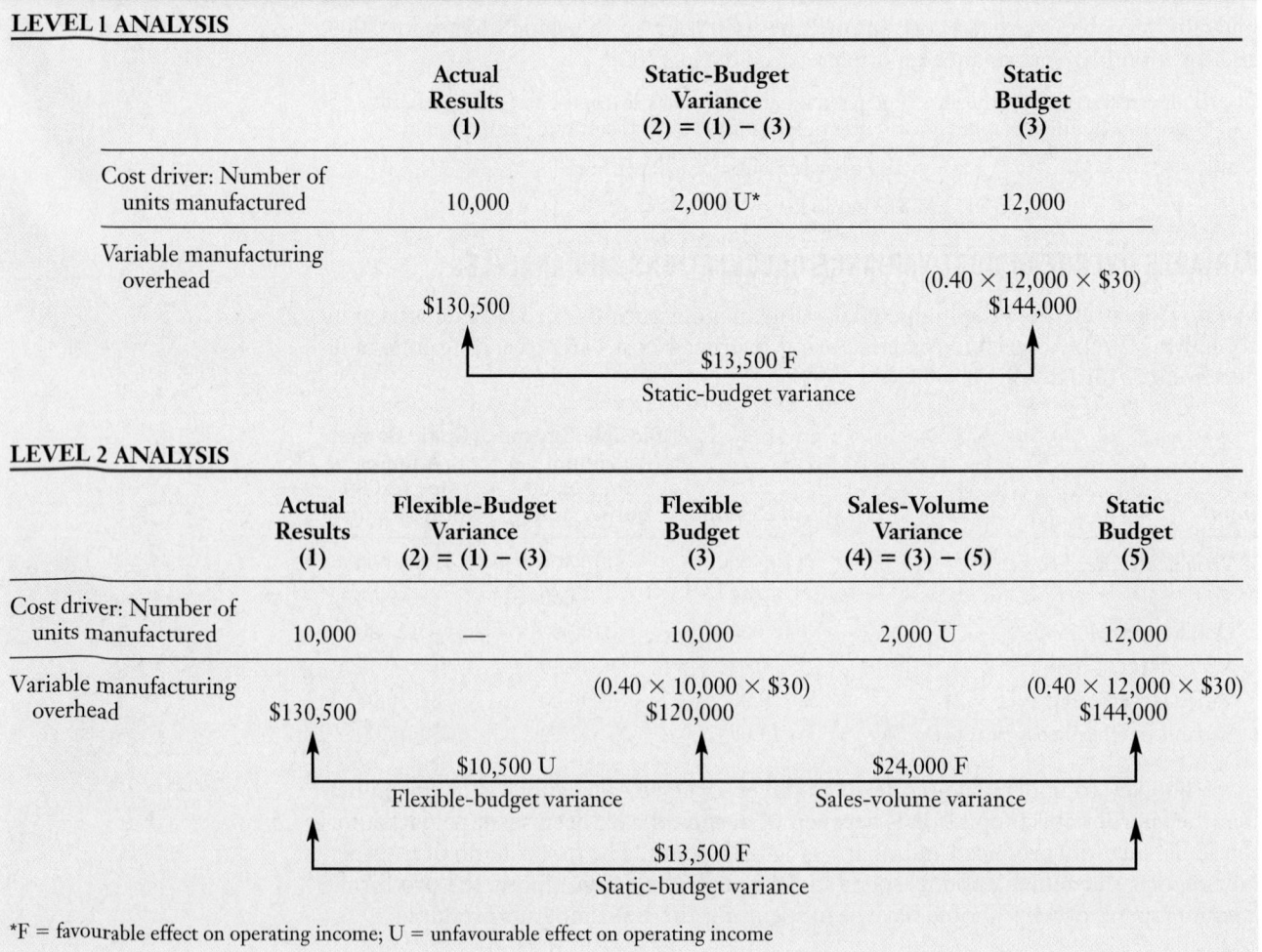

LEVEL 1 ANALYSIS

	Actual Results (1)	Static-Budget Variance (2) = (1) − (3)	Static Budget (3)
Cost driver: Number of units manufactured	10,000	2,000 U*	12,000
Variable manufacturing overhead	$130,500		(0.40 × 12,000 × $30) $144,000

$13,500 F
Static-budget variance

LEVEL 2 ANALYSIS

	Actual Results (1)	Flexible-Budget Variance (2) = (1) − (3)	Flexible Budget (3)	Sales-Volume Variance (4) = (3) − (5)	Static Budget (5)
Cost driver: Number of units manufactured	10,000	—	10,000	2,000 U	12,000
Variable manufacturing overhead	$130,500		(0.40 × 10,000 × $30) $120,000		(0.40 × 12,000 × $30) $144,000

$10,500 U
Flexible-budget variance

$24,000 F
Sales-volume variance

$13,500 F
Static-budget variance

*F = favourable effect on operating income; U = unfavourable effect on operating income

The variable manufacturing overhead flexible-budget variance arises because Webb's actual variable manufacturing overhead cost differs from that budgeted for the actual output units sold:

$$\text{Variable overhead flexible-budget variance} = \text{Actual result} - \text{Flexible-budget amount}$$

$$= \$130,500 - \$120,000$$

$$= \$10,500 \text{ U}$$

This $10,500 unfavourable flexible-budget variance shows that Webb's actual variable manufacturing overhead exceeded the flexible-budget amount by $10,500 for the 10,000 jackets actually produced in April 2009. While this can focus attention on what happened, Webb's managers will want to explain why the variance arose to help them solve any production problems.

In Chapter 7 we illustrated how subdividing the flexible-budget variance for direct-cost items into efficiency and price variances provided additional insight into the causes of variance. We now discuss how managers can gain additional insight into the causes of flexible-budget variances for indirect-cost items by splitting the Level 2 variable manufacturing overhead flexible-budget variance into its Level 3 efficiency and spending variances. Exhibit 8-7 on page 379 is the columnar presentation of these Level 3 efficiency and spending variances.

VARIABLE OVERHEAD EFFICIENCY VARIANCE

The **variable overhead efficiency variance** measures the efficiency with which the cost-allocation base is used. This is a comparison of costs per MH input shown in the table on page 375. The formula is:

$$\text{Variable overhead efficiency variance} = \left(\begin{array}{c} \text{Actual units of} \\ \text{variable overhead} \\ \text{cost-allocation base} \\ \text{used for actual output} \\ \text{units achieved} \end{array} - \begin{array}{c} \text{Budgeted units of} \\ \text{variable overhead} \\ \text{cost-allocation base} \\ \text{allowed for actual} \\ \text{output units achieved} \end{array} \right) \times \begin{array}{c} \text{Budgeted} \\ \text{variable overhead} \\ \text{cost-allocation rate} \end{array}$$

$$= [4,500 \text{ MH} - (10,000 \text{ units} \times 0.40 \text{ MH/unit})] \times \$30 \text{ per MH}$$

$$= (4,500 \text{ MH} - 4,000 \text{ MH}) \times \$30 \text{ per MH}$$

$$= 500 \text{ MH} \times \$30 \text{ per MH}$$

$$= \$15,000 \text{ U}$$

For indirect costs, efficiency variances for variable overhead costs are based on the efficiency with which the cost-allocation base is used. Webb's unfavourable variable overhead efficiency variance of $15,000 means that actual MH used (the cost-allocation base) was 500 MH higher than the MH budgeted to manufacture 10,000 jackets. There are several possible causes for this variance and it is incorrect to assume that workers were simply inefficient. The possible causes and appropriate management responses to this higher-than-budgeted machine-hour usage include the following:

Possible Causes for Exceeding Budget	Potential Management Responses
1. Workers were less skilled than expected in using machines.	1. Encourage the human resources function to implement better employee-hiring practices and procedures.
2. Production scheduler inefficiently scheduled jobs, resulting in more machine-hours than budgeted.	2. Improve plant operations by installing production-scheduling software.
3. Machines were not maintained in good operating condition.	3. Ensure preventive maintenance is done on all machines.
4. Webb's sales staff promised a distributor a rush delivery, which resulted in more machine-hours used than budgeted.	4. Coordinate production schedules with sales staff and distributors, and share information with them.
5. Budgeted machine-time standards were set too tight.	5. Commit more resources to develop appropriate standards.

Management's response to this $15,000 unfavourable variance would be guided by whichever cause(s) best describe(s) the April 2009 results.

In Chapter 7, the direct-cost variance analyses included only direct manufacturing materials and labour price, and spending and efficiency variances. From these, Webb could understand where it had overconsumed direct inputs. Selecting direct machine-hours as the cost allocation base for both fixed and variable overhead costs provided the managers with additional relevant information about overconsumption of direct inputs, specifically the 500 direct machine-hours indicated by the production-volume variance analysis of fixed overhead costs. This also generated a considerable cost overrun, calculated by the variable overhead efficiency variance.

Knowing about this overconsumption of direct machine-hours presents another possible reason for the labour efficiency variance—simply that as long as the machines run an additional 500 machine-hours, people must be working on those machines. Even though Webb is using a straightforward, traditional method of cost assignment by assigning indirect costs to each jacket, the indirect-cost variance analyses of overhead provide additional insight into how to ensure the flexible-budget allocations are met or improved upon in future.

Let us assume that Webb's managers discovered one reason the machines operated below budgeted efficiency levels in April 2009 was that insufficient maintenance was performed in the prior two months. A former plant manager delayed maintenance to meet monthly budget cost targets. As we discussed in Chapter 6, managers should not be focused on meeting short-run budget targets if it is likely to result in harmful long-run consequences. Webb has since strengthened its internal maintenance procedures so that failure to do monthly maintenance as required raises a "red flag" that must be immediately explained to management. Underskilled workers were another reason for actual machine-hours exceeding budgeted machine-hours. As a result, Webb initiated steps to improve hiring and training practices.

VARIABLE OVERHEAD SPENDING VARIANCE

The **variable overhead spending variance** is the difference between actual variable overhead cost per unit of the cost-allocation base and budgeted variable overhead cost per unit of the cost-allocation base, multiplied by actual quantity of variable overhead cost-allocation base used for actual output. This variance compares costs per input unit, or MH, that should have arisen from consuming 4,500 MH with the costs per MH that actually were reported.

The formula for the variable overhead spending variance is

$$\begin{pmatrix} \text{Variable overhead} \\ \text{spending variance} \end{pmatrix} = \begin{pmatrix} \text{Actual variable} & \text{Budgeted variable} \\ \text{overhead cost} & \text{overhead cost per} \\ \text{per unit of cost} - \text{unit of cost-} \\ \text{allocation base} & \text{allocation base} \end{pmatrix} \times \begin{pmatrix} \text{Actual quantity of variable} \\ \text{overhead cost-allocation} \\ \text{base used for actual} \\ \text{output units achieved} \end{pmatrix}$$

$$= (\$29 \text{ per MH} - \$30 \text{ per MH}) \times 4{,}500 \text{ MH}$$

$$= -\$1 \text{ per MH} \times 4{,}500 \text{ MH}$$

$$= \$4{,}500 \text{ F}$$

Webb operated in April 2009 with a lower-than-budgeted variable overhead cost per MH. Hence, there is a favourable variable overhead spending variance. The two level 3 variances are illustrated in Exhibit 8-7.

EXHIBIT 8-7
Columnar Presentation of Variance Analysis: Variable Manufacturing Overhead for
Webb Company

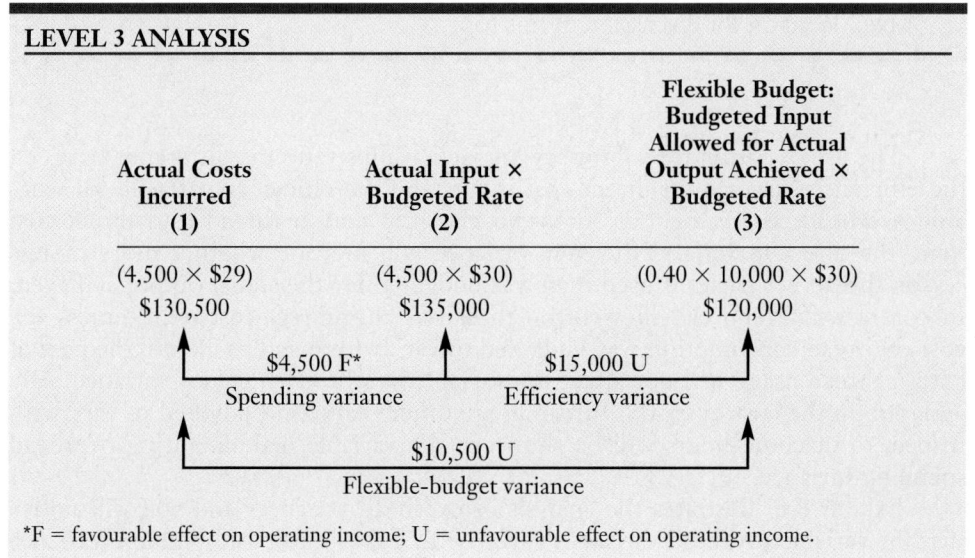

LEVEL 3 ANALYSIS

Actual Costs Incurred (1)	Actual Input × Budgeted Rate (2)	Flexible Budget: Budgeted Input Allowed for Actual Output Achieved × Budgeted Rate (3)
(4,500 × $29)	(4,500 × $30)	(0.40 × 10,000 × $30)
$130,500	$135,000	$120,000

$4,500 F* $15,000 U

Spending variance   Efficiency variance

$10,500 U

Flexible-budget variance

*F = favourable effect on operating income; U = unfavourable effect on operating income.

The variable overhead spending variance is computed similarly to the price variance described in Chapter 7 for direct-cost items such as direct materials. The reasons for the direct-cost price variances differ from those of the indirect-cost spending variances. The former refers to a cost traced directly to an input unit. The latter refers to a cost per unit in an allocation base. Not all costs in a variable overhead cost pool arise from consuming the same input unit, but Webb's managers have decided on an input unit that explains most of the variability in this cost pool.

Webb's managers now want to explain why the actual variable overhead cost per MH is lower than the budgeted variable overhead per MH. Two main causes could explain a variable overhead spending variance of $4,500 F at Webb:

1. The actual prices of individual items included in variable overhead differ from their budgeted prices—for example, the April 2009 purchase prices of energy, indirect materials, or indirect manufacturing labour were less than the budget prices. The price effects could be the result of skillful negotiation on the part of the purchasing manager, oversupply in the market, or lower quality of inputs such as indirect materials. Webb's response would depend on what was discovered to be the cause of the variance. For example, if the concerns are about quality, Webb would seek to put in place new quality management systems.

2. The actual usage of individual items included in variable overhead differs from the budgeted usage—for example, the budgeted usage of energy, indirect materials, or indirect manufacturing labour was less than the usage assumed in setting the $30 budgeted variable manufacturing overhead rate per machine-hour. If the actual energy consumed was 32,400 kilowatt-hours (KWH) compared to a flexible budget amount of 30,000 KWH then the 8% increase [(32,400 KWH − 30,000 KWH) ÷ 30,000 KWH = 8%] powered a 12.5% increase in MH [(4,500 MH − 4,000 MH) ÷ 4,000 MH = 12.5%). The cost of additional energy supported proportionally more MH and this gave rise to the favourable spending variance.

Cause 1 has implications for the purchasing area of Webb. Cause 2 has implications for the production area of Webb. Distinguishing between these two causes for a variable overhead spending variance requires detailed information about the budgeted prices and the budgeted quantities of the individual line items in the variable overhead cost pool.

The use of cotton thread for sewing jackets illustrates the difference between the efficiency variance for direct-cost inputs and the efficiency variance for variable overhead cost categories. If Webb classifies cotton thread as a direct-cost item, the direct materials efficiency variance will indicate whether more or less cotton thread per jacket is used than was budgeted for the actual output achieved. In contrast, if Webb classifies cotton thread as an indirect-cost item, unless the cost of thread consumption was budgeted to vary with machine-hours, the cost of cotton thread usage will not affect the variable overhead efficiency variance. Any variation in the cost of cotton thread usage other than that budgeted to vary with respect to machine-hours will be shown in the variable manufacturing overhead spending variance.

Exhibit 8-8 illustrates the analysis of overhead variances and you will notice that the variable overhead variances gave rise to a favourable sales-volume variance of $24,000, as also shown in Exhibit 8-6. The static budget variance includes only indirect overhead, excluding all direct variances, thus does not sum to the flexible and sales volume variance amount of $41,500 U. In Chapter 7, Exhibit 7-2, the variable manufacturing overhead is $120,000 and fixed manufacturing overhead is $276,000 for 10,000 jackets—these have been analyzed in this chapter. For simplicity, we have excluded discussion of the $50,000 in variable marketing (or period) overhead and the $434,000 of fixed marketing (or period) overhead. The favourable variance between the actual and budgeted marketing costs can be explained in part by period overhead variance and other factors discussed in Chapter 16.

EXHIBIT 8-8
Static-Budget and Flexible-Budget Analysis of Fixed and Variable Manufacturing Overhead
Costs for Webb Company for April 2009

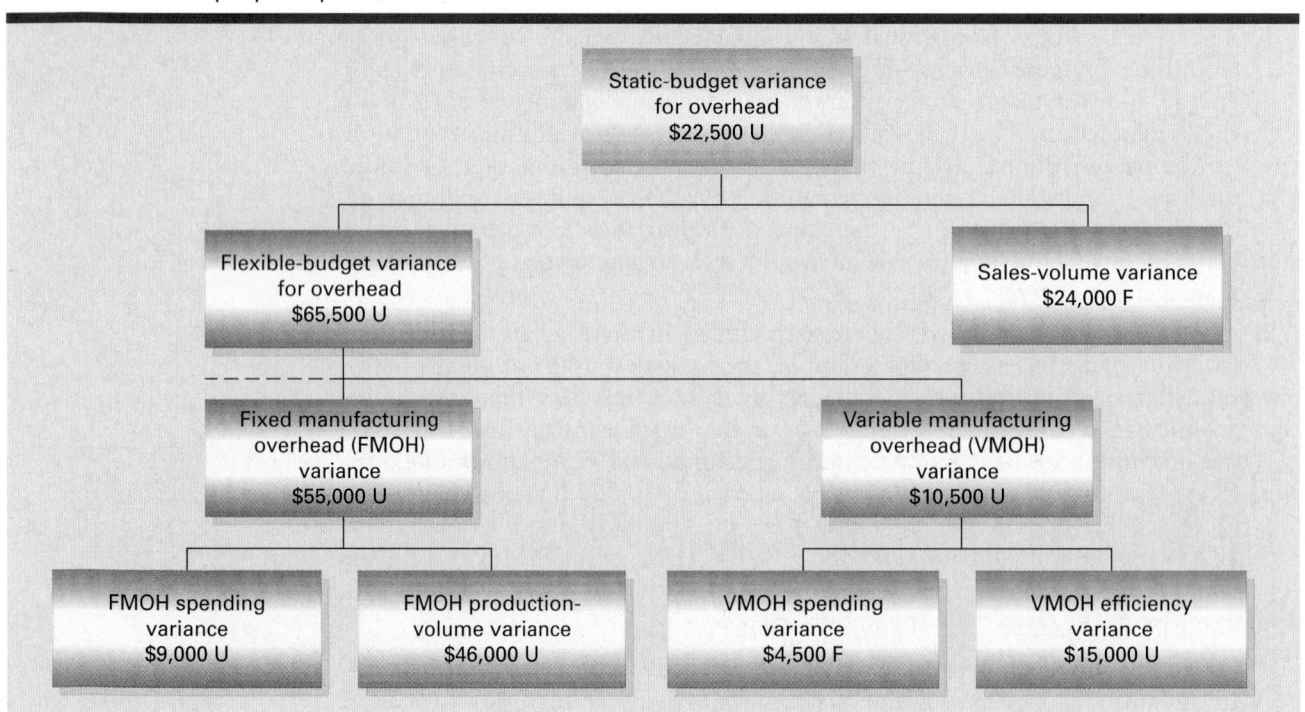

Managers must always explore why a variance has occurred before concluding that the label of unfavourable or favourable necessarily indicates, respectively, poor or good management performance. Understanding the reasons for a variance also helps managers decide on future courses of action. Should they try to reduce capacity, increase sales, or do nothing? Based on their analysis of the situation, the key cause of Webb's unfavourable flexible-budget variance is that the actual use of machine-hours is higher than budgeted. Webb's managers decided to reduce some capacity use but had to maintain excess capacity, which could perhaps be utilized for production outsourced to them by other manufacturers.

Throughout this chapter, it is assumed that companies have made a distinction between those costs that are variable and those costs that are fixed. However, some companies do not segregate their costs into these two categories, particularly within overhead costs. For these companies, the variable manufacturing overhead variances are not determined, and all overhead costs are assumed to be fixed. Any interpretation of the variance analysis for these companies will be limited due to the selection of this type of cost system.

JOURNAL ENTRIES FOR VARIABLE OVERHEAD COSTS AND VARIANCES

Variable Overhead Control and the contra account Variable Overhead Allocated are used for the journal entries for April 2009 (Exhibit 8-7):

1. Variable Overhead Control   130,500
        Utilities, wages, and other accounts payable   130,500
      Records actual variable overhead costs incurred

2. WIP Control   120,000
        Variable Overhead Allocated   120,000
      To record variable overhead costs allocated
      (0.40 MH/jacket × 10,000 jackets × $30/MH)

      The costs accumulated in WIP control are transferred
      to Finished Goods Control when production is completed
      and into Cost of Goods Sold Control when the goods
      are sold (Ch. 4)

3. Variable Overhead Allocated   120,000
      Variable Overhead Efficiency Variance   15,000
        Variable Overhead Control   130,500
        Variable Overhead Spending Variance   4,500
      Records variances for the accounting period

The variances arise because of underallocated or overallocated variable overhead costs. At the end of the fiscal year, the treatment of a variance depends on whether it is material or immaterial. If the variances are not material, then the variance accounts are written off to cost of goods sold. If the variances are material, then they are prorated among WIP Control, Finished Goods Control, and Cost of Goods Sold accounts on the basis of the variable overhead allocated to these accounts (see Chapter 4, Learning Objective 5). Only the unavoidable costs are prorated and all avoidable variances are written off in the period. Assume that the April 2009 variances are also those at the end of the fiscal year and are immaterial. The following journal entry records the write-off of the variance accounts to cost of goods sold:

     Cost of Goods Sold   10,500
     Variable Overhead Spending Variance   4,500
       Variable Overhead Efficiency Variance   15,000

ASSESS YOUR MASTERY

To check your understanding of the material in Learning Objective ❷, go to the *Mastery Questions* section at the end of this chapter and complete Learning Objective ❷ questions 1, 2, and 3.

ACTIVITY-BASED COSTING AND VARIANCE ANALYSIS

3   Calculate ABC overhead variances

ABC systems classify costs of various activities into a cost hierarchy: output-unit level, batch level, product sustaining, and facility sustaining. The basic principles and concepts for variable and fixed manufacturing overhead costs presented earlier in the chapter can be extended to ABC systems. In this section, we illustrate variance analysis for variable and fixed batch-level setup overhead costs. Batch-level costs are resources sacrificed on activities that are related to a group of units of product(s) or service(s) rather than to each individual unit of product or service.

We will use the example of Lyco Brass Works, which manufactures Jacutaps, a line of decorative brass faucets for Jacuzzis. Lyco manufactures Jacutaps in batches. To manufacture a batch of Jacutaps, Lyco must set up the machines and moulds to ensure the correct colour is injected into each batch. Setup is a skilled activity. Hence, a separate setup department is responsible for setting up machines and moulds for different types of Jacutaps. Lyco regards setup costs as overhead costs of products.

> ### THINKING CRITICALLY
>
> How might setup time impact idle capacity? Explain in a sentence or two. Read on for discussion of this topic.

Lyco wants to ensure that the cost of productive capacity, the standard hours to produce a product, is appropriately assigned to each output. Idle capacity is time lost when the machines cannot be used in production, time used when machines must rework damaged finished goods, and time scheduled for maintenance. Machines cannot be setup for batches of, say, black taps when they are used to produce batches of white taps. Setup requires that the machines be idle. Nevertheless, companies like Lyco cannot run batches of different coloured taps unless they idle the machines to set them up. The setup time is essential, but it is not a direct cost of a batch of white or black taps; it is an overhead cost. The setup cost is incurred each time a new batch of product is going to be produced and that is why in the ABC cost hierarchy it is neither a unit nor a product cost, but a batch cost.

Setup costs consist of some costs that are variable and some costs that are fixed with respect to the number of setup-hours. Variable costs of setups consist of wages paid to hourly setup labour and indirect support labour, costs of maintenance of setup equipment, and costs of indirect materials and energy used during setups. Fixed setup costs consist of salary costs of engineers, supervisors, and setup equipment leases.

Information regarding Jacutaps for 2010 follows:

	Static-Budget Amounts	Actual Amounts
1. Units of Jacutaps produced and sold	180,000	151,200
2. Batch size (units/batch)	150	140
3. Number of batches (Line 1 ÷ Line 2)	1,200	1,080
4. Setup-hours per batch	6	6.25
5. Total setup-hours (Line 3 × Line 4)	7,200	6,750
6. Variable overhead cost per setup-hour	$ 20	$ 21
7. Variable setup overhead costs (Line 5 × Line 6)	$144,000	$141,750
8. Total fixed setup overhead costs	$216,000	$220,000

FLEXIBLE-BUDGET AND VARIANCE ANALYSIS FOR VARIABLE SETUP OVERHEAD COSTS

To prepare the flexible budget for variable setup overhead costs, Lyco starts with the actual units of output produced (151,200 units), then undertakes a series of interdependent processes. Exhibit 8-9 illustrates the process of developing variable setup overhead rates.

EXHIBIT 8-9
Developing Variable Setup Overhead Rates

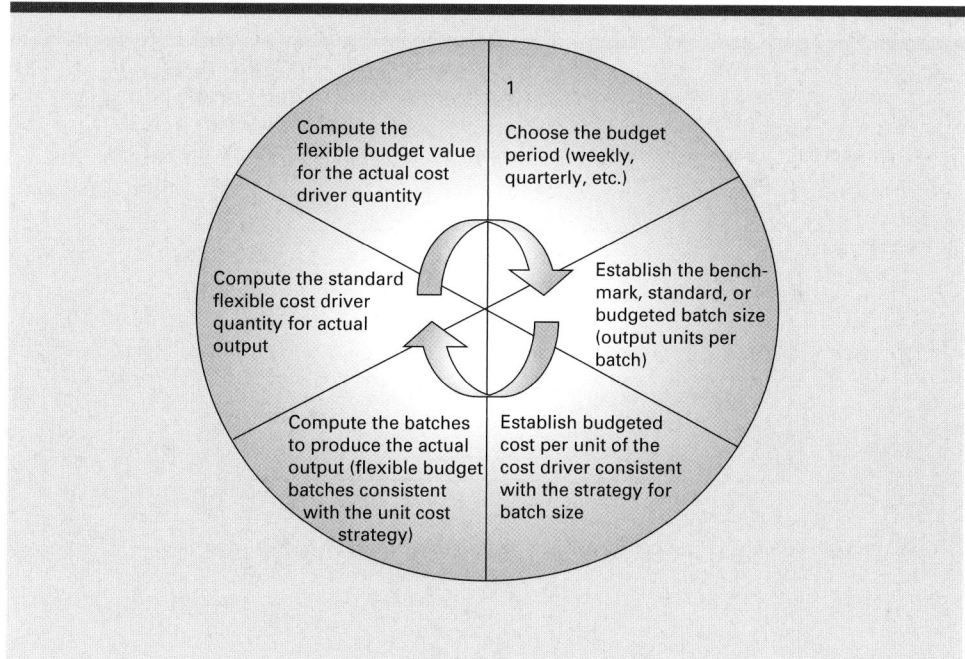

Developing ABC systems is a complex process and we have assumed the cost driver for a batch has been decided upon by the managers at Lyco. The cost driver will be the benchmark, standard, or budgeted quantity of setup-hours per batch. It is also assumed that the batch cost pool has been decided consistent with how Lyco chose its quantity of setup-hours per batch. Lyco's managers also must establish a batch size consistent with how it chose its setup-hours per batch. Based on these data, the managers can calculate the benchmark, standard, or budgeted variable overhead setup cost-driver rate per setup-hour. Lyco can also calculate how many batches are required to produce an actual quantity of output units (e.g., blue taps) during a specified time period. Lyco should have manufactured the 151,200 units of output in 1,008 batches (151,200 ÷ 150).

Based on the quantity of setups, Lyco's managers calculate the quantity of setup-hours (cost driver) that should have been consumed for the actual number of batches during a specified time period. At the budgeted quantity of 6 setup-hours per batch, 1,008 batches should have required 6,048 setup-hours (1,008 × 6). Notice that this is a flexible-budgeting approach to establishing variable overhead cost variances. What has changed is that the unit of measure is a different level in the cost hierarchy.

At this stage in the process, it is relatively straightforward to multiply the variable overhead setup cost driver rate by the budgeted (standard or benchmark) flexible quantity of setup-hours for the actual output produced. The flexible-budget amount is 6,048 setup-hours × $20 per setup-hour = $120,960.

$$\begin{aligned} \text{Flexible-budget variance for variable setup overhead costs} &= \text{Actual costs} - \text{Flexible-budget costs} \\ &= \begin{array}{c} 6{,}750 \text{ setup-hours} \\ \times\ \$21/\text{setup-hour} \end{array} - \begin{array}{c} 6{,}048 \text{ setup-hours} \\ \times\ \$20/\text{setup-hour} \end{array} \\ &= \$141{,}750 - \$120{,}960 \\ &= \$20{,}790\ \text{U} \end{aligned}$$

Exhibit 8-10 presents the variances for variable setup overhead costs in columnar form.

EXHIBIT 8-10
Columnar Presentation of Variable Setup Overhead Variance Analysis for
Lyco Brass Works for 2010

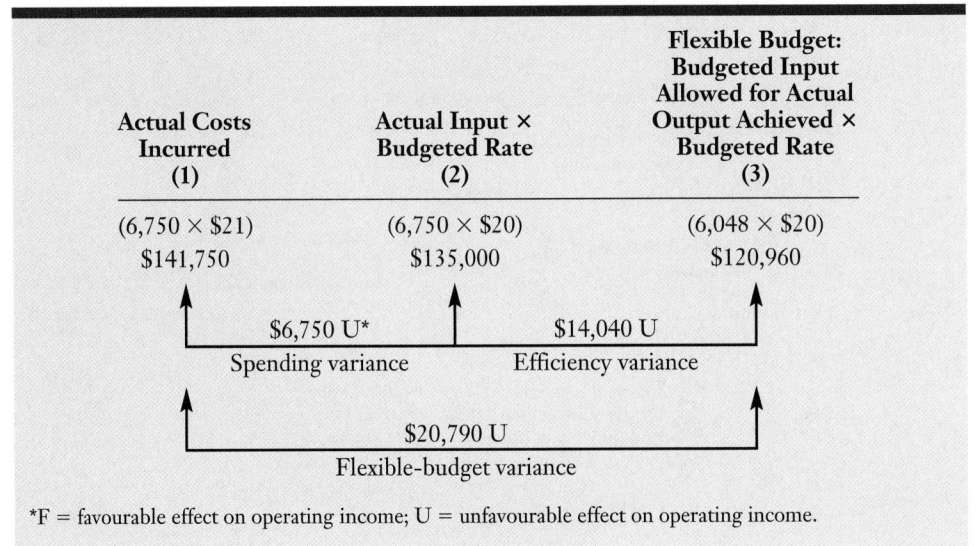

*F = favourable effect on operating income; U = unfavourable effect on operating income.

The flexible-budget variance for variable setup overhead costs can be subdivided into efficiency and spending variances.

$$\begin{matrix} \text{Variable setup} \\ \text{overhead efficiency} \\ \text{variance} \end{matrix} = \left(\begin{matrix} \text{Actual units of} \\ \text{variable overhead} \\ \text{cost-allocation base} \\ \text{used for actual output} \end{matrix} - \begin{matrix} \text{Budgeted units of} \\ \text{variable overhead cost-} \\ \text{allocation base allowed} \\ \text{for actual output} \end{matrix} \right) \times \begin{matrix} \text{Budgeted} \\ \text{variable} \\ \text{overhead rate} \end{matrix}$$

$$= (6{,}750 \text{ setup-hours} - 6{,}048 \text{ setup-hours}) \times \$20/\text{setup-hour}$$

$$= 702 \text{ setup-hours} \times \$20/\text{setup-hour}$$

$$= \$14{,}040 \text{ U}$$

The unfavourable variable setup overhead efficiency variance of $14,040 arises because the actual number of setup-hours (6,750) exceeds the number of setup-hours that Lyco should have used (6,048) for the number of units it produced.

Two reasons for the unfavourable efficiency variance are (1) smaller actual batch sizes of 140 units instead of budgeted batch sizes of 150 units, which results in Lyco producing the 151,200 units in 1,080 batches instead of 1,008 batches, and (2) higher actual setup-hours per batch of 6.25 hours instead of the budgeted setup-hours per batch of 6 hours.

Explanations for smaller-than-budgeted batch sizes could include (1) quality problems if batch sizes exceed 140 faucets or (2) high costs of carrying inventory. Explanations for longer actual setup-hours per batch could include (1) problems with equipment, (2) unmotivated or inexperienced employees, or (3) inappropriate setup-time standards.

$$\begin{matrix} \text{Variable setup} \\ \text{overhead spending} \\ \text{variance} \end{matrix} = \left(\begin{matrix} \text{Actual variable} \\ \text{overhead cost} \\ \text{per unit of cost-} \\ \text{allocation base} \end{matrix} - \begin{matrix} \text{Budgeted variable} \\ \text{overhead cost per} \\ \text{unit of cost-} \\ \text{allocation base} \end{matrix} \right) \times \begin{matrix} \text{Actual quantity of variable} \\ \text{overhead cost-allocation} \\ \text{base used for actual output} \\ \text{units achieved} \end{matrix}$$

$$= (\$21/\text{setup-hour} - \$20/\text{setup-hour}) \times 6{,}750 \text{ setup-hours}$$

$$= \$1/\text{setup-hour} \times 6{,}750 \text{ setup-hours}$$

$$= \$6{,}750 \text{ U}$$

The unfavourable spending variance indicates that Lyco operated in 2010 with higher-than-budgeted variable overhead cost per setup-hour. Two main reasons that could contribute to the unfavourable spending variance are (1) the actual prices of individual items included in variable overhead, such as setup labour, indirect support labour, or energy, are higher than the budgeted prices, and (2) the actual quantity usage of individual items such as indirect support labour and energy increases more than the increase in setup-hours, due perhaps to setups becoming more complex because of equipment problems. Thus, equipment problems could lead to an unfavourable efficiency variance because setup-hours increase, but they could also lead to an unfavourable spending variance because each setup-hour requires more resources from the setup-cost pool than the budgeted amounts.

Identifying the reasons for the variances is important because it helps managers plan for corrective action. We now consider fixed setup overhead costs.

FLEXIBLE-BUDGET AND VARIANCE ANALYSIS FOR FIXED SETUP OVERHEAD COSTS

For fixed setup overhead costs, the flexible-budget amount equals the static-budget amount of $216,000; there is no "flexing" of fixed costs over a relevant range of production.

$$\begin{array}{l} \text{Fixed setup overhead} \\ \text{flexible-budget variance} \end{array} = \begin{array}{l} \text{Actual} \\ \text{costs} \end{array} - \begin{array}{l} \text{Flexible-budget} \\ \text{costs} \end{array}$$
$$= \$220,000 - \$216,000$$
$$= \$4,000 \text{ U}$$

The fixed setup overhead spending variance is the same amount as the fixed overhead flexible-budget variance (because fixed overhead costs have no efficiency variance).

$$\begin{array}{l} \text{Fixed setup overhead} \\ \text{spending variance} \end{array} = \begin{array}{l} \text{Actual} \\ \text{costs} \end{array} - \begin{array}{l} \text{Flexible-budget} \\ \text{costs} \end{array}$$
$$= \$220,000 \text{ U} - \$216,000$$
$$= \$4,000$$

The unfavourable fixed setup overhead spending variance could be due to lease costs of new setup equipment or higher salaries paid to engineers and supervisors. Lyco may have incurred these costs to alleviate some of the difficulties it was having in setting up machines.

To calculate the production-volume variance, Lyco first computes the budgeted cost-allocation rate for fixed setup overhead costs. This process does not differ from that used for fixed overhead allocation already illustrated. With a reference time period of one fiscal year, Lyco has identified its cost allocation base for fixed overhead as setup-hours. The setup-hours (using a benchmark, standard, or budget strategy) are 7,200 for the year. The fixed overhead cost pool for setups has also been identified as $216,000. The fixed overhead cost rate is $30 per setup hour ($216,000 ÷ 7,200 setup-hours = $30/setup-hour).

$$\begin{array}{l} \text{Budgeted fixed setup} \\ \text{overhead cost rate} \end{array} = \frac{\text{Budgeted total costs in overheaf cost pool}}{\text{Budgeted total quantity of cost-allocation base}} = \frac{\$216,000}{7,200 \text{ setup-hours}}$$

Exhibit 8-11 presents the variance analysis of fixed setup overhead in columnar form.

During 2010, Lyco planned to produce 180,000 units of Jacutaps but actually produced only 151,200 units. The unfavourable production-volume variance measures the amount of extra fixed setup costs that Lyco incurred for setup capacity it planned to use but did not.

$$\begin{array}{l} \text{Production-volume} \\ \text{variance for fixed} \\ \text{setup overhead costs} \end{array} = \begin{array}{l} \text{Budgeted fixed} \\ \text{setup overhead} \\ \text{costs} \end{array} - \begin{array}{l} \text{Fixed setup overhead allocated} \\ \text{using budgeted input allowed for} \\ \text{actual output units produced} \end{array}$$
$$= \$216,000 - (1,008 \text{ batches} \times 6 \text{ hours per batch}) \times \$30/\text{setup-hour}$$
$$= \$216,000 - (6,048 \text{ setup-hours} \times \$30/\text{setup-hour})$$
$$= \$216,000 - \$181,440$$
$$= \$34,560 \text{ U}$$

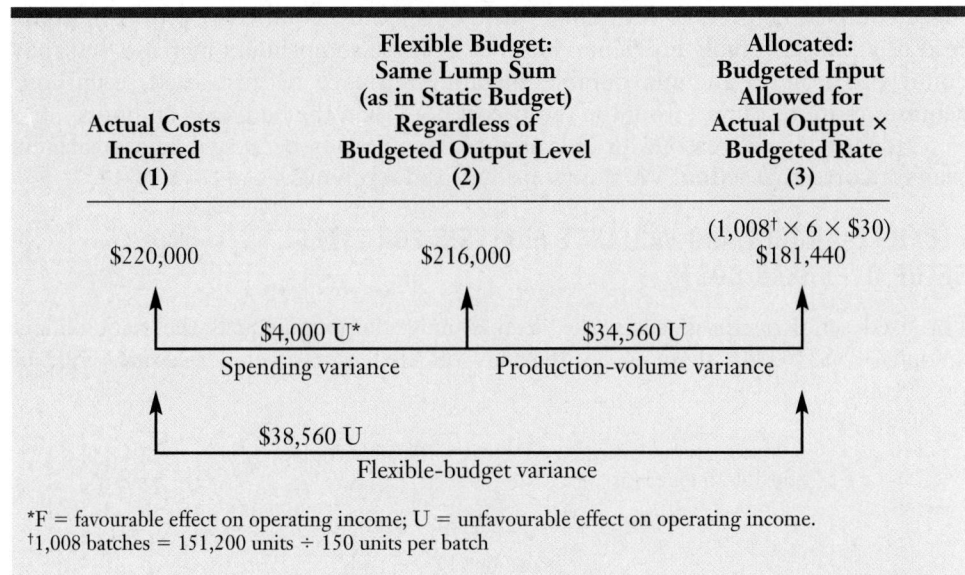

Actual Costs Incurred (1)	Flexible Budget: Same Lump Sum (as in Static Budget) Regardless of Budgeted Output Level (2)	Allocated: Budgeted Input Allowed for Actual Output × Budgeted Rate (3)
		$(1,008^\dagger \times 6 \times \$30)$
$220,000	$216,000	$181,440

$4,000 U* → Spending variance

$34,560 U → Production-volume variance

$38,560 U → Flexible-budget variance

*F = favourable effect on operating income; U = unfavourable effect on operating income.
†1,008 batches = 151,200 units ÷ 150 units per batch

One interpretation is that the unfavourable $34,560 production-volume variance represents inefficient utilization of setup capacity. However, Lyco may have earned higher operating income by selling 151,200 units at a higher price than what it would have earned by selling 180,000 units at a lower price. The production-volume variance should be interpreted cautiously because it does not consider such information.

ASSESS YOUR MASTERY

To check your understanding of the material in Learning Objective ③, go to the *Mastery Questions* section at the end of this chapter and complete Learning Objective ③ questions 1 and 2.

OVERVIEW OF OVERHEAD-COST VARIANCES

④ Integrate the fixed and variable overhead cost variance analyses to reconcile the actual overhead incurred with overhead allocated

For Webb Company, the variances that have been discussed so far are presented in Exhibit 8-12: Panel A for variable costs and Panel B for fixed costs. In total, the flexible-budget variance for overhead costs is $65,500 U, the sum of the $10,500 U variable overhead variance and the $55,000 U fixed overhead variance. Reporting overhead variances at this level of detail assists managers in large and complex businesses, such as Barrick Gold Corporation, to focus attention on where actual or realized results did not meet expectations. In smaller and less complex businesses, managers might choose not to distinguish the variable from fixed overhead because they are very familiar with the causes of cost overruns.

In tabular form, the four-variance analysis appears as:

Four-Variance Analysis

	Spending Variance	Efficiency Variance	Production-Volume Variance
Variable Manufacturing Overhead	$4,500 F	$15,000 U	(Never a variance)
Fixed Manufacturing Overhead	$9,000 U	(Never a variance)	$46,000 U

EXHIBIT 8-12
Variance Analysis: Variable and Fixed Manufacturing Overhead for Webb Company

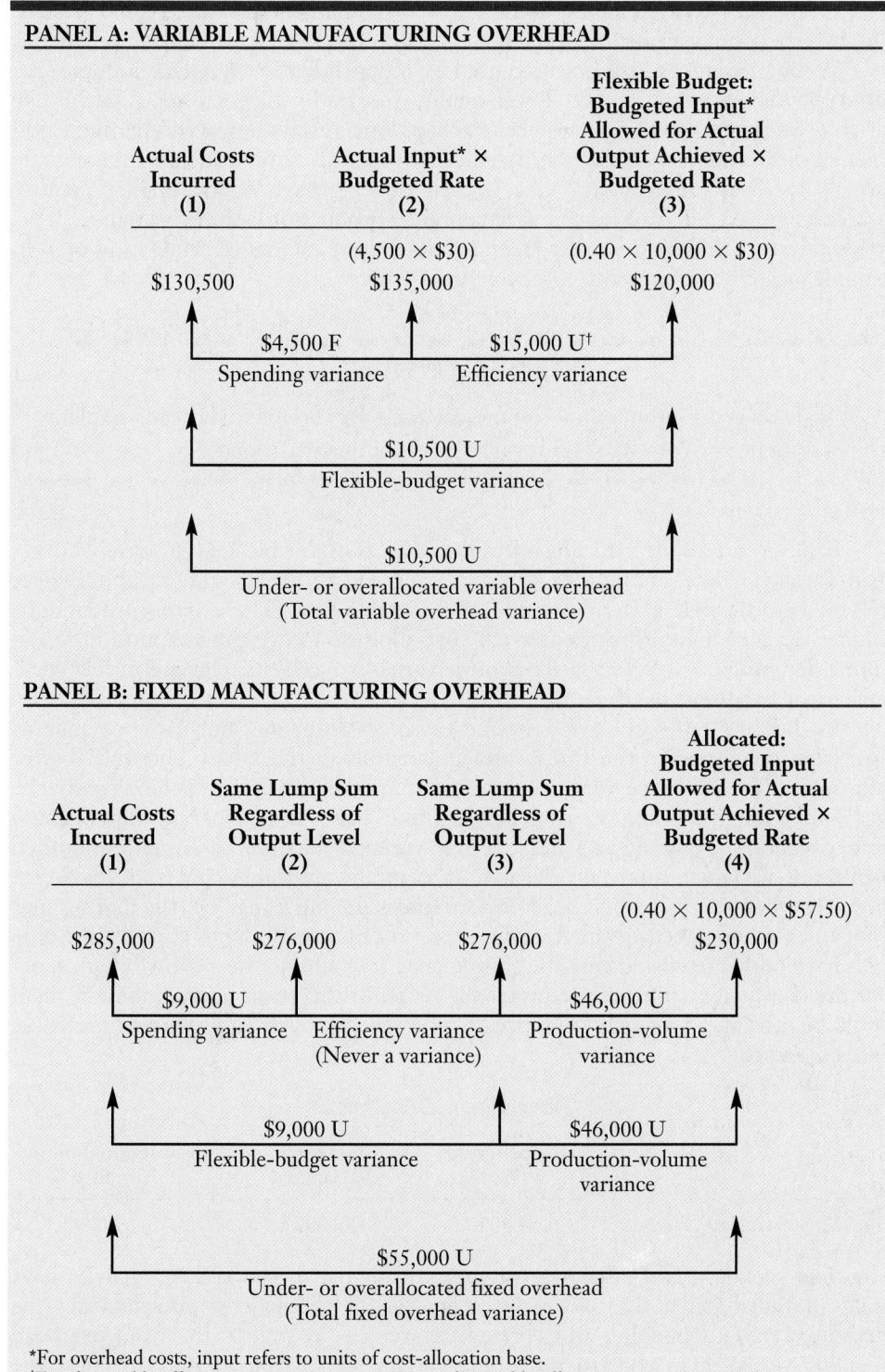

PANEL A: VARIABLE MANUFACTURING OVERHEAD

Actual Costs Incurred (1)	Actual Input* × Budgeted Rate (2)	Flexible Budget: Budgeted Input* Allowed for Actual Output Achieved × Budgeted Rate (3)
	(4,500 × $30)	(0.40 × 10,000 × $30)
$130,500	$135,000	$120,000

$4,500 F ← Spending variance

$15,000 U[†] ← Efficiency variance

$10,500 U ← Flexible-budget variance

$10,500 U ← Under- or overallocated variable overhead
(Total variable overhead variance)

PANEL B: FIXED MANUFACTURING OVERHEAD

Actual Costs Incurred (1)	Same Lump Sum Regardless of Output Level (2)	Same Lump Sum Regardless of Output Level (3)	Allocated: Budgeted Input Allowed for Actual Output Achieved × Budgeted Rate (4)
			(0.40 × 10,000 × $57.50)
$285,000	$276,000	$276,000	$230,000

$9,000 U ← Spending variance

Efficiency variance (Never a variance)

$46,000 U ← Production-volume variance

$9,000 U ← Flexible-budget variance

$46,000 U ← Production-volume variance

$55,000 U ← Under- or overallocated fixed overhead
(Total fixed overhead variance)

*For overhead costs, input refers to units of cost-allocation base.
[†]F = favourable effect on operating income; U = unfavourable effect on operating income.

The four variances in this table are the two variable manufacturing overhead variances and the two fixed manufacturing overhead variances. Note also that two areas show "Never a variance" and it is clear why there is no efficiency variance for fixed overhead cost pools. The table is a compact report of Webb's overhead variances.

The $65,500 unfavourable total manufacturing overhead variance for Webb Company in April 2009 is largely the result of the $46,000 unfavourable production-volume variance. Using the four-variance analysis presentation, the next-largest amount (after the $46,000) is the $15,000 unfavourable variable overhead efficiency variance. This variance arises from the additional 500 machine-hours used in April 2009 above the 4,000 machine-hours allowed to manufacture the 10,000 jackets. The two spending variances ($4,500 F and $9,000 U) partially offset each other.

Webb's variances may not be caused by independent events. For example, the company may have purchased lower-quality lubricants that caused a favourable variable overhead spending variance. Perhaps one result, however, was increased machine-hours per jacket, since the needles moved more slowly, and an unfavourable variable overhead efficiency variance. In turn, this may have led to a smaller quantity of jackets produced, causing an unfavourable production-volume variance. This brief analysis highlights the interdependencies among factors of production even in a simple jacket manufacturing company like Webb.

> **THINKING CRITICALLY**
>
> Why is there no production-volume variance for variable overhead? Explain in a sentence or two. Read on for discussion of this situation.

Panel A in Exhibit 8-12 illustrates the sources of flexible-budget variable overhead variance. The amount of variable overhead is always the flexible-budget amount because that is the definition of a variable cost. There is no production-volume variance arising from an actual cost-allocation base consumption different from a denominator-level capacity choice. Variable overhead costs are unrelated to capacity or fixed-cost overhead.

In the next table, the two *spending* variances from the four-variance analysis have been combined in the three-variance analysis in the table. The only loss of information in the three-variance analysis is in the overhead spending variance area—only one spending variance is reported instead of separate variable and fixed overhead spending variances. Three-variance analysis is sometimes called **combined-variance analysis**, because it combines variable-cost and fixed-cost variances when reporting overhead cost variances. While it may be true that simpler companies do not need detailed analyses, as you may recall from Chapter 2, some costs have both a fixed and variable component. It would not be worthwhile to separate the components of these semivariable or semifixed costs, and combining them would be sensible. This may well explain why the two overhead spending variances were combined.

Three-Variance Analysis

	Spending Variance	Efficiency Variance	Production-Volume Variance
Total Manufacturing Overhead	$4,500 U	$15,000 U	$46,000 U

The spending and efficiency variances from the three-variance analysis have been combined under the two-variance analysis. The first cost pool includes the variable overhead spending and efficiency variances as well as the fixed overhead spending variance. In constructing these variances, it is unnecessary to know the actual machine-hours because no efficiency variance is calculated.

Two-Variance Analysis

	Flexible-Budget Variance	Production-Volume Variance
Total Manufacturing Overhead	$19,500 U	$46,000 U

The single variance of $65,500 U in one-variance analysis is the sum of the flexible-budget variance and the production-volume variance under two-variance analysis. This simply reports the flexible budget variance between the $415,500

Interdependencies Are Everywhere

Throughout the discussion of Webb Company's potential management responses to the management accounting reports on variance, the materiality of unfavourable variance values has been the guide. There is also a question of internal interdependence, especially when there is a single cost allocation base for all variances. Machine-hours is certainly measurable and is a required resource, but in the value chain there are business functions beyond production. This cost-allocation base measure provided additional useful insight regarding interdependencies internal to production.

Strategic cost management requires an approach to managing costs that moves beyond a single business function in an organization. Competitive benchmarking instead of standards, ABC instead of traditional cost allocation, supply-chain management, and customer cost management are all strategic approaches to cost management. These approaches to costing and cost management either focus on interdependencies across the value chain of business functions, or compare performance measures of a target business to those with which it competes.

($130,500 + $285,000 = $415,500) total overhead actually realized in April and the $350,000 ($120,000 + $230,000 = $350,000) budgeted overhead allocated to produce 10,000 jackets (actual output) during that month.

One-Variance Analysis

	Total Overhead Variance
Total Manufacturing Overhead	$65,500 U

A **value-added cost** is one that, if eliminated, would reduce the value customers obtain from using the product or service. For example, Webb's customers expect the jackets to last; therefore, managers consider sewing an essential value-added activity, and the costs of supplies such as sewing needles and maintenance of the sewing machines are considered value-added overhead costs. A **non–value-added cost** is one that, if eliminated, would not reduce the value customers obtain from using the product or service.

For example, to offset problems that arise if suppliers fail to meet their delivery schedule, Webb also undertakes the activity of storing rolls of cloth in its warehouse. To the customer, a jacket sewn from cloth stored in a warehouse is no different from a jacket sewn from cloth delivered by a supplier directly to the production floor. Therefore, the activity of storing cloth is non-value-added for the customer, and managers view the costs associated with warehousing as non–value-added costs. There is a continuum between value-added costs and non–value-added costs. Many overhead cost items are in a grey, uncertain area between value-adding and non-value-adding costs.

DIFFERENT PURPOSES OF MANUFACTURING OVERHEAD COST ANALYSIS

Different types of cost analysis may be appropriate for different purposes. Webb's variable manufacturing overhead is shown in Exhibit 8-3 as being variable, with respect to output units (jackets) produced, for both the planning and control purpose (p. 370) and the inventory costing purpose. The greater the number of output units manufactured, the higher the budgeted total variable manufacturing overhead costs and the total variable manufacturing overhead costs allocated to output units.

Exhibit 8-3 also shows that, for the planning and control purpose, fixed overhead costs do not change in the 1,000-to-14,000-unit output range. Consider a monthly leasing cost of $20,000 for a building under a three-year leasing agreement. Managers control this fixed leasing cost at the time the lease is signed. During any month in the leasing period, management can do little to change this $20,000 lump sum payment. Contrast this description of fixed overhead with how these costs are depicted for the inventory costing purpose. Under generally accepted accounting principles, fixed manufacturing costs are capitalized as part of inventory on a unit-of-output basis. Every output unit that Webb manufactures will increase the fixed overhead allocated to products by $23/jacket ($57.50/MH × 0.40 MH/jacket). Managers should not use this unitization of fixed manufacturing overhead costs for their planning and control.

NONFINANCIAL AND NONMANUFACTURING PERFORMANCE MEASURES

5 Analyze nonfinancial and nonmanufacturing variance

NONFINANCIAL PERFORMANCE MEASURES

The overhead variances discussed in this chapter are examples of *financial* performance measures. Managers also find that nonfinancial measures provide useful information. Examples of such measures that Webb Company would likely find useful in planning and controlling its overhead costs are as follows:

1. Actual indirect materials usage in metres per machine-hour, compared with budgeted indirect materials usage in metres per machine-hour
2. Actual energy usage per machine-hour, compared with budgeted energy usage per machine-hour
3. Actual machining time per job, compared with budgeted machining time per job.

NONMANUFACTURING OVERHEAD COST ANALYSIS

Services ranging from passenger air transportation, to recuperative health care, to management accounting, are also provided by for-profit companies. The focus of profitable service provision is the customer's satisfaction. Management accountants have applied their techniques to estimating and managing costs according to the factors contributing most to customers' satisfaction. The value proposition for customers changes, and yet to retain customers service providers must remain agile and responsive as well as profitable. Service companies need to know how effectively they have fulfilled the value proposition and how efficiently they have done so.

Effective and efficient customer response or **agility** implies a process of service design, implementation, and delivery with flexible performance indicators. Agility means the service company has the ability to excel simultaneously in quality, delivery time, customization, and cost in a co-ordinated way.[4] Strategically, service companies must not only differentiate their product but also exercise cost leadership strategies to maintain profitability. In a competitive context where service demands change (e.g., demand for environmental sustainability and corporate social responsibility reporting), providers who cannot fulfil new value propositions will not thrive.

One possible strategic response is to develop or purchase human resources with superior competencies—a knowledge or intellectual-capital approach for core competencies. Another strategic response may be to outsource some competencies in joint venture or partnership with other providers (e.g., luxury hotel and spa management). This response is constrained by anti-trust laws preventing companies from creating monopolies. A third strategic response is to develop new competencies (e.g., a bank providing insurance services).

Service companies can segment their services by types of customers. It is important to understand the profitability of types of customers and factors such as purchasing preference (rush orders, standing contracts), delivery (face-to-face,

[4] L.J. Menor, A.V. Roth, and C.H. Mason, "Agility in Retail Banking: A Numerical Taxonomy of Strategic Service Groups," *Manufacturing and Service Operations Management*, 3.4 (Fall 2001): 273–292.

Variance Analysis and Control Decisions

There is widespread usage of the variances discussed in Chapters 7 and 8 across the globe. A survey of companies in the United Kingdom reported the following percentages:[a]

In addition, a recent survey of 270 Danish chief management accountants found that 74% consider variance analysis "important" or "very important."[b] Another survey of U.K. and New Zealand manufacturers found that after adopting modern management techniques, including just-in-time and advanced manufacturing technologies, 87% of U.K. and 84% of New Zealand respondents experienced either no change or an increased importance in the role of variance analysis in their control systems.[c]

[a] C.S. Drury, S. Braund, P. Osborne, and M. Tayles, *A Survey of Management Accounting Practices in UK Manufacturing Companies* (London: Chartered Association of Certified Accountants, 1993).

[b] J. Mouritsen, "Five Aspects of Accounting Departments' Work," *Management Accounting Research* (1996).

[c] C. Guilding, D. Lamminmaki, and C. Drury, "Budgeting and Standard Costing Practices in New Zealand and the United Kingdom," *The International Journal of Accounting* (1998).

Variance	Percentage of Companies Computing Variance	Percentage of Companies Viewing the Variance as "Above Average Importance" or "Vitally Important" in Control Decisions
Sales volume	77%	70%
Selling price	75	69
Materials price	94	69
Materials efficiency	80	66
Labour price	63	36
Labour efficiency	73	65
Overhead spending	89	69
Production volume	41	28

electronic), range of services (core, facilitating, peripheral), service provision (the vice-president, managers), and after-sale support. Overall, service companies can also examine a value chain beginning with the business acquisition and marketing, development of relationships, customer account maintenance, and customer account administration overhead. Overhead or backroom operations would include contract management, billing, collections, and general administration such as technical and legal support.

Within the service sector, the selection of standards is difficult to reconcile with the need for agility. On the one hand, standards of common resource input consumption permit ready comparability between service providers for different types of customers. On the other hand, agility requires solutions to problems that were not imagined when the standards were chosen. In addition, agility is multi-dimensional and suggests at a minimum that at least four standards are required for quality, timeliness, customization, and cost.

Starbucks lost its place as first in customer loyalty in 2007 to Dunkin' Donuts and, after analysis of the competition, decided that its strategic approach had been inappropriate. The company had removed the roasting process and automated espresso and cappuccino delivery, which reduced the time customers spent chatting with baristas. The relentless focus on controlling costs by changing internal processes did not conform to the value proposition of customers: Starbucks customers wanted the coffee "experience" rather than fast-food delivery.[5] Starbucks had improved the time and cost of service delivery but the quality of its service from the customers' point of view had deteriorated. One analytical approach is shown below:

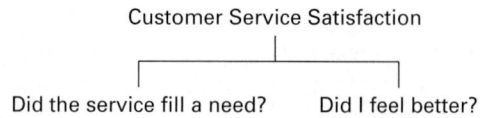

The two dimensions of satisfaction include a thoughtful or cognitive dimension and an emotional or affective dimension. For a Starbucks customer, a cognitive response to satisfaction could be that a beverage quenched thirst in the anticipated way. The affective response could be delight, happiness, or contentment from being pampered at an affordable price. The chairman of Revlon once was quoted as saying "We don't sell cosmetics. We sell hope." in an attempt to characterize the difference between the cognitive and affective dimensions of Revlon's products.

Service attributes such as timeliness appeal to cognitive satisfaction, while those such as quality and customization appeal to affective satisfaction. The smell of roasting and fresh ground coffee delighted the Starbucks customers who left to quench their thirst elsewhere when this perk was eliminated. More careful analysis of the multidimensional nature of what a cup of Starbucks meant to customers could have given managers information relevant to their decision, which changed the experience and meaning of purchasing a cup of Starbucks coffee.

NONFINANCIAL PERFORMANCE MEASURES

Nonfinancial performance measures include market share, on-time delivery performance (e.g., Purolator), customer acquisition rate, customer retention rate, and order time to completion. These measures will vary from one service industry to another. In the hospitality industry, a hotel would track nonfinancial measures of: satisfaction with hotel location; room availability and reservations; check-in; room security, quietness, cleanliness, and amenities; restaurant and bar services; spa services; entertainment; and concierge services.[6] While the core services of a hotel are lodging and food, other ancillary services contribute to the customer's positive experience and satisfaction.

A service company such as an airline would likely analyze nonfinancial measures of satisfaction with the personal space per seat, seat comfort, food, and baggage handling, as well as flight availability, on-time take-off and arrival, and convenient connections with other flights. Few costs can be traced to these outputs in a cost-effective way. The majority of costs are fixed overhead costs (for example, costs of equipment, buildings, and staff). Using capacity effectively is the key to profitability, and fixed overhead variances can help managers in this task. For airlines, the nonfinancial capacity measure is available seat miles (ASM) while the financial measures are revenue per ASM and costs per ASM.

Consider the following data for United Airlines for the years 2000, 2003, and 2006. Available Seat Miles (ASM) are the actual seats in a plane multiplied by the distance travelled.

Year	Total ASMs (Millions) (1)	Revenue per ASM (2)	Cost per ASM (3)	Operating Income per ASM (4) = (2) − (3)
2000	175,485	$0.1103	$0.1066	0.0037
2003	136,630	$0.1006	$0.1104	(0.0098)
2006	143,095	$0.1352	$0.1320	0.0032

[5]K.A. Gjerde and S.B. Hughes, "Tracking Performance: When Less is More," *Management Accounting Quarterly*, 9.1 (2007): 1–12.

[6]A. Cuigini, A. Carù, and F. Zerbini, "The Cost of Customer Satisfaction: A Framework for Strategic Cost Management in Service Industries," *European Accounting Review*, 16.3 (2007): 499–530.

After September 11, 2001, as air travel declined, United's revenues decreased but a majority of its costs comprising fixed costs of airport facilities, equipment, and personnel did not. United had a large unfavourable production-volume variance as its capacity remained unutilized. As column 1 of the preceding table indicates, United responded by reducing its capacity from 175,485 million ASMs to 136,630 million in 2003 but, unable to fill even the planes it was left with, revenue per ASM declined (column 2) and cost per ASM increased (column 3) in 2003. United filed for Chapter 11 bankruptcy protection and began seeking government guarantees to obtain the loans it needed to bring it out of bankruptcy.

More recently, strong demand for airline travel and yield improvement from more efficient use of United's resources and networks have meant increased volume. Airlines generally have increased their prices per ticket and therefore the total revenue has increased, providing improved operating income. With a disciplined approach to capacity and tight control over growth, United saw a 34.4% increase in its revenue per ASM between 2003 and 2006. While the increase in aviation fuel accounted for a large part of the 19.6% increase in cost per ASM, United improved enough to emerge from bankruptcy protection on February 1, 2006.

In other service-sector companies such as banking, measures of output are more difficult to identify. Banks provide a variety of services to their customers, such as chequing accounts, loans, credit cards, and retirement or other investment accounts. Most costs of these activities are overhead costs. Technology has made it easier to trace overhead costs to activities. For example, when employees record the time they spend on each activity in an activity database, a computer-generated report of total labour-hours and costs per activity can be provided to managers. Standard costing techniques can then be applied to manage the overhead costs of activities.

Variance analysis of fixed nonmanufacturing overhead costs is also important for companies that work on a full-actual-cost-plus basis—that is, where it is reimbursed for its full actual costs plus an additional percentage of those costs. Here, information on these variances enables more accurate estimates of actual costs to be computed. In many other cases, however, managers do not conduct detailed variance analysis of fixed nonmanufacturing costs. Most believe little information is gained by computing spending or efficiency variances for these fixed nonmanufacturing costs.

ASSESS YOUR MASTERY

To check your understanding of the material in Learning Objective ⑤, go to the *Mastery Questions* section at the end of this chapter and complete Learning Objective ⑤ question 1.

MyAccountingLab

PULLING IT ALL TOGETHER—PROBLEM FOR SELF-STUDY

PROBLEM

Dawn Smith is the newly appointed president of Laser Products. She is examining the May 2010 results for the Aerospace Products division. This division manufactures wing parts for satellites. Smith's current concern is with manufacturing overhead costs at the Aerospace Products division. Both variable and fixed manufacturing overhead costs are allocated to the wing parts based on laser-cutting-hours. The budgeted cost rates are variable manufacturing overhead of $200 per hour and fixed manufacturing overhead of $240 per hour. The budgeted laser-cutting time per wing part is 1.50 hours. Budgeted production and sales for 2010 are 5,000 wing parts. Budgeted fixed manufacturing overhead costs for May 2010 are $1,800,000.

Wing parts produced and sold	4,800 units
Laser-cutting-hours used	8,400 units
Variable manufacturing overhead costs	$1,478,400
Fixed manufacturing overhead costs	$1,832,200

REQUIRED

1. Compute the spending variance and the production-volume variance for fixed manufacturing overhead.
2. Compute the spending variance and the efficiency variance for variable manufacturing overhead.
3. Give explanations for the variances in requirements 1 and 2 to illustrate how fixed and variable overhead cost variances provide integrated relevant information.
4. What nonfinancial variables could Laser Products use as performance measures?
5. What customer-satisfaction measures would be important to Laser Products?

SOLUTION

1. and **2.** See Exhibit 8-13.

3. a. Variable manufacturing overhead spending variance ($201,600 F). One possible reason is that the actual prices of individual items included in variable overhead (such as utilities cost) are lower than the budgeted prices. A second possible reason is that the percentage increase in the actual quantity usage of individual items in the variable overhead cost pool is less than the percentage increase in machine-hours compared to the flexible budget.

  b. Variable manufacturing overhead efficiency variance ($240,000 U). One possible reason is inadequate maintenance of laser machines, causing them to take more laser time per wing part. A second possible reason is use of less-trained workers with the laser-cutting machines, resulting in longer laser time per wing part.

  c. Fixed manufacturing overhead spending variance ($32,200 U). One possible reason is that the actual prices of individual items in the fixed-cost pool unexpectedly increased from those budgeted (such as an unexpected increase in the manager's salary). Overhead also includes maintenance supplies and labour, inspection labour, taxes, and insurance costs. It could be that an unanticipated increase in taxes or inspection time caused the spending variance for the month.

  d. Production-volume variance ($72,000 U). Actual production of wing parts is 4,800 units compared with the 5,000 units budgeted. One possible reason is demand factors, such as a decline in the aerospace program that led to a decline in the demand for satellite wings. What is known with certainty is that the use of the laser time exceeded what would have been budgeted for 4,800 wing parts. An actual inefficiency may have caused this increased consumption of laser hours or the company could have chosen an inappropriate denominator level. The increased use of laser hours could have several causes from ill-trained operators who took more time and caused waste, to an improperly functioning machine. It may also have been a smart decision by the company not to produce 5,000 wing parts if quality control was an issue or if demand has fallen.

4. Laser Products is already measuring nonfinancial variables when it measures the actual quantity consumed of the cost-allocation base. Other nonfinancial variables that could be important would depend upon the competitive environment. If, for example, the environment is becoming increasingly competitive, Laser Products may want to plan ways of becoming more agile. For a manufacturing company, this could involve cross-training equipment operators, and some measure of hours of training would be needed. As those purchasing Laser Products parts become more demanding and request more customization, the

PANEL A: VARIABLE MANUFACTURING OVERHEAD

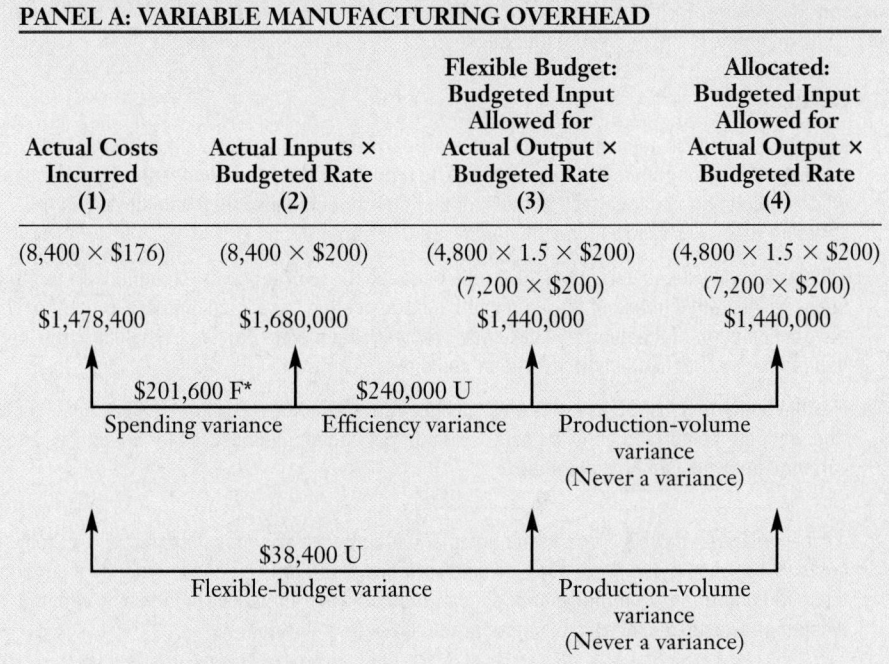

PANEL B: FIXED MANUFACTURING OVERHEAD

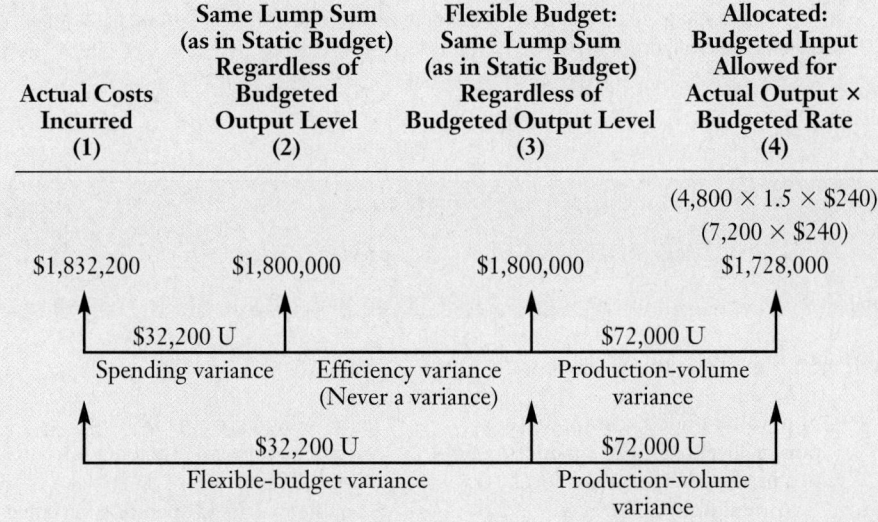

*F = favourable effect on operating income; U = unfavourable effect on operating income.

company may choose to analyze the types of customers it may be able to serve according to the attributes of the products they demand such as physical size, fragility, complexity, and so on.

5. Customers for wing parts are unlikely to have an affective response to receiving these products. They are focused on how useful the product is, how well it meets engineering specifications, and if it is delivered on time within the costs stated in the contract. These are cognitive measures of customer satisfaction appropriate to this manufacturing setting.

The following decision guidelines use a question-and-answer format to summarize the chapter's main points. Each decision presents a key question. The guideline is the answer to that question.

DECISIONS	GUIDELINES
1. How do managers budget pro forma fixed overhead cost rates and analyze fixed overhead variances?	Managers establish some standard fixed overhead cost rate based on either internal or external engineering or competitor information. The terms *standard* and *budget* are interchangeable when calculating variance. The actual calculation is not complex but the value-added of variance reports is ascertaining the cause(s) of the variance.
2. How do managers budget pro forma variable overhead cost rates and analyze variable overhead variances?	The variable overhead variances may arise because the indirect costs exceeded pro forma or because the consumption of the input in the cost-allocation base exceeded pro forma. Analyzing the consumption of the overhead variance cost-allocation base provides insight into the interdependencies that cause both overhead and direct variances.
3. Can the flexible-budget variance approach for analyzing overhead costs be used in activity-based costing?	Flexible budgeting in ABC systems gives insight into why actual overhead activity costs differ from budgeted overhead activity costs. Using output and input measures for an activity, a four-variance analysis can be conducted.
4. How does increasing detail of variance analyses help reconcile actual with budgeted overhead costs?	A four-variance analysis presents spending and efficiency variances for variable overhead costs and spending and production-volume variances for fixed overhead costs. By analyzing these four variances together, managers can reconcile the actual overhead costs with the amount of overhead allocated to output produced during a period.
5. Of what use are nonfinancial and nonmanufacturing performance measures?	Increasingly, companies must simultaneously manage costs, quality, customization, and timely delivery. The separation of cost leadership from product or service differentiation strategies will not accomplish this goal. Nonfinancial measures of customer satisfaction and comparisons to some standard or benchmark are relevant to important management decisions that will affect revenue.

TERMS TO LEARN

This chapter contains definitions of the following important terms:

agility (p. 390)
capacity (p. 365)
capacity cost (p. 365)
combined-variance analysis (p. 388)
denominator-level variance (p. 369)
fixed overhead spending variance (p. 368)

non–value-added cost (p. 389)
output-level overhead variance (p. 369)
production denominator level (or volume) (p. 367)
production-volume variance (p. 369)
specific production-volume variance (p. 367)

value-added cost (p. 389)
variable overhead efficiency variance (p. 377)
variable overhead spending variance (p. 378)

MASTERY QUESTIONS

The Mastery Questions are rated by proficiency level—elementary, intermediate, and advanced. The solutions appear in the Mastery Question Solutions section of MyAccountingLab.

LEARNING OBJECTIVE 1
1. **Fixed overhead variance—Elementary.** French Bread Company has two direct-cost categories: direct materials and direct manufacturing labour. Fixed manufacturing overhead is allocated to products on the basis of standard direct manufacturing labour hours (DMLH).

Baguettes are baked in batches of 100 loaves. Following are some pertinent data for French Bread Company:

Direct manufacturing labour use	2.00 DMLH per batch
Fixed manufacturing overhead	$4.00 per DMLH

French Bread Company recorded the following additional data for the year ended December 31, 2010:

Planned (budgeted) output	3,840,000 baguettes
Actual production	3,360,000 baguettes
Direct manufacturing labour	50,400 DMLH
Actual fixed MOH	$326,400

REQUIRED
1. Prepare a variance analysis of fixed manufacturing overhead costs.
2. Is fixed overhead underallocated or overallocated? By how much?
3. Comment on your results. Discuss the various variances and explain what may be driving them.

2. Fixed overhead variance—Intermediate. Consider each of the following situations—cases A, B, and C—independently. Data refer to operations for April 2009. For each situation, assume standard costing. Also assume the use of a flexible budget for control of variable and fixed manufacturing overhead based on machine-hours.

	Cases		
	A	**B**	**C**
1. Fixed manufacturing overhead incurred	$26,500	—	$30,000
2. Variable manufacturing overhead incurred	$15,000	—	—
3. Denominator level in machine-hours	1,250	—	2,750
4. Standard machine-hours allowed for actual output achieved	—	1,625	—
5. Fixed manufacturing overhead (per standard machine-hour)	—	—	—
Flexible-budget data:			
6. Variable manufacturing overhead (per standard machine-hour)	—	$ 8.50	$ 5.00
7. Budgeted fixed manufacturing overhead	$25,000	—	$27,500
8. Budgeted variable manufacturing overhead[a]	—	—	—
9. Total budgeted manufacturing overhead[a]	—	$ 31,313	—
Additional data:			
10. Standard variable manufacturing overhead allocated	$18,750	—	—
11. Standard fixed manufacturing overhead allocated	$25,000	—	—
12. Production-volume variance	—	$ 1,250 U	$ 1,250 F
13. Variable manufacturing overhead spending variance	$ 4,875 F	$ 0	$ 875 U
14. Variable manufacturing overhead efficiency variance	—	$ 0	$ 250 U
15. Fixed manufacturing overhead spending variance	—	$ 750 F	—
16. Actual machine-hours used	—	—	—

[a]For standard machine-hours allowed for actual output produced.

REQUIRED
Fill in the blanks under each case. [Hint: Prepare a worksheet similar to that in Exhibit 8-12 (p. 387). Fill in the knowns and then solve for the unknowns.]

3. Fixed overhead variance—Advanced. Carvelli Company is a manufacturer of housewares. In its job-costing system, manufacturing overhead (both variable and fixed) is allocated to products based on budgeted machine-hours. The budgeted amounts are taken from Carvelli's standard-costing system. The budget for 2010 included:

Variable manufacturing overhead	$10.80 per machine-hour
Fixed manufacturing overhead	$86,400,000
Denominator level	4,000,000

1. Prepare four graphs, two for variable manufacturing overhead and two for fixed manufacturing overhead. Each pair of graphs should display how total manufacturing overhead costs of Carvelli will be depicted for the purpose of (a) planning and control and (b) inventory costing.
2. Suppose that 3,500,000 machine-hours were allowed for actual output achieved in 2010, but 3,800,000 machine-hours were used. Actual manufacturing overhead was variable, $43,320,000; fixed, $86,640,000. Compute (a) variable manufacturing overhead spending and efficiency variances and (b) the fixed manufacturing overhead spending and production-volume variances. Use the columnar presentation illustrated in Exhibit 8-7 (p. 379).
3. What is the amount of the underallocated or overallocated variable manufacturing overhead? Of the underallocated or overallocated fixed manufacturing overhead? Why are the flexible-budget variance and the underallocated or overallocated overhead amount always the same for variable manufacturing overhead but rarely the same for fixed manufacturing overhead?
4. Suppose the denominator level was 3,000,000 rather than 4,000,000 machine-hours. What variances in requirement 2 would be affected? Recompute them.

LEARNING OBJECTIVE 2

1. **Variable overhead variance—Elementary.** French Bread Company bakes baguettes for distribution to upscale grocery stores. The company has two direct-cost categories: direct materials and direct manufacturing labour. Variable manufacturing overhead is allocated to products based on standard direct manufacturing labour-hours (DMLH). Baguettes are baked in batches of 100 loaves. Following are some pertinent data for French Bread Company:

Direct manufacturing labour use	2.00 DMLH per batch
Variable manufacturing overhead	$12.00 per DMLH

French Bread Company recorded the following additional data for the year ended December 31, 2010:

Planned (budgeted) output	3,200,000 baguettes
Actual production	2,800,000 baguettes
Direct manufacturing labour	50,400 DMLH
Actual fixed MOH	$816,480

REQUIRED

1. What is the denominator used for allocating manufacturing overhead (i.e., how many DMLH is French Bread budgeting for)?
2. Prepare a complete analysis of variable manufacturing overhead (Levels 1 through 3). Use the exhibits in this chapter for reference.
3. Discuss the variances you have calculated. Provide possible explanations for these variances.

2. **Variable overhead variance—Intermediate.** Sarah Beth's Art Supply Company produces various types of paints. Actual direct manufacturing labour hours (DMLH) in the factory that produces paint have been higher than budgeted hours for the last few months and the owner, Sarah B. Jones, is concerned about the effect this has had on the company's cost overruns. Because variable manufacturing overhead is allocated to units produced using DMLH, Sarah feels that the mismanagement of labour will have a twofold effect on company profitability. Following are the relevant budgeted and actual results for the second quarter of 2010.

	Budget Information	Actual Results
Paint set production	10,000	13,000
Direct manufacturing labour-hours (DMLH) per paint set	0.5 DMLH	0.75 DMLH
Direct manufacturing labour rate	$20.00/DMLH	$20.20/DMLH
Variable manufacturing overhead rate	$ 10/DMLH	$ 9.75/DMLH

REQUIRED

1. Calculate the direct manufacturing labour price and efficiency variances and indicate whether each is favourable (F) or unfavourable (U).
2. Calculate the variable manufacturing overhead spending and efficiency variances and indicate whether each is favourable (F) or unfavourable (U).
3. For both direct manufacturing labour and variable manufacturing overhead, do the price/spending variances help Sarah explain the efficiency variances?
4. Is Sarah correct in her assertion that the mismanagement of labour has a twofold effect on cost overruns? Why might the variable manufacturing overhead efficiency variance not be an accurate representation of the effect of labour overruns on variable manufacturing overhead costs?

3. **Overhead variances, governance—Advanced.** Zuller Company uses standard costing. The company prepared its static budget for 2009 at 2,500,000 machine-hours for the year. Total budgeted overhead cost is $31,250,000. The variable overhead rate is $10 per machine-hour ($20 per unit). Actual results for 2009 follow:

Machine-hours	2,400,000 hours
Output	1,245,000 units
Variable overhead	$25,200,000
Fixed overhead spending variance	$ 1,500,000 U

REQUIRED

1. Compute for the fixed overhead:
   a. Budgeted amount
   b. Budgeted cost per machine-hour
   c. Actual cost
   d. Production-volume variance
2. Compute the variable overhead spending variance and the variable overhead efficiency variance.
3. Jack Remich, the controller, prepares the variance analysis. It is common knowledge in the company that he and Ronald Monroe, the production manager, are not on the best of terms. In a recent executive committee meeting, Monroe had complained about the lack of usefulness of the accounting reports he receives. To get back at him, Remich manipulated the actual fixed overhead amount by assigning a greater-than-normal share of allocated costs to the production area. And, he decided to amortize all of the newly acquired production equipment using the double-declining-balance method rather than the straight-line method, contrary to company practice. As a result, there was a sizable unfavourable fixed overhead spending variance. He boasted to one of his confidants, "I am just returning the favour." Discuss Remich's actions and their ramifications.

LEARNING OBJECTIVE 3

1. **ABC overhead variances—Intermediate.** Asma Surgical Instruments Inc. makes a special line of forceps, SFA, in batches. Asma randomly selects forceps from each SFA batch for quality-testing purposes. Quality-testing costs are batch-level costs. A separate quality-testing section is responsible for SFA quality testing.

Quality-testing costs consist of some variable and some fixed costs in relation to the quality-testing hours. The following information is for 2010:

	Static-Budget Amounts	Actual Amounts
Units of SFA produced and sold	21,000	22,000
Batch size (number of units per batch)	500	550
Testing-hours per batch	5.5	5.4
Variable overhead cost per testing-hour	$ 48.00	$ 50.40
Total fixed testing overhead costs	$32,650.00	$32,659.00

REQUIRED

1. For variable testing overhead costs, compute the efficiency and spending variances. Comment on the results.
2. For fixed testing overhead costs, compute the spending and the production-volume variances. Comment on the results.

2. **ABC overhead variances—Advanced.** CellOne is a cellular phone service reseller, contracting with major cellular operators for airtime in bulk and then reselling service to retail customers. Having adopted an ABC system last year, CellOne has defined the following activity areas—contracting, marketing, technical service, and customer service.

   The technical service area has one major cost driver—technical support hours. One hour of technical support is budgeted for every 5,000 minutes of airtime sold. For the month ended August 31, 2010, CellOne budgeted to sell 6,850,000 minutes; however, actual minutes sold totalled 7,350,000. During August 2010, 1,500 actual technical support hours were logged. Some additional data follow:

	Actual	Budget
Variable technical service activity cost	$37,800	$39,456
Fixed technical service activity costs	$81,000	$83,844

Budgeted input allowed for actual output achieved totalled 1,470 hours of technical support.

REQUIRED
1. What is the actual variable technical service activity area cost per technical support hour? Budgeted cost per hour?
2. What is the allocated fixed technical service area overhead?
3. Calculate the spending variance, the efficiency variance, and the flexible-budget variance for variable overhead costs. Explain these variances based on the data provided.
4. Has CellOne management underallocated or overallocated fixed overhead for August 2010? Show how you calculate the underallocation or overallocation.

LEARNING OBJECTIVE 4

1. **Integrate and reconcile all overhead variances—Intermediate.** FlatScreen manufactures flat-panel LCD displays. The displays are sold to major PC manufacturers. Following are some manufacturing overhead data for FlatScreen for the year ended December 31, 2010:

	Actual	Flexible Budget	Allocated Amount
Variable manufacturing overhead	$1,838,592	$1,843,200	$1,843,200
Fixed manufacturing overhead	$8,404,992	$8,354,304	$9,031,680

FlatScreen's budget was based on the assumption that 17,760 units (panels) will be manufactured during 2010. The planned allocation rate was two machine-hours per unit. FlatScreen uses machine-hours as the cost driver. Actual number of machine-hours used during 2010 was 36,480. The budgeted variable manufacturing overhead costs equal $1,704,960.

REQUIRED
Compute the following quantities (you should be able to do so in the prescribed order):
1. Budgeted number of machine-hours planned
2. Budgeted fixed manufacturing overhead costs per machine-hour
3. Budgeted variable manufacturing overhead costs per machine-hour
4. Budgeted number of machine-hours allowed for actual output achieved
5. Actual number of output units
6. Actual number of machine-hours used per panel
7. Allocated amount for fixed manufacturing overhead

2. **Integrate and reconcile all overhead variances—Advanced.** (Continuation of Mastery Question 1, above).

REQUIRED
1. Prepare appropriate journal entries for variable and fixed manufacturing overhead (you will need to calculate the different variances to accomplish this).
2. Overhead variances may be used to reconcile the Cost of Goods Sold account at the end of the fiscal year. Cost of goods sold (COGS) is then entered on the income statement. Show how COGS is reconciled through journal entries.

LEARNING OBJECTIVE 5

1. Nonfinancial and nonmanufacturing variances—Advanced. Daisy Canine Products produces high-quality dog food distributed only through veterinary offices. To ensure that the food is of the highest quality and has taste appeal, Daisy has a rigorous inspection process. For quality-control purposes, Daisy has a standard based on the number of kilograms inspected per hour and the number of kilograms that pass or fail the inspection.

Daisy expects that for every 10,000 kilograms of food produced, 1,000 kilograms of food will be inspected. Inspection of 1,000 kilograms of dog food should take 1 hour. Daisy also expects that 2% of the food inspected will fail the inspection. During the month of May, Daisy produced 2,250,000 kilograms of food and inspected 200,000 kilograms of food in 210 hours. Of the 200,000 kilograms of food inspected, 3,500 kilograms of food failed to pass the inspection.

REQUIRED

1. Compute two variances that help determine whether the time spent on inspections was more or less than expected. (Follow a format similar to the one used for the variable overhead spending and efficiency variances, but without prices.)
2. Compute two variances that can be used to evaluate the percentage of the food that fails the inspection.

ASSIGNMENT MATERIAL

Make the grade with MyAccountingLab: The questions, exercises, and problems marked in red can be found on MyAccountingLab at **www.myaccountinglab.com**. You can practise them as often as you want, and most feature step-by-step guided instructions to help you find the right answer. Exercises and problems with an Excel icon in the margin have an accompanying Excel template on MyAccountingLab.

SHORT-ANSWER QUESTIONS

8-1 Describe the difference in planning the pro forma fixed and variable overhead cost rates.

8-2 How do budgeting, standard, and benchmark costing differ?

8-3 Why is there never a sales-volume variance arising from fixed overhead spending variances?

8-4 How does a variable overhead variance also result in a sales-volume variance?

8-5 The spending variance for variable manufacturing overhead is affected by several factors. Explain.

8-6 Assume variable manufacturing overhead is allocated using machine-hours. Give three possible reasons for a $30,000 favourable variable overhead efficiency variance.

8-7 Describe the difference between a direct materials efficiency variance and a variable manufacturing overhead efficiency variance.

8-8 What are the issues with proration and writeoff methods?

8-9 Why is the flexible-budget variance the same amount as the spending variance for fixed manufacturing overhead?

8-10 Explain how the analysis of fixed overhead costs differs for (a) planning and control on the one hand and (b) inventory costing for financial reporting on the other.

8-11 Describe one caveat that will affect whether a production-volume variance is a good measure of the economic cost of unused capacity.

8-12 Of what use are nonfinancial performance measures and variances?

8-13 Explain how four-variance analysis differs from one-, two-, and three-variance analysis.

8-14 Explain how variance analysis provides relevant information for nonmanufacturing firms.

8-15 How can the Levels 1 to 3 variance-analysis approach be used in control of costs in activity areas?

8-16 Variable manufacturing overhead, variance analysis. Esquire Clothing is a manufacturer of designer suits. The cost of each suit is the sum of three variable costs (direct materials costs, direct manufacturing labour costs, and manufacturing overhead costs) and one fixed-cost category (manufacturing overhead costs). Variable manufacturing overhead cost is allocated to each suit based on budgeted direct manufacturing labour-hours (DMLH) per suit. For June 2010, each suit is budgeted to take 4 labour-hours. Budgeted variable manufacturing overhead costs per labour-hour are $12.00. The budgeted number of suits to be manufactured in June 2010 is 1,040.

Actual variable manufacturing overhead costs in June 2010 were $52,164 for 1,080 suits started and completed. There was no beginning or ending inventory of suits. Actual direct manufacturing labour-hours for June were 4,536 DMLH.

REQUIRED

1. Compute the flexible-budget variance, the spending variance, and the efficiency variance for variable manufacturing overhead.
2. Comment on the results.

8-17 Fixed manufacturing overhead variance analysis (continuation of 8-16). Esquire Clothing allocates fixed manufacturing overhead to each suit using budgeted direct manufacturing labour-hours (DMLH) per suit. Data pertaining to fixed manufacturing overhead costs for June 2010 are $62,400 budgeted and $63,916 actual.

REQUIRED

1. Compute the spending variance for fixed manufacturing overhead. Comment on these results.
2. Compute the production-volume variance for June 2010. What inferences can Esquire Clothing draw from this variance?

8-18 Manufacturing overhead, variance analysis. Solutions Corporation is a manufacturer of centrifuges. Fixed and variable manufacturing overheads are allocated to each centrifuge using budgeted assembly-hours. Budgeted assembly time is two hours per unit. The following table shows the budgeted amounts and actual results related to overhead for June 2009.

Solutions Corporation (June 2009)	Actual Results	Static Budget
Number of centrifuges assembled and sold	216	200
Hours of assembly time	411	
Variable manufacturing overhead cost per hour of assembly time		$ 30.00
Variable manufacturing overhead costs	$12,420	
Fixed manufacturing overhead costs	$20,560	$19,200

REQUIRED

1. Prepare an analysis of all variable manufacturing overhead and fixed manufacturing overhead variances using the columnar approach in Exhibit 8-12, p. 387.
2. Prepare journal entries for Solutions' June 2009 variable and fixed manufacturing overhead costs and variances; write off these variances to cost of goods sold for the quarter ended June 30, 2009.
3. How does the planning and control of variable manufacturing overhead costs differ from the planning and control of fixed manufacturing overhead costs?

8-19 Overhead variances, service sector. Meals on Wheels (MOW) operates a meal home-delivery service. It has agreements with 20 restaurants to pick up and deliver meals to customers who phone or fax orders to MOW. MOW allocates variable and fixed overhead costs on the basis of delivery time. MOW's owner, Josh Carter, obtains the following information for May 2009 overhead costs:

Meals on Wheels (May 2009)	Actual Results	Static Budget
Output units (number of deliveries)	8,800	10,000
Hours per delivery		0.70
Hours of delivery time	5,720	
Variable overhead cost per hour of delivery time		$ 1.50
Variable overhead costs	$10,296	
Fixed overhead costs	$38,600	$35,000

1. Compute spending and efficiency variances for MOW's variable overhead in May 2009.
2. Compute the spending variance and production-volume variance for MOW's fixed overhead in May 2009?
3. Comment on MOW's overhead variances and suggest how Josh Carter might manage MOW's variable overhead differently from its fixed overhead costs.

8-20 Spending and efficiency overhead variances, service sector. TimeSavers (TS) operates a personal home meal delivery service. It has agreements with 20 restaurants to pick up and deliver meals to customers who phone or fax in orders. TS is currently examining its overhead costs for May 2010. Customers are charged $12 per delivery. The delivery driver is paid $7 per delivery. TS receives a 10% commission on the meal costs that the restaurants charge the customers who use TS.

1. Variable MOH spending variance, $3,580 U

Variable overhead costs for May 2010 were budgeted at $2 per hour of home delivery time. Fixed overhead costs were budgeted at $28,800. The budgeted number of home deliveries in May 2010 was 9,600. Delivery time, the allocation base for variable and fixed overhead costs, is budgeted to be 0.80 hour per delivery.

Actual results for May 2010 were as follows:

Variable overhead	$17,008
Fixed overhead	$33,120
Number of home deliveries	8,952
Hours of delivery time	6,714

REQUIRED
1. Compute spending and efficiency variances for TS's variable and fixed overhead in May 2010. Comment on the results.
2. How might TS manage its variable overhead costs differently from the way it manages its fixed overhead costs?

8-21 4-variance analysis, fill in the blanks. Pandom Inc. produces chemicals for large biotech companies. It has the following data for manufacturing overhead costs during August 2010:

1. (a) Variable MOH spending variance, $4,200 U

	Variable	Fixed
Actual costs incurred	$35,700	$18,000
Costs allocated to products	27,000	14,400
Flexible budget: Budgeted input allowed for actual output produced × budgeted rate	27,000	15,000
Actual input × budgeted rate	31,500	15,000

REQUIRED
Fill in the variances in the table below. Use F for favourable and U for unfavourable.

	Variable	Fixed
1. Spending variance	$____	$____
2. Efficiency variance	$____	$____
3. Production-volume variance	$____	$____
4. Flexible-budget variance	$____	$____
5. Underallocated (overallocated) manufacturing overhead	$____	$____

8-22 Spending and efficiency overhead variances, distribution. Speciality Delivery Service (SDS) operates a parcel delivery service. In 2010 it charged retail companies and mail-order catalogue companies $18 per delivery. Delivery drivers in 2010 were contracted at $6.00 per delivery. Variable delivery overhead for September 2010 was budgeted at $2.40 per hour of delivery time. Budgeted fixed delivery overhead in September 2010 was $144,000. SDS budgeted 100,000 deliveries for September 2010. Delivery time, the allocation base for variable and fixed overhead costs, is budgeted to be 0.25 hours per delivery. SDS's costing system has one direct-cost category (delivery driver payments) and two overhead categories—variable delivery overhead and fixed delivery overhead.

1. Variable MOH spending variance, $2,880 U

Actual results for September 2010 were as follows:

Variable delivery overhead	$ 72,000
Fixed delivery overhead	$154,080
Number of deliveries	96,000
Hours of delivery time	28,800

REQUIRED

1. Compute the spending and efficiency variances for SDS's variable delivery overhead costs in September 2010. Compute the spending and production-volume variances for SDS's fixed delivery overhead costs in September 2010. Comment on the results.
2. What problems might SDS face in managing (a) its direct costs, (b) its variable delivery overhead costs, and (c) its fixed delivery overhead costs?

1. Variable MOH spending variance, $17,800 U

8-23 **Straightforward four-variance overhead analysis.** Lopez Company uses a standard-cost system in its manufacturing plant for auto parts. The standard cost of a particular auto part, based on a denominator level of 4,000 output units per year, included 6 machine-hours of variable manufacturing overhead at $8 per hour and 6 machine-hours of fixed manufacturing overhead at $15 per hour. Actual output achieved was 4,400 units. Variable manufacturing overhead incurred was $245,000. Fixed manufacturing overhead incurred was $373,000. Actual incurred machine-hours were 28,400.

REQUIRED

1. Prepare an analysis of all variable manufacturing overhead and fixed manufacturing overhead variances, using the four-variance analysis in Exhibit 8-12, p. 387.
2. Prepare journal entries using the four-variance analysis.
3. Describe how individual variable manufacturing overhead items are controlled from day to day. Also, describe how individual fixed manufacturing overhead items are controlled.

1. Variable MOH spending variance, $43,704 F

8-24 **Straightforward coverage of manufacturing overhead, standard cost system.** The Singapore division of a Canadian telecommunications company uses a standard cost system for its machine-based production of telephone equipment. Data regarding production during June are as follows:

Variable manufacturing overhead costs incurred	$186,120
Variable manufacturing overhead costs allocated (per standard machine-hour allowed for actual output achieved)	$ 14.40
Fixed manufacturing overhead costs incurred	$481,200
Fixed manufacturing overhead budgeted	$468,000
Denominator level in machine-hours	15,600
Standard machine-hours allowed per unit of output	0.30
Units of output	49,200
Actual machine-hours used	15,960
Ending work-in-process inventory	0

REQUIRED

1. Prepare an analysis of all manufacturing overhead variances. Use the four-variance analysis framework illustrated in Exhibit 8-12, p. 387.
2. Prepare journal entries for manufacturing overhead without explanations.
3. Describe how individual variable manufacturing overhead items are controlled from day to day. Also, describe how individual fixed manufacturing overhead items are controlled.

1. Direct manufacturing labour efficiency variance, $1,920 U

8-25 **Total overhead, 3-variance analysis.** Furniture Inc. specializes in the production of futons. It uses standard costing and flexible budgets to account for the production of a new line of futons. For 2010, budgeted variable overhead at a level of 3,200 standard monthly direct labour-hours was $25,600; budgeted total overhead at 4,000 standard monthly direct labour-hours was $79,040. The standard cost allocated to each output included a total overhead rate of 120% of standard direct labour costs. For October, Furniture Inc. incurred total overhead of $99,600 and direct labour costs of $80,976. The direct labour price variance was $3,856 unfavourable. The direct labour flexible-budget variance was $5,776 unfavourable. The standard labour price was $16 per hour. The production-volume variance was $5,600, favourable.

REQUIRED

1. Compute the direct labour efficiency variance, and the spending and efficiency variances for overhead. Also, compute the denominator level.
2. Describe how individual variable overhead items are controlled from day to day. Also, describe how individual fixed overhead items are controlled.

8-26 **Overhead variances, missing information.** Dvent budgets 18,000 machine-hours for the production of computer chips in August 2009. The budgeted variable overhead rate is $6 per machine-hour. At the end of August, there is a $375 favourable spending variance for variable overhead and a $1,575 unfavourable spending variance for fixed overhead. For the computer chips produced, 14,850 machine-hours are budgeted and 15,000 machine-hours are actually used. Total actual overhead costs are $120,000.

REQUIRED

1. Compute efficiency and flexible-budget variances for Dvent's variable overhead in August 2009. Will variable overhead be overallocated or underallocated? By how much?
2. Compute production-volume and flexible-budget variances for Dvent's fixed overhead in August 2009. Will fixed overhead be overallocated or underallocated? By how much?

8-27 **Identifying favourable and unfavourable variances.** Purdue Inc. manufactures tires for large auto companies. It uses standard costing and allocates variable and fixed manufacturing overhead based on machine-hours.

REQUIRED

For each independent scenario given, indicate whether each of the manufacturing variances will be favourable or unfavourable or, in case of insufficient information, indicate "cannot be determined."

Scenario	Variable Overhead Spending Variance	Variable Overhead Efficiency Variance	Fixed Overhead Spending Variance	Fixed Overhead Production-Volume Variance
Production output is 5% more than budgeted, and actual fixed manufacturing overhead costs are 6% more than budgeted				
Production output is 10% more than budgeted; actual machine-hours are 5% less than budgeted				
Production output is 8% less than budgeted				
Actual machine-hours are 15% greater than flexible-budget machine-hours				
Relative to the flexible budget, actual machine-hours are 10% greater, and actual variable manufacturing overhead costs are 15% greater				

8-28 **Four-variance analysis, working backwards.** Lookmeup.com is striving to become a Web portal. The site allows surfers to find anything they want to look up—be it a person, a site, a company, or news article—through one interactive and easy-to-use interface. Most of Lookmeup.com's operating overhead is due to Internet connection costs. Lookmeup.com faces both fixed and variable Internet connection charges. Following is the four-variance analysis of Lookmeup.com's operations overhead:

	Spending Variance	Efficiency Variance	Production-Volume Variance
Variable Operating Overhead	$44,400 F	$28,800 F	Never a variance
Fixed Operating Overhead	$16,800 U	Never a variance	$20,400 U

REQUIRED

1. For total operating overhead, compute the following:
   a. Spending variance
   b. Efficiency variance
   c. Production-volume variance

d. Flexible-budget variance

e. Total overhead variance

Present your results in a suitable format for presenting three-variance, two-variance, and one-variance analyses.

2. If Lookmeup.com's total actual operating overhead was $420,000, what was the operating overhead allocated to actual output units provided?

3. Can you say whether fixed operating overhead was underallocated or overallocated? If so, by what amount?

4. Are Lookmeup.com's different variances in the four-variance analysis above necessarily independent? Explain and provide an example.

1. a. Direct materials price variance, $100,000 U

8-29 Flexible-budget variances, review of Chapters 7 and 8. David James is a cost accountant and business analyst for Doorknob Design Company (DDC), which manufactures expensive brass doorknobs. DDC uses two direct cost categories: direct materials and direct manufacturing labour. James feels that manufacturing overhead is most closely related to material usage. Therefore, DDC allocates manufacturing overhead to production based upon kilograms of materials used.

At the beginning of 2009, DDC budgeted production of 100,000 doorknobs and adopted the following standards for each doorknob:

	Input	Cost/Doorknob
Direct materials (brass)	0.5 kg @ $20/kg	$10.00
Direct manufacturing labour	0.25 hours @ $30/hour	7.50
Manufacturing overhead:		
Variable	$10/kg × 0.5 kg	5.00
Fixed	$ 5/kg × 0.5 kg	2.50
Standard cost per doorknob		$25.00

Actual results for April 2009 were:

Production	95,000 doorknobs
Direct materials purchased	50,000 kg at $22/kg
Direct materials used	45,000 kg
Direct manufacturing labour	20,000 hours for $650,000
Variable manufacturing overhead	$400,000
Fixed manufacturing overhead	$350,000

REQUIRED

1. For the month of April, compute the following variances, indicating whether each is favourable (F) or unfavourable (U).

a. Direct materials price variance (based on purchases)

b. Direct materials efficiency variance

c. Direct manufacturing labour price variance

d. Direct manufacturing labour efficiency variance

e. Variable manufacturing overhead spending variance

f. Variable manufacturing overhead efficiency variance

g. Production-volume variance

h. Fixed manufacturing overhead spending variance

2. Can James use any of the variances to help explain any of the other variances? Give examples.

1. Direct materials sales-volume variance, $14,400 U

8-30 Comprehensive review of Chapters 7 and 8, flexible budget. *The Monthly Herald* budgets to produce 300,000 copies of its monthly newspaper for August 2010. It is budgeted to run 15,000,000 print pages in August with 50 print pages per newspaper. Actual production in August 2010 was 320,000 copies with 17,280,000 print pages run. Each paper was only 50 print pages, but quality problems with paper led to many pages being unusable.

Variable costs comprise direct materials, direct labour, and variable indirect costs. Variable and fixed indirect costs are allocated to each copy on the basis of print pages. The driver for all variable costs is the number of print pages. Data pertaining to August 2010 are as follows:

	Budgeted	Actual
Direct materials	$216,000	$269,568
Direct labour costs	54,000	60,134
Variable indirect costs	72,000	76,723
Fixed indirect costs	108,000	116,400

Data pertaining to revenues *for The Monthly Herald* in August 2010 are:

	Budgeted	Actual
Circulation revenue	$168,000	$184,800
Advertising revenue	432,000	473,520

The Monthly Herald sells for $0.60 per copy in 2010. No change from this budgeted price of $0.60 per copy occurred in August 2010. The actual direct labour rate in August 2010 was $34.80 per hour. Actual and budgeted pages produced per direct labour-hour in August 2010 was 10,000 print pages. Copies produced but not sold have no value. Advertising revenue covers payments from all advertising sources.

REQUIRED

1. Prepare a comprehensive set of variances for each of the four categories of cost of *The Monthly Herald.*
2. Comment on the results in requirement 1. What extra insights are available with a flexible-budget analysis over that of a static-budget analysis?

PROBLEMS

8-31 **Comprehensive variance analysis.** Kitchen Whiz manufactures premium food processors. The following is some manufacturing overhead data for Kitchen Whiz for the year ended December 31, 2010.

④

1. 1,776 machine-hours

Manufacturing Overhead	Actual Results	Flexible Budget	Amount Allocated
Variable	$ 76,608	$ 76,800	$ 76,800
Fixed	350,208	348,096	376,320

Budgeted number of output units: 888

Planned allocation rate: 2 machine-hours per unit

Actual number of machine-hours used: 1,824

Static-budget variable manufacturing overhead costs: $71,040

REQUIRED

Compute the following quantities (you should be able to do so in the prescribed order):

1. Budgeted number of machine-hours planned
2. Budgeted fixed manufacturing overhead costs per machine-hour
3. Budgeted variable manufacturing overhead costs per machine-hour
4. Budgeted number of machine-hours allowed for actual output achieved
5. Actual number of output units
6. Actual number of machine-hours used per output unit

8-32 **Journal entries (continuation of 8-31).**

① ② ④

Refer to Problem 8–31.

REQUIRED

1. Prepare journal entries for variable and fixed manufacturing overhead (you will need to calculate the various variances to accomplish this).
2. Overhead variances are written off to the Cost of Good Sold (COGS) account at the end of the fiscal year. Show how COGS is adjusted through journal entries.

8-33 **Graphs and overhead variances.** Fresh Inc. is a manufacturer of vacuums and uses standard costing. Manufacturing overhead (both variable and fixed) is allocated to products on the basis of budgeted machine-hours. In 2009, budgeted fixed manufacturing overhead cost was $18,000,000. Budgeted variable manufacturing overhead was $9 per machine-hour. The denominator level was 1,000,000 machine-hours.

① ② ④

2. Variable MOH spending variance, $475,000 U

REQUIRED

1. Prepare a graph for fixed manufacturing overhead. The graph should display how Fresh Inc.'s fixed manufacturing overhead costs will be depicted for the purposes of (a) planning and control and (b) inventory costing.
2. Suppose that 875,000 machine-hours were allowed for actual output produced in 2009, but 950,000 actual machine-hours were used. Actual manufacturing overhead

was $9,025,000, variable, and $18,050,000, fixed. Compute (a) the variable manufacturing overhead spending and efficiency variances and (b) the fixed manufacturing overhead spending and production-volume variances. Use the columnar presentation illustrated in Exhibit 8-12, p. 387.

3. What is the amount of the underallocated or overallocated variable manufacturing overhead and the underallocated or overallocated fixed manufacturing overhead? Why are the flexible-budget variance and the underallocated or overallocated overhead amount always the same for variable manufacturing overhead but rarely the same for fixed manufacturing overhead?

4. Suppose the denominator level was 750,000 rather than 1,000,000 machine-hours. What variances in requirement 2 would be affected? Recompute them.

1 2

1. Variable MOH spending variance, $280 U

8-34 Causes of indirect variances. Heather's Horse Spa (HHS) is an establishment that boards, trains, and pampers horses while their owners are on vacation. Heather sells her service as an "enchanting vacation experience for your horse while you vacation elsewhere." Horse feed, shampoos, ribbons, and other supplies are treated as variable indirect costs. Consequently, there are no direct materials involved in the vacation service. Other overhead costs including indirect labour, amortization on the barn, and advertising are fixed. Both variable and fixed overhead are allocated to each horse guest-week using the weight of the horse in pounds (lbs.) as the basis of allocation.

HHS budgeted amounts for August 2009 were:

Horse guest-weeks	40
Average weight per horse	900 lbs
Variable overhead cost per pound of horse	$0.20/lb
Fixed overhead rate	$1.50/lb

Actual results for August 2009 were:

Horse guest-weeks	38
Average weight per horse	950 lbs
Actual variable overhead	$7,500
Actual fixed overhead	$50,000

REQUIRED

1. Calculate the variable overhead spending and efficiency variances and indicate whether each is favourable (F) or unfavourable (U).
2. Calculate the fixed overhead spending and production-volume variances and indicate whether each is favourable (F) or unfavourable (U).
3. Explain what the variable overhead spending variance means. What factors could have caused it?
4. What factors could have caused the variable overhead efficiency variance?
5. If fixed overhead is, in fact, fixed, how could a fixed overhead spending variance occur?
6. What caused the fixed overhead production-volume variance? What does it mean? What are the negative implications, if any, of the production-volume variance?

3

1. Static budget number of crates, 20,000

8-35 Activity-based costing, batch-level variance analysis. Rica's Fleet Feet Inc. produces dance shoes for stores all over the world. While the pairs of shoes are boxed individually, they are crated and shipped in batches. The shipping department records both variable and fixed overhead costs. The following information pertains to shipping costs for 2009.

	Static-Budget Amounts	Actual Results
Pairs of shoes shipped	240,000	180,000
Average number of pairs of shoes per crate	12	10
Packing hours per crate	1.2 hours	1.1 hours
Variable overhead cost per hour	$20	$21
Fixed overhead cost	$60,000	$55,000

REQUIRED

1. What is the static budget number of crates for 2009?
2. What is the flexible budget number of crates for 2009?
3. What is the actual number of crates shipped in 2009?
4. Assuming fixed overhead is allocated using crate-packing hours, what is the predetermined fixed overhead allocation rate?

5. For variable overhead costs, compute the spending and efficiency variances.
6. For fixed overhead costs, compute the spending and the production-volume variances.

8-36 Flexible budgets, four-variance analysis. (CMA, adapted) Fireside Enterprises, which uses a standard-costing system, allocates manufacturing overhead (both variable and fixed) based on standard direct manufacturing labour-hours (DMLH). Fireside calculates its manufacturing overhead rate from the current annual budget. The manufacturing overhead budget for 2010 is based on budgeted output of 720,000 units requiring 3,600,000 direct manufacturing labour-hours. The company is able to schedule production uniformly throughout the year.

A total of 66,000 output units requiring 315,000 direct labour-hours were produced during May 2010. Manufacturing overhead (MOH) costs incurred for May amounted to $433,000. The actual costs as compared with the annual budget and 1/12 of the annual budget are shown below.

Annual Manufacturing Overhead Budget 2010

	Annual Budget	Per Output Unit	Per DMLH Input Unit	Monthly MOH Budget May 2010	Actual MOH Costs for May 2010
Variable MOH:					
Indirect manufacturing labour	$1,080,000	$1.50	$0.300	$ 90,000	$ 90,000
Supplies	1,476,000	2.05	0.410	123,000	133,000
Fixed MOH:					
Supervision	777,600	1.08	0.216	64,800	61,200
Utilities	648,000	0.90	0.180	54,000	64,800
Amortization	1,209,600	1.68	0.336	100,800	84,000
Total	$5,191,200	$7.21	$1.442	$432,600	$433,000

REQUIRED

Calculate the following amounts for Fireside Enterprises for May 2010:

1. Fixed manufacturing overhead costs allocated and flexible budget for variable manufacturing overhead
2. Variable manufacturing overhead spending variance
3. Fixed manufacturing overhead spending variance
4. Variable manufacturing overhead efficiency variance
5. Production-volume variance

Be sure to identify each variance as favourable (F) or unfavourable (U).

8-37 Overhead analysis. The following information for 2010 is for Morgan Corporation, which uses standard costing:

2. Variable MOH spending variance, $720,000 U

Static-budget machine-hours	33,000
Fixed overhead budget costs	$ 5,940,000
Fixed overhead actual costs	$ 5,400,000
Variable overhead actual costs	$11,520,000
Variable overhead rate per machine-hour	$ 360
Actual machine-hours used	30,000
Budgeted machine-hours allowed for actual output	35,000

REQUIRED

1. Calculate variable overhead spending variance and efficiency variance.
2. Compute fixed overhead spending variance and production-volume variance.

8-38 Activity-based costing, batch-level variance analysis. Jo Nathan Publishing Company specializes in printing specialty textbooks for a small but profitable college market. Due to the high setup costs for each batch printed, Jo Nathan holds the book requests until demand for a book is approximately 500. At that point Jo Nathan will schedule the setup and production of the book. For rush orders, Jo Nathan will produce smaller batches for an additional charge of $700 per setup.

1. Static budget number of setups, 400

Budgeted and actual costs for the printing process for 2009 were:

	Static-Budget Amounts	Actual Results
Number of books produced	200,000	216,000
Average number of books per setup	500	480
Hours to set up printers	6 hours	6.5 hours
Variable overhead cost per setup-hour	$100	$90
Total fixed setup overhead costs	$72,000	$79,000

REQUIRED

1. What is the static budget number of setups for 2009?
2. What is the flexible budget number of setups for 2009?
3. What is the actual number of setups in 2009?
4. Assuming fixed setup overhead costs are allocated using setup-hours, what is the predetermined fixed setup overhead allocation rate?
5. Does Jo Nathan's charge of $700 cover the budgeted variable overhead cost of an order? The budgeted total overhead cost?
6. For variable setup overhead costs, compute the spending and efficiency variances.
7. For fixed setup overhead costs, compute the spending and the production-volume variances.
8. What qualitative factors should Jo Nathan consider before accepting or rejecting a special order?

④

1. Fixed overhead spending variance, 200 U

8-39 **Production-volume variance analysis and sales-volume variance.** Dawn Floral Creations Inc. makes jewellery in the shape of flowers. Each piece is hand-made and takes an average of 1.5 hours to produce because of the intricate design and scrollwork. Dawn uses direct labour hours to allocate the overhead cost to production. Fixed overhead costs, including rent, amortization, supervisory salaries, and other production expenses, are budgeted at $9,000 per month. These costs are incurred for a facility large enough to produce 1,000 pieces of jewellery a month.

During the month of February, Dawn produced 600 pieces of jewellery and actual fixed costs were $9,200.

REQUIRED

1. Calculate the fixed overhead spending variance and indicate whether it is favourable (F) or unfavourable (U).
2. If Dawn uses direct labour hours available at capacity to calculate the budgeted fixed overhead rate, what is the production-volume variance? Indicate whether it is favourable (F) or unfavourable (U).
3. An unfavourable production-volume variance is a measure of the underallocation of fixed overhead cost caused by production levels at less than capacity. It therefore could be interpreted as the economic cost of unused capacity. Why would Dawn be willing to incur this cost? Your answer should separately consider the following two unrelated factors:

   a. Demand could vary from month to month while available capacity remains constant.
   b. Dawn would not want to produce at capacity unless it could sell all the units produced. What does Dawn need to do to raise demand and what effect would this have on profit?
4. Dawn's budgeted variable cost per unit is $25 and it expects to sell the jewellery for $55 apiece. Compute the sales-volume variance and reconcile it with the production-volume variance calculated in requirement 2. What does each concept measure?

④

1. a. Total direct materials purchased, 160,000 kg

8-40 **Comprehensive review of Chapters 7 and 8, working backward from given variances.** Mancusco Company uses a flexible budget and standard costs to aid planning and control of its machining manufacturing operations. Its costing system for manufacturing has two direct-cost categories (direct materials and direct manufacturing labour—both variable) and two overhead-cost categories (variable manufacturing overhead and fixed manufacturing overhead, both allocated using direct manufacturing labour-hours (DMLH)).

At the 40,000 budgeted DMLH level for August, budgeted direct manufacturing labour is $800,000, budgeted variable manufacturing overhead is $480,000, and budgeted fixed manufacturing overhead is $640,000.

The following actual results are for August:

Direct materials price variance (based on purchases)	$176,000 F
Direct materials efficiency variance	69,000 U
Direct manufacturing labour costs incurred	522,750
Variable manufacturing overhead flexible-budget variance	10,350 U

Variable manufacturing overhead efficiency variance		18,000 U
Fixed manufacturing overhead incurred		597,460
Fixed manufacturing overhead spending variance		42,540 F

The standard cost per kilogram of direct materials is $11.50. The standard allowance is three kilograms of direct materials for each unit of product. During August, 30,000 units of product were produced. There was no beginning inventory of direct materials. There was no beginning or ending work in process. In August, the direct materials price variance was $1.10 per kilogram.

In July, labour unrest caused a major slowdown in the pace of production, resulting in an unfavourable direct manufacturing labour efficiency variance of $45,000. There was no direct manufacturing labour price variance. Labour unrest persisted into August. Some workers quit. Their replacements had to be hired at higher wage rates, which had to be extended to all workers. The actual average wage rate in August exceeded the standard average wage rate by $0.50 per hour.

REQUIRED

1. Compute the following for August:
   a. Total kilograms of direct materials purchased
   b. Total number of kilograms of excess direct materials used
   c. Variable manufacturing overhead spending variance
   d. Total number of actual DMLH used
   e. Total number of standard DMLH allowed for the units produced
   f. Production-volume variance
2. Describe how Mancusco's control of variable manufacturing overhead items differs from its control of fixed manufacturing overhead items.

8-41 Review of Chapters 7 and 8, three-variance analysis. (CPA, adapted) Beal Manufacturing Company's costing system has two direct-cost categories: direct materials and direct manufacturing labour. Manufacturing overhead (both variable and fixed) is allocated to products on the basis of standard direct manufacturing labour hours (DMLH). At the beginning of 2010, Beal adopted the following standards for its manufacturing costs:

2. Direct materials price variance, $5,000 U

	Input	Cost per Output Unit
Direct materials	3 kg at $5 per kg	$ 15
Direct manufacturing labour	5 hours at $15 per hour	75
Manufacturing overhead:		
Variable	$6 per DMLH	30
Fixed	$8 per DMLH	40
Standard manufacturing cost per output unit		$160

The denominator level for total manufacturing overhead per month in 2010 is 40,000 DMLH. Beal's flexible budget for January 2010 was based on this denominator level. The records for January indicate the following:

Direct materials purchased	25,000 kg at $5.20/kg
Direct materials used	23,100 kg
Direct manufacturing labour	40,100 hours at $14.60/hour
Total actual manufacturing overhead (variable and fixed)	$600,000
Actual production	7,800 output units

REQUIRED

1. Prepare a schedule of total standard manufacturing costs for the 7,800 output units in January 2010.
2. For January 2010, compute the following variances, indicating whether each is favourable (F) or unfavourable (U):
   a. Direct materials price variance, based on purchases
   b. Direct materials efficiency variance
   c. Direct manufacturing labour price variance
   d. Direct manufacturing labour efficiency variance
   e. Total manufacturing overhead spending variance
   f. Variable manufacturing overhead efficiency variance
   g. Production-volume variance

8-42 Nonfinancial performance measures. Rollie Manufacturing makes, among other things, wheels for roller skates. Manufacturing Department B receives plastic wheel casings from Manufacturing Department A and puts them on axles along with some ball bearings. The wheel casings have been inspected in Department A and should be free from major defects.

Most of the work in Department B is done by machine, but before the wheels are sent to the Packaging Department they are inspected for defects. Poorly made wheels are disassembled by hand and sent back to the beginning of the Department B line for rework. Thus any wheel that was made incorrectly and fixed takes more than twice as long to finish as a wheel that was made correctly the first time. Any wheels still not useable after rework are thrown away.

The same amount of ball bearings is requisitioned from the materials storeroom daily. Any leftover ball bearings at the end of the day are discarded. Ball bearings are measured by weight.

The machines in Department B are serviced only at night after the manufacturing run is over to save on intentional downtime. There are three machines in Department B, so if one does go down during processing there are still two workable machines until the next day. Rollie's goal in Department B is to produce 400 usable wheels per day.

REQUIRED
1. Under what circumstance would you consider ball bearings indirect rather than direct materials? Would you consider them direct materials or overhead in this problem?
2. What nonfinancial measures can Rollie use in Department B to control overhead costs?
3. Suggest some ways Rollie can better plan for and reduce overhead costs, given your answer to requirement 2.

COLLABORATIVE LEARNING CASES

8-43 Overhead variances, four-variance analysis. A large metropolitan health-care complex, General Hospital, has had difficulty controlling its accounts receivable. Costs currently available from the information system are inaccurate and have led to gross errors in reports to the various government funding agencies which has indicated that the hospital appears to be operating at a deficit. The hospital administration is concerned that the poor quality of information could lead to their replacement.

With the participation of the billing department, a set of standard costs and standard amounts was developed for 2010. These standard costs can be used in a flexible budget with separate variable-cost and fixed-cost categories. The output unit is defined to be a single bill.

The accountant of General Hospital provides you with the following for April 2010:

Variable overhead costs, allowance per standard hour	$ 12
Fixed overhead flexible budget variance	$ 240 F
Total budgeted overhead costs for the bills prepared	$ 27,000
Production-volume variance	$ 1,080 F
Variable cost spending variance	$ 2,400 U
Variable cost efficiency variance	$ 2,400 F
Standard hours allowed for the bills prepared	1,800 labour-hours

REQUIRED
Compute the following:
1. Actual hours of input used
2. Fixed overhead budget
3. Fixed overhead allocated
4. Budgeted fixed overhead rate per hour
5. Denominator level in hours

8-44 Standard setting, benchmarking, governance (continuation of 8-43). Ira Stone, the president of General Hospital, has a meeting with the Medical Economics Group (MEG). MEG is a consulting firm in the health services sector. It reports that General's billing operations are grossly inefficient. Its standard costing per bill is above 90% of the 130 hospitals MEG tracks in its benchmarking database.

Stone suspects the billing group deliberately "padded" its standard costs and standard amounts. Despite large investment in new information systems, the standards for 2010 were not below actual results for 2009. Stone does not want to institute a witch hunt, but he does want to eliminate the fat in General's cost structure.

REQUIRED
1. How might General's billing operations group have "padded" its standard costs and standard amounts? Why might they do this padding?
2. What steps should Stone take to "reduce the fat" in the overhead costs of the billing operations at General Hospital?

Income Effects of Denominator Level on Inventory Valuation

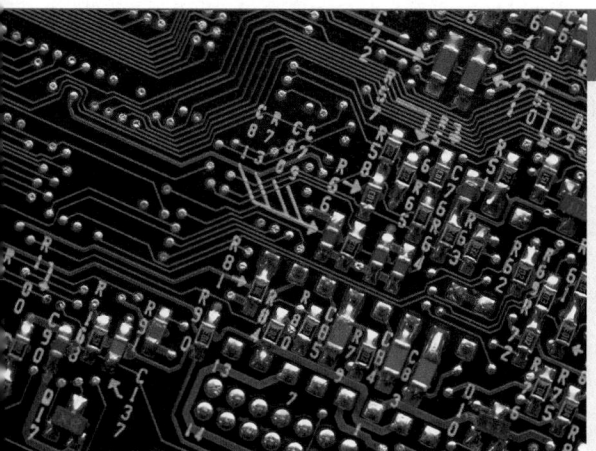

BUSINESS MATTERS

Capacity-Level Choices

Intel is a high-operating-leverage company. When it operates at full capacity, the higher the production output, the lower the unit fixed cost rate per unit. There is, however, a limit or constraint on just how many chips Intel can produce without purchasing more capacity.

The cost of goods sold includes only the fixed costs of units sold, not units produced, and the difference remains in the valuation of finished goods inventory. The decision about what capacity will be in the denominator level used to calculate the fixed cost overhead rate affects the reported operating income because it affects both the inventory values and cost of goods sold.

LEARNING OBJECTIVES

After studying this chapter, you should be able to

1 Identify the factors important to choosing the denominator level used to calculate fixed overhead allocation rates

2 Explain how the choice of denominator affects capacity management, costing, pricing, and performance evaluation

3 Distinguish absorption from variable costing; prepare and explain the differences in operating income under each costing policy

4 Distinguish throughput costing from variable costing and absorption costing, and explain differences in operating income under each costing policy

5 Explain productivity measurement under each of the three costing policies

In this chapter we examine the capacity choices available to managers who decide on the denominator level used to calculate fixed overhead rates. The capacity choice managers make will be the denominator level. This decision affects product costing and pricing, capacity management, governance (compliance with external reporting regulations), and performance evaluation. This is one of the most strategically important and complex decisions managers face. The decision to acquire too much capacity relative to demand will incur idle, unproductive capacity costs that must be recovered from the sale of output to keep the company profitable. Too little capacity relative to demand means companies will incur the cost of lost market share as competitors serve their customers, who may never return.

DENOMINATOR LEVELS: A COMPLEX DECISION WITH COMPLEX EFFECTS

1 Identify the factors important to choosing the denominator level used to calculate fixed overhead allocation rates

Each of the four choices for denominator level constrains output produced through either supply or demand capacity. The first two denominator-level choices constrain output because of the supply that can be provided by existing capacity:

◆ **Theoretical capacity** is the amount of output theoretically possible if there were never any delays or interruptions in production—a 24/7/365 quantity.

◆ **Practical capacity** is the amount of output practically possible after taking into account required idle time for maintenance, safety inspections, holidays, and other relevant factors.

Theoretical capacity must always be greater than practical capacity because practical capacity excludes any volume lost through idle time.

The following two denominator-level choices constrain output produced because of the existing demand level for the output:

◆ **Normal capacity** is the level of output that will satisfy average customer demand over a specified time period and complies with GAAP.

◆ **Master-budget capacity** is the level of output that will satisfy customer demand for a single budget cycle and complies with Canada Revenue Agency (CRA) for tax purposes.

Exhibit 9-1 illustrates the four potential choices of capacity and the implications of using each capacity option as the denominator level. The decision process itself is in orange. There are two pairs of denominator-level choices. The pair of choices based on production capacity is illustrated in blue and the pair based on non-production factors in gold.

The issues arising from the selection of the denominator level based on either a supply or demand measure of capacity affect both the balance sheet and the income statement. Although high-operating-leverage companies rely more heavily on machines (or capital) than labour in the production process, the capacity level will also entail changes to labour supply. Assume that managers have good business intelligence about the level of demand (market size) in the industry and how well their competitors do (market share).

The first decision is whether to acquire all the forecast capacity required to supply growth in the company's market share, or to make many acquisitions as the need arises. Chapter 22 presents analyses of this decision in detail. Bear in mind that most capacity is purchased in large increments. This means for acquisition purposes, capacity costs are a step function or semi-fixed. The demand, however, is usually a continuous growth curve that peaks then tapers off as the life cycle of the product ends. In the relationship between demand and capacity illustrated in Exhibit 9-2, the two lines never intersect. Intersection would indicate capacity less than demand and a missed opportunity to maximize market share. There is no perfect capacity choice to ensure a perfect denominator level because the behaviour of fixed costs, demand, and inventory values differs.

The semi-fixed costs of capacity acquisition behave according to fixed added increments of capacity. As growth in demand accelerates, the increments must be added more quickly. Exhibit 9-2 illustrates two types of rates of change. The blue dashed line is a stepped or discontinuous rate of change for capacity. The curved gold line is the rate

EXHIBIT 9-1
Stage in the Denominator Level Choice Process

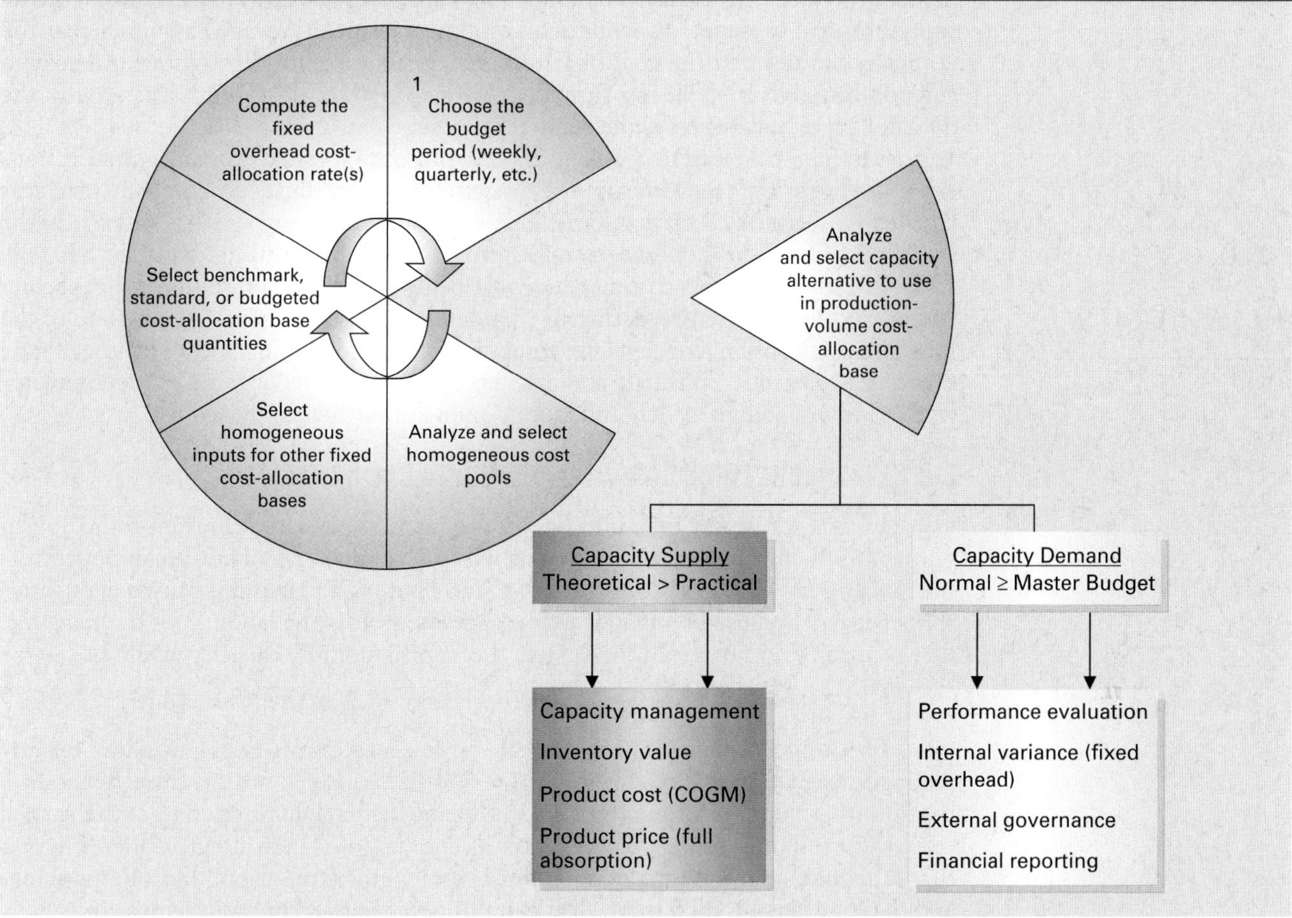

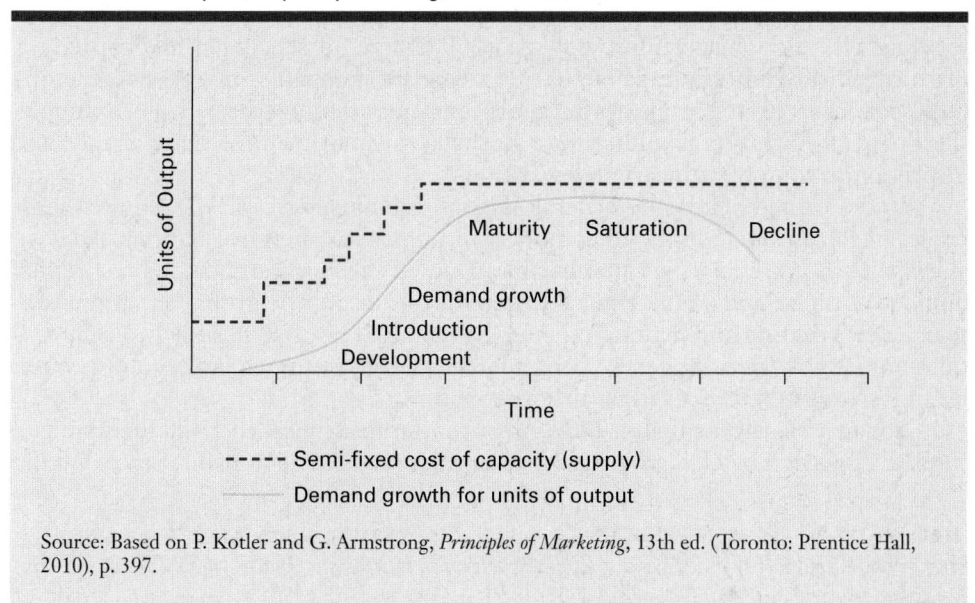

1. Choose the budget period (weekly, quarterly, etc.)

Compute the fixed overhead cost-allocation rate(s)

Select benchmark, standard, or budgeted cost-allocation base quantities

Select homogeneous inputs for other fixed cost-allocation bases

Analyze and select homogeneous cost pools

Analyze and select capacity alternative to use in production-volume cost-allocation base

Capacity Supply
Theoretical > Practical

Capacity Demand
Normal ≥ Master Budget

Capacity management

Inventory value

Product cost (COGM)

Product price (full absorption)

Performance evaluation

Internal variance (fixed overhead)

External governance

Financial reporting

of change in demand assumed over time for the product life cycle. The different rates and patterns of change make it unlikely the lines will intersect. Practically speaking, this means that you will almost always have a production-volume variance. For internal management purposes, the dollar value of that production-volume variance will depend on the capacity measure—the denominator level chosen by managers.

EXHIBIT 9-2
The Product Life Cycle, Capacity Planning, and Production-Volume Variance

Units of Output

Maturity   Saturation   Decline

Demand growth

Introduction

Development

Time

- - - - Semi-fixed cost of capacity (supply)
——— Demand growth for units of output

Source: Based on P. Kotler and G. Armstrong, *Principles of Marketing*, 13th ed. (Toronto: Prentice Hall, 2010), p. 397.

Notice in Exhibit 9-2, where the horizontal lines shorten on the stepped growth of capacity, the demand curve line is steeper. Notice the space between the demand growth curve and the semi-fixed capacity growth. This distance visually represents the presence of production-volume variance. We have assumed that the company has decided the cost of temporary excess capacity throughout the growth stage is bearable in order to sustain growth in market share and that is why the demand curve never crosses the semi-fixed costs.

We will use an iced tea bottling plant to illustrate several alternative capacity concepts and begin with the two supply capacity alternatives. Bushells Company produces labelled bottles of iced tea for Tazo. The variable manufacturing costs of each bottle are $0.35. The fixed monthly manufacturing costs of the bottling plant are $50,000. Bushells uses absorption costing (discussed below) for its monthly internal reporting system and for financial reporting to shareholders. Bushells could use any one of the four different capacity concepts for computing the fixed manufacturing overhead rate: theoretical, practical, normal, and master-budget capacity utilization (denominator level). Bushells defines its denominator in output units (bottles of iced tea).

SUPPLY: THEORETICAL CAPACITY OR PRACTICAL CAPACITY?

Capacity is a constraint or limit. Theoretical capacity is based on the production of output at full efficiency all the time. Bushells can produce 2,400 bottles an hour when the bottling lines are operating at full speed. There is a maximum of two eight-hour shifts per day because of a labour union agreement. It is the labour, not the machine, that constrains output for Bushells. The theoretical monthly capacity would be:

$$2,400 \text{ bottles per hour} \times 16 \text{ hours per day} \times 30 \text{ days} = 1,152,000 \text{ bottles}$$

Theoretical capacity is theoretical in the sense that it does not allow for any plant maintenance or interruptions from bottle breakages on the filling lines or a host of other factors. Although it is a rare plant that is able to operate at theoretical capacity, it can represent a goal or target level of usage. The strategic tradeoff here is that scheduled idle time for maintenance can lengthen the useful life of equipment and the long-term total output, or it can improve short-term cost savings.

Assume that the financial-accounting reporting method is used to estimate cost of goods manufactured and sold, which includes fixed overhead costs as well as variable manufacturing costs. This is called *absorption costing* or *full absorption costing* (see p. 424 for further discussion). No idle time results in the highest possible supply-side denominator level, the lowest fixed overhead cost rate, and the lowest inventory valuation. If, however, actual production is less than theoretical capacity because there is no demand or production is interrupted, the production-volume variance will be high and indicates the cost of idle productive capacity.

Practical capacity is the capacity concept that reduces theoretical capacity for unavoidable operating interruptions such as scheduled maintenance time, shutdowns for holidays, safety inspections, and so on. This type of scheduled idle capacity is often called **off-limits idle capacity**.[1] Strategically, companies might schedule off-limits idle capacity to comply with regulations and safety legislation. For example, the Board of Directors would require Bushells to shut down for maintenance and inspection to comply with certain legislation.

In the United States, the Federal Aviation Administration (FAA) requires companies in the airline industry to comply with numerous safety regulations. After an aircraft has flown a specified number of air miles, taken off and landed a specified number of times, and so on, the FAA requires the aircraft be grounded and its systems, such as wiring and hydraulics, must be rebuilt. The goal of these procedures is to minimize risk to passengers. After a rebuild, the aircraft must undergo inspection by an FAA agent before it can be airborne again.

You may remember that in 2008, American Airlines cancelled 2,500 flights after a surprise inspection by U.S. government authorities revealed poor maintenance. Wiring

[1]Parvez, R. Sopariwala, "Capacity Utilization: Using the CAM-I Capacity Model in a Multi-Hierarchical Manufacturing Environment," *Management Accounting Quarterly*, 7.2 (Winter 2006): p. 17–34.

in the landing gear was a potential fire hazard and the planes were grounded. American subsequently scrapped 570 aircraft in its fleet. The FAA also fined Southwest Airlines $10.2 million for failing to comply with inspection schedules. This illustrates why companies in some industries must plan for off-limits idle capacity.

Another reason for idle capacity may be due to downtime for setups. Usually bottling companies have several customers, each with different shaped bottles, labels, and contents. An important job for the production manager is to schedule setups to minimize **non-productive idle capacity**. This type of capacity is not off-limits because it can be minimized with either excellent scheduling or deployed in other ways. Bushells may also acquire idle capacity to provide some excess resources required if there are unexpected delays in obtaining materials or unscheduled interruptions to fill rush orders. Practical capacity is not constant over the life of equipment. Process redesign can improve labour efficiency, wait-time for materials, and scheduling, which would increase practical capacity. At Bushells, assume that the practical hourly production rate including non-productive and off-limits idle capacity is 2,000 bottles an hour and that the plant can operate 25 days a month.

The practical monthly capacity is:

$$2{,}000 \text{ bottles per hour} \times 16 \text{ hours} \times 25 \text{ days} = 800{,}000 \text{ bottles}$$

Engineers at the Bushells plant can provide input on the technical capabilities of machines for filling bottles. Human safety factors are important, such as increased risk of injury when the line operates at faster speeds. Also, the likelihood of bottles shattering and the hazard of bottling broken glass with the tea increases as the line speed increases. In some cases, an increase in capacity may be technically possible but not economically sound. For example, the labour union may actually permit a third shift per day but only at unusually high wage rates that clearly do not make financial sense in the bottling market.

DEMAND: NORMAL CAPACITY OR MASTER-BUDGET CAPACITY?

Normal capacity utilization and master-budget capacity utilization measure the denominator level in terms of demand for the output. In many cases, demand is well below the supply available, as was illustrated in Exhibit 9-2. In such cases, the semi-fixed costs do not intersect the demand line, indicating the presence of idle non-productive capacity.

Strategically, Bushells' managers have likely concluded that the excess non-productive capacity can be used in other revenue-generating ways (see Chapters 11 and 12) until demand growth accelerates. Increased demand by customers may be not only for product, but also for services customized to their needs. Bushells may also have made this decision as an agility-response strategy: The managers may have seen the ability to provide faster delivery (using increased capacity) as a competitive advantage in acquiring new customers, and considered the benefit greater than the cost of excess capacity.

Normal capacity utilization is the capacity concept based on the level of capacity utilization that satisfies average customer demand over a period (say, of two to three years) that includes seasonal, cyclical, or other trend factors. Master-budget capacity utilization is the capacity concept based on the anticipated level of capacity utilization for the next operating budget period of a month, a quarter, or a year. The key difference is the *time period* under consideration, long (normal) or short (master) term. These two denominator levels will differ when an industry has cyclical periods of high and low demand or when management believes that the budgeted production for the coming period is unrepresentative of "long-term" demand.

Consider our Bushells example. The master budget for 2010 is based on production of 400,000 bottles per month. Hence, the master budget denominator level is 400,000 bottles. However, Bushells' senior management believes that over the next one to three years, the normal monthly production level will be 500,000 bottles. This also explains the distance between the demand and semi-fixed cost lines in Exhibit 9-2. GAAP external reporting requires the use of normal capacity in the denominator taking into account off-limits idle capacity. Unallocated overhead (variance) is recognized in the time period incurred. GAAP also permits the use of actual production level if it is not materially different from normal capacity.

Bushells' master-budget denominator level of 400,000 is a short-term estimate of market share for the year 2010. The managers have competitive information that a major competitor has sharply reduced its price and increased advertising. Bushells expects that the lower prices and advertising blitz will be a short-run phenomenon and that in 2011 the market share it has lost to this competitor will be regained. The Canada Revenue Agency (CRA) requires companies to use the master-budget denominator level (along with full proration of variances between inventories and cost of goods sold) for income tax reporting. CRA income tax rulings effectively prohibit using either theoretical capacity or practical capacity denominator-levels. Both typically result in companies taking writeoffs of fixed manufacturing overhead as tax deductions more quickly than desired by the CRA.

MyAccountingLab

ASSESS YOUR MASTERY

To check your understanding of the material in Learning Objective ❶, go to the *Mastery Questions* section at the end of this chapter and complete Learning Objective ❶ questions 1, 2, and 3.

EFFECTS ON REPORTING, COSTING, PRICING, AND EVALUATION

❷ Explain how the choice of denominator affects capacity management, costing, pricing, and performance evaluation

Bushells has budgeted fixed manufacturing costs of $50,000 per month. Assume the actual costs are also $50,000. To keep this example simple, we assume all fixed manufacturing costs are indirect. The budgeted fixed manufacturing overhead rates in May 2010 for the four alternative capacity concepts discussed are as follows:

Capacity Concept (1)	Budgeted Fixed Manufacturing Overhead per Month (2)	Budgeted Capacity Level (in Bottles) (3)	Budgeted Manufacturing Overhead Cost Rate (4) = (2) ÷ (3)
Theoretical capacity	$50,000	1,152,000	$0.0434
Practical capacity	50,000	800,000	0.0625
Normal capacity utilization	50,000	500,000	0.1000
Master-budget capacity utilization	50,000	400,000	0.1250

The budgeted fixed manufacturing overhead rate based on master-budget capacity utilization ($0.1250) represents an increase of more than 188% from the rate based on theoretical capacity ($0.0434). The fixed cost pool is $50,000 over the relevant range of 400,000 to 1,152,000 bottles.

Exhibit 9-3 illustrates the four possible fixed overhead cost rates per bottle as the denominator-level choice changes. If the managers decide to use only one system for

EXHIBIT 9-3
Fixed Cost Overhead Rate Per Bottle at Bushells

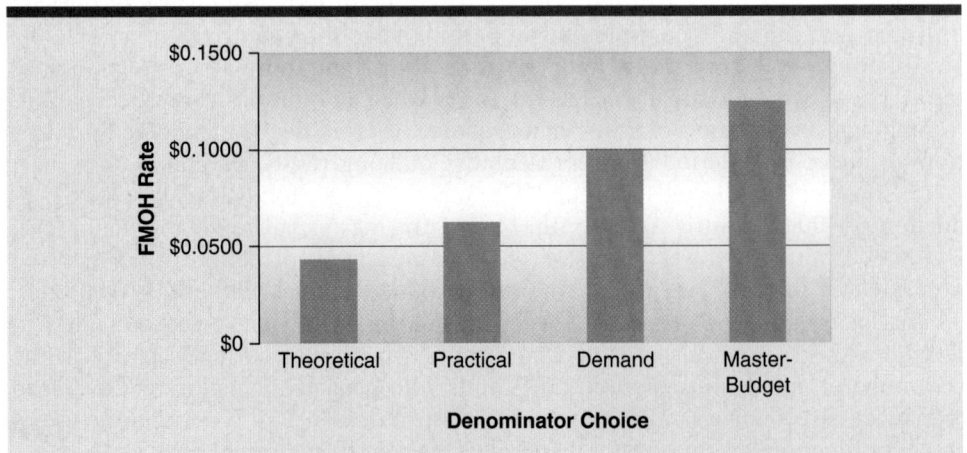

both internal management and external financial reporting purposes, then they will choose 500,000 as the denominator level. This will guarantee a short-run 2010 unfavourable production-volume variance. But the company will also be consistent with GAAP and use full absorption costing to estimate inventory value and cost of goods sold. This will lead to applying the full cost of $0.1000 of all idle capacity of 752,000 bottles (1,152,000 − 400,000 bottles) when pricing each of the 400,000 bottles actually sold.

Assume now that Bushells' actual production in May 2010 is 460,000 bottles. Actual sales are 420,000 bottles. Also assume no beginning inventory on May 1, 2010, and no price, spending, or efficiency variances for May 2010. The manufacturing plant sells bottles of iced tea to another division for $0.50 per bottle. Its only costs are variable manufacturing costs of $0.35 per bottle and $50,000 per month for fixed manufacturing overhead. Bushells writes off all variances to cost of goods sold each month.

The budgeted manufacturing costs per bottle of iced tea for each capacity concept are the sum of $0.35 in variable manufacturing costs and the budgeted fixed manufacturing overhead costs (shown from the preceding table).

Capacity Concept (1)	Variable Manufacturing Costs (2)	Fixed Manufacturing Overhead Cost Rate (3)	Total Manufacturing Costs (4) = (2) + (3)
Theoretical capacity	$0.3500	$0.0434	$0.3934
Practical capacity	0.3500	0.0625	0.4125
Normal capacity utilization	0.3500	0.1000	0.4500
Master-budget capacity utilization	0.3500	0.1250	0.4750

Each capacity concept will result in a different production-volume variance.

$$\text{Production-volume variance} = \left(\begin{array}{c} \text{Denominator} \\ \text{level in} \\ \text{output units} \end{array} - \begin{array}{c} \text{Actual} \\ \text{output units} \end{array} \right) \times \begin{array}{c} \text{Budgeted fixed} \\ \text{manufacturing overhead} \\ \text{rate per output unit} \end{array}$$

$$\text{Theoretical capacity} = (1,152,000 - 460,000) \times \$0.0434$$
$$= \$30,033 \text{ U}$$

$$\text{Practical capacity} = (800,000 - 460,000) \times \$0.0625$$
$$= \$21,250 \text{ U}$$

$$\text{Normal capacity utilization} = (500,000 - 460,000) \times \$0.1000$$
$$= \$4,000 \text{ U}$$

$$\text{Master-budget capacity utilization} = (400,000 - 460,000) \times \$0.1250$$
$$= 7,500 \text{ F}$$

Exhibit 9-4 shows how the choice of a denominator affects Bushells' operating income for May 2010. Using the master-budget denominator will mean assigning the highest amount of fixed manufacturing overhead costs per bottle to the 40,000 bottles in ending inventory. Accordingly, operating income is highest using the master-budget capacity utilization denominator. Recall that Bushells had no beginning inventory on May 1, 2010, production in May of 460,000 bottles, and sales in May of 420,000 bottles. Hence, the ending inventory on May 31 is 40,000 bottles. The differences between the operating incomes for the four denominator-level concepts in Exhibit 9-4 are due to different amounts of fixed manufacturing overhead costs being inventoried:

Fixed Manufacturing Overhead May 31, 2010 Pro Forma Inventory Valuation

Denominator Level (1)	Pro Forma Quantity (2)	Fixed Overhead Rate (3)	Pro Forma Inventory (4) = (2) × (3)
Theoretical	40,000	$0.0434	$1,736
Practical	40,000	0.0625	2,500
Normal	40,000	0.1000	4,000
Master-budget	40,000	0.1250	5,000

Thus, in Exhibit 9-4 the difference in operating income between the master-budget capacity utilization concept and the normal capacity utilization concept of $1,000 ($8,000 − $7,000) is due to the difference in fixed manufacturing overhead inventoried ($5,000 − $4,000 = $1,000).

PRODUCT COSTING

Cost data from a standard-costing system are often used in pricing or product-mix decisions. As the Bushells example illustrates, the use of theoretical capacity results in an unachieveably small fixed manufacturing overhead cost per bottle because it is based on an unattainable level of capacity utilization. Theoretical

EXHIBIT 9-4
Bushells Company: Income Statement Effects of Alternative Denominator Levels for May 2010

Actual sales volume (bottles)	420,000			
Actual output (bottles)	460,000			
Variable manufacturing overhead rate	$0.3500			

	Denominator-Level Alternatives			
	Theoretical	**Practical**	**Normal**	**Master-Budget**
Capacity alternative (denominator level)	1,152,000	800,000	500,000	400,000
Fixed overhead cost rate	$0.0434	$0.0625	$0.1000	$0.1250
Sales, $0.50 × 420,000	$210,000	$210,000	$210,000	$210,000
Cost of goods sold (COGS)				
Beginning inventory	0	0	0	0
Variable manufacturing costs*	161,000	161,000	161,000	161,000
Fixed manufacturing overhead costs†	19,964	28,750	46,000	57,500
Cost of goods available for sale	180,964	189,750	207,000	218,500
Ending inventory‡	15,736	16,500	18,000	19,000
Total COGS (at standard)	165,228	173,250	189,000	199,500
Adjustments for variances§	30,033U	21,250U	4,000U	(7,500)F
Total COGS	195,261	194,500	193,000	192,000
Gross margin	14,739	15,500	17,000	18,000
Marketing, other expenses	10,000	10,000	10,000	10,000
Operating income	$ 4,739	$ 5,500	$ 7,000	$ 8,000

*$ 0.35 × 460,000 = $161,000

†Fixed manufacturing overhead costs

	Production		Rate		Cost
	460,000	×	$0.0434	=	$19,964
	460,000	×	$0.0625	=	$28,750
	460,000	×	$0.1000	=	$46,000
	460,000	×	$0.1250	=	$57,500

‡Ending inventory costs

	Variable		Fixed		Production		Sales		Value
	($0.3500	+	$0.0434)	×	(460,000	−	420,000)	=	$ 15,736
	($0.3500	+	$0.0625)	×	(460,000	−	420,000)	=	$ 16,500
	($0.3500	+	$0.1000)	×	(460,000	−	420,000)	=	$ 18,000
	($0.3500	+	$0.1250)	×	(460,000	−	420,000)	=	$ 19,000

§The production-volume variance is calculated on p. 419. It is the only variance Bushells incurred in May 2010.

capacity is rarely used to calculate the budgeted fixed manufacturing overhead cost rate per bottle because it departs significantly from the real capacity available to a company.

Many companies favour practical capacity as the denominator to calculate the budgeted fixed manufacturing cost per bottle. Practical capacity in the Bushells example represents the maximum number of bottles that Bushells intends to produce per year. If Bushells had consistently planned to produce fewer bottles of iced tea, it would have built a smaller plant and incurred lower costs. The drawback is that neither GAAP nor CRA accept this denominator for external reporting purposes.

Bushells budgets $0.0625 in fixed manufacturing overhead cost per bottle based on the $50,000 it costs to acquire the capacity to produce 800,000 bottles. This plant capacity is acquired well before Bushells uses the capacity and even before Bushells knows how much of the capacity it will actually use. That is, the budgeted fixed manufacturing cost of $0.0625 per bottle measures the *cost per bottle of supplying the capacity.*

Demand for Bushells' iced tea in 2010 is expected to be 400,000 bottles lower than practical capacity. The cost of *supplying* the capacity needed to make bottles is still $0.0625 per bottle. That's because capacity is acquired in "lumpy" amounts, and it costs $50,000 per year to acquire the capacity to make 800,000 bottles. The capacity and its cost are fixed in the *short run*; the capacity supplied cannot be reduced to match the capacity needed in 2010. As a result, not all of the capacity supplied at $0.0625 per bottle will be needed or used in 2010.

Using practical capacity will include the cost of idle capacity in the fixed overhead cost rate. Highlighting the cost of capacity acquired but not used directs managers' attention to managing unused capacity, perhaps by designing new products to fill unused capacity or leasing out unused capacity to others. In contrast, using either of the capacity levels based on the demand for Bushells' iced tea—master-budget capacity utilization or normal capacity utilization—hides the amount of unused capacity.

If Bushells had used the master-budget capacity utilization as the capacity level to conform with CRA, it would have calculated the budgeted fixed manufacturing cost per bottle as $0.1250 ($50,000 ÷ 400,000 bottles). This calculation does not use data about practical capacity, so it does not separately identify the cost of unused capacity. Note, however, that the cost of $0.1250 per bottle includes a charge for unused capacity—the $0.0625 fixed manufacturing resource that would be used to produce each bottle at practical capacity plus the cost of unused capacity allocated to each bottle, $0.0625 per bottle.

The next section illustrates how the use of normal capacity utilization or master-budget capacity utilization results in setting selling prices that are not competitive.

STRATEGY

The Denominator Level Is a Strategic Choice

If Bushells has adequate business intelligence data to benchmark its fixed overhead to become at least as good as or better than its competitors, the $0.0625 rate is more aggressive than the $0.1250 master-budget rate yet remains possible to achieve, which the $0.0434 theoretical rate is not. Practical capacity focuses on the supply constraint on production and does not include any non-productive idle capacity cost. In a competitive market where gross margins are very slim, the cost of idle capacity is non-value-added to the customer who expects Bushells to either manage its capacity or bear the cost of ineffectiveness itself. By definition, this denominator level is associated with long-term costs incurred in the capacity decision.

PRODUCT PRICING: THE DOWNWARD DEMAND SPIRAL

The easiest way to understand the **downward demand spiral** is via an example. The downward demand spiral is a progressive reduction in sales, which leads to an increase in the fixed overhead rate. As sales decrease, the realized quantity in the master-budget denominator of any fixed overhead cost rate decreases but the fixed cost pool is constant. The master-budget fixed overhead rate increases each time the master budget denominator decreases. A decreased quantity of forecast sales must bear higher costs per unit—which lead to an increased unit sales price to cover full costs. In a competitive market, all else being equal, this will further decrease sales. At the extreme, if Bushells sold only one bottle, its share of fixed overhead cost would be $50,000. This is a drawback of using master-budget as the denominator level.

Assume Bushells uses master-budget capacity utilization of 400,000 bottles for full product costing in 2010. The resulting manufacturing cost is $0.4750 (0.35 + 0.125) per bottle. Assume in December 2009 a competitor, Lipton Iced Tea, offers to supply a major customer of Bushells at $0.45 per bottle. Bushells' forecast of sales to this customer was 100,000 bottles in 2010. The Bushells manager, not wanting to show a loss on the account of $0.025 per bottle and wanting to recoup all costs in the long run, does not match the competitor's price and the account is lost. The lost account means budgeted fixed manufacturing costs of $50,000 will be spread over the remaining master-budget volume of 300,000 bottles. This means the unitized rate will increase to $0.167 ($50,000 ÷ 300,000 bottles) from $0.125 ($50,000 ÷ 400,000). The variable mOH rate remains at $0.35. The new full absorption cost, all other things equal, will be $0.517 per bottle ($0.35 + $0.167 = $0.517).

Suppose then another customer of Bushells—also accounting for 100,000 bottles of budgeted volume—receives a bid from a competitor priced at $0.45. The Bushells manager compares this bid with his revised unit cost of $0.517, declines to match the competition, and the account is lost. The planned output would shrink further to 200,000 units. The budgeted fixed manufacturing cost per unit for the remaining 200,000 now would be $0.25 ($50,000 ÷ 200,000 bottles). With the variable costs remaining at $0.35, the new full absorption cost will be $0.60.

THINKING CRITICALLY

Why use practical capacity for internal-pricing purposes? Explain in a sentence or two. Read on for an assessment of this situation.

The use of practical capacity as the denominator to calculate the budgeted fixed manufacturing cost per bottle avoids the recalculation of unit costs when expected demand levels change. This is because the fixed-cost rate is calculated based on the capacity available rather than the capacity used to meet demand. Managers who use reported unit costs in a mechanical way to set prices are less likely to promote a downward demand spiral when they use practical capacity concepts than when they use the normal capacity or master-budget capacity-utilization concepts.

PERFORMANCE EVALUATION

Consider how the choice between normal capacity utilization, master-budget capacity utilization, and practical capacity affects how a marketing manager is evaluated. Normal capacity utilization is often used as a basis for long-term plans. The normal capacity utilization depends on the time span selected and the forecasts made for each year. *However, normal capacity utilization is an average that provides no meaningful feedback to the marketing manager for a particular year.* Using normal capacity utilization as a reference for judging current performance of a marketing manager is an example of misusing a long-run measure for a short-run purpose.

The master-budget capacity utilization, rather than normal capacity utilization or practical capacity, is what should be used for evaluating a marketing manager's performance in the current year. This is because the master budget is the principal short-run planning and control tool. Managers feel more obligated to reach the levels specified in the master budget, which should have been carefully set in relation to the maximum opportunities for sales in the current year.

When large differences exist between practical capacity and master-budget capacity utilization, several companies classify part of the large difference as *planned unused capacity.* One reason for this approach is performance evaluation. Consider our Bushells iced-tea example. The managers in charge of capacity planning usually do not make pricing decisions. Top management decided to build an iced-tea plant with 800,000 bottles of practical capacity, focusing on demand over the next five years.

Bushells' marketing managers, who are mid-level managers, make the pricing decisions. This group believes it should be held accountable only for the manufacturing overhead costs related to the potential customer base in 2010. The master-budget capacity utilization suggests a customer base in 2010 of 400,000 bottles. Using responsibility accounting principles, part of the budgeted total fixed manufacturing costs would be attributed to the fixed capacity costs of meeting 2010 demand. The remaining costs would be separately shown as the capacity cost of meeting long-run demand increases expected to occur beyond 2010.

CAPACITY COSTS AND DENOMINATOR-LEVEL ISSUES

The choice of any denominator level introduces rigidity into the budgeting and costing system. Standard cost systems do not recognize fluctuations and uncertainty. The managers must make a choice despite their knowledge that they will almost certainly be wrong. Managers know that both supply of and demand for capacity is uncertain, if only due to random events. Bushells' plant has estimated practical capacity of 800,000 bottles. The estimated master-budget capacity utilization for 2010 is 400,000 bottles. These estimates are uncertain. To deal with uncertainty, Bushells more than likely built its current plant with an 800,000-bottle practical capacity in part to provide the capability to meet unexpected surges in growth in demand. For example, consumers are increasingly aware of the waste from plastic bottles and producers are switching back to glass despite the increased weight, fragility, and transportation costs.

Challenging issues also arise in measuring the numerator, the fixed-cost pool. For example, deregulation of the electric utility industry has resulted in many electric utilities becoming unprofitable. This situation has led to write-downs in the values of their plant and equipment. The write-downs reduce the numerator via the amortization used to compute fixed capacity cost per kilowatt-hour of electricity produced.

In nonmanufacturing value-chain functions, capacity costs also arise. Bushells may acquire a fleet of vehicles capable of distributing the practical capacity of its iced-tea plant. When actual production is below the practical capacity, there will be unused capacity cost issues with the distribution function, as well as with the manufacturing function.

As you saw in Chapter 8, capacity cost issues are prominent in many service-sector companies, such as airlines, hospitals, railroads, and banks, even though these companies carry no inventory and so have no inventory-costing issues. For example, in calculating the fixed overhead cost per patient-day in its obstetrics and gynecology department, a hospital must decide what denominator to use—practical capacity, normal utilization, or master-budget utilization. Its decision may have implications for capacity management, as well as pricing and performance evaluation.

The Bushells example assumed that all fixed manufacturing overhead costs had a single cost driver: bottles of iced tea produced. As you saw in Chapter 5, ABC systems have multiple overhead cost pools at the output-unit, batch, product-sustaining, and facility-sustaining levels, each with its own cost driver. In calculating the activity cost rates (for setups and materials handling, say), management must choose a capacity level for the quantity of the cost driver (setup-hours or loads moved). Should it use practical, normal, or master-budget capacity utilization? For all the reasons described in the chapter, most proponents of ABC argue that practical capacity should be used as the denominator to calculate activity cost rates.

Prorate or Writeoff: CRA versus Internal Evaluation

Good governance is in part about adopting costing policies that comply with external reporting standards and legislation. It is also crucial, however, to provide relevant cost information to inform important managerial decisions. Strategic choices have practical implications. The strategic choice to undertake ABC and use either theoretical or practical denominator levels as appropriate to the activities measured by the cost driver will lead to overallocation and underallocation. CRA requires the use of the master-budget denominator level for tax purposes. GAAP requires the use of the normal capacity denominator. Overallocations or underallocations, which will show as variances, must be prorated according to the CRA and GAAP—but each requires a different denominator. This will lead to a tax COGS estimate and estimate of inventory values that differs from the GAAP COGS estimate and the estimate of inventory values. For internal purposes, writing off even material variances may provide more relevant information for strategic and operating decisions than proration. Management accountants are often called upon to provide the cost estimates and to translate the benefits of, for example, ABC into dollar values. The common language of benefit and cost is dollars, and by doing this in a thoughtful way, management accountants contribute relevant information crucial to choosing the denominator level and other financial policy decisions.

MyAccountingLab

ASSESS YOUR MASTERY

To check your understanding of the material in Learning Objective ❷, go to the *Mastery Questions* section at the end of this chapter and complete Learning Objective ❷ questions 1, 2, and 3.

DENOMINATOR LEVEL AND INVENTORY VALUATION

❸ Distinguish absorption from variable costing; prepare and explain the differences in operating income under each costing policy

From the standpoint of Canadian and international financial accounting standards, there is only one method to value inventory: Full absorption based on the normal-capacity denominator level. It is the most conservative of the three overhead cost assignment and inventory valuation policy choices available for internal management purposes. Inventory must also be valued on a first-in, first-out (FIFO) basis. For internal management purposes, the two most commonly encountered methods of inventory valuation are variable costing and absorption costing. A third option is throughput costing.

ABSORPTION AND VARIABLE INVENTORY VALUATION ASSUMPTIONS

Throughout Chapter 9, we assume that the chosen allocation base for calculating the variable and fixed manufacturing overhead allocation rates is a production-output-related variable, for example, direct labour-hours or direct machine-hours per unit of output produced. The variable and fixed manufacturing overhead cost pools are assumed to be reasonably associated with a measure of a homogeneous manufacturing input. This association is what permits managers to explain variances in cost on the basis of changes in the consumption of the cost allocation base, making it sensible to calculate efficiency and production-volume variances.

Absorption costing (also called **full absorption costing**) is a method of inventory valuation in which inventory "absorbs" both variable and fixed manufacturing costs as inventoriable costs but classifies all nonmanufacturing costs as period costs. A variety of costs such as tax, insurance premiums, and amortization of manufacturing plant and equipment will be included in the fixed overhead cost rate assigned to each unit remaining in inventory. The important event transferring costs of production from the inventory on the balance sheet to the cost of goods sold (COGS) expense on the income statement is a sale. The timing of recognition of COGS is matched to incoming revenue.

Variable costing is a method of inventory valuation in which only *variable manufacturing* costs are included as inventoriable costs. All fixed and all nonmanufacturing costs are classified as period costs expensed during the specific time period they are incurred. Under variable costing, for example, no amortization of manufacturing plant and equipment will be included in the overhead rate assigned to each unit remaining in inventory. These costs will be recognized as period costs when incurred as cost of goods available for sale. The important event transferring fixed costs of production from inventory on the balance sheet to period expenses on the income statement is the end of the budget period.

The key distinguishing factors of these two valuation policies are:

◆ classification of fixed manufacturing overhead as an inventoriable (COGS) or a period cost

◆ the classification of variable nonmanufacturing overhead as an inventoriable (COGS) or period cost

◆ the event that triggers recognition of fixed overhead expense

◆ the timing of expensing fixed manufacturing overhead

We will illustrate differences between the two costing methods using Radius Company, which manufactures specialty industrial belts. Radius allocates costs using a normal costing system. That is, its direct costs are traced to products using actual prices multiplied by the actual inputs used, but its indirect (overhead) costs are allocated using budgeted indirect-cost rate(s) multiplied by actual inputs used. The allocation base for all manufacturing costs is units of output produced. The allocation base for all marketing costs is units of output sold. We assume the following for 2010:

◆ The budgeted equals the actual number of units produced (1,100,000 units).

◆ The budgeted equals the actual number of units sold (1,000,000 units).

◆ The budgeted equals actual fixed costs.

◆ Work in process is minimal.

◆ No beginning inventory on January 1, 2010.

◆ All variable costs are driven by an output-unit–related variable. (We assume, for example, batch-level and product-sustaining costs are zero.)

With 2010 production of 1,100,000 units and sales of 1,000,000 units, the ending inventory on December 31, 2010, is 100,000 units. The per unit and total actual costs for 2010 are as follows:

	Per Unit	Total Costs
Variable costs:		
Direct materials	$3.50	$3,850,000
Direct manufacturing labour	1.60	1,760,000
Indirect manufacturing costs	0.90	990,000
Manufacturing costs	6.00	6,600,000
Direct marketing costs	0.80	800,000
Indirect marketing costs	1.60	1,600,000
Marketing costs	2.40	2,400,000
Total variable costs	$8.40	$9,000,000
Fixed costs:		
Direct manufacturing costs	$0.30	$ 330,000
Indirect manufacturing costs	1.70	1,870,000
Manufacturing costs	2.00	2,200,000
Direct marketing costs	2.10	2,100,000
Indirect marketing costs	3.40	3,400,000
Marketing costs	5.50	5,500,000
Total fixed costs	$7.50	$7,700,000

The heart of the difference between variable and absorption costing for financial reporting is accounting for fixed manufacturing and variable nonmanufacturing costs. There is no difference in how variable manufacturing overhead costs are recognized, which is as inventoriable (COGS) expenses. A direct manufacturing cost could be supervision of production of a product line but the supervisors' salaries are fixed irrespective of the quantity of individual outputs produced. This is a fixed direct cost of production. The straight-line amortization expense on a machine is also a fixed cost but it is an indirect cost of producing the output that is established based on useful life, not quantity of outputs produced.

		Direct	Indirect
Same under Both Methods }	Variable	Direct manufacturing cost	Indirect manufacturing cost
Differs under the Two Methods }	Fixed	Direct manufacturing cost	Indirect manufacturing cost

THINKING CRITICALLY

Do budgeting, static, master, and inventory-valuation policies relate? Explain in a sentence or two. Read on for an assessment of this situation.

In budgeting (Chapter 6), all the fixed overhead manufacturing costs including amortization of plant and equipment used exclusively in converting raw materials to finished goods were included in COGS. In variance analysis (Chapter 8), this was also true for budgeting the pro forma fixed cost manufacturing overhead rate for the static budget. The static budget assumed an unvarying output, the denominator level used to calculate the fixed cost manufacturing overhead rate. The denominator level could have been the theoretical, normal, practical, or master-budget level. The important point is that the denominator level for the static budget be used to calculate the pro forma fixed overhead rate. The internal inventory valuation policy is a choice of where and when to recognize the fixed manufacturing overhead, the overallocated or underallocated fixed manufacturing overhead (the variance), and the variable nonmanufacturing costs as an expense. If included in COGS, they are inventoriable; if included in period costs, they are not inventoriable. Notice that by including fixed manufacturing overhead and variance in the COGS, managers slow down the timing of recognizing this expense and capitalize this dollar value according to the rate at which units are sold.

Both absorption and variable inventory valuation methods capitalize all fixed costs (both manufacturing and nonmanufacturing). Capitalizing means acquisition costs are recorded as an asset on the balance sheet when incurred. This value is methodically decreased as amortization, most often on the units-of-production or via the straight-line method. The dollar value, amortization (an expense), is methodically transferred to the income statement. Under the absorption valuation method, there is a second stage of capitalization of fixed manufacturing overhead. This value is capitalized according to the units of finished goods sold using FIFO. The variable costing method deducts the amortization expense associated with fixed costs (both manufacturing and nonmanufacturing) as a period cost of the period in which they are incurred.

An example of a fixed indirect manufacturing cost is the annual lease cost of a building where multiple products are assembled. The lease cost is allocated over the different products. If the building had been used for manufacturing only one product, it would be a fixed direct cost of that product.

Inspect the classification of inventoriable costs under the two methods for Radius as shown below and it is clear that under absorption costing the total unit inventoriable cost is higher than under the variable costing method. Accurately classifying the costs determines both the appropriate inventory valuation and estimates of cost of goods sold expense using each method.

	Variable Costing		Absorption Costing	
Variable manufacturing costs:				
Direct materials	$3.50		$3.50	
Direct manufacturing labour	1.60		1.60	
Indirect manufacturing costs	0.90	$6.00	0.90	$6.00
Fixed manufacturing costs:				
Direct manufacturing costs	–		0.30	
Indirect manufacturing costs	–	–	1.70	2.00
Total inventoriable costs		$6.00		$8.00

Exhibit 9-5 presents the variable costing and absorption costing income statements for Radius Company in 2010. The absorption costing income statement uses the gross margin format introduced in Chapter 2. The variable costing income statement uses the contribution format introduced in Chapter 3.

┌───┐
│ **THINKING CRITICALLY**

Why have more than one format to report costs? Explain in a sentence or two. Read on for a discussion of this topic.
└───┘

The contribution format highlights the distinction between variable and fixed costs, whereby all fixed costs are period costs and excluded from calculating the variable cost of goods sold. The gross-margin format highlights the distinction between manufacturing and nonmanufacturing costs, whereby all nonmanufacturing costs are period costs and excluded from calculating the absorption cost of goods sold. Many companies using absorption costing find it unnecessary to design a cost accounting system that distinguishes between variable and fixed costs.

Highlight the fixed manufacturing costs of $2,200,000 in Exhibit 9-5. The income statement under variable costing deducts the $2,200,000 lump sum as a period cost in 2010. In contrast, the income statement under absorption costing regards each finished unit as absorbing $2 of fixed manufacturing costs. Under absorption costing, the $2,200,000 is initially capitalized as an inventoriable cost in 2010. Given the preceding data for Radius, $2,000,000 subsequently becomes an expense in 2010, and $200,000 remains an asset—part of ending finished goods inventory (100,000 units × $2) at December 31, 2010. The variable manufacturing costs are accounted for in the same way in both income statements in Exhibit 9-5.

Compare sales of 900,000, 1,000,000, and 1,100,000 units by Radius Company in 2010. Fixed manufacturing costs would be included in the 2010 expense as follows:

	Fixed Manufacturing Costs Treated as an Expense in 2010
Variable costing, where	
◆ Sales are 900,000, 1,000,000, or 1,100,000 units	$2,200,000
Absorption costing, where	
◆ Sales are 900,000 units, $400,000 (200,000 × $2) held back in inventory	$1,800,000
◆ Sales are 1,000,000 units, $200,000 (100,000 × $2) held back in inventory	$2,000,000
◆ Sales are 1,100,000 units, $0 held back in inventory	$2,200,000

EXHIBIT 9-5
Comparison of Variable Costing and Absorption Costing Income Statements for the Year Ended December 31, 2010, for Radius Company (quantity of units and dollar values are reported in thousands)

	A	B	C
1	PANEL A: VARIABLE COSTING		
2	Revenues $17 × 1,000 units (in thousands)		$17,000
3	Variable costs:		
4	Beginning inventory	$ 0	
5	Variable manufacturing costs: $6 × 1,100 units	6,600	
6	Cost of goods available for sale	6,600	
7	Deduct ending inventory: $6 × 100 units	(600)	
8	Variable cost of goods sold	6,000	
9	Variable marketing costs: $2.40 × 1,000 units sold	2,400	
10	Adjustment for variable cost variances	0	
11	Total variable costs		8,400
12	Contribution margin		8,600
13	Fixed costs:		
14	Fixed manufacturing costs $2 × 1,100	2,200	
15	Fixed marketing costs $5.50 × 1,000 units sold	5,500	
16	Adjustment for fixed cost variances	0	
17	Total fixed costs		7,700
18	Operating income		$ 900
19			
20	PANEL B: ABSORPTION COSTING		
21	Revenues $17 × 1,000 units (in thousands)		$17,000
22	Cost of goods sold:		
23	Beginning inventory	$ 0	
24	Variable manufacturing costs: $6 × 1,100 units	6,600	
25	Allocated fixed manufacturing costs $2 × 1,100	2,200	
26	Cost of goods available for sale	8,800	
27	Deduct ending inventory: $8 × 100 units	(800)	
28	Adjustment for manufacturing variances	0	
29	Cost of goods sold		8,000
30	Gross margin		9,000
31	Marketing costs:		
32	Variable marketing costs $2.40 × 1,000 units sold	2,400	
33	Fixed marketing costs $5.50 × 1,000 units sold	5,500	
34	Adjustment for marketing variances	0	
35	Total marketing costs		7,900
36	Operating income		$ 1,100

Some companies use the term **direct costing** to inaccurately describe the inventory costing method we call *variable costing*. This is unfortunate terminology:

◆ Variable and absorption inventory valuation treat direct *manufacturing variable* costs identically as COGS expense.

◆ Variable inventory valuation includes direct nonmanufacturing and variable nonmanufacturing costs as COGS expense.

◆ Variable inventory valuation excludes both direct *fixed* manufacturing and nonmanufacturing costs (such as general administration) from COGS.

COMPARISON OF STANDARD VARIABLE COSTING AND ABSORPTION COSTING

Our next example explores the implications of accounting for fixed manufacturing costs in more detail. Stassen Company manufactures and markets telescopes for military use. Stassen uses a standard costing system for both its manufacturing and its marketing costs.[2] Stassen began business on January 1, 2010, and it is now March 2010. The president asks you to prepare comparative income statements for January 2010 and February 2010. The following simplified data are available:

A	B	C
Unit Data	**January 2010**	**February 2010**
Beginning inventory	0	200
Production	600	650
Sales	400	750
Ending inventory	200	100
Other data		
Selling price	$ 99	per unit sold
Standard variable unit manufacturing costs	$ 20	per unit produced
Standard variable unit marketing costs	$ 19	per unit sold
Standard fixed monthly manufacturing costs	$12,800	
Standard fixed monthly marketing costs	$10,400	
Budgeted denominator level of monthly production	800	output units

The total standard variable manufacturing costs per unit of $20 includes $11 for direct materials. For simplicity, we assume all fixed manufacturing costs are indirect product costs.

We assume work in process is minimal. There were no beginning or ending inventories of materials. On January 1, 2010, there was no beginning inventory of finished goods. To highlight the effect of the production-volume variance, we assume there were no price, efficiency, or spending variances for any costs in either January or February of 2010. The standard fixed manufacturing cost per unit is $16 ($12,800 ÷ 800). Thus, the key standard cost data per units of denominator-level capacity are:

Variable costs:
Standard variable manufacturing costs	$20
Standard variable marketing costs	19
Total variable costs	$39

Manufacturing costs:
Standard variable manufacturing costs	$20
Standard fixed manufacturing costs ($12,800 ÷ 800)	16
Total manufacturing costs	$36

Stassen expenses all variances to cost of goods sold in the accounting period in which they occur.

Assume that managers at Stassen receive a bonus based on reported monthly income. The following points illustrate how the choice between variable and

---

[2]For simplicity, we assume that Stassen Company uses a standard-costing system for all its operating costs—that is, it uses standards for both variable and fixed costs in both its manufacturing and marketing.

absorption costing will affect Stassen's reported monthly income and hence the bonuses its managers will receive.

COMPARATIVE INCOME STATEMENTS

Exhibit 9-6 contains the comparative income statements under variable costing (Panel A) and absorption costing (Panel B) for Stassen Company in January 2010 and February 2010. The operating income numbers are:

In Panel A, Variable Costing, all variable-cost line items are at standard cost except the adjustment for variances. This item would include all price, spending, and efficiency variances related to variable cost items (which are zero in our Stassen example).

	January 2010	February 2010
(1) Absorption costing	$4,000	$ 20,200
(2) Variable costing	800	21,800
(3) Difference = (1) − (2)	$3,200	$(1,600)

In Panel B, Absorption Costing, all cost of goods sold line items are at standard cost except the adjustment for variances. This item includes all manufacturing cost variances—price, spending, efficiency, and production-volume variances. Only the production-volume variance is nonzero in our Stassen example.

Keep the following points about absorption costing in mind as you study Panel B of Exhibit 9-6:

◆ The inventoriable costs are $36 per unit, not $20, because fixed manufacturing costs ($16), as well as variable manufacturing costs ($20), are assigned to each unit of product.

◆ The $16 fixed manufacturing cost rate was based on a denominator level of 800 units per month ($12,800 ÷ 800 = $16). Whenever actual *production* (not sales) volume varies from the denominator level of 800 units, a production-volume variance arises. This variance is the difference between actual and denominator-level volumes multiplied by $16, the rate.

◆ The production-volume variance, which relates to fixed manufacturing overhead, exists only under absorption costing and not under variable costing because fixed costs are not allocated in the variable costing method. All other variances exist under both absorption costing and variable costing.

◆ The absorption costing income statement classifies costs primarily by *business function*, such as manufacturing and marketing. In contrast, the variable costing income statement features *cost behaviour* (variable or fixed) as the basis of classification. Absorption costing income statements need not differentiate between the variable and fixed costs. Exhibit 9-6 does make this differentiation for Stassen Company to highlight how individual line items are classified differently under variable and absorption costing formats.

EXPLAINING DIFFERENCES IN OPERATING INCOME

If the inventory level increases during an accounting period, the value of total ending inventory increases more under the full absorption than variable valuation policy. The period cost, however, will be lower under the full absorption than variable valuation policy. The difference between operating income under absorption costing and variable costing can be computed by Formula 1, which is illustrated with Exhibit 9-6 data:[3]

[3]This formula assumes that the amounts used for beginning and ending inventory are after proration of manufacturing overhead variances.

EXHIBIT 9-6
Stassen Company: Comparison of Variable Costing and Absorption Costing Income
Statements for January 2010 and February 2010

	A	B	C
1	**PANEL A: VARIABLE COSTING**		
2		**January 2010**	**February 2010**
3	Revenue $99 × 400; 750 units	$39,600	$74,250
4	Variable costs:		
5	Beginning inventory $20 × 0; 200 units	0	4,000
6	Variable cost of goods manufactured $20 × 600; 650 units	12,000	13,000
7	Cost of goods available for sale	12,000	17,000
8	Ending inventory $20 × 200; 100 units	(4,000)	(2,000)
9	Variable manufacturing cost of goods sold	8,000	15,000
10	Variable marketing costs $19 × 400; 750 units	7,600	14,250
11	Total standard variable costs	15,600	29,250
12	Contribution margin (standard)	24,000	45,000
13	Adjustment for variable cost variances to COGS	0	0
14	Total variable costs	15,600	29,250
15	Contribution margin	24,000	45,000
16	Fixed costs:		
17	Fixed manufacturing costs	12,800	12,800
18	Fixed marketing costs	10,400	10,400
19	Total standard fixed costs	23,200	23,200
20	Adjustment for fixed cost variances	0	0
21	Total fixed costs	23,200	23,200
22	Operating income	$ 800	$21,800
23			
24	**PANEL B: ABSORPTION COSTING**		
25		**January 2010**	**February 2010**
26	Revenue $99 × 400; 750 units	$39,600	$74,250
27	Cost of goods sold		
28	Beginning inventory $36 × 0; 200 units	0	7,200
29	Variable manufacturing costs $20 × 600; 650 units	12,000	13,000
30	Allocated fixed manufacturing costs $16 × 600; 650 units	9,600	10,400
31	Cost of goods available for sale	21,600	30,600
32	Deduct ending inventory: $36 × 200; 100 units	(7,200)	(3,600)
33	Total standard cost of goods sold	14,400	27,000
34	Gross margin at standard	25,200	47,250
35	Adjustment for manufacturing variances to COGS*	3,200 U	2,400 U
36	Cost of goods sold	17,600	29,400
37	Gross margin	22,000	44,850
38	Marketing costs:		
39	Variable marketing costs $19 × 400; 750 units sold	7,600	14,250
40	Fixed marketing costs	10,400	10,400
41	Total standard marketing costs	18,000	24,650
42	Adjustment for marketing variances	0	0
43	Total marketing costs	18,000	24,650
44	Operating income	$ 4,000	$20,200
45			
46	*Production volume variance for January $16 × 200 where the denominator of 800 units exceeds the volume produced and the allocation rate is $12,800 ÷ 800 = $16/unit. Similarly, the production-volume variance for February is $16 × 150.		

Formula 1

$$\begin{pmatrix}\text{Absorption costing}\\\text{operating}\\\text{income}\end{pmatrix} - \begin{pmatrix}\text{Variable costing}\\\text{operating}\\\text{income}\end{pmatrix} = \begin{pmatrix}\text{Fixed manufacturing}\\\text{costs in}\\\text{ending inventory}\end{pmatrix} - \begin{pmatrix}\text{Fixed manufacturing}\\\text{costs in}\\\text{beginning inventory}\end{pmatrix}.$$

January 2010 $\qquad\qquad \$4,000 - \$800 = (200 \times \$16) - (0 \times \$16)$
$$\$3,200 = \$3,200$$
February 2010 $\qquad\quad \$20,200 - \$21,800 = (100 \times \$16) - (200 \times \$16)$
$$-\$1,600 = -\$1,600$$

Fixed manufacturing costs in ending inventory are a current-period expense under variable costing that absorption costing defers to future periods.

Two alternative formulas can be used if we assume that all manufacturing variances are written off as period costs, that no change occurs in work-in-process inventory, and that no change occurs in the budgeted fixed manufacturing overhead rate between accounting periods:

Formula 2

$$\begin{pmatrix}\text{Absorption costing}\\\text{operating}\\\text{income}\end{pmatrix} - \begin{pmatrix}\text{Variable costing}\\\text{operating}\\\text{income}\end{pmatrix} = \begin{pmatrix}\text{Units}\\\text{produced} - \text{Units}\\\text{sold}\end{pmatrix} \times \begin{pmatrix}\text{Budgeted fixed}\\\text{manufacturing}\\\text{cost rate}\end{pmatrix}$$

January 2010 $\qquad\qquad \$4,000 - \$800 = (600 - 400) \times \$16$
$$\$3,200 = \$3,200$$
February 2010 $\qquad\quad \$20,200 - \$21,800 = (650 - 750) \times \$16$
$$-\$1,600 = -\$1,600$$

Formula 3

$$\begin{pmatrix}\text{Absorption costing}\\\text{operating}\\\text{income}\end{pmatrix} - \begin{pmatrix}\text{Variable costing}\\\text{operating}\\\text{income}\end{pmatrix} = \begin{pmatrix}\text{Ending}\\\text{inventory} - \text{Beginning}\\\text{inventory}\\\text{in units}\quad\text{in units}\end{pmatrix} \times \begin{pmatrix}\text{Budgeted fixed}\\\text{manufacturing}\\\text{cost rate}\end{pmatrix}.$$

January 2010 $\qquad\qquad \$4,000 - \$800 = (200 - 0) \times \$16$
$$\$3,200 = \$3,200$$
February 2010 $\qquad\quad \$20,200 - \$21,800 = (100 - 200) \times \$16$
$$-\$1,600 = -\$1,600$$

EFFECT OF SALES AND PRODUCTION ON OPERATING INCOME

The period-to-period change in operating income under variable costing is driven solely by changes in the unit level of sales, given a constant contribution margin per unit. Consider for Stassen the variable costing operating income in February 2010 versus that in January 2010:

$$\begin{matrix}\text{Change in}\\\text{operating income}\end{matrix} = \begin{matrix}\text{Contribution}\\\text{margin}\end{matrix} \times \begin{matrix}\text{Change in unit}\\\text{sales level}\end{matrix}$$
$$\$21,800 - \$800 = (\$99 - \$39) \times (750 - 400)$$
$$\$21,000 = \$60 \times 350$$
$$\$21,000 = \$21,000$$

Note that under variable costing, Stassen managers cannot increase operating income (and hence their bonuses) by producing for inventory.

Under absorption costing, however, period-to-period change in operating income is driven by variations in *both* the unit level of sales and the unit level of production. Exhibit 9-7 illustrates this point. The exhibit shows how absorption costing operating income for February 2010 changes as the production level in February 2010 changes. This exhibit assumes that all variances (including the production-volume variance) are written off to cost of goods sold at the end of each accounting period. The beginning inventory in February 2010 of 200 units and the February sales of 750 units are unchanged. Exhibit 9-7 shows that production of only 550 units meets February 2010 sales of 750. Operating income at

EXHIBIT 9-7

Stassen Company: Effect on Absorption Costing Operating Income of Different Production Levels Holding the Unit Sales Level Constant—Data for February 2010 with Sales of 750 Units

	February 2010 Production Level				
	550	650	700	800	850
Unit data:					
Beginning inventory	200	200	200	200	200
Production	550	650	700	800	850
Goods available for sale	750	850	900	1,000	1,050
Sales	750	750	750	750	750
Ending inventory	0	100	150	250	300
Income statement:					
Revenues	$74,250	$74,250	$74,250	$74,250	$74,250
Beginning inventory	7,200	7,200	7,200	7,200	7,200
Variable manufacturing costs*	11,000	13,000	14,000	16,000	17,000
Fixed manufacturing costs[†]	8,800	10,400	11,200	12,800	13,600
Cost of goods available for sale	27,000	30,600	32,400	36,000	37,800
Ending inventory[‡]	0	3,600	5,400	9,000	10,800
Cost of goods sold (at standard cost)	27,000	27,000	27,000	27,000	27,000
Adjustment for manufacturing variances[§]	4,000 U	2,400 U	1,600 U	0	800 F
Total cost of goods sold	31,000	29,400	28,600	27,000	26,200
Gross margin	43,250	44,850	45,650	47,250	48,050
Total marketing and administrative costs	24,650	24,650	24,650	24,650	24,650
Operating income	$18,600	$20,200	$21,000	$22,600	$23,400

*$20 per unit.
[†]Assigned at $16 per unit.
[‡]$36 per unit.
[§](Production in units − 800) × $16. All written off to cost of goods sold at end of the accounting period.

this production level (column 1) is $18,600. By producing more than 550 units in February 2010, Stassen increases absorption costing operating income.

Each unit in February 2010 ending inventory will increase February operating income by $16. For example, if 800 units are produced, ending inventory will be 250 units and operating income will be $22,600. This amount is $4,000 more than what operating income is with zero ending inventory (250 units × $16 = $4,000) on February 28, 2010. Recall that Stassen's managers receive a bonus based on monthly operating income. Absorption costing enables them to increase operating income (and hence their bonuses) by producing for inventory.

Exhibit 9-7 illustrates how a Stassen manager could increase February 2010 operating income from $18,600 to $22,600 by producing an additional 250 units for inventory. This will increase the costs of doing business without an attendant increase in revenue obtained from additional sales. Managers whose performance evaluation and compensation are based on absorption costing income have incentives to increase production solely to increase reported income. Each additional unit produced absorbs fixed manufacturing costs that would otherwise have been written off as a cost of the period.

PERFORMANCE EVALUATION: UNDESIRABLE BUILDUP OF INVENTORIES

Absorption costing is the required inventory valuation method for external reporting in Canada, and to avoid any internal confusion that could arise by using a different valuation method for internal planning and control, most companies use one method for both internal and external purposes (see the Real Companies feature on p. 435). Using the same method for valuation and performance evaluation helps avoid situations wherein managers take action that enhances their individual evaluation but harms overall corporate performance. Absorption costing includes all production costs when valuing inventory that has been sold, and better informs the long-run pricing and product mix decisions. In the long run, the revenue must cover total costs plus generate profit if a company is to thrive.

Unfortunately, absorption costing can lead managers to increase operating income in the short run by increasing the production schedule independent of customer demand. In practice this is a well-known possibility and can be controlled either by monitoring the inventory levels or choosing a variable cost method for internal performance evaluation of the efficiency and effectiveness of manufacturing activities. See the Governance Issues feature (p. 436) to understand some external controls of inventory valuation practices and revenue recognition. The added advantage of variable costing is to reveal the cost–volume–profit relationships that improve the quality of information upon which managers make short-run decisions. Exhibit 9-8 compares the key differences between variable and absorption costing.

The undesirable effects of an increase in production in order to increase operating income in the short run by increasing end-of-period inventory may be sizable, and they can arise in several ways, as the following examples show:

◆ A plant manager may switch production to those orders that absorb the highest amount of fixed manufacturing costs, irrespective of the customer demand for these products (called "cherry picking" the production line). Some difficult-to-manufacture items may be delayed, resulting in failure to meet promised customer delivery dates.

◆ A plant manager may accept a particular order to increase production, even though another plant in the same company is better suited to handle that order.

◆ To meet increased production, a manager may defer maintenance beyond the current accounting period. Although operating income may increase now, future operating income will probably decrease because of increased repairs and less-efficient equipment.

EXHIBIT 9-8
Comparative Income Effects of Variable Costing and Absorption Costing

Question	Variable Costing	Absorption Costing	Comment
Are fixed manufacturing costs inventoried?	No	Yes	Basic theoretical question when these costs should be expensed as period costs.
Is there a production-volume variance?	No	Yes	Choice of denominator level affects measurement of operating income under absorption costing only.
How are the other variances treated?	Same	Same	Highlights that the basic difference is the accounting for fixed manufacturing costs, not the accounting for any variable manufacturing costs.
Are classifications between variable and fixed costs routinely made?	Yes	Not always	Absorption costing can be easily modified to obtain subclassifications for variable and fixed costs, if desired (for example, see Exhibit 9-5, Panel B).
How do changes in unit inventory levels affect operating income?			
Production = sales	Equal	Equal	Differences are attributable to the timing of when fixed manufacturing costs become period costs
Production > sales	Lower*	Higher†	
Production < sales	Higher	Lower	
What are the effects on cost-volume-profit relationships?	Driven by unit sales level	Driven by unit sales level and unit production level	Management control benefit: Effects of changes in production level on operating income are easier to understand under variable costing.

*That is, lower operating income than under absorption costing.
†That is, higher operating income than under variable costing.

Usage of Variable Costing and Absorption Costing by Companies

Surveys of company practice in the United States, Scandinavia, and Asia report that approximately 20% to 55% of companies use variable costing in their internal accounting systems. In addition, up to 30% of companies use both variable costing and absorption costing:

Surveys to date have not extensively examined the usage of throughput costing.

Many companies using variable costing for internal reporting, short-run decisions, and performance evaluation also use absorption costing for external reporting or tax reporting. Companies that use variable costing for internal accounting make an adjustment at the end of the quarter (for quarterly reporting) or at the end of the fiscal year (for annual reporting) to prorate fixed manufacturing overhead to inventory and cost of goods sold to prepare absorption-costing statements for external reporting. The most common problem reported by companies using variable costing is the difficulty of classifying costs into fixed or variable categories.

	China[a]	Estonia[b]	Finland[c]	India[d]	Malaysia[e]	Norway[f]	United States[g]
Variable costing used	32%	39%	42%	50%	23%	55%	24%
Absorption costing used	68	55	31	48	46	29	76
Both systems used	6	28	2	31	16	—	—

[a] M. Firth, "The Diffusion of Managerial Accounting Procedures in the People's Republic of China and the Influence of Foreign Partnered Joint Ventures," *Accounting Organizations and Society* (1996).

[b] T. Haldma and K. Lääts, "Contingencies Influencing the Management Accounting Practices of Estonian Manufacturing Companies," *Management Accounting Research* (2002).

[c] K. Lukka and M. Granlund, "Cost Accounting in Finland: Current Practice and Trends of Development," *The European Accounting Review* (1996).

[d] P. Joshi, "The International Diffusion of New Management Accounting Practices: The Case of India," *Journal of International Accounting, Auditing & Taxation* (2001).

[e] L.Chun, N. Kassim, and B. Minai, "Are Management Accounting Systems in Malaysia Outmoded?" *Singapore Management Review* (2000).

[f] T. Bjornenak, "Conventional Wisdom and Costing Practices," *Management Accounting Research* (1997).

[g] Ernst & Young, *2003 Survey of Management Accounting* (New York: Ernst & Young, March 2003).

Early criticisms of absorption costing concentrated on whether fixed manufacturing overhead qualified as an asset under GAAP. However, current criticisms of absorption costing have increasingly emphasized its potentially undesirable incentives for managers. Indeed, one critic labels absorption costing as "one of the black holes of cost accounting," in part because it may induce managers to make decisions "against the long-run interests" of the company.

PROPOSALS FOR REVISING PERFORMANCE EVALUATION

Critics of absorption costing have made a variety of proposals for revising how managers are evaluated. Their proposals include the following:

1. *Change the accounting system.* As discussed previously and will be shown later in this chapter, both variable and throughput costing reduce the incentives of managers to build up inventory.

2. *Careful budgeting and inventory planning* to reduce management's freedom to build up excess inventory. For example, the budgeted monthly balance sheets

have estimates of the dollar amount of inventories. If actual inventories exceed these dollar amounts, top management can investigate the inventory buildups.

3. *Incorporate a carrying charge for inventory* in the internal accounting system. For example, an inventory carrying charge of 1% per month could be assessed for the investment tied up in inventory, and for spoilage and obsolescence when evaluating a manager's performance.

4. *Change the time period used to evaluate performance.* Critics of absorption costing give examples where managers take actions that maximize quarterly or annual income at the potential expense of long-run income. By evaluating performance over a three-to-five-year period, the incentive to take short-run actions that reduce long-term income is reduced.

5. *Include nonfinancial as well as financial variables in the measures used to evaluate performance.* Companies currently are using nonfinancial variables, such as the following, drawn from the Stassen data:

(a) $\dfrac{\text{Ending inventory in units February 2010}}{\text{Beginning inventory in units February 2010}} = \dfrac{100}{200} = 0.5$

(b) $\dfrac{\text{Units produced in February 2010}}{\text{Units sold in February 2010}} = \dfrac{650}{750} = 0.867$

A good report of manufacturing performance would show not only stable inventory ratios of outputs over time for each product, but also a production to sales-volume ratio very close to 1 to indicate all production and inventory was sold during the period it was produced. Of course, these nonfinancial ratios would also be interpreted in light of, for example, fluctuations due to seasonal demand, perishability, and other factors appropriate to a specific manufacturing situation.

GOVERNANCE ISSUES

Inventory Strategy Bites Back

Answers to denominator-level policy and costing policy issues are not clear-cut. Management accountants may face pressure from managers to make choices that increase (or sometimes decrease) operating income. Between 1999 and 2001, Bristol-Myers Squibb (BMS) produced much more product than it sold to consumers. This action increased operating income under absorption costing. But BMS went much further, by offering incentives to wholesalers to build their inventories and then recording deliveries to wholesalers as revenues—an illegal practice called channelling. This step allowed BMS to meet its quarterly revenue forecasts. Following an investigation, the U.S. Department of Justice and the Securities and Exchange Commission concluded that the loading of inventories onto wholesalers could not be recognized as revenue. BMS was charged with overstating revenues by US$2.5 billion from 1999 through 2001. In a 2004 interview, chief financial officer Andrew Bonfield stated that the company was working to "improve the transparency and quality of its financial disclosures." The Board of Directors failed in its corporate governance duty to BMS, but this does not remove responsibility from management accountants who also had a professional obligation not to produce misleading reports.

Source: Barbara Martinez, "Bristol-Myers Again Restates Results," *Wall Street Journal*, March 16, 2004.

MyAccountingLab

ASSESS YOUR MASTERY

To check your understanding of the material in Learning Objective ③, go to the *Mastery Questions* section at the end of this chapter and complete Learning Objective ③ questions 1, 2, and 3.

Distinguish throughput costing from variable costing and absorption costing, and explain differences in operating income under each costing policy

4

Some critics of existing costing systems maintain that even variable costing materially overstates operating income and provides a perverse incentive to produce into inventory to decrease the COGS expense. They argue that only direct materials are "truly variable" with respect to volume (quantity) of units produced, and ideally the quantity of units produced should meet the quantity demanded by customers. Production managers can rarely control direct materials and labour prices, or fixed manufacturing overhead, but they can control direct materials efficiency variances by matching volumes produced as closely as possible to volumes demanded.

To reward efficient and effective production, **throughput costing** (also called **super-variable costing**) treats all costs except variable direct materials as period costs that are expensed when they are incurred. Only variable direct materials costs are inventoriable. All overhead and labour costs are not considered as a source of future benefit for internal planning and control purposes. All other things equal, this method is most conservative and leads to the lowest internally reported operating income in comparison to either variable or absorption costing. As you can see from Exhibit 9-9, each unsold unit reduces the throughput contribution by $88, a decrease of $11 in cost, but a larger decrease of $99 in lost revenue for a net loss of $88. It is the difference in rate of change of revenue and cost that reduces operating income by another $88.

When innovation cycles are very short, obsolescence can occur almost overnight and the assumption that unsold production is unlikely to produce future benefit may be appropriate. In situations such as this, achieving expected profit

EXHIBIT 9-9
Throughput Costing for Stassen Company

A	B	C
1		January 2010	February 2010
2	**Unit Data Production:**	600	650
3	**Unit Data Sales:**	400	750
4 Income Statement:		
5 Revenue $99 × 400; 750	$39,600	$74,250
6 Variable direct materials costs:		
7 Beginning inventory $11 × 0; 200 units	0	2,200
8 Direct materials in goods manufactured $11 × 600; 650	6,600	7,150
9 Cost of goods available for sale	6,600	9,350
10 Ending inventory $11 × 200; 100	(2,200)	(1,100)
11 Direct materials standard cost	4,400	8,250
12 Adjustment for direct materials variances	0	0
13 Total variable direct materials costs	4,400	8,250
14 Throughput contribution*	35,200	66,000
15 Other costs:		
16 Manufacturing $12,800 + ($9 × 600; 650)	18,200	18,650
17 Marketing $10,400 + ($19 × 400; 750)	18,000	24,650
18 Adjustment for variances	0	0
19 Total other costs	36,200	43,300
20 Operating income	$ (1,000)	$22,700
21		
22 *Throughput contribution is the difference between revenues and variable direct materials costs		

targets requires an intense focus on minimizing period costs incurred due to the production of unsold units. This is a more recently designed method of inventory valuation and is not widely adopted.[4]

Exhibit 9-9 is the throughput costing income statement for Stassen Company. Compare the operating income amounts reported with those for absorption and variable costing:

	Absorption Costing	Variable Costing	Throughput Costing
January 2010	$ 4,000	$ 800	$ (1,000)
February 2010	20,200	21,800	22,700

Only the $11 direct materials cost per unit is inventoriable under throughput costing (compared with $36 for absorption costing and $20 for variable costing). Where production exceeds sales (as in January 2010), throughput costing results in the largest amount of costs being expensed to the current period. Throughput contribution in Exhibit 9-9 is revenues minus all variable direct materials costs.

Advocates of throughput costing maintain there is reduced incentive for building up excess inventories compared to when variable or (especially) absorption costing is used. Reducing inventory levels means less funds are tied up in inventory and hence more funds are available to invest in productive outlets. Moreover, reducing inventory levels typically means reducing inventory spoilage and obsolescence costs.

OVERVIEW OF THREE COSTING POLICIES

Variable costing, absorption costing, and throughput costing may be combined with actual, normal, or standard costing. Exhibit 9-10 presents a capsule comparison of a job-costing record under nine alternative inventory costing systems:

Variable Costing	Absorption Costing	Throughput Costing
1. Actual costing	4. Actual costing	7. Actual costing
2. Normal costing	5. Normal costing	8. Normal costing
3. Standard costing	6. Standard costing	9. Standard costing

The data in Exhibit 9-10 represent the debits to job-costing account(s) (that is, the amounts assigned to products) under alternative inventory costing systems.

Variable costing has been a controversial subject among accountants—not so much because there is disagreement about the need for delineating between variable and fixed costs for management planning and control, but because there is a question about using variable costing for external reporting. Those favouring variable costing for external reporting maintain that the fixed portion of manufacturing costs is more closely related to the capacity to produce than to the production of specific units. Supporters of absorption costing maintain that inventories should carry a fixed manufacturing cost component. Why? Since both variable and fixed manufacturing costs are necessary to produce goods, both types of costs should be inventoriable, regardless of their having different behaviour patterns.

Absorption costing (or variants close to it) is the method required to achieve the external regulatory purpose of accounting systems. For example, when companies whose shares are traded on the Toronto Stock Exchange report financial results to the Ontario Securities Commission, generally accepted accounting principles as stated in the *CICA Handbook* must be followed. Thus, all manufacturing costs plus some product overhead must be included as inventoriable costs. Overhead costs must be allocated between those costs related to manufacturing activities (inventoriable costs) and those not related to manufacturing activities. For external reporting to shareholders, companies around the globe tend to follow the generally accepted accounting principle that all manufacturing overhead is inventoriable.

[4]See E. Goldratt, *The Theory of Constraints* (New York: North River Press, 1990); E. Noreen, D. Smith, and J. Mackey, *The Theory of Constraints and Its Implications for Management Accounting* (New York: North River Press, 1995).

		Actual Costing	Normal Costing	Standard Costing
Absorption Costing → Variable Costing → Throughput Costing	Variable Direct Materials Costs	Actual prices × Actual quantity of inputs used	Actual prices × Actual quantity of inputs used	Standard prices × Standard quantity of inputs allowed for actual output achieved
	Variable Direct Conversion* Costs	Actual prices × Actual quantity of inputs used	Actual prices × Actual quantity of inputs used	Standard prices × Standard quantity of inputs allowed for actual output achieved
	Variable Manufacturing Overhead Costs	Actual variable overhead rate × Actual quantity of cost-allocation bases used	Budgeted variable overhead rates × Actual quantity of cost-allocation bases used	Standard variable overhead rates × Standard quantity of cost-allocation bases allowed for actual output achieved
	Fixed Direct Manufacturing Costs	Actual prices × Actual quantity of inputs used	Actual prices × Actual quantity of inputs used	Standard prices × Standard quantity of inputs allowed for actual output achieved
	Fixed Manufacturing Overhead Costs	Actual fixed overhead rates × Actual quantity of cost-allocation bases used	Budgeted fixed overhead rates × Actual quantity of cost-allocation bases used	Standard fixed overhead rates × Standard quantity of cost-allocation bases allowed for actual output achieved

*Conversion costs are all manufacturing costs minus direct materials costs.

Throughput costing is not permitted for the external regulatory purpose of accounting systems if it results in materially different numbers to those reported by absorption costing. Advocates of throughput costing emphasize the internal purposes of management accounting data.

ASSESS YOUR MASTERY

To check your understanding of the material in Learning Objective ④, go to the *Mastery Questions* section at the end of this chapter and complete Learning Objective ④ questions 1, 2, and 3.

MyAccountingLab

PRODUCTIVITY UNDER EACH COST POLICY

> Explain productivity measurement under each of the three costing policies ⑤

Chapter 3 introduced cost-volume-profit analysis. If variable costing is used, the breakeven point (operating income of $0) is computed in the usual manner. There is only one breakeven point in this case, and it is a function of

◆ fixed costs,
◆ contribution margin per unit, and
◆ unit level of sales.

Holding fixed cost and unit contribution margin constant, operating income rises as the level of sales rises. The formula for computing the breakeven point with variable costing is a special case of the more general target operating income formula from Chapter 3 (pp. 96–97):

$$Q = \frac{\text{Total fixed costs} + \text{Target operating income}}{\text{Contribution margin per unit}}$$

$$= \text{Number of units sold to earn the target operating income}$$

Breakeven occurs when the target operating income is $0. In our Stassen illustration for 2010 (see p. 431):

$$Q = \frac{(\$12,800 + \$10,400) + \$0}{\$99 - (\$20 + \$19)} = \frac{\$23,200}{\$60}$$

$$= 387 \text{ units (rounded)}[5]$$

If absorption costing is used, the required number of units sold to achieve a specific target operating income is not unique because of the number of variables involved. The following formula highlights the factors that will affect the target operating income under absorption costing:

$$Q = \frac{\begin{array}{c}\text{Total} \\ \text{fixed} \\ \text{costs}\end{array} + \begin{array}{c}\text{Target} \\ \text{operating} \\ \text{income}\end{array} + \left[\begin{array}{c}\text{Fixed} \\ \text{manufacturing} \\ \text{cost rate}\end{array} \times \left(\begin{array}{c}\text{Breakeven} \\ \text{sales} \\ \text{in units}\end{array} - \begin{array}{c}\text{Units} \\ \text{produced}\end{array}\right)\right]}{\text{Contribution margin per unit}}$$

This formula has three terms in the numerator compared with two terms in the numerator of the variable-costing formula stated earlier. In this formula, total fixed costs include all manufacturing and nonmanufacturing fixed costs. The extra term added to the numerator under absorption costing is as follows:

$$\left[\begin{array}{c}\text{Fixed manufacturing} \\ \text{cost rate}\end{array} \times \left(\begin{array}{c}\text{Breakeven sales} \\ \text{in units}\end{array} - \begin{array}{c}\text{Units} \\ \text{produced}\end{array}\right)\right]$$

This term captures the additional amount of target operating income in the numerator due to absorption costing moving fixed manufacturing costs to inventory from cost of goods sold under variable costing for all units produced that exceed the breakeven sales quantity. The breakeven point is defined as the quantity for which the target operating income is $0. This formula shows that under absorption costing there is still a unique breakeven point for each quantity of units produced.

There is also an inverse relationship (as one goes up the other goes down) between the quantity of units produced and the required quantity of units sold to breakeven. The higher the quantity of units produced, the higher the level of fixed manufacturing overhead costs absorbed into finished goods inventory and the higher the COGS. The period costs remain unchanged, therefore the quantity of units that must be sold to cover these costs too (and break even) will decrease.

Consider Stassen Company in 2010. One breakeven point under absorption costing for production of 500 units is as follows:

$$Q = \frac{(\$12,800 + \$10,400) + \$0 + [\$16(Q - 500)]}{\$99 - (\$20 + \$19)}$$

$$= \frac{\$23,200 + \$16Q - \$8,000}{\$60}$$

$$\$60Q = \$15,200 + \$16Q$$
$$\$44Q = \$15,200$$
$$Q = 346 \text{ (rounded)}$$

The breakeven point under absorption costing depends on the:

◆ fixed costs,
◆ contribution margin per unit,

[5]Operating income is not $0 because the breakeven number of units is rounded up to 387 from 386.67.

Proof of breakeven point:

Revenues, $99 × 387	$38,313
Variable costs, $39 × 387	15,093
Contribution margin, $60 × 387	23,220
Fixed costs	23,200
Operating income	$ 20

- unit level of sales,
- unit level of production, and
- overhead cost rate.

For Stassen in 2010, a combination of 346 units sold, 500 units produced, and an 800-unit denominator level would result in an operating income of $0.[6] Note, however, that there are many combinations of these five factors that would give an operating income of $0. For example, a combination of 291 units sold, 650 units produced, and an 800-unit denominator level also results in an operating income of $0 under absorption costing.

Suppose in our illustration that actual production in 2010 was equal to the denominator level, 800 units. Also suppose that there were no units sold and no fixed operating costs. All the production would be placed in inventory, and so all the fixed manufacturing overhead would be included in inventory. There would be no production-volume variance. Thus, the company would break even with no sales whatsoever! In contrast, under variable costing the operating loss would be equal to the fixed manufacturing costs of $12,800.

REAL COMPANIES

Inventory Valuation—External versus Internal

Analog Devices, Inc. (ADI) produces integrated circuits and systems used in computers, broadband modems, medical instruments, and consumer electronics. It is a leading semiconductor company with 2007 revenues of over US$2.5 billion and 50,000 customers worldwide.

Improving yield—the quantity of good die produced on a silicon wafer divided by the total number of die that could be printed and produced on the wafer—is critical to delivering high-quality products at low cost. For internal-reporting purposes, ADI uses variable costing. For external reporting, fixed costs are allocated to products. The denominator level used to allocate standard fixed overhead costs to products is practical machine capacity assuming efficient operations (e.g., machines work six hours per day). What if

four hours will fill actual demand because of improved yield? Financially, this will cause an unfavourable production-volume variance. The higher the yields, the fewer machine hours will be required (see Chapter 10 for a discussion of learning curve effects). With less spoilage and waste, fewer silicon wafers need to be started to get the desired output. Costs in inventory decrease but the unfavourable production-volume variance increases. As the production-volume variance is written off to cost of goods sold at year-end, profit margins decline. Thus, quality improvements can have negative operating-income effects!

The performance of planners at ADI was evaluated more on satisfying customer orders than reducing inventory levels. As yields improved, they waited to reduce the number of wafer starts in the denominator-level until they were sure higher yields would continue. ADI's chairman and president warned, "Unless quality improvement and other more-fundamental performance measures are elevated to the same level of importance as financial measures, when conflicts arise, financial considerations win out." ADI continued to improve yield and it also developed performance measures that gave incentives to planners and managers to avoid producing to inventory simply to absorb more fixed overhead costs. This strategy has proven very successful.

Source: Analog Devices: The Half-Life System, Harvard Business School case number 9-190-061; Analog Devices, Inc., 2007 Annual Report; and discussions with company management.

ASSESS YOUR MASTERY

To check your understanding of the material in Learning Objective ⑤ , go to the *Mastery Questions* section at the end of this chapter and complete Learning Objective ⑤ question 1.

---

[6]Operating income is not $0 because the breakeven number of units is rounded up to 346 from 345.45.

PROBLEM

Suppose that Bushells Company from our chapter example is computing the operating income for May 2011. This month is identical to May 2010, the results of which are in Exhibit 9-4 (p. 420), except that master-budget capacity utilization for 2011 is 600,000 bottles per month instead of 400,000 bottles. There was no beginning inventory on May 1, 2011, and no variances other than the production-volume variance. Bushells writes off this variance to cost of goods sold each month.

REQUIRED

1. Identify the four potential denominator levels and calculate each fixed overhead rate.
2. Calculate the new production-volume variance for the new master-budget denominator level and explain the CRA effect of the production-volume variance.
3. How would the financial results in Exhibit 9-4 for Bushells Company be different if the month is May 2011 rather than May 2010? Show your computations.
4. Explain what the higher master-budget denominator level means.
5. What changes would adopting a variable inventory valuation method mean to the internal reports of COGS and period expense?
6. What change would adopting a throughput inventory valuation method mean to the internal reports of COGS and period expense?
7. Calculate a breakeven for Bushells (there is no unique solution).

SOLUTION

1. The four possible levels are theoretical, practical, normal, and master budget. The rates are calculated by dividing $50,000 by 1,152,000, 800,000, 500,000, and 600,000. All but the master-budget rate are in Exhibit 9-4. The rates are $0.0434, $0.0625, $0.1000, and $0.0833.

$$\frac{\$50,000}{600,000 \text{ bottles}} = \$0.0833 \text{ per bottle}$$

2. The manufacturing cost per bottle becomes $0.4333 ($0.3500 + $0.0833). In turn, the production volume variance for May 2011 becomes:

$$(600,000 - 460,000) \times (\$0.0833) = \$11,662 \text{ U}$$

The master-budget level conforms with CRA regulations. The unfavourable production-volume variance must be prorated over the inventory remaining in finished goods. The unfavourable variance increases the finished goods inventory value, which is subtracted from COGS. A lower COGS will be reported for tax purposes and therefore a higher taxable income.

3. The income statement for May 2011 is now

Revenues	$210,000
Cost of goods sold:	
Beginning inventory	0
Variable manufacturing costs:	
$0.35 × 460,000	161,000
Fixed manufacturing costs:	
$0.0833 × 460,000	38,318
Cost of goods available for sale	199,318
Ending inventory:	
$0.4333 × (460,000 − 420,000)	17,332
Total cost of goods sold (at standard costs)	181,986
Adjustment for variances	11,662 U
Total cost of goods sold	193,648
Gross margin	16,352
Marketing, other expenses	10,000
Operating income	$ 6,352

4. The higher denominator level in the 2011 master budget means that a temporary set of circumstances has led Bushells to expect a higher than normal denominator-level of sales and production in 2011. The normal denominator-level is based on a longer-term expected average demand.

5. For purposes of external reporting, the use of variable inventory valuation does not comply either with GAAP or with CRA, which both require absorption inventory valuation. Variable inventory valuation collects all manufacturing and nonmanufacturing costs incurred during a production time period and allocates this total variable cost pool to each unit remaining in finished goods inventory. All fixed manufacturing and nonmanufacturing costs are deducted as period expenses. This method will make it easier for Bushells to calculate a breakeven volume.

6. Throughput inventory valuation collects only the direct materials costs during a production time period and these are traced to each unit of output remaining in finished goods inventory. All other costs are treated as period costs. Very likely, the immediate recognition of all variable and fixed cost pools during the period they were incurred will reduce the internally reported operating income.

7. There is no *unique* solution—the answer will depend on assumptions made.

DECISION POINTS

The following decision guidelines use a question-and-answer format to summarize the chapter's main points. Each decision presents a key question. The guideline is the answer to that question.

DECISIONS	GUIDELINES
1. What are the various capacity levels a company can use to calculate budgeted fixed manufacturing cost rate?	Capacity levels can be measured in terms of what a plant can supply—theoretical capacity or practical capacity. Capacity can also be measured in terms of demand for the output of a plant—normal capacity utilization or master-budget capacity utilization. When the chosen capacity level exceeds the actual production level, there will be an unfavourable production-volume variance; when the chosen capacity level is less than the actual production level, there will be a favourable production-volume variance.
2. What are the major factors managers consider when choosing the capacity level to compute the budgeted fixed overhead cost rate?	The major factors managers consider when choosing the capacity level to compute the budgeted fixed manufacturing cost per unit are (a) the effect on product costing and capacity management, (b) the effect on pricing decisions, (c) the effect on performance evaluation, (d) the effect on financial statements, (e) regulatory requirements, and (f) difficulties in forecasting chosen capacity-level concepts.
3. How do level of sales and level of production affect operating income under variable costing and absorption costing?	Under variable costing, operating income is driven by the unit level of sales. Under absorption costing, operating income is driven by the unit level of production, as well as by the unit level of sales.
4. How does throughput costing differ from variable costing and absorption costing?	Throughput costing treats all costs except direct materials as costs of the period in which they are incurred. Throughput costing results in a lower amount of manufacturing costs being inventoried than either variable or absorption costing.
5. How is a breakeven calculation affected by using absorption costing?	The target operating income at breakeven is $0 and there is no unique solution because a number of values change at the same time, including fixed costs, contribution margin per unit, sales quantity, production quantity, and the overhead cost rates. Many values for these factors can combine to give an operating income of $0.

This chapter contains definitions of the following important terms:

absorption costing (p. 424)	non-productive idle capacity (p. 417)	theoretical capacity (p. 414)
direct costing (p. 429)	normal capacity (p. 414)	throughput costing (p. 437)
downward demand spiral (p. 422)	off-limits idle capacity (p. 416)	variable costing (p. 425)
full absorption costing (p. 424)	practical capacity (p. 414)	
master-budget capacity (p. 414)	super-variable costing (p. 437)	

MASTERY QUESTIONS

The Mastery Questions are rated by proficiency level—elementary, intermediate, and advanced. The solutions appear in the Solutions to Mastery Questions section of MyAccountingLab.

LEARNING OBJECTIVE 1

1. **Capacity-level (denominator) choices—Elementary.** Each of the following items is identified by a number:

   1. Should be used for performance evaluation
   2. Measures the denominator level in terms of demand for the output of the plant
   3. Represents the expected level of capacity utilization for the next budget period
   4. Is based on producing at full efficiency all the time
   5. Takes into account seasonal, cyclical, and trend factors
   6. Measures the denominator level in terms of what a plant can supply
   7. Represents an ideal benchmark
   8. Highlights the cost of capacity acquired but not used
   9. Hides the cost of capacity acquired but not used
   10. Should be used for long-term pricing purposes
   11. If used as the denominator-level concept, would avoid the restatement of unit costs when expected demand levels change

   REQUIRED
   Match each of the items above with one or more of the following denominator-level capacity concepts by putting appropriate letter(s) by each number:
   a. Theoretical capacity
   b. Practical capacity
   c. Normal capacity utilization
   d. Master-budget capacity utilization

2. **Capacity-level (denominator) choices—Intermediate.** Finn and Sawyer Company employs five individuals for its bill-processing activity. Each of the employees is paid an annual salary of $36,000. The budgeted annual activity output of bill processing is 6,000 bills per employee. All other costs in the bill-processing activity are variable and are budgeted at $27,000 for the year. During the year, 26,000 bills were actually processed.

   REQUIRED
   1. Calculate the budgeted fixed rate, budgeted variable rate, and the budgeted rate for bill-processing activity.
   2. Compute the total capacity available in bill-processing activity in units.
   3. Compute the unused capacity in bill-processing activity in units.
   4. Calculate the total cost of bill-processing capacity supplied, the cost of used capacity of bill-processing activity, and the cost of unused capacity of bill-processing activity.

3. **Capacity-level (denominator) choices—Advanced.** Lucky Lager recently purchased a brewing plant from a bankrupt company. It was constructed only two years ago. The plant has budgeted fixed manufacturing overhead of $50 million per year ($4.167 million each month) in 2010. Paul Vautin, the controller of the brewery, must decide on the denominator-level concept to use in its absorption costing system for 2010. The options available to him are

   a. Theoretical capacity: 600 barrels an hour for 24 hours a day for 365 days = 5,256,000 barrels
   b. Practical capacity: 500 barrels an hour for 20 hours a day for 350 days = 3,500,000 barrels

c. Normal capacity utilization for 2010: 400 barrels an hour for 20 hours a day for 350 days = 2,800,000 barrels

d. Master-budget capacity utilization for 2010 (separate rates computed for each half-year):

- ◆ January to June 2010 budget—320 barrels an hour for 20 hours a day for 175 days = 1,120,000 barrels
- ◆ July to December 2010 budget—480 barrels an hour for 20 hours a day for 175 days = 1,680,000 barrels

Variable standard manufacturing costs per barrel are $51.40 (variable direct materials, $38.40; variable manufacturing labour, $6.00; and variable manufacturing overhead, $7.00). The brewery "sells" its output to the sales division of Lucky Lager at a budgeted price of $82.00 per barrel.

REQUIRED

1. Compute the budgeted fixed manufacturing overhead rate using each of the four denominator-level concepts for (a) beer produced in March 2010 and (b) beer produced in September 2010. Explain why any differences arise.
2. Explain why the theoretical capacity and practical capacity concepts are different.
3. Which denominator-level concept would the plant manager of the brewery prefer when senior management of Lucky Lager is judging plant manager performance during 2010? Explain.

LEARNING OBJECTIVE 2

1. Effects of denominator—Elementary. Shen Company is a manufacturer of MP3 players. It implemented standard costs and a flexible budget on January 1, 2009. The president has been pondering how fixed manufacturing overhead should be allocated to products. Machine-hours have been chosen as the allocation base. Her remaining uncertainty is the denominator level for machine-hours. She decides to wait for the first month's results before making a final choice of what denominator level should be used from that day forward.

In January 2009, the actual units of output had a standard of 28,000 machine-hours allowed. If the company used practical capacity as the denominator level, the fixed manufacturing overhead spending variance would be $4,000, unfavourable, and the production-volume variance would be $14,400, unfavourable. If the company used normal capacity utilization as the denominator level, the production-volume variance would be $8,000, favourable. Budgeted fixed manufacturing overhead was $48,000 for the month.

REQUIRED

1. Compute the denominator level, assuming that the normal-capacity-utilization concept is chosen.
2. Compute the denominator level, assuming that the practical-capacity concept is chosen.
3. Suppose you are the executive vice president. You want to maximize your 2009 bonus, which depends on 2009 operating income. Assume that the production-volume variance is written off to cost of goods sold at year end. Which denominator level would you favour? Why?

2. Effects of denominator—Intermediate (continuation of Mastery Question 3 for Learning Objective 1). In 2010, the brewery of Lucky Lager showed these results:

Unit data in barrels:

Beginning inventory, January 1, 2010	0
Production	2,600,000
Ending inventory, December 31, 2010	200,000

The brewery had actual costs of

Cost data:

Variable manufacturing	$144,456,000
Fixed manufacturing overhead	$ 48,758,400

The sales division of Lucky Lager purchased 2,400,000 barrels in 2010 at the $82 per barrel rate. All manufacturing variances are written off to cost of goods sold in the period in which they are incurred.

REQUIRED

1. Compute the operating income of the brewery using the following: (a) theoretical capacity, (b) practical capacity, and (c) normal capacity utilization denominator-level capacity concepts. Explain any differences between (a), (b), and (c).

2. What denominator-level concept would Lucky Lager prefer for income tax reporting? Explain.
3. Explain the ways in which the Canada Revenue Agency might restrict the flexibility of a company like Lucky Lager, which uses absorption costing to reduce its reported taxable income.

3. **Effects of denominator—Advanced.** Deli One operates a chain of 10 retirement homes in the Toronto area. Its central food-catering facility, Deliman, prepares and delivers meals to the retirement homes. It has the capacity to deliver up to 1,460,000 meals a year. In 2009, based on estimates from each retirement-home controller, Deliman budgeted for 1,022,000 meals a year. Budgeted fixed costs in 2009 were $1,533,000. Each retirement home was charged $6.00 per meal—$4.50 variable costs plus $1.50 allocated budgeted fixed cost.

Recently, the retirement homes have been complaining about the quality of Deliman's meals and their rising costs. In mid-2009, Deli One's president announces that all Deli One retirement homes and support facilities will be run as profit centres. Retirement homes will be free to purchase quality-certified services from outside the system. Ron Smith, Deliman's controller, is preparing the 2010 budget. He hears that three retirement homes have decided to use outside suppliers for their meals; this will reduce the 2010 estimated demand to 876,000 meals. No change in variable cost per meal or total fixed costs is expected in 2010.

In 2010, only 806,840 Deliman meals were produced and sold to the retirement homes. Smith suspects that retirement-home controllers had systematically inflated their 2010 meal estimates.

REQUIRED
1. Deliman uses the master-budget capacity utilization to allocate fixed costs and to price meals. What was the effect of production-volume variance on Deliman's operating income in 2010?
2. Why might retirement-home controllers deliberately overestimate their future meal counts?
3. What other evidence should Deli One's controller seek to investigate his concerns?
4. Suggest two specific steps that Deli One's controller might take to reduce retirement-home controllers' incentives to inflate their estimated meal counts.

LEARNING OBJECTIVE 3

1. **Absorption from variable inventory costing—Elementary.** Nascar Motors assembles and sells motor vehicles. It uses an actual costing system, in which unit costs are calculated each month. Data relating to April and May of 2010 are:

	April	May
Unit data:		
Beginning inventory	0	150
Production	500	400
Sales	350	520
Variable cost data:		
Manufacturing costs per unit produced	$12,000	$12,000
Marketing costs per unit sold	3,000	3,000
Fixed cost data:		
Manufacturing costs	$2,000,000	$2,000,000
Marketing costs	600,000	600,000

The selling price per vehicle is $28,800.

REQUIRED
1. Present income statements for Nascar Motors in April and May of 2010 under (a) variable costing and (b) absorption costing.
2. Prepare a numerical reconciliation and explanation of the difference between operating income for each month under absorption costing and variable costing.

2. **Absorption from variable inventory costing—Intermediate.** Sonnenheim Bamberger is a German pharmaceutical company that provides a single drug—Mimic™—for the treatment of hair loss in men. Sonnenheim began commercial production of Mimic on January 1, 2010. Patients use three pills per day (365 days a year). Sonnenheim marketing analysts estimate 50,000 patients will use Mimic in 2010. Production in 2010 is 54,750,000 units (pills). However, only 44,800 patients are prescribed Mimic during 2010. Each patient used three pills per day for 365 days a year. The average wholesale selling price (the price Sonnenheim receives from distributors) is $1.44 per pill. Sonnenheim's actual costs are as follows:

Variable costs per unit	
Manufacturing costs *per pill produced*	$0.06
Direct materials	0.04

Direct manufacturing labour	0.11	
Manufacturing overhead	0.07	
Marketing costs *per pill sold*		
Fixed costs		
Manufacturing costs	$ 7,358,400	
R&D	4,905,000	
Marketing	19,622,400	

REQUIRED

1. What is the number of Mimic pills actually sold in 2010, assuming all patients began using the drug on January 1 and used it through December 31? What is Sonnenheim's ending inventory on December 31, 2010?

2. Calculate operating income under variable costing and absorption costing for Sonnenheim Bamberger for the year ended December 31, 2010. The allocation base for fixed manufacturing costs under absorption costing is $0.15 per unit (pill) produced. All variances are written off to cost of goods sold.

3. Explain differences in operating income in requirement 2.

3. Absorption from variable inventory costing—Advanced. Iotera Inc. manufactures flash drives for the portable personal computer market. Iotera's products are very popular and have attracted an almost cult-like following among laptop warriors and PDA (personal digital assistant) junkies. Iotera's chief competitor, Sybest, is based in Silicon Valley, California. Iotera is currently engaged in a vicious price war with Sybest. Unfortunately, Iotera must also contend with rapidly dropping prices for high-tech consumer products.

Iotera manufactures three products—Duda, a 2 Gb flash drive; Rock, a 5 Gb flash drive that comes in novelty shapes; and Funky, a 10 Gb flash drive. Once the darling of Wall Street, bad times have come to Iotera. Management is now questioning the profitability of each product and would like to discontinue any product that has a gross profit margin percentage lower than 10%.

Iotera's current cost-accounting system is rather simplistic. The single overhead allocation base is direct labour-hours. The allocation rate per hour is calculated by summing variable and fixed overhead costs and dividing by the number of direct labour-hours. Product cost is calculated by multiplying the number of direct labour-hours required to manufacture the product by the overhead rate and adding this amount to the direct labour and direct materials costs.

Budgeted cost data for 2010 for Iotera are:

Budgeted Cost Data for Iotera Inc. in 2010

Total overhead costs	$5,191,690	
Total labour-hours	60,089	
Allocation rate per labour-hour	?	

	Duda	Rock	Funky	Iotera Inc.
Product characteristics				
Direct labour-hours per 10 units	1	?	10	
Total units produced	123,190	72,600	?	?
Total labour-hours spent	?	?	4,210	60,089
Product costs				
Direct materials per unit	$19.44	$107.76	$221.52	
Direct labour per unit @ $21.60 per hour	?	?	?	
Allocated overhead per unit	?	?	?	
Total product costs	?	?	?	
Average selling price	$47.76	$190.80	$384.00	
Gross margin per unit	?	?	?	
Total revenues	?	?	?	?
Total costs	?	?	?	?
Operating income	?	?	?	?

REQUIRED

1. What is the overhead allocation rate per labour-hour? Will Iotera discontinue any product? Iotera would redirect all available capacity freed up from dropping a product to the most profitable product in total dollar terms that is retained. Complete the budgeted cost data table to answer this question.

2. Consider the products Iotera will produce after any decisions in requirement 1. It now considers average selling prices for 2010 as follows: Duda, $52.20; Rock, $210.50; and Funky, $468.00. Compute the profitability of each product using the new selling prices; will Iotera discontinue any product?

3. Consider what products Iotera will produce after any decisions in requirements 1 and 2. Assume that anything produced can be sold, and that total overhead is unchanged at $5,191,690. Due to packaging and warehouse constraints, Iotera's capacity is limited to the production of 200,000 units in 2010 (each product produced constitutes a single unit, regardless of product type).
   a. Recalculate costs and gross margins under this scenario.
   b. Will Iotera consider dropping any additional products?
   c. How has the overhead allocation rate changed?
   d. What has happened to the profit margins on the remaining products, and how has this affected Iotera's total gross profits?

4. What recommendations would you make to management regarding the current product-costing system and product decision policies?

LEARNING OBJECTIVE 4

1. **Throughput—Elementary.** Refer to Mastery Question 1 for Learning Objective 3. The unit variable manufacturing costs of Nascar Motors are:

	April	May
Direct materials	$8,040	$8,040
Direct manufacturing labour	1,500	1,500
Manufacturing overhead	1,800	1,800

REQUIRED

1. Present income statements for Nascar Motors in April and May of 2010 under throughput costing.
2. Give one motivation for Nascar Motors to adopt throughput costing.

2. **Throughput—Intermediate.** Refer to Mastery Question 2 for Learning Objective 3. Sonnenheim is concerned with the inventory buildup in 2010. It receives advice from a consultant to use throughput costing.

REQUIRED

1. Calculate operating income under throughput costing for the year ended December 31, 2010.
2. Why might use of throughput costing reduce inventory buildup?

3. **Throughput—Advanced.** (CMA) Byrd Company is a manufacturer of appliances for both residential and commercial use. The company's accounting and financial reporting system is primarily designed to meet external reporting requirements in accordance with generally accepted accounting principles. For inventory costing purposes, Byrd uses the absorption costing method in conjunction with a standard costing system. Costs are allocated to products on a units-produced basis. The denominator of fixed manufacturing costs is normal capacity utilization in production units. Relevant information on Byrd's steam cooker appliance for the last two years is as follows:

Unit Data	2009	2010
Beginning inventory	900	1,400
Production	2,000	400
Sales	1,500	1,700
Normal capacity utilization	2,000	2,000

The standard costs for this product are the same in 2008, 2009, and 2010.

Financial Data	2009	2010
Selling price per unit	$ 120	$ 120
Standard variable direct manufacturing costs per unit*	48.70	48.70
Standard variable indirect manufacturing costs per unit	15	15
Variable marketing costs per unit sold	1	1
Total budgeted (and actual) fixed manufacturing costs	10,000	10,000
Total fixed marketing costs	3,000	3,000
Net unfavourable variance† pertaining to variable manufacturing costs	1,000	1,000

*Standard variable direct materials costs are $28 per unit.

†All variances are written off to cost of goods sold in the period incurred.

Currently, Byrd evaluates the performance of its product-line managers and calculates their bonuses based on operating income computed on an absorption-costing basis. It has been suggested that the use of variable costing for internal reporting purposes would more accurately reflect the performance of each product-line manager.

REQUIRED
1. Calculate Byrd Company's operating income on its steam cooker appliance line for 2009 and 2010 using (a) absorption costing, (b) variable costing, and (c) throughput costing.
2. Discuss the features of variable costing that allow it to reflect the performance of Byrd's product-line managers more accurately. Be sure to include in your discussion how absorption costing may influence a product-line manager's behaviour differently from the way variable costing would.
3. What are the pros and cons of adopting throughput costing?

LEARNING OBJECTIVE 5

1. **Variable and absorption costing, and breakeven points—Advanced.** Shasta Hills, a winery in British Columbia, manufactures a premium white cabernet and sells primarily to distributors. Wine is sold in cases of one dozen bottles. In the year ended December 31, 2010, Shasta Hills sold 242,400 cases at an average selling price of $112.80 per case. The following additional data are for Shasta Hills for the year ended December 31, 2010 (assume constant unit costs and no price, spending, or efficiency variances):

Beginning inventory, January 1, 2010	32,600 cases
Ending inventory, December 31, 2010	24,800 cases
Fixed manufacturing overhead	$4,504,320
Fixed operating costs	$7,882,560
Variable costs per case:	
Direct materials	
Grapes	$19.20 per case
Bottles, corks, and crates	$12.00 per case
Direct labour	
Bottling	$7.20 per case
Winemaking	$16.80 per case
Aging	$2.40 per case

On December 31, 2010, the unit costs per case for closing inventory are $55.20 for variable costing and $73.20 for absorption costing.

REQUIRED
1. Calculate cases of production for Shasta Hills in 2010.
2. Find the breakeven point (number of cases) in 2010:
   a. under variable costing
   b. under absorption costing

3. Grape prices are expected to increase 25% in 2011. Assuming all other data remain constant, what is the minimum number of cases Shasta Hills must sell in 2011 to break even? Calculate the breakeven point:
   a. under variable costing
   b. under absorption costing
4. Assume the owners of Shasta Hills want to increase 2011 operating income 10% over 2010 levels. Using the same data as in requirement 3, recalculate the target quantity of cases under variable and absorption costing. Use approximation method re absorption costing.

ASSIGNMENT MATERIAL

 Make the grade with MyAccountingLab: The questions, exercises, and problems marked in red can be found on MyAccountingLab at **www.myaccountinglab.com**. You can practise them as often as you want, and most feature step-by-step guided instructions to help you find the right answer. Exercises and problems with an Excel icon in the margin have an accompanying Excel template on MyAccountingLab.

SHORT-ANSWER QUESTIONS

9-1 "Differences in operating income between variable and absorption costing are due solely to accounting for fixed costs." Do you agree? Explain.

9-2 Why is the term *direct costing* a misnomer?

9-3 Do companies in either the service sector or the merchandising sector make choices about absorption costing versus variable costing?

9-4 Explain the main conceptual issue under variable and absorption costing regarding the proper timing for the release of fixed manufacturing overhead as expense.

9-5 "Companies that make no variable cost/fixed cost distinctions must use absorption costing and those that do make variable cost/fixed cost distinctions must use variable costing." Do you agree? Explain.

9-6 "The main trouble with variable costing is that it ignores the increasing importance of fixed costs in modern manufacturing." Do you agree? Why?

9-7 Give an example of how, under absorption costing, operating income could fall even though the unit sales level rises.

9-8 What are the factors that affect the breakeven point under (a) variable costing and (b) absorption costing?

9-9 Why might throughput costing also be called super-variable costing?

9-10 Critics of absorption costing have increasingly emphasized its potential for promoting undesirable incentives for managers. Give an example.

9-11 What are two ways of reducing the negative aspects associated with using absorption costing to evaluate the performance of a plant manager?

9-12 Describe the downward demand spiral and its implications for pricing decisions.

9-13 Will the financial statements of a company always differ when different choices at the start of the period are made regarding the denominator-level capacity concept?

9-14 Which denominator-level concepts emphasize what a plant can supply? Which denominator-level concepts emphasize what customers demand for products produced by a plant?

9-15 "The difference between practical capacity and master-budget capacity utilization is the best measure of management's ability to balance the costs of having too much capacity and having too little capacity." Do you agree? Explain.

EXERCISES

9-16 Variable and absorption costing; explaining operating-income differences. Zippy Motors assembles and sells motor vehicles, and uses standard costing. Actual data relating to April and May 2010 are:

1. a. Operating income, April 2010, $1,250,000

	April	May
Unit data:		
Beginning inventory	0	150
Production	500	400
Sales	350	520
Variable costs:		
Manufacturing cost per unit produced	$10,000	$10,000
Operating (marketing) cost per unit sold	3,000	3,000
Fixed costs:		
Manufacturing costs	$2,000,000	$2,000,000
Operating (marketing) costs	600,000	600,000

The selling price per vehicle is $24,000. The budgeted level of production used to calculate the budgeted fixed manufacturing cost per unit is 500 units. There are no price, efficiency, or spending variances. Any production-volume variance is written off to cost of goods sold in the month in which it occurs.

REQUIRED

1. Prepare April and May 2010 income statements for Zippy Motors under (a) variable costing and (b) absorption costing.
2. Prepare a numerical reconciliation and explanation of the difference between operating income for each month under variable costing and absorption costing.

9-17 Throughput costing (continuation of 9-16). The variable manufacturing costs per unit of Zippy Motors are:

1. Operating income, April 2010, $755,000

	April	May
Direct material cost per unit	$6.700	$6,700
Direct manufacturing labour cost per unit	1,500	1,500
Manufacturing overhead cost per unit	1,800	1,800

REQUIRED

1. Prepare income statements for Zippy Motors in April and May of 2010 under throughput costing.
2. Contrast the results in requirement 1 with those in requirement 1 of Exercise 9-16.
3. Give one motivation for Zippy Motors to adopt throughput costing.

9-18 Variable and absorption costing, explaining operating-income differences. BigScreen Corporation manufactures and sells 50-inch television sets and uses standard costing. Actual data relating to January, February, and March of 2009 are:

1. a. Operating income, January 2009, $160,000

	January	February	March
Unit data:			
Beginning inventory	0	300	300
Production	1,000	800	1,250
Sales	700	800	1,500
Variable costs:			
Manufacturing cost per unit produced	$900	$900	$900
Operating (marketing) cost per unit sold	600	600	600
Fixed costs:			
Manufacturing costs	$400,000	$400,000	$400,000
Operating (marketing) costs	140,000	140,000	140,000

The selling price per unit is $3,000.

1. Present income statements for BigScreen Corporation in January, February, and March of 2009 under (a) variable costing and (b) absorption costing.
2. Explain the difference in operating income for January, February, and March under variable costing and absorption costing.

9-19 Throughput costing (continuation of 9-18). The variable manufacturing costs per unit of BigScreen Corporation are:

	January	February	March
Direct material cost per unit	$500	$500	$500
Direct manufacturing labour cost per unit	100	100	100
Manufacturing overhead cost per unit	300	300	300
	$900	$900	$900

REQUIRED

1. Prepare income statements for BigScreen Corporation in January, February, and March of 2009 under throughput costing.
2. Contrast the results in requirement 1 with those in requirement 1 of Exercise 9-18.
3. Give one motivation for BigScreen to adopt throughput costing.

9-20 Absorption and variable costing. (CMA) Osawa Inc. planned and actually manufactured 200,000 units of its single product in 2009, its first year of operation. Variable manufacturing cost was $20 per unit produced. Variable operating (nonmanufacturing) cost was $10 per unit sold. Planned and actual fixed manufacturing costs were $600,000. Planned and actual fixed operating (nonmanufacturing) costs totalled $400,000. Osawa sold 120,000 units of product at $40 per unit.

REQUIRED

1. Osawa's 2009 operating income using absorption costing is (a) $440,000, (b) $200,000, (c) $600,000, (d) $840,000, or (e) none of these. Show supporting calculations.
2. Osawa's 2009 operating income using variable costing is (a) $800,000, (b) $440,000, (c) $200,000, (d) $600,000, or (e) none of these. Show supporting calculations.

9-21 Comparison of actual costing methods. Rehe Company sells its razors at $3 per unit. The company uses a first-in, first-out actual costing system. A fixed manufacturing cost rate is computed at the end of each year by dividing the actual fixed manufacturing costs by the actual production units. The following data are related to its first two years of operation:

	2008	2009
Sales	1,000 units	1,200 units
Production	1,400 units	1,000 units
Costs:		
Variable manufacturing	$ 700	$ 500
Fixed manufacturing	700	700
Variable operating (marketing)	1,000	1,200
Fixed operating (marketing)	400	400

REQUIRED

1. Prepare income statements based on variable costing for each of the two years.
2. Prepare income statements based on absorption costing for each of the two years.
3. Prepare a numerical reconciliation and explanation of the difference between operating income for each year under absorption costing and variable costing.
4. Critics have claimed that a widely used accounting system has led to undesirable buildups of inventory levels. (a) Is variable costing or absorption costing more likely to lead to such buildups? Why? (b) What can be done to counteract undesirable inventory buildups?

9-22 Absorption versus variable costing. Electron Inc. is a semiconductor company based in Winnipeg. In 2009, it produced a new router system for its corporate clients. The average wholesale selling price of the system is $1,200 each. For 2009, Electron estimates that it will sell 10,000 router systems and so produces 10,000 units. Actual 2009 sales are 8,960 units. Electron's actual 2009 costs are:

1. Operating income, $2,531,520

Variable costs per unit:	
Manufacturing cost per unit produced	
Direct materials	$ 55
Direct manufacturing labour	45
Manufacturing overhead	120
Marketing cost per unit sold	75
Fixed costs:	
Manufacturing costs	$1,471,680
R&D	981,120
Marketing	3,124,480

REQUIRED
1. Calculate the operating income under variable costing.
2. Each router unit produced is allocated $165 in fixed manufacturing costs. If the production-volume variance is written off to cost of goods sold, and there are no price, spending, or efficiency variances, calculate the operating income under absorption costing.
3. Explain the differences in operating incomes obtained in requirement 1 and requirement 2.
4. Electron's management is considering implementing a bonus for the supervisors based on gross margin under absorption costing. What incentives will this create for the supervisors? Do you think this new bonus plan is a good idea? Explain briefly.

9-23 Capacity management, denominator-level capacity concepts.

REQUIRED
Match each of the following numbered items with one or more of the denominator-level capacity concepts by putting the appropriate letter(s) by each item:
a. Theoretical capacity
b. Practical capacity
c. Normal capacity utilization
d. Master-budget capacity utilization

1. Measures the denominator level in terms of what a plant can supply
2. Is based on producing at full efficiency all the time
3. Represents the expected level of capacity utilization for the next budget period
4. Measures the denominator level in terms of demand for the output of the plant
5. Takes into account seasonal, cyclical, and trend factors
6. Should be used for performance evaluation
7. Represents an ideal benchmark
8. Highlights the cost of capacity acquired but not used
9. Should be used for long-term pricing purposes
10. Hides the cost of capacity acquired but not used
11. If used as the denominator-level concept, would avoid the restatement of unit costs when expected demand levels change

9-24 Income statements. (SMA) Mass Company manufactures and sells a single product. The denominator level is 30,000 output units per year. Mass Company's accounting records produce variable costing information, and year-end adjustments are made to produce external reports showing absorption-costing information.

1. Variable costing operating income, $207,500

The following data cover the two latest years of operations:

	2009	2010
Unit data:		
Sales	25,000	25,000
Beginning inventory	2,000	2,000
Ending inventory	2,000	6,000
Selling price per unit	$ 48	$ 48
Cost data:		
Standard fixed costs		
Manufacturing overhead	$120,000	$120,000
Marketing and administrative	$190,000	$190,000

Standard variable costs per unit:

Direct materials	$12.60
Direct manufacturing labour	9.50
Manufacturing overhead	4.00
Marketing and administrative	1.20

All variances are insignificant and thus are charged to cost of goods sold.

REQUIRED

1. Prepare two income statements for 2010, one under variable costing and one under absorption costing.
2. Explain briefly why the operating income figures computed in requirement 1 agree or do not agree.
3. Give two advantages and two disadvantages of using variable costing for internal reporting.

PROBLEMS

1. Selling price per unit, $800

9-25 Downward demand spiral. Network Company is a large manufacturer of optical storage systems based in British Columbia. Its practical annual capacity is 7,500 units, and, for the past few years, its budgeted and actual sales and production volume have been 7,500 units per year. Network's budgeted and actual variable manufacturing costs are $100 per unit, and budgeted and actual total fixed manufacturing costs are $2,250,000 per year. Network calculates full manufacturing cost per unit as the sum of the variable manufacturing cost per unit and the fixed manufacturing costs allocated to the budgeted units produced. Selling price is set at a 100% markup to full manufacturing cost per unit.

REQUIRED

1. Compute Network's selling price.
2. Recent competition from abroad has caused a drop in budgeted production and sales volume to 6,000 units per year, and analysts are predicting further declines. If Network continues to use budgeted production as the denominator level, calculate its new selling price.
3. Comment on the effect that changes in budgeted production have on selling price. Suggest another denominator level that Network might use for its pricing decision. Justify your choice.
4. Network has received an offer to buy identical storage units for $400 each instead of manufacturing the units in-house. Shutting down the manufacturing plant would reduce fixed costs to $450,000 per year. At what level of expected annual sales (in units) should Network accept this offer? Explain your answer.

1. Theoretical inventoriable cost per unit, $3.75

9-26 Absorption costing and production-volume variance—alternative capacity bases. Earth Light First (ELF), a producer of energy-efficient light bulbs, expects that demand will increase markedly over the next decade. Due to the high fixed costs involved in the business, ELF has decided to evaluate its financial performance using absorption costing income. The production-volume variance is written off to cost of goods sold. The variable cost of production is $2.50 per bulb. Fixed manufacturing costs are $1,000,000 per year. Variable and fixed selling and administrative expenses are $0.25 per bulb sold and $250,000, respectively. Because its light bulbs are currently popular with environmentally conscious customers, ELF can sell the bulbs for $9.00 each.

ELF is deciding whether to use, when calculating the cost of each unit produced:

Theoretical capacity	800,000 bulbs
Practical capacity	500,000 bulbs
Normal capacity	250,000 bulbs (average production for the next three years)
Master-budget capacity	200,000 bulbs produced this year

REQUIRED

1. Calculate the inventoriable cost per unit using each level of capacity to compute fixed manufacturing cost per unit.
2. Calculate the production-volume variance using each level of capacity to compute the fixed manufacturing overhead allocation rate and this year's production of 220,000 bulbs.

3. Assuming ELF has no beginning inventory, calculate operating income for ELF using each type of capacity to compute fixed manufacturing cost per unit and this year's sales of 200,000 bulbs.

9-27 Operating income effects of denominator-level choice and disposal of production-volume variance (continuation of 9-26).

1. Theoretical operating income, $125,000

REQUIRED

1. If ELF sells all 220,000 bulbs produced, what would be the effect on operating income of using each type of capacity as a basis for calculating manufacturing cost per unit?

2. Compare the results of operating income at different capacity levels when 200,000 bulbs are sold and when 220,000 bulbs are sold. What conclusion can you draw from the comparison?

3. Using the original data (that is, 220,000 units produced and 200,000 units sold), if ELF had used the proration approach to allocate the production-volume variance, what would operating income have been under each method? (Assume that there is no ending work in process.)

9-28 Variable costing versus absorption costing. Proteus Company uses an absorption costing system based on standard costs.

1. Operating income for 2010, $223,000

Total variable manufacturing costs, including direct materials costs, were $3.60 per unit; the standard production rate was ten units per machine-hour. Total budgeted and actual fixed manufacturing overhead costs were $420,000.

Fixed manufacturing overhead was allocated at $7 per machine-hour ($420,000 ÷ 60,000 machine-hours of denominator level). The selling price is $6 per unit. Variable marketing and administrative costs, which are driven by units sold, were $1 per unit. Fixed marketing and administrative costs were $120,000.

Beginning inventory in 2010 was 30,000 units; ending inventory was 40,000 units. Sales in 2010 were 540,000 units. The same standard unit costs persisted throughout 2009 and 2010. For simplicity, assume that there were no price, spending, or efficiency variances.

REQUIRED

1. Prepare an income statement for 2010 assuming that all underallocated or overallocated overhead is written off directly at year end as an adjustment to cost of goods sold.

2. The president has heard about variable costing. She asks you to recast the 2010 income statement as it would appear under variable costing. Explain the difference in operating income as calculated in requirements 1 and 2.

3. Graph how fixed manufacturing overhead is accounted for under absorption costing. There will be two lines, one for the budgeted fixed overhead (which is equal to the actual fixed manufacturing overhead in this case) and one for the fixed overhead allocated. Show how the overallocated or underallocated manufacturing overhead might be indicated on the graph.

9-29 Breakeven under variable and absorption costing (continuation of 9-28).

1. Breakeven point, 385,714 units

REQUIRED

1. Compute the breakeven point in units under variable costing.

2. Compute the breakeven point in units under absorption costing.

3. Suppose that production were exactly equal to the denominator level, but no units were sold. Fixed manufacturing costs are unaffected. Assume, however, that all marketing and administrative costs were avoided. Compute operating income under (a) variable costing and (b) absorption costing. Explain the difference between your answers.

9-30 Variable and absorption costing, sales, and operating-income changes. Headsmart, a three-year-old company, has been producing and selling a single type of bicycle helmet. Headsmart uses standard costing. After reviewing the income statements for the first three years, Stuart Weil, president of Headsmart, commented, "I was told by our accountants—and in fact, I have memorized—that our breakeven volume is 50,000 units. I was happy that we reached that sales goal in each of our first two years. But, here's the strange thing: in our first year, we sold 50,000 units and indeed we broke even. Then, in our second year we sold the same volume and had a positive operating income. I didn't complain, of course . . . but here's the bad part. In our third year, we sold 20% more helmets, but our operating income fell by more than 80% relative to the second year! We didn't change our selling price or cost structure over the past three years and have no price, efficiency, or spending variances . . . so what's going on?!"

3. Operating income for 2008, $0

Absorption Costing	2008	2009	2010
Sales (units)	50,000	50,000	60,000
Revenues	$2,100,000	$2,100,000	$2,520,000
Cost of goods sold:			
Beginning inventory	0	0	380,000
Production	1,900,000	2,280,000	1,900,000
Available for sale	1,900,000	2,280,000	2,280,000
Deduct ending inventory	0	(380,000)	0
Adjustment for production-volume variance	0	(240,000)	0
Cost of goods sold	1,900,000	1,660,000	2,280,000
Gross margin	200,000	440,000	240,000
Selling and administrative expenses (all fixed)	200,000	200,000	200,000
Operating income	$ 0	$ 240,000	$ 40,000
Beginning inventory	0	0	10,000
Production (units)	50,000	60,000	50,000
Sales (units)	50,000	50,000	60,000
Ending inventory	0	10,000	0
Variable manufacturing cost per unit	$ 14	$ 14	$ 14
Fixed manufacturing overhead costs	$1,200,000	$1,200,000	$1,200,000
Fixed manufacturing costs allocated per unit produced	$ 24	$ 24	$ 24

REQUIRED

1. What denominator level is Headsmart using to allocate fixed manufacturing costs to the bicycle helmets? How is Headsmart disposing of any favourable or unfavourable production-volume variance at the end of the year? Explain your answer briefly.
2. How did Headsmart's accountants arrive at the breakeven volume of 50,000 units?
3. Prepare a variable-costing–based income statement for each year. Explain the variation in variable costing operating income for each year based on contribution margin per unit and sales volume.
4. Reconcile the operating incomes under variable costing and absorption costing for each year, and use this information to explain to Stuart Weil the positive operating income in 2009 and the drop in operating income in 2010.

1. Theoretical budgeted fixed manufacturing overhead cost rate, $1,388.89

9-31 Denominator-level problem. Speedy Inc. is a manufacturer of the very popular G36 motorcycles. The management at Speedy has recently adopted absorption costing and is debating which denominator level concept to use. The G36 motorcycles sell for an average price of $8,500. Budgeted fixed manufacturing overhead costs for 2009 are estimated at $4,000,000. Speedy Inc. uses subassembly operators that provide component parts. The following are the denominator-level options that management has been considering:

a. Theoretical capacity—based on two shifts, completion of four motorcycles per shift, and a 360-day year—2 × 4 × 360 = 2,880.
b. Practical capacity—theoretical capacity adjusted for unavoidable interruptions, breakdowns, and so forth—2 × 3 × 320 = 1,920.
c. Normal capacity utilization—estimated at 1,200 units.
d. Master-budget capacity utilization—the growing popularity of motorcycles have prompted the Marketing Department to issue an estimate for 2009 of 1,500 units.

REQUIRED

1. Calculate the budgeted fixed manufacturing overhead cost rates under the four denominator-level concepts.
2. What are the benefits to Speedy Inc. of using either theoretical capacity or practical capacity?
3. Under a cost-based pricing system, what are the negative aspects of a master-budget denominator level? What are the positive aspects?

9-32 Cost allocation, downward demand spiral. Deli One operates a chain of 10 retirement homes in the Toronto area. Its central food-catering facility, Deliman, prepares and delivers meals to the retirement homes. It has the capacity to deliver up to 1,460,000 meals a year. In 2009, based on estimates from each retirement-home controller, Deliman budgeted for 1,022,000 meals a year. Budgeted fixed costs in 2009 were $1,533,000. Each retirement home was charged $6.00 per meal—$4.50 variable costs plus $1.50 allocated budgeted fixed cost.

Recently, the retirement homes have been complaining about the quality of Deliman's meals and their rising costs. In mid-2009, Deli One's president announces that all Deli One retirement homes and support facilities will be run as profit centres. Retirement homes will be free to purchase quality-certified services from outside the system. Ron Smith, Deliman's controller, is preparing the 2010 budget. He hears that three retirement homes have decided to use outside suppliers for their meals; this will reduce the 2010 estimated demand to 876,000 meals. No change in variable cost per meal or total fixed costs is expected in 2010.

2. Budgeted cost per meal, $6.25

REQUIRED
1. How did Smith calculate the budgeted fixed cost per meal of $1.50 in 2009?
2. Using the same approach to calculating budgeted fixed cost per meal and pricing as in 2009, how much would retirement homes be charged for each Deliman meal in 2010? What would their reaction be?
3. Suggest an alternative cost-based price per meal that Smith might propose and that might be more acceptable to the retirement homes. What can Deliman and Smith do to make this price profitable in the long run?

9-33 **Effects of differing production levels on absorption costing income: Metrics to minimize inventory buildups.** University Press produces textbooks for university courses. They recently hired a new editor, Leslie White, to handle production and sales of books for an introduction to accounting course. Leslie's compensation depends on the gross margin associated with sales of this book. Leslie needs to decide how many copies of the book to produce. The following information is available for the fall semester 2010:

1. Expected gross margin for 10,000 books, $280,000

Estimated sales	10,000 books
Beginning inventory	0 books
Average selling price	$100 per book
Variable production costs	$60 per book
Fixed production costs	$120,000 per semester

The fixed cost allocation rate is based on expected sales and is therefore equal to $120,000 ÷ 10,000 books = $12 per book

REQUIRED
Leslie must decide whether to produce 10,000, 12,000, or 16,000 books.
1. Calculate expected gross margin if Leslie produces 10,000, 12,000, or 16,000 books. (Make sure you include the production-volume variance as part of cost of goods sold.)
2. Calculate ending inventory in units and in dollars for each production level.
3. Managers who are paid a bonus that is a function of gross margin may be inspired to produce product in excess of demand to maximize their own bonus. The chapter suggested metrics to discourage managers from producing products in excess of demand. Do you think the following metrics will accomplish this objective? Show your work.
   a. Incorporate a charge of 10% of the cost of the ending inventory as an expense for evaluating the manager.
   b. Include nonfinancial measures (such as the ones recommended on pp. 435–436) when evaluating management and rewarding performance.

9-34 **Variable costing and absorption costing, The All-Fixed Company.** (R. Marple, adapted) It is the end of 2010. The All-Fixed Company began operations in January 2009. The company is so named because it has no variable costs. All its costs are fixed.

All-Fixed is located on the bank of a river and has its own hydroelectric plant to supply power, light, and heat.

The company manufactures a synthetic fertilizer from air and river water and sells its product at a price that is not expected to change. It has a small staff of employees, all hired on a fixed annual salary. The output of the plant can be increased or decreased by adjusting a few dials on a control panel.

Management adopted the policy effective January 1, 2010, of producing only as much product as was needed to fill sales orders. During 2010, sales were the same as 2009 and were filled entirely from beginning inventory at the start of 2010.

1. (a) Operating income for 2009, ($20,000)

The following are data regarding the operations of The All-Fixed Company:

	2009	2010
Sales (tonnes)	10,000	10,000
Production (tonnes)	20,000	0
Selling price per tonne	$30	$30
Costs (all fixed):		
Manufacturing	$280,000	$280,000
Marketing and administrative	$40,000	$40,000

REQUIRED

1. Prepare income statements with one column for 2009, one column for 2010, and one column for the two years together, using (a) variable costing and (b) absorption costing.
2. What is the breakeven point under (a) variable costing and (b) absorption costing?
3. What inventory costs would be carried on the balance sheets at December 31, 2009, and 2010, under each method?
4. Assume that the performance of the top manager of the company is evaluated and rewarded largely on the basis of reported operating income. Which costing method would the manager prefer? Why?

9-35 The Semi-Fixed Company. The Semi-Fixed Company also began operations in 2009 and differs from The All-Fixed Company (described in Problem 9-34) by having both variable and fixed manufacturing costs.

The variable manufacturing costs are $8.40 per tonne, and the fixed manufacturing costs are $140,000 per year. The denominator level is 20,000 tonnes per year.

REQUIRED

1. Using the same data as in Problem 9-34 except for the change in manufacturing cost behaviour, prepare income statements with adjacent columns for 2009, 2010, and the two years together, under (a) variable costing and (b) absorption costing.
2. Explain the differences in operating income for The Semi-Fixed Company and The All-Fixed Company.
3. What inventory costs would be carried on the balance sheets at December 31, 2009 and 2010 under each method?
4. Assume that the performance of the top manager of the company is evaluated and rewarded largely based on reported operating income. Which costing method would the manager prefer? Why?

9-36 Comparison of variable costing and absorption costing. Consider the following data:

Monk Company
Income Statement for the Year Ended December 31, 2010

	Variable Costing	Absorption Costing
Revenues	$8,400,000	$8,400,000
Costs of goods sold (at standard)	4,392,000	5,490,000
Fixed manufacturing overhead	1,200,000	—
Manufacturing variances (all unfavourable):		
Direct materials price and efficiency	60,000	60,000
Direct manufacturing labour price and efficiency	72,000	72,000
Variable manufacturing overhead spending and efficiency	36,000	36,000
Fixed manufacturing overhead:		
Spending	120,000	120,000
Production volume	—	480,000
Total marketing costs (all fixed)	1,200,000	1,200,000
Total administrative costs (all fixed)	600,000	600,000
Total costs	7,680,000	8,058,000
Operating income	$ 720,000	$ 342,000

The inventories, carried at standard costs, were

	Variable Costing	Absorption Costing
December 31, 2009	$1,584,000	$1,980,000
December 31, 2010	72,000	90,000

REQUIRED

1. Tim Monk, president of Monk Company, has asked you to explain why the operating income for 2010 is less than for 2009, even though sales have increased 40% over last year. What will you tell him?
2. At what percentage of denominator level was the plant operating during 2010?
3. Prepare a numerical reconciliation and explanation of the difference between the operating incomes under absorption costing and variable costing.
4. Critics have claimed that a widely used accounting system has led to undesirable buildups of inventory levels.
   a. Is variable costing or absorption costing more likely to lead to such buildups? Why?
   b. What can be done to counteract undesirable inventory buildups?

9-37 **Inventory costing and management planning.** It is November 30, 2010. Consider the income statement (shown below) for the operations of Multi-Products Inc. for January through November 2010.

Production in the past three months has been 100 units monthly. Practical capacity is 125 units monthly. To retain a stable nucleus of key employees, management never schedules monthly production at fewer than 40 units.

Maximum available storage space for inventory is regarded as 200 units. The sales outlook for the next four months is 70 units monthly. Inventory is never to be fewer than 50 units.

Multi-Products Inc.
Income Statement for 11 Months Ended November 30, 2010

	Units	Costs	Total Values
Revenues @ $1,200	1,000		$1,200,000
Cost of goods sold:			
Beginning inventory, December 31, 2009, @ $960	50	$ 48,000	
Manufacturing costs @ $960, including $720 per unit for fixed manufacturing overhead	1,100	1,056,000	
Total standard cost of goods available for sale	1,150	1,104,000	
Ending inventory, November 30, 2010, @ $960	150	144,000	
Standard cost of goods sold*	1,000		960,000
Gross margin			240,000
Marketing, distribution, and customer-service costs:			
Variable, 1,000 units @ $60		60,000	
Fixed, @ $12,000 monthly		132,000	192,000
Operating income			$ 48,000

*There are no variances for the 11-month period considered as a whole.

The company uses a standard absorption costing system. The denominator production level is 1,200 units annually. All variances are disposed of at year end as an adjustment to cost of goods sold.

1. The division manager is given an annual bonus that is geared to operating income. Assume that the manager wants to maximize the company's operating income for 2010. How many units should the manager schedule for production in December? Note that you do not have to (nor should you) compute the operating income for 2010 in this or in subsequent parts of this problem.

2. Assume that standard variable costing is in use rather than standard absorption costing. Would variable costing operating income for 2010 be higher, lower, or the same as standard absorption costing income, assuming that production for December is 80 units and sales are 70 units? Why?

3. If standard variable costing were used, what production schedule should the division manager set? Why?

4. Assume that the manager is interested in maximizing his performance over the long run and that performance is being judged based on net income. Assume that the company's income tax rate will be substantially reduced in 2011 and that the year-end writeoffs of variances are acceptable for income tax purposes. Assume that standard absorption costing is used. How many units should be scheduled for production in December? Why?

5. Assume that the total production and total sales for 2009 and 2010, taken together, will be unchanged by the specific decision in requirement 4. Assume also that the standards will be unchanged in 2011. Suppose the decision in requirement 4 is to schedule 50 units instead of an originally scheduled 120 units. By how much will operating income in 2011 be affected by the decision to schedule 50 units in December 2010? (That is, how much operating income is shifted from 2010 to 2011?)

9-38 Absorption costing and production-volume variances (continuation of Problem 9-37).

1. What operating income will be reported for 2010 as a whole, assuming that the implied cost behaviour patterns will continue in December as they did in January through November (without regard to your answer to requirement 1 in Problem 9-37), and that production for December is 80 units and sales are 70 units?

2. Assume the same conditions as in requirement 1 except that a monthly denominator level of 125 units (practical capacity) was used in setting fixed manufacturing overhead rates for inventory costing throughout 2010. What production volume variance would be reported for 2010?

9-39 Alternative denominator-level capacity concepts, effect on operating income. Lissom Lager has just purchased Austin Brewery. The brewery is two years old and uses absorption costing. It will "sell" its product to Lissom Lager at $45 per barrel. Paul Brandon, Lissom Lager's controller, obtains the following information about Austin Brewery's capacity and budgeted fixed manufacturing costs for 2009:

Denominator-Level Capacity Concept	Budgeted fixed manufacturing overhead per period	Days of Production per Period	Hours of Production per Day	Barrels per Hour
Theoretical capacity	$28,000,000	360	24	540
Practical capacity	$28,000,000	350	20	500
Normal capacity utilization	$28,000,000	350	20	400
Master-budget capacity for each half year				
(a) January–June 2009	$14,000,000	175	20	320
(b) July–December 2009	$14,000,000	175	20	480

REQUIRED

1. Compute the budgeted fixed manufacturing overhead rate per barrel for each of the denominator-level capacity concepts. Explain why they are different.

2. In 2009, Austin Brewery reported these production results:

Beginning inventory in barrels, January 1, 2009	0
Production in barrels	2,600,000
Ending inventory in barrels, December 31, 2009	200,000
Actual variable manufacturing costs	$78,520,000
Actual fixed manufacturing overhead costs	$27,088,000

There are no variable cost variances. Fixed manufacturing overhead cost variances are written off to cost of goods sold in the period in which they occur. Compute Austin Brewery's operating income when the denominator-level capacity is (a) theoretical capacity, (b) practical capacity, and (c) normal capacity utilization.

9-40 Variable and absorption costing, and breakeven points. Tammy Cat Tree Co. (TCTC) builds luxury cat trees and sells them through the Internet to cat owners who want to provide their cats with a more natural environment. At the start of 2009, TCTC carried no inventory. During the year, it produced 1,000 cat trees and sold 800 cat trees for $300 each. Fixed production costs were $100,000 and variable production costs were $75 per cat tree. Fixed advertising, website, and other general and administrative expenses were $50,000 and variable shipping costs were $25 per tree.

1. a. Operating income, $10,000

REQUIRED
1. Prepare an income statement assuming TCTC uses:
   a. Variable costing
   b. Absorption costing
2. Compute the breakeven point in units assuming TCTC uses:
   a. Variable costing
   b. Absorption costing
3. Due to recent changes in local conservation laws, the price of the wood used in the cat trees is expected to increase by $25 for each tree. What effect would this have on the breakeven points calculated above?
4. Using the original data in the problem and the breakeven/target income formulas, show that it would be necessary to sell 800 cat trees to earn the income calculated in requirements 1a and 1b above.

9-41 Absorption costing, standard costs, governance. Advanced Engineering Company (AEC) is a multinational business selling metal products used in the assembly of many cars, trucks, and planes. AEC has more than 50 manufacturing divisions worldwide and is listed on the Toronto Stock Exchange. AEC has consistently reported annual earnings growth rates of 15% or more for each of the past ten years.

1. Absorption-costing operating income, $2,407,200

Division managers at AEC receive an annual bonus of 30% of their annual salary if the plant operating income increases 15% or more over the previous year's operating income. Division managers who increase operating income more than 10% but less than 15% receive a bonus of 5% of their annual salary. Division managers who do not achieve a 10% increase in operating income receive no bonus. Instead, they receive a visit from the AEC corporate consulting team.

Bob Wood is manager of the Mississauga, Ontario, division, which manufactures crankshafts for sale to automobile manufacturers. Wood has just received a 30% bonus for 2010. Mary Easson, head of the AEC corporate consulting team, is less than impressed by Wood's performance. She suspects him of producing for inventory and collects the following information on the Mississauga division for 2010:

Unit data in crankshafts:	
Beginning inventory	0
Production	480,000
Ending inventory	30,000
Sales	450,000
Selling price per unit	$79.20
Cost data:	
Standard variable costs per crankshaft:	
Direct materials	$24.00
Direct manufacturing labour	6.00
Manufacturing overhead	14.40
Variable marketing	4.80
Standard fixed costs:	
Manufacturing overhead	$10,800,000
Marketing	1,200,000

Manufacturing overhead is allocated to each crankshaft based on standard machine-hours. Each crankshaft has a standard machining time of 30 minutes. The denominator level in 2010 was the master-budget capacity utilization for the Mississauga plant, 500,000 crankshafts. A standard absorption-costing system is used for each AEC plant. All variances are recorded as a cost of the period in which they are incurred.

All auto companies require suppliers to deliver on a just-in-time basis (that is, just before the crankshafts are required for assembly). The last four months of 2010 saw a reduction in the orders auto companies placed for crankshafts.

The price, spending, and efficiency manufacturing variances for 2010 were $360,000, unfavourable. The total marketing variances were $187,200, favourable (variable $156,000 favourable and fixed $31,200 favourable).

Operating income for the Mississauga division in 2010 was $1,712,412.

REQUIRED

1. Compute the absorption-costing operating income for the Mississauga division in 2010.
2. Why might Easson believe that in 2010 Wood engaged in behaviour not in the best interests of AEC? How might Wood respond to any charges Easson might make about producing for inventory?
3. Is the problem Easson raised likely to be eliminated by her talking to Wood about management ethics? Explain.

9-42 Absorption costing, governance (continuation of 9-41). Mary Easson decides to undertake a systematic investigation of how the combination of the existing division manager bonus plan and absorption costing may be causing division managers to make decisions not in the best interests of Advanced Engineering Company (AEC). She will first visit the Morristown division of AEC, which manufactures more than 100 different metal products.

REQUIRED

1. Name three types of behaviour that Easson should look for that would suggest problems for AEC with the existing bonus plan and accounting system.
2. What possible changes might Easson consider if her investigation produces widespread evidence of systematic poor decision making by division managers at AEC?

COLLABORATIVE LEARNING CASE

9-43 Absorption, variable, and throughput costing. EnRG Inc. produces trail mix packaged for sale in convenience stores across Canada. At the beginning of April 2010, EnRG has no inventory of trail mix. Demand for the next three months is expected to remain constant at 50,000 bags per month. EnRG plans to produce to demand, 50,000 bags in April. However, many of the employees take vacation in June, so EnRG plans to produce 70,000 bags in May and only 30,000 bags in June.

Costs for the three months are expected to remain unchanged. The costs and revenues for April, May, and June are expected to be:

Sales revenue	$6.00 per bag
Direct material cost	$0.80 per bag
Direct manufacturing labour cost	$0.45 per bag
Variable manufacturing overhead cost	$0.30 per bag
Variable selling cost	$0.15 per bag
Fixed manufacturing overhead cost	$105,000 per month
Fixed administrative costs	$ 35,000 per month

Suppose the actual costs, market demand, and levels of production for April, May, and June are as expected.

REQUIRED

1. Compute operating income for April, May, and June under variable costing.
2. Compute operating income for April, May, and June under absorption costing. Assume that the denominator level for each month is that month's expected level of output.
3. Compute operating income for April, May, and June under throughput costing.
4. Discuss the benefits and problems associated with using throughput costing.

Quantitative Analyses of Cost Functions

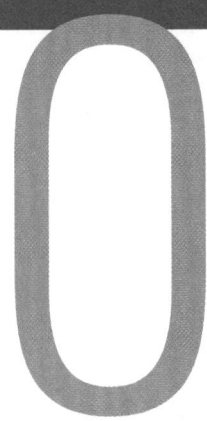

BUSINESS MATTERS

Statistics Are Your Best Friend

Understanding what causes costs to vary is essential to controlling costs. As Chapters 4 and 5 indicated, however, it is often not cost-effective to be able to explain 100% of changes in costs. Fortunately, quantitative tools exist to indicate clearly just how much suspected causesdo explain cost behaviour.

As an example, examine the handmede rugs shown above. These rugs are wool and each length of yarn has been inserted into the backing (tufted), knotted, and then cut to a specific length by hand. In the making of rugs like these, differences in use of direct labour cause most of the changes in cost, and there are few indirect costs. In contrast, broadloom carpet is mass produced by machines that tuft, knot, and shear the four- to five-metre-wide rolls. Changes in direct labour do not explain much of any changes in cost. If there is one indirect cost pool, then changes in resources such as utilities, materials handling, and security will each explain some of the change in cost.

LEARNING OBJECTIVES

After studying this chapter, you should be able to

1 Assess the appropriateness and quality of the data set proposed for use in the ordinary least squares (OLS) method of analysis

2 Apply standardized mathematical manipulations to a set of data points and produce the results of an OLS simple linear regression analysis with benchmark statistics testing reliability

3 Identify and explain data problems encountered in estimating cost functions

4 Extend the analysis of data sets to include discontinuous linear cost functions within a relevant range

5 Distinguish between the curvilinear cumulative average time learning model and incremental unit time learning model

This chapter focuses on tools for analyzing how changes in consumption of a resource affect costs. However, it is important to understand the limitations of such analyses—these limitations mean there will be a level of uncertainty in any analysis. Direct cost control is more straightforward because the relationship between the input consumed and the cost is readily and economically observable. It would be reasonable to expect that changes in the cost driver would explain almost 100% of changes in the direct cost pool (see Chapter 4) with some small amount of variance caused by random events. But direct costs comprise a small percentage of total costs and not all costs are variable. Explaining changes or variance in either indirect or fixed costs is less straightforward (see Chapters 8 and 9).

Problems arise in understanding relationships between consumption of resources and indirect cost pools well enough to reliably reduce costs. Indirect costs are often a far higher proportion of total costs throughout the value chain than are direct costs. If the indirect cost pool varies, then one key question is "varies with what?" Fortunately, **ordinary least squares (OLS)** linear regression is a well-established statistical method to analyze past data and provide an explanation of why indirect cost pools vary. The purpose of OLS is to model a relationship among events and objectively assess the reliability of the model. Another method of analysis, called high-low, is less reliable because it uses only two of all the available relevant data points and provides no information to managers on how confident they can be in the result. Managers may also either pool their opinions about cost behaviour, which is primarily a qualitative approach, or undertake work-measurement to set standards rather than work with actual data.

We will begin with OLS because it is a straightforward method that uses all the relevant information at hand and clearly informs managers of the limitations of the result.

GOOD DATA IN, GOOD EXPLANATIONS OUT[1]

① Assess the appropriateness and quality of the data set proposed for use in the ordinary least squares (OLS) method of analysis

Regression analysis identifies a standard series of mathematical manipulations used to analyze the presence of any relationship among sets of data recorded from past events. Linear regression analysis identifies the proposed relationship as linear. It is possible to graph a straight line through data points obtained after the mathematical manipulations are complete. Ordinary least squares (OLS) specifies the path of the straight line (the regression line), which arithmetically minimizes the sum of the squared difference between the actual data points in the original data set and the estimated data points on the line. OLS linear regression describes an objective, standardized method of data analysis, the benchmark statistical indicators of reliability, and graphs of results. OLS is unnecessary for purely variable direct cost pools and purely fixed cost pools. It is extremely useful when analyzing the causes of either heterogeneous costs accumulated in an indirect cost pool or mixed costs.

In Exhibit 10-1, all the relationships between the resource(s) consumed and the size of the cost pool are linear. The solid sloped line is a pure variable cost pool with its beginning at 0 resources consumed and $0 in the cost pool. As the consumption of resources increases, the cost pool increases at a steady rate. This is clear because the slope of the straight line is constant. The dashed line has no slope at all. This indicates a fixed cost that remains at $10,000 regardless of whether 0 units or 6,000 units of the resource are consumed. Fixed costs are caused by some measure of capacity available, not capacity used (Chapter 9). The dotted sloped line is a mixed cost pool. When no resources are consumed the lowest cost is $10,000. This component of mixed cost is caused by available capacity. But as consumption of a different resource increases, the cost pool also increases at a steady rate, which is the variable component. The consumption of resources explains only part of the change in the financial value of this mixed cost pool.

Consider the example of producing rugs. The machines, for which the acquisition cost is known, are amortized. Assume the amortization is straight-line and results

[1]Thank you to David Growing, who revised the presentation of the statistical material in this chapter.

EXHIBIT 10-1
Variable, Fixed, and Mixed Cost Behaviour

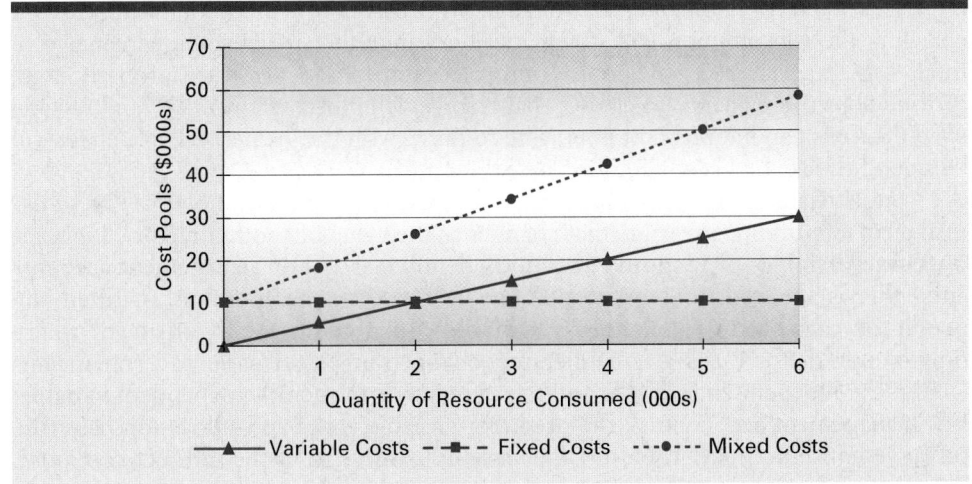

in a constant amortization expense each year. This expense is a fixed cost throughout the relevant range of practical capacity of the machines. There are, however, other readily measurable causes of variable costs such as utilities, which may vary from one week or month to another throughout the year. This expense is a variable cost and when summed with the amortization expense gives rise to a mixed cost. There are indirect costs such as lubricants and maintenance, quality control, security, and so on, for which it is more costly and less feasible to accurately record resource consumption per machine.

The indirect cost pool is an accumulation of several heterogeneous costs. This means that changes to consumption of any single cause of one of the costs will explain only part of the overall change to the cost pool. Whereas changes to the kilowatt hours of energy consumption will explain almost 100% of the change to a homogeneous variable cost pool, this is not the case for a heterogeneous cost pool. The power of OLS is to identify the change in a resource consumed that will provide a predictable level of explanation or explanatory power for the change in the financial value of the indirect cost pool. If a change in the resource consumed caused a 30% change in the cost pool, we would say that change in resource consumption has a level of explanation (or explanatory power) of 30%. If the decrease is $100, then $30 is explained by the decrease in the resource consumed. This often provides enough relevant information to guide managers towards successfully controlling this indirect cost. Managers who are dissatisfied with explaining only 30% of changes in an indirect cost pool based on changes to a single resource consumed may choose to measure more than one cause.

Remember, however, that the reason different costs have been accumulated and allocated is that it was either not feasible or too costly to identify and measure their causes. Doing so is the strategy of ABC. If the strategy of traditional cost allocation has been adopted, then it is important that managers know how confident they can be that controlling consumption of a specific resource will make a difference to the size of the indirect cost pool.

Confidence is different from explanatory power. A manager might prefer to be 95% confident of an explanation of 30% of a cost change, rather than 5% confident of an explanation of 80% of a cost change. In the first instance, the manager can expect the explanation of a change of $0.30 for every $1.00 in the indirect cost pool will be true 95 times out of 100. In the second instance, the manager can only expect the explanation will be true 5 times out of 100. Output from an OLS regression analysis gives managers this relevant information. Managers will know, for example, that they can be 95% confident or more.

Standard software packages, including Excel, SPSS, and SAS, make this type of rigorous analysis straightforward, quick, affordable, and available even to very small companies. The software packages not only complete all the calculations and graph the results but also present various statistics or benchmarks that inform a knowledgeable user of the limitations of the results. The smaller the scope of limitations, the more confidence a management accountant can have that if quantities of a resource consumed is one data set and corresponding sizes of an indirect cost pool is the second data set, then changing the consumption will systematically change the size of some percentage of total costs in an indirect cost pool. Appropriate statistical tools, when properly used, provide objective evidence to clarify what change will most systematically and reliably *affect* the size of an indirect cost pool. The resource with the greatest reliable effect will be a good choice for a cost-allocation base.

Statisticians are not accountants and they use different terminology. The statistical term identifying any value that changes as the value of another factor changes is **outcome variable** (or **response variable**), denoted as Y. For management accountants, this is the indirect cost pool. The factor that changes first is called the **predictor variable** (or **explanatory variable**),[2] denoted as X. In situations where only one predictor variable is deliberately changed in a systematic way, statisticians label it the independent variable and the outcome is termed the dependent variable. For management accountants, the predictor variable is the cost-allocation base (the resource consumed) and the outcome variable is the size of the indirect cost pool. The underlying relationship between the predictor and outcome variable is, to some degree, causal and the OLS analysis in part tests the extent to which the apparent causality is reliably modeled by the regression line.

In this chapter we will assume values of the indirect cost pool are always Y, the outcome variable; and values of the quantities consumed of each resource that is a candidate for the cost-allocation base are always X, the predictor variable. It is important to understand that no one deliberately changes the value of the predictor variable X, but rather simply measures and records whatever changes are observed for both X and Y. Managers can systematically collect these measures of resources consumed and size of the indirect cost pools (X,Y) at the same location but at different times. Data collected in this way are called *time-series data*. Managers can also choose to systematically collect these data points simultaneously at many different locations. Data collected this way are called cross-sectional data. Sometimes it is difficult to tell what causes what—the chicken-and-egg problem. In these cases, the Granger causality test can be used to assess which is the predictor and which is the outcome variable in a time series.

Without controlled experimentation, it is difficult to assert with certainty that a cause–effect relationship between X and Y exists. If trials are conducted, the terminology changes, although the techniques do not. Practically, however, it is highly disruptive and risky to experiment with a production process for a good or service. One ready example is a continuous process situation described in Chapter 17. In a milk processing facility, stopping the pasteurization process to conduct an experiment would destroy all the inputs (milk) currently in process and create costly waste (the improperly pasteurized milk would have to be discarded).

The sacrifice or cost of experimentation needs to be weighed against any benefit that could be obtained from establishing causality rather than conducting an OLS regression analysis of cost-pool changes based on an observed association with the consumption of resources. The OLS tells managers a stable relationship exists between the predictor and the outcome variable. It means changes in the predictor are associated with changes in the outcome—but OLS can never define what is causing what. Remember, for accountants, tracing is the technique for determining what is causing what; this chapter is about allocation. OLS is a useful tool to statistically justify the choice of an allocation base from alternatives.

THINKING CRITICALLY

Benjamin Disraeli is quoted as having said "There are three kinds of lies: lies, damned lies, and statistics." What do you think he was trying to caution people against? Explain in a sentence or two. Read on for a discussion of this topic.

---

[2]P.C. Abrami, P. Cholmsky, and R. Gordon, *Statistical Analysis for the Social Sciences An Interactive Approach* (Boston: Allyn & Bacon, 2001).

Numbers, including statistics, are powerful ways to persuade others that an apparent relationship really does exist. For example, as alcohol consumption increases, so too does attendance at places of worship. The reverse is also true: as attendance increases, so too does alcohol consumption. The explanation lies in another fact: the population is increasing. With this increase comes an increase in both alcohol consumption and attendance. Statistics are the results of manipulating data—if the input data are nonsense, then the statistics will also be nonsense. A succinct way of saying this is: garbage in, garbage out. The goal of management accountants is to provide information useful for decision making, and nonsense does not qualify. Management accountants need to understand OLS well enough to check whether or not specific assumptions about the data and the data collection process have been met to ensure the quality of the input data.

ASSUMPTIONS

Management accountants must assure themselves that the data sets they use meet the following four key assumptions before undertaking OLS linear regression:

- Economic plausibility implies that a real relationship, not a coincidental one, exists between the quantity of the resource consumed and the size of the indirect cost pool
- Linearity best describes the economic relationship between the quantity of the resource consumed and the size of the indirect cost pool
- Normality of the distribution of residuals tells you that the differences between actual measurements and their average occur due to random events
- Uniformity of residuals assures that the error terms or distances of the actual data points from the regression line are not systematically changing around that line

Specification analysis is the process of testing these assumptions of the quality of input data used in regression analysis. Any OLS software will automatically report the results of specification analysis. If the assumptions are met, then the output—a regression equation, graphs, and benchmark statistics—will indicate the regression model is reliable. Reliability in large part depends upon whether or not the statistical result reflects reality in a systematic way, not an accidental or random way. Reliability is essential if information is to be useful for decision making. The first step in producing reliable statistical output is to assure the quality of data input.

Economic Plausibility   *Economic plausibility* means that resources being considered as predictor variables are actually consumed when the indirect costs are incurred. Among other things, OLS provides useful evidence that one resource is preferable to another as a cost-allocation base with respect to understanding changes in a specific indirect cost pool. Recall that an indirect manufacturing cost pool is a grouping of types of indirect costs incurred but the resources consumed are not readily and economically traced directly to a unique cause. Materials handling, custodial labour, security, equipment maintenance, quality control, rework labour, overtime, idle time, fringe and statutory benefits, and managers' salaries might all be combined into a single indirect manufacturing labour cost pool often called *manufacturing overhead*. Manufacturing overhead is an inventoriable cost and part of cost of goods sold reported on the income statement. An input common to all these activities can, at best, explain only part of the change in costs in the indirect cost pool often because the wage rates differ for different types of indirect labour.

Often the choice of consumption of a resource, or the predictor variable X, is an input that has already been measured, such as direct machine hours or direct manufacturing labour hours. These become cost-allocation bases because they are economically and readily measurable, not because their relationship to the size of indirect cost pools (Y) is well understood. If management accountants must allocate indirect costs on the basis of second-best choices for the cost-allocation base, then all other things equal, they should choose the resource for which changes in consumption most reliably explain the greatest proportion of the change in the size of an indirect cost pool. It is the best choice because by controlling the quantity of the resource consumed, managers can be somewhat confident they will control the size of the indirect cost pool.

When two events vary together, they exhibit **correlation**, also called *covariance*. At Elegant Rugs, normally, but not always, as the direct machine hours (DMH) are consumed, the wages for materials handling will also increase because materials have to be delivered to the machinery for conversion into finished goods. Materials handlers also have to remove finished goods from the production area to the warehousing area. Similar reasoning can be presented for custodial, security, quality control, maintenance, and other indirect labour costs. There is an economically plausible relationship between the consumption of DMH and the size of the indirect manufacturing labour cost pool, but the relationship is indirect. Perhaps if machines manufacturing the rugs at Elegant Rugs do not run, then the materials handlers do not have to spend time transferring inputs to and outputs off the machines. But a union contract may require the fork lift truck operators be paid for idle time, which means the consumption of DMH does not always covary perfectly with the wages paid to materials handlers.

Before undertaking an activity-based costing (ABC) effort that would clarify the relationship between components of the cost pool and inputs consumed, the management accountant can use OLS linear regression analysis to assess the proportion of the cost pool explained by consumption of DMH. If the explanatory power of DMH meets particular statistical benchmarks, then the management accountant may recommend the use of DMH as the cost-allocation base for this cost pool. While this choice is second best compared to an ABC effort to identify cost drivers, if no material difference can be gained in controlling costs, then it is not worthwhile to undertake ABC. The objective of OLS is not to assess simply if a change in resource consumption changes the size of the indirect cost pool, but rather whether by controlling resource consumption, managers can reliably control the size of the indirect cost pool. It is worth emphasizing that with indirect cost pools, no single resource will explain a lot of change. If it did, then managers could readily undertake an ABC strategy and create a separate direct cost pool.

One measure or statistic used to convey the strength of the relationship between consumption of a resource and the size of the indirect cost pool is the **coefficient of determination, r^2**. The r^2 reports the proportion or percentage of the change in the size of the indirect cost pool that can be explained by the change in consumption of the resource if the model is reliable. **Goodness of fit** is the term statisticians use to describe explanatory power, and r^2 is the statistic or measure of goodness of fit. The benchmark or threshold for a reliable model is $r^2 \geq |0.30|$. If $r^2 \geq 0.30$, then increases in consumption of a resource will explain at least 30% of the increase in the size of the indirect cost pool and this identifies a relationship between the predictor and outcome variables. If $r^2 \geq -0.30$ then increases in consumption of a resource will explain at least 30% of the decrease in the size of the indirect cost pool, and this identifies an inverse relationship between the predictor and outcome variables.

Linearity *Linearity* means that the relationship between the consumption of a resource and the change in an indirect cost pool can best be graphed as a straight line. Mathematicians and statisticians call this relationship a **cost function**. A **linear cost function** is depicted on a graph as a straight line for the equation $y = a + bX$. The *a* **coefficient** is the value of y when $X = 0$, and it is a constant referred to as the *intercept*. The value of *a* is the proportion of the total cost pool that cannot be explained by changes in consumption of the resource X. Be careful in cases of purely variable indirect cost pools, as *a* is *not* a fixed cost but an unexplained cost. In mixed indirect cost pools, some of the unexplained cost may indeed be fixed.

The value of *b* is the slope of the line. A non-zero value of *y* when $X = 0$ will remind the management accountant that some proportion of the total indirect cost pool cannot be explained by the consumption of a specific resource. Note that the linear-regression line is a mathematical estimate of a straight line. An analysis program does not know whether the underlying relationship is indeed linear. The value-added of management accountants is not that they can perform a few mouse clicks to run a linear regression, but rather that they have used professional judgment. Their best judgment is that a straight line, not a curved line, is economically plausible.

Notation is very important—notice that on the left of the equation $y = a + bX$, it is *y*, not *Y*. This is because *Y* represents an actual data point measured at the same time as *X* was measured. The forecast of the outcome value (*y*), based on historical values of *X*, is the result of the OLS mathematical manipulation and is an *estimated* value. The size of the estimated indirect cost pool (*y*) is calculated such that absolute error between all the actual values of $Y = a + bX$ of the real data points and the forecast values of $y = a + bX$ on the graph of the results of the mathematical manipulation is minimized. This line $y = a + bX$ is called the **regression line**. A regression line combines the actual historical values of *X* with the forecast values of *y* obtained from the OLS analysis. The actual values of *X* may not indicate normal values because they may include the effects of either random (unexpected) events or effects of changes in predictor variables not yet included in the model. This is why the forecast value of the outcome variable, *y*, at each time period is calculated to minimize the overall sum of the squares of these differences $\Sigma(Y - y)^2$ between actual (*Y*) and forecast (*y*) values of the outcome variable. That is why it is called the *ordinary least squares method*.

The choices to improve explanatory power include regressing consumption of a different resource against the values of the total indirect cost pool, or adding consumption of different resources to the equation. If more predictor variables are added, then the management accountant is undertaking a multiple linear regression. One problem is that simply adding another predictor will improve explanatory power but part of the improvement may be that the original effect is being measured twice. The test for goodness of fit for a multiple linear regression is a mathematically **adjusted r^2**. The adjusted r^2 uses the ratio between the number of predictor variables (*k*) and the number of observations (*n*) to improve on the measure r^2.

Normality **Normality** means that if the **residual** values were plotted they would differ little from a plot of random values with a mean of 0 and a constant variance, producing the familiar bell-shaped curve (shown in Exhibit 10-2). "Random" simply means that the probability of a specific error value occurring is no higher or lower than any other. The importance of normality is that the linear model of the relationship between the outcome and predictor variables will not systematically overestimate or underestimate the value of the outcome variable. In accounting, this means the indirect cost pool values predicted by the OLS regression will be unbiased. Neutrality, or lack of bias, is one characteristic of reliability in financial accounting, as it is in management accounting.

The bell curve is a convenient way to display the dispersion or spread of observed errors around μ, the arithmetic mean of the values for an entire population. The standard deviation (σ) is calculated using a specific arithmetic formula. The numeric value of σ will depend on each distribution. The normal curve that is like an envelope around all the observed errors and their frequencies is symmetric; therefore, the observed measures will be either higher or lower than μ but they must sum to zero in a normal distribution.

The curve also tells you that for a normal distribution, 34.1% of error values will be higher and 34.1% lower than μ. More importantly, these proportions will be within one standard deviation of μ. An additional 13.6% of error values will be included under the curve if you count those that are both one and two standard deviations from the mean. An additional 2.15% will be included if you count all

EXHIBIT 10-2
A Bell Curve

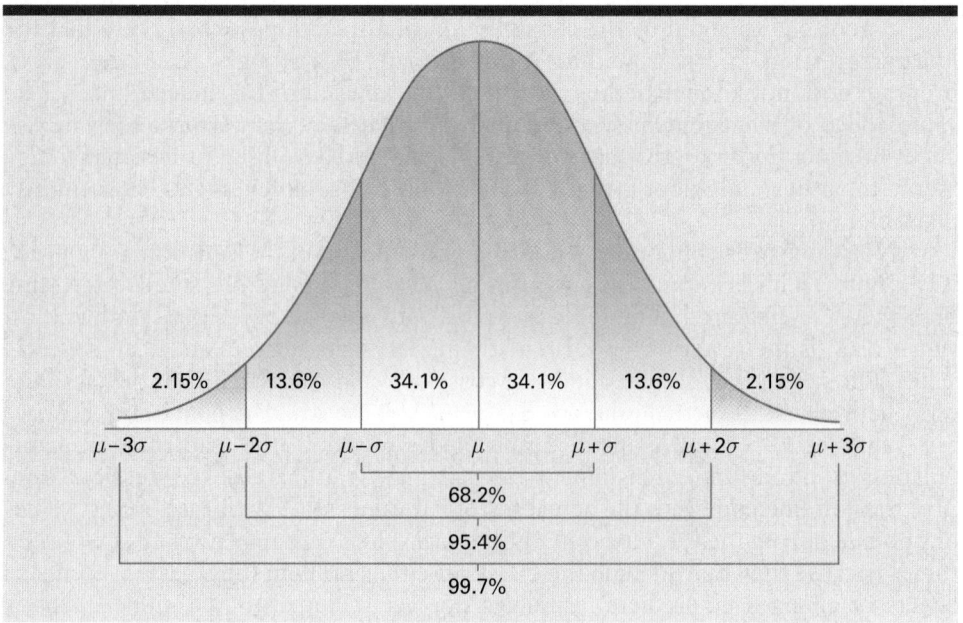

observations which are 1 σ, 2 σ, and 3 σ from the mean. Notice that at ± 3 σ that 99.7% of the observed values are included.

The likelihood of an observed error value greater or less than three standard deviations from the mean is very small, only 0.3%, a fraction of 1%. When an error value of this type is observed during some time period, it tells you that something out of the ordinary has happened. These values are often called *outliers*. From a management accountant's perspective, an outlier would tell you that there is some event or series of events that has biased the error of measured values. When there is bias in the errors, the OLS is no longer a reliable indicator of the best predictor variable (cost-allocation base).

The **residual term *u*** is also called either the *disturbance* or the *error term*. The sum of residuals is zero. The residual is calculated as $u = Y - y$ and graphically it appears as the vertical deviation of the estimated data point (X, y) from the actual data point (X, Y). The importance of normality is that the linear model of the relationship between the outcome and predictor variables will not systematically overestimate or underestimate the value of the outcome variable. The regression line will be unbiased. Neutrality, or lack of bias, is one characteristic of reliability in financial accounting, as it is in management accounting.

Uniformity of Residuals   *Uniformity of residuals* means that if the vertical distance between the forecast y and the actual Y bears no relationship to the value of X, then the value of X does not affect the residual value. When the data set is cross-sectional, this uniformity is called **homoskedasticity**. If there is some systematic pattern between the size of the residuals and the predictor variable, this is called **heteroskedasticity**. If the data points in the data set were measured at one factory at different times, then managers have a time-series data set. When the data set is time series, this uniformity is called **serial correlation**. When a residual value at one point in time differs systematically from the residual value at another point in time, serial correlation is present. This means, again, that the error or residual term in the straight-line equation is not neutral—it is either too high or too low because of the effect of the error term at an earlier point in time.

One type of systematic dependence is called **autocorrelation**, which arises when the current residual value depends upon the residual value either immediately prior (lagged) to it or immediately after it in time (leading). The scatterplots in

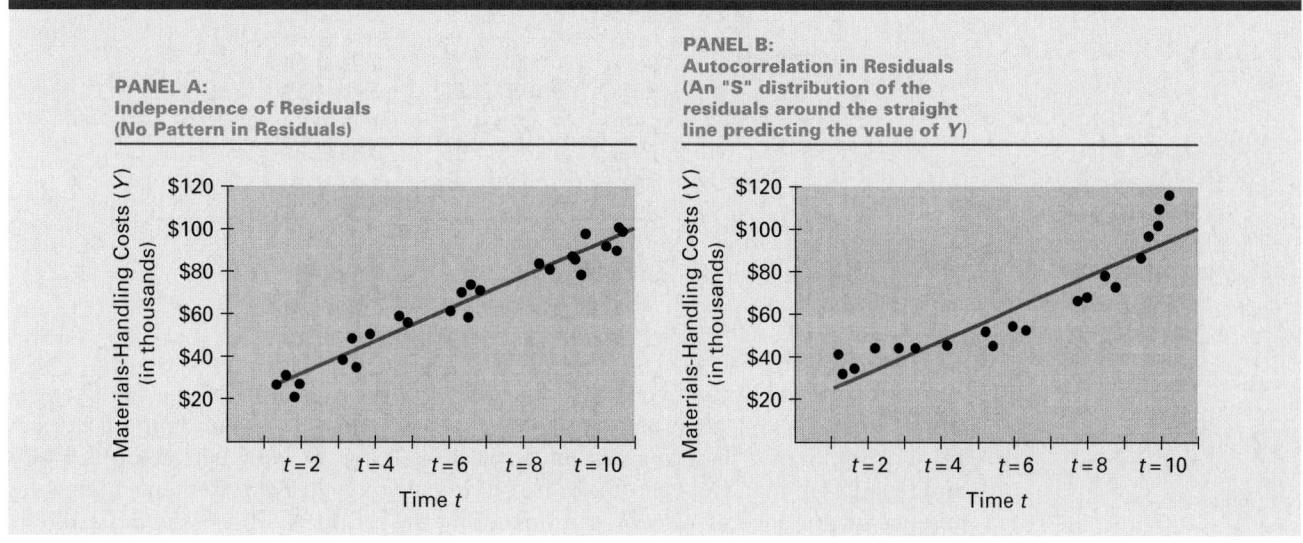

PANEL A:
Independence of Residuals
(No Pattern in Residuals)

PANEL B:
Autocorrelation in Residuals
(An "S" distribution of the
residuals around the straight
line predicting the value of Y)

Exhibit 10-3 illustrate independence among the residuals in Panel A, and autocorrelation in Panel B.

In this example, the size of the indirect cost pool is being measured at several different time periods. Time is the horizontal axis rather than the value of the predictor variable. When actual measures of the size of the indirect cost pool differ unsystematically from the measures estimated using OLS linear regression, then the regression line is a good model of the relationship between the predictor (X) and outcome variable (y). If, however, there is a systematic pattern to the residuals, for example the oscillating pattern illustrated in Panel B, then an unidentified factor is affecting the size of the indirect cost pool. The regression line is still precisely estimated but the management accountant cannot be confident that this line represents how the predictor variable affects the size of the indirect materials handling cost pool, if at all.

The **Durbin-Watson statistic, d,** tests for the presence of serial correlation among residuals of a linear regression model using ordinary least squares (OLS). Formally, the Durbin-Watson statistic is calculated as:

$$d = \frac{\sum_{t=2}^{n}(e_t - e_{t-1})^2}{\sum_{t=1}^{n}(e^2)}$$

where,
d = Durbin-Watson statistic
e = residuals (forecast minus actual value)
t = time period

The Durbin-Watson statistic d can confirm the presence or absence of autocorrelation in the measures of the predictor variable (X). To use d, we must start with a **null hypothesis, H_0.** A null hypothesis is a statement to be rejected if an analysis of the data fails a specified statistical test. In the case of a time series, the null hypothesis (H_0) is that no autocorrelation exists among the residuals. H_0 will be rejected if, using an appropriate analysis, the data fail to meet a benchmark value. The critical or benchmark values for d range from 0 to 4. When H_0 cannot be rejected, $d \approx 2$. We can state our null hypothesis quantitatively as H_0: $d \approx 2$. When lagged values of the independent variable(s) are used to explain changes in the dependent variable (Y), then d is biased toward not rejecting H_0: $d \approx 2$. The table of critical values, below, shows the lower range (D-L) and upper range (D-U) of critical values for the case of one ($X = 1$) and two ($X = 2$) independent variables for specific numbers of observations at both the 95% and 99% confidence levels.

There are three possible outcomes that must be considered after calculating the d statistic. If, after calculating d, the value ranges between 0 and 1, then positive

Durbin-Watson Table of Critical Values

Observations N Confidence		X = 1 D–L D–U		X = 2 D–L D–U	
15	95%	1.08	1.36	0.95	1.54
	99%	0.81	1.07	0.70	1.25
20	95%	1.20	1.71	1.10	1.54
	99%	0.95	1.15	0.86	1.27
25	95%	1.29	1.45	1.21	1.55
	99%	1.05	1.21	0.98	1.30
30	95%	1.35	1.49	1.28	1.57
	99%	1.13	1.26	1.07	1.34

Source: http://hadm.sph.sc.edu/courses/J716/Dw.html

autocorrelation exists and you must reject H_0. If, after calculating d, the value ranges from (4 – D-L) to 4, then negative autocorrelation exists and again you must reject H_0. For values of d that range either between D-L and D-U or between (4 – D-U) and (4 – D-L), managers can make no statistically conclusive statements about the absence or presence of autocorrelation among the residuals. To use the table above, the calculated value of d when there are 15 observations of a single independent variable ($X = 1$) must be compared to the critical values in the table for D-L and D-U. If managers are satisfied being 95% confident of their conclusion, then the following would be the case:

d (Calculated)	H_0	Critical Value(s)	Reason
0 to 1.08 (D-L)	reject	$d < 2$	positive autocorrelation
1.08 to 1.36 or	inconclusive*	$\text{D-U} < d < \text{D-L}$	
2.64 to 2.69	inconclusive	$(4\text{–D-U}) < d < (4\text{–D-L})$	
2.92 to 4	reject	$(4\text{–D-L}) < d < 4$	negative autocorrelation

*inconclusive means managers can neither accept nor reject H_0 with 95% confidence.

A picture is worth thousands of words, and the best test to determine uniformity is a scatterplot of the residuals showing reasonably small random variation of the actual data points from those on the regression line. Exhibit 10-4 illustrates homoskedasticity of the residual or error terms on the left and heteroskedasticity on

EXHIBIT 10-4

Constant Variance of Residuals Assumption in Cross-Sectional Data Sets

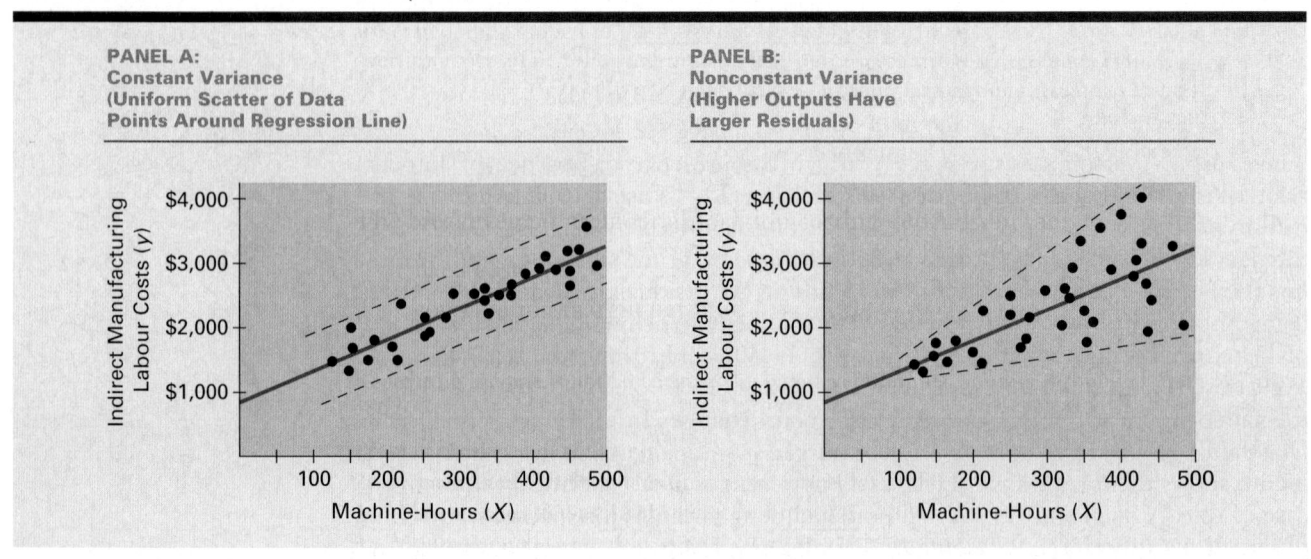

PANEL A:
Constant Variance
(Uniform Scatter of Data
Points Around Regression Line)

PANEL B:
Nonconstant Variance
(Higher Outputs Have
Larger Residuals)

the right. Assume that the data points illustrated in Exhibit 10-4 were measured at many different factories at the same point in time, a cross-sectional data set. The predictor variable X is direct machine hours consumed (DMH), which is a resource consumed that indirectly gives rise to many of the indirect manufacturing labour costs in the cost pool, the outcome variable Y.

In Panel A on the left, the estimated values of (X,y) fall on the regression line. Notice that the actual values of (X,Y) are fairly close to and scattered in a random manner around the regression line. In contrast, Panel B illustrates a very different pattern. If this was the data set collected in the factories, then the larger the quantity of DMH, the greater is the distance between the estimated values of (X,y) on the regression line from the actual values of (X,Y). The management accountant should interpret this to mean that, as the quantity of DMH consumed increases, the proportion of the increase in the indirect manufacturing labour cost pool explained decreases. From Panel B, the good news is that the regression line has still been precisely estimated given the data provided. The bad news is that the residual was supposed to arise due to random factors and this is not true. A systematic increase in the size of the residual strongly suggests there is another input, an unspecified predictor variable, systematically affecting the size of the indirect cost pool.

Statistical Significance   *Statistical Significance* is based on a mathematical manipulation of the raw measure of random error called the *standard error* of the estimate. The standard error is used in the denominator of a benchmark statistic to assess whether or not the calculated values of a (the intercept) and b (the slope of the regression line) are likely to have arisen by coincidence. This benchmark is called the **student t-statistic.** If the value of t calculated from the input data does not meet a critical or threshold value, then management accountants have no confidence that the calculated values of a and b that specify the linear-regression line are not simply random values.

Random values of a and b mean that the management accountant is as well off drawing a line through the data points while blindfolded. An unreliable linear-regression line provides no relevant information about how the value of the indirect cost pool would change if the quantity of the consumption of the resource changed. Not all is lost. Even if the calculated t-value does not meet the critical value, management accountants have at least identified an irrelevant candidate for the cost-allocation base of a specific indirect cost pool.

Like accounting, statistics is a conservative process. Statisticians assume that the estimated values of the coefficients a and b are random values, then conduct a test to provide evidence of whether or not they can reject this assumption. This assumption is the null hypothesis or H_0. **Statistically significant** means the value of the coefficients a and b are probably different from random values. If true, then the regression line has some predictive power. But statistical analysis is never a sure thing, and there is always a probability, despite results that support rejecting H_0, that the results are false. Management accountants have to choose the **confidence level** they prefer, usually either 95% or 99%. In keeping with conservatism, however, the benchmark above which H_0 can be rejected is the probability that the results are wrong. Probability is denoted as p, and the thresholds are usually reported at $p = 0.05$ (a 5% probability of failing to reject H_0 when you should) and $p = 0.01$ (a 1% probability of failing to reject a false H_0). This is a Type 2 error. A Type 1 error is rejecting a true H_0. Confidence level is the probability that the conclusion based on comparing a calculated student t-value to the critical value of a student t-statistic is wrong.

Critical Values   A **critical value** is a benchmark value for the student t-statistic. If the calculated value of t for the values of the coefficients a and b exceed the critical value, then at a specific confidence level, the values of a and b are not due to chance. Rejecting H_0 is good news. The management accountant can be confident (within specific limits) that values of a and b are related to the change in value of the indirect cost pool. Unfortunately, only b relates to the explanatory power of the predictor variable. The coefficient a refers to changes in all the variables other than the predictor variable that could explain changes in the value of the indirect cost pool.

In practice, the management accountant could assure users of the analysis that the results were not good luck arising from the data points used. Below is a table of critical values for the student *t*-statistic reporting different values at different degrees of freedom and confidence levels.

Table of Critical Values — *t*-Statistic

Degrees of Freedom	95% Confidence Level	99% Confidence Level
1	12.706	63.657
2	4.303	9.925
3	3.182	5.841
4	2.776	4.604
5	2.571	4.032
6	2.447	3.707
7	2.365	3.499
8	2.306	3.355
9	2.262	3.250
10	2.228	3.169
11	2.201	3.106
12	2.179	3.055
15	2.131	2.947
25	2.060	2.787
40	2.021	2.704
60	2.000	2.660
infinity	1.960	2.576

Source: From Appendix C of Philip C. Abrami, Paul Cholmsky, and Robert Gordon, *Statistical Analysis for the Social Sciences* (Boston, MA: Allyn & Bacon, 2001).

Mathematically, the student *t*-statistic is the ratio of how large the estimated value of the coefficient is relative to its standard error. The use of less than 30 data points increases the probability that the estimated value of the coefficient (for example, *b*) is biased. In the example shown in the next section in Exhibit 10-5, there are only 12 data points. *Bias* means the estimate is almost always too high or too low relative to the actual value. Graphically, the slope would be too steep or too shallow. If the slope was too steep, then the forecast cost would almost always be too high relative to the observed cost. Mathematically, bias in the standard error can be eliminated and the unbiased value is used to calculate the student *t*. This is important in choosing the threshold or critical value of student *t* above which H_0 can be rejected.

Degrees of Freedom   *Degrees of freedom* is a way to properly classify a critical value for each sample size. For our purposes, the number of observed measures recorded is the sample size. The critical value changes with the **degrees of freedom (*d.f.*)** in the set of data points and the confidence level the management accountant prefers. The degrees of freedom for a set of *n* data points is *d.f.* = *n* − *k*. In the case shown in Exhibit 10-5, *n* = 12, and there is only one predictor variable *X* with one coefficient *b*; therefore, *k* = 1 and the *d.f.* = 11. The comparison of the student *t*-statistics for *a* and *b* to their critical values will be completed in Objective 3 of this chapter.

MyAccountingLab

ASSESS YOUR MASTERY

To check your understanding of the material in Learning Objective ❶, go to the *Mastery Questions* section at the end of the chapter and complete Learning Objective ❶ questions 1, 2, and 3.

474 CHAPTER 10

EXCEL DOES THE MATH: VALUE ADDED FROM INTERPRETING THE RESULTS

Exhibit 10-5 shows 12 actual values or observations for X, the predictor variable direct machine hours (DMH); an alternative X, the predictor variable direct manufacturing labour hours (DMLH); and Y, the outcome variable indirect manufacturing labour costs for Elegant Rugs. Notice that in column A these values are measured one week apart; therefore the values are a time-series data set. Column B reports the weekly values of the first resource consumed, DMH. Column C reports the weekly values of the size of the indirect manufacturing labour cost pool (security, custodial, quality control costs, etc.). Column D reports the actual weekly values of direct manufacturing labour hours (DMLH).

Before calculating r^2, however, there are three further tests of the data set that must be undertaken. The next test answers whether or not a straight line is the best description of any relationship between either of the predictor variables and the outcome variable. This is a test of linearity, which requires actually calculating the estimated values of the constant or intercept a and the slope b using the mathematical manipulations required by the OLS method. Exhibit 10-6 illustrates the actual data points (X,Y) in blue, and the forecast data points from the linear regression calculation (X,y) in red for both the DMH on the left and DMLH on the right, which are the predictor variables (X).

Assuming that consumption of DMH is independent of consumption of DMLH, there are two resources that may be used as a cost-allocation base. It appears that the distances between the actual values (X,Y) and the forecast values (X,y) for DMLH are greater than the distances for DMH. It also appears that the a value for the DMLH regression line (in red) is greater than that of DMH, which means that the proportion of the total cost pool that cannot be explained by changes in consumption of the resource is higher for DMLH than DMH. Finally, the slope b of the regression line appears less steep for DMLH than for DMH. This means a unit increase in consumption of DMLH will explain a smaller proportion of the change in size of the indirect cost pool than will an increase in unit consumption of DMH.

Fortunately, if Excel is used in these analyses, the program provides arithmetic values to improve the precision of comparisons of the suitability of DMLH or DMH

Apply standardized mathematical manipulations to a set of data points and produce the results of an OLS simple linear regression analysis with benchmark statistics testing reliability

EXHIBIT 10-5
Actual Time-Series Data Points at Elegant Rugs

	A	B	C	D
1			Indirect	Direct
2		Direct	Manufacturing	Manufacturing
3	Week	Machine-Hours	Labour Costs	Labour-Hours
4		(X)	(Y)	Alternative (X)
5	1	68	$ 1,190	30
6	2	88	1,211	35
7	3	62	1,004	36
8	4	72	917	20
9	5	60	770	47
10	6	96	1,456	45
11	7	78	1,180	44
12	8	46	710	38
13	9	82	1,316	70
14	10	94	1,032	30
15	11	68	752	29
16	12	48	963	38
17	Total	862	$12,501	462

EXHIBIT 10-6
The Linear Regression Illustrating the Relationship Between Each Predictor and Outcome Variable

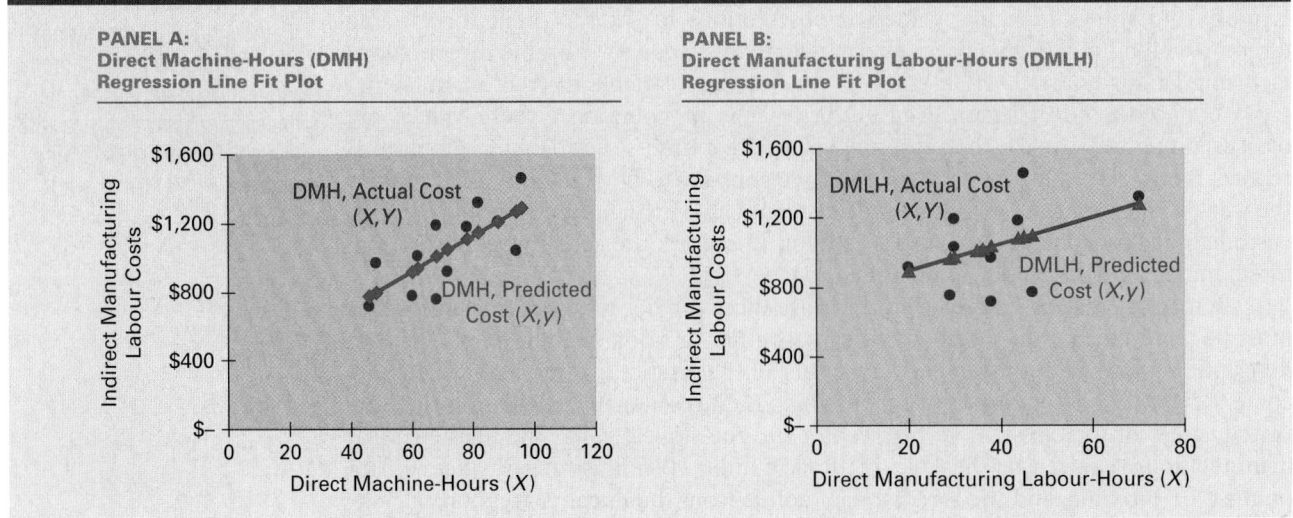

PANEL A:
Direct Machine-Hours (DMH)
Regression Line Fit Plot

PANEL B:
Direct Manufacturing Labour-Hours (DMLH)
Regression Line Fit Plot

as a cost-allocation base. Part of Excel's output includes a table of the residuals (the distances between actual measures of DMH and the average DMH), as shown below. Notice for the third data point, the predicted outcome is $1,022.46 (rounded) and this is $18.46 (rounded) lower than the average:

Observation	Residual Output Predicted (y)	Residuals
1	976.160704	213.839296
2	1,014.742643	196.2573572
3	1,022.459031	−18.45903058
4	898.9968263	18.00317369
5	1,101.339296	−337.339296

Exhibit 10-7 illustrates the results of all the arithmetic manipulations done by the computer to estimate the regression line such that the sum of the squared difference between each (X,Y) and (X,y) is least. The first three columns are report values identical to those in the first three columns of Exhibit 10-5. After all the mathematics are complete, the output reports the estimated value of a, the constant or intercept (X,y) when $X = 0$. The value is measured in dollars because it reports the total in the indirect manufacturing labour cost pool when no direct machine-hours are consumed.

There are, however, two further tasks in the specification analysis. We are reassured that there is an economically plausible relationship between the outcome variable and each of the two predictor variables, and that a straight line can describe the relationship. We do not yet know if the residuals are either distributed normally, or if they are of uniform distribution. The statistical analysis used to test for normality is beyond the scope of this text. There is, however, a graph of the residuals that can be analyzed to assess if the residuals in this time series display any autocorrelation.

Exhibit 10-8 presents the graphs of the pattern of the residuals around a straight line. A management accountant actually hopes to find *no* pattern in the plot. The left panel of Exhibit 10-8 depicts the residuals for the outcome variable direct machine-hours (DMH), and the right panel depicts the residuals for the outcome variable direct manufacturing labour-hours (DMLH).

Simple inspection of the two graphs does not suggest any systematic change in the value of the residuals as the values of each outcome variable change. There is neither a funnel shape nor an oscillating curve through the data points. The residuals for DMH appear to be more closely clustered around the straight line than do those of DMLH. The calculation of the residual values is also part of the output produced by Excel. A sample of output for the first 3 observations is shown in Exhibit 10-7.

EXHIBIT 10-7
Results of Calculations of the Residuals Derived ($y - Y$) for Each Outcome Variable

	Residual Output Outcome Variable DMH, (X)			Residual Output Outcome Variable DMLH, Alternate (X)	
Observation	Predicted (y)	Residuals	Observation	Predicted (y)	Residuals
1	1002.219152	187.780848	1	976.160704	213.8393
2	1208.467054	2.53294552	2	1014.742643	196.25763
3	940.3447813	63.6552187	3	1022.459031	–18.45903

The Residuals columns show the results of subtracting the forecast value, y (forecast using the linear regression equation), from the actual value, Y. The actual values of the data points of Y are shown in Exhibit 10-5. The result (the residual) for the first data point is \$187.78. Calculating the Durbin-Watson statistic d for the residuals for DMH results in $d = 2.05$. A comparison with critical values in the Durbin-Watson Table of Critical Values indicates there is no statistical basis on which to reject H_0: $d \approx 2$. Therefore, managers of Elegant Rugs can say with 95% confidence (there is still a 5% probability they will be incorrect) there is no auto-correlation among the residuals. The linear-regression line or model will provide reliable forecasts of future indirect manufacturing cost pool values.

d (Calculated)	H_0	Critical Value(s)	Reason
2.05	accept	$d > 2$	no evidence of autocorrelation

Having used the computer output in the specification analysis and concluded that the input data set meets all four assumptions, we can now examine the goodness of fit of the regression line for each predictor variable. The objective is to select the best resource for use as a cost-allocation base to assign indirect manufacturing labour costs to each rug. The management accountant is looking for $r^2 \geq |0.30|$; otherwise there will not be enough evidence that either predictor variable has adequate explana-tory power. If r^2 is too low, then neither of the predictor variables would be a wise choice as a cost-allocation base. The results of the mathematical manipulations used to calculate r^2 are shown in Exhibit 10-9. The predictor variable is direct machine hours (DMH), and r^2 measures how closely the line based on the estimated value of y differs from the actual value of Y. The coefficient of determination (r^2) indicates the proportion of the variance of Y, the outcome variable explained by changes in the pre-dictor varialble X. The outcome variable Y is calculated as $(\overline{Y})^2 \div n$, where n is the number of observations (12), where $\overline{Y} = \Sigma Y \div n$. It is more convenient to express the coefficient of determination as 1 minus the proportion of total variance that is *not*

EXHIBIT 10-8
Scatterplot of the Residuals For Predictor Variable DMH and Alternative Predictor Variable DMLH

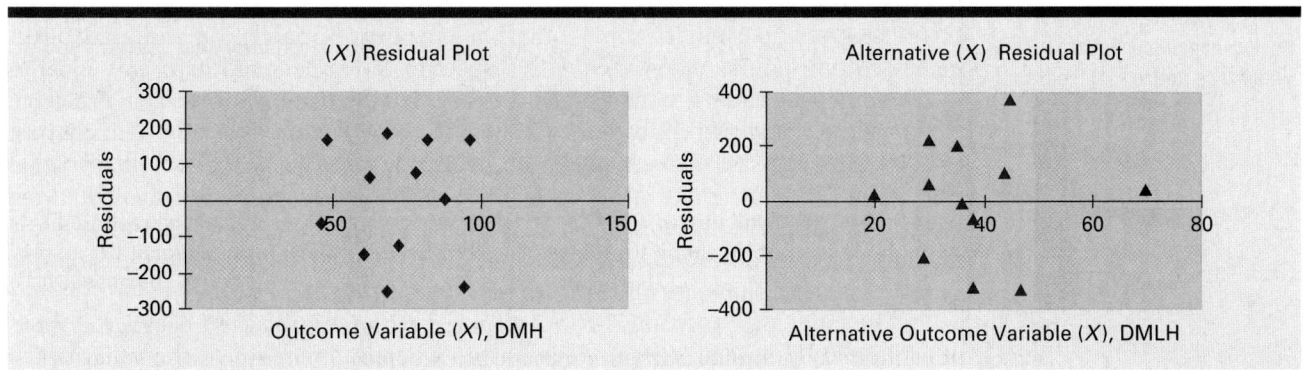

explained by the independent variable. The data to calculate r^2 are in Exhibit 10-5 as well as the results of key calculations to solve the following:

$$r^2 = 1 - \frac{\text{Unexplained variation}}{\text{Total variation}} = 1 - \frac{\Sigma (Y - y)^2}{\Sigma (Y - \overline{Y})^2}$$

$\Sigma Y = 12,501$ and $\overline{Y} = 12,501 \div 12 = 1,041.75$. Therefore, to obtain the total variation,

$$\Sigma (Y - \overline{Y})^2 = (1,190 - 1,041.75)^2 + (1,211 - 1,041.75)^2 + \cdots + (963 - 1,041.75)^2$$

$$= 607,699$$

Each value of X generates a forecast, y. For example, in week 1, $y = \$300.98 + (\$10.31 \times 68) = \$1,002.06$. Therefore, to obtain the unexplained variation,

$$\Sigma (Y - y)^2 = (1,190 - 1,002.06)^2 + (1,211 - 1,208.26)^2 + \cdots + (963 - 795.86)^2$$

$$= 35,321 + 8 + \cdots + 27,936 = 290,824$$

$$r^2 = 1 - \frac{290,824}{607,699} = 0.52$$

The r^2 of 0.52 indicates that 52% of the changes in the forecast values of the outcome variable y can be explained by the corresponding changes in X, the actual values of direct machine hours. The blue data points in Panel A of Exhibit 10-6 illustrate this actual relationship. If some other independent variable, for example direct manufacturing-hours, were tested with respect to the same y and its r^2 was equal to 0.169, you could safely say the changes in the second independent variable explained far less of the changes in the forecast values of the outcome variable, 16.9% in contrast to 52%. The contrast of these two r^2 on its own justifies the initial observation that changes in DMH are more closely associated with changes in indirect manufacturing labour cost than are changes in DMLH. The last line in Exhibit 10-9 reports the number of paired observations of (X,Y), which is 12. For the moment, focus on one statistic, r^2, in the summary table in Exhibit 10-9.

The range of r^2 is from –1 to +1 denoted arithmetically as $-1 \leq r^2 \leq +1$. An r^2 of –1 implies a perfect negative relationship whereby increases in the value of the predictor variable perfectly explain 100% of the decreases in value of the outcome variable. An r^2 of 0 implies that the predictor variable has no explanatory power. An r^2 of +1 implies that increases in the value of the predictor variable perfectly explain

EXHIBIT 10-9
Summary Output of Regression Statistics

Direct Machine-Hours (DMH)

Regression Statistics		Coefficients		t-stat	p-value
		Intercept a	300.97628	1.3099936	0.219491
r^2	0.5214333	Standard Error a	170.53566		
Adjusted r^2	0.4735767	Slope b	10.312395	3.3008681	0.0080018
Observations	12	Standard error b	3.1241464		

Direct Manufacturing Labour-Hours (DMLH)

Regression Statistics		Coefficients		t-stat	p-value
		Intercept a	744.66907	3.4219846	0.0065257
r^2	0.1698004	Standard Error a	224.61319		
Adjusted r^2	0.0867804	Slope b	7.7163878	1.4301384	0.1831701
Observations	12	Standard Error b	5.3955532		

100% of the increases in the value of the outcome variable. When $r^2 = 1$, the forecast cost values (y) would be exactly equal to the actual cost values (Y), and no random factors or other predictor variables would improve on the current explanatory power. The management accountant would have to conclude that the model actually traced a direct cost relationship. Visually, on a regression-line graph, the blue and red points would perfectly overlap each other.

The smaller the sample, the higher the r^2 required to justify a conclusion that this statistic correctly measures the association between the outcome and predictor variables. In this example, 12 observations is a small sample, and 52% is only a partial, not a full, correlation. One possibility is to take more measurements, but this could be costly to accomplish if the time periods represented years rather than weeks. Moreover, most equipment is obsolete well before 12 years and has been replaced. Another way to improve explanatory power of the linear model of the relationships between the outcome variable and predictor is to add more predictor variables. The arithmetic good news about this method of measuring the strength of association between the outcome and predictor variable(s) is that as predictor variables are added, the r^2 increases. The bad news is that this is true no matter what the new predictor variable is.

Recall that we have 12 data points (see Exhibit 10-5) and one coefficient for one predictor variable X, DMH, in this simple linear regression; therefore, $k = 1$ and $d.f. = 11$. The critical value of student $t = 3.106$ for $d.f. = 11$ at the 99% confidence level. The student-t for the slope coefficient, b, is calculated as $10.31 \div \$3.12 = 3.30; 3.30 > 3.106$. The **p value**, or probability it is wrong to reject H_0, is approximately 8 in 1,000 or p = 0.008. Management accountants can recommend with 99% confidence that the coefficient of b lies between –$0.62 and $20.00. This range is calculated as $10.31 \pm (3.106 \times \$3.12)$ or $10.31 \pm \$9.69$. This seems to be a wide range of error for the true value of b that could be improved by obtaining more clean data points. Contrast this with the result of testing the value $a = \$300.98 \div \$224.61 = 1.34; 1.34 < 2.20$, therefore the value of the constant term is not significantly different from a random value. You will recall that this indirect cost pool comprises indirect labour costs arising from many activities ranging from custodial and security to materials handling, maintenance, and quality control. In contrast, for the predictor variable DMLH, the t-statistic for a implies it is significantly different from a random value while the t-statistic for b implies it is not.

The results suggest that if it is important to obtain a better estimate of a and b, Elegant Rugs must at the very least obtain more data points. It may be more important, however, to discuss how to improve the specification of this cost function. It is unlikely that simply adding more predictor variables to the current model will improve the explanatory power of DMH to forecast the size of the indirect cost pool. The first steps would be to take the effort and time to produce a more homogeneous cost pool that is more closely associated with consumption of a resource. But time and effort cost money, as does accessing or creating new data on cost pools and quantity of inputs consumed. The initial reason for using a cost-allocation base for indirect costs was because the causes of these costs were not readily or economically measurable. A good management accountant would be sure to highlight the limitations of these statistical results to help managers understand the limits of reliability for any forecasts of cost-pool size based on forecast values of DMH consumed.

> ### THINKING CRITICALLY
>
> If you were a management accountant with a goal to provide high-quality information to help managers make good decisions about cost-allocation base selection, why would you be concerned with an increase in the value of r^2 after adding a predictor variable? Explain in a sentence or two, then read on for further discussion of this topic.

Relevant information is crucial to choosing the best cost-allocation base to allocate an indirect cost pool. If OLS is used appropriately, then the practical result will be that by controlling the predictor variable(s), costs will be controlled. The expected decrease in costs will be reliably forecast by the equation of the regression line. Underlying regression is the assumption there actually is some systematic relationship to be measured. If this is not the case, just adding predictor variables without reason may increase the r^2, but it decreases the likelihood that controlling that factor will control an indirect cost. Results from misapplied statistical methods are unreliable and have no relevance.

In a simple world, the best outcome of OLS linear regression analysis would be a reliable linear-regression line with the values of both a and b with t-statistics that meet or improve upon the critical value for a specified confidence level and degrees of freedom. In our example, we have been more realistic. Notice that the critical value of the t-statistic for 11 $d.f.$ and a confidence level of 95% is 2.20. Selecting DMH as the cost-allocation base will mean that the calculated t-value for the slope coefficient b exceeds the critical value; therefore, the management accountant can be confident in rejecting the H_0. In fact, the probability of being wrong is very small, approximately 8 in 1,000, as shown by the p-value of 0.008. The calculated t-value for the intercept a, however, is only 1.31, which means it is likely this is a random value. In fact, the probability that the management accountant would be wrong rejecting H_0 is very high, more than 1 in 5 or $p = 0.22$. The reverse is the case for using DMLH as the cost-allocation base. The slope coefficient b is likely to be a random value but this is highly unlikely for the value of the intercept a.

With ambiguous results, the management accountant must explain the limitations of the results of the OLS linear regression analysis. One consolation is that it takes about five minutes, including data input time, to run the regression; therefore, it would be difficult to justify an accusation that OLS is a waste of time. In fact, managers now know more about the limitations of using a direct cost driver as an indirect cost-allocation base than they did before the five minutes were consumed. The managers may still decide to use either DMH or DMLH as the cost-allocation base. In this situation, the steeper-sloped model is preferable because the shallower the slope, the more difficult it is to explain changes in the indirect cost pool on the basis of changes in the consumption of the resource in the cost-allocation base. At a slope of 0, the consumption changes have no power to explain the indirect cost pool changes. Bear in mind, however, that consumption of resources explain approximately 52% and 17% of the change in size of the indirect cost pool, and this may be adequate to suit the managers' needs.

There are, however, other possible courses of action. One is to subdivide the very heterogeneous costs in the current indirect cost pool. One approach illustrated in Chapter 4 was to consider the indirect costs, such as the employer's statutory contributions that were directly caused by the direct wage levels, as a separate indirect cost pool from other costs. If this did not result in a material improvement in the managers' ability to control a material proportion of costs in the indirect cost pool, then the next step could be a more extensive activity-based costing (ABC) project to further refine the causes of different components of the indirect cost pool. Bear in mind, however, that these projects take both time and money to complete, and the benefit may not outweigh the cost.

ASSESS YOUR MASTERY

To check your understanding of the material in Learning Objective ② , go to the *Mastery Questions* section at the end of the chapter and complete Learning Objective ② questions 1, 2, and 3.

MyAccountingLab

DATA COLLECTION AND ADJUSTMENT ISSUES

The ideal database for estimating cost functions quantitatively has two characteristics:

> **Identify and explain data problems encountered in estimating cost functions** ③

◆ It contains at least 31 reliably measured observations of the predictor variables (the resource consumed) and the outcome variable (the indirect cost pool). Measurement errors impair the quality of data input, resulting in a very statistically precise but wrong model of how the consumption of the resource affects the size of the indirect cost pool.

◆ It includes values for the predictor variable over a wide range. Using only a few values that are grouped closely together considers too small a segment of the relevant range and reduces confidence in the estimates obtained.

Unfortunately, management accountants rarely have the advantage of working with a database having both characteristics. This section outlines some frequently encountered data problems and steps a management accountant can take to overcome them.

1. The time period for measuring the outcome variable (for example, indirect manufacturing labour costs) does not properly match the period for measuring the predictor variable(s), for example direct machine-hours (DMH) and direct manufacturing labour-hours (DMLH). This problem often arises when financial accounting records are not kept on an accrual basis. Consider a cost function with machine lubricant costs as the outcome variable and machine-hours as the predictor. Assume that the lubricant is purchased sporadically and stored for later use. Records maintained on a cash basis will indicate no lubricant consumption in many months and sizable lubricant consumption in other months. This is an obviously inaccurate picture of what is actually taking place. The management accountant should encourage the use of accrual accounting to measure consumption of machine lubricants to better match costs with the consumption of a resource.

2. Fixed costs are allocated as if they were variable (see Chapter 2 for a full discussion of unitized costs). Costs such as amortization, insurance, or rent may be allocated to products to calculate costs per unit of output. The danger is to misunderstand these costs as variable rather than as fixed. Apparent variability is the result of calculating a unit fixed cost, then multiplying it by some actual quantity of input consumed to arrive at a total fixed cost. In fact, over a relevant range the total fixed cost does not vary. To avoid this problem, management accountants must distinguish carefully between fixed and variable costs, and avoid treating allocated fixed costs per unit as they would a unit variable cost. Separating fixed from variable cost pools is not as straightforward as it first appears.

EXHIBIT 10-10
Examples of Direct Linear Cost Functions

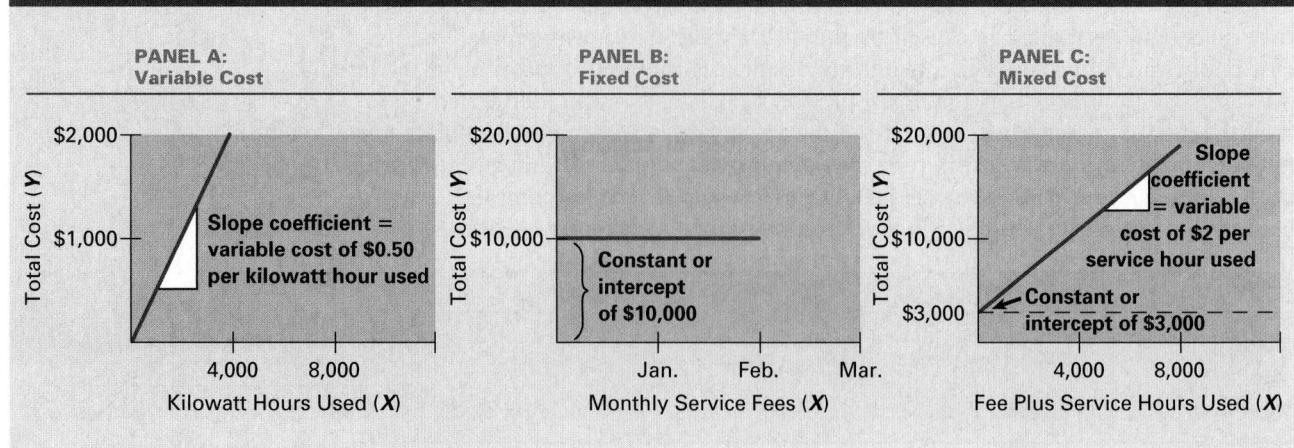

Cost functions may be purely variable, purely fixed, or mixed. Exhibit 10-10 illustrates these three types of costs. Panel A illustrates a purely variable cost pool case where, when the quantity of the resource consumed (X) is zero, the size of the cost pool (Y) is also zero. The intercept value a for this linear cost function will also be zero. As the quantity of the resource consumed increases, so too does the size of the cost pool and at a predictable, constant rate. The resource could be kilowatt-hours of electricity. This rate of increase will be a non-zero, positive value of b, the slope coefficient. Panel B illustrates a fixed cost where the slope b is zero over the relevant range but the intercept value a is non-zero and positive if the relevant range includes zero quantity of an input consumed. An example would be a monthly administration fee of $10,000 to service all machines of a specific type. Panel C illustrates a mixed cost where both the intercept a and slope b values are positive and non-zero. When zero is included in the relevant range of inputs consumed, costs are still incurred. An example would be a maintenance service contract at Elegant Rugs that included a flat monthly rate for a range of service hours up to a maximum plus some incremental cost per unit for any service hours beyond the maximum.

3. Data are either not available for all observations or are not uniformly reliable. Missing cost observations often arise from a failure to record a cost or from classifying a cost incorrectly. Data on predictor variables often originate outside the internal accounting system. For example, the accounting department may get data on testing times for medical instruments from the company's manufacturing department and data on the number of items shipped to customers from the distribution department. The reliability of such data varies greatly among organizations. In some systems, data are still recorded manually rather than electronically. Manually recorded data typically have a higher percentage of missing observations and erroneously entered observations than electronically entered data. To minimize this problem, the management accountant can recommend new data reports that regularly and routinely obtain the required data and should follow up immediately whenever data are missing.

4. Extreme values of observations occur from errors in recording costs (for example, a misplaced decimal point); from nonrepresentative time periods (for example, from a period in which an unusual major machine breakdown occurred); or from observations being outside the relevant range. Management accountants should adjust or eliminate unusual observations, called outliers,

before estimating a cost function to reduce the effect of extraordinary occurrences and improve the reliability of the forecast regression line.

5. There is no homogeneous, economically plausible relationship between the individual cost items in the dependent variable pool and the cost driver. A homogeneous relationship exists when each activity whose costs are included in the outcome variable, or indirect cost pool, consumes the same resource (predictor variable). Consider materials procurement overhead costs. This overhead cost account can include a diverse set of activities (for example, new vendor negotiations, materials ordering, incoming inspection, and materials handling). If each activity consumes the same resource, the homogeneous relationship principle suggests that a single cost function can be estimated for the entire indirect cost pool. Where resource consumption for each activity is different, separate cost functions, each with its own resource, would be estimated for each activity.

6. The relationship between predictor and outcome variables is not stationary; that is, the underlying process that generated the observations has not remained stable over time. For example, the relationship between manufacturing overhead costs and machine-hours is unlikely to be stationary if the data cover a period in which new technology was introduced. One way to test whether the relationship is stationary in this case is to split the sample into two parts and estimate separate cost relationships for the before- and after-technology-change periods. If the estimated coefficients for regression lines during the two periods are similar, then the management accountant can pool all the data to estimate a single cost relationship. Pooling data provides a larger data set for the estimation, which increases the confidence in the cost forecasts being made.

7. Inflation has affected the outcome variable, the predictor variable(s), or both. For example, inflation may cause costs to change even when there is no change in the quantity of the resource consumed. To study the underlying cause-and-effect relationship between the predictor and outcome variables, the management accountant should specify inflation as a second predictor variable.

Often, management accountants must expend a lot of effort to "clean up the data" and reduce the effect of these problems before estimating a cost function.

Activity-Based Costing: Identifying Cost and Revenue Drivers

Many cost-estimation methods presented in this chapter are essential to service-sector and retail-sector implementations of activity-based costing (ABC). In a statistical context, if ABC is to improve cost control, there should be a simple linear relationship between a single input or cost driver and the size of the cost pool. Ideally, a management accountant would expect a very high r^2, a low intercept value relative to total cost, and a steep slope for the ABC regression results compared to the traditional-system results. If the ABC cost driver perfectly forecasts the size of the cost pool, then a straight line such as that illustrated in Panels A or C of Exhibit 10-10 should be depicted with very little dispersion of blue data points from the estimated red data points on the regression line. Based on the comparison of the two regression results, managers could assess if the improved explanatory power of an ABC costing system appeared to be worth the expense to redesign the cost control system.

ASSESS YOUR MASTERY

To check your understanding of the material in Learning Objective ③, go to the *Mastery Questions* section at the end of the chapter and complete Learning Objective ③ questions 1 and 2.

STEP FIXED COST FUNCTION

④ Extend the analysis of data sets to include discontinuous linear cost functions within a relevant range

The linear cost function introduced the concept of partial explanations perhaps being the most cost-effective, and regression analysis as a rigorous and objective method to model a linear cost function. Often, however, costs are not linear with the consumption of a resource. Exhibit 10-11 illustrates three types of non-linear cost functions. A **non-linear cost function** arises when, within the relevant range of production inputs, the graph of total costs with a single resource consumed does not form a straight line. Nonlinear graphs illustrate the well-known effect from economies of scale. A change in an indirect nonmanufacturing overhead cost example would arise when an enterprise doubles the number of advertisements for less than double the costs. An indirect manufacturing cost example is the quantity discount available on indirect materials such as lubricants, as shown in Exhibit 10-11, Panel A. For quantities between 1 and 1,000 units of machine lubricants purchased, $b = \$25$; but for quantities between 1,001 and 2,000 units purchased, $b = \$15$; and for quantities in excess of 2,000 units purchased, $b = \$10$ with an intercept a of $\$0$ for all ranges. At each quantity point where the unit price decreases, the total cost for indirect materials rises but at a slower rate. The result is a straight line with varying slopes over the relevant range of indirect materials purchased.

Panel B of Exhibit 10-11 illustrates a step variable cost function. A **step variable cost function** is a function in which the cost is constant over various ranges of capacity, but the cost increases by discrete amounts (that is, in steps) as the range of the resource consumed changes from one relevant range to another. Step variable cost functions are discontinuous and therefore do not result in a sloped straight line. The step variable cost function is a series of short vertical lines. The indirect cost or outcome variable is constant over one relevant range of the resource consumed. This step pattern behaviour occurs when people are hired to undertake production scheduling, product design, and process engineering. People are hired in entire, not fractional, quantities but their labour may be used in fractional quantities. For example, during a

EXHIBIT 10-11
Three Examples of Non-Linear Cost Functions

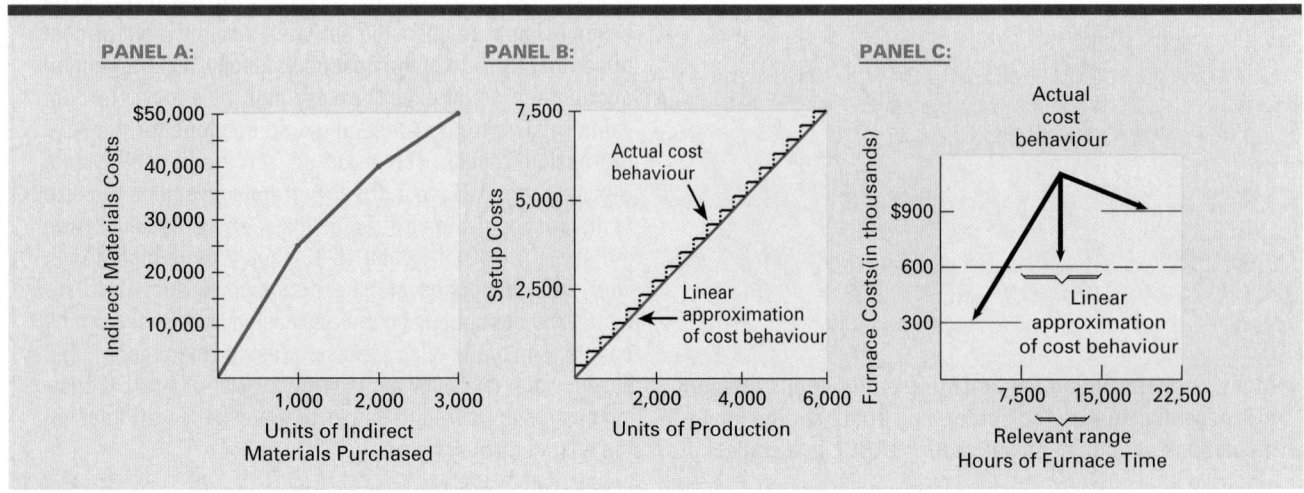

one-year period, a process engineer may work to improve manufacturing on several product lines. The engineer's actual salary would be divided and allocated to each product line based on the fraction of time spent improving each process.

Panel C of Exhibit 10-11 illustrates a *step fixed cost function* for Crofton Steel, a company that operates large heat treatment furnaces to harden steel parts. The key difference between a step fixed cost function and a step variable cost function is that the cost in a step fixed cost function is constant over a relevant range of consumption, or capacity. The relevant ranges indicate the number of furnaces being used. Assume the acquisition cost of each furnace is constant with each furnace costing $300,000. The cost from one relevant range to the next changes when the hours of furnace time required exceeds the capacity supplied by one furnace. For the relevant range of 7,500 to 15,000 hours of furnace time required, the company expects to operate with two furnaces at a cost of $600,000. Effective cost management utilizes a particular level of step fixed costs as fully as possible (on a particular step, operate as far to the right side as feasible). In this example, demand for 15,000 hours will consume the full capacity of two furnaces.

When the underlying relationship between a resource consumed and indirect costs cannot be modeled as a continuous straight line over a relevant range, OLS linear regression is inappropriate. There are four alternative approaches:

◆ Industrial engineering method
◆ Conference method
◆ Account analysis method
◆ Quantitative analyses

These approaches differ in the costs of conducting the analysis, the assumptions made, and the reliability of the estimated cost function. They are not mutually exclusive. Many organizations use a combination of these approaches.

Industrial engineering method (work measurement method) begins with identifying a measure of a specific output, then works back to identify and assess cost effectiveness of a configuration of transformation activities. These methods often generate imaginary cost-allocation bases analogous to an indirect cost pool. One example is a workload unit, once used in hospitals as an aggregate measure of groups of similar nursing activities. Where cost pools are the sum of similar costs, a workload unit is the sum of similar causes of cost.

Consider, for example, Elegant Rugs, the carpet manufacturer discussed earlier. It uses inputs of cotton, wool, dyes, direct labour, machine time, and power. Production output is square metres of carpet (m^2). Assume a time-and-motion study is used to analyze time and materials required to perform the various conversion activities to produce the carpet. The industrial engineering study concludes that 20 m^2 of carpet requires two bales of cotton and eleven litres of dye. Assume the new combined resource consumption is called a bale-litre. The combined measure can be used as a cost-allocation base and the costs of the bales of cotton and litres of dye can be combined into a cost pool. Dividing the cost pool by the quantity of the new total bale-litres consumed results in a standard unit cost measured as $/bale-litre. When multiplied by the m^2 per carpet, Elegant Rugs can forecast part of the materials cost of any carpet.

Important limitations of this method include its high cost of hiring external work-measurement specialists, eventual obsolescence as conversion activities change, and increasingly tenuous cause–effect links between consumption of a few resources and the number of costs in the cost pool. Attenuated cause and effect reduces economic plausibility and the reliability of the forecast effect of controlling resource consumption on the size of a cost pool.

The conference method develops cost estimates based on analysis and opinions gathered from various departments of an organization (purchasing, process engineering, manufacturing, employee relations, and so on). The Co-operative Bank in the United Kingdom has a cost estimating department that develops cost functions for its retail banking products (current accounts, VISA cards, mortgages, and so on) based on a consensus of estimates from the relevant departments. The bank uses this information to price products, to adjust its product mix to the products that are most profitable, and to monitor and measure cost improvements over time.

The conference method allows cost functions and cost estimates to be developed quickly. The pooling of expert knowledge from each value-chain area gives the conference method credibility. The accuracy of the cost estimates largely depends on the care and detail taken by the people providing the inputs.[3]

The account analysis method classifies cost accounts in the ledger as variable, fixed, or mixed with respect to the cost driver. Typically, qualitative rather than quantitative analysis is used in making these classification decisions. The account analysis approach is widely used.[4]

Consider indirect manufacturing labour costs for a small production area (or cell) at Elegant Rugs, which weaves carpets for homes and offices and uses state-of-the-art automated weaving machines. These costs include maintenance, quality control, and setup costs for the machines. During the most recent 12-week period, Elegant Rugs worked the machines for a total of 862 hours and incurred total indirect manufacturing labour costs of $12,501. Management wants the cost analyst to use the account analysis method to estimate a linear cost function for indirect manufacturing labour costs with machine-hours as the cost driver.

From experience and training, the management accountant identifies and separates total indirect manufacturing labour costs ($12,501) into costs that are fixed ($2,157) and costs that are variable ($10,344), given the cost driver is the number of machine-hours worked. Variable costs per machine-hour are $10,344 ÷ 862 = $12. The general cost equation, $y = a + bX$, is:

$$\text{Indirect manufacturing labour costs} = \$2,157 + (\$12 \times \text{number of machine-hours})$$

The indirect manufacturing labour cost per machine-hour is $12,501 ÷ 862 = $14.50. Management at Elegant Rugs can use the cost function to estimate the indirect manufacturing labour costs of using 950 machine-hours to produce carpet in the next 12-week period. Using the cost function, estimated costs = $2,157 + (950 × 12) = $13,557. The indirect manufacturing labour costs per machine-hour decrease to $13,557 ÷ 950 = $14.27, as fixed costs are spread over a greater number of machine hours.

Organizations differ with respect to the care taken in implementing account analysis. In some organizations, individuals thoroughly knowledgeable about the operations make the cost classification decisions. For example, costs such as machine lubricants and materials-handling labour would usually be classified by manufacturing managers, whereas costs such as advertising brochures and sales salaries would

---

GOVERNANCE ISSUES

Statistics Are Evidence

Determining the appropriate resource to use for a cost-allocation base or as a cost driver requires considerable judgment. When management compensation is based on performance measures that may change unfavourably with the introduction of a new allocation method, managers can exert pressure to make more favourable selections. The management accountant, using a rigorous quantitative analysis of clean data, is in a strong position to readily obtain evidence to support or resist any biased recommendation. For those enterprises with shareholders, the larger the management compensation, the lower will be profits available for distribution to the owners. The use of objective evidence is also more persuasive for shareholders of the enterprise that compensation packages provide reasonable incentives for obtaining cost-control targets.

---

[3]The conference method is further described in W. Winchell, *Realistic Cost Estimating for Manufacturing*, 2nd ed. (Dearborn, Mich.: Society for Manufacturing Engineers, 1991).

[4]Survey evidence appears in M. M. Mowen, *Accounting for Costs as Fixed and Variable* (Montvale, N.J.: National Association of Accountants, 1986).

usually be classified by marketing managers. In other organizations, only cursory analysis is conducted, sometimes by individuals with limited knowledge of operations, before cost classification decisions are made. Clearly, the former approach would provide more accurate cost classifications, and hence estimates of the fixed and variable components of the cost, than the latter. Supplementing the account analysis method with the conference method improves its credibility.

ESTIMATING A COST FUNCTION

Any analysis begins with identifying the target cost pool to be forecast and choosing consumption of an economically plausible resource or set of resources, which have in the past affected the size of the cost pool. Both the cost pool and resource values must be collected and, using the experience of managers and the management accountant's conservatism, extraordinary data points must be removed. The reason for cleaning up the data is not to bias the results but rather to avoid biasing the results by including data points that will probably never recur. The data points should be plotted, then the cost function estimated. The picture of the data points will provide a quick way to assess if the cost function is linear, discontinuous and linear, or curvilinear.

Management accountants need to decide if cross-sectional or time-series data are most appropriate, bearing in mind the cost of collecting the data. If the consumption of an appropriate resource has been identified, then it is likely the experienced people in operations have made this decision through conferencing. The information or data upon which the decision was based may have been obtained from electronic or documentary records, internal interviews, or perhaps consulting studies. Once extraordinary data points have been eliminated, the list of data points can be plotted graphically.

Plotting the data can provide insight into whether the relationship is approximately linear and what the relevant range of the cost function is. The data from the indirect manufacturing labour costs for Elegant Rugs has already been statistically analyzed. If, however, the skills to undertake OLS linear regression were unavailable, then an alternative would be a simpler but less rigorous, and therefore less reliable, estimation using the high-low method. Given that the causal direction is from resource consumption to the size of the cost pool in a cost function, choosing the highest and lowest observation of the consumption measured is appropriate. Exhibit 10-12 plots the weekly data from columns B and C of Exhibit 10-5. Inspection of the plot of data points provides the visual insight but what is missing is the quantitative evidence required to choose the most reliable straight line. While the evidence may be adequate to persuade managers there is a linear relationship, there is little evidence that the

EXHIBIT 10-12
Plot of Weekly Indirect Manufacturing Labour Costs and Machine-Hours for Elegant Rugs

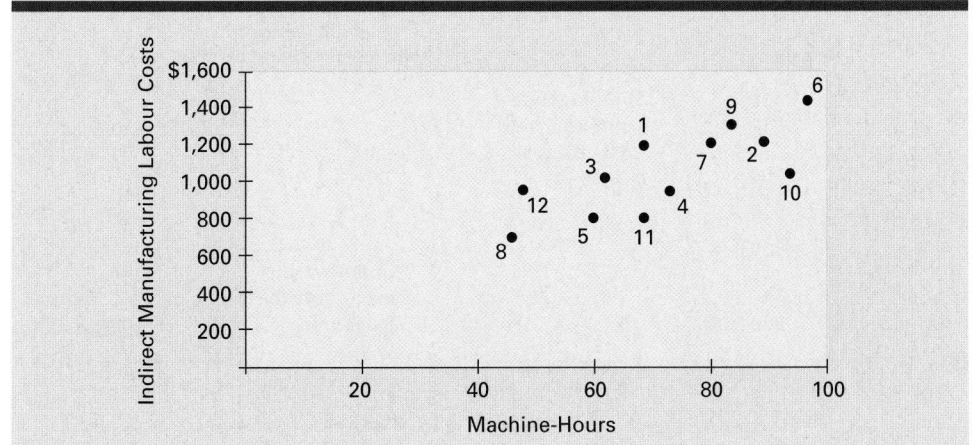

specification of the equation between the estimated indirect manufacturing labour costs, y, and machine-hours, X, is adequate to forecast with reasonable accuracy what would happen if consumption of machine hours changed.

The **high-low method** uses only the highest and lowest observed values of the consumed resource within the relevant range. The line connecting these two points becomes the estimated cost function. High-low method, while simple, is not a rigorous statistical analysis and when used will not reveal discontinuities in linearity. In the discussion that follows, the lack of quantitative evidence can make a decision as to just what the high and low values are difficult to justify. The estimated high-low lines in Exhibit 10-13 illustrate two possible linear relationships between the indirect manufacturing cost pool and consumption of the resource.

The slope coefficient, b, is calculated as:

$$\text{Slope coefficient } b = \frac{\Delta y}{\Delta X}$$

$$= \$746 \div 50 = \$14.92 \text{ per machine-hour}$$

To compute the constant, we can use either the highest or the lowest actual value of recorded resource consumption. The two calculations yield the same answer (because the solution technique solves two linear equations with two unknowns, the slope coefficient and the constant).

$$y = a + bX, \ a = y - bX$$

At the highest observation of the consumption,

$$\text{Constant } a = \$1,456 - (\$14.92 \times 96) = \$23.68$$

At the lowest observation of the consumption,

$$\text{Constant } a = \$710 - (\$14.92 \times 46) = \$23.68$$

Therefore, the high-low estimate of the cost function is

$$y = a + bX$$

$$= \$23.68 + \$14.92X$$

The lower line in Exhibit 10-13 shows the estimated cost function using the high-low method. The estimated cost function is a straight line joining the observations with the highest and lowest data points (X,Y). The constant or intercept term signals the proportion of costs that cannot be explained by changes in the consumption of a specified resource. If managers control consumption, there remains a proportion of costs that will not change. Consumption of another resource may be causing those costs, or the linear model may not correctly specify the relationship between consumption and the cost pool. One issue is externalities. An externality cannot be controlled

EXHIBIT 10-13
Alternate High-Low Linear Relationships for Elegant Rugs

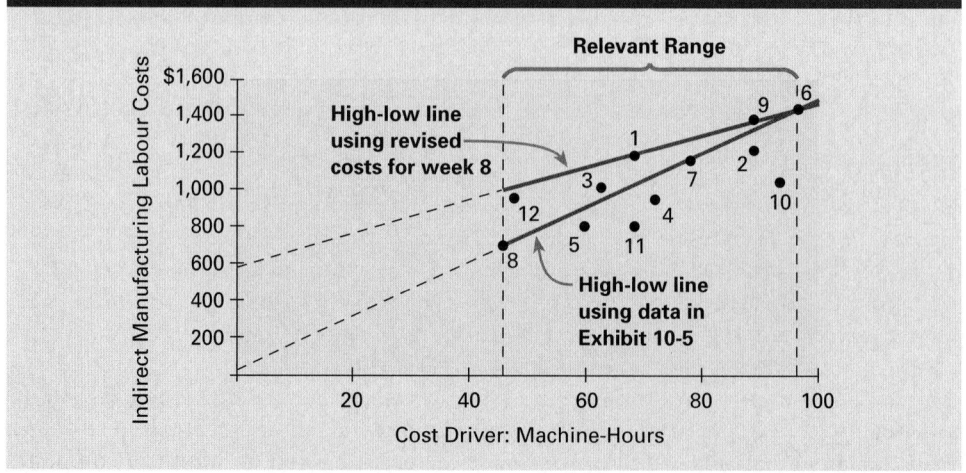

by a manager. For example, a labour contract guaranteeing minimum payments for idle time resulted in indirect manufacturing labour costs in week 8 of $1,000 instead of $710 when only 46 machine-hours were worked. This type of event contributes to the dollar value of the intercept.

Exhibit 10-13, however, illustrates two lines. The second, the top line, is based on a change in the data points in week 8 from data point 9 (96, $1,456) to data point 2 (96, $1,280). Now, the highest observation of the cost driver (machine-hours of 96 in week 6) does not coincide with the next highest value of the actual indirect cost pool of $1,316 in week 9. The high-low method would estimate the new cost function still using data from weeks 6 and 8. Notice, however, the top line joining the highest and lowest data points lies above the remaining data. Inspection suggests a better line could be drawn and sometimes an intuitive response is to modify the high-low method to a *representative* high and a *representative* low pair of data points. This is a practical way to exclude values that arise from extraordinary events, the outliers, but produces no justification for choosing any pair of data points over any other, whereas an OLS does provide quantitative justification for the regression line.

Compare the regression equation $y = \$300.98 + \$10.31X$ with the initial high-low equation $\$23.68 + \$14.92X$. For 90 machine-hours, the forecast cost based on the high-low equation is $\$23.68 + (\$14.92 \times 90) = \$1,366.48$. Assume that over the next 12-week period, Elegant Rugs runs its machines for 90 hours each week for three weeks and incurs average indirect manufacturing labour costs for those three weeks of $1,300. Based on the high-low forecast of $1,366.48, Elegant Rugs would conclude it has performed well. But based on the $1,228.88 forecast of the regression model, Elegant Rugs would undertake ways to improve its cost performance.

ASSESS YOUR MASTERY

To check your understanding of the material in Learning Objective ❹, go to the Mastery Questions section at the end of the chapter and complete Learning Objective ❹ questions 1 and 2.

LEARNING CURVES AND NONLINEAR COST FUNCTIONS

> **❺** Distinguish between the curvilinear cumulative average time learning model and incremental unit time learning model

The nonlinear or curvilinear relationship of total output produced relative to quantity of labour input reflects progress in producing outputs. The plot of this time series of data illustrates the effect of the **learning curve**. The learning curve reflects the common intuition that practice makes perfect. People take less time to do familiar than unfamiliar tasks. The learning curve is a curvilinear mathematical production function that shows how the ratio of quantity produced increases at a faster rate than the rate at which the time spent in activities of production decreases (Q_t output $\div Q_t$ DLH).

Management accountants whose task is to analyze costs would be more interested in the **experience curve**. The experience curve reflects common intuition that part of learning comes from doing. The experience curve is a cost function that shows how full product costs per unit (including manufacturing, marketing, distribution, and so on) decrease as total quantity produced increases. Whereas Boeing first documented the learning-curve effect, the Boston Consulting Group first popularized the experience-curve effect. The relationship is, roughly stated, at each point when cumulative production doubles, costs decrease by a predictable percentage ranging from 10% to 30% depending on the industry. Understanding the experience curve explains in part what is meant by the first-mover advantage. The first company to market with a successful output will grow as demand grows. As the volume of output grows, the unit cost will decrease because people have learned how to avoid and resolve errors, and simply complete tasks more quickly.

To fully understand the experience curve, however, management accountants need to understand the mechanics of the learning curve as well. The strategic benefits of the learning curve only arise if the learning stays within the company.

Knowledge Reduces Production Costs

Cost leadership can be a very successful strategy for the first mover (the first entrant into a market) if the first-mover's cost savings are passed on to buyers. Lowering prices to maintain profit will make it difficult for new entrants, who lack experience, to compete profitably. Sustaining high prices will give new entrants incentive to enter the market, and worse, they will be able to achieve a higher entry-level profit margin than if the prices had been lowered. Assuming demand continues to grow, the new entrants then have the time they need to gain experience as their volume increases. New entrants can take the initiative to lower prices and lure buyers to the same quality of product at a lower price and further increase their volumes. As volumes double again, costs decrease and the new entrant can capture market leadership from the first mover. Management accountants who understand the experience-curve effect can gather and use data to deliberately achieve cost leadership.

In a broader perspective, the learning-curve effect illustrates how important good training and low turnover are to the long-term profitability of a company. The quantitative effects of the learning-curve and experience-curve effects can be reliably modelled and provide objective evidence based on past data of future cost savings. Better cost forecasts that are free of bias improve both budgeting and pricing outcomes in organizations. In not-for-profit organizations where the goal is to break even, as learning-curve and experience-curve effects are realized, the breakeven amount decreases, and reliable plans can be made to expand the benefits provided on the same revenue base.

The underlying assumption of the learning-curve relationship is that direct manufacturing labour-hours (DMLH) necessary to complete a unit of production will decrease by a constant percentage each time the production quantity is doubled. This is a long-term accumulation of quantity produced from the inception of production. It is a strategy that requires long-term data to implement; a single year or even two years of data is inadequate. The reason is that quantity must double for the learning-curve effect to be observable, and as the cumulative quantity increases, the time to double also increases. A single year of data often is not a long-enough time horizon to observe the doubling and, therefore, the constant rate of cost reduction.

This concept was defined mathematically years ago by an engineer at Boeing. We begin with Exhibit 10-14, which graphs the comparison of two types of nonlinear or learning-curve relationships. Panel A illustrates an incremental unit time learning model while Panel B illustrates a cumulative average time learning model. In both panels, the top line illustrates how incremental learning affects the nonlinear relationship between quantity produced and quantity of DMLH input. The lower line illustrates how cumulative learning affects the nonlinear relationship between quantity produced and quantity of DMLH input. In both examples, we assume that there is a constant rate of decrease in DMLH of 20% each time quantity of output doubles.

To model the nonlinear relationship between a faster rate of change in output (the outcome variable y) relative to input (the cause or predictor variable x) requires the use of natural logarithms ($\ln x$), one of the two common types of logarithms. The natural logarithm uses a base e = 2.71828 . . . when modeling a relationship. The other common logarithm uses the more familiar base of 10.[5]

---

[5]Logarithm is the inverse of exponentiation, e.g., let $x = 100$: $10^2 = 100$
$$2 = \log_{10}100$$
when using the logarithm of base 10. When using the natural logarithmic function the basis of the calculation of the exponent is e = 2.71828. . . . If you raise 2.71828 to the exponent 4.605170. . . ($2.71828^{4.605170}$) the answer is 99.99996. . . rounded to 100, e.g., let $x = 100$ then $\ln(x)$ is:
$$e^{4.605170} = 100$$
$$4.605170 = \ln(100)$$
Most mathematics texts provide tables of logarithmic and natural logarithmic values.

EXHIBIT 10-14
Plots for Incremental Unit Time Learning Model

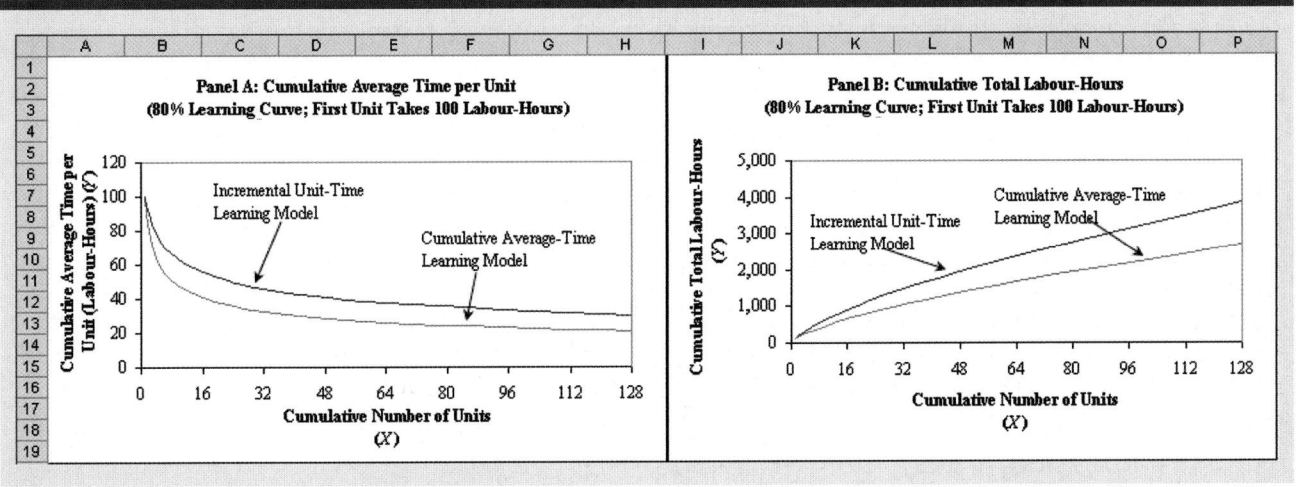

Panel A: Cumulative Average Time per Unit
(80% Learning Curve; First Unit Takes 100 Labour-Hours)

Panel B: Cumulative Total Labour-Hours
(80% Learning Curve; First Unit Takes 100 Labour-Hours)

INCREMENTAL UNIT TIME LEARNING MODEL

In the **incremental unit time learning model**, the incremental unit time (the time needed to produce the last unit) declines by a constant percentage each time the cumulative quantity of units produced doubles. Exhibits 10-14 and 10-15 illustrate the incremental unit time learning model with an 80% learning curve. We assume that there is a constant rate of decrease in DMLH of 20% each time quantity of output doubles. It is counterintuitive, but a higher percentage learning rate (e.g., 90% rather than 80%) indicates a slower rate of learning. Consider in Exhibit 10-15 the row for two cumulative units. Under this 80% learning curve, the cumulative average time per unit is 80 labour-hours. If the rate of learning had been 90%, the cumulative average time per unit would have been 90 labour-hours (100 × 0.90).

The incremental unit time model forecasts that when quantity of output doubles from 2 to 4 units, it will take on average 80 DMLH (80% × 100 DMLH) to produce the second unit. When output doubles again from 4 to 8 units it will take on average 64 DMLH (80% × 80 DMLH) to produce the fourth unit, and so on. Panel A in Exhibit 10-14 shows the cumulative *average* time per unit when the first unit requires 100 DMLH to produce but each subsequent unit takes only 80% of the time required for its predecessor. The mathematical function and calculations are shown in Exhibit 10-15. This model forecasts that it will take 180 DMLH to produce a total of 2 units; 250.21 DMLH to produce a total of 3 units; and 314.21 DMLH to produce a total of 4 units. Panel B in Exhibit 10-14 shows the cumulative *total* DMLH to produce total quantities of outputs when learning has an incremental effect on DMLH required.

The more preferable model is the one that more accurately approximates the behaviour of manufacturing DMLH consumption as production levels increase. The choice can be decided only on a case-by-case basis. Engineers, plant managers, and workers are good sources of information on the amount and type of learning actually occurring as production increases. Plotting this information is helpful in selecting the appropriate model.

The Problem for Self Study on page 495 illustrates the cumulative average time learning model and the incremental unit time learning model in a job-costing situation.

CUMULATIVE AVERAGE TIME LEARNING MODEL

The **cumulative average time learning model** depicts a relationship such that the cumulative average time per unit declines by a constant percentage each time the cumulative quantity of units produced doubles. Exhibit 10-16 illustrates the cumulative average time learning model with an 80% learning curve. The 80% means that when the quantity of units produced is doubled from X to $2X$, the cumulative average time *per unit* for the $2X$ units is 80% of the cumulative average time *per unit* for the X units. In other words, average time per unit drops by 20%. Panel A in Exhibit 10-14 shows

EXHIBIT 10-15
Incremental Unit Time Learning Model

	A	B	C	D	E	F
1		**80% Learning Curve**				
2						
3	**Cumulative**	**Individual Unit Time**		**Cumulative**	**Cumulative**	
4	**Number of**	**for Xth Unit $(y)^{-b}$:**		**Total Time:**	**Average Time per**	
5	**Units (X)**	**Labour-Hours**		**Labour-Hours**	**Unit: Labour-Hours**	
6	**(1)**	**(2)**		**(3)**	**(4) = (3) ÷ (1)**	
7	1	100.00		100.00	100.00	E9 = D9 ÷ A9
8	2	80.00 = (100 × 0.8)		180.00	90.00	
9	3	70.21		250.21	83.40	
10	4	64.00 = (80 × 0.8)		314.21	78.55	
11	5	59.56		373.77	74.75	
12	6	56.17		429.94	71.66	
13	7	53.45		483.39	69.06	
14	8	51.20 = (64 × 0.8)		534.59	66.82	
15	9	49.29		583.88	64.88	
16	10	47.65		631.53	63.15	
17	11	46.21		677.74	61.61	
18	12	44.93		722.67	60.22	
19	13	43.79		766.46	58.96	
20	14	42.76		809.22	57.80	
21	15	41.82		851.04	56.74	
22	16	40.96 = (51.2 × 0.8)		892.00	55.75	
23						
24	*The mathematical relationship underlying the incremental unit-time learning model is:					
25	$y = aX^{-b}$					
26	where y = Time (labour-hours) taken to produce the last single unit					
27	X = Cumulative number of units produced					
28	a = Time (labour-hours) required to produce the first unit					
29	b = Factor used to calculate incremental unit time to produce units					
30	$= \dfrac{\ln (\text{learning-curve \% in decimal form})}{\ln 2}$					
31	For an 80% learning curve, $b = \ln 0.8 ÷ \ln 2 = -0.2231 ÷ 0.6931 = -0.3219$					
32	When $X = 3$, $a = 100$, $b = -0.3219$					
33	$y = 100 \times 3^{0.3219} = 70.21$ labour-hours					
34	The cumulative total time when $X = 3$ is $100 + 80 + 70.21 = 250.21$ labour-hours.					
35	Numbers in the table may not be exact because of rounding.					

the cumulative average time per unit for this model of the effect of learning on DMLH required in the lower curved line. Notice that the total labour time is accumulating at a slower rate (column D in Exhibit 10-16). This is because the effect of learning is modelled differently for the cumulative than the incremental model.

The cumulative model uses the average time per unit based on the most recent quantity of units produced. While the first unit took 100 DMLH, the first two took on average only 80 DMLH to produce each one. Therefore the total time to produce two units is only 160 DMLH (2 × 80 DMLH). When three units were produced, it took on average 70.21 DMLH to produce each one. The total time to produce three units was 210.63 DMLH (3 × 71.21 DMLH). It took, on average, 64 DMLH to produce each of four units for a total of 256 DMLH (4 × 64 labour hours), and so on. Panel B of Exhibit 10-14 illustrates the cumulative *total* DMLH to produce total quantities of outputs when learning has a cumulative effect on DMLH required (100 + 80 + 70.21 + 64 + 51.20). Simply put, people are learning faster using this model than under the incremental unit time model.

EXHIBIT 10-16
Cumulative Average Time Learning Model

	A	B	C	D	E	F
1		**80% Learning Curve**				
2						
3	**Cumulative**	**Cumulative**		**Cumulative**	**Individual Unit**	
4	**Number**	**Average Time**		**Total Time:**	**Time for Xth**	
5	**of Units (X)**	**Per Unit (y)*: Labour-Hours**		**Labour-Hours**	**Unit: Labour-Hours**	
6	**(1)**	**(2)**		**(3) = (1) × (2)**	**(4)**	
7	1	100.00		100.00	100.00	E9=D9−D8=210.63−160.00
8	2	80.00	= (100 × 0.8)	160.00	60.00	
9	3	70.21		210.63	50.63	
10	4	64.00	= (80 × 0.8)	256.00	45.37	
11	5	59.56		297.80	41.80	
12	6	56.17		337.02	39.22	
13	7	53.45		374.15	37.13	
14	8	51.20	= (64 × 0.8)	409.60	35.45	
15	9	49.29		443.61	34.01	
16	10	47.65		476.50	32.89	
17	11	46.21		508.31	31.81	
18	12	44.93		539.16	30.85	
19	13	43.79		569.27	30.11	
20	14	42.76		598.64	29.37	
21	15	41.82		627.30	28.66	
22	16	40.96	= (51.2 × 0.8)	655.36	28.06	
23						
24	*The mathematical relationship underlying the cumulative average time learning model is:					
25		$y = aX^b$				
26	where y = Cumulative average time (labour-hours) per unit					
27	X = Cumulative number of units produced					
28	a = Time (labour-hours) required to produce the first unit					
29	b = Factor used to calculate cumulative average time to produce units					
30	1. The value of b is calculated as					
31	$\dfrac{\text{ln (learning-curve \% in decimal form)}}{\text{ln 2}}$					
32	For an 80% learning curve, $b = \ln 0.8 \div \ln 2 = -0.2231 \div 0.6931 = -0.3219$.					
33	When $X = 3$, $a = 100$, $b = -0.3219$,					
34	$y = 100 \times 3^{-0.3219} = 70.21$ labour-hours					
35	2. The cumulative total time when $X = 3$ is $70.21 \times 3 = 210.63$ labour-hours					
36	3. The individual unit times in column E are calculated using the data in column D. For example, the individual unit time for the third unit is 50.63 labour-hours (210.63 − 160.00) Numbers in the table may not be exact because of rounding.					

SETTING PRICES, BUDGETS, AND STANDARDS

Forecasts of costs should allow for learning. Consider the data in Exhibit 10-16 for the cumulative average time learning model. Suppose the variable costs subject to learning effects consist of direct manufacturing labour ($20 per DLH)

EXHIBIT 10-17
Forecasting Costs Using Learning Curves

	A	B	C	D	E	F
1		Cumulative				
2	Cumulative	Average Time	Cumulative	Cumulative Costs		Additions to
3	Number of	per Unit:	Total Time:	at $50 per		Cumulative
4	Units	Labour-Hours[a]	Labour-Hours[a]	Labour-Hour		Costs
5	1	100.00	100.00	$ 5,000	(100.00 × $50)	$ 5,000
6	2	80.00	160.00	8,000	(160.00 × $50)	3,000
7	4	64.00	256.00	12,800	(256.00 × $50)	4,800
8	8	51.20	409.60	20,480	(409.60 × $50)	7,680
9	16	40.96	655.36	32,768	(655.36 × $50)	12,288
10						
11	[a]Based on the cumulative average time learning model. See Exhibit 10-16 (p. 493) for the computation of these amounts.					

and related overhead ($30 per DLH). Management should forecast the costs shown in Exhibit 10-17.

These data show that the effects of the learning curve could have a major influence on decisions. For example, a company might set an extremely low selling price on its product to generate high demand. As the company's production increases to meet this growing demand, costs per unit drop. The company rides the product costs down the learning curve as it establishes a higher market share. Although the company may have earned little on its first unit sold—it may actually have lost money—the company earns more profit per unit as output increases.

Alternatively, subject to legal and other considerations, the company might set a low price on just the final eight units. After all, the labour and related overhead costs per unit are forecast to be only $12,288 for these final eight units ($32,768 − $20,480). The per-unit costs of $1,536 on these final eight units ($12,288 ÷ 8) are much lower than the $5,000 costs per unit of the first unit produced. The learning and experience curve effects on costs are highest in a labour-intensive process.

REAL COMPANIES

Curvilinear Cost Functions: Statistics and Good Forecasts

Many companies incorporate learning-curve effects when evaluating performance. For example, the Nissan Motor Company sets assembly labour efficiency standards for new models of cars after taking into account the learning that will occur as more units are produced. Other companies have developed models to explain how quality improves as workers learn to produce new products. Organizing people into specialized groups or training people in several phases of the production process and rotating them periodically to perform different tasks has been shown to help improve the quality of products.

PULLING IT ALL TOGETHER—PROBLEM FOR SELF-STUDY

PROBLEM

The Helicopter Division of Aerospatiale is examining helicopter assembly costs at its plant in Marseilles, France. It has received an initial order for eight of its new land-surveying helicopters. Aerospatiale can adopt one of two methods of assembling the helicopters:

	A	B	C	D	E
1		**Labour-Intensive Assembly**		**Machine-Intensive Assembly**	
2		**Method**		**Method**	
3	Direct material cost per helicopter	$40,000		$36,000	
4	Direct assembly labour time for first helicopter	2,000	labour-hours	800	labour-hours
5	Learning curve for assembly labour time per helicopter	85%	cumulative average time[a]	90%	incremental unit time[b]
6	Direct assembly labour cost	$ 30	per hour	$ 30	per hour
7	Equipment-related indirect manufacturing cost	$ 12	per direct-assembly labour-hour	$ 45	per direct-assembly labour-hour
8	Materials-handling-related indirect manufacturing cost	50%	of direct material cost	50%	of direct material cost
9					
10	[a]Using the formula for an 85% learning curve, $b = \dfrac{\ln 0.85}{\ln 2} = \dfrac{-0.162519}{0.693147} = -0.234465$				
11	[b]Using the formula for a 90% learning curve, $b = \dfrac{\ln 0.90}{\ln 2} = \dfrac{-0.105361}{0.693147} = -0.152004$				

REQUIRED

1. How many direct-assembly labour-hours are required to assemble the first eight helicopters under (a) the labour-intensive method and (b) the machine-intensive method? ⑤
2. What is the total cost of assembling the first eight helicopters under (a) the labour-intensive method and (b) the machine-intensive method? ⑤

SOLUTION

1. a. The following calculations show the labour-intensive assembly method based on an 85% cumulative average-time learning model (using Excel):

	A	B	C	D
1		Cumulative		Incremental
2	Cumulative	Average Time	Cumulative	Time for
3	Number	per Unit (y):	Total Time:	Xth Unit:
4	of Units	Labour-Hours	Labour-Hours	Labour-Hours
5	(1)	(2)	(3) = (1) × (2)	(4)
6	1	2,000	2,000	2,000
7	2	1,700 (2,000 × 0.85)	3,400	1,400
8	3	1,546	4,638	1,238

(continued)

(continued)

9	4	1,445 (1,700 × 0.85)	5,780	1,142
10	5	1,371	6,855	1,075
11	6	1,314	7,884	1,029
12	7	1,267	8,869	985
13	8	1,228.25 (1,445 × 0.85)	9,826	957

Cumulative average-time per unit for the Xth unit in column 2 is calculated as $y = aX^b$; see Exhibit 10-16 (p. 493).

For example, when $X = 3$, $y = 2,000 \times 3^{-0.234465} = 1,546$ labour-hours.

b. The following calculations show the machine-intensive assembly method based on a 90% incremental unit-time learning model:

	A	B	C	D	E
1		**Incremental**			**Cumulative**
2	**Cumulative**	**Unit Time**		**Cumulative**	**Average Time**
3	**Number**	**for Xth Unit (y):**		**Total Time:**	**per Unit:**
4	**of Units**	**Labour-Hours**		**Labour-Hours**	**Labour-Hours**
5	**(1)**	**(2)**		**(3)**	**(4) = (3) ÷ (1)**
6	1	800		800	800
7	2	720	(800 × 0.9)	1,520	760
8	3	677		2,197	732
9	4	648	(720 × 0.9)	2,845	711
10	5	626		3,471	694
11	6	609		4,080	680
12	7	595		4,675	668
13	8	583	(648 × 0.9)	5,258	657

Individual unit time for the Xth unit in column 2 is calculated as $y = aX^b$; see Exhibit 10-15 (p. 492). For example, when $X = 3$, $y = 800 \times 3^{-0.105361} = 677$ labour-hours.

2. Total costs of assembling the first eight helicopters are:

	A	B	C
1		**Labour-Intensive**	**Machine-Intensive**
2		**Assembly Method**	**Assembly Method**
3		**(using data from part la)**	**(using data from part lb)**
4	Direct materials:		
5	8 helicopters × $40,000, $36,000 per helicopter	$320,000	$288,000
6	Direct assembly labour:		
7	9,826 hours: 5,258 hours × $30/hour	294,780	157,740
8	Indirect manufacturing costs		
9	Equipment related		
10	9,826 hours × $12/hour; 5,258 hours × $45/hour	117,912	236,610
11	Materials-handing-related		
12	0.50 × $320,000; $288,000	160,000	144,000
13	Total assembly costs	$892,692	$826,350

The machine-intensive method's assembly costs are $66,342 lower than the labour-intensive method ($892,692 − $826,350).

The following decision guidelines use a question-and-answer format to summarize the chapter's main points. Each decision presents a key question. The guideline is the answer to that question.

DECISIONS	GUIDELINES
1. Of what importance is a specification analysis?	Careful specification analysis assures the management accountant that the data points used as input represent an economically plausible linear relationship between the quantity consumed of a resource and the size of an indirect cost pool. The differences between the actual and estimated data point are due to random events and there is no relationship between the quantity of a resource consumed and the size of the error.
2. Of what importance is an ordinary least squares (OLS) linear regression analysis?	An OLS linear regression analysis describes an objective and rigorous statistical analysis of a set of data points. The analysis includes specific and standardized manipulation of the data input to estimate the equation of a straight line called the linear-regression line. Outputs include both graphs and results of tests of reliability against statistical benchmarks. If the data points meet the standards set in the specification analysis, then the OLS linear regression analysis provides objective evidence of whether a regression line is the result of a systematic relationship between the predictor and output variable or simply coincidence.
3. What common data problems arise that make analyses of costs difficult?	Collecting enough properly measured and reliable data on the quantity of a resource consumed and the size of the indirect cost pool is difficult in most companies. Common problems include too few data points, inaccurate measures, missing data, and extreme values.
4. What are discontinuous linear cost functions and how do they arise?	Discontinuous linear cost functions are illustrated by graphs with bends where the slope of the line changes or has discontinuities in it. Within the relevant range of consumption, the indirect cost pool values are not continuous. Discontinuous costs take the form of step functions and bent lines.
5. What are the different curvilinear learning curve models a company can use to improve its cost leadership strategy?	The two types are cumulative and incremental learning curve. The cumulative learning curve models the decrease in average direct labour-time consumed per unit each time the total quantity produced doubles. The rate of decrease is constant. The incremental learning curve models the decrease in the time needed to produce the last unit of production. The rate of decrease is also a constant but is different from the rate for the cumulative learning curve model.

APPENDIX: MULTIPLE LINEAR REGRESSION ANALYSIS AND ABC

For linear regression to provide the best information, there should be only a few independent predictor variables that affect the value of the outcome variable. Independence means that the presence of and change in the value of one predictor variable has no effect on the change in value of a second predictor variable. If this is true, then each predictor variable independently measures a different effect on the outcome variable. **Multiple linear regression** is the technique used to measure the strength of relationships among at least two predictor variables and the outcome variable.

Care must be taken to ensure the predictor variables both meet the specification analysis and measure different effects on the outcome variable. In the Elegant Rugs example, many different types of labour arose as a consequence of the machine and labour time directly consumed in production. Each type of labour caused some portion of the indirect labour cost pool to increase. Depending on how well the consumption of either direct labour or direct machine hours explained the change in the size of the indirect labour cost pool, it could be worthwhile for the management accountant to seek a second or third predictor variable. Multiple regression analysis is extremely useful for estimating total costs when different levels of the cost hierarchy are involved. The example in this Appendix uses number of machine-hours (an output-unit-level cost driver) and number of production batches (a batch-level cost driver).

MULTIPLE REGRESSION AND COST HIERARCHIES

In some cases, a satisfactory estimation of a cost function may be based on only one independent variable, such as machine-hours. In many cases, however, basing the estimation on more than one independent variable is economically plausible and improves the reliability of the linear regression. The most widely used equations to express relationships between two or more independent variables and a dependent variable are linear in the form:

$$y = a + b_1X_1 + b_2X_2 \cdots + u$$

where:

y = cost pool or outcome variable

$X_1, X_2, \ldots$ = predictor variables on which the estimate of the outcome variable is based

$a, b_1, b_2, \ldots$ = estimated coefficients of the regression model

u = residual term that includes the net effect of other factors not in the model, and measurement errors in the predictor and outcome variables

Example: Consider the Elegant Rugs data in Exhibit 10-18. Indirect manufacturing labour costs include sizable costs incurred for setup and changeover costs when production on one carpet batch is stopped and production on another batch is started. Management believes that, in addition to machine-hours (an output-unit-level cost driver), indirect manufacturing labour costs are also affected by the number of different batches of carpets produced during each week (a batch-level driver). Elegant Rugs estimates the relation between two independent variables, machine-hours and number of separate carpet jobs worked on during the week, and indirect manufacturing labour costs.

Exhibit 10-19 presents results for the following multiple regression model, using data in columns B, C, and E of Exhibit 10-18:

$$y = \$42.58 + \$7.60X_1 + \$37.77X_2$$

where X_1 is the number of machine-hours and X_2 is the number of production batches. It is economically plausible that both machine-hours and production batches would help explain variations in indirect manufacturing labour costs at Elegant Rugs. The r^2 of 0.52 for the simple regression using machine-hours (from Exhibit 10-9) increases to 0.72 with the multiple regression in Exhibit 10-19. (Note that Excel expresses "r^2" as "R Square" in its output.) The *t*-values suggest that the independent

EXHIBIT 10-18

Weekly Indirect Manufacturing Labour Costs, Machine-Hours, Direct Manufacturing Labour-Hours, and Number of Production Batches for Elegant Rugs

	A	B	C	D	E
1			Number of	Direct	Indirect
2			Production	Manufacturing	Manufacturing
3	Week	Machine-Hours	Batches	Labour-Hours	Labour-Costs
4		(X_1)	(X_2)		(Y)
5	1	68	12	30	$ 1,190
6	2	88	15	35	1,211
7	3	62	13	36	1,004
8	4	72	11	20	917
9	5	60	10	47	770
10	6	96	12	45	1,456
11	7	78	17	44	1,180
12	8	46	7	38	710
13	9	82	14	70	1,316
14	10	94	12	30	1,032
15	11	68	7	29	752
16	12	48	14	38	963
17	Total	862	144	462	$12,501

variable coefficients of both machine-hours and production batches are significantly different from zero ($t = 2.74$ for the coefficient on machine-hours, and $t = 2.48$ for the coefficient on production batches). The multiple regression model in Exhibit 10-19 satisfies both economic and statistical criteria, and it explains much greater variation in indirect manufacturing labour costs than does the simple regression model using only machine-hours as the independent variable. The information in Exhibit 10-19 indicates that both machine-hours and production batches are important cost drivers of monthly indirect manufacturing labour costs at Elegant Rugs.

EXHIBIT 10-19

Multiple Regression Results with Indirect Manufacturing Labour Costs and Two Independent Variables or Cost Drivers (Machine-Hours and Production Batches) for Elegant Rugs

	A	B	C	D	E	F	G
1		Coefficients	Standard Error	t-Statistic			
2		(1)	(2)	(3) = (1) ÷ (2)			
3	Intercept	$42.58	$213.91	0.20			
4	Independent variable 1: Machine-hours (X_1)	$ 7.60	$ 2.77	2.74 ⟶	= Coefficient/Standard Error = B4/C4 = 7.60/2.77		
5	Independent variable 2: Number of production batches (X_2)	$37.77	$ 15.25	2.48			
6							
7	Regression Statistics						
8	R Square	0.72					
9	Durbin-Watson Statistic	2.49					

In Exhibit 10-19, the slope coefficients—$7.60 for machine-hours and $37.77 for production batches—measure the change in indirect manufacturing labour costs associated with a unit change in an independent variable (assuming that the other independent variable is held constant). For example, indirect manufacturing labour costs increase by $37.77 when one more production batch is added, assuming that the number of machine-hours is held constant.

An alternative approach would be to create two separate cost pools—one for costs tied to machine-hours and another for costs tied to production batches. Elegant Rugs would then estimate the relationship between the cost driver (predictor variable) and overhead costs separately for each cost pool. The difficult task under that approach would be properly dividing overhead costs into the two cost pools.

MULTICOLLINEARITY

A major concern that arises with multiple linear regression is multicollinearity. **Multicollinearity** exists when two or more predictor variables are highly correlated with each other. The rule of thumb is if the correlation between X_1 and X_2 is 0.70, then there is no issue of correlated predictor variables. If the correlation is ≥ 0.70, then one of the predictor variables must be dropped. Multicollinearity increases the standard errors of the coefficients of the individual predictor variables. The result is that there is greater uncertainty about the underlying value of the coefficients of each predictor variable. That is, variables that are economically and statistically significant will appear insignificant.

The coefficients of correlation between the potential independent variables for Elegant Rugs in Exhibit 10-19 are:

Coefficient of Pairwise Combinations	Correlation
Machine-hours and direct manufacturing labour-hours	0.12
Machine-hours and production batches	0.40
Direct manufacturing labour-hours and production batches	0.31

These results indicate that multiple regressions using any pair of the independent variables in Exhibit 10-19 are not likely to encounter multicollinearity problems.

If severe multicollinearity exists, try to obtain new data that do not suffer from multicollinearity problems. Do not drop an independent variable (cost driver) that should be included in a model because it is correlated with another independent variable. Omitting such a variable will cause the estimated coefficient of the independent variable included in the model to be biased away from its true value.

TERMS TO LEARN

This chapter contains definitions of the following important terms:

industrial engineering method (p. 485)
learning curve (p. 489)
linear cost function (p. 468)
multicollinearity (p. 500)
multiple linear regression (p. 497)
non-linear cost function (p. 484)
normality (p. 469)
null hypothesis, H_0 (p. 471)

ordinary least squares regression (p. 464)
outcome (response) variable (p. 466)
predictor (explanatory) variable (p. 466)
p value (p. 479)
regression analysis (p. 464)
regression line (p. 469)
residual (p. 469)
residual term u (p. 470)

serial correlation (p. 470)
specification analysis (p. 467)
statistically significant (p. 473)
step variable cost function
  (p. 484)
student t-statistic (p. 473)
work measurement method
  (p. 485)

MASTERY QUESTIONS

The Mastery Questions are rated by proficiency level—elementary, intermediate, and advanced. The solutions appear in the Solutions to Mastery Questions section of MyAccountingLab.

LEARNING OBJECTIVE 1

1. **Specification analysis—Elementary.** The graph below illustrates the OLS linear-regression line between quantity of output produced and sold, and the size of the indirect manufacturing labour cost.

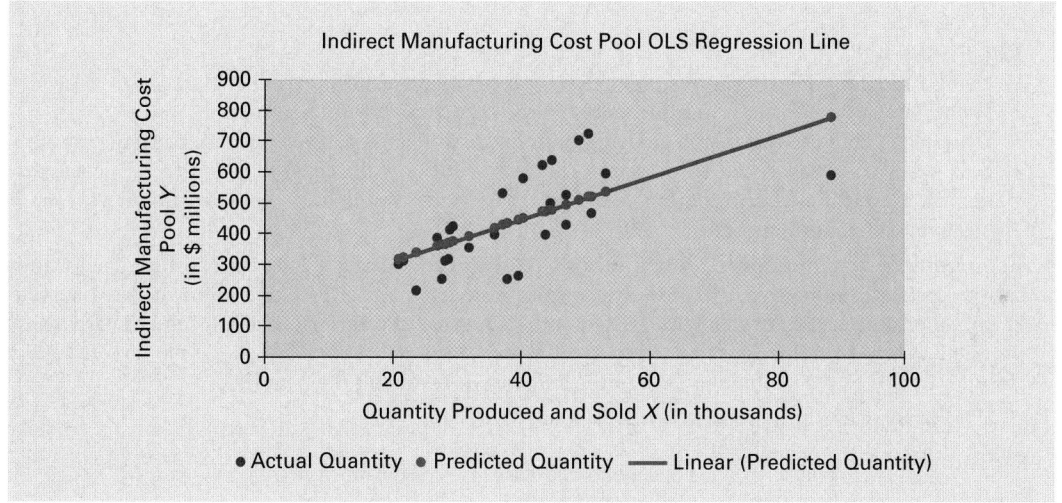

Indirect Manufacturing Cost Pool OLS Regression Line

● Actual Quantity ● Predicted Quantity —— Linear (Predicted Quantity)

REQUIRED
What does this graph confirm for the management accountant who understands the importance of the specification analysis?

2. **Regression analysis, service company—Intermediate.** (CMA, adapted) Bob Jones owns a catering company that prepares banquets and parties for both individual and business functions throughout the year. Jones's business is seasonal, with a heavy schedule during the summer months and the year-end holidays and a light schedule at other times. During peak periods there are extra costs.

   One of the major events Jones's customers request is a cocktail party. He offers a standard cocktail party and has developed the following cost structure on a per-person basis.

Food and beverages	$18.00
Labour (0.5 hour × $12.00 per hour)	6.00
Overhead (0.5 hour × $16.80 per hour)	8.40
Total costs per person	$32.40

Jones is quite certain about his estimates of the food, beverages, and labour costs but is not as comfortable with the overhead estimate. This estimate was based on the actual data for the past 12 months, presented below. These data indicate that overhead expenses vary with the direct labour-hours expended. The $16.80-per-hour estimate was determined by dividing total overhead expended for the 12 months by total labour-hours.

Month	Labour Hours	Overhead Costs
January	2,500	$ 66,000
February	2,700	70,800
March	3,000	72,000
April	4,200	76,800
May	7,500	92,400
June	5,500	85,200
July	6,500	88,800
August	4,500	80,400
September	7,000	90,000
October	4,500	81,600
November	3,100	74,400
December	6,500	87,600
Total	57,500	$966,000

Jones has recently become aware of regression analysis. He estimated the following regression equation with overhead costs as the dependent variable (y) and labour-hours as the independent variable (X):

$$y = \$57,925 + \$4.71X$$

REQUIRED
1. Using Excel, complete a regression analysis and complete a specification analysis.
2. What important information is presented in the r^2, t-statistic, and p-values?
3. Using data from the regression analysis, find the variable cost per person for a cocktail party.
4. Bob Jones has been asked to prepare a bid for a 200-person cocktail party to be given next month. Determine the minimum bid price that Jones would be willing to submit to earn a positive contribution margin.

3. **Estimating a cost function, two methods—Advanced.** Laurie Daley is examining customer service costs in the Southern Region of Capitol Products. Capitol Products has over 200 separate electrical products that are sold with a six-month guarantee of full repair or replacement with a new product. When a product is returned by a customer, a service report is made. This service report includes details of the problem and the time and cost of resolving the problem.

Weekly data for the most recent ten-week period are

Week Number	Customer Service Department Costs	Number of Service Reports
1	$16,614	201
2	24,750	276
3	15,530	122
4	22,142	386
5	17,810	274
6	26,268	436
7	20,198	321
8	25,715	328
9	21,920	243
10	20,198	161

REQUIRED
1. Using the regression function in Excel, plot the relationship between customer service costs and number of service reports.
2. Is the relationship between the predictor and outcome variable economically plausible?
3. What do the r^2, t, and p values tell the management accountant about this estimated regression line?
4. Is the relationship between the predictor and outcome variables linear?

5. Use the high-low method to plot the cost function, relating customer service costs to the number of service reports.
6. What predictor variables, in addition to number of service reports, might be causes of monthly customer service costs of Capitol Products?

LEARNING OBJECTIVE 2

1. Linear cost approximation—Elementary. Terry Lawler, managing director of the Winnipeg Consulting Group, is examining how overhead costs behave with variations in monthly professional labour-hours billed to clients. Assume the following historical data:

Total Overhead Costs	Professional Labour-Hours Billed to Clients
$408,000	3,000
480,000	4,000
522,000	5,000
572,400	6,000
634,800	7,000
704,400	8,000

REQUIRED
1. Use OLS linear regression to assess how well the data sets conform to the four assumptions of the specification analysis.
2. As a management accountant, would you have any reservations about using these results to justify professional direct labour-hours as a cost-allocation base for the overhead cost pool?
3. Compute the linear cost function, relating total overhead cost to professional labour-hours, using the representative observations of 4,000 and 7,000 hours. Plot the linear cost function. Does the constant component of the cost function represent the fixed overhead costs of the Winnipeg Consulting Group? Why?
4. What would be the predicted total overhead costs for (a) 5,000 hours and (b) 8,000 hours using the cost function estimated in requirement 3? Plot the predicted costs and actual costs for 5,000 and 8,000 hours.
5. Lawler had a chance to accept a special job that would have boosted professional labour-hours from 4,000 to 5,000 hours. Suppose Lawler, guided by the linear cost function, rejected this job because it would have brought a total increase in contribution margin of $45,600, before deducting the predicted increase in total overhead cost, $51,600. What is the actual total contribution margin forgone?

2. OLS linear regression—Intermediate. Below are the input and results of an OLS linear regression. The president of a specialty fruit juice company believed that for every one-degree-Celsius drop in

Table of Data Points Used			Output Statistics	
Observations	**Predictor X**	**Outcome Y**	**Regression Statistics**	
1993	22.6	$1,219	r^2	0.011852065
1994	24.3	1,568	adjusted r^2	−0.05872993
1995	25.5	1,731	standard error	975.122693
1996	28.1	1,395	observations	16
1997	29.3	1,421		
1998	31.0	1,320	**Coefficients Value**	
1999	30.1	2,101	intercept a	1169.697572
2000	26.9	1,795	standard error a	2718.027151
2001	31.0	2,300	t-statistic a	0.430348009
2002	28.3	2,152	p-value a	0.673493531
2003	29.1	2,487	slope b	39.60026518
2004	29.8	2,104	standard error b	96.6380257
2005	31.2	3,307	t-statistic b	0.409779327
2006	28.6	3,502	p-value b	0.688169092
2007	24.5	3,862		
2008	27.9	4,200		

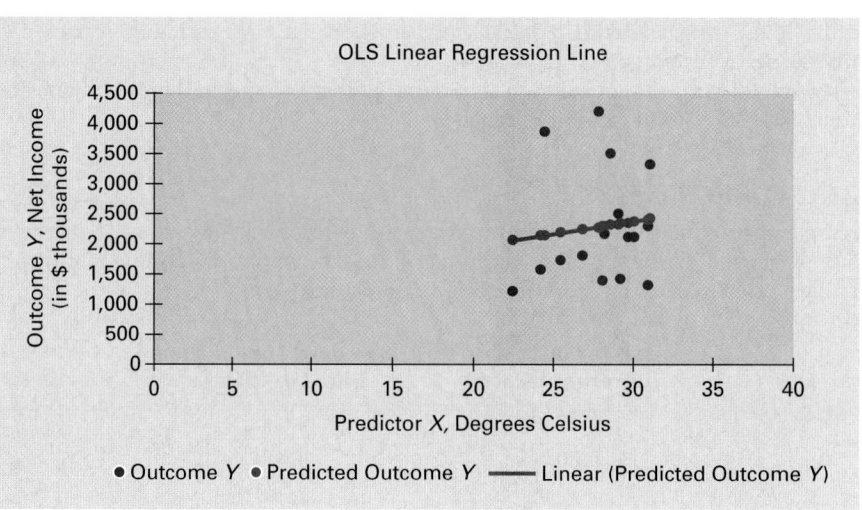

OLS Linear Regression Line

● Outcome *Y* ● Predicted Outcome *Y* ⸺ Linear (Predicted Outcome *Y*)

average temperature during the summer months, the profit would decline 3%. This information was used to prepare budgets. The president obtained forecasts of the average summer temperature and then requested the budget be adjusted accordingly. The table of values above presents the raw data for temperatures (predictor variable X) and net income (outcome variable Y).

REQUIRED
1. What do the coefficients of the OLS linear-regression line $y = a + bX$, where $a = \$1,169.70$ and $b = \$39.60$ tell you about the relationship between these two sets of data?
2. What does the r^2 tell you about the explanatory power of temperature to predict net income?
3. What does the t-statistic and the p-value tell you about whether or not the coefficients a and b could arise by accident?
4. What recommendations would you make to the president?

3. **Regression computations, governance—Advanced.** Cambridge Engineering manufactures small electric motors. Data on manufacturing labour costs and units produced for the last four quarters are as follows:

Quarter	Manufacturing Labour Costs	Units Produced
1	$211,200	9,000
2	208,800	10,000
3	198,000	9,000
4	246,000	12,000
Total	$864,000	40,000

Peter Smith, the manufacturing manager, is evaluated on how labour costs in a quarter compare with labour costs in the previous four quarters. In the recently concluded Quarter 5, Cambridge Engineering produced 12,000 motors and incurred manufacturing labour costs of $249,600. Smith is very happy with the results. Over the previous four quarters, the average manufacturing labour cost per unit was $21.60 ($864,000 ÷ 40,000 units), resulting in a benchmark for Quarter 5 of $21.60 × 12,000 = $259,200. Just as Smith is thinking about what he might do with the bonus, Allison Hart, the plant controller, knocks on Smith's door.

Allison: I'm sorry that we couldn't beat the benchmark over the last four quarters. We certainly gave it our best shot.

Peter: What do you mean we didn't beat the benchmark? Here are the numbers I just calculated. Against a benchmark of $259,200, we achieved $249,600.

Allison: No, that's not how the calculations are done. Some of the labour costs are fixed and others vary with production. My analysis here first separates out the fixed from the variable components. My calculations then show that our Quarter 5 performance was worse than the previous quarters.

Peter: Please review your calculations. I am sure you can report better numbers than that. This approach you are using is subject to estimation error. You should make some adjustment for that. If we don't show senior management that we are succeeding in reducing labour costs, they might shut us down because they don't believe we're competitive. I'm sure no one in this plant wants that to happen.

1. Verify, either by using the actual formulae given in the chapter, or by using a software program on a computer, that the regression equation is given by

$$y = \$78{,}000 + (\$13.80 \times \text{units produced})$$
with an $r^2 = 0.88$; adjusted $r^2 = 0.819$

2. What is the benchmark for Quarter 5 that Allison Hart calculated?
3. Why is there a difference between the benchmark calculated by Peter Smith and the benchmark calculated in requirement 2? Which benchmark do you prefer? Explain your answer.
4. Identify the steps that Allison Hart should follow in attempting to resolve the situation created by Peter Smith's comment about adjusting the benchmark.

LEARNING OBJECTIVE 3

1. **OLS regression analysis, activity-based costing, choosing cost drivers—Intermediate.** Larry Chu, the plant controller at Rohan Plastics, wants to identify cost drivers for support overhead cost.

Indirect support consists of skilled staff responsible for the efficient functioning of all aspects (setup, production, maintenance, and quality control) of the plastic injection-moulding facility. In talking to the support staff, Chu has the impression that they spend a good portion of their time ensuring that the equipment is set up correctly and checking that the first units of production in each batch are of good quality.

Chu has collected the following monthly data for the past 12 months:

Month	Support Overhead	Machine-Hours	Number of Batches
January	$100,800	2,250	309
February	49,200	2,400	128
March	75,600	2,850	249
April	52,800	2,100	159
May	52,800	2,700	216
June	57,600	2,250	174
July	79,200	3,800	264
August	55,200	3,600	162
September	39,600	1,850	147
October	79,200	3,300	219
November	97,200	3,750	303
December	68,400	2,000	106
Total	$807,600	32,850	2,436

Chu estimates the following regression equations:

$$y = \$33{,}707 + (\$12.27 \times \text{machine-hours})$$
$$\text{and} \quad y = \$19{,}237 + (\$236.76 \times \text{number of batches})$$

where y is the monthly support overhead.

REQUIRED
1. Present plots of the monthly data and the regression lines underlying each of the following cost functions. Which cost driver for support overhead costs would you choose?
   a. Support overhead costs $= a + (b \times \text{machine-hours})$
   b. Support overhead costs $= a + (b \times \text{number of batches})$
2. Chu anticipates 2,600 machine-hours and 300 batches will be run next month. Using the cost driver you chose in requirement 1, what should Chu budget for support overhead costs?
3. a. Chu adds 20% to costs as a first cut for determining target revenues (and hence prices). Costs other than support overhead are expected to equal $150,000 next month. Compare the target revenue numbers obtained if (i) machine-hours and (ii) number of batches is used as the cost driver. Discuss what would happen if Chu picked the "wrong" cost driver—the cost driver other than the one you chose in requirement 1—to set target revenues and prices.
   b. Describe any other implications of choosing the "wrong" cost driver and cost function.

2. **Purchasing department cost drivers, activity-based costing, simple regression analysis— Advanced.** Fashion Flair operates a chain of ten retail department stores. Each department store makes its own purchasing decisions. Barry Lee, assistant to the president of Fashion

Flair, is interested in better understanding the drivers of purchasing department costs. For many years, Fashion Flair has allocated purchasing department costs to products on the basis of the dollar value of merchandise purchased. An item costing $120 is allocated ten times as much overhead costs associated with the purchasing department as an item costing $12 is allocated.

Lee recently attended a seminar titled "Cost Drivers in the Retail Industry." In a presentation at the seminar, Couture Fabrics, a leading competitor that implemented activity-based costing, reported the number of purchase orders and the number of suppliers to be the two most important cost drivers of purchasing department costs. The dollar value of merchandise purchased on each purchase order was not found to be a significant cost driver by Couture Fabrics. Lee interviewed several members of the purchasing department at the Fashion Flair store in Victoria. These people told Lee that they believed that Couture Fabrics' conclusions also applied to their purchasing department.

Lee collects the following data for the most recent year for the ten retail department stores of Fashion Flair:

y Department Store	X_1 Purchasing Department Costs (PDC)	X_2 Dollar Value of Merchandise Purchased (MP$)	X_3 Number of Purchase Orders (no. of POs)	Number of Suppliers (no. of Ss)
Saskatoon	$1,827,600	$ 81,978,000	4,357	132
Chicago	1,320,000	40,147,200	2,550	222
Victoria	656,400	145,392,000	1,433	11
Miami	2,458,800	143,479,200	5,944	190
New York	1,267,200	40,206,000	2,793	23
Calgary	634,800	35,824,800	1,327	33
Seattle	1,845,600	123,450,000	7,586	104
St. Louis	2,104,800	46,408,800	3,617	119
Toronto	1,934,400	167,174,400	1,707	208
Vancouver	1,508,400	157,132,800	4,731	201

Lee decides to use simple regression analysis to examine whether one or more of three variables (the last three columns in the table) are cost drivers of purchasing department costs. Summary results for these regressions are as follows:

◆ **Regression 1.** PDC = $a + (b \times \text{MP\$})$; $n = 10$, $d.f. = 9$

Variable	Coefficient	Standard Error	t-Value
Constant	$1,246,873	$412,127	3.03
Independent variable 1: MP$	0.0031	0.0037	0.84

$r^2 = 0.08$; Durbin-Watson statistic = 2.43; adjusted $r^2 = 20.03$

◆ **Regression 2.** PDC = $a + (b \times \text{no. of POs})$; $n = 10$, $d.f. = 9$

Variable	Coefficient	Standard Error	t-Value
Constant	$876,858	$318,502	2.75
Independent variable 1: no. of POs	$ 188.36	$ 77.62	2.43

$r^2 = 0.42$; Durbin-Watson statistic = 2.016; adjusted $r^2 = 0.352$

◆ **Regression 3.** PDC = $a + (b \times \text{no. of Ss})$; $n = 10$, $d.f. = 9$

Variable	Coefficient	Standard Error	t-Value
Constant	$977,833.99	$297,385.63	3.29
Independent variable 1: no. of Ss	$ 4,649.77	$ 2,036.75	2.28

$r^2 = 0.39$; Durbin-Watson statistic = 2.056; adjusted $r^2 = 0.3187$

1. Compare and evaluate the three simple regression models estimated by Lee. Graph each one. Evaluate the information summarized in the three outputs from the three regressions.
2. Do the regression results support the Couture Fabrics presentation about purchasing department cost drivers? Which of these cost drivers would you recommend in designing an activity-based cost system?
3. How might Lee gain additional evidence on drivers of purchasing department costs at each store of Fashion Flair?

LEARNING OBJECTIVE 4

1. **Matching graphs with appropriate cost functions—Intermediate.** (D. Green, adapted) Shown below are a number of charts, each indicating some relationship between cost and a cost driver. No attempt has been made to draw these charts to any particular scale; the absolute numbers on each axis may be closely or widely spaced.

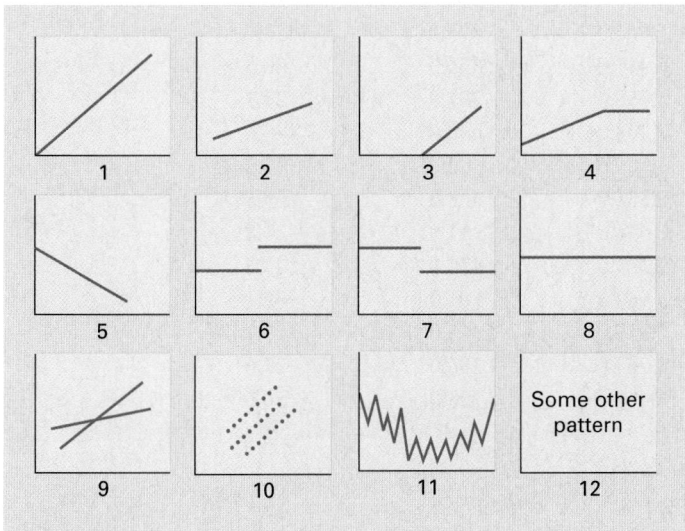

   The horizontal axis represents the units produced over the year and the vertical axis represents *total cost or revenue*. Indicate by number which one of the charts best fits each of the situations or items described. Each situation or item is independent of all the others; all factors not stated are assumed to be irrelevant. Some charts will be used more than once; some may not apply to any of the situations.
   a. Direct materials costs
   b. Supervisors' salaries for one shift and two shifts
   c. A cost-volume-profit chart
   d. Mixed costs—for example, a car rental fixed charge plus a rate per kilometre driven
   e. Amortization of plant, computed on a straight-line basis
   f. Data supporting the use of a variable cost rate, such as manufacturing labour cost of $14 per unit produced
   g. Incentive bonus plan that pays managers $0.10 for every unit produced above some level of production
   h. Interest expense on $2 million borrowed at a fixed rate of interest
2. **Discontinuous linear cost functions—Advanced.** Below are the input and results of an OLS linear regression. The managers have asked you, the management accountant, to undertake a study of any systematic change to the size of the indirect manufacturing cost pool. They have provided you with quarterly data. After you run the regression, you are quite pleased with the r^2, which indicates about a 42% explanatory power for quantity sold and produced to explain the change in the size of the indirect manufacturing cost pool. The actual t for the intercept a, is above the critical value for the 95% confidence interval and $d.f.$ 25 with about a 2% probability the a value is random. For the slope coefficient b, however, the actual t-statistic implies that this value is random. Also, examining the residuals plot raises questions for you.

Observation	Cumulative Sales and Production	Indirect Manufacturing Cost Pool	Quantity Sold and Produced	Regression Statistics	
1	252.0	$252.0	37.8	r^2	0.423167
2	516.0	264.0	39.6	adjusted r^2	0.399132
3	1,107.0	591.0	88.7	standard error	113.7238
4	1,505.0	398.0	43.8	observations	26
5	1,721.0	216.0	23.8		
6	1,973.0	252.0	27.7	**Coefficients Value**	
7	2,437.0	464.0	51.0		
8	2,866.0	429.0	47.2	intercept a	173.4348
9	3,221.0	355.0	32.0	t-statistic a	2.560119
10	3,539.0	318.0	28.6	p-value a	0.017181
11	4,062.0	523.0	47.1		
12	4,558.0	496.0	44.6	slope b	6.821927
13	4,956.0	398.0	35.8	t-statistic b	4.19601
14	5,268.0	312.0	28.1	p-value b	0.000321
15	5,861.0	593.0	53.4		
16	6,437.0	576.0	40.3		
17	6,738.0	301.0	21.1		
18	7,378.0	640.0	44.8		
19	7,910.0	532.0	37.2		
20	8,332.0	422.0	29.5		
21	8,643.0	311.0	21.8		
22	9,263.0	620.0	43.4		
23	964.0	701.0	49.1		
24	10,379.0	415.0	29.1		
25	10,765.0	386.0	27.0		
26	11,488.0	723.0	50.6		

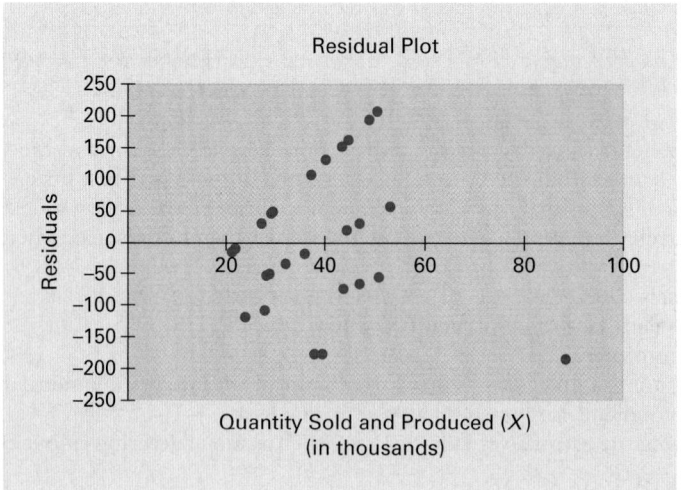

REQUIRED

1. Compare the values of the t-statistic calculated for both *a* (the intercept) and *b* (the slope) coefficients of the estimated regression line to the critical value at the 99% confidence level. What can you conclude from this comparison?
2. What does the graph of the residuals help a management accountant assess?
3. What does the graph of the residuals alert the management accountant to investigate?

LEARNING OBJECTIVE 5

1. **Curvilinear relationships—Advanced.** There are several non-linear relationships that could improve the model of a relationship between two variables, measured as quantity of common input consumed (or output produced) and the size of an indirect cost pool. Consider the data shown below.

Observation (quarter)	Cumulative Sales and Production	Quantity Sold and Produced	Indirect Manufacturing Cost Pool
1	198	198	$277.20
2	398	200	196.00
3	792	394	270.28
4	1,153	361	247.65
5	1,317	164	112.50
6	1,584	267	128.21
7	2,296	712	341.90
8	2,816	520	249.70
9	2,933	117	56.18
10	3,168	235	78.99
11	3,852	684	229.92
12	4,348	496	166.73
13	4,551	203	68.24
14	4,812	261	87.73
15	5,515	703	236.31
16	6,091	576	193.62
17	6,336	245	57.65
18	6,587	251	59.06
19	7,274	687	161.65
20	7,846	572	134.59
21	8,102	256	60.24
22	8,303	201	47.29
23	9,026	723	170.12
24	9,709	683	160.71
25	10,001	292	68.71
26	10,255	254	59.77

REQUIRED

1. Refer to the data above, and calculate the points at which cumulative sales and production double. In what quarters does this occur? What are the average unit costs in each quarter when cumulative sales and production double?

2. Plot the average-cost-per-unit curve including a trendline using Excel.

3. Calculate the constant percentage by which the size of the indirect cost pool declines each time the cumulative output doubles. How would the management accountant change the model of the relationship between quantity produced and sold, and the indirect manufacturing cost pool?

4. What non-linear relationship linked to quantity produced might provide a better model?

CHAPTER 10 APPENDIX

1. Evaluating alternative simple regression models, not-for-profit—Intermediate. Kathy Hanks, executive assistant to the president of Eastern University, is concerned about the overhead costs at her university. Cost pressures are severe, so controlling and reducing overhead is very important. Hanks believes overhead costs incurred are generally a function of the number of different academic programs (including different specializations, degrees, and majors) that the university has and the number of enrolled students. Both have grown significantly over the years. She collects the following data:

Year	Overhead Costs (in thousands)	Number of Academic Programs	Enrolled Students
1	$16,200	29	3,400
2	23,040	36	5,000
3	20,160	49	2,600
4	24,120	53	4,700
5	23,400	54	3,900
6	27,720	58	4,900

Year	Overhead Costs (in thousands)	Number of Academic Programs	Enrolled Students
7	28,440	88	5,700
8	24,120	72	3,900
9	27,360	83	3,500
10	35,640	73	3,700
11	37,440	101	5,600
12	45,720	103	7,600

◆ **Regression 1.** Overhead costs = $a + (b \times$ number of academic programs)

Variable	Coefficient	Standard Error	t-Value
Constant	$8,553.30	$4,002.41	2.14
Independent variable 1: number of academic programs	$ 288.76	$ 56.80	5.08

$r^2 = 0.72$; Durbin-Watson statistic $= 2.07$; adjusted $r^2 = 0.693$

◆ **Regression 2.** Overhead costs = $a + (b \times$ number of enrolled students)

Variable	Coefficient	Standard Error	t-Value
Constant	$7,190.10	$6,081.45	1.18
Independent variable 1: number of enrolled students	$ 4.53	$ 1.29	3.52

$r^2 = 0.55$; Durbin-Watson statistic $= 0.82$; adjusted $r^2 = 0.509$

REQUIRED

1. Plot the relationship between overhead costs and each of the following variables: (a) number of academic programs and (b) number of enrolled students.
2. Compare and evaluate the two simple regression models estimated by Hanks and summarized in the regression output.
3. What insights do the analyses provide about controlling and reducing overhead costs at the University?

2. **Evaluating multiple regression models, not-for-profit—Advanced.** (Continuation of Mastery Question 1.)

REQUIRED

1. Given your findings in Mastery Question 1, should Hanks use multiple regression analysis to better understand the cost drivers of overhead costs? Explain your answer.
2. Hanks decides that the simple regression analysis in Mastery Question 1 should be extended to a multiple regression analysis. She finds the following result:

◆ **Regression 3.** Overhead costs = $a + (b_1 \times$ number of academic programs) + $(b_2 \times$ number of enrolled students)

Variable	Coefficient	Standard Error	t-Value
Constant	$3,335.54	$4,344.06	0.77
Independent variable 1: number of academic programs	$ 214.04	$ 61.84	3.46
Independent variable 2: number of enrolled students	$ 2.24	$ 1.11	2.02

$r^2 = 0.81$; Durbin-Watson statistic $= 1.91$; adjusted $r^2 = 0.766$

The coefficient of correlation between number of academic programs and number of students is 0.60. Use the format in Exhibit 10-19 to evaluate the multiple regression model. (Assume linearity, and constant variance and normality of residuals.) Should Hanks choose the multiple regression model over the two simple regression models of Mastery Question 1?

3. How might the president of Eastern University use these regression results to manage overhead costs?

MyAccountingLab Make the grade with MyAccountingLab: The questions, exercises, and problems marked in red can be found on MyAccountingLab at **www.myaccountinglab.com.** You can practise them as often as you want, and most feature step-by-step guided instructions to help you find the right answer. Exercises and problems with an Excel icon in the margin have an accompanying Excel template on MyAccountingLab.

SHORT-ANSWER QUESTIONS

10-1 What two assumptions are frequently made when estimating a cost function?

10-2 What is ordinary least squares linear regression? What is the goal of an OLS linear regression?

10-3 What types of data points are needed for an OLS analysis? What is the first step in any statistical analysis?

10-4 What are the four assumptions that must be met to assure good quality input data? What data measurement problems can cause poor data quality?

10-5 "High correlation between two variables means that one is the cause and the other is the effect." Do you agree? Explain.

10-6 What is a linear cost function? Describe three alternative linear cost functions.

10-7 Name four approaches to estimating a cost function.

10-8 When using the high-low method, should you base the high and low observations on the dependent variable or on the cost driver?

10-9 What is the difference between the coefficient of determination, r^2, and the goodness of fit? What does explanatory power mean?

10-10 What is a residual?

10-11 How do the null hypothesis H_0, the degrees of freedom (*d.f.*) relate to one another? How do the student-*t*, confidence level, and critical value relate to *d.f.* and H_0?

10-12 Describe three criteria for evaluating cost functions and choosing cost drivers.

10-13 "All independent variables in a cost function estimated with regression analysis are cost drivers." Do you agree?

10-14 What is a discontinuous linear cost function? What types of analyses can be done to improve cost control when the data sets indicate a discontinuous linear cost function?

10-15 Define *learning curve*. Outline two models that can be used when incorporating learning into the estimation of cost functions.

EXERCISES

10-16 OLS linear regression. The results of an OLS linear regression analysis are below. The predictor variable used is the quantity produced and sold. The explanatory power of this variable to explain changes in the size of the indirect manufacturing cost pool is approximately 38%. This exceeds the threshold value for r^2 for a reliable relationship of 30%. As a management accountant familiar with OLS linear regression modelling, you are uneasy with the results.

Observation	Cumulative Sales and Production	Quantity Sold and Produced	Indirect Manufacturing Cost Pool	Regression Statistics	
1	198	198	$277.20	r^2	0.383655
2	398	200	196.00	adjusted r^2	0.357974
3	792	394	270.28	standard error	84.16542
4	1,153	361	247.65	observations	26
5	1,317	164	112.50		
6	1,584	267	128.21	**Coefficients Value**	
7	2,296	712	341.90		
8	2,816	520	249.70	intercept a	36.48440218
9	2,933	117	56.18	t-statistic a	1.005959215
10	3,168	235	78.99	p-value a	0.324470437
11	3,852	684	229.92		
12	4,348	496	166.73	slope b	0.304644864
13	4,551	203	68.24	t-statistic b	3.865131137
14	4,812	261	87.73	p-value b	0.000740362
15	5,515	703	236.31		
16	6,091	576	193.62		
17	6,336	245	57.65		
18	6,587	251	59.06		
19	7,274	687	161.65		
20	7,846	572	134.59		
21	8,102	256	60.24		
22	8,303	201	47.29		
23	9,026	723	170.12		
24	9,709	683	160.71		
25	10,001	292	68.71		
26	10,255	254	59.77		

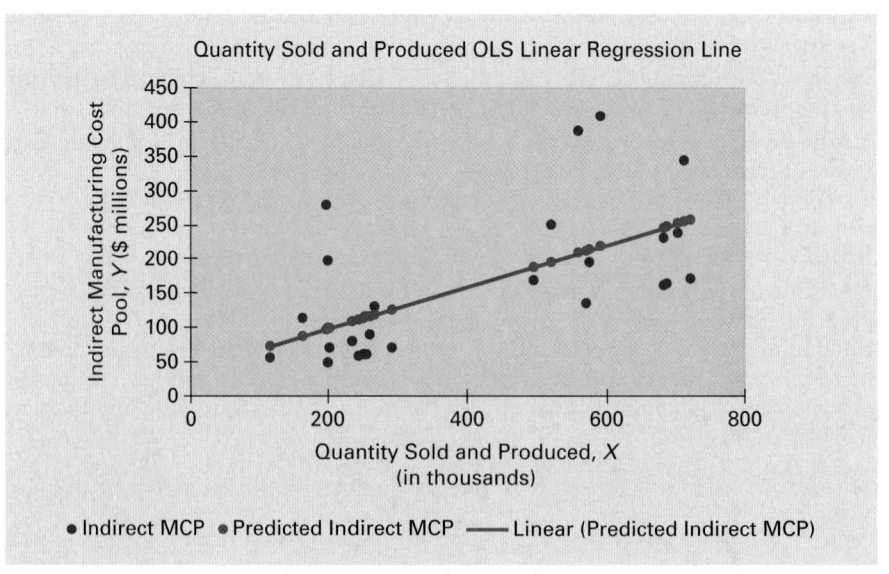

Quantity Sold and Produced OLS Linear Regression Line

● Indirect MCP ● Predicted Indirect MCP —— Linear (Predicted Indirect MCP)

REQUIRED
1. What output causes your unease?
2. What step did you miss, and what should you do at this point?

10-17 OLS linear regression (continuation of Exercise 10-16). Using Excel, plot the actual values of the predictor variable Y (in $ millions) from Exercise 10-16 as a bar chart and add a trendline.

REQUIRED
1. What does this step of the specification analysis tell a management accountant?
2. How would a management accountant interpret this new information? What is the next step?
3. Below is the plot of the residuals. How would a management accountant interpret this new information?

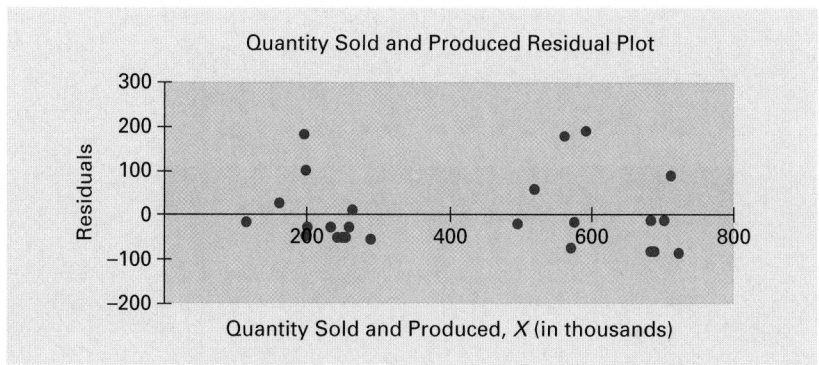

10-18 Estimating a cost function. The controller of the Ijiri Company wants you to estimate a cost function from the following two observations in a general ledger account called Maintenance:

Month	Machine-Hours	Maintenance Costs Incurred
January	6,000	$4,000
February	10,000	5,400

REQUIRED
1. Estimate the cost function for maintenance.
2. Can the constant in the cost function be used as an estimate of fixed maintenance cost per month? Explain.

10-19 Identifying variable, fixed, and mixed cost functions. The Pacific Corporation operates car rental agencies at more than 20 airports. Customers can choose from one of three contracts for car rentals of one day or less:
- Contract 1: $50 for the day
- Contract 2: $30 for the day plus $0.20 per kilometre traveled
- Contract 3: $1 per kilometre traveled

REQUIRED
1. Plot separate graphs for each of the three contracts, with costs on the vertical axis and kilometres traveled on the horizontal axis.
2. Express each contract as a linear cost function of the form $y = a + bX$.
3. Identify each contract as a variable, fixed, or mixed cost function.

10-20 Discontinuous linear cost functions. (CPA, adapted) Select the graph that matches the numbered manufacturing cost data. Indicate by letter which of the graphs best fits each of the situations or items described.

  The vertical axes of the graphs represent total dollars of cost, and the horizontal axes represent production output during a calendar year. In each case, the zero point of dollars and production is at the intersection of the two axes. The graphs may be used more than once.
1. Annual amortization of equipment, where the amount of amortization charged is computed by the machine-hours method.
2. Electricity bill—a flat fixed charge, plus a variable cost after a certain number of kilowatt-hours are used, where the quantity of kilowatt-hours used varies proportionately with quantity of production output.

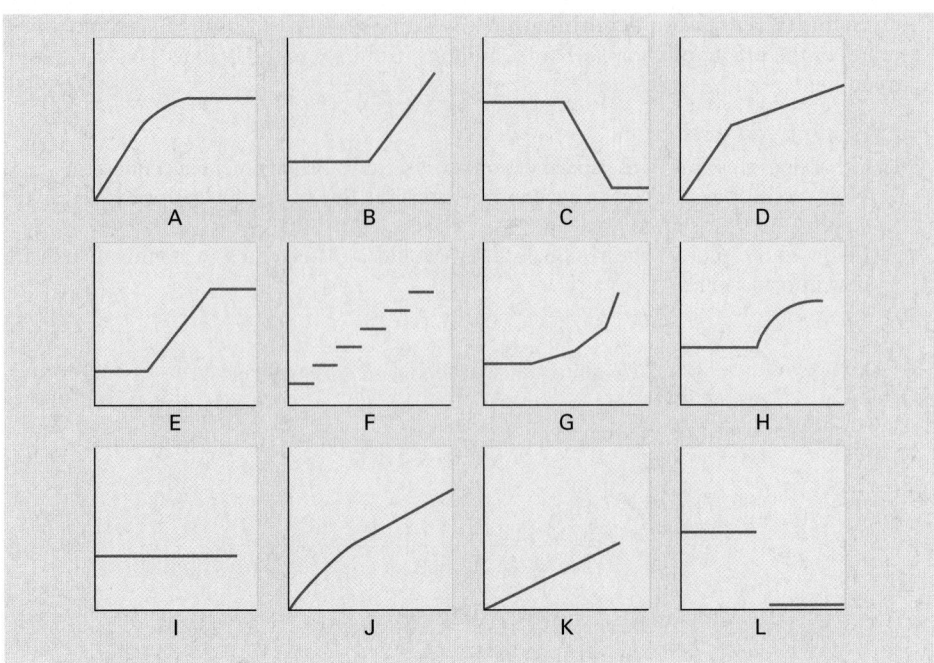

3. City water bill, which is computed as follows:

First 1,000,000 litres or less	$1,000 flat fee
Next 10,000 litres	$0.003 per litre used
Next 10,000 litres	$0.006 per litre used
Next 10,000 litres	$0.009 per litre used
And so on	And so on

The litres of water used vary proportionately with the quantity of production output.

4. Cost of lubricant for machines, where cost per unit decreases with each kilogram of lubricant used (for example, if one kilogram is used, the cost is $10; if two kilograms are used, the cost is $19.98; if three kilograms are used, the cost is $29.94) with a minimum cost per kilogram of $9.20.

5. Annual amortization of equipment, where the amount is computed by the straight-line method. When the amortization rate was established, it was anticipated that the obsolescence factor would be greater than the wear-and-tear factor.

6. Rent on a manufacturing plant donated by the city, where the agreement calls for a fixed fee payment unless 200,000 labour-hours are worked, in which case no rent need be paid.

7. Salaries of repair personnel, where one person is needed for every 1,000 machine-hours or less (that is, 0 to 1,000 hours requires one person, 1,001 to 2,000 hours requires two people, etc.).

8. Cost of direct materials used (assume no quantity discounts).

9. Rent on a manufacturing plant donated by the county, where the agreement calls for rent of $100,000 reduced by $1 for each direct manufacturing labour-hour worked in excess of 200,000 hours, but a minimum rental fee of $20,000 must be paid.

10-21 **Account analysis method.** Lorenzo operates a brushless car wash. Incoming cars are put on an automatic, continuously moving conveyor belt. Cars are washed as the conveyor belt carries the car from the start station to the finish station. After the car moves off the conveyor belt, the car is dried manually. Workers then clean and vacuum the inside of the car. Lorenzo serviced 80,000 cars in 2009. Lorenzo reports the following costs for 2009:

Account Description	Costs
Car wash labour	$260,000
Soap, cloth, and supplies	42,000
Water	38,000
Electric power to move conveyor belt	72,000
Amortization	64,000
Salaries	46,000

1. Classify each account as variable or fixed with respect to cars washed. Explain.
2. Lorenzo expects to wash 90,000 cars in 2010. Use the cost classification you developed in requirement 1 to estimate Lorenzo's total costs in 2010. Amortization is computed on a straight-line basis.

10-22 Interpreting results of regression analysis. In the example of Elegant Rugs in the chapter, the student-t showed that for direct machine-hours (DMH) as the predictor variable, the intercept a was not statistically different from a random value but the slope b was very probably not random. For direct manufacturing labour-hours (DMLH) as the predictor variable, the intercept a was very probably not random but the slope b was not statistically different from a random value.

REQUIRED
1. What other statistics would the management accountant review before recommending which of these two should be the cost-allocation base?
2. What other alternatives could Elegant Rugs pursue if the decision was to improve on explanatory power?

10-23 Account analysis method. Gower Inc., a manufacturer of plastic products, reports the following manufacturing costs and account analysis classification for the year ended December 31, 2009.

Account	Classification	Amount
Direct materials	All variable	$300,000
Direct manufacturing labour	All variable	225,000
Power	All variable	37,500
Supervision labour	20% variable	56,250
Materials-handling labour	50% variable	60,000
Maintenance labour	40% variable	75,000
Amortization	0% variable	95,000
Rent, property taxes, and administration	0% variable	100,000

Gower Inc., produced 75,000 units of product in 2009. Gower's management is estimating costs for 2010 based on 2009 numbers. The following additional information is available for 2010:
a. Direct materials prices in 2010 are expected to increase by 5% compared with 2009.
b. Under the terms of the labour contract, direct manufacturing labour wage rates are expected to increase by 10% in 2010 compared with 2009.
c. Power rates and wage rates for supervision, materials-handling, and maintenance are not expected to change from 2009 to 2010.
d. Amortization costs are expected to increase by 5%, and rent, property taxes, and administration costs are expected to increase by 7%.
e. Gower, Inc. expects to manufacture and sell 80,000 units in 2010.

REQUIRED
1. Prepare a schedule of variable, fixed, and total manufacturing costs for each account category in 2010. Estimate total manufacturing costs for 2010.
2. Calculate Gower's total manufacturing cost per unit in 2009 and estimated total manufacturing cost per unit in 2010.
3. How can you get better estimates of fixed and variable costs? Why would these better estimates be useful to Gower?

10-24 Linear cost approximation. Sandy Smith, managing director of the Calgary Consulting Group, is examining how overhead costs behave with changes in monthly professional labour-hours billed to clients. Assume the following historical data:

Total Overhead Costs	Professional Labour-Hours Billed to Clients
$340,000	3,000
400,000	4,000
435,000	5,000
477,000	6,000
529,000	7,000
587,000	8,000

REQUIRED

1. Compute the linear cost function, relating total overhead cost to professional labour-hours, using the representative observations of 4,000 and 7,000 hours. Plot the linear cost function. Does the constant component of the cost function represent the fixed overhead costs of the Calgary Consulting Group? Why?

2. What would be the predicted total overhead costs for (a) 5,000 hours and (b) 8,000 hours using the cost function estimated in requirement 1? Plot the predicted costs and actual costs for 5,000 and 8,000 hours.

3. Smith had a chance to accept a special job that would have boosted professional labour-hours from 4,000 to 5,000 hours. Suppose Smith, guided by the linear cost function, rejected this job because it would have brought a total increase in contribution margin of $38,000, before deducting the predicted increase in total overhead cost, $43,000. What is the actual total contribution margin forgone?

1. a. Average cost per frame, $30

10-25 Cost-volume-profit and regression analysis. Garvin Corporation manufactures a children's bicycle, model CT8. Garvin currently manufactures the bicycle frame. During 2009, Garvin made 30,000 frames at a total cost of $900,000. Ryan Corporation has offered to supply as many frames as Garvin wants at a cost of $28.50 per frame. Garvin anticipates needing 36,000 frames each year for the next few years.

REQUIRED

1. **a.** What is the average cost of manufacturing a bicycle frame in 2009? How does it compare to Ryan's offer?

   b. Can Garvin use the answer in requirement 1a to determine the cost of manufacturing 36,000 bicycle frames? Explain.

2. Garvin's cost analyst uses annual data from past years to estimate the following regression equation with total manufacturing costs of the bicycle frame as the dependent variable and bicycle frames produced as the independent variable:

$$y = \$432{,}000 + \$15X$$

During the years used to estimate the regression equation, the production of bicycle frames varied from 28,000 to 36,000. Using this equation, estimate how much it would cost Garvin to manufacture 36,000 bicycle frames. How much more or less costly is it to manufacture the frames rather than to acquire them from Ryan?

3. What other information would you need to be confident that the equation in requirement 2 accurately predicts the cost of manufacturing bicycle frames?

10-26 Regression analysis, activity-based costing, choosing cost drivers. Jill Goldstein has been collecting data over the last year in an effort to understand the cost drivers of distribution costs at Waterloo Corporation, a manufacturer of brass door handles. Distribution costs include the costs of organizing different shipments as well as physically handling and moving packaged units. Goldstein believes that, because the product is heavy, number of units moved will affect distribution costs significantly but she is not certain that this is the case. Goldstein collects the following monthly data for the past 12 months.

Month Made	Distribution Costs	Number of Packaged Units Moved	Number of Shipments Made
January	$ 33,600	51,000	200
February	24,000	43,000	210
March	20,400	28,000	185
April	38,400	67,000	315
May	48,000	73,000	335
June	28,800	54,000	225
July	26,400	37,000	190
August	42,000	72,000	390
September	50,400	71,000	280
October	27,600	56,000	360
November	39,600	52,000	380
December	26,400	45,000	270
Total	$405,600	649,000	3,340

Goldstein estimates the following regression equations:

$$y = \$1{,}618.45 + (\$0.595 \times \text{Number of packaged units moved})$$
$$y = \$12{,}500.57 + (\$76.52 \times \text{Number of shipments made})$$

1. Using Excel, produce plots of the monthly data and the regression lines underlying each of the following cost functions:

   a. Distribution costs $= a + (b \times$ number of packaged units moved$)$
   b. Distribution costs $= a + (b \times$ number of shipments made$)$

   Which cost driver for support overhead costs would you choose? Explain your answer briefly based on the statistics provided by the analysis.
2. Goldstein anticipates moving 40,000 units in 220 shipments next month. Using the cost function you chose in requirement 1, what distribution costs should Goldstein budget?
3. If Goldstein chose the wrong cost function—the cost function other than the one you chose in requirement 1—and 40,000 units were moved in 220 shipments, would you expect actual costs to be lower than, to be greater than, or to closely approximate the predictions made using the "wrong" cost driver and cost function? Explain your answer briefly and discuss any other implications of choosing the "wrong" cost driver and cost function.

10-27 Learning curve, cumulative average-time learning model. Global Defence manufactures radar systems. It has just completed the manufacture of its first newly designed system, RS-32. Manufacturing data for the RS-32 follow:

Total variable costs of
producing 2 units, $376,000

Direct material cost	$80,000	per unit of RS-32
Direct manufacturing labour time for first unit	3,000	direct manufacturing labour-hours (DMLH)
Learning curve for manufacturing labour time per radar system	90%	cumulative average time[a]
Direct manufacturing labour cost	$ 25	per direct manufacturing labour-hour (DMLH)
Variable manufacturing overhead cost		$ 15 per direct manufacturing labour-hour (DMLH)

[a]Using the formula for a 90% learning curve,

$$b = \frac{\ln 0.90}{\ln 2} = \frac{-0.105361}{0.693147} = -0.152004$$

REQUIRED
Calculate the total variable costs of producing 2, 4, and 8 units.

10-28 Learning curve, incremental unit-time learning model. Assume the same information for Global Defence as in Exercise 10-27, except that Global Defence uses a 90% incremental unit-time learning model as a basis for predicting direct manufacturing labour-hours. (A 90% learning curve means $b = -0.152004$.)

1. Total variable costs of
producing 2 units, $388,000

REQUIRED
1. Calculate the total variable costs of producing 2, 3, and 4 units.
2. If you solved Exercise 10-27, compare your cost predictions in the two exercises for 2 and 4 units. Why are the predictions different? How should Global Defence decide which model it should use?

PROBLEMS

10-29 Organizing data, high-low method. Ken Howard, financial analyst at JVR Corporation, a manufacturer of precision parts, is examining the behaviour of quarterly maintenance costs for budgeting purposes. Howard collects the following data on machine-hours worked and maintenance costs for the past 13 quarters:

Quarter	Machine-Hours	Maintenance Costs
1	90,000	$282,000
2	110,000	222,000
3	100,000	264,000
4	120,000	240,000
5	85,000	288,000
6	105,000	204,000
7	95,000	258,000
8	115,000	234,000

Quarter	Machine-Hours	Maintenance Costs
9	95,000	282,000
10	115,000	228,000
11	105,000	270,000
12	125,000	216,000
13	90,000	300,000

REQUIRED

1 **a.** Using Excel, do a regression analysis to estimate and plot the quarterly data underlying the cost function: Maintenance costs = $a + (b \times \text{Machine-hours})$.

   b. Estimate the cost function for the data represented by the plots in requirement 1(a) using the high-low method.

   c. How well does each cost function fit the data?

2 **a.** Using Excel, do a regression analysis to estimate and plot the quarterly data relating machine-hours in a quarter (t, say) to maintenance costs in the following quarter ($t + 1$). That is, plot machine-hours in quarter 1 against maintenance costs in quarter 2, machine-hours in quarter 2 against maintenance costs in quarter 3, and so on.

   b. Estimate the cost function for the data represented by the plots in requirement 2(a) using the high-low method.

   c. How well does each cost function fit the data?

3. Howard anticipates that JVR will operate machines for 95,000 hours in quarter 14. Calculate the predicted maintenance costs in quarter 14 using the cost functions estimated in requirements 1(b) and 2(b). What maintenance costs should Howard budget for quarter 14? Explain your answer briefly.

3. a. Increase in revenues, $8,723

10-30 High-low versus regression method. (CIMA, heavily adapted) Anna Martinez, the financial manager at the Casa Real restaurant, is working with Jan Brown, the marketing manager, to establish whether there is any relationship between newspaper advertising and sales revenue at the restaurant. They obtain the following monthly data for the past 10 months:

Month	Revenues	Advertising Expense
March	$60,000	$2,400
April	84,000	3,600
May	66,000	1,800
June	78,000	4,200
July	66,000	1,200
August	78,000	2,400
September	54,000	1,800
October	96,000	4,800
November	66,000	3,000
December	72,000	3,000

They estimate the following regression equation:

$$y = \$47,402 + (8.723 \times \text{Advertising Expense}), \text{ where } y \text{ is the monthly revenue}$$

REQUIRED

1. Using Excel, do a regression analysis to estimate and plot the relationship between advertising expense and revenues, and interpret the results.

2. Use the high-low method to compute the cost function, relating advertising expense and revenues.

3. Using (a) the regression equation and (b) the high-low equation, what is the increase in revenues for each $1,000 spent on advertising within the relevant range?

4. Should Martinez and Brown use the cost function estimated from the regression method or the high-low method to predict the effect of advertising on revenues? Explain briefly.

1. Predicted total costs, $2,949,975

10-31 Cost estimation, cumulative average-time learning curve. Nautilus Company, which is under contract to the Canadian Navy, assembles troop deployment boats. As part of its research program, it completes the assembly of the first of a new model (PT109) of deployment boats. The Navy is impressed with the PT109. It requests that Nautilus submit a proposal on the cost of producing another seven PT109s.

Nautilus reports the following cost information for the first PT109 assembled and uses an 85% cumulative average-time learning model as a basis for forecasting direct manufacturing labour-hours (DMLH) for the next seven PT109s. (An 85% learning curve means $b = -0.234465$.):

Direct materials	$100,000	
Direct manufacturing labour time for first boat	10,000	labour-hours (DMLH)
Direct manufacturing labour rate	$ 30	per direct manufacturing labour-hour (DMLH)
Variable manufacturing overhead cost	$ 20	per direct manufacturing labour-hour (DMLH)
Other manufacturing overhead	25%	of direct manufacturing labour costs
Tooling costs[a]	$500,000	
Learning curve for manufacturing labour time per boat	85%	cumulative average time[b]

[a]Tooling can be reused at no extra cost because all of its cost has been assigned to the first deployment boat.

[b]Using the formula for an 85% learning curve,

$$b = \frac{\ln 0.85}{\ln 2} = \frac{-0.162519}{0.693147} = -0.234465$$

REQUIRED

1. Calculate predicted total costs of producing the seven PT109s for the Navy. (Nautilus will keep the first deployment boat assembled, costed at $725,000, as a demonstration model for potential customers.)
2. What is the dollar amount of the difference between (a) the predicted total costs for producing the seven PT109s in requirement 1, and (b) the predicted total costs for producing the seven PT109s, assuming that there is no learning curve for direct manufacturing labour? That is, for (b) assume a linear function for units produced and direct manufacturing labour-hours.

10-32 Cost estimation, incremental unit-time learning model. Assume the same information for Nautilus Company as in Problem 10-31 with one exception. This exception is that Nautilus uses an 85% incremental unit-time learning model as a basis for predicting direct manufacturing labour-hours (DMLH) in its assembling operations. (An 85% learning curve means $b = -0.234465$.)

1. Predicted total costs, $3,538,085

REQUIRED

1. Prepare a prediction of the total costs for producing the seven PT109s for the Navy.
2. If you solved requirement 1 of Problem 10-31, compare your cost prediction there with the one you made here. Why are the predictions different? How should Nautilus decide which model it should use?

10-33 Promotion of a new product, simple and multiple regression analysis. (Chapter Appendix, S. Stickel, adapted) "What does all this mean. All I really want to know is whether I should advertise or not, and where?" said Rick Savalas, the sales manager of Cleanhair Products Inc. Rick has asked for your help to understand the results of regression analyses that have been prepared by his assistants for a new product, Glowbright, that Cleanhair Products recently introduced. The notation used is as follows:

y estimated sales of Glowbright
X_1 dollars incurred on discount coupons placed in magazines
X_2 dollars spent on advertising Glowbright on television

Standard errors of the coefficients (not t-statistics) are in parentheses.

1. $y = \$457,200 + \$4.78 X_1$ $r^2 = 0.47$
      ($2.08)

2. $y = \$560,400 + \$5.08 X_2$ $r^2 = 0.53$
      ($2.23)

3. $y = \$902,760 + \$1.04 X_1 + \$1.09 X_2$ $r^2 = 0.88$
    ($0.95)   ($1.19)

1. For each of the regressions, perform a statistical test and indicate whether sales are affected by discount coupons and television advertising.
2. Contrast the multiple regression results (equation 3) with the simple regression results (equations 1 and 2) in terms of the statistical tests that you performed in requirement 1. Suggest a possible explanation for any differences in the results of the statistical tests.
3. Interpret the $4.78, the $5.08, the $1.04, and the $1.09 coefficients in the regression equations. Specifically, explain briefly what the coefficients imply about whether and how Rick should advertise.

10-34 Regression; choosing among models (Chapter Appendix). Tilbert Toys (TT) makes the popular Floppin' Freddy Frog and Jumpin' Jill Junebug dolls in batches. TT has recently adopted activity-based costing. TT incurs setup costs for each batch of dolls that it produces. TT uses "number of setups" as the cost driver for setup costs.

TT has just hired Bebe Williams, an accountant. Bebe thinks that "number of setup hours" might be a better cost driver because the setup time for each product is different. Bebe collects the following data.

Month	Number of setups	Number of setup hours	Setup costs
1	195	920	$52,300
2	240	1,340	63,850
3	100	580	28,740
4	220	1,900	118,420
5	140	1,840	89,440
6	230	1,950	106,880
7	210	1,490	104,810
8	150	600	45,040
9	185	1,640	110,520

REQUIRED

1. Estimate the regression equation for (a) setup costs and number of setups and (b) setup costs and number of setup hours. You should obtain the following results:

◆ Regression 1: Setup costs $= a + (b \times \text{Number of setups})$

Variable	Coefficient	Standard Error	t-Value
Constant	$3,905	$41,439	0.09
Independent variable 1: No. of setups	$ 410	$ 217	1.89

$r^2 = 0.34$; Durbin-Watson statistic $= 1.12$

◆ Regression 2: Setup costs $= a + (b \times \text{Number of setup-hours})$

Variable	Coefficient	Standard Error	t-Value
Constant	$ 3,349	$12,879	0.26
Independent variable 1: No. of setup-hours	$56.270	$ 8.85	6.36

$r^2 = 0.85$; Durbin-Watson statistic $= 1.50$

2. On two different graphs plot the data and the regression lines for each of the following cost functions.
   a. Setup costs $a + (b \times \text{Number of setups})$
   b. Setup costs $a + (b \times \text{Number of setup hours})$
3. Evaluate the regression models for "Number of setups" and "Number of setup-hours" as the cost driver according.
4. Based on your analysis, which cost driver should Tilbert Toys use for setup costs, and why?

10-35 Purchasing department cost drivers, activity-based costing, simple regression analysis. Flashy Fashion operates a chain of ten retail department stores. Each department store makes its own purchasing decisions. Sherry Jones, assistant to the president of Flashy Fashion, is interested in better understanding the drivers of purchasing department costs. For many years, Flashy Fashion has allocated purchasing department costs to products on the basis of the dollar value of merchandise purchased. An item costing $100 is allocated ten times as much overhead costs associated with the purchasing department as an item costing $10 is allocated.

Jones recently attended a seminar titled "Cost Drivers in the Retail Industry." In a presentation at the seminar, Couture Fabrics, a leading competitor that implemented activity-based costing, reported the number of purchase orders and the number of suppliers to be the two most important cost drivers of purchasing department costs. The dollar value of merchandise purchased on each purchase order was not found to be a significant cost driver. Jones interviewed several members of the purchasing department at the Flashy Fashion store in Toronto. These people told Jones that they believed that Couture Fabrics' conclusions also applied to their purchasing department.

Jones collects the following data for the most recent year for Flashy Fashion's ten retail department stores:

y Department Store	X_1 Purchasing Department Costs (PDC)	X_2 Dollar Value Merchandise Purchased (MP$)	X_3 Number Purchase Orders (no. of POs)	Number of Suppliers (no. of Ss)
Saskatoon	$1,523,000	$ 68,315,000	4,357	132
Chicago	1,100,000	33,456,000	2,550	222
Victoria	547,000	121,160,000	1,433	11
Miami	2,049,000	119,566,000	5,944	190
New York	1,056,000	33,505,000	2,793	23
Calgary	529,000	29,854,000	1,327	33
Seattle	1,538,000	102,875,000	7,586	104
St. Louis	1,754,000	38,648,000	3,617	119
Toronto	1,612,000	139,312,000	1,707	208
Vancouver	1,257,000	130,944,000	4,731	201

Jones decides to use simple regression analysis to examine whether one or more of three variables (the last three columns in the table) are cost drivers of purchasing department costs. Summary results for these regressions are as follows:

◆ **Regression 1.** PDC $= a + (b \times$ MP$)$; $n = 10$, d.f. $= 9$

Variable	Coefficient	Standard Error	t-value
Constant	$1,039,061	$343,439	3.03
Independent variable 1:			
MP$	0.0031	0.0037	0.84

$r^2 = 0.08$; Durbin-Watson statistic $= 2.41$

◆ **Regression 2.** PDC $= a + (b \times$ no. of POs$)$; $n = 10$, d.f. $= 9$

Variable	Coefficient	Standard Error	t-Value
Constant	$730,716	$265,419	2.75
Independent variable 1:			
no. of POs	$ 56.97	$ 64.69	2.43

$r^2 = 0.42$; Durbin-Watson statistic $= 1.98$

◆ **Regression 3.** PDC $= a + (b \times$ no. of Ss$)$; $n = 10$, d.f. $= 9$

Variable	Coefficient	Standard Error	t-Value
Constant	$814,862	$247,821	3.29
Independent variable 1:			
no. of Ss	$ 3,875	$ 1,697	2.28

$r^2 = 0.39$; Durbin-Watson statistic $= 1.97$

1. Compare and evaluate the three simple regression models estimated by Jones. Graph each one. Evaluate the information summarized in the three outputs from the three regressions.
2. Do the regression results support the Couture Fabrics presentation about purchasing department cost drivers? Which of these cost drivers would you recommend in designing an activity-based cost system?
3. How might Jones gain additional evidence on drivers of purchasing department costs at each of Flashy Fashion's stores?

10-36 Purchasing department cost drivers, multiple regression analysis (continuation of Problem 10-35). Sherry Jones decides that the simple regression analysis used in Problem 10-35 could be extended to a multiple regression analysis. She finds the following results for several multiple regressions:

◆ **Regression 4.** PDC $= a + (b_1 \times$ no. of POs$) + (b_2 \times$ no. of Ss$)$

Variable	Coefficient	Standard Error	t-Value
Constant	$485,384	$257,477	1.89
Independent variable 1: no. of POs	$ 123.22	$ 57.69	2.14
Independent variable 2: no. of Ss	$ 2,952	$ 1,476	2.00

$r^2 = 0.63$; Durbin-Watson statistic $= 1.90$

◆ **Regression 5.** PDC $= a + (b_1 \times$ no. of POs$) + (b_2 \times$ no. of Ss$) + (b_3 \times$ MP$\$)$

Variable	Coefficient	Standard Error	t-Value
Constant	$494,684	$310,205	1.59
Independent variable 1: no. of POs	$ 124.05	$ 63.49	1.95
Independent variable 2: no. of Ss	$ 2,984	$ 1,622	1.84
Independent variable 3: MP$	−0.0002	0.0030	−0.07

$r^2 = 0.63$; Durbin-Watson statistic $= 1.90$

The coefficients of correlation between combinations of pairs of the variables are

	PDC	MP$	No. of POs
MP$	0.29		
No. of POs	0.65	0.27	
No. of Ss	0.63	0.34	0.29

REQUIRED

1. Evaluate regression 4 using the economic plausibility, goodness of fit, significance of independent variables, and specification analysis criteria. Compare regression 4 with regressions 2 and 3 in Problem 10-35. Which model would you recommend that Jones use? Why?
2. Compare regression 5 with regression 4. Which model would you recommend that Jones use? Why?
3. Jones estimates the following data for the Saskatoon store for next year: dollar value of merchandise purchased, $75,000,000; number of purchase orders, 3,900; number of suppliers, 110. How much should Jones budget for purchasing department costs for the Saskatoon store for next year?
4. What difficulties may arise in multiple regressions that do not arise in simple regressions? Is there evidence of such difficulties in either of the multiple regressions presented in this problem?
5. Give two examples of decisions where the regression results reported here (and in Problem 10-35) could be informative.

10-37 Data analysis and governance. Nordic Wind makes downhill skis. Sales of the skis have been very steady over the past ten years. Helen Gibbs, the manager of the department that manufactures the skis, is keen on introducing robots into the department to improve production quality. To obtain funding, Gibbs knows that she will need to justify the investment in terms of labour cost savings. Gibbs estimates average annual labour costs in the department of $1,449,000 over the past ten years. Labour costs over the past three years have averaged

① ② ⑤

1. a. Labour cost savings, $780,000

$960,000. If robots are introduced, labour costs would decrease to $660,000 per year. Average savings in labour costs of at least $480,000 per year are needed to justify the investment in robots. Gibbs uses the $1,440,000 number in her analysis. She then asks Joan Mistry, the management accountant, to review her calculations before she submits the robot proposal to senior management.

Mistry has a problem with Gibbs's analysis. She feels that by using a long time period of ten years, Gibbs was able to show larger labour cost savings than was justified. Mistry knew that Gibbs would be unhappy with these findings.

Mistry also felt that the robot investment was good for the company. She tried to redo the analysis in a way that might show larger cost savings, even though she knew that the assumptions she was using were not appropriate. Nothing she tried could change the conclusion that the cost savings were not large enough to justify the investment in robots. Gibbs is upset when she sees Mistry's report. She tells Mistry, "Try something else. I am sure you can come up with a set of assumptions under which this investment can be justified. You and I both know this is a good investment for the company to make. Quality is essential if we are to compete."

REQUIRED
1. Calculate the labour cost savings if Gibbs uses average labour costs incurred (a) over the past ten years and (b) over the past three years. Does it make a difference in terms of justifying the robot investment?
2. Why do you think the average labour costs over the past ten years differ significantly from the average labour costs over the past three years?
3. Explain whether Joan Mistry's initial attempts to redo the data analysis to justify the robot investment were ethical.
4. Identify the steps that Joan Mistry should follow in attempting to resolve this situation.

10-38 **High-low method and regression analysis.** Happy Business College has recently opened a restaurant as part of its hospitality major. For the first 10 weeks the manager did not estimate any costs, but instead hoped revenues would cover costs. One of the new waiters, who happens to be taking a cost accounting class, suggests that the manager take the past known weekly costs and try to determine a cost equation by relating the cost to the number of customers served. The cost and customer data are as follows:

Week	Number of Customers per Week	Weekly Total Cost of Restaurant
1	751	$16,800
2	745	16,597
3	810	17,800
4	833	18,600
5	825	17,900
6	876	19,600
7	855	18,900
8	897	18,500
9	925	20,305
10	910	20,000

The manager gives this information to the waiter, who runs a regression and gets the following equation:

Weekly total restaurant costs = $2,453 + ($19.04 × Number of customers per week)

REQUIRED
1. Plot the relationship between number of customers per week and weekly total restaurant costs.
2. Estimate the cost equation using the high-low method, and draw this line on your graph.
3. Draw the regression line on your graph. Use your graph to evaluate the regression line using the criteria of economic plausibility, goodness of fit, and significance of the independent variable. Is the cost function estimated using the high-low method a close approximation to the cost function estimated using the regression method? Explain briefly.
4. At what point (number of customers) will the expected total cost based on the high-low equation equal the expected total cost based on the regression equation?

10-39 **Regression, activity-based costing, choosing cost drivers.** Newroute Manufacturing has been using activity-based costing to determine the cost of product X-678. One of the activities, "Inspection," occurs just before the product is finished. Newroute inspects every 10th unit, and has been using "number of units inspected" as the cost driver for inspection costs. A significant component of inspection costs is the cost of the test kit used in each inspection.

Neela McFeen, the line manager, is wondering if inspection labour-hours might be a better cost driver for inspection costs. Neela gathers information for weekly inspection costs, units inspected, and inspection labour-hours as shown below:

Week	Units Inspected	Inspection Labour-Hours	Inspection Costs
1	1,500	200	$3,900
2	500	80	2,000
3	1,800	240	4,700
4	2,500	250	6,000
5	2,200	220	5,500
6	800	90	2,600
7	1,000	120	3,100

Neela runs regressions on each of the possible cost drivers and estimates these cost functions:

$$\text{Inspection Costs} = \$1,004 + (\$2.02 \times \text{Number of units inspected})$$

$$\text{Inspection Costs} = \$626 + (\$19.51 \times \text{Inspection labour-hours})$$

REQUIRED

1. Explain why number of units inspected and inspection labour-hours are plausible cost drivers of inspection costs.
2. Plot the data and regression line for units inspected and inspection costs. Plot the data and regression line for inspection labour-hours and inspection costs. Which cost driver of inspection costs would you choose? Explain.
3. Neela expects inspectors to work 150 hours next period and to inspect 1,200 units. Using the cost driver you chose in requirement 2, what amount of inspection costs should Neela budget? Explain any implications of Neela choosing the cost driver you did not choose in requirement 2 to budget inspection costs.

COLLABORATIVE LEARNING CASE

10-40 High-low method, alternative regression functions, accrual accounting adjustments. Trevor Kennedy, the cost analyst at a can manufacturing plant of United Packaging, is seeking to examine the relationship between total engineering support costs reported in the plant records and machine-hours. These costs have two components: (1) labour (which is paid monthly) and (2) materials and parts (which are purchased from an outside vendor every three months). After further discussion with the operating manager, Kennedy discovers that the materials and parts numbers reported in the monthly records are on an "as purchased" basis and not on an "as used" or accrual accounting basis. By examining materials and parts usage records, Kennedy is able to restate the materials and parts costs to an "as used" basis. (No restatement of the labour costs was necessary.) The reported and restated costs are as follows:

Month	Labour: Reported Costs (1)	Materials and Parts: Reported Costs (2)	Materials and Parts: Restated Costs (3)	Total Engineering Support: Reported Costs (4) = (1) + (2)	Total Engineering Support: Restated Costs (5) = (1) + (3)	Machine-Hours (6)
March	$416	$1,016	$218	$1,432	$ 634	30
April	625	0	493	625	1,118	63
May	478	0	322	478	800	49
June	426	1,153	274	1,579	700	38
July	568	0	418	568	986	57
August	740	0	419	740	1,159	73
September	294	985	150	1,279	444	19
October	584	0	437	584	1,021	53
November	517	0	348	517	865	42

The regression results, when total engineering support reported costs (column 4) are used as the dependent variable, are:

◆ **Regression 1.** Engineering support reported costs = $a + (b \times$ machine-hours)

Variable	Coefficient	Standard Error	*t*-Value
Constant	$1,671.41	$366.60	4.56
Independent variable 1: machine-hours	$ (17.08)	$ 7.38	−2.31

$r^2 = 0.43$; Durbin-Watson statistic = 2.48. Adjusted $r^2 = 0.35$

The regression results, when total engineering support restated costs (column 5) are used as the dependent variable, are

◆ **Regression 2.** Engineering support restated costs = $a + (b \times$ machine-hours)

Variable	Coefficient	Standard Error	*t*-Value
Constant	$211.52	$64.46	3.28
Independent variable 1: machine-hours	$ 13.73	$ 1.30	10.59

$r^2 = 0.94$; Durbin-Watson statistic = 1.54. Adjusted $r^2 = 0.933$

INSTRUCTIONS
Form groups of two or more students to complete the following requirements.

REQUIRED
1. Present a plot of the data for the cost function relating the *reported costs* for total engineering support to machine-hours. Present a plot of the data for the cost function relating the *restated costs* for total engineering support to machine-hours. Comment on the plots.
2. Compute estimates of the cost functions ($y = a + bX$) for reported engineering support costs and machine-hours and restated engineering support costs and machine-hours using the high-low method.
3. Contrast and evaluate the cost function estimated with regression using restated data for materials and parts with the cost function estimated with regression using the data reported in the plant records. Use the comparison format employed in Exhibit 10-19 (p. 499).
4. Of all the cost functions estimated in requirements 2 and 3, which one would you choose to best represent the relationship between engineering support costs and machine-hours? Why?
5. Kennedy expects 50 machine-hours to be worked in December. What engineering support costs should Kennedy budget for December?
6. What problems might Kennedy encounter when restating the materials and parts costs recorded to an "as used" or accrual accounting basis?
7. Why is it important for Kennedy to pick the correct cost function? That is, illustrate two potential problems Kennedy could run into, by choosing a cost function other than the one you chose in requirement 4.

11

Decision Making and Relevant Information

BUSINESS MATTERS

Different Information for Different Decisions

Gildan Activewear is a multinational company that markets and manufactures various kinds of apparel. The company sells clothing to wholesale distributors as undecorated "blanks," which are then decorated by screenprinters with designs and logos. Consumers ultimately purchase Gildan's products in places like sporting goods stores, entertainment venues, and tourism destinations. The company is also a leading supplier of private-label and Gildan-branded socks to mass-market retailers. The company's managers require excellent information to decide what quantities of material to purchase, where to manufacture products, and whether to expand or close manufacturing facilities.

LEARNING OBJECTIVES

After studying this chapter, you should be able to

1 Contrast relevant and irrelevant costs and revenues as well as quantitative and qualitative information influencing decisions

2 Identify the differences among relevant costs for short-term and long-term production output decisions

3 Explain why opportunity cost is relevant and book value is irrelevant in decision making

4 Identify key concepts and apply them to product and customer mix decisions

5 Explain how to reduce the negative effects and conflicts arising in relevant-cost analyses

In Chapter 11 we focus on common internal decisions—process change, output level, product, and customer mix. Using a common measure of value, such as operating income, enables managers to make comparisons of expected profitability among either similar or very dissimilar management decisions. The accounting profession is often called upon to apply its expertise in measuring outcomes to improve the reliability and relevance of available information used to identify what we know and what we need to know to make a reasonable decision. We especially stress the importance of distinguishing between relevant and irrelevant financial information when making these decisions.

Reliable and relevant information is essential to good decision making. The presence of high quality information alone, however, does not guarantee good decisions if managers do not understand how to use it, or ignore it and take impulsive actions. Decisions affect future outcomes but the future is uncertain (see Chapter 3). Forecasting outcomes is the heart of a decision but requires that managers make informed assumptions about what may happen in the future. There will almost always be a gap between what was expected and what is actually realized. A good decision process includes a post-implementation assessment and explanation of the key causes of differences between expected and actual outcomes. This is how managers learn from their experiences.

RELEVANCE OF INFORMATION IN A DECISION PROCESS

1 Contrast relevant and irrelevant costs and revenues as well as quantitative and qualitative information influencing decisions

A *decision model* illustrates processes in making a choice. Good choices depend on good information. However, perfect and complete information is never available. If it were, no decision would be necessary; it would be obvious what should be done. Information comes from many sources:

- ◆ qualitative data from relevant past experience or relevant stories of the past experience of others
- ◆ executive, managerial, and line expertise about processes and outcomes
- ◆ analyses of both current and historical internal MIS quantitative data
- ◆ analyses of both current and historical external data about uncontrollable factors in the competitive environment
- ◆ advice and forecasts of experts in an area

While some operating decisions can and should be made on the spot by a single decision maker, far-reaching business decisions are made by teams of top management. In Chapter 2 the concepts of uncertainty and risk were introduced. Uncertainty refers to outcomes that are not imagined during a decision-making process. Risk refers to an array of outcomes that are imagined. Probabilities are risks that can be quantified. A team of experts will consider some outcomes to be more likely than others and quantify risks as probabilities. The process of having experts pool their expertise to agree on probabilities and other assumptions about the future is often referred to as a **Delphic process**.

In Chapter 3 we illustrated a specific model of decision-making called a Bayesian model because it has a common-sense appeal. It is a recursive model, which means the decision-makers update initial assumptions when new, relevant information becomes known. An important step in this process is to quantify the team's assumptions about the likelihood of different profitability outcomes. The measure used is probability, and probability measures risk.

THINKING CRITICALLY

This seems to be very complicated. Of what use are these probabilities? Explain in a sentence or two. Read on to understand the importance of transforming a "gut feeling" into a quantity.

The use of probabilities not only helps a team calculate the likelihood of different financial outcomes, but also records assumptions about the future that can be checked at a later date. If changes in the assumptions must be made, then it is very straightforward to input changes to a spreadsheet to provide a new forecast. Notice that the management process is in the discussion and achievement of consensus on what assumptions must be changed, not in using a probability value. The number itself is not capable of thought. The quantities such as $p = 0.01$ compared to $p = 0.87$ tell a team something about how likely it is an outcome will arise. A big shift over a short time, such as $p = 0.01$ to $p = 0.87$, also tells the team that something very dramatic and unexpected happened. This helps management teams learn to apply experience to assess risk.

Often the straightforward discipline of attaching numbers to beliefs leads to very fruitful discussions justifying those numbers and helps team members think more clearly about what future outcomes are more and less likely. Once a quantity is attached to a belief, often people find discussions are less emotional, because while people have strong commitment to their beliefs, they tend not to have strong commitments to numbers. This is especially helpful if a company is facing difficulties, because it can be made apparent through the probabilities agreed upon by a team just how probable it is the company will survive. Quantifying risk helps bring clarity to situations where either fear or overconfidence would lead managers to make decisions to the detriment of the company.

There are realities that complicate decision making. One is that many factors are beyond the control of any team of experts, such as whether the economy is robust and thriving or recessionary and weak. The thriving economy is good news and the weak economy is bad news for most companies. To simplify the decision model, we consider four assumptions: the possibilities are mutually exclusive, random, independent, and mutually exhaustive. Assume that only one possibility or the other can occur (the possibilities are mutually exclusive). Also assume no one can predict which one will occur in a specific time period because the likelihood of either outcome is equal (random). The outcome in one time period will not influence the outcome in the next (independent). What you know with certainty, however, is that *only* one of two outcomes is possible (mutually exhaustive). If the economic outcomes are mutually exclusive, random, independent, and exhaustive, their probabilities must sum to 1.00. If the probabilities are equal and sum to 1.00, then the probability of a thriving economy is $p = 0.50$ and the probability of a weak economy is also $p = 0.50$ ($1.00 - p = 1.00 - 0.50 = 0.50$).

Clearly the fortunes of a single company will rise or fall to some extent with the economic state. The outcome of the economy influences the outcome for the company. This means that when experts analyze available information they must take into account that the company's outcomes depend, or are conditional, on the economic state that will be realized. The experts must therefore forecast two types of outcomes conditional on a thriving or weak economy. The conditional probability assigned to the outcome is called a **prior probability**.[1] In Exhibit 11-1 this influence of one outcome (the economy's performance) on another (the company's performance) is shown in the first set of influence arrows between A and B. (Outcomes are contained in circles.)

As new, relevant information becomes available, the expert team of decision makers will revise their prior probabilities to take the new information into account. The experts make new decisions about risk for the outcomes for the company. In Exhibit 11-1 the second influence pair models how a decision (the conditional probability) influences the expected outcome (the company's financial strength). Decisions are contained in boxes.

The first influence pair of A and B illustrates our example explained above. The probability of a bad or recessionary economy influences the probability of a low profit for a company. The higher the risk of a recession, the higher the risk of low profit, and vice versa. The second influence pair of C and D illustrates a normal choice situation typical of most of the examples in this chapter. The managers have alternatives and need to decide which one to take. The risk of a high or low profit will depend on what choice is made.

---

[1] W. R. Scott, *Financial Accounting Theory* (Toronto: Prentice Hall, 2009). Chapter 3 expands on and provides an excellent discussion and numerical examples of Bayesian decision theory and conditional probability.

EXHIBIT 11-1
A Decision Process and Influence Model

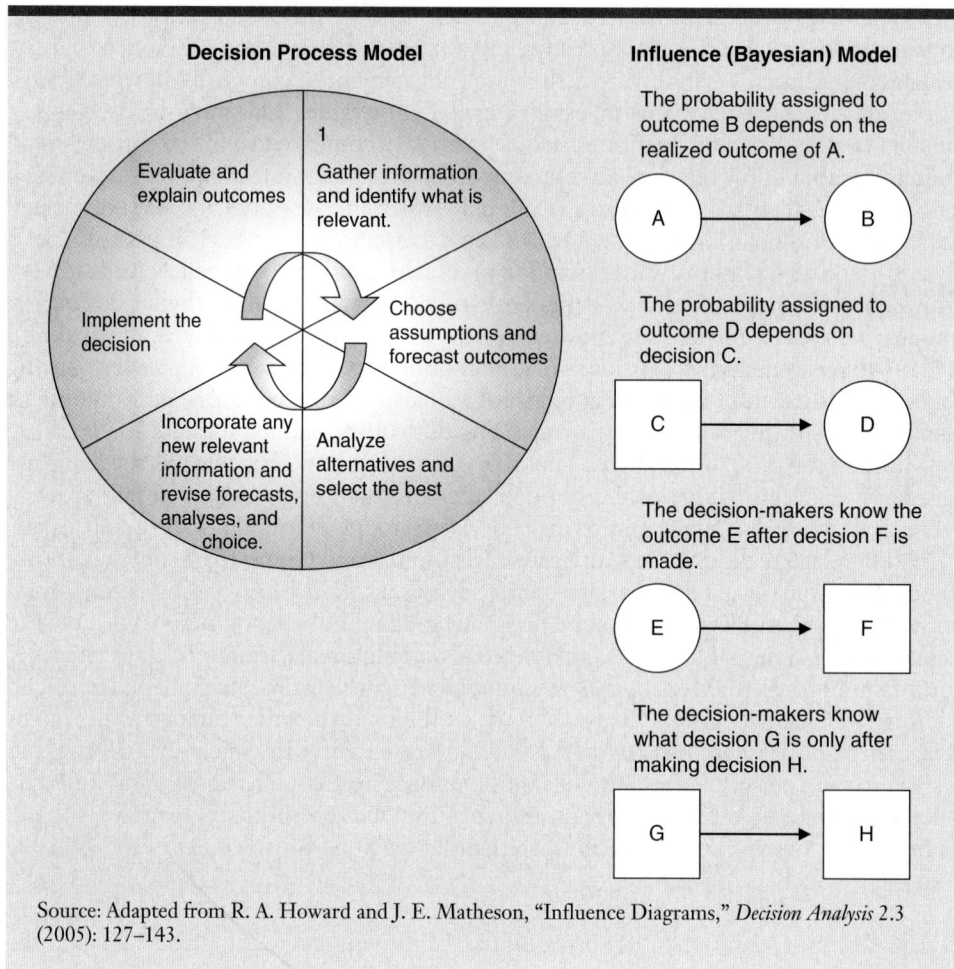

Source: Adapted from R. A. Howard and J. E. Matheson, "Influence Diagrams," *Decision Analysis* 2.3 (2005): 127–143.

It is quite important to understand that a good decision may be risky. Generally, the higher the risk of a course of action, the higher the return you expect. If this is not the case, then it is foolish to take the risk. Generally, exceptional managers do not try to avoid risk but rather try to take sensible risks. One criterion of a sensible risk is that the probable reward will be higher than the other less risky choices. It would be a rare and desperate management team who would "bet the farm" and choose an alternative which, if it fails, carries the risk of destroying the company.

The third influence pair, E and F, illustrates a common-sense situation where the decision F makes the outcome E more likely. This is what we normally expect decisions to do. Even in situations of high uncertainty where the risks of doing anything are high, the risk of doing nothing can be higher. Excellent management teams do not often know what they must do, but they do know they must do something. In the fourth influence pair, G and H, there are a series of decisions to be made. Only after the first choice is made will the managers know the series of decisions that must follow. An example would be when a decision about the key cause of failure leads to a new decision about remedial action.

In this chapter we assume a Bayesian process that gives relevant information a central role in decision making. Relevant information is that which *changes* a decision. Without relevant information, good decisions become a matter of luck, not thoughtfulness.

The modelling does not stop with estimating expected financial outcomes from different management decisions. Action must be taken or nothing will change. A decision is made with the intent to improve the strength of a company. If the decision is good, failure to achieve the expected improvement can happen at the action stage because of poor implementation (or execution). Exhibit 11-2 illustrates the complex interactions among elements that influence the implementation of a business process change decision. The exhibit was adapted from an actual map of elements at a manufacturing company.

The complex interdependencies among the elements of management decision making are depicted by the arrows. This is an **enterprise risk management (ERM)** perspective. Enterprise risk management analyzes interdependencies among processes and systems in an enterprise. In Exhibit 11-2, a failure in supply-chain management, for example, could be affected directly or indirectly by failure in one of several other areas. A direct cause of failure might be poor recruitment and training, a human resources process failure. An indirect cause might be failure to develop a relevant performance-measurement system to clearly signal when the supply-chain management process is out of control. This failure in measurement tools and skills would directly affect capacity management, which would then indirectly affect supply-chain management.

Poor execution of a good decision can occur because of failure in one element or in a combination of interdependent elements. The explanation of failure depends on reliable and relevant (accurate and timely) reports of actual outcomes (see Chapters 7 and 8 on variance analysis) in comparison to what was expected. This new relevant information should enable decision makers to pinpoint the causes of failure and decide on appropriate action to remedy the situation.

As you examine Exhibit 11-2, focus on *systems-management skill* (computer services) at the bottom of the exhibit. During implementation of a change, assume there is delay installing and running new software. This delay influences supply-chain management at the top of the exhibit as well as capacity and demand management just to the left. Both systems management and capacity management influence process improvement. Systems management, supply-chain management, and process improvement all influence the outcome in the grey box to the right.

EXHIBIT 11-2
Interdependencies Affecting the Outcome of a Business Process Change

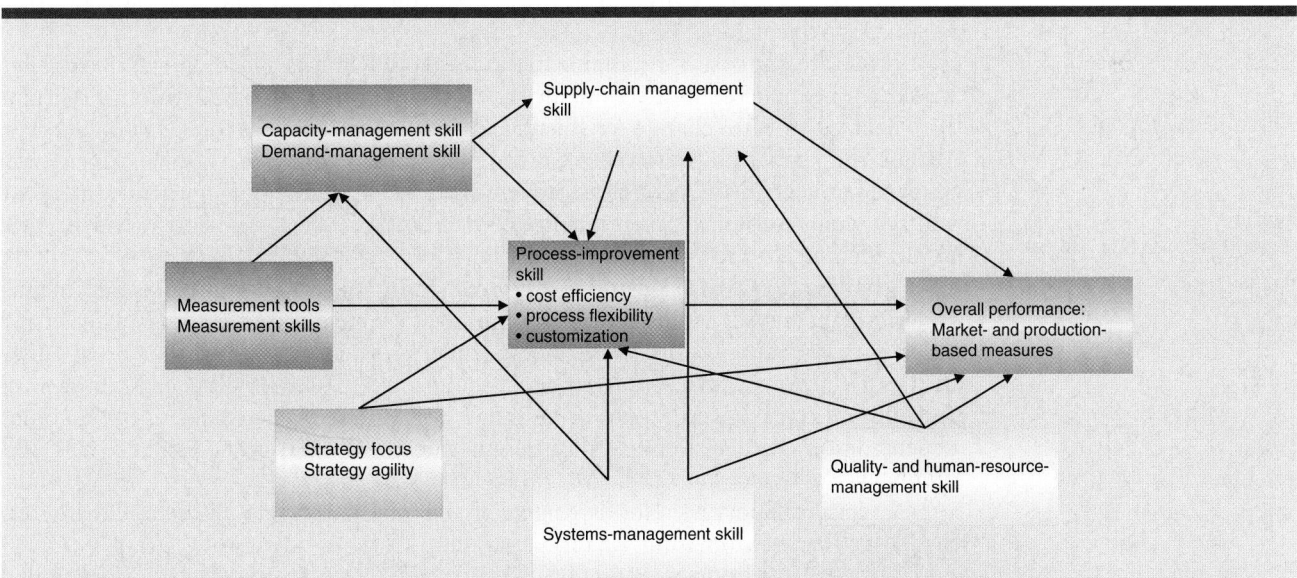

Source: Adapted from A. J. Scavarda, T. Chameeva, S. M. Goldstein, J. M. Hays, and A. V. Hill, "A Methodology for Constructing Collective Causal Maps," *Decision Sciences* 37.2 (2006): 263–279; M. Swink, R. Narasimhan, and S. W. Kim, "Manufacturing Practices and Strategy Integration: Effects on Cost Efficiency, Flexibility, and Market-Based Performance," *Decision Sciences* 36.3 (2005): 427.

Top managers must make timely decisions despite conditions of uncertainty and missing or low-quality information. Decisions are intended to solve problems. **"Paralysis by analysis"** describes situations where managers decide to wait and wait for more information. The danger is that the opportunity to actually remedy problems can disappear faster than relevant information can appear. In the following example of Precision Sporting Goods, we will simplify the decision process by presenting a complete and perfect set of information, and we will hold most outcomes constant (all other things equal).

Consider a strategic decision confronting Precision Sporting Goods, a manufacturer of golf clubs: Should it reorganize a manufacturing assembly line to reduce manufacturing labour costs? For simplicity, assume:

◆ The only alternatives are do not reorganize (do nothing) and reorganize.

◆ The reorganization will eliminate all manual handling of materials; hence, equipment (a long-term capacity decision) must be acquired.

◆ The MIS and accountants can provide relevant, high-quality financial and non-financial information about the proposed process.

◆ All outcome data are already weighted using probabilities (see Chapter 2) and are therefore the expected financial result.

◆ Interdependencies are held constant.

The current manufacturing line uses 20 workers—15 workers operate machines and 5 workers handle materials. Installing the new equipment will eliminate the task of materials handling and the need for these 5 workers. The historical wage rate of $14 per hour has been renegotiated and will increase to $16 immediately. The standard is 2,000 labour hours annually per worker. Precision Sporting Goods is facing a permanent increased labour cost of $4,000, which the top managers believe is avoidable. From their competitive intelligence reports, Precision knows that it cannot pass this on to consumers through a price increase, and the price will remain at $250 per unit. The predicted production output of 25,000 units for the next year will not be affected by the decision. Some of this information will affect the decision, and some is not relevant. The first step for the top management team is to sort out what will differ, depending on their decision, and what will not. If their decision will not change a cost, or revenue, or another performance measure, then the information about that measure is irrelevant.

The forecast cost of reorganization is $90,000. This is a new one-time cost that would not be incurred if the company did nothing. Given the competition, Precision also decides not to change its historical marketing expense of $2,000,000. We assume the supply chain remains unchanged, and so too does the direct materials costs per unit of $50. The results of analysis indicate that acquiring new equipment will not change other manufacturing overhead of $750,000. The cost driver is units of production.

A straightforward calculation using the existing information predicts that manufacturing labour cost under the "do nothing" alternative is $640,000 (20 workers × 2,000 hours × $16 per hour = $640,000). Predicted manufacturing labour cost under the "reorganize" alternative is $480,000 (15 workers × 2,000 hours × $16 per hour = $480,000). Both financial values are estimates. They are expected financial outcomes depending on the decision taken, represented in the second influence pair (C, D) in Exhibit 11-1.

Precision Sporting Goods' management compares the predicted savings of $160,000 from eliminating materials-handling labour costs (5 workers × 2,000 hours × $16 per hour = $160,000) to the $90,000 cost of reorganization, which includes any retraining costs. After a decision is made, the financial value of these two expected outcomes can be calculated. This is represented in the third decision pair (E, F) in Exhibit 11-1.

At this stage, assume the top executives have taken into account other qualitative considerations, such as the effect that reducing the number of workers will have on employee morale. The difference in total cost between two alternatives is a

differential or **net relevant cost**. The differential cost between alternatives 1 and 2 is $70,000 ($160,000 − $90,000 = $70,000) in favour of alternative 2. The forecast change in operating income is an increase of $70,000 because all other factors have been held equal. With good-quality, relevant information, clearly the decision is to reorganize the process to improve the financial strength of Precision by $70,000.

It is important to realize, however, that the numbers do not dictate the decision. This is only one of many relevant pieces of information which must be considered by the top management team. This is another situation where the decision team must take an enterprise-wide view, as illustrated in Exhibit 11-2, to carefully assess any interdependencies within their enterprise. Reflection on the indirect consequences of alternative 2 will help the enterprise avoid unintended and negative consequences. Some unintended consequences can also be very positive. An improvement in profitability is, nevertheless, a persuasive but not a decisive indication of a reasonable course of action.

RELEVANT COSTS AND RELEVANT REVENUES

Exhibit 11-3 is a table that reports all the forecast and historical financial information for this decision by Precision Sporting Goods. This format has the virtue of brevity, but it hides all the complexity faced by top executives who must consider the interdependencies illustrated in Exhibit 11-2 and the chain of influence among decisions and outcomes in Exhibit 11-1. The financial values have meaning beyond simple arithmetic operations.

The first pair of columns reports all the financial information for each alternative. Notice how much of this information, which is historical, is unchanged irrespective of the decision made. Identical information may reassure top management that the change will do no harm. It depicts the situation where in fact all the interdependencies are held constant and equal between the two alternatives.

High-quality historical information is a useful basis upon which to analyze and forecast future outcomes. There is a big difference, however, between information that is reassuring and that which is relevant or useful. Historical cost and revenue is past and cannot be changed by any current decision Precision's top

EXHIBIT 11-3
Determining Relevant Revenues and Relevant Costs for Precision Sporting Goods

	All Revenues and Costs		Relevant Revenues and Costs	
	Alternative 1: Do Not Reorganize	Alternative 2: Reorganize	Alternative 1: Do Not Reorganize	Alternative 2: Reorganize
Revenues[a]	$6,250,000	$6,250,000	—	—
Costs:				
Direct materials[b]	1,250,000	1,250,000	—	—
Manufacturing labour	640,000[c]	480,000[d]	$ 640,000[c]	$ 480,000[d]
Manufacturing overhead	750,000	750,000	—	—
Marketing	2,000,000	2,000,000	—	—
Reorganization costs	—	90,000	—	90,000
Total costs	4,640,000	4,570,000	640,000	570,000
Operating income	$1,610,000	$1,680,000	$(640,000)	$(570,000)

$70,000 Difference $70,000 Difference

[a]25,000 units × $250 per unit = $6,250,000   [c]20 workers × 2,000 hours per worker × $16 per hour = $640,000
[b]25,000 units × $50 per unit = $1,250,000   [d]15 workers × 2,000 hours per worker × $16 per hour = $480,000

management makes. As useful as high-quality historical cost information is, it is irrelevant to the process decision. The past manufacturing labour rate of $14 per hour and total past manufacturing labour costs of $560,000 (2,000 hours × 20 workers × $14 per hour) are not relevant to understanding future costs, which are known to be $16 per hour. In particular, the quantity of total labour-hours per year is irrelevant; however, the future manufacturing labour rate of $16 per hour and quantity of 15 workers is relevant because these cause future total labour costs to change.

If there is no difference in financial values between the two alternatives, then the information is irrelevant. The second pair of columns reports only the financial values that differ between the two alternatives. Reading down the columns you can readily see the influence of the manufacturing and reorganization costs (outcomes) of each decision on the operating income (outcome). Reading across the columns you can readily see the influence of the decision about "do nothing" or "reorganize" (decision) on the costs (outcomes).

It is clear that the reduction in manufacturing labour cost ($640,000 − $480,000 = $160,000) by choosing alternative 2 is higher than the cost of the "reorganize" decision ($90,000). The total cost of alternative 2 is less than the "do nothing" alternative. **Relevant costs** are those forecast future costs that *differ* because of a decision. **Relevant revenues** are those forecast future revenues that *differ* because of a decision.

Precision decides to reorganize the process and purchase the new equipment. New relevant information will be the actual results. It turns out not to be good news. The realized new manufacturing labour costs are reported as $550,000 rather than the forecast $480,000. The forecast saving realized from reorganization has decreased to zero ($550,000 + $90,000 = $640,000). The value added comes from finding an explanation. Exhibit 11-2 provides an idea of where the implementation may have failed; however, remember that the interdependencies have been held constant. The relevant information is the unfavourable manufacturing labour costs:

◆ The skills of remaining workers did not match those required for the new process; the result was overtime, suggesting a failure in either recruitment or placement.

◆ The training programs failed to provide adequate opportunity for workers to learn new skills; the result was lower-than-expected productivity, suggesting a human resources failure, or a failure to communicate new training needs.

◆ The equipment installation did not go well, and the batch sizes had to be reduced until repairs could be made; the result was excess non-productive idle time for setups and overtime for workers, suggesting a failure to foresee and fulfill the need for process improvement.

◆ The layoffs affected morale and productivity; the result was more workers had to be hired to meet production commitments, suggesting a failure to foresee and fulfill human resource management needs.

◆ The assumptions top management used in their forecast were incorrect, suggesting a weakness in either performance measurement or in strategic processes.

QUANTITATIVE AND QUALITATIVE RELEVANT INFORMATION

We divide new relevant information about outcomes into two broad categories: *quantitative* and *qualitative*. **Quantitative factors** can be measured numerically. Some quantitative factors can be readily expressed in financial terms. Examples include the risks, costs of direct materials, direct manufacturing labour, and marketing. Other quantitative factors are nonfinancial. They can be measured numerically, but they are not expressed in financial terms. Examples include amounts of labour-hours, direct materials, or units produced. **Qualitative factors** are outcomes that cannot be measured in numerical terms. Examples include ineffective training, employee morale, and incorrect assumptions made by top management.

Cost analysis emphasizes quantitative factors that can be expressed in financial terms. Despite the difficulty, and sometimes the impossibility, of measuring qualitative and nonfinancial quantitative factors in financial terms, these factors remain important. Management accountants often make an extremely important contribution by developing rough relative measures of qualitative information like morale using scales such as –1 (very low) through +5 (very high). Gathering information directly from surveys of employees, it is straightforward to estimate average scores to the questions.

The unexpected $70,000 labour cost overrun ($550,000 − $480,000 = $70,000 U) could then be divided by the average score (ranging from −1 to +5), for example +1. If low morale from the layoffs was the problem and the goal was +5 on the scale, then it cost Precision approximately $17,500 per lost morale point ($70,000 ÷ (5 − 1) = $17,500). The remedy to ensure the savings are realized in future is to undertake a program to restore morale—the layoffs are in the past and cannot be changed. Notice how quantifying the qualitative factor of morale into a roughly estimated financial value provides relevant information to assist in the reassessment of the decision.

THINKING CRITICALLY

This is a bit disturbing. Is it necessary to quantify everything into dollars and cents to make a business decision? Explain in a sentence or two. Read on for a discussion of this topic.

It is unnecessary to try to estimate the financial value of qualitative factors. There are some factors that usually are not priced, such as health and safety. Insurance companies, however, do so all the time and provide the benefit of insurance to us if we are willing to pay the price. Excellent and responsible management teams will go to experts outside their enterprise to help them more clearly understand the risks a particular decision may pose to their employees, customers, and other stakeholders without assessing financial value. The idea of putting a price or a cost on that factor is often enough to make the decision team aware it will not make that particular choice, regardless of the financial benefits of doing so.

Managers must at times give more weight to either qualitative or nonfinancial quantitative factors than to financial factors. For example, Precision Sporting Goods may, upon further investigation, determine that it can purchase pre-assembled materials from an outside supplier at a price that is lower than what it costs to manufacture them in-house. The company may still choose to manufacture in-house because it feels that the supplier is unlikely to meet the demanding delivery schedule—a quantitative nonfinancial factor—and because purchasing the part from outside may adversely affect employee morale—a qualitative factor. Trading off nonfinancial and financial considerations is seldom easy.

Concepts presented in Chapters 2, 6, 7, and 8 are applied in this analysis of Precision's decision from its inception through implementation and, finally, evaluation. From Chapter 2 it is clear that risk is not a qualitative factor, but it is subjective. It can be analyzed and quantified. The probability of an internal business outcome conditioned by an economic outcome, multiplied by the pro forma financial value of the business outcome, provides a mathematically sound estimate of the expected financial value of future outcomes. The expected financial value is a budgeted value and is reported in financial statement format in Exhibit 11-3 to highlight the effect of change on operating income—the key measure of financial strength. Finally, the feedback in financial statement format focuses management attention on any material, unfavourable, and unanticipated variance between the realized and budgeted outcome of the change.

Variance Analysis and Control Decisions

In 2007, *The Economist* surveyed 154 executives around the world to find out how they rated the management decision making at their firm and why. Of the total, 61% said the process was only moderately efficient or worse and almost 20% (25% in North America) said frequently the wrong decisions were made. It seems that in reality decision making is informal, unstructured, and largely a Delphic process among top executives. But most noted poor data, not poor structure, was the cause of poor decisions. For strategic decisions 78% ranked data as the single most important input, and 79% said the same for operational decisions. More than half said their available data were usually faulty, inaccurate, or incomplete (56%). The executives had more confidence in financial information than in any other kind of internally available information. Not only accuracy or quality, but also timeliness was an issue. Only 10% reported that information was available when it was needed; 40% said they had to delay decisions until updated data were available. Failure, 56% reported, was due to poor implementation rather than poor organizational structure or processes. This survey information emphasizes how critical timely information is to good decisions.

Source: "In Search of Clarity: Unravelling the Complexities of Executive Decision Making," *The Economist.* London: The Economist Intelligence Unit, 2007, available at http://graphics.eiu.com/upload/EIU_In_search_of_clarity.pdf.

MyAccountingLab

ASSESS YOUR MASTERY

To check your understanding of the material in Learning Objective ❶, go to the *Mastery Questions* section at the end of this chapter and complete Learning Objective ❶ questions 1, 2, and 3.

CHANGING OUTPUT LEVEL—SHORT- AND LONG-TERM DECISIONS

❷ Identify the differences among relevant costs for short-term and long-term production output decisions

Managers often make decisions that affect output levels. For example, managers must choose whether to introduce a new product or sell more units of an existing product. Some decisions are short term and have no capacity-management effects, such as accepting or rejecting one-time-only special orders when there is idle production capacity and when the order has no long-run implications. To simplify this short-term decision process and the identification of relevant costs, assume:

◆ No variable marketing costs are incurred to obtain the special one-time order.

◆ All costs can be classified as either variable with respect to a single driver (units of output) or fixed.

◆ All outcome data have already been weighted by their respective probabilities.

Crucial to understanding this decision is to understand the different information provided by either full-absorption or variable-costing policies (Chapter 9). The use of absorption costing provides yet another example of how unitizing fixed costs can mislead managers about the effect that temporarily increasing output within a relevant range has on operating income. In the short run, focusing on unit sales price, variable costs per unit, and contribution margin per unit can provide key information for decisions about the choice of output level.

Example 1: Surf Gear manufactures quality beach towels at its highly automated plant. The plant has a production capacity of 48,000 towels each month. Current monthly production is 30,000 towels. Retail department stores account for all existing sales. Expected results for the coming month (August) are shown in Exhibit 11-4. (These amounts are forecasts based on past costs.) Exhibit 11-4 presents data in an absorption costing format: In this exhibit, the manufacturing cost of $12 per unit and the marketing cost of $7 per unit include both variable and fixed costs.

The sum of all costs (variable and fixed) in a *particular* business function of the value chain, such as manufacturing costs or marketing costs, are called *business function costs*. The sum of all variable and fixed costs in *all* business functions of the value chain (R&D, design, production, marketing, distribution, and customer service) equal the absorption or full product costs, in this case $19 per unit.

As a result of a strike at its existing towel supplier, a luxury hotel chain has offered to buy 5,000 towels from Surf Gear in August at $11 per towel. No subsequent sales to this hotel chain are anticipated. The denominator level for fixed manufacturing costs is normal capacity of 30,000 towels and the additional 5,000 is within the relevant range of current capacity. But the practical capacity is 48,000 towels (see Chapter 9). Fixed manufacturing costs will not change if Surf Gear accepts the special order. Surf Gear will use existing idle capacity to produce the 5,000 towels.

No **incremental** marketing **costs** are necessary for the 5,000-unit one-time-only special order because the customer has already approached Surf Gear. Incremental **out-of-pocket** or **outlay costs** are additional costs made to obtain either additional resources or sales. Accepting this special order is not expected to affect the selling price or the quantity of towels sold to regular customers. The assumption of no long-run implications is crucial in the analysis we present for the one-time-only special-order decision. Suppose, for example, that Surf Gear is concerned that the

EXHIBIT 11-4
Budgeted Income Statement for August, Absorption-Costing Format for Surf Gear[a]

	A	B	C
1		Total	Per Unit
2	Units sold	30,000	
3			
4	Revenues	$ 600,000	$20.00
5	Cost of goods sold (COGS)		
6	Variable manufacturing costs	225,000	7.50[b]
7	Fixed manufacturing costs	135,000	4.50[c]
8	Total COGS	360,000	12.00
9	Marketing costs		
10	Variable marketing costs	150,000	5.00
11	Fixed marketing costs	60,000	2.00
12	Total marketing costs	210,000	7.00
13	Full costs of the product	570,000	19.00
14	Operating income	$ 30,000	$ 1.00
15			
16	[a]Surf Gear incurs no R&D, product-design, distribution, or customer-service costs		

17	[b]Variable manufacturing = Direct material + Direct manufacturing + Variable manufacturing
	    cost per unit cost per unit labour cost per unit overhead per unit
	    = $6.00 + $0.50 + $1.00 = $7.50		

18	[c]Fixed manufacturing = Fixed direct manufacturing + Fixed manufacturing
	    cost per unit labour cost per unit overhead per unit
	    = $1.50 + $3.00 = $4.50		

retail department stores (its regular customers) will demand a lower price if it sells towels at $11 a towel to the luxury hotel chain. In this case, the analysis of the luxury hotel chain order must be modified to consider both the short-term benefits from accepting the order and the long-term consequences on Surf Gear's business and profitability. Assuming no long-term implications, should Surf Gear accept the hotel chain's order?

Marketing costs, both variable and fixed, are clearly not relevant because they are both unchanged whether Surf Gear accepts the order or not. Based on the manufacturing cost per unit of $12—which is greater than the $11-per-unit price offered by the hotel chain—the manager might decide to reject the offer. But consider Exhibit 11-5, which presents the data using a variable costing policy. The data are in a contribution income statement format (see Exhibit 9-4, p. 420). Consistent throughout all the examples, the relevant costs are the expected future costs that differ between the alternatives—the variable manufacturing costs of $37,500 ($7.50 per unit × 5,000 units).

The fixed manufacturing costs and all marketing costs (including variable marketing costs) are irrelevant in this case; they will not change in total whether or not the special order is accepted. Therefore, the only relevant items here are sales revenues and variable manufacturing costs. Given the $11 relevant revenue per unit (the special-order price) and the $7.50 relevant costs per unit, Surf Gear would gain an additional $17,500 [($11 − $7.50) × 5,000] in operating income per month by accepting the special order. In this case, by using a variable costing policy, comparisons based on either total amounts or relevant amounts (Exhibit 11-5) avoid the misleading implication of the absorption cost per unit (Exhibit 11-4).

Contrast the two outcomes using an absorption costing policy in Exhibit 11-4 and a variable costing policy in Exhibit 11-5. The full cost per towel of $19 is $8 higher than the price the hotel is willing to pay of $11. As noted before, this does not cover even the manufacturing costs. The unit cost, however, includes two fixed cost allocation rates that are treated as if they vary. As discussed in Chapter 2, this is a

EXHIBIT 11-5

Comparative Income Statements for August, Contribution Income Statement Format for Surf Gear

	Variable Costing Policy: Reject the Special Order		Variable Costing Policy: Accept the Special Order		
	Per unit	Total	Per unit	Total	Difference
Output level		30,000		35,000	5,000
Sales	$ 20.00	$ 600,000	$ 11.00	$ 655,000	$ 55,000 F
Costs:					
Variable costs:					
Manufacturing[a]	7.50	225,000	7.50	262,500	(37,500) U
Marketing[b]	5.00	150,000	5.00	150,000	—
Total variable costs	12.50	375,000	12.50	412,500	(37,500) U
Contribution margin	7.50	225,000		242,500	(17,500) F
Fixed costs:					
Manufacturing[c]	4.00	135,000		135,000	—
Marketing	2.00	60,000		60,000	—
Total fixed costs	6.50	195,000		195,000	—
Operating income	$ 1.00	$ 30,000		$ 47,500	$ (17,500) F

[a]Variable manufacturing costs = direct materials ($6) + direct manufacturing labour ($0.50) + manufacturing overhead ($1) = $7.50

[b]No additional (incremental) variable marketing costs are incurred for the special order of 5,000 towels at a price of $11/towel.

[c]Fixed manufacturing costs = direct manufacturing labour + manufacturing overhead ($3) = $4.50. These are unaffected by the special order.

mistake because fixed costs never vary over a relevant range. The implications for standard costing and variance analysis were further discussed in Chapters 8 and 9. The unitizing of a cost pool that will remain constant whether or not Surf Gear accepts the special order generates an irrelevant cost. Surf Gear will pay the $195,000 of fixed costs regardless of the decision made.

The second reason fixed costs are irrelevant is that these were costs committed to long ago when a capacity decision was made (see Chapter 9). The capacity costs are sunk costs. Sunk costs such as the acquisition costs of capacity cannot be retrieved. The fixed marketing costs are also the result of market share decisions made in the past. They are committed costs which are not retrieved in the short run, regardless of whether this special order is accepted or not.

The incremental costs of $7.50 per unit that Surf Gear will incur if it accepts the special order for 5,000 towels would be avoided if Surf Gear did not accept the special order. Surf Gear incurs no incremental fixed manufacturing costs if it accepts the special order. Fixed manufacturing costs do not change in Exhibit 11-4 because the analysis assumes that the 5,000-towel special order will use already acquired capacity that will otherwise remain idle for August and the two months following. For the same reason, fixed marketing costs remain unchanged. The final column of figures reports the differential cost between the two choices. A differential cost is the difference in total costs between alternatives. **Incremental revenue** is any additional total revenue from one alternative, whereas **differential revenue** is the difference between the total revenue of two or more alternatives. The difference (F) or (U) is relative to the effect of each choice on operating income. The comparison indicates that accepting the special order will increase operating income by $17,500.

OUTSOURCING—MAKE OR BUY—AND IDLE FACILITIES

Another output-level decision is long term. This is the decision either to expand existing capacity to **insource**, and produce more output in-house, or to **outsource** the additional production externally. Another term to describe this decision is **make/buy decision**. Outsourcing is the process of purchasing goods and services from outside vendors rather than producing the same goods or providing the same services within the organization, which is called insourcing.

Kodak prefers to manufacture its own digital cameras (insourcing) but has IBM do its data processing (outsourcing). British Air outsources almost all its activities, including reservations, food services, baggage handling, information technology, and legal services. It even leases aircraft with pilots, ground crew, and maintenance. Dell Computers must buy the Pentium chip for its personal computers from Intel (outsourcing) because it does not have the know-how and technology to make the chip itself.

Insourcing implies a strategy of **vertical integration**. The oil and gas industry is made up of the very different activities of oil and gas exploration, extraction, refining, and retailing. Petro-Canada, for example, is a vertically integrated company that controls all of these various activities. It explores for new raw materials, extracts them, and transports them to its own refineries where the direct materials are inputs for gasoline, home heating oil, and other petroleum products. It sells gasoline and other automotive products at its Petro-Canada stations. Vertical integration means a company incorporates as much of the value chain as possible within itself.

Sometimes a company decides to protect its competitive advantage by protecting the secure supply of key inputs. For other companies, making the product in-house retains control of the product and technology. For example, to safeguard Coca-Cola's formula, the company does not outsource the manufacture of its concentrate. What are the most important factors in the make/buy decision? Surveys of company practices indicate they are quality, dependability of supplies, and cost.

Example 2: The Soho Company manufactures a digital flat-screen television system, which includes an MP3 player, a Blu-ray high-definition DVD player, and a spectacular sound system. Columns 1 and 2 of the following table show the current costs for manufacturing the MP3-player unit based on an analysis of various manufacturing activities:

	Total Current Costs of Production, 1,000,000 Units in 2,500 Batches (1)	Current Cost per Unit (2) = (1) ÷ 1,000,000	Expected Total Costs of Production, 1,000,000 Units in 5,000 Batches Next Year (3)	Expected Cost per Unit (4) = (3) ÷ 1,000,000
Direct materials	$ 9,000,000	$ 9.00	$ 9,000,000	$ 9.00
Direct manufacturing labour	2,400,000	2.40	2,400,000	2.40
Variable manufacturing overhead costs of power and utilities	1,600,000	1.60	1,600,000	1.60
Materials (variable and fixed) manufacturing overhead costs of materials handling and setup	1,750,000	1.75	2,000,000	2.00
Fixed manufacturing overhead costs of plant lease, insurance, and administration	3,000,000	3.00	3,000,000	3.00
Total manufacturing costs	$17,750,000	$17.75	$18,000,000	$18.00

Currently, materials-handling and setup activities occur each time a batch of MP3 players is made. Soho produces 1,000,000 MP3 players in 2,500 batches, with 400 units in each batch. The number of batches is the cost driver for these costs. Total materials-handling costs and setup costs equal fixed costs of $500,000 plus variable costs of $500 per batch [$500,000 + (2,500 batches × $500 per batch) = $1,750,000]. Soho is considering whether to produce MP3 players in smaller batch sizes. Soho anticipates producing the 1,000,000 MP3 players next year in 5,000 batches of 200 units per batch. Through continuous improvement, the company expects to reduce variable costs for materials handling and setup to $300 per batch. No other changes in variable cost per unit or fixed costs are anticipated.

Another manufacturer offers to sell Soho 1,000,000 MP3 players next year for $16 per unit on as flexible a delivery schedule as Soho wants. Assume that financial factors will be the basis of this make/buy decision. Should Soho make or buy the MP3 players?

Columns 3 and 4 of the preceding table indicate the expected total costs and expected cost per unit of producing 1,000,000 MP3 players next year. Direct material costs, direct manufacturing labour costs, and variable manufacturing overhead costs (M/OH) that vary with units produced are not expected to change because Soho plans to continue to produce 1,000,000 units next year at the same variable cost per unit as this year. Materials-handling and setup costs are expected to increase, even with no change in total production quantity. That's because these costs will vary with the number of batches, not the number of units produced.

Soho's managers expect total materials-handling costs and setup costs to be $2,000,000 [$500,000 + (5,000 batches × the cost per batch of $300)]. Soho expects fixed manufacturing overhead costs to remain the same. The expected manufacturing cost per unit for next year is $18. At first glance, it appears that the company should buy MP3 players because the expected $18-per-unit cost of making the MP3 player is more than the $16 per unit to buy it. But often a make/buy decision is not obvious. A good decision depends on the answer to the question: What is the difference in relevant costs between the alternatives? Assume:

◆ The capacity now used to make the MP3 players will become idle next year if the MP3 players are purchased.

◆ The $3,000,000 of fixed manufacturing overhead will continue to be incurred next year, regardless of the decision made.

◆ The $500,000 in fixed salaries to support materials handling and setup will not be incurred if the manufacture of MP3 players is completely shut down.

Exhibit 11-6 presents the relevant cost computations. Note that Soho will save $1,000,000 by making MP3 players rather than buying them from the outside supplier. Making MP3 players is the preferred alternative. The values in Exhibit 11-6 are valid only if the released facilities remain idle. There is a different analysis needed if the MP3 player is bought from the outside supplier and the released facilities can potentially be used for other, more profitable purposes.

More generally, then, the choice in our example is not fundamentally whether to make or buy; it is how best to use available capacity. The notation of (U) or (F) beside the difference in the final column indicates the effect on operating income. In this case, operating income would decrease by $1,000,000 if the company outsourced. Soho will save $1,000,000 by insourcing the MP3 players. We use relevance to assess which costs to consider, as noted below.

◆ Current cost data in columns 1 and 2 (see table, p. 540) play no role in the analysis in Exhibit 11-6 because for next year's make/buy decision these costs are past costs and, hence, irrelevant. Their usefulness lies in helping to predict future costs.

◆ Exhibit 11-6 shows $2,000,000 of future materials-handling and setup costs under the make alternative but not under the buy alternative. Buying MP3 players rather than manufacturing them will eliminate $2,000,000 in future variable costs per batch and avoidable fixed costs of non-productive idle capacity incurred during setups. The $2,000,000 represents future costs that differ between the alternatives and therefore is relevant to the make/buy decision.

◆ Exhibit 11-6 excludes the $3,000,000 of plant-lease, insurance, and administration costs under both alternatives. These future fixed manufacturing overhead costs will not differ between the alternatives; therefore, they are irrelevant.

In this example the incremental cost of making the MP3 players is the additional absorption cost of $15,000,000 that Soho will incur if it decides to manufacture rather than outsource the players. Similarly, the incremental cost of outsourcing the MP3 players is the additional variable cost of $16,000,000 that Soho will incur from the buy decision. A *differential cost* is the difference in total cost between two alternatives. In Exhibit 11-6, the differential cost ($16,000,000 − $15,000,000) is $1,000,000. Note that *incremental* and *differential cost* are sometimes interchanged in practice. When these terms are used, ensure you know what they mean.

EXHIBIT 11-6
Relevant (Incremental) Items for Make/Buy Decision for MP3 Players at Soho

Total units: 1,000,000

	Relevant Costs: Make		Relevant Costs: Buy		
	Per unit	Total	Per unit	Total	Difference
Purchase (buy)	—	—	$16.00	$16,000,000	$(16,000,000) U
Direct materials (make)	$ 9.00	$ 9,000,000	—	—	9,000,000 F
Direct labour (make)	2.40	2,400,000	—	—	2,400,000 F
Direct M/OH (make)	1.60	1,600,000	—	—	1,600,000 F
Mixed handling and setup	2.00	2,000,000	—	—	2,000,000 F
Total costs*	$ 15.00	$15,000,000	$16.00	$16,000,000	$ (1,000,000) U

*The $3,000,000 of plant-lease, insurance, and administration costs could be included under both alternatives. But these costs remain unchanged irrespective of the decision that is made. Therefore they are not relevant costs. One reason managers may prefer to see this $3,000,000 is to have a complete set of costs to be reassured of those, which remain unchanged between the alternatives.

MyAccountingLab

ASSESS YOUR MASTERY
To check your understanding of the material in Learning Objective ② , go to the *Mastery Questions* section at the end of this chapter and complete Learning Objective ② questions 1, 2, and 3.

OPPORTUNITY COST, BOOK VALUE—ONE RELEVANT, ONE IRRELEVANT

③ Explain why opportunity cost is relevant and book value is irrelevant in decision making

The calculations in Exhibit 11-6 assumed that the capacity currently used to make MP3 players will remain idle if Soho purchases the parts from the outside manufacturer. However, the released capacity can be used for other, more profitable purposes. The choice Soho's managers are then faced with is not whether to make or buy, but how best to use available production capacity.

Deciding to use a resource in a particular way causes a manager to give up the opportunity to use the resource in alternative ways. The lost opportunity is a cost that the manager must take into account when making a decision. **Opportunity cost** is the contribution to income that is forgone (rejected) by not using a limited resource in its next-best alternative use. Opportunity costs are not incorporated into formal financial accounting records. Financial historical record keeping is limited to transactions involving alternatives that were *actually selected*, rather than alternatives that were rejected. A transaction must occur. Rejected alternatives do not produce transactions and so they are not recorded.

Example 3: Suppose that if Soho decides to buy MP3 players for its HDTVs from the outside supplier, then Soho's best use of the capacity that becomes available is to produce 500,000 standalone converters that convert input from low-definition DVDs and TV cable into a viewing format that fills the screen. The converter is a standalone unit that can be attached readily to any HDTV. With help from operating managers, John Marquez, Soho's management accountant, estimates the following future revenues and costs if Soho decides to manufacture and sell converters:

Incremental future revenue		$8,000,000
Incremental future costs		
Direct materials	$3,400,000	
Direct manufacturing labour	1,000,000	
Variable overhead (utilities)	600,000	
Materials handling and setup overhead	500,000	
Total incremental future costs		5,500,000
Incremental future operating income		$2,500,000

Because of capacity constraints, Soho can make either MP3 players and Blu-ray DVD players or HD converters and Blu-ray DVD players. Which of the following three alternatives should Soho choose?

◆ Make MP3 players and do not make HD converters.

◆ Buy MP3 players and do not make HD converters.

◆ Buy MP3 players and make HD converters.

Exhibit 11-7, Panel A, summarizes the "total alternatives" approach—the incremental expected future costs and expected future revenues for all alternatives. Alternative 3, buying MP3 players and using the available capacity to make and sell HD converters, is the preferred alternative. The effect is clear from Panel A because the total relevant cost is lowest in the third column. The forgone incremental operating income from selling HD converters is treated as a reduction to the incremental cost of alternative 3. In Panel B it is treated as an added cost of not selling HD converters.

It does not matter how the relevant costs are listed; the cost of alternative 3 is $1,500,000 ($17,500,000 − $16,000,000 = $1,500,000 Panel B) less than the cost of

EXHIBIT 11-7
Total-Alternatives Approach and Opportunity-Cost Approach to Make/Buy Decisions for Soho Company

	Alternatives for Soho		
Relevant Items	**1. Make MP3 Players and Do Not Make HD Converters**	**2. Buy MP3 Players and Do Not Make HD Converters**	**3. Buy MP3 Players and Make HD Converters**
PANEL A: Total-Alternatives Approach to Make/Buy Decisions			
Total incremental future costs of making/buying MP3 players (from Exhibit 11-6)	$15,000,000	$16,000,000	$16,000,000
Deduct future operating income from selling HD Converts	0	0	(2,500,000)
Total relevant costs under total-alternatives approach	$15,000,000	$16,000,000	$13,500,000
PANEL B: Opportunity-Cost Approach to Make/Buy Decisions			
Total incremental future costs of making/buying MP3 players (from Exhibit 11-6)	$15,000,000	$16,000,000	$16,000,000
Add foregone future operating income from not selling HD Converts	2,500,000	2,500,000	0
Total relevant costs under opportunity-cost approach	$17,500,000	$18,500,000	$16,000,000

Note that the differences in costs across the columns in Panels A and B are the same: The cost of alternative 3 is $1,500,000 less than the cost of alternative 1, and $2,500,000 less than the cost of alternative 2.

alternative 1, and $2,500,000 less than the cost of alternative 2 ($18,500,000 − $16,000,000 = $2,500,000 Panel B). The key difference between Soho and Surf Gear is that Soho could put its idle capacity to long-term use. If Soho fails to do so it incurs the opportunity cost of not using this idle capacity, which is the next best use of its capacity after all MP3s are produced. Surf Gear had no alternative use for its idle capacity.

Both the approach of Panel A and Panel B are consistent approaches to decision making with capacity constraints. Panel B, however, highlights the idea that when capacity is constrained, the relevant revenues and costs of any alternative *must* include the opportunity cost. That said, when more than two alternatives are being considered simultaneously, it is generally easier to use the total-alternatives approach. If opportunity costs are not considered, on the basis of only the incremental costs systematically recorded in the accounting system because no HD converters are being produced, it is less costly for Soho to make rather than buy stereo MP3 players. Recognizing the opportunity cost of $2,500,000, however, leads to the conclusion that it is preferable to buy MP3 players.

Suppose Soho has sufficient capacity to make HD converters even if it makes MP3 players. In this case, Soho has a fourth alternative: make stereo MP3 players and make HD converters. For this alternative, the opportunity cost of making MP3 players is $0 because Soho does not give up the $2,500,000 operating income from making HD converters because there is enough capacity to make both. The relevant costs are $15,000,000 (incremental costs of $15,000,000 plus opportunity cost of $0). Under these conditions, Soho would prefer to make MP3 players rather than buy them, and also make HD converters.

Besides quantitative considerations, the make/buy decision should consider strategic and qualitative factors as well. If Soho decides to buy MP3 players from an outside supplier, it should consider factors indicated in Exhibit 11-2 such as the supplier's reputation for quality and timely delivery. This is a supply-chain management skill. Other factors include process improvements and strategic factors such as agility, product differentiation, and cost leadership.

CARRYING COSTS OF INVENTORY

The notion of opportunity cost can also be illustrated using Soho. Soho will pay cash for the stereo MP3 players it buys. Based on the information below, which purchasing alternative is more economical for Soho?

Annual estimated stereo MP3 player requirements for next year	1,000,000 units
Cost per unit when each purchase is equal to 10,000 units	$ 16.00
Cost per unit when each purchase is equal to or greater than 500,000 units; $16 minus 1% discount	$ 15.84
Cost of a purchase order	$ 500.00

Alternatives under consideration:
  A. Make 100 purchases of 10,000 units each during the next year
  B. Make 2 purchases of 500,000 units each during the next year

Average investment in inventory:

A. *(10,000 units × $16.00 per unit)/2	$ 80,000
B. *(500,000 units × $15.84 per unit)/2	$3,960,000
Annual rate of return if the cash is invested elsewhere (e.g., bonds or shares) at the same level of risk as the investment in inventory	9.0%

*The example assumes that MP3-player purchases will be used up uniformly throughout the year. The average investment in inventory during the year is the cost of inventory when a purchase is received plus the cost of inventory just prior to the delivery of the next purchase (in this example zero) divided by 2.

The following table presents two alternatives:

	Alternative A: Make 100 Purchases of 10,000 Units Each During the Year (1)	Alternative B: Make 2 Purchases of 500,000 Units Each During the Year (2)	Difference (3) = (1) − (2)
Annual purchase-order costs (100 purchase orders × $500/purchase order; 2 purchase orders × $500/ purchase order	$ 50,000	$ 1,000	$ 49,000
Annual purchase costs (1,000,000 units × $16.00/unit; 1,000,000 × $15.84/unit)	16,000,000	15,840,000	160,000
Annual rate of return that could be earned if investment in inventory were invested elsewhere at the same level of risk (opportunity cost) (0.09 × $80,000; 0.09 × $3,960,000)	7,200	356,400	(349,200)
Relevant costs	$16,057,200	$16,197,400	$(140,200)

The opportunity cost of holding inventory is the income forgone by tying up money in inventory and not investing it elsewhere. The opportunity cost would not be recorded in the accounting system because, once the alternative of investing money elsewhere is rejected, there are no transactions related to this alternative to record. On the basis of the costs recorded in the accounting system (purchase-order costs and purchase costs), Soho would erroneously conclude that making two purchases of 500,000 units each is the least costly alternative. Column 3, however, indicates that, consistent with the trends toward holding smaller inventories, purchasing smaller quantities of 10,000 units 100 times a year is preferred to purchasing 500,000 units twice during the year. The lower opportunity cost of holding smaller inventory exceeds the higher purchase and ordering costs. If the opportunity cost of money tied up in inventory were greater than 9% per year, or if other incremental benefits of holding lower inventory were considered—such as lower insurance, materials-handling, storage, obsolescence, and breakage costs—making 100 purchases would be even more economical.

STRATEGIC AND QUALITATIVE FACTORS

Strategic and qualitative factors affect outsourcing decisions. For example, Soho may prefer to manufacture MP3 players in-house to retain control over the design, quality, reliability, and delivery schedules of the MP3 players it uses in its stereos. Conversely, despite the cost advantages documented in Exhibit 11-6, Soho may prefer to outsource, become a smaller and leaner organization, and focus on areas of its core competencies—the manufacture and sale of HD components. As an example of focus, advertising companies, such as J. Walter Thompson, do only the creative and planning aspects of advertising (their core competencies), and they outsource production activities, such as film, photography, and illustration.

Of course, outsourcing is not without its risks. As a company's dependence on its suppliers increases, suppliers could increase prices and let quality and delivery performance slip. For example, raw material outsourced for manufacturing of pet food was found to be contaminated with melamine. This chemical is toxic to humans and animals because it causes kidney failure if consumed in large enough doses. It was the autopsies of deceased pets in North America that revealed the contamination. These suppliers subsequently were found to have exported contaminated powered raw milk. The problem was discovered when infants fell ill and some died in the exporting country.

To minimize risks, companies generally enter into long-term contracts with their suppliers that specify costs, quality, and delivery schedules. Intelligent managers will build close partnerships or alliances with a few key suppliers, teaming with suppliers on design and manufacturing decisions and building a culture of and commitment to quality and timely delivery. Toyota goes so far as to send its own engineers to improve suppliers' processes (see Real Companies).

Outsourcing decisions invariably have a long-run horizon in which the financial costs and benefits of outsourcing become more uncertain. Almost always, strategic and qualitative factors such as those described here become important determinants of the outsourcing decision. Weighing all these factors requires the exercise of considerable management judgment and care.

REAL COMPANIES

Outsourcing

Outsourcing has been global for decades. Familiar examples are the shift of manufacturing and assembly to Taiwan; of customer software technical support anywhere; of garment manufacturing to the Philippines, Honduras, and Haiti. This is also called either *offshoring* or *nearshoring*. The reason for offshoring is expected cost savings. Within the high-tech sector, for example, a software developer for IBM in the United States costs US$56 an hour, whereas one in China costs only US$12.50 an hour, including salary and benefits. By 2003, US companies had offshored more than US$10 billion in software development. But in 2006 *InformationWeek* reported that only half the companies offshoring software development rated their projects as successes, and almost one in six said they were disasters. One common reason, 34% of the respondents reported, is the failure to measure and value the work done in-house and the cost of the knowledge that walks out the door as engineers resign to work for competitors. Companies also fail to fully understand the effect of higher taxes in countries where they offshore tasks, most do not consider supply chain effects, and walking away from a contract can cause termination costs of $50 million to $120 million. Companies underestimate the added complexity and communications costs and overestimate the agility and flexibility of the supplier.

Sources: InfoWorld.com, June 15, 2004, available at www.infoworld.com/article/04/06/15/HNoffshorebacklash_1.html; *InformationWeek,* June 19, 2006, "In Depth: When Outsourcing Goes Bad," available at www. informationweek.com/story/showArticle.jhtml?articleID=189500043.

IRRELEVANCE OF BOOK VALUE IN EQUIPMENT REPLACEMENT DECISIONS

The illustrations in this chapter have shown that expected future costs that do not differ among alternatives are irrelevant. Now we return to the idea that all past costs are irrelevant. Consider an example of equipment replacement. The irrelevant cost illustrated here is the **book value** (original cost minus accumulated amortization) of the existing equipment. Assume that the Tormart Company is considering replacing a metal-cutting machine for aircraft parts with a more technically advanced model. The new machine has an automatic quality-testing capability and is more efficient than the old machine. The new machine, however, has a shorter life. The Tormart Company uses the straight-line amortization method. Sales of aircraft parts ($1.1 million per year) will be unaffected by the replacement decision. Summary data on the existing machine and the replacement machine are as follows:

	Existing Machine	Replacement Machine
Original cost	$1,000,000	$600,000
Useful life	5 years	2 years
Current age	3 years	0 years
Remaining useful life	2 years	2 years
Accumulated amortization	$600,000	Not acquired yet
Book value	$400,000	Not acquired yet
Current disposal value (in cash)	$40,000	Not acquired yet
Terminal disposal value (in cash 2 years from now)	$0	$0
Annual operating costs (maintenance, energy, repairs, coolants, and so on)	$800,000	$460,000

To focus on the main concept of relevance, we ignore the time value of money in this illustration.

Exhibit 11-8 presents a cost comparison of the two machines. Some managers would not replace the old machine because it would entail recognizing a $360,000 "loss on disposal" ($400,000 book value minus $40,000 current disposal price); retention would allow spreading the $400,000 book value over the next two years in the form of "amortization expense" (a term more appealing than "loss on disposal").

EXHIBIT 11-8

Cost Comparison—Replacement of Machinery, Including Relevant and Irrelevant Items for the Tormart Company

	Two Years Together		
	Keep	Replace	Difference
Sales	$2,200,000	$2,200,000	—
Operating costs:			
Cash operating costs	1,600,000	920,000	$680,000
Old machine book value:			
Periodic writeoff as amortization	400,000	—	—
or Lump sum writeoff	—	400,000*	
Current disposal price of old machine	—	(40,000)*	40,000
New machine cost, written off periodically as amortization	—	600,000	(600,000)
Total operating costs	2,000,000	1,880,000	120,000
Operating income	$ 200,000	$ 320,000	$120,000

*In a formal income statement, these two items would be combined as "loss on disposal of machine" of $360,000.

We can apply our definition of relevance to four commonly encountered items in equipment replacement decisions such as the one facing Tormart Company:

1. *Book value of old machine.* Irrelevant—it is a past (historical) cost. All past costs are "down the drain." Nothing can change what has already been spent or what has already happened.

2. *Current disposal price of old machine.* Relevant—because it is an expected future cash inflow that differs between alternatives.

3. *Gain or loss on disposal.* This is the algebraic difference between items 1 and 2. It is a meaningless combination blurring the distinction between the irrelevant book value and the relevant disposal price. Each item should be considered separately.

4. *Cost of new machine.* Relevant—it is an expected future cash outflow that will differ between alternatives.

Exhibit 11-8 should clarify these four assertions. The difference column in Exhibit 11-8 shows that the book value of the old machine is not an element of difference between alternatives and could be completely ignored for decision-making purposes. No matter what the timing of the charge against revenue, the amount charged is still $400,000 regardless of the alternative chosen because it is a past (historical) cost. The advantage of replacing is $120,000 for the two years together.

In either event, the unamortized cost will be written off with the same ultimate effect on operating income. The $400,000 enters into the income statement either as a $400,000 offset against the $40,000 proceeds to obtain the $360,000 loss on disposal in the current year or as $200,000 amortization in each of the next two years. But how it appears in the income statement is irrelevant to the replacement decision. In contrast, the $600,000 cost of the new machine is relevant because it can be avoided by deciding not to replace.

Past costs that are unavoidable because they cannot be changed no matter what action is taken are sometimes described as **sunk costs**. In our example, old equipment has a book value of $400,000 and a current disposal price of $40,000. What are the sunk costs in this case? The entire $400,000 is sunk and down the drain because it represents an outlay made in the past that cannot be changed. Past costs and sunk costs are synonyms.

Exhibit 11-9 concentrates on relevant items only. Note that the same answer (the $120,000 net difference) will be obtained even though the book value is completely omitted from the calculations. The only relevant items are the cash operating costs, the disposal price of the old machine, and the cost of the new machine (represented as amortization in Exhibit 11-9).

Decision makers vary in their preference between the formats presented in Exhibits 11-8 and 11-9. Some prefer the format used in Exhibit 11-8, because it illustrates why some items are irrelevant to the decision. Other managers prefer the format used in Exhibit 11-9, because it is concise.

EXHIBIT 11-9
Cost Comparison—Replacement of Machinery, Relevant Items Only for the Tormart Company

	Two Years Together		
	Keep	**Replace**	**Difference**
Cash operating costs	$1,600,000	$ 920,000	$680,000
Current disposal price of old machine	—	(40,000)	40,000
New machine, written off periodically as amortization	—	600,000	(600,000)
Total relevant costs	$1,600,000	$1,480,000	$120,000

PRODUCT AND CUSTOMER DECISIONS

④ Identify key concepts and apply them to product and customer mix decisions

Companies with capacity constraints, such as Soho, must decide which products to make and in what quantities. When a multiple-product plant operates at full capacity, managers must choose how to use the available capacity and which products to emphasize. These decisions frequently have a short-run focus. For example, General Mills must continually adapt the mix of its different products to short-run fluctuations in materials costs, selling prices, and demand. Throughout this section, we assume that as short-run changes in product mix occur, the only costs that change are those that are variable with respect to the number of units produced (and sold).

Analysis of individual product contribution margins provides insight into the product mix that maximizes operating income. This is the same approach taken in Chapter 3. Consider Power Engines, a company that manufactures engines for a broad range of commercial and consumer products. At its Calgary, Alberta, plant, it assembles two engines—a snowmobile engine and a boat engine. Information on these products is as follows:

	Snowmobile Engine	Boat Engine
Selling price	$800	$1,000
Variable costs per unit	560	625
Contribution margin per unit	$240	$ 375

At first glance, boat engines appear more profitable than snowmobile engines. The product to be emphasized, however, is not necessarily the product with the higher individual contribution margin per unit. Rather, managers should aim for the *highest contribution margin per unit of the constraining factor*—that is, the scarce, limiting, or critical factor. The constraining factor restricts or limits the production or sale of a given product. (See also Chapter 19 on the theory of constraints.)

Assume that only 600 machine-hours are available daily for assembling engines. Additional capacity cannot be obtained in the short run. Power Engines can sell as many engines as it produces. The constraining factor, then, is machine-hours. It takes two machine-hours to produce one snowmobile engine and five machine-hours to produce one boat engine.

	Snowmobile Engine	Boat Engine
Contribution margin per engine	$240	$375
Machine-hours required to produce one engine	2 machine-hours	5 machine-hours
Contribution margin per machine-hour (240 ÷ 2; 375 ÷ 5)	$120	$75
Total contribution margin for 600 machine-hours ($120 × 600; $75 × 600)	$72,000	$45,000

Producing snowmobile engines contributes more margin per machine-hour, which is the constraining factor in this example. Therefore, choosing to emphasize snowmobile engines is the correct decision. Other constraints in manufacturing settings can be the availability of direct materials, components, or skilled labour, as well as financial and sales considerations. In a retail department store, the constraining factor may be linear metres of display space. The greatest possible contribution margin per unit of the constraining factor yields the maximum operating income.

As you can imagine, in many cases a manufacturer or retailer must meet the challenge of trying to maximize total operating income for a variety of products, each with more than one constraining factor. The problem of formulating the most profitable production schedules and the most profitable product mix is essentially that of maximizing the total contribution margin in the face of many constraints. Optimization techniques, such as the linear programming technique discussed in this chapter beginning on page 553, help solve these complicated problems.

Finally, there is the question of managing the bottleneck constraint to increase output and, therefore, contribution margin:

- Can the available machine-hours for assembling engines be increased beyond 600, for example by reducing idle time?
- Can the time needed to assemble each snowmobile engine (two machine-hours) and each boat engine (five machine-hours) be reduced, for example by reducing setup time and processing time of assembly?
- Can quality be improved so that constrained capacity is used to produce only good units rather than some good and some defective units? Can some of the assembly operations be outsourced to allow more engines to be built?

Implementing any of these options will likely require Power Engines to incur incremental costs. Power Engines will implement only those options whose benefits of higher contribution margins exceed the costs. Instructors and students who, at this point, want to explore these issues in more detail can go to the section in Chapter 19 titled "Theory of Constraints and Throughput Contribution Analysis" (pp. 938–943) and then return to this chapter without any loss of continuity.

RELEVANT-COST ANALYSIS OF CUSTOMER BASE CHANGES—ABC APPROACH

In addition to making choices among products, companies must often decide whether they should add some customers and drop others. This section illustrates relevant-revenue and relevant-cost analysis when different cost drivers are identified for different activities in activity-based costing. The cost object in our example is customers. The analysis focuses on customer profitability at Allied West, the west coast sales office of Allied Furniture, a wholesaler of specialized furniture.

Allied West supplies furniture to three local retailers, Vogel, Brenner, and Wisk. Exhibit 11-10 presents representative revenues and costs of Allied West by customers for the year 2010. Additional information on Allied West's costs for different activities at various levels of the cost hierarchy is as follows:

1. Materials-handling labour costs vary with the number of units of furniture shipped to customers.

2. Different areas of the warehouse stock furniture for different customers. Materials-handling equipment in an area and amortization costs on the equipment are identified with individual customer accounts. Any equipment not used remains idle. The equipment has a one-year useful life and zero disposal price.

3. Allied West allocates rent to each customer account based on the amount of warehouse space occupied by the products to be shipped to that customer.

4. Marketing costs vary with the number of sales visits made to customers.

5. Purchase order costs vary with the number of purchase orders received; delivery processing costs vary with the number of shipments made.

6. Allied West allocates fixed general administration costs to customers based on dollar sales made to each customer.

EXHIBIT 11-10
Customer Profitability Analysis for Allied West

	Vogel	Brenner	Wisk	Total
Sales	$500,000	$300,000	$ 400,000	$1,200,000
Cost of goods sold	370,000	220,000	330,000	920,000
Materials-handling labour	41,000	18,000	33,000	92,000
Materials-handling equipment cost written off as amortization	10,000	6,000	8,000	24,000
Rent	14,000	8,000	14,000	36,000
Marketing support	11,000	9,000	10,000	30,000
Purchase orders and delivery processing	13,000	7,000	12,000	32,000
General administration	20,000	12,000	16,000	48,000
Total operating costs	479,000	280,000	423,000	1,182,000
Operating income	$ 21,000	$ 20,000	$ (23,000)	$ 18,000
Allocated corporate costs				24,000
				$ (6,000)

RELEVANT-COST ANALYSIS OF DISCONTINUING A CUSTOMER

Exhibit 11-10 indicates a loss of $23,000 on sales to Wisk. Allied West's manager believes this loss occurred because Wisk places many low-volume orders with Allied, resulting in high purchase order, delivery processing, materials-handling, and marketing activity. Allied West is considering several possible actions with respect to the Wisk account—reducing its own costs of supporting Wisk by becoming more efficient, cutting back on some of the services it offers Wisk, charging Wisk higher prices, or dropping the Wisk account. The following analysis focuses on the operating income effect of dropping the Wisk account.

The key question is what are the relevant costs and relevant revenues? The following information about the effect of reducing various activities related to the Wisk account is available.

1. Dropping the Wisk account will save cost of goods sold, materials-handling labour, marketing support, purchase order, and delivery processing costs incurred on the Wisk account.

2. Dropping the Wisk account will mean that the warehouse space currently occupied by products for Wisk and the materials-handling equipment used to move them will become idle.

3. Dropping the Wisk account will have no effect on fixed general administration costs.

Exhibit 11-11 presents the relevant-cost computations. Allied West's operating income will be $15,000 lower if it drops the Wisk account, so Allied decides to keep the Wisk account. The last column in Exhibit 11-11 shows that the cost savings from dropping the Wisk account, $385,000, is not enough to offset the loss of $400,000 in revenue. The key reason is that amortization, rent, and general administration costs will not decrease if the Wisk account is dropped.

Now suppose that if Allied drops the Wisk account, it could lease the extra warehouse space to the Sanchez Corporation, which has offered $20,000 per year for it. Then the $20,000 that Allied would receive would be the opportunity cost of continuing to use the warehouse to service Wisk. Allied would gain $5,000 by dropping the Wisk account ($20,000 from lease revenue minus lost operating income of $15,000). Before reaching a final decision, however, Allied must examine whether Wisk can be made more profitable so that supplying products to Wisk earns more than the $20,000 from leasing to Sanchez. Allied must also consider qualitative factors such as the effect of the decision on Allied's reputation for developing stable, long-run business relationships.

EXHIBIT 11-11
Relevant-Cost Analysis for Allied West Dropping the Wisk Account

	Amount of Total Revenues and Total Costs		Difference: Incremental (Loss in Revenue and Savings in Costs from Dropping Wisk Account)
	Keep Wisk Account	Drop Wisk Account	
Sales	$1,200,000	$800,000	$(400,000)
Cost of goods sold	920,000	590,000	330,000
Materials-handling labour	92,000	59,000	33,000
Materials-handling equipment cost written off as amortization	24,000	24,000	—
Rent	36,000	36,000	—
Marketing support	30,000	20,000	10,000
Purchase orders and delivery processing	32,000	20,000	12,000
General administration	48,000	48,000	—
Total operating costs	1,182,000	797,000	385,000
Operating income	$ 18,000	$ 3,000	$ (15,000)

RELEVANT-COST ANALYSIS OF ADDING A CUSTOMER

Suppose that in addition to dropping the Wisk account, Allied is evaluating the profitability of substituting a customer, Loral. Allied is already paying rent of $36,000 for the warehouse and is incurring general administration costs of $48,000. These costs will not change if Loral is added as a customer. Loral is a customer with a profile much like Wisk's. Suppose Allied predicts other revenues and costs of doing business with Loral to be the same as those described under the Wisk column of Exhibit 11-10. Should Allied substitute Loral as a customer? Exhibit 11-12 shows incremental revenues exceed incremental costs by $7,000. Allied would prefer to substitute Loral as a customer for Wisk. One key point is that the cost of acquiring new equipment to support the Loral order (written off as amortization of $8,000 in Exhibit 11-10) is included as a relevant cost. Why? Because this cost can be avoided if Allied decides not to do business with Loral. Note the critical distinction here. Amortization cost is irrelevant in deciding whether to drop Wisk as a customer (because it is a past cost), but the purchase cost of the new equipment that will then be written off as amortization in the future is relevant in deciding whether to add Loral as a new customer.

RELEVANT-REVENUE AND RELEVANT-COST ANALYSIS OF DISCONTINUING OR ADDING BRANCHES OR SEGMENTS

Companies periodically confront decisions about discontinuing or adding branches or business segments. For example, given Allied West's expected loss of $6,000 (see Exhibit 11-10), should it be closed? Assume that closing Allied West will have no effect on total corporate-office costs.

Exhibit 11-13, column 1, presents the relevant-revenue and relevant-cost analysis using data from the Total column in Exhibit 11-10. The revenue losses of $1,200,000 will exceed the cost savings of $1,158,000, leading to a decrease in operating income of $42,000. Allied West should not be closed down. The key reasons are that closing Allied West will not save amortization costs of $24,000, which is a past or sunk cost (see above), or actual total corporate costs. Corporate costs allocated to various sales offices will change but not decline in total. The $24,000 no longer allocated to Allied West will be allocated to other sales offices. Therefore, the $24,000 of allocated corporate costs should not be included as expected cost savings from closing Allied West.

EXHIBIT 11-12
Relevant-Cost Analysis for Dropping the Wisk Account and Adding the Loral Account

	(Loss in Revenues) and Savings in Costs from Dropping Wisk Account (1)	Incremental Revenues and (Incremental Costs) from Adding Loral Account (2)
Revenues	$(400,000)	$400,000
Cost of goods sold	330,000	(330,000)
Furniture-handling labour	33,000	(33,000)
Furniture-handling equipment cost written off as amortization	0	(8,000)
Rent	0	0
Marketing support	10,000	(10,000)
Purchase-order and delivery processing	12,000	(12,000)
General administration	0	0
Corporate-office costs	0	0
Total costs	385,000	(393,000)
Effect on operating income (loss)	$ (15,000)	$ 7,000

Now suppose Allied Furniture has the opportunity to open another sales office, Allied South, whose revenues and costs would be identical to Allied West's costs, including a cost of $25,000 to acquire materials-handling equipment with a one-year useful life and zero disposal value. Opening this office will have no effect on total corporate costs. Should Allied Furniture open Allied South? Exhibit 11-13, column 2, indicates that it should do so because opening Allied South will increase operating income by $17,000. As before, the cost of new equipment (written off as amortization) is relevant. But the point here is to ignore allocated corporate costs and focus on actual total corporate-office costs. Total corporate costs will not change if Allied South is opened and, hence, these costs are irrelevant.

EXHIBIT 11-13
Relevant-Revenue and Relevant-Cost Analysis for Closing Allied West and Opening Allied South

	(Loss in Revenues) and Savings in Costs from Closing Allied West (1)	Incremental Revenues and (Incremental Costs) from Opening Allied South (2)
Revenues	$(1,200,000)	$1,200,000
Cost of goods sold	920,000	(920,000)
Furniture-handling labour	92,000	(92,000)
Furniture-handling equipment cost written off as amortization	0	(25,000)
Rent	36,000	(36,000)
Marketing support	30,000	(30,000)
Purchase-order and delivery processing	32,000	(32,000)
General administration	48,000	(48,000)
Corporate-office costs	0	0
Total costs	1,158,000	(1,183,000)
Effect on operating income (loss)	$ (42,000)	$ 17,000

LINEAR PROGRAMMING

Linear programming (LP) is an **optimization technique** used to maximize total contribution margin (the objective function), given multiple constraints. Optimization techniques are ways to find the best answer using a mathematical model. LP models typically assume that all costs can be classified as either variable or fixed with respect to a single driver (units of output). LP models also require certain other linear assumptions to hold. When these assumptions fail, other decision models should be considered.[2]

Consider again the example of Power Engines (pp. 548–549). Suppose that both the snowmobile and boat engines must be tested on a very expensive machine before they are shipped to customers. The available testing machine time is limited. Production data are as follows:

Department	Available Daily Capacity in Hours	Use of Capacity in Hours per Unit of Product		Daily Maximum Production in Units	
		Snowmobile Engine	Boat Engine	Snowmobile Engine	Boat Engine
Assembly	600 machine-hours	2.0	5.0	300*	120
Testing	120 testing-hours	1.0	0.5	120	240

*For example, 600 machine-hours ÷ 20 machine-hours per snowmobile engine = 300, the maximum number of snowmobile engines that the assembly department can make if it works exclusively on snowmobile engines.

Exhibit 11-14 summarizes these and other relevant data. Note that snowmobile engines have a contribution margin of $240 and that boat engines have a contribution margin of $375. Material shortages for boat engines will limit production to 110 boat engines per day. How many engines of each type should be produced daily to maximize operating income?

STEPS IN SOLVING AN LP PROBLEM

We use the data in Exhibit 11-14 to illustrate the three steps in solving an LP problem. Throughout this discussion, S equals the number of units of snowmobiles produced and B equals the number of units of boat engines produced.

◆ **Step 1: Determine the objective.** The **objective function** of a linear program expresses the objective or goal to be maximized (for example, operating income) or minimized (for example, operating costs). In our example, the objective is to find the combination of products that maximizes total contribution margin in the short run. Fixed costs remain the same regardless of the product mix chosen and are therefore irrelevant. The linear function expressing the objective for the total contribution margin (TCM) is

$$\text{TCM} = \$240S + \$375B$$

◆ **Step 2: Specify the constraints.** A **constraint** is a mathematical inequality or equality that must be satisfied by the variables in a mathematical model. The following linear inequalities depict the relationships in our example:

Assembly department constraint	$2S + 5B \leq 600$
Testing department constraint	$1S + 0.5B \leq 120$
Material shortage constraint for boat engines	$B \leq 110$
Negative production is impossible	$S \geq 0$ and $B \geq 0$

A line means the constraint never appears with an exponent or square root. If it did then the line would curve and the relationship would be curvilinear. In Exhibit 11-14 all the constraints are labelled and appear as straight lines. The coefficients of the constraints are often called *technical coefficients*. For example, in the assembly

[2]Other decision models are described in G. Eppen, F. Gould, and C. Schmidt, *Quantitative Concepts for Management* (Englewood Cliffs, N.J.: Prentice-Hall, 1991); and S. Nahmias, *Production and Operations Analysis* (Homewood, Ill.: Irwin, 1993).

EXHIBIT 11-14
Operating Data for Power Engines

	Department Capacity (per Day) in Product Units			Variable Cost per Unit	Contribution Margin per Unit
Product	Assembly	Testing	Selling Price		
Only snowmobile engines	300	120	$ 800	$560	$240
Only boat engines	120	240	$1,000	$625	$375

department, the technical coefficient is two machine-hours for snowmobile engines and five machine-hours for boat engines.

The three solid lines on the graph in Exhibit 11-15 show the existing constraints for assembly and testing and the material shortage constraint.[3]

The feasible alternatives are those combinations of quantities of snowmobile engines and boat engines that satisfy all the constraining factors. The shaded "Area of feasible solutions" in Exhibit 11-15 shows the boundaries of those product combinations that are feasible, or technically possible.

◆ **Step 3: Compute the optimal solution.** We present two approaches for finding the optimal solution: the trial-and-error approach and the graphic approach. These approaches are easy to use in our example, because there are only two variables in the objective function and a small number of constraints. An understanding of these two approaches provides insight into LP modelling. In most real-world LP applications, however, managers use computer software packages to calculate the optimal solution.[4]

Trial-and-Error Approach The optimal solution can be found by trial and error, by working with coordinates of the corners of the area of feasible solutions. The approach is simple.

First, select any set of corner points and compute the total contribution margin. Five corner points appear in Exhibit 11-15. It is helpful to use simultaneous equations to obtain the exact graph coordinates. To illustrate, the point ($S = 75$, $B = 90$) can be derived by solving the two pertinent constraint inequalities as simultaneous equations:

$$2S + 5B = 600 \tag{1}$$
$$1S + 0.5B = 120 \tag{2}$$

Multiplying (2) by 2.0, we get
$$2S + 1B = 240 \tag{3}$$

Subtracting (3) from (1)
$$4B = 360$$

Therefore
$$B = 360 \div 4 = 90$$

Substituting B in (2)
$$1S + 0.5(90) = 120$$
$$S = 120 - 45 = 75$$

Given $S = 75$ and $B = 90$, TCM = $240(75) + $375(90) = $51,750.

---

[3]For an example of how the lines are plotted in Exhibit 11-15, use equal signs instead of inequality signs and assume for the assembly department that $B = 0$; then $S = 300$ (600 machine-hours ÷ 2 machine-hours per snowmobile engine). Assume that $S = 0$; then $B = 120$ (600 machine-hours ÷ 5 machine-hours per boat engine). Connect those two points with a straight line.

[4]Although the trial-and-error and graphic approaches can be useful for two or possibly three variables, they are impractical when many variables exist. Standard computer software packages rely on the *simplex method*, an interactive step-by-step procedure for determining the optimal solution to an LP problem. It starts with a specific feasible solution and then tests it by substitution to see whether the result can be improved. These substitutions continue until no further improvement is possible and the optimal solution is obtained.

Second, move from corner point to corner point, computing the total contribution margin at each corner point. The total contribution margin at each corner point is as follows:

Trial	Corner Point (S, B)	Snowmobile Engines (S)	Boat Engines (B)	Total Contribution Margin		
1	(0, 0)	0	0	$240(0)	+ $375(0)	= $ 0
2	(0, 110)	0	110	$240(0)	+ $375(110) =	41,250
3	(25,110)	25	110	$240(25)	+ $375(110) =	47,250
4	(75, 90)	75	90	$240(75)	+ $375(90) =	51,750*
5	(120, 0)	120	0	$240(120) + $375(0)		= 28,800

*Indicates the optimal solution

The optimal product mix is the mix that yields the highest total contribution—75 snowmobile engines and 90 boat engines.

Graphic Approach   Consider all possible combinations that will produce an equal total contribution margin of, say, $12,000. That is

$$\$240S + \$375B = \$12,000$$

This set of $12,000 contribution margins is a straight dashed line in Exhibit 11-15 through ($S = 50$, $B = 0$) and ($S = 0$, $B = 32$). Other equal total contribution margins can be represented by lines parallel to this one. In Exhibit 11-15, we show three dashed lines. The equal total contribution margins increase as the lines get farther from the origin because lines drawn farther from the origin represent more sales of both snowmobile and boat engines.

The optimal line is the one farthest from the origin but still passing through a point in the area of feasible solutions. This line represents the highest contribution margin. The optimal solution is the point at the corner ($S = 75$, $B = 90$). This solution will become apparent if you put a ruler on the graph and move it outward from the

EXHIBIT 11-15
Linear Programming—Graphic Solution for Power Engines

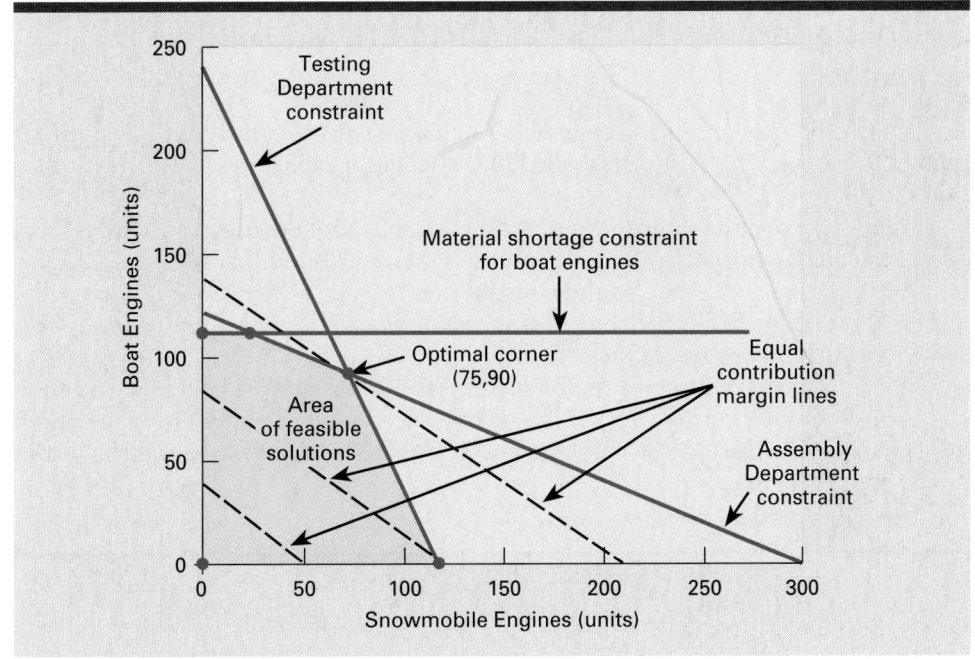

origin and parallel with the $12,000 line. The idea is to move the ruler as far away from the origin as possible (that is, to increase the total contribution margin) without leaving the area of feasible solutions. In general, the optimal solution in a maximization problem lies at the corner where the dashed line intersects an extreme point of the area of feasible solutions. Moving the ruler out any farther puts it outside the feasible region.

The key to the optimal solution is exchanging a given contribution margin per unit of scarce resource for some other contribution margin per unit of scarce resource. Examine Exhibit 11-15 and consider moving from corner ($S = 25$, $B = 110$) to corner ($S = 75$, $B = 90$). In the assembly department, each machine-hour devoted to 1 unit of boat engines (B) may be given up (sacrificed or traded) for 2.5 units of snowmobile engines (S) (5 hours required for 1 boat engine ÷ 2 hours required for 1 snowmobile engine). Will this exchange add to profitability? Yes, as shown here:

Total contribution margin at ($S = 25$, $B = 110$): $240 × 25 + $375 × 110		$47,250
Added contribution margin from product S by moving to corner ($S = 75$, $B = 90$): (75 − 25) × $240	$12,000	
Lost contribution margin from product B by moving to corner ($S = 75$, $B = 90$): (110 − 90) × $375	(7,500)	
Net additional contribution margin		4,500
Total contribution margin at ($S = 75$, $B = 90$): $240 × 75 + $375 × 90		$51,750

As we move from corner ($S = 25$, $B = 110$) to corner ($S = 75$, $B = 90$), we are contending with the assembly department constraint. In this department, there is a net advantage of trading 1 unit of B for 2.5 units of S. At corner ($S = 25$, $B = 110$), the testing department constraint comes into effect. Should we move to corner ($S = 120$, $B = 0$) along the testing department constraint? No. An analysis (not presented) similar to the one here will show that such a move is not worthwhile.

SENSITIVITY ANALYSIS

Sensitivity analysis was discussed in Chapter 2 in a different context. In the Power Engines example, large changes in the contribution margin per unit may not affect the optimal product mix if there are no nearby corner points. What are the implications of uncertainty about the accounting or technical coefficients used in the LP model? Changes in coefficients affect the slope of the objective function (the equal contribution margin lines) or the area of feasible solutions. Consider how a change in the contribution margin of snowmobile engines from $240 to $300 per unit might affect the optimal solution. Assume the contribution margin for boat engines remains unchanged at $375 per unit. The revised objective function will be:

$$\text{TCM} = \$300S + \$375B$$

Using the trial-and-error approach, calculate the total contribution margin for each of the five corner points described in the table on page 555. The optimal solution is still ($S = 75$, $B = 90$).

Now suppose the contribution margin of snowmobile engines is lower than $240 per unit. By repeating the preceding steps, you will find that the optimal solution will not change so long as the contribution margin of the snowmobile engine does not fall below $150. *Big changes in the contribution margin per unit of snowmobile engines have no effect on the optimal solution.*

What happens if the contribution margin falls below $150? The optimal solution will then shift to the corner ($S = 25$, $B = 110$). Snowmobile engines now generate so little contribution margin per unit that Power Engines will choose to shift its mix in favour of boat engines.

MyAccountingLab

ASSESS YOUR MASTERY

To check your understanding of the material in Learning Objective ④, go to the *Mastery Questions* section at the end of this chapter and complete Learning Objective ④ question 1.

UNIT COSTS CAN MISLEAD

Unit-cost data can often help in the cost analysis. Nevertheless, they can also mislead decision makers in two major ways:

1. *When irrelevant costs are included.* Consider the $4.50 per unit allocation of fixed direct manufacturing labour and manufacturing overhead costs in the one-time-only special-order decision for Surf Gear (see Exhibit 11-5). This $4.50 per unit cost is irrelevant given the assumptions of our example and therefore should be excluded.

2. *When unit costs at different output levels are compared.* Generally, managers use total fixed costs rather than unit costs. Then, if desired, the total fixed costs can be unitized. Machinery sales personnel, for example, may brag about the low unit costs of using their new machines. However, they sometimes neglect to say that the unit costs are based on outputs far in excess of their prospective customers' current or anticipated production levels.

Consider, for example, a new machine that costs $100,000, is capable of producing 100,000 units over its useful life, and has a zero terminal disposal price. The salesperson may represent the machine-related costs per unit to be $1. This amount is incorrect if the company anticipates a total demand of, say, only 50,000 units over the useful life of the machine (unit cost would be $100,000 ÷ 50,000 = $2). Unitized fixed costs over different production levels can be particularly misleading.

PITFALLS IN RELEVANT-COST ANALYSIS

One pitfall in relevant-cost analysis is to assume that all variable costs are relevant. In the Surf Gear example, the marketing costs of $5 per unit are variable but not relevant because for the special-order decision Surf Gear incurs no incremental marketing costs—the business "walked in the door."

A second pitfall is to assume that all fixed costs are irrelevant. Consider fixed manufacturing costs. In our example, we assume that the extra production of 5,000 towels per month does not affect fixed manufacturing costs. That is, we assume that the relevant range is at least from 30,000 to 35,000 towels per month. In some cases, however, the extra 5,000 towels might increase fixed manufacturing costs.

Assume that Surf Gear would have to run three shifts of 16,000 towels per shift to achieve full capacity of 48,000 towels per month. Increasing the monthly production from 30,000 to 35,000 would require a partial third shift, because two shifts alone could produce only 32,000 towels. This extra shift would probably increase fixed manufacturing costs, thereby making any incremental fixed manufacturing costs relevant for this decision.

The best way to avoid these two pitfalls is to focus first and foremost on the relevance concept. Always require each item included in the analysis to be:

◆ an expected future revenue or cost
◆ different between the alternatives.

CONFUSING TERMINOLOGY

Many different terms are used to describe the costs of specific products and services. Exhibit 11-16 presents several different unit-cost numbers using the data from column 1 of Exhibit 11-5. **Business function costs** are the sum of all the costs (variable costs and fixed costs) in a particular business function in the value chain. For example, manufacturing costs are $12 per unit, and marketing costs are $7 per unit. For inventory costing purposes, absorption costs are often used as a synonym for manufacturing costs.

Full product costs refer to the sum of all the costs in all the business functions in the value chain (R&D, design, production, marketing, distribution, and customer service). Full product costs in Exhibit 11-5 are $19 per unit.

EXHIBIT 11-16
Variety of Cost Terms for Surf Gear* Using Unit-Cost Data from Exhibit 11-5

	A	B	C	D	E	F
		Variable	Fixed	Manufacturing		Full
1		Product	Product	(Absorption)	Marketing	Product
2		Costs	Costs	Costs**	Costs**	Costs
3						
4	Variable manufacturing costs	$ 7.50		$ 7.50		$ 7.50
5	Variable marketing costs	5.00			$5.00	5.00
6	Fixed manufacturing costs		$4.50	4.50		4.50
7	Fixed marketing costs	—	2.00	—	2.00	2.00
8		$12.50	$6.50	$12.00	$7.00	$19.00
9						
10	*In this example marketing costs include distribution and customer service costs, and there are no R&D or product design costs.					
11	**Business function costs					

Managers use terms such as *business function costs* and *full product costs* differently. To avoid being confused, you must understand their exact meanings in a given situation.

DECISIONS AND PERFORMANCE EVALUATION

Consider our equipment replacement example in light of Exhibit 11-1 (p. 530). If the decision model demands choosing the alternative that will minimize total costs over the life span of the equipment, then the analysis in Exhibits 11-8 and 11-9 dictates replacing rather than keeping. In the real world, however, would the manager replace? The answer depends on the manager's perceptions of whether the decision model is consistent with the performance evaluation model. The performance evaluation model describes the basis on which the manager's performance is judged. This is illustrated by the final influence pair (G, H).

Managers tend to favour the alternative that makes their performance look best. If the performance evaluation model conflicts with the decision model, the performance evaluation model often prevails in influencing a manager's behaviour.

For example, the decision model in Exhibit 11-8, based on a relevant-cost analysis over the life of the two machines, favours replacing the machine. But if the manager's promotion or bonus hinges on the first year's operating income performance under accrual accounting, the manager's temptation not to replace will be overwhelming. Why? Because the accrual accounting model for measuring performance will show a higher first-year operating income if the old machine is kept than if it is replaced (as the following table shows):

	First-Year Results: Accrual Accounting			
	Keep		**Replace**	
Revenues		$1,100,000		$1,100,000
Operating costs				
Cash operating costs	$800,000		$460,000	
Amortization	200,000		300,000	
Loss on disposal	—		360,000	
Total operating costs		1,000,000		1,120,000
Operating income (loss)		$ 100,000		$ (20,000)

Even if top management's goals are long term (and consistent with the decision model), the subordinate manager's concern is more likely to be short term if his or her evaluation is based on short-run measures such as operating income.

Resolving the conflict between the decision model and the performance evaluation model is frequently a baffling problem in practice. In theory, resolving the difficulty seems obvious—merely design consistent models. Consider our replacement example. Year-by-year effects on operating income of replacement can be budgeted over the planning horizon of two years. The manager would be evaluated on the understanding that the first year would be expected to be poor, the next year much better.

THINKING CRITICALLY

How can conflict be resolved? Explain in a sentence or two. Read on for further discussion of this topic.

Many companies—such as Cisco Systems, General Electric, and Novartis—design systems that seek to align decision-making models and performance-evaluation models. They integrate strategy with performance evaluation. Accountants who understand opportunity cost can implement this type of solution too. In a profit centre, for example, the manager is evaluated on operating income less the imputed interest cost of holding assets such as accounts receivable and inventory, and the opportunity cost of not collecting the cash or not selling the finished goods. This is one way to remove the incentive to produce into inventory to make short-term operating income look good. Even though the financial accounting system cannot record opportunity costs, they are nevertheless calculated for performance evaluation. This removes conflicting incentives when managers make decisions.

In practice, accounting systems rarely track each decision separately. Performance evaluation focuses on responsibility centres for a specific time period, not on projects or individual items of equipment for their entire useful lives. Therefore, the impacts of many different decisions are combined in a single performance report. Top management, through the reporting system, is rarely aware of particular desirable alternatives that were not chosen by subordinate managers. One solution, with the inexpensive technology now available, is to add project performance to the MIS.

Consider another conflict between the decision model and the performance evaluation model. Suppose a manager buys a particular machine only to discover that a better machine could have been purchased in its place. The decision model clearly indicates that replacing the existing machine with the better machine will improve operating income. The manager is reluctant to take action because replacing the machine so soon after its purchase may reflect badly on the manager's capabilities and performance. If the manager's superiors have no knowledge of the better machine, the manager may prefer to keep, rather than replace, the existing

---

GOVERNANCE ISSUES

Management Accounting—Asking the Right Questions

By getting up and "walking around," management accountants can gain a better understanding of the interdependencies depicted in Exhibit 11-2. They are in a position to ask questions other managers will not, and can explain why the answers are relevant to good costing. Questions such as, "What can be done with idle capacity if a part is outsourced?" "What is the contribution margin of the constrained resource?" "How would total costs change if we dropped a product line or a group of customers?"

They also become familiar with the potential conflicts that top managers face when making decisions. There is no room for an accounting professional to conceal any conflict, and indeed the profession has a duty to reveal actions that may be taken which are not in the company's best interests.

machine (see Governance Issues). Of course, one reason why decisions of this type are made by a team of top managers is to make it more difficult to hide mistakes. The objective is to learn from mistakes, not blame individuals.

MyAccountingLab

ASSESS YOUR MASTERY

To check your understanding of the material in Learning Objective ⑤, go to the *Mastery Questions* section at the end of this chapter and complete Learning Objective ⑤ question 1.

PULLING IT ALL TOGETHER—PROBLEM FOR SELF-STUDY

PROBLEM
Wally Lewis is manager of the engineering development division of Mainland Products. Lewis has just received a proposal signed by all 10 of his engineers to replace the office computers (PCs) with newer models. Lewis is not enthusiastic about the proposal.

	Old PCs	New PCs
Original cost	$300,000	$135,000
Useful life	5 years	3 years
Current age	2 years	0 years
Remaining useful life	3 years	3 years
Accumulated amortization	$120,000	Not acquired yet
Current book value	$180,000	Not acquired yet
Current disposal value (in cash)	$95,000	Not acquired yet
Terminal disposal value (in cash 3 years from now)	$0	$0
Annual computer-related cash operating costs	$40,000	$10,000
Annual revenues	$1,000,000	$1,000,000
Annual non–computer-related operating costs	$880,000	$880,000

Lewis's annual bonus includes a component based on division operating income. He has a promotion possibility next year that would make him a group vice-president of Mainland Products.

REQUIRED
1. Compare the costs of the old PCs and new PC options. Consider the cumulative results for the three years together, ignoring the time value of money. What is the best alternative?
2. Use Exhibit 11-2 to suggest important interdependencies that should be considered.
3. Explain how this is either a short-term or a long-term decision.
4. Explain how the table indicates how book value should be considered in this replacement decision.
5. Why might Lewis be reluctant to purchase the 10 new computers?

SOLUTION

1. The following table considers all cost items when comparing future costs of the old and new PC options:

All Items	Three Years Together		
	Old PCs	New PCs	Difference
Revenues	$3,000,000	$3,000,000	—
Operating costs:			
Non-computer-related operating costs	2,640,000	2,640,000	—
Computer-related cash operating costs	120,000	30,000	$ 90,000
Old PC book value:			
Periodic writeoff as amortization	180,000	—	
or Lump sum writeoff	—	180,000	
Current disposal price of PCs	—	(95,000)	95,000
New PCs, written off periodically as amortization		135,000	(135,000)
Total operating costs	2,940,000	2,890,000	50,000
Operating income	$ 60,000	$ 110,000	$ 50,000

Alternatively, the analysis could focus on only those items in the preceding table that differ across the alternatives.

Relevant Items	Three Years Together		
	Old PCs	New PCs	Difference
Computer-related cash operating costs	$120,000	$ 30,000	$ 90,000
Current disposal price of old PCs	—	(95,000)	95,000
New PCs, written off periodically as amortization	—	135,000	(135,000)
Total relevant costs	$120,000	$ 70,000	$ 50,000

The conclusion from this analysis is that operating income would be strengthened by $50,000 if the old PCs were replaced with new PCs.

2. This is a system management decision about how engineers can best gather and communicate various types of engineering nonfinancial data. Systems management affects areas of capacity management, process improvement, and overall financial performance. This manager should not be making this decision on his own but rather as part of a team that includes the managers of these other areas.

3. One reason why this is a long-term decision is that the useful life of the PCs is longer than one year, although likely less than three years for an engineer whose productivity improves when the best equipment and software is available.

4. In the table, the old PC book value appears as $180,000 in both alternatives; one is a line below the other. Book value is irrelevant because the acquisition cost of the old PCs is a historical cost and will remain unchanged irrespective of this decision. The book value of the old machines is not an element of difference between alternatives and could be completely ignored for decision-making purposes.

5. The accrual accounting operating incomes for the first year under the "keep old PCs" versus the "buy new PCs" alternatives are as follows:

		Keep Old PCs		Buy New PCs
Revenues		$1,000,000		$1,000,000
Operating costs:				
Non–computer-related operating costs	$880,000		$880,000	
Computer-related operating costs	40,000		10,000	
Amortization	60,000		45,000	
Loss on disposal of old PCs	—		85,000*	
Total operating costs		980,000		1,020,000
Operating income		$ 20,000		$ (20,000)

*$85,000 = book value of old PCs, $180,000 − current disposal price, $95,000.

Lewis would probably react negatively to the expected operating loss of $20,000 if the old PCs are replaced as compared to an operating income of $20,000 if the old PCs are kept. The decision would eliminate the component of his bonus based on operating income. He might also perceive the $20,000 operating loss as reducing his chances of being promoted to a group vice-president. This, however, is not in the best interests of Mainland Products because the obsolete PCs are slowing down the production of his engineers.

Engineers represent capacity—labour capacity—and their time is constrained. The extra time they spend on projects because they have no access to modern equipment is also a waste of money for Mainland. Fewer projects can be undertaken and completed, which affects the top line of the company. If engineering salaries are fixed then any incremental revenue that could be gained if the engineers could work more effectively would go straight to operating income. Wally needs an accountant to point out important relevant information that remains unconsidered in this decision.

DECISION POINTS

The following question-and-answer format summarizes the chapter's learning objectives. Each decision presents a key question related to a learning objective. The guidelines are the answer to that question.

DECISIONS	GUIDELINES
1. How do decision processes unfold?	Decisions are made by top management teams using a Delphic process as they pool their expertise to analyze existing incomplete but relevant information about the general economic outlook and the probable or expected outcomes of the company conditioned on the economic outcome. Their preliminary decisions on risk are changed by incoming relevant information as it arrives as they update risks in a Bayesian process. Both quantitative and qualitative information is relevant. Relevant information changes a decision, differs among the alternatives, and is information about the future. Historical information about the past is useful but not relevant.
2. How does relevance differ for short- and long-term decisions about production output level?	In the short term fixed costs cannot change between alternatives, while long-term decisions are almost always capacity decisions that will change fixed costs. In the short term there must be idle capacity to ensure existing production is not changed or interrupted by any added commitment to new production.

3. Why is opportunity cost relevant and book value irrelevant?	Opportunity cost is the contribution to income that is forgone or rejected by not using a limited resource in its next-best alternative use. Opportunity cost is included in decision making because it represents the best alternative way in which an organization could have used its resources had it not made the decision it did. Book value is a historical cost that cannot be changed irrespective of any decision, therefore it is irrelevant.
4. What are the key concepts when making product and customer mix decisions?	The product, branch, segment, or customer group yielding the highest contribution margin per *constrained* resource should be selected. Managers should ignore allocated overhead costs when making decisions about discontinuing and adding customers, branches, and segments. They should focus instead on how total costs differ among alternatives
5. What potential problems should be avoided in relevant-cost analysis?	Two potential problems to avoid in relevant-cost analysis are (a) making incorrect general assumptions—such as all variable costs are relevant and all fixed costs are irrelevant—and (b) losing sight of grand totals, focusing instead on unit amounts. Top management also faces a persistent challenge—that is, making sure that the performance evaluation model of subordinate managers is consistent with the decision model. A common inconsistency is to tell subordinate managers to take a multiple-year view in their decision making but then judge their performance only on the basis of the current year's operating income.

TERMS TO LEARN

This chapter contains definitions of the following important terms:

book value (p. 546)
business function costs (p. 557)
constraint (p. 553)
Delphic process (p. 528)
differential cost (p. 534)
differential revenue (p. 539)
enterprise risk management
   (ERM) (p. 531)
full product costs (p. 557)
incremental costs (p. 537)

incremental revenue (p. 539)
insource (p. 539)
make/buy decisions (p. 539)
net relevant cost (p. 534)
objective function (p. 553)
opportunity cost (p. 542)
optimization technique
   (p. 553)
out-of-pocket costs (p. 537)
outlay costs (p. 537)

outsource (p. 539)
paralysis by analysis (p. 532)
prior probability (p. 529)
qualitative factors (p. 534)
quantitative factors (p. 534)
relevant costs (p. 534)
relevant revenues
   (p. 534)
sunk costs (p. 547)
vertical integration (p. 539)

The Mastery Questions are rated by proficiency level—elementary, intermediate, and advanced. The solutions appear in the Solutions to Mastery Questions section of MyAccountingLab.

LEARNING OBJECTIVE 1

1. **Relevance, quantitative and qualitative—Elementary.** Louisville Corporation produces baseball bats for kids that it sells for $32 each. At capacity, the company can produce 50,000 bats a year. The costs of producing and selling 50,000 bats are as follows:

	Cost per Bat	Total Costs
Direct materials	$12	$ 600,000
Direct manufacturing labour	3	150,000
Variable manufacturing overhead	1	50,000
Fixed manufacturing overhead	5	250,000
Variable selling expenses	2	100,000
Fixed selling expenses	4	200,000
Total costs	$27	$1,350,000

REQUIRED

1. Suppose Louisville is currently producing and selling 40,000 bats. At this level of production and sales, its fixed costs are the same as given in the table above. Ripkin Corporation wants to place a one-time special order for 10,000 bats at $25 each. Louisville will incur no variable selling costs for this special order. Should Louisville accept this one-time special order? Show your calculations.
2. Now suppose Louisville is currently producing and selling 50,000 bats. If Louisville accepts Ripkin's offer it will have to sell 10,000 fewer bats to its regular customers.
   a. On financial considerations alone, should Louisville accept this one-time special order? Show your calculations.
   b. On financial considerations alone, at what price would Louisville be indifferent between accepting the special order and continuing to sell to its regular customers at $32 per bat?
   c. What other factors should Louisville consider in deciding whether to accept the one-time special order?

2. **Relevance, quantitative and qualitative—Intermediate.** The Department of National Defence has the difficult decision of deciding which military bases to close down. Military and political factors obviously matter, but cost savings are also an important factor. Consider two naval bases— one in Vancouver, British Columbia, and one in Halifax, Nova Scotia. National Defence has decided that it needs only one of those two bases permanently, so one must be shut down. The decision regarding which base to shut down will be made on cost considerations alone. The following information is available:
   a. The Vancouver base was built at a cost of $110 million. The operating costs of the base are $440 million per year. The base is built on land owned by National Defence, so it pays nothing for the use of the property. If the base is closed, the land will be sold to developers for $550 million.
   b. The Halifax base was built at a cost of $165 million on land leased by National Defence from private citizens. National Defence can choose to lease the land permanently for an annual lease payment of $3.3 million per year. If it decides to keep the Halifax base open, National Defence plans to invest $66 million in a fixed income note, which at 5% interest will earn the $3.3 million the government needs for the lease payments. The land and buildings will immediately revert to the owner if the base is closed. The operating costs of the base, excluding lease payments, are $330 million per year.
   c. If the Vancouver base is closed down, National Defence will have to transfer some personnel to the Halifax facility. As a result, the yearly operating costs at Halifax will increase by $110 million per year. If the Halifax facility is closed down, no extra costs will be incurred to operate the Vancouver facility.

REQUIRED

The British Columbia delegation argues that it is cheaper to close down the Halifax base, for two reasons: (1) it would save $110 million per year in additional costs required to operate the Halifax base, and (2) it would save $3.3 million per year in lease payments. (Recall that the Vancouver base requires no cash payments for use of the land because the land is owned by National Defence.) Do you agree with the British Columbia delegation's arguments and conclusions? In your answer, identify and explain all costs that you consider relevant and all costs that you consider irrelevant for the base-closing decision.

3. **Relevance, quantitative and qualitative—Comprehensive.** Aristide Corporation has four operating divisions. During the first quarter of 2009, the company reported total income from operations of $61,000 and the following results for each division:

	Division			
	A	**B**	**C**	**D**
Sales	$530,000	$730,000	$920,000	$450,000
Cost of goods sold	450,000	480,000	576,000	390,000
Selling, general, and administrative expenses	100,000	207,000	246,000	120,000
Operating income/loss	$ (20,000)	$ 43,000	$ 98,000	$ (60,000)

Further analysis of costs reveals the following percentages of variable costs in each division

Cost of goods sold	90%	80%	90%	95%
Selling, general, and administrative expenses	60%	60%	70%	80%

Closing down any division would result in savings of 60% of the fixed costs of that division. Top management is very concerned about the unprofitable divisions (A and D) and is considering shutting them down.

REQUIRED
1. Calculate the contribution margin for the two unprofitable divisions (A and D).
2. On the basis of financial considerations alone, should the top management of Aristide shut down Division A? Division D?
3. What other factors should the top management of Aristide consider before making a decision?

LEARNING OBJECTIVE 2

1. **Relevance, short-term—Elementary.** (CMA, adapted) Today Design Ltd. sells three types of specialized paint to withstand different ranges of temperatures, cool, warm, and hot. Estimated sales demand, unit selling prices, and production requirements are:

	Cool	**Warm**	**Hot**
Estimated demand	600	500	400
Unit sales price	$ 16	$ 18	$ 14
Production requirements per unit			
Material Y9 (kilograms)	8	5	2
Heat-sensitive paint (litres)	6	12	8

The company has existing inventories of 300 units of cool and 200 units of hot, but is adopting just-in-time inventory management and expects to reduce inventory to zero by the end of this year.

All three products use the same direct materials and next year the available supply of materials will be restricted to 5,000 kilograms of material Y9 and 12,000 litres of heat-sensitive paint. Material Y9 costs $0.95 per kilogram and the heat-sensitive paint costs $0.50 per litre. All other costs are fixed.

REQUIRED
Calculate the number of units of each product Today Design Ltd. should produce next year to maximize operating income.

2. **Relevance, short-term—Intermediate.** (A. Atkinson) Oxford Engineering manufactures small engines. The engines are sold to manufacturers who install them in such products as lawn mowers. The company currently manufactures all the parts used in these engines but is considering a proposal from an external supplier who wants to supply the starter assembly used in

these engines. The starter assembly is currently manufactured in Division 3 of Oxford Engineering. The costs relating to Division 3 for the past 12 months were as follows:

Direct materials	$220,000
Direct manufacturing labour	165,000
Manufacturing overhead	440,000
Total	$825,000

Over the past year, Division 3 manufactured 165,000 starter assemblies; the average cost for the starter assembly is computed as $5 ($825,000 ÷ 165,000).

Further analysis of manufacturing overhead revealed the following information. Of the total manufacturing overhead reported, only 25% is considered variable. Of the fixed portion, $165,000 is an allocation of general overhead that would remain unchanged for the company as a whole if production of the starter assembly is discontinued. A further $110,000 of the fixed overhead is avoidable if self-manufacture of the starter assembly is discontinued. The balance of the current fixed overhead, $55,000, is the division manager's salary. If self-manufacture of the starter assembly is discontinued, the manager of Division 3 will be transferred to Division 2 at the same salary. This move will allow the company to save the $44,000 salary that would otherwise be paid to attract an outsider to this position.

REQUIRED

1. Tidnish Electronics, a reliable supplier, has offered to supply starter assembly units at $4 per unit. Since this price is less than the current average cost of $5 per unit, the vice-president of manufacturing is eager to accept this offer. Should the outside offer be accepted? (*Hint:* Production output in the coming year may be different from production output in the last year.)
2. How, if at all, would your response to requirement 1 change if the company could use the vacated plant space for storage and, in so doing, avoid $55,000 of outside storage charges currently incurred? Why is this information relevant or irrelevant?
3. **Relevance, short-term—Advanced.** Hernandal Corporation is bidding on a new construction contract, here called Contract No. 1. If the bid is accepted, work will begin in a few days, on January 1, 2010. Contract No. 1 requires a special cement. Hernandal has already purchased 10,000 kilograms of the special cement for $20,000. The current purchase cost of the cement is $2.40 per kilogram. The company could sell the cement now for $1.60 per kilogram after all selling costs. Hernandal will also bid on Contract No. 2 one month from now. If Contract No. 1 is not landed, the special cement will be available for Contract No. 2. If Contract No. 1 is landed, Hernandal will need to buy 10,000 kilograms of another grade of cement for $2.50 per kilogram to fulfill Contract No. 2.

    If it is not used in either of these two ways, the special cement would be of no use to the company and would be sold a little more than a month from now for $1.50 per kilogram after all selling costs.

    The president of Hernandal, Julio Grand, is puzzled about the appropriate total cost of the special cement to be used in bidding on Contract No. 1. Competition is intense and markups are very thin, so determining the relevant material costs when bidding on Contract No. 1 is crucial.

REQUIRED

1. Suppose Grand is certain that Hernandal will land Contract No. 2; what (relevant) cost figure should Grand use for the special cement when bidding on Contract No. 1?
2. This part requires knowledge of the material on decision making under uncertainty, which was covered in Chapter 3. Suppose Grand estimates a probability of 0.7 that Hernandal will land Contract No. 2. What (relevant) cost figure should Grand use for the special cement when bidding on Contract No. 1?
3. Suppose Hernandal could sell the special cement now for $2.30 per kilogram after all selling costs (instead of $1.60 per kilogram as described in paragraph 1). Suppose Grand is certain that Hernandal will land Contract No. 2. What (relevant) cost figure should Grand use for the special cement when preparing a bid on Contract No. 1?

LEARNING OBJECTIVE 3

1. **Opportunity costs, book value—Intermediate.** Larry Miller, the general manager of Basil Software, scheduled a meeting on June 2, 2010 with Nicole Nguyen, sales manager, Andy Ayim, accountant, and Ellen Eisner, software operations manager, to discuss the development and release

of Basil Software's new version of its spreadsheet package, Easyspread 2.0. It is only a question of time before other software firms have a package that matches Easyspread 2.0. Nicole Nguyen, the sales manager, could hardly control her enthusiasm for the new product.

Nicole Nguyen: This product is exactly what the market has been waiting for. We should not delay, by even a single day, the introduction of this product. Let's make July 1, 2010, the sales release date.

Ellen Eisner: I don't disagree with Nicole's assessment of the market potential for this product, but I have a problem. The threatened strike by our printers caused us to purchase large quantities of user's manuals for Easyspread 1.0. We don't like to store the manuals separately, so we also got extra diskettes duplicated. The manuals and diskettes were then packaged and shrink-wrapped. We are currently holding 60,000 completed packages, which equals the expected sales for July, August, and September 2010 of Easyspread 1.0. I think we should make October 1, 2010, the expected release date of Easyspread 2.0. This date would enable us to sell all of our inventory of Easyspread 1.0.

Larry Miller: Nicole, do you see any problem with Ellen's suggestion? Our inventory of Easyspread 1.0 seems rather large for us to ignore. If we introduce Easyspread 2.0 on July 1, what would we do with the inventory of Easyspread 1.0 that we currently hold?

Nicole Nguyen: We currently sell Easyspread 1.0 to our wholesalers and distributors for $165.00 each. The additional optimization features in Easyspread 2.0 mean that we should be able to sell Easyspread 2.0 to our distributors for about $203.50. We should not ignore the higher profit margins from Easyspread 2.0. It is true, though, that each time we sell one unit of Easyspread 2.0, we forgo the sale of one unit of Easyspread 1.0. Since the expected demand for Easyspread 2.0 is at least as large as the demand for Easyspread 1.0, we may have to throw away the existing inventory of Easyspread 1.0 once we introduce Easyspread 2.0.

Larry Miller: Andy, you've heard what Nicole and Ellen have to say. I would like you to do a detailed analysis of the alternatives, and let me know within a week what you come up with. We need to make a decision on this one way or another, and we need to do so soon.

When Andy Ayim returned to his office, he pulled out the cost records he had developed for Easyspread 1.0 and Easyspread 2.0. The unit costs for the two products could be summarized as follows:

	Easyspread 1.0	Easyspread 2.0
Manuals, diskettes	$ 22.00	$ 27.50
Development costs	82.50	115.50
Marketing and administration costs	27.50	33.00
Total cost per unit	$132.00	$176.00

The following additional facts are available:
a. Basil contracts with outside vendors to print manuals and duplicate diskettes.
b. Development costs are allocated on the basis of the total costs of developing the software and the anticipated unit sales over the life of the software.
c. Marketing and administration costs are fixed costs in 2010, incurred to support all activities of Basil Software. Marketing and administration costs are allocated to products on the basis of the budgeted revenues from each of the products. The preceding unit costs assume Easyspread 2.0 will be introduced on July 1, 2010.

REQUIRED
1. Based on financial considerations only, is Basil Software better off introducing Easyspread 2.0 immediately or waiting? Explain your conclusion, clearly identifying relevant and irrelevant costs.
2. What other factors might Nicole Nguyen and Ellen Eisner raise? What factors might Larry Miller consider important?

2. **Opportunity costs, book value—Advanced.** Todd and Smale Company Ltd. (T&S) is a small manufacturer of auto parts. The total production capacity is 100,000 units per year. T&S currently produces and sells 80,000 units, which completely satisfies current market

demand. This demand has been constant for 5 years and with the current downturn in the auto industry it is not likely that demand will change in the near future. The unit price has also been constant for the last 5 years. Below is a flexible budget statement over the relevant range of 80,000 to 100,000 units.

	80,000		90,000		100,000	
Unit price: $10.00						
Total units produced and sold:	Unit Cost	Total	Unit Cost	Total	Unit Cost	Total
Revenue		$800,000		$900,000		$1,000,000
Production:						
Direct materials	$1.50	120,000	$1.50	135,000	$1.50	150,000
Direct manufacturing labour	1.00	80,000	1.00	90,000	1.00	100,000
Manufacturing overhead:						
Variable	1.50	120,000	1.50	135,000	1.50	150,000
Fixed	3.50	280,000	3.11	279,900	2.80	280,000
Total inventoriable cost	7.50	600,000	7.11	639,900	6.80	680,000
Period costs:						
Variable	0.80	64,000	0.80	72,000	0.80	80,000
Fixed	0.70	56,000	0.62	55,800	0.56	56,000
Total period costs	1.50	120,000	1.42	127,800	1.36	136,000
Total costs	$9.00	720,000	$8.53	767,700	$8.16	816,000
Operating income		$ 80,000		$132,300		$ 184,000

T&S uses standards based on engineering information available from specialized industry databases. These standards are shown below:

		Rate ($)	
Direct materials in kilograms per unit	1.5	$ 1.00	$1.50
Direct labour (DLH)	0.1	10.00	1.00
Variable manufacturing overhead (DLH)	0.1	15.00	1.50
Fixed manufacturing overhead (DLH)	0.1	35.00	3.50
Standard inventoriable cost per unit			$7.50

T&S purchased machine C last year for $230,000. Its remaining useful life is 3 years and the net book value is $180,000. Now it can be sold for $120,000 or it can be used for another 3 years and sold for a scrap value of $30,000.

A new machine S from Singapore is available with a capacity of 100,000 units per year. Its useful life is 3 years with a scrap value of $24,000. It requires a more expensive and higher-quality direct material and will eliminate some direct manufacturing labour, which is paid hourly. Machine S can be operated by one full-time salaried person. The seller requires a licensing fee of $1.00 per unit produced and the price of machine S is $210,000. Projected annual costs of purchasing machine S are:

Production volume in units	80,000	100,000
Direct materials	$152,000	$190,000
Direct labour	—	—
Amortization	62,000	62,000
Licensing fee	80,000	100,000
Other overhead	280,000	310,000
Total	$574,000	$662,000

1. Identify the costs relevant to the decision of whether or not to purchase machine S.
2. If T&S decides to purchase machine S, what is the annual saving in each of the next 3 years if production is 80,000 units?
3. What is the net cash outflow if T&S decides to purchase machine S?

LEARNING OBJECTIVE 4

1. Product, customer mix—Advanced. (N. Melumad, adapted) Pendleton Engineering makes cutting tools for metal-working operations. It makes two types of tools: R3, a regular cutting tool, and HP6, a high-precision cutting tool. R3 is manufactured on a regular machine but HP6 must be worked on both the regular machine and a high-precision machine. The following information is available:

	R3	HP6
Selling price	$ 20	$ 180
Variable manufacturing costs per unit	$ 72	$ 120
Variable marketing costs per unit	$ 18	$ 42
Budgeted total fixed overhead costs	$350,000	$550,000
Hours required to produce 1 unit on the regular machine	1	.5

The following additional information is available:
a. Pendleton faces a capacity constraint on the regular machine of 50,000 hours per year.
b. Pendleton has no capacity constraint on the high-precision machine.
c. Of the $550,000 budgeted fixed overhead costs of HP6, $360,000 is for lease payments for the high-precision machine. This cost is charged entirely to HP6 because Pendleton uses the machine exclusively to produce HP6. The leasing agreement for the high-precision machine can be cancelled at any time without penalties.
d. All other fixed overhead costs cannot be changed.

REQUIRED
1. What product mix—that is, how many units of R3 and HP6—will maximize Pendleton's operating income?
2. Suppose Pendleton can increase the annual capacity of the regular machine by 15,000 hours at a cost of $180,000. Should Pendleton increase the capacity of the regular machine by 15,000 machine-hours? By how much will Pendleton's operating income increase?
3. Suppose that the capacity of the regular machine has been increased to 65,000 hours. Pendleton has been approached by Carter Corporation to supply 20,000 units of another cutting tool, S3, for $144 per unit. S3 is exactly like R3 except that its variable manufacturing costs are $84 per unit. What product mix should Pendleton choose to maximize operating income?

LEARNING OBJECTIVE 5

1. Reduce conflict—Advanced. The Pastel Company must reach a make/buy decision with respect to a high-volume, easily made metal tool, RG1. Sean Gray, the cost analyst, estimates the following costs and production information for the 50,000 units of RG1 that are expected to be put into production.

Total direct materials costs	$660,000
Direct manufacturing labour costs (all variable)	$220,000
Manufacturing overhead costs (all fixed)	$440,000
Good units of RGI manufactured and sold	40,000 units
Units of RGI scrapped for zero revenue	10,000 units

York Corporation has offered to supply as many units of RG1 as Pastel needs for $23.10 per unit. If Pastel buys RG1 from York instead of manufacturing it in-house, Pastel would be able to save $263,450 of the $440,000 fixed manufacturing overhead costs. (There is no alternative use for the capacity currently used to make RG1.)

Gray shows his analysis to Jim Berry, the controller. Berry does not like what he sees. He asks Gray to review all his assumptions and calculations with the comment, "The yield assumptions you made are very low. I think this plant can achieve much better quality than we have in the past. Better quality will reduce our costs and make them competitive with the outside purchase price." Gray knows that Berry is very concerned about purchasing RG1 from an outside supplier because it will mean that some of his close friends who work on the RG1 line will be laid off. Berry had played a key role in convincing management to produce RG1 in-house.

Gray rechecks his calculations. He believes it is unlikely that the plant can achieve the quality levels it would take for the make alternative to be superior to the buy alternative.

REQUIRED

1. Based on the information Gray obtains, should Pastel make or buy RG1?
2. For what levels of scrap would the make alternative be preferred to purchasing from outside?
3. Evaluate whether Jim Berry's suggestion to Gray to review his estimates is unethical. Will it be unethical for Gray to change his analysis to support the make alternative? What steps should Gray take next?

 Make the grade with MyAccountingLab: The questions, exercises, and problems marked in red can be found on MyAccountingLab at **www.myaccountinglab.com.** You can practise them as often as you want, and most feature step-by-step guided instructions to help you find the right answer. Exercises and problems with an Excel icon in the margin have an accompanying Excel template on MyAccountingLab.

SHORT-ANSWER QUESTIONS

11-1 Provide examples of interdependencies and relate them to Exhibit 11-1.

11-2 Define *relevant cost*. Why are historical costs irrelevant?

11-3 Why is book value irrelevant to equipment purchase decisions?

11-4 Distinguish between *quantitative* and *qualitative* factors in decision making.

11-5 Describe two ways in which unit-cost data can mislead a decision maker.

11-6 When are variable costs irrelevant?

11-7 "A component part should be purchased whenever the purchase price is less than its total unit manufacturing cost." Do you agree? Why?

11-8 Define opportunity cost.

11-9 "Managers should always buy inventory in quantities that result in the lowest purchase cost per unit." Do you agree? Why?

11-10 "Management should always maximize sales of the product with the highest contribution margin per unit." Do you agree? Why?

11-11 "A customer, branch, or business segment that shows negative operating income should be shut down." Do you agree? Explain briefly.

11-12 "Cost written off as amortization is always irrelevant." Do you agree? Why?

11-13 "Managers will always choose the alternative that maximizes operating income or minimizes costs in the decision model." Do you agree? Why?

11-14 Describe the three steps in solving a linear programming problem.

11-15 How might the optimal solution of a linear programming problem be determined?

EXERCISES

11-16 **Relevant and irrelevant costs.** Answer the following questions.

REQUIRED

1. Dalton Computers makes 5,000 units of a circuit board, CB76, at a cost of $230 each. Variable cost per unit is $180 and fixed cost per unit is $50. Peach Electronics offers to

supply 5,000 units of CB76 for $210. If Dalton buys from Peach it will be able to save $20 per unit of fixed costs but continues to incur the remaining $30 per unit. Should Dalton accept Peach's offer? Explain.

2. AP Manufacturing is deciding whether to keep or replace an old machine. It obtains the following information:

	Old Machine	New Machine
Original cost	$10,000	$ 8,000
Useful life	10 years	4 years
Current age	6 years	0 years
Remaining useful life	4 years	4 years
Accumulated amortization	$6,000	Not acquired yet
Book value	$4,000	Not acquired yet
Current disposal value (in cash)	$2,500	Not acquired yet
Terminal disposal value (4 years from now)	$0	$0
Annual cash operating costs	$20,000	$12,000

AP Manufacturing uses straight-line amortization. Ignore the time value of money and income taxes. Should AP replace the old machine? Explain.

11-17 The careening personal computer. (W. A. Paton) An employee in the accounting department of a certain business was moving a personal computer from one room to another. As he came alongside an open stairway, he slipped and let the computer get away from him. It went careening down the stairs with a great racket and wound up at the bottom, completely wrecked. Hearing the crash, the office manager came rushing out and turned rather pale when he saw what had happened. "Someone tell me quickly," the manager yelled, "if that is one of our fully amortized items." A check of the accounting records showed that the smashed computer was, indeed, one of those items that had been written off. "Thank God!" said the manager.

REQUIRED
Explain and comment on the point of this anecdote.

11-18 Equipment upgrade versus replacement. (A. Spero, adapted) TechMech Company produces and sells 6,000 modular computer desks per year at a selling price of $500 each. Its current production equipment, purchased for $1,500,000 and with a five-year useful life, is only two years old. It has a terminal disposal value of $0 and is amortized on a straight-line basis. The equipment has a current disposal price of $600,000. However, the emergence of a new moulding technology has led TechMech to consider either upgrading or replacing the production equipment. The following table presents expected costs under the upgrade and replace alternatives:

	Upgrade	Replace
One-time equipment costs	$2,700,000	$4,200,000
Variable manufacturing costs per desk	$ 140	$ 80
Remaining useful life of equipment	3 years	3 years
Terminal disposal value of equipment	$ 0	$ 0

All equipment costs will continue to be amortized on a straight-line basis. For simplicity, ignore income taxes, interest, and present value considerations.

REQUIRED
1. Should TechMech upgrade its production line or replace it? Show all calculations.
2. Now suppose the capital expenditure needed to replace the production line is somewhat negotiable. All other data are as given previously. What is the maximum price that TechMech would be willing to pay for the new line to prefer replacing the existing line over upgrading it?
3. Assume that the capital expenditures needed to replace and upgrade the production line are as given in the original question, but that the expected production and sales

quantity is not known. For what production and sales quantity would TechMech prefer to (i) upgrade the line, (ii) replace the line?

4. Consider again the basic information given in this exercise. Suppose Dan Doria, the manager of TechMech, is evaluated on operating income. Because he is likely to relocate after about a year, his current bonus is his primary concern. Which alternative would Doria choose? Explain.

11-19 Relevance of equipment costs. Sparkles Ltd. has just today paid for and installed a special machine for polishing cars at one of its several outlets. It is the first day of the company's fiscal year. The machine cost $25,000. Its annual operating costs total $18,200, exclusive of amortization. The machine will have a four-year useful life and a zero terminal disposal price.

After the machine has been used for a day, a machine salesperson offers a different machine that promises to do the same job at a yearly operating cost of $10,250, exclusive of amortization. The new machine will cost $28,700 cash, installed. The "old" machine is unique and can be sold outright for only $12,000, minus $2,400 removal cost. The new machine, like the old one, will have a four-year useful life and zero terminal disposal price.

Sales, all in cash, will be $170,000 annually, and other cash costs will be $123,000 annually, regardless of this decision.

For simplicity, ignore income taxes, interest, and present value considerations.

REQUIRED

1. **a.** Prepare a statement of cash receipts and disbursements for each of the four years under both alternatives. What is the cumulative difference in cash flow for the four years taken together?

   b. Prepare income statements for each of the four years under both alternatives. Assume straight-line amortization. What is the cumulative difference in operating income for the four years taken together?

   c. What are the irrelevant items in your presentations in requirements a and b? Why are they irrelevant?

2. Suppose the cost of the "old" machine was $1.1 million rather than $25,000. Nevertheless, the old machine can be sold outright for only $11,000, minus $2,200 removal cost. Would the net differences in requirements 1a and 1b change? Explain.

3. "To avoid a loss, we should keep the old machine." What is the role of book value in decisions about replacement of machines?

11-20 Closing and opening stores. Sundry Corporation runs two convenience stores, one in Vancouver and one in Surrey. Operating income for each store in 2010 follows:

	Vancouver	Surrey
Revenues	$1,070,000	$860,000
Operating costs:		
Cost of goods sold	750,000	660,000
Lease rent (renewable each year)	90,000	75,000
Labour (paid on an hourly basis)	42,000	42,000
Amortization of equipment	25,000	22,000
Utilities (electricity, heating)	43,000	46,000
Allocated corporate overhead	50,000	40,000
Total operating costs	1,000,000	885,000
Operating income (loss)	70,000	(25,000)

The equipment has a remaining useful life of one year and zero disposal price. In a senior management meeting, Maria Lopez, the management accountant at Sundry Corporation, makes the following comment: "Sundry can increase its profitability by closing down the Surrey store or by adding more stores like it."

REQUIRED

Answer the following questions referring to the preceding data.

1. Calculate Sundry's operating income if it closes down the Surrey store. By closing down the store, Sundry can reduce overall corporate overhead costs by $44,000. Is Maria Lopez correct? Explain.

2. Calculate Sundry's operating income if it opens another store with revenues and costs identical to the Surrey store (including a cost of $22,000 to acquire equipment with a one-year useful life and zero disposal price). Opening this store will increase corporate overhead costs by $4,000. Is Maria Lopez correct? Explain.

11-21 Open a store. (CMA, adapted) Voltaire, a renowned pastry chef employed at a four-star hotel, has decided to open his own exclusive pastry shop. He has $100,000 to invest and the information he has obtained is as follows:

1. Market size, 532,500 units

◆ There is a 55% probability the market size in the area will be 600,000 pastries per year and a 45% chance it will be 450,000 pastries per year.

◆ Price per pastry is assumed to be $4.00 and this is the basis for predicting Voltaire's market share.

◆ Variable costs are $2.60 per pastry.

The market share Voltaire will capture depends on where he locates. There are two possibilities:

◆ Location A costs $38,000 annual rent where Voltaire will capture 30% of the pastry market (his market share). Fixed costs excluding rent are estimated at $90,000 per year.

◆ Location B costs $12,000 annual rent where Voltaire will capture 22% of the pastry market (his market share). Fixed costs excluding rent are estimated at $54,000 per year.

REQUIRED

1. Based on your quantitative analysis what is the best choice of location for Voltaire?
2. There is a consultant who sells industry market information. How much should Voltaire be willing to pay to know with certainty what the total market size is?

	Estimated Demand (Units)	Selling Price	Direct Material Cost per Unit	Variable Machining Cost per Unit
Nealy	1,800	$3,000	$750	$600
Tersa	4,500	$2,100	$500	$500
Pelta	39,000	$ 800	$100	$200

11-22 Product mix, constrained resource. Taylor Furniture produces and sells specialty mattresses. Production is a machine-intensive process. Taylor's variable costs are direct material costs, variable machining costs, and sales commissions. Marion Taylor, the owner, is planning production for the coming year and collects the following data:

1. Machine hours demanded, Tersa mattress, 11,250

Salespeople are paid a 5% commission on each Nealy or Tersa sold, and a 10% commission on each Pelta sold. All other marketing and administrative costs are fixed and, along with the fixed manufacturing costs, total $8,750,000. Annual capacity is 50,000 machine-hours, which is limited by the availability of machines. Variable machining costs are $200 per hour. Taylor Furniture holds negligible inventories to minimize business risk.

REQUIRED

1. Calculate the machine-hours required to satisfy the estimated demand for each type of mattress.
2. What is the contribution margin earned from each type of mattress?
3. Advise Marion Taylor about the most profitable production levels of the three products.
4. Suppose Taylor Furniture can lease additional machining capacity on an as-needed basis. What is the maximum amount that Marion Taylor would be willing to pay for each hour of additional machining capacity in the coming year?

11-23 Sell or process further. (J. Watson) Xylon Processing Limited is a chemical manufacturer. Two chemicals, Aardyn and Gargaton, are produced from the common chemical xylon. The joint process requires 15,000 litres of xylon to be processed at a cost of $21,500 (including the cost of the chemical itself). From these 15,000 litres, the company produces 9,600 litres of Aardyn and 5,400 litres of Gargaton. The joint costs of $21,500 are allocated $13,760 to Aardyn and $7,740 to Gargaton. The company can sell the Aardyn and the Gargaton at the split-off point for $15,360 and $8,748, respectively. Alternatively, the company can process the Aardyn further to produce 9,600 litres of Anardyn. The Anardyn sells for $2.38 per litre and additional processing costs are $6,945.

Incremental revenues from further processing, $22,848

REQUIRED

Should Xylon sell Aardyn, or should it process it further to product Anardyn?

11-24 Special order. Swat Corporation produces tennis racquets for kids that it sells for $16 each. At capacity, the company can produce 50,000 racquets per year. The costs of producing and selling 50,000 racquets are as follows:

	Cost per Racquet	Total Costs
Direct materials	$ 6	$300,000
Direct manufacturing labour	2	100,000
Variable manufacturing overhead	1	50,000
Fixed manufacturing overhead	2	100,000
Variable selling expenses	1	50,000
Fixed selling expenses	1	50,000
Total costs	$13	$650,000

REQUIRED

1. Suppose Swat is currently producing and selling 40,000 racquets. At this level of production and sales, its fixed costs are the same as given in the table above. Lanny Corporation wants to place a one-time special order for 10,000 racquets at $11 each. Swat will incur no variable selling costs for this special order. Should Swat accept this one-time special order? Show all calculations.
2. Now suppose Swat is currently producing and selling 50,000 racquets. If Swat accepts Lanny's order, it will have to sell 10,000 fewer racquets to its regular customers.
   a. On financial considerations alone, should Swat accept this one-time special order? Show all calculations.
   b. On financial considerations alone, at what price would Swat be indifferent between accepting the special order and continuing to sell to its regular customers at $16 per racquet?
   c. What other factors should Swat consider in deciding whether to accept the one-time special order?

11-25 Make or buy. (J. Watson) Mitchell Ltd. manufactures electronic components used in producing appliances. Data relating to the unit cost of manufacturing one of its components are provided below:

Direct material	$8.00
Direct manufacturing labour	$3.00
Variable manufacturing overhead	$4.00
Fixed manufacturing overhead	$2.50

The unit fixed manufacturing overhead cost is based on a denominator volume of 100,000 units. Since the component is used internally, there are no associated selling costs.

Phillips Corporation has offered to supply the component at a price of $16.25 per unit. Mitchell believes that if it purchases the component, it will save $62,000 a year in fixed manufacturing salaries. It has been assured that the quality of the purchased component is consistent with its own product.

Mitchell is planning to produce 100,000 units of the component for the upcoming year.

REQUIRED

Should Mitchell continue to manufacture the component or should it purchase from Phillips Corporation? What nonfinancial factors should be considered by Mitchell?

11-26 Product mix, constrained resource. Westford Company produces three products, A110, B382, and C657. Unit data for the three products follow:

	Product		
	A110	**B382**	**C657**
Selling price	$84	$56	$70
Variable costs:			
Direct materials	24	15	9
Other variable costs	28	27	40

All three products use the same direct material, Bistide. The demand for the products far exceeds the direct material available to produce the products. Bistide costs $3 per kilogram and a maximum of 5,000 kilograms is available each month. Westford must produce a minimum of 200 units of each product.

REQUIRED

1. How many units of product A110, B382, and C657 should Westford produce?
2. What is the maximum amount Westford would be willing to pay for another 1,000 kilograms of Bistide?

11-27 Linear programming. (J. Watson) Purcell Ltd. manufactures two models of regulators, the X900 and the P330. The assembly process for each is similar in that both require a certain amount of wiring and soldering. The X900 requires 3 hours of wiring and 2 hours of soldering, and the P330 requires 2 hours of wiring and 1 hour of soldering. During the next production period, 360 hours of wiring time are available and up to 210 hours of soldering time may be used. The X900 sells for $352 with costs of $322. The P330 sells for $248 with costs of $230.

P330 contribution margin per unit, $18

REQUIRED

Formulate and solve this linear programming production mix situation and find the best combination of X900 and P330 that yields the highest profit.

11-28 Closing down divisions. Patterson Corporation has four operating divisions. During the first quarter of 2010, the company reported total income from operations of $55,000 and the following results for each division:

1. Division A variable cost of goods sold, $416,500

	Division			
	A	**B**	**C**	**D**
Sales	$550,000	$780,000	$970,000	$460,000
Cost of goods sold	490,000	520,000	575,000	390,000
Selling and admin expenses	140,000	230,000	240,000	120,000
Operating income (loss)	$ (80,000)	$ 30,000	$155,000	$ (50,000)

Further analysis of costs reveals the following percentages of variable costs in each division:

	Division			
	A	**B**	**C**	**D**
Cost of goods sold	85%	84%	94%	96%
Selling and admin expenses	64%	64%	70%	78%

Closing down any division would result in savings of 50% of the fixed costs of that division.

Top management is very concerned about the unprofitable divisions (A and D) and is considering shutting them down.

REQUIRED

1. Calculate the contribution margin for the two unprofitable divisions (A and D).
2. On the basis of financial considerations alone, should the top management of Patterson shut down Division A? Division D?
3. What other factors should the top management of Patterson consider before making a decision?

PROBLEMS

11-29 Multiple-choice comprehensive problem on relevant costs. The following are the Class Company's unit costs of manufacturing and marketing a high-style pen at a level of 25,000 units per month:

Manufacturing costs:	
Direct materials	$1.30
Direct manufacturing labour	$1.48
Variable manufacturing overhead	$0.92
Fixed manufacturing overhead	$0.75
Marketing costs:	
Variable	$1.72
Fixed	$1.10

REQUIRED

The following situations refer only to the preceding data; there is no connection between the situations. Unless stated otherwise, assume a regular selling price of $7.50 per unit.

Choose the best answer to each of the seven questions. Support each answer with summarized computations.

1. In an inventory of 10,000 units of the high-style pen presented on the balance sheet, the unit cost used is

   a. $3.70
   b. $2.72
   c. $6.17
   d. $4.45
   e. $7.27

2. The pen is usually produced and sold at the rate of 300,000 units per year (an average of 25,000 per month). The selling price is $7.50 per unit, which yields total annual sales of $2,250,000. Total costs are $2,181,000, and operating income is $69,000, or $0.23 per unit. Market research estimates that unit sales could be increased by 15% if prices were cut to $7.22. Assuming the implied cost behaviour patterns are correct, this action, if taken, would

   a. Decrease operating income by a net of $66,000.
   b. Decrease operating income by $0.10 per unit ($30,000) but increase operating income by 15% ($10,350) for a net decrease of $19,650.
   c. Decrease unit fixed costs by 15%, or $0.2775, per unit, and thus decrease operating income by $0.1775 ($0.10 − $0.2775) per unit.
   d. Increase unit sales to 345,000 units, which at the $7.22 price would give total sales of $2,490,900; costs at $7.27 per unit for 345,000 units would be $2,508,150; and a loss of $17,250 would result.
   e. None of these.

3. A cost contract with the government for 5,000 units of the pens calls for the reimbursement of all manufacturing costs plus a fixed fee of $1,500. No variable marketing costs are incurred on the government contract. You are required to compare the following two alternatives:

	Alternative A	Alternative B
Regular customers	20,000 units	20,000 units
Government	0 units	5,000 units

   Operating income under alternative B is greater than that under alternative A by

   a. $1,500
   b. $5,250
   c. $3,750
   d. $5,500
   e. none of these.

4. Assume the same data with respect to the government contract as in requirement 3 except that the two alternatives to be compared are:

	Alternative A	Alternative B
Regular customers	25,000 units	20,000 units
Government	0 units	5,000 units

Operating income under alternative B relative to that under alternative A is

a. $10,400 less
b. $13,750 greater
c. $5,150 less
d. $115 greater
e. none of these.

5. The company wants to enter a foreign market in which price competition is keen. The company seeks a one-time-only special order for 10,000 units on a minimum-unit-price basis. It expects that shipping costs for this order will amount to only $0.86 per unit, but the fixed costs of obtaining the contract will be $5,200. The company incurs no variable marketing costs other than shipping costs. Domestic business will be unaffected. The selling price to break even is

a. $4.45
b. $4.56
c. $5.08
d. $3.70
e. $5.31

6. The company has an inventory of 1,400 units of pens that must be sold immediately at reduced prices. Otherwise, the inventory will be worthless. The unit cost that is relevant for establishing the minimum selling price is

a. $4.45
b. $3.70
c. $5.42
d. $6.17
e. $1.72

7. A proposal is received from an outside supplier who will make and ship these high-style pens directly to the Class Company's customers as sales orders are forwarded from Class's sales staff. Class's fixed marketing costs will be unaffected, but its variable marketing costs will be slashed by 20%. Class's plant will be idle, but its fixed manufacturing overhead will continue at 50% of present levels. How much per unit would the company be able to pay the supplier without decreasing operating income?

a. $5.451
b. $4.075
c. $4.825
d. $5.925
e. none of these.

11-30 Make or buy (continuation of 11-29). Assume that, as in requirement 7 of Problem 11-29, a proposal is received from an outside supplier who will make and ship high-style pens directly to the Class Company's customers as sales orders are forwarded from Class's sales staff. If the supplier's offer is accepted, the present plant facilities will be used to make a new pen whose unit costs will be:

New pen sales, $1,537,500

Variable manufacturing costs	$5.80
Fixed manufacturing costs	$1.50
Variable marketing costs	$1.80
Fixed marketing costs for the new pen	$0.75

Total fixed manufacturing overhead will be unchanged from the original level given at the beginning of Problem 11-29. Fixed marketing costs for the new pens are over and above the fixed marketing costs incurred for marketing the high-style pens at the beginning of Problem 11-29. As in the previous problem, the variable marketing expenses will be reduced by 20%. The new pen will sell for $10.25. The minimum desired operating income on the two pens taken together is $75,000 per year. New pen sales will be 150,000 units.

REQUIRED
What is the maximum purchase cost per unit that the Class Company would be willing to pay for subcontracting the production of the high-style pens?

11-31 Discontinuing a product line, selling more product. The Northern Furniture Division of Grossman Corporation makes and sells tables and beds. The following revenue and cost information from the division's activity-based costing system is available:

a. On January 1, 2010, the equipment has a book value of $110,000 and zero disposal price. Any equipment not used remains idle.

b. Fixed marketing and distribution costs of a product line can be avoided if the line is discontinued.

c. Fixed general administration costs of the division and corporate office costs will not change if sales of individual product lines are increased or decreased, or if product lines are added or dropped.

	4,000 Tables	5,000 Beds	Total
Selling price/unit	$ 187.50	$ 225.00	
Revenues	$750,000	$1,125,000	$1,875,000
Variable direct materials and direct labour cost per unit	$ 125.00	$ 140.00	
Total variable direct costs	$500,000	$ 700,000	$1,200,000
Amortization on equipment used exclusively by each product line	$ 58,000	$ 62,000	$ 120,000
Fixed marketing costs	$ 65,000	$ 70,000	$ 135,000
Variable @ $850 per shipment	$ 34,000	$ 85,000	$ 119,000
Fixed general administration costs allocated to product lines on the basis of revenues	$ 72,000	$ 108,000	$ 180,000
Allocated corporate head office costs (allocated on the basis of revenues)	$104,000	$ 156,000	$ 260,000
Total costs	$833,000	$1,181,000	$2,014,000
Operating income (loss)	($83,000)	($56,000)	($139,000)

REQUIRED

1. Should the Furniture Division discontinue the tables product line assuming the released facilities remain idle? Show all calculations.
2. Should the Furniture Division sell 4,000 more tables? Assume that to do so the division would have to acquire equipment costing $48,500 with a one-year useful life and zero terminal disposal value. Assume further that the fixed marketing and distribution costs will not change but that the number of shipments will double. Show all calculations.

11-32 Opportunity cost. (H. Schaefer) Wolverine Corporation is working at full production capacity producing 10,000 units of a unique product, Rosebo. Manufacturing costs per unit for Rosebo are as follows:

Direct materials	$2.00
Direct manufacturing labour	$3.00
Manufacturing overhead	$5.00
Total manufacturing cost	$10.00

The unit manufacturing overhead cost is based on a variable cost per unit of $2.00 and fixed costs of $30,000 (at full capacity of 10,000 units). The selling costs, all variable, are $4.00 per unit, and the selling price is $20 per unit.

A customer, the Miami Company, has asked Wolverine to produce 2,000 units of Orangebo, a modification of Rosebo. Orangebo would require the same manufacturing processes as Rosebo. Miami Company has offered to pay Wolverine $15.00 for a unit of Orangebo and half the selling costs per unit.

REQUIRED

1. What is the opportunity cost to Wolverine of producing the 2,000 units of Orangebo? (Assume that no overtime is worked.)
2. Buckeye Corporation has offered to produce 2,000 units of Rosebo for Wolverine so that Wolverine may accept the Miami offer. That is, if Wolverine accepts the Buckeye offer, Wolverine would manufacture 8,000 units of Rosebo and 2,000 units of Orangebo and

purchase 2,000 units of Rosebo from Buckeye. Buckeye would charge Wolverine $14.00 per unit to manufacture Rosebo. Should Wolverine accept the Buckeye offer? (Support your conclusions with specific analysis.)

3. Suppose Wolverine had been working at less than full capacity, producing 8,000 units of Rosebo at the time the Orangebo offer was made. What is the minimum price Wolverine should accept for Orangebo under these conditions? (Ignore the previous $15.00 selling price.)

11-33 Influences on decisions. (CMA) Windsor Headlights Ltd. sells its products into a very competitive North American market. Sales have been steady for about three years and the company's capacity has been 60,000 machine-hours per month. This is 60% of its practical capacity. There are two contracts Windsor's top management team is considering with the intent to increase sales.

④ ⑤

1. Unit variable cost, $1.40

The first contract is with Mitsubishi, a Japanese manufacturer. The contract is going to be awarded to the lowest bidder who meets the contract specifications. Mitsubishi requires 100,000 units of Y-95 headlights per month and Windsor currently supplies this model to one of its North American customers. The North American contract is for two years at $3.25 per unit. Not many North American suppliers have been awarded contracts with Japanese companies. The table illustrates various potential bid prices and the probability the contract will be awarded at each bid price:

Probability of Acceptance	Bid Price per Unit, CDN $
100%	$2.00
80%	2.50
50%	3.00
25%	3.25
0%	3.50

The second contract is with Chrysler in the U.S., which is currently a very important customer with Windsor. Chrysler has offered a contract to purchase 800,000 units of model Y-95 headlights to be delivered in 5 months. Windsor, however, must agree to discount its price of CDN $3.60 per unit by 30%. Chrysler normally deals in very small quantities on a monthly basis with Windsor and this is the first time it has ordered the Y-95 headlight from Windsor.

The standard manufacturing cost of one unit of model Y-95 is:

	Units	Cost per Headlight
Direct materials	kilograms	$0.90
Direct labour	labour-hours	0.20
Factory overhead	0.1 machine-hour	1.50
Total standard cost		$2.60

The overhead rate is based on the current capacity of 60,000 machine-hours per month and 80% of this rate represents fixed costs.

REQUIRED

1. Based on your quantitative analysis of relevant costs and revenue, which bid price for the Mitsubishi contract would have the highest favourable effect on Windsor's operating income?
2. What other factors should influence Windsor's decision on the bid price for the Mitsubishi contract?
3. What factors should influence Windsor's decision on the bid price for the Chrysler contract?
4. Assume Windsor's practical capacity increases to 80,000 machine-hours per month throughout the next 12 months. If all other production data remain unchanged, calculate the total standard manufacturing cost per unit of model Y-95 headlights for next year.

11-34 Optimal production mix. (CMA, adapted) Della Simpson Inc. sells two popular brands of cookies, Della's Delight and Bonny's Bourbon. Della's Delight goes through the Mixing and Baking Departments and Bonny's Bourbon, a filled cookie, goes through the Mixing, Filling, and Baking departments.

④

Michael Shirra, vice-president for sales, believes that at the current price, Della Simpson can sell all of its daily production of Della's Delight and Bonny's Bourbon. Both cookies are made in batches of 3,000 cookies. The batch times (in minutes) for producing each type of cookie and the minutes available per day are as follows:

	Department Minutes		
	Mixing	**Filling**	**Baking**
Della's Delight	30	0	10
Bonny's Bourbon	15	15	15
Minutes available per day	660	270	300

Revenue and cost data for each type of cookie are:

	Della's Delight	Bonny's Bourbon
Revenue per batch	$ 475	$ 375
Variable cost per batch	$ 175	$ 125
Contribution margin per batch	$ 300	$ 250
Monthly fixed costs (allocated to each product)	$18,650	$22,350

REQUIRED
1. Using D to represent the batches of Della's Delight and B to represent the batches of Bonny's Bourbon made and sold each day, formulate Shirra's decision as a linear programming model.
2. Compute the optimal number of batches of each type of cookie that Della Simpson Inc. should make and sell each day to maximize operating income.

11-35 Special order. (J. Watson) Butler Ltd. manufactures one product in its Waterloo factory. Currently, Butler has capacity for 80,000 units per month and normally produces 50,000 units per month. The regular selling price for its product is $9.00.

Recently, Butler has been approached to provide a special order to a customer outside its normal distribution channels. The customer has requested a 40% price reduction on an order for 10,000 units.

The accountant for Butler has provided the following information regarding the average cost per unit at different production volumes:

Monthly Unit Production	Average Cost per Unit
50,000 units	$8.50
60,000 units	$7.75
70,000 units	$7.375
80,000 units	$6.953

If the company exceeds 64,000 units per month, it must hire additional factory supervision and cleanup staff, increasing the monthly fixed costs by $11,250.

REQUIRED
1. Assuming the company is producing at the normal volume of 50,000 units per month, should it accept the special order at the 40% discounted price? What is the minimum price Butler would be willing to accept?
2. Assume the company is producing at a monthly volume of 55,000 units per month. What is the minimum price per unit it should charge the customer for this special order?
3. Assume the company is producing at a monthly volume of 73,000 units. Should the special order be accepted? Assume the order must be filled in full (all 10,000 units). Fully support your answer.

11-36 Make versus buy, governance. (CMA, adapted) Lynn Hardt, a management accountant with the Paibec Corporation, is evaluating whether a component, MTR-85, should continue to be manufactured by Paibec or purchased from Marley Company, an outside supplier. Marley has submitted a bid to manufacture and supply the 35,000 units of MTR-85 that Paibec will need for 2011 at a unit price of $22.20 to be delivered according to Paibec's production specifications and needs. While the contract price of $22.20 is applicable only in 2011, Marley is interested in entering into a long-term arrangement beyond 2011.

Hardt has collected the following additional information related to manufacturing 32,000 units of MTR-85 in the previous year.

Direct materials	$243,200
Direct manufacturing labour	152,000
Plant space rental costs	98,000
Equipment leasing costs	45,000
Other manufacturing overhead costs	320,000
Total manufacturing costs	$858,200

◆ Direct materials used in the production of MTR-85 are expected to increase 6% in 2011.
◆ Paibec's direct manufacturing labour contract calls for an 8% increase in 2011.
◆ Paibec can withdraw from the plant space rental agreement without any penalty. Paibec will have no need for this space if MTR-85 is not manufactured.
◆ The equipment lease can be terminated by paying $8,500.
◆ Sixty percent of the other manufacturing overhead is considered variable. Variable overhead changes with the number of units produced. The rate per unit is not expected to change in 2011. The fixed manufacturing overhead costs are not expected to change whether or not MTR-85 is manufactured.

John Porter, plant manager at Paibec Corporation, is concerned that Hardt's analysis may lead to the closing down of the MTR-85 line. Porter indicates to Hardt that the current performance of the plant can be significantly improved on and that the price increases she is assuming are unlikely to occur. Hence, the analysis should be done assuming costs will be considerably below current levels. Hardt knows that Porter is concerned about outsourcing MTR-85 because it will mean that some of his close friends will be laid off. Furthermore, Porter had played a key role in convincing management to produce MTR-85 in-house.

Hardt believes that it is unlikely the plant will achieve the lower costs Porter describes. She is very confident about the accuracy of the information she has collected, but she is unhappy about laying off employees.

REQUIRED
1. Based on the information Hardt has obtained, should Paibec make MTR-85 or buy it? Show all calculations.
2. What other factors should Paibec consider before making a decision?
3. What should Lynn Hardt do in response to John Porter's comments?

11-37 Linear programming. (CMA, adapted) Cape Breton Manufacturing Ltd. (CBML) produces two products, Smart and Supersmart. The company has a just-in-time (JIT) inventory policy, therefore the direct materials, work-in-process, and finished goods inventories are not materially different from $0. Careful planning and production schedules are needed to ensure the success of this JIT policy. In the coming month, the sales manager estimates that the maximum demand will be 2,500 units of Smart and 2,000 units of Supersmart. CBML's contract with its supplier of direct materials states that in the coming month it will deliver a maximum of 38,000 kilograms at $1.25/kg. Employee vacations will limit direct labour to 900 hours in the coming month and the direct labour wage is $20/hour. Price and production data available are:

	Smart	Supersmart
Selling price per unit	$30.00	$32.00
Direct materials (kg) for each unit	10.00	8.00
Direct labour (minutes) for each unit	12.00	18.00
Variable overhead (direct labour-hours)	7.00	8.50

REQUIRED
1. Formulate and solve the linear programming problem to determine the production mix that will maximize the total contribution margin in the coming month for CBML.
2. Calculate the overtime premium CBML should be willing to pay per hour to increase its direct labour capacity by an added 50 hours in the coming month.

11-38 Optimal production plan, computer manufacturer. Information Technology, Inc. assembles and sells two products: printers and desktop computers. Customers can purchase either (a) a computer or (b) a computer plus a printer. The printers are not sold without the computer. The result is that the quantity of printers sold is equal to or less than the quantity of desktop computers sold. The contribution margins are $250 per printer and $140 per computer.

Each printer requires 7.2 hours' assembly time on production line 1 and 12 hours' assembly time on production line 2. Each computer requires 4.8 hours' assembly time on production line 1 only. (Many of the components of each computer are preassembled by external vendors.) Production line 1 has 28.8* hours of available time per day. Production line 2 has 24 hours of available time per day.

Let X represent units of printers and Y represent units of desktop computers. The production manager must decide on the optimal mix of printers and computers to manufacture.

*Line 1 is actually two parallel lines, each used 14.4 hours per day. To simplify calculations count as one line with 28.8 hours.

REQUIRED
1. Express the production manager's problem in an LP format.
2. Which combination of printers and computers will maximize the operating income of Information Technology? Use both the trial-and-error and the graphic approach.

11-39 One-time orders. (CMA, adapted) Edmonton Precision Tool Ltd. (EPTL) has a maximum practical capacity of 4,000 laser machine-hours and 1,000 imaging machine-hours. The direct costs per hour to operate each machine are $15 and $20, respectively. A prospective customer has offered EPTL $35,000 to build a custom tool. The expected cost of direct materials for this one-time contract is $5,000. The contract will require 200 laser machine-hours and 10 image machine-hours to complete. Indirect overhead is allocated based on the following regression (see Chapter 10):

$$y = 200,000 + 50x + 10z$$

where y is the total overhead costs, x is laser machine-hours, and z is image machine-hours.

REQUIRED
1. Assume that EPTL will just reach its operating capacity if it decides to accept this offer. Calculate the change in operating income if this offer is accepted.
2. Assume now that both machines are operating at 90% capacity and all current units are sold at $1,500 per unit. Each unit requires direct materials costing $250, 4 laser machine-hours, and 1 image machine-hour to produce. Indirect variable overhead costs are $200 per unit and the indirect fixed overhead costs are $225 per unit based on full capacity.

A second prospective customer offers to purchase 240 units at $1,350 per unit. If EPTL accepts this offer it must deliver all 240 units by year-end. Calculate the opportunity cost if EPTL accepts this offer.
3. Assume the same data as in requirement 2. EPTL, however, can lease machinery to accept the second customer's offer at a cost of $76,000. Calculate the change in operating income if the offer was accepted and the equipment was leased.

11-40 Optimal product mix. (CMA, adapted) OmniSport's Plastics Department is currently manufacturing 5,000 pairs of skates annually, making full use of its machine capacity. Presented below are the selling price and costs associated with OmniSport's skates.

Selling price per pair of skates		$145
Costs per pair of skates:		
Moulded plastic	$10	
Other direct materials	14	
Variable machine costs ($24 per hour)	36	
Manufacturing overhead costs	30	
Marketing and administrative costs*	20	110
Operating income per pair of skates		$ 35

*an allocated $8 of fixed overhead is included in the marketing and administrative costs

OmniSport believes it could sell 8,000 pairs of skates annually if it had sufficient manufacturing capacity. Colcott Inc., a steady supplier of quality products, has agreed to provide 6,000 pairs of skates per year at a price of $105 per pair delivered to OmniSport's facility.

Jack Petrone, OmniSport's product manager, has suggested that the company can make better use of its Plastics Department by manufacturing snowboard bindings. Petrone believes that OmniSport could expect to sell 12,000 snowboard bindings annually at a price of $80 per binding. Petrone's estimate of the costs to manufacture the bindings is presented next.

Selling price per snowboard binding		$80
Costs per snowboard binding:		
Moulded plastic	$20	
Other direct materials	6	
Variable machine costs ($24 per hour)	12	
Manufacturing overhead costs	8	
Marketing and administrative costs*	18	64
Operating income per pair of skates		$16

*an allocated $8 of fixed overhead is included in the marketing and administrative costs

Other information pertinent to OmniSport's operations is presented below.

◆ An allocated $8.00 fixed overhead cost per unit is included in the marketing and administrative cost for all the purchased and manufactured products. Total fixed and variable marketing and administrative costs for the purchased skates would be $14 per pair ($14 − $8 = $6 selling and administrative costs).

◆ In the Plastics Department, OmniSport uses machine-hours as the allocation base for other manufacturing overhead costs. The fixed manufacturing overhead component of these costs for the current year is the $36,000 of fixed plantwide manufacturing overhead that has been allocated to the Plastics Department.

REQUIRED

Which product or products should OmniSport manufacture and/or purchase to maximize operating income? Show all calculations.

11-41 **Linear programming.** (J. Watson) Vulcan Ltd. produces and sells two products, the Spock and the Vorick:

	Spock	Vorick
Selling price per unit	$120	$200
Direct materials	$ 30	$ 40
Direct labour	$ 30	$ 60
Variable overhead	$ 15	$ 25
Fixed overhead	$ 15	$ 20

Each unit of Spock requires 1.5 direct labour-hours and 2.0 machine-hours. The Vorick requires 3.0 direct labour-hours and 2.0 machine-hours per unit. Vulcan has a total of 30,000 direct labour-hours available and 25,000 machine-hours. The market for the products is unlimited within the volumes that the constraints will allow to be produced.

Vulcan currently has firm orders for 5,000 units of each product for the next period. Last period, Vulcan produced 10,000 units of each product and had no under- or overapplied overhead.

REQUIRED

Formulate and solve the linear programming problem required to determine the optimum production plan for next period. Calculate the total contribution margin assuming this optimum production plan.

11-42 **Optimal sales mix for a retailer, sensitivity analysis.** Always Open Inc. operates a chain of food stores open 24 hours a day. Each store has a standard 48,000 square metres of floor space available for merchandise. Merchandise is grouped in two categories: grocery products and dairy products. Always Open requires each store to devote a minimum of 12,000 square metres to grocery products and a minimum of 9,600 square metres to dairy products. Within these restrictions, each store manager can choose the mix of products to carry.

The manager of the Winnipeg store estimates the following weekly contribution margins per square metre: grocery products, $12; dairy products, $3.60.

1. Formulate the decision facing the store manager as an LP model. Use G to represent square metres of floor space for grocery products and D to represent square metres of floor space for dairy products.
2. Why might Always Open set minimum bounds on the floor space devoted to each line of products?
3. Compute the optimal mix of grocery products and dairy products for the Winnipeg store.
4. Will the optimal mix determined in requirement 3 change if the contribution margins per square metre change to grocery products, $9.60, and dairy products, $6?

11-43 **Make versus buy.** (J. Watson) Strudwick Ltd. is a distributor of canvas, leather, and synthetic products including backpacks, luggage, and computer carrying cases. It currently manufactures approximately 70% of its products, and outsources the remainder. It is reviewing whether it should continue to manufacture or outsource one of its models of nylon laptop carrying cases. This bag is designed to fit widescreen laptops and Strudwick has capacity to produce only 9,000 units per year. It believes it could sell 13,000 if it had sufficient capacity. The selling price and costs for each bag are:

Selling price		$88.00
Direct materials (nylon)	$ 6.00	
Direct labour ($16/hour)	20.00	
Zippers, handle, inserts	2.00	
Manufacturing overhead	30.00	
Selling and administration	9.00	67.00
Profit per bag		$21.00

It can purchase the laptop bags for $57 per unit. Strudwick estimates that its total selling costs on the purchased bags would be $7.80 per unit.

Besides the capacity issue, Strudwick believes it could make better use of the production capacity by manufacturing a wheeled hockey goalie bag. It believes it could sell 14,200 of these bags at a price of $99. The costs to manufacture the bag would be:

Direct materials	$24.00
Direct labour ($16/hour)	12.00
Wheels, handles, zippers	15.60
Manufacturing overhead	18.00
Selling and administration	12.00
Total costs	$81.60

The company applies its manufacturing overhead on the basis of direct labour-hours. The manufacturing overhead rate includes $45,000 of factorywide overhead that has been allocated to the product line. The remainder of the manufacturing overhead is variable. The selling and administration cost includes a $6 per unit fixed cost allocation, regardless of whether the product is manufactured or outsourced.

REQUIRED

1. Which products should Strudwick manufacture and/or purchase to maximize operating income?
2. What qualitative factors would impact this decision?

Pricing Decisions, Product Profitability Decisions, and Cost Management

Engineering
a Higher
Quality of Life

Parker Hannifin Corporation Annual Report 2008
The Premier Diversified Motion & Control Company

Parker

ENGINEERING **YOUR** SUCCESS.

BUSINESS MATTERS

Relevant Costs Inform Price Decisions

For years Parker Hannifin, a global industrial parts maker, priced its 800,000 different products at total cost plus 30%. In 2001, after touring the company's 221 facilities, the new CEO changed this strategy to target pricing. The CEO focused on the customers' willingness to pay (similar to the retail industry) and found that 28% of Parker's products were priced too low. Overnight, Parker raised its prices an average of 5%, ranging from 3% to as high as 60%. The company then focused on selling products with the highest price premiums and added $200 million to operating income by 2006 on revenues of $9.4 billion.

LEARNING OBJECTIVES

After studying this chapter, you should be able to

1. Discuss the major influences on both short- and long-run pricing decisions

2. Understand the pricing of products using the target-costing approach

3. Contrast pricing of products using the cost-plus approach, pricing of products using life-cycle budgeting, and pricing of products using the target-pricing approach

4. Explain the importance of non-cost factors, including environmental sustainability, in pricing practices

5. Explain how corporate social responsibility differs from corporate governance

This chapter describes how managers integrate relevant information about consumer demand at different prices to manage their costs to influence supply and earn a profit. Managers make pricing decisions about the products and services their companies deliver. These decisions affect the revenues a company earns, which must exceed total costs if profits are to be achieved. Consequently, determining current and forecasting future new product cost information are both highly relevant to making pricing decisions. There is no universal principle of relevant cost selection for product and service pricing. Customers demand different value propositions from different products and services, competition varies, influences of costs vary among products and services, and decisions differ greatly in both their time horizons and their contexts. Understanding relevant cost behaviour patterns as well as both cost and revenue drivers is central to profitable pricing decisions.

Economic theory indicates that companies should produce and sell units until the marginal revenue (the incremental revenue from selling an incremental unit based on the demand for a product) equals the marginal or variable cost to supply an incremental unit. In practice, what is key to profitability is that companies sell units at the price a customer is willing to pay.

MAJOR INFLUENCES ON PRICING

1 Discuss the major influences on both short- and long-run pricing decisions

Three pricing strategies are discussed in this chapter:

- ◆ Target pricing, where the price is based on what customers are willing to pay.
- ◆ Cost-plus, where a flat-rate percentage is added to the full cost of products.
- ◆ Life-cycle costing and pricing for each product.

None of these strategies is the best choice for all products or services. Customers, costs, and competitors as well as legislation and ability to pay will influence which of the three strategies is most appropriate. Increasingly, customers have enlarged the scope of their demands on manufacturers worldwide to consider the environmental costs of their outputs as well. Finally, pricing decisions also depend on the time horizon—relevant information for the short run will differ from relevant information for the long-run pricing decision. Some factors can be controlled by managers of a company and the negative consequences avoided, while others, such as the nature of the competition, are uncontrollable. In Chapter 12 it becomes apparent that pricing decisions are as complex as the output decisions considered in Chapter 11.

There are three major influences on pricing decisions: customers, competitors, and costs.

- ◆ **Customers.** Managers must always examine pricing problems through the eyes of their customers. A price increase may cause customers to reject a company's product and choose a competing or substitute product because they perceive the substitute provides more value or benefit in use for the price they are willing to pay. Availability, customization, and quality all affect willingness to pay.

   A second strategic consideration is the customer's ability to pay and corporate social responsibility. Pharmaceutical companies in particular, although they are for profit, price the same medications differently in different countries. HIV-AIDS is a high-profile example in which the price of medication in developing countries such as those in Africa is far lower than the identical medication in developed countries such as Canada. With its not-for-profit health-care system, Canada also pays less than its for-profit US counterpart for identical medications.

   These pricing decisions reflect in part the difference between full, variable, and throughput pricing strategies (see Chapter 9), which have long-term implications. Pharmaceutical companies have decided to trade off some profit to present themselves as compassionate and sensitive to the suffering their products are intended to alleviate. To those countries that can afford to pay full absorption cost, including the research and development of the pharmaceuticals used to combat HIV-AIDS, the price is far higher than to those countries which cannot. The strategic tradeoff between the intangible realization of corporate social responsibility and financial responsibility to shareholders has been made by these companies.

◆ **Costs.** Companies price products to exceed the costs of making them. The study of cost behaviour patterns gives insight into the income that results from different combinations of price and output quantities sold for a particular product. Companies with many product lines, however, may be unable to apply absorption costing to all of them. This is why understanding variable and throughput costing and the relevant information provided by their respective contribution margins is so important. When it comes to pricing in a competitive market, the best strategy may be to adopt a variable costing policy for some products but not others.

◆ **Competitors.** Competitors' reactions influence pricing decisions. At one extreme, a business without a rival in a given situation can set higher prices. This is a monopoly. Even where there are only a few rivals high prices can be charged, as in the oil industry. This is an oligopoly. At the other extreme, where there are many rivals, no single company can cause a price increase and must take the price the customers will pay. This is competition. In competitive markets one single company can lower its prices to temporarily capture more volume and start a price war. To sustain market share in the short run, its rivals must follow or provide to the customer an improved value proposition that justifies their higher prices.

Both economic theory and surveys of how executives actually make pricing decisions reveal that companies weigh customers, costs, and competitors differently. Companies selling commodity products such as steel, wheat, and rice have many competitors, each offering identical products. The market sets the price, but cost data can help these sellers decide on the output levels that best meet a company's particular profit objective.

In less competitive markets, where features can distinguish one product from another (for example, automobiles, mobile communication devices, flat-screen televisions, and laptop computers), managers have some discretion in setting prices. For these differentiated products the pricing decision depends on three factors:

◆ How much customers value the product.
◆ The costs of the product.
◆ The pricing strategies of competitors.

The price of a product or service is the outcome of the interaction between demand for the product or service and its supply. Customers influence prices through their effect on demand. Costs influence prices through their effect on supply. Competitors offer alternative or substitute products and thereby affect supply, demand, and price.

Competition spans international borders. For example, when companies have excess capacity in their domestic markets, they often take an aggressive pricing policy in their export markets. Today, managers readily take a global viewpoint, and it is increasingly common for them to consider both domestic and international rivals when making pricing decisions. In the global market, cost and pricing decisions are also affected by fluctuations in the exchange rates of currencies among different countries, as well as tax regimes. These considerations become extremely important for companies manufacturing components in different parts of the world and transferring them to a plant where they are assembled into the final product.

Competitor analysis takes different forms. Many companies, including Research In Motion (RIM), Rogers, Bombardier, and Bank of Montreal, have departments devoted to searching out information on their competitors' financial performance, patents, technologies, revenue and cost structures, and strategic alliances. Competitors themselves, their customers, suppliers, and even former employees are important sources of competitive intelligence. Another form of obtaining information is reverse engineering—a process of analyzing and tearing apart competitors' products—to incorporate the best features, materials, and technology in a company's own designs. Managers of a company who know about its rival's technology, plant capacity, and operating policies are able to estimate a rival's costs, which is valuable information in setting competitive prices.

PRODUCT COST CATEGORIES AND TIME HORIZON

Chapter 1 described customer satisfaction, continuous improvement, and the dual internal/external focus as important, newly evolving themes in management. Pricing is an area where these themes explicitly converge. For example, charging lower prices for high-quality products is important for customer satisfaction, an external focus. But when prices are lower, costs must be reduced as well. Continuous improvement, an internal focus, is one way to keep costs down.

When reducing costs, a company must consider costs in all six value-chain business functions, from R&D to customer service. In computing the costs within these functions that are relevant in a pricing decision, the time horizon of the decision is critical. Most pricing decisions are either short run or long run. Short-run decisions include both pricing for a one-time-only special order with no long-term implications and adjusting product mix and output volume in a competitive market.

The time horizon used to compute those costs that differ among the alternatives for short-run decisions is typically six months or less but sometimes as long as a year. Long-run decisions include pricing a product in a major market where price setting has considerable leeway. A time horizon of a year or longer is used when computing relevant costs for these long-run decisions. Many pricing decisions have both short-run and long-run implications. Two key differences affect pricing for the long run versus the short run:

◆ Fixed costs that remain unchanged in the short run—for example, the cost of permanently increasing or decreasing capacity—will be relevant only in the long run because they can be altered only over a long time horizon.

◆ Profit margins in long-run pricing decisions are often set to earn a reasonable return on investment. Short-run pricing is opportunistic, whereby prices are decreased when demand decreases and increased when demand increases.

We next examine short-run pricing decisions.

SHORT-RUN PRICING DECISIONS: A SPECIAL ORDER, RELEVANT COSTS

Consider a one-time-only special order from a customer to supply products for the next four months. Acceptance or rejection of the order will not affect the revenues (units sold or the selling price per unit) from existing sales outlets. The customer is unlikely to place any future sales orders.

Consider a short-run pricing decision facing the management team at Astel Computers. Datatech Corporation has asked Astel to bid on supplying 5,000 Provalue computers over the next three months. After this three-month period, Datatech is unlikely to place any future sales orders with Astel. Datatech will sell Provalue computers under its own brand name in regions and markets where Astel does not sell Provalue. Whether Astel accepts or rejects this order will not affect Astel's revenues—neither the units sold nor the selling price—from existing sales channels.

Before Astel can bid on Datatech's offer, Astel's managers must first estimate how much it will cost to supply the 5,000 computers. Similar to the Surf Gear example in Chapter 11, the relevant costs Astel's managers must focus on include all direct and indirect costs throughout the value chain that will change in total by accepting the one-time-only special order from Datatech. Astel's managers outline the relevant costs in the following table:

Direct materials ($460 × 5,000 computers)	$2,300,000
Direct manufacturing labour ($64 per computer × 5,000 computers)	320,000
Fixed costs of additional capacity to manufacture Provalue	250,000
Total costs	$2,870,000*

*No additional costs will be required for R&D, design, marketing, distribution, or customer service.

The relevant cost per computer is $574 ($2,870,000 ÷ 5,000). Therefore, any selling price above $574 will improve Astel's profitability in the short run. Astel's managers also know that one of its competitors with a highly efficient plant has significant idle capacity and is eager to win the Datatech contract. Armed with all this information, Astel's managers must set a bid price for a one-time order.

Astel manufactures two brands of laptops—Deskpoint and Provalue. Deskpoint is Astel's top-of-the-line product sold through computer dealers to large organizations and government accounts. Our analysis focuses on pricing Provalue, a less powerful machine sold through catalogues and mass merchandisers to individual consumers and small organizations.

The manufacturing costs of Provalue are calculated using the activity-based costing (ABC) approach described in Chapter 5. Astel has three direct manufacturing cost categories (direct materials, direct manufacturing labour, and direct machining costs) and three indirect manufacturing cost pools (ordering and receiving, testing and inspection, and rework) in its accounting system. Astel treats machining costs as a direct fixed cost of Provalue because it is manufactured on machines that are used for no other products. The following table summarizes the activity cost pools, the cost driver for each activity, and the cost per unit of the cost driver that Astel uses to allocate manufacturing overhead costs to products.

Manufacturing Activity	Description of Activity	Cost Driver	Cost per Unit of Cost Driver
1. Ordering and receiving	Placing orders, receiving, and paying for components	Number of orders	$80 per order
2. Testing and inspection	Testing components and final product	Testing hours	$2 per testing-hour
3. Rework	Correcting and fixing errors and defects	Units reworked	$40 per unit reworked

Astel uses a long-run time horizon to price Provalue. Over this horizon, Astel's management views direct materials costs and direct manufacturing labour costs as variable with respect to the units of Provalue produced, and manufacturing overhead costs as variable with respect to their chosen cost drivers. For example, ordering and receiving costs vary with the number of orders. Staff members responsible for placing orders can be reassigned or laid off in the long run if fewer orders need to be placed. Direct machining costs (rent paid on leased machines) do not vary over this time horizon for the relevant range of production; they are fixed long-run costs.

Astel has no beginning or ending inventory of Provalue in 2010 and manufactures and sells 150,000 units. Astel's decision team calculates Provalue's manufacturing costs using the following information (summarized in the spreadsheet on the next page), which indicates the resources used to manufacture Provalue in 2010.

The direct materials costs per finished unit of Provalue are $460. There are 22,500 orders placed to purchase the components required, and we assume that the Provalue has 450 components supplied by different suppliers. For each component 50 orders are placed to match the JIT production schedule. The direct manufacturing labour costs per finished unit of Provalue are $64. Although Astel manufactures several products, some equipment is used exclusively to manufacture Provalue, giving rise to direct fixed costs of $11,400,000. Astel has an 8% defect rate at the output level of 150,000 units; therefore, there are 12,000 rework units per year

	A	B	C	D	E	F	G	H
1				PROVALUE MANUFACTURING COST DATA				
2	Output Level: 150,000 units							
3		Cost					Quantity of	Cost
4		Driver	Quantity	Unit of	Quantity	Unit of	Cost Driver	Driver
5		(1)	(2)	Measure	(3)	Measure	(4) = (2) × (3)	Rate
6	**Direct Costs**							
7	Direct materials	No. of kits	1.0	kit per output unit	150,000	output units	150,000	$460
8	Direct manufacturing labour (DMLH)	DMLH	3.2	DMLH per output unit	150,000	output units	480,000	$ 20
9	Direct machining, fixed (DMH)	DMH hours	2.0	DMH per output unit	150,000	output units	300,000	$ 38
10	**Overhead Costs**							
11	Ordering and receiving	No. of orders	50.0	orders per component	450	components	22,500	$ 80
12	Testing and inspection (TH)	Testing hours	30.0	TH per output unit	150,000	output units	4,500,000	$ 2
13	Rework (RMH)	Rework hours	2.5	RMH per defective unit*	12,000	defective units	30,000	$ 40
14	Defect rate				8.0%	defect rate		
15	*8% defect rate × 150,000 output units = 12,000 defective units							

(8% × 150,000 = 12,000). The testing hours for inspection of the Provalue are 4,500,000, or 30 hours per unit (30 hours/unit × 150,000 units = 4,500,000 hours).

Exhibit 12-1 indicates that the total cost of manufacturing Provalue is $102,000,000 and the manufacturing cost per unit is $680. Manufacturing, however, is only one business function of the value chain. To set long-run prices that will cover all the costs of doing business and achieve a target profit, Astel's managers must calculate the *full cost* of producing and selling Provalue.

For its nonmanufacturing business functions in the value chain, Astel's managers identify direct costs and choose cost drivers and cost pools for indirect costs that measure cause-and-effect relationships. Astel's managers allocate costs to Provalue based on the quantity of cost-driver units that Provalue uses. Exhibit 12-2 summarizes the operating income for Provalue for 2010 based on an activity-based analysis of costs in all business functions. (For brevity, supporting calculations for nonmanufacturing business functions are not given.) Astel earns $15 million from Provalue, or $100 per unit sold in 2010.

STRATEGIC AND OTHER FACTORS IN SHORT-RUN PRICING

In choosing how much to bid, Astel's managers must be strategic. If, based on its market intelligence, Astel believes its competitor will bid between $596 and $610 per computer, Astel could bid $595 per computer and still increase operating income by $105,000 (relevant revenues, $595 × 5,000 = $2,975,000 minus relevant costs, $2,870,000). Management's strategy is to bid as high above $574 as possible while remaining lower than competitors' bids.

Astel's managers also carefully reconsidered the probability Datatech would decide to undercut Astel's selling price in the current markets. If Astel's managers believe this is a significant risk, the relevant costs of the bidding decision should

EXHIBIT 12-1
Manufacturing Costs of Provalue for 2010 Using Activity-Based Costing

	A	B	C
		Total	
		Manufacturing	
		Costs for	Manufacturing
		150,000 Units	Cost per Unit
		(1)	(2) = (1) ÷ 150,000
6	Direct manufacturing costs:		
7	Direct materials costs (150,000 units × $460)	$ 69,000,000	$460
8	Direct manufacturing labour costs (150,000 units × $64)	9,600,000	64
9	Direct machining costs (fixed costs of $11,400,000)	11,400,000	76
10	Direct manufacturing costs	90,000,000	600
11	Manufacturing overhead costs:		
12	Ordering and receiving costs (22,500 orders × $80)	1,800,000	12
13	Testing and inspection costs (4,500,000 hours × $2)	9,000,000	60
14	Rework costs (12,000 units × $100)	1,200,000	8
15	Manufacturing overhead costs	12,000,000	80
16	Total manufacturing costs	$102,000,000	$680

EXHIBIT 12-2
Product Profitability of Provalue for 2010 Using Value-Chain Activity-Based Costing

	A	B	C
		Total Amounts	
		for 150,000 Units	Per Unit
		(1)	(2) = (1) ÷ 150,000
4	Revenue	$150,000,000	$1,000
5	Cost of goods sold[a] (from Exhibit 12-1)	102,000,000	680
6	Operating costs[b]		
7	R&D costs	5,400,000	36
8	Design costs of product and process	6,000,000	40
9	Marketing costs	15,000,000	100
10	Distribution costs	3,600,000	24
11	Customer-service costs	3,000,000	20
12	Operating costs	33,000,000	220
13	Full cost of the product	135,000,000	900
14	Operating income	$ 15,000,000	$ 100
15			
16	[a]Cost of goods sold = Total manufacturing costs because there is no beginning or ending inventory of Provalue in 2010		
17	[b]Numbers for operating-cost line items are assumed without supporting calculations.		

include the contribution margin lost on sales to existing customers. If Astel's managers view the threat to its existing business from accepting the Datatech order to be serious enough, they may decide not to bid for the Datatech business, or they may quote Datatech a price close to the price Astel charges its other customers. After carefully evaluating the situation, Astel's managers conclude that Datatech will not undercut prices to Astel's customers, so Astel makes a bid to supply Provalue computers at a price of $595 each.

Astel's short-run pricing decision focused on identifying a sufficiently low price at which Astel would still make a profit. That's because we assumed (a) Astel has access to extra capacity and (b) a competitor with an efficient plant and idle capacity was likely to make a low bid. However, short-run pricing does not always work this way. Companies may experience strong demand for their products in the short run, but they may have limited capacity. In these cases, companies strategically increase prices in the short run to as much as the market will bear. We observe high short-run prices in the case of new products or new models of older products, such as microprocessors, computer chips, cellular telephones, and software.

Many pricing decisions are made for the long run. Buyers—whether a person buying a litre of milk; a construction company, such as Bechtel Corporation, buying a fleet of tractors; or General Foods Corporation buying audit services—prefer stable prices over an extended time horizon. A stable price reduces the need for continuous monitoring of suppliers' prices. Greater price stability also improves planning and builds long-run buyer–seller relationships.

Obtaining accurate product cost information is essential to a manager making a pricing decision. In industries such as oil and gas and mining, competitive forces set the price for a product, and knowledge of long-run product costs can guide decisions about entering or remaining in the market. In other industries, such as specialized machines, appliances, and automobiles, managers have some control over the price charged for a product, and long-run product costs can be used as a base for setting that price.

MyAccountingLab

ASSESS YOUR MASTERY

To check your understanding of the material in Learning Objective ❶, go to the *Mastery Questions* section at the end of this chapter and complete Learning Objective ❶ questions 1, 2, and 3.

TARGET PRICING USING TARGET COSTING

❷ Understand the pricing of products using the target-costing approach

ALTERNATIVE LONG-RUN PRICING APPROACHES

The starting point for pricing decisions can be

◆ Market-based (target pricing)
◆ Cost-based (also called cost-plus)
◆ Life-cycle

The market-based approach to pricing *starts* by asking: Given what our customers want and how our competitors will react to what we do, what price should we charge? The cost-based approach to pricing *starts* by asking: What does it cost us to make this product, and hence what price should we charge that will recoup our costs and produce a desired profit? Both approaches consider customers, competitors, and costs. Only their starting points differ.

Companies may take one of two approaches. Some companies start by anticipating customer and competitor reactions and then examine costs—the market-based approach. In very competitive markets (for example, steel, petroleum products, wheat, and rice) the market-based approach is logical. The items produced or services provided by one company are almost identical to those produced or provided by others, so companies have no influence over the prices customers are willing to pay.

In contrast, other companies first look at costs and then consider customers or competitors—the cost-based approach. Companies in non-competitive markets favour this approach because they do not need to respond either to competitors' prices or consumers' reactions. In industries where there is more product differentiation (for example, automobiles, consumer electronics, management consulting, and professional services), firms have more discretion over prices, products, and services.

Notice that all companies consider all three factors but their starting points differ. A final decision on price, product, and service is made after evaluating these external influences on pricing along with the costs to produce and sell the product. We will begin by considering the market-based approach.

TARGET PRICING AND TARGET COSTING

Market-based pricing starts with a target price. A **target price per unit** is the estimated price for a product or service that potential customers will pay. This estimate is based on an understanding of customers' perceived value for a product or service and how competitors will price competing products or services. A **target operating income per unit** is the operating income that a company wants to earn on each unit of a product (or service) sold (see Chapter 2). The operating income is calculated by:

◆ agreeing upon an operating margin percentage (Chapter 3: operating income per unit ÷ target price per unit = operating margin percentage)

◆ multiplying the target price per unit by (1 – operating margin percentage) to calculate the target cost.

A company's sales and marketing organization, through close contact and interaction with customers, is usually in the best position to identify customers' needs and their perceived value for a product or service. Companies also conduct market research studies about product features that customers want and the prices they are willing to pay for those features. Increasingly, through statistical analyses of data (often referred to as *data mining*) provided by cards such as Air Miles and personal profiles on social networking services such as Facebook, companies identify the characteristics of their typical customers and how well these match with their intended customer base.

This target pricing approach is particularly difficult when products are highly differentiated and have a very short consumer life cycle. Personal electronic devices are one example where innovation in technology drives the introduction of audio-visual playback devices, cell phones, devices like the BlackBerry, and products combining attributes of all three. The life cycle prior to the introduction of a new product is approximately six months. The process of target pricing requires a lot of retracing between relevant customer-preference data and value engineering (see Exhibit 12-3). One result may be that the operating margin percentage (OM%) must change and Astel would have to revisit whether the new OM% is adequate to support this project. This is an example of an influence pair (Chapter 11), where one decision changes a previous decision.

The process itself is Bayesian and recursive, which means people will revisit prior decisions as new data become available (refer to Exhibit 11-1, p. 530). In reality, as more relevant information is acquired, it will influence previous decisions about probable outcomes. The customer's value proposition is most definitely relevant information because a likely target operating income will be estimated. To estimate target operating income requires estimating target revenue, which in turn requires estimating the price and the volume.

The unit price and total volume of a product or service will depend on how closely the supplier can meet the customer's value proposition and still earn a reasonable profit. The unit price the customer is willing to pay is another piece of relevant information. This will determine the extent to which a company will make a commitment to product development. If the decision is to go ahead with development, then the forecast price the customer is willing to pay becomes the target price. The company also needs to estimate the market size and its share of that market

EXHIBIT 12-3
Target Pricing and Costing Decision Process

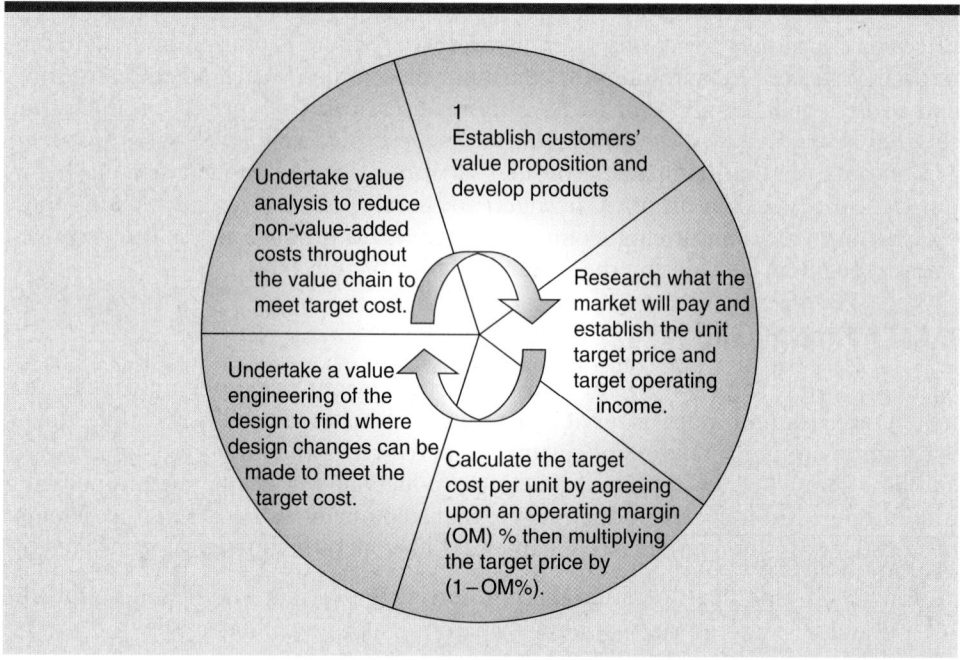

(see Chapter 16) to obtain the likely volume and therefore the target revenue from the product.

A **target cost per unit** is the estimated long-run cost per unit of a product (or service) that, when sold at the target price, enables the company to achieve the target operating income per unit. Having this understanding of customers and competitors has become important for three reasons:

◆ Competition from lower-cost producers has meant that prices cannot be increased.

◆ Products are on the market for shorter periods of time, leaving less time and opportunity to recover from pricing mistakes.

◆ Customers have become more knowledgeable and demand quality products at reasonable prices.

The target pricing process begins with the customer. Astel's team must determine the attributes of the laptop that will meet the needs of potential customers. For example, the existing Provalue design accommodates various upgrades that can make the laptop run faster and perform calculations more quickly. It also comes with special audio features. Customer feedback indicates that customers do not need Provalue's extra features. They want Astel to redesign Provalue into a no-frills laptop and sell it at a much lower price.

At this point the team can reach a preliminary agreement on the target operating income. It is straightforward to fix operating income as a percentage of the target price. This percentage is the operating margin percentage, introduced in Chapter 3. OM% = operating income ÷ revenue. The *target cost* is derived from the target price and OM%, and if full absorption costing is appropriate then COGS and period costs (operating expenses) will be included in the target cost. If variable costing is appropriate, then only the *variable* COGS and period costs will be included for this product development project.

The current design must be changed, and customers have pointed the way to redesign that might also reduce costs. A thorough **value analysis** will help the team pinpoint how to eliminate superfluous design features, but this is an absorption costing challenge involving all business functions. Value analysis focuses on the product design stage, where there is the greatest opportunity to change design, materials, and manufacturing processes to reduce costs. For example, the reliability of the computer can be enhanced by using a simpler motherboard. The newly designed computer will not support the top-of-the-line video card, but this is of little concern to Astel because video quality is not important to Astel's targeted customers. The decisions made at the design stage will lock in some costs, for example the lower cost of the simpler motherboard. This is an example of how a decision will affect a future outcome, the target cost.

Value engineering encompasses the entire value chain of all business functions to determine where non-value-added costs can be eliminated.[1] Using the approach of value engineering, Astel can review the business functions with the goal of eliminating or at least reducing all the activities with no value added to the customer. Again the customer drives this value engineering process. A value-added cost is a cost that customers perceive as adding value, or utility (usefulness), to a product or service. For Provalue, value-added attributes include the laptop's features and its price. Activities and the costs of these activities do not always fall neatly into value-added or non-value-added categories. Some costs fall in the grey area in between, and include both value-added and non-value-added components.

UNDERSTANDING TARGET PRICING FOR PROVALUE

Astel's initial market research establishes that $800 is the most probable target price for Provalue under current economic and competitive conditions. The attributes preferred by customers exclude both the audio features and the ease of upgrading to increase the speed of the laptop. The target market prefers reliability in a laptop that can perform basic input, illustration, arithmetic, and communication functions.

The market is very competitive, however, and the most probable response to a new product introduction is that competitors will lower their prices to $850, which will be less than the current unit price estimate of $1,000 for Provalue. Astel would beat the lower price and estimates the most probable long-term price for Provalue will be $800 per unit, not $1,000. The good news, however, is that the top marketing executives on Provalue's team expect that they will win this price war and capture more market share, selling 200,000 rather than only 150,000 units.

To gauge how competitors might react to a prospective price, a company needs to understand competitors' technologies, products or services, costs, and financial conditions. For example, knowing competitors' technologies and products helps a company (a) to evaluate how distinctive its own products or services will be in the market and (b) to determine the prices it might be able to charge as a result of being distinctive. Where does a company obtain information about its competitors? Usually from customers, suppliers, and employees of competitors; large companies such as Chrysler employ people whose sole purpose is to analyze competitors. Another source of information is *reverse engineering*—that is, disassembling and analyzing competitors' products to determine product designs and materials and to become acquainted with the technologies competitors use.

The top management team has agreed on an operating margin percentage of 10%, given the current economic and competitive conditions. The target cost percentage must be 90% (100% − 10% = 90%) and the target cost is therefore $720 per unit based on absorption costing ($800 × 90% = $720). The next task is to design a Provalue II that can be manufactured at or below the target cost. For Astel this is a challenge because its current internal information has indicated the current absorption cost for the product will be $900 per unit.

The goal is to find ways to reduce the cost per unit of Provalue by $180, from $900 to $720, yet include the attributes and reliability preferred by customers. The challenge is to achieve the target cost through value engineering and value analysis. The data are summarized as follows: The attributes of a product will drive its design, and generally the simpler the design that meets the customer's value proposition by providing the number and quality of attributes, the lower the cost will be. Many

[1]B. R. A. McConachy, "Decision Process for Value Management Proposals," *2000AACE International Transactions* ABI/INFORM Global (2000): pp. RISK 11.01–11.06.

decisions about insourcing and outsourcing will be made to establish where non-value-added costs can be eliminated and the target cost achieved.

Total target revenues	=	$800 × 200,000 = $160,000,000
Operating margin %	=	10.00% × $800 = $80 per unit
Total cost %	=	90.00% × $800 = $720 per unit
Current absorption cost	=	$900 (from Exhibit 12-2)
Target reduction	=	$180 per unit

Astel's target cost per unit is $180 lower than the existing absorption cost per unit. To achieve the target cost per unit and the target operating income per unit, the organization must improve its products and processes. Before undertaking a pilot to construct the new product, the team needs to validate its calculations and continue to gather relevant information prior to implementing manufacture and launch of the product.

THINKING CRITICALLY

What costs are relevant for target costing? Explain in a sentence or two. Read on for an analysis of this topic.

Astel is considering a new product introduction, which is a long-term decision. New design may require new, different capacity and labour skills or at the very least changes in existing capacity management. New suppliers may be needed as well as new information added to the MIS. *All* costs, both variable and fixed, are relevant because the company must recover all the costs of the project. If Astel has no alternative but to succeed in this project and its best estimates indicate it cannot compete, then the company's best alternative is to shut down. Regarding the shutting-down alternative, all costs, whether fixed or variable, are relevant.

VALUE-ANALYSIS AND CROSS-FUNCTIONAL TEAMS

Usually a value-analysis team consists of top management experts in marketing, product design and engineering, process improvement, supply-chain management, distribution, customer service, and management accounting. The team evaluates the impact of design innovations and modifications on all business functions of the value chain. They choose modifications that have the greatest value to their customers relative to the costs required to provide those features. Here are some of the team's ideas:

- Use a simpler, more reliable motherboard without complex features.
- Design Provalue so that various parts snap-fit together rather than solder together, to decrease direct manufacturing labour-hours, related direct materials costs, and indirect MOH such as utilities costs.
- Simplify the Provalue design and use fewer components to decrease ordering and receiving costs and also decrease testing and inspection costs.
- Design Provalue to be lighter and smaller to reduce distribution and packaging costs.
- Design Provalue to reduce repair costs at customer sites to lower customer-service costs.

Key concepts in value analysis are *cost incurrence* and *locked-in costs*. **Cost incurrence** arises when a resource is sacrificed or consumed. Financial reporting systems recognize and record costs only when costs are incurred, and this transactions logic ensures reliability. Astel's costing system, for example, recognizes the direct materials costs of the finished laptop as each unit of Provalue is assembled. But Provalue's direct materials costs per unit are determined much earlier, when designers finalize the components that will go into Provalue. Direct materials costs per unit of Provalue are *locked in* (or *designed in*) at the product design stage. **Locked-in costs (designed-in costs)** are those costs that have not yet been incurred but that will be incurred in the future on the basis of decisions that have already been made. In Exhibit 11-1 this is illustrated in the second influence pair, where the design decision affects the probable cost of direct materials incurred in the future.

Locked-in costs become unavoidable. For example, rework costs incurred during manufacturing could be locked in by a faulty design. Similarly, in the software industry, costs of producing software are often locked in at the design and analysis stage. Costly and difficult-to-fix errors that appear during coding and testing are frequently locked in by bad designs.

Other examples of how Astel's design decisions affect costs include the following:

◆ Design decisions influence direct materials costs through the choices of printed circuit boards and add-on features used in Provalue. Better designs also reduce both product failures in the plant and the time it takes to rework defective products.

◆ Designing Provalue so that it is easy to manufacture and easy to assemble decreases direct manufacturing labour costs. For example, designing Provalue so that various parts snap-fit together (rather than having various parts soldered together) saves manufacturing labour time.

◆ Designing Provalue with fewer components reduces ordering and materials-handling costs.

◆ Simplifying the Provalue design decreases the time required for testing and inspection.

◆ Designing Provalue to reduce the need for repairs as well as the time it takes to service and repair Provalue at customer sites reduces customer service costs.

Costs are *not* always locked in at the design stage. In some industries (such as bulk chemical manufacturing, legal, and consulting) costs are locked in and incurred at about the same time. If costs are not locked in early, cost reduction can be achieved right up to the time when costs are incurred. In these cases, costs are lowered through improved operating efficiency and productivity (for example, reducing the time it takes to do a task) rather than better design. Many companies combine value engineering with *kaizen*, or continuous improvement methods that seek to improve productivity and eliminate waste during production and delivery of products.

Management accountants use their understanding of the technical and business aspects of the entire value chain to quickly estimate cost savings and to explain to the team the cost implications of alternative design choices. These cost estimates are based on the parts and processes required by the new design. Having finished the value analysis, Astel's management team feels it has two alternatives: respond less aggressively to its competitors, or replace Provalue with a newly designed computer that has fewer complex features and therefore is less costly to make. Astel decides to go with the second alternative.

Exhibit 12-4 illustrates how the locked-in cost curve and the cost-incurrence curve might appear in the case of Provalue. (The numbers underlying the graph are assumed.) The bottom curve plots the cumulative costs per unit incurred in different business functions. The top curve plots the cumulative costs locked in. Both curves deal with the same total cumulative costs per unit. The graph emphasizes the wide divergence between the time when costs are locked in and the time when those costs are incurred. In our example, once the product and processes are designed, nearly 87% ($780 ÷ $900) of the unit costs of Provalue are locked in when only about 8% ($76 ÷ $900) of the unit costs are actually incurred. For example, at the end of the design stage, costs such as direct materials, direct manufacturing labour, direct machining, and many manufacturing, marketing, distribution, and customer-service overheads are all locked in. To reduce total costs, Astel must act to modify the design before costs get locked in.

EXHIBIT 12-4
Pattern of Cost Incurrence and Locked-in Costs for Provalue

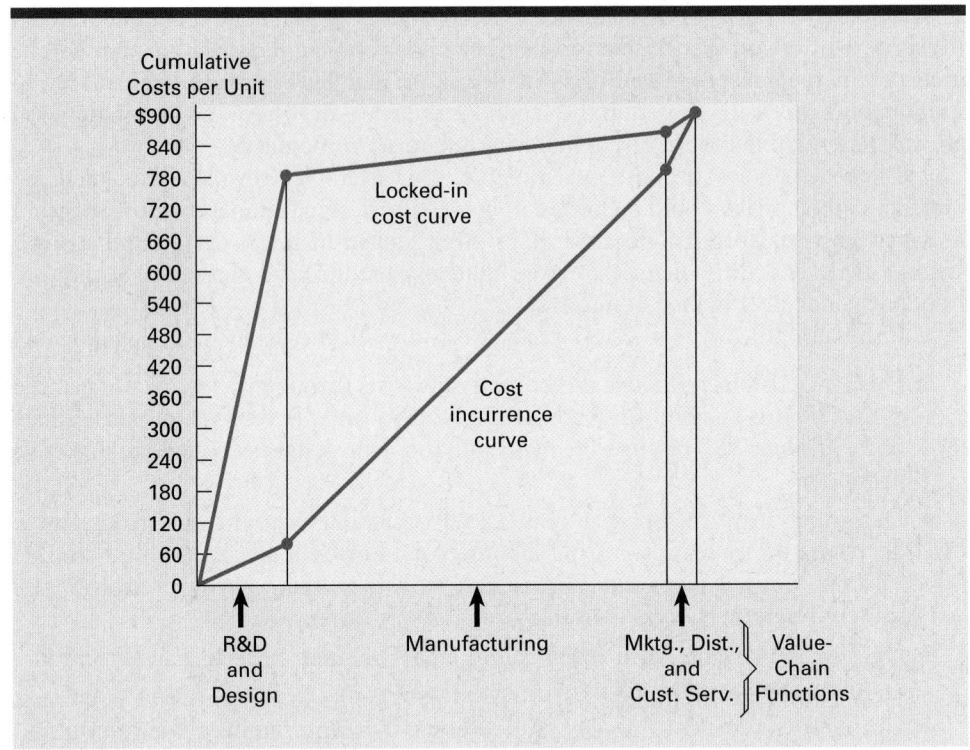

VALUE ENGINEERING

In the Provalue example, direct materials, direct manufacturing labour, and machining costs are value-added costs; ordering and testing costs fall in the grey area (customers perceive some portion, but not all, of these costs as necessary for adding value); and rework costs are non-value-added costs. Astel's goal is to reduce and, if possible, eliminate non-value-added costs such as ordering, quality control, and rework costs by reducing the defect rate.

Eliminating or reducing the defect rate may entail process improvement, but another reason to re-examine the production process is the anticipated volume of production. The higher the volume produced and sold, the lower will be Astel's fixed-cost allocation rate per unit and the more readily it will achieve its target cost. But this brings with it the temptation to produce excess inventory, especially under absorption costing. Changing performance evaluation can reduce or eliminate this perverse incentive. It may also be possible to design Provalue in a way that reduces the proportion of fixed costs.[2] This illustrates the interdependence among value-chain functions where the interdependence is caused by conflicting policies.

Reducing variable costs requires reducing unit input costs, which may be achieved by good negotiation or changing suppliers, or by reducing the quantity of the input consumed. Other factors such as appropriate training, production scheduling, and maintenance also contribute to reduced direct labour costs. The variable direct and indirect costs throughout the value chain are interdependent. For example, replacing the motherboard with a simpler, less expensive component will reduce direct material costs per unit but may require a more complex assembly that will increase variable manufacturing labour costs. In itself the more complex assembly may cause an increase in defects. This is an example of one outcome, driven

[2]P. Woodlock, "Does It Matter How Targeted Costs Are Achieved?" *The Journal of Corporate Accounting & Finance*, 11.3 (2000): 43–52.

Extreme Target Pricing at IKEA

IKEA is the world's largest furniture retailer with 186 stores in 31 countries. Products are known for unpronounceable names, flat packaging, and do-it-yourself assembly instructions. IKEA uses aggressive target pricing and relentless cost management. Their prices typically run 30% to 50% below the competition. IKEA identifies gaps in the current product portfolio, surveys competitors to discover the market price, and then sets a target price that is 30% to 50% less than the market. A brief describing the new target cost and basic product specifications is submitted for bidding among IKEA's 1,800 suppliers in 55 countries who compete to present the lowest bid. Finally, internal and freelance designers compete to determine the product's final design based on price, function, and materials to be used. This value-engineering process promotes volume-based cost efficiencies throughout the design and production process. All IKEA products can be shipped unassembled in flat packages, which reduces shipping costs to 1/6th that of competitors. IKEA stores' customer service is sparse, with few salespeople and no free product delivery. Founder Ingvar Kamprad once noted, "Waste of resources is a mortal sin at IKEA. Expensive solutions are often a sign of mediocrity, and an idea without a price tag is never acceptable."

Sources: L. Margonelli, "How IKEA Designs Its Sexy Price Tags," *Business 2.0* (October 2002); R. Cooper and W. Chew, "Control Tomorrow's Costs Through Today's Designs," *Harvard Business Review* (January–February 1996); Ingvar Kamprad and IKEA, Harvard Business School case number 9–F390–132; O. Burkeman, "The Miracle of Älmhult," *The Guardian* (June 17, 2004).

externally by customer preference, affecting two other outcomes driven internally by the consumption of labour in a more complex process.

Value engineering and target costing have some undesirable effects if these processes are mismanaged:

♦ Decreased morale if employees fail to attain performance targets.

♦ A poorly designed product as the cross-functional team compromises among itself on the various customer attributes.

♦ A protracted development cycle causing a missed market opportunity.

♦ Conflict among business functions as the goal is to remove non-value-added costs wherever they arise. The burden of cost reduction will be unequal.

Strong employee participation in the new project and realistic expectations regarding the difficulties of full manufacturing of new products using new processes will encourage employees. Keeping the focus on the customer's priorities among the attributes will reduce the problem of compromises within the pricing team. Disciplined progress towards the goal of a timely introduction of a new product will reduce the problem of paralysis by analysis. Nourishing a co-operative corporate culture of cost reduction and providing incentives to celebrate each improvement will reduce conflict.

ACHIEVING THE TARGET COST PER UNIT FOR PROVALUE

Astel's value-analysis team focused on selecting a design to reduce the costs of Provalue. The new product design is sufficiently different that it acquires a new name. Astel decides to discontinue the existing Provalue and introduce Provalue II. Provalue II has fewer components than does Provalue and is easier to manufacture and test. The spreadsheet on page 600 compares the direct costs and the manufacturing overhead costs and cost drivers of Provalue and Provalue II. In place of the

PROVALUE MANUFACTURING COST DATA

Output Level: 150,000

	Cost Driver (1)	Quantity (2)	Unit of Measure	Quantity (3)	Unit of Measure	Total Quantity of Cost Driver (4) = (2) × (3)	Input Cost Driver Rate
Direct Costs							
Direct materials	No. of kits	1.0	kit per output unit	150,000	output units	150,000	$460
Direct manufacturing labour (DMLH)	DMLH	3.2	DMLH per output unit	150,000	output units	480,000	$ 20
Direct machining-fixed (DMH)	DMH hours	2.0	DMH per output unit	150,000	output units	300,000	$ 38
Overhead Costs							
Ordering and receiving	No. of orders	50.0	orders per component	450	components	22,500	$ 80
Testing and inspection (TH)	Testing hours	30.0	TH per output unit	150,000	output units	4,500,000	$ 2
Rework (RMH)	Rework hours	2.5	RMH per defective unit*	12,000	defective units	30,000	$ 40
Defect rate				8.0%	defect rate		

*8% defect rate × 1500,000 output units = 12,000 defective units

PROVALUE II MANUFACTURING COST DATA

Output Level: 200,000

	Cost Driver (1)	Quantity (2)	Unit of Measure	Quantity (3)	Unit of Measure	Total Quantity of Cost Driver (4) = (2) × (3)	Input Cost Driver Rate
Direct Costs							
Direct materials	No. of kits	1.0	kit per output unit	200,000	output units	200,000	$385
Direct manufacturing labour (DMLH)	DMLH	2.65	DMLH per output unit	200,000	output units	530,000	$ 20
Direct machining - fixed (DMH)	DMH hours	1.5	DMH per output unit	200,000	output units	300,000	$ 38
Overhead Costs							
Ordering and receiving	No. of orders	50.0	orders per component	425	components	21,250	$ 80
Testing and inspection (TH)	Testing hours	15.0	TH per output unit	200,000	output units	3,000,000	$ 2
Rework (RMH)	Rework hours	2.5	RMH per defective unit†	13,000	defective units	32,500	$ 40
Defect rate				6.5%	defect rate		

†6.5% defect rate × 200,000 output units = 13,000 defective units

150,000 Provalue units manufactured and sold in 2010, Astel expects to make and sell 200,000 Provalue II units in 2011.

Note that value-engineering activities reduce both value-added and non-value-added costs. For example, direct manufacturing labour cost per unit, a value-added cost, is reduced by designing a product that requires fewer direct manufacturing labour-hours (the cost driver for direct manufacturing labour costs). Rework cost per unit, a non-value-added cost, is reduced by simplifying the design to reduce defects during manufacturing and hence rework-hours (the cost driver for rework costs).

Exhibit 12-5 presents the target manufacturing costs of Provalue II, assuming no change in the cost per unit of the cost drivers. (The Problem for Self-Study on page 618 considers changes in the cost per unit of the cost drivers.) For comparison, Exhibit 12-5 also reproduces the manufacturing costs per unit of Provalue from Exhibit 12-1. Exhibit 12-5 shows that the new design is expected to reduce the manufacturing cost per unit by $140, to $540 from $680. A similar analysis (not presented) estimates the expected effect of the new design on costs in other value-chain business functions.

Exhibit 12-6 shows that the estimated full product cost per unit equals $720—the target cost per unit for Provalue II. Astel's goal is to sell Provalue II at the target price, achieve target cost, and earn the target operating income.

EXHIBIT 12-5
Target Manufacturing Costs of Provalue II for 2011

A	B	C	D
1		PROVALUE II		PROVALUE
2		Estimated	Estimated	Manufacturing
3		Manufacturing Costs	Manufacturing	Cost per Unit
4		for 200,000 Units	Cost per Unit	(Exhibit 12-1)
5		(1)	(2) = (1) ÷ 200,000	(3)
6 Direct manufacturing costs:				
7 Direct material costs (200,000 units × $385 per unit)	$ 77,000,000	$385.00	$460.00
8 Direct manufacturing labour costs (300,000 hours × $20 per hour)	10,600,000	$ 53.00	64.00
9 Direct machining costs (fixed) (530,000 machine-hours × $38 per machine-hour)	11,400,000	57.00	76.00
10 Direct manufacturing costs	99,000,000	495.00	600.00
11 Manufacturing overhead costs:				
12 Ordering and receiving costs (21,250 orders × $80 per order)	1,700,000	8.50	12.00
13 Testing and inspection costs (3,000,000 hours × $2 per hour)	6,000,000	30.00	60.00
14 Rework costs (32,500 rework hours × $40 per hour)	1,300,000	6.50	8.00
15 Manufacturing overhead costs	9,000,000	45.00	80.00
16 Total manufacturing costs	$108,000,000	$540.00	$680.00

EXHIBIT 12-6
Target Product Profitability of Provalue II in 2011

	A	B	C
		Estimated	**Estimated**
		Total Amounts	**Total Amount**
		for 200,000 Units	**per Unit**
		(1)	**(2) = (1) ÷ 200,000**
5	Revenues	$160,000,000	$800
6	Cost of goods sold[a] (from Exhibit 12-5)	108,000,000	540
7	Operating costs[b]		
8	R&D costs	4,000,000	20
9	Design costs of product and process	6,000,000	30
10	Marketing costs	18,000,000	90
11	Distribution costs	4,400,000	22
12	Customer-service costs	3,600,000	18
13	Total operating costs	36,000,000	180
14	Full cost of the product	144,000,000	720
15	Operating income	$ 16,000,000	$ 80
16			
17	[a]Cost of goods sold = Total manufacturing costs because there is no beginning or inventory for Provalue II in 2011.		
18	[b]Numbers of operating-cost line items are assumed without supporting calculations		

ALTERNATIVE PRICING STRATEGIES: COST-PLUS AND LIFE CYCLE

Contrast pricing of products using the cost-plus approach, pricing of products using life-cycle budgeting, and pricing of products using the target-pricing approach

In the previous section, Astel used an external market-based approach in its long-run pricing decisions. One alternative strategy has an internal focus to determine a cost-based price. This is the cost-plus pricing strategy. Managers can turn to numerous pricing formulas based on cost. The starting point is not relevant information about attributes and price but rather costs. The general formula for setting a price adds a markup to the cost base:

Cost base	$	X
Markup component		Y
Prospective selling price		$X + Y

Consider a cost-based pricing formula that Astel could use for Provalue II. Assume that Astel's engineers have redesigned Provalue into Provalue II as described earlier and that Astel uses a 12% markup on the full product cost per unit in developing the prospective selling price.

Cost base (full product cost per unit, from Exhibit 12-6)	$720.00
Markup component (12% × $720)	86.40
Prospective selling price	$806.40

The markup was obtained by first estimating the **target rate of return on investment (ROI).** The target ROI is the target operating income that an organization must earn divided by invested capital. Invested capital in this chapter is defined as total assets (long-term or fixed assets plus current assets). Companies usually specify their target ROI. Suppose Astel's (pretax) target ROI is 18%.

Assume that the capital investment needed for Provalue II is $96 million. The target operating income that Astel must earn from Provalue II can then be calculated as follows:

Invested capital	$96,000,000
Target rate of return on investment	18%
Total target operating income (18% × $96,000,000)	$17,280,000
Target operating income per unit of Provalue II ($17,280,000 ÷ 200,000 units)	$ 86.40

The calculation indicates that Astel would like to earn a target operating income of $86.40 on each unit of Provalue II. The $86.40 expressed as a percentage of the full product cost per unit of $720 equals 12% ($86.40 ÷ $720).

The ROI cost-plus pricing method is often used when prices are regulated. In Canada examples include milk, hydro-electric power, and telecommunications. The government regulators examine the absorption costs of the supplier and negotiate a target ROI. The new price is established on this cost-plus basis for a specified time period with periodic, regulated increases. Suppliers may not charge consumers a rate higher than the contracted rate.

Do not confuse the 18% target ROI with the 12% markup percentage. The 18% target rate of return on investment expresses Astel's expected operating income as a percentage of investment. The 12% markup expresses operating income per unit as a percentage of the full product cost per unit. Astel establishes the target ROI and calculates its dollar value for the Provalue project, then determines the markup percentage on the cost base required to obtain the dollar value of ROI.

Companies sometimes find it difficult to determine the capital invested to support a product. Computing invested capital requires allocations of investments in equipment and buildings (used for design, production, marketing, distribution, and customer service) to individual products—a difficult and sometimes arbitrary task. Some companies therefore prefer to use alternative cost bases and markup percentages that do not require calculations of invested capital to set price.

ALTERNATIVE COST-PLUS METHODS

We illustrate these alternatives using the Astel example. Exhibit 12-7 separates the cost per unit for each value-chain business function into its variable and fixed components (without providing details of the calculations). The following table illustrates some alternative cost bases and markup percentages.

Cost Base	Estimated Cost per Unit of Provalue II (1)	Markup Percentage (2)	Markup Component for Provalue II (3) = (1) × (2)	Forecast Selling Price For Provalue II (4) = (1) + (3)
Variable manufacturing cost	$483.00	65%	$313.95	$796.95
Variable product cost	547.00	45	246.15	793.15
Manufacturing cost (COGS)	540.00	50	270.00	810.00
Absorption cost	720.00	12	86.40	806.40

To illustrate the markup calculations, we have assumed (but not derived) the markup percentages in the table. The different cost bases and markup percentages that we use in the table give prospective selling prices that are relatively close to one another. In practice, a company will choose a cost base that it regards as reliable, and a markup percentage on the basis of its experience in pricing products, to recover its costs and earn a desired return on investment. For example, a company may choose a full product cost base if it is unsure about variable and fixed cost distinctions.

EXHIBIT 12-7
Estimated Cost Structure of Provalue II for 2011

Business Function	Estimated Variable Cost per Unit	Estimated Fixed Cost per Unit[a]	Business-Function Cost per Unit
R&D	$ 8	$ 12	$ 20
Design of product/process	10	20	30
Manufacturing	483	57	540
Marketing	25	65	90
Distribution	13	9	22
Customer service	8	10	18
Total	$547	$173	$720
	↑	↑	↑
	Per-unit variable cost of the product	Per-unit fixed cost of the product	Per-unit full cost of the product

[a]Based on budgeted annual capacity of 200,000 units.

THINKING CRITICALLY

Why do the markup percentages vary? Explain in a sentence or two. Read on for an analysis of this topic.

The markup percentages in the table vary a great deal, from a high of 65% on variable manufacturing costs to a low of 12% on absorption costs. The reason is that the company still must cover all costs even though it is using variable COGS as its cost base. The higher the operating leverage (see Chapter 3) the higher are fixed costs, both COGS and period, as a percentage of total costs. To set a price high enough to cover both total period costs and fixed COGS requires that a higher percentage of variable costs be added. The markup percentage on absorption costs is much lower because this cost already includes all period and fixed COGS. The desired markup percentage may need to be adjusted depending on the competitiveness of the product market. Markups and profit margins tend to be lower in more competitive markets.

Surveys indicate that most managers use absorption costing (see Chapter 9)— that is, they include both fixed costs per unit and variable costs per unit in the cost base when making their pricing decisions. The advantages cited for including fixed costs per unit for pricing decisions include the following:

◆ **Full product cost recovery.** For long-run pricing decisions, absorption costing informs managers of the bare minimum costs they need to recover to continue in business rather than shut down. Using variable costs as a base does not give managers this information. There is then a temptation to engage in excessive long-run price cutting as long as prices give a positive contribution margin. Long-run price cutting, however, may result in long-run revenues being less than long-run full product costs, resulting in the company going out of business.

◆ **Price stability.** Managers believe that an absorption cost policy for pricing promotes price stability, because it limits the ability of managers to cut prices. Managers prefer price stability because it facilitates planning.

◆ **Simplicity.** An absorption cost policy for pricing does not require a detailed analysis of cost behaviour patterns to separate costs into fixed and variable components for each product. Calculating variable costs for each product is expensive and prone to errors. For these reasons, many managers believe that absorption formula pricing meets the cost-benefit test.

Including unit fixed costs when pricing is not without its problems. Allocating fixed costs to products can be somewhat arbitrary. Calculating fixed cost per unit requires an estimate of expected future sales quantities. If actual sales fall short of this estimate, the actual full product cost per unit could exceed price.

COST-PLUS PRICING CONTRASTED AGAINST TARGET PRICING

The selling prices computed under cost-plus pricing are *prospective* or forecast prices. Forecasts are probable, not exact amounts. For example, suppose Astel's initial product design results in a $750 cost for Provalue II. Assuming a 12% markup, Astel sets a prospective price of $840 [$750 + (12% × $750)]. Since the personal computer market is reasonably competitive, customer and competitor reactions to this price may force Astel to reduce the markup percentage and reduce the price to $800. Alternatively, Astel may redesign Provalue II to reduce cost to $720 per unit, as in our example, and achieve a markup of $80 per unit. The eventual design and cost-plus price balance the conflicting tensions among costs, markup, and customer reactions.

The target-pricing approach eliminates the need to go back and forth among cost-plus prospective prices, customer reactions, and design and cost modifications. Instead, the target-pricing approach first determines product characteristics and price on the basis of customer preferences and competitor responses. The target price then serves to focus and motivate managers to achieve the target cost to earn the target operating income. Sometimes the target cost is not achieved. Managers must then redesign the product, adjust the price, or work with a smaller margin.

Suppliers who provide relatively unique products and services—accountants and management consultants, for example—frequently use cost-plus pricing. Professional service firms set prices on the basis of hourly cost-plus billing rates of partners, managers, and support staff. These prices are, however, reduced in competitive situations. Professional service firms also consider a multiyear client perspective when choosing prices. Chartered accountants, for example, may charge a client a low price initially and higher prices later, a practice called *lowballing*. By capturing clients initially, perhaps even at a loss, the service provider expects to make higher profits later when providing additional services. Supermarket chains engage in the same practice but the product sold at the low price is called a loss leader.

Refined cost driver and cost information play an important role in both cost-plus pricing and target costing and pricing. The identification of cost drivers is critical as managers do value engineering to *cost down* their products—to reduce the cost of a product while still satisfying customer expectations. Service companies such as home repairs, automobile repairs, and architectural firms use a cost-plus pricing method called the *time and materials method*. Individual jobs are priced based on materials and labour time. The price charged for materials equals the cost of materials plus a markup. The price charged for labour represents the cost of labour, allocated overhead, and a markup. Therefore, the price charged for each cost item includes its own markup.

THINKING CRITICALLY

Why is variable costing misleading in the long run? Relate your response to the concept of the downward demand spiral. Explain in a sentence or two. Read on for an analysis of this topic.

Assume that the full cost of a product is $50, of which $20 is fixed and avoidable if the product is discontinued and $30 is a variable cost per unit. Also assume that the fixed cost rate is based on sales of 1,000 units. Avoidable costs are those that will not be incurred if a company stops the activity that causes the cost. At a unit sales price of $35 there will still be a positive contribution margin of $5 per unit ($35 unit sales price − $30 unit variable cost = $5 unit contribution margin). The total contribution margin will be $5,000 if the sales volume is 1,000 units ($5 unit contribution margin × 1,000 units = $5,000 total contribution margin).

The remaining avoidable costs are incurred and total $20,000 ($20 avoidable per unit × 1,000 units = $20,000) because the product has *not* been discontinued. This phenomenon is called the downward demand spiral. There will be an unrecovered cost of $15,000 using absorption costing ($20,000 − $5,000 = $15,000). This company will have to sell a minimum of 4,000 units to cover the fixed cost of $20,000 ($5 unit contribution margin × 4,000 units sold = $20,000) and be profitable in the long run.

LIFE-CYCLE PRICING AND COSTING

The meaning of a **product life cycle** can be viewed differently by different stakeholders. From the internal view of the company the product life cycle spans the time from initial R&D to the time at which support to customers is withdrawn. If the company is purchasing an asset then its life cycle begins with the acquisition, through maintenance to disposal. This view is evolving, however, to include recycling and reclamation costs of disposing of obsolete finished products.

From a consumer's view the time span of a product's life cycle is similar to that of a corporate purchase of an asset, but the life span of the products and services purchased varies. For motor vehicles, this time span may range from five to ten years and the costs include acquisition, operating and maintenance, and disposal. Recently Chrysler offered a guaranteed price of $2.50 per US gallon of gasoline (converted is $0.66 per litre) for two years with any purchase of a Chrysler vehicle. This pricing strategy reduces the operating costs and thus the life-cycle costs of Chrysler's vehicles. For some pharmaceutical products, the time span may be 15 to 20 years. These products are usually unique in application, and incentives may be offered to health-care organizations such as Shoppers Drug Mart pharmacies, but not to individuals. For fashion clothing products and computer games the time span may be less than four weeks.

As with target pricing, life-cycle pricing and costing assumes that good planning by companies can affect future costs before a single unit of product is manufactured. In the next section we will examine the product life cycle from the external view, which considers the social costs of waste and scrap disposal, pollution, recycling, reclamation, and remediation.

Life-cycle costing tracks and accumulates the actual costs attributable to each product from start to finish. The terms "cradle-to-grave costing" and "womb-to-tomb costing" convey the sense of fully capturing all costs associated with the product. Clearly, in this long-term approach the past, current, and expected cost behaviour for a specific product will change as technology and other factors affect the product. Throughout its life cycle, improvements will need to be made to the product simply to keep costs and price within a competitive range. This is particularly important if the company has focused on a strategy of agility and customization to differentiate their product.

Life-cycle budgeted costs can provide important information for pricing decisions. For some products, the development period is relatively long, and many costs are incurred before manufacturing. Consider Insight Inc., a computer software company developing a new accounting package, General Ledger. Assume the following budgeted amounts for General Ledger over a six-year product life cycle:

	Years 1 and 2
R&D costs	$240,000
Design costs	160,000

	Years 3 to 6	
	Total Fixed Costs	Variable Unit Costs
Production costs	$100,000	$25
Marketing costs	70,000	24
Distribution costs	50,000	16
Customer-service costs	80,000	30

To be profitable, Insight must generate revenues to cover costs in all six business functions. A product life cycle budget highlights the importance of setting prices and budgeting revenues to recover costs in all the value-chain business functions rather than costs in only some of the functions (such as production). The life-cycle budget also indicates the costs to be incurred over the life of the product. Exhibit 12-8 presents the life-cycle budget for General Ledger. The sensitivity analysis reports on three sets of assumptions about selling price and sales quantity combinations. These alternatives reflect the general economic principle that, in a competitive market, as the price of a commodity increases the demand or quantity sold decreases.

A sensitivity analysis (see Chapter 2) of three combinations of prospective selling price per package and demand is shown. The high nonproduction costs at Insight are readily apparent in Exhibit 12-8. For example, R&D and product design costs constitute more than 30% of total costs for each of the three combinations of selling price and predicted sales quantity. At 5,000 in sales the costs in years 1 and 2 are 34% of total life-cycle costs ($400,000 ÷ $1,175,000 = 0.34 or 34%) and at 2,500 in sales this increases to 42.7%. Insight should put a premium on having as accurate a set of revenue and cost predictions for General Ledger as possible, given the high percentage of total life-cycle costs incurred before any production begins and before any revenue is received.

EXHIBIT 12-8
Budgeted Life-Cycle Revenues and Costs for General Ledger Software Package of Insight, Inc.*

	Alternative Selling Price/ Sales Quantity Combinations		
	1	2	3
Selling price per package	$ 400	$ 480	$ 600
Sales quantity in units	5,000	4,000	2,500
Life-cycle revenues ($400 × 5,000; $480 × 4,000; $600 × 2,500)	$2,000,000	$1,920,000	$1,500,000
Life-cycle costs:			
R&D costs	240,000	240,000	240,000
Design costs of product/process	160,000	160,000	160,000
Production costs:			
$100,000 + ($25 × 5,000); $100,000 + ($25 × 4,000); $100,000 + ($25 × 2,500)	225,000	200,000	162,500
Marketing costs:			
$70,000 + ($24 × 5,000); $70,000 + ($24 × 4,000); $70,000 + ($24 × 2,500)	190,000	166,000	130,000
Distribution costs:			
$50,000 + ($16 × 5,000); $50,000 + ($16 × 4,000); $50,000 + ($16 × 2,500)	130,000	114,000	90,000
Customer-service costs:			
$80,000 + ($30 × 5,000); $80,000 + ($30 × 4,000); $80,000 + ($30 × 2,500)	230,000	200,000	155,000
Total life cycle costs	1,175,000	1,080,000	937,500
Life-cycle operating income	$ 825,000	$ 840,000	$ 562,500

*This exhibit does not take into consideration the time value of money when computing life-cycle revenues or life-cycle costs. Chapters 22 and 23 outline how this important factor can be incorporated into such calculations.

Exhibit 12-8 assumes that the selling price per package is the same over the entire life cycle. For strategic reasons, however, Insight may choose to "skim the market" by charging higher prices to customers eager to try General Ledger when it first comes out and lower prices to customers who are willing to wait. The life-cycle budget will then express this strategy.

DEVELOPING LIFE-CYCLE REPORTS

Most accounting systems emphasize reporting on a calendar basis—monthly, quarterly, and annually. In contrast, product life-cycle reporting does not have this calendar-based focus. Consider the life spans of four Insight products shown below:

	Year 1	Year 2	Year 3	Year 4	Year 5	Year 6
General Ledger package						
Law package						
Payroll package						
Engineering package						

Each product spans more than one calendar year.

Developing life-cycle reports for each product requires tracking costs and revenues on a product-by-product basis over several calendar periods. For example, the R&D costs included in a product life-cycle cost report are often incurred in different calendar years. When R&D costs are tracked over the entire life cycle, the total magnitude of these costs for each individual product can be computed and analyzed.

A product life-cycle reporting format offers at least three important benefits:

1. The full set of revenues and costs associated with each product becomes visible. Manufacturing costs are highly visible in most accounting systems. However, the costs associated with upstream areas (for example, R&D) and downstream areas (for example, customer service) are frequently less visible on a product-by-product basis.

2. Differences between products in the percentage of their total costs incurred at early stages in the life cycle are highlighted. The higher this percentage, the more important it is for managers to develop, as early as possible, accurate predictions of the revenues for that product.

3. Interrelationships among business function cost categories are highlighted. For example, companies that cut back their R&D and product design costs may experience major increases in customer-service costs in subsequent years. Those costs arise because products fail to meet promised quality-performance levels. A life-cycle revenue and cost report prevents such causally related changes among business function costs from being hidden (buried) as they are in annual income statements.

Life-cycle costs further reinforce the importance of locked-in costs, target costing, and value engineering in pricing and cost management. For products with long life cycles, a very small fraction of the total life-cycle costs are actually incurred at the time when costs are locked in. But locked-in costs will determine how actual costs will be incurred later. For example, poor product design can lock in very costly rework and quality control activities at the production stage.

MyAccountingLab

Consider the prices airlines charge for a round-trip flight from Toronto to Beijing. Booking prior to the opening day of the Olympics, a direct Air Canada one-week return flight was listed on Expedia.ca as CDN $1,772 for coach class. Booking the opening day of the Olympics and returning one week later cost $2,809, and during the last week of the Olympics a ticket cost $2,799. Can the price differences be explained by the difference in the cost to Air Canada of these round-trip flights? No: it costs the airline the same amount of money to transport the passenger from Toronto to Beijing and back regardless of whether the passenger flew on August 1, 8, or 18, 2008.

Price discrimination is the practice of charging some customers a higher price than is charged to other customers. In the airline example, the demand for airline tickets comes from two main sources: business travellers and pleasure travellers. Business travellers need to travel in order to conduct business on behalf of their companies. They generally travel to their destinations and return home within the same week immediately after completing their work, because time is very important to them. These aspects make business travellers' demand for air travel relatively insensitive to prices. The insensitivity of demand to price changes is called *demand inelasticity*. Airlines can charge business travellers higher fares because the higher fares have little effect on demand and earn higher operating income for the airlines.

Pleasure travellers have a less pressing need to return home during the week—in fact, they generally prefer to spend weekends at their destinations. Since they pay for their tickets themselves, they are much more sensitive to price than the business traveller (demand is more price-elastic). For pleasure travellers, it is profitable for the airlines to keep fares low to stimulate demand. Requiring a Saturday-night stay distinguishes between the two customer segments. The airline company price-discriminates between the two market segments to take advantage of the different sensitivities to prices exhibited by the business and pleasure travellers. Price differences exist even though there is no cost difference in serving the two segments.

In addition to price discrimination, pricing decisions also consider other non-cost considerations such as capacity constraints. **Peak-load pricing** is the practice of charging a higher price for the same product or service when demand approaches physical capacity limits. That is, the prices charged during busy periods (when loads on the system are high) are greater than the prices charged when slack or excess capacity is available. Peak-load pricing can be found in the telephone, telecommunication, hotel, car rental, and electric utility industries. The following are the daily rental rates charged by Discount Car Rental for compact cars rented at 8 a.m. and returned the next day at noon:

Weekdays (Monday–Thursday)	$39 per day
Weekends (Friday–Sunday)	$32 per day

Discount's incremental costs of renting a car are the same whether the car is rented on a weekday or a weekend. What, then, explains the difference in prices? We offer two separate but related explanations. One explanation is that there is a greater demand for cars during weekdays because of business activity. Faced with capacity limits, Discount raises rental rates to levels that the market will bear.

A second explanation is that the rental rates are a form of price discrimination. During weekdays, the demand for cars comes largely from business travellers who need to rent cars to conduct their business and who are relatively insensitive to prices. Charging higher rental rates during weekdays is profitable because it has little effect on demand. In contrast, the demand for weekend rentals comes largely from nonbusiness or pleasure travellers who are more price-sensitive. Lower rates stimulate demand from these individuals and increase Discount's operating income. Under either explanation, the pricing decision is not driven by cost considerations.

Environmental sustainability and *life-cycle costing* touch on the increasing social concern about what constitutes the end of a product's life cycle. The internal view of companies begins with the research, development, and design of a product and ends with its full production. Concerns about environmental sustainability are extending that view. Costs of anti-pollution measures, responsible waste disposal during production, and disposal of obsolete products now must be included in the life-cycle costs. Decisions about materials also affect environmental sustainability, as illustrated in Chapter 7. These choices did not lock in disposal and recycling costs in the past, but in Germany, for example, new legislation requires manufacturers to pay for recycling of products and reclamation of materials from their obsolete products.

The enactment of strict environmental laws for resource extraction and refining industries has introduced tougher environmental standards and increased the penalties and fines for polluting the air and contaminating subsurface soil and groundwater. The goal is to include ecological responsibility as a *value-added cost* engineered in at the design phase.[3] Environmental costs are often locked in at the product and process design phase. Companies are developing a better understanding of how to design products, processes, and procedures to prevent and reduce pollution over the product's life cycle and eliminate avoidable environmental life-cycle costs.

Beyond the walls of the producer, for electronic products in particular, there are considerable disposal costs for lithium and nickel-cadmium batteries, plastic casings, and metal components. Computer manufacturers HP and Apple, for example, have recently introduced costly recycling programs to ensure that nickel-cadmium batteries powering their laptops are disposed of in an environmentally safe way at the end of the product's life. But other recycling opportunities are available. For example, approximately 1.36 billion kilograms of high-value plastics are produced from petroleum products. High-value plastics are direct materials for injection moulding for plastic cases used for cell phones, BlackBerry devices, laptops, HD players and converters, and TVs. Manufacturers can reclaim the high-value plastic products and maximize the recovery of this value through recycling in a plastics-to-plastics supply chain.

Telus, now part of Rogers Communications, recycled 17,024 tonnes of materials of which 6% arose from electronic products. At a disposal cost of $70 per tonne, Telus estimated it avoided approximately $2 million in landfill fees. Used, recycled, and surplus equipment produced $4.8 million revenue that would not have otherwise been realized.[4] Currently, less than 1% of the high-value plastic consumed in manufacture of electronic products is recovered. A new industry will not evolve on its own, however, until profitable yields of appropriate high-value plastic can be reasonably anticipated from a low- or negative-value mixed input of reclaimable and recyclable plastics. One straightforward value-added solution is to design a recycling process that begins with disassembly and sorting of the high- from low-value plastics.

To achieve high yields, the mixed input must be separated from the disassembled products before the reprocessing process begins.[5] Benefits to producers from reusing and remoulding the reprocessed plastic casings arise not only from reduced direct material cost, but also reduced impact on the environment as the demand for newly produced high-value plastics decreases. The reclamation of mixed input, for example obsolete laptop computers, requires careful separation. Both the plastic and metal must be reclaimed using different processes. The high price of some

---

[3]E. Westkämper, J. Niemann, and A. Dauensteiner, "Economic and Ecological Aspects in Product Life Cycle Evaluation," *Proceedings of the Institute of Mechanical Engineers* 215.B (2001): 673–681.

[4]TELUS, *Leading the Telecommunications Sector in CSR* at www.nrcan-rncan.gc.ca/sd-dd/pubs/csr-rse/pdf/cas/telus_e.pdf.

[5]P. Rios, J. A. Stuart, and E. Grant, "Plastics Disassembly versus Bulk Recycling: Engineering Design for End-of-Life Electronics Resource Recovery," *Environmental Science & Technology*, 37 (2003): 5463–5470.

metals makes reclamation not only central in environmental sustainability but also profitable.

One example is gold. As little as approximately 26 grams of gold per tonne of ore can be profitable at February 2009's price of $1,224 Canadian per ounce (28.3 grams). Over 90% of gold production is direct material for the jewellery industry. Refining raw ore involves the use of sulphuric acid, cyanide, and heavy metals such as arsenic, lead, cadmium, and mercury that can leak into groundwater from the residue (tailings) left after refining the ore. Cyanide is lethal to humans in a solution of 2 parts per million (ppm). Canada has adopted the World Health Organization (WHO) standard permitting 0.2 ppm. The US Environmental Protection Agency (EPA) has estimated over 40% of the western US watersheds are already affected by water pollution from mining, and the remediation costs will be in the hundreds of millions of dollars. Reclamation of even very small amounts of gold from obsolete finished products carries with it a far smaller potential environmental cost than refining. The demand for gold, however, exceeds the supply available from recycled gold.

Responsible companies such as Barrick continue to develop refining techniques to avoid environmental pollution. Not all mining companies are like Barrick. Some use an extraction method called heap leaching. Minute amounts of gold are extracted from the ore which is dumped in a pit lined with plastic (either polyvinyl chloride (PVC) or polyethylene) or clay and sprayed with sodium cyanide of 250–500 ppm. Today in the US over 1 billion tons of tailings per year are produced from heap leaching. Tailings can reach a height exceeding 90 metres.

During the decade ending in 1992, at one site close to the Alamosa River–Rio Grande watershed in Colorado, at least nine leakages of cyanide from the same mine into the groundwater were detected. The US Environmental Protection Agency (EPA) demanded penalties of US $40 million in fines from the mine. The Canadian owner, Cambior, declared bankruptcy and was sued by the US government for US $150 million and, in a plea bargain settled in 1996, Cambior paid a maximum fine of US $20 million. Reclamation costs paid by US taxpayers to date have exceeded US $100 million.

The same company also controlled a heap leach operation in Guyana on the Omai River. In 1995 over 3.17 billion litres of liquid at 25 ppm flushed into the river and flowed to the Essequibo, a principal river in South America. The company abandoned the mine, which the government closed in 2008.

Leakage and spills continue. In 2000, a spill of 100 million litres into the Tisza River from the Baia Mara mine in Romania flowed to the Danube. The spill polluted the river waters of Romania, Hungary, and the former Yugoslavia. Under legislation in place at the time, the Australian company Arul operating the mine could not be held liable for damages outside of Romania. New European legislation now holds companies responsible for transborder pollution in Europe. For example, a spill of 80 tonnes of cyanide would incur a fine of US $50 million.

Most of the technologies to prevent leakage and failure are far younger than heap leaching. While some companies are bearing the full cost of research to make the refining of gold more ecologically sound for all, others leave behind chemicals and heavy metals that eventually contaminate the land and water and all the organisms dependent upon them. A key question is the extent to which consumers, who demand environmental sustainability, will pay the real life-cycle costs of gold jewellery. With few exceptions, remediation of abandoned mine pits is paid from tax revenues collected from the general population, not from either the producers or consumers of the product.

Some companies such as Barrick and Apple adopt proactive strategies to remedy the environmental effects of production. Others adopt a reactive strategy of minimal compliance with health, safety, and environmental regulations. Still others ignore the problems they create until confronted in court. Their legal costs, including fines, comprise part of the life-cycle costing of the risks of environmental degradation, being caught, and successfully prosecuted. For yet other companies, excellent environmental practices can generate revenue through the sale of

Environmental Sustainability, Ecological Friendliness—Who Cares?

A survey of 167 U.K. companies indicated that 58% expressed concern with reducing consumption of non-renewable energy, 57% with appropriate waste disposal, and 41% with reducing or eliminating emissions and pollution. These percentages, however, varied widely from one industry to another. For example 83% in the food industry expressed concern about energy consumption, in contrast to 36% of those in retail of which 64% were concerned with waste. Taxes on landfill use and energy costs have increased. Only half the companies, however, had adopted formal environmental policies, 16% explicit environmental targets, and only 48% had decided upon systematic certification such as the EU's Eco-Management and Audit Scheme (EMAS) or the Responsible Care system in the chemical industry. Management accountants, with their specific expertise in applying sound costing techniques, can improve life-cycle costing techniques by providing reliable estimates of relevant environmental costs.

Source: F. Dahlmann, S. Brammer, and A. Millington, "Environmental Management in the United Kingdom: New Survey Evidence," *Management Decision,* 46.2 (2008): 264–283.

emissions credits on global exchanges in Chicago and Montreal. Those unable or unwilling to adopt benchmark practices can incorporate the purchase of emissions credits into their environmental sustainability strategy.[6]

MyAccountingLab

ASSESS YOUR MASTERY

To check your understanding of the material in Learning Objective ④, go to the *Mastery Questions* section at the end of this chapter and complete Learning Objective ④ question 1.

CORPORATE SOCIAL RESPONSIBILITY AND CORPORATE GOVERNANCE

⑤ Explain how corporate social responsibility differs from corporate governance

CORPORATE SOCIAL RESPONSIBILITY

Corporate social responsibility (CSR) includes but is not confined to responsible environmental practices. As one global aquaculture business, Nutreco, remarked, "A company should be judged on more than its financial performance. Characteristics such as openness to, and regard for, the communities in which it operates are also important factors if a company is to earn a sustainable place in society."[7] As a global force in a controversial industry, Nutreco's CSR policy in British Columbia

[6]Much of this section was based on information from S. Fields, "Tarnishing the Earth: Gold Mining's Dirty Secret," *Environmental Health Perspectives* 109.10 (2001): A474–481 at www.jstor.org/sici?sici=0091-6765(200110)109:10%3CA474:TTEGMD%3E2.0.CO;2-4; I. M. Kiss, "The Bond Is Dead," *Central Europe Review* 2.7 (2000) at www.ce-review.org/00/7/kiss7.html; S. G. Vick, "Failure of the Omai Tailings Dam," *Geotechnical News,* September (1996): 34–40 at www.infomine.com/publications/docs/Vick1996.pdf; N. Langerman, "Cyanide Spill," *Chemical Health and Safety,* 7.3 May–June (2000): 41–42 at www.sciencedirect.com/science?_ob=HomePageURL&_method=userHomePage&_btn=Y&_acct=C000050221&_version=1&_urlVersion=0&_userid=10&md5=6b8f8a0bb11c4ebe676f09e6d7da52c8; and L. Loopnarine, "Wounding Guyana: Gold Mining and Environmental Degradation," *Revista Europea de Estudios Latinoamericanos y del Caribe,* 73 October (2002): 83–90 at www.cedla.uva.nl/60_publications/PDF_files_publications/73RevistaEuropea/73Loopnarine.pdf.

[7]Government of Canada CSR Case Study, "Marine Harvest Canada: Taking Leadership" at www.nrcan-rncan.gc.ca/sd-dd/pubs/csr-rse/pdf/cas/mh_e.pdf.

has led to awards for exemplary leadership. This company provides a comprehensive report of its CSR achievements voluntarily under the Global Reporting Initiative. None of the measures reported are financial measures.

Chemical companies such as DuPont Canada belong to the Canadian Chemical Producers' Association, which has a formal code of practice. The CCPA members have adopted the Responsible Care program as their industry standard and the program is composed of six management codes: community awareness and emergency response (CAER), research and development, manufacturing, transportation, distribution, and hazardous waste management. R&D, manufacturing, transportation, and distribution are familiar elements of the business function value chain. Others such as CAER and hazardous waste management are specialized parts of the chemical industry.

Canada's National Pollutant Release Inventory (NPRI), which is publicly accessible, requires that companies such as Dow Chemical Company report the type and amount of industrial chemicals they emit. Dow's commitment to sustainable growth is tracked using many nonfinancial measures, as illustrated in Exhibit 12-9. The improvements shown by companies such as Dow will affect many industries. For example, a new refrigeration fluid that is currently in testing may reduce energy consumption by up to 24%. This would benefit a huge number of companies using refrigeration systems.

Dow is also changing its own processes to reduce pollutants. They are working to reduce CO_2 emission by 85% in the manufacturing of polyethylene. To reduce landfill, the company is using new technology to recover and reuse discarded carpet, and they are working to extend the life of asphalt roofing material from 10 to over 30 years. Dow has won the European Responsible Care Award, as well as an award for corporate social responsibility for its use of recycled, decontaminated municipal watsewater, which reduced energy use by 65%.

Dow uses financial measures to report what it has returned to the communities in which it operates each year. In 2008, Dow contributed approximately $17.4 million in charitable donations and an additional $20.8 million in special disaster relief projects. A further $38.2 million was donated to support community programs and advance education in science and sustainability. For the second consecutive year, the

EXHIBIT 12-9
Dow Chemical Company's Progress Toward Selected 2015 Sustainability Goals*

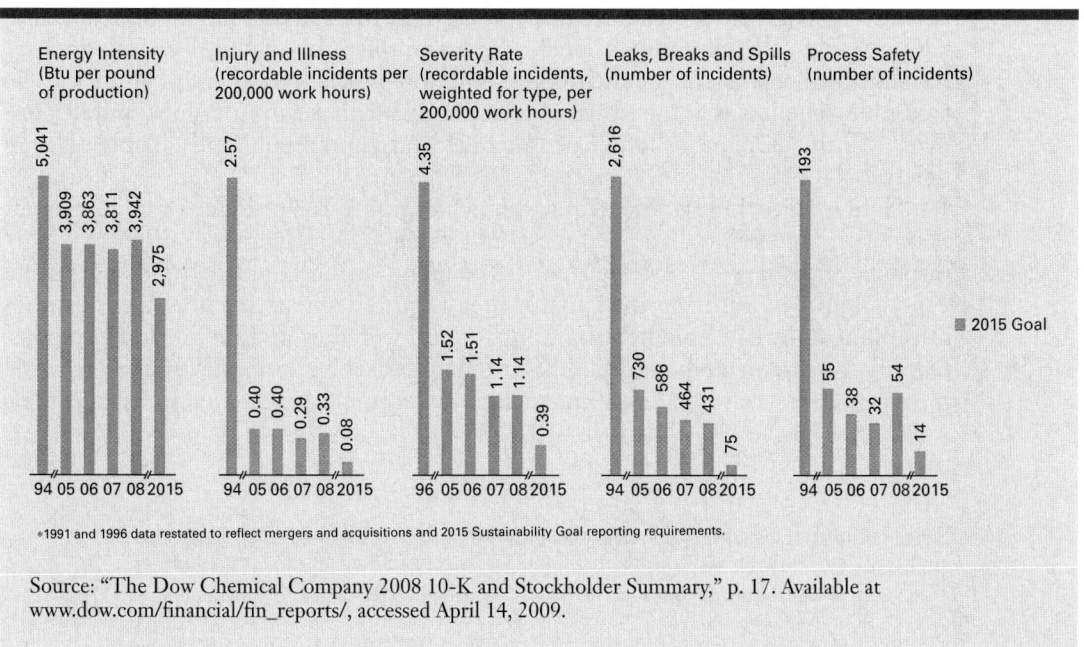

*1991 and 1996 data restated to reflect mergers and acquisitions and 2015 Sustainability Goal reporting requirements.

Source: "The Dow Chemical Company 2008 10-K and Stockholder Summary," p. 17. Available at www.dow.com/financial/fin_reports/, accessed April 14, 2009.

company was awarded "Working Mother 100 Best Companies" award by *Working Mother* magazine. Dow has also been recognized for the excellence of its corporate governance. Sustainability for Dow has many factors—environmental, social, and governance improvements are part of the company's global strategy.[8]

The output of the food industry affects the safety of almost all societies. In the realm of CSR, fast food retailers are particularly vulnerable. Three examples are McDonald's, Kentucky Fried Chicken, and Burger King. McDonald's has been widely criticized for using plastic clamshell containers and changed to paper wrapping. Kentucky Fried Chicken (KFC) Canada has been criticized for its treatment of chickens. The People for Ethical Treatment of Animals (PETA), a global advocacy group, successfully sued KFC in the US for deceitful advertising that reassured consumers about its humane treatment of chickens. The campaign gained international publicity.

PETA complained publicly about how chickens for KFC were housed and slaughtered. In May 2005, PETA claimed that the slaughtering process whereby chickens were supposed to be slaughtered and the remains scalded to sterilize them and make it easier to remove feathers did not work. Many animals were still alive when dipped into scalding tanks. In Canada there are approximately 2,800 farms, housing up to 50,000 birds each. The farms provide chicken for meat. PETA received support from animal welfare experts at both the University of Guelph and the Ontario Society for the Prevention of Cruelty to Animals.

In June 2008, KFC Canada, owned by Priszm Income Fund, had closed 120 of its original 461 outlets and lost over half its 2005 market value. The CEO announced that KFC was phasing in a new supply-chain strategy. It would purchase chickens only from suppliers who slaughtered chickens using controlled atmosphere process. The U.K. has already legislated this process which, while more humane, is more expensive. CSR, however, illustrates how serious financial consequences arise when companies offend widely held social values.

KFC is not the only fast food retailer to respond to PETA. In 2007 Burger King announced its new supply-chain strategy. In general the direct material for food chains is raised on industrial farms and the animals—hogs, cattle, and chickens— are confined to cages for their lifetimes. Burger King promised suppliers would be rewarded if they used controlled atmosphere slaughtering process and to purchase 2% of their eggs and 10% of their pork from animals that had not been caged.

The scope of social concern for corporate practices is very wide. While it will cost these chains more to acquire direct materials, the benefits should be realized in increased sales, all other things equal. Moreover, the public should be willing to pay the additional costs associated with new and more ethical treatment of animals. The intangible benefit is that the two chains responded with regard for global public concerns over the humane slaughter of animals to earn and retain a sustainable place in society.[9]

The monitoring and control systems integral to the practice of management accounting are essential to producing and using CSR-effective nonfinancial performance measures. As external parties demand an enlarged scope of corporate responsibility, monitoring the gap between required and actual practices becomes more important to implementing appropriate remedies and measuring progress. Beyond the financial benefits, CSR reporting is one example of the growing importance of relevant nonfinancial information. Management accountants

[8]Based on information from "The Dow Chemical Company 2008 10-K and Stockholder Summary," available at www.dow.com/financial/fin_reports/, accessed April 14, 2009.

[9]This section based on information from "KFC Gains Praise from Its Opponents,"
June 3, 2008, *TheGlobe and Mail*; "Burger King Takes 'Historic' Step Towards Animal Welfare" at http://veg.ca/content/view/352/101/; and "KFC vs PETA" at http://veg.ca/content/view/167/101/.

working with cross-functional teams not only develop nonfinancial measures but often translate them into estimates of expected financial benefit relevant to life-cycle costing.

CORPORATE GOVERNANCE[10]

Corporate governance is, at a minimum, compliance with existing laws, regulations, and standards. Corporate governance refers to the responsibility of the Board of Directors (BOD), legal officers of the company such as the CEO, and others in top management. The BOD must adequately supervise those within companies to ensure they are managing in a responsible way. Regular performance evaluation to ensure the corporation is in full legal and regulatory compliance is essential, ranging from timely tax remittance to employee and product safety regulations. If the officers of the company do undertake wrongful acts and the BOD has not supervised them in a prudent and appropriate manner, the BOD members can be held legally liable for the wrongful acts of top management.

Legal liability is a complex area because federal and provincial common, contract, and statutory laws differ depending on the industry. Often, legal action for negligence is brought simultaneously with a civil liability lawsuit. A conviction for negligence (failure to exercise duty of care towards one to whom this duty is legally owed) in itself carries with it large financial penalties and in some cases mandatory minimum time in jail. The failure to fulfill a duty of care can be applied towards harms of a financial, physical, and emotional nature endured by those harmed, and penalties will vary.

Convictions for one offence make it extremely difficult to defend against civil action taken by third parties who have indirectly suffered harm as a result of negligence. Most punitive of these is what is known as a class action lawsuit, where large groups of individuals suffering harm take action against a company. Class action lawsuits, while often settled out of court, range from employees suing because of unequal, unsafe, or illegal treatment to groups injured by the sale of products without adequate warning about the limits of safe use. It is prudent that members of the BOD, often including the officers of the company, purchase liability insurance. But there is no affordable insurance policy that covers all possible, or even all probable, liability risks.

Pricing practices in most industries are governed by the *Competition Act* (the Act). The purpose of the legislation and its predecessors is to "protect the specific public interest in free competition."[11] This concept is founded on the belief that unrestricted competition improves the performance of industries as a whole and protects the public from unfair pricing practices. Each of the sections discussed below creates criminal offences for contravening the Act.

Under section 50(1)(a) of the Act, a manufacturer cannot price-discriminate between two customers if the intent is to lessen or prevent competition between customers. Four key elements of the price discrimination laws are (1) they apply to manufacturers and not service providers; (2) price discrimination is permissible if differences in prices can be justified by differences in costs; (3) price discrimination is illegal only if the intent is to discriminate between competitors; and (4) it is not an offence to discriminate in pricing, unless doing so is part of a practice of discrimination.[12]

---

[10]This section is provided with assistance from Russell Hoffman, LL.B., MBA.

[11]See *Weidman v. Schragge* (1912), 20 CCC 177 at 147, where the Supreme Court of Canada first considered the rationale for regulating trades and industries.

[12]Although a "practice" is not specifically defined, more than one sale is likely required. Further, it should be noted that, in order to contravene this section of the Act, a practice of price discrimination does not have to actually have an adverse effect on competition.

To comply with section 50(1)(c) of the Act, pricing must not be predatory. Section 50(1) of the Act states that a business engages in **predatory pricing** when it sells products at unreasonably low prices that either tend to substantially lessen competition or were designed to have that effect.

However, it is difficult to state with certainty what the legal thresholds are, as only three cases have ever been decided under this section.[13] In light of the lack of judicial consideration, and to further clarify matters, the Director of Investigation and Research (the Director) released the *Predatory Pricing Enforcement Guidelines* (the *Guidelines*) on May 21, 1992. In these *Guidelines* the Director defined predatory pricing as "a situation where a dominant firm charges low prices over a long enough period of time so as to drive a competitor from the market or deter others from entering and raises prices to recoup its losses."[14] According to these *Guidelines*, the predator must account for more than 35% of the market and be able to sustain a pricing increase for more than two years after the period of low pricing in order for its actions to be considered predatory pricing.

In determining whether pricing is "unreasonably low," courts draw a distinction between pricing a product above average variable cost and below. It is likely that as long as a product is sold above average variable cost (even if below average total cost), and it cannot be established that the accused would have made a greater total contribution to overhead by raising prices, a court will not find the price "unreasonably low."

In a 1981 case, *R. v. Consumers Glass Co.*,[15] the accused, which sold small plastic lids before 1975, had faced reduced demand for its products. When the accused's competition cut prices by 2% to 3%, it responded by cutting prices by 16% and then a further 5%, which still enabled the accused to cover its average variable costs but not its total costs. The Court held that "it is better for a manufacturer to produce and sell at a loss, than to cease production and suffer the loss of having to bear all the fixed overhead."[16] The Court went on to hold that there was no evidence of predatory pricing, as the accused had lowered its price to retain market share and maximize its contribution to fixed overhead.

In contrast, pricing below average variable costs will be tolerated by the courts only in limited circumstances. In *R. v. Hoffmann-La Roche Ltd.*,[17] the Ontario Court of Appeal affirmed the trial judge's decision of an "unreasonably low" price. In this trial it was held that a pharmaceutical firm that chose to combat new competition in the hospital market by giving away Valium was "selling" its products at an unreasonably low price. The year-long Valium giveaways were in response to the new competitor's price reductions of 25% to 50% of the accused's price. The Court stated that in determining the reasonableness or unreasonableness of a particular price it will "take into account all the economic costs, which include the direct production costs as well as any potential future savings or benefits."[18] This includes looking at benefits that derive to related markets, or future markets.

The trial judge then went on to state that the court should look to four general considerations in determining whether the actual price is unreasonably low. First, the difference between the average variable cost and the sale price is important, as the greater the reduction in price, the more likely it is that it will be seen as unreasonable. Second, the length of time during which sales take place at the questionable price is significant; the longer the "deal" continues the more unreasonable the price becomes. Third, the circumstances of the price cut should be considered; defensive price-cutting may be justifiable where offensive price-cutting is not.

---

[13]Although the Supreme Court of Canada has never considered a case under this section, the most recent of these cases, *R. v. Hoffmann-La Roche Ltd.* (1980), 28 O.R. (2d) 164, was affirmed by the Ontario Court of Appeal in 1981, 125 D.L.E. (3d) 607 (C.A.).

[14]Director of Investigation and Research, "Executive Summary," *Predatory Pricing Enforcement Guidelines* (Ottawa: Consumer and Corporate Affairs Canada, 1992).

[15]*R. v. Consumers Glass Co.* (1981), 33 (.R. (2d) 228 (H.C.).

[16]Ibid, p. 238.

[17]See n. 12 *supra*.

[18]*R. v. Hoffmann-La Roche Ltd.*, p. 199.

Pricing Decisions Are Not Arbitrary

As we have seen many times before, the role of the management accountant also includes potential ethical obstacles. As it relates to pricing decisions, management accountants must always be careful that their pricing proposals are ethical and legal—no matter how profitable such actions might be in the short run. As a member of the accounting profession, management accountants must protest illegal or unethical pricing actions. Failure to do so can result in multi-million-dollar fines and significant damage to a company's reputation. With respect to CSR, management accountants have the expertise to translate the needs of various stakeholders and the benefits of satisfying those needs into performance measures and justifiable cost-benefit measures. The quantification and estimation of the financial benefits from actions that will most certainly increase costs is a key contribution made by the profession.

Lastly, consideration must be given to any accruals of external or long-term benefits to the seller that result from pricing below costs.[19]

Managers and accountants who are concerned with their conformance to the competition laws would be prudent to have a system that incorporates the following procedures:

◆ Collect data in a manner that permits relatively easy compilation of variable costs.

◆ Keep detailed records of variable costs for all value-chain business functions and review all proposed prices below variable costs in advance, with a presumption of claims of predatory intent.

Closely related to predatory pricing is dumping. Under Canadian laws, **dumping** occurs when a non-Canadian company sells goods in Canada at a price below the market value in the home country or receives a government subsidy and this action materially injures or threatens to materially injure an industry in Canada. If dumping is proven, under section 42(I)(c)(ii) of the *Special Import Measures Act* (SIMA) the Canadian International Trade Tribunal (the Tribunal) has the power to impose a countervailing duty on the goods to prevent the recurrence of the material injury.

Cases related to dumping have occurred in the agricultural and automotive industries. In 1990, the Supreme Court of Canada considered an appeal of the Tribunal's decision that the subsidization of corn imports from the United States had caused, was causing, and would likely cause material injury to the production of like goods in Canada. The Supreme Court held that the Tribunal's decision was final in this case and that decisions are generally final unless the Tribunal acts outside the scope of its mandate or its interpretation of the SIMA is patently unreasonable.[20]

Another violation of the Act is collusive pricing. **Collusive pricing** occurs when companies in an industry conspire in their pricing and output decisions to achieve a price above the competitive price. Section 45 of the Act makes it a criminal offence to conspire, agree, or combine with another person to prevent, lessen, or restrain competition unduly. Collusive pricing violates the Act because an agreement with respect to pricing and output levels prevents competition between the companies in an industry.

ASSESS YOUR MASTERY

MyAccountingLab

To check your understanding of the material in Learning Objective ⑤, go to the *Mastery Questions* section at the end of this chapter and complete Learning Objective ⑤ question 1.

[19] *R. v. Hoffmann-La Roche Ltd.*, pp. 200–204.
[20] See *American Farm Bureau Federation v. Canadian Import Tribunal* (1990), 74 D.L.R. (4th) 449.

Reconsider the Astel Computer example (pp. 588–604). Astel's marketing manager realizes that a further reduction in prices is necessary to sell 200,000 units of Provalue II. To maintain a target profitability of $16 million, or $80 per unit (the same amounts shown in Exhibit 12-6, p. 602), Astel will need to reduce costs of Provalue II by $6 million, or $30 per unit. Astel targets a reduction of $4 million, or $20 per unit, in manufacturing costs, and $2 million, or $10 per unit, in marketing, distribution, and customer-service costs. The cross-functional team assigned to this task proposes the following changes to manufacture a different version of Provalue, called Provalue III:

1. Reduce direct materials and ordering costs by purchasing subassembled components rather than individual components.
2. Reengineer ordering and receiving. Reduce ordering and receiving costs per order.
3. Reduce testing time and the labour and power required per hour of testing.
4. Develop new rework procedures to reduce rework costs per hour.

No changes are proposed in direct manufacturing labour costs per unit and in total machining costs. The spreadsheet on page 619 summarizes the cost-driver quantities and the cost per unit of each cost driver for Provalue III compared with Provalue II.

REQUIRED
1. What long-term factors are relevant in target pricing?
2. Will the proposed changes achieve the target cost of $20 per output unit for a total cost reduction of $4 million to manufacture Provalue III? Show your calculations, using Exhibit 12-5 as an example.
3. As a producer of electronics, what environmental factors should Astel consider?
4. Identify four factors Astel could use to measure its progress in CSR.
5. What corporate governance problems can a management accountant alert Astel to?

SOLUTION
1. Astel must consider fixed as well as variable costs and use absorption costing to ensure the target price will cover all costs of production including period costs.
2. Exhibit 12-10 (p. 620) presents the manufacturing costs for Provalue III based on the proposed changes. Manufacturing costs will decline from $108 million, or $540 per unit (Exhibit 12-5), to $104 million, or $520 per unit (Exhibit 12-10), and will achieve the target reduction of $4 million, or $20 per unit.
3. Electronics producers can recycle high-value plastic covers and other components. Recycling is more environmentally sustainable than new plastics production, can avoid disposal costs, and can improve revenue. These recycling costs and benefits can be locked in at the design stage of Provalue III. In addition, Astel could consider price discrimination if it has a global customer base. The ability to pay could determine that a lower price would be charged to customers in developing countries than in developed countries. Astel views its product life cycle from an internal perspective without considering the needs of groups other than its customers. In fact, if Astel were producing in Europe, the life cycle of Provalue III would extend to disposal of the obsolete product.
4. CSR is broader in scope than environmental sustainability and was characterized as social sustainability by one global company. Important factors include the engagement of stakeholders, integration of local communities and service to them, reduction of poverty, and workplace diversity. Management accountants develop nonfinancial measures to monitor progress in CSR.
5. Whether Astel uses target, cost-plus, or life-cycle pricing, the company cannot engage in predatory pricing with the intent to lower competition by deterring others from entering. Basing a price on variable costs is not predatory pricing

PROVALUE II MANUFACTURING COST DATA

Output Level: 200,000

	Cost Driver (1)	Quantity (2)	Unit of Measure	Quantity (3)	Unit of Measure	Total Quantity of Cost Driver (4) = (2) × (3)	Input Cost Driver Rate
Direct Costs							
Direct materials	No. of kits	1.0	kit per output unit	200,000	output units	200,000	$385
Direct manufacturing labour (DMLH)	DMLH	2.65	DMLH per output unit	200,000	output units	530,000	$ 20
Direct machining - fixed (DMH)	DMH hours	1.5	DMH per output unit	200,000	output units	300,000	$ 38
Overhead Costs							
Ordering and receiving	No. of orders	50.0	orders per component	425	components	21,250	$ 80
Testing and inspection (TH)	Testing hours	15.0	TH per output unit	200,000	output units	3,000,000	$ 2
Rework (RMH)	Rework hours	2.5	RMH per defective unit*	13,000	defective units	32,500	$ 40
Defect rate				6.5%	defect rate		

*6.5% defect rate × 200,000 output units = 13,000 defective units

PROVALUE III MANUFACTURING COST DATA

Output Level: 200,000

	Cost Driver (1)	Quantity (2)	Unit of Measure	Quantity (3)	Unit of Measure	Total Quantity of Cost Driver (4) = (2) × (3)	Input Cost Driver Rate
Direct Costs							
Direct materials	No. of kits	1.0	kit per output unit	200,000	output units	200,000	$ 375
Direct manufacturing labour (DMLH)	DMLH	2.65	DMLH per output unit	200,000	output units	530,000	$ 20
Direct machining - fixed (DMH)	DMH hours	1.5	DMH per output unit	200,000	output units	300,000	$ 38
Overhead Costs							
Ordering and receiving	No. of orders	50.0	orders per component	400	components	20,000	$ 60
Testing and inspection (TH)	Testing hours	14.0	TH per output unit	200,000	output units	2,800,000	$1.70
Rework (RMH)	Rework hours	2.5	RMH per defective unit*	13,000	defective units	32,500	$ 32
Defect rate				6.5%	defect rate		

	A	B	C
1		Estimated	Estimated
2		Manufacturing Costs	Manufacturing
3		for 200,000 Units	Cost per Unit
4		(1)	(2) = (1) ÷ 200,000
5	Direct manufacturing costs:		
6	Direct material costs (200,000 units × $375 per unit)	$ 75,000,000	$375.00
7	Direct manufacturing labour costs (530,000 hours × $20 per hour)	10,600,000	53.00
8	Direct machining costs (fixed) (300,000 machine-hours × $38 per machine-hour)	11,400,000	57.00
9	Direct manufacturing costs	97,000,000	485.00
10			
11	Manufacturing overhead costs:		
12	Ordering and receiving costs (20,000 orders × $60 per order)	1,200,000	6.00
13	Testing and inspection costs (2,800,000 hours × $1.70 per hour)	4,760,000	23.80
14	Rework costs (32,500 rework hours × $32 per hour)	1,040,000	5.20
15	Manufacturing overhead costs	7,000,000	35.00
16	Total manufacturing costs	$104,000,000	$520.00

unless the intent was to eliminate or reduce the competition. In Canada, Astel could not price its products substantially lower than the market value in its home country (dumping). Finally, Astel cannot conspire to combine with another company to price the product in a way that would prevent the two from competing. This is collusive pricing.

DECISION POINTS

The following question-and-answer format summarizes the chapter's learning objectives. Each decision presents a key question related to a learning objective. The guidelines are the answer to that question.

DECISIONS	GUIDELINES
1. What are the three major influences on pricing decisions?	Customers, competitors, and costs influence prices through their effects on demand and supply—customers and competitors affect demand, and costs affect supply. These factors will differ depending on the time horizon of the pricing decision. The time horizon affects the set of costs that are relevant to ensure profitability.
2. How do companies price products using target costing?	Target pricing is one response to a decision with a long-term time horizon. Target price is driven by the customer in the market place. It is the estimated price that potential customers are willing to pay for a product or service. Given the OM%, the target cost is [(1 − OM%) × target price]. Target cost per unit is the estimated long-run cost of a product or service that when sold enables the company to achieve target operating income per unit. The challenge for the organization is to make the necessary cost improvements through value analysis and value-engineering methods to achieve the target cost.

3. How do companies price products using either the cost-plus or life-cycle costing approach?	The cost-plus approach to pricing adds a markup component to a cost base as the starting point for pricing decisions. Many different costs, such as full cost of the product or manufacturing cost, can serve as the cost base in applying the cost-plus formula. Prices are then modified on the basis of customers' reactions and competitors' responses. Therefore, the size of the "plus" is determined by the market. Life-cycle budgeting and costing estimate, track, and accumulate the costs (and revenues) attributable to a product from its initial R&D to its final customer servicing and support.
4. How do non-cost factors, including environmental sustainability, affect pricing decisions?	There is no legal requirement to charge each customer the same price for the same good or service although costs are identical or very similar. Price discrimination is charging some customers a higher price for a given product or service than other customers. Peak-load pricing is charging a higher price for the same product or service when demand approaches physical capacity limits. In life-cycle pricing, the legal requirement to recycle and reclaim is increasing. Companies must include the costs of environmental rehabilitation and waste disposal in their life-cycle costs to be in compliance.
5. How do corporate social responsibility (CSR) and corporate governance differ?	CSR includes but is not limited to minimum compliance with laws. Corporate governance is limited to compliance issues. CSR refers to decisions that ensure the company's actions are socially acceptable, such as humane slaughter of animals, community awareness and philanthropy, and voluntary disclosure. Important corporate governance issues include compliance with laws against predatory pricing, dumping, or collusive pricing, which lessen competition, put another company at a competitive disadvantage, or harm consumers.

TERMS TO LEARN

This chapter contains definitions of the following important terms:

collusive pricing (p. 617)
cost incurrence (p. 596)
designed-in costs (p. 597)
dumping (p. 617)
life-cycle costing (p. 606)
locked-in costs (p. 597)
peak-load pricing (p. 609)

predatory pricing (p. 615)
price discrimination (p. 609)
product life cycle (p. 606)
target cost per unit (p. 594)
target operating income per unit (p. 593)

target price per unit (p. 593)
target rate of return on investment (ROI) (p. 602)
value analysis (p. 594)
value engineering (p. 595)

MASTERY QUESTIONS

Mastery Questions are rated by proficiency level—elementary, intermediate, and advanced. The solutions appear in the Solutions to Mastery Questions section of MyAccountingLab.

LEARNING OBJECTIVE 1

1. Major influences—Elementary. Dill Company produces specialized videotape for the film industry. The following financial data apply to its videotape production plant for October 2010:

	Budgeted Manufacturing Costs per Videotape
Direct materials	$1.80
Direct manufacturing labour	0.96
Variable manufacturing overhead	0.84
Fixed manufacturing overhead	1.20
Total manufacturing costs	$4.80

Variable manufacturing overhead varies with respect to units produced. Fixed manufacturing overhead of $1.20 per tape is based on budgeted fixed manufacturing overhead of $180,000 per month and budgeted production of 150,000 tapes per month. The Dill Company sells each tape for $6.

Marketing costs have two components:

◆ Variable marketing costs (sales commissions) of 5% of dollar sales
◆ Fixed monthly costs of $65,000

During October 2010, Lyn Randell, a Dill Company salesperson, asked the president for permission to sell 1,000 tapes at $4.56 per tape to a customer not in Dill's normal marketing channels. The president refused this special order on the grounds that the order would show a loss because the selling price was below the total budgeted manufacturing cost.

REQUIRED
1. What would have been the effect on monthly operating income of accepting the special order?
2. Comment on the president's "below manufacturing costs" reasoning for rejecting the special order.
3. What factors would you recommend that the president consider when deciding whether to accept or reject a special order?

2. **Major influences—Intermediate.** The Marino Repair Shop repairs and services machine tools. A summary of its costs (by activity) for 2010 is as follows:

a. Materials and labour for servicing machine tools	$ 960,000
b. Rework costs	90,000
c. Expediting costs caused by work delays	72,000
d. Materials-handling costs	60,000
e. Materials procurement and inspection costs	42,000
f. Preventive maintenance of equipment	18,000
g. Breakdown maintenance of equipment	66,000
	$1,308,000

REQUIRED
1. Classify each of the seven costs as value-added, non-value-added, or in the grey area in between.
2. For any costs classified in the grey area, assume 65% of the costs are value-added and 35% are non-value-added. How much of the total costs are value-added and how much are non-value-added?
3. Marino is considering the following changes at the shop: (a) introducing quality improvement programs whose net effect will be to reduce rework and expedite costs by 75% and materials and labour costs by 5%, (b) working with suppliers to reduce materials procurement and inspection costs by 20% and materials-handling costs by 25%, and (c) increasing preventive maintenance costs by 50% to reduce breakdown maintenance costs by 40%. What effect would each of these programs have on value-added costs, non-value-added costs, and total costs as calculated in requirement 2? Comment briefly.

3. **Major influences—Advanced.** Stardom Inc. cans peaches for sale to food distributors. All costs are classified as either manufacturing or marketing. Stardom prepares monthly budgets. The March 2010 budgeted absorption costing income statement is as follows:

Revenues (1,000 crates × $120 per crate)	$120,000	100%
Cost of goods	72,000	60
Gross margin	48,000	40
Marketing costs	36,000	30
Operating income	$ 12,000	10%
Normal markup percentage:		
$48,000 ÷ $72,000 = 66.7% of absorption cost		

Monthly costs are classified as fixed or variable (with respect to the cans produced for manufacturing costs and with respect to the number of crates sold for marketing costs):

	Fixed	Variable
Manufacturing	$24,000	$48,000
Marketing	19,200	16,800

Stardom has the capacity to can 1,500 crates per month. The relevant range in which monthly fixed manufacturing costs will be "fixed" is from 500 to 1,500 crates per month.

REQUIRED

1. Calculate the normal markup percentage based on total variable costs.
2. Assume that a new customer approaches Stardom to buy 200 crates at $66 per crate. The customer does not require additional marketing effort. Additional manufacturing costs of $2,400 (for special packaging) will be required. Stardom believes that this is a one-time-only special order, because the customer is discontinuing business in six weeks' time. Stardom is reluctant to accept this 200-crate special order because the $66 per crate price is below the $72 per crate absorption cost. Do you agree with this reasoning? Explain.
3. Assume that the new customer decides to remain in business. How would this longevity affect Stardom's willingness to accept the $66 per crate offer? Explain.

LEARNING OBJECTIVE 2

1. **Target price—Elementary.** Carasco Associates is a small structural-design firm that prepares architectural drawings that focus on structural safety for various clients. The architectural plans are then submitted to local government departments for approval. Carasco's income statement for 2010 follows:

Revenues	$816,000
Salaries of professional staff	
(8,000 hours × $60 per hour)	480,000
Travel	21,600
Administration and support	192,000
Total costs	693,600
Operating income	$122,400

An analysis of the percentage of time spent by professional staff on various activities is as follows:

Doing calculations and preparing drawings for clients	75%
Checking calculations and drawings	4
Correcting drawings	7
Making changes in response to client requests	6
Making corrections required by government officials before they give approval	8
Total	100%

Further assume that administration and support costs vary with professional labour-hours.

REQUIRED

1. How much of the total costs in 2010 are value-added, non-value-added, or in the grey area in between? Explain your answers briefly. What actions can Carasco take to reduce its costs?
2. If Carasco can eliminate all corrections and proportionately reduce professional labour-hours, how much will Carasco's operating income be?

2. **Target price—Elementary.** Carasco would like to double operating income in 2011. Carasco can take on as much business as it can get done but it cannot add more professional staff.

REQUIRED

By how much will Carasco be able to increase its operating income if all corrections are eliminated and the time saved is used to increase revenues proportionately? Assume travel expenses for 2011 will remain at $21,600.

3. **Target price—Intermediate.** Snappy Tiles is a small distributor of marble tiles. Snappy identifies its three major activities and cost pools as ordering, receiving and storage, and shipping, and reports the following details for 2010:

Activity	Cost Driver	Quantity of Cost Driver	Cost per Unit of Cost Driver
1. Placing and paying for orders of marble tiles	Number of orders	500	$60 per order
2. Receiving and storage	Number of loads moved	4,000	$36 per load
3. Shipping marble tiles to retailers	Number of shipments	1,500	$48 per shipment

Snappy buys 250,000 marble tiles at an average cost of $3.60 per tile and sells them to retailers at an average price of $4.80 per tile. Fixed costs are $48,000.

REQUIRED

1. Calculate Snappy's operating income for 2010.

2. For 2011, retailers are demanding a 5% discount off the 2010 price. Snappy's suppliers are willing to give only a 4% discount. Snappy expects to sell the same quantity of marble tiles in 2011 as it did in 2010. If all other costs and cost driver information remain the same, what will be Snappy's operating income in 2011?

3. Suppose further that Snappy decides to make changes in its ordering and receiving and storing practices. By placing long-term orders with its key suppliers, it expects to reduce the number of orders to 200 and the cost per order to $30 per order. By redesigning the layout of the warehouse and reconfiguring the crates in which the marble tiles are moved, Snappy expects to reduce the number of loads moved to 3,125 and the cost per load moved to $33.60. Will Snappy achieve its target operating income of $0.36 per tile in 2011? Show your calculations.

4. **Target price—Advanced.** Cutler Electronics makes a Blu-ray player, CE100, that has 80 components. Cutler sells 7,000 units each month for $84 each. The costs of manufacturing CE100 are $54 per unit, or $378,000 per month. Monthly manufacturing costs incurred are as follows:

Direct materials costs	$218,400
Direct manufacturing labour costs	33,600
Machining costs (fixed)	37,800
Testing costs	42,000
Rework costs	16,800
Ordering costs	4,032
Engineering costs (fixed)	25,368
Total manufacturing costs	$378,000

Cutler's management identifies the activity cost pools, the cost drivers for each activity, and the cost per unit of cost driver for each overhead cost pool as follows:

Manufacturing Activity	Description of Activity	Cost Driver	Cost per Unit of Cost Driver
1. Machining costs	Machining components	Fixed costs	No cost driver
2. Testing costs	Testing components and final product (each unit of CE100 is tested individually)	Testing-hours	$2.40 per testing-hour
3. Rework costs	Correcting and fixing errors and defects	Units of CE100 reworked	$24 per unit
4. Ordering costs	Ordering of components	Number of orders	$25.20 per order
5. Engineering costs	Designing and managing of products and process	Fixed costs	No cost driver

Over a long-run time horizon, Cutler's management views direct materials costs and direct manufacturing labour costs as variable with respect to the units of CE100 manufactured. Each overhead cost described in the preceding table varies, as described, with the chosen cost drivers.

The following additional information describes the existing design:

a. Testing and inspection time per unit is 2.5 hours.

b. Ten percent of the CE100s manufactured are reworked.

c. Cutler places two orders with each component supplier each month. Each component is supplied by a different supplier. It takes one hour to place an order.

To respond to competitive pressures, Cutler must reduce its price to $74.40 per unit and reduce its costs by $9.60 per unit. No additional sales are anticipated at this lower price. However, Cutler stands to lose significant sales if it does not cut its price. Manufacturing has been asked to reduce its costs by $7.20 per unit. Improvements in manufacturing efficiency are expected to yield net savings of $1.80 per Blu-ray player, but that is not enough. The chief engineer has proposed a new modular design that reduces the number of components to 50 and also simplifies testing. The newly designed Blu-ray player, called "New CE100," will replace CE100.

The expected effects of the new design are as follows:

a. Direct materials costs for New CE100 are expected to be lower by $2.64 per unit.

b. Direct manufacturing labour costs for New CE100 are expected to be lower by $0.60 per unit.

c. Machining time required to manufacture New CE100 is expected to be 20% less. It currently takes one hour to manufacture one unit of CE100.

d. Time required for testing New CE100 is expected to be lower by 20%.

e. Rework is expected to decline to 4% of New CE100s manufactured.

Assume that the cost per unit of the cost driver for CE100 continues to apply to New CE100.

REQUIRED

1. Calculate Cutler's manufacturing cost per unit of New CE100.
2. Will the new design achieve the per-unit cost reduction targets that have been set for the manufacturing costs of New CE 100?
3. The problem describes two strategies to reduce costs: (a) improving manufacturing efficiency and (b) modifying the design. Which strategy has a bigger impact on costs? Why? Explain briefly.

LEARNING OBJECTIVE 3

1. Cost plus and life cycle—Advanced. (S. Sridhar, adapted) Waterbury Inc. manufactures and sells RF17, a specialty raft used for whitewater rafting. In 2009, it reported the following:

	2009
Units produced and sold	20,000
Investment	$2,400,000
Full cost per unit	$300
Rate of return on investment	20%
Markup percentage on variable cost	50%

REQUIRED

1. What was the selling price in 2009? What was the percentage markup on full cost? What was the variable cost per unit?
2. Waterbury is considering raising its selling price to $348. However, at this price, its sales volume is predicted to fall by 10%. If Waterbury's cost structure (variable cost per unit and total fixed costs) remains unchanged and if its demand forecast is accurate, should it raise the selling price to $348?
3. In 2010, due to increased competition, Waterbury must reduce its selling price to $315 in order to sell 20,000 units. The manager of the rafts division reduces annual investment to $2,100,000 but still demands a 20% target rate of return on investment. If fixed costs cannot be changed in this time frame, what is the target variable cost per unit?

2. Cost plus and life cycle—Advanced. (S. Sridhar, adapted) Waterford Inc. manufactures and sells 15,000 units of a raft, RF17, in 2010. The full cost per unit is $240. Waterford earns a 20% return on an investment of $2,160,000 in 2010. Ignore any income tax effects.

REQUIRED

1. Calculate the selling price of RF17 in 2010. Calculate the markup percentage on the full cost per unit of RF17 in 2010.
2. If the markup percentage on variable costs per unit is 40%, calculate the variable cost per unit of RF17 in 2010.
3. Calculate Waterford's operating income if it sold 13,500 units of RF17 at a price of $276 per unit in 2010. Assume no change in total fixed costs for 2010.
4. In response to competitive pressures, Waterford must reduce the price of RF17 to $252 in 2011 to achieve sales of 15,000 units. Waterford plans to reduce its investment to $1,980,000. If Waterford wants to maintain a 20% return on investment, what is the target cost per unit in 2011?

LEARNING OBJECTIVE 4

1. Non-cost factors—Advanced. Examples of prices charged by Phones-R-Us for long-distance telephone calls within Canada at different times of the day and week are as follows:

Peak period (8 a.m. to 6 p.m., Monday through Friday)	Basic rate
Evenings (6 p.m. to 11 p.m., Monday through Friday)	35% savings
Nights and weekends	60% savings

REQUIRED

Are there differences in incremental or outlay costs per minute for Phones-R-Us for telephone calls made during peak hours compared with telephone calls made at other times of the day?

LEARNING OBJECTIVE 5

1. **Corporate social responsibility and corporate governance—Advanced.** A recent study by Schnietz and Epstein (2005)[21] reported that during a crisis, a reservoir of goodwill that has been generated by good corporate governance and social responsibility protects financial returns to shareholders. Their study of decreases in returns of Fortune 500 firms following the World Trade Organization (WTO) failure in Seattle in 1999 accumulates the decrease in return from November 26 to 29, 1999.

◆ Firms in industries with reputations for irresponsible environmental or labour practices (primarily natural resource extraction and processing companies) suffered, on average, declines in share price exceeding 3% or US$418 million. Within this group, however, those with good reputations for responsible practices saw no share price decrease attributable to the failure of the WTO in Seattle.

◆ The group of firms in the industries with good reputations for responsible conduct of their businesses experienced no significant negative return. Within this group of well-reputed firms, those lacking a positive reputation for social responsibility endured a decline of 1.77% or US$85 million in lost market capitalization compared to no decrease for firms with good reputations for social responsibility.

◆ In the regression analysis, corporate social responsibility was positively and significantly correlated with the company's stock return; with a probability of as small as 1 in 1,000 the result was purely random. Difference in corporate social responsibility explained 16.7% of the difference in lost market capitalization (total common shares issued and outstanding × share price).

REQUIRED

1. What was the difference in lost financial returns to shareholders for the companies with poor reputations in the socially irresponsible industries compared to companies with poor reputations in the socially responsible industries?

2. As a shareholder who has estimated risk, including sustainability risk, would a decrease of 3% of the value of your investment be of concern?

3. What is the percentage difference in lost financial returns to shareholders in companies with good reputations in irresponsible industries and those with good reputations in responsible industries?

4. As a shareholder would you care about goodwill arising from a good reputation for corporate social responsibility when it explains only 16.7% of the change in return?

5. What is the difference between corporate social responsibility and corporate governance?

ASSIGNMENT MATERIAL

 Make the grade with MyAccountingLab: The questions, exercises, and problems marked in red can be found on MyAccountingLab at **www.myaccountinglab.com**. You can practise them as often as you want, and most feature step-by-step guided instructions to help you find the right answer. Exercises and problems with an Excel icon in the margin have an accompanying Excel template on MyAccountingLab.

SHORT-ANSWER QUESTIONS

12-1 What are the three major influences on pricing decisions?

12-2 Are there any circumstances when a firm would offer a price on a product or service that is below full cost? Explain.

12-3 Give two examples of pricing decisions with a short-run focus.

12-4 How is activity-based costing useful for pricing decisions?

12-5 Describe two alternative approaches to long-run pricing decisions.

12-6 What is a target cost per unit?

12-7 Describe value engineering and its role in target costing.

---

[21]K. E. Schnietz and M. J. Epstein, "Exploring the Financial Value of a Reputation for Corporate Social Responsibility During a Crisis," *Corporate Reputation Review*, 7.4 (2005): 327–345.

12-8 Give two examples each of a value-added cost and a non-value-added cost.

12-9 "It is not important for a firm to distinguish between cost incurrence and locked-in costs." Do you agree? Explain.

12-10 What is cost-plus pricing?

12-11 Describe three alternative cost-plus methods.

12-12 Give two examples where the difference in the costs of two products or services is much smaller than the difference in their prices.

12-13 What is life-cycle budgeting?

12-14 What are three benefits of using a product-life-cycle reporting format?

12-15 Define predatory pricing, dumping, and collusive pricing.

EXERCISES

12-16 Cost-plus target return on investment pricing. John Beck is the managing partner of a partnership that has just finished building a 60-room motel. Beck anticipates that he will rent these rooms for 16,000 nights next year (or 16,000 room-nights). All rooms are similar and will rent for the same price. Beck estimates the following operating costs for next year:

Variable operating costs	$4 per room-night
Fixed costs:	
Salaries and wages	$177,000
Maintenance of building and pool	$ 40,000
Other operating and administration costs	$141,000
Total fixed costs	$358,000

2

1. Target contribution per room-night, $38

The capital invested in the motel is $1,000,000. The partnership's target return on investment is 25%. Beck expects demand for rooms to be about uniform throughout the year. He plans to price the rooms at full cost plus a markup on full cost to earn the target return on investment. Ignore any income tax effects.

REQUIRED

1. What price should Beck charge for a room-night? What is the markup as a percentage of the full cost of a room-night?
2. Beck's market research indicates that if the price of a room-night determined in requirement 1 were reduced by 10%, the expected number of room-nights Beck could rent would increase by 10%. Should Beck reduce prices by 10%?

12-17 Cost-plus pricing, different definitions of costs. Wellington Ltd. manufactures bedroom furniture. Its primary customers are hotel chains, and the company manufactures large quantities of products per customer specification. It recently has received a request from Holiday Hotels to bid on a contract to supply a multipurpose cabinet. The cabinet will be designed to house a TV, mini fridge, and coffee maker as well as provide some storage. Holiday Hotels is interested in purchasing 10,000 units for its 50 hotels across Ontario. The estimated manufacturing costs per cabinet are:

1

Direct materials	$45.00
Direct labour, 1.5 hours @ $18	$27.00
Variable overhead rate	$6 per direct labour hour
Fixed overhead rate	$8 per direct labour hour

Variable selling costs are $4 per unit. The company has determined that fixed administration charges of $25,000 should be allocated to this contract.

REQUIRED

1. Calculate the total cost of this order under each of the following definitions of "cost":
   i. Absorption manufacturing cost
   ii. Variable manufacturing cost
   iii. Total variable product cost
   iv. Total (full) product cost.
2. Calculate the estimated bid prices assuming the following pricing policies:
   i. 210% of absorption manufacturing cost
   ii. 240% of variable manufacturing cost

iii. 225% of total variable cost

iv. 200% of total cost.

3. Compare your prices calculated in part 2. Under what circumstances would you recommend each of the pricing policies?

12-18 Target costs, effect of product-design changes on product costs. Medical Instruments manufactures many products. To compute manufacturing costs, it uses an accounting system with one direct-cost category (direct materials) and three indirect-cost categories:

1. Batch-related setup, production order, and material-handling costs, all which vary with the number of batches.

2. Manufacturing operations costs that vary with machine-hours.

3. Costs of engineering changes that vary with the number of engineering changes made.

In response to competitive pressures, product designers at Medical Instruments have employed value-engineering methods to reduce manufacturing costs. Actual information for 2010 and budgeted information for 2011 follow:

	Actuals for 2010	Budgeted for 2011
Total setup, production order, and material-handling costs	$ 8,858,750	$ 9,200,000
Total number of batches	950	1,000
Total manufacturing operations costs	$15,255,000	$16,250,000
Total quantity of machine-hours worked	226,000	250,000
Total costs of engineering changes	$ 2,864,160	$ 2,500,000
Total number of engineering changes	216	200

The management of Medical Instruments wants to evaluate whether value engineering has succeeded in reducing the target cost per unit of one of its products, HJ6, by 12%. Actual data for 2010 and budgeted data for 2011 for HJ6 follow:

	Actuals for 2010	Budgeted for 2011
Units of HJ6 produced	3,600	4,000
Direct materials costs per unit	$ 1,500	$ 1,410
Total number of batches required to produce HJ6	72	85
Total machine hours to produce HJ6	21,600	22,440
Number of engineering changes	15	10

REQUIRED

1. Calculate the actual manufacturing cost per unit of HF6 in 2010.

2. Calculate the estimated manufacturing cost per unit of HF6 in 2011.

3. Did Medical Instruments achieve the target cost per unit for HF6?

4. Comment briefly on how Medical Instruments was able to reduce the estimated cost per unit of HF6 in 2011.

12-19 Cost-plus pricing, missing data. Information relating to the costs of Brigham Ltd.'s only product is summarized below:

Direct materials cost per unit	$145.00
Direct labour cost per unit	$110.00
Variable overhead cost per unit	$ 90.00
Applied fixed manufacturing cost per unit	?
Variable selling and administrative cost per unit	$ 50.00
Allocated fixed selling and administrative cost per unit	$ 30.00

The company has established a target price of $575, which is a 15% markup on total product cost.

REQUIRED

1. What is the amount of fixed manufacturing overhead applied (allocated) to each unit?

2. Determine the percentage markup that would be necessary to achieve the target price of $575 under each of the following cost definitions:

i. Absorption manufacturing cost

ii. Total variable product cost

iii. Variable manufacturing cost

12-20 Life-cycle product costing, product emphasis. Starlight Systems Ltd. is examining the profitability and pricing policies of its software division. Starlight develops software for a variety of clients. Currently it is examining three of its products used by engineering firms. Data regarding these products follow:

◆ Power—software for electrical engineers

◆ Mecha—software for mechanical engineers

◆ Solutions—software for chemical engineers

Summary details on each software package over its two-year "cradle-to-grave" product life are as follows:

2. Mecha operating income, $2,225,500

Software	Selling Price	Number of Units Sold	
		Year 1	Year 2
Power	$420	2,500	8,400
Mecha	$525	2,500	5,000
Solutions	$300	5,000	2,500

Assume that no inventory remains on hand at the end of year 2.

Starlight is deciding which product lines to emphasize in its software division. In the past two years, the profitability of this division has been mediocre and Starlight is particularly concerned with the increase in R&D costs in several of its divisions. An analyst in the software division pointed out that, for one of its most recent packages (Solutions), major efforts had been made to cut back R&D costs.

Last week Nancy Sullivan, the software division manager, attended a seminar on product life-cycle management. Sullivan decides to use life-cycle reporting. She collects the following life-cycle cost information for the engineering software packages:

	Power		Mecha		Solutions	
	Year 1	Year 2	Year 1	Year 1	Year 2	Year 1
Revenues	$1,050,000	$3,528,000	$1,312,500	$2,625,000	$1,500,000	$750,000
R&D	950,000	0	690,000	0	430,000	0
Product design	246,000	22,000	156,000	11,000	145,000	27,000
Manufacturing	120,000	336,000	130,000	130,000	180,000	70,000
Marketing	217,500	462,000	150,000	190,000	300,000	250,000
Distribution	20,000	75,000	30,000	45,000	75,000	45,000
Customer service	50,000	400,000	60,000	120,000	280,000	470,000

REQUIRED

1. How does a product-life-cycle income statement differ from an income statement that is fiscal year–based? What are the benefits of using a product-life-cycle reporting format?

2. Present a product-life-cycle income statement for each software package. Which package is the most profitable, and which is the least profitable?

3. How do the three software packages differ in their cost structure (the percentage of total costs in each cost category)?

12-21 Target prices, target costs. Hogan Ltd. is about to introduce a new product to the market. Hogan has established a target 40% return on sales. The costs of the new product are estimated as follows:

2. Total product cost per unit, $61

Direct materials per unit	$16
Direct labour per unit	$12
Variable overhead per unit	$18
Fixed overhead applied per unit	$15

Hogan has received an order for 15,000 units of this product at a price of $70 per unit.

REQUIRED

1. At a price of $70, what is the target cost per unit?

2. What is the total profit from the order assuming full product costing?

3. What would be the profit if the company achieved its target cost and maintained the $70 price?

4. Should the order be accepted? Fully explain.

12-22 Life-cycle product costing. Intentical Inc. manufactures game systems. Intentical has decided to create and market a new system with wireless controls and excellent video graphics. Intentical's managers are thinking of calling this system the Yew. Based on experience, they expect the total life cycle of the Yew to be four years. They budget the following costs for the Yew:

		Total Fixed Costs Over 4 Years	Variable Cost per Unit
Year 1	R&D costs	$ 6,590,000	Not applicable
	Design costs	$ 1,450,000	Not applicable
Years 2–4	Production costs	$19,560,000	$50 per unit
	Marketing and distribution costs	$ 5,242,000	$10 per unit
	Customer-service costs	$ 2,900,000	Not applicable

REQUIRED

1. Suppose the managers price the Yew game at $110 per unit. How many units do they need to sell to break even?

2. The managers are reviewing two alternative pricing strategies:
   a. Sell the Yew at $110 each from the outset. At this price they expect to sell 1,500,000 units over its life cycle.
   b. Boost the selling price of the Yew in year 2 when it first comes out to $240. At this price, they expect to sell 100,000 units in year 2. In years 3 and 4, they will drop the price to $110 per unit and believe unit sales will be 1,200,000.
   What pricing strategy would you recommend? Explain.

3. What other factors should Intentical consider in choosing its pricing strategy?

12-23 Cost-plus pricing, bidding, corporate social responsibility. Wilson Ltd. manufactures promotional items (pens, mechanical pencils, buttons, etc.). Recently, it has been approached by a large charity to supply 2 million pens. The charity is obligated to receive at least three bids before selecting a supplier. The charity also specifies that the maximum price it will pay is total cost plus 12%. Total cost is defined to include all variable costs of production and distribution as well as a reasonable allocation of fixed manufacturing and fixed administrative costs. The charity has also indicated that any cost over $1.50 per pen will be rejected.

The controller for Wilson has determined the following costs would be applicable to the order:

Direct material	$122 per 100 pens
Direct labour	$20 per direct labour-hour
Variable overhead	$15 per direct labour-hour
Fixed overhead	$18 per direct labour-hour
Incremental administrative costs	$8,000 per order

The company will produce the units at a rate of 2,500 units per hour.

REQUIRED

1. Calculate the maximum price the charity will pay for the order.

2. What is the minimum price that Wilson could accept?

3. Independent of your answer to part 1, assume the maximum price under the charity guideline of total cost plus 12% works out to $1.20. The manager of the division points out that the charity is willing to pay $1.50 per pen and argues that any price quoted below $1.50 is "leaving profits on the table." He argues that Wilson should inflate its costs so that its price under the cost-plus formula will work out to $1.50. Do you agree with the manager? Fully explain your position.

12-24 Target rate of return on investment, activity-based costing. Electronic Arts (EA) distributes video games to retail stores and video-game arcades. It has a simple business model: order the video games, catalogue the games on the company's website, deliver and provide

1. Total fixed costs over life, $35,742,000

1. Total costs, $2,490,400

on-site support, and bill and collect from the customers. EA reported the following costs in April 2009:

Activity	Cost Driver	Quantity	Cost per Unit of Cost Driver
Ordering	Number of game vendors	40	$250 per vendor
Cataloguing	Number of new titles	20	$100 per title
Delivery and support	Number of deliveries	400	$15 per delivery
Billing and collection	Number of customers	300	$50 per customer

In April 2009, EA purchased 12,000 video-game discs at an average cost of $15 per disc, and sold them at an average price of $22 per disc. The catalogue on the website and the customer interactions that occur during delivery are EA's main marketing inputs. EA incurs no other costs.

REQUIRED

1. Calculate EA's operating income for April 2009. If the monthly investment in EA is $300,000, what rate of return on investment does the business earn?
2. The current crop of game systems is maturing, and prices for games are beginning to decline. EA anticipates that from May onward, it will be able to sell 12,000 game discs each month for an average of $18 per disc and can purchase the discs at a cost of $12 each. Assuming other costs are the same as in April, will EA be able to earn its 15% target rate of return on investment?
3. EA's small workforce gathers as a team and considers process improvements. They recommend "firing" the marginal vendors—those who need a lot of hand-holding but whose titles are not very popular. They agree that they should shift some of their resources from vendor relationships and cataloguing to delivery and customer relationships. In May 2009, EA reports the following support costs:

Activity	Cost Driver	Quantity	Cost per Unit of Cost Driver
Ordering	Number of game vendors	30	$200 per vendor
Cataloguing	Number of new titles	15	$100 per title
Delivery and support	Number of deliveries	450	$20 per delivery
Billing and collection	Number of customers	300	$50 per customer

At a selling price of $18 and a cost of $12 per disc, how many game discs must EA sell in May to earn its 15% target rate of return on investment?

12-25 **Pricing of special orders, corporate social responsibility.** Taylor Ltd. manufactures cosmetic bags. The average selling price of the bag is $15. Each bag has variable manufacturing costs of $7.20 per unit and applied fixed production costs of $4.60. These cosmetic bags are sold through specialty gift shops, and Taylor's salespeople earn a 10% commission for sales to these distributors. Fixed selling and administrative costs are $150,000 per year.

One of Taylor's sales staff has obtained a request to bid on an order for 1,500 units. Taylor is currently operating above the breakeven point.

REQUIRED

1. Assuming that Taylor has sufficient capacity, what is the minimum selling price Taylor should charge on the order?
2. Assume that Taylor requires a target return of 12%. What is the bid price for the order?
3. Now assume that Taylor will have to incur setup costs of $7,950. What is the bid price for the order if Taylor requires a 10% return?
4. Return to the original data. Assume the cosmetic bags produced for this order will be sold through a number of retailers. The customer would like to retail the bags for $16 and donate excess profits to a local women's shelter. The customer has proposed that Taylor supply the bags at incremental cost plus $0.25 profit per bag. The customer will take a $0.10 profit per bag and donate the rest to the charity. Under this proposal, the salesperson would receive a $0.50 commission per unit.
   i. What will be Taylor's rate of return if it agrees to the customer's proposal?
   ii. How much money will be raised for the charity assuming all bags are sold?
   iii. Should Taylor accept the customer's proposal? Discuss the financial and corporate social responsibility issues raised.

12-26 Cost-plus and market-based pricing. Alberta Temps, a large labour contractor, supplies contract labour to building construction companies. For 2009, Alberta has budgeted to supply 80,000 hours of contract labour. Its variable costs are $12 per hour, and its fixed costs are $240,000. Roger Mason, the general manager, has proposed a cost-plus approach for pricing labour at full cost plus 20%.

REQUIRED
1. Calculate the price per hour that Alberta Temps should charge based on Mason's proposal.
2. The marketing manager supplies the following information on demand levels at different prices:

Price per Hour	Demand (Hours)
$16	120,000
$17	100,000
$18	80,000
$19	70,000
$20	60,000

Alberta can meet any of these demand levels. Fixed costs will remain unchanged for all the demand levels. On the basis of the additional information, calculate the price per hour that Alberta should charge to maximize operating income.
3. Comment on your answers to requirements 1 and 2. Why are they the same or different?

PROBLEMS

12-27 Pricing dispute. Urban Solutions manufactures bicycle parking systems. With the push towards environmentally friendly modes of transportation, it sees a huge opportunity to expand its business by selling these systems to large cities and private downtown businesses such as hotels. It sees its bicycle storage solutions as being replacements to the downtown car parkades. It is currently preparing a bid for the City of Vancouver. The city is interested in purchasing 1,400 of these bicycle parking systems. The City has agreed to a cost plus 25% price. The company has capacity to produce 15,000 units and is currently operating at 70% of its capacity. Cost data for the production of the order for the City of Vancouver are as follows:

Direct materials	$175,000
Direct labour	$245,000
Indirect materials (variable)	$161,000
Fixed overhead allocated	$168,000
Variable selling and distribution costs	$ 42,000
Variable administration costs	$ 35,700
Fixed administration costs (indirect)	$ 58,100

On completion of the order, Urban Solutions billed the City of Vancouver $1,106,000 (based on 1,400 at a unit price of $790). The City is disputing the charge, and argues that the unit price under the contract should be $588.13.

REQUIRED
1. How did the company determine the unit selling price of $790?
2. How did the City determine its unit selling price of $588.13?
3. What price do you recommend should be charged by Urban Solutions and how would you resolve this dispute?

12-28 Cost-plus, target pricing, working backward. The new CEO of Roile Manufacturing has asked for a variety of information about the operations of the firm from last year. The CEO is given the following information, but with some data missing:

Total sales revenue	?
Number of units produced and sold	500,000
Selling price	?
Operating income	$ 225,000
Total investment in assets	$2,500,000
Variable cost per unit	$ 2.50
Fixed costs for the year	$3,250,000

1. Find (a) total sales revenue, (b) selling price, (c) rate of return on investment, and (d) markup percentage on full cost for this product.
2. The new CEO has a plan to reduce fixed costs by $250,000 and variable costs by $0.50 per unit. Using the same markup percentage as in requirement 1, calculate the new selling price.
3. Assume the CEO institutes the changes in requirement 2, including the new selling price, expecting to sell more units of product because of the lower price. However, the reduction in variable costs has resulted in lower product quality, leading to 10% fewer units being sold compared to before the change. Calculate operating income (loss).

12-29 Product costs, activity-based costing systems. Executive Power (EP) manufactures and sells computers and computer peripherals to several nationwide retail chains. Johan Farnham is the manager of the printer division. Its two largest-selling printers are P-41 and P-63.

The manufacturing cost of each printer is calculated using EP's activity-based costing system. EP has one direct manufacturing cost category (direct materials) and the following five indirect manufacturing cost pools:

Indirect Manufacturing Cost Pool	Allocation Base	Allocation Rate
1. Materials-handling	Number of parts	$1.38 per part
2. Assembly management	Hours of assembly time	$60 per assembly hour
3. Machine insertion of parts	Number of machine-inserted parts	$0.80 per machine-inserted part
4. Manual insertion of parts	Number of manually inserted parts	$3.20 per manually inserted part
5. Quality testing	Inspection hours	$40 per inspection hour

Product characteristics of P-41 and P-63 are as follows:

	P-41	P-63
Direct materials cost	$525	$375
Number of parts	90 parts	48 parts
Assembly hours	3.5 hours	1.8 hours
Number of machine-inserted parts	48 parts	28 parts
Number of manually inserted parts	36 parts	12 parts
Inspection hours	1.6 hours	0.9 hours

REQUIRED
What is the manufacturing cost of P-41? of P-63?

12-30 Target cost, activity-based costing systems (continuation of 12-29). Assume all the information in Problem 12-29. Farnham has just received some bad news. A foreign competitor has introduced products very similar to P-41 and P-63. Given their announced selling prices, Farnham estimates the P-41 clone to have a manufacturing cost of approximately $975 and the P-63 clone to have a manufacturing cost of approximately $560. He calls a meeting of product designers and manufacturing personnel at the printer division. They all agree to have the $975 and $560 figures become target costs for redesigned versions of EP's P-41 and P-63, respectively. Product designers examine alternative ways of designing printers with comparable performance but lower cost. They come up with the following revised designs for P-41 and P-63 (termed P-41 REV and P-63 REV, respectively):

	P-41 REV	P-63 REV
Direct materials cost	$505.20	$347.62
Number of parts	76 parts	41 parts
Assembly hours	2.9 hours	1.5 hours
Number of machine-inserted parts	60 parts	30 parts
Number of manually inserted parts	15 parts	8 parts
Inspection hours	1.5 hours	0.8 hours

Total indirect manufacturing product costs for P-63, $271.04

Total indirect manufacturing product costs P-63 REV, $228.18

REQUIRED

1. Define *target cost per unit.*
2. Using the activity-based costing system outlined in Problem 12-29, compute the manufacturing costs of P-41 REV and P-63 REV. How do they compare with the target costs per unit?
3. Explain the differences between P-41 and P-41 REV and between P-63 and P-63 REV.
4. Assume now that Johan Farnham has achieved major cost reductions in one of the activity areas. As a consequence, the allocation rate in the assembly management activity area will be reduced from $60 to $49.40 per assembly-hour. How will this activity-area cost reduction affect the manufacturing costs of P-41 REV and P-63 REV? Comment on the results.

1. Total direct costs Deluxe, $12,400

12-31 Cost-plus pricing, activity-based costing, target pricing. Plume Ltd. manufactures two models of its product, Standard and Deluxe. In reviewing its operations it has identified five different types of overhead and their associated costs:

Purchasing	$1,125,000
Receiving	$ 630,000
Setups	$ 450,000
Machine-related costs	$1,620,000
Shipping	$ 675,000

Under its current costing system, Plume allocates overhead on the basis of machine-hours. The plant has a capacity of 250,000 machine-hours and is fully utilized. Information regarding each of its products is summarized below:

	Standard	Deluxe
Number of units produced	660	540
Direct materials per unit	$ 7,300	$ 9,650
Direct labour per unit	$ 2,400	$ 2,750
Number of items purchased	1,440	2,160
Number of setups	150	100
Number of incoming shipments	60	60
Kilometres of outgoing shipments	5,500	7,000
Machine-hours	125,000	125,000

REQUIRED

1. The company's current policy is to price at 130% of direct costs. Is this pricing policy appropriate?
2. The company has examined the marketplace for its Deluxe product. It believes the maximum it can charge is $20,000 per unit. Can Plume earn a target 15% return at this price?

12-32 Cost-plus and market-based pricing. (CMA, adapted) Best Test Laboratories evaluates the reaction of materials to extreme increases in temperature. Much of the company's early growth was attributable to government contracts. Recent growth has come from diversification and expansion into commercial markets. Environmental testing at Best Test now includes:

2. HTT test pool labour costs, $186,000

Heat testing (HTT)	Arctic condition testing (ACT)
Air turbulence testing (ATT)	Aquatic testing (AQT)
Stress testing (SST)	

Currently, all the budgeted operating costs are collected in a single overhead pool. All the estimated testing hours are also collected in a single pool. One rate per test-hour is used for all five types of testing. This hourly rate is marked up by 40% to recover administrative costs, taxes, and profit in the selling price.

Rick Shaw, Best Test's controller, believes that there is enough variation in the test procedures and cost structure to establish separate costing and billing rates. He also believes that the inflexible rate structure currently being used is inadequate in today's competitive environment. After analyzing the following data, he has recommended new rates for Best Test's upcoming fiscal year.

The budgeted total test laboratory costs for the coming year are

Test-pool labour (10 employees)	$ 620,000
Supervision	90,000
Equipment amortization	225,000
Heat	210,000
Electricity	150,000
Water	98,000
Setup	75,000
Indirect materials	240,000
Operating supplies	62,000
Total test lab costs	$1,770,000
Total estimated test-hours	120,000

Shaw has determined the resource usage by test type in the following table:

	HTT	ATT	SST	ACT	AQT
Test-pool labour employees	3	2	2	1	2
Supervision	40%	15%	15%	15%	15%
Amortization	$63,000	$27,000	$45,000	$33,750	$56,250
Heat	50%	5%	5%	30%	10%
Electricity	30%	10%	10%	40%	10%
Water	0%	0%	20%	20%	60%
Setup	25%	10%	30%	15%	20%
Indirect materials	12%	18%	30%	20%	20%
Operating supplies	10%	10%	24%	20%	36%
Test-hours	33,600	14,400	31,200	25,200	15,600
Competitors' hourly billing rate	$ 20.30	$ 23.60	$ 20.00	$ 18.50	$ 26.00

REQUIRED

1. Compute the single-pool hourly cost and hourly billing rate for Best Test Laboratories.
2. Compute the five separate hourly billing rates for Best Test Laboratories.
3. Discuss what effect the new cost-plus method will have on the pricing structure for each of the five test types. Given the competitors' hourly billing rates, how might Best Test modify its pricing?
4. In general, identify at least three other internal or external factors that influence pricing structure.

12-33 Pricing of a special order. Fane Industries Ltd. has been approached by a customer who wishes to purchase 50,000 units of its product at $52 per unit. The customer requires delivery within one month. The company has capacity to produce 350,000 units per month and has 5,000 units currently in stock. Sales to Fane's regular customers are forecast at 325,000 units for the upcoming month. The sales manager has indicated that if the company accepts the special order, it would be able to recover 30% of the sales lost to regular customers. Units sold through normal distribution channels have a selling price of $70 per unit and the gross margin earned on each unit is $24. Selling and administration costs total $16 per unit.

A further analysis determined that the variable manufacturing costs of the regular units are $35 per unit with variable selling costs of $12 per unit. Because of the nature of the special order, the selling costs will be reduced to $8.00 per unit.

1. Total lost sales, 14,000

REQUIRED

1. Should Fane accept the offer from the customer?
2. What is the minimum price Fane should charge for this order?
3. What factors should be considered in pricing special orders?

12-34 Life-cycle product costing, activity-based costing. Destin Products makes digital watches. Destin is preparing a product-life-cycle budget for a new watch, MX3. Development on the new watch with features such as a calculator and a daily diary is to start shortly. Destin expects the watch to have a product life cycle of three years. Estimates about MX3 are as follows:

	Year 1	Year 2	Year 3
Unitsmanufactured and sold	50,000	200,000	150,000
Price per watch	$ 55	$ 50	$ 45
R&D costs	$1,200,000	$150,000	$ 0
Manufacturing costs:			
Variable cost per unit	$ 20.00	$ 18.00	$ 18.00
Variable cost per batch	$ 860	$ 750	$ 750
Watches per batch	400	500	500
Fixed costs	$ 800,000	$800,000	$800,000
Marketing:			
Variable cost per watch	$ 4.20	$ 3.75	$ 3.50
Fixed costs	$ 400,000	$320,000	$320,000
Distribution:			
Variable cost per watch	$ 1.50	$ 1.50	$ 1.50
Variable cost per batch	$ 160	$ 200	$ 150
Watches per batch	200	160	150
Fixed costs	$ 300,000	$300,000	$300,000
Customer-service costs per watch	$ 3.00	$ 2.40	$ 2.00

REQUIRED
(Ignore the time value of money in your answers.)

1. Calculate the budgeted life-cycle operating income for the new watch.
2. What percentage of the budgeted product-life-cycle costs will be incurred at the end of the R&D and design stages?
3. An analysis reveals that 80% of the total product-life-cycle costs of the new watch will be locked in at the end of the R&D and design stages. What implications would this finding have on managing MX3's costs?
4. Destin's market research department estimates that reducing MX3's price by $3.50 each year will increase sales by 10% each year. If sales increase by 10%, Destin will increase the batch size for manufacturing in year 1 by only 10%. Assume that all variable costs per watch, variable costs per batch, and fixed costs will remain the same. Should Destin reduce MX3's price by $3.50?

④ ⑤

12-35 Governance, corporate social responsibility, and sustainability. Clarke Ltd. is a Canadian company with its headquarters and Canadian manufacturing plant located in Mississauga, Ontario. The company also has a plant in Tianjin, China. The company manufactures a variety of medical products, including oxygen masks, feeding tubes, catheters, and other plastic hoses used in a variety of applications. Clarke has been asked to bid on a contract for the Hope Children's Hospital, located in London, Ontario. If Clarke wins the bid, it would be the exclusive supplier of these medical supplies to the hospital for a two-year period.

As a public institution, the hospital will award the contract to the lowest bidder, but will factor in quality of the product in reviewing the bids.

The management of Clarke Ltd. is keen to win this order. It has lost recent bids and is currently operating well below capacity in its Mississauga plant. Without this contract, Clarke anticipates it will have to lay off workers in Canada.

The Tianjin plant is operating near capacity. Clarke knows its costs to manufacture in China are significantly less than in Canada for several reasons:

a. Labour costs are 40% lower.
b. Due to more stringent environmental regulations in Canada, the fixed costs allocated per unit are approximately 30% lower in China (assuming both plants operate at long-run normal capacity).
c. Energy costs are 20% lower in China due to the use of coal as the primary fuel.

Clarke is considering how it should approach the bid for this contract. It is deciding whether it should produce in China or in Mississauga. It believes that although the Tianjin plant is near capacity, it will be able to accommodate this order without a significant effect on its existing sales. It is also considering whether it should negotiate with its workers in Mississauga to reduce their wages by 20% to make the plant more competitive.

Clarke also knows that one of the ways to reduce its costs (and hence improve its chance of being successful on its bid) is to use a lower grade of plastic in production of the masks and tubes. This lower grade of plastic would save 25% of the direct materials costs. It is known, however, to puncture more easily and have a shorter useful life. This means that a patient who has an extended stay at the hospital would require the tubes and masks be replaced more frequently.

REQUIRED

1. Discuss the ethical and corporate social responsibility issues raised.
2. Discuss the sustainability issues raised.
3. What are your recommendations to Clarke on how it should proceed with the bid?

12-36 Cost-plus, target return on investment pricing. Vend-o-licious makes candy bars for vending machines and sells them to vendors in cases of 30 bars. Although Vend-o-licious makes a variety of candy, the cost differences are insignificant and the cases all sell for the same price.

2. Contribution margin, $3,500,000

Vend-o-licious has a total investment in capital of $13,000,000. It expects to sell 500,000 cases of candy next year as it has had relatively constant sales over the past few years. The company requires a 10% target return on investment. Expected costs for next year are:

Variable production costs	$3.50 per case
Variable marketing and distribution costs	$1.50 per case
Fixed production costs	$ 1,000,000
Fixed marketing and distribution costs	$ 700,000
Other fixed costs	$ 500,000

Vend-o-licious prices the cases of candy at full cost plus markup to generate profits equal to the target return on capital.

REQUIRED

1. What is the target operating income?
2. What is the selling price the company needs to charge to earn the target operating income? Calculate the markup percentage on full cost.
3. Vend-o-licious's closest competitor has just increased its candy case price to $15, although it sells 36 candy bars per case. Vend-o-licious is considering increasing its selling price to $14 per case. Assuming sales decrease by 5%, calculate the company's return on investment. Is increasing the selling price a good idea?

12-37 Product life cycle and pricing. (J. Watson) Neptune Ltd. is an established manufacturer of robotic equipment used in industrial applications. Recently it has faced increased competition, primarily from companies in India, and its market share has eroded and profits are declining.

1. Total life-cycle revenues, $57,050,000

To restore its position in the industry, it established a new division to research new applications of the equipment and to design and develop these new products. The inaugural product from the division is the Triton, to be used in the aerospace industry. The costs expended in the preliminary stages of the product were as follows:

R&D costs	$1,800,000
Design	$1,600,000

In order to manufacture these specialized robots, the company had to adapt existing production equipment at a cost of $900,000. It also invested $400,000 in startup marketing costs, $250,000 in distribution, and $350,000 in establishing a separate customer-service department. Neptune believes that in Year 1 it will have to spend another $125,000 on design-related costs.

Neptune realizes that technology rapidly becomes obsolete, so it predicts that the Triton will have a four-year life (post-development). It estimates the following sales:

	Year 1	Year 2	Year 3	Year 4
Units sold	150	400	250	100
Selling price	$62,000	$65,000	$63,000	$60,000

Additional information regarding the production of the Triton follows:
a. Direct materials costs for the Triton are expected to be $16,000 per unit.
b. Direct manufacturing labour costs for the Triton are estimated at $7,000 per unit.

c. Overhead per unit is estimated at $15,000 per unit, of which 60% is fixed. The fixed overhead rate is based on a normal capacity of 250 units per year.

d. The Triton is costly to ship to customers due to its weight and packaging needs. Distribution costs will average $3,200 per unit. Distribution costs are variable.

e. Marketing costs are predicted at $1,800 per unit, all variable.

f. Customer-service costs will be $2,400 per unit plus fixed costs of $250,000 per year.

REQUIRED

1. Prepare a product-life-cycle costing report.

2. Triton is considering dropping its price by 10%. It believes this will increase units sold in each year by 20%. Should Triton drop its price?

3. What are the advantages of using product-life-cycle reporting when setting prices?

COLLABORATIVE LEARNING CASE

③ ④

1. Tvez total ABC overhead allocation, $548,000

12-38 Target prices, target costs, value engineering. Avery Inc. manufactures two component parts for the television industry:

◆ Tvez, with annual production and sales of 50,000 units at a selling price of $56.35 per unit
◆ Premia, with annual production and sales of 25,000 units at a selling price of $78 per unit

Avery includes all R&D and design costs in engineering costs. Assume that Avery has no marketing, distribution, or customer-service costs.

The direct and overhead costs incurred by Avery on Tvez and Premia are described as follows:

	Tvez	Premia	Total
Direct materials costs (variable)	$1,200,000	$800,000	$2,000,000
Direct manufacturing labour costs (variable)	400,000	250,000	650,000
Direct machining costs (fixed)	200,000	150,000	350,000
Manufacturing overhead costs:			
Machine setup			120,000
Testing costs			600,000
Engineering cost			480,000
Total overhead costs			1,200,000
Total costs			$4,200,000

Avery's management identifies the following activity cost pools, cost drivers for each activity, and the costs per unit of cost driver for each overhead cost pool:

Activity	Description	Cost Driver	Cost per Unit of Cost Driver
Setup	Preparing machine to manufacture a new batch of products	Setup hours	$32 per setup-hour
Testing	Testing components and final product (each unit is tested individually)	Testing hours	$2.40 per testing-hour
Engineering	Designing products and processes and ensuring their smooth functioning	Complexity of product and process	Costs assigned to products by special study

Over a long-run time horizon, Avery's management views direct materials costs and direct manufacturing labour costs as variable with respect to the units of Tvez and Premia produced. Direct machining costs for each product do not vary over this time horizon and are fixed long-run costs. Overhead costs vary with respect to their chosen cost drivers. For example, setup costs vary with the number of setup-hours. Additional information is as follows:

	Tvez	Premia
Production batch size	500 units	200 units
Setup time per batch	15 hours	18 hours
Testing and inspection time per unit of product produced	2.5 hours	5 hours
Engineering costs incurred on each product	$200,000	$280,000

Avery is facing competitive pressure to reduce the price of Tvez and has set a target price of $48.00, well below its current price of $52.50. The challenge for Avery is to reduce the cost of Tvez. Avery's engineers have proposed a new product design and process improvements for the "New Tvez" to replace Tvez. The new design would improve product quality, and reduce scrap and waste. The reduction in prices will not enable Avery to increase its current sales. (However, if Avery does not reduce prices, it will lose sales.)

The expected effects of the new design relative to Tvez are as follows:

a. Direct materials costs for New Tvez are expected to decrease by $2.50 per unit.
b. Direct manufacturing labour costs for New Tvez are expected to decrease by $0.70 per unit.
c. Time required for testing each unit of New Tvez is expected to be reduced by 0.5 hours.
d. Machining time required to make New Tvez is expected to decrease by 20 minutes. It currently takes one hour to manufacture one unit of Tvez. The machines are dedicated to the production of New Tvez.
e. New Tvez will take seven setup-hours for each setup.
f. Engineering costs are unchanged.

Assume that the batch sizes are the same for New Tvez as for Tvez. If Avery requires additional resources to implement the new design, it can acquire these additional resources in the quantities needed. Further assume the costs per unit of cost driver for the New Tvez are the same as those described for Tvez.

INSTRUCTIONS

Form groups of two students to complete the following requirements.

REQUIRED

1. Develop full product costs per unit for Tvez and Premia, using an activity-based product-costing approach.
2. What is the markup on the full product cost per unit for Tvez?
3. What is Avery's target cost per unit for New Tvez if it is to maintain the same markup percentage on the full product cost per unit as it had for Tvez?
4. Will the New Tvez design achieve the cost-reduction targets that Avery has set?
5. What price would Avery charge for New Tvez if it used the same markup percentage on the full product cost per unit for New Tvez as it did for Tvez?
6. What price should Avery charge for New Tvez, and what next steps should Avery take regarding New Tvez? Address sustainability in your response.

Strategy, Balanced Scorecard, and Strategic Profitability Analysis

13

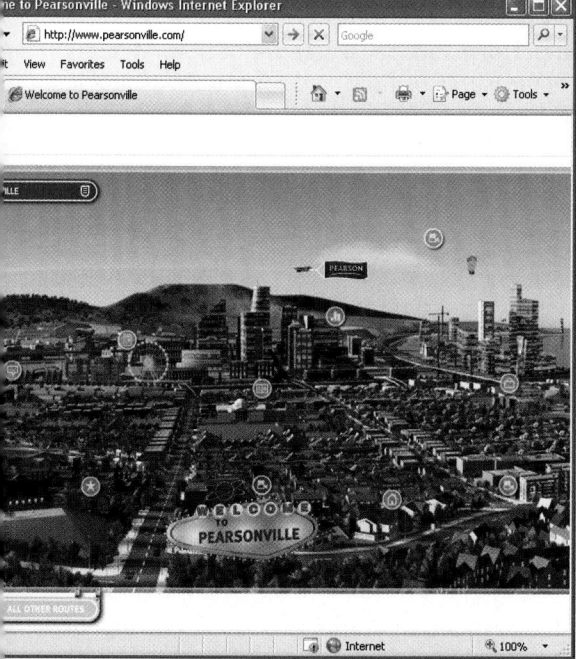

Balanced Performance Measures of Social and Financial Results

Pearson PLC is a global media company with a 2007 net profit of $617 million, of which 60% was generated by textbook sales. The company presents financial results, employee development policies, philanthropic projects, and an annual report on its financial, business, and society goals and achievements. These perspectives comprise a balanced score-card (BSC) report of financial and social success. Pearson PLC has won recognition for its environmental achievements including recycling and reuse of 95% of its textbooks. The company has also been recognized as a global leader in corporate sustainability.

After studying this chapter, you should be able to

1. Explain how short-term measures evaluate the success of long-term strategies

2. Apply the BSC to enterprise risk management (ERM) and explain the link between corporate governance and corporate competitiveness

3. Interpret the BSC in the context of enterprise risk management (ERM) of corporate and environmental sustainability

4. Implement and apply the BSC in a comprehensive analysis

5. Analyze specific productivity and capacity control strategies to achieve BSC expectations

Strategy is "a way of thinking that relies on hypothesis generation and testing. In hypothesizing, you ask the creative 'what if' questions. To test your hypothesis, you ask the analytic 'if . . . , then . . .' questions. You adopt a mindset that treats your method of accomplishing your purpose as an experiment. If that experiment fails, you try something else. . . . It is intelligently opportunistic in search of its goals . . . while leaving room for new and unintended strategies to emerge" (see Chapter 2). While it is open and flexible, strategy is the outcome of a deliberate, rational, reflective process.

This chapter presents an important tool to measure the success of competitive corporate strategy—the **balanced scorecard (BSC)**.[1] The BSC translates an organization's mission and strategy into a comprehensive set of performance measures that provide the framework for implementing its strategy. Competition itself is a definition of the external and uncontrollable environment in which a business operates either for profit or not for profit. An alternative environment is defined by cooperation while a third is defined by hierarchy, neither competitive nor cooperative but rather coerced by legislation and regulation. In this chapter we will focus on competitive strategy.

The BSC applies familiar management accounting techniques and measures of short-term operating success to evaluate the success of long-term strategy. The use of quantitative financial and nonfinancial performance measures is not new. What is new is their successful implementation as measures of how well long-term strategic goals have been achieved. The BSC began as a four-factor measure of corporate strategic achievement. It has expanded into multi-dimensional measurement of complex factors such as corporate social responsibility.

USEFULNESS OF BALANCED SCORECARDS

1 Explain how short-term measures evaluate the success of long-term strategies

Strategies have been classified in many different ways, but what is common is to set the business within its external environment. Strategic analysis highlights how, given its internal constraints, a business can respond best to change. The BSC introduced by Kaplan and Norton a decade ago comprised four distinct but interdependent perspectives contributing to financial profitability. They are financial, customer, internal business process, and learning and growth.

Financial Perspective The **financial perspective** highlights achievement of financially strategic goals. Among others, measures of financial achievement include operating and net profit margins, percentage increase in operating cash flow, return on capital employed (ROCE), return on either equity (ROE) or assets (ROA), and percentage increase in share price. Financial success, however, cannot be achieved in isolation.

Customer Perspective The **customer perspective** identifies the targeted market segments and measures the company's success in these segments. To measure its growth objectives, companies use market share, percentage growth in revenue, new segments reached, number of new customers, and customer satisfaction. Success with customers, however, depends on how well the company does relative to its competitors. The threats and opportunities presented in a competitive environment change.

Internal Business Process Perspective The **internal business process perspective** requires analysis of how to improve internal operations, which implicates the entire

[1]See R. S. Kaplan and D. P. Norton, *The Balanced Scorecard* (Cambridge: Harvard Business School Press, 1996); R. S. Kaplan and D. P. Norton, *The Strategy-Focused Organization: How Balanced Scorecard Companies Thrive in the New Business Environment* (Boston: Harvard Business School Press, 2001); and R. S. Kaplan and D. P. Norton, *Strategy Maps: Converting Intangible Assets into Tangible Outcomes* (Boston: Harvard Business School Press, 2004).

value chain of business functions. Measures of success have been discussed in Chapters 7 and 8 (variance analysis) and also include short- and long-term measures of capacity management (Chapter 9). Companies use public and private databases to understand both their competitive stature in an industry and any changes in the competitive environment. To meet competitive challenges, companies may physically take apart competitors' products to compare them with their own designs, with the goal of reverse engineering improvements to their own products and improving their management of costs.

Learning and Growth Perspective The **learning and growth perspective** has expanded to become a field of study of its own on the identification, development, retention, and valuation of **intellectual capital**. Intellectual capital comprises human, structural, and relational capital.

Human capital is the skill, expertise, experience, and innovativeness of employees measured as the number of suggestions for improvements or new products. *Structural capital* includes outputs such as patents and databases. It also includes internal routines and MIS which store knowledge. Retention of knowledge means retention of satisfied employees measured as reduced turnover, increased internal promotions, and fulfillment of external certifications. *Relational capital* arises from experience in business relationships with both clients and suppliers, measured as management of brands.

An intangible asset, intellectual capital is difficult to identify, let alone value.[2] In an increasingly knowledge-based economy, the BSC enables measurement of the effective management of intellectual capital because that capital is an important source of competitive advantage. In the long term, effective management of intellectual capital reduces costs of labour in a systematic way by enhancing the rate of learning of its labour force (Chapter 10).

The BSC recognizes not only interdependence among corporate business functions (see Exhibit 11-2 on p. 531), but also interdependence among corporate activities and the external environment. The BSC incorporates customers, costs, and competition (Chapter 12) in financial and nonfinancial performance measures that include intangibles. The relevant and reliable measures of achievement provide feedback on how well execution or implementation of strategy is progressing. The measures reflect reasonable cause–effect relationships.

Exhibit 13-1 illustrates the interdependencies among the four perspectives and strategic decision making. The central pie chart illustrates the strategic decision-making process. The boxes around the perimeter illustrate the four perspectives. Exhibit 13-1 incorporates interactions among customers, costs, and competitors when making strategic decisions such as pricing in the dotted lines among the perspectives. M. Porter pioneered strategy classification in his books *Competitive Strategy* (1980) and *Competitive Advantage* (1985). Porter simplified strategy into two generic alternatives for growth: product differentiation or cost leadership.[3]

In the strategic decision-making pie chart, the dynamic between setting strategic goals will fail without relevant input provided by BSC measures. The measures, however, must reflect some reasonable cause–effect assumption. This strategic decision making is an example of the Bayesian influence model in Exhibit 11-1. The information about outcomes (customer expectations) provided by BSC measurements influences top management's assumption about the probability of delivering a satisfactory service.

The more superior the intellectual capital in the company, the more able the managers are to understand these complex and interdependent causal chains. Excellent MIS, well-trained employees, and communication of successful customer relationship building all improve the quality of data that informs the selection of strategic goals.

[2]T. Sällebrant, J. Hansen, N. Bontis, and P. Hofman-Bang, "Managing Risk with Intellectual Capital Statements," *Management Decision* 45.9 (2007): 1470–1483.

[3]M. Porter, *Competitive Strategy* (New York: Free Press, 1980); M. Porter, *Competitive Advantage* (New York: Free Press, 1985); M. Porter, "What Is Strategy?" *Harvard Business Review* (November–December 1996): 61–78.

EXHIBIT 13-1
The Kaplan and Norton Balanced Scorecard

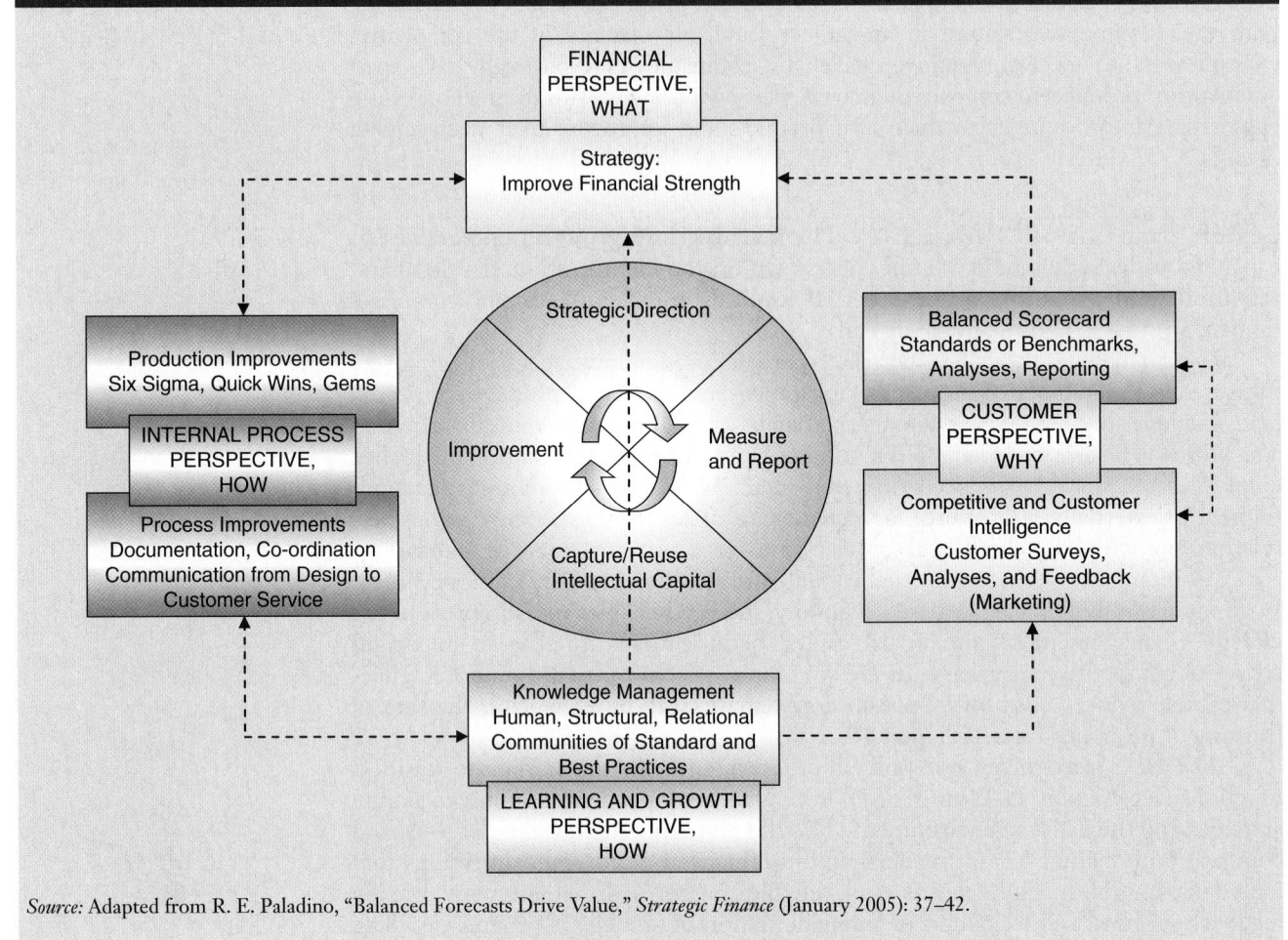

FINANCIAL PERSPECTIVE, WHAT

Strategy: Improve Financial Strength

Strategic Direction

Improvement

Measure and Report

Capture/Reuse Intellectual Capital

Production Improvements Six Sigma, Quick Wins, Gems

INTERNAL PROCESS PERSPECTIVE, HOW

Process Improvements Documentation, Co-ordination Communication from Design to Customer Service

Balanced Scorecard Standards or Benchmarks, Analyses, Reporting

CUSTOMER PERSPECTIVE, WHY

Competitive and Customer Intelligence Customer Surveys, Analyses, and Feedback (Marketing)

Knowledge Management Human, Structural, Relational Communities of Standard and Best Practices

LEARNING AND GROWTH PERSPECTIVE, HOW

Source: Adapted from R. E. Paladino, "Balanced Forecasts Drive Value," *Strategic Finance* (January 2005): 37–42.

The changes to service delivery (the internal processes) are responses to relevant information and are undertaken after strategic decisions are made. The *what*—improved growth and profitability—are decided in the context of *why* growth is a reasonable objective based on customers and competition. The management of intellectual capital and of change to internal processes are *how* the company will succeed. Note that the answer to *how* requires understanding cause and effect.

Companies such as Apple increase their market share in mobile communications by creating new product attributes such as novelty, versatility, and ease of use, which delight their customers—*product differentiation*. Apple most certainly surveys its potential customers to learn about desirable attributes, but its products have always been differentiated by ease of use or intuitiveness. Apple has developed and applied its superior intellectual capital when designing innovative products in a knowledge-based industry. A high-tech giant, Apple continues to surprise customers with products that meet their needs and continues to expand its market share against formidable competitors such as Toshiba (laptops) and RIM (mobile communication).

In contrast, companies such as Wal-Mart increase their market share in retail sales by providing standard products at the lowest cost—*cost leadership*. Wal-Mart pioneered practices of offshore supply-chain partnerships to drive down the costs of sales and exploited technology to improve internal processes of procurement. Customers, however, increasingly demand both differentiation and low prices, and many companies combine both generic strategies into a strategy called *agility*. Agility requires clear understanding of what the company was, is, and can be, given the limitations and opportunities in its competitive environment.

There are as many measures of cause and effect in each quadrant in the BSC as there are management teams and strategic objectives. In selecting measures, top management must understand how increases and decreases in these measures indicate effective or ineffective control of resources. While this text has focused on cost behaviour, the genius of the BSC was to provide a straightforward way to extend concepts of causality into other domains. The complexity of the most important causal chains within each company can be mapped using BSC measures.

INTERNAL BUSINESS PROCESS—RELEVANCE OF CUSTOMERS

The essence of a good BSC is that it represents well the "how"—the cause and effect both internal and external. That is why we start this discussion with the internal business process. In a case study, Paladino (2005) reported how one company improved profit through customer satisfaction.[4] The installation company surveyed customers and discovered the expected cycle time from order to completed installation was 21 days. The customers were most concerned with tasks completed in a timely way, earlier rather than later in the cycle. Accurate customer intelligence gave managers the basis upon which to establish a more relevant nonfinancial performance target—percentage of completion of all installation tasks undertaken earlier in the three-week cycle. Once this target was set, internal processes were redesigned to reach the new timeliness targets and improve customer satisfaction.

An unexpected result was to shorten the installation cycle time, which provided an opportunity to increase the volume of customers served. With a higher percentage of satisfied customers, increased volume followed. The company shortened the *cash-to-cash cycle*—between signing the contract and realizing the cashflow from rent of the installed product—to fewer days. Internal business process requires understanding how the company must change to fulfill the customers' needs.

This example illustrates the high relevance of customer information in the establishment of strategic goals. In Exhibit 13-1, the arrow between the financial and BSC box is continued with a double-directional arrow linking BSC measures to one uncontrollable external factor, the customer's expectations. In a competitive environment, if the company is unresponsive to changes relative to its competition, it will fail. At the root or bottom of the exhibit is intellectual capital management. It takes learning from past successes and mistakes to recognize and respond effectively to the changing needs of customers in a dynamic competitive environment. It also takes education, imagination, and communication to preserve the lessons learned—all of which are dimensions of intellectual capital.

CUSTOMER PERSPECTIVE—FINANCIAL AND NONFINANCIAL MEASURES

Market share, increased new-product acceptance, market size, and customer satisfaction are all nonfinancial measures of cause and effect. Ultimately higher volume of sales should result in increased revenue. This is a reasonable causal chain.

The measures of market share (and, from time to time, market size) need to be consistent with the revenue growth strategy. Companies can grow by improving efficiency and delivering at a lower cost, or by innovating to differentiate their offerings from those of competitors. Measures of success, such as reducing the gap between the customer's demand for and company's supply of product attributes, on-time delivery, increased customer satisfaction, and increased market share, provide the feedback needed to evaluate a company's responsiveness to its customers. An example of growth by increasing market size is Southwest Airlines, a discount service in the US. This management team decided to price its transportation service to compete with bus, train, and automobile transportation; in so doing it expanded the market for air transportation services to the destinations it served.

The internal business process perspective arguably includes the greatest number of performance measures. These are measures of achievement across all the business functions. Top management, adopting a strategy of eliminating non-value-added activities, can pursue this objective in many ways. Recall that value-added is an activity perceived by the customer as adding value. For example, customers prize convenient

[4]R. E. Paladino, "Balanced Forecasts Drive Value," *Strategic Finance* (January 2005): 37–42.

and accessible offerings, but the costs of inventory storage and rush delivery by air are not value-added. Customers expect effective business management to minimize inventory and transportation costs. As mentioned in Chapter 9, customers also do not perceive the gap between practical and normal capacity as value-added, and this affects the fixed overhead rate assigned to each output. Customers will not be willing to pay these non-value-added costs when they purchase product and service offerings.

The discussion of ABC cost allocation and variance analysis provided some insight into the complexity of internal business process measures. Improved service response time in the example of affixing antennae to communication towers is one way to measure internal process improvement. Shortening either a production or a cash-to-cash cycle is another. On-time deliveries, yield, low rework hours, and improved productivity are also widely used. Increasingly, however, changes in process are responses to external customer needs as well as internal management needs for efficiency and effectiveness.

LEARNING AND GROWTH—MANAGING INTELLECTUAL CAPITAL

The most intangible target of management is represented in the learning and growth perspective. There must be knowledge to learn and, as indicated by the arrow on the left side of Exhibit 13-2, learning, applying, and producing knowledge enables improvement in all the other functions in the value chain. Once people learn, the goal of intellectual capital management is to apply, retain, and expand knowledge to improve long-term competitive success.

Levels of educational accomplishment measure knowledge acquisition, while the number of successful innovations measures knowledge application. The Karolinska Center for Molecular Medicine (CMM) in Sweden, for example, measures inputs as the percentage of research professionals who are doctoral or postdoctoral students and those who are doctoral graduates. This organization is a global leader in medical research, and its nonfinancial measures of human capital include output such as quantity of new patents, students graduated per year, publications in international journals, and prizes and awards for excellence. CMM also reports financial measures of percentage of revenue and funding generated by new patents as well as return on research and development investment.

Another European institution, the Austrian Central Bank (Oesterreichische Nationalbank, OeNB), which is responsible for advising the government on macroeconomic and financial policy, also publishes an intellectual capital report.[5] Its 16 measures of human capital include the number of people on expert career paths relative to total expert career positions available, number of internal job rotations, number of employees obtaining new credentials of expertise, and number of training days per employee. The cost of training per employee trained and travel expenses per training episode are also reported.[6]

Among its 26 measures of relational capital, the number of external job rotations to other regulatory agencies and central banks, number of memberships in international groups and on task forces, webpages accessed, and visits to OeNB's website act as an index of confidence in the bank. The CMM has 12 measures of knowledge transfer including quantity of collaborations within and external to Sweden, service on Nobel and other award committees, number of researchers who practise medicine, and the percentage of their time in practice (to measure knowledge transfer). Other measures include the quantity of public debates, media interviews, retention of doctoral graduates, medical treatment programs in progress, and spin-off companies created.

Structural capacity at CMM is measured using a financial indicator of the percentage of the total budget met by external funding donations. Donors include pharmaceutical companies, governments, and specific disease foundations. The number

[5]Source: Intellectual Capital Report 2004, CMM, www.cmm.ki.se/omCMM/rapporter/intellect_report_04.pdf.
[6]Source: Intellectual Capital Report 2007, www.oenb.at/en/img/wissensbilanz_07_e_screen_tcm 16-85369.pdf.

EXHIBIT 13-2
Specific Short-Term Measures Linked to Long-Term Success

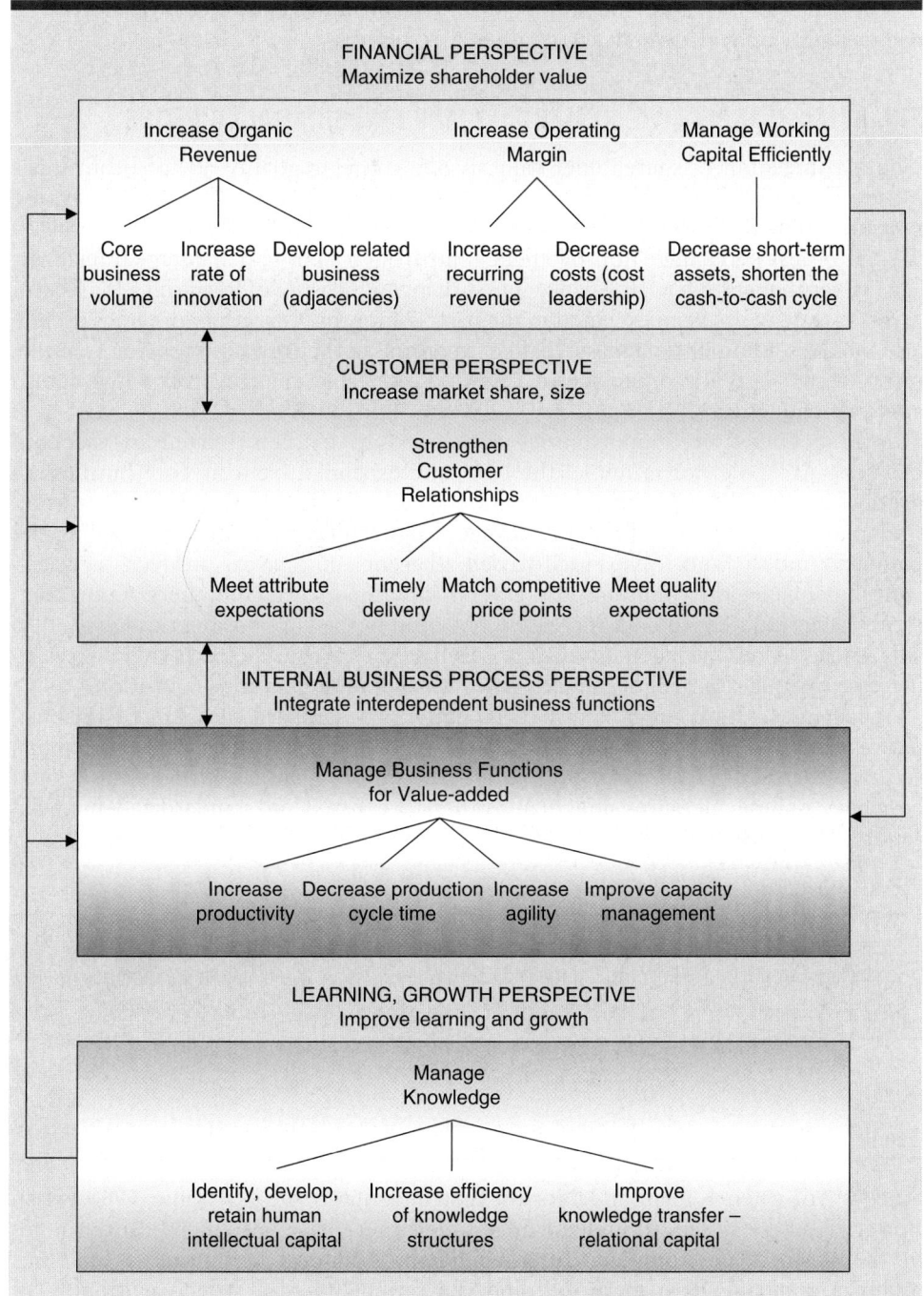

of laboratory testing methods for which advanced technology is available, the number of medical fields in which research is conducted, and the time spent on research are nonfinancial measures of structural intellectual capital. The OeNB's 17 measures of structural capital (patents, internal processes, and so on) include percentage of on-time publication of monetary statistics, quantity of products per product manager, number of internal areas of expertise with outside certification, quantity of languages in which databases are maintained, and quantity of information technology systems provided by OeNB.

In previous chapters, reference often has been made to financial accounting information. It is a reliable and standardized base to which management accounting techniques can be applied to improve relevance. Intellectual capital, however, is not reported unless an economic transfer has occurred. Patents, customer lists, regulatory quotas, marketing rights, and licences, among others, represent intangible assets for which the costs, or value, cannot be reliably measured. Until these outputs are sold, the tasks of performance measurement and estimation of financial value are the responsibility of management accountants.

FINANCIAL PERSPECTIVE, RELIABILITY, AND FINANCIAL ACCOUNTING

The maximization of shareholder value is one strategic goal of all for-profit businesses. From financial information come a host of effectiveness measures. **Organic revenue growth** is obtained without mergers or acquisitions (see Exhibit 13-2). A year-to-year percentage improvement compared to a target percentage transforms a short-term operating performance measure into a measure of how well a long-term growth strategy has been executed in the past 12 months. Growth in organic revenue also includes nonfinancial measures, like expansion in the core business (for example, introducing a product or service in a new country) and changes in revenue due to a new revenue mix.

Adjacencies are opportunities to expand to markets related to the core business. At Apple, for example, the company expanded from its core business of producing and selling personal computers to mobile communications devices using the same technology in a different package. Logitech's core business was selling the computer mouse, and it expanded to sell adjacent audio-visual products as accessories to enhance the communications versatility of personal computers. Companies rarely have resources to both increase innovation in the core business and expand to adjacencies. A top management team must make a strategic choice as to how best to increase organic revenue, or pursue growth through mergers and acquisition.

Change in operating margin percentage is a standard measure of financial performance. Various other financial ratios such as quick ratio, aging of accounts receivable, inventory turnover, and so on are familiar measures of working capital efficiency. These measures and many others are based on standardized financial reports of income.

MyAccountingLab

BSC VERSATILITY

2 Apply the BSC to enterprise risk management (ERM) and explain the link between corporate governance and corporate competitiveness

Since 1996, when Kaplan and Norton first introduced the BSC, and 1980, when Porter created a system to understand strategy, there have been significant changes in the business environment. Interdependencies among the business functions within a company have increased, and the rationality of a strict partitioning of successful competitive strategies has decreased. For example, quality control of production has transformed in some companies into a strategy of quality throughout the value chain. Successful growth strategies through globalization have expanded opportunities not only to expand markets but also to access high-quality resources at lower costs. On the supply side, globalization has also increased risk of disruption to the flow of those resources.

Differences in environmental, employment, and governance regulations worldwide have increased the exposure of individual companies to regulatory risk. For example, in some countries it is taken for granted that individuals and groups essential to economic processes will obtain special financial consideration (bribes and kickbacks). Other countries regard any special consideration beyond the scope of what is explicitly in a contract as illegal. Siemens, an international company, is now enduring the consequences of the legal and reputation risks taken when it allegedly created a formal global bribery network. Within countries, changes in political regimes can result in regulatory change such as new employment, financial reporting, or environmental remediation standards.

Beyond regulatory risk, consumers boycott the products of companies such as Nike to protest employment practices undertaken by its offshore suppliers and manufacturers. Tyson Foods, a global food processor, found its slaughtering practices at one plant in Alabama posted by PETA on YouTube. Tyson is under investigation by the US Department of Agriculture. The company has since fired the employees concerned and is investigating an alternative slaughtering method.

These examples represent only a few of many sources of operating and financial risk to a global enterprise. Each example is an alleged breach of compliance with laws and regulations. Mandatory compliance is the minimum criterion of good governance. These governance requirements emphasize the importance of a coherent **enterprise risk management (ERM)** strategy. The purpose of ERM is to align strategy with risk management and evaluate how management initiatives have improved the overall risk profile of the company.

The financial accounting profession has already contributed towards improved ERM through the Committee of Sponsoring Organizations of the Treadway Commission (COSO). COSO identified eight elements of ERM as:[7]

- Internal identification and communication of the enterprise's risk appetite, integrity, and risk management philosophy.
- Objective setting in a formal process to align objectives with the enterprise's mission and its risk appetite.
- Event identification of triggers in a chain of events that should alert managers to new internal and external opportunities and threats.
- Risk assessment arising from formal analysis of likelihood and planned response.
- Risk response analysis to avoid, reduce, share, or accept risk to align the response with the enterprise's risk appetite.
- Control activities comprising policies and procedures that monitor the effective implementation of risk responses.
- Information capture and communication to ensure those accountable receive relevant and timely information.
- Monitoring processes and feedback of actual risk management practices.

The BSC can be successfully applied to assessing the success of an ERM strategy. The following example focuses on managing the risk of the **supply-chain strategy**.

The supply-chain strategy transforms external suppliers into internal partners with the buyer. The popular view of the relationship of buyer and seller has been that both compete to obtain the most benefit for the least cost. This competition to maximize self-interest is in high contrast to the cooperation strategy within a company among its various business functions. A company changing to partnerships in a supply chain has extended its corporate boundaries to include trusted suppliers. The costs and benefits of competition against individual suppliers for the highest quality and quantity must be compared to the costs and benefits of cooperation. This strategy affects the speed and amount of confidential information communicated between partners in the supply chain. Each partner must assess the cost of identifiable risks and appropriate control strategies, as well as the effect of partnership failure on the enterprise.[8]

The strategic goals from the financial perspective are to improve profit margin, cash flow, and revenue growth; however, these are measured with respect to the supply-chain partner's estimated contribution. The **return on supply chain assets (ROSCA)** is a cost-benefit ratio. The numerator is the difference between revenue

[7]Committee of Sponsoring Organizations of the Treadway Commission, "Enterprise Risk Management–Integrated Framework," September 2004, www.coso.org/Publications/ERM/COSO_ERM_ExecutiveSummary.pdf.
[8]M. Beasley, A. Chen, K. Nunez, and L. Wright, "Working Hand in Hand: Balanced Scorecards and Enterprise Risk Management," *Strategic Finance* (March 2006): 49–56.

arising from incremental sales obtained by using the supply chain minus the expenses (often sacrificed profit margin) of the supply chain. The denominator is the assets in which the company has invested to use the supply chain.[9]

Assume a buyer's annual quantity of a resource is 10,000 units with a cost of $100 per order. The cost per unit to store inventory is $10. The supplier's setup cost to produce a batch of units is $300 and the total annual cost will depend on the quantity ordered. The best reorder quantity for the buyer is 445 units and the best batch quantity for the supplier is double the buyer's, 890 units. If the buyer can dominate the supplier, then 23 orders will be placed each year (10,000 units ÷ 445 = 22.47 rounded to 23 orders). The buyer will receive 10,235 units. Orders will be placed approximately every 2-1/4 weeks. The total cost to the buyer will be $4,650. The cost of ordering will be $2,300 (23 orders × $100/order = $2,300) and of storage will be $2,350 (235 units × $10/unit = $2,350), totalling $4,650 ($2,300 + $2,350 = $4,650). The supplier's cost will be $6,900, making the **total channel cost** of this strategy $11,550. Total channel cost is the sum of the costs to the supplier and the buyer.

If the supplier could dominate the seller, then the supplier's cost would decrease to the cost of 12 orders (10,000 units ÷ 890 = 11.24 rounded to 12 orders), or $3,600 annually (12 orders × $300/order = $3,600). This is a cost saving of $3,300 for the supplier. The buyer would receive 10,680 units (12 orders × 890 units/order = 10,680 units). The total cost to the buyer would be $8,000, including both order and storage costs. The order cost would decline to $1,200 (12 orders × $100/order = $1,200) and the storage cost would increase to $6,800 (680 units × $10/unit = $6,800). This is a cost increase of $3,350. The total channel cost would be $11,600. These facts are summarized in the table:

| | Domination | | |
Costs	Supplier	Buyer	Difference
Order	$ 1,200	$ 2,300	$(1,100)
Inventory Storage	6,800	2,350	4,450
Buyer Cost	8,000	4,650	$ 3,350
Batch	3,600	6,900	(3,300)
Total Channel	$11,600	$11,550	$ 50

If neither the buyer nor the supplier can dominate the other, then through negotiation the two can arrive at a total cost that will decrease for both. This is the financial incentive to adopt a supply-chain strategy of cooperation. The buyer wants a cost less than the maximum of $8,000, and the supplier wants a cost less than the maximum of $6,900. By sharing information about batch, ordering, and storage costs the two parties can partner to reduce the costs incurred by each.

THINKING CRITICALLY

What does good governance contribute to ERM? Explain in a sentence or two. Read on for an assessment of this situation.

Reflect quickly on whom you would trust—someone with a good reputation for integrity or someone without? The foundation of supply-chain management is an intangible asset called *trust*. One high-profile measure of trust is the public information available about non-compliance with mandatory regulations and laws. Without trust in good governance, neither the buyer nor the supplier will have the opportunity to undertake a supply-chain strategy. Learning from governance mistakes is one form of capturing human intellectual capital that in the long run will change the opportunities

[9]R. H. Ballou, "The Evolution and Future of Logistics and Supply Chain Management," *Produção* 16.3 (2006): 375–386.

for a buyer or seller in a competitive environment to include a strategy of cooperation with one another.

Measures from the customer perspective include measures of order process time and satisfaction, as well as the average incremental sales per customer. Other financial ratios, such as either the inventory turnover ratio or days' supply on hand, as well as shortening the cash outflow to inflow time (cash-to-cash cycle), are short-term measures of the internal business processes associated with the supply-chain strategy. They also provide readily accessible and reliable performance measures upon which future goals can be set and measured against actual performance. Learning and growth measures include comparisons with actual to expected disruptions and changes to the content and frequency of information exchange among partners.

In an analysis of 104 international companies, Ho (2005) produced quantitative evidence that good corporate governance practices strengthen global competitiveness for an enterprise.[10] Five elements of good practice include board of directors (BOD) structure, stewardship processes, strategic leadership role, ownership concentration, and discharging social responsibilities. BOD structure includes the balance of insider and outsider directors, board committee responsibilities, independence from management influence, and audit and internal control. Exhibit 13-3 illustrates the BSC approach to the dimensions of corporate governance and their effects on three factors of corporate competitiveness.

Stewardship includes measures of controls and safeguards on corporate resources including internal audit controls. Strategic leadership includes measures of how well strategic goals are implemented in day-to-day operations, the quality and appropriateness of the measures (for example, a BSC), and the frequency and timeliness of corporate responsiveness to changes. Ownership concentration is a strategy measured by the presence of policies directed towards obtaining stable, long-term investors. Corporate social responsibility refers to, among other things, measures of responsiveness to environmental, philanthropic, and community concerns. Employment equity, environmental protection, and community development practices all can be measured.

Measures of corporate competitiveness include productivity, cost leadership, business risk management, financial risk management, business process success in marketing and capacity utilization, as well as measures of value creation. Using regression analysis (see Chapter 10), Ho reported strong correlations, illustrated by the black arrows on the left of Exhibit 13-3, among the factors measuring good corporate governance, which means that as one factor improves it has a measurable effect on improving the others. Good corporate governance is a matter of implementing these practices as a whole, not piecemeal.

The different-coloured lines on the right indicate the influence of different corporate governance practices on measures of corporate competitiveness. Changes in the level of good corporate governance explain changes in improved corporate competitiveness. The adjusted r^2 describes explanatory power for these measures that range from approximately 42% for financial performance measured as ROE, to 40% for improvements in intellectual capital management, to 48% for customer and process management (see Chapter 10). This means the change in level of corporate governance can be partially explained by changes in these three factors. The coloured lines on the right of Exhibit 13-3 illustrate the influence or correlations among the three measures of corporate competitiveness. Again, this means that as the company improves on one measure it will have a measurable effect on improving the other two measures. Ho noted that not all measures of either corporate governance or competitiveness were tested; nevertheless, he reported persuasive evidence that good governance improves profitability.

One standardized Corporate Governance Scorecard is free and was developed in the context of Germany's corporate code.[11] First published in 2000 by the German

---

[10]Chi-Kun Ho, "Corporate Governance and Corporate Competitiveness: An International Analysis," *Corporate Governance and Corporate Competitiveness* 13.2 (March 2005): 211–253.

[11]"Corporate Governance," *International Finance Corporation*, www.ifc.org/ifcext/corporategovernance.nsf.

EXHIBIT 13-3
BSC, Corporate Governance, and Corporate Competitiveness

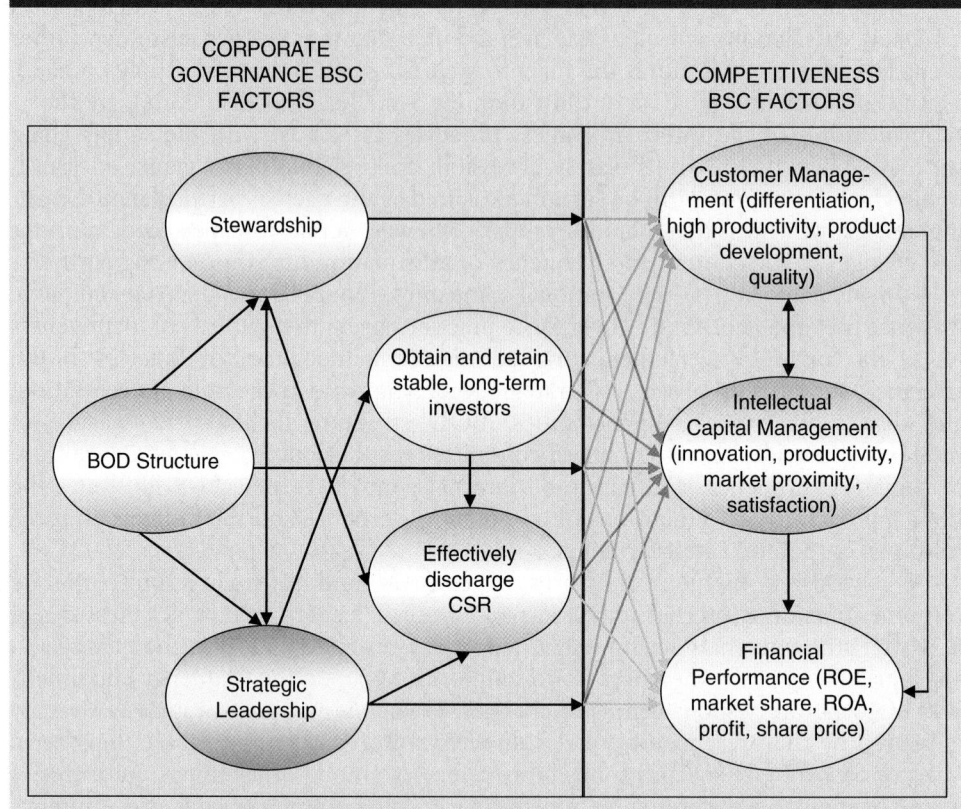

CORPORATE GOVERNANCE BSC FACTORS

COMPETITIVENESS BSC FACTORS

Source: Adapted Chi-Kun Ho, "Corporate Governance and Corporate Competitiveness: an International Analysis," *Corporate Governance and Corporate Competitiveness* 13.2 (March 2005): 239.

Society of Financial Analysts, it is intended for use in Excel and sets thresholds or standards of achievement in each of seven factors. The factors are:

♦ Corporate governance commitment including the appointment of a governance officer and a process to adapt quickly to changes in the governance environment (stewardship and BOD structure).

♦ Structure of communication to shareholders including equal treatment policies, full voting rights, and right of first refusal (preemptive rights) for existing shareholders due to increases in capital (strategic leadership).

♦ Cooperation between management and corporate supervisory boards (BOD structure).

♦ Management boards that develop executive compensation linked to shareholder value creation (strategic leadership, stewardship).

♦ Supervisory boards such as audit and compensation committees, which reduce conflict of interest and increased reliance on external expertise when appropriate (stewardship and BOD structure).

♦ Transparency of all information to external parties in full compliance with fair disclosure legislation (stewardship).

♦ Auditor independence and full compliance with various standards of accounting, reporting, and auditing worldwide (stewardship).

This scorecard, although it has been criticized, has gained acceptance not only in Germany but also in countries with a less comprehensive governance infrastructure.[12]

---

[12]C. Strenger, "The Corporate Governance Scorecard: A Tool for the Implementation of Corporate Governance," *Corporate Governance* 12.1 (January 2004): 11–15.

RESPONSIVE BUSINESS SCORECARD AND CORPORATE SUSTAINABILITY

Interpret the BSC in the context of enterprise risk management (ERM) of corporate and environmental sustainability ❸

The BSC focuses on transactions in the marketplace, and the overarching strategic goal is economic or financial corporate sustainability. The link among the four perspectives of the BSC is that transactions giving rise to measures of performance are undertaken in a competitive market. **Corporate sustainability** is a business approach that creates long-term shareholder value by embracing opportunities and managing risks deriving from economic, environmental, and social developments.[13] This definition is globally applied in the Dow Jones Sustainability Indexes (DJSI).

The Dow Jones Sustainability Indexes are stock indexes that include companies based on a specific set of sustainability-related criteria. There are several indexes, including the DJSI World, DJSI North America, and DJSI Asia Pacific. The DJSI World includes the top 10% of the leading sustainability companies out of the biggest 2,500 companies in the Dow Jones Global Total Stock Market Index. Information on the sustainability analysis and further information on the companies included in the DJSI are available on the DJSI website (www.sustainability-indexes.com). Examples of four companies that are considered the best in their industry are shown in Exhibit 13-4. In publishing is Pearson PLC (the publisher of this text), in automotive BMW AG, in high-tech industry is Intel Corp., and in transportation is TNT.

EXHIBIT 13-4
Selected DJSI Exemplary (Benchmark) Performers

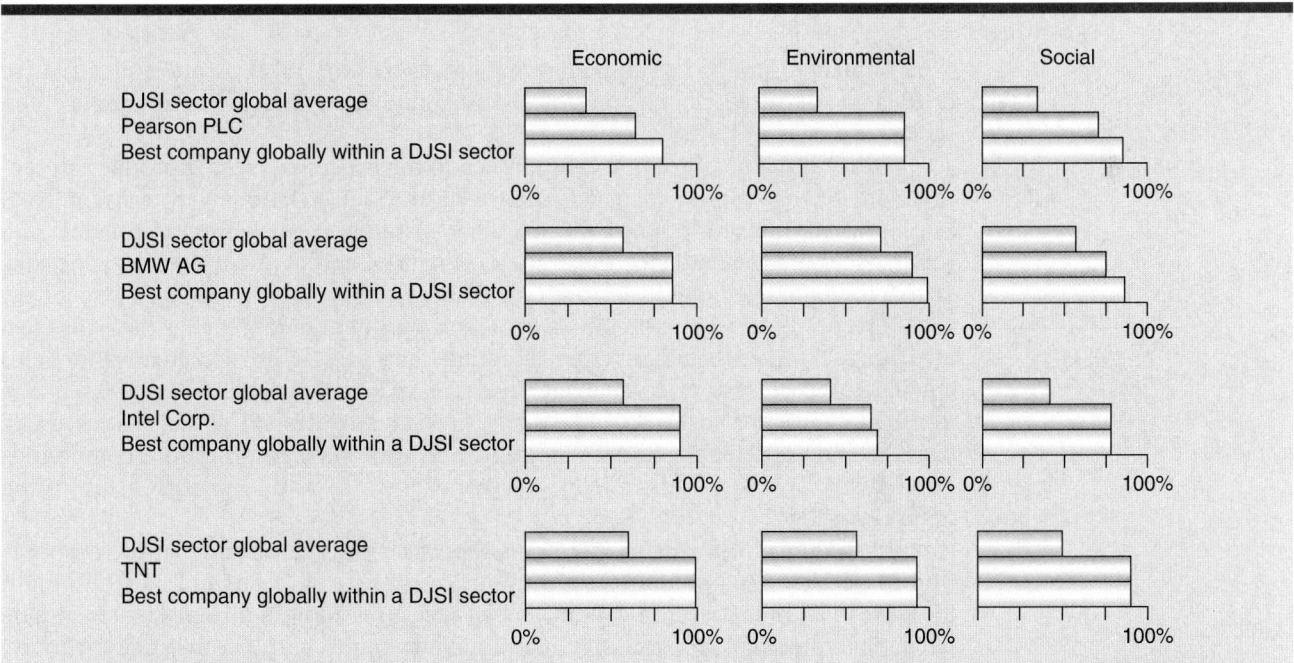

Sources: Based on information from "Global Supersector Leaders,"*Dow Jones Sustainability Indexes,* www.sustainability-index.com/07_htmle/ indexes/djsiworld_supersectorleaders_08.html; "Sustainability Leader: Bayerische Motoren Werke AG (BMW), AUT Automobiles," www.sustainability-index.com/djsi_pdf/Bios09/BMW_09.pdf; "Sustainability Leader: Pearson Plc., PUB Media," www.sustainability-index.com/djsi_pdf/Bios09/Pearson_09.pdf; "Sustainability Leader: Intel Corp., SEM Semiconductors," www.sustainability-index.com/djsi_pdf/Bios09/Intel_09.pdf; and "Sustainability Leader: TNT N.V., TRA Industrial Transportation," www.sustainability-index.com/djsi_pdf/Bios09/TNT_09.pdf.

[13]"Corporate Sustainability Assessment," *Dow Jones Sustainability Indexes*, www.sustainability-indexes.com/07_htmle/assessment/overview.html.

The DJSI measures vary from industry to industry. Economic measures for Intel include customer relationship management, corporate governance, innovation management, product quality, and recall management. For Pearson PLC, measures cover product piracy, lobbying, brand management, and corporate governance. The table provides examples of the assessment criteria for each of the four companies on each of the three dimensions of corporate sustainability:

	Economic	Environmental	Social
Pearson PLC	Product piracy	Env. policy/management system	Stakeholder engagement
	Lobbying activities	Volatile organic compounds	Labour practices
	Brand management	Hazardous substances	Protection of children
	Corporate governance	Operational eco-efficiency	Human-capital development
BMW AG	Codes of conduct	Env. policy/management system	Stakeholder engagement
	Brand management	Low-carbon strategy	Labour practices
	Risk and crisis management	Closed loops*	Standards for suppliers
	Corporate governance	Environmental reporting	Human-capital development
Intel Corp	Customer relationship management	Env. policy/management system	Stakeholder engagement
	Innovation management	Environmental reporting	Labour practices
	Product quality and recall management	Climate strategy	Standards for suppliers
	Corporate governance		Human-capital development
TNT	Customer relationship management	Env. policy/management system	Labour practices
	Risk and crisis management	Fuel efficiency	Talent attraction and retention
	Codes of conduct, compliance	Climate strategy	Corporate citizenship
	Corporate governance	Biodiversity	Human-capital development

*"Closed loops" refers to practices of life-cycle management including reclamation and recycling.

Similar to the BSC, the underlying analysis of the DJSI captures quantitative criteria in all three dimensions of sustainability: economic, environmental, and social.

Other BSC measures of important economic processes include product protection, intellectual capital management (structural and relational), internal process improvement (innovation and R&D), and customer responsiveness (quality and recall). The interdependence of economic financial success with many competitive factors is emphasized, but legislative compliance or corporate governance is required.

The responsiveness of companies to sustaining and conserving their physical environment is reflected in environmental measures. The presence of policies and an internal system to manage industry-specific environmental risks is the minimum measure in every industry. Other measures such as hazardous waste disposal, fuel efficiency, climate strategy, and use of volatile organic compounds are industry-specific. This dimension situates a corporation in relationship to the natural world.

In the social dimension, measures report on the relationship of the corporation to people. This dimension places human capital development as a minimum measure in all industries. In general, social measures address difficult issues such as fair labour practices (for example, employment equity and labour-force diversity) and elimination of both child and forced labour. These appear to be non-issues in developed Western democracies but in other countries these practices are locally accepted and even encouraged as a means to improve the economic status of families. Other broader issues are also addressed on an industry basis, such as respect for indigenous rights, freedom of association, and elimination of corruption and bribery.

Does Anyone Really Do Triple Bottom Lines?

Yes. Petro-Canada publishes an online annual scorecard on corporate sustainability, covering all aspects of its commitment and achievements in economic, environmental, and social domains. The Report to the Community includes details of its inclusive business practices with indigenous people, environmental responses, labour practices, and commitment to human rights. There is also a website reporting specific measures of past environmental goals, current achievements, and future goals as well as a site for the company's annual report. Environmental measures include those of emissions, waste, yield, energy intensity, noise, waste heat, land and water use, and, in some cases, radiation control. Social measures include monitoring the elimination of bribery and corruption, advocacy and support of freedom of association and speech, social equity, fair labour practices, and ethical investment by both Petro-Canada and its suppliers.

Sources: Petro-Canada, *Report to the Community*, www.petro-canada.ca/en/socialresp/912.aspx?2005report2; Petro-Canada, "Environment and Society," www.petro-canada.ca/en/environment/112.aspx; Petro-Canada, "Human Rights," www.petro-canada.ca/en/socialresp/932.aspx; and Petro-Canada, *2007 Annual* Report, http://annualreport.petro-canada.ca/default.aspx.

Strengthening the association between sustainability and financial value is the presence of global standards, the Global Reporting Initiative (GRI). Since the release of new standards, the G3 Reporting Framework, in 2006, the pace of companies issuing corporate sustainability reports has accelerated.[14] The term to describe a formal response to the GRI is **triple bottom line** reporting. The standard financial statements, notes, and the management discussion and analysis (MD&A) of strategic response as required in annual reports are now augmented with specific environmental and social sustainability reports.

Preliminary quantitative evidence has been published confirming that the interdependence among economic, environmental, and social best practices is recognized by investors. In their article, Lo and Sheu (2007) measured the market valuation of the firm using Tobin's q. **Tobin's q** is the sum of the balance sheet value of debt, plus all equity divided by the total assets.

The researchers conducted many tests of the robustness of their result. They reported a statistically significant difference in the average value of Tobin's q between sustainable and other firms (see Chapter 10). Moreover, there is a significant interaction between sustainability and sales growth. When sales growth is high, sustainability influences firm value more strongly than when sales growth is low.[15] These results confirm that competitive strategies incorporating both financial and ethical goals are rewarded by higher market values.

[14]B. Ballou, D. L. Heitger, and C. E. Landes, "The Future of Corporate Sustainability Reporting," *Journal of Accountancy* (December 2006): 65–74.

[15]S-F. Lo, H-J. Sheu, "Is Corporate Sustainability a Value-Increasing Strategy for Business?" *Corporate Governance* 15.2 (March (2007): 345–358.

IMPLEMENTATION OF THE BSC

❹ Implement and apply the BSC in a comprehensive analysis

We illustrate five forces using the example of Chipset Inc. The core business for Chipset is manufacturing integrated circuit devices (ICDs) used in modems and communication networks. Chipset produces a single specialized product, CX1. This standard, high-performance microchip can be used in multiple applications that require instant processing of **real-time data**. CX1 was designed with extensive inputs from key customers. Real-time data is instantaneous and continuous data about process parameters such as temperature and pressure that must be maintained within tight ranges.

Competitors Chipset has many competitors as eager as Chipset is to grow market share. The infrastructure costs in this industry are high (fixed costs of capacity); therefore one of Chipset's strengths would be its ability to utilize capacity fully and reduce selling prices (see Chapter 9 for a discussion of allocating capacity costs). Reducing prices of products is critical for industry growth because it allows ICDs to be incorporated into digital subscriber lines (DSL) for major corporations such as Earth-Link and Verizon. CX1 has slightly superior product features relative to competitive products, but competition is severe along the dimensions of price, timely delivery, and quality. Quality is important because ICD failure disrupts the communication network.

Potential Entrants into the Market The integrated circuits industry does not attract potential new entrants because of high capacity costs, short product life cycles, and small profit margins. Companies that have already been making ICDs are farther down the learning curve and hence are likely to have lower costs (see Chapter 10 for a discussion of the learning curve effects on cost). Existing companies also have the advantage of close relationships with customers and suppliers that they have built over the years.

Equivalent Products Chipset uses a technology that allows its customers to use CX1 flexibly to best meet their needs. The flexible design of CX1, and the fact that it is closely integrated into end-products made by Chipset's customers, reduce the potential for equivalent products or new technologies to replace CX1 during the next few years. This risk is reduced even further if Chipset continuously improves CX1's design and processes to decrease costs.

Bargaining Power of Customers Customers such as EarthLink and Verizon have bargaining power because each buys large quantities of product. Customers can also obtain microchips from other potential suppliers. Signing a contract to deliver microchips is very important to Chipset. Recognizing this fact, customers negotiate hard to keep prices down.

Bargaining Power of Input Suppliers Chipset maintains its superior quality in part because it purchases high-quality materials such as silicon wafers, pins for connectivity, and plastic or ceramic packaging from its suppliers. Chipset also employs skilled engineers, technicians, and manufacturing labour. Materials suppliers and employees have some bargaining power to demand higher prices and wages. Strong competition and the bargaining powers of customers and suppliers put significant pressure on prices. Chipset can respond to these challenges by adopting one of two basic strategies: differentiating its product or achieving cost leadership.

Product differentiation is a company's ability to offer products or services perceived by its customers as being superior and unique relative to those of its competitors. For example, Samsung has successfully differentiated its products in the electronics industry, as have Merck in the pharmaceutical industry and Coca-Cola in the soft-drinks industry. Through innovative product research and development, and by developing processes that bring products to market rapidly, each of these companies has been able to provide better and differentiated products. This differentiation increases brand loyalty and the prices that customers are willing to pay.

Cost leadership is an organization's ability to achieve low costs relative to competitors through productivity and efficiency improvements, elimination of waste, and tight cost control. Some cost leaders in their respective industries are Home Depot (building products), Samsung (consumer electronics), and Magna International (automotive parts). These companies all provide products and services that are similar to, not differentiated from, those of their competitors, but at a lower cost to the customer. Lower selling prices—rather than unique products or services— provide a competitive advantage for these cost leaders.

What strategy should Chipset follow? CX1 is already somewhat differentiated from competing products. Differentiating CX1 further will be costly but it may allow Chipset to charge a higher price. Conversely, reducing the cost of manufacturing and selling CX1 will allow Chipset to reduce the price of CX1 and spur growth. The CX1 technology allows Chipset's customers to achieve different performance levels by simply altering the number of CX1 units in their products. This solution is more cost effective than designing new customized microchips for different applications. Customers want Chipset to keep the current design of CX1 but to lower its price. Chipset's current engineering talent is also oriented more towards making product and process improvements than creatively designing brand-new products and technologies. Chipset concludes that it should pursue a cost leadership strategy. Of course, successful cost leadership generally would increase Chipset's market share and help the company to grow.

To be successful, a company must both formulate an effective strategy and implement it vigorously. In the next section, we focus on the balanced scorecard as a tool for implementing strategy. The first is an increased emphasis on compliance with existing legislation and regulation—satisfactory corporate governance. The board of directors and other responsible corporate officers develop a strategy designed to identify risks potentially affecting the company and how best to manage those risks. Financial fraud is certainly one risk, and new securities regulations such as Sarbanes-Oxley section 404 and Canada's Multilateral Instrument 52-11 have introduced new and stringent accounting and accountability standards. Consistent with the scorekeeping function, the management accountant has an important role to play by developing BSC measures to assist managers as they track a company's progress in implementing strategy.

To understand the measures Chipset uses to monitor progress under each perspective of the BSC, it is important to recognize key elements of Chipset's cost leadership strategy—improve quality and reengineer processes. As a result of these initiatives, Chipset plans to reduce costs, downsize, and eliminate capacity in excess of that needed to support future growth. However, it does not want to make deep cuts in personnel that would adversely affect employee morale and hinder future growth.

IMPLEMENTING A BALANCED SCORECARD

To successfully implement a balanced scorecard requires commitment and leadership from top management. At Chipset, the team building the balanced scorecard (headed by the vice-president of strategic planning) conducted interviews with senior managers, probed executives about customers, competitors, and technological developments, and sought proposals for balanced scorecard objectives across the four perspectives. The team then met to discuss the responses and build a prioritized list of objectives.

Chipset's top management team sought to achieve consensus on the scorecard objectives and to establish a cause-and-effect linkage across the chosen objectives. Senior management was then divided into four groups, with each group responsible for one of the perspectives. In addition, representatives from the next lower levels of management and key functional managers were included in each group to broaden the base of inputs. The groups identified measures for each objective and the sources of information for each measure. The groups then met to finalize BSC objectives, measures, targets, and the initiatives to achieve the targets. The final BSC was communicated and used both to evaluate the performance of managers throughout the company and to ensure widespread engagement and alignment.

FEATURES OF A GOOD BALANCED SCORECARD

A good BSC design has several features:

♦ It tells the story of a company's strategy by articulating a limited sequence of critical or cause-and-effect relationships.

People have cognitive limits; therefore, a good BSC focuses on a limited set of measures. For example, measures in the learning and growth perspective could lead to improvements in internal business processes. These, in turn, lead to increased customer satisfaction and market share, as well as higher operating income and shareholder value. Each measure in the BSC is part of a critical cause-and-effect chain, a linkage from strategy formulation to financial outcome.

♦ It helps to communicate the strategy to all members of the organization by translating the strategy into a coherent and linked set of understandable and measurable operational targets.

Guided by the BSC, managers and employees take actions and make decisions that aim to achieve the company's strategy. To focus these actions, some companies, such as Mobil and Bank of Montreal, have pushed down and developed scorecards at the division and department levels.

♦ In for-profit companies, the balanced scorecard places strong emphasis on financial objectives and measures.

Managers sometimes tend to focus too much on innovation, quality, and customer satisfaction as ends in themselves, even if they do not lead to tangible payoffs. A BSC also emphasizes nonfinancial measures as a part of a program to achieve future financial performance. In not-for-profit enterprises, nonfinancial factors measure the achievement of almost all key objectives.

♦ The BSC limits the number of measures used by identifying only the most critical ones.

Avoiding a proliferation of measures focuses management's attention on those that are key to the implementation of strategy. These critical success elements change over time and so too must the BSC.

♦ The BSC highlights suboptimal tradeoffs that managers may make when they fail to consider operational and financial measures together.

For example, a company for which innovation is a key strategy could achieve superior short-run financial performance by reducing money spent on R&D. A good BSC would signal that the short-run financial performance may have been achieved by taking actions that hurt future financial performance because a leading indicator of that performance, R&D spending and R&D output, has declined.

PITFALLS WHEN IMPLEMENTING A BALANCED SCORECARD

Pitfalls to avoid when implementing a balanced scorecard include the following:

♦ Strategy comprises sets of hypotheses about cause–effect links (see Chapter 10 for a discussion of causal models).

A critical challenge is to identify the strength and speed of the causal linkages among the nonfinancial and financial measures. Management must gather evidence of these linkages over time. Evolving the BSC over time avoids the paralysis by analysis associated with trying to design the "perfect" scorecard at the outset.

- Scarce corporate resources mean tradeoffs or priority setting must occur among various strategic goals.

For example, emphasizing quality and on-time performance beyond a point may not be worthwhile—improving these objectives may be inconsistent with profit maximization.

- BSC includes the intangible achievement of good management of intellectual capital.

Qualitative or subjective measures such as interviews and surveys to assess intellectual and corporate sustainability achievements provide a rich basis upon which to progress.

- Intangible costs are extremely difficult to estimate, but intangible benefits even more so.

Nonfinancial measures of the benefits of improved information technology, advocacy of human rights, and reduction of carbon emission are not standardized. Management accountants play a large liaison role translating quantitative measures made by technical experts into financial measures of benefit.

- Managers tend to focus on what their performance is measured by.

Excluding nonfinancial measures when evaluating performance will reduce the significance and importance given to managing nonfinancial BSC measures. Many of the nonfinancial measures serve as leading indicators of future financial performance. The Chipset example will show how improvements in nonfinancial factors lead to improvements in financial factors.

QUALITY IMPROVEMENT AND REENGINEERING AT CHIPSET

One key element of Chipset's strategy to reduce costs is improving quality (that is, reducing defects and improving yields in its manufacturing process). High quality and reliability is the minimum the company's customers demand, a customer perspective. Chipset needs real-time data about manufacturing process parameters in order to implement advanced process control methods, an internal process perspective. Chipset must also train its front-line workers in quality management techniques to help them identify and resolve defects and problems. Following this training, Chipset needs to empower its workforce to make timely decisions and continuously improve the process, a learning and growth perspective.

THINKING CRITICALLY

How does reengineering relate to value engineering and the BSC? Explain in a sentence or two. Read on for an assessment of this topic.

Reengineering focuses on redesigning business processes to improve performance and satisfy customers. Value engineering (Chapter 12) relies on changes including those in product design and material specifications to improve performance and satisfy customers. Measures of corporate sustainability are in essence measures of the quality of a company's interaction with the natural, social, and economic world. Product and process quality are ways to implement economic competitive strategies based on a system of assuring high quality. Measures of achievement arising from quality strategies include volume growth relative to the industry, maximized capacity utilization, and the resulting reduction in allocation of unit fixed costs and prices. Customer satisfaction measures include the frequency and speed of response to customer-service demands and reduction in after-sales replacements and repairs. Internal measures include availability, conformance, timeliness, excellent global supply-chain management, and improved productivity and yield. Learning and growth measures include reduced absenteeism and turnover, increased career opportunities, increased patents, and so on.

Another key element of Chipset's strategy to reduce costs is reengineering its order delivery process. **Reengineering** is the fundamental rethinking and redesign of business processes to achieve improvements in critical measures of performance such as cost, quality, service, speed, and customer satisfaction.[16] To illustrate the concept of reengineering, we examine the order delivery system at Chipset Inc. in 2009. Chipset's salespeople work with customers to identify and plan customer needs. A copy of each purchase order received from a customer is sent to manufacturing, where a production scheduler begins the planning for manufacturing the order.

Frequently, there is a long waiting time before production begins. After manufacturing is complete, the CX1 chips are sent to the shipping department, which matches the quantities of CX1 to be shipped against customer purchase orders. Often, the completed CX1 chips are held in inventory until a truck is available for shipment to the customer. If the quantity shipped does not match the number of chips requested by the customer, a special shipment is scheduled. The shipping documents are sent to the billing department for issuing of invoices. Special staff in the accounting department follow up with customers for payments.

Chipset discovered that the many transfers across departments (sales, manufacturing, shipping, billing, and accounting) to satisfy a customer order slowed down the process and created delays. A multifunction team from the various departments has reengineered the order delivery process for 2010. Its goal is to make the entire organization more customer-focused and reduce delays by eliminating the number of interdepartment transfers.

Under the new system, a customer relationship manager is responsible for the entire customer relationship. Chipset has entered into long-term contracts with customers that specify quantities and prices. The customer relationship manager will work closely with the customer and with manufacturing to specify delivery schedules for CX1 one month in advance. The schedule of customer orders will be sent electronically to manufacturing. Completed chips will be shipped directly from the manufacturing plant to customer sites. Each shipment will automatically trigger an invoice that will be sent electronically to the customer.

The experiences of many companies, such as Royal Bank, Ford Motor, and Siemens AG, indicate that the benefits from reengineering are the most significant when reengineering cuts across functional lines to focus on an entire business process (as in the Chipset example). Reengineering only the shipping or invoicing activity at Chipset rather than the entire order delivery process would not be particularly beneficial. Successful reengineering efforts involve changing roles and responsibilities, eliminating unnecessary activities and tasks, using information technology, and developing employee skills. Chipset's balanced scorecard for 2010 must track Chipset's progress in reengineering the order delivery process from both a nonfinancial and financial perspective.

ALIGNING THE BSC TO STRATEGY

Different strategies call for different scorecards. Suppose that Visilog, another company in the microchip industry, follows a product differentiation strategy by designing custom chips for the communication networks business. Visilog designs its scorecard to fit its strategy. For example, in the financial perspective, Visilog evaluates how much of its operating income comes from charging premium prices for its products. In the customer perspective, Visilog measures the percentage of its revenues from new products (and new customers). In the internal business

[16]See M. Hammer and J. Champy, *Reengineering the Corporation: A Manifesto for Business Revolution* (New York: Harper, 1993); Ruhli, Treichler, and Schmidt, "From Business Reengineering to Management Reengineering—A European Study," *Management International Review* (1995): pp. 361–371; and K. Sandberg, "Reengineering Tries a Comeback—This Time for Growth, Not Just for Cost Savings," *Harvard Management Update* (November 2001).

process perspective, Visilog measures the development of advanced manufacturing capabilities to produce custom chips. In the learning and growth perspective, Visilog measures new-product development time.

Of course, Visilog uses some of the measures described in the balanced scorecard in Exhibit 13-1. For example, revenue growth, customer satisfaction ratings, order delivery time, on-time delivery, percentage of front-line workers empowered to manage processes, and employee satisfaction ratings are important measures under the new strategy. The key point, though, is to align the balanced scorecard to company strategy.[17]

EVALUATING STRATEGIC SUCCESS—FOCUS ON OPERATING INCOME

To evaluate how successful it has been in implementing its strategy, Chipset compares the target and actual performance columns of its BSC. Exhibit 13-5 illustrates the strategic mapping of both forecast and actual short-term measures onto each BSC perspective. This comparison indicates that Chipset met most of the targets it had set on the basis of competitor benchmarks.

Meeting the targets suggests that the strategic initiatives that Chipset had identified and measured for learning and growth resulted in improvements in internal business processes, customer measures, and financial performance. The financial measures show that Chipset achieved targeted cost savings and growth. The key question is, how does Chipset isolate operating income from specific sources such as cost savings and growth instead of focusing on the change in total operating income?

Some companies might be tempted to gauge the success of their strategies by measuring the change in their operating incomes from one year to the next, but this approach is inadequate. For example, operating income can increase simply because entire markets are expanding, not because a specific strategy has been successful. Also, changes in operating income might be caused by factors outside the strategy. For example, a company such as Chipset that has chosen a cost leadership strategy may find that operating income increases have instead been caused incidentally by, say, some degree of product differentiation. The success of a strategy must be evaluated on the basis of whether the sources of operating income increases are the result of implementing the chosen strategy.

To use operating income numbers to evaluate the success of a strategy, a company needs to isolate the operating income due to cost leadership from the operating income due to product differentiation. Of course, successful cost leadership or product differentiation generally increases market share and helps a company to grow. To evaluate the success of a company's strategy, we subdivide changes in operating income into components that can be identified with growth, product differentiation, and cost leadership.

Subdividing the change in operating income to evaluate the success of a company's strategy resembles variance analysis discussed in Chapters 7 and 8. The growth component is similar to calculating sales-volume variance. Price recovery is similar to calculating price and spending variances. The productivity component resembles calculating efficiency variances for direct and indirect costs.

The focus here is on comparing actual operating performance over two different time periods and explicitly linking that performance to strategic choices. A company is considered successful in implementing its strategy when the amounts of the product differentiation, cost leadership, and growth components align closely with its strategy. At this point, management accountants have expertise in understanding how these

---

[17]For simplicity, we have presented the balanced scorecard in the context of companies that have followed either a cost leadership or a product differentiation strategy. Of course, a company may have some products for which cost leadership is critical and other products for which product differentiation is important. The company will then develop separate scorecards to implement the different product strategies. In still other contexts, product differentiation may be of primary importance but some cost leadership must also be achieved. The BSC measures would then link to this strategy.

EXHIBIT 13-5
The Balanced Scorecard for Chipset Inc. for 2010

Objectives	Measures	Initiatives	Target Performance	Actual Performance
Financial Perspective				
Increase shareholder value	Operating income from productivity gain	Manage costs and unused capacity	$2,000,000	$2,012,500
	Operating income from growth	Build strong customer relationships	$3,000,000	$3,420,000
	Revenue growth		6%	6.48%[a]
Customer Perspective				
Increase market share	Market share in communication-networks segment	Identify future needs of customers	6%	7%
Increase customer satisfaction	Number of new customers	Identify new target-customer segments	1	1[b]
	Customer-satisfaction ratings	Increase customer focus of sales organization	90% of customers give top two ratings	87% of customers give top two ratings
Internal Business Process Perspective				
Improve manufacturing quality and productivity	Yield	Identify root causes of problems and improve quality	78%	79.3%
Reduce delivery time to customers	Order-delivery time	Reengineer order-delivery process	30 days	30 days
Meet specified delivery dates	On-time delivery	Reengineer order-delivery process	92%	90%
Improve postsales service	Service response time	Improve customer-service process	Within 4 hours	Within 3 hours
Improve processes	Number of major improvements in manufacturing and business processes	Organize teams from manufacturing and sales to modify processes	5	5
Improve manufacturing capability	Percentage of processes with advanced controls	Organize R&D/manufacturing teams to implement advanced controls	75%	75%
Learning and Growth Perspective				
Align employee and organization goals	Employee-satisfaction ratings	Employee participation and suggestions program to build teamwork	80% of employees give top two ratings	88% of employees give top two ratings
Develop process skill	Percentage of employees trained in process and quality management	Employee training programs	90%	92%
Empower workforce	Percentage of line workers empowered to manage processes	Have supervisors act as coaches rather than decision makers	85%	90%
Enhance information-system capabilities	Percentage of manufacturing processes with real-time feedback	Improve online and offline data gathering	80%	80%

[a](Revenues in 2010 − Revenues in 2009) ÷ Revenues in 2009 = ($28,750,000 − $27,000,000) ÷ $27,000,000 = 6.48%.

[b]Number of customers increased from seven to eight in 2010.

measures were developed and can readily advise on how the results should be interpreted to be consistent with the intent of the measures.

The following simplified example illustrates how operating-income changes between two years can be divided into components that can describe how successful a company has been with regard to cost leadership, product differentiation, and growth.[18]

	2009	2010
1. Good units of CX1 produced and sold	1,000,000	1,150,000
2. Defective units of CX1 produced and disposed of at zeronet disposal price	500,000	300,000
3. Selling price	$ 27	$ 25
4. Direct materials (square centimetres of silicon wafer)	3,000,000	2,900,000
5. Direct materials cost per square centimetre	$ 1.40	$ 1.50
6. Manufacturing capacity	1,875,000 units	1,750,000 units
7. Total manufacturing conversion costs	$11,250,000	$10,850,000
8. Manufacturing conversion cost per unit of capacity (Row 7 ÷ Row 6)	$ 6	$ 6.20
9. Selling and customer-service capacity	60 customers	55 customers
10. Total selling and customer-service costs	$ 4,800,000	$ 4,400,000
11. Cost per customer of selling and customer-service capacity (Row 10 ÷ Row 9)	$ 80,000	$ 80,000
12. R&D employees	40	39
13. Total R&D costs	$ 4,000,000	$ 3,900,000
14. R&D costs per employee (Row 13 ÷ Row 12)	$ 100,000	$ 100,000

Chipset provides the following additional information:

◆ Manufacturing conversion costs for each year depend on production capacity defined in terms of the number of units of CX1 that can be produced. Such costs do not vary with the actual quantity of CX1 units produced. Because direct manufacturing labour costs are small (and tied to capacity, not production), Chipset includes these costs and other manufacturing costs as part of manufacturing conversion costs rather than as a separate cost category. To reduce manufacturing conversion costs, management would have to reduce capacity by selling some of the manufacturing equipment and laying off some manufacturing personnel.

◆ Most of Chipset's marketing costs are costs of selling chips to customers. Selling and customer-service costs for each year depend on the number of customers that the selling and customer-service functions are designed to support. These costs do not vary with the actual number of customers Chipset sells to in each year. Chipset had 40 customers in 2009 and 46 customers in 2010. To reduce selling and customer-service costs, Chipset management would have to lay off selling and customer-service staff.

◆ At the start of each year, management uses its discretion to determine the amount of R&D to be done. The amount of R&D is independent of the actual quantity of CX1 produced or the number of customers to whom CX1 is sold.

◆ The investment base and asset structure are not materially different in the years 2009 and 2010.

[18]For other details, see R. Banker, S. Datar, and R. Kaplan, "Productivity Measurement and Management Accounting," *Journal of Accounting, Auditing and Finance* (1989): 528–554; and A. Hayzen and J. Reeve, "Examining the Relationships in Productivity Accounting," *Management Accounting Quarterly* (2000).

Operating income for each year is as follows:

	2009	2010
Revenues ($27 × 1,000,000; $25 × 1,150,000)	$27,000,000	$28,750,000
Costs		
Direct materials costs		
($1.40 × 3,000,000; $1.50 × 2,900,000)	4,200,000	4,350,000
Manufacturing conversion costs		
($6 × 1,875,000; $6.20 × 1,750,000)	11,250,000	10,850,000
Selling and customer-service costs		
($80,000 × 60; $80,000 × 55)	4,800,000	4,400,000
R&D costs ($100,000 × 40; $100,000 × 39)	4,000,000	3,900,000
Total costs	24,250,000	23,500,000
Operating income	2,750,000	5,250,000
Increase in operating income		$2,500,000

The goal of managers at Chipset is to evaluate how much of this $2,500,000 increase in operating income was caused by the successful implementation of the company's strategy. To do so, they must examine three main analysis components: growth, price recovery, and productivity. Exhibit 13-6 provides a summary of the following analysis of the growth, price-recovery, and productivity effects.

THE GROWTH COMPONENT

The growth component measures the increase in revenues minus the increase in costs from selling more units of CX1 in 2010 (1,150,000 units) than in 2009 (1,000,000 units), assuming nothing else has changed. That is, the output prices, input prices, efficiencies, and capacities of 2009 are assumed to continue into 2010.

Revenue Effect of Growth

$$\begin{array}{c}\text{Revenue effect}\\\text{of growth}\\\text{component}\end{array} = \left(\begin{array}{c}\text{Actual units of output}\\\text{sold in 2010}\end{array} - \begin{array}{c}\text{Actual units of output}\\\text{sold in 2009}\end{array} \right) \times \begin{array}{c}\text{Selling price}\\\text{in 2009}\end{array}$$

This component is favourable (F) because it increases operating income. Decreases in operating income are unfavourable (U).

Note that we keep the 2009 price of CX1 unchanged and focus only on the increase in output sold between 2009 and 2010. The objective of the revenue effect

EXHIBIT 13-6
Strategic Analysis of Profitability

	Income Statement Amounts in 2009 (1)	Revenue and Cost Effects of Growth Component in 2010 (2)	Revenue and Cost Effects of Price-Recovery Component in 2010 (3)	Cost Effect of Productivity Component in 2010 (4)	Income Statement Amounts in 2010 (5) = (1) + (2) + (3) + (4)
Revenues	$27,000,000	$4,050,000 F	$2,300,000 U	—	$28,750,000
Costs	24,250,000	630,000 U	720,000 U	$2,100,000 F	23,500,000
Operating income	$ 2,750,000	$3,420,000 F	$3,020,000 U	$2,100,000 F	$ 5,250,000

$2,500,000 F
Change in operating income

of the growth component is to isolate the increase in revenues between 2009 and 2010 due solely to the change in the quantity sold. The analysis assumes that in this highly competitive environment the 2009 selling price continues into 2010.

Cost Effect of Growth Of course, to produce the higher output sold in 2010, more inputs would be needed. The cost increase from growth measures the amount by which costs in 2010 would have increased (1) if the relationship between inputs and outputs that existed in 2009 had continued in 2010, and (2) if prices of inputs in 2009 had continued in 2010.

$$
\begin{pmatrix} \text{Cost effect} \\ \text{of growth} \\ \text{component} \end{pmatrix} = \left(\begin{array}{c} \text{Actual units of input or capacity} \\ \text{that would have been used to} \\ \text{produce year 2010 output} \\ \text{assuming the same input--output} \\ \text{relationship that existed in 2009} \end{array} - \begin{array}{c} \text{Actual units of input} \\ \text{capacity to produce} \\ \text{2009 output} \end{array} \right) \times \begin{array}{c} \text{Input} \\ \text{prices in} \\ \text{2009} \end{array}
$$

We use 2009 input–output relationships and 2009 input prices because the goal is to isolate the increase in costs caused solely by the growth in the units of CX1 sold between 2009 and 2010. As our example assumes that the manufacturing conversion costs, selling and customer-service costs, and R&D costs are fixed, then only the direct materials costs will change with the change in volumes from 2009 to 2010.

To produce 1,150,000 units of CX1 in 2010, as compared to the 1,000,000 units produced in 2009 (15% more), assuming the same rework rate, Chipset would require a proportionate increase in the 3,000,000 square centimetres of direct materials used in 2009. Note that variable direct materials costs are distinguished from fixed costs that include conversion and R&D costs. Fixed costs do not change proportionately as long as the increase in production is within the relevant range, while variable costs will. The quantity of direct materials that would be required equals 3,450,000 square centimetres $\left(3,000,000 \times \frac{1,150,000}{1,000,000}\right)$.

Thus, the cost effects of the growth component are

Direct materials costs	$(3,450,000 - 3,000,000) \times \$1.40$	= \$630,000 U
Manufacturing conversion costs	$(1,875,000 - 1,875,000) \times \$6$	= 0
Selling and customer-service costs	$(60 - 60) \times \$80,000$	= 0
R&D costs	$(40 - 40) \times \$100,000$	= 0
Cost effects of growth component		\$630,000 U

In summary, the net increase in operating income as a result of growth equals

Revenue effect of growth component		\$4,050,000 F
Cost effect of growth		
Direct materials costs	630,000 U	
Manufacturing conversion costs	0	
Selling and customer-service costs	0	
R&D costs	0	630,000 U
Increase in operating income due to growth component		\$3,420,000 F

THE PRICE-RECOVERY COMPONENT

The price-recovery component of operating income measures the change in revenues and the change in costs to produce the 1,150,000 units of CX1 manufactured in 2010 as a result of the change in the prices of CX1 and the change in the prices of inputs required to make CX1, assuming that the relationship between inputs and outputs that existed in 2009 continued in 2010.

Revenue Effect of Price Recovery

$$
\begin{pmatrix} \text{Revenue effect} \\ \text{of product differentiation} \\ \text{component} \end{pmatrix} = \left(\begin{array}{c} \text{Selling price} \\ \text{in 2010} \end{array} - \begin{array}{c} \text{Selling price} \\ \text{in 2009} \end{array} \right) \times \begin{array}{c} \text{Actual units of} \\ \text{output sold in} \\ \text{2010} \end{array}
$$

$$
= (\$25 - \$27) \times 1,150,000 = \$2,300,000 \text{ U}
$$

Note that the calculation focuses on the decrease in the price of CX1 between 2009 and 2010 because the objective of the revenue effect of price recovery is to isolate the change in revenues between 2009 and 2010 due solely to the change in selling prices.

Cost Effect of Price Recovery This calculation focuses on the effect of changes in the prices of inputs. Because of the anticipated change in manufacturing conversion costs, these fixed costs must be considered in order to capture the full cost effect of price recovery.

$$
\begin{pmatrix} \text{Cost effect} \\ \text{of product} \\ \text{differentiation} \\ \text{component} \end{pmatrix} = \left(\begin{array}{c} \text{Input prices} \\ \text{in year 2010} \end{array} - \begin{array}{c} \text{Input prices} \\ \text{in year 2009} \end{array} \right) \times \begin{array}{c} \text{Actual units of inputs/capacity} \\ \text{that would have been used} \\ \text{to produce year 2010 output} \\ \text{assuming the same input–output} \\ \text{relationship that existed in 2009} \end{array}
$$

Direct materials costs	($1.50 − $1.40) × 3,450,000	= $345,000 U
Manufacturing conversion costs	($6.20 − $6.00) × 1,875,000	= 375,000 U
Selling and customer-service costs	($80,000 − $80,000) × 60	= 0
R&D costs	($100,000 − $100,000) × 40	= 0
Total cost effect of price-recovery component		= $720,000 U

Note that the quantity of inputs that would have been needed to produce the output in year 2010 (assuming the relationship between inputs and outputs that existed in 2009 continued in 2010) has already been determined when calculating the cost effects of growth. The calculation focuses on the change in costs caused solely by the change in the prices of inputs between 2009 and 2010.

In summary, the net decrease in operating income attributable to price recovery (measured by the change in output prices relative to the change in input prices) is

Revenue effect of price recovery		$2,300,000 U
Cost effect of price recovery		
Direct materials cost	$345,000 U	
Manufacturing conversion costs	375,000 U	
Selling and customer-service costs	0	
R&D costs	0	720,000 U
Decrease in operating income due to price-recovery component		$3,020,000 U

The price-recovery analysis indicates that, even as the prices of its inputs increased, Chipset could not pass these increases on to its customers via higher prices of CX1.

THE PRODUCTIVITY COMPONENT

The productivity component of operating income compares how costs have decreased as a result of using fewer inputs, a better mix of inputs, and less capacity to produce year 2010 output, assuming year 2010 input prices.

$$
\begin{pmatrix} \text{Productivity/} \\ \text{cost leadership} \\ \text{component} \end{pmatrix} = \left(\begin{array}{c} \text{Actual units of} \\ \text{input/capacity to} \\ \text{produce year} \\ \text{2010 input} \end{array} - \begin{array}{c} \text{Actual units of inputs/capacity that} \\ \text{would have been used to produce} \\ \text{year 2010 output assuming the} \\ \text{same input–output relationship that} \\ \text{existed in 2009} \end{array} \right) \times \begin{array}{c} \text{Year} \\ \text{2010} \\ \text{prices} \end{array}
$$

Note that the calculations use year 2010 prices and year 2010 output. The objective of the productivity component is to isolate the change in costs between 2009 and 2010 caused solely by the change in the quantities, mix, and capacities of inputs.

The actual units of capacity that would have been used to produce year 2010 output, assuming the same input–output relationship that existed in 2009, have already been calculated and explained when computing the growth component (p. 664–665). The actual units of input or capacity to produce year 2010 output is given in the basic data for Chipset on page 663. By using 2010 prices and output, the change in costs between 2009 and 2010 caused solely by change in the quantities, mix, and/or capacity of inputs is isolated.[19]

The productivity component of cost changes is

Direct materials costs	$(2,900,000 - 3,450,000) \times \$1.50$	= $	825,000 F
Manufacturing conversion costs	$(1,750,000 - 1,875,000) \times \$6.20$	=	775,000 F
Selling and customer-service costs	$(55 - 60) \times \$80,000$	=	400,000 F
R&D costs	$(39 - 40) \times \$100,000$	=	100,000 F
Increase in operating income due to productivity component			$2,100,000 F

The productivity component indicates that Chipset was able to increase operating income by improving quality and productivity, eliminating capacity, and reducing costs.

Exhibit 13-6 (p. 664) summarizes the growth, price-recovery, and productivity components of the changes in operating income. At a basic level, companies that have been successful at cost leadership will show large favourable productivity and growth components; companies that have successfully differentiated their products will show large favourable price-recovery and growth components. In Chipset's case, productivity contributed $2,100,000 to the increase in operating income and growth contributed $3,420,000. Operating income suffered because Chipset was unable to pass along increases in input prices. Had Chipset been able to differentiate its product, the price effects may have been less unfavourable.

FURTHER ANALYSIS OF GROWTH, PRICE-RECOVERY, AND PRODUCTIVITY COMPONENTS

As in all variance and profit analysis, the thoughtful analyst will want to analyze the sources of operating income more closely. For instance, in the Chipset example, growth may have been helped by an increase in industry market size. Therefore, at least a part of the increase in operating income may be attributable to favourable economic conditions in the industry rather than to any successful implementation of strategy. Some of the growth may also have come as a result of a management decision at Chipset to take advantage of its productivity gains by cutting prices. In this case, the increase in operating income from cost leadership equals the productivity gain plus any increase in operating income from growth in market share attributable to productivity improvements minus any decrease in operating income from a strategic decision to lower prices.

To illustrate these ideas, consider again the Chipset example and the following additional information.

◆ The market growth rate in the industry is 10%. That is, of the 150,000 (1,150,000 − 1,000,000) units of increase in sales of CX1 between 2009 and 2010, 100,000 (10% × 1,000,000) units are due to an increase in industry market size (which Chipset would have benefited from regardless of its productivity gains) and the remaining 50,000 units are due to an increase in market share.

[19] The productivity-component calculation uses actual 2010 input prices, whereas its counterpart, the efficiency variance in Chapters 7 and 8, uses budgeted prices. This chapter assumes the forecast year is unfolding as this analysis occurs. Year 2010 prices are used in the productivity calculation because it is real-time information and not a forecast. Chipset wants managers to choose input quantities to minimize costs in 2010 based on currently prevailing prices. If the forecast prices were used, the quantities chosen would be based on outdated, irrelevant prices estimated for use in the 2010 budget. In Chapters 7 and 8 the pro forma price is a forecast that can be changed as the year unfolds to match those prices experienced by the company.

◆ Of the $2 decrease in the selling price of CX1, $1.25 is due to a general decline in the market prices of chips in the industry. The further decrease of $0.75 is the result of a management decision to lower prices to take advantage of its productivity gains, which increased market share by 50,000 units.

Chipset would compute the increase in operating income from cost leadership as follows:

Productivity component	$2,100,000 F
Decrease in price of CX1 ($0.75 × 1,150,000 units)	862,500 U
Growth in market share due to productivity improvement and lower prices $3,420,000 (from Exhibit 13-6, col. 2) × $\frac{50,000\ units}{150,000\ units}$	1,140,000 F
Change in operating income due to cost leadership	$2,377,500 F

Further, suppose that the growth in market size was the result of a decrease in industrywide market prices. Then the effect on Chipset's operating income from industrywide effects rather than specific strategic actions is

Change in operating income due to growth in industry market size $3,420,000 (Exhibit 13-6, col. 2) × $\frac{100,000}{150,000}$	$2,280,000 F

Change in operating income due to decline in industrywide selling prices	
$1.25 × 1,150,000	1,437,500 U
Effect on operating income of industrywide factors	$ 842,500 F

Lacking a differentiated product, Chipset is unable to pass along increases in input prices to its customers. The effect of product differentiation on operating income is:

Increase in market prices of inputs (cost effect of price recovery)	$720,000 U

The change in operating income between 2009 and 2010 can be summarized as follows:

Change due to cost leadership	$2,377,500 F
Change due to industrywide factors	842,500 F
Change due to product differentiation	720,000 U
Change in operating income	$2,500,000 F

Under different assumptions of how changes in prices affect the quantity of CX1 sold, the analyst will attribute different amounts to the different strategies. The important point, though, is that, consistent with its cost leadership strategy, the productivity gains of $2,100,000 Chipset made in 2010 were key to the operating income increases in 2010. The Problem for Self-Study on page 667 describes the analysis of the growth, price-recovery, and productivity components for a company following a product-differentiation strategy.

The BSC methodology can be used in both for-profit and not-for-profit organizations. The Canadian Institute for Health Information analyzes information received from hospitals in Ontario that permits a comparison of each hospital across multiple dimensions of hospital performance. Using a balanced scorecard approach, performance indicators across the four perspectives were identified based on their scientific soundness, relevance, and feasibility. Exhibit 13-7 provides the report of one hospital, which details the specific indicators used and a comparison of this hospital with the other hospitals being analyzed.

EXHIBIT 13-7
Hospital Balanced Scorecard

Clinical Utilization and Outcomes

Acute Myocardial Infarction
Use of Selected Diagnostic Technologies ▶
Complications ▶
Readmissions ▶

Asthma
Readmissions ▶

Pneumonia
Complications ▶

Stroke
Length of Stay ▶

Cholecystectomy
Percent Day Surgery ○
Complications ●

Hysterectomy
Length of Stay NR
Complications NR
Readmissions NR

Prostatectomy
Readmissions ▶

Above-average performance refers to lower complication rates, lower readmission rates, shorter length of stay, greater use of technology, and higher percentage of day surgery.

Below-average performance refers to higher complication rates, higher readmission rates, longer length of stay, less use of technology, and lower percentage of day surgery.

Financial Performance and Condition

Financial Viability
Total Margin ▶

Efficiency
Unit Cost Performance ▶
Corporate Services ▶
Days in Inventory ▶

Liquidity
Current Ratio ▶
Working Capital ▶

Capital
Equipment Expense ▶

Human Resources
Nursing Care Hours as Percentage of Total Inpatient Nursing Hours ▶
Patient Care Hours as a Percentage of Total Staff Hours ▶

Above-average performance refers to higher values for indicators of financial viability, liquidity, capital, and human resources and lower values for indicators of efficiency.

Below-average performance refers to lower values for indicators of financial viability, liquidity, capital, and human resources and higher values for indicators of efficiency.

Patient Satisfaction

Global Quality ▶
Process Quality ▶
Outcome ▶
Nursing Care ▶
Physician Care ▶
Ancillary Patient Care Staff ▶
Support Services ▶
Housekeeping ▶

Above-average performance refers to higher scores on each indicator.

Below-average performance refers to lower scores on each indicator.

(Continued)

EXHIBIT 13-7   Continued

System Integration and Change

Above-average performance refers to higher scores on each indicator.	**Information Use**
	Clinical Information Technology ●
	Clinical Data-Collection, Dissemination, and Benchmarking ●
	Intensity of Information Use ●
Below-average performance refers to lower scores on each indicator.	**Internal Coordination of Care**
	Development and Use of Clinical Pathways ●
	Coordination of Care ▶
	Hospital-Community Integration
	Hospital-CCAC Relationships ▶
	Hospital-Community Relationships ▶
	Continuity of Care ▶
	Strategies for Managing ALC Patients ▶

Legend

Above Average Performance	●
Average Performance	▶
Below Average Performance	○
Nonreportable	NR

MyAccountingLab

ASSESS YOUR MASTERY

To check your understanding of the material in Learning Objective ④, go to the *Mastery Questions* section at the end of this chapter and complete Learning Objective ④ questions 1 and 2.

SPECIFIC CONTROL STRATEGIES

⑤ Analyze specific productivity and capacity control strategies to achieve BSC expectations

As we saw in our discussion of the productivity component, fixed costs are tied to capacity. Unlike variable costs, fixed costs do not change automatically with changes in the level of the cost driver (such as units started into production, in the case of manufacturing overhead costs). Productivity improvements never occur automatically when costs are fixed. The only way to reduce these costs is to reduce capacity (plant, equipment, or the balance in the use of human and machine-intensive conversion processes). This analysis begins with control strategies for variable costs.

PRODUCTIVITY CONTROL MEASURES

Productivity measures the relationship between actual inputs used (both quantities and costs) and actual outputs produced. The lower the quantity of inputs for a given quantity of outputs (the higher the outputs for a given quantity of inputs) the higher the level of productivity. Measuring productivity improvements over time highlights the specific input–output relationships that contribute to cost leadership.

Partial productivity, the most frequently used productivity measure, compares the quantity of output produced with the quantity of an individual input used. In its most common form, partial productivity is expressed as a ratio:

$$\text{Partial productivity} = \frac{\text{Quantity of output produced}}{\text{Quantity of input used}}$$

The higher the ratio the greater the productivity.

Consider direct materials productivity at Chipset in the year 2010.

$$\frac{\text{Direct materials}}{\text{partial productivity}} = \frac{\text{Quantity of CX1 units produced during 2010}}{\text{Direct materials quantity used to produce CX1 in 2010}}$$

$$= \frac{1{,}150{,}000 \text{ units of CX1}}{2{,}900{,}000 \text{ cm}^2 \text{ of direct materials}}$$

$$= 0.4 \text{ units of CX1 per cm}^2 \text{ of direct materials}$$

Note that the direct materials partial productivity ignores Chipset's other inputs, manufacturing conversion, selling and customer service, and R&D. Partial productivity measures become meaningful when comparisons are made that examine productivity changes over time, either across several facilities or relative to a benchmark. Exhibit 13-8 presents partial productivity measures for Chipset's various inputs for 2009 and 2010 using information from the productivity calculations on page 667. These measures compare the actual inputs used in the year 2010 to produce 1,150,000 units of CX1 with the inputs that would have been used in 2010 had the input–output relationship from 2009 continued in 2010.

It is important to distinguish between the partial productivity effects of variable- and fixed-cost components because for variable-cost elements, such as direct materials, productivity improvements automatically result in using fewer input resources. For example, Chipset's improvements in direct materials productivity in 2010 resulted in 2,900,000 cm² of direct materials being acquired and used rather than the 3,450,000 cm² that would have been required to produce 1,150,000 units of output in 2010 at the 2009 productivity level. On the other hand, for fixed-cost elements such as manufacturing conversion costs, using less of the available fixed-capacity resources will not lead automatically to lowering the cost of these resources. To improve partial productivity in these cases, management must take actions to release workers or reduce capacity. These actions are often more difficult to implement and, as in Exhibit 13-8, result in lower partial productivity gains for fixed-cost categories than for variable-cost categories.

Consider, for example, manufacturing conversion partial productivity. At the 2009 productivity levels, Chipset would need to start 1,725,000 units of CX1 to produce 1,150,000 units. Chipset has manufacturing capacity of 1,875,000 units. Efficiency improvements in 2010 result in Chipset having to start 1,450,000 units in 2010. Reducing the number of units started into production, however, does not automatically lead to a decrease in manufacturing capacity. Partial productivity increases because Chipset's managers take actions to release workers and reduce manufacturing capacity to 1,750,000 units.

A major advantage of partial productivity measures is that they focus on a single input. As a result, they are simple to calculate and easily understood by operations personnel. Managers and operators examine these numbers to understand the reasons underlying productivity changes from one period to the next. For example, Chipset's managers will evaluate whether the lower defect rates (that resulted in

EXHIBIT 13-8
Comparing Chipset's Partial Productivities in 2009 and 2010

Input (1)	Partial Productivity in 2010 (2)	Comparable Partial Productivity Based on 2009 Input–Output Relationships (3)	Percentage Change from 2009 to 2010 (4)
Direct materials	$\frac{1{,}150{,}000}{2{,}900{,}000} = 0.397$	$\frac{1{,}150{,}000}{3{,}450{,}000} = 0.333$	$\frac{0.397 - 0.333}{0.333} = 19.2\%$
Manufacturing conversion capacity	$\frac{1{,}150{,}000}{1{,}750{,}000} = 0.657$	$\frac{1{,}150{,}000}{1{,}875{,}000} = 0.613$	$\frac{0.657 - 0.613}{0.613} = 7.2\%$
Selling and customer service	$\frac{1{,}150{,}000}{55} = 20{,}909$	$\frac{1{,}150{,}000}{60} = 19{,}167$	$\frac{20{,}909 - 19{,}167}{19{,}167} = 9.1\%$
R&D	$\frac{1{,}150{,}000}{39} = 29{,}487$	$\frac{1{,}150{,}000}{40} = 28{,}750$	$\frac{29{,}487 - 28{,}750}{28{,}750} = 2.6\%$

management's being able to reduce capacity and increase manufacturing conversion partial productivity from 2009 to 2010) were caused by better training of workers, lower absenteeism, lower labour turnover, better incentives, improved methods, or substitution of materials for labour. Isolating the relevant factors is important because it helps Chipset implement and sustain these practices in the future. Chipset can then set targets for gains in manufacturing conversion productivity and monitor planned productivity improvements.

For all their advantages, partial productivity measures also have some serious drawbacks. Because partial productivity focuses on only one input at a time rather than on all inputs simultaneously, it does not allow managers to evaluate the effect of input substitutions on overall productivity. For example, manufacturing conversion partial productivity may increase from one period to the next while direct materials partial productivity may decrease. Partial productivity measures cannot evaluate whether the increase in manufacturing conversion partial productivity offsets the decrease in direct materials partial productivity. Total factor productivity (TFP) or total productivity is a technique for measuring productivity that considers all inputs simultaneously.

Total factor productivity (TFP) is the ratio of the quantity of output produced to the costs of all inputs used, where the inputs are combined on the basis of current period prices.

$$\text{Total factor productivity} = \frac{\text{Quantity of output produced}}{\text{Costs of all inputs used}}$$

TFP considers all inputs simultaneously and also considers the tradeoffs across inputs based on current input prices. Do not be tempted to think of all productivity measures as physical measures lacking financial content—how many units of output are produced per unit of input. Total factor productivity is intricately tied to minimizing total cost—a financial objective. We next measure changes in TFP at Chipset from 2009 to 2010.

CALCULATING AND COMPARING TOTAL FACTOR PRODUCTIVITY

We first calculate Chipset's TFP in 2010, using 2010 prices and 1,150,000 units of output produced (using information from the first column of the productivity component calculations on p. 667).

$$\frac{\text{Total factor productivity}}{\text{for 2010 using 2010 prices}} = \frac{\text{Quantity of outputs produced in 2010}}{\text{Costs of inputs used in 2010 based on 2010 prices}}$$

$$= \frac{1,150,000}{2,900,000 \times \$1.50 + 1,750,000 \times \$6.20 + 55 \times \$80,000 + 39 \times \$100,000}$$

$$= \frac{1,150,000}{\$23,500,000}$$

$$= 0.048936 \text{ units of output per dollar of input}$$

By itself, the 2010 TFP of 0.048936 units of CX1 per dollar of input is not particularly helpful. We need something to compare the 2010 TFP against. One alternative is to compare TFPs of other similar companies in 2010. However, finding similar companies and obtaining accurate comparable data is often difficult. Companies therefore usually compare their own TFP over time. In the Chipset example, we use as a benchmark TFP calculated using the inputs that Chipset would have used in 2009 to produce 1,150,000 units of CX1 at 2010 prices (that is, we use the costs calculated from the second column in the productivity component calculations on p. 667). The 2010 prices are used because using the current year's (2010) prices in both calculations controls for input price differences and focuses the analysis on the adjustments the manager made in the quantities of inputs in response to changes in prices.

$$\text{Benchmark TFP} = \frac{\text{Quantity of output produced in 2010}}{\text{Costs of inputs that would have been used in 2009 to produce 2010 output}}$$

$$= \frac{1,150,000}{3,450,000 \times \$1.50 + 1,875,000 \times \$6.20 + 60 \times \$80,000 + 40 \times \$100,000}$$

$$= \frac{1,150,000}{\$25,600,000}$$

$$= 0.044922 \text{ units of output per dollar of inputs}$$

Using year 2010 prices, total factor productivity increased 8.94% [(0.048936 − 0.044922) ÷ 0.044922] from 2009 to 2010. Note that the 8.94% increase in TFP equals the $2,100,000 gain (Exhibit 13-6, column 4, p. 664) divided by the $23,500,000 of actual costs incurred in 2010 (Exhibit 13-6, column 5). Total factor productivity increased because Chipset produced more output per dollar of input in 2010 relative to 2009, measured in both years using 2010 prices. The gain in TFP occurs because Chipset increases the partial productivities of individual inputs and, consistent with its strategy, seeks the least expensive combination of inputs to produce CX1. Note that TFP increases cannot be due to differences in input prices because we used year 2010 prices to evaluate both the inputs that Chipset would have used in 2009 to produce 1,150,000 units of CX1 and the inputs actually used in 2010.

A major advantage of TFP is that it measures the combined productivity of all inputs used to produce output. Therefore, it explicitly considers gains from using fewer physical inputs as well as substitution among inputs. Managers can analyze these numbers to understand the reasons for changes in TFP. For example, Chipset's managers will try to evaluate whether the increase in TFP from 2009 to 2010 was due to better human resource management practices, higher quality of materials, or improved manufacturing methods. Chipset will adopt the most successful practices and use TFP measures to implement and evaluate strategy by setting targets and monitoring trends.

Many companies, such as Monsanto, a manufacturer of fibres, and Motorola, a microchip manufacturer, use both partial productivity and total factor productivity to evaluate performance. *Partial productivity and TFP measures work best together because the strengths of one are the weaknesses of the other.*

Although TFP measures are comprehensive, operations personnel find financial TFP measures more difficult to understand and less useful than physical partial productivity measures in performing their tasks. Physical measures of manufacturing labour partial productivity, for example, provide direct feedback to workers about output produced per labour-hour worked by focusing on factors within the workers' control. Manufacturing labour partial productivity also has the advantage that it can be easily compared across time periods because it uses physical inputs rather than inputs that are weighted by the prices prevailing in different periods. Workers, therefore, often prefer to tie productivity-based bonuses to gains in manufacturing labour partial productivity. Unfortunately, this situation creates incentives for workers to substitute materials (and capital) for labour, which improves their own productivity measure while possibly decreasing overall productivity of the company as measured by TFP. To overcome the possible incentive problems of partial productivity measures, some companies—for example, TRW and Whirlpool—explicitly adjust bonuses based on manufacturing labour partial productivity for the effects of other factors such as investments in new equipment and higher levels of scrap. That is, they combine partial productivity with TFP-like measures.

CAPACITY CONTROL MEASURES

How, then, can managers reduce capacity-based fixed costs? The key is in understanding and managing unused capacity. To understand unused capacity, managers find it useful to classify costs into *engineered* and *discretionary* categories.

Engineered costs arise specifically from a clear cause-and-effect relationship between output (or cost driver) and the (direct or indirect) resources used to produce that output. In the Chipset example, direct materials costs are an example of direct engineered costs. Manufacturing conversion costs are an example of indirect engineered costs. Consider the year 2010. The output of 1,150,000 units of CX1 and the efficiency with which inputs are converted into outputs result in 1,450,000 units of CX1 started into production. Manufacturing conversion resources needed and used to process 1,450,000 units of CX1 equal $8,990,000 ($6.20 × 1,450,000), assuming that the cost of resources used increases proportionately with the number of units started.

Of course, total manufacturing conversion costs are higher ($10,850,000) because they are related to the manufacturing capacity of 1,750,000 units ($6.20 × 1,750,000 = $10,850,000). These costs are fixed in the short run, but, over time, there is a clear cause-and-effect relationship among output, manufacturing capacity required, and manufacturing conversion costs needed. Thus, engineered costs can be either variable or fixed in the short run. Selling and customer-service costs are also examples of engineered costs that are fixed in the short run. There is, however, a clear cause-and-effect relationship between selling and customer-service resources used and the number of customers served.

Discretionary costs have two important features:

◆ they arise from periodic (usually yearly) decisions regarding the maximum amount to be incurred, and
◆ they have no clearly measurable cause-and-effect relationship between output and resources used.

There is often a delay between the acquisition of a resource and its eventual use. Examples of discretionary costs include advertising, executive training, R&D, health care, and corporate staff department costs such as legal, human resources, and public relations. The most noteworthy aspect of discretionary costs is that managers are seldom confident that the "correct" amounts are being spent. The founder of Lever Brothers, an international consumer-products company, once noted, "Half the money I spend on advertising is wasted; the trouble is, I don't know which half." In the Chipset example, R&D costs are discretionary costs because there is no measurable cause-and-effect relationship between output of 1,450,000 units produced and R&D resources needed or used.

Infrastructure costs arise from having property, plant, equipment, and a functioning organization. Examples are amortization, long-run lease rental, and the acquisition of long-run technical capabilities. These costs are generally fixed costs, because they are committed to and acquired before they are used. Infrastructure costs can be engineered or discretionary.

For instance, manufacturing overhead costs incurred at Chipset to acquire manufacturing capacity are an infrastructure cost that is an example of an engineered cost. In the long run, there is a clear cause-and-effect relationship between output and lease rental costs needed to produce that output. R&D costs incurred to acquire technical capability are an infrastructure cost that is an example of a discretionary cost. There is no clear cause-and-effect relationship between output and R&D costs incurred.

Engineered costs differ from discretionary costs along two key dimensions

◆ the type of process and
◆ the level of uncertainty.

Engineered costs pertain to processes that are detailed, physically observable, and repetitive, such as manufacturing or customer-service activities. In contrast, discretionary costs are associated with processes that are sometimes called *black boxes*, because they are less precise and not well understood.

Uncertainty refers to the possibility that an actual amount will deviate from an expected amount. The higher the level of uncertainty about the relationship between resources used and outputs, the less likely a cause-and-effect relationship will exist, leading the cost to be classified as a discretionary cost. R&D costs have an uncertain effect on output because other factors such as overall market conditions, competitors' R&D investments, and new-product introductions also affect the level of output produced.

In contrast, there is a low level of uncertainty about the effect of output on manufacturing conversion resources used because other factors do not affect this relationship. Uncertainty is greater in the case of discretionary costs such as R&D because, in most cases, R&D resources are committed well before any output is produced. Exhibit 13-9 summarizes these key distinctions between engineered and discretionary costs.

EXHIBIT 13-9
Differences between Engineered Costs and Discretionary Costs

	Engineered Costs (Examples: Manufacturing, Distribution)	Discretionary Costs (Examples: R&D, Advertising, Public Relations)
Type of process or activity	a. Detailed and physically observable	a. Black box (knowledge of process is sketchy or unavailable)
	b. Repetitive	b. Nonrepetitive or nonroutine
Level of uncertainty (the possibility that actual costs will deviate from expected costs)	Moderate or small (for example, shipping or manufacturing settings)	Large (for example, R&D or advertising settings)

Source: This exhibit is a modification of one suggested by H. Itami.

How does the distinction between engineered and discretionary costs help a manager to understand and manage unused capacity? Actually, the different types of costs have very different relationships to capacity. Consider first the engineered manufacturing conversion costs. Chipset management indicates that manufacturing capacity can be added or reduced in increments of 125,000 units. Adding capacity, however, takes time. Manufacturing conversion costs are a step function, as shown in Exhibit 13-10. Each step represents increments of 125,000 units of capacity at a cost of $775,000. At each step, manufacturing conversion costs are fixed. For example, manufacturing conversion costs are fixed at $9,300,000 if Chipset wants enough capacity to process between 1,375,000 and 1,500,000 units.

At the start of the year 2010, Chipset has the capacity to process 1,875,000 units. Quality and productivity improvements made during 2010 enable Chipset to

EXHIBIT 13-10
Engineered Costs and Unused Capacity at Chipset Inc. in 2010

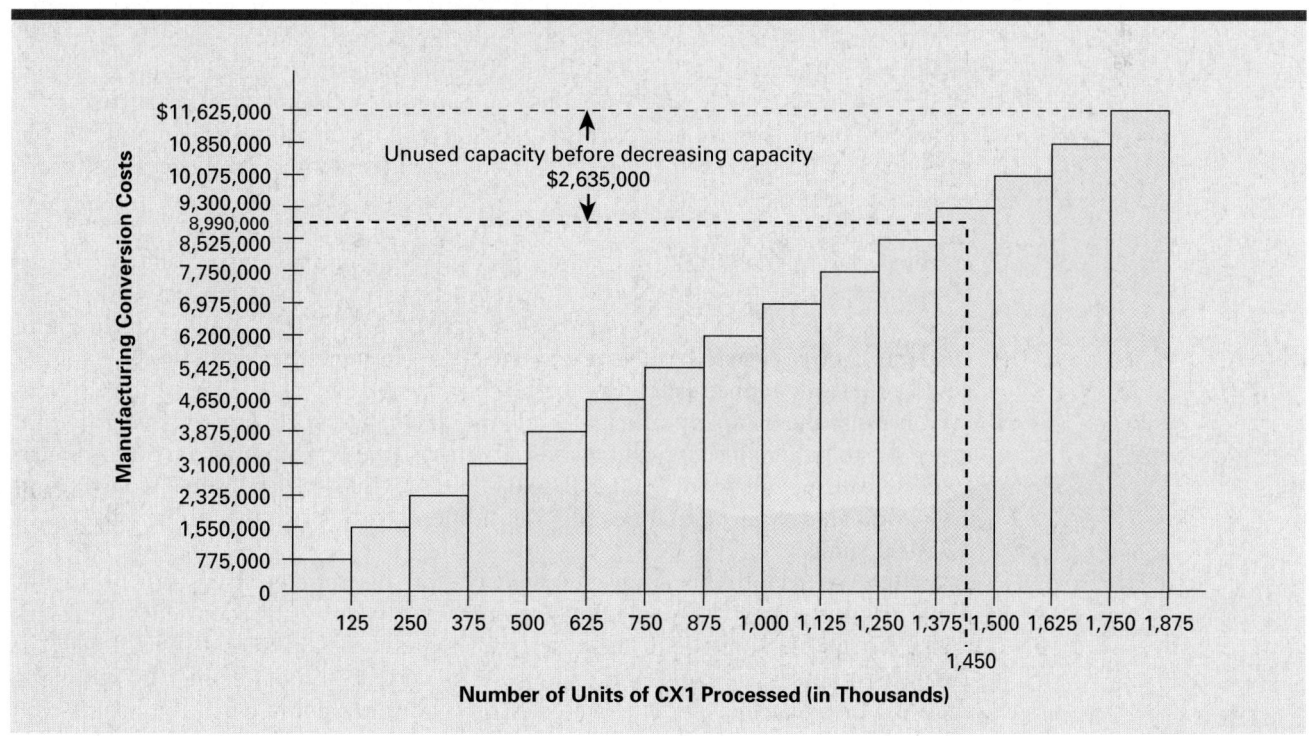

produce 1,150,000 units of CX1 by processing 1,450,000 units. Chipset calculates its unused manufacturing capacity as 425,000 (1,875,000 − 1,450,000) units for 2010, which corresponds to manufacturing conversion costs of $2,635,000 ($6.20 × 425,000 units). As shown in Exhibit 13-10, this unused capacity of $2,635,000 can also be calculated as $11,625,000 (manufacturing overhead costs for 1,875,000 units) minus $8,990,000 ($6.20 × 1,450,000, the manufacturing resources used to process 1,450,000 units).

The absence of a cause-and-effect relationship makes identifying unused capacity for discretionary costs much more difficult. Management cannot determine the R&D resources used for the actual output produced to compare R&D capacity against. Consequently, they cannot compute unused capacity as they did in the case of the engineered manufacturing conversion costs.

MANAGING UNUSED CAPACITY

What actions can Chipset management take when it identifies unused capacity? In general, it has two options. It can attempt to eliminate the unused capacity, or it can attempt to use the unused capacity to grow revenues.

In recent years, many companies have tried to *downsize* in an attempt to eliminate their unused capacity. **Downsizing** (also called **rightsizing**) is an integrated approach to configure processes, products, and people to match costs to the activities needed to be performed to operate efficiently and effectively in the present and future. Companies such as Nortel, General Motors, and IBM have downsized to focus on their core businesses and have instituted organization changes to increase efficiency, reduce costs, and improve quality. Downsizing often means eliminating jobs, which can have an adverse effect on employee morale and the culture of the organization. It is important that downsizing be done in the context of the organization's overall strategy and by retaining individuals with key management, leadership, and technical skills.

Consider Chipset's options with respect to its unused manufacturing capacity. Because it needs to process 1,450,000 units in 2010, it could potentially reduce capacity to 1,500,000 units (recall that manufacturing conversion capacity can be added or reduced only in increments of 125,000 units), resulting in cost savings of $2,325,000 [(1,875,000 − 1,500,000) × $6.20]. Chipset's strategy, however, is not only to cut costs but also to grow its business. So Chipset only reduces its manufacturing capacity by 125,000 units, from 1,875,000 units to 1,750,000 units, saving $775,000 ($6.20 × 125,000). It retains some unused capacity for future growth. By avoiding deep cuts in capacity, it also maintains the morale of its skilled and capable work force. The success of this strategy will depend on Chipset achieving the future growth it has projected.

Chipset makes similar decisions with respect to the engineered selling and customer-service costs. At the start of 2010, Chipset has the capacity to serve 60 customers. Chipset currently has 46 customers, resulting in unused service capacity of 14 customers, which corresponds to $1,120,000 ($80,000 × 14) in selling and customer-service costs. (Recall that it costs $80,000 to support each customer.) Chipset could potentially reduce selling and customer-service capacity by 10 customers. However, because the company anticipates adding nine more customers in the near future, it decides to only reduce its selling and customer-service capability from 60 to 55 customers, realizing savings of $400,000 ($80,000 × 5). Chipset's goal is to align its selling and customer-service capabilities of 55 customers with its manufacturing capacity of 1,750,000 units.

Because identifying unused capacity for discretionary costs is difficult, downsizing or otherwise managing this unused capacity is also difficult. Chipset's management uses judgment and discretion to reduce R&D costs by $100,000 in 2010. Its rationale is to cut R&D costs without significantly affecting the output of the R&D activity. Deeper cuts in R&D costs, however, could harm the business by slowing down critically needed product and process improvements. The key is to balance the need for cost reductions without compromising quality, continuous improvement, and future growth.

Growth Outpaces Profitability

Google is one of the most successful web services. It charges nothing to users of its search engine. Rather it monetizes its service by selling space to advertisers. YouTube is one of Google's services, purchased in November 2006 for approximately $1.65 billion. The infrastructure for YouTube currently includes 45 terabytes of storage (about 5,000 home computers) and millions of dollars of purchased bandwidth access each month. Although Google's net income was roughly $3.1 billion in 2006, the company

must generate millions of dollars in revenue each month to remain profitable. Sources of revenue for web-based services include:

- subscriptions for use of specific interest sites (e.g. ESPN.com, Salesforce.com)
- advertising on popular sites such as MySpace and Google itself
- transactions fees for sites such as eBay and PayPal

YouTube in particular presents unobtrusive mini commercial advertising at the bottom of its videos. Companies such as Fox, Warner Brothers, and BMW purchase advertising according to videos selected by users of YouTube. This is a highly differentiated service offered by YouTube to its advertisers.

Sources: YouTube Fact Sheet (July 2007) available from YouTube, www.youtube.com/t/fact_sheet; H. Green, "YouTube: Waiting for the Payoff," *BusinessWeek*, September 18, 2006; L. Gomes "Will All of Us Get Our 15 Minutes On a YouTube Video?" *The Wall Street Journal*, August 30, 2006; K. Delaney, "YouTube Sketches a Path to Profitability," *The Wall Street Journal*, June 29, 2006; A. Edgecliffe-Johnson, "Google Unveils YouTube Advertising Format," *Financial Times*, August 22, 2007.

ASSESS YOUR MASTERY

To check your understanding of the material in Learning Objective ⑤ go to the *Mastery Questions* section at the end of this chapter and complete Learning Objective ⑤ questions 1 and 2.

MyAccountingLab

PULLING IT ALL TOGETHER—PROBLEM FOR SELF-STUDY

Following a strategy of product differentiation, Westwood Corporation makes a high-end kitchen range hood, KE8. Westwood presents the following data for the years 2009 and 2010.

	2009	2010
1. Units of KE8 produced	40,000	42,000
2. Selling price	$100	$110
3. Direct materials (square metres)	120,000	123,000
4. Direct materials costs per square metre	$10	$11
5. Manufacturing capacity for KE8	50,000 units	50,000 units
6. Total manufacturing conversion costs	$1,000,000	$1,100,000
7. Manufacturing conversion costs per unit of capacity (Row 6 ÷ Row 5)	$20	$22
8. Selling and customer-service capacity	30 customers	29 customers
9. Total selling and customer-service costs	$720,000	$725,000
10. Cost per customer of selling and customer-service capacity (Row 9 ÷ Row 8)	$24,000	$25,000

Westwood produces no defective units but it wants to reduce direct materials usage per unit of KE8 in 2010. Manufacturing conversion costs in each year depend on production capacity defined in terms of KE8 units that can be produced. Selling and customer-service costs depend on the number of customers that the customer and service functions are designed to support. Westwood has 23 customers in 2009 and 25 customers in 2010. The industry market size for high-end kitchen range hoods increased 5% from 2009 to 2010.

REQUIRED

1. Describe briefly key elements that you would include in Westwood's balanced scorecard.
2. How would improved corporate governance improve Westwood's corporate competitiveness?
3. How would BSC measures of environmental sustainability contribute to West-wood's enterprise risk management?
4. Calculate the growth, price-recovery, and productivity components of changes in operating income between 2009 and 2010.
5. Without doing any more calculations, explain in a few sentences whether West-wood was successful in implementing its strategy.

SOLUTION

1. Key elements that Westwood should include in its balanced scorecard are

   ◆ *Financial perspective.* Operating income growth from charging higher prices on KE8.
   ◆ *Customer perspective.* Market share in high-end kitchen range market and customer satisfaction.
   ◆ *Internal business perspective.* Manufacturing quality, order delivery time, on-time delivery, and new product features added.
   ◆ *Learning and growth perspective.* Development time for designing new products and improving manufacturing processes.

2. Improving any one of the five dimensions of corporate governance improves the others. Improved corporate governance also improves competitiveness because all the factors affect customer, financial, and intellectual capital management.

3. Increasingly countries are enacting legislation that requires reclamation, recycling, and remediation activities be paid for by companies causing the need for these activities. The risk to the enterprise is that their current life-cycle pricing practices fail to include reasonable estimates of environmental life-cycle costs. Global companies need to measure their performance in a BSC format to provide relevant information to improve their strategy to respond to mandatory compliance with new legislation—good corporate governance.

4. Operating income for each year is as follows:

	2009	2010
Revenues ($100 × 40,000; $110 × 42,000)	$4,000,000	$4,620,000
Costs		
Direct materials costs ($10 × 120,000; $11 × 123,000)	1,200,000	1,353,000
Manufacturing conversion costs ($20 × 50,000; $22 × 50,000)	1,000,000	1,100,000
Selling and customer-service costs ($24,000 × 30; $25,000 × 29)	720,000	725,000
Total costs	2,920,000	3,178,000
Operating income	$1,080,000	$1,442,000
Change in operating income	↓ $362,000 F ↓	

The Growth Component

$$\begin{array}{c}\text{Revenue effect}\\\text{of growth}\\\text{component}\end{array} = \left(\begin{array}{c}\text{Actual units}\\\text{of output sold}\\\text{in 2010}\end{array} - \begin{array}{c}\text{Actual units of}\\\text{output sold in}\\2009\end{array}\right) \times \begin{array}{c}2009\\\text{output}\\\text{price}\end{array}$$

$$= (42{,}000 - 40{,}000) \times \$100 = \$200{,}000 \text{ F}$$

$$\begin{array}{c}\text{Cost effect}\\\text{of growth}\\\text{component}\end{array} = \left(\begin{array}{c}\text{Actual units of input/capacity that}\\\text{would have been used to produce}\\\text{year 2010 output assuming the}\\\text{same input–output relationship}\\\text{that existed in 2009}\end{array} - \begin{array}{c}\text{Actual units of}\\\text{input/capacity to}\\\text{produce 2009}\\\text{output}\end{array}\right) \times \begin{array}{c}\text{Year}\\2009\\\text{prices}\end{array}$$

Direct materials costs that would be required in 2010 to produce 42,000 units instead of the 40,000 units produced in 2009, assuming the 2009 input–output relationship continued into 2010, equal 126,000 square metres (120,000/40,000 × 42,000). Manufacturing conversion costs and selling and customer-service costs will not change since adequate capacity exists in 2009 to support year 2010 output and customers.

The cost effects of growth component are

Direct materials costs	$(126{,}000 - 120{,}000) \times \$10$	$=$	\$60,000 U
Manufacturing conversion costs	$(50{,}000 - 50{,}000) \times \$20$	$=$	0
Selling and customer-service costs	$(30 - 30) \times \$24{,}000$	$=$	0
Cost effect of growth component			\$60,000 U

In summary, the net increase in operating income as a result of the growth component equals

Revenue effect of growth component	\$200,000 F
Cost effect of growth component	60,000 U
Increase in operating income due to growth component	\$140,000 F

The Price-Recovery Component

$$\begin{array}{c}\text{Revenue effect of}\\\text{product differentiation}\\\text{component}\end{array} = \left(\begin{array}{c}\text{Output price}\\\text{in 2010}\end{array} - \begin{array}{c}\text{Output price}\\\text{in 2009}\end{array}\right) \times \begin{array}{c}\text{Actual units of}\\\text{output sold}\\\text{in 2010}\end{array}$$

$$= (\$110 - \$100) \times 42{,}000 = \$420{,}000 \text{ F}$$

$$\begin{array}{c}\text{Cost effect}\\\text{of product}\\\text{differentiation}\end{array} = \left(\begin{array}{c}\text{Input price}\\\text{in 2010}\end{array} - \begin{array}{c}\text{Input price}\\\text{in 2009}\end{array}\right) \times \begin{array}{c}\text{Actual units of input/capacity that}\\\text{would have been used to produce}\\\text{year 2010 output assuming the}\\\text{same input–output relationship}\\\text{that existed in 2009}\end{array}$$

Direct materials costs	$(\$11 - \$10) \times 126{,}000$	$=$	\$126,000 U
Manufacturing conversion costs	$(\$22 - \$20) \times 50{,}000$	$=$	100,000 U
Selling and customer-service costs	$(\$25{,}000 - \$24{,}000) \times 30$	$=$	30,000 U
Total cost effect of price-recovery component			\$256,000 U

In summary, the net increase in operating income as a result of the price-recovery component equals

Revenue effect of price-recovery component	\$420,000 F
Cost effect of price-recovery component	256,000 U
Increase in operating income due to price-recovery component	\$164,000 F

The Productivity Component

$$\text{Productivity/} \atop \text{cost leadership} \atop \text{component} = \left(\begin{array}{c} \text{Actual units of} \\ \text{input/capacity to} \\ \text{produce year} \\ \text{2010 input} \end{array} - \begin{array}{c} \text{Actual units of inputs/capacity} \\ \text{that would have been used to} \\ \text{produce year 2010 output} \\ \text{assuming the same input–} \\ \text{output relationship that} \\ \text{existed in 2009} \end{array} \right) \times \begin{array}{c} \text{Year} \\ \text{2010} \\ \text{prices} \end{array}$$

The productivity component of cost changes are

Direct materials costs	$(123,000 - 126,000) \times \$11$	=	$33,000 F
Manufacturing conversion costs	$(50,000 - 50,000) \times \$20$	=	0
Selling and customer-service costs	$(29 - 30) \times \$25,000$	=	25,000 F
Increase in operating income due to productivity component			$58,000 F

The change in operating income between 2009 and 2010 can be analyzed as follows:

	Income Statement Amounts in 2009 (1)	Revenue and Cost Effects of Growth Component in 2010 (2)	Revenue and Cost Effects of Price-Recovery Component in 2010 (3)	Cost Effect of Productivity Component in 2010 (4)	Income Statement Amounts in 2010 (5) = (1) + (2) + (3) + (4)
Revenues	$4,000,000	$200,000 F	$420,000 F	—	$4,620,000
Costs	2,920,000	60,000 U	256,000 U	$58,000 F	3,178,000
Operating income	$1,080,000	$140,000 F	$164,000 F	$58,000 F	$1,442,000

$362,000 F

Change in operating income

5. The analysis of operating income indicates that Westwood was successful in implementing its product differentiation strategy. The company was able to continue to charge a premium price for KE8. Westwood was also able to earn additional operating income from improving its productivity. The growth in units (from 40,000 to 42,000) was attributable entirely to the 5% increase in market size rather than Westwood's product differentiation strategy.

DECISION POINTS

The following decision guidelines use a question-and-answer format to summarize the chapter's main points. Each decision presents a key question. The guideline is the answer to that question.

DECISIONS	GUIDELINES
1. How does a set of short-term operating measures contribute to evaluating the success of long-term strategies?	Short-term financial and nonfinancial measures of internal business processes, customer satisfaction and growth in market share, and learning and growth of intellectual capital ultimately link to improved financial results. The balanced scorecard (BSC) is a way to combine these measures in an orderly way to highlight key interdependencies among them. The BSC links strategic decision making to execution of strategy.

2. How versatile is the BSC in enterprise risk management, (ERM) and corporate governance? Is there a link to corporate competitiveness?	The BSC is extremely versatile because it measures successful performance from many different perspectives. ERM is a strategy consistent with BSC measures because it requires understanding how external risks affect the entire company. One important risk is failure of corporate governance—failure to comply with laws and regulations. This failure reduces trust and opportunities to pursue cost leadership strategies such as supply-chain management. Changes in corporate governance explain changes in corporate competitiveness.
3. How does the BSC apply to economic, environmental, and social sustainability?	Economic, environmental, and social sustainability are an alternative set of BSC perspectives. Within each are measures of success. This BSC approach measures how well companies respond to demands from both shareholders and nonfinancial stakeholders to advocate for and support a healthy planet and a healthy social community. Success at corporate sustainability improves the value of a company.
4. How can a company analyze changes in operating income to evaluate strategy?	Strategic success can be measured by growth, price-recovery, and productivity components of improved operating income. The growth component measures the change in revenues and costs from selling greater or fewer units, assuming no changes in prices, efficiencies, or capacities. The price-recovery component measures changes in revenues and costs as a result solely of changes in the prices of outputs and inputs. The productivity component measures the decrease in costs from using fewer inputs and from reducing capacity. A company is considered successful in implementing its strategy when changes in operating income align closely with that strategy.
5. What cost control strategies are important?	Productivity improvement and capacity utilization are two key cost control strategies.

TERMS TO LEARN

This chapter contains definitions of the following important terms:

adjacencies (p. 648)
balanced scorecard (BSC) (p. 642)
corporate sustainability (p. 653)
cost leadership (p. 657)
customer perspective (p. 642)
discretionary costs (p. 674)
downsizing (p. 676)
engineered costs (p. 673)
enterprise risk management (ERM)
   (p. 649)

financial perspective (p. 642)
infrastructure costs (p. 674)
intellectual capital (p. 643)
internal business process
   perspective (p. 642)
learning and growth perspective (p. 643)
organic revenue (p. 648)
partial productivity (p. 670)
product differentiation (p. 656)
productivity (p. 670)

real-time data (p. 656)
reengineering (p. 660)
return on supply chain assets (p. 649)
rightsizing (p. 676)
supply-chain strategy (p. 649)
Tobin's q (p. 655)
total channel cost (p. 650)
total factor productivity (p. 672)
(TFP) (p. 672)
triple bottom line (p. 655)

MASTERY QUESTIONS

Mastery Questions are rated by proficiency level—elementary, intermediate, and advanced. The solutions appear in the Solutions to Mastery Questions section of MyAccountingLab.

LEARNING OBJECTIVE 1

1. BSC measures—Intermediate. Pearson PLC makes the following statements on its About Us webpage:

> We lead our markets in quality, innovation and in profitability, . . . With more than 30,000 employees based in 60 countries, we are a family of businesses that draws on common assets, processes and shares a common purpose: to help our customers live and learn . . .
> In everything we do, we aspire to be **brave, imaginative** and **decent** . . .
>   **Our people** are our most important asset. We choose them for what they can do, not who they are; we expect a lot out of them and reward them well.

Our customers are always right, even when they're wrong, and we watch their changing needs and tastes closely.

Our shareholders own our business. We number ourselves among them, and we want as many Pearson staff to be shareholders as possible. We are running the company for the owners.

Our suppliers are our partners and important sources of both ideas and efficiencies. We require them to provide competitive prices and service, but we treat them with respect and deal honestly with them.

Our communities are home to our companies and people. They are where we work and to which we have responsibilities; we take those responsibilities seriously.

Our assets consist of intellectual property. We respect the rights of the creators of this property, and we respect the rights of others to the materials they have created.

REQUIRED

1. What is the mission of Pearson PLC?
2. What is the strategic goal of Pearson PLC's customer perspective?
3. What is one strategic goal of Pearson PLC's learning and growth perspective?
4. What is a second strategic goal of Pearson PLC's learning and growth perspective?

2. **BSC measures—Advanced.** In the Business Review that begins Pearson PLC's annual report for 2007, the company says:

> We create and manage intellectual property, which we promote and sell to our customers under well-known brand names, to inform, educate and entertain. We deliver our content in a variety of forms and through a variety of channels, including books, newspapers and online services. We increasingly offer services as well as content, from test administration and processing to teacher development and school software . . .
>
> Our goal is to produce sustainable growth on our three key financial measures—adjusted earnings per share, cash flow and return on invested capital—which we believe are, together, good indicators that we are building the long-term value of Pearson.
>
> In Education (64% of 2007 sales and operating profit), we expect another year of good profit growth, benefiting once again from the unique breadth of our education business—from pre-school to adult learning; across publishing, testing and technology; and in the US and around the world.
>
> In our School business, integration of our recently-acquired Harcourt businesses is progressing well. In 2008, we expect School margins to be similar to 2007, after expensing integration costs relating to the acquisition. In 2009, we expect School margins to rise to around 15% as the majority of the integration costs fall away and as we realise the financial benefits of the acquisition . . . Aside from the Harcourt deal, we also announced the acquisition of eCollege in 2007, a key provider of e-learning and enrolment services to post-secondary education.
>
> In 2007, Pearson's sales increased by 6% to £4.2bn and adjusted operating profit by 14% to a record £634m. Every part of Pearson contributed to this profit increase, with adjusted operating profit at Pearson Education up 9%, Penguin up 20% and the FT Group up 30%.

REQUIRED

1. What did Pearson PLC report as an increase in organic revenue?
2. What adjacencies does Pearson PLC exploit?
3. Where did Pearson PLC obtain non-organic growth and what is the strategic goal?

LEARNING OBJECTIVE 2

1. **BSC and ERM—Intermediate.** Pengor, a manufacturer, is investigating how to reduce its purchasing costs of materials. The company has a reputation for honesty and has had excellent past experience with its current supplier, Irish, who provides a crucial component. Pengor's best quantity to order, given its current conversion process, is 600 per order and the company requires 14,000 components annually. It costs Pengor $300 per order and $25 per unit to store inventory. Pengor places 24 orders per year. For Irish, each time it responds to an order, it must set up its conversion process at a cost of $800 per setup. The best batch size is 1,225 for Irish, and Irish is trying to change its sales policy to reduce setup costs. Ideally Irish would prefer that Pengor placed only 12 orders per year.

REQUIRED

1. If Irish can dominate the seller and require 12 orders per year of 1,200 units each, what would be the cost to Pengor?
2. What would be the total channel costs if Irish dominated?

3. What is the advantage of a supply-chain partnership for both Pengor and Irish?

4. If Pengor did not have a good reputation, how much cost savings would it lose because Irish would not consider a supply-chain partnership?

2. **BSC and ERM—Advanced.** One important governance factor is stewardship. Factors indicating good stewardship include controls and safeguards of corporate resources. Sarbanes-Oxley section 404 is US legislation to increase assurance of high-quality financial reporting. All companies listed on stock exchanges in the US must comply.

Average compliance costs for large companies in 2006 were estimated at $2.92 million per company. On average, external audit costs are $1.2 million to provide assurance that internal controls are effective at safeguarding corporate resources. One CFO estimated about half the costs were to implement best practices and the rest was documentation for audit purposes. In effect, the deadweight or non-value-added cost of compliance averages about $1.46 million.

Ho (2005) provided evidence that stewardship, BOD composition, strategic leadership, recruitment and retention of long-term investors, and good execution of corporate social responsibility commitments all interacted to improve corporate competitiveness (customer, intellectual capital, and financial management).

REQUIRED

Explain why deadweight compliance costs are an issue.

LEARNING OBJECTIVE 3

1. **BSC, ERM, and corporate sustainability—Intermediate.** Corporate sustainability comprises measures of economic, environmental, and social sustainability. The following is a statement of commitment:

Harrah's is committed to

♦ recruiting, retaining and developing the best employees regardless of race, colour, religion, sex, sexual orientation, age, disability or national origin. We encourage a diverse work environment that fully capitalizes on the talents, skills and potential of all our employees.

♦ making charitable contributions to a wide range of community interests and encouraging employees to volunteer to make their communities better places to live.

♦ procuring its goods, products and services from a diversified pool of vendors, contractors and professional service providers, and working with developing businesses to help them grow.

A commitment to all our communities to help make them healthy and vibrant places to live and work:

♦ We conduct our business with honesty and integrity, and act in accordance with the highest ethical and legal standards.

♦ We recognize the importance of being responsible stewards of the environment, and we're committed to environmental sustainability and energy conservation.

♦ We share our financial success with our communities by donating a proportion of company profits to community and charitable causes.

♦ We encourage our employees to volunteer in community and charitable causes.

♦ We value the diversity and vitality of the communities in which we operate, and are committed to supporting a wide range of local businesses, charitable organizations, and community groups.

REQUIRED

1. What corporate sustainability measures are included in these statements of commitment and what phrases identify each element?

2. In your opinion does this company have a basis to measure its corporate sustainability? Why?

3. You may not be aware that the core business of Harrah's is running gambling casinos. Does this affect your opinion and if so why?

2. **BSC, ERM, and corporate sustainability—Advanced.** United Technologies Corporation (UTC) issued a 25-page Corporate Responsibility Report in 2007 which included a section on governance, environment, customers and suppliers, communities, and people. Among other things, UTC reported that 95% of all employees were aware of UTC's code of ethics, an 8% improvement over awareness measured in 2005. UTC's goal is to improve by 3% the positive response to the statement "My managers comply with the UTC Code of Ethics." The company has incorporated ethics awareness and compliance into its annual appraisals. It also pays tuition and education fees for its employees who choose to improve their education totalling $688 million since 1996 and its employees have earned 23,819 degrees.

UTC reduced its greenhouse gas emissions 5% and water consumption 6%, exceeding its targets of 3% and 2.5% annually from 2007 to 2010. UTC's goal is to continue reducing greenhouse gas emissions 3% and water consumption 2.5% in 2008 and invest $100 million in energy conservation projects over three years as well as improve energy efficiency and reduce packaging 10%. It will adopt the US Green Building Council's Leadership in Energy and Environmental Design (LEED) for all its buildings and reduce its energy consumption by 25% with 12.5% of energy from renewable resources.

The company is working to effect global change, leading the World Business Council for Sustainable Development, and has signed the Bali Communiqué to work with international governments and reduce greenhouse gas emissions by investing in low-carbon technologies. The company has won US Environmental Protection Agency awards, best diversity company awards, and has manufactured a geothermal (power from hot springs) power system that was recognized as one of the most technologically significant products of 2007.

The company reduced its lost-workday incident rate and met its 2007 goals but suffered four work incident fatalities while the goal is zero. UTC provides details about the structure of its BOD and noted it participates in government and international affairs and industry organizations. UTC was first included in the DJSI in 2006 as well as the Dow Jones Sustainable Asset Management (SAM) index.

REQUIRED

1. In your opinion does this company have a basis to measure its corporate sustainability? Why?
2. You may not be aware that one key business of UTC is armament invention and manufacture. Does this fact change your opinion of UTC's commitment to social responsibility?

LEARNING OBJECTIVE 4

1. **BSC comprehensive analysis—Intermediate.** Winchester Corporation manufactures special ball bearings. In 2009, it plans to grow and increase operating income by capitalizing on its reputation for manufacturing a product that is superior to that of its competitors. An analysis of Winchester's operating income changes between 2008 and 2009 shows the following:

Operating income for 2008	$4,140,000
Add growth component	360,000
Add price-recovery component	480,000
Add productivity component	420,000
Operating income for 2009	$5,400,000

Further analysis of these components indicates that the entire growth component is accounted for by an increase in the market size for ball bearings in 2009 and that 90% of the price-recovery component is accounted for by an increase in the market prices of ball bearings in 2009. Input prices did not change from 2008 to 2009.

REQUIRED

1. Is Winchester's 2009 strategy one of product differentiation or cost leadership? Explain briefly.
2. Was Winchester's gain in operating income in 2009 consistent with the strategy you identified in requirement 1? Explain briefly.
3. Assume the effect of the industry-marketing factor is $900,000 F. Illustrate Winchester's performance in chart form and discuss the company's performance based on its strategy of product differentiation, specifically with the increase in operating income from 2008 to 2009.

2. **BSC comprehensive analysis—Advanced.** Rowland Corporation manufactures gears using turning machines. In 2009, Rowland's turning machines operated for 80,000 hours. Rowland employed four workers in its repairs and maintenance area to fix and repair machines that had broken down or were functioning improperly. In 2009, each repairs and maintenance person was paid a fixed annual salary of $48,000 for 250 days of work at eight hours per day. During 2009, the workers spent 6,000 hours on repairs and maintenance.

REQUIRED

1. Do you think repairs and maintenance costs at Rowland Corporation are engineered costs or discretionary costs? Explain your answer.
2. Assume repairs and maintenance costs are engineered costs. Calculate the cost of unused repairs and maintenance capacity in 2009. Would you recommend that Rowland downsize its repairs and maintenance capacity? Explain your answer briefly.
3. Assume repairs and maintenance costs are discretionary costs. Calculate the cost of unused repairs and maintenance capacity in 2009.

LEARNING OBJECTIVE 5

1. **BSC-specific control strategies—Intermediate.** Berkshire Corporation makes small steel parts. Berkshire management has some ability to substitute direct materials for direct manufacturing labour. If workers cut the steel carefully, Berkshire can manufacture more parts out of a metal sheet, but this will require more direct manufacturing labour-hours. Alternatively, Berkshire can use fewer direct manufacturing labour-hours if it is willing to tolerate a larger quantity of direct materials waste. Berkshire operates in a very competitive market. Its strategy is to produce a quality product at a low cost. Berkshire produces no defective products. It reports the following data for the last two years of operations:

	2008	2009
Output units	375,000	525,000
Direct material used, kg	450,000	610,000
Direct material cost per kg	$1.44	$1.50
Direct manufacturing labour-hours used	7,500	9,500
Wages per hour	$24	$30
Manufacturing capacity in output units	600,000	582,000
Manufacturing capacity-related fixed costs	$1,245,600	$1,222,200
Fixed manufacturing costs per unit of capacity	$2.076	$2.10

REQUIRED

1. Compute the partial productivity ratios for 2008 and 2009.
2. On the basis of the partial productivity ratios alone, can you conclude whether and by how much productivity improved overall in 2009 relative to 2008? Explain.
3. How might the management of Berkshire Corporation use the partial productivity analysis?

2. **BSC-specific control strategies—Advanced.** Use the data given for Berkshire Corporation in Question 1, above.

REQUIRED

1. Compute Berkshire Corporation's total factor productivity in 2009.
2. Compare Berkshire Corporation's total factor productivity performance in 2009 relative to that in 2008.
3. What does total factor productivity tell you that partial productivity measures do not?

ASSIGNMENT MATERIAL

MyAccountingLab Make the grade with MyAccountingLab: The questions, exercises, and problems marked in red can be found on MyAccountingLab at **www.myaccountinglab.com**. You can practise them as often as you want, and most feature step-by-step guided instructions to help you find the right answer. Exercises and problems with an Excel icon in the margin have an accompanying Excel template on MyAccountingLab.

SHORT-ANSWER QUESTIONS

13-1 What are the four key perspectives in the balanced scorecard?

13-2 What are the key benefits of using a BSC?

13-3 How does the BSC relate to strategic decision making?

13-4 How does intellectual capital management relate to the learning and growth perspective of the BSC?

13-5 What is the difference between organic growth and an adjacency?

13-6 How does enterprise risk management (ERM) relate to a supply-chain strategy?

13-7 What is the relationship among corporate governance, corporate social responsibility, environmental sustainability, and corporate sustainability?

13-8 Describe three key components in doing a strategic analysis of operating income.

13-9 What is the difference between a stakeholder and a shareholder?

13-10 How does an engineered cost differ from a discretionary cost?

13-11 "The distinction between engineered and discretionary costs is irrelevant when identifying unused capacity." Do you agree? Comment briefly.

13-12 What is downsizing?

13-13 What is a partial productivity measure?

13-14 What is total factor productivity?

13-15 "We are already measuring total factor productivity. Measuring partial productivities would be of no value." Do you agree? Comment briefly.

EXERCISES

13-16 Balanced scorecard. La Quinta Corporation manufactures corrugated cardboard boxes. It competes and plans to grow by producing high-quality boxes at a low price that are delivered to customers in a timely manner. Many other manufacturers produce similar boxes. La Quinta believes that continuously improving its manufacturing processes and having satisfied employees are critical to implementing its strategy in 2009.

REQUIRED
1. Is La Quinta's 2009 strategy one of product differentiation or cost leadership? Explain briefly.
2. Indicate two measures you would expect to see under each perspective on La Quinta's balanced scorecard for 2009. Briefly explain your answer.

13-17 Analysis of growth, price-recovery, and productivity components (continuation of Exercise 13-16). An analysis of La Quinta's operating income changes between 2008 and 2009 shows the following:

Operating income for 2008	$1,700,000
Add growth component	70,000
Deduct price-recovery component	(60,000)
Add productivity component	140,000
Operating income for 2009	$1,850,000

The industry market size for corrugated boxes did not grow in 2009, input prices did not change, and La Quinta reduced the price of its boxes in line with the market.

REQUIRED
1. Was La Quinta's gain in operating income in 2009 consistent with the strategy you identified in requirement 1 of Exercise 13-16?
2. Explain the productivity component. In general, does it represent savings in only variable costs, only fixed costs, or both variable and fixed costs?

13-18 Strategy, balanced scorecard. Meredith Corporation makes a special-purpose D4H machine used in the textile industry. Meredith has designed the D4H machine for 2009 to be distinct from its competitors. It has been generally regarded as a superior machine. Meredith presents the following data for the years 2008 and 2009.

	2008	2009
1. Units of D4H produced	200	210
2. Selling price	$ 40,000	$ 42,000
3. Direct materials (kilograms)	300,000	310,000
4. Direct material cost per kilogram	$ 8.00	$ 8.50
5. Manufacturing capacity (units of D4H)	250	250
6. Total conversion costs	$2,000,000	$2,025,000
7. Conversion cost per unit of capacity	$8,000	$ 8,100
8. Selling and customer-service capacity	100 customers	95 customers
9. Total selling and customer-service costs	$1,000,000	$ 940,500
10. Selling and customer-service capacity cost per customer	$ 10,000	$ 9,900
11. Design staff	12	12
12. Total design costs	$1,200,000	$1,212,000
13. Design cost per employee	$ 100,000	$ 101,000

Meredith produces no defective machines, but it wants to reduce direct materials usage per D4H machine in 2009. Manufacturing conversion costs in each year depend on production capacity defined in terms of D4H units that can be produced, not the actual units of D4H produced. Selling and customer-service costs depend on the number of customers that Meredith can support, not the actual number of customers Meredith serves. Meredith has 75 customers in 2008 and 80 customers in 2009. At the start of each year, management uses its discretion to determine the number of design staff for the year. The design staff and costs have no direct relationship with the quantity of D4H produced or the number of customers to whom D4H is sold.

REQUIRED

1. Is Meredith's strategy one of product differentiation or cost leadership? Explain briefly.
2. Describe briefly key elements that you would include in Meredith's balanced scorecard and the reasons for doing so.

13-19 **Strategic analysis of operating income.** Refer to the information in Exercise 13-18.

④

1. 2008 total costs, $6,600,000

REQUIRED

1. Calculate the operating income of Meredith Corporation in 2008 and 2009.
2. Calculate the growth, price-recovery, and productivity components of changes in operating income between 2008 and 2009.
3. Comment on your answer in requirement 2. What do these components indicate?

13-20 **Analysis of growth, price-recovery, and productivity components (continuation of Exercise 13-19).** Suppose that between 2008 and 2009 the market for Meredith's special-purpose machines grew at 3%. All increases in market share (that is, sales increases greater than 3%) are the result of Meredith's strategic actions.

⑤

Change in operating income from industry market-size factor, $168,000 F

REQUIRED

Calculate how much of the change in operating income between 2008 and 2009 is due to industry market-size factors, cost leadership, and product differentiation. How successful has Meredith been in implementing its strategy? Explain.

13-21 **Identifying and managing unused capacity.** Refer to the Meredith Corporation information in Exercise 13-18.

⑤

1. Amount of unused manufacturing capacity, 40

REQUIRED

1. Where possible, calculate the amount and cost of unused capacity for (a) manufacturing, (b) selling and customer service, and (c) design at the beginning of 2009 based on 2009 production. If you could not calculate the amount and cost of unused capacity, indicate why not.
2. Suppose Meredith can add or reduce its manufacturing capacity in increments of 30 units. What is the maximum amount of costs that Meredith could save by downsizing manufacturing capacity?
3. Meredith, in fact, does not eliminate any of its unused manufacturing capacity. Why might Meredith not downsize?

13-22 **Balanced scorecard.** Following is a random-order listing of perspectives, strategic objectives, and performance measures for the balanced scorecard.

③

Perspectives	Performance Measures
Internal business process	Percentage of defective product units
Customer	Return on assets
Learning and growth	Number of patents
Financial	Employee turnover rate
	Net income
Strategic Objectives	Customer profitability
Acquire new customers	Percentage of processes with real-time feedback
Increase shareholder value	Return on sales
Retain customers	Average job-related training hours per employee
Improve manufacturing quality	Return on equity
Develop profitable customers	Percentage of on-time deliveries by suppliers
Increase proprietary products	Product cost per unit
Increase information-system capabilities	Profit per salesperson
Enhance employee skills	Percentage of error-free invoices
On-time delivery by suppliers	Customer cost per unit

Increase profit generated by each salesperson	Earnings per share
Introduce new product	Number of new customers
Minimize invoice error rate	Percentage of customers retained

REQUIRED

For each perspective, select those strategic objectives from the list that best relate to it. For each strategic objective, select the most appropriate performance measure(s) from the list.

13-23 Strategy, balanced scorecard, service company. Snyder Corporation is a small information systems consulting firm that specializes in helping companies implement sales management software. The market for Snyder's products is very competitive. To compete, Snyder must deliver quality service at a low cost. Snyder bills clients in terms of units of work performed, which depends on the size and complexity of the sales management system. Snyder presents the following data for the years 2008 and 2009.

	2008	2009
1. Units of work performed	80	90
2. Selling price	$ 80,000	$ 77,200
3. Software implementation labour-hours	40,000	44,000
4. Cost per software implementation labour-hour	$ 80	$ 82
5. Software implementation support capacity (units of work)	100	100
6. Total cost of software implementation support	$540,000	$547,000
7. Software implementation support capacity cost per unit of work	$ 5,400	$ 5,470
8. Number of employees doing software development	4	4
9. Total software development costs	$620,000	$640,000
10. Software development cost per employee	$155,000	$160,000

Software implementation labour-hour costs are variable costs. Software implementation support costs for each year depend on the software implementation support capacity (defined in terms of units of work) that Snyder chooses to maintain each year. It does not vary with the actual units of work performed each year. At the start of each year, management uses its discretion to determine the number of software-development employees. The software-development staff and costs have no direct relationship with the number of units of work performed.

REQUIRED

1. Is Snyder Corporation's strategy one of product differentiation or cost leadership?
2. Describe briefly key elements that you would include in Snyder's balanced scorecard and your reasons for doing so.

13-24 Strategic analysis of operating income. Refer to the information in Exercise 13-23.

REQUIRED

1. Calculate the operating income of Snyder Corporation in 2008 and 2009.
2. Calculate the growth, price-recovery, and productivity components of changes in operating income between 2008 and 2009.
3. Comment on your answer in requirement 2. What do these components indicate?

13-25 Analysis of growth, price-recovery, and productivity components (continuation of Exercise 13-24). Suppose that during 2009 the market for implementing sales management software increased by 5%, and that Snyder experiences a 1% decline in prices. Assume that any further decreases in selling prices and increases in market share are strategic choices by Snyder's management to implement Snyder's cost leadership strategy.

REQUIRED

Calculate how much of the change in operating income between 2008 and 2009 is due to industry market-size factors, cost leadership, and product differentiation. How successful has Snyder been in implementing its strategy?

13-26 Identifying and managing unused capacity. Refer to the Snyder Corporation information in Exercise 13-23.

REQUIRED

1. Where possible, calculate the amount and cost of unused capacity for (a) software implementation support and (b) software development at the beginning of 2009, based on units of

work to be performed in 2009. If you could not calculate the amount and cost of unused capacity, indicate why not.

2. Suppose Snyder can add or reduce its software implementation support capacity in increments of 5 units. What is the maximum amount of costs that Snyder could save by downsizing software implementation support capacity?

3. Snyder, in fact, does not eliminate any of its unused software implementation support capacity. Why might Snyder not downsize?

13-27 Balanced scorecard, sustainability. Okanagan Orchard Products Ltd. is a manufacturer of jams and jellies. It distributes its products to food retailers across Canada. Okanagan's objective is to be the #1 distributor of its product lines in Canada. Okanagan competes against a limited number of Canadian companies, but also must compete against several large American food manufacturers. It seeks to increase market share through the delivery of quality products. It believes it can achieve its objectives through high quality control in its manufacturing processes, improved efficiency (particularly relating to yields), and innovation of its products.

Okanagan has had problems with employee turnover, both in production and administration. It pays competitive wages, but still has struggled managing employee turnover. Employee surveys have determined that employees do not believe the company provides adequate training or support and that employees are unaware of opportunities for advancement.

REQUIRED

1. Create a balanced scorecard for Okanagan Orchard Products Ltd. using the traditional four perspectives.
2. What types of sustainability measures would you recommend for Okanagan?
3. What specific measures could Okanagan take to address its employee turnover issues?

13-28 Growth, price-recovery, and productivity components. Oceano T-Shirt Company sells a variety of T-shirts. Oceano presents the following data for its first two years of operations, 2008 and 2009. For simplicity, assume that all purchasing and selling costs are included in the average cost per T-shirt and that each customer buys one T-shirt.

1. Revenue effect of growth component, $141,400 F

	2008	2009
Number of T-shirts purchased	25,000	32,000
Number of T-shirts lost	420	350
Number of T-shirts sold	24,580	31,650
Average selling price	$ 20.00	$ 18.00
Average cost per T-shirt	$ 13.00	$ 11.10
Administrative capacity in terms of number of customers that can be served	40,000	36,000
Administrative costs	$100,000	$82,080
Administrative cost per customer	$ 2.50	$ 2.28

REQUIRED

1. Calculate the growth, price-recovery, and productivity components of changes in operating income between 2008 and 2009.
2. Comment on your results in requirement 1.

PROBLEMS

13-29 Balanced scorecard, non-profit, governance. Sunset Heights Animal Rescue & Protection Society (SHARP) is a non-profit organization dedicated to the rescue and protection of domestic animals. It operates several animal shelters in the Sunset Heights area (including animal adoption services), rescues injured or abused domestic animals, and educates volunteers, pet owners, and potential pet owners on animal guardianship.

As with all charitable organizations, it is facing increased competition in raising funds and recruiting volunteers. It is also experiencing greater demands for accountability from its donors. Recently it was unable to respond to its board of directors on the costs of running each of its programs and its allocation of funds received to various programs. Although SHARP is expected to operate with a balanced budget, it reported an operating deficit last year.

REQUIRED

1. Create a balanced scorecard for SHARP. In your answer, consider the various programs/services SHARP provides.
2. What are the corporate governance issues raised, and how might they be addressed?

13-30 Balanced scorecard and strategy. Dransfield Company manufactures an electronic component ZP98. This component is significantly less expensive than similar products sold by Dransfield's competitors. Order processing is very short; however, approximately 10% of products are defective and returned by the customer. Returns and refunds are handled promptly. Yorunt Manufacturing, Dransfield's main competitor, has a higher-priced product with almost no defects but a longer order-processing time.

REQUIRED
1. Is Dransfield's current strategy one of product differentiation or cost leadership?
2. Dransfield would like to improve quality without significantly increasing costs or order-processing time. Dransfield's managers believe the increased quality will increase sales. What elements should Dransfield include in its balanced scorecard?

13-31 Strategic analysis of operating income (continuation of Problem 13-30). Assume that in 2009, Dransfield has changed its processes and trained workers to recognize quality problems and fix them before products are finished and shipped to customers. Quality is now at an acceptable level. Cost per kilogram of materials is about the same as before, but conversion costs are higher and Dransfield has raised its selling price in line with the market. Sales have increased and returns have decreased. Dransfield's managers attribute this to higher quality and a price that is still less than Yorunt's. Information about the current period and prior period follows:

	2008	2009
1. a. Units of ZP98 produced and sold	5,000	6,250
b. Units of ZP98 returned	500	225
c. Net sales in units	4,500	6,025
2. Selling price	$ 44	$ 50
3. Direct materials (kilograms) used	2,500	3,125
4. Direct material cost per kilogram	$ 10	$ 10
5. Manufacturing capacity in units of ZP98	8,000	8,000
6. Total conversion costs	$128,000	$184,000
7. Conversion cost per unit of capacity	$ 16	$ 23
8. Selling and customer-service capacity	60 customers	60 customers
9. Total selling and customer-service costs	$ 4,000	$ 4,180
10. Total selling and customer-service capacity cost per customer	$ 66.67	$ 69.67
11. Advertising staff	1	1
12. Total advertising costs	$ 20,000	$ 24,000
13. Advertising cost per employee	$ 20,000	$ 20,000

Conversion costs in each year depend on production capacity defined in terms of ZP98 units that can be produced, not the actual units produced. Selling and customer-service costs depend on the number of customers that Dransfield can support, not the actual number of customers it serves. Dransfield has 50 customers in 2008 and 60 customers in 2009. At the start of each year, management uses its discretion to determine the number of advertising staff for the year. Advertising staff and its costs have no direct relationship with the quantity of ZP98 units produced and sold or the number of customers who buy ZP98.

REQUIRED
1. Calculate the operating income of Dransfield Company for 2008 and 2009.
2. Calculate the growth, price-recovery, and productivity components that explain the change in operating income from 2008 to 2009.
3. Comment on your answer in requirement 2. What do these components indicate?

13-32 Analysis of growth, price-recovery, and productivity components (continuation of Problem 13-31). Suppose that during 2009 the market for ZP98 grew 8%. All increases in market share (that is, sales increases greater than 8%) are the result of Dransfield's strategic actions.

REQUIRED
Calculate how much of the change in operating income from 2008 to 2009 is due to the industry market-size factor, product differentiation, and cost leadership. How does this relate to Dransfield's strategy and its success in implementation? Explain.

13-33 Identifying and managing unused capacity (continuation of Problem 13-31). Refer to the information for Dransfield Company in Problem 13-31.

1. Amount of unused manufacturing capacity, 1,750

REQUIRED

1. Calculate the amount and cost of unused capacity for:

   a. Manufacturing
   b. Sales and customer service
   c. Advertising

   If you are unable to calculate the amount and cost of unused capacity, explain why.

2. State two reasons why Dransfield might downsize and two reasons why it might not downsize.

3. Assume Dransfield has several product lines, of which ZP98 is only one. The manager for the ZP98 product line is evaluated on the basis of manufacturing and customer sales and service costs, but not advertising costs. The manager wants to increase his capacity for customers because he thinks the market is growing, and this will cost an additional $1,098. However, the manager is not going to use this extra capacity immediately, so he classifies it as advertising cost rather than customer sales and service cost. How will the deliberate misclassification of this cost affect:

   a. The operating income overall?
   b. The growth, price-recovery, and productivity components?
   c. The evaluation of the ZP98 manager?

13-34 Balanced scorecard. Caltex Inc. refines gasoline and sells it through its own Caltex Gas Stations. On the basis of market research, Caltex determines that 60% of its customers (medium- to high-income individuals) are willing to pay a higher price for its gas if the gas stations can provide excellent customer service such as a clean facility, a convenience store, friendly employees, quick turnaround, the ability to pay by credit card, and high-octane premium fuel. Marketwide prices for inputs and outputs and the market size did not change in 2009. Caltex's balanced scorecard for 2009 follows. For brevity, the initiatives taken under each objective are omitted.

Objectives	Measures	Target Performance	Actual Performance
Financial Perspective			
Increase shareholder value	Operating income changes from price recovery	$108,000,000	$114,000,000
	Operating income changes from growth	$ 78,000,000	$ 80,400,000
Customer Perspective			
Increase market share	Market share of total gasoline market	10%	9.8%
Internal Business Process Perspective			
Improve gasoline quality	Quality index	94 points	95 points
Improve refinery performance	Refinery reliability index (%)	92%	92%
Ensure gasoline availability	Product availability index (%)	99%	100%
Learning and Growth Perspective			
Increase refinery process capability	Percentage of refinery processes with advanced controls	88%	90%

REQUIRED

1. Was Caltex successful in implementing its strategy in 2009? Explain your answer.
2. Would you have included some measure of employee satisfaction and employee training in the learning and growth perspective? Are these objectives critical to Caltex for implementing its strategy? Why or why not? Explain briefly.
3. Explain how Caltex did not achieve its target market share in the total gasoline market but still exceeded its financial targets. Is "market share of total gasoline market" the correct measure of market share? Explain briefly.
4. Is there a clear cause-and-effect linkage between improvements in the measures in the internal business process perspective and the measures in the customer

perspective? That is, would you add other measures to the internal business process perspective or the customer perspective? Why or why not? Explain briefly.

5. Do you agree with Caltex's decision not to include measures of changes in operating income from productivity improvements under the financial perspective of the balanced scorecard? Explain briefly.

13-35 **Engineered and discretionary overhead costs, unused capacity, customer help-desk.** BrightStar, a cable television operator, had 900,000 subscribers in 2009. The company employs eight customer-help-desk representatives to respond to customer questions and problems. During 2009, each customer-help-desk representative worked eight hours per day for 250 days at a fixed annual salary of $48,000. The company received 72,000 telephone calls from its customers in 2009. Each call took an average of 10 minutes.

REQUIRED

1. Do you think customer-help-desk costs at BrightStar are engineered costs or discretionary costs? Explain your answer.
2. Calculate the cost of unused customer-help-desk capacity in 2009 under each of the following two assumptions: (a) customer-help-desk costs are engineered costs and (b) customer-help-desk costs are discretionary costs.
3. Assume that BrightStar had 1,020,000 subscribers in 2010 and that the 2009 percentage of telephone calls received to total subscribers continued into 2010. Customer-help-desk capacity in 2010 was the same as it was in 2009. Calculate the cost of unused customer-help-desk capacity in 2010 under each of the following two assumptions: (a) customer-service costs are engineered costs and (b) customer-service costs are discretionary costs.

13-36 **Balanced scorecard, governance.** John Emburey, division manager of the Household Product Division, a maker of kitchen dishwashers, had just seen the balanced scorecard for his division for 2009. He immediately called Patricia Conley, the management accountant for the division, into his office for a meeting. "I think the employee satisfaction and customer satisfaction numbers are way too low. These numbers are based on a random sample of subjective assessments made by individual managers and customer representatives. My own experience indicates that we are doing well on both these dimensions. Until we do a formal survey of employees and customers sometime next year, I think we are doing a disservice to ourselves and this company by reporting such low scores for employee and customer satisfaction. These scores will be an embarrassment for us at the division managers' meeting next month. We need to get these numbers up."

Patricia knew that the employee and customer satisfaction scores were subjective but the procedure she had used was identical to the procedures she had used in the past. She believed the scores represented the unhappiness of employees with the latest work rules and the unhappiness of customers with missed delivery dates. She also knew that these problems would be corrected in time.

REQUIRED

1. Do you think that Household Product Division should include subjective measures of employee satisfaction and customer satisfaction in its balanced scorecard? Explain.
2. What should Patricia Conley do?

13-37 **Partial productivity measurement.** Guble Company manufactures wallets from fabric. In 2008, Guble made 2,500,000 wallets using 1,875,000 metres of fabric. In 2009, Guble plans to make 2,650,000 wallets and wants to make fabric use more efficient. At the same time, Guble wants to reduce capacity. Capacity in 2008 was 3,000,000 wallets at a total cost of $9,000,000. Guble wants to reduce capacity to 2,800,000 wallets, at a total cost of $8,680,000 in 2009.

Suppose that in 2009 Guble makes 2,650,000 wallets, uses 1,669,500 metres of fabric, and reduces capacity to 2,800,000 units and costs to $8,680,000.

REQUIRED

1. Calculate the partial-productivity ratios for materials and conversion (capacity costs) for 2009, and compare them to a benchmark for 2008 calculated based on 2009 output.
2. How can Guble Company use the information from the partial-productivity calculations?

13-38 **Total factor productivity (continuation of Problem 13-37).** Refer to the data for Problem 13-37. Assume the fabric costs $4 per metre in 2009 and $4.10 per metre in 2008.

REQUIRED

1. Compute Guble Company's total factor productivity (TFP) for 2009.
2. Compare TFP for 2009 with a benchmark TFP for 2008 inputs based on 2009 output.
3. What additional information does TFP provide that partial productivity measures do not?

13-39 Downsizing. (CMA, adapted) Mayfair Corporation currently subsidizes cafeteria services for its 250 employees. Mayfair is in the process of reviewing the cafeteria services as cost-cutting measures are needed throughout the organization to keep the prices of its products competitive. Two alternatives are being evaluated: downsize the cafeteria staff and offer a reduced menu or contract with an outside vendor.

The current cafeteria operation has five employees with a combined annual salary of $155,000 plus additional employee benefits at 25% of salary. The cafeteria operates 260 days each year, and the costs for utilities and equipment maintenance average $52,000 annually. The daily sales include 100 entrées at $7.20 each, 90 sandwiches or salads at an average price of $4.50 each, plus an additional $300 for beverages and desserts. The cost of all cafeteria supplies is 62% of revenues.

The plan for downsizing the current operation envisions retaining two of the current employees whose combined base annual salaries total $94,000. An entrée would no longer be offered, and prices of the remaining items would be increased slightly. Under this arrangement, Mayfair expects daily sales of 160 sandwiches or salads at a higher average price of $5.10. The revenue for beverages and desserts is expected to increase to $340 each day. Because of the elimination of the entrée, the cost of all cafeteria supplies is expected to drop to 52% of revenues. All other conditions of operation would remain the same. Mayfair is willing to continue to subsidize this reduced operation but will not spend more than 20% of the current subsidy.

A proposal has been received from Wilco Foods, an outside vendor that is willing to supply cafeteria services. Wilco has proposed to pay Mayfair $1,300 per month for use of the cafeteria and utilities. Mayfair would be expected to cover equipment repair costs. In addition, Wilco would pay Mayfair 8% of all revenues received above the breakeven point; this payment would be made at the end of the year. All other costs incurred by Wilco to supply the cafeteria services are variable and equal 75% of revenues. Wilco plans to charge $7.80 for an entrée, and the average price for the sandwich or salad would be $5.50. All other daily sales are expected to average $370. Wilco expects daily sales of 70 entrées and 98 sandwiches or salads.

REQUIRED

1. Determine whether the plan for downsizing the current cafeteria operation would be acceptable to Mayfair Corporation. Show all calculations.
2. Is the Wilco Foods proposal more advantageous to Mayfair Corporation than the downsizing plan? Show all calculations.

COLLABORATIVE LEARNING CASE

13-40 Analysis of growth, price-recovery, and productivity components. Tilson Ltd. sells men's clothing. Corporate strategy is to offer a wide selection of clothes and excellent customer service, and to charge a premium price. Tilson presents the following data for the years 2009 and 2010. For simplicity, assume that each customer purchases one piece of clothing.

	2009	2010
1. Number of items of clothing purchased and sold	60,000	60,000
2. Average selling price	$ 75.00	$ 73.80
3. Average cost per item of clothing	$ 51.00	$ 52.00
4. Selling and customer-service capacity	72,000 customers	61,000 customers
5. Selling and customer-service costs	$594,000	$494,100
6. Purchasing and administrative capacity	950 designs	820 designs
7. Purchasing and administrative costs	$308,750	$258,300

Total selling and customer-service costs depend on the number of customers that Tilson has created capacity to support, not the actual number of customers served. Total purchasing and administrative costs depend on purchasing and administrative capacity that the company has created (defined in terms of the number of distinct clothing designs that Tilson can purchase and administer). Purchasing and administration costs do not depend on the actual number of clothing pieces purchased.

Actual results for 2009 showed that Tilson purchased 920 distinct designs. This number dropped to 800 distinct designs in 2010.

1. Downsizing plan subsidy, $25,231

2. 2010 total costs, $3,872,400

Marketwide prices for clothes and the market size were unchanged in 2009 and 2010. At the start of 2010, the company had targeted a 10% increase in operating income over the previous year.

REQUIRED

1. Is Tilson's strategy one of product differentiation or cost leadership?
2. Calculate the company's operating income in 2009 and 2010.
3. Calculate the growth, price-recovery, and productivity components of changes in operating income between 2009 and 2010.
4. Does the strategic analysis of operating income indicate the company was successful in implementing its strategy in 2010? Explain.

Cost Allocation

Good Period Overhead Cost-Allocation Methods Lead to Good Cost Management

Best Buy is firing customers. The angels purchase and keep products. The devils purchase the same products, apply for rebates, return the purchase, then repurchase the product at an open-box discount and sell it at a higher price on eBay. To discourage them Best Buy now enforces a 15% restocking fee on returned merchandise. Revenue and costs differ between the angels and devils. The extent of the difference depends in part on how rational Best Buy is when it allocates its overhead period costs to each product and to each customer.

After studying this chapter, you should be able to

1. Apply relevance as a criterion to guide decisions related to allocation of support costs

2. Apply cost-allocation procedures to period overhead cost allocation of support departments' cost pools

3. Analyze and select appropriate cost-allocation procedures to assign support costs to operating departments

4. Analyze and select appropriate cost-allocation procedures to assign support costs to other support and operating departments

5. Analyze cost-allocation procedures to assign common costs and justify contractual reimbursement

The purpose of this chapter and Chapter 15 is to explain and apply techniques to allocate support department, or period overhead, costs. Support department cost allocation is treated separately in part because most period costs are excluded from inventoriable costs by the CICA standard. Yet under absorption costing, *all* costs must be recovered from selling the finished goods or the services. Cost allocation is only an estimation. The techniques often unitize fixed costs, but with all the inaccuracies of that process it is a reasonable alternative to spending too much to obtain information of too little improved relevance. Managers must always decide where the cost of improved accuracy exceeds the benefit. One useful criterion is relevance. You may recall that relevance means the additional information that will change a decision. Relevant information will differ among alternatives (Chapters 11 and 12).

From Chapters 4 and 5, allocation techniques for operating departments and for the production function were developed. It is seldom clear what the right answer is regarding how to allocate indirect costs, and there are several appropriate techniques from which to choose. Support costs are particularly challenging because often support departments provide resources to one another as well as to operating departments. As a manager you will be faced with many cost-allocation questions in your career; understanding and applying relevance as a criterion will improve your competence at making sound professional judgments.

PURPOSES OF COST ALLOCATION

1 Apply relevance as a criterion to guide decisions related to allocation of support costs

The core of the allocation problem is that activities giving rise to indirect costs benefit either many products, business functions, or departments—the *cost objects*. For example, no single operating department causes all the accounting costs of an enterprise. Most support activities are interdependent: to the extent that if one activity consumes more overhead period costs, it may well reduce the period costs of all other activities dependent upon it. In this context it is difficult to imagine an effective legal department without an effective accounting department. It is more difficult to imagine how either could be effective without an effective MIS. The added challenge is that how to allocate costs depends on what problem managers are solving. Exhibit 14-1 illustrates this decision-making process.

The allocation of one particular cost need not satisfy all purposes simultaneously. Four possible reasons for allocating period costs with examples are:

1. To provide information for economic decisions
2. To motivate managers and employees
3. To justify costs or compute reimbursement
4. To measure income and assets for reporting to external parties

The salary of an aerospace scientist in a central research department of Boeing or Airbus may be allocated as part of central research costs to satisfy purpose 1 (economic decisions). Under generally accepted accounting principles it must not be allocated to inventory to satisfy purpose 4 (income and asset measurement). This period cost may or may not be allocated to satisfy purpose 2 (motivation). It may or may not be allocated to a government contract to justify a cost to be reimbursed to satisfy purpose 3 (cost reimbursement).

The same combination of costs in the six business functions typically will not satisfy each of the four purposes listed. For economic decision purposes, the costs in all six functions should be included. For motivation purposes, costs from more than one function are often included to emphasize to managers how costs in different functions are related to each other and encourage teamwork. For example, some Japanese companies require product designers to incorporate costs farther down the chain than design (such as distribution, customer service, and manufacturing) into their product cost estimates. The aim is to focus attention on how different product design options affect the total costs of the organization.

EXHIBIT 14-1
Cost-Allocation Decision Process—The Procedure Depends on the Purpose

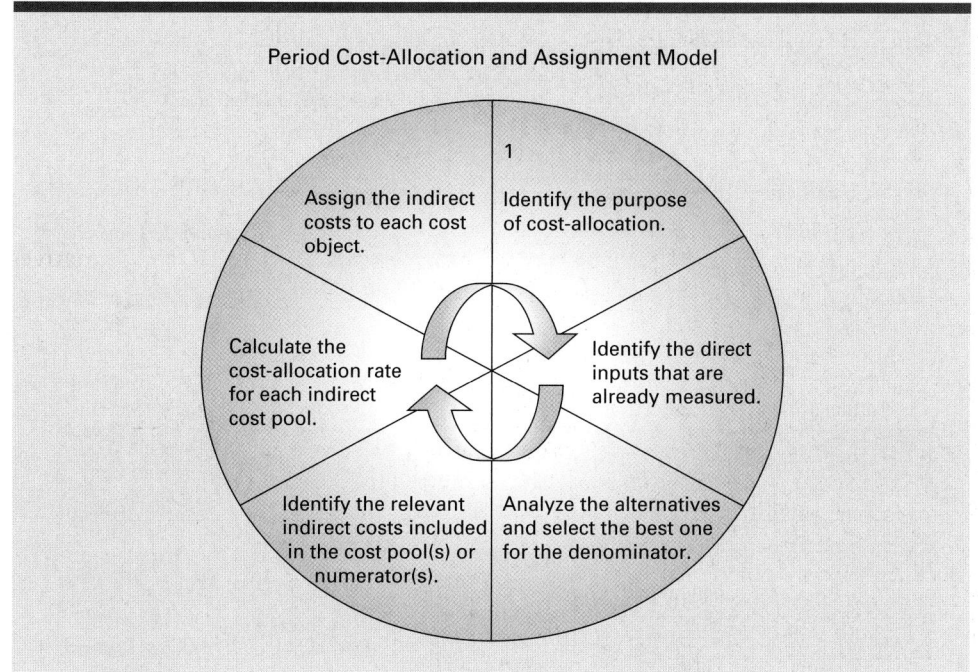

Period Cost-Allocation and Assignment Model

For cost reimbursement purposes, the particular contract will often stipulate whether all six of the business functions or only a subset of them are to be reimbursed. For instance, cost reimbursement rules governing government contracts may explicitly exclude marketing costs. For purposes of income and asset measurement for reporting to external parties, inventoriable costs under generally accepted accounting principles include only manufacturing costs (and product design costs in some cases). In Canada, research costs are expensed to the accounting period in which they are incurred, while some development costs may be capitalized and charged to future periods.

Exhibit 14-2 may look familiar because it is very similar to Exhibit 4-4 (p. 145). The difference is that in Chapter 4 the generic term for cost object was *job*. In this chapter we will deal with the product first as cost object, then with departments. For simplicity, we will assume that inventoriable overhead costs (manufacturing overhead MOH) have been assigned and focus on the allocation and assignment of period costs. In Chapter 4, the focus was on how to allocate the inventoriable cost portion of the total green indirect cost pool to a cost object generically identified as a job. In the exhibits in this chapter, the overhead or indirect period costs are signified by green, the element of cost allocation which is the focus of Chapter 14.

Exhibit 14-2 illustrates a period overhead allocation process. It is still necessary to identify and separate direct from indirect and inventoriable from period costs. In this chapter, however, understand that the direct inputs are those causing the orange period, not the blue inventoriable costs. Of course both the blue direct inventoriable costs and the orange direct period costs will be actual costs traced to the cost object. Only the indirect costs will be assigned.

We will begin with period cost allocation to products, then move to period cost allocation to departments to illustrate allocation techniques appropriate to accomplishing two different costing objectives. In contrast to Chapters 4 and 5, in Chapter 14 the choice of period cost-allocation methods depends upon the nature of the management decision that must be made. The same period overhead cost pool can be assigned using different allocation bases depending upon the management situation for which cost assignment is required. Relevance is relative to the reason for period cost allocation.

EXHIBIT 14-2
Period Cost Allocation—One Part of the Big Picture

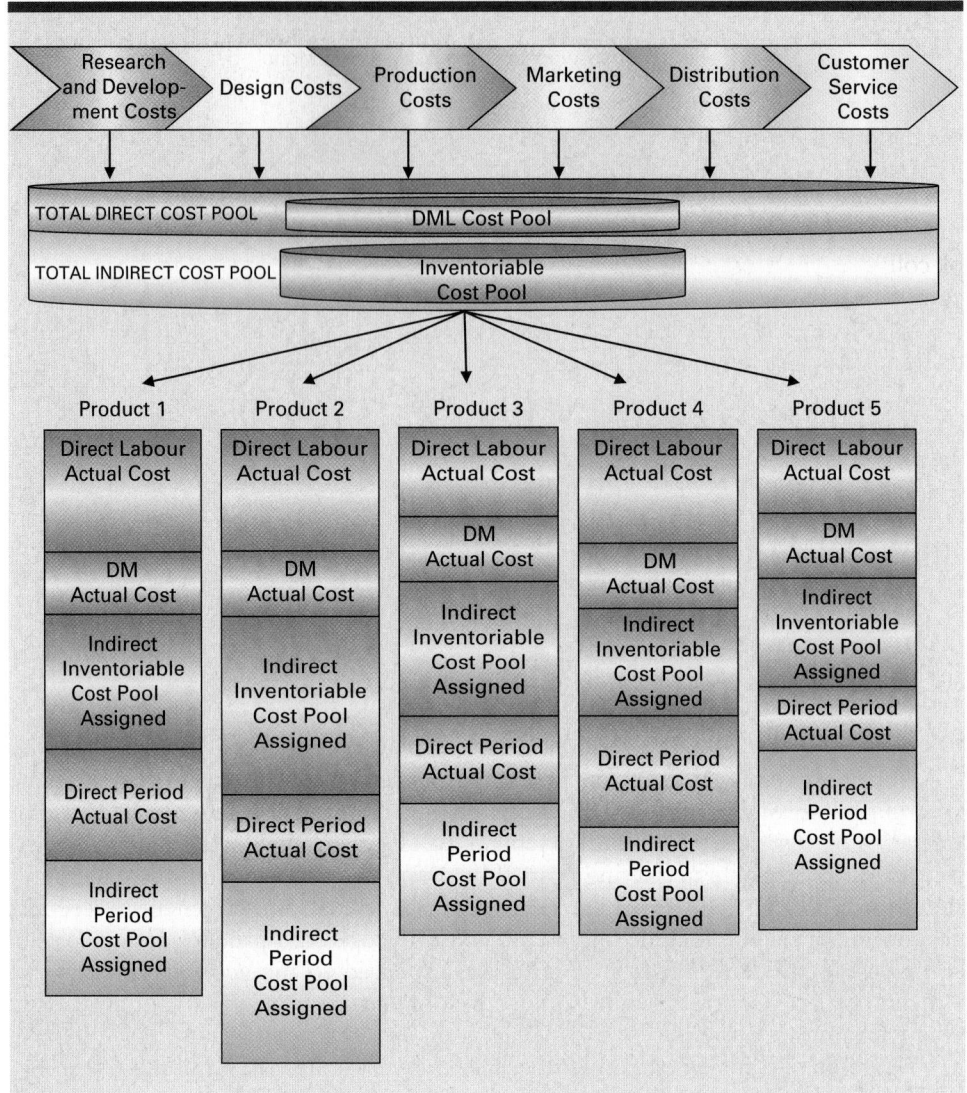

THE RELEVANCE CRITERION

Managers will decide upon the number of period cost pools and their cost-allocation bases based on relevance. Having made some reasonable assumptions about what period costs are relevant, the justification for the choice can be made using cause-and-effect and benefits-received criteria, especially when the purpose for cost allocation is related to either economic decisions or motivation. The reason is that clear causal chains improve the probability that changes to causes will change the costs. Benefits received ensures that those receiving little or no material benefit from the consumption of overhead during a specified time period will not be burdened with its cost. Two other justifications are fairness and ability to bear the cost burden.

For government contract purposes the fairness criterion may be more relevant. For example, the Department of National Defence requires facilities to full-cost their services in any proposal to offer unused capacity for sale. Although it would be financially beneficial to sell any unused capacity of a facility as long as the price exceeds the incremental cost, the government does not want to be seen as competing unfairly in the private sector. Thus the price must cover all costs, including allocations of overhead costs.

Fairness and ability to bear are used less frequently than either cause and effect or benefits received. Fairness is a difficult criterion on which to obtain agreement.[1] Some issues that arise when using the ability-to-bear criterion emerge if you consider a product that consumes a large amount of indirect costs but whose selling price is currently below its direct costs for competitive purposes. This product has no ability to bear any indirect costs of the services it uses. If this proportion of indirect costs is allocated to other products, then their selling prices will subsidize the product that is losing money.

When deciding upon period cost-allocation methods, managers must weigh the overall costs and benefits. With rapid advances in technology, the financial costs of collecting and processing timely cost information have rapidly declined. Many companies have either adopted or developed costing systems that use multiple cost-allocation bases where the benefits of improved information for decision making make this task worthwhile.

THE JUSTIFICATION OF CAUSE-EFFECT

In practice, the strength of the cost-benefit justification for adopting a specific procedure of cost allocation depends upon how clear the cause-effect relationship is. If it is possible to implement ABC, for example, many indirect costs contained in one or two heterogeneous overhead cost pools will be separated into several homogeneous overhead cost pools. A homogeneous cost pool will change in value as a specific quantity of the cost driver consumed changes. It is a variable overhead cost pool. The same cost driver can cause different costs across different functions in the value chain. The key to understanding homogeneous cost pools is the cost driver in the denominator, not the various costs in the numerator.

The cost-allocation base will be a cost driver, and this means that changes in the cost driver will explain a very large percentage of the change in the value of the cost pool. In statistical terms the r^2 will be very high, with random events explaining any remaining change (see Chapter 10). If activities, their frequency, duration, or intensity provide a justifiable cause-effect relationship, then ABC is an effective strategy. ABC will improve the relevance of information used for cost control and reduction, pricing, performance measurement, cost modelling, and budgeting.

ABC, however, can be expensive and difficult to implement because it requires a coalition of managers across the functions of the value chain. The team is necessary because the goal is to identify all costs caused by one activity at either the unit of output, batch, product, or facilities level in the cost hierarchy. This strategy also reveals clearly where products cross-subsidize each other, and this can create performance evaluation issues for managers whose products are not profitable. Moreover, improving profitability of a single product in a multiproduct company requires careful planning to ensure that the entire enterprise is considered. Thus, implementing an improved allocation system to clarify cause-effect relationships must be cost-beneficial.

THE JUSTIFICATION OF COST-BENEFIT

Many companies place great importance on cost-benefit considerations when designing their cost-allocation systems. Companies incur costs not only in gathering data, but also in taking the time necessary to educate management about the chosen system. The more sophisticated the system, in general, the higher these education costs. The costs of designing and implementing sophisticated cost-allocation systems are highly visible, and most companies work to reduce them.

---

[1]Kaplow and Shavell, for example, in a review of the legal literature observed that "notions of fairness are many and varied. They are analyzed and rationalized by different writers in different ways, and they also typically depend upon the circumstances under consideration. Accordingly, it is not possible to identify a consensus view on these notions. . . . " See L. Kaplow and S. Shavell, "Fairness versus Welfare," *Harvard Law Review*, February 2001.

In contrast, the benefits from using a well-designed cost-allocation system—being able to make better-informed make/buy decisions, pricing decisions, cost control decisions, and so on—are difficult to measure and are frequently less visible. Still, designers of cost-allocation systems should consider these benefits as well as costs. Once the benefits are identified, management accountants work with the team to estimate financial values. When benefits are intangible, such as increased teamwork and cooperation, these values are often presented in the form of anticipated cost savings.

Spurred by rapid reductions in the costs of collecting and processing information, organizations today are moving toward more detailed cost-allocation systems. Many companies have now developed manufacturing or distribution overhead costing systems that use more than 10 different cost-allocation bases. Also, some businesses have state-of-the-art information technology already in place for operating their plants or distribution networks. Applying this existing technology to the development and operation of a cost-allocation system is less expensive—and thus more inviting—than starting up such a system from scratch.

THE JUSTIFICATION OF FAIRNESS

Not all costs are either variable or fixed. Especially with respect to fixed costs it is sometimes simpler to select a cost-allocation base and rate that pleases no one rather than establish a cost assignment considered fair. Organizational research on the concept of justice or fairness has advanced considerably. Two distinguishable dimensions are distributive and procedural fairness. What is perceived as distributive fairness of burdens such as a proportion of fixed cost, and benefits such as a bonus, depends largely on the procedure undertaken before the distributive decisions were made.

Generally speaking, if people

◆ believe the decision makers and the decision process is undertaken in good faith,

◆ are given the opportunity to participate in distributive decision making,

◆ have access to relevant information about the consequences, and

◆ are treated with respect and sensitivity when they are not beneficiaries,

then they will accept that the distribution was fair although it was burdensome for them but not others. These factors, when present in the procedure of deciding how costs and benefits will be distributed, generate trust that any harm is not intentional.[2] There is, unfortunately, no standardized procedure to fit all situations. How people perceive the fairness of a decision depends on a complex interaction of perceptions about procedural and distributive justice which arise from specific situations.

THE JUSTIFICATION OF ABILITY TO BEAR

The question of the ability to bear the burden of cost has already been presented in Chapter 12 in a discussion of pricing. Global companies, and in particular pharmaceutical companies, often make widely different pricing decisions depending on the geographical location of their buyers. Although retroviral treatments that make the difference between a very short and longer lifespan for HIV-AIDS victims was an example, the principle is generalizable. In this example it seems repugnant to withhold beneficial and medically necessary treatment from people in Africa simply because they cannot pay. At the same time, pharmaceutical companies incur huge costs in the hundreds of millions of dollars to develop

[2]S. M. Hopkins and B. L. Weatherington, "The Relationships between Justice Perceptions, Trust, and Employee Attitudes in a Downsized Organization," *The Journal of Psychology*, v. 140 (2006): 477–498.

effective and safe treatments. These companies are not charitable organizations but for profit, and the creditors and shareholders have risked their cash on development, not society in general.

The decision made globally by this industry was to supply treatments at approximately 1/2% of the cost per dose charged to developed nations. In a formal treaty, pharmaceutical companies have contracted different costs to different consumers based on their ability to bear the cost. This principle can be applied within a corporation when justifying methods of cost allocation and cost assignment. In particular, for fixed costs it may be impossible to sustain innovation and research when the departments responsible are charged under absorption costing for services such as distribution and customer service. To thrive, these risky but competitively important activities must be cross-subsidized. This is a strategic decision and the employees affected by it will assess its fairness or appropriateness.

SUPPORT DEPARTMENT COST ALLOCATION

Apply cost-allocation procedures to period overhead cost allocation of support departments' cost pools ❷

The top management team at Computer Horizons Inc. (CHI) needs relevant information on product costs to make a strategic pricing decision. The purpose of cost allocation is an economic one. The company has decided to adopt target costing for the product to compete effectively.

This is a long-term decision; therefore, they require absorption costing (see Chapter 12). Absorption costing means all corporate costs must be recovered from the sales of CHI's products. Pricing is an economic decision. To simplify the example, we will assume this is the only reason why the top managers must decide upon the number of cost pools and their allocation bases. In Exhibit 14-3, the cost allocation for products is represented in the vertical boxes. Process costing is represented in the horizontal boxes.

In this example we will begin by examining how overhead period cost pools, in gold, are allocated to each of CHI's two divisions, Personal Computers and Peripherals. These two divisions provide support to all of CHI's other value-chain functions. CHI manufactures, sells, and services three types of personal computers. It is a global company, and costs incurred in different parts of an organization can be assigned and then reassigned when costing products, services, customers, or contracts. Its manufacturing plants are located in Canada, the United States, Mexico, Singapore, and the United Kingdom. It has marketing operations in more than 20 countries. Every month it consolidates accounting information from each of its operations to use in its planning and control decisions.

CHI has two manufacturing divisions. The Personal Computer Division manufactures its Plum, Plum Laptop, and Super Plum products. The Plum and Plum Laptop are assembled at its St. Louis, Birmingham, and Singapore plants. The Super Plum is assembled at its Vancouver plant. The Peripheral Equipment Division manufactures printers, cables, and other items used with its computer products. It has plants in St. Louis and Toronto. Exhibit 14-4 presents an overview of the costing system at CHI.

The divisional costing overview is only one part of a larger costing system. This larger costing system can be for a product, a plant, or even a whole company with multiple plants and divisions in many countries. A detailed costing overview of this companywide system would be sizably more complex than what has been illustrated. The exhibit illustrates the costing system for the Personal Computer Division.

EXHIBIT 14-3
Cost Allocation for Either Product or Process

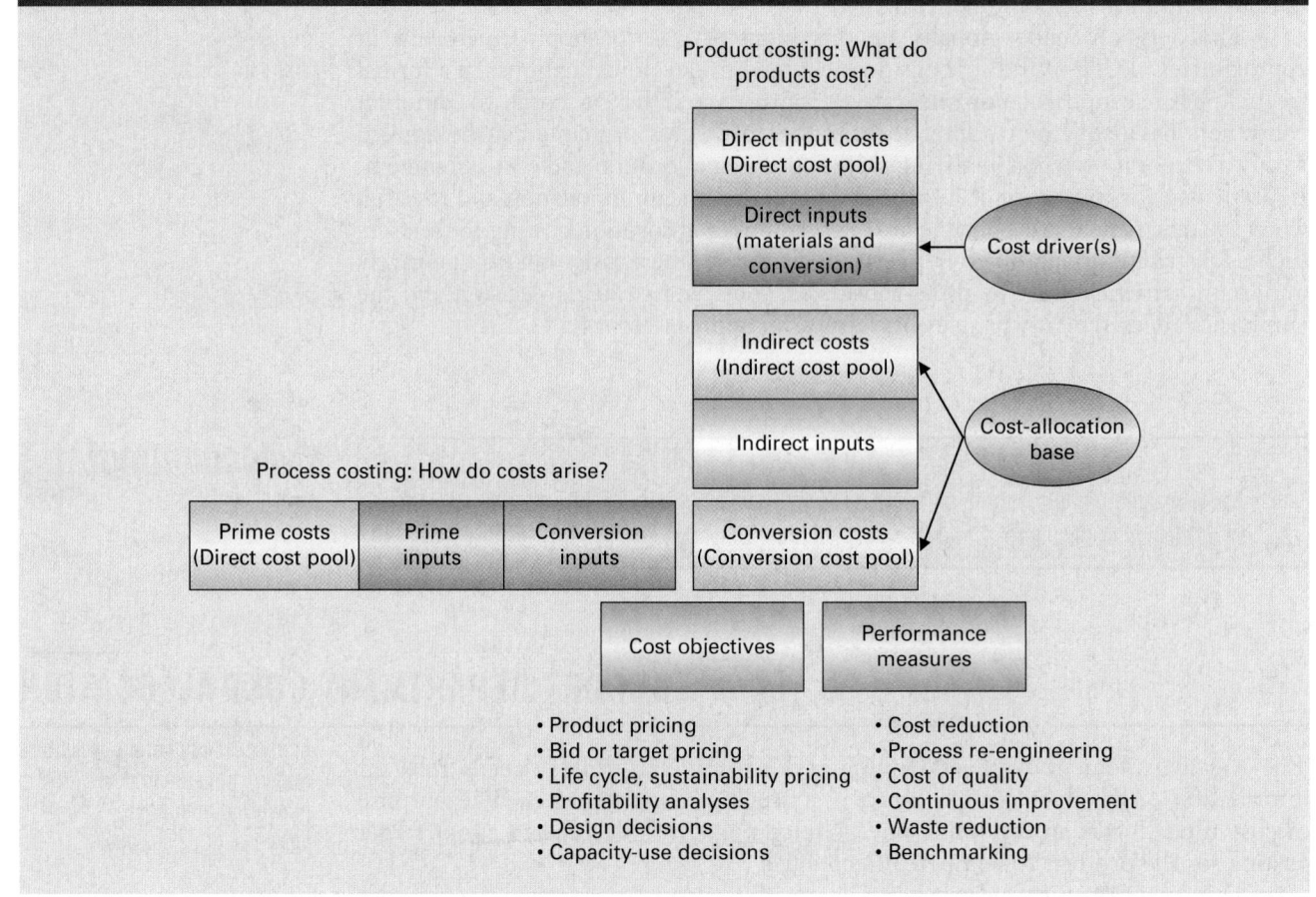

Notice in Exhibit 14-4 that the cost of purchasing the new assembly equipment is a corporate period overhead cost because the financing decision was made at the corporate level, not in the manufacturing plant. The capacity or acquisition cost, however, is a fixed manufacturing overhead cost. Similarly, the indirect salary and labour comprising Corporate Human Resource Costs (CHRM) and other Corporate Administration Costs (e.g. information technology, accounting, legal) are incurred at the corporate level for the benefit of the two operating divisions. The dashed lines indicate that these corporate costs are allocated to the two divisions. Allocations and cost-allocation bases for only one, the Personal Computer Division, are illustrated. Costs are colour-coded based on colours used in previous chapters.

The costing system for the Personal Computer Division portrayed in Exhibit 14-4 highlights two important points. First, it highlights how there are multiple cost objects in most costing systems. The three indirect period cost pools representing corporate overhead costs indicate ABC is used at CHI, otherwise only one cost pool or perhaps two would be indicated. The seven indirect cost pools within the Personal Computer Division confirm this. Secondly, including all corporate and divisional operating overhead costs as well as direct costs at the bottom of the exhibit indicates that this system is providing absorption costing information for the pricing decision. All period and inventoriable overhead has been allocated.

The corporate cost-allocation bases are very different from the division cost-allocation bases, as should be the case in ABC costing. Changes in each of these cost drivers should explain all but a small percentage of changes in the financial value of the cost pool. Indirect costs allocated to the products (Plum, Plum Laptop, and Super Plum) are partitioned into the red period overhead and the green inventoriable overhead costs.

EXHIBIT 14-4
Cost Tracing and Cost Allocation at the St. Louis Assembly Plant of Computer Horizons

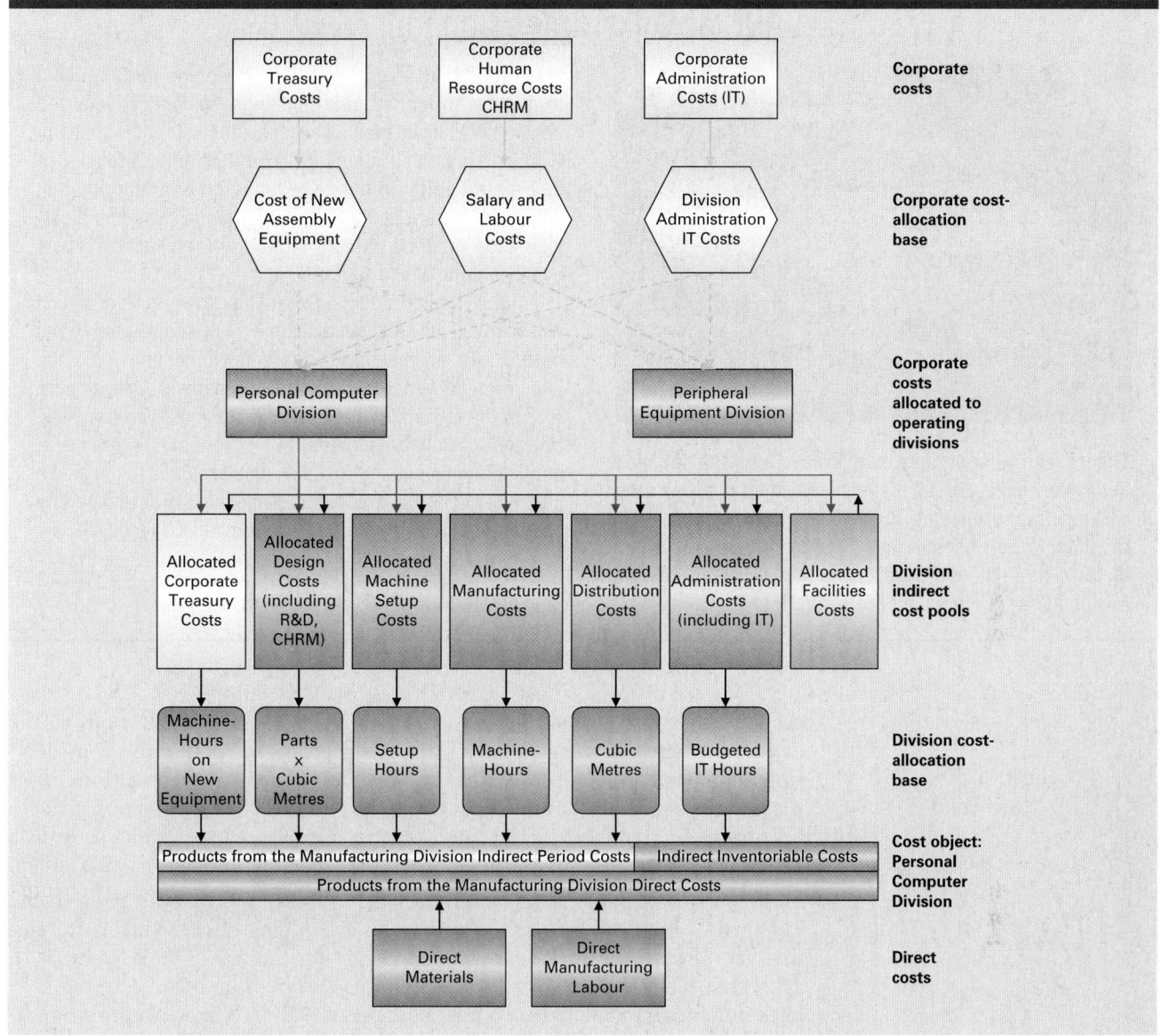

The allocation of indirect costs to each product is not illustrated but would look similar. All overhead now residing in each division would be allocated on some reasonable basis to each product. The indirect costs of products assembled at the manufacturing plants of CHI include (1) costs incurred at corporate headquarters and (2) costs incurred at the manufacturing plants. Exhibit 14-4 illustrates cost pools at both levels.

It is extremely important to remember that this cost-allocation process is valid for internal use in a pricing decision. According to the CICA standard, corporate costs cannot be allocated to units of product output for reporting purposes, nor is it permitted by CRA for tax purposes.

CHOICES RELATED TO INDIRECT COSTS

Computer Horizons has several key choices to make when accumulating and subsequently allocating the indirect costs to products of the Personal Computer Division:

◆ Which cost categories from corporate headquarters and the other divisions should be included in the indirect costs of the Personal Computer Division?

◆ Should all the corporate headquarters cost pools in Exhibit 14-4 be allocated, or should only a subset of them be allocated? For example, some companies

ABC at Volkswagen Canada

The reason accountants can assess costs a lot more accurately using ABC is that it allows them to break down overheads and allocate them to the right products. The revelations can be startling. Take an ABC pilot project undertaken in the die-cast engine parts area of the Volkswagen Canada Inc. plant in Barrie, Ontario. Volkswagen was ripe for ABC: it made about 25 engine parts ranging from mass-produced gear housings to highly specialized camshaft-bearing caps. The cost analysis indicated the whole die-cast operation was profitable only because 5 or 6 of all the parts produced a very high operating margin while the rest lost money. One reason was the cost-allocation method which spread all inspection costs evenly among all the parts.

The engine mounting brackets, every one of which was X-rayed for defects because a failure could be a safety hazard, are an example. Before implementing ABC, the labour-intensive gear housing that was never X-rayed bore 50% of the inspection costs. It was the mounting brackets, however, which consumed 80% of the machine resource, and after implementing ABC this was assigned to the single part. Now Volkswagen Canada samples 25 brackets per bin and only if one is rejected is the entire bin X-rayed.

Source: J. Southerst, "Suddenly, It All Makes Sense," *Canadian Business.* Reprinted by permission of Canadian Business Magazine.

---

exclude corporate public relations from any corporate cost allocations to the divisions; division managers have little say in corporate public relations decisions and would object to allocations as "taxation without representation." This is a fairness argument; however, all costs must be absorbed if the company is to be profitable. Judicious selection of a cost-allocation base could provide a persuasive justification based on ability to bear or even perhaps on cause-effect.

◆ How many cost pools should be used when allocating corporate costs to the Personal Computer Division? A cost pool is a grouping of individual cost items that vary due to the variations in what is causing the cost. One extreme is to aggregate all corporate costs into a single cost pool. The other extreme is to have numerous individual corporate cost pools (ABC). The concept of homogeneity (described in the following section) is important in making this decision.

◆ Which allocation base should be used for each of the corporate cost pools when allocating corporate costs to the Personal Computer Division? Examples include the following:

Cost Pools	Possible Cost Drivers
Corporate executive salaries	Sales, assets employed, operating margin
Treasury, financial management	Sales, assets employed, estimated duration of management activity
Legal department	Sales, assets employed, estimated duration of legal activity
Marketing department	Sales volume, sales personnel
Payroll department (CHRM)	Number of employees, financial value of payroll
CHRM	Number of employees, financial value of payroll, number of new hires

◆ Which allocation base should be used when allocating the indirect-cost pools at each manufacturing plant to the products assembled in those plants? Examples include number of parts assembled in each product, direct manufacturing labour-hours, machining-hours, and testing-hours.

These allocation bases for both corporate and plant indirect costs are illustrative only. Managers' choices of allocation bases depend on the purpose served by the cost allocation, the criteria used to guide the cost allocation, and the costs of implementing the different allocation bases.

A homogeneous cost pool is one in which all the activities whose costs are included in the pool have the same or a similar cause-and-effect relationship or benefits-received relationship between the cost allocator and the costs of the activity. Homogeneity is important because the assignment of costs will be more accurate. A consequence of using a homogeneous cost pool is that the cost allocations using that pool will be *identical* to allocations made if costs of each individual activity in that pool *were allocated separately*. The greater the degree of homogeneity, the fewer cost pools required to explain accurately the differences in how products use resources of the organization.

Assume that CHI wants to use the cause-and-effect criterion to guide cost-allocation decisions. The company should aggregate only those cost pools that have the same cause-and-effect relationship to the cost object. For example, if the number of employees in a division is the cause for incurring both corporate payroll department costs and CHRM costs, the payroll cost pool and the human resources cost pool could be aggregated before determining the combined payroll and human resources cost rate per unit of the allocation base. That is, the combined rate per unit of the allocation base is the same as the sum of the rates if the individual cost pools were allocated separately.

THINKING CRITICALLY

Why not stay with one or two ABC pools? Explain in a sentence or two. Read on for an analysis of this topic.

A variety of factors may prompt managers to consider recognizing multiple cost pools where a single cost pool is currently being used. One factor is the purpose of the cost allocation. Another is the views of line managers and personnel. These employees know what is happening in real time, and they communicate that differences exist in how costs are driven or how products use the facilities not currently being recognized using a single cost pool. It will improve relevance to listen to their advice, provided the cost of change is reasonable. Changes made in plant layout, general operations, and so on are undertaken on a continuous basis. Products do not use the facility in an equivalent way. Changes in product or services mix will change the way those products or services use the resources in the cost pool. Changes in information-gathering technology are increasing the opportunities to increase the number of cost pools at very little incremental cost.

A given cost item or amount may be included or excluded from a cost pool depending on the purpose at hand. Consider a consulting firm whose purpose is to price jobs for (1) a commercial client and (2) a government client. When pricing for a commercial client, the consulting firm may include the cost of beer and wine at meals that have a clear business-related rationale. In contrast, when billing the government under a contract, the contract may state that no cost amount for any alcoholic beverage is permitted to enter the cost pools from which costs are allocated to the government.

ASSESS YOUR MASTERY

To check your understanding of the material in Learning Objective ❷, go to the *Mastery Questions* section at the end of this chapter and complete Learning Objective ❷ questions 1 and 2.

3 Analyze and select appropriate cost-allocation procedures to assign support costs to operating departments

In many cases, the costs of a department will include costs allocated from other departments. Three key issues that arise when allocating costs from one department to another are (1) whether to use a single-rate method or a dual-rate method, (2) whether to use budgeted rates or actual rates, and (3) whether to use budgeted quantities or actual quantities. In the following example, nonproduction facilities sustaining costs (see Chapter 5) incurred at corporate headquarters are being allocated to the two production departments of the organization.

OPERATING DEPARTMENTS AND SUPPORT DEPARTMENTS

Many organizations distinguish between operating or core departments and support departments. An **operating** or **core department** (also called a **production department** in manufacturing companies) adds value to a product or service that is observable by a customer. A **support department** (also called a **service department**) provides the services that maintain other internal departments (operating departments and other support departments) in the organization. These are *facilities sustaining costs*. Support departments at CHI include the Treasury Department and the CHRM at corporate headquarters.

SINGLE-RATE AND DUAL-RATE METHODS

A **single-rate cost-allocation method** pools all costs in one cost pool and allocates them to cost objects using the same rate per unit of the single allocation base. There is no distinction between costs in the cost pool in terms of cost variability (such as fixed costs versus variable costs). A **dual-rate cost-allocation method** first classifies costs in the cost pool into two pools (typically into a variable-cost pool and a fixed-cost pool). Each pool has a different allocation rate or base.

Consider the Information Technology Department (IT) at the corporate headquarters of CHI. For simplicity, assume that the only users of this facility are the Personal Computer Division and the Peripheral Equipment Division. The following data apply to the coming budget year:

Fixed costs of operating the facility	$300,000 per year
Total capacity available	1,500 hours
Budgeted long-term usage (quantity) in hours	
Personal Computer Division	800 hours
Peripheral Equipment Division	400 hours
Total	1,200 hours
Budgeted variable costs per hour in the 1,000- to 1,500-hour relevant range	$ 200 per hour used

Based on budgeted usage as the quantity in the cost-allocation base and budgeted cost-allocation rates, under the single-rate method, the costs of the IT Department would be allocated as follows:

Total cost pool: $300,000 + (1,200 budgeted hours × $200)	$540,000 per year
Budgeted usage	1,200 hours
Budgeted total per hour rate: $540,000 ÷ 1,200 hours	$ 450 per hour used
Allocation rate for Personal Computer Division	$ 450 per hour used
Allocation rate for Peripheral Equipment Division	$ 450 per hour used

The rate of $450 per hour differs sizably from the $200 budgeted variable cost per hour. The $450 rate includes an allocated amount of $250 per hour ($300,000 ÷ 1,200 hours) for the fixed costs of operating the facility. These fixed costs will be incurred whether the computer runs its 1,500-hour capacity, its 1,200-hour budgeted usage, or even only 600 hours' usage.

Using the $450 per hour single-rate method (combined with the budgeted usage allocation base) transforms what is a fixed cost to the IT Department (and to CHI) into a variable cost to users of that facility. This presents a problem if internal users decide to purchase computer time outside the company. The downward demand spiral will arise (see Chapter 9). Consider an external vendor that charges less than $450 per hour but more than $200 per hour. A division of CHI that uses this vendor rather than the IT Department may decrease its own division costs, but the overall costs to CHI are increased. For example, suppose the Personal Computer Division uses an external vendor that charges $360 per hour when the IT Department has excess capacity. In the short run, CHI incurs an extra $160 per hour, because this external vendor is used ($360 external purchase price per hour minus the $200 internal variable costs per hour) instead of its own IT department.

When the dual-rate method is used, allocation bases for each of the fixed and variable cost pools must be chosen. Assume that the budgeted rates are used. The allocation quantities chosen are budgeted rates and usage for fixed costs and budgeted rates with actual usage for variable costs. The total budgeted usage of 1,200 hours comprises 800 hours for the Personal Computer Division and 400 hours for the Peripheral Equipment Division. The costs allocated to the Personal Computer Division would be as follows:

Fixed-cost function (800 hours ÷ 1,200 hours) × $300,000	$200,000 per year
Variable-cost function	$ 200 per hour used

The costs allocated to the Peripheral Equipment Division would be

Fixed-cost function (400 hours ÷ 1,200 hours) × $300,000	$100,000 per hour used
Variable-cost function	$ 200 per hour used

Assume now that during the coming year the Personal Computer Division actually uses 900 hours but the Peripheral Equipment Division uses only 300 hours. The costs allocated to these two divisions would be computed as follows:

Under the Single-Rate Method

Personal Computer Division	900 × $450 = $405,000
Peripheral Equipment Division	300 × $450 = $135,000

Under the Dual-Rate Method

Personal Computer Division	$200,000 + (900 × $200) = $380,000
Peripheral Equipment Division	$100,000 + (300 × $200) = $160,000

Should actual costs of the IT Department differ from the allocated costs, the company would account for over- or underallocated costs using methods described in Chapter 4. One obvious benefit of using the single-rate method is the low cost of implementation. It avoids the expensive analysis necessary to classify the individual cost items of a department into fixed and variable categories. The difficulty is that the single-rate method unitizes fixed costs and a careless manager could perceive this unitized rate as if it were a variable rate. The single-rate method may lead divisions to take actions that appear to be in their own best interests but are not in the best interests of the organization as a whole.

An important benefit of the dual-rate method is that it signals to division managers the different behaviour of variable costs and fixed costs. This important information guides division managers into making decisions that benefit the corporation as well as each division. For example, it would signal that using a third-party computer provider who charges more than $200 per hour results in CHI being worse off than if it had used its own IT department, which has a variable cost of $200 per hour.

BUDGETED VERSUS ACTUAL RATES

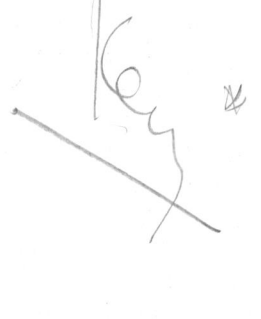

The decision on whether to use budgeted cost rates or actual cost rates affects the level of uncertainty user departments face. Budgeted rates let the user departments know in advance the cost rates they will be charged. Users are then better equipped to determine the amount of the service to request and—if the option exists— whether to use the internal department source or outsource to an external vendor. In contrast, when actual rates are used, the user department will not know the rates charged until the end of the period.

Budgeted rates also help motivate the manager of the support department (for example, the IT Department) to improve efficiency. During the budget period, the support department, not the user departments, bears the risk of any unfavourable cost variances. This asymmetric risk arises because user departments do not pay for any costs that exceed the budgeted rates. The manager of the support department, IT, would likely view the use of budgeted rates negatively, especially when unfavourable cost variances occur, because of price increases outside the department's control.

Some organizations recognize that it may not always be best to impose all the risks of variances from budgeted amounts completely on the support department (as when costs are allocated using budgeted rates) or completely on the user departments (as when costs are allocated using actual rates). One corporate response has been to identify uncontrollable factors and relieve the supplier-department manager of responsibility for these variances. Another response has been to have the two departments agree to share the risk (through an explicit formula) of a large, uncontrollable increase in the price of materials used by the support department.

BUDGETED VERSUS ACTUAL USAGE ALLOCATION BASES

The choice between actual usage and budgeted usage for allocating department fixed costs also can affect a manager's behaviour. Consider the budget of $300,000 fixed costs at the IT Department of CHI. Assume that actual and budgeted fixed costs are equal. Assume also that the actual usage by the Personal Computer Division is always equal to the budgeted usage. We now look at the effect on allocating the $300,000 in total fixed costs when actual usage by the Peripheral Equipment Division equals (case 1), is greater than (case 2), and is less than (case 3) the budgeted usage. Recall that the budgeted usage is 800 hours for the Personal Computer Division and 400 hours for the Peripheral Equipment Division. Exhibit 14-5 presents the allocation of total fixed costs of $300,000 to each division for these three cases.

In case 1, the fixed-cost allocation equals the expected amount. In case 2, the fixed-cost allocation is $40,000 less to the Personal Computer Division than expected ($160,000 vs. $200,000). In case 3, the fixed-cost allocation is $40,000 more

EXHIBIT 14-5
Effect of Variations in Actual Usage on Departmental Cost Allocations

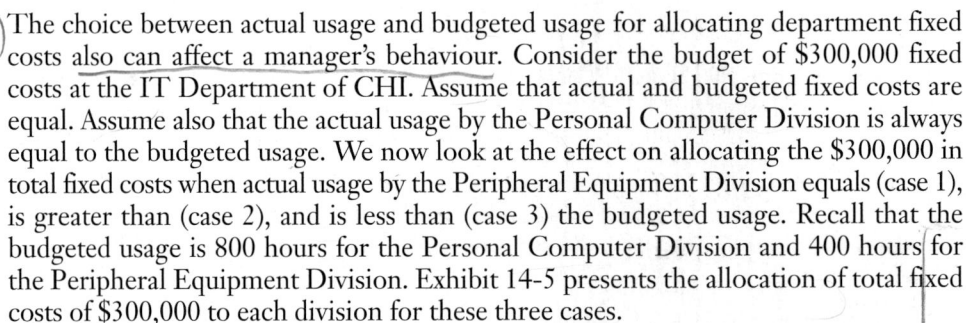

	Actual Usage		Budgeted Usage as Allocation Base		Actual Usage as Allocation Base	
Case	Personal Computer Division	Peripheral Equipment Division	Personal Computer Division	Peripheral Equipment Division	Personal Computer Division	Peripheral Equipment Division
1	800 hours	400 hours	$200,000*	$100,000†	$200,000*	$100,000†
2	800 hours	700 hours	$200,000*	$100,000†	$160,000‡	$140,000
3	800 hours	200 hours	$200,000*	$100,000†	$240,000§	$ 60,000#

$$ {}^{*}\ \frac{800}{(800 + 400)} \times \$300{,}000 \qquad {}^{\dagger}\ \frac{400}{(800 + 400)} \times \$300{,}000 \qquad {}^{\ddagger}\ \frac{800}{(800 + 700)} \times \$300{,}000 $$

$$ {}^{\S}\ \frac{800}{(800 + 200)} \times \$300{,}000 \qquad \frac{700}{(800 + 700)} \times \$300{,}000 \qquad {}^{\#}\ \frac{200}{(800 + 200)} \times \$300{,}000 $$

Wrong Choice! Bad Judgment!

Cost allocations require good professional judgment when deciding on a single- or dual-rate method and appropriate allocation bases. Period cost allocations to operating divisions will differ according to the method used. Division managers may try to convince management accountants to recommend a cost-allocation method that is most favourable to their division. As an accountant, professional judgment will support a confident and legitimate justification of why a method was chosen and the limitations of the use of information based on the purpose for the allocation. At Boeing in October 2002, Darleen Druyun, a senior U.S. Air Force acquisition officer, negotiated a multi-million-dollar NATO aircraft order that Boeing won. She had also been working on a multi-billion-dollar contract to lease and buy Boeing aircraft that would serve as refuelling planes. In November 2002, as Ms. Druyun prepared for retirement from the Air Force, she removed herself from discussions involving Boeing, and in

January 2003 she joined Boeing as an executive in its defence business operations.

In December 2003, *The Wall Street Journal* reported, "Actions related to Ms. Druyun's hiring in January 2003 are now the subject of Pentagon and Justice Department probes as well as Congressional scrutiny into the nation's number one defense contractor. Boeing fired both Mr. Sears (Boeing's chief financial officer who had allegedly discussed employment opportunities at Boeing with Ms. Druyun while she still had authority over contracts in which Boeing had an interest) and Ms. Druyun for what it called 'unethical' conduct in late November [2002]. Their dealings were a major factor in the resignation a week later of the company's chairman and chief executive, Phil Condit."

Source: A. M. Squeo and J. L. Lunsford, "How Two Officials Got Caught by Pentagon's Revolving Door," *The Wall Street Journal*, December 18, 2003, p. A1.

than expected ($240,000 vs. $200,000). Consider case 3. Why is there an increase of $40,000 even though the Personal Computer Division's actual and budgeted usage are exactly equal? Because the fixed costs are spread over fewer hours of usage. Variations in usage in another division will affect the fixed costs allocated to the Personal Computer Division when fixed costs are allocated on the basis of actual usage. When actual usage is the allocation base, user divisions will not know how much cost is allocated to them until the end of the budget period.

When budgeted usage is the allocation base, user divisions will know their allocated costs in advance. This information helps the user divisions with both short-run and long-run planning. The main justification given for the use of budgeted usage to allocate fixed costs relates to long-run planning. Organizations commit to infrastructure costs (such as the fixed costs of a support department) on the basis of a long-run planning horizon. Organizations commit to infrastructure costs (such as the fixed costs of a support department) on the basis of a long-run planning horizon; the use of budgeted usage to allocate these fixed costs is consistent with this long-run horizon usage. Alternatively, some organizations impose cost penalties for under-estimating long-run usage. For instance, a higher cost rate may be charged after a division exceeds its budgeted usage.

If fixed costs are allocated on the basis of estimated long-run use, some managers may be tempted to underestimate their planned usage. In this way, they will bear a lower fraction of the total costs (assuming all other managers do not similarly under-estimate). Some organizations offer rewards in the form of salary increases and promotions to managers who make accurate forecasts of long-run usage. Alternatively, some organizations impose cost penalties for underestimating long-run usage. For instance, a higher cost rate may be charged after a division exceeds its budgeted usage.

SUPPORT COSTS ALLOCATED TO OTHER SUPPORT AND OPERATING DEPARTMENTS

Analyze and select appropriate cost-allocation procedures to assign support costs to other support and operating departments

We now examine three methods of allocating the facilities sustaining costs of support departments: *direct*, *step-down*, and *reciprocal*. Support departments, which generate period overhead costs, create special accounting problems when they provide reciprocal support to each other as well as support to operating departments. An example of reciprocal support at CHI would be the Treasury Department providing services to CHRM (such as economic forecasts of labour demand) and the CHRM providing support to the Treasury Department (such as recruitment and training of corporate finance employees).

To obtain accurate product, service, and customer costs, CHI must include support department or period overhead costs as well as operating department costs. This section illustrates alternative ways to allocate period overhead costs. More accurate support department cost allocations result in more accurate product, service, and customer costs. In this section we will examine a new company, Castleford Engineering (CE).

Be aware that organizations differ in the departments located at the corporate and division levels; therefore, their facilities sustaining costs will differ. Some departments located at corporate headquarters of CHI (for example, R&D) are located at the division level in other organizations. Second, organizations differ in their definitions of *operating department* and *support department*. Always try to ascertain the precise meaning of these terms when analyzing data that include allocations of operating department costs and support department costs. Third, organizations differ in the percentage of total support costs allocated using the methods described in this section. Some companies allocate all support department costs using one of the methods outlined in this section. Other companies allocate only *indirect* support department costs using these methods, with all *direct* support costs traced to the appropriate operating department.

CE manufactures engines used in electric power generating plants. CE's current cost system includes two support departments and two operating departments in its manufacturing facility:

Support Departments	Operating Departments
Plant Maintenance	Machining
Information Systems	Assembly

Costs are accumulated in each department for planning and control purposes. For inventory costing, however, the support department costs of CE must be allocated to the operating departments. The data for our example are listed in Exhibit 14-6. Only the period costs contributing to the production of its units can be allocated to inventory and COGS, according to the *CICA Handbook*. For internal purposes, however, CE can assign the proportion of cost pools relevant to achieving the purpose for the cost allocation in the first place.

The percentages in this table can be illustrated by reference to the Plant Maintenance Department (PM). This support department provides a total of 8,000 hours of support work: 20% (1,600 ÷ 8,000) goes to the Information Systems (IS) support department; 30% (2,400 ÷ 8,000) to the Machining Department (M); and 50% (4,000 ÷ 8,000) to the Assembly Department (A). These costs happen to be inventoriable manufacturing overhead (MO/H) costs.

DIRECT ALLOCATION METHOD

The **direct allocation method** (often called the **direct method**) is the most widely used method of allocating support department costs. This method allocates each support department's costs directly to the operating departments. The pro forma

EXHIBIT 14-6
Data for Allocating Support Department Costs at Castleford Engineering for 2010

	A	B	C	D	E	F
1		SUPPORT		OPERATING		
2		DEPARTMENTS		DEPARTMENTS		
3		Plant	Information			
4		Maintenance	Systems	Machining	Assembly	Total
5	Budgeted manufacturing overhead costs before any interdepartment cost allocations	$600,000	$116,000	$400,000	$200,000	$1,316,000
6	Support work furnished:					
7	By Plant Maintenance					
8	Budgeted labour-hours	—	1,600	2,400	4,000	8,000
9	Percentage	—	20%	30%	50%	100%
10	By Information Systems					
11	Budgeted computer hours	200	—	1,600	200	1,800
12	Percentage	10%	—	80%	10%	100%

unallocated cost pools for both the support and operating departments as well as the budgeted nonfinancial data and the cost allocation expressed as a percentage are summarized in Exhibit 14-6. Exhibit 14-7 illustrates the direct allocation method using the data in Exhibit 14-6.

This method, although simple, ignores both the 1,600 hours of support time rendered by PM to IS and the 200 hours of support time rendered by IS to PM. The base used to allocate PM is the budgeted total maintenance labour-hours worked in the operating departments: 2,400 + 4,000 = 6,400 hours. This amount excludes the 1,600 hours of support time provided by PM to IS. For PM, 1,600 of the total of 8,000 hours is provided to IS. The unallocated period cost is $120,000 (1,600 hours ÷ 8,000 hours = 0.20 × $600,000 = $120,000). The denominator is understated and the cost-allocation rate will be overstated. Similarly, the base used for allocation of IS costs is 1,600 + 200 = 1,800 hours of computer time. The financial and non-financial information provided by IS to PM provides benefit equal to 10% of the IS budgeted cost, or $11,600 (200 hours ÷ 2,000 hours = 0.10 × $116,000 = $11,600). Again the denominator will be understated and the cost-allocation rate overstated leading inevitably to either a write-off or proration of overallocated MO/H to the operating departments, M and A. Of course for tax purposes this overallocated over-head must be prorated (see Chapter 4).

The issue is one of fairness. One support department is providing services to the other but there is no internal recognition of this transaction between the support departments. The operating departments M and A are bearing more overhead period cost burden than they should because the cost-allocation rate is higher than it should be and inventory values will be overstated. Whether this is an issue depends upon the purpose of the cost allocation. If the purpose is pricing it is irrelevant as long as all costs are included. If, however, the purpose is performance evaluation and minimizing the value of finished goods inventory is a performance measure, then the managers may consider this overstatement as relevant. The top management team may, during discussion, use either ability to bear, cause-effect, or cost-benefit justifications of this decision.

In Exhibit 14-7 the diagram illustrates how the costs are assigned from the support to the two operating departments using the direct method. Notice that there is no dual-directional arrow between PM and IS. The absence of this arrow reflects the failure of this method to account for the use of support department resources by the support departments themselves.

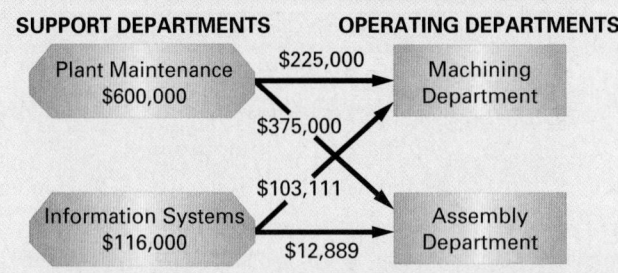

	SUPPORT DEPARTMENTS		OPERATING DEPARTMENTS		
A	B	C	D	E	F
	Plant Maintenance	Information Systems	Machining	Assembly	Total
Budgeted manufacturing overhead costs before any interdepartment cost allocations	$600,000	$116,000	$400,000	$200,000	$1,316,000
Allocation of Plant Maintenance (3/8, 5/8)[a]	(600,000)		225,000	375,000	
Allocation of Information Systems (8/9, 1/9)[b]		(116,000)	103,111	12,889	
Total budgeted manufacturing overhead of operating departments	$ 0	$ 0	$728,111	$587,889	$1,316,000

[a]Base is (2,400 + 4,000) or 6,400 hours; 2,400 ÷ 6,400 = 3/8; 4,000 ÷ 6,400 = 5/8. An equivalent approach is to calculate a budgeted rate for allocating Plant Maintenance Department costs, $600,000 ÷ 6,400 hours = $93.75 per hour. The Machining Department would then be allocated $225,000 ($93.75 per hour × 2,400 hours) and the Assembly Department $375,000 ($93.75 per hour × 4,000 hours)

[b]Base is (1,600 + 200), or 1,800 hours; 1,600 ÷ 1,800 = 8/9; 200 ÷ 1,800 = 1/9. An equivalent approach is to calculate a budgeted rate for allocating Information Systems Department Costs, $116,000 ÷ 1,800 hours = $64.444 per hour. The Machining Department would then be allocated $103,111 ($64.444 per hour × 1,600 hours) and the Assembly Department $12,889 ($64.444 per hour × 200 hours). For ease of exposition throughout this section, we will use the fraction of the support department services used by other departments to allocate support department costs to other departments rather than calculate budgeted rates to allocate costs.

STEP-DOWN ALLOCATION METHOD

The **step-down allocation method** (sometimes called the **step allocation method**, or **sequential allocation method**) allows for *partial* recognition of the services rendered by support departments to other support departments. This method requires the support departments to be sequenced (ranked) in the order in which the step-down allocation is to proceed. The costs in the first-ranked support department are allocated to the other support departments and to the operating departments.

The costs in the second-ranked department are allocated to those support departments not yet allocated and to the operating departments. This procedure is followed until the costs in the last-ranked support department have been allocated to the operating departments. Two ways to determine the sequence to allocate support department costs are as follows:

◆ **Approach A.** Rank support departments on the percentage of the support department's total support provided to other support departments. The support department with the highest percentage is allocated first. The support department with the lowest percentage is allocated last. In our CE example, the chosen order would be

	Percentage of Total Service Provided to Other Support Departments
1. Plant Maintenance	20%
2. Information Systems	10%

◆ **Approach B.** Rank support departments on the total dollars of service provided to other support departments. In our CE example, the chosen order would be

	Dollar Amount of Total Service Provided to Other Support Departments
1. Plant Maintenance (0.20 × $600,000)	$120,000
2. Information Systems (0.10 × $116,000)	$ 11,600

Exhibit 14-8 shows the step-down method where the PM costs of $600,000 are allocated first: $120,000 is allocated to IS (20% of $600,000); $180,000 to M (30% of $600,000); and $300,000 to A (50% of $600,000). The costs in IS now total $236,000 ($116,000 + $120,000 from the first-round allocation). This $236,000 amount is then allocated between the two operating departments—$209,778 (8/9 × $236,000) to M and $26,222 (1/9 × $236,000) to A. The improvement is illustrated in the diagram at the top of this exhibit. Notice that now there is an allocation of PM to IS as well as to M and A. This means the cost-allocation rate is more accurate, because for PM the denominator is no longer understated in the cost-allocation base. This is not true, however, for IS.

In the step-down method, once a support department's costs have been allocated, no subsequent support department costs are allocated or circulated back to it. Thus, once the PM costs are allocated, they receive no further allocation from other (lower-ranked) support departments.

EXHIBIT 14-8
Step-Down Method of Allocating Support Department Costs at Castleford Engineering for 2010

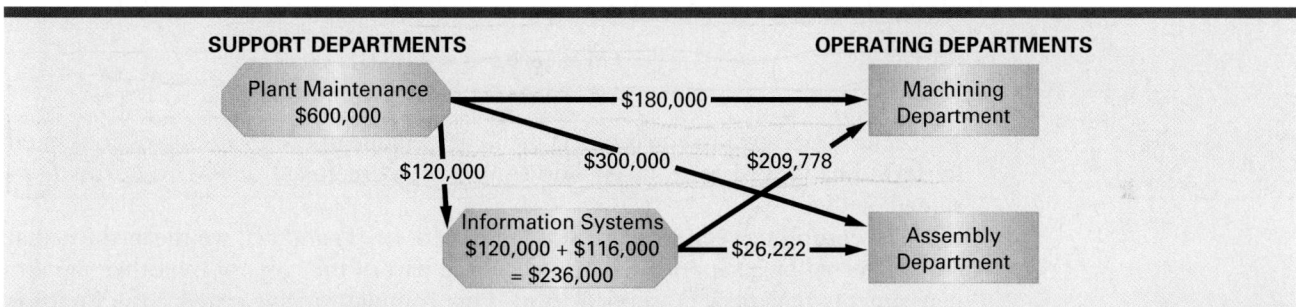

	A	B	C	D	E	F
1		**SUPPORT**		**OPERATING**		
2		**DEPARTMENTS**		**DEPARTMENTS**		
3		**Plant**	**Information**			
4		**Maintenance**	**Systems**	**Machining**	**Assembly**	**Total**
5	Budgeted manufacturing overhead costs before any interdepartment cost allocations	$600,000	$116,000	$400,000	$200,000	$1,316,000
6	Allocation of Plant Maintenance (2/10, 3/10, 5/10)ᵃ	(600,000)	120,000	180,000	300,000	
7			236,000			
8	Allocation of Information Systems (8/9, 1/9)ᵇ		(236,000)	209,778	26,222	
9	Total budgeted manufacturing overhead of operating departments	$ 0	$ 0	$789,778	$526,222	$1,316,000
10						
11	ᵃBase is (1,600 + 2,400 + 4,000), or 8,000 hours; 1,600 ÷ 8,000 = 2/10; 2,400 ÷ 8,000 = 3/10; 4,000 ÷ 8,000 = 5/10. Instead of using fractions, we could have calculated a budgeted rate for allocating plant maintenance costs to the other departments as described in Exhibit 14-7.					
12	ᵇBase is (1,600 + 200), or 1,800 hours; 1,600 ÷ 1,800 = 8/9; 200 ÷ 1,800 = 1/9.					

RECIPROCAL ALLOCATION METHODS—LINEAR EQUATION, MATRIX ALGEBRA[3]

The **reciprocal allocation method** allocates costs by explicitly including the mutual services provided among all support departments. Theoretically, the direct method and the step-down method are less accurate when support departments provide services to one another reciprocally. For example, the PM maintains all the computer equipment in IS. Similarly, IS provides database support for PM.

The reciprocal allocation method enables us to incorporate interdepartmental relationships *fully* into the support department cost allocations. That is, PM is allocated to IS, and IS is allocated to PM. Each support department cost pool is allocated to the operating departments M and A as well. No simultaneous equations are needed at this stage of this method.

Implementing the reciprocal allocation method can be done using simultaneous linear equations or matrix algebra. The drawback of using the linear equation method is that it quickly becomes unwieldy beyond examples of two support departments and two operating departments. The matrix algebra method can readily be input in Excel and extended to as many support and operating departments as needed. Using matrix algebra it is only the reciprocal support department allocations that require this treatment and the goal is to obtain the *artificial costs* in a more efficient manner than using simultaneous equations. No matrix algebra is required to calculate the allocations of support department costs to the two operating departments.

LINEAR EQUATION METHOD

The simultaneous linear equation method requires three steps.[4]

♦ **Step 1:** *Express support department costs and reciprocal relationships in linear equation form.* Let PM be the complete reciprocated costs of PM and IS be the complete reciprocated costs of IS. We then express the data in Exhibit 14-6 (p. 711) as follows:

$$PM = \$600,000 + 0.1IS \ (1)$$
$$IS = \$116,000 + 0.2PM \ (2)$$

The 0.1IS term in equation (1) is the percentage of the IS resources consumed by PM. The 0.2PM term in equation (2) is the percentage of PM resources consumed by IS.

By **complete reciprocated cost** in equations (1) and (2), we mean the actual costs incurred by a support department plus a part of the costs of the other support departments that provide service to it. This complete reciprocated costs figure is sometimes called the **artificial costs** of the support department; it is always larger than the actual costs.

♦ **Step 2:** *Solve the system of simultaneous equations to obtain the complete reciprocated costs of each support department.* Where there are two support departments, the following substitution approach can be used. Substituting equation (2) into equation (1):

$$PM = \$600,000 + [0.1(\$116,000 + 0.2PM)]$$
$$PM = \$600,000 + \$11,600 + 0.02PM$$
$$0.98PM = \$611,600$$
$$PM = \$624,082$$

Substituting into equation 2:

$$IS = \$116,000 + 0.2(\$624,082) = \$240,816$$

---

[3]David Gowing (P. Eng., MSc Finance) developed the matrix algebra functions and examples. D. Franz, "Using Matrix Algebra Functions in Spreadsheet Modifications," AAA Western Regional Conference, May 2, 2008 and online at http://papers.ssrn.com/sol3/papers.cfm?abstract_id=1001542.

[4]The reciprocal allocation method requires iteration. Iteration is a mathematical approach to solving a problem that requires an estimate of the answer to begin solving a system of linear equations. By repeatedly substituting improved estimates, the error term in the equations converges to zero, or the best answer. Undertaking reciprocal allocation in Excel, the iteration is automatic.

Where more than two support departments have reciprocal relationships, computer programs can be used to calculate the complete reciprocated costs of each support department.

◆ **Step 3:** *Allocate the complete reciprocated costs of each support department to all other departments (both support and operating departments) on the basis of the usage proportions (based on total units of service provided to all departments).* Consider the Information Systems Department, which has a complete reciprocated cost of $240,816. This amount would be allocated as follows:

To Plant Maintenance ($1/_{10} \times$ $240,816)	=	$ 24,082
To Machining ($8/_{10} \times$ $240,816), rounded	=	192,652
To Assembly ($1/_{10} \times$ $240,816)	=	24,082
Total		$240,816

Exhibit 14-9 presents summary data pertaining to the reciprocal method.

One source of confusion to some managers using the reciprocal cost-allocation method is why the complete reciprocated costs of the support departments of $864,898 ($624,082 and $240,816 in Exhibit 14-9) exceed their budgeted amount of $716,000 ($600,000 and $116,000 in Exhibit 14-6). The excess of $148,898 ($24,082

EXHIBIT 14-9
Reciprocal Method of Allocating Support Department Costs Using Linear Equations at Castleford Engineering for 2010

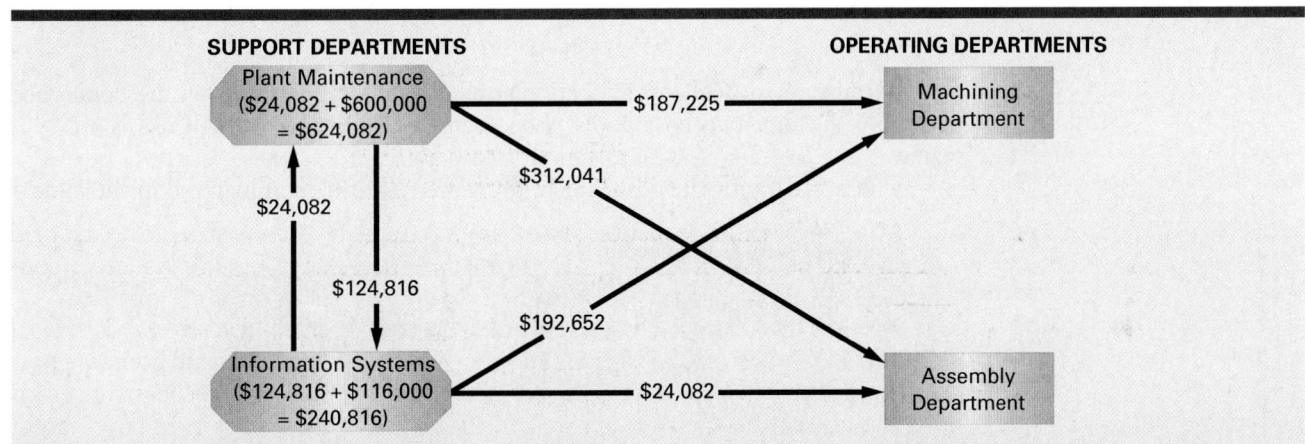

	A	B	C	D	E	F
1		**SUPPORT**		**OPERATING**		
2		**DEPARTMENTS**		**DEPARTMENTS**		
3		**Plant**	**Information**			
4		**Maintenance**	**Systems**	**Machining**	**Assembly**	**Total**
5	Budgeted manufacturing overhead costs before any interdepartment cost allocations	$600,000	$116,000	$400,000	$200,000	$1,316,000
6	Allocation of Plant Maintenance (2/10, 3/10, 5/10)[a]	(624,082)	124,816	187,225	312,041	
7	Allocation of Information Systems (1/10, 8/10, 1/10)[b]	24,082	(240,816)	192,652	24,082	
8	Total budgeted manufacturing overhead of operating departments	$ 0	$ 0	$779,877	$536,123	$1,316,000
9						
10	[a]Base is (1,600 + 2,400 + 4,000), or 8,000 hours; 1,600 ÷ 8,000 = 2/10; 2,400 ÷ 8,000 = 3/10; 4,000 ÷ 8,000 = 5/10					
11	[b]Base is (200 + 1,600 + 200), or 2,000 hours; 200 ÷ 2,000 = 1/10, 1,600 ÷ 2,000 = 8/10; 200 ÷ 2,000 = 1/10.					

for PM and $124,816 for IS) is the total of costs that are allocated among support departments. The total costs allocated to the operating departments under the reciprocal allocation method remain only $716,000.

MATRIX ALGEBRA METHOD

A **matrix** is a way of succinctly communicating relevant information in rows and columns. You have created a matrix each time you have entered data into an Excel spreadsheet. Excel provides a matrix algebra function as readily usable as its linear regression function. Once the raw data are entered, a simple click of the mouse will produce the results as the Excel program completes all the calculations necessary. This method enables management accountants to almost instantaneously provide the reciprocal cost allocations for complex systems such as the one illustrated in Exhibit 14-4.

There is a bit of terminology to learn. The multiplier is referred to as the **vector** of constants. A vector is a matrix with one or more rows and one single column. There are four departments. Therefore the matrix for this example of departmental costs is referred to as a 4×1 matrix, or, alternatively, a vector. This particular vector comprises a single column of costs. For simplicity, the cost pools are expressed in thousands of dollars. The vector of constants appears in Excel as:

	Cost Pool
PM	$600
IS	116
M	400
A	200

Because reciprocal cost allocation applies only to PM and IS we are concerned with only the first two cost pools. The vector of constants we will use is a 2×1 matrix.

The raw data for the cost-allocation percentages are summarized in the table.

% Costs used by:

Supplied by:	PM	IS	M	A
PM	0	0.2	0.3	0.5
IS	0.1	0	0.8	0.1
M	0	0	1	0
A	0	0	0	1

The matrix above is referred to as a 4×4 matrix; however, we want to focus on only the first two rows and the first two columns of this matrix, a 2×2 matrix, because that is where the data regarding support departments have been entered. We also use only the support department cost pools, which is a 2×1 matrix or a vector.

This is important because it determines the order in which the two matrices are multiplied. The 2×2 matrix must be multiplied by the 2×1 vector and the notation is $(2 \times 2) \cdot (2 \times 1)$. Notice the $\times$ multiplication sign is replaced by $\cdot$ and that the last number in the first set of parentheses is identical to the first number in the last set of parentheses—both are 2s indicating that matrix multiplication can occur. The final set of artificial costs will be a matrix of 2×1 as indicated by the first number in the first set of parentheses and the last number in the second set. This is important because it tells you how to highlight the cells in Excel to successfully multiply the matrices. This implies, for example, that you can multiply a (3×2) matrix by a (2×1) matrix and the solution matrix will be (3×1).

The first step in this matrix multiplication is to input the **coefficient matrix**. The coefficient matrix summarizes the coefficients or cost-allocation percentages to solve the equations to calculate the complete reciprocated costs. In this example it is a 2×2 matrix where the entries are the coefficients of the equations (1) and (2) for each of the support department costs allocated reciprocally to one another.

Consumption of Support

Supplier of Support Service	PM	IS	Cost Pool	
PM	0	0.2	$600	PM = $600 + (0 × PM) + (0.1 × IS) (1)
IS	0.1	0	$116	IS = $116 + (0.2 × PM) + (0 × IS) (2)

Artificial Costs > Cost Pool

Transpose the allocated costs for PM in 1:	1.0 × PM − 0.1 × IS = $600
Transpose the allocated costs for IS in 2:	−0.2 × PM + 1.0 × IS = $116

Therefore the coefficient matrix and vector of constants must be:

	Coefficient Matrix		**Vector of Constants**
	PM	IS	Cost Pools
PM	1	−0.1	$600
IS	−0.2	1	$116

The equations shown in the first two lines of the Excel table are a restatement of equations 1 and 2 which you have already produced. You must manually input the coefficient matrix based on the information in the two transposed equations. The first matrix algebra function to calculate the artificial costs is to create the inverse of the coefficient matrix, which is also a 2×2 matrix.[5]

Do this by highlighting a set of destination cells first: 2 columns and 2 rows:. Place the cursor in the f_x dialog box at the top of the spreadsheet and type: "= minverse(" (without quotations). At this point the program will ask you what the source matrix is. You simply move the cursor to the coefficient matrix and highlight the four numerical entries. Press Ctrl + Shift + Enter; hold them down simultaneously then release them simultaneously. The inverse matrix will appear with the values shown:

Inverse of Coefficient Matrix

	PM	IS
PM	1.020408163	0.1020408
IS	0.204081633	1.0204082

This matrix will be now multiplied by the vector of constants, the original two cost pools for PM and IS. Do this by first highlighting the two numerical values in the vector of constants and then placing the cursor in the f_x dialog box. Type in: "=mmult(" (without quotations). At this point the program will ask for two pieces of information. The first is what you're going to multiply, which is the inverse matrix. Highlight the four numerical quantities in the inverse matrix and type a comma, then highlight the destination cells. There are only two artificial costs related to the vector of constants which comprise the two support cost pools. Highlight two cells and close the parentheses. To complete the matrix multiplication press Ctrl + Shift + Enter and hold simultaneously, then release all three simultaneously. The solution, the artificial costs, will appear in the destination cells as shown:

Artificial Cost Pools

PM	$624.082
IS	240.816
	$864.898

[5]It is not necessary for you to know what the inverse matrix is or how to calculate it manually, although this can be done readily. For those who are interested, an excellent text on matrix algebra is *Modern Matrix Algebra* by David R. Hill and Bernard Kolman.

As with the linear equation method, no more is required than the artificial cost pools be allocated to the operating departments.

	Operating Departments		
Supplier	**M**	**A**	**Artificial Costs > Cost Pool**
PM	0.3	0.5	$642.082 PM = (0.3 × PM) + (0.8 × IS) + $400
IS	0.8	0.1	$240.816 IS = (0.5 × PM) + (0.1 × IS) + $200

In this situation, the PM and IS costs are the artificial costs.

	Artificial Costs > Cost Pool
Transpose the allocated costs for PM:	−0.3 × PM − 0.8 × IS = $400
Transpose the allocated costs for IS:	−0.5 × PM − 0.1 × IS = $200

Therefore the final cost allocations must be:

Artificial Cost Pools		**Original Cost Pools**	
M	$ 779.878	PM	$ 600
A	536.122	IS	116
	$1,316.000	M	400
		A	200
		Total	$1,316

Notice that of course the costs allocated to the operating departments using the artificial cost pools sum to the original cost pool total. The allocation dollar values are identical to those calculated using the linear equation method. The benefit of knowing how to use the matrix algebra function for reciprocal allocation of support department costs is that far more complex cost allocations can be readily done.

OVERVIEW OF METHODS

Assume that the total budgeted overhead costs of each operating department in the example in Exhibits 14-7 to 14-9 are allocated to individual products on the basis of budgeted machine-hours for operating department M (4,000 hours) and budgeted direct labour-hours for operating department A (3,000 hours). The budgeted overhead allocation rates associated with each support department allocation method (rounded to the nearest dollar) are:

Support Department Cost-Allocation Method	Total Budgeted Costs after Support Overhead Allocation of All Department Costs		Budgeted Overhead Rate per Hour for Product Costing Purposes	
	Machining	**Assembly**	**Machining 4,000 Machine-Hours**	**Assembly 3,000 Labour-Hours**
Direct	$728,111	$587,889	$182	$196
Step-down	789,778	526,222	197	175
Reciprocal	779,877	536,123	195	179

These differences in budgeted overhead rates with alternative support department cost-allocation methods can be important to managers. For example, consider a cost reimbursement contract that uses 100 machine-hours and 15 assembly labour-hours. The support department costs allocated to this contract would be

Direct	$21,140	$182 × 100 + $196 × 15
Step-down	22,325	$197 × 100 + $175 × 15
Reciprocal	22,185	$195 × 100 + $179 × 15

Use of the step-down method would result in the highest cost reimbursement to the contractor. To avoid disputes in cost-reimbursement contracts, managers should always clarify the method that will be used for allocation.

The reciprocal method, while conceptually preferable, is not widely used. The advantage of the direct and step-down methods is that they are relatively simple to compute and understand (see Real Companies, below). However, with the ready availability of computer software to solve sets of simultaneous equations, the extra costs of using the reciprocal method will, in most cases, be minimal. Another advantage is that this method highlights the complete reciprocated costs of support departments and makes clear how these costs differ from either the budgeted or actual costs of the departments. This improved information leads to more informed decisions about what services of a support department to outsource.

For example, assume all of CE's support department costs are variable over the period of a potential outsourcing contract. The third party bids to provide all the Information Systems (IS) services currently provided internally to CE. The bid price must be compared to the complete reciprocated costs for this service of $240,816, not the reported departmental cost of $116,000, because the complete reciprocated costs include the services PM provides to deliver 2,000 hours of computer time to all other departments at CE.

The hourly rate for the complete reciprocated costs is $120.41 ($240,816 ÷ 2,000 hours). To be competitive, the third party must bid less than either the hourly rate of $120.41 or the total reciprocated cost of $240,816 to improve the company's operating income. In this case the relevant costs of shutting down IS are $116,000 plus $124,816 of PM costs because these will no longer be incurred to support IS, making the total relevant cost savings $240,816. Neither the direct nor step-down methods will provide this relevant information for outsourcing decisions.[6]

The more likely roadblocks to the reciprocal method being widely adopted are (1) many managers find it difficult to understand and (2) the numbers obtained by using the reciprocal method differ little, in some cases, from those obtained by using the direct or step-down method. The mechanical process of creating and solving simultaneous equations was a barrier, but that barrier is now removed by the very

REAL COMPANIES

Allocation of Support Department Costs

Support Department Cost-Allocation Method	Australia	Japan	United Kingdom	Poland
1. Direct method	43%	58%	64%	19%
2. Step-down method	3%	27%	6%	39%
3. Reciprocal method	5%	10%	14%	33%
4. Other method	15%	1%	8%	6%
5. Not allocated	34%	4%	8%	3%

Use of the direct method of allocating support department costs is widespread in many nations, whereas the step-down and reciprocal methods are gaining popularity in others. Surveys of support department cost-allocation methods are available for Australia, Japan, the United Kingdom, and Poland.[a,b]

[a]P. Blaney, and I. Yokohama, *Comparative Analysis of Japanese and Australian Cost Accounting and Management Practices*, Working Paper, The University of Sydney, Australia, 1991.

[b]A. Szychta, "The Scope and Application of Management Accounting Methods in Polish Enterprises," *Management Accounting Research*, 2002.

[6]Technical issues when using the reciprocal method in outsourcing decisions are discussed in R. S. Kaplan and A. A. Atkinson, *Advanced Management Accounting*, 3rd ed. (Upper Saddle River, N.J.: Prentice Hall, 1998), pp. 73–81.

simple-to-use matrix function in Excel. With only a bit of technical input on matrix algebra, management accountants can readily input a coefficient matrix, provided they can create the linear equation of each of the cost functions. The vector of constants is simply the cost pools of each support and operating department.

MyAccountingLab

ASSESS YOUR MASTERY

To check your understanding of the material in Learning Objective ❹, go to the *Mastery Questions* section at the end of this chapter and complete Learning Objective ❹ question 1.

ALLOCATING COMMON COSTS

❺ Analyze cost-allocation procedures to assign common costs and justify contractual reimbursement

We next consider two methods used to allocate **common costs**. A common cost is a cost of operating a facility, operation, activity, or like cost object that is shared by two or more users. Consider Jason Stevens, a graduating student in Winnipeg who has been invited to an interview with an employer in Halifax. The round-trip Winnipeg–Halifax airfare is $1,200. A week before leaving, Stevens is also invited to an interview with an employer in Montreal. The round-trip Winnipeg–Montreal fare is $800. Stevens decides to combine the two recruiting stops into a Winnipeg–Montreal–Halifax trip that will cost $1,500 in airfare. The $1,500 is a common cost that benefits both employers. Two methods for allocating this common cost between the two potential employers are now discussed: the stand-alone method and the incremental method.

STAND-ALONE COST-ALLOCATION METHOD

The **stand-alone cost-allocation method** uses information pertaining to each cost object as a separate operating entity to determine the cost-allocation weights. For the airfare common cost of $1,500, information about the separate (stand-alone) return airfares ($1,200 and $800) is used to determine the allocation weights:

$$\text{Halifax employer:} \quad \frac{\$1,200}{\$1,200 + \$800} \times \$1,500 = 0.60 \times \$1,500 = \$900$$

$$\text{Montreal employer:} \quad \frac{\$800}{\$800 + \$1,200} \times \$1,500 = 0.40 \times \$1,500 = \$600$$

Advocates of this method often emphasize an equity or fairness rationale. That is, fairness occurs because each employer bears a proportionate share of total costs in relation to its individual stand-alone costs.

INCREMENTAL COST-ALLOCATION METHOD

The **incremental cost-allocation method** ranks the individual cost objects and then uses this ranking to allocate costs among those cost objects. The first-ranked cost object is termed the *primary party* and is allocated costs up to its cost as a stand-alone entity. The second-ranked cost object is termed the *incremental party* and is allocated the additional cost that arises from there being two users instead of only the primary user. If there are more than two parties, the nonprimary parties will need to be ranked.

Consider Jason Stevens and his $1,500 airfare cost. Assume that the Halifax employer is viewed as the primary party. Stevens's rationale was that he had already committed to go to Halifax. The cost allocations would then be:

Party	Cost Allocated	Costs Remaining to Be Allocated to Other Parties
Halifax (primary)	$1,200	$300 = $1,500 − $1,200
Montreal (incremental)	300	0

The Halifax employer is allocated the full Winnipeg–Halifax airfare. The nonallocated part of the total airfare is allocated to the Montreal employer. Had the Montreal employer been chosen as the primary party, the cost allocations would have been Montreal, $800 (the stand-alone Winnipeg–Montreal return airfare), and Halifax, $700 ($1,500 − $800). Where there are more than two parties, this method requires them to be ranked and the common costs allocated to those parties in the ranked sequence.

Under the incremental method, the primary party typically receives the highest allocation of the common costs. Not surprisingly, most users in common cost situations propose themselves as the incremental party. In some cases, the incremental party is a newly formed "organization" such as a new product line or a new sales territory. Chances for its short-term survival may be enhanced if it bears a relatively low allocation of common costs.

A caution is appropriate here as regards Stevens's cost-allocation options. His chosen method must be acceptable to each prospective employer. Indeed, some prospective employers may have guidelines that recruiting candidates must follow. For example, the Montreal employer may have a policy that the maximum reimbursable airfare is a seven-day advance booking price in economy class. If this amount is less than the amount that Stevens would receive under (say) the stand-alone method, then the employer's upper-limit guideline would govern how much could be allocated to that interviewer. Stevens should obtain approval before he purchases his ticket as to what cost-allocation method(s) each potential employer views as acceptable.

Disputes over how to allocate common costs are often encountered. The final section of this chapter discusses the role of cost data in contracting. This is also an area where disputes about cost allocation frequently arise.

THE PURPOSE IS TO JUSTIFY REIMBURSEMENT COSTS

Many commercial contracts include clauses that require the use of cost accounting information. Examples include

1. A contract between the Department of National Defence and a company designing and assembling a new fighter plane. The price paid for the plane is based on the contractor's costs plus a preset fixed fee.

2. A research contract between a university and a government agency. The university is reimbursed its direct costs plus an overhead rate that is a percentage of direct costs.

3. A contract between an energy-consulting firm and a hospital. The consulting firm receives a fixed fee plus a share of the energy-cost savings arising from the consulting firm's recommendations.

Contract disputes arise with some regularity, often with respect to cost allocation. The areas of dispute between the contracting parties can be reduced by making the "rules of the game" explicit and in writing at the time the contract is signed. Such rules of the game include the definition of cost items allowed, the permissible cost-allocation bases, and how differences between budgeted and actual costs are to be handled.

CONTRACTING

There are two main approaches to reimbursing costs as determined by a contract.

1. The *contractor is paid a set price without analysis of actual contract cost data*. This approach is used, for example, where there is competitive bidding, where there is adequate price competition, or where there is an established catalogue with prices quoted for items sold in substantial quantities to the general public.

2. The *contractor is paid after analysis of actual contract cost data*. In some cases, the contract will explicitly state that reimbursement is based on actual allowable costs plus a set fee. This arrangement is a cost-plus contract.

FAIRNESS OF PRICING

When uncertainty is high, as in many defence contracts involving new weapons and equipment, contracts are rarely subject to competitive bidding. Why? Because no contractor is willing to assume all the risk. Hence, market-based fixed-price setting fails to attract a contractor, or the resulting price is too outrageously high for the government. So the government assumes a major share of the risks. It negotiates contracts by using costs as a substitute for selling prices as ordinarily set by suppliers in open markets. In this contracting arena, a cost allocation may be difficult to defend on the basis of any cause-and-effect reasoning. Nonetheless, the contracting parties may still view it as a "reasonable" or "fair" means to help establish a selling price. Some costs become "allowable," but others are "unallowable." An **allowable cost** is a cost that the contract parties agree to include in the costs to be reimbursed. Some contracts specify how allowable costs are to be determined. For example, only economy-class airfares may be allowable in a contract. Other contracts identify cost categories that are nonallowable. For example, the costs of lobbying activities and the costs of alcoholic beverages are not allowable costs on some contracts.

MyAccountingLab

ASSESS YOUR MASTERY

To check your understanding of the material in Learning Objective ⑤, go to the *Mastery Questions* section at the end of this chapter and complete Learning Objective ⑤ question 1.

PULLING IT ALL TOGETHER—PROBLEM FOR SELF-STUDY

This problem illustrates how the costs of two corporate support departments are allocated to operating divisions.

Computer Horizons budgets the following amounts for its two central corporate support departments (Legal and Human Resources) in supporting each other and the two manufacturing divisions, the Laptop Division (LTD) and the Work Station Division (WSD):

	A	B	C	D	E	F
		SUPPORT		OPERATING		
1		Legal	Human Resources			
2		Department	Department	LTD	WSD	Total
3						
4	**BUDGETED USAGE**					
5	Legal (hours)	—	250	1,500	750	2,500
6	(Percentages)	—	10%	60%	30%	100%
7	Human Resources (hours)	2,500	—	22,500	25,000	50,000
8	(Percentages)	5%	—	45%	50%	100%
9						
10	**ACTUAL USAGE**					
11	Legal (hours)	—	400	400	1,200	2,000
12	(Percentages)	—	20%	20%	60%	100%
13	Human Resources (hours)	2,000	—	26,600	11,400	40,000
14	(Percentages)	5%	—	66.5%	28.5%	100%
15	Budgeted fixed overhead costs before any interdepartment cost allocations	$360,000	$475,000	—	—	$835,000
16	Actual variable overhead costs before any interdepartment cost allocations	$200,000	$600,000	—	—	$800,000

The company needs to improve the accuracy of its cost allocations to improve the competitiveness of its prices.

REQUIRED

1. What are the other possible reasons why a company would undertake improved cost allocation?

2. What are the possible cost drivers of the Legal Department?

3. Why might Computer Horizons choose budgeted rather than actual cost-allocation rates for this project?

4. What amount of support department costs for Legal and Human Resources will be allocated to LTD and WSD using (a) the direct method, (b) the step-down method (allocating the Legal Department costs first), and (c) the reciprocal method using linear equations?

5. If Computer Horizons were justifying reimbursement from a contract, how would this project improve its position?

SOLUTION

1. One objective may be to motivate employees through challenging performance targets accompanied by substantial compensation if they are achieved. The effectiveness of using period cost allocation to accomplish this depends on what is perceived as fair by those affected. Generally speaking, if people

   ◆ believe the decision makers and the decision process is undertaken in good faith,
   ◆ are given the opportunity to participate in distributive decision making,
   ◆ have access to relevant information about the consequences, and
   ◆ are treated with respect and sensitivity when they are not beneficiaries, but bear burdens,

   then they will accept that the distribution was fair although it was burdensome for them but not others.

   A second reason is legal, to verify and justify that particular period cost is allowable per specific contract terms. The methods of cost allocation in this chapter can be used to justify beyond reasonable doubt a cost is allowable. Nevertheless, the same principles of fairness apply and the preferable approach is that the parties of the contract negotiate the allocation method and the specifics of its implementation.

   A third reason is to measure income and assets. An additional burden is imposed, however, that the allocation method chosen be justifiable within GAAP if the values of income and assets are publicized. Different methods will impose different costs on different departments and this in turn will be reported in segmented statements of income.

2. Cost drivers should be chosen on the basis of their capacity to explain a reasonable proportion of total change in the cost pool (see Chapter 13). Choices include sales, assets employed, estimated duration of legal activity. Notice that these choices include an output measure of activity (sales), a capacity input measure (assets employed), and a measure of time (duration of legal activity).

3. The choice of rates can affect managers' behaviour. When budgeted rates are used, the consumers of support resources will know in advance what the pro forma costs will be and this improves their planning.

4. Exhibit 14-7 (p. 712) presents the computations for allocating the fixed and variable support department costs. A summary of these costs follows:

	Laptop Division (LTD)	Work Station Division (WSD)
(a) Direct Method		
Fixed costs	$465,000	$370,000
Variable costs	470,000	330,000
	$935,000	$700,000

(b) Step-Down Method

Fixed costs	$458,053	$376,947
Variable costs	488,000	312,000
	$946,053	$688,947

(c) Reciprocal Method

Fixed costs	$462,513	$372,487
Variable costs	476,364	323,636
	$938,877	$696,123

5. Contractors may price their job prior to it being undertaken and they establish what costs are allowable. An accurate cost-allocation project will enable Computer Horizons to understand and separate allowable from other costs. The company will be better able to justify its claim for reimbursement is fair and within the terms of the contract.

DECISION POINTS

The following decision guidelines use a question-and-answer format to summarize the chapter's main points. Each decision presents a key question. The guideline is the answer to that question.

DECISIONS	GUIDELINES
1. What are the four purposes for allocating costs to cost objects?	The four purposes of cost allocation are (a) to provide information for economic decisions, (b) to motivate managers and employees, (c) to justify costs or compute reimbursement, and (d) to measure income and assets for reporting to external parties.
2. What are the key decisions managers must make when collecting costs in indirect-cost pools?	Two key decisions related to indirect-cost pools are the number of pools to form and the individual items of cost to be included to ensure each cost pool is homogeneous. Homogeneity is assured if all items in the cost pool change as the quantity in the cost-allocation base changes.
3. Should a manager use the single-rate or the dual-rate cost-allocation method?	The single-rate cost-allocation method allocates costs in each cost pool to cost objects using the same rate per unit of the single allocation base. In the dual-rate method, costs are grouped into a variable-cost pool and a fixed-cost pool; each pool uses a different cost-allocation base. If costs can be easily separated into variable and fixed costs, the dual-rate cost-allocation method should be used because it provides better information for making decisions.
4. What methods can a manager use to allocate costs of multiple support departments to operating departments?	The three methods are direct, step-down, and reciprocal. The direct method ignores any reciprocal services among support departments and allocates support department costs directly to operating departments. The step-down method allows for partial recognition of services among support departments. The reciprocal method provides full recognition of those services, but it is more complex than the direct or step-down methods.
5. What methods can a manager use to allocate common costs to two or more users?	Common costs are the costs of operating a facility, of an activity, or of a cost object that are shared by two or more users. The stand-alone cost-allocation method uses information pertaining to each user of the cost object to determine cost-allocation weights. The incremental cost-allocation method ranks individual users of the cost object and allocates common costs first to the primary user and then to the other incremental users.

This chapter contains definitions of the following important terms:

allowable cost (p. 722)
artificial costs (p. 714)
coefficient matrix (p. 716)
common cost (p. 720)
complete reciprocated cost (p. 714)
core department (p. 706)
direct allocation method (p. 710)
direct method (p. 710)
dual-rate cost-allocation method
  (p. 706)

incremental cost-allocation method
  (p. 720)
matrix (p. 716)
operating department (p. 706)
production department (p. 706)
reciprocal allocation method
  (p. 714)
sequential allocation method
  (p. 712)
service department (p. 706)

single-rate cost-allocation method
  (p. 706)
stand-alone cost-allocation method
  (p. 720)
step allocation method (p. 712)
step-down allocation method
  (p. 712)
support department (p. 706)
vector (p. 716)

MASTERY QUESTIONS

Mastery Questions are rated by proficiency level—elementary, intermediate, and advanced. The solutions appear in the Solutions to Mastery Questions section of MyAccountingLab.

LEARNING OBJECTIVE 1

1. Criteria of cost-allocation decisions—Intermediate. Dave Meltzer went to Lake Tahoe for his annual winter vacation. Unfortunately, he broke his ankle severely while skiing and had to spend two days at the Tahoe General Hospital. Meltzer's insurance company received a $4,800 bill for his two-day stay. One item that caught Meltzer's eye was a $10.62 charge for a roll of cotton. Meltzer was a salesman for Johnson & Johnson and knew that the cost to the hospital of the roll of cotton would be in the $2.20 to $3 range. He asked for a breakdown of how the $10.62 charge was derived. The accounting office of the hospital sent him the following information:

a. Invoiced cost of cotton roll	$ 2.30	
b. Processing of paperwork for purchase	0.50	
c. Supplies room management fee	0.60	
d. Operating-room and patient-room handling charge	1.50	
e. Administrative hospital costs	1.00	
f. Research-related recoupment	0.50	
g. Malpractice insurance costs	1.10	
h. Cost of treating uninsured patients	2.62	
i. Profit component	0.50	
Total	$10.62	

Meltzer believes the overhead charge is obscene. He comments, "There was nothing I could do about it. When they come in and dab your stitches, it's not as if you can say, 'Keep your cotton roll. I brought my own.'

REQUIRED
1. Compute the overhead rate Tahoe General Hospital charged on the cotton roll.
2. What criteria might Tahoe General use to justify allocation of each of the overhead items (b) through (i) in the preceding list? Examine each item separately, and use the allocation justifications in your answer.
3. What should Meltzer do about the $10.62 charge for the cotton roll?

2. Criteria of allocation decisions—Advanced. Rembrandt Hotel and Casino is situated in Ontario. The complex includes a 300-room hotel, a casino, and a restaurant. As Rembrandt's new controller, you are asked to recommend the basis used for allocating fixed overhead costs to the three divisions in 2010. You are presented with the following income statement for the year 2010:

	Hotel	Restaurant	Casino
Revenue	$16,625,000	$5,456,000	$12,540,000
Direct costs	10,019,260	3,949,172	4,448,768
Segment margin	$ 6,605,740	$1,506,828	$ 8,091,232

You are also given the following data on the three segments:

	Hotel	Restaurant	Casino
Square metres	80,000	16,000	64,000
# of employees	200	50	250

You may choose to allocate costs based on direct costs, floor space (in square metres), or the number of employees. Total fixed overhead for 2010 was $14,550,000.

REQUIRED

1. Calculate segment margins in percentage terms before allocating fixed overhead costs.
2. Allocate indirect costs to the three divisions using each of the three allocation bases suggested. Calculate segment margins in dollar and percentage terms.
3. Discuss the results. What is your preferred basis for allocating indirect costs to the divisions?
4. Would you recommend shutting any of the three divisions (and possibly reallocating resources to other divisions) as a result of your analysis? If so, which division would you close, and why?

LEARNING OBJECTIVE 2

1. **Support cost-allocation processes—Intermediate.** Environ Petroleum Company is engaged in all phases of exploring, refining, and marketing of oil and petrochemical products. To ensure full compliance with all applicable laws, the company has a legal department staffed by lawyers who have expertise in a variety of legal areas. The top management of Environ wants to motivate all operating managers to seek legal counsel from the in-house lawyers whenever necessary to avoid violation of any laws during the course of its operations.

Currently, users of the Legal Department are allocated cost at a $400 standard hourly rate based on actual usage. The chief financial officer has suggested that department managers would make more use of the Legal Department's services, and thus avoid potential legal pitfalls, if services were provided free of cost to their departments.

REQUIRED

Comment on the proposal of the chief financial officer. Do you have any alternative suggestion(s)?

2. **Support cost-allocation processes—Advanced.** (CMA, adapted) Bulldog Inc. is a large manufacturing company that runs its own electrical power plant from the excess steam produced in its manufacturing process. Power is provided to two production departments—Department A and Department B. The capacity of the power plant was originally determined by the expected peak demands of the two production departments. The expected average usage and peak demands are, respectively, 60 percent and 66,000,000 kilowatt hours (kwh) for Department A and 40 percent and 44,000,000 kwh for Department B.

The budgeted monthly costs of producing power, based on normal usage of 100,000,000 kwh, are $30,500,000 in fixed costs and $8,000,000 in variable costs. For November, the actual kwh used was 60,000,000 by Department A and 20,000,000 by Department B. Actual fixed costs were $30,500,000, and actual variable costs were $8,000,000.

Terry Lamb, the controller, prepared the following monthly report:

Bulldog Inc.
Monthly Allocation Report
November 2010

Power plant usage	80,000,000 kwh
Actual costs:	
Fixed	$30,500,000
Variable	8,000,000
Total	$38,500,000

Rate per kwh	($38,500,000 ÷ 80,000,000 kwh)	$ 0.48125
Allocations		
To Department A	(60,000,000 kwh × $0.48125)	$28,875,000
To Department B	(20,000,000 kwh × $0.48125)	9,625,000
Total allocated		$38,500,000

Lamb fully allocated all power plant costs on the basis of actual kwh used by each production department. This report will be submitted to the two production department operating managers.

REQUIRED

1. Discuss at least two problems with the monthly allocation report prepared by Lamb for November 2010 at Bulldog Inc.
2. Prepare a revised monthly allocation report for November 2009 using a flexible budget approach.
3. Discuss the behavioural implications of Lamb's monthly allocation report for November 2010 on the production managers of Department B at Bulldog Inc.

LEARNING OBJECTIVE 3

1. **Support cost-allocation to operations—Advanced.** Fruit Juice Inc. processes orange juice at its East Miami plant and grapefruit juice at its West Miami plant. It purchases oranges and grapefruit from growers' cooperatives in the Orlando area. It owns its own trucking fleet. Both Miami plants are the same distance from Orlando. The trucking fleet is run as a cost centre. Each Miami plant is billed for the direct costs and the indirect costs of each return trip.

The trucking fleet costs include direct costs (labour costs of drivers, fuel, and toll charges) and indirect costs. Indirect costs include wear and tear on tires and the vehicles, leasing costs, insurance, and state registration fees.

At the start of 2010, the Orange Juice Division budgeted for 150 Orlando to East Miami truck trips, while the Grapefruit Juice Division budgeted for 100 Orlando to West Miami truck trips. On the basis of these 250 budgeted trips, the Trucking Fleet Division budgeted trucking fleet indirect costs of $590,000. The following actual results occurred for 2010:

Trucking fleet indirect costs	$660,000
Trips to East Miami plant	200
Trips to West Miami plant	100

The Trucking Fleet Division uses a single-rate method when allocating indirect trucking costs. The costs charged to each plant equal this rate times the actual number of trips made.

REQUIRED

1. What is the indirect-cost rate per truck trip when (a) budgeted costs and budgeted quantities (trips) are used and (b) actual costs and actual quantities (trips) are used? What dollar amount will be allocated to the Orange Juice Division and the Grapefruit Juice Division for (a) and for (b)?
2. From the viewpoint of the Orange Juice Division, what are the effects of using budgeted costs/quantities rather than actual costs/quantities?

LEARNING OBJECTIVE 4

1. **Support cost-allocation to support and operations—Advanced.** Magnum T.A. Inc. specializes in the assembly and installation of high-quality security systems for the home and business segments of the market. The four departments at its highly automated state-of-the-art assembly plant are as follows:

Service Departments	Assembly Departments
Engineering Support	Home Security Systems
Information Systems Support	Business Security Systems

The budgeted level of service relationships at the start of the year was

	Used by			
Supplied by	Engineering Support	Information Systems Support	Home Security Systems	Business Security Systems
Engineering Support	—	0.10	0.40	0.50
Information Systems Support	0.20	—	0.30	0.50

The actual level of service relationships for the year was

		Used by		
Supplied by	Engineering Support	Information Systems Support	Home Security Systems	Business Security Systems
Engineering Support	—	0.15	0.30	0.55
Information Systems Support	0.25	—	0.15	0.60

Magnum collects fixed costs and variable costs of each department in separate cost pools. The actual costs (in thousands) in each pool for the year were

	Fixed-Cost Pool	Variable-Cost Pool
Engineering Support	$2,800	$8,500
Information Systems Support	8,100	3,750

Fixed costs are allocated on the basis of the budgeted level of service. Variable costs are allocated on the basis of the actual level of service.

The support department costs allocated to each assembly department are allocated to products on the basis of units assembled. The units assembled in each department during the year were

Home Security Systems	7,950 units
Business Security Systems	3,750 units

REQUIRED

1. Allocate the support department costs to the assembly departments using a dual-rate system and (a) the direct method, (b) the step-down method (allocate Information Systems Support first), (c) the step-down method (allocate Engineering Support first), and (d) the reciprocal method. Present results in a format similar to that of Exhibit 14-10.
2. Compare the support department costs allocated to each Home Security Systems unit assembled and each Business Security Systems unit assembled under (a), (b), (c), and (d) in requirement 1.
3. What factors might explain the very limited adoption of the reciprocal method by many organizations?

LEARNING OBJECTIVE 5

1. **Common cost allocation and contracts—Advanced.** Jason Miller and Eric Jackson would like to lease an office building to open their separate law offices. The building has a total of 1,700 square metres of office space. Miller and Jackson need 1,000 square metres and 700 square metres, respectively. If each rents the space on his own, the rent will be $1 per square metre. If they rent the space together, the rent will decrease to $0.80 per square metre.

REQUIRED

1. Calculate Miller and Jackson's respective share of the rent under the stand-alone cost-allocation method.
2. Do requirement 1 using the incremental cost-allocation method. Assume Miller to be the primary party.
3. What method would you recommend Miller and Jackson use to share the rent?

EXHIBIT 14-10
Alternative Methods of Allocating Corporate Support Department Costs to Operating Divisions of Computer Horizons: Dual-Rate Method

	A	B	C	D	E	F
1		CORPORATE SUPPORT		OPERATING		
2		DEPARTMENTS		DIVISIONS		
3			Human			
4		Legal	Resources			
5	Allocation Method	Department	Department	LTD	WSD	Total
6	**A. DIRECT METHOD**					
7	Fixed Costs	$360,000	$475,000			
8	Legal (1,500 ÷ 2,250; 750 ÷ 2,250)	(360,000)		$240,000	$120,000	
9	Human resources (22,500 ÷ 47,500; 25,000 ÷ 47,500)		(475,000)	225,000	250,000	
10	Corporate support dept. fixed costs allocated to operating divisions	$ 0	$ 0	$465,000	$370,000	$835,000
11	Variable Costs	$200,000	$600,000			
12	Legal (400 ÷ 1,600; 1,200 ÷ 1,600)	(200,000)		$ 50,000	$150,000	
13	Human resources (26,600 ÷ 38,000; 11,400 ÷ 38,000)		(600,000)	420,000	180,000	
14	Corporate support dept. variable costs allocated to operating divisions	$ 0	$ 0	$470,000	$330,000	$800,000
15	**B. STEP-DOWN METHOD**					
16	(Legal Department First)					
17	Fixed Costs	$360,000	$475,000			
18	Legal (250 ÷ 2,500; 1,500 ÷ 2,500; 750 ÷ 2,500)	(360,000)	36,000	$216,000	$108,000	
19	Human resources (22,500 ÷ 47,500; 25,000 ÷ 47,500)		(511,000)	242,053	268,947	
20	Corporate support dept. fixed costs allocated to operating divisions	$ 0	$ 0	$458,053	$376,947	$835,000
21	Variable Costs	$200,000	$600,000			
22	Legal (400 ÷ 2,000; 400 ÷ 2000; 1,200 ÷ 2000)	(200,000)	40,000	$ 40,000	$120,000	
23	Human resources (26,600 ÷ 38,000; 11,400 ÷ 38,000)		(640,000)	448,000	192,000	
24	Corporate support dept. variable costs allocated to operating divisions	$ 0	$ 0	$488,000	$312,000	$800,000
25	**C. RECIPROCAL METHOD**					
26	Fixed Costs	$360,000	$475,000			
27	Legal (250 ÷ 2,500; 1,500 ÷ 2,500; 750 ÷ 2,500)	(385,678)[a]	38,568	$231,407	$115,703	
28	Human resources (2,500 ÷ 50,000; 22,500 ÷ 50,000; 25,000 ÷ 50,000)	25,678	(513,568)[a]	231,106	256,784	
29	Corporate support dept. fixed costs allocated to operating divisions	$ 0	$ 0	$462,513	$372,487	$835,000
30	Variable Costs	$200,000	$600,000			
31	Legal (400 ÷ 2,000; 400 ÷ 2,000; 1,200 ÷ 2,000)	(232,323)[b]	46,465	$ 46,465	$139,393	
32	Human resources (2,000 ÷ 40,000; 26,600 ÷ 40,000; 11,400 ÷ 40,000)	32,323	(646,465)[b]	429,899	184,243	
33	Corporate support dept. variable costs allocated to operating divisions	$ 0	$ 0	$476,364	$323,636	$800,000
34						
35	[a]FIXED COSTS		[b]VARIABLE COSTS			

36	Letting *LF* = Legal Department Fixed Costs, and *HRF* = Human Resources Department Fixed Costs, the simultaneous equations for the reciprocal method for fixed costs are	Letting *LV* = Legal Department Variable Costs, and *HRV* = Human Resources Department Variable Costs, the simultaneous equations for the reciprocal method for variable costs are	
37	$LF = \$360,000 + 0.05\ HRF$	$LV = \$200,000 + 0.05\ HRV$	
38	$HRF = \$475,000 + 0.10\ LF$	$HRV = \$600,000 + 0.20\ LV$	
39	$LF = \$360,000 + 0.05\ (\$475,000 + 0.10\ LF)$	$LV = \$200,000 + 0.05\ (\$600,000 + 0.20\ LV)$	
40	$LF = \$385,678$	$LV = \$232,323$	
41	$HRF = \$475,000 + 0.10\ (\$385,678) = \$513,568$	$HRV = \$600,000 + 0.20\ (\$232,323) = \$646,465$	

SHORT-ANSWER QUESTIONS

14-1 "I am going to focus on the customers of my business and leave cost-allocation issues to my accountant." Do you agree with this comment by a division president?

14-2 How can an individual cost item, such as the salary of a plant security guard, be both a direct cost and an indirect cost at the same time?

14-3 What are four purposes of cost allocation?

14-4 What criteria might be used to justify cost-allocation decisions? Which are the dominant criteria?

14-5 Identify six reasons why Canadian executives allocate costs to divisions and departments.

14-6 How do cost-benefit considerations affect choices by a company about the allocation of indirect costs to products, services, or customers?

14-7 Name three decisions managers face when designing the cost-allocation component of an accounting system.

14-8 Give examples of bases used to allocate corporate cost pools to the operating divisions of an organization.

14-9 Why might a manager prefer that budgeted rather than actual indirect cost-allocation rates be used for costs being allocated to her department from another department?

14-10 "To ensure unbiased cost allocations, fixed indirect costs should be allocated on the basis of estimated long-run use by user department managers." Do you agree? Why?

14-11 Specify the strengths and weaknesses among the three methods of allocating the costs of service departments to production departments.

14-12 What is theoretically the most defensible method for allocating service department costs?

14-13 Distinguish between two methods of allocating common costs.

14-14 What is one key way to reduce cost-allocation disputes arising with government contracts?

14-15 How might a dispute over the allocation of revenues of a bundled product be resolved?

EXERCISES

14-16 Single-rate versus dual-rate cost-allocation methods. (W. Crum, adapted) An Ontario-based company has a power plant that was designed and built to serve its three factories. Data for 2010 are as follows:

| | Usage in Kilowatt-Hours | |
Factory	Budget	Actual
Mississauga	100,000	80,000
Cambridge	60,000	120,000
Burlington	40,000	40,000

Actual fixed costs of the power plant were $1.1 million in 2010; actual variable costs were $2.2 million.

REQUIRED

1. Compute the amount of power costs that would be allocated to Cambridge using a single-rate method for both budgeted and actual usage.

2. Compute the amount of power costs that would be allocated to Cambridge using a dual-rate method for both budgeted and actual usage.

1. Allocation to Cambridge based on budgeted usage, $990,000

14-17 Single-rate versus dual-rate methods, support department. The Ontario power plant that services all manufacturing departments of Ontario Engineering has a budget for the coming year. This budget has been expressed in the following monthly terms:

1. a. Costs allocated to Rockford under single-rate method based on practical capacity, $3,000

Manufacturing Department	Needed at Practical Capacity Production Level (kilowatt-hours)	Average Expected Monthly Usage (kilowatt-hours)
Rockford	10,000	8,000
Peoria	20,000	9,000
Hammond	12,000	7,000
Kanakee	8,000	6,000
Total	50,000	30,000

The expected monthly costs for operating the power plant during the budget year are $15,000: $6,000 variable and $9,000 fixed.

1. Assume that a single cost pool is used for the power plant costs. What budgeted amounts will be allocated to each manufacturing department if (a) the rate is calculated based on practical capacity and costs are allocated based on practical capacity and (b) the rate is calculated based on expected monthly usage and costs are allocated based on expected monthly usage?
2. Assume the dual-rate method is used with separate cost pools for the variable and fixed costs. Variable costs are allocated on the basis of expected monthly usage. Fixed costs are allocated on the basis of practical capacity. What budgeted amounts will be allocated to each manufacturing department? Why might you prefer the dual-rate method?

14-18 Single-rate method, budgeted versus actual costs and quantities. Chocolat Inc. is a producer of premium chocolate based in Owen Sound. The company has a separate division for each of its two products: dark chocolate and milk chocolate. Chocolat purchases ingredients from Toronto for its Dark Chocolate division and from Barrie for its Milk Chocolate division. Both locations are the same distance from Chocolat's Owen Sound plant.

1. a. Budgeted rate, $2,300 per round trip

Chocolat Inc. operates a fleet of trucks as a cost centre that charges the divisions for variable costs (drivers and fuel) and fixed costs (vehicle amortization, insurance, and registration fees) of operating the fleet. Each division is evaluated on the basis of its operating income. For 2009, the trucking fleet had a practical capacity of 50 round trips between the Owen Sound plant and the two suppliers. It recorded the following information:

	Budgeted	Actual
Costs of truck fleet	$115,000	$96,750
Number of round trips for Dark Chocolate Division (Owen Sound plant–Toronto)	30	30
Number of round trips for Milk Chocolate Division (Owen Sound plant–Barrie)	20	15

REQUIRED

1. Using the single-rate method, allocate costs to the Dark Chocolate Division and the Milk Chocolate Division in these three ways:
   a. Calculate the budgeted rate per round trip and allocate costs based on round trips budgeted for each division.
   b. Calculate the budgeted rate per round trip and allocate costs based on actual round trips used by each division.
   c. Calculate the actual rate per round trip and allocate costs based on actual round trips used by each division.
2. Describe the advantages and disadvantages of using each of the three methods in requirement 1. Would you encourage Chocolat Inc. to use one of these methods? Explain and indicate any assumptions you made.

14-19 Dual-rate method, budgeted versus actual costs, and practical capacity versus actual quantities (continuation of 14-18). Chocolat Inc. decides to examine the effect of using the dual-rate method for allocating truck costs to each round trip. At the start of 2009, the budgeted costs were:

1. Variable indirect cost rate, $1,500 per round trip

Variable cost per round trip	$ 1,500
Fixed costs	$40,000

The actual results for the 45 round trips made in 2009 were:

Variable costs	$60,750
Fixed costs	$36,000
	$96,750

Assume all other information to be the same as in Exercise 14-18.

REQUIRED
1. Using the dual-rate method, what are the costs allocated to the Dark Chocolate Division and the Milk Chocolate Division when (a) variable costs are allocated using the budgeted rate per round trip and actual round trips used by each division, and when (b) fixed costs are allocated based on the budgeted rate per round trip and round trips budgeted for each division.
2. From the viewpoint of the Dark Chocolate Division, what are the effects of using the dual-rate method rather than the single-rate method?

1. a. Costs allocated to Govt., $1,120,000

14-20 Support department cost allocation; direct and step-down methods. Phoenix Partners provides management consulting services to government and corporate clients. Phoenix has two support departments—Administrative Services (AS) and Information Systems (IS)—and two operating departments—Government Consulting (Govt.) and Corporate Consulting (Corp.). For the first quarter of 2010, Phoenix's cost records indicate the following:

	Support		Operating		
	AS	IS	Govt.	Corp.	Total
Budgeted overhead costs before any interdepartment cost allocations	$600,000	$2,400,000	$8,756,000	$12,452,000	$24,208,000
Support work supplied by AS (budgeted head count)	—	25%	40%	35%	100%
Support work supplied by IS (budgeted computer time)	10%	—	30%	60%	100%

REQUIRED
1. Allocate the two support departments' costs to the two operating departments using the following methods:
   a. Direct method
   b. Step-down method (allocate AS first)
   c. Step-down method (allocate IS first)
2. Compare and explain differences in the support department costs allocated to each operating department.
3. What approaches might be used to decide the sequence in which to allocate support departments when using the step-down method?

1. a. Allocation of AS costs to Govt., $344,615

14-21 Support department cost allocation, reciprocal method (continuation of 14-20). Refer to the data given in Exercise 14-20.

REQUIRED
1. Allocate the two support departments' costs to the two operating departments using the reciprocal method. Use (a) linear equations and (b) repeated iterations.
2. Compare and explain differences in requirement 1 with those in requirement 1 of Exercise 14-20. Which method do you prefer? Why?

1. Allocate building and grounds expenses at $0.10/sq. m.

14-22 Allocating costs of support departments; step-down and direct methods. The Central Valley Company has prepared department overhead budgets for budgeted-volume levels before allocations as follows:

Support departments:		
Building and grounds	$10,000	
Personnel	1,000	
General plant administration	26,090	
Cafeteria: operating loss	1,640	
Storeroom	2,670	$ 41,400

Operating departments:

Machining	34,700	
Assembly	48,900	83,600
Total for support and operating departments		$125,000

Management has decided that the most appropriate inventory costs are achieved by using individual department overhead rates. These rates are developed after support department costs are allocated to operating departments.

Bases for allocation are to be selected from the following:

Department	Direct Manufacturing Labour-Hours	Number of Employees	Square Metres of Floor Space Occupied	Manufacturing Labour-Hours	Number of Requisitions
Building and grounds	0	0	0	0	0
Personnel[a]	0	0	2,000	0	0
General plant administration	0	35	7,000	0	0
Cafeteria: operating loss	0	10	4,000	1,000	0
Storeroom	0	5	7,000	1,000	0
Machining	5,000	50	30,000	8,000	2,000
Assembly	15,000	100	50,000	17,000	1,000
Total	20,000	200	100,000	27,000	3,000

[a]Basis used is number of employees.

REQUIRED

1. Using the step-down method, allocate support department costs. Develop overhead rates per direct manufacturing labour-hour for machining and assembly. Allocate the costs of the support departments in the order given in this problem. Use the allocation base for each support department you think is most appropriate.
2. Using the direct method, rework requirement 1.
3. Based on the following information about two jobs, determine the total overhead costs for each job by using rates developed in (a) requirement 1 and (b) requirement 2.

	Direct Manufacturing Labour-Hours	
	Machining	Assembly
Job 88	18	2
Job 89	3	17

4. The company evaluates the performance of the operating department managers on the basis of howwell they managed their total costs, including allocated costs. As the manager of the MachiningDepartment, which allocation method would you prefer from the results obtained in requirements 1 and 2? Explain.

14-23 **Stand-alone revenue allocation.** Funland is an amusement park complex in southern Florida. Funland is divided into three autonomous divisions: a water park, a superhero theme park with rides, and an animal park. In addition to selling a daily entrance ticket for each park, Funland has decided to sell a three-day ticket that would allow entrance into each of the parks for one day. The ticket selling price and the costs associated with each entrant into a park are:

Park	Ticket Price	Daily Cost per Entrant
Water park	$40	$15
Superhero theme park	$60	$25
Animal park	$20	$10
Three-day ticket	$90	

REQUIRED

1. Allocate the revenue from the three-day ticket to each park using the stand-alone method based on ticket price.
2. Allocate the revenue from the three-day ticket to each park using the stand-alone method based on cost per entrant.

1. Revenue allocation to water park, $30

3. Allocate the revenue from the three-day ticket to each park using the stand-alone method based on physical units (that is, number of tickets received for each park).

4. Which basis of allocation makes the most sense in this situation? Explain your answer.

14-24 Direct and step-down allocation. E-books, an online book retailer, has two operating departments—Corporate Sales and Consumer Sales—and two support departments—Human Resources and Information Systems. Each sales department conducts merchandising and marketing operations independently. E-books uses number of employees to allocate Human Resources costs and processing time to allocate Information Systems costs. The following data are available for September 2010:

	Support Departments		Operating Departments	
	Human Resources	**Information Systems**	**Corporate Sales**	**Consumer Sales**
Budgeted costs incurred before any interdepartment cost allocations	$72,700	$234,400	$998,270	$489,860
Support work supplied by Human Resources Department				
Budgeted number of employees	—	21	42	28
Support work supplied by Information Systems Department				
Budgeted processing time (in minutes)	320	—	1,920	1,600

REQUIRED

1. Allocate the support departments' costs to the operating departments using the direct method.

2. Rank the support departments based on the percentage of their services provided to other support departments. Use this ranking to allocate the support departments' costs to the operating departments based on the step-down method.

3. How could you have ranked the support departments differently?

14-25 Reciprocal cost allocation (continuation of 14-24). Consider E-books again. The controller of E-books reads a widely used textbook that states "the reciprocal method is conceptually the most defensible." He seeks your assistance.

REQUIRED

1. Describe the key features of the reciprocal method.

2. Allocate the support departments' costs (Human Resources and Information Systems) to the two operating departments using the reciprocal method.

3. In the case presented in this exercise, which method (direct, step-down, or reciprocal) would you recommend? Why?

PROBLEMS

14-26 Single-rate, dual-rate, and practical capacity allocation. Beauty Department Store has a new promotional program that offers a free gift-wrapping service for its customers. Beauty's customer-service department has practical capacity to wrap 7,500 gifts at a budgeted fixed cost of $6,750 each month. The budgeted variable cost to gift wrap an item is $0.50. Although the service is free to customers, a gift-wrapping service cost allocation is made to the department where the item was purchased. The customer-service department reported the following for the most recent month:

Department	**Actual Number of Gifts Wrapped**	**Budgeted Number of Gifts to Be Wrapped**	**Practical Capacity Available for Gift-Wrapping**
Women's face wash	2,100	2,475	2,625
Men's face wash	750	825	938
Fragrances	1,575	1,800	1,969
Body wash	525	450	656
Hair products	1,050	1,200	1,312
Total	6,000	6,750	7,500

1. Using the single-rate method, allocate gift-wrapping costs to different departments in these three ways:

   a. Calculate the budgeted rate based on the budgeted number of gifts to be wrapped and allocate costs based on the budgeted use (of gift-wrapping services).

   b. Calculate the budgeted rate based on the budgeted number of gifts to be wrapped and allocate costs based on actual usage.

   c. Calculate the budgeted rate based on the practical gift-wrapping capacity available and allocate costs based on actual usage.

2. Using the dual-rate method, compute the amount allocated to each department when (a) the fixed-cost rate is calculated using budgeted costs and the practical gift-wrapping capacity, (b) fixed costs are allocated based on budgeted usage of gift-wrapping services, and (c) variable costs are allocated using the budgeted variable-cost rate and actual usage.

3. Comment on your results in requirements 1 and 2. Discuss the advantages of the dual-rate method.

14-27 Allocating costs to divisions. Gether Corporation manufactures appliances. It has four divisions: Refrigerator, Stove, Dishwasher, and Microwave Oven. Each division is located in a different city and the headquarters is located in Mississauga, Ontario. Headquarters incurs a total of $14,255,000 in costs, none of which are direct costs of any of the divisions. Revenues, costs, and facility space for each division are as follows:

1. Allocation to stove based on square metres, $3,207,375

	Refrigerator	Stove	Dishwasher	Microwave Oven
Revenue	$10,900,000	$18,800,000	$11,500,000	$6,780,000
Direct costs	5,700,000	10,400,000	6,200,000	3,220,000
Segment margin	5,200,000	8,400,000	5,300,000	3,560,000
Square metres of floor space occupied	130,000	90,000	80,000	100,000

Gether wants to allocate the indirect costs of headquarters on the basis of either square metres or segment margin for each division.

REQUIRED

1. Allocate the indirect headquarters costs to each division, first using square metres of space and then using segment margin as the allocation base. Calculate the division operating margins after each allocation in dollars and as a percentage of revenues.

2. Which allocation base do you prefer? Why?

3. Should any of the divisions be dropped based on your calculations? Why or why not?

14-28 Support department cost allocations; single-department cost pools; direct, step-down, and reciprocal methods. The Manes Company has two products. Product 1 is manufactured entirely in Department X. Product 2 is manufactured entirely in Department Y. To produce these two products, the Manes Company has two support departments: A (a materials-handling department) and B (a power-generating department).

An analysis of the work done by departments A and B in a typical period follows:

1. Allocation of A to X, $62,500

	Used By			
Supplied By	A	B	X	Y
A	—	100	250	150
B	500	—	100	400

The work done in Department A is measured by the direct labour-hours of materials-handling time. The work done in Department B is measured by the kilowatt-hours of power. The budgeted costs of the support departments for the coming year are:

	Department A (Materials Handling)	Department B (Power Generation)
Variable indirect labour and indirect materials costs	$ 70,000	$10,000
Supervision	10,000	10,000
Amortization	20,000	20,000
	$100,000	$40,000
	+ Power costs	+ Materials-handling costs

The budgeted costs of the operating departments for the coming year are $1,500,000 for Department X and $800,000 for Department Y.

Supervision costs are salary costs. Amortization in Department B is the straight-line amortization of power-generation equipment in its 19th year of an estimated 25-year useful life; the equipment is old but well maintained.

REQUIRED

1. What are the allocations of costs of support departments A and B to operating departments X and Y using (a) the direct method, (b) the step-down method (allocate Department A first), (c) the step-down method (allocate Department B first), and (d) the reciprocal method?
2. An outside company has offered to supply all the power needed by the Manes Company and to provide all the services of the present power department. The cost of this service will be $40 per kilowatt-hour of power. Should Manes accept? Explain.

14-29 **Common costs.** Wright Inc. and Brown Inc. are two small clothing companies that are considering leasing a dyeing machine together. The companies estimated that in order to meet production, Wright needs the machine for 900 hours and Brown needs it for 600 hours. If each company rents the machine on its own, the fee will be $40 per hour of usage. If they rent the machine together, the fee will decrease to $32 per hour of usage.

1. Allocation to Wright Inc. under stand-alone cost allocation method, $28,800

REQUIRED

1. Calculate Wright's and Brown's respective share of fees under the stand-alone cost-allocation method.
2. Calculate Wright's and Brown's respective share of fees using the incremental cost-allocation method. Assume Wright to be the primary party.
3. Which method would you recommend Wright and Brown use to share the fees?

14-30 **Cost allocation to divisions.** Lenzig Corporation has three divisions: Pulp, Paper, and Fibres. Lenzig's new controller, Ari Bardem, is reviewing the allocation of fixed corporate-overhead costs to the three divisions. He is presented with the following information for each division for 2009:

Pulp division margin percentage, 12.63157%

	Pulp	Paper	Fibres
Revenues	$8,500,000	$17,500,000	$24,000,000
Direct manufacturing costs	4,100,000	8,600,000	11,300,000
Division administrative costs	2,000,000	1,800,000	3,200,000
Division margin	$2,400,000	$ 7,100,000	$ 9,500,000
Number of employees	350	250	400
Floor space (square metres)	35,000	24,000	66,000

Until now, Lenzig Corporation has allocated fixed corporate-overhead costs to the divisions on the basis of division margins. Bardem asks for a list of costs that comprise fixed corporate overhead and suggests the following new allocation bases:

Fixed Corporate-Overhead Costs		**Suggested Allocation Bases**
Human resource management	$1,800,000	Number of employees
Facility	2,700,000	Floor space (square metres)
Corporate administration	4,500,000	Division administrative costs
Total	$9,000,000	

REQUIRED

1. Allocate 2009 fixed corporate-overhead costs to the three divisions using division margin as the allocation base. What is each division's operating margin percentage (division margin minus allocated fixed corporate-overhead costs as a percentage of revenues)?
2. Allocate 2009 fixed costs using the allocation bases suggested by Bardem. What is each division's operating margin percentage under the new allocation scheme?
3. Compare and discuss the results of requirements 1 and 2. If division performance is linked to operating margin percentage, which division would be most receptive to the new allocation scheme? Which division would be the least receptive? Why?
4. Which allocation scheme should Lenzig Corporation use? Why? How might Bardem overcome any objections that may arise from the divisions?

14-31 Allocation of corporate costs to divisions. Dusty Rhodes, controller of Richfield Oil Company, is preparing a presentation to senior executives about the performance of its four divisions. Summary data (dollar amounts in millions) related to the four divisions for the most recent year are:

2. Oil & Gas upstream division operating income, $4,193

	Divisions				
	Oil & Gas Upstream	Oil & Gas Downstream	Chemical Products	Copper Mining	Total
Revenues	$ 8,000	$16,000	$4,800	$3,200	$32,000
Operating costs	3,000	15,000	3,800	3,500	25,300
Operating income	$ 5,000	$ 1,000	$1,000	$ (300)	6,700
Identifiable assets	$14,000	$ 6,000	$3,000	$2,000	$25,000
Number of employees	9,000	12,000	6,000	3,000	30,000

Under the existing accounting system, costs incurred at corporate headquarters are collected in a single cost pool ($3,228 million in the most recent year) and allocated to each division on the basis of its actual revenues. The top managers in each division share in a division-income bonus pool. Division income is defined as operating income less allocated corporate costs.

Rhodes has analyzed the components of corporate costs and proposes that corporate costs be collected in four cost pools. The components of corporate costs for the most recent year (dollar amounts in millions) and Rhodes' suggested cost pools and allocation bases are:

Corporate Cost Category	Amount	Suggested Cost Pool	Suggested Allocation Base
Interest on debt	$2,000	Cost pool 1	Identifiable assets
Corporate salaries	150	Cost pool 2	
Accounting and control	110	Cost pool 2	
General marketing	200	Cost pool 2	Division revenues
Legal	140	Cost pool 2	
Research and development	200	Cost pool 2	
Public affairs	203	Cost pool 3	Positive operating income*
Personnel and payroll	225	Cost pool 4	Number of employees
Total	$3,228		

*Since public affairs includes the cost of public relations staff, lobbyists, and donations to environmental charities, Rhodes proposes that this cost be allocated using operating income (if positive) of divisions, with only divisions with positive operating income included in the allocation base.

REQUIRED
1. Discuss two reasons why Richfield Oil should allocate corporate costs to each division.
2. Calculate the operating income of each division when all corporate costs are allocated based on revenues of each division.
3. Calculate the operating income of each division when all corporate costs are allocated using the four cost pools.
4. How do you think the new proposal will be received by the division managers? What are the strengths and weaknesses of Rhodes' proposal relative to the existing single-cost-pool method?

14-32 Cost allocation to divisions. Forber Bakery makes baked goods for grocery stores, and has three divisions: Bread, Cake, and Doughnuts. Each division is run and evaluated separately, but the main headquarters incurs costs that are indirect costs for the divisions. Costs incurred in the main headquarters are:

2

1. Bread operating income, $4,700,000

Human resources (HR) costs	$1,900,000
Accounting department costs	1,400,000
Rent and amortization	1,200,000
Other	600,000
Total costs	$5,100,000

The Forber upper management currently allocates this cost to the divisions equally. One of the division managers has done some research on activity-based costing and proposes the use of different allocation bases for the different indirect costs—number of employees for HR costs, total revenues for accounting department costs, square metres of space for rent and amortization costs, and equal allocation among the divisions of "other" costs. Information about the three divisions follows:

	Bread	Cake	Doughnuts
Total revenues	$20,900,000	$4,500,000	$13,400,000
Direct costs	14,500,000	3,200,000	7,250,000
Segment margin	$ 6,400,000	$1,300,000	$ 6,150,000
Number of employees	400	100	300
Square metres of space	10,000	4,000	6,000

REQUIRED

1. Allocate the indirect costs of Forber to each division equally. Calculate division operating income after allocation of headquarters costs.
2. Allocate headquarters costs to the individual divisions using the proposed allocation bases. Calculate the division operating income after allocation. Comment on the allocation bases used to allocate headquarters costs.
3. Which division manager do you think suggested this new allocation? Explain briefly. Which allocation do you think is "better"?

14-33 Matrix algebra. A firm that manufactures specialized scientific equipment, Nominal Engineering Inc. (NEI), has decided to implement a new costing system to more accurately allocate its support costs. The company anticipates this will improve the competitiveness of its bids for design contracts and provide solid justification when it claims reimbursement for contracted costs. NEI has four support departments: Engineering (design), Accounting, Information Systems (IS), and Human Resources Administration (HR). NEI's two operating divisions are geographically separate. One is national and the other international. The table summarizes the five cost pools and the percentage of costs allocated to each department and division. The four support departments are interdependent and each uses the resources of the others. Because the goal of NEI is improved accuracy of cost allocation, the top management team decides to use the reciprocal cost-allocation method for the support department costs. The table summarizes the cost pools and the percentage of each cost pool to be allocated to each department. The cost pools are reported in $millions.

4

2. Engineering artificial costs, $47.32112

Supplier of Support Service	Vector of Constants Cost Pools	Consumption of Support: Support Depts.				Operating Divisions		Check
		Engineering	Accounting	IS	HR	National	International	
Engineering	$ 36	0	0.1	0.2	0.05	0.35	0.3	1
Accounting	20	0.1	0	0.1	0.05	0.45	0.3	1
IS	20	0.2	0.1	0	0.05	0.4	0.25	1
HR	10	0.1	0.1	0.1	0	0.4	0.3	1

Operating Divisions	
National	30
International	22
	$138

REQUIRED

1. Use the matrix algebra function in Excel to calculate the inverse of the coefficient matrix for support departments.
2. Multiply the inverse of the coefficient matrix by the vector of constants to obtain the artificial costs.
3. Calculate the allocation of costs to the support departments and the two divisions.

14-34 Matrix algebra. Computer retailer Lowest Price Bargains Ltd. (LPBL) sells computers of all models and sizes at low prices. The company can keep its costs down with very careful cost allocation of both its three operating departments and its three support departments, which are interdependent and consume one another's resources. The three support departments are Corporate Treasury, Corporate Human Resource Management (CHRM), and Information Technology (IT). The three core operating departments are Sales & Marketing, Purchasing, and Consumer Services & Returns. LPBL uses reciprocal cost allocation for its support departments. A table summarizes the cost pools and the cost allocations among all six departments:

2. Corporate Treasury artificial costs, $162.30043

Supplier of Support Service	Vector of Constants	Consumption of Support: Support Depts.			Operating Departments			
	Cost Pools	Corporate Treasury	CHRM	IS	Sales & Mktg.	Purchasing	Consumer Services & Returns	Check
Corporate Treasury	$ 96	0	0.2	0.25	0.15	0.2	0.2	1
CHRM	49	0.1	0	0.2	0.25	0.25	0.2	1
IT	156	0.25	0.15	0	0.2	0.2	0.2	1

Operating Departments	
Sales & Marketing	84
Purchasing	203
Consumer Services & Returns	36
	$624

REQUIRED

1. Use the matrix algebra function in Excel to calculate the inverse of the coefficient matrix for support departments.
2. Multiply the inverse of the coefficient matrix by the vector of constants to obtain the artificial costs.
3. Calculate the allocation of costs all departments.

COLLABORATIVE LEARNING CASE

14-35 Revenue allocation, bundled products. Heavenly Resorts operates a five-star hotel with a world-recognized championship golf course. Heavenly has a decentralized management structure with three divisions:

5

1. Lodging stand-alone revenue, $582

- ◆ Lodging (rooms, conference facilities)
- ◆ Food (restaurants and in-room service)
- ◆ Recreation (golf course, tennis courts, and so on)

Starting next month, Heavenly Resorts will offer a two-day, two-person "getaway package" for $1,000. This deal includes:

- ◆ Two nights' stay for two in an ocean-view room—separately priced at $800 ($400 per night for two).
- ◆ Two rounds of golf—separately priced at $375 ($187.50 per round). One person can do two rounds, or two people can do one round each.
- ◆ Candlelight dinner for two at the exclusive Heavenly Resorts Restaurant—separately priced at $200 ($100 per person).

Jenny Lee, president of the Recreation Division, recently asked the CEO of Heavenly Resorts how her division would share in the $1,000 revenue from the package. The golf course was operating at 100% capacity. Under the getaway-package rules, participants who booked one week in advance were guaranteed access to the golf course. Lee noted that every "getaway" booking would displace $375 of golf bookings. She emphasized that the high demand reflected the devotion of her team to keeping the golf course rated one of the "Best 10 Courses in the World" by *Golf Monthly*. As an aside, she also noted that the Lodging and Food divisions had to turn away customers only during "peak-season events such as the New Year's period."

REQUIRED

1. Using selling prices, allocate the $1,000 getaway-package revenue to the three divisions using:
   a. The stand-alone revenue-allocation method
   b. The incremental revenue-allocation method (with Recreation first, then Lodging, and then Food)
2. What are the pros and cons of the two methods in requirement 1?

Cost Allocation: Joint Products and Byproducts

BUSINESS MATTERS

Challenges of Joint Cost Allocation

The Hibernia offshore oil field project off the coast of Newfoundland is a joint venture among many companies, including ExxonMobil Canada, Chevron Canada Resources, and Petro-Canada. The costs of this project are shared among the companies investing in this project. Ultimately, the cost of the oil produced and the ultimate costs of processing the oil into a range of products will involve an allocation of these costs to the various products produced.

LEARNING OBJECTIVES

After studying this chapter, you should be able to

1. Apply cost-allocation methods to the allocation of joint costs

2. Analyze alternative cost-allocation methods to assign joint costs to individual products

3. Explain the irrelevance of joint costs in deciding to sell or further process inputs

4. Understand the governance challenges of joint costing

5. Account for byproducts using two different methods

rior chapters have emphasized costing for either single-product companies or companies in which individual products are separately produced. The shared consumption of resources was confined to support departments. We now consider costing for the more complex case where two or more products are simultaneously produced. Shared consumption extends to operating departments and the activities shared give rise to joint costs. Joint costs arise from a single act of resource consumption that yields multiple products. This chapter examines methods for allocating joint costs to products and services.

JOINT-COST BASICS

1 Apply cost-allocation methods to the allocation of joint costs

There are many contexts that require the allocation of joint costs to individual products or services. Examples include:

- Computation of inventoriable costs and cost of goods sold for external financial statements and reports for income tax authorities.
- Computation of inventoriable costs and cost of goods sold for internal financial reporting. Such reports are used in division profitability analysis when determining compensation for division managers.
- Cost reimbursement under contracts when only a portion of a business's products or services is sold or delivered to a single customer (such as a government agency).
- Customer profitability analysis where individual customers purchase varying combinations of joint products or byproducts as well as other products of the company.
- Insurance settlement computations when damage claims made by businesses with joint products, main products, or byproducts are based on cost information.
- Rate regulation when one or more of the jointly produced products or services is subject to price regulation.
- Contract litigation in which costs of joint products are key inputs.

Many companies such as ExxonMobil Canada produce two or more products simultaneously using the same processes. The distillation of coal, for example, gives us coke, gas, and other products. The cost of this distillation process would be called a joint cost. The juncture in the process when one or more products in a joint cost setting become separately identifiable is called the **splitoff point**. An example is the point where coal becomes coke, gas, and other products. **Separable costs** are costs incurred beyond the splitoff point—for example, manufacturing, marketing, and distribution costs—that can be assigned to one or more individual products. At or beyond the splitoff point, decisions relating to sale or further processing of individual products can be made independently of decisions about other products.

Various terms have arisen in conjunction with production processes. A **product** is any output that has a positive sales value (or an output used internally that enables an organization to avoid incurring costs). **Joint products** all have relatively high sales value but are not separately identifiable as individual products until the splitoff point. When a single process yielding two or more products yields only one product with a relatively high sales value, that product is termed a **main product**.

A **byproduct** has a low sales value compared with the sales value of the main or joint product(s). **Scrap** has minimal sales value. Some outputs can have a negative revenue when their disposal costs (for example, the costs of handling nonsaleable toxic substances) are considered. These disposal costs must be added to the joint production costs that are allocated to the main and joint products. The classification of products as main, joint, byproduct, or scrap can change over time, especially for

EXHIBIT 15-1
Classification of Products of a Joint Production Process

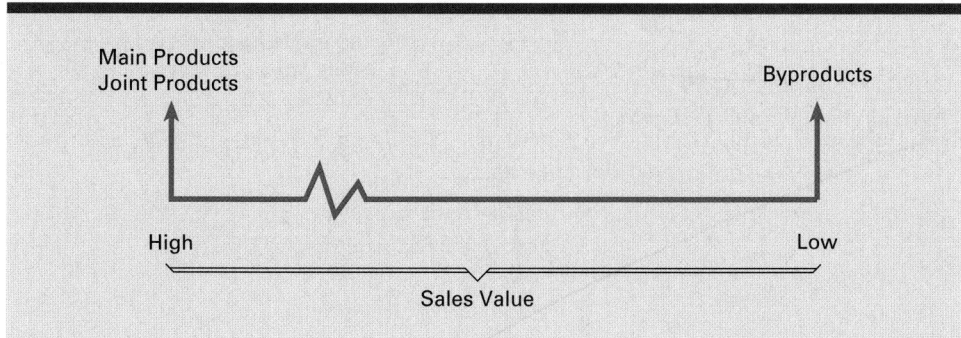

products (such as tin) whose market price can increase or decrease by, say, 30% or more in any one year.

For example, if logs are processed into standard lumber and wood chips, standard lumber is a main product and wood chips are the byproducts, because standard lumber has a high total sales value compared to the sales value of wood chips. If the logs are processed into fine grade lumber, standard lumber, and wood chips, then both the fine and standard grade lumber with high sales values are joint products while the wood chips with low sales values are the byproducts.

Exhibit 15-1 shows the relationship between the terms defined in the preceding paragraph. Be careful; these distinctions are not firm in practice. The variety of terminology and accounting practice is bewildering. Always gain an understanding of the terms as used by the particular organization with which you are dealing. Throughout this chapter we will use the following notation:

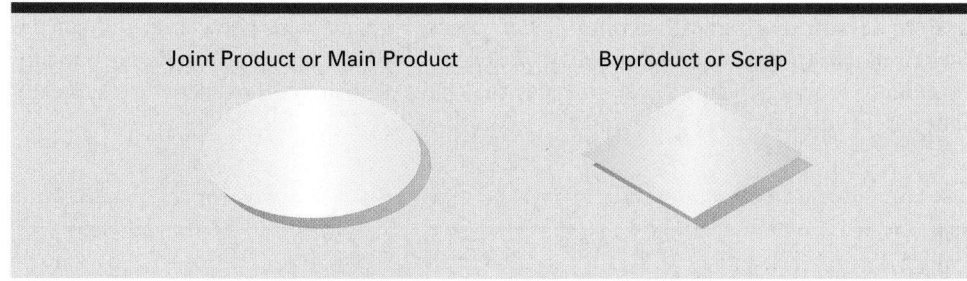

Industries abound in which single processes simultaneously yield two or more products. Exhibit 15-2 presents examples of joint-cost situations in diverse industries. In each example in Exhibit 15-2, no individual product can be produced without the accompanying products appearing, although sometimes the proportions can be varied. A poultry farm cannot kill a turkey wing; it has to kill a whole turkey, which yields breasts, thighs, drumsticks, digest, feather meal, and poultry meal in addition to wings. In this example, the focus is on building up costs of individual products as disassembly occurs. This focus contrasts with that of prior chapters that emphasize building up costs of individual products as assembly occurs.

In some joint-cost settings, the number of outputs produced exceeds the number of products. This situation can occur where an output, produced as an inherent part of the joint-production process, is recycled without any value being added by its production.

For example, the offshore processing of hydrocarbons to yield oil and gas also yields water as an output, which is recycled back into the ocean. Similarly, the processing of mineral ore to yield gold and silver also yields dirt as an output, which is recycled back into the ground. The water and dirt in these examples typically are not classified as products, but they are outputs. No entries are made in the accounting

EXHIBIT 15-2
Examples of Joint Cost Situations

Industry	Separable Products at the Splitoff Point
Agriculture and Food Processing	
Cocoa beans	Cocoa butter, cocoa powder, cocoa drink mix, tanning cream
Lambs	Lamb cuts, tripe, hides, bones, fat
Hogs	Bacon, ham, spare ribs, pork roast
Raw milk	Cream, liquid skim
Lumber	Lumber of varying grades and shapes
Turkeys	Breasts, wings, thighs, drumsticks, digest, feather meal, poultry meal
Extractive Industries	
Coal	Coke, gas, benzol, tar, ammonia
Copper ore	Copper, silver, lead, zinc
Petroleum	Crude oil, natural gas, raw LPG
Salt	Hydrogen, chlorine, caustic soda
Chemical Industries	
Raw LPG (liquefied petroleum gas)	Butane, ethane, propane
Crude oil	Gasoline, kerosene, benzene, naphtha
Semiconductor Industry	
Fabrication of silicon-wafer chips	Memory chips of different quality (as to capacity), speed, life expectancy, and temperature tolerance

system to record their processing. The physical quantity of these outputs can be large relative to the physical quantity of outputs that are recorded in the accounting system as products. Only those outputs that have a positive sales value are typically labelled products.

MyAccountingLab

ASSESS YOUR MASTERY

To check your understanding of the material in Learning Objective **1**, go to the *Mastery Questions* section at the end of this chapter and complete Learning Objective **1** questions 1 and 2.

APPROACHES TO ALLOCATING JOINT COSTS

1 Analyze alternative cost-allocation methods to assign joint costs to individual products

The seven areas mentioned on page 742 are illustrative rather than exhaustive. Their wide-ranging natures illustrate why it is important to master methods for allocating joint costs.

There are two basic approaches to allocating joint costs:

Approach 1: *Allocate costs using market-based data (for example, revenues).* Three methods that can be used in applying this approach are the:

◆ Sales value at splitoff method

◆ Estimated net realizable value (NRV) method

◆ Constant gross margin percentage NRV method

Approach 2: *Allocate costs using physical-measure-based data such as weight or volume.*

In prior chapters we emphasized both the cause-and-effect and the benefits-received criteria (see Exhibit 14-2, p. 698) for guiding cost-allocation decisions. In joint cost settings, it is not feasible to use the cause-and-effect criterion to guide individual product cost allocations. Joint costs, by definition, cannot be the subject of cause-and-effect analysis at the individual product level. The cause-and-effect relationship exists only at the joint process level. The benefits-received criterion leads to a preference for methods under the first approach.[1] Revenues, in general, are a better indicator of benefits received than are physical measures such as weight or volume.

In the simplest situation, the joint products are sold at the splitoff point without further processing. We use this case first (termed Example 1) to illustrate two methods: first the sales value at splitoff method and second the physical measures method using volume as the metric. Then we consider situations involving further processing beyond the splitoff point (termed Example 2) to illustrate our final two methods: the estimated NRV method and the constant gross margin percentage NRV method. To enable comparisons across the methods, we report for each method individual gross margin percentages for individual products.

> *Example 1:* Farmers' Dairy purchases raw milk from individual farms and processes it up to the splitoff point, where two products (cream and liquid skim) are obtained. These two products are sold to an independent company, which markets and distributes them to supermarkets and other retail outlets.

Exhibit 15-3 presents an overview of the basic relationships in this example. Summary data for May 2010 are as follows:

◆ **Raw milk processed:** 4,400 hectolitres (hL) of fluid raw milk with a 10% shrinkage of 400 hL due to evaporation and spillage, to net 4,000 hL of cream and liquid cream for sale. One hectolitre equals 100 litres. After the raw milk is received at the Farmers' Dairy processing plant it is separated in machines.

EXHIBIT 15-3
Farmers' Dairy: Example 1 Overview

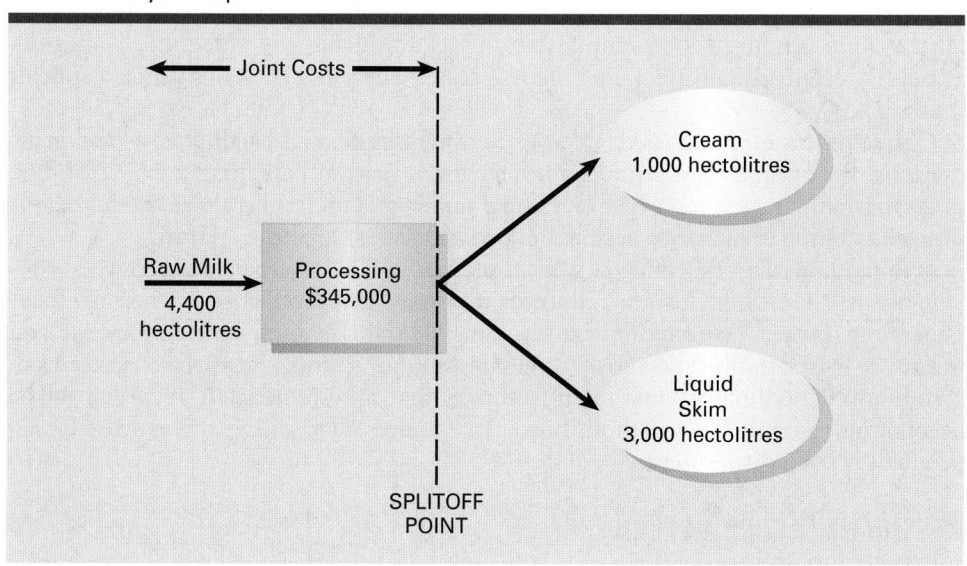

[1]See J. Crespi and J. Harris, "Joint Cost Allocation Under the Natural Gas Act: An Historical Review," *Journal of Extractive Industries Accounting*, 2.2 (1983): 133–142. Also see International Accounting Standards Committee Foundation, *IASC Issues Paper: Extractive Industries* (London, United Kingdom: IASB, 2000).

- **Inventories:** The inventory amounts are shown in the table below.
- Cost of processing 4,400 hL of fluid raw milk and processing it up to the splitoff point to yield 1,000 hL of cream and 3,000 hL of liquid skim: $345,000

	A	B	C
1		Joint Costs	
2	Joint costs (costs of 4,400 hectolitres of raw milk and processing to splitoff point)		$345,000
3		Cream	Liquid Skim
4	Beginning Inventory (hectolitres)	0	0
5	Production (hectolitres)	1,000	3,000
6	Sales (hectolitres)	800	900
7	Ending Inventory (hectolitres)	200	2,100
8	Selling price per hectolitre	$155.00	$ 75.00

How much of the joint costs of $345,000 should be allocated to the ending inventory of 200 hL of cream and 2,100 hL of liquid skim? The joint production costs of $345,000 cannot be uniquely identified with or traced to either product. The reason is that the products themselves were not separated before the splitoff point. The joint cost allocation methods we now discuss can be used for costing the inventory of cream and liquid skim as well as determining cost of goods sold.

SALES VALUE AT SPLITOFF METHOD

The **sales value at splitoff method** allocates joint costs on the basis of the relative sales value at the splitoff point of the total production in the accounting period for each product. In Exhibit 15-4, Panel A, the sales value at splitoff of the May 2010 production is $155,000 for cream and $225,000 for liquid skim. We then assign a weighting to each product, which is a percentage of total sales value. Using this weighting, we allocate the joint costs to the individual products. This approach uses the sales value of the *entire production of the accounting period* (1,000 hL of cream and 3,000 hL of liquid skim). Why? Because joint costs were incurred on all the units produced, not simply the units sold during the current sales period. Panel B presents the product-line income statement using the sales value at splitoff method.

Use of this method has enabled us to obtain individual product costs and gross margins. Both cream and liquid skim have gross margin percentages of 9.2%. The gross margin percentages are always equal under this method if there are no beginning and ending inventories because all products are sold at the splitoff.

Note how the sales value at splitoff method follows the benefits-received criterion of cost allocation: Costs are allocated to products in proportion to their revenue-generating power (expected revenue). This method is both straightforward and intuitive. The cost-allocation base (total sales value at splitoff) is expressed in terms of a common denominator (amount of revenue) that is systematically recorded in the accounting system. This method, however, requires that selling prices exist for all products at the splitoff point.

PHYSICAL MEASURE METHOD

The **physical measure method** allocates joint costs on the basis of their relative proportions at the splitoff point, using a common physical measure such as weight or volume of the total production of each product. In Example 1, the $345,000 joint costs produced 1,000 hL of cream and 3,000 hL of liquid skim.

Exhibit 15-5 presents the product-line income statement using this method of joint cost allocation. Panel A illustrates the allocation of joint costs to individual products to

EXHIBIT 15-4

Farmers' Dairy Product Line Income Statement for May 2010: Joint Costs Allocated Using Sales Value at Splitoff Method

	A	B	C	D
1	**PANEL A: Allocation of Joint Costs Using Sales Value at Splitoff Method**			
2		**Cream**	**Liquid Skim**	**Total**
3	Sales value of total production at splitoff point (1,000 hL × $155/hL; 3,000 hL × $75/hL).	$155,000	$225,000	$380,000
4	Weighting ($155,000 ÷ $380,000; $225,000 ÷ $380,000)	40.789%	59.211%	
5	Joint costs allocated (0.40789 × $345,000; 0.59211 × $345,000)	140,724	204,276	345,000
6	Joint production cost per hectolitre	$140.724	$ 68.092	
7				
8	**PANEL B: Product-Line Income Statement Using Sales Value at Splitoff Method for May 2010**			
9		**Cream**	**Liquid Skim**	**Total**
10	Revenue (800 hL × $155/hL; 900 hL × $75.00/hL)	$124,000	$ 67,500	$191,500
11	Cost of goods sold (joint costs) Production costs (0.40789 × $345,000; 0.59211 × $345,000)	140,724	204,276	345,000
12	Deduct ending inventory (200 hL × $140.724/hL; 2,100 hL × $68.092/hL)	(28,145)	(142,993)	(171,138)
13	Cost of goods sold (joint costs)	112,579	61,283	173,862
14	Gross margin	$ 11,421	$ 6,217	$ 17,638
15	Gross margin percentage (Gross margin ÷ Revenue)	9.2%	9.2%	9.2%
16				
17	Suppose Farmers' Dairy has beginning inventory of cream and liquid skim milk in May 2010. Suppose further that when this inventory is sold, Farmers' earns a gross margin different from 9.2%. Then the gross-margin percentage for cream and liquid skim milk will be different from the figures shown. The actual value of the gross-margin percentage depends on the proportion of sales of each product from beginning inventory and the proportion from current period production.			

EXHIBIT 15-5

Farmers' Dairy Product-Line Income Statement for May 2010: Joint Costs Allocated Using Physical Measure Method

	A	B	C	D
1	**PANEL A: Allocation of Joint Costs Using Physical Measure Method**			
2		**Cream**	**Liquid Skim**	**Total**
3	Physical measure of total production (hectolitres)	1,000	3,000	4,000
4	Weighting (1,000 ÷ 4,000; 3,000 ÷ 4,000)	0.25	0.75	
5	Joint costs allocated (0.25 × $345,000; 0.75 × $345,000)	$ 86,250	$258,750	$345,000
6	Joint production cost per hectolitre	$ 86.25	$ 86.25	
7				
8	**PANEL B: Product-Line Income Statement Using Physical Measure Method for May 2010**			
9				
10		**Cream**	**Liquid Skim**	**Total**
11	Revenues (800 hL × $155/hL; 900 hL × $75/hL)	$124,000	$ 67,500	$191,500
12	Cost of goods sold (joint costs)			
13	Production costs (0.25 × $345,000; 0.75 × $345,000)	86,250	258,750	345,000
14	Deduct ending inventory (200 hL × $86.25/hL; 2,100 hL × $86.25/hL)	(17,250)	(181,125)	(198,375)
15	Cost of goods sold (joint costs)	69,000	77,625	146,625
16	Gross margin	$ 55,000	$ (10,125)	$ 44,875
17	Gross margin percentage (Gross margin ÷ Revenue)	44.4%	−15.0%	23.4%

calculate cost per hectolitre of cream and liquid skim for ending inventory valuation. This method allocates joint costs on the basis of total hectolitres; therefore, the cost per hectolitre is the same for both products. Panel B presents the product-line income statement using the physical measure method. The gross margin percentages are 44.4% for cream and a *loss* of 15% for liquid skim.

Under the benefits-received criterion, this method is less desirable than the sales value at splitoff method because the physical weights used for allocating joint costs may have no relationship to the revenue-producing power of the individual products.

Consider a mine that extracts ore containing gold, silver, and lead. Use of a common physical measure (tonnes) would result in almost all the costs being allocated to the product that weighs the most—lead, which has the lowest revenue-producing power. This costing method not only is inconsistent with the revenue objective, which is to earn revenue from sales of gold and silver, but also distorts the profit per tonne of the three products. The profit per tonne of gold and silver will be overstated while that of lead will show a sizeable loss.

Another issue arises if the physical measures of output are not straightforward. For example, oil, a liquid, and natural gas, a vapour, are both outputs from production. The physical measure for oil is barrels, but gas is not measured in barrels; therefore, a common measure of equivalent units, such as British Thermal Units (BTU), must be calculated. Most accountants will have to rely on outside technical expertise to complete this calculation. Finally, byproducts and outputs with zero sales value (such as dirt in gold mining) will be excluded from the physical measure used in the denominator.

> *Example 2:* Assume the same situation as in Example 1 except that both cream and liquid skim can be processed further:
>
> ◆ **Cream → buttercream:** 1,000 hL of cream are further processed to yield 800 hL of buttercream at additional processing (separable) costs of $135,000. Buttercream is sold for $385 per hL
>
> ◆ **Liquid skim → condensed milk:** 3,000 hL of liquid skim are further processed to yield 2,000 hL of condensed milk at additional processing costs of $270,000. Condensed milk is sold for $310 per hL.

Sales during the accounting period were 720 hL of buttercream and 1,800 hL of condensed milk. Exhibit 15-6 presents an overview of the basic relationships. Panel A illustrates both the basic relationships in the conversion process from raw milk into cream and liquid skim in a joint production process and the separate processing of cream into buttercream as well as liquid skim into condensed milk. Panel B provides the data for Example 2.

ESTIMATED NET REALIZABLE VALUE (NRV) METHOD

The **estimated net realizable value (NRV) method** allocates joint costs on the basis of the *relative estimated net realizable value* (expected final sales value in the ordinary course of business minus the expected separable costs of production and marketing of the total production of the period). This method is an alternative when selling prices for one or more products at splitoff do not exist. Using this method for Example 2, Exhibit 15-7, Panel A illustrates how joint costs are allocated to individual products to calculate the cost per hectolitre of buttercream and condensed milk for ending inventory valuation. Panel B presents the product-line income statement using the NRV method. Gross margin percentages are 19.2% for both buttercream and condensed milk.

The NRV method is often used for joint products that have no market value at splitoff. This method always requires assumptions about events occurring after the splitoff point. Examples are the quantities or volume of product produced, the unit selling price for each product, and the dollar value of separable costs.

EXHIBIT 15-6
Farmers' Dairy: Example 2 Overview

PANEL A: Graphical Presentation of Processing for Example 2

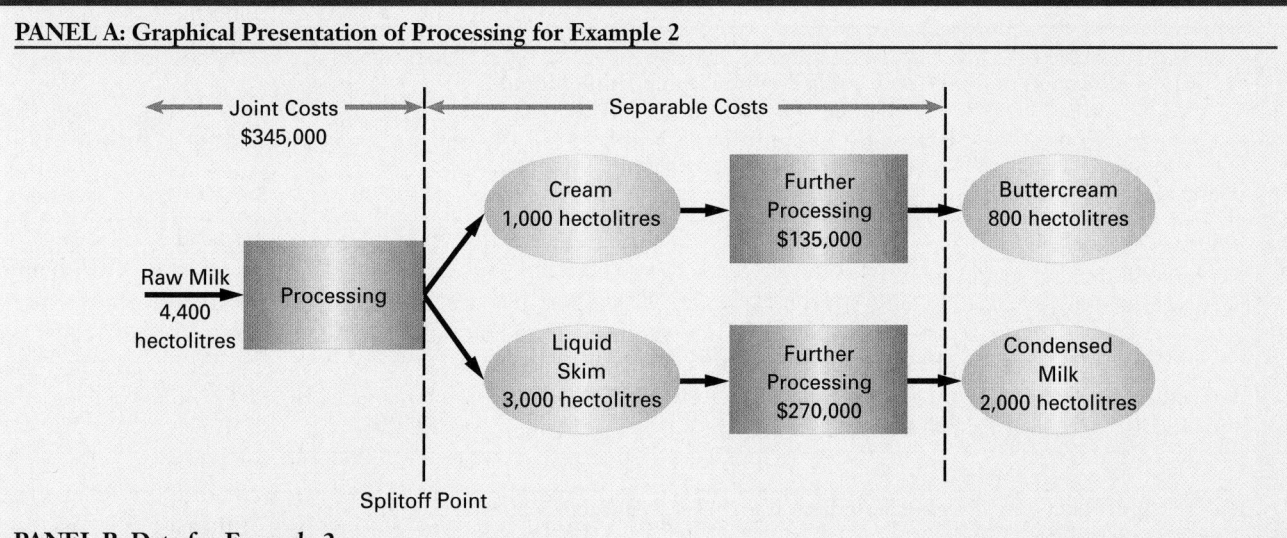

Splitoff Point

PANEL B: Data for Example 2

	A	B	C	D	E
1		Joint Costs		Buttercream	Condensed Milk
2	Joint costs (costs of 4,400 hL fluid milk and processing to splitoff point)	$345,000			
3	Separable cost of processing 1,000 hL cream into 800 hL of buttercream			$135,000	
4	Separable cost of processing 3,000 hL liquid skim into 2,000 hL condensed milk				$270,000
5					
6		Cream	Liquid Skim	Buttercream	Condensed Milk
7	Beginning inventory (hectolitres)	0	0	0	0
8	Production (hectolitres)	1,000	3,000	800	2,000
9	Transfer for further processing (hectolitres)	1,000	3,000		
10	Sales (hectolitres)			720	1,800
11	Ending inventory (hectolitres)	0	0	80	200
12	Selling price per hectolitre	$ 155.00	$75.00	$ 385.00	$ 310.00

Estimating the net realizable value of each product at the splitoff point requires information about the subsequent processing steps to be taken (and their expected separable costs). This is not straightforward because, for example in petrochemical plants, there are alternatives among possible subsequent steps. Companies will frequently change further processing to exploit fluctuations in the separable costs of each processing stage or in the selling prices of individual products. Under the estimated NRV method, each such change would affect the joint cost allocation percentages. In practice, a set of standard subsequent steps is assumed at the start of the accounting period when using the estimated NRV method. Another consideration is that the estimated NRV method is clear-cut when there is only one splitoff point. When there are multiple splitoff points, however, additional allocations may be required if processes subsequent to the initial splitoff point subsequently converge with each other to create a second joint-cost situation.

EXHIBIT 15-7
Joint-Cost Allocation and Product-Line Income Statement Using NRV Method: Farmers' Dairy for May 2010

	A	B	C	D
1	**PANEL A: Allocation of Joint Costs Using Net Realizable Value Method**			
2		**Buttercream**	**Condensed Milk**	**Total**
3	Final sales value of total production during the accounting period (800 hL × $385/hL; 2,000 hL × $310/hL)	$308,000	$620,000	$928,000
4	Deduct separable costs	135,000	270,000	405,000
5	Net realizable value at splitoff point	$173,000	$350,000	$523,000
6	Weighting ($173,000 ÷ $523,000; $350,000 ÷ $523,000)	0.33	0.67	
7	Joint costs allocated (0.33 × $345,000; 0.67 × $345,000)	$113,850	$231,150	$345,000
8	Production cost per hectolitre ([$113,850 + $135,000] ÷ 800 hL [$231,150 + $270,000] ÷ 2,000 hL)	$311.063	$250.575	
9				
10	**PANEL B: Product-Line Income Statement Using Net Realizable Value Method for May 2010**			
11		**Buttercream**	**Condensed Milk**	**Total**
12	Revenue (720 hL × $385/hL; 1,800 hL × $310/hL)	$277,200	$558,000	$835,200
13	Cost of goods sold Joint costs (0.33 × $345,000; 0.67 × $345,000)	113,850	231,150	345,000
14	Separable costs	135,000	270,000	405,000
15	Production costs	248,850	501,150	750,000
16	Deduct ending inventory (80 hL × $311.063; 200 hL × $250.575)	(24,885)	(50,115)	(75,000)
17	Cost of goods sold	223,965	451,035	675,000
18	Gross margin	$ 53,235	$106,965	$160,200
19	Gross margin percentage (Gross margin ÷ Revenue)	19.2%	19.2%	19.2%

The sales value at splitoff method is less complex than the estimated NRV method, as it does not require knowledge of the subsequent steps in processing. However, it is not always feasible to use the sales value at splitoff method. Why? Because there may not be any market prices at the splitoff point for one or more individual products. Market prices may not first appear until after processing beyond the splitoff point has occurred.

Consider two chicken processing companies, Northern and West Coast (disguised names). Northern classifies white breast meat as the only main product and all others are byproducts. The revenue from byproducts will reduce the main product chicken processing costs. White breast meat is often further processed into many individual products (such as trimmed chicken and marinated chicken). The separable cost of this further processing is added to the cost per kilogram of deboned white breast meat to obtain the cost of further-processed products.

West Coast classifies any product sold to a retail outlet as a joint product. Such products include breast fillets, half-breasts, thighs, whole legs, and wings. Products not sold to a retail outlet are classified as byproducts. Revenue that will be earned from byproducts is offset against the chicken-processing cost before that cost is allocated among the joint products. Average selling prices of products sold to retail outlets are used to allocate net chicken processing cost to the individual joint products. Distribution costs of transporting the chicken products from the processing plants to retail outlets are not taken into account when determining weights for joint cost allocation.[2]

---

[2]Adapted from conversations with executives of poultry firms.

CONSTANT GROSS MARGIN PERCENTAGE NRV METHOD

The **constant gross margin percentage NRV method** works in reverse. For each product, the gross margin (based on the overall gross margin percentage) and separable costs are deducted from the final sales value of units produced. The residual amount for each product is its allocation of joint costs.

The constant gross margin percentage NRV method allocates joint costs in such a way that the overall gross margin percentage is identical for all the individual products. This method entails three steps:

◆ **Step 1.** Compute the overall gross margin percentage.

◆ **Step 2.** Use the overall gross margin percentage and deduct the gross margin from the final sales values to obtain the total costs that each product should bear.

◆ **Step 3.** Deduct the expected separable costs from the total costs to obtain the joint cost allocation.

Exhibit 15-8, Panel A illustrates these three steps for allocating the $345,000 joint costs between buttercream and condensed milk in the Farmers' Dairy example to calculate the cost per hectolitre of buttercream and condensed milk for valuation of ending inventory. Panel B presents the product-line income statement for the constant gross margin percentage NRV method.

The tenuous assumption underlying the constant gross margin percentage NRV method is that all the products have the same ratio of cost to sales value. A constant ratio of cost to sales value across products is rarely seen in companies that produce multiple products but have no joint costs.

> ### THINKING CRITICALLY
>
> What does this method mean? Explain in a sentence or two. Read on for a discussion of this topic.

This variation on the NRV method means the gross margin percentage will be identical for each product, irrespective of its separable costs. In effect, products with relatively high separable costs are subsidized because they are assigned a lower proportion of joint costs. This seems counter-intuitive if the purpose of cost allocation is to avoid cross-subsidization.

	A	B	C	D
1	**PANEL A: Allocation of Joint Costs Using Constant Gross Margin Percentage NRV Method**			
2	**Step 1**			
3	Final sales value of total production during the accounting period (800 hL × $385/hL; 2,000 hL × $310)	$928,000		
4	Deduct joint and separable costs ($345,000 + $135,000 + $270,000)	750,000		
5	Gross margin	$178,000		
6	Gross margin percentage (Gross margin ÷ Revenue)	19.181%		
7				
8	**Step 2**	**Buttercream**	**Condensed Milk**	**Total**
9	Final sales value of total production during accounting period (800 hL × $385/hL; 2,000 hL × $310)	$308,000	$620,000	$928,000
10	Deduct gross margin, using constant gross margin percentage (19.181% × $308,000; 19.181% × $620,000)	59,078	118,922	178,000
11	Total production costs	248,922	501,078	750,000
12	**Step 3**			
13	Deduct separable costs	(135,000)	(270,000)	(405,000)
14	Joint costs allocated	$113,922	$231,078	$345,000
15				
16	**PANEL B: Product-Line Income Statement Using Constant Gross Margin Percentage NRV Method for May 2010**			
17		**Buttercream**	**Condensed Milk**	**Total**
18	Revenue (720 hL × $385/hL; 1,800 hL × $310/hL)	$277,200	$558,000	$835,200
19	Cost of goods sold Joint costs (from PANEL A, Step 3)	113,922	231,078	345,000
20	Separable costs	135,000	270,000	405,000
21	Production costs	248,922	501,078	750,000
22	*Deduct ending inventory (80 hL × $311.15/hL; 200 hL × $250.54)	(24,892)	(50,108)	(75,000)
23	Cost of goods sold	224,030	450,970	675,000
24	Gross margin	$ 53,170	$107,030	$160,200
25	Gross margin percentage (Gross margin ÷ revenue)	19.2%	19.2%	19.2%
26				
27	*Total production cost of buttercream ÷ Total production of buttercream	$ 311.15/hL		
28	Total production cost of condensed milk ÷ Total production of condensed milk		$ 250.54/hL	

COMPARISON OF METHODS

Which method of allocating joint costs should be chosen? Because the costs are joint in nature, managers cannot use the cause-and-effect criterion in making this choice. Managers cannot be sure what causes what cost when examining joint costs. The benefits-received criterion leads to a preference for the sales value at splitoff point method (or other related revenue or market-based methods). Additional benefits of this method include the following:

◆ **No anticipation of subsequent management decisions.** The sales value at splitoff method does not presuppose an exact number of subsequent steps undertaken for further processing.

◆ **Availability of meaningful common denominator to compute the weighting factors.** The denominator of the sales value at splitoff method (dollars) is a meaningful one. In contrast, the physical measure method may lack a meaningful common denominator for all the separable products (for example, when some products are liquids and other products are solids).

◆ **Simplicity.** The sales value at splitoff method is simple. In contrast, the estimated NRV method can be very complex in operations with multiple products and multiple splitoff points. The total sales value at splitoff is unaffected by any change in the production process after the splitoff point.

The purpose of the joint cost allocation is important. Consider rate regulation. Market-based measures are difficult to use in this context. It is circular to use selling prices as a basis for setting prices (rates) and at the same time use selling prices to allocate the costs on which prices (rates) are based. Physical measures represent one joint cost allocation approach appropriate for rate regulation.

Market-based measures are preferred for joint cost allocation, with the net realizable value method the predominant choice. The most common alternative market-based measure was a variation of the net realizable value method, in which the final sales value of each product is used as the allocation base without any deduction for the expected separable costs of production and marketing. This variation illustrates how companies may make their own adjustment to the basic methods described in this chapter, often on the grounds of a perceived cost-benefit basis.

ASSESS YOUR MASTERY

MyAccountingLab

To check your understanding of the material in Learning Objective ❷, go to the *Mastery Questions* section at the end of this chapter and complete Learning Objective ❷ questions 1 and 2.

REAL COMPANIES

Challenges of Joint Costing

The petroleum industry is an example of an industry with joint costs. Petroleum mining and processing start with extracting hydrocarbons. During this process, petroleum companies frequently obtain multiple products from the same field, such as crude oil, natural gas, and raw liquefied petroleum gas (LPG). One survey of European petroleum-producing companies found that 46% allocate joint costs to gas and oil extracted from the same field.[a] Of those companies, 33% use market-based methods, 50% use the physical-measure method, and 17% use other methods. For American companies, among market-based methods, the NRV method was the predominant choice. The most

common other market-based choice was a variation of the NRV method in which the final sales value of each product was used as the allocation base without any deduction for the expected separable costs.[b] This variation illustrates how companies make adjustments to the basic methods described in this chapter, often on the grounds of a perceived cost-benefit basis.

Market-based methods methods	
Net realizable value	46%
Other	20%
Physical-measure method	
Volume (barrels, litres, or cubic metres)	27%
Mass (weight or molecular mass)	2%
Other	5%
	100%

[a] Coopers & Lybrand, *Survey of Accounting Practices in the European Oil and Gas Industry* (Denton, TX: Coopers & Lybrand/University of North Texas, February 1997).

[b] R. Koester and D. Barnett, "Petroleum Refinery Joint Cost Allocation," Working Paper, California State University, Dominguez Hills, 1996.

IRRELEVANCE OF JOINT COSTS FOR DECISION MAKING

3 Explain the irrelevance of joint costs in deciding to sell or further process inputs

All the preceding methods of allocating joint costs to individual products are subject to criticism. As a result, some companies refrain from joint cost allocation entirely. Instead, they carry all inventories at estimated net realizable value. Income on each product is recognized when production is completed. Industries that use variations of this approach include meat packing, canning, and mining.

Accountants ordinarily criticize carrying inventories at estimated net realizable values because income is recognized before sales are made. Partly in response to this criticism, some companies using this no-allocation approach carry their inventories at estimated net realizable values minus a normal profit margin.

Exhibit 15-9 presents the product-line income statement with no allocation of joint costs for Example 2. The separable costs are assigned first, which highlights for managers the cause-and-effect relationship between individual products and the costs incurred on them. The joint costs are not allocated to buttercream and condensed milk as individual products.

No technique for allocating joint product costs should guide management decisions regarding whether a product should be sold at the splitoff point or processed beyond splitoff. When a product is an inevitable result of a joint process, the decision to further process should not be influenced either by the size of the total joint costs or by the portion of the joint costs allocated to particular products. Instead, managers should use the relevant cost concepts introduced in Chapter 11.

SELL OR FURTHER PROCESS?

The decision to incur additional costs beyond splitoff should be based on the incremental operating income attainable beyond the splitoff point. Example 2 assumed that it was profitable for both cream and liquid skim to be further processed into buttercream and condensed milk, respectively. The incremental analysis for these decisions to further process is as follows:

	Buttercream	Condensed Milk	Total
Incremental revenue (buttercream–cream; liquid skim–condensed milk)[3]	$153,200	$490,500	$643,700
Incremental costs (buttercream–cream; liquid skim–condensed milk)	135,000	270,000	405,000
Incremental operating income	$ 18,200	$220,500	$238,700

EXHIBIT 15-9
Farmers' Dairy Product-Line Income Statement for May 2010: No Allocation of Joint Costs

	A	B	C	D
1		**Buttercream**	**Condensed Milk**	**Total**
2	Produced and sold (buttercream, 720 hL × $385/hL; 1,800 hL × $310/hL)	$277,200	$558,000	$835,200
3	Produced but not sold (buttercream 80 hL × $385/hL; 200 hL × $310/hL)	24,892	50,108	75,000
4	Total sales value of production	302,092	608,108	910,200
5	Separable costs (given)	135,000	270,000	405,000
6	Contribution to joint costs and operating income	$167,092	$338,108	505,200
7	Joint costs (given)			345,000
8	Gross margin			$160,200
9	Gross margin percentage (Gross margin ÷ Revenue)			19.2%

[3]Buttercream is a further processing of cream. Cream revenue was $124,000 (Exh. 15-5) for 500 hL at $155/hL. The new unit cost is $385/hL and the new quantity is 720 hL, resulting in Buttercream revenue of $277,200. The difference between the Buttercream and Cream revenue is $153,200.

The amount of joint costs incurred up to splitoff ($345,000)—and how it is allocated—is irrelevant in deciding whether to process further cream or liquid skim. Why? Because the joint costs of $345,000 are the same whether or not further processing is done.

Incremental costs are those costs that differ between the alternatives being considered (such as sell or process further). Do not assume that all separable costs in our joint cost allocations for product-costing purposes are always incremental costs. For example, some separable costs may be allocated costs that do not differ between the specific alternatives being considered.

ASSESS YOUR MASTERY

To check your understanding of the material in Learning Objective ③, go to the *Mastery Questions* section at the end of this chapter and complete Learning Objective ③ question 1.

MyAccountingLab

CHALLENGES FOR MANAGEMENT ACCOUNTANTS

Understand the governance challenges of joint costing ④

The potential conflict between the cost concepts used for decision making and those used for evaluating the performance of managers is a key theme of this book. If managers make process (and process or sell) decisions using an incremental revenue/incremental cost approach, the resulting budgeted product-line income statement using any of the three methods under the market-based approach (sales value at splitoff, estimated NRV, and constant gross margin percentage NRV) will all show each individual product budgeted to have a positive (or zero) operating income (as long as the incremental costs do not exceed the incremental revenues). In contrast, allocating joint costs using a physical measure can show a manager being responsible for one or more products budgeted to have losses even though the company has higher operating income by producing those products in a joint-product setting.

Consider again Example 1 (Farmers' Dairy) with the following change. The selling price per hL of liquid skim increases by 20%. This change would not affect the joint costs allocated and the cost of goods computed using the physical measure method (see Exhibit 15-5, p. 747). However, it would affect the revenues of the liquid skim product. The revised product-line income statement for May 2010 using the physical measure method is

	A	B	C	D
1	**PANEL B: Product-Line Income Statement Using Physical Measure Method for May 2010**			
2		**Cream**	**Liquid Skim**	**Total**
3	Revenues (800 hL × $155/hL; 900 hL × $90/hL)	$124,000	$81,000	$205,000
4	Cost of goods sold (joint costs)			
5	Production costs (0.25 × $345,000; 0.75 × $345,000)	86,250	258,750	345,000
6	Deduct ending inventory (200 hL × $86.25/hL; 2,100 hL × $86.25/hL)	(17,250)	(181,125)	(198,375)
7	Cost of goods sold (joint costs)	69,000	77,625	146,625
8	Gross margin	$ 55,000	$ 3,375	$ 58,375
9	Gross margin percentage (Gross margin ÷ Revenue)	44.4%	4.2%	28.5%

Note that the liquid skim product now has a positive gross margin percentage of 4.2% (highly improved from the former loss of 15%). On the basis of the initial

Management Accountants: Overcoming the Pitfalls of Allocating Joint Costs

When you think of companies such as the Hershey Company, Oscar Mayer (a subsidiary of Kraft Foods Inc.), and Petro-Canada, perhaps the first thing that comes to mind is a chocolate bar, a hot dog at a hockey game, or the high cost of gasoline. Chances are you don't think about the accounting challenges the management accountants at these companies face on a daily basis. Unfortunately, this process is somewhat arbitrary, which means product managers, who are evaluated on product profitability, invariably favour joint cost allocations that assign the lowest joint costs to their department. However, allocating joint costs in the way that product managers want may not be in the best interests of the company as a whole. Management accountants' decisions should never be influenced by product managers who might be more concerned with their own performance. Challenges with joint cost allocations can also arise when two separate companies, such as Petro-Canada and British Petroleum, enter into a joint venture to produce crude oil and natural gas from petroleum, with one company processing primarily the crude oil and the other company processing primarily the natural gas. The contract terms often spell out how joint costs—such as labour and manufacturing overhead—are to be allocated. It is the responsibility of the management accountants to ensure that both sides adhere to the terms of the contract when allocating joint costs to the two companies. When circumstances arise that are not specifically covered by the contract clauses, management accountants must have the integrity to make decisions in a fair and unbiased manner.

loss reported using the physical measure method, a manager who is evaluated on the basis of product-by-product gross margin information will be reluctant to process the raw milk into cream and liquid skim to avoid having to explain why liquid skim is being produced at a negative gross margin. This also obscures the opportunity to exploit added profitability from processing further into buttercream and condensed milk. Under this method, a price change, which is beyond the processing manager's control, is crucial to improving profitability. Use of a market-based joint cost allocation method avoids this situation.

MyAccountingLab

ASSESS YOUR MASTERY

To check your understanding of the material in Learning Objective **4**, go to the *Mastery Questions* section at the end of this chapter and complete Learning Objective **4** question 1.

ACCOUNTING FOR BYPRODUCTS

5 Account for byproducts using two different methods

Processes that yield joint products often also yield what are frequently called byproducts—products that have relatively low sales value compared with the sales value of the main or joint product(s). We now discuss accounting for byproducts. To simplify the discussion, consider a two-product example consisting of a main product and a byproduct.

Joint production processes may yield not only joint products and main products but byproducts as well. Although byproducts have low total sales values compared with total sales values of joint or main products, the presence of byproducts in a joint production process can affect the allocation of joint costs. Let's consider a two-product example consisting of a main product and a byproduct.

Example 3: The Westlake Corporation processes timber into fine-grade lumber and wood chips that are used as mulch in gardens and lawns. Information about these products follows:

- Fine-grade lumber (the main product)—sells for $505 per thousand board feet (MBF), or $0.505 per board foot
- Wood chips (the byproduct)—sell for $86 per oven-dried tonne

Data for 2010 are:

	A	B	C	D	E
1		Beginning Inventory	Production	Sales	Ending Inventory
2	Fine grade lumber, million board feet (MMBF)	0	4,000	3,950	50
3	Wood chips, thousands of oven-dried tonnes	0	700	450	250
4		Softwood	Chips		
5	Prices (per MBF, lumber, per tonne, chips)	$505	$ 86		
6		Direct Materials	Conversion	Total	
7	Joint manufacturing costs ($ millions)	$356	$1,068	$1,424	
8	Note: MBF = thousand board feet; MMBF = million board feet				

Joint manufacturing costs for these products were $1,424 million, comprising $356 million for direct materials and $1,068 million for conversion costs. Both products are sold at the splitoff point without further processing, as Exhibit 15-10 shows.

Two byproduct accounting methods will be presented. Method A (the production byproduct method) recognizes byproducts in the financial statements at the time their production is completed. Method B (the sale byproduct method) delays recognition of byproducts until the time of their sale.[4] Recognition of byproducts at the time of production is conceptually correct. Where recognition at the time of sales occurs in practice, it is usually rationalized on the grounds that the dollar amounts of byproducts are immaterial. Exhibit 15-11 presents the income statement of the Westlake Corporation under both methods.

EXHIBIT 15-10
Example 3: Overview of Westlake Corporation

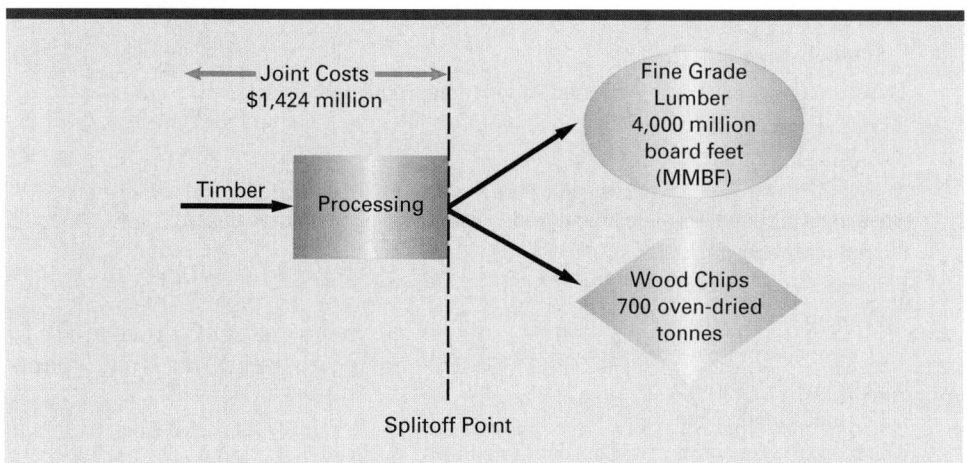

[4]Further discussion on byproduct accounting methods is in C. Cheatham and M. Green, "Teaching Accounting for Byproducts," *Management Accounting News & Views* (Spring 1988): 14–15; and D. Stout and D. Wygal, "Making Byproducts a Main Product of Discussion: A Challenge to Accounting Educators," *Journal of Accounting Education* (1989): 219–233. See also P. D. Marshall and R. F. Dombrowski, "A Small Business Review of Accounting for Primary Products, Byproducts and Scrap," *The National Public Accountant* (February/March 2003): 10–13.

EXHIBIT 15-11

Income Statements of Westlake Corporation for July 2010 Using the Production and Sales Methods for Byproduct Accounting

	Production Method	Sales Method
Revenues ($ millions)		
Main product fine grade lumber (3,950 MMBF × $505/MBF)	$1,995	$1,995
Byproduct pulp quality wood chips (450 tonnes × $86/tonne)	—	39
Total revenue	1,995	2,034
Cost of goods sold		
Total manufacturing costs	1,424	1,424
Deduct byproduct sales value (700 tonnes × $86/tonne)	(60)	$ —
Net manufacturing costs	1,364	1,424
Deduct main product ending inventory	(17)	(18)
Cost of goods sold	1,347	1,406
Gross margin	$ 649	$ 628
Gross margin percentage	32.5%	30.9%
Inventoriable costs (end of the period)		
Main product fine grade lumber	$17.05[a]	$ 17.80[b]
Byproduct pulp quality wood chips	$86.00[c]	$ 0[d]

[a]$1,364 × 50 ÷ 4,000 = $17.05
[b]$1,424 × 50 ÷ 4,000 = $17.80
[c]$86 × 250 = $21,500 total for remaining tonnes in inventory
[d]zero inventory value carried in books for byproduct not sold under sales method

METHOD A: BYPRODUCTS RECOGNIZED AT TIME PRODUCTION IS COMPLETED

This method recognizes in the financial statements the byproduct—700 tonnes of wood chips—as it is produced in 2010. The estimated net realizable value from the byproduct is offset against the costs of the main (or joint) products. The following journal entries illustrate this method (all amounts in million $):

1. Work in Process	$ 356	
Accounts Payable		$ 356

To record direct materials purchased and used in production.

2. Work in Process	$1,068	
Various accounts		$1,068

To record conversion costs in the joint process during 2010; examples include energy, manufacturing supplies, all manufacturing labour, and plant amortization.

3. Byproduct Inventory: Chips	$ 60	
Finished goods: Softwood ($1,424 − $60)	$1,364	
Work in Process ($356 + 1,068)		$1,424

To record cost of goods completed during 2010.

4a. Cost of Goods Sold	$1,347	
Finished Goods: Softwood		$1,347

To record the cost of the main product sold during 2010.

4b. Cash or Accounts Receivable (3,950/MMBF × $505/MBF)	$1,995	
Revenues: Softwood		$1,995

To record the sale of the main product during 2010.

5. Cash or Accounts Receivable (450 × $86)	$ 39	
Byproduct Inventory: Chips		$ 39

To record the sale of the byproduct during 2010.

This method reports the byproduct inventories of oven-dried wood chips on the balance sheet at their per-tonne selling price.

One variant of this method would be to report byproduct inventory at its estimated net realizable value reduced by a normal profit margin. When the byproduct inventory is sold in a subsequent period, the income statement would match the selling price with the "net" selling price repor8ted for the byproduct inventory.

METHOD B: BYPRODUCTS RECOGNIZED AT TIME OF SALE

This method makes no journal entries until sale of the byproduct occurs. Revenues of the byproduct are reported as a revenue item in the income statement at the time of sale. In the Westlake Corporation example, byproduct revenues in 2010 would be $39 million because only 450,000 tonnes of chips are sold in 2010.

All amounts in million $:

1. Work in Process	$ 356	
Accounts Payable		$ 356
To record direct materials purchased and used in production.		
2. Work in Process	$1,068	
Various accounts		$1,068
To record conversion costs in the joint process during 2010; examples include energy, manufacturing supplies, all manufacturing labour, and plant amortization.		
3. Finished goods: Softwood	$1,424	
Work in Process ($356 + 1,068)		$1,424
To record cost of goods completed during 2010.		
4a. Cost of Goods Sold	$1,406	
Finished Goods: Softwood		$1,406
To record the cost of the main product sold during 2010.		
4b. Cash or Accounts Receivable (3,950/MMBF × $505/MBF)	$1,995	
Revenues: Softwood		$1,995
To record the sale of the main product during 2010.		
5. Cash or Accounts Receivable (450 × $86)	$ 39	
Revenues: Chips		$ 39
To record the sale of the byproduct during 2010.		

Method B is rationalized in practice primarily on the grounds that the dollar amounts of byproducts are immaterial. However, this method permits managers to "manage" reported earnings by timing when they sell byproducts. Managers may stockpile byproducts so that they have the flexibility to give revenues a boost" at opportune times.

PULLING IT ALL TOGETHER—PROBLEM FOR SELF-STUDY

Inorganic Chemicals (IC) processes salt into various industrial products. In July 2010, IC incurred joint costs of $100,000 to purchase salt and convert it into two saleable products: caustic soda and chlorine. Although there is an active outside market for chlorine, IC processes all 800 tonnes of chlorine it produces into 500 tonnes of PVC (polyvinyl chloride), which is then sold. There were no beginning or ending inventories of salt, caustic soda, chlorine, or PVC in July. Information for July 2010 production and sales follows:

	A	B	C	D
1		**Joint Costs**		**PVC**
2	Joint costs (costs of salt and processing to splitoff point)	$100,000		
3	Separable cost of processing 800 tonnes chlorine into 500 tonnes PVC			$20,000
4				
5		**Caustic Soda**	**Chlorine**	**PVC**
6	Beginning inventory (tonnes)	0	0	0
7	Production (tonnes)	1,200	800	500
8	Transfer for further processing (tonnes)		800	
9	Sales (tonnes)	1,200	—	500
10	Ending inventory (tonnes)	0	0	0
11	Selling price per tonne in active outside market (for products not actually sold)		$ 75	
12	Selling price per tonne for products sold	$ 50		$ 200

REQUIRED

1. Allocate the joint costs of $100,000 between caustic soda and chlorine under (a) the sales value at splitoff method and (b) the physical measure method.
2. Allocate the joint costs of $100,000 between caustic soda and PVC under the estimated NRV method.
3. What is the gross margin percentage of (a) caustic soda and (b) PVC under the estimated three allocation methods?
4. Lifetime Swimming Pool Products offers to purchase 800 tonnes of chlorine in August 2010 at $75 per tonne. Assume all other production and sales data are the same for August as they were for July. This sale of chlorine to Lifetime would mean that no PVC would be produced by IC in August. How would accepting this offer affect IC's August 2010 operating income?

SOLUTION

1a. Sales value at splitoff method

	A	B	C	D
1	**Allocation of Joint Costs Using Sales Value at Splitoff Method**	**Caustic Soda**	**Chlorine**	**Total**
2	Sales value of total production at splitoff point (1,200 tonnes × $50 per tonne; 800 tonnes × $75 per tonne)	$60,000	$60,000	$120,000
3	Weighting ($60,000 ÷ $120,000; $60,000 ÷ $120,000)	0.50	0.50	
4	Joint costs allocated (0.50 × $100,000; 0.50 × $100,000)	$50,000	$50,000	$100,000

1b. Physical-measure method

	A	B	C	D
1	**Allocation of Joint Costs Using Physical Measure Method**	**Caustic Soda**	**Chlorine**	**Total**
2	Physical measure of total production (tonnes)	1,200	800	2,000
3	Weighting (1,200 tonnes ÷ 2,000 tonnes; 800 tonnes ÷ 2,000 tonnes)	0.60	0.40	
4	Joint costs allocated (0.60 × $100,000; 0.40 × $100,000)	$60,000	$40,000	$100,000

2. Estimated net realizable value method

Allocation of Joint Costs Using Estimated Net Realizable Value Method	Caustic Soda	PVC	Total
Final sales value of total production during accounting period (1,200 tonnes × $50 per tonne; 500 tonnes × $200 per tonne)	$60,000	$100,000	$160,000
Deduct separable costs to complete and sell	0	20,000	20,000
Net realizable value at splitoff point	$60,000	$ 80,000	$140,000
Weighting ($60,000 ÷ $140,000; $80,000 ÷ $140,000)	$\frac{3}{7}$	$\frac{4}{7}$	
Joint costs allocated (caustic, $\frac{3}{7}$ × $100,000; chlorine, $\frac{4}{7}$ × $100,000)	$42,857	$ 57,143	$100,000

3a. Caustic soda

	Sales Value at Splitoff	Physical Measure	Estimated Net Realizable Value
Sales	$60,000	$60,000	$60,000
Joint costs	50,000	60,000	42,857
Gross margin	$10,000	$ 0	$17,143
Gross margin percentage	16.67%	0%	28.57%

3b. PVC

	Sales Value at Splitoff	Physical Measure	Estimated Net Realizable Value
Sales	$100,000	$100,000	$100,000
Joint costs	50,000	40,000	57,143
Separable costs	20,000	20,000	20,000
Gross margin	$ 30,000	$ 40,000	$ 22,857
Gross margin percentage	30.00%	40.00%	22.86%

4. Incremental revenue from further processing of chlorine into PVC

(500 tonnes × $200 per tonne) − (800 tonnes × $75 per tonne)	$40,000
Incremental costs of further processing chlorine into PVC	20,000
Incremental operating income from further processing	$20,000

The operating income of Inorganic Chemicals would be reduced by $20,000 if it sold 800 tonnes of chlorine to Lifetime Swimming Pool Products instead of further processing the chlorine into PVC for sale.

The following decision guidelines use a question-and-answer format to summarize the chapter's main points. Each decision presents a key question. The guideline is the answer to that question.

DECISIONS	GUIDELINES
1. How do joint products differ from byproducts?	Joint products have high total sales value at the splitoff point. A byproduct has a low total sales value at the splitoff point compared with the sales value of a joint or main product. Products can change from byproducts to joint products when their total sales values significantly increase; they can change from joint products to byproducts when their total sales values significantly decrease. The splitoff point is the juncture in a joint production process when the products become separately identifiable.
2. What methods can be used to allocate joint costs to individual products?	The methods available to allocate joint costs to products are sales value at splitoff, estimated NRV, constant gross margin percentage NRV, and physical measure.
3. Are joint costs relevant in a sell-or-process-further analysis?	No, joint costs and how they are allocated are irrelevant in deciding whether to process further because joint costs are the same whether or not further processing occurs.
4. What challenges do management accountants face?	Often information relevant for decision making about products is also used for performance evaluation of managers. Some allocation methods result in a higher gross margin for a product than others. Managers whose performance depends on maximizing gross margin will prefer biased allocation methods.
5. What methods can be used to account for byproducts?	Byproduct accounting methods differ on whether byproducts are recognized in financial statements at the time of production or at the time of sale. Recognition at the time of production is conceptually correct. Recognition at the time of sale is often used in practice because dollar amounts of byproducts are immaterial.

TERMS TO LEARN

This chapter contains definitions of the following important terms

byproduct (p. 742)
constant gross margin percentage NRV method (p. 751)
estimated net realizable value (NRV) method (p. 748)

joint products (p. 742)
main product (p. 742)
physical measure method (p. 746)
product (p. 742)
sales value at splitoff method (p. 746)

scrap (p. 742)
separable costs (p. 742)
splitoff point (p. 742)

MASTERY QUESTIONS

Mastery Questions are rated by proficiency level—elementary, intermediate, and advanced. The solutions appear in the Solutions to Mastery Questions section of MyAccountingLab.

LEARNING OBJECTIVE 1

1. **Usefulness of joint cost allocation—Intermediate.** In the US, organ procurement organizations (OPOs), transplant centres, and the medical professions co-ordinate the organ donation process. The US government pays for this treatment through its Medicare program. What price should the US government pay for these organs from the taxes it collects from all citizens? Often multiple organs are removed from a single donor, meaning that there are joint costs such as operating room time, surgeons' fees, and medications to preserve the organs. The OPOs insist all costs be allocated to each organ, irrespective of whether the organ is actually collected for transplant. For example, lung and kidney donations may be planned but the surgeon discovers post-mortem that the lungs are not viable. A portion of joint costs will still be assigned to the lungs; otherwise, total costs of the donation would be assigned to the kidneys.

The payer, the US government, does not want to pay the joint costs assigned to the lungs. The Medicare program pays only for transplanted organs. Over 62% of all kidney transplants are paid for by Medicare. Two years ago, a government audit revealed that of the total of $80 million in organ acquisition costs, $47 million were unallowable and unsupported.*

*Sources: Department of Health and Human Services Centers for Medicare & Medicaid Services, "Ruling No.: CMS-1543-R," December 21, 2006; Department of Health and Human Services, Office of Inspector General, "Review of Organ Acquisition Costs Claimed by Certified Transplant Centers (A-09-05-00034)," September 28, 2006; and Jim Warren, "CMS Enforcement of Rule Covering Organ Acquisition Fees Could Shut Down SomeOPOs, Transplant Centers,"*Transplant News*, April 28, 2003.

REQUIRED

Of the reasons to use acceptable methods to allocate joint costs, which ones are relevant in this case?

2. **Usefulness of joint cost allocation—Advanced.** Some organs, such as one kidney, part of a liver, part of a lung, bone marrow, and stem cells, can be recovered from live donors. The recovery of these organs requires major surgery and patients are anaesthetized. The surgeon ensures the donor's organs are suffused with a protective chemical and removes the organ. The donated organ is preserved in a chemical and placed in a refrigerated container for immediate transport. The donor often recovers after two to five days in hospital.

In contrast, stem cells are recovered from live donors who receive medication to increase the number of stem cells in the blood for four to five days prior to the transplant. The process is similar to a blood donation. The stem cells are extracted from whole blood removed intravenously from the donor's arm. The rest of the blood is returned to the donor while the stem cells are sealed in plastic packs, placed in a special container, and transported to the recipient. The donor usually returns home to rest for the remainder of the day before resuming normal life. The stem cells are injected intravenously into the recipient's arm.

REQUIRED

1. What costs are incurred beyond the splitoff point that differ between these two types of donations?
2. What would the separable costs be?
3. In Canada, where all medically necessary care is paid for from tax revenue, of what relevance is joint cost allocation?

LEARNING OBJECTIVE 2

1. **Usefulness of joint cost allocation—Intermediate.** Roundtree Chocolates manufactures and distributes chocolate products. It purchases cocoa beans and processes them into two intermediate products:

◆ Chocolate powder liquor base
◆ Milk chocolate liquor base

These two intermediary products become separately identifiable at a single splitoff point. Every 500 kilograms of cocoa beans yields 20 four-litre containers of chocolate powder liquor base and 30 four-litre containers of milk chocolate liquor base.

The chocolate powder liquor base is further processed into chocolate powder. Every 20 containers of chocolate powder liquor base yields 200 kilograms of chocolate powder. The milk chocolate liquor base is further processed into milk chocolate. Every 30 containers of milk chocolate liquor base yields 340 kilograms of milk chocolate.

The following is an overview of the manufacturing operations at Roundtree Chocolates:

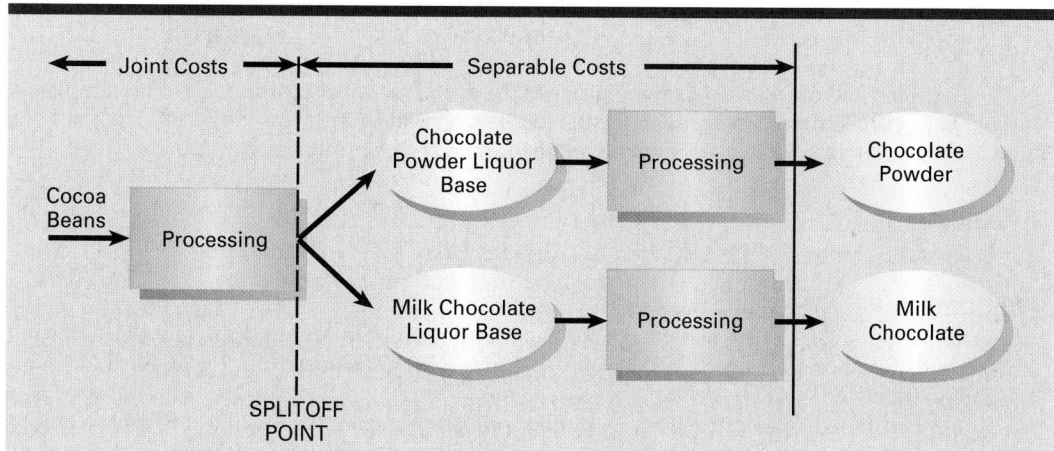

Production and sales data for August 2010 are as follows:

♦ Cocoa beans processed, 5,000 kilograms
♦ Costs of processing cocoa beans to splitoff point (including purchase of beans) = $12,000

	Production	Sales	Unit Selling Price
Chocolate powder	2,000 kilograms	2,000 kilograms	$4.80 per kilogram
Milk chocolate	3,400 kilograms	3,400 kilograms	$6.00 per kilogram

The August 2010 separable costs of processing chocolate powder liquor base into chocolate powder are $5,100. The August 2010 separable costs of processing milk chocolate liquor base into milk chocolate are $10,500.

Roundtree fully processes both of its intermediate products into chocolate powder or milk chocolate. There is an active market for these intermediate products. In August 2010, Roundtree could have sold chocolate powder liquor base for $25.20 a container and milk chocolate liquor base for $31.20 a container.

REQUIRED

1. Calculate how the joint costs of $12,000 would be allocated between chocolate powder liquor base and milk chocolate liquor base under each of the following methods: (a) sales value at splitoff, (b) physical measure (containers), (c) estimated NRV, and (d) constant gross margin percentage NRV.
2. What is the gross margin percentage of chocolate powder and milk chocolate under methods (a), (b), (c), and (d) in requirement 1?
3. Could Roundtree Chocolates have increased its operating income by a change in its decision to fully process both of its intermediate products?

2. **Usefulness of joint cost allocation—Advanced.** The Sunshine Oil Company buys crude vegetable oil. Refining this oil results in four products at the splitoff point: A, B, C, and D. Product C is fully processed at the splitoff point. Products A, B, and D can be individually further refined into Super A, Super B, and Super D. In the most recent month (December), the output at the splitoff point was

Product A	300,000 litres
Product B	100,000 litres
Product C	50,000 litres
Product D	50,000 litres

The joint cost of purchasing the crude vegetable oil and processing it was $120,000.

Sunshine had no beginning or ending inventories. Sales of product C in December were $60,000. Total output of products A, B, and D was further refined and then sold. Data related to December are as follows:

	Separable Processing Costs to Make Super Products	Sales
Super A	$240,000	$360,000
Super B	96,000	120,000
Super D	108,000	144,000

Sunshine had the option of selling products A, B, and D at the splitoff point. This alternative would have yielded the following sales for the December production:

Product A	$60,000
Product B	36,000
Product D	84,000

REQUIRED

1. What is the gross margin percentage for each product sold in December, using the following methods for allocating the $120,000 joint costs: (a) sales value at splitoff, (b) physical measure, and (c) estimated NRV?
2. Could Sunshine have increased its December operating income by making different decisions about the further refining of products A, B, or D? Show the effect on operating income of any changes you recommend.

LEARNING OBJECTIVE 3

1. Irrelevance of joint costs—Advanced. The Wood Spirits Company produces two products, turpentine and methanol (wood alcohol), by a joint process. Joint costs amount to $144,000 per batch of output. Each batch totals 40,000 litres: 25% methanol and 75% turpentine. Both products are processed further without gain or loss in volume. Separable processing costs are methanol, $0.90 per litre; turpentine, $0.60 per litre. Methanol sells for $6.30 per litre. Turpentine sells for $4.20 per litre.

REQUIRED

1. How much joint cost per batch should be allocated to turpentine and to methanol, assuming that joint costs are allocated on a physical-measure (number of litres at splitoff point) basis?
2. If joint costs are to be assigned on an NRV basis, how much joint cost should be assigned to turpentine and to methanol?
3. Prepare product-line income statements per batch for requirements 1 and 2. Assume no beginning or ending inventories.
4. The company has discovered an additional process by which the methanol (wood alcohol) can be made into laboratory ethanol. The selling price of this product would be $18 a litre. Additional processing would increase separate costs $2.70 per litre (in addition to the $0.90 per litre separable cost required to yield methanol). The company would have to pay excise taxes of 20% on the selling price of the product. Assuming no other changes in cost, what is the joint cost applicable to the ethanol (using the NRV method)? Should the company produce the ethanol? Show your computations.

LEARNING OBJECTIVE 4

1. Byproduct, disposal costs, governance. Chemtech Chemicals, a multinational company, has a subsidiary located in a small East European country. The country has only a few environmental protection laws, and even those that exist are not strictly enforced. The subsidiary's three major products emerge at splitoff point from a common input. The joint costs are allocated to each product using the sales values at splitoff method. In addition to the three joint products, another product that emerges at splitoff point is a hazardous material. The hazardous material can be dumped into the Gulf at zero cost to the company. Alternatively, it can be processed further and sold as a cleaning liquid.

The cost accountant responsible for joint cost allocation presented the following comparative analysis to you, the controller:

	Alternatives	
	Dump in the Gulf	**Process Further**
Revenue	$0	$ 600,000
Costs:		
Further processing	0	360,000
Allocated joint costs	0	300,000
Marketing and distribution	0	60,000
Total costs	0	720,000
Net realizable value	$0	$(120,000)

REQUIRED

1. Comment on the comparative analysis prepared by the cost accountant purely from a financial perspective. Show any supporting computations.
2. Assume, regardless of your conclusion in requirement 1, that adopting the process-further alternative would lead to a decrease in the company's operating income. Disposal of the hazardous waste in a manner different than dumping it into the Gulf would also be costly. Discuss the legal and ethical implications of dumping the hazardous material into the Gulf.

LEARNING OBJECTIVE 5

1. Accounting for byproducts—Advanced. (Cheatham and Green, adapted) Bill Dundee is the owner and operator of Western Bottling, a bulk soft drink producer. A single production process yields two bulk soft drinks, Rainbow Dew (the main product) and Resi-Dew (the byproduct). Both products are fully processed at the splitoff point, and there are no separable costs.

Summary data for September 2010 are as follows:

◆ Cost of soft drink operations = $144,000
◆ Production and sales data:

	Production (in Litres)	Sales (in Litres)	Selling Price per Litre
Main product (Rainbow Dew)	10,000	8,000	$24.00
Byproduct (Resi-Dew)	2,000	1,400	2.40

There were no beginning inventories on September 1, 2010. The following is an overview of operations:

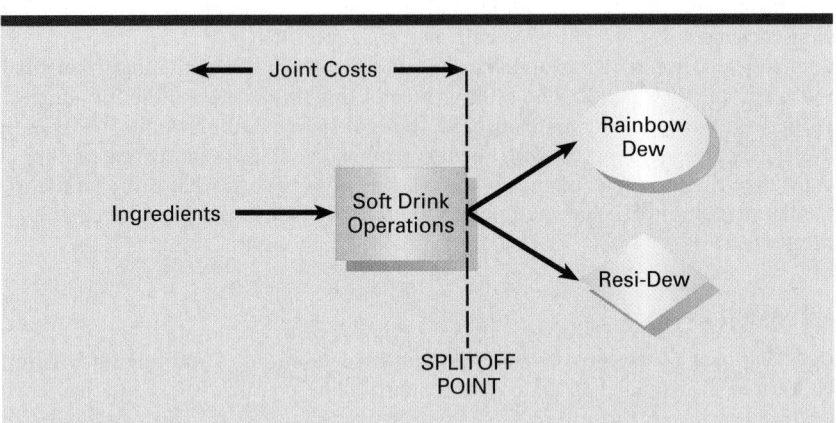

REQUIRED

1. What is the gross margin for Western Bottling under methods A and B of byproduct accounting?
2. What are the inventory amounts reported in the balance sheet on September 30, 2010, for Rainbow Dew and Resi-Dew under each of the two methods of byproduct accounting cited in requirement 1?
3. Which method would you recommend Western Bottling use? Explain.

SHORT-ANSWER QUESTIONS

15-1 Give two examples of industries in which joint costs are found. For each example, what are the individual products at or beyond the splitoff point?

15-2 What is a joint cost? What is a separable cost?

15-3 Distinguish between a joint product and a byproduct.

15-4 Why might the number of products in a joint-cost setting differ from the number of outputs? Give an example.

15-5 Provide three reasons for allocating joint costs to individual products or services.

15-6 Why does the sales value at splitoff method use the sales value of the total production in the accounting period and not just the sales value of the products sold?

15-7 Describe a situation where the sales value at splitoff method cannot be used but the estimated NRV method can be used for joint cost allocation.

15-8 Distinguish between the sales value at splitoff method and the estimated NRV method.

15-9 Give two limitations of the physical measure method of joint cost allocation.

15-10 How might a company simplify its use of the estimated NRV method when the final selling prices can vary sizably in an accounting period and management makes frequent changes to the point at which it sells individual products?

15-11 Why is the constant gross margin percentage NRV method sometimes called a "joint cost and a profit allocation" method?

15-12 "Managers must decide whether a product should be sold at splitoff or processed further. The sales value at splitoff method of joint cost allocation is the best method for generating the information managers need." Do you agree? Why?

15-13 "Managers should consider only additional revenues and separable costs when making decisions about selling now or processing further." Do you agree? Why?

15-14 Describe two major methods to account for byproducts.

15-15 Why might managers with a monthly bonus payment based on attaining a target operating income prefer a byproduct accounting method that recognizes byproducts at the time of sale rather than production?

EXERCISES

15-16 **Joint cost allocation, insurance settlement.** Quality Chicken grows and processes chickens. Each chicken is disassembled into five main parts. Information pertaining to production in July 2009 is:

1. a. Joint costs allocated to breasts, $33.75

Parts	Kilograms of Product	Wholesale Selling Price per Kilogram When Production Is Complete
Breasts	100	$0.55
Wings	20	0.20
Thighs	40	0.35
Bones	80	0.10
Feathers	10	0.05

Joint cost of production in July 2009 was $50.

A special shipment of 40 kilograms of breasts and 15 kilograms of wings has been destroyed in a fire. Quality Chicken's insurance policy provides reimbursement for the cost of the items destroyed. The insurance company permits Quality Chicken to use a joint cost allocation method. The splitoff point is assumed to be at the end of the production process.

REQUIRED
1. Compute the cost of the special shipment destroyed using
   a. Sales value at splitoff method
   b. Physical-measure method (kilograms of finished product)
2. What joint cost allocation method would you recommend Quality Chicken use? Explain.

15-17 **Joint products and byproducts (continuation of 15-16).** Quality Chicken is computing the ending inventory values for its July 31, 2009, balance sheet. Ending inventory amounts on July 31 are 15 kilograms of breasts, 4 kilograms of wings, 6 kilograms of thighs, 5 kilograms of bones, and 2 kilograms of feathers.

1. Wings ending inventory, $0.49

Quality Chicken's management wants to use the sales value at splitoff method. However, they want you to explore the effect on ending inventory values of classifying one or more products as a byproduct rather than a joint product.

REQUIRED
1. Assume Quality Chicken classifies all five products as joint products. What are the ending inventory values of each product on July 31, 2009?
2. Assume Quality Chicken uses the production method of accounting for byproducts. What are the ending inventory values for each joint product on July 31, 2009, assuming breasts and thighs are the joint products and wings, bones, and feathers are byproducts?
3. Comment on differences in the results in requirements 1 and 2.

15-18 Net realizable value cost-allocation method, further process decision. (W. Crum) A crushing and refining process for mineral ore is performed by Montore Inc. It creates three main products, Alco, Devo, and Holo, in a joint-cost operation. Costs and production information for 2010 are as follows:

◆ **Department 1,** at initial joint costs of $504,000, produces 20,000 kilograms of Alco, 60,000 kilograms of Devo, and 100,000 kilograms of Holo.
◆ **Department 2** processes Alco further at a cost of $120,000.
◆ **Department 3** processes Devo further at a cost of $240,000.

Results for 2010 are
◆ **Alco:** 20,000 kilograms completed; 19,000 kilograms sold for $24 per kilogram; ending inventory, 1,000 kilograms.
◆ **Devo:** 60,000 kilograms completed; 59,000 kilograms sold for $7.20 per kilogram; ending inventory, 1,000 kilograms.
◆ **Holo:** 100,000 kilograms completed; 99,000 kilograms sold for $1.20 per kilogram; ending inventory, 1,000 kilograms; Holo required no further processing.

REQUIRED
1. Compute the total costs and unit costs of the ending inventories using the NRV method to allocate the joint costs to the three products.
2. Determine the individual gross margin percentages of the three products.
3. Montore receives an offer to sell all its Devo product for a price of $2.40 per kilogram at the splitoff point before going through Department 3, just as it comes off the production line in Department 1. Using last year's figures, would Montore be better off by selling Devo that way, or processing it through Department 3 and selling it? Show computations to support your answer. Disregard all other factors not mentioned in the problem.

15-19 Process further or sell, joint cost allocation. (R. Capettini) Three products are produced in a joint process by the Maxxim Company. The products are denoted as A, B, and C. The joint costs are composed of a fixed cost of $6,000 and a variable cost of $2.40 per input unit. Each product can be either processed further or, at the splitoff point, it (1) can be sold or (2) must be disposed of at a cost. Out of each input unit, Maxxim Company produces 1 unit of A, 3 units of B, and 2 units of C. In addition, the company has selling and administrative costs of $16,800.

REQUIRED
1. Given the table below, for each product, should Maxxim Company process the product further or dispose of it (or sell it) at the splitoff point, if Maxxim Company inputs 5,000 units? Show, for each product, how much better off Maxxim would be if it followed your advice versus making the alternative decision. Assume that if Maxxim does not further process a product, it does not incur any of the further processing costs.

Product	Selling Price per Unit at Splitoff Point	Cost per Unit to Dispose of Product at Splitoff Point	Further Processing Costs		Selling Price per Unit after Further Processing
			Fixed	**Variable per Unit**	
A	—	$0.24	$ 7,200	$1.08	$1.80
B	$0.60	—	1,200	1.20	1.80
C	—	1.08	12,000	1.32	6.48

2. What is Maxxim Company's gross margin at the 5,000-unit input level?

15-20 Estimated net realizable value method. Divco Inc. produces two joint products, cooking oil and soap oil, from a single vegetable oil refining process. In July 2010, the joint costs of this process were $28,800,000. Separable processing costs beyond the splitoff point were cooking oil, $36,000,000, and soap oil, $9,000,000. Cooking oil sells for $60 per drum. Soap oil sells for $30 per drum. Divco produced and sold 1,000,000 drums of cooking oil and 500,000 drums of soap oil. There are no beginning or ending inventories of cooking oil or soap oil.

REQUIRED
Allocate the $28,800,000 joint costs using the estimated NRV method.

15-21 **Net realizable value method.** Convad Company is one of the world's leading corn refiners. It produces two joint products, corn syrup and corn starch, using a common production process. In July 2009, Convad reported the following production and selling price information:

	Corn Syrup	Corn Starch	Joint Costs
Joint costs (costs of processing corn to splitoff point)			$325,000
Separable cost of processing beyond splitoff point	$375,000	$93,750	
Beginning inventory (cases)	0	0	
Production and sales (cases)	12,500	6,250	
Ending inventory (cases)	0	0	
Selling price per case	$50	$25	

REQUIRED

Allocate the $325,000 joint costs using the NRV method.

15-22 **Joint cost allocation, sales value, physical measure, NRV methods.** Instant Foods produces two types of microwavable products—beef-flavoured ramen and shrimp-flavoured ramen. The two products share common inputs such as noodles and spices. The production of ramen results in a waste product referred to as stock, which Instant dumps at negligible costs in a local drainage area. In June 2009, the following data were reported for the production and sales of beef-flavoured and shrimp-flavoured ramen:

	Joint Costs	
Joint costs (costs of noodles, spices, and other inputs and processing to splitoff point)		$240,000

	Beef Ramen	Shrimp Ramen
Beginning inventory (tonnes)	0	0
Production (tonnes)	10,000	20,000
Sales (tonnes)	10,000	20,000
Selling price per tonne	$10	$15

Due to the popularity of its microwavable products, Instant decides to add a new line of products that targets dieters. These new products are produced by adding a special ingredient to dilute the original ramen and are to be sold under the names Special B and Special S, respectively. The monthly data for all the products follow:

	Joint Costs	Special B	Special S
Joint costs (costs of noodles, spices, and other inputs and processing to splitoff point)	$240,000		
Separable costs of processing 10,000 tonnes of beef ramen into 12,000 tonnes of Special B		$48,000	
Separable cost of processing 20,000 tonnes of shrimp ramen into 24,000 tonnes of Special S			$168,000

	Beef Ramen	Shrimp Ramen	Special B	Special S
Beginning inventory (tonnes)	0	0	0	0
Production (tonnes)	10,000	20,000	12,000	24,000
Transfer for further processing (tonnes)	10,000	20,000		
Sales (tonnes)			12,000	24,000
Selling price per tonne	$ 10	$15	$18	$25

1. Calculate Instant's gross margin percentage for Special B and Special S when joint costs are allocated using:
   a. Sales value at splitoff method
   b. Physical-measure method
   c. Net realizable value method

2. Recently, Instant discovered that the stock it is dumping can be sold to cattle ranchers at $5 per tonne. In a typical month with the production levels shown above, 4,000 tonnes of stock are produced and can be sold by incurring marketing costs of $10,800. Sherrie Dong, a management accountant, points out that in treating the stock as a joint product and using the sales value at splitoff method the stock product would lose about $2,228 each month, so it should not be sold. How did Dong arrive at that final number, and what do you think of her analysis? Should Instant sell the stock?

1. a. Crude oil joint costs allocated, $270

15-23 Joint cost allocation, process further. Sinclair Oil & Gas, a large energy conglomerate, jointly processes purchased hydrocarbons to generate three nonsaleable intermediate products: ICR8, ING4, and XGE3. These intermediate products are further processed separately to produce Crude Oil, Natural Gas Liquids (NGL), and Natural Gas (measured in liquid equivalents). An overview of the process and results for August 2009 is shown here (*Note:* The numbers are small to keep the focus on key concepts):

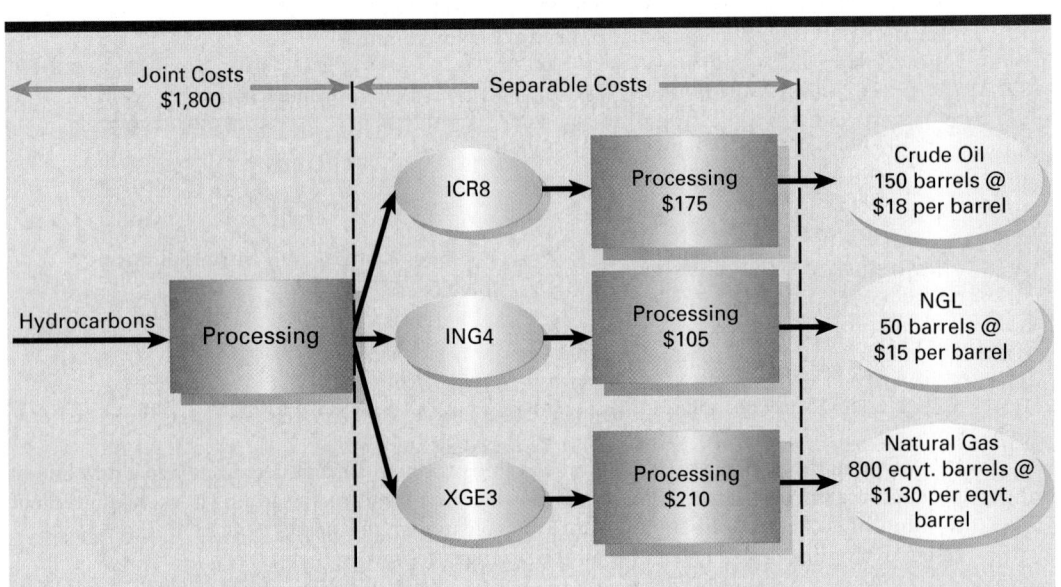

A federal law has recently been passed that taxes crude oil at 30% of operating income. No new tax is to be paid on natural gas liquid or natural gas. Starting August 2009, Sinclair Oil & Gas must report a separate product-line income statement for crude oil. One challenge facing Sinclair Oil & Gas is how to allocate the joint cost of producing the three separate saleable outputs. Assume no beginning or ending inventory.

REQUIRED

1. Allocate the August 2009 joint cost among the three products using
   a. Physical-measure method
   b. NRV method
2. Show the operating income for each product using the methods in requirement 1.
3. Which, if any, method would you use for product emphasis? Explain.
4. Draft a letter to the taxation authorities on behalf of Sinclair Oil & Gas that justifies the joint cost allocation method you recommend Sinclair use.

15-24 Alternative methods of joint cost allocation, ending inventories. The Darl Company operates a simple chemical process to convert a single material into three separate items, referred to here as X, Y, and Z. All three end products are separated simultaneously at a single splitoff point.

Products X and Y are ready for sale immediately upon splitoff without further processing or any other additional costs. Product Z, however, is processed further before being sold. There is no available market price for Z at the splitoff point.

The selling prices quoted here are expected to remain the same in the coming year. During 2009, the selling prices of the items and the total amounts sold were:

1. a. Z net realizable value at splitoff point, $150,000

◆ X—120 tonnes sold for $1,500 per tonne
◆ Y—340 tonnes sold for $1,000 per tonne
◆ Z—475 tonnes sold for $700 per tonne

The total joint manufacturing costs for the year were $400,000. Darl spent an additional $200,000 to finish product Z.

There were no beginning inventories of X, Y, or Z. At the end of the year, the following inventories of completed units were on hand: X, 180 tonnes; Y, 60 tonnes; Z, 25 tonnes. There was no beginning or ending work in process.

REQUIRED

1. Compute the cost of inventories of X, Y, and Z for balance sheet purposes and the cost of goods sold for income statement purposes as of December 31, 2009, using the following joint cost allocation methods:
   a. NRV method
   b. Constant gross margin percentage NRV method.

2. Compare the gross margin percentages for X, Y, and Z using the two methods given in requirement 1.

15-25 Process further or sell, byproduct. (CMA, adapted) Newcastle Mining Company (NMC) mines coal, puts it through a one-step crushing process, and loads the bulk raw coal onto river barges for shipment to customers.

1. Incremental sales revenue, $68,400,000

NMC's management is currently evaluating the possibility of further processing the raw coal by sizing and cleaning it and selling it to an expanded set of customers at higher prices. The option of building a new sizing and cleaning plant is ruled out as being financially infeasible. Instead, Amy Kimbell, a mining engineer, is asked to explore outside contracting arrangements for the cleaning and sizing process. Kimbell puts together the following summary:

Selling price of raw coal	$27	per tonne
Cost of producing raw coal	$22	per tonne
Selling price of sized and cleaned coal	$36	per tonne
Annual raw coal output	10,000,000	tonnes
Percentage of material weight loss in sizing/cleaning coal	6%	

	Incremental Costs of Sizing and Cleaning Processes	
Direct labour	$800,000	per year
Supervisory personnel	$200,000	per year
Heavy equipment: rental, operating, maintenance costs	$ 25,000	per month
Contract sizing and cleaning	$ 3.50	per tonne of raw coal
Outbound rail freight	$ 240	per 60-tonne rail car

Kimbell also learns that 75% of the material loss that occurs in the cleaning and sizing process can be salvaged as coal fines, which can be sold to steel manufacturers for their furnaces. The sale of coal fines is erratic and NMC may need to stockpile it in a protected area for up to one year. The selling price of coal fines ranges from $15 to $24 per tonne and costs of preparing coal fines for sale range from $2 to $4 per tonne.

REQUIRED

1. Prepare an analysis to show whether it is more profitable for NMC to continue selling raw bulk coal or to process it further through sizing and cleaning. (Ignore coal fines in your analysis.)

2. How would your analysis be affected if the cost of producing raw coal could be held down to $20 per tonne?

3. Now consider the potential value of the coal fines and prepare an addendum that shows how their value affects the results of your analysis prepared in requirement 1.

1. Total revenues under sales method, $668,000

15-26 Accounting for a main product and a byproduct. (Cheatham and Green, adapted) Yum Inc. is a producer of potato chips. A single production process at Yum Inc. yields potato chips as the main product and a byproduct that can also be sold as a snack. Both products are fully processed by the splitoff point, and there are no separable costs.

For September 2009, the cost of operations is $480,000. Production and sales data are as follows:

	Production (in kg)	Sales (in kg)	Selling Price per kg
Main product: Potato chips	40,000	32,000	$20
Byproduct	8,000	5,600	$ 5

There were no beginning inventories on September 1, 2009.

REQUIRED

1. What is the gross margin for Yum Inc. under the production method and the sales method of byproduct accounting?

2. What are the inventory costs reported in the balance sheet on September 30, 2009, for the main product and byproduct under the two methods of byproduct accounting in requirement 1?

1. Net joint costs to be allocated, $131,000

15-27 Joint costs and byproducts. (W. Crum) Royston Inc. is a large food processing company. It processes 120,000 kilograms of peanuts in the Peanuts Department at a cost of $160,000 to yield 10,000 kilograms of product A, 60,000 kilograms of product B, and 20,000 kilograms of product C.

◆ Product A is processed further in the Salting Department to yield 10,000 kilograms of salted peanuts at a cost of $20,000 and sold for $10 per kilogram.
◆ Product B (Raw Peanuts) is sold without further processing at $2 per kilogram.
◆ Product C is considered a byproduct and is processed further in the Paste Department to yield 20,000 kilograms of peanut butter at a cost of $10,000 and sold for $3 per kilogram.

The company wants to make a gross margin of 10% of revenues on product C and needs to allow 25% of revenues for marketing costs on product C. An overview of operations follows:

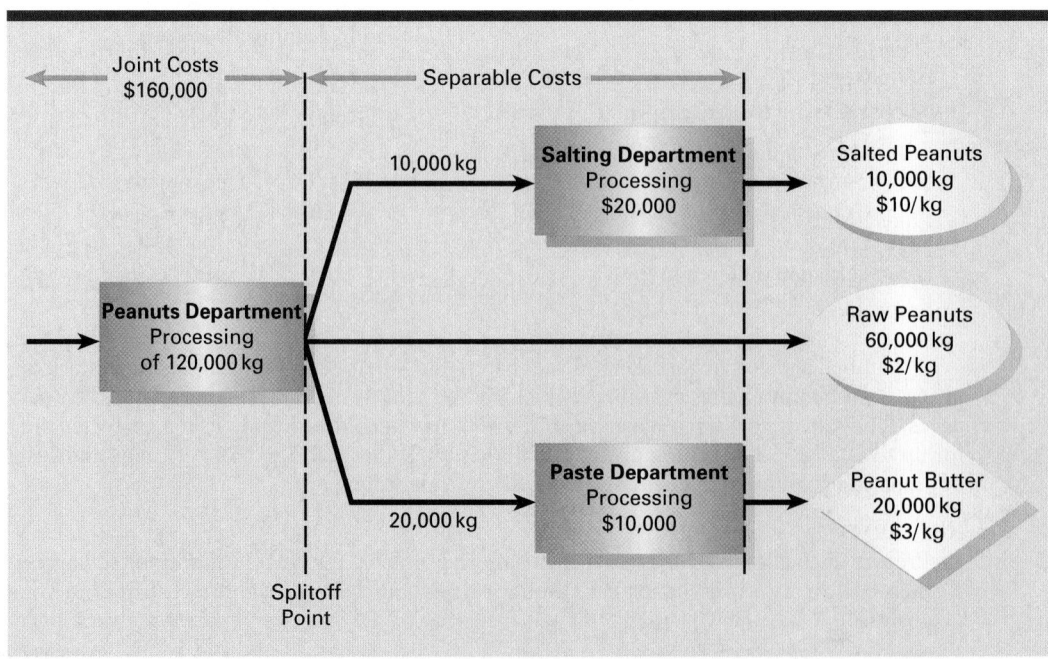

1. Compute unit costs per kilogram for products A, B, and C, treating C as a byproduct. Use the NRV method for allocating joint costs. Deduct the NRV of the byproduct produced from the joint cost of products A and B.

2. Compute unit costs per kilogram for products A, B, and C, treating all three as joint products and allocating joint costs by the NRV method.

15-28 Comparison of alternative joint cost allocation methods, further-processing decision. The Chocolate Factory manufactures and distributes chocolate products. It purchases cocoa beans and processes them into two intermediate products: chocolate powder liquor base and milk chocolate liquor base. These two intermediate products become separately identifiable at a single splitoff point. Every 1,500 kilograms of cocoa beans yields 60 litres of chocolate powder liquor base and 90 litres of milk chocolate liquor base.

1. a. Joint costs allocated to milk chocolate, $19,500

The chocolate powder liquor base is further processed into chocolate powder. Every 60 litres of chocolate powder liquor base yield 600 kilograms of chocolate powder. The milk chocolate liquor base is further processed into milk chocolate. Every 90 litres of milk chocolate liquor base yield 1,020 kilograms of milk chocolate.

Production and sales data for August 2009 are (assume no beginning inventory):

◆ Cocoa beans processed, 15,000 kilograms
◆ Costs of processing cocoa beans to splitoff point (including purchase of beans), $30,000

	Production	Sales	Selling Price	Separable Processing Costs
Chocolate powder	6,000 kg	6,000 kg	$4 per kg	$12,750
Milk chocolate	10,200 kg	10,200 kg	$5 per kg	$26,250

Chocolate Factory fully processes both of its intermediate products into chocolate powder or milk chocolate. There is an active market for these intermediate products. In August 2009, Chocolate Factory could have sold the chocolate powder liquor base for $21 a litre and the milk chocolate liquor base for $26 a litre.

REQUIRED

1. Calculate how the joint costs of $30,000 would be allocated between chocolate powder and milk chocolate under the following methods:
   a. Sales value at splitoff
   b. Physical-measure (litres)
   c. NRV
   d. Constant gross margin percentage NRV

2. What are the gross margin percentages of chocolate powder and milk chocolate under each of the methods in requirement 1?

3. Could Chocolate Factory have increased its operating income by a change in its decision to fully process both of its intermediate products? Show your computations.

15-29 Joint cost allocation, process further or sell. (CMA, adapted) Sonimad Sawmill Inc. (SSI) purchases logs from independent timber contractors and processes the logs into three types of lumber products:

1. a. Joint costs allocated to posts, $307,692

◆ Studs for residential buildings (walls, ceilings)
◆ Decorative pieces (fireplace mantels, beams for cathedral ceilings)
◆ Posts used as support braces (mine support braces, braces for exterior fences on ranch properties)

These products are the result of a joint sawmill process that involves removal of bark from the logs, cutting the logs into a workable size, and then cutting the individual products from the logs.

The joint process results in the following costs of products for a typical month:

Direct materials (rough timber logs)	$ 500,000
Debarking (labour and overhead)	50,000
Sizing (labour and overhead)	200,000
Product cutting (labour and overhead)	250,000
Total joint costs	$1,000,000

Product yields and average sales values on a per-unit basis from the joint process are as follows:

Product	Monthly Output of Materials at Splitoff Point	Fully Processed Selling Price
Studs	75,000 units	$ 8
Decorative pieces	5,000 units	100
Posts	20,000 units	20

The studs are sold as rough-cut lumber after emerging from the sawmill operation without further processing by SSI. Also, the posts require no further processing beyond the splitoff point. The decorative pieces must be planed and further sized after emerging from the sawmill. This additional processing costs $100,000 per month and normally results in a loss of 10% of the units entering the process. Without this planing and sizing process, there is still an active intermediate market for the unfinished decorative pieces in which the selling price averages $60 per unit.

REQUIRED

1. Based on the information given for Sonimad Sawmill, allocate the joint processing costs of $1,000,000 to the three products using:

   a. Sales value at splitoff method
   b. Physical-measure method (volume in units)
   c. NRV method

2. Prepare an analysis for Sonimad Sawmill that compares processing the decorative pieces further, as they currently do, with selling them as a rough-cut product immediately at split-off.

3. Assume Sonimad Sawmill announced that in six months it will sell the unfinished decorative pieces at splitoff due to increasing competitive pressure. Identify at least three types of likely behaviour that will be demonstrated by the skilled labour in the planing-and-sizing process as a result of this announcement. Include in your discussion how this behaviour could be influenced by management.

PROBLEMS

15-30 Alternative methods of joint cost allocation, product-mix decision. The Northwest Forestry Products Company processes lumber products for sale to lumber wholesalers. Its most popular line is oak products. Oak tree growers sell Northwest Forestry whole trees. These trees are jointly processed up to the splitoff point at which raw select oak, raw white oak, and raw knotty oak become separable products. Each of these raw products is then separately further processed by Northwest Forestry into finished products (select oak, white oak, and knotty oak) that are sold to lumber wholesalers. Data for August 2010 are

a. Joint processing costs (including cost of oak trees) $360,000
b. Separable product at splitoff point

   ◆ Raw select oak   30,000 board feet
   ◆ Raw white oak   50,000 board feet
   ◆ Raw knotty oak   20,000 board feet

c. Final product produced and sold

   ◆ Select oak   25,000 board feet at $19.20 per board foot
   ◆ White oak   40,000 board feet at $10.80 per board foot
   ◆ Knotty oak   15,000 board feet at $8.40 per board foot

d. Separable processing costs

   ◆ For select oak $72,000
   ◆ For white oak $108,000
   ◆ For knotty oak $18,000

There is an active market for raw oak products. Selling prices available in August 2010 were raw select oak ($9.60 per board foot), raw white oak ($4.80 per board foot), and raw knotty oak ($3.60 per board foot).

There were no beginning or ending inventories for August 2010.

REQUIRED

1. Allocate the joint costs to the three products using the

    a. sales value at splitoff method.

    b. physical-measure method.

    c. estimated net realizable value method.

2. Assume that not all final product produced in August 2010 was sold. Ending inventory for August 2010 was select oak (1,000 board feet), white oak (2,000 board feet), and knotty oak (500 board feet). What would be the ending inventory values in the August 31 balance sheet under each product for each of the three methods in requirement 1?

3. Is Northwest Forestry maximizing its total August 2010 operating income by fully processing each raw oak product into its finished product form? Show computations.

15-31 Alternative methods of joint cost allocation, product-mix decisions. The Sunshine Oil Company buys crude vegetable oil. Refining this oil results in four products at the splitoff point: A, B, C, and D. Product C is fully processed by the splitoff point. Products A, B, and D can individually be further refined into Super A, Super B, and Super D. In the most recent month (December), the output at the splitoff point was:

1. a. Joint costs allocated to C, $25,000

- ◆ Product A, 300,000 litres
- ◆ Product B, 100,000 litres
- ◆ Product C, 50,000 litres
- ◆ Product D, 50,000 litres

The joint costs of purchasing and processing the crude vegetable oil were $100,000. Sunshine had no beginning or ending inventories. Sales of product C in December were $50,000. Products A, B, and D were further refined and then sold. Data related to December are:

	Separable Processing Costs to Make Super Products	Sales
Super A	$200,000	$300,000
Super B	80,000	100,000
Super D	90,000	120,000

Sunshine had the option of selling products A, B, and D at the splitoff point. This alternative would have yielded the following revenues for the December production:

- ◆ Product A, $50,000
- ◆ Product B, $30,000
- ◆ Product D, $70,000

REQUIRED

1. Compute the gross margin percentage for each product sold in December, using the following methods for allocating the $100,000 joint costs:

    a. Sales value at splitoff

    b. Physical-measure

    c. NRV

2. Could Sunshine have increased its December operating income by making different decisions about the further processing of products A, B, or D? Show the effect on operating income of any changes you recommend.

15-32 Joint cost allocation, relevant costs. (R. Capettini, adapted) Consider the following scenario. Each day a butcher buys a 200-kilogram pig for $360. The pig can be processed to yield the following three products:

2. Joint costs allocated to Ham, $130.43

	Selling Price per kg	Weight (kg)
Pork chops	$4.80	30
Ham	$3.60	50
Bacon	$1.44	120
		200

Day 1 The butcher buys a pig. The $360 joint cost of the pig is allocated to individual products based on the relative weights of the products.

	Selling Price	Weight (kg)	Revenues	−	Joint Costs Allocated	=	Operating Income
Pork chops	$4.80	30	$144.00	−	$ 54.00	=	$ 90.00
Ham	3.60	50	180.00	−	90.00	=	90.00
Bacon	1.44	120	172.80	−	216.00	=	(43.20)
			$496.80	−	$360.00	=	$136.80

Day 2   The butcher buys an identical pig and throws out the bacon because it has been shown to lose money. She now has 80 kilograms of "good output."

	Selling Price	Weight (kg)	Revenues	−	Joint Costs Allocated	=	Operating Income
Pork chops	$4.80	30	$144.00	−	$135.00	=	$ 9.00
Ham	3.60	50	180.00	−	225.00	=	(45.00)
			$324.00	−	$360.00	=	$(36.00)

Day 3   The butcher buys an identical pig and throws out the ham and the bacon because they have been shown to lose money. She now has 30 kilograms of "good output."

	Selling Price	Weight (kg)	Revenues	−	Joint Costs Allocated	=	Operating Income
Pork chops	$4.80	30	$144.00	−	$360.00	=	$(216.00)
			$144.00	−	$360.00	=	$(216.00)

Day 4   The butcher buys an identical pig and throws out the whole pig because each product has been shown to lose money. Therefore, she loses $360.

REQUIRED

1. Comment on the preceding series of decisions.
2. How would the joint costs be allocated to all three products using the sales value at splitoff method?
3. Should the operating income numbers from requirement 2 be used to determine whether the butcher is better off by selling or not selling individual products? Explain briefly.

1. Inventoriable cost of main product, $3.60 per container

15-33 **Accounting for a byproduct.** West-Coast Oceanic Water (WOW) desalinates and bottles sea water. The desalinated water is in high demand from a large group of environmentally conscious people on the west coast of Canada. During March, WOW processes 1,000 litres of sea water and obtains 800 litres of drinking water and 50 kilograms of sea salt (the rest of the sea water evaporates in the desalinization process). Processing the 1,000 litres of water costs WOW $1,500. WOW sells 600 litres of the desalinated water in 2-litre containers for $8 per container. In addition, WOW sells 40 kilograms of sea salt for $1.20 per kilogram. Due to the relatively small proportion of sea salt, WOW has decided to treat it as a byproduct.

REQUIRED

1. Assuming WOW accounts for the byproduct using the production method, what is the inventoriable cost for each product and WOW's gross margin?
2. Assuming WOW accounts for the byproduct using the sales method, what is the inventoriable cost for each product and WOW's gross margin?
3. Discuss the difference between the two methods of accounting for byproducts.

1. a. Joint costs allocated to butter, $4,000

15-34 **Joint cost allocation.** Elsie Dairy Products Corp buys one input, full-cream milk, and refines it in a churning process. From each gallon of milk Elsie produces two cups (one pound) of butter and two quarts (8 cups) of buttermilk. During May 2008, Elsie bought 10,000 gallons of milk for $15,000. Elsie spent another $5,000 on the churning process to separate the milk into butter and buttermilk. Butter could be sold immediately for $2 per pound and buttermilk could be sold immediately for $1.50 per quart.

Elsie chooses to process the butter further into spreadable butter by mixing it with canola oil, incurring an additional cost of $0.50 per pound. This process results in 2 tubs of spreadable butter for each pound of butter processed. Each tub of spreadable butter sells for $2.50.

REQUIRED

1. Allocate the $20,000 joint cost to the spreadable butter and the buttermilk using the
   a. Physical-measure method (using cups) of joint cost allocation
   b. Sales value at splitoff method of joint cost allocation

    c. NRV method of joint cost allocation

    d. Constant gross margin percentage NRV method of joint cost allocation

2. Each of these measures has advantages and disadvantages; what are they?

3. Some claim that the sales value at splitoff method is the best method to use. Discuss the logic behind this claim.

15-35 Further-processing decision (continuation of 15-34). Elsie has decided that buttermilk may sell better if it were marketed for baking and sold in pints. This would involve additional packaging at an incremental cost of $0.25 per pint. Each pint could be sold for $0.90. (*Note:* 1 quart = 2 pints.)

①

1. Process further
NRV—butter, $45,000

REQUIRED

1. If Elsie uses the sales value at splitoff method, what combination of products should Elsie sell to maximize profits?

2. If Elsie uses the physical-measure method, what combination of products should Elsie sell to maximize profits?

3. Explain the effect that the different cost allocation methods have on the decision to sell the products at splitoff or to process them further.

15-36 Joint cost allocation with a byproduct. The Cumberland Mine is a small mine that extracts coal in central Alberta. Each tonne of coal mined is 40% Grade A coal, 40% Grade B coal, and 20% coal tar. All output is sold immediately to a local utility. In May, Cumberland mined 1,000 tonnes of coal. It spent $10,000 on the mining process. Grade A coal sells for $100 per tonne. Grade B coal sells for $60 per tonne. Cumberland gets one-quarter of a vat of coal tar from each tonne of coal tar processed. The coal tar sells for $60 per vat. Cumberland treats Grade A and Grade B coal as joint products, and treats coal tar as a byproduct.

⑤

1. Joint costs to be charged to
joint products, $7,000

REQUIRED

1. Assume that Cumberland allocates the joint costs to Grade A and Grade B coal using the sales value at splitoff method and accounts for the byproduct using the production method. What is the inventoriable cost for each product and Cumberland's gross margin?

2. Assume that Cumberland allocates the joint costs to Grade A and Grade B coal using the sales value at splitoff method and accounts for the byproduct using the sales method. What is the inventoriable cost for each product and Cumberland's gross margin?

3. Discuss the difference between the two methods of accounting for byproducts, focusing on what conditions are necessary to use each method.

15-37 Byproduct-costing journal entries (continuation of 15-36). Cumberland's accountant needs to record the information about the joint products and byproducts in the general journal, but is not sure what the entries should be. Cumberland Mines has hired you as a consultant to help its accountant.

⑤

1. DR WIP inventory, 10,000;
CR A/P, etc., 10,000

REQUIRED

1. Show journal entries at the time of production and at the time of sale assuming Cumberland accounts for the byproduct using the production method.

2. Show journal entries at the time of production and at the time of sale assuming Cumberland accounts for the byproduct using the sales method.

15-38 Accounting for a byproduct. Sanjana's Silk Shirts (SSS) hand-makes blouses and sells them to high-end department stores. SSS buys bolts of silk for $300 each. Out of each bolt it gets 30 blouses, which it sells for $90 each. SSS's new manager has suggested taking the scraps left after cutting out the blouses and using them to make scarves. By carefully cutting the blouses, SSS can produce 6 scarves from each bolt, which it can sell for $25 each. During September, SSS buys 50 bolts of silk and spends an additional $10,000 on the cutting and sewing process. By the end of the month, SSS sells 1200 blouses and 260 scarves made from these bolts. Because the scarves are lower in value than the blouses, SSS decides to treat the scarves as a byproduct.

⑤

1. Inventoriable cost of main
product, $11.67 per blouse

REQUIRED

1. Assuming SSS accounts for the byproduct using the production method, what is the inventoriable cost of each product and SSS's gross margin?

2. Assuming SSS accounts for the byproduct using the sales method, what is the inventoriable cost of each product and SSS's gross margin?

3. Show all journal entries for the month of September assuming SSS accounts for the byproduct using (a) the production method and (b) the sales method.

15-39 Estimated net realizable value method, byproducts. (CMA, adapted) The Princess Corporation grows, processes, packages, and sells three joint apple products: (a) sliced apples that are used in frozen pies, (b) applesauce, and (c) apple juice. The skin of the

①

apple, processed as animal feed, is treated as a byproduct. Princess uses the estimated NRV method to allocate costs of the joint process to its joint products. The byproduct is inventoried at its selling price when produced; the net realizable value of the byproduct is used to reduce the joint production costs before the splitoff point. Details of Princess's production process are presented here:

◆ The apples are washed and the skin is removed in the Cutting Department. The apples are then cored and trimmed for slicing. The three joint products and the byproduct are recognizable after processing in the Cutting Department. Each product is then transferred to a separate department for final processing.

◆ The trimmed apples are forwarded to the Slicing Department, where they are sliced and frozen. Any juice generated during the slicing operation is frozen with the slices.

◆ The pieces of apple trimmed from the fruit are processed into applesauce in the Crushing Department. The juice generated during this operation is used in the applesauce.

◆ The core and any surplus apple pieces generated from the Cutting Department are pulverized into a liquid in the Juicing Department. There is a loss equal to 8% of the weight of the good output produced in this department.

◆ The outside skin is chopped into animal feed and packaged in the Feed Department. It can be kept in cold storage until needed.

A total of 270,000 kilograms of apples entered the Cutting Department during November. The following schedule shows the costs incurred in each department, the proportion by weight transferred to the four final processing departments, and the selling price of each end product.

Processing Data and Costs, November 2010

Departments	Costs Incurred	Proportion of Transferred to Department	Selling Price per Kilogram of Final Product
Cutting	$ 72,000		
Slicing	13,536	33%	$0.96
Crushing	10,260	30	0.66
Juicing	3,600	27	0.48
Feed	840	10	0.12
Total	$100,236	100%	$2.22

REQUIRED

1. The Princess Corporation uses the estimated NRV method to determine inventory cost of its joint products; byproducts are reported on the balance sheet at their selling price when produced. For the month of November 2010, calculate the following:

   a. The output for apple slices, applesauce, apple juice, and animal feed, in kilograms.
   b. The estimated NRV at the splitoff point for each of the three joint products.
   c. The amount of the cost of the Cutting Department assigned to each of the three joint products and the amount assigned to the byproduct in accordance with corporate policy.
   d. The gross margins in dollars for each of the three joint products.

2. Comment on the significance to management of the gross margin dollar information by joint product for planning and control purposes, as opposed to inventory costing purposes.

15-40 **Joint product/byproduct distinctions, governance (continuation of 15-39).** The Princess Corporation classifies animal feed as a byproduct. The byproduct is inventoried at its selling price when produced; the net realizable value of the product is used to reduce the joint production costs before the splitoff point. Before 2010, Princess classified both apple juice and animal feed as byproducts. These byproducts were not recognized in the accounting system until sold. Revenues from their sale were treated as a revenue item at the time of sale.

The Princess Corporation uses a "management by objectives" basis to compensate its managers. Every six months, managers are given "stretch" operating-income-to-revenue ratio targets. They receive no bonus if the target is not met and a fixed amount if the target is met or exceeded.

REQUIRED

1. Assume that Princess managers aim to maximize their bonuses over time. What byproduct method (the pre-2010 method or the 2010 method) would the manager prefer?

2. How might a controller gain insight into whether the manager of the Apple Products division is "abusing" the accounting system in an effort to maximize his or her bonus?

3. Describe an accounting system for the Princess Corporation that would reduce "gaming" behaviour by managers with respect to accounting rules for byproducts.

COLLABORATIVE LEARNING CASES

15-41 Joint cost allocation, process further or sell byproducts. (CMA) The Remarkable Pharmaceutical Company manufactures three joint products from a joint process: Alpha, Beta, and Delta. Data regarding these products for the fiscal year ended May 31, 2010, are as follows:

②

1. Estimated net realizable value at splitoff point of Beta, $1,320,000

	Alpha	Beta	Delta
Units produced	170,000	500,000	330,000
Selling price per unit at splitoff	$ 4.20	—	$ 2.40
Separable costs	—	$1,680,000	—
Final selling price per unit	—	$ 6.00	—

The joint production cost up to the splitoff point where Alpha, Beta, and Delta become separable products is $2,160,000 (which includes the $21,000 disposal costs for Dorzine as described below).

The president of Remarkable, Martha Wellington, is reviewing an opportunity to change the way in which these three products are processed and sold. Proposed changes for each product are as follows:

♦ Alpha is currently sold at the splitoff point to a manufacturer of vitamins. Alpha can also be refined for use as a medication to treat high blood pressure; however, this additional processing would cause a loss of 20,000 units of Alpha. The separable costs to further process Alpha are estimated to be $300,000 annually. The final product would sell for $6.60 per unit.

♦ Beta is currently processed further after the splitoff point and sold by Remarkable as a cold remedy. The company has received an offer from another pharmaceutical company to purchase Beta at the splitoff point for $2.70 per unit.

♦ Delta is an oil produced from the joint process and is currently sold at the splitoff point to a cosmetics manufacturer. Remarkable's research department has suggested that the company process this product further and sell it as an ointment to relieve muscle pain. The additional processing would cost $90,000 annually and would result in 25% more units of product. The final product would be sold for $2.16 per unit.

The joint process currently used by Remarkable also produces 50,000 units of Dorzine, a hazardous chemical waste product. The company pays $0.42 per unit to dispose of the Dorzine properly. Dietriech Mills Inc. is interested in using the Dorzine as a solvent; however, Remarkable would have to refine the Dorzine at an annual cost of $51,600. Dietriech would purchase all the refined Dorzine produced by Remarkable and is willing to pay $0.90 for each unit.

INSTRUCTIONS

Form groups of two or more students to complete the following requirements.

REQUIRED

1. Allocate the $2,160,000 joint production cost to Alpha, Beta, and Delta using the estimated NRV method.

2. Identify which of the three joint products Remarkable should sell at the splitoff point in the future and which of the three main products the company should process further to maximize profits. Support your decisions with appropriate calculations.

3. Assume that Remarkable has decided to refine the waste product Dorzine for sale to Dietriech Mills Inc. and will treat Dorzine as a byproduct of the joint process in the future.

   a. Evaluate whether Remarkable made the correct decision regarding Dorzine. Support your answer with appropriate calculations.

   b. Explain whether the decision to treat Dorzine as a byproduct will affect the decisions reached in requirement 2.

15-42 Joint cost allocation. Memory Manufacturing Company (MMC) produces memory modules in a two-step process: chip fabrication and module assembly.

In chip fabrication, each batch of raw silicon wafers yields 500 standard chips and 500 deluxe chips. Chips are classified as standard or deluxe on the basis of their density (the number of memory bits on each chip). Standard chips have 500 memory bits per chip, and deluxe chips have 1,000 memory bits per chip. Joint costs to process each batch are $24,000.

In module assembly, each batch of standard chips is converted into standard memory modules at a separately identified cost of $1,000 and then sold for $8,500. Each batch of deluxe chips is converted into deluxe memory modules at a separately identified cost of $1,500 and then sold for $25,000.

REQUIRED

1. Allocate joint costs of each batch to deluxe modules and standard modules using (a) the NRV method, (b) the constant gross margin percentage NRV method, and (c) the physical-measure method, based on the number of memory bits. Which method should MMC use?
2. MMC can process each batch of 500 standard memory modules to yield 400 DRAM modules at an additional cost of $1,600. The selling price per DRAM module would be $26. Assume MMC uses the physical-measure method. Should MMC sell the standard memory modules or the DRAM modules?

Revenues, Sales Variances, and Customer Profitability Analysis

BUSINESS MATTERS

Allocation—Again? Yes—for Revenue.

Royalty contracts are by and large revenue-sharing contracts. Oil companies pay a percentage of revenue to governments from whom they lease the mineral development rights. Publishers pay royalties to their authors. Movie studios and recording companies pay royalties to creative artists. How revenue is allocated can mean millions of dollars received or withheld and the legal costs associated with settling disputes. Often, too, government allocates revenue to non-profit service organizations such as universities and hospitals.

LEARNING OBJECTIVES

After studying this chapter, you should be able to

1. Apply revenue-allocation methods to individual products in a bundled package

2. Analyze product profitability using level 3 and 4 sales and level 4 cost variances

3. Evaluate the relevance of information obtained from revenue and cost variance analyses

4. Analyze customer profitability by applying ABC cost hierarchy concepts

5. Prepare a customer profitability profile

REVENUE ALLOCATION AND BUNDLED PRODUCTS

> **1** Apply revenue-allocation methods to individual products in a bundled package

Revenues are inflows of assets (almost always cash or accounts receivable) received for products or services provided to customers. Just as costs can be allocated to specific products, services, customers, or some other more relevant cost object, so too can revenues. **Revenue allocation** occurs when revenues that can be related to, but not traced to, individual revenue objects (products, services, divisions, customers, and so on) are assigned to those individual products. Revenue tracing results in a more accurate assignment of revenues to products than does revenue allocation. Just as with cost data, more accurate information is believed to result in better decisions. Revenue allocation is undertaken when it is neither economically nor practically feasible to trace revenue.

Governments also use revenue-allocation formulas to distribute tax revenue to various social welfare programs such as university education and health care. Their choice of how revenue is allocated will make a significant difference to people who require those services. In the Real Companies example, the allocation of casino revenue retained by one First Nations band illustrates how allocation can affect individuals in a group. Generally, the band retains only about 30% of total casino revenue net of prizes paid out. This band makes quarterly payments to its eligible members.

REAL COMPANIES

Revenue Allocation

First Nations casinos on reserves in Alberta are regulated under the Alberta Gaming and Liquor Commission (AGLC).

Gaming license fees pay for the commission's operating costs. Net of winnings paid, commissions, and a percentage paid to the federal government, the Alberta Lottery Fund (ALF) and the First Nations Development Fund Grant Program (FNDF) share the proceeds from slot machines. Of the net revenue, 30% is allocated to the FDNF and 70% goes to the ALF. The revenue allocation does not stop here. Of the 70% going to the ALF, the province returns 40% to the FNDF. There are two types of First Nations groups, identified as either host or other First Nations. The host First Nations receive 75% of revenue allocated to by the ALF and the other First Nations receive the remaining 25%. The revenue flowing from the slot machines to the two First Nations groups is considered charitable gaming proceeds. There are regulations regarding how these proceeds should be allocated to the First Nations groups. Safety, addiction treatment, subsidized housing and services, seniors and elder support, cultural events, and life skills training are among the FNDF programs funded by the allocated charitable gaming revenue. The AGLC estimated total revenue of $1.5 billion for 2008–2009. In 2007–2008, approximately $325 million in revenue was obtained from charitable gaming.

Source: Alberta Gaming Research Institute, "Revenue Allocation," May 1, 2007, www.abgaminginstitute.ualberta.ca/Alberta_casinos_revenue_allocation.cfm, accessed March 23, 2009; Alberta Gaming Research Institute, "Quick Facts — Gaming," www.gaming.gov.ab.ca/pdf/quickfacts/quickfacts_gaming.pdf, accessed March 23, 2009.

Turning to an internal consideration of revenue allocation to provide information for making operating and strategic decisions, we will use an example of a software company. The Superhighway Group (SG), a computer software company, will be used to illustrate the issues that arise from decisions to allocate revenue. SG develops, sells, and supports three software packages:

1. **WordMaster.** Current version is WordMaster 5.0, which was released 36 months ago. WordMaster was the company's initial product.
2. **SpreadMaster.** Current version is SpreadMaster 3.0, which was released 18 months ago.
3. **FinanceMaster.** Current version is FinanceMaster 2.0. This product, the company's most recent, has been its most successful. The 2.0 version was released 2 months ago.

Superhighway sells these three products individually and also sells them as bundled products. A **bundled product** is a package of two or more products or services, sold for a single price, whose individual components may also be sold as separate items, each with its own stand-alone price. The single price for the bundled product is typically less than the sum of the prices of two or more products if purchased separately.

One example is the way Cogeco bundles its high-speed Internet access with its television service at a price lower than the cost of the two sold separately. Another example is a resort hotel that offers, for a single price, a weekend package that includes services from its lodging (the room), food (the restaurant), and recreational (golfing) divisions. Where individual department or division managers have revenue or profit responsibilities, the issue becomes how to allocate the single bundled revenue amount among the individual products in that bundle.

SG encounters revenue-allocation decisions with its bundled product sales (termed "suite sales"). Here, two or more of the software products are sold as a single package. SG's managers are keenly interested in individual-product profitability figures. There are separate managers for each product who are responsible for the operating income of that product. Moreover, its Software Department engineers are organized on a product-by-product basis and receive a percentage of product profitability as part of their bonus.

How should Superhighway allocate suite revenues to individual products? The following table summarizes information pertaining to its three suite sales and the stand-alone prices of its individual products. The two main classes of revenue-allocation methods are the stand-alone method and the incremental method. We will discuss each in turn. Both methods are analogous to cost-allocation methods discussed in Chapter 14.

Product	Sales Price	Manufacturing Cost per Unit
Stand-alone		
WordMaster	$125	$18
SpreadMaster	150	20
FinanceMaster	225	25
Suite		
Word + Spread	$220	
Word + Finance	280	
Finance + Spread	305	
Word + Finance + Spread	380	

STAND-ALONE REVENUE-ALLOCATION METHODS

The **stand-alone revenue-allocation method** uses product-specific information pertaining to products in the bundle to determine the weights used to allocate the bundled revenues to those individual products. The term *stand-alone* refers to the product as a separate (nonsuite) item, not bundled. Consider the Word and Finance suite, which sells for $280. Four stand-alone sources of weights are as follows:

1. **Selling prices.** The individual selling prices are $125 for WordMaster and $225 for FinanceMaster. The weights for allocating the $280 between the two products are

$$\text{Word:} \quad \frac{\$125}{\$125 + \$225} \times \$280 = 0.357 \times \$280 = \$100$$

$$\text{Finance:} \quad \frac{\$225}{\$125 + \$225} \times \$280 = 0.643 \times \$280 = \$180$$

2. **Unit manufacturing costs.** This method uses costs of individual products to determine the weights to allocate revenues. Assume unit manufacturing costs are used to determine the weights to allocate Word and Finance suite revenues of $280:

$$\text{Word:} \quad \frac{\$18}{\$18 + \$25} \times \$280 = 0.419 \times \$280 = \$117$$

$$\text{Finance:} \quad \frac{\$25}{\$18 + \$25} \times \$280 = 0.581 \times \$280 = \$163$$

This method does not recognize differences in the willingness of customers to purchase individual products.

3. **Physical units.** This method gives each product unit in the suite the same weight when allocating suite revenue to individual products. Thus, with two products in the Word plus Finance suite, each product gets 50% of the suite revenues allocated to it.

$$\text{Word:} \quad \frac{1}{1 + 1} \times \$280 = 0.50 \times \$280 = \$140$$

$$\text{Finance:} \quad \frac{1}{1 + 1} \times \$280 = 0.50 \times \$280 = \$140$$

THINKING CRITICALLY

When is it appropriate to use the physical units method? Explain in a sentence or two. Read on for a discussion of this topic.

It is most appropriate to use physical units when the sales values of the individual products in the bundle are approximately equal. Using physical units for, say, a bundle that includes a washing machine and a box of detergent would be inappropriate because it makes no sense to allocate half of the revenue to the box of detergent. The disproportionate amount of cost compared to the revenue generated by the sale of a box of detergent is what makes this method inappropriate for this product bundle. This method would also be inappropriate when the retailer bundles special insurance with the product because the components of the bundle are not both physical units.

4. **Stand-alone product revenues.** Stand-alone product revenues will capture the quantity of each product sold as well as their selling prices. Assume that the stand-alone revenues are WordMaster, $28 million; SpreadMaster, $15 million; and FinanceMaster, $7 million. The weights for the Word and Finance suites would be

$$\text{Word:} \quad \frac{\$28 \text{ million}}{\$28 \text{ million} + \$7 \text{ million}} \times \$280 = 0.80 \times \$280 = \$224$$

$$\text{Finance:} \quad \frac{\$7 \text{ million}}{\$28 \text{ million} + \$7 \text{ million}} \times \$280 = 0.20 \times \$280 = \$56$$

The lower revenue allocation to FinanceMaster is, in part, due to it being released only partway through the year.

These four approaches to determining weights with the stand-alone method yield the following revenue allocations to individual products:

Revenue-Allocation Weights	WordMaster	FinanceMaster
Selling prices	$100	$180
Unit manufacturing costs	117	163
Physical units	140	140
Stand-alone product revenues	224	56

The unit selling price weights are advantageous in that they frequently are the best available external indicator of the benefits companies receive from selling products. Market-based weighting schemes that are closer to the customer better capture a benefits-received notion in a bundled product allocation setting than do cost-based or unit-based weights. Unit-based revenue allocation is typically rationalized on the basis of ease of use or limitations of alternative methods (such as unit selling prices being unstable, or unit manufacturing costs being difficult to calculate at the individual product level).

INCREMENTAL REVENUE-ALLOCATION METHOD

The **incremental revenue-allocation method** ranks the individual products in a bundle and then uses this ranking to allocate the bundled revenues to these individual products. The first-ranked product is termed the *primary product* in the bundle. The second-ranked product is termed the *first incremental product*, the third-ranked product is the *second incremental product*, and so on.

Who decides on the ranking of products in the incremental revenue-allocation method? One approach is to survey customers on the relative importance of individual products in their decision to purchase the bundled products. A second approach is to use data on recent stand-alone performance of the individual products in the bundle. A third approach is for top management to decide the rankings based on their knowledge or intuition.

Consider again the Word and Finance suite of Superhighway. Assume WordMaster is designated as the primary product. If the suite revenue exceeds the stand-alone revenue of the primary product, the primary product is allocated 100% of its stand-alone revenue. This is the case for the Word and Finance suite. The suite revenue of $280 exceeds the stand-alone revenue of $125 for WordMaster; WordMaster is allocated revenues of $125, with the remaining or residual revenue of $155 ($280 – $125) allocated to FinanceMaster:

Product	Revenue Allocated	Cumulative Revenue Allocated
WordMaster	$125	$125
FinanceMaster ($280 – $125)	155	$280
Total	$280	

Clearly, the ranking of the individual products in the suite is a key factor in determining the revenues allocated to individual products.

THINKING CRITICALLY

Who wants to be first in a zero-sum game? Explain in a sentence or two. Read on for a discussion of this topic.

Under the incremental revenue-allocation method, all users of the revenue object want to be the first-ranked user. The first-ranked user will be allocated a larger portion of the revenues. If FinanceMaster were the primary product, the revenue allocated would be $225, not $155. WordMaster would be allocated $55, not $125. The differences between these two allocations are material for managers who may be paid on the basis of new revenue generated or total revenue generated. This is called a zero-sum game, which is a game where what one gains the other loses. This is another example where the purpose of allocation must be clear and one allocation method is not satisfactory to achieve all purposes.

If Superhighway sells equal quantities of WordMaster and FinanceMaster, then the *Shapley value* method allocates to each product the average of the revenues allocated as the primary and first incremental products:

$$\text{WordMaster:} \qquad \frac{\$125 + \$55}{2} = \$180 \div 2 = \$90$$

$$\text{FinanceMaster:} \qquad \frac{(\$125 + \$155)}{2} = \$380 \div 2 = \$190$$

$$\text{Total} \qquad\qquad\qquad = \$280$$

But what if, in the most recent quarter, Superhighway sells 80,000 units of WordMaster and 20,000 units of FinanceMaster? Because Superhighway sells four times as many units of WordMaster, its managers believe that the sales of the Word + Finance suite are four times more likely to be driven by WordMaster as the primary product. The *weighted Shapley value* method takes this into account by weighting the revenue allocations when WordMaster is the primary product four times as much as when FinanceMaster is the primary product:

$$\text{WordMaster:} \qquad \frac{(\$125 \times 4 + \$55 \times 1)}{(4 + 1)} = \frac{\$555}{5} = \$111$$

$$\text{Finance Master:} \qquad \frac{(\$225 \times 1 + \$155 \times 4)}{(4 + 1)} = \frac{\$845}{5} = \$169$$

$$\text{Total} \qquad\qquad\qquad = \$280$$

When there are more than two products in the suite, the incremental revenue-allocation method allocates suite revenues sequentially. Assume WordMaster is the primary product in Superhighway's three-product suite (Word + Finance + Spread). FinanceMaster is the first incremental product, and SpreadMaster is the second incremental product. This suite sells for $380. The allocation of the $380 suite revenues proceeds as follows:

Product	Revenue Allocated	Cumulative Revenue Allocated
WordMaster	$125	$125
FinanceMaster ($280 − $125)	155	$280 (price of Word + Finance suite)
SpreadMaster ($380 − $280)	100	$380 (price of Word + Finance + Spread suite)
Total	$380	

Now suppose WordMaster is the primary product, SpreadMaster is the first incremental product, and FinanceMaster is the second incremental product.

Product	Revenue Allocated	Cumulative Revenue Allocated
WordMaster	$125	$125
SpreadMaster ($220 − $125)	95	$220 (price of Word + Spread suite)
FinanceMaster ($380 − $220)	160	$380 (price of Word + Spread + Finance suite)
Total	$380	

The ranking of the individual products in the suite determines the revenues allocated to them. Product managers at Superhighway likely would differ on how they believe their individual products contribute to sales of the suite products. It is possible that each product manager would claim to be responsible for the primary product in the Word + Finance + Spread suite!

Calculating the Shapley value mitigates this problem because each product is considered as a primary, first-incremental, and second-incremental product. Assuming equal weights on all products, the revenue allocated to each product is an average of the revenues calculated for each product under these different assumptions: FinanceMaster, $180; WordMaster, $87.50; and SpreadMaster, $112.50:

Order			Revenues Allocated to Each Product		
Primary	**First Incremental**	**Second Incremental**	**FinanceMaster**	**WordMaster**	**SpreadMaster**
FinanceMaster	WordMaster	SpreadMaster	$225	$ 55 ($280 − $225)	$100 ($380 − $225 − $55)
FinanceMaster	SpreadMaster	WordMaster	$225	$ 75 ($380 − $225 − $80)	$ 80 ($305 − $225)
WordMaster	FinanceMaster	SpreadMaster	$155 ($280 − $125)	$125	$100 ($380 − $125 − $155)
WordMaster	SpreadMaster	FinanceMaster	$160 ($380 − $125 − $95)	$125	$ 95 ($220 − $125)
SpreadMaster	FinanceMaster	WordMaster	$155 ($305 − $150)	$ 75 ($380 − $150 − $155)	$150
SpreadMaster	WordMaster	FinanceMaster	$160 ($380 − $150 − $70)	$ 70 ($220 − $150)	$150
Total:			$1,080	$525	$675
Average Revenue Allocated:			$1,080 ÷ 6 = $180	$525 ÷ 6 = $87.50	$675 ÷ 6 = $112.50

Because the stand-alone revenue-allocation method does not require rankings of individual products in the suite, this method is less likely to cause debates among product managers.

STRATEGY

Not-for-Profit Revenue Allocation—A Long-Term Policy

Provision of health care is a complex managerial process of quality improvement. The government allocates revenue to preventive, acute, and non-acute programs to serve all the medically necessary requirements of its citizens. While relatively few people are hospitalized, treatments are very expensive to fund, but the services provided more often than not will save lives. Currently the Ontario Ministry of Health and Long-Term Care has proposed a change in revenue allocation. The annual budget allocation is now based largely on the historical spending pattern of each hospital. The proposed change is to fund hospitals on the basis of the quantity and type of services that they actually deliver. In 2008 the budget to fund Ontario's 150 hospitals was $14.4 billion.

Many issues have an impact on funding. One of these is what measure of unit of service will be used. Acute-care hospitals provide outpatient and inpatient services. Treatments range from kidney dialysis to heart transplants. One possible measure is the case mix group (CMG). The CMG approach is conceptually the same as the unit manufacturing approach. A drawback of this measure is insufficient and poor-quality information that compromises the accuracy of the rate calculated for reimbursement per CMG. A second issue is what services each hospital will provide and what

(continued)

(continued)

analysis can be undertaken to justify each operating budget upon which resource allocation for the impending year will be provided. Finally, hospitals respond to imminent and changing medical needs. If hospitals do not service quantity and mix according to the budget but do achieve the financial performance targets, then on what basis will they be held accountable for the service gaps?

There are no Canadian market prices for medically necessary care, and service is neither a physical unit nor do services stand alone. Often patients must be extremely ill before they are admitted and many suffer from several ailments known as comorbidities. The incremental method could be useful if comorbidities could be ranked in order of priority of treatment. Unfortunately the restoration or partial restoration of the quality of health is holistic, and frequently one medical goal cannot be accomplished without accomplishing another simultaneously. The CMG is a default method.

Sources: "Advancing Accountability through Hospital Funding Reform: A Policy Framework to Promote Greater Access, Efficiency and Quality of Care," Ontario Hospital Association www.oha.com/oha/reports.nsf/($Att)/pspr5y8nzb/$FILE/Advancing_Accountability_Through Hospital_FundingReform.pdf?OpenElement; CNW: MOHLTC Funding Boost for Ontario Hospitals Backgrounder, April 13, 2008 at http://ogov.newswire.ca/ontario/GPOE/2008/04/13/c5003. html?lmatch=&lang=_e.html.

OTHER REVENUE-ALLOCATION METHODS

Management's judgment that is not explicitly based on a specific formula is an alternative method of revenue allocation. In one case, the president of a software company decided to issue a set of revenue-allocation weights after the managers of the three products in the bundled suite could not themselves agree on a set of weights. The weights chosen by the president for the three products were 45% for Product A, 45% for Product B, and 10% for Product C.

The factors the president considered included stand-alone selling prices (all three were very similar), stand-alone unit sales (A and B were over 10 times more than C), product ratings by independent experts, and consumer awareness. The Product C manager complained that his 10% weighting dramatically short-changed the contribution of Product C to suite revenues. The president responded that its inclusion in the suite greatly increased consumer exposure to Product C with the result that Product C's total revenues would be far larger (even with only 10% of suite revenues) than had it not been included in the suite.

Part One of this chapter has discussed revenue allocation. Part Two analyzes profitability by combining level 3 and 4 sales variances as well as level 4 cost variances.

GOVERNANCE ISSUES

Management Accountants: Choice of Revenue-Allocation Method

Recently the Canadian Securities Administrators (CSA) enacted National Instrument NI 52-109, which is the Canadian equivalent to Sarbanes-Oxley section 302. This requires that an internal control system be designed and implemented to reasonably assure any public financial disclosure be materially free of misstatement. One key goal is to ensure those at the top are held accountable for internal management control. Revenue allocation has an important management control function. The appropriate choice of allocation method will affect important strategic and operational choices. An inappropriate method will bias and degrade the usefulness of internal information for decision making. In the design of a defensible internal control system it is key to assess how appropriate allocation method choices have been. The Chief Executive and Chief Financial Officers must sign the certification required under NI 52-109. The Board of Directors, with oversight function, ultimately is held responsible for accepting an inadequate internal control system.

PROBLEM

Business Horizons (BH) produces and markets videos for sale to the business community. It hires well-known business speakers to present new developments in their area of expertise in video format. The compensation paid to each speaker is individually negotiated. It always has a component based on the percentage of revenues from the sale of the video, but that percentage is not uniform across speakers. Moreover, some speakers negotiate separate fixed-dollar payments or multiple-video deals.

BH sells most videos as separate items. However, there is a growing trend for videos also to be sold as part of bundled packages. BH offered bundled packages of its three best-selling videos in 2010. Individual and bundled sales of these three videos for 2010 are

Individual Sales

Speaker	Title	Units Sold	Selling Price	Speaker Royalty
Jeannett Smith	Negotiating for Win–Win (N)	25,000	$150	24%
Mark Coyne	Marketing for the Internet (M)	17,000	$120	16%
Laurie Daley	Electronic Commerce (E)	8,000	$130	19%

Bundled Product Sales

Titles in Bundle	Units Sold	Selling Price
Negotiating for Win–Win + Marketing for the Internet	12,000	$210
Negotiating for Win–Win + Electronic Commerce	5,000	$220
Marketing for the Internet + Electronic Commerce	4,000	$190
Negotiating + Marketing + Electronic	11,000	$280

REQUIRED

1. Allocate the bundled product revenues to the individual videos using the stand-alone revenue-allocation method (using selling prices as the weights).
2. Describe (without computations) an alternative method of allocating the bundled product revenues to that in requirement 1.

SOLUTION

1. The weights in the stand-alone method are based on the stand-alone selling prices of the videos in the bundled package. The following table details these weights, which are then used to allocate the revenues of each bundled package to the three individual videos.

	Allocation Formula	Negotiating	Marketing	Electronic
N + M:	($150 ÷ $270) × $210 × 12,000	$1,400,000		
N + E:	($150 ÷ $280) × $220 × 5,000	589,286		
N + M + E:	($150 ÷ $400) × $280 × 11,000	1,155,000		
Total		$3,144,286		
M + N:	($120 ÷ $270) × $210 × 12,000		$1,120,000	
M + E:	($120 ÷ $250) × $190 × 4,000		364,800	
M + N + E:	($120 ÷ $400) × $280 × 11,000		924,000	
Total			$2,408,800	
E + N:	($130 ÷ $280) × $220 × 5,000			$ 510,714
E + M:	($130 ÷ $250) × $190 × 4,000			395,200
E + N + M:	($130 ÷ $400) × $280 × 11,000			1,001,000
Total				$1,906,914

2. An alternative approach to allocating the bundled product revenues is the incremental revenue-allocation method. Here the individual videos in the bundle are ranked in order of importance, and the revenues are allocated to each product using stand-alone selling prices until all the bundled revenue has been fully allocated. Use of this approach would likely create some friction among the three business speakers. It would be in each speaker's interest to claim to be the primary speaker driving sales of the bundle. The actual 2010 units-sold figures would enable Business Horizons to give a market-success-based ranking of individual business speakers if it used the incremental revenue-allocation method.

MyAccountingLab

◆ PART TWO: PRODUCT PROFITABILITY ANALYSES

PROFITABILITY VARIANCE COMPONENTS

2 Analyze product profitability using level 3 and 4 sales and level 4 cost variances

In Part Two we examine how to calculate variances that use revenue information as a key input. Profitability analyses require thorough understanding of the causes of both revenue and costs. The finer or more detailed the analyses of what caused unexpected outcomes, the more relevant the information available to managers who must remedy the situation. Feedback is essential in complex and ongoing decision-making where new information changes the likelihood of future outcomes. This is an example of the Bayesian process discussed in Chapter 11. We begin with a finer analysis of revenue variances, then proceed to cost variances.

SALES VOLUME VARIANCE—LEVELS 3 AND 4

Special attention is paid to companies with multiple products or services and to companies selling the same product or service in multiple distribution channels. Companies such as Cisco, GE, and Hewlett-Packard perform similar analyses because they sell their products through multiple distribution channels, for example via the Internet, over the telephone, and in retail stores.

Spring Distribution Company sells bottled water. It has two distribution channels: (1) a wholesale distribution channel, in which the wholesaler sells to supermarkets, drugstores, and other stores, and (2) a retail distribution channel for a small number of business customers. Spring classifies all customer-level costs as variable costs and distribution-channel and corporate-sustaining costs as fixed costs. To simplify the sales-variance analysis and calculations, we assume that all these variable costs are variable with respect to units (cases) sold. (This means, for example, that average batch sizes remain the same as the total cases sold vary.) Without this assumption, the analysis would become more complex and would have to be done using the ABC-variance analysis approach described in Chapter 7.

The basic insights, however, would not change. Budget data for June 2010 are shown in the table below:

Budget Data for June 2010

	Selling Price per Unit (1)	Variable Cost per Unit (2)	Contribution Margin per Unit (3) = (1) − (2)	Sales Volume in Units (4)	Sales Mix (Based on Units) (5)	Contribution Margin (6) = (3) × (4)
Wholesale channel	$13.37	$12.88	$0.49	712,000	80%[a]	$348,880
Retail channel	14.10	13.12	0.98	178,000	20%	174,440
Total				890,000	100%	$523,320

"Unit" in the column headings refers to a case of 24 bottles
[a]Percentage of unit sales to wholesale channel = 712,000 units ÷ 890,000 total units = 80%.

Actual Data for June 2010

	Selling Price per Unit (1)	Variable Cost per Unit (2)	Contribution Margin per Unit (3) = (1) − (2)	Sales Volume in Units (4)	Sales Mix (Based on Units) (5)	Contribution Margin (6) = (3) × (4)
Wholesale channel	$13.37	$12.88	$0.49	756,000	84%	$370,440
Retail channel	14.10	13.17	0.93	144,000	16%	133,920
Total				900,000	100%	$504,360

The budgeted and actual fixed distribution-channel costs and corporate-sustaining costs are $160,500 and $263,000, respectively.

Recall that the levels of detail introduced in Chapter 7 included the static-budget variance (level 1), the flexible-budget variance (level 2), and the sales-volume variance (level 2). The sales-quantity and sales-mix variances are level 3 variances that subdivide the sales-volume variance.[1]

STATIC-BUDGET VARIANCE

The *static-budget variance* is calculated as:

Static-budget variance = Actual results − Static-budget amount

Our analysis focuses on the difference between actual and budgeted contribution margins (column 6 in the preceding tables). The total static-budget variance is $18,960 U (actual contribution margin of $504,360 − budgeted contribution margin of $523,320). Exhibit 16-1 (columns 1 and 3) uses the columnar format introduced in Chapter 7 to show detailed calculations of the static-budget variance. Managers can gain more insight about the static-budget variance by subdividing it into the flexible-budget variance and the sales-volume variance.

FLEXIBLE-BUDGET AND SALES-VOLUME VARIANCES

The *flexible-budget variance* is calculated as:

Flexible-budget variance = Actual results − Flexible-budget amount

The *flexible-budget variance* is the difference between an actual result and the corresponding flexible-budget amount based on actual output level in the budget

[1]The presentation of the variances in this chapter draws on teaching notes prepared by J. K. Harris.

period. The flexible-budget contribution margin is equal to budgeted contribution margin per unit (case) times actual units (cases) sold of each product. Exhibit 16-1, column 2, shows the flexible-budget calculations. The flexible budget measures the contribution margin that Spring would have budgeted for the actual quantities of cases sold. The flexible-budget variance is the difference between columns 1 and 2 in Exhibit 16-1.

The only difference between columns 1 and 2 is that actual units sold of each product is multiplied by actual contribution margin per unit in column 1 and budgeted contribution margin per unit in column 2. The $7,200 U flexible-budget variance arises because actual contribution margin on retail sales of $0.93 per case is lower than the budgeted amount of $0.98 per case. Spring's management is aware that this difference of $0.05 per case resulted from excessive price discounts, and they have put in place controls to reduce discounts in the future.

The *sales-volume variance* is calculated as:

$$\text{Sales-volume variance} = \left(\begin{array}{c} \text{Actual sales} \\ \text{quantity in units} \end{array} - \begin{array}{c} \text{Static-budget sales} \\ \text{quantity in units} \end{array} \right) \times \begin{array}{c} \text{Budgeted contribution} \\ \text{margin per unit} \end{array}$$

The *sales-volume variance* shows the effect of the difference between the actual and budgeted quantity of the variable used to "flex" the flexible budget. The sales-volume variance of $11,760 U is the difference between columns 2 and 3 in Exhibit 16-1. Spring's managers can gain substantial insight into the sales-volume variance by subdividing it into the sales-mix variance and the sales-quantity variance.

Exhibit 16-2 shows how both the sales-mix and sales-quantity variances can be calculated using the columnar approach introduced in Chapter 7. Please refer to this exhibit when reading the following discussion of these two variances.

EXHIBIT 16-1
Flexible-Budget and Sales-Volume Variance Analysis of Spring Distribution for June 2010

	A	B	C	D	E	F	G
1		**Actual Results:**		**Flexible Budget:**		**Static Budget:**	
2		**Actual Units of**		**Actual Units of**		**Budgeted Units of**	
3		**All Products Sold ×**		**All Products Sold ×**		**All Products Sold ×**	
4		**Actual Sales Mix ×**		**Actual Sales Mix ×**		**Budgeted Sales Mix ×**	
5		**Actual Contribution**		**Budgeted Contribution**		**Budgeted Contribution**	
6		**Margin per Unit**		**Margin per Unit**		**Margin per Unit**	
7		**(1)**		**(2)**		**(3)**	
8	Wholesale	900,000 × 0.84 × $0.49 =	$370,440	900,000 × 0.84 × $0.49 =	$370,440	890,000 × 0.80 × $0.49 =	$348,880
9	Retail	900,000 × 0.16 × $0.93 =	133,920	900,000 × 0.16 × $0.98 =	141,120	890,000 × 0.20 × $0.98 =	174,440
10			$504,360		$511,560		$523,320
11			↑	$7,200 U	↑	$11,760 U	↑
12	Level 2			Flexible-budget variance		Sales-volume variance	
13			↑		$ 18,960 U		↑
14	Level 1			Static budget variance			
15							
16	F = favourable effect on operating income; U = unfavourable effect on operating income						

	A	B	C	D	E	F	G
1		**Flexible Budget:**				**Static Budget:**	
2		**Actual Units of**		**Actual Units of**		**Budgeted Units of**	
3		**All Products Sold ×**		**All Products Sold ×**		**All Products Sold ×**	
4		**Actual Sales Mix ×**		**Budgeted Sales Mix ×**		**Budgeted Sales Mix ×**	
5		**Budgeted Contribution**		**Budgeted Contribution**		**Budgeted Contribution**	
6		**Margin per Unit**		**Margin per Unit**		**Margin per Unit**	
7		**(1)**		**(2)**		**(3)**	
8	Wholesale	900,000 × 0.84 × $0.49 =	$370,440	900,000 × 0.80 × $0.49 =	$352,800	890,000 × 0.80 × $0.49 =	$348,880
9	Retail	900,000 × 0.16 × $0.98 =	141,120	900,000 × 0.20 × $0.98 =	176,400	890,000 × 0.20 × $0.98 =	174,440
10			$511,560		$529,200		$523,320
11				$17,640 U		$5,880 F	
12	Level 3			Sales-mix variance		Sales-quantity variance	
13					$ 11,760 U		
14	Level 2				Sales-volume variance		

SALES-MIX VARIANCE

The **sales-mix variance** is the difference between two amounts: (1) the budgeted amount for the actual sales mix and (2) the budgeted amount for the budgeted sales mix. The formula for computing the sales-mix variance in terms of the contribution margin for Spring is

$$\begin{array}{l} \text{Sales mix} \\ \text{variance} \end{array} = \begin{array}{l} \text{Actual units of} \\ \text{all products sold} \end{array} \times \left(\begin{array}{l} \text{Actual sales} \\ \text{mix percentage} \end{array} - \begin{array}{l} \text{Budgeted sales} \\ \text{mix percentage} \end{array} \right) \times \begin{array}{l} \text{Budgeted} \\ \text{contribution} \\ \text{margin per unit} \end{array}$$

	Actual Units of All Products Sold	×	(Actual Sales-Mix Percentage	−	Budgeted Sales-Mix Percentage)	×	Budgeted Contribution Margin per Unit	=	Sales-Mix Variance
Wholesale	900,000 units	×	(84.00%	−	80.00%)	×	$0.49 per unit	=	$ 17,640 F
Retail	900,000 units	×	(16.00%	−	20.00%)	×	$0.98 per unit	=	$(35,280) U
Total sales-mix variance									$(17,640) U

A favourable sales-mix variance arises for the wholesale channel because the 84% actual sales-mix percentage exceeds the 80% budgeted sales-mix percentage. In contrast, the retail channel has an unfavourable variance because the 16% actual sales-mix percentage is less than the 20% budgeted sales-mix percentage. The sales-mix variance is unfavourable because actual sales mix shifted towards the less-profitable wholesale channel relative to budgeted sales mix.

The concept underlying the sales-mix variance is best explained in terms of budgeted contribution margin per composite unit of the sales mix. A **composite unit** is a hypothetical unit with weights based on the mix of individual units. For actual sales mix, the composite unit consists of 0.84 units of sales to the wholesale channel and 0.16 units of sales to the retail channel. For budgeted sales mix, the composite unit consists of 0.80 units of sales to the wholesale channel and 0.20 units of sales to the retail channel. In the following table, budgeted contribution margin per composite unit is computed in column 3 for actual mix and in column 5 for budgeted mix:

	Budgeted Contribution Margin per Unit (1)	Actual Sales-Mix Percentage (2)	Budgeted Contribution Margin per Unit for Actual Mix (3) = (1) × (2)	Budgeted Sales-Mix Percentage (4)	Budgeted Contribution Margin per Composite Unit for Budgeted Mix (5) = (1) × (4)
Wholesale	$0.49	84.00%	$0.4116	80.00%	$0.3920
Retail	0.98	16.00%	0.1568	20.00%	0.1960
			$0.5684		$0.5880

Actual sales mix has a budgeted contribution margin per composite unit of $0.5684. Budgeted sales mix has a budgeted contribution margin per composite unit of $0.5880. Budgeted contribution margin per composite unit can be computed in another way by dividing total budgeted contribution margin of $523,320 by total budgeted units of 890,000: $523,320 ÷ 890,000 units = $0.5880 per unit. The effect of the sales-mix shift for Spring is to decrease budgeted contribution margin per composite unit by $0.0196 ($0.5880 − $0.5684). For the 900,000 units actually sold, this decrease translates to a $17,640 U sales-mix variance ($0.0196 per unit × 900,000 units).

Managers should probe why the $17,640 U sales-mix variance occurred in June 2010. Is the shift in sales mix because, as the analysis in the previous section showed, profitable retail customers proved to be more difficult to find? Is it because of a competitor in the retail channel providing better service at a lower price? Or is it because the initial sales-volume estimates were made without adequate analysis of the potential market?

SALES-QUANTITY VARIANCE

The **sales-quantity variance** is the difference between two amounts: (1) the budgeted contribution margin based on actual units sold of all products and the budgeted mix, and (2) the contribution margin in the static budget (which is based on the budgeted units to be sold of all products and the budgeted mix). The formula for calculating the sales-quantity variance in terms of contribution margin is

$$\text{Sales-quantity variance} = \left(\begin{array}{c} \text{Actual units of} \\ \text{all products sold} \end{array} - \begin{array}{c} \text{Budgeted units of} \\ \text{all products sold} \end{array} \right) \times \begin{array}{c} \text{Budgeted sales-} \\ \text{mix percentage} \end{array} \times \begin{array}{c} \text{Budgeted} \\ \text{contribution} \\ \text{margin per unit} \end{array}$$

	(Actual Units of All Products Sold	−	Budgeted Units of All Products Sold)	×	Budgeted Sales- Mix Percentage	×	Budgeted Contribution Margin per Unit	=	Quantity Variance
Wholesale	(900,000	−	890,000)	×	80.00%	×	$0.49 per unit	=	$ 3,920 F
Retail	(900,000	−	890,000)	×	20.00%	×	$0.98 per unit	=	1,960 F
Total sales-quantity variance									$ 5,880 F

This variance is favourable when actual units of all products sold exceed budgeted units of all products sold. Spring sold 10,000 more cases than were budgeted, resulting in a $5,880 F sales-quantity variance (also equal to budgeted contribution margin per composite unit for the budgeted sales mix times additional cases sold, $0.5880 × 10,000). Managers would want to probe the reasons for the increase in sales. Did higher sales come as a result of a competitor's distribution problems? Better customer service? Or growth in the overall market? Further insight into the causes of the sales-quantity variance can be gained by analyzing changes in Spring's share of the total industry market and in the size of that market.

Sales depend on overall demand for the industry's products as well as the company's share of the market for bottled water. Assume that Spring derived its total unit sales budget for 2010 from a management estimate of a 25% market share and a total industry sales forecast of 3,560,000 units ($0.25 \times 3,560,000$ units = 890,000 units). For June 2010 actual industry sales were 4,000,000 and Spring's actual market share was 22.5% ($900,000 \div 4,000,000 = 0.225$ or 22.5%). Exhibit 16-3 shows the columnar presentation of the market-share and market-size variances of Spring.

MARKET-SHARE VARIANCE

The **market-share variance** is the difference between two amounts: (1) the budgeted amount based on actual market size in units, *actual market share*, and budgeted contribution margin per composite unit for the budgeted mix, and (2) the budgeted amount based on actual market size in units, *budgeted market share*, and budgeted contribution margin per composite unit for the budgeted mix. The formula for computing the market-share variance in terms of contribution margin for Spring is

$$\begin{array}{l} \text{Market-share} \\ \text{variance} \end{array} = \begin{array}{l} \text{Actual market} \\ \text{size in units} \end{array} \times \left(\begin{array}{l} \text{Actual} \\ \text{market share} \end{array} - \begin{array}{l} \text{Budgeted} \\ \text{market share} \end{array} \right) \times \begin{array}{l} \text{Budgeted contribution} \\ \text{margin per composite} \\ \text{unit for budgeted mix} \end{array}$$

$$= 4{,}000{,}000 \text{ units (cases)} \times (0.225 - 0.25) \times \$0.5880 \text{ per unit (case)}$$
$$= \$58{,}800 \text{ U}$$

The budgeted contribution margin per composite unit for the budgeted mix (also known as budgeted average contribution margin per unit) can be calculated using the approach outlined earlier in this chapter.

EXHIBIT 16-3
Market-Share and Market-Size Variance Analysis of Spring Distribution for June 2010

	A	B	C	D	E	F
1						**Static Budget:**
2		**Actual Market Size ×**		**Actual Market Size ×**		**Budgeted Market Size ×**
3		**Actual Market Share ×**		**Budgeted Market Share ×**		**Budgeted Market Share ×**
4		**Budgeted Average**		**Budgeted Average**		**Budgeted Average**
5		**Contribution Margin**		**Contribution Margin**		**Contribution Margin**
6		**per Unit**		**per Unit**		**per Unit**
7		$4{,}000{,}000 \times 0.225^a \times \$0.5880^b$		$4{,}000{,}000 \times 0.25^c \times \$0.5880^b$		$3{,}560{,}000 \times 0.25^c \times \$0.5880^b$
8		$\$529{,}200$		$\$588{,}000$		$\$523{,}320$
9		↑		↑		↑
10			$\$58{,}800$ U		$\$64{,}680$ F	
11	Level 4		Market-share variance		Market-size variance	
12		↑				↑
13				$\$5{,}880$ F		
14	Level 3			Sales-quantity variance		
15						
16	F = favourable effect on operating income U = unfavourable effect on operating income					
17	^{a}Actual market share: 900,000 units ÷ 4,000,000 units = 0.225 or 22.5%					
18	^{b}Budgeted average contribution margin per unit: $523,320 ÷ 890,000 units = $0.5880 per unit					
19	^{c}Budgeted market share: 890,000 ÷ 3,560,000 units = 0.25 or 25%					

MARKET-SIZE VARIANCE

The **market-size variance** is the difference between two amounts: (1) the budgeted amount based on *actual market size in units*, budgeted market share, and budgeted contribution margin per composite unit for budgeted mix, and (2) the static budget amount based on the *budgeted market size in units*, budgeted market share, and budgeted contribution margin per composite unit for budgeted mix. The formula for computing the market-size variance in terms of contribution margin for Spring is

$$
\begin{array}{l}
\text{Market-size} \\
\text{variance}
\end{array}
= \left(
\begin{array}{l}
\text{Actual market} \\
\text{size in units}
\end{array}
-
\begin{array}{l}
\text{Budgeted market} \\
\text{size in units}
\end{array}
\right)
\times
\begin{array}{l}
\text{Budgeted} \\
\text{market share}
\end{array}
\times
\begin{array}{l}
\text{Budgeted contribution} \\
\text{margin per composite} \\
\text{unit for budgeted mix}
\end{array}
$$

$$
= 4,000,000 \text{ units (cases)} - 3,560,000) \times 0.25 \times \$0.5880
$$
$$
= \$64,680 \text{ F}
$$

The market-size variance is favourable because actual market size, or total consumer demand, increased 440,000 cases or 12.4%[2] compared to budgeted market size. Managers should probe the reasons for the market-share and market-size variances for June 2010. Was the $58,800 unfavourable market-share variance because of competitors providing better service and offering a lower price? Did Spring's products experience quality-control problems that were the subject of negative media coverage? Is the $64,680 F market-size variance because of an increase in market size that can be expected to continue in the future? If yes, Spring has much to gain by attaining or exceeding its budgeted 25% market share.

Some companies place more emphasis on the market-share variance than the market-size variance when evaluating their managers. That's because they believe the market-size variance is influenced by economywide factors and shifts in consumer preferences that are outside the managers' control, whereas the market-share variance measures how well managers performed relative to their peers. Be cautious when computing the market-size variance and the market-share variance. Reliable information on market size and market share is available for some, but not all, industries. The automobile, computer, and television industries are cases in which market-size and market-share statistics are widely available. In other industries, such as management consulting and personal financial planning, information about market size and market share is far less reliable.

Exhibit 16-4 presents an overview of the level 1 to level 4 variances. The next discussion describes mix and quantity variances for production outputs.

The sales-mix variance, sales-quantity variance, market-share variance, and market-size variance can also be calculated in a multiproduct company, in which each individual product has a different contribution margin per unit. The Problem for Self-Study calculates these level 3 and level 4 sales variances in a multiproduct company.

COST-MIX AND YIELD LEVEL 4 VARIANCES FOR SUBSTITUTABLE INPUTS

Profitability analysis requires not only revenue analysis but also cost analysis. We began by extending the Chapter 7 coverage of sales volume variance. The mix and quantity framework already presented can also be applied to the analysis of production-input variances. In Chapter 7 the input variances were presented assuming they were *nonsubstitutable*. Consider a company assembling voyager satellites for NASA's space program.

Once a product design for a satellite is approved, there is a mandate that it be adhered to. The contractor cannot substitute a different combination of doors and door locks, irrespective of price movements of alternative doors and locks. In other cases, however, managers have some leeway in combining inputs. For example, Del Monte can combine material inputs (such as pineapples, cherries, and grapes) in varying proportions for its cans of fruit salad. Within limits, these individual fruits are *substitutable* inputs in making a fruit salad.

[2](4,000,000 − 3,560,000) ÷ 3,560,000 = 0.124 or 12.4%

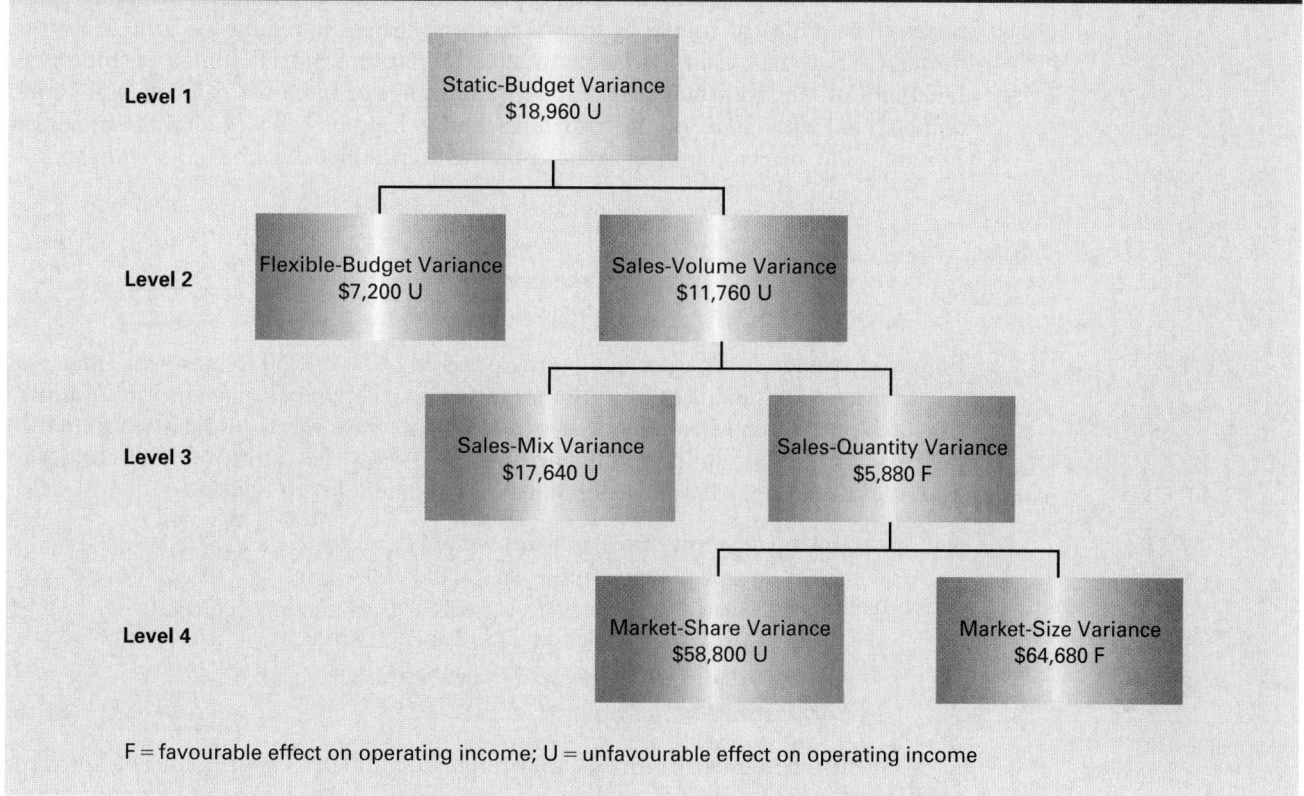

F = favourable effect on operating income; U = unfavourable effect on operating income

When inputs are substitutable, the decisions managers make will have financial implications for profitability which are highlighted by the presentation of mix and yield variances. These variances separate the components of the efficiency variance that was discussed in Chapter 7. To illustrate mix and yield variances, we examine Delpino Corporation, which makes tomato ketchup. Our example focuses on direct

REAL COMPANIES

Revenue Allocation

Using data from public sources, Mudde and Sopariwala used the methods in this section and augmented by Sopariwala to analyze the sources of increased revenue for Southwest Airlines (SWA) from 2004 to 2005. They determined that a revenue increase of $70 million resulted from a 4.55% increase in the market size of

domestic travel in the US. This market trend was not within SWA's control; however, it *was* within management's control to increase flights to take advantage of the trend. As a result, SWA earned an additional $126 million. When you compare the $70 million in growth that was due to the "good luck" of market growth to the $126 million of growth due to good management, it is clear that superior management played an important role in the company's earnings. The authors do a more detailed analysis of cost efficiencies to provide additional evidence supporting this conclusion.

Source: P. A. Mudde and P. R. Sopariwala, "Examining Southwest Airlines' Strategic Execution: A Strategic Variance Analysis," *Management Accounting Quarterly,* 9.4 (2008): 20–32.

material inputs and substitution among three of these inputs. The same approach can also be used to examine substitutable direct labour inputs.

To produce ketchup of the desired consistency, colour, and taste, Delpino mixes three types of tomatoes grown in three different regions—Latin American tomatoes (Latoms), California tomatoes (Caltoms), and Florida tomatoes (Flotoms). Delpino's production standards require 1.60 tonnes of tomatoes to produce 1 tonne of ketchup, with 50% of the tomatoes being Latoms, 30% Caltoms, and 20% Flotoms. The direct materials input standards to produce 1 tonne of ketchup are:

0.80 (50% of 1.6) tonne of Latoms at $70 per tonne	$ 56.00
0.48 (30% of 1.6) tonne of Caltoms at $80 per tonne	38.40
0.32 (20% of 1.6) tonne of Flotoms at $90 per tonne	28.80
Total standard cost of 1.6 tonnes of tomatoes	$123.20

Budgeted average cost per tonne of tomatoes is $123.20 ÷ 1.60 tonnes = $77.00.

Because Delpino uses fresh tomatoes to make ketchup, no inventories of tomatoes are kept. Purchases are made as needed, so all price variances relate to tomatoes purchased and used. Actual results for June 2010 show that a total of 6,500 tonnes of tomatoes were used to produce 4,000 tonnes of ketchup:

3,250	tonnes of Latoms at actual cost of $70 per tonne	$227,500
2,275	tonnes of Caltoms at actual cost of $82 per tonne	186,550
975	tonnes of Flotoms at actual cost of $96 per tonne	93,600
6,500	tonnes of tomatoes	$507,650
	Standard cost of 4,000 tonnes of ketchup at $123.20	492,800
	Total variance to be explained	$ 14,850 U

Given the standard ratio of 1.60 tonnes of tomatoes to 1 tonne of ketchup, 6,400 tonnes of tomatoes should be used to produce 4,000 tonnes of ketchup. At the standard mix, the quantities of each type of tomato required are

Latoms	0.50 × 6,400 = 3,200 tonnes
Caltoms	0.30 × 6,400 = 1,920 tonnes
Flotoms	0.20 × 6,400 = 1,280 tonnes

DIRECT MATERIALS PRICE AND EFFICIENCY VARIANCES

Exhibit 16-5 presents the columnar analysis of the flexible-budget variance for direct materials discussed in Chapter 7. The direct materials price and efficiency variances are calculated separately for each input material and then added together. The variance analysis prompts Delpino to investigate the unfavourable price and efficiency variances—why did they pay more for the tomatoes and use greater quantities than they should have? Causes could include a higher market price for tomatoes or poor negotiation by the Purchasing Department. One is uncontrollable, the other is controllable. Inefficiency could also have been due to poor-quality tomatoes with too much water content or issues with the processing.

DIRECT MATERIALS MIX AND DIRECT MATERIALS YIELD VARIANCES

Managers sometimes do have discretion to substitute one material for another. For example, the manager of Delpino's ketchup plant has some leeway in combining Latoms, Caltoms, and Flotoms without affecting quality. We will assume that to maintain quality, the mix percentages of each type of tomato can vary only up to 5% from the standard mix. For example, the percentage of Caltoms in the mix can vary between 25% and 35% (30% ± 5%).

When inputs are substitutable, direct materials efficiency improvement relative to budgeted costs can come from two sources: (1) using a cheaper mix to produce a given quantity of output and (2) using less input to achieve a given quantity of output. The direct materials yield and mix variances divide the efficiency variance into two variances: the mix variance focuses on how the multiple types of substitutable materials or labour are combined and the yield variance focuses on how much of those inputs are used.

EXHIBIT 16-5
Direct Materials Price and Efficiency Variances for the Delpino Corporation for June 2010*

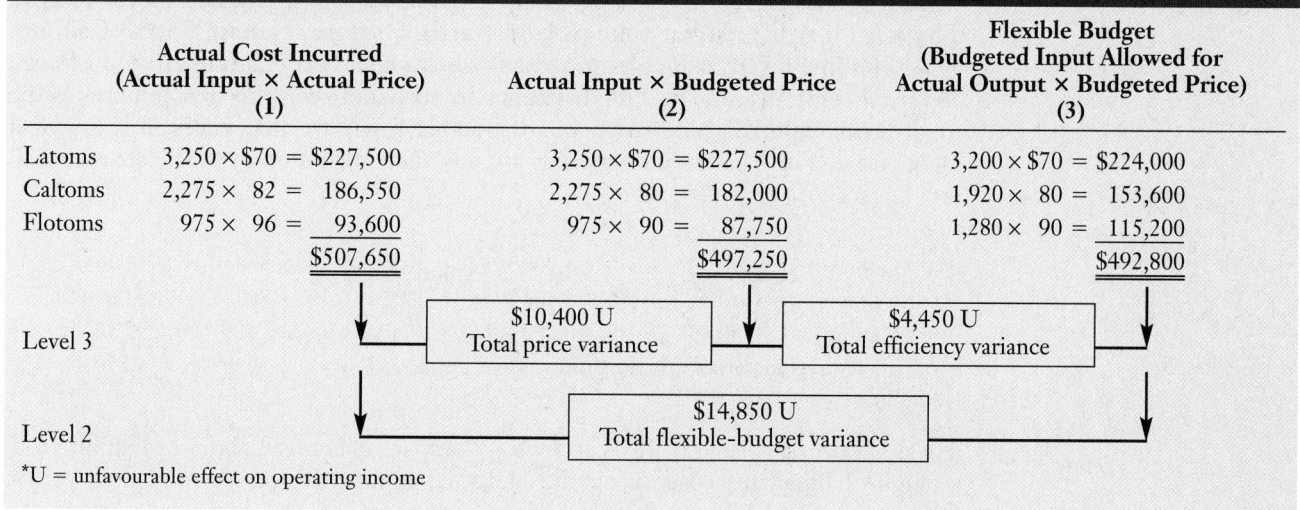

	Actual Cost Incurred (Actual Input × Actual Price) (1)	Actual Input × Budgeted Price (2)	Flexible Budget (Budgeted Input Allowed for Actual Output × Budgeted Price) (3)
Latoms	3,250 × $70 = $227,500	3,250 × $70 = $227,500	3,200 × $70 = $224,000
Caltoms	2,275 × 82 = 186,550	2,275 × 80 = 182,000	1,920 × 80 = 153,600
Flotoms	975 × 96 = 93,600	975 × 90 = 87,750	1,280 × 90 = 115,200
	$507,650	$497,250	$492,800

Level 3: $10,400 U Total price variance $4,450 U Total efficiency variance

Level 2: $14,850 U Total flexible-budget variance

*U = unfavourable effect on operating income

Holding constant the actual total quantity of all direct materials inputs used, the total **direct materials mix variance** is the difference between two amounts: (1) the budgeted cost for the actual mix of the total quantity of direct materials used, and (2) the budgeted cost of the budgeted mix of the actual total quantity of direct materials used. Holding the budgeted input mix constant, the **direct materials yield variance** is the difference between two amounts: (1) the budgeted cost of direct materials based on the actual total quantity of all direct materials inputs used, and (2) the flexible-budget cost of direct materials based on the budgeted total quantity of direct materials inputs for the actual output.

Exhibit 16-6 presents the total direct materials mix and yield variances for the Delpino Corporation.

EXHIBIT 16-6
Total Direct Materials Mix and Yield Variances for the Delpino Corporation for June 2010*

	Actual Total Quantity of All Inputs Used × Actual Input Mix Budgeted Price × (1)	Actual Total Quantity of All Inputs Used × Budgeted Input Mix Budgeted Price × (2)	Flexible Budget (Budgeted Total Quantity of All Inputs Allowed for Actual Output Budgeted Input Mix × Budgeted Price) × (3)
Latoms	6,500 × 0.50[a] × $70 = $227,500	6,500 × 0.50 × $70 = $227,500	6,400 × 0.50 × $70 = $224,000
Caltoms	6,500 × 0.35[b] × 80 = 182,000	6,500 × 0.30 × 80 = 156,000	6,400 × 0.30 × 80 = 153,600
Flotoms	6,500 × 0.15[c] × 90 = 87,750	6,500 × 0.20 × 90 = 117,000	6,400 × 0.20 × 90 = 115,200
	$497,250	$500,500	$492,800

Level 4: $3,250 F Total mix variance $7,700 U Total yield variance

Level 3: $4,450 U Total efficiency variance

[a]3,250 ÷ 6,500
[b]2,275 ÷ 6,500
[c]975 ÷ 6,500

*F = favourable effect on operating income; U = unfavourable effect on operating income

Direct Materials Mix Variance   Compare columns 1 and 2 in Exhibit 16-6. Both columns calculate cost using the actual total quantity of all inputs used (6,500 tonnes) and budgeted input prices (Latoms, $70; Caltoms, $80; and Flotoms, $90). The *only* difference is that column 1 uses *actual input mix* (Latoms, 50%; Caltoms, 35%; Flotoms, 15%), and column 2 uses *budgeted input mix* (Latoms, 50%; Caltoms, 30%; and Flotoms, 20%). The difference in costs between the two columns is the total direct materials mix variance, attributable solely to differences in the mix of inputs used. The total direct materials mix variance is the sum of the direct materials mix variances for each input.

Latoms $(0.50 - 0.50) \times 6{,}500 \times \$70 = 0.00 \times 6{,}500 \times \$70$ $= \$\quad 0$

Caltoms $(0.35 - 0.30) \times 6{,}500 \times \$80 = 0.05 \times 6{,}500 \times \$80$ $= \quad 26{,}000 \text{ U}$

Flotoms $(0.15 - 0.20) \times 6{,}500 \times \$90 = (0.05) \times 6{,}500 \times \$90$ $= \quad \underline{29{,}250} \text{ F}$

Total direct materials mix variance $\underline{\underline{\$\ 3{,}250}} \text{ F}$

Total Direct Materials Yield Variance   Compare columns 2 and 3 of Exhibit 16-6. Column 2 calculates costs using the budgeted input mix and the budgeted prices. Column 3 calculates the flexible-budget cost based on the budgeted cost of the budgeted total quantity of all inputs used (6,400 tonnes of tomatoes) for the actual output achieved (4,000 tonnes of ketchup) times the budgeted input mix (Latoms, 50%; Caltoms, 30%; Flotoms, 20%).

The only difference in the two columns is that column 2 uses the actual total quantity of all inputs used (6,500 tonnes), while column 3 uses the budgeted total quantity of all inputs used (6,400 tonnes). Hence, the difference in costs between the two columns is the total direct materials yield variance, due solely to differences in actual and budgeted total input quantity used. The total direct materials yield variance is the sum of the direct materials yield variances for each input.

Latoms $(6{,}500 - 6{,}400) \times 0.50 \times \$70 = 100 \times 0.50 \times \$70 = \$3{,}500 \text{ U}$

Caltoms $(6{,}500 - 6{,}400) \times 0.30 \times \$80 = 100 \times 0.30 \times \$80 = \quad 2{,}400 \text{ U}$

Flotoms $(6{,}500 - 6{,}400) \times 0.20 \times \$90 = 100 \times 0.20 \times \$90 = \quad \underline{1{,}800} \text{ U}$

Total direct materials yield variance $\underline{\underline{\$7{,}700}} \text{ U}$

The total direct materials yield variance is unfavourable because Delpino used 6,500 tonnes of tomatoes rather than the 6,400 tonnes that it should have used to produce 4,000 tonnes of ketchup. Holding the budgeted mix and budgeted prices of tomatoes constant, the budgeted cost per tonne of tomatoes in the budgeted mix is $77 per tonne. The unfavourable yield variance represents the budgeted cost of using 100 more tonnes of tomatoes: $(6{,}500 - 6{,}400) \times \$77 = \$7{,}700 \text{ U}$.

The direct materials variances computed in Exhibits 16-5 and 16-6 can be summarized as follows:

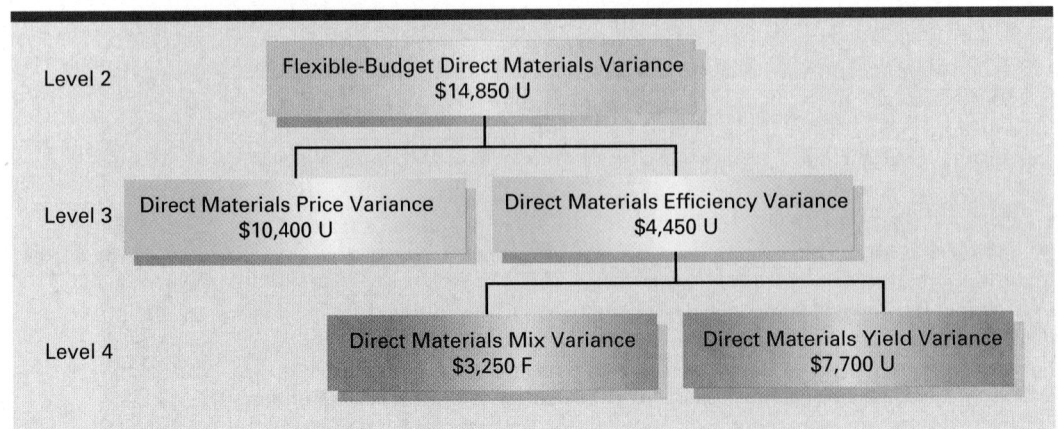

Reduced Waste and Spoilage from Yield Variance Analysis

Sandoz is the generic manufacturing division of Novartis, a global pharmaceutical company. Success requires delivering quality product at the lowest price. The successful strategy is cost leadership. Sandoz uses standard costs, based on the recipes for each product, to predict the costs associated with producing batches of each generic drug.

To monitor and control costs weekly, the plant controller reviews detailed materials variances and yield loss analyses to improve operations. The materials with the highest cost and highest yield loss are priorities. Along with year-to-date trends, the variance analyses are forwarded to the engineers and scientists in production and their task is to remedy the unfavourable variances. The remedy may be a change in material, equipment, suppliers, process, or even the standard quantity used for each batch.

Direct manufacturing labour in the blending, mixing, tableting, and packaging processes are also closely analyzed and suggestions to improve yield are implemented. Over the years, Sandoz has decreased yield and destruction losses. This has shortened cycle times, reduced backorders, and improved Sandoz's ability to meet its customers' expectations and improve its own profitability.

Source: Conversations with and documents prepared by Eric Evans and Erich Erchr (of Sandoz US) on March 20, 2004 and May 28, 2004.

PULLING IT ALL TOGETHER—PROBLEM FOR SELF-STUDY

PROBLEM

The Payne Company manufactures two types of vinyl flooring. Budgeted and actual operating data for 2010 are:

	Static Budget			Actual Results		
	Commercial	Residential	Total	Commercial	Residential	Total
Unit sales in rolls	20,000	60,000	80,000	25,200	58,800	84,000
Contribution margin	$10,000,000	$24,000,000	$34,000,000	$11,970,000	$24,696,000	$36,666,000

In late 2009, a marketing research firm estimated industry volume for commercial and residential vinyl flooring for 2010 at 800,000 rolls. Actual industry volume for 2010 was 700,000 rolls.

REQUIRED

1. Compute the sales-mix variance and the sales-quantity variance by type of vinyl flooring and in total. (Compute all variances in terms of contribution margins.)
2. Compute the market-share variance and the market-size variance.
3. What insights do the variances calculated in 1 and 2 provide about Payne Company's performance in 2010?

SOLUTION

1. Actual sales-mix percentage:

$$\text{Commercial} = 25{,}200 \div 84{,}000 = 0.30, \text{ or } 30\%$$
$$\text{Residential} = 58{,}800 \div 84{,}000 = 0.70, \text{ or } 70\%$$

Budgeted sales-mix percentage:

$$\text{Commercial} = 20{,}000 \div 80{,}000 = 0.25, \text{ or } 25\%$$
$$\text{Residential} = 60{,}000 \div 80{,}000 = 0.75, \text{ or } 75\%$$

	Actual Units of All Products Sold	×	(Actual Sales-Mix Percentage − Budgeted Sales-Mix Percentage)	×	Budgeted Contribution Margin per Unit	=	Sales-Mix Variance
Commercial	84,000 units	×	(0.30 − 0.25)	×	$500 per unit	=	$2,100,000 F
Residential	84,000 units	×	(0.70 − 0.75)	×	$400 per unit	=	1,680,000 U
Total sales-mix variance							$ 420,000 F

	(Actual Units of All Products Sold − Budgeted Units of All Products Sold)	×	Budgeted Sales-Mix Percentage	×	Budgeted Contribution Margin per Unit	=	Sales-Quantity Variance
Commercial	(84,000 units − 80,000 units)	×	0.25	×	$500 per unit	=	$ 500,000 F
Residential	(84,000 units − 80,000 units)	×	0.75	×	$400 per unit	=	1,200,000 F
Total sales-quantity variance							$1,700,000 F

2. Actual market share = $84{,}000 \div 700{,}000 = 0.12$, or 12%
Budgeted market share = $80{,}000 \div 800{,}000 = 0.10$, or 10%
Budgeted contribution margin
   per composite unit = $\$34{,}000{,}000 \div 80{,}000$ units = $425 per unit
      of budgeted mix

Budgeted contribution margin per composite unit of budgeted mix can also be calculated as:

$$\text{Commercial:} \quad \$500 \text{ per unit} \times 0.25 = \$125 \text{ per unit}$$
$$\text{Residential:} \quad \$400 \text{ per unit} \times 0.75 = \underline{\$300} \text{ per unit}$$
$$\underline{\underline{\$425}} \text{ per unit}$$

$$\begin{aligned}
\text{Market-share variance} &= \text{Actual market size in units} \times \left(\text{Actual market share} - \text{Budgeted market share} \right) \times \text{Budgeted contribution margin per composite unit for budgeted mix} \\
&= 700{,}000 \text{ units} \times \quad (0.12 - 0.10) \quad \times \quad \$425 \text{ per unit} \\
&= \$5{,}950{,}000 \text{ F}
\end{aligned}$$

$$\begin{aligned}
\text{Market-size variance} &= \left(\text{Actual market size in units} - \text{Budgeted market size in units} \right) \times \text{Budgeted market share} \times \text{Budgeted contribution margin per composite unit for budgeted mix} \\
&= (700{,}000 \text{ units} - 800{,}000 \text{ units}) \times \quad 0.10 \quad \times \quad \$425 \text{ per unit} \\
&= \$4{,}250{,}000 \text{ U}
\end{aligned}$$

Note that the algebraic sum of the market-share variance and the market-size variance is equal to the sales-quantity variance: $5,950,000 F + $4,250,000 U = $1,700,000 F.

3. Both the sales-mix variance and the sales-quantity variance are favourable. The favourable sales-mix variance occurred because the actual mix comprised more of the higher-margin commercial vinyl flooring. The favourable sales-quantity variance occurred because the actual total quantity of rolls sold exceeded the budgeted amount. The company's large favourable market-share variance is due to a 12% actual market share compared with a 10% budgeted market share. The market-size variance is unfavourable because the market size was 100,000 rolls less than the budgeted amount. Payne's performance in 2010 appears to be very good. Although overall market size declined, the company sold more units than budgeted by gaining market share.

RELEVANCE

❸ Evaluate the relevance of information obtained from revenue and cost variance analyses

Managers solve problems—where there are no problems there is no need to manage anything. The quality of the remedies managers invent or simply reapply from past experience depends on the knowledge at their disposal. Knowledge in the form of information is the basis of their decisions when they can identify alternative remedies. Decisions are made continuously and in response to unexpected events in a context of intense competition characterized emphatically by uncertainty.

Beginning with Chapters 2 and 3, then formally presented in Chapter 11, the importance of high-quality information to this Bayesian process has been highlighted throughout the text. High-quality information is reliable and relevant, hence the dependence on standardized financial information as the basis for reconfiguring the information to be improve its relevance. If management were not essentially a Bayesian process then relevance would be a meaningless term because no one would be making informed decisions. Levels 3 and 4 variance analyses are important to understand for this reason. The essential management problem is neither cost nor revenue control, but rather profitability control.

The decomposition of the sales-volume variance into sales-mix and sales-quantity variance illustrates the signalling or attention-getting purpose of managerial accounting. In essence the management team has already decided upon the bundle of outputs or the budgeted composite unit for sale. Their decision was in part based on historical information and in part on assumptions about the future, in particular the demand for their bundle. The quantity demanded in the short run may or may not be the basis of estimating the allocation of fixed costs (see Chapter 9).

While managers understand that there will be random events that cause actual performance to vary from expected, timely feedback alerts them when a variance may have a non-random cause. The sales-mix variance helps direct attention to a non-random change in variable costs or unit price which has reduced the contribution margin. The sales-quantity variance isolates and directs attention towards a non-random change in quantities produced and sold. Recall that using the contribution margin approach implies zero ending inventory of finished goods (Chapter 3). Knowing actual demand did not meet the pro forma will also alert managers to expect an unfavourable production volume variance.

The managerial task, based on this feedback, is to decide upon the best response. The unfavourable variances have only revealed what occurred, not how it occurred. If there is a controllable cause, then the team will find an operating remedy. If there is an uncontrollable cause, then the best decision may be to change the budget and deal with a new set of expectations, as unfavourable as they may be.

The realized outcome has caused managers to reassess their prior assessments about the likelihood of achieving some targeted quantity of sales. Based on their reassessment, a new decision is made about the utilization of capacity. After this decision is made a new denominator is chosen for the fixed overhead allocations. This interdependent series of influences among outcomes and decisions was illustrated in Exhibit 11-1 (p. 530).

Market-share and market-size variances reveal generally what variances are controllable and uncontrollable. In a competitive market it is rare that a single company can control market size. The demand for a product or a service depends on consumer preference. In classical economic models, preferences are formed prior to and independently of specific consumption decisions. Once consumers express their preference, demand or market size is known and suppliers attempt to influence the proportion of that market they serve, or market share.

Thus an unfavourable market size variance has strategic implications. For example the reduced demand for SUVs implies a long-term decision to change capacity. The cause of the reduced market size, high fuel prices, is beyond the control of vehicle manufacturers. Another potential remedy is innovative use of alternative, less expensive fuels, which requires redesign of the internal combustion engine. Still a third alternative would be to expand using adjacencies and simply harvest the benefits of the capacity already in place.

In contrast, an unfavourable market share variance has operating implications. The reduced demand for products made by a specific company with no accompanying reduction in market size provides different relevant information. Remedies include improved understanding of the value proposition, improved product attributes, or improved timeliness. In some cases a strategic remedy is required. This was true for the reduction in demand for Kentucky Fried Chicken as a result of a candid video on YouTube of slaughtering practices by the supplier of chicken. There is an increasing influence of corporate and environmental sustainability issues on the operations of for-profit companies.

The fourth level direct material variance analyses of mix and yield extends efficiency and effective analysis to substitutable inputs. For perishable food processing such as ketchup, olive oil, and imperishable processing of ethanol from corn, an inescapable economic fact is that the higher the yield, the lower the price. In June of any year, ethanol fuel inventory from last year's harvest will be almost gone.

Those who planted corn early this year will harvest early and be first to provide input to refineries. The uncertainty of the weather means uncertainty about the total available supply of corn in the current growing season, and not all farmers will risk planting corn early only to lose the crop. If the early yield is high relative to the expected total seasonal yield, then prices will not be as high as when the immediate yield is relatively low. Corn producers know this, and the effect of both market size and market share on their revenue. As demand for ethanol as a fuel (market size) increases, all other things equal, price for corn will increase, unless supply grows as well.

Olive oil is produced primarily in Mediterranean countries. In Turkey, a yield of olives in 1997 that was 40% lower than the yield in 2001 resulted in a 1997 price of olive oil that was higher by 68%.[3] Olives pressed for their oil cannot be sold for eating. Each has a different taste and texture. The oil is pressed within 48 hours of obtaining the olives. Most producers lease land from farmers because they can reduce production costs through economies of scale. Their costs include pruning, stem cutting, fertilization, and weed and insect and disease management of mature trees, and the growing cycle is fixed at two years.

But the producer who leases olive farms is directly exposed to uncertainty about the yield of olives during the two-year growth cycle. Yield depends on the oil content of olives, which depends on the weather and therefore is random within some range. Producers can enter into purchase agreements with other farmers for additional olives to supply their practical capacity should it appear yield will be low from the leased property. Producers need to decide on the mix of purchased and harvested

[3]B. Kazaz, "Production Planning Under Yield and Demand Uncertainty with Yield-Dependent Cost and Price," *Manufacturing & Service Operations Management*, 6.3 (2004): 209–224.

olives at the beginning of each cycle. If the leased crop yield is high, then any olives which cannot be pressed within 48 hours of harvest will be a byproduct. Supply conditions are identical; therefore the make/buy decision and the market share of supply chosen by producers will affect their relative profitability.

In this industry, the oil is not inventoried from year to year because its acidity increases and quality decreases. Thus excess, aged olive oil has only very low salvage value. The oil yielded by any specific quantity of olives depends on the quality of the olives. The higher the yield, the lower will be the price of high-quality oil because supply will be abundant. All other things equal, the higher the yield, the higher will be inventoried byproduct oil and the lower revenue gleaned from total output. Understanding the variance in substitutable (harvested or purchased) input mix and yield will inform the decisions made by managers undertaking financial contracts to manage risk and protect profitability throughout the two-year cycle.

Parts One and Two of this chapter have discussed revenue allocation and sales viances. Part Three discusses customer profitability analysis.

♦ PART THREE: CUSTOMER PROFITABILITY ANALYSIS

CUSTOMER REVENUES AND CUSTOMER COSTS

Analyze customer profitability by applying ABC cost hierarchy concepts

Prosperous companies have a strong customer focus in their decisions. Management accountants are giving increased attention to **customer profitability analysis**, which is the reporting and analysis of customer revenues and customer costs. Armed with this information, managers can ensure that customers contributing sizably to the profitability of an organization receive a comparable level of attention from the organization.

An analysis of customer differences on both revenues and costs can provide important insight into why differences in customer profitability exist. Returning to the example of Spring Distribution Company, we will focus mainly on customer profitability analysis in Spring's retail distribution channel. The list selling price in this channel is $14.40 per case (unit), while the purchase cost to Spring is $12 per case. If every bottle is sold at its list price in this distribution channel, Spring would earn a gross margin of $2.40 per case.

CUSTOMER REVENUE ANALYSIS

Let us first consider customer revenues. Data for four of Spring's customers in June 2010 are:

	A	B	C	D	E
1			CUSTOMER		
2		A	B	G	J
3 Cash sold		42,000	33,000	2,900	2,500
4 List selling price		$ 14.40	$ 14.40	$ 14.40	$ 14.40
5 Price discount		$ 0.96	$ 0.24	$ 1.20	$ –
6 Invoice price		$ 13.44	$ 14.16	$ 13.20	$ 14.40
7 Revenues (Row 3 × Row 6)		$564,480	$467,280	$38,280	$36,000

Customer revenue analysis is enhanced by tracking as much detail as possible to explain why customers differ in their revenues. Two variables explain revenue differences across these four customers: (a) the volume of bottles purchased and (b) the magnitude of price discounting. **Price discounting** is the reduction of selling prices below listed levels to encourage an increase in purchases by customers. Companies that record only the invoice price in their information system would not be able to readily track the magnitude of their price discounting (except in the extreme case of a single-product company with a constant list price in the accounting period).[4]

Price discounts are a function of multiple factors, including the volume of product purchased (higher-volume customers receive higher discounts) and the desire to sell to a customer who might help promote sales to other customers. Discounts could also be due to poor negotiating by a salesperson or the unwanted effect of an incentive plan based only on revenues. At no time should price discounts run afoul of the law by way of price discrimination, predatory pricing, or collusive pricing. Price discounts can also be unethical—for example, when discounts are given by pharmaceutical representatives to doctors to encourage them to prescribe a particular drug.

Tracking discounts by customer, and by salesperson, can provide valuable information about ways to improve customer profitability. For example, Spring Distribution may institute a corporate policy to ensure that any volume-based price discounting policy is enforced for customers with decreasing volume as well as those with increasing volume. It may also require its salespeople to obtain approval before giving large discounts to customers not normally qualifying for them. In addition, it could track the future sales of customers that its salespeople argue warrant a sizable price discount due to their predicted "high growth potential." Salespeople who have a poor track record in predicting the future growth of customers may be given additional training in sales forecasting (or may even be encouraged to seek employment elsewhere). For example, Spring should track future sales to customer G to confirm that the $1.20-per-case discount translated into higher future sales.

Customer revenues are one element of customer profitability. The other is customer costs.

CUSTOMER COST ANALYSIS

Chapters 5 and 14 discussed the *cost hierarchy* concept, in which costs are categorized into different cost pools on the basis of different types of cost drivers (or cost-allocation bases) or different degrees of difficulty in determining cause-and-effect (or benefits received) relationships. Spring Distribution has an activity-based costing system that classifies its costs into four categories:

- ◆ **Customer output unit-level costs**—costs of activities to sell each unit (case) to a customer. An example is product-handling costs of each case sold.

- ◆ **Customer batch-level costs**—costs of activities that are related to a group of units (cases) sold to a customer. Examples are costs incurred to process orders or to make deliveries.

- ◆ **Customer-sustaining costs**—costs of activities to support individual customers, regardless of the number of units or batches of product delivered to the customer. Examples are costs of visits to customers or costs of displays at customer sites.

- ◆ **Distribution-channel costs**—costs of activities related to a particular distribution channel rather than to each unit of product, each batch of product, or specific customers. An example is the salary of the manager of Spring's retail distribution channel.

- ◆ **Corporate-sustaining costs**—costs of activities that cannot be traced to individual customers or distribution channels. Examples are top-management and general-administration costs.

[4]Further analysis of customer revenues could distinguish between gross revenues and net revenues. This approach would highlight differences across customers in sales returns. Additional discussion of ways to analyze revenue differences across customers is in R. S. Kaplan and R. Cooper, *Cost and Effect* (Boston, Mass.: Harvard Business School Press, 1998), Chapter 10.

Spring uses its customer-cost hierarchy to assist managers in decisions made at different levels in this hierarchy. We will now consider decisions made at the individual customer level. Note from these descriptions that four of the five levels of Spring's cost hierarchy closely parallel the cost hierarchy described in Chapter 5, except that Spring focuses on *customers* whereas the cost hierarchy in Chapter 5 focused on *products*. Spring has one additional cost hierarchy category—distribution-channel costs, for the costs it incurs to support its wholesale and retail distribution channels.

CUSTOMER-SPECIFIC COSTS

Spring includes cost of goods sold and selling-related costs for individual customers in this category. Spring is particularly interested in analyzing customer-level indirect costs that are incurred in the first three categories of the customer-cost hierarchy: customer output unit-level costs, customer batch-level costs, and customer-sustaining costs. Spring believes that it can work with customers to reduce these costs. It believes that customer actions will have less impact on distribution-channel and corporate-sustaining costs. The five activity areas used to collect costs for selling-related costs, cost drivers, and rates are as follows:

Activity Area	Cost Rate and Driver	Cost Hierarchy Category
Product handling	$0.50 per case sold	Customer output-unit-level costs
Order taking	$ 100 per purchase order	Customer batch-level costs
Delivery vehicles	$ 2 per delivery kilometre travelled	Customer batch-level costs
Rush deliveries	$ 300 per expedited delivery	Customer batch-level costs
Visits to customers	$ 80 per sales visit	Customer-sustaining costs

The table below provides information on the quantity of cost driver consumed or used by each customer:

	Customer			
	A	B	G	J
Number of purchase orders	30	25	15	10
Number of deliveries	60	30	20	15
Kilometres travelled per delivery	5	12	20	6
Number of rush deliveries	1	–	2	–
Number of visits to customers	6	5	4	3

Spring Distribution can use the information underlying Exhibit 16-7 to assist its customers in reducing their consumption of the cost drivers. Consider in Exhibit 16-7 a comparison of Customer G, with total purchases (2,900 cases) only 7% the size of Customer A (42,000 cases). Customer G, however, requires one-half the number of purchase orders, two-thirds the number of visits to customers, one-third the number of deliveries, and double the number of rush deliveries. To improve the profitability of Customer G Spring must encourage this customer to request fewer customer visits and rush deliveries as well as larger but fewer purchases.

The ABC system underlying Exhibit 16-7 provides a road-map to facilitate less use of cost drivers by a customer in order to promote cost reduction. Another advantage of ABC is that it highlights a second way cost reduction can be promoted by Spring Distribution. Spring can take actions to reduce the costs in each of its own activity areas. For example, order taking currently is estimated to cost $100 per purchase order. By making its own ordering process more efficient (such as having its customers order electronically), Spring can reduce its costs even if its customers make the same number of orders.

Exhibit 16-8 shows a monthly operating income statement for Spring Distribution. The customer-level operating income of customers A and B in Exhibit 16-7 are shown in columns 8 and 9 of Exhibit 16-8 and information for the remaining

EXHIBIT 16-7
Customer Profitability Analysis for Four Customers of Spring Distribution for June 2010

	A	B	C	D	E
1			**CUSTOMER**		
2		**A**	**B**	**G**	**J**
3	Revenues at list price: $14.40 × 42,000; 33,000; 2,900; 2,500	$604,800	$475,200	$41,760	$36,000
4	Price discount: $0.96 × 42,000; $0.24 × 33,000; $1.20 × 2,900; $0 × 2,500	40,320	7,920	3,480	–
5	Revenues at actual price	564,480	467,280	38,280	36,000
6	Cost of goods sold: $12 × 42,000; 33,000; 2,900; 2,500	504,000	396,000	34,800	30,000
7	Gross margin	60,480	71,280	3,480	6,000
8	Customer-level operating costs				
9	Product handling: $0.50 × 42,000; 33,000; 2,900; 2,500	21,000	16,500	1,450	1,250
10	Order taking: $100 × 30; 25; 15; 10	3,000	2,500	1,500	1,000
11	Delivery vehicles: $2 × (5 × 60); (12 × 30); (20 × 20); (6 × 15)	600	720	800	180
12	Rush deliveries: $300 × 1; 0; 2; 0	300	–	600	–
13	Visits to customers: $80 × 6; 5; 4; 3	480	400	320	240
14	Total customer-level operating costs	25,380	20,120	4,670	2,670
15	Customer-level operating income	$ 35,100	$ 51,160	$ (1,190)	$ 3,330

customers in Exhibit 16-9. Wholesale customers comprise new data, as do the distribution-channel costs and corporate-sustaining costs. The format of Exhibit 16-8 is based on Spring's cost hierarchy.

All costs incurred to serve customers are not included in customer-level costs and therefore are not allocated to customers in Exhibit 16-8. For example, distribution-channel costs such as the salary of the manager of the retail distribution channel are not included in customer-level costs and are not allocated to customers. Instead, these costs are identified as costs of the distribution channel as a whole. That is

EXHIBIT 16-8
Income Statement for Spring Distribution in 2010

	A	B	C	D	E	F	G	H	I	J	K	L	M	N
1				**CUSTOMER DISTRIBUTION CHANNELS**										
2			**Wholesale Customers**					**Retail Customers**						
3		Total	Total	A1	A2	A3	•	Total	Aᵃ		Bᵃ		Gᵃ	Jᵃ
4		(1) = (2) + (7)	(2)	(3)	(4)	(5)	(6)	(7)	(8)		(9)		(10)	(11)
5	Revenues (at actual prices)	$12,138,120	$10,107,720	$1,946,000	$1,476,000	•	•	$2,030,400	$564,480		$467,280		•	•
6	Customer-level costs	11,633,760	9,737,280	1,868,000	1,416,000	•	•	1,896,480	529,380	ᵇ	416,120	ᵇ	•	•
7	Customer-level operating income	504,360	370,440	78,000	60,000	•	•	133,920	$35,100		$ 51,160		•	•
8	Distribution-channel costs	160,500	102,500					58,000						
9	Distribution-channel operating income	343,860	$267,940					$ 75,920						
10	Corporate-sustaining costs	263,000												
11	Operating income	$80,860												
12														
13	ᵃFull details are presented in Exhibit 16-7													
14	ᵇCost of goods sold + Total customer-level operating costs from Exhibit 16-7													

EXHIBIT 16-9
Customer-Profitability Analysis for Retail Channel Customers: Spring Distribution, June 2010

	A	B	C	D	E	F
1						Cumulative
2						Customer-Level
3		Customer-				Operating Income
4		Level		Customer-Level	Cumulative	as a % of Total
5		Operating	Customer	Operating Income	Customer-Level	Customer-Level
6	Customer	Income	Revenue	Divided by Revenue	Operating Income	Operating Income
7	Code	(1)	(2)	(3) = (1) – (2)	(4)	(5) = (4) ÷ $133,920
8	B	$ 51,160	$ 467,280	10.95%	$ 51,160	38.20%
9	A	35,100	564,480	6.22	86,260	64.41
10	C	21,070	255,640	8.24	107,330	80.14
11	D	17,580	277,000	6.35	124,910	93.27
12	F	7,504	123,500	6.08	132,414	98.88
13	J	3,330	36,000	9.25	135,744	101.36
14	E	3,176	193,000	1.65	138,920	103.73
15	G	(1,190)	38,280	–3.11	137,730	102.84
16	H	(1,690)	38,220	–4.42	136,040	101.58
17	I	(2,120)	37,000	–5.73	133,920	100.00
18		$133,920	$2,030,400			

because Spring's management believes that changes in the retail channel manager's salary will not affect the behaviour of a specific customer.

Distribution-channel costs will be affected only by decisions pertaining to the whole channel, such as a decision to discontinue retail distribution. Another reason Spring does not allocate distribution-channel costs to customers is motivation. Spring's managers contend that salespersons responsible for managing individual customer accounts would lose motivation if their bonuses were affected by the

GOVERNANCE ISSUES

Is the Customer Always Right?

What are some of the most important aspects of a business? The bottom line? Shareholders' perception of a company? The quality of a product or service offered? What about customers? Customers are essential to any business, but unfortunately some customers are not always profitable, which makes customer-profitability analysis a complex issue for management accountants. Consider Fidelity Investments. Fidelity's customer-profitability analysis revealed that some of its customers were unprofitable because of the ways they communicated with the company. Armed with this information, managers made changes to the company's processes. For example, telephone calls from unprofitable customers were placed in a long waiting queue, which was intended to discourage these customers from calling service representatives and to encourage them to instead use less-costly Internet and automated phone-line services. Fidelity's management was concerned that, unhappy with these changes, customers would leave; however, 96% of the targeted customers stayed, switched to lower-cost channels, and became profitable.[a] These short-term successes were shared with other managers, and the company grew more confident about the actions it needed to take. Teamwork, communication, and careful management of the changes were critical to the success of the customer-profitability implementation and the positive results that followed.

[a]See L. Seldon and G. Colvin, "Will This Customer Sink Your Stock?" Fortune, September 30, 2003.

allocation to customers of distribution-channel costs over which they have almost no influence.

Once an organization decides to measure customer profitability, management accountants are responsible for articulating the benefits of such measurements. This can be problematic for management accountants because the sales organizations in most companies are compensated on the basis of revenues, not customer profits. Therefore, the sales force may be reluctant to follow a strategy of serving only profitable customers and taking actions to change the behaviour and buying patterns of those that are unprofitable. Management accountants need to communicate to the sales force why measuring customer profits is critical to the organization. For example, they need to explain what might happen if change does not occur and how customer-profitability analysis can help the company reallocate resources to increase both revenues and profits.

When it comes to customer-profitability analysis, the sales force is not the only part of an organization that may pose challenges for management accountants. Line managers are sometimes surprised by which customers are profitable and which are not, because they may assume a company's largest customer is profitable. However, this customer may consume high levels of customer support and actually be unprofitable. For this reason, management accountants must make it a point to team up with line managers when designing the system to calculate customer profitability. Customer-profitability analysis should always be based on a thorough understanding of business processes so that it correctly represents the costs incurred to support different customers.

Now, consider corporate-sustaining costs such as top-management and general-administration costs. Spring's managers have concluded that there is neither a cause-and-effect nor a benefits-received relationship between any cost-allocation base and corporate-sustaining costs. Consequently, allocation of corporate-sustaining costs serves no useful purpose in decision making, performance evaluation, or motivation. For example, suppose Spring allocated the $263,000 of corporate-sustaining costs to its distribution channels: $173,000 to the wholesale channel and $90,000 to the retail channel. Using information from Exhibit 16-8, the retail channel would then show a loss of $14,080 ($75,920 – $90,000).

If this same situation persisted in subsequent months, should Spring shut down the retail distribution channel? No, because if retail distribution were discontinued, corporate-sustaining costs would be unaffected. Allocating corporate-sustaining costs to distribution channels could give the misleading impression that the potential cost savings from discontinuing a distribution channel would be greater than the likely amount.

Consider a distributor of medical supplies to hospitals. It strategically prices each of its services separately. For example, if a hospital wants a rush delivery or special packaging, the distributor charges the hospital an additional price for each particular service. Hospitals that value these services continue to demand them and pay for them while hospitals that do not value these services drop them, saving the distributor some costs. This is how the distributor's pricing strategy influences customer behaviour in a way that increases the distributor's revenues or decreases its costs.

Some managers and management accountants advocate fully allocating all costs to customers and distribution channels so that (1) the sum of operating incomes of all customers in a distribution channel (segment) equals the operating income of the distribution channel, and (2) the sum of the distribution-channel operating incomes equals companywide operating income. These managers and management accountants argue that customers and products must eventually be profitable on a full-cost basis. For some decisions, such as pricing, allocating all costs ensures that long-run prices are set at a level to cover the cost of all resources used to produce and sell products.

The hierarchical format in Exhibit 16-8 distinguishes among various degrees of objectivity when allocating costs, and it dovetails with the different levels at which decisions are made and performance is evaluated. The issue of when and what costs to allocate is another example of the "different costs for different purposes" theme emphasized throughout the book.

ASSESS YOUR MASTERY

MyAccountingLab

To check your understanding of the material in Learning Objective ④, go to the *Mastery Questions* section at the end of this chapter and complete Learning Objective ④ question 1.

CUSTOMER PROFITABILITY PROFILES

Prepare a customer profitability profile ⑤

Managers find customer profitability analysis useful for several reasons. First, it frequently highlights how vital a small set of customers is to total profitability. Managers need to ensure that the interests of these customers receive high priority. Microsoft uses the phrase "not all revenue dollars are endowed equally in profitability" to stress this key point. Second, when a customer is ranked in the "loss category," managers can focus on ways to make future business with this customer more profitable.

This high-percentage contribution by a small number of customers is a common finding in many studies. It highlights the importance of Spring Distribution maintaining good relations with this pivotal set of customers.

Exhibit 16-9 ranks customers on revenue (after price discounts). Three of the four smallest customers (based on revenue) are unprofitable. Moreover, customer E, with revenues of $193,000, is only marginally profitable. Further analysis revealed that a former sales representative gave customer E excessive discounts in an attempt to meet a monthly sales-volume target.

Managers often find the bar chart presentation in Exhibit 16-10 to be the most intuitive way to visualize customer profitability. The highly profitable customers clearly stand out. Moreover, the number of loss-customers and the magnitude of their losses are apparent and focus management attention on how to improve the profitability of these loss-customers.

ASSESSING CUSTOMER VALUE

The "80-20" rule also prevails among customers. Of total profit, 80% will come from 20% of the customers. Customer-profitability analysis is attention-getting and directs management attention on maintaining the best possible retention ratio of

EXHIBIT 16-10
Bar Chart Presentation of Customer Profitability for Spring Distribution

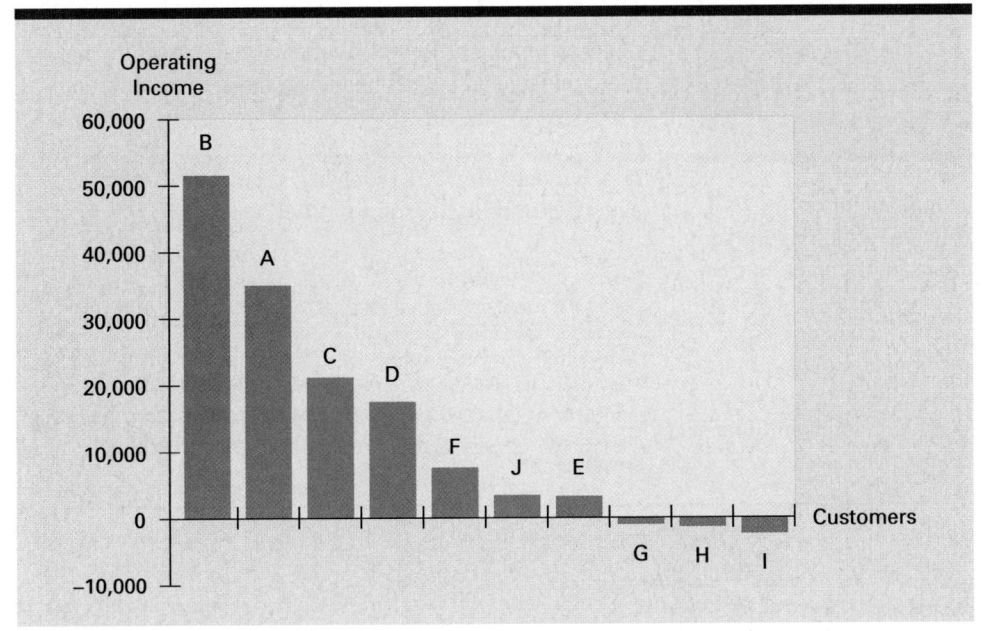

these customers and transforming the remainder into more profitable customers. The information in Exhibits 16-8 (p. 808) and 16-9 (p. 809) relates to customer profitability in a single accounting period. This is one of several factors that managers should consider in deciding how to allocate resources across customers. Other factors include:

1. **Short-run and long-run customer profitability.** This factor will be influenced by factors 2 and 3 below as well as by the level of resources likely to be required to retain the accounts.

2. **Customer retention likelihood.** The more likely a customer is to continue doing business with a company, the more valuable the customer. Customers can differ in their loyalty and their willingness to "shop their business" on a frequent basis.

3. **Customer growth potential.** This factor will be influenced by the likely growth of the industry of the customer and the likely growth of the customer (due to, say, its ability to develop new products). This factor will also be influenced by cross-selling opportunities—that is, when a customer of one of the company's products becomes a customer of one or more of the company's other products.

4. **Increases in overall demand from having well-known customers.** Some customers are highly valuable because they have established reputations that make them very useful to mention in sales visits. Other customers are valuable because of their willingness to provide product endorsements.

5. **Ability to learn from a customer.** Customers can be an important source of ideas about new products or ways to improve existing products. Customers willing to provide such input can be especially valuable.

REAL COMPANIES

Verizon Wireless Bundled Services—Customer Profitability

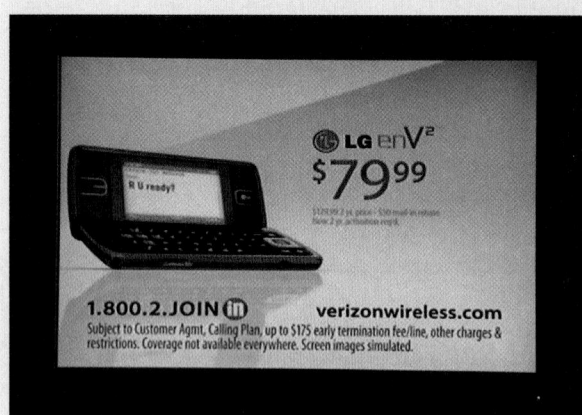

Verizon, a leading wireless-communications provider, offers a variety of services to businesses, government agencies, and individuals. Each product bundle is carefully costed and priced to increase the likelihood of customer profitability. During standard office hours, costs of transmission are high because customers demand large amounts of data bandwidth and suppliers use peak-load pricing. In contrast, individuals use bandwidth most extensively on evenings and weekends and download added features such as text messaging, music ringtones, and video game features. Some customers are urban and others rural. People using bare bones services very sparingly can select a limited service plan which is least expensive, while business customers can select guaranteed service and reliability plans which are more expensive. In 2007 base plans ranged from $39.99/month to $239.99/month, with additional charges for additional features such as video games. Careful analysis of customer profitability informs Verizon's managers of how profitable each service bundle is relative to expectations and how to expand in the most profitable customer segment. Verizon has the highest customer-retention rate, wireless-network reliability, and overall profitability among all wireless carriers.

Sources: J. Biln, *U.S. Wireless Carrier Data Services 3Q06-3Q07 Vendor Analysis: Q View Summary and Analysis* (IDC, January 23, 2007); R. Dineen, *Verizon Communications* (HSBC, June 14, 2007); Verizon Wireless Web site, http://investor.verizon.com/ accessed July 2, 2008; C. Osborn, "Customer Retention: Can Wireless Data Make ‘Em Stay Put?" in *The Future of Wireless: Business Strategies, Broadband Technologies, and Network Operations* (Chicago: International Engineering Consortium, 2004).

How Important Is Customer Profitability Analysis?

A survey of US and Australian managers[a] asked respondents about "the three most important general management priorities that your organization faces today." The top-ranked priorities were

1. Customer profitability/satisfaction
2. Cost management/cost control
3. Quality
4. Growth

A growing number of companies are now developing customer profitability systems to reinforce this strategic focus on customers. A survey of United Kingdom companies[b] found that 50% had "embarked on customer profitability analysis . . . A further 12% planned to pursue it in future." The uses of customer profitability analysis were ranked as follows (most important = 1):

1. Guidance for pricing policies
2. Renegotiation of customer contracts
3. Guidance for customer relations policies
4. Influence cost control in respect of customers.

"The 80/20 rule applied (that is, 20% of their customers were generating 80% of the profits)" to 60% of those who had examined cumulative contributions of customers to total profits.

[a]G. Foster and S. M. Young, "Frontiers of Management Accounting Research," *Journal of Management Accounting Research* (1997).

[b]J. Innes and F. Mitchell, "A Survey of Activity-Based Costing in the U.K.'s Largest Companies," *Management Accounting Research*, Vol. 6 (1995): 137–154.

Managers should be particularly cautious when deciding to drop customers. Short-run profitability reports may provide misleading signals about their long-run profitability. Moreover, not all costs assigned to a customer may be variable with respect to short-run reductions in purchases by customers. It is typically *not* the case that a policy of dropping any currently unprofitable customer (sometimes called "revenue shedding") will eliminate in the short run all the costs assigned to that customer.

PULLING IT ALL TOGETHER—PROBLEM FOR SELF-STUDY

PROBLEM

Spring Distribution is concerned with the level of its profitability. Its June 2010 operating income of $78,000 is less than 1% of sales ($78,000 ÷ $12,470,000 = 0.63%). Suppose that July 2010 is identical to June 2010 with one exception. In July 2010, Spring conducts an extensive efficiency analysis of its activity areas and is able to reduce their costs to the levels shown below:

Activity Area	Cost Driver Rate
Order taking	$60 per purchase order
Sales visits	$50 per visit
Delivery vehicles	$1.50 per delivery kilometre travelled
Product handling	$0.015 per bottle sold
Expedited deliveries	$200 per expedited delivery

REQUIRED

1. What is the effect of these activity-area cost reductions on the July 2010 profitability (customer-specific contribution) of customers A, B, G, and J in Exhibit 16-7 (p. 808)?
2. What are additional ways Spring could seek to improve the profitability of customers A, B, G, and J?

SOLUTION

1. The July 2010 activity-area cost rate reductions affect only the customer-specific operating costs in Exhibit 16-7. The revised customer-specific contributions to operating income are

	Customer			
	A	B	G	J
Gross margin	$60,480	$71,280	$3,480	$6,000
Customer-specific operating costs				
Order taking[a]	1,800	1,500	900	600
Sales visits[b]	300	250	200	150
Delivery vehicles[c]	450	540	600	135
Product handling[d]	15,120	11,880	1,044	900
Expedited deliveries[e]	200	0	400	0
Total	17,870	14,170	3,144	1,785
Customer-specific contribution	$42,610	$57,110	$ 336	$4,215

[a]$60 × 30; $60 × 25; $60 × 15; $60 × 10
[b]$50 × 6; $50 × 5; $50 × 4; $50 × 3
[c]$1.50 × (5 × 60); $1.50 × (12 × 30); $1.50 × (20 × 20); $1.50 × (6 × 15)
[d]$0.015 × 1,008,000[f]; $0.015 × 792,000[g]; $0.015 × 69,600[h]; $0.015 × 60,000[i]
[e]$200 × 1; $200 × 0; $200 × 2; $200 × 0
[f]42,000 cases × 24 = 1,008,000 bottles
[g]33,000 cases × 24 = 792,000 bottles
[h]2,900 cases × 24 = 69,600 bottles
[i]2,500 cases × 24 = 60,000 bottles

The customer-specific contribution has increased for each customer. The total contribution from these four customers is $104,271 in July 2010 compared to $88,400 in June 2010, an increase of 18%.

2. Spring could seek to improve the profitability of its customers by reducing its cost of goods sold through better negotiating with its supplier. It could also explore the effect of a list price increase, a reduction in price discounts, or encouraging customers to use fewer service units from its five activity areas. The challenge here is to retain, or possibly increase, the customer's willingness to purchase from Spring given the new pricing and cost parameters.

MyAccountingLab

ASSESS YOUR MASTERY

To check your understanding of the material in Learning Objective ⑤, go to the *Mastery Questions* section at the end of this chapter and complete Learning Objective ⑤ question 1.

The following decision guidelines use a question-and-answer format to summarize the chapter's main points. Each decision presents a key question. The guideline is the answer to that question.

DECISIONS	GUIDELINES
1. What is product bundling and why does it give rise to revenue-allocation issues?	Bundling occurs when a package of two or more products (or services) is sold for a single price. Revenue allocation of the bundled price is required when managers of the individual products in the bundle are evaluated on product revenues or product operating incomes. Revenues can be allocated for a bundled product using the stand-alone method, the incremental method, or management judgment.
2. How can level 3 and 4 revenue variances and level 4 cost variances be explained?	The calculation of variances themselves is a straightforward exercise in arithmetic. The reason for calculating these variances is to direct attention to what has actually happened relative to what was expected. The actual causes require cooperation among those who know best how the processes work. Revenue variances are best explained by marketing while materials mix and yield variances are best explained by production.
3. Of what relevance are these variance analyses?	Unfavourable variances are a form of feedback that information managers use to revise their understanding of what causes decreases in profitability. Management is never required when there are no problems—hence, the essence of management is problem-solving. Without timely, relevant feedback neither the nature of the problem nor the most likely remedy can be well understood.
4. Why does profitability differ across customers purchasing the same product?	Revenues can differ due to differences in the quantity purchased and discounts given from the list selling price. Different customers place different demands on a company's resources in terms of processing purchase orders, making deliveries, and customer support. Companies should be aware of and devote sufficient resources to maintaining and expanding relationships with key contributors to profitability.
5. What is the advantage of using a customer cost hierarchy?	Customer cost hierarchies highlight how some costs can be reliably assigned to individual customers whereas other costs can be reliably assigned only to distribution channels or to corporatewide activities.

This chapter contains definitions of the following important terms:

bundled product (p. 783)
composite unit (p. 793)
customer profitability analysis (p. 805)
direct materials mix variance (p. 799)
direct materials yield variance (p. 799)

incremental revenue-allocation
　method (p. 785)
market-share variance (p. 795)
market-size variance (p. 796)
price discounting (p. 806)

revenue allocation (p. 782)
sales-mix variance (p. 793)
sales-quantity variance (p. 794)
stand-alone revenue-allocation
　method (p. 783)

Mastery Questions are rated by proficiency level—elementary, intermediate, and advanced. The solutions appear in the Solutions to Mastery Questions section of MyAccountingLab.

LEARNING OBJECTIVE 1

1. **Revenue allocation for bundled products—Intermediate**. Pebble Resorts operates a five-star hotel with a world-recognized championship golf course. It has a decentralized management structure. There are three divisions:
   ◆ Lodging (rooms, conference facilities)
   ◆ Food (restaurants and in-room service)
   ◆ Recreation (the golf course, tennis courts, and so on)

   Starting next month, Pebble will offer a two-day, two-person "getaway package" deal for $770. This deal includes

   ◆ Two nights' stay for two in an ocean-view room—separately priced at $704 ($352 per night for two).
   ◆ Two rounds of golf separately priced at $330 ($165 per round). One person can do two rounds, or two can do one round each.
   ◆ Candlelight dinner for two at the exclusive Pebble Pacific Restaurant—separately priced at $88 per person.

   Samantha Lee, president of the Recreation Division, recently asked the CEO of Pebble Resorts how her division would share in the $770 revenue from the package. The golf course was operating at 100% capacity (and then some). Under the "getaway package" rules, participants who booked one week in advance were guaranteed access to the golf course. Lee noted that every "getaway" booking would displace a $165 booking. She stressed that the high demand reflected the devotion of her team to keeping the golf course rated in the "Best 10 Courses in the World" listings in Golf Monthly magazine. As an aside she also noted that the Lodging and Food divisions only had to turn away customers on "peak-season events such as the New Year's period."

   REQUIRED
   1. Allocate the $770 "getaway package" revenue to the three divisions using
      a. The stand-alone revenue-allocation method.
      b. The incremental revenue-allocation method (with Recreation first, then Lodging, and then Food).
      Use unit selling prices as the weights in (a) and (b).
   2. What are the pros and cons of (a) and (b) in requirement 1?

2. **Revenue allocation for bundled products—Advanced**. Pétale Parfum (PP) manufactures and sells upscale perfumes. In recent months, PP has started selling its products in bundled form, as well as in individual form. Sales in 2010 of three products that have been sold individually are as follows:

	Retail Price	Units Sold
Stand-alone		
Fraîche	$110	20,000
Désarmer	88	37,500
Innocence	275	20,000
Suite		
Fraîche + Désarmer	165	
Fraîche + Innocence	308	

REQUIRED
1. Compute the weights for allocating revenues to each division for each of the bundled products using:
   a. The stand-alone revenue-allocation method based on total revenues of individual products.
   b. The incremental revenue-allocation method, with Innocence ranked 1; Désarmer, 2; and Fraîche, 3, based on retail prices of individual products. According to this ranking, the primary product in a suite has the highest rank, and so on.
2. Recalculate the allocation using the Shapley and the weighted Shapley value methods. What method would you recommend and why?

LEARNING OBJECTIVE 2

1. **Product sales variance analyses—Intermediate.** The Penguins play in the North American Ice Hockey League. The Penguins play in the Downtown Arena, which has a capacity of 30,000 seats (10,000 lower-tier seats and 20,000 upper-tier seats). The Downtown Arena charges the Penguins a per-ticket charge for use of the facility. All tickets are sold by the Reservation Network, which charges the Penguins a reservation fee per ticket. The Penguins' budgeted net revenue for each type of ticket in 2010 is computed as follows:

	Lower-Tier Tickets	Upper-Tier Tickets
Selling price	$35.00	$14.00
Downtown arena fee	11.00	6.60
Reservation network fee	5.50	3.30
Contribution margin	$18.50	$ 4.10

The budgeted and actual average attendance figures per game in the 2010 season are

	Budgeted Seats Sold	Actual Seats Sold
Lower-tier	8,000	6,600
Upper-tier	12,000	15,400
Total	20,000	22,000

There was no difference between the budgeted and actual net revenue for lower-tier or upper-tier seats.

The manager of the Penguins was delighted that actual attendance was 10% above budgeted attendance per game, especially given the depressed state of the local economy in the past six months.

REQUIRED

1. Compute the sales-volume variance for individual "product" net revenues and total net revenues for the Penguins in 2010.
2. Compute the sales-quantity and sales-mix variances for individual "product" net revenues and total net revenues in 2010.
3. Write a brief analysis of the variances in requirements 1 and 2. Comment on the results.

2. **Product input mix and yield variance—Advanced.** Tropical Fruits Inc. processes tropical fruit into a fruit salad mix, which it sells to a food-service company. Tropical Fruits has in its budget the following standards for the direct materials inputs to produce a batch of 80 kilograms of tropical fruit salad:

50 kilograms of pineapple at $1.05 per kilogram	$52.50
30 kilograms of watermelon at $0.55 per kilogram	16.50
20 kilograms of strawberries at $0.80 per kilogram	16.00
100	$85.00

Note that 100 kilograms of input quantities are required to produce 80 kilograms of fruit salad. No inventories of direct materials are kept. Purchases are made as needed, so all price variances are related to direct materials used. The actual direct materials inputs used to produce 54,000 kilograms of tropical fruit salad for October were

36,400 kilograms of pineapple at $0.95 per kilogram	$34,580
18,200 kilograms of watermelon at $0.65 per kilogram	11,830
15,400 kilograms of strawberries at $0.75 per kilogram	11,550
70,000	$57,960

REQUIRED

1. Compute the total direct materials price and efficiency variances in October.
2. Compute the total direct materials mix and yield variances for October.

3. Comment on your results in requirements 1 and 2.
4. How might the management of Tropical Fruits Inc. use information about the direct materials mix and yield variances?

LEARNING OBJECTIVE 3

1. **Relevance of variance analyses—Advanced.** As a producer of wine in the Niagara region you have the opportunity to either lease vineyards from local grape-growers or to purchase grapes from other farmers. In the past you have purchased grapes from the Okanagan Valley in British Columbia, and from the Sonoma Valley in California.

   The quality of wine depends in part on the quality of grapes input to the fermenting process, but your fermenting machinery has a fixed capacity. Any unused capacity in one year cannot be applied to a different use. To obtain the best return your preference is to operate at practical capacity even if projected demand or normal capacity is higher. An interesting opportunity in the industry is the ability to enter into a contract in the spring to pay a specific dollar value for grapes harvested in the fall.

   Financial experts call this a hedging contract because you are protecting yourself against the risk that actual prices in the fall (the spot price) will be higher than your spring contracted price (the strike price). The quantity and quality of grapes harvested each year depends largely on a single uncontrollable factor—the weather. In spring you must decide on the input mix of harvested and purchased grapes that you believe is most likely to make the best use of available practical capacity—but you have no idea what the weather will be in the months before harvest.

   A supplier approaches you in the spring with a proposition to sell you grapes and specifies the strike price. This supplier from the Okanagan provides you with a historical trend chart which summarizes the association between weather and yield from the vineyard for the last 8 years.

   REQUIRED
   1. Explain your reasons for your contracting decision.
   2. Of what use would similar information on your own market share be?

LEARNING OBJECTIVE 4

1. **Customer profitability and ABC hierarchy—Advanced.** The Sherriton Hotels chain embarked on a new customer loyalty program in 2010. The 2010 year-end data have been collected, and it is now time for you to determine whether the loyalty program should be continued, discontinued, or perhaps altered to improve loyalty and profitability levels at Sherriton.

   Sherriton's loyalty program consists of three different customer loyalty levels. All new customers can sign up for the Sherriton Bronze Card—this card provides guests with a complimentary bottle of wine (cost to the chain is $5 per bottle) and $20 in restaurant coupons each night (cost to the chain is $10). Bronze customers also receive a 10% discount off the nightly rate. The program enables the chain to track a member's stays and activities. Once a customer has stayed and paid for 20 nights at any of the chain's locations worldwide, he or she is upgraded to Silver Customer status. Silver benefits include the bottle of wine (cost to the chain is $5 per bottle), $30 in restaurant coupons (cost to the chain is $15), and 20% off every night from the 21st night on. A customer who reaches the 50-night level is upgraded to Gold Customer status. Gold status increases the nightly discount to 30% and replaces the $5 bottle of wine with a bottle of champagne (cost to the chain is $20 per bottle). As well, $40 in restaurant coupons are granted (cost to the chain is $20).

   The average full price for one night's stay is $200. The chain incurs variable costs of $65 per night, exclusive of loyalty program costs. Total fixed costs for the chain are $140,580,000. Sherriton operates ten hotels with, on average, 500 rooms each. All hotels are open for business 365 days a year, and approximate average occupancy rates are around 80%. Following are some loyalty program characteristics:

Loyalty Program	Number of Customers	Average Number of Nights per Customer
Gold	2,673	60
Silver	9,174	35
Bronze	88,330	10
No program	240,900	1

   Note that an average Gold Customer would have received the 10% discount for his or her first 20 stays, received the 20% discount for the next 30 stays, and the 30% discount only for the last ten nights. Assume that all program members signed on to the program the first time they stayed with one of the chain's hotels. Also, assume the restaurants are managed by a 100%-owned subsidiary of Sherriton.

REQUIRED

1. Calculate the program contribution margin for each of the three programs, as well as for the group of customers not subscribing to the loyalty program. Which program is the most profitable? Which is the least profitable? Do not allocate fixed costs to individual rooms or specific loyalty programs.
2. Develop an income statement for Sherriton for the year ended December 31, 2010.
3. What is the average room rate per night? What are average variable costs per night inclusive of the loyalty program?
4. Explain what drives the profitability (or lack thereof) of the most and least profitable loyalty programs (again, one of these may be the "no program" option).

LEARNING OBJECTIVE 5

1. **Customer profitability report—Advanced.** Ramish Electronics has two retail customers and two wholesale customers. Pertinent information relating to each customer for 2011 follows (all amounts are in thousands of dollars):

	WHOLESALE		RETAIL	
	North America Wholesaler	South America Wholesaler	Big Sam Stereo	World Market
Cost of goods sold	$325,000	$490,000	$112,000	$92,000
Delivery costs:				
Regular	300	450	150	80
Expedited	120	200	10	5
Order processing	800	1,000	200	130
Product handling	5,000	6,000	800	900
Sales visits	480	550	240	165
Revenues at list prices	440,000	660,000	143,000	110,000
Discounts from list prices	30,000	50,000	7,000	0

REQUIRED

Ramish's distribution-channel costs are $30 million for wholesale customers and $10 million for retail customers. Its corporate-sustaining costs are $60 million.

1. Calculate customer-level operating income using the format in Exhibit 16-7.
2. Prepare a customer cost hierarchy report using the format in Exhibit 16-8.

ASSIGNMENT MATERIAL

SHORT-ANSWER QUESTIONS

16-1 Describe how companies are increasingly facing revenue-allocation decisions.

16-2 Distinguish between the stand-alone revenue-allocation method and the incremental revenue-allocation method.

16-3 Identify and discuss arguments individual product managers may put forward to support their preferred revenue-allocation method.

16-4 How might a dispute over the allocation of revenues of a bundled product be resolved?

16-5 Show how managers can gain insight into the causes of a sales-volume variance by drilling down into the components of this variance.

16-6 How can the concept of a composite unit be used to explain why an unfavourable total sales-mix variance of contribution margin occurs?

16-7 Explain why a favourable sales-quantity variance occurs.

16-8 Distinguish between a market-size variance and a market-share variance.

16-9 Why might some companies choose not to compute market-size and market-share variances?

16-10 Why is customer profitability analysis a vitally important topic to managers?

16-11 How can the extent of price discounting be tracked on a customer-by-customer basis?

16-12 "A customer profitability profile highlights those customers that should be dropped to improve profitability." Do you agree?

16-13 Give an example of three types of different levels of costs in a customer cost hierarchy.

16-14 Distinguish between processes where the inputs are nonsubstitutable and where they are substitutable.

16-15 Explain how the direct materials, mix, and yield variances provide additional information about the direct materials efficiency variance.

EXERCISES

1. a. Allocation to St. Anne, $1,500

16-16 Allocation of common costs. The cities of St. Anne, St. Teresa, and St. Steven are considering the implementation of a new program to handle disposal of hazardous waste to comply with a new, more stringent provincial law. Because of the close proximity of the three cities, a joint program has been suggested. The annual cost of separate programs and a joint program are:

City	Capacity	Cost
St. Anne	100,000 tonnes	$2,100,000
St. Teresa	25,000 tonnes	$1,400,000
St. Steven	175,000 tonnes	$3,500,000
Joint Program	300,000 tonnes	$5,000,000

REQUIRED

1. Allocate the $5,000,000 cost of the joint program to each of the three cities using:
   a. The stand-alone method
   b. The incremental-allocation method (in the order of the most waste to the least waste).
2. How do you think the citizens of each community would feel about each of the two methods of allocation?

1. a. Allocated to RCC, $36

16-17 Revenue allocation. Lee Shu-yu Inc. produces and sells DVDs to business people and students who are planning extended stays in China. It has been very successful with two DVDs: Beginning Mandarin and Conversational Mandarin. It is introducing a third DVD, Reading Chinese Characters. It has decided to market its new DVD in two different packages grouping the Reading Chinese Characters DVD with each of the other two language DVDs. Information about the separate DVDs and the packages follow.

DVD	Selling Price
Beginning Mandarin (BegM)	$60
Conversational Mandarin (ConM)	$50
Reading Chinese Characters (RCC)	$40
BegM + RCC	$90
ConM + RCC	$72

REQUIRED

1. Using the selling prices, allocate revenues from the BegM + RCC package to each DVD in that package using (a) the stand-alone method (b) the incremental method, in either order (c) the Shapley value method.

2. Using the selling prices, allocate revenues from the ConM + RCC package to each DVD in that package using (a) the stand-alone method (b) the incremental method, in either order (c) the Shapley value method.
3. Which method is most appropriate for allocating revenues among the DVDs? Why?

16-18 **Variance analysis, multiple products.** The Penguins play in the North American Ice Hockey League. The Penguins play in the Downtown Arena (owned and managed by the City of Downtown), which has a capacity of 15,000 seats (5,000 lower-tier seats and 10,000 upper-tier seats). The Downtown Arena charges the Penguins a per-ticket charge for use of the facility. All tickets are sold by the Reservation Network, which charges the Penguins a reservation fee per ticket. The Penguins' budgeted contribution margin for each type of ticket in 2010 is computed as follows:

2 3
1. Lower-tier tickets, $14,000 U

	Lower-Tier Tickets	Upper-Tier Tickets
Selling price	$35	$14
Downtown Arena fee	10	6
Reservation Network fee	5	3
Contribution margin per ticket	$20	$ 5

The budgeted and actual average attendance figures per game in the 2010 season are:

	Budgeted Seats Sold	Actual Seats Sold
Lower tier	4,000	3,300
Upper tier	6,000	7,700
Total	10,000	11,000

There was no difference between the budgeted and actual contribution margin for lower-tier or upper-tier seats.

The manager of the Penguins was delighted that actual attendance was 10% above budgeted attendance per game, especially given the depressed state of the local economy in the past six months.

REQUIRED
1. Compute the sales-volume variance for each type of ticket and in total for the Penguins in 2010. (Calculate all variances in terms of contribution margins.)
2. Compute the sales-quantity and sales-mix variances for each type of ticket and in total in 2010.
3. Present a summary of the variances in requirements 1 and 2. Comment on the results.

16-19 **Variance analysis, working backward.** The Jinwa Corporation sells two brands of wine glasses, Plain and Chic. Jinwa provides the following information for sales in the month of June 2009:

2 3
1. Sales mix, 80% Plain, 20% Chic

Static-budget total contribution margin	$5,600
Budgeted units to be sold of all glasses	2,000 units
Budgeted contribution margin per unit of Plain	$2 per unit
Budgeted contribution margin per unit of Chic	$6 per unit
Total sales-quantity variance	$1,400 U
Actual sales-mix percentage of Plain	60%

All variances are to be computed in contribution-margin terms.

REQUIRED
1. Calculate the sales-quantity variances for each product for June 2009.
2. Calculate the individual-product and total sales-mix variances for June 2009. Calculate the individual-product and total sales-volume variances for June 2009.
3. Briefly describe the conclusions you can draw from the variances.

16-20 Variance analysis, multiple products. Soda-King manufactures and sells three soft drinks: Kola, Limor, and Orlem. Budgeted and actual results for 2010 are as follows:

	Budget for 2010			Actual for 2010		
Product	**Selling Price**	**Variable Cost per Carton**	**Cartons Sold**	**Selling Price**	**Variable Cost per Carton**	**Cartons Sold**
Kola	$6.00	$4.00	400,000	$6.20	$4.50	480,000
Limor	$4.00	$2.80	600,000	$4.25	$2.75	900,000
Orlem	$7.00	$4.50	1,500,000	$6.80	$4.60	1,620,000

REQUIRED

1. Compute the total sales-volume variance, the total sales-mix variance, and the total sales-quantity variance. (Calculate all variances in terms of contribution margin.) Show results for each product in your computations.
2. What inferences can you draw from the variances computed in requirement 1?

16-21 Market-share and market-size variances (continuation of 16-20). Soda-King prepared the budget for 2010 assuming a 10% market share based on total sales in the western region of Canada. The total soft drinks market was estimated to reach sales of 25 million cases in the region. However, actual total sales volume in the western region was 24 million cases.

REQUIRED

Calculate the market-share and market-size variances for Soda-King in 2010. (Calculate all variances in terms of contribution margin.) Comment on the results.

16-22 Customer profitability, service company. Instant Service (IS) repairs printers and photocopiers for five multisite companies in a tri-city area. IS's costs consist of the cost of technicians and equipment that are directly traceable to the customer site and a pool of office overhead. Until recently, IS estimated customer profitability by allocating the office overhead to each customer based on share of revenues. For 2010, IS reported the following results:

	Avery	Okie	Wizard	Grainger	Duran	Total
Revenues	$260,000	$200,000	$322,000	$122,000	$212,000	$1,116,000
Technician and equipment cost	182,000	175,000	225,000	107,000	178,000	867,000
Office overhead allocated	31,859	24,507	39,457	14,949	25,978	136,750
Operating income	$ 46,141	$ 493	$ 57,543	$ 51	$ 8,022	$ 112,250

Tina Sherman, IS's new controller, notes that office overhead is more than 10% of total costs, so she spends a couple of weeks analyzing the consumption of office overhead resources by customers. She collects the following information:

Activity Area	Cost Driver Rate
Service-call handling	$75 per service call
Parts ordering	$80 per web-based parts order
Billing and collection	$50 per bill (or reminder)
Customer database maintenance	$10 per service call

	Avery	Okie	Wizard	Grainger	Duran
Number of service calls	150	240	40	120	180
Number of web-based parts orders	120	210	60	150	150
Number of bills (or reminders)	30	90	90	60	120

1. Sales mix, 16% Kola, 24% Limor, 60% Orlem

Actual market share, 12.5%

1. Avery customer-level operating income, $54,150

REQUIRED

1. Compute customer-level operating income using the new information that Sherman has gathered.
2. Prepare exhibits for IS similar to Exhibits 16-8 and 16-9. Comment on the results.
3. What options should IS consider, with regard to individual customers, in light of the new data and analysis of office overhead?

16-23 **Customer profitability, distribution.** Figure Four is a distributor of pharmaceutical products. Its ABC system has five activities:

4 5
1. Order processing costs for Chapelville Pharmacy, $400

Activity Area	Cost Driver Rate in 2009
1. Order processing	$40 per order
2. Line-item ordering	$3 per line item
3. Store deliveries	$50 per store delivery
4. Carton deliveries	$1 per carton
5. Shelf-stocking	$16 per stocking-hour

Rick Flair, the controller of Figure Four, wants to use this ABC system to examine individual customer profitability within each distribution market. He focuses first on the Ma and Pa single-store distribution market. Two customers are used to exemplify the insights available with the ABC approach. Data pertaining to these two customers in August 2009 are as follows:

	Charlesville Pharmacy	Chapelville Pharmacy
Total orders	13	10
Average line items per order	9	18
Total store deliveries	7	10
Average cartons shipped per store delivery	22	20
Average hours of shelf-stocking per store delivery	0	0.5
Average revenue per delivery	$2,400	$1,800
Average cost of goods sold per delivery	$2,100	$1,650

REQUIRED

1. Use the ABC information to compute the operating income of each customer in August 2009. Comment on the results and what, if anything, Flair should do.
2. Flair ranks the individual customers in the Ma and Pa single-store distribution market on the basis of monthly operating income. The cumulative operating income of the top 20% of customers is $55,680. Figure Four reports operating losses of $21,247 for the bottom 40% of its customers. Make four recommendations that you think Figure Four should consider in light of this new customer-profitability information.

16-24 **Direct materials efficiency, mix, and yield variances.** (CMA, adapted) The Energy Products Company produces a gasoline additive, Gas Gain, that increases engine efficiency and improves gasoline mileage. The actual and budgeted quantities (in litres) of materials required to produce Gas Gain and the budgeted prices of materials in August 2010 are as follows:

2 3
1. Echol actual mix percentage, 0.28

Chemical	Actual Quantity	Budgeted Quantity	Budgeted Price
Echol	24,080	25,200	$0.22
Protex	15,480	16,800	0.47
Benz	36,120	33,600	0.17
CT-40	10,320	8,400	0.32

REQUIRED

1. Calculate the total direct materials efficiency variance for August 2010.
2. Calculate the total direct materials mix and yield variances for August 2010.
3. What conclusions would you draw from the variance analysis?

16-25 Direct materials price, efficiency, mix, and yield variances. Greenwood Inc. manufactures apple products such as apple jelly and applesauce. It makes applesauce by blending Tolman, Golden Delicious, and Ribston apples. Budgeted costs to produce 100,000 kilograms of applesauce in November 2010 are as follows:

45,000 kilograms of Tolman apples at $0.32 per kilogram	$14,400
180,000 kilograms of Golden Delicious apples at $0.28 per kilogram	50,400
75,000 kilograms of Ribston apples at $0.24 per kilogram	18,000

Actual costs in November 2010 are

62,000 kilograms of Tolman apples at $0.30 per kilogram	$18,600
155,000 kilograms of Golden Delicious apples at $0.28 per kilogram	43,400
93,000 kilograms of Ribston apples at $0.22 per kilogram	20,460

REQUIRED
1. Calculate the total direct materials price and efficiency variances for November 2010.
2. Calculate the total direct materials mix and yield variances for November 2010.
3. Comment on your results in requirements 1 and 2.

PROBLEMS

16-26 Revenue allocation for bundled products. Yves Parfum Company blends and sells designer fragrances. It has a Men's Fragrances Division and a Women's Fragrances Division, each with different sales strategies, distribution channels, and product offerings. Yves is now considering the sale of a bundled product consisting of a men's cologne and a women's perfume. For the most recent year, Yves reported the following:

Product	Retail Price
Monaco (men's cologne)	$ 80
Innocence (women's perfume)	120
L'Amour (Monaco + Innocence)	180

REQUIRED
1. Allocate revenue from the sale of each unit of L'Amour to Monaco and Innocence using:
   a. The stand-alone revenue-allocation method based on selling price of each product
   b. The incremental revenue-allocation method, with Monaco ranked as the primary product
   c. The incremental revenue-allocation method, with Innocence ranked as the primary product
   d. The Shapley value method, assuming equal unit sales of Monaco and Innocence.
2. Of the four methods in requirement 1, which one would you recommend for allocating L'Amour's revenues to Monaco and Innocence? Explain.

16-27 Variance analysis, sales-mix, and sales-quantity variances. Aussie Infonautics Inc. produces handheld Windows CE–compatible organizers. Aussie Infonautics markets three different handheld models. PalmPro is a souped-up version for the executive on the go; PalmCE is a consumer-oriented version; and PalmKid is a stripped-down version for the young adult market. You are Aussie Infonautics' senior vice president of marketing. The CEO has discovered that the total contribution margin came in lower than budgeted, and it is your responsibility to explain to him why actual results are different from the budget. Budgeted and actual operating data for the company's third quarter of 2010 are as follows:

Budgeted Operating Data, Third Quarter 2010

	Selling Price	Variable Cost per Unit	Contribution Margin per Unit	Sales Volume in Units
PalmPro	$379	$182	$197	12,500
PalmCE	269	98	171	37,500
PalmKid	149	65	84	50,000
				100,000

Actual Operating Data, Third Quarter 2010

	Selling Price	Variable Cost per Unit	Contribution Margin per Unit	Sales Volume in Units
PalmPro	$349	$178	$171	11,000
PalmCE	285	92	193	44,000
PalmKid	102	73	29	55,000
				110,000

REQUIRED

1. Compute the actual and budgeted contribution margins in dollars for each product and in total for the third quarter of 2010.
2. Calculate the actual and budgeted sales mixes for the three products for the third quarter of 2010.
3. Calculate total sales-volume, sales-mix, and sales-quantity variances for the third quarter of 2010. (Calculate all variances in terms of contribution margins.)
4. Given that your CEO is known to have temper tantrums, you want to be well prepared for this meeting. In order to prepare, write a paragraph or two comparing actual results to budgeted amounts.

16-28 **Market-share and market-size variances (continuation of 16-27).** Aussie Infonautics' senior vice president of marketing prepared his budget at the beginning of the third quarter assuming a 25% market share based on total sales. The total handheld-organizer market was estimated by Foolinstead Research to reach sales of 400,000 units worldwide in the third quarter. However, actual sales in the third quarter were 500,000 units.

1. Budgeted average contribution margin per unit, $130.75

REQUIRED

1. Calculate the market-share and market-size variances for Aussie Infonautics in the third quarter of 2010 (calculate all variances in terms of contribution margins).
2. Explain what happened based on the market-share and market-size variances.
3. Calculate the actual market size, in units, that would have led to no market-size variance (again using budgeted contribution margin per unit). Use this market-size figure to calculate the actual market share that would have led to a zero market-share variance.

16-29 **Variance analysis, multiple products.** Debbie's Delight Inc. operates a chain of cookie stores. Budgeted and actual operating data for its three Calgary stores for August 2010 are as follows:

1. Chocolate chip sales-volume variance, $25,200 F

Budget for August 2010

	Selling Price per kg	Variable Cost per kg	Contribution Margin per kg	Sales Volume in kg
Chocolate chip	$4.50	$2.50	$2.00	45,000
Oatmeal raisin	5.00	2.70	2.30	25,000
Coconut	5.50	2.90	2.60	10,000
White chocolate	6.00	3.00	3.00	5,000
Macadamia nut	6.50	3.40	3.10	15,000
				100,000

Actual for August 2010

	Selling Price per kg	Variable Cost per kg	Contribution Margin per kg	Sales Volume in kg
Chocolate chip	$4.50	$2.60	$1.90	57,600
Oatmeal raisin	5.20	2.90	2.30	18,000
Coconut	5.50	2.80	2.70	9,600
White chocolate	6.00	3.40	2.60	13,200
Macadamia nut	7.00	4.00	3.00	21,600
				120,000

Debbie's Delight focuses on contribution margin in its variance analysis.

REQUIRED

1. Compute the total sales-volume variance for August 2010.
2. Compute the total sales-mix variance for August 2010.
3. Compute the total sales-quantity variance for August 2010.
4. Comment on your results in requirements 1, 2, and 3.

16-30 Market-share and market-size variances (continuation of 16-29). Debbie's Delight attains a 10% market share based on total sales of the Calgary market. The total Calgary market is expected to be 1,000,000 kilograms in sales volume for August 2010. The actual total Calgary market for August 2010 was 960,000 kilograms in sales volume.

REQUIRED

Compute the market-share and market-size variances for Debbie's Delight in August 2010. Calculate all variances in contribution-margin terms. Comment on the results.

16-31 Direct materials efficiency, mix, and yield variances. Flavr-Wave Company makes candy. Their most popular product is the toe pop, a large lollipop shaped like a toe. The direct materials used in the toe pop are sugar, flavouring, and colouring. For each batch of 100 pops, the budgeted quantities and budgeted prices of direct materials are as follows:

	Quantity for One Batch	Price of Input
Sugar	7 litres	$1 per litre
Flavouring	2 litres	$3 per litre
Colouring	1 litres	$2 per litre

Changing the standard mix of direct material quantities slightly does not significantly affect the overall end product, particularly for the flavouring and colouring.

In the current period, Flavr-Wave made 2,300 toe pops in 23 batches with the following actual quantity, cost, and mix of inputs:

	Actual Quantity	Actual Cost	Actual Mix (rounded)
Sugar	165 litres	$165	70%
Flavouring	45 litres	135	19%
Colouring	25 litres	50	11%
Total actual	235 litres	$350	100%

REQUIRED

1. What is the budgeted cost of direct materials for the 2,300 toe pops?
2. Calculate the total direct materials efficiency variance.
3. Why is the total direct materials price variance zero?
4. Calculate the total direct materials mix and yield variances. What are these variances telling you about the 2,300 toe pops produced this period? Are the variances large enough to investigate?

16-32 Materials variances: price, efficiency, mix, and yield. PDS Manufacturing makes wooden furniture. One of their products is a wooden dresser. The exterior and some of the shelves are made of oak, a high-quality wood, but the interior drawers are made of pine, a less expensive wood. The budgeted direct materials quantities and prices for one dresser are:

	Quantity	Price per Unit of Input	Cost for One Dresser
Oak	8 board feet	$6 per board foot	$48
Pine	12 board feet	2 per board foot	24

That is, each dresser is budgeted to use 20 board feet of wood, comprised of 40% oak and 60% pine, although sometimes more pine is used in place of oak with no obvious change in the quality or function of the dresser.

During the month of May, PDS manufactures 3,000 dressers. Actual direct materials costs are:

Oak (23,180 board feet)	$141,398
Pine (37,820 board feet)	68,076
Total actual direct materials cost	$209,474

1. What is the budgeted cost of direct materials for 3,000 dressers?

2. Calculate the total direct materials price and efficiency variances.

3. For the 3,000 dressers, what is the total actual amount of oak and pine used? What is the actual direct materials input mix percentage? What is the budgeted amount of oak and pine that should have been used for the 3,000 dressers?

4. Calculate the total direct materials mix and yield variances. How do these numbers relate to the total direct materials efficiency variance? What do these variances tell you?

16-33 **Customer profitability, customer-cost hierarchy.** Ramish Electronics has only two retail and two wholesale customers. Information relating to each customer for 2009 follows (in thousands):

1. North America wholesaler customer-level operating income, $58,150

	Wholesale Customers		Retail Customers	
	North America Wholesaler	South America Wholesaler	Big Sam Stereo	World Market
Revenues at list price	$420,000	$580,000	$130,000	$100,000
Discounts from list prices	30,000	40,000	7,000	500
Cost of goods sold	325,000	455,000	118,000	90,000
Delivery costs	450	650	200	125
Order processing costs	800	1,000	200	130
Costs of sales visits	5,600	5,500	2,300	1,350

Ramish's annual distribution-channel costs are $38 million for wholesale customers and $7 million for retail customers. Its annual corporate-sustaining costs, such as salary for top management and general administration costs, are $65 million. There is no cause-and-effect or benefits-received relationship between any cost-allocation base and corporate-sustaining costs. That is, corporate-sustaining costs could be saved only if Ramish Electronics were to completely shut down.

REQUIRED

1. Calculate customer-level operating income using the format in Exhibit 16-7.

2. Prepare a customer-cost hierarchy report, using the format in Exhibit 16-8.

3. Ramish's management decides to allocate all corporate-sustaining costs to distribution channels: $51 million to the wholesale channel and $14 million to the retail channel. As a result, distribution channel costs are now $89 million ($38 million + $51 million) for the wholesale channel and $21 million ($7 million + $14 million) for the retail channel. Calculate the distribution-channel-level operating income. On the basis of these calculations, what actions, if any, should Ramish's managers take? Explain.

16-34 **Customer profitability in a manufacturing firm.** Bizzan Manufacturing makes a component they call P14-31. This component is manufactured only when ordered by a customer, so Bizzan keeps no inventory of P14-31. The list price is $100 per unit, but customers who place "large" orders receive a 10% discount on price. Currently, the salespeople decide whether an order is large enough to qualify for the discount. When the product is finished, it is packed in cases of 10. When a customer order is not a multiple of 10, Bizzan uses a full case to pack the partial amount left over (e.g., if Customer C orders 25 units, three cases will be required). Customers pick up the order so Bizzan incurs costs of holding the product in the warehouse until customer pickup. The customers are manufacturing firms; if the component needs to be exchanged or repaired, customers can come back within 10 days for free exchange or repair.

The full cost of manufacturing a unit of P14-31 is $80. In addition, Bizzan incurs customer-level costs.

Customer-level cost-driver rates are:

Order taking	$380 per order
Product handling	$ 10 per case
Warehousing (holding finished product)	$ 55 per day
Rush order processing	$520 per rush order
Exchange and repair costs	$ 40 per unit

Information about Bizzan's five biggest customers follows:

	A	B	C	D	E
Number of units purchased	5,000	2,400	1,200	4,000	8,000
Discounts given	10%	0	10%	0	10% on half the units
Number of orders	10	12	48	16	12
Number of cases	500	240	144	400	812
Days in warehouse (total for all orders)	13	16	0	12	120
Number of rush orders	0	2	0	0	5
Number of units exchanged/repaired	0	30	5	20	95

The salesperson gave customer C a price discount because, although Customer C ordered only 1,200 units in total, only 12 orders (one per month) were placed. The salesperson wanted to reward customer C for repeat business. All customers except E ordered units in the same order size. Customer E's order quantity varied, so E got a discount some of the time but not all the time.

REQUIRED

1. Calculate the customer-level operating income for these five customers. Use the format in Exhibit 16-7. Prepare a customer profitability analysis by ranking the customers from most to least profitable, as in Exhibit 16-9.
2. Discuss the results of your customer profitability analysis. Does Bizzan have unprofitable customers? Is there anything Bizzan should do differently with its five customers?

④

1. Customer 02 customer-level operating income, $900

16-35 Customer profitability. Ring Delights is a new company that manufactures custom jewellery. Ring Delights currently has six customers referenced by customer number: 01, 02, 03, 04, 05, and 06. Besides the costs of making the jewellery, the company has the following activities:

1. Customer orders. The salespeople, designers, and jewellery makers spend time with the customer. The cost driver rate is $40 per hour spent with a customer.
2. Customer fittings. Before the jewellery piece is completed the customer may come in to make sure it looks right and fits properly. Cost driver rate is $25 per hour.
3. Rush orders. Some customers want their jewellery quickly. The cost driver rate is $100 per rush order.
4. Number of customer return visits. Customers may return jewellery up to 30 days after the pickup of the jewellery to have something refitted or repaired at no charge. The cost driver rate is $30 per return visit.

Information about the six customers follows. Some customers purchased multiple items. The cost of the jewellery is 70% of the selling price.

Customer number	01	02	03	04	05	06
Sales revenue	$600	$4,200	$300	$2,500	$4,900	$700
Cost of item(s)	$420	$2,940	$210	$1,750	$3,430	$490
Hours spent on customer order	2	7	1	5	20	3
Hours on fittings	1	2	0	0	4	1
Number of rush orders	0	0	1	1	3	0
Number of return visits	0	1	0	1	5	1

REQUIRED

1. Calculate the customer-level operating income for each customer. Rank the customers in order of most to least profitable and prepare a customer profitability analysis, as in Exhibit 16-7.
2. Are any customers unprofitable? What is causing this? What should Ring Delights do with respect to these customers?

④

1. GM customer-level operating income, $2,340

16-36 Customer profitability and governance. Glat Corporation manufactures a product called the glat, which it sells to merchandising firms such as International House of Glats (IHoG), Glats-R-Us (GRU), Glat Marcus (GM), Glat City (GC), Good Glats (GG), and Glat-mart (Gmart). The list price of a glat is $40, and the full manufacturing costs are $30. Salespeople receive a commission on sales, but the commission is based on number of orders taken, not on sales revenue generated or number of units sold. Salespeople receive a commission of $20 per order (in addition to regular salary).

Glat Corporation makes products based on anticipated demand. Glat Corporation carries an inventory of glats so rush orders do not result in any extra manufacturing costs over and above the $30 per glat. Glat Corporation ships finished product to the customer at no additional charge to the customer for either regular or expedited delivery. Glat incurs significantly higher costs for expedited deliveries than for regular deliveries.

Expected and actual customer-level cost driver rates are:

Order taking (excluding sales commission)	$28 per order
Product handling	$1 per unit
Delivery	$1 per km driven
Expedited (rush) delivery	$300 per shipment

Because salespeople are paid $20 per order, they break up large orders into multiple smaller orders. This practice reduces the actual order taking cost by $16 per smaller order (from $28 per order to $12 per order) because the smaller orders are all written at the same time. This lower cost rate is not included in budgeted rates because salespeople create smaller orders without telling management or the accounting department. Also, salespeople offer customers discounts to entice them to place more orders; GRU and Gmart each receive a 5% discount off the list price of $40.

Information about Glat's clients follows:

	IHG	GRU	GM	GC	GG	Gmart
Total number of units purchased	200	540	300	100	400	1,000
Number of actual orders	2	12	2	2	4	10
Number of written orders per actual order	2	1*	3	2	4	2
Total number of km driven to deliver all products	80	120	72	28	304	100
Number of expedited deliveries	0	4	0	0	1	3

*Because GRU places 12 separate orders, its order costs are $28 per order. All other orders are multiple smaller orders and so have actual order costs of $12 each.

REQUIRED

1. Using the information above, calculate the expected customer-level operating income for the six customers of Glat Corporation. Use the number of written orders at $28 each to calculate expected order costs.
2. Recalculate the customer-level operating income using the number of written orders but at their actual $12 cost per order instead of $28 (except for GRU, whose actual cost is $28 per order). How will Glat Corporation evaluate customer-level operating cost performance this period?
3. Recalculate the customer-level operating income if salespeople had not broken up actual orders into multiple smaller orders. Don't forget to also adjust sales commissions.
4. How is the behaviour of the salespeople affecting the profit of Glat Corporation? Is their behaviour ethical? What could Glat Corporation do to change the behaviour of the salespeople?

COLLABORATIVE LEARNING CASE

16-37 **Cost allocation and decision making.** Greenbold Manufacturing has four divisions named after its locations: Ontario, Alberta, Yukon, and Saskatchewan. Corporate headquarters is in Manitoba. Greenbold corporate headquarters incurs $5,600,000 per period, which is an indirect cost of the divisions. Corporate headquarters currently allocates this cost to the divisions based on the revenues of each division. The CEO has asked each division manager to suggest an allocation base for the indirect headquarters costs from among revenues, segment margin, direct costs, and number of employees. Below is relevant information about each division:

2 3

1. Ontario operating margin after allocating headquarter costs, $940,000

	Ontario	Alberta	Yukon	Saskatchewan
Revenues	$7,800,000	$8,500,000	$6,200,000	$5,500,000
Direct costs	$5,300,000	$4,100,000	$4,300,000	$4,600,000
Segment margin	$2,500,000	$4,400,000	$1,900,000	$900,000
Number of employees	2,000	4,000	1,500	500

1. Allocate the indirect headquarters costs of Greenbold Manufacturing to each of the four divisions using revenues, direct costs, segment margin, and number of employees as the allocation bases. Calculate operating margins for each division after allocating headquarters costs.
2. Which allocation base do you think the manager of the Saskatchewan division would prefer? Explain.
3. What factors would you consider in deciding which allocation base Greenbold should use?
4. Suppose the Greenbold CEO decides to use direct costs as the allocation base. Should the Saskatchewan division be closed? Why or why not?

Process Costing

Allocation Affects Net Income—Reliable Estimates Are Important

Royal Dutch Shell is a global explorer and developer of energy sources. In 2004, the company disclosed it had overstated its oil reserves by almost 20%, and as a result its restated earnings decreased by $432 million. Accounting improprieties regarding some gas contracts resulted in overstatement of profits. Upon restatement, the profits increased. The reason is that Shell switched from last-in, first-out (LIFO) to first-in, first-out (FIFO) to account for inventory. The cost of goods sold decreased more than the $156 million of overstated profits.

One result of these revelations was that Chairman Sir Philip Watts was dismissed in March 2005. The company settled with the US Securities and Exchange Commission on June 3, 2008, for US $117.85 million plus the European settlement for US $52.6 million to non-US investors, bringing the total reparations payout to shareholders to US $170.45 million.

After studying this chapter, you should be able to

1. Analyze process costing in contrast to job costing and apply the weighted-average method of inventory valuation when the beginning work-in-process inventory is zero

2. Contrast the journal entries for a process-costing system when there is and when there is not ending work-in-process inventory using the weighted-average method of inventory valuation

3. Apply the weighted-average method of process costing to calculate the cost of goods manufactured and transferred out when there is both beginning and ending work-in-process inventory

4. Analyze weighted-average, FIFO, and standard-costing methods of inventory valuation of cost of goods manufactured and transferred out

5. Apply process-costing methods to report transferred-in costs and operations costing

This chapter introduces the procedure of process cost allocation. To simplify the concept of process costing, we will assume a two-part process-costing system (see Chapter 4). Direct materials will comprise the homogeneous costs in the direct materials cost pool. This is a prime cost pool. The second cost pool consists of all direct labour and other indirect manufacturing overhead (MOH) of conversion. This is the conversion cost pool. We assume that the conversion process is only partially complete, and this means that valuation estimates of work-in-process (WIP) ending inventory must be made. There is only one MOH conversion cost pool, so there is only one cost allocation base to calculate prior to assigning costs of goods manufactured (COGM) and transferred out for either sale or further processing.

A process-costing system is a costing system appropriate when the output is a large volume of identical or very similar units. Either the units of service or units of product output are homogeneous. Examples include industries that output gasoline, wine, salt, milk, or gold, in which one unit of finished goods is indistinguishable from another. Each unit processed requires very similar inputs, and the conversion process for each unit is materially identical. This means the conversion costs should be applied evenly to all WIP and finished goods, depending on the degree or percentage of completion. The percentage of completion is probably a familiar concept to you from financial accounting, where it is one method used to match revenue and expenses of long-term contracts.

PROCESS-COSTING CALCULATIONS

1 Analyze process costing in contrast to job costing and apply the weighted-average method of inventory valuation when the beginning work-in-process inventory is zero

Industries using process costing in their manufacturing area include chemical processing, oil refining, pharmaceuticals, plastics, brick and tile manufacturing, semiconductor chips, beverages, and breakfast cereals.[1]

There are two principal differences between process costing and job costing. The first difference is that there is no controversy about the cost object—it is always the process. The second difference is that there is no controversy about the cost allocation base, or denominator—it is always equivalent units (EU), which will be explained in detail in this chapter. **Equivalent units (EU)** measures physical input units not yet completely converted in terms of the hypothetical quantity required to equal a single completely converted physical output unit. All completely converted input units are 100% complete; therefore, the conversion factor to EU is 100%.

In process costing, the average cost per EU is the basis of cost allocation. As Chapter 5 illustrated, when there are several differences in quantities of different inputs consumed, the cost-allocation process becomes more complex. Many different cost pools and cost drivers need to be chosen to appropriately assign the indirect costs. In process costing, there is only one indirect cost pool, consisting of both direct labour and all conversion costs. This makes sense because each output unit is consuming identical amounts of both types of inputs.

The managerial logic of cost allocation in a job-costing system was to assign proportions of an indirect cost pool or several indirect cost pools to individual jobs that consume different quantities of direct and indirect materials and labour. The larger the difference in the quantities of inputs consumed, the more incorrect it would be to cost each job at the same average production cost. In contrast, the logic of process costing is that the output consumes almost identical amounts of inputs; therefore, the goal of process costing is to calculate an average production cost for all units produced. Process costing is strongly similar to traditional or peanut butter costing but with a logical reason for selecting only a single indirect cost pool and a single cost allocation base, EU.

[1]Sources: Shell press release www.shell.com/home/content/media/news_and_library/ press_releases/2007/shell_claims_non_us_investors_11042007.html, accessed July 18, 2008; Shell press release www.shell.com/home/content/media/news_and_library/press_releases/2008/ us_reserves_settlement_06032008.html, accessed July 18, 2008; S. Labaton and J. Garth, "At Shell, New Accounting and Rosier Oil Outlook," *The New York Times*, March 12, 2004, p. A1.

Unit costs are computed by dividing total costs incurred by the number of units of equivalent output from the production process. Some processes, such as clothes manufacturing, have aspects of both process costing (cost per unit of each operation, such as cutting or sewing, is identical) and job costing (different materials are used in different batches of clothing, say, wool versus cotton). Costing systems that combine process costing and job costing are described later in this chapter.

ILLUSTRATING PROCESS COSTING

The characteristics of the products and services provided by a corporation will determine how the costing system is designed. The objectives of a costing system, as you will recall from Chapter 4, are to:

◆ Estimate as accurately as possible the costs of products and services to assist in decisions such as pricing and product mix

◆ Value inventory and cost of goods sold in compliance with external reporting requirements

◆ Manage costs and evaluate actual against expected performance to assist in redesigning the processes that make up the value chain

In Chapter 4 the single traditional cost-allocation technique was introduced, and in Chapter 5 the ABC technique was introduced for job costing. In deciding about what costs were combined into cost pools, the issue of variable and fixed costs was considered in detail. In Chapters 7 and 8, the issue of mixing variable and fixed costs was addressed as problematic when the time came to interpret feedback on cost variation between what was expected and what costs were actually incurred. Thus, decisions about cost pools and cost allocation bases affect the quality of information used to assess what variance reports mean and how best to control costs.

In this chapter, the cost object is referred to generically as a process. There is only one direct cost pool. Direct costs pose no challenge because direct costs can be traced directly to each output unit. In addition, we begin by assuming this one direct cost pool is 100% consumed at the point direct materials resources are input into the conversion process.

With respect to indirect costs, no analysis is necessary because we assume only one indirect cost pool. There is no decision to make about the variable-cost and fixed-cost components of the sole indirect cost pool. Both the direct and indirect cost pools refer to inventoriable cost pools; therefore, the allocation choices will affect COGS. Finally, the cost allocation base is always EU. Examples of indirect inventoriable costs in the conversion cost pool would include variable costs such as utilities, custodial wages, and rework, and fixed costs such as the amortization on the physical plant and equipment (refer to Exhibit 2-6). The allocation goals remain to:

◆ Estimate as accurately as possible the costs of products and services to assist in decisions such as pricing and product mix

◆ Value inventory and cost of goods sold in compliance with external reporting requirements

The key challenge is the allocation of all MOH, including direct manufacturing labour. This was the indirect cost pool identified in the two-part classification system in Chapter 4 as the conversion cost pool. Adding to the challenge is that during conversion the process cannot be observed without disrupting conversion and destroying the possibility of obtaining finished goods available for sale. A large amount of non-value-added spoilage costs will be incurred (Chapter 18). Another challenge is that a physical count of WIP inventory is not possible because the process cannot be interrupted. Even if WIP inventory could be observed, one output unit is identical to the other. There is no way to tell a unit that is 98% complete from a unit that is 25% complete.

Although it is impossible to observe how complete each unit is during each phase of conversion or to count the WIP units in inventory, to comply with GAAP, inventory valuation must be estimated and reported according to GAAP standards.

Inventory valuation is also necessary to estimate COGM, cost of goods available for sale (COGAS), and finished goods inventory. More importantly, the cost of goods sold (COGS) expense must be reported on the income statement.

Oil and metal refining, juice production, milk pasteurization, and alcohol fermentation are continuous processes. They are also machine intensive, not labour intensive, and that explains the use of a two-part costing system that includes direct manufacturing labour in the conversion cost pool. Labour cost is not considered sufficiently material to merit its own prime cost pool. Once the direct materials are fed into the first phase of conversion, the machines work 24/7, although downtime is scheduled for maintenance.

Process engineers are specialists who have developed methods to estimate how complete the conversion is at each of its stages. First the engineers estimate both the physical units of WIP and the degree of completion obtained at some point in time. Then, it is the management accountant's task to implement a cost procedure estimating the financial value of both the incomplete units in WIP inventory as well as finished goods completed during a specific time period. The estimate, however, must withstand the scrutiny of auditors who will attest that there is no material misstatement in the financial disclosure.

Costs are allocated to the output unit referred to generically as a process. The estimation of the total inventory value is based on either the first-in, first-out (FIFO) method or the weighted-average method used by financial accountants to value inventory. The **weighted-average process-costing method** calculates the average equivalent unit (EU) cost of the work done to date (regardless of the period in which it was done) and assigns it to units completed and transferred out, and to EU in ending work-in-process inventory (EI WIP).

The **first-in, first-out (FIFO) process-costing method** assigns the cost of the prior accounting period's EUs in beginning work-in-process inventory (BI WIP) to the first units completed and transferred out, and assigns the cost of EUs worked on during the current period first to complete beginning inventory, then to start and complete new units, and finally to units in EI WIP. Under the new CICA accounting standards, last-in, first-out (LIFO) is no longer permitted for inventory valuation for any purpose. It is the financial valuation of WIP where management accountants focus on how to classify and allocate the direct prime cost pool comprising costs of direct materials and the indirect conversion cost pool (direct manufacturing labour plus all indirect MOH).

Consider the pasteurization phase of industrial mass production of raw milk. Milk is pasteurized to remove pathogens and ensure that what is sold to retail customers is safe, a standard product that meets government standards of quality. The Canadian government regulates the supply of raw milk and its price. Therefore, the price of direct materials is standardized across all producers.

The contribution of milk manufacturing to the Canadian economy is approximately $13 billion per year. The government also sets standards of quality. For example, one litre of vitamin-fortified 2% milk is regulated with respect to the quantity of butterfat and safety. This ensures customers, the consumers, are guaranteed their value proposition by federal law and producers are guaranteed a rate of return (see Chapter 22). In economic terms, strategically, milk is a commodity, and cost leadership becomes the strategy of choice in order to improve profits in the industry. Without periodic reports of cost, however, it is impossible to manage profit. With regulated prices of raw and processed milk, the only way for a milk manufacturer to improve profit is to reduce conversion costs. Conversion costs cannot be reduced if they are not known.

The cost allocation base for the direct material cost pool is quantity of physical units input, and the assumption is that these are 100% consumed at the point of input although they are *not* 100% converted. With regulated raw milk prices, there will be little variation in the delivered cost of direct or raw materials inventory. As long as the unit price variation is not extreme, the use of an average unit input cost over some specified time period multiplied by the quantity of milk in direct materials inventory will not materially misstate the value of either what remains in ending direct materials inventory or what has been transferred out to WIP during the time period. Assume the total of DM purchased is transferred into conversion. The total cost pool of $2,000 of direct materials is transferred out of direct materials inventory and there is no EI of direct materials.

The raw milk is transported to the factory in stainless steel tanker trucks and the contents are pumped into chilled storage tanks. The conversion process requires several stages including pasteurizing, homogenizing, and vitamin fortification before packaging and distribution of the finished goods. Raw milk continuously flows into and out of the various stages of conversion. At the end of the pathway through the various tanks and pipes, the input is far closer to conversion into pasteurized, homogenized, fortified milk than the input at the beginning of the process.

If you could withdraw processed milk during pasteurization, you could not tell simply by looking at the milk the difference between the 1% and 99% pasteurized output. Milk, however, cannot be withdrawn without compromising the pasteurization process that guarantees its safety. Compromising the process is not an option because it would not comply with government safety regulations. All the WIP would have to be destroyed. A different measurement of percentage of completion and a different costing procedure is required to estimate the financial value of WIP. It is the milk process engineers who have devised non-invasive methods to infer the average percentage of conversion of all partially converted input units remaining in each stage of the conversion process.

The final challenge is that during conversion—say, pasteurization—the quantity of hectolitres transferred to the next conversion stage of homogenization is directly measurable—but the quantity remaining in the ending WIP inventory, although measurable, is difficult to cost. The reason is that the total volume of the machine that pasteurizes raw milk is known but the stage from 0% to almost 100% pasteurized of any given hectolitre of milk is not known and cannot be observed.

The management accountant may know that in total 1,000 hectolitres of milk is in the pasteurization process because that is what the tanks and pipes hold. What the management accountant will not know is how pasteurized each hectolitre is, nor in reality does a partially pasteurized hectolitre of milk have any financial value in the marketplace. It does, however, have value to the milk processor as WIP.

A partially pasteurized hectolitre of raw milk is not yet ready to proceed to homogenization, the next stage of processing. Therefore, a partially pasteurized hectolitre of raw milk does *not* have the same financial value as a fully pasteurized hectolitre of raw milk to the milk processor. This means all the costs of pasteurization have not yet been incurred by WIP but rather only some proportion of those costs have. The task of the management accountant who knows the total in the indirect conversion cost pool for the time period is $2,500 is to allocate that cost logically to the fully and partially pasteurized milk processed during the time period.

COST ALLOCATION BASE—EQUIVALENT UNITS (EU)

The incompletely converted input units represent the financial value of the ending inventory (EI) of WIP for a specific time period—and of course also the beginning inventory (BI) of WIP for the next time period. To begin the example, assume there was zero EI WIP from the previous time period. The conversion cost pool or numerator is known, and the total hectolitres of milk both transferred out and remaining in EI WIP for the current time period is known. Where the problem arises is deciding on the cost allocation base that measures units for the EI WIP that is not ready to be transferred out. The key is to establish some reasonable way to equate the partially pasteurized raw milk to fully pasteurized raw milk to give a common denominator for the conversion cost pool, yet retain the distinction between them.

The unit of measurement is equivalent units (EU). Equivalent units measures incompletely converted physical input units in terms of the hypothetical quantity required to equal a single completely converted physical output unit. The equivalence must be done in a way that reflects the lower financial value of input units remaining in the ending inventory of work in process. The cost allocation rate for the conversion cost pool is stated as $/EU both remaining in WIP and transferred out to the next phase.

By assuming a uniform rate of conversion for all raw input units transferred into pasteurization, a hypothetical equivalence can be calculated. A physical unit is 100% converted or, in decimal notation, 1.00. Therefore 1 physical unit $\times$ 1.00 = 1 EU. The process engineer has informed the management accountant that the raw milk remaining in WIP is 50% pasteurized. The accountant knows from various source documents that in total 250 hectolitres of raw milk (direct materials) were added to the pasteurization process during the specified time period. The same source materials reveal that 150 hectolitres were completely pasteurized and transferred out to the homogenization process. What remains in EI WIP is 100 hectolitres measured in physical units (250 hL – 150 hL = 100 hL). This volume of milk is neither raw nor pasteurized milk.

WEIGHTED-AVERAGE METHOD OF ASSIGNING CONVERSION COSTS

One WIP physical unit that is 50% converted will hypothetically equal 0.50 of one physical output unit transferred out. How many partially converted input units are required to be equivalent to one transferred, fully converted output unit? The answer of course is 2 (1 transferred output unit ÷ 0.50 EU input units = 2). The total EU remaining in the ending inventory of WIP is 50 EU (100 physical units $\times$ 0.50 = 50 EU).

In equivalent units, the cost allocation base for the conversion cost pool of $2,500 is 200 EU. The cost allocation base includes both all raw milk fully converted plus the raw milk only 50% converted, all measured using a common measure. The total is 200 EU (150 EU + 50 EU = 200 EU). Now the conversion cost pool can be divided by the total EU in the cost allocation base to calculate the cost allocation rate. Notice the difference between the 200 EU, the input of 250 physical units or hectolitres of raw milk, and the 150 physical units or hectolitres of completely pasteurized milk ready to be transferred out. This should make clear that the cost allocation base in this example is *not* physical units but rather EU.

THINKING CRITICALLY

What is another term to describe the 200 EU? Explain in a sentence or two. Read on for further discussion of this topic.

The 200 EU in the cost allocation base is a weighted average of 100% of those hectolitres of fully pasteurized raw milk, and those hectolitres of raw milk only 50% pasteurized. When these quantities are used to assign costs transferred out and costs remaining in ending WIP inventory, the costs too are a weighted average of all indirect costs in the conversion cost pool.

Exhibit 17-1 records flow of production in units. The Physical Units column records the hectolitres of milk in beginning WIP inventory and the quantity started in the specific time period, giving the total physical units to account for. For the quantity 100% pasteurized and transferred out, the physical units and EU are identical; therefore, the 150 units reappear in all three columns. The ending physical units in ending WIP inventory are obtained by subtracting the total physical units complete and transferred out from the total physical units input (250 hectolitres – 150 hectolitres = 100 hectolitres). Simply adding the two provides the total physical units accounted for.

The Equivalent Units columns report the EU for the direct materials cost pool and the EU for the indirect conversion costs pool for the 150 EU of milk completed and transferred out. For the incomplete units, recall that we assumed all direct materials were immediately consumed or, alternatively, there is absolutely no raw milk in the ending WIP inventory. This means that for the direct materials cost pool, the physical units and EU are an identical quantity of 100 because 100% of the direct materials costs have been consumed.

Of the physical units remaining in WIP, it would be incorrect to calculate the average conversion cost based on the physical units. The reason is that the milk is not

EXHIBIT 17-1
Summarizing the Flow of Production in Physical Units and Equivalent Units for Pasteurization of Raw Milk for a Particular Month

	A	B	C	D
			Equivalent Units	
		Physical	Direct	Conversion
3	Flow of Production	Units	Materials	Costs
4	Work in process, beginning	0		
5	Started during current period	250		
6	To account for	250		
7	Completed and transferred out during current period	150	150	150
8	Work in process, ending[a]	100		
9	(100 × 100%; 100 × 50%)		100	50
10	Accounted for	250		
11	Work done in current period only		250	200
12				
13	[a]Degree of completion in this department: direct materials, 100%; conversion costs, 50%.			

yet 100% pasteurized although 100% of conversion costs have been consumed. To obtain an appropriate higher unit average cost per unit remaining in WIP, the percentage-completion rate must be used. Multiplying the physical units of 100 in WIP by the percentage of completion, we obtain the EU that will be added to the fully complete EU and used as the total in the cost allocation base. Summing the EU completed and transferred out and the EU in ending WIP inventory equals the quantity of EU in the cost allocation base for the work done in the current period only.

Exhibit 17-2 shows the calculation of costs per EU and then the assignment of costs to both milk pasteurized and transferred out, and partially pasteurized milk remaining in EI WIP. At the top of Exhibit 17-2, the Direct Materials column shows that $2,000 is the direct materials cost pool incurred when 250 hectolitres of raw milk was added to the pasteurization process during the month. To simplify the example, we have assumed all beginning inventories were zero. The Conversion Costs column shows the conversion cost pool incurred for the month given as $2,500. The total production costs to be accounted for during the month are the sum of the direct materials and conversion costs, or $4,500.

Each cost pool will have its specific cost allocation base. The cost allocation base for the conversion cost pool is 200 EU; therefore, the cost allocation rate (average cost per EU remaining in EI WIP) is $12.50/EU ($2,500 ÷ 200 EU = $12.50/EU). The direct materials of 250 EU (equal to the 250 physical units) were 100% at the beginning of the time period; therefore, this is the quantity in the cost allocation base for the $2,000 direct materials cost pool. The cost allocation rate for this cost pool is $8.00/EU ($2,000 ÷ 250 EU = $8.00/EU). The weighted-average cost allocation rate for the total cost pool is the sum of the two rates, which is $20.50 ($12.50/EU + $8.00/EU = $20.50/EU).

The bottom section of Exhibit 17-2 illustrates how to use the cost allocation rates (the management accounting information) to assign costs according to GAAP. The costs must be apportioned to both the units completed and transferred out and to WIP to correctly calculate COGM, COGAS, and most importantly COGS. Without excellent process costing, the audited financial reports could contain material misstatement.

The units completed and transferred out include both the direct materials cost of $2,000 (250 EU of raw milk × $8.00/EU = $2,000) and the conversion costs of $1,875 for the 150 EU completed and transferred out to the next process in the current time period (150 EU × $12.50/EU = $1,875). The total costs of the EU completed and transferred out is $3,875 ($2,000 prime + $1,875 conversion = $3,875).

NI 52-109—Internal Control System Design

At all levels of management, managers owe a duty of care or stewardship to those whose assets they control. The Canadian Securities Administrators have recently passed a new national regulation NI 52-109. This regulation applies to companies listed on any Canadian stock exchange. Every quarter that a company reports its financial results, the Chief Executive Officer (CEO) must sign a certificate attesting to the quality of the disclosure.

The CEOs certify they have either supervised or designed an internal control system that provides reasonable assurance there has been no material misstatement in the financial disclosure. Process cost allocation affects the COGS, and ultimately the net income reported, as well as inventory on the balance sheet. By applying process costing thoughtfully, management accountants establish a sound foundation for internal control.

This sum is the COGM of pasteurization for the month, which is transferred out to the next phase of processing. For the ending WIP inventory, there are $0 of direct materials and $625 of conversion costs for the 50 EU of partially pasteurized milk remaining in EI WIP (50 EU from Exhibit 17-1 × $12.50/EU = $625). The completed and transferred-out amount of $3,875 and the ending WIP inventory amount of $625 sum to $4,500, the total costs of pasteurization to account for.

More is required to comply with *CICA Handbook* standards for inventory valuation. Either the weighted-average or first-in, first-out (FIFO) method must be used to ensure no material misstatement of the financial value of EI WIP. For the moment, assuming the valuation process complies with financial accounting requirements, the amounts on the bottom of Exhibit 17-2 would be used to report the

EXHIBIT 17-2

Calculating Equivalent Unit Costs and Assigning Costs to Completed Units and Ending WIP Inventory for Pasteurization of Raw Milk for a Particular Month

	A	B	C	D
		Total		
1		Total		
2		Production	Direct	Conversion
3		Costs	Materials	Costs
4	Cost added during the month	$4,500	$2,000	$2,500
5	Divide by equivalent units of work done in current period (Exhibit 17-1)		÷ 250	÷ 200
6	Cost per equivalent unit		$ 8.00	$ 12.50
7	Total costs to account for	$4,500		
8	Assignment of costs:			
9	Completed and transferred out			
10	Direct materials (250 EU × $8.00)	$2,000		
11	Conversion costs (150 EU from Exhibit 17-1 × $12.50)	1,875		
12	Total units completed and transferred out	3,875		
13	Work-in-process ending inventory (50 EU from Exhibit 17-1 × $12.50)	625		
14	Total costs accounted for	$4,500		
15				

financial results on a statement of cost of goods manufactured for the pasteurization process for the month for this milk manufacturing company.

The simplifying assumption of this example is that all direct materials costs are 100% consumed at the moment the raw milk is transferred in to the pasteurization process. This also explains why, when calculating the dollar value of ending WIP inventory, there is no cost of direct materials included. Irrespective of whether the pasteurization of raw milk is 100% or 50% complete, all raw materials costs are already reported as costs transferred out. The ending WIP inventory includes only a portion of the conversion cost pool that was *not* transferred out. The conversion cost allocation rate multiplied by the EU of ending WIP inventory becomes the financial value of this WIP inventory reported on the balance sheet. As a current asset, this inventory value must be realized within 12 months or one business cycle to comply with CICA standards. Any impairment to inventory must be reported immediately and the inventory revalued to the lower of cost or net realizable value.

WEIGHTED-AVERAGE METHOD WITH NO BEGINNING WIP INVENTORY

The easiest way to learn process costing is by example. Consider the following illustration, which is somewhat different from the first.

> **Example:** Global Defence Inc. manufactures thousands of components for missiles and military equipment. We will focus on the production of one of these components, DG-19. The difference between milk pasteurization and this example is the process itself and when the direct materials are added. The DG-19 is a critical part in a defence system. Global Defence assembles and tests the DG-19.

A subcomponent printed circuit arrives for assembly, but prior to adding the circuit to the DG-19, thorough quality control and inspection must be done as part of the conversion. These costs are indirect costs of conversion and are done by robots in a clean room. The results are transmitted directly to a computer and back to the robots, which discard substandard parts. The standard parts move along a conveyor to be inserted into a circuit board by hand along with two other elements of direct materials. This all happens in the Assembly Department. The circuit board then moves to the Testing Department for the final testing phase. Either the final two elements are inserted into the circuit board or they are not; therefore, only those circuit boards completely converted use direct materials. Nevertheless the direct materials are 100% consumed prior to the testing phase.

The product-costing system for DG-19 has a single direct-cost category (direct materials) and a single indirect-cost category (conversion costs). Each DG-19 unit passes through two departments—the Assembly Department and the Testing Department. Every effort is made to ensure that all DG-19 units are identical and meet a set of demanding performance specifications. Direct materials are added at the end of the process in Assembly and 100% consumed.

Contrast the journal entries for a process-costing system when there is and when there is not ending work-in-process inventory using the weighted-average method of inventory valuation

2

Conversion costs are added evenly during both processes. Conversion costs are all manufacturing costs other than direct materials costs. Conversion costs include manufacturing labour, indirect materials, energy, plant amortization, and so on. When the Testing Department finishes work on each DG-19 component, more direct materials are added and then the completed DG-19 is immediately transferred to Finished Goods. The following graphic summarizes these facts:

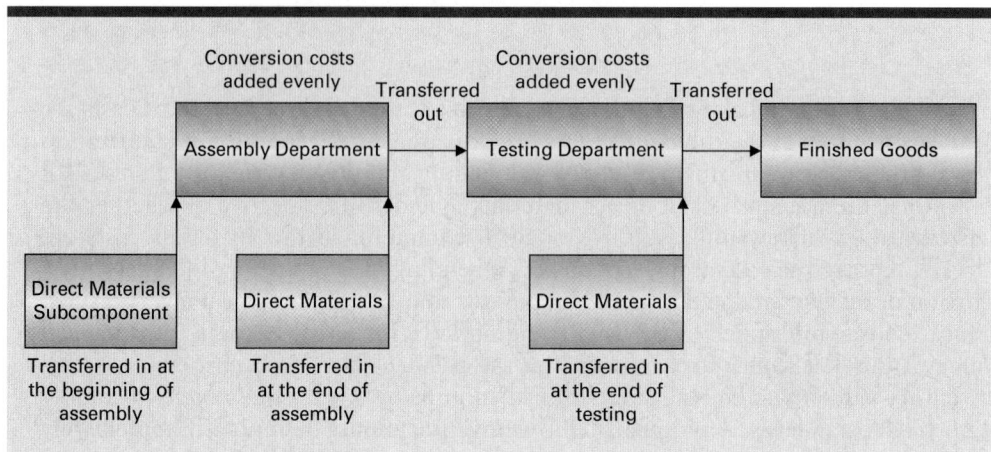

We will use the manufacture of the DG-19 component to illustrate three cases:

◆ **Case 1:** Process costing with no beginning inventory (BI) or ending inventory (EI) WIP of DG-19—that is, all units are started and fully completed by the end of the accounting period. This case illustrates the basic averaging-of-costs idea that is a key feature of process-costing systems.

◆ **Case 2:** Process costing with no BI WIP but an EI WIP of DG-19—that is, some units of DG-19 started during the accounting period are incomplete at the end of the period. This means that no direct materials have been added to the incomplete circuit boards at the end of assembly.

◆ **Case 3:** Process costing with both BI WIP and EI WIP of DG-19.

For *Case 1*, on January 1, 2010, the value is $0 for BI WIP of DG-19 circuit boards and all direct materials. During January 2010, Global Defence started, completed assembly of, and transferred out to the Testing Department 400 DG-19 units. The total costs for January 2010 were:

Direct materials costs added during January	$32,000
Conversion costs added during January	24,000
Total Assembly Department costs added during January	$56,000

With zero BI and EI WIP, no inventory valuation is necessary. By averaging, the assembly cost per unit of DG-19 would simply be $56,000 ÷ 400 units = $140, itemized as follows:

Direct materials ($32,000 ÷ 400) cost per unit	$ 80
Conversion costs ($24,000 ÷ 400) cost per unit	60
Assembly Department cost per unit	$140

This case shows that in a process-costing system, unit costs can be averaged by dividing total cost in a given accounting period by total units produced in the period. The facts of the specific situation permit a simple average cost per physical unit calculation for both the direct and indirect cost pools. Because each unit is identical, there is no reason to believe any single unit would cost more to produce than the other units. All units receive the identical amount of direct materials and conversion costs. If organizations mass-produce standard units, then they can use this simple average-costing approach when there are no incomplete units at the end of each accounting period. Here is another way to summarize this situation.

Global Defence Inc., January 2010—Case 1 (No Beginning and No Ending WIP Inventory)

| | Physical Units | Calculating the Cost Allocation Base in EU | | Cost Pools | | |
		Conversion Rate	Equivalent Units (EU)	Direct Materials	Conversion	Total
BI WIP	0			$ 0	$ 0	
Started (added) this month	400			32,000	24,000	
Units to account for	400					
Good units completed and transferred out this month	400	100%	400			
EI WIP this month	0	0%	0			
Units accounted for	400		400			
Total costs to date				$32,000	$24,000	$56,000
Cost per EU (cost allocation rate $/EU)				$ 80.00	$60.00	$140.00
				($32,000 ÷ 400 EU)	($24,000 ÷ 400 EU)	

REAL COMPANIES

Real Practices Worldwide

Process costing is used extensively at corporations around the world. One survey noted that 52% of Australian companies and 46% of Japanese companies use process costing, making it the most popular product-costing system in both countries.[a] Additional findings from Eastern Europe show that 66% of all Estonian manufacturing companies also use process costing.[b] Another Australian survey examines the widespread use of process costing across a variety of industries.[c] (The reported percentages exceed 100% because several companies surveyed used more than one product-costing system.)

	Food	Textiles	Metals	Chemicals	Refining
Process costing	96%	91%	92%	75%	100%
Job costing	4	18	25	25	25
Other	—	—	8	12	—

Process costing is widely used in mass-production industries that manufacture homogeneous products, including food, textiles, primary metals, chemicals, and refining. In contrast, job costing is favoured over process costing in industries that produce many distinct products—for example, in printing and publishing, furniture and fixtures, machinery and computers, and electronics. Among artisan-based enterprises in Nigeria, 49% of respondents use job costing, whereas only 10% rely on process costing for product-costing purposes.[d]

	Printing and Publishing	Furniture and Fixtures	Machinery and Computers	Electronics
Process costing	20%	38%	43%	55%
Job costing	73	63	65	58
Other	13	—	9	10

[a]H. Wijewardena and A. De Zoysa, "A Comparative Analysis of Management Accounting Practices in Australia and Japan: An Empirical Investigation," *International Journal of Accounting* (1999).

[b]T. Haldma and K. Lääts, "Contingencies Influencing the Management Accounting Practices in Estonian Manufacturing Companies," *Management Accounting Research* (2002).

[c]M. Joye and P. Blayney, "Cost and Management Accounting Practices in Australian Manufacturing Companies: Survey Results" (Accounting Research Centre, The University of Sydney, 1991).

[d]L. Obara and N. Ukpai, "Cost Accounting Practice in the Information Sector of Nigeria: A Survey of Eastern Business Zone" (Tangier, Morocco: African Training and Research Centre in Administration for Development, 2001).

GLOBAL DEFENCE—ENDING WIP INVENTORY VALUATION USING THE WEIGHTED-AVERAGE METHOD

We now examine *Case 2*. In February 2010, Global Defence places another 400 units of DG-19 into production. Recall there is no beginning inventory of partially completed units in the Assembly Department on February 1, 2010, because all units placed into production in January were fully completed by February 1. During February, however, customer delays in placing orders for DG-19 prevented the complete assembly of all units started in February. Only 175 units were completed and transferred out to the Testing Department. This means that 225 units remained in the Assembly Department's EI WIP and no direct materials were added to these units as at February 28, 2010. The production engineers estimated that the conversion of the 225 units in EI WIP was 60% complete.

The total costs for the Assembly Department for February 2010 were:

Direct materials costs added during February	$32,000
Conversion costs added during February	18,600
Total Assembly Department costs added during February	$50,600

Exhibit 17-3 records flow of production in units. The Physical Units column records the units in beginning WIP inventory (which was 0) and the quantity started in February (which was 400), giving the 400 total units to account for. The quantity completed and transferred out of the Assembly Department (175 physical units) and the EI WIP (225 physical units) are then recorded, giving the 400 total quantity accounted for. The Equivalent Units columns report the EU for both the direct materials and indirect conversion costs pools for the EU completed and transferred out and the units remaining in EI WIP. Multiplying percentage of completion by the physical units in the first column of numbers results in the EU. Summing the EU completed and transferred out and the EU in ending WIP inventory equals the quantity of EU in the cost allocation base for the work done only in February (400 EU for direct materials and 135 EU for conversion costs).

Exhibit 17-4 shows the calculation of costs per EU and then the assignment of costs to units completed and transferred out, and to partially completed units remaining in ending WIP inventory. At the top of Exhibit 17-4, the Direct Materials column shows that $32,000 of direct materials was purchased and should have been

EXHIBIT 17-3
Summarizing the Flow of Production in Physical Units and Equivalent Units for the Assembly Department of Global Defence Inc. for February 2010—Case 2 (Ending WIP Inventory but No Beginning WIP Inventory)

	A	B	C	D
1				Equivalent Units
2		Physical	Direct	Conversion
3	**Flow of Production**	**Units**	**Materials**	**Costs**
4	Work in process, beginning	0		
5	Started during February	400		
6	To account for	400		
7	Completed and transferred out during February	175	175	175
8	Work in process, ending[a]	225		
9	(225 × 100%; 225 × 60%)		225	135
10	Accounted for	400		
11	Work done in February only		400	310
12				
13	[a]Degree of completion in this department: direct materials, 100%; conversion costs, 60%.			

EXHIBIT 17-4

Calculating Equivalent Unit Costs and Assigning Costs to Completed Units and Ending
WIP Inventory for the Assembly Department of Global Defence Inc. for February
2010—Case 2 (Ending WIP Inventory but No Beginning WIP Inventory)

	A	B	C	D
		Total		
		Production	Direct	Conversion
		Costs	Materials	Costs
4	Cost added during February	$50,600	$32,000	$18,600
5	Divide by equivalent units of work done in current period (Exhibit 17-3)		÷ 400	÷ 310
6	Cost per equivalent unit		$ 80	$ 60
7	Total costs to account for	$50,600		
8	Assignment of costs:			
9	Work in process ending inventory (225 units)			
10	Direct materials	$18,000	(225 × $80)	
11	Conversion costs	8,100	(135 EU from Exh. 17-3 × $60)	
12	Total work in process	26,100		
13	Completed and transferred out (175 units from Exh. 17-3)	24,500	(175 × ($80 + $60))	
14	Total costs accounted for	$50,600		
15				

added to the 400 units started during February. There was no direct materials BI
WIP. Thus the cost per EU for direct materials was $80 ($32,000 ÷ 400 EU from
Exhibit 17-3 = $80/EU). The Conversion Costs column shows the conversion cost
pool for the Assembly Department for February was $18,600. Thus the cost per EU
for conversion costs was $60 ($18,600 ÷ 310 EU from Exhibit 17-3 = $60/EU).
The total production costs to be accounted for during the month are the sum of the
direct materials and conversion costs, or $50,600.

The bottom section of Exhibit 17-4 uses the costs per EU to assign costs to
units completed and transferred out and to EI WIP. The costs are assigned using the
weighted-average method. Recall that the weighted average is very straightforward
because the weights have already been provided in transforming the physical into
equivalent units. The cost allocation rates are already weighted. In the case of the
direct materials cost pool, the weights for both complete and incomplete physical
units are 1, but this will not always be the case; it is simply the way the facts of this
specific case have been presented. The weights for the conversion cost pool are 1 for
those transferred out and 0.60 for those in EI WIP.

Exhibit 17-4 shows the COGM for the 175 completed units is $24,500 (175 ×
$80/EU for direct materials + 175 × $60/EU for conversion costs). The value of
EI WIP is not quite as straightforward to calculate. The direct materials remain
100% unused for the 225 units in EI WIP; therefore, this cost is $18,000 (225 EU ×
$80/EU = $18,000). The conversion cost for the 135 EU in EI WIP is $8,100 (135
EU × $60 = $8,100). The total value of EI WIP at the end of February is $26,100
($18,000 + $8,100 = $26,100). The completed and transferred-out amount of
$24,500 and the EI WIP amount of $26,100 sum to $50,600, the total costs of the
Assembly Department to account for. These amounts would appear on the COGM,
which is illustrated above.

In the pasteurization example, the direct materials (raw milk) were 100% input at the beginning of the pasteurization process. Therefore, irrespective of how many hectolitres of raw milk was actually pasteurized, 100% of the direct materials would be completely consumed in pasteurization and so too would be the costs. In the Case 2 DG-19 Assembly Department example, the direct materials are either added or not at the end of the assembly process. Therefore, only that proportion of circuit boards 100% converted will consume the direct materials inputs and the costs of those inputs. Only the costs consumed by the completed circuit boards will be transferred out to the Testing Department. Allocation of conversion and direct materials costs differs according to the facts of the process.

Process-costing systems separate costs into cost categories according to the timing of when costs are introduced into the process. Only two cost pools are required in the Global Defence example because direct materials are all added at the same time, and all conversion costs are assumed to be added to the process at an even rate over time. If, however, direct manufacturing labour were added to the process at different times than all other conversion costs, then a third cost pool would be necessary. In this situation, we could no longer assume all conversion activities occur at a uniform rate; therefore, separate estimates of equivalent units would be required for the manufacturing labour and the quality-control assembly processes.

The costs transferred out as reported in the bottom section of Exhibit 17-4 is an accounting process wherein the costs follow the EU through conversion. The methods to value EI WIP are constrained for external reporting purposes by GAAP to either the weighted-average or the FIFO (first-in, first-out) method. At this point in the Global Defence example, no decision need be made because the BI WIP was $0 in both January and February. The choice of methods will make a difference in Case 3, however, because there is BI WIP to be converted and transferred out.

JOURNAL ENTRIES

Process-costing journal entries are basically like those made in the job-costing system. That is, direct materials and conversion costs are accounted for as in job-costing systems. The main difference is that, in process costing, there is often more than one WIP—in our Global Defence example, there is Work in Process—Assembly and Work in Process—Testing. Global Defence purchases direct materials as needed. These materials are delivered directly to the Assembly Department. Using dollar amounts from Exhibit 17-4, summary journal entries for the month of February at Global Defence Inc. are as follows:

1. Work in Process—Assembly $32,000
       Accounts Payable $32,000
      To record direct materials purchased and used in
         production during February.

2. Work in Process—Assembly $18,600
       [Various accounts] $18,600
      To record Assembly Department conversion costs for
         February; examples include energy, manufacturing supplies,
         all manufacturing labour, and plant amortization.

3. Work in Process—Testing $24,500
       Work in Process—Assembly $24,500
      To record cost of goods completed and transferred
         from Assembly to Testing during February.

Exhibit 17-5 shows a general sketch of the flow of costs through the T-accounts. The key T-account, Work in Process—Assembly, shows an ending balance of $26,100.

EXHIBIT 17-5
Flow of Costs in a Process-Costing System, Assembly Department of Global Defence Inc. for February 2010

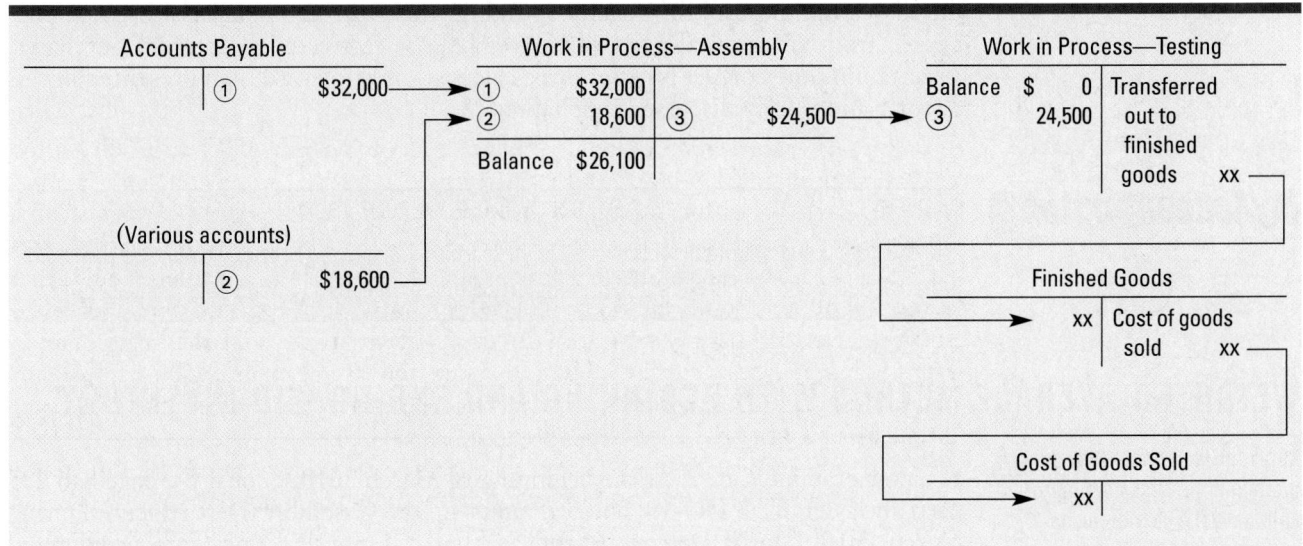

For presentation in correct financial-reporting format, the dollar values presented in Exhibit 17-4 (and the journal entries) for the Assembly Department are reported below in the same format as in Chapter 2, Exhibit 2-10 (p. 52):

Global Defence Inc. Schedule of Cost of Goods Manufactured, Assembly Department For the Month Ended:	January 31, 2010 (Case 1) Weighted Average		February 28, 2010 (Case 2) Weighted Average	
Direct Materials				
Beginning inventory of direct materials	$ 0		$ 0	
Purchases of direct materials during the month	32,000		32,000	
Cost of direct materials available for use	32,000		32,000	
Ending inventory of direct materials for the month	0		0	
Direct materials used during the month		$32,000		$ 32,000
All conversion costs	24,000		18,600	
Total conversion costs		24,000		18,600
Manufacturing costs incurred during the month		56,000		50,600
Beginning work-in-process inventory		0		0
Total manufacturing costs to account for		56,000		50,600
Ending work-in-process inventory		0		(26,100)
Cost of goods manufactured—transferred out to Testing Department		$56,000		$ 24,500

> ## THINKING CRITICALLY
>
> What inventory does the COGM transferred out to Testing Department represent? Explain in a sentence or two. Read on for further discussion of this topic.

In double-entry bookkeeping, this report from the Assembly Department represents only half the transaction. The other half is the receipt into inventory of both the physical units and the COGM by the Testing Department. The physical units received by the Testing Department from the Assembly Department are subcomponents, which are direct materials. The dollar value of the monthly COGM represents the direct materials transferred in or added to the Testing Department's purchases for the month. Strictly speaking, these direct materials were not purchased from an external party but nevertheless are treated as internal purchases. Ascertaining the correct transfer price is less straightforward than presented in this chapter and is fully discussed in Chapter 23.

WEIGHTED-AVERAGE METHOD WITH BEGINNING AND ENDING WIP INVENTORY

③ Apply the weighted-average method of process costing to calculate the cost of goods manufactured and transferred out when there is both beginning and ending work-in-process inventory

We now examine *Case 3*. At the beginning of March 2010, Global Defence had 225 partially assembled DG-19 physical units in the Assembly Department. During March 2010, Global Defence placed another 275 physical units into production. The total physical units in various stages of production during March was 500 (225 beginning physical units + 275 physical units = 500 physical units), of which 400 were completed and transferred out to the Testing Department. At the end of March 2010, there were 100 physical units remaining in Assembly that were 50% complete. During March, direct materials costs of $19,800 and conversion costs of $16,380 were added in the Assembly Department, for total costs of $36,180 added during March. With a non-zero BI WIP, a choice must be made with respect to how the costs will flow when BI WIP is fully converted and transferred out to the Testing Department—weighted average or FIFO.

The EU calculation in the weighted-average method is only concerned with total equivalent units of work done to date regardless of (a) whether the work was done during the preceding period and is part of beginning work in process or (b) whether it was done during the current period. That is, the weighted-average method merges equivalent units in beginning inventory (work done before March) with equivalent units of work done in the current period. Thus, the stage of completion of the current-period beginning work in process is irrelevant and not used in the computation. The flow of physical units and the calculation of equivalent units for the Assembly Department for March 2010 are shown in Exhibit 17-6.

The weighted-average cost is the total of all costs entering the WIP account (regardless of whether it is from beginning work in process or from work started during the period) divided by total equivalent units of work done to date:

$$\text{EU in BI WIP} + \frac{\text{EU of work done}}{\text{in current period}} = \frac{\text{EU completed and transferred}}{\text{out in current period}} + \text{EU in EI WIP}$$

Exhibit 17-7 shows the calculation of the direct materials and conversion cost per equivalent unit, and the assignment of costs to units completed and transferred out and to EI WIP. The dollars follow the EU, which are either 100% converted and transferred out to the Testing Department, or remain 50% complete in the EI WIP of the Assembly Department, allocated on a weighted-average cost per EU. The total costs of March EI WIP are calculated in Exhibit 17-7 as follows:

Direct materials:	
100 equivalent units × weighted-average cost per equivalent unit of $75.60	$ 7,560
Conversion costs:	
50 equivalent units × weighted-average cost per equivalent unit of $54.40	2,720
Total costs of ending work in process	$10,280

EXHIBIT 17-6

Summarizing the Flow of Production in Physical Units and Equivalent Units for the Assembly Department of Global Defence Inc. for March 2010—Case 3, Weighted-Average Method with Beginning and Ending WIP Inventory

	A	B	C	D
1			Equivalent Units	
2		Physical	Direct	Conversion
3	Flow of Production	Units	Materials	Costs
4	Work in process, beginning (February EI WIP, Exh. 17-3)	225		
5	Started during current period (given, p. 846)	275		
6	To account for	500		
7	Completed and transferred out during March	400	400	400
8	Work in process, ending ^a (given, p. 846)	100		
9	(100 × 100%; 100 × 50%)		100	50
10	Accounted for	500		
11	Work done to date		500	450
12				
13	^aDegree of completion in this department: direct materials, 100%; conversion costs, 50%.			

The completed and transferred-out amount of $52,000 and the EI WIP amount of $10,280 sum to $62,280, the total costs of the Assembly Department to account for in March.

It is important to note that the factor for direct materials EU is 100%, or 1, but that is not always the case. It is entirely possible to encounter a conversion process wherein the direct materials of partially converted units are also only partially consumed.

EXHIBIT 17-7

Calculating Equivalent Unit Costs and Assigning Costs to Completed Units and Ending WIP Inventory for the Assembly Department of Global Defence Inc. for March 2010—Case 3, Weighted-Average Method with Beginning and Ending WIP Inventory

	A	B	C	D
1		Total		
2		Production	Direct	Conversion
3		Costs	Materials	Costs
4	Work in process, beginning (February EI WIP, Exh. 17-4)	$26,100	$18,000	$ 8,100
5	Costs added in current period (given, p. 846)	36,180	19,800	16,380
6	Costs incurred to date		$37,800	$24,480
7	Divide by equivalent units of work done to date (Exhibit 17-6)		÷ 500	÷ 450
8	Cost per equivalent unit of work done to date		$ 75.60	$ 54.40
9	Total costs to account for	$62,280		
10	Assignment of costs:			
11	Completed and transferred out (400 units)	$52,000	(400^a × $75.60) + (400^a × $54.40)	
12	Work in process, ending (100 units)	10,280	(100^b × $75.60) + (50^b × $54.40)	
13	Total costs accounted for	$62,280		
14				
15	^aEquivalent units completed and transferred out from Exhibit 17-6.			
16	^bEquivalent units in ending work in process from Exhibit 17-6.			

The factor for direct materials consumption is unique and unrelated to the conversion factor. Thus it is possible for partially converted units to have consumed 20% of direct materials and 75% of conversion inputs or vice versa, 75% of direct materials and 20% of conversion inputs. The actual conversion factors from physical to equivalent units are independent and will be given in each situation.

The following table summarizes the total costs to account for and the $62,280 accounted for in Exhibit 17-7. The arrows indicate that costs of units completed and transferred out, and costs of units in ending work in process are calculated using average total costs obtained after merging costs of beginning work in process and costs added in the current period.

Costs to Account For		Costs Accounted For Calculated at Weighted-Average Cost	
Beginning work in process	$26,100	Completed and transferred out	$52,000
Costs added in current period	36,180	Ending work in process	10,280
Total costs to account for	$62,280	Total costs accounted for	$62,280

Before proceeding, please pause and review Exhibits 17-6 and 17-7 carefully to check your understanding of the weighted-average method. The information Global Defence has calculated for the month of March based on the weighted-average method of inventory valuation is summarized below in the accounting format illustrated in Exhibit 2-10 (p. 52):

Global Defence Inc.
Schedule of Cost of Goods Manufactured,
Assembly Department
For the Month Ended: **March 31, 2010**
Weighted Average

Direct materials		
Beginning inventory of direct materials	$ 0	
Purchases of direct materials during the month	19,800	
Cost of direct materials available for use	19,800	
Ending inventory of direct materials for the month	0	
Direct materials used during the month		$19,800
All conversion costs	16,380	
Total conversion costs		16,380
Manufacturing costs incurred during the month		36,180
Beginning work-in-process inventory		26,100
Total manufacturing costs to account for		62,280
Ending work-in-process inventory		(10,280)
Costs of goods manufactured—transferred out to Testing Department		$52,000

Using dollar amounts from Exhibit 17-7, summary journal entries for the month of March at Global Defence Inc. are

1. Work in Process—Assembly $19,800
       Accounts Payable $19,800
   To record direct materials purchased and used in production during March.

2. Work in Process—Assembly $16,380
       [Various accounts] $16,380
   To record Assembly Department conversion costs for March; examples include energy, manufacturing supplies, all manufacturing labour, and plant amortization.

3. Work in Process—Testing $52,000
       Work in Process—Assembly $52,000
   To record cost of units completed and transferred from Assembly to Testing during March.

The key T-account, Work in Process—Assembly, would show the following:

Work in Process—Assembly			
Beginning inventory, March 1	$26,100	③ Transferred out to Work in	
① Direct materials	19,800	Process—Testing	$52,000
② Conversion costs	16,380		
Ending inventory, March 31	$10,280		

FIRST-IN, FIRST-OUT AND STANDARD-COST METHODS

Analyze weighted-average, FIFO, and standard-costing methods of inventory valuation of cost of goods manufactured and transferred out

④

In contrast to the weighted-average method, the first-in, first-out (FIFO) process-costing method assigns the cost of the prior accounting period's equivalent units in beginning work-in-process inventory to the first units completed and transferred out. It assigns the cost of equivalent units worked on during the current period first to complete beginning inventory, then to start and complete new units, and finally to units in ending work-in-process inventory. This method assumes that the earliest EU in the WIP—Assembly account are completed first.

A distinctive feature of the FIFO process-costing method is that *the costs* of work done on BI WIP before the current period are kept separate from work done in the current period. Costs incurred in the *current period* and units produced in the *current period* are used to calculate costs per EU of work done in the current period. In contrast, EU and cost-per-EU calculations in the weighted-average method merge the units and costs in BI WIP with units and costs of work done in the current period, and make no distinction between the units.

The following observations help explain the physical units calculations in Exhibit 17-8:

◆ The first physical units assumed to be completed and transferred out during the period are the 225 units from the BI WIP.

◆ From the March data given on page 846, 400 physical units were completed during March. The FIFO method assumes that the first 225 of these units were from BI WIP; thus 175 physical units (400 physical units – 225 physical units) must have been started and completed during March.

◆ EI WIP consists of 100 physical units (275 physical units – 175 physical units) partially converted in March.

◆ Note that the physical units "to account for" equal the physical units "accounted for" (500 units).

Under the FIFO method, the EU calculations focus on only what has been converted in March. Under the FIFO method, the work done in the current period is assumed to first complete the 225 units in beginning work in process. The EU of work done in March on the BI WIP are computed by multiplying the 225 physical units by the percentage of work remaining to be done to complete these units: 0% for direct materials because the beginning work in process is 100% complete with respect to direct materials, and 40% for conversion costs, because the beginning work in process is 60% complete with respect to conversion costs. The results are 0 (225 physical units × 0.0 = 0) EU of work for direct materials and 90 EU (225 physical units × 0.40 = 90 EU) for conversion costs.

Next, the work done in the current period is assumed to start and complete the next 175 units. The EU of work done on the 175 physical units started and completed are computed by multiplying 175 units by 100% for both direct materials and

EXHIBIT 17-8
Summarizing the Flow of Production in Physical Units and Equivalent Units for the Assembly Department of Global Defence Inc. for March 2010—Case 3, FIFO Method with Beginning and Ending WIP Inventory

	A	B	C	D
			Equivalent Units	
		Physical	Direct	Conversion
3	Flow of Production	Units	Materials	Costs
4	Work in process, beginning (February EI WIP, Exh. 17-3)	225	(Work done before current period)	
5	Started during current period (given, p. 846)	275		
6	To account for	500		
7	Completed and transferred out during current period:			
8	From beginning work in process[a]	225		
9	[225 × (100% − 100%); 225 × (100% − 60%)]		0	90
10	Started and completed	175[b]		
11	(175 × 100%; 175 × 100%)		175	175
12	Work in process, ending[c] (given, p. 846)	100		
13	(100 × 100%; 100 × 50%)		100	50
14	Accounted for	500		
15	Work done in March only		275	315
16				
17	[a]Degree of completion in this department: direct materials, 100%; conversion costs, 60%.			
18	[b]400 physical units completed and transferred out minus 225 physical units completed and transferred out from beginning work-in-process inventory.			
19	[c]Degree of completion in this department: direct materials, 100%; conversion costs, 50%.			

conversion costs, because all work on these units is done in the current period. Therefore, there are 175 EU (175 physical units × 1.0 = 175 EU) started and completed in March.

Finally, the work done in the current period is assumed to start but leave incomplete the final 100 physical units as EI WIP. The EU of work done on the 100 physical units of EI WIP are calculated by multiplying 100 physical units by 100% for direct materials (because all direct materials have been added for these units in the current period) and 50% for conversion costs (because 50% of conversion and corresponding costs have been undertaken and consumed in the current period). The flow of production in physical units and EU is summarized in Exhibit 17-8.

THINKING CRITICALLY

What kind of cost behaviour applies to the conversion cost pool? Explain in a sentence or two. Read on for further discussion of this topic.

This cost pool is most likely a fixed cost pool because the material element of MOH for Global Defence is equipment costs. According to GAAP, Global Defence must use either the master budget capacity or normal capacity in the denominator as the cost allocation base. The quantity appears to be 400 physical units for the month, or 4,800 physical units per year. The budgeted cost allocation rate for conversion costs is most likely to be $60/physical unit. The budgeted cost per physical unit of direct materials is most likely $80/physical unit. To the extent actual cost allocation rates differ from the pro forma rate, a production volume variance will arise for the conversion cost pool, and a quantity or price (or both) variance for the direct materials cost pool.

In FIFO, the logic of the flow of costs is that all of February's costs must be transferred out first. The EI WIP from February is 60% converted, which means the remaining 40% conversion must be paid from the conversion cost pool for March. The total conversion cost for March is given as $16,380. The actual conversion EU comprise the 90 (225 physical units × 0.40 = 90 EU) remaining from February, the 175 (175 physical units × 1.0 = 175 EU) begun and completed in March, and the 50 (100 physical units × 0.50 = 50 EU) remaining in Assembly. The actual cost allocation rate for March, based on only those conversion costs incurred in March, is $52.00 ($16,380 ÷ (90 + 175 + 50) = $52.00).

Finally, the work done in the current period is assumed to start but leave incomplete the final 100 units as ending work in process. The equivalent units of work done on the 100 units of ending work in process are calculated by multiplying 100 physical units by 100% for direct materials (because all direct materials have been added for these units in the current period) and 50% for conversion costs (because 50% of conversion work has been done on these units in the current period). Under FIFO, the EI WIP comes from physical units that were started but not fully completed during the current period. The total cost of the 100 partially assembled physical units in ending work in process consists of

Direct materials:	
100 equivalent units × cost per equivalent unit in March of $72	$7,200
Conversion costs:	
50 equivalent units × cost per equivalent unit in March of $52	2,600
Total costs of work in process on March 31	$9,800

Exhibit 17-9 shows the calculation of the direct materials and conversion cost per equivalent unit, and the assignment of costs to units completed and transferred out and to EI WIP using the FIFO method of process costing. The completed and transferred out amount of $52,480 and the EI WIP amount of $9,800 sum to $62,280, the total costs of the Assembly Department to account for in March.

The following table summarizes the total costs to account for and the costs accounted for of $62,280 in Exhibit 17-9. Notice how under the FIFO method, the layers of beginning work in process and costs added in the current period are kept separate. The arrows indicate where the costs in each layer go (that is, to units completed and transferred out, or to ending work in process). Be sure to include the costs of beginning work in process ($26,100) when calculating the costs of units completed from beginning inventory.

Costs to Account For		Costs Accounted For Calculated on a FIFO Basis	
		Completed and transferred out:	
Beginning work in process	$26,100	Beginning work in process	$26,100
Costs added in current period	36,180	Used to complete beginning work in process	4,680
		Started and completed	21,700
		Completed and transferred out	52,480
		Ending work in process	9,800
Total costs to account for	$62,280	Total costs accounted for	$62,280

Before proceeding, please pause and review Exhibits 17-8 and 17-9 carefully to check your understanding of the FIFO method. The information Global Defence

EXHIBIT 17-9

Calculating Equivalent Unit Costs and Assigning Costs to Completed Units and Ending WIP Inventory for the Assembly Department of Global Defence Inc. for March 2010—Case 3, FIFO Method with Beginning and Ending WIP Inventory

	A	B	C	D
		Total		
		Production	Direct	Conversion
		Costs	Materials	Costs
4	Work in process, beginning (February EI WIP, Exh. 17-4)	$26,100	(costs of work done before current period)	
5	Costs added in current period (given, p. 846)	36,180	$19,800	$16,380
6	Divide by equivalent units of work done in current period (Exhibit 17-8)		÷ 275	÷ 315
7	Cost per equivalent unit of work done in current period		$ 72	$ 52
8	Total costs to account for	$62,280		
9	Assignment of costs:			
10	Completed and transferred out (400 units):			
11	Work in process, beginning (225 units)	$26,100		
12	Costs added to beginning work in process in current period	4,680	$(0^a \times \$72) + (90^a \times \$52)$	
13	Total from beginning inventory	30,780		
14	Started and completed (175 units)	21,700	$(175^b \times \$72) + (175^b \times \$52)$	
15	Total costs of units completed and transferred out	52,480		
16	Work in process, ending (100 units)	9,800	$(100^c \times \$72) + (50^c \times \$52)$	
17	Total costs accounted for	$62,280		
18				
19	ᵃEquivalent units used to complete beginning work in process from Exhibit 17-8.			
20	ᵇEquivalent units started and completed from Exhibit 17-8.			
21	ᶜEquivalent units in ending work in process from Exhibit 17-8.			

calculated for the month of March based on the FIFO method of valuation of inventory is summarized in the same accounting format as illustrated in Exhibit 2-10 and compared to the amounts obtained using the weighted-average method:

Global Defence Inc.
Schedule of Cost of Goods Manufactured,
Assembly Department
For the Month Ended:

	March 31, 2010 Weighted Average	March 31, 2010 FIFO
Direct Materials		
Beginning inventory of direct materials	$ 0	$ 0
Purchases of direct materials during the month	19,800	19,800
Cost of direct materials available for use	19,800	19,800
Ending inventory of direct materials for the month	0	0
Direct materials used during the month	$19,800	$ 19,800
All conversion costs	16,380	16,380
Total conversion costs	16,380	16,380
Manufacturing costs incurred during the month	36,180	36,180
Beginning work-in-process inventory	26,100	26,100
Total manufacturing costs to account for	62,280	62,280
Ending work-in-process inventory	(10,280)	(9,800)
Cost of goods manufactured—transferred out to Testing Department	$52,000	$ 52,480

The journal entries under the FIFO method parallel the journal entries under the weighted-average method. The only difference is that the entry to record the cost of goods completed and transferred out would be for $52,480 under the FIFO method instead of for $52,000 under the weighted-average method.

Only rarely is an application of pure FIFO ever encountered in process costing. As a result, it should really be called a modified or departmental FIFO method because FIFO is applied within a department to compile the cost of units transferred out, but the units transferred in during a given period usually are carried at a single average unit cost as a matter of convenience. For example, the average cost of units transferred out of the Assembly Department is $52,480 ÷ 400 units = $131.20 per DG-19 unit. The Assembly Department uses FIFO to distinguish between monthly batches of production. The succeeding department, Testing, however, costs these units (that consist of costs incurred in February and March) at one average unit cost ($131.20 in this illustration). If this averaging were not done, the attempt to track costs on a pure FIFO basis throughout a series of processes would be unduly cumbersome, if not impossible.

COMPARE WEIGHTED-AVERAGE AND FIFO METHODS

The following table summarizes the costs assigned to units completed and those still in process under the weighted-average and FIFO process-costing methods for our example:

	Weighted Average (from Exhibit 17-7)	FIFO (from Exhibit 17-9)	Difference
Cost of units completed and transferred out	$52,000	$52,480	+$480
Work in process, ending	10,280	9,800	−$480
Total costs accounted for	$62,280	$62,280	

The weighted-average ending inventory is higher than the FIFO ending inventory by $480, or 4.9% ($480 ÷ $9,800). This is a significant difference when aggregated over the many thousands of components that Global Defence makes. The weighted-average method in our example also results in lower COGS and hence higher operating income and higher tax payments than the FIFO method. Differences in EU costs of BI WIP and work done during the current period account for the differences in weighted-average and FIFO costs. Recall that the cost per EU of BI WIP was greater than the cost per EU of work done during the period.

For the Assembly Department, FIFO assumes that all the higher-cost prior-period units in BI WIP are the first to be completed and transferred out while EI WIP consists of only the lower-cost current-period units. The weighted-average method, however, smoothes out cost per EU by assuming that more of the lower-cost units are completed and transferred out, while some of the higher-cost units are placed in EI WIP. Hence, in this example, the weighted-average method results in a lower cost of units completed and transferred out and a higher EI WIP relative to FIFO.

Unit costs can differ materially between the weighted-average and FIFO methods when (1) the direct materials or conversion costs per unit vary from period to period and (2) the physical inventory levels of work in process are large in relation to the total number of units transferred out. This means that both gross margin and operating income will differ materially between the two approaches. As companies move towards long-term procurement contracts that smooth out the unit cost differences from one time period to another, and towards eliminating inventory, the difference between these two cost estimates will decrease.

For example, suppose BI WIP for March were 125 physical units (instead of 225) with a total value of $14,500, and the number of units started during the period were 375. Suppose costs per EU of work completed in the current period (March) consisted of direct materials unit cost of $75/EU and unit conversion costs of $55/EU. Assume no other changes in the data in the example. Under our new assumptions, the cost of units completed and transferred out would be $52,833 under the weighted-average method and $53,000 under the FIFO method. The EI WIP would be $10,417 under the weighted-average method and $10,250 under the FIFO method. These differences are $167 and ($167) respectively, far smaller than in the original example.

Managers need feedback about their most recent performance (March in this illustration) in order to plan and improve their future performance. A major advantage of FIFO is that it gives managers actual information from which they can judge their performance in the current period independently from that in the preceding period. Work done during the current period is vital information for these planning and control purposes.

```
┌─ ─ ─ ─ ─ ─ ─ ─ ─ ─ ─ ─ ─ ─ ─ ─ ─ ─ ─ ─ ─ ─ ─ ─ ─ ─ ─ ─ ─ ┐
                        THINKING CRITICALLY
  What GAAP method would managers prefer—weighted average or FIFO?
  Explain in a sentence or two. Read on for further discussion of this topic.
└─ ─ ─ ─ ─ ─ ─ ─ ─ ─ ─ ─ ─ ─ ─ ─ ─ ─ ─ ─ ─ ─ ─ ─ ─ ─ ─ ─ ─ ┘
```

Managers in operations often receive cash bonuses based on minimizing costs. The weighted-average method reports the lowest COGM transferred out for the Assembly Department. Notice that irrespective of the GAAP method chosen, for purposes of deducting COGM to arrive at taxable income, the total cost is identical. What is added to EI WIP is deducted from COGM completed and transferred out. There is no tax benefit to either choice. The manager, however, would prefer to report lower rather than higher COGM and without accounting training could choose FIFO over the weighted-average method. However, as those trained in financial accounting know, this benefit will most likely reverse out in the next accounting time period—the iron law of accruals. Managers who know this should be indifferent between the two GAAP methods of process costing.

COMPUTATIONS UNDER STANDARD COSTING

This section assumes that you have already studied Chapters 7 and 8. If you have not, proceed to the next section, "Hybrid-Costing Systems," on page 857.

As we have mentioned, companies that use process-costing systems produce numerous like or similar units of output. Setting standard quantities for inputs is often relatively straightforward in such companies. Standard costs per input unit may then be assigned to the physical standards to develop standard costs.

The major difference between standard costing and the other two methods is that standard costing is not a GAAP method for inventory and COGM valuation for external-reporting purposes. The overallocation or underallocation of process costs must be prorated prior to the calculation of taxable income.

Weighted-average and FIFO methods become very complicated when used in industries that produce a variety of products. For example, a steel rolling mill uses various steel alloys and produces sheets of various sizes and of various finishes. The items of direct materials are not numerous nor are the operations performed. But used in various combinations, they yield so great a variety of products that inaccurate costs for each product result if the broad averaging procedure of historical process costing is used. Similarly complex conditions are frequently found, for example in plants that manufacture rubber products, textiles, ceramics, paints, and packaged food products. As we shall see, standard costing is especially useful in these situations.

The intricacies of weighted-average and FIFO historical costing methods and the conflicts between them are also eliminated by using standard costs. We again use the Assembly Department of Global Defence Inc. as an example, except this time we assign standard costs to the process. The same standard costs apply in February and March of 2010.

EXHIBIT 17-10

Summarizing the Flow of Production in Physical Units and Equivalent Units for the Assembly Department of Global Defence Inc. for March 2010—Standard Costing with Beginning and Ending WIP Inventory

	A	B	C	D
1			Equivalent Units	
2		Physical	Direct	Conversion
3	Flow of Production	Units	Materials	Costs
4	Work in process, beginning (February EI WIP, Exh. 17-3)	225		
5	Started during current period (given, p. 846)	275		
6	To account for	500		
7	Completed and transferred out during current period:			
8	From beginning work in process[a]	225		
9	[225 × (100% − 100%); 225 × (100% − 60%)]		0	90
10	Started and completed	175[b]		
11	(175 × 100%; 175 × 100%)		175	175
12	Work in process, ending[c] (given, p. 846)	100		
13	(100 × 100%; 100 × 50%)		100	50
14	Accounted for	500		
15	Work done in March only		275	315
16				
17	[a]Degree of completion in this department: direct materials, 100%; conversion costs, 60%.			
18	[b]400 physical units completed and transferred out minus 225 physical units completed and transferred out from beginning work-in-process inventory.			
19	[c]Degree of completion in this department: direct materials, 100%; conversion costs, 50%.			

We have incomplete units in both BI and EI WIP. Exhibit 17-8 presented the results of the FIFO method. Exhibit 17-10 summarizes the flow of production in both physical units and EU for the standard-costing method of process costing. Notice in Exhibit 17-10 that the standard-costing method also assumes that the earliest EU in BI WIP are completed first. Work done in the current period for direct materials is 275 equivalent units. Work done in the current period for conversion costs is 315 equivalent units.

Exhibit 17-11 shows the standard cost per EU, and the assignment of costs to units completed and transferred out and to EI WIP using the standard-costing method of process costing, ending with a summary of variances. The standard-costing method requires no calculation of the cost allocation rates for either direct materials purchases or conversion costs. Costs per equivalent unit are already given as standard costs: direct materials, $74, and conversion costs, $54. These rates have been decided upon using one of the approaches described in Chapter 4. The bookkeeping to adjust the COGM and EI WIP for overallocation or underallocation is straightforward and this method has the added advantage of drawing a manager's attention to unfavourable cost variances. This method provides an opportunity to apply management-accounting analyses of variance to ascertain where the costs of a process require explanation and perhaps remedy.

The total debits to WIP—Assembly differ from total debits to WIP—Assembly under the actual-cost-based weighted-average and FIFO methods. That's because, as in all standard-costing systems, the debits to the WIP account are at standard costs, rather than actual costs. Notice in comparing Exhibit 17-9 to Exhibit 17-11 that all the quantities are identical; it is the rates that change. In Exhibit 17-9 the direct materials cost allocation rate is $72/EU and the conversion cost allocation rate is

EXHIBIT 17-11

Standard Costs per Equivalent Unit and Assigning Costs to Completed Units and Ending WIP Inventory for the Assembly Department of Global Defence Inc. for March 2010—Standard-Costing Method with Beginning and Ending WIP Inventory

	A	B	C	D	E	F
		Total				
		Production	Direct		Conversion	
		Costs	Materials		Costs	
5	Standard cost per equivalent unit (given, p. 855)		$ 74		$ 54	
6	Work in process, beginning (given, Exhibit 17-10)					
7	Direct materials, 225 × $74; Conversion costs, 135 × $54	$23,940	$16,650		$ 7,290	
9	Costs added in current period at standard costs					
10	Direct materials, 275 × $74; Conversion costs, 315 × $54	37,360	$20,350		$17,010	
11	Total costs to account for	$61,300				
12	Assignment of costs at standard costs:					
13	Completed and transferred out (400 units):					
14	Work in process, beginning (225 units)	$23,940				
15	Costs added to beginning work in process in current period	4,860	$(0^a × $74)$	+	$(90^a × $54)$	
16	Total from beginning inventory	28,800				
17	Started and completed (175 units)	22,400	$(175^b × $74)$	+	$(175^b × $54)$	
18	Total costs of units completed and transferred out	51,200				
19	Work in process, ending (100 units):	10,100	$(100^c × $74)$	+	$(50^c × $54)$	
20	Total costs account for	$61,300				
21	Summary of variances for current performance:					
22	Costs added in current period at standard costs (see above)		$20,350		$17,010	
23	Actual costs incurred (given, p. 846)		$19,800		$16,380	
24	Variance		$ 550	F	$ 630	F
25						
26	[a]Equivalent units used to complete beginning work in process from Exhibit 17-10.					
27	[b]Equivalent units started and completed from Exhibit 17-10.					
28	[c]Equivalent units in ending work in process from Exhibit 17-10.					

$52/EU, while the direct materials standard cost rate is $74/EU in Exhibit 17-11 and standard conversion cost rate is $54/EU. The standard costs total $61,300 in Exhibit 17-11.

ACCOUNTING FOR VARIANCES

Process-costing systems using standard costs usually accumulate actual costs separately from the inventory accounts. The following is an example. The actual data are recorded in the first two entries. Recall that Global Defence purchases direct materials as needed and that these materials are delivered directly to the Assembly Department. The total variances are recorded in the next two entries. The final entry transfers out the completed goods at standard costs.

1. Assembly Department Direct Materials Control (at actual) $19,800
       Accounts Payable $19,800
     To record direct materials purchased and used in production during March.

This cost control account is debited with actual costs and credited later with standard costs assigned to the units worked on.

2. Assembly Department Conversion Costs Control (at actual)	$16,380	
[Various accounts]		$16,380
To record Assembly Department conversion costs for March.		

(Entries 3, 4, and 5 use standard-cost dollar amounts from Exhibit 17-11)

3. Work in Process—Assembly (at standard costs)	$20,350	
Direct Materials Variances		$ 550
Assembly Department Direct Materials Control		19,800
To record actual direct materials used and total direct materials variances.		
4. Work in Process—Assembly (at standard costs)	$17,010	
Conversion Costs Variances		$ 630
Assembly Department Conversion Costs Control		16,380
To record actual conversion costs and total conversion costs variances.		
5. Work in Process—Testing (at standard costs)	$51,200	
Work in Process—Assembly (at standard costs)		$51,200
To record cost of units completed and transferred at standard cost from Assembly to Testing.		

Variances arise under the standard-costing method, as in entries 3 and 4, because the standard costs assigned to products on the basis of work done in the current period do not usually equal the actual costs incurred in the current period. Variances can be measured and analyzed in little or great detail for feedback, control, and decision-making purposes, in the same manner as described in Chapters 7 and 8. Exhibit 17-12 illustrates how the costs flow using T-accounts.

HYBRID-COSTING SYSTEMS

Product-costing systems do not always fall neatly into the categories of job costing or process costing. A **hybrid-costing system** blends characteristics from both job-costing

EXHIBIT 17-12
Flow of Standard Costs in a Process-Costing System, Assembly Department of Global Defence Inc. for March 2010

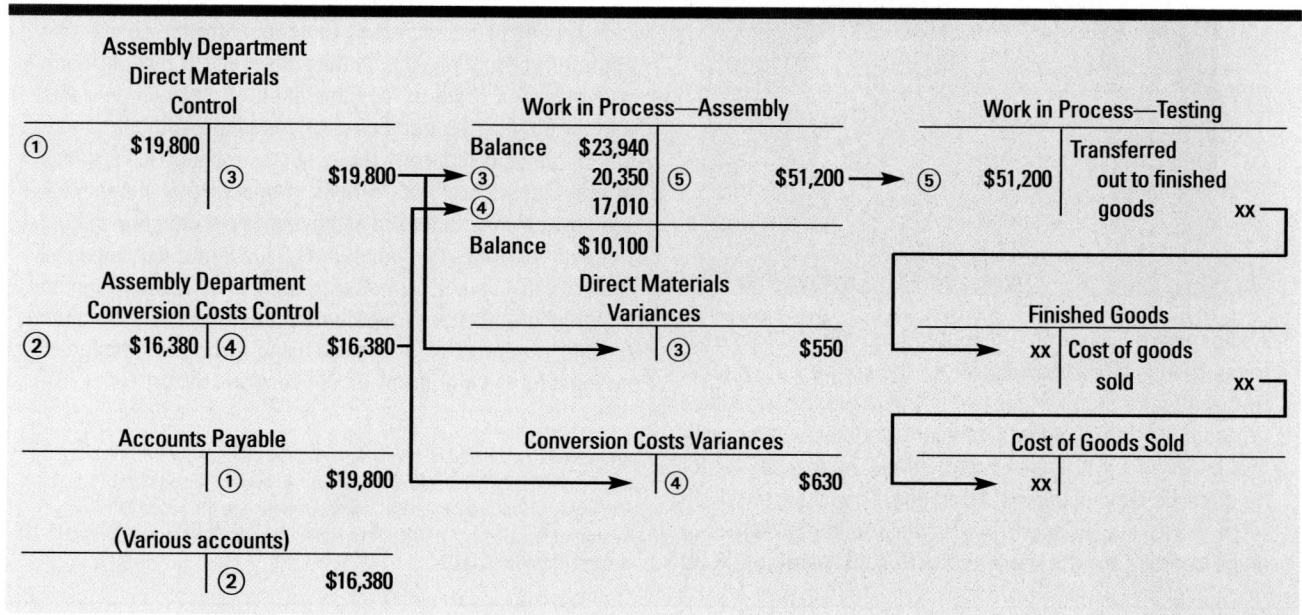

systems and process-costing systems. Job-costing and process-costing systems are best viewed as ends of a continuum:

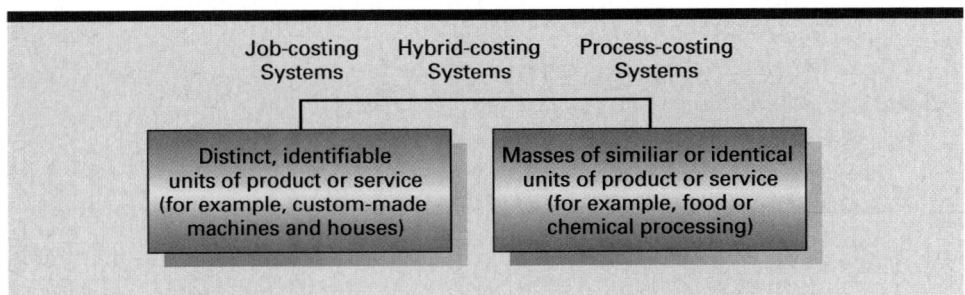

Job-costing Systems	Hybrid-costing Systems	Process-costing Systems
Distinct, identifiable units of product or service (for example, custom-made machines and houses)		Masses of similiar or identical units of product or service (for example, food or chemical processing)

Product-costing systems must often be designed to fit the particular characteristics of different production systems. Many production systems are a hybrid—they have some features of custom-order manufacturing and other features of mass-production manufacturing. Manufacturers of a relatively wide variety of closely related standardized products tend to use a hybrid system. Consider Ford Motor Company. Automobiles may be manufactured in a continuous flow, but each may be customized with a special combination of engine size, transmission, music system, and so on. Companies develop hybrid-costing systems to meet these individual needs.

REAL COMPANIES

Hybrid Costing for Customized Shoes at Adidas

Adidas has designed and manufactured athletic footwear for more than 80 years. Adidas took the concept of specialized crafting a step further when it initiated the mi adidas program. Using mi adidas, customers worldwide can create and order shoes to their exact personal specifications for function, fit, and aesthetics. Mi adidas is available in 100 US retail stores and at specialized mobile units that travel to major sporting events, such as the Boston Marathon. A 3D computer scanner transmits data on the customer's feet as well as the selection from 100 different styles. These data are transferred to an Adidas plant, where small, multiskilled teams produce the customized shoe.

Historically, costs associated with individually customized products have fallen into the domain of job costing. Adidas uses a hybrid-costing system—job costing for the material and customizable components, which customers choose, and process costing to account for the conversion costs of production. Calculating the cost of making each pair of shoes requires accumulating all production costs and dividing by the number of shoes made. Although each pair of shoes is different, the cost is identical. This process is mass customization. Various products that companies are now able to customize within a mass-production setting (for example, personal computers, blue jeans, bicycles) still require job costing of materials and considerable human intervention. However, as manufacturing systems become flexible, companies are also using process costing to account for the standardized conversion costs.

Sources: "The 'mi adidas' Mass Customization Initiative," IMD case number IMD159; N. Tait, "How 'mi adidas' Provides Personalized Style, Fit," *Apparel* (January 1, 2004); "Adidas America to Introduce Running Customization Shoe at 2002 LaSalle Bank Chicago Marathon," *Chicago Athlete* (October 2, 2002).

ASSESS YOUR MASTERY

To check your understanding of the material in Learning Objective ④, go to the *Mastery Questions* section at the end of this chapter and complete Learning Objective ④ question 1.

MyAccountingLab

TRANSFERRED-IN COSTS IN PROCESS COSTING

Apply process-costing methods to report transferred-in costs and operations costing ⑤

Financial accounting is a double-entry system and to this point we have only illustrated how to estimate and report the COGM transferred out of the Assembly Department and value the EI WIP of the Assembly Department. Many process-costing systems have two or more departments or processes in the cycle, as does Global Defence Inc. Ordinarily, as units move from department to department, related costs are also transferred by monthly journal entries. If standard costs are used, the accounting for such transfers is relatively simple. However, if weighted average or FIFO is used, the accounting can become more complex. To illustrate, we now extend our Global Defence Inc. example to encompass the Testing Department.

Recall that the Assembly Department of Global Defence transfers DG-19 units to its Testing Department. Here the units receive further quality-control testing and inspection (conversion costs that are primarily MOH), and additional direct materials, such as the housing for the closed circuit, completing the unit in readiness for shipment to the customer. Assume conversion costs are added evenly during the Testing Department's process. As units are completed in Testing, they are immediately transferred to Finished Goods. The COGM become cost of goods available for sale (COGAS) and upon sale will become cost of goods sold (COGS).

Similar to the Assembly Department, subcomponents are transferred into the Testing Department. The difference is that the Assembly Department received subcomponents from an external supplier for conversion while the Testing Department receives subcomponents from an internal supplier. Conceptually, however, the units transferred into the Testing Department are direct materials. The costs of all the transferred-in physical units from the Assembly Department are, however, called transferred-in costs, not direct materials costs, for the Testing Department. These costs will differ depending upon the choice of weighted average ($52,000) or FIFO ($52,480) to estimate the Assembly Department's COGM and EI WIP.

Direct materials costs for the Testing Department will consist of only those costs incurred to acquire direct materials from external third parties. With respect to the physical units of transferred-in costs, they are 100% complete as BI WIP for the Testing Department. They are not complete with respect to any conversion or any direct materials added by the Testing Department. Unless the transferred-in physical units are 100% converted, no direct materials will be added by the Testing Department. That is, no unfinished circuits will be placed in their housing unless they successfully pass all tests and quality inspections.

Data for the Testing Department for March 2010 are shown on the next page.

Transferred-in costs (or **previous department costs**) are costs incurred in a previous department that are carried forward as part of the product's cost as it moves to a subsequent department for processing. That is, as the physical units move from one department to the next, their costs per EU move with them. Thus, computations of Testing Department costs must include transferred-in costs, as well as any additional direct materials costs and conversion costs added in Testing.

TRANSFERRED-IN COSTS AND THE WEIGHTED-AVERAGE METHOD

To examine the weighted-average process-costing method with transferred-in costs, we need to add calculations to the process illustrated in Exhibits 17-6 and 17-7 for the weighted-average method in the Assembly Department.

	A	B	C	D	E
1		**Physical Units**	**Transferred-in**	**Direct**	**Conversion**
2		**(DG-19s)**	**Costs**	**Materials**	**Costs**
3	Work in process, beginning inventory (March 1)	240	$33,600	$ 0	$18,000
4	Degree of completion, beginning work in process		100%	0%	62.5%
5	Transferred-in during March	400			
6	Completed and transferred out during March	440			
7	Work in process, ending inventory (March 31)	200			
8	Degree of completion, ending work in process		100%	0%	80%
9	Total costs added during March				
10	Direct materials and conversion costs			$13,200	$48,600
11	Transferred-in (Weighted-average from Exhibit 17-7)[a]		$52,000		
12	Transferred-in (FIFO from Exhibit 17-9)[a]		$52,480		
13					
14	[a] The transferred-in costs during March are different under the weighted-average method (Exhibit 17-7) and the FIFO method (Exhibit 17-9). In our example, beginning work-in-process inventory of $51,600 ($33,600 + $0 + $18,000) is the same under both the weighted-average and FIFO inventory methods because we assume costs per equivalent unit to be the same in both January and February. If costs per equivalent unit had been different in the two months, work-in-process inventory at the end of February (beginning of March) would be costed differently under the weighted-average and FIFO methods. The basic approach to process costing with transferred-in costs, however, would still be the same as what we describe in this section.				

Exhibit 17-13 shows the flow of production in both physical units and EU. The computations are basically the same as the calculations of EU under the weighted-average method for the Assembly Department in Exhibit 17-6, except for the addition of transferred-in costs.

Exhibit 17-14 has been expanded to illustrate the allocation of the Direct Materials cost pool using the conversion rates appropriate to the BI WIP of the Testing Department and the good units completed and transferred out this month. The addition of this calculation of the quantity in the cost allocation base for this cost pool is quite straightforward in an all-or-nothing process and was excluded in the Assembly Department analysis for this reason. It is more frequently the case that direct materials are assumed to be added evenly throughout a process. The cost allocation base is always the EU, not the physical units.

EXHIBIT 17-13
Summarizing the Flow of Production in Physical Units and Equivalent Units Using the Weighted-Average Method of Process Costing for the Testing Department of Global Defence Inc. for March 2010

	A	B	C	D	E
1			**Equivalent Units**		
2		**Physical**	**Transferred-in**	**Direct**	**Conversion**
3	**Flow of Production**	**Units**	**Costs**	**Materials**	**Costs**
4	Work in process, beginning (given above)	240	(work done before current period)		
5	Transferred-in during current period (given above)	400			
6	To account for	640			
7	Completed and transferred out during current period:	440	440	440	440
8	Work in process, ending[a] (given above)	200			
9	(200 × 100%; 200 × 0%; 200 × 80%)		200	0	160
10	Accounted for	640			
11	Work done to date		640	440	600
12					
13	[a]Degree of completion in this department: transferred-in costs, 100%; direct materials, 0%; conversion costs, 80%.				

For example, had the conversion rate for direct materials been 75% in the Testing Department because materials were added continuously, then it would have been important to transform the physical units to equivalent units in Exhibit 17-13. Under the weighted-average method, the total EU completed would have remained 440. Of the total of 640 physical units, the EI WIP of 200 units 75% complete with respect to direct materials would have been 150 EU (200 physical units × 0.75 = 150 EU). The cost allocation base would have been 590 EU and the direct materials cost allocation rate approximately $22.37/EU ($13,200 ÷ 590 EU = $22.37/EU).

Exhibit 17-14 also reports the new cost pool to be considered, the costs transferred in to the Testing Department from physical units transferred out by the Assembly Department. The transferred-in cost pool consists of two cost elements. The first is the EI WIP of the Testing Department, which was 62.5% converted, and 0% of direct materials had been added to these 240 physical units. These units were all transferred into the Testing Department from the Assembly Department during the month of February. The transferred-in costs remaining in BI WIP of the Testing Department at the beginning of March equal $33,600. No direct materials were added; therefore, there is $0 reported in the first line of Exhibit 17-14 for direct materials. The dollar value of conversion costs for the EI WIP in February and therefore BI WIP of March for the Testing Department is also given as $18,000, and this is reported in the final column of cost pools in Exhibit 17-14.

In fact the BI WIP for March has only been 62.5% converted, thus 37.5% of the conversion process remains to be completed before these circuit boards will be housed. The physical units in BI WIP for March are 240 and this equals 90 EU (240 physical units × 0.375 = 90 EU) to be completed in March from BI WIP. The timing of the completion of the 440 physical units completed and transferred out of the Testing Department during the month of March is irrelevant when the weighted-average method is used; however, it will be relevant when we consider the FIFO method.

EXHIBIT 17-14

Calculating Equivalent Unit Costs and Assigning Costs to Completed Units and Ending WIP Inventory for the Testing Department of Global Defence Inc. for March 2010—Weighted-Average Method with Beginning and Ending WIP Inventory

	A	B	C	D	E
1		Total			
2		Production	Transferred-in	Direct	Conversion
3		Costs	Costs	Materials	Costs
4	Work in process, beginning (given, p. 860)	$ 51,600	$33,600	$ 0	$18,000
5	Costs added in current period (given, p. 860)	113,800	52,000	13,200	48,600
6	Costs incurred to date		$85,600	$13,200	$66,600
7	Divide by equivalent units of work done to date (Exhibit 17-13)		÷ 640	÷ 440	÷ 600
8	Cost per equivalent unit of work done to date		$133.75	$ 30	$ 111
9	Total costs to account for	$165,400			
10	Assignment of costs:				
11	Completed and transferred out (440 units)	$120,890	(440* × $133.75) + (440* × $30) + (440* × $111)		
12	Work in process, ending (200 units)	44,510	(200† × $133.75) + (0† × $30) + (160† × $111)		
13	Total costs accounted for	$165,400			
14					
15	*Equivalent units completed and transferred out from Exhibit 17-13.				
16	†Equivalent units in ending work in process from Exhibit 17-13.				

The information in Exhibit 17-7 illustrating the March weighted-average costs for the Assembly Department reported the total COGM transferred out for the 400 completed physical units was $52,000, which appears as the dollar value of physical units transferred in to the Testing Department on the second line of Exhibit 17-14 in the Transferred-in Costs column. The total transferred-in, direct materials, and conversion costs in the Testing Department for those 440 fully completed units are $165,400 for the month of March. The dollar amounts in the Testing direct materials and Testing conversion cost pools are given as shown.

In Exhibit 17-14, the cost assignment is based on the cost allocation rates shown in the top section of the exhibit. The first line refers to the EU completed and transferred out to Finished Goods and the second refers to the EU remaining in EI WIP. Notice that 0 EU remaining in EI WIP consumed any direct materials, the housing for the circuit boards during March. Using the dollar amount from Exhibit 17-14, the journal entry for the transfer out of the Testing Department to Finished Goods inventory is

Finished Goods	$120,890	
Work in Process—Testing		$120,890
To transfer units to Finished Goods inventory.		

Entries to the key T-account, Work in Process—Testing, follow, using information from Exhibit 17-14:

Work in Process—Testing			
Beginning inventory, March 1	$51,600	Transferred out	$120,890
Transferred-in costs	52,000		
Direct materials	13,200		
Conversion costs	48,600		
Ending inventory, March 31	$44,510		

TRANSFERRED-IN COSTS AND THE FIFO METHOD

To examine the FIFO process-costing method with transferred-in costs, we must refer back to Exhibit 17-9 on page 852 for both the transferred-out COGM from the Assembly Department and the physical units completed and transferred out. It is important to understand that in a series of interdepartmental transfers, each department is regarded as being separate and distinct for accounting purposes. All costs transferred in during a given accounting period are carried at one unit cost figure regardless of whether previous departments used the weighted-average or the FIFO method.

Exhibit 17-15 shows the flow of production in both physical units and EU under the FIFO method of process costing. Other than considering transferred-in costs, the computations of equivalent units are basically the same as those under the FIFO method for the Assembly Department shown in Exhibit 17-8 on page 850.

Exhibit 17-16 shows the calculation of the transferred-in, direct materials, and conversion cost per equivalent unit, and the assignment of costs to units completed and transferred out and to EI WIP using the FIFO method of process costing. Although under FIFO the transferred-in cost allocation rate is calculated as a simple average of the cost pool of transferred-in costs for the month of March divided by the total of 400 physical units, this is not the case for the remaining two cost pools. The direct materials costs added in the Testing Department are calculated based on the 440 EU completed and transferred out this month. Conversion costs of Testing are divided by the total equivalent units finished in the current time period, which have been calculated in Exhibit 17-15 as 450 EU.

The reasoning for using only $52,480 in the Transferred-in, $13,200 in the Direct Materials, and $48,600 in the Conversion cost pools is that these are the only

EXHIBIT 17-15

Summarizing the Flow of Production in Physical Units and Equivalent Units Using the FIFO Method of Process Costing for the Testing Department of Global Defence Inc. for March 2010

	A	B	C	D	E
				Equivalent Units	
1		Physical	Transferred-in	Direct	Conversion
2	Flow of Production	Units	Costs	Materials	Costs
3					
4	Work in process, beginning (given, p. 860)	240	(work done before current period)		
5	Transferred-in during current period (given, p. 860)	400			
6	To account for	640			
7	Completed and transferred out during current period:				
8	From beginning work in process[a]	240			
9	[240×(100% − 100%); 240×(100% − 0%); 240×(100% − 62.5%)]		0	240	90
10	Started and completed	200[b]			
11	(200 × 100%; 200 × 100%; 200 × 100%)		200	200	200
12	Work in process, ending[c] (given, p. 860)	200			
13	(200 × 100%; 200 × 0%; 200 × 80%)		200	0	160
14	Accounted for	640			
15	Work done in current period only		400	440	450
16					
17	[a]Degree of completion in this department: Transferred-in costs, 100%; direct materials, 0%; conversion costs, 62.5%.				
18	[b]440 physical units completed and transferred out minus 240 physical units completed and transferred out from beginning work-in-process inventory.				
19	[c]Degree of completion in this department: transferred-in costs, 100%; direct materials, 0%; conversion costs, 80%.				

EXHIBIT 17-16

Calculating Equivalent Unit Costs and Assigning Costs to Completed Units and Ending WIP Inventory for the Testing Department of Global Defence Inc. for March 2010—FIFO Method with Beginning and Ending WIP Inventory

	A	B	C	D	E
1		Total			
2		Production	Transferred-in	Direct	Conversion
3		Costs	Costs	Materials	Costs
4	Work in process, beginning (given, p. 861)	$ 51,600	(costs of work done before current period)		
5	Costs added in current period (given, p. 861)	114,280	$52,480	$13,200	$48,600
6	Divide by equivalent units of work done in current period (Exhibit 17-15)		÷ 400	÷ 440	÷ 450
7	Cost per equivalent unit of work done in current period		$131.20	$ 30	$ 108
8	Total costs to account for	$165,880			
9	Assignment of costs:				
10	Completed and transferred out (440 units)				
11	Work in process, beginning (240 units)	$ 51,600			
12	Costs added to beginning work in process in current period	16,920	(0[a] × $131.20) + (240[a] × $30) + (90[a] × $108)		
13	Total from beginning inventory	68,520			
14	Started and completed (200 units)	53,840	(200[b] × $131.20) + (200[b] × $30) + (200[b] × $108)		
15	Total costs of units completed and transferred out	122,360			
16	Work in process, ending (200 units)	43,520	(200[c] × $131.20) + (0[c] × $30) + (160[c] × $108)		
17	Total costs accounted for	$165,880			
18					
19	[a]Equivalent units used to complete beginning work in process from Exhibit 17-15.				
20	[b]Equivalent units started and completed from Exhibit 17-15.				
21	[c]Equivalent units in ending work in process from Exhibit 17-15.				

relevant costs for the month of March in the Testing Department using FIFO. Based on the appropriate cost allocation rates, the costs are assigned using the appropriate EU beginning with the 90 EU to be converted from BI WIP first (240 physical units $\times$ 0.375 = 90 EU). Notice that direct materials are added to 240 EU because these 240 physical units must be 100% converted before the Testing Department adds any direct materials at all.

In Exhibit 17-16, the total costs to account for and accounted for of $165,880 under the FIFO method differ from the corresponding amounts under the weighted-average method of $165,400 because of the different costs of completed units transferred in from the Assembly Department under the two methods ($52,480 under FIFO and $52,000 under weighted average).

Using the dollar amount from Exhibit 17-16, the journal entry for the transfer out to Finished Goods inventory is

Finished Goods	$122,360	
Work in Process—Testing		$122,360
To transfer units to Finished Goods inventory.		

Entries to the key T-account, Work in Process—Testing, follow, using information from Exhibit 17-16:

Work in Process—Testing

Beginning inventory, March 1	$51,600	Transferred out	$122,360
Transferred-in costs	52,480		
Direct materials	13,200		
Conversion costs	48,600		
Ending inventory, March 31	$43,520		

The information from Exhibit 17-16 is presented in the financial format of Exhibit 2-10 (see p. 52). The dollar values using the weighted-average and FIFO methods reported in Exhibits 17-14 and 17-16 for the Testing Department are summarized and compared for the month of March.

Global Defence Inc. Schedule of Cost of Goods Manufactured, Testing Department For the Month Ended:	March 31, 2010 Weighted Average		March 31, 2010 FIFO	
Direct Materials				
Beginning inventory of direct materials	$ 0		$ 0	
Purchases of direct materials during the month	13,200		13,200	
Cost of direct materials available for use	13,200		13,200	
Ending inventory of direct materials for the month	0		0	
Direct materials used during the month		$13,200		$ 13,200
All conversion costs	48,600		48,600	
Total conversion costs		48,680		48,600
Manufacturing costs incurred during the month		61,800		61,800
Beginning work-in-process inventory	33,600		33,600	
Transferred-in cost of goods manufactured from Assembly	52,000		52,480	
Total manufacturing costs to account for		85,600		86,080
Ending work-in-process inventory		(44,510)		(48,520)
Cost of goods manufactured—transferred out to Finished Goods		$130,110		$129,600

COMMON MISTAKES WITH TRANSFERRED-IN COSTS

Here are some common pitfalls to avoid when accounting for transferred-in costs:

1. Remember that transferred-in costs from previous departments are cost pools that must be added into your calculations.

2. In calculating costs to be transferred on a FIFO basis, do not overlook the costs assigned at the beginning of the period to units that were in process but are now included in the units transferred out. For example, do not overlook the $51,600 in Exhibit 17-16.

3. The cost allocation rates most likely will fluctuate from month to month because they are based on actual costs incurred. Therefore, transferred units may contain batches accumulated at different unit costs. For example, the 400 units transferred in at $52,480 in Exhibit 17-16 using the FIFO method consist of units that have different unit costs for direct materials and conversion costs when these units were worked on in the Assembly Department (see Exhibit 17-9, p. 852). Remember, however, that when these units are transferred in to the Testing Department, they are at one average unit cost of $131.20 ($52,480 ÷ 400), as in Exhibit 17-16.

4. Units may be measured in different terms in different departments. Consider each department separately. Unit costs could be based on kilograms in the first department and litres in the second; therefore, as units are received by the second department, their measurements must be converted to litres to ensure comparable cost allocation bases and rates.

OVERVIEW OF OPERATION-COSTING SYSTEMS

An example will illustrate key calculations and journal entries in operation-costing systems. An **operation** is a standardized method or technique that is performed repetitively regardless of the distinguishing features of the finished goods. Operations are usually conducted within departments. The Global Defence example illustrates a departmentalized process; however, it could have been presented as a quality-control operation (in both Assembly and Testing) and two additional operations to add direct materials, one in each department.

A suit maker may have a cutting operation and a hemming operation within a single department. The term operation, however, is often used loosely. It may be a synonym for a department or process. For example, some companies may call their finishing department a finishing process or a finishing operation.

An **operation-costing system** is a hybrid-costing system applied to batches of similar products. Each batch of products is often a variation of a single design and proceeds through a sequence of selected, though not necessarily the same, activities or operations. The Adidas example in the Real Companies box on page 858 illustrated the hybrid process of mass customization. Within each operation, all product units are treated as being exactly alike, using identical amounts of the operation's resources. Batches are also termed production runs.

Consider a business that makes suits. Management may select a single basic design for every suit that the company manufactures. Depending on specifications, batches of suits vary from each other. One batch may use wool; another batch, silk. One batch may require special hand stitching; another batch, machine stitching. Other products that are likewise often manufactured in batches are semiconductors, sweet beverages, and shoes.

An operation-costing system uses work orders that specify the needed direct materials and step-by-step operations. Product costs are compiled for each work order. Direct materials that are unique to different work orders are specifically identified with the appropriate work order as in job-costing systems. The conversion cost, however, is identical for every output unit because each unit is assumed to use the identical resources during conversion within a single operation. A single average conversion cost per EU is calculated as in process costing. For each operation, this amount is computed by aggregating conversion costs and dividing them by all EU passing through that operation. Our examples assume only two cost categories, direct materials and conversion costs. Of course, operation costing can have more than two cost categories. The costs in each category are identified with work orders using job-costing or process-costing methods as appropriate.

Operation costing focuses on the physical processes, or operations, of a given production system. Operation costing captures the financial impact of the control of physical processes. Feedback from an operation-costing system can therefore provide essential insight into the control of physical processes and the management of operation costs.

ILLUSTRATION OF OPERATION-COSTING SYSTEM

Consider Baltimore Company, a clothing manufacturer that produces two lines of blazers for department stores. Wool blazers use better-quality materials and undergo more operations than do polyester blazers. Let's look at the following operations in 2010:

	Work Order 423	Work Order 424
Direct materials	Wool	Polyester
	Satin full lining	Rayon partial lining
	Bone buttons	Plastic buttons
Operations		
1. Cutting cloth	Use	Use
2. Checking edges	Use	Do not use
3. Sewing body	Use	Use
4. Checking seams	Use	Do not use
5. Machine sewing of collars and lapels	Do not use	Use
6. Hand sewing of collars and lapels	Use	Do not use

Suppose work order 423 is for 50 wool blazers and work order 424 is for 100 polyester blazers. The following costs are assumed for these two work orders, which were started and completed in March 2010:

	Work Order 423	Work Order 424
Number of blazers	50	100
Direct materials costs	$6,000	$3,000
Conversion costs allocated:		
Operation 1	580	1,160
Operation 2	400	—
Operation 3	1,900	3,800
Operation 4	500	—
Operation 5	—	875
Operation 6	700	—
Total manufacturing costs	$10,080	$8,835

As in process costing, all product units in any work order are assumed to consume identical amounts of conversion costs of a particular operation. Baltimore Company's operation-costing system uses a budgeted rate to calculate the conversion costs of each operation. For example, the costs of operation 1 might be budgeted as follows (amounts assumed):

$$\begin{array}{c} \text{Operation 1 budgeted} \\ \text{conversion cost rate} \\ \text{in 2010} \end{array} = \frac{\begin{array}{c}\text{Operation 1 budgeted} \\ \text{conversion costs in 2010}\end{array}}{\begin{array}{c}\text{Operation 1 budgeted} \\ \text{product units in 2010}\end{array}}$$

$$= \$232,000 \div 20,000 \text{ units}$$

$$= \$11.60 \text{ per unit}$$

The budgeted conversion costs of operation 1 include labour, power, repairs, supplies, amortization, and other overhead of this operation. If some units have not been completed, so that all units in operation 1 have not received the same amounts of conversion costs, the conversion cost rate is computed by dividing budgeted conversion costs by the EU, not the physical units, as in process costing. We have assumed that every jacket will be converted in an identical manner in Operation 1; therefore, it is appropriate to use the total units produced, disregarding whether they are wool or polyester blazers.

As goods are manufactured, conversion costs are allocated to the work orders processed in operation 1 by multiplying the $11.60 conversion costs per unit by the number of product units processed. The conversion costs of operation 1 for 50 wool blazers (work order 423) are $11.60 × 50 = $580, and for 100 polyester blazers (work order 424) are $11.60 × 100 = $1,160. If work order 424 had contained 75 units, its total costs in operation 1 would have been $870 ($11.60 × 75). If EU has been used to calculate the conversion cost rate, costs would have been allocated to work orders by multiplying the conversion cost per EU by the number of EU in the work order. Direct materials costs of $6,000 for the 50 wool blazers (work order 423) and $3,000 for the 100 polyester blazers (work order 424) are specifically identified with each order as in a job-costing system. Note that operation unit costs are assumed to be the same regardless of the work order but direct materials costs vary across orders as the materials themselves vary.

JOURNAL ENTRIES

Actual conversion costs for operation 1 in March 2010 (assumed to be $24,400, of which $580 are on work order 423 and $1,160 are on work order 424) are entered into a Conversion Costs Control account:

1. Conversion Costs Control	$24,400	
Various accounts (such as Wages Payable and Accumulated Amortization)		$24,400

Summary journal entries for assigning costs to the polyester blazers (work order 424) follow. Entries for the wool blazers would be similar.

Of the $3,000 of direct materials for work order 424, $2,975 are used in Operation 1. The journal entry for the use of direct materials, which are traced directly to particular batches, for the 100 polyester blazers is as follows:

2. Work in Process, Operation 1	$2,975	
Materials Inventory Control		$2,975

The allocation of conversion costs to products in operation costing uses the budgeted rate $11.60 times the 100 units processed, or $1,160.

3. Work in Process, Operation 1	$1.160	
Conversion Costs Allocated		$1,160

The transfer of the polyester blazers from operation 1 to operation 2 (recall that the polyester blazers do not go through operation 2) would be journalized as follows:

4. Work in Process, Operation 3	$4,135	
Work in Process, Operation 1		$4,135

After posting, the Work in Process, Operation 1 account appears as follows:

Work in Process, Operation 1

2. Direct materials	$2,975	4. Transferred to Operation 3	4,135
3. Conversion costs allocated	1,160		

The costs of the blazers are transferred through the pertinent operations and then to finished goods in the usual manner. Costs are added throughout the year in the accounts Conversion Costs Control and Conversion Costs Allocated. Any over-allocation or underallocation of conversion costs is disposed of in the same way as overallocated or underallocated manufacturing overhead in a job-costing system.

MyAccountingLab

PULLING IT ALL TOGETHER—PROBLEM FOR SELF-STUDY

Allied Chemicals operates a thermo-assembly process as the second of three processes at its plastics plant. Direct materials in thermo-assembly are added at the end of the process. Conversion costs are added evenly during the process. The following data pertain to the Thermo-Assembly Department for 2010.

	A	B	C	D	E
1		Physical	Transferred-in	Direct	Conversion
2		Units	Costs	Materials	Costs
3	Work in process, beginning inventory	50,000			
4	Degree of completion, beginning work in process		100%	0%	80%
5	Transferred in during current period	200,000			
6	Completed and transferred out during current period	210,000			
7	Work in process, ending inventory	?			
8	Degree of completion, ending work in process		100%	0%	40%

REQUIRED
Compute equivalent units under (1) the weighted-average method and (2) the FIFO method.

SOLUTION
1. The weighted-average method uses equivalent units of work done to date to compute cost per equivalent unit. The calculation of equivalent units follows:

	A	B	C	D	E
1			**Equivalent Units**		
2		Physical	Transferred-in	Direct	Conversion
3	**Flow of Production**	Units	Costs	Materials	Costs
4	Work in process, beginning (given)	50,000			
5	Transferred in during current period (given)	200,000			
6	To account for	250,000			
7	Completed and transferred out during current period	210,000	210,000	210,000	210,000
8	Work in process, ending[a]	40,000[b]			
9	(40,000 × 100%; 40,000 × 0%; 40,000 × 40%)		40,000	0	16,000
10	Accounted for	250,000			
11	Work done to date		250,000	210,000	226,000
12					
13	[a]Degree of completion in this department: transferred-in costs, 100%; direct materials, 0%; conversion costs, 40%.				
14	[b]250,000 physical units to account for minus 210,000 physical units completed and transferred out.				

2. The FIFO method uses equivalent units of work done in the current period only to compute cost per equivalent unit. The calculations of equivalent units follows:

	A	B	C	D	E
			Equivalent Units		
		Physical	Transferred-in	Direct	Conversion
	Flow of Production	Units	Costs	Materials	
4	Work in process, beginning (given)	50,000			
5	Transferred in during current period (given)	200,000			
6	To account for	250,000			
7	Completed and transferred out during current period:				
8	From beginning work in process[a]	50,000			
9	[50,000 × (100% − 100%); 50,000 × (100% − 0%); 50,000 × (100% − 80%)]		0	50,000	10,000
10	Started and completed	160,000[b]			
11	(160,000 × 100%; 160,000 × 100%; 160,000 × 100%)		160,000	160,000	160,000
12	Work in process, ending[c]	40,000[d]			
13	(40,000 × 100%; 40,000 × 0%; 40,000 × 40%)		40,000	0	16,000
14	Accounted for	250,000			
15	Work done in current period only		200,000	210,000	186,000
16					
17	[a]Degree of completion in this department: transferred-in costs, 100%; direct materials, 0%; conversion costs, 80%.				
18	[b]210,000 physical units completed and transferred out minus 50,000 physical units completed and transferred out from beginning work-in-process inventory.				
19	[c]Degree of completion in this department: transferred-in costs, 100%; direct materials, 0%; conversion costs, 40%.				
20	[d]250,000 physical units to account for minus 210,000 physical units completed and transferred out.				

DECISION POINTS

The following decision guidelines use a question-and-answer format to summarize the chapter's main points. Each decision presents a key question. The guideline is the answer to that question.

DECISIONS	GUIDELINES
1. What is the weighted-average method of process costing?	The weighted-average method computes unit costs by dividing the total costs to date by the total equivalent units completed to date and assigns this average cost to units completed and to any units in ending work-in-process inventory.
2. How are costs assigned to units completed and units in ending WIP using the weighted-average method?	The cost allocation base is equivalent units, and all cost allocation rates are calculated on a cost per equivalent unit. Each cost pool is assigned on the basis of the equivalent units either completed or remaining in ending WIP inventory. Journal entries in a process-costing system are similar to journal entries in a job-costing system. The main difference is that in a process-costing system, there is a separate WIP account for each department.
3. What is a transferred-out cost?	After the cost of goods manufactured is assigned using an acceptable process-costing method, the costs of the completed goods follows the physical units to the next stage of conversion in the process.

4. What are the first-in, first-out method and standard-costing method of process costing?	The first-in, first-out (FIFO) method computes unit costs based on costs incurred during the period and equivalent units of work done in the current period. It assigns the costs of the beginning work-in-process inventory to the first units completed and assigns the costs of the equivalent units worked on during the current period first to complete beginning inventory, next to started and completed new units, and finally to units in ending work-in-process inventory. Under the standard-costing method, cost allocation rates are already in place as standard costs per unit when assigning cost to units completed and to units in ending work-in-process inventory.
5. What is a transferred-in cost and what is operations costing?	The costs of goods manufactured, those physical units completed in a prior conversion process, are transferred out of the prior department at the end of a specified time period. These become the beginning balance of transferred-in costs for the next department in the conversion process. Some companies choose to separate and track their cost of goods manufactured using operations rather than departments. The cost object for process costing is an operation rather than a department.

TERMS TO LEARN

This chapter contains definitions of the following important terms:

equivalent unit (EU)   (p. 832)
first-in, first-out (FIFO)
   process-costing method   (p. 834)
hybrid-costing system   (p. 857)

operation   (p. 865)
operation-costing system   (p. 865)
previous department costs   (p. 860)
transferred-in costs   (p. 860)

weighted-average process-costing
   method   (p. 834)

MASTERY QUESTIONS

Mastery Questions are rated by proficiency level—elementary, intermediate, and advanced. The solutions appear in the Solutions to Mastery Questions section of MyAccountingLab.

LEARNING OBJECTIVE 1

1. **Weighted-average costing, zero beginning inventory—Intermediate.** International Electronics manufactures microchips in large quantities. Each microchip undergoes assembly and testing. The total assembly costs during January 2010 were

Direct materials used	$ 740,000
Conversion costs	780,000
Total manufacturing costs	$1,520,000

REQUIRED

1. Assume there was no beginning inventory on January 1, 2010. During January, 10,000 microchips were placed into production and all 10,000 microchips were fully completed at the end of January. What is the unit cost of an assembled microchip in January 2010?
2. Assume that during February 10,000 microchips were placed into production. Further assume the same total assembly costs for January are also incurred in February 2010, but only 9,000 microchips are fully completed at the end of February. All direct materials had been added to the remaining 1,000 microchips. However, on average, these remaining 1,000 microchips were only 50% complete as to conversion costs. (a) What are the equivalent units for direct materials and conversion costs and their respective equivalent unit costs for February? (b) What is the unit cost of an assembled microchip in February 2010?
3. Explain the difference in your answers to requirements 1 and 2.

2. Weighted-average costing, zero beginning inventory—Advanced. Vaasa Chemicals has a mixing department and a refining department. Its process-costing system in the mixing department has two direct materials cost categories (chemical P and chemical Q) and one conversion costs pool. The following data pertain to the mixing department for July 2010:

Physical Units:	
Work in process, July 1	0
Units started	55,000
Completed and transferred to refining department	38,500
Costs:	
Chemical P	$275,000
Chemical Q	77,000
Conversion costs	148,500

Chemical P is introduced at the start of operations in the mixing department, and chemical Q is added when the product is three-fourths completed in the mixing department. Conversion costs are added uniformly during the process. The ending work in process in the mixing department is two-thirds completed.

REQUIRED

1. Compute the equivalent units in the mixing department for July 2010 for each cost element.
2. Compute (a) the cost of goods completed and transferred to the refining department during July and (b) the cost of work in process as of July 31, 2010.

LEARNING OBJECTIVE 2

1. Weighted-average method, ending work-in-process inventory—Intermediate. Global Defence Inc. is a manufacturer of military equipment. Its Halifax plant manufactures the Interceptor missile under contract to the Canadian government and friendly countries. All Interceptors go through an identical manufacturing process. Every effort is made to ensure that all Interceptors are identical and meet many demanding performance specifications. The product-costing system at the Halifax plant has a single direct-cost category (direct materials) and a single indirect-cost category (conversion costs). Each Interceptor passes through two departments—the Assembly Department and the Testing Department. Direct materials are added at the beginning of the process in Assembly. Conversion costs are added evenly throughout the two departments. When the Assembly Department finishes work on each Interceptor, it is immediately transferred to Testing.

Global Defence uses the weighted-average method of process costing. Data for the Assembly Department for October 2010 are

	Physical Units (missiles)	Direct Materials	Conversion Costs
Work in process, October 1*	25	$ 506,000	$ 132,000
Started during October 2010	85		
Completed during October 2010	95		
Work in process, October 31†	15		
Costs added during October 2010		$2,200,000	$1,028,500

*Degree of completion: direct materials, ?%; conversion costs, 60%.
†Degree of completion: direct materials, ?%; conversion costs, 70%.

REQUIRED

1. For each cost element, compute equivalent units of work done in October 2010 in the Assembly Department. Show physical units in the first column.
2. For each cost element, calculate cost per equivalent unit of beginning work in process and of work done in October 2010.
3. Summarize the total Assembly Department costs for October 2010, and assign these costs to units completed (and transferred out) and to units in ending work in process using the weighted-average method.

2. Journal entries, weighted-average method, ending work-in-process inventory—Advanced. Refer to Learning Objective 2, Question 1, above.

REQUIRED

Prepare a set of summarized journal entries for all October 2010 transactions affecting Work in Process—Assembly. Set up a T-account for Work in Process—Assembly, and post the entries to it.

LEARNING OBJECTIVE 3

1. **Journal entries, weighted-average method, beginning and ending work-in-process inventory—Advanced.** Star Toys manufactures one type of wooden toy figure. It buys wood as its direct material for the Forming Department of its Fredericton plant. The toys are transferred to the Finishing Department, where they are hand-shaped and metal is added to them.

Star Toys uses the weighted-average method of process costing. Consider the following data for the Forming Department in April 2010:

	Physical Units (Toys)	Direct Materials	Conversion Costs
Work in process, April 1*	350	$ 7,500	$ 2,125
Started during April 2010	2,250		
Completed during April 2010	2,050		
Work in process, April 30†	550		
Costs added during April 2010		$70,000	$42,500

*Degree of completion: direct materials, 100%; conversion costs, 40%.
†Degree of completion: direct materials, 100%; conversion costs, 25%.

REQUIRED

Summarize the total Forming Department costs for April 2010, and assign these costs to units completed (and transferred out) and to units in ending work in process using the weighted-average method.

2. **Journal entries, weighted-average method, ending work-in-process inventory—Advanced.** Refer to Learning Objective 3, Question 1, above.

REQUIRED

Prepare a set of summarized journal entries for all April 2010 transactions affecting Work in Process—Forming. Set up a T-account for Work in Process—Forming, and post the entries to it.

LEARNING OBJECTIVE 4

1. **Analyze weighted-average, FIFO, and standard-costing methods—Advanced.** Refer to Learning Objective 3, Question 1, above.

REQUIRED

Do Learning Objective 3, Question 1, using FIFO and three decimal places for unit costs. Explain any difference between the cost of work completed and transferred out and cost of ending work in process in the Forming Department under the weighted-average method and the FIFO method.

LEARNING OBJECTIVE 5

1. **Transferred-in costs and operations costing—Intermediate.** Frito-Lay Inc. manufactures convenience foods, including potato chips and corn chips. Production of corn chips occurs in four departments: Cleaning, Mixing, Cooking, and Drying and Packaging. Consider the Drying and Packaging Department, where direct materials (packaging) is added at the end of the process. Conversion costs are added evenly during the process. Suppose the accounting records of a Frito-Lay plant provided the following information for corn chips in its Drying and Packaging Department during a weekly period (week 37):

	Physical Units (cases)	Transferred-in Costs	Direct Materials	Conversion Costs
Beginning work in process, week 37*	1,300	$29,000	$ 0	$ 9,060
Transferred in during week 37 from Cooking Department	5,050			
Completed during week 37	5,300			
Ending work in process, week 37†	1,050			
Costs added during week 37		$96,000	$25,200	$38,400

*Degree of completion: transferred-in costs, 100%; direct materials, ?%; conversion costs, 80%.
†Degree of completion: transferred-in costs, ?%; direct materials, ?%; conversion costs, 40%.

1. For each cost element, compute equivalent units of work done in week 37 in the Drying and Packaging Department. Show physical units in the first column.
2. Summarize the total Drying and Packaging Department costs for week 37, and assign these costs to units completed (and transferred out) and to units in ending work in process using the weighted-average method.
3. Assume that the FIFO method is used for the Drying and Packaging Department. The transferred-in costs for work-in-process beginning inventory are $28,920. The transferred-in costs during the week from the Cooking Department are $94,000. All other data are unchanged. Summarize the total Drying and Packaging Department costs for week 37 and assign these costs to units completed (and transferred out) and to units in ending work in process using the FIFO method.

2. **Transferred-in costs and operations costing—Advanced.** Victoria Corporation uses a standard-costing system for its manufacturing operations. Standard costs for the cooking process are $5.143 per unit for direct materials and $2.571 per unit for conversion costs. All direct materials are introduced at the beginning of the process, but conversion costs are added uniformly during the process. The operating summary for May 2010 included the following data for the cooking process:

> Work-in-process inventories:
> May 1: 3,500 units*
>   (direct materials $18,000; conversion costs $5,400)
>   May 31: 5,000 units†
> Units started in May: 20,500
> Units completed and transferred out of cooking in May: 19,000
> Additional actual costs incurred for cooking during May:
>   Direct materials: $125,000
>   Conversion cost: $57,000

> *Degree of completion: direct materials, 100%; conversion costs, 60%.
> †Degree of completion: direct materials, 100%; conversion costs, 50%.

REQUIRED

1. Compute the total standard costs of units transferred out in May and the total standard costs of the May 31 inventory of work in process.
2. Compute the total May variances for direct materials and conversion costs.

ASSIGNMENT MATERIAL

SHORT-ANSWER QUESTIONS

17-1 Give three examples of industries that often use process-costing systems.

17-2 In process costing, why are costs often divided into two main classifications?

17-3 Explain equivalent units. Why are equivalent-unit calculations necessary in process costing?

17-4 Name the key steps in process costing when equivalent units are computed.

17-5 State two conditions under which computing equivalent units will make a material difference to reported inventory amounts.

17-6 Name the three inventory methods commonly associated with process costing.

17-7 Describe the distinctive characteristic of weighted-average computations in assigning costs to units completed and ending work in process.

17-8 Describe the distinctive characteristic of FIFO computations in assigning costs to units completed and ending work in process.

17-9 Why should the FIFO method be called the *modified* or *departmental* FIFO method?

17-10 Identify a major advantage of the FIFO method for purposes of planning and control.

17-11 Identify the main difference between journal entries in process costing and the ones in job costing.

17-12 "Standard-cost procedures are particularly applicable to process-costing situations." Do you agree? Why?

17-13 Why should the accountant distinguish between transferred-in costs and additional direct material costs for each subsequent department in a process-costing system?

17-14 "Transferred-in costs are those incurred in the preceding accounting period." Do you agree? Explain.

17-15 "There's no reason for me to get excited about the choice between the weighted-average and FIFO methods in my process-costing system. I have long-term contracts with my materials suppliers at fixed prices." State the conditions under which you would (a) agree and (b) disagree with this statement, made by a plant controller. Explain.

EXERCISES

17-16 Equivalent units, zero beginning inventory. Nihon Inc. is a manufacturer of digital cameras. It has two departments: Assembly and Testing. In January 2010, the company incurred $750,000 on direct materials and $798,000 on conversion costs, for a total manufacturing cost of $1,548,000.

REQUIRED

1. Assume there was no beginning inventory of any kind on January 1, 2010. During January, 10,000 cameras were placed into production and all 10,000 were fully completed at the end of the month. What is the unit cost of an assembled camera in January 2010?
2. Assume that during February 10,000 cameras were placed into production. Further assume the same total assembly costs for January are also incurred in February 2010, but only 9,000 cameras are fully completed at the end of February. All direct materials have been added to the remaining 1,000 cameras. However, on average, these remaining 1,000 cameras are only 50% complete as to conversion costs. (a) What are the equivalent units for direct materials and conversion costs and their respective costs per equivalent unit for February? (b) What is the unit cost of an assembled camera in February 2010?
3. Explain the difference in your answers to requirements 1 and 2.

17-17 Journal entries (continuation of 17-16). Refer to requirement 2 of Exercise 17-16.

REQUIRED

Prepare summary journal entries for the use of direct materials and incurrence of conversion costs. Also prepare a journal entry to transfer out the cost of goods completed. Show the postings to the Work-in-Process account.

17-18 Zero beginning inventory, materials introduced in middle of process. Roary Chemicals has a Mixing Department and a Refining Department. Its process-costing system in the Mixing Department has two direct materials cost categories (Chemical P and Chemical Q) and one conversion costs pool. The following data pertain to the Mixing Department for July 2010:

Physical Units:	
Work in process, July 1	0
Units started	50,000
Completed and transferred to refining department	35,000
Costs:	
Chemical P	$250,000
Chemical Q	70,000
Conversion costs	135,000

Chemical P is introduced at the start of operations in the Mixing Department, and Chemical Q is added when the product is three-fourths completed in the Mixing Department. Conversion costs are added evenly during the process. The ending work in process in the Mixing Department is two-thirds completed.

REQUIRED
1. Compute the equivalent units in the Mixing Department for July 2010 for each cost category.
2. Compute (a) the cost of goods completed and transferred to the Refining Department during July and (b) the cost of work in process as of July 31, 2010.

17-19 **Weighted-average method, assigning costs.** Bio Doc Corporation is a biotech company based in Milpita. It makes a cancer-treatment drug in a single processing department. Direct materials are added at the start of the process. Conversion costs are added evenly during the process. Bio Doc uses the weighted-average method of process costing. The following information for July 2010 is available:

③
1. Direct materials cost per equivalent unit, $6.80

	Equivalent Units		
	Physical Units	Direct Materials	Conversion Costs
Work in process, July 1*	12,500	12,500	8,750
Started during July	50,000		
Completed and transferred out during July	42,500	42,500	42,500
Work in process, July 31†	20,000	20,000	10,000

*Degree of completion: direct materials, 100%; conversion costs, 70%.
†Degree of completion: direct materials, 100%; conversion costs, 50%.

Total Costs for July 2010

Work in process, beginning		
Direct materials	$75,000	
Conversion costs	87,500	$162,500
Direct materials added during July		350,000
Conversion costs added during July		463,750
Total costs to account for		$976,250

REQUIRED
1. Calculate the cost per equivalent unit for direct materials and conversion costs.
2. Summarize total costs to account for, and assign total costs to units completed (and transferred out) and to units in ending work in process.

17-20 **FIFO method, assigning costs.** Refer to the information in Exercise 17-19.

REQUIRED
Do Exercise 17-19 using the FIFO method. Note that you first need to calculate the equivalent units of work done in the current period (for direct materials and conversion costs) to complete beginning work in process, to start and complete new units, and to produce ending work in process.

④
1. Direct materials cost per equivalent unit, $7.00

17-21 **Standard-costing method, assigning costs.** Refer to the information in Exercise 17-19. Suppose Bio Doc determines standard costs of $6.60 per equivalent unit for direct materials and $10.40 per equivalent unit for conversion costs for both beginning work in process and work done in the current period.

④
2. Total direct materials cost variance, $20,000 U

REQUIRED
1. Do Exercise 17-19 using the standard-costing method. Note that you first need to calculate the equivalent units of work done in the current period (for direct materials and conversion costs) to complete beginning work in process, to start and complete new units, and to produce ending work in process.
2. Compute the total direct materials and conversion costs variances for July 2010.

17-22 Weighted-average method, equivalent units and unit costs. Consider the following data for the Assembly Division of a satellite manufacturer:

	Physical Units (Satellites)	Direct Materials	Conversion Costs
Beginning work in process (May 1)*	8	$ 5,426,960	$ 1,001,440
Started in May 2010	55		
Completed during May 2010	51		
Ending work in process (May 31)†	12		
Costs added during May 2010		$35,420,000	$15,312,000

*Degree of completion: direct materials, 90%; conversion costs, 40%.
†Degree of completion: direct materials, 60%; conversion costs, 30%.

The Assembly Division uses the weighted-average method of process costing.

REQUIRED
1. Compute equivalent units for direct materials and conversion costs. Show physical units in the first column of your schedule.
2. Calculate cost per equivalent unit for direct materials and conversion costs.

17-23 Weighted-average method, assigning costs (continuation of 17-22).

REQUIRED
For the data in Exercise 17-22, summarize total costs to account for, and assign these costs to units completed (and transferred out) and to units in ending work in process.

17-24 FIFO method, equivalent units and unit costs. Refer to the information in Exercise 17-22. Suppose the Assembly Division uses the FIFO method of process costing instead of the weighted-average method.

REQUIRED
1. Compute equivalent units for direct materials and conversion costs. Show physical units in the first column of your schedule.
2. Calculate cost per equivalent unit for direct materials and conversion costs.

17-25 FIFO method, assigning costs (continuation of 17-24).

REQUIRED
For the data in Exercise 17-22, use the FIFO method to summarize total costs to account for, and assign these costs to units completed and transferred out, and to units in ending work in process.

17-26 Standard-costing method, assigning costs. Refer to the information in Exercise 17-22. Suppose the Assembly Division uses the standard-costing method of process costing. Suppose further that the Assembly Division determines standard costs of $700,000 per equivalent unit for direct materials and $300,000 per equivalent unit for conversion costs for both beginning work in process and work done in the current period.

REQUIRED
1. Compute equivalent units for direct materials and conversion costs. Show physical units in the first column of your schedule.
2. Summarize total costs to account for, and assign these costs to units completed and transferred out, and to units in ending work in process.
3. Compute the total direct material and conversion cost variances for May 2010.

17-27 Transferred-in costs, weighted-average method. Asaya Clothing Inc. is a manufacturer of winter clothes. It has a Knitting Department and a Finishing Department. This exercise focuses on the Finishing Department. Direct materials are added at the end of the process. Conversion costs are added evenly during the process. Asaya uses the weighted-average method of process costing. The following information for June 2010 is shown on the next page

REQUIRED
1. Calculate equivalent units (tonnes) of transferred-in costs, direct materials, and conversion costs.
2. Summarize total costs to account for, and calculate the cost per equivalent unit for transferred-in costs, direct materials, and conversion costs.
3. Assign total costs to units completed (and transferred out) and to units in ending work in process.

	Physical Units (tonnes)	Transferred-in Costs	Direct Materials	Conversion Costs
Work in process, beginning inventory (June 1)	75	$75,000	$ 0	$30,000
Degree of completion, beginning work in process		100%	0%	60%
Transferred in during June	135			
Completed and transferred out during June	150			
Work in process, ending inventory (June 30)	60			
Degree of completion, ending work in process		100%	0%	75%
Total costs added during June		$142,500	$37,500	$78,000

17-28 Transferred-in costs, FIFO method. Refer to the information in Exercise 17-27. Suppose that Asaya uses the FIFO method instead of the weighted-average method in all of its departments. The only changes to Exercise 17-27 under the FIFO method are that the total transferred-in costs of beginning work in process on June 1 are $60,000 (instead of $75,000) and total transferred-in costs added during June are $130,800 (instead of $142,500).

3. Total cost of work in process, $81,534

REQUIRED

Do Exercise 17-27 using the FIFO method. Note that you first need to calculate the equivalent units of work done in the current period (for transferred-in costs, direct materials, and conversion costs) to complete beginning work in process, to start and complete new units, and to produce ending work in process.

17-29 Weighted-average method, equivalent units and unit costs. Consider the following data for the Assembly Division of Fenton Watches Inc.:

Direct materials equivalent units, 532

	Physical Units	Direct Materials	Conversion Costs
Beginning work in process (May 1)*	80	$ 493,360	$ 91,040
Started in May 2010	500		
Completed during May 2010	460		
Ending work in process (May 31)†	120		
Costs added during May 2010		$3,220,000	$1,392,000

*Degree of completion: direct materials, 90%; conversion costs, 40%.
†Degree of completion: direct materials, 60%; conversion costs, 30%.

The Assembly Division uses the weighted-average method of process costing.

REQUIRED
Compute equivalent units for direct materials and conversion costs. Show physical units in the first column of your schedule.

17-30 Weighted-average method, assigning costs (continuation of 17-29).

Total cost of work in process, $610,200

REQUIRED
For the data in Exercise 17-29, summarize total costs to account for, calculate cost per equivalent unit for direct materials and conversion costs, and assign total costs to units completed (and transferred out) and to units in ending work in process.

17-31 FIFO method, equivalent units. Refer to the information in Exercise 17-29. Suppose the Assembly Division at Fenton Watches Inc. uses the FIFO method of process costing instead of the weighted-average method.

Direct materials equivalent units, 460

REQUIRED
Compute equivalent units for direct materials and conversion costs. Show physical units in the first column of your schedule.

17-32 FIFO method, assigning costs (continuation of 17-31).

Total cost of work in process, $612,000

REQUIRED
For the data in Exercise 17-29, use the FIFO method to summarize total costs to account for, calculate cost per equivalent unit for direct materials and conversion costs, and assign total costs to units completed (and transferred out) and to units in ending work in process.

④

2. Total cost of work in process, $411,240

17-33 Standard-costing method, assigning costs. Bucky's Boxes makes boxes for moving. It sells its boxes to major national moving companies. Because of the simple nature of the production process, Bucky's uses standard costing. The following information for July 2010 is available.

	Physical Units	Direct Materials	Conversion Costs
Standard cost per equivalent unit		$ 1.30	$ 2.10
Work in process, beginning inventory (July 1)	185,000	$240,500	$ 97,125
Degree of completion of beginning work in process		100%	25%
Started during July	465,000		
Completed and transferred out	512,000		
Work in process, ending inventory (July 31)	138,000		
Degree of completion of ending work in process		100%	80%
Actual total costs added during July		$607,500	$1,207,415

REQUIRED
1. Compute equivalent units for each cost category.
2. Summarize total costs to account for, and assign total costs to units completed and transferred out and to units in ending work in process.

④

4. Total cost of beginning work in process inventory, $6,325,575

17-34 Standard-costing method. Ozumo's Gardening makes several different kinds of mulch. Its busy period is in the summer months. In August, the controller suddenly quits due to a stress-related disorder. He takes with him the standard costing results for RoseBark, Ozumo's highest-quality mulch. The controller had already completed the assignment of costs to finished goods and work in process, but the company does not know standard costs or the completion levels of inventory. The following information is available:

Ozumo's Gardening
Standard Costing Calculations for RoseBark
For the Month Ended August 31, 2010

	Equivalent Units (m³)		
	Physical Units (m³ of mulch)	Direct Materials	Conversion Costs
Complete beginning work in process	965,000	0	434,250
Start and complete	845,000	845,000	845,000
Start ending work in process†	1,817,000	1,817,000	1,090,200
		2,662,000	2,369,450
Units to account for	3,627,000		

	Costs
Cost of units completed from beginning work in process	$ 7,671,750
Cost of new units started and completed	6,717,750
Cost of units completed in August	14,389,500
Cost of ending work in process	12,192,070
Total costs accounted for	$26,581,570

REQUIRED
1. Calculate completion percentages of beginning work in process with respect to the two inputs.
2. Calculate completion percentages of ending work in process with respect to the two inputs.
3. Determine the standard costs per unit for the two inputs.
4. Determine the cost of beginning work in process inventory.

PROBLEMS

17-35 Weighted-average method. Larsen Corp. manufactures car seats in its Sarnia plant. Each car seat passes through the Assembly Department and the Testing Department. This problem focuses on the Assembly Department. The process-costing system at Larsen Corp. has a single direct-cost category (direct materials) and a single indirect-cost category (conversion costs). Direct materials are added at the beginning of the process. Conversion costs are added evenly during the process. When the Assembly Department finishes work on each car seat, it is immediately transferred to Testing.

Larsen Corp. uses the weighted-average method of process costing. Data for the Assembly Department for October 2010 are:

②

3. Total cost of work in process, $772,750

	Physical Units (car seats)	Direct Materials	Conversion Costs
Work in process, October 1*	5,000	$1,250,000	$ 402,750
Started during October 2010	20,000		
Completed during October 2010	22,500		
Work in process, October 31†	2,500		
Total costs added during October 2010		$4,500,000	$2,337,500

*Degree of completion: direct materials, ?%; conversion costs, 60%.
†Degree of completion: direct materials, ?%; conversion costs, 70%.

REQUIRED
1. For each cost category, compute equivalent units of work done in October 2010 in the Assembly Department. Show physical units in the first column of your schedule.
2. For each cost category, summarize total Assembly Department costs for October 2010 and calculate the cost per equivalent unit.
3. Assign total costs to units completed and transferred out and to units in ending work in process.

17-36 Journal entries (continuation of 17-35).

②

REQUIRED
Prepare a set of summarized journal entries for all October 2010 transactions affecting Work in Process—Assembly. Set up a T-account for Work in Process—Assembly, and post the entries to it.

17-37 FIFO method (continuation of 17-35).

④

3. Total cost of work in process, $755,000

REQUIRED
Do Problem 17-35 using the FIFO method of process costing. Explain any difference between the cost per equivalent unit in the Assembly Department under the weighted-average method and the FIFO method.

17-38 Transferred-in costs, weighted-average method (related to 17-35 to 17-37). Larsen Corp., as you know, is a manufacturer of car seats. Each car seat passes through the Assembly Department and Testing Department. This problem focuses on the Testing Department. Direct materials are added when the Testing Department process is 90% complete. Conversion costs are added evenly during the Testing Department's process. As work in Assembly is completed, each unit is immediately transferred to Testing. As each unit is completed in Testing, it is immediately transferred to Finished Goods.

⑤

3. Total cost of work in process, $1,686,460

Larsen Corp. uses the weighted-average method of process costing. Data for the Testing Department for October 2010 are:

	Physical Units (car seats)	Transferred-in Costs	Direct Materials	Conversion Costs
Work in process, October 1*	7,500	$2,932,500	$0	$835,460
Transferred in during October 2010	?			
Completed during October 2010	26,300			
Work in process, October 31†	3,700			
Costs added during October 2010		$7,717,500	$9,704,700	$3,955,900

*Degree of completion: transferred-in costs, ?%; direct materials, ?%; conversion costs, 70%.
†Degree of completion: transferred-in costs, ?%; direct materials, ?%; conversion costs, 60%.

REQUIRED

1. What is the percentage of completion for (a) transferred-in costs and direct materials in beginning work-in-process inventory and (b) transferred-in costs and direct materials in ending work-in-process inventory?
2. For each cost category, compute equivalent units in the Testing Department. Show physical units in the first column of your schedule.
3. For each cost category, summarize total Testing Department costs for October 2010, calculate the cost per equivalent unit, and assign total costs to units completed (and transferred out) and to units in ending work in process.
4. Prepare journal entries for October transfers from the Assembly Department to the Testing Department, and from the Testing Department to Finished Goods.

17-39 Transferred-in costs, FIFO-costing method (continuation of 17-38). Refer to the information in Problem 17-38. Suppose that Larsen Corp. uses the FIFO method instead of the weighted-average method in all of its departments. The only changes to Problem 17-38 under the FIFO method are that total transferred-in costs of beginning work in process on October 1 are $2,881,875 (instead of $2,932,500) and that total transferred-in costs added during October are $7,735,250 (instead of $7,717,500).

REQUIRED

Using the FIFO process-costing method, address the requirements of Problem 17-38.

17-40 Weighted-average method. Porter Handcraft is a manufacturer of picture frames for large retailers. Every picture frame passes through two departments: the Assembly Department and the Finishing Department. This problem focuses on the Assembly Department. The process-costing system at Porter has a single direct-cost category (direct materials) and a single indirect-cost category (conversion costs). Direct materials are added when the Assembly Department process is 10% complete. Conversion costs are added evenly during the Assembly Department's process.

Porter uses the weighted-average method of process costing. Consider the following data for the Assembly Department in April 2010:

	Physical Units (frames)	Direct Materials	Conversion Costs
Work in process, April 1*	75	$ 1,775	$ 135
Started during April 2010	550		
Completed during April 2010	500		
Work in process, April 30†	125		
Costs added during April 2010		$17,600	$10,890

*Degree of completion: direct materials, 100%; conversion costs, 40%.
†Degree of completion: direct materials, 100%; conversion costs, 20%.

REQUIRED

Summarize the total Assembly Department costs for April 2010, and assign total costs to units completed (and transferred out) and to units in ending work in process.

17-41 Journal entries (continuation of 17-40).

REQUIRED

Prepare a set of summarized journal entries for all April transactions affecting Work in Process—Assembly. Set up a T-account for Work in Process—Assembly, and post the entries to it.

17-42 FIFO method (continuation of 17-40).

REQUIRED

Do Problem 17-40 using the FIFO method of process costing. If you did Problem 17-40, explain any difference between the cost of work completed and transferred out and the cost of ending work in process in the Assembly Department under the weighted-average method and the FIFO method.

17-43 Transferred-in costs, weighted-average method. Publish Inc. has two departments: Printing and Binding. Each department has one direct-cost category (direct materials) and one indirect-cost category (conversion costs). This problem focuses on the Binding Department.

Margin notes:

⑤ 3. Total cost of work in process, $1,649,419

③ Total cost of work in process, $4,400

③

④ Total cost of work in process, $4,550

Books that have undergone the printing process are immediately transferred to the Binding Department. Direct material is added when the binding process is 80% complete. Conversion costs are added evenly during binding operations. When those operations are done, the books are immediately transferred to Finished Goods. Publish Inc. uses the weighted-average method of process costing. The following is a summary of the April 2010 operations of the Binding Department.

1. Total cost of work in process, $38,463

	Physical Units (books)	Transferred-in Costs	Direct Materials	Conversion Costs
Beginning work in process	900	$32,775	$ 0	$15,000
Degree of completion, beginning work in process		100%	0%	40%
Transferred in during April 2010	2,700			
Completed and transferred out during April	3,000			
Ending work in process (April 30)	600			
Degree of completion, ending work in process		100%	0%	60%
Total costs added during April		$144,000	$26,700	$69,000

REQUIRED
1. Summarize the total Binding Department costs for April 2010, and assign these costs to units completed (and transferred out) and to units in ending work in process.
2. Prepare journal entries for April transfers from the Printing Department to the Binding Department and from the Binding Department to Finished Goods.

17-44 Transferred-in costs, FIFO costing (continuation of 17-43). Refer to the information in Problem 17-43. Suppose that Publish Inc. uses the FIFO method instead of the weighted-average method in all of its departments. The only changes to Problem 17-43 under the FIFO method are that total transferred-in costs of beginning work in process on April 1 are $27,855 (instead of $32,775) and that total transferred-in costs added during April are $141,750 (instead of $144,000).

1. Total cost of work in process, $39,780

REQUIRED
1. Using the FIFO process-costing method, do Problem 17-43.
2. If you did Problem 17-43, explain any difference between the cost of work completed and transferred out and the cost of ending work in process in the Binding Department under the weighted-average method and the FIFO method.

17-45 Transferred-in costs, weighted-average and FIFO. Frito-Lay Inc. manufactures convenience foods, including potato chips and corn chips. Production of corn chips occurs in four departments: Cleaning, Mixing, Cooking, and Drying and Packaging. Consider the Drying and Packaging Department, where direct materials (packaging) is added at the end of the process. Conversion costs are added evenly during the process. Suppose the accounting records of a Frito-Lay plant provided the following information for corn chips in its Drying and Packaging Department during a weekly period (week 37):

1. Total cost of work in process, $23,360

	Physical Units (cases)	Transferred-in Costs	Direct Materials	Conversion Costs
Beginning work in process, week 37*	1,250	$29,000	$ 0	$9,060
Transferred in during week 37 from Cooking Department	5,000			
Completed during week 37	5,250			
Ending work in process, week 37†	1,000			
Costs added during week 37		$96,000	$25,200	$38,400

*Degree of completion: transferred-in costs, 100%; direct materials, ?%; conversion costs, 80%.
†Degree of completion: transferred-in costs, ?%; direct materials, ?%; conversion costs, 40%.

REQUIRED
1. Using the weighted-average method, summarize the total Drying and Packaging Department costs for week 37, and assign total costs to units completed (and transferred out) and to units in ending work in process.

2. Assume that the FIFO method is used for the Drying and Packaging Department. Under FIFO, the transferred-in costs for work-in-process beginning inventory in week 37 are $28,920 (instead of $29,000 under the weighted-average method), and the transferred-in costs during the week from the Cooking Department are $94,000 (instead of $96,000 under the weighted-average method). All other data are unchanged. Summarize the total Drying and Packaging Department costs for week 37 and assign total costs to units completed and transferred out and to units in ending work in process using the FIFO method.

17-46 Standard costing with beginning and ending work in process. Paquita's Pearls Company (PPC) is a manufacturer of knock-off jewellery. Paquita attends Fashion Week in New York City every September and February to gauge the latest fashion trends in jewellery. She then makes trendy jewellery at a fraction of the cost of those designers who participate in Fashion Week. This Fall's biggest item is triple-stranded pearl necklaces. Because of her large volume, Paquita uses process costing to account for her production. In October, she had started some of the triple strands. She continued to work on those in November. Costs and output figures are as follows:

Paquita's Pearls Company Process Costing
For the Month Ended November 30, 2010

	Units	Direct Materials	Conversion Costs
Standard cost per unit		$2.50	$10.00
Work in process, beginning inventory (November 1)	25,000	$62,500	$ 187,500
Degree of completion of beginning work in process	100%	100%	75%
Started during October	126,250		
Completed and transferred out	125,000		
Work in process, ending inventory (November 30)	26,250		
Degree of completion of ending work in process		100%	50%
Actual total costs added during November		$327,500	$1,207,415

REQUIRED

1. Compute equivalent units for direct materials and conversion costs. Show physical units in the first column of your schedule.
2. Compute the total standard costs of pearls transferred out in November and the total standard costs of the November 30 inventory of work in process.
3. Compute the total November variances for direct materials and conversion costs.

17-47 Operation costing. Two styles of men's shoes are manufactured by the Comfort Fit Shoe Company: Designer and Regular. Designer style is made from leather, and Regular style uses synthetic materials. Three operations—cutting, sewing, and packing—are common to both styles, but only Designer style passes through a lining operation. The conversion cost rates for 2010 are:

	Cutting	Sewing	Lining	Packing
Rate per unit (pair)	$11	$16	$9	$3

Details of two work orders processed in August are:

	Work Order 815	Work Order 831
Style	Designer	Regular
Number of units (pairs)	1,000	5,000
Direct materials costs	$30,000	$50,000

REQUIRED

Calculate the total costs and the total cost per unit of work order 815 and work order 831.

17-48 Operation costing, equivalent units. (CMA, adapted) Plastco Industries manufactures a variety of plastic products, including a series of moulded chairs. The three models of moulded chairs, which are all variations of the same design, are Standard (can be stacked), Deluxe (with arms), and Executive (with arms and padding). The company uses batch manufacturing and has an operation-costing system.

Plastco has an extrusion operation and subsequent operations to form, trim, and finish the chairs. Plastic sheets are produced by the extrusion operation, some of which are sold directly to other manufacturers. During the forming operation, the remaining plastic sheets are moulded into chair seats and the legs are added. The Standard model is sold after this operation. During the trim operation, the arms are added to the Deluxe and Executive models and the chair edges are smoothed. Only the Executive model enters the finish operation, where the padding is added. All of the units produced receive the same steps within each operation.

The May production run had a total manufacturing cost of $898,000. The units of production and direct materials costs incurred are as follows:

	Units Produced	Extrusion Materials	Form Materials	Trim Materials	Finish Materials
Plastic sheets	5,500	$ 60,000	$ 0	$ 0	$ 0
Standard model	6,500	72,000	24,000	0	0
Deluxe model	3,500	36,000	12,000	9,000	0
Executive model	2,500	24,000	8,000	6,000	12,000
	18,000	$192,000	$44,000	$15,000	$12,000

Manufacturing costs of production assigned during the month of May were:

	Extrusion Operation	Form Operation	Trim Operation	Finish Operation
Direct manufacturing labour	$152,000	$60,000	$30,000	$18,000
Manufacturing overhead	240,000	72,000	39,000	24,000

REQUIRED

1. For each product produced by Plastco Industries during May, determine (a) the unit cost and (b) the total cost. Be sure to account for all costs incurred during the month, and support your answer with appropriate calculations.
2. Without considering your answer in requirement 1, assume that 1,500 units of the Deluxe model produced during May remained in work in process at the end of the month. These units were 100% complete as to materials costs and 60% complete in the trim operation. Determine the cost of the 1,500 units of the Deluxe model in the work-in-process inventory at the end of May.

17-49 Equivalent-unit computations, benchmarking, governance. Susan Draco is the corporate controller of Comfort Suits. Comfort Suits has 20 plants worldwide that manufacture basic suits for retail stores. Each plant uses a process-costing system. At the end of each month, each plant manager submits a production report and a production cost report. The production report includes the plant manager's estimate of the percentage of completion of the ending work in process as to direct materials and conversion costs. Draco uses these estimates to compute the equivalent units of work done in each plant and the cost per equivalent unit of work done for both direct materials and conversion costs in each month. Plants are ranked from 1 to 20 in terms of (a) cost per equivalent unit of direct materials and (b) cost per equivalent unit of conversion costs. Each month Draco publishes a report that she calls "Benchmarking for Efficiency Gains at Comfort Suits." The three top-ranked plants on each category receive a bonus and are written up as the best in their class in the company newsletter.

Draco has been pleased with the success of her benchmarking program. However, she has heard some disturbing news. She has received some unsigned letters stating that two plant managers have been manipulating their monthly estimates of percentage of completion in an attempt to obtain "best in class" status.

REQUIRED

1. How and why might plant managers "manipulate" their monthly estimates of percentage of completion?
2. Draco's first instinct is to contact each plant controller and discuss the problem raised by the unsigned letters. Is that a good idea?
3. Assume that the plant controller's primary reporting responsibility is to the plant manager and that each plant controller receives the phone call from Draco mentioned in requirement 2. What is the ethical responsibility of each plant controller (a) to Susan Draco and (b) to Comfort Suits in relation to the equivalent unit information each plant provides for the "Benchmarking for Efficiency" report?
4. How might Draco gain some insight into whether the equivalent-unit figures provided by particular plants are being manipulated?

COLLABORATIVE LEARNING CASES

17-50 Transferred-in costs, equivalent-unit costs, working backwards. Ottawa Plastics Corp. has two processes—extrusion and thermo-assembly. Consider the June 2010 data for physical units in the thermo-assembly process:

Beginning work in process	16,000 units
Transferred in from the Extruding Department during the month	10,000 units
Ending work in process	6,000 units

Direct materials are added when the process in the Thermo-Assembly Department is 80% complete. Conversion costs are added evenly during the process. Ottawa Plastics uses the FIFO method of process costing. The following information is available:

	Transferred-in Costs	Direct Materials	Conversion Costs
Beginning work in process	$90,000	$ 0	$45,000
Percentage completion of beginning work in process	100%	0%	60%
Costs added in current period	$58,500	$57,000	$57,200
Cost per equivalent unit of work done in current period	$5.85	$2.85	$4.931

INSTRUCTIONS

Form pairs of students to complete the following requirements.

REQUIRED

1. For each cost category, compute equivalent units of work done in the current period.
2. For each cost category, compute equivalent units of work done to complete beginning work-in-process inventory, to start and complete new units, and to produce ending work in process.
3. For each cost category, calculate the percentage of completion of ending work-in-process inventory.
4. Summarize total costs to account for, and assign these costs to units completed (and transferred out) and to units in ending work in process.

17-51 Operation costing. Farkas Shoes, a high-end shoe manufacturer, produces two lines of shoes for women. The shoes are identical in design, but differ in the materials used and the trim added to the shoes. The basic shoes are made from a synthetic leather, have a synthetic insole, and have plain buttons decorating the upper. The elaborate shoes are made from genuine leather, have a special insole, and have creative buttons applied to the upper. Each shoe is assumed to use an identical amount of conversion costs for a given operation. Work orders 10399 and 10400 are representative work orders for the two types of shoes.

Farkas Shoes
Selected Work Orders
For the Month Ended February 28, 2010

	Work Order 10399	Work Order 10400
Quantity (pairs of shoes)	1,000	150
Direct materials	Synthetic leather	Genuine leather
	Synthetic insole	FitDry insole
	Plain buttons	Creative buttons
Operations		
1. Cut leather	Use	Use
2. Shape leather	Use	Use
3. Treat leather	Do not use	Use
4. Sew shoes	Use	Use
5. Machine application of buttons	Use	Do not use
6. Hand application of buttons	Do not use	Use

Selected budget information for February follows:

	Basic	Elaborate	Total
Units	30,000	2,250	32,250
Direct material costs	$390,000	63,000	$453,000

Budgeted conversion costs for each operation for February follow:

Operation 1	$145,125	Operation 4	$67,725
Operation 2	58,050	Operation 5	13,500
Operation 3	4,275	Operation 6	2,025

REQUIRED

1. Using budgeted pairs of shoes as the denominator, calculate the budgeted conversion cost rates for each of the six operations.
2. Using the information in requirement 1, calculate the budgeted cost of goods manufactured for the two February work orders.
3. Based on the two representative work orders for February, calculate the budgeted cost of each pair of shoes.

18

Spoilage, Rework, and Scrap

Allocation of Spoilage, Rework, and Scrap— Profit Means Revenue Exceeds All Costs

Undelivered planes cannot earn revenue. During the manufacture of the new A380, Airbus minimized the environmental impact of this aircraft for its entire life cycle. From contractual agreements to transportation of parts and finished product to decommissioning the A380, Airbus has insisted on implementation of best environmental practices.

The jetliner exceeds the minimum required by international environmental standards set out in ISO 14001. The cargo planes can carry 150 tonnes over 5,600 kilometres with 21% lower operating costs.

But manufacturing problems in wiring the aircraft plagued production on this $14 billion project. Poorly fitted wiring on 20 finished aircraft had to be ripped out and scrapped, and new wiring installed. This caused a huge delay in delivery, and FedEx cancelled a $3 billion order for 10 planes as a result.[1]

After studying this chapter, you should be able to

1. Distinguish among spoilage, rework, and scrap, and apply the appropriate methods to account for the costs of normal and abnormal costs

2. Apply process-costing methods to account for spoilage using weighted average and first-in, first-out (FIFO) methods

3. Apply the standard-costing method to account for spoilage in process costing using the standard-costs method, and allocate costs of normal spoilage

4. Apply job cost allocation procedures to account for spoilage in job costing

5. Apply cost allocation procedures to account for reworked units and scrap

[1]Nelson D. Schwartz, "Big Plane, Big Problems," *Fortune,* March 1, 2007; Michelle Dunlop, "Airbus Delivers First A380 Today, More Than a Year Late," *HeraldNet,* October 15, 2007, available at www.heraldnet.com/article/20071015NEWS0/710150041&news01ad51; Airbus website: www.airbus.com/en/aircraftfamilies/a380/freight.html accessed July 4, 2008.

This chapter examines three costs that arise as a result of defects—spoilage, rework, and scrap—and ways to account for them. Chapter 19 discusses other aspects of quality with greater emphasis on cost management and control. Managing spoilage, rework, and scrap is a challenge for many companies, regardless of a company's size or the products it manufactures. To control costs, managers are more intensely focused on improving quality and reducing defects. Many managers believe that reducing defects both reduces costs and improves customer satisfaction, which makes their company more competitive.

The timely and accurate recording of these costs will direct prompt attention towards eliminating the causes of both the defects and their costs. Using this information, managers have several cost-reduction alternatives: design better products and processes, invest in production systems such as just-in-time (JIT) and computer-integrated manufacturing (CIM), train and motivate workers, and maintain machines properly.

TERMINOLOGY

1 Distinguish among spoilage, rework, and scrap, and apply the appropriate methods to account for the costs of normal and abnormal costs

The terms spoilage, rework, and scrap are not interchangeable. For a financial accountant the costs must be classified differently because different transactions give rise to each type of cost. Exhibit 18-1 illustrates the differences. Often these costs are locked in during the design of a product (see Chapter 12).

Spoilage refers to unacceptable units of production that are either discarded or salvaged and sold for net disposal proceeds. Partially completed or fully completed units of output may be spoiled. Examples are defective shirts, jeans, shoes, and carpets sold as "seconds," and defective aluminum cans sold to aluminum manufacturers to be melted down and recycled into other aluminum products. **Reworked units** are unacceptable units of production that are subsequently reworked and sold as acceptable

EXHIBIT 18-1
Classification of Spoilage, Rework, and Scrap

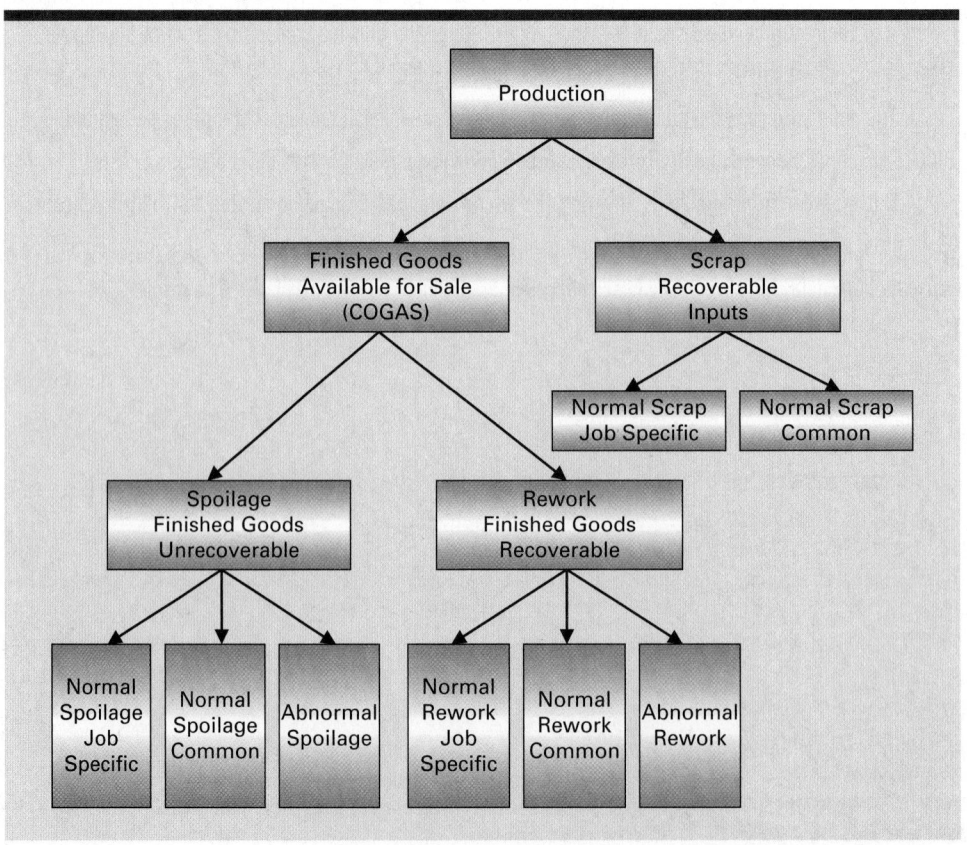

finished goods. For example, defective units of products such as pagers, computer disk drives, and aircraft can sometimes be reworked and sold as good products. **Scrap** is a residual material that results from manufacturing a product. It has low total sales value compared with the total sales value of the product. Examples are short lengths from woodworking operations, edges from plastic moulding operations, and frayed cloth and end cuts from suit-making operations.

Some amount of spoilage, rework, or scrap is an inherent part of many production processes. One example is semiconductor manufacturing, where the products are so complex and delicate that some spoiled units are invariably produced and cannot be reworked. For manufacturers of precision tools such as Siemens, the exacting tolerances and specifications result in occasional spoilage and rework. Spoiled units can be reworked to meet standards but only at a considerable cost. In the case of Airbus, the spoiled wiring had to be scrapped, but careful attention to the design and manufacturing process can decrease scrap.

Two key objectives when accounting for spoilage (illustrated under Finished Goods in Exhibit 18-1) are determining the magnitude of the costs of spoilage, and distinguishing between the costs of normal and abnormal spoilage (illustrated under Spoilage in Exhibit 18-1). Managers use this information both to cost products and to control and reduce costs by improving the quality of the product and process.

Normal spoilage is spoilage that arises under efficient operating conditions; it arises from the nature of a particular production process, often a locked-in cost. Management must decide the rate of spoilage it is willing to accept as normal. Costs of normal spoilage are typically viewed as a part of the costs of good units manufactured (COGM), when good units cannot be made without the simultaneous appearance of spoiled units. Normal spoilage rates should be computed using the total *good* units completed as the base, not the total *actual* units started because total actual units started also include any abnormal spoilage in addition to normal spoilage.

Abnormal spoilage is spoilage that is unexpected under efficient operating conditions; it is not an inherent part of the chosen production process. Most abnormal spoilage is usually regarded as avoidable and controllable. Line operators and other plant personnel can generally decrease abnormal spoilage by minimizing machine breakdowns, accidents, and the like. Abnormal spoilage costs are written off as losses of the accounting period in which detection of the spoiled units occurs. For the most informative feedback, the Loss from Abnormal Spoilage account should appear in a detailed income statement as a separate line item and not be buried as an indistinguishable part of the COGM.

Many companies, such as Toyota Motor Corporation, adhere to a perfection standard as a part of their emphasis on total quality control. Their ideal goal is zero defects. Hence, all spoilage would be treated as abnormal. Issues about accounting for spoilage arise in both process-costing and job-costing systems. We first present the accounting for spoilage in process-costing systems because it is an extension of the discussion of process costing introduced in Chapter 17.

PROCESS COSTING AND SPOILAGE

A key issue in accounting for spoilage in process-costing systems is how to count spoiled units. As we have already discussed, units of abnormal spoilage should be counted and recorded separately. But what about units of normal spoilage? These units can either be recognized (approach A) or not counted (approach B) when computing output units—actual or equivalent—in a process-costing system. Approach A makes visible the costs associated with spoilage. Approach B spreads the spoilage costs over good units, potentially resulting in less accurate product costs.

An **inspection point** is the stage of the production process at which products are examined to determine whether they are acceptable or unacceptable units. In the situation of process costing, spoilage is typically assumed to occur at the stage of completion where inspection takes place. That's because spoilage is not detected until inspection and inspection cannot occur prior to completion. In our example, the inspection point is at the end of the process. As a result, the spoiled units are assumed to be 100% complete with respect to direct materials.

Example 1: Chipmakers Inc. manufactures computer chips for television sets. All direct materials are added at the beginning of the chip-making process. To highlight issues that arise with spoilage, we assume no beginning inventory. In May 2010 the following data are available:

	A	B	C
		Physical	Direct
		Units	Material
1			
2			
3	Work in process, beginning inventory (May 1)	0	
4	Started during May	10,000	
5	Good units completed and transferred out during May	5,000	
6	Units spoiled (all normal spoilage)	1,000	
7	Work in process, ending inventory (May 31)	4,000	
8	Degree of completion of ending work in process		100%
9	Direct materials costs added in May		$270,000

Exhibit 18-2 calculates and assigns cost per unit of direct materials using approach A and approach B. Approach A shows 10,000 equivalent units of output: 5,000 equivalent units in good units completed (5,000 physical units × 100%), 4,000 units in ending work in process (4,000 physical units × 100%), and 1,000 equivalent units in normal spoilage (1,000 physical units × 100%). Approach B shows 9,000 equivalent units of output: 5,000 equivalent units in good units completed and 4,000 equivalent units in ending work in process. Not counting the equivalent units for normal spoilage in approach B decreases equivalent units, resulting in a higher cost of each good unit. A $30 equivalent-unit cost in approach B (by not measuring actual spoiled units), instead of a $27 equivalent-unit cost in approach A (by measuring spoiled units), is assigned to work in process that has not reached the inspection point.

EXHIBIT 18-2
Effect of Recognizing Equivalent Units in Spoilage for Direct Materials Costs for Chipmakers Inc. for May 2010

	A	B	C
		Approach A:	Approach B:
		Counting Spoiled	Not Counting Spoiled
		Units When Computing	Units When Computing
		Output in Equivalent	Output in Equivalent
		Units	Units
6	Costs to account for	$270,000	$270,000
7	Divide by equivalent units of output	÷ 10,000	÷ 9,000
8	Cost per equivalent units of output	$ 27	$ 30
9	Assignment of costs:		
10	Good units completed (5,000 units × $27 per unit; 5,000 units × $30 per unit)	$135,000	$150,000
11	Add normal spoilage (1,000 units × $27 per unit)	27,000	0
12	Total costs of good units completed and transferred out	162,000	150,000
13	Work in process, ending (4,000 units × $27 per unit; 4,000 units × $30 per unit)	108,000	120,000
14	Cost accounted for	$270,000	$270,000

Managing Toxic Waste—Environmental and Corporate Sustainability

The DuPont Corporation manufactures a wide range of chemicals and chemical products, and calls the spoilage and scrap it generates *waste*. Chemical waste, often toxic, impacts the environment, and legislation requires environmentally safe disposal. Special disposal costs increase the cost of generating waste. DuPont calculates the full costs of waste to include (1) the costs of materials lost in the chemical process minus their disposal value; (2) the full costs of semi-finished and finished products spoiled; (3) the full costs of disposing of or treating the waste, such as site charges for hazardous waste or costs of scrubbers and biotreatment plants to treat the waste; and (4) the costs of any solvents used to clean plant and equipment as a result of generating waste.

The company focuses on avoidance of waste altogether as the best way to achieve profitability and environmental performance, and it rewards managers for reducing waste. The company's new process for Terathane® significantly reduces environmental emissions and energy use. Relative to the old technology, the new technology reduced air emissions by 91,000 kilograms, solid waste by 11 million kilograms, aqueous waste by 11 million kilograms, and steam use by more than 68 million kilograms, while generating cost savings of more than US $5 million a year.

Sources: Adapted from Environmental Respect Awards, DuPont Corporation, and based on discussions with Dale Martin, manager, Environmental Effectiveness; C. Holliday, "Sustainable Growth, the DuPont Way," *Harvard Business Review,* September 2001, pp. 129–134.

Under approach B, the direct material costs assigned to good units completed and transferred out, which include the costs of normal spoilage, are understated by $12,000—$150,000 instead of $162,000. The 4,000 units in ending work in process contain costs of normal spoilage of $12,000 ($120,000 − $108,000) that do not pertain to the 4,000 units in ending work in process because they have not yet been inspected. That $12,000 belongs with the good units completed and transferred out. The 4,000 units in ending work in process undoubtedly include some units that will be detected as spoiled when they are inspected upon completion in the subsequent accounting period.

In effect, under approach B, these units will bear two charges for spoilage. The ending work in process is being charged for spoilage in the current period, and it will be charged again when inspection occurs as the units are completed. Such cost distortions do not occur when spoiled units are recognized in the computation of equivalent units. Approach A has a further advantage. It highlights the cost of normal spoilage to management and thereby focuses management's attention on reducing spoilage. Therefore, we will use approach A to present process costing with spoilage.

ASSESS YOUR MASTERY

To check your understanding of the material in Learning Objective ❶, go to the *Mastery Questions* section at the end of this chapter and complete Learning Objective ❶ questions 1 and 2.

PROCESS COSTING WITH SPOILAGE FOR WEIGHTED-AVERAGE AND FIFO METHODS

② Apply process-costing methods to account for spoilage using weighted average and first-in, first-out (FIFO) methods

We illustrate process costing with spoilage using the following example.

Example 2: Anzio Company manufactures a wooden recycling container in its Processing Department. Direct materials for this product are introduced at the beginning of the production cycle. At the start of production, all direct materials required to make one output unit are bundled together in a single kit. Conversion costs are added evenly during the cycle. Some units of this product are spoiled as a result of defects only detectable at inspection of finished units. Normally, the spoiled units are 10% of the good output. Summary data for July 2010 are as follows:

A	B	C	D	E
	Physical	**Direct**	**Conversion**	**Total**
	Units	**Materials**	**Costs**	**Costs**
	(1)	**(2)**	**(3)**	**(4) = (2) + (3)**
4 Work in process, beginning inventory (July 1)	1,500	$12,000	$ 9,000	$ 21,000
5 Degree of completion of ending work in process		100%	60%	
6 Started during July	8,500			
7 Good units completed and transferred out during July	7,000			
8 Work in process, ending inventory (July 31)	2,000			
9 Degree of completion of ending work in process		100%	50%	
10 Total costs added during July		$76,500	$89,100	$165,600
11 Normal spoiling as a percentage of good units	10%			
12 Degree of completion of normal spoilage		100%	100%	
13 Degree of completion of abnormal spoilage		100%	100%	

The approach used in Chapter 17 needs only slight modification to accommodate spoilage. The key change is in calculating the number of spoiled units as you organize the data for the flow of physical units of output. The conversion and direct material costs must be given, and we assume direct materials are converted 100%. The calculation of conversion costs is based on equivalent units (EU), not physical units, and the total equivalent units converted is the conversion cost allocation base. The cost allocation rate is simply the total conversion cost pool divided by the total EU. Then the direct materials and conversion costs must be assigned, which will provide a statement of COGM and transferred out.

◆ *Summarize the flow of physical units of output.* Identify both normal and abnormal spoilage.

The number of total spoiled units is computed as follows:

$$\text{Total spoilage} = \left(\begin{array}{c} \text{Units in beginning} \\ \text{work-in-process} \\ \text{inventory} \end{array} + \text{Units started} \right) - \left(\begin{array}{c} \text{Good units} \\ \text{completed and} \\ \text{transferred out} \end{array} + \begin{array}{c} \text{Units in ending} \\ \text{work-in-process} \\ \text{inventory} \end{array} \right)$$

$$= (1,500 + 8,500) - (7,000 + 2,000)$$

$$= 10,000 - 9,000$$

$$= 1,000 \text{ units}$$

Normal spoilage at Anzio's Processing Department is 10% of the 7,000 units of good output, or 700 units. Thus:

$$\text{Abnormal spoilage} = \text{Total spoilage} - \text{Normal spoilage}$$

$$= 1,000 - 700$$

$$= 300 \text{ units}$$

- *Compute conversion cost allocation base in equivalent units (EU).* Compute equivalent units for spoilage in the same way as for good units. Because Anzio inspects at the completion point, the same amount of work will be done on each spoiled unit and each completed good unit.

- *Compute conversion cost allocation rate per equivalent unit ($/EU).* The details of this step do not differ from those in Chapter 17. We assume that spoiled units are included in the computation of output units.

- *Summarize total costs to account for.* These are all the costs debited to Work in Process. The details of this step do not differ from those in Chapter 17.

- *Assign these costs to units completed, spoiled units, and units in ending work in process (EI WIP).* This step now includes computation of the cost of spoiled units and the cost of good units.

To proceed, we first need to specify the inventory costing method—weighted average, FIFO, or standard costing. We illustrate process costing under each of these inventory methods and show how the computations incorporate normal and abnormal spoilage.

WEIGHTED-AVERAGE METHOD AND SPOILAGE

Exhibit 18-3 summarizes the production data and includes calculations of equivalent units (EU) of normal and abnormal spoilage based on the information provided for Anzio Company. All good and spoiled units are considered 100% completed. Remember that we assume the direct materials (DM) are 100% consumed during conversion. Panel A of Exhibit 18-3 summarizes the flow of production in physical units and equivalent units, and includes calculations of equivalent units of normal and abnormal spoilage. Panel B begins with the calculation of the cost per equivalent unit, then applies the costs to the units completed and transferred out, including normal spoilage, as well as the abnormal spoilage and EI WIP.

In Panel B, notice how, for each cost category, the costs of beginning work in process and costs of work done in the current period are totalled and divided by the equivalent units of all work done to date to calculate the weighted-average cost. These unit costs are multiplied by the equivalent units calculated in Panel A to assign costs to the completed units, spoiled units, and EI WIP. Note how the costs of normal spoilage of $13,825 are added to the DM (700 units × $8.85 = $6,195) and added to the conversion costs (700 × $10.90 = $7,630) of the good units (7,000 units × ($8.85 + $10.90) = $138,250). Hence, the cost per good unit completed and transferred out equals the total costs transferred out (including the costs of normal spoilage) divided by the number of good units produced, $152,075 ÷ 7,000 = $21.725. It is *not* equal to $19.75, the sum of the costs per EU of direct materials, $8.85, and conversion costs, $10.90. Instead, the cost per good unit is equal to the total cost of DM and conversion costs per EU, $19.75, *plus* a share of the normal spoilage, $1.975 ($13,825 ÷ 7,000 = $1.975), for a total of $21.725 per good unit. The $5,925 costs of abnormal spoilage are assigned to the Loss from Abnormal Spoilage account and do not appear in the good-unit costs.[2]

The total costs to account for of $186,600 are recorded in a journal entry as a debit to the Work-in-Process (WIP) Inventory account. This account must also be credited with the costs of abnormal spoilage of $5,925 and the cost of good units converted and transferred out of $152,075, which includes costs of normal spoilage of $13,825. The total EI WIP will be $28,600.

FIFO METHOD AND SPOILAGE

Exhibit 18-4 uses the FIFO method: Panel A focuses on equivalent units of work done in the current period and Panel B keeps the costs of the beginning work-in-process

[2]The actual costs of spoilage (and rework) are often greater than the costs recorded in the accounting system because opportunity costs of disruption of the production line, storage, and lost contribution margins are not recorded in accounting systems. Chapter 19 discusses these opportunity costs from a management viewpoint.

EXHIBIT 18-3
Weighted-Average Method of Process Costing with Spoilage—Forming Department of Anzio Company for July 2010

	A	B	C	D	E
1		**PANEL A: Summarize Output in Physical Units and Compute Equivalent Units**			
2				**Equivalent Units**	
3			**Physical**	**Direct**	**Conversion**
4		**Flow of Production**	**Units**	**Materials**	**Costs**
5		Work in process, beginning (given, p. 892)	1,500		
6		Started during current period (given, p. 892)	8,500		
7		To account for	10,000		
8		Good units completed and transferred out during the current period	7,000	7,000	7,000
9		Normal spoilage[a]	700		
10		(700 × 100%; 700 × 100%)		700	700
11		Abnormal spoilage[b]	300		
12		(300 × 100%; 300 × 100%)		300	300
13		Work in process, ending[c] (given, p. 892)	2,000		
14		(2,000 × 100%; 2,000 × 50%)		2,000	1,000
15		Accounted for	10,000		
16		Work done to date		10,000	9,000
17					
18		[a]Normal spoilage is 10% of good units transferred out: 10% × 7,000 = 700 units. Degree of completion of normal spoilage in this			
19		department: direct materials, 100%; conversion costs, 100%.			
20		[b]Abnormal spoilage = Total spoilage − Normal spoilage = 1,000 − 700 = 300 units. Degree of completion of abnormal spoilage			
21		in this department: direct materials, 100%; conversion costs, 100%.			
22		[c]Degree of completion in this department: direct materials, 100%; conversion costs, 50%.			
23					
24		**PANEL B: Compute Cost per Equivalent Unit, Summarize Total Costs to Account For, and Assign**			
25		**Total Costs to Units Completed, to Spoiled Units, and to Units in Ending Work in Process**			
26			**Total**		
27			**Production**	**Direct**	**Conversion**
28			**Costs**	**Materials**	**Costs**
29		Work in process, beginning (given, p. 892)	$ 21,000	$12,000	$ 9,000
30		Costs added in the current period (given, p. 892)	165,600	76,500	89,100
31		Costs incurred to date		$88,500	$98,100
32		Divide by equivalent units of work done to date		÷10,000	÷9,000
33		Cost per equivalent unit		$ 8.85	$ 10.90
34		Total costs to account for	$186,600		
35		Assignment of costs:			
36		Good units completed and transferred out (7,000 units):			
37		Costs before adding normal spoilage	$138,250	(7,000[d] × $8.85) + (7,000[d] × $10.90)	
38		Normal spoilage (700 units)	13,825	(700[d] × $8.85) + (700[d] × $10.90)	
39 (A)		Total costs of good units completed and transferred out	152,075		
40 (B)		Abnormal spoilage (300 units)	5,925	(300[d] × $8.85) + (300[d] × $10.90)	
41 (C)		Work in process, ending (2,000 units)	28,600	(2,000[d] × $8.85) + (1,000[d] × $10.90)	
42 (A+B+C)		Total costs accounted for	$186,600		
43					
44		[d]Equivalent units of direct materials and conversion costs calculated in Panel A			

inventory separate and distinct from the costs of work done in the current period when assigning costs.

Panel A of Exhibit 18-4 summarizes the flow of production in physical units and equivalent units, including calculations of equivalent units of normal and abnormal spoilage. Panel B begins with the calculation of the cost per equivalent unit, then applies the costs to the units completed and transferred out, including normal spoilage, as well as the abnormal spoilage and EI WIP. All spoilage costs are assumed to be related to units completed during this period, using the unit costs of the current period.

In Exhibit 18-4, there are several items that are different from what was shown for the weighted-average method in Exhibit 18-3. First, the BI WIP for the FIFO method includes good units that were 60% completed in the previous month. This means they must be 40% converted in the current month. These BI WIP units must be the first to be accounted for with respect to costs transferred out each month. Because DM is 100% consumed at the beginning of conversion, the current month's DM costs assigned to BI WIP of 600 EU (1,500 physical units × 0.4 = 600 EU) already 60% converted last month will be zero. The added DM costs for the current month will be assigned to only the 8,500 physical units started; hence, the DM cost per unit is $9.00/EU ($76,500 ÷ 8,500 EU = $9.00/EU). The added conversion costs for this month will be assigned to only the 8,100 EU, including the 1,000 EU in EI WIP (2,000 physical units × 0.5 = 1,000 EU). The cost allocation rate for the conversion cost pool is $11.00/EU ($89,100 ÷ 8,100 EU = $11.00/EU). All the spoilage for this month will be calculated at these two rates and spoiled units are 100% converted.

If the FIFO method were used in its purest form, normal spoilage costs would be split between the goods started and completed during the current period and those completed from BI WIP—using the appropriate unit costs of the period in which the units were worked on. The simpler, modified FIFO method, as illustrated in Exhibit 18-4, in effect uses the unit costs of the current period for assigning normal spoilage costs to the goods completed from BI WIP. This modified FIFO method assumes that all normal spoilage traceable to the BI WIP was started and completed during the current period.

ASSESS YOUR MASTERY

To check your understanding of the material in Learning Objective ② , go to the *Mastery Questions* section at the end of this chapter and complete Learning Objective ② questions 1 and 2.

MyAccountingLab

PROCESS COSTING STANDARD COSTS

This section assumes you have studied Chapters 7 and 8 and the standard costs method in Chapter 17. Otherwise, omit this section.

Standard-costing methods can also be used to account for normal and abnormal spoilage. We illustrate how much simpler the calculations of conversion costs become by continuing our Anzio Company example; however, journal entries must be made to account for the variances between standard and actual costs.

Suppose Anzio Company develops standard costs for the Forming Department. Assume the same standard costs apply to the beginning inventory and to work done in July 2010.

Apply the standard-costing method to account for spoilage in process costing using the standard-costs method, and allocate costs of normal spoilage ③

Standard Costs for Forming Department

Direct materials	$ 8.50
Conversion costs	10.50
Total manufacturing cost	$19.00

EXHIBIT 18-4
First-In, First-Out (FIFO) Method of Process Costing with Spoilage—Forming Department of Anzio Company for July 2010

	A	B	C	D
1	**PANEL A: Summarize Output in Physical Units and Compute Equivalent Units**			
2			**Equivalent Units**	
3		**Physical**	**Direct**	**Conversion**
4	**Flow of Production**	**Units**	**Materials**	**Costs**
5	Work in process, beginning balance (given)	1,500		
6	Started during current period (given)	8,500		
7	To account for	10,000		
8	Good units completed and transferred out during the current period			
9	From beginning work in process inventory[a]	1,500		
10	$1,500 \times (100\% - 100\%)$; $1,500 \times (100\% - 60\%)$		—	600
11	Started and completed[b]	5,500		
12	$5,500 \times 100\%$; $5,500 \times 100\%$		5,500	5,500
13	Normal spoilage[c]	700		
14	$700 \times 100\%$; $700 \times 100\%$		700	700
15	Abnormal spoilage[d]	300		
16	$300 \times 100\%$; $300 \times 100\%$		300	300
17	Work in process, ending balance[e] (given)	2,000		
18	$2,000 \times 100\%$; $2,000 \times 50\%$		2,000	1,000
19	Accounted for	10,000		
20	Work done in current period only		8,500	8,100
21				
22	[a]Degree of completion in this department: direct materials, 100%; conversion costs, 60%.			
23	[b]7,000 physical units completed and transferred out minus 1,500 physical units completed and transferred from BI WIP			
24	[c]Normal spoilage is 10% of good units transferred out: $10\% \times 7,000 = 700$ units. Degree of completion of normal spoilage in this			
25	department: direct materials, 100%; conversion costs, 100%.			
26	[d]Abnormal spoilage = Actual spoilage − Normal spoilage = $1,000 - 700 = 300$ units. Degree of completion of abnormal spoilage			
27	in this department: direct materials, 100%; conversion costs, 100%.			
28	[e]Degree of completion in this department: direct materials, 100%; conversion costs, 50%.			
29	**PANEL B: Compute Cost per Equivalent Unit, Summarize Total Costs to Account For,**			
30	**and Assign Total Costs to Units Completed, to Spoiled Units, and to Units in Ending Work in Process**			
31		**Total**		
32		**Production**	**Direct**	**Conversion**
33		**Costs**	**Materials**	**Costs**
34	Work in process, beginning balance (given)	$ 21,000		
35	Costs added in the current period (given)	165,600	$76,500	$89,100
36	Divide by equivalent units of work done in the current period		÷8,500	÷8,100
37	Cost per equivalent unit		$ 9	$ 11
38	Total costs to account for	$186,600		
39	Assignment of costs:			
40	Good units completed and transferred out (7,000 units):			
41	Work in process beginning balance (1,500 units)	$ 21,000		
42	Costs added in current period[f]	6,600	=	$(0^f \times \$9) + (600^f \times \$11)$
43	Total from beginning inventory before normal spoilage	27,600		
44	Started and completed before normal spoilage (5,500 units)	110,000	=	$(5,500^f \times \$9) + (5,500^f \times \$11)$
45	Normal spoilage (700 units)	14,000	=	$(700^f \times \$9) + (700^f \times \$11)$
46 A	Total costs of good units completed and transferred out	151,600		
47 B	Abnormal spoilage (300 units)	6,000	=	$(300^f \times \$9) + (300^f \times \$11)$
48 C	Work in process, ending balance (2,000 units)	29,000	=	$(2,000^f \times \$9) + (1,000^f \times \$11)$
49 A + B + C	Total costs accounted for	$186,600		
50				
51	[f]Equivalent units of direct materials and conversion costs calculated in Panel A			

Assume the same standard costs per unit also apply to the beginning inventory: 1,500 (1,500 × 100%) equivalent units of direct materials and 900 (1,500 × 60%) equivalent units of conversion costs. Hence, the beginning inventory at standard costs is:

Direct materials: 1,500 × $8.50/unit	$12,750
Conversion costs: 900 × $10.50/unit	9,450
Total manufacturing cost	$22,200

Exhibit 18-5, Panel A, shows the flow of production in physical units and equivalent units, including normal spoilage and abnormal spoilage. The steps are the same as for the FIFO method described in Exhibit 18-4. Panel B shows the cost per equivalent unit and the assignment of costs to units completed and transferred out (including normal spoilage), to abnormal spoilage, and to EI WIP. Panel B contains no calculation of a cost allocation rate because this rate is already given as a standard cost. The actual costs were provided in the initial table on page 892 but the total standard, or pro forma, costs must be assigned. Using the methods of Chapters 7 and 8, variances have been calculated and indicate unfavourable variances for both DM and conversion. This approach directs management attention to the impairment to gross margin, and, all other things equal, operating income this month. There is, as yet, no explanation for these variances.

Regardless of the method managers choose to assign conversion costs, the COGM, COGAS, and COGS must conform to the CICA standard for valuation of inventory. The three methods presented are in conformance, but all three methods arrive at the identical actual costs added during the month of July.

JOURNAL ENTRIES

The information from Panel B in Exhibits 18-3, 18-4, and 18-5 supports the following journal entries:

	Weighted Average		FIFO		STANDARD	
1. Finished Goods	$152,075		$151,600		$146,300	
Work in Process—Forming		$152,075		$151,600		$146,300
To transfer good units completed in July.						
2. Loss from Abnormal Spoilage	$ 5,925		$ 6,000		$ 5,700	
Work in Process—Forming		$ 5,925		$ 6,000		$ 5,700
To recognize abnormal spoilage detected in July.						
3. Work in Process—Forming (at standard costs)					$ 72,250	
Direct Materials Variances					4,250	
Forming Department Direct Materials Control						$ 76,500
To record actual direct materials used and total direct materials variances						
4. Work in Process—Forming (at standard costs)					$ 85,050	
Conversion Costs Variance					4,050	
Forming Department Conversion Costs Control						$ 89,100
To record actual conversion costs and total conversion cost variances						

ALLOCATING COSTS OF NORMAL SPOILAGE

Spoilage might actually occur at various points or stages of the production cycle, but spoilage is typically not detected until one or more specific points of inspection. The cost of spoiled units is assumed to be all costs incurred by spoiled units before

EXHIBIT 18-5
Use of Standard Cost in Process Costing with Spoilage—Forming Department of Anzio Company for July 2010

	A	B	C	D
1	**PANEL A: Summarize Output in Physical Units and Compute Equivalent Units**			
2			**Equivalent Units**	
3		**Physical**	**Direct**	**Conversion**
4	**Flow of Production**	**Units**	**Materials**	**Costs**
5	Work in process, beginning balance (given)	1,500		
6	Started during current period (given)	8,500		
7	To account for	10,000		
8	Good units completed and transferred out during the current period			
9	From beginning work in process inventory[a]	1,500		
10	$1,500 \times (100\% - 100\%)$; $1,500 \times (100\% - 60\%)$		–	600
11	Started and completed[b]	5,500		
12	$5,500 \times 100\%$; $5,500 \times 100\%$		5,500	5,500
13	Normal spoilage[c]	700		
14	$700 \times 100\%$; $700 \times 100\%$		700	700
15	Abnormal spoilage[d]	300		
16	$300 \times 100\%$; $300 \times 100\%$		300	300
17	Work in process, ending balance[e] (given)	2,000		
18	$2,000 \times 100\%$; $2,200 \times 50\%$		2,000	1,000
19	Accounted for	10,000		
20	Work done in current period only		8,500	8,100
21				
22	[a]Degree of completion in this department: direct materials, 100%; conversion costs, 60%.			
23	[b]7,000 physical units completed and transferred out minus 1,500 physical units completed and transferred from BI WIP			
24	[c]Normal spoilage is 10% of good units transferred out: $10\% \times 7,000 = 700$ units. Degree of completion of			
25	normal spoilage in this department: direct materials 100%; conversion costs 100%.			
26	[d]Abnormal spoilage = Actual spoilage – Normal spoilage = $1,000 - 700 = 300$ units. Degree of completion			
27	of abnormal spoilage in this department: direct materials 100%; conversion costs 100%.			
28	[e]Degree of completion in this department: direct materials 100%; conversion costs 50%.			
29	**PANEL B: Standard Cost per Equivalent Unit, Summarize Total Costs to Account For,**			
30	**and Assign Total Costs to Units Completed, to Spoiled Units, and to Units in Ending Work in Process**			
31		**Total**		
32		**Production**	**Direct**	**Conversion**
33		**Costs**	**Materials**	**Costs**
34	Standard cost per equivalent unit (given)	$ 19.00	$ 8.50	$ 10.50
35	Work in process, beginning balance (given)	$ 22,200		
36	Costs added in the current period (at standard)	157,300 =	72,250[g] +	85,050[h]
37	Total costs to account for	$179,500		
38	Cost per equivalent unit (at standard)		$ 8.50	$ 10.50
39	Assignment of costs:			
40	Good units completed and transferred out (7,000 units):			
41	Work in process beginning balance (1,500 units)	$ 22,200		
42	Costs added in current period[f] $(0 \times \$8.50; 600 \times \$10.50)$	6,300 =	$ – +	$ 6,300
43	Total from beginning inventory before normal spoilage	28,500		
44	Started and completed before normal spoilage (5,500 units)	104,500 =	46,750 +	57,750
45	Normal spoilage (700 units)	13,300 =	5,950 +	7,350
46 A	Total costs of good units completed and transferred out	146,300		
47 B	Abnormal spoilage (300 units)	5,700 =	2,550 +	3,150
48 C	Work in process, ending balance $(2,000 \times \$8.50; 1,000 \times \$10.50)$	27,500 =	17,000 +	10,500
49 A + B + C	Total costs accounted for:	$179,500	$ 72,250	$85,050
50	Summary of variances for current performance:			
51	Costs added in current period at standard costs (see above)		$ 72,250	$85,050
52	Actual costs incurred (given p. 892)		76,500	89,100
53	Variance		$ (4,250) U	$ (4,050) U
54				
55	[f]Equivalent units of direct materials and conversion costs calculated in Panel A			
56	[g]8,500 equivalent units × \$8.50			
57	[h]8,100 equivalent units × \$10.50			

inspection. When spoiled goods have a disposal value, the net cost of spoilage is computed by deducting disposal value from the costs of the spoiled goods accumulated to the point of inspection.

The unit costs of abnormal and normal spoilage are the same when the two are detected simultaneously. However, situations might arise when abnormal spoilage is detected at a different point from normal spoilage. In such cases, the unit cost of abnormal spoilage would differ from the unit cost of normal spoilage. Costs of abnormal spoilage are separately accounted for as losses for the period. Recall, however, that normal spoilage costs are added to costs of good units.

Accounting for normal spoilage, therefore, raises an additional issue: Should normal spoilage costs be allocated between completed units and ending WIP inventory? One approach is to presume that normal spoilage occurs at the inspection point in the production cycle and to allocate its cost over all units that have passed that point. In the Anzio Company example, spoilage is assumed to occur when finished units are inspected, so no cost of normal spoilage is allocated to EI WIP.

Whether the cost of normal spoilage is allocated to the units in EI WIP, in addition to completed units, depends strictly on whether they have passed the point of inspection. For example, if the inspection point is presumed to be the halfway stage of the production cycle, work in process that is more than 50% completed is allocated a full measure of normal spoilage costs, calculated on the basis of all costs incurred before the point of inspection. But work in process that is less than 50% completed is not allocated any normal spoilage costs. Additional discussion concerning various assumptions about spoilage appears in the next section.

INSPECTION AND SPOILAGE AT INTERMEDIATE STAGES OF COMPLETION

Consider how the timing of inspection at various stages of completion affects the amount of normal and abnormal spoilage. Assume that normal spoilage is 10% of the good units passing inspection in the Forging Department of Dana Corporation, a manufacturer of automobile parts. Direct materials are added at the start of production in the Forging Department. Conversion costs are allocated evenly during the process.

Suppose inspection had occurred at the 20%, 50%, or 100% completion stage. Spoilage totals 8,000 units in all cases. Note how the number of units of normal spoilage and abnormal spoilage change. Normal spoilage is computed on the number of *good units* that pass the inspection point *in the current period*. The following data are for October 2010.

Flow of Production	Physical Units Inspection at Stage of Completion		
	at 20%	at 50%	at 100%
Work in process, beginning (25%)[a]	11,000	11,000	11,000
Started during October	74,000	74,000	74,000
To account for	85,000	85,000	85,000
Good units completed and transferred out (85,000 − 8,000 spoiled − 16,000 ending)	61,000	61,000	61,000
Normal spoilage	6,600[b]	7,700[c]	6,100[d]
Abnormal spoilage (8,000 − normal spoilage)	1,400	300	1,900
Work in process, ending balance[a]	16,000	16,000	16,000
Accounted for	85,000	85,000	85,000

[a]Degree of completion for conversion costs of this department at the dates of the work-in-process inventories is 75%.

[b]10% × (74,000 units started − 8,000 units spoiled), since only the units started passed the 20% completion inspection point in the current period. Beginning work in process is excluded from this calculation because it is already 25% complete.

[c]10% × (85,000 units − 8,000 units spoiled), since *all* units passed the 50% completion inspection point in the current period.

[d]10% × 61,000 since 61,000 units were fully completed and inspected in the current period.

To see the number of units passing each inspection point, focus on the vertical lines at the 20%, 50%, and 100% inspection points in the diagram below. Note that the vertical line at 20% cuts two horizontal lines: 50,000 good units started and completed and 16,000 units in ending work in process, for a total of 66,000 good units. (It does not cut the line representing work done on the 11,000 good units completed from beginning work in process because these units were already 25% complete at the start of the period and hence were not inspected this period.) Normal spoilage equals 10% × 66,000 = 6,600 units. Similarly, the vertical line at the 50% point cuts all three horizontal lines, indicating that 11,000 + 50,000 + 16,000 = 77,000 good units pass this point. Normal spoilage in this case is 10% × 77,000 = 7,700 units. At the 100% point, normal spoilage = 10% × (11,000 + 50,000) = 6,100 units.

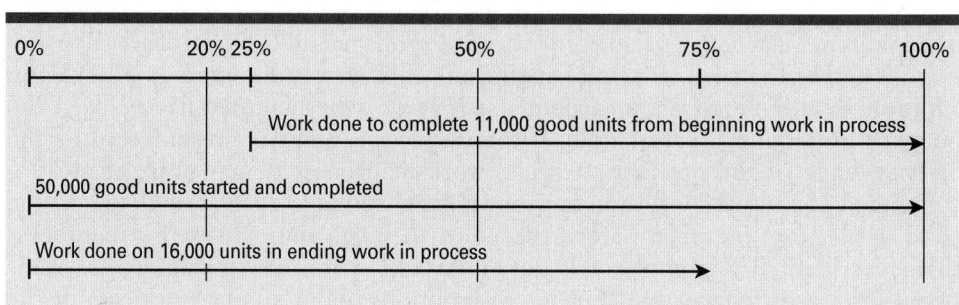

Exhibit 18-6 illustrates the computation of equivalent units assuming inspection at the 50% completion stage. The calculations depend on how much of the direct materials and conversion costs were incurred to get the units to the point of inspection. The spoiled units, in this case, have a full measure of direct materials and a 50% measure of conversion costs. The computations of equivalent-unit costs and the assignments of total costs to units completed and in ending work in process would be similar to those in previous illustrations. Since ending

EXHIBIT 18-6

Computing Equivalent Units with Spoilage Using Weighted-Average Method of Process Costing with Inspection at 50% of Completion for the Forging Department of Dana Corporation for October 2010

		Equivalent Units	
Flow of Production	**Physical Units**	**Direct Materials**	**Conversion Costs**
Work in process, beginning[a]	11,000		
Started during current period	74,000		
To account for	85,000		
Good units completed and transferred out	61,000	61,000	61,000
Normal spoilage	7,700		
(7,700 × 100%; 7,700 × 50%)		7,700	3,850
Abnormal spoilage	300		
(300 × 100%; 300 × 50%)		300	150
Work in process, ending[b]	16,000		
(16,000 × 100%; 16,000 × 75%)		16,000	12,000
Accounted for	85,000		
Total work done to date		85,000	77,000

[a]Degree of completion: direct materials, 100%; conversion costs, 25%.
[b]Degree of completion: direct materials, 100%; conversion costs, 75%.

work in process has passed the inspection point in this example, these units would bear normal spoilage costs, just like the units that have been completed and transferred out.

ASSESS YOUR MASTERY

To check your understanding of the material in Learning Objective ③, go to the *Mastery Questions* section at the end of this chapter and complete Learning Objective ③ questions 1, 2, and 3.

MyAccountingLab

JOB COSTING AND SPOILAGE

> Apply job cost allocation procedures to account for spoilage in job costing
>
> ④

The concepts of normal and abnormal spoilage also apply to job-costing systems. Abnormal spoilage is usually regarded as controllable by the manager. It is separately identified with the goal of eliminating it altogether. Costs of abnormal spoilage are not considered as product manufacturing costs and are written off as costs of the period in which detection occurs. Normal or planned spoilage in job-costing systems, however, is considered part of normal manufacturing costs, although increasingly, managements are tolerating only small amounts of spoilage as normal. The costs are then assigned to individually distinct jobs, a step unnecessary in process costing since masses of similar units are manufactured.

We illustrate the accounting for spoilage in job costing using the following example:

Example 3: In Hull Machine Shop, 5 aircraft parts out of a job lot of 50 aircraft parts are spoiled. Costs assigned up to the point of inspection are $100 per unit. Hull calculates these costs on the basis of its inventory costing assumptions—weighted average, FIFO, or standard costs. We do not, however, emphasize cost-flow assumptions in our presentation here or in subsequent sections. The current disposal price of the spoiled parts is estimated to be $30 per part. When the spoilage is detected, the spoiled goods are inventoried at $30 per unit.

Normal Spoilage Attributable to a Specific Job When normal spoilage occurs because of the specifications of a specific job, that job bears the cost of the spoilage reduced by the current disposal value of that spoilage. The journal entry to recognize the disposal value of the salvage (items in parentheses indicate subsidiary postings) is as follows:

Materials Control (spoiled goods at current disposal value): 5 × $30	$150	
Work-in-Process Control (specific job): 5 × $30		$150

The effect of this accounting is that the net cost of the normal spoilage, $350 ($500 – $150), becomes a direct cost of the 45 (50 – 5) good units produced.

Normal Spoilage Common to All Jobs In some cases, spoilage may be considered a normal characteristic of a given production cycle. The spoilage inherent in the process only coincidentally occurs when a specific job is being worked on. The spoilage then is not attributable, and hence is not charged, to the specific job. Instead, it is costed as manufacturing overhead. The budgeted manufacturing overhead allocation rate includes a provision for normal spoilage cost. Therefore, normal spoilage cost is spread, through overhead allocation, over all jobs rather than loaded on particular jobs only.[3]

---

[3]Note that costs *already assigned to products* are being charged back to Manufacturing Overhead Control, which generally accumulates only costs incurred, not both costs incurred and costs already assigned.

Materials Control (spoiled goods at current disposal value): 5 × $30	$150	
Manufacturing Department Overhead Control (normal spoilage): 5 × $70	350	
Work-in-Process Control (specific job): 5 × $100		$500

Abnormal Spoilage   If the spoilage is abnormal, the net loss is highlighted to management by charging the loss to an abnormal loss account:

Materials Control (spoiled goods at current disposal value): 5 × $30	$150	
Loss from Abnormal Spoilage: 5 × $70	350	
Work-in-Process Control (specific job): 5 × $100		$500

MyAccountingLab

ASSESS YOUR MASTERY

To check your understanding of the material in Learning Objective ④, go to the *Mastery Questions* section at the end of this chapter and complete Learning Objective ④ question 1.

REWORKED UNITS AND SCRAP

⑤ Apply cost allocation procedures to account for reworked units and scrap

Reworked units are unacceptable units of production that are subsequently reworked into good units and sold. The cost of rework is frequently material and therefore included in COGM.

Consider the Hull Machine Shop data (Example 3). Assume that the five spoiled parts used in our Hull Machine Shop illustration are reworked. The journal entry for the $500 of total costs (details of costs assumed) assigned to the five spoiled units before considering rework costs is as follows:

Work-in-Process Control	$500	
Materials Control		$200
Wages Payable		200
Manufacturing Overhead Allocated		100

Assume that rework costs equal $190 (direct materials, $40; direct labour, $100; manufacturing overhead, $50).

Normal Rework Attributable to a Specific Job   If the rework is normal but occurs because of the requirements of a specific job, the rework costs are charged to that job. The journal entry is as follows:

Work-in-Process Control (specific job)	$190	
Materials Control		$ 40
Wages Payable		100
Manufacturing Overhead Allocated		50

Normal Rework Common to All Jobs   When rework is normal and not attributable to any specific job, the costs of rework are charged to manufacturing overhead and spread, through overhead allocation, over all jobs.

Manufacturing Department Overhead Control (rework)	$190	
Materials Control		$ 40
Wages Payable		100
Manufacturing Overhead Allocated		50

Notice that the Manufacturing Overhead Control (MOH Control) and Manufacturing Overhead (MOH) are allocated in the same journal entry. MOH Control is debited because the normal rework is common to all jobs and is not attributable to a specific job. In this case, the additional MOH costs incurred to rework the units (for example, utilities, materials handling, inspection) are spread over all jobs by including an allowance for estimated rework in the pro forma MOH. This allowance is credited to MOH allocated.

Abnormal Rework   If the rework is abnormal, it is highlighted to management by charging abnormal rework to a separate loss account.

Loss from Abnormal Rework	$190	
Materials Control		$ 40
Wages Payable		100
Manufacturing Overhead Allocated		50

Accounting for rework in process costing only requires abnormal rework to be distinguished from normal rework. Abnormal rework is accounted for as in job costing. Since masses of similar units are manufactured, accounting for normal rework follows the accounting described for normal rework common to all jobs.

Costing rework highlights the resources wasted on activities that would not have to be undertaken if the product were made correctly. It prompts management to seek ways to reduce rework—for example, by designing new products or processes, training workers, or investing in new machines. Calculating rework costs helps management perform cost-benefit analyses for various alternatives. To emphasize the importance of eliminating rework and to simplify the accounting, some companies expense all rework, including the costs of normal rework, as an expense of the current period.

ACCOUNTING FOR SCRAP

Scrap is a product that has minimal (frequently zero) sales value compared with the sales value of the main or joint product(s).

There are two major aspects of accounting for scrap:

◆ Planning and control, including physical tracking
◆ Inventory costing, including when and how to affect operating income

Initial entries to scrap records are most often in physical or nonfinancial terms such as in kilograms or units. In various industries, items such as stamped-out metal sheets are quantified by weighing, counting, or some other expedient means. Scrap records not only help measure efficiency, but also often focus on a tempting source for theft. Scrap reports are prepared as source documents for periodic summaries of the amount of actual scrap compared with budgeted norms or standards. Scrap is either sold or disposed of quickly, or stored in some routine way for later sale, disposal, or reuse.

The tracking of scrap often extends into the financial records. For example, in one survey, 60% of the companies maintained a distinct cost for scrap somewhere in their cost accounting system.[4] The issues here are similar to those discussed in Chapter 15 regarding the accounting for byproducts:

◆ When should any value of scrap be recognized in the accounting records: at the time of production of scrap or at the time of sale of scrap?
◆ How should revenue from scrap be accounted for?

[4]Price Waterhouse, *Survey of the Cost Management Practices of Selected Midwest Manufacturers* (Cleveland: Price Waterhouse, 1989), p. 10.

To illustrate, we extend our Hull Machine Shop example by assuming that the manufacture of aircraft parts generates scrap. We further assume that the normal scrap from a job lot has a total sales value of $45.

RECOGNIZING SCRAP AT THE TIME OF SALE OF SCRAP

When scrap is sold, the simplest accounting is to regard scrap sales as a separate line item of other revenues. The journal entry is

Sale of scrap:	Cash or Accounts Receivable	$45	
	Sales of Scrap		$45

> ### THINKING CRITICALLY
>
> Why is there a difference in recording rework and scrap? Explain in a sentence or two. Read on for a discussion of this topic.

Rework costs are recorded when incurred because they tend to be material in their amount. Scrap has minimal salvage value and is not material. Scrap may not be recorded and included in COGM but rather recorded at the time of sale as COGS.

Scrap Attributable to a Specific Job Job-costing systems sometimes trace the sales of scrap to the jobs that yielded the scrap. This method is used only when the tracing can be done in an economically feasible way. For example, Hull Machine Shop and particular customers may reach an agreement that provides for charging specific jobs with all rework or spoilage costs, and for crediting these jobs with all scrap sales that arise from them. The journal entry is

Scrap returned to storeroom:	[No journal entry. Memo of quantity received and related job is entered in the inventory record.]		
Sale of scrap:	Cash or Accounts Receivable	$45	
	Work-in-Process Control		$45
	Posting made to specific job record.		

Unlike spoilage and rework, there is no cost attached to the scrap, and hence no normal or abnormal scrap. All scrap sales, whatever the amount, are credited to the specific job. Scrap sales reduce the costs of the job.

> ### THINKING CRITICALLY
>
> Why is this the timing of the scrap journal entry? Explain in a sentence or two. Read on for a discussion of this topic.

In job costing, the cost of scrap is already in the WIP account for each job generating the scrap. These costs are already accounted for, and therefore no journal entry is necessary. When the scrap is sold, however, the WIP account must be decreased (credited) to reduce the cost of the job by the amount of the scrap's disposal value.

Scrap Common to All Jobs In this case,

Scrap returned to storeroom:	[No journal entry. Memo of quantity received and related job is entered in the inventory record.]	

Managing Waste and Environmental Costs at Toyota

Currently, Toyota has reduced its landfill waste to less than 50% of the level in 1995 to approximately 59,000 tonnes per year from 160,000 tonnes per year, excluding recycled material. The volume of waste remaining in landfill after incineration and recycling was 8,900 tonnes. Yield improvements (reduction of scrap and waste of inputs) and the use of returnable and recyclable packaging have helped Toyota achieve this reduction. Currently the company has a vehicle recovery rate of 98% through design changes to create easy-to-remove components. Toyota has also eliminated the use of cadmium and chromium, reduced the use of PVC, and eliminated the use of asbestos in its vehicles.

Toyota's president defined waste as "anything other than the minimum amount of equipment, materials, parts, space, and workers' time which are absolutely essential to add value to the product."

Sources: J. Newberry, "A Goal of Zero," *Cincinnati Post* (June 30, 2003); Toyota Sustainability Report, 2006 www.toyota.co.jp/en/environmental_ rep/06/download/index.html accessed July 11, 2008.

This method does not link scrap with any particular physical product. Instead, all products bear regular production costs without any credit for scrap sales except in an indirect manner: The sales of scrap are considered when setting budgeted manufacturing overhead rates. Thus, the budgeted overhead rate is lower than it would be if no credit for scrap sales were allowed in the overhead budget. This accounting for scrap is used in both process-costing and job-costing systems.

RECOGNIZING SCRAP AT THE TIME OF PRODUCTION OF SCRAP

Our preceding illustrations assume that scrap returned to the storeroom is sold or disposed of quickly and hence not assigned an inventory cost figure. Scrap, however, sometimes has a significant market value, and the time between storing it and selling or reusing it can be quite long. Under these conditions, the company is justified in inventorying scrap at a conservative estimate of net realizable value so that production costs and related scrap recovery may be recognized in the same accounting period. Some companies tend to delay sales of scrap until the market price is most attractive. Volatile price fluctuations are typical for scrap metal. If scrap inventory becomes significant, it should be inventoried at some "reasonable value"—a difficult task in the face of volatile market prices.

Scrap Attributable to a Specific Job The journal entry in the Hull Machine Shop example is

Scrap returned to storeroom:
Materials Control	$45	
Work-in-Process Control		$45

Scrap Common to All Jobs The journal entry in this case is

Scrap returned to storeroom:
Materials Control	$45	
Manufacturing Department Overhead Control		$45

Observe that the Materials Control account is debited in place of Cash or Accounts Receivable.

When this scrap is sold, the journal entry is

| Sale of scrap: | Cash or Accounts Receivable | $45 | |
| | Materials Control | | $45 |

Scrap is sometimes reused as direct materials rather than sold as scrap. Then it should be debited to Materials Control as a class of direct materials and carried at its estimated net realizable value. For example, the entries when the scrap generated is common to all jobs are

Scrap returned to storeroom:	Materials Control	$45	
	Manufacturing Department Overhead Control		$45
Reuse of scrap:	Work-in-Process Control	$45	
	Materials Control		$45

The accounting for scrap under process costing follows the accounting for jobs when scrap is common to all jobs since process costing is used to cost the mass manufacture of similar units. The high cost of scrap focuses management's attention on ways to reduce scrap and to use it more profitably. For example, General Motors has redesigned its plastic injection moulding processes to reduce the scrap plastic that must be broken away from its moulded parts. General Motors also regrinds and reuses the plastic scrap as direct materials, saving substantial input costs.

MyAccountingLab

ASSESS YOUR MASTERY

To check your understanding of the material in Learning Objective 5, go to the *Mastery Questions* section at the end of this chapter and complete Learning Objective 5 question 1.

PULLING IT ALL TOGETHER—PROBLEM FOR SELF-STUDY

PROBLEM

Burlington Textiles has some spoiled goods that had an assigned cost of $40,000 and zero net disposal value.

REQUIRED

Prepare a journal entry for each of the following conditions under (a) process costing (Department A) and (b) job costing:

1. Abnormal spoilage of $40,000
2. Normal spoilage of $40,000 regarded as common to all operations
3. Normal spoilage of $40,000 regarded as attributable to specifications of a particular job

SOLUTION

(a) Process Costing			(b) Job Costing		
1. Loss from Abnormal Spoilage	$40,000		Loss from Abnormal Spoilage	$40,000	
Work in Process—Dept. A		$40,000	Work-in-Process Control (specific job)		$40,000
2. No entry until units are complete and transferred out; then the normal spoilage costs are transferred as part of the cost of good units.			Manufacturing Overhead Control	$40,000	
			Work-in-Process Control (specific job)		$40,000
Work in Process—Dept. B	$40,000				
Work in Process—Dept. A		$40,000			
3. Not applicable			No entry. Normal spoilage cost remains in Work-in-Process Control (specific job)		

The following decision guidelines use a question-and-answer format to summarize the chapter's main points. Each decision presents a key question. The guideline is the answer to that question.

DECISIONS	GUIDELINES
1. What are spoilage, rework, and scrap?	Spoilage is units of production that do not meet the standards required by customers for good units and that are discarded or sold for reduced prices. Rework is unacceptable units that are subsequently repaired and sold as acceptable finished goods. Scrap is material left over when making a product; it has low sales value compared with the sales value of the main product. Normal spoilage is inherent in a particular production process and arises even under efficient operating conditions. Abnormal spoilage would not arise under efficient operating conditions. Generally, accounting systems explicitly recognize both types of spoilage when computing the number of output units. Normal spoilage is typically included in the cost of good output units; abnormal spoilage is recorded as a loss for the accounting period in which it is detected.
2. How do the weighted-average method and FIFO method of process costing differ in calculating the costs of good units and spoilage?	The weighted-average method combines costs in beginning inventory with costs of the current period when determining the costs of good units (which include a normal spoilage amount) and the costs of abnormal spoilage. The FIFO method keeps separate the costs in beginning inventory from the costs of the current period when determining the costs of good units (which include a normal spoilage amount) and the costs of abnormal spoilage.
3. How does the standard-costing method of process costing calculate the costs of good units and spoilage?	The standard-costing method uses standard costs to determine the costs of good units (which include a normal spoilage amount) and the costs of abnormal spoilage.

4. How do job-costing systems account for spoilage and rework?	Normal spoilage specific to a job is assigned to that job, or, if common to all jobs, it is allocated as part of manufacturing overhead. Loss from abnormal spoilage is recorded as a cost of the accounting period in which it is detected. Completed reworked units should be indistinguishable from nonreworked good units. Normal rework can be assigned to a specific job, or, if common to all jobs, as part of manufacturing overhead. Abnormal rework is written off as a cost of the accounting period in which it is detected.
5. How is scrap accounted for?	Scrap is recognized in the accounting records either at the time of its sale or at the time of its production. Sale of scrap, if immaterial, is often recognized as other revenue. If material, the sale of scrap or its net realizable value reduces the cost of a specific job, or, if common to all jobs, reduces manufacturing overhead.

TERMS TO LEARN

This chapter contains definitions of the following important terms:

abnormal spoilage (p. 889)   normal spoilage (p. 889)   scrap (p. 889)
inspection point (p. 889)   reworked units (p. 888)   spoilage (p. 888)

MASTERY QUESTIONS

Mastery Questions are rated by proficiency level—elementary, intermediate, and advanced. The solutions appear in the Solutions to Mastery Questions section of MyAccountingLab.

LEARNING OBJECTIVE 1

1. **Recognition of loss from spoilage—Elementary.** Arokia Electronics manufactures cell phone models in its Saskatoon plant. Suppose the company provides you with the following information regarding operations for September 2010:

Total cell phones manufactured	10,000
Phones rejected as spoiled units	500
Total manufacturing cost	$209,000

Assume the spoiled units have no disposal value.

REQUIRED
1. What is the unit cost of making the 10,000 cell phones?
2. What is the total cost of the 500 spoiled units?
3. If the spoilage is considered normal, what is the increase in the unit cost of good phones manufactured as a result of the spoilage?

2. **Normal and abnormal spoilage in units—Intermediate.** The following data, in physical units, describe a grinding process for January:

Work in process, beginning	22,800
Started during current period	180,000
To account for	202,800

Spoiled units		14,400
Good units completed and transferred out		158,400
Work in process, ending		30,000
Accounted for		202,800

Inspection occurs at the 100% completion stage. Normal spoilage is 5% of the good units passing inspection.

REQUIRED

1. Compute the normal and abnormal spoilage in units.
2. Assume that the equivalent unit cost of a spoiled unit is $12. Compute the amount of potential savings if all spoilage were eliminated, assuming that all other costs would be unaffected. Comment on your answer.

LEARNING OBJECTIVE 2

1. **Weighted-average method, spoilage—Intermediate.** Superchip specializes in the manufacture of microchips for aircraft. Direct materials are added at the start of the production process. Conversion costs are added evenly during the process. Some units of this product are spoiled as a result of defects not detectable before inspection of finished goods. Normally, the spoiled units are 15% of the good units transferred out. Spoiled units are disposed of at zero net disposal price.

Superchip uses the weighted-average method of process costing. Summary data for September 2010 are

	Physical Units (microchips)	Direct Materials	Conversion Costs
Work in process, September 1*	400	$ 76,800	$ 12,240
Started during September 2010	1,700		
Good units completed and transferred out during September 2010	1,400		
Work in process, September 30†	300		
Costs added during September 2010		$453,600	$184,320

*Degree of completion: direct materials, 100%; conversion costs, 30%.
†Degree of completion: direct materials, 100%; conversion costs, 40%.

REQUIRED

1. For each cost element, compute the equivalent units. Show physical units in the first column.
2. For each cost element, calculate the cost per equivalent unit.
3. Summarize the total costs to account for, and assign these costs to units completed and transferred out (to normal spoilage), to abnormal spoilage, and to units in ending work in process.

2. **FIFO method, spoilage—Intermediate.** Refer to the information in Learning Objective 2, Question 1.

REQUIRED

Do Learning Objective 2, Question 1 using the FIFO method of process costing.

LEARNING OBJECTIVE 3

1. **Standard costing method, spoilage—Elementary.** Refer to the information in Learning Objective 2, Question 1. Suppose Superchip determines standard costs of $246 per (equivalent) unit for direct materials and $96 per (equivalent) unit for conversion costs for both beginning work in process and work done in the current period.

REQUIRED

Do Learning Objective 2, Question 1 using standard costs.

2. **Standard-costing method, spoilage, and journal entries—Intermediate.** Jordan Inc. is a manufacturer of vents for water heaters. The company uses a process-costing system to account for its

work-in-process inventories. When Job 852 was being processed in the machining department, a piece of sheet metal was off centre in the bending machine and two vents were spoiled. Because this problem occurs periodically, it is considered normal spoilage and is consequently recorded as an overhead cost. Because this step comes first in the procedure for making the vents, the only costs incurred were $575 for direct materials. Assume the sheet metal cannot be sold, and its cost has been recorded in work-in-process inventory.

REQUIRED
Prepare the journal entries to record the spoilage incurred.

3. **Physical units, inspection at various stages of completion—Advanced.** Normal spoilage is 8% of the good units passing inspection in a forging process. In March, a total of 10,000 units were spoiled. Other data include units started during March, 120,000; work in process, beginning, 14,000 units (23% completed for conversion costs); work in process, ending, 11,000 units (69% completed for conversion costs).

REQUIRED
In columnar form, compute the normal and abnormal spoilage in units, assuming inspection at 15%, 40%, and 100% stages of completion.

LEARNING OBJECTIVE 4

1. **Spoilage and job costing—Advanced.** (L. Bamber) COOP Foods produces a variety of items in accordance with special job orders from hospitals, plant cafeterias, and university dormitories. An order for 2,500 cases of green beans costs $7.20 per case: direct materials, $3.60; direct manufacturing labour, $2.40; and manufacturing overhead allocated, $1.20. The manufacturing overhead rate includes a provision for normal spoilage. Consider each requirement independently.

REQUIRED
1. Tasters at the company reject 200 of the 2,500 cases. The 200 cases are disposed of for $480. Assume that this rejection rate is considered normal. Prepare a journal entry to record this event, and calculate the unit cost if
   a. The rejection is attributable to exacting specifications of this particular job.
   b. The rejection is characteristic of the production process and is not attributable to this specific job.
   c. Are unit costs the same in requirements 1(a) and 1(b)? Explain your reasoning briefly.
2. Refer to the original data. Assume that a labourer dropped 200 cases. Suppose that part of the 200 cases could be sold to a nearby prison for $240 cash. Prepare a journal entry to record this event. Calculate and explain briefly the unit cost of the remaining 2,300 cases.
3. Refer to the original data. Tasters rejected 200 cases that had insufficient salt. The product can be placed in a vat, salt added, and reprocessed into cans. This operation, which is considered normal, will cost $240. Prepare a journal entry to record this event, and calculate the unit cost of all the cases if:
   a. This additional cost was incurred because of the exacting specifications of this particular job.
   b. This additional cost occurs regularly because of difficulty in seasoning.
   c. Are unit costs the same in requirements 3(a) and 3(b)? Explain your reasoning briefly.

LEARNING OBJECTIVE 5

1. **Job costing, scrap—Advanced.** Wheels Corporation makes two different types of hubcaps for cars—models HM3 and JB4. Circular pieces of metal are stamped out of steel sheets (leaving the edges as scrap), formed, and finished. The stamping operation is identical for both types of hubcaps. During May, Wheels manufactured 20,000 units of HM3 and 10,000 units of JB4. In May, manufacturing costs per unit of HM3 and JB4 before accounting for the scrap are as follows:

	HM3	JB4
Direct materials	$12.00	$18.00
Direct manufacturing labour	3.60	4.80
Materials-related manufacturing overhead (materials handling, storage, etc.)	2.40	3.60
Other manufacturing overhead	7.20	9.60
Unit manufacturing costs	$25.20	$36.00

Materials-related manufacturing costs are allocated to products at 20% of direct materials costs. Other manufacturing overhead is allocated to products at 200% of direct manufacturing labour costs. Since the same metal sheets are used to make both types of hubcaps, Wheels maintains no records of the scrap generated by the individual products. Scrap generated during manufacturing is accounted for at the time it is returned to the storeroom as an offset to materials-related manufacturing overhead. The value of scrap generated during May and returned to the storeroom was $8,400.

REQUIRED

1. Prepare a journal entry to summarize the accounting for scrap during May.
2. Suppose the scrap generated in May was sold in June for $8,400. Prepare a journal entry to account for this transaction.
3. What adjustments, if any, would you make for scrap when calculating the manufacturing cost per unit for HM3 and JB4 in May? Explain.

ASSIGNMENT MATERIAL

MyAccountingLab

Make the grade with MyAccountingLab: The questions, exercises, and problems marked in red can be found on MyAccountingLab at **www.myaccountinglab.com.** You can practise them as often as you want, and most feature step-by-step guided instructions to help you find the right answer. Exercises and problems with an Excel icon in the margin have an accompanying Excel template on MyAccountingLab.

SHORT-ANSWER QUESTIONS

18-1 Why is there an unmistakable trend in manufacturing to improve quality?

18-2 Distinguish among spoilage, reworked units, and scrap.

18-3 "Normal spoilage is planned spoilage." Discuss.

18-4 "Costs of abnormal spoilage are losses." Explain.

18-5 "What has been regarded as normal spoilage in the past is not necessarily acceptable as normal spoilage in the present or future." Explain.

18-6 "Units of abnormal spoilage are inferred rather than identified." Explain.

18-7 "In accounting for spoiled goods, we are dealing with cost assignment rather than cost incurrence." Explain.

18-8 "Total input includes abnormal as well as normal spoilage and is, therefore, inappropriate as a basis for computing normal spoilage." Do you agree? Explain.

18-9 "The point of inspection is the key to the allocation of spoilage costs." Do you agree? Explain.

18-10 "The unit cost of normal spoilage is the same as the unit cost of abnormal spoilage." Do you agree? Explain.

18-11 "In job costing, the costs of normal spoilage that occur while a specific job is being done are charged to the specific job." Do you agree? Explain.

18-12 "The costs of reworking defective units are always charged to the specific jobs where the defects were originally discovered." Do you agree? Explain.

18-13 "Abnormal rework costs should be charged to a loss account, not to manufacturing overhead." Do you agree? Explain.

18-14 When is a company justified in inventorying scrap?

18-15 How do managers use information about scrap?

EXERCISES

18-16 Normal and abnormal spoilage in units. The following data, in physical units, describe a grinding process for January:

1. Normal spoilage, 6,600 units

Work in process, beginning	19,000
Started during current period	150,000
To account for	169,000
Spoiled units	12,000
Good units completed and transferred out	132,000
Work in process, ending	25,000
Accounted for	169,000

Inspection occurs at the 100% completion stage. Normal spoilage is 5% of the good units passing inspection.

REQUIRED
1. Compute the normal and abnormal spoilage in units.
2. Assume that the equivalent-unit cost of a spoiled unit is $10. Compute the amount of potential savings if all spoilage were eliminated, assuming that all other costs would be unaffected. Comment on your answer.

18-17 Weighted-average method, spoilage, equivalent units. (CMA, adapted) Consider the following data for November 2010 from Grey Manufacturing Company, which makes silk pennants and uses a process-costing system. All direct materials are added at the beginning of the process, and conversion costs are added evenly during the process. Spoilage is detected upon inspection at the completion of the process. Spoiled units are disposed of at zero net disposal price. Grey Manufacturing Company uses the weighted-average method of process costing.

Total equivalent units for conversion costs, 9,750 units

	Physical Units (pennants)	Direct Materials	Conversion Costs
Work in process, November 1*	1,000	$ 1,423	$ 1,110
Started during November 2010	?		
Good units completed and transferred out during November 2010	9,000		
Normal spoilage	100		
Abnormal spoilage	50		
Work in process, November 30†	2,000		
Total costs added during November 2010		$12,180	$27,750

*Degree of completion: direct materials, 100%; conversion costs, 50%.
†Degree of completion: direct materials, 100%; conversion costs, 30%.

REQUIRED
Compute the equivalent units of work done in the current period for direct materials and conversion costs. Show physical units in the first column of your schedule.

18-18 Weighted-average method, assigning costs (continuation of 18-17).

Conversion cost per equivalent unit, $2.96

REQUIRED
For the data in Exercise 18-17, summarize total costs to account for, calculate the cost per equivalent unit for direct materials and conversion costs, and assign total costs to units completed and transferred out (including normal spoilage), to abnormal spoilage, and to units in ending work in process.

18-19 FIFO method, spoilage, equivalent units. Refer to the information in Exercise 18-17. Suppose Grey Manufacturing Company uses the FIFO method of process costing instead of the weighted-average method.

Total equivalent units for conversion costs in current period only, 9,250 units

REQUIRED
Compute equivalent units for direct materials and conversion costs. Show physical units in the first column of your schedule.

18-20 FIFO method, assigning costs (continuation of 18-19).

Conversion cost per equivalent unit, $3.00

REQUIRED
For the data in Exercise 18-19, use the FIFO method to summarize total costs to account for, calculate the cost per equivalent unit for direct materials and conversion costs, and assign total costs to units completed and transferred out (including normal spoilage), to abnormal spoilage, and to units in ending work in process.

18-21 Weighted-average method, spoilage. Appleton Company makes wooden toys in its Forming Department, and it uses the weighted-average method of process costing. All direct materials are added at the beginning of the process, and conversion costs are added evenly during the process. Spoiled units are detected upon inspection at the end of the process and are disposed of at zero net disposal value. Summary data for August 2010 are:

2

1. Total equivalent units for conversion costs, 11,550 units

	Physical Units (pennants)	Direct Materials	Conversion Costs
Work in process, November 1*	2,000	$17,700	$ 10,900
Started during November 2010	?		
Good units completed and transferred out during November 2010	9,000		
Normal spoilage	900		
Abnormal spoilage	300		
Work in process, November 30†	1,800		
Total costs added during November 2010		$12,000	$11,550

*Degree of completion: direct materials, 100%; conversion costs, 50%.
†Degree of completion: direct materials, 100%; conversion costs, 30%.

REQUIRED
1. For each cost category, calculate equivalent units. Show physical units in the first column of your schedule.
2. Summarize total costs to account for, calculate cost per equivalent unit for each cost category, and assign total costs to units completed and transferred out (including normal spoilage), to abnormal spoilage, and to units in ending work in process.

18-22 Standard costing method, spoilage, and journal entries. Aaron Inc. is a manufacturer of vents for water heaters. The company uses a process-costing system to account for its work-in-process inventories. When Job 512 was being processed in the machining department, a piece of sheet metal was off centre in the bending machine and two vents were spoiled. Because this problem occurs periodically, it is considered normal spoilage and is consequently recorded as an overhead cost. Because this step comes first in the procedure for making the vents, the only costs incurred were $250 for direct materials. Assume the sheet metal cannot be sold, and its cost has been recorded in work-in-process inventory.

3

REQUIRED
Prepare the journal entries to record the spoilage incurred.

18-23 Weighted-average method, spoilage. Chipcity Inc. is a fast-growing manufacturer of computer chips. Direct materials are added at the start of the production process. Conversion costs are added evenly during the process. Some units of this product are spoiled as a result of defects not detectable before inspection of finished goods. Spoiled units are disposed of at zero net disposal value. Chipcity uses the weighted-average method of process costing. Summary data for September 2010 are:

2

1. Total equivalent units for conversion costs, 2,880 units

	Physical Units (computer chips)	Direct Materials	Conversion Costs
Work in process, beginning inventory (Sept. 1)	600	$ 96,000	$ 15,300
Degree of completion of beginning WIP		100%	30%
Started during September	2,550		
Good units completed and transferred out during September	2,100		
Work in process, ending inventory (Sept. 30)	450		
Degree of completion of ending WIP		100%	40%
Total costs added during September		$567,000	$230,400
Normal spoilage as a percentage of good units	15%		
Degree of completion of normal spoilage		100%	100%
Degree of completion of abnormal spoilage		100%	100%

1. Total equivalent units for conversion costs in current period only, 2,700 units

2. Total costs to account for, $846,000

Normal spoilage at 15%, 8,190 units; abnormal spoilage at 40%, 2,690 units

1. Unit cost of remaining cases, $6.00

REQUIRED
1. For each cost category, compute equivalent units. Show physical units in the first column of your schedule.
2. Summarize total costs to account for, calculate cost per equivalent unit for each cost category, and assign total costs to units completed and transferred out (including normal spoilage), to abnormal spoilage, and to units in ending work in process.

18-24 FIFO method, spoilage. Refer to the information in Exercise 18-23.

REQUIRED
Do Exercise 18-23 using the FIFO method of process costing.

18-25 Standard-costing method, spoilage. Refer to the information in Exercise 18-23. Suppose Chipcity determines standard costs of $200 per equivalent unit for direct materials and $75 per equivalent unit for conversion costs for both beginning work in process and work done in the current period.

REQUIRED
Do Exercise 18-23 using the standard-costing method.

18-26 Physical units, inspection at various stages of completion. Normal spoilage is 7% of the good units passing inspection in a forging process. In March, a total of 12,000 units were spoiled. Other data include units started during March, 129,000; work in process, beginning, 16,000 units (20% completed for conversion costs); work in process, ending, 13,000 units (70% completed for conversion costs).

REQUIRED
In columnar form, compute the normal and abnormal spoilage in units, assuming inspection at 15%, 40%, and 100% stages of completion.

18-27 Spoilage and job costing. (L. Bamber) Bamber Kitchens produces a variety of items in accordance with special job orders from hospitals, plant cafeterias, and university dormitories. An order for 2,500 cases of mixed vegetables costs $6.00 per case: direct materials, $3.00; direct manufacturing labour, $2.00; and manufacturing overhead allocated, $1.00. The manufacturing overhead rate includes a provision for normal spoilage. Consider each requirement independently.

REQUIRED
1. Assume that a labourer dropped 200 cases. Suppose that part of the 200 cases could be sold to a nearby prison for $200 cash. Prepare a journal entry to record this event. Calculate and explain briefly the unit cost of the remaining 2,300 cases.
2. Refer to the original data. Tasters at the company reject 200 of the 2,500 cases. The 200 cases are disposed of for $400. Assume that this rejection rate is considered normal. Prepare a journal entry to record this event, and:
   a. Calculate the unit cost if the rejection is attributable to exacting specifications of this particular job.
   b. Calculate the unit cost if the rejection is characteristic of the production process and is not attributable to this specific job.
   c. Are unit costs the same in requirements 2(a) and 2(b)? Explain your reasoning briefly.
3. Refer to the original data. Tasters rejected 200 cases that had insufficient salt. The product can be placed in a vat, salt added, and reprocessed into jars. This operation, which is considered normal, will cost $200. Prepare a journal entry to record this event, and:
   a. Calculate the unit cost of all the cases if this additional cost was incurred because of the exacting specifications of this particular job.
   b. Calculate the unit cost of all the cases if this additional cost occurs regularly because of difficulty in seasoning.
   c. Are unit costs the same in requirements 3(a) and 3(b)? Explain your reasoning briefly.

18-28 Reworked units, costs of rework. Grey Goods assembles washing machines at its Cambridge plant. In February 2010, 60 tumbler units that cost $44 each from a new supplier were defective and had to be disposed of at zero disposal price. That new supplier is now bankrupt. Grey Goods was able to rework all 60 washing machines by substituting new tumbler units purchased from one of its existing suppliers. Each replacement tumbler cost $50.

REQUIRED
1. What alternative approaches are there to account for the materials costs of reworked units?
2. Should Grey Goods use the $44 or $50 amount as the costs of materials reworked? Explain.
3. What other costs might Grey Goods include in its analysis of the total costs of rework due to the tumbler units purchased from the (now) bankrupt supplier?

18-29 Scrap, job-order costing. Mendola Corp. has an extensive job-costing facility that uses a variety of metals. Consider each requirement independently.

REQUIRED
1. Job 372 uses a particular metal alloy that is not used for any other job. Assume that scrap is material in amount and sold for $490 quickly after it is produced. Prepare the journal entry.
2. The scrap from Job 372 consists of a metal used by many other jobs. No record is maintained of the scrap generated by individual jobs. Assume that scrap is accounted for at the time of its sale. Scrap totalling $4,000 is sold. Prepare two alternative journal entries that could be used to account for the sale of scrap.
3. Suppose the scrap generated in requirement 2 is returned to the storeroom for future use, and a journal entry is made to record the scrap. A month later, the scrap is reused as direct material on a subsequent job. Prepare the journal entries to record these transactions.

PROBLEMS

18-30 Weighted-average method, spoilage. Lang Manufacturing Company uses the weighted-average method of process costing. All direct materials are added at the beginning of the process, and conversion costs are added evenly during the process. Spoiled units are detected upon inspection at the end of the process and are disposed of at zero net disposal value. Summary data for March 2010 are

1. Total equivalent units for conversion costs, 72,000 units

	Physical Units	Direct Materials	Conversion Costs
Work in process, March 1*	30,000	$288,000	$216,000
Started during March 2010	50,000		
Good units completed and transferred out during March 2010	40,000		
Normal spoilage	6,000		
Abnormal spoilage	2,000		
Work in process, March 31†	32,000		
Total costs added during March 2010		$504,000	$699,840

*Degree of completion: direct materials, 100%; conversion costs, 60%.
†Degree of completion: direct materials, 100%; conversion costs, 75%.

REQUIRED
1. For each cost category, compute equivalent units. Show physical units in the first column of your schedule.
2. For each cost category, calculate cost per equivalent unit.
3. Summarize total costs to account for, and assign these costs to units completed and transferred out (including normal spoilage), to abnormal spoilage, and to units in ending work in process.

18-31 FIFO method, spoilage. Refer to the information in Problem 18-30.

1. Total equivalent units for conversion costs in current period only, 54,000 units

REQUIRED
Do Problem 18-30 using the FIFO method. Note that you first need to calculate the equivalent units of work done in the current period (for direct materials and conversion costs) to complete beginning work in process, to start and complete new units, for normal and abnormal spoilage units, and to produce ending work in process.

18-32 Standard-costing method, spoilage. Refer to the information in Problem 18-30. Suppose Lang determines standard costs of $9.60 per equivalent unit for direct materials and $12.00 per equivalent unit for conversion costs for both beginning work in process and work done in the current period.

2. Total costs to account for, $1,632,000

REQUIRED
Do Problem 18-30 using the standard-costing method. Note that you first need to calculate the equivalent units of work done in the current period (for direct materials and conversion costs) to complete beginning work in process, to start and complete new units, for normal and abnormal spoilage units, and to produce ending work in process.

18-33 Weighted-average method, spoilage. Windsor Company is a food-processing company. It operates under the weighted-average method of process costing and has two departments, Cleaning and Packaging. For the Cleaning Department, conversion costs are added uniformly throughout the processes, and direct materials are added at the beginning of the process. Spoiled units are detected upon inspection at the end of the process and are disposed of at zero net disposal value. All completed work is transferred to the Packaging Department. Summary data for May follow:

	Physical Units	Direct Materials	Conversion Costs
Work in process, beginning inventory (May 1)	2,500	$ 2,500	$ 2,000
Degree of completion of beginning WIP		100%	80%
Started during May	22,500		
Good units completed and transferred out during May	18,500		
Work in process, ending inventory (May 30)	4,000		
Degree of completion of ending WIP		100%	25%
Total costs added during May		$22,500	$20,000
Normal spoilage as a percentage of good units	10%		
Degree of completion of normal spoilage		100%	100%
Degree of completion of abnormal spoilage		100%	100%

REQUIRED

For the Cleaning Department, summarize total costs to account for, and assign total costs to units completed and transferred out (including normal spoilage), to abnormal spoilage, and to units in ending work in process. Carry unit-cost calculations to four decimal places when necessary. Calculate final totals to the nearest dollar. (Problem 18-35 explores additional facets of this problem.)

18-34 FIFO method, spoilage. Refer to the information in Problem 18-33.

REQUIRED

Do Problem 18-33 using the FIFO method of process costing. (Problem 18-36 explores additional facets of this problem.)

18-35 Weighted-average method, Packaging Department (continuation of 18-33). In Windsor Company's Packaging Department, conversion costs are added evenly during the process, and direct materials are added at the end of the process. Spoiled units are detected upon inspection at the end of the process and are disposed of at zero net disposal value. All completed work is transferred to the next department. The transferred-in costs for May equal the total cost of good units completed and transferred out in May from the Cleaning Department, which were calculated in Problem 18-33 using the weighted-average method of process costing. Summary data for May follow:

	Physical Units	Transferred-in Costs	Direct Materials	Conversion Costs
Work in process, beginning inventory (May 1)	7,500	$16,125	$ 0	$ 6,125
Degree of completion of beginning WIP		100%	0%	80%
Started during May	18,500			
Good units completed and transferred out during May	15,000			
Work in process, ending inventory (May 30)	10,000			
Degree of completion of ending WIP		100%	0%	25%
Total costs added during May		?	$1,600	$12,375
Normal spoilage as a percentage of good units	5%			
Degree of completion of normal spoilage			100%	100%
Degree of completion of abnormal spoilage			100%	100%

REQUIRED

For the Packaging Department, use the weighted-average method to summarize total costs to account for, and assign total costs to units completed and transferred out (including normal spoilage), to abnormal spoilage, and to units in ending work in process.

18-36 FIFO method, Packaging Department (continuation of 18-34). Refer to the information in Problem 18-35 except for the transferred-in costs for May, which equal the total cost of good units completed and transferred out in May from the Cleaning Department, which were calculated in Problem 18-34 using the FIFO method of process costing.

1. Total equivalent units for conversion costs in current period only, 12,500 units

REQUIRED

For the Packaging Department, use the FIFO method to summarize total costs to account for, and assign total costs to units completed and transferred out (including normal spoilage), to abnormal spoilage, and to units in ending work in process.

18-37 Physical units, inspection at various stages of completion. Normal spoilage is 6% of the good units passing inspection in a forging process. In March, a total of 10,000 units were spoiled. Other data include units started during March, 120,000; work in process, beginning, 14,000 units (20% completed for conversion costs); work in process, ending, 11,000 units (70% completed for conversion costs).

(a) Normal spoilage at 15%, 6,600 units;

(b) Abnormal spoilage at 40%, 2,560 units

REQUIRED

In columnar form, compute the normal and abnormal spoilage in units, assuming the inspection point is at (a) the 15% stage of completion, (b) the 40% stage of completion, and (c) the 100% stage of completion.

18-38 Weighted-average method, inspection at 80% completion. (A. Atkinson) Ottawa Manufacturing is a furniture manufacturer with two departments: moulding and finishing. The company uses the weighted-average method of process costing. In August, the following data were recorded for the Finishing Department:

Total equivalent units for conversion costs, 96,250 units

Units of beginning work-in-process inventory	12,500
Percentage completion of beginning work-in-process units	25%
Cost of direct materials in beginning work in process	$ 0
Units started	87,500
Units completed	62,500
Units in ending inventory	25,000
Percentage completion of ending work-in-process units	95%
Spoiled units	12,500
Total costs added during current period:	
Direct materials	$819,000
Direct manufacturing labour	$794,500
Manufacturing overhead	$770,000
Work in process, beginning:	
Transferred-in costs	$103,625
Conversion costs	$ 52,500
Cost of units transferred in during current period	$809,375

Conversion costs are added evenly during the process. Direct materials costs are added when production is 90% complete. The inspection point is at the 80% stage of production. Normal spoilage is 10% of all good units that pass inspection. Spoiled units are disposed of at zero net disposal value.

REQUIRED

For August, summarize total costs to account for, and assign these costs to units completed and transferred out (including normal spoilage), to abnormal spoilage, and to units in ending work in process.

18-39 Job-cost spoilage and scrap. (F. Mayne) Canadian Metal Fabricator Ltd. has a large job, No. 2734, that calls for producing various ore bins, chutes, and metal boxes for enlarging a copper concentrator. The following charges were made to the job in November 2010:

Direct materials	$40,400
Direct manufacturing labour	22,600
Manufacturing overhead	11,300

The contract with the customer called for the total price to be based on a cost-plus approach. The contract defined cost to include direct materials, direct manufacturing labour costs, and manufacturing overhead to be allocated at 50% of direct manufacturing labour costs. The contract also provided that the total costs of all work spoiled were to be removed from the billable cost of the job and that the benefits from scrap sales were to reduce the billable cost of the job.

REQUIRED

1. In accordance with the stated terms of the contract, prepare journal entries for the following two items:

   a. A cutting error was made in production. The up-to-date job cost record for the batch of work involved showed materials of $975, direct manufacturing labour of $600, and allocated overhead of $300. Because fairly large pieces of metal were recoverable, the company believed that the scrap value was $800 and that the materials recovered could be used on other jobs. The spoiled work was sent to the warehouse.

   b. Small pieces of metal cuttings and scrap in November 2010 amounted to $1,995, which was the price quoted by a scrap dealer. No journal entries were made with regard to the scrap until the price was quoted by the scrap dealer. The scrap dealer's offer was immediately accepted.

2. Consider normal and abnormal spoilage. Suppose the contract described above had contained the clause "a normal spoilage allowance of 1% of the job costs will be included in the billable costs of the job."

   a. Is this clause specific enough to define exactly how much spoilage is normal and how much is abnormal? Explain.

   b. Repeat requirement 1(a) with this "normal spoilage of 1%" clause in mind. You should be able to provide two slightly different journal entries.

18-40 Spoilage in job costing. Whitefish Machine Shop is a manufacturer of motorized carts for vacation resorts. Pat Cruz, the plant manager of Whitefish, obtains the following information for Job #10 in August 2010. A total of 40 units were started, and 5 spoiled units were detected and rejected at final inspection, yielding 35 good units. The spoiled units were considered to be normal spoilage. Costs assigned prior to the inspection point are $1,000 per unit. The current disposal price of the spoiled units is $200 per unit. When the spoilage is detected, the spoiled goods are inventoried at $200 per unit.

REQUIRED

1. What is the normal spoilage rate?
2. Prepare the journal entries to record the normal spoilage, assuming:
   a. The spoilage is related to a specific job.
   b. The spoilage is common to all jobs.
   c. The spoilage is considered to be abnormal spoilage.

18-41 Rework in job costing, journal entry (continuation of 18-40). Assume that the five spoiled units of Whitefish Machine Shop's Job #10 can be reworked for a total cost of $1,800. A total cost of $5,000 associated with these units has already been assigned to Job #10 before the rework.

REQUIRED

Prepare the journal entries for the rework, assuming:
a. The rework is related to a specific job.
b. The rework is common to all jobs.
c. The rework is considered to be abnormal.

18-42 Scrap at time of sale or at time of production, journal entries (continuation of 18-40). Assume that Job #10 of Whitefish Machine Shop generates normal scrap with a total sales value of $300 (it is assumed that the scrap returned to the storeroom is sold quickly).

REQUIRED

Prepare the journal entries for the recognition of scrap, assuming:
a. The value of scrap is immaterial and scrap is recognized at the time of sale.
b. The value of scrap is material, is related to a specific job, and is recognized at the time of sale.
c. The value of scrap is material, is common to all jobs, and is recognized at the time of sale.
d. The value of scrap is material, scrap is recognized as inventory at the time of production, and is recorded at its net realizable value.

18-43 Job costing, rework. Solutions Corporation is a manufacturer of computer chips based in Nepean. It manufactures two types of computer chips, CS1 and CS2. The costs of manufacturing each CS1 chip, excluding rework costs, are direct materials, $60; direct manufacturing labour, $12; and manufacturing overhead, $38. Defective units are sent to a separate rework area. Rework costs per CS1 chip are direct materials, $12; direct manufacturing labour, $9; and manufacturing overhead, $15.

⑤

In August 2010, Solutions manufactured 1,000 CS1 chips and 500 CS2 chips; 80 of the CS1 chips and none of the CS2 chips required rework. Solutions classifies 50 of the CS1 chips reworked as normal rework caused by inherent problems in its production process that coincidentally occurred only during the production of CS1. Hence the rework costs for these 50 CS1 chips are normal rework costs not specifically attributable to the CS1 product. Solutions classifies the remaining 30 units of CS1 chips reworked as abnormal rework. Solutions allocates manufacturing overhead on the basis of machine-hours required to manufacture CS1 and CS2. Each CS1 and CS2 chip requires the same number of machine-hours.

REQUIRED

1. Prepare journal entries to record the accounting for the cost of the spoiled chips and for rework.
2. What were the total rework costs of CS1 chips in August 2010?

18-44 Job costing, spoilage, governance. (CMA, adapted) Richmond Company manufactures products that often require specification changes or modifications to meet customers' needs. Still, Richmond has been able to establish a normal spoilage rate of 2.5% of normal input. Normal spoilage is recognized during the budgeting process and classified as a component of manufacturing overhead when determining the overhead rate.

④

1. Normal spoilage, 3,000 units

Rose Drummond, one of Richmond's inspection managers, obtains the following information for Job No. R1192-122 that was recently completed. A total of 122,000 units were started, and 5,000 units were rejected at final inspection yielding 117,000 good units. Drummond noted that 900 of the first units produced were rejected because of a design defect that was considered very unusual; this defect was corrected immediately, and no further units were rejected for this reason. These units were disposed of after incurring an additional cost of $1,440. Drummond was unable to identify a rejection pattern for the remaining 4,100 rejected units. These units can be sold at $8.40 per unit.

Direct materials	$2,635,200
Direct manufacturing labour	2,196,000
Manufacturing overhead	3,513,600
Total manufacturing costs	$8,344,800

The total costs for all 122,000 units of Job No. R1192-122 are presented here. The job has been completed, but the costs have yet to be transferred to finished goods.

REQUIRED

1. Calculate the unit quantities of normal and abnormal spoilage.
2. Prepare the appropriate journal entry (or entries) to properly account for Job No. R1192-122 including spoilage, disposal, and transfer of costs to finished goods control.
3. Richmond Company has small profit margins and is anticipating very low operating income for the year. The controller, Thomas Rutherford, tells Martha Perez, the management accountant responsible for Job No. R1192-122, the following: "This was an unusual job. I think all 5,000 spoiled units should be considered normal." Martha knows that similar jobs had been done in the past and that the spoilage levels for Job R1192-122 were much greater than in the past. She feels Thomas made these comments because he wants to show higher operating income for the year.
   a. Prepare the journal entry (or entries), similar to the journal entry (or entries) prepared in requirement 2, to account for Job No. R1192-122 if all spoilage were considered normal. By how much will Richmond's operating income be affected if all spoilage is considered normal?
   b. What should Martha Perez do?

COLLABORATIVE LEARNING CASE

18-45 FIFO method, spoilage, working backward. The Cooking Department of Spicier Inc. uses a process-costing system. Direct materials are added at the beginning of the cooking process. Conversion costs are added evenly during the cooking process. Consider the following data for the Cooking Department of Spicier Inc. for January:

	Physical Units	Direct Materials	Conversion Costs
Work in process, January 1*	10,000	$ 264,000	$ 36,000
Started during January	74,000		
Good units completed and transferred out during January	61,000		
Spoiled units	8,000		
Work in process, January 31†	15,000		
Costs added during January		$1,776,000	$1,130,400
Cost per equivalent unit of work done in January		$ 24	$ 14.40

*Degree of completion: direct materials, 100%; conversion costs, 60%.
†Degree of completion: direct materials, 100%; conversion costs, 75%.

Spicier uses the FIFO method of process costing. Inspection occurs when production is 100% completed. Normal spoilage is 11% of good units completed and transferred out during the current period.

INSTRUCTION
Form pairs of students to complete the following requirements.

REQUIRED
1. For each cost category, compute equivalent units of work done in the current period (January).
2. For each cost category, compute equivalent units of work done to complete beginning work-in-process inventory, to start and complete new units, for normal and abnormal spoilage units, and to produce ending work-in-process inventory.
3. For each cost category, calculate the percentage of completion of ending work-in-process inventory.
4. Summarize total costs to account for, and assign these costs to units completed (and transferred out), normal spoilage, abnormal spoilage, and ending work in process.

Cost Management: Quality, Time, and the Theory of Constraints

BUSINESS MATTERS

Improve Poor Quality

Defective components can cause dramatic consequences. One flawed component used in computers that control space shuttle engines caused a space shuttle engine to shut down 1.5 seconds into its ignition sequence. The defect, discovered during a firing test with an empty shuttle, did not threaten any lives. Testing revealed an undisclosed flaw. After an extensive investigation, approximately 1,600 components were purged from the controllers.

LEARNING OBJECTIVES

After studying this chapter, you should be able to

1. Apply balanced scorecard (BSC) concepts to the analysis of quality

2. Analyze quality-control problems using three methods

3. Analyze the benefits of using both financial and nonfinancial measures of quality

4. Evaluate methods using time as a competitive tool

5. Evaluate the strengths and weaknesses of the theory of constraints (TOC) and activity-based costing (ABC) for managing bottlenecks

This chapter applies the concepts of the balanced scorecard (Chapter 13) to illustrate how managers can improve quality, time, and internal processes as competitive tools. Global competition and increasing customer intolerance for long wait times and poor quality means managers must work hard to remove obstructions to achieving on-time deliveries and satisfactory standards of quality. This chapter examines how management accounting information assists managers to take the initiative in the quality and time areas, and to improve the decisions they must make when faced with many constraints. Chapter 19 expands on the discussion of the balanced scorecard introduced in Chapter 13. The balanced scorecard is a set of performance measures that provide a framework for implementing an organization's mission and strategy. The focus will be on those measures that relate to using quality, time, and increased throughput to satisfy customers and gain competitive advantage.

◆ PART ONE

QUALITY AS A COMPETITIVE TOOL

1 Apply balanced scorecard (BSC) concepts to the analysis of quality

In an increasingly challenging world of global competition, most companies view quality management as one of the most important strategies for success. Quality on the production line (conformance to technical specifications) reduces costs and high-quality outputs increase customer satisfaction. Several prestigious, high-profile awards—for example, the Malcolm Baldrige Quality Award in North America, the Deming Prize in Japan, and the Premio Nacional de Calidad in Mexico—have been instituted to recognize exceptional quality.

Global companies can readily access international standards on everything from graphical symbols to nuclear power plants. The ISO certification is confirmation that a company is conforming to a specific level of quality. ISO 9001 is the international benchmark for global quality systems management, and ISO 14001 for environmental management.

The Standards Council of Canada issues accreditation to companies meeting the ISO 14001 standards of environmental management. This ISO standard describes principles and frameworks for (1) environmental management systems to improve the environmental impact of an organization's activities, products, and services and (2) environmental auditing and performance evaluation systems to review and provide feedback on how well an organization has achieved its environmental goals. Canada also has formal environmental legislation. Corporate governance failures to conform can result in multi-million-dollar fines.

ISO 14064 standards for greenhouse gas accounting (GHG), reporting, and emissions trading are actively promoted by the World Resources Institute (WRI) and the World Business Council for Sustainable Development (WBCSD). ISO 22000 set standards on food safety management, ISO 22005 on traceability, and ISO/TS 22003 on auditing and certification of these standards. The ISO 28000 standards on supply-chain security management address security issues at all stages of the supply process to manage threats such as terrorism, fraud, and piracy. Among other projects, ISO is currently developing standards on social responsibility (ISO 26000).[1]

THE BSC—FOUR PERSPECTIVES TO MEASURE THE COSTS OF QUALITY

The term *quality* refers to a wide variety of factors—fitness for use, the degree to which a product satisfies the needs of a customer, and the degree to which a product conforms to design specification and engineering requirements. We discuss two basic aspects of quality—**quality of design** and **conformance quality**. Both aspects of quality can be addressed throughout the functions of the business value chain because quality of design, for example, applies equally to production, supply-chain management, and corporate governance systems.

[1]ISO Annual Report 2007 at www.iso.org/iso/annual_report_2007.pdf, accessed July 11, 2008.

Quality of design measures how closely the characteristics of products or services match the needs and wants of customers. Suppose customers of photocopying machines want copiers that combine copying, faxing, scanning, and electronic printing. Photocopying machines that fail to meet these needs fail in the quality of their design. Similarly, if customers of a bank want an automated payment system for their monthly bills, not providing this facility would be a quality of design failure.

Conformance quality is the performance of a product or service according to design and production specifications. For example, if a photocopying machine mishandles paper or breaks down, it will have failed to satisfy conformance quality. Products not conforming to specifications must be repaired, reworked, or scrapped at an additional cost to the organization (see Chapter 18).

Uncorrected nonconformance errors by producers and suppliers through changes to design, production, and inspection will result in product or service failure in the customer's hands. One such situation occurred when the space shuttle *Challenger* exploded shortly after takeoff. Lives were lost in this event televised worldwide. The engineering company, Morton Thiokol, responsible for manufacturing the part which did not conform to technical specifications had no second chance to recover business. An investigation revealed not only a failure in production but also a failure in quality management because top executives had been informed of conformance problems and failed to respond. Morton Thiokol eventually declared bankruptcy. In the banking industry, depositing a customer's cheque into the wrong bank account is an example of conformance quality failure. The following diagram illustrates our framework for quality of conformance and design:

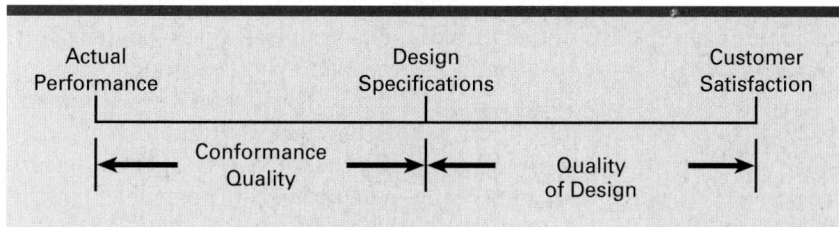

Within this framework are the tasks of managing quality such as identifying quality problems, estimating the costs of quality failures, and estimating the costs of different actions taken to improve quality. In fact, quality-management systems are one part of an overall enterprise risk management (ERP) assessment. We use the Photon Corporation as an example. Photon makes many products. Our presentation focuses on Photon's photocopying machines, which earned an operating income of $24 million on sales of $300 million (20,000 copiers) in 2010.

In Chapter 13, four perspectives from the balanced scorecard (BSC) were introduced: financial, customer, internal business process, and learning and growth. This discussion begins with financial measures of quality, in particular the costs of conformance quality. The financial costs of poor design quality are primarily the opportunity costs of future lost sales if Photon fails to design a product that meets its customers' demands at a price they are willing to pay.

Objective measures of opportunity costs—of something that does not occur—are notoriously difficult, which is why Photon highlights the customer perspective when estimating its opportunity costs. Remedies, however, are found primarily in changes to improve the internal business process of quality control. Thus the perspectives of the BSC are interdependent for successful execution of a quality-management strategy.

FINANCIAL PERSPECTIVE

The financial perspective of Photon's balanced scorecard includes measures such as revenue growth and operating income—financial measures that are likely to be affected by quality-improvement programs. Photon measures **costs of quality (COQ)**. The COQ are costs incurred to prevent or rectify the production of a low-quality product. Management accountants who apply various techniques to measure these costs are producing a means to an end. The costs are important relevant information to managers who must decide on what action to take to achieve conformance targets. These costs focus on conformance quality and are incurred in all areas of the value chain. They are classified into four categories:

1. **Prevention costs.** Costs incurred to preclude the production of products that do not conform to specifications

2. **Appraisal costs.** Costs incurred to detect which of the individual units of products do not conform to specifications

3. **Internal failure costs.** Costs incurred to detect a nonconforming product before it is shipped to customers

4. **External failure costs.** Costs incurred to detect a nonconforming product after it is shipped to customers

Exhibit 19-1 presents examples of individual cost of quality items in each of these four categories reported on COQ reports.

The items in Exhibit 19-1 are all derived from the business functions comprising the value chain and expand on the internal failure costs of spoilage, rework, and scrap described in Chapters 15 and 18. Photon determines the costs of quality of its photocopying machines using the costing process illustrated in Exhibit 4-2 on page 143.

The top management team will be implementing ABC and for this overhead cost has selected the photocopying machines as the cost object. There are 20,000 photocopiers and the goal is to calculate the total costs of quality for these machines. There are no direct costs of quality. To implement a full quality-management system, the indirect costs of quality will pertain to prevention, appraisal, internal failure, and external failure. Failure costs in the form of spoilage and rework (Chapter 18) are only a part of total internal failure costs of the photocopier manufacturing process.

The costs incurred in the internal system of production are summarized in Exhibit 19-2. The costs include either cost driver or allocation rates, the quantity of either the cost driver or the cost allocation base, the total costs, and the performance measure of cost as a percentage of revenue. The term cost driver refers to the ABC allocation method, whereas cost allocation base is used when non-ABC allocation methods are chosen to assign indirect costs (see Chapters 4 and 5). Photon uses the ABC method. For example, Photon's team chose as the cost driver the inspection hours rather than inspections for the inspection activity. Inspection hours has a better cause-and-effect relationship with inspection costs, which means change in the quantity of inspection hours can explain most of the change in the value of this cost pool.

The team must also decide on what costs, both fixed and variable, constitute a homogeneous cost pool (see Chapter 14) for each activity throughout all the business functions of the value chain. This is one reason why the ABC strategy fits well with BSC. Both ABC and BSC require understanding interdependence. A quality-management strategy includes all internal business functions, not merely production.

EXHIBIT 19-1
Items Pertaining to Cost-of-Quality Reports

Prevention Costs	Appraisal Costs	Internal Failure Costs	External Failure Costs
Design engineering	Inspection	Spoilage	Customer support
Process engineering	Online product manufacturing and process inspection	Rework	Manufacturing/ process engineering for external failures
Supplier evaluations		Scrap	
Preventive equipment maintenance		Machine repairs	
Quality training	Product testing	Manufacturing/process engineering on internal failures	Warranty repair costs
Testing of new materials			Liability claims

EXHIBIT 19-2
Analysis of Activity-Based Costs of Quality (COQ) for Photocopying Machines at Photon Corporation

	A	B	C	D	E	F	G
1	**PANEL A: COQ REPORT**						**Percentage of**
2		**Cost Allocation**		**Quantity of Cost**		**Total**	**Revenues**
3	**Cost of Quality and Value-Chain Category**	**Rate**[a]		**Allocation Base**		**Costs**	**(5) = (4) ÷**
4	(1)	(2)		(3)		(4) = (2) × (3)	**$300,000,000**
5	*Prevention costs*						
6	Design engineering (R & D/Design)	$ 80	per hour	40,000	hours	$ 3,200,000	1.1%
7	Process engineering (R & D/Design)	$ 60	per hour	45,000	hours	2,700,000	0.9
8	Total prevention costs					5,900,000	2.0
9	*Appraisal costs*						
10	Inspection (Manufacturing)	$ 40	per hour	240,000	hours	9,600,000	3.2
11	Total appraisal costs					9,600,000	3.2
12	*Internal failure costs*						
13	Rework (Manufacturing)	$100	per hour	100,000	hours	10,000,000	3.3
14	Total internal failure costs					10,000,000	3.3
15	*External failure costs*						
16	Customer support (Marketing)	$ 50	per hour	12,000	hours	600,000	0.2
17	Transportation (Distribution)	$240	per load	3,000	loads	720,000	0.2
18	Warranty repair (Customer service)	$110	per hour	120,000	hours	13,200,000	4.4
19	Total external failure costs					14,520,000	4.8
20	Total costs of quality					$40,020,000	13.3
21							
22	[a]Amounts assumed.						
23							
24	**PANEL B: OPPORTUNITY COST ANALYSIS**						
25						**Total Estimated**	**Percentage**
26						**Contribution**	**of Revenues**
27	**Cost of Quality Category**					**Margin Lost**	**(3) = (2) ÷**
28	(1)					(2)	**$300,000,000**
29	*External failure costs*						
30	Estimated forgone contribution margin						
31	and income on lost sales					$12,000,000[b]	4.0%
32	Total external failure costs					$12,000,000	4.0
33							
34	[b]Calculated as total revenues minus all variable costs (whether output-unit, batch, product-sustaining, or facility-sustaining) on lost sales in 2010. If poor quality causes Photon to lose sales in subsequent years as well, the opportunity costs will be even greater.						

Having established the activities, cost drivers, and cost pools it is straightforward to calculate each cost driver rate and assign cost to the photocopying machines. The quantities of each activity consumed are in column 3 of Exhibit 19-2. For example, photocopying machines use 240,000 inspection-hours. Column 4 of Exhibit 19-2, Panel A, shows the indirect costs of quality of the photocopying machines. The indirect costs of quality of the photocopying machines (column 4, Panel A) equal the total quantity of the cost allocation base used by the photocopying machines for each activity (column 3) multiplied by the cost allocation rate (column 2).

Photon's total cost of quality in the COQ report for photocopying machines is $40.02 million (bottom of column 4, Panel A), or 13.3% of current revenues (bottom of column 5). Costs reported on this COQ do not represent the total costs of quality for a company's photocopying process. COQ reports typically exclude opportunity costs, such as forgone contribution margins and income from lost sales, lost production, or lower prices, that result from poor quality. Opportunity costs (potential cost savings) are difficult to estimate and are generally not recorded in financial accounting systems. Nevertheless, opportunity costs can be substantial. Managerial accountants should provide information about opportunity costs to direct management's attention toward key items to remedy with quality-improvement programs. Neglecting such change will probably cause financial loss.

CUSTOMER-SERVICE PERSPECTIVE

Using data from the Market Research Department, Photon Corporation's management team estimates the financial value of probable lost sales of 2,000 photocopying machines because of external failures. The forgone contribution and operating income of $12 million measures the financial costs from dissatisfied customers who have returned machines to Photon and from sales lost because potential new customers become aware of quality problems. Total costs of quality (including opportunity costs) equal $52.02 million (Panel A, $40.02 million + Panel B, $12 million), or 17.34% of current sales. Opportunity costs account for 23% ($12 million ÷ $52.02 million) of Photon's total costs of quality.

The COQ report and the opportunity cost analysis highlight Photon's high internal and external failure costs. The advantage of the balanced scorecard framework is that Photon does not have to wait for this opportunity cost to arise nor to analyze its financial results to estimate the costs of quality failure. The nonfinancial measures of the customer perspective in the balanced scorecard provide advance warning of the potential costs of internal and external failure.

Even if products and services are defect-free and fully satisfy conformance quality, they will not be effective or sell well unless they also have design quality—that is, unless they satisfy customer needs. Usually management accountants are responsible for maintaining and reporting nonfinancial measures. Similar to companies such as Toyota, Photon measures customer satisfaction trends over time. Measures include:

◆ Market research information on customer preferences and satisfaction with specific attributes and the overall value proposition
◆ Market share
◆ Percentage of customers giving high customer satisfaction ratings
◆ Number of customer complaints (companies estimate that for every customer who actually complains, there are 10 to 20 others who have had bad experiences with the product but have not complained)
◆ Percentage of products that fail soon after delivery
◆ Customer-response time (the difference between scheduled delivery date and date requested by the customer)
◆ On-time delivery rate (percentage of shipments made on or before the scheduled delivery date)

Often customer complaints arise because of technical non-conformance, an internal production process failure frequently measured as defect rate or mean time between failures (MTBF). Federal Express, for example, tracks measures of customer satisfaction similar to those listed above in its overnight delivery business. Management steps in and investigates if, over time, these numbers deteriorate below standard performance thresholds.

In addition to these routine nonfinancial measures, many companies such as Procter & Gamble conduct surveys to measure customer satisfaction. Surveys serve two objectives. First, they provide a deeper perspective into customer experiences and preferences. Second, they provide a glimpse into features that customers would like future products to have.

MyAccountingLab

ASSESS YOUR MASTERY

To check your understanding of the material in Learning Objective ❶, go to the *Mastery Questions* section at the end of this chapter and complete Learning Objective ❶ questions 1 and 2.

Tools such as statistical quality control (SQC) or statistical process control (SPC) provide relevant nonfinancial quantitative information. These data are a formal means of distinguishing between random variation and nonrandom variation in an operating process. A key method of reporting SQC results is a **control chart**. A control chart illustrates in a graph a time series (see Chapter 10) of successive observations of a particular step, procedure, or operation taken at regular time intervals. In addition to actual results, the expected range of specified results is also presented. Only **outliers**, those observations outside the specified limits, are ordinarily regarded as nonrandom and worth investigating.

Exhibit 19-3 presents control charts for the daily defect rates observed at Photon's three production lines. Defect rates in the prior 60 days for each plant were assumed to provide a good basis from which to calculate the distribution of daily defect rates. The arithmetic mean (μ, read "mu") and standard deviation (σ, read "sigma") are the two parameters of the distribution that are used in the control charts in Exhibit 19-3. On the basis of experience, the company decides that any observation outside the $\mu \pm 2\sigma$ range should be investigated.

In a standard normal distribution, the arithmetic mean of the population or μ is simply the sum of all observed values divided by the number of observations made. The standard deviation measures how much each actual observation deviates from the mean. If the deviation is caused by random factors then 68.27% of all observed values will fall within one standard deviation (either + or –) from the mean.

Approximately 95.45% will fall within two, 99.73% within three, 99.994% within four, 99.9994% within five, and 99.9999998% within six standard deviations of the mean. Companies with a reputation for the highest quality achieve what is known as sigma6 quality. That is to say their failure rate is less than or equal to 1 in 10 million. Photon's goal is to achieve less than or equal to 4.55 or approximately 5 failures out of every 100 photocopiers produced. While this may be a measure of high quality for a photocopier, for a heart valve used to replace a damaged human valve this is not a satisfactory failure rate.

In Exhibit 19-3 all observations for production line A are within the range of $\pm 2\sigma$ from the mean. The report signals no investigation is necessary. The last two observations for production line B signal that an out-of-control occurrence is highly probable. Given the $\pm 2\sigma$ rule, this would lead to an investigation. Production line C illustrates a process that would not prompt an investigation under the $\pm 2\sigma$ rule but may well be out of control. Note that the last eight observations show a clear

EXHIBIT 19-3
Statistical Quality Control Charts: Daily Defect Rate at the Photon Corporation

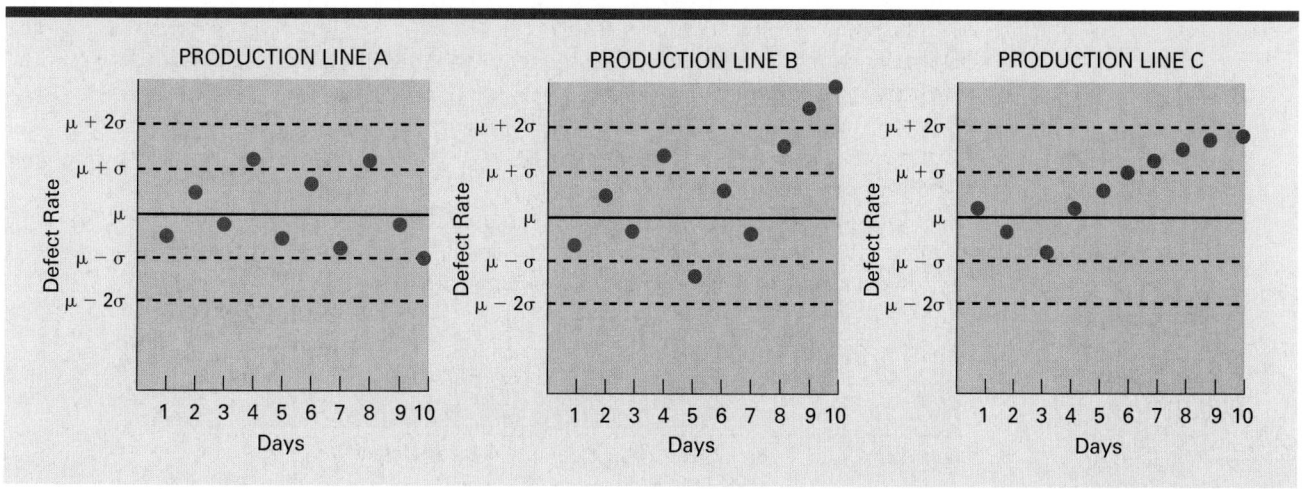

direction and that the direction by day 5 is away from the mean. Statistical procedures have been developed using the trend as well as the level of the variable in question to evaluate whether a process is out of control.

PARETO DIAGRAMS

Observations outside control limits serve as inputs to *Pareto diagrams*. A **Pareto diagram** or frequency chart indicates how frequently each type of failure (defect) occurs. Exhibit 19-4 presents a Pareto diagram for Photon's quality problems. Fuzzy and unclear copies are the most frequently recurring problem.

The fuzzy-copy problem results in high rework costs, because, in many cases, Photon discovers the fuzzy image problem only after the copier has been built. Sometimes fuzzy images occur at customer sites, resulting in high warranty and repair costs. This Pareto diagram is another attention-directing report but the real value added arises from determining the cause(s) of the defect rate.

The SQC signalled where the quality problem is most likely to arise: Production lines B and C. The Pareto diagram signalled what the most probable quality problem is because, of the total possible quality problems, "fuzzy and unclear copies" occurs most frequently. These two reports indicate where managers should investigate further to ascertain what is causing the quality problem.

CAUSE-AND-EFFECT DIAGRAMS

The most frequently occurring problems identified by the Pareto diagram are analyzed using *cause-and-effect diagrams*. A **cause-and-effect diagram** identifies potential causes of failures or defects. As a first step, Photon analyzes the causes of the most frequently occurring failure, fuzzy and unclear copies. Exhibit 19-5 presents the cause-and-effect diagram for this problem. The exhibit identifies four major categories of potential causes of failure: human factors, methods and design factors, machine-related factors, and materials and components factors. As additional arrows are added for each cause, the general appearance of the diagram begins to resemble a fishbone (hence, cause-and-effect diagrams are also called *fishbone diagrams*).[2]

The analysis of quality problems is aided by automated equipment and computers that record the number and types of defects and the operating conditions that existed at the time the defects occurred. Using these inputs, computer programs simultaneously prepare control charts, Pareto diagrams, and cause-and-effect diagrams.

EXHIBIT 19-4
Pareto Diagram for the Photon Corporation

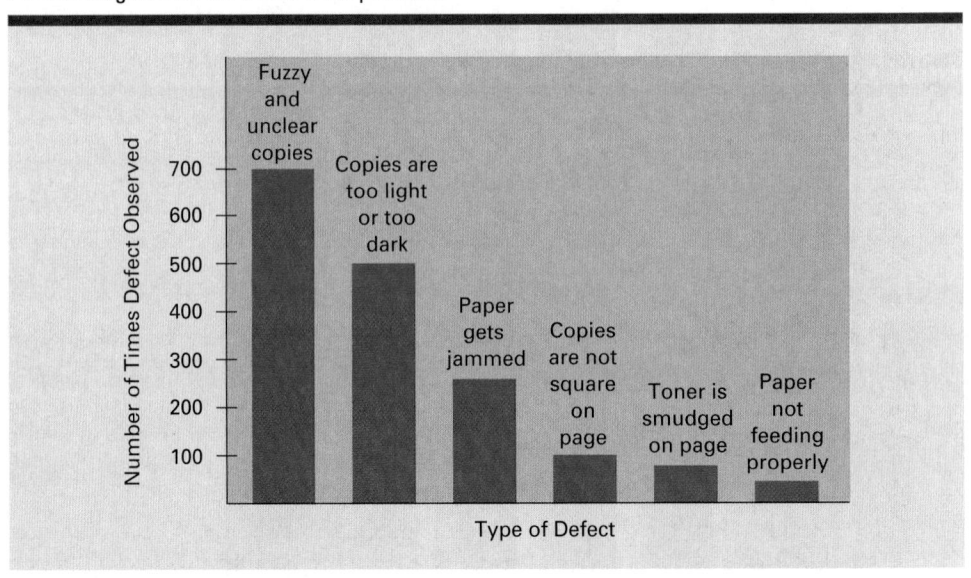

[2] See P. Clark, "Getting the Most from Cause-and-Effect Diagrams," *Quality Progress* (June 2000).

EXHIBIT 19-5
Cause-and-Effect Diagram for Fuzzy and Unclear Copies at the Photon Corporation

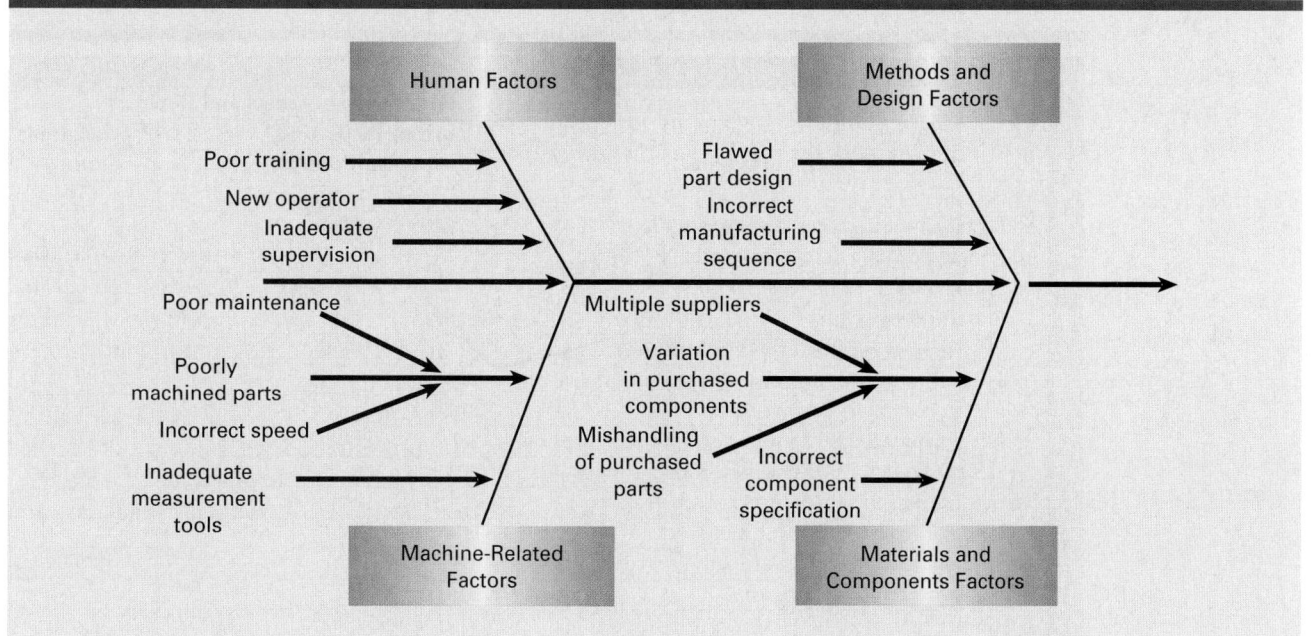

ASSESS YOUR MASTERY

To check your understanding of the material in Learning Objective ②, go to the *Mastery Questions* section at the end of this chapter and complete Learning Objective ② questions 1 and 2.

MyAccountingLab

RELEVANT COSTS AND BENEFITS OF QUALITY IMPROVEMENT

Careful analysis of the cause-and-effect diagram reveals that the steel frame (or chassis) of the copier is often mishandled as it travels from the suppliers' warehouses to Photon's plant. The frame must satisfy very precise specifications and tolerances; otherwise, various copier components (such as drums, mirrors, and lenses) attached to the frame will be improperly aligned. Mishandling causes the dimensions of the frame to vary from specifications, resulting in fuzzy images.

The team of engineers working to solve the fuzzy-image problem offers two alternative solutions: (1) to improve the inspection of the frame immediately upon delivery or (2) to redesign and strengthen the frame and the containers used to transport them to better withstand mishandling during transportation.

Should Photon inspect incoming frames more carefully or redesign them and their containers? Exhibit 19-6 shows the costs and benefits of each choice.

1. **Estimated incremental costs:** $400,000 for the inspection alternative; $460,000 for the redesign alternative including $300,000 process engineering and $160,000 design engineering.

2. **Cost savings from less rework, customer support, and repairs:** Exhibit 19-6, lines 9 and 10, shows that reducing rework results in savings of $40 per hour. Exhibit 19-2, Panel A, column 2, line 13 (see page 925), shows total rework cost per hour of $100. Why the difference? Because Photon concludes that as it improves quality, it will save only the $40 variable cost per rework-hour, not the $60 fixed cost per rework-hour.

   Exhibit 19-6, line 9, shows the inspection alternative is expected to eliminate 24,000 rework-hours and therefore save variable costs of $960,000 ($40 per hour × 24,000 rework-hours). The redesign alternative (Exhibit 19-6, line 10) is expected to eliminate 32,000 rework-hours and therefore save variable costs of

Analyze the benefits of using both financial and nonfinancial measures of quality ③

A	B	C	D
	Relevant Costs and Benefits of		
	Further Inspecting		**Redesigning**
Relevant Items	**Incoming Frames**		**Frames**
(1)	(2)		(3)
Additional inspection and testing costs	$(400,000)		–
Additional process engineering costs	–		$ (300,000)
Additional design engineering costs	–		(160,000)
Savings in rework costs			
($40 per hour × 24,000 fewer rework-hours)	960,000		
($40 per hour × 32,000 fewer rework-hours)			1,280,000
Savings in customer-support costs			
($20 per hour × 2,000 fewer customer-support hours)	40,000		
($20 per hour × 2,800 fewer customer-support hours)			56,000
Savings in transportation costs for repair parts			
($180 per load × 500 fewer loads moved)	90,000		
($180 per hour × 700 fewer loads moved)			126,000
Savings in warranty repair costs			
($45 per hour × 20,000 fewer repair-hours)	900,000		
($45 per hour × 28,000 fewer repair-hours)			1,260,000
Total contribution margin from additional sales			
(250 additional copiers × $6,000 per copier)	1,500,000		
(300 additional copiers × $6,000 per copier)			1,800,000
Net cost savings and additional contribution margin	$3,090,000		$4,062,000
Difference in favour of redesigning frame	↑	$972,000	↑

$1,280,000 ($40 per rework-hour × 32,000 rework-hours). Exhibit 19-6 also shows expected variable-cost savings in customer support, transportation, and warranty repair for the two alternatives.

3. **Increased contribution margin from higher sales as a result of building a reputation for quality and performance** (Exhibit 19-6, lines 21 and 22): $1,500,000 for 250 copiers under the inspection alternative and $1,800,000 for 300 copiers under the redesign alternative. This benefit is important because quality improvements cannot always be translated into lower costs. For example, laying off workers (as a result of quality improvements) to reduce costs can adversely affect the morale of employees and limit future quality initiatives. Management should always look for opportunities to generate higher revenues from quality improvements.

Exhibit 19-6 shows that both the inspection and the redesign alternatives yield net benefits relative to the status quo. However, the net benefits from the redesign alternative are expected to be $972,000 greater. The costs of a poorly designed frame appear in the form of higher manufacturing, marketing, distribution, and customer-service costs, as internal and external failures begin to mount. But these costs are locked in when the frame is designed. Thus, it is not surprising that redesign will yield significant savings.

In the Photon example, lost contribution margin occurs because Photon's repeated external failures damage its reputation for quality, resulting in lost sales. Lost contribution margin can also occur as a result of internal failures. Suppose Photon's manufacturing capacity is fully used. In this case, rework uses up valuable manufacturing capacity and causes the company to forgo contribution margin from producing and selling additional copiers. Suppose Photon could produce and (subsequently) sell an additional 600 copiers by improving quality and reducing rework. The costs of internal failure would then include lost contribution margin of

$3,600,000 ($6,000 contribution margin per copier × 600 copiers). This $3,600,000 is the opportunity cost of poor quality.

Photon can use its COQ report to examine interdependencies across the four categories of quality-related costs. In our example, redesigning the frame increases costs of prevention activities (design and process engineering), decreases costs of internal failure (rework), and decreases costs of external failure (warranty repairs).

Costs of quality give more insight when managers compare trends over time. In successful quality programs, the costs of quality as a percentage of sales and the costs of internal and external failure as a percentage of total costs of quality should decrease over time. Many companies, for example, Digital Equipment Corporation, Solectron, and Toyota, believe they should eliminate all failure costs and have zero defects.

COSTS OF DESIGN QUALITY

Our discussion so far has focused on measuring the cost of conformance quality and the methods that companies use to reduce these costs. In addition to conformance quality, companies must also pay attention to quality of design by designing products that satisfy customer needs. The **costs of design quality** refer to costs incurred to prevent, or costs arising from, low quality of design. These costs include the costs of designing a product, and the production, marketing, distribution, and customer-service costs wasted on supporting a poorly designed product. A significant component of these costs is the opportunity cost of sales lost from not producing a product that customers want. Many of these costs are very difficult to measure precisely. For this reason, most companies do not measure the financial costs of design quality.

BSC—NONFINANCIAL MEASURES OF INTERNAL-BUSINESS-PROCESS QUALITY

Prevention costs, appraisal costs, and internal failure costs are examples of financial measures of quality performance inside the company. Most companies monitor both financial and nonfinancial measures of internal quality.

Photon measures internal-business-process quality using the following non-financial measures:

- ◆ Defect rate—the percentage of defective to total units
- ◆ Average repair time to fix machines at the customer's site
- ◆ Rework rate—the percentage of reworked to total units
- ◆ Number of different types of defects analyzed using control charts, Pareto diagrams, and cause-and effect diagrams
- ◆ Number of design and process changes made

By themselves, nonfinancial measures of quality have limited meaning. They are more informative when management examines trends over time. To prepare this report, the management accountant must review the numbers to ensure that non-financial measures are calculated accurately and consistently, and must then present the information to help management evaluate internal quality performance. Management accountants help companies improve quality in multiple ways—they compute the costs of quality, assist in developing cost-effective solutions to quality problems, and provide feedback about quality improvement.

BSC—LEARNING AND GROWTH NONFINANCIAL MEASURES OF QUALITY

Photon's managers have analyzed performance to determine the drivers of internal-business-process quality. Photon measures the following factors in the learning and growth perspective in the balanced scorecard:

- ◆ Employee turnover ratio (number of employees who leave compared with the average total number of employees)
- ◆ Employee empowerment ratio (number of processes in which employees have the right to make decisions without consulting supervisors compared with the total number of processes)

- Employee satisfaction ratio (employees indicating high satisfaction ratings compared with the total employees surveyed)
- Employee training rate (percentage of employees trained in different quality-enhancing methods)

These quality-related balanced scorecard measures provide the best information when managers examine trends and relationships (across the learning and growth, the internal business process, the customer, and the financial perspectives) over time as they seek to improve performance. To provide information on trends, management accountants must review the nonfinancial measures for accuracy and consistency.

BSC—EVALUATING QUALITY—FINANCIAL AND NONFINANCIAL MEASURES

Measuring the financial costs of quality and measuring the nonfinancial aspects of quality have distinctly different advantages.

The advantages of the costs of quality (COQ) measures are as follows:

- COQ focuses attention on how costly poor quality can be throughout all business functions of a value chain, including communication.
- Financial COQ measures are a useful way of comparing different quality improvement programs and setting priorities for achieving maximum cost reduction.
- Financial COQ measures serve as a common denominator for evaluating tradeoffs among prevention and failure costs. COQ provides a single, summary measure of quality performance.

The advantages of nonfinancial measures of quality are that they:

- Are often easy to quantify and easy to understand.
- Direct attention to physical processes and hence focus attention on the precise problem areas that need improvement.
- Provide immediate short-run feedback on whether quality-improvement efforts have, in fact, succeeded in improving quality.
- Are useful indicators of long-run performance.

Most organizations use both financial and nonfinancial quality measures to measure quality performance.

GOVERNANCE ISSUES

The Cost of Quality Failure at Firestone

Company and division managers undoubtedly feel pressure to meet quarterly and annual financial performance targets, but it is as important to achieve both product and service quality. Quality-control and assurance activities carry significant costs, but quality failures can cost far more. As Bridgestone/Firestone, Inc., makers of Firestone tires, learned during a widely publicized recall of 6.5 million tires in 2000, the financial, public-relations, and legal effects of quality failure can be disastrous. Firestone received thousands of unfavourable news stories, more

than 200 lawsuits from angry customers, and high-profile congressional inquiries about tire failures. On May 22, 2001, Ford announced the further recall of 13 million tires. Ford ended its relationship with Firestone. Firestone suffered 40% revenue declines in key segments and a US $510 million loss in 2000. It also paid out over US $1 billion in recall-related costs (including new tires, claim settlements, and lawsuits), lost US $10 billion in stock market capitalization, and dismissed most Bridgestone/Firestone corporate executives in the United States and Japan.

(continued)

(continued)

The production quality control issue was made worse because top management was fully aware of the problem and failed to remedy it. In the US, the National Highway Traffic Safety Administration (NHSTA) requires companies and suppliers to report unusual vehicle failures. The investigation revealed neither Ford nor Firestone conformed to this legislation. It was the NHSTA which informed Ford of an unusual frequency of rollover accidents involving its Ford Explorer.

Ford Motor Company—Firestone's largest US customer for a century—conducted an analysis that indicated that tires from Firestone's Decatur, Illinois, plant exhibited tendencies to come apart at high speeds, which caused vehicles, especially Ford's popular Explorer sports utility vehicle, to roll over. At this point Firestone failed to prevent failure prior to the product reaching the customer's hands. Although both companies displayed public remorse and began working together in handling the recall, Firestone responded to Ford's study by stating:

> We are confident in the quality of our tires and in the effectiveness of our inspection processes at the Decatur, Illinois, plant and at all of our plants . . . Like all Bridgestone/Firestone production facilities, the Decatur plant adheres to stringent standards of quality control where every tire is subject to strict inspection by both people and machines at every step of the manufacturing process, from raw material through finished tire. And, every production employee, at each of our plants, receives substantial training before they work on the line. . . . The plant also has received quality awards from our customers, including Ford, General Motors, and Nissan.

Scrutiny of quality practices at Firestone told a different story. In late 1999, it was found that tread separation among light-truck tires had risen 18.6% during the previous year. This change led Firestone engineers to investigate tread separation. They identified tread separation as a critical performance issue at their October 2000 quarterly quality meeting. Another investigation at Firestone reported that the number of warranty claims for ATX and ATXII tires made at the Decatur facility between 1994 and 1996 were three to six times higher than claims for tires made at all other US Firestone plants. Although quality improved after 1996, claim rates remained significantly higher for the Decatur plant than at all other facilities.

These findings—coupled with news that tread separation caused Ford to replace the same, or similar, tires on nearly 50,000 of its vehicles in 16 South American and Asian countries starting in 1999—led most observers to conclude that the rollovers were being caused by Firestone tire defects. A Harvard Business School case notes:

> Although the rising cost of claims and lawsuits regarding the Firestone ATX tire was apparently discussed at some quarterly financial meetings beginning in 1997, the matter did not go beyond the finance area which maintained information on claims costs. As [Vice President Gary] Crigger explained: "Claims and lawsuits are not considered to be representative throughout a line . . . [but] individual cases that occur for a variety of reasons. So they have never been part of [tire] performance evaluation."

Both companies had the relevant nonfinancial and financial information indicating quality failure. Neither company calculated cost of quality failure and implemented remedies. Firestone failed to incorporate both the opportunity cost of legal proceedings and the loss of Ford as their customer. With an ERP strategy, and using the process described in this chapter, Firestone's executives could have recognized the interdependence of legal, financial, and production nonfinancial information and made decisions to better protect the company's most valuable asset—its customers.

Sources: L. S. Payne, "Recall 2000: Bridgestone Corp. (A)," HBS Case No. 9-302-013 (Boston: Harvard Business School Publishing, 2003); S. Govindaraj and B. Jaggi, "Market Overreaction to Product Recall Revisited—The Case of Firestone Tires and the Ford Explorer," *Review of Quantitative Finance and Accounting* (July 2004); D. Welch, "Firestone: Is This Brand Beyond Repair?" *BusinessWeek*, June 11, 2001; "Firestone Decatur Tire Plant Inspection—Defective Tires," Bridgestone America Holdings press release (Nashville, TN: August 13, 2001).

ASSESS YOUR MASTERY

To check your understanding of the material in Learning Objective ③, go to the *Mastery Questions* section at the end of this chapter and complete Learning Objective ③ questions 1 and 2.

Companies increasingly view time as a key variable in competition.[3] Doing things faster helps to increase revenues and decrease costs. For example, a moving company such as United Van Lines will be able to generate more revenues if it can move goods from one place to another faster and on time. Companies such as Wal-Mart also report lower costs from their emphasis on time. They cite, for example, the need to carry less inventory because of their ability to respond rapidly to customer demands.

We focus on *operational measures of time*, which reveal how quickly companies respond to customers' demands for their products and services and the reliability with which these companies meet scheduled delivery dates. Two common operational measures of time are customer-response time and on-time performance.

CUSTOMER-RESPONSE TIME

Customer-response time is the amount of time between when a customer places an order for a product or requests a service and when the product or service is delivered to the customer. A timely response to customer requests is a key competitive factor in many industries. Exhibit 19-7 illustrates components of customer-response time which can be measured. In the case of Airbus, **order receipt time** is the time it takes the Marketing Department to send engineering and other specifications to the Manufacturing Department. One remedy implemented by Airbus was to install a new software system enabling engineers in Toulouse to communicate directly with those in Hamburg. This improved conformance.

Manufacturing lead time is the time between when the order is ready to start on the production line (ready to be set up) and when it becomes a finished good. Manufacturing lead time includes waiting time plus manufacturing time for the order. An order may be delayed because the equipment the order requires is busy processing orders that arrived earlier. **Manufacturing cycle time** refers to the sum of waiting time plus production cycle time. Some companies evaluate their response time improvement using a measure called **manufacturing cycle efficiency (MCE)**. MCE is the ratio of value-added manufacturing cycle time divided by the total manufacturing cycle time:

$$MCE = (\text{Value-added manufacturing time} \div \text{Manufacturing cycle time})$$

EXHIBIT 19-7
Components of Customer-Response Time

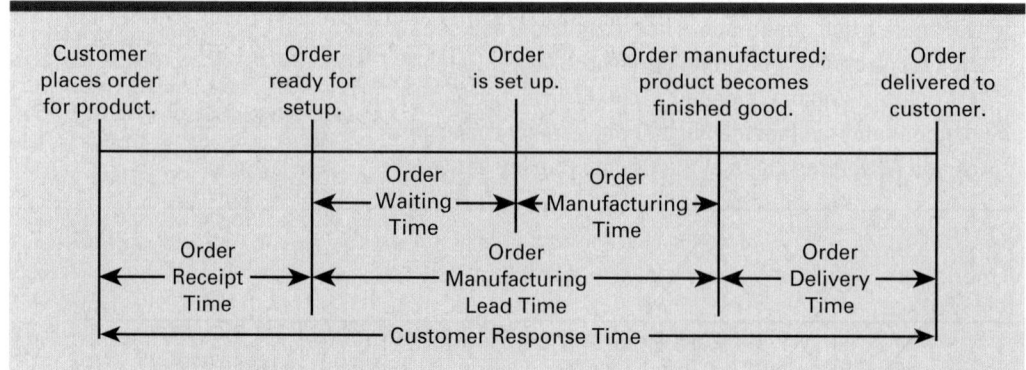

[3]See G. Stalk and T. Hout, *Competing Against Time* (New York: Free Press, 1990); K. Eisenhardt and S. Brown, "Time Pacing: Competing in Strategic Markets That Won't Stand Still," *Harvard Business Review* (March–April 1998); and T. Willis and A. Jurkus, "Product Development: An Essential Ingredient of Time-Based Competition," *Review of Business* (2001).

As discussed in Chapter 12, wait time is not value-added; therefore, this measure is a time yield measure of value-added time divided by total time of manufacture. Wait time or non-value-added time includes that spent by the manufacturer waiting for parts, inspection time, rework and repair time, and materials-handling time.

Order delivery time is the time it takes distribution to pick up the order from manufacturing and deliver it to the customer. The new software system at Airbus also avoided delays due to rewiring and shortened the order delivery time to meet the customer's requirements. For retail catalogue companies the time from the placement of the order to the customer's receipt of the product is often shorter than the 7 to 10 day delivery delay of retail stores such as The Brick and The Bay. Retail catalogue companies delivering in less than 7 days use time as a competitive advantage for their service.

On-time performance refers to situations in which the product or service is actually delivered at the time it is scheduled to be delivered. Consider Federal Express, which specifies a price per package and a next-day delivery time of 10:30 a.m. for its overnight courier service. Federal Express measures on-time performance by how often it meets its stated delivery time of 10:30 a.m. On-time performance is an important element of customer satisfaction because customers want and expect on-time deliveries.

Commercial airlines gain loyal passengers from consistent on-time service. Note that there is a tradeoff between customer-response time and on-time performance. Simply scheduling longer customer-response times, such as Federal Express scheduling deliveries at 1 p.m. instead of 10:30 a.m., or airlines lengthening scheduled arrival times, makes it easier to achieve on-time performance (although this tactic could displease customers).

UNCERTAINTY AND BOTTLENECKS AS DRIVERS OF TIME

A **time driver** is any factor where change in the factor causes a change in the speed with which an activity is undertaken. What are the drivers of time? We consider two of the most important: (1) *Uncertainty about when customers will order products or services.* For example, the more randomly a company receives orders for its machine tools, the more likely that queues will form and delays will occur. (2) *Limited capacity and bottlenecks.* A **bottleneck** is an operation where the work required to be performed approaches or exceeds the available capacity. For example, a bottleneck is created when products that need to be processed at a particular machine arrive while the machine is busy processing other products.

Consider the example of Falcon Works (FW), which uses one turning machine to convert steel bars into one specialty component, A22. FW makes this component only after FW's customers order the component. To focus on manufacturing lead time, we assume that FW's order receipt time and order delivery time are minimal. FW acquires direct materials when it receives an order, rather than waiting until just before manufacturing is scheduled to start, because of uncertainty about (1) how long it will take to obtain materials from suppliers and (2) when manufacturing will start.

FW expects it will receive 30 orders, but it could actually receive 10, 20, or 50 orders of A22. Each order is for 1,000 units. Each order will take 100 hours of manufacturing time (8 hours of setup time to clean and prepare the machine, and 92 hours of processing time). The annual capacity of the machine is 4,000 hours. If FW receives the number of orders it expects, the total amount of manufacturing time required on the machine will be 3,000 (100×30) hours, which is within the available machine capacity of 4,000 hours. Even though expected capacity utilization is not strained, queues and delays will still occur because uncertainty about when FW's customers will place an order may cause the order to be received while the machine is processing another order.

In the single-product case, under certain assumptions about the pattern of customer orders and how orders will be processed, the **average waiting time**, the average amount of time that an order will wait in line before it is set up and processed, equals:

$$\frac{\text{Average number of orders of A22} \times \left(\text{Manufacturing time for A22}\right)^2}{2 \times \left[\text{Annual machine capacity} - \left(\text{Average number of orders of A22} \times \text{Manufacturing time for A22}\right)\right]}$$

$$= \frac{30 \times (100)^2}{2 \times [4,000 - (30 \times 100)]} = \frac{30 \times 10,000}{2 \times (4,000 - 3,000)} = \frac{300,000}{2 \times 1,000} = \frac{300,000}{2,000} = 150 \text{ hours}$$

The precise technical assumptions are (a) that customer orders for the product follow a Poisson distribution with a mean equal to the expected number of orders (30 in our example) and (b) that orders are processed on a first-in, first-out (FIFO) basis. The Poisson arrival pattern for customer orders has been found to be reasonable in many real-world settings. The FIFO assumption can be modified. Under the modified assumptions, the basic queuing and delay effects will still occur, but the precise formulas will be different.

Our formula describes only the average waiting time. A particular order may happen to arrive when the machine is free, in which case manufacturing will start immediately. In other situations, FW may receive an order while two other orders are waiting to be processed. In this case, the delay will be longer than 150 hours. The average manufacturing lead time for an order of A22 is 250 hours (150 hours of average waiting time + 100 hours of manufacturing time). Note that manufacturing time per order is a squared term in the numerator. It indicates the disproportionately large impact manufacturing time has on waiting time. (See Real Companies, page 942.)

The longer the manufacturing time, the greater the probability that the machine will be in use when an order arrives. This leads to longer delays. The denominator in this formula measures excess capacity or **cushion**. The smaller the cushion, the greater the probability of delay because the higher is the probability the machine will be processing an earlier order. Throughout this section, we use manufacturing lead time to refer to manufacturing lead time for an order.

FW is considering whether to introduce a new product, C33. FW expects to receive 10 orders of C33 (each order for 800 units) in the coming year. Each order will take 50 hours of manufacturing time (3 hours of setup time and 47 hours of processing time). The expected demand for A22 will be unaffected whether or not FW introduces C33.

The average waiting time before an order is set up and processed is given by the following formula, which is an extension of the formula described earlier for the single-product case.

$$\frac{\left[\text{Average number of orders of A22} \times \left(\text{Manufacturing time for A22}\right)^2\right] + \left[\text{Average number of orders of C33} \times \left(\text{Manufacturing time for C33}\right)^2\right]}{2 \times \left[\text{Annual machine capacity} - \left(\text{Average number of orders of A22} \times \text{Manufacturing time for A22}\right) - \left(\text{Average number of orders of C33} \times \text{Manufacturing time for C33}\right)\right]}$$

$$= \frac{[30 \times (100)^2] + [10 \times (50)^2]}{2 \times [4,000 - (30 \times 100) - (10 \times 50)]} = \frac{(30 \times 10,000) + (10 \times 2,500)}{2 \times (4,000 - 3,000 - 500)}$$

$$= \frac{300,000 + 25,000}{2 \times 500} = \frac{325,000}{1,000} = 325 \text{ hours}$$

Introducing C33 causes average waiting time to more than double, from 150 hours to 325 hours. To understand why, think of excess capacity as a cushion for absorbing the shocks of variability and uncertainty in the arrival of customer orders. Introducing C33 causes excess capacity to shrink, increasing the chance that at any point in time, new orders will arrive while existing orders are being manufactured. The cushion is cut in half from 1,000 to 500 hours, doubling the average wait time by halving the denominator. The product introduction also increases demand on capacity by 25,000 hours which increases the numerator but at a slower rate than the increase in the denominator. The total effect of introducing the C33 is to increase average waiting time by 117% [(325 − 150) ÷ 150].

With the addition of another product, average manufacturing lead time for A22 is 425 hours (325 hours of average waiting time + 100 hours of manufacturing time), and for C33 it is 375 hours (325 hours of average waiting time + 50 hours of manufacturing time). Note that C33 spends 86.67% (325 ÷ 375) of its manufacturing lead time just waiting for manufacturing to start!

RELEVANT REVENUES AND COSTS OF TIME

Should FW introduce product C33? Consider the following information:

Product	Annual Average Number of Orders	Average Selling Price per Order If Average Manufacturing Lead Time per Order Is		Direct Material Cost per Order	Inventory Carrying Cost per Order per Hour
		Less than 300 Hours	More than 300 Hours		
A22	30	$22,000	$21,500	$16,000	$1.00
C33	10	10,000	9,600	8,000	0.50

Note that manufacturing lead times affect both revenues and costs in our example. Revenues are affected because customers are willing to pay a slightly higher price for faster delivery. Direct materials costs and inventory carrying costs are the only costs affected by the decision to introduce C33. Inventory carrying costs usually consist of the opportunity costs of investment tied up in inventory (see Chapter 11) and the relevant costs of storage such as space rental, spoilage, deterioration, and materials handling. Companies usually calculate inventory carrying costs on a per-order-per-year basis. To simplify computations, we express inventory carrying costs on a per-order-per-hour basis. FW incurs inventory carrying costs for the duration of the wait time and manufacturing time.

Exhibit 19-8 presents relevant revenues and relevant costs that the management accountant would calculate for this decision. The preferred alternative is not to introduce C33. Note that C33 is rejected despite having a positive contribution margin of at least $1,600 ($9,600 − $8,000) per order. Recall, too, that FW's machine has the capacity to process C33 because the machine will, on average, use only 3,500 of the available 4,000 hours. *The key to the decision is to recognize the relevant negative*

EXHIBIT 19-8

Determining Expected Relevant Revenues and Relevant Costs for Falcon Works' Decision to Introduce C33

Relevant Items	Alternative 1: Introduce C33 (1)	Alternative 2: Do Not Introduce C33 (2)	Difference (3) = (1) − (2)
Expected revenues	$741,000[a]	$660,000[b]	$ 81,000
Expected variable costs	560,000[c]	480,000[d]	(80,000)
Expected inventory carrying costs	14,625[e]	7,500[f]	(7,125)
Expected total costs	574,625	487,500	(87,125)
Expected revenues minus expected costs	$166,375	$172,500	$ (6,125)

[a]($21,500 × 30) + ($9,600 × 10) = $741,000; average manufacturing lead time will be more than 300 hours.
[b]($22,000 × 30) = $660,000; average manufacturing lead time will be less than 300 hours.
[c]($16,000 × 30) + ($8,000 × 10) = $560,000.
[d]$16,000 × 30 = $480,000.
[e](Average manufacturing lead time for A22 × Inventory carrying cost per order for A22 × Expected number of orders for A22) + (Average manufacturing lead time for C33 × Inventory carrying cost per order for C33 × Expected number of orders for C33) = (425 × $1.00 × 30) + (375 × $0.50 × 10) = $12,750 + $1,875 = $14,625.
[f]Average manufacturing lead time for A22 × Inventory carrying cost per order for A22 × Expected number of orders for A22 = 250 × $1.00 × 30 = $7,500.

effects of C33 on the existing product A22. The following table presents the expected loss in revenues and expected increase in costs of using up extra capacity on the turning machine to manufacture C33.

Effect of Increasing Average Manufacturing Lead Time

Product	Expected Loss in Revenues for A22 (1)	Expected Increase in Carrying Costs for All Products (2)	Expected Increase in Carrying Costs of Introducing C33 (3) = (1) + (2)
A22	$15,000[a]	$5,250[b]	$20,250
C33	—	1,875[c]	1,875
Total	$15,000	$7,125	$22,125

[a]($22,000 − $21,500) per order × 30 expected orders = $15,000.
[b](425 − 250) hours per order × $1.00 per hour × 30 expected orders = $5,250.
[c](375 − 0) hours per order × $0.50 per hour × 10 expected orders = $1,875.

Introducing C33 causes the average manufacturing lead time of A22 to increase from 250 hours to 425 hours. This increases inventory carrying costs. Introducing C33 also causes A22's revenues to decrease because it would, on average, take more than 300 hours to manufacture A22. The expected costs of introducing C33 equals $22,125, which exceeds C33's expected contribution margin of $16,000 ($1,600 per order × 10 expected orders). FW should choose not to produce C33.

We have described a simple setting to explain the effects of uncertainty and capacity constraints and the relevant revenues and relevant costs of time.[4] Delays can be reduced by increasing the capacity at the bottleneck to reduce queues, delays, and inventories. When demand uncertainty is high, *some* cushion is desirable. Companies can increase capacity in several ways. One is to reduce setup time by improving the efficiency of the setup process. Another is to invest in new equipment. Many companies are investing in flexible manufacturing systems that can be programmed to quickly switch from producing one product to producing another. Delays can also be reduced through careful scheduling of orders on machines—for example, by batching similar jobs together for processing.

MyAccountingLab

ASSESS YOUR MASTERY

To check your understanding of the material in Learning Objective 4, go to the *Mastery Questions* section at the end of this chapter and complete Learning Objective 4 question 1.

◆ PART THREE

THEORY OF CONSTRAINTS AND THROUGHPUT CONTRIBUTION ANALYSIS

5 Evaluate the strengths and weaknesses of the theory of constraints (TOC) and activity-based costing (ABC) for managing bottlenecks

The **theory of constraints (TOC)** describes methods to maximize operating income when faced with some bottleneck and some nonbottleneck operations. It defines three measurements:[5]

◆ *Throughput contribution* equals sales revenue minus direct materials costs (see Chapter 9)

[4]Other complexities such as analyzing a network of machines, priority scheduling, and allowing for uncertainty in processing times are beyond the scope of this book. In these cases, the basic queuing and delay effects persist, but the precise formulas are more complex.
[5]See E. Goldratt and J. Cox, *The Goal* (New York: North River Press, 1986); E. Goldratt, *The Theory of Constraints* (New York: North River Press, 1990); E. Noreen, D. Smith, and J. Mackey, *The Theory of Constraints and Its Implications for Management Accounting* (New York: North River Press, 1995); and M. Woeppel, *Manufacturers' Guide to Implementing the Theory of Constraints* (Boca Raton, FL: Lewis Publishing, 2000).

◆ *Investments (inventory)* equals the sum of materials costs of direct materials inventory, work-in-process inventory, and finished goods inventory; R&D costs; and costs of equipment and buildings

◆ *Operating costs* equals all operating costs (other than direct materials) incurred to earn throughput contribution; includes salaries and wages, rent, utilities, and amortization

The objective of TOC is to increase throughput contribution while decreasing investments and operating costs. *The theory of constraints considers short-run time horizons and assumes other current operating costs to be fixed costs.* The management process is illustrated in Exhibit 19-9. The bottleneck must be located within the production process because this capacity constraint will determine the entire plant's throughput contribution. The general manager can enlist the line managers to reveal where large quantities of direct or WIP inventory await further processing. The immediate remedy is to maximize the capacity of the bottleneck. This means the flow of all nonbottlenecked resources will be determined by the bottleneck capacity.

Maximizing the bottleneck is an important example of the concept presented in Chapter 11: To maximize overall contribution margin, the plant must maximize contribution margin (in this case, throughput contribution) of the constrained or bottleneck resource. For this reason, the bottleneck machine must always be kept running, not waiting for jobs. To achieve this, companies often maintain a small buffer inventory of jobs waiting for the bottleneck machine. The bottleneck machine sets the pace for all nonbottleneck machines. That is, the output at the nonbottleneck operations is tied or linked to the needs of the bottleneck machine. For example, workers at nonbottleneck machines are not motivated to improve their productivity if the additional output cannot be processed by the bottleneck machine. Producing more nonbottleneck output only creates excess inventory; it does not increase throughput contribution.

In the longer term, top management must take actions to increase bottleneck efficiency and capacity—the objective is to increase throughput contribution minus the incremental costs of taking such actions. The management accountant plays a key role by calculating throughput contribution, identifying relevant and irrelevant costs, and doing a cost-benefit analysis of alternative actions to increase bottleneck efficiency and capacity.

EXHIBIT 19-9
The Debottleneck Management Process

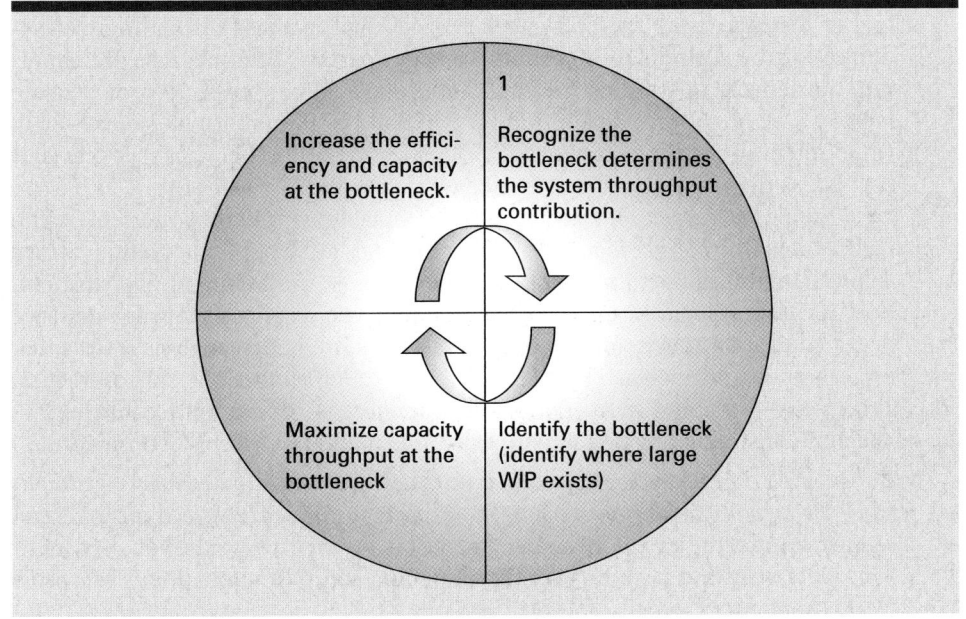

We illustrate debottlenecking with the example of Cardinal Industries (CI). CI manufactures car doors in two operations—stamping and pressing. Additional information is as follows:

	Stamping	Pressing
Capacity per hour	20 units	15 units
Annual capacity (6,000 hours of capacity available in each operation; 6,000 hours × 20 units/hour; 15 units/hour)	120,000 units	90,000 units
Annual production and sales	90,000 units	90,000 units
Other fixed operating costs (excluding direct materials)	$720,000	$1,080,000
Other fixed operating costs per unit produced ($720,000 ÷ 90,000 units; $1,080,000 ÷ 90,000 units)	$8 per unit	$12 per unit

Each door sells for $100 and has direct materials costs of $40. Variable costs in other functions of the value chain—R&D, design of products and processes, marketing, distribution, and customer service—are negligible. CI's output is constrained by the capacity of 90,000 units at the pressing operation. The actions taken to maximize the bottleneck capacity include:

- *Eliminate idle time (time when the pressing machine is neither being set up to process products nor actually processing products) at the bottleneck operation.* CI is considering permanently positioning two workers at the pressing operation.

  The sole responsibility of additional direct manufacturing labourers would be to unload finished units as soon as one batch of units is processed and to set up the machine to process the next batch. Suppose the annual cost of this action is $48,000 and the effect of this action is to increase bottleneck output by 1,000 units per year. CI should incur this additional cost because based on incremental cost and revenue analysis, CI's relevant throughput contribution increases by $60,000 [1,000 units × (selling price, $100 − direct materials costs, $40)], which exceeds the additional cost of $48,000. All other costs are irrelevant.

- *Process only those parts or products that increase sales and throughput contribution, not parts or products that remain in finished goods or spare parts inventory.* Manufacturing products that sit in inventory does not increase throughput contribution.

- *Shift products that do not have to be made on the bottleneck machine to nonbottleneck machines or to outside facilities. Suppose the Spartan Corporation, an outside contractor, offers to press 1,500 doors at $15 per door from direct materials that CI supplies.* This is a standard make/buy decision for CI.

  Spartan's quoted price is greater than CI's own operating costs in the Pressing Department of $12 per door. On an incremental basis the cost is higher but increasing the bottleneck capacity will increase throughput contribution for the entire plant. CI should accept Spartan's offer because pressing is the bottleneck operation. Getting additional doors pressed from outside increases throughput contribution by $90,000 [($100 − $40) × 1,500 doors], while relevant costs increase by $22,500 ($15 × 1,500). The fact that CI's unit cost is less than Spartan's quoted price is irrelevant.

  Suppose Gemini Industries, another outside contractor, offers to stamp 2,000 doors from direct materials that CI supplies at $6 per door. Gemini's price is lower than CI's operating cost of $8 per door in the Stamping Department. For CI, other operating costs such as stamping are fixed costs. CI will not save by subcontracting the stamping operations. An incremental analysis reveals that total costs would increase by $12,000 ($6 × 2,000) under the subcontracting alternative. Stamping more doors will not increase throughput contribution, which is constrained by pressing capacity. CI should not accept Gemini's offer.

- *Reduce setup time and processing time at bottleneck operations (for example, by simplifying the design or reducing the number of parts in the product).* Suppose CI can reduce setup time at the pressing operation by incurring additional costs of $55,000 a year. Suppose further that reducing setup time enables CI to press 2,500 more doors a year.

CI should incur the costs to reduce setup time because throughput contribution increases by $150,000 [($100 − $40) × 2,500], which exceeds the additional costs incurred of $55,000. It would not be worthwhile for CI to incur any incremental costs to reduce machining time consumed at the stamping operation. Other operating costs will increase, but throughput contribution will remain unaffected. Throughput contribution increases only by increasing bottleneck output. Machine time is not bottlenecked and increasing nonbottleneck output has no effect.

◆ *Improve the quality of parts or products manufactured at the bottleneck operation.* Poor quality is often more costly at a bottleneck operation than it is at a nonbottleneck operation. The cost of poor quality at a nonbottleneck operation is the cost of materials wasted.

If CI produces 1,000 defective doors at the stamping operation, the cost of poor quality is $40,000 (direct materials cost per unit, $40 × 1,000 doors). No throughput contribution is forgone because stamping has excess capacity. Despite the defective production, stamping can produce and transfer 90,000 doors to the pressing operation. At a bottleneck operation, the cost of poor quality is the cost of materials wasted plus the opportunity cost of lost throughput contribution.

Bottleneck capacity not wasted in producing defective units could be used to generate additional sales and throughput contribution. If CI produces 1,000 defective units at the pressing operation, the cost of poor quality is $100,000: direct materials cost of $40,000 (direct materials cost per unit, $40 × 1,000 units) plus forgone throughput contribution of $60,000 [($100 − $40) × 1,000 doors].

The high costs of poor quality at the bottleneck operation mean that bottleneck time should not be wasted processing units that are defective. That is, inspection should be done before processing parts at the bottleneck to ensure that only good-quality units are transferred to the bottleneck operation. Also, quality-improvement programs should focus on ensuring that bottlenecks produce minimal defects.

If the remedies are successful, the capacity of the pressing operation will increase and eventually exceed the capacity of the stamping operation. The bottleneck will then shift to the stamping operation. CI should then focus continuous-improvement actions on increasing stamping efficiency and capacity. For example, the contract with Gemini Industries to stamp 2,000 doors at $6 per door from direct materials supplied by CI becomes attractive now because throughput contribution increases by ($100 − $40) × 2,000 − $120,000, while costs increase by $12,000 ($6 × 2,000). TOC emphasizes the management of bottlenecks as the key to improving the performance of the system as a whole. It focuses on the short-run maximization of throughput contribution—revenues minus materials costs.

TOC is less useful for the long-run management of costs, because it does not model the behaviour of costs or identify individual activities and cost drivers. Instead, it regards operating costs as given and fixed. ABC is an alternative strategy that takes a longer-run perspective when more costs can be managed; the focus is on improving processes by eliminating non-value-added activities and reducing the costs of performing value-added activities. ABC systems, therefore, are more useful for long-run pricing, long-run cost control and profit planning, and capacity management. The short-run TOC emphasis on maximizing throughput contribution by managing bottlenecks complements the long-run strategic-cost-management focus of ABC.[6]

BSC AND TIME-RELATED MEASURES

In this section, we use the balanced scorecard to summarize how financial and nonfinancial measures of time relate to one another. We classify these measures under the four perspectives of the balanced scorecard—financial, customer, internal business

[6]For an excellent evaluation of TOC, operations management, cost accounting, and the relationship between TOC and activity-based costing, see A. Atkinson, "Cost Accounting, the Theory of Constraints, and Costing" (Issue Paper, CMA Canada, December 2000).

Overcoming Bottlenecks on the Internet

In 2004, Intel's chief technology officer, Patrick Gelsinger, warned that the World Wide Web was becoming so overloaded with traffic that it might eventually collapse. In 2007 Deloitte & Touche confirmed that exponential growth in web use was creating online bottlenecks as too many people were trying to simultaneously access the same information on the same server. This is a particularly serious problem for companies that take orders online because more than 40% of online shoppers abandon a transaction if response time is too slow. In 2006, Wal-Mart, Disney, and Amazon.com lost millions in sales because their sites crashed during the busiest shopping day of the year in the US, Thanksgiving. In 2007, a 2-day crash in voice-over IP (VoIP) telephone service company Skype reduced the market value of shares of its parent company, e-Bay, by over $1 billion.

Debottlenecking remedies include remote caching (storing duplicated data) and remote mirroring. Social-networking site MySpace stores its seldom-updated content on Akamai's third-party global network of over 15,000 servers.

Each MySpace user's request for content is routed to the Akamai's server that is geographically closest and results in the fastest data transmission or cycle time between request for content and its delivery. Remote mirroring is the storage of huge databases in different geographically remote locations. Using redundant arrays of inexpensive disks (RAID) each extra copy is not only a backup in the event of system crashes but relieves traffic congestion by enabling rerouting around bottlenecks to data RAID sites with lower traffic and faster response times. Both remedies relieve bottleneck constraints, increase capacity, and reduce customer-response time to improve the profitability of the Internet's most popular sites.

Sources: Risk Management (May 2001); The Wall Street Journal (March 20, 2001); Business Wire (October 4, 1999); and a poll conducted by www.esearch.com in 1999; "‘Beware of the End of the World (Wide Web),' Says Intel," Fortune.com, September 10, 2004, www.forbes.com/execpicks/feeds/general/2004/09/10/generalcomtex_2004_09_10_ir_0000-5884-KEYWORD.Missing.html, accessed September 13, 2004; "Downtime and Lost Revenue," NetSource America, www.netsourceamerica.com/welcome.html, accessed June 5, 2006; D. Shand, "Banish Bottlenecks," Computer World, April 10, 2000, www.computerworld.com/news/2000/story/0,11280,44371,00.html, accessed September 17, 2004; T. Wilson, "The Cost of Downtime," http://internetweek.cmp.com/lead/lead073099.htm, accessed June 5, 2006; D. Riley, "EBay Sees $1 billion Knocked Off Market Cap; Skype Outages Continue," Techcrunch.com (August 16, 2007), www.techcrunch.com/2007/08/15/ebay-sees-1-billion=knocked-off=market-cap-as-skype-outages-continue/, accessed September 10, 2007; Telecommunications Predictions: TMT Trends 2007. Deloitte Touche Tohmatsu (January 2007); E. Schuman, "Black Friday Turns Servers Dark at Wal-Mart, Macy's" eWeek.com, www.eweek.com/article2/0,1759,206354,00.asp?kc=EWRSS03119TX1K0000.594, accessed September 12, 2007; "If You're Going to Plan Online Doorbusters, Shouldn't You Plan Ahead for the Traffic?" Techdirt.com, www.techdirt.com/articles/20061127/003210.shtml, accessed September 12, 2007.

processes, and learning and growth. Managers use the balanced scorecard measures to reduce delays and to increase throughput of their bottleneck operations.

Financial measures
Revenue losses or price discounts attributable to delays
Carrying cost of inventories
Throughput contribution minus operating costs

Customer measures
Customer-response time (the time it takes to fulfill a customer order)
On-time performance (delivering a product or service by the scheduled time)

Internal-business-process measures
Average manufacturing time for key products
Idle time at bottleneck operations
Defective units produced at bottleneck operations
Average reduction in setup time and processing time at bottleneck operations

Learning and growth measures
Employee satisfaction
Number of employees trained in managing bottleneck operations

Note the cause-and-effect linkages across these measures. For example, better employee training leads to better management of bottleneck operations, which in turn leads to better customer-response times and higher revenues and throughput contributions. Managers use time-related measures in the balanced scorecard to help them identify actions that improve customer-response times and create long-run competitive advantage.

ASSESS YOUR MASTERY

To check your understanding of the material in Learning Objective ⑤ , go to the *Mastery Questions* section at the end of this chapter and complete Learning Objective ⑤ question 1.

MyAccountingLab

PULLING IT ALL TOGETHER—PROBLEM FOR SELF-STUDY

PROBLEM

The Sloan Corporation is a moving company that transports household goods from one city to another within North America. It measures quality of service in terms of (a) time required to transport goods, (b) on-time delivery (within two days of agreed-upon delivery date), and (c) number of lost or damaged shipments. Sloan is considering investing in a new scheduling and tracking system costing $160,000 per year, which should help it improve performance with respect to items (b) and (c). The following information describes Sloan's current performance and the expected performance if the new system is implemented:

	Current Performance	Expected Future Performance
On-time delivery performance	85%	95%
Variable costs per carton lost or damaged	$60	$ 60
Fixed cost per carton lost or damaged	$40	$ 40
Number of cartons lost or damaged per year	3,000 cartons	1,000 cartons

Sloan expects that each percentage point increase in on-time performance will result in revenue increases of $20,000 per year. Sloan's contribution margin percentage is 45%.

REQUIRED

1. Should Sloan acquire the new system?
2. What is the minimum amount of revenue increase that needs to occur for the benefits from the new system to exceed the costs?
3. What nonfinancial measures may be important?
4. What other nonfinancial benefits may be obtained?

SOLUTION

1. Additional costs of the new scheduling and tracking system are $160,000 per year.
   Additional annual benefits of the new scheduling and tracking system are

Additional annual sales from improving on-time performance $20,000 (95% − 85% or 10 percentage points)	$200,000
Contribution margin from additional annual revenues 45% × $200,000	$ 90,000
Reduction in costs per year from fewer cartons lost or damaged (only variable costs are relevant) $60 (3,000 − 1,000)	120,000
Total additional benefits	$210,000

Therefore, since benefits outweigh costs, Sloan should acquire the new system.

2. As long as Sloan earns a contribution margin of $40,000 (to cover incremental costs of $160,000—relevant variable cost savings of $120,000) from additional annual sales, investing in the new system is beneficial. This contribution margin corresponds to additional sales of $40,000 ÷ 0.45 = $88,889.

3. The new system performance provides Sloan with the time to serve more customers without expanding its fleet. This nonfinancial measure will help assess whether the anticipated benefits were realized. It also affords Sloan a new opportunity, perhaps, to tell its customers where in the transportation system the product is. This non-financial measure of effectiveness may also help Sloan identify opportunities to improve its internal business process. It enables Sloan to identify bottlenecks and devise remedies.

4. The longer-term benefits to Sloan include opportunities such as providing tracking services for others in the supply chain as a new source of revenue. This new service may require some additional infrastructure such as a website but the cost is low relative to the cost of increasing the fleet. The tracking service to customers could reduce the number of customer complaints in two ways. First, tracking enables Sloan to debottleneck and actually reduce transportation time. Second, customers observing the transport process improve their own understanding of where unavoidable delays can occur. By using nonfinancial measures, Sloan can more carefully target its service to meet or exceed the value proposition of its customers and improve its competitiveness.

DECISION POINTS

The following decision guidelines use a question-and-answer format to summarize the chapter's main points. Each decision presents a key question. The guideline is the answer to that question.

DECISIONS	GUIDELINES
1. What are the four categories of a cost-of-quality program?	Four cost categories in a cost-of-quality program are prevention costs (costs incurred to preclude the production of products that do not conform to specifications), appraisal costs (costs incurred to detect which of the individual units of products do not conform to specifications), internal failure costs (costs incurred by a nonconforming product before it is shipped to customers), and external failure costs (costs incurred by a nonconforming product after it is shipped to customers).
2. What methods can managers use to identify quality problems and improve quality?	Three methods to identify quality problems and to improve quality are (a) control charts, to distinguish random from nonrandom variations in an operating process; (b) Pareto diagrams, which indicate how frequently each type of failure occurs; and (c) cause-and-effect diagrams, which identify potential causes of failure.
3. How do managers augment the relevant costs and benefits of quality improvements?	The relevant costs of quality improvements are the incremental costs to implement the quality program. The relevant benefits are the cost savings and the estimated increase in contribution margin from the higher sales due to quality improvements. Nonfinancial measures of customer satisfaction include number of customer complaints and on-time delivery rate. Nonfinancial measures of internal quality performance include product defect levels and process yields. Financial data helps managers decide on tradeoffs among prevention, appraisal, and failure costs where nonfinancial measures direct attention to problems.

4. What is customer-response time? What are the reasons for and the costs of delays?	Customer-response time is the duration between the time a customer places an order for a product or service and the time the product or service is delivered to the customer. Delays occur because of (a) uncertainty about when customers will order products or services and (b) bottlenecks due to limited capacity. Bottlenecks are operations at which the work to be performed approaches or exceeds the available capacity. The costs of delays include lower revenues and increased inventory carrying costs.
5. What three measures do managers need to implement the theory of constraints?	The three measures in the theory of constraints are (a) throughput contribution (equal to revenues minus direct materials cost of the goods sold); (b) investments (equal to the sum of materials costs in direct materials, and work-in-process and finished goods inventories, R&D costs, and costs of equipment and buildings); and (c) operating costs (equal to all operating costs, other than direct materials costs, incurred to earn throughput contribution).

TERMS TO LEARN

This chapter contains definitions of the following important terms:

appraisal costs (p. 924)
average waiting time (p. 935)
bottleneck (p. 935)
cause-and-effect diagram (p. 928)
conformance quality (p. 922)
control chart (p. 927)
costs of design quality (p. 931)
costs of quality (COQ) (p. 923)

cushion (p. 936)
customer-response time (p. 934)
external failure costs (p. 924)
internal failure costs (p. 924)
manufacturing cycle efficiency (p. 934)
manufacturing cycle time (p. 934)
manufacturing lead time (p. 934)
on-time performance (p. 935)

order delivery time (p. 935)
order receipt time (p. 934)
outliers (p. 927)
Pareto diagram (p. 928)
prevention costs (p. 924)
quality of design (p. 922)
theory of constraints (TOC) (p. 938)
time driver (p. 935)

MASTERY QUESTIONS

Mastery Questions are rated by proficiency level—elementary, intermediate, and advanced. The solutions appear in the Solutions to Mastery Questions section of MyAccountingLab.

LEARNING OBJECTIVE 1

1. **BSC analysis of quality—Intermediate.** (CMA, adapted) Bergen Inc. produces cell phones at its London plant. In recent years, the company's market share has been eroded by stiff competition from Asian and European competitors. Price and product quality are the two key areas in which companies compete in this market.

   Jerry Holman, Bergen's president, decided to devote more resources to the improvement of product quality after learning that his company's products had been ranked fourth in product quality in a 2009 survey of telephone equipment users. He believed that Bergen could no longer afford to ignore the importance of product quality.

   Bergen's quality improvement program has now been in operation for two years, and the cost report shown below has recently been issued.

   As they were reviewing the report, Sheila Haynes, manager of sales, asked Tony Reese, production manager, what he thought of the quality program. "The work is really moving through the Production Department," replied Reese. "We used to spend time helping the Customer Service Department solve their problems but they are leaving us alone these days."

Semi-Annual Costs of Quality Report, Bergen Inc.
(in Thousands)

	6/30/2010	12/31/2010	6/30/2011	12/31/2011
Prevention costs				
Machine maintenance	$ 258	$ 258	$ 228	$ 192
Training suppliers	6	54	24	18
Design reviews	24	122	120	114
Total prevention costs	288	434	372	324
Appraisal costs				
Incoming inspection	54	64	43	26
Final testing	192	192	168	113
Total appraisal costs	246	256	211	139
Internal failure costs				
Rework	144	127	106	74
Scrap	82	77	50	48
Total internal failure costs	226	204	156	122
External failure costs				
Warranty repairs	83	37	30	28
Customer returns	314	301	139	96
Total external failure costs	397	338	169	124
Total quality costs	$1,157	$1,232	$ 908	$ 709
Total production and sales	$4,944	$5,448	$5,580	$5,412

REQUIRED

1. By analyzing the Cost of Quality Report presented, determine whether Bergen Inc.'s quality-improvement program has been successful. List specific evidence to support your answer.

2. Jerry Holman believed that the quality-improvement program was essential and that Bergen Inc. could no longer afford to ignore the importance of product quality. Discuss how Bergen could measure the opportunity cost of not implementing the quality-improvement program.

2. **BSC analysis of quality—Advanced.** Ontario Industries manufactures two types of refrigerators, Olivia and Solta. Information on each refrigerator is as follows:

	Olivia	Solta
Units manufactured and sold	10,000 units	5,000 units
Selling price	$2,400	$1,800
Variable costs per unit	$1,440	$ 960
Hours spent on design	6,000	1,000
Testing and inspection hours per unit	1	0.5
Percentage of units reworked in plant	5%	10%
Rework costs per refrigerator	$ 600	$ 480
Percentage of units repaired at customer site	4%	8%
Repair costs per refrigerator	$ 720	$ 540
Estimated lost sales from poor quality	—	300 units

The labour rates per hour for various activities are as follows:

Design	$90 per hour
Testing and inspection	$48 per hour

REQUIRED

1. Calculate the costs of quality for Olivia and Solta classified into prevention, appraisal, internal failure, and external failure categories.

2. For each type of refrigerator, calculate the ratio of each COQ item as a percentage of sales. Compare and comment on the costs of quality for Olivia and Solta.

3. Give two examples of nonfinancial quality measures that Ontario Industries could monitor as part of a total quality-control effort.

LEARNING OBJECTIVE 2

1. **Methods of analyzing quality-control problems—Intermediate.** Peoples Skyway operates daily round-trip flights on the London–Vancouver route using a fleet of three 747s, the *Spirit of Birmingham*, the *Spirit of Glasgow*, and the *Spirit of Manchester*. The budgeted quantity of fuel for each round-trip flight is the mean (average) fuel usage. Over the past 12 months, the average fuel usage per round trip is 120 litre-units with a standard deviation of 12 litre-units. A litre-unit is 1,000 litres.

Cilla Black, the operations manager of Peoples Skyway, uses a statistical quality control (SQC) approach in deciding whether to investigate fuel usage per round-trip flight. She investigates those flights with fuel usage greater than two standard deviations from the mean.

In October, Black receives the following report for round-trip fuel usage by the three planes operating on the London–Vancouver route:

Flight	Spirit of Birmingham (Litre-Units)	Spirit of Glasgow (Litre-Units)	Spirit of Manchester (Litre-Units)
1	124.8	123.6	116.4
2	112.8	112.8	124.8
3	116.4	115.2	133.2
4	121.2	128.4	124.8
5	126.0	110.4	146.4
6	128.4	135.6	141.6
7	133.2	118.8	151.2
8	134.2	127.2	136.8
9	138.0	121.2	140.4
10	142.8	111.6	147.6

REQUIRED

1. Using the $\pm 2\sigma$ rule, what variance investigation decisions would be made?
2. Present SQC charts for round-trip fuel usage for each of the three 747s in October. What inferences can you draw from them?
3. Some managers propose that Peoples Skyway present its SQC charts in monetary terms rather than in physical quantity terms (litre-units). What are the advantages and disadvantages of using monetary fuel costs rather than litre-units in the SQC charts?

2. **Methods of analyzing quality-control problems—Advanced.** The Murray Corporation manufactures, sells, and installs photocopying machines. Murray has placed heavy emphasis on reducing defects and failures in its production operations. Murray wants to apply the same total quality management (TQM) principles to managing its accounts receivables.

REQUIRED

1. On the basis of your knowledge and experience, what would you classify as failures in accounts receivables?
2. Give examples of prevention activities that could reduce failures in accounts receivables.
3. Draw a Pareto diagram of the types of failures in accounts receivables and a fishbone diagram of possible causes of one type of failure in accounts receivables.

LEARNING OBJECTIVE 3

1. **Financial and nonfinancial analysis of quality—Intermediate.** The Hartono Corporation manufactures and sells industrial grinders. The following table presents financial information pertaining to quality in 2010 and 2011 (in thousands):

	2010	2011
Sales	$10,000	$12,500
Line inspection	110	85
Scrap	250	175
Design engineering	100	240
Cost of returned goods	60	145
Product-testing equipment	50	50
Customer support	40	30
Rework costs	160	135

(Continued)

(Continued)

	2010	2011
Preventive equipment inspection	35	90
Product liability claims	200	100
Incoming materials inspection	20	40
Breakdown maintenance	90	40
Product-testing labour	220	75
Training	45	120
Warranty repair	300	200
Supplier evaluations	20	50

REQUIRED

1. Classify the cost items in the table into prevention, appraisal, internal failure, or external failure categories.
2. Calculate the ratio of each COQ category to sales in 2010 and 2011. Comment on the trends in costs of quality between 2010 and 2011.
3. Give two examples of nonfinancial quality measures that Hartono Corporation could monitor as part of a total quality control effort.

2. **Financial and nonfinancial analysis of quality—Advanced.** Pacific-Dunlop supplies tires to major automotive companies. It has two tire plants in Ontario, in Kitchener and Napanee. The quarterly bonus plan for each plant manager has three components:

   a. **Profitability performance.** Add 2% of operating income.
   b. **On-time delivery performance.** Add $12,000 if on-time delivery performance to the 10 most important customers is 98% or better. If on-time performance is below 98%, add nothing.
   c. **Product quality performance.** Deduct 50% of cost of sales returns from the 10 most important customers.

   Quarterly data for 2010 on the Kitchener and Napanee plants are as follows:

	January–March	April–June	July–September	October–December
Kitchener				
Operating income	$ 960,000	$1,020,000	$ 840,000	$1,080,000
On-time delivery*	98.4%	98.6%	97.1%	97.9%
Cost of sales returns*	$ 21,600	$ 31,200	$ 12,000	$ 30,000
Napanee				
Operating income	$1,920,000	$1,800,000	$2,160,000	$2,280,000
On-time delivery*	95.6%	97.1%	97.9%	98.4%
Cost of sales returns*	$ 42,000	$ 40,800	$ 33,600	$ 26,400

*For the ten most important customers.

REQUIRED

1. Compute the bonuses paid in each quarter of 2010 to the plant managers of the Kitchener and Napanee plants.
2. Discuss the three components of the bonus plan as measures of profitability, on-time delivery, and product quality.
3. Why would you want to evaluate plant managers on the basis of both operating income and on-time delivery?
4. Give one example of what might happen if on-time delivery were dropped as a performance evaluation measure.

LEARNING OBJECTIVE 4

1. **Customer-response time, on-time delivery.** Pizzafest Inc. makes and delivers pizzas to homes and offices in the Vancouver area. Fast, on-time delivery is one of Pizzafest's key strategies. Pizzafest provides the following information for the year 2010 about its customer-response time— the amount of time between when a customer calls to place an order and when the pizza is delivered to the customer.

	January–June	July–December
1. Pizzas delivered in 30 minutes or less	120,000	180,000
2. Pizzas delivered in between 31 and 45 minutes	240,000	312,000
3. Pizzas delivered in between 46 and 60 minutes	96,000	84,000
4. Pizzas delivered in between 61 and 75 minutes	24,000	24,000
Total pizzas delivered	480,000	600,000

REQUIRED

1. For January–June 2010 and July–December 2010, calculate the percentage of pizzas delivered in each of the four time intervals (less than 30 minutes, 31 to 45 minutes, 46 to 60 minutes, and 61 to 75 minutes). On the basis of these calculations, has customer-response time improved in July–December 2010 compared with January–June 2010?
2. When customers call Pizzafest, they often ask how long it will take for the pizza to be delivered to their home or office. If Pizzafest quotes a long time interval, customers will often not place the order. If Pizzafest quotes too short a time interval and the pizza is not delivered on time, customers get upset and Pizzafest will lose repeat business. Based on the January–June 2010 data, what maximum customer-response time should Pizzafest quote to its customers if (a) it wants to have an on-time delivery performance of at least 75%? (b) it wants to have an on-time delivery performance of at least 95%?
3. If Pizzafest had quoted the maximum customer-response times you calculated in requirements 2(a) and 2(b), would it have met its on-time delivery performance targets of 75% and 95% respectively for the period July–December 2010?

LEARNING OBJECTIVE 5

1. Theory of constraints—Advanced. Aardee Industries manufactures pharmaceutical products in two departments—Mixing and Tablet-Making. Additional information on the two departments follows. Each tablet contains 0.5 gram of direct materials.

	Mixing	Tablet-Making
Capacity per hour	150 grams	200 tablets
Monthly capacity (2,000 hours available in each of mixing and tablet-making)	300,000 grams	400,000 tablets
Monthly production	200,000 grams	390,000 tablets
Fixed operating costs (excluding direct materials)	$ 19,200	$ 46,800
Fixed operating costs per unit ($19,200 ÷ 200,000; $46,800 ÷ 390,000)	$ 0.096 per gram	$ 0.12 per tablet

The Mixing Department makes 200,000 grams of direct materials mixture (enough to make 400,000 tablets) because the Tablet-Making Department has only enough capacity to process 400,000 tablets. All direct materials costs are incurred in the Mixing Department. Aardee incurs $187,200 in direct materials costs. The Tablet-Making Department manufactures only 390,000 tablets from the 200,000 grams of mixture processed; 2.5% of the direct materials mixture is lost in the tablet-making process. Each tablet sells for $1.20. All costs other than direct materials costs are fixed costs. The following requirements refer only to the preceding data; there is no connection between the situations.

REQUIRED

1. An outside contractor makes the following offer: if Aardee will supply the contractor with 10,000 grams of mixture, the contractor will manufacture 19,500 tablets for Aardee (allowing for the normal 2.5% loss during the tablet-making process) at $0.144 per tablet. Should Aardee accept the contractor's offer?
2. Another firm offers to prepare 20,000 grams of mixture a month from direct materials Aardee supplies. The company will charge $0.084 per gram of mixture. Should Aardee accept the company's offer?
3. Aardee's engineers have devised a method that would improve quality in the tablet-making operation. They estimate that the 10,000 tablets currently being lost would be saved. The modification would cost $8,400 a month. Should Aardee implement the new method?
4. Suppose that Aardee also loses 10,000 grams of mixture in its mixing operation. These losses can be reduced to zero if the company is willing to spend $10,800 per month in quality-improvement methods. Should Aardee adopt the quality-improvement methods?
5. What are the benefits of improving quality at the mixing operation compared with the benefits of improving quality at the tablet-making operation?

SHORT-ANSWER QUESTIONS

19-1 Describe two benefits of improving quality.

19-2 How does conformance quality differ from quality of design? Explain.

19-3 Name two items classified as prevention costs.

19-4 Distinguish between internal failure costs and external failure costs.

19-5 Describe three methods that companies use to identify quality problems.

19-6 "Companies should focus on financial measures of quality because these are the only measures of quality that can be linked to bottom-line performance." Do you agree? Explain.

19-7 Give two examples of nonfinancial measures of customer satisfaction.

19-8 Give two examples of nonfinancial measures of internal performance.

19-9 Distinguish between customer-response time and manufacturing lead time.

19-10 There is no tradeoff between customer-response time and on-time performance." Do you agree? Explain.

19-11 Give two reasons why delays occur.

19-12 "Companies should always make and sell all products whose selling prices exceed variable costs." Do you agree? Explain.

19-13 Describe the three main measures used in the theory of constraints.

19-14 Describe the four key steps in managing bottleneck resources.

19-15 Describe three ways to improve the performance of a bottleneck operation.

EXERCISES

1. 6/30/2009 total quality costs % of revenues, 24.7%

19-16 Costs of quality. (CMA, adapted) Costen Inc. produces cell phone equipment. Jessica Tolmy, Costen's president, decided to devote more resources to the improvement of product quality after learning that her company had been ranked fourth in product quality in a 2008 survey of cell phone users. Costen's quality-improvement program has now been in operation for two years, and the cost report shown on the next page has recently been issued.

REQUIRED

1. For each period, calculate the ratio of each COQ category to revenues and to total quality costs.
2. Based on the results of requirement 1, would you conclude that Costen's quality program has been successful? Prepare a short report to present your case.
3. Based on the 2008 survey, Jessica Tolmy believed that Costen had to improve product quality. In making her case to Costen management, how might Tolmy have estimated the opportunity cost of not implementing the quality-improvement program?

19-17 Costs of quality analysis. Safe Rider produces car seats for children from newborn to 2 years old. The company is worried because one of its competitors has recently come under public scrutiny because of product failure. Historically, Safe Rider's only problem with its car seats was stitching in the straps. The problem can usually be detected and repaired during an internal inspection. The cost of the inspection is $5, and the repair cost is $1. All 100,000 car seats were inspected last year and 5% were found to have problems with the stitching in the straps during the internal inspection. Another 2% of the 100,000 car seats had problems with the stitching, but the internal inspection did not discover them.

Semi-Annual COQ Report, Costen Inc.
(in thousands)

	6/30/2009	12/31/2009	6/30/2010	12/31/2010
Prevention costs				
Machine maintenance	$ 440	$ 440	$ 390	$ 330
Supplier training	20	100	50	40
Design reviews	50	214	210	200
Total prevention costs	510	754	650	570
Appraisal costs				
Incoming inspections	108	123	90	63
Final testing	332	332	293	203
Total appraisal costs	440	455	383	266
Internal failure costs				
Rework	231	202	165	112
Scrap	124	116	71	67
Total internal failure costs	355	318	236	179
External failure costs				
Warranty repairs	165	85	72	68
Customer returns	570	547	264	188
Total external failure costs	735	632	336	256
Total quality costs	$2,040	2,159	$1,605	$1,271
Total revenues	$8,240	$9,080	$9,300	$9,020

Defective units that were sold and shipped to customers needed to be shipped back to Safe Rider and repaired. Shipping costs are $10, and repair costs are $1. However, the out-of-pocket costs (shipping and repair) are not the only costs of defects not discovered in the internal inspection. For 20% of the external failures, negative word of mouth will result in a loss of sales, lowering the following year's contribution margin by $500 for each of the 20% of units with external failures.

REQUIRED
1. Calculate appraisal cost.
2. Calculate internal failure cost.
3. Calculate out-of-pocket external failure cost.
4. Determine the opportunity cost associated with the external failures.
5. What are the total costs of quality?
6. Safe Rider is concerned with the high up-front cost of inspecting all 100,000 units. It is considering an alternative internal inspection plan that will cost only $1.50 per car seat inspected. During the internal inspection, the alternative technique will detect only 2.5% of the 100,000 car seats that have stitching problems. The other 4.5% will be detected after the car seats are sold and shipped. What are the total costs of quality for the alternative technique?
7. What factors other than cost should Safe Rider consider before changing inspection techniques?

19-18 Costs of quality analysis, ethical considerations. Refer to information in Exercise 19-17 in answering this question. Safe Rider has discovered a more serious problem with the plastic core of its car seats. An accident can cause the plastic in some of the seats to crack and break, resulting in serious injuries to the occupant. It is estimated that this problem will affect about 200 car seats in the next year. This problem could be corrected by using a higher quality of plastic that would increase the cost of every car seat produced by $25. If this problem is not corrected, Safe Rider estimates that out of the 200 accidents, customers will realize that the problem is due to a defect in the seats in only two cases. Safe Rider's legal team has estimated that each of these two accidents would result in a lawsuit that could be settled for about $750,000. All lawsuits settled would include a confidentiality clause, so Safe Rider's reputation would not be affected.

1. Cost of improving quality of plastic, $2,500,000

REQUIRED

1. Assuming that Safe Rider expects to sell 100,000 car seats next year, what would be the cost of increasing the quality of all 100,000 car seats?
2. What will be the total cost of the lawsuits next year if the problem is not corrected?
3. Safe Rider has decided not to increase the quality of the plastic because the cost of increasing the quality exceeds the benefits (saving the cost of lawsuits). What do you think of this decision? (*Note:* Because of the confidentiality clause, the decision will have no effect on Safe Rider's reputation.)
4. Are there any other costs or benefits that Safe Rider should consider?

1. 2009 percentage of defective units shipped, 5%

19-19 Nonfinancial measures of quality and time. Worldwide Cell Phones (WCP) has developed a cell phone that can be used anywhere in the world (even in countries like Japan that have a relatively unique cell phone system). WCP has been receiving complaints about the phone. For the past two years, WCP has been test marketing the phones and gathering nonfinancial information related to actual and perceived aspects of the phone's quality. They expect that, given the lack of competition in this market, increasing the quality of the phone will result in higher sales and thereby higher profits.

Quality data for 2009 and 2010 include the following:

	2009	2010
Cell phones produced and shipped	2,000	10,000
Number of defective units shipped	100	400
Number of customer complaints	150	250
Units reworked before shipping	120	700
Manufacturing lead time	15 days	16 days
Average customer-response time	30 days	28 days

REQUIRED

1. For each year, 2009 and 2010, calculate:
   a. Percentage of defective units shipped.
   b. Customer complaints as a percentage of units shipped.
   c. Percentage of units reworked during production.
   d. Manufacturing lead time as a percentage of total time from order to delivery.
2. Referring to the information computed in requirement 1, explain whether WCP's quality and timeliness have improved.
3. Why would manufacturing lead time have increased while customer-response time decreased? (It may be useful to first describe what is included in each time measurement—see Exhibit 19-7 on p. 934.)

1. Relevant costs of choosing new printing presses, $1,100,000

19-20 Quality improvement, relevant costs, relevant revenues. TechnoPrint manufactures and sells 20,000 high-technology printing presses each year. The variable and fixed costs of rework and repair are as follows:

	Variable Costs	Fixed Cost	Total Cost
Rework cost per hour	$ 80	$120	$200
Repair costs			
Customer support cost per hour	40	60	100
Transportation cost per load	360	120	480
Warranty repair cost per hour	90	130	220

TechnoPrint's current presses have a quality problem that causes variations in the shade of some colours. Its engineers suggest changing a key component in each press. The new component will cost $55 more than the old one. In the next year, however, TechnoPrint expects that with the new component it will (1) save 12,875 hours of rework, (2) save 900 hours of customer support, (3) move 200 fewer loads, (4) save 7,000 hours of warranty repairs, and (5) sell an additional 150 printing presses, for a total contribution margin of $1,800,000. TechnoPrint believes that even as it improves quality, it will not be able to save any of the fixed costs of rework or repair. TechnoPrint uses a one-year time horizon for this decision, because it plans to introduce a new press at the end of the year.

REQUIRED
1. Should TechnoPrint change to the new component? Show your calculations.
2. Suppose the estimate of 150 additional printing presses sold is uncertain. What is the minimum number of additional printing presses that TechnoPrint needs to sell to justify adopting the new component?

19-21 Manufacturing cycle time, manufacturing cycle efficiency. (CMA, adapted) Torrance Manufacturing evaluates the performance of its production managers based on a variety of factors, including cost, quality, and cycle time. The following information relates to the average amount of time needed to complete an order for its one product:

Wait time:	
From order being placed to start of production	8 days
From start of production to completion	6 days
Inspection time	2 days
Process time	4 days
Move time	2 days

1. Total manufacturing time, 22 days

REQUIRED
1. Compute the manufacturing cycle efficiency for an order.
2. Compute the manufacturing cycle time (or lead time) for an order.

19-22 Nonfinancial quality measures, on-time delivery. Checkers Pizza promises to deliver pizzas in 25 minutes or less. If pizzas are not delivered on time, then the customer receives $5 off the price of the order. Some store managers, who receive bonuses based on store profits, believe that the guarantee is a win-win situation for Checkers. Because the average pizza sells for $9 but has a marginal cost of $2.25, the store makes a profit no matter what the delivery time. If a pizza is delivered on time, then the store earns $6.75 ($9 − $2.25) per pizza. If a pizza is delivered late, then the store still earns $1.75 ($9 − $5 − $2.25) per pizza. If more than one pizza is ordered, then Checkers makes even more money because it only gives one $5 discount per order.

2. Slope coefficient, −0.10

   The head of the Checkers chain is worried that this perceived win-win situation may encourage a complacent attitude in store managers with respect to on-time deliveries. While short-run profits are still earned with late deliveries, repeated late deliveries could lead to annoyance on the part of customers and eventually to a loss of customers. Therefore, the Checkers corporate headquarters has decided to gather information about late deliveries and customer satisfaction. It has developed a survey that asks delivery customers to rate their satisfaction based on three attributes: delivery service, value for money, and overall satisfaction with Checkers. Responses can range from 1 to 5, where 1 is "Awful" and 5 is "Excellent." The following responses were gathered from stores in a single city.

	Store 1	Store 2	Store 3	Store 4
Percentage of deliveries that were late	10%	5%	12%	25%
Average rating of delivery service	4	4.5	3.8	2
Average rating of value received	3.5	4.1	3.5	1.5
Average overall satisfaction with Checkers	3.6	4	3	2

REQUIRED
1. Examine the relationship between the percentage of deliveries that were late and average responses to the three survey questions. Do the data provide any support for Checkers headquarters' concerns?
2. Estimate the effect of changes in the late-delivery percentage on average overall satisfaction with Checkers. Use the customer satisfaction score as the dependent variable. Based on this analysis, compute the impact of a change from 5% late deliveries to 7% late deliveries on overall customer satisfaction.
3. What factors would Checkers need to consider when determining whether the delivery guarantee is actually beneficial for the company?

19-23 Waiting time, service industry. The registration advisers at a small university (SU) help 4,000 students develop each of their class schedules and register for classes each semester. Each adviser works for 10 hours a day during the registration period. SU currently has 10 advisers. While advising an individual student can take anywhere from 2 to 30 minutes, it takes an average of 12 minutes per student. During the registration period, the 10 advisers see an average of 300 students a day.

REQUIRED

1. Using the formula on p. 936, calculate how long the average student will have to wait in the adviser's office before being advised.
2. The head of the registration advisers would like to increase the number of students seen each day, because at 300 students a day it would take 14 working days to see all of the students. This is a problem because the registration period lasts for only two weeks (10 working days). If the advisers could advise 400 students a day, it would take only two weeks (about 10 days). However, they want to make sure that the waiting time is not excessive. What would be the average waiting time if 400 students were seen each day?
3. SU wants to know the effect of reducing the average advising time on the average wait time. If SU can reduce the average advising time to 10 minutes, what would be the average waiting time if 400 students were seen each day?

19-24 Waiting time, cost considerations, customer satisfaction. Refer to the information presented in Exercise 19-23. The head of the registration advisers at SU has decided that the advisers must finish their advising in two weeks and therefore must advise 400 students a day. However, the average waiting time given a 12-minute advising period will result in student complaints, as will reducing the average advising time to 10 minutes. SU is considering two alternatives:

A. Hire two more advisers for the two-week (10-working-day) advising period. This will increase the available number of advisers to 12 and therefore lower the average waiting time.

B. Increase the number of days that the advisers will work during the two-week registration period to 6 days a week. If SU increases the number of days worked to six per week, then the 10 advisers need only see 350 students a day to advise all the students in two weeks.

REQUIRED

1. What would the average wait time be under each alternative described above?
2. If advisers earn $100 per day, which alternative would be cheaper for SU (assume that if advisers work 6 days in a given work week, they will be paid time and a half for the sixth day)?
3. From a student satisfaction point of view, which of the two alternatives would be preferred? Why?

19-25 Theory of constraints, throughput contribution, relevant costs. The Mayfield Corporation manufactures filing cabinets in two operations: machining and finishing. It provides the following information:

	Machining	Finishing
Annual capacity	100,000 units	80,000 units
Annual production	80,000 units	80,000 units
Fixed operating costs (excluding direct materials)	$640,000	$400,000
Fixed operating costs per unit produced ($640,000 ÷ 80,000; $400,000 ÷ 80,000)	$8 per unit	$5 per unit

Each cabinet sells for $72 and has direct material costs of $32 incurred at the start of the machining operation. Mayfield has no other variable costs. Mayfield can sell whatever output it produces. The following requirements refer only to the preceding data. There is no connection between the requirements.

REQUIRED

1. Mayfield is considering using some modern jigs and tools in the finishing operation that would increase annual finishing output by 1,000 units. The annual cost of these jigs and tools is $30,000. Should Mayfield acquire these tools? Show your calculations.
2. The production manager of the Machining Department has submitted a proposal to do faster setups that would increase the annual capacity of the Machining Department by 10,000 units and would cost $5,000 per year. Should Mayfield implement the change? Show your calculations.

3. An outside contractor offers to do the finishing operation for 12,000 units at $10 per unit, double the $5 per unit that it costs Mayfield to do the finishing in-house. Should Mayfield accept the subcontractor's offer? Show your calculations.

4. The Hunt Corporation offers to machine 4,000 units at $4 per unit, half the $8 per unit that it costs Mayfield to do the machining in-house. Should Mayfield accept Hunt's offer? Show your calculations.

19-26 Theory of constraints, throughput contribution, quality. Refer to the information in Exercise 19-25 in answering the following requirements. There is no connection between the requirements.

⑤

2. Forgone throughput contribution, $80,000

REQUIRED

1. Mayfield produces 2,000 defective units at the machining operation. What is the cost to Mayfield of the defective items produced? Explain your answer briefly.

2. Mayfield produces 2,000 defective units at the finishing operation. What is the cost to Mayfield of the defective items produced? Explain your answer briefly.

PROBLEMS

19-27 Quality improvement, relevant costs, and relevant revenues. The Thomas Corporation sells 300,000 V262 valves to the automobile and truck industry. Thomas has a capacity of 110,000 machine-hours and can produce 3 valves per machine-hour. V262's contribution margin per unit is $8. Thomas sells only 300,000 valves because 30,000 valves (10% of the good valves) need to be reworked. It takes one machine-hour to rework 3 valves, so 10,000 hours of capacity are used in the rework process. Thomas's rework costs are $210,000. Rework costs consist of:

②

1. Contribution margin per machine-hour for V262, $24

◆ Direct materials and direct rework labour (variable costs): $3 per unit
◆ Fixed costs of equipment, rent, and overhead allocation: $4 per unit

   Thomas's process designers have developed a modification that would maintain the speed of the process and ensure 100% quality and no rework. The new process would cost $315,000 per year. The following additional information is available:

◆ The demand for Thomas's V262 valves is 370,000 per year.
◆ The Jackson Corporation has asked Thomas to supply 22,000 T971 valves (another product) if Thomas implements the new design. The contribution margin per T971 valve is $10. Thomas can make two T971 valves per machine-hour with 100% quality and no rework.

REQUIRED

1. Suppose Thomas's designers implement the new design. Should Thomas accept Jackson's order for 22,000 T971 valves? Show your calculations.

2. Should Thomas implement the new design? Show your calculations.

3. What nonfinancial and qualitative factors should Thomas consider in deciding whether to implement the new design?

19-28 Quality improvement, relevant costs, and relevant revenues. The Tan Corporation uses multicolour moulding to make plastic lamps. The moulding operation has a capacity of 200,000 units per year. The demand for lamps is very strong. Tan will be able to sell whatever output quantities it can produce at $40 per lamp.

②

1. Additional direct materials cost, $800,000

   Tan can start only 200,000 units into production in the Moulding Department because of capacity constraints on the moulding machines. If a defective unit is produced at the moulding operation, it must be scrapped at a net disposal value of zero. Of the 200,000 units started at the moulding operation, 30,000 defective units (15%) are produced. The cost of a defective unit, based on total (fixed and variable) manufacturing costs incurred up to the moulding operation, equals $25 per unit, as follows:

Direct materials (variable)	$16 per unit
Direct manufacturing labour, setup labour, and materials-handling labour (variable)	3 per unit
Equipment, rent, and other allocated overhead, including inspection and testing costs on scrapped parts (fixed)	6 per unit
Total	$25 per unit

   Tan's designers have determined that adding a different type of material to the existing direct materials would result in no defective units being produced, but it would increase the variable costs by $4 per lamp in the Moulding Department.

REQUIRED

1. Should Tan use the new material? Show your calculations.
2. What nonfinancial and qualitative factors should Tan consider in making the decision?

19-29 **Statistical quality control, airline operations.** Jetrans Airlines operates daily round-trip flights on the London–Vancouver route using a fleet of three 747s: the *Spirit of Birmingham*, the *Spirit of Glasgow*, and the *Spirit of Manchester*. The budgeted quantity of fuel for each round-trip flight is the 12-month mean (average) round-trip fuel consumption of 200 litre-units, with a standard deviation of 20 litre-units. A litre-unit is 1,000 litres.

Using a statistical quality control (SQC) approach, Shirley Watson, the Jetrans operations manager, investigates any round trip with fuel consumption that is greater than two standard deviations from the mean. In October, Watson receives the following report for round-trip fuel consumption for the three planes on the London–Vancouver route:

Flight	*Spirit of Birmingham* (Litre-Units)	*Spirit of Glasgow* (Litre-Units)	*Spirit of Manchester* (Litre-Units)
1	208	206	194
2	187	188	208
3	194	192	221
4	202	214	208
5	211	184	242
6	215	226	234
7	216	198	249
8	218	212	227
9	221	202	232
10	232	186	244

REQUIRED

1. Using the $\pm 2\sigma$ rule, what variance-investigation decisions would be made?
2. Present SQC charts for round-trip fuel usage for each of the three 747s in October. What inferences can you draw from the charts?
3. Some managers propose that Jetrans Airlines present its SQC charts in monetary terms rather than in physical-quantity terms (litre-units). What are the advantages and disadvantages of using monetary fuel costs rather than litre-units in the SQC charts?

19-30 **Compensation linked with profitability, waiting time, and quality measures.** Mid-Atlantic Healthcare USA operates two medical groups, one in Philadelphia and one in Baltimore. The semi-annual bonus plan for each medical group's president has three components:

a. *Profitability performance.* Add 1% of operating income.
b. *Average patient waiting time.* Add $50,000 if the average waiting time for a patient to see a doctor after the scheduled appointment time is less than 15 minutes. If average patient waiting time is more than 15 minutes, add nothing.
c. *Patient satisfaction performance.* Deduct $50,000 if patient satisfaction (measured using a survey asking patients about their satisfaction with their doctor and their overall satisfaction with Mid-Atlantic Healthcare) falls below 70 on a scale from 0 (lowest) to 100 (highest). No additional bonus is awarded for satisfaction scores of 70 or more.

Semi-annual data for 2009 for the Philadelphia and Baltimore groups are as follows:

	January–June	July–December
Philadelphia		
Operating income	$10,650,000	$10,600,000
Average waiting time	14 minutes	16 minutes
Patient satisfaction	79	82
Baltimore		
Operating income	$9,000,000	$950,000
Average waiting time	17 minutes	14.5 minutes
Patient satisfaction	66	70

REQUIRED

1. Compute the bonuses paid in each half year of 2009 to the Philadelphia and Baltimore medical group presidents.
2. Discuss the validity of the components of the bonus plan as measures of profitability, waiting-time performance, and patient satisfaction. Suggest one shortcoming of each measure and how it might be overcome (by redesign of the plan or by another measure).
3. Why do you think Mid-Atlantic Healthcare USA includes measures of both operating income and waiting time in its bonus plan for group presidents? Give one example of what might happen if waiting time were dropped as a performance measure.

19-31 Waiting times, manufacturing lead times. The SRG Corporation uses an injection moulding machine to make a plastic product, Z39. SRG makes products only after receiving firm orders from its customers. SRG estimates that it will receive 50 orders for Z39 (each order is for 1,000 units) during the coming year. Each order of Z39 will take 80 hours of machine time. The annual capacity of the machine is 5,000 hours.

④

1. Average order waiting time for Z39, 160 hours

REQUIRED

1. Calculate (a) the average amount of time that an order for Z39 will wait in line before it is processed and (b) the average manufacturing lead time per order for Z39.
2. SRG is considering introducing a new product, Y28. SRG expects it will receive 25 orders of Y28 (each order for 200 units) in the coming year. Each order of Y28 will take 20 hours of machine time. The average demand for Z39 will be unaffected by the introduction of Y28. Calculate (a) the average waiting time for an order received and (b) the average manufacturing lead time per order for each product, if SRG introduces Y28.

19-32 Waiting times, relevant revenues, and relevant costs (continuation of 19-31). SRG is still deciding whether it should introduce Y28. The following table provides information on selling prices, variable costs, and inventory carrying costs for Z39 and Y28. SRG will incur additional variable costs and inventory carrying costs for Y28 only if it introduces Y28. Fixed costs equal to 40% of variable costs are allocated to all products produced and sold during the year.

④

1. Additional contribution per order of Y28, $3,000

| | | Selling Price per Order If Average Manufacturing Lead Time per Order Is | | | |
Product	Annual Average Number of Orders	Less than 320 Hours	More than 320 Hours	Variable Cost per Order	Inventory Carrying Cost per Order per Hour
Z39	50	$27,000	$26,500	$15,000	$0.75
Y28	25	8,400	8,000	5,000	0.25

REQUIRED

1. Should SRG manufacture and sell Y28? Show your calculations.
2. Should SRG manufacture and sell Y28 if the data are changed as follows: Selling price per order is $6,400, instead of $8,400, if average manufacturing lead time per order is less than 320 hours; and $6,000, instead of $8,000, if average manufacturing lead time per order is more than 320 hours? All other data for Y28 are the same.

19-33 Manufacturing lead times, relevant revenues, and relevant costs. The Brandt Corporation makes wire harnesses for the aircraft industry. Brandt is uncertain about when and how many customer orders will be received. The company makes harnesses only after receiving firm orders from its customers. Brandt has recently purchased a new machine to make two types of wire harnesses, one for Boeing airplanes (B7) and the other for Airbus Industries airplanes (A3). The annual capacity of the new machine is 6,000 hours. The following information is available for next year:

④

1. a. Average order waiting time for B7, 100 hours

| | Annual Average Number of Orders | Manufacturing Time Required | Selling Price per Order If Average Manufacturing Lead Time per Order Is | | Variable Cost per Order | Inventory Carrying Cost per Order per Hour |
Customer			Less than 200 Hours	More than 200 Hours		
B7	125	40 hours	$15,000	$14,400	$10,000	$0.50
A3	10	50 hours	13,500	12,960	9,000	0.45

REQUIRED
1. Calculate the average manufacturing lead times per order (a) if Brandt manufactures only B7 and (b) if Brandt manufactures both B7 and A3.
2. Even though A3 has a positive contribution margin, Brandt's managers are evaluating whether Brandt should (a) make and sell only B7 or (b) make and sell both B7 and A3. Which alternative will maximize Brandt's operating income? Show your calculations.
3. What other factors should Brandt consider in choosing between the alternatives in requirement 2?

2. Additional relevant costs of new direct materials, $640,000

19-34 Theory of constraints, throughput contribution, relevant costs. Cabano Industries manufactures electronic testing equipment. Cabano also installs the equipment at customers' sites and ensures that it functions smoothly. Additional information on the Manufacturing and Installation Departments is as follows (capacities are expressed in terms of the number of units of electronic testing equipment):

	Equipment Manufactured	Equipment Installed
Annual capacity	400 units per year	300 units per year
Equipment manufactured and installed	300 units per year	300 units per year

Cabano manufactures only 300 units per year because the Installation Department has only enough capacity to install 300 units. The equipment sells for $40,000 per unit (installed) and has direct material costs of $15,000. All costs other than direct material costs are fixed. The following requirements refer only to the preceding data. There is no connection between the requirements.

REQUIRED
1. Cabano's engineers have found a way to reduce equipment manufacturing time. The new method would cost an additional $50 per unit and would allow Cabano to manufacture 20 additional units a year. Should Cabano implement the new method? Show your calculations.
2. Cabano's designers have proposed a change in direct materials that would increase direct material costs by $2,000 per unit. This change would enable Cabano to install 320 units of equipment each year. If Cabano makes the change, it will implement the new design on all equipment sold. Should Cabano use the new design? Show your calculations.
3. A new installation technique has been developed that will enable Cabano's engineers to install 10 additional units of equipment a year. The new method will increase installation costs by $50,000 each year. Should Cabano implement the new technique? Show your calculations.
4. Cabano is considering how to motivate workers to improve their productivity (output per hour). One proposal is to evaluate and compensate workers in the Manufacturing and Installation Departments on the basis of their productivities. Do you think the new proposal is a good idea? Explain briefly.

1. Direct materials costs per tablet, $0.40

19-35 Theory of constraints, throughput contribution, quality, relevant costs. Aardee Industries manufactures pharmaceutical products in two departments: Mixing and Tablet-Making. Additional information on the two departments follows. Each tablet contains 0.5 gram of direct materials.

	Mixing	Tablet Making
Capacity per hour	150 grams	200 tablets
Monthly capacity (2,000 hours available in each department)	300,000 grams	400,000 tablets
Monthly production	200,000 grams	390,000 tablets
Fixed operating costs (excluding direct materials)	$ 16,000	$ 39,000
Fixed operating cost per tablet ($16,000 ÷ 200,000 grams; $39,000 ÷ 390,000 tablets)	$ 0.08 per gram	$ 0.10 per tablet

The Mixing Department makes 200,000 grams of direct materials mixture (enough to make 400,000 tablets) because the Tablet-Making Department has only enough capacity to process 400,000 tablets. All direct material costs are incurred in the Mixing Department.

Aardee incurs $156,000 in direct material costs. The Tablet-Making Department manufactures only 390,000 tablets from the 200,000 grams of mixture processed; 2.5% of the direct materials mixture is lost in the tablet-making process. Each tablet sells for $1. All costs other than direct material costs are fixed costs. The following requirements refer only to the preceding data. There is no connection between the requirements.

REQUIRED

1. An outside contractor makes the following offer: If Aardee will supply the contractor with 10,000 grams of mixture, the contractor will manufacture 19,500 tablets for Aardee (allowing for the normal 2.5% loss of the mixture during the tablet-making process) at $0.12 per tablet. Should Aardee accept the contractor's offer? Show your calculations.

2. Another company offers to prepare 20,000 grams of mixture a month from direct materials Aardee supplies. The company will charge $0.07 per gram of mixture. Should Aardee accept the company's offer? Show your calculations.

3. Aardee's engineers have devised a method that would improve quality in the Tablet-Making Department. They estimate that the 10,000 tablets currently being lost would be saved. The modification would cost $7,000 a month. Should Aardee implement the new method? Show your calculations.

4. Suppose that Aardee also loses 10,000 grams of mixture in its Mixing Department. These losses can be reduced to zero if the company is willing to spend $9,000 per month in quality-improvement methods. Should Aardee adopt the quality-improvement method? Show your calculations.

5. What are the benefits of improving quality in the Mixing Department compared with improving quality in the Tablet-Making Department?

19-36 **Governance and quality.** Information from a quality report for 2010 prepared by Lindsey Williams, assistant controller of Citocell, a manufacturer of electric motors, is as follows:

1. Appraisal costs, $300,000

Revenues	$10,000,000
Inspection of production	$ 90,000
Warranty liability	$ 260,000
Product testing	$ 210,000
Scrap	$ 230,000
Design engineering	$ 200,000
Percentage of customer complaints	5%
On-time delivery rate	93%

Davey Evans, the plant manager of Citocell, is eligible for a bonus if the total costs of quality as a percentage of revenues are less than 10%, the percentage of customer complaints is less than 4%, and the on-time delivery rate exceeds 92%. Evans is unhappy about the customer complaints of 5% because, when preparing her report, Williams actually surveyed customers regarding customer satisfaction. Evans expected Williams to be less proactive and to wait for customers to complain. Evans's concern with Williams's approach is that it introduces subjectivity into the results and also fails to capture the seriousness of customers' concerns. "When you wait for a customer to complain, you know he is complaining because it is something important. When you do customer surveys, customers mention whatever is on their mind, even if it is not terribly important."

John Roche, the controller, asks Williams to see him. He tells her about Evans's concerns. "I think Davey has a point. See what you can do." Williams is confident that the customer complaints are genuine and that customers are concerned about quality and service. She believes it is important for Citocell to be proactive and obtain systematic and timely customer feedback, and then to use this information to make improvements. She is also well aware that Citocell has not done customer surveys in the past, and that, except for her surveys, Evans would probably be eligible for the bonus. She is confused about how to handle Roche's request.

REQUIRED

1. Calculate the ratio of each cost-of-quality category (prevention, appraisal, internal failure, and external failure) to revenues in 2010. Are the total costs of quality as a percentage of revenues less than 10%?

2. Would it be unethical for Williams to modify her analysis? What steps should Williams take to resolve this situation?

19-37 Theory of constraints, contribution margin, sensitivity analysis. Low Tech Toys (LTT) produces dolls in two processes: moulding and assembly. LTT is currently producing two models: Chatty Chelsey and Talking Tanya. Production in the Moulding Department is limited by the amount of materials available. Production in the Assembly Department is limited by the amount of trained labour available. The only variable costs are materials in the Moulding Department and labour in the Assembly Department. Following are the requirements and limitations by doll model and department.

	Moulding Materials	Assembly Time	Selling Price
Chatty Chelsey	1.5 kg per doll	20 minutes per doll	$35 per doll
Talking Tanya	2 kg per doll	30 minutes per doll	$45 per doll
Materials/Labour Available	30,000 kg	8,400 hours	
Cost	$10 per kg	$12 per hour	

REQUIRED

1. If LTT sold only one type of doll, which doll would it produce? How many of these dolls would it make and sell?
2. If LTT sells two Chatty Chelseys for each Talking Tanya, how many dolls of each type would it produce and sell? What would be the total contribution margin?
3. If LTT sells two Chatty Chelseys for each Talking Tanya, how much would production and contribution margin increase if the Moulding Department could buy 10 more kilograms of materials for $10 per kilogram?
4. If LTT sells two Chatty Chelseys for each Talking Tanya, how much would production and contribution margin increase if the Assembly Department could get 10 more labour-hours at $12 per hour?

COLLABORATIVE LEARNING CASE

19-38 Quality improvement, theory of constraints. The Wellesley Corporation makes printed cloth in two departments: Weaving and Printing. Direct material costs are Wellesley's only variable costs. The demand for Wellesley's cloth is very strong. Wellesley can sell whatever output quantities it produces at $1,250 per roll to a distributor who markets, distributes, and provides customer service for the product. Wellesley provides the following information.

	Weaving	Printing
Monthly capacity	10,000 rolls	15,000 rolls
Monthly production	9,500 rolls	8,550 rolls
Direct material cost per roll of cloth processed at each operation	$ 500	$ 100
Fixed operating costs	$2,850,000	$427,500
Fixed operating cost per roll ($2,850,000, 9,500 rolls; $427,500, 8,550 rolls)	$ 300 per roll	$ 50 per roll

Wellesley can start only 10,000 rolls of cloth in the Weaving Department because of capacity constraints of the weaving machines. If the Weaving Department produces defective cloth, the cloth must be scrapped and yields zero net disposal value. Of the 10,000 rolls of cloth started in the Weaving Department, 500 (5%) defective rolls are produced. The cost of a defective roll, based on total (fixed and variable) manufacturing cost per roll incurred up to the end of the weaving operation, equals $785 per roll, as follows:

Direct material cost per roll (variable)	$500
Fixed operating cost per roll ($2,850,000 ÷ 10,000 rolls)	285
Total manufacturing cost per roll in Weaving Department	$785

The good rolls from the Weaving Department (called grey cloth) are sent to the Printing Department. Of the 9,500 good rolls started at the printing operation, 950 (10%) defective rolls are produced and scrapped at zero net disposal value. The cost of a defective roll based on total (fixed and variable) manufacturing cost per unit incurred up to the end of the printing operation, equals $930 per roll, calculated as follows:

Total manufacturing cost per roll in Weaving Department		$785
Printing Department manufacturing cost per roll		
Direct material cost per roll (variable)	$100	
Fixed operating cost per roll ($427,500 ÷ 9,500 rolls)	45	
Total manufacturing cost per roll in Printing Department		145
Total manufacturing cost per roll		$930

The Wellesley Corporation's total monthly sales of printed cloth equal the Printing Department's output. Each requirement refers only to the preceding data. There is no connection between the requirements.

REQUIRED

1. The Printing Department is considering buying 5,000 additional rolls of grey cloth from an outside supplier at $900 per roll. The Printing Department manager is concerned that the cost of purchasing the grey cloth is much higher than Wellesley's cost of manufacturing it. The quality of the grey cloth acquired from the outside supplier is very similar to that manufactured in-house. The Printing Department expects that 10% of the rolls obtained from the outside supplier will result in defective products. Should the Printing Department buy the grey cloth from the outside supplier? Show your calculations.

2. Wellesley's engineers have developed a method that would lower the Printing Department's rate of defective products to 6% at the printing operation. Implementing the new method would cost $350,000 per month. Should Wellesley implement the change? Show your calculations.

3. The design engineering team has proposed a modification that would lower the Weaving Department's rate of defective products to 3%. The modification would cost the company $175,000 per month. Should Wellesley implement the change? Show your calculations.

Supply-Chain Strategies: JIT, MRP, and Backflush Costing

20

Inventory Cost Management Strategies

Customers are demanding lower lead time between their orders and receipt of the finished product. Therefore, manufacturers are demanding more frequent deliveries with shorter purchase order lead times from their suppliers. To better service the companies who use its automotive products, Challenger Freight invested in information systems. The technology improved coordination and response times so that Challenger Freight could help its customers reduce inventory levels and costs.

After studying this chapter, you should be able to

1. Analyze five categories of costs associated with goods for sale and balance ordering costs and carrying costs using the economic order quantity (EOQ) decision model

2. Analyze and reduce conflicts that can arise between EOQ decision models and models used for performance evaluation

3. Analyze the relevant benefits and costs of JIT alternatives

4. Differentiate a materials requirements planning (MRP) strategy from ERP strategy of supply-chain management

5. Analyze how backflush costing can simplify traditional job-costing systems

In this chapter, three supply-chain strategies are presented, compared, and contrasted. Supply-chain management is a strategy. The buyer and suppliers act in partnership, sharing otherwise sensitive and confidential information to reduce partnership costs below what could be achieved separately (Chapter 13). There are several alternatives and the goal is to manage and control the cost of inventory yet ensure a smooth flow of production. Retail and manufacturing companies alike need to manage their COGS as well as revenue as they meet the demand of customers and maximize revenue. Under just-in-time, materials requirement planning, and backflush costing methods of accounting for inventory, the tradeoffs among various costs differ but the goals remain constant.

Inventory management is a pivotal part of profit planning for manufacturing and merchandising companies. Materials costs can account for more than 50% of total costs in some manufacturing companies and more than 70% of total costs in retail companies. Unused material is unsold product, and the carrying costs to retain material in various inventories can represent up to 35% of annual manufacturing costs. Accounting information has a key role in inventory valuation and cost control strategies.

INVENTORY MANAGEMENT

1 Analyze five categories of costs associated with goods for sale and balance ordering costs and carrying costs using the economic order quantity (EOQ) decision model

Inventory management is the planning, coordinating, and control activities related to the flow of inventory into, through, and from the organization. Costs associated with goods for resale include opportunity costs of which the management accountant is aware but which are not recorded in the financial accounting management information system (MIS). Consider retailers where the cost of goods sold constitutes the largest single cost item. The following breakdown of operations for two major retailers is illustrative:

	Loblaw Companies	Sobeys Inc.
Sales	100.0%	100.0%
Cost of sales and other expenses	91.9%	95.9%
Depreciation and amortization	1.8%	1.4%
Interest and taxes	2.6%	1.1%
Net income	3.7%	1.6%

With a high level of perishable inventory and low net income percentage, managers in the grocery retail industry must make accurate decisions regarding the purchasing and managing of goods for sale or incur avoidable costs of spoilage. Dry good inventories also require a cash outflow to suppliers, and the shorter the cash-to-cash cycle the higher will be the revenue for these retailers.

COSTS ASSOCIATED WITH GOODS FOR SALE

The descriptions of the cost categories indicate that some of the relevant costs for making inventory decisions and managing goods for sale are not available in existing accounting systems. The following cost categories are important when managing inventories and goods for sale:

◆ **Purchasing costs** consist of the acquisition costs of goods acquired from suppliers including freight in, the transportation costs.

These direct costs usually make up the largest single cost category of goods for sale. Supplier credit terms, discounts for different purchase order sizes, and frequency of ordering affect purchasing costs.

- **Ordering costs** consist of the costs to prepare and issue a purchase order.

  These support department overhead costs vary with the number of purchase orders processed, special processing, receiving, inspection, and payment costs.

- **Carrying costs** arise when a business holds inventories of goods for sale.

  These manufacturing overhead costs include the costs associated with storage, such as storage space rental and insurance, obsolescence, and spoilage, which are reported by the financial accounting management information system (MIS). Also relevant for managers are the opportunity costs of the investment tied up in inventory (see Chapter 11), assessed by applying managerial accounting techniques.

- **Stockout costs** occur when a company runs out of an item for which there is customer demand. A company may respond to the shortfall or stockout by expediting an order from a supplier.

  Expediting costs of a stockout include the additional ordering costs plus any associated transportation costs. Alternatively, the company may lose a sale due to the stockout. In this case, stockout costs include the opportunity cost of the lost contribution margin on the sale plus any contribution margin lost on future sales hurt by customer ill-will caused by the stockout.

- **Costs of quality (COQ)** were defined and discussed in Chapter 19.

  Four categories of costs of quality are often distinguished: (a) prevention costs, (b) appraisal costs, (c) internal failure costs, and (d) external failure costs.

- **Shrinkage costs** arise from theft, embezzlement, misclassifications, and clerical errors.

  This cost is measured by the difference between the cost of inventory recorded without theft or other incidents, and the cost of inventory physically counted. Shrinkage is often an important performance measure by which management effectiveness is evaluated. In grocery retail the operating margin is very small, approximately 2%. Control of inventory shrinkage is one of a store manager's prime responsibilities. To make up for a loss of $1,000 due to shrinkage, a store would have to earn an additional $50,000 in revenues ($1,000 ÷ 0.02 = $50,000).

Information technology such as the scheduling, inventory control, and costing system software provided by Seradex, and bar code and radio-frequency identification (RFID) on items, increases reliability and timeliness of inventory data. For example, bar-coding technology is a low-cost way to capture purchases and sales of individual units. This creates an instantaneous record of inventory movements and helps in the management of purchasing, carrying, and stockout costs. In the sections that follow, we consider how to calculate relevant costs for different inventory-related decisions.

ECONOMIC ORDER QUANTITY DECISION MODEL

The first major decision in managing goods for sale is deciding how much of a given product to order. The **economic order quantity (EOQ)** decision model calculates the optimal quantity of inventory to order. The simplest version of this model incorporates only ordering costs and carrying costs into the calculation. It assumes the following:

- The same fixed quantity is ordered at each reorder point.

- Demand, ordering costs, and carrying costs are certain. **The purchase order lead time**—the time between the placement of an order and its delivery—is also certain.

- Purchasing costs per unit are unaffected by the quantity ordered. This assumption makes purchasing costs irrelevant to determining EOQ, because purchasing costs of all units acquired will be the same, whatever the order size in which the units are ordered.

♦ No stockouts occur. One justification for this assumption is that the costs of a stockout are prohibitively high. We assume that to avoid these potential costs, management always maintains adequate inventory so that no stockout can occur.

♦ In deciding the size of the purchase order, management considers the COQ and shrinkage only to the extent that these costs affect ordering costs or carrying costs.

Given these assumptions, EOQ analysis ignores purchasing costs, stockout costs, and quality costs. To determine EOQ, we minimize the relevant ordering and carrying costs (those ordering and carrying costs that are affected by the quantity of inventory ordered):

Total relevant costs = Total relevant ordering costs + Total relevant carrying costs

Example: CDWorld, a retailer, sells packages of blank CDs to its customers. It purchases packages of CDs from Sontek at $14 a package. Sontek pays all incoming freight. No incoming inspection is necessary, as Sontek has a superb reputation for delivering quality merchandise. Annual demand is 13,000 packages, at a rate of 250 packages per week. CDWorld requires a 15% annual return on investment. The purchase order lead time is two weeks. The following cost data are available:

Relevant ordering costs per purchase order		$200.00
Relevant carrying costs per package per year:		
Required annual return on investment, 15% × $14	$2.10	
Relevant insurance, materials handling, breakage, etc. per year	3.10	$ 5.20

Carrying costs are higher than you may think. In many companies, average annual carrying costs exceed 30% of purchasing costs. In the CDWorld example, annual carrying costs are 37% ($5.20 ÷ $14.00) of purchasing costs. What is the economic order quantity of packages of CDs? The formula underlying the EOQ model is:

$$EOQ = \sqrt{\frac{2DP}{C}}$$

Where:

EOQ = Economic order quantity

D = Demand in units for a specified time period (one year in this example)

P = Relevant ordering costs per purchase order

C = Relevant carrying costs of one unit in stock for the time period used for D (one year in this example)

The formula indicates that EOQ increases with demand and ordering costs and decreases with carrying costs. Notice the square root in this equation. Either an exponent or a square root signals that the relationship is non-linear—it is a curve, as illustrated in Exhibit 20-1. You may be familiar with calculating EOQ, reorder point, and safety stock from finance or production courses. In those courses, costs for the formulas are assumed. Here you will see that management accountants help (1) decide what costs to include in the formulas and (2) estimate the dollar value of the costs. We can use this formula to determine the EOQ for CDWorld as follows:

$$EOQ = \sqrt{\frac{2 \times 13,000 \times \$200}{\$5.20}} = \sqrt{1,000,000} = 1,000 \text{ packages}$$

Therefore, CDWorld should order 1,000 CD packages each time to minimize total ordering and carrying costs.

The total annual relevant costs (TRC) for any order quantity Q can be calculated using the following formula:

$$\text{TRC} = \begin{array}{c}\text{Total annual relevant} \\ \text{ordering costs}\end{array} + \begin{array}{c}\text{Total annual relevant} \\ \text{carrying costs}\end{array}$$

$$= \begin{array}{c}\text{Number of} \\ \text{purchase orders} \\ \text{per year}\end{array} \times \begin{array}{c}\text{Relevant} \\ \text{ordering costs per} \\ \text{purchase order}\end{array} + \begin{array}{c}\text{Average inventory} \\ \text{in units}\end{array} \times \begin{array}{c}\text{Annual relevant} \\ \text{carrying costs of} \\ \text{1 unit for a year}\end{array}$$

$$= \left(\frac{D}{Q}\right) \times P + \left(\frac{Q}{2}\right) \times C = \frac{DP}{Q} + \frac{QC}{2}$$

(Note that in this formula, Q can be any order quantity, not just the EOQ.) When Q = 1,000 units,

$$\text{TRC} = \frac{13,000 \times \$200}{1,000} + \frac{1,000 \times \$5.20}{2}$$

$$= \$2,600 + \$2,600 = \$5,200$$

The number of deliveries each time period (in our example, one year) is:

$$\frac{D}{\text{EOQ}} = \frac{13,000}{1,000} = 13 \text{ deliveries}$$

Exhibit 20-1 shows a graph analysis of the total annual relevant costs of ordering (DP/Q) and carrying inventory ($QC/2$) under various order sizes (Q), and illustrates the tradeoff between the two types of costs. The larger the order quantity, the higher the annual relevant carrying costs, but the lower the annual relevant ordering costs. *The total annual relevant costs are at a minimum where total relevant ordering costs and total relevant carrying costs are equal* (in the CDWorld example, each equals $2,600).

EXHIBIT 20-1
Ordering Costs and Carrying Costs for CDWorld

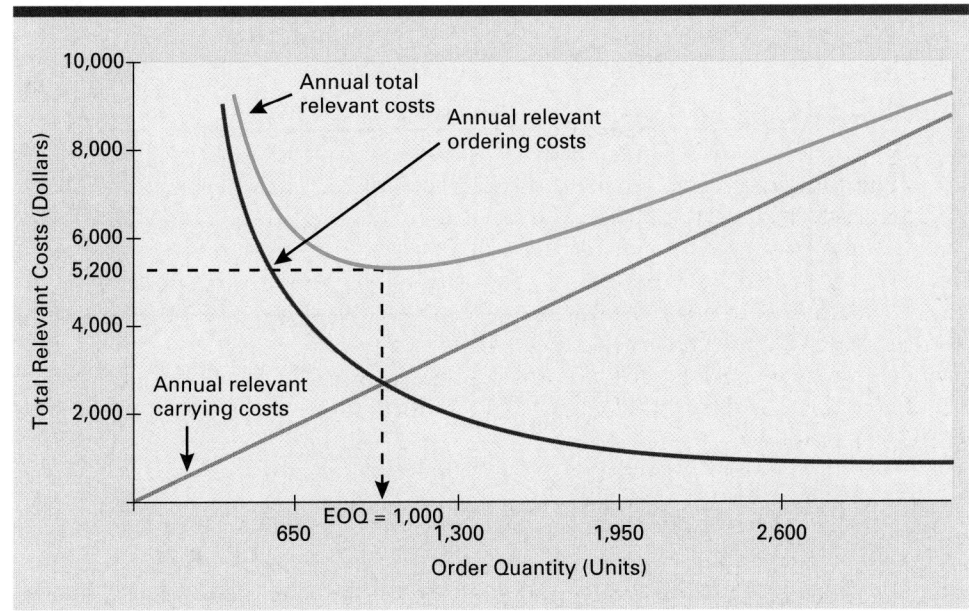

WHEN TO ORDER, ASSUMING CERTAINTY

The second major decision in dealing with cost of goods available for sale is when to order. The **reorder point** is the quantity level of the inventory on hand that triggers a new order. The reorder point is simplest to compute when both demand and lead time are certain:

$$\text{Reorder point} = \frac{\text{Number of units sold}}{\text{per unit of time}} \times \text{Purchase order lead time}$$

Consider our CDWorld example. We choose a week as the unit of time:

Economic order quantity	1,000 packages
Number of units sold per week	250 packages
Purchase order lead time	2 weeks

Thus:

$$\text{Reorder point} = \frac{\text{Number of units sold}}{\text{per unit of time}} \times \text{Purchase order lead time}$$

$$= 250 \times 2 = 500 \text{ packages}$$

CDWorld will order 1,000 packages of CDs each time its inventory stock falls to 500 packages. The intuition for the reorder point is that CDWorld must reorder when inventory on hand falls to the level at which it equals the amount needed for sales that will occur during the purchase-order lead time.

The graph in Exhibit 20-2 presents the behaviour of the inventory level of CD packages, assuming demand occurs uniformly throughout each week.[1] If the purchase order lead time is two weeks, a new order will be placed when the inventory level reaches 500 CD packages so that the 1,000 packages ordered are received at the time inventory reaches zero.

EXHIBIT 20-2
Inventory Level of CD Packages for CDWorld*

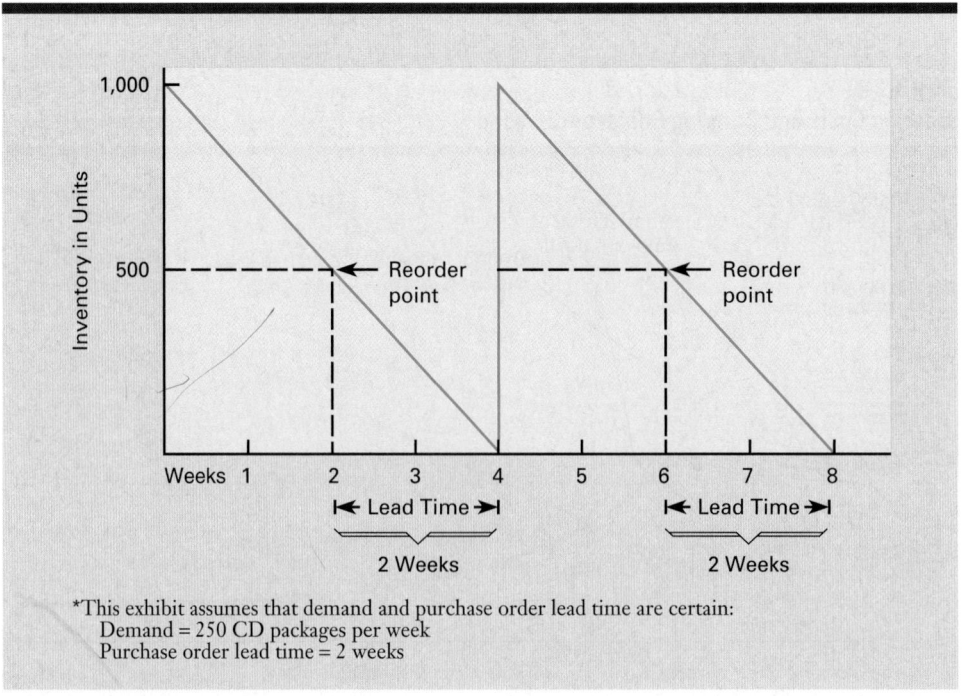

*This exhibit assumes that demand and purchase order lead time are certain:
Demand = 250 CD packages per week
Purchase order lead time = 2 weeks

---

[1]This handy but special formula does not apply when the receipt of the order fails to increase inventory to the reorder-point quantity (for example, when the lead time is three weeks and the order is a one-week supply). In these cases, orders will overlap.

SAFETY STOCK

So far, we have assumed that demand and purchase order lead time are certain. When retailers are uncertain about the demand, the lead time, or the quantity that suppliers can provide, they often hold safety stock. **Safety stock** is inventory held at all times regardless of inventory ordered using EOQ. Like a capacity cushion, safety stock is a buffer against unexpected increases in demand or lead time and unavailability of stock from suppliers.

In the CDWorld example, stockout costs include only the cost of rush orders, because rush orders are assumed to fully satisfy customer demand. However, stockouts can result in opportunity costs—lost contribution margin on lost current sales and lost future sales—and some companies adopt safety stock policy. Safety stock, like unused capacity cushions, also creates opportunity costs.

In our example, expected demand is 250 packages per week, but the company's managers feel that a maximum demand of 400 packages per week may occur. If the managers decide that the costs of stockout are prohibitive, they may decide to hold safety stock of 300 packages. The opportunity cost of stockouts must also exceed the opportunity cost of holding safety stock. This amount is the maximum excess demand of 150 packages per week for the two weeks of purchase order lead time. The computation of safety stock hinges on demand forecasts. Managers will have some notion—usually based on experience—of the range of weekly demand. When calculating safety stock, the tradeoff is between stockout costs and carrying costs. Columns G and H in Exhibit 20-3 illustrate this tradeoff.

A frequency distribution based on prior daily or weekly levels of demand provides data for computing the associated costs of maintaining safety stock. Assume

EXHIBIT 20-3
Computation of Safety Stock for CDWorld When Reorder Point is 500 Units

	A	B	C	D	E	F	G	H	I
1	Safety	Demand							
2	Stock	Levels			Relevant	Number	Expected	Relevant	Relevant
3	Level	Resulting	Stockout	Probability	Stockout	of Orders	Stockout	Carrying	Total
4	in Units	in Stockouts	in Units[a]	of Stockout	Costs[b]	per Year[c]	Costs[d]	Costs[e]	Costs
5	(1)	(2)	(3) = (2) − 500 − (1)	(4)	(5) = (3) × \$4	(6)	(7) = (4) × (5) × (6)	(8) = (1) × \$5.20	(9) = (7) + (8)
6	0	600	100	0.20	\$ 400	13	\$1,040		
7		700	200	0.09	800	13	936		
8		800	300	0.06	1,200	13	936		
9							\$2,912	\$ 0	\$2,912
10	100	700	100	0.09	400	13	\$ 468		
11		800	200	0.06	800	13	624		
12							\$1,092	\$ 520	\$1,612
13	200	800	100	0.06	400	13	\$ 312	\$1,040	\$1,352
14	300	–	–	–	–	–	\$ 0[f]	\$1,560	\$1,560
15									
16	[a]Demand level resulting in stockouts − Inventory available during lead time (excluding safety stock), 500 units − safety stock.								
17	[b]Stockout in units × Relevant stockout costs of \$4 per unit.								
18	[c]Annual demand, 13,000 ÷ 1,000 EOQ = 13 orders per year.								
19	[d]Probability of stockout × Relevant stockout costs × Number of orders per year.								
20	[e]Safety stock × Annual relevant carrying costs of \$5.20 per unit (assumes that safety stock is on hand at all times and that there is no overstocking caused by decreases in expected usage).								
22	[f]At a safety stock level of 300 units, no stockouts will occur and, hence, expected stockout costs = \$0.								

that one of seven different levels of demand will occur over the two-week purchase order lead time at CDWorld.

Total Demand for Two Weeks	Units						
	200	300	400	500	600	700	800
Probability (sums to 1.00)	0.06	0.09	0.20	0.30	0.20	0.09	0.06

We see that 500 is the most likely level of demand for two weeks, because it is assigned the highest probability of occurrence. We also see that there is a 0.35 probability that demand will be between 600, 700, and 800 packages (0.20 + 0.09 + 0.06 = 0.35).

If a customer calls CDWorld to buy CDs, and the store has none in stock, it can rush order them to the customer at a cost to CDWorld of $4 per package. The relevant stockout costs in this case are $4 per package. The optimal safety stock level is the quantity of safety stock that minimizes the sum of the relevant annual stockout and carrying costs. Recall that the relevant carrying costs for CDWorld are $5.20 per unit per year.

Exhibit 20-3 presents the total annual relevant stockout and carrying costs when the reorder point is 500 units. We need only consider safety stock levels of 0, 100, 200, and 300 units, since demand will exceed the 500 units of stock available at reordering by 0 if demand is 500, by 100 if demand is 600, by 200 if demand is 700, and by 300 if demand is 800. The total annual relevant stockout and carrying costs would be minimized at $1,352 when a safety stock of 200 packages is maintained. Think of the 200 units of safety stock as extra stock that CDWorld maintains. For example, CDWorld's total inventory of CDs at the time of reordering its EOQ of 1,000 units would be 700 units (the reorder point of 500 units plus the safety stock of 200 units).

JUST-IN-TIME PURCHASING (JIT)

Just-in-time (JIT) purchasing is a strategy to purchase goods or materials such that a delivery immediately precedes demand or use. It is a demand-pull strategy. JIT requires organizations to restructure their relationships with suppliers and place smaller, more frequent purchase orders. JIT can be implemented in both the retail and manufacturing sectors of the economy.

JIT PURCHASING AND EOQ MODEL PARAMETERS

Companies moving toward JIT purchasing argue that the cost of carrying inventories (parameter C in the EOQ model) has been dramatically underestimated in the past. This cost includes storage costs, spoilage, obsolescence, and opportunity costs such as investment tied up in inventory. The cost of placing a purchase order (parameter P in the EOQ model) has also been reevaluated. Three factors are causing sizable reductions in P:

◆ Companies increasingly are establishing long-run purchasing arrangements in which price and quality dimensions that apply over an extended period are agreed to by both parties. Individual purchase orders occur without any additional negotiation over price or quality in this period.

◆ Companies have increased their use of electronic links, such as the Internet, to place purchase orders. Electronic commerce (e-commerce) is one of the fastest growing areas of the Internet. The cost of placing some orders on the Internet is estimated at as much as one one-hundredth the cost of placing orders by telephone or by mail.

◆ Companies are increasing the use of purchase cards (similar to consumer credit cards like VISA and MasterCard). Purchasing personnel are given total dollar limits or individual transaction dollar limits. As long as personnel stay within these limits, the traditional labour-intensive procurement approval mechanisms are not required.

Both increases in the carrying cost (C) and decreases in the ordering cost per purchase order (P) result in smaller EOQ amounts.

Exhibit 20-4 analyzes the sensitivity of CDWorld's EOQ to illustrate the economics of smaller and more frequent purchase orders. The analysis presented in Exhibit 20-4 supports JIT purchasing—that is, having a smaller EOQ and placing more frequent orders—as relevant carrying costs increase and relevant ordering costs per purchase order decrease.

JIT STRATEGY AND MANUFACTURING

Consider JIT purchasing by Chrysler, which has 15 assembly plants in North America. Parts and supplies are flown in from 2,000 locations, with each plant off-loading up to 600 truckloads per day. Physical inventory count in the plants is measured in "a couple of hours." The company's central tracking group monitors and responds 24/7 to automated alerts signalling glitches in the supply chain. Supply analysts use a production control portal which extends into the software systems of suppliers and shippers as well as those of Chrysler itself.

The production control portal provides access to information on the status of parts and the likelihood of a stockout well in advance. Suppliers failing to ship according to an agreed-upon schedule are alerted that a shipment should have been made but was not. Suppliers who fail to deliver components on time, or components that fail to meet agreed-upon quality standards, can cause a failure in Chrysler's assembly plant to meet its own scheduled deliveries for vehicles.

JIT strategy means companies do not have large amounts of material inventories on hand to provide a cushion to the production line if deliveries are late or parts are defective. Recent delays at border crossings between the US and Canada have caused some suppliers to rethink whether JIT remains a viable strategy. The costs of stockouts are reaching the point of exceeding the carrying costs for holding inventory. Some suppliers have changed their supply strategy to include safety stock inventoried on the customer side of borders, which has already cleared customs, to ensure they meet the customer's JIT requirements.

JIT requires a high level of information sharing with suppliers who commit to deliver components in narrow time windows. We now explore the relationship between JIT purchasing and the EOQ decision model already discussed in this chapter.

Just-in-time (JIT) production (also called **lean production**) is a demand-pull system in which each component in a production line is produced immediately as the next step in the production line needs the component. The goals are to eliminate non-value-added spoilage and scrap, reduce carrying costs, and improve customer satisfaction. In a JIT production line, manufacturing activity at any particular workstation is prompted by the need for that station's output at the following station.

Demand triggers each step of the production process, starting with customer demand for a finished product at the end of the process and working all the way back to the demand for direct materials at the beginning of the process. In this way,

EXHIBIT 20-4
Sensitivity of EOQ to Variations in Relevant Ordering and Carrying Costs for CDWorld

	A	B	C	D	E
1	**Relevant Carrying**	**Annual Demand (D) = 13,000 units**			
2	**Costs per Package**	**Relevant Ordering Costs per Purchase Order (P)**			
3	**per Year (C)**	**$200**	**$150**	**$100**	**$30**
4	$ 5.20	EOQ = 1,000	EOQ = 866	EOQ = 707	EOQ = 387
5	7.00	862	746	609	334
6	10.00	721	624	510	279
7	15.00	589	510	416	228

demand pulls an order through the production line. The demand-pull feature of JIT production systems achieves close coordination among workstations. It smoothes the flow of goods, despite low quantities of inventory. JIT production systems aim to simultaneously meet customer demand (a) in a timely way, (b) with high-quality products, and (c) at the lowest possible total cost. JIT is most financially feasible when availability and prices of resource inputs are relatively constant and production cycles are well controlled.

Companies implementing JIT production systems manage inventories by eliminating (or at least minimizing) them. The main features in a JIT production system are:

◆ Production is organized in **manufacturing cells**, a grouping of all the different types of equipment used to make a given product. Materials move from one machine to another where various operations are performed in sequence. Materials-handling costs are minimized.

◆ Workers are hired and trained to be multiskilled and capable of performing a variety of operations and tasks including minor repairs and routine maintenance of equipment. This training adds greatly to the flexibility of the plant.

◆ Defects are aggressively eliminated (TQM). Because of the tight links between stages in the production line, and the minimal inventories at each stage, defects arising at one stage quickly affect other stages in the line. JIT creates an urgency

---

REAL COMPANIES

JIT—Retailing Meets Manufacturing

Each year, hundreds of thousands of rock music fans flock to Dave Matthews Band concerts. Although many of them stop by the merchandise stand to pick up a T-shirt or poster after the show ends, soon they will have another option . . . buying a multiple-CD set that contains a professional recording of the entire concert they just saw! A JIT strategy, enabled by recent advances in digital audio and CD-burning technology, now allows fans to relive the live concert experience as soon as 10 minutes after the final chord is played. Clear Channel Entertainment uses an army of high-speed CD burners to produce concert recordings. As soon as each song is complete, Instant Live's engineers burn the track onto hundreds of CDs using the digital signals heard live through the audio mixing hardware and software and broadcast live to fans at the concert. Of course no editing or remastering can be done. At the end of the show one last song is burned and the CDs packaged. In smaller venues the logistics of distribution to merchandisers are less difficult than in large amphitheatres. During Instant Live's initial testing, up to 20% of concertgoers bought these CDs, to the tune of US$15 to US$30 each. The artists got US$6 to US$8 from each CD sold, with the remaining money split among the record label, the concert venue, and the recording company.

Digital recording has changed how artists release official live albums between studio releases. The old technology required a complex remastering and album-production process. Recordings took months, if not years, to reach fans. Further, live albums typically sold few copies, and retail outlets that profit from volume-driven merchandise turnover were somewhat reluctant to carry them. Digital technology assures better sound quality, near-immediate production turnaround, and low finished-goods carrying costs. Further, these recordings can also be distributed through retailers and artist websites.

Sources: S. Chartland, "How to Take the Concert Home," *The New York Times,* May 3, 2004; S. Humphries, "Get Your Official 'Bootleg' Here," *Christian Science Monitor,* November 21, 2003; S. Knopper, "Live Discs a Hit with Fans," *Rolling Stone,* November 7, 2003; S. Galupo, "Death of the Live Concert Album?" *Washington Times,* July 9, 2004.

for solving problems immediately and eliminating the root causes of defects as quickly as possible. TQM is an essential component of any JIT production system.

◆ *Setup time*, which is the time required to get equipment, tools, and materials ready to start the production of a component or product, is reduced. Simultaneously *manufacturing lead time*, which is the amount of time from when an order is ready to start on the production line (ready to be set up) to when it becomes a finished good, is reduced. Reducing setup time makes production in smaller batches economical, which in turn reduces inventory levels. Reducing manufacturing lead time enables a company to respond faster to changes in customer demand (see Real Companies).

◆ Suppliers are selected on the basis of their ability to deliver quality materials in a timely manner. Most companies implementing *JIT production* also implement the *JIT purchasing methods* described earlier in this chapter. JIT plants expect JIT suppliers to provide high-quality goods and make frequent deliveries of the exact quantities specified on a timely basis. Suppliers often deliver materials directly to the plant floor to be immediately placed into production.

ASSESS YOUR MASTERY

MyAccountingLab

To check your understanding of the material in Learning Objective ❶, go to the *Mastery Questions* section at the end of this chapter and complete Learning Objective ❶ question 1.

CHALLENGES IN SUPPLY-CHAIN COST MANAGEMENT

> ❷ Analyze and reduce conflicts that can arise between EOQ decision models and models used for performance evaluation

The level of inventories held by retailers is influenced by demand patterns of their customers and supply relationships with their distributors, manufacturers, and suppliers, and so on. The term *supply chain* describes the flow of goods, services, and information from cradle to grave (womb to tomb), regardless of whether those activities occur in the same organizations or other organizations. Chapter 1 introduced this concept using the example of a supply chain in the beverage industry. One point well documented in supply-chain analysis is that there are significant total gains to companies in this supply chain from coordinating their activities and sharing information.

Procter & Gamble's (P&G) experience with their Pampers product illustrates the gains from supply-chain coordination. Retailers selling Pampers encounter some variability in weekly demand, despite babies consuming diapers at a relatively steady rate. However, there was pronounced variability in retailers' orders to the manufacturer (P&G), and even more variability in orders by P&G to its own suppliers. Trade promotions worsened the situation because retailers took advantage of lower prices to increase their inventory for future sales. One result was that high levels of inventory are often held at various stages in the supply chain.

P&G responded by sharing information as well as planning and coordinating activities throughout its supply chain. The retailers shared their daily sales information about Pampers with P&G, their distributors, and their suppliers. This updated sales information reduced the level of uncertainty that manufacturers and the manufacturers' suppliers had about retail demand for Pampers. This reduction in demand uncertainty led to fewer stockouts at the retail level, reduced manufacture of Pampers not subsequently demanded by retailers, a reduction in expedited manufacturing orders, and lower inventories being held by each company in the supply chain. The benefits of supply-chain coordination at P&G have been so great that retailers such as Wal-Mart have contracted with P&G to manage Wal-Mart's retail inventories on a just-in-time basis. This practice is called *supplier- or vendor-managed inventory*. Supply-chain management, however, is not without its challenges.

A supply chain is one way for manufacturers to start managing their own inventory better. Of course, the need to produce high-quality products at competitive cost levels leads managers at manufacturing companies to also seek out additional ways to manage their inventories. Numerous systems have been developed to help managers plan and implement production and inventory activities. We now consider two widely used types of systems—materials requirements planning (MRP) and just-in-time (JIT) production.

ESTIMATING RELEVANT COSTS OF A SUPPLY CHAIN

Obtaining accurate estimates of the cost parameters used in the EOQ decision model is a challenging task. For example, the relevant annual carrying costs of inventory consist of *incremental or outlay costs plus the opportunity cost of capital.* Calculating the cost of capital is taught in finance.

What are the relevant incremental costs of carrying inventory? Only those costs that vary with the quantity of inventory held—for example, insurance, property taxes, costs of obsolescence, and costs of breakage, shrinkage, warehouse rent, and salaries paid to warehouse workers. Salaries paid to clerks, storekeepers, and materials handlers, however, are irrelevant if they are unaffected by changes in inventory levels.

If as inventories decrease these salary costs also decrease as the clerks, storekeepers, and materials handlers are transferred to other activities or laid off, then these salaries are relevant incremental costs of carrying inventory. Similarly, the costs of storage space owned that cannot be used for other profitable purposes as inventories decrease are irrelevant. But if the space has other profitable uses, or if rental cost is tied to the amount of space occupied, storage costs are relevant incremental costs of carrying inventory.

What is the relevant opportunity cost of capital? It is the return forgone by investing capital in inventory rather than elsewhere. It is calculated as the required rate of return multiplied by those costs per unit that vary with the number of units purchased and that are incurred at the time the units are received. Examples of these costs per unit are purchase price, incoming freight, and incoming inspection.

Opportunity costs are not calculated on investments, say, in buildings, if these investments are unaffected by changes in inventory levels. In the case of stockouts, calculating the relevant opportunity costs requires an estimate of the lost contribution margin on that sale as well as on future sales hurt by customer ill-will resulting from the stockout. Relevant ordering costs are only those ordering costs that change with the number of orders placed (for example, costs of preparing and issuing purchase orders and receiving and inspecting materials).

COST OF A PREDICTION ERROR

Our discussion suggests that predicting relevant costs requires care and is difficult. Managers understand that their projections will seldom be flawless. This leads to the question: What is the cost of an incorrect prediction when actual relevant costs are different from the relevant predicted costs used for decision making?

Continuing our example, suppose CDWorld's relevant ordering costs per purchase order are $100 instead of the predicted $200. We can calculate the cost of this prediction error in a logical manner as follows:

◆ *Compute the monetary outcome from the best action that could have been taken, given the actual amount of the cost input.* The appropriate inputs are D = 13,000 units, P = $100, and C = $5.20. The economic order quantity size is:

$$EOQ = \sqrt{\frac{2DP}{C}}$$

$$= \sqrt{\frac{2 \times 13,000 \times \$100}{\$5.20}} = \sqrt{500,000}$$

$$= 707 \text{ packages (rounded)}$$

The total annual relevant cost when EOQ = 707 is:

$$TRC = \frac{DP}{Q} + \frac{QC}{2}$$

$$= \frac{13{,}000 \times \$100}{707} + \frac{707 \times \$5.20}{2}$$

$$= \$1{,}839 + \$1{,}838 = \$3{,}677$$

◆ *Compute the monetary outcome from the best action on the basis of the incorrect amount of the predicted cost input.* The planned action when the relevant ordering costs per purchase order are predicted to be \$200 is to purchase 1,000 packages in each order. The total annual relevant costs using this order quantity when D = 13,000 units, P = \$100, and C = \$5.20 are:

$$TRC = \frac{13{,}000 \times \$100}{1{,}000} + \frac{1{,}000 \times \$5.20}{2}$$

$$= \$1{,}300 + \$2{,}600 = \$3{,}900$$

◆ *Compute the difference between the monetary outcomes.*

	Monetary Outcome
Step 1	\$3,677
Step 2	3,900
Difference	\$ (223)

The cost of the prediction error is only \$223, or just over 6% of the relevant total costs of \$3,677 because the total annual relevant costs curve in Exhibit 20-1 (p. 967) is relatively flat over the range of order quantities from 650 to 1,300. *An important feature of the EOQ model is that the total relevant costs are rarely sensitive to minor variations in cost predictions. The square root in the EOQ model reduces the sensitivity of the decision to errors in predicting its inputs.*

In the following section we consider a planning-and-control and performance-evaluation issue that frequently arises when managing inventory.

GOAL-CONGRUENCE ISSUES

Goal-congruence issues can arise when there is an inconsistency between the decision model and the model used to evaluate the performance of the person implementing the decision. For example, the absence of recorded opportunity costs in conventional accounting systems raises the possibility of a conflict between the EOQ model's optimal order quantity and the order quantity that the purchasing manager, evaluated on conventional accounting numbers, regards as optimal.

If annual carrying costs are excluded when evaluating the performance of managers, the managers may favour purchasing a larger order quantity than the EOQ decision model indicates is optimal. Companies such as Coca-Cola and Wal-Mart resolve this conflict by designing the performance evaluation system so that the carrying costs, including a required return on investment, are charged to the appropriate manager.

The opportunity cost of the investment tied up in inventory can be reduced by reducing inventory levels. We now discuss just-in-time purchasing, an approach that has led to dramatic reductions in inventories being held by some companies.

Inventory Valuation and JIT Implementation

Trouble erupts when companies seeking increases in income overstate values of inventories. Aware of this perverse incentive to managers, management accountants must pay careful attention to, and correctly record, both the physical quantity of inventories and values ascribed to them. A recent survey by *CFO Magazine* found that since 2001, one-fifth of financial executives said they felt more pressure to use accounting methods to "make results appear more favourable" and that 47% have felt pressure from superiors to use aggressive accounting techniques.

El Paso Corporation, a leading provider of natural gas in North America, reported "outside investigation had found that some employees might have deliberately overstated oil and gas reserves and that it would need to restate five years of results . . . and take a [US]$1 billion charge [to earnings]. . . . The company said certain employees . . . provided reserve estimates that they knew, or should have known, were incorrect . . . ." Many management accountants, as internal auditors, have the authority and expertise to either prevent or curtail this abuse.

One remedy is to adopt a JIT strategy. Inventory overstatement is not a danger with a JIT strategy because the value of inventory is immaterial. A JIT system brings on different challenges for management accountants. To successfully implement JIT, management accountants must be comfortable working in a changing and ambiguous environment and balance the demands of different managers. Marketing managers may seek greater levels of customization and customer responsiveness that production and purchasing managers find burdensome. Several of the rewards of moving to a JIT system—more reliable deliveries to customers and greater customer responsiveness—may be difficult to quantify in the short run. Management accountants must therefore motivate their teams to focus on long-term successes. At Cessna, for example, it wasn't until its third year of using lean manufacturing for its single-engine aircraft and business jets that the company began to see productivity gains in the 40% to 60% range.

Source: T. Damos, "CFO Pressure Cooker," *Fortune,* June 28, 2004. H. Timmons, "El Paso Says Reserves May Have Been Falsified," *The New York Times,* May 4, 2004, p. C14

MyAccountingLab

RELEVANCE AND THE JIT STRATEGY OF SUPPLY-CHAIN MANAGEMENT

③ Analyze the relevant benefits and costs of JIT alternatives

The JIT purchasing model is not guided solely by the EOQ model. As discussed earlier (pp. 965–967), the EOQ model is designed to emphasize only the tradeoff between carrying and ordering costs. Inventory management extends beyond ordering and carrying costs to include purchasing costs, stockout costs, and quality costs. The quality of materials and goods and timely deliveries are important motivations for using JIT purchasing, and stockout costs are an important concern. We add these features as we move from the EOQ decision model to present the JIT purchasing model.

CDWorld has recently established an Internet business-to-business (B2B) purchase-order link with Sontek. CDWorld triggers a purchase order for CDs by a single computer entry. Payments are made electronically for batches of deliveries, rather than for each individual delivery. These changes reduce the ordering cost from $200 to only $2 per purchase order! CDWorld will use the Internet purchase-order link whether or not it shifts to a JIT strategy. CDWorld is negotiating to have Sontek deliver 100 packages of CDs 130 times per year (5 times every 2 weeks), instead of delivering 1,000 packages 13 times per year, as shown in Exhibit 20-1 (p. 967). Sontek is willing to make these frequent deliveries, but it would add $0.02 to the price per CD package. CDWorld's required rate of return on investment remains at 15%. Assume the annual relevant carrying cost of insurance, materials handling, shrinkage, breakage, and the like remains at $3.10 per package per year.

Suppose that CDWorld incurs no stockout costs under its current purchasing policy because demand and purchase order lead times over each four-week period are certain. CDWorld's major concern is that lower inventory levels from implementing JIT purchasing will lead to more stockouts because demand variations and delays in supplying CDs are more likely to occur in the short time intervals between supplies under JIT purchasing. Sontek assures CDWorld that its new manufacturing processes enable it to respond rapidly to changing demand patterns. Consequently, stockouts may not be a serious problem. CDWorld expects to incur stockout costs on 150 CD packages each year under a JIT purchasing policy. In the event of a stockout, CDWorld will have to rush-order CD packages at a cost of $4 per package. Should CDWorld implement JIT purchasing?

Exhibit 20-5 compares (1) the incremental costs CDWorld incurs when it purchases CDs from Sontek under its current purchasing policy with (2) the incremental costs CDWorld would incur if Sontek supplied CDs under a JIT policy. The difference in the two incremental costs is the relevant savings of JIT purchasing. In other methods of comparing the two purchasing policies, the analysis would include only the relevant costs—those costs that differ between the two alternatives. Exhibit 20-5 shows a net cost savings of $1,789 per year from shifting to a JIT purchasing policy.

EXHIBIT 20-5
Annual Relevant Costs of Current Purchasing Policy and JIT Purchasing Policy for CDWorld

	A	B	C
1		**Relevant Costs Under**	
2		**Current**	**JIT**
3		**Purchasing**	**Purchasing**
4	**Relevant Item**	**Policy**	**Policy**
5	Purchasing costs		
6	$14 per unit $\times$ 13,000 units per year	$182,000	
7	$14.02 per unit $\times$ 13,000 units per year		$182,260
8	Ordering costs		
9	$200 per order $\times$ 13 orders per year	2,600	
10	$2 per order $\times$ 130 orders per year		260
11	Opportunity carrying costs, required return on investment		
12	0.15 per year $\times$ $14 cost per unit $\times$ 250[a] units of average inventory per year	525	
13	0.15 per year $\times$ $14.02 cost per unit $\times$ 250[b] units of average inventory per year		526
14	Other carrying costs (insurance, materials handling, breakage, and so on)		
15	$3.10 per unit per year $\times$ 250[a] units of average inventory per year	775	
16	$3.10 per unit per year $\times$ 150[c] units of average inventory per year		465
17	Stockout costs		
18	$4 per unit $\times$ 0 units per year	—	
19	$4 per unit $\times$ 150 units per year	—	600
20	Total annual relevant costs	$185,900	$ 184,111
21	Annual difference in favour of JIT purchasing		$1,789
22	[a]Average inventory = 1,000 $\div$ 52/13 = 250		
23	[b]Average inventory = 100/week $\times$ 2.5 orders/week = 250		
24	[c]Maximum demand 400/week − average inventory 250/week = 150		

RELEVANT COSTS OF QUALITY AND TIMELY DELIVERIES

The timely delivery of quality products is particularly crucial in JIT purchasing environments. Defective materials and late deliveries often bring the whole plant to a halt, resulting in forgone contribution margin on lost sales. Companies that implement JIT purchasing choose their suppliers carefully and pay special attention to developing long-run supplier partnerships. Some suppliers are very cooperative with a business's attempts to adopt JIT purchasing. For example, Frito-Lay, which has a large market share in potato chips and other snack foods, makes more frequent deliveries to retail outlets than many of its competitors. The company's corporate strategy emphasizes service to retailers and consistency, freshness, and quality of the delivered product.

What are the relevant costs when choosing suppliers? Consider again our CDWorld example. The Denton Corporation also supplies CDs. It offers to supply all of CDWorld's CD needs at a price of $13.80 per package (less than Sontek's price of $14.02) under the same JIT delivery terms that Sontek offers. Denton proposes an electronic hookup identical to Sontek's that would make CDWorld's ordering costs $2.00 per purchase order. CDWorld's relevant outlay carrying costs of insurance, materials handling, breakage, and so on per package per year is $3.10 if it purchases CDs from Sontek and $3.00 if it purchases from Denton. Should CDWorld buy from Denton? Not before considering the relevant costs of quality and also the relevant costs of failing to deliver on time.

CDWorld has used Sontek in the past and knows that Sontek fully deserves its reputation for delivering quality merchandise on time. In fact CDWorld does not even inspect the CD packages that Sontek supplies, therefore incurring zero inspection costs. Denton, however, does not enjoy as sterling a reputation for quality. When evaluating and choosing suppliers, quality and on-time delivery become increasingly important as the emphasis shifts away from minimizing purchasing costs towards minimizing costs across the entire value chain of business functions. CDWorld anticipates the following negative aspects of using Denton:

◆ CDWorld would incur additional inspection costs of $0.05 per package.

◆ Average stockouts of 360 CD packages each year would occur, largely resulting from late deliveries. Denton cannot rush-order CD packages to CDWorld on short notice, causing an additional cost of $4 per package

◆ Customers would likely return 2.5% of all packages sold owing to poor quality of the CDs. CDWorld estimates its additional costs to handle each returned package at $10.

Exhibit 20-6 presents the relevant costs of purchasing from Sontek and from Denton. Even though Denton is offering a lower price per package, the total relevant costs of purchasing goods from Sontek are lower by $1,847 per year. Selling high-quality merchandise also has nonfinancial and qualitative benefits. For example, offering Sontek's high-quality CDs enhances CDWorld's reputation and increases customer goodwill, which may lead to higher future profitability.

JIT'S EFFECT ON COSTING SYSTEMS

In reducing the need for materials handling, warehousing, and incoming inspection, JIT systems reduce overhead costs. JIT systems also facilitate the direct tracing of some costs that were formerly classified as overhead. For example, the use of manufacturing cells makes it easy to trace materials handling and machine operating costs to specific products or product families made in specific cells. These costs then become direct costs of those products. Also, the use of multiskilled workers in these cells allows the costs of setup, minor maintenance, and quality inspection to become easily traced direct costs.

FINANCIAL BENEFITS OF JIT AND RELEVANT COSTS

Early advocates say the benefit of JIT production is lower carrying costs of inventory. But there are other benefits to lower inventories, such as intensifying emphasis

EXHIBIT 20-6
Annual Relevant Costs of Purchasing from Sontek and Denton

	A	B	C
1		**Relevant Costs of Purchasing from**	
2	**Relevant Item**	**Sontek**	**Denton**
3	Purchasing costs		
4	$14.02 per unit × 13,000 units per year	$182,260	
5	$ 13.80 per unit × 13,000 units per year		$179,400
6	Ordering costs		
7	$2.00 per order × 130 orders per year	260	
8	$2.00 per order × 130 orders per year		260
9	Inspection costs		
10	No inspection necessary	–	
11	$0.05 per unit × 13,000 units per year		650
12	Opportunity carrying costs, required return on investment		
13	0.15 per year × $14.02 × 250[a] units of average inventory per year	526	
14	0.15 per year × $13.80 × 250[a] units of average inventory per year		518
15	Other carrying costs (insurance, materials handling, breakage, etc.)		
16	$3.10 per unit per year × 250[a] units of average inventory per year	775	
17	$3.00 per unit per year × 250[a] units of average inventory per year		750
18	Stockout costs		
19	$4 per unit × 150 units per year	600	
20	$4 per unit × 360 units per year		1,440
21	Customer returns costs		
22	No customer returns	–	
23	$10 per unit returned × 2.5% units returned × 13,000 units		3,250
24	Total annual relevant costs	$184,421	$186,268
25	Annual difference in favour (disfavour) of Sontek	$1,847	
26	[a]Average inventory = 100/week × 2.5 orders per week = 250		

on improved quality (by eliminating scrap, rework, and spoilage), and reduced manufacturing lead times. Management accounting provides the information required for managers to calculate the relevant benefits and costs of reduced inventories in JIT systems.

Consider the Emco Corporation, a manufacturer of brass fittings. Emco is considering implementing a JIT production system. Suppose that to implement JIT production, Emco must incur $100,000 in annual tooling costs to reduce setup times. Suppose further that JIT will reduce average inventory by $500,000. Also, relevant costs of insurance, space, materials-handling, and setup will decline by $30,000 per year. The company's required rate of return on inventory investments is 10% per year. Should Emco implement JIT? On the basis of the numbers provided, we would be tempted to say no because annual relevant cost savings in carrying costs amount to $80,000 [($500,000 × 0.10) + $30,000], which is less than the additional annual tooling costs of $100,000.

Our analysis, however, has not considered other benefits of lower inventories in JIT production. For example, Emco estimates that implementing JIT will reduce rework on 500 units each year, resulting in savings of $50 per unit. Also, better quality and faster delivery will allow Emco to charge $2 more per unit on the 20,000 units that it sells each year. The annual relevant quality and delivery benefits from JIT and lower inventory levels equal $65,000 (rework savings, $50 × 500 + additional contribution margin, $2 × 20,000). Total annual relevant benefits and cost savings equal $145,000

($80,000 + $65,000), which exceeds annual JIT implementation costs of $100,000. Therefore, Emco should implement a JIT production system. Management accountants face challenges when valuing inventory and implementing JIT.

PERFORMANCE MEASURES AND CONTROL

To manage and reduce inventories, the management accountant must also design performance measures to evaluate and control JIT production. Examples of information the management accountant may use are

- Personal observation by production line workers and team leaders
- Financial performance measures such as the inventory turnover ratio (cost of goods sold ÷ average inventory), which is expected to increase
- Nonfinancial performance measures of time, inventory, and quality, such as manufacturing lead time, units produced per hour, and days inventory is on hand
- Manufacturing lead time is expected to decrease
- Units produced per hour, expected to increase
- Total setup time for machines, expected to decrease total manufacturing time
- Number of units requiring rework or scrap, expected to decrease total number of units started and completed

Personal observation and nonfinancial performance measures are the dominant methods of control. These methods are the most timely, intuitive, and easy-to-comprehend measures of plant performance. Rapid, meaningful feedback is critical because the lack of buffer inventories in a demand-pull system creates added urgency to detect and solve problems quickly.

MyAccountingLab

> ### ASSESS YOUR MASTERY
> To check your understanding of the material in Learning Objective ③, go to the *Mastery Questions* section at the end of this chapter and complete Learning Objective ③ question 1.

INVENTORY MANAGEMENT: MRP AND ERP

④ Differentiate a materials requirements planning (MRP) strategy from ERP strategy of supply-chain management

A key feature of MRP is its push-through approach, whereas JIT is a demand-pull approach.

Materials requirements planning (MRP) is a demand push-through system that manufactures finished goods for inventory on the basis of demand forecasts. MRP uses (a) demand forecasts for the final products; (b) a bill of materials outlining the materials, components, and subassemblies for each final product; and (c) the quantities of materials, components, finished products, and product inventories to predetermine the necessary outputs at each stage of production.

Panasonic Corporation of North America is a supply-chain partner with Best Buy Co. Panasonic used to wait for orders from Best Buy and then initiate the process of filling the order. Now, Best Buy collects information on sales of all Panasonic items at its stores' point-of-sale (POS) checkout stations. Best Buy's computers transmit this information to a unit of i2 Technologies Inc. in India. i2 Technologies provides forecasting and other supply-chain analytics to Panasonic. The forecast of demand, modelled on Best Buy's actual sales of Panasonic products, is now transmitted electronically from i2 to Panasonic. i2 Technologies' forecasts are the basis for Panasonic's production schedule. This the way in which forecast demand pushes production.

Taking into account the lead time required to purchase materials and to manufacture components and finished products, a master production schedule specifies the quantity and timing of each item to be produced. Once scheduled production starts, the output of each department is pushed through the production line whether it is needed or not. The result is often an accumulation of inventory at workstations that receive work they are not yet ready to process.

Inventory management is a key challenge in an MRP system. The management accountant can play several important roles in meeting this challenge. A key role is maintaining accurate and timely information pertaining to materials, work in process, and finished goods inventories. A major cause of unsuccessful attempts to implement MRP systems has been the problem of collecting and updating inventory records. Calculating the full cost of carrying finished goods inventory motivates other actions. For example, instead of storing product at multiple (and geographically dispersed) warehouses, National Semiconductor contracted with Federal Express to airfreight its microchips from a central location in Singapore to customer sites worldwide. The change enabled National to move products from plant to customer in 4 days rather than 45, and to reduce distribution costs from 2.6% to 1.9% of revenues. These benefits subsequently led National to outsource all its logistics to Federal Express, including shipments among its own plants in the United States, Scotland, and Malaysia.

A second role of the management accountant is providing estimates of the setup costs for each production run at a plant, the downtime costs, and carrying costs of inventory. Costs of setting up a production run are analogous to ordering costs in the EOQ model. When the costs of setting up machines or sections of the production line are high (for example, as with a blast furnace in an integrated steel mill), processing larger batches of materials and incurring larger inventory carrying costs is the optimal approach, because it reduces the number of setups that must be made. When setup costs are small, processing smaller batches is optimal because it reduces carrying costs. Similarly, when the costs of downtime are high, there can be sizable benefits from maintaining continuous production.

ENTERPRISE RESOURCE PLANNING (ERP) SYSTEMS[2]

For both MRP and JIT supply-chain strategies, the most important resource is effective and efficient communication of relevant information. The speed of information flow from buyers to suppliers is a problem for large companies with fragmented information systems. Systems to program and control manufacturing do not communicate with those tracking inventory, for example. These incompatible systems are spread across the business functions of the value chain.

Enterprise resource planning (ERP) systems improve internal business process flows of information enabling effective inventory cost control. An ERP system is an integrated set of software modules including accounting, distribution, manufacturing, purchasing, human resources, and other functions. These interdependencies are illustrated in Exhibit 11-2 (page 531). An ERP system integrates all the information from a company into a single database that collects data and feeds it into applications supporting all of a company's business activities. All internal software operations receive data in real time, heightening the visibility of the interdependencies and bottlenecks in the entire business process. With an ERP system, companies can choose a supply-chain strategy that demands accurate and timely sharing of information to parties external to the company.

For example, using an ERP system, a salesperson can generate a contract for a customer in Germany, verify the customer's credit limits, and place a production order. The system schedules manufacturing in, say, Brazil, requisitions materials from inventory, orders components from suppliers, and schedules shipment. It also credits sales commissions to the salesperson and records all the costing and financial accounting information.

ERP systems give low-level managers, workers, customers, and suppliers access to operating information. This benefit, coupled with tight coordination across business functions, enables ERP systems to rapidly shift manufacturing and distribution

[2]For an excellent discussion, see T. H. Davenport, "Putting the Enterprise into the Enterprise System," *Harvard Business Review*, July–August 1998; also see A. Cagilo, "Enterprise Resource Planning Systems and Accountants: Towards Hybridization?" *European Accounting Review*, May 2003.

plans in response to changes in supply and demand. Companies believe that an ERP system is essential to support JIT and MRP initiatives because of the effect it has on lead times. Using an ERP system, Autodesk, a maker of computer-aided design software, reduced order lead times from 2 weeks to 1 day; Fujitsu reduced lead times from 18 to 1.5 days. ERP systems are the basis for demand forecasts and MRP as part of their operations and logistics modules.

Although the tight coupling of systems throughout a business streamlines administrative and financial processes and saves costs, it can also make the system large and unwieldy. Because of their complexity, suppliers of ERP systems such as SAP, Baan, Peoplesoft, and Oracle provide software packages that are standard but that can be customized, although at considerable cost. Without some customization, unique and distinctive features that confer strategic advantage will not be available. The challenge when implementing ERP systems is to strike the right balance between systems that are common across all of a company's business and geographical locations and systems that for strategic reasons are designed to be unique.

Adopting an MRP or JIT supply-chain approach requires diverse organizations to cooperate and communicate on a broad set of issues. Respondents emphasized this challenge was not always successfully met. Not surprisingly, not all supply-chain initiatives have delivered the initially met projected financial and operating benefits. The next section discusses *backflush costing*, which is a job-costing system that dovetails with JIT production and is less costly to operate than most traditional costing systems described in Chapters 4, 7, 8, and 9.

REAL COMPANIES

Challenge: Securing the Benefits of Good Supply-Chain Management

	North America	Europe	Asia
Exceeds expectations	1.5%	0.0%	9.7%
Meets expectations	43.9%	57.5%	67.7%
Below expectations	48.5%	32.5%	19.4%
Far below expectations	6.1%	10.0%	3.2%

A sample of 220 retailers and manufacturers lists key issues requiring remedy if companies are to benefit from adopting a supply-chain strategy.[b] Manufacturers reported the following preferences for information from retailers ranked in importance and obstacles to be overcome:

Preferred Information	Obstacles and Challenges
Retail sales forecasts	Unwillingness to share information
Sales information (e.g., daily sales per outlet)	Supply-chain partners will fail in commitments to share data
Pricing and advertising strategies	Incompatible information system software
Inventory levels at each outlet	Limited resources to implement a supply-chain strategy

Supply-chain benefits include fewer stockouts, reduced manufacture of items not subsequently demanded at the retail level, reduced quantities of rush orders, and lower inventory levels. One recent survey found that 78% of global managers identified the supply-chain function as "very important" or "somewhat important" to their organization's business strategy.[a]

One principal challenge is to manage the information flow in order for supply-chain partners to share timely, accurate, relevant information The table summarizes the assessment of communication management by global companies:

[a]ITtoolbox/Oracle, "2004 ITtoolbox Supply Chain Survey" (Scottsdale, Arizona, 2004).

[b]Research Incorporated, "Synchronizing the Supply Chain Through Collaborative Design" (Alpharetta, Georgia, 1998).

ASSESS YOUR MASTERY

To check your understanding of the material in Learning Objective ④, go to the *Mastery Questions* section at the end of this chapter and complete Learning Objective ④ question 1.

MyAccountingLab

BACKFLUSH COSTING

A unique production system such as JIT leads to its own unique costing system. Organizing manufacturing in cells, reducing defects and manufacturing lead time, and ensuring timely delivery of materials enables purchasing, production, and sales to occur in quick succession with minimal inventories. The absence of inventories makes choices about cost flow assumptions (such as weighted average or first-in, first-out) or inventory costing methods (such as absorption or variable costing) unimportant—all manufacturing costs of a period flow directly into cost of goods sold. The rapid conversion of direct materials to finished goods that are immediately sold simplifies job costing.

Analyze how backflush costing can simplify traditional job-costing systems ⑤

SIMPLIFIED NORMAL OR STANDARD COSTING

Traditional and standard costing systems (discussed in Chapters 4, 7, and 8) use **sequential tracking** (also called **synchronous tracking**), which is any product costing method in which the accounting system entries occur in the same order as actual purchases and production. These traditional systems track costs sequentially as products pass from direct materials, to work in process, to finished goods, and finally to sales, as shown here. Some have called this the "just in case" system.

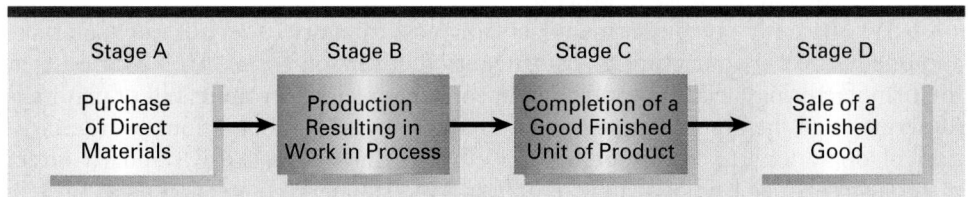

A sequential tracking costing system would have four trigger points, corresponding to separate journal entries being made at Stages A, B, C, and D. The term **trigger point** refers to a stage in the cycle (beginning with purchase of direct materials (Stage A) to sale of finished goods (Stage D) at which journal entries are made in the accounting system.

An alternative approach to sequential tracking is backflush costing. **Backflush costing** is a costing system that omits recording some or all journal entries relating to the cycle from purchase of direct materials to the sale of finished goods. It is a single-step costing process initiated by the production of a finished good. The manufacturer simply labels the finished product with either a bar code or RFID and scans the unit. This initiates a computer program that attributes quantities of direct materials to appropriate inventories. The program, using either standard or normal costs, will both assign material and conversion costs and allocate indirect costs to the finished unit.

Some programs both inform the distributor that the product is ready for pickup and delivery to the customer and inform the customer of the status of their order(s) as well as calculate variances using data from other information systems such as payroll and purchasing. Scrap, rework, and spoilage costs can be entered when appropriate to provide accurate unit costing. Where journal entries for one or more stages in the cycle are omitted, the journal entries for a subsequent stage use normal or standard costs to work backward to flush out the costs in the cycle for which journal entries were not made.

The following three examples illustrate backflush costing. To underscore basic concepts, we assume no direct materials variances in any of the examples. The three examples differ in the number and placement of trigger points at which journal entries are made in the accounting system:

	Number of Journal Entry Trigger Points	Location in Cycle Where Journal Entries Made
Example 1	3	Stage A. Purchase of direct materials (called "raw materials")
		Stage C. Completion of unspoiled good finished units of product
		Stage D. Sale of finished goods.
Example 2	2	Stage A. Purchase of direct materials (called "raw materials")
		Stage D. Sale of finished goods.
Example 3	2	Stage C. Completion of unspoiled good finished units of product
		Stage D. Sale of finished goods.

In all three examples, there are no journal entries in the accounting system for work in process (Stage B). These three examples of backflush costing are typically used where the amounts of work in process are small. With just-in-time production, sizable reductions in work in process have occurred.

EXAMPLE 1: TRIGGER POINTS ARE STAGES A, C, AND D

This example uses three trigger points to illustrate how backflushing can eliminate the need for a separate Work-in-Process account. Champion International uses a method similar to Example 1 in its specialty papers plant. A hypothetical company, Silicon Valley Computer (SVC), produces keyboards for personal computers. For April, there were no beginning inventories of raw materials. Moreover, there is zero beginning and ending work in process.

SVC has only one direct manufacturing cost category (direct or raw materials) and one indirect manufacturing cost category (conversion costs). All labour costs at the manufacturing facility are included in conversion costs. From its bill of materials (description of the types and quantities of materials) and an operations list (description of operations to be undergone), SVC determines the April standard direct materials costs per keyboard unit of $19 and the standard conversion costs of $12. SVC has two inventory accounts:

Type	Account Title
Combined direct materials and any direct material in work in process	Inventory: Raw and In-Process Control
Finished goods	Finished Goods Control

Trigger point 1 occurs when materials are purchased. These costs are charged to Inventory: Raw and In-Process Control.

Actual conversion costs are recorded as incurred under backflush costing, just as in other costing systems, and charged to Conversion Costs Control. Conversion costs are allocated to products at trigger point 2—the transfer of units to Finished Goods. This example assumes that under- or overallocated conversion costs are written off to cost of goods sold monthly. This flow of costs is analogous to job costing in Chapter 4, except backflush costing bypasses the WIP Control account.

SVC undertakes the following analysis and journal entries of the costs to units sold and to inventories:

1. Record the direct materials purchased during the accounting period. Assume April purchases of $1,950,000:

Entry (a)	Inventory: Raw and In-Process Control	$1,950,000	
	Accounts Payable Control		$1,950,000

2. Record the incurrence of conversion costs during the accounting period. Assume that conversion costs are $1,260,000:

Entry (b)	Conversion Costs Control	$1,260,000	
	[Various accounts (such as Accounts Payable Control and Wages Payable)]		$1,260,000

3. Determine the number of finished units manufactured during the accounting period. Assume that 100,000 keyboard units were manufactured in April.

4. *Compute the budgeted or standard costs of each finished unit.* The standard cost is $31 ($19 direct materials + $12 conversion costs) per unit.

5. *Record the cost of finished goods completed during the accounting period.* In this case, 100,000 units × $31 = $3,100,000. This step gives backflush costing its name.

   Up to this point in the operations, the costs have not been recorded sequentially with the flow of product along its production route. Instead, the output trigger reaches back and pulls the standard costs of direct materials from Inventory: Raw and WIP and the standard conversion costs for manufacturing the finished goods.

Entry (c)	Finished Goods Control	$3,100,000	
	Inventory: Raw and In-Process Control		$1,900,000
	Conversion Costs Allocated		1,200,000

6. *Record the cost of goods sold during the accounting period.* Assume that 99,000 units were sold in April (99,000 units × $31 = $3,069,000).

Entry (d)	Cost of Goods Sold	$3,069,000	
	Finished Goods Control		$3,069,000

7. *Record under- or overallocated conversion costs.* Actual conversion costs may be under- or overallocated in any given accounting period. Chapter 4 discussed various ways to account for under- or overallocated manufacturing overhead costs. Many companies write off underallocations or overallocations to cost of goods sold only at year-end; other companies, like SVC, do so monthly.

Companies that use backflush costing typically have low inventories, so proration of under- or overallocated costs between finished goods and cost of goods sold is less often necessary. The journal entry for the $60,000 difference between actual conversion costs incurred and standard conversion costs allocated would be:

Entry (e)	Conversion Costs Allocated	$1,200,000	
	Cost of Goods Sold	60,000	
	Conversion Costs Control		$1,260,000

The April ending inventory balances are

Inventory: Raw and In-Process	$50,000	
Finished Goods, 1,000 units × $31	31,000	
Total inventories	$81,000	

Exhibit 20-7, Panel A, on page 986 summarizes the journal entries for this example. Exhibit 20-8 (p. 987) provides an overview of this version of backflush costing. The elimination of the typical WIP account reduces the amount of detail in the accounting system.

Units on the production line may still be tracked in physical terms, but there is "no attaching of costs" to specific work orders as they flow along the production cycle. In fact, there are no work orders or labour time tickets in the accounting system.

EXHIBIT 20-7
Journal Entries in Backflush Costing

PANEL A, EXAMPLE 1: THREE TRIGGER POINTS—PURCHASE OF DIRECT MATERIALS, COMPLETION OF UNSPOILED GOOD FINISHED UNITS, AND SALE OF FINISHED GOODS

Transactions

(a) Purchase of direct materials[a]	Inventory: Raw and In-Process Control	$1,950,000	
	Accounts Payable Control		$1,950,000
(b) Incur conversion costs	Conversion Costs Control	1,260,000	
	Various Accounts		1,260,000
(c) Completion of good finished units[a]	Finished Goods Control	3,100,000	
	Inventory: Raw and In-Process Control		1,900,000
	Conversion Costs Allocated		1,200,000
(d) Sale of finished goods[a]	Cost of Goods Sold	3,069,000	
	Finished Goods Control		3,069,000
(e) Underallocated or overallocated conversion costs	Conversion Costs Allocated	1,200,000	
	Cost of Goods Sold	60,000	
	Conversion Costs Control		1,260,000

PANEL B, EXAMPLE 2: TWO TRIGGER POINTS—PURCHASE OF DIRECT MATERIALS AND SALE OF FINISHED GOODS

Transactions

(a) Purchase of direct materials[a]	Inventory Control	$1,950,000	
	Accounts Payable Control		$1,950,000
(b) Incur conversion costs	Conversion Costs Control	1,260,000	
	Various Accounts		1,260,000
(c) Completion of good finished units	No entry		
(d) Sale of finished goods[a]	Cost of Goods Sold	3,069,000	
	Inventory Control		1,881,000
	Conversion Costs Allocated		1,188,000
(e) Underallocated or overallocated conversion costs	Conversion Costs Allocated	1,188,000	
	Cost of Goods Sold	72,000	
	Conversion Costs Control		1,260,000

PANEL C, EXAMPLE 3: TWO TRIGGER POINTS—COMPLETION OF UNSPOILED GOOD FINISHED UNITS AND SALE OF FINISHED GOODS

Transactions

(a) Purchase of direct materials	No entry		
(b) Incur conversion costs	Conversion Costs Control	$1,260,000	
	Various Accounts		$1,260,000
(c) Completion of good finished units[a]	Finished Goods Control	3,100,000	
	Accounts Payable Control		1,900,000
	Conversion Costs Allocated		1,200,000
(d) Sale of finished goods[a]	Cost of Goods Sold	3,069,000	
	Finished Goods Control		3,069,000
(e) Underallocated or overallocated conversion costs	Conversion Costs Allocated	1,200,000	
	Cost of Goods Sold	60,000	
	Conversion Costs Control		1,260,000

[a]A trigger point.

The use of three triggers to make journal entries in Example 1 will result in SVC's backflush costing system reporting costs similar to sequential tracking when SVC has minimal work-in-process inventory. In Example 1, any inventories of raw materials or finished goods are recognized in SVC's backflush costing system when they first appear (as would be done in a costing system using sequential tracking).

ACCOUNTING FOR VARIANCES

The accounting for variances between actual costs incurred and standard costs allowed and the disposition of variances is basically the same under all standard costing

EXHIBIT 20-8
General-Ledger Overview of Backflush Costing

PANEL A, EXAMPLE 1: THREE TRIGGER POINTS—PURCHASE OF DIRECT MATERIALS, COMPLETION OF UNSPOILED GOOD FINISHED UNITS, AND SALE OF FINISHED GOODS

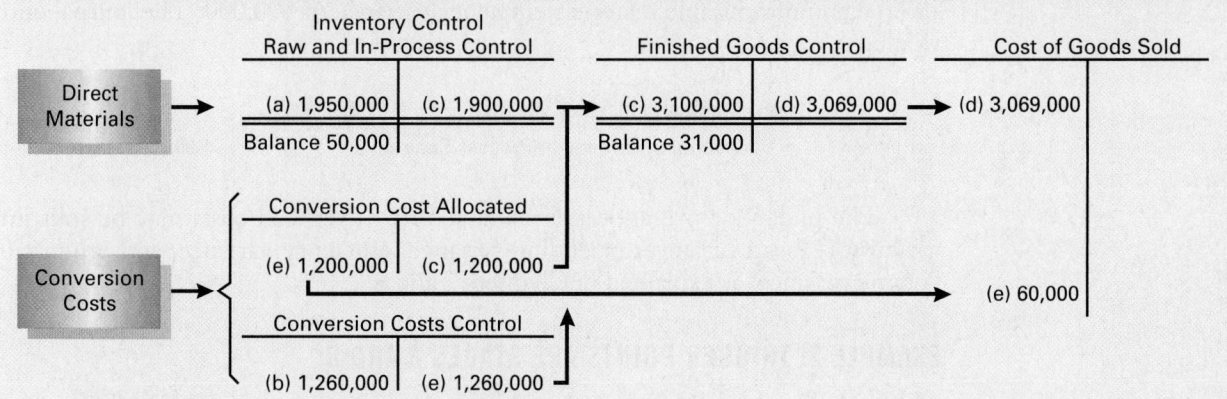

PANEL B, EXAMPLE 2: TWO TRIGGER POINTS—PURCHASE OF DIRECT MATERIALS AND SALE OF FINISHED GOODS

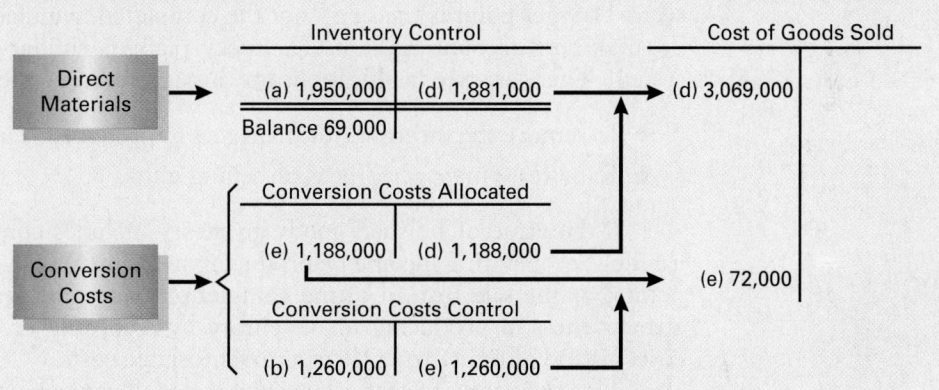

PANEL C, EXAMPLE 3: TWO TRIGGER POINTS—COMPLETION OF UNSPOILED GOOD FINISHED UNITS AND SALE OF FINISHED GOODS

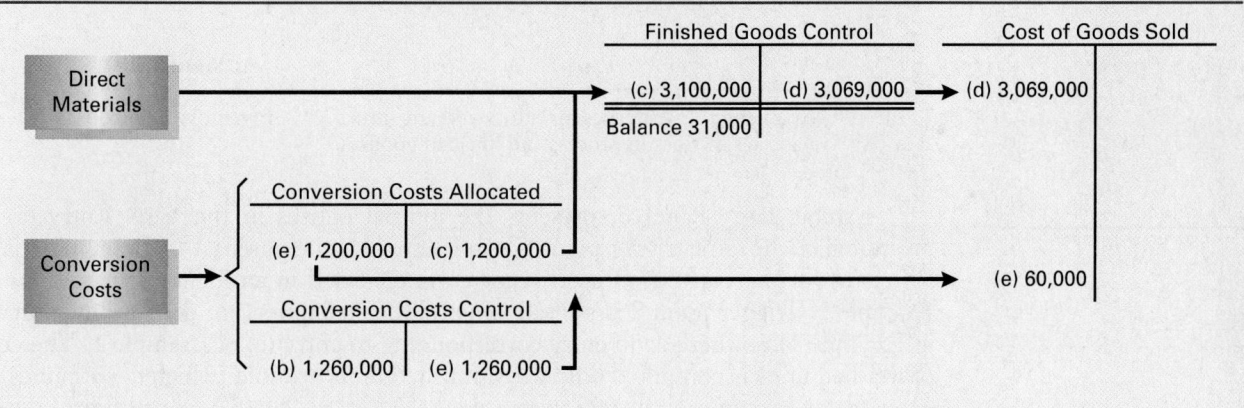

systems. The procedures are described in Chapters 7 and 8. In Example 1, suppose the direct materials purchased had an unfavourable price variance of $42,000. Entry (a) would then be

Inventory: Raw and In-Process Control	$1,950,000	
Raw Materials Price Variance	42,000	
Accounts Payable Control		$1,992,000

Direct materials are often a large proportion of total manufacturing costs, sometimes over 60%. Consequently, many companies will at least measure the direct materials efficiency variance in total by physically comparing what remains in direct materials inventory against what should be remaining, given the output of finished goods for the accounting period. In our example, suppose that such a comparison showed an unfavourable materials efficiency variance of $90,000. The journal entry would be:

Raw Materials Efficiency Variance	$90,000	
Inventory: Raw and In-Process Control		$90,000

The under- or overallocated manufacturing overhead costs may be split into various overhead variances (spending variance, efficiency variance, and production volume variance) as explained in Chapters 7 and 8.

EXAMPLE 2: TRIGGER POINTS ARE STAGES A AND D

This example, also based on SVC and using the same data, presents a backflush costing system that, relative to Example 1, is a more dramatic departure from a sequential tracking inventory costing system. The first trigger point in this example is the same as the first trigger point in Example 1 (the purchase of direct materials), but the second trigger point is the sale—not the completed manufacture—of finished units. Toyota's cost accounting at its Kentucky plant is similar to this type of costing system. There are two justifications for this accounting system:

◆ To remove the incentive for managers to produce for inventory.
◆ To increase managers' focus on selling units.

If the value of finished goods inventory includes conversion costs, managers can bolster operating income by producing more units than are sold. Having trigger point 2 as the sale instead of the completion of production, however, reduces the attractiveness of producing for inventory by recording conversion costs as period costs instead of capitalizing them as inventoriable costs.

This variation of backflush costing treats all conversion costs as period costs.

The inventory account in this example is confined solely to direct materials (whether they are in storerooms, in process, or in finished goods). There is only one inventory account:

Type	Account Title
Combined direct materials inventory and any direct materials in work in process and finished goods	Inventory Control

Exhibit 20-7, Panel B, presents the journal entries in this case. Entry (a) is prompted by the same trigger point 1 as in Example 1, the purchase of direct materials. Entry (b) for the conversion costs incurred is recorded in an identical manner as in Example 1. Trigger point 2 is the sale of good finished units (not their production, as in Example 1), so there is no entry corresponding to entry (c) of Example 1. The cost of finished units is computed only when finished units are sold (which corresponds to entry (d) of Example 1): 99,000 units sold × $31 = $3,069,000, consisting of direct materials (99,000 × $19 = $1,881,000) and conversion costs allocated (99,000 × $12 = $1,188,000).

No conversion costs are inventoried. That is, compared to Example 1, Example 2 does not attach $12,000 ($12 per unit × 1,000 units) of conversion costs to finished goods inventory. Hence, Example 2 allocates $12,000 less in conversion costs than Example 1. Of the $1,260,000 in conversion costs, $1,188,000 is allocated at standard cost to the units sold. The remaining $72,000 ($1,260,000 – $1,188,000) of conversion costs is underallocated. Entry (e) in Exhibit 20-7, Panel B, presents the journal entry if SVC, like many companies, writes off these underallocated costs monthly as additions to cost of goods sold.

The April ending balance of Inventory Control is $69,000 ($50,000 direct materials still on hand + $19,000 direct materials embodied in the 1,000 units manufactured but not sold during the period). Exhibit 20-8 provides an overview of this version of backflush costing. Entries are keyed to Exhibit 20-7, Panel B. The approach described in Example 2 closely approximates the costs computed using sequential tracking when a company holds minimal work in process and finished goods inventories.

EXAMPLE 3: TRIGGER POINTS ARE STAGES C AND D

This example presents an extreme and simpler version of backflush costing. It has only one trigger point for making journal entries to inventory. The trigger point is SVC's completion of finished units. Exhibit 20-7, Panel C, presents the journal entries in this case, using the same data as in Examples 1 and 2. Note that since the purchase of direct materials is not a trigger point, there is no entry corresponding to entry (a)—purchases of direct materials. Exhibit 20-8 provides an overview of this version of backflush costing. Entries are keyed to Exhibit 20-7, Panel C.

Compare entry (c) in Exhibit 20-7, Panel C, with entries (a) and (c) in Exhibit 20-7, Panel A. The simpler version in Example 3 ignores the $1,950,000 purchases of direct materials (entry (a) of Example 1). At the end of April, $50,000 of direct materials purchased has not yet been placed into production ($1,950,000 – $1,900,000 = $50,000), nor has it been entered into the inventory costing system.

Example 3 does not record accounts payable for direct materials until the products being manufactured are completely through the production process! As a result, this version of backflush costing is feasible only if there is a very short lag between receipt of direct materials and completion of the finished goods. Other journal entries must be made in addition to the trigger-point entries. Journal entries must be made for conversion costs incurred and for disposing of underallocated or overallocated conversion costs.

Extending Example 3, backflush costing systems could also use the sale of finished goods (instead of the production of finished goods) as the only trigger point. This version of backflush costing would be most suitable for a JIT production system with minimal direct materials, work-in-process, and finished goods inventories because this backflush costing system would maintain no inventory accounts.

SPECIAL CONSIDERATIONS IN BACKFLUSH COSTING

The accounting illustrated in Examples 1, 2, and 3 does not strictly adhere to the GAAP of external reporting. For example, WIP (an asset) exists but is not recognized in the accounting system. Advocates of backflush costing, however, cite the materiality concept in support of these versions of backflushing. They claim that if inventories are low or their total costs are not subject to significant change from one accounting period to the next, operating income and inventory costs developed in a backflush costing system will not differ materially from the results generated by a system that adheres to generally accepted accounting principles.

Suppose material differences in operating income and inventories do exist between the results of a backflush costing system and those of a conventional standard costing system. An adjustment can be recorded to make the backflush numbers satisfy external reporting requirements. For example, the backflush entries in Example 2 would result in expensing all conversion costs as a part of COGS ($1,188,000 at standard costs + $72,000 writeoff of underallocated conversion costs = $1,260,000). But suppose conversion costs were regarded as sufficiently material in amount to be included in Inventory Control. Then entry (e), closing the Conversion Costs accounts, would change as shown below:

Original entry (e)	Conversion Costs Allocated	$1,188,000	
	Cost of Goods Sold	72,000	
	Conversion Costs Control		$1,260,000
Revised entry (e)	Conversion Costs Allocated	$1,188,000	
	Inventory Control (1,000 units × $12)	12,000	
	Cost of Goods Sold	60,000	
	Conversion Costs Control		$1,260,000

Criticisms of backflush costing focus mainly on the absence of audit trails—the ability of the accounting system to pinpoint the uses of resources at each step of the production process. The absence of large amounts of materials and WIP inventory means that managers can keep track of operations by personal observations, computer monitoring, and nonfinancial measures.

What are the implications of JIT and backflush costing systems for ABC systems? Simplifying the production process, as in a JIT system, makes more of the costs direct and so reduces the extent of overhead cost allocations. Simplified ABC systems are often adequate for companies implementing JIT. But even these simpler ABC systems can enhance backflush costing. Costs from ABC systems give relatively more accurate budgeted conversion costs per unit for different products, which are then used in the backflush costing system. The activity-based cost data are also useful for product costing, decision making, and cost management.

MyAccountingLab

ASSESS YOUR MASTERY

To check your understanding of the material in Learning Objective 5, go to the *Mastery Questions* section at the end of this chapter and complete Learning Objective 5 question 1.

PULLING IT ALL TOGETHER—PROBLEM FOR SELF-STUDY

PROBLEM 1

Lee Company has a Singapore plant that manufactures MP3 players. One component is an XT chip. Expected demand is for 5,200 of these chips in March 2010. Lee estimates the ordering cost per purchase order to be $250. The monthly carrying cost for one unit of XT in stock is $5.

REQUIRED
1. Compute the EOQ for the XT chip.
2. Compute the number of deliveries of XT in March 2010.
3. What are some conflicts that can arise from the use of an EOQ model?
4. Identify relevant costs and benefits of a JIT strategy.
5. What is the key difference between MRP and JIT supply-chain management strategies?
6. What resource is essential to successful implementation of either MRP or JIT strategies?

SOLUTION

1.

$$\text{EOQ} = \sqrt{\frac{2 \times 5{,}200 \times \$250}{\$5}}$$

$$= 721 \text{ chips (rounded)}$$

2. Number of deliveries = 5,200 ÷ 721 = 8 (rounded up)

3. The EOQ model focuses on the tradeoff between carrying and ordering costs but ignores purchasing, stockout, and quality costs. A performance measure for the purchasing manager could be a purely financial accounting measure which excludes the opportunity cost of misstating the EOQ. The EOQ optimal solution and the optimal performance threshold will not match because opportunity cost is included in considering the best EOQ. A similar problem arises if annual carrying costs of excess inventory are excluded from the performance measure for purchasing managers.

4. Relevant costs include purchasing, ordering, carrying, stockout, and opportunity costs. Financial accounting standards determine the methods of accounting for all but opportunity costs for purposes of external reporting. COGS and inventory valuation methods are standardized. For internal purposes, however, tradeoffs are required between incurring one type versus another of opportunity costs. Management accountants have the expertise required to provide this relevant information.

5. A JIT supply-chain management strategy is based on demand push. The demand, an order for goods, initiates the system to supply goods. An MRP supply-chain management strategy is based on demand pull wherein a forecast of demand is sent directly to the supplier rather than an order. The demand forecast initiates the system to supply goods.

6. Both the JIT and MRP supply-chain strategies require effective information sharing. Often the information stored by one business function software in a company cannot be readily transmitted to another, which incurs delay. An ERP information system collects information from different computer systems into a single database and removes delay.

PROBLEM 2

Littlefield Company uses a backflush costing system with three trigger points:

◆ Purchase of direct materials
◆ Completion of good finished units of product
◆ Sale of finished goods

There are no beginning inventories. Information for April 2010 is:

Direct materials purchased	$ 880,000
Direct materials used	$ 850,000
Conversion cost incurred	$ 422,000
Conversion costs allocated	$ 400,000
Costs transferred to finished goods	$1,250,000
Cost of goods sold	$1,190,000

REQUIRED

1. Prepare journal entries for April (without disposing of underallocated or overallocated conversion costs). Assume there are no direct materials variances.

2. Under an ideal JIT production system, how would the amounts in your journal entries differ from the journal entries in requirement 1?

SOLUTION

1. Journal entries for April are:

Entry (a)	Inventory: Materials and In-Process Control	$ 880,000	
	Accounts Payable Control		$ 880,000
	(direct materials purchased)		
Entry (b)	Conversion Costs Control	$ 422,000	
	Various accounts (such as		
	Wages Payable Control)		$ 422,000
	(conversion costs incurred)		
Entry (c)	Finished Goods Control	$1,250,000	
	Inventory: Materials and In-Process Control		$ 850,000
	Conversion Costs Allocated		400,000
	(standard cost of finished goods completed)		
Entry (d)	Cost of Goods Sold	$1,190,000	
	Finished Goods Control		$1,190,000
	(standard costs of finished goods sold)		

2. Under an ideal JIT production system, if the manufacturing lead time per unit is very short, there could be zero inventories at the end of each day. Entry (c) would be $1,190,000 finished goods production [to match finished goods sold in entry (d)], not $1,250,000. If the Marketing Department could only sell goods costing $1,190,000, the JIT production system would call for direct materials purchases and conversion costs of lower than $880,000 and $422,000, respectively, in entries (a) and (b).

DECISION POINTS

The following decision guidelines use a question-and-answer format to summarize the chapter's main points. Each decision presents a key question. The guideline is the answer to that question.

DECISIONS	GUIDELINES
1. How do managers use the EOQ model?	The economic order quantity (EOQ) decision model calculates the optimal quantity of inventory to order by balancing ordering and carrying costs. The larger the order quantity, the higher the annual carrying costs and the lower the annual ordering costs. The EOQ model includes both costs recorded in the financial accounting system and opportunity costs not recorded in the financial accounting system.
2. How can companies reduce the conflict between the EOQ decision model and the models used for performance evaluation?	The opportunity cost of investment tied up in inventory is a key input in the EOQ decision model. Some companies include opportunity costs when evaluating managers so that the EOQ decision model is consistent with the performance evaluation model.
3. What are the features of a JIT strategy of supply-chain management?	A JIT strategy is based on demand push. Five features of a JIT production system are (a) organizing production in manufacturing cells, (b) hiring and training multiskilled workers, (c) emphasizing total quality management, (d) reducing manufacturing lead time and setup time, and (e) building strong supplier relationships.
4. How do materials requirement planning (MRP) systems differ from ERP systems?	Materials requirement planning (MRP) systems use a "push-through" approach that manufactures finished goods for inventory on the basis of demand forecasts. ERP systems are information management systems that consolidate data from different incompatible computer systems into a single database.
5. How does backflush costing simplify job costing?	Backflush costing delays recording some of the journal entries relating to the cycle from purchase of direct materials to the sale of finished goods. Traditional job-costing systems use sequential tracking, in which recording of the journal entries occurs in the same order as actual purchases and progress in production. Most backflush costing systems do not record journal entries for the work-in-process stage of production. Some backflush costing systems also do not record entries for either the purchase of direct materials or the completion of finished goods.

This chapter contains definitions of the following important terms:

backflush costing (p. 983)
carrying costs (p. 965)
cost of quality (COQ) (p. 965)
economic order quantity (EOQ) (p. 965)
enterprise resource planning (ERP)
  (p. 981)
inventory management (p. 964)
just-in-time (JIT) production (p. 971)

just-in-time (JIT) purchasing
  (p. 969)
lean production (p. 971)
manufacturing cells (p. 972)
materials requirements planning
  (MRP) (p. 980)
ordering costs (p. 965)
purchase order lead time (p. 965)

purchasing costs (p. 964)
reorder point (p. 968)
safety stock (p. 969)
sequential tracking (p. 983)
shrinkage costs (p. 965)
stockout costs (p. 965)
synchronous tracking (p. 983)
trigger point (p. 983)

MASTERY QUESTIONS

Mastery Questions are rated by proficiency level—elementary, intermediate, and advanced. The solutions appear in the Solutions to Mastery Questions section of MyAccountingLab.

LEARNING OBJECTIVE 1

1. EOQ—Advanced. Koala Blue retails a broad line of Australian merchandise at its London store. It sells 26,000 Ken Done linen bedroom packages (two sheets and two pillowcases) each year. Koala Blue pays Ken Done Merchandise Inc. $124.80 per package. Its ordering costs per purchase order are $86.40. The carrying costs per package are $12.48 per year.

　　　Liv Carrol, manager of the London store, seeks your advice on how ordering costs and carrying costs vary with different order quantities. Ken Done Merchandise Inc. guarantees the $124.80 purchase cost per package for the 26,000 units budgeted to be purchased in the coming year.

REQUIRED

1. Compute the annual ordering costs, the annual carrying costs, and their sum for purchase order quantities of 300, 500, 600, 700, and 900, using the formulas described in this chapter. What is the economic order quantity? Comment on your results.
2. Assume that Ken Done Merchandise Inc. introduces a computerized ordering network for its customers. Liv Carrol estimates that Koala Blue's ordering costs will be reduced to $48 per purchase order. How will this reduction in ordering costs affect the EOQ for Koala Blue on its linen bedroom packages?

LEARNING OBJECTIVE 2

1. EOQ conflicts—Advanced. Ralph Menard is the owner of a truck repair shop. He uses an EOQ model for each of his truck parts. He initially predicts the annual demand for heavy-duty tires to be 2,000. Each tire has a purchase price of $60. The incremental ordering costs per purchase order are $48. The incremental carrying costs per year are $4.80 per unit plus 10% of the supplier's purchase price.

REQUIRED

1. Calculate the EOQ for heavy-duty tires, along with the sum of annual relevant ordering costs and carrying costs.
2. Suppose Menard is correct in all his predictions except the purchase price. (He ignored a new law that abolished tariff duties on imported heavy-duty tires, which led to lower prices from foreign competitors.) If he had been a faultless predictor, he would have foreseen that the purchase price would drop to $36 at the beginning of the year and would be unchanged throughout the year. What is the cost of the prediction error?

LEARNING OBJECTIVE 3

1. JIT strategy—Advanced. (CMA, adapted) The Margro Corporation is an automotive supplier that uses automatic turning machines to manufacture precision parts from steel bars. Margro's inventory of raw steel averages $720,000. John Oates, president of Margro, and

Helen Gorman, Margro's controller, are concerned about the costs of carrying inventory. The steel supplier is willing to supply steel in smaller lots at no additional charge. Helen Gorman identified the following effects of adopting a JIT inventory program to virtually eliminate steel inventory:

◆ Without scheduling any overtime, lost sales due to stockouts would increase by 35,000 units per year. However, by incurring overtime premiums of $48,000 per year, the increase in lost sales could be reduced to 20,000 units. This would be the maximum amount of overtime that would be feasible for Margro.

◆ Two warehouses currently used for steel bar storage would no longer be needed. Margro rents one warehouse from another company under a cancellable leasing arrangement at an annual cost of $72,000. The other warehouse is owned by Margro and contains 12,000 square metres. Three-quarters of the space in the owned warehouse could be rented for $1.80 per square metre per year.

◆ Insurance and property tax costs totalling $16,800 per year would be eliminated.

Margro's projected operating results for the 2010 calendar year follow. Long-term capital investments by Margro are expected to produce a rate of return of 20%.

Margro Corporation Budgeted Income Statement
For the Year Ending December 31, 2010
(in thousands)

Revenues (900,000 units)		$12,960
Cost of goods sold:		
Variable costs	$4,860	
Fixed costs	1,740	
Total costs of goods sold:		6,600
Gross margin		6,360
Marketing and distribution costs:		
Variable costs	$1,080	
Fixed costs	1,800	
Total marketing and distribution costs		2,880
Operating income		$ 3,480

REQUIRED

1. Calculate the estimated dollar savings (loss) for the Margro Corporation that would result in 2010 from the adoption of the JIT inventory control method.
2. Identify and explain other factors that Margro should consider before deciding whether to install a JIT system.

LEARNING OBJECTIVE 4

1. MRP and ERP—Advanced. MacroHard Corp. produces J-Pods, music players that can download thousands of songs. MacroHard forecasts that demand in 2010 will be 48,000 J-Pods. The variable production cost of each J-Pod is $50. Due to the large $50,000 cost per setup, MacroHard plans to produce J-Pods once a month in batches of 4,000 each. The carrying cost of a unit in inventory is $20 per year.

REQUIRED

1. Using an MRP system, what is the annual cost of producing and carrying J-Pods in inventory? (Assume that, on average, half of the units produced in a month are in inventory.)
2. A new manager at MacroHard has suggested that the company use the EOQ model to determine the optimal batch size to produce. (To use the EOQ model, MacroHard needs to treat the setup cost in the same way it would treat ordering cost in a traditional EOQ model.) Determine the optimal batch size and number of batches. Round up the number of batches to the nearest whole number. What would be the annual cost of producing and carrying J-Pods in inventory if it uses the optimal batch size?
3. MacroHard is also considering switching from an MRP system to a JIT system. This will result in producing to demand in batch sizes of 500 J-Pods. The frequency of production batches will force MacroHard to reduce setup time and will result in a reduction in setup cost. The new setup cost will be $5,000 per setup. What is the annual cost of producing and carrying J-Pods in inventory under the JIT system?
4. Compare the models analyzed in the previous parts of the problem. What are the advantages and disadvantages of each?

LEARNING OBJECTIVE 5

1. **Backflush—Advanced.** The Ronowski Company produces telephones. For June, there were no beginning inventories of raw materials and no beginning and ending work in process. Ronowski uses a JIT production system and backflush costing with three trigger points for making entries in its accounting system:
   ◆ Purchase of direct (raw) materials
   ◆ Completion of good finished units of product
   ◆ Sale of finished goods

   Ronowski's June standard cost per unit of telephone product is direct materials, $31.20; conversion costs, $18. There are three inventory accounts:
   ◆ Inventory: Raw
   ◆ Inventory: In-Process Control
   ◆ Finished Goods Control

   The following data apply to June manufacturing:

Raw materials purchased	$6,360,000
Conversion costs incurred	$3,696,000
Number of finished units manufactured	200,000
Number of finished units sold	192,000

REQUIRED

1. Prepare summary journal entries for June (without disposing of under- or overallocated conversion costs). Assume no direct materials variances.
2. Post the entries in requirement 1 to T-accounts for applicable Inventory Control, Conversion Costs Control, Conversion Costs Allocated, and Cost of Goods Sold.

ASSIGNMENT MATERIAL

Make the grade with MyAccountingLab: The questions, exercises, and problems marked in red can be found on MyAccountingLab at **www.myaccountinglab.com**. You can practise them as often as you want, and most feature step-by-step guided instructions to help you find the right answer. Exercises and problems with an Excel icon in the margin have an accompanying Excel template on MyAccountingLab.

SHORT-ANSWER QUESTIONS

20-1 Why do better decisions regarding the purchasing and managing of goods for sale frequently cause dramatic percentage increases in net income?

20-2 Name five cost categories that are important in managing goods for sale in a retail organization.

20-3 What assumptions are made when using the simplest version of the economic order quantity (EOQ) decision model?

20-4 Give examples of costs included in annual carrying costs of inventory when using the EOQ decision model.

20-5 Give three examples of opportunity costs that typically are not recorded in accounting systems, although they are relevant to the EOQ model.

20-6 What are the steps in computing the cost of a prediction error when using the EOQ decision model?

20-7 Why might goal-congruence issues arise when an EOQ model is used to guide decisions on how much to order?

20-8 Describe just-in-time (JIT) purchasing and its benefits.

20-9 What are three factors causing reductions in the cost to place purchase orders of materials?

20-10 Describe how the Internet can be used to reduce the costs of placing purchase orders.

20-11 What is supply-chain analysis and how can it benefit manufacturers and retailers?

20-12 What are some obstacles to companies adopting a supply-chain approach?

20-13 What are the main features in a JIT production system?

20-14 Distinguish job-costing systems using sequential tracking from backflush costing.

20-15 Describe three different versions of backflush costing.

EXERCISES

20-16 Economic order quantity for retailer. Fan Base (FB) operates a megastore featuring sports merchandise. It uses an EOQ decision model to make inventory decisions. It is now considering inventory decisions for its Los Angeles Galaxy soccer jerseys product line. This is a highly popular item. Data for 2009 are:

Expected annual demand for Galaxy jerseys	10,000
Ordering cost per purchase order	$ 200
Carrying cost per year	$ 7 per jersey

Each jersey costs FB $40 and sells for $80. The $7 carrying cost per jersey per year comprises the required return on investment of $4.80 (12% × $40 purchase price) plus $2.20 in relevant insurance, handling, and theft-related costs. The purchasing lead time is 7 days. FB is open 365 days a year.

REQUIRED
1. Calculate the EOQ.
2. Calculate the number of orders that will be placed each year.
3. Calculate the reorder point.

20-17 Economic order quantity, effect of parameter changes (continuation of 20-16). Athletic Textiles (AT) manufactures the Galaxy jerseys that Fan Base (FB) sells to its customers. AT has recently installed computer software that enables its customers to conduct "one-stop" purchasing using state-of-the-art website technology. FB's ordering cost per purchase order will be $30 using this new technology.

REQUIRED
1. Calculate the EOQ for the Galaxy jerseys using the revised ordering cost of $30 per purchase order. Assume all other data from Exercise 20-16 are the same. Comment on the result.
2. Suppose AT proposes to "assist" FB. AT will allow FB customers to order directly from the AT website. AT would ship directly to these customers. AT would pay $10 to FB for every Galaxy jersey purchased by one of FB's customers. Comment qualitatively on how this offer would affect inventory management at FB. What factors should FB consider in deciding whether to accept AT's proposal?

20-18 EOQ for a retailer. The Cloth Centre sells fabrics to a wide range of industrial and consumer users. One of the products it carries is denim cloth, used in the manufacture of jeans and carrying bags. The supplier for the denim cloth pays all incoming freight. No incoming inspection of the denim is necessary because the supplier has a track record of delivering high-quality merchandise. The purchasing officer of the Cloth Centre has collected the following information:

Annual demand for denim cloth	20,000 metres
Ordering cost per purchase order	$160
Carrying cost per year	20% of purchase costs
Safety-stock requirements	None
Cost of denim cloth	$8 per metre

The purchasing lead time is 2 weeks. The Cloth Centre is open 250 days a year (50 weeks for 5 days a week).

REQUIRED
1. Calculate the EOQ for denim cloth.
2. Calculate the number of orders that will be placed each year.
3. Calculate the reorder point for denim cloth.

20-19 EOQ for manufacturer. Lakeland Company, which produces lawn mowers, purchases 18,000 units of a rotor blade part each year at a cost of $60 per unit. Lakeland requires a 15% annual rate of return on investment. In addition, the relevant carrying cost (for insurance, materials handling, breakage, and so on) is $6 per unit per year. The relevant ordering cost per purchase order is $150.

1. Required annual return on investment, $9

REQUIRED
1. Calculate Lakeland's EOQ for the rotor blade part.
2. Calculate Lakeland's annual relevant ordering costs for the EOQ calculated in requirement 1.
3. Calculate Lakeland's annual relevant carrying costs for the EOQ calculated in requirement 1.
4. Assume that demand is uniform throughout the year and known with certainty so that there is no need for safety stocks. The purchase-order lead time is half a month. Calculate Lakeland's reorder point for the rotor blade part.

20-20 Sensitivity of EOQ to changes in relevant ordering and carrying costs. Alyia Company's annual demand for Model X253 is 10,000 units. Alyia is unsure about the relevant carrying cost per unit per year and the relevant ordering cost per purchase order. This table presents six possible combinations of carrying and ordering costs.

1. EOQ (C = $10; P = $300) 775

Relevant Carrying Cost per Unit per Year	Relevant Ordering Cost per Purchase Order
$10	$300
$10	$200
$15	$300
$15	$200
$20	$300
$20	$200

REQUIRED
1. Determine EOQ for Alyia for each of the relevant ordering and carrying-cost alternatives.
2. How does your answer to requirement 1 give insight into the impact on EOQ of changes in relevant ordering and carrying costs?

20-21 Economic order quantity for retailer, ordering and carrying costs. Office Emporium (OE) is deciding the purchase order quantity for a new modem product. Annual demand is 24,000 units. Ordering costs per purchase order are $144. Carrying costs per modem unit are $12 per year. OE uses an economic-order-quantity model in its purchasing decisions. OE is open 360 days a year.

REQUIRED
1. Calculate OE's EOQ for modems.
2. Calculate OE's total ordering and carrying costs.
3. Assume that demand is known with certainty and the purchasing lead time is five days. Calculate OE's reorder point for modems.

20-22 Purchase order size for retailer, EOQ, just-in-time purchasing. The 24-Hour Mart operates a chain of supermarkets. Its best-selling soft drink is Fruitslice. Demand (D) in April for Fruitslice at its Regina supermarket is estimated to be 7,200 cases (24 cans in each case). In March, the Regina supermarket estimated the ordering costs per purchase order (P) for Fruitslice to be $36. The carrying costs (C) of each case of Fruitslice in inventory for a month were estimated to be $1.20. At the end of March, the Regina 24-Hour Mart reestimated its carrying costs to be $1.80 per case per month to take into account an increase in warehouse-related costs.

1. a. EOQ (D = 7,200; P = $36; C = $1.20) 658 cases

During March, 24-Hour Mart restructured its relationship with suppliers. It reduced the number of suppliers from 600 to 180. Long-term contracts were signed only with those suppliers that agreed to make product quality checks before shipping. Each purchase order would be made by linking into the suppliers' computer network. The Regina 24-Hour Mart estimated that these changes would reduce the ordering costs per purchase order to $6. The 24-Hour Mart is open 30 days in April.

REQUIRED
1. Calculate the economic order quantity in April for Fruitslice. Use the EOQ model, and assume in turn that
   a. D = 7,200; P = $36; C = $1.20
   b. D = 7,200; P = $36; C = $1.80
   c. D = 7,200; P = $6; C = $1.80

20-23 JIT production, relevant benefits, relevant costs. The Champion Hardware Company manufactures specialty brass door handles at its Kitchener plant. Champion is considering implementing a JIT production system. The following are the estimated costs and benefits of JIT production.

a. Annual additional tooling costs would be $100,000.

b. Average inventory would decline by 80% from the current level of $1,000,000.

c. Insurance, space, materials handling, and setup costs, which currently total $300,000 annually, would decline by 25%.

d. The emphasis on quality inherent in JIT production would reduce rework costs by 30%. Champion currently incurs $200,000 in annual rework costs.

e. Improved product quality under JIT production would enable Champion to raise the price of its product by $4 per unit. Champion sells 40,000 units each year.

Champion's required rate of return on inventory investment is 15% per year.

REQUIRED

1. Calculate the net benefit or cost to Champion if it adopts JIT production at the Kitchener plant.

2. What nonfinancial and qualitative factors should Champion consider when making the decision to adopt JIT production?

3. Suppose Champion implements JIT production at its Kitchener plant. Give examples of performance measures Champion could use to evaluate and control JIT production. What would be the benefit of Champion implementing an enterprise resource planning (ERP) system?

20-24 Backflush costing and JIT production. Road Warrior Corporation assembles handheld computers that have scaled-down capabilities of laptop computers. Each handheld computer takes 6 hours to assemble. Road Warrior uses a JIT production system and a backflush costing system with three trigger points:

◆ Purchase of direct materials

◆ Completion of good finished units of product

◆ Sale of finished goods

There are no beginning inventories of materials or finished goods. The following data are for August 2008:

Direct materials purchased	$2,754,000
Direct materials used	$2,733,600
Conversion costs incurred	$ 723,600
Conversion costs allocated	$ 750,400

Road Warrior records direct materials purchased and conversion costs incurred at actual costs. When finished goods are sold, the backflush costing system "pulls through" standard direct material cost ($102 per unit) and standard conversion cost ($28 per unit). Road Warrior produced 26,800 finished units in August 2010 and sold 26,400 units. The actual direct material cost per unit in August 2010 was $102, and the actual conversion cost per unit was $27.

REQUIRED

1. Prepare summary journal entries for August 2010 (without disposing of under- or overallocated conversion costs).

2. Post the entries in requirement 1 to T-accounts for applicable Inventory: Materials and In-Process Control, Finished Goods Control, Conversion Costs Control, Conversion Costs Allocated, and Cost of Goods Sold.

3. Under an ideal JIT production system, how would the amounts in your journal entries differ from those in requirement 1?

20-25 Backflush costing, two trigger points, materials purchase and sale (continuation of 20-24). Assume the same facts as in Exercise 20-24, except that Road Warrior now uses a backflush costing system with the following two trigger points:

◆ Purchase of direct materials

◆ Sale of finished goods

The Inventory Control account will include direct materials purchased but not yet in production, materials in work in process, and materials in finished goods but not sold. No conversion costs are inventoried. Any under- or overallocated conversion costs are written off monthly to Cost of Goods Sold.

REQUIRED

1. Prepare summary journal entries for August, including the disposition of under- or over-allocated conversion costs.
2. Post the entries in requirement 1 to T-accounts for Inventory Control, Conversion Costs Control, Conversion Costs Allocated, and Cost of Goods Sold.

20-26 Backflush costing, two trigger points, completion of production and sale (continuation of 20-24). Assume the same facts as in Exercise 20-24, except now Road Warrior uses only two trigger points, the completion of good finished units of product and the sale of finished goods. Any under- or overallocated conversion costs are written off monthly to Cost of Goods Sold.

1. Conversion Costs Allocated DR., $750,400

REQUIRED

1. Prepare summary journal entries for August, including the disposition of under- or over-allocated conversion costs.
2. Post the entries in requirement 1 to T-accounts for Finished Goods Control, Conversion Costs Control, Conversion Costs Allocated, and Cost of Goods Sold.

20-27 Inventory management and the balanced scorecard. Devin Sports Cars (DSC) has implemented a balanced scorecard to measure and support its just-in-time production system. In the learning and growth category, DSC measures the percentage of employees who are cross-trained to perform a wide variety of production tasks. Internal business process measures are inventory turns and on-time delivery. The customer perspective is measured using a customer satisfaction measure, and financial performance using operating income. DSC estimates that if it can increase the percentage of cross-trained employees by 5%, the resulting increase in labour productivity will reduce inventory-related costs by $100,000 per year and shorten delivery times by 10%. The 10% reduction in delivery times, in turn, is expected to increase customer satisfaction by 5%, and each 1% increase in customer satisfaction is expected to increase revenues by 2% due to higher prices.

1. Increased revenue from higher customer satisfaction, $500,000

REQUIRED

1. Assume that budgeted revenues in the coming year are $5,000,000. Ignoring the costs of training, what is the expected increase in operating income in the coming year if the number of cross-trained employees is increased by 5%?
2. What is the most DSC would be willing to pay to increase the percentage of cross-trained employees if it is only interested in maximizing operating income in the coming year?
3. What factors other than short-term profits should DSC consider when assessing the benefits from employee cross-training?

PROBLEMS

20-28 Effect of different order quantities on ordering costs and carrying costs, EOQ. Koala Blue, a retailer of bed and bath linen, sells 234,000 packages of Mona Lisa designer sheets each year. Koala Blue incurs an ordering cost of $81 per purchase order placed with Mona Lisa Enterprises and an annual carrying cost of $11.70 per package. Liv Carrol, purchasing manager at Koala Blue, seeks your help: She wants to understand how ordering and carrying costs vary with order quantity.

1. Total relevant costs, scenario 1, $26,325

	Scenario				
	1	2	3	4	5
Annual demand (packages)	234,000	234,000	234,000	234,000	234,000
Cost per purchase order	$ 81	$ 81	$ 81	$ 81	$ 81
Carrying cost per package per year	$ 11.70	$ 11.70	$ 11.70	$ 11.70	$ 11.70
Quantity (packages) per purchase order	900	1,500	1,800	2,100	2,700
Number of purchase orders per year					
Annual relevant ordering costs					
Annual relevant carrying costs					
Annual total relevant costs of ordering and carrying inventory					

REQUIRED

1. Complete the preceding table for Liv Carrol. What is the EOQ? Comment on your results.
2. Mona Lisa is about to introduce a Web-based ordering system for its customers. Liv Carrol estimates that Koala Blue's ordering costs will be reduced to $49 per purchase order. Calculate the new EOQ and the new annual relevant costs of ordering and carrying inventory.
3. Liv Carrol estimates that Koala Blue will incur a cost of $2,000 to train its two purchasing assistants to use the new Mona Lisa system. Help Liv Carrol present a case to upper management showing that Koala Blue will be able to recoup its training costs within the first year of adoption.

②

2. Weekly demand, 2,500 pairs of shoes

20-29 EOQ, uncertainty, safety stock, reorder point. Clarkson Shoe Co. produces and sells excellent quality walking shoes. After production, the shoes are distributed to 20 warehouses around the country. Each warehouse services approximately 100 stores in its region. Clarkson uses an EOQ model to determine the number of pairs of shoes to order for each warehouse from the factory. Annual demand for Warehouse OR2 is approximately 120,000 pairs of shoes. The ordering cost is $250 per order. The annual carrying cost of a pair of shoes is $2.40 per pair.

REQUIRED

1. Use the EOQ model to determine the optimal number of pairs of shoes per order.
2. Assume each month consists of approximately 4 weeks. If it takes 1 week to receive an order, at what point should warehouse OR2 reorder shoes?
3. Although OR2's average monthly demand is 10,000 pairs of shoes (120,000 ÷ 12 months), demand each month may vary from the average by up to 20%. To handle the variation in demand Clarkson has decided that OR2 should maintain enough safety stock to cover any demand level. How much safety stock should Warehouse OR2 hold? How will this affect the reorder point and reorder quantity?
4. What is the total relevant ordering and carrying costs with safety stock and without safety stock?

③

1. Total incremental costs, JIT purchasing policy, $156,500

20-30 JIT purchasing, relevant benefits, relevant costs. (CMA, adapted) The Margro Corporation is an automotive supplier that uses automatic turning machines to manufacture precision parts from steel bars. Margro's inventory of raw steel averages $600,000. John Oates, president of Margro, and Helen Gorman, Margro's controller, are concerned about the costs of carrying inventory. The steel supplier is willing to supply steel in smaller lots at no additional charge. Gorman identifies the following effects of adopting a JIT inventory program to virtually eliminate steel inventory:

◆ Without scheduling any overtime, lost sales due to stockouts would increase by 35,000 units per year. However, by incurring overtime premiums of $40,000 per year, the increase in lost sales could be reduced to 20,000 units per year. This would be the maximum amount of overtime that would be feasible for Margro.

◆ Two warehouses currently used for steel bar storage would no longer be needed. Margro rents one warehouse from another company under a cancellable leasing arrangement at an annual cost of $60,000. The other warehouse is owned by Margro and contains 12,000 square metres. Three-fourths of the space in the owned warehouse could be rented for $1.50 per square metre per year. Insurance and property tax costs totalling $14,000 per year would be eliminated.

Margro's required rate of return on investment is 20% per year. Margro's budgeted income statement for the year ending December 31, 2010 (in thousands) is as follows:

Revenues (900,000 units)		$10,800
Cost of goods sold		
Variable costs	$4,050	
Fixed costs	1,450	
Total costs of goods sold		5,500
Gross margin		5,300
Marketing and distribution costs		
Variable costs	$ 900	
Fixed costs	1,500	
Total marketing and distribution costs		2,400
Operating income		$ 2,900

1. Calculate the estimated dollar savings (loss) for the Margro Corporation that would result in 2010 from the adoption of JIT purchasing.
2. Identify and explain other factors that Margro should consider before deciding whether to adopt JIT purchasing.

20-31 Backflush costing and JIT production. The Acton Corporation manufactures electrical meters. For August, there were no beginning inventories of direct materials and no beginning or ending work in process. Acton uses a JIT production system and backflush costing with three trigger points for making entries in the accounting system:

1. Finished Goods Control DR., $945,000

◆ Purchase of direct materials—debited to Inventory: Materials and In-Process Control
◆ Completion of good finished units of product—debited to Finished Goods Control
◆ Sale of finished goods

Acton's August standard cost per metre is direct material, $25; and conversion cost, $20. The following data apply to August manufacturing:

Direct materials purchased	$550,000
Conversion costs incurred	$440,000
Number of finished units manufactured	21,000
Number of finished units sold	20,000

REQUIRED

1. Prepare summary journal entries for August (without disposing of under- or overallocated conversion costs). Assume no direct materials variances.
2. Post the entries in requirement 1 to T-accounts for Inventory: Materials and In-Process Control, Finished Goods Control, Conversion Costs Control, Conversion Costs Allocated, and Cost of Goods Sold.

20-32 Backflush, two trigger points, materials purchase and sale (continuation of 20-31). Assume that the second trigger point for Acton Corporation is the sale—rather than the completion—of finished goods. Also, the inventory account is confined solely to direct materials, whether these materials are in a storeroom, in work in process, or in finished goods. No conversion costs are inventoried. They are allocated to the units sold at standard costs. Any under- or overallocated conversion costs are written off monthly to Cost of Goods Sold.

1. Cost of Goods Sold DR., $900,000

REQUIRED

1. Prepare summary journal entries for August, including the disposition of under- or overallocated conversion costs. Assume no direct materials variances.
2. Post the entries in requirement 1 to T-accounts for Inventory Control, Conversion Costs Control, Conversion Costs Allocated, and Cost of Goods Sold.

20-33 Backflush, two trigger points, completion of production and sale (continuation of 20-31). Assume the same facts as in Problem 20-31 except now there are only two trigger points: the completion of good finished units of product and the sale of finished goods.

1. Conversion Costs Allocated DR., $420,000

REQUIRED

1. Prepare summary journal entries for August, including the disposition of under- or overallocated conversion costs. Assume no direct materials variances.
2. Post the entries in requirement 1 to T-accounts for Finished Goods Control, Conversion Costs Control, Conversion Costs Allocated, and Cost of Goods Sold.

20-34 Relevant benefits and costs of JIT purchasing. Hardesty Medical Instruments is considering JIT implementation in 2010. Hardesty's annual demand for product XJ-200, a surgical scalpel, is 20,000 units. If Hardesty implements JIT, the purchase price of the scalpel is expected to increase from $12 to $12.06 because of frequent deliveries by Morrison Manufacturing Inc. Morrison enjoys a sterling reputation for quality and reliability. Ordering costs will remain at $6 per order. However, the annual number of orders placed will be 200 instead of the current 20. As a result of frequent ordering, Hardesty's order size will decrease proportionally. Hardesty's required rate of return on investment is 20%. Other carrying costs (insurance, materials handling, and so on) will remain at $5.40 per unit. Currently, Hardesty has no stockout costs. Lower inventory levels from implementing JIT will lead to $3.60 per unit stockout costs on 100 units during the year due to rush orders being required.

1. Total annual relevant costs, current purchasing policy, $244,020

REQUIRED

1. Calculate the estimated dollar savings (loss) for Hardesty Medical Instruments from the adoption of JIT purchasing using the format of Exhibit 20-5 (p. 977).
2. Under what conditions would it be beneficial for Hardesty to have Morrison manage all inventories in the supply chain?

20-35 Supplier evaluation and relevant costs of quality and timely deliveries (continuation of 20-34). Hardesty Medical Instruments installed a JIT purchasing system in 2010 and selected Morrison Manufacturing Inc. as its supplier. Herriott Manufacturing Corporation also manufactures XJ-200. It offers to supply all of Hardesty's XJ-200 needs at a price of $11.70 per unit (less than Morrison's price of $12.06) under the same JIT delivery terms that Morrison offers. Hardesty's relevant carrying costs of insurance, material handling, and so on would be $5.28 per unit per year if it purchases from Herriott. Due to the lower quality of Herriott's product, Hardesty anticipates the following negative consequences of purchasing from Herriott:

◆ Hardesty would incur inspection costs of $0.096 per unit.
◆ Average stockouts of 800 units per year would occur from late deliveries, requiring rush orders at a cost of $3.60 per unit.
◆ Customers would likely return 10% of all units sold due to poor quality of the product. Hardesty estimates its additional costs to handle each returned unit are $7.20.

REQUIRED
Calculate the relevant costs of purchasing (1) from Morrison and (2) from Herriott using the format of Exhibit 20-6 (p. 979). From whom should Hardesty buy XJ-200?

20-36 Supplier evaluation and relevant costs of quality and timely deliveries. Copeland Sporting Goods is evaluating two suppliers of footballs, Big Red and Quality Sports. Pertinent information about each potential supplier follows:

Relevant Item	Big Red	Quality Sports
Purchase price per unit (case)	$ 60.00	$ 61.20
Ordering costs per order	$ 7.20	$ 7.20
Inspection costs per unit	$ 0.02	$ 0.00
Insurance, material handling, and so on per unit per year	$ 4.00	$ 4.50
Annual demand	12,000 units	12,000 units
Average quantity of inventory held during the year	100 units	100 units
Required return on investment	15%	15%
Stockout costs per unit	$ 24	$ 12
Stockout units per year	350 units	60 units
Customer returns	300 units	25 units
Customer-return costs per unit	$ 30	$ 30

REQUIRED
Calculate the relevant costs of purchasing (1) from Big Red and (2) from Quality Sports using the format of Exhibit 20-6 (p. 979). From whom should Copeland buy footballs?

20-37 Effect of management evaluation criteria on EOQ model. Computers 4 U is an online company that sells computers to individual consumers. The annual demand for one model that will be shipped from the northeast distribution centre is estimated to be 500,000 computers. The ordering cost is $800 per order. The cost of carrying a computer in inventory is $50 per year, which includes $20 in opportunity cost of investment. The average purchase cost of a computer is $200.

REQUIRED
1. Compute the optimal order quantity using the EOQ model.
2. Compute the number of orders per year and the annual relevant total cost of ordering and holding inventory.
3. Assume that the benchmark that is used to evaluate distribution centre managers includes only the out-of-pocket costs incurred (that is, managers' evaluations do not include the opportunity cost of investment tied up in holding inventory). If the manager makes the EOQ decision based upon the benchmark, the order quantity would be calculated using a carrying cost of $30, not $50. How would this affect the EOQ amount and the actual annual relevant cost of ordering and carrying inventory?
4. What will the inconsistency between the actual carrying cost and the benchmark used to evaluate managers cost the company? Why do you think the company currently excludes

the opportunity costs from the calculation of the benchmark? What could the company do to encourage the manager to make decisions more congruent with the goal of reducing total inventory costs?

20-38 Effect of EOQ ordering on supplier costs (continuation of 20-37). IMBest Computers supplies computers to Computers 4 U. Terry Moore, the president of IMBest, is pleased to hear that Computers 4 U will be ordering 500,000 computers. Moore has asked his accounting and production departments to team up and determine the best production schedule to meet Computers 4 U's desired delivery schedule. Assume that the computers would be ordered in batches of 2,000 and that there would be 250 orders annually. Because Computers 4 U's employees work a 5-day workweek for 50 weeks a year, they would expect to receive an order every day. They have developed the following two production alternatives:

A. IMBest could produce the 10,000 units demanded per week (2,000 × 5) in one large run on Mondays. Shipments would be made each day. If this option is chosen then IMBest would have to set up the machines only once a week, but would incur carrying cost to hold the computers in inventory until Computers 4 U's desired delivery date.

B. IMBest could rearrange its production schedule during the week and produce 2,000 computers each day of the week, totalling 10,000 computers per week. Shipments would be made at the end of each production day. If it chooses this alternative it will incur setup costs every day, but carrying costs would be negligible and are assumed to be zero.

1. Setup cost, Alternative A $50,000

REQUIRED
1. If setup costs are $1,000 per setup and carrying costs are $50 per computer per year, what would be the annual cost of each alternative?
2. How much would carrying costs have to increase before the preferred alternative would change?

20-39 Supply-chain effects on total relevant inventory cost. Cow Spot Computer Co. outsources the production of motherboards for its computers. It has narrowed down its choice of suppliers to two companies: Maji and Induk. Maji is an older company with a good reputation, while Induk is a newer company with cheaper prices. Given the difference in reputation, 5% of the motherboards will be inspected if they are purchased from Maji, but 25% of the motherboards will be inspected if they are purchased from Induk. The following data refer to costs associated with Maji and Induk.

1. Total cost, Maji, $935,930

	Maji	Induk
Number of orders per year	50	50
Annual motherboards demanded	10,000	10,000
Price per motherboard	$ 93	$ 90
Ordering cost per order	$ 10	$ 8
Inspection cost per unit	$ 5	$ 5
Average inventory level	100 units	100 units
Expected number of stockouts	100	300
Stockout cost (cost of rush order) per stockout	$ 5	$ 8
Units returned by customers for replacing motherboards	50	500
Cost of replacing each motherboard	$ 25	$ 25
Required annual return on investment	10%	10%
Other carrying costs per unit per year	$ 2.50	$ 2.50

REQUIRED
1. What is the relevant cost of purchasing from Maji and Induk?
2. What factors other than cost should Cow Spot consider?

20-40 Lean accounting. Flexible Security Devices (FSD) has introduced a just-in-time production process and is considering the adoption of lean accounting principles to support its new production philosophy. The company has two product lines: Mechanical Devices and Electronic Devices. Two individual products are made in each line. The company's traditional cost accounting system allocates all plant-level overhead costs to individual products. Product-line overhead costs are traced directly to product lines, and then allocated to

2. Value stream operating income, Mechanical Devices, $227

the two individual products in each line. Equipment costs are directly traced to products. The latest accounting report using traditional cost accounting methods included the following information (in thousands of dollars).

	Mechanical Devices		Electronic Devices	
	Product A	Product B	Product C	Product D
Sales	$700	$500	$900	$450
Direct materials (based on quantity used)	200	100	250	75
Direct manufacturing labour	150	75	200	60
Equipment costs	90	125	200	100
Allocated product-line overhead	110	60	125	50
Allocated plant-level overhead	50	35	80	25
Operating income	$100	$105	$ 45	$140

FSD has determined that each of the two product lines represents a distinct value stream. It has also determined that $120,000 of the allocated plant-level overhead costs represents occupancy costs. Product A occupies 20% of the plant's square footage, Product B occupies 20%, Product C occupies 30%, and Product D occupies 15%. The remaining square footage is occupied by plant administrative functions or is not being used. Finally, FSD has decided that direct material should be expensed in the period it is purchased, rather than when the material is used. According to purchasing records, direct material purchase costs during the period were:

	Mechanical Devices		Electronic Devices	
	Product A	Product B	Product C	Product D
Direct materials (purchases)	$190	$125	$250	$90

REQUIRED

1. What are the cost objects in FSD's lean accounting system? Which of FSD's costs would be excluded when computing operating income for these cost objects?
2. Compute operating income for the cost objects identified in requirement 1 using lean accounting principles. Why does operating income differ from the operating income computed using traditional cost accounting methods?

20-41 Supply-chain analysis, company viewpoints. Manufacturing companies participating in a supply-chain initiative linking manufacturers and retailers recently made the following comments on the benefits of the initiative:

- ◆ "Receiving better information has allowed us to forecast and reduce inventory levels . . . "
- ◆ "You produce only what you need and that keeps the product and floor cost down."
- ◆ "There is more accuracy with the retailer's needs so that we can fine-tune our production scheduling."
- ◆ "The inventory levels are lower and we have less waste by not overstocking the warehouses."

Manufacturing companies highlighted the following information from retailers as most valuable to them:

- ◆ "We would like to see [the retailers] forward planning expectations of their sales."
- ◆ "We could use retail store level data on a daily basis and better scanner information."
- ◆ "Better forecasts, decisions about shelving and shelf allocations by retailers would help."
- ◆ "I wish we had access to each retailer's sales forecasts and the advertisements that they will be running next."

REQUIRED

1. What are the major benefits from adopting a supply-chain approach? Use the comments above as a prompt to a more detailed discussion. Explain how these benefits can lead to increased operating income.
2. What are the key obstacles to a manufacturer adopting a supply-chain approach?

20-42 Backflush costing, income manipulation, governance. Shira Honig, the chief financial officer of Silicon Valley Computer, is an enthusiastic advocate of just-in-time production.

The SVC Keyboard Division that produces keyboards for personal computers has made dramatic improvements in its operations by a highly successful JIT implementation. The Keyboard Division president now wants to adopt backflush costing.

Honig discusses the backflush costing proposal with Ralph Strong, the controller of SVC. Strong is totally opposed to backflush costing. He argues that it will open up "Pandora's box" as regards allowing division managers to manipulate reported division operating income. A member of Strong's group outlines the three possible variations of backflush costing shown in Exhibits 20-7 and 20-8. Strong notes that none of these three methods track work in process. He asserts that this omission would allow managers to "artificially change" reported operating income by manipulating work-in-process levels. He is especially scathing about the backflush costing where no entries are made until a sale occurs. He comments:

> Suppose the Division has already met its target operating income and wants to shift some of this year's income to next year. Under backflush costing with sale of finished goods as the trigger point, the Division will have an incentive to not make sales this year of goods produced this year. This is a bizarre incentive. I rest my case about why we should stay with a job-costing system using sequential tracking.

Strong concludes that as long as reported accounting numbers are central to SVC's performance and bonus reviews, backflush costing should never be adopted.

REQUIRED
1. What factors should SVC consider in deciding whether to adopt a version of backflush costing?
2. Are Strong's concerns about income manipulation sufficiently important for SVC to not adopt backflush costing?
3. What other ways has SVC to motivate managers to not "artificially change" reported income?

COLLABORATIVE LEARNING CASE

20-43 Backflushing. The following conversation occurred between Brian Richardson, plant manager at Glendale Engineering, and Charles Cheng, plant controller. Glendale manufactures automotive component parts, such as gears and crankshafts, for automobile manufacturers. Richardson has been very enthusiastic about implementing JIT and about simplifying and streamlining production and other business processes.

"Charles," Richardson began, "I would like to substantially simplify our accounting in the new JIT environment. Can't we just record one journal entry at the time we ship products to our customers? I don't want to have our staff spending time tracking inventory from one stage to the next, when we have as little inventory as we do."

"Brian," Cheng said, "I think you are right about simplifying the accounting, but we still have a fair amount of direct materials and finished goods inventory that varies from period to period, depending on the demand for specific products. Doing away with all inventory accounting may be a problem."

"Well," Richardson replied, "you know my desire to simplify, simplify, simplify. I know that there are some costs of oversimplifying, but I believe that, in the long run, simplification pays dividends. Why don't you and your staff study the issues involved, and I will put it on the agenda for our next management meeting."

REQUIRED
1. What version of backflush costing would you recommend that Cheng adopt? Remember Richardson's desire to simplify the accounting as much as possible. Develop support for your recommendation.
2. Think about the three versions of backflush costing shown in this chapter. These versions differ with respect to the number and types of trigger points used. Suppose your goal of implementing backflush costing is to simplify the accounting, but only if it closely matches the sequential-tracking approach. Which version of backflush costing would you propose if:
   a. Glendale had no direct materials and no work-in-process inventories but did have finished goods inventory?
   b. Glendale had no work in process and no finished goods inventories but did have direct materials inventory?
   c. Glendale had no direct materials, no work-in-process, and no finished goods inventories?

3. Backflush costing has its critics. In an article in the magazine *Management Accounting* titled "Beware of the New Accounting Myths," R. Calvasina, E. Calvasina, and G. Calvasina state:

> The periodic (backflush) system has never been reflective of the reporting needs of a manufacturing system. In the highly standardized operating environments of the present JIT era, the appropriate system to be used is a perpetual accounting system based on an up-to-date, realistic set of standard costs. For management accountants to backflush on an actual cost basis is to return to the days of the outdoor privy (toilet).

Comment on this statement.

Capital Budgeting: Methods of Investment Analysis

Investment Decisions and Relevant Costs

Capital budgeting for projects such as the Confederation Bridge linking Prince Edward Island to New Brunswick reflects a company's long-term strategic plans. Construction took almost four years at a cost of $1 billion. Throughout construction over 5,000 people were employed, but at its peak almost 2,100 construction and 415 staff workers were employed.

After studying this chapter, you should be able to

1 Apply the concept of the time value of money to capital budgeting decisions

2 Evaluate discounted cash flow (DCF) and non-DCF methods to calculate rate of return (ROR)

3 Apply the concept of relevance to DCF methods of capital budgeting

4 Assess the complexities in capital budgeting within an interdependent set of value-chain business functions

5 Apply the concept of defensive strategic investment to the capital budgeting process

This chapter introduces long-term **investment decision** and internal cost control methods. An investment is a long-term cash allocation decision. Comparisons of expected and actual outcomes from long-term investments (also called **investment programs** or **projects**) affect the balance sheet as well as the income statement and cash flow statement of companies. Projects often require long-term financing, although corporate financing decisions are beyond the scope of this text. The Confederation Bridge project, for both providers and investors, produced a capital asset with an estimated useful life of many decades. For the providers this long-term asset was the contract; for the investors it is the bridge itself. The investors expect that they will earn more over the estimated useful life of the bridge than the opportunity cost of their investment.

The providers have received payment for their service, but prior to entering into the contract, needed to carefully estimate what the relevant costs would be for the duration of the project as well as the revenues. Multi-year projects of this type require careful planning and control over several years, and the capital budget is one means to direct attention towards potential problems that may require remedy. **Capital budgeting** is the process of collating information in a familiar pro forma financial accounting format. To fully grasp the importance of capital budgeting, the differences between the capital and operating budgets, each of which has its particular section on the cash flow statement, must be well understood. The capital budget provides a basis for evaluating how appropriate have been the strategic choices made by top management. Strategies are usually long-term plans for future growth, although in sunset industries the best strategy may be to simply harvest the rewards of past investment without making new investments for the future. The outflow of cash from new investment or inflow from liquidating investments is reported in the cash flow statement as cash flow to (from) investments. The outflow of cash to repay long-term financing or inflow from new long-term financing is reported on the cash flow statement as cash flow from (to) financing. Both of these are separate from the operating cash flow on the cash flow statement.

APPLY THE CONCEPT OF THE TIME VALUE OF MONEY TO CAPITAL BUDGETING

1 Apply the concept of the time value of money to capital budgeting decisions

Different costs are appropriate for different purposes. Capital budgeting decisions focus on the project, which spans multiple time periods. The uncertainty associated with future outcomes means that it is unwise to base long-term capital budgeting decisions on the income statement of the current period. The current period's income does not report any effects of future investment projects or programs. Investment in a long-term project almost always will decrease the reported operating income in the near term but is expected to increase both operating cash flow and operating income over the longer term.

ACCRUALS ARE NOT CASH

It is important to understand that accrual accounting estimates of value are reported on the income statement and balance sheet. Theoretically, income is the residual from changes to assets and liabilities. Neither long-term assets nor liabilities are debits or credits to the cash account of any company. The financial estimates of value for these long-term accounts are accruals made according to GAAP standards and reported on the balance sheet. On the income statement, GAAP requires recognition of revenue from sales and recognition of expenses in the period the sale was made or the current obligation was incurred. The financial values of recognized revenue and expenses are reported on the income statement irrespective of whether or not they have been realized in cash inflow or outflow. Special standards apply to the recognition and reporting of long-term contracted inflows of revenue.

As the current assets section of the balance sheet makes clear, revenue and expenses do not equal cash paid to or by the company. The cash account, a current asset, is reported on the balance sheet and the difference between the prior and current period balance will not equal either operating or net income for the current period. Accounts receivable reports cash payments owing to the company within the following 12 months, while accounts payable reports cash payments owed by the company within the following 12 months. Unfortunately, companies cannot pay their obligations with accounts receivable; they must pay in cash. Companies without cash to fulfill their contractual obligations are either insolvent or bankrupt.

The cash flow statement reconciles the prior year's ending cash balance reported on the balance sheet with the current year's ending cash balance. The realized cash inflow of revenue and cash outflow of expense payments is reported in the operating cash flow portion of the cash flow statement using either the direct or indirect method.[1] A quick glance at any set of financial statements will quickly confirm that neither operating income nor net income equals operating cash flow.

The cash flow statement, however, also reports long-term sources of cash such as new debt issued by the company in the form of bonds and debentures or incurred by the company in the form of long-term loans and mortgages. Payments against old debt obligations are cash flow out within the reporting time period, to repay principal amounts on the financing incurred in the past. Like long-term debt, investments also generate cash inflows from long-term assets. Indeed this is the definition of an asset—that which generates future benefits—and those benefits are conventionally measured as cash flow. In this chapter, methods of measuring the cash flows of different alternative future investments will be presented with their strengths and weaknesses in different situations.

The sum of the operating cash flow, the cash flow from or to financing and from or to investments, comprises a full cash flow statement reporting the realized net cash flow for the reporting time period. The realized net cash flow reconciles the cash balance on the prior period's balance sheet to the cash balance reported on the current period's balance sheet.

CAPITAL BUDGETING IS A DECISION PROCESS

Our focus is on the decision process leading to changes in the long-term asset accounts intended to affect core operations of a company. Identification of the relevant costs and benefits of investing in or divesting long-term assets (or projects) begins with a discussion of cost analysis. The capital budgeting decision process model illustrated in Exhibit 21-1 is, like other decision models, a series of interdependent decisions. The process is called capital budgeting in large part because there are insufficient corporate resources, including access to financing, to pursue all attractive investments. The capital budget represents a selection of long-term investments that fall within a specified budget constraint.

It is a Bayesian process wherein relevant information will change prior expectations about likely outcomes. As prior expectations change, so too will previous decisions. We have assumed that the corporate strategy is in place, but what must be decided is the best investment or investments to implement the strategy. Strategic investments include those made for ERP systems, supply-chain management, or agility to incorporate both cost leadership and product differentiation. A revenue growth strategy could be achieved by expanding core business or into adjacencies. Investments would differ depending on the strategy chosen.

Many alternatives could be chosen to implement a growth strategy, and each will draw upon and contribute to corporate resources in different ways. What will be constant among the alternative investments is the large capital expenditures which must be made to provide capacity to implement a strategy. The top management team must demonstrate due diligence in exploring the risk and the return associated with each expenditure.

---

[1]To review these financial accounting concepts, refer to any introductory financial accounting textbook.

EXHIBIT 21-1
Capital Budgeting Decision Process Model

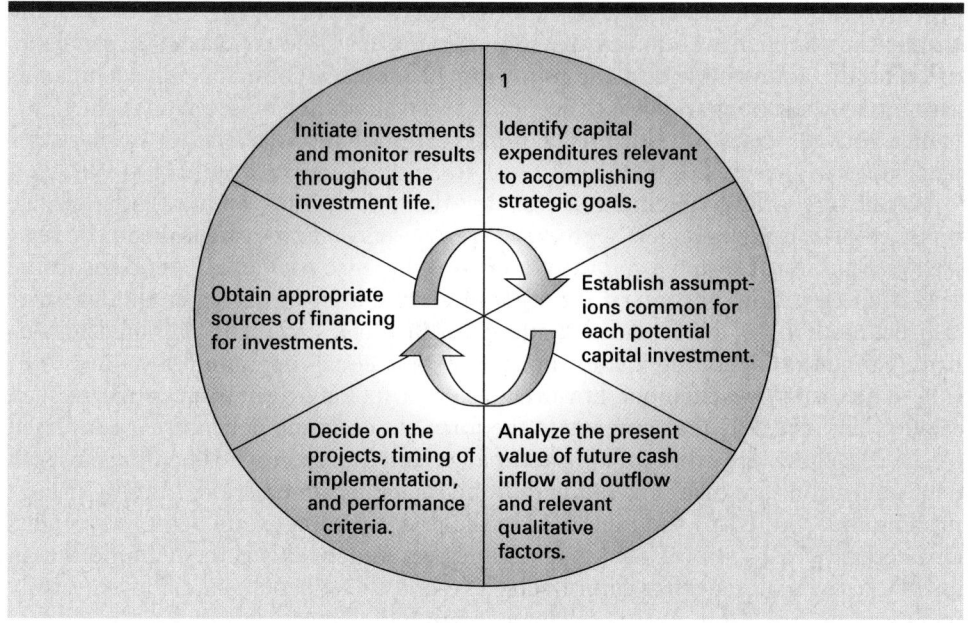

Risk and return analysis is presented fully in introductory finance courses. One widely taught model is called the Capital Asset Pricing Model (CAPM), which depicts an investing universe where the risk-return relationship is linear. The risk is the predictor and the return is the outcome variable in this regression (see Chapter 10). Risk models themselves are complex and our focus is on estimating return. To estimate the return over time on an investment, using discounted cash flow (DCF) models, information on the most likely relevant cash outflows and inflows as well as their timing must be gathered.

Capital budgeting emphasizes the role of financial information in investment decisions; however, both nonfinancial and qualitative factors must also be considered. Nonfinancial factors include the effect of an investment on market share, revenue mix, yield, and environmental sustainability. Qualitative factors could include the effect of an investment on corporate governance and perceived corporate social responsibility.

Organizations choose those projects whose likely, predicted long-term benefits exceed costs by the greatest amount. Formal analyses under any method include only predicted outcomes quantified in financial terms. Managers use managerial judgment to take into account nonfinancial and qualitative considerations. Evaluating costs and benefits is often the responsibility of the management accountant. The ratio of the predicted cost inflow minus outflow divided by the total outflow for the investment is one measure of the **rate of return (ROR)**. It is similar to calculating an operating margin percentage but total cash flows replace accruals as the basis for the calculation.

Long-term investments are appropriately financed by long-term debt to avoid the opportunity costs of spending too much cash immediately and jeopardizing the solvency of the corporation. At a minimum, opportunity cost includes interest forgone on risk-free investments. Sources of financing include internally generated cash flow from operations (within the organization) and externally generated cash flow from capital markets (equity and debt instruments). Notice the relevance of operating cash flow, a short-term performance indicator, to the financing decision. Internally generated cash flow must be adequate to cover any working capital outlays in the first year of a long-term investment because rarely do long-term investments generate cash inflow in their early years. In capital budgeting, working capital is recovered at the end of the project's life cycle.

Financing is most often the treasury function of an organization. Once the investment decision is made, then the financing must be acquired. Again this is an information-gathering process, and if financing is unavailable at a reasonable cost, then this relevant information will change the investment decision. In reality financing opportunities are often investigated simultaneously with the formal analyses of the costs and benefits of various investments. One reason is that interest expense is a cash cost of any investment financed by debt.

As the project is implemented, the company must evaluate whether capital investments are being made as scheduled and within the budget. Integral to the selection of investments is the selection of appropriate performance criteria such as ROR. As the project generates cash inflows, monitoring and control may include a postinvestment audit, in which the predictions made at the time the project was selected are compared with the actual results.

This chapter emphasizes the information acquisition, selection, implementation, and control stages of capital budgeting because these are the stages in which the management accountant is most involved. Beyond the numbers, however, the ability of individual managers to "sell" their own projects to senior management is often pivotal in the acceptance or rejection of projects.

Exhibit 21-2 illustrates two different dimensions of cost analysis:

◆ the project dimension, for which life-cycle costing should be used (Chapter 12)
◆ the time dimension, for which the time value of money must be considered

Each project is represented in Exhibit 21-2 as a distinct horizontal rectangle. The life of each project is longer than one accounting period. Capital budgeting focuses on the entire life of the project in order to consider all cash inflows or cash savings from the investment. The white area in Exhibit 21-2 illustrates the accounting-period focus on income determination and routine planning and control. This cross-section emphasizes the company's performance for the 2010 accounting period.

Accounting operating income is of particular interest to the manager because bonuses are frequently based on this value. Both operating cash flow and net income reported in an accounting period are important because they affect a public company's share price. Excessive focus on short-run income and operating cash flow, however, can cause a company to forgo long-term profitability. Successful managers balance short-term accounting-period considerations and longer-term project considerations in their decision process.

The accounting system that corresponds to the project dimension in Exhibit 21-2 is termed *life-cycle costing*. This system, described in Chapter 12, accumulates revenues

EXHIBIT 21-2
The Project and Time Dimensions of Capital Budgeting

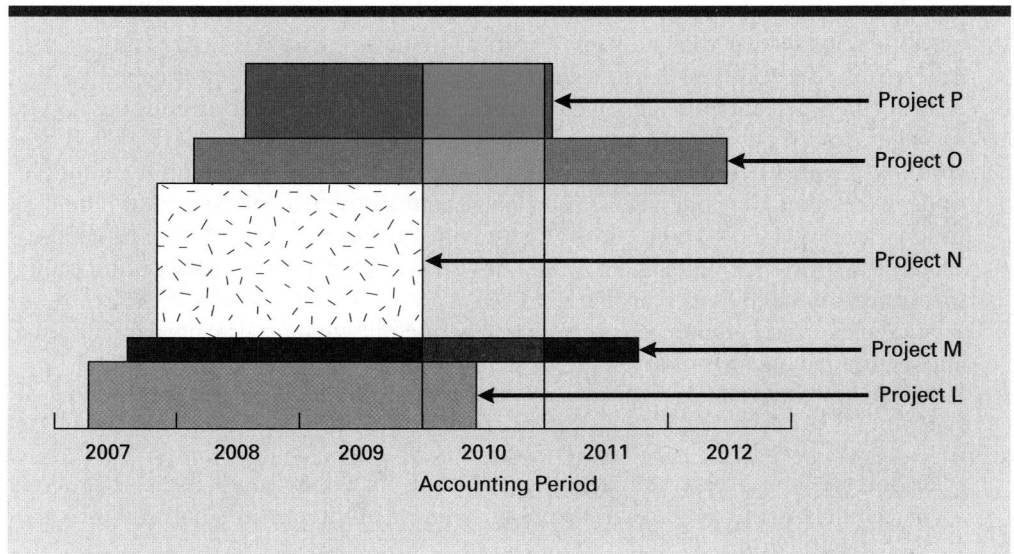

and costs on a project-by-project basis. For example, a life-cycle costing statement for a new car project at Toyota could encompass a four-year period during which the costs of business activities throughout the value chain would be accumulated for the project. This accumulation is a management, not a financial, accounting effort to measure income on a period-by-period basis for internal management purposes. External reporting must conform to GAAP.

Any system that focuses on the life span of a project must cover several years and thus must consider the time value of money. The *time value of money* takes into account the fact that a dollar (or any other monetary unit) received today is worth more than a dollar received tomorrow. The reason is that $1 received today can be invested to start earning a risk-free return of perhaps 3.55% per year so that it grows to $1.0355 at the end of the year. The time value of money is the opportunity cost (the return of $0.0355 forgone) from not having the money today to invest. Capital budgeting focuses on projects that can be accounted for using life-cycle costing and that must be evaluated taking into consideration the time value of money.

We use information from Lifetime Care Hospital to illustrate capital budgeting. Lifetime Care is a not-for-profit organization that is not subject to taxes. Chapter 22 introduces tax considerations in capital budgeting.

One of Lifetime Care's goals is to improve the productivity of its X-ray Department. To achieve this goal, the manager of Lifetime Care identifies a need to purchase a new state-of-the-art X-ray machine to replace an existing machine. The search stage yields several alternative models, but the hospital's technical staff focuses on one machine, XCAM8, as being particularly suitable. They next begin to acquire information for a more detailed evaluation. Quantitative financial information for the formal analysis follows.

Revenue will remain unchanged regardless of whether the new X-ray machine is acquired. Lifetime Care charges a fixed rate for a particular diagnosis, regardless of the number of X-rays taken. The only relevant financial benefit in evaluating Lifetime's decision to purchase the X-ray machine is the cash savings in operating costs. The existing X-ray machine can operate for another five years and will have a disposal price of zero at the end of five years. The initial investment will be $379,100, which is calculated as follows:

Cost of new machine	$372,890
Investment in working capital (supplies and spare parts for the new machine)	10,000
Cash flow from disposal of the old machine (after tax)	(3,790)
Net initial investment for the new machine	$379,100

The manager expects the new machine to have a five-year useful life and a disposal price of zero at the end of five years. The new machine is faster and easier to operate, has the ability to X-ray a larger area, and will reduce the average number of X-rays taken per patient. This will decrease labour, power, and utilities costs. The manager expects the investment to result in annual cash inflows of $100,000. These cash flows will generally occur throughout the year; however, to simplify computations, we assume that operating cash flows occur at the end of each year. The cash inflows are expected to come from cash savings in operating costs of $100,000 for each of the first four years and $90,000 in year five plus recovery of working capital investment of $10,000 in year five.

Managers at Lifetime Care also identify the following nonfinancial quantitative and qualitative benefits of investing in the new X-ray equipment:

1. **Quality:** Higher-quality X-rays will lead to improved diagnoses and better patient treatment.
2. **Safety:** The greater efficiency of the new machine would mean that X-ray technicians and patients are exposed to fewer of the possibly harmful effects of X-ray radiation.

These nonfinancial benefits are not considered in the formal financial analysis.

In the *selection* stage, managers must decide whether Lifetime Care should purchase the new X-ray machine.

DISCOUNTED CASH FLOW (DCF) METHODS

Discounted cash flow (DCF) methods are net present value (NPV) and internal rate of return (IRR). The payback method and the accrual accounting rate of return method do not consider the time value of money. DCF measures the cash inflows and outflows of a project as if they occurred at a single point in time so that they can be compared in an appropriate way. These DCF methods recognize that the use of money has an opportunity cost—return forgone. The intuition of DCF is that a dollar in the treasury today is certain and therefore worth more than a dollar collected in the future because the future is uncertain. Because the DCF methods explicitly and routinely weight cash flows by the time value of money, they are usually the best (most comprehensive) methods to use for long-run decisions.

DCF focuses on *cash* inflows and outflows rather than on *operating income* as used in conventional accrual accounting. Cash is invested now with the expectation of receiving a greater amount of cash in the future. Avoid injecting accrual concepts of accounting into DCF analysis. For example, amortization is deducted as an accrual expense when calculating operating income under accrual accounting. It is not deducted in DCF analysis because this expense entails no cash outflow.

The compound interest tables and formulas used in DCF analysis are included in Appendix A of this textbook. (Appendix A will be used frequently in Chapters 21 and 22.)

There are two main DCF methods:

◆ Net present value (NPV)
◆ Internal rate of return (IRR)

NPV is calculated using the **required rate of return (RRR)**, which is the minimum acceptable rate of return on an investment. It is the return that the organization could expect to receive elsewhere for an investment of comparable risk. This rate is also called the **discount rate, hurdle rate,** or **(opportunity) cost of capital**. When working with IRR, the RRR is used as a point of comparison. Chapter 22 discusses issues encountered in estimating this rate.

Assume that the required rate of return, or discount rate, for the Lifetime Care X-ray machine project is 8%.

NET PRESENT VALUE (NPV) METHOD

The **net present value (NPV)** method calculates the expected net monetary gain or loss from a project by discounting all expected future cash inflows and outflows to the present point in time, using the required rate of return. Only projects with a positive net present value are acceptable because the return from these projects exceeds the cost of capital (the return available by investing the capital elsewhere). Managers prefer projects with higher NPVs to projects with lower NPVs, if all other things are equal. Using the NPV method entails the following:

◆ *Sketch the relevant cash inflows and outflows.* The right side of Exhibit 21-3 shows how these cash flows are portrayed. Outflows appear in parentheses. The sketch helps the decision maker organize the data in a systematic way. Note that Exhibit 21-3 includes the outflow for the new machine at year 0, the time of the acquisition. The NPV method focuses only on cash flows. NPV analysis is indifferent to where the cash flows come from (operations, purchase or sale of equipment, or investment or recovery of working capital) and to the accrual accounting treatments of individual cash flow items (for example, amortization costs on equipment purchases).

◆ *Choose the correct compound interest table from Appendix A.* In our example, we can discount each year's cash flow separately using Table 2 (Appendix A), or we can compute the present value of an annuity using Table 4 (Appendix A). If we use Table 2, we find the discount factors for periods 1–5 under the 8% column. Approach 1 in Exhibit 21-3 presents the five discount factors. Because the investment produces an annuity, a series of equal cash flows at equal intervals, we may use Table 4. We find the discount factor for five periods under the 8%

column. Approach 2 in Exhibit 21-3 shows that this discount factor is 3.993 (3.993 is the sum of the five discount factors used in approach 1). To obtain the present value figures, multiply the discount factors by the appropriate cash amounts in the sketch in Exhibit 21-3.

◆ *Sum the present value figures to determine the net present value.* If the sum is zero or positive, the NPV model indicates that the project should be accepted. That is, its expected rate of return equals or exceeds the required rate of return. If the total is negative, the project is undesirable. Its expected rate of return is below the required rate of return.

Assumptions about the timing and amount of cash flows are extremely important. For example, if you use a programmable calculator or a popular spreadsheet program to calculate NPV, you often obtain a slightly different answer than if you use a compound interest table. The first reason is that the compound interest table in Appendix A assumes the cash inflow all occurs at the end of each year whereas many programs assume the inflow occurs at the beginning of each year. The second reason is rounding. The tables in Appendix A round to 3 decimal places in contrast to 8 or more used by programmable calculators and computer spreadsheet programs. Many programs include an option to choose your assumption about the timing of cash inflows.

Exhibit 21-3 indicates an NPV of $20,200 at the required rate of return of 8%; the expected return from the project exceeds the 8% required rate of return.

EXHIBIT 21-3
Net Present Value Method: Lifetime Care Hospital's New X-Ray Machine

	A	B	C	D	E	F	G	H	I
1			Net initial investment	$379,100					
2			Useful life	5 years					
3			Annual cash inflow	$100,000					
4			Required rate of return	8%					
5									
6		**Present Value**	**Present Value of**	**Sketch of Relevant Cash Flows at End of Each Year**					
7		**of Cash Flow**	**$1 Discounted at 8%**	0	1	2	3	4	5
8	**Approach 1: Discounting Each Year's Cash Flow Separately**[a]								
9	Net initial investment	$(379,100) ←	1.000 ←	$(379,100)					
10		92,600 ←	0.926 ←		$100,000				
11		85,700 ←	0.857 ←			$100,000			
12	Annual cash inflow	79,400 ←	0.794 ←				$100,000		
13		73,500 ←	0.735 ←					$100,000	
14		68,100 ←	0.681 ←						$100,000
15	NPV if new machine purchased	$ 20,200							
16									
17	**Approach 2: Using Annuity Table**[b]								
18	Net initial investment	$(379,100) ←	1.000 ←	$(379,100)					
19					$100,000	$100,000	$100,000	$100,000	$100,000
20									
21	Annual cash inflow	399,300 ←	3.993 ←						
22	NPV if new machine purchased	$ 20,200							
23									
24	*Note:* Parentheses denote relevant cash outflows throughout all exhibits in Chapter 21.								
25	[a]Present values from Table 2, Appendix A at the end of the book. For example, 0.857 = 1 ÷ (1.08)².								
26	[b]Annuity present value from Table 4, Appendix A. The annuity table value of 3.993 is the sum of the individual discount rates 0.926 + 0.857 + 0.794 + 0.735 + 0.681, subject to rounding.								

Therefore, the project is desirable. The cash flows from the project are adequate to (1) recover the net initial investment in the project and (2) earn a return greater than 8% on the investment tied up in the project from period to period. Had the NPV been negative, the project would have been undesirable on the basis of financial considerations.

Of course, the manager of the hospital must also weigh nonfinancial factors. Consider the reduction in the average number of individual X-rays taken per patient with the new machine. This reduction is a qualitative benefit of the new machine given the health risks to patients and technicians. Other qualitative benefits of the new machine are the better diagnoses and treatments that patients receive. Had the NPV been negative, the manager would need to judge whether the nonfinancial benefits outweigh the negative NPV.

It is important that you not proceed until you thoroughly understand Exhibit 21-3. Compare approach 1 with approach 2 in Exhibit 21-3 to see how Table 4 in Appendix A merely aggregates the present value factors of Table 2. That is, the fundamental table is Table 2; Table 4 reduces calculations when there is an annuity—a series of equal cash flows at equal intervals. The DCF approach answers the question of whether a project will break even or generate positive cash flow over its lifetime but does not answer the question of what the return on the investment will be. This question is answered by using the internal rate of return method.

EVALUATE TWO DCF AND TWO NON-DCF METHODS TO CALCULATE THE ROR

The **internal rate of return (IRR)** is the discount rate at which the present value of expected cash inflows from a project equals the present value of expected cash outflows of the project. That is, the IRR is the discount rate that makes NPV = $0. IRR is sometimes called the **time-adjusted rate of return**. As in the NPV method, the sources of cash flows and the accrual accounting treatment of individual cash flows are irrelevant to the IRR calculations. We illustrate the computation of the IRR using the X-ray machine project of Lifetime Care. Exhibit 21-4 presents the cash flows and shows the calculation of the NPV using a 10% discount rate. At a 10% discount rate, the NPV of the project is zero. Therefore, the IRR for the project is 10%. All qualitative and nonfinancial considerations being equal, managers will choose projects with the IRR exceeding the required rate of return by the greatest amount.

How do we determine the 10% discount rate that yields NPV = $0? In most cases, analysts solving capital budgeting problems have a calculator or computer programmed to provide the internal rate of return. Without a calculator or computer program, a trial-and-error approach can provide the answer.

◆ Try a discount rate and calculate the NPV of the project using that discount rate.

◆ If the NPV is less than zero, try a lower discount rate. (A lower discount rate will increase the NPV; remember, we are trying to find a discount rate for which NPV = $0.) If the NPV is greater than zero, try a higher discount rate to lower the NPV.

Keep adjusting the discount rate until NPV = $0. In the Lifetime Care example, a discount rate of 8% yields NPV of +$20,200 (see Exhibit 21-4). A discount rate of 12% yields NPV of –$18,600 (3.605, the present value annuity factor from Table 4, × $100,000 – $379,100). Therefore, the discount rate that makes NPV = $0 must lie

Evaluate discounted cash flow (DCF) and non-DCF methods to calculate rate of return (ROR)

2

	A	B	C	D	E	F	G	H	I
1			Net initial investment	$379,100					
2			Useful life	5 years					
3			Annual cash inflow	$100,000					
4			Annual Discount rate	10%					
5									
6		**Present Value**	**Present Value of**	**Sketch of Relevant Cash Flows at End of Each Year**					
7		**of Cash Flow**	**$1 Discounted at 10%**	**0**	**1**	**2**	**3**	**4**	**5**
8	**Approach 1: Discounting Each Year's Cash Flow Separately[b]**								
9	Net initial investment	$(379,100) ←	1.000 ←	$(379,100)					
10		90,900 ←	0.909 ←		$100,000				
11		82,600 ←	0.826 ←			$100,000			
12	Annual cash inflow	75,100 ←	0.751 ←				$100,000		
13		68,300 ←	0.683 ←					$100,000	
14		62,100 ←	0.621 ←						$100,000
15	NPV if new machine purchased[c] (the zero difference proves that the internal rate of return is 10%)	$ 0							
16									
17	**Approach 2: Using Annuity Table**								
18	Net initial investment	$(379,100) ←	1.000 ←	$(379,100)					
19					$100,000	$100,000	$100,000	$100,000	$100,000
20									
21	Annual cash inflow	379,100 ←	3.791[d] ←						
22	NPV if new machine purchased	$ 0							
23									
24	*Note:* Parentheses denote relevant cash outflows throughout all exhibits in Chapter 21.								
25	[a]The internal rate of return is computed by methods explained on pp. 1015–1017.								
26	[b]Present values from Table 2, Appendix A at the end of the book.								
27	[c]Sum is $(100) due to rounding. We round to $0.								
28	[d]Annuity present value from Table 4, Appendix A. The annuity table value of 3.791 is the sum of the individual discount rates 0.909 + 0.826 + 0.751 + 0.683 + 0.621, subject to rounding.								

between 8% and 12%. We happen to try 10% and get NPV = $0. Hence, the IRR is 10%.

The step-by-step computations of an internal rate of return are easier when the cash inflows are equal, as in our example. Information from Exhibit 21-4 can be expressed in the following equation:

$$\$379,100 = \text{Present value of annuity of } \$100,000 \text{ at } x\% \text{ for 5 years}$$

Or, using Table 4 (Appendix A), what factor F will satisfy the following equation?

$$\$379,100 = \$100,000F$$

$$F = 3.791$$

On the five-period line of Table 4, find the percentage column that is closest to 3.791. It is exactly 10%. If the factor F falls between the factors in two columns, straight-line interpolation is used to approximate the IRR. (For an illustration of interpolation, see requirement 1 of the Problem for Self-Study on page 1031.)

A project is accepted only if the internal rate of return exceeds the required rate of return (the opportunity cost of capital). In the Lifetime Care example, the X-ray machine has an IRR of 10%, which is greater than the required rate of return of 8%. On the basis of financial factors, Lifetime Care should invest in the new machine. If the IRR exceeds the RRR, then the project has a positive NPV when project cash flows are discounted at the RRR. If the IRR equals the RRR, NPV = $0. If the IRR is less than the RRR, NPV is negative. Obviously, managers prefer projects with higher IRRs to projects with lower IRRs, if all other things are equal. The IRR of 10% means that the cash inflows from the project are adequate to:

◆ recover the net initial investment in the project
◆ earn a return of exactly 10% on investment tied up in the project over its useful life.

Despite the limitations of the IRR method, surveys report its widespread use, probably not only because managers find the IRR method easier to understand, but also because in most instances their decisions would be unaffected by using IRR or NPV. In some cases, however, as when comparing two projects with unequal lives or unequal investments, the two methods will not indicate the same decision.

This text emphasizes the NPV method, which has the important advantage that the end result of the computations is dollars, not a percentage. We can therefore add the NPVs of individual independent projects to estimate the effect of accepting a combination of projects. In contrast, the IRRs of individual projects cannot be added or averaged to derive the IRR of the combination of projects.

A second advantage of the NPV method is that we can use it in situations where the required rate of return varies over the life of the project. For example, suppose in the X-ray machine example Lifetime Care has a required rate of return of 8% in years 1, 2, and 3 and 12% in years 4 and 5. The total present value of the cash inflows is as follows:

Year (1)	Cash Inflows (2)	Required Rate of Return (3)	Present Value of $1 Discounted at Required Rate (4)	Total Present Value of Cash Inflows (5) = (4) × (2)
1	$100,000	8%	0.926	$ 92,600
2	100,000	8	0.857	85,700
3	100,000	8	0.794	79,400
4	100,000	12	0.636	63,600
5	100,000	12	0.567	56,700
				$378,000

Given the net initial investment of $379,100, NPV calculations indicate that the project is unattractive: it has a negative NPV of –$1,100 ($378,000 – $379,100). However, it is not possible to use the IRR method to infer that the project should be rejected. The existence of different required rates of return in different years (8% for years 1, 2, and 3 versus 12% for years 4 and 5) means there is not a single RRR that the IRR (a single figure) must exceed for the project to be acceptable.

SENSITIVITY ANALYSIS

To highlight the basic differences between the NPV and IRR methods, we have assumed that the expected values of cash flows will occur for certain. Obviously, managers know that their predictions are imperfect and thus uncertain. To examine how a result will change if the predicted financial outcomes are not achieved or if an underlying assumption changes, managers can use sensitivity analysis, a what-if technique first introduced in Chapter 3.

Sensitivity analysis can take various forms. For example, suppose Lifetime Care management believes forecast savings are uncertain and difficult to predict. Management could then ask: What is the minimum annual cash savings that will cause us to invest in the new X-ray machine (that is, for NPV = $0)? For the data in Exhibit 21-4, let ACI = annual cash inflows and let NPV = $0. The net initial investment is $379,100, and the present-value factor at the 8% required rate of return for a five-year annuity of $1 is 3.993. Then:

$$NPV = \$0$$
$$3.993A - \$379,100 = \$0$$
$$3.993A = \$379,100$$
$$A = \$94,941$$

Thus, at the discount rate of 8%, annual cash inflows can decrease to $94,941 (a decline of $100,000 – $94,941 = $5,059) before NPV falls below zero. If management believes it can attain annual cash savings of at least $94,941, it could justify investing in the new X-ray machine on financial grounds alone.

Computer spreadsheets enable managers to conduct systematic, efficient sensitivity analysis. Exhibit 21-5 shows how the net present value of the X-ray machine project is affected by variations in (1) the annual cash inflows and (2) the required rate of return. NPVs can also vary with the useful life of a project. Sensitivity analysis helps a manager focus on those decisions that are most sensitive, and it eases the manager's mind about those decisions that are not so sensitive. For the X-ray machine project, Exhibit 21-5 shows that variations in either the annual cash inflows or the required rate of return have sizable effects on NPV.

NON-DCF CAPITAL BUDGETING METHODS

We now consider two methods for capital budgeting. Neither method accounts for the time value of money. If forgone interest in a risk-free investment is immaterial then the time value of money can be ignored. This is appropriate if cash inflow will begin within a short time and repay the initial investment quickly. These are short-term projects in a managerial, not financial, accounting context. The project life cycle is less than three to five years. What is considered short term will vary from one company to another. One non-DCF method assumes uniform cash flow throughout the project life cycle; the other method assumes non-uniform cash flows.

UNIFORM CASH FLOWS

The **payback method** measures the time it will take to recoup, in the form of net cash inflows, the net initial investment in a project. Like NPV and IRR, the payback method does not distinguish the sources of cash inflows (operations, disposal of equipment, or recovery of working capital). It does, however, assume *uniform cash flows* through the expected life cycle. In the Lifetime Care example, the X-ray

EXHIBIT 21-5
Net Present Value Calculations for Lifetime Care Hospital Under Different Assumptions of Annual Cash Flows and Required Rates of Return[a]

	A	B	C	D	E	F
1	**Required**	**Annual Cash Flow**				
2	**Rate of Return**	**$80,000**	**$90,000**	**$100,000**	**$110,000**	**$120,000**
3	6%	$(42,140)	$ (20)	$42,100	$84,220	$126,340
4	8%	$(59,660)	$(19,730)	$20,200	$60,130	$100,060
5	10%	$(75,820)	$(37,910)	$ 0	$37,910	$ 75,820
6						
7	[a]All calculated amounts assume the project's useful life is five years.					

machine costs $379,100, has a five-year expected useful life, and generates a $100,000 uniform cash inflow each year. The payback calculations[2] are as follows:

$$\text{Payback} = \frac{\text{Net initial investment}}{\text{Uniform increase in annual cash flows}}$$

$$= \frac{\$379,100}{100,000} = 3.791 \text{ years}$$

Under the payback method, organizations often choose a cutoff period for a project. The greater the risks of a project, the smaller the cutoff period. Why? Because faced with higher risks, managers would like to more quickly recover the investments they have made. For example, a software development company may use a payback period of one to two years for investment decisions. Projects with a payback period less than the cutoff period are acceptable. Those with a payback period greater than the cutoff period are rejected. If Lifetime's cutoff period under the payback method is three years, Lifetime will reject the new machine. If Lifetime uses a cutoff period of four years, Lifetime will consider the new machine to be acceptable.

The payback method highlights liquidity, which is often an important factor in capital budgeting decisions. Managers prefer projects with shorter paybacks (more liquid) to projects with longer paybacks, if all other things are equal. Projects with shorter payback periods give the organization more flexibility because funds for other projects become available sooner. Also, managers are less confident about cash flow predictions that stretch far into the future. The shorter the payback, the more confident managers can feel that their forecasts are on target.

The major strength of the payback method is that it is easy to understand. Like the DCF methods described previously, the payback method is not affected by accrual accounting conventions such as amortization. Advocates of the payback method argue that it is a handy measure when (1) estimates of profitability are not crucial and preliminary screening of many proposals is necessary and (2) the predicted cash flows in later years of the project are highly uncertain.

Two major weaknesses of the payback method are (1) it neglects the time value of money and (2) it neglects to consider project cash flows after the net initial investment is recovered. Consider an alternative to the $379,100 X-ray machine mentioned earlier. Assume that another X-ray machine, with a three-year useful life and zero terminal disposal price, requires only a $300,000 net initial investment and will also result in cash inflows of $100,000 per year. First, compare the two payback periods:

$$\text{Payback period for machine 1:} = \frac{\$379,100}{\$100,000} = 3.791 \text{ years}$$

$$\text{Payback period for machine 2:} = \frac{\$300,000}{\$100,000} = 3.000 \text{ years}$$

The payback criterion would favour buying the $300,000 machine, because it has a shorter payback. In fact, if the cutoff period is three years, then Lifetime Care would not acquire machine 1, because it fails to meet the payback criterion. Consider next the NPV of the two investment options using Lifetime Care's 8% required rate of return for the X-ray machine investment. At a discount rate of 8%, the NPV of machine 2 is −$42,300 (2.577, the present value annuity factor for three years at 8% from Table 4 × $100,000 = $257,700, the net initial investment of $300,000). Machine 1, as we know, has a positive NPV of $20,200 (from Exhibit 21-3). The NPV criterion suggests that Lifetime Care should acquire machine 1. Machine 2,

[2]Cash savings from the new X-ray machine occur *throughout* the year, but for simplicity in calculating NPV and IRR, we assume they occur at the *end* of each year. A literal interpretation of this assumption would imply a payback of four years because Lifetime Care will only recover its investment when cash inflows occur at the end of the fourth year. The calculations shown in this chapter, however, better approximate Lifetime Care's payback on the basis of uniform cash flows throughout the year.

with a negative NPV, would fail to meet the NPV criterion. The payback method gives a different answer from the NPV method because the payback method (1) does not consider cash flows after the payback period and (2) does not discount cash flows.

An added problem with the payback method is that choosing too short a cutoff period for project acceptance may promote the selection of only short-lived projects. The organization will tend to reject long-term, positive-NPV projects. Companies often use both the payback and DCF method to select positive NPV projects with an acceptably short payback period.

NON-UNIFORM CASH FLOWS

The payback formula is designed for uniform annual cash inflows. When payback is short term, the opportunity cost of money, interest forgone, is immaterial. This is why the time value of money is ignored. When annual cash inflows are *not uniform*, the payback computation takes a cumulative form. The years' net cash inflows are accumulated until the amount of the net initial investment has been recovered. Assume that Venture Law Group is considering the purchase of video-conferencing equipment for $150,000. The equipment is expected to provide total cash savings of $380,000 over the next five years, due to reduced travel costs and more effective use of associates' time. The cash savings occur uniformly throughout each year, but non-uniformly across years. Payback occurs during the third year:

Year	Cash Savings	Cumulative Cash Savings	Net Initial Investment Yet to Be Recovered at the End of the Year
0	—	—	$150,000
1	$ 50,000	$ 50,000	100,000
2	60,000	110,000	40,000
3	80,000	190,000	—
4	90,000	280,000	—
5	100,000	380,000	—

Straight-line interpolation within the third year, which has cash savings of $80,000, reveals that the final $40,000 needed to recover the $150,000 investment (that is, $150,000 − $110,000 recovered by the end of year 2) will be achieved halfway through year 3 (in which $80,000 of cash savings occur):

$$\text{Payback} = 2 \text{ years} + \left(\frac{\$40,000}{\$80,000} \times 1 \text{ year} \right) = 2.5 \text{ years}$$

The videoconferencing example has a single cash outflow of $150,000 at year 0. Where a project has multiple cash outflows occurring at different points in time, these outflows are added to derive a total cash outflow figure for the project. No adjustment is made for the time value of money when adding these cash outflows in computing the payback period.

The **accrual accounting rate of return (AARR)** is an accounting measure of income divided by an accounting measure of investment. It is also called **accounting rate of return** or **return on investment (ROI)**. Note that NPV, IRR, and payback are all based on cash flows whereas AARR is based on accrual accounting. We illustrate AARR for the Lifetime Care example using the project's net initial investment as the denominator:

$$\text{AARR} = \frac{\text{Increase in expected average annual operating income}}{\text{Net initial investment}}$$

If Lifetime Care purchases the new X-ray machine, the increase in expected average annual savings in operating costs will be $98,000. This amount is the total operating savings of $490,000 ($100,000 for four years and $90,000 in year 5) ÷ 5.

The new machine has a zero terminal disposal price. Straight-line amortization on the new machine is $372,890 ÷ 5 = $74,578. The net initial investment is $379,100.

The accrual accounting rate of return is equal to

$$\text{AARR} = \frac{\$98,000 - \$74,578}{\$379,100} = \frac{\$23,422}{\$379,100} = 6.18\%$$

In practice there are variations on this formula. Some companies use "increase in expected average annual operating income" in the numerator and/or "average investment per year" in the denominator. The AARR method focuses on how investment decisions affect operating income numbers routinely reported by organizations. The AARR of 6.18% indicates the rate at which a dollar of investment generates operating income.

THINKING CRITICALLY

With non-uniform cash flows how can analyses be biased? Explain in a sentence or two. Read on for an analysis of this situation.

Timing affects both total cash inflow and total cash outflow under DCF analyses and payback. As the years advance from the point at which the investment was made, the multiplier to calculate the present value decreases. The result of the arithmetic is that the farther out in time is a cash outflow, the less will be its discounted value. The closer in time to the initial investment is a cash inflow, the greater will be its discounted value. Knowing this simple manipulation can occur, a management accountant must exercise professional judgment in both producing and evaluating the financial analyses of alternative long-term investments. As little as a one-year advance in cash inflow and a one-year delay in cash outflow can make the difference in attaining a hurdle rate. The same tactics will shorten the payback.

ASSESS YOUR MASTERY

To check your understanding of the material in Learning Objective ② , go to the *Mastery Questions* section at the end of this chapter and complete Learning Objective ② question 1.

ASSESSING RELEVANCE IN DCF ANALYSES

Apply the concept of relevance to DCF methods of capital budgeting ③

The key point of discounted cash flow methods is to focus exclusively on differences in expected future cash flows that result from implementing a project. All cash flows are treated the same, whether they arise from operations, purchase or sale of equipment, or investment in or recovery of working capital. The opportunity cost and the time value of money are tied to the cash flowing in or out of the organization, not to the source of the cash.

One of the biggest challenges in DCF analysis is determining those cash flows that are relevant to making the decision. One reason is that rapid technological change can dramatically shorten the predicted lifetime of an investment after the investment has been made. Estimating a reasonable useful life is one of the biggest challenges in capital budgeting.

Relevant cash flows are expected future cash flows that differ between the alternatives. At Lifetime Care, the alternatives are either to continue to use the old X-ray machine or to replace it with the new machine. The relevant cash flows are the differences in cash flows between continuing to use the old machine and purchasing the new one. *When reading this section, focus on identifying future expected cash flows of each alternative and differences in cash flows between alternatives.*

Capital investment projects (for example, purchasing a new machine) typically have five major categories of cash flows: (1) initial investment in machine and working capital, (2) cash flow from current disposal of the old machine, (3) recurring operating cash flows, (4) cash flow from terminal disposal of machine and recovery of working capital, and (5) income tax impacts on cash flows. We discuss the first four categories here, using Lifetime Care's purchase decision of the X-ray machine as an illustration. Income tax effects are described in Chapter 22.

1. **Initial investment.** Two components of investment cash flows are (a) the cash outflow to purchase the machine and (b) the working capital cash outflows.

   a. *Initial machine investment.* These outflows, made for purchasing plant, equipment, and machines, occur in the early periods of the project's life and include cash outflows for transporting and installing the item. In the Lifetime Care example, the $372,890 cost (including transportation and installation costs) of the X-ray machine is an outflow in year 0. These cash flows are relevant to the capital budgeting decision because they will be incurred only if Lifetime decides to purchase the new machine.

   b. *Initial working capital investment.* Investments in plant, equipment, machines, and in the sales promotions for product lines are invariably accompanied by incremental investments in working capital. These investments take the form of current assets, such as receivables and inventories (supplies and spare parts for the new machine in the Lifetime Care example), minus current liabilities, such as accounts payable. Working capital investments are similar to machine investments. In each case, available cash is tied up.

   The Lifetime Care example assumes a $10,000 incremental investment in working capital (supplies and spare parts inventory) if the new machine is acquired. The incremental working capital investment is the difference between the working capital required to operate the new machine (say $15,000) and the working capital required to operate the old machine (say $5,000). The $10,000 additional investment in working capital is a cash outflow in year 0.

2. **Current disposal price of old machine.** Any cash received from disposal of the old machine is a relevant cash inflow (in year 0) because it is an expected future cash flow that differs between the alternatives of investing and not investing in the new project. If Lifetime Care invests in the new X-ray machine, it will be able to dispose of its old machine for $3,790. These proceeds are included as cash inflow in year 0.

   Recall from Chapter 11 that the book value (original cost minus accumulated amortization) of the old equipment is irrelevant. It is a sunk cost. Nothing can change what has already been spent or what has already happened.

   The net initial investment for the new X-ray machine, $379,100, is the initial machine investment plus the initial working capital investment minus current disposal price of the old machine: $372,890 + $10,000 – $3,790 = $379,100.

3. **Recurring operating cash flows.** This category includes all recurring operating cash flows that differ among the alternatives. Organizations make capital investments to generate cash inflows in the future. These inflows may result from producing and selling additional goods or services, or, as in the Lifetime Care example, from savings in operating cash costs. Recurring operating cash flows can be net outflows in some periods. For example, oil production may require large expenditures every five years (say) to improve oil extraction rates. Focus on operating cash flows, not on accrued revenues and costs.

   To underscore this point, consider the following additional facts about the Lifetime Care X-ray machine example:

   ◆ Total X-Ray Department overhead costs will not change whether the new machine is purchased or the old machine is kept.

The X-Ray Department overhead costs are allocated to individual X-ray machines—Lifetime has several—on the basis of the labour costs for operating each machine. Because the new X-ray machine will have lower labour costs, overhead allocated to it will be $30,000 less than the amount allocated to the machine it is replacing.

◆ Amortization on the new X-ray machine using the straight-line method is $74,578 [(original cost, $372,890 – expected terminal disposal price, $0) ÷ useful life, 5 years].

The savings in operating cash flows (labour and materials) of $100,000 in each of the first four years and $90,000 in the fifth year are clearly relevant because they are expected future cash flows that will differ between the alternatives of investing and not investing in the new machine. But what about the decrease in allocated overhead costs of $30,000? What about amortization of $74,578?

a. *Overhead costs*. The key question is do total overhead cash flows decrease as a result of acquiring the new machine? In our example, they do not.

Total X-Ray Department overhead costs remain the same whether or not the new machine is acquired. They are fixed costs such as insurance. What changes is the overhead allocated to individual machines. The overhead costs allocated to the new machine are $30,000 less but this additional $30,000 will simply be assigned to *other* machines in the department. No cash flow savings in total overhead occur. Therefore, the $30,000 should not be included as part of recurring operating cash inflows.

b. *Amortization*. Amortization is irrelevant because it is a noncash allocation of costs, whereas DCF is based on inflows and outflows of cash.

In DCF methods, the initial cost of equipment is regarded as a *lump sum* outflow of cash at year 0. Deducting amortization from operating cash inflows would be counting the lump sum amount twice. What we will examine in the following chapter is the cash flow effect of tax regulations on capital budgeting.

4. **Terminal disposal price of investment.** The disposal of the investment at the date of termination of a project generally increases cash inflow in the year of disposal. Errors in forecasting the terminal disposal price are seldom critical on long-duration projects, because the present value of amounts to be received in the distant future is usually small. Two components of the terminal disposal price of an investment are (a) the terminal disposal price of the machine and (b) the recovery of working capital.

a. *Terminal disposal price of machine*. At the end of the useful life of the project, the initial machine investment may not be recovered at all, or it may be only partially recovered in the amount of the terminal disposal price.

The relevant cash inflow is the difference in expected terminal disposal prices at the end of five years under the two alternatives—the terminal disposal price of the new machine (zero in the case of Lifetime Care) minus the terminal disposal price of the old machine (also zero in the Lifetime Care example).[3]

b. *Recovery of working capital*. The initial investment in working capital is usually fully recouped when the project is terminated. At that time, inventories and receivables necessary to support the project are no longer needed.

The relevant cash inflow is the difference in the expected working capital recovered under the two alternatives. If the new X-ray machine is

[3]The Lifetime Care example assumes that both the new and the old machine have a future useful life of five years. If instead the old machine had a useful life of only four years, management could choose to evaluate the investment decision over a four-year horizon. In this case, Lifetime's management would need to predict the terminal disposal price of the new machine at the end of four years.

purchased, Lifetime Care will recover $15,000 of working capital in year 5. If the new machine is not acquired, Lifetime will recover $5,000 of working capital in year 5, at the end of the useful life of the old machine. The relevant cash inflow in year 5 if Lifetime invests in the new machine is $10,000 ($15,000 – $5,000).

Some capital investments *reduce* working capital. Assume that a computer-integrated manufacturing (CIM) project with a seven-year life will reduce inventories and hence working capital by $20 million from, say, $50 million to $30 million. This reduction will be represented as a $20-million cash inflow for the project at year 0. At the end of seven years, the recovery of working capital will show a relevant cash outflow of $20 million because the company recovers only $30 million of working capital under CIM rather than the $50 million of working capital it would have recovered had it not implemented CIM.

Exhibit 21-6 presents the relevant cash inflows and outflows for Lifetime Care's decision to purchase the new machine as described in items in the preceding list.

The total relevant cash flows for each year are the same as the relevant cash flows used in Exhibits 21-3 and 21-4 to illustrate the NPV and IRR methods.

While there is no uniform method of calculating AARR, the interpretation in any situation is that the greater the positive difference between the AARR of a project and the AARR hurdle rate, the more preferable is the project. This method is similar to the IRR method because it provides the answer to the question "what is the rate of return on this project," but the AARR uses operating income rather than cash flow. Because cash flow and time value of money are central to investment project decisions, both the IRR and NPV methods are preferred over the AARR method.[4] On the other hand, AARR calculations use numbers reported in the financial statements and provide managers with forecasts of operating income on the statement of earnings if a project is accepted. In contrast to the payback method, AARR includes income earned throughout the lifetime of a project whereas the payback method includes cash flows only up to the point of payback. Many companies worldwide use more than one capital budgeting method to analyze alternatives.

EXHIBIT 21-6
Relevant Cash Inflows and Outflows for Lifetime Care Hospital

		A / B	C	D	E	F	G	H
1					**Sketch of Relevant Cash Flows**			
2								
3		End of Year:	0	1	2	3	4	5
4	1a	Initial machine investment	$(372,890)					
5	b	Initial working capital investment	(10,000)					
6	2	Current disposal price of old machine	3,790					
7		Net initial investment	$(379,100)					
8	3	Recurring operating cash flows		$100,000	$100,000	$100,000	$100,000	$ 90,000
9	4a	Terminal disposal price of new machine						–
10	b	Recovery of working capital						10,000
11		Total relevant cash inflows and outflows						
12		as shown in Exhibits 21-3 and 21-4	$(379,100)	$100,000	$100,000	$100,000	$100,000	$100,000

[4]Note that if amortization is calculated as economic amortization (the decline in the present value of future cash flows) under the AARR method, and if operating income and investment are adjusted each year for this amortization, the AARR each year will equal the project's IRR. In practice, however, the book amortization and investment value used in AARR computations are not calculated in this way.

Real Practices Worldwide

What methods do companies around the world use for analyzing capital investment decisions? The percentages in the table below indicate how frequently particular capital budgeting methods are used in eight countries. The reported percentages exceed 100% because many companies surveyed use more than one method.

The payback method is popular in all countries. The AARR method lags behind DCF methods in all surveyed countries except Japan, where it is preferred over IRR and NPV. Companies in the US, Australia, Canada, Poland, Scotland, and the UK tend to use more than one capital budgeting method. (The sum of the capital budgeting percentages in the columns for each of these countries ranges from approximately 150% to 300%.) Companies in these countries use DCF (IRR and NPV) extensively. In contrast, Japanese and Cypriot companies tend to use one method. (The sum of

the capital budgeting percentages for Japan and Cyprus are approximately 100%.) Japanese companies use the payback method as their primary method of analysis in their capital budgeting decisions. In addition to Canada and the UK, IRR is the most-used capital-budgeting method in Singapore and Thailand.[a, b]

[a]G. Kester and T. Chong, "Capital Budgeting Practices of Listed Firms in Singapore," *Singapore Management Review* (1998).

[b]O. Arsiraphongphisit, G. Kester, and T. Skully, "Financial Policies and Practices of Listed Firms in Thailand: Capital Structure, Capital Budgeting, Cost of Capital, and Dividends," *Journal of Business Administration* (2000).

[c]P. Blayney and I. Yokohama, "Comparative Analysis of Japanese and Australian Cost Accounting and Management Practices" (Working Paper, The University of Sydney, Australia, 1991).

[d]V. Jog, and A. Srivastava, "Corporate Financial Decision Making in Canada," *Revue Canadienne des Sciences de l'Administration* (1994).

[e]I. Lazaridis, "Capital Budgeting Practices: A Survey of Firms in Cyprus," *Journal of Small Business Management* (2004).

[f]A. Szychta "The Scope and Application of Management Accounting Methods in Polish Enterprises," *Management Accounting Research* (2002).

[g]A. Sangster, "Capital Investment Appraisal Techniques: A Survey of Current Usage," *Journal of Business, Finance & Accounting* (April 1993).

[h]G. Arnold and P. Hatzopoulos, "The Theory-Practice Gap in Capital Budgeting: Evidence from the United Kingdom," *Journal of Business, Finance & Accounting* (2000).

[i]P. Ryan and G. Ryan, "Capital Budgeting Practices of the Fortune 1000: How Have Things Changed?" *Journal of Business and Management* (2002).

	Australia[c]	Canada[d]	Cyprus[e]	Japan	Poland[f]	Scotland[g]	United Kingdom[h]	United States[i]
Payback	61%	50%	37%	52%	40%	78%	70%	35%
IRR	37%	62%	9%	4%	25%	58%	81%	45%
NPV	45%	41%	11%	6%	30%	48%	80%	50%
AARR	24%	17%	4%	36%	—	31%	56%	5%
Other	7%	8%	49%	5%	50%	—	31%	8%

ASSESS YOUR MASTERY

To check your understanding of the material in Learning Objective ③, go to the *Mastery Questions* section at the end of this chapter and complete Learning Objective ③ question 1.

MyAccountingLab

COMPLEXITIES IN CAPITAL BUDGETING APPLICATIONS

In this section, we consider some challenging aspects of predicting outcomes in the information acquisition stage and of choosing projects.

Apply the concept of the time value of money to capital budgeting decisions — ④

PREDICTING THE FULL SET OF BENEFITS AND COSTS

The factors that companies consider in making computer-integrated manufacturing (CIM) decisions are far broader than costs alone. For example, the reasons for introducing CIM technology—faster response time, higher product quality, and greater flexibility in meeting changes in customer preferences—are often to increase revenues and contribution margins. Ignoring the revenue effects underestimates the financial benefits of CIM investments. As we describe below, however, the revenue benefits of technology investments are often difficult to quantify in financial terms. Nevertheless, competitive and revenue advantages are important managerial considerations when introducing CIM.

Exhibit 21-7 presents examples of the broader set of factors that companies in the United States, Australia, Japan, and the United Kingdom weigh in evaluating CIM technology. The benefits include

1. **Faster response to market changes.** An automated plant can, for example, make major design modifications (such as switching from a two-door to a four-door car) relatively quickly. To quantify this benefit requires some notion of consumer demand changes that may occur many years in the future and of the manufacturing technology choices made by competitors (defensive investment).

2. **Increased worker knowledge of automation.** If workers have a positive experience with CIM, the company can implement other automation projects more quickly and more successfully. Quantifying this benefit requires a prediction of the company's subsequent automation plans. Survey evidence emphasizes the importance of linking CIM decisions to a company's overall competitive strategies (intellectual capital management).

Predicting the full set of costs also presents problems. Three classes of costs are difficult to measure and are often underestimated:

1. Costs associated with a reduced competitive position in the industry. If other companies in the industry are investing in CIM, a company not investing in CIM will probably suffer a decline in market share because of its inferior quality and slower delivery performance. Several companies in the machine tool industry that continued to use a conventional manufacturing approach experienced rapid drops in market share after their competitors introduced CIM.

2. Costs of retraining the operating and maintenance personnel to handle the automated facilities.

3. Costs of developing and maintaining the software and maintenance programs to operate the automated manufacturing activities.

RECOGNIZING THE FULL TIME HORIZON OF THE PROJECT

The time horizon of CIM projects can stretch well beyond ten years. Many of the costs are incurred and are highly visible in the early years of adopting CIM. In contrast, important benefits may not be realized until many years after the adoption of CIM. A long time horizon should be considered when evaluating CIM investments.

EXHIBIT 21-7
Factors Considered in Making Capital Budgeting Decisions for CIM Projects

Examples of Financial Outcomes	Examples of Nonfinancial and Qualitative Outcomes
Lower direct labour costs	Reduction in manufacturing cycle time
Lower hourly support labour costs	Increase in manufacturing flexibility
Less scrap and rework	Increase in business risk due to higher fixed cost structure
Lower inventory costs	Improved product delivery and service
Increase in software and related costs	Reduction in product development time
Costs of retraining personnel	Faster response to market changes
	Increased learning by workers about automation
	Improved competitive position in the industry

Difficulties in predicting the full set of benefits and costs and long time horizons also arise in other investment decisions—for example, R&D projects and oil exploration.

PERFORMANCE EVALUATION AND THE SELECTION OF PROJECTS

The use of the accrual accounting rate of return for evaluating performance can often deter a manager from using DCF methods for capital budgeting decisions. Consider Peter Costner, the manager of the X-Ray Department at Lifetime Care Hospital. The NPV method for capital budgeting indicates that Peter should purchase the new X-ray machine, since it has a positive NPV of $20,200.

Suppose top management of Lifetime Care uses the AARR for judging the X-Ray Department's performance. Peter Costner may consider not purchasing the new X-ray machine if the AARR of 6.18% on the investment reduces his overall AARR and so negatively affects his department's performance. The AARR on the new X-ray machine is low because the investment increases the denominator and, as a result of amortization, also reduces the numerator (operating income) in the AARR computation.

Obviously, there is an inconsistency between citing DCF methods as being best for capital budgeting decisions and then using a different method to evaluate subsequent performance. As long as such practice continues, managers will be tempted to make capital budgeting choices on the basis of accrual accounting rates of return, even though such choices are not in the best interests of the organization. Such temptations become more pronounced if managers are frequently transferred (or promoted), or if annual operating income is important in their evaluations and their compensation plans. The reason is that the manager's performance is being evaluated over short time horizons. The manager has no motivation to use a DCF model to take into account cash flows that will occur in the distant future. Those cash flows will not influence the manager's performance evaluation.

MANAGEMENT CONTROL OF THE INVESTMENT ACTIVITY

Some initial investments such as purchasing X-ray or videoconferencing equipment are relatively easy to implement. Other initial investments such as building shopping malls or new manufacturing plants are more complex and take more time. In the

---

GOVERNANCE ISSUES

Long-Term Contracts and Performance Evaluation at Enron

Publicly listed companies often announce their long-term projects. If people who may buy or already own the shares believe the projects are of high quality and the anticipated return is commensurate with risk, then it is likely the share price will increase as more people choose to purchase shares than sell them. Like the managers within Enron, purchasers of shares do so in anticipation of future cash flows. When Enron entered into a long-term contract to sell gas to the Chicago-based Peoples Gas, Light & Coke Co., Enron's share price rose to represent the financial market's assessment of the deal.

Enron's performance management system ranked all employees within a business group from the best to the worst performers. Employees in the bottom 20% were warned about their performance and were terminated if they showed no significant improvement. Enron recorded the total NPV of all future cash flows for long-term contracts as revenue in the year the contract was signed and compensated managers on this basis. With no postinvestment audit process in place, when anticipated future cash flow failed to materialize, there was no attention-directing report. This pressure to perform coupled with the opportunity to report higher operating income based on optimistic assumptions about future natural gas prices created a strong temptation to inflate estimates of future cash flows and managers did so. Among other duties, accountants are expected to detect and remedy internal control-system weaknesses of this nature.

Source: M. Salter, L. Levesque, and M. Ciampa, "The Rise and Fall of Enron," Harvard Business School working paper, 2002.

latter case, monitoring and controlling the investment schedules and budgets is critical to the success of the overall project.

Assumptions made by managers of a company drive the evaluation of alternative investments. A company may develop a simple DCF analysis using, for example, a 12% discount rate for all projects. As a company grows globally, risks of otherwise identical projects can vary widely and the issue of currency repatriation (reporting foreign revenue and cost in domestic currency) and political instability affect many countries. Expansion by a Canadian energy producer into Argentina or Somalia, for example, carries higher risk than expansion into the Gulf of Mexico.

Failing to adjust assumptions about the required rate of return to account for higher risk, such as regulatory and currency risk, produces a biased valuation of investment alternatives. Another factor that creates fundamental difficulties for applying analytic models of domestic investments to overseas expansion is the increasing complexity of international financing. Global expansion strategies require a capital budgeting process which evaluates each proposed investment as a distinct opportunity with unique risks. A single discount rate does not fit all alternatives.

An approach could begin by considering representatives from various countries and deriving a weighted average cost of capital (WACC) for each project. WACC is covered in introductory finance courses. Briefly, WACC calculations require measuring all of the constituent parts of financing for projects: the cost of debt, the target capital structure, the local-country tax rates, and an appropriate cost of equity.[5]

To capture the country-specific risks in foreign markets one approach is to calculate a cost of debt and a cost of equity for each representative project using domestic data. The risk-free investment is assessed using the difference between the yield on local government bonds and the yield on corresponding domestic government Treasury bonds to both the cost of debt and the cost of equity. The difference,

---

REAL COMPANIES

Globalizing Capital Budgeting at AES Corporation

AES Corporation is a leading global electricity producer with more than US$31 billion in assets stretched across the world. AES has also expanded into many adjacencies including power plant construction, energy generation, and power distribution The global economic downturn that began in late 2000 devastated AES, weakening cash flow and the ability to service debt. The share price collapsed and its market capitalization fell nearly 95%,

from US$28 billion in December 2000 to US$1.6 billion just two years later. In 2008, market capitalization was approximately US$11.9 billion The AES board of directors requested the development of new methods to improve AES's assessment of opportunities in countries that were significantly different from the US. New methods improved AES accuracy in evaluating capital projects and protected against overleveraging its assets. Subsequent changes to the model's calculations and methodology were made. Improved capital budgeting helped AES regain its financial footing through the re-evaluation and restructuring of existing capital projects while ensuring that the company only selected new capital projects that met these revised criteria. AES anticipates growth in earnings of 14% to 20% from 2007–2011.

Sources: Based on "Globalizing the Cost of Capital and Capital Budgeting at AES," Harvard Business School Case No. 9-204-109; "AES Provides Guidance through 2011" (BusinessWire: May 25, 2007), GoogleFinance: June 8, 2007; AES 2007 10-k http://media.corporate-ir.net/media_files/irol/76/76149/reports/AES4Q0710K.pdf, accessed July 9, 2008; and discussions with the case writer and company management.

---

[5]Based on "Globalizing the Cost of Capital and Capital Budgeting at AES," Harvard Business School Case No. 9-204-109.

or *sovereign spread*, can approximate the incremental borrowing costs (and market risk) in the local country. This approach is a more sophisticated way to think about capital budgeting risk and its cost of capital around the world.

MANAGEMENT CONTROL OF THE PROJECT—POSTINVESTMENT AUDIT

A postinvestment audit compares the predictions of investment costs and outcomes made at the time a project was selected to the actual results. It provides management with feedback about the investment's performance. Suppose, for example, that actual outcomes (operating cash savings from the new X-ray machine in the Lifetime Care example) are much lower than predicted outcomes. Management must then investigate whether this occurred because the original estimates were overly optimistic or because there were problems in implementing the project. Both types of problems are a concern.

Optimistic estimates are a concern because they may result in the acceptance of a project that would otherwise have been rejected. To discourage optimistic estimates, companies such as DuPont maintain records comparing actual performance to the estimates made by individual managers when seeking approval for capital investments. DuPont believes that postinvestment audits discourage managers from making unrealistic forecasts. Problems in implementing a project are an obvious concern because the returns from the project will not meet expectations. Postinvestment audits can point to areas requiring corrective action.

Care should be exercised when performing a postinvestment audit. It should be done only after project outcomes have stabilized. Doing the audit early may give a misleading picture. Obtaining actual data to compare against estimates is often not easy. For example, actual labour cost savings from the new X-ray machine may not be comparable to the estimated savings, because the actual number and types of X-rays taken may be different from the quantities assumed during the capital budgeting process. Postinvestment audits of capital projects require information about project-specific costs and benefits. It can be extremely costly, however, to disentangle these actual outcomes as if they were independent from, instead of interdependent with, overall corporate outcomes.

The absence of postinvestment audits can lead managers to overstate project cash inflows and to accept projects that should never have been undertaken. Implementation problems, such as not achieving budgeted revenues or exceeding budgeted costs, are a concern because the returns from the project will then be inadequate. Postinvestment audits can point to areas of implementation that need improvement (such as better quality-control processes). Other benefits, such as the impact on patient treatment, may be difficult to quantify.

It is interesting that the convergence to new international accounting board (IAB) regulations in both Canada and the US require an annual postinvestment review. Upon review, if the carrying value (acquisition cost less accumulated amortization) materially misstates the long-term investment or liability values, then an impairment must be reported. The reported values must also be adjusted along with explanatory notes informing readers of the key changes in assumptions that explain the impairment. Should a reversal happen in subsequent years to the impairment, then the values must be readjusted to reflect their higher value. In this change to financial accounting standards is a new demand for the skills in applying management accounting methods long used in capital budgeting and forecasts to retrospective reporting of performance on the balance sheet.

ASSESS YOUR MASTERY

To check your understanding of the material in Learning Objective ❹, go to the *Mastery Questions* section at the end of this chapter and complete Learning Objective ❹ question 1.

DEFENSIVE STRATEGY IN CAPITAL BUDGETING

A company's strategy is the source of its strategic capital budgeting decisions. Strategic investments may be undertaken offensively to grow market share and profitability or defensively to avoid impairing a company's competitive advantage. A defensive strategy will mean that quantitative factors, while somewhat important, are secondary to the qualitative choice to defend market share.

Offensive strategies have been exhibited in many industries. Strategic decisions by WestJet, such as expansion to fly to US and European destinations, required capital investments be made in several countries. The strategic decision by Chapters Indigo to support book sales over the Internet required capital investments creating chapters.indigo.ca and an Internet infrastructure. Bell Canada Enterprises' decision to enter the media industry resulted in a big investment to acquire both *The Globe and Mail* and CTV.

Defensive strategies include cell phone companies such as Motorola, Nokia, and Samsung adding features that provide Internet access, e-mail, and text-messaging to their phone capabilities. Companies that fail to provide these product attributes will suffer a decline in market share. The capital investment may be higher than the benefit but prevents a long-term decline in revenue and profit. This type of investment is extremely difficult to quantify because the opportunity cost, and likelihood, of lost market share are very difficult to predict.

Capital investment decisions that are strategic in nature require managers to consider a broad range of factors that may be difficult to estimate. Consider some of the difficulties of justifying investments in computer-integrated manufacturing (CIM) technology made by companies such as Mitsubishi, Sony, and Audi. In CIM, computers give instructions that quickly and automatically set up and run equipment to manufacture many different products. Quantifying these benefits requires some notion of consumer-demand changes that may occur many years in the future because limitations of the machinery lock in limitations to designs flexible enough to respond to changing consumer preferences.

Initially, the first investors in CIM took an offensive strategy to improve the quality and the market share of their products. Very quickly, however, the investment for subsequent companies became a defensive strategy to stop erosion of their existing market share to higher-quality, lower-cost vehicles. CIM technology also increases worker knowledge of and experience with automation; however, the benefit of this knowledge and experience is difficult to measure. Managers need to develop judgment and intuition to make these decisions.

CUSTOMER VALUE AND CAPITAL BUDGETING

To remain viable, companies must keep their profitable customers and gain new ones. Consider Potato Supreme, which makes potato products for sale to retail outlets. It is currently analyzing two of its customers: Shine Stores and Always Open. Potato Supreme predicts the following cash flow from operations, net of income taxes (in thousands), from each customer account for the next five years:

	2010	2011	2012	2013	2014
Shine Stores	$1,450	$1,305	$1,175	$1,058	$ 950
Always Open	690	1,160	1,900	2,950	4,160

Which customer is more valuable to Potato Supreme? Looking at only the first year, 2010, Shine Stores provides more than double the cash flow compared to Always Open ($1,450 versus $690). A different picture emerges, however, when looking over the entire five-year horizon. Using Potato Supreme's 10% RRR, the NPV of the Always Open customer is $7,610, compared to $4,591 for Shine Stores (computations not shown). These NPV amounts are calculated using the 10% NPV of $1,318 ($1,450 × 0.909) for Shine Stores and $627 ($690 × 0.909) for Always Open.

Note how NPV captures in its estimate of customer value the future growth of Always Open. Potato Supreme uses this information to allocate more resources and salespersons to service the Always Open account. Potato Supreme can also use NPV calculations to examine the effects of alternative ways of increasing customer loyalty and retention, such as introducing frequent-purchaser cards.

A comparison of year-to-year changes in customer NPV estimates highlights whether managers have been successful in maintaining long-run profitable relationships with their customers. Suppose the NPV of Potato Supreme's customer base declines 15% in one year. Management can then examine the reasons for the decline, such as aggressive pricing by competitors, and devise new product development and marketing strategies for the future.

Capital One, a financial-services company, uses NPV to estimate the value of different credit-card customers. Cellular telephone companies such as Rogers and Telus attempt to sign up customers for multiple years of service. The objective is to prevent "customer churn," customers switching frequently from one company to another. The higher the probability of customer churn, the lower the NPV of the customer to the telecommunications company.

INVESTMENT IN RESEARCH AND DEVELOPMENT

Companies such as Research In Motion (RIM), a global leader in designing, manufacturing, and marketing innovative wireless mobile communications such as the BlackBerry, regard R&D projects as important strategic investments. R&D payoffs not only are more uncertain than other investment projects, but also will often occur far into the future. Most companies engaged in these types of investment projects stage their R&D so they have the choice to increase or decrease their investment at different points in time based on its success. This option feature of R&D investments—called *real options*—is an important aspect of R&D investments and increases the NPV of these investments. That's because a company can limit its losses when things are going badly and take advantage of new opportunities when things are going well.

ASSESS YOUR MASTERY

MyAccountingLab

To check your understanding of the material in Learning Objective ⑤, go to the *Mastery Questions* section at the end of this chapter and complete Learning Objective ⑤ question 1.

PULLING IT ALL TOGETHER—PROBLEM FOR SELF-STUDY

PROBLEM

Let us revisit the Lifetime Care X-ray machine project. Assume that the expected annual cash inflows are $130,000 instead of $100,000. All other facts are unchanged: a $379,100 net initial investment, a five-year useful life, a zero terminal disposal price, and an 8% required rate of return. Year 5 cash inflows include a $10,000 recovery of working capital. When calculating breakeven time, assume that the investment in the X-ray machine will occur immediately after management approves the project.

REQUIRED

Compute the following:
1. Discounted cash flow
   a. Net present value
   b. Internal rate of return

2. Payback period

3. Accrual accounting rate of return on net initial investment

4. Non-uniform cash flows. Assume (for calculation purposes) that cash outflows and cash inflows occur at the end of each period.

5. To what five areas would you direct your attention when assessing relevant from irrelevant cash flows for two alternative long-term investments?

6. What prominent change in financial accounting standards has contributed to the importance of the interconnection of management accounting and financial reporting processes?

7. Aside from a growth strategy, for what other reason might managers undertake new investment?

SOLUTION

1. a. NPV = ($130,000 × 3.993) − $379,100
= $519,090 − $379,100 = $139,990

b. There are several approaches to computing the IRR. One is to use a calculator with an IRR function; this gives an IRR of 21.16%. An alternative approach is to use Table 4 in Appendix A:

$$\$379,100 = \$130,000\,F$$

$$F = \frac{\$379,100}{\$130,000} = 2.916$$

On the five-period line of Table 4, the column closest to 2.916 is 22%. To obtain a more accurate number, straight-line interpolation can be used:

	Present Value	Factors
20%	2.991	2.991
IRR	—	2.916
22%	2.864	—
Difference	0.127	0.075

$$\text{IRR} = 20\% + \frac{0.075}{0.127}(2\%) = 21.18\% \quad \begin{array}{l}\text{(difference due to rounding of PV}\\ \text{factor to 3 decimals)}\end{array}$$

2.
$$\text{Payback} = \frac{\text{Net initial investment}}{\text{Uniform increase in annual cash flows}}$$

$$= \$379,100 \div \$130,000 = 2.92 \text{ years}$$

3.
$$\text{AARR} = \frac{\text{Increase in expected average annual operating income}}{\text{Net initial investment}}$$

$$\text{Increase in expected average annual operating savings} = [(\$130,000 \times 4) + \$120,000] \div 5$$

$$= \$128,000$$

$$\text{Average annual amortization} = \$372,890 \div 5 = \$74,578$$

$$\text{Increase in expected average annual operating income} = \$128,000 - \$74,578$$

$$= \$53,422$$

$$\text{AARR} = \frac{\$53,422}{\$379,100} = 14.09\%$$

4. Non-uniform cash flow computations are as follows:

Year	PV Discount Factor at 8% (1)	Investment Cash Outflows (2)	PV of Investment Cash Outflows* (3) = (1) × (2)	Cumulative PV of Investment Cash Outflows* (4)	Cash Inflows (5)	PV of Cash Inflows* (6) = (1) × (5)	Cumulative PV of Cash Inflows* (7)
0	1.000	$379,100	$379,100	$379,100			
1	0.926				$130,000	$120,380	$120,380
2	0.857				130,000	111,410	231,790
3	0.794				130,000	103,220	335,010
4	0.735				130,000	95,550	430,560
5	0.681				130,000	88,530	519,090

*At year 0.

$$\text{BET} = 3 \text{ years} + \frac{(\$379,100 - \$335,010)}{95,550}$$

$$= 3 \text{ years} + \frac{44,090}{95,550}$$

$$= 3.46 \text{ years}$$

5. The five areas where cash flows may differ are the cost of initial investment including working capital requirements, liquidation values of any old investments, recurring cash flows, overhead costs including amortization (or CCA), and the terminal disposal price.

6. The convergence from national to international financial accounting and reporting standards now requires an annual postinvestment audit. In addition, new standards for long-term liabilities require an annual review of their carrying value as well as an annual impairment test for long-term assets. The methods of capital budgeting are now recommended for use in valuation for financial reporting purposes.

7. Strategically, if competitors are undertaking specific types of long-term investments, it is highly likely to put a firm at a competitive disadvantage to fail to do so as well. An example is upgrading management information and control systems. A defensive strategy is to upgrade if all competitors are doing so. Thus, investments may be for growth or defence.

DECISION POINTS

The following decision guidelines use a question-and-answer format to summarize the chapter's main points. Each decision presents a key question. The guideline is the answer to that question.

DECISIONS	GUIDELINES
1. What does the term "time value of money" recognize?	The term recognizes that money received earlier is worth more because of the returns that can be generated sooner.
2. What are the disadvantages of DCF and non-DCF capital budgeting analyses (payback and AARR) methods of capital budgeting?	The NPV method computes a result in dollars not percentages and can be used where the required rates of return vary over the life of the project. The payback method neglects any cash flow after the payback period and the time value of money. The AARR is an after-tax operating income divided by a measure of the investment. The AARR does not consider the time value of money. The payback and AARR methods are nondiscounted cash flow methods whereas the NPV and IRR are discounted cash flow methods.

3. What does relevance mean in DCF analyses?	Relevance in this context means cash flow. No accruals, sunk cost, or cash flows unchanged by alternatives are relevant when these capital budgeting methods are applied. All cash flow is treated identically irrespective of its source from operations, financing, or disinvestment.
4. What conflicts can arise between using discounted cash flow methods for capital budgeting decisions and accrual accounting for performance evaluation? How can these conflicts be reduced?	Frequently, the decision made using a DCF method will not report good "operating income" results in the project's early years under accrual accounting. For this reason, managers are tempted not to use DCF methods even though the decisions based on them would be the best for the company over the long run. This conflict can be reduced by evaluating managers on a project-by-project basis, looking at their ability to achieve the amounts and timing of forecast cash flows.
5. What are the implications of a defensive long-term investment?	A defensive strategic or long-term investment is made for purposes of defending market-share. The quantitative and non-quantitative factors are secondary to this purpose. One very great difficulty is properly identifying and assessing the long-term opportunity cost of lost market-share.

TERMS TO LEARN

This chapter contains definitions of the following important terms:

accounting rate of return (p. 1020)
accrual accounting rate of return (AARR) (p. 1020)
capital budgeting (p. 1008)
discount rate (p. 1013)
discounted cash flow (DCF) (p. 1013)
hurdle rate (p. 1013)

internal rate of return (IRR) (p. 1015)
investment decision (p. 1008)
investment program (p. 1008)
investment project (p. 1008)
net present value (NPV) method (p. 1013)

(opportunity) cost of capital (p. 1013)
payback method (p. 1018)
rate of return (ROR) (p. 1010)
required rate of return (RRR) (p. 1013)
return on investment (ROI) (p. 1020)
time-adjusted rate of return (p. 1015)

MASTERY QUESTIONS

Mastery Questions are rated by proficiency level—elementary, intermediate, and advanced. The solutions appear in the Solutions to Mastery Questions section of MyAccountingLab.

LEARNING OBJECTIVE 1

1. **NPV—Advanced.** (CMA, adapted) Fox Valley Healthcare Inc. is a not-for-profit organization that operates eight nursing homes and ten assisted-living facilities. The company has grown considerably over the last three years and expects to continue to expand in the years ahead, particularly in the area of assisted-living facilities for seniors.

Jim Ruffalo, president of Fox Valley, has developed a plan to add a new building for top management and the administrative staff. He has selected a building contractor, Vukacek Construction Co., and has reached agreement on the building and its construction. Vukacek is ready to start as soon as the contract is signed and will complete the work in two years.

The building contractor has offered Fox Valley a choice of three payment plans:

◆ **Plan I:** Payment of $240,000 on the signing of the contract and $3,600,000 at the time of completion.

◆ **Plan II:** Payment of $1,200,000 on the signing of the contract and $1,200,000 at the end of each of the two succeeding years. The end of the second year is the completion date.

◆ **Plan III:** Payment of $120,000 on the signing of the contract and $1,200,000 at the end of each of the three succeeding years.

Ruffalo is not sure which payment plan he should accept. He has asked the treasurer, Lisa Monroe, for her assessment and advice. Fox Valley will finance the construction with a long-term loan and has a borrowing rate of 10%.

REQUIRED

1. Using the net present value method, calculate the comparative cost of each of the three payment plans being considered by Fox Valley Healthcare Inc.
2. Which payment plan should the treasurer recommend? Explain.
3. Discuss the financial factors, other than the cost of the plan, and nonfinancial factors that should be considered in selecting an appropriate payment plan.

LEARNING OBJECTIVE 2

1. **DCF and non-DCF—Advanced.** Eastern Cola is considering the purchase of a special-purpose bottling machine for $33,600. It is expected to have a useful life of seven years with a zero terminal disposal price. The plant manager estimates the following savings in cash operating costs:

Year	Amount
1	$12,000
2	9,600
3	7,200
4	6,000
5	4,800
6	3,600
7	3,600
Total	$46,800

Eastern Cola uses a required rate of return of 14% in its capital budgeting decisions.

REQUIRED

1. Compute the payback period.
2. Compute the net present value.
3. Compute the internal rate of return.
4. Compute the accrual accounting rate of return based on net initial investment. Assume straight-line amortization. Use the average annual savings in cash operating costs when computing the numerator of the accrual accounting rate of return.

LEARNING OBJECTIVE 3

1. **Relevance and DCF—Advanced.** The Strubel Company currently makes as many units of Part No. 789 as it needs. David Lin, general manager of the Strubel Company, has received a bid from the Gabriella Company for making Part No. 789. Current plans call for Gabriella to supply 1,000 units of Part No. 789 per year at $60 a unit. Gabriella can begin supplying on January 1, 2010, and continue for five years, after which time Strubel will not need the part. Gabriella can accommodate any change in Strubel's demand for the part and will supply it for $60 a unit, regardless of quantity.

Jack Tyson, the controller of the Strubel Company, reports the following costs for manufacturing 1,000 units of Part No. 789:

Direct materials	$26,400
Direct manufacturing labour	13,200
Variable manufacturing overhead	8,400
Amortization on machine	12,000
Product and process engineering	4,800
Rent	2,400
Allocation of general plant overhead costs	6,000
Total costs	$73,200

The following additional information is available:

a. Part No. 789 is made on a machine used exclusively for the manufacture of Part No. 789. The machine was acquired on January 1, 2009, at a cost of $72,000. The machine has a useful life of six years and zero terminal disposal price. Amortization is calculated on the straight-line method.
b. The machine could be sold today for $18,000.
c. Product and process engineering costs are incurred to ensure that the manufacturing process for Part No. 789 works smoothly. Although these costs are fixed in the short

run, with respect to units of Part No. 789 produced, they can be saved in the long run if this part is no longer produced. If Part No. 789 is outsourced, product and process engineering costs of $4,800 will be incurred for 2010 but not thereafter.

d. Rent costs of $2,400 are allocated to products on the basis of the floor space used for manufacturing the product. If Part No. 789 is discontinued, the space currently used to manufacture it would become available. The company could then use the space for storage purposes and save $1,200 currently paid for outside storage.

e. General plant overhead costs are allocated to each department on the basis of direct manufacturing labour dollars. These costs will not change in total. But no general plant overhead will be allocated to Part No. 789 if the part is outsourced.

Assume that Strubel requires a 12% rate of return for this project.

REQUIRED

1. Should David Lin outsource Part No. 789? Prepare a quantitative analysis.
2. Describe any sensitivity analysis that seems advisable, but you need not perform any sensitivity calculations.
3. What other factors should Lin consider in making a decision?
4. Lin is particularly concerned about his bonus for 2010. The bonus is based on Strubel's accounting income. What decision will Lin make if he wants to maximize his bonus in 2010?

LEARNING OBJECTIVE 4

1. **Complexities—Advanced.** Ibrahim Asafi, the general manager of the Coronado Company, is contemplating replacing the existing assembly-line equipment in the Assembly Department with automated assembly equipment. Production output and revenues will be unaffected by the replacement decision. Transactions related to the capital investment are cash transactions that would occur today.

	Existing Assembly Equipment	New Automated Assembly Equipment
Original cost	$1,320,000	$1,440,000
Useful life	11 years	5 years
Current age	6 years	0 years
Useful life remaining	5 years	5 years
Accumulated amortization	$ 720,000	$ 0
Book value	$ 636,000	Not acquired yet
Current disposal price (in cash)	$ 240,000	Not acquired yet
Terminal disposal price (in cash, in 5 years)	$ 0	$ 0
Average working capital needed	$ 144,000	$ 84,000

Current annual Assembly Department costs are as follows:

Direct materials	$720,000
Direct manufacturing labour	480,000
Amortization	120,000
Maintenance and repairs	180,000
Other operating costs	60,000
Supervision (allocated as 10% of direct manufacturing labour costs)	48,000
Allocated rent (based on space used)	48,000
Allocated corporate overhead (based on direct manufacturing labour costs)	144,000
Total	$1,800,000

ADDITIONAL INFORMATION

a. Coronado uses straight-line amortization calculated on the difference between the initial equipment investment and the terminal disposal price of the equipment.

b. The new equipment will produce output more swiftly. Therefore, the average working capital investment, if the new equipment is purchased, will decrease.

c. Of the total direct materials costs, $144,000 is waste and scrap. The new equipment is expected to reduce scrap costs to $24,000.

d. The new equipment is expected to reduce direct manufacturing labour costs by $180,000 each year.

e. Maintenance and repairs on the old equipment have been excessive. If the new equipment is acquired, maintenance and repair costs are expected to decrease to $120,000.

f. Coronado collects all supervision costs for all manufacturing departments in the plant into one cost pool. These costs are then allocated to departments on the basis of direct manufacturing labour costs. The Assembly Department has only one supervisor currently. The supervisor will continue in her current position if the new equipment is purchased.

g. The new equipment will reduce the space required for assembly operations by 20%, reducing allocated rent by $9,600. The Coronado Company has no alternative uses for this extra space.

h. Corporate overhead costs are allocated to each department at 30% of direct manufacturing labour costs of each department.

Asafi estimates a required rate of return of 12% for this project.

REQUIRED

1. On the basis of the net present value method, should Asafi replace the existing assembly equipment?

2. Suppose that next year is the last year Coronado will offer the attractive bonus plan currently in place. Asafi's bonus hinges on short-run accrual accounting income for that year. Will Asafi be inclined to replace the Assembly Department equipment? Provide quantitative support for your answer.

3. What nonfinancial and qualitative factors should Asafi consider in coming to a decision?

LEARNING OBJECTIVE 5

1. **Defensive strategy—Advanced.** Christen Granite sells granite counter tops to the construction industry. Christen Granite has three customers: Homebuilders, a small construction company that builds private luxury homes; Kitchen Constructors, a company that designs and builds kitchens for hospitals and hotels; and Subdivision Erectors, a construction company that builds large subdivisions in major metro suburbs. Following are Christen Granite's revenue and cost data by customer for the year ended December 31, 2010.

	Homebuilders	Kitchen Constructors	Subdivision Erectors
Revenues	$54,000	$390,000	$1,032,000
Cost of goods sold	26,400	216,000	660,000
Operating costs	12,000	90,000	282,000

Operating costs include order processing, sales visits, delivery, and special delivery costs. Christen estimates that revenue and costs will increase as follows on an annual basis:

	Homebuilders	Kitchen Constructors	Subdivision Erectors
Revenues	5%	15%	8%
Cost of goods sold	4%	4%	4%
Operating costs	4%	4%	4%

REQUIRED

1. Calculate operating income per customer for 2010 and for each year of the 2011–2015 period.

2. Christen estimates the value of each customer by calculating the customer's projected NPV over the next five years (2011–2015). Use the operating incomes calculated above to compute the value of all three customers. Christen uses a 10% discount rate.

3. Recently, Kitchen Constructors (KC), Christen's most valuable customer, has been threatening to leave. Lawson Tops, Christen's fiercest competitor, has offered KC a greater discount. KC demands a 20% discount from Christen if the latter wants to keep its business. At the same time, Christen re-evaluates the KC account and anticipates annual revenue increases of only 5% thereafter. Should Christen grant KC the 20% discount? What is the five-year value of KC after incorporating the 20% discount? What other factors should Christen consider before making a final decision?

4. What are the possible adverse effects of caving in to KC's pressure?

MyAccountingLab Make the grade with MyAccountingLab: The questions, exercises, and problems marked in red can be found on MyAccountingLab at **www.myaccountinglab.com**. You can practise them as often as you want, and most feature step-by-step guided instructions to help you find the right answer. Exercises and problems with an Excel icon in the margin have an accompanying Excel template on MyAccountingLab.

SHORT-ANSWER QUESTIONS

21-1 "Capital budgeting has the same focus as accrual accounting." Do you agree? Explain.

21-2 List and briefly describe each of the six parts in the capital budgeting decision process.

21-3 What is the essence of the discounted cash flow method?

21-4 "Only quantitative outcomes are relevant in capital budgeting analyses." Do you agree? Explain.

21-5 How can sensitivity analysis be incorporated in DCF analysis?

21-6 What is the payback method? What are its main strengths and weaknesses?

21-7 Describe the accrual accounting rate-of-return method. What are its main strengths and weaknesses?

21-8 "The trouble with discounted cash flow techniques is that they ignore amortization costs." Do you agree? Explain.

21-9 "Let's be more practical. DCF is not the gospel. Managers should not become so enchanted with DCF that strategic considerations are overlooked." Do you agree? Explain.

21-10 "The net present value method is the preferred method for capital budgeting decisions. Therefore, managers will always use it." Do you agree? Explain.

21-11 "All overhead costs are relevant in NPV analysis." Do you agree? Explain.

21-12 List and briefly describe the five major categories of cash flows included in capital investment projects.

21-13 "Managers' control of job projects generally focuses on four critical success factors." Identify those factors.

21-14 Bill Watts, president of Western Publications, accepts a capital-budgeting project advocated by Division X. This is the division in which the president spent his first 10 years with the company. On the same day, the president rejects a capital-budgeting project proposal from Division Y. The manager of Division Y is incensed. She believes that the Division Y project has an internal rate of return at least 10 percentage points above that of the Division X project. She comments, "What is the point of all our detailed DCF analysis? If Watts is panting over a project, he can arrange to have the proponents of that project massage the numbers so that it looks like a winner." What advice would you give the manager of Division Y?

21-15 How can capital budgeting tools assist in evaluating a manager who is responsible for retaining customers of a cellular telephone company?

EXERCISES

Throughout the assignment material, ignore the effects of income taxes.

21-16 Exercises in compound interest. To be sure that you understand how to use the tables in Appendix A at the end of this book, solve the following exercises. Ignore income tax considerations. (The correct answers, rounded to the nearest dollar, appear on pp. 1049–1050.)

REQUIRED
1. You have just won $5,000. How much money will you have at the end of 10 years if you invest it at 5% compounded annually? at 12%? (Interpolate the value.)
2. Ten years from now, the unpaid principal of the mortgage on your house will be $95,650. How much do you have to invest today at 5% interest compounded annually to accumulate the $95,650 in 10 years? (Interpolate the value.)
3. If the unpaid mortgage on your house in 10 years will be $95,650, how much money do you have to invest annually at 8% to have exactly this amount on hand at the end of the 10th year?

4. You plan to save $6,000 of your earnings at the end of each year for the next 10 years. How much money will you have at the end of the 10th year if you invest your savings compounded at 12% per year?

5. You have just turned 65, and an endowment insurance policy has paid you a lump sum of $240,000. If you invest the sum at 4%, how much money can you withdraw from your account in equal amounts at the end of each year so that at the end of 10 years (age 75) there will be nothing left?

6. You have estimated that for the first 10 years after you retire you will need an annual cash inflow of $60,000. How much money must you invest at 8% at your retirement age to obtain this annual cash inflow? at 18%?

7. The following table shows two schedules of prospective operating cash inflows, each of which requires the same net initial investment of $12,000 now:

	Annual Cash Inflows	
Year	Plan A	Plan B
1	$ 1,000	$ 5,000
2	2,000	4,000
3	3,000	3,000
4	4,000	2,000
5	5,000	1,000
Total	$15,000	$15,000

The required rate of return is 8% compounded annually. All cash inflows occur at the end of each year. In terms of net present value, which plan is more desirable? Show your computations.

21-17 Comparison of approaches in capital budgeting. A company is considering a project that requires purchasing a particular asset. Data pertaining to the purchase are shown below.

① ②
2. Discount factor, 4.00

Net initial investment to acquire the asset	$400,000
Useful life of the acquired asset	5 years
Recurring cash flow per year generated by the acquired asset	$125,000
Required rate of return	8%

REQUIRED
1. Determine the payback period in years.
2. Determine the present value of total recurring cash flows.
3. Determine the net present value of the project.
4. Do you estimate that the IRR of the project is higher or lower than 8%?
5. Do you accept the project?

21-18 New assets: comparison of approaches in capital budgeting. Panayiotis, the owner and manager of Micos Ltd., is evaluating the acquisition of new equipment needed to attend a new line of business. He has two alternatives: either buy two small machines or one large and more automatic machine:

① ②
2. Discount factor,
2 small machines, 3.5460

	Buy 2 Small Machines	Buy 1 Large Machine
Net initial investment to acquire the asset	$100,000 per machine	$250,000
Useful life of the acquired asset	4 years both machines	5 years
Recurring cash inflow per year	$ 70,000	$ 70,000
Recurring cash outflow per year	$ 5,000 per machine	$ 15,000
Required rate of return for both projects	5%	

REQUIRED
1. Determine the payback period in years.
2. Determine the present value of total recurring cash flows.
3. Determine the net present value of the project.
4. Do you estimate that the IRR of the project is higher or lower than 5%?
5. If both projects were independent, would you accept them?

2. Discount factor, 5.216

21-19 Comparison of approaches to capital budgeting. Oshawa Contractors is thinking of buying, at a cost of $300,000, a new crane that is expected to save $80,000 in cash operating costs per year. Its estimated useful life is 10 years, and it will have zero terminal disposal price. The required rate of return is 14%.

REQUIRED
1. Compute the payback period.
2. Compute the net present value.
3. Compute the internal rate of return.
4. Compute the accrual accounting rate of return based on net initial investment. Assume straight-line amortization.

2. Discount factor, 5.650

21-20 Comparison of approaches to capital budgeting. GTA Financial Services estimates that it can save $20,000 a year in cash operating costs for the next 10 years if it redesigns the layout of its office at a cost of $60,000. A zero terminal disposal price is expected. GTA's required rate of return is 12%.

REQUIRED
1. Compute the payback period.
2. Compute the net present value.
3. Compute the internal rate of return.
4. Compute the accrual accounting rate of return based on net initial investment. Assume straight-line amortization.

1. Plan 1 NPV, ($3,901,725)

21-21 Comparison of projects, no income taxes. (CMA, adapted). New Bio Corporation is a rapidly growing biotech company that has a required rate of return of 12%. It plans to build a new facility in Mississauga, Ontario. The building will take two years to complete. The building contractor offered New Bio a choice of three payment plans, as follows:

◆ **Plan I:** Payment of $375,000 at the time of signing the contract and $4,425,000 upon completion of the building. The end of the second year is the completion date.
◆ **Plan II:** Payment of $1,500,000 at the time of signing the contract and $1,500,000 at the end of each of the two succeeding years.
◆ **Plan III:** Payment of $150,000 at the time of signing the contract and $1,500,000 at the end of each of the three succeeding years.

REQUIRED
1. Using the net present value method, calculate the comparative cost of each of the three payment plans being considered by New Bio.
2. Which payment plan should New Bio choose? Explain.
3. Discuss the financial factors, other than the cost of the plan, and the nonfinancial factors that should be considered in selecting an appropriate payment plan.

Salvage NPV, $12,830

21-22 Payback period, net present value. A company is considering buying a $250,000 production machine. It estimates that the machine would cost $12,000 per year to operate, but would save $65,000 annually in labour costs. The machine has a seven-year life and a salvage value of $25,000. Assume all cash flows occur at the end of each year. The company evaluates capital projects using the payback period and net present value (discount rate of 10%). For a project to be acceptable, it must have a payback period of five years or less, and generate a positive net present value.

REQUIRED
Based on the company's criteria, is this an acceptable investment? Explain.

1. a. Discount factor, 3.6048

21-23 Net present value, internal rate of return, sensitivity analysis. Muskoka Landscaping Ltd. is planning to buy equipment costing $25,000 to improve its services. The equipment is expected to save $8,000 in cash operating costs per year. Its estimated useful life is five years, and it will have zero terminal disposal price. The required rate of return is 12%.

REQUIRED
1. Compute the net present value. Compute the internal rate of return.
2. What is the minimum annual cash savings that will make the equipment desirable on a net present value basis?
3. When might a manager calculate the minimum annual cash savings described in requirement 2 rather than use the $8,000 savings in cash operating costs per year to calculate the net present value or internal rate of return?

21-24 Equipment replacement, net present value, relevant costs, payback. Edgeley Inc., a logistics operator located in Concord, Ontario, is considering replacing one of its tractor trailers (informally known as a 53' truck). The truck was purchased for $64,800 two years ago, has a current book value of $45,600, and a remaining useful life of four years. Its current disposal price is $31,200; in four years its terminal disposal price is expected to be $7,200. The annual cash operating costs of the truck are expected to be $42,000 for each of the next three years and $48,000 in year 4.

Edgeley is considering the purchase of a new 53' truck for $67,200. Annual cash operating costs for the new truck are expected to be $30,000. The new truck has a useful life of four years and a terminal disposal price of $9,600.

Edgeley Inc. amortizes all its trucks using straight-line amortization calculated on the difference between the initial cost and the terminal disposal price divided by the estimated useful life. Edgeley uses a rate of return of 12% in its capital budgeting decisions.

REQUIRED
1. Using a net present value criterion, should Edgeley Inc. purchase the new truck?
2. Compute the payback period for Edgeley Inc. if it purchases the new 53' truck.

②
1. NPV, keep old truck, $126,833

21-25 **Payback and NPV methods, no income taxes.** (CMA, adapted) Portage Transportation Services is analyzing capital expenditure proposals for the improvement of its cross-docking facilities. The capital budget is limited to $300,000, which Portage believes is the maximum capital it can borrow from financial institutions.

Leslie O'Connor, an external consultant, is preparing an analysis of four projects that Karl Luften, Portage's president, is considering. O'Connor has projected the future cash flows for each potential purchase. The information concerning the four projects is given below.

②
1. b. Project A payback, 4 years

	Project A	Project B	Project C	Project D
Projected cash outflow				
Net initial investment	$240,000	$228,000	$300,000	$252,000
Projected cash inflows				
Year 1	$ 60,000	$ 48,000	$ 90,000	$ 90,000
2	60,000	60,000	90,000	90,000
3	60,000	84,000	72,000	72,000
4	60,000	90,000	96,000	48,000
5	60,000	90,000	120,000	24,000

REQUIRED
1. Since Portage's cash is limited, Karl Luften thinks that the payback method of calculating investments would be the best method for choosing capital-budgeting projects.
   a. Explain what the payback method measures and how it is used. Include in your explanation several benefits and limitations of the payback method.
   b. Calculate the payback period for each of the four projects. Ignore income tax considerations.
2. O'Connor would like to compare the projects using the net present value method. The required rate of return for Portage is 10%. All cash flows occur at the end of the year. Calculate the net present value for each project. Ignore income tax considerations.
3. Which projects, if any, would you recommend funding? Briefly state your reasons why.

21-26 **DCF, accrual accounting rate of return, working capital, evaluation of performance.** Edilcan Inc. has been offered an automated special-purpose welder (robot) for $60,000. The machine is expected to have a useful life of eight years with a terminal disposal price of $12,000. Savings in cash operating costs are expected to be $15,000 per year. However, additional working capital is needed to keep the welder running efficiently and without stoppages. Working capital includes mainly argon gas, wires, and tips. These items must continually be replaced so that an investment of $5,000 must be maintained in them at all times, but this investment is fully recoverable (will be "cashed in") at the end of the useful life. Edilcan's required rate of return is 14%.

③
1. a. Present value of annuity of savings in cash operating costs, $69,583

REQUIRED
1. a. Compute the net present value.
   b. Compute the internal rate of return.
2. Compute the accrual accounting rate of return based on the net initial investment. Assume straight-line amortization.
3. You have the authority to make the purchase decision. Why might you be reluctant to base your decision on the DCF model?

21-27 Selling a plant, IRR, and AARR. (CMA, adapted) The Crossroad Company is an international clothing manufacturer. Its Santa Monica plant will become idle on December 31, 2008. Peter Laney, the corporate controller, has been asked to look at three options regarding the plant.

- ◆ **Option 1:** The plant, which has been fully amortized, can be sold immediately for $340,000.
- ◆ **Option 2:** The plant can be leased to the Austin Corporation, one of Crossroad's suppliers, for four years. Under the lease terms, Austin would pay Crossroad $96,000 rent per year (payable at year-end) and would grant Crossroad an $18,960 annual discount off the normal price of fabric purchased by Crossroad (assume discount received at year-end for each of the four years). Austin would bear all of the plant's ownership costs. Crossroad expects to sell this plant for $80,000 at the end of the four-year lease.
- ◆ **Option 3:** The plant could be used for four years to make souvenir jackets for the Olympics. Fixed overhead costs (a cash outflow) before any equipment upgrades are estimated to be $8,000 annually for the four-year period. The jackets are expected to sell for $42 each. Variable cost per unit is expected to be $33. The following production and sales of jackets are expected: 2009, 8,000 units; 2010, 12,000 units; 2011, 16,000 units; 2012, 4,000 units. In order to manufacture the jackets, some of the plant equipment would need to be upgraded at an immediate cost of $60,000. The equipment would be amortized using the straight-line amortization method and zero terminal disposal value over the four years it would be in use. Because of the equipment upgrades, Crossroad could sell the plant for $120,000 at the end of four years. No change in working capital would be required.

Crossroad treats all cash flows as if they occur at the end of the year, and it uses a required rate of return of 12%. Crossroad is subject to a 40% tax rate on all income, including capital gains.

REQUIRED
1. Calculate net present value of each of the options and determine which option Crossroad should select using the NPV criterion.
2. What nonfinancial factors should Crossroad consider before making its choice?

21-28 New equipment purchase. Norberto Garcia, general manager of the Argentinean subsidiary of Innovation Inc., is considering the purchase of new industrial equipment to improve efficiency at its Cordoba plant. The equipment has an estimated useful life of five years. The estimated cash flows for the equipment are shown in the table that follows, with no anticipated change in working capital. Innovation has a 12% required rate of return. Assume amortization is calculated on a straight-line basis. Assume all cash flows occur at year-end except for initial investment amounts.

Initial investment:	$80,000
Annual cash flow from operations (excluding the amortization effect):	$31,250
Cash flow from terminal disposal of equipment:	$ 0

REQUIRED
1. Calculate (a) net present value, (b) payback period, and (c) internal rate of return.
2. Compare and contrast the capital budgeting methods in requirement 1.
3. The controller of Innovation Inc. received Garcia's estimates but adjusted them to capture the added risk of doing the project in Argentina. Recalculate item 1 with a required rate of return of 20% and explain if the project will be approved by Innovation Inc. for its Argentinean subsidiary.

21-29 NPV and customer profitability. Ready Ink and Paper Ltd. sells and distributes office supplies for printers and photocopy machines; its overall margin on sales is 10%. Ready Ink and Paper has customers of two kinds: low and high volume. Low-volume customers on average generate sales for $5,000 per year and the average tenure is four years. High-volume customers on average generate sales for $18,000. Their average tenure is seven years but they require an initial investment of $8,000 (comprised mostly of legal fees paid to lawyers to review the long-term contract and upgrades in the software to allow customers to place purchase orders online).

REQUIRED
1. Calculate operating income per customer in each year.
2. Ready Ink and Paper Ltd. estimates the value of each kind of customer by calculating the customer's projected NPV over the total expected time of the contract. Use the operating incomes calculated above to compute the value of each kind of customer.
3. Indicatewhichtype of customer is more profitable for Ready Ink and Paper Ltd.

PROBLEMS

21-30 DCF, sensitivity analysis, no income taxes. (CMA, adapted) Applewood Manufacturing Ltd. produces a variety of hand tools that are directly sold to local hardware stores in Alberta. The company's manager of sales has come up with a business plan to export tools to the United States, particularly to underserved states such as Montana and Wyoming.

The following information for the business plan was developed from the best estimates of the sales, production, and administrative managers.

Annual sales volume	100,000 units
Selling price	$12 per unit
Cash variable costs	$4.80 per unit
Cash fixed costs	$250,000 per year
Investment required	$380,000
Length of first contract	3 years

① ②

1. Cash inflow from operations, $470,000

The business plan starts with a three-year contract and at the end of the three years the investment made will have a zero terminal disposal price.

Applewood Manufacturing uses discounted cash flow analysis in its decision making. Its required rate of return on this project is 20%.

The US is a new market for Applewood, and management is concerned about the reliability of the estimates and the proper consideration of all costs involved in the decision. The controller has proposed applying sensitivity analysis to selected factors, and is investigating some alternatives. Ignore income taxes in your calculations.

REQUIRED
1. What is the net present value of this investment proposal?
2. What is the effect on the net present value of the following three changes in assumptions? Treat each item independently of the others.
   a. 10% reduction in the selling price.
   b. 10% reduction in annual sales in units.
   c. 10% reduction in the variable cost per unit.
3. Discuss how management would use the data developed in requirements 1 and 2 in its consideration of the proposed capital investment.

21-31 DCF, sensitivity analysis, no income taxes. (CMA, adapted) Landom Corporation is an international manufacturer of fragrances for women. Management at Landom is considering expanding the product line to men's fragrances. From the best estimates of the marketing and production managers, annual sales (all for cash) for this new line is 1,000,000 units at $25 per unit; cash variable cost is $10 per unit; cash fixed cost is $5,000,000 per year. The investment project requires $30,000,000 of cash outflow and has a project life of five years.

① ②

1. Cash inflow from operations, $10,000,000

At the end of the five-year useful life, there will be no terminal disposal value. Assume all cash flows occur at year-end except for initial investment amounts.

Men's fragrance is a new market for Landom, and management is concerned about the reliability of the estimates. The controller has proposed applying sensitivity analysis to selected factors. Ignore income taxes in your computations. Landom's required rate of return on this project is 14%.

REQUIRED
1. Calculate the net present value of this investment proposal.
2. Calculate the effect on the net present value of the following two changes in assumptions. (Treat each item independently of the other.)
   a. 5% reduction in the selling price
   b. 5% increase in the variable cost per unit
3. Discuss how management would use the data developed in requirements 1 and 2 in its consideration of the proposed capital investment.

21-32 NPV, IRR, and sensitivity analysis. Crumbly Cookie Company is considering expanding by buying a new (additional) machine that costs $42,000, has zero terminal disposal value, and has a 10-year useful life. It expects the annual increase in cash revenues from the expansion to be $23,000 per year. It expects additional annual cash costs to be $16,000 per year. Its cost of capital is 6%. Ignore taxes.

① ②

1. Present value of net cash inflows, $51,520

REQUIRED
1. Calculate the net present value and internal rate of return for this investment.
2. Assume the finance manager of Crumbly Cookie Company is not sure about the cash revenues and costs. The revenues could be anywhere from 10% higher to

10% lower than predicted. Assume cash costs are still $16,000 per year. What are NPV and IRR at the high and low points for revenue?

3. The finance manager thinks that costs will vary with revenues, and if the revenues are 10% higher, the costs will be 7% higher. If the revenues are 10% lower, the costs will be 10% lower. Recalculate the NPV and IRR at the high and low revenue points with this new cost information.

4. The finance manager has decided that the company should earn 2% more than the cost of capital on any project. Recalculate the original NPV in requirement 1 using the new discount rate.

① ②

1. Net annual cash inflow, $30,000

21-33 **Payback, even and uneven cash flows.** You have the opportunity to expand your business by purchasing new equipment for $159,000. You expect to incur fixed costs of $96,000 per year to use this new equipment, and you expect to incur variable costs in the amount of approximately 10% of annual revenues.

REQUIRED

1. Calculate the payback period for this investment assuming you will generate $140,000 in cash revenues every year.
2. Assume you expect the following revenue stream for this investment:

Year 1: $ 90,000	Year 4: 155,000	Year 7: 140,000
Year 2: 115,000	Year 5: 170,000	Year 8: 125,000
Year 3: 130,000	Year 6: 180,000	Year 9: 80,000

Based on this estimated revenue stream, what is the payback period for this investment?

① ② ④

1. Present value of initial investments, ($325,000)

21-34 **NPV and AARR, goal-congruence issues.** Nate Stately, a manager of the Plate Division for the Great Slate Manufacturing company, has the opportunity to expand the division by investing in additional machinery costing $320,000. He would amortize the equipment using the straight-line method, and expects it to have no residual value. It has a useful life of six years. The firm mandates a required rate of return of 16% on investments. Nate estimates annual net cash inflows for this investment of $100,000 and an investment in working capital of $5,000.

REQUIRED

1. Calculate the net present value of this investment.
2. Calculate the accrual accounting rate of return for this investment.
3. Should Nate accept the project? Will Nate accept the project if his bonus depends on achieving an accrual accounting rate of return of 16%? How can this conflict be resolved?

② ③

1. New cash flow, $9.6

21-35 **Payback, net present value, relevant costs, sensitivity analysis.** The Students' Association of Your University has been operating a cafeteria, but it is considering converting it to a completely automated set of vending machines. If the change is made, the old equipment would be sold now for whatever cash it might bring.

The vending machines would be purchased immediately for cash. A catering firm would take complete responsibility for servicing and replenishing the vending machines and would pay the Student Association a predetermined percentage of the gross vending receipts.

The present cafeteria equipment has 10 years of remaining useful life. The new vending machines have a 10-year useful life. The following data are available (in thousands):

Cafeteria cash revenues per year	$144
Cafeteria cash costs per year	$149
Present cafeteria equipment:	
Net book value	$101
Annual amortization cost	$ 7
Current disposal price	$ 5
Terminal disposal price (10 years from now)	$ 0
New vending machines:	
Initial machine investment	$ 77
Terminal disposal price	$ 6

Expected annual gross receipts	$ 96
Students' percentage share of receipts	10%
Expected annual cash costs (negligible)	
Present values at 10%:	
$1 due in 10 years	$0.3815
Annuity of $1 a year for 10 years	$6.1445

Your University Students' Association has a 10% required rate of return.

REQUIRED

Compute the following for the vending machine investment:

1. Expected increase in net annual operating cash inflows as a result of investing in the vending machines
2. Payback period
3. Net present value
4. Point of indifference (zero NPV) in terms of annual gross vending machine receipts

21-36 Recognizing cash flows for capital investment projects. Ludmilla Quagg owns a fitness centre and is thinking of replacing the old Fit-O-Matic machine with a brand new Flab-Buster 3000. The old Fit-O-Matic has a historical cost of $50,000 and accumulated amortization of $46,000, but has a trade-in value of $5,000. It currently costs $1,200 per month in utilities and another $10,000 a year in maintenance to run the Fit-O-Matic. Ludmilla feels that the Fit-O-Matic can be used for another 10 years, after which it would have no salvage value.

2. Annual cash flow from operations, $9,320

The Flab-Buster 3000 would reduce the utilities costs by 30% and cut the maintenance cost in half. The Flab-Buster 3000 costs $98,000, has a 10-year life, and an expected disposal value of $10,000 at the end of its useful life. Ludmilla charges customers $10 per hour to use the fitness centre. Replacing the fitness machine will not affect the price of service or the number of customers she can serve.

Ludmilla also looked at replacing the Fit-O-Matic with a Walk-N-Pull Series 3, which costs $78,000. However, she prefers the Flab-Buster 3000.

REQUIRED

1. Ludmilla wants to evaluate the Flab-Buster 3000 project using capital budgeting techniques, but does not know how to begin. To help her, read through the problem and separate the cash flows into four groups: (1) net initial investment cash flows, (2) cash flow savings from operations, (3) cash flows from terminal disposal of investment, and (4) cash flows not relevant to the capital budgeting problem.
2. Assuming a required rate of return of 8%, and straight-line amortization over remaining useful life of machines, should Ludmilla buy the Flab-Buster 3000?

21-37 Recognizing cash flows for capital investment projects, NPV. Met-All Manufacturing manufactures over 20,000 different products made from metal, including building materials, tools, and furniture parts.

1. Annual cash flow from operations with new equipment, $760,000

The manager of the furniture parts division has proposed that his division expand into bicycle parts as well.

The furniture parts division currently generates cash revenues of $4,700,000 and incurs cash costs of $3,600,000, with an investment in assets of $12,090,000. One-fourth of the cash costs are direct labour.

The manager estimates that the expansion of the business will require an investment in working capital of $45,000. Because the company already has a facility, there would be no additional rent or purchase costs for a building, but the project would generate an additional $390,000 in annual cash overhead.

Moreover, the manager expects annual materials cash costs for bicycle parts to be $1,700,000, and labour for the bicycle parts to be about the same as the labour cash costs for furniture parts.

The Controller of Met-All, working with various managers, estimates that the expansion would require the purchase of equipment with a $5,000,000 cost and an expected disposal value of $400,000 at the end of its 10-year useful life. Amortization would occur on a straight-line basis.

The CFO of Met-All determines the firm's cost of capital as 12%. The CFO's salary is $460,000 per year.

Adding another division will not change that. The CEO asks for a report on expected revenues for the project, and is told by the marketing department that it might be able to achieve cash revenues of $3,750,000 annually from bicycle parts.

1. Separate the cash flows into four groups: (1) net initial investment cash flows, (2) cash flows from operations, (3) cash flows from terminal disposal of investment, and (4) cash flows not relevant to the capital budgeting problem.

2. Calculate the NPV of the expansion project and comment on your analysis.

1. Total relevant operating cash outflows, developed machine, $660,000

21-38 Equipment replacement, relevant costs, sensitivity analysis. The engineering department of an automotive supplier specialized in manufacturing seating systems has developed a $600,000 machine for assembling school bus recliners. The machine has been used to produce only one batch of 1,000 units so far (prototypes). The company will amortize the $600,000 initial machine investment evenly over five years, after which production of the recliners will be stopped. The company's expected annual costs will be direct materials, $300,000; direct manufacturing labour, $120,000; and variable manufacturing overhead, $240,000. Variable manufacturing overhead varies with direct manufacturing labour costs. Fixed manufacturing overhead, exclusive of amortization, is $90,000 annually, and fixed marketing and administrative costs are $45,000 annually.

A German manufacturer of special-purpose machines informs the engineering department manager that in two weeks he can deliver a new machine that is ideally suited for assembling recliners. This new machine is clearly superior because it reduces the use of direct materials by 10% and produces twice as many units per hour. It will cost $500,000 and will have a zero terminal disposal price at the end of five years.

Production and sales of 25,000 units per year (sales of $1,200,000) will be the same whether the company uses the old machine or the new machine. The current disposal price of the internally developed machine is $60,000. Its terminal disposal price in four years will be $30,000.

REQUIRED

1. Assume that the required rate of return is 16%. Using the net present value method, show whether the new machine should be purchased. What is the role of the book value of the old machine in the analysis?

2. What is the payback period for the new machine?

3. As the manager who developed the $600,000 old machine, you are trying to justify not buying the new $500,000 machine. You question the accuracy of the expected cash operating savings. By how much must these cash savings fall before the point of indifference—the point where the net present value of investing in the new machine reaches zero?

1. Net incremental benefit per car from accepting special order, $39.60

21-39 Special order, relevant costs, capital budgeting. (A. Spero, adapted) Toys Inc. sells neon-coated Nightglow cars to several local toy stores. It has the capacity to make 250,000 of these units per year, but during the year ending December 31, 2010, it made and sold 130,000 cars to its existing customers. It makes these cars by dipping its highly unsuccessful Gander model plastic toy cars into a vat of neon paint. It originally purchased 780,000 of the Ganders but has been unable to sell them as Ganders. These plastic cars originally cost $24 per unit, and 650,000 of them remain in inventory.

Toys' accountant has prepared the following cost sheet per Nightglow car:

Selling price per car			$70.80
Manufacturing costs per car:			
Direct materials:			
Plastic cars	$24.00		
Neon paint	7.20		
Boxes	3.60	34.80	
Direct manufacturing labour		9.60	
Vat amortization		12.00	
Allocated plant manager's salary		6.00	
Manufacturing costs per car			62.40
Gross margin per car			8.40
Marketing costs per car ($2.40 of which is variable)			7.20
Operating margin per car			$ 1.20

On December 31, 2010, the Tiny Tot chain asked Toys Inc. to provide 100,000 Nightglow cars at a special price of $60 per car. Toys Inc. will not need to incur any marketing cost for the Tiny Tot sale.

Toys Inc. expected to sell the Nightglow cars to its existing customers for the next four years at the current level of demand of 130,000 units per year and none thereafter. At the end of four years, Toys Inc. will dispose of the vat and whatever cars remain at zero net disposal price. If Toys accepts the Tiny Tot order, it is certain that its other customers will refuse to pay the current price of $70.80 and will demand a discount. Toys estimates a required rate of return of 16%.

REQUIRED

1. Should Toys accept the special order if it must also offer the same price of $60 to its existing customers for the next four years?
2. Suppose Toys is uncertain about the discount the existing customers would demand. Determine the price that Toys Inc. would have to offer its existing customers for the next four years to be indifferent between accepting and rejecting Tiny Tot's special order.

21-40 Capital budgeting, computer-integrated manufacturing, sensitivity. Locomotive Engines Inc. is planning to replace the process control system in all of its three production lines. The current system uses mechanical process controls, which have a remaining useful life of 10 years, book value of $10.8 million, a current disposal price of $6 million, and a negligible terminal disposal value 10 years from now. The average investment in working capital is $7.2 million.

1. Total present value, recurring operating cash savings for 10 years, $25.037 million

Locomotive Engines Inc. plans to replace all mechanical controls with electronic controls that automatically feed a computer-integrated manufacturing (CIM) system at a cost of $54 million. Norbert Grass, the production manager, estimates the following annual cash flow effects of implementing CIM:

a. Cost of maintaining software programs and CIM equipment, $1.8 million
b. Reduction in technicians' fees due to reduced maintenance requirements, $1.2 million
c. Fewer product defects and reduced rework, $5.4 million

In addition, Grass estimates the average investment in working capital will decrease to $2.4 million. The estimated disposal price of the CIM equipment is $16.8 million at the end of 10 years. Locomotive uses a required rate of return of 14%.

REQUIRED

1. Compute the net present value of the CIM proposal. On the basis of this criterion, should Locomotive adopt CIM?
2. Grass argues that the higher quality and faster production resulting from CIM will also increase Locomotive's revenues. He estimates additional cash revenues net of cash-operating costs from CIM of $3.6 million per year. Compute the net present value of the CIM proposal under this assumption.
3. Management is uncertain if the cash flows from additional revenues will occur. Compute the minimum annual cash flow from additional revenues that will cause Locomotive to invest in CIM on the basis of the net present value criterion.
4. Discuss the effects of reducing the investment horizon for CIM to five years, Locomotive's usual time period for making investment decisions. Assume disposal prices at the end of five years of the CIM line, $24 million; old production line, $4.8 million. Also assume additional cash revenues net of cash operating costs from CIM of $3.6 million per year.

21-41 Defensive and offensive strategies in capital budgeting. (CMA, adapted) The management of Kleinburg Industrial Bakery is analyzing two competing investment projects and they must decide which one can be done immediately and which one can be postponed for at least a year. The details of each proposed investment are shown on the next page.

1. Present value, years 1–9 cash inflows, increase capacity project, $2,131,200

The Bakery has a 12% required rate of return to evaluate all investments that directly impact operations and amortizes the investment in plant and equipment using straight-line amortization over 10 years on the difference between the initial investment and terminal disposal price.

REQUIRED

1. Calculate the net present value of each proposal.
2. Which project should the Bakery choose on the basis of the NPV calculations?
3. Mention which strategic factors must be considered by the managers when ranking the projects.

	Project: Increase Capacity to Serve New Markets	Project: Upgrade Customer Service
Proposed by	Production manager	Sales and marketing manager
Rationale	Assets are operating at full capacity and we are unable to attend to all the demand, therefore we need to expand our facilities to produce more kilograms.	The fleet of trucks and vans need to be upgraded with tracking devices and remote connexions to flex the planning of routes. The new software will allow the company to be paperless and respond faster to customers' requests.
Investment	$600,000	$345,000
Working capital	$ 50,000	$150,000
Terminal disposal value	$60,000	None
Expected useful life	10 years	5 years
Expected increase in operating income	$400,000	$80,000
Expected savings in administrative costs	None	$40,000

COLLABORATIVE LEARNING CASES

1. Annual net cash inflows, periods 1–12, $74,000

21-42 Net present value, internal rate of return, sensitivity analysis. Francesca Freed wants a Burg-N-Fry franchise. The buy-in is $500,000. Burg-N-Fry headquarters tells Francesca that typical annual operating costs are $160,000 (cash) and that she can bring in "as much as" $260,000 in cash revenues per year. Burg-N-Fry headquarters also wants her to pay 10% of her revenues to them per year. Francesca wants to earn at least 8% on the investment, because she has to borrow the $500,000 at a cost of 6%. Use a 12-year window, and ignore taxes.

INSTRUCTIONS

Form groups of three students to complete the following requirements.

1. Find the NPV and IRR of this investment, given the information that Burg-N-Fry has given Francesca.
2. Francesca is nervous about the "as much as" statement from Burg-N-Fry, and worries that the cash revenues will be lower than $260,000. Repeat requirement 1 using revenues of $240,000 and $220,000.
3. Francesca thinks she should try to negotiate a lower payment to the Burg-N-Fry headquarters, and also thinks that if revenues are lower than $260,000 her costs might also be lower by about 10,000. Repeat requirement 2 using $150,000 as annual cash operating cost and a payment to Burg-N-Fry of only 6% of sales revenues.
4. Discuss how the sensitivity analysis will affect Francesca's decision to buy the franchise. Why don't you have to recalculate the internal rate of return if you change the desired (discount) interest rate?

1. Top Line unit contribution margin, $20

21-43 Relevant costs, capital budgeting, strategic decision. (M. Porporato, adapted) Wilcox is a family-owned company that has been making microwaves for almost 20 years. The company's production line includes 10 models, ranging from a basic model to a deluxe stainless steel model. Most of its sales are through independently owned retailers in medium-sized towns in central Canada, giving the microwaves an image of high quality and price. However, industry sales have been stagnant and those of Wilcox have been falling in the past two years due to the Asian brands. Currently Wilcox sells 75,000 units per year at an average price of $120 each with variable unit costs of $60 (of which materials is $30). As a result Wilcox is operating its plant at about 75% of a one-shift capacity, although in their "golden years" in the early 1990s they were operating at 75% of a two-shifts capacity.

   In the spring of 2009 Oh Mart, a chain of large supermarkets, approached Wilcox's CEO and asked about the possibility of producing microwaves for them. The microwaves will be sold under the Oh Mart house brand, called Top Line. They are offering a five-year contract that could be automatically extended on a year-to-year basis, unless one party gives the other at least three months' notice that it does not wish to extend the contract. The deal is for

24,000 units per year with a unit price of $90 each. Oh Mart does not want title on a microwave to pass from Wilcox to Oh Mart until the microwave is shipped to a specific Oh Mart store. Additionally Oh Mart wants the Top Line microwaves to be somewhat different in appearance from Wilcox's other microwaves. These requirements would increase Wilcox's purchasing, inventorying, and production costs.

In order to be able to give an answer to Oh Mart, knowing that they had no room to negotiate, Wilcox managers gathered the following information:

1. First-year costs of producing Top Line microwaves

Materials (includes items specific to Oh Mart models)	$40
Labour (same as with regular microwaves)	$20
Overhead at 100% of labour (50% is variable; the 100% rate is based on a volume of 100,000 units per year)	$20
Total unit cost	$80

2. Related added inventories (the cost of financing them is estimated to be close to 15% per year)

Materials:	two-month supply (a total of 4,000 units)
Work in process:	1,000 units, half completed (but all materials for them issued)
Finished goods:	500 units (awaiting next carload lot shipment to an Oh Mart central warehouse in Concord, Ontario)

3. Impact on Wilcox's regular sales. Wilcox's sales over the next two years are expected to be about 75,000 units a year if they forgo the Oh Mart deal, based on the CEO estimates after launching a new "top of the line" microwave. If Wilcox accepts the deal, it would lose about 5,000 units of the regular sales volume a year, since their retail distribution is quite strong in Oh Mart market regions. These estimates do not include the possibility that a few of Wilcox's current dealers might drop their line if they find out that Wilcox is making microwaves for Oh Mart with a lower selling price.

INSTRUCTIONS
Form groups of three students to complete the following requirements.

REQUIREMENTS
1. Determine if the proposal of Oh Mart will increase Wilcox's net income in the next year.
2. Calculate the total value of the contract (suppose there is no renewal after the 5th year).
3. On the basis of the net present value criterion, should Wilcox Microwaves accept the offer?
4. Estimate the strategic consequences of accepting the proposal (consider the current situation of the industry, Wilcox positioning, image, distribution, and production issues).

ANSWERS TO EXERCISES IN COMPOUND INTEREST (EXERCISE 21-16)
The general approach to these exercises centres on a key question: Which of the four tables in Appendix A should be used? No computations should be made until after this basic question has been answered with confidence.

1. **From Table 1.** The $5,000 is the present value P of your winnings. Their future value S in 10 years will be:

$$S = P(1 + r)^n$$

The conversion factor, $(1 + r)^n$, is on line 10 of Table 1.

Substituting at 5%: $S = 5,000 \times 1.629 = \$8,145$

Substituting at 12%: $S = 5,000 \times 3.106 = \$15,530$

2. **From Table 2.** The $95,650 is an *amount of future worth*. You want the present value of that amount, which is $P = S \div (1 + r)^n$.
The conversion factor, $1 \div (1 + r)^n$, is on line 10 of Table 2. Substituting

$$P = \$95,650 \times 0.614 = \$58,729.10$$

3. **From Table 3.** The $95,650 is *future worth*. You are seeking the uniform amount (annuity) to set aside annually. Note that $1 invested each year for 10 years at 8% has a future worth F of $14.487 after 10 years, from line 10 of Table 3.

$$S_n = \text{Annual deposit} \times F$$
$$\$95,650 = \text{Annual deposit} \times 14.487$$
$$\text{Annual deposit} = \frac{\$95,650}{14.487} = \$6,602.47$$

4. **From Table 3.** You are seeking the *amount of future worth* of an annuity of $6,000 per year. Note that $1 invested each year for 10 years at 12% has a future worth F of $17.549 after 10 years.

$$S_n = \$6,000F \quad \text{where } F \text{ is the conversion factor}$$
$$= \$6,000 \times 17.549 = \$105,294$$

5. **From Table 4.** When you reach age 65, you will get $240,000, a present value at that time. You must find the annuity that will exactly exhaust the invested principal in 10 years. To pay yourself $1 each year for 10 years when the interest rate is 4% requires you to have $8.111 today, from line 10 of Table 4.

$$P_n = \text{Annual withdrawal} \times F$$
$$\$240,000 = \text{Annual withdrawal} \times 8.111$$
$$\text{Annual withdrawal} = \frac{\$240,000}{8.111} = \$29,589.45$$

6. **From Table 4.** You need to find the present value of an annuity for 10 years. At 8%:

$$P_n = \text{Annual withdrawal} \times F$$
$$= \$60,000 \times 6.710$$
$$= \$402,600$$

At 18%:

$$P_n = \$60,000 \times 4.494$$
$$= \$269,640, \text{ a much lower figure}$$

7. Plan B is preferable. The net present value of plan B exceeds that of plan A by $1,224 ($591 + $633):

Year	PV Factor at 8%	Plan A Cash Inflows	Plan A PV of Cash Inflows	Plan B Cash Inflows	Plan B PV of Cash Inflows
0	1.000	$(12,000)	$(12,000)	$(12,000)	$(12,000)
1	0.926[a]	1,000	926	5,000	4,630
2	0.857[b]	2,000	1,714	4,000	3,428
3	0.794	3,000	2,382	3,000	2,382
4	0.735	4,000	2,940	2,000	1,470
5	0.681	5,000	3,405	1,000	681
			$ (633)		$ 591

[a] $1 \div (1.08)^1 = 0.926$
[b] $1 \div (1.08)^2 = 0.857$

Even though plan B and plan A have the same total cash inflows over the five years, plan B is preferred to plan A because it has greater cash inflows occurring earlier.

Capital Budgeting:
A Closer Look

Tax Is a Relevant Cost

Investment projects such as a major year-round destination resort require managers to consider several dimensions of the decision, including tourism trends, economic cycles, the environment, and, ultimately, discounted cash flows. One of the key considerations is the effect on cash of tax paid when investments are made in projects of this type. Intrawest ULC has developed year-round destination resorts such as Whistler-Blackcomb in British Columbia and Mont Tremblant in Quebec, pictured here, at costs exceeding $200 million.

After studying this chapter, you should be able to

1. Analyze the impact of income taxes on operating and capital cash flows and calculate the after-tax NPV of investments

2. Apply the total-project approach and the differential approach appropriately to different capital budgeting decisions

3. Apply the concepts of real and nominal ROR to account for inflation in capital budgeting

4. Analyze alternative approaches used to recognize the degree of risk in capital budgeting projects and explain the usefulness of excess present value index in capital budgeting

5. Implement capital budgeting in not-for-profit organizations and explain why IRR and NPV may rank projects differently

In this chapter the focus is on an exceptionally important cash outflow—income tax. Different tax regimes affect different types of capital investments. The Canada Revenue Agency (CRA) enforces the Canadian Income Tax Act. Managers must analyze the effects of both tax and inflation as they make capital budgeting decisions. Tax and inflation are considered external factors affecting corporate decisions to undertake investment projects because no single corporation can initiate or change either the rate of taxation or the rate of inflation. We discuss risk and uncertainty in capital budgeting, capital budgeting in not-for-profit organizations, and issues in implementing the NPV and IRR decision methods.

The Income War Tax Act became legislation in 1917. This was the first time in Canada's history that the federal government was given the legal right to tax income. In 1942, automatic deduction at source began. In 1946 the Income Tax Appeal Board was born, and by 1983 it became the Tax Court of Canada, although it was 1993 before this court achieved sole jurisdiction over income tax appeals processes. Today Canadian federal and most provincial governments impose both sales and value-added taxes (PST and GST), corporate surtax (a percentage of tax paid), land transfer tax, and large corporations tax. Our discussion will be confined to the effect of capital cost allowance (CCA) on cash paid in corporate income tax.

INCOME TAXES AND CAPITAL BUDGETING

1 Analyze the impact of income taxes on operating and capital cash flows and calculate the after-tax NPV of investments

Income taxes are mandatory cash disbursements and therefore an important cash flow consideration. Income taxes almost always influence the amount and/or the timing of cash flows. Their basic role in capital budgeting is no different from that of any other cash disbursement. Payment of income tax tends to narrow the cash differences between projects. The Canadian federal and provincial governments raise money through corporate income taxes. Income tax rates differ considerably, and thus overall corporate income tax rates can vary widely.

Income tax rates are progressive and depend on the amount of pretax income. Larger pretax income is taxed at higher rates. In capital budgeting, the relevant rate is the **marginal income tax rate**; that is, the tax rate paid on additional amounts of pretax income. Suppose corporations pay income taxes of 15% on the first $50,000 of pretax income and 30% on pretax income over $50,000. What is the *marginal income tax* rate of a company with $75,000 of pretax income? It is 30%, because 30% of any *additional* income over $50,000 will be paid in taxes. In contrast, the company's *average income tax rate* is only 20% (that is, 15% × $50,000 + 30% × $25,000 = $15,000 ÷ $75,000 of pretax income). When we assess tax effects of capital budgeting decisions, we will always use the *marginal* tax rate because that is the rate applied to the additional cash flows generated by a proposed project.

THINKING CRITICALLY

Why isn't the average tax rate 22.5%? Explain in a sentence or two. Read on for further discussion of this topic.

The more arithmetically accurate term is the *weighted* average corporate tax rate. As you can see, each increment of pretax income is weighted or multiplied by its respective tax rate to provide the dollar values. The dollar values are summed then divided by the total pretax income. The result is referred to as the average tax rate.

Organizations that pay income taxes report their net income to the public using the CICA standards in order to obtain a clean audit opinion. These standards allow managers to choose among amortization methods and, when necessary, change from one method to another. The amortization expense deducted to calculate pretax income would be at the discretion of corporate managers. This the Canadian Revenue Agency (CRA) does not permit. This is why governments have created laws that, for purposes of paying tax, require corporations to deduct capital cost allowance (CCA) when calculating their taxable income.

Legally, the taxable income reported to CRA on a confidential basis differs from mandatory public disclosure under CICA standards. This means that the tax expense on the statement of income, an accrual, will differ from the cash tax paid to the government. The difference between the accrual and the cash flow amounts accumulates as future tax liabilities, which will eventually be paid. This means that the CCA that affects cash flow in the form of corporate income tax paid each year is relevant to assessing investment projects. Amortization, however, is not. In this chapter we are concerned with effects on the cash outflows for taxes. We focus on the tax *reporting rules*, not those for public financial reporting.

TAX EFFECT ON OPERATING CASH FLOWS

Recognizing the impact of income taxes on operating cash flows is straightforward. If a capital proposal results in a reduction in costs, for example an annual cost saving of $60,000, then the company's taxable income will increase by $60,000 all other things being equal. If the company has a marginal tax rate of 40%, then the company's income taxes will increase by $24,000 ($60,000 × 0.40). A net annual after-tax savings of $36,000 results ($60,000 − $24,000). This means the after-tax savings can be calculated quickly as $60,000 × (1 minus the tax rate) or $60,000 × 0.60 = $36,000.

If operating expenses increase by $250,000, then the taxable income will decrease by $250,000. If the company has a 40% marginal tax rate, then the tax saving will be $100,000 ($250,000 × 0.40). An after-tax cost increase of $150,000 results [$250,000 × (1 − 0.40)]. Thus, to incorporate the impact of income taxes on operating cash flows poses no real difficulty. The difficulty occurs in the recognition of the tax effects of investment expenditures in capital equipment.

TAX EFFECT ON INVESTMENT CASH FLOWS

In financial reporting, the expenditure on capital equipment results in the recording of the asset and the related amortization expense over the asset's useful economic life. Amortization rates and policies are determined by the company's management and vary from company to company even for the same asset.

GOVERNANCE ISSUES

Tax Is Mandatory

The CRA is authorized to investigate and undertake both civil and criminal proceedings against those who fail to accurately report taxable income and pay the appropriate amount of tax. Criminal investigations of tax evasion or fraud in 2005–2006 achieved a 94% conviction rate. The 293 convictions resulted in approximately $14.4 million in fines and over 33 years of jail sentences. Fines imposed by the courts can be as high as 200% of the amount owing, and taxpayers must still pay the taxes owed and any other civil penalties and interest imposed by CRA. The Special Enforcements Program specializes in audits of people suspected of criminal activity. Proceeds from crime are also taxable. The 1,349 audits undertaken identified an additional $80 million in taxes owed. All prosecutions are public documents, and CRA itself ensures media coverage of convictions to deter criminal activity.

Source: Canada Revenue Agency Fact Sheet www.cra-arc.gc.ca/nwsrm/fctshts/2006/nv/fs061123-eng.html, accessed July 10, 2008.

To apply a consistent set of regulations and to provide a means to implement government initiatives, the federal government has implemented its own system of **capital cost allowance (CCA)**. The Income Tax Act (ITA) does not permit a company to deduct amortization expense in determining taxable income, but rather a company is allowed to deduct CCA. If you like, CCA is the legally required income tax counterpart to annual amortization expense in financial reporting.

The income tax statutes for intangible assets such as patents, copyrights, goodwill, and trademarks differ as does the terminology. The **eligible capital expenditure** is the acquisition cost of the intangible asset. The **eligible capital property** is 75% of the acquisition cost of the intangible asset. The full cost is not deductible because the asset is considered to provide indefinite benefit. Intangible assets, by definition, have an indefinite useful life, and the annual deduction is called the **cumulative eligible capital amount (CECA)**, calculated at 7% on a declining balance basis. The balance remaining after deducting CECA is called the **cumulative eligible capital (CEC)** pool. If the intangible asset is assigned a definite life, then it is not an eligible capital property, and CCA must be deducted for tax purposes.[1]

CAPITAL COST ALLOWANCE—DECLINING BALANCE CLASSES

The ITA assigns all capital purchases to a CCA class. For example, a desk would qualify as a Class 8 asset that includes all furniture and fixtures. Class 8 has a predetermined rate of 20% declining balance capital cost allowance. Exhibit 22-1 depicts the calculation of CCA for a desk that costs $10,000.

A number of years ago, a company could deduct a full year's worth of CCA on any asset acquired during the year, as long as the company had been in business the entire year. Thus, companies with a December 31 year-end would buy assets on or about December 31 and claim a full year's deduction even though the asset had not really been used to generate the income. To minimize this problem, the government implemented the so-called "half-year rule."

The **half-year rule** assumes that all net additions are purchased in the middle of the year, and thus only one-half of the stated CCA rate is allowed in the first year. Thus in year 1 of the example in Exhibit 22-1, the CCA is $1,000 or 1/2 times 20% multiplied by the $10,000 capital expenditure. This leaves a balance of $9,000 ($10,000 – $1,000), which is known as the **unamortized capital cost (UCC)**.

In year 2 and all succeeding years, the rate of 20% is applied to the UCC of the previous year. This results in a declining amount of capital cost allowance for each year. Even after the 25 years shown in Exhibit 22-1, a UCC of $42 remains and will require 15 more years to get to a zero balance (which in practice can only be obtained by rounding to the nearest dollar).

The CCA of each year is deducted in the calculation of a company's taxable income. Thus, the CCA is not a cash flow. Rather we must multiply the CCA of each year by the company's marginal tax rate to calculate the actual tax savings in each year. In Chapter 21, we recognized the time value of money. Thus, to determine the present value of the tax savings, we would need to multiply the tax savings of each year by the present value factor from the CCA list for each year at the company's required rate of return (say 10%).

This, as you could well imagine, would be a long and labourious task to perform for each capital proposal. An efficient way to calculate the present value of the tax savings is to use the following **tax shield formula**:

$$\text{Present value of tax savings} = \left(\text{Investment} \times \text{marginal tax rate} \right) \left(\frac{\text{CCA rate}}{\text{CCA rate} + \text{required rate of return}} \right) \frac{(2 + \text{required rate of return})}{2\,(1 + \text{required rate of return})}$$

[1]Canada Revenue Agency, "What Is? Eligible Capital Property," www.cra-arc.gc.ca/tx/bsnss/tpcs/slprtnr/rprtng/ece-dca/whts-eng.html, accessed July 8, 2008.

EXHIBIT 22-1
Capital Cost Allowance Illustration

CCA—Class 8 Rate is 20% Declining Balance (rounded to the nearest dollar)			
Year 1 (day 1) addition	$10,000	Year 13 UCC	618
CCA year 1 (10%)	1,000	CCA year 14 (20%)	124
Year end UCC	9,000	Year 14 UCC	494
CCA year 2 (20%)	1,800	CCA year 15 (20%)	99
Year 2 UCC	7,200	Year 15 UCC	395
CCA year 3 (20%)	1,440	CCA year 16 (20%)	79
Year 3 UCC	5,760	Year 16 UCC	316
CCA year 4 (20%)	1,152	CCA year 17 (20%)	63
Year 4 UCC	4,608	Year 17 UCC	253
CCA year 5 (20%)	922	CCA year 18 (20%)	51
Year 5 UCC	3,686	Year 18 UCC	202
CCA year 6 (20%)	737	CCA year 19 (20%)	40
Year 6 UCC	2,949	Year 19 UCC	162
CCA year 7 (20%)	590	CCA year 20 (20%)	32
Year 7 UCC	2,359	Year 20 UCC	130
CCA year 8 (20%)	472	CCA year 21 (20%)	26
Year 8 UCC	1,887	Year 21 UCC	104
CCA year 9 (20%)	377	CCA year 22 (20%)	21
Year 9 UCC	1,510	Year 22 UCC	83
CCA year 10 (20%)	302	CCA year 23 (20%)	17
Year 10 UCC	1,208	Year 23 UCC	66
CCA year 11 (20%)	242	CCA year 24 (20%)	13
Year 11 UCC	966	Year 24 UCC	53
CCA year 12 (20%)	193	CCA year 25 (20%)	11
Year 12 UCC	773	Year 25 UCC	$42
CCA year 12 (20%)	155		

In the case of the $10,000 desk, the present value of the tax savings from deducting CCA, commonly referred to as the tax shield, is $2,548, computed as follows assuming a 10% required rate of return:

$$\text{Tax shield} = (\$10,000 \times 40\%) \left(\frac{20\%}{20\% + 10\%} \right) \left(\frac{(2 + 10\%)}{2(1 + 10\%)} \right)$$

$$= \$4,000 \times 0.667 \times 0.955$$
$$= \$2,668 \times 0.955$$
$$= \$2,548$$

Therefore, the net after-tax cost of the desk is $7,452, or $10,000 less $2,548.

A detailed proof of the tax shield formula is not necessary for our purposes, but some explanation will be useful. The first component of the formula, investment times the marginal tax rate, computes the total tax savings over the life of the asset from the CCA deduction. The $4,000, however, does not incorporate any time value of money considerations.

The second component, the CCA rate divided by the sum of the CCA rate plus the required rate of return, calculates the present values of all the annual tax savings assuming the half-year rule did not exist. This is important to note when residual values are discussed later in the chapter.

The third component incorporates an adjustment for the half-year rule. For example, in the above scenario, the tax shield was reduced to 95.5% of the benefit that existed before the introduction of the half-year rule. Most CCA classes use the declining balance method. However, occasionally the straight-line method is used, in which the CCA is the same for each year except the first and last years, which have one-half of the CCA due to the half-year rule. It is also important to note that CCA applies only to tangible assets.

CCA CLASSES AND RATES

Companies may claim up to the percentages shown of the UCC in any year for the specified class of tangible assets (see the table below). The legislation regarding CCA allows this annual deduction only if the asset can be classified under the act; otherwise no deduction is permitted. In establishing the initial value of the asset, if the company has or is entitled to receive financial assistance to acquire the asset, then the dollar value of this assistance may reduce the asset's initial value. In addition, if during the useful life of the asset its value is reappraised downwards, then the UCC must also decrease.

Class	Maximum CCA	Tangible Assets in Pool
1	4%	Buildings or other structures, including component parts acquired after 1987
3	5%	Buildings or other structures, including component parts acquired before 1988
8	20%	Miscellaneous tangible capital property and machinery or equipment not included in another class
9	25%	Electrical generating equipment, radar and radio equipment acquired before 1976
10	30%	Automotive equipment and general-purpose electronic data processing equipment with its systems software
12	100%	Tools or utensils costing less than $200, videotape, certified feature films, computer software
29		Property used in manufacturing or processing acquired before 1988 (2 years straight-line)
39		Property used in manufacturing or processing acquired after 1987 (1988–40%; 1989–35%; 1990–30%; after 1990–25%)

Source: Canada Revenue Agency, "Sources of Depreciable Property," www.cra-arc.gc.ca/tx/bsnss/tpcs/slprtnr/rprtng/cptl/dprcbl-eng.html#buildings, accessed July 8, 2008.

TRADEINS AND DISPOSALS OF CAPITAL ASSETS

When a capital asset is traded in on another asset or is sold, we do not need to concern ourselves with the net tax book value of the asset.

Assume that a company's Class 8 UCC for all of its furniture and fixtures is $50,000, as shown in Exhibit 22-2, at the end of year 3. Let us also assume that included in the $50,000 is the remaining UCC on the desk of $5,760.

If in year 4 the desk was traded in on a new desk, where the price of the new desk is $12,000, and $4,000 was allowed as a tradein, the Class 8 UCC would increase by $8,000. Note that the CCA system works on a pool basis, in that we are not concerned with the UCC of the specific desk being sold. Rather we are concerned only with the net cash flows. The UCC of the class that existed before the disposal is reduced only by the amount of the cash received. Thus, the actual amount of the UCC of the specific asset is irrelevant to the decision. In this example, the net capital expenditure of $8,000 is the relevant cash flow.

Continuing with the example in Exhibit 22-2, the CCA for year 4 is $10,800. This is a combination of the CCA at the rate of 20% on the opening UCC of $50,000 ($10,000) and the CCA at the half-year-rule rate of 10% on the net addition of $8,000 ($800).

EXHIBIT 22-2
Tradein of a Capital Asset

CCA—Class 8	
Ending UCC—year 3	$50,000
Purchase	12,000
Less: Tradein	(4,000)
Net change in UCC	8,000
Revised UCC	58,000
Year 4—CCA	
20% × $50,000	10,000
10% × $8,000	800
Total CCA	10,800
UCC—year 4	$47,200

Thus, as shown in Exhibit 22-3, the net after-tax present value of the cost of the new desk is $5,964. This amount recognizes the fact that the tax shield of $2,036 on the net addition of $8,000 must recognize the half-year rule.

If in the above scenario a new desk had not been purchased, but rather the old desk was sold for $4,000, the CCA would be 20% of $46,000 or $9,200. Note the half-year rule does not apply to net disposals; that is, where the amount of disposals exceeds the amount of additions during a given year.

From Exhibit 22-3, note that the sale of $4,000 reduces the future CCA and results in a lost tax shield of $1,067. Thus, the net after-tax present value of the sale is $2,933.

SIMPLIFYING ASSUMPTIONS

It is useful to note that a number of simplifying assumptions have been made when using the tax shield formula:

1. We have assumed that the company's marginal tax rate will remain the same (at 40% in the above examples). Further, the above examples also assume that the company will have a taxable income each year.

2. Although it is uncommon, governments can change the CCA rates that we have assumed to be constant.

EXHIBIT 22-3
Net Capital Cash Flow of Tradeins and Disposals

Tradein:	Purchase price	$12,000
	Tradein	(4,000)
	Net cash payment	8,000
	Tax shield[a]	2,036
	NPV cash outflow	$ 5,964
Disposal:	Sales price	4,000
	Lost tax shield[b]	1,067
	NPV cash inflow	$ 2,933

[a]Includes the half-year adjustment:

$$(\$8,000 \times 40\%) \times \left(\frac{20\%}{20\% + 10\%} \right) \times \left(\frac{2 + 10\%}{2(1 + 10\%)} \right)$$

[b]Excludes the half-year adjustment

$$(\$4,000 \times 40\%) \times \left(\frac{20\%}{20\% + 10\%} \right)$$

3. We have also assumed that all CCA tax savings occur at the year-end. In reality, companies make monthly instalments. However, the additional cost of attempting to be more precise is not warranted, given the degree of uncertainty that already exists in the estimation of the cash flows.

INCOME TAX COMPLICATIONS

In the foregoing illustrations, we deliberately avoided many possible income tax complications. As all taxpaying citizens know, income taxes are affected by many intricacies, including progressive tax rates, loss carrybacks and carryforwards, varying provincial income taxes, capital gains, distinctions between capital assets and other assets, offsets of losses against related gains, exchanges of property of like kind, exempt income, and so forth. Keep in mind that changes in the tax law occur each year. Always check the current tax law before calculating the tax consequences of a decision.

The meanings of amortization and book value are widely misunderstood. Pause and consider their role in decisions. Suppose a bank has some printing equipment with a book value of $30,000, an expected terminal disposal value of zero, a current disposal value of $12,000, and a remaining useful life of three years. For simplicity, assume that straight-line amortization of $10,000 yearly will be taken.

In particular, note that the inputs to the decision model are the predicted income tax effects on cash. The book loss of $18,000 or the amortization of $10,000 may be necessary for making *predictions*. By themselves, however, they are not inputs to DCF decision models.

The following points summarize the role of amortization regarding the replacement of equipment:

◆ **Initial investment.** The amount paid for (and hence amortization on) old equipment is irrelevant except for its effect on tax cash flows. In contrast, the amount paid for new equipment is relevant, because it is an expected future cost that will not be incurred if replacement is rejected.

◆ **Do not double-count.** The investment in equipment is a one-time outlay at time zero, so it should not be double-counted as an outlay in the form of amortization. Amortization by itself is irrelevant; it is not a cash outlay.

◆ **Relation to income tax cash flows.** Relevant quantities were defined in Chapter 4 as expected future data that will differ among alternatives. Given this definition, book values and past amortization are irrelevant in all capital budgeting decision models. The relevant item is the *income tax cash effect*, not the book value or the amortization.

MyAccountingLab

ALTERNATIVE APPROACHES TO CAPITAL BUDGETING

❷ Apply the total-project approach and the differential approach appropriately to different capital budgeting decisions

We turn now to a fuller discussion of how income taxes can affect cash inflows and outflows and also how they influence managers' decisions. We focus on the information-acquisition and selection stages of capital budgeting, highlight the effect of income taxes, and use the net present value method for the formal financial analysis.

Example: Potato Supreme produces potato products for sale to supermarkets and other retail outlets. It is considering replacing an old packaging machine (purchased three years ago) with a new, more efficient packaging machine that has recently been introduced. The new machine is less labour-intensive and has lower operating costs than the old machine. For simplicity, we assume the following:

1. All cash outflows or inflows occur at the end of the year (even though cash operating costs generally occur throughout the year).

2. The tax effects of cash inflows and outflows occur at the same time that the inflows and outflows occur.

3. The income tax rate is 30% each year.

4. The equipment is one of several assets that qualify as CCA Class 8, with a CCA rate of up to 20% declining balance. Potato Supreme takes the maximum rate each year.

5. Both the old and the new machine have the same working capital requirements.

6. Potato Supreme is a profitable company.

Summary data for the two machines are as follows:

	Old Machine	New Machine
Original cost	$ 87,500	$200,000
Accumulated amortization	$ 37,500	—
Current book value	$ 50,000	—
Current disposal price	$ 26,000	—
Proceeds of disposition, 4 years from now	$ 6,000	$ 20,000
Annual cash operating costs	$250,000	$150,000
Remaining useful life	4 years	4 years
After-tax required rate of return	10%	10%
Capital cost allowance rate	20% (declining balance)	20% (declining balance)

Potato Supreme uses the net present value method to evaluate whether it should replace the old with the new packaging machine immediately or in four years' time. As in the Lifetime Care example of Chapter 21, the key point in net present value analysis is to identify the relevant cash flows. To emphasize the ideas of relevance, Chapter 21 used the **differential approach**, which analyzes only relevant cash flows—those future cash outflows and inflows that differ between alternatives. The differential approach is generally faster when there are only two alternatives.

When the number of alternatives is more than two, the differential approach becomes unwieldy because it forces the analyst into difficult calculations of differences among multiple alternatives. Companies then use the *total-project approach*.

The **total-project approach** calculates the present value of *all* future cash inflows and outflows under each alternative separately. It does not require the identification of cash flows that differ among alternatives. The total-project approach requires the following:

1. Calculate the present value of all cash inflows and outflows under the status quo alternative.

2. Separately calculate the present value of all cash inflows and outflows under another alternative.

We use the Potato Supreme example to illustrate the two steps of the total-project approach. We then use the differential approach to show that both approaches give the same net present value. The following categories of cash flows are considered in both approaches:

a. Initial machine investment
b. Tax shield on initial investment
c. Cash flow from current disposal of old machine
d. Lost tax shield from current disposal of machine

e. Recurring after-tax cash operating flows
f. Cash flow from proceeds of disposition of old machine. Other assets remain in this asset class.
g. Lost tax shield from terminal disposal of machine

TOTAL-PROJECT APPROACH

1. *Calculate the present value of total cash flows of replacing the old packaging machine in four years' time.* Under this alternative, cash flow categories that specifically pertain to the new machine are not relevant. But the purchase price is relevant when calculating item g, the lost tax shield. If the purchase price of new equipment exceeds proceeds of disposition of the old equipment, **net addition**, the half-year rule applies.

   a. *Initial machine investment.* No new investment is necessary if Potato Supreme keeps the old packaging machine. Exhibit 22-4, item a, shows an initial machine investment of $0 in year 0.

   b. *Tax shield on initial investment.* As there is no new investment, there is no additional tax shield.

   c. *Cash flow from current disposal of old machine.* Since the old machine is kept and not disposed of, Exhibit 22-4, item c, shows after-tax cash flow from current disposal of old machine of $0 in year 0.

   d. *Lost tax shield from current disposal of machine.* As the old machine is not sold, no tax shield adjustments are required.

   e. *Recurring after-tax cash operating flows.*

Recurring cash operating flows (costs) for the old machine	$(250,000)
Deduct: Income tax savings at 30% of $250,000	75,000
Recurring after-tax cash operating flows	$(175,000)

   After-tax cash operating flows of $(175,000) in years 1 to 4 appear as relevant cash outflows in Exhibit 22-4, item e. Our example assumes that Potato Supreme's income tax rate is 30% each year. When future tax rates are uncertain, analysts must predict the tax rate applicable for each year of a project.

   f. *Cash flow from proceeds of disposition of old machine. Other assets remain in this asset class.*

Proceeds of disposition at end of year 4	$6,000

   The cash flow of $6,000 from the proceeds of disposition of the old machine appears as a cash inflow in year 4 of Exhibit 22-4, item f.

   g. *Lost tax shield.* The proceeds of disposition of $6,000 would reduce the CCA pool by $6,000, and thus reduce the future cash savings from capital cost allowance deductions by $1,145.

   $$(\$6,000 \times 0.30) \times \frac{0.20}{(0.20 + 0.10)} \times \frac{(2 + 0.10)}{2(1 + 0.10)}$$
   $$= \$1,800 \times 2 \div 3 \times 0.955 = \$1,146$$

   Exhibit 22-4 presents all after-tax cash flows that would arise if Potato Supreme continued to use the old packaging machine. Each cash flow is multiplied by its corresponding present value discount factor to give its present value. The total present value is $(551,435).

2. Calculate the present value of total cash flows of immediately replacing the old packaging machine.

   a. *Initial machine investment.* The original cost of the new packaging machine is $200,000. This amount appears as a cash outflow in year 0 in Exhibit 22-5, item a.

EXHIBIT 22-4

Total-Project Approach for Potato Supreme: After-Tax Analysis of Replacing Old Machine in Four Years' Time

	Total Present Value	Present Value Discount Factors at 10%	Sketch of Relevant After-Tax Cash Flows				
End of Year:			0	1	2	3	4
Explanations for the after-tax cash flow amounts are given on pp. 1060–1062.							
a. Initial machine investment	$ 0 ← 1.000 ←		$0				
c. After-tax cash flow from immediate proceeds of disposition	0 ← 1.000 ←		0				
e. Recurring after-tax cash operating flows	(554,750) ← 3.170 ←--------------			$(175,000)	$(175,000)	$(175,000)	$(175,000)
f. Cash flow from proceeds of disposition in four years' time	4,098 ← 0.683 ←---						6,000
g. Lost tax shield from the disposal in four years' time	(783) ← 0.683 ←---						($1,146)
Total present value of all cash flows if Potato Supreme replaces the old machine in four years' time	$(551,435)						

Note: Parentheses denote relevant cash outflows throughout all exhibits in this chapter.

EXHIBIT 22-5

Total-Project Approach for Potato Supreme: After-Tax Analysis of Immediately Purchasing the New Machine

	Total Present Value	Present Value Discount Factors at 10%	Sketch of Relevant After-Tax Cash Flows				
End of Year:			0	1	2	3	4
Explanations for the after-tax cash flow amounts are given on pp. 1060–1062.							
a. Initial machine investment	$(200,000) ← 1.000 ←		$(200,000)				
b. Tax shield	38,200 ← 1.000 ←		$ 38,200				
	$(161,800)						
c. Cash flow from immediate proceeds of disposition of old machine	26,000 ← 1.000 ←		$ 26,000				
d. Lost tax shield from immediate disposal of old machine	$ (4,966) ← 1.000 ←		$ (4,966)				
Net investment	$(140,766)						
e. Recurring after-tax cash operating flows	(332,850) ← 3.170 ←--------------			$(105,000)	$(105,000)	$(105,000)	$(105,000)
f. Cash flow from proceeds of disposition of the new machine in four years' time	13,660 ← 0.683 ←---						$20,000
g. Lost tax shield from disposal of the new machine in four years' time	(2,732) ← 0.683 ←---						(4.000)
Total present value of all cash flows if Potato Supreme immediately replaces the old machine	$(462,688)						

b. *Tax shield.* The original cost of $200,000 will generate a cash savings from capital cost allowance of $38,160. This amount is determined by using the tax shield formula.

$$(\$200,000 \times 0.30) \times \frac{0.20}{(0.20 + 0.10)} \times \frac{(2 + 0.10)}{2(1 + 0.10)}$$

$$= \$60,000 \times \frac{2}{3} \times \frac{2.1}{2.2}$$

$$= \$40,000 \times 0.955 = \$38,200$$

Recall that the tax shield formula calculates the present value of the cash flows.

c. *Cash flow from immediate proceeds of disposition.*

Immediate proceeds of disposition	$26,000

Review what is included in the present value analysis. It is the immediate *cash inflow* from the proceeds of disposition of the asset. The book value of the old machine and the loss on disposal do not themselves affect cash flow. The book value, however, enters into the calculation of the loss on disposal of the asset, which in turn affects the accounting net income.

d. *Lost tax shield from immediate disposal of old machine.* The current disposal of $26,000 would reduce the cash savings from future capital cost allowance by $4,966.

$$(\$26,000 \times 0.30) \times \frac{0.20}{(0.20 + 0.10)} \times \frac{(2 + 0.10)}{2(1 + 0.10)}$$

$$= \$7,800 \times \frac{2}{3} \times 0.955$$

$$= \$4,966$$

In this case, the half-year rule applies to the calculation of the tax shield formula because the net addition is a positive number ($200,000 – $26,000).

e. *Recurring after-tax cash operating flows.*

Recurring cash operating flows (costs) for the new machine	$(150,000)
Deduct: Income tax savings (30% × $150,000)	45,000
Recurring after-tax cash operating flows	$(105,000)

The after-tax cash operating flows of $(105,000) in years 1 to 4 appear as relevant cash outflows in Exhibit 22-5, item e.

f. *Cash flow from proceeds of disposition of new machine. Other assets remain in this asset class.*

Proceeds from disposition of new machine	$20,000

g. *Lost tax shield from disposition of new machine in four years' time.* Assume no future replacement for the new machine. Therefore, the net addition ($0 – $20,000) will be negative and the half-year rule will not apply. The proceeds of disposition of $20,000 would reduce the future cash savings from CCA at the maximum rate of 20% by $2,732.

$$(\$20,000 \times 0.30) \times \frac{0.20}{(0.20 + 0.10)}$$

$$= \$6,000 \times \frac{2}{3} = \$4,000$$

Exhibit 22-5 summarizes the relevant after-tax cash flows that would occur if Potato Supreme replaced its old machine immediately. Present values are derived by multiplying cash flows by the corresponding present value discount factors. The total present value of cash flows equals $(462,688). Recall from Exhibit 22-4 that the present value of after-tax cash flows of replacing the old machine in four years' time is $(551,435). The decision to replace the old machine with the new machine immediately has a positive net present value of $88,747 ($551,435 – $462,688) and is therefore preferred.

DIFFERENTIAL APPROACH

Unlike the two-step total-project approach, the differential approach is a one-step method that includes only those cash inflows and outflows that *differ* between the two alternatives. The differential approach compares the cash outflows arising from replacing the old machine with the savings in future cash outflows resulting from using the new machine rather than the old machine. We will now examine the differences in cash flows between the keep and replace alternatives in the Potato Supreme example using the categories of cash flows that we described earlier.

a. *Initial machine investment* of $200,000 for the new machine (see Exhibit 22-5) appears as a cash outflow in year 0 in Exhibit 22-6, item a.

c. *Cash flow from immediate proceeds of disposition of old machine* of $26,000 (see Exhibit 22-5) appears as a cash inflow in year 0 in Exhibit 22-6, item c. The initial machine investment, $200,000, minus the cash flow from current disposal of the old machine, $26,000, is the net initial investment of $174,000, shown as a cash outflow in year 0 in Exhibit 22-6.

b. net of d. *Tax shield.* The net initial investment of $174,000 would increase the CCA pool by this amount and thus would generate cash savings from

EXHIBIT 22-6
Differential Approach for Potato Supreme: After-Tax Analysis of Replacing Old Machine

	Total Present Value	Present Value Discount Factors at 10%	Sketch of Relevant After-Tax Cash Flows				
		End of Year:	0	1	2	3	4
Explanations for the after-tax inflow amounts are given on p. 1062.							
a. Initial machine investment	$(200,000) ← 1.000 ←		$(200,000)				
c. Cash flow from immediate proceeds of disposition of old machine	26,000 ← 1.000 ←		26,000				
Net initial investment	(174,000)		(174,000)				
b. net of d. Tax shield (Exhibit 22-5)	33,234 ← 1.000 ←		33,234				
	(140,766)						
e. Recurring after-tax cash operating flows	221,900	3.170		$70,000	$70,000	$70,000	$70,000
f. Cash flow from proceeds of disposition of old machine in four years' time	(4,098) ← 0.683 ◄-------						$ (6,000)
g. Lost tax shield from disposal of old machine in four years' time	783 ← 0.683 ◄-------						$ 1,146
	(3,315)						
f. Cash flow from proceeds of disposition of new machine in four years' time = ($551,435 − $462,688) = $88,747	13,660 ← 0.683 ◄-------						$20,000
g. Lost tax shield from disposal of new machine in four years' time	(2,732) ← 0.683 ◄-------						$ (4,000)
	10,928						
Net present value if old machine is replaced immediately	$ 88,747						

CCA from now to infinity. The cash savings would be $33,234, a figure determined by using the tax shield formula:

$$(\$174,000 \times 0.30) \times \frac{0.20}{(0.20 + 0.10)} \times \frac{(2 + 0.10)}{2(1 + 0.10)}$$

$$= \$52,200 \times \frac{2}{3} \times 0.955$$

$$= \$33,234$$

e. *Recurring after-tax cash operating flows.* Replacing the old machine results in lower after-tax cash operating costs, as follows:

Recurring after-tax cash operating costs if old machine kept (Exhibit 22-4, item e)	$175,000
Deduct: Recurring after-tax cash operating costs if machine replaced (Exhibit 22-5, item e)	105,000
Savings in recurring after-tax cash operating costs if machine replaced	$ 70,000

Exhibit 22-6, item e, shows this $70,000 increase in recurring after-tax cash operating flows in years 1–4.

f. **net of g.** *Cash flow from proceeds of disposition of each machine in four years' time, net of the lost tax shield of each respective disposal.* The immediate disposition of the old machine results in no disposition of this machine in four years' time. This opportunity cost for the old machine based on Exhibit 22-4 is $3,315 ($4,098 − $793) for the old machine. The opportunity cost for the new machine based on Exhibit 22-5 is $10,928 ($13,550 − $2,732).

In Exhibit 22-5, the terminal disposal of the new machine for $20,000 will result in a lost tax shield of $2,732, the net of which is $10,928.

Both the total-project approach (Exhibits 22-4 and 22-5) and the differential approach (Exhibit 22-6) result in a net present value of $88,747 in favour of immediately replacing the old packaging machine with the new one. When comparing alternatives, these two approaches will always give the same net present value.

MyAccountingLab

ASSESS YOUR MASTERY

To check your understanding of the material in Learning Objective ❷, go to the *Mastery Questions* section at the end of this chapter and complete Learning Objective ❷ question 1.

CAPITAL BUDGETING AND INFLATION

❶ Apply the concepts of real and nominal ROR to account for inflation in capital budgeting

It is important to account for **inflation** in capital budgeting because declines in the general purchasing power of the monetary unit (say, dollars) will inflate future cash flows above what they would have been had there been no inflation. Inflation can be defined as the decline in the general purchasing power of the monetary unit (for example, the dollar in Canada or the yen in Japan). We present how inflation can be explicitly recognized in capital budgeting analysis. Because of inflation, the cash inflows for future periods will be measured in dollars that have less value than the dollars invested in the project in year 0. Failure to take inflation into account will overstate the financial return of the project.

An inflation rate of 10% in one year means that what you could buy with $100 (say) at the start of the year will cost you $110 [$100 + (10% × $100)] at the end of the year. Prices increase as more money chases fewer goods. Some countries—for example, Brazil, Israel, Mexico, and Russia—have experienced annual inflation rates of 15% to more than 100%. Even an annual inflation rate of 5% over, say, a five-year period can result in sizable declines in the general purchasing power of the monetary unit over that time.

REAL AND NOMINAL RATES OF RETURN

When analyzing inflation, distinguish between the real rate of return and the nominal rate of return:

- ◆ **Real rate of return** is the rate of return required to cover only investment risk.
- ◆ **Nominal rate of return** is the rate of return required to cover investment risk and the anticipated decline, due to inflation, in the general purchasing power of the cash that the investment generates. The rates of return (or interest) earned on the financial markets are nominal rates, because they compensate investors for both risk and inflation.

We next describe the relationship between real and nominal rates of return. Assume that the real rate of return for investments in high-risk cellular data transmission equipment at Network Communications is 20% and that the expected inflation rate is 10%. The nominal rate of return is:[2]

$$\text{Nominal rate} = (1 + \text{Real rate})(1 + \text{Inflation rate}) - 1$$
$$= (1 + 0.20)(1 + 0.10) - 1$$
$$= [(1.20)(1.10)] - 1 = 1.32 - 1 = 0.32$$

The nominal rate of return is also related to the real rate of return and the inflation rate as follows:

Real rate of return	0.20
Inflation rate	0.10
Combination (0.20 × 0.10)	0.02
Nominal rate of return	0.32

Note that the nominal rate is slightly higher than the real rate (0.20) plus the inflation rate (0.10). The reason is that the nominal rate recognizes that inflation also decreases the purchasing power of the real rate of return earned during the year.

THINKING CRITICALLY

How does inflation differ from foreign-currency exchange fluctuation? Explain in a sentence or two. Read on for further discussion of this topic.

Foreign-currency exchange rates determine the domestic dollar value of cash flows from non-domestic investments. Foreign-currency exchange rates are based on nominal dollar values. The foreign-currency exchange rate tells you how much foreign money you can purchase with your Canadian dollar. The effect of inflation considered in this chapter applies to the erosion or improvement to the purchasing power of the domestic currency. There is a relationship therefore between inflation and the quantity of foreign currency a Canadian dollar will purchase because inflation erodes all purchasing power. If the cash flow from foreign investments has already been translated into nominal Canadian dollars, the quantity of Canadian dollar–denominated foreign cash flow has already been calculated. What remains in the capital budgeting process is to convert the rate of return from nominal to the inflation-adjusted real rate of return.

---

[2]The real rate of return can be expressed in terms of the nominal rate of return as follows:

$$\text{Real rate} = \frac{(1 + \text{Nominal rate})}{(1 + \text{Inflation rate})} - 1 = \frac{(1 + 0.32)}{(1 + 0.10)} - 1 = 0.20$$

NET PRESENT VALUE METHOD AND INFLATION

The watchword when incorporating inflation into the net present value (NPV) method is *internal consistency*. There are two internally consistent approaches:

◆ *Nominal approach*. Predict cash inflows and outflows in nominal monetary units and use a nominal rate as the required rate of return.

◆ *Real approach*. Predict cash inflows and outflows in real monetary units and use a real rate as the required rate of return.

Consider an investment that is expected to generate sales of 100 units and a net cash inflow of $1,000 ($10 per unit) each year for two years *absent inflation*. If inflation of 10% is expected each year, net cash inflows from the sale of each unit would be $11 ($10 × 1.10) in year 1 and $12.10 [$11 × 1.10 or $10 × (1.10)²] in year 2—resulting in net cash inflows of $1,100 in year 1 and $1,210 in year 2. The net cash inflows of $1,100 and $1,210 are nominal cash inflows because they include the impact of inflation. *These are the cash flows recorded by the accounting system*. The cash inflows of $1,000 each year are real cash flows because they exclude inflationary effects. Note that the real cash flows equal the nominal cash flows discounted for inflation, $1,000 = $1,100 ÷ 1.10 = $1,210 ÷ (1.10)². Many managers find the nominal approach easier to understand and use, because they observe nominal cash flows in their accounting systems and the nominal rates of return on financial markets.

Let's revisit Network Communications, which is deciding whether to invest in equipment to make and sell a cellular data transmission product. The equipment would cost $750,000 immediately. It is expected to have a four-year useful life with a zero terminal disposal price. An annual inflation rate of 10% is expected over this four-year period. Network Communications requires an after-tax real rate of return of 20% from this project or an after-tax nominal rate of return of 32%.

The following table presents the predicted amounts of real (assuming no inflation) and nominal (after considering cumulative inflation) net cash inflows from the equipment over the next four years (excluding the $750,000 investment in the equipment and before any income tax payments):

Year	Before-Tax Cash Inflows in Real Dollars (1)	Cumulative Inflation Rate Factor* (2)	Before-Tax Cash Inflows in Nominal Dollars (3) = (1) × (2)
1	$500,000	$(1.10)^1 = 1.1000$	$550,000
2	600,000	$(1.10)^2 = 1.2100$	726,000
3	600,000	$(1.10)^3 = 1.3310$	798,600
4	300,000	$(1.10)^4 = 1.4641$	439,230

*1.10 = 1.00 + 0.10 inflation rate.

The income tax rate is 40%. For tax purposes, the equipment will be amortized using a capital cost allowance rate of 30%, declining balance method.

Exhibit 22-7 presents the capital budgeting approach for predicting cash flows in nominal dollars and using a nominal discount rate.[3] The calculations in Exhibit 22-7 exactly follow the calculations used in the Potato Supreme example for initial machine investment, tax shields, and recurring after-tax cash operating flows. Under the nominal approach, first express all amounts in terms of *future-year dollars* (using cumulative inflation rate factors), then discount the resulting amounts to their present value using *nominal discount-rate factors*.

Exhibit 22-8 presents the approach of predicting cash flows in real terms and using a real discount rate. The calculations for item 3, recurring after-tax cash operating

---

[3]The present value discount factors in the example are calculated using six decimal digits to eliminate doubt about the equivalence of the two approaches. In practice, the present value discount factors (to three decimal digits) can be obtained using Table 2 (present value of $1) of Appendix A at the end of the text. The Problem for Self-Study at the end of this chapter uses Table 2.

EXHIBIT 22-7
Nominal Approach to Inflation for Network Communications: Predict Cash Inflows and Outflows in Nominal Dollars and Use a Nominal Discount Rate*

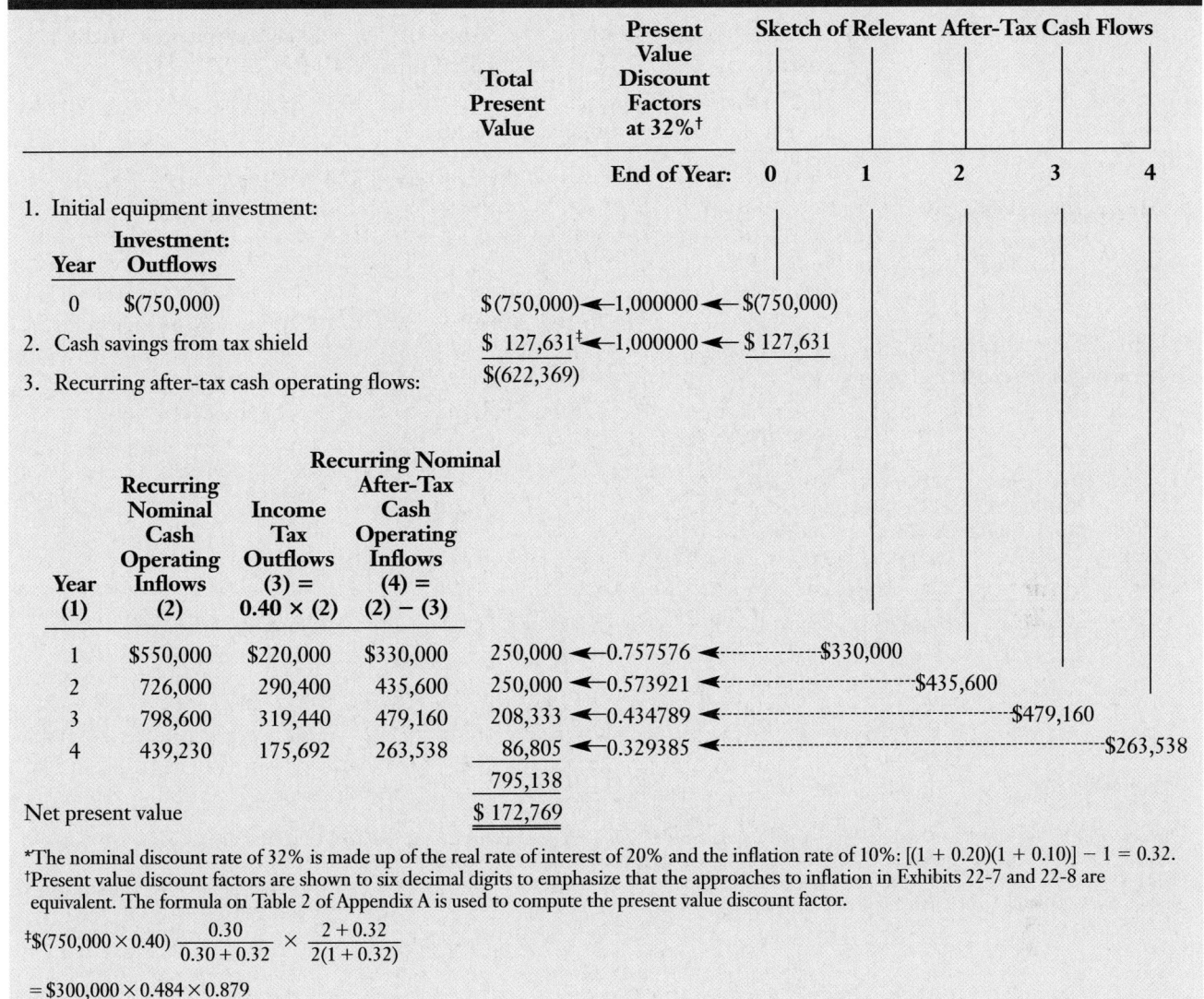

1. Initial equipment investment:

Year	Investment: Outflows
0	$(750,000)

$(750,000) ◄— 1.000000 ◄— $(750,000)

2. Cash savings from tax shield

$ 127,631[‡] ◄— 1.000000 ◄— $ 127,631

$(622,369)

3. Recurring after-tax cash operating flows:

Year (1)	Recurring Nominal Cash Operating Inflows (2)	Income Tax Outflows (3) = 0.40 × (2)	Recurring Nominal After-Tax Cash Operating Inflows (4) = (2) − (3)
1	$550,000	$220,000	$330,000
2	726,000	290,400	435,600
3	798,600	319,440	479,160
4	439,230	175,692	263,538

250,000 ◄— 0.757576 ◄-------------- $330,000
250,000 ◄— 0.573921 ◄----------------------------- $435,600
208,333 ◄— 0.434789 ◄--- $479,160
86,805 ◄— 0.329385 ◄--- $263,538
795,138

Net present value **$ 172,769**

*The nominal discount rate of 32% is made up of the real rate of interest of 20% and the inflation rate of 10%: $[(1 + 0.20)(1 + 0.10)] − 1 = 0.32$.

[†]Present value discount factors are shown to six decimal digits to emphasize that the approaches to inflation in Exhibits 22-7 and 22-8 are equivalent. The formula on Table 2 of Appendix A is used to compute the present value discount factor.

$$[‡]\$(750,000 \times 0.40)\frac{0.30}{0.30 + 0.32} \times \frac{2 + 0.32}{2(1 + 0.32)}$$

$$= \$300,000 \times 0.484 \times 0.879$$

$$= \$127,631.$$

flows, are basically the same as before except that the cash inflows are measured in real terms and discounted at real rates.

Both approaches show that the project has a net present value of $172,769 and should therefore be accepted. The two approaches give the same answer because, for example, in going from the real approach to the nominal approach, the cash flows are multiplied by and the discount rates are divided by the same cumulative inflation factor.[4]

The most frequently encountered error when accounting for inflation in capital budgeting is stating cash inflows and outflows in real monetary units and using a nominal discount rate. This error understates the discounted present value of cash flows that occur in the future and therefore creates a bias against the acceptance of many worthwhile capital investment projects.

[4]For example, recurring after-tax *real* cash operating flow in year 2 of $360,000 in Exhibit 22-8 is multiplied by $(1.10)^2$ to give $435,600 in after-tax *nominal* cash operating flows in year 2 in Exhibit 22-7. The *real* discount rate of 0.694444 in year 2 in Exhibit 22-8 is divided by $(1.10)^2$ to give the nominal discount rate of 0.573921 in year 2 in Exhibit 22-7.

EXHIBIT 22-8
Real Approach to Inflation for Network Communications: Predict Cash Inflows and Outflows in Real Dollars
and Use a Real Discount Rate

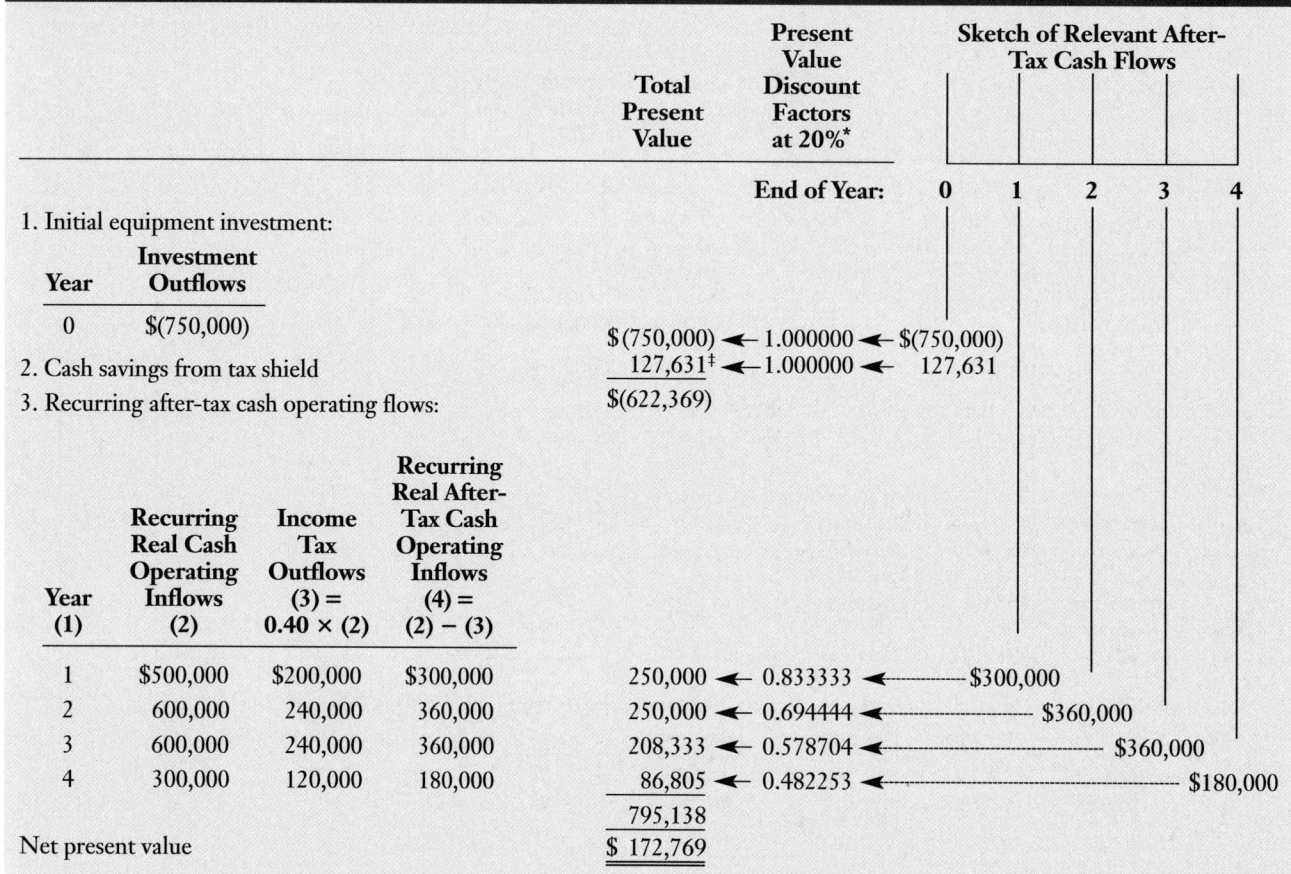

*Present value factors are shown to six decimal digits and the present value calculations rounded to emphasize that the approaches to inflation in Exhibits 22-7 and 22-8 are equivalent. The formula on Table 2 of Appendix A is used to compute the present value discount factor.
†The tax shield formula has used the nominal rate of 32% for demonstration purposes. It is common for companies to use a nominal rate, even though capital cost allowance amounts are not inflated.

MyAccountingLab

ASSESS YOUR MASTERY

To check your understanding of the material in Learning Objective ③, go to the *Mastery Questions* section at the end of this chapter and complete Learning Objective ③ question 1.

PROJECT RISK AND ROR

④ Analyze alternative approaches used to recognize the degree of risk in capital budgeting projects and explain the usefulness of excess present value index in capital budgeting

The *required rate of return (RRR)*, which we discussed in Chapter 21, is a critical variable in discounted cash flow analysis. It is the rate of return that the organization forgoes by investing in a particular project rather than in an alternative project of comparable risk. Risk here refers to the business risk of the project, *independent* of the specific manner in which the project is financed—whether with debt or with equity. Here is a safe generalization: The higher the risk, the higher the required rate of return and the faster management would want to recover the net initial investment. The reason is that higher risk means a greater chance that the project may lose money. Management would be willing to take this added risk only if it was compensated with a higher expected return.

Real Practices Worldwide

How do companies around the globe adjust for risk when evaluating capital investments? The percentages in the following table indicate how frequently particular risk adjustment methods are used in capital budgeting in four countries. The reported percentages exceed 100% because some companies use more than one risk adjustment method. Dashes indicate information was not disclosed in the survey.

The surveys indicate that the specific methods managers use vary among countries. A common feature, however, is that managers appear to favour simpler methods (for example, sensitivity analysis, shortening the payback period, increasing the required rate of return, and subjective, nonquantitative assessments) rather than more sophisticated techniques (for example, estimating the probability distribution of future cash flows).

Adapted from: *V. Jog and A. Srivastava, "Corporate Financial Decision Making in Canada," *Canadian Journal of Administrative Sciences* (1994); [†]C. Sullivan and K. Smith, "Capital Investment Justification for U.S. Factory Automation Projects," *Journal of the Midwest Finance Association*; [‡]M. Freeman and G. Hobbes, "Capital Budgeting: Theory versus Practice," *Australian Accountant*; [§]S. Ho and R. Pike, "Risk Analysis in Capital Budgeting Contexts: Simple or Sophisticated?" *Accounting and Business Research*; [‖]S. Ho and L. Yang, "Managerial Risk Taking and Handling in Corporate Investment: An Exploratory Study in Taiwan," Proceedings of the Second International Conference on Asian-Pacific Financial Markets; [#]D. Zarzecki and T. Wisniewski, "Investment Appraisal Practice in Poland" (Working Paper, Szcecin University, Szcecin, Poland).

	Canada*	United States[†]	Australia[‡]	United Kingdom[§]	Taiwan[‖]	Poland[#]
Sensitivity analysis	59%	29%	57%	63%	—	10%
Increase the required rate of return	31%	18%	—	42%	61%	13%
Shorten payback period	24%	17%	—	34%	72%	25%
Estimate probability distribution of future cash flows	18%	12%	11%	15%	—	13%
Compare optimistic and pessimistic forecasts	—	—	63%	—	—	—
Make subjective, nonquantitative assessment	29%	54%	37%	22%	69%	4%
Make no adjustments	10%	37%	—	—	—	—

The RRR used in discounted cash flow analysis should be internally consistent with the approach applied to predict cash inflows and outflows. The options include various combinations of (1) the real rate and the nominal rate and (2) the pretax and the after-tax rate. The differences among these rates can be sizable, given estimates of inflation that may exceed 10% and corporate tax rates of 30% or more.

Organizations typically use at least one of the following approaches in dealing with the risk factor of projects:

1. **Varying the required payback time.** Companies such as Nissan that use payback as a project selection criterion vary the required payback to reflect differences in project risk. The higher the risk, the shorter the required payback time.

   When faced with higher risk, companies also evaluate how to minimize their downside risk if the project is prematurely abandoned before the full cash inflows can be realized. A reason for abandoning a project prematurely arises (as it did for Ontario Power Generation) when government policies regarding environmental protection change and current projects in operation, such as a coal-fired electricity-generating plant, cannot be refurbished.[5]

2. **Adjusting the required rate of return.** Companies such as DuPont and Shell Oil use a higher required rate of return when the risk is higher. Estimating a precise risk factor for each project is difficult.

   Some organizations simplify the task by having three or four general-risk categories (for example, very high, high, average, and low). Each project under consideration is assigned to a specific category. Management uses a predetermined discount rate, assigned to each category, as the required rate of return for projects in that category.

3. **Adjusting the estimated future cash inflows.** Some companies, such as Dow Chemical, reduce the estimated future cash inflows of riskier projects. For example, they may systematically reduce the predicted cash inflows of very-high-risk projects by 30%, high-risk projects by 20%, average-risk projects by 10%, and make no change to the projected cash inflows of low-risk projects.

   This approach is called the *certainty equivalent approach*. Since the cash flows for higher-risk projects have already been adjusted downward for their increased riskiness, the RRR used to evaluate those projects is the same as the RRR for low-risk projects. Note how this approach contrasts with adjusting the required rate of return. In that approach, the cash flows are not adjusted for risk, but the RRR is. In the certainty equivalent approach, the cash flows are adjusted for risk, but the RRR is not. Both adjusting the cash flows for risk and then using risk-adjusted RRRs would double-count the risk adjustment.

REAL COMPANIES

Risk Analysis in Capital Budgeting at Consumers Energy Company

Consumers Energy Company (CEC) owns pipelines to distribute natural gas to its customers. About 1,609 of the 32,186 kilometres of CEC's main pipelines are cast iron, although most of the pipelines are made of cathodically protected coated and wrapped steel or of plastic. Gas leaks from cast-iron pipes are almost ten times higher than from the other materials. An important capital budgeting decision for CEC is how much of the cast-iron pipes it should replace and when. The benefits of replacing the pipes include lower repairs and maintenance costs and

fewer claims following gas leaks, but the dollar value is uncertain. CEC estimates a range of quantitative values for key factors—the number of times the pipeline might leak, the quantity of gas that may leak, the dollar claims that may have to be paid, and the repairs and maintenance costs that may be incurred—under each replacement alternative. Sensitivity analysis identifies the factors most likely to affect the decision and those that do not. Probability distributions for the key factors are based on actual data obtained from structured interviews with experts in different subject areas. Discounting expected returns by the risk-adjusted ROR gives the NPVs for the different alternatives. CEC computes NPVs on an after-tax basis, using nominal cash flows and nominal discount rates to consistently consider the effects of inflation. CEC's analysis indicated that the optimal program was to replace the worst cast-iron pipes first and all cast-iron pipes over a 40-year period. In the absence of this detailed and thorough risk-based analysis, CEC's managers would have favoured replacing the cast-iron pipes sooner.

Source: Adapted from K. L. Elenbars and D. O'Neill, "Formal Decision Analysis Process Guides Maintenance Budgeting," *Pipeline Industry*, October 1994.

---

[5] See J. Grinyer and N. Daing, "The Use of Abandonment Values in Capital Budgeting—A Research Note," *Management Accounting Research 4* (1993).

4. **Sensitivity (what-if) analysis.** Companies such as Consumers Energy Company use this approach to examine the consequences of changing key assumptions underlying a capital budgeting project.

5. **Estimating the probability distribution of future cash inflows and outflows for each project.** Companies such as Niagara Mohawk use the approach to uncertainty that was discussed in Chapter 3.

The approach gives due weight to all possible cash flow outcomes to arrive at an expected cash flow and then discounts this amount at the risk-adjusted required rate of return for the investment. Estimating these probability distributions is difficult, but a practical guideline is to limit the number of outcomes under consideration to a small, manageable set. Consider another benefit of estimating the probability distribution of future cash inflows and outflows. Suppose a project has a 60% likelihood of very high cash inflows and a 40% likelihood of minimal cash inflows in its early years. This 40% probability may prompt managers to establish lines of credit with a bank. If the low outcome occurs, these lines of credit would enable the company to avoid a short-run cash flow crisis.

ASSESS YOUR MASTERY

To check your understanding of the material in Learning Objective ❹, go to the *Mastery Questions* section at the end of this chapter and complete Learning Objective ❹ question 1.

IMPLEMENTING CAPITAL BUDGETING

> **⑤** Implement capital budgeting in not-for-profit organizations and explain why IRR and NPV may rank projects differently

Discounted cash flow analysis applies to both profit-seeking and not-for-profit organizations. Almost all organizations must decide which investments in long-term assets will accomplish various tasks at the least cost.

Studies of the capital budgeting practices of government agencies at various levels (federal, provincial, and local) and in several countries report that, as in the profit-oriented sector, the following prevails:

1. Urgency is an important factor when allocating funds. For example, capital budgeting for roads is often motivated by physical deficiencies in an existing highway rather than a systematic analysis of alternative road construction projects.

2. Project estimates are sometimes systematically biased. For example, studies report overestimates of the benefits, underestimates of the costs, and underestimates of the time it takes to construct dams and other irrigation infrastructures.

3. There is a tendency to cut capital-budget projects first when there is a strong push to balance a budget or reduce a deficit. Consider the effect of efforts to contain health-care costs in Canada. As a result of these changes and the increased emphasis on controlling hospital charges through competition and regulation, hospitals are increasingly using analytical capital budgeting methods (such as discounted cash flow methods) and are also more carefully auditing the benefits of capital expenditures.

IMPLEMENTING THE NPV DECISION RULE

Executives in both profit-seeking and not-for-profit organizations must frequently work within an overall capital budget limit. This section discusses problems in using the net present value method when there is a restriction on the total funds available for capital spending.

The **excess present value index** (sometimes called the **profitability index**) is the total present value of future net cash inflows of a project divided by the total present value of the net initial investment. The following table illustrates this index for two software graphics packages—Superdraw and Masterdraw—that Business Systems is evaluating:

Project	Present Value at 10% (1)	Net Initial Investment (2)	Excess Present Value Index (3) = (1) ÷ (2)	Net Present Value (4) = (1) − (2)
Superdraw	$1,400,000	$1,000,000	140%	$400,000
Masterdraw	3,900,000	3,000,000	130%	900,000

The excess present value index or profitability index measures the cash flow return per dollar invested. The index is viewed as particularly helpful in choosing between projects when investment funds are limited. The reason is that profitability indexes can identify the projects that will generate the most money from the limited capital available.

Suppose the developers of each package require that Business Systems market only one software graphics package, so accepting one software package automatically means rejecting the other—that is, the packages are mutually exclusive. Which package should Business Systems choose?

Using the profitability index, Superdraw will be preferred over Masterdraw, because it has a profitability index of 140%, which is higher than the 130% for Masterdraw. But the profitability index analysis assumes that all other things, such as risk and alternative use of funds, are equal. For example, it assumes that choosing between Superdraw and Masterdraw has no effect on the other projects that Business Systems plans to implement. If "all other things" are not "equal," which is often the case, the profitability index may not result in the optimal choice of investment projects.

Continuing the Business Systems example, assume that Business Systems has a total capital budget limit of $5,000,000 for the coming year. It is considering investing in Superdraw or Masterdraw and in any one or more of eight other projects (coded B, C, . . . , H, I). Exhibit 22-9 presents two alternative combinations of these projects. Note that the project portfolio in alternative 2 is superior to that

EXHIBIT 22-9
Allocation of $5,000,000 Capital Budget: Comparison of Two Alternatives for Business Systems

Alternative 1				Alternative 2			
Project	Net Initial Investment	Excess Present Value Index	Total Present Value at 10%	Project	Net Initial Investment	Excess Present Value Index	Total Present Value at 10%
C	$ 600,000	167%	$1,002,000	C	$ 600,000	167%	$1,002,000
Superdraw	1,000,000	140%	1,400,000				
D	400,000	132%	528,000	D	400,000	132%	528,000
				Masterdraw	3,000,000	130%	3,900,000
F	1,000,000	115%	1,150,000	F	1,000,000	115%	1,150,000
					$5,000,000*		$6,580,000‡
E	800,000	114%	912,000	E	$ 800,000	114%	Reject
B	1,200,000	112%	1,344,000	B	1,200,000	112%	Reject
	$5,000,000*		$6,336,000†				
H	$ 550,000	105%	Reject	H	550,000	105%	Reject
G	450,000	101%	Reject	G	450,000	101%	Reject
I	1,000,000	90%	Reject	I	1,000,000	90%	Reject

*Total budget constraint.
†Net present value = $6,336,000 − $5,000,000 = $1,336,000.
‡Net present value = $6,580,000 − 5,000,000 = $1,580,000.

in alternative 1, despite the greater cash flow return per dollar invested in Super-draw than in Masterdraw. The reason is that the $2,000,000 incremental invest-ment in Masterdraw increases net present value (NPV) by $500,000. The $2,000,000 would otherwise be invested in projects E and B, which have a lower combined NPV of $256,000:

	Present Value	Net Initial Investment	Increase in Net Present Value
Masterdraw	$3,900,000	$3,000,000	
Superdraw	1,400,000	1,000,000	
Increment	$2,500,000	$2,000,000	$500,000
Project E	$ 912,000	$ 800,000	
Project B	1,344,000	1,200,000	
Total	$2,256,000	$2,000,000	$256,000

Note that other than Superdraw, alternative 2 includes projects with the highest excess present value indexes and excludes those with the lowest excess present value indexes. The excess present value index is a useful guide for identifying and choosing projects that will offer the best return on limited capital and that will thereby maximize net present value. But managers cannot base decisions involving mutually exclusive investments of different sizes solely on the excess present value index. The net present value method is the best general guide.

DIFFERENT METHODS GIVE DIFFERENT RANKINGS

The NPV method always indicates the project (or set of projects) that maximizes the NPV of future cash flows. However, surveys of practice report widespread use of the internal rate of return (IRR) method. The most probable reason is that managers find this method easier to understand and because, in most instances, their decisions would be unaffected by using one method or the other. In some cases, however, the two methods will not indicate the same decision.

Where mutually exclusive projects have unequal lives or unequal investments, the IRR method can rank projects differently from the NPV method. Consider Exhibit 22-10.[6] The ranking by the IRR method favours project X, while the ranking by the NPV method favours project Z. The projects ranked in Exhibit 22-10 differ in both life (5, 10, and 15 years) and net initial investment ($286,400, $419,200, and $509,200).

Managers using the IRR method implicitly assume that the reinvestment rate is equal to the indicated rate of return for the shortest-lived project. Managers using the NPV method implicitly assume that the funds obtainable from competing projects

EXHIBIT 22-10

Ranking of Projects Using Internal Rate of Return and Net Present Value

Project	Life	Net Initial Investment	Annual Cash Flow from Operations, Net of Income Taxes	IRR Method		NPV Method $r = 10\%$*		
				IRR	Ranking	PV of Annual Cash Flow from Operations, Net of Income Taxes	NPV	Ranking
X	5	$286,400	$100,000	22%	1	$379,100	$ 92,700	3
Y	10	419,200	100,000	20	2	614,500	195,300	2
Z	15	509,200	100,000	18	3	760,600	251,400	1

*If the r is changed to 20%, the NPV rankings will change to $NPV_X = \$12,660$ (first); $NPV_Y = \$50$ (second); $NPV_Z = -\$41,650$ (not considered at all because it is negative).

[6]Exhibit 22-10 concentrates on differences in project lives. Similar conflicting results can occur when the terminal dates are the same but the sizes of the net initial investments differ.

Capital Budgeting Methods and the Balanced Scorecard (BSC)

Capital budgeting is about the financial perspective of the BSC. While those undertaking investment analyses must gather relevant information about the customer, internal business, and learning and growth perspective prior to estimating the cash inflows and outflows, the DCF and non-DCF methods of calculating the rate of return apply to these financial estimates. Most investment initiatives are motivated by an offensive strategy of growth; however, other strategies include harvest in a sunset industry or a defensive strategy to protect existing market share. Capital budgeting makes good strategic sense for a defensive strategy to provide information on the opportunity cost of undertaking a low ranking investment, and to quantity and probable loss. In reality, ranking based on ROR will not be the sole factor in capital budgeting decisions.

can be reinvested at the company's required rate of return. The NPV method is generally regarded as conceptually superior. Students should refer to corporate finance texts for more details on these issues, and on the problems of ranking projects with unequal lives or unequal investments.

MyAccountingLab

ASSESS YOUR MASTERY

To check your understanding of the material in Learning Objective ⑤, go to the *Mastery Questions* section at the end of this chapter and complete Learning Objective ⑤ question 1.

PULLING IT ALL TOGETHER—PROBLEM FOR SELF-STUDY

This is a comprehensive review problem. It illustrates both income tax factors and capital budgeting with inflation.

PROBLEM

Stone Aggregates (SA) operates 92 plants producing a crushed stone that is used in many construction projects. Transportation is a major cost item. A scale clerk weighs the products and, on a delivery ticket, records details of the product shipped: its weight, its freight charges, and whether or not it is taxed.

SA is considering a proposal to use computerized delivery ticket–writing equipment at each of its 92 plants. One plant has used the equipment as a pilot site for the past 12 months, generating cash operating cost savings (before taxes) of $300,000 by improving productivity and by reducing plant operating costs and excess shipments to customers. The cost analyst estimates that if the equipment had been in use at all of the company's plants for the past year, net cost savings would have been $25 million (expressed in today's dollars).

The cost of the equipment for all 92 plants is $45 million, which would be payable immediately. This equipment has an expected useful life of four years and a terminal disposal price of $10 million (expressed in today's dollars). The equipment qualifies for a capital cost allowance rate of 25% declining balance. Stone Aggregates expects a 30% income tax rate in each of the next four years.

REQUIRED

1. Does the proposal for the computerized delivery ticket–writing equipment meet SA's 16% after-tax required rate-of-return criterion? This rate of return includes an 8% inflation component. (The real rate of return is 7.4%; recall that nominal rate of return = $[(1 + 0.074)(1 + 0.08)] - 1 = 0.16$.) This 8% inflation

prediction applies to both the cost savings and the terminal disposal price of the equipment. Compute the NPV using nominal dollars and a nominal required rate of return.

2. What other factors would you recommend that SA consider when evaluating the computerized delivery ticket–writing equipment?

SOLUTION

1. Exhibit 22-11 shows the NPV computations. To illustrate an alternative presentation found in practice, the format of Exhibit 22-11 differs from that of Exhibits 22-4, 22-5, and 22-6 (pp. 1061 and 1063). The proposal for computerized delivery ticket–writing equipment has an NPV of $29,560 million, indicating that—on the basis of financial factors—it is an attractive investment.

2. The analysis in Exhibit 22-11 assumes that net cash savings are $25 million each year. However, operating and implementation costs in the year of changeover to new computerized equipment are often 200% higher than in subsequent years. Consequently, net cash savings may be lower in the first year.

EXHIBIT 22-11

Net Present Value Analysis of Computerized Delivery Ticket-Writing System for Stone Aggregates (in Thousands; n.d. = Nominal Dollars)

	A	B	C	D	E	F
		Total	End of	End of	End of	End of
1						
2		Present Value	Year 1	Year 2	Year 3	Year 4
3	**Recurring After-Tax Cash Operating Flows**					
4	1. Recurring cash operating savings (real dollars)	$ –	$25,000	$25,000	$25,000	$25,000
5	2. Cumulative inflation factor (from Table 1, Appendix A for 8%)	–	1.080	1.166	1.260	1.360
6	3. Cash operating savings (n.d.): 1×2		$27,000	$29,150	$31,500	$34,000
7	4. Tax payments: $30\% \times 3$		8,100	8,745	9,450	10,200
8	5. Recurring after-tax cash operating savings (n.d.): $3 - 4$		$18,900	$20,405	$22,050	$23,800
9	6. Present value discount factor (16% nominal)		0.862	0.743	0.641	0.552
10	7. P.V. of recurring after-tax cash operating savings (n.d.): 5×6	$ 58,725	$16,292	$15,161	$14,134	$13,138
11						
12	**Initial Equipment Investment**					
13	New equipment	$(45,000)				
14	Tax shield	7,664*				
15	After tax cash flow effect of equipment investment	(37,336)				
16	Terminal disposal	10,000				
17	Lost tax shield	(1,829)[†]				
18	After tax cash flow effect of terminal disposal	8,171				
19	Net present value	$ 29,560				
20						
21	*Tax shield $= (\$45,000 \times 0.30) \times \dfrac{0.25}{0.25 + 0.16} \times \dfrac{(2 + 0.16)}{2(1 + 0.16)} = \$7,664$					
22	[†]Lost tax shield $= (\$10,000 \times 0.30) \times \dfrac{0.25}{0.25 + 0.16} = \$1,829$					
23	(Half-year rule does not apply to disposals.)					

The following decision guidelines use a question-and-answer format to summarize the chapter's main points. Each decision presents a key question. The guideline is the answer to that question.

DECISIONS	GUIDELINES
1. What is a tax shield?	Operating cash flows are multiplied by a rate of (1 minus the tax rate) to obtain the after-tax operating cash flows. Capital cost allowance (CCA) is the ITA equivalent of amortization. It is the only legally allowable deduction when a corporation calculates the net taxable income on which income taxes will be based. The CCA on investments shields some taxable income from income tax.
2. What is the essential difference between the total-project approach and the differential approach to capital budgeting decisions?	The essential difference is that the total-project approach compares the sum of all the cash flows between two projects while the differential approach examines the differences in cash flows for each type of cash flow that varies between two projects.
3. What is included in the nominal rate of return that is not in the real rate of return?	The nominal rate of return includes the anticipated rate of inflation due to changes in the general purchasing power of the cash flows.
4. Why is it important to recognize risk when evaluating capital budgeting projects?	Risk is an important consideration because riskier projects should require a higher rate of return to compensate for the additional risk.
5. Under what condition can the internal rate of return (IRR) and the net present value (NPV) methods rank projects differently?	Different rankings of projects can arise when mutually exclusive projects have unequal lives or unequal investments.

TERMS TO LEARN

This chapter contains definitions of the following important terms:

capital cost allowance (CCA) (p. 1054)
cumulative eligible capital (CEC) (p. 1054)
cumulative eligible capital amount (CECA) (p. 1054)
differential approach (p. 1059)
eligible capital expenditure (p. 1054)

eligible capital property (p. 1054)
excess present value index (p. 1071)
half-year rule (p. 1054)
inflation (p. 1064)
marginal income tax rate (p. 1052)
net addition (p. 1060)
nominal rate of return (p. 1065)

profitability index (p. 1071)
real rate of return (p. 1065)
tax shield formula (p. 1054)
total-project approach (p. 1059)
unamortized capital cost (UCC) (p. 1054)

MASTERY QUESTIONS

Mastery Questions are rated by proficiency level—elementary, intermediate, and advanced. The solutions appear in the Solutions to Mastery Questions section of MyAccountingLab.

LEARNING OBJECTIVE 1

1. **After-tax NPV—Advanced.** (CPA, adapted) The Apex Company is evaluating a capital budgeting proposal for the current year. Deal with operating cash flow, not operating income. The relevant data are as follows:

Year	Present Value of an Annuity of $1 in Arrears at 15%
1	$0.870
2	1.626
3	2.284
4	2.856
5	3.353
6	3.785

The initial equipment investment would be $36,000. Apex would amortize the equipment for accounting purposes on a straight-line basis over six years with a zero terminal disposal price. The before-tax annual cash inflow arising from this investment is $12,000. The income tax rate is 40%, and income tax is paid the same year as incurred. The capital investment qualifies for a capital cost allowance rate of 20%, declining balance. The after-tax required rate of return is 15%. Choose the best answer for each question and show your computations.

REQUIRED

1. What is the after-tax accrual accounting rate of return on Apex's initial equipment investment? (a) 10%, (b) 16⅔%, (c) 26⅔%, (d) 33⅓%.
2. What is the after-tax payback period (in years) for Apex's capital budgeting proposal? (a) 5, (b) 2.6, (c) 3, (d) 2.
3. What is the net present value of Apex's capital budgeting proposal? (a) $(7,290), (b) $(1,056), (c) $7,850, (d) $11,760.
4. How much would Apex have had to invest five years ago at 15% compounded annually to have $36,000 now? (a) $12,960, (b) $17,892, (c) $20,592, (d) cannot be determined from the information given.

LEARNING OBJECTIVE 2

1. **Alternative approaches—Advanced.** (CMA, adapted) Waterford Specialties Corporation, a clothing manufacturer, has a plant that will become idle on December 31, 2009. John Landry, corporate controller, has been asked to look at three options regarding the disposal of the plant.

◆ **Option 1:** The plant, which has been fully amortized for financial reporting, can be sold immediately for $10.8 million.
◆ **Option 2:** The plant can be leased to Auburn Mills, one of Waterford's suppliers, for four years. Under the terms of the lease, Auburn would pay Waterford $240,000 per month in rent and would grant Waterford a special 10% discount off the normal price of $2.40 per metre on 2.37 million metres of fabric purchased by another Waterford plant. Auburn would cover all the plant's ownership costs including property taxes. Waterford expects to sell this plant for $2.4 million at the end of the four-year lease.
◆ **Option 3:** The plant could be used for four years to make souvenir jackets for the Olympics. Fixed overhead, before any equipment upgrades, is estimated to be $240,000 annually for the four-year period. The jackets are expected to sell for $50.40 each. Unit variable costs are expected to be as follows: direct materials, $24.96; direct manufacturing, marketing, and distribution labour, $7.68; variable manufacturing, marketing, and distribution overhead, $6.96.

The following production and sales of jackets is expected: 2010, 200,000 units; 2011, 300,000 units; 2012, 400,000 units; 2013, 100,000 units. To manufacture the souvenir jackets, some of the plant equipment would have to be upgraded at an immediate cost of $1.8 million to be amortized for financial reporting purposes using straight-line amortization over the four years it will be in use. Because of the modernization of the equipment, Waterford could sell the plant for $3.6 million at the end of four years. The equipment qualifies for a 25% declining balance capital cost allowance rate.

Waterford treats all cash flows as if they occur at the end of the year and uses an after-tax cost of capital of 12%. Waterford is subject to a 40% tax rate.

REQUIRED

1. Would you use the total-project approach or the differential approach to choose among the three options? Why?
2. Calculate the net present value of each of the options available to Waterford and determine which option Waterford should select using the net present value criterion.
3. What nonfinancial and qualitative factors should Waterford consider before making its choice?

LEARNING OBJECTIVE 3

1. Inflation—Advanced. (J. Fellingham, adapted) Sapna Patel is manager of the customer-service division of an electrical appliance store. Sapna is considering buying a repairing machine that costs $12,000 on December 31, 2010. The machine will last five years. Sapna estimates that the incremental pretax cash savings from using the machine will be $3,600 annually. The $3,600 is measured at current prices and will be received at the end of each year. For tax purposes, the machinery qualifies for a capital cost allowance rate of 25%, declining balance. Sapna requires a 10% after-tax real rate of return (that is, the rate of return is 10% when all cash flows are denominated in December 31, 2010, dollars). Use the 10% after-tax real rate of return when answering all four requirements.

REQUIRED

Treat each of the following cases independently.
1. Sapna lives in a world without income taxes and without inflation. What is the net present value of the machine in this world?
2. Sapna lives in a world without inflation, but there is an income tax rate of 40%. What is the net present value of the machine in this world?
3. There are no income taxes, but the annual inflation rate is 20%. What is the net present value of the machine? The cash savings each year will be increased by a factor equal to the cumulative inflation rate.
4. The annual inflation rate is 20%, and the income tax rate is 40%. What is the net present value of the machine?

LEARNING OBJECTIVE 4

1. Assessing risk—Advanced. (CMA, adapted) The WRL Company operates a snack food centre at the Hartsfield Airport. On January 2, 2008, WRL purchased a special cookie-cutting machine, which has been used for three years. WRL is considering purchasing a newer, more efficient machine. If purchased, the new machine would be acquired today on January 2, 2011. WRL expects to sell 300,000 cookies in each of the next four years. The selling price of each cookie is expected to average $0.60.

WRL has two options: (1) continue to operate the old machine or (2) sell the old machine and purchase the new machine. The seller of the new machine offered no tradein.

The following information has been assembled to help management decide which option is more desirable:

	Old Machine	New Machine
Initial machine investment	$96,000	$144,000
Terminal disposal price at the end of useful life assumed for amortization purposes	$12,000	$24,000
Useful life from date of acquisition	7 years	4 years
Expected annual cash operating costs:		
Variable cost per cookie	$0.24	$0.168
Total fixed costs	$18,000	$16,800
Amortization method used for accounting purposes	Straight-line	Straight-line
Estimated disposal prices of machines:		
January 2, 2011	$48,000	$144,000
December 31, 2014	$8,400	$24,000
Capital cost allowance rate (declining balance)	25%	25%

WRL has a 40% income tax rate and an after-tax required rate of return of 16%.

REQUIRED

1. Use the net present value method to determine whether WRL should retain the old machine or acquire the new machine.
2. How much more or less would the recurring after-tax variable cash operating savings have to be for WRL to exactly earn the 16% after-tax required rate of return? Assume all other data about the investment do not change.
3. Assume that the financial differences between the net present values of the two options are so slight that WRL is indifferent between the two proposals. Identify and discuss the nonfinancial and qualitative factors that WRL should consider.

LEARNING OBJECTIVE 5

1. **Different methods, different ranking—Advanced.** (Adapted from NAA Research Report No. 35, pp. 83–85) Assume that six projects, A to F in the table that follows, have been submitted for inclusion in the coming year's budget for capital expenditures:

		Project Cash Flows					
	Year	A	B	C	D	E	F
Investment	0	$(120,000)	$(120,000)	$(240,000)	$(240,000)	$(240,000)	$(60,000)
	1	0	24,000	84,000	0	6,000	27,600
	2	12,000	24,000	84,000	0	18,000	24,000
	3	24,000	24,000	84,000	0	36,000	12,000
	4	24,000	24,000	84,000	0	60,000	12,000
	5	24,000	24,000	84,000	0	60,000	
Per year	6–9	24,000	24,000		240,000	60,000	
	10	24,000	24,000			60,000	
Per year	11–15	24,000					
Internal rate of return		14%	?	?	?	12.6%	12.0%

REQUIRED

1. Compute the internal rates of return (to the nearest half-percent) for projects B, C, and D. Rank all projects in descending order in terms of the internal rate of return. Show your computations.
2. On the basis of your answer in requirement 1, state which projects you would select, assuming a 10% required rate of return (a) if $600,000 is the limit to be spent, (b) if $660,000 is the limit, and (c) if $780,000 is the limit.
3. Assuming a 16% required rate of return and using the net present value method, compute the net present values and rank all the projects. Which project is more desirable, C or D? Compare your answer with your ranking in requirement 1.
4. What factors other than those considered in requirements 1 to 3 would influence your project rankings? Be specific.

SHORT-ANSWER QUESTIONS

22-1 Describe three types of cash flows affected by income taxes.

22-2 "It doesn't matter what accounting amortization method is used. The total-dollar tax bills are the same." Do you agree? Explain.

22-3 Give examples of four categories of cash flows considered in capital budgeting analyses.

22-4 Distinguish between the total-project approach and the differential approach to choosing between two capital budgeting projects.

22-5 "Accounting amortization is an irrelevant factor in deciding whether to replace an existing delivery vehicle with a more energy-efficient vehicle." Do you agree? Explain.

22-6 "Income taxes only play a role in capital budgeting because of capital cost allowance tax savings." Do you agree? Explain.

22-7 What are the two basic types of capital cost allowance classes?

22-8 Distinguish between the nominal rate of return and the real rate of return.

22-9 What are the two internally consistent approaches to incorporating inflation into DCF analysis?

22-10 What approaches might be used to recognize risk in capital budgeting?

22-11 "In practice there is no single rate that a given company can use as a guide for sifting among all projects." Do you agree? Explain.

22-12 "Discounted cash flow techniques are relevant only to profit-seeking organizations." Do you agree? Explain.

22-13 "The excess present value index or profitability index is a useful guide when allocating limited funds among projects." Do you agree? Explain.

22-14 "The net present value method and the internal rate-of-return method always rank different projects identically." Do you agree? Explain.

EXERCISES

1. a. Total present value of recurring after-tax operating savings, $90,846

22-15 **New equipment purchase.** Presentation Graphics prepares slides and other aids for individuals making presentations. It estimates it can save $42,000 a year in cash operating costs for the next five years if it buys a special-purpose colour-slide workstation at a cost of $90,000. The workstation qualifies for a capital cost allowance rate of 25%, declining balance, and will have a zero terminal disposal price at the end of year 5. Presentation Graphics has a 12% after-tax required rate of return. Its income tax rate is 40% each year for the next five years.

REQUIRED
Compute (a) net present value, (b) payback period, and (c) internal rate of return.

1. a. Total present value of recurring after-tax operating savings, $5,466,600

22-16 **Automated materials-handling capital project, income taxes, sensitivity analysis.** Just-in-Time Distributors, an operator of a large distribution network of health-related products, is considering an automated materials-handling system for its major warehouse in Toronto to reduce storage space, labour costs, and product damage. The automation equipment will cost $7,375,000 payable at the time of acquisition. The equipment has a useful life of four years and no residual disposal price. The lease on the warehouse will expire in four years and is not expected to be renewed. The company has a marginal income tax rate of 40% and an after-tax required rate of return of 12%. Under existing tax laws, the $7,375,000 of the equipment cost will qualify for a capital cost allowance rate of 30%, declining balance. The before-tax net cash operating savings from the automation are estimated to be $3,000,000 a year.

REQUIRED
1. Compute (a) the net present value and (b) the payback period on the automated materials-handling project.
2. Calculate the minimum annual before-tax net cash operating savings that will make the automated material handling equipment desirable from a net present value standpoint.
3. What other factors should Just-in-Time Distributors consider in its decision?

1. a. Total present value of recurring after-tax cash operating costs, ($78,019)

22-17 **Total-project versus differential approach, income taxes.** A specialized automobile parts manufacturer is considering the acquisition of a new machine. The new machine is far more efficient than the present machine. It would cost $87,600, would cut annual cash operating costs from $72,000 to $48,000, and would have zero terminal disposal price at the end of its useful life of three years. The applicable income tax rate is 30%. The after-tax required rate of return is 14%.

The current machine has been used for one year. It will have no useful economic life after three more years. It cost $105,600 when acquired, has a current disposal price of $39,200, and has a residual disposal price of $7,200.

These machines qualify for a capital cost allowance rate of 20%, declining balance.

REQUIRED
Using the net present value method, show whether the new machine should be purchased (a) under a total-project approach and (b) under a differential approach.

1. Total present value of tax shield, $227,335

22-18 **Project risk, required rate of return.** Northern Petroleum is considering two capital projects. The first project, viewed as a high-risk investment, is drilling equipment for oil exploration activities. Northern expects the drilling equipment to cost $1,185,000 and result in operating cash flows before taxes of $448,000 per year for five years. The drilling equipment has a five-year life and a terminal disposal price of zero.

The second project, viewed as a low-risk investment, is for production equipment that will improve the yield in Northern's refinery. Northern expects the production equipment to cost $850,000 and result in operating cash flows before taxes of $355,000 per year for four years. The equipment has a four-year life and a terminal disposal price of zero. Northern's income tax rate is 30%. The production and drilling equipment capital cost allowance rate is 25%, declining balance.

REQUIRED

1. Which project has the higher net present value if Northern uses an after-tax required rate of return (RRR) of 12% for both projects?
2. A manager at Northern objects to the calculations in requirement 1 arguing that riskier investments should have a higher RRR. Suppose Northern requires an 18% after-tax RRR for high-risk investments and a 12% after-tax RRR for low-risk investments. Which project has the higher net present value?
3. Which project do you favour? Why?

22-19 Income taxes and inflation. An investment of $254,200 in special tools, with a life expectancy of four years and a residual price of $24,000, is being examined at December 31, 2010 by StrengthCo. The tools will enable StrengthCo to manufacture drill bits to very high tolerances without incurring any incremental costs, and to earn additional cash flows of $2.40 per unit in 2011, $2.54 in 2012, $2.70 in 2013, and $2.86 in 2014. StrengthCo expects to sell 37,500 units each year for the next four years. StrengthCo is subject to a 40% tax rate. The after-tax required rate of return determined by the plant manager, James Marco, is 18%. The tools qualify for a capital cost allowance rate of 35%, declining balance.

1. a. Total present value of recurring cash flows from drill bits, $156,974

REQUIRED

1. Compute the net present value of the project.
2. Marco feels that inflation will persist for the next four years at the rate of 6% per year. However, the 18% minimum desired rate of return already includes a return required to cover the effects of anticipated inflation. Repeat requirement 1 to take inflationary effects into consideration.
3. Could you have taken inflation into account in a way different from what you did in requirement 2? Broadly describe how without actually performing any calculations.

22-20 Inflation and not-for-profit institution, no tax aspects. KopiPro is considering the purchase of a photocopying machine for $5,500 on December 31, 2010. It has a useful life of five years and a zero residual disposal price. Amortization will be applied on a straight-line basis. The cash operating savings are expected to be $1,350 annually, measured in December 31, 2010, dollars. The discount factor is 18.8%, which includes the effects of anticipated inflation of 10%. The KopiPro pays no taxes due to being a non-profit organization. The present values of $1 discounted at 18.8% received at the end of 1, 2, 3, 4, and 5 periods are 0.842, 0.709, 0.596, 0.502, and 0.423.

1. Present value of recurring cash operating savings, $5,390

REQUIRED

1. A KopiPro official computed the net present value of the project using an 18.8% discount rate without adjusting the cash operating savings for inflation. What net present value figure did he compute? Is this approach correct? If not, how would you redo the analysis?
2. (a) What is the real rate of return required by KopiPro for investing in the photocopying machine? (b) Calculate the net present value using the real rate of return approach to incorporating inflation.
3. Compare your analyses in requirements 1 and 2. Present generalizations that seem applicable about the analysis of inflation in capital budgeting.

22-21 Excess present value index. The ChipTech Company is considering the acquisition of four capital investment projects. The projects under consideration are mutually exclusive. The company is considering buying new design equipment for which each project is identified as Design Pro and Easychip. Also under consideration are two other capital investments which internally are referenced as projects C and D.

1. Excess present value index, Design Pro, 150%

The following table describes the financial characteristics of these projects:

Project	Present Value of Cash Inflows at 14% Required Rate of Return	Net Initial Investment
Design Pro	$ 900,000	$600,000
Easychip	1,260,000	900,000
Project C	702,000	540,000
Project D	384,000	240,000

1. For each project, calculate (a) the net present value and (b) the excess present value index. On the basis of the excess present value index only, should ChipTech choose Design Pro or Easychip?

2. Supposing ChipTech must choose one of Design Pro or Easychip, and supposing ChipTech has a capital investment budget of $1,140,000, which projects should ChipTech choose?

3. Comment on your answers to requirements 1 and 2.

⑤

1. Present value factor,
Project 1, 0.833

22-22 Comparison of projects with unequal lives. Melanie Leblanc, the general manager of Worldwide Foods Inc., has asked Frank Devine, the management accountant, to prepare an analysis for two mutually exclusive capital projects. The after-tax required rate of return of this company is 10%.

The anticipated cash flows are as follows:

		Cash Inflows			
Project No.	Investment Required Now	Year 1	Year 2	Year 3	Year 4
1	$12,000	$14,400	$0	$0	$ 0
2	12,000	0	0	0	21,000

REQUIRED

1. Compute the internal rate of return of both projects. Which project is preferable?

2. Compute the net present value of both projects. Which project is preferable?

3. Comment briefly on the results in requirements 1 and 2. Be specific in your comparisons.

①

1. a. Total present value
of recurring after-tax
operating savings,
$65,599

22-23 New equipment purchase, income taxes. Anna's Bakery plans to purchase a new oven for its store. The oven has an estimated useful life of four years. The estimated pretax cash flows for the oven are as shown in the table that follows, with no anticipated change in working capital. Anna's Bakery has a 12% after-tax required rate of return and a 40% income tax rate. Assume ammortization is calculated on a straight-line basis for tax purposes using the initial oven investment and estimated terminal disposal value of the oven. Assume all cash flows occur at year-end except for initial investment amounts. Equipment is subject to 20% CCA rate declining balance for income tax purposes.

	Relevant Cash Flows at End of Each Year					
	0	**1**	**2**	**3**	**4**	**5**
Initial motor investment	$(88,000)					
Annual cash flow from operations (excluding the amortization effect)		$36,000	$36,000	$36,000	$36,000	$36,000
Cash flow from terminal disposal of motor						8,000

REQUIRED

1. Calculate (a) net present value, (b) payback period, and (c) internal rate of return.

2. Compare and contrast the capital budgeting methods in requirement 1.

①

1. a. Total present value
of recurring after-tax
operating savings,
$67,594

22-24 New equipment purchase, income taxes. Innovation Inc. is considering the purchase of a new industrial electric motor to improve efficiency at its Fremont plant. The motor has an estimated useful life of five years. The estimated pretax cash flows for the motor are shown in the table that follows, with no anticipated change in working capital. Innovation has a 12% after-tax required rate of return and a 40% income tax rate. Assume amortization is calculated on a straight-line basis for tax purposes. Assume all cash flows occur at year-end except for initial investment amounts. Equipment is subject to 20% CCA rate declining balance for income tax purposes.

	Relevant Cash Flows at End of Each Year					
	0	**1**	**2**	**3**	**4**	**5**
Initial motor investment	$(62,500)					
Annual cash flow from operations (excluding the amortization effect)		$31,250	$31,250	$31,250	$31,250	$31,250
Cash flow from terminal disposal of motor						$ 0

1. Calculate (a) net present value, (b) payback period, and (c) internal rate of return.
2. Compare and contrast the capital budgeting methods in requirement 1.

22-25 Selling a plant, income taxes. (CMA, adapted) The Crossroad Company is an international clothing manufacturer. Its Winnipeg plant will become idle on December 31, 2008. Peter Laney, the corporate controller, has been asked to look at three options regarding the plant.

1. Total present value of lost tax shield, Option 1, ($40,000)

- ◆ **Option 1:** The plant, which has been fully amortized for tax purposes, can be sold immediately for $340,000.
- ◆ **Option 2:** The plant can be leased to the Austin Corporation, one of Crossroad's suppliers, for four years. Under the lease terms, Austin would pay Crossroad $96,000 rent per year (payable at year-end) and would grant Crossroad a $18,960 annual discount off the normal price of fabric purchased by Crossroad (assume discount received at year-end for each of the four years). Austin would bear all of the plant's ownership costs. Crossroad expects to sell this plant for $80,000 at the end of the four-year lease.
- ◆ **Option 3:** The plant could be used for four years to make souvenir jackets for the Olympics. Fixed overhead costs (a cash outflow) before any equipment upgrades are estimated to be $8,000 annually for the four-year period. The jackets are expected to sell for $42 each. Variable cost per unit is expected to be $33. The following production and sales of jackets are expected: 2009, 8,000 units; 2010, 12,000 units; 2011, 16,000 units; 2012, 4,000 units. In order to manufacture the jackets, some of the plant equipment would need to be upgraded at an immediate cost of $60,000. The equipment would be amortized using the straight-line amortization method and zero terminal disposal value over the four years it would be in use. Because of the equipment upgrades, Crossroad could sell the plant for $120,000 at the end of four years. No change in working capital would be required.

Crossroad treats all cash flows as if they occur at the end of the year, and it uses an after-tax required rate of return of 12%. Crossroad is subject to a 40% tax rate on all income, including capital gains. The plant is subject to 5% CCA rate declining balance for income tax purposes.

REQUIRED

1. Calculate net present value of each of the options and determine which option Crossroad should select using the NPV criterion.
2. What nonfinancial factors should Crossroad consider before making its choice?

PROBLEMS

22-26 Equipment replacement, income taxes. (CMA, adapted) Microvac is considering the purchase of a new, more efficient pump on January 1, 2012 (four years later). The new pump costs $807,500. The pump qualifies for a capital cost allowance rate of 25%, declining balance. The new pump is expected to have a terminal disposal price of $96,000 at the end of four years. At current rates of production, the new pump's greater efficiency will result in annual cash savings of $175,000.

1. Total present value of recurring cash flows from additional manufacturing, $115,517

On January 1, 2008, Microvac bought a vacuum pump for $480,000. This pump will be fully amortized for accounting purposes by December 31, 2011, but it can still be used for another four years. It has a current disposal price of $72,600. If it is used for another four years, the pump's residual disposal price will be zero.

Microvac is able to sell all the testing instruments for microcircuits it produces. These instruments sell for $4,480 each. Microvac incurs cash operating costs of $3,220 to manufacture these instruments. Because of the increased speed of the new pump, output is expected to increase by 30 units in 2012, 50 units in 2013 and 2014, and 70 units in 2015. Over and above the annual cash savings at current production levels, Microvac's cash manufacturing costs will decrease by $180 per unit on all additional units produced.

Microvac is subject to a 40% tax rate. Microvac's after-tax required rate of return is 16%.

REQUIRED

1. Determine whether Microvac should purchase the new pump by calculating the net present value at January 1, 2012, of the estimated after-tax cash flows that would result from the acquisition.
2. Describe the nonfinancial and qualitative factors that Microvac should consider before making the pump replacement decision.

22-27 Capital budgeting, make versus buy, income taxes, relevant costs. (CMA, adapted) The equipment owned and operated by the Protect-it Company and used to

manufacture waste containers must be replaced because it is irreparable. The old equipment has a current salvage price of $1,800. The new equipment would cost $1,373,700. The equipment would go into service on January 1, 2010, and would have a five-year useful life. Under the prevailing income tax laws, capital cost allowance is calculated on the declining-balance method at a rate of 25%. The terminal disposal price at the end of five years is estimated at $14,400.

Protect-it estimates the following number of waste containers will be needed over the next five years: 2010, 50,000; 2011, 50,000; 2012, 52,000; 2013, 55,000; 2014, 55,000 for its products.

Protect-it's current manufacturing costs for waste containers are as follows:

Direct materials		$12.00
Direct manufacturing labour		9.60
Variable manufacturing overhead		4.80
Fixed manufacturing overhead:		
Supervision	$ 2.40	
Amortization on old equipment	3.60	
General administrative overhead	7.20	13.20
Total manufacturing cost per unit		$39.60

An outside supplier has offered to supply all the containers that Protect-it needs over the next five years at a fixed price of $35.75 per container. If the supplier's offer is accepted, Protect-it would not need to replace the equipment.

If the waste containers are purchased outside, the salary and benefits of one supervisor, included in the fixed overhead at $62,000, would be eliminated. There would, however, be no change in general administrative overhead. Protect-it has no alternative use for the extra space that would become available if the containers were purchased from outside. Working capital requirements are approximately the same whether the containers are made or purchased.

Protect-it has a 40% marginal income tax rate. Its after-tax required rate of return on new equipment is 12%.

REQUIRED

1. Use a net present value analysis to determine whether Protect-it should purchase the waste containers from the outside supplier or purchase the new equipment.
2. What nonfinancial and qualitative factors should Protect-it consider before coming to a decision?

22-28 Capital budgeting, inventory changes. (M. Wolfson, J. Harris, adapted) Comfort Footwear Inc. is considering whether to add a new line of running shoes to be sold to its retail customers. To produce these shoes, special machines costing a total of $131,040 must be acquired. The machines will have a useful life of four years, with a combined terminal residual price of $21,600. The new line of shoes would be dropped at the end of four years. The estimates for the new product line are as follows:

Year	Units Produced	Units Sold	Variable Selling Price	Manufacturing Costs per Unit
1	7,000	6,000	$30.00	$14.40
2	6,500	6,200	30.00	15.60
3	6,500	7,700	28.80	16.80
4	3,000	3,100	26.40	18.00
	23,000	23,000		

For tax purposes, the machines qualify for a capital cost allowance rate of 25%, declining balance. Manufacturing costs are deductible for tax purposes in the year when the related goods are sold. The company uses the first-in, first-out inventory method for accounting purposes. Marketing, distribution, and customer-service costs are deductible for tax purposes in the year when they are incurred. Assume a 40% marginal tax rate. Also, assume that all operating cash flows and income tax payments occur at the end of the year. The after-tax nominal required rate of return is 16%.

Variable marketing, distribution, and customer-service costs are estimated at $3.60 per unit and are not expected to change over the four-year period. The selling-price data and all cost estimates are expressed in nominal dollars. Accounts receivable and current liabilities are expected to be minimal.

Absorption costing must be used for tax purposes. Amortization is allocated on the basis of the estimates of the units produced each year.

REQUIRED

1. Prepare a schedule of relevant cash flows, including income taxes, for each year.
2. Compute the net present value of adding the new line of running shoes.

22-29 **Mining, income taxes, inflation, sensitivity analysis.** (CMA, adapted) Frank Hart, Sparkling Enterprises' controller, has gathered the following data to analyze an investment in new mining equipment which will allow the company to extract gold ore from once inaccessible sections of the Mountain Creek Mining Facility.

1. Recurring operating cash flows, $1,229,000

Acquiring and installing the equipment will involve an investment of $3,600,000. The useful life of the specialized equipment is estimated to be five years with no residual value at the end of this period. Sparkling uses the straight-line amortization method for this equipment for financial reporting purposes.

Using the equipment, Sparkling estimates that an additional 400 troy pounds of gold (12 troy ounces per pound) will be extracted annually for the next five years. Hart plans to use an estimated market price of $490 per troy ounce of gold in his analysis based on expert information. A significant risk factor is represented by the price of gold projected due to the numerous factors that could influence the value per troy ounce.

Variable costs to extract, sort, and pack the gold are $175 per troy ounce. Allocated fixed overhead costs are $48 per ounce.

Three skilled technicians will be hired to operate the new equipment. The total salary and fringe benefit costs for these three employees will be $198,000 annually over the next five years. Periodic maintenance on the equipment is expected to cost $85,000 per annum.

Sparkling requires a 12% after-tax required rate of return and is subject to a 40% tax rate. The equipment qualifies for a 30% declining balance capital cost allowance rate.

REQUIRED

1. Determine the payback period.
2. Calculate the after-tax net present value for Sparkling's proposed acquisition of the extraction equipment.
3. Determine the revenue per ounce of gold at which Sparkling's acquisition of the extraction equipment will break even from a net present value perspective where Sparkling earns the 12% after-tax required rate of return.
4. Hart feels that inflation will occur and persist for the next five years at the rate of 2% per year. Assume all the data given in the problem are already in nominal dollars and that the 12% minimum desired rate of return already includes an element attributable to anticipated inflation. Repeat requirement 2, to take inflationary effects into consideration.

22-30 **Capital project, inflation, income taxes.** Pipe-it Inc. wishes to modernize its facilities which refurbish used pipeline equipment. Robotic machinery appears to be the best option for the spot-welding process. The investment will cost $12,750,000 payable immediately. The introduction of the new equipment is expected to reduce labour costs, worker insurance costs, and materials usage costs by a total of $8.4 million (in January 1, 2010, dollars) a year. At the same time, the robots will require an addition to annual cash operating costs of $3.6 million (in January 1, 2010, dollars) a year. As a bonus, Pipe-it believes that using the robots will eliminate industrial accidents involving workers at the spot-welding activity.

2. Total present value of proceeds from disposal, $921,167

The robots have a four-year useful life with a terminal disposal price of $1,350,000 (in January 1, 2010, dollars). The robots qualify for a 25% declining balance capital cost allowance rate. Pipe-it anticipates inflation in its operating costs and in the terminal disposal price of the robots of 20% per year. It uses a 10% after-tax required rate of return for investments expressed in real dollars. Pipe-it's income tax rate is 40%.

REQUIRED

1. What is the nominal after-tax required rate of return of Pipe-it for investments expressed in nominal dollars?
2. What is the net present value of the $12-million investment in robots? Use the approach of predicting cash inflows and outflows in nominal dollars and using a nominal discount rate.
3. What are the advantages of the approach to capital budgeting for inflation in requirement 2 relative to the approach of predicting real cash inflows and outflows and using a real discount rate?
4. What factors other than the net present value figure in requirement 2 should Pipe-it consider in deciding whether or not to invest in robots?

22-31 **Ranking of capital budgeting projects, alternative selection methods, capital rationing.** (CMA, adapted) Conglomerates has not yet told Sam Pilon what the total amount of funds available for capital projects at Firthing Manufacturing will be, except for the after-tax required rate of return being 12%.

Pilon, division president of Firthing, is preparing the 2011 capital budget for submission to corporate headquarters at Conglomerates Inc. Each project is considered to have the same degree of risk. Projects A and D are mutually exclusive: either one can be chosen, not both.

When analyzing projects, Firthing assumes that any budgeted amount not spent on the identified projects will be invested at the after-tax required rate of return, and funds released at the end of a project can be reinvested at the hurdle rate. Further information about each of these projects is presented in the following schedule:

Firthing Manufacturing Proposed Capital Projects

	Project A	Project B	Project C	Project D	Project E	Project F
Capital investment	$127,200	$240,000	$168,000	$192,000	$172,800	$156,000
Net present value at 12%	$ 83,620	$ 28,528	$(12,274)	$ 89,249	$ 7,232	$ 83,416
Excess present value index (profitability index)	1.66	1.12	0.93	1.46	1.04	1.53
Internal rate of return	35%	15%	9%	22%	14%	26%
Payback period	2.2 years	4.5 years	3.9 years	4.3 years	2.9 years	3.3 years
Economic life	6 years	8 years	5 years	8 years	6 years	8 years

REQUIRED
1. Assume that Firthing Manufacturing has no budget restrictions for capital expenditures and wants to maximize its value to Conglomerates. Identify the capital investment projects that Firthing should include in the capital budget it submits to Conglomerates Inc. Explain the basis for your selection.
2. Ignore your response to requirement 1. Assume that Conglomerates Inc. has specified that Firthing Manufacturing will have a restricted budget for capital expenditures, and that Firthing should select the projects that maximize the company's value. Identify the capital investment projects Firthing should include in its capital expenditures budget, and explain the basis for your selections, if the budget is (a) $540,000 and (b) $600,000.

22-32 NPV and inflation. Cost-Less Foods is considering replacing all of its old cash registers with new ones. The old registers are fully depreciated and have no disposal value. The new registers cost $600,000 (in total). Because the new registers are more efficient than the old registers, Cost-Less will have annual incremental cash savings from using the new registers in the amount of $140,000 per year. The registers have a six-year useful life, and are depreciated using the straight-line method with no disposal value. Cost-Less requires a 10% real rate of return. Ignore taxes.

③

1. Present value of annuity of annual cash savings, $609,700

REQUIRED
1. Given the information above, what is the net present value of the project?
2. Assume the $140,000 cost savings is in current real dollars, and the inflation rate is 5.5%. Find the NPV of the project assuming inflation.
3. Should Cost-Less buy the new cash registers?

22-33 NPV, inflation and taxes (continuation of 22-32). Refer to the information in the preceding problem, but now assume that the tax rate is 30% and that you are not ignoring taxes. Equipment is subject to 20% CCA rate declining balance for income tax purposes.

①

1. Total present value of tax shield, $114,545

REQUIRED
1. Calculate the NPV of the project without inflation.
2. Calculate the NPV of the project with inflation.
3. Should Cost-Less buy the new cash registers?

22-34 Governance, discounted cash-flow analysis. Claude Marchand, the manager of Homestead Products, a wholly owned division of Crosslink Inc., has asked Thandie Ng, the management accountant, to analyze the possibility of introducing a new product referenced as CL2009-6. Through the years the company has found that its products have a useful life of six years, after which the product is dropped and replaced by another new product.

④

1. Total present value of tax shield, $293,521

Marchand is trying to decide whether to launch the product. He is particularly excited about this proposal, because it calls for producing the product in the company's old plant at Kelowna, Marchand's home town. During the last recession, Crosslink had to shut down this plant and lay off its workers, many of whom had grown up with Marchand and were his friends. Marchand had been very upset when the plant was closed down. If CL2009-6 were produced in the new plant, most of the laid-off workers would be rehired.

Ng gathers the following data:

a. CL2009-6 will require new special-purpose equipment costing $1,275,000. The useful life of the equipment is six years, with a $360,000 estimated terminal disposal price at that time. The equipment qualifies for a capital cost allowance rate of 25%, declining balance.

b. The old plant has a book value of $300,000 and is being amortized for accounting purposes on a straight-line basis at $30,000 annually. The plant is currently being leased to another company. This lease has six years remaining at an annual rental of $60,000. The lease contains a cancellation clause whereby the landlord can obtain immediate possession of the premises upon payment of $42,000 cash (fully deductible for income tax purposes).

c. Certain nonrecurring market research studies and sales promotion activities will amount to a cost of $375,000 at the end of year 1. The entire amount is deductible in full for income tax purposes in the year of expenditure.

d. Additions to working capital will require $260,000 at the outset and an additional $240,000 at the end of two years. This total is fully recoverable at the end of six years.

e. Net cash inflow from operations before amortization and income taxes is expected to be $480,000 in years 1 and 2, $720,000 in years 3 to 5, and $400,000 in year 6.

The after-tax required rate of return is 12%. The income tax rate is 36%.

REQUIRED

1. Use a net present value analysis to determine whether Ng should recommend launching CL2009-6.

2. Ng subsequently learns that the new special-purpose equipment required to make CL2009-6 may only be available at a cost of $1.68 million. All other data would remain unchanged. He revises his analysis and presents it to Marchand. Marchand is very unhappy with what he sees. He tells Ng, "Try different assumptions and redo your analysis. I have no doubt that this project should be worth pursuing on financial grounds." Ng is aware of Marchand's interest in supporting his hometown community. There is also the possibility that Marchand may be hired as a consultant by the new plant management after he retires next year. Why is Marchand unhappy with Ng's revised analysis? How should Ng respond to Marchand's suggestions? Identify the specific steps that Ng should take to resolve this situation.

22-35 Introduction of new product, income taxes. (W. Bruns, adapted) Sales of a new product line for Petrus S.A. as of December 2010 are forecast at SFr. 2,400,000 per year, from which a sales commission of 15% would be paid to sales agents. Actual sales are to be made in several different currencies, but all money measurements are stated in Swiss francs, the currency of the head office.

1. Present value factor, 3.0

To add the new line of moulded plastic products to those already manufactured and distributed by Petrus S.A., the company, under the direction of Andre Andros, would have to buy new injection moulding equipment in order to maintain manufacturing quality control; none of the existing equipment could be adapted to perform the necessary operation.

Direct manufacturing costs are budgeted at SFr. 720,000 for materials and SFr. 1,080,000 for labour, leaving an annual cash flow before tax of SFr. 240,000. The new equipment would cost SFr. 720,000 delivered and installed, and was expected to have a useful life of 10 years, with a zero terminal disposal value. Petrus is able to borrow money at 8%.

REQUIRED

1. Ignoring the effect of taxes, what is the internal rate of return (IRR) on the proposed investment? Assume the new equipment would be installed by January 1, 2011, and begin producing on that date.

2. Assume for tax purposes, the equipment is amortized on a straight-line basis over 10 years. The tax rate is expected to be 45%. What is the IRR on an after-tax basis?

3. Andros has stated that Petrus should be willing to purchase this machine as long as it yielded a return of 12% after taxation. Should he make the investment? Show your calculations.

4. Actually, to stimulate industrial development, the tax rules allow for amortization deductions up to one-third of the cost of any such investment to be deducted from reported earnings in the first year after the investment, and up to one-fifth of the remainder of the unamortized investment amount can be deducted in the second year. Thereafter, annual deductions are computed on a straight-line basis such that no more than the original cost of the equipment is amortized over its useful life. How, if at all, does this affect the attractiveness of the investment?

5. Petrus has learned that investment in working capital (receivables and inventories, less payables) amounts to approximately 15% of revenues. Will the additional SFr. 360,000 investment for the new line decrease the rate of return on investment to less than the 12% criterion Andros has been using?

6. In late December 2010 Petrus purchased the equipment, and the operating results turned out as forecast. A year later, Andros learned that the manufacturer of the new equipment had introduced new models that were more automated. The new equipment costs SFr. 1,200,000 and would permit labour savings of SFr. 240,000 per year, thus doubling the net operating cash flow on the product. As a result of the technological advance, Andros expected the one-year-old machine could be sold for only SFr. 240,000 despite the fact that its book value was SFr. 480,000. If Petrus buys the new machine and amortizes it using allowed tax amortization over 10 years, would the investment meet the 12% after-tax criterion? Show your calculations.

7. If the one-year-old machine has a zero disposal price, would replacing it with the new machine still be desirable? Show your calculations.

8. Andros was loath to throw away a nearly new machine and thought he might be better off to keep it one more year and then replace it. Would he be better off? How would you go about addressing this issue? Explain.

9. During 2011 the rate of inflation remained low, and it was expected that it would average about 4% for the year. Andros wondered how Petrus's analysis should reflect this rate of inflation, which he expected might continue for several years. Should an assumed inflation rate change his decision? Explain.

COLLABORATIVE LEARNING CASE

22-36 Equipment replacement, income taxes, unequal project lives, governance. (CMA, adapted) Mark Hatcher, CFO, was instrumental in convincing the board of directors of Modern Food Services (MFS), preparers of microwaveable frozen foods, to open the Western Plant. Now, unless significant improvements in cost control and production efficiency are achieved, the Western Plant may be sold. Hatcher is anxious to have the Western Plant continue to operate to maintain his credibility with the board and also to help Western's production manager, a longtime friend of Hatcher.

MFS is considering purchasing an automated materials-handling system (AMHS) for its Western Plant. Hatcher has asked Simon Palmer, the assistant controller, to prepare a net present value analysis for the proposal.

The AMHS could replace a number of forklift trucks, eliminate the need for a number of materials handlers, and increase the output capacity of the Western plant.

Hatcher has given Palmer the following information regarding the AMHS investment for the net present value analysis:

Projected useful life	10 years
Purchase/installation	$5,490,500
Increased working capital needed	1,125,000
Increased annual operating costs (excluding amortization) over current costs	240,000
Reduction in annual manufacturing costs over current costs	480,000
Reduction in annual maintenance costs over current costs	360,000
Increase in cash flow from higher sales revenue	840,000
Estimated disposal price at end of useful life	1,150,000
Estimated recovery of working capital at end of useful life	1,125,000

MFS uses the straight-line method of amortization for financial reporting purposes for all its equipment assuming a zero terminal disposal price. The forklift trucks have a net book value of $576,000 with a remaining useful life of eight years and a zero terminal disposal price. If MFS purchases AMHS now, it can sell the forklift trucks for $155,000. To make the 10-year project life of AMHS comparable to that of the forklift alternative, Palmer estimates that if MFS does not buy the AMHS, the company will lease new forklift trucks for the Western Plant for years 9 and 10 at a cost of $105,000 per year.

MFS has a 40% marginal tax rate and requires a 12% after-tax rate of return on this project. Assume that tax effects and cash flows from equipment acquisition and disposal occur at the time of the transaction and that tax effects and cash flows from operations occur at the end of each year. The equipment qualifies for a 30% declining balance capital cost allowance rate.

Hatcher was pleased with Palmer's initial analysis. After the initial analysis was completed and additional information became available, Palmer discovered that the estimated terminal disposal price of the AMHS should be $120,000, not $1,150,000, and that the useful life of the system was expected to be 8 years, not 10 years. Palmer prepared a revised, second analysis based on this new information. On seeing the second analysis, Hatcher told Palmer to discard the revised analysis and not to discuss it with anyone at MFS or with the board of directors.

INSTRUCTIONS
Assume that because the terminal disposal value is zero, there are no assets remaining in the pool.

REQUIRED
1. What is the net present value of the decision to replace forklifts with the AMHS based on the original estimates Hatcher gave to Palmer?
2. Using net present value analysis, determine whether MFS should purchase and install the AMHS on the basis of the revised estimates that Palmer obtained.
3. Explain how Palmer, a management accountant, should evaluate Hatcher's directives to conceal the revised analysis.
4. Identify the specific steps Palmer should take to resolve this situation.

Management Control Systems, Transfer Pricing, and Multinational Considerations

BUSINESS MATTERS

Global Governance and Transfer Pricing—It's Complicated

Transfer prices are the prices at which all assets and services are traded by related parties such as corporate subsidiaries. Tax laws as well as internal factors such as goal-congruence, incentives, and autonomy are important considerations in transfer pricing. Transfer prices affect the profits reported in each division and are therefore of interest to both division managers, who may receive bonuses based on the division's financial performance, and tax officials in the different countries, who must ensure their government receives its fair share of taxes.

LEARNING OBJECTIVES

After studying this chapter, you should be able to

1. Evaluate the CoCo framework in the context of existing legislation and professional accounting standards

2. Apply transfer pricing processes

3. Assess the market-based transfer price method

4. Apply relevant costs and tax considerations to evaluate the selection of cost-based and negotiated transfer prices

5. Analyze income tax considerations in multinational transfer pricing

This chapter develops the link between strategy, internal control systems, and governance. With the implementation of cooperative regulation and legislation throughout the globe, organizational structure is a response to mandated governance requirements. Transfer pricing is only one example of an area of corporate decision making where legislation, in this case tax legislation, has severely curtailed managerial discretion. Global governance requirements for multinational corporations (MNCs) often make what used to be an internal decision a complex negotiation with tax authorities who wish to protect their country's tax revenue.

To organize is to arrange elements into an orderly structure comprehensible by others. External legislation, regulation, and standards constrain decisions managers can make about how to structure their organizations. Legislation increasingly holds top managers accountable for organizing management accounting control systems (MACS) that ensure people within the organization have relevant information so they know what they are supposed to do and have the resources to achieve the organization's goals. The mandated dimensions of internal control for companies listed on Canadian stock exchanges include public disclosure of internal control deficiencies in the Management Discussion and Analysis (MD&A) of the Annual Report.

MANAGEMENT CONTROL SYSTEMS

> **1** Evaluate the CoCo framework in the context of existing legislation and professional accounting standards

In Canada, the most recent legislation of publicly listed companies, National Instrument 52-109 (NI52-109), formalizes the importance of a balanced scorecard (BSC) approach to management control.[1] This legislation holds the chief executive (CEO) and chief financial (CFO) officers responsible for ensuring the effectiveness of a company's internal control systems, without specifying what constitutes compliance. NI52-109 was designed to improve the quality of financial reporting, from which none of the business functions of the value chain are exempt. The top management team must evaluate the effectiveness of the corporate internal control systems annually and report deficiencies to their audit committee, the external auditors, and to the shareholders in the MD&A section of the annual report.

In effect, the CEO and CFO must attest by signing a statutory declaration each year that they have received all relevant information from others necessary to provide an opinion about the internal control system's design and operation. The accounting profession developed coherent compliance and control frameworks as well as formal and informal guidance regarding what constitutes compliance with NI52-109. The Criteria and Control Board (CoCo) of the Canadian Institute of Chartered Accountants (CICA) defines control as "comprising those elements of an organization (including its resources, systems, processes, culture, structure and tasks) that, taken together, support people in the achievement of the organization's objectives."

Effective control means that members of an organization have a basis upon which to ensure any risk the organization will fail to achieve its objectives is acceptable. The impact of the full NI52-109, effective December 31, 2007, was to formalize the need for a **management accounting control system (MACS)** which provides relevant information as a basis for assurance of effective control. The CoCo provided further guidance in the form of a framework for control as shown in Exhibit 23-1.

An important feature of the framework is the emphasis on the interdependence of reliable financial reporting, coherent and directed organizational structures, and communication of relevant nonfinancial and financial information. Appropriate control systems developed within this framework would include the following characteristics:[2]

◆ diagnostic control to provide exception reports to deliver feedback on actual and expected achievement when goals are either unmet or exceeded

◆ interactive control systems to identify strategic feedback sources and attention-directing relevant information on expectations and achievements

---

[1] M. Ferris, *CMA Management*, 81.4 June/July (2007): 30–34.
[2] Certified Management Accountants, *Internal Control Bridging Manual*, 2008.

EXHIBIT 23-1
CoCo Control Framework

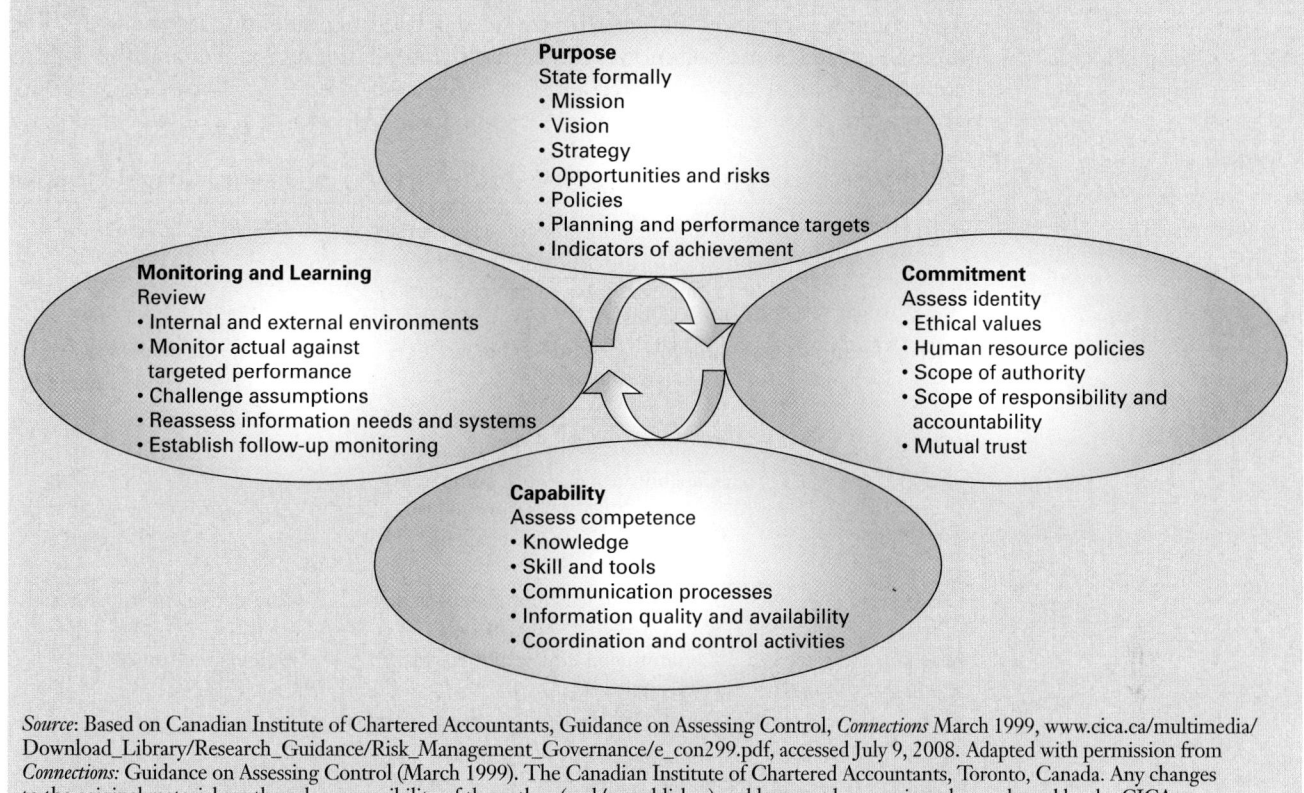

Source: Based on Canadian Institute of Chartered Accountants, Guidance on Assessing Control, *Connections* March 1999, www.cica.ca/multimedia/ Download_Library/Research_Guidance/Risk_Management_Governance/e_con299.pdf, accessed July 9, 2008. Adapted with permission from *Connections: * Guidance on Assessing Control (March 1999). The Canadian Institute of Chartered Accountants, Toronto, Canada. Any changes to the original material are the sole responsibility of the author (and/or publisher) and have not been reviewed or endorsed by the CICA.

◆ boundary systems defining the scope of acceptable behaviour, tasks, responsibility, and accountability

◆ belief systems defining the core values and ethics to which senior managers are committed and within which business is conducted

While the CICA and CMA guidance recommends appropriate control over financial reporting, the development of intellectual capital, customer intelligence, and internal process control as elements of competent stewardship, in an MNC there is ample room for conflict. On the one hand, social responsibility and appropriate organizational identity require tolerance for and support of diversity. Indeed, belief systems, ethics, and values are diverse; thus there is an inherent conflict for MNCs in managing diversity and yet establishing core values. The implementation of effective internal control systems in itself raises profound ethical issues about what constitutes corporate social responsibility.

A MACS comprises formal and informal components. The formal MACS includes those explicit rules, procedures, performance measures, and incentive plans that guide the behaviour of its managers and employees. The formal control system itself consists of several systems including financial and management accounting systems, human resource systems (providing information on compensation, benefits, recruiting, training, absenteeism, and safety), and quality systems (providing information on scrap, defects, rework, and late deliveries to customers). The informal part of the MACS includes such aspects as shared values, loyalties, mutual commitments among members of the organization, and the unwritten norms about acceptable behaviour for promotion that also influence employee behaviour. Criteria of acceptable control specified by CoCo include the extent to which external parties have been made aware of the corporation's ethical standards.

National Instrument 58-201 (NI58-201), in place since 2005 for companies listed on the Toronto Stock Exchange (TSX), includes guidance from the Ontario

Securities Commission (OSC). While companies are not obliged to comply with the OSC guidelines (including formal adoption by the Board of Directors (BOD) of a corporate code of ethics and monitoring), they are obliged to publicly disclose if they comply, if not, why not, and if not, what substitute guidelines are in place.[3] The table illustrates some commonalities across the BSC, the legislative, and the MACS concepts:

BSC Perspectives	NI58-201	Internal Control Elements
Financial	Purpose: indicators of achievement	Diagnostic control
	Monitoring, learning: appropriate information and communication systems	
Internal business	Purpose: mission, vision, strategy, policies, planning	Diagnostic control systems Interactive control systems
	Commitment: scope of responsibility, authority, accountability, HR policies	Boundary systems
	Capability: skill, tools, competence, communication, coordination	
	Monitoring, learning: challenge assumptions	
Customer	Monitoring, learning: feedback on external environment	Interactive control systems
Learning and growth (intellectual capital)	Commitment: ethics, mutual trust, HR policies	Boundary systems Belief systems
	Capability: knowledge, communication	

EVALUATING A MACS

An effective MACS is an intervention with the purpose of constraining behaviour. One constraint is **motivation**, the desire to attain a selected goal (the goal-congruence aspect) combined with the resulting drive or pursuit toward that goal (the effort aspect). Motivation implies, however, both that the goal is worthy and that the means to achieve it are known. In this context, the commitment by senior managers to goals and ethical practices, now formalized in CoCo and NI58-201, are to some extent a means to adapt to new assumptions about employee motivation and remedy new problems arising when motivation is absent.

Goal-congruence exists when individuals and groups work toward the publicly declared organization goals. Employees sacrifice their personal interest to achieve what is best for the organization as a whole. It is difficult to remember that organizations, whether profit, non-profit, or governmental, are entities whose existence is intended to benefit society as a whole. It is equally difficult to ignore opportunities to use the organizational structure for personal gain. Formal, public statements in an Annual Report of mission, vision, and code of ethics are a means to alert individuals of social goals broader in scope than immediate self-interest. Voluntary compliance is the least costly control process, but it depends in large part on consensus of beliefs, values, and ethics that are difficult to obtain in an MNC. The explosion of regulations, laws, certification, and attestation processes worldwide provide a more costly means to enforce behaviour.

Effort is defined as exertion toward a goal. Effort goes beyond physical exertion, such as a worker producing at a faster rate, to include all conscientious actions (physical and mental). Once people are formally advised of goals and expected behaviour, it takes effort to comply because formal legislation and regulation reduce individual discretion or freedom, a highly regarded value in Western democracies.

---

[3]C. Carnaghan and S. P. Gunz, "Recent Changes in the Regulation of Financial Markets and Reporting in Canada," *Accounting Perspectives*, 6.1 (2007): 55–94.

ORGANIZATIONAL STRUCTURE—CENTRALIZED OR DECENTRALIZED?

Control structures are interventions in the form of constraints, enforcement, and penalties. The interventions may be structural. For example, if the control issue is too broad a scope of discretion, then one remedy is to eliminate the **decentralization** which enables individual discretion. Decentralization itself is a strategic response made by organizations that face great uncertainties in their diverse environments, require detailed local knowledge for performing various jobs, and have few interdependencies among subunits such as geographic divisions.

One way to manage the risks of a decentralized structure is to replace people with machines as a way to centralize an activity or sets of activities. Machines have a predetermined scope of activity and no discretion. Another structural remedy is to reduce an individual's scope of authority over the range of decisions that can be made without consulting and obtaining formal agreement from a higher level of management. A third remedy is to formalize processes through the implementation of new policies and procedures to document activity. Meetings, forms to authorize activity, and so on are structural responses to issues rising from decentralization. A fourth structural remedy is to provide formal incentives in employment contracts to reward the appropriate exercise of discretion. Rewards such as cash bonuses, perquisites (perks), and increased scope of discretion are positive incentives to behave appropriately in a decentralized structure of subunits within an organization.

Total decentralization *means minimum constraints and maximum freedom for managers to make decisions at the lowest levels of an organization. Total centralization means maximum constraints and minimum freedom for managers at the lowest levels.* Most companies' structures fall somewhere in between these two extremes.

BENEFITS OF DECENTRALIZATION

From a practical standpoint, top managers can seldom quantify either the benefits or the costs of decentralization. Still, using a cost-benefit approach focuses on the central issues. Advocates of decentralized decision making and granting responsibilities to managers of subunits claim the following benefits:

◆ *Segregates duties.* Centralization, and in particular the grouping of key functions within one subunit, provides opportunities for people to intentionally or inadvertently make errors and then conceal them within the normal scope of their tasks and authority.

   Segregation of duties is a principle of internal control that has been formalized in Generally Accepted Auditing Standards (GAAS). It is a mandatory element of good governance. Operating responsibility, reporting of asset transactions, and custody of assets must be segregated or decentralized. Limiting the scope of tasks performed by one subunit and one individual depends not only on capability but also on commitment to stewardship.

◆ *Creates greater responsiveness to local needs.* Information is the key to intelligent decisions.

   Compared with executives, subunit managers are better informed about their customers, competitors, suppliers, employees, and factors that affect the performance of their jobs, such as ways to decrease costs and improve quality in response to customer demand.

◆ *Leads to quicker decision making.* An organization that gives lower-level managers the responsibility for making decisions can make decisions quickly, creating a competitive advantage over organizations that are slower because they send the decision-making responsibility upward through layer after layer of management.

   Interlake, a manufacturer of materials-handling equipment, notes this important benefit of increased decentralization: "We have distributed decision-making powers more broadly to the cutting edge of product and market

Structure Cannot Replace Commitment and Capability

Internal control failure costs are often embarrassingly public. One high-profile example occurred in 2008 in a London, Ontario, Tim Hortons when an employee exercised discretion and provided a $0.16 Timbit to a regular customer's child without charging the customer or paying herself. Managers, reviewing stored video security data, called the employee into the office. They noted the store's policy was to give away no free food and dismissed the employee, who was rehired by the franchise owner a day later. Despite knowing the policy, the employee did not comply; the franchisee, however, disagreed with the policy implemented by the managers. This example illustrates the importance of both communication by the manager to the franchisee and capability or competence at management tasks. Boundary systems and centralized structures cannot replace common sense, belief systems, and commitment to core values.

Sources: www.cbc.ca/consumer/story/2008/05/08/timbit-lilliman. html?ref=rss, accessed July 11, 2008; www.theglobeandmail.com/servlet/story/RTGAM.20080507.wtimbit0507/BNStory/National/home, accessed July 11, 2008.

opportunity." Interlake's materials-handling equipment must often be customized to fit individual customers' needs. Delegating decision making to the sales force allows Interlake to respond quickly to changing customer requirements. Delegation must be accompanied, however, by capability and competence to ensure appropriate decisions are made.

◆ *Increases motivation.* Subunit managers are usually more highly motivated when they can exercise greater individual initiative.

Johnson & Johnson, a highly decentralized company, maintains that "Decentralization = Creativity = Productivity." Decentralization provides flexibility to deal with diversity in an MNC.

◆ *Aids management development and learning.* Giving managers more responsibility promotes the development of an experienced pool of management talent—a pool that the organization can draw from to fill higher-level management positions.

The organization also learns how to hone the skills of properly identifying issues of knowledge, storage of knowledge, and communication of knowledge. Intellectual capital management is enhanced by coherent control systems. Tektronix, an electronics instruments company, expressed this benefit as follows: "Decentralized units provide a training ground for general managers, and a visible field of combat where product champions may fight for their ideas."

◆ *Sharpens the focus of managers.* In a decentralized setting, the manager of a small subunit has a concentrated focus.

A small subunit is more flexible and nimble than a larger subunit and is better able to adapt itself quickly to a fast-opening market opportunity. In a competitive environment where agility may be the optimal strategy, decentralization is essential. Also, top management, relieved of the burden of day-to-day operating decisions, can spend more time and energy on strategic planning for the entire organization.

COSTS OF DECENTRALIZATION

Advocates of more centralized decision making point out the following costs of decentralizing decision making:

◆ *Leads to suboptimal decision making.* **Suboptimal decision making** (also called either **goal-incongruent** or **dysfunctional decision making**) arises when a decision's benefit to one subunit is more than offset by the costs or loss of benefits to the organization as a whole.

This cost arises because top subunit management has lost sight of the interdependence among subunits. Interdependence means that subunit managers must cooperate with one another to realize organizational goals. Cooperation, however, best exists when relevant information is readily accessible and communicated effectively among subunits. The belief that each subunit serves a larger organizational purpose is also crucial to ensuring a functional team.

Suboptimal decision making may occur when (1) there is a lack of harmony or congruence among the overall organization goals, the subunit goals, and the individual goals of decision makers, (2) subunit managers lack competence, or (3) subunit managers lack the guidance necessary to evaluate the effects of their decisions on other parts of the organization. Suboptimal decision making is most likely to occur when the subunits in the organization are highly interdependent, such as when the end product of one subunit is the direct material of another subunit.

◆ *Results in redundant activities.* Several individual subunits of the organization may undertake the same activity separately. For example, there may be a duplication of staff functions (accounting, employee relations, and legal) if an organization is highly decentralized.

Centralizing these support functions, which are crucial to effective management but non-value-added for a customer, helps to reduce their costs through internal operational redesign or downsizing.

◆ *Decreases loyalty toward the organization as a whole.* Individual subunit managers may regard the managers of other subunits in the same organization as external parties.

In a decentralized structure, managers may be unwilling to either share relevant information or assist when another subunit is in need. Instead of internal co-operation, managers act as if other managers were competitors. One remedy is to provide contractual incentives based on explicit performance criteria and reward managers for effective and efficient communication of relevant information.

◆ *Increases costs of gathering information.* Managers may spend too much time negotiating the prices for internal products or services transferred among subunits.

The outsourcing of resources as well as their internal transfer raises issues of not only cost but also revenue allocation among subunits. Many alternative allocation techniques have been presented in this text to remedy these issues. All rely on the availability of relevant information for excellent implementation.

The Canadian body of legislation and regulation is only one example of the increasing requirement of managers to account for their choices of organizational structures. These new constraints have been developed in cooperation with global regulatory and advisory agencies such as ISO and the Organisation for Economic Co-operation and Development (OECD). The nationally and provincially mandated governance practices are congruent with international benchmarks. This international cooperation among legislators and regulators helps establish a stable foundation for MNC governance.

Surveys of North American and European companies report that the decisions made most frequently at the decentralized level and least frequently at the corporate level are related to sources of supplies, products to manufacture, and product advertising. Decisions related to the type and source of long-term financing are made least frequently at the decentralized level and most frequently at the corporate level.[4]

DECISIONS ABOUT RESPONSIBILITY CENTRES

To measure the performance of subunits in centralized or decentralized organizations, the management accounting control system uses one or a mix of the four types of responsibility centres presented in Chapter 6:

◆ *Cost centre:* Manager accountable for costs only
◆ *Revenue centre:* Manager accountable for revenues only
◆ *Profit centre:* Manager accountable for revenues and costs
◆ *Investment centre:* Manager accountable for investments, revenues, and costs

Notice that a profit centre would require particular attention to desegregation of duties to reduce opportunities to manipulate both revenue and cost. With desegregation, however, comes the tendency to ignore interdependence and behave in ways that fail to achieve overall corporate objectives.

A common misconception is that the term *profit centre* (and, in some cases, *investment centre*) is a synonym for a decentralized subunit and that *cost centre* is a synonym for a centralized subunit. *Profit centres can be coupled with a highly centralized organization, and cost centres can be coupled with a highly decentralized organization.* For example, managers in a division organized as a profit centre may have little leeway in making decisions. They may need to obtain approval from corporate headquarters for any expenditure over, say, $10,000 and may be forced to accept central staff "advice." In another company, divisions may be organized as cost centres, but their managers may have great latitude on capital expenditures and on where to purchase materials and services. In short, the labels "profit centre" and "cost centre" are independent of the degree of decentralization in an organization.

MyAccountingLab

ASSESS YOUR MASTERY

To check your understanding of the material in Learning Objective **1**, go to the *Mastery Questions* section at the end of this chapter and complete Learning Objective **1** question 1.

GOVERNANCE ISSUES

Internal Control Systems—Catastrophic Failure

Most corporations deploy resources paid for by the money of others, either creditors or equity holders. The assets are considered under the control of corporate managers although they are not legally owned by these managers. Decentralization of MNCs without the development and successful implementation of appropriate control systems is bad governance. Barings PLC, a British investment banking firm, went bankrupt and had to be sold when one of its traders in Singapore caused the firm to lose over £1 billion on unauthorized trades. Barings attributed the bankruptcy to rogue trading activity beyond the scope of anticipated behaviour. In part, however, a good internal control system requires the periodic identification of potential risks and not mere review of known, probable risks.

[4]*Evaluating the Performance of International Operations* (New York: Business International, 1989), p. 4; and *Managing the Global Finance Function* (London: Business International, 1992), p. 31.

For both job and process costing, **intermediate products** in a multi-stage production process are transferred from one production stage to another. An intermediate product is an unfinished product transferred from one subunit to another subunit of the same organization. The cost of goods manufactured (COGM), a large proportion of which is allocated manufacturing overhead (MOH), is also transferred (see Chapter 2).

In large decentralized MNCs, individual subunits of an organization acting as autonomous units transfer intermediate goods not only among individual subunits at COGM but also across geographical boundaries at a **transfer price** (not at COGM). A transfer price is the price one subunit of an organization charges for a product (tangible or intangible) or service supplied to another subunit of the same organization. The transfer price more closely approximates absorption costs incurred from all business functions in the value chain.

Strategically, the goal within an MNC is good governance guided formally by the OECD pricing guidelines and known as the **arm's-length principle**. The principle maintains that a transfer price should be the same as it would be if the two subunits were independent companies.[5] In the age of supply-chain management, however, partnerships to increase interdependence and reduce channel costs are often undertaken. Cooperation among subunits to maximize net profit could include deliberate over- or understatement of the transfer price to minimize tax.

The problem is that in this related-party transaction, the cost to the purchasing subunit is deductible from taxable income, and the transfer price received by the supplying subunit is revenue added to taxable income. Transfer prices affect the cash taxes collected by each country. A taxable income of $100 million in Canada would result in approximately $40 million in tax, but the same $100 million in Barbados would incur approximately $2.7 million of tax.

If the Barbados' subunit transferred nearly finished goods to Canada at, for example, $90 million, the MNC's taxable income in Canada would decrease to $10 million and the tax liability would be only $4 million, for a saving in Canada of approximately $36 million.[6] The CRA, along with other national tax authorities, is vitally interested in internal transfer prices for this reason. In the transfer pricing process, national tax authorities are dominant partners and can enforce their opinion of the appropriate price.

ALTERNATIVE TRANSFER PRICING METHODS

The CRA has adopted the OECD Hierarchy of Methods for transfer pricing, which ranks in preference the methods of transfer pricing. First we will discuss transfer of goods and services among divisions in the same country. Transfers of intellectual property, related-party loans, leases, and intragroup (centralized support) services are as subject to transfer pricing scrutiny by CRA when the transfers are interprovincial as are MNC transfers across national boundaries. For example, in 2005 the Ministry of Finance of Ontario noted that as a result of 25 Advanced Tax Rulings by the CRA, approximately $200 million in provincial tax revenue could be lost.[7] Increased scrutiny by Ontario is intended to prevent transfer pricing for the purpose of tax avoidance, which is not considered a good-faith intent, and penalize companies that do so.

There are three general methods for determining transfer prices:

1. *Market-based transfer prices.* Upper management may choose to use the price of a similar product or service publicly listed in, say, a trade journal.

    Also, upper management may select, for the internal price, the external price that a subunit charges to outside customers. Notice that the CRA method is consistent with current pricing methods that are the basis of many financial

[5] M. E. Battersby, "Transfer Pricing Strategies Begin at Home," *The Bottom Line*, 3.1 (2008): 37–39.
[6] D. C. Hill, *CMA Management*, 81.1 (2007): 36–39.
[7] M. Przysuski, "Canada Begins Provincial Transfer Pricing Enforcement," *Corporate Business Taxation Monthly*, 7.2 (2005): 17–20.

US$3.4 Billion Is an Incentive

On May 30, 2008, the Tax Court of Canada decided that the Canadian subsidiary GlaxoSmithKline Inc. (GSKI), of the UK parent company Glaxo Group Ltd., had used an inappropriate transfer pricing method during the years 1990–1993. The values involved decreased GSKI's taxable Canadian income by hundreds of millions of dollars.

The active ingredient of the drug product Zantac was purchased by GSKI from a Swiss affiliate. The Canadian manufacturers produced the drug for approximately $190 to $305 per kilogram, whereas the price paid to the Swiss affiliate was approximately $1,500 to $1,650 per kilogram. A 6% royalty on each purchase was remitted by GSKI to the UK parent under a licensing agreement. The UK parent then paid a 25% withholding tax to the UK. This exceeds the UK/Canada tax treaty amount of 10%.

The Canada Revenue Agency (CRA) successfully argued that the comparable uncontrolled price (CUP) method should have applied to the transfer price estimate where GSKI had applied the resale price method (RSP).

The decision hinged on two facts: first, what a reasonable price would have been in an arm's-length transaction; second, if the additional 6% royalty paid to the UK parent should be included in the transfer price.

In this case it was successfully argued by CRA that "reasonable" meant the highest generic price for which the ingredient was sold in Canada. It also argued successfully to separate the supply and licensing contracts to consider the supply contract on its own and exclude the royalty from the total transfer price. The CRA has proposed an adjustment of $51.5 million payable by GSKI, which has appealed the decision to the Federal Court of Appeal.

The US Internal Revenue Service (IRS) has already settled a 14-year claim against the US affiliate of this company. At issue again was the use of inappropriate transfer pricing for ingredients for various drugs, including Zantac. This case was settled September 11, 2006, with a negotiated settlement of $3.4 billion.

First, the decision upholds the use of the OECD hierarchy of transfer pricing methods. Second, the court successfully narrowed the case to a decision on the supply price and excluded other contracts as relevant in assessing the appropriate transfer price. Third, the court decided that the analysis by GSKI's Canadian tax experts was unreasonable, relying instead on US and Canadian Crown experts.

The Economist, January 29, 2004; KPMG, "GlaxoSmithKline—Tax Court Prescribes Bitter Pill in Transfer Pricing Case," www.kpmg.ca/en/services/tax/tp60/tp60_0803.html, June 13, 2008; Fasken Martineau, "Tax Court of Canada issues *GlaxoSmithKline* decision," www.fasken.com/tax-court-of-canada-issues-iglaxosmithklinei-decision-07-11-2008/, July 2008; Fraser Milner Casgrain LLP, "Focus on Tax—*GlaxoSmithKline Inc. v. The Queen*," www.fmc-law.com/Publications/Tax_SteevesC_Focus_On_Tax_June2008.aspx, June 17, 2008.

accounting valuation standards. Only when market prices are unavailable is a fair-value model used. In principle, the CRA and GAAP can be readily reconciled by professional accountants.

2. *Cost-based transfer prices.* Upper management may choose a transfer price based on the costs of producing the product in question.

Examples include variable manufacturing costs, manufacturing (absorption) costs, and full product costs. "Full product costs" include all production costs as well as costs from other business functions (R&D, design, marketing, distribution, and customer service). The costs used in cost-based transfer prices can be actual costs or budgeted costs.

3. *Negotiated transfer prices.* In some cases, the subunits of a company are free to negotiate the transfer price between themselves and then to decide whether to buy and sell internally or deal with outside parties.

Subunits may use information about costs and market prices in these negotiations, but there is no requirement that the chosen transfer price bear any specific relationship to either cost or market price data. Negotiated transfer prices are often employed when market prices are volatile and change occurs constantly. The negotiated transfer price is the outcome of a bargaining process between the selling and the buying divisions. Ideally, the chosen transfer pricing method should lead each subunit manager to make optimal decisions for the organization as a whole.

We present an example of internal transfer pricing policies, Northern Petroleum of Calgary, Alberta, which operates its Transportation and Refining Divisions as profit centres. The Transportation Division manages the operation of a pipeline that transports crude oil from the Calgary area to the Refining Division in Sarnia, Ontario. The Refining Division processes crude oil into gasoline. (For simplicity, assume that gasoline is the only saleable product the refinery makes and that it takes two barrels of crude oil to yield one barrel of gasoline.)

Variable costs in each division are assumed to be variable with respect to a single cost driver in each division: barrels of crude oil produced by the Production Division, barrels of crude oil transported by the Transportation Division, and barrels of gasoline produced by the Refining Division. The fixed costs per unit are based on the budgeted annual output of crude oil to be produced and transported and the amount of gasoline to be produced. Northern Petroleum reports all costs and revenues of its non-Canadian operations in Canadian dollars using the prevailing exchange rate.

◆ The Production Division can sell crude oil to outside parties in the Calgary area at $72 per barrel.

◆ The Transportation Division "buys" crude oil from the Production Division, transports it to Sarnia, and then "sells" it to the Refining Division. The pipeline from Calgary to Sarnia has the capacity to carry 40,000 barrels of crude oil per day.

◆ The Refining Division has been utilizing its total practical capacity, operating at 30,000 barrels of crude oil a day, using oil delivered by both the Transportation Division (an average of 10,000 barrels per day) and other external suppliers who also deliver to the Sarnia Refinery (an average of 20,000 barrels per day, at $85 per barrel).

◆ The Refining Division sells the gasoline it produces at $190 per barrel.

Exhibit 23-2 summarizes Northern Petroleum's variable and fixed costs per unit of the cost driver in each division, the external market prices of buying and selling

EXHIBIT 23-2
Operating Data for Northern Petroleum

	A	B	C	D	E	F	G	H
1								
2				**Transportation Division**				
3				Variable cost per barrel of crude oil	$1			
4	Contact price per barrel of crude oil supplied in Calgary =	$72	→	Fixed cost per barrel of crude oil	3			
5				Full cost per barrel of crude oil	$4			
6								
7								
8				Barrels of crude oil transferred				
9								
10								
11				**Refining Division**				
12				Variable cost per barrel of gasoline	$ 8		Market price per barrel of gasoline sold to external parties =	
13	Market price per barrel of crude oil supplied to Sarnia refinery =	$85	→	Fixed cost per barrel of gasoline	6	→		$190
14				Full cost per barrel of gasoline	$14			
15								

crude oil, and the external market prices of selling gasoline. Consider the division operating income resulting from three transfer pricing methods applied to a series of transactions involving 100 barrels of crude oil produced by Northern's Production Division.

- ◆ **Method A.** Market-based transfer prices
- ◆ **Method B.** Cost-based transfer prices at 105% of full costs, where full costs are the cost of the transferred-in product plus the division's own variable and fixed costs
- ◆ **Method C.** Negotiated transfer prices

The transfer prices per barrel of crude oil under each method are as follows.

- ◆ **Method A:** Market-Based Transfer Prices
- ◆ From Production Division to Transportation Division = $72
- ◆ From Transportation Division to Refining Division = $85
- ◆ **Method B:** Cost-Based Transfer Prices at 105% of Full Costs
- ◆ Full cost of crude oil plus the Transportation Division's = 1.05($72 + $1 + $3) full costs = $79.80
- ◆ **Method C:** Transfer Prices Negotiated by Divisions to Be between Market-Based and Cost-Based Transfer Prices
- ◆ Negotiated transfer price of $83.00 per barrel of crude oil (a price within the range of the market-based and cost-based transfer prices).

Exhibit 23-3 presents division operating incomes per 100 barrels of crude oil reported under each transfer pricing method. Transfer prices create income for the "selling" division and corresponding costs for the "buying" division that cancel out when divisional results are consolidated. The exhibit assumes that the different transfer pricing methods have no effect on the decisions made and actions taken by the division managers. Northern Petroleum's total operating income from producing, transporting, and refining the 100 barrels of crude oil is therefore the same, $1,200, regardless of internal transfer prices used:

$$\frac{\text{Operating}}{\text{income}} = \text{Revenues} - \frac{\text{Cost of}}{\text{crude oil}} - \frac{\text{Transporation}}{\text{costs}} - \frac{\text{Refining}}{\text{costs}}$$

$$= (\$190 \times 50 \text{ barrels of gasoline}) - (\$72 \times 100 \text{ barrels of crude oil})$$
$$- (\$4 \times 100 \text{ barrels of crude oil}) - (\$14 \times 50 \text{ barrels of gasoline})$$

$$= 9,500 - \$7,200 - \$400 - \$700 = \$1,200$$

When operating income is constant, we can focus on the effects of different transfer pricing methods on division operating incomes. These incomes differ under the three methods. Analyzing the high and low operating incomes for each division, this exhibit readily shows that the operating income of the Transportation Division benefits most when the market-based method is used ($900 − $380 = $520), whereas the Refining Division benefits most when the full-cost method is used ($820 − $300 = $520). This means that each division would choose a different transfer pricing method if its sole criterion were to maximize its own division operating income: the Transportation Division would favour market pricing, and the Refining Division would choose 105% of full costs. Clearly this is why managers whose compensation or promotion directly depends on operating division income take considerable interest in the setting of transfer prices.

Exhibit 23-3 maintains companywide operating income at $1,200 and illustrates how the choice of a transfer pricing method divides the companywide operating income pie among individual divisions. The transfer price methods do not change the size of the total pie but rather how it is divided between the two divisions. If Northern Petroleum failed to obtain a long-term contract for the crude oil transported to its refinery, then the revenues and operating income would also fluctuate for each division and for the company as a whole, although the proportions or operating income for each division under each transfer pricing method would not fluctuate.

EXHIBIT 23-3
Division Operating Income of Northern Petroleum for 100 Barrels of Crude Oil under Alternative Transfer Pricing Methods

	A	B	C	D	E	F	G
1	**Production and Sales Data**						
2	Barrels of crude transferred =	100					
3	Barrels of gasoline sold =	50					
4		**Internal Transfers**			**Internal Transfers at**		**Internal Transfers at**
5		**at Market Price of**			**105% of Full Cost =**		**Negotiated Price of**
6		**$85.00**			**$79.80**		**$83.00**
7		**per Barrel**			**per Barrel**		**per Barrel**
8	**Transportation Division**						
9	Revenue: 100 × $85; $79.80; $83.00	$8,500			$7,980		$8,300
10	Costs						
11	Crude oil						
12	$72 × 100 barrels of crude oil	7,200			7,200		7,200
13	Division variable costs						
14	$1 × 100 barrels of crude oil	100			100		100
15	Division fixed costs						
16	$3 × 100 barrels of crude oil	300			300		300
17	Total division costs	7,600			7,600		7,600
18	Division operating income	$ 900			$ 380		$ 700
19	Operating margin	10.59%			4.76%		8.43%
20							
21	**Refining Division**						
22	Revenues: $190 × 50	$9,500			$9,500		$9,500
23	Costs						
24	Transferred-in costs: 100 × $85; $79.80; $83.00	8,500			7,980		8,300
25	Division variable costs						
26	$8 × 50 barrels of gasoline	400			400		400
27	Division fixed costs						
28	$6 × 50 barrels of gasoline	300			300		300
29	Total division costs	9,200			8,680		9,000
30	Division operating income	$ 300			$ 820		$ 500
31	Operating margin	3.16%			8.63%		5.26%
32	Total operating income for Northern Petroleum	$1,200			$1,200		$1,200

The more volatile the market price, the more difficult it would be for Northern Petroleum to predict its future revenues upon which to base its strategic and operating plans. Subsequent sections of this chapter illustrate that the choice of a transfer pricing method can also affect the decisions that individual division managers make and hence the size of the operating income pie itself. We consider this effect as we expand our discussion of market-based, cost-based, and negotiated transfer prices.

INTERPROVINCIAL TRANSFERS AND TAXES

Top management at Northern Petroleum transferred intermediate goods interprovincially. The corporate tax rates in Alberta are the lowest in Canada, whereas Ontario has the highest provincial corporate tax rates in the country. From the company's perspective, the split of taxable income between the provinces would make a difference in both operating cash flow and net income. It would also make a difference to the taxes collected by each province.

The operating margin if the market price is used will be 10.59% for the Transportation Division in Alberta and 3.16% for the Refining Division in Ontario. This would be the best after-tax choice for Northern Petroleum. The second-best choice would be at the negotiated transfer price which will leave 8.43% of the operating income in Alberta and transfer 5.26% to Ontario. The least preferred choice from the company's perspective is to use full cost because that leaves only 4.76% of operating income in the provincial jurisdiction with the lowest tax rates and transfers 8.63% to the provincial jurisdiction with the highest tax rates in Canada.

Fortunately, the first choice from the company's perspective also ranks first in the transfer price hierarchy of the OECD. The national and provincial governments prefer transfer prices at the market price because it is assured this transfer price is an arm's-length price. In this situation there is no need for Northern Petroleum to approach either tax authority to obtain an **advance transfer price arrangement (APA)**. APAs are a substitute for dispute resolution wherein the company and the tax authority can cooperate to prospectively agree on a transfer price method.[8]

APAs are exceptionally important to sustain good corporate governance. As you must realize, in disputes between the tax authorities and corporations, fines alone reach billions. This excludes legal expenses and opportunity costs of diverting resources to dispute resolution. Most MNCs will approach the tax authorities in all countries (or provinces) where related-party transfers of intermediate goods will occur. Most tax authorities including CRA will negotiate a tax method acceptable to them for some specified future time period. Companies voluntarily undertake APAs but the agreement is legally binding.

The APA process is costly; however, complex, high-dollar-value related-party transactions should be negotiated in advance because it is exactly these transactions which tax authorities will most likely audit. The opportunity cost of a CRA transfer price audit is very high, especially if the company has failed internally to produce ongoing documentation. All related-party transfers are reportable in the corporate tax return. The maximum late-filing penalty is $10,000 and the maximum failure to file penalty is $12,000 for *each* infraction. Legislation authorizes provinces to levy the same penalties domestically.[9] When companies fail to provide acceptable documentation, a 10% penalty can be added to any transfer pricing adjustment. The penalty is applied only if the transfer price adjustment exceeds 10% of the gross revenue prior to any transfer pricing adjustments or $5 million.[10]

MyAccountingLab

ASSESS YOUR MASTERY

To check your understanding of the material in Learning Objective ➋, go to the *Mastery Questions* section at the end of this chapter and complete Learning Objective ➋ question 1.

MARKET-BASED TRANSFER PRICES

➌ Assess the market-based transfer price method

Transferring products or services at market prices generally leads to optimal decisions when three conditions are satisfied: (1) the intermediate market is perfectly competitive, (2) interdependencies of subunits are minimal, and (3) there are no additional costs or benefits to the corporation as a whole in using the market instead of transacting internally. A **perfectly competitive market** exists when there is a homogeneous product with equivalent buying and selling prices and no individual

[8]M. Przysuski, "Advance Pricing Arrangements (APAs) in Canada," *Corporate Business Taxation Monthly*, 6.2 (2004): 11–16.

[9]M. Przysuski, S. Lalapet, and H. Swaneveld, "Transfer Pricing Filing in Canada," *Corporate Business Taxation Monthly*, 6.7 (2005): 25–28.

[10]S. J. Smith and P. L. Kelley, "It's an Art, Not a Science," *camagazine*, 138.8 (2005): 44–46.

buyers or sellers can affect those prices by their own actions. By using market-based transfer prices in perfectly competitive markets, a company can meet the criteria of goal-congruence, management effort, optimal subunit performance, and (if desired) subunit autonomy.

Reconsider the Northern Petroleum example, assuming that there is a perfectly competitive market for crude oil in the Calgary area, and that the market price is $85 per barrel. As a result, the Transportation Division can sell and the Refining Division can buy as much crude oil as each wants at $85 per barrel. Northern, however, would like its managers to buy or sell crude oil internally. Think about the decisions that Northern's division managers would make if each had the option to sell or buy crude oil externally.

If the transfer price between Northern's Transportation and Refining Divisions is set below $85, the manager of the Transportation Division will be motivated to sell all production to outside buyers at $85 per barrel. If the transfer price is set above $85, the manager of the Refining Division will be motivated to purchase all its crude oil requirements from outside suppliers. A current market value transfer price of $85 could motivate both the Transportation and Refining Division to buy and sell internally.

Suppose each division manager is motivated to maximize his or her own division operating income. The Transportation Division will sell (either internally or externally) as much crude oil as it can profitably sell, and the Refining Division will buy (either internally or externally) as much crude oil as it can profitably transport. At a transfer price of $85, the actions that maximize division operating income are also the actions that maximize operating income of Northern Petroleum as a whole. Market prices also serve to evaluate the economic performance and profitability of each division individually.

In perfectly competitive markets, the minimum price the selling division is willing to accept from the buying division is the market price, because the selling division can always sell its output in the external market at that price. The maximum price the buying division is willing to pay to the selling division is the market price, because the buying division can always buy its input in the external market at that price.

DISTRESS PRICES

When supply outstrips demand, market prices may drop well below their historical average. If the drop in prices is expected to be temporary, these low market prices are sometimes called "distress prices." Deciding whether a current market price is a distress price is often difficult. The market prices of several agricultural commodities, such as wheat and oats, have stayed for many years at what observers initially believed were temporary distress levels.

Which transfer pricing method should be used for judging performance if distress prices prevail? Some companies use the distress prices themselves, but others use long-run average prices, or "normal" market prices. In the short run, the manager of the supplier division should meet the distress price as long as it exceeds the incremental costs of supplying the product or service; if not, the supplying division should stop producing, and the buying division should buy the product or service from an outside supplier. These actions would increase overall companywide operating income. If the long-run average market price is used, forcing the manager to buy internally at a price above the current market price will hurt the buying division's short-run performance and understate its profitability. If, however, prices remain low in the long run, the manager of the supplying division must decide whether to dispose of some manufacturing facilities or shut down and have the buying division purchase the product from outside.

```
┌ ─ ─ ─ ─ ─ ─ ─ ─ ─ ─ ─ ─ ─ ─ ─ ─ ─ ─ ─ ─ ─ ─ ─ ─ ─ ─ ┐
         THINKING CRITICALLY
  Why is related-party conflict something to watch out for? Explain in a sentence
  or two. Read on for a discussion of this topic.
└ ─ ─ ─ ─ ─ ─ ─ ─ ─ ─ ─ ─ ─ ─ ─ ─ ─ ─ ─ ─ ─ ─ ─ ─ ─ ─ ┘
```

Be aware of the conflict distress prices can cause. Because the selling division receives very low revenues from distress prices, managers may decide to produce other products that would not be in the company's best interest in the long run. Alternatively, if the transfer price is based on the long-run average market price, the buying division will prefer to buy externally or outsource. If top management requires buying internally (at the long-run average market price), subunit autonomy is violated in a decentralized structure.

MyAccountingLab

COST-BASED TRANSFER PRICES

❹ Apply relevant costs and tax considerations to evaluate the selection of cost-based and negotiated transfer prices

Cost-based transfer prices are helpful when market prices are unavailable, inappropriate, or too costly to obtain. For example, the product may be specialized or unique, price lists may not be widely available, or the internal product may be different from the products available externally in terms of quality and service.

FULL-COST BASES

In practice, many companies use transfer prices based on full costs. These prices, however, can lead to suboptimal decisions. Assume that Northern Petroleum makes internal transfers at 105% of full cost. The Sarnia Refining Division purchases, on average, 30,000 barrels of crude oil per day from a local Sarnia supplier, who delivers the crude oil to the refinery. Freight-on-board (FOB) cost is $85 per barrel. To reduce crude oil costs, the Refining Division has located an independent producer in Calgary who is willing to sell 30,000 barrels of crude oil per day at $79 per barrel, delivered to Northern's pipeline in Calgary.

Given Northern's organization structure, the Transportation Division would purchase the 20,000 barrels of crude oil in Calgary, transport it to Sarnia, and then sell it to the Refining Division. The pipeline has excess capacity and can ship the 20,000 barrels at its variable costs of $1 per barrel. Will Northern Petroleum incur lower costs by purchasing crude oil from the independent producer in Calgary or by purchasing crude oil from the Sarnia supplier? Will the Refining Division show lower crude oil purchasing costs by using oil from the Calgary producer or by using its current Sarnia supplier?

The following analysis shows that operating income of Northern Petroleum as a whole would be maximized by purchasing oil from the independent Calgary producer. The analysis compares the incremental costs in all divisions under the two alternatives:

- ◆ **Alternative 1:** Buy 20,000 barrels from the Sarnia supplier at $85 per barrel. Total costs to Northern Petroleum = 20,000 × $85 = $1,700,000.
- ◆ **Alternative 2:** Buy 20,000 barrels in Calgary at $79 per barrel and transport it to Sarnia at $1 per barrel variable costs or $80/bbl. Total costs to Northern Petroleum = 20,000 × $80 = $1,600,000.

There is a reduction in total costs to Northern Petroleum of $100,000 by using the independent producer in Calgary ($1,700,000 – $1,600,000).

In turn, suppose the Transportation Division's transfer price to the Refining Division is 105% of full cost. The Refining Division will see its reported division costs increase if the crude oil is purchased from the independent producer in Calgary:

$$\text{Transfer price} = 1.05 \times \left(\begin{array}{c} \text{Purchase price} \\ \text{from Calgary} \\ \text{producer} \end{array} + \begin{array}{c} \text{Unit variable cost} \\ \text{of Transportation} \\ \text{Division} \end{array} + \begin{array}{c} \text{Unit fixed cost} \\ \text{of Transportation} \\ \text{Division} \end{array} \right)$$

$$= 1.05 \times (\$79 + \$1 + \$3) = 1.05 \times \$83 = \$87.15 \text{ per barrel}$$

◆ **Alternative 1:** Buy 20,000 barrels from the Sarnia supplier at $85 per barrel. Total costs to Refining Division = 20,000 × $85 = $1,700,000.

◆ **Alternative 2:** Buy 20,000 barrels from the Transportation Division of Northern Petroleum that are purchased from the independent producer in Calgary. Total costs to Refining Division = 20,000 × $87.15 = $1,743,000.

As a profit centre, the Refining Division can maximize its short-run division operating income by purchasing from the Sarnia supplier ($1,700,000 versus $1,743,000).

The transfer pricing method has led the Refining Division to regard the fixed cost(and the 5% markup) of the Transportation Division as a variable cost. The reason is that the Refining Division looks at each barrel that it obtains from the Transportation Division as a variable cost of $87.15—if 10 barrels are transferred, it costs the Refining Division $871.50; if 100 barrels are transferred, it costs $8,715. From the point of view of Northern Petroleum as a whole, its variable costs per barrel are $80 ($79 to purchase the oil from the independent producer and $1 to transport it to Sarnia).

The remaining $7.15 ($87.15 – $80) per barrel is seen by the Refining Division as a fixed cost and markup of the Transportation Division. Buying crude oil in Sarnia costs Northern Petroleum $85 per barrel. For the company, it is cheaper to buy from Calgary. Goal-incongruence is induced by the transfer price based on full cost plus a markup.

Should Northern's top management interfere and force the Refining Division to buy from the Transportation Division? Top management interference would undercut the philosophy of decentralization, so Northern's top management would probably view the decision by the Refining Division to purchase crude oil from external suppliers as an inevitable cost of decentralization and not interfere. Of course, some interference may occasionally be necessary to prevent costly blunders. But recurring interference and constraints would simply transform Northern from a decentralized company into a centralized company.

What transfer price will promote goal-congruence for both the Transportation Division and the Refining Division? The minimum transfer price is $80 per barrel; a transfer price below $80 does not provide the Transportation Division with an incentive to purchase crude oil from the independent producer in Calgary while a transfer price above $80 generates contribution margin to cover fixed costs. The maximum transfer price is $85 per barrel; a transfer price above $85 will cause the Refining Division to purchase crude oil from the external market rather than from the Transportation Division.

A transfer price between the minimum and maximum transfer prices of $80 and $85 respectively will promote goal-congruence—both divisions will increase their own reported division operating income by purchasing crude oil from the independent producer in Calgary. In particular, a transfer price based on the full costs of $83 without a markup will achieve goal-congruence. The Transportation Division will show no operating income and will be evaluated as a cost centre. Surveys indicate that managers prefer to use full-cost transfer pricing because it yields relevant costs for long-run decisions and because it facilitates pricing on the basis of full product costs.

Using full-cost transfer prices that include an allocation of fixed overhead costs raises other issues. How are indirect costs allocated to products? Have the correct activities, cost pools, and cost drivers been identified? Are the chosen overhead rates actual or budgeted rates? The issues here are similar to the issues that arise in allocating fixed costs (Chapter 14). Full-cost-based transfer prices calculated using ABC cost drivers can provide more refined allocation bases for allocating costs to products. Using budgeted costs and budgeted rates lets both divisions know the transfer price in advance.

Some companies calculate budgeted rates based on practical capacity rather than master-budget capacity utilization levels (Chapter 9). For tax purposes, however, the CRA requires the use of normal capacity, a long-term measure of demand. Using budgeted rates and practical capacity overcomes the problem of inefficiencies in actual costs and costs of unused capacity being passed along from the selling to the buying division. In negotiation with the CRA, the use of normal capacity as the allocation base for fixed cost pool is unlikely to provide the same cost allocation rate. To maximize tax revenue, the CRA prefers the lower cost allocation rate to maximize taxable income. For CRA purposes, using budgeted fixed-cost allocation rates based on normal capacity will eliminate variations in full-cost transfer prices caused by variation in the actual quantity of units produced.

VARIABLE COST BASES

Transferring 20,000 barrels of crude oil from the Transportation Division to the Refining Division at the variable cost of $80 per barrel achieves goal-congruence, as shown in the preceding section. The Refining Division would buy from the Transportation Division because the Transportation Division's variable cost (which is also the relevant incremental cost for Northern Petroleum as a whole) is less than the $85 price charged by outside suppliers.

At the $80 per barrel transfer price, the Transportation Division would record an operating loss and the Refining Division would show large profits because it would be charged only for the variable costs of the Transportation Division. One approach to addressing this problem is to have the Refining Division make a lump-sum transfer payment to cover fixed costs and generate some operating income for the Transportation Division while the Transportation Division continues to make transfers at variable cost. The fixed payment is the price the Refining Division pays for using the capacity of the Transportation Division. The income earned by each division can then be used to evaluate the performance of each division and its manager.

PRORATING THE DIFFERENCE BETWEEN MINIMUM AND MAXIMUM TRANSFER PRICES

An alternative cost-based approach is for Northern Petroleum to choose a transfer price that splits the $5 difference between the maximum transfer price the Refining Division is willing to pay and the minimum transfer price the Transportation Division wants on some equitable basis. Suppose Northern Petroleum allocates the $5 difference on the basis of the budgeted variable costs incurred by the Transportation Division and the Refining Division for a given quantity of crude oil. Using the data in Exhibit 23-3 (p. 1103), the variable costs are as follows:

Transportation Division's variable costs to transport 100 barrels of crude oil ($1 × 100)	$100
Refining Division's variable costs to refine 100 barrels of crude oil and produce 50 barrels of gasoline ($8 × 50)	400
Total variable costs	$500

The Transportation Division gets to keep $100/$500 × $5 = $1.00, and the Refining Division gets to keep $400/$500 × $5 = $4.00 of the $5 difference. That is, the transfer price between the Transportation Division and the Refining Division would be $81 per barrel of crude oil ($79 purchase cost + $1 variable costs + $1 that the Transportation Division gets to keep). Essentially, this approach is a budgeted variable cost plus transfer price; the "plus" indicates the setting of a transfer price above variable costs.

To decide on the $1 and $4 allocation of the $5 contribution to total corporate operating income per barrel, the divisions must share information about their variable costs. In effect, each division does not operate (at least for this transaction) in a totally decentralized manner. Because most organizations are hybrids of centralization and decentralization anyway, this approach deserves serious consideration when transfers are significant. Note, however, that each division has an incentive to overstate its variable costs in order to receive a more favourable transfer price.

DUAL PRICING

There is seldom a *single* transfer price that simultaneously meets the criteria of goal-congruence, management effort, and subunit autonomy. Some companies turn to **dual pricing**, using two separate transfer pricing methods to price each interdivision transaction. An example of dual pricing arises when the selling division receives a full cost plus markup–based price and the buying division pays the market price for the internally transferred products. Assume that Northern Petroleum purchases crude oil from the independent producer in Calgary at $79 per barrel. One way of recording the journal entry for the transfer between the Transportation Division and the Refining Division is the following:

1. Credit the Transportation Division (the selling division) with the 105%-of-full-cost transfer price of $87.15 per barrel of crude oil.

2. Debit the Refining Division (the buying division) with the market-based transfer price of $85 per barrel of crude oil.

3. Debit a corporate cost account for the $2.15 ($87.15 − $85.00) difference between the two transfer prices for the cost of crude oil borne by corporate rather than the Refining Division.

The dual-price method promotes goal-congruence because it makes the Refining Division no worse off if it purchases the crude oil from the Transportation Division rather than from the outside supplier. In either case, the Refining Division's cost is $85 per barrel of crude oil. This dual-price system essentially gives the Transportation Division a corporate subsidy. One result of dual pricing is that the operating income for Northern Petroleum as a whole is less than the sum of the operating incomes of the divisions.

THINKING CRITICALLY

What is the likely response of tax authorities to dual pricing? Explain in a sentence or two. Read on for a discussion of this topic.

Managers, irrespective of how decentralized their corporate structure, must conform to tax legislation. It is unlikely the CRA would object as long as there was no decrease in corporate taxable income and the method complied with legislation. The OECD hierarchy of preference, however, places current market value as the most preferred method and a competitive market is assumed where there is only one homogeneous price, not two. Interprovincially, and in an MNC situation, when dual rates do affect taxable income in more than one jurisdiction there is risk. Overall the consolidated taxable income would be unaffected but the distribution of tax revenue would be affected by dual rates. The amounts are not trivial. Nations as well as provinces will dispute what are perceived as tax avoidance strategies, especially if a current market price can be used instead.

Dual pricing is not widely used in practice even though it reduces the goal-congruence problems associated with a pure cost plus–based transfer pricing method. One concern of top management is that the manager of the supplying division does not have sufficient incentive to control costs with a dual-price system. A second concern is that the dual-price system confuses division managers about the level of decentralization top management seeks. Above all, dual pricing tends to insulate managers from the frictions of the marketplace. Managers should know as much as possible about their subunits' buying and selling markets, and dual pricing reduces the incentive to gain this knowledge.

ASSESS YOUR MASTERY

To check your understanding of the material in Learning Objective ④, go to the *Mastery Questions* section at the end of this chapter and complete Learning Objective ④ question 1.

NEGOTIATED TRANSFER PRICES AND MNC ISSUES

⑤ Analyze income tax considerations in multinational transfer pricing

Negotiated transfer prices arise as the outcome of a bargaining process between selling and buying divisions. Consider again the choice of a transfer price between the Transportation and Refining Divisions of Northern Petroleum. The Transportation Division has excess capacity that it can use to transport oil from Calgary to Sarnia. The Transportation Division will be willing to "sell" oil to the Refining Division only if the transfer price equals or exceeds $80 per barrel of crude oil (its variable costs). The Refining Division will be willing to "buy" crude oil from the Transportation Division only if the cost equals or is below $85 per barrel (the price at which the Refining Division can buy crude oil in Sarnia).

Given the Transportation Division's unused capacity, Northern Petroleum as a whole maximizes operating income if the Refining Division purchases from the Transportation Division rather than from the Sarnia market (incremental costs of $80 per barrel versus incremental costs of $85 per barrel). Both divisions would be interested in transacting with each other if the transfer price is set between $80 and $85. For example, a transfer price of $83 per barrel will increase the Transportation Division's operating income by $83 − $80 = $3.00 per barrel. It will increase the Refining Division's operating income by $85 − $83 = $2.00 per barrel because Refining can now "buy" the oil for $83 inside rather than for $85 outside.

The key question is where between $80 and $85 the transfer price will be. The answer depends on the bargaining strengths of the two divisions. The Transportation Division has more information about the price less incremental marketing costs of supplying crude oil to outside refineries while the Refining Division has more information about its other available sources of oil. Negotiations become particularly sensitive if Northern evaluates each division's performance on the basis of divisional operating income.

The price negotiated by the two divisions will, in general, have no specific relationship to either costs or market price. But cost and price information are often useful starting points in the negotiation process. Exhibit 23-4 compares the three methods of transfer pricing discussed. The full-cost-based transfer price is the most used and negotiated prices are the least frequently used transfer pricing method worldwide.

A GENERAL GUIDELINE FOR TRANSFER PRICING SITUATIONS

There exists no pervasive rule for transfer pricing that leads towards optimal decisions for the organization as a whole because the three criteria of goal-congruence, management effort, and subunit autonomy must all be considered simultaneously. The following general guideline, however, has proven to be a helpful first step in setting a minimum transfer price in many specific situations:

$$\begin{array}{c} \text{Minimum} \\ \text{transfer price} \end{array} = \begin{array}{c} \text{Additional } \textit{incremental} \text{ or } \textit{outlay costs} \text{ per unit} \\ \text{incurred up to the point of transfer} \end{array} + \begin{array}{c} \textit{Opportunity costs} \text{ per unit} \\ \text{to the supplying division} \end{array}$$

The term *incremental* or *outlay costs* in this context represents the additional costs that are directly associated with the production and transfer of the products or services. *Opportunity costs* are defined here as the maximum contribution forgone by the supplying division if the products or services are transferred internally. For example, if the supplying division is operating at capacity, the opportunity cost of

Real Practices Worldwide

Transfer pricing remains an important accounting priority for managers around the world. A recent survey of managers in 22 countries, including the United States, Australia, Canada, and Japan, found that 86% of all respondents believed transfer pricing was important to their group's operations.[a]

What transfer pricing methods are used around the world? The following tables indicate how extensively particular transfer pricing methods are used in different countries.

A. Domestic Transfer-Pricing Methods

Methods	Australia[b]	Canada[c]	Japan[d]	New Zealand[e]	United Kingdom[f]	United States[d]
Market-based	13%	34%	34%	18%	26%	26%
Cost-based:						
Variable cost	—	6	2	10	10	3
Absorption or full cost	—	37	44	61	38	49
Other	—	3	—	—	1	1
Total	65%	46%	46%	71%	49%	53%
Negotiated	11%	18%	19%	11%	24%	17%
Other	11%	2%	1%	—	1%	4%
	100%	100%	100%	100%	100%	100%

B. Multinational Transfer-Pricing Methods

Methods	Australia	Canada[c]	Japan[d]	New Zealand	United Kingdom	United States[d]
Market-based	—	37%	37%	—	—	35%
Cost-based:						
Variable cost	—	5	3	—	—	0
Absorption or full cost	—	26	38	—	—	42
Other	—	2	—	—	—	1
Total	—	33%	41%	—	—	43%
Negotiated	—	26%	22%	—	—	14%
Other	—	4%	—	—	—	8%
	—	100%	100%	—	—	100%

Note: Dashes indicate information was not disclosed in survey.

In all countries, managers use cost-based more often than market-based transfer prices for domestic transfers. Managers use cost-based only slightly more often than market-based methods for international transfers and many use market-based transfer prices in some divisions and cost-based transfer prices in others. Managers consider the following factors important when making domestic transfer pricing decisions (in order of importance): (1) maximizing consolidated after-tax profits, (2) performance evaluation, and (3) management motivation. Factors ranked in importance for multinational transfer pricing decisions include: (1) income tax rate and other tax differences among countries, (2) total income of the company, and (3) income- or dividend-repatriation restrictions.[c,g]

[a] Ernst & Young, *Transfer Pricing 2003 Global Survey* (New York: Ernst & Young, November 2003).

[b] M. Joye and P. Blayney, "Cost and Management Accounting Practices in Australian Manufacturing Companies: Survey Results" (Accounting Research Centre, The University of Sydney, 1991).

[c] R. Tang, "Canadian Transfer Pricing in the 1990s," *Management Accounting* (1992).

[d] R. Tang, *Transfer Pricing Systems Management: Practical Issues and Cases* (Montvale, NJ: Institute of Management Accountants, 2001).

[e] Z. Hoque and M. Alam, "Organization Size, Business Objectives, Managerial Autonomy, Industry Conditions, and Management's Choice of Transfer Pricing Methods: A Contextual Analysis of New Zealand Companies" (Working Paper, Victoria University of Wellington, New Zealand, 1998).

[f] C. Drury, S. Braund, P. Osborne, and M. Tayles, *A Survey of Management Accounting Practices in UK Manufacturing Companies* (London: Chartered Association of Certified Accountants, 1993).

[g] J. Elliot, "International Transfer Pricing: A Survey of U.K. and Non-U.K. Groups," *Management Accounting* (1998).

transferring a unit internally rather than selling it externally is equal to the market price minus variable costs. We distinguish incremental costs from opportunity costs because the accounting system typically records incremental costs but not opportunity costs. We illustrate the general guideline in some specific situations using data from the Production and Transportation Divisions of Northern Petroleum.

1. **A perfectly competitive market for the intermediate product exists, and the selling division has no unused capacity.** If the market for crude oil in Calgary is perfectly competitive, the Transportation Division can sell all the

EXHIBIT 23-4
Comparison of Different Transfer-Pricing Methods

Criteria	Market-Based	Cost-Based	Negotiated
Achieves goal-congruence	Yes, when markets are competitive	Often but not always	Yes
Useful for evaluating subunit performance	Yes, when markets are competitive	Difficult unless transfer price exceeds full cost and even then is somewhat arbitrary	Yes, but transfer prices are affected by bargaining strengths of the buying and selling divisions
Motivates management effort	Yes	Yes, when based on budgeted costs; less incentive to control costs if transfers are based on actual costs	Yes
Preserves subunit autonomy	Yes, when markets are competitive	No, because it is rule based	Yes, because it is based on negotiations between subunits
Other factors	Market may not exist, or markets may be imperfect or in distress	Useful for determining full cost of products and services; easy to implement	Bargaining and negotiations take time and may need to be reviewed repeatedly as conditions change

crude oil it transports to the external market at $85 per barrel, and it will have no unused capacity.

The Transportation Division's incremental cost (as shown in Exhibit 23-2, p. 1101) is either $73 per barrel (purchase cost of $72 per barrel plus variable transportation cost of $1 per barrel) for oil purchased under the long-term contract or $80 per barrel (purchase cost of $79 plus variable transportation cost of $1) for oil purchased at current market prices from the Calgary producer. The Transportation Division's opportunity cost per barrel of transferring the oil internally is the contribution margin per barrel forgone by not selling the crude oil in the external market: $12 for oil purchased under the long-term contract (market price, $85, minus variable cost, $73) and $5 for oil purchased from the Calgary producer (market price, $85, minus variable cost, $80). In either case,

$$\text{Minimum transfer price per barrel} = \text{Incremental cost per barrel} + \text{Opportunity costs per barrel}$$

$$= \$73 + 12 = \$85$$

$$\text{or}$$

$$= \$80 + \$5 = \$85$$

Market-based transfer prices are ideal in perfectly competitive markets when there is no idle capacity.

2. **An intermediate market exists that is not perfectly competitive, and the selling division has unused capacity.** In markets that are not perfectly competitive, capacity utilization can only be increased by decreasing prices. Unused capacity exists because decreasing prices is often not worthwhile—it decreases operating income. If the Transportation Division has unused capacity, its opportunity cost of transferring the oil internally is zero because the division does not forgo any external sales or contribution margin from internal transfers. In this case:

$$\text{Minimum transfer price per barrel} = \text{Incremental cost per barrel} + \begin{array}{l}\text{\$73 per barrel for oil purchased under the} \\ \text{long-term contract or \$80 per barrel for oil} \\ \text{purchased from the Calgary producer}\end{array}$$

Any transfer price above incremental cost but below $85—the price at which the Refining Division can buy crude oil in Sarnia—motivates the Transportation Division to transport crude oil to the Refining Division and the Refining Division to buy crude oil from the Transportation Division. In this situation, the company could either use a cost-based transfer price or allow the two divisions to negotiate a transfer price between themselves.

In general, though, in markets that are not perfectly competitive, the potential to influence demand and operating income through prices makes measuring opportunity costs more complicated. The transfer price depends on constantly changing levels of supply and demand. There is not just one transfer price; rather, a transfer pricing schedule yields the transfer price for various quantities supplied and demanded, depending on the incremental costs and opportunity costs of the units transferred.

Consider the following situation: Suppose the Refining Division receives an order to supply specially processed gasoline. The Refining Division will profit from this order only if the Transportation Division can supply crude oil at a price not exceeding $82 per barrel. Suppose the incremental cost to purchase and supply crude oil is $80 per barrel. In this case, the transfer price that would benefit both divisions must be greater than $80 but less than $82 (rather than $85).

3. **No market exists for the intermediate product.** This would occur, for example, in the Northern Petroleum case if oil from the production well flows directly into the pipeline and cannot be sold to outside parties.

Here, the opportunity cost of supplying crude oil internally is zero because the inability to sell crude oil externally means no contribution margin is forgone. At the Transportation Division of Northern Petroleum, the minimum transfer price under the general guideline would be the incremental costs per barrel of either $73 or $80. As in the previous case, any transfer price between the incremental cost and $85 will achieve goal-congruence. Knowledge of the incremental cost per barrel of crude oil would be helpful to the Refining Division for many decisions, such as short-run pricing.

In transfer pricing situations, opportunity cost is the profit the selling division (SD) forgoes by selling internally rather than externally. Assume the SD has no idle capacity for a particular product and can sell all it produces at $4 per unit. Incremental cost is $1 per unit. If the SD sells internally, the opportunity cost is $3 per unit ($4 revenue per unit – $1 incremental cost per unit). In contrast, if the SD has unused capacity with no alternative use, no profit is forgone by selling internally (opportunity cost is $0).

MNC TRANSFER PRICING AND TAX CONSIDERATIONS

Now we will consider factors affecting transfer prices among corporate subunits in different countries. Sales between corporate subunits are called sales between **related parties**, in contrast to external sales between a subunit and a nonrelated party termed **arm's-length transactions**. The transfer prices have tax implications and therefore affect the government revenues of each country involved. Tax factors include income taxes, payroll taxes, customs duties, tariffs, sales taxes, value-added taxes, environment-related taxes, and other government levies. We focus on income tax factors as a key consideration in transfer pricing decisions.

The Income Tax Act of Canada (section 247) sets out the laws regarding transfer pricing. The most recent rules were introduced in 1998 after legislative changes in the US and the publication of transfer price guidelines by the OECD. The CRA intends to achieve harmonization with OECD and US laws to reduce the costs of tax compliance for multinational corporations. The most important laws limit how companies set transfer prices to one of five methods.

Transfer prices also have tax implications, particularly when products are transferred across country borders. Setting transfer prices is almost always a matter of judgment. At no time, however, should management accountants choose transfer

Once Again—Tax Is Mandatory—They Will Get You

Transfer pricing requires one subunit manager to earn revenues and another subunit manager to incur costs. Managers are frequently evaluated on the basis of subunit profits. Little wonder, then, that subunit managers care deeply about how transfer prices are set. It is natural for subunit managers to argue for transfer prices that make their own performance look good. Management accountants must ensure that the transfer prices set are in the best interests of the company as a whole. This requires management accountants to understand business issues and the external market environment within which the businesses function. They must also never cave in to pressure from managers that will make a subunit's performance look good while hurting the corporation as a

whole. Consider Motorola, the electronics products manufacturer. In 2004, the US Internal Revenue Service (IRS) notified the company that it was disputing the way Motorola calculated earnings from 1996 to 2000, resulting in an additional tax liability of US$500 million. The underlying issue was related to transfer pricing involving Motorola's 67 tax entities around the world. The IRS claimed too much profit was left in the company's tax entities abroad and that not enough income was recognized in the US. Motorola must convince the IRS that its practices are within the law.

Source: R. Crockett, "Motorola's Taxing Dispute," *Business Week Online,* August 12, 2004, www.businessweek.com/bwdaily/dnflash/aug2004/nj20040812_8175_db016.htm, accessed September 17, 2004.

prices that do not adhere to the tax codes of different countries. The time and cost to resolve transfer pricing disputes can be very high.

Traditional transaction methods include the **comparable uncontrolled price (CUP), resale price method (RPM)**, and **cost-plus method (CPM)**. The CUP is analogous to the internal market-based price. The related-party transfer price reported by a corporation is compared to prices for similar transactions among arm's-length (nonrelated) parties and must fall within the middle two quartiles of this range of prices. The CRA has confidential comparable tables in its ever-growing database that it uses to make these comparisons.

The RPM requires a company calculate the arm's-length resale price. Distributors of finished goods typically use this method when the cost of distribution is low relative to the value of the finished goods (that is, almost non-value-added). Again the CRA compares the estimated transfer price to a range of prices for similar arm's-length transactions and usually accepts transfer prices in the two mid-quartiles of this range. The CPM highlights the effect of the transfer price on the pretax income of each subunit. This method permits corporations the greatest discretion and most readily justified transfer price to the CRA because of the quality of information provided by management accounting and control systems.

The transactional profit methods of setting a transfer price are the **profit split method (PSM)** and **transactional net margin method (TNMM)**. The PSM requires understanding the value added by the functions performed by each related party and the resulting allocation of profit and loss to each subunit. The fifth method, TNMM, is based on the return on assets (ROA) of the corporation as a whole and provides maximum discretion for establishing a transfer price.

Establishing the arm's-length price for value-added services such as marketing or intangible contributions such as research and development knowledge is difficult. The role of the management accountant has increased in importance as has the role of the internal data on pricing already produced by the management accounting and control system because companies must produce contemporaneous documentation for every transfer price transaction or be subject to an automatic financial penalty for failing to do so. Companies are obligated to comply with Canada's tax laws. This audit trail, which justifies in detail the transfer price used, provides the CRA with evidence companies have made reasonable effort to do what they should to establish the price is arm's length. The CRA auditors may still disagree with and adjust the transfer price despite the documentation provided, but no penalty will be imposed for failing to make a reasonable effort to establish an arm's-length transfer price.

Corporations may choose a tax minimization strategy by establishing a legitimate subsidiary in a tax haven (e.g., Andorra, Liechtenstein, Monaco). **Tax havens** have no tax agreements with Canada and share no information, which will increase the costs to the company of any tax audit. A second strategy is to establish a legitimate subsidiary in an **international financial centre** with very low income tax rates (e.g., Barbados or Ireland). These centres have tax treaties with Canada. Consider an example of a Canadian company that manufactures and sells products from Ireland. Tax and other incentives offered there result in the Irish division paying lower taxes on its income in Ireland. Therefore, the company has an incentive to set the transfer price for transfers into Canada as high as possible. Why? To maximize income reported in Ireland where tax rates are lower and reduce income reported in Canada that is taxed at rates as high as 40%. Nevertheless, to make sound transfer pricing decisions, managers must remember that penalties for noncompliance with transfer pricing tax laws can be substantial.

In Canada the CRA has indicated it will aggressively challenge transfer prices based on costs allocated proportionally to revenues of the related parties, management services to Canadian companies at cost plus, and any dual product prices. While the CRA has published transfer pricing guidelines (IC87-2R), when disputes arise the final decision on the transfer price is often negotiated among the tax authorities involved in the dispute. This resolution process not only is costly but also can take as long as two years, and any penalties imposed are retroactive and accumulate interest during the process. To avoid costly disputes, companies may choose a third strategy—to request an advance pricing arrangement with all involved tax authorities.

Consider the Northern Petroleum data in Exhibit 23-3 (p. 1103). Assume that Northern operates a Transportation Division in Mexico that pays Mexican income taxes at 30% of operating income and that both the Transportation and Refining Divisions based in Canada pay income taxes at 20% of operating income. Northern Petroleum would minimize its total income tax payments with the 105% of full costs transfer pricing method, as shown in the following table:

| Transfer-Pricing Method | Operating Income for 100 Barrels of Crude Oil | | | Income Tax on 100 Barrels of Crude Oil | | |
	Transportation Division (Mexico) (1)	Refining Division (Canada) (2)	Total (3) = (1) + (2)	Transportation Division (Mexico) (4) = 0.30 × (1)	Refining Division (Canada) (5) = 0.20 × (2)	Total (6) = (4) + (5)
Market price	$900	$300	$1,200	$270	$ 60	$330
105% of full costs	380	820	1,200	114	164	278
Negotiated price	650	550	1,200	195	110	305

Tax considerations raise additional issues that may conflict with other objectives of transfer pricing. Suppose that the market for crude oil in Calgary is perfectly competitive. In this case, the market-based transfer price achieves goal-congruence and provides effort incentives. It also helps Northern to evaluate the economic profitability of the Transportation Division. But it is costly from an income tax standpoint.

Northern Petroleum would favour using 105% of full costs for tax reporting. Tax laws in Canada and Mexico constrain this option. In particular, the Mexican tax authorities are fully aware of Northern Petroleum's incentives to minimize income taxes by reducing the income reported in Mexico. They would challenge any attempts to shift income to the Refining Division through a low transfer price.

The perfectly competitive market for crude oil in Mexico would probably force Northern Petroleum to use the market price for transfers from the Production Division to the Transportation Division. Northern Petroleum might successfully argue that the transfer price should be set below the market price because the Production

Real Practices Worldwide

Tax authorities and government officials around the world pay close attention to taxes paid by multinational companies operating within their boundaries. At the heart of the issue are the transfer prices that companies use to transfer products from one country to another. The US Internal Revenue Service (IRS) and the Japanese National Tax Agency (NTA) have been among the most active agencies pursuing international transfer pricing disputes. For example, in 1993 the IRS investigated and concluded that Nissan Motor Company had understated US taxes by setting transfer prices on passenger cars and trucks imported from Japan at "unrealistically" high levels. Nissan argued that it had maintained low margins in the United States to increase long-run market share in a very competitive market. Eventually, Nissan agreed to pay the IRS US$170 million, but the company suffered no loss. That's because

the Japanese NTA refunded Nissan the full amount of the IRS payment. In 2000, Japan's NTA and the IRS had to settle another dispute regarding transfer prices. This time Coca-Cola's Japanese subsidiary had to record an additional US$450 million in taxable income from 1993 through 1999, which meant that it owed approximately US$170 million to Japan's NTA in back taxes and penalties. To avoid double taxation, the IRS refunded Coca-Cola the tax it had already paid to the United States.

Historically, disputes arise between governments over what constitutes a "fair" transfer price because of the absence of an easily observable market price for the transferred product. In 2003, the United States and Japan signed a new tax treaty that, among other things, stipulates that future transfer pricing disputes be addressed in accordance with the OECD's Transfer Pricing Guidelines. This development has eased tax disputes between the United States and Japan. The IRS and NTA remain actively engaged in transfer pricing conflicts with other nations.

Sources: Adapted from C. Pass, "Transfer Pricing in Multinational Companies," *Management Accounting* (September 1994); "Coca-Cola Gets 10 Billion Yen Reprieve in Back Taxes," *Yomiuri Shimbun* (February 24, 1998); *Financial Times* (September 3, 1999); *Daily Yomiuri* (February 24, 1998, and April 30, 2000); Morrison & Foster, LLP, *New United States–Japan Tax Treaty Enters into Force: New Withholding Rates Take Effect on July 1, 2004.*

Division incurs no marketing and distribution costs when "selling" crude oil to the Transportation Division. Northern Petroleum could obtain advance approval of the transfer pricing arrangements from the appropriate tax authorities.

To meet multiple transfer pricing objectives, a company may choose to keep one set of accounting records for tax reporting and a second set for internal management reporting. The difficulty here is that tax authorities may interpret two sets of books as suggestive of the company manipulating its reported taxable income to avoid tax payments. Additional factors that arise in multinational transfer pricing include tariffs and customs duties levied on imports of products into a country. The issues here are similar to the income tax considerations discussed earlier—companies will have incentives to lower transfer prices for products imported into a country to reduce the tariffs and customs duties that those products will attract. MNC transfer prices are sometimes influenced by restrictions that some countries place on the payment of income or dividends to parties outside their national borders. By increasing the prices of goods or services transferred into divisions in these countries, companies can increase the funds paid out of these countries without appearing to violate income or dividend restrictions.

MyAccountingLab

ASSESS YOUR MASTERY

To check your understanding of the material in Learning Objective 5, go to the *Mastery Questions* section at the end of this chapter and complete Learning Objective 5 question 1.

PROBLEM

The Pillercat Corporation is a highly decentralized company. Each division manager has full authority for sourcing and selling decisions. The Machining Division of Pillercat has been the major supplier of the 2,000 crankshafts that the Tractor Division needs each year.

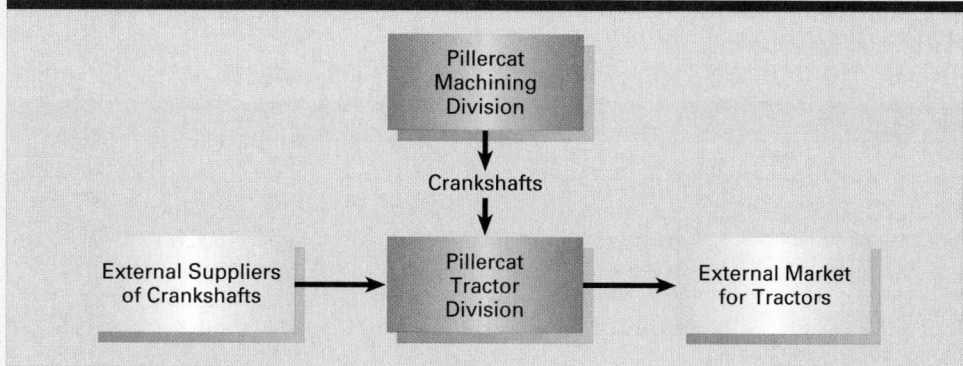

The Tractor Division, however, has just announced that it plans to purchase all its crankshafts in the forthcoming year from two external suppliers at $200 per crankshaft. The Machining Division of Pillercat recently increased its price for the forthcoming year to $220 per unit (from $200 per unit in the current year).

Juan Gomez, manager of the Machining Division, feels that the 10% price increase is fully justified. It results from a higher amortization charge on some new specialized equipment used to manufacture crankshafts and an increase in labour costs. Gomez wants the president of Pillercat Corporation to direct the Tractor Division to buy all its crankshafts from the Machining Division at the price of $220. The additional incremental costs per unit that Pillercat incurs to produce each crankshaft are the Machining Division's variable costs of $190. Fixed cost per crankshaft in the Machining Division equals $20.

	A	B
1	Number of crankshafts purchased by Tractor Division	2,000
2	External supplier's market price per crankshaft	$ 200
3	Variable cost per crankshaft in Machining Division	$ 190
4	Fixed cost per crankshaft in Machining Division	$ 20

REQUIRED

1. Compute the advantage or disadvantage (in terms of monthly operating income) to the Pillercat Corporation as a whole if the Tractor Division buys crankshafts internally from the Machining Division under each of the following cases:
   a. The Machining Division has no alternative use for the facilities used to manufacture crankshafts.
   b. The Machining Division can use the facilities for other production operations, which will result in monthly cash operating savings of $29,000.
   c. The Machining Division has no alternative use for the facilities, and the external supplier drops its price to $185 per crankshaft.

2. As the president of Pillercat, how would you respond to Juan Gomez's request to order the Tractor Division to purchase all of its crankshafts from the Machining Division? Would your response differ according to the scenarios described in parts (a), (b), and (c) of requirement 1? Why?

3. Discuss the tax implications if the Machining and Tractor division were located in different countries. Pillercat management's best transfer price choice would be

the current market price or CUP because it conforms with the OECD hierarchy. The managers would be wise to negotiate an advance transfer price arrangement with tax authorities in both countries (APA). If there were no market for the inter-mediate product then profit split (PSM) or transactional net margin methods (TNMM) could be negotiated.

4. The best transfer price for performance evaluation may not be the most acceptable to tax authorities. In terms of good governance what option is available to managers?

SOLUTION

1. Computations for the Tractor Division buying crankshafts internally for cases (a), (b), and (c) are:

	A	B	C	D
1			Case	
2		a	b	c
3	Number of crankshafts purchased by Tractor Division	2,000	2,000	2,000
4	External supplier's market price per crankshaft	$ 200	$ 200	$ 185
5	Incremental cost per crankshaft in Machining Division	$ 190	$ 190	$ 190
6	Opportunity costs of the Machining Division supplying	–	$ 29,000	–
7	crankshafts to the Tractor Division			
8				
9	Total purchase costs if buying from an external supplier			
10	(2,000 shafts × $200, $200, $185 per shaft)	$400,000	$400,000	$370,000
11	Incremental costs of buying from the Machining Division			
12	(2,000 shafts × $190 per shaft)	380,000	380,000	380,000
13	Total opportunity costs of the Machining Division	–	29,000	–
14	Total relevant costs	380,000	$409,000	380,000
15	Annual operating income advantage (disadvantage) to			
16	Pillercat of buying from the Machining Division	$ 20,000	$ (9,000)	$ (10,000)
17				

The general guideline introduced on page 1110 as a first step in setting a transfer price highlights the alternatives:

	A	B	C	D	E	F	G
1		Incremental Cost			Opportunity Cost				External
2		per Unit Incurred to			per Unit to the		Transfer	Market
3	Case	Point of Transfer	+	Supplying Division	=	Price	Price
4	a	$190	+	$ 0	=	$190.00	$200
5	b	$190	+	$14.50[a]	=	$204.50	$200
6	c	$190	+	$ 0	=	$190.00	$185
7							
8	[a]Opportunity per unit = Total opportunity costs ÷ Number of crankshafts = $29,000 ÷ 2,000 = $14.50						

The Tractor Division will maximize monthly operating income of Pillercat Corporation as a whole by purchasing from the Machining Division in case (a) and by purchasing from the external suppliers in cases (b) and (c).

2. Pillercat Corporation is a highly decentralized company. If no forced transfer were made, the Tractor Division would use an external supplier, resulting in an optimal decision for the company as a whole in cases (b) and (c) of requirement 1, but not in case (a).

Suppose that in case 1(a), the Machining Division refuses to meet the price of $200. This decision means that the company will be $20,000 worse off in the short run. Should top management interfere and force a transfer at $200? This interference would undercut the philosophy of decentralization. Many top management teams would not interfere because they would view the $20,000 as an inevitable cost of a suboptimal decision that occasionally occurs under decentralization. But how high must this cost be before the temptation to interfere would be irresistible? $30,000? $40,000?

Any top management interference with lower-level decision making weakens decentralization. Of course, such interference may occasionally be necessary to prevent costly blunders. But recurring interference and constraints simply transform a decentralized organization into a centralized organization.

3. Pillercat management's best transfer price choice would be the current market price or CUP because it conforms with the OECD hierarchy. The managers would be wise to negotiate an advance transfer price arrangement with tax authorities in both countries (APA). If there were no market for the intermediate product, then profit split (PSM) or transactional net margin methods (TNMM) could be negotiated.

4. Assuming that managers do achieve satisfactory standards of good governance, they will have access to relevant information as described in the CoCo framework. This implies the presence of coordinated information systems which enable the development of dual accounting records. One management accounting system reports values used for performance evaluation purposes over which tax authorities have no concern. The second reports performance according to methods of transfer pricing acceptable to tax authorities.

DECISION POINTS

The following decision guidelines use a question-and-answer format to summarize the chapter's main points. Each decision presents a key question. The guideline is the answer to that question.

DECISIONS	GUIDELINES
1. What is a control system and how should it be designed?	A control system is a means to organize or arrange elements into an orderly structure. Choices of organizational structure are constrained by legislation such as NI52-109 and NI58-201 in Canada as well as CRA tax legislation. The goal of control systems is to nurture and sustain good governance.
2. How are transfer pricing methods ranked?	To ease the compliance burden on MNCs, most countries worldwide have adopted the OECD Hierarchy of Methods for transfer pricing. The principle upon which the ranking is based is the arm's-length principle. The most preferred transfer price is current market price of intermediate products. Other alternatives for internal control include cost-based and negotiated prices.
3. What are the benefits of transferring products at current market price?	Optimal internal management decisions to benefit the entire corporation are made if the intermediate market is perfectly competitive (homogeneous product and prices) and interdependencies among subunits are minimal.
4. How does cost-plus transfer pricing lead to suboptimal internal management decisions?	A transfer price based on full cost plus a markup may lead to suboptimal decisions because it leads the buying division to regard the fixed costs and the markup of the selling division as variable costs. The buying division may then purchase products from an outside vendor expecting savings in variable costs that, in fact, will not occur.
5. What constraints are externally imposed to internal guidelines for determining a minimum transfer?	Transfer prices can reduce income tax payments by recognizing more income in low-tax-rate countries and less income in high-tax-rate countries. However, tax regulations of different countries restrict the transfer prices that companies can choose. Internal guidelines state that the minimum transfer price equals the incremental cost per unit incurred up to the point of transfer plus the opportunity cost per unit to the supplying division resulting from transferring products or services internally.

This chapter contains definitions of the following important terms:

advance transfer price arrangement
    (APA) (p. 1104)
arm's-length principle (p. 1099)
arm's-length transaction (p. 1113)
comparable uncontrolled price method
    (CUP) (p. 1114)
cost-plus method (CPM) (p. 1114)
decentralization (p. 1095)
dual pricing (p. 1109)
dysfunctional decision making (p. 1097)

effort (p. 1094)
goal-congruence (p. 1094)
goal-incongruent decision making
    (p. 1097)
intermediate products (p. 1099)
international financial centre (p. 1115)
management accounting control system
    (MACS) (p. 1092)
motivation (p. 1094)
perfectly competitive market (p. 1104)

profit split method (PSM) (p. 1114)
related parties (p. 1113)
resale price method (RPM)
    (p. 1114)
suboptimal decision making
    (p. 1097)
tax haven (p. 1115)
transactional net margin method
    (TNMM) (p. 1114)
transfer price (p. 1099)

MASTERY QUESTIONS

Mastery Questions are rated by proficiency level—elementary, intermediate, and advanced. The solutions appear in the Solutions to Mastery Questions section of MyAccountingLab.

LEARNING OBJECTIVE 1

1. **Evaluate CoCo—Advanced.** Hexton Chemicals consists of seven operating divisions that each operate independently. The operating divisions are supported by a number of support divisions such as R&D, labour relations, and environmental management. The environmental management group consists of 20 environmental engineers. These engineers must seek out business from the operating divisions—that is, the projects they work on must be mutually agreed to and paid for by one of the operating divisions. Under Hexton's rules, the environmental group is required to charge the operating divisions for environmental services at cost.

REQUIRED
1. Is the environmental management organization centralized or decentralized?
2. What type of responsibility centre is the environmental management group?
3. What benefits and problems do you see in structuring the environmental management group the way Hexton has? Does it lead to goal-congruence and motivation?

LEARNING OBJECTIVE 2

1. **Apply transfer pricing methods—Advanced.** Blue Ribbon Fisheries is a fishing company located on the Canadian Pacific coast. It has three divisions:
   a. Harvesting—operates a fleet of 20 trawling vessels.
   b. Processing—processes the raw fish into fillets.
   c. Marketing—packages fillets in two-kilogram packets that are sold to wholesale distributors at $15 each on average.

   The Processing Division has a yield of 500 kilograms of processed fish fillets from 1,000 kilograms of raw fish provided by the Harvesting Division. The Marketing Division has a yield of 300 two-kilogram packets from every 500 kilograms of processed fish fillets provided by the Processing Division (the weight of the packaging material is included in the two-kilogram weight). Cost data for each division are as follows:

Fish Harvesting Division	
Variable costs per kilogram of raw fish	$0.24
Fixed costs per kilogram of raw fish	$0.48
Fish Processing Division	
Variable costs per kilogram of processed fish	$0.96
Fixed costs per kilogram of processed fish	$0.72
Fish Marketing Division	
Variable costs per two-kilogram packet	$0.36
Fixed costs per two-kilogram packet	$0.84

Fixed costs per unit are based on the estimated quantity of raw fish, processed fish, and two-kilogram packets to be produced during the current fishing season.

Blue Ribbon Fisheries has chosen to process internally all raw fish brought in by the Harvesting Division. Other fish processors on the Pacific Coast purchase raw fish from boat operators at $1.70 per kilogram on average. Blue Ribbon has also chosen to process internally all fish fillets into the two-kilogram packets sold by the Marketing Division. Several fish marketing companies on the Pacific Coast purchase fish fillets at $7 per kilogram on average.

REQUIRED

1. Compute the overall operating income to Blue Ribbon Fisheries of harvesting 1,000 kilograms of raw fish, processing it into fillets, and then selling it in two-kilogram packets.
2. Compute the transfer prices that will be used for internal transfers (i) from the Harvesting Division to the Processing Division and (ii) from the Processing Division to the Marketing Division under each of the following transfer pricing methods:
   a. 200% of variable costs. Variable costs are the costs of the transferred-in product (if any) plus the division's own variable costs.
   b. 150% of full costs. Full costs are the costs of the transferred-in product (if any) plus the division's own variable and fixed costs.
   c. Market price.
3. Blue Ribbon Fisheries rewards each division manager with a bonus, calculated as 1% of division operating income (if positive). What is the amount of the bonus that will be paid to each division manager under each of the three transfer pricing methods in requirement 2? Which transfer pricing method will each division manager prefer to use?

LEARNING OBJECTIVE 3

1. **Market-based transfer price method—Advanced.** Mark's division had been judged on the basis of its profit and return on investment. Top management had been working to gain effective results from a policy of decentralizing responsibility for all decisions except those relating to overall company policy. Top management felt that the concept of decentralization had been successfully applied and that the company's profits and competitive position had definitely improved in the last two years.

Mark is considering two alternative bids to submit for a very large project that will represent 50% of his division's activity. He plans to apply the usual 10% profit markup on full costs to both bids.

◆ **Alternative 1:** Price of $55 per piece (will yield a ROI of 20% and the probability of winning the bid is 80%)

About 60% of Mark's cost represents the cost of parts manufactured by another division of the same company that had been running below capacity and had excess inventory but quoted the market price. The costs of the supplying division are about 50 percent of the selling price quoted to Mark.

◆ **Alternative 2:** Price of $52.80 per piece (will yield a ROI of 18% and the probability of winning the bid is 90%)

A reduction in prices can be obtained if part of the job is outsourced. The parts that Mark's division needs can be bought at $28 from an external supplier.

Mark knows that they sell in a very competitive market, where higher costs cannot be passed on. His preference for alternative 2 is opposite to company's guidelines of buying internally, so he asked the CEO, "How can we be expected to show a decent profit and return on investment if we have to buy our supplies internally at more than the market price?"

Knowing that the supplying division had on occasion in the past few months been unable to operate at capacity, Mark asserted that it was odd to add the full overhead and profit charge to his costs. In particular, the portion that belonged to corporate overhead that is allocated to all divisions at a rate of 10% of total own costs.

REQUIRED

1. Calculate the profit per piece in dollars for each division under each alternative.
2. Calculate the transfer price at which the parts are being transferred from the internal supplier to Mark's division. Explain if it is the most adequate in this situation.
3. Explain which alternative is best for Mark.
4. Explain which alternative is best for the whole corporation.

LEARNING OBJECTIVE 4

1. **Apply relevant costs and tax—Advanced.** The Ottawa Valley Instrument Company (OVIC) consists of the Semiconductor Division and the Process-Control Division, each which operates as an independent profit centre. The Semiconductor Division employs

craftsmen who produce two different electronic components, the new high-performance Super-chip and an older product called Okay-chip. These two products have the following cost characteristics:

	Super-chip	Okay-chip
Direct materials	$ 2.40	$ 1.20
Direct manufacturing labour		
2 hours × $16.80; 0.5 hours × $16.80	33.60	8.40

Annual overhead in the Semiconductor Division totals $400,000, all fixed. Owing to the high skill level necessary for the craftsmen, the semiconductor division's capacity is set at 50,000 hours per year.

One customer orders a maximum of 15,000 Super-chips per year, at a price of $72 per chip. If OVIC cannot meet this entire demand, the customer curtails its own production. The rest of the Semiconductor Division's capacity is devoted to the Okay-chip, for which there is unlimited demand at $14.40 per chip.

The Process-Control Division provides only one product, a process-control unit with the following cost structure:

Direct materials (circuit board)	$72
Direct manufacturing labour (5 hours × $12)	60

Fixed overhead costs of the Process-Control Division are $96,000 per year. The current market price of the control unit is $158.40 per unit.

A joint research project has just revealed that a single Super-chip could be substituted for the circuit board currently used to make the process-control unit. Using Super-chip would require an extra hour of labour per control unit for a new total of 6 hours per control unit.

REQUIRED

1. Calculate the contribution margin per hour of selling Super-chip and Okay-chip. If no transfers of Super-chip were made to the Process-Control Division, how many Super-chips and Okay-chips should the Semiconductor Division sell?
2. The Process-Control Division expects to sell 5,000 control units this year. From the viewpoint of Ottawa Valley Instruments as a whole, should 5,000 Super-chips be transferred to the Process-Control Division to replace circuit boards? Show all calculations.
3. If demand for the control unit is sure to be 5,000 units, but its price is uncertain, what should be the transfer price of Super-chip to ensure that the division managers' actions maximize operating income for OVIC as a whole? (All other data are unchanged.)
4. If demand for the control unit is sure to be 12,000 units, but its price is uncertain, what should be the transfer price of Super-chip to ensure the division managers' actions maximize operating income for OVIC as a whole? (All other data are unchanged.)

LEARNING OBJECTIVE 5

1. **Transfer prices and excess capacity—Advanced.** Italian Sausages Inc. is still a family-owned company located in Maple, Ontario. It has experienced significant growth in the last 10 years, and nowadays it employs more than 100 persons in production-related activities and another 20 persons in support activities such as selling, administrative, health and safety, and so on. Italian Sausages manufactures and sells high-quality sausages and is organized along two divisions: (Meat) Grinding/Mixing and (Sausage) Stuffing.

The first step in the production of sausages is done in the Grinding/Mixing Division, where the meat is ground in special machines and then several spices and additives are added to the mixture. The mixture is transferred to the Stuffing Division in 50-kilogram metal containers. Each container is directed to a particular stuffing machine, whether vertical or horizontal, where sausages of different diameters are assembled. In Maple and vicinity there are active markets for both the mixture and the sausages. Each division is evaluated as a profit centre. The transfer price for the mixture has been set at the long-run average market price. The following data per kilogram are available to each division:

Estimated selling price of 1 kg of sausages	$5.00
Long-run average selling price for 1 kg of mixture	$3.25
Incremental costs for completion in Stuffing Division	$2.00
Incremental costs for preparing the mixture in Grinding/Mixing Division	$1.00

The manager of the Stuffing Division has made the following calculation:

Estimated selling price of 1 kg of sausages	$ 5.00
Transferred-in costs at market price	$ 3.25
Incremental costs for completion in Stuffing Division	$ 2.00
Contribution (loss) on 1 kg of sausage	$(0.25)

REQUIRED

1. Should transfers be made to Stuffing if there is no excess capacity in Grinding/Mixing? Is the market price the correct transfer price?
2. Assume that Grinding/Mixing's maximum capacity is 10,000 kilograms per week and sales to the intermediate market are now 5,000 kilograms. Should 5,000 kilograms be transferred to Stuffing? At what transfer price? Assume that for a variety of reasons, Grinding/Mixing will maintain the $3.25 selling price indefinitely; that is, Grinding/Mixing is not considering lowering the price to outsiders even if idle capacity exists.
3. Suppose Grinding/Mixing quoted a transfer price of $3 for up to 5,000 kilograms. What would be the contribution to the company as a whole if the transfer were made? As manager of Stuffing, would you be inclined to buy at $3?

ASSIGNMENT MATERIAL

MyAccountingLab Make the grade with MyAccountingLab: The questions, exercises, and problems marked in red can be found on MyAccountingLab at **www.myaccountinglab.com**. You can practise them as often as you want, and most feature step-by-step guided instructions to help you find the right answer. Exercises and problems with an Excel icon in the margin have an accompanying Excel template on MyAccountingLab.

SHORT-ANSWER QUESTIONS

23-1 What is a management control system?

23-2 Describe three criteria you would use to evaluate whether a management control system is effective.

23-3 What is the relationship among motivation, goal-congruence, and effort?

23-4 Name three benefits and two costs of decentralization.

23-5 "Organizations typically adopt a consistent decentralization or centralization philosophy across all their business functions." Do you agree? Explain.

23-6 "Transfer pricing is confined to profit centres." Do you agree? Why?

23-7 What are the three general methods for determining transfer prices?

23-8 What properties should transfer pricing systems have?

23-9 "All transfer pricing methods give the same division operating income." Do you agree? Explain.

23-10 Under what conditions is a market-based transfer price optimal?

23-11 What is one potential limitation of full-cost-based transfer prices?

23-12 Give two reasons why a dual-price approach to transfer pricing is not widely used.

23-13 "Cost and price information play no role in negotiated transfer prices." Do you agree? Explain.

23-14 "Under the general transfer pricing guideline, the minimum transfer price will vary depending on whether or not the supplying division has idle capacity." Do you agree? Explain.

23-15 Why should managers consider income tax issues when choosing a transfer pricing method?

EXERCISES

23-16 **Decentralization, responsibility centres.** Corporate Express manufactures and sells stationery products. Corporate Express's sales and marketing divisions are organized by customer type—government, large corporations, SMEs, NPOs and others. The manufacturing division produces stationery products for all the divisions.

During the planning process, each sales and marketing division specifies the quantity of each product to be manufactured. Senior management then assigns the task of manufacturing the products to different plants in the manufacturing division. Because manufacturing capacity is limited, some production is also outsourced. Senior management determines the manufacturing schedule on the basis of detailed studies that have been done to measure the time and cost of manufacturing different types of products. Manufacturing managers are evaluated based on achieving target output within budgeted costs.

REQUIRED
1. Are the manufacturing plants in the Manufacturing Division cost centres or profit centres? Explain.
2. Corporate Express is considering decentralizing its marketing and manufacturing decisions by letting manufacturing and marketing managers directly negotiate the prices for manufacturing various products.
   a. How should Corporate Express evaluate manufacturing plant managers under this proposal?
   b. Would you recommend that Corporate Express decentralize its marketing and manufacturing decisions? Explain.

23-17 Decentralization, goal-congruence, responsibility centres. Toronto Appliances Corporation (TAC) is an integrated manufacturer of several types of home appliances. TAC has a decentralized, divisional organization consisting of four product divisions, four manufacturing divisions, and four support offices. The product divisions designed, engineered, assembled, and sold various home appliances directly to large customers both in Canada and the US. They are evaluated on ROI. They assembled the appliances from parts purchased either from the manufacturing divisions or from outside vendors. The manufacturing divisions made approximately 80% of their sales to the product divisions and their managers are compensated on achieving profit targets. Parts made by the manufacturing divisions were generally designed by the product divisions; the manufacturing divisions merely produced the parts to specifications provided to them.

The divisions were instructed to deal with one another as if they were independent companies. The prices for the parts transferred between manufacturing and product divisions were based on the actual prices paid to outside suppliers for the same or comparable parts, but they were adjusted to capture the differences in design. The same rule did not apply for support offices (finance, purchasing, marketing, and industrial relations); they were required to charge the product and manufacturing divisions for their services at cost.

REQUIRED
1. Is TAC a centralized or decentralized organization?
2. What type of responsibility centre should be:
   a. the product divisions?
   b. the manufacturing divisions?
   c. the support offices?
3. What benefits and problems do you see in the TAC structure? Does it lead to goal-congruence and motivation?

23-18 Cost centres, profit centres, decentralization, transfer prices. Fenster Corporation manufactures windows with wood and metal frames. Fenster has three departments: Glass, Wood, and Metal. The Glass Department makes the window glass and sends it to either the Wood or Metal Department where the glass is framed. The window is then sold. Upper management sets the production schedules for the three departments and evaluates them on output quantity, cost variances, and product quality.

REQUIRED
1. Are the three departments cost centres, revenue centres, or profit centres?
2. Are the three departments centralized or decentralized?
3. Can a centralized department be a profit centre? Why or why not?
4. Suppose the upper management of Fenster Corporation decides to let the three departments set their own production schedules, buy and sell products in the external market, and have Wood and Metal negotiate with Glass for the glass panes using a transfer price.
   a. Will this change your answers to requirements 1 and 2?
   b. How would you recommend upper management evaluate the three departments if this change is made?

23-19 Effect of alternative transfer pricing methods on division operating income. (CMA, adapted) Liuanha Chemical Co. has two divisions. The Raw Chemicals Division makes zinc oxide 99%, which is then transferred to the Medicinal Division. The zinc oxide is further processed by the Medicinal Division and is sold to customers at a price of $2,800 per tonne.

The Raw Chemical Division is currently required by Liuanha to transfer its total yearly output of 2,000 tonnes of zinc oxide 99% to the Medicinal Division at 110% of full manufacturing cost. Unlimited quantities of zinc oxide can be purchased and sold on the outside market at $2,330 per tonne. To sell the zinc oxide it produces at $2,000 per tonne on the outside market, the Medicinal Division would have to incur variable marketing and distribution costs of $70 per unit. Similarly, if the Medicinal Division purchased zinc oxide from the outside market, it would have to incur variable purchasing costs of $35 per tonne.

The following table gives the manufacturing costs per tonne in the Raw Chemical and Medicinal Divisions for the year 2010:

1. a. Revenues, Raw Chemicals Division, $4,660,000

	Raw Chemicals Division	Medicinal Division
Direct materials	$ 200	$ 50
Direct manufacturing labour costs	$ 250	$ 250
Manufacturing overhead costs	$ 400*	$ 300**
Manufacturing costs per unit	$ 850	$ 600

*Manufacturing overhead costs in the Raw Chemical Division are 25% fixed and 75% variable.
**Manufacturing overhead costs in the Medicinal Division are 60% fixed and 40% variable.

REQUIRED

1. Calculate the operating incomes for the Raw Chemicals and Medicinal Divisions for the 2,000 tonnes of zinc oxide transferred under each of the following transfer pricing methods: (a) market price and (b) 110% of full manufacturing costs.
2. Suppose Liuanha rewards each division manager with a bonus, calculated as 1% of division operating income (if positive). What is the amount of bonus that will be paid to each division manager under each of the transfer pricing methods in requirement 1? Which transfer pricing method will each division manager prefer to use?
3. What arguments would the manager of the Raw Chemicals Division make to support the transfer pricing method that he prefers?

23-20 Multinational transfer pricing, effect of alternative transfer pricing methods, global income tax minimization. User Friendly Computer Inc., with headquarters in Nepean, Ontario, manufactures and sells a premium desktop computer system. User Friendly has three divisions, each of which is located in a different country:
a. China Division—manufactures memory devices and keyboards
b. South Korea Division—assembles desktop computers using internally manufactured parts and memory devices and keyboards from the China Division
c. Canadian Division—packages and distributes desktop computer packages

1. a. China division after-tax operating income, $60

Each division is run as a profit centre. The costs for the work done in each division for a single desktop computer system are as follows:

China Division	Variable costs = 1,000 yuan
	Fixed costs = 1,800 yuan
South Korea Division	Variable costs = 360,000 won
	Fixed costs = 480,000 won
Canadian Division	Variable costs = 100 CAD
	Fixed costs = 200 CAD

Chinese income tax rate on China Division's operating income	40%
South Korean income tax rate on South Korea Division's operating income	20%
Canadian income tax rate on Canadian Division's operating income	30%

Each desktop computer package is sold to retail outlets in Canada for $3,200. Assume that the current foreign exchange rates are:

$$8 \text{ yuan} = \$1 \text{ Cdn.}$$
$$1,200 \text{ won } = \$1 \text{ Cdn.}$$

Both the China and South Korea Divisions sell part of their production under a private label. The China Division sells the comparable memory/keyboard package used in each User Friendly desktop computer to a Chinese manufacturer for 3,600 yuan. The South Korea division sells the comparable desktop computer package to a South Korean distributor for 1,560,000 won.

1. Calculate the after-tax operating income per unit earned by each division under each of the following transfer-pricing methods: (a) market price, (b) 200% of full cost, and (c) 300% of variable cost. (Income taxes are not included in the computation of the cost-based transfer prices.)
2. Which transfer-pricing method(s) will maximize the after-tax operating income per unit of User Friendly Computer Inc.?

23-21 Transfer pricing methods, goal-congruence. BlackoilCorp. has two divisions, Refining and Production. The company's primary product is Clean Oil. Each division's costs are provided below:

Refining:	Variable costs per litre of oil	$30
	Fixed costs per litre of oil	$24
Production:	Variable costs per litre of oil	$ 6
	Fixed costs per litre of oil	$ 4

The Production Division is able to sell the oil to other areas for $24 per litre. The Refining Division has been operating at a capacity of 80,000 barrels a day, purchasing 50,000 barrels of oil, on average, from the Production Division and 30,000 barrels, on average, from other suppliers at $40 per barrel.

REQUIRED

1. What is the transfer price per litre assuming the method used to place a value on each barrel of oil is 175% of variable costs?
2. What is the transfer price per litre from the Production Division to the Refining Division assuming the method used to place a value on each barrel of oil is 120% of full costs?
3. What is the transfer price that makes the production division indifferent to sell internally or to outside customers?

23-22 Transfer pricing methods, goal congruence. British Columbia Lumber has a Raw Lumber Division and a Finished Lumber Division. The variable costs are:
◆ Raw Lumber Division: $100 per 100 board-feet of raw lumber
◆ Finished Lumber Division: $125 per 100 board-feet of finished lumber

Assume that there is no board-feet loss in processing raw lumber into finished lumber. Raw lumber can be sold at $200 per 100 board-feet. Finished lumber can be sold at $275 per 100 board-feet.

REQUIRED

1. Should British Columbia Lumber process raw lumber into its finished form? Show your calculations.
2. Assume that internal transfers are made at 110% of variable cost. Will each division maximize its division operating-income contribution by adopting the action that is in the best interests of British Columbia Lumber as a whole? Explain.
3. Assume that internal transfers are made at market prices. Will each division maximize its division operating-income contribution by adopting the action that is in the best interests of British Columbia Lumber as a whole? Explain.

23-23 Transfer price dispute: market or distress price. Zanello Inc., manufacturer of home appliances, is organized along decentralized lines, with each manufacturing division operating as a separate profit centre (refrigeration, cooking, dishwashers, laundry, and minor appliances).

Each division manager has been delegated full authority on all decisions involving the sale of that division's output both to outsiders and to other divisions of Zanello. The Laundry Division has in the past always purchased its requirement of a particular engine from the Engines Division that produces various types of engines for several appliances. However, when informed that the Engines Division is increasing its selling price to $20, the Laundry Division's manager decides to purchase the engine component from outside suppliers.

The Laundry Division can purchase the component for $17 on the open market. The Engines Division insists that, because of the recent installation of some highly specialized equipment and the resulting high amortization charges, it will not be able to earn an adequate return on its investment unless it raises its price. The Laundry Division's manager appeals to top management of Zanello for support in the dispute with the Engines Division and supplies the following operating data:

Laundry Division's annual purchase of engines:	10,000 units	
Engine Division's variable cost per engine:	$	12
Engine Division's fixed costs per engine:	$	7

2. Full cost of Production Division, $10

1. Savings in variable costs if buy outside, $120,000

REQUIRED

1. What are the operating incomes of the two divisions and the company as a whole for the year?
2. Explain why the company operating income is less than the sum of the two divisions' total income.

23-27 **General guideline, transfer pricing.** Shamrock Company manufactures and sells television sets. Its Assembly Division (AD) buys television screens from the Screen Division (SD) and assembles the TV sets. The SD, which is operating at capacity, incurs an incremental manufacturing cost of $80 per screen. The SD can sell all its output to the outside market at a price of $120 per screen, after incurring a variable marketing and distribution cost of $5 per screen. If the AD purchases screens from outside suppliers at a price of $120 per screen, it will incur a variable purchasing cost of $3 per screen. Shamrock's division managers can act autonomously to maximize their own division's operating income.

REQUIRED

1. What is the minimum transfer price at which the SD manager would be willing to sell screens to the AD?
2. What is the maximum transfer price at which the AD manager would be willing to purchase screens from the SD?
3. Now suppose that the SD can sell only 80% of its output capacity of 10,000 screens per month on the open market. Capacity cannot be reduced in the short run. The AD can assemble and sell more than 10,000 sets per month.
   a. What is the minimum transfer price at which the SD manager would be willing to sell screens to the AD?
   b. From the point of view of Shamrock's management, how much of the SD output should be transferred to the AD?
   c. What transfer-pricing policy will achieve the outcome desired in requirement 3b?

23-28 **Transfer pricing, general guideline, goal congruence.** (CMA, adapted) Quest Motors Inc. operates as a decentralized multidivision company. The Tivo Division of Quest Motors purchases most of its airbags from the Airbags Division. The Airbag Division's incremental cost for manufacturing the airbags is $90 per unit. The Airbag Division is currently working at 80% of capacity. The current market price of the airbags is $125 per unit.

REQUIRED

1. Using the general guideline presented in the chapter, what is the minimum price at which the Airbag Division would sell airbags to the Tivo Division?
2. Suppose that Quest Motors requires that whenever divisions with unused capacity sell products internally, they must do so at the incremental cost. Evaluate this transfer-pricing policy using the criteria of goal congruence, evaluating division performance, motivating management effort, and preserving division autonomy.
3. If the two divisions were to negotiate a transfer price, what is the range of possible transfer prices? Evaluate this negotiated transfer-pricing policy using the criteria of goal congruence, evaluating division performance, motivating management effort, and preserving division autonomy.
4. Do you prefer the transfer pricing policy in requirement 2 or requirement 3? Explain your answer briefly.

23-29 **Transfer pricing dispute.** Tokoyama Corporation manufactures small appliances such as coffee-makers and toasters. It is organized along decentralized lines, with each manufacturing division operating as a separate profit centre. Each division manager has been delegated full authority on all decisions involving the sale of that division's output both to outsiders and to other divisions of Tokoyama. The Coffee Machines Division has in the past always purchased its requirement of a particular timer component from Timers and Thermostats Division. However, when informed that Timers and Thermostats Division is increasing its selling price to $10, Coffee Machines Division's manager decides to purchase the timer component from outside suppliers.

Coffee Machines Division can purchase the component for $8.50 on the open market. Timers and Thermostats Division insists that, because of the recent transfer of its operations to a newly built facility and the resulting high amortization charges, it will not be able to earn an adequate return on its investment unless it raises its price. Timers and Thermostats Division's manager appeals to top management of Tokoyama for support in the dispute with Coffee Machines Division and supplies the following operating data:

Coffee Machines Division's annual purchase of timers:	1,000 units
Timers and Thermostats Division's variable cost per timer:	$ 6
Timers and Thermostats Division's fixed costs per timer:	$ 3

1. Savings in variable costs if buy outside, $6,000

REQUIRED

1. Assume there are no alternative uses for internal facilities. Determine whether the company as a whole will benefit if Coffee Machines Division purchases the timer component from outside suppliers for $8.50 per unit.
2. Assume internal facilities of Timers and Thermostats Division would not otherwise be idle. By not producing the 1,000 units for Coffee Machines Division, the Timers and Thermostats Division equipment and other facilities would be used for other production operations that would result in annual cash operating savings of $3,000. Should Coffee Machines Division purchase from outside suppliers?
3. Assume there are no alternative uses for Timers and Thermostats Division internal facilities and that the price from outsiders drops by 20%. Should Coffee Machines Division purchase from outside suppliers?

23-30 Transfer pricing problem (continuation of 23-29). Refer to Exercise 23-29. Assume that Timers and Thermostats Division can sell the 1,000 units to other customers at $10 per unit with variable marketing costs of $0.50 per unit.

⑤

Net costs to company from buying outside, $2,500

REQUIRED

Determine whether Tokoyama will benefit if Coffee Machines Division purchases the 1,000 components from outside suppliers at $8.50 per unit.

PROBLEMS

23-31 Governance, transfer pricing. The Caledonia plant of Melrose Automotive Inc. manufactures recliners for car seats that are assembled in the Alliston Plant. The recliners are transferred at 300% of variable costs. The currently reported variable cost of each recliner is $2.54. John Cross, the production manager of Caledonia Plant, required the controller to revise the variable costs reported for each recliner. Cross said to the controller: "I am not sure about the fixed and variable cost distinctions you are making. I think the variable costs are higher than $2.54 per recliner."

②

1. a. Transfer price, $7.62 per recliner

The controller knows that showing higher variable costs will increase Caledonia Plant's profits and lead to higher bonuses for all the employees, and particularly for the managers. The controller is uncomfortable about making any changes because he has used the same method to classify costs as either fixed or variable over the last few years. But both John Cross and the controller know that fixed and variable cost distinctions are not always clear cut.

REQUIRED

1. Calculate Caledonia Plant's contribution margin from transferring 10,000 recliners if (a) variable costs are $2.54 per recliner, and (b) variable costs are $3 per recliner.
2. Evaluate whether John Cross's suggestion to the controller regarding variable costs is ethical. Would it be ethical for the controller to revise the variable cost per unit? What steps should the controller take to resolve this situation?

23-32 Effect of alternative transfer pricing methods on division operating income. Crango Products is a cranberry cooperative that operates two divisions: a Harvesting Division and a Processing Division. Currently, all of Harvesting's output is converted into cranberry juice by the Processing Division, and the juice is sold to large beverage companies that produce cranberry juice blends. The Processing Division has a yield of 500 litres of juice per 1,000 kg of cranberries. Cost and market price data for the two divisions are as follows:

②

2. a. Harvesting Division manager's bonus, $7,000

Harvesting Division		Processing Division	
Variable cost per kg of cranberries	$0.10	Variable processing cost per litre of juice produced	$0.20
Fixed cost per kg of cranberries	$0.25	Fixed cost per litre of juice produced	$0.40
Selling price per kg of cranberries in outside market	$0.60	Selling price per litre of juice	$2.10

REQUIRED

1. Compute Crango's operating income from harvesting 400,000 kilograms of cranberries during June 2010 and processing them into juice.

2. Crango rewards its division managers with a bonus equal to 5% of operating income. Compute the bonus earned by each division manager in June 2010 for each of the following transfer pricing methods:
   a. 200% of full cost
   b. Market price
3. Which transfer-pricing method will each division manager prefer? How might Crango resolve any conflicts that may arise on the issue of transfer pricing?

2. Harvesting Division operating income, $140,000

23-33 Goal-congruence problems with cost-plus transfer pricing methods, dual-pricing system (continuation of 23-32). Assume that Pat Borges, CEO of Crango, had mandated a transfer price equal to 200% of full cost. Now he decides to decentralize some management decisions and sends around a memo that states: "Effective immediately, each division of Crango is free to make its own decisions regarding the purchase of direct materials and the sale of finished products."

REQUIRED

1. Give an example of a goal-congruence problem that will arise if Crango continues to use a transfer price of 200% of full cost and Borges' decentralization policy is adopted.
2. Borges feels that a dual transfer-pricing policy will improve goal congruence. He suggests that transfers out of the Harvesting Division be made at 200% of full cost and transfers into the Processing Division be made at market price. Compute the operating income of each division under this dual transfer pricing method when 400,000 kilograms of cranberries are harvested during June 2010 and processed into juice.
3. Why is the sum of the division operating incomes computed in requirement 2 different from Crangro's operating income from harvesting and processing 400,000 kilograms of cranberries?
4. Suggest two problems that may arise if Crango implements the dual transfer prices described in requirement 2.

3. Corn Division contribution margin, $13,000

23-34 Effect of market prices oscillations. Green Energy Corp. makes biodiesel from corn. It is organized into two operating divisions. The Corn Division leases large farms to grow the varieties of corn needed by the Ethanol Division. The biodiesel produced by the Ethanol Division is sold to corporate customers at a price of $1.50 per litre; each tonne of corn yields 500 litres of biodiesel. The Corn Division transfers its total output of 200,000 tonnes of corn to the Ethanol Division at market price. The market price is determined twice a year (November 5 and May 5 or the immediately previous day if it is a holiday), one per harvesting season, and it is the price of "Maize (corn), US No. 2 Yellow, FOB Gulf of Mexico, US price, US$ per metric tonne" set at the Chicago Board of Trade. For the current season the price determined is $250; however, unlimited quantities of corn can be purchased and sold on the outside market at prices that change on a daily basis. To sell the corn on the outside market, the Corn Division would have to incur variable distribution costs of $5 per tonne. Similarly, if the Ethanol Division purchased corn from the open market, it would have to incur variable purchasing costs of $3 per tonne.

The following table provides a detail of costs per tonne in both divisions:

	Corn Division (tonnes)	Ethanol Division (litres)
Direct materials	$ 60	Corn
Direct manufacturing labour costs	$ 50	$ 0.10
Manufacturing overhead costs	$ 100*	$ 0.80**
Manufacturing costs per unit	$ 210	$ 0.90+ corn

*Manufacturing overhead costs in the Corn Division are 25% fixed and 75% variable.

**Manufacturing overhead costs in the Ethanol Division are 75% fixed and 25% variable.

REQUIRED

1. Calculate the operating incomes for both divisions operating at a volume of 200,000 tonnes of corn transferred.
2. Suppose Green Energy rewards each division manager with a bonus, calculated as 1% of division operating income (if positive). What is the amount of bonus that will be paid to each division manager?
3. Suppose that an independent farmer contacts the Ethanol Division and offers to sell 50,000 tonnes, at $220 each, delivered at the door of the processing plant because it has been an extremely good season for corn and the excess of supply is driving its market price down. If the Corn Division can sell its excess in the market at the Chicago price of $220,

determine if it is convenient for Green Energy to accept the offer of the independent farmer. Determine the bonuses of each manager.

23-35 Multinational transfer pricing, global tax minimization. Golden Bars Inc. has two divisions:

1. Market price of ore in Montana, $2,151/kg CAD

a. **Shelby Mining Division.** Operates a gold mine in the northern portion of the state of Montana in the United States. This division extracts ore of high quality with a gold-to-ore ratio of 1:10.

b. **Lethbridge Processing Division.** Processes the ore coming from Shelby to extract gold. The processing plant, located in Canada, is 100 kilometres north from Shelby.

The costs of the Shelby Mining Division are:

◆ Variable costs, US$1,000 per kilogram of ore.
◆ Fixed costs, US$500 per kilogram of ore.

Regardless of the international availability of ore for processing, Golden Bars has the policy of processing in Lethbridge 100% of the ore extracted in Shelby. Several gold processing companies in Montana buy ore from other local mining companies at US$2,000 per kilogram of ore. Assume that the current foreign-exchange rate is US$0.93 = $1 Cdn.

The costs of the Lethbridge Processing Division are:

◆ Variable costs, $1,700 per kilogram of gold.
◆ Fixed costs, $1,800 per kilogram of gold.

The kilogram of gold is sold for $27,800.

REQUIRED

1. Compute the transfer price (in $Cdn.) for one kilogram of ore transferred from the Shelby Mining Division to the Lethbridge Processing Division under two methods: (a) 140% of full costs and (b) market price.

2. Assume a world of no income taxes. Ten kilograms of ore are mined by the Shelby Division and then processed and sold by the Lethbridge Processing Division. Compute the operating income (in $Cdn.) for each division under each transfer pricing method in requirement 1.

3. Assume that the corporate income tax rate is 30% in the United States and 35% in Canada. Compute the after-tax operating income (in $Cdn.) for each division under each transfer pricing method in requirement 1. (Income taxes are not included in the computation of the cost-based transfer price. Golden Bars does not pay Canadian taxes on income already taxed in the United States.)

4. Which transfer pricing method in requirement 1 will maximize the total after-tax operating income of Golden Bars?

5. What factors, in addition to global tax minimization, might Golden Bars consider in choosing a transfer pricing method for transfers between its two divisions?

23-36 Multinational transfer pricing and taxation. (Richard Lambert, adapted) Deutschland Machines Inc., headquartered in Canada, manufactures special-purpose welding machines. It has two marketing subsidiaries, one in Vietnam and one in Spain, which sell its products. Deutschland Machines is building one new machine, at a cost of $600,000. There is no market for the equipment in Canada. The equipment can be sold in Vietnam for $1,200,000, but the subsidiary would incur transportation and modification costs of $240,000. Alternatively, the equipment can be sold in Spain for $1,140,000, but the subsidiary would incur transportation and modification costs of $300,000. The Canadian company can sell the equipment to either its Vietnamese subsidiary or its Spanish subsidiary but not to both. Deutschland Machines and its subsidiaries operate in a very decentralized manner. Managers in each subsidiary have considerable autonomy, with each manager interested in maximizing company income.

1. Operating income if sold in Vietnam, $360,000

REQUIRED

1. From the viewpoint of Deutschland Machines and its subsidiaries taken together, should the company manufacture the equipment? If it does, where should it sell the equipment to maximize total operating income? What would be the operating income for Deutschland Machines and its subsidiaries from the sale? Ignore any income tax effects.

2. What range of transfer prices will result in achieving the actions determined to be optimal in requirement 1? Explain your answer.

3. The effective income tax rates for this transaction are as follows: 40% in Canada, 20% in Vietnam, and 60% in Spain. The tax authorities in the three countries are uncertain about the cost of the intermediate product and will allow any transfer price between $600,000 and $840,000. If Deutschland Machines and its subsidiaries want to maximize after-tax operating income, (a) should the equipment be manufactured and (b) where and at what price should it be transferred?

4. Now suppose managers act autonomously to maximize their own subsidiary after-tax operating income. The tax authorities will allow transfer prices only between $600,000 and $840,000. Which subsidiary will get the product and at what price? Is your answer the same as your answer in requirement 3? Explain why or why not.

④

1. Opportunity cost, $0

23-37 International transfer pricing, taxes, goal-congruence. Argone Division of Gemini Corporation is located in the United States. Its effective income tax rate is 20%. Another division of Gemini, Calcia, is located in Canada, where the income tax rate is 38%. Calcia manufactures, among other things, an intermediate product for Argone called IP-2007. Calcia operates at capacity and makes 20,000 units of IP-2007 for Argone each period, at a variable cost of $80 per unit. Assume that there are no outside customers for IP-2007. Because the IP-2007 must be shipped from Canada to the United States, it costs Calcia an additional $2 per unit to ship the IP-2007 to Argone. There are no direct fixed costs for IP-2007. Calcia also manufactures other products. A product similar to IP-2007 that Argone could use as a substitute is available in the United States for $100 per unit.

REQUIRED

1. What are the minimum and maximum transfer prices that would be acceptable to Argone and Calcia for IP-2007, and why?
2. What transfer price would minimize income taxes for Gemini Corporation as a whole? Would Calcia and Argone want to be evaluated on operating income using this transfer price?
3. Suppose Gemini uses the transfer price from requirement 2, and each division is evaluated on its own after-tax division operating income. Now suppose Calcia has an opportunity to sell 10,000 units of IP-2007 to an outside customer for $95 each. Calcia will not incur shipping costs because the customer is nearby and offers to pay for shipping. Assume that if Calcia accepts the special order, Argone will have to buy 10,000 units of the substitute product in the United States at $100 per unit.
   a. Will accepting the special order maximize after-tax operating income for Gemini Corporation as a whole?
   b. Will Argone want Calcia to accept this special order? Why or why not?
   c. Will Calcia want to accept this special order? Explain.
   d. Suppose Gemini Corporation wants to operate in a decentralized manner. What transfer price should Gemini set for IP-2007 so that each division acting in its own best interest takes actions with respect to the special order that are in the best interests of Gemini Corporation as a whole?

⑤

1. Incremental cost in Seats Division, $180

23-38 Pertinent transfer price. ITS Automotive plant in Bradford manufactures car seats. It has two divisions, Frames and Seats. The Frames Division produces the structural frame of the seat, and the Seats Division assembles all the parts and mechanisms onto the frame. There is a market for both the subassembly and the final product. Each division has been designated as a profit centre. The transfer price for the subassembly has been set at $240 and includes all intermediate products (engines, recliners, frames, etc.), while the long-run average market price for the assembled seat is estimated at $360. The manager of Seats Division has made the following calculation:

Estimated selling price of the assembled seat		$360
Transferred-in costs at market price	$240	
Incremental costs for completion in the Division	180	
Contribution (loss) on product		$(60)

REQUIRED

1. Should transfers be made to Seats Division if there is no excess capacity in Frames Division? Is the market price the correct transfer price?
2. Assume that the maximum capacity of the Frames Division for this product is 1,000 units per month and sales to the intermediate market are now 800 units. Should 200 units be transferred to Seats Division? At what transfer price? Assume that, for a variety of reasons, Frames Division will maintain the $240 selling price indefinitely; that is, Frames Division is not considering lowering the price to outsiders even if idle capacity exists.
3. Suppose Frames Division quoted a transfer price of $180 for up to 200 units. What would be the contribution to the company as a whole if the transfer were made? As manager of Seats Division, would you be inclined to buy at $180?

23-39 Pricing in imperfect markets (continuation of 23-38). Refer to Problem 23-38.

Refer to Problem 23-38.

1. Contribution from external sale, $90,000

REQUIRED

1. Suppose the manager of Frames Division has the option of (a) cutting the external price to $234 with the certainty that sales will rise to 1,000 units or (b) maintaining the outside price of $240 for the 800 units and transferring the 200 units to Seats Division at some price that would produce the same operating income for Frames Division. What transfer price would produce the same operating income for Frames Division? Does that price coincide with that recommended by the general guideline in the chapter so that the desirable decision for the company as a whole would result?

2. Suppose that if the selling price for the intermediate products is dropped to $234, outside sales can be increased to 900 units. Seats Division wants to acquire as many as 200 units if the transfer price is acceptable. For simplicity, assume there is no outside market for the final 100 units of Frames Division's capacity.
   a. Using the general guideline, what is (are) the minimum transfer price(s) that should lead to the correct economic decision? Ignore performance evaluation considerations.
   b. Compare the total contributions under the alternatives to show why the transfer price(s) recommended lead(s) to the optimal economic decision.

23-40 Transfer pricing, goal-congruence. Johnson Farming Equipment Corp. manufactures and sells heavy farm equipment. One of its divisions assembles 1,000 tractors per year. It buys the wheels from another division. The Wheels Division is operating at capacity and producing 1,200 wheels. The demand for special-dimension wheels is strong. Any wheel not sold to the Tractors Division can be sold in the outside market for $420 per unit. The Wheels Division currently sells 1,000 wheels to the Tractor Division and 200 wheels in the outside market. The incremental cost of manufacturing each wheel is $300.

1. a. Net costs, buy wheels at $444, $228,000

A crucial component for producing good-quality wheels is the rubber component. The Wheels Division thermoforms the rubber component for its wheels. Many outside suppliers have offered to supply the rubber component already thermoformed to Johnson. To ensure quality, Johnson requires that any outside supplier wanting to supply wheels to Johnson's divisions must purchase the thermoformed rubber component from the Wheels Division. The Wheels Division's incremental cost of thermoforming the rubber component is $144 per unit. The Wheels Division will charge $216 per unit for the wheels' rubber component. The Wheels Division has excess manufacturing capacity for thermoforming the rubber component of wheels. That is, even if the Wheels Division thermoforms wheels' rubber components for outside suppliers, it will still be able to manufacture and sell 1,200 wheels in the outside market at $420 per unit.

Molson Corporation, an outside supplier, is currently negotiating to supply 1,000 wheels to the Tractor Division for a price in the range of $444 to $516. If Molson gets the business it will buy the wheels' rubber component from the Wheels Division for $216 per unit.

REQUIRED

1. From the standpoint of Johnson Farming Equipment as a whole, should the Tractor Division accept Molson's offer at (a) a price of $444 per wheel? (b) a price of $516 per wheel? Show all calculations.

2. What transfer price for wheels will result in the Wheels Division and the Tractor Division taking actions that are optimal for Johnson Corporation as a whole? Explain your answer.

23-41 Transfer pricing, goal-congruence. The Orsilo Corporation makes and sells 10,000 multisystem music players each year. Its Assembly Division purchases components from other divisions of Orsilo or from external suppliers and assembles the multisystem music players. In particular, the Assembly Division can purchase the CD player from the Compact Disc Division of Orsilo or from Johnson Corporation. Johnson agrees to meet all of Orsilo's quality requirements and is currently negotiating with the Assembly Division to supply 10,000 CD players at a price between $38 and $45 per CD player.

1. Incremental costs of supplying 10,000 CD players to Assembly Division, $250,000

A critical component of the CD player is the head mechanism that reads the disc. To ensure the quality of its multisystem music players, Orsilo requires that if Johnson wins the contract to supply CD players, it must purchase the head mechanism from Orsilo's Compact Disc Division for $20 each.

The Compact Disc Division can manufacture at most 12,000 CD players annually. It also manufactures as many additional head mechanisms as can be sold. The incremental cost of manufacturing the head mechanism is $15 per unit. The incremental cost of manufacturing a CD player (including the cost of the head mechanism) is $25 per unit, and any number of CD players can be sold for $35 each in the external market.

1. What are the incremental costs minus revenues from sales to external buyers for the company as a whole if the Compact Disc Division transfers 10,000 CD players to the Assembly Division and sells the remaining 2,000 CD players on the external market?

2. What are the incremental costs minus revenues from sales to external buyers for the company as a whole if the Compact Disc Division sells 12,000 CD players on the external market and the Assembly Division accepts Johnson's offer at (a) $38 per CD player or (b) $45 per CD player?

3. What is the minimum transfer price per CD player at which the Compact Disc Division would be willing to transfer 10,000 CD players to the Assembly Division?

4. Suppose that the transfer price is set to the minimum computed in requirement 3 plus $1, and the division managers at Orsilo are free to make their own profit-maximizing sourcing and selling decisions. Now, Johnson offers 10,000 CD players for $40.50 each.

    a. What decisions will the managers of the Compact Disc Division and Assembly Division make?

    b. Are these decisions optimal for Orsilo as a whole?

    c. Based on this exercise, at what price would you recommend the transfer price be set?

COLLABORATIVE LEARNING CASES

1. Contribution margin from new frame, $272

23-42 Goal-congruence, taxes, different market conditions. TECA Halifax makes kids' bicycles. The Frames Division makes and paints the frames and supplies them to the Assembly Division where the bicycles are assembled. TECA is a successful and profitable corporation that attributes much of its success to its decentralized operating style. Each division manager is compensated on the basis of division operating income.

    The Assembly Division currently acquires all its frames from the Frames Division. The Assembly Division manager could purchase similar frames in the market for $480.

    The Frames Division is currently operating at 80% of its capacity of 4,000 frames (units) and has the following particulars:

Direct materials ($150 per unit × 3,200 units)	$480,000
Direct manufacturing labour ($60 per unit × 3,200 units)	192,000
Variable manufacturing overhead costs ($30 per unit × 3,200 units)	96,000
Fixed manufacturing overhead costs	624,000

All the Frames Division's 3,200 units are currently transferred to the Assembly Division. No frames are sold in the outside market.

    The Frames Division has just received an order for 2,000 units at $450 per frame that would utilize half the capacity of the plant. The order has to be either taken in full or rejected totally. The order is for a slightly different frame than what the Frames Division currently makes but takes the same amount of manufacturing time. To produce the new frame would require direct materials per unit of $100, direct manufacturing labour per unit of $48, and variable manufacturing overhead costs per unit of $30.

INSTRUCTIONS

Form groups of two or three students to complete the following requirements.

REQUIRED

1. From the viewpoint of TECA Halifax as a whole, should the Frames Division accept the order for the 2,000 units?

2. What range of transfer prices result in achieving the actions determined to be optimal in requirement 1, if division managers act in a decentralized manner?

3. The manager of the Assembly Division has proposed a transfer price for the frames equal to the full cost of the frames including an allocation of overhead costs. The Frames Division allocates overhead costs to engines on the basis of the total capacity of the plant used to manufacture the frames.

    a. Calculate the transfer price for the frames transferred to the Assembly Division under this arrangement.

    b. Do you think that the transfer price calculated in requirement 3(a) will result in achieving the actions determined to be optimal in requirement 1, if division managers act in a decentralized manner?

    c. Comment in general on one advantage and one disadvantage of using full costs of the producing division as the basis for setting transfer prices.

4. Now consider the effect of income taxes.
   a. Suppose the Assembly Division is located in a country that imposes a 10% tax on income earned within its boundaries, while the Frames Division is located in a country that imposes no tax on income earned within its boundaries. What transfer price would be chosen by TECA to minimize tax payments for the corporation as a whole? Assume that only transfer prices that are greater than or equal to full manufacturing costs and less than or equal to the market price of "substantially similar" engines are acceptable to the taxing authorities.
   b. Suppose that TECA announces the transfer price computed in requirement 4(a) to price all transfers between the Frames and Assembly Divisions. Each division manager then acts autonomously to maximize division operating income. Will division managers acting in a decentralized manner achieve the actions determined to be optimal in requirement 1?
5. Consider your responses to requirements 1 to 4 and assume the Frames Division will continue to have opportunities for outside business as described in requirement 1. What transfer pricing policy would you recommend TECA use and why? Would you continue to evaluate division performance on the basis of division operating incomes?

23-43 Transfer prices, goal-congruence, capacity. The Bottle Division of Orange Fresh Inc. is the only source of bottles to contain the orange flavour soda that is mixed, bottled, and packaged by the Mixing Division to be sold in southern Ontario. A substantial part of the Bottle Division's costs are fixed. For any output up to 1,000 bottles a day, its total costs are $500 a day. Total costs increase by $100 a day for every additional 1,000 bottles made. Bottle Division judges that its own results will be optimized if it sets its price at $0.40 a bottle, and it acts accordingly.

The Mixing Division incurs additional costs to mix, bottle, and pack the premium soda. These costs are $1,250 for any output up to 1,000 bottles, and $250 per thousand for outputs in excess of 1,000 bottles. On the revenue side, the Mixing Division can increase its revenue only by spending more on sales promotion and by reducing selling prices.

Table 1 compares the Mixing Division's costs and revenues at various levels of output while considering both its own processing costs and what it is charged by the Bottle Division for the intermediates that it will supply. Table 1 makes it clear that the most profitable policy for the Mixing Division is to set its output at either 2,000 or 3,000 bottles a day and to accept a profit of $350 a day. If its output is more than 3,000 bottles or less than 2,000 bottles it will make less profit.

Table 1: Mixing Division—Costs and Revenues Forecasts

Division B's Output (Units) (1)	B's Own Processing Costs (2)	A's Charge to B for Intermediate at $0.40 a Unit (3)	B's Total Costs (2) + (3) = (4)	B's Revenue (Net of Setting Costs) per 1,000 Units (5)	B's Total Revenue (1) × (5) = (6)	B's Profit (Loss) (6) − (4) = (7)
1,000	$1,250	$ 400	$1,650	$1,750	$1,750	$100
2,000	$1,500	$ 800	$2,300	$1,325	$2,650	$350
3,000	$1,750	$1,200	$2,950	$1,100	$3,300	$350
4,000	$2,000	$1,600	$3,600	$ 925	$3,700	$100
5,000	$2,250	$2,000	$4,250	$ 800	$4,000	($250)
6,000	$2,500	$2,400	$4,900	$ 666	$4,000	($900)

The Mixing Division decided to sell 3,000 bottles a day. The Bottle Division transfers each bottle at $0.40 making total revenues of $1,200 with total cost of $700. Therefore, the Bottle Division profit is $500 a day. Adding this to Mixing Division's profit of $350 a day, Orange Fresh Inc. gets an aggregate profit of $850 a day.

The controller of Orange Fresh Inc. was studying the company's figures trying to find ways to maximize profit. The controller assumed that the company abandoned its divisionalized structure and, instead of having two profit centres, Bottle and Mixing, the two were combined into a single profit centre with responsibility for the complete processing. The controller assumed that all the other conditions previously presented continued to apply, and prepared a forecast of costs and revenues for the single profit centre as shown in Table 2.

Table 2: Orange Fresh Inc.—Costs and Revenues Forecasts

Output (Units) (1)	Cost of Producing Intermediates (2)	Cost of Processing to Completion (3)	Total Cost (2) + (3) = (4)	Total Revenue (5)	Profit (5) − (4) = (6)
1,000	$ 500	$1,250	$1,750	$1,750	0
2,000	$ 600	$1,500	$2,100	$2,650	$550
3,000	$ 700	$1,750	$2,450	$3,330	$850
4,000	$ 800	$2,000	$2,800	$3,700	$900
5,000	$ 900	$2,250	$3,150	$4,000	$850
6,000	$1,000	$2,500	$3,500	$4,000	$500

INSTRUCTIONS

Form groups of two or three students to complete the following requirements.

REQUIRED

1. What level of output maximizes Orange Fresh Inc.'s profit?
2. What is the lowest price that Bottle Division should be willing to accept from Mixing Division for 4,000 bottles?
3. What is the highest price at which Mixing Division should be willing to buy 4,000 bottles from Bottle Division?
4. If Bottle Division does sell 4,000 bottles to Mixing Division, what should be the transfer price?
5. Explain why the divisions were transferring 3,000 units between them.

Performance Measurement, Compensation, and Multinational Considerations

BUSINESS MATTERS

Qualitative and Nonfinancial Measures Are Relevant

Home Depot publicizes its corporate goals and values on its website. Some of its values include "taking care of our people," "giving back to our communites," and "excellent customer service."[1] Measuring achievement, however, requires considerable expertise and professional skill to select appropriate financial and nonfinancial performance measures. Performance measures are applied to evaluate and compensate people. But raising CEO compensation as share prices fall also raises the ire of shareholders. Former Home Depot CEO Bob Nardelli's compensation increased to $38.1 million as share price decreased 6% and rival Lowe's share price increased 200%. Mr. Nardelli's retirement package when he left Home Depot exceeded $210 million.

LEARNING OBJECTIVES

After studying this chapter, you should be able to

1. Analyze and evaluate alternative measures of financial performance

2. Evaluate current-cost and historical-cost asset measurement methods

3. Analyze the technical difficulties that arise when comparing the performance of divisions operating in different countries

4. Evaluate the behavioural effects of salaries and incentives in compensation arrangements

5. Apply strategic concepts to analyze the four levers of control and evaluate their usefulness

[1] See http://corporate.homedepot.com for more details.

This chapter examines technical, governance, and behavioural issues in designing and implementing appropriate financial and nonfinancial performance measures. We have discussed multi-dimensional BSC performance measurement as a strategy. Performance measures are also a central component of a management accounting control system (MACS). To be effective, however, MACS must motivate not only internal goal congruence but also external governance achievements.

Performance measurement of managers is used in decisions about their salaries, bonuses, future assignments, and career advancement. Moreover, the very act of measuring their performance can motivate managers to strive for the goals used in their evaluation and ignore achieving other equally important goals. At a higher level of analysis, performance measurement of an organization's subunits is a prerequisite for allocating resources within that organization. At the highest corporate level of analysis, the corporation forecasts revenues, costs, and investments and periodically compares actual achievements with pro forma expected targets. Feedback then guides top management's decisions about future allocations.

FINANCIAL AND NONFINANCIAL PERFORMANCE MEASURES

1 Analyze and evaluate alternative measures of financial performance

Chapters 13 and 23 noted how the information used in a MACS can be financial or nonfinancial. Many common financial performance measures, such as operating income, rely on internal financial and accounting information. Increasingly complex governance legislation, however, means companies must supplement internal financial with nonfinancial measures (for example, manufacturing lead time) and external nonfinancial information (such as customer satisfaction). In addition, companies often benchmark their financial and nonfinancial measures against other companies that are regarded as the "best performers." To compete effectively in the global market, companies need to perform at or near the "best of the breed."

An increasing number of organizations present both financial and nonfinancial performance measures for various organization subunits in a single report called the *balanced scorecard* (BSC; see Chapter 13).[2] Most BSC include the financial, internal business process, customer, and learning and growth (intellectual capital management) perspectives. Improving relevant information essential to managing intellectual capital enables improved identification and interpretation of relevant external information on customers and information on internal business processes. Such information ultimately informs improvements in financial performance.

Some performance measures, such as the number of new patents developed, are structural changes to intellectual capital, which have a long-run time horizon. Other measures, such as direct materials efficiency variances, overhead spending variances, and yield, have a short-run time horizon. We focus on the most widely used performance measures covering an intermediate to long-run time horizon. These are internal financial measures based on accounting numbers routinely maintained by organizations.

ACCOUNTING-BASED PERFORMANCE MEASURES

Performance measurement is another example of a complex decision process wherein each decision informs and is interdependent with others (see Exhibit 24-1).

◆ *Decide those accounting measures best aligned with top management's financial goals.* For example, does operating income, net income, return on assets, or revenues best measure a subunit's financial performance?

[2] R. S. Kaplan and D. P. Norton, *The Strategy-Focused Organization: How Balanced Scorecard Companies Thrive in the New Business Environment* (Boston: Harvard Business School Press, 2001); and R. S. Kaplan and D. P. Norton, *Strategy Maps: Converting Intangible Assets into Tangible Outcomes* (Boston: Harvard Business School Press, 2004).

EXHIBIT 24-1
Performance Measures Decision Process Model

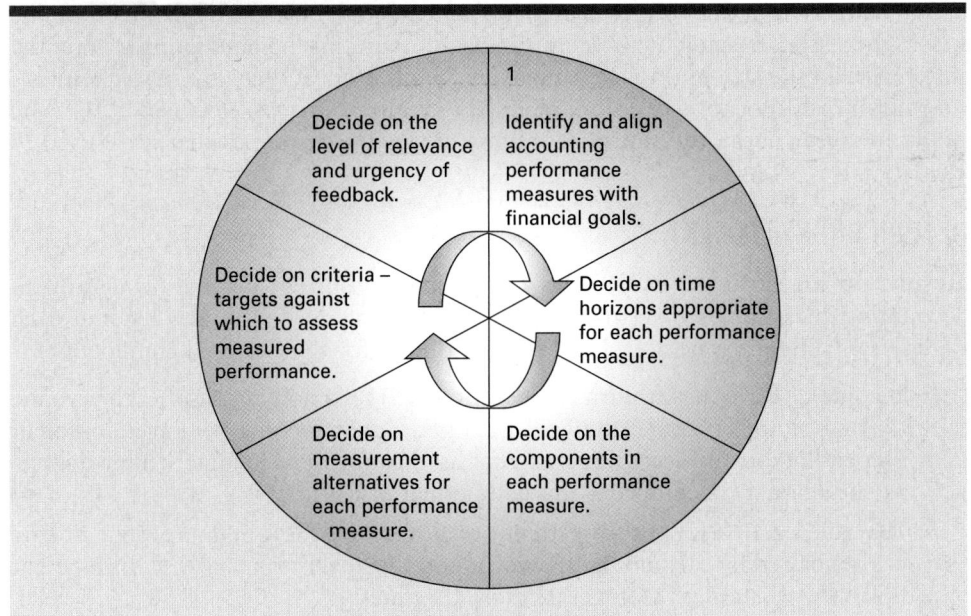

- *Decide the time horizons of each performance measure, short or long term, strategic, or operating.* For example, should performance measures such as return on assets be calculated for one year or for a multiyear horizon?
- *Decide how to define the components of performance measure.* For example, should assets be defined as total assets or net assets (total assets minus total liabilities)?
- *Decide the appropriate measurement method.* For example, should assets be measured at historical cost, current cost, or present value?
- *Decide criteria—the target against which to gauge level of performance.* For example, should all subunits have as a target the same required rate of return on assets?
- *Decide the timing of feedback.* For example, should manufacturing performance reports be sent to top management daily, weekly, or monthly?

The decisions are not sequential and the decision makers often must retrace their decisions prior to implementing accounting performance measures of financial achievement.

Issues with which a decision team must cope will depend on top management's beliefs about how well proposed measures achieve both cost-effectiveness and goal congruence, how well they provide incentives for employee effort, and whether they preserve an appropriate level of subunit autonomy as discussed in Chapter 23. Formal structures such as statements of mission, vision, strategy, and beliefs all clarify how coherent the corporate foundations are for selecting performance measures.

Four measures are commonly used to evaluate the financial performance of organization subunits. These performance measures all use financial accounting information:

- return on investment (ROI)
- residual income (RI)
- economic value added (EVA®)
- return on sales (ROS).

We illustrate these measures using the example of Hospitality Inns. Hospitality Inns owns and operates three motels, located in Saskatoon, Saskatchewan; Brandon, Manitoba; and Hull, Quebec. Exhibit 24-2 summarizes data for each of the three motels for the most recent year (2009). At present, Hospitality Inns does not allocate to the three separate motels the total long-term debt of the company.

Exhibit 24-2 indicates that the Hull motel generates the highest operating income, $510,000. The Brandon motel generates $300,000; the Saskatoon motel, $240,000. But can the results be reliably interpreted that the Hull motel is the most "successful"? Actually, the comparison of operating income ignores potential differences in the size of the investments in the different motels. An investment is a long-term cash allocation decision intended to realize returns (see Chapter 21). The question is how large the return should be, given the resources that were used to earn it.

RETURN ON INVESTMENT

Return on investment (ROI) is an accounting measure of income divided by an accounting measure of investment. ROI tells managers how much income each dollar of investment generates. Here is the intuition for the two ROI components:

1. Income ÷ Revenues (return on sales or ROS) tells how much of each revenue dollar becomes income; the goal is to get higher income per revenue dollar. Depending on the accounting accrual used to measure income, either operating or net margin comprises this component of ROI.

2. Revenues ÷ Investment (investment turnover) tells how many revenue dollars are generated by each dollar of investment; the goal is to make each investment dollar "work harder" to generate more revenues.

$$\text{Return on investment (ROI)} = \frac{\text{Income}}{\text{Investment}}$$

ROI is the most popular approach to incorporating the investment base into a performance measure. ROI appeals conceptually because it blends all the major ingredients of profitability (revenues, costs, and investment) into a single number. ROI can be compared with the rate of return on opportunities elsewhere, inside or

EXHIBIT 24-2
Annual Financial Data for Hospitality Inns for 2009

A	B	C	D	E
	Saskatoon	Brandon	Hull	Total
	(1)	(2)	(3)	(4) = (1) + (2) + (3)
3 Motel revenues	$1,200,000	$1,400,000	$3,185,000	$5,785,000
4 Motel variable costs	310,000	375,000	995,000	1,680,000
5 Motel fixed costs	650,000	725,000	1,680,000	3,055,000
6 Motel operating income	240,000	300,000	510,000	1,050,000
7 Interest costs on long-term debt at 10%				450,000
8 Income before income taxes				600,000
9 Income tax at 30%				180,000
10 Net income				$ 420,000
11 Net book values at the end of 2009:				
12 Current assets	$ 400,000	$ 500,000	$ 600,000	$1,500,000
13 Long-term assets	600,000	1,500,000	2,400,000	4,500,000
14 Total assets	$1,000,000	$2,000,000	$3,000,000	$6,000,000
15 Current liabilities	$ 50,000	$ 150,000	$ 300,000	$ 500,000
16 Long-term debt	—	—	—	4,500,000
17 Shareholders' equity	—	—	—	1,000,000
18 Total liabilities and shareholders' equity				$6,000,000

outside the company. Like any single performance measure, however, ROI should be used cautiously and in conjunction with other performance measures.

ROI is also called the accounting rate of return or the accrual accounting rate of return (see Chapter 21) because accruals are included in both the numerator and denominator of this performance measure. Managers usually use the term ROI in the context of evaluating the performance of a division or subunit, and accrual accounting rate of return (AARR) when evaluating a project. Companies vary in the way they define both the numerator and the denominator of the ROI. For example, some firms use operating income for the numerator. Other firms use net income. Some firms use total assets in the denominator. Others use total assets minus current liabilities.

Hospitality Inns can increase ROI by increasing revenues or decreasing costs (both these actions increase the numerator), or by decreasing investments (decreases the denominator). ROI can often provide more insight into performance when it is divided into the following components:

$$\frac{\text{Revenues}}{\text{Investment}} \times \frac{\text{Income}}{\text{Revenues}} = \frac{\text{Income}}{\text{Investment}}$$

This approach is widely known as the *DuPont method of profitability analysis*. The DuPont approach recognizes that there are two basic ingredients in profit making: using assets to generate more revenue and increasing income per dollar of revenue. An improvement in either ingredient without changing the other increases return on investment.

Consider the ROI of each of the three Hospitality motels in Exhibit 24-2. For our calculations, we are using the operating income of each motel for the numerator and total assets of each motel for the denominator.

Motel	Operating Income	÷	Total Assets	=	ROI
Saskatoon	$240,000	÷	$1,000,000	=	24%
Brandon	$300,000	÷	$2,000,000	=	15%
Hull	$510,000	÷	$3,000,000	=	17%

Using these ROI figures, the Saskatoon motel appears to make the best use of its total assets.

Assume that the top management at Hospitality Inns adopts a 30% target ROI for the Saskatoon motel. How can this return be attained? The DuPont method illustrates the present situation and three alternatives:

	Operating Income (1)	Revenue (2)	Total Assets (3)	Operating Income ÷ Revenue (4) = (1) ÷ (2)	×	Revenue ÷ Total Assets (5) = (2) ÷ (3)	=	Operating Income ÷ Total Assets (6) = (1) ÷ (3)
Current Situation	$240,000	$1,200,000	$1,000,000	0.20	×	1.2	=	24%
Alternatives								
A. Decrease assets (e.g., receivables). Revenue and operating income per dollar of revenue remain constant	$240,000	$1,200,000	$ 800,000	0.20	×	1.5	=	30%
B. Increase revenues (e.g., sell more rooms). Assets and operating income per dollar of revenue remain constant.	$300,000	$1,500,000	$1,000,000	0.20	×	1.5	=	30%
C. Decrease costs (e.g., efficient maintenance) to increase operating income per dollar of revenue; assets remain constant.	$300,000	$1,200,000	$1,000,000	0.25	×	1.2	=	30%

Other alternatives, such as increasing the selling price per room, could increase both the revenue per dollar of total assets and the operating income per dollar of revenue. Managers vary in their judgment of how best to define income (for example, operating income or net income) and investment (for example, total assets employed or total assets employed minus current liabilities).

ROI highlights the benefits that managers can obtain by reducing their investments in current or fixed assets. Some managers are conscious of the need to boost revenues or to control costs but pay less attention to reducing their investment base. Reducing investments means decreasing idle cash, managing credit judiciously, determining proper inventory levels, and spending carefully on fixed assets.

> **THINKING CRITICALLY**
>
> Why not use net income for ROI? Explain in a sentence or two. Read on for a discussion of this topic.

Operating income or earnings before interest and taxes (EBIT) is a measure of how well managers have deployed assets to generate an operating return. Incurring interest is not a result of any operating decisions made from day to day but rather a strategic decision made by the CFO and the team in the finance subunit. The expanded DuPont measure of ROI does contain a specific ratio to measure the effectiveness and efficiency of financial management. Tax is also the responsibility of the CFO and the management team in finance, not the operating managers. Again, the expanded DuPont measure of ROI contains another specific ratio to measure the effectiveness and efficiency of tax management.

To use net income (after-tax earnings) in the numerator could misstate by a material amount the actual operating return generated by the operating investments. This is why the operating income is more appropriate than either earnings before tax or net income.

RESIDUAL INCOME (RI)

Residual income (RI) is income minus a required dollar return on the investment.[3]

$$\text{Residual income} = \text{Income} - (\text{Required rate of return} \times \text{Investment})$$

The required rate of return (ROR) multiplied by investment is also called the **imputed cost** of the investment. Imputed costs are costs recognized in particular situations that are not regularly recognized by accrual accounting procedures. An imputed cost is not recognized in accounting records because it is not an incremental cost but instead represents the return forgone by Hospitality Inns as a result of tying up cash in various investments of similar risk. The ROR management should use to calculate residual income is the company's **weighted-average cost of capital (WACC)**. WACC equals the after-tax average cost of all the long-term funds used.

Conceptually, it would be better to use the cost of capital based on each subunit's risk level. For example, an oil-exploration division would warrant a higher required rate of return than an oil-refining division because the risk of failing to find oil is far higher than the risks of refining oil already being produced. Generally, the cost of capital based on each subunit's risk level is not externally available.

Assume that each motel faces similar risks. Hospitality Inns defines residual income for each motel as motel operating income minus a required rate of return of 12% of the total assets of the motel:

Motel	Operating Income	−	Required Rate of Return	×	Investment	=	Residual Income
Saskatoon	$240,000	−	12%	×	$(1,000,000)	=	$120,000
Brandon	$300,000	−	12%	×	$(2,000,000)	=	$ 60,000
Hull	$510,000	−	12%	×	$(3,000,000)	=	$150,000

[3]Just as in the case of ROI, companies using RI vary in the way they define income (for example, operating income, pretax income, or net income) and investment (for example, total assets or total assets minus current liabilities).

Given the 12% ROR, the Hull motel is performing best in terms of residual income. Generally, residual income is more likely than ROI to induce goal congruence. This preference for RI over ROI parallels the preference for NPV over IRR when managers produce a capital budget.

Some firms favour the residual-income approach because managers will concentrate on maximizing an absolute amount (dollars of residual income) rather than a percentage (return on investment). The objective of maximizing residual income assumes that as long as a division earns a rate in excess of the ROR that specific division should expand.

The objective of maximizing ROI may induce managers of highly profitable divisions to reject projects that, from the viewpoint of the organization as a whole, should be accepted. To illustrate, assume that Hospitality's required ROR is 12%. Assume also that an expansion of the Saskatoon motel will increase its operating income by $160,000 and increase its total assets by $800,000. The ROI for the expansion is 20% ($160,000 ÷ $800,000), which makes it attractive to Hospitality Inns as a whole. By making this expansion, however, the Saskatoon manager will see the motel's ROI decrease:

$$\text{Preexpansion ROI} = \frac{\$240,000}{\$1,000,000} = 24\%$$

$$\text{Postexpansion ROI} = \frac{(\$240,000 + \$160,000)}{(\$1,000,000 + \$800,000)} = \frac{\$400,000}{\$1,800,000} = 22.2\%$$

The annual bonus paid to the Saskatoon manager may decrease if ROI is a key component in the bonus calculation and the expansion option is selected. In contrast, if the annual bonus is a function of residual income, the Saskatoon manager will view the expansion favourably:

Preexpansion residual income = $240,000 − (12% × $1,000,000) = $120,000
Postexpansion residual income = $400,000 − (12% × $1,800,000) = $184,000

Goal congruence is more likely to be promoted by using residual income rather than ROI as a measure of the division manager's performance.

ECONOMIC VALUE ADDED (EVA®)

Economic value added (EVA®) is a specific type of residual income calculation that attracted considerable attention during the dot-com boom of the late 1990s.[4] The difference between this and other accounting performance measures is that this measure does not use a reported GAAP accrual in the numerator. Economic value added (EVA®) substitutes the following numbers in the residual-income calculations: (1) income equal to after-tax operating income, (2) a required rate of return equal to the weighted-average cost of capital, and (3) investment equal to total assets minus current liabilities.[5] We use the Hospitality Inns data in Exhibit 24-2 to illustrate EVA®.

$$\begin{matrix} \text{Economic} \\ \text{value added} \\ \text{(EVA®)} \end{matrix} = \begin{matrix} \text{After-tax} \\ \text{operating income} \end{matrix} - \left[\begin{matrix} \text{Weighted-average} \\ \text{cost of capital} \end{matrix} \times \left(\begin{matrix} \text{Total} \\ \text{assets} \end{matrix} - \begin{matrix} \text{Current} \\ \text{liabilities} \end{matrix} \right) \right]$$

The key calculation is the weighted-average cost of capital (WACC). Hospitality Inns has two sources of long-term funds—long-term debt with a market and book

---

[4]O'Byrne and D. Young, *EVA and Value-Based Management: A Practical Guide to Implementation* (New York: McGraw-Hill, 2000); J. Stein, J. Shiely, and I. Ross, *The EVA Challenge: Implementing Value Added Change in an Organization* (New York: John Wiley and Sons, 2001).

[5]When implementing EVA®, companies make several adjustments to the operating income and asset numbers reported under generally accepted accounting principles (GAAP). For example, when calculating EVA®, costs such as R&D, restructuring costs, and leases that have long-run benefits are recorded as assets (which are then amortized), rather than as current operating costs. The goal of these adjustments is to obtain a better representation of the economic assets, particularly intangible assets, used to earn income. Of course, the specific adjustments applicable to a company will depend on its individual circumstances.

value of $4.5 million issued at an interest rate of 10%, and equity capital that has a market value of $3 million (and a book value of $1 million).[6] Because interest costs are tax-deductible, the after-tax cost of debt financing equals $0.10 \times (1 - \text{tax rate}) = 0.10 \times (1 - 0.30) = 0.10 \times 0.70 = 0.07$, or 7%. The cost of equity capital is the opportunity cost to investors of not investing their capital in another investment that is similar in risk to Hospitality Inns. Suppose that Hospitality's cost of equity capital is 15%.[7] The WACC computation, which uses market values of debt and equity, is as follows:

$$\text{WACC} = \frac{(0.07 \times \$4,500,000) + (0.15 \times \$3,000,000)}{\$4,500,000 + \$3,000,000}$$

$$= \frac{(\$315,000 + \$450,000)}{\$7,500,000} = \frac{\$765,000}{\$7,500,000}$$

$$= 0.102 \text{ or } 10.2\%$$

The company applies the same WACC to all its motels, since each motel faces similar risks.

Total assets minus current liabilities (see Exhibit 24-2, p. 1140) can also be computed as:

$$\text{Total assets} - \text{Current liabilities} = \text{Long-term assets} + \text{Current assets} - \text{Current liabilities}$$
$$= \text{Long-term assets} + \text{Working capital}$$

where working capital = current assets − current liabilities. After-tax motel operating income is:

$$\frac{\text{Motel operating}}{\text{income}} \times (1 - \text{Tax rate}) = \frac{\text{Motel operating}}{\text{income}} \times (1 - 0.30) = \frac{\text{Motel operating}}{\text{income}} \times 0.70$$

EVA® calculations for Hospitality Inns are as follows:

Motel	After-Tax Operating Income −	Weighted Average Cost of Capital ×	Total Assets	Current − Liabilities =	EVA®
Saskatoon	$240,000 × 0.70 −	[10.2%	× ($1,000,000 −	$ 50,000)] =	$71,100
Brandon	$300,000 × 0.70 −	[10.2%	× ($2,000,000 −	$150,000)] =	$21,300
Hull	$510,000 × 0.70 −	[10.2%	× ($3,000,000 −	$300,000)] =	$81,600

The Hull motel has the highest EVA®. EVA®, like residual income, charges managers for the cost of their investments in long-term assets and working capital. Value is created only if after-tax operating income exceeds the cost of investing the capital. To improve EVA®, managers must earn more operating income with the same capital, use less capital, or invest capital in high-return projects.

After implementing EVA®, CSX, a railroad company, began running trains with three locomotives instead of four by scheduling arrivals just in time for unloading, rather than having trains arrive at their destination several hours in advance. The idle time decreased as the capital utilization rate increased, without affecting service to the customer. The result is higher profits because of lower fuel costs, and less capital invested in locomotives. Chief executive officers of companies such as AT&T, Briggs & Stratton, Coca-Cola, CSX, Equifax, FMC, and Quaker Oats credit the EVA® concept with motivating decisions that have increased shareholder value.

RETURN ON SALES

The income-to-revenue (sales) ratio—often called **return on sales (ROS)**—is a frequently used financial performance measure. ROS is one component of ROI in the

---

[6]The market value of Hospitality Inns' equity exceeds book value because book value, based on historical cost, does not measure the current value of the company's assets, and because various intangible assets, such as the company's brand name, are not shown at current value in the balance sheet under GAAP.

[7]For details on calculating cost of equity capital adjusted for risk, see J. Van Horne, *Financial Management and Policy*, 12th ed. (Upper Saddle River, NJ: Prentice Hall, 2002).

DuPont method of profitability analysis. To calculate the ROS of each of Hospitality's motels, we use operating income divided by revenues. The ROS for each motel is

Motel	Operating Income	÷	Revenues	=	ROS
Saskatoon	$240,000	÷	$1,200,000	=	20.00%
Brandon	$300,000	÷	$1,400,000	=	21.43%
Hull	$510,000	÷	$3,185,000	=	16.01%

The Brandon motel has the highest ROS, whereas its performance is rated worse than the other motels using performance measures such as ROI, RI, and EVA®.

The following table summarizes the performance and ranking of each motel under each of the four performance measures:

Motel	ROI	Rank	Residual Income	Rank	EVA®	Rank	ROS	Rank
Saskatoon	24%	1	$120,000	2	$71,100	2	20.00%	2
Brandon	15%	3	$ 60,000	3	$21,300	3	21.43%	1
Hull	17%	2	$150,000	1	$81,600	1	16.01%	3

The residual-income and EVA® rankings differ from the ROI and ROS rankings. Consider the ROI and residual-income rankings for the Saskatoon and Hull motels. The Hull motel has a smaller ROI. Although its operating income is only slightly more than twice that of the Saskatoon motel ($510,000 versus $240,000), its total assets are three times as large ($3 million versus $1 million). The return on assets invested in the Hull motel is not as high as the return on assets invested in the Saskatoon motel. The Hull motel has a higher residual income because it earns a higher operating income after covering the 12% required return on investment.

The Brandon motel has the highest ROS but the lowest ROI, because although it earns very high income per dollar of revenue, it generates very low revenues per dollar of assets invested. None of the methods is superior to the others because each evaluates a slightly different aspect of performance. For example, in markets where revenue growth is limited, return on sales is the most meaningful indicator of a sub-unit's performance.

ROS measures how effectively costs are managed; ROI measures which investment yields the highest return. To evaluate overall aggregate performance, ROI or residual-income-based measures are more appropriate, since they consider both income earned and investments made. Residual-income and EVA® measures overcome some of the goal-congruence problems that ROI measures might introduce. Some managers favour EVA® because it explicitly considers tax effects, while pretax residual-income measures do not. Other managers favour pretax residual-income because it is easier to compute and because it often leads to the same conclusions as EVA®. Generally, companies use multiple financial measures to evaluate performance.

SELECT THE TIME HORIZON

Another consideration in designing accounting-based performance measures is choosing the time horizon of the performance measures. The ROI, RI, EVA®, and ROS calculations represent the results for a single time period, a year in our example. Managers could take actions that cause short-run increases in these measures but are in conflict with the long-run interests of the organization. For example, managers may curtail R&D and plant maintenance in the last three months of a fiscal year to achieve a target level of annual operating income. For this reason, many companies evaluate subunits on the basis of ROI, RI, EVA®, and ROS over multiple years.

Another reason for evaluating subunits over a multiyear time horizon is that the benefits of actions taken in the current period may not show up in short-run performance measures such as the current year's ROI or RI. For example, the investment in a new motel may adversely affect ROI and RI in the short run but benefit ROIs and RIs in the long run.

Real Practices Worldwide

Country	Key Financial Performance Measures
Australia	ROI, income
Germany[f]	Revenue, contribution margin (on a per-unit basis)
India	ROI, income
Japan	ROS, ROI
Netherlands	ROI, cash flow, income
Singapore[g]	ROI
United States	Income, ROI, EVA®

Multiple global surveys indicate extensive use of financial performance measures. The percentage of the largest US companies that view specific financial performance measures as most important are income in comparison with budget, 49%; return on investment (ROI), 29%; economic value added (EVA®), 14%; return on sales (ROS), 3%; and other measures, 5%.[a] Similar to many US companies, Australian, Indian, and Dutch corporations also focus on ROI and income.[b,c,d] In contrast, 82% of Japanese companies use return on sales (ROS), whereas only 37% use ROI in measuring financial performance.[e] Some researchers argue that Japanese managers favour ROS because it is easier to calculate, lessens the emphasis on short-term profitability, and is a market-oriented measure that provides more-useful insights for making pricing and target costing decisions. The following table presents the key financial performance measures (in order of importance) used by companies in seven different countries.

[a]R. Tang, "Canadian Transfer Pricing in the 1990s," *Management Accounting* (1992).

[b]R. Crenhall, R., and K. Smith, "Adoption and Benefits of Management Accounting Practices: An Australian Study," *Management Accounting Research* (1998).

[c]P. Joshi, "The International Diffusion of New Management Accounting Practices: The Case of India," *Journal of International Accounting, Auditing & Taxation* (2001).

[d]T. Groot, "Managing Costs in The Netherlands: Past Theory and Current Practice," in A. Bhimani (ed.) *Management Accounting: European Perspectives* (Oxford: Oxford University Press, 1996).

[e]H. Wijewardena and A. De Zoysa, "A Comparative Analysis of Management Accounting Practices in Australia and Japan: An Empirical Investigation," *International Journal of Accounting* (1999).

[f]G. Scherrer, "Management Accounting: A German Perspective," in A. Bhimani (ed.) *Management Accounting: European Perspectives* (Oxford: Oxford University Press, 1996).

[g]B. Ghosh and Y. Chan, "Management Accounting in Singapore—Well in Place?" *Managerial Auditing Journal* (1997).

A multiyear analysis highlights another advantage of the RI measure. The net present value of all the cash flows over the life of an investment equals the net present value of RIs.[8] This means that if managers use net present value analysis to make investment decisions (as prescribed in Chapter 21), using multiyear RI to evaluate managers' performances achieves goal congruence.

[8]We are grateful to S. Reichelstein for pointing this out. To see this equivalence, suppose a $400,000 investment in the Brandon motel increases operating income by $70,000 per year as follows: Increase in operating cash flows of $150,000 each year for five years minus amortization of $80,000 per year ($400,000 ÷ 5), assuming straight-line amortization and zero terminal disposal price. Amortization reduces the investment amount by $80,000 each year. Assuming a required rate of return of 12%, net present values of cash flows and residual incomes are as follows:

Year	0	1	2	3	4	5	Net Present Value
(1) Cash flow	−$400,000	$150,000	$150,000	$150,000	$150,000	$150,000	
(2) Present value of $1 discounted at 12%	1	0.89286	0.79719	0.71178	0.63552	0.56743	
(3) Present value: (1) × (2)	−$400,000	$133,929	$119,578	$106,767	$ 95,328	$ 85,115	$140,717
(4) Operating income		$ 70,000	$ 70,000	$ 70,000	$ 70,000	$ 70,000	
(5) Assets at start of year		$400,000	$320,000	$240,000	$160,000	$ 80,000	
(6) Capital charge: (5) × 12%		$ 48,000	$ 38,400	$ 28,800	$ 19,200	$ 9,600	
(7) Residual income: (4) − (6)		$ 22,000	$ 31,600	$ 41,200	$ 50,800	$ 60,400	
(8) Present value of RI: (7) × (2)		$ 19,643	$ 25,191	$ 29,325	$ 32,284	$ 34,273	$140,716

Another way that companies motivate managers to take a long-run perspective is by compensating them on changes in the market price of the company's shares (in addition to using multiyear accounting-based performance measures). Why does this approach help to extend managers' time horizons? Because share prices more rapidly incorporate the expected future period effects of current decisions.

SELECT THE TIME HORIZON

We use the different definitions of investment that companies use to illustrate the second phase of designing accounting-based performance measures. Definitions include the following:

◆ *Total assets available.* Includes all business assets, regardless of their particular purpose.

◆ *Total assets employed.* Defined as total assets available minus idle assets and minus assets purchased for future expansion. For example, if the Hull motel in Exhibit 24-2 (p. 1140) has unused land set aside for potential expansion, the total assets employed by the motel would exclude the cost of that land.

◆ *Working capital (current assets minus current liabilities) plus long-term assets.* This definition excludes that portion of current assets financed by short-term creditors.

◆ *Shareholders' equity.* Use of this definition for each individual motel in Exhibit 24-2 requires allocation of the long-term liabilities of Hospitality Inns to the three motels, which would then be deducted from the total assets of each motel.

Most companies that employ ROI, residual income, or EVA® for performance measurement use either total assets available or working capital plus long-term assets as the definition of investment. However, when top management directs a division manager to carry extra assets, total assets employed can be more informative than total assets available. The most common rationale for using working capital plus long-term assets is that the division manager often influences decisions on the short-term debt of the division.

ASSESS YOUR MASTERY

To check your understanding of the material in Learning Objective ❶, go to the *Mastery Questions* section at the end of this chapter and complete Learning Objective ❶ question 1.

MyAccountingLab

EVALUATE PERFORMANCE MEASUREMENT ALTERNATIVES

Evaluate current-cost and historical-cost asset measurement methods ❷

To illustrate the decision on performance measurement alternatives, we examine present value and accrual methods of historical cost, current cost, and current disposal price. We also examine the relevance of gross book value in contrast to net book value for depreciable assets. Managers have already chosen the accrual method of ROI, RI, or EVA® and now must select the most appropriate, relevant accruals to estimate dollar values in the numerator and denominator.

CURRENT COST

Current cost is the cost of purchasing an asset today identical to the one currently held. It is the cost of purchasing the services provided by that asset if an identical asset cannot currently be purchased. Of course, measuring assets at current costs will result in different ROIs compared to the ROIs calculated based on historical costs.

We illustrate the current-cost ROI calculations using the Hospitality Inns example (see Exhibit 24-2) and then compare current- and historical-cost-based ROIs. Assume the following information about the long-term assets of each motel:

	Saskatoon	Brandon	Hull
Age of facility (at end of 2009)	8 years	4 years	2 years
Gross book value of long-term assets	$1,400,000	$2,100,000	$2,800,000
Accumulated amortization (straight-line)	800,000	600,000	400,000
Net book value (at end of 2009)	$ 600,000	$1,500,000	$2,400,000
Amortization expense for 2009	$ 100,000	$ 150,000	$ 200,000

Hospitality Inns assumes a 14-year estimated useful life, assumes no terminal disposal price for the physical facilities, and calculates amortization on a straight-line basis.

An index of construction costs for the eight-year period that Hospitality Inns has been operating (year 0 = 100) is as follows:

Year	1	2	3	4	5	6	7	8
Construction cost index	110	122	136	144	152	160	174	180

Earlier in this chapter, we computed an ROI of 24% for Saskatoon, 15% for Brandon, and 17% for Hull (see p. 1141). One possible explanation of the high ROI for Saskatoon is that this motel's long-term assets are expressed in terms of year 0 construction price levels (eight years ago) and that the long-term assets for the Brandon and Hull motels are expressed in terms of the higher, more recent construction price levels, which depress ROIs for these motels.

Exhibit 24-3 illustrates a step-by-step approach for incorporating current-cost estimates for long-term assets and amortization into the ROI calculation. The aim is to approximate what it would cost today to obtain assets that would produce the same expected operating income as the subunits currently earn. (Similar adjustments to represent current costs of capital employed and amortization can also be made in the residual income and EVA calculations.) The current-cost adjustment dramatically reduces the ROI of the Saskatoon motel.

	Historical-Cost ROI	Current-Cost ROI
Saskatoon	24%	10.81%
Brandon	15%	11.05%
Hull	17%	14.70%

Adjusting for current costs negates differences in the investment base caused solely by differences in construction price levels. Consequently, compared to historical-cost ROI, current-cost ROI is a better measure of the current economic returns from the investment. For example, current-cost ROI indicates that taking into account current construction price levels, investing in a new motel in Saskatoon will result in an ROI closer to 10.8% than to 24%. If Hospitality Inns were to invest in a new motel today, investing in one like the Hull motel offers the best ROI.

A drawback of the current-cost method is that obtaining current-cost estimates for some assets can be difficult because the estimate requires a company to consider technological advances when determining the current cost of assets needed to earn today's operating income.[9]

[9]When a specific cost index (such as the construction cost index) is not available, companies use a general index (such as the consumer price index) to approximate current costs.

Step 1: Restate long-term assets from gross book value at historical cost to gross book value at current cost as of the end of 2009:

Motel	Gross Book Value of Long-Term Assets at Historical Cost	×	Construction Cost Index in 2009	÷	Construction Cost Index in Construction Year	=	Gross Book Value of Long-Term Assets at Current Cost at End of 2009
Saskatoon	$1,400,000	×	(180	÷	100)	=	$2,520,000
Brandon	$2,100,000	×	(180	÷	144)	=	$2,625,000
Hull	$2,800,000	×	(180	÷	160)	=	$3,150,000

Step 2: Derive net book value of long-term assets at current cost as of the end of 2009. (Assume estimated useful life of each motel is 14 years.)

Motel	Gross Book Value of Long-Term Assets at Current Cost at End of 2009	×	(Estimated Remaining Useful Life	÷	Estimated Total Useful Life)	=	Net Book Value of Long-Term Assets at Current Cost at End of 2009
Saskatoon	$2,520,000	×	(6	÷	14)	=	$1,080,000
Brandon	$2,625,000	×	(10	÷	14)	=	$1,875,000
Hull	$3,150,000	×	(12	÷	14)	=	$2,700,000

Step 3: Calculate the current cost of total assets at the end of year 8. (Assume the current assets of each motel are expressed in year 8 dollars.)

Motel	Current Assets at end of 2009 (from Exhibit 24-2)	+	Long-Term Assets Derived in Step 2 (above)	=	Current Cost of Total Assets at End of 2009
Saskatoon	$400,000	+	$1,080,000	=	$1,480,000
Brandon	$500,000	+	$1,875,000	=	$2,375,000
Hull	$600,000	+	$2,700,000	=	$3,300,000

Step 4: Calculate current-cost amortization expense in 2009 dollars.

Motel	Gross Book Value of Long-Term Assets at Current Cost at End of 2009	÷	Estimated Total Useful Life	=	Current Cost of Amortization Expense in 2009 Dollars
Saskatoon	$2,520,000	÷	14	=	$180,000
Brandon	$2,625,000	÷	14	=	$187,500
Hull	$3,150,000	÷	14	=	$225,000

Step 5: Calculate year 8 operating income using year 8 current cost amortization.

Motel	Historical Cost Operating Income	−	Current Cost of Amortization Expense in 2009 Dollars	−	Historical Cost Amortization Expense	=	Operating Income for 2009 Using Current Cost Amortization Expense in 2009 Dollars
Saskatoon	$240,000	−	($180,000	−	$100,000)	=	$160,000
Brandon	$300,000	−	($187,500	−	$150,000)	=	$262,500
Hull	$510,000	−	($225,000	−	$200,000)	=	$485,000

Step 6: Calculate ROI using current cost estimates for long-term assets and amortization expense.

Motel	Operating Income for 2009 Using Current Cost Amortization Expense in 2009 Dollars	÷	Current Cost of Total Assets at End of 2009	=	ROI Using Current Cost Estimate
Saskatoon	$160,000	÷	$1,480,000	=	10.81%
Brandon	$262,500	÷	$2,375,000	=	11.05%
Hull	$485,000	÷	$3,300,000	=	14.70%

LONG-TERM ASSETS: GROSS OR NET BOOK VALUE?

Because historical-cost investment measures are used often in practice, there has been much discussion about the relative merits of using gross book value (original cost) or net book value (original cost minus accumulated amortization). Using the data in Exhibit 24-2 and page 1140, the ROI calculations using net book values and gross book values of plant and equipment are as follows:

	Operating Income (from Exhibit 24-2)	Net Book Value of Total Assets (from Exhibit 24-2)	Accumulated Amortization (from p. 1148)	Gross Book Value of Total Assets	2009 ROI Using Net Book Value of Total Assets	2009 ROI Using Gross Book Value of Total Assets
	(1)	(2)	(3)	(4) = (2) + (3)	(5) = (1) ÷ (2)	(6) = (1) ÷ (4)
Saskatoon	$240,000	$1,000,000	$800,000	$1,800,000	24%	13.33%
Brandon	$300,000	$2,000,000	$600,000	$2,600,000	15%	11.54%
Hull	$510,000	$3,000,000	$400,000	$3,400,000	17%	15.00%

Using the gross book value, the ROI of the older Saskatoon motel (13.33%) is lower than that of the newer Hull motel (15%). Those who favour using gross book value claim that it enables more accurate comparisons across subunits. For example, using gross book value calculations, the return on the original plant and equipment investment is higher for the newer Hull motel than for the older Saskatoon motel. This probably reflects the decline in earning power of the Saskatoon motel. In contrast, using the net book value masks this decline in earning power, because the constantly decreasing base results in a higher ROI (24%); this higher rate may mislead decision makers into thinking that the earning power of the Saskatoon motel has not decreased.

The proponents of using net book value as a base maintain that it is less confusing because (1) it is consistent with the total assets shown on the conventional balance sheet and (2) it is consistent with net income computations that include deductions for amortization. Surveys of company practice report net book value to be the dominant asset measure used by companies in their internal performance evaluations. When using net book value, the declining denominator increases ROI as an asset ages, all other things equal. Evaluating managers based on assets at net book value rather than gross book value increases incentives for retaining old property, plant, and equipment. Because older assets valued at net book value inflate ROI (particularly if investment is defined as net book value rather than gross book value), top management may set higher target ROIs for divisions with older assets.

SELECTING PERFORMANCE GOALS AND TIMING OF FEEDBACK

We next consider the selection of criteria, those accounting-based measures against which to compare actual performance. Recall that book value accounting measures are often inadequate for evaluating economic returns on new investments and sometimes create disincentives for new expansion. Despite these problems, book value ROIs can be used to evaluate current performance by adjusting target ROIs. Consider our Hospitality Inns example. The key is to recognize that the motels were built at different times, which in turn means they were built at different levels of the construction cost index. Top management could adjust the target accordingly, perhaps setting Saskatoon's ROI at 26%, Brandon's at 18%, and Hull's at 19%.

Nevertheless, the alternative of comparing actual to target performance is frequently overlooked in the literature. Critics of book value have indicated how high rates of return on old assets may erroneously induce a manager not to replace assets. Regardless, the manager's mandate is often "Go forth and attain the budgeted results." The budget, then, should be carefully negotiated with full knowledge of book value measurement bias. *The desirability of tailoring a budget* to a particular subunit and a particular accounting system cannot be overemphasized. For example, many problems of asset valuation and income measurement (whether based on book value or current cost) can be satisfactorily solved if top management gets everybody to focus on what is attainable in the forthcoming budget period—regardless of whether the financial measures are based on book value or some other measure, such as current costs.

Top management often sets continuous improvement targets. Consider companies implementing EVA®. These companies have generally found it cost-effective to use net book value rather than estimates of market or replacement values. Why? Because top management evaluates operations on year-to-year changes in EVA®, not on absolute measures of EVA®. Evaluating performance on the basis of improvements in EVA® makes the initial method of calculating EVA® less important.

SELECT LEVEL OF RELEVANCE—THE TIMING OF FEEDBACK

The final selection is the timing of feedback. Timing of feedback depends largely on how critical the information is for the success of the organization, the specific level of management that is receiving the feedback, and the sophistication of the organization's information technology. For example, motel managers responsible for room sales will want information on the number of rooms sold each day on a daily or, at most, weekly basis; a large percentage of motel costs are fixed costs, so achieving high room sales and taking quick action to reverse any declining sales trends are critical to the financial success of each motel. Supplying managers with daily information about room sales would be much easier if Hospitality Inns had a computerized room reservation and check-in system. Senior management, on the other hand, in their oversight role may look at information about daily room sales only on a monthly basis. In some instances (for example, because of concern about the low sales to total assets ratio of the Brandon motel), they may want the information weekly.

ASSESS YOUR MASTERY

To check your understanding of the material in Learning Objective ❷, go to the *Mastery Questions* section at the end of this chapter and complete Learning Objective ❷ question 1.

PERFORMANCE MEASUREMENT IN MULTINATIONAL COMPANIES

Comparing the performance of divisions of a multinational company operating in different countries creates additional difficulties:[10]

Analyze the technical difficulties that arise when comparing the performance of divisions operating in different countries

- ◆ The economic, legal, political, social, and cultural environments differ significantly across countries.

- ◆ Governments in some countries limit selling prices and impose controls on a company's products. For example, developing countries in Asia, Latin America, and Eastern Europe impose tariffs and duties to restrict the import of certain goods. Beginning in 2005, the General Agreement on Tariffs and Trade (GATT) seeks to reduce and eliminate tariffs and duties imposed.

- ◆ Availability of materials and skilled labour, as well as costs of materials, labour, and infrastructure (power, transportation, and communication) may also differ significantly across countries.

- ◆ Divisions operating in different countries keep score of their performance in different currencies. Issues of inflation and fluctuations in foreign currency exchange rates then become important.

We focus on the last of these issues next.

---

[10]M. Z. Iqbal, T. Melcher, and A. Elmallah, *International Accounting—A Global Perspective* (Cincinnati: Southwestern ITP, 2002).

CALCULATING THE FOREIGN DIVISION'S ROI IN THE FOREIGN CURRENCY

Suppose Hospitality Inns invests in a motel in Mexico City. The investment consists mainly of the costs of buildings and furnishings. The following information is available:

◆ The exchange rate at the time of Hospitality's investment on December 31, 2009, is 3 pesos = $1.

◆ During 2010, the Mexican peso suffers a steady and steep decline in its value.

◆ The exchange rate on December 31, 2010, is 6 pesos = $1.

◆ The average exchange rate during 2010 is [(3 + 6) ÷ 2] = 4.5 pesos = $1.

◆ The investment (total assets) in the Mexico City motel = 9,000,000 pesos.

◆ The operating income of the Mexico City motel in 2010 = 1,800,000 pesos.

What is the historical-cost-based ROI for the Mexico City motel in 2010? Some specific questions arise. Should we calculate the ROI in pesos or in dollars? If we calculate the ROI in dollars, what exchange rate should we use? How does the ROI of Hospitality Inns Mexico City (HIMC) compare with the ROI of Hospitality Inns Hull (HIH), which is also a relatively new motel of roughly the same size? Hospitality Inns may be interested in this information for making future investment decisions.

$$\text{HIMC's ROI (calculated using pesos)} = \frac{\text{Operating income}}{\text{Total assets}} = \frac{1,800,000 \text{ pesos}}{9,000,000 \text{ pesos}} = 20\%$$

HIMC's ROI of 20% is higher than HIH's ROI of 17% (computed on p. 1141). Does this mean that HIMC outperformed HIH on the ROI criterion? Not necessarily, because HIMC operates in a very different economic environment than does HIH.

The peso has declined steeply in value relative to the dollar in 2010. Research studies show that the peso's decline is correlated with correspondingly higher inflation in Mexico relative to Canada.[11] A consequence of the higher inflation in Mexico is that HIMC will charge higher prices for its motel rooms, which will increase HIMC's operating income and lead to a higher ROI. Inflation clouds the real economic returns on an asset and makes ROI calculated on historical cost of assets unrealistically high. The reason is that had there been no inflation, HIMC's room rates and hence operating income would have been much lower. Differences in inflation rates between the two countries make a direct comparison of HIMC's peso-denominated ROI with HIH's dollar-denominated ROI misleading.

CALCULATING THE FOREIGN DIVISION'S ROI IN CANADIAN DOLLARS

One way to achieve a more meaningful comparison of historical-cost-based ROIs is to restate HIMC's performance in dollars. But what exchange rate(s) should be used to make the comparison meaningful? Assume operating income was earned evenly throughout 2010. We use the average exchange rate of 4.5 pesos = $1 to convert the operating income from pesos to dollars: 1,800,000 pesos ÷ 4.5 = $400,000. The effect of dividing the operating income in pesos by the higher pesos-to-dollars exchange rate is that any increase in operating income in pesos as a result of inflation is undone when converting back to dollars.

At what rate should we convert HIMC's total assets of 9,000,000 pesos? At the exchange rate prevailing when the assets were acquired on December 31, 2009, namely 3 pesos = $1, because HIMC's book value of assets is recorded at the December 31, 2009, cost and is not revalued as a result of inflation in Mexico in 2010. Since the book value of assets is unaffected by subsequent inflation, so should the

[11]W. Beaver and M. Wolfson, "Foreign Currency Translation Gains and Losses: What Effect Do They Have and What Do They Mean?" *Financial Analysts Journal* (March–April 1984); F. D. S. Choi, "Resolving the Inflation/Currency Translation Dilemma," *Management International Review*, Vol. 34, Special Issue, 1994; H. Louis, "The Value Relevance of the Foreign Translation Adjustment," *TheAccounting Review* (October 2003).

exchange rate used to convert it into dollars. Using exchange rates after December 31, 2009, would be incorrect, because these rates incorporate the higher inflation in Mexico in 2010. Total assets would be converted to 9,000,000 pesos ÷ 3 = $3,000,000. Then:

$$\text{HIMC's ROI (calculated using dollars)} = \frac{\text{Operating income}}{\text{Total assets}} = \frac{\$400,000}{\$3,000,000} = 13.33\%$$

These adjustments make the historical-cost-based ROIs of the two motels comparable because they negate the effects of any differences in inflation rates between the two countries. HIMC's ROI of 13.33% is less than HIH's ROI of 17%.

Residual income calculated in pesos suffers from the same problems as ROI calculated using pesos. Instead, calculating HIMC's residual income in dollars adjusts for changes in exchange rates and facilitates comparisons with Hospitality's other motels:

$$\begin{aligned}
\text{HIMC's residual income} &= \$400,000 - (12\% \times \$3,000,000) \\
&= \$400,000 - \$360,000 \\
&= \$40,000
\end{aligned}$$

which is also less than HIH's residual income of $150,000. In interpreting HIMC's and HIH's ROI and residual income, note that they are historical-cost-based calculations. They do, however, pertain to relatively new motels.

LEVELS OF ANALYSIS DIFFER BETWEEN MANAGERS AND SUBUNITS[12]

The performance evaluation of a manager should be distinguished from the performance evaluation of an organization subunit, such as a division of a company. For example, historical-cost-based ROIs for a particular division can be used to evaluate a manager's performance relative to a budget or over time, even though historical-cost ROIs may be unsatisfactory for evaluating economic returns earned by the subunit. But using historical-cost ROIs to compare the performance of managers of different subunits can be misleading.

In the Hospitality Inns example, Hospitality Inns Hull's (HIH's) ROI of 17% exceeds Hospitality Inns Mexico City's (HIMC's) ROI of 13.33% after adjusting for the higher inflation in Mexico. The ROIs may give some indication of the economic returns from each motel but do not mean that the manager of HIH performed better than the manager of HIMC. The reason is that among other factors, HIMC's ROI may have been adversely affected relative to HIH's ROI because of externalities beyond the HIMC manager's control, such as legal, political, and government regulations as well as economic conditions in Mexico.

Consider another example. Companies often put the most skillful division manager in charge of the weakest division in an attempt to change its fortunes. Such an effort may take years to bear fruit. Furthermore, the manager's efforts may result merely in bringing the division up to a minimum acceptable ROI. The division may continue to be a poor profit performer in comparison with other divisions, but it would be a mistake to conclude from the poor performance of the division that the manager is necessarily performing poorly.

What dictates the intensity of the incentives? That is, how large should the incentive component be relative to salary? A key question is: How well does the performance measure capture the manager's ability to influence the desired results? Measures of performance that are superior change significantly with the manager's performance and not very much with changes in factors that are beyond the manager's control. We presented this justification for using operating margin instead of either pretax or net margin when measuring ROI.

Superior performance measures motivate the manager but limit the manager's exposure to uncontrollable risk and hence reduce the cost of providing incentives to get the manager to accept the incentive program. When possible, owners use performance evaluation measures that are tightly linked to managers' efforts. Managers

[12]The presentations here draw (in part) on teaching notes prepared by S. Huddart, N. Melumad, and S. Reichelstein.

are evaluated based on things they can affect, even if they are not completely controllable. For example, salespeople often earn commissions based on the amount of sales revenues they generate. Salespeople can affect the amount of sales they generate by working harder, but they cannot control other factors (such as the economy and competitors' products) that also affect the amount of their sales.

Sally Fonda owns the Hospitality Inns chain of motels. Roger Brett manages the Hospitality Inns Saskatoon (HIS) motel. Suppose Brett has no authority to determine investments. Further suppose revenue is determined largely by external factors such as the local economy. Brett's actions influence only costs. Using RI as a performance measure in these circumstances subjects Brett's bonus to excessive risk, because two components of the performance measure (investments and revenues) are unrelated to his actions. The management accountant might suggest that, to create stronger incentives, Fonda consider using a different performance measure for Brett—perhaps HIS's costs—that more closely captures Brett's effort. Note that in this case, RI may be a perfectly good measure of the economic viability of HIS, but it is not a good measure of Brett's performance.

The salary component of compensation dominates when performance measures sensitive to a manager's effort are unavailable (as in the case of some corporate staff and government officials). This is not to say, however, that incentives are completely absent; promotions and salary increases do depend on some overall measure of performance, but the incentives are less direct. Employers give stronger incentives when superior measures of performance are available to them and when monitoring the employee's effort is very difficult (real estate agencies, for example, reward employees mainly on commissions on houses sold).

In evaluating Brett, Fonda uses measures from multiple perspectives of the BSC because nonfinancial measures on the BSC—employee satisfaction and the time taken for check-in, cleaning rooms, and providing room service—are more sensitive to Brett's actions. Financial measures such as RI are less sensitive to Brett's actions because they are affected by external factors such as local economic conditions that are beyond Brett's control.

Another reason for using nonfinancial measures in the BSC is that these measures follow Hospitality Inns' strategy and are drivers of future performance. Evaluating managers on these nonfinancial measures motivates them to take actions that will sustain long-run performance. Therefore, evaluating performance in all four perspectives of the BSC promotes both short- and long-run actions. Surveys show that division managers' compensation plans include a mix of salary, bonus, and long-term compensation tied to earnings and share price of the company. The goal is to balance division and companywide, as well as short-term and long-term incentives.

If managers are evaluated on a single performance measure, they will treat other critical success factors as secondary to that single measure. For example, managers might curtail advertising and maintenance to increase the current year's ROI. This is why performance evaluation needs to be based on a variety of critical success factors such as those sustained by the BSC strategy.

BENCHMARKS AND RELATIVE PERFORMANCE EVALUATION

Owners can use benchmarks to evaluate performance. Benchmarks representing best practice may be available inside or outside the overall organization. In our Hospitality Inns example, benchmarks could be other similar motels, either within or outside the Hospitality Inns chain. Suppose Brett has authority over revenues, costs, and investments. In evaluating Brett's performance, Fonda would want to use as a benchmark a motel of a similar size that is influenced by the same uncontrollable factors—for example, location, demographic trends, and economic conditions—that affect HIS. *Differences* in performances of the two motels occur only because of differences in the two managers' performances, not because of random factors. Thus, benchmarking, also called *relative performance evaluation*, "filters out" the effects of the common noncontrollable factors.

Can the performance of two managers responsible for running similar operations within a company be benchmarked against one another? Yes, but one problem is that the use of these benchmarks may reduce incentives for these managers to help one another. That is, a manager's performance-evaluation measure improves either by doing a better job or by making the other manager look bad. Failing to work together as a team is not in the best interests of the organization as a whole. In this case, using benchmarks for performance evaluation can lead to goal incongruence.

ASSESS YOUR MASTERY

To check your understanding of the material in Learning Objective ③, go to the *Mastery Questions* section at the end of this chapter and complete Learning Objective ③ question 1.

MyAccountingLab

EXECUTIVE PERFORMANCE MEASURES AND COMPENSATION

The performance evaluation of managers and employees often affects their compensation. Compensation arrangements run the range from a flat salary with no direct performance-based bonus (as in the case of government officials) to rewards based only on performance (as in the case of employees of real estate agencies). Most often, however, a manager's total compensation includes some combination of salary and a performance-based bonus. An important consideration in designing compensation arrangements is the tradeoff between creating incentives and imposing risk. We illustrate this tradeoff in the context of our Hospitality Inns example.

> Evaluate the behavioural effects of salaries and incentives in compensation arrangements **4**

Insurance companies possess extraordinary expertise at modelling risk because their core business is to profitably enter into contracts to share risk. All other things equal, some people purchase insurance while others do not. One explanation is difference in risk preference. Risk-averse people want to minimize the probability of enduring financial or other harms and are willing to pay to avoid bearing risk alone. Some people, however, are not risk averse. What this means is that in a competitive market, when faced with the same array of probabilities, outcomes, and financial penalties or rewards, people with different risk preferences will make different choices.

People who become entrepreneurs (owners) are generally more risk-tolerant than those who decide to work for others (managers). The reason is that an entrepreneur has no guaranteed return on investment. Entrepreneurs assume that all other things equal, their reward is linked to their effort—the harder they work the higher the reward. What the entrepreneur receives is the residual after all contracted obligations have been paid.

Managers or employees, on the other hand, prefer the security of a salary and are willing to accept a lower but certain return for their hard work. Unfortunately, effort is no guarantee because uncontrollable factors also affect return. Whether or not compensation is well designed depends in large part on how well the performance measures reflect the manager's efforts. In the case of Mr. Nardelli of Home Depot (page 1137), shareholders complained that the CEO was collecting reward for misdirected effort that failed to produce increases in the price of their shares. The shareholders' wealth is represented in the residual after all contracted obligations are paid. The more Mr. Nardelli received, the smaller was their residual.

It is more cost-efficient for owners to bear risk than managers, because managers demand a premium (extra compensation) for bearing risk. For risk-averse managers, an incentive is required to take the same level of risk as would an entrepreneurial owner. The objective of many compensation plans is to provide managers with incentives to work hard while minimizing the risk placed on them.

Assume that Fonda uses RI to measure performance. To achieve good results as measured by RI, Fonda would like Brett to control costs, provide prompt and courteous service, and reduce receivables. But even if Brett did all those things, good results are by no means guaranteed. HIS's RI is affected by many factors outside

Fonda's and Brett's control, such as a recession in the Saskatoon economy, or weather that might negatively affect HIS. Alternatively, noncontrollable factors might have a positive influence on HIS's RI. Noncontrollable factors make HIS's profitability uncertain and risky.

Fonda is an entrepreneur (the owner) who does not mind bearing risk, but Brett does not like being subject to risk; that is why he chose to be an employee rather than an owner. One way of insuring Brett against risk is to pay Brett a flat salary, regardless of the actual amount of residual income attained. All the risk would then be borne by Fonda. There is a problem here, however, because the effort that Brett puts in is difficult to monitor. The absence of performance-based compensation provides Brett with no incentive to work harder or undertake extra physical and mental effort beyond the minimum necessary to retain his job or to uphold his own personal values.

Moral hazard[13] describes contexts in which, once risk is shared, the individual fails to make as much effort to avoid harm as when risk was not shared. Effort is generally not observable in employees in management because it is primarily mental, not physical. Assume that managers prefer to exert less effort (or report biased measures of effort) than the effort (or unbiased measures) desired by the owner because the employee's effort (or reported measures) cannot be accurately monitored and enforced. In employment contracting with managers, what the owner wants is performance measures highly correlated with effort (see Chapter 10). The finer the measures, the more completely will variation in those measures explain variation in effort.

Paying no salary and rewarding Brett *only* on the basis of some performance measure—RI, in our example—raises different concerns. Brett would now be motivated to strive to increase RI because his rewards would increase with increases in RI. But compensating Brett on RI also subjects Brett to risk because HIS's RI depends not only on Brett's effort, but also on external factors such as inflation or other changes in the economy over which Brett has no control. More succinctly, Brett's management effort may be overwhelmed by good or bad luck associated with these changes in externalities.

To compensate Brett, who is risk averse, for taking on the consequences of uncontrollable risk, Fonda must pay Brett some extra compensation within the structure of the RI-based arrangement. Thus, using performance-based incentives will cost Fonda more money, *on average*, than paying Brett a flat salary. "On average" is appropriate because Fonda's compensation payment to Brett will vary with RI outcomes. When averaged over these outcomes, the RI-based compensation will cost Fonda more than would paying Brett a flat salary. The motivation for having some salary and some performance-based bonus in compensation arrangements is to balance the benefits of incentives against the extra costs of imposing uncontrollable risk on the manager.

The BSC approach is important because Brett can be compensated for satisfactory performance measured in more than one way. This means that if, due to an uncontrollable factor, performance decreases according to one measure it may increase on another and Brett will be spreading his risk of financial loss over several measures. As a manager, moreover, Brett performs many business functions in the value chain. While the functions may be interdependent, if he excels at them all, he should be rewarded more than another manager who excels at only a few. From Fonda's perspective, greater reliance can be placed on a performance report where several measures converge to report the same level of performance.

---

[13]The term *moral hazard* originated in insurance contracts to represent situations where insurance coverage, which relieves the owner of assets of part of the risks of loss and/or damage, caused insured parties to take less care of their properties than they would if they bore the full costs of replacement and/or repair. One response to moral hazard in insurance contracts is the system of deductibles (that is, the insured pays for damages below a specified amount). You are familiar with the concept if you have worked in teams to obtain marks for your output. The presence of a team spreads the risk of a low mark among the team's members.

Output or Effort—Measure One or Both?

Suppose the employer can easily measure the quantity of auto repairs but not their quality. If the employer rewards workers on a piece-rate system—which pays workers only on the basis of the number of repairs actually performed—mechanics will increase the number of repairs they make to maximize income. Sears experienced a problem when it introduced by-the-job rates for their mechanics because quantity soared but quality sank. To address the problem, Sears's management changed the performance measures and the compensation system. The piece-rate system was replaced with an hourly salary to reduce the importance of quantity of output. In addition, promotions and pay increases were determined on the basis of assessing each mechanic's overall performance on both quantity and quality of repairs. Performance measures from customer satisfaction surveys, the number of complaints, and dissatisfied customers were implemented. From time to time repairs would be audited for quality on a random basis. Nonfinancial measures (such as customer satisfaction measures) were central in motivating mechanics to balance quantity and quality by rewarding both.

TEAM-BASED COMPENSATION ARRANGEMENTS

Many manufacturing, marketing, and design problems require employees with multiple skills, experiences, and judgments to pool their talents. In these situations, a team of employees achieves better results than employees acting on their own.[14]

Team-based incentive compensation encourages employees to work together to achieve common goals. This approach encourages cooperation among interdependent subunits. Individual-based incentive compensation rewards employees for their own performance, consistent with responsibility accounting. This approach encourages competition to excel and be the best. A mix of both types of incentives encourages employees to maximize their own performance while working together in the best interest of the company as a whole.

Some companies balance the need for competition among employees to excel against cooperation by giving incentives and bonuses to individuals on the basis of team performance. Team incentives encourage cooperation, with individuals helping one another as they strive towards a common goal. The blend of knowledge and skills needed to change methods and improve efficiency puts a team in a better position than a lone individual to respond to incentives.[15] TRW, Whirlpool, and Monsanto in the United States, Novartis (a Swiss pharmaceutical company), and Nissan Motors in Japan are examples of companies that use some form of team-based incentives.

---

[14]J. Katzenbach and D. Smith, *The Wisdom of Teams* (Boston: The Harvard Business School Press, 1993).

[15]*Teams That Click: The Results-Driven Manager Series* (Boston: Harvard Business School Press, 2004).

Whether team-based compensation is desirable depends, to a great extent, on the culture and management style of a particular organization. One criticism of teams is that individual incentives to excel are dampened, harming overall performance. This problem becomes more acute when effort cannot be monitored. Unproductive team members contribute less than the effort expected (shirk); nevertheless, they share equally in the team's reward. Shirking is a pervasive problem and you have probably experienced shirking at least once when you have worked with teams of students to obtain shared marks for output.

The principles of performance evaluation apply to executive compensation plans at the total-organization level. Executive compensation plans are based on both financial and nonfinancial performance measures and consist of a mix of (1) base salary; (2) annual incentives (for example, cash bonus based on yearly net income); (3) long-term incentives (for example, stock options based on achieving a specified return by the end of a five-year period); and (4) fringe benefits (for example, life insurance, an office with a view, or a personal secretary).[16] Designers of executive compensation plans emphasize three factors: achievement of organizational goals, administrative ease, and the likelihood that affected managers will perceive the plan as fair.

Well-designed plans use a compensation mix that carefully balances risk and short- and long-term incentives. For example, evaluating performance on the basis of annual ROI would sharpen an executive's short-term focus. Using ROI and stock option plans over, say, five years would motivate the executive to take a long-term view as well. Stock options are covered in detail in finance courses; however, they are not difficult to understand. Stock options give executives and employees the right to buy company shares at a specified price (called the exercise price) within a specified period. Suppose that on September 16, 2009, BP gave its CEO the option to buy 200,000 shares of the company at any time before June 30, 2015, at the September 16, 2009, market price of $49 per share. Let's say BP's share price rises to $69 per share on March 24, 2010; these options are "in the money." If the CEO exercises share options on all 200,000 shares, the CEO would earn $20 ($69 − $49) per share on 200,000 shares, or $4 million. If BP's share price remains below $49 during the entire period, these shares will be "out of the money" and the CEO will simply forgo the right to buy the shares.

By linking CEO compensation to increases in the company's share price, the stock option plan motivates the CEO to improve the company's long-run performance and share price. Accounting rules require Canadian companies to recognize stock option expense in their income statements according to standards published by the CICA. The International Accounting Standards Board requires the same disclosure, as does the Financial Accounting Standards Board (FASB) in the United States. Companies also provide full note disclosure of how the equivalent value of compensation expense for stock options was calculated as at the grant date of compensation. All relevant assumptions must also be disclosed.[17]

The Ontario Securities Commission (OSC) and the US Securities and Exchange Commission (SEC) require detailed disclosures of the compensation arrangements of top-level executives. Investors use this information to evaluate the relationship between compensation and performance across companies generally, across companies of similar sizes, and across companies operating in similar industries. In recent years both regulators have investigated companies that backdated stock option exercise prices prior to the contract date. The executives and boards of directors signing these contracts knew at the date of signing what their profits would be. This is not legal, and convicted companies have paid multi-million-dollar fines for this practice.

[16]*The Wall Street Journal*/Mercer Human Resource Consulting, *2003 CEO Compensation Survey and Trends* (May, 2004).

[17]If the exercise price is less than the market price of the shares on the date the options are granted, the company must recognize compensation cost equal to the difference between the two prices. This difference is less than the fair market value of the options. See http://asc.fasb.org.

STRATEGY AND LEVERS OF CONTROL[18]

Given the management accounting focus of this book, this chapter has emphasized the role of quantitative financial and nonfinancial performance evaluation measures that companies use to implement their strategies. These measures—such as ROI, RI, EVA®, ROS, customer satisfaction, and employee satisfaction—monitor critical performance factors that help managers monitor progress towards attaining the company's strategic goals. Because these measures help diagnose whether a company is performing to expectations, they are collectively called **diagnostic control systems**.

> Apply strategic concepts to analyze the four levers of control and evaluate their usefulness
>
> ⑤

Companies motivate managers to achieve these goals by holding managers accountable for and by rewarding them for meeting these goals. Recently, however, it has become clear that sometimes one consequence of the pressure to perform is that managers materially misstate financial measures to obscure actual performance (e.g., Nortel, Parmalat, WorldCom). Avoiding unethical and illegal behaviour requires that companies balance the push for performance resulting from diagnostic control systems, the first of four levers of control, with three other levers: *boundary systems*, *belief systems*, and *interactive control systems*.

Boundary systems describe standards of behaviour and codes of conduct expected of all employees, especially actions that are off-limits. Ethical behaviour on the part of managers is paramount. In particular, numbers that subunit managers report should be free of overstated assets, understated liabilities, fictitious revenues, and understated costs. In Canada, the Canadian Securities Administrators (CSA) withdrew their proposed guidelines, Multilateral Instrument 52–111, covering corporate governance and internal control regulations for any company listed on a Canadian stock exchange.

The CSA reasoned that most large Canadian companies were already compliant with the **Sarbanes-Oxley Act**, which became law in the US in 2002, because these companies are listed on both US and Canadian stock exchanges. Currently, the CICA has proposed it will adopt the International Accounting Standards Board standards. For these reasons and others, the CSA amended its Multilateral Instrument 52–109 to include internal control regulations effective 2007 (see Chapter 23).

Most large Canadian companies are already listed on US stock exchanges and, because they have already taken the steps needed to comply with Sarbanes-Oxley, will not have to incur additional costs. Costs of compliance have averaged approximately US$4.3 million, but have been reported as high as US$40 million.[19] The broad scope of Canadian legislation on corporate governance includes the requirement that the CEO accept full responsibility for any material misstatement of financial information. Under Sarbanes-Oxley, companies must publish their codes of ethics and of conduct as part of the material audited for their annual report. Regulations are one set of boundary systems which mandate specific actions.

Belief systems articulate the mission, purpose, and core values of a company. They describe the accepted norms and patterns of behaviour expected of all managers and employees with respect to each other, shareholders, customers,

---

[18] For a more detailed discussion see R. Simons, "Control in an Age of Empowerment," *Harvard Business Review* (March–April 1995).

[19] "SOX Causes Jump in Audit Costs, But Benefits Seen," www.accountingweb.com/ cgi-bin/ item.cgi? id5100788&d5815&h5817&f5816&dateformat5%B%20e,%20Y, accessed June 6, 2006.

and communities. Johnson & Johnson describes its values and norms in its credo statement:

> We believe our first responsibility is to the doctors, nurses and patients, to mothers and fathers and all others who use our products and services. . . . Everything we do must be of high quality.
>
> We are responsible to our employees. . . . We must respect their dignity and recognize their merit. They must have a sense of security in their jobs. . . . We must be mindful of ways to help our employees fulfill their family responsibilities and provide opportunity for development and advancement. . . . Our actions must be just and ethical.
>
> We are responsible to the communities in which we live. . . . We must support good works and charities and bear our fair share of taxes. . . . We must encourage better health and education.
>
> Our final responsibility is to our stockholders. Business must make a sound profit. . . . We must experiment with new ideas . . . develop innovative programs and pay for mistakes.

Johnson & Johnson's credo is intended to inspire managers and employees to do their best. Values and culture generate organizational commitment, pride, and belonging and are an important source of **intrinsic motivation**. Intrinsic motivation is the desire to achieve self-satisfaction from good performance regardless of external rewards such as bonuses or promotion. Intrinsic motivation comes from being given greater responsibility, doing interesting and creative work, having pride in doing that work, establishing commitment to the organization, and developing personal bonds with co-workers. High intrinsic motivation enhances performance because managers and workers have a sense of achievement, feel satisfied with their jobs, and see opportunities for personal growth.

GOVERNANCE ISSUES

Courage—Boundaries and Beliefs

The managers of for-profit corporations face intense pressures. Not the least of these are the contractual requirements to achieve performance measures such as those specified in long-term debt covenants and compensation contracts and the more informal requirements in operating and capital budgets. Banks and bondholders are not charitable institutions, and the intent of covenants is to alert creditors of possible risk to their investment. These covenants are often based on ratios derived from accrual accounting such as times interest earned, operating cash flow, and debt to equity.

What can be the harm in, say, calling a supplier and asking for a few days' delay in sending an invoice to prevent reporting the additional expense in a quarterly statement of earnings if it avoids contravening a times interest earned ratio and gives the corporation another 90 days to recover? It would postpone recognizing the expense on the actual operating performance report as well and avoid a negative variance. If the cause of the shortfall is uncontrollable, surely the company's owners and managers should not be penalized by a contract rigidity, especially if the only issue is one of timing.

This type of reasoning leads to earnings management, whereby managers use their discretion to bias both internal and external performance reports. The ethical problem is clear—it is the professional duty of accountants to present unbiased reports—but their managers who may not be accountants are not bound to the same ethical standard. The logical problem is also clear—if uncontrollable factors have caused the shortfall in revenue over expenses—how can managers be assured time will fix the problem? They cannot be sure, nor can accountants avoid their professional duty to act in the best interests of the public, not the corporate managers. Where boundary systems fail, professional belief systems can prevail.[a]

[a]For a full discussion of earnings management refer to Chapter 11 of W. R. Scott, *Financial Accounting Theory* 5th edition (Toronto: Prentice Hall, 2009).

Codes of business conduct signal appropriate and inappropriate individual behaviour. The following is a portion of Caterpillar Tractor's "Code of Worldwide Business Conduct and Operating Principles":

> We must not engage in activities that create, or even appear to create, conflict between our personal interests and the interests of the company. [. . .] A conflict of interest or the appearance of a conflict of interest very often arises where an employee is offered a gift, favour, or entertainment. While some of this activity is part of a normal business relationship, we do not accept gifts, favours, or entertainment that have a value greater than we could reasonably reciprocate or that obligate or appear to obligate us to act in any way contrary to the law, Caterpillar business interests or Caterpillar's ethical business practices.[20]

Division managers often cite enormous pressure from top management "to make the budget" as excuses or rationalizations for not adhering to ethical accounting policies and procedures. A healthy amount of motivational pressure is desirable, as long as both the "tone from the top" and the codes of conduct communicate the absolute need for all managers to behave ethically at all times. Managers should train employees to behave ethically, and promptly and severely reprimand unethical conduct, regardless of the benefits that might accrue to the company from unethical actions. Some companies, such as Lockheed-Martin, emphasize ethical behaviour by routinely evaluating employees against a business code of ethics.

Many organizations also set explicit boundaries precluding actions that harm the environment. Environmental violations (such as water and air pollution) carry heavy fines and are prison offences under Canadian laws and those of other countries. But in many companies, environmental responsibilities extend beyond legal requirements. There are also many international indices of environmental performance, such as the Dow Jones Sustainability Index (see Chapter 14). Some companies, such as TransCanada Corporation (a Canadian natural gas transportation company), and Unilever Group (a US manufacturer of consumer products), believe that a high ranking on this index is sufficiently important to positively affect share price, and they announce their rankings on the Internet and in formal press releases.

Socially responsible companies, such as Starbucks, also report specific performance measures to affirm their commitment to human rights and fair pricing. German, Swiss, Dutch, and Scandinavian companies also report on social responsibility disclosures such as employee welfare and community development activities. Many existing sets of global principles, such as the **Sullivan Principles**, can be used to compare corporate performance in the area of social responsibility.

Interactive control systems are formal information systems that managers use to focus organization attention and learning on key strategic issues. An excessive focus on diagnostic control systems and critical performance variables can cause an organization to ignore emerging threats and opportunities—changes in technology, customer preferences, regulations, and industry competition that can undercut a business.

Interactive control systems track strategic uncertainties that businesses face, such as the emergence of digital imaging in the case of Kodak and Fujifilm, airline deregulation in the case of American Airlines and Southwest Airlines, and the shift in customer preferences for mini- and microcomputers in the case of IBM. The result is ongoing discussion and debate about assumptions and action plans. New strategies emerge from the dialogue and debate surrounding the interactive process. Interactive control systems force busy managers to step back from the actions needed to manage the business today and to shift their focus forward to positioning the organization for the opportunities and threats of tomorrow.

---

[20]Caterpillar, "Caterpillar's Worldwide Code of Conduct: Integrity: Conflicts of Interest," www.cat.com/cda/layout?m=209561&x=7, accessed April 16, 2008.

Measuring and rewarding managers for achieving critical performance variables is an important driver of corporate performance. But these diagnostic control systems must be counterbalanced by the other levers of control—boundary systems, belief systems, and interactive control systems—to ensure that proper business ethics, inspirational values, and attention to future threats and opportunities are not sacrificed to achieve business results.

MyAccountingLab

> **ASSESS YOUR MASTERY**
>
> To check your understanding of the material in Learning Objective ⑤, go to the *Mastery Questions* section at the end of this chapter and complete Learning Objective ⑤ question 1.

PULLING IT ALL TOGETHER—PROBLEM FOR SELF-STUDY

PROBLEM

Budgeted data of the baseball manufacturing division of Home Run Sports for February 2010 are as follows:

Current assets	$ 400,000
Long-term assets	600,000
Total assets	$1,000,000
Production output	200,000 baseballs per month
Target ROI (operating income ÷ total assets)	30%
Fixed costs	$ 400,000 per month
Variable costs	$ 4 per baseball

REQUIRED

1. Compute the minimum unit selling price necessary to achieve the 30% target ROI, assuming ROI is based on total assets.

2. Using the selling price from requirement 1, separate the target ROI into its two components using the DuPont method.

3. Pamela Stephenson, division manager, receives 5% of the monthly residual income of the baseball manufacturing division as a bonus. Compute her bonus for February 2010, using the selling price from requirement 1. Home Run Sports uses a 12% required rate of return on total division assets when computing division residual income.

4. What behavioural issues arise from compensation contracts based on a single performance measure?

5. If Pamela recommends an investment in new equipment and for reasons beyond her control revenue is not realized but she has the opportunity to postpone recognition of expenses until the next reporting period, what levers of control can reduce the likelihood she will do so?

SOLUTION

1.

$$\text{Target operating income} = 30\% \text{ of } \$1,000,000$$
$$= \$300,000$$
$$\text{Let } P = \text{Selling price}$$
$$\text{Sales} - \text{Variable costs} - \text{Fixed costs} = \text{Operating income}$$
$$200,000P - (200,000 \times \$4) - \$400,000 = \$300,000$$
$$200,000P = \$300,000 + \$800,000 + \$400,000 = \$1,500,000$$
$$P = \$7.50$$

Proof:	Sales, 200,000 × $7.50	$1,500,000
	Variable costs, 200,000 × $4	800,000
	Contribution margin	700,000
	Fixed costs	400,000
	Operating income	$ 300,000

2.

$$\frac{\text{Revenues}}{\text{Investment}} \times \frac{\text{Income}}{\text{Revenues}} = \frac{\text{Income}}{\text{Investment}}$$

$$\frac{\$1,500,000}{\$1,000,000} \times \frac{\$300,000}{\$1,500,000} = \frac{\$300,000}{\$1,000,000}$$

$$1.5 \quad \times \quad 0.2 \quad = 0.30 \text{ or } 30\%$$

3.

$$\text{Residual income} = \text{Operating income} - \text{Required return on investment}$$
$$= \$300,000 - (0.12 \times \$1,000,000)$$
$$= \$300,000 - \$120,000$$
$$= \$180,000$$

Stephenson's bonus is $9,000 (5% of $180,000)

4. This bonus is a cash bonus based on short-term operations. Should Pamela have the opportunity to invest in more efficient equipment, the investment will reduce ROI in the short term in two ways. First, the operating costs will increase before the revenues are realized because there is a lag between production and sales. Operating income will decrease and it is possible revenue will also decrease. Investment will increase, and in combination with reduced revenue and income it is unlikely that the 30% ROI will be achieved. If Pamela cares about her bonus she will not invest.

5. If Pamela is a professional accountant, the belief system embodied in the professional ethical code is one lever of control to constrain the likelihood she will manage earnings. If she is not, then a public statement of the corporate code of ethics, its core values, and the tone at the top from examples set by top management can also constrain her.

DECISION POINTS

The following decision guidelines use a question-and-answer format to summarize the chapter's main points. Each decision presents a key question. The guideline is the answer to that question.

DECISIONS	GUIDELINES
1. What financial and nonfinancial measures do companies use?	Financial measures such as return on investment (ROI), residual income (RI), and economic value added (EVA®) measure aspects of both manager performance and organization-subunit performance. In many cases, financial measures are supplemented with nonfinancial measures of performance, such as customer satisfaction ratings, number of defects, and productivity.
2. What is the current cost of an asset?	The current cost of an asset is the cost now of purchasing an asset identical to the one currently held. Historical-cost measurement methods consider the original cost of the asset net of accumulated amortization.

	3. What difficulties arise when comparing the performance of divisions in different countries?	Comparing the performance of divisions operating in different countries is difficult because of legal, political, social, economic, and currency differences. ROI calculations for subunits operating in different countries need to be adjusted for differences in inflation between the two countries and changes in exchange rates.
	4. How do salaries and incentives work together in compensation arrangements?	Organizations create incentives by rewarding managers on the basis of performance. But managers may face risks because random factors beyond the managers' control may also affect performance. Owners choose a mix of salary and incentive compensation to trade off the incentive benefit against the cost of imposing risk.
	5. What are the levers of control and why does a company need to implement them?	The four levers of control are diagnostic control systems, boundary systems, belief systems, and interactive control systems. Implementing the four levers of control helps a company simultaneously strive for performance, behave ethically, inspire employees, and respond to strategic threats and opportunities.

TERMS TO LEARN

This chapter contains definitions of the following important terms:

belief systems (p. 1159)	imputed costs (p. 1142)	return on investment (ROI) (p. 1140)
boundary systems (p. 1159)	interactive control systems (p. 1161)	return on sales (ROS) (p. 1144)
current cost (p. 1147)	intrinsic motivation (p. 1160)	Sarbanes-Oxley Act (p. 1159)
diagnostic control systems (p. 1159)	moral hazard (p. 1156)	Sullivan Principles (p. 1161)
economic value added (EVA®) (p. 1143)	residual income (RI) (p. 1142)	weighted-average cost of capital (p. 1142)

MASTERY QUESTIONS

Mastery Questions are rated by proficiency level—elementary, intermediate, and advanced. The solutions appear in the Solutions to Mastery Questions section of MyAccountingLab.

LEARNING OBJECTIVE 1

1. **Analyze financial performance measures—Advanced.** The Media Group has three major divisions:
   a. Newspapers—owns leading newspapers on four continents
   b. Television—owns major television networks on three continents
   c. Film studios—owns one of the five largest film studios in the world

   Summary financial data for 2009 and 2010 are as follows (in millions):

	Operating Income		Revenue		Total Assets	
	2009	2010	2009	2010	2009	2010
Newspapers	$1,080	$1,320	$5,400	$5,520	$5,280	$5,880
Television	156	192	7,200	7,680	3,240	3,600
Film studios	264	240	1,920	1,980	3,000	3,120

The manager of each division has an annual bonus plan based on division return on investment (ROI). ROI is defined as operating income divided by total assets. Senior executives from divisions reporting increases in ROI from the prior year are automatically eligible for a bonus. Senior executives of divisions reporting a decline in the division ROI have to provide persuasive explanations for the decline to be eligible for a limited bonus.

Ken Kearney, manager of the Newspapers Division, is considering a proposal to invest $240 million in high-speed printing presses with colour-print options. The estimated increment to 2011 operating income would be $36 million. The Media Group has a 12% required rate of return for investments in all three divisions.

REQUIRED

1. Use the DuPont method to explain differences among the three divisions in their 2010 division ROI. Use 2010 total assets as the investment base.
2. Why might Kearney be less than enthusiastic about the high-speed printing press investment proposal?
3. Rupert Prince, chairman of the Media Group, receives a proposal to base senior executive compensation at each division on division residual income. Compute the residual income of each division in 2010.
4. Would adoption of a residual income measure reduce Kearney's reluctance to adopt the high-speed printing press investment proposal?

LEARNING OBJECTIVE 2

1. **Evaluate accrual measures—Advanced.** Mineral Waters Ltd. operates three divisions that process and bottle sparkling mineral water. The historical-cost accounting system reports the following data for 2010:

	Calistoga Division	Alpine Springs Division	Rocky Mountains Division
Revenues	$600,000	$ 840,000	$1,320,000
Operating costs (excluding amortization	360,000	456,000	720,000
Plant amortization	84,000	120,000	144,000
Operating income	$156,000	$ 264,000	$ 456,000
Current assets	$240,000	$ 300,000	$ 360,000
Fixed assets—plant	168,000	1,080,000	1,584,000
Total assets	$408,000	$1,380,000	$1,944,000

Mineral Waters estimates the useful life of each plant to be 12 years with a zero terminal disposal price. The straight-line amortization method is used. At the end of 2010, the Calistoga plant is 10 years old, Alpine Springs plant is 3 years old, and Rocky Mountains plant is 1 year old.

An index of construction costs of plants for mineral water production for the 10-year period that Mineral Waters has been operating (2000 year-end = 100) is:

2000	2007	2008	2009	2010
100	136	149	160	170

Given the high turnover of current assets, management believes that the historical-cost and current-cost measures of current assets are approximately the same.

REQUIRED

1. Compute the ROI (operating income to total assets) ratio of each division using historical-cost measures. Comment on the results.
2. Use the approach in Exhibit 24-3 (p. 1149) to compute the ROI of each division, incorporating current-cost estimates as of 2010 for amortization and fixed assets. Comment on the results.
3. What advantages might arise from using current-cost asset measures as compared with historical-cost measures for evaluating the performance of the managers of the three divisions?

LEARNING OBJECTIVE 3

1. **Analyze MNC performance—Advanced.** The Sandvik Corporation manufactures electric motors in Canada and Sweden. The Canadian and Swedish operations are organized as decentralized divisions. The following information is available for 2010:

	Canadian Division	Swedish Division
Operating income	$1,440,000	7,862,400 kronor
Total assets	$9,600,000	50,400,000 kronor

REQUIRED

1. Calculate the Canadian Division's return on investment for 2010.
2. Calculate the Swedish Division's return on investment for 2010 in kronor.
3. Senior management at Sandvik want to know which division earned a better return on investment in 2010. What would you tell them? Explain your answer. Assume that the exchange rate at the time of the Swedish division investment was 6 kronor per dollar and the average exchange rate during 2010 was 6.5 kronor per dollar.

LEARNING OBJECTIVE 4

1. **Evaluate behavioural effects—Advanced.** The Dexter Division of AMCO sells car batteries. AMCO's corporate management gives Dexter management considerable operating and investment autonomy in running the division. AMCO is considering how it should compensate Jim Marks, the general manager of the Dexter Division. Proposal 1 calls for paying Marks a fixed salary. Proposal 2 calls for paying Marks no salary and compensating him only on the basis of the division's ROI (calculated on the basis of operating income before any bonus payments). Proposal 3 calls for paying Marks some salary and some bonus based on ROI. Assume that Marks does not like bearing risk.

REQUIRED

1. **a.** Evaluate each of the three proposals, specifying the advantages and disadvantages of each.
   b. Suppose that AMCO competes against Tiara Industries in the car battery business. Tiara is roughly the same size and operates in a business environment that is very similar to Dexter's. The senior management of AMCO is considering evaluating Marks on the basis of Dexter's ROI minus Tiara's ROI. Marks complains that this approach is unfair because the performance of another firm, over which he has no control, is included in his performance evaluation measure. Is Marks's complaint valid? Why or why not?
2. Now suppose that Marks has no authority for making capital investment decisions. Corporate management makes these decisions. Is return on investment a good performance measure to use to evaluate Marks? Is return on investment a good measure to evaluate the economic viability of the Dexter Division? Explain.
3. Dexter's salespersons are responsible for selling and providing customer service and support. Sales are easy to measure. Although customer service is very important to Dexter in the long run, it has not yet implemented customer service measures. Marks wants to compensate his sales force only on the basis of sales commissions paid for each unit of product sold. He cites two advantages to this plan: (a) it creates very strong incentives for the sales force to work hard, and (b) the company pays salespersons only when the company itself is earning revenues and has cash. Do you like his plan? Why or why not?

LEARNING OBJECTIVE 5

1. **Strategic levers of control—Advanced (continuation of Learning Objective 1, question 1).** Rupert Prince seeks your advice on revising the existing bonus plan for division managers of the Media Group. Assume division managers do not like bearing risk. He is considering three ideas:

- Make all of each division manager's compensation depend on division ROI.
- Make all of each division manager's compensation depend on companywide ROI.
- Use benchmarking, and compensate each division manager on the basis of his or her own division's ROI minus the average ROI of the other two divisions.

REQUIRED

Evaluate each of the three ideas Prince has put forth using performance evaluation concepts described in this chapter. Indicate the positive and negative features of each proposal.

SHORT-ANSWER QUESTIONS

24-1 Give two examples of financial performance measures and two examples of nonfinancial performance measures.

24-2 What are the six steps in designing an accounting-based performance measure?

24-3 What factors affecting ROI does the DuPont method highlight?

24-4 "Residual income is not identical to ROI although both measures incorporate income and investment into their computations." Do you agree? Explain.

24-5 Describe economic value added.

24-6 Give three definitions of investment used in practice when computing ROI.

24-7 Distinguish between measuring assets based on present value, current cost, and historical cost.

24-8 What special problems arise when evaluating performance in multinational companies?

24-9 Why is it important to distinguish between the performance of a manager and the performance of the organization subunit for which the manager is responsible? Give examples.

24-10 Describe moral hazard.

24-11 Explain the management accountant's role in helping organizations design stronger incentive systems for their employees.

24-12 Explain the role of benchmarking in evaluating managers.

24-13 Explain the incentive problems that can arise when employees have to perform multiple tasks as part of their jobs.

24-14 List four components of executive compensation plans.

24-15 Describe each of the levers of control and their interrelation with strategy.

EXERCISES

24-16 **Return on investment; comparisons of three companies.** (CMA, adapted) Return on investment is often expressed as follows:

$$\frac{\text{Income}}{\text{Investment}} = \frac{\text{Revenues}}{\text{Investment}} \times \frac{\text{Income}}{\text{Revenues}}$$

2. Blue ROI, 20%
Orange investment
turnover, 2.0

REQUIRED

1. What advantages are there in the breakdown of the computation into two separate components?
2. Fill in the following blanks:

	Blue	**Green**	**Orange**
	\multicolumn{3}{c}{**Companies in the Same Industry**}
Revenue	?	$ 600,000	$12,000,000
Income	?	$ 60,000	$ 60,000
Investment	$600,000	$6,000,000	?
Income as a percentage of revenue	10.0%	?	?
Investment turnover	2.00	?	?
Return on investment	?	?	1.0%

After filling in the blanks, comment as thoroughly as the data permit on the relative performance of these companies.

24-17 Analysis of return on invested assets, comparison of three divisions. Easy Paints Inc. is a manufacturer of paints. It has three divisions: indoor paints, outdoor paints, and special purpose paints. Results for the past three years are as follows (in thousands):

		Indoor	Outdoor	Special Purpose	Total Easy Paints
2008	Revenues	$15,000	$ 8,000	$12,000	$35,000
	Operating Income	1,500	800	1,800	4,100
	Total Assets	30,000	20,000	15,000	65,000
2009	Revenues	16,000	8,000	8,000	32,000
	Operating Income	1,600	750	900	3,250
	Total Assets	28,000	20,000	14,000	62,000
2010	Revenues	17,000	8,000	5,000	30,000
	Operating Income	1,800	700	1,000	3,500
	Total Assets	25,000	15,000	10,000	50,000

REQUIRED
Use the DuPont method to explain changes in the operating income to total assets ratio over the 2008 to 2010 period for each division. Comment on the results.

24-18 ROI and RI. (D. Kleespie) Speed Logistics provides transportation services to a wide variety of companies in southern Ontario. One of its divisions, the Concord Division, offers the service to pick up containers at the CN railway interchange and deliver them within Ontario. The demand for its services is relatively insensitive to price changes. The Concord Division is considered to be an investment centre and in recent years has averaged a return on investment of 20%. The Concord Division has a total of annual fixed costs of $1,200,000, the variable cost per km is $3.60, the average number of kilometres travelled per year is 1,000,000, and the average operating assets invested in the division are $1,920,000.

REQUIRED
1. What is the minimum selling price that the Concord Division could charge for a 100-km trip if the division manager wants to get a favourable performance rating? Management considers an ROI below 20% to be unfavourable.
2. Assume that Speed Logistics judges the performance of its investment centre managers on the basis of residual income rather than ROI, as was assumed in requirement 1. The company's required rate of return is considered to be 15%. What is the minimum selling price per a 100-km trip that the Concord Division should charge to receive a favourable performance rating?

24-19 Pricing and return on investment. Orilla Exhaust Systems Co. produces exhaust systems for SUVs that are assembled in vehicles manufactured by various customers in several car assembly plants located within 500 km. Orilla Exhaust Systems uses long-run (defined as three to five years) average demand to set the budgeted production level and costs for pricing. Prices are then adjusted only for large changes in production wage rates or direct materials prices. In the last budgeted period, direct materials assembly wages and other variable costs are $15.84 per exhaust system. The plant fixed costs are $3,600,000 per year and are prorated by the normal utilization of capacity (average output) of 1,000,000 exhaust systems. The investment (total net assets) is $20,000,000 and the minimum expected return on investment is 20%.

REQUIRED
1. What operating income percentage on revenues is needed to attain the minimum expected (target) return on investment of 20%? What is the selling price per unit?
2. Using the selling price per unit calculated in requirement 1, what rate of return on investment will be earned if Orilla Exhaust Systems assembles and sells 1,500,000 units? 500,000 units?
3. The company has a management bonus plan based on yearly division performance. Assume that Orilla Exhaust Systems assembled and sold 1,000,000, 1,500,000, and 500,000 units in three successive years. Each of three people served as division manager for one year before being killed in an automobile accident. As the principal heir of the third manager, comment on the bonus plan.

24-20 Goal incongruence and ROI. Bleefl Corporation manufactures furniture in several divisions, including the Patio Furniture division. The manager of the Patio Furniture division plans to retire in two years. The manager receives a bonus based on the division's ROI, which is currently 11%.

1

2. ROI 5: year 5: 12.12%

One of the machines that the Patio Furniture division uses to manufacture the furniture is rather old, and the manager must decide whether to replace it. The new machine would cost $30,000 and would last 10 years. It would have no salvage value. The old machine is fully amortized and has no tradein value. Bleefl uses straight-line amortization for all assets. The new machine, being new and more efficient, would save the company $5,000 per year in cash operating costs. The only difference between cash flow and net income is amortization. The internal rate of return of the project is approximately 11%. Bleefl Corporation's weighted-average cost of capital is 6%. Bleefl is not subject to any income taxes.

REQUIRED

1. Should Bleefl Corporation replace the machine? Why or why not?
2. Assume that "investment" is defined as average net long-term assets after amortization. Compute the project's ROI for each of its first five years. If the Patio Furniture manager is interested in maximizing his bonus, would he replace the machine before he retires? Why or why not?
3. What can Bleefl do to entice the manager to replace the machine before retiring?

24-21 ROI and RI with manufacturing costs. Superior Motor Company makes electric cars and has only two products, the Simplegreen and the Superiorgreen. To produce the Simplegreen, Superior Motor employed assets of $13,500,000 at the beginning of the period, and $13,400,000 of assets at the end of the period. Other costs to manufacture the Simplegreen include:

1

1. ROI, 16.50%

Direct materials	$3,000 per unit
Setup	$1,300 per setup-hour
Production	$ 415 per machine-hour

General administration and selling costs total $7,340,000 for the period. In the current period, Superior Motor produced 10,000 Simplegreen cars using 6,000 setup-hours and 175,200 machine-hours. Superior Motor sold these cars for $12,000 each.

REQUIRED

1. Assuming that Superior Motor defines investment as average assets during the period, what is the return on investment for the Simplegreen division?
2. Calculate the residual income for the Simplegreen if Superior Motor has a required rate of return of 12% on investments.

24-22 ROI, RI, EVA®. (D. Solomons, adapted) Agile Transportation has two divisions which are treated as profit centres. Consider the following data for the two divisions:

1

1. Railway, 15%

	Railway Connection Division	Maritime Connection Division
Total Assets	$6,000,000	$1,200,000
Current Liabilities	1,800,000	300,000
Operating Income	900,000	240,000

REQUIRED

1. Calculate the return on investment (ROI) using operating income as the measure of income and using total assets as the measure of investment.
2. Agile Transportation has used residual income as a measure of management success, the variable it wants a manager to maximize. Using this criterion, what is the residual income for each division using operating income and total assets if the required rate of return on investment is 12%?
3. Agile Transportation has two sources of funds: long-term debt with a market value of $4,200,000 and an interest rate of 10%, and equity capital with a market value of $4,200,000 at a cost of equity of 14%. Agile Transportation's income tax rate is 40%. Agile Transportation applies the same weighted-average cost of capital to both divisions, since each division faces similar risks. Calculate the economic value added for each division. Which of the measures calculated in requirements 1, 2, and 3 would you recommend Agile Transportation use? Why? Explain briefly.

24-23 **RI, EVA®.** Toys for All is a small company that manufactures old-fashioned, high-quality toys in two divisions: wood and metal. Results reported for the last year are as follows:

	Wood Toys Division	Metal Toys Division
Total Assets	$80,000	$130,000
Current Liabilities	$ 8,000	$ 15,000
Operating Income before tax	$12,000	$ 24,000

REQUIRED
1. Calculate the residual income for each division using operating income before tax and investment equal to total assets minus current liabilities. The required rate of return on investments is 12%.
2. The company has two sources of funds: long-term debt with a market value of $18,000 at an interest rate of 10% and equity capital with a market value of $12,000 at a cost of equity of 15%. Toys for All's income tax rate is 40%. Toys for All applies the same weighted-average cost of capital to both divisions, since each division faces similar risks. Calculate the economic value added (EVA®) for each division.
3. Using your answers to requirements 1 and 2, what would you conclude about the performance of each division? Explain briefly.

24-24 **ROI, RI, measurement of assets.** (CMA, adapted) Carter Corporation recently announced a bonus plan to be awarded to the manager of the most profitable division. The three division managers are to choose whether ROI or RI will be used to measure profitability. In addition, they must decide whether investment will be measured using gross book value or net book value of assets. Carter defines income as operating income and investment as total assets. The following information is available for the year just ended:

Division	Gross Book Value of Assets	Accumulated Amortization	Operating Income
Radnor	$1,200,000	$645,000	$142,050
Easttown	1,140,000	615,000	137,550
Marion	750,000	420,000	92,100

Carter uses a required rate of return of 10% on investment to calculate RI.

REQUIRED
Each division manager has selected a method of bonus calculation that ranks his or her division Number 1. Identify the method for calculating profitability that each manager selected, supporting your answer with appropriate calculations. Comment on the strengths and weaknesses of the methods chosen by each manager.

24-25 **ROI, RI, measurement of assets.** Direct Sales Corporation is analyzing the implementation of a bonus plan for its direct salespersons. Currently each salesperson has a target of net income of $5,000; if it is achieved, then a lump sum is paid. Each salesperson is provided with a company car, each car has a useful life of five years, and 20% of amortization is applied in the year of purchase. To test the idea, the General Manager estimated that the required rate of return of assets is 12%. He also obtained the 2009 data of three salespersons as follows:

Salesperson	Gross Book Value of the Car	Year of Purchase of the Car	Operating Income
Eshrat	$15,000	2008	$5,000
Faheem	$15,000	2009	$5,000
Georgy	$15,000	2007	$5,000

REQUIRED
The General Manager has to select a method of bonus calculation that ranks the three salespersons without overlaps (having two or more salespersons showing the same performance). Identify the method for calculating profitability that the general manager selected, supporting your answer with appropriate calculations.

24-26 **Various measures of profitability.** As a way to incentcompetition between divisions, the president of Industrial Products told the division managers that a quarterly bonus would be paid only to the most profitable division. However, absolute division operating income as conventionally computed would not be used. Instead, the ranking would be affected by the relative investments in the three divisions. Options available include ROI and residual income. Investment can be measured using gross book value or net book value. Each manager has now written a memorandum claiming entitlement to the bonus. The following data are available:

Division	Gross Book Value of Division Assets	Division Operating Income
Ontario	$1,000,000	$150,000
Quebec	$1,000,000	$120,000
Alberta	$ 350,000	$ 55,000

All the assets are fixed assets that were purchased 10 years ago and have 10 years of useful life remaining. A zero terminal disposal price is predicted. Industrial Products' required rate of return on investment used for computing residual income is 12% of investment.

REQUIRED
Which method for computing profitability did each manager choose? Make your description specific and brief. Show supporting computations. Where applicable, assume straight-line amortization.

24-27 ROI, RI, measurement of assets. (CMA, adapted) Leeds Corporation recently announced a bonus plan to be awarded to the manager of the most profitable division. The three division managers are to choose whether ROI or RI will be used to measure profitability. In addition, they must decide whether investment will be measured using gross book value or net book value of assets. Leeds defines income as operating income and investment as total assets. The following information is available for the year just ended:

Division	Gross Book Value of Assets	Net Book Value of Assets	Operating Income
Dales	$500,000	$300,000	$61,000
Reeds	$520,000	$330,000	$66,000
Holms	$275,000	$250,000	$35,000

Leeds uses a required rate of return of 12% on investment to calculate RI.

REQUIRED
Each division manager has selected a method of bonus calculation that ranks his or her division Number 1. Identify the method for calculating profitability that each manager selected, supporting your answer with appropriate calculations.

24-28 Multinational performance measurement, ROI, RI. The Grandlund Corporation manufactures similar products in Canada and Norway. The Canadian and Norwegian operations are organized as decentralized divisions. The following information is available for 2011; ROI is calculated as operating income divided by total assets.

1. a. $1,200,000

	Canadian Division	Norwegian Division
Operating income	?	8,100,000 kroner
Total assets	$8,000,000	52,500,000 kroner
ROI	15%	?

Both investments were made on December 31, 2010. The exchange rate at the time of Grandlund's investment in Norway on December 31, 2010, was 6 kroner = $1. During 2011, the Norwegian kroner increased steadily in value so that the exchange rate on December 31, 2011, is 7 kroner = $1. The average exchange rate during 2011 is [(6 + 7) / 2] = 6.5 kroner = $1.

REQUIRED
1. **a.** Calculate the Canadian division's operating income for 2011.
   b. Calculate the Norwegian division's ROI for 2011 in kroner.
2. Top management wants to know which division earned a better ROI in 2011. What would you tell them? Explain your answer.
3. Which division do you think had the better RI performance? Explain your answer. The required rate of return on investment (calculated in Canadian dollars) is 12%.

24-29 Multinational performance measurement, ROI, RI. Fabulous Skin has been manufacturing sun lotions for six decades and currently has a very solid position in the industry. It has two divisions that manufacture and market sun lotions, one located in Spain that attends the Mediterranean market, and the other in Halifax that attends the Caribbean market (including the US). The following information is available for 2009. The required rate of return on investments is 15%.

	Canadian Division	Spanish Division
Operating income	$918,000	648,000 euros
Total assets	$5,400,000	3,600,000 euros

Investments in both divisions were made on December 31, 2008. The exchange rate at the time of investment in Spain on December 31, 2008, was 0.60 euros = $1. During 2009, the euro declined steadily in value, reaching an exchange rate on December 31, 2009, of 0.75 euros = $1. The average exchange rate during 2009 is [(0.60 + 0.75) ÷ 2] = 0.675 euros = $1.

REQUIRED
1. **a.** Calculate the Canadian Division's return on investment for 2009.
   b. Calculate the Spanish Division's return on investment for 2009 in euros.
   c. Which division earned a better return on investment in 2009? Explain.
2. Senior management wants to compare the performance of the two divisions using residual income. Which division do you think had the better residual-income performance? Explain your answer.
3. On the basis of your answers to requirements 1 and 2, which division is performing better? If you had to promote one of the division managers to vice-president, which would you choose? Explain.

24-30 Financial and nonfinancial performance measures, goal-congruence. (CMA, adapted) Summit Equipment specializes in the manufacture of medical equipment, a field that has become increasingly competitive. Approximately two years ago, Ben Harrington, president of Summit, decided to revise the bonus plan (based, at the time, entirely on operating income) to encourage division managers to focus on areas that were important to customers and that added value without increasing cost. In addition to a profitability incentive, the revised plan includes incentives for reduced rework costs, reduced sales returns, and on-time deliveries. Bonuses are calculated and awarded semi-annually on the following basis: A base bonus is calculated at 2% of operating income; this amount is then adjusted as follows:

a. (i) Reduced by excess of rework costs over and above 2% of operating income.
   (ii) No adjustment if rework costs are less than or equal to 2% of operating income.
b. (i) Increased by $5,000 if more than 98% of deliveries are on time, and by $2,000 if 96% to 98% of deliveries are on time.
   (ii) No adjustment if on-time deliveries are below 96%.
c. (i) Increased by $3,000 if sales returns are less than or equal to 1.5% of sales.
   (ii) Decreased by 50% of excess of sales returns over 1.5% of sales.

Note: If the calculation of the bonus results in a negative amount for a particular period, the manager simply receives no bonus, and the negative amount is not carried forward to the next period.

Results for Summit's Charter Division and Mesa Division for 2009, the first year under the new bonus plan, follow. In 2008, under the old bonus plan, the Charter Division manager earned a bonus of $27,060 and the Mesa Division manager a bonus of $22,440.

	Charter Division		Mesa Division	
	January 1, 2009 to June 30, 2009	July 1, 2009 to Dec. 31, 2009	January 1, 2009 to June 30, 2009	July 1, 2009 to Dec. 31, 2009
Revenues	$4,200,000	$4,400,000	$2,850,000	$2,900,000
Operating income	$ 462,000	$ 440,000	$ 342,000	$ 406,000
On-time delivery	95.4%	97.3%	98.2%	94.6%
Rework costs	$ 11,500	$ 11,000	$ 6,000	$ 8,000
Sales returns	$ 84,000	$ 70,000	$ 44,750	$ 42,500

1. Why did Harrington need to introduce these new performance measures? That is, why does Harrington need to use these performance measures in addition to the operating-income numbers for the period?
2. Calculate the bonus earned by each manager for each six-month period and for 2009.
3. What effect did the change in the bonus plan have on each manager's behaviour? Did the new bonus plan achieve what Harrington desired? What changes, if any, would you make to the new bonus plan?

24-31 Financial and nonfinancial performance measures, goal-congruence. (CMA, adapted) Leader Automotive Canada is a Tier 1 supplier in the automotive industry (direct supplier to car assemblies), an industry that is considered the most competitive in the manufacturing sector. A couple of years ago the CEO decided to revise the bonus plan (based, at the time, entirely on operating income) to encourage plant managers to focus on areas that were important to customers and that added value without increasing cost. In addition to a profitability incentive, the revised plan also includes incentives for reduced rework costs, reduced rejections (sales returns), and on-time deliveries. Bonuses are calculated and awarded semi-annually on the following basis. A base bonus is calculated at 2% of operating income. The bonus amount is then adjusted by the following amounts:

2. Alliston Plant bonuses: June, $0; December, $7,920

a. i. Reduced by excess of rework costs over 2% of operating income.
    ii. No adjustment if rework costs are less than or equal to 2% of operating income.
b. Increased by $6,000 if over 98% of deliveries are on time, by $2,400 if 96–98% of deliveries are on time, and by $0 if on-time deliveries are below 96%.
c. i. Increased by $3,600 if rejections are less than or equal to 1.5% of sales.
    ii. Decreased by 50% of excess of rejections over 1.5% of sales.

Note: If the calculation of the bonus results in a negative amount for a particular period, the manager simply receives no bonus, and the negative amount is not carried forward to the next period.

Results for Leader Automotive Canada's plants for the year 2010, the first year under the new bonus plan, follow. In the previous year, 2009, under the old bonus plan, the Alliston Plant manager earned a bonus of $32,472 and the Oshawa Plant manager a bonus of $26,928.

	Alliston Plant		Oshawa Plant	
	January 1, 2010 to June 30, 2010	**July 1, 2010 to Dec. 31, 2010**	**January 1, 2010 to June 30, 2010**	**July 1, 2010 to Dec. 31, 2010**
Revenues	$5,040,000	$5,280,000	$3,420,000	$3,480,000
Operating income	$554,400	$528,000	$410,400	$487,000
On-time delivery	95.4%	97.3%	98.2%	94.6%
Rework costs	$13,800	$13,200	$7,200	$8,600
Sales returns	$100,800	$84,000	$53,750	$51,000

REQUIRED
1. Why did the Leader Automotive CEO introduce these new performance measures? That is, why does he need to use these performance measures over and above the operating income numbers for the period?
2. Calculate the bonus earned by each manager for each six-month period and for the year 2010.
3. What effect did the change in the bonus plan have on each manager's behaviour? Did the new bonus plan achieve what the CEO desired? What changes, if any, would you make to the new bonus plan?

24-32 Financial performance measures with uncertainty. (CMA, adapted) The following forecast variable costing income statement was prepared for Electric Machines Ltd. for the year ending April 2012:

Sales	$100,000,000
Variable costs	45,000,000
Contribution margin	55,000,000
Fixed costs	25,000,000
Net income	30,000,000

The General Manager is interested in buying a leisure boat with a tag price of $30,000 with the bonus he will collect in May 2012 (based on the net income of the year ending in April 2012). To estimate his bonus he developed a probabilistic model for a range of possible outcomes for these financial parameters. He collected the following information from various managers within the firm:

1. The likelihood that the worst-case scenario for sales would occur (drop of 25%) was set at 15%. The likelihood that the best-case scenario for sales would occur (an increase of 25%) was set at 10%. Finally, the likelihood that the most likely scenario would occur (sales of $100,000,000) was set at 75%.
2. The likelihood that the worst-case scenario for fixed costs would occur (increase of 20%) was set at 20%. The likelihood that the best-case scenario for fixed costs would occur (a decrease of 20%) was set at 20%. Finally, the likelihood that the most likely scenario would occur (fixed costs of $25,000,000) was set at 60%.
3. Variable costs will always run at 45% of sales.

The General Manager's compensation is composed of a flat salary of $75,000 plus 1% of net income that is in excess of the target for the year. The target for the year ending April 2012 was $26,500,000.

REQUIRED

1. Determine if the manager will be able to buy the boat with the bonus he will collect in May 2012.
2. Suppose the owners of Electric Machines propose to change the remuneration to the General Manager and they offer a flat salary of $100,000. Explain why the General Manager would be interested in accepting the offer or not. What is more convenient in the long term for the General Manager?

24-33 Nonfinancial performance and levers of control. (CMA, adapted). Light Seating Canada produces recliners, the device inside car seats that allows the seats to recline to a position comfortable to the driver but prevents the seat from trapping the driver in the case of a front crash. The company has always been associated with high-quality, expensive products, but this has limited their sales to manufacturers of sports cars.

About one year ago, the Production Manager, Bill Jones, identified an opportunity for Light Seating Canada to enter the low-cost, high-volume segment of the market. Up to that point, Light Seating Canada had used expensive materials assembled automatically using a special-purpose machine. Jones, considered a competent manager, felt certain a new, cheaper machine with intensive use of direct labour would allow for the manufacture of an inexpensive recliner allowing the firm to enter the low-cost, high-volume segment of the market. Jones vocally championed this idea and eventually received permission to purchase one of these machines to begin stamping recliner parts and assembling them manually on a trial basis. If the trial were successful, about 10 more of these machines would have to be purchased for Light Seating Canada to be an effective competitor.

The test machine had been installed approximately eight months ago, and it was time for senior management to review its performance and consider the decision to make the additional investment necessary to enter this new market segment. To aid in this review the Vice-President of operations asked Emily Chang, the Assistant Controller, to conduct a post-audit report on the operations of the stamping machine and manual assembly.

Chang collected information from numerous sources in the preparation of her report. Her efforts unearthed a number of items that were in contrast with the original estimates provided by Jones to justify this investment. For example, the amount of time necessary to train production staff on the use of the stamping machine and manual assembly was more than four times greater than the one month originally forecast. Even then, with Jones describing the staff as now fully competent on the stamping machine and assembly process, the quality of the output was far below the acceptable level, and scrap rates were running double from the original plan. In addition to scrap rates, the throughput volume had failed to meet the levels expected. Chang concluded the report by describing all of these issues as significant and clearly sufficient grounds to reconsider the viability of the new initiative that would redirect the firm's market strategy.

As was standard practice at Light Seating Canada, Chang's report was reviewed by the Controller, Paul James, in advance to its presentation to senior management. The day after James had received a copy of Chang's report, he approached her to discuss its findings. James and Jones had both been with Light Seating Canada for many years, and James was Jones's brother-in-law. He explained to Chang that he had reviewed the findings of her report with Jones. He explained that while she had certainly identified some disappointing events in the past, he was unconvinced that these items warranted the cautionary tone of the report. He raised the issue of training delays and suggested that this entire item could be dropped from the report, as it was unlikely that training delays would persist since some staff were now familiar with the stamping machine and assembly process. Additionally, he asked Chang to rewrite the sections of the report dealing with scrap rates and throughput, as they were quite negative, and Jones believed that both of these items were likely to improve with more organizational experience with the machine and manual assembly process.

Finally, James mentioned that Jones was widely seen as the champion of this new initiative. He suggested to Chang that perhaps she should be particularly cautious in producing a report that might reflect negatively on Jones and impact his career and subjective portion of the bonus. James reminded Chang that at Light Seating Canada all managers and employees have an annual bonus that is mostly subjective and determined by his/her immediate superior.

REQUIRED
1. Put yourself in Emily Chang's position and consider the ethical dimensions of the situation in which you find yourself. How would you resolve this situation?
2. Which levers of control need to be activated at Light Seating Canada?

PROBLEMS

24-34 Evaluating managers, ROI, value-chain analysis of cost structure. Integrated Automatic Solutions is one of the largest and most successful companies that design, implement, and maintain integrated systems of process controllers in the petrochemical industry. The board of directors met urgently several times during the last weeks to decide on the appointment of its new president after its president and CEO died in an airplane accident. An executive search firm recommends that the board consider appointing Louise Reinhold (current president of Flexible Systems) or John Cross (current president of Rigid Structures). You collect the following financial information on Flexible Systems and Rigid Structures for 2008 and 2009 (in millions):

1
1. Flexible Systems ROI
2009 = 9.8%

	Flexible Systems		Rigid Structures	
	2008	**2009**	**2008**	**2009**
Total assets	$432.0	$408.0	$192.0	$288.0
Revenues	$400.0	$320.0	$200.0	$350.0
Costs:				
R&D	36.0	16.8	18.0	43.5
Design	15.0	8.4	3.6	11.6
Production	102.0	112.0	82.8	98.6
Marketing	75.0	92.4	36.0	66.7
Distribution	27.0	22.4	18.0	23.2
Customer service	45.0	28.0	21.6	46.4
Total costs	300.0	280.0	180.0	290.0
Operating income	$100.0	$ 40.0	$ 20.0	$ 60.0

In early 2010, an industry publication ranked Rigid Structures as the best of its class among a list of 16 companies, while Flexible systems was ranked fifth, down two positions from a year ago because of customer-service problems. The publication also ran an article on innovative solutions; Rigid Structures received high marks in 2009, while Flexible Systems' performance was called "mediocre." One "unnamed insider" of Flexible Systems commented: "Our innovative solutions cupboard is empty."

REQUIRED
1. Use the DuPont method to analyze the ROI of Flexible Systems and Rigid Structures in 2008 and 2009. Comment on the results.
2. Compute the percentage of costs in each of the six business-function cost categories for Flexible Systems and Rigid Structures in 2008 and 2009. Comment on the results.
3. Rank Reinhold and Cross as potential candidates for president of Integrated Automatic Solutions.

24-35 ROI, RI, ROS, management incentives. (CMA, adapted) Soft Drinks Inc. is a company organized in several business units, each one dedicated to a particular type or flavour of soft drinks. The Ginger Ale Division produces and bottles ginger ale flavoured drinks, and its general manager is considering building a new plant in 2010 to expand capacity given the increasing and sustained demand experienced in the last 10 years. The investment will cost $3.0 million. The annual expected contribution margin is $1.5 million with revenues of $2.5 million; fixed costs for the new plant in 2010 will be $980,000.

1

Ginger Ale Division's ROI in 2009 is 20% and its return on sales (ROS) is 20%. ROI is defined as operating income divided by total assets. The bonuses of Adrian Shiling, the division manager of Ginger Ale, and other Soft Drinks managers are based on division ROI.

REQUIRED
1. If Soft Drinks uses ROI to evaluate division managers, explain why the Ginger Ale Division would be reluctant to build the new plant. Show all calculations.
2. Suppose Soft Drinks uses RI as the basis for awarding bonuses to Ginger Ale managers. Suppose further that the required rate of return on investment is 15%. Would Ginger Ale Division be more willing to build the new plant? Explain.
3. Calculate the ROS for the new plant. What are the advantages and disadvantages of using this measure to determine the bonuses paid to Ginger Ale managers?

24-36 Historical-cost and current-cost ROI measures. World of 1 Dollar Ltd. owns and manages three convenience stores. The following information has been collected for the year 2010:

	Jane and Rutherford	Major Mackenzie and Keele	Weston and Langstaff
Operating income	28,000	33,000	15,000
Historical cost of investment	50,000	100,000	30,000
Current cost of investment	120,000	135,000	80,000
Age of store	5	2	4

REQUIRED
1. Compute the ROI for each store where investment is measured at (a) historical cost and (b) current cost.
2. How would you judge the performance of each store?

24-37 ROI performance measures based on historical cost and current cost. Nature's Elixir Corporation operates three divisions that process and bottle natural fruit juices. The historical-cost accounting system reports the following information for 2008:

	Passion Fruit Division	Kiwi Fruit Division	Mango Fruit Division
Revenues	$1,000,000	$1,400,000	$2,200,000
Operating costs (excluding plant amortization)	600,000	760,000	1,200,000
Plant amortization	140,000	200,000	240,000
Operating income	$ 260,000	$ 440,000	$ 760,000
Current assets	$ 400,000	$ 500,000	$ 600,000
Long-term assets—plant	280,000	1,800,000	2,640,000
Total assets	$ 680,000	$2,300,000	$3,240,000

Nature's Elixir estimates the useful life of each plant to be 12 years, with no terminal disposal value. The straight-line amortization method is used. At the end of 2008, the Passion Fruit plant is 10 years old, the Kiwi Fruit plant is 3 years old, and the Mango Fruit plant is 1 year old. An index of construction costs over the 10-year period that Nature's Elixir has been operating (1998 year-end = 100) is:

1998	2005	2007	2008
100	136	160	170

Given the high turnover of current assets, management believes that the historical-cost and current-cost measures of current assets are approximately the same.

REQUIRED
1. Compute the ROI ratio (operating income to total assets) of each division using historical-cost measures. Comment on the results.
2. Use the approach in Exhibit 24-3 (p. 1149) to compute the ROI of each division, incorporating current-cost estimates as of 2008 for amortization expense and long-term assets. Comment on the results.

3. What advantages might arise from using current-cost asset measures as compared with historical-cost measures for evaluating the performance of the managers of the three divisions?

24-38 Relevant costs, performance evaluation, goal-congruence. Soccer Fifa Inc. has three operating divisions. The managers of these divisions are evaluated on their divisional operating income, a figure that includes an allocation of corporate overhead proportional to the revenues of each division. The operating income statement (in thousands) for the first quarter of 2010 is as follows:

1. Azurro operating income, $364,000

	Azurro Division	Orange Division	Canarinha Division	Total
Revenues	$2,400	$1,440	$1,920	$5,760
Cost of goods sold	$1,260	$ 648	$ 768	$2,676
Gross margin	$1,140	$ 792	$1,152	$3,084
Division overhead	$ 300	$ 150	$ 192	$ 642
Corporate overhead	$ 480	$ 288	$ 384	$1,152
Division operating income	$ 360	$ 354	$ 576	$1,290

The manager of the Azurro Division is unhappy that his profitability is about the same as the Orange Division's and is much less than the Canarinha Division's, even though his revenues are much higher than either of these other two divisions. The manager knows that he is carrying one line of products with very low profitability. He was going to replace this line of business as soon as more profitable product opportunities became available, but he has kept it because the line is marginally profitable and uses facilities that would otherwise be idle. That manager now realizes, however, that the sales from this product line are attracting a fair amount of corporate overhead because of the allocation procedure, and maybe the line is already unprofitable for him. In the first quarter of 2010 this low-margin line of products had a gross margin of $250,000 (with revenues for $960,000) and avoidable division overhead of $120,000.

REQUIRED
1. Prepare the operating income statement for Soccer Fifa Inc. for the second quarter of 2010. Assume that revenues and operating results are identical to those of the first quarter except that the manager of the Azurro Division has dropped the low-margin product line from his product group.
2. Is Soccer Fifa better off from this action?
3. Is the Azurro Division manager better off from this action?
4. Suggest changes for Soccer Fifa's system of division reporting and evaluation that will motivate division managers to make decisions that are in the best interests of Soccer Fifa Inc. as a whole. Discuss any potential disadvantages of your proposal.

24-39 ROI, RI, and multinational firms. Konekopf Corporation has a division in Canada and another in France. The investment in the French assets was made when the exchange rate was $1.20 per euro. The average exchange rate for the year was $1.30 per euro. The exchange rate at the end of the fiscal year was $1.38 per euro. Income and investment for the two divisions are:

1. RI France in dollars, $58,320

	Canada	France
Investment in assets	$3,490,000	2,400,000 euros
Income for current year	$ 383,900	266,400 euros

REQUIRED
1. The required return for Konekopf is 10%. Calculate ROI and RI for the two divisions. For the French division, calculate these measures using both dollars and euros. Which division is doing better?
2. What are the advantages and disadvantages of translating the French division information from euros to dollars?

24-40 Multinational firms, differing risk, comparison of profit, ROI, and RI. Zzwuig Multinational Inc. has divisions in Canada, Germany, and New Zealand. The Canadian division is the oldest and most established of the three, and has a cost of capital of 6%. The German division was started three years ago when the exchange rate for euros was 1€ = $1.25. Although it is a large and powerful division of Zzwuig Inc., its cost of capital is 10%. The New Zealand division was started this year, when the exchange rate was 1 New Zealand

Dollar (NZD) = $0.64. Its cost of capital is 13%. Average exchange rates for the current year are 1€ = $1.32 and 1 NZD = $0.67. Other information for the three divisions includes:

1. New Zealand, $696,800

	Canada	Germany	New Zealand
Long-term assets	$14,845,000	9,856,000 euros	9,072,917 NZD
Operating revenues	$10,479,000	5,200,000 euros	4,800,000 NZD
Operating expenses	$ 7,510,000	3,600,000 euros	3,500,000 NZD
Income tax rate	40%	30%	20%

REQUIRED

1. Translate the German and New Zealand information into dollars to make the divisions comparable. Find the after-tax operating income for each division and compare the profits.
2. Calculate ROI using after-tax operating income. Compare among divisions.
3. Use after-tax operating income and the individual cost of capital of each division to calculate residual income and compare.
4. Redo requirement 2 using pretax operating income instead of net income. Why is there a big difference, and what does it mean for performance evaluation?

1. Income South American Div., 1,300,000 pesos

24-41 Multinational firms, comparison of profit, ROI, RI, and EVA. Kase Tractor Company, a multinational company, allows its divisions to operate as autonomous units. In the year 2008 it established a division in a South American country as a subsidiary corporation, with an initial investment in total assets of 6.5 million pesos (the local currency), which cost the company $3,250,000 Canadian at the time. The company sent an experienced manager to run the division, and gave her a target of 13% required rate of return, promising a bonus if this was met and/or exceeded. At the end of the first year (2008), the subsidiary manager was pleased to report a 20% ROI with sales of 1,000,000 Canadian dollars. The current exchange rate as of the end of the year 2009 was 3 pesos to 1 Canadian dollar. The exchange rate at the end of 2008 was the same as when the initial investment was made.

The tax rate for the two Canadian divisions is 35% and for the South American division is 20%. Other operating data for 2009 follow:

	Ontario (in Cdn dollars)	Quebec (in Cdn dollars)	South America (in pesos)
Revenues	$2,250,000	$500,000	$3,900,000
Accounts receivable	800,000	152,500	1,435,000
Total assets	1,000,000	400,000	5,500,000
Accounts payable	250,000	100,000	500,000
Net operating income	220,000	60,000	1,000,000
Taxable income	165,000	90,000	850,000
WACC	11.5%	11.5%	7.5%

REQUIRED

1. Compute the return on investment for each division in 2009 and calculate the South American subsidiary's income in pesos for the year 2008.
2. Compute the EVA for each division.
3. What other ratio could be calculated for performance evaluation? Explain why it would be beneficial.
4. Calculate the RI of the South American subsidiary in Canadian dollars for the years 2008 and 2009.
5. Explain at least two factors that may have contributed to the increase or decrease in RI between 2008 and 2009 in the South American division.

24-42 Risk-sharing, incentives, benchmarking, multiple tasks. Acme Inc. is a diversified multidivisional corporation. One of its business units manufactures and sells industrial pumps. Acme's corporate management gives Industrial Pumps management considerable operating and investment autonomy in running the division. Cynthia Franco is an exceptional manager with a brilliant career within Industrial Pumps division and Acme will offer her the opportunity to become the new vice-president of industrial products. Acme has a handful of candidates to become the general manager of Industrial Pumps, but all of them lack the internal motivation that Cynthia has shown. Acme Inc. is considering how it should compensate the new general manager of the division.

- *Proposal 1:* Pay a fixed salary.
- *Proposal 2:* Pay no salary and compensate the manager only on the basis of the division's RI (calculated on the basis of operating income before any bonus payments).
- *Proposal 3:* Pay some salary and some bonus based on ROI.
- *Proposal 4:* Pay some salary and some bonus based on the difference between the ROI of Industrial Pumps division and the ROI of Pumps-for-All Ltd. Pumps-for-All is roughly the same size, operates in a very similar business environment, and half of its customers also buy from Industrial Pumps division of Acme Inc.

REQUIRED

1. Evaluate each of the four proposals, specifying the advantages and disadvantages of each.
2. One of the candidates complains that the fourth proposal is unfair because the performance of another firm, over which he has no control, is included in his performance evaluation measure. Is his complaint valid? Why or why not?
3. Now suppose the Industrial Pumps manager has no authority for making capital investment decisions. Corporate management makes these decisions. Is return on investment a good performance measure to use to evaluate the divisional manager? Is return on investment a good measure to evaluate the economic viability of the Industrial Pumps division? Explain.
4. Industrial Pumps' salespersons are responsible for selling and providing customer service and support. Sales are easy to measure. Although customer service is very important to Industrial Pumps in the long run, it has not yet implemented customer-service measures. Cynthia Franco recommended compensating her sales force only on the basis of sales commissions paid for each pump sold. She cites two advantages to this plan: (a) it creates very strong incentives for the sales force to work hard and (b) the company pays salespersons only when the company itself is earning revenues and has cash. Do you like her plan? Why or why not?

24-43 Executive performance measurement and compensation. The Vaughan Speed Taxi company is a young company that operates a fleet of six taxis in the Greater Toronto Area. The owner relies on the abilities of two managers to run each business: Airport and York. At the end of each month, the owner evaluates the performances of each business. His evaluations determine the size of the manager bonus. If the business achieved an annual ROA of 20% then the manager gets $1,000. The bonus is also augmented by $1 for every $10 the business exceeded its profit target.

However, the bonus contract gives the owner the right to make subjective adjustments for the effects of factors he deems outside the control of the managers. In the past few months he had made such adjustments for the adverse effects on revenue of having major construction and delays in the airport. By far the largest uncontrollable factor for the business at York is the weather. In particular, rides and sales volume increase sharply when it rains or snows. The budget, which was updated monthly, was prepared based on an assumption of hours of good weather. Inevitably, though, those assumptions were not accurate.

The month of November 2010 was not a typical month, and it did not snow and rain as much as had been assumed in the budget. Actual profits for the York business were below the budgeted profit level as shown in Table 1. Table 2 shows some operating assumptions and statistics for the month. The York line of business has $60,000 of total assets and is available every day, 10 hours per day. The taxi drivers are paid the legally required minimum wage plus a fixed amount for each trip completed, so labour costs are highly variable with revenues.

Table 1: York Business, November 2010

	Budget	**Actual**	**Variance**
Revenue	$5,400	$4,590	(810)
Variable expenses (50% of revenues)	2,700	2,295	405
Fixed expenses	1,000	1,195	(195)
Profit	1,700	1,100	(600)

Table 2: York Business Operating Statistics, November 2010

	Budgeted	**Actual**
Average number of trips in a bad-weather hour	2	3
Average revenue per trip	$10	$9
Hours of bad weather	270	170
Hours of good weather	30	130

1. How large will be the bonus for the York business line manager in November 2010?
2. Was the York business line properly managed in November 2010? Support your arguments with numbers.

24-44 Governance, levers of control. (R. Madison, adapted, *Strategic Finance*, January 2000). United Forest Products (UFP) is a large timber and wood processing plant. UFP's performance-evaluation system pays its managers substantial bonuses if the company achieves annual budgeted profit numbers. In the last quarter of 2009, Amy Kimbell, UFP's controller, noted a slight increase in output and a significant decrease in the purchase cost of raw timber.

One day when Kimbell was at the log yard where timber is received and scaled (weighed and checked for quality) to determine what UFP pays for it, she noted that a timber contractor was quite aggravated when he was given the scale report (board feet and quality). When she asked one of the scale employees what was bothering the contractor, he revealed that the scalers had received instructions from their supervisors to deliberately "lowball" evaluations of timber quantity and quality. This reduced the price paid to timber suppliers, which also reduced direct material costs, helping UFP to meet its profit target.

REQUIRED

1. What should Kimbell do?
2. Which lever of control is UFP emphasizing? What changes, if any, should be made?

24-45 Division manager's compensation, risk sharing, incentives (continuation of 24-30). The management of Summit Equipment is having problems implementing a complex bonus scheme and was forced to award only the base bonus calculated as 2% of operating income. For the immediate future management is considering the following alternative compensation arrangements:

◆ Make the managers' compensation a fixed salary without any bonuses. Ben Harrington, Summit's president, believes that one advantage of this arrangement is that the division managers will be less inclined to reject future investments just because of their impact on operating income.

◆ Make all of division managers' compensation depend on the division's RI. The benefit of this arrangement is that it creates incentives for them to aggressively seek and accept all proposals that increase the divisional RI.

◆ Evaluate managers' performance using benchmarking by comparing the divisional RI against the RI achieved by managers of other similar companies in terms of size, volume, products, and investment. Harrington believes that the advantage of benchmarking is that it focuses attention on divisional performance relative to peers rather than on the division's absolute performance.

REQUIRED

1. Assume that the divisional managers are risk averse. Using concepts of performance evaluation described in this chapter, evaluate each of the three proposals that Harrington is considering. Indicate the positive and negative features of each proposal.
2. What compensation arrangement would you recommend? Explain briefly.

24-46 Governance, manager's performance evaluation. (A. Spero, adapted) Schomberg Milk Products manufactures and sells organic Balkanic-style yogurt. Each box of 48 yogurts is sold for $30. Schomberg's manufacturing costs per box of 48 yogurts consist of the following:

Raw milk	$ 8.00
Fruits and flavours	1.50
Other variable costs	6.50
Total variable costs	$16.00

Schomberg Milk Products calculates operating income using absorption costing—that is, Schomberg Milk Products calculates fixed manufacturing costs per box by dividing total manufacturing costs by actual production. Schomberg Milk Products costs all units in inventory at this rate and expenses the costs in the income statement only when the units in inventory are sold. The details of fixed costs per quarter are as follows:

Fixed manufacturing costs	$1,000,000
Fixed administrative costs	150,000
Fixed marketing costs	300,000
Total fixed costs	$1,450,000

1. a. Operating income, ($50,000)

The next quarter appears to be a difficult one for Schomberg Milk Products. It expects to sell only 100,000 boxes. The demand for this specialty yogurt fluctuates considerably with general economic conditions. Schomberg Milk Products, like most of the companies in this industry, usually holds minimal inventory.

REQUIRED

1. Calculate Schomberg Milk Products' operating income in the next quarter if it manufactures (a) 100,000 boxes and (b) 125,000 boxes.
2. Would it be unethical for the general manager of Schomberg Milk Products to produce more boxes than can be sold in order to show better operating results? The manager's compensation has a bonus component based on operating income. Explain your answer.
3. Would it be unethical for the manager to ask distributors to buy more product than they need? Schomberg Milk Products follows the industry practice of booking sales when products are shipped to distributors. Explain your answer.

COLLABORATIVE LEARNING CASES

24-47 ROI, RI division manager's compensation, nonfinancial measures. In 2010 the Mandarin Division of Key Products Corporation generated an operating income of $3,000,000 from $20,000,000 of sales revenues and using assets worth $15,000,000.

1. ROS, 15%

Mandarin managers are evaluated and rewarded on the basis of ROI defined as operating income divided by total assets. Key Products Corporation expects its divisions to increase ROI each year.

The year 2011 appears to be a difficult year for Mandarin. Mandarin Division had planned new investments to improve quality but, in view of poor economic conditions, has postponed the investment. ROI for 2011 was certain to decrease had Mandarin made the investment. Management is now considering ways to meet its target ROI of 22% for next year. It anticipates revenues to be steady at $20,000,000 in 2011.

INSTRUCTIONS

Form groups of two or more students to complete the following requirements.

1. Calculate Mandarin Division return on sales (ROS) and ROI for 2010.
2. **a.** By how much would Mandarin have to cut costs in 2011 to achieve its target ROI of 22% in 2011, assuming no change in total assets between 2010 and 2011?
   b. By how much would Mandarin have to decrease total assets in 2011 to achieve its target ROI of 22% in 2011, assuming no change in operating income between 2010 and 2011?
3. Calculate Mandarin's RI in 2010 assuming a required rate of return on investment of 18%.
4. Mandarin wants to increase RI by 30% in 2011. Assuming it could cut costs by $30,000 in 2011, by how much would Mandarin have to decrease total assets in 2011?
5. Key Products Corporation is concerned that the focus on cost cutting and asset sales will have an adverse long-run effect on Mandarin's customers. Yet Key Products Corporation wants Mandarin to meet its financial goals. What other measurements, if any, do you recommend that Key Products use? Explain briefly.

24-48 ROI, RI, division manager's compensation, nonfinancial measures. (CGA, adapted) General Appliance (GA) builds coffeemakers and battery-powered small tools. For a long time, GA held a reputation for strong, durable, and reliable appliances. This reputation began to decline, however, when increased competition forced GA to cut costs, and this was handled poorly. For a moderate period following the cost cutting, as long as they were able to take advantage of their reputation, GA's sales remained relatively steady. This effect then all but disappeared. The loss of reputation, coupled with increased overseas competition, caused GA's sales to plummet sharply.

Electronic, $75,000

On January 1, 2008, GA began a massive effort directed towards rewarding for quality. In the two years that followed, sales failed to go up, but remained steady at around $10 million per year. A significant amount of money was spent on testing equipment, increasing inspection, setting up a statistical process control system, reworking or throwing out defective items, and paying incentives. The results of the effort are presented in the following exhibit:

Quality Costs as a % of Sales for the Years Ended:	2007	2008	2009
External Failure Costs	8.20	2.40	1.15
Internal Failure Costs	2.80	4.00	3.40
Appraisal Costs	2.00	3.20	3.39
Prevention Costs	1.20	2.60	2.79
Total Quality Costs	14.20	12.20	10.73

Also on January 1, 2008, GA organized into three divisions: electronic circuits, coffee-makers, and battery-powered small tools. Electronic circuits were used by the other two divisions, and 100% of its production was transferred at full cost plus an 8% markup (this is the standard practice in the electronic components industry) to coffeemakers and battery-powered small tools. All rejections made by coffeemakers and small tools were treated in the quality control system as internal failures, but most of the time they were not reported simply because electronic circuits replaced them immediately in the production lines.

Each division had a bonus pool with 50% based on quality performance and 50% based on financial performance. The 50% based on financial performance is equal to 20% of the divisional residual income (the minimum required rate of return is the ROI of the worst-performing division). The 50% based on quality performance is calculated as: (Internal Failures as % of sales − External Failures as % of sales) × GA's net profit.

Given the results of last year, the manager of the coffeemaker division asked the top managers to review the current compensation system, because he was having the feeling that his division had been subsidizing those "lazy" fellows of electronic circuits. He supported his claim with the following:

2009	Electronic Circuits	Coffeemakers	Battery-Powered Small Tools
Net profit	$ 500,000	$ 700,000	$ 660,000
Investment	$2,500,000	$7,000,000	$6,000,000
External failures	0% of sales	1.2% of sales	2.4% of sales
Internal failures	5% of sales	2% of sales	3.2% of sales
Appraisal costs	0% of sales	5.2% of sales	3.1% of sales
Prevention costs	1% of sales	7% of sales	4.2% of sales

INSTRUCTIONS
Form groups of two or more students to complete the following requirement.

Calculate the bonus paid to each division. Explain to the upper management if the money is being spent effectively and if the claims of the divisional manager are correct.

Notes on Compound Interest and Interest Tables

Interest is the cost of using money. It is the rental charge for funds, just as renting a building and equipment entails a rental charge. When the funds are used for a period of time, it is necessary to recognize interest as a cost of using the borrowed ("rented") funds. This requirement applies even if the funds represent ownership capital and if interest does not entail an outlay of cash. Why must interest be considered? Because the selection of one alternative automatically commits a given amount of funds that could otherwise be invested in some other alternative.

Interest is generally important, even when short-term projects are under consideration. Interest looms correspondingly larger when long-run plans are studied. The rate of interest has significant enough impact to influence decisions regarding borrowing and investing funds. For example, $100,000 invested now and compounded annually for 10 years at 8% will accumulate to $215,900; at 20%, the $100,000 will accumulate to $619,200.

INTEREST TABLES

Many computer programs and pocket calculators are available that handle computations involving the time value of money. You may also turn to the following four basic tables to compute interest.

TABLE 1—FUTURE AMOUNT OF $1

Table 1 shows how much $1 invested now will accumulate in a given number of periods at a given compounded interest rate per period. Consider investing $1,000 now for three years at 8% compound interest. A tabular presentation of how this $1,000 would accumulate to $1,259.70 follows:

Year	Interest per Year	Cumulative Interest Called Compound Interest	Total at End of Year
0	$ —	$ —	$1,000.00
1	80.00 (0.08 × $1,000)	80.00	1,080.00
2	86.40 (0.08 × $1,080)	166.40	1,166.40
3	93.30 (0.08 × $1,166.40)	259.70	1,259.70

This tabular presentation is a series of computations that could appear as follows, where S is the future amount and the subscripts 1, 2, and 3 indicate the number of time periods.

$$S_1 = \$1,000(1.08)^1$$
$$S_2 = \$1,000(1.08)^2$$
$$S_3 = \$1,000(1.08)^3$$

The formula for the "amount of 1," often called the "future value of $1" or "future amount of $1," can be written

$$S = P(1 + r)^n$$
$$S = \$1,000(1 + 0.08)^3 = \$1,259.70$$

S is the future value amount; P is the present value, $1,000 in this case; r is the rate of interest; and n is the number of time periods.

Fortunately, tables make key computations readily available. A facility in selecting the *proper* table will minimize computations. Check the accuracy of the preceding answer using Table 1.

TABLE 2—PRESENT VALUE OF $1

In the previous example, if $1,000 compounded at 8% per year will accumulate to $1,259.70 in 3 years, then $1,000 must be the present value of $1,259.70 due at the end of 3 years. The formula for the present value can be derived by reversing the process of *accumulation* (finding the future amount) that we just finished.

If $$S = P(1 + r)^n$$

then $$P = \frac{S}{(1 + r)^n}$$

$$P = \frac{\$1,259.70}{(1.08)^3} = \$1,000$$

Use Table 2 to check this calculation.

When accumulating, we advance or roll forward in time. The difference between our original amount and our accumulated amount is called *compound interest*. When discounting, we retreat or roll back in time. The difference between the future amount and the present value is called *compound discount*. Note the following formulas (where $P = \$1,000$):

$$\text{Compound interest} = P[(1 + r)^n - 1] = \$259.70$$

$$\text{Compound discount} = S\left[1 - \frac{1}{(1 + r)^n}\right] = \$259.70$$

TABLE 3—AMOUNT OF ANNUITY OF $1

An (ordinary) *annuity* is a series of equal payments (receipts) to be paid (or received) at the *end* of successive periods of equal length. Assume that $1,000 is invested at the end of each of 3 years at 8%:

End of Year	Amount
1st payment	$1,000.00 ➤ $1,080.00 ➤ $1,166.40, which is $1,000(1.08)^2$
2nd payment	$1,000.00 ➤ 1,080.00, which is $1,000(1.08)^1$
3rd payment	1,000.00
Accumulation (future amount)	$3,246.40

The preceding arithmetic may be expressed algebraically as the amount of an ordinary annuity of $1,000 for 3 years = $1,000(1 + r)^2 + $1,000(1 + r)^1 + $1,000.

We can develop the general formula for S_n, the amount of an ordinary annuity of $1, by using the example above as a basis:

1. $S_n = 1 + (1 + r)^1 + (1 + r)^2$

2. Substitute: $S_n = 1 + (1.08)^1 + (1.08)^2$

3. Multiply (2) by $(1 + r)$: $(1.08)S_n = (1.08)^1 + (1.08)^2 + (1.08)^3$

4. Subtract (2) from (3): $1.08S_n - S_n = (1.08)^3 - 1$
Note that all terms on the right-hand side are removed except $(1.08)^3$ in equation (3) and 1 in equation (2).

5. Factor (4): $S_n(1.08 - 1) = (1.08)^3 - 1$

6. Divide (5) by $(1.08 - 1)$: $S_n = \dfrac{(1.08)^3 - 1}{1.08 - 1} = \dfrac{(1.08)^3 - 1}{.08}$

7. The general formula for the amount of an ordinary annuity of $1 becomes: $S_n = \dfrac{(1 + r)^n - 1}{r}$ or $\dfrac{\text{Compound interest}}{\text{Rate}}$

This formula is the basis for Table 3. Look at Table 3 or use the formula itself to check the calculations.

TABLE 4—PRESENT VALUE OF AN ORDINARY ANNUITY OF $1

Using the same example as for Table 3, we can show how the formula of P_n, *the present value of an ordinary annuity*, is developed.

| | 0 | 1 | 2 | 3 |

End of Year

1st payment	$\dfrac{1,000}{(1.08)^1} = \$ 925.93$ ◄——— $1,000
2nd payment	$\dfrac{1,000}{(1.08)^2} = \$ 857.34$ ◄———— $1,000
3rd payment	$\dfrac{1,000}{(1.08)^3} = \$ 793.83$ ◄————— $1,000
Total present value	$2,577.10

For the general case, the present value of an ordinary annuity of $1 may be expressed as:

1. $P_n = \dfrac{1}{1 + r} + \dfrac{1}{(1 + r)^2} + \dfrac{1}{(1 + r)^3}$

2. Substitute $P_n = \dfrac{1}{1.08} + \dfrac{1}{(1.08)^2} + \dfrac{1}{(1.08)^3}$

3. Multiply by $\dfrac{1}{1.08}$: $P_n \dfrac{1}{1.08} = \dfrac{1}{(1.08)^2} + \dfrac{1}{(1.08)^3} + \dfrac{1}{(1.08)^4}$

4. Subtract (3) from (2): $P_n - P_n\dfrac{1}{1.08} = \dfrac{1}{1.08} - \dfrac{1}{(1.08)^4}$

5. Factor: $P_n\left(1 - \dfrac{1}{(1.08)}\right) = \dfrac{1}{1.08}\left[1 - \dfrac{1}{(1.08)^3}\right]$

6. or $P_n\left(\dfrac{.08}{1.08}\right) = \dfrac{1}{1.08}\left[1 - \dfrac{1}{(1.08)^3}\right]$

7. Multiply by $\frac{1.08}{0.08}$:

$$P_n = \frac{1}{0.08}\left[1 - \frac{1}{(1.08)^3}\right]$$

The general formula for the present value of an annuity of $1.00 is:

$$P_n = \frac{1}{r}\left[1 - \frac{1}{(1+r)^n}\right] = \frac{\text{Compound discount}}{\text{Rate}}$$

Solving,

$$P_n = \frac{0.2062}{0.08} = 2.577$$

The formula is the basis for Table 4. Check the answer in the table. The present value tables, Tables 2 and 4, are used most frequently in capital budgeting.

The tables for annuities are not essential. With Tables 1 and 2, compound interest and compound discount can readily be computed. It is simply a matter of dividing either of these by the rate to get values equivalent to those shown in Tables 3 and 4.

TABLE 1

Compound Amount of $1.00 (The Future Value of $1.00).

$S = P(1 - r)^n$. In this table $P = \$1.00$.

Periods	2%	4%	6%	8%	10%	12%	14%	16%	18%	20%	22%	24%	26%	28%	30%	32%	40%	Periods
1	1.020	1.040	1.060	1.080	1.100	1.120	1.140	1.160	1.180	1.200	1.220	1.240	1.260	1.280	1.300	1.320	1.400	1
2	1.040	1.082	1.124	1.166	1.210	1.254	1.300	1.346	1.392	1.440	1.488	1.538	1.588	1.638	1.690	1.742	1.960	2
3	1.061	1.125	1.191	1.260	1.331	1.405	1.482	1.561	1.643	1.728	1.816	1.907	2.000	2.097	2.197	2.300	2.744	3
4	1.082	1.170	1.262	1.360	1.464	1.574	1.689	1.811	1.939	2.074	2.215	2.364	2.520	2.684	2.856	3.036	3.842	4
5	1.104	1.217	1.338	1.469	1.611	1.762	1.925	2.100	2.288	2.488	2.703	2.932	3.176	3.436	3.713	4.007	5.378	5
6	1.126	1.265	1.419	1.587	1.772	1.974	2.195	2.436	2.700	2.986	3.297	3.635	4.002	4.398	4.827	5.290	7.530	6
7	1.149	1.316	1.504	1.714	1.949	2.211	2.502	2.826	3.185	3.583	4.023	4.508	5.042	5.629	6.275	6.983	10.541	7
8	1.172	1.369	1.594	1.851	2.144	2.476	2.853	3.278	3.759	4.300	4.908	5.590	6.353	7.206	8.157	9.217	14.758	8
9	1.195	1.423	1.689	1.999	2.358	2.773	3.252	3.803	4.435	5.160	5.987	6.931	8.005	9.223	10.604	12.166	20.661	9
10	1.219	1.480	1.791	2.159	2.594	3.106	3.707	4.411	5.234	6.192	7.305	8.594	10.086	11.806	13.786	16.060	28.925	10
11	1.243	1.539	1.898	2.332	2.853	3.479	4.226	5.117	6.176	7.430	8.912	10.657	12.708	15.112	17.922	21.199	40.496	11
12	1.268	1.601	2.012	2.518	3.138	3.896	4.818	5.936	7.288	8.916	10.872	13.215	16.012	19.343	23.298	27.983	56.694	12
13	1.294	1.665	2.133	2.720	3.452	4.363	5.492	6.886	8.599	10.699	13.264	16.386	20.175	24.759	30.288	36.937	79.371	13
14	1.319	1.732	2.261	2.937	3.797	4.887	6.261	7.988	10.147	12.839	16.182	20.319	25.421	31.691	39.374	48.757	111.120	14
15	1.346	1.801	2.397	3.172	4.177	5.474	7.138	9.266	11.974	15.407	19.742	25.196	32.030	40.565	51.186	64.359	155.568	15
16	1.373	1.873	2.540	3.426	4.595	6.130	8.137	10.748	14.129	18.488	24.086	31.243	40.358	51.923	66.542	84.954	217.795	16
17	1.400	1.948	2.693	3.700	5.054	6.866	9.276	12.468	16.672	22.186	29.384	38.741	50.851	66.461	86.504	112.139	304.913	17
18	1.428	2.026	2.854	3.996	5.560	7.690	10.575	14.463	19.673	26.623	35.849	48.039	64.072	85.071	112.455	148.024	426.879	18
19	1.457	2.107	3.026	4.316	6.116	8.613	12.056	16.777	23.214	31.948	43.736	59.568	80.731	108.890	146.192	195.391	597.630	19
20	1.486	2.191	3.207	4.661	6.727	9.646	13.743	19.461	27.393	38.338	53.358	73.864	101.721	139.380	190.050	257.916	836.683	20
21	1.516	2.279	3.400	5.034	7.400	10.804	15.668	22.574	32.324	46.005	65.096	91.592	128.169	178.406	247.065	340.449	1171.356	21
22	1.546	2.370	3.604	5.437	8.140	12.100	17.861	26.186	38.142	55.206	79.418	113.574	161.492	228.360	321.184	449.393	1639.898	22
23	1.577	2.465	3.820	5.871	8.954	13.552	20.362	30.376	45.008	66.247	96.889	140.831	203.480	292.300	417.539	593.199	2295.857	23
24	1.608	2.563	4.049	6.341	9.850	15.179	23.212	35.236	53.109	79.497	118.205	174.631	256.385	374.144	542.801	783.023	3214.200	24
25	1.641	2.666	4.292	6.848	10.835	17.000	26.462	40.874	62.669	95.396	144.210	216.542	323.045	478.905	705.641	1033.590	4499.880	25
26	1.673	2.772	4.549	7.396	11.918	19.040	30.167	47.414	73.949	114.475	175.936	268.512	407.037	612.998	917.333	1364.339	6299.831	26
27	1.707	2.883	4.822	7.988	13.110	21.325	34.390	55.000	87.260	137.371	214.642	332.955	512.867	784.638	1192.533	1800.927	8819.764	27
28	1.741	2.999	5.112	8.627	14.421	23.884	39.204	63.800	102.967	164.845	261.864	412.864	646.212	1004.336	1550.293	2377.224	12347.670	28
29	1.776	3.119	5.418	9.317	15.863	26.750	44.693	74.009	121.501	197.814	319.474	511.952	814.228	1285.550	2015.381	3137.935	17286.737	29
30	1.811	3.243	5.743	10.063	17.449	29.960	50.950	85.850	143.371	237.376	389.758	634.820	1025.927	1645.505	2619.996	4142.075	24201.432	30
35	2.000	3.946	7.686	14.785	28.102	52.800	98.100	180.314	327.997	590.668	1053.402	1861.054	3258.135	5653.911	9727.860	16599.217	130161.112	35
40	2.208	4.801	10.286	21.725	45.259	93.051	188.884	378.721	750.378	1469.772	2847.038	5455.913	10347.175	19426.689	36118.865	66520.767	700037.697	40

TABLE 2 *(Place a clip on this page for easy reference.)*
Present Value of $1.00.

$P = \dfrac{S}{(1+r)^n}$. In this table $S = \$1.00$.

Periods	2%	4%	6%	8%	10%	12%	14%	16%	18%	20%	22%	24%	26%	28%	30%	32%	40%	Periods
1	0.980	0.962	0.943	0.926	0.909	0.893	0.877	0.862	0.847	0.833	0.820	0.806	0.794	0.781	0.769	0.758	0.714	1
2	0.961	0.925	0.890	0.857	0.826	0.797	0.769	0.743	0.718	0.694	0.672	0.650	0.630	0.610	0.592	0.574	0.510	2
3	0.942	0.889	0.840	0.794	0.751	0.712	0.675	0.641	0.609	0.579	0.551	0.524	0.500	0.477	0.455	0.435	0.364	3
4	0.924	0.855	0.792	0.735	0.683	0.636	0.592	0.552	0.516	0.482	0.451	0.423	0.397	0.373	0.350	0.329	0.260	4
5	0.906	0.822	0.747	0.681	0.621	0.567	0.519	0.476	0.437	0.402	0.370	0.341	0.315	0.291	0.269	0.250	0.186	5
6	0.888	0.790	0.705	0.630	0.564	0.507	0.456	0.410	0.370	0.335	0.303	0.275	0.250	0.227	0.207	0.189	0.133	6
7	0.871	0.760	0.665	0.583	0.513	0.452	0.400	0.354	0.314	0.279	0.249	0.222	0.198	0.178	0.159	0.143	0.095	7
8	0.853	0.731	0.627	0.540	0.467	0.404	0.351	0.305	0.266	0.233	0.204	0.179	0.157	0.139	0.123	0.108	0.068	8
9	0.837	0.703	0.592	0.500	0.424	0.361	0.308	0.263	0.225	0.194	0.167	0.144	0.125	0.108	0.094	0.082	0.048	9
10	0.820	0.676	0.558	0.463	0.386	0.322	0.270	0.227	0.191	0.162	0.137	0.116	0.099	0.085	0.073	0.062	0.035	10
11	0.804	0.650	0.527	0.429	0.350	0.287	0.237	0.195	0.162	0.135	0.112	0.094	0.079	0.066	0.056	0.047	0.025	11
12	0.788	0.625	0.497	0.397	0.319	0.257	0.208	0.168	0.137	0.112	0.092	0.076	0.062	0.052	0.043	0.036	0.018	12
13	0.773	0.601	0.469	0.368	0.290	0.229	0.182	0.145	0.116	0.093	0.075	0.061	0.050	0.040	0.033	0.027	0.013	13
14	0.758	0.577	0.442	0.340	0.263	0.205	0.160	0.125	0.099	0.078	0.062	0.049	0.039	0.032	0.025	0.021	0.009	14
15	0.743	0.555	0.417	0.315	0.239	0.183	0.140	0.108	0.084	0.065	0.051	0.040	0.031	0.025	0.020	0.016	0.006	15
16	0.728	0.534	0.394	0.292	0.218	0.163	0.123	0.093	0.071	0.054	0.042	0.032	0.025	0.019	0.015	0.012	0.005	16
17	0.714	0.513	0.371	0.270	0.198	0.146	0.108	0.080	0.060	0.045	0.034	0.026	0.020	0.015	0.012	0.009	0.003	17
18	0.700	0.494	0.350	0.250	0.180	0.130	0.095	0.069	0.051	0.038	0.028	0.021	0.016	0.012	0.009	0.007	0.002	18
19	0.686	0.475	0.331	0.232	0.164	0.116	0.083	0.060	0.043	0.031	0.023	0.017	0.012	0.009	0.007	0.005	0.002	19
20	0.673	0.456	0.312	0.215	0.149	0.104	0.073	0.051	0.037	0.026	0.019	0.014	0.010	0.007	0.005	0.004	0.001	20
21	0.660	0.439	0.294	0.199	0.135	0.093	0.064	0.044	0.031	0.022	0.015	0.011	0.008	0.006	0.004	0.003	0.001	21
22	0.647	0.422	0.278	0.184	0.123	0.083	0.056	0.038	0.026	0.018	0.013	0.009	0.006	0.004	0.003	0.002	0.001	22
23	0.634	0.406	0.262	0.170	0.112	0.074	0.049	0.033	0.022	0.015	0.010	0.007	0.005	0.003	0.002	0.002	0.000	23
24	0.622	0.390	0.247	0.158	0.102	0.066	0.043	0.028	0.019	0.013	0.008	0.006	0.004	0.003	0.002	0.001	0.000	24
25	0.610	0.375	0.233	0.146	0.092	0.059	0.038	0.024	0.016	0.010	0.007	0.005	0.003	0.002	0.001	0.001	0.000	25
26	0.598	0.361	0.220	0.135	0.084	0.053	0.033	0.021	0.014	0.009	0.006	0.004	0.002	0.002	0.001	0.001	0.000	26
27	0.586	0.347	0.207	0.125	0.076	0.047	0.029	0.018	0.011	0.007	0.005	0.003	0.002	0.001	0.001	0.001	0.000	27
28	0.574	0.333	0.196	0.116	0.069	0.042	0.026	0.016	0.010	0.006	0.004	0.002	0.002	0.001	0.001	0.000	0.000	28
29	0.563	0.321	0.185	0.107	0.063	0.037	0.022	0.014	0.008	0.005	0.003	0.002	0.001	0.001	0.000	0.000	0.000	29
30	0.552	0.308	0.174	0.099	0.057	0.033	0.020	0.012	0.007	0.004	0.003	0.002	0.001	0.001	0.000	0.000	0.000	30
35	0.500	0.253	0.130	0.068	0.036	0.019	0.010	0.006	0.003	0.002	0.001	0.001	0.000	0.000	0.000	0.000	0.000	35
40	0.453	0.208	0.097	0.046	0.022	0.011	0.005	0.003	0.001	0.001	0.000	0.000	0.000	0.000	0.000	0.000	0.000	40

TABLE 3
Compound Amount of Annuity of $1.00 in Arrears* (Future Value of Annuity).

$$S_n = \frac{(1+r)^n - 1}{r}$$

Periods	2%	4%	6%	8%	10%	12%	14%	16%	18%	20%	22%	24%	26%	28%	30%	32%	40%	Periods
1	1.000	1.000	1.000	1.000	1.000	1.000	1.000	1.000	1.000	1.000	1.000	1.000	1.000	1.000	1.000	1.000	1.000	1
2	2.020	2.040	2.060	2.080	2.100	2.120	2.140	2.160	2.180	2.200	2.220	2.240	2.260	2.280	2.300	2.320	2.400	2
3	3.060	3.122	3.184	3.246	3.310	3.374	3.440	3.506	3.572	3.640	3.708	3.778	3.848	3.918	3.990	4.062	4.360	3
4	4.122	4.246	4.375	4.506	4.641	4.779	4.921	5.066	5.215	5.368	5.524	5.684	5.848	6.016	6.187	6.362	7.104	4
5	5.204	5.416	5.637	5.867	6.105	6.353	6.610	6.877	7.154	7.442	7.740	8.048	8.368	8.700	9.043	9.398	10.946	5
6	6.308	6.633	6.975	7.336	7.716	8.115	8.536	8.977	9.442	9.930	10.442	10.980	11.544	12.136	12.756	13.406	16.324	6
7	7.434	7.898	8.394	8.923	9.487	10.089	10.730	11.414	12.142	12.916	13.740	14.615	15.546	16.534	17.583	18.696	23.853	7
8	8.583	9.214	9.897	10.637	11.436	12.300	13.233	14.240	15.327	16.499	17.762	19.123	20.588	22.163	23.858	25.678	34.395	8
9	9.755	10.583	11.491	12.488	13.579	14.776	16.085	17.519	19.086	20.799	22.670	24.712	26.940	29.369	32.015	34.895	49.153	9
10	10.950	12.006	13.181	14.487	15.937	17.549	19.337	21.321	23.521	25.959	28.657	31.643	34.945	38.593	42.619	47.062	69.814	10
11	12.169	13.486	14.972	16.645	18.531	20.655	23.045	25.733	28.755	32.150	35.962	40.238	45.031	50.398	56.405	63.122	98.739	11
12	13.412	15.026	16.870	18.977	21.384	24.133	27.271	30.850	34.931	39.581	44.874	50.895	57.739	65.510	74.327	84.320	139.235	12
13	14.680	16.627	18.882	21.495	24.523	28.029	32.089	36.786	42.219	48.497	55.746	64.110	73.751	84.853	97.625	112.303	195.929	13
14	15.974	18.292	21.015	24.215	27.975	32.393	37.581	43.672	50.818	59.196	69.010	80.496	93.926	109.612	127.913	149.240	275.300	14
15	17.293	20.024	23.276	27.152	31.772	37.280	43.842	51.660	60.965	72.035	85.192	100.815	119.347	141.303	167.286	197.997	386.420	15
16	18.639	21.825	25.673	30.324	35.950	42.753	50.980	60.925	72.939	87.442	104.935	126.011	151.377	181.868	218.472	262.356	541.988	16
17	20.012	23.698	28.213	33.750	40.545	48.884	59.118	71.673	87.068	105.931	129.020	157.253	191.735	233.791	285.014	347.309	759.784	17
18	21.412	25.645	30.906	37.450	45.599	55.750	68.394	84.141	103.740	128.117	158.405	195.994	242.585	300.252	371.518	459.449	1064.697	18
19	22.841	27.671	33.760	41.446	51.159	63.440	78.969	98.603	123.414	154.740	194.254	244.033	306.658	385.323	483.973	607.472	1491.576	19
20	24.297	29.778	36.786	45.762	57.275	72.052	91.025	115.380	146.628	186.688	237.989	303.601	387.389	494.213	630.165	802.863	2089.206	20
21	25.783	31.969	39.993	50.423	64.002	81.699	104.768	134.841	174.021	225.026	291.347	377.465	489.110	633.593	820.215	1060.779	2925.889	21
22	27.299	34.248	43.392	55.457	71.403	92.503	120.436	157.415	206.345	271.031	356.443	469.056	617.278	811.999	1067.280	1401.229	4097.245	22
23	28.845	36.618	46.996	60.893	79.543	104.603	138.297	183.601	244.487	326.237	435.861	582.630	778.771	1040.358	1388.464	1850.622	5737.142	23
24	30.422	39.083	50.816	66.765	88.497	118.155	158.659	213.978	289.494	392.484	532.750	723.461	982.251	1332.659	1806.003	2443.821	8032.999	24
25	32.030	41.646	54.865	73.106	98.347	133.334	181.871	249.214	342.603	471.981	650.955	898.092	1238.636	1706.803	2348.803	3226.844	11247.199	25
26	33.671	44.312	59.156	79.954	109.182	150.334	208.333	290.088	405.272	567.377	795.165	1114.634	1561.682	2185.708	3054.444	4260.434	15747.079	26
27	35.344	47.084	63.706	87.351	121.100	169.374	238.499	337.502	479.221	681.853	971.102	1383.146	1968.719	2798.706	3971.778	5624.772	22046.910	27
28	37.051	49.968	68.528	95.339	134.210	190.699	272.889	392.503	586.481	819.223	1185.744	1716.101	2481.586	3583.344	5164.311	7425.699	30366.674	28
29	38.792	52.966	73.640	103.966	148.631	214.583	312.094	456.303	669.447	984.068	1447.608	2128.965	3127.798	4587.680	6714.604	9802.923	43214.343	29
30	40.568	56.085	79.058	113.263	164.494	241.333	356.787	530.312	790.948	1181.882	1767.081	2640.916	3942.026	5873.231	8729.985	12940.859	60501.081	30
35	49.994	73.652	111.435	172.317	271.024	431.663	693.573	1120.713	1816.652	2948.341	4783.645	7750.225	12527.442	20188.966	32422.868	51869.427	325400.279	35
40	60.402	95.026	154.762	259.057	442.593	767.091	1342.025	2360.757	4163.213	7343.858	12936.535	22728.803	39792.982	69377.460	120392.883	207874.272	1750091.741	40

*Payments (or receipts) at the end of each period.

TABLE 4 (Place a clip on this page for easy reference.)
Present Value of Annuity $1.00 in Arrears.*

$$P_n = \frac{1}{r}\left[1 - \frac{1}{(1+r)^n}\right]$$

Periods	2%	4%	6%	8%	10%	12%	14%	16%	18%	20%	22%	24%	26%	28%	30%	32%	40%	Periods
1	0.980	0.962	0.943	0.926	0.909	0.893	0.877	0.862	0.847	0.833	0.820	0.806	0.794	0.781	0.769	0.758	0.714	1
2	1.942	1.886	1.833	1.783	1.736	1.690	1.647	1.605	1.566	1.528	1.492	1.457	1.424	1.392	1.361	1.331	1.224	2
3	2.884	2.775	2.673	2.577	2.487	2.402	2.322	2.246	2.174	2.106	2.042	1.981	1.923	1.868	1.816	1.766	1.589	3
4	3.808	3.630	3.465	3.312	3.170	3.037	2.914	2.798	2.690	2.589	2.494	2.404	2.320	2.241	2.166	2.096	1.849	4
5	4.713	4.452	4.212	3.993	3.791	3.605	3.433	3.274	3.127	2.991	2.864	2.745	2.635	2.532	2.436	2.345	2.035	5
6	5.601	5.242	4.917	4.623	4.355	4.111	3.889	3.685	3.498	3.326	3.167	3.020	2.885	2.759	2.643	2.534	2.168	6
7	6.472	6.002	5.582	5.206	4.868	4.564	4.288	4.039	3.812	3.605	3.416	3.242	3.083	2.937	2.802	2.677	2.263	7
8	7.325	6.733	6.210	5.747	5.335	4.968	4.639	4.344	4.078	3.837	3.619	3.421	3.241	3.076	2.925	2.786	2.331	8
9	8.162	7.435	6.802	6.247	5.759	5.328	4.946	4.607	4.303	4.031	3.786	3.566	3.366	3.184	3.019	2.868	2.379	9
10	8.983	8.111	7.360	6.710	6.145	5.650	5.216	4.833	4.494	4.192	3.923	3.682	3.465	3.269	3.092	2.930	2.414	10
11	9.787	8.760	7.887	7.139	6.495	5.938	5.453	5.029	4.656	4.327	4.035	3.776	3.543	3.335	3.147	2.978	2.438	11
12	10.575	9.385	8.384	7.536	6.814	6.194	5.660	5.197	4.793	4.439	4.127	3.851	3.606	3.387	3.190	3.013	2.456	12
13	11,348	9.986	8.853	7.904	7.103	6.424	5.842	5.342	4.910	4.533	4.203	3.912	3.656	3.427	3.223	3.040	2.469	13
14	12.106	10.563	9.295	8.244	7.367	6.628	6.002	5.468	5.008	4.611	4.265	3.962	3.695	3.459	3.249	3.061	2.478	14
15	12.849	11.118	9.712	8.559	7.606	6.811	6.142	5.575	5.092	4.675	4.315	4.001	3.726	3.483	3.268	3.076	2.484	15
16	13.578	11.652	10.106	8.851	7.824	6.974	6.265	5.668	5.162	4.730	4.357	4.033	3.751	3.503	3.283	3.088	2.489	16
17	14.292	12.166	10.477	9.122	8.022	7.120	6.373	5.749	5.222	4.775	4.391	4.059	3.771	3.518	3.295	3.097	2.492	17
18	14.992	12.659	10.828	9.372	8.201	7.250	6.467	5.818	5.273	4.812	4.419	4.080	3.786	3.529	3.304	3.104	2.494	18
19	15.678	13.134	11.158	9.604	8.365	7.366	6.550	5.877	5.316	4.843	4.442	4.097	3.799	3.539	3.311	3.109	2.496	19
20	16.351	13.590	11.470	9.818	8.514	7.469	6.623	5.929	5.353	4.870	4.460	4.110	3.808	3.546	3.316	3.113	2.497	20
21	17.011	14.029	11.764	10.017	8.649	7.562	6.687	5.973	5.384	4.891	4.476	4.121	3.816	3.551	3.320	3.116	2.498	21
22	17.658	14.451	12.042	10.201	8.772	7.645	6.743	6.011	5.410	4.909	4.488	4.130	3.822	3.556	3.323	3.118	2.498	22
23	18.292	14.857	12.303	10.371	8.883	7.718	6.792	6.044	5.432	4.925	4.499	4.137	3.827	3.559	3.325	3.120	2.499	23
24	18.914	15.247	12.550	10.529	8.985	7.784	6.835	6.073	5.451	4.937	4.507	4.143	3.831	3.562	3.327	3.121	2.499	24
25	19.523	15.622	12.783	10.675	9.077	7.843	6.873	6.097	5.467	4.948	4.514	4.147	3.834	3.564	3.329	3.122	2.499	25
26	20.121	15.983	13.003	10.810	9.161	7.896	6.906	6.118	5.480	4.956	4.520	4.151	3.837	3.566	3.330	3.123	2.500	26
27	20.707	16.330	13.211	10.935	9.237	7.943	6.935	6.136	5.492	4.964	4.524	4.154	3.839	3.567	3.331	3.123	2.500	27
28	21.281	16.663	13.406	11.051	9.307	7.984	6.961	6.152	5.502	4.970	4.528	4.157	3.840	3.568	3.331	3.124	2.500	28
29	21.844	16.984	13.591	11.158	9.370	8.022	6.983	6.166	5.510	4.975	4.531	4.159	3.841	3.569	3.332	3.124	2.500	29
30	22.396	17.292	13.765	11.258	9.427	8.055	7.003	6.177	5.517	4.979	4.534	4.160	3.842	3.569	3.332	3.124	2.500	30
35	24.999	18.665	14.498	11.655	9.644	8.176	7.070	6.215	5.539	4.992	4.541	4.164	3.845	3.571	3.333	3.125	2.500	35
40	27.355	19.793	15.046	11.925	9.779	8.244	7.105	6.233	5.548	4.997	4.544	4.166	3.846	3.571	3.333	3.125	2.500	40

*Payments (or receipts) at the end of each period.

Cost Accounting in Professional Examinations

This appendix describes the role of cost accounting in professional examinations. We use professional examinations in Canada, the United States, Australia, Japan, and the United Kingdom to illustrate the role. A conscientious reader who has solved a representative sample of the problems at the end of the chapters will be well prepared for the professional examination questions dealing with cost accounting. This appendix aims to provide perspective, instill confidence, and encourage readers to take the examinations.

CANADIAN PROFESSIONAL EXAMINATIONS

Three professional accounting designations are available in Canada:

Designation	Sponsoring Organization
Certified Management Accountant (CMA)	Society of Management Accountants (SMA)
Certified General Accountant (CGA)	Certified General Accountants' Association (CGA)
Chartered Accountant (CA)	Canadian Institute of Chartered Accountants (CICA)

The CMA represents over 40,000 certified management accountants, and 10,000 students and candidates employed globally in business, industry, and government.

To obtain certification, CMA applicants must have completed a university degree, passed the CMA entrance examination, and completed a two-year strategic leadership program simultaneously as they gain two years of appropriate work experience. Accounting, management, and strategy are the three pillars of the CMA program of certification.

The CMA is a competency-based program. The functional competencies include strategic risk management, risk management and governance, performance management and measurement, as well as financial management and reporting. Augmenting these are enabling competencies of problem solving and decision making, leadership and group dynamics, professionalism and ethical behaviour, and communication. Each competency can be tested progressively through four levels: acquisition, basic proficiency, advanced proficiency, and mastery. Detailed information may be accessed at www.cma-canada.org/index.cfm/ci_id/2544/la_id/1/document/1/re_id/0.

CMA Canada publishes *CMA: The Management Accounting Magazine* monthly. This magazine includes details of courses that assist students in preparing for the CMA examination.

AMERICAN PROFESSIONAL EXAMINATIONS

CPA AND CMA DESIGNATIONS

Many American readers may eventually take the Certified Public Accountant (CPA) examination or the Certified Management Accountant (CMA) examination. Certification is important to professional accountants for many reasons, such as the following:

1. Recognition of achievement and technical competence by fellow accountants and by users of accounting services
2. Increased self-confidence in one's professional abilities
3. Membership in professional organizations offering programs of career-long education
4. Enhancement of career opportunities
5. Personal satisfaction

The CPA certificate is issued by individual states; it is necessary for obtaining a state's licence to practise as a Certified Public Accountant. A prominent feature of public accounting is the use of independent (external) auditors to give assurance about the reliability of the financial statements supplied by managers. These auditors are called Certified Public Accountants in the United States and Chartered Accountants in many other English-speaking nations. The major U.S. professional association in the private sector that regulates the quality of external auditing is the American Institute of Certified Public Accountants (AICPA).

The CMA designation is offered by the Institute of Management Accountants (IMA). The IMA is the largest association of management accountants in the world. The major objective of the CMA certification is to enhance the development of the management accounting profession. In particular, focus is placed on the modern role of the management accountant as an active contributor to and a participant in management. The CMA designation is gaining increased stature in the business community as a credential parallel to the CPA designation.

The CMA examination is given in a computer-based format and has four parts. The questions are carefully constructed multiple-choice and written-response questions that test all levels of cognitive skills. The CMA exam consists of:

Part 1: Business Analysis
- Global Business
- Internal Controls
- Quantitative Methods
- Financial Statement Analysis
- Business Economics

Part 2: Management Accounting and Reporting
- Budget Preparation
- Cost Management
- Information Management
- Performance Measurement
- External Financial Reporting

Part 3: Strategic Management
- Strategic Planning
- Strategic Marketing

- ◆ Corporate Finance
- ◆ Decision Analysis
- ◆ Investment Decision Analysis

Part 4: Business Application
- ◆ All topics from Parts 1, 2, and 3, plus:
- ◆ Organization Management
- ◆ Organization Communication
- ◆ Behavioural Issues
- ◆ Ethical Considerations

A person who has successfully completed the U.S. CPA examination is exempt from Part 1. For more information, visit the IMA website at www.imanet.org.

Cost/management accounting questions are prominent in the CMA examination. The CPA examination also includes such questions, although they are less extensive than questions regarding financial accounting, auditing, and business law. On the average, cost/managerial accounting represents 35% to 40% of the CMA examination and 5% of the CPA examination. This book includes many questions and problems used in past CMA and CPA examinations. Careful study of appropriate topics in this book will give candidates sufficient background for succeeding in the cost accounting portions of the professional examinations.

The IMA publishes *Management Accounting* monthly. Each issue includes advertisements for courses that help students prepare for the CMA examination.

AUSTRALIAN PROFESSIONAL EXAMINATIONS

CPA Australia is the largest body representing accountants in Australia. Their professional designation is termed a CPA (Certified Practising Accountant). The basic entry requirement for Associate membership of the Society is an approved Bachelors degree. Associates of the Society can advance to CPA status by passing the CPA program and having the required amount of relevant work experience. There are three compulsory core segments in the program: Reporting and Professional Practice, Corporate Governance and Accountability, and Business Strategy and Leadership. Candidates must also take three of nine elective subjects. These subjects are assurance services and auditing, financial accounting, financial reporting and disclosure, financial risk management, insolvency and reconstruction, knowledge management, personal financial planning and superannuation, strategic management accounting, and taxation.

The strategic management accounting segment topics include:

1. Management accounting: supporting the value creation process
2. Creating organizational value
3. Managing performance measures
4. Techniques for managing value
5. Project management

INTHEBLACK, published monthly, includes advertisements for courses that help students prepare for the CPA examination.

The Institute of Chartered Accountants in Australia (ICAA) offers the Chartered Accountant (CA) certification that has membership requirements including passing five modules: Financial Accounting and Reporting, Management Accounting and Analysis, Audit and Assurance, Taxation, and Ethics and Business Application.

The *Management Accounting & Analysis* module includes topics such as forecasting and budgeting with decision tools, investment analysis tools and techniques, risk management, strategic planning and analysis, ethics, and performance reporting.

JAPANESE PROFESSIONAL EXAMINATIONS

There are two major management accounting organizations in Japan—Japanese Industrial Management and Accounting Association (JIMMA) and Enterprise Management Association. The JIMAA is the oldest, largest, and most authoritative accounting organization of its kind in Japan. It directs a School of Cost Control and a School of Corporate Tax Accounting. There are two courses in the School of Cost Control—Preparatory Course and Cost Control Course. These courses are taught by university professors and executives from member corporations. The Enterprise Management Association is the Japanese chapter of the U.S.-based Institute of Management Accountants.

The Japanese Institute of Certified Public Accountants (JICPA) is the organization of the CPA profession in Japan. The CPA exam, conducted by the Certified Public Accountants Board, consists of three stages. The second stage covers cost accounting.

UNITED KINGDOM PROFESSIONAL EXAMINATIONS

The Chartered Institute of Management Accountants (CIMA) is the largest professional management accounting body in the United Kingdom. CIMA provides a wide range of services to members in commerce, education, government, and the accounting profession.

The syllabus for the CIMA examination consists of three learning streams:

◆ *Business Management*: includes papers on organizational management and information systems, integrated management, and business strategy
◆ *Management Accounting*: includes papers on performance evaluation, decision making, and risk control and strategy
◆ *Financial Management*: includes papers on financial accounting and tax principles, financial analysis, and financial strategy.

Management Accounting, published monthly by CIMA, includes details of courses assisting students in preparing for their examinations. Management accounting topics are also covered by several other professional bodies. The syllabus for the examinations of the Association of Chartered Certified Accountants (ACCA) has three distinct parts. Skills examined include information for control, decision making, management, strategy, reporting, taxation, and overall strategic financial management.

Other accounting bodies include the Institute of Chartered Accountants in England and Wales (ICAEW) and the Institute for Chartered Accountants of Scotland (ICAS). Both Institutes have requirements that cover proficiency in "general management" topics as well as professional accounting topics.

a The coefficient, a is the value of y when $X = 0$ and it is a constant referred to as the intercept.

Abnormal spoilage   Spoilage that would not arise under efficient operating conditions; it is not inherent in a particular production process.

Absorption costing (or *full absorption costing*) A method of inventory valuation in which inventory "absorbs" both variable and fixed manufacturing costs as inventoriable costs, but all nonmanufacturing costs are classified as period costs.

Account analysis method   Cost accounts are classified in the ledger as variable, fixed, or mixed with respect to the cost driver.

Accounting rate of return   Also known as *accrual accounting rate of return (AARR)*, or *return on investment (ROI)*; an accounting measure of income divided by an accounting measure of investment.

Accrual accounting rate of return (AARR)   Also known as *accounting rate of return*, or *return on investment (ROI)*; An accounting measure of income divided by an accounting measure of investment.

Actions   Include choices made by management.

Activity   An event, task, or unit of work with a specified purpose.

Activity-based budgeting   A strategy to identify and control costs that focuses on the cost of activities necessary to produce and sell products and services.

Activity-based costing (ABC)   A refined costing system that focuses on activities as the fundamental cost objects.

Activity-based management (ABM)   A cost-leadership strategy to eliminate non-value-added activities, which are those activities failing to add value for which customers will pay.

Activity cost driver   In activity-based costing (ABC) systems, these are cost allocation bases.

Activity cost pool   The dollar value of the cost of activities at a specified level.

Activity cost rate   The activity cost pool divided by the total quantity consumed of the activity cost driver.

Activity level   The cost object that specifies the scope of changes in cost, which may cause a change in the cost of single units, batches, and entire products.

Actual cost   Cost incurred (a historical or past cost), as distinguished from a budgeted or forecasted cost.

Actual costing   Tracing direct costs to each job by multiplying each actual unit direct cost rate by the quantity of the direct input used.

Adjacencies   Opportunities to expand to markets related to the core business.

Adjusted r^2   Uses the ratio between the number of predictor variables and the number of observations to improve on the measure of r^2 for small samples.

Advance transfer price arrangement (APA)   A substitute for dispute resolution wherein the company and the tax authority can cooperate to prospectively agree on a transfer price method.

Agility   The ability for a service company to excel simultaneously in quality, delivery time, customization, and cost in a coordinated way.

Allowable cost   A cost that the contract parties agree to include in the costs to be reimbursed.

Appraisal costs   Costs incurred to detect which of the individual units of products do not conform to specifications.

Arm's-length principle   A transfer price should be the same as it would be if the two subunits were independent companies.

Arm's-length transactions   Transactions between a corporate subunit and a nonrelated party.

Artificial costs (also called *complete reciprocated costs*) The actual costs incurred by a support department plus a part of the costs of the other support departments that provide service to it.

Attention directing   Clarifying and sorting out situations that require management attention from those that do not.

Autocorrelation   A type of systematic dependence that arises when the current residual value depends upon the residual value either immediately prior (lagged) to it or immediately after (leading) it in time.

Average waiting time   The average amount of time that an order will wait in line before it is set up and processed.

b The value of b is the slope of the line.

Backflush costing   A costing system that omits recording some or all journal entries relating to the cycle from purchase of direct materials to the sale of finished goods.

Balanced scorecard (BSC)   A document that translates an organization's mission and strategy into a comprehensive set of performance measures that provide the framework for implementing its strategy.

Batch-level costs   Resources sacrificed on activities that are related to a group of units.

Bayesian decision models   Multi-stage mathematical models of the establishment and revision of probable outcomes conditioned by other outcomes.

Belief systems An articulation of the mission, purpose, and core values of a company.

Benchmarking A strategy of establishing ideal standards as the baseline against which to measure actual performance.

Book value The original acquisition cost of a long-term asset minus accumulated amortization.

Bottleneck An operation where the work required to be performed approaches or exceeds the available capacity.

Boundary systems An articulation of standards of behaviour and codes of conduct expected of all employees, especially actions that are off-limits.

Breakeven point (BEP) Quantity of output at which total revenues and total costs are equal; that is, where the operating income is zero.

Breakeven revenue Level of sales in dollars at which total revenues and total costs are equal; that is, where the operating income is zero.

Breakeven volume Level of sales in units at which total revenues and total costs are equal; that is, where the operating income is zero.

Budget A quantitative expression for a set time period of a proposed (future) plan of action by management.

Budget constraint The combination of limitations on nonfinancial and financial resources within a company's management control.

Budgetary slack The practice of underestimating budgeted revenues (or overestimating budgeted costs) to make budgeted targets easier to achieve.

Budgeted cost Predicted or forecasted cost (future cost) as distinguished from an actual or historical cost.

Budgeting cycle The process of budgeting: planning performance, providing a frame of reference, investigating variations from plans, and adjusting plans as necessary.

Bundled product A package of two or more products or services, sold for a single price, whose individual components may also be sold as separate items, each with its own stand-alone price.

Business function costs The sum of all the costs (variable costs and fixed costs) in a particular business function in the value chain.

Byproduct A product that has a low sales value compared with the sales value of the main or joint product(s).

Capacity The quantity of outputs that can be produced from long-term resources available to the company.

Capacity cost The cost of maintaining a certain plant capacity—a fixed overhead cost. It is often a cost pool grouping all fixed overhead costs.

Capital budgeting The process of collating information in a familiar pro forma financial accounting format.

Capital Cost Allowance (CCA) The legally required income tax counterpart to annual amortization expense in financial reporting.

Carrying costs These costs arise when a business holds inventories of goods for sale.

Cash budget A schedule of expected cash receipts and disbursements.

Cash cycle Also known as a *self-liquidating cycle*, *working capital cycle*, or *operating cycle*; the movement of cash to inventories, to receivables, and back to cash.

Cause-and-effect diagram A diagram that identifies potential causes of failures or defects.

Certified Management Accountant (CMA) The designation given by the Society of Management Accountants of Canada (SMAC) to management accountants who have passed admission criteria and demonstrated the competency of technical knowledge and skills required by the SMAC.

Chief financial officer (CFO) Also called the *finance director*, this is the senior officer empowered with overseeing the financial operations of an organization.

Choice criterion A reason to choose one alternative over another, which is usually based on an agreed-upon quantitative threshold or goal.

Coefficient of determination r^2 Measures the percentage of variation in an outcome variable explained by one or more predictor variables.

Coefficient matrix Summarizes the cost-allocation percentages to solve the equations of each complete reciprocated cost.

Collusive pricing Companies in an industry conspire in their pricing and output decisions to achieve a price above the competitive price.

Combined-variance analysis (also called *three-variance analysis*) Combines variable-cost and fixed-cost variances when reporting overhead cost variances.

Common cost A cost of operating a facility, operation, activity, or like cost object that is shared by two or more users.

Comparable uncontrolled price method (CUP) A transfer price that is analogous to the internal market-based price.

Complete reciprocated costs (also called *artificial costs*) The actual costs incurred by a support department plus a part of the costs of the other support departments that provide service to it.

Composite unit A hypothetical unit with weights based on the mix of individual units.

Conference method Develops cost estimates based on analysis and opinions gathered from various departments of an organization.

Confidence level The probability that the conclusion based on the student *t*-statistic is wrong.

Conformance quality The performance of a product or service according to design and production specifications.

Constant gross margin percentage NRV method The gross margin (based on the overall gross margin percentage) and separable costs deducted from the final sales value of units produced for each product. The residual amount for each product is its allocation of joint costs.

Constraint In linear programming techniques, a mathematical inequality or equality that must be satisfied by the variables in a mathematical model.

Continuous improvement A strategy whereby a budgeted cost is successively reduced over succeeding time periods.

Contribution income statement Income statement that groups line items by cost-behaviour pattern to highlight the contribution margin.

Contribution margin (TCM) Revenues minus all costs of the output (a product or service) that vary with respect to the number of output units.

Contribution margin percentage (CM%, contribution margin ratio) Contribution margin per unit divided by unit selling price, or total contribution margin divided by total revenue.

Control Coordinated action that companies take to implement their planning decisions, evaluate actual against expected performance, and provide timely feedback on current results.

Control chart Graphs a time series of successive observations of a particular step, procedure, or operation taken at regular time intervals. In addition to actual results, the expected range of specified results is also presented.

Controllability The degree of authority that a specific manager has over costs, revenues, or other items in question.

Controllable cost Any cost that is primarily subject to the authorization of a specific manager of a specific responsibility centre for a specific time span.

Controller The financial executive primarily responsible for both management accounting and financial accounting.

Controllership Providing financial information for both internal reports to managers and external reports to investors, as well as overseeing the overall operations of the accounting system.

Conversion cost Any manufacturing cost (may include direct labour) other than direct material cost.

Core or operating department (also called a *production department* in manufacturing companies) A department that adds value that is observable by a customer to a product or service.

Corporate governance Mandatory compliance with existing laws, regulations, and standards.

Corporate social responsibility The voluntary integration by companies of social and environmental concerns into their business operation.

Corporate sustainability A business approach that creates long-term shareholder value by embracing opportunities and managing risks deriving from economic, environmental, and social developments.

Correlation (or *covariance*) Identifies two events that systematically vary together.

Cost Resource sacrificed or forgone to achieve a specific objective.

Cost accounting Measures, analyzes, and reports financial and nonfinancial information relating to the costs of acquiring or using resources in an organization. It provides information for both management accounting and financial accounting.

Cost allocation (or *cost application*) A method to attribute or assign relevant indirect costs to each job.

Cost-allocation base An input factor that systematically links some proportion of each indirect cost pool to each job or cost object.

Cost-allocation rate A unit average cost of an input common to all jobs. It is the result of dividing a cost pool by its cost-allocation base.

Cost application (or *cost allocation*) A method to attribute or assign relevant indirect costs to each job.

Cost-application base A synonym for *cost-allocation base*.

Cost assignment The multiplication of the cost-allocation rate by the specific quantity of inputs in the denominator that is consumed by the specific job.

Cost-benefit approach Promotes decision making in which the perceived net benefits from spending corporate resources should exceed their perceived expected costs.

Cost centre A responsibility centre for which managers are accountable for costs only, not revenue lost or gained.

Cost cross-subsidization A result that arises when at least one miscosted product results in miscosting at least one other product in the organization.

Cost driver A variable, such as the level of activity or volume, that causally affects costs over a given time span.

Cost function Describes in arithmetic notation the relationship between factors and costs.

Cost incurrence Costs are incurred when a resource is sacrificed or consumed.

Cost hierarchy The name given to the management-accounting logic used to separate one indirect cost pool into one of four possible cost pools according to the level at which activities contribute to producing output.

Cost leadership An organization's ability to achieve low costs relative to competitors through productivity and efficiency improvements, elimination of waste, and tight cost control.

Cost management The approaches and activities of managers who undertake both short-run and long-run planning and control decisions to increase value to customers and to achieve organizational goals.

Cost object Anything for which it is desirable to measure the costs.

Cost of goods available for sale (COGAS) The accumulation of all costs incurred to manufacture the finished products that are available to be sold to customers.

Costs of goods manufactured (COGM) Cost of goods brought to completion, whether they were started before or during the current accounting period.

Costs of goods sold (COGS) The accumulation of all costs incurred to manufacture the finished products that have been sold during a specific time period.

Costs of sales (COS) The accumulated purchase costs for merchandise sold by merchandising companies.

Cost-plus method (CPM) A method of determining a transfer price that highlights the effect of the transfer price on the pretax income of each subunit.

Cost pool The accumulation of relevant costs from general ledger accounts.

Cost smoothing A costing system that spreads the costs of conversion and inputs uniformly.

Cost-volume-profit (CVP) Examines the behaviour of total revenues, total costs, and operating income as changes occur in the output level, selling price, variable costs per unit, or fixed costs; a single revenue driver and a single cost driver are used in this analysis.

Costs of design quality Costs incurred to prevent, or costs arising from, low quality of design.

Costs of quality (COQ)   Costs incurred to prevent or rectify the production of a low-quality product.

Critical value   A benchmark value for the student t-statistic such that if the calculated value of t for the values of the coefficients a, and b exceed the critical value, then at a specific confidence level, the values of a and b are not due to chance.

Cumulative average time learning model   Depicts a relationship such that the cumulative average time per unit declines by a constant percentage each time the cumulative quantity of units produced doubles.

Cumulative eligible capital (CEC)   This pool is the balance of the eligible capital property remaining after deducting CECA.

Cumulative eligible capital amount (CECA)   The annual CRA deduction permitted on intangible assets, calculated at 7% on a declining-balance basis.

Current cost   The cost of purchasing an asset today identical to the one currently held.

Cushion   Excess capacity.

Customer perspective   This perspective identifies the targeted market segments and measures the company's success in these segments.

Customer profitability analysis   The reporting and analysis of customer revenues and customer costs.

Customer-response time   The amount of time between when a customer places an order for a product or requests a service and when the product or service is delivered to the customer.

Customer service   Providing after-sale support to customers.

Decentralization   A strategic response made by organizations that enables individual discretion. Primarily useful to organizations that face great uncertainties in their diverse environments, require detailed local knowledge for performing various jobs, and have few interdependencies among subunits.

Decision model   Outlines formally how to make a choice using both quantitative and qualitative analysis.

Decision table   A summary of the contemplated actions, events, and probabilities of events, as well as outcomes, for each decision.

Degree of operating leverage   Contribution margin divided by operating income.

Delphic process   The process of having experts pool their expertise to agree on probabilities and other assumptions about the future.

Denominator-level variance   A production-volume or output-level variance equal to the difference between budgeted fixed overhead and the assigned fixed overhead for the actual quantity of outputs.

Design of products, services, or processes   The detailed planning and engineering of products, services, or processes.

Designed-in costs   (or *locked-in costs*) Costs that have not yet been incurred but that will be incurred in the future on the basis of decisions that have already been made.

Diagnostic control systems   Measures that help diagnose whether a company is performing to expectations.

Differential approach   This approach analyzes only relevant cash flows—those future cash outflows and inflows that differ between alternatives.

Differential cost   (or *net relevant cost*) The difference in total cost between two alternatives.

Differential revenue   The difference between the total revenue of two or more alternatives.

Direct cost   A cost related to a particular cost object that can be traced to that object in an economically feasible way.

Direct cost-allocation rate   The result of dividing a direct cost pool by the quantity of resources in the direct cost-allocation base (also called cost driver). It is a unit direct cost of an input.

Direct costing   Inaccurately describes the inventory costing (valuation) method we call *variable costing*.

Direct labour (DL)   The compensation of all period labour that can be traced to a cost object in an economically feasible way but are *not* part of cost of goods sold.

Direct manufacturing labour (DML)   The compensation of all manufacturing labour that can be traced to a cost object (work in process and then finished goods) in an economically feasible way.

Direct materials (DM)   Acquisition costs of all materials that eventually become part of the cost object (work in process and then finished goods), and that can be traced to the cost object in an economically feasible way.

Direct materials mix variance   The difference between two amounts: (1) the budgeted cost for the actual mix of the total quantity of direct materials used, and (2) the budgeted cost of the budgeted mix of the actual total quantity of direct materials used.

Direct materials yield variance   The difference between two amounts: (1) the budgeted cost of direct materials based on the actual total quantity of all direct materials inputs used, and (2) the flexible-budget cost of direct materials based on the budgeted total quantity of direct materials inputs for the actual output, holding the budgeted input mix constant.

Direct method   (also called the *direct allocation method*) Allocates each support department's costs directly to the operating departments.

Discount rate   Also known as *hurdle rate, (opportunity) cost of capital*, or *required rate of return (RRR)*; the minimum acceptable rate of return on an investment.

Discounted cash flow (DCF)   Two methods are net present value (NPV) and internal rate of return (IRR).

Discretionary costs   These costs arise from periodic (usually yearly) decisions regarding the maximum amount to be incurred; they have no clearly measurable cause-and-effect relationship between output and resources used.

Distribution   Delivering products or services to customers.

Downsizing (rightsizing)   An integrated approach to configure processes, products, and people to match costs to the activities needed to be performed to operate efficiently and effectively in the present and future.

Downward demand spiral   A progressive reduction in sales and production that leads to an increase in the fixed overhead rate. As sales decrease, the realized quantity in the denominator of any fixed overhead cost rate decreases but the fixed cost pool is constant. Diminishing sales must bear higher costs per unit, which leads to diminishing sales.

Dual pricing   Using two separate transfer pricing methods to price each interdivision transaction.

Dual-rate cost-allocation method This method first classifies costs in the cost pool into two pools (typically into a variable-cost pool and a fixed-cost pool), and each pool has a different allocation rate or base.

Dumping A non-Canadian company sells goods in Canada at a price below the market value in the home country or receives a government subsidy and this action materially injures or threatens to materially injure an industry in Canada.

Durbin-Watson statistic *d* Tests for the presence of serial correlation among residuals of a linear regression model using ordinary least squares (OLS).

Dysfunctional decision making Also known as *goal-incongruent decision making*, or *suboptimal decision making*; arises when a decision's benefit to one subunit is more than offset by the costs or loss of benefits to the organization as a whole.

Economic order quantity (EOQ) A decision model that calculates the optimal quantity of inventory to order.

Economic value added (EVA®) A calculation that substitutes the following numbers in the residual-income calculations: (1) income equal to after-tax operating income, (2) a required rate of return equal to the weighted-average cost of capital, and (3) investment equal to total assets minus current liabilities.

Effectiveness The degree to which a predetermined objective or target is met.

Efficiency The relative amount of inputs used to achieve a given level of output.

Efficiency variance The difference between the actual quantity of input used and the budgeted quantity of input that should have been used multiplied by the budgeted input price.

Effort Exertion towards a goal. Effort goes beyond physical exertion, such as a worker producing at a faster rate, to include all conscientious actions (physical and mental).

Eligible capital expenditure The acquisition cost of an intangible asset.

Eligible capital property 75% of the acquisition cost of an intangible asset.

Engineered costs These costs arise specifically from a clear cause-and-effect relationship between output (or cost driver) and the (direct or indirect) resources used to produce that output.

Enterprise resource planning (ERP) Systems that improve internal business process flows of information enabling effective inventory cost control.

Enterprise risk management (ERM) Aligns strategy with risk management and evaluates how management initiatives have improved the overall risk profile of the company.

Equivalent units (EU) Derived amount of output units that (a) takes the quantity of each input (factor of production) in units completed and in incomplete units of work in process and (b) converts the quantity of input into the amount of completed output units that could be produced with that quantity of input.

Estimated net realizable value (NRV) method A method that allocates joint costs on the basis of the *relative estimated net realizable value* (expected final sales value in the ordinary course of business minus the expected separable costs of production and marketing of the total production of the period).

Events Occurrences that management cannot control and often called externalities.

Excess present value index (or *profitability index*) The total present value of future net cash inflows of a project divided by the total present value of the net initial investment.

Exhaustive No event in addition to those specified can possibly occur.

Expected monetary value The sum of the weighted outcomes as measured in monetary terms.

Expected value The sum of multiplying each cash inflow, a_i, by the probability or $\sum_{a=1}^{i} E\,(a) = \sum (p_i) \times a_i$.

Experience curve A cost function that shows how full product costs per unit (including manufacturing, marketing, distribution, and so on) decrease as total quantity produced increases.

Explanatory variable(s) *X* (or *predictor variable*) Variables measured first for changes. Then associated changes are measured for the outcome variable *Y*.

External failure costs Costs incurred to detect a nonconforming product after it is shipped to customers.

Facility-sustaining costs The cost of activities that cannot be traced to individual products or services but support the organization as a whole.

Favourable (F) variance A favourable variance results when actual operating income exceeds the budgeted amount.

Finance director (or *chief financial officer*) The senior officer empowered with overseeing the financial operations of an organization.

Financial accounting Measures and records business transactions and provides financial statements that are based on generally accepted accounting principles. It focuses on reporting to external parties such as investors and banks.

Financial budget That part of the master budget that comprises the capital budget, cash budget, budgeted balance sheet, and budgeted statement of cash flows.

Financial perspective This perspective highlights achievement of financially strategic goals.

Fineness A characteristic of reliable information that enables users of that information to better predict how one factor will change with a change in another factor.

First-in, first-out (FIFO) process-costing method A method of process costing that assigns the cost of the previous accounting period's equivalent units in beginning work-in-process inventory to the first units completed and transferred out of the process, and assigns the cost of equivalent units worked on during the current period first to complete beginning inventory, next to start and complete new units, and finally to units in ending work-in-process inventory.

Fixed cost A cost that remains unchanged in total for a particular time period despite wide changes in the related level of total activity or volume.

Fixed overhead spending variance Indicates whether more or less was spent on fixed manufacturing overhead than the lump-sum pro forma (budgeted) amount.

Flexible budget A budget that is adjusted in accordance with ensuing changes in either actual output or actual revenue and cost drivers.

Flexible-budget variance The difference between the actual (realized) results and the flexible-budget (pro forma) amount for the actual levels of the revenue and cost drivers.

Full absorption costing A method of inventory valuation in which inventory "absorbs" both variable and fixed manufacturing costs as inventoriable costs, but all nonmanufacturing costs are classified as period costs.

Full product costs The sum of all the costs in all the business functions in the value chain (R&D, design, production, marketing, distribution, and customer service).

Goal-congruence Exists when individuals and groups work towards the publicly declared organization goals.

Goal-incongruent decision making Also known as *dysfunctional decision making*, or *suboptimal decision making*; arises when a decision's benefit to one subunit is more than offset by the costs or loss of benefits to the organization as a whole.

Goodness of fit The term statisticians use to describe the proportion of change in an outcome variable Y that is explained by a predictor variable X. r^2 is the statistic or measure of goodness of fit.

Governance A minimum compliance with laws, regulations, standards, conventions, traditions, and norms to avoid doing harm in pursuit of profit.

Gross margin Revenue minus cost of goods sold (or cost of sales); TRev – COGS (or COS).

Gross margin percentage (GM%) The result obtained from dividing the gross margin by the total revenue.

Half-year rule Assumes that all net additions are purchased in the middle of the year, and thus only one-half of the stated CCA rate is allowed in the first year.

Heteroskedasticity A systematic pattern between the size of the residuals and the predictor variable X.

High-low method Uses only the highest and lowest observed values of the common input within the relevant range. The line connecting these two points becomes the estimated cost function.

Homoskedasticity The value of the predictor variable X does not affect the residual value.

Hurdle rate Also known as *discount rate, (opportunity) cost of capital*, or *required rate of return (RRR)*; the minimum acceptable rate of return on an investment.

Hybrid-costing system Costing system that blends characteristics from both job-costing systems and process-costing systems.

Idle time Wages paid for unproductive time caused by lack of orders, machine breakdowns, material shortages, poor scheduling, and the like that interrupt production.

Imputed costs Costs recognized in particular situations that are not regularly recognized by accrual accounting procedures.

Incremental cost-allocation method This method ranks the individual cost objects and then uses this ranking to allocate costs among those cost objects.

Incremental costs Also known as *out-of-pocket costs*, or *outlay costs*; additional costs made to obtain either additional resources or sales.

Incremental revenue Any additional total revenue from one alternative.

Incremental revenue-allocation method A method that ranks the individual products in a bundle and then uses this ranking to allocate the bundled revenues to these individual products. The first-ranked product is termed the *primary product* in the bundle.

Incremental unit time learning model The incremental unit time (the time needed to produce the last unit) declines by a constant percentage each time the cumulative quantity of units produced doubles.

Indirect cost A cost related to a particular cost object that cannot be traced to that object in an economically feasible way.

Indirect cost-allocation rate The result of dividing an indirect cost pool by the quantity of resources in the indirect cost-allocation base. It is the estimated unit or average cost of indirect inputs.

Intermediate products Unfinished products transferred from one subunit to another subunit of the same organization in a multi-stage production process.

Inflation The decline in the general purchasing power of the monetary unit.

Infrastructure costs These costs arise from having property, plant, and equipment and a functioning organization.

Input-efficiency variance The difference between the actual quantity of input used and the budgeted quantity of input that should have been used multiplied by the budgeted input price.

Input-price variance The difference between the actual price and the budgeted price multiplied by the actual quantity of input in question.

Insource To produce goods or provide services within the organization.

Inspection point Stage of the production process at which products are examined to determine whether they are acceptable or unacceptable units. In the situation of process costing, spoilage is typically assumed to occur at the stage of completion where inspection takes place.

Intellectual capital This is comprised of human, structural, and relational capital.

Interactive control systems Formal information systems that managers use to focus organization attention and learning on key strategic issues.

Internal business process perspective This perspective requires analysis of how to improve internal operations, which implicates the entire value chain of business functions.

Internal failure costs Costs incurred to detect a nonconforming product before it is shipped to customers.

Internal rate of return (IRR) (or *time-adjusted rate of return*) The discount rate at which the present value of expected cash inflows from a project equals the present value of expected cash outflows of the project.

International financial centres Countries with very low income tax rates that have tax treaties with Canada.

Intrinsic motivation The desire to achieve self-satisfaction from good performance regardless of external rewards such as bonuses or promotion.

Inventoriable cost All costs of a product that are considered as assets in the balance sheet when they are incurred and that become cost of goods sold only when the product is sold.

Inventory management The planning, coordinating, and control activities related to the flow of inventory into, through, and from the organization.

Investment centre A responsibility centre for which managers are accountable for investments, revenues, and costs.

Investment decision Also known as *investment program*, or *investment project*; a long-term cash allocation decision.

Investment program Also known as *investment*, or *investment project*; A long-term cash allocation decision.

Investment project Also known as *investment*, or *investment program*; A long-term cash allocation decision.

Investor relations The function in a corporation that responds to and interacts with shareholders.

Job A distinct output unit or set of units.

Job cost record (or *job cost sheet*) The document where the costs for a job are recorded and accumulated. Jobs usually require some type of direct materials input.

Job cost sheet See *job cost record*.

Job costing system A system where costs are assigned to a distinct unit, or set of units, of a product or service called a job.

Joint products Products that have relatively high sales value but are not separately identifiable as individual products until the splitoff point.

Just-in-time (JIT) production (also called *lean production*) A demand-pull system in which each component in a production line is produced immediately as the next step in the production line needs the component.

Just-in-time (JIT) purchasing A strategy to purchase goods or materials such that a delivery immediately precedes demand or use.

Kaizen budgeting Budgeting to implement a strategy of systematic elimination of waste in every business process.

Key success factor A strategic factor that requires close attention and control to assure an organization will survive and thrive.

Labour time record A source document recording the type of labour, quantity of time, unit labour rate, and total cost of labour for each job.

Lean management Reducing or preferably eliminating those activities that fail to add value for customers.

Lean production (also called *JIT production*) A demand-pull system in which each component in a production line is produced immediately as the next step in the production line needs the component.

Learning and growth perspective A field of study on the identification, development, retention, and valuation of intellectual capital, which comprises human, structural, and relational capital.

Learning curve A curvilinear mathematical production function that shows how the ratio of quantity produced increases at a faster rate than the rate at which the time spent in activities of production decreases (Q_t output $\div$ Q_t DLH).

Life-cycle costing This process tracks and accumulates the actual costs attributable to each product from start to finish.

Line management Managers (for example, in production, marketing, or distribution) who are directly responsible for attaining the goals of the organization.

Linear cost function Can be depicted on a graph as a straight line of the equation $y = a + bX$.

Locked-in costs (or *designed-in costs*) Costs that have not yet been incurred but that will be incurred in the future on the basis of decisions that have already been made.

Main product One product with a high sales value relative to the other products that a single process yields.

Make/buy decision The decision whether to insource or outsource a business service or product.

Management accounting Measures, analyzes, and reports financial and nonfinancial information that helps managers make decisions to fulfill the goals of an organization. It focuses on internal reporting.

Management accounting control system (MACS) A system that provides relevant information as a basis for assurance of effective control.

Management by exception The practice of focusing management attention on areas not operating as expected (such as a cost overrun on a project) and giving less attention to areas operating as expected.

Manufacturing cells A grouping of all the different types of equipment used to make a given product.

Manufacturing cycle efficiency (MCE) The ratio of value-added manufacturing cycle time divided by the total manufacturing cycle time.

Manufacturing cycle time The sum of waiting time plus production cycle time.

Manufacturing lead time The sum of waiting time plus manufacturing time for the order.

Manufacturing overhead See *indirect cost*.

Margin of safety The excess of forecasted or budgeted revenues over the breakeven revenues.

Marginal income tax rate The tax rate paid on additional amounts of pretax income.

Market-share variance The difference between two amounts: (1) the budgeted amount based on actual market size in units, *actual market share*, and budgeted contribution margin per composite unit for the budgeted mix, and (2) the budgeted amount based on actual market size in units, *budgeted market share*, and budgeted contribution margin per composite unit for the budgeted mix.

Market-size variance The difference between two amounts: (1) the budgeted amount based on *actual market size in units*, budgeted market share, and budgeted contribution margin per composite unit for budgeted mix, and (2) the static budget amount based on the *budgeted market size in units*, budgeted market share, and budgeted contribution margin per composite unit for budgeted mix.

Marketing Promoting and selling products or services to customers or prospective customers.

Master budget Summarizes the financial projections of all the organization's individual schedules and sub-unit budgets required to produce an operating budget.

Master-budget capacity The level of output that will satisfy customer demand for a single budget cycle and complies with Canada Revenue Agency (CRA) for tax purposes.

Materials requirements planning (MRP) A demand push-through system that manufactures finished goods for inventory on the basis of demand forecasts.

Materials requisition record A source document recording the job for which materials are needed.

Matrix A way of succinctly communicating relevant information in rows and columns.

Moral hazard Describes contexts in which, once risk is shared, the individual fails to make as much effort to avoid harm as when risk was not shared.

Motivation The desire to attain a selected goal (the goal-congruence aspect) combined with the resulting drive or pursuit towards that goal (the effort aspect).

Multicollinearity When two or more predictor variables are highly correlated with each other.

Multiple linear regression The technique used to measure the strength of relationships among at least two predictor variables and the outcome variable.

Mutually exclusive Two (or more) events that cannot occur simultaneously.

Net addition Arises when the purchase price of new equipment exceeds proceeds of disposition of the old equipment.

Net income (NI) *Operating income* plus nonoperating revenues (such as interest revenue) minus nonoperating costs (such as interest cost) minus income taxes.

Net present value (NPV) method A method that calculates the expected net monetary gain or loss from a project by discounting all expected future cash inflows and outflows to the present point in time, using the required rate of return.

Net relevant cost or differential cost The difference in total cost between two alternatives.

Nominal rate of return The rate of return required to cover investment risk and the anticipated decline, due to inflation, in the general purchasing power of the cash that the investment generates.

Non-linear cost function Arises when, within the relevant range of production inputs, the graph of total costs with a single cost driver does not form a straight line.

Non-productive idle capacity A capacity level that incorporates downtime for setups.

Non-value-added activity An activity that fails to contribute to the customer's value proposition.

Non-value-added cost A cost that, if eliminated, would not reduce the value customers obtain from using the product or service.

Normal capacity The level of output that will satisfy average customer demand over a specified time period and complies with GAAP.

Normal costing The use of standard or predetermined or budgeted indirect cost-allocation rates to assign overhead costs but actual direct cost rates to assign direct costs.

Normal spoilage Spoilage inherent in a particular production process that arises even under efficient operating conditions; often a locked-in cost.

Normality Residual values are distributed normally.

Null hypothesis H_0 Will be rejected if, using an appropriate analysis, the data fail to meet a benchmark value.

Objective function The objective or goal to be maximized expressed by a linear program.

Off-limits idle capacity A capacity level that accounts for unavoidable operating interruptions such as scheduled maintenance time, shutdowns for holidays, safety inspections, and so on.

On-time performance Situations in which the product or service is actually delivered at the time it is scheduled to be delivered.

Operating budget (or *pro forma net income statement*) When the income statement refers to the future and not the past, it is an *operating budget*, also referred to as a *pro forma net income statement*. The operating budget presents the results of operations in many value-chain business functions prior to financing and taxes.

Operating cycle Also known as a *self-liquidating cycle*, *working capital cycle*, or *cash cycle*; the movement of cash to inventories, to receivables, and back to cash.

Operating department Or *core department* (also called a *production department* in manufacturing companies) A department that adds value that is observable by a customer to a product or service.

Operating income (OI) Total revenues from operations minus total costs from operations (excluding interest and income tax expenses) including inventoriable and period costs.

Operating leverage The effects that different fixed costs (FC) have on changes in operating income (OI) as changes occur in the quantity (Q) available and sold, and hence either the unit or total contribution margin.

Operating Margin (OM, operating margin percentage) The result obtained from dividing the operating income by the total revenue.

Operation A standardized method or technique that is performed repetitively, often on different materials, resulting in different finished goods. Operations are usually conducted within departments.

Operation-costing system A hybrid-costing system applied to batches of similar, but not identical, products. Each batch of products is often a variation of a single design, and it proceeds through a sequence of operations, but each batch does not necessarily move through the same operations as other batches. Within each operation, all product units use identical amounts of the operation's resources.

Opportunity cost The contribution to income that is forgone (rejected) by not using a limited resource in its next-best alternative use.

Opportunity cost of capital Also known as *discount rate*, *hurdle rate*, or *required rate of return (RRR)*; the minimum acceptable rate of return on an investment.

Optimization technique A way to find the best answer using a mathematical model.

Order delivery time The time it takes distribution to pick up the order from manufacturing and deliver it to the customer.

Order receipt time The time it takes the Marketing Department to send engineering and other specifications to the Manufacturing Department.

Ordering costs The costs to prepare and issue a purchase order.

Ordinary least squares regression A method that computes a formal measure of goodness of fit, called the *coefficient of determination*.

Organic revenue Growth obtained without mergers or acquisitions.

Organizational structure An arrangement of centres of responsibility within an entity.

Out-of-pocket costs Also known as *incremental costs*, or *outlay costs*; additional costs made to obtain either additional resources or sales.

Outcome variable Any value (Y), that increases and decreases after a change in the value of another factor (X).

Outcomes Refer to the company and are uncertain if they are possible-but-unidentified consequences from different combinations of actions and events.

Outlay costs Also known as *incremental costs*, or *out-of-pocket costs*; additional costs made to obtain either additional resources or sales.

Outliers Actual observations outside the specified limits that are ordinarily regarded as nonrandom and worth investigating.

Output level overcosting A unit, batch, or product consumes a relatively low level of input materials and conversion activities but is reported to have a relatively high total cost.

Output-level overhead variance A production-volume or denominator-level variance equal to the difference between budgeted fixed overhead and the assigned fixed overhead for the actual quantity of outputs.

Output level undercosting A unit, batch, or product consumes a relatively high level of input materials and conversion activities but is reported to have a relatively low total cost.

Output unit-level costs Costs that arise when activities contribute to the cost of each unit of a product or service.

Outsource The process of purchasing goods and services from outside vendors rather than producing the same goods or providing the same services within the organization.

Overallocated indirect costs (*overapplied indirect costs*, *overabsorbed indirect costs*) Costs that occur when the allocated amount of indirect costs in an accounting period is greater than the actual (incurred) amount in that period.

Overtime cost Cost of wages paid to workers (for both direct labour and indirect labour) in excess of their straight-time wages.

Padding The practice of underestimating budgeted revenues (or overestimating budgeted costs) to make budgeted targets easier to achieve.

Paralysis by analysis A phrase that describes situations where managers delay making a decision because they decide to wait for more information.

Pareto diagram (frequency chart) This diagram indicates how frequently each type of failure (defect) occurs.

Pareto principle Expresses materiality in a straightforward way—for many events, 80% of effects arise from 20% of the causes.

Partial productivity This most frequently used productivity measure compares the quantity of output produced with the quantity of an individual input used.

Payback method A method that measures the time it will take to recoup, in the form of net cash inflows, the net initial investment in a project.

Peak-load pricing The practice of charging a higher price for the same product or service when demand approaches physical capacity limits.

Peanut butter costing A costing system that spreads the costs of conversion and inputs uniformly.

Perfectly competitive market Exists when there is a homogeneous product with equivalent buying and selling prices and no individual buyers or sellers can affect those prices by their own actions.

Period costs All costs incurred to generate revenue during a specific time period except the costs of manufacturing accumulated as cost of goods sold.

Perverse incentive Rewards inappropriate management behaviour to present the appearance of cost-effective performance instead of to achieve actual cost-effective performance.

Physical measure method This method allocates joint costs on the basis of their relative proportions at the splitoff point, using a common physical measure such as weight or volume of the total production of each product.

Planning Selecting organizational goals, predicting results under various ways of achieving those goals, deciding how to attain the desired goals, and communicating the goals and how to attain them to the entire organization.

Practical capacity The amount of output possible if idle time for maintenance, safety inspections, and holidays is scheduled.

Predatory pricing A company sells products at unreasonably low prices that either tend to substantially lessen competition or were designed to have that effect.

Predictor variable(s) X Measured first for changes then associated changes are measured for the outcome variable Y.

Prevention costs Costs incurred to preclude the production of products that do not conform to specifications.

Previous department costs (or *transferred-in costs*) Costs incurred in previous departments that are carried forward as the product's costs when it moves to a subsequent process in the production cycle.

Price discounting The reduction of selling prices below listed levels to encourage an increase in purchases by customers.

Price discrimination The practice of charging some customers a higher price than is charged to other customers.

Price variance The difference between the actual price and the budgeted price multiplied by the actual quantity of input in question.

Prime cost May include only direct materials, or may include all direct manufacturing costs including direct labour.

Prior probability The conditional probability assigned to an expected outcome.

Pro forma income statement Classifies and reports predicted revenue and costs in the standardized format of a financial accounting income statement.

Pro forma net income statement See *operating budget*.

Probability Likelihood an actual or realized value, event or outcome will differ from an expected or budgeted value, event, or outcome.

Probability distribution The likelihood or probability that each of the mutually exclusive and exhaustive set of events will occur.

Problem solving Comparative analysis to reduce the scope of and identify the best available alternatives to achieve the company's goals.

Process costing system A system where costs are assigned to masses of similar units produced during a specific time period.

Product Any output that has a positive sales value (or an output used internally that enables an organization to avoid incurring costs).

Product cost Sum of the costs assigned to a product for a specific purpose.

Product differentiation A company's ability to offer products or services perceived by its customers as being superior and unique relative to those of its competitors.

Product life cycle From the viewpoint of the producer, the product life cycle spans the time from initial R&D to the time at which support to customers is withdrawn.

Product-sustaining costs (or *service-sustaining costs*) Resources sacrificed on activities undertaken to support product lines, not batches of product lines or units of product.

Production Acquiring, coordinating, and assembling resources to produce a product or deliver a service.

Production cost Cost of acquiring, coordinating, and assembling resources to produce a product or deliver a service.

Production denominator level (or *Production denominator volume*) A measure of capacity. The denominator can be one of four choices.

Production department (or *core or operating department*) In manufacturing companies, a department that adds value that is observable by a customer to a product or service.

Production-volume variance A denominator-level or output-level variance equal to the difference between budgeted fixed overhead and the assigned fixed overhead for the actual quantity of outputs.

Productivity Measurement of the relationship between actual inputs used (both quantities and costs) and actual outputs produced.

Profit centre A responsibility centre for which managers are accountable for revenues and costs and have some authority over others who decide upon key factors affecting both revenue and cost.

Profit split method (PSM) A transactional profit method of setting a transfer price that requires understanding the value added by the functions performed by each related party and the resulting allocation of profit and loss to each subunit.

Profit-volume (PV) graph Shows how changes in the quantity of units sold affect operating income.

Profitability index (or *excess present value index*) The total present value of future net cash inflows of a project divided by the total present value of the net initial investment.

Proration An allocation method that uses the percentages of manufacturing overhead allocated based on normal costing to allocate the underallocation or overallocation among the relevant accounts.

Purchase order lead time The time between the placement of an order and its delivery.

Purchasing costs The acquisition costs of goods acquired from suppliers including freight in, the transportation costs.

Qualitative factors Outcomes that cannot be measured in numerical terms.

Quality of design Measures how closely the characteristics of products or services match the needs and wants of customers.

Quantitative factors Outcomes that are measured in numerical terms.

Rate of return (ROR) The ratio of the predicted cost inflow minus outflow divided by the total outflow for the investment.

Rate variance The difference between the actual price and the budgeted price multiplied by the actual quantity of input in question.

Real rate of return The rate of return required to cover only investment risk.

Real-time data Instantaneous and continuous data about process parameters such as temperature and pressure that must be maintained within tight ranges.

Reciprocal allocation method Allocates costs by explicitly including the mutual services provided among all support departments.

Reengineering The fundamental rethinking and redesign of business processes to achieve improvements in critical measures of performance such as cost, quality, service, speed, and customer satisfaction.

Related parties Corporate subunits conducting sales activity between one another.

Relevant costs Forecast future costs that *differ* because of a decision.

Relevant information Information that will change a decision.

Relevant range Band of normal activity level or volume in which there is a specific relationship between the level of activity or volume and the cost in question.

Relevant revenues Forecast future revenues that *differ* because of a decision.

Refined costing system A costing system that results in a better measure of the nonuniformity in the use of an organization's resources by products and customers.

Regression analysis The name of one standard series of mathematical manipulations used to analyze two sets of data recorded from past events.

Regression line Comprises the actual historical values of X with the predicted values of y obtained from the statistical analysis.

Reorder point The quantity level of the inventory on hand that triggers a new order.

Required rate of return (RRR) Also known as *discount rate, hurdle rate,* or *(opportunity) cost of capital*; the minimum acceptable rate of return on an investment.

Resale price method (RPM) This transaction method requires a company calculate the arm's-length resale price.

Research and development (R&D) Generating and experimenting with ideas related to new products, services, or processes.

Residual income (RI) Income minus a required dollar return on the investment.

Residual term u Also called the *disturbance* or the *error* term. The residual is calculated as $u = Y - y$ and graphically it appears as the vertical deviation of the actual data point (X,Y) from the estimated data point (X,y).

Response variable (or *outcome variable*) Any value (Y), that increases and decreases after a change in the value of another factor (X).

Responsibility accounting A system that measures the plans (by budgets) and actions (by actual results) of each responsibility centre.

Responsibility centre A part, segment, or sub-unit of an organization whose manager is accountable for a specified set of activities.

Return on investment (ROI) Also known as *accounting rate of return*, or *accrual accounting rate of return (AARR)*; an accounting measure of income divided by an accounting measure of investment.

Return on sales (ROS) The income-to-revenue (sales) ratio and a frequently used financial performance measure.

Return on supply-chain assets (ROSCA) A cost-benefit ratio that measures the difference between revenue arising from incremental sales obtained by using the supply chain minus the expenses (often sacrificed profit margin) of the supply chain divided by the assets in which the company has invested to use the supply chain.

Revenue An actual or promised inflow of assets, most often cash or accounts receivable, received for products or services provided to customers.

Revenue centre A responsibility centre for which managers are accountable for revenues only, not costs incurred to generate the revenues.

Revenue driver Any factor that affects revenues.

Revenue mix (or *sales mix*) The relative contribution of quantities of products or services that constitutes total revenues.

Reworked units Units of production that do not meet the specifications required by customers for finished units that are subsequently repaired and sold as good finished units.

Rightsizing (or *downsizing*) An integrated approach to configure processes, products, and people to match costs to the activities needed to be performed to operate efficiently and effectively in the present and future.

Risk The probability that actual future results will differ from budgeted or expected results. Risk is uncertainty quantified as a probability.

Rolling budget A budget or plan that is always available for a specified future period by adding a month, quarter, or year in the future as the month, quarter, or year just ended is dropped.

Safety stock Inventory held at all times regardless of inventory ordered using EOQ.

Sales mix The relative contribution of quantities of products or services that constitutes total revenues.

Sales-mix variance The difference between two amounts: (1) the budgeted amount for the actual sales mix and (2) the budgeted amount for the budgeted sales mix.

Sales-quantity variance The difference between two amounts: (1) the budgeted contribution margin based on actual units sold of all products and the budgeted mix, and (2) the contribution margin in the static budget (which is based on the budgeted units to be sold of all products and the budgeted mix).

Sales value at splitoff method This method allocates joint costs on the basis of the relative sales value at the splitoff point of the total production in the accounting period for each product.

Sales-volume variance The difference between the flexible-budget amount and the static-budget amount; unit selling prices, unit variable costs, and fixed costs are held constant.

Sarbanes-Oxley Act A law that took effect in the US in 2002 and that is the US equivalent of Canada's MI52-109.

Scorekeeping Accumulating data and reporting reliable results to all levels of management.

Scrap Outputs that have minimal sales value, or, residual material left over when making a product. Some outputs can have a negative revenue when their disposal costs are considered.

Self-liquidating cycle Also known as a working *capital cycle*, *cash cycle*, or *operating cycle*; the movement of cash to inventories, to receivables, and back to cash.

Selling-price variance The difference between the actual selling price and the budgeted selling price of a good or service.

Sensitivity analysis Uses percentage changes to understand what changes cause the largest effect on profit.

Separable costs Costs incurred beyond the splitoff point that can be assigned to one or more individual products.

Sequential allocation method Often called the *step-down* or *step allocation method*; allows for *partial* recognition of the services rendered by support departments to other support departments.

Sequential tracking (or *synchronous tracking*) Any product costing method in which the accounting system entries occur in the same order as actual purchases and production.

Serial correlation Present when a residual value at one point in time differs systematically from the residual value at another point in time.

Service department (or *support department*) Provides the services that maintain other internal departments (operating departments and other support departments) in the organization.

Service-sustaining costs Resources sacrificed on activities undertaken to support service lines, not batches of service lines or units of service.

Shrinkage costs Costs that arise from theft, embezzlement, misclassifications, and clerical errors.

Single-rate cost-allocation method Pools all costs in one cost pool and allocates them to cost objects using the same rate per unit of the single allocation base.

Society of Management Accountants of Canada (SMAC) The largest association of management accountants in Canada.

Source document An original record, such as a time sheet for an employee where the hours worked per job are recorded as well as the cost per hour.

Specific production-volume variance A production-volume variance that results from choosing a particular denominator to represent capacity.

Specification analysis The process of testing four assumptions of the quality of input data used in regression analysis.

Splitoff point The juncture in the process when one or more products in a joint cost setting become separately identifiable.

Spoilage Units of production that do not meet the specifications required by customers for good units and that are discarded or sold at reduced prices. Partially completed or fully completed units of output may be spoiled.

Staff management Staff, such as management accountants and human resources managers, who provide advice and assistance to line management.

Stand-alone cost-allocation method Uses information pertaining to each cost object as a separate operating entity to determine the cost-allocation weights.

Stand-alone revenue-allocation method An allocation method that uses product-specific information pertaining to products in the bundle to determine the weights used to allocate the bundled revenues to those individual products. The term *stand-alone* refers to the product as a separate (nonsuite) item.

Standard   A carefully determined price, cost, or quantity used for judging performance; frequently refers to amounts estimated from either engineering or time-motion studies. Standard and budgeted amounts are often interchangeable for the purpose of calculating variance.

Standard cost   A carefully predetermined cost. Standard costs can relate to units of inputs or units of outputs.

Standard input   A carefully predetermined quantity of inputs (such as kilograms of materials or hours of labour time) required for one unit of output.

Static budget   A budget that is based on one level of output; it is not adjusted or altered after it is set, regardless of ensuing changes in either actual output or actual revenue and cost drivers.

Statistically significant   The value of the coefficients *a* and *b* are probably different from random values.

Step-down allocation method   Sometimes called the *step allocation method*, or *sequential allocation method*; allows for *partial* recognition of the services rendered by support departments to other support departments.

Step variable cost function   A function in which the cost is constant over various ranges of the predictor variable, but the cost increases by discrete amounts (that is, in steps) as the range of the predictor variable changes from one set of values to another set of values.

Stockout costs   Costs that occur when a company runs out of an item for which there is customer demand.

Strategic analysis   Evaluation of how well an organization has combined its own capabilities with the competitive environment to progress towards its future.

Strategic management   Cost management that focuses on strategic issues.

Strategy   Specifies how an organization matches its own capabilities with the opportunities in the marketplace to accomplish its objectives.

Student *t*-statistic   The ratio of how large the estimated value of the coefficient is relative to its standard error.

Suboptimal decision making   Also known as *dysfunctional decision making*, or *goal-incongruent decision making*; arises when a decision's benefit to one subunit is more than offset by the costs or loss of benefits to the organization as a whole.

Sullivan Principles   A set of principles that can be used to compare corporate performance in the area of social responsibility.

Sunk costs   Past costs that cannot be changed, no matter what action is taken.

Super-variable costing   (or *throughput costing*) A costing method that treats all costs except variable direct materials as period costs that are expensed when they are incurred. Only variable direct materials costs are inventoriable.

Supply-chain strategy   A strategy that transforms external suppliers into internal partners with the buyer.

Support department   (or *service department*) Provides the services that maintain other internal departments (operating departments and other support departments) in the organization.

Supply chain   An integrated system of suppliers, subcontractors, manufacturers, distributors, and retailers collaborating with the purpose of adding value to the output for the customer.

Target cost per unit   The estimated long-run cost per unit of a product (or service) that, when sold at the target price, enables the company to achieve the target operating income per unit.

Target operating income per unit   The operating income that a company wants to earn on each unit of a product (or service) sold.

Target price per unit   The estimated price for a product or service that potential customers will pay.

Target rate of return on investment (ROI)   The target operating income that an organization must earn divided by invested capital.

Tax   Fees levied by various levels of government; includes income taxes, sales taxes, and domestic and international tax planning.

Tax havens   Countries that have no tax agreements with Canada and share no information, which will increase the costs of any tax audit for the company.

Tax shield formula   An efficient way to calculate the present value of the tax savings as a result of deducting CCA.

Theoretical capacity   The amount of output theoretically possible if there were never any delays or interruptions; a 24/7/365 quantity.

Theory of constraints (TOC)   This theory describes methods to maximize operating income when faced with some bottleneck and some nonbottleneck operations.

Throughput costing   (or *super-variable costing*) A costing method that treats all costs except variable direct materials as period costs that are expensed when they are incurred. Only variable direct materials costs are inventoriable.

Time-adjusted rate of return   (or *internal rate of return (IRR)*) The discount rate at which the present value of expected cash inflows from a project equals the present value of expected cash outflows of the project.

Time driver   Any factor where change in the factor causes a change in the speed with which an activity is undertaken.

Tobin's q   The sum of the balance sheet value of debt, plus all equity divided by the total assets.

Total channel cost   The sum of the costs to the supplier and the buyer.

Total costs   The sum of all variable plus all fixed costs; TVC = TVC + FC.

Total factor productivity (TFP)   The ratio of the quantity of output produced to the costs of all inputs used, where the inputs are combined on the basis of current period prices.

Total fixed costs (FC)   The sum of all costs that remain unchanged in total for a given time period, despite wide changes in the related level of total activity or volume.

Total-project approach   Calculates the present value of *all* future cash inflows and outflows under each alternative separately.

Total variable costs (TVC)   The sum of all costs that change in total in proportion to changes in the related level of total activity or volume. Calculated by multiplying the quantity of input by its unit cost (or price).

Traditional costing   Also known as *cost smoothing*, or *peanut butter costing*; a costing system that spreads the costs of conversion and inputs uniformly.

Transactional net margin method (TNMM) A transactional profit method of setting a transfer price that is based on the return on assets (ROA) of the corporation as a whole and provides maximum discretion for establishing a transfer price.

Transfer price The price one subunit of an organization charges for a product (tangible or intangible) or service supplied to another subunit of the same organization.

Transferred-in costs (or *previous department costs*) Costs incurred in previous departments that are carried forward as the product's costs when it moves to a subsequent process in the production cycle.

Treasury The department responsible for short-term and long-term financing and investments, banking, and cash, foreign exchange, and derivatives management.

Triple bottom line This type of reporting is a formal response to the Global Reporting Initiative (GRI) and augments standard financial reports with specific environmental and social sustainability reports.

Unamortized capital cost (UCC) The balance of a capital expenditure after the allowable CCA has been deducted.

Uncertainty The possibility that an actual amount will deviate from an expected amount.

Underallocated indirect costs (*underapplied indirect costs, underabsorbed indirect costs*) Costs that occur when the allocated amount of indirect costs in an accounting period is less than the actual (incurred) amount in that period.

Unfavourable (U) variance A variance that results in an actual operating income that is less than the budgeted amount.

Unit contribution margin (UCM) The selling price per unit less the variable costs per unit; UCM = USP − UVC.

Usage variance The difference between the actual quantity of input used and the budgeted quantity of input that should have been used multiplied by the budgeted input price.

Value The usefulness a customer gains from a company's good or service.

Value-added activity An activity that contributes directly to the customer's value proposition.

Value-added cost A cost that, if eliminated, would reduce the value customers obtain from using the product or service.

Value analysis With the purpose of reducing costs, an analysis that focuses on the product design stage, where there is the greatest opportunity to change design, materials, and manufacturing processes.

Value chain The sequence of business functions in which customer usefulness is added to products or services.

Value engineering An analysis of the entire value chain of all business functions to determine where non-value-added costs can be eliminated.

Value proposition A distinct benefit for which customers will pay.

Variable cost A cost that changes in total in proportion to changes in the related level of total activity or volume.

Variable-cost percentage Total variable costs (with respect to the quantity (Q) units available and sold) divided by total revenue.

Variable costing A method of inventory valuation in which only *variable manufacturing* costs are included as inventoriable costs. All fixed and all nonmanufacturing costs are classified as period costs expensed during the specific time period they are incurred.

Variable overhead efficiency variance A measure of the efficiency with which the cost allocation base is used.

Variable overhead spending variance The difference between actual variable overhead cost per unit of the cost-allocation base and budgeted variable overhead cost per unit of the cost-allocation base.

Variance The difference between actual (realized) and budgeted (pro forma) results.

Variance analysis An exceptions-based approach to management.

Vector A matrix with one or more rows and one single column.

Vertical integration A company that incorporates as much of the value chain as possible within itself is vertically integrated.

Weighted-average cost of capital (WACC) Equals the after-tax average cost of all the long-term funds used.

Weighted-average process-costing method Method of process costing that assigns the equivalent-unit cost of the work done to date (regardless of the accounting period in which it was done) to equivalent units completed and transferred out of the process and to equivalent units in ending work-in-process inventory.

Working capital cycle Also known as a *self-liquidating cycle, cash cycle,* or *operating cycle*; the movement of cash to inventories, to receivables, and back to cash.

estimated net realizable value (NRV) method, 748–750, 748f
fairness criterion, 698, 700
fairness of pricing, 721–722
fixed overhead cost variances, 364–373
governance issues, 709
guidelines, 724
homogeneous cost pool, 705
inaccurate cost-allocation procedures, 154
incremental cost-allocation method, 720–721
indirect cost-allocation rate, 144
indirect cost pool allocation procedure, 158–161
indirect costs, choices related to, 703–705
joint cost allocation. See joint cost allocation
linear equation method, 714–715, 715f
matrix algebra method, 716–718
mechanical aspect of, 144
and net income, 831
period cost allocations to operating divisions, 709
period costs, 696, 698f
physical measure method, 744–748, 747f, 753, 755–756
predetermined indirect cost-allocation rates, 163
process cost allocation. See process costing
product or process, 702f
purposes of, 696–701
reciprocal allocation method, 714, 715f–716f
reimbursement costs, 721
relevance criterion, 698–699
sales value at splitoff method, 746, 747f
selection of cost allocation base, 373
sequential allocation method, 712–713, 713f
single-rate cost-allocation method, 706–707
stand-alone cost-allocation method, 720
standard cost-allocation rates, 163
step-down allocation method, 712–713, 713f
support costs allocated to operating divisions, 706–709
support costs allocated to other departments, 710–720
support department cost allocation, 701–705, 719–720
under- and over-allocation of indirect costs, 166–172
cost-allocation bases, 144
see also cost allocation
corporate *vs.* division, 702–703
as cost driver, 699
multiple cost-allocation bases, 162
percentages, in six countries, 162
process costing, 835–836
and regression analysis, 498
selection of, 152
cost-allocation rate, 144
cost application, 144
cost-application base, 144
cost assignment, 145
for direct cost pool, 150f
as fiduciary duty, 219
materially inaccurate cost assignment, 151
cost-based transfer prices
dual pricing, 1109
full-cost bases, 1106–1108

generally, 1100
prorating difference between minimum and maximum transfer prices, 1108
usefulness of, 1106
variable cost bases, 1108
cost behaviour
average fixed costs, 59f
fixed costs, 55–58, 57f, 465f
major assumptions, 55–59
mixed cost, 465f
production-volume allocated cost behaviour, 370f
total inventoriable costs, 57f
variable costs, 55–58, 57f, 465f
cost-benefit approach, 14
cost-benefit considerations, 699–700
cost centre, 274
cost classification
activity-based costing, 325
different costs for different purposes, 60–62
direct and indirect costs, 42–45
financial-cost classifications, 38f
fixed costs *vs.* variable costs, 54–55
flexibility in, 50, 53
governance issues, 53
and imaginary costs, 53
labour cost classification, 50
logics of, 35, 36
management-cost classifications, 38f
period and inventoriable costs, 36–42
prime costs and conversion costs, 45–47
strategy, 47–49
two-part classification systems, 47
cost-control-problems, 60, 62
cost cross-subsidization, 203–205, 204f
cost drivers, 54
and activity-based costing (ABC), 483
activity cost drivers, 208, 211
cost-allocation base, 699
generally, 54–55
multiple cost drivers, 114–115
number of units manufactured, 310
number of units sold, 310
variable cost driver, 88
cost effect
of growth, 665
of price recovery, 666
cost function, 468
see also quantitative analyses of cost functions; statistics
curvilinear cost functions, 494
data collection and adjustment issues, 481–483
estimate of, 481, 487–489
linear cost function, 468
non-linear cost function, 484, 484f
nonlinear cost functions, 489–494
step fixed cost function, 484–487
step variable cost function, 484–485
types of, 482, 482f
cost hierarchy, 207
customer cost analysis, 806
customer-cost hierarchy, 807
and management-accounting logic, 207–210
and multiple linear regression, 498–500
cost incurrence, 596–597
cost-incurrence curve, 597, 598f

cost leadership, 99, 140, 478, 490, **657**
cost management, 3–4, 55
broad focus, 4
cost classification as accounting logic, 35
generally, 55
strategic cost management, 389
cost-mix and yield level 4 variances, 796–798
cost object, 41, 140
activity level, 202
in job costing system, 141
in process costing, 833
use of, 42
cost of capital, 1013, 1142
cost of design quality, 931
cost of goods available for sale (COGAS), 37
cost of goods manufactured (COGM), 37
cost of goods sold budget, 261–262
cost of goods sold (COGS), 36
see also inventoriable costs
accounting and managing, 37
and GAAP, 3, 60, 424
on income statement, 2
manufacturing variable costs, 428
variable inventory valuation, 428
write-off to cost of goods sold approach, 175–176
cost of sales (COS), 37
cost outflow, 37
cost-plus method (CPM), 1114
cost-plus pricing
alternative cost-plus methods, 603–605
generally, 602
ROI cost-plus pricing method, 602–603
vs. target pricing, 605–606
cost pools, 141
activity cost pool, 208, 213f
and allocation rates, 144f
artificial cost pools, 717, 718
cost assignment for direct cost pool, 150f
direct labour cost pool, 149
homogeneous cost pool, 705
indirect cost pool, 465, 466, 480
see also ordinary least squares (OLS)
indirect cost pools, 143
indirect-cost pools, 211
in job costing system, 141
as mix, 202
selection of, 152
separation of, 144–145
cost-reduction decision, 217–218
cost smoothing, 203
cost structures
alternative cost structures, 106–111
influence on, and risk-return tradeoff, 111–112
cost tracing, 703f
direct-cost tracing, 211
direct materials, ease of tracing, 47
production costs, 42–43
tracing to output unit, 45
cost variance analysis, 803–805
cost variances, 309
cost-volume-profit (CVP), 85–86
analysis procedures, 86–87
assumptions, 88
breakeven point, determination of, 92–98

LIST OF ABBREVIATIONS